McDougal Littell

CLASSZONE

Visit classzone.com and get connected.

ClassZone resources provide instruction, practice and learning support for students and parents.

Literature and Reading Center

- Selection-specific content includes vocabulary practice, research links, and extension activities for writing and critical thinking
- Author Online provides information about each author, as well as in-depth author studies on selected writers
- English Learner support for a variety of languages includes audio summaries of selections and a Multi-Language Academic Glossary

Vocabulary Center

- Vocabulary practice and games reinforce skills

Writing and Grammar Center

- Quick-Fix Editing Machine provides grammar help in a student-friendly format
- Writing Templates and graphic organizers promote clear, orderly communication

Media Center

- Media Analysis Guides encourage critical thinking skills
- Project Ideas, Storyboards, and Production Templates inspire creative media projects

Access the online version of your textbook at **classzone.com**

Your complete text is available for immediate use!

McDougal Littell

Where Great Lessons Begin

McDougal Littell

WORLD LITERATURE

TEACHER'S EDITION

McDougal Littell
EVANSTON, ILLINOIS • BOSTON • DALLAS

Printed in the United States of America

ISBN 13: 978-0-547-11647-1 ISBN 10: 0-547-11647-0

1 2 3 4 5 6 7 8 9 – DWO – 12 11 10 09 08

Senior Consultants

The senior consultants guided the conceptual development for *The Language of Literature* series. They participated actively in shaping prototype materials for major components, and they reviewed completed prototypes and/or completed units to ensure consistency with current research and the philosophy of the series.

Arthur N. Applebee Professor of Education, State University of New York at Albany; Director, Center for the Learning and Teaching of Literature; Senior Fellow, Center for Writing and Literacy

Andrea B. Bermúdez Professor of Studies in Language and Culture; Director, Research Center for Language and Culture; Chair, Foundations and Professional Studies, University of Houston–Clear Lake

Sheridan Blau Senior Lecturer in English and Education and former Director of Composition, University of California at Santa Barbara; Director, South Coast Writing Project; Director, Literature Institute for Teachers; Former President, National Council of Teachers of English

Rebekah Caplan Senior Associate for Language Arts for middle school and high school literacy, National Center on Education and the Economy, Washington, D.C.; served on the California State English Assessment Development Team for Language Arts; former co-director of the Bay Area Writing Project, University of California at Berkeley

Peter Elbow Emeritus Professor of English, University of Massachusetts at Amherst; Fellow, Bard Center for Writing and Thinking

Susan Hynds Professor and Director of English Education, Syracuse University, Syracuse, New York

Judith A. Langer Professor of Education, State University of New York at Albany; Co-director, Center for the Learning and Teaching of Literature; Senior Fellow, Center for Writing and Literacy

James Marshall Professor of English and English Education; Chair, Division of Curriculum and Instruction, University of Iowa, Iowa City

Contributing Consultants

Linda Diamond Executive Vice President, Consortium on Reading Excellence (CORE); co-author of *Building a Powerful Reading Program*

Lucila A. Garza ESL Consultant, Austin, Texas

Jeffrey N. Golub Assistant Professor of English Education, University of South Florida, Tampa

William L. McBride, Ph.D. Reading and Curriculum Specialist; former middle and high school English instructor

Sharon Sicinski-Skeans, Ph.D. Assistant Professor of Reading, University of Houston–Clear Lake; primary consultant on *The InterActive Reader*

THE LANGUAGE OF LITERATURE

Experience the Language of Literature

I want to change people's minds...

I want to love what I do...

I want to make a statement...

Experience

THE LANGUAGE OF

LITERATURE

Seeing the World Through World Literature

World Literature helps students experience the daily lives and traditions of other peoples through a wide variety of literature selections from around the world.

World Literature Classics with Real-World Connections

Specific examples demonstrate how the work, language, politics, and traditions of other cultures relate to students' everyday lives.

Comparing Literature Across Cultures

Students learn to compare and contrast literature selections from different genres or cultures, gaining a better understanding and appreciation of what each selection offers.

Literary Milestones, Translations, and Legacies

A detailed look into the lives of featured authors and famous works teaches students how the context of an era can impact a writer's choices and how language shapes meaning.

Integrated Writing, Assessment, and Internet

Writing workshops, technology options, and flexible assessment practice are integrated with the selections to help students be better prepared and more successful.

Experience the possibilities. Experience the success. Experience *The Language of Literature.*

I want to see the world...

I want to create a memory...

World Literature Classics with Real-World Connections

Specific examples show students how the work, language, politics, and traditions of other cultures relate to modern, everyday life in the United States.

I want to try new things...

Connect to Today helps students identify with other cultures and relate what they read to their own lives.

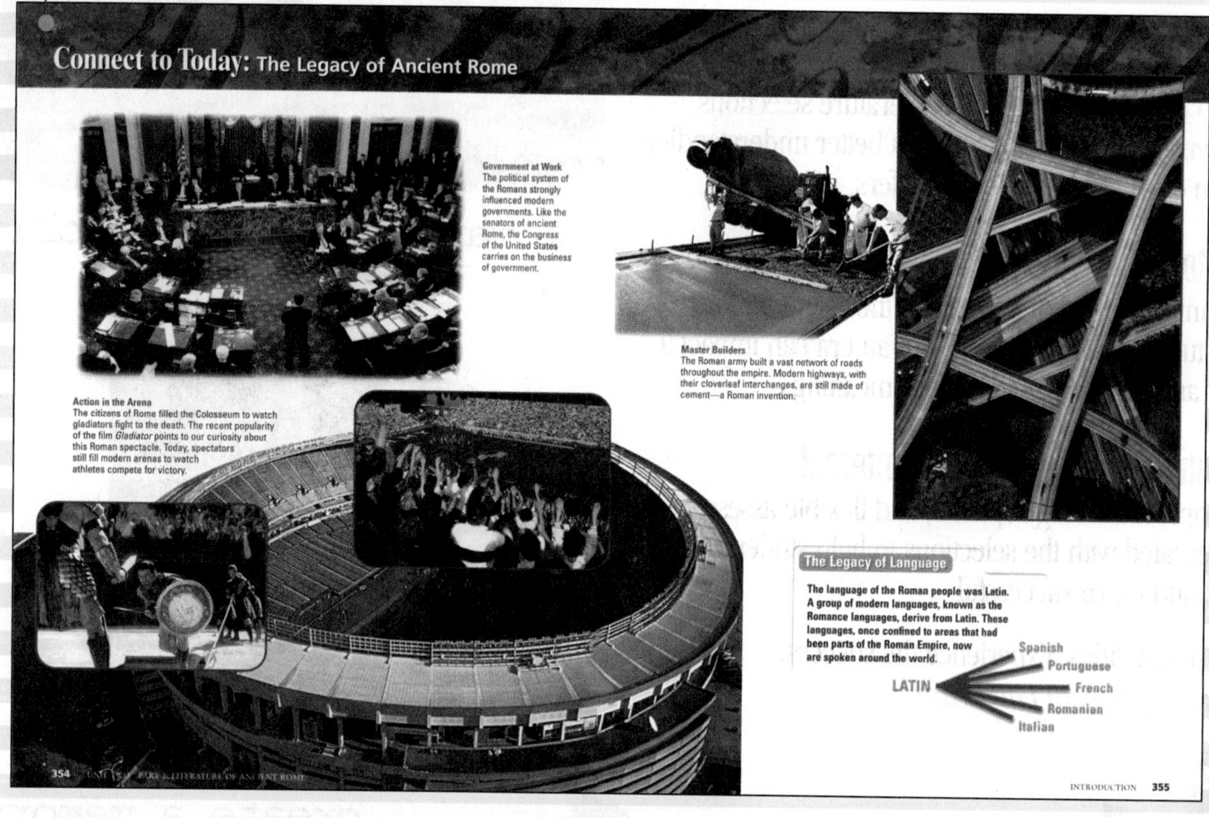

Connect to Today: The Legacy of Ancient Rome

Government at Work
The political system of the Romans strongly influenced modern governments. Like the senators of ancient Rome, the Congress of the United States carries on the business of government.

Action in the Arena
The citizens of Rome filled the Colosseum to watch gladiators fight to the death. The recent popularity of the film *Gladiator* points to our curiosity about this Roman spectacle. Today, spectators still fill modern arenas to watch athletes compete for victory.

Master Builders
The Roman army built a vast network of roads throughout the empire. Modern highways, with their cloverleaf interchanges, are still made of cement—a Roman invention.

The Legacy of Language

The language of the Roman people was Latin. A group of modern languages, known as the Romance languages, derive from Latin. These languages, once confined to areas that had been parts of the Roman Empire, now are spoken around the world.

354

INTRODUCTION 355

Connections

Comparing Literature Across Cultures

Students learn how to compare and contrast two literature selections from different genres or cultures and place the literature into historical context.

COMPARING LITERATURE ACROSS CULTURES

Trickster Tales

OVERVIEW

The **trickster tale** is a genre of literature found in West Africa and all over the world. It is a humorous folktale in which an animal or person creates mischief by trying to outwit others. Usually a culture will have a whole cycle of stories about the same trickster character. Famous tricksters include the Native American Coyote, the African-American Brer Rabbit (who descended from a West African trickster hare), and even the cartoon character Bugs Bunny.

In the pages that follow, you will read trickster tales from West African and Native American cultures. You will compare and contrast Anansi the spider, a West African trickster, and the Native American spider known as Iktomi, and you will decide how well each character displays the qualities of a trickster. Through this comparison, you will decide if the two tricksters are basically the same character.

Points of Comparison

The trickster is a complex character with both admirable and terrible qualities. He can be a **culture hero** who brings good things to people and teaches them to live properly. He can be a **clever deceiver** who uses trickery to capture or humiliate others. He can also be a **fool** whose greed or arrogance leads to his own downfall. The chart below lists some common characteristics of tricksters.

Analyzing Trickster Tales As you read the Anansi stories, keep track of the trickster characteristics you see in Anansi on a chart similar to this one. Later you will do the same for Iktomi.

Trickster Characteristics	Anansi (West African)	Iktomi (Native American)
clever		
heroic		
supernaturally powerful		
greedy, selfish		
lying, deceitful		
proud, self-important		
foolish		

Standardized Test Practice: Comparison-and-Contrast Essay After you have finished reading all the stories, you will have the information you need to write a comparison-and-contrast essay. Your notes will help you include details and examples from the stories.

650 UNIT FOUR PART 2: WEST AFRICAN ORAL LITERATURE

Graphic organizers help students prepare for standardized tests with a compare-and-contrast focus.

PREPARING to *Read*

SELECTION 1 COMPARING LITERATURE

Connect to Your Life
How would you get someone to do what you wanted him or her to do, without that person's realizing what you were up to? Share a strategy that worked for you.

Build Background

West African Tricksters There are several tricksters in African folklore. In east, central, and southern Africa and the western Sudan, the trickster is the hare. Among the Yoruba, Edo, and Ibo of Nigeria, the trickster is the tortoise. Anansi the spider is the famous trickster of the Ashanti people, who live in Ghana. All Ashanti folktales are referred to as *anansesem*, or "spider tales," whether Anansi appears in them or not.

Hundreds of stories have been told about Anansi; his wife, Aso; and his sons, Kweku Tsin and Intikuma. Traditionally, the stories are told only after dark. Anansi is a culture hero to the Ashanti, responsible for scattering wisdom throughout the world and otherwise making things as they are today. He is also a model for bad behavior, however. Through Anansi stories, the Ashanti make fun of human faults.

Anansi Abroad Anansi stories were brought to the Americas as a result of the slave trade. Many Ashanti were enslaved in Jamaica, and Anansi stories are told there as Anancy or Aunt Nancy stories. Stories told in Jamaica are almost identical to the original West African stories, although modern writers such as Andrew Salkey have invented new Anansi stories to comment on today's world.

Focus Your Reading

LITERARY ANALYSIS: TRICKSTER TALE
A **trickster tale** involves a human or animal character who engages in clever deceit, physical harm, or magic to try to get what he or she desires. Sometimes the trickster fools others; sometimes he or she is fooled. Trickster tales are usually humorous, and often they explain how some feature of the world or society came to be. Look for these qualities in the Anansi tales you are about to read.

ACTIVE READING: INTERPRETING THEMES
Often, the beginning or end of a trickster tale will state outright what feature of the world the story explains. The first story, for example, tells you:

"In this way Anansi . . . became the owner of all stories."

The more important theme of a trickster tale is usually unstated, however. Frequently it is a moral lesson that can be inferred from what is rewarded or punished in the story. One unstated theme of the first story might be "If you let yourself be flattered, you might suffer."

READER'S NOTEBOOK. As you read each Anansi tale, take notes following the model below.

__________ is rewarded for __________.
__________ is punished for __________.
Lesson: __________.

COMPARING LITERATURE ACROSS CULTURES 651

Literary Analysis provides the definitions of specific literary terms and supports those definitions with literary examples.

Key literary concepts such as **Interpreting Themes** "bookend" the selection. The concepts are introduced before reading, and reinforced and practiced after reading.

The **Active Reading** strand prepares students to focus on a concept they will encounter in the selection and incorporates graphic organizers through the **Reader's Notebook**.

Comparisons

Literary Milestones, Translations, and Legacies

A detailed look into the lives of featured authors and famous works teaches students how the context of an era can impact a writer's choices and how language shapes meaning.

The Translator at Work helps students learn the process involved in translating some of the world's best-known works.

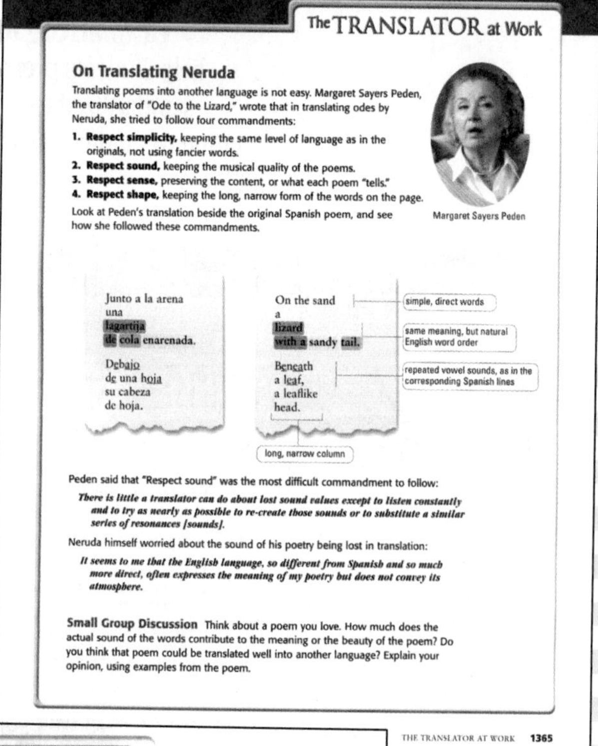

The TRANSLATOR at Work

On Translating Neruda

Translating poems into another language is not easy. Margaret Sayers Peden, the translator of "Ode to the Lizard," wrote that in translating odes by Neruda, she tried to follow four commandments:

1. **Respect simplicity,** keeping the same level of language as in the originals, not using fancier words.
2. **Respect sound,** keeping the musical quality of the poems.
3. **Respect sense,** preserving the content, or what each poem "tells."
4. **Respect shape,** keeping the long, narrow form of the words on the page.

Look at Peden's translation beside the original Spanish poem, and see how she followed these commandments.

Margaret Sayers Peden

Junto a la arena
una
lagartija
de cola enarenada.

Debajo
de una hoja
su cabeza
de hoja.

On the sand
a
lizard
with a sandy tail.

Beneath
a leaf,
a leaflike
head.

Peden said that "Respect sound" was the most difficult commandment to follow:

There is little a translator can do about lost sound values except to listen constantly and to try as nearly as possible to re-create those sounds or to substitute a similar series of resonances [sounds].

Neruda himself worried about the sound of his poetry being lost in translation:

It seems to me that the English language, so different from Spanish and so much more direct, often expresses the meaning of my poetry but does not convey its atmosphere.

Small Group Discussion Think about a poem you love. How much does the actual sound of the words contribute to the meaning or the beauty of the poem? Do you think that poem could be translated well into another language? Explain your opinion, using examples from the poem.

THE TRANSLATOR AT WORK 1365

Milestones in World Literature highlight important, longer works that are a part of our cultural heritage.

MILESTONES IN WORLD LITERATURE

Lady Murasaki Shikibu

The Tale of Genji

Yasunari Kawabata, a Japanese writer who won the Nobel Prize in literature in 1968, has called *The Tale of Genji* (gĕn′jē) "the highest pinnacle of Japanese literature." However, this 11th-century masterpiece, which is considered the world's first novel, was almost totally unfamiliar to Western readers until English translations of the work were published in the 20th century. To this day, little is known about the author of the work, Murasaki Shikibu.

Born around 978, Murasaki was the daughter of a provincial governor who was also a scholar of Chinese and a renowned poet. As a child, Murasaki eavesdropped on her brother's lessons and learned Chinese more quickly than he did. Murasaki's brilliance led her father to regret that she had not been born a boy. In 998, she married a middle-aged man with whom she had a daughter in the following year. Four years after her husband's death in 1001, Murasaki was appointed a lady in waiting to Empress Akiko. Many believe that she penned *The Tale of Genji* while she was in service at the imperial court.

Written at the height of the highly cultured Heian period, *The Tale of Genji* relates the many romances of its hero, Prince Genji, the handsome son of an emperor. Known as "the Shining Prince," Genji embodies the

Phoenix Hall, built during the Heian period by the noble Fujiwara family

508

The Legacy of Language

Words and Phrases

You may not know how to speak Greek, but many of the words you use have Greek origins. For example, the word **democracy** comes from the Greek root *demo,* meaning "people," and *crat,* meaning "rule." Here are just a few examples of English words that have Greek roots.

Root	Meaning	English Words
astra	star	astronaut, asterisk, astronomy
biblio	book	bibliography, Bible
log	word	dialogue, monologue, eulogy
polis	city, state	police, political, metropolis

The Legacy of Language feature teaches word origin and usage.

Literary

I want a challenge...

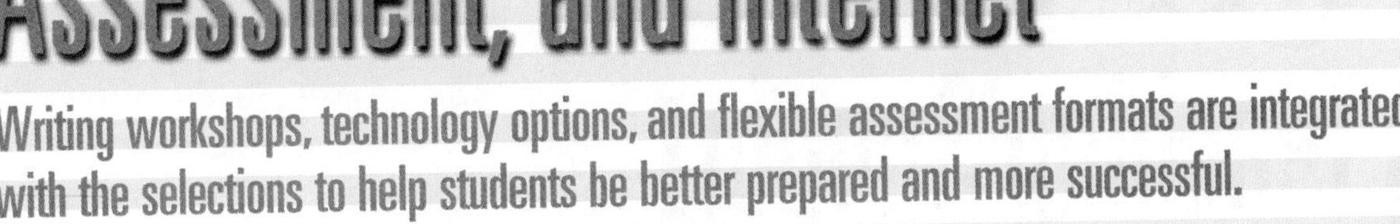
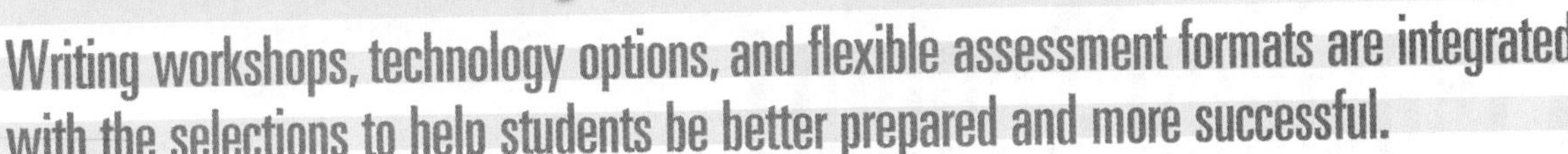

Writing workshops, technology options, and flexible assessment formats are integrated with the selections to help students be better prepared and more successful.

Assessment practice and strategies are supported in each unit of the *Pupil's Edition.*

Standardized Test Practice

Reading & Writing for Assessment

Throughout high school, you will be tested on your ability to read and understand different kinds of reading selections. The tests will assess your basic understanding of ideas and knowledge of vocabulary. They will also assess your ability to analyze and evaluate the messages of the selections, along with the techniques the writers use in getting their messages across.

Some useful test-taking strategies are presented in this lesson. Practice applying the strategies by working through each of the models provided.

PART 1 How to Read a Test Selection

Sometimes a test requires you to read a passage and then answer multiple-choice questions about it. Applying these test-taking strategies, taking notes, and marking important passages as you read can help you focus on information.

STRATEGIES FOR READING A TEST SELECTION

- **Before you begin reading, skim the questions that follow the passage.** These can help focus your reading.
- **Think about the title.** What does it suggest about the overall message or theme of the selection?
- **Use active reading strategies, such as analyzing, predicting, and questioning.** Take notes in the margin or highlight important words and passages to help you focus your reading. (Do not do this, however, if the test directions forbid you to mark on the test.)
- **Look for main ideas.** You will often find them stated at the beginning or end of paragraphs. Sometimes they are implied rather than directly stated. After reading each paragraph, ask yourself, "What was this passage about?"
- **Note the literary elements and techniques used by the writer.** You might, for example, consider the writer's tone or use of comparison and contrast. Then ask yourself what effect is created by each element or technique.
- **Examine the sequence of ideas.** Are the ideas developed in chronological order, presented in order of importance, or organized in some other way—as causes and effects, for instance, or as problems and solutions?
- **Think about the writer's purpose and message.** What questions does the selection answer? What new questions does it raise? What generalizations can you make about the subject?

PART 2: LITERATURE OF ANCIEN

Reading Selection

❶Ancient Greece Revived in Rome; Colosseum Reopens as Theater with Staging of *Oedipus Rex*
by Sarah Delaney

1 ❷ More than 15 centuries after its last gladiators saluted Caesar, the Roman Colosseum reopened tonight as a place of public entertainment, this time for a small, cultured audience rather than tens of thousands of plebeians screaming for blood. The draw for tonight's 500 people . . . was a Greek-language performance of the ancient Greek drama *Oedipus Rex*. As spotlights illuminated chambers and walls of the giant ruin, actors played out the classic story of love and incest.

2 Costas Galanakis, cast as the old blind seer, Tiresias, declared it "a great, emotional moment to perform here."

3 ❸Concetta Notardonato, 47, a Roman and an avid theatergoer, said from her standing position on the third tier of the arena that "it's a great idea, and the setting is fantastic." But she felt ticket prices, about $25, were too high. And, she objected to the language. "We don't all know Greek," she lamented. "A unique performance like this should be more accessible to everybody; the Colosseum is a symbolic place for the people."

4 Opened in the year 80 as a venue for Rome's beloved spectacles, the grand stone structure closed and descended into ruin in the centuries after the fall of the empire. But this evening, courtesy of government agencies here, it reopened for a show ❹that could not have been less like the mayhem of Ridley Scott's film *Gladiator*.

5 A large helium balloon floa arena; the chorus, loosely clad ghostly white plaster statues the distance came the sounds

6 The stage was a newly buil created the arena's long-lost o cells where exotic beasts and and entertain Romans of ever Greek National Theater, was Sophocles' *Oedipus* trilogy, inc based on *Oedipus at Colonus.*

STRATEGIES IN ACTION

❶ Look at the title.
ONE STUDENT'S THOUGHTS
"The title tells me that this article deals with ancient Greek culture and the Roman Colosseum."

❷ Look for main ideas.
"This selection is about the reopening of the Roman Colosseum after more than 1,500 years."
YOUR TURN
Look at the end of the article for other stated main ideas.

❸ Evaluate sources of information.
"The person being quoted lives in Rome and goes to the theater often. She probably knows what she's talking about, and maybe her views are shared by other theatergoers."

TEST PRACTICE

413

Teacher's Guide to Assessment and Portfolio Use
McDougal Littell
THE LANGUAGE OF LITERATURE

McDougal Littell
THE LANGUAGE OF LITERATURE
TEST GENERATOR

ClassZone
THE LANGUAGE OF LITERATURE

The Teacher's Guide to Assessment and Portfolio Use includes portfolio assessment, writing rubrics, and other forms of open-ended assessment.

The **Test Generator CD-ROM** contains a variety of pre-made tests and a test bank of items that allows teachers to create customized tests.

classzone.com is *The Language of Literature*'s companion Web site that offers links correlated to the textbook, a research tutorial, activities, and assessment practice.

The **Formal Assessment** and **Integrated Assessment** booklets provide selection tests, part tests, a mid-year test, and end-of-year tests, plus writing rubrics, and practice questions for standardized tests.

THE LANGUAGE OF LITERATURE

Time-Saving Teaching Support

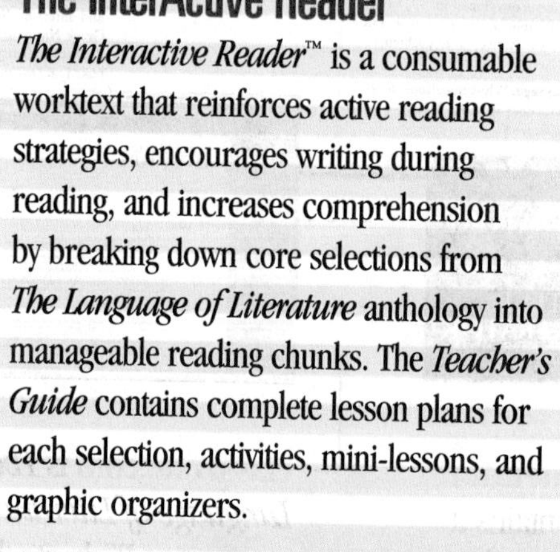

The Language of Literature Comprehensive Teacher's Edition

The annotated *Teacher's Edition* serves as a complete reference tool for the classroom. Each page contains a wealth of information that includes a lesson overview, teaching strategies, background information, and references to ancillary materials.

The InterActive Reader™

The Interactive Reader™ is a consumable worktext that reinforces active reading strategies, encourages writing during reading, and increases comprehension by breaking down core selections from *The Language of Literature* anthology into manageable reading chunks. The *Teacher's Guide* contains complete lesson plans for each selection, activities, mini-lessons, and graphic organizers.

The Reading Toolkit

The *Reading Toolkit* is a valuable collection of teacher tools, mini-lessons, copymasters, and transparencies that helps teachers diagnose students' abilities and provides them with guidelines for direct instruction in reading comprehension skills and strategies.

Literature Connections

Each *Literature Connections* volume contains a complete novel or play with five to eight theme-related readings that represent a variety of genres. Each title is supported by a *Teacher's SourceBook* that includes background material, author biographies, discussion starters, and suggested essay questions.

Unit Resource Books

The *Unit Resource Books,* one per unit, provide additional skills work and extensions of activities and exercises. Contents include a family and community involvement section; a selection summary; SkillBuilders in active reading, literary analysis, vocabulary, grammar, and spelling; a selection quiz; a Writing Workshop; a reflect and assess segment; and answer keys.

Lesson Planning Guide

This booklet helps teachers organize resources, keep track of daily objectives and activities, and track standards met.

Formal Assessment

This booklet offers selection tests, part tests, a mid-year test, an end-of-year test, writing rubrics, and standardized test practice questions.

Integrated Assessment

Features of this booklet include Unit Integrated Assessments, an End-of-Year Integrated Assessment, and a record of student thinking and planning.

Teacher's Guide to Assessment and Portfolio Use

This guide includes portfolio assessment, writing rubrics, and other forms of open-ended assessment.

English Learners/Students Acquiring English Resources

The Language of Literature offers solid support for the English Learner.

EL/SAE Spanish Study Guide

EL/SAE Teacher's SourceBook for Language Development

Writing Research Papers

This booklet provides students with a complete guide to the process of writing a research paper, from finding a topic to preparing the final manuscript.

History from Visuals: World Art & Cultures

This set of full-color transparencies features paintings, sculptures, artifacts, and architecture that represent the many world cultures explored in the literature selections.

THE LANGUAGE OF LITERATURE

Integrated Technology

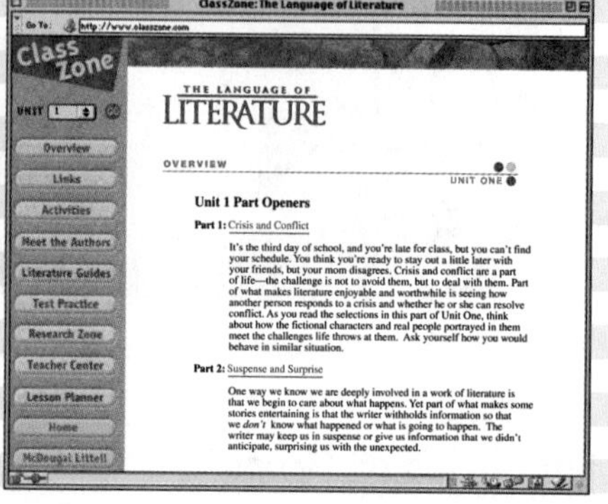

classzone.com

ClassZone is an online guide to *The Language of Literature* that provides access to a variety of Internet resources. This companion Web site offers links correlated to the textbook, an Internet research tutorial, vocabulary flipcards and other activities, author background, spelling practice, a *Teacher Center* and access to the *Online Lesson Planner.*

Online Lesson Planner

The *Online Lesson Planner* allows teachers to conveniently create, edit, and customize lesson plans on the Internet. Lessons can be modified to incorporate activities from the *Teacher's Edition* or customized to meet specific classroom needs. A correlation feature allows the plans to be correlated to specific state standards or guidelines.

Test Generator

This CD-ROM contains a variety of pre-made tests and a test bank of items that allows teachers to create customized tests. The program provides tools that walk the user through the searching and editing steps and help correlate the tests to national and state standards.

NetActivities

This CD-ROM contains extension activities for each Author Study in the text and offers additional information about featured authors through links to related Web sites.

Electronic Library

This CD-ROM collection lets teachers customize instruction by choosing the works of a favorite author from over 200 additional pieces of classic literature.

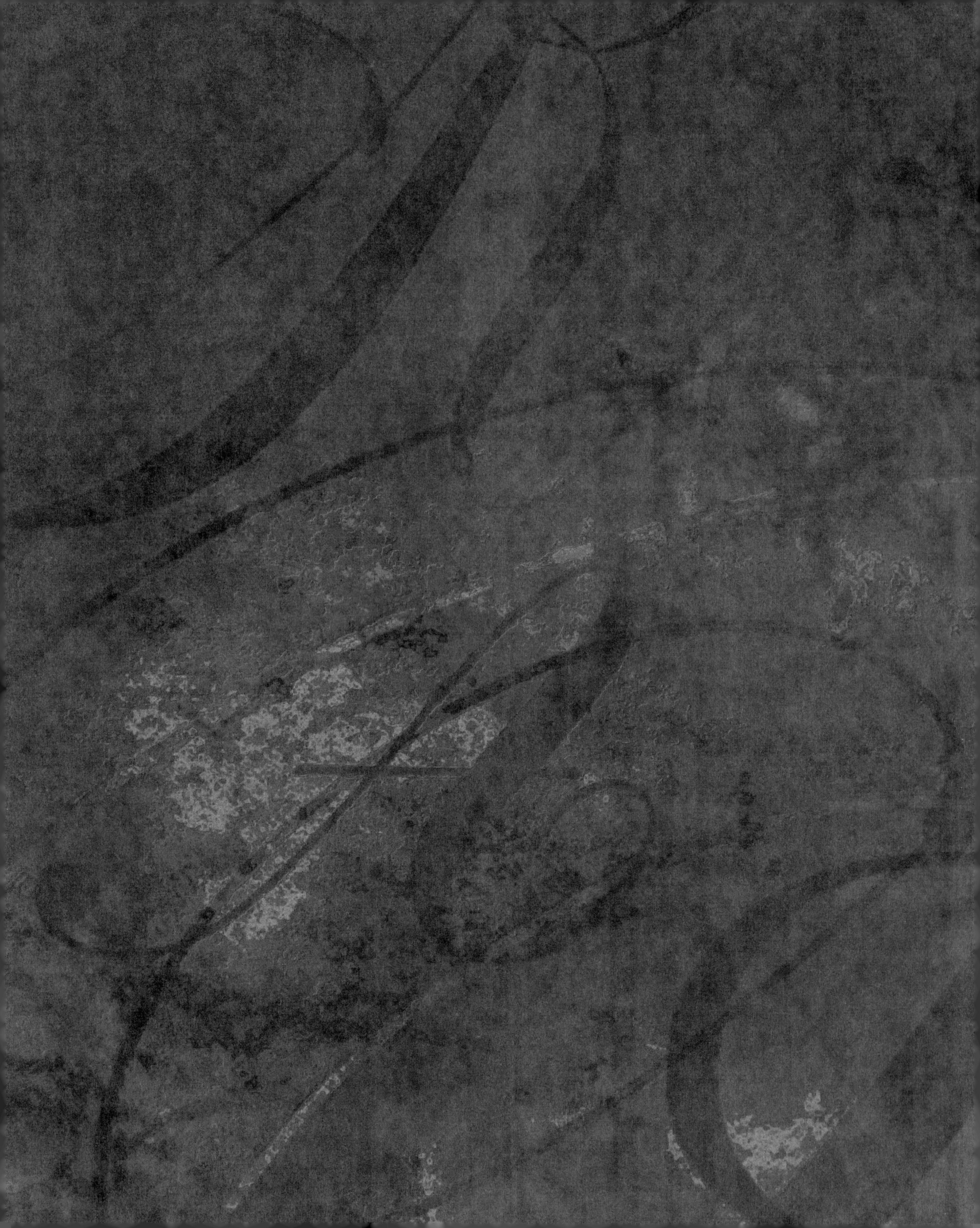

McDougal Littell

WORLD LITERATURE

McDougal Littell

WORLD LITERATURE

Arthur N. Applebee
Andrea B. Bermúdez
Sheridan Blau
Rebekah Caplan
Peter Elbow
Susan Hynds
Judith A. Langer
James Marshall

McDougal Littell
EVANSTON, ILLINOIS • BOSTON • DALLAS

ACKNOWLEDGMENTS

READING MODEL

Parabola and Paul Jordan-Smith: "Green Willow," retold by Paul Jordan-Smith, from *Parabola: The Magazine of Myth and Tradition* 8.1 (January 1983). Copyright © 1983 by Paul Jordan-Smith. Reprinted by permission of Parabola and the author.

UNIT ONE

Penguin Books: Excerpts from *The Epic of Gilgamesh,* translated by N. K. Sandars (Penguin Classics, 1960; third edition, 1972). Copyright © 1960, 1964, 1972 by N. K. Sandars. Reproduced by permission of Penguin Books Ltd.

"Creation Hymn" and "Burial Hymn," from *The Rig Veda,* translated by Wendy Doniger O'Flaherty (Penguin Classics, 1981). Copyright © 1981 by Wendy Doniger O'Flaherty. Reproduced by permission of Penguin Books Ltd.

Henry Holt and Company: Excerpt from the Book of the Dead, from *Wings of the Falcon,* translated by Joseph Kaster. Copyright © 1968 by Joseph Kaster. Reprinted by permission of Henry Holt and Company, LLC.

University of Texas Press: "I'm going downstream on Kingswater Canal" and "Whenever I leave you, I go out of breath," from *Love Songs of the New Kingdom,* translated from the ancient Egyptian by John L. Foster. Copyright © 1969, 1970, 1971, 1972, 1973, 1974 by John L. Foster. Reprinted by permission of the University of Texas Press.

Simon & Schuster: Excerpts from the Book of Genesis and the Book of Psalms, from *The Bible, Designed to Be Read as Living Literature,* edited by Ernest Sutherland Bates. Copyright © 1936 by Simon and Schuster, Inc. Copyright renewed © 1964 by Simon and Schuster, Inc. Reprinted with the permission of Simon & Schuster.

Continued on page R180

ART CREDITS

Maps © GeoNova LLC.

COVER, FRONTISPIECE

Illustration © 2002 Glenn Harrington.

Continued on page R187

Printed in the United States of America

ISBN 13: 978-0-547-11648-8 ISBN 10: 0-547-11648-9

1 2 3 4 5 6 7 8 9—DWO—12 11 10 09 08

iv

Senior Consultants

The senior consultants guided the conceptual development for *The Language of Literature* series. They participated actively in shaping prototype materials for major components, and they reviewed completed prototypes and/or completed units to ensure consistency with current research and the philosophy of the series.

Arthur N. Applebee Professor of Education, State University of New York at Albany; Director, Center for the Learning and Teaching of Literature; Senior Fellow, Center for Writing and Literacy

Andrea B. Bermúdez Professor of Studies in Language and Culture; Director, Research Center for Language and Culture; Chair, Foundations and Professional Studies, University of Houston–Clear Lake

Sheridan Blau Senior Lecturer in English and Education and former Director of Composition, University of California at Santa Barbara; Director, South Coast Writing Project; Director, Literature Institute for Teachers; Former President, National Council of Teachers of English

Rebekah Caplan Senior Associate for Language Arts for middle school and high school literacy, National Center on Education and the Economy, Washington, D.C.; served on the California State English Assessment Development Team for Language Arts; former co-director of the Bay Area Writing Project, University of California at Berkeley

Peter Elbow Emeritus Professor of English, University of Massachusetts at Amherst; Fellow, Bard Center for Writing and Thinking

Susan Hynds Professor and Director of English Education, Syracuse University, Syracuse, New York

Judith A. Langer Professor of Education, State University of New York at Albany; Co-director, Center for the Learning and Teaching of Literature; Senior Fellow, Center for Writing and Literacy

James Marshall Professor of English and English Education; Chair, Division of Curriculum and Instruction, University of Iowa, Iowa City

Contributing Consultants

Linda Diamond Executive Vice President, Consortium on Reading Excellence (CORE); co-author of *Building a Powerful Reading Program*

Lucila A. Garza ESL Consultant, Austin, Texas

Jeffrey N. Golub Assistant Professor of English Education, University of South Florida, Tampa

William L. McBride, Ph.D. Reading and Curriculum Specialist; former middle and high school English instructor

Sharon Sicinski-Skeans, Ph.D. Assistant Professor of Reading, University of Houston–Clear Lake; primary consultant on *The InterActive Reader*

v

Multicultural Advisory Board

The multicultural advisors reviewed literature selections for appropriate content and made suggestions for teaching lessons in a multicultural classroom.

Julie A. Anderson English Department Chairperson, Dayton High School, Dayton, Oregon

Vikki Pepper Ascuena Meridian High School, Meridian, Idaho

Dr. Joyce M. Bell Chairperson, English Department, Townview Magnet Center, Dallas, Texas

Linda F. Bellmore Livermore High School, Livermore, California

Dr. Eugenia W. Collier Author; lecturer; Chairperson, Department of English and Language Arts; Teacher of Creative Writing and American Literature, Morgan State University, Maryland

Dr. Bill Compagnone English Department Chairperson, Lawrence High School, Lawrence, Massachusetts

Kathleen S. Fowler President, Palm Beach County Council of Teachers of English, Boca Raton Middle School, Boca Raton, Florida

Jan Graham Cobb Middle School, Tallahassee, Florida

Barbara J. Kuhns Camino Real Middle School, Las Cruces, New Mexico

Patricia J. Richards Prior Lake, Minnesota

Continued on page R168

Teacher Review Panels

The following educators provided ongoing review during the development of the tables of contents, lesson design, and key components of the program.

CALIFORNIA

Steve Bass 8th Grade Team Leader, Meadowbrook Middle School, Ponway Unified School District

Cynthia Brickey 8th Grade Academic Block Teacher, Kastner Intermediate School, Clovis Unified School District

Karen Buxton English Department Chairperson, Winston Churchill Middle School, San Juan School District

Bonnie Garrett Davis Middle School, Compton School District

Sally Jackson Madrona Middle School, Torrance Unified School District

Sharon Kerson Los Angeles Center for Enriched Studies, Los Angeles Unified School District

Continued on page R168

Manuscript Reviewers

The following educators reviewed prototype lessons and tables of contents during the development of *The Language of Literature* program.

David Adcox Trinity High School, Euless, Texas

Carol Alves English Department Chairperson, Apopka High School, Apopka, Florida

Jacqueline Anderson James A. Foshay Learning Center, Los Angeles, California

Kathleen M. Anderson-Knight United Township High School, East Moline, Illinois

Anita Arnold Thomas Jefferson High School, San Antonio, Texas

Cassandra L. Asberry Dean of Instruction, Carter High School, Dallas, Texas

Jolene Auderer Pine Tree High School, Longview, Texas

Don Baker English Department Chairperson, Peoria High School, Peoria, Illinois

Continued on page R169

World Literature Teacher Panel

The following educators provided guidance during the initial development of this book.

Renee Bartholomew Crystal Lake Central High School, Crystal Lake, Illinois

Johanna Brocker Wells Community Academy, Chicago, Illinois

Ken Filas Round Lake High School, Round Lake, Illinois

Elizabeth Kenny Adlai E. Stevenson High School, Lincolnshire, Illinois

Allan Ruter Glenbrook South High School, Glenview, Illinois

Margaret Sinclair Glenbard High School, Carol Stream, Illinois

Judith Soltis, Ph.D. Homewood-Flossmoor High School, Flossmoor, Illinois

Patty Van Lehn St. Charles High School, St. Charles, Illinois

Charles Venegoni, Ph.D. John Hersey High School, Arlington Heights, Illinois

Suzanne Zweig Sullivan High School, Chicago, Illinois

The following people provided assistance with Lakota and West African pronunciations.

Jim Green Lakota Instructor, Language Department, South Dakota State University

Robert Launay Professor or Anthropology, Northwestern University

Elikem Tomety Consultant from Ghana

vii

World Literature

Overview

UNIT ONE Literature of the Ancient World 3000 B.C.–A.D. 500

Part 1 Mesopotamian, Egyptian & Hebrew Literature

Part 2 Literature of India

LITERARY FOCUS	SKILL FOCUS
The Epic	**Writing Workshop:** Autobiographical Incident **Grammar:** Using Elements in a Series **Vocabulary:** Words with Multiple Meanings

UNIT TWO The Classical Age of Greece and Rome 800 B.C.–A.D. 200

Part 1 Literature of Ancient Greece

Part 2 Literature of Ancient Rome

LITERARY FOCUS	SKILL FOCUS
The Epics of Greece and Rome	**Communication Workshop:** Writing and Staging a Scene **Grammar:** Using Participles **Vocabulary:** Analyzing Word Parts—Greek and Latin Roots

UNIT THREE Traditions in Chinese and Japanese Literature 1500 B.C.–A.D. 1800

Part 1 Literature of Ancient China

Part 2 Literature of Japan

LITERARY FOCUS	SKILL FOCUS
Moral Teaching Through Literature	**Writing Workshop:** Lyric Poetry, Problem-Solution Essay **Grammar:** Using Parallelism for Effect, Creating Compound and Complex Sentences **Vocabulary:** Homophones, Homonyms, and Homographs; Using Reference Tools

UNIT FOUR Literature of the Middle East and Africa A.D. 300–1900

Part 1 Persian and Arabic Literature

Part 2 West African Oral Literature

SKILL FOCUS
Writing Workshop: Personality Profile **Grammar:** Using Adverbs and Adverb Phrases **Vocabulary:** Using Context Clues

UNIT FIVE Europe in Transition 400–1789

Part 1 Literature of the Middle Ages

Part 2 Literature of the Renaissance & Enlightenment

LITERARY FOCUS	SKILL FOCUS
The Sonnet	**Writing Workshop:** Subject Analysis **Communication Workshop:** Persuasive Speech **Grammar:** Changing Word Order for Sentence Variety, Using Noun Clauses **Vocabulary:** Understanding Analogies, Analyzing Word Parts—Affixes

UNIT SIX 19th-Century European Literature 1789–1899

Part 1 The Age of Romanticism

Part 2 The Emergence of Realism

LITERARY FOCUS	SKILL FOCUS
Romanticism **Realism**	**Writing Workshop:** Cause-and-Effect Essay **Grammar:** Using Adverb Clauses **Vocabulary:** Recognizing Denotations and Connotations

UNIT SEVEN Modern and Contemporary Literature 1900–Present

Part 1 Expressions of Modernism

Part 2 Responses to War and Conflict

Part 3 Contemporary Nobel Prize Winners

LITERARY FOCUS	SKILL FOCUS
Modernism **Magical Realism**	**Writing Workshops:** Literary Interpretation, Research Report **Grammar:** Using Adjective Phrases and Clauses, Varying Sentence Length **Vocabulary:** Recognizing Word Families, Choosing Word Attack Strategies

viii

Table of Contents

Student Resource Bank

Literature Connections

Each of the books in the *Literature Connections* series combines a novel or play with related readings—poems, stories, plays, personal essays, articles—that add new perspectives on the theme or subject matter of the longer work.

Listed below are some of the titles that can be used along with this World Literature anthology:

The Tempest by William Shakespeare
Hamlet by William Shakespeare
Macbeth by William Shakespeare
Julius Caesar by William Shakespeare
Canterbury Tales by Geoffrey Chaucer
Tess of the d'Urbervilles by Thomas Hardy
1984 by George Orwell
Kaffir Boy by Mark Mathabane
Nervous Conditions by Tsitsi Dangarembga
A Place Where the Sea Remembers by Sandra Benítez
Things Fall Apart by Chinua Achebe
The Underdogs by Mariano Azuela
When Rain Clouds Gather by Bessie Head

THE LANGUAGE OF
LITERATURE

Reading Strategies

UNIT ONE

Literature of the Ancient World

2500 B.C.–A.D. 300

x

Sacred and Practical Teachings

Part 2 Literature of Ancient India

xi

UNIT TWO

The Classical Age of *Greece* and *Rome*

xii

The Tradition Continues

Part 2 Literature of Ancient Rome

xiii

UNIT THREE

Traditions in Chinese and Japanese Literature

xiv

xv

UNIT FOUR

Literature of the Middle East and Africa

A.D. 300–1900

xvi

Giving Guidance, Praising Greatness

Part 2 West African Oral Literature

xvii

UNIT FIVE

Europe in *Transition* 400–1789

xviii

Human Possibility

Part 2 Literature of the Renaissance & Enlightenment

INTERNET CONNECTION

xix

UNIT SIX

19th-Century European Literature 1798–1899

xx

xxi

UNIT SEVEN

Modern and Contemporary Literature 1900–PRESENT 1094

xxii

xxiii

Critics and Dreamers

Part 3 Contemporary Nobel Prize Winners

xxiv

Student *Resource Bank*

xxv

Selections by Genre

Epic

Myths, Tales, and Legends

Romance

Scripture

Fiction

xxvi

Nonfiction

Poetry

xxvii

Drama

xxviii

Special Features of This Book

Author Study

Comparing Literature Across Cultures

Learning the Language of Literature

Milestones in World Literature

Connect to Today

xxix

The Translator at Work

Writing Workshop

Communication Workshop

Building Vocabulary

Sentence Crafting

Assessment Pages

xxx

Why Study World Literature?

To Become Culturally Literate

What is the story behind the Trojan horse? What's the name of Chinua Achebe's most famous novel? Someday you may need to know this, for an exam or even a quiz show. If you read world literature, you'll be ready.

To Experience the World—Past and Present

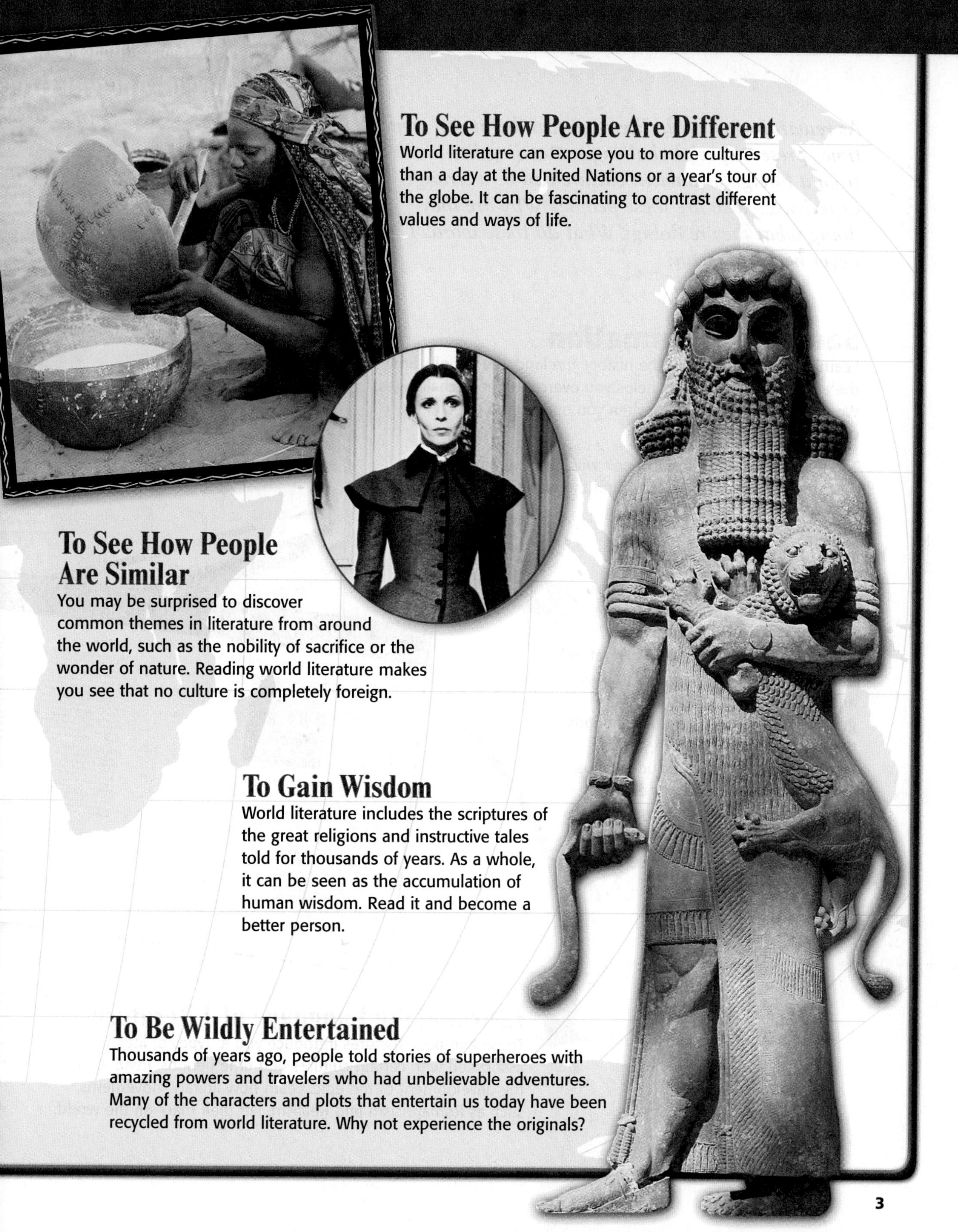

To See How People Are Different

World literature can expose you to more cultures than a day at the United Nations or a year's tour of the globe. It can be fascinating to contrast different values and ways of life.

To See How People Are Similar

You may be surprised to discover common themes in literature from around the world, such as the nobility of sacrifice or the wonder of nature. Reading world literature makes you see that no culture is completely foreign.

To Gain Wisdom

World literature includes the scriptures of the great religions and instructive tales told for thousands of years. As a whole, it can be seen as the accumulation of human wisdom. Read it and become a better person.

To Be Wildly Entertained

Thousands of years ago, people told stories of superheroes with amazing powers and travelers who had unbelievable adventures. Many of the characters and plots that entertain us today have been recycled from world literature. Why not experience the originals?

Understanding World Literature

As rewarding as world literature can be, it can sometimes present special challenges. Reading literature from a foreign or ancient culture can be a strange experience. Who are these people? Why are they doing what they're doing? What do these words I never heard of mean?

PART 1 In the Name of Honor

Literature of Ancient Gree

Why It Matters
Greece is a small mountainous country, yet it gave birth to some of the most cherished ideas of Western civilization. The Greeks championed individual freedom, developed an early form of democracy, and demonstrated the power of rational thought. Greek ideals of beauty and justice have spread throughout the world. Greek literature, especially poetry and drama, continues to inspire writers today.

For Links to Ancient Greece, click on:

HUMANITIES
CLASSZONE.COM

Ionian Sea
Ithaca
MACEDONIA
Mt. Olympus
GREECE
Delphi
Corinth
Olympia
Sparta
PELOPONNESUS

Seek Out Information

Learning something about the history, the land, the people, and the author before you read helps you overcome these challenges. World literature comes alive when you understand the context in which it was written.

The following features in this book will help you open new doors to literature from around the world:

Introductions

Why did stories from Ancient Greece often tell of long voyages across the sea? Why is storytelling such an important part of West African literature? Introductions provide answers to these and other questions. They are quick guides to the cultures and time periods that produced the literature you will read. Each introduction includes maps, information about history and society, a time line of important events, and a feature showing the contributions of that culture or period to today's world.

LEARNING *the Language of Literature*

The Epics of Greece and Rome

Literary Style

Epic Conventions

The Importance of Honor

The Power of Fate

Learning the Language of Literature

These two-page features introduce you to types of literature associated with certain cultures and time periods. Read about the development of the epic. Learn how literary movements, such as Romanticism and Realism, left their mark on the world.

Author Biography and Build Background

Prereading pages give background that will help you understand each selection more fully. Learn about an author's life, study important terms, and find out more about the history and culture of the selection you're about to read.

Online Background

Background information doesn't stop there. Visit our Web site to learn even more about the cultural contributions of each time and place.

HUMANITIES
CLASSZONE.COM

Reader's Notebook

Putting your thoughts on paper can help you understand and connect with literature. Many readers record their ideas in a **READER'S NOTEBOOK**. You can use almost any kind of notebook for this purpose. Below are two ways you can use your notebook.

1 IMPROVE YOUR READING SKILLS

Complete the **READER'S NOTEBOOK** activity on the **Preparing to Read** page of each selection. This activity will help you apply an important skill as you read.

Connect to Your Life
Would you give your last dollar to your friend? to a stranger? Discuss the idea of giving with your classmates. Then create a few moral guidelines that people could use when making decisions about giving.

Focus Your Reading
LITERARY ANALYSIS: FORESHADOWING
Foreshadowing is a writer's use of hints or clues to suggest what will happen later. For example, in "How Much Land Does a Man Need?" Pakhom's dream in section VII foreshadows his fate at the end. As you read, look for clues that foreshadow what's to come.

ACTIVE READING: PREDICTING
Predicting what will happen next in a story can alert you to foreshadowing. Keep in mind what you know about Tolstoy, and always use your own ability to figure things out in making your predictions.

READER'S NOTEBOOK "What Men Live By" has many strange events that are not explained until the end of the story. As you come across each event in your reading, write a question about it and then a brief **prediction** that might answer the question. Use a chart like this one to keep track of your predictions.

Question	Prediction
1. Who's the stranger that appears in section I?	1.

Question	Prediction
1. Who's the stranger that appears in section one?	1. He'll turn out to be someone who's the opposite of what he seems to be.

2 RECORD YOUR THOUGHTS

Write down ideas, responses, connections, and questions before you read, while you read, and after you read a selection. Summarize important passages, and collect any ideas that may later be a springboard to your own writing.

Working Portfolio

Artists and writers keep portfolios to store their works in progress or the works they are most proud of. Create your own **Working Portfolio**, using a folder, a box, or a notebook. As the year progresses, fill it with examples of your papers, your creative writing, your summaries of projects, and your own goals and accomplishments as a reader and writer.

Tasha Edwards
PORTFOLIO

Date	Project	Comments
10/6	Essay on Tolstoy's stories	Finished
11/19	Report on realism	Best paper I've written
12/8	Essay on "A Doll's House"	Need more supporting details

Strategies for Reading

Reading world literature presents special challenges and often requires more background than what you need to read literature from your own culture. However, once you begin reading, you apply the same reading strategies that you would for any piece of literature. Don't forget to **monitor** how well you're using these strategies during reading.

Predict Try to figure out what will happen next and how the selection might end. Then read on to see how accurate your guesses were.

Visualize Visualize characters, events, and setting to help you understand what's happening. Use the art to help you imagine faraway places. Pay attention to the images that form in your mind as you read.

Connect Connect personally with what you read. Think of similarities between the descriptions in the selection and what you have personally experienced, heard about, and read about. In spite of the obvious differences, you may find you have things in common with people from other times and cultures.

Question While you read, question what happens. Searching for reasons behind events and characters' feelings can help you feel closer to literature from another time and place.

Clarify Stop occasionally to review your understanding of what you read. You can do this by **summarizing** what you have read, identifying the **main idea**, and **making inferences**—drawing conclusions from the information you are given. As necessary, reread passages and background information. Also watch for answers to questions you had earlier.

Evaluate Form opinions about what you read, both while you're reading and after you've finished. Develop your own ideas about characters, events, time periods, and cultures.

On the following pages, you will see how one reader tackles a World Literature selection—how she uses background information and the Strategies for Reading above to understand literature from a different time and culture.

Build Background

The story you are about to read is a folk tale from 19th-century Japan. The main character is a samurai, a member of an elite class of professional soldiers. Known for their skill in battle, samurai lived by a strict code of honor. The code stressed the values of courage and loyalty to the regional lord, or *daimyo*.

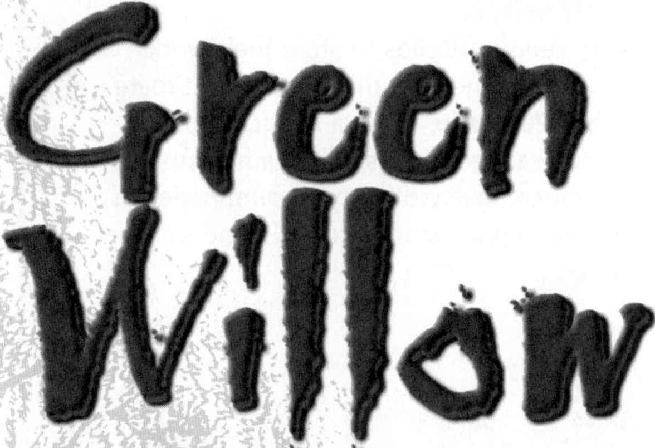

Japanese Folk Tale

Retold by Paul Jordan-Smith

8 STRATEGIES FOR READING

In the era of Bummei there lived a young samurai, Tomotada, in the service of the daimyo of Noto. He was a native of Echizen, but had been accepted at a young age into the palace of the Lord of Noto, where he proved himself a good soldier and a good scholar as well, and enjoyed the favor of his prince. Handsome and amiable, he was admired also by his fellow samurai.

One day, the Lord of Noto called for Tomotada and sent him on a special quest to the Lord of Kyoto. Being ordered to pass through Echizen, Tomotada asked and was granted permission to visit his widowed mother. And so he set out on his mission.

Winter had already come; the countryside was covered with snow, and though his horse was among the most powerful in the Lord of Noto's stable, the young man was forced to proceed slowly. On the second day of his journey, he found himself in mountain districts where settlements were few and far between. His anxiety was increased by the onslaught of a heavy snowstorm, and his horse was showing signs of extreme fatigue. In the very moment of his despair, however, Tomotada caught sight of a cottage among the willows on a nearby hill. Reaching the dwelling, he knocked loudly on the storm doors which had been closed against the wind. Presently the doors opened, and an old woman appeared, who cried out with compassion at the sight of the noble Tomotada, "Ah, how pitiful! Traveling in such weather, and alone! Come in, young sir, come in!"

"What a relief to find a welcome in these lonely passes," thought Tomotada, as he led his horse to a shed behind the cottage. After seeing that his horse was well sheltered and fed, Tomotada entered the cottage, where he beheld the old woman and her husband, and a young girl as well, warming themselves by a fire of bamboo splints. The old couple respectfully requested that he be seated, and proceeded to warm some rice wine and prepare food for the warrior. The young girl, in the meantime, disappeared behind a screen, but not before Tomotada had observed with astonishment that she was extremely beautiful, though dressed in the meanest attire. He wondered how such a beautiful creature could be living in such a lonely and humble place. His thoughts, however, were interrupted by the old man, who had begun to speak.

"Honored Sir," he began. "The next village is far from here and the road is unfit for travel. Unless your quest is of such importance that it cannot be delayed, I would advise you not to force yourself and your horse beyond your powers of endurance. Our hovel is perhaps unworthy of your presence, and we have no comforts to offer; nevertheless, please honor us by staying under this miserable roof."

Strategies in Action

Alongside this story are comments that high school student **Nicola Shorobura** made as she read the story for the first time. Her comments will give you a glimpse into the mind of a reader actively engaged in the process of reading. To get the most from this reading model, first read the story on you own and record your responses to it in your READER'S NOTEBOOK. Then read Nicola's comments below and respond to each of the prompts labeled "YOUR TURN."

Nicola: *This sets the mood really well and helps you picture what's happening.*
VISUALIZING/EVALUATING

Nicola: *I'm wondering who the old woman is. Maybe it'll say further on in the story.*
QUESTIONING

Nicola: *I bet that the girl will be a main character in this story.*
PREDICTING

Nicola: *He doesn't even know these people. They're being really nice to him and taking him in. They're apologizing for their place.*
EVALUATING

GREEN WILLOW 9

Tomotada was touched by the old man's words—and secretly, he was glad of the chance afforded him to see more of the young girl. Before long, a simple meal was set before him, and the girl herself came from behind the screen to serve the wine. She had changed her dress, and though her clothes were still of homespun, her long loose hair was neatly combed and smoothed. As she bent to fill his cup, Tomotada was amazed to see that she was even more beautiful than he had at first thought: she was the most beautiful creature he had ever seen. She moved with a grace that captivated him, and he could not take his eyes from her. The old man spoke apologetically, saying, "Please forgive the clumsy service of our daughter, Green Willow. She has been raised alone in these mountains and is only a poor, ignorant girl." But Tomotada protested that he considered himself lucky indeed to be served by so lovely a maiden. He saw that his admiring gaze made her blush, and he left his wine and food untasted before him. Suddenly struck by inspiration, he addressed her in a poem.

As I rode through the winter
I found a flower and thought,
"Here I shall spend the day."
But why does the blush of dawn appear
When the dark of night is still around us?

Without a moment's hesitation, the girl replied:

If my sleeve hides the faint color of dawn,
Perhaps when morning has truly come
My lord will remain.

➤ **YOUR TURN**
What details help you form a mental picture of the girl?
VISUALIZING

Nicola: Her reply kind of seems like she's asking him to stay on.
CLARIFYING

➤ **YOUR TURN**
Do you agree with Nicola?
CLARIFYING

Then Tomotada knew that the girl had accepted his admiration, and he was all the more taken by the art of her verse and the feelings it expressed. "Seize the luck that has brought you here!" he thought to himself, and he resolved to ask the old couple to give him the hand of their daughter in marriage.

Alas for the Lord of Noto's quest!

The old couple were astonished by the request of Tomotada, and they bowed themselves low in gratitude. After some moments of hesitation, the father spoke: "Honored master, you are a person of too high a degree for us to consider refusing the honor your request brings. Indeed our gratitude is immeasurable. But this daughter of ours is merely a country girl, of no breeding and manners, certainly not fit to become the wife of a noble samurai such as yourself. But since you find the girl to your liking, and have condescended to overlook her peasant origins, please accept her as a gift, a humble handmaid. Deign, O Lord, to regard her henceforth as yours, and act towards her as you will."

Nicola: In this culture, I guess the parents have control over the girl's future.
EVALUATING/QUESTIONING

10 STRATEGIES FOR READING

Now a samurai was not allowed to marry without the consent of his lord, and Tomotada could not expect permission until his quest was finished. When morning came, Tomotada resumed his journey, but his heart grew more apprehensive with every footfall of his horse. Green Willow rode behind her lord, saying not a word, and gradually the progress of the young man slowed to a halt. He could not tear his thoughts from the girl, and did not know whether he should bring her to Kyoto. He was afraid, moreover, that the Lord of Noto would not give him permission to marry a peasant girl, and afraid also that his daimyo might be likewise captivated by her beauty and take her for himself. And so he resolved to hide with her in the mountains, to settle there and become himself a simple farmer. Alas for the Lord of Noto's quest!

Nicola: *Why is the quest so important to him? He says he wants to marry the girl. Why not just do it? Maybe this has something to do with the samurai code of honor mentioned in* ***Build Background*** *at the beginning.*
QUESTIONING/CLARIFYING

Nicola: *It seems Tomotada doesn't have a lot of confidence in what he does. He's scared of what's going to happen because in this society, his lord has total control of his life.*
EVALUATING/CLARIFYING

Tsukiji at Akashi (1913), Kaburaki Kiyokata. Photo © Peter Harholdt/Corbis.

For five happy years, Tomotada and Green Willow dwelt together in the mountains, and not a day passed that did not bring them both joy and delight in each other and their life together. Forgotten was the time before Green Willow had come into his life. But one day, while talking with her husband about some household matter, Green Willow uttered a loud cry of pain, and became very white and still. "What is it, my wife?" cried Tomotada as he took her in his arms. "Forgive me, my lord, for crying out so rudely, but the pain was so sudden . . . My dear husband, hold me to you and listen—do not let me go! Our union has been filled with great joy, and I have known with you a happiness that cannot bear description. But now it is at an end: I must beg of you to accept it."

Nicola: *The kind of love he has for her reminds me of* Romeo and Juliet. *Their love is more important than anything else.*
CONNECTING

Nicola: *They brought each other joy and happiness. Why does it have to come to an end? Why is she ending it?*
QUESTIONING

GREEN WILLOW 11

Toba (Su Dongpo) (1820–1832), Katsushika Hokusai. Woodblock print, 516 mm × 227 mm. Honolulu (Hawaii) Academy of Arts, gift of James A. Michener, 1970 (15, 943).

12 STRATEGIES FOR READING

"Ah!" cried Tomotada, "It cannot be so. What wild fancies are these? You are only a little unwell, my darling. Lie down and rest, and the pain shall pass."

"No, my dearest, it cannot be. I am dying—I do not imagine it. It is needless to hide from you the truth any longer, my husband. I am not a human being. The soul of a tree is my soul, the heart of a tree my heart, the sap of a willow is my life. And some one, at this most cruel of moments, has cut down my tree—even now its branches have fallen to the ground. And this is why I must die! I have not even the strength left to weep, nor the time . . ."

With another cry of pain, Green Willow turned her head and tried to hide her face behind her sleeve. In the same moment, her form seemed to fold in upon itself, and before Tomotada's astonished and grief-stricken eyes, her robes crumpled in the air and fell empty to the ground.

Many years after this, an itinerant monk came through the mountain passes on his way to Echizen. He stopped for water beside a stream, on the banks of which stood the stumps of three willow trees—two old and one young. Nearby, a rude stone memorial had been set up, which showed evidence of regular care unusual in such a remote place. He inquired about it from an old priest who lived in the neighborhood and was told the story of Green Willow.

"And what of Tomotada?" asked the mendicant, when the priest had finished his tale. But the old man had fallen into a reverie and gazed at the shrine, oblivious of his guest.

"Alas for the Lord of Noto's quest!" the old man sighed to himself and fell silent. The air grew chill as the evening drew on. At length, the old priest shook himself from his dreams.

"Forgive me!" he told his guest. "As age creeps upon me, I sometimes find myself lost in the memories of a young samurai."

Nicola: *Is this really happening, or is she just comparing herself to a tree that's been cut down? Her name is Green Willow, so maybe this is for real. Folk tales sometimes have unusual things happen.*
Questioning/Clarifying

➤ YOUR TURN
What's your take on what has just happened?
Clarifying

Nicola: *Who is this monk? Why is he inquiring of the priest? What's the significance?*
Questioning

➤ YOUR TURN
Who do you think the old priest might be?
Predicting

Nicola: *By the process of elimination, I figure that the priest was the samurai. He must have set up the memorial. This ending is really good. It's kind of magical.*
Clarifying/Evaluating

GREEN WILLOW 13

Literature of the Ancient World
In Unit One, students will read literature from the ancient Middle East and ancient India. These works are among the world's oldest, most beloved, and most influential. Some of them, such as the Hebrew Bible and the Indian *Ramayana* epic, continue to shape modern cultures.

Part 1
Spiritual Beginnings: Mesopotamian, Egyptian, and Hebrew Literature This part will introduce students to writings from the oldest known civilizations: Mesopotamian and Egyptian. Excerpts from the *Epic of Gilgamesh* and the *Egyptian Book of the Dead* reveal the spiritual beliefs of these ancient cultures. The part also contains selections from the Hebrew Bible, one of the foundations of Western literature. A feature, **Comparing Literature Across Cultures,** allows students to compare biblical accounts of the Creation and the Flood with similar stories from the *Popol Vuh,* an ancient Mayan scripture.

Part 2
Sacred and Practical Teachings: Literature of Ancient India This part includes important Hindu scriptures: Aryan hymns from the *Rig Veda* and the later *Mahabharata* and *Ramayana* epics, which present religious ideals. The part also includes secular stories from the *Panchatantra*, a collection of folk tales arranged as a practical guide for living.

Literature of the Ancient World

3000 B.C.–A.D. 500

Nakht hunting with his family (18th Dynasty, 16th–14th centuries B.C.). From the tomb of Nakht, scribe and priest under Pharaoh Tuthmosis IV, in the cemetery of Sheikh Abd al-Qurnan, Luxor-Thebes, Egypt. Photograph copyright © Erich Lessing/Art Resource, New York.

UNIT ONE

"Man dies, his body is dust,
his family all brought low to the earth;
But writing shall make him remembered,
alive in the mouths of any who read."

—Papyrus Inscription
(c. 1300–1100 B.C.)

Making Connections

Ask: In what way might writing make a dead man, or a dead civilization, "alive in the mouths of any who read"?

Possible Response: Reading a burial inscription or the preserved words of a dead person conjures up his or her memory. Reading the literature of a past civilization, such as that of the ancient Egyptians, enables people to imagine its gods, rituals, and way of life—making it exist again in the reader's mind.

PART 1 SKILLS TRACE

Features and Selections	Literary Analysis	Reading and Critical Thinking	Writing Opportunities
Literature of the Ancient World 3000 B.C.–A.D. 500			
Spiritual Beginnings: Mesopotamian, Egyptian, and Hebrew Literature		Interpreting the Text, 17, 22 Using the Time Line, 26	
Learning the Language of Literature Foundations of Early Literature	Foundations of Early Literature, 30, 31	Strategies for Reading, 31	
EPIC POETRY *from* The Epic of Gilgamesh	The Quest Story, 33, 47 The Quest Story, 34, 38, 40	Cause and Effect, 33, 47 Cause and Effect, 34, 36, 38, 42 Cylinder Seals, 35 Views of Life After Death, 36–37 Treasures from the Royal Tombs of Ur, 38–39 Flood Stories, 41 The Fertile Crescent?, 42 Mythology, 46	Definition of Heroism, 48 Gilgamesh Adventure, 48
Connect to Today The Quest to Find *Gilgamesh*		Small Group or Whole Class Discussion, 49	
SCRIPTURE/POETRY *from the* Book of the Dead Adoration of the Disk New Kingdom Poetry I'm going downstream on Kingswater Canal Whenever I leave you, I go out of breath	Speaker, 51, 59 Speaker, 52, 54	Identifying Cultural Characteristics, 51, 59 Identifying Cultural Characteristics, 52, 56	Autobiographical Papyrus Scroll, 60 Praise Poem, 60
The Translator at Work Decoding Hieroglyphics			
Comparing Literature Across Cultures Creation Literature	Creation Literature Plot Structure, 62, 75, 86	Compare and Contrast, 62, 75, 86	Comparison-and-Contrast Essay, 62 Standardized Test Practice (Comparison-and-Contrast Essay), 62
SCRIPTURE *from* Genesis Creation and the Fall Noah and the Flood	Sacred Literature, 64, 74 Sacred Literature, 64, 68, 72	Reading Sacred Literature, 64, 74 Reading Sacred Literature, 68, 72 The Face of the Deep, 66 The World Tree, 68 Comparing Arks, 70	Guide-for-Living Comparison, 75
MYTH *from* Popol Vuh		The Mayan Calendar, 79	
Comparing Literature Standardized Test Practice			Comparison-and-Contrast Essay, 87 Standardized Test Practice (Responding to a Writing Prompt), 87

LEGEND **Black type – Pupil Edition**
Green type – Teacher's Edition
DLS – Daily Language SkillBuilder

Speaking and Listening Viewing and Representing	Inquiry and Research	Grammar, Usage, and Mechanics	Vocabulary
Using the Map, 16			
Gilgamesh Illustration, 48 City Plan, 48 Art Appreciation, 44 Small Group or Whole Class Discussion, 49	Report on a Lost Civilization, 48	DLS, 32 Diagnostic: Parts of Speech, 43 Concrete and Abstract Nouns, 45	Synonyms, 48 Context Clues, 34
Pyramid Cutaway, 60 Dramatic Monologue, 52 Art Appreciation, 53, 55, 56 Oral Interpretation, 58 Activity (design picture-signs), 61	Papyrus Demonstration, 60	DLS, 50 Common and Proper Nouns, 57	
Bible Storyboard, 75 Good vs. Evil Debate, 75 Reading the Map, 63 Art Appreciation, 65, 69, 72	Bible Report, 75 Genesis in the Arts, 75	DLS, 63 Plural and Possessive Nouns, 71 Action and Linking Verbs, 73	Multiple Meaning Words, 67
Art Appreciation, 77, 80, 83		DLS, 76 Auxiliary Verbs, 78 Pronoun Case, 82	Context Clues, 81

LEGEND **Black type – Pupil Edition**
Green type – Teacher's Edition
DLS – Daily Language SkillBuilder

UNIT ONE
PART 1 SKILLS TRACE

Features and Selections	Literary Analysis	Reading and Critical Thinking	Writing Opportunities
SCRIPTURE Psalm 23 Psalm 104 The Book of Ruth	Description, 88, 97 Description, 88, 90, 94	Visualizing, 88, 97 Visualizing, 88, 90, 94 Shepherds and Flocks, 89	
Reflect and Assess	Reflecting on the Literature (Being Human), 100 Reviewing Literary Concepts (Kinds of Heroes), 100		Building Your Portfolio, 100

UNIT ONE
PART 2 SKILLS TRACE

Features and Selections	Literary Analysis	Reading and Critical Thinking	Writing Opportunities
Sacred and Practical Teachings: Literature of Ancient India		Interpreting the Text, 105, 108–9 Using the Time Line, 110	
SCRIPTURE *from the* Rig Veda Creation Hymn Burial Hymn	Paradox, 114, 119 Paradox, 114	Making Inferences, 114, 119 Making Inferences, 116, 118	
Learning the Language of Literature The Development of the Epic	The Development of the Epic, 120, 121	Strategies for Reading, 121	
EPIC *from the* Mahabharata Arjuna, the Mighty Archer	Characterization in an Epic, 123, 126 Characterization in an Epic, 124	Seeing Contrasts, 123, 126 Seeing Contrasts, 124	Dramatic Monologue, 127 Remembering a Teacher, 127 Paragraph on Excellence, 127
EPIC *from the* Ramayana Rama and Ravana in Battle **Related Reading** *from* Arrow of the Blue-Skinned God: Retracing the Ramayana Through India **Connect to Today** Modern Views of Rama and Sita	Conflict in an Epic, 131, 143 Conflict in an Epic, 132, 134, 136, 138 Informal Assessment (Story Maps), 140–141	Classifying Characters, 131, 143 Classifying Characters, 134, 136 Rama and Indian Politics, 139 Group Discussion, 145	Comparison Essay, 144 Battle Lines, 144 Definition Essay, 144
Writing Workshop Autobiographical Incident Standardized Test Practice Building Vocabulary Sentence Crafting		Analyzing a Student Model, 151–152 Patterns of Organization, 151	Autobiographical Incident, 150, 153 Maintaining a Clear Focus, 154 Choosing an Incident, 153 Planning Your Autobiographical Incident, 153 Organizing the Draft, 153
Reflect and Assess	Reflecting on the Literature (Teaching Stories), 158 Reviewing Literary Concepts (Developing Characters), 158		Building Your Portfolio, 158

LEGEND **Black type – Pupil Edition**
Green type – Teacher's Edition
DLS – Daily Language SkillBuilder

Speaking and Listening Viewing and Representing	Inquiry and Research	Grammar, Usage, and Mechanics	Vocabulary
		DLS, 88 Adjectives and Adverbs, 94–95	Word Origins, 91
			Self Assessment, 100 Self Assessment, 100
Using the Map, 103			
Art Appreciation, 116, 118		DLS, 114	
Dramatic Reading, 127 Cover Illustration, 127 Art Appreciation, 125	More *Mahabharata,* 127	DLS, 122	Synonyms and Antonyms, 127 Multisyllabic Words, 124
Battle Scene, 144 Comic Book, 144 Art Appreciation, 133, 137, 142 Dramatic Reading, 135 Group Discussion, 145	The Epic Performed, 144	DLS, 130 Prepositions, 134 Interjections, 138	Context, 144 Root Words, 132
		Run-on Sentences, 154, 155 Capitalization, 155 Fragments, 155 Pronoun Cases, 155 Elements in a Series, 157 Pronoun Case, 154–155	Multiple Meanings, 156 Context Clues, 156 Dictionary, 156
			Self Assessment, 159 Self Assessment, 159

LEGEND **Black type – Pupil Edition**
Green type – Teacher's Edition
DLS – Daily Language SkillBuilder

UNIT ONE
RESOURCE MANAGEMENT GUIDE
PART 1

	Unit Resource Book	Assessment	Integrated Technology and Media	Additional Support
Spiritual Beginnings **Mesopotamian, Egyptian, and Hebrew Literature**			Humanities classzone.com	**World Art and Cultures Transparencies** • AT2 Upper Sumerian artifacts • AT3 The Great Sphinx • AT4 Egyptian tomb painting
from **The Epic of Gilgamesh** *pp. 32–49*	• Summary p. 4 • Active Reading p. 5 • Literary Analysis p. 6 • Words to Know p. 7 • Selection Quiz p. 8	• Selection Test, Formal Assessment pp. 7–8 • Teacher's Guide to Assessment and Portfolio Use Test Generator	Humanities Activity classzone.com Research Starter classzone.com	This selection is included in the *World Literature InterActive Reader™*.
from the **Book of the Dead** **Adoration of the Disk** **New Kingdom Poetry** **I'm going downstream on Kingswater Canal** **Whenever I leave you, I go out of breath** *pp. 50–61*	• Active Reading p. 9 • Literary Analysis p. 10	• Selection Test, Formal Assessment pp. 9–10 • Teacher's Guide to Assessment and Portfolio Use Test Generator	Humanities Activity classzone.com Research Starter classzone.com	
from **Genesis** **Creation and the Fall** **Noah and the Flood** *pp. 62–75* *from* **Popol Vuh** *pp. 76–87*	• Comparison Chart p. 11 • Summary p. 12 • Active Reading p. 13 • Literary Analysis p. 14 • Selection Quiz p. 15 • Summary p. 16 • Glossary p. 17 • Selection Quiz p. 18 • Compare/contrast Essay, p. 19	• Selection Test, Formal Assessment pp. 11–12 • Teacher's Guide to Assessment and Portfolio Use Test Generator	Research Starter classzone.com	
Psalm 23 **Psalm 104** **The Book of Ruth** *pp. 88–97*	• Summary p. 20 • Active Reading p. 21 • Literary Analysis p. 22 • Selection Quiz p. 23	• Selection Test, Formal Assessment pp. 13–14 • Teacher's Guide to Assessment and Portfolio Use Test Generator		
		Unit Assessment	***Unit Technology***	
		• Unit One, Part 1 Test, Formal Assessment pp. 15–16 Test Generator	classzone.com	

UNIT ONE
RESOURCE MANAGEMENT GUIDE
PART 2

	Unit Resource Book	Assessment	Integrated Technology and Media	Additional Support
Sacred and Practical Teachings **Literature of Ancient India**			Humanities classzone.com	**World Art and Cultures Transparencies** • AT6 Indian mother goddess • AT15 Subjugation of the Furious Elephant [detail]
from the **Rig Veda** **Creation Hymn** **Burial Hymn** *pp. 114–119*	• Active Reading p. 25 • Literary Analysis p. 26	• Selection Test, Formal Assessment pp. 17–18 • Teacher's Guide to Assessment and Portfolio Use Test Generator		
from the **Mahabharata** **Arjuna, the Mighty Archer** *pp. 122–127*	• Summary p. 27 • Active Reading p. 28 • Literary Analysis p. 29 • Words to Know p. 30 • Selection Quiz p. 31	• Selection Test, Formal Assessment pp. 19–20 • Teacher's Guide to Assessment and Portfolio Use Test Generator	Research Starter classzone.com	
Milestones in World Literature **Bhagavad-Gita** *pp. 128–129*			Milestone Links classzone.com	
from the **Ramayana** **Rama and Ravana in Battle** *pp. 130–145*	• Summary p. 32 • Active Reading p. 33 • Literary Analysis p. 34 • Words to Know p. 35 • Selection Quiz p. 36	• Selection Test, Formal Assessment pp. 21–22 • Teacher's Guide to Assessment and Portfolio Use Test Generator	Humanities Activity classzone.com Research Starter classzone.com	This selection is included in the *World Literature InterActive Reader™*.

Writing Workshop: Autobiographical Incident *pp. 150–157*		*Unit Assessment*	*Unit Technology*
Unit One Resource Book • Prewriting p. 37 • Drafting and Elaboration p. 38 • Peer Response Guide pp. 39–40 • Revising, Editing, and Proofreading p. 41 • Student Models pp. 42–47 • Rubric p. 48	Publishing Options classzone.com **Teacher's Guide to Assessment and Portfolio Use**	• Unit One, Part 2 Test, Formal Assessment pp. 23–24 Test Generator • Unit One, Integrated Assessment Test, Integrated Assessment pp. 1–6	classzone.com

UNIT ONE
DAILY LANGUAGE SKILLBUILDERS

Selection	SkillBuilder Sentences	Suggested Answers
from The Epic of Gilgamesh	**1.** scholars believe Gilgamesh was a real king who lives around 2700 B.C. **2.** According too legend, Gilgamesh were part god and part human.	**1.** **S**cholars believe Gilgamesh was a real king who live**d** around 2700 B.C. **2.** According **to** legend, Gilgamesh **was** part god and part human.
from the Book of the Dead Adoration of the Disk New Kingdom Poetry	**1.** The Egyptians believes in life after death, tara said. **2.** "Whose assigned to read the article on the pharaoh's asked ms. Edwards.	**1.** "The Egyptians believe**d** in life after death," **T**ara said. **2.** "**Who's** assigned to read the article on the **pharaohs?"** asked **M**s. Edwards. (Students should remove the apostrophe from *pharaohs.)*
from Genesis Creation and the Fall Noah and the Flood	**1.** Why where Adam and Eve cent away from Eden. **2.** Our Teacher explained that "Legends about a flood can be found in many different cultures."	**1.** Why **were** Adam and Eve **sent** away from Eden? **2.** Our **t**eacher explained that **l**egends about a flood can be found in many different cultures. (Students should remove the quotation marks before *legends* and after *cultures.*)
from Popol Vuh	**1.** According to mayan myth, it took several trys to make human beings. **2.** By around 1550, spanish explorers had conquer the mayan civilization.	**1.** According to **M**ayan myth, it took several tr**ies** to make human beings. **2.** By around 1550, **S**panish explorers had conquer**ed** the **M**ayan civilization.
Psalms 23, 104 The Book of Ruth	**1.** Psalms describes the relationship between God and people I really like Psalm 23. **2.** how much should a person depend on the kindness of others asked Michael?	**1.** Psalms describ**e** the relationship between God and people**.** I really like Psalm 23. **2.** **"H**ow much should a person depend on the kindness of others**?"** asked Michael**.**
from the Rig Veda Creation Hymn Burial Hymn	**1.** The Rig Veda mentions thirty three gods that the aryan people beleived in. **2.** "By reading this sacred text what did you learned about these ancient people," asked Maggie.	**1.** The **<u>Rig Veda</u>** mentions thirty**-**three gods that the **A**ryan people bel**ie**ved in. **2.** "By reading this sacred text**,** what did you lear**n** about these ancient people**?**" asked Maggie.
from the Mahabharata Arjuna, the Mighty Archer	**1.** Drona gave Arjuna a powerful weapon. To use against his enemys. **2.** I think the Mahabharata is the longest epic ever written? answered James.	**1.** Drona gave Arjuna a powerful weapon **t**o use against his enem**ies**. (Students should remove the period after *weapon.)* **2.** "I think the **<u>Mahabharata</u>** is the longest epic ever written**,"** answered James.
from the Ramayana Rama and Ravana in Battle	**1.** I like the Ramayana better then I thought I would Joe explained. **2.** Well, Lee replied, it was a good action story but I still like the Star Wars movies better.	**1.** "I like the **<u>Ramayana</u>** better th**a**n I thought I would," Joe explained. **2.** "Well," Lee replied, "it was a good action story, but I still like the **<u>Star Wars</u>** movies better."

INTEGRATING GRAMMAR AND LITERATURE: GRAMMAR PLANNER

Grammar Focus by Unit	Unit One	Unit Two	Unit Three	Unit Four	Unit Five	Unit Six	Unit Seven
	Parts of Speech	The Sentence and Its Parts	Using Verbs	Using Modifiers	Using Phrases	Clauses and Sentence Structure	Clauses and Sentence Structure

The Language of Literature offers several options for integrating grammar instruction and literature.

- Each unit has a grammar focus. The Teacher's Edition includes Mini Lessons for the selections that help develop the grammar focus for the unit and spring from the content of the specific literature.
- The Pupil Edition includes several full-page lessons on Sentence Crafting. These lessons are related to both the literature and the grammar focus for a unit and help students use proper grammar in their own writing.
- Daily Language SkillBuilders in the Teacher's Edition provide students with ongoing proofreading practice and reinforce correct punctuation, spelling, grammar and usage, and capitalization.

Black type — Pupil Edition
Green type — Teacher's Edition

Part 1

Parts of Speech

Diagnostic
from *The Epic of Gilgamesh,* p. 43

Concrete and Abstract Nouns
from *The Epic of Gilgamesh,* p. 45

Common and Proper Nouns
from the *Book of the Dead, Adoration of the Disk, New Kingdom Poetry,* p. 57

Plural and Possessive Nouns
"Creation and the Fall," "Noah and the Flood" from *Genesis,* p. 71

Action and Linking Verbs
"Creation and the Fall," "Noah and the Flood" from *Genesis,* p. 73

Auxiliary Verbs
from *Popol Vuh,* p. 78

Pronoun Case
from *Popol Vuh,* p. 82

Adjectives and Adverbs
Psalm 23, Psalm 104, The Book of Ruth, pp. 94–95

Part 2

Parts of Speech

Prepositions
"Rama and Ravana in Battle," from the *Ramayana,* p. 134

Interjections
"Rama and Ravana in Battle," from the *Ramayana,* p. 138

The Sentence and Its Parts

Run-on Sentences
Writing Workshop, p. 154
Standardized Test Practice, p. 155

Fragments
Standardized Test Practice, p. 155

Pronoun Usage

Pronoun Cases
Writing Workshop, pp. 154-155
Standardized Test Practice, p. 155

Capitalization

Capitalization Errors
Standardized Test Practice, p. 155

Punctuation

Elements in a Series
Sentence Crafting, p. 157

Unit One, Part 1, includes literature from three cultures of the ancient Middle East that occupied a region called the Fertile Crescent. Two of the cultures–the Mesopotamian and the Egyptian–are the oldest civilizations known. The third–the Hebrew–produced a body of literature that has been instrumental in shaping Western civilization. The three cultures have many things in common and, because they interacted over the centuries, their histories often intersect.

World Art and Cultures Transparencies

AT2 Upper Sumerian artifacts
AT3 The Great Sphinx
AT4 Egyptian tomb painting

You may use the listed transparencies to acquaint students with art from these early civilizations.

Pronunciations

Mesopotamia (mĕs′ə-pə-tā′mē-ə)
Canaan (kā′nən)
Tigris (tī′grĭs)
Euphrates (yo͞o-frā′tēz)
Giza (gē′zə)
Thebes (thēbz)
Sumerians (so͞o-mîr′ē-ənz)
Assyrians (ə-sîr′ē-ənz)
Nineveh (nĭn′ə-və)
ziggurat (zĭg′ə-răt′)
Ur (o͝or)
Uruk (o͞o′ro͝ok′)
Torah (tôr′ə)

PART 1 Spiritual Beginnings

Mesopotamian, Egyptian, and Hebrew Literature

Why It Matters
The ancient Middle East is often called the cradle of civilization. In prehistoric times, people gathered in the fertile river valleys of Mesopotamia, Canaan, and Egypt— the Fertile Crescent—to farm. From their interactions arose the basic elements of civilization: law, commerce, arts, religion, education, and literature. On this foundation were built many later cultures, including our own.

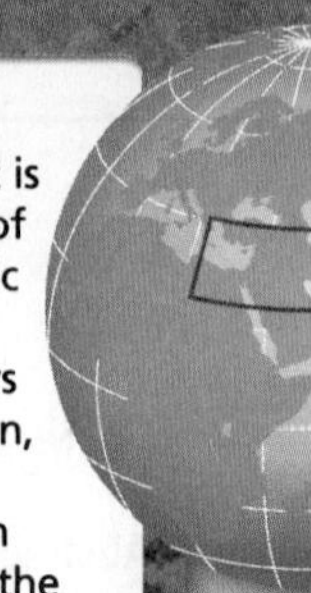

1 River Cultures The earliest civilizations in the arid Middle East grew up around rivers. Rivers provided water necessary for people, livestock, and agriculture. The **Nile, Tigris,** and **Euphrates Rivers** flooded each year, depositing silt that produced a rich topsoil good for planting. Rivers also provided an easy means of travel, promoting commerce and social interaction.

For Links to the Ancient Middle East, click on:
HUMANITIES CLASSZONE.COM

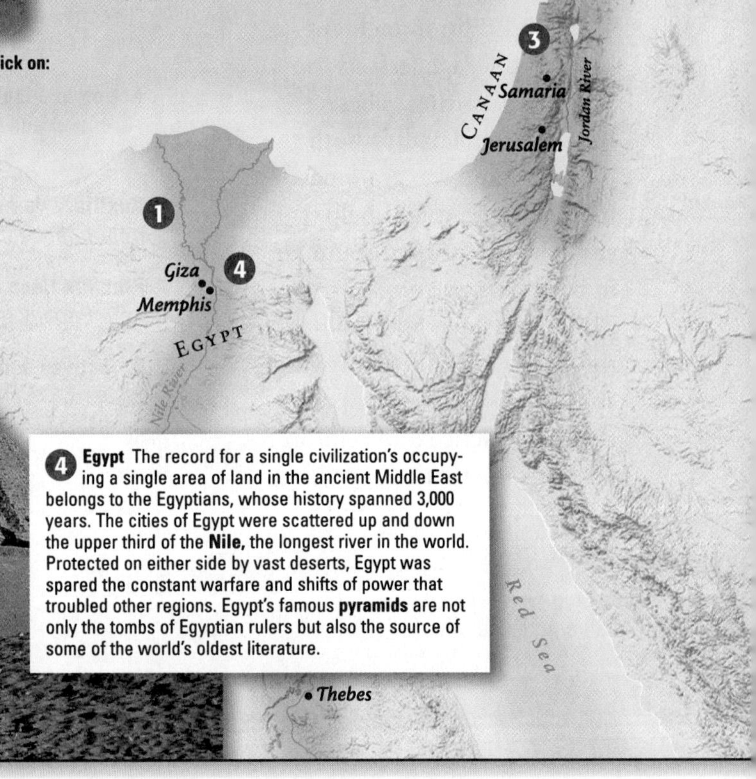

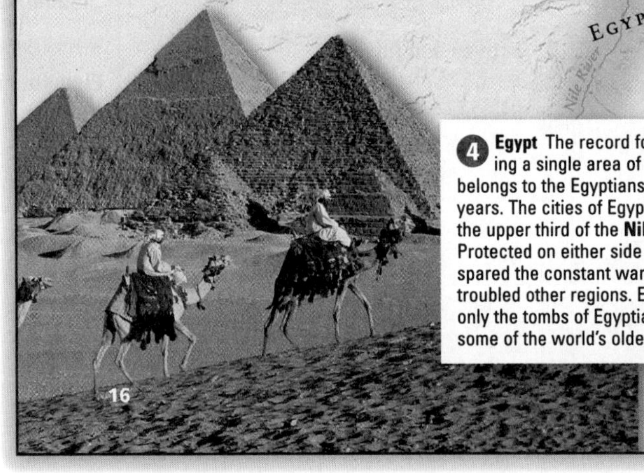

4 Egypt The record for a single civilization's occupying a single area of land in the ancient Middle East belongs to the Egyptians, whose history spanned 3,000 years. The cities of Egypt were scattered up and down the upper third of the **Nile,** the longest river in the world. Protected on either side by vast deserts, Egypt was spared the constant warfare and shifts of power that troubled other regions. Egypt's famous **pyramids** are not only the tombs of Egyptian rulers but also the source of some of the world's oldest literature.

16

MINI LESSON Using the Map

Have students read the information in the numbered boxes on pages 16–17 and answer the following questions:

- Why might the Jordan River have been less important to the Hebrews than the Nile to the Egyptians or the Tigris and Euphrates to the Mesopotamians? *(The Jordan is smaller; Canaan has a large body of open water nearby–the Mediterranean; Canaan is small and travel distances not so great as in the other two regions of the Middle East.)*
- How far apart did the Mesopotamian cities of Ur and Uruk lie? *(approximately 50 miles)*
- How many miles did the first Hebrews cover in their migration from Ur to Haran and then from Haran to Canaan? *(about a thousand miles)*
- Is the Egyptian city of Memphis closer to Thebes or to Jerusalem? *(Jerusalem)*

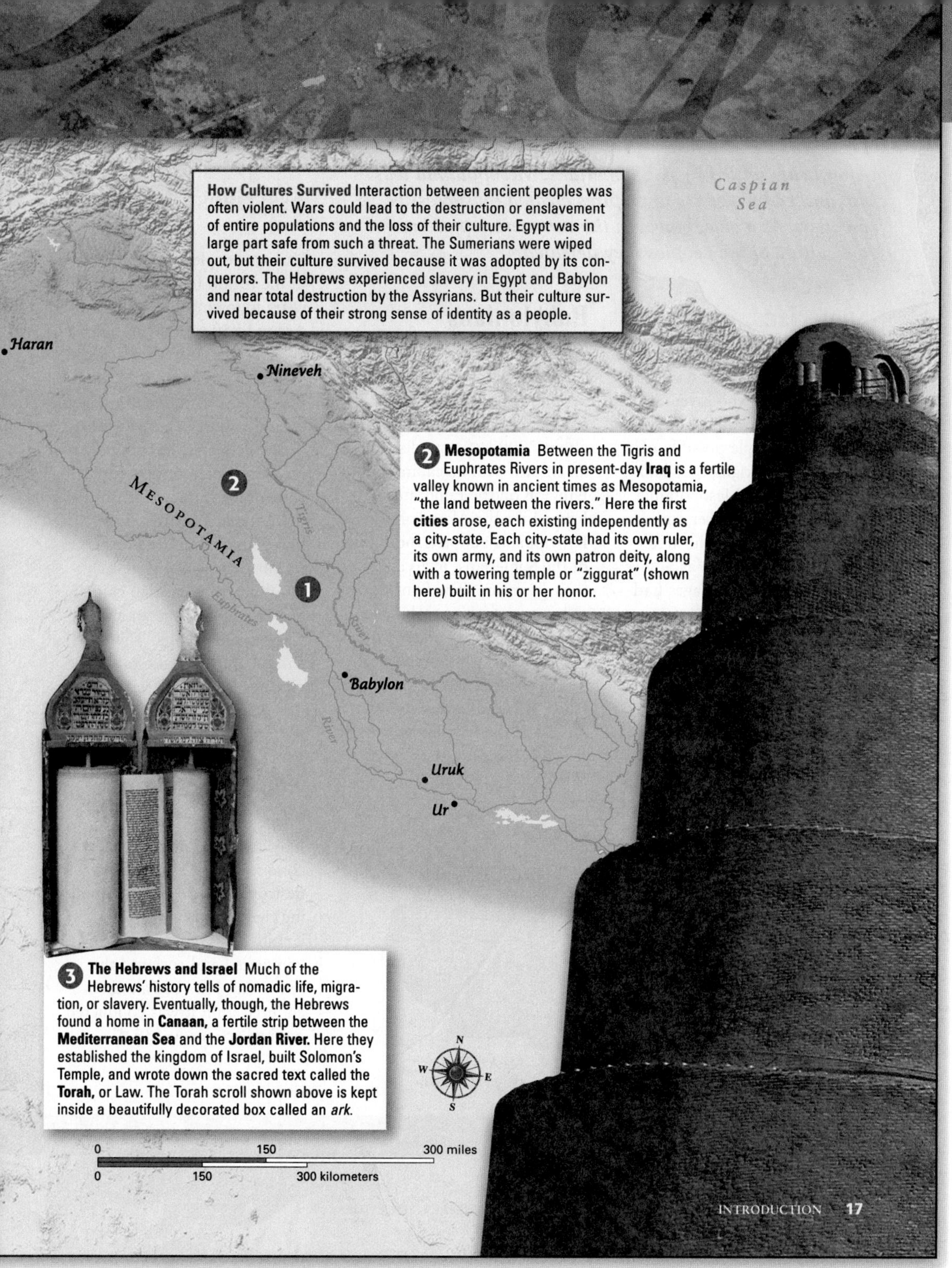

READING FOR INFORMATION
Reading Skills and Strategies
ANALYZING STRUCTURE

Explain to students that in the pages that follow they are going to read an essay on each of three cultures covered in this part of Unit One: Mesopotamian (pages 18–19), Egyptian (pages 20–21), and ancient Hebrew (pages 22–23). Have students scan the heads of all three essays and tell you what structure they have in common. *(Each is divided up into a historical section, a section on arts and culture, and a section on people and society.)*

MINI LESSON Interpreting the Text

After students have read pages 16 and 17, draw their attention to the text box **How Cultures Survived** at the top of page 17. Explain that each culture's way of existing in the region was radically different from that of the other two. The Egyptians were a single ethnic group in a single geographic area, the Mesopotamians different ethnic groups in a single area, and the Hebrews one ethnic group in a number of areas. Use a chart like the one shown to illustrate these differences. Suggest that, as students read the rest of this part introduction, they look for causes for these differences and ways the differences affected the cultures.

CULTURE	GEOGRAPHIC STABILITY	ETHNIC STABILITY
Egyptian	X	X
Mesopotamian	X	
Hebrew		X

READING FOR INFORMATION
Reading Skills and Strategies
PATTERN OF ORGANIZATION

Point out to students the introductory paragraph at the top of this page, which gives an overview of the historical section. Ask students to scan the heads on the page and tell you what pattern of organization is used in the subsections of the historical section. *(chronological order)*

Pronunciations

Sumer (so͞o′mər)
Semites (sĕm′īts′)
Sargon (sär′gŏn′)
Akkad (ăk′ăd′)
Akkadian (ə-kā′dē-ən)
Babylonians (băb′ə-lō′nē-ənz)
Hammurabi (hăm′ə-rä′bē)
Kassite (kăs′īt′)
Ashurbanipal (ä′sho͞or-bä′nə-päl′)
Chaldean (kăl-dē′ən)
shaduf (shä-do͞of′)
cuneiform (kyo͞o′nē-ə-fôrm′)

Mesopotamia: History, Arts, and Culture

After being settled by the Sumerians, Mesopotamia was dominated by a series of empires created by successive invaders. As a rule, however, the conquerors preserved the culture of the peoples they defeated.

Sumerians

c. 3500–2350 B.C.

Recorded history began with the Sumerians, who invented writing around 3000 B.C. A mysterious people possibly of central-Asian origin, they had settled southern Mesopotamia about 500 years earlier and taken up farming in the area, which became known as **Sumer.** By 3000 B.C. their villages had grown into large city-states, such as **Ur** and **Uruk.** Each had a different ruler and worshiped a different god or goddess.

Akkadians

c. 2350–2000 B.C.

Around 2350 B.C. a group of **Semites**—people who spoke a language related to Hebrew and Arabic—invaded Sumer from the north. Led by Sargon of Akkad, the **Akkadians** conquered the city-states of Sumer and unified them and the adjoining regions into the world's first empire. The Akkadians adopted much of Sumerian culture, including its religion and literature.

Babylonians

c. 2000–1570 B.C.

The Babylonians, a Semitic people who spoke Akkadian, conquered Mesopotamia in about 2000 B.C., establishing an empire with its capital of Babylon on the Euphrates River. Like the Akkadians, the Babylonians adopted the culture of the Sumerians, including their literature. The Babylonian empire reached its peak from 1792 to 1750 B.C. under **King Hammurabi,** who established one of the first sets of laws—the **Code of Hammurabi.** Around 1570 B.C. the Babylonian empire fell to Kassite invaders, who ruled for more than 400 years.

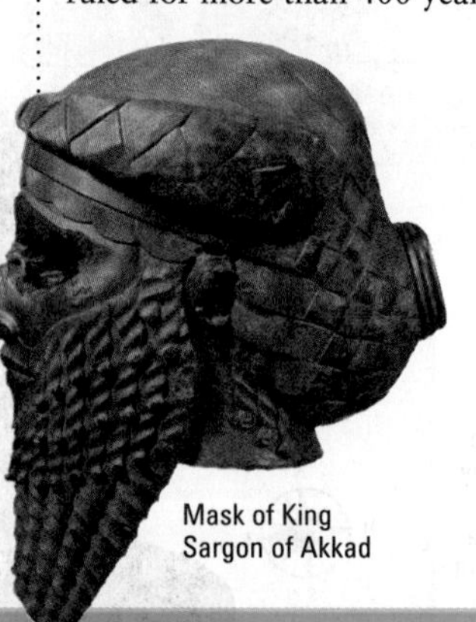
Mask of King Sargon of Akkad

Assyrians

c. 850–612 B.C.

Various peoples vied for control of the region for the next 300 years following Kassite rule. Around 850 B.C. one of these groups—the Assyrians, a warlike people from northern Mesopotamia—began to consolidate a great empire. They extended their rule from Mesopotamia to Egypt and present-day Turkey. Known for ruthlessness in battle, the Assyrians destroyed the kingdom of Israel and dispersed its inhabitants (see page 22). However, the Assyrian capital of **Nineveh** became an important learning center. There **King Ashurbanipal** established an early library, preserving many Sumerian and Babylonian writings.

Neo-Babylonians

c. 612–539 B.C.

In 612 B.C. Chaldean invaders conquered the Assyrians, destroying Nineveh and founding the second Babylonian empire. This empire, which conquered and enslaved the remaining Jews of Palestine, endured until it was conquered by the Persians in 539 B.C.

SUMERIANS

c. 3500 B.C.

Cities, Civilization, and Culture

The Development of Cities Mesopotamian agriculture had begun well before the Sumerians arrived in about 3500 B.C. However, it was their effort to control the flooding of the Tigris and Euphrates for regular irrigation that forced people to become more organized, encouraging the growth of cities. This led to the following developments:

Architecture Some ancient Mesopotamian cities had magnificent buildings and gardens. A towering ziggurat could be seen from miles away. Walls, city gates, and thoroughfares were often decorated with impressive relief carvings or mosaics.

Technology The *shaduf*—a long pole on a fulcrum with a bucket on one end and a weight on the other—made it possible to lift water above river level and create terraced or "hanging" gardens and even fountains. Other Mesopotamian inventions include the wheel, the sail, and the plow.

Law Established sets of laws like the Code of Hammurabi made justice more consistent and made it easier for large groups of people to live together in harmony.

Writing The Sumerians invented the world's first writing. Known as **cuneiform**, or "wedge-shaped" script, it was made by pressing the ends of reeds into clay, which was then hardened by baking. Writing was essential to the development of commerce, law, government, religion, and literature.

Math and Science Using arithmetic, geometry, and astronomy, the Mesopotamians developed a calendar to help with irrigation needs and even a "map of the world," shown at left.

People and Society

The Upper Class
In most Mesopotamian cities, the aristocracy, or upper class, included members of the ruling family, high-ranking government officials, military leaders, priests, large landowners, and some very wealthy merchants.

The Common Folk
Lower on the social scale were merchants and farmers; artisans skilled in crafts, such as toolmakers, stonemasons, and potters; and scribes, who kept records of religious events and trade or government transactions.

The Slaves
On the bottom rung of the social ladder, slaves performed society's lowliest tasks. Some slaves were foreigners conquered in war; others were locals sold into slavery by impoverished parents.

The Women
Sumerian women had far more opportunities than women in most other ancient civilizations. They could farm, take up crafts, become merchants, even join the priesthood. Some of the world's oldest surviving written poetry is a series of sacred hymns composed by a moon priestess named Enheduanna, daughter of King Sargon of Akkad. (A)

NEO-BABYLONIANS ▼

AKKADIANS	BABYLONIANS	ASSYRIANS	
c. 2350 B.C.	c. 2000 B.C.	c. 1570 B.C. c. 850 B.C.	539 B.C.

READING FOR INFORMATION
Reading Skills and Strategies
INTERPRETING IMAGES
Have students study the painting on this page. Ask them to identify the following items mentioned in the paragraphs under **Architecture** and **Technology:** a decorated building, a garden, a ziggurat, a city wall, a city gate, a thoroughfare, a hanging garden, a fountain, a sail. Then draw students' attention to the cuneiform writing at the top of the photograph of the clay tablet. Ask them how the symbols are formed. *(They are composed of different arrangements of a single wedge-shaped impression.)*

Historical Note
(A) **Enheduanna** Enheduanna (ĕn-hĕd′o͞o-ä′nə) can be thought of as the world's first author, because her writings are the earliest ones known to be connected with a particular person.

READING FOR INFORMATION
Reading Skills and Strategies
CLARIFYING

Students may assume that the three kingdoms refer to three different places or three different kings. After students have read the historical section on this page, ask for volunteers to explain the meaning of kingdom as it is used here. *(A "kingdom" is a period in Egyptian history during which the country was unified and ruled by a series of strong dynasties.)*

Reading Skills and Strategies
CONNECTING

Ask students how the history of Egypt is connected to the history of Mesopotamia as described on page 18. *(Egypt is invaded by the Assyrians in 671 B.C.)*

Pronunciations

Menes (mē′nēz)
Khafre (kăf′rā)
Amenemhet (äm′ən-ĕm-hĕt′)
Nubia (no͞o′bē-ə)
Hyksos (hĭk′sōs)
Thutmose (to͞ot-mō′sə)
Ramses (răm′sēz′)
Hittites (hĭt′ īts′)
Indo-European (ĭn′dō-yo͝or′ə-pē′ən)
Akhenaten (ä′kə-nät′n)
Aten (ät′n)
Nefertiti (nĕf′ər-tē′tē)
Tutankhamen (to͞ot′äng-kä′mən)
Ahhotep (ä-hō′tĕp′)
Hatshepsut (hăt-shĕp′so͞ot′)

Egypt: History, Arts, and Culture

Egyptian history is divided into three "kingdoms." Each consisted of several dynasties, or successions of rulers from the same family or line.

Old Kingdom

c. 2660–2180 B.C.

By 3200 B.C., farming villages along the upper and lower Nile had organized into two separate kingdoms, Upper Egypt and Lower Egypt. These were united in about 3100 B.C. by **King Menes,** who established the first dynasty. Little is known of the first two dynasties, but extensive records were kept in the third, which begins the Old Kingdom. During this time, powerful pharaohs built gigantic **pyramids** to serve as royal tombs. The Old Kingdom ended about 2180 B.C. Five weak dynasties followed in the first Intermediate Period.

Pharaoh Khafre (Fourth Dynasty), builder of the second of the great pyramids at Giza

Middle Kingdom

c. 2080–1640 B.C.

The Middle Kingdom began when a family of ruling nobles in Thebes emerged victorious in its struggles with the rulers of other cities, seized control of the entire kingdom, and established a powerful central government in Thebes. Amenemhet I, founder of the 12th dynasty, and his heirs strengthened the realm both politically and commercially, conquering the African kingdom of Nubia in the south and trading with Asian neighbors in the east. After the prosperity of the Middle Kingdom, weak rulers and internal strife allowed Semitic invaders called the **Hyksos** to conquer Egypt.

New Kingdom

c. 1570–1075 B.C.

The New Kingdom began when native Egyptian rulers banded together to drive out the dreaded Hyksos. Fighting with bronze weapons and two-wheeled chariots, New Kingdom pharaohs went on to make Egypt the world's strongest power. Thutmose III expanded his kingdom farther into Africa; Ramses II fought and later formed an alliance with the Hittites, an Indo-European people living in what today is Turkey. The weak rule of the 20th dynasty marks the end of the New Kingdom and the beginning of a long period of decline that culminated when Egypt was invaded and sacked by the Assyrians in 671 B.C.

History to Literature

EVENT IN HISTORY	EVENT IN LITERATURE
Ancient Egyptians believe in an afterlife.	Egyptian hymns, poems, and spells are collected in the *Book of the Dead.*
New-Kingdom pharaoh Akhenaten institutes exclusive worship of the sun god Aten.	Akhenaten and his wife, Nefertiti, compose the *Hymn to Aten,* or *Adoration of the Disk.*

OLD KINGDOM — MIDDLE KINGDOM

c. 2660 B.C. — c. 2180 B.C. — c. 2080 B.C.

Life and the Afterlife

The culture of the ancient Egyptians was dominated by a religious outlook focused on preparation for the afterlife. Much of their technology and craftsmanship went into this effort. The construction of the great pyramids utilized the Egyptians' skill in mathematics and engineering, and the art of mummification benefited from their advances in medicine. The Egyptians' vision of paradise was an idealized version of life on earth. For this reason, preparations for the afterlife became a focal point for Egyptian artistic creativity as well.

This multimedia work of art was found in a pyramid containing the tomb of King Tutankhamen. The image decorates the back of a throne included for the king's use in the afterlife. The scene depicts the queen anointing the king with perfume. Overlooking the couple is the sun god, one of the most important Egyptian deities, who blesses them with hands extended on rays of light. The Egyptians believed that pictures and words describing their hopes for the afterlife could help make those hopes come true.

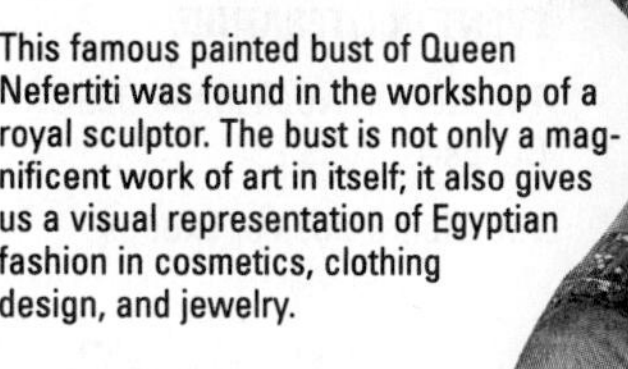

This famous painted bust of Queen Nefertiti was found in the workshop of a royal sculptor. The bust is not only a magnificent work of art in itself; it also gives us a visual representation of Egyptian fashion in cosmetics, clothing design, and jewelry.

People and Society

The Upper Class
In addition to the ruling family, who were considered divine, the upper class included wealthy landowners, government officials, high-ranking priests, and military leaders. Medicine was quite advanced, and most doctors were also in the upper class.

The Middle Class
This group included merchants, craftspeople, artisans, and other skilled workers. These people could sometimes move into the upper class through marriage.

The Lower Class
Farm laborers, who formed the bulk of the Egyptian lower class, also worked on building projects such as the pyramids. Even lower on the social scale were slaves. Though assigned heavy labor and lowly chores, slaves could marry, own property, and sometimes even buy their freedom.

The Women
Upper- and middle-class women had almost the same rights as men. They could own land, run businesses, and even propose marriage. Women in ruling families sometimes took the reins of power. Queen Ahhotep helped drive out the Hyksos, and a woman named Hatshepsut even reigned successfully as pharaoh. (A)

NEW KINGDOM

c. 1640 B.C. c. 1570 B.C. c. 1075 B.C.

Historical Note

(A) Hatshepsut When Hatshepsut's husband, the pharoah Thutmose II, died in about 1490 B.C., she was expected to act as regent for the pharaoh's young son, who was next in line for the throne. Instead, she declared herself pharoah and, since women could not be pharoahs, ruled as a man. She had herself sculpted with a masculine build and the artificial chin-beard worn by the king on ceremonial occasions and produced a document in which the god Amen (ä′ mən) endorsed her rule. Hatshepsut ruled efficiently for about twenty years, and her reign was distinguished as a time of peace, free trade, and the building of beautiful monuments.

Pronunciations
Nebuchadnezzar (nĕb′ə-kəd-nĕz′ər)
Cyrus (sī′rəs)

The Ancient Hebrews: History, Arts, and Culture

Hebrew civilization is associated more with a particular people than a geographical region. At different times, the Hebrews occupied nearly every part of the ancient Middle East and interacted with many of its other civilizations.

The Early Hebrews
c. 2000–1200 B.C.

The Semitic people known as the Hebrews or Jews trace their history to **Abraham,** a shepherd who lived in the Mesopotamian city of Ur in about 2000 B.C. According to the Bible, he and his family crossed over the Euphrates River (the word *Hebrew* means "cross over"), wandered along the Fertile Crescent to Egypt, and eventually settled in the land of Canaan. Abraham's son Isaac had a son named **Jacob,** also called **Israel,** whose twelve sons are the ancestors of the Twelve Tribes of Israel.

The Exodus
c. 1200–1020 B.C.

To escape famine, the Hebrews migrated once again to Egypt. There they multiplied over the centuries but were enslaved and forced into hard labor. Finally **Moses** brought them across the Sinai Desert back to Canaan. The Hebrews fought for two centuries to establish themselves and grew as a military power.

The Kingdom of Israel
c. 1020–922 B.C.

In about 1020 B.C. the Hebrews united under a king named **Saul** to form the nation called Israel. Saul was succeeded by his son-in-law, **David,** a popular king who established **Jerusalem** as Israel's capital; David was succeeded by his son **Solomon,** a powerful king who built the great Temple of Solomon in Jerusalem.

After Solomon's death, internal fighting divided the nation into two kingdoms—Israel in the north and Judah in the south.

The Divided Kingdom
c. 922–539 B.C.

Over the next 200 years, Israel and Judah sometimes fought each other and sometimes allied against outside enemies. The most powerful of these enemies were the Assyrians, to whom Israel fell in 722 B.C. About 150 years later, Judah fell to the Babylonian king Nebuchadnezzar II, who vanquished Jerusalem and destroyed the temple in 586 B.C. Most of the surviving Jews were exiled to Babylon, where they stayed until King Cyrus the Great of Persia conquered Babylonia in 539 B.C. and let the Jews return to Jerusalem and rebuild the Temple.

King Solomon, Anagni Cathedral, Italy/The Art Archive/Dagli Orti.

History to Literature

EVENT IN HISTORY	EVENT IN LITERATURE
A flood devastates the Middle East.	The story of Noah in the Bible's Book of Genesis
Moses leads the Hebrews out of captivity in Egypt.	The Bible's Book of Exodus

THE EARLY HEBREWS
c. 2000 B.C.

MINI LESSON Interpreting the Text

After students have read the historical overview on this page, ask them to identify connections between the history of the ancient Hebrews and that of the Mesopotamians and Egyptians. *(Abraham migrated from the Mesopotamian city of Ur about the time the Babylonians took Sumer from the Akkadians. The Hebrews migrated to Egypt during the New Kingdom period, became enslaved there, and were brought out of Egypt by Moses after the end of the New Kingdom. Israel was destroyed by the Assyrians. The Babylonians conquered Judah and took the Jewish people as slaves back to Mesopotamia.)*

The Center of Cultural Life

The Hebrews' change from nomads to city dwellers and citizens of a kingdom had a tremendous impact on their culture. Nomadic life does not encourage the creation of beautiful buildings or works of art or promote the development of technology. With their own land, the Hebrews had more opportunities for cultural expression.

The Temple A dramatic example of this expression is the construction of Solomon's Temple in Jerusalem. For many years the Hebrews carried their holiest relic, the tablets on which were inscribed the Ten Commandments, in a special chest with handles that was called the Ark of the Covenant. When the Temple was built, the tablets were permanently housed in its most sacred area, the "Holy of Holies."

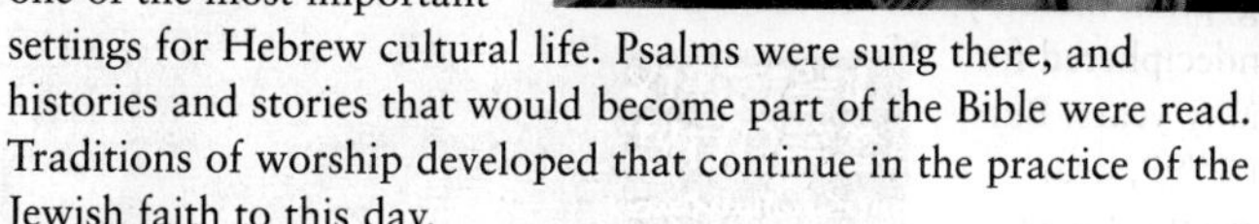

In addition to being a monumental work of architecture, the Temple provided one of the most important settings for Hebrew cultural life. Psalms were sung there, and histories and stories that would become part of the Bible were read. Traditions of worship developed that continue in the practice of the Jewish faith to this day.

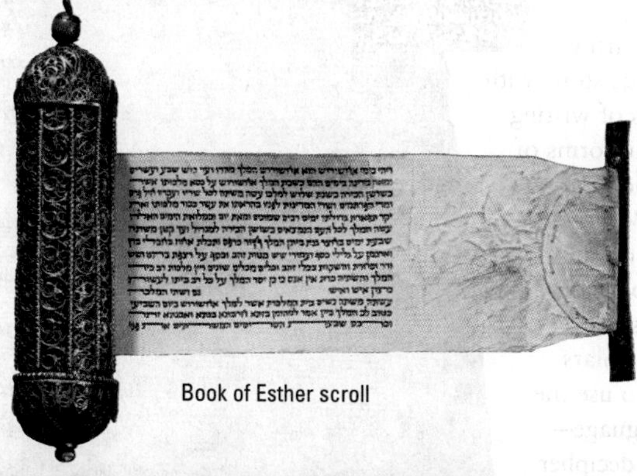

Book of Esther scroll

People and Society

The Most Powerful
The early Hebrews followed tribal patriarchs, or "fathers," similar to tribal chiefs; later, judges presided as important military leaders; still later, the Hebrews united under a king. In a society dominated by faith, however, prophets and priests wielded great influence, even over judges and kings.

In the Middle
Landowners and warriors formed something of a middle class, which merchants and artisans gradually joined with the growth of Hebrew cities.

The Least Powerful
Most Hebrews were simple herders and farmers or worked as servants or hired help. During periods of military conquest, the Hebrews also made slaves of conquered peoples, as was the custom of the day.

The Women
Like most cultures of the ancient Middle East, Jewish society was dominated by males, and. women had few rights and privileges outside the home. Nevertheless, they occasionally rose to positions of influence. For example, one of the most powerful military leaders was a female judge named Deborah.

THE EXODUS	THE KINGDOM OF ISRAEL	THE DIVIDED KINGDOM	
c. 1200 B.C.	c. 1020 B.C.	c. 922 B.C.	539 B.C.

READING FOR INFORMATION
Reading Skills and Strategies
MAKING INFERENCES
Ask students which categories of people mentioned in **People and Society** would be affected by the Hebrews' settling in Canaan. *(A king would have a land to rule over; people could own land and become landowners; merchants and artisans would have a place to set up shop and store their merchandise; women would have homes to manage.)*

Historical Note

The Temple After Cyrus freed the Jews from Babylonian captivity, his successor Darius I allowed them to return to Jerusalem and rebuild the Temple. Darius also returned sacred objects stolen from the Temple by the Babylonian king Nebuchadnezzar, but the Ark of the Covenant and the tablets of Moses were lost forever.

The second Temple still existed during the time of Jesus at the beginning of the first century A.D., and many incidents from his life narrated in the New Testament take place there. The second Temple was destroyed by the Roman general Titus in A.D. 70.

Part of the original Temple wall remains today and is one of the holiest sites of Judaism. At dusk on Friday, Jews gather at the site, known as the Wailing Wall, to welcome the sabbath with song and prayer.

Searching for the Past

READING FOR INFORMATION
Reading Skills and Strategies
SETTING A PURPOSE
Each of the six short essays on this page and the next describes a problem and explains how it was solved. Ask students to identify the problem or problems in each essay. Point out that not all of the problems were solved intentionally.

- How Writing Was Invented *(No one understood the purpose of the clay tokens or why tablets were rounded.)*
- Breaking the Code *(No one could read Egyptian hieroglyphics.)*
- A Library in the Sand *(The Gilgamesh epic was lost.)*
- King Tut's Tomb *(Most pyramids had been looted, so their contents could not be studied.)*
- The Dead Sea Scrolls *(Bible texts from the time of Jesus did not exist; the scrolls were not widely available for study.)*
- The Search Continues *(Only broken tablets had been found.)*

Here are some of the major breakthroughs in the quest to reconstruct the history of ancient Middle Eastern cultures.

Tokens representing different items of trade

Clay envelope showing both impressions made with tokens and drawn images

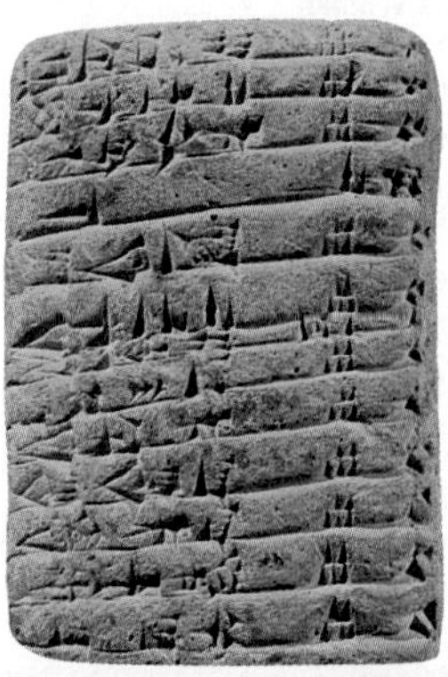
Rounded clay tablet showing the more advanced cuneiform script

How Writing Was Invented

For years mysterious clay tokens had been found in the Middle East, some of them from as early as 8000 B.C. Researchers also noticed another mystery: many cuneiform tablets were curved rather than flat. Then in the 1990s archaeologist Denise Schmandt-Besserat hypothesized that the small images were a very early form of writing. Sumerian merchants used the tokens to record shipments of goods. For every sheep or jar of oil loaded on a boat, a token would be sealed into a clay envelope. The recipient could break the envelope to make sure a shipment was complete. In time, people also made impressions with the tokens on the outside of the envelopes so that they could be "read" without being broken. Eventually, pictures drawn on the clay with a reed replaced tokens altogether. These pictures in turn evolved into cuneiform, and scribes continued to make tablets rounded like the outside of an envelope.

Breaking the Code

Egyptian hieroglyphics remained undeciphered for many years. But in 1799, near Rosetta, Egypt, soldiers in Napoleon's army found a large stone with three bands of writing on it: two in forms of hieroglyphics and one in Greek. Because the three texts on the **Rosetta Stone** contained the same message, scholars were able to use the known language—Greek—to decipher hieroglyphics.

The Rosetta Stone

A Library in the Sand

While serving as a British diplomat in the Middle East, Austen Henry Layard grew fascinated with the possibility of locating lost cities mentioned in the Bible. In 1849 he located the ruins of Nineveh, capital of ancient Assyria, and unearthed the once-magnificent library of Ashurbanipal, the seventh-century-B.C. Assyrian king. Housing some 25,000 broken clay tablets, the library was a virtual gold mine of early Mesopotamian literature, including the Gilgamesh epic, which had been lost for 24 centuries.

King Tut's Tomb

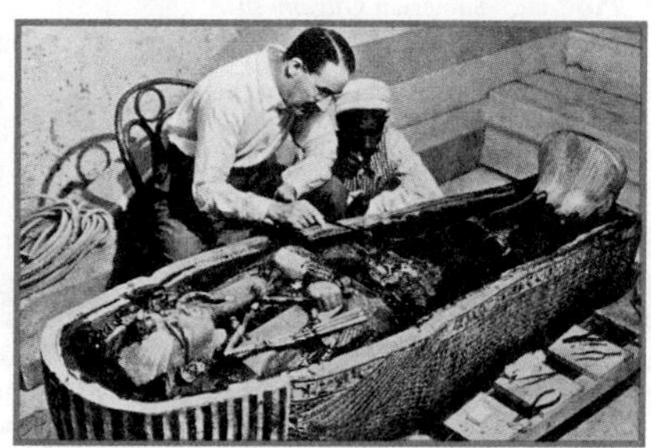

Although most Egyptian royal tombs were looted over the centuries, the tomb of the young king Tutankhamen survived with many of its riches intact. Its discovery by a British expedition in 1922 captured the world's imagination. In the burial chamber was a coffin of solid gold where the mummy of the young pharaoh rested, wearing a magnificent golden mask. Decorative hieroglyphic inscriptions identifying and honoring the dead king were meant to ease his way into the afterlife. In the treasury area was an array of valuables also aimed at making the king's afterlife comfortable—boats, thrones, golden goddess figurines, and even a chariot.

The Dead Sea Scrolls

In 1947 a young shepherd hunting for a lost goat in the desert near the Dead Sea came upon some caves that no one had entered for centuries. The caves contained earthenware jars that stored ancient scrolls carefully wrapped in linen to preserve them from the elements. Some of the scrolls turned out to be the oldest surviving texts of many sections of the Bible. Scholars date the scrolls to the time of Jesus. Most think the scrolls were likely the work of the Essenes, a Jewish sect living in the area at that time, possibly in contact with early Christians. To prevent damage, the Israeli government has allowed only a few experts to handle the scrolls, but their contents are now available for reading on the Internet.

The Search Continues

The library of King Ashurbanipal had been destroyed, and in its remains were found only broken tablets. However, in 1986 near Sippar, Iraq, an ancient library was discovered that contained unbroken tablets still on their shelves. The Gulf War and subsequent UN sanctions have prevented this find from being fully explored. But the library at Sippar may one day yield up literary treasures from the ancient world that we now can only imagine.

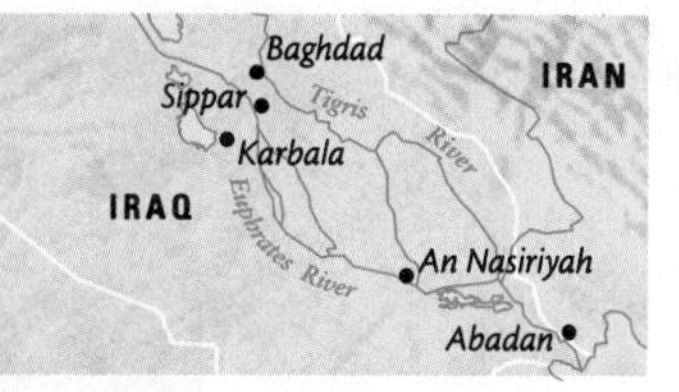

Pronunciations
Essenes (ĕs′ēnz′)
Sippar (sĭ-pär′)

INTRODUCTION 25

READING FOR INFORMATION
Reading Skills and Strategies
READING A TIME LINE
Make sure students understand that the time line is broken into three separate sections: **Events in Literature, Events in the Ancient Middle East,** and **Events in World History.** Read horizontally left to right, each section moves forward chronologically from 3000 B.C. to A.D. 1.

Pronunciations
Beaker (bē′kər)
Indus (ĭn′dəs)
Minoan (mĭ-nō′ən)
Huang He (hwäng′ hŭ′)
Shang (shäng)
Hellenistic (hĕl′ə-nĭs′tĭk)
Aryans (âr′ē-ənz)
Olmec (ŏl′mĕk)
Zhou (jō)
Aksum (äk′so͞om′)
Siddharta Gautama (sĭd-där′tə gô′tə-mə)
Nok (nŏk)
Zapotec (zä′pə-tĕk′)
Shi Huangdi (shĭ′ hwäng′dē′)
Augustus (ô-gŭs′təs)
Octavian (ŏk-tā′vē-ən)

Time Line

ANCIENT MIDDLE EAST (3000 B.C.–A.D. 70)

3000 B.C. | A.D. 1 | PRESENT

c. approximately
B.C. before Christ
A.D. after Christ

EVENTS IN LITERATURE

3000 B.C.	2500 B.C.	2000 B.C.
c. 2700 B.C. Earliest pyramid texts in Egypt	**c. 2500 B.C.** Earliest legends of Gilgamesh orally composed **c. 2275 B.C.** Enheduanna, priestess daughter of King Sargon, records some of the world's earliest surviving written poems **c. 2100 B.C.** Sumerian *Gilgamesh* epics begin to be composed **c. 2040 B.C.** Earliest versions of the Egyptian "Tale of the Shipwrecked Sailor"	**c. 2000 B.C.** First coffin texts in Egyptian tombs **c. 1700 B.C.** Old Babylonian version of *Gilgamesh* epic

EVENTS IN THE ANCIENT MIDDLE EAST

3000 B.C.	2500 B.C.	2000 B.C.
c. 3000 B.C. Sumerians develop cuneiform writing **c. 3000 B.C.** Egyptians begin using hieroglyphic writing **c. 2750 B.C.** Gilgamesh is king in Sumerian city-state of Uruk **c. 2556 B.C.** Great Pyramid of Giza is built during Egypt's Old Kingdom	**c. 2350 B.C.** Sargon of Akkad conquers and unites city-states of Sumer **c. 2180 B.C.** Egypt's Old Kingdom ends in an intermediate period of weak rulers **c. 2080 B.C.** Beginning of Egypt's Middle Kingdom (to c. 1600 B.C.)	**c. 2000 B.C.** Babylonians conquer Akkadians in Mesopotamia; Hebrews migrate to Canaan **c. 1790 B.C.** Babylonian King Hammurabi issues ➢ his code of laws **c. 1570 B.C.** Beginning of Egypt's New Kingdom (to c. 1075 B.C.) **c. 1550 B.C.** Hittites of present-day Turkey conquer Babylonians

Inscription of code

EVENTS IN WORLD HISTORY

3000 B.C.	2500 B.C.	2000 B.C.
c. 3000 B.C. New Stone Age in northern Europe **c. 2750 B.C.** Beaker People of Britain build Stonehenge ➢	**c. 2500 B.C.** First cities in India's Indus Valley	**c. 2000 B.C.** Late Bronze Age in Greece; Minoan civilization flourishes on Crete **c. 2000 B.C.** First cities emerge along China's Huang He River **c. 1600 B.C.** Mycenean culture flourishes on the Greek mainland **c. 1600 B.C.** Beginning of China's Shang Dynasty

MINI LESSON Using the Time Line

Have students answer the following questions based on the time line:

1. What was taking place in Britain at about the same time that Gilgamesh ruled as king in Uruk? *(The Beaker people were building Stonehenge.)*
2. How long after the Egyptians began using hieroglyphics did they create the earliest pyramid texts? *(about 300 years)*
3. What parts of the Bible would it have been possible for King Ashurbanipal to put in his library? *(the Torah and many of the Psalms)*
4. Could King Solomon have attended the first Olympic games? *(No; he died over 160 years earlier.)*
5. How many years elapsed between the earliest written versions of the Gilgamesh epic and the standard version? *(800 years)*

1500 B.C.	1000 B.C.	500 B.C.
c. 1500 B.C. Egyptian *Book of the Dead* assembled from earlier texts **c. 1375 B.C.** *Adoration of the Disk (Hymn to Aten)* composed **c. 1300 B.C.** Standard version of *Gilgamesh* written down **c. 1300 B.C.** Oldest New Kingdom love lyrics composed	**c. 1000 B.C.** Hebrew Torah assembled; many biblical psalms composed **c. 650 B.C.** *Gilgamesh* epic collected or copied for Ashurbanipal's library **c. 612 B.C.** Ashurbanipal's library buried; *Gilgamesh* epic lost for next 24 centuries **c. 600 B.C.** Bible's Book of Ruth	**c. 300 B.C.** Entire Hebrew Bible assembled **c. A.D. 100** New Testament Gospels completed

1500 B.C.	1000 B.C.	500 B.C.
c. 1472 B.C. Hatshepsut is female pharaoh of Egypt **c. 1365 B.C.** Amenhotep IV (Akhenaten) briefly establishes a monotheistic religion in Egypt **c. 1350 B.C.** Tutankhamen (King Tut) succeeds Akhenaten as pharaoh **c. 1205 B.C.** Moses leads Hebrew people from captivity in Egypt **c. 1020 B.C.** Hebrews establish kingdom of Israel, with Saul as first king	**922 B.C.** Death of King Solomon; Hebrew kingdom divided into Israel and Judah **650 B.C.** Assyrian Empire at its peak **586 B.C.** Nebuchadnezzar II captures Jerusalem; Hebrews' Babylonian captivity begins **539 B.C.** Persia's Cyrus the Great conquers the Babylonians and ends Babylonian captivity	**c. 332–331 B.C.** Alexander the Great conquers Egypt and Persia and brings the Hebrews under Hellenistic (Greek) control **63 B.C.** Romans gain control of Judah, which they call Judea **c. A.D. 29** Crucifixion of Jesus **c. A.D. 70** Fall of Jerusalem; Jews dispersed in the Diaspora

1500 B.C.	1000 B.C.	500 B.C.
c. 1500 B.C. Aryans, Indo-European speakers of central Asia, invade India **c. 1200 B.C.** Olmec civilization flourishes on Mexico's Gulf Coast **c. 1050 B.C.** City of Troy defeated by ancient Greeks **c. 1050 B.C.** The Chou overthrow China's Shang Dynasty and establish their own	**c. 1000 B.C.** Kingdom of Aksum is established in East Africa **776 B.C.** First recorded Greek Olympic Games **c. 563 B.C.** Birth of Siddhartha Gautama, founder of Buddhism **551 B.C.** Birth of Chinese philosopher Confucius	**c. 500 B.C.** Nok culture develops iron-making technology in West Africa **c. 500 B.C.** Zapotec civilization at its height in Mexico **c. 204 B.C.** Emperor Shi Huangdi completes first Great Wall of China **27 B.C.** Augustus (Octavian) becomes emperor of Rome

INTRODUCTION 27

Connect to Today: The Legacy of the Ancient Middle East

Modern Hebrew
Over the centuries, Jews continued to study the Hebrew language and use it in worship. When the modern state of Israel was proclaimed in 1948, a modernized form of Hebrew became one of its official everyday languages.

Law
The Code of Hammurabi and the Mosaic Code of the Torah are the ancestors of all Western laws. The Ten Commandments— the most important laws of the Torah—remain basic to both Jewish and Christian moral teachings.

28

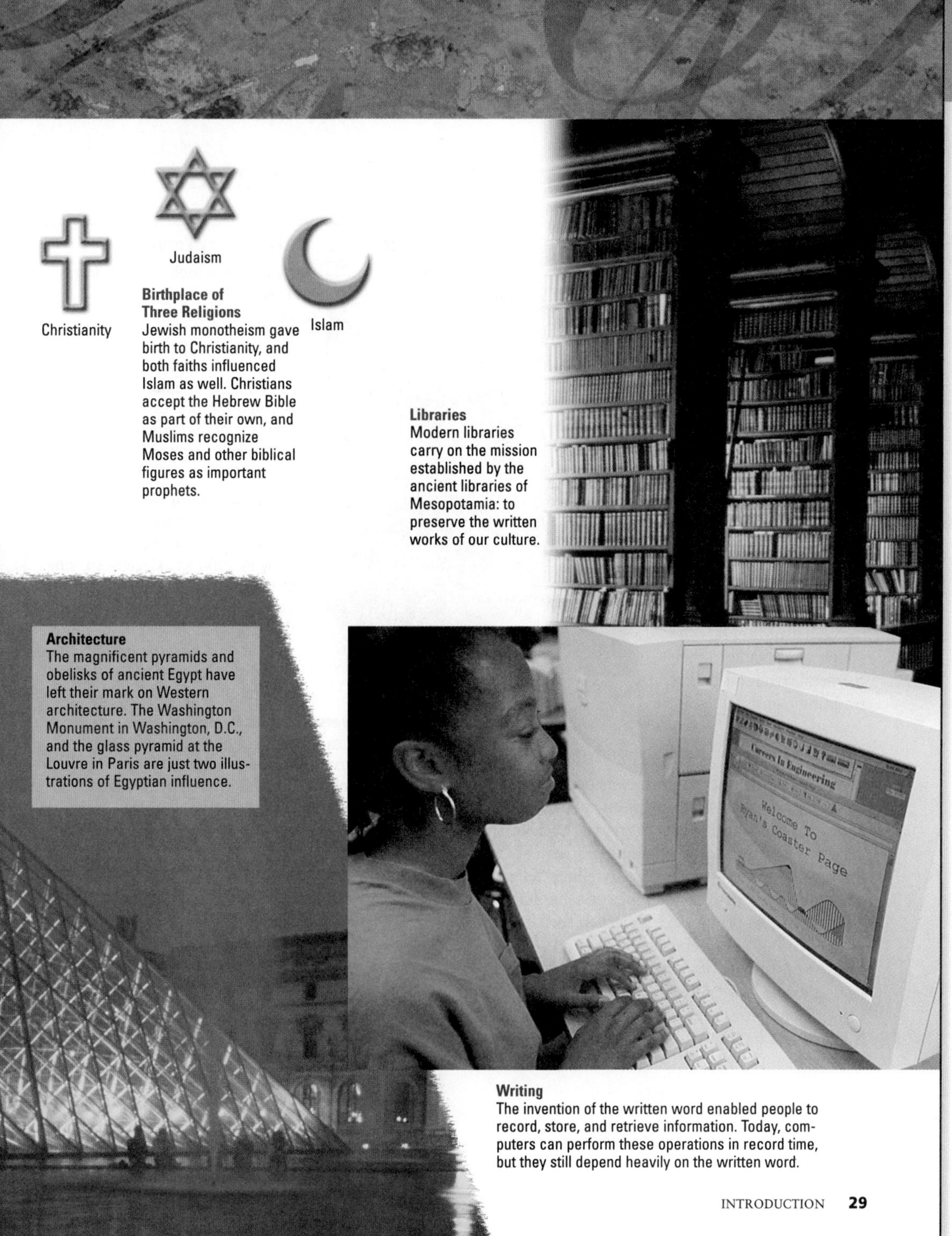

Christianity

Judaism

Islam

Birthplace of Three Religions
Jewish monotheism gave birth to Christianity, and both faiths influenced Islam as well. Christians accept the Hebrew Bible as part of their own, and Muslims recognize Moses and other biblical figures as important prophets.

Libraries
Modern libraries carry on the mission established by the ancient libraries of Mesopotamia: to preserve the written works of our culture.

Architecture
The magnificent pyramids and obelisks of ancient Egypt have left their mark on Western architecture. The Washington Monument in Washington, D.C., and the glass pyramid at the Louvre in Paris are just two illustrations of Egyptian influence.

Writing
The invention of the written word enabled people to record, store, and retrieve information. Today, computers can perform these operations in record time, but they still depend heavily on the written word.

READING FOR INFORMATION

Reading Skills and Strategies

MAKING INFERENCES

Remind students that the medium used in writing has played a critical role in the survival of ancient texts. Ask students what the advantages and disadvantages might be of using electronic media to store text digitally.

Possible Responses: (Advantages) It's easy to make many copies of a digitalized text; electronic files can easily be sent to other locations to be stored; since they don't exist only on paper, digital texts are less likely to be destroyed by fire or decay. (Disadvantages) Texts that don't exist in hard-copy form can easily be lost; it only takes a push of a button to destroy an electronic file; electronic documents cannot be accessed without the right equipment, which can be expensive or break down and which might not even exist in the distant future.

Objectives
- understand the following literary terms:
  - myth
  - heroic literature
  - sacred verse
  - wisdom literature
  - folk tales
  - archetype
- understand the important function of literature in early societies
- recognize types of early literature across cultures

Why It Matters
Have students discuss the following questions:
- What kinds of literature probably existed in early societies?
- What purposes would these kinds of literature serve?
- What similar literary forms exist in our own culture?

From Oral to Written Literature
Ask students to think of examples of literary forms in use today that exist primarily in the form of writing and examples of those that usually exist in other forms.
Possible Responses: (Writing) Novels, stories, poems, nonfiction of all kinds, bumper stickers, T-shirts. (Other) Songs, plays, movies, prayers, religious rituals, testimonials, jokes.

Early Literary Forms
As you go through the descriptions of early literary forms listed in the box on this page, have students suggest examples from their own experience.

Foundations of Early Literature

Why It Matters

To explain the world's mysteries, to sing praise and express one's faith, to impart wisdom, to record great deeds and landmark events—these are some of the universal human needs and desires that gave rise to early literature. It is hard for us today to understand the importance of literature in early societies. We tend to think of literature as something far removed from real life. Yet in early societies, literature was at the center of life. It connected people to their cultures' strongest beliefs, traditions, and values.

Detail from *Moses Receiving the Ten Commandments* (15th century), Raphael

From Oral to Written Literature

The world's earliest literature was oral, passed along by word of mouth from one person to another and from one generation to the next. This literature was always connected with some important activity—singing, storytelling, religious or social ritual, prayer, teaching, or even magic. As civilizations progressed, however, they began to use writing to preserve their literature. This had the advantage of giving works a stable and lasting form. But it often separated the works from the activities they were related to, so that it is harder for us today to fully appreciate their importance.

Early Literary Forms

Early literature took different forms to serve different purposes:

- **Myths** are traditional stories—often about gods and goddesses—that serve to explain natural phenomena, the human situation, or the origin of a belief or ritual. *The Epic of Gilgamesh* incorporates several Sumerian myths into its plot.
- **Heroic literature** records and celebrates the great deeds of heroes and heroines. Probably as early as 2500 B.C., Gilgamesh, king of Uruk, was celebrated in Sumerian oral **legends.** In time, these evolved into an **epic,** a long poem celebrating the exploits of this important hero in Sumerian culture.
- **Sacred verse,** such as **hymns, prayers,** and **psalms,** expresses religious faith and is usually written to be chanted or sung. Some of the world's oldest surviving written poems are hymns praising Sumerian gods and goddesses. The Egyptian *Book of the Dead* contains hymns to the god Osiris.
- **Wisdom literature** instructs or advises human beings about wise and moral behavior. Sometimes it takes the form of memorable sayings, like the **proverbs** of the Bible. At other times, brief stories are used to illustrate moral messages, as in the New Testament **parables.**
- **Folk tales** focus on ordinary people having extraordinary experiences. Often they feature magic, exaggeration, and humor. Ancient Egypt produced one of the world's oldest folk tales about a shipwrecked sailor. The tale probably inspired the famous tales of Sindbad that appear in *The Thousand and One Nights.*

Literature Across Time and Cultures

The literature of every culture reflects the culture's distinctive qualities. Yet when we look at many works from different cultures over the ages, we find some startling similarities. Certain types of situations, characters, and images seem to occur again and again, even in works from cultures having no knowledge of one another.

For example, *The Epic of Gilgamesh* and the Book of Genesis both tell of a great flood that nearly destroyed humanity. The *Popol Vuh,* which could not have been influenced by either of the other two works, tells of a similar event. Another recurring story element is a **quest,** a journey to find a treasure, achieve a goal, or undergo a personal transformation. Many ancient works of literature are quest stories, including *The Epic of Gilgamesh,* the *Iliad,* the *Odyssey,* the *Aeneid,* and the biblical stories of Abraham and Moses.

Archetypes

Common elements such as situations, characters, or images that appear again and again in literature and art are called **archetypes.** Scholars sometimes explain archetypes in terms of psychology. Stories about quests, for example, may be common because a quest is a good analogy for life. A journey to the underworld or to the bottom of the sea can stand for a person's exploration of hidden parts of his or her psyche. Archetypes reflect universal characteristics of human experience. They apply to all people, regardless of time or culture.

YOUR TURN Can you think of recent books or movies that tell stories about quests?

Armand Assante in TV production of the *Odyssey*

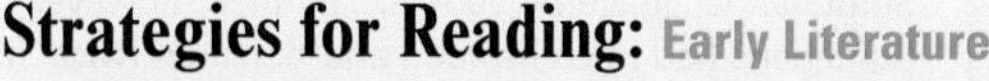

Strategies for Reading: Early Literature

1. Before reading, learn as much as you can about the culture and time from which the work comes.
2. Notice what the literary form of the work is—for example, myth, heroic literature, or sacred verse. Think about the purposes of the form, and look for ways in which the work fulfills them.
3. If the work is lengthy, use a list or diagram to help keep track of characters and major events.
4. If a passage confuses you, go back and summarize its main idea.
5. If the work is a short one, such as a song or a prayer, read it through once without stopping, then read it again carefully line by line.
6. When reading *The Epic of Gilgamesh* (page 32) and the *Popol Vuh* (page 76), use the accompanying Guides for Reading to help clarify meaning.
7. Monitor your reading strategies, and modify them when your understanding breaks down. Remember to use the strategies for active reading: **predict, visualize, connect, question, clarify,** and **evaluate.**

Literature Across Time and Cultures

Tell students that in studying world literature they will be simultaneously learning about how other cultures are different and about what they have in common.

Archetypes

Tell students that archetypes (är′kĭ-tīps′) are found not only in literature, but also in visual arts, dreams, religious and other symbols, architecture, and even advertising.

YOUR TURN To help students think of examples of quest stories, tell them that in our time quest stories often take place in outer space, in the form of road trips across the United States, or in the form of a metaphorical journey of the mind or the heart. Included in the latter category are many stories about growing up or coming of age.

Strategies for Reading

Make sure students understand that these strategies for reading are resources that they can turn to for help, not rules they have to follow. Assure students that they will be able to read, understand, and enjoy the early works of literature in this part of the book.

This selection is included in the **World Literature InterActive Reader™.**

Objectives

- appreciate one of the world's oldest great **epics (Literary Analysis)**
- learn about the **quest story** and **quest hero (Literary Analysis)**
- analyze **cause-and-effect** relationships in a text **(Active Reading)**

Summary

This selection begins with the story of a dream told to Gilgamesh by his friend Enkidu. After Enkidu dreams about death, he sickens and dies. Gilgamesh, grieving for his friend and afraid of his own mortality, begins a quest to find Utnapishtim. Because Utnapishtim is immortal, Gilgamesh hopes to learn from him the secret of eternal life. On his quest Gilgamesh encounters several figures who test him before he can proceed: lions, scorpion people, the god Shamash, the goddess Siduri, and Urshanabi the ferryman. Urshanabi brings Gilgamesh to Utnapishtim, who tells how he survived a great flood and became immortal. Utnapishtim then tests Gilgamesh to see if he is worthy of immortality. Gilgamesh must remain awake for a week, but he falls asleep and fails the test. Utnapishtim then sends Gilgamesh home with a consolation prize—knowledge of where to find a magic plant that makes the old young again. Gilgamesh finds the plant, but loses it when it is stolen by a serpent. Gilgamesh then returns with Urshanabi to Uruk.

Use **Unit One Resource Book,** p. 4, for additional support.

Thematic Link

The **spiritual beginnings** of literature are nowhere clearer than in *The Epic of Gilgamesh.* When Gilgamesh learns about death and the afterlife, he journeys to the realm of the gods to get answers about his destiny.

Use **Unit One Resource Book,** p. 7, for practice with Words to Know.

5-Minute Warm-Up

Daily Language SkillBuilder

Have students **proofread** the display sentences on page 15g and write them correctly.

PREPARING to *Read*

Build Background

What Is The Epic of Gilgamesh?

The Epic of Gilgamesh is one of the oldest works of literature in existence. The earliest versions of the story date back over 4,000 years to a time more than 1,000 years before the *Iliad* and the *Odyssey* or the first books of the Bible. Yet the story is one that modern readers can understand and enjoy because it deals with concerns that still matter to people today: friendship, heroism, mortality, and the desire to control one's destiny.

Gilgamesh is two parts god and one part human. In the first half of the story, Gilgamesh explores his godlike side. Using superhuman powers, he performs amazing feats and even defies the gods. But along with his extraordinary abilities come extraordinary flaws. Gilgamesh is arrogant, boastful, selfish, and destructive; he represents both the best and the worst that a person can be.

In the second half of the story, Gilgamesh explores the human side of his character as he faces unexpected limitations of his power. These limitations not only show his human weaknesses; they also give him the opportunity to develop human strengths. This part of the epic also contains a flood story remarkably like the one in the Bible.

How the Epic Evolved *The Epic of Gilgamesh,* like most epics, is based to some degree on fact. Scholars believe that Gilgamesh was a Sumerian king who ruled over the city-state of Uruk around 2700 B.C. In the centuries following his death, stories about him circulated orally and tales of his adventures grew. Through this oral tradition of storytelling, Gilgamesh developed over time into a figure of legendary proportions.

The evolution of this oral tradition into the written epic that we have today was the work of nearly 1,000 years. Written stories about Gilgamesh existed in the Sumerian language by 2000 B.C. By then, however, the Sumerians had been invaded and defeated twice, first by the Akkadians and then by the Babylonians. The Babylonians put an end to Sumerian civilization. However, they valued the culture of the Sumerians and integrated it into their own. Using the older culture's cuneiform script, the Babylonians preserved and translated the Gilgamesh texts and continued to develop them. The "standard" version of the epic that we have today was put together and written down by a Babylonian scribe around 1300 B.C.

For a humanities activity, click on:

LESSON RESOURCES

UNIT ONE RESOURCE BOOK, pp. 4–8

ASSESSMENT RESOURCES
Formal Assessment, pp. 7–8
Teacher's Guide to Assessment and Portfolio Use
Test Generator

INTEGRATED TECHNOLOGY
Visit our Web site: classzone.com

ADDITIONAL RESOURCES
Lesson Planning Guide, pp. 1–2
Teacher's Sourcebook for Language Development

How the Epic Survived The Assyrian King Ashurbanipal (668–627 B.C.) set out to compile a world's first great library at his capital city of Nineveh. He sent representatives all over the ancient Middle East to collect, copy, and translate famous texts. Among these were at least 35 copies of *The Epic of Gilgamesh.* However, when the Assyrian Empire fell to its enemies in 612 B.C., Nineveh was leveled. The library was destroyed, and *The Epic of Gilgamesh* lost.

Nearly 2,500 years later, in 1849, a young archaeologist named Austen Henry Layard unearthed the remains of the buried library. What he found was more than 25,000 broken tablets. It was not until the mid-1850s that scholars Henry Rawlinson and George Smith deciphered the cuneiform script found on the broken tablets. Years later, Smith announced a remarkable discovery: among the newly excavated writings was a story of a great flood like the one described in the Bible, but much older. What Smith had discovered was part of *The Epic of Gilgamesh.*

To date, none of the 11 Gilgamesh tablets have been completely restored, but by comparing fragments of different copies, scholars have been able to fill in many gaps in the text. Much of the epic is still missing, however. Translators must use their imaginations, their literary skills, and their knowledge of cuneiform to bring this masterpiece to the modern reader.

Archaeological excavation in progress at the site of the ancient city of Ebla in Syria. Cuneiform tablets found at this site reveal a civilization that flourished in the third millennium B.C. To date, more than half a million tablets have been found in the Middle East.

Connect to Your Life

In this story the main character experiences a loss that he finds hard to accept. Think of some disappointments or defeats that you or people you know have experienced; for example, moving away from friends to a new town, or breaking up with a boyfriend or girlfriend. In each case, how easy was it to accept the situation?

Focus Your Reading

LITERARY ANALYSIS: THE QUEST STORY

The Epic of Gilgamesh may be the oldest quest story in existence. On page 31, you learned that a **quest story** is a kind of story that is common to many cultures. In a quest story, a hero goes on a journey and tries to achieve a goal, such as bringing back a valuable object or acquiring knowledge. Usually, a **quest hero** has special powers or special friends that help (or hinder) him or her on the journey. As you read this story, notice what powers or friends Gilgamesh has and the roles they play in his quest.

ACTIVE READING: CAUSE AND EFFECT

Events in a plot are often related by **cause and effect.** One event in the story can cause another event, which is the effect. The effect may in turn cause another event, and so on. For example, on page 35, Gilgamesh's behavior causes people to complain about him. As a result of these complaints, the gods take action against him.

READER'S NOTEBOOK As you read this story, keep track of cause-and-effect relationships by using a chart. Remember that some events may appear first as an effect and then again as a cause.

Causes	Effects
	→
	→

WORDS TO KNOW **Vocabulary Preview**

allot	musing	presumption	teem
incantation	ominous	prevail	transit
lament	ordain	stupor	

READING FOR INFORMATION

Reading Skills and Strategies

PREVIEWING

Help students with the **Build Background** essay by going over with them the three subheads and the information covered in each section:

What Is The Epic of Gilgamesh? Gives an overview of the Gilgamesh story itself.

How the Epic Evolved Tells the story of the writing and development of the Gilgamesh story in epic form.

How the Epic Survived Tells the story of what happened to the epic after it was written and how it has come down to us today.

TIME MANAGEMENT

If your schedule requires that you cover the lesson objectives in a shorter time, use . . .

- Preparing to Read, p. 32
- Thinking Through the Literature, p. 47
- Vocabulary in Action, p. 48

If you want to take advantage of longer blocks of class time, use . . .

- TE Teaching Options: Viewing and Representing, p. 44; Vocabulary Strategy, p. 34; Cross Curricular Link, pp. 35, 36, 38, 41, 42, 46; Grammar, pp. 43, 45
- Choices & Challenges, p. 48
- Connect to Today, p. 49

Reading and Analyzing

Reading Skills and Strategies
CLARIFYING

Point out the list on page 34 of **Characters and Places in the Epic.** Suggest that students refer to this list as needed to keep the names in the story straight.

Guide for Reading

The Guide for Reading notes in this selection are intended to help students read the text by dividing it into manageable sections. Each section begins with a **Focus** suggestion to help students read actively and with a purpose. Between sections, a **Pause & Reflect** question gives students an opportunity to stop and review what they have read and understood so far.

Reading Skills and Strategies
PREDICTING

A Have students read the three introductory paragraphs on page 35. Then ask them to predict what will happen in the part of the epic they are going to read.

Literary Analysis THE QUEST STORY

Remind students that, like many quest heroes, Gilgamesh has both human and superhuman qualities. Have them look for examples of each kind of quality as they read the selection.

 Use **Unit One Resource Book,** p. 6, for more practice.

Reading Skills and Strategies
VISUALIZING

To help students understand the significance of Enkidu's dream, have them visualize his description of the underworld and describe their visualizations to each other.

Active Reading CAUSE AND EFFECT

Ask students to note the effect that Enkidu's dream, illness, and death have on Gilgamesh.

 Use **Unit One Resource Book,** p. 5, for more practice.

from The Epic of Gilgamesh

Translated by N. K. Sanders

• CHARACTERS AND PLACES IN THE EPIC •

Anu (ā′no͞o): Father of the gods, who had an important temple in Uruk.

Anunnaki (ä-no͞o-nä′kē): gods who judge the dead and control destinies.

Belit-Sheri (bĕl′ēt shĕr′ē): Scribe and recorder of the underworld gods.

Dilmun (dĭl′mən): a paradise in the world of the gods.

Ea (ā′ä): God of waters and of wisdom, and one of the creators of mankind, toward whom he is usually well-disposed.

Enkidu (ĕn′kē-do͞o): Gilgamesh's friend; molded by Aruru, goddess of creation, out of clay, he is wild or natural man.

Enlil (ĕn′lĭl): God of earth, wind, and spirit; carries out tasks for Anu.

Ereshkigal (ĕ-rĕsh′kē′gäl): The queen of the underworld.

Gilgamesh (gĭl′gə-mĕsh′): The king of Uruk and the hero of the epic.

Irkalla (ĭr-kä′lə): Another name for Ereshkigal, the queen of the underworld.

Ishtar (ĭsh′tär): Goddess of love, fertility, and war, called the Queen of Heaven.

Nergal (nĕr′gäl): husband of Ereshkigal and co-ruler of the underworld.

Ninurta (nə-nĕr′tə): A warrior and god of war, wells, and irrigation.

Shamash (shä′mäsh): The sun god, judge and giver of laws.

Siduri (sə-do͞o′rē): The divine winemaker and brewer, who lives on the shore of the sea in the garden of the sun.

Urshanabi (ûr′shə-nä-bē): The boatman of Utnapishtim who ferries daily across the waters of death that divide the garden of the sun from the paradise where Utnapishtim lives.

Uruk (o͞o′ro͝ok′): Biblical Erech, modern Warka, in southern Babylonia between Fara and Ur. Shown by excavation to have been an important city from very early times, with great temples to the gods Anu and Ishtar.

Utnapishtim (o͞ot′nə-pēsh′təm): Friend of the god Ea, with whose help he survives the flood, together with his family and with "the seed of all living creatures." He and his wife are the only mortals to be granted the gift of eternal life.

MINI LESSON Vocabulary Strategy

CONTEXT CLUES Remind students that they can often understand the meaning of an unfamiliar word from the context in which it is used. Use the model below to demonstrate.

Model: The science teacher *allotted* five test tubes to each pair of students.

Instruction

- Ask a volunteer to summarize the meaning of the model sentence.
- Have students use the meaning of the sentence to infer the meaning of *allotted.*
- Ask another volunteer to use *allotted* in a sentence.

Practice Have students use context clues to infer the meanings of the italicized words.

1. When the bell rings and classes change, the school hallways *teem* with students.
2. Jake was able to *prevail* against sleep and continue studying through the night.
3. The school board *ordained* that all students would wear uniforms to school.

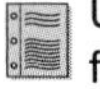 Use **Unit One Resource Book,** p. 7, for more practice.

A lesson on context clues appears on p. 674 in the Pupil's Edition.

Gilgamesh and Enkidu slaying Humbaba. Photograph courtesy of the Royal Ontario Museum, ©ROM.

GUIDE FOR READING

FOCUS In this section, Enkidu tells Gilgamesh about a dream of a visit to the Underworld, the place where people go after they die. As you read, look for passages that help you understand what the ancient Mesopotamians expected the afterlife to be like.

THE DEATH OF ENKIDU

A *The hero Gilgamesh, king of Uruk, is "two-thirds a god, one-third a man." In this epic, we see him exploring both sides of his character.*

Gilgamesh is first presented as a superhuman ruler who has let his power go to his head. He has begun taking advantage of his subjects rather than taking care for them. The gods hear the people's complaints and create Enkidu, "hairy-bodied wild man" equal in strength to Gilgamesh, to fight him. Instead of fighting, however, Enkidu and Gilgamesh become best friends. Together they fight and defeat Humbaba, a monster created by the gods to guard a sacred grove.

After the victory, the goddess Ishtar falls in love with Gilgamesh. When he rejects her, she has her father, Anu, send the Bull of Heaven to punish him. Together, Gilgamesh and Enkidu kill the bull. For this and other offenses, the gods decree, one of the two heroes must die. Enkidu, who is not part god, is chosen. Before he dies, Enkidu has a dream of what waits for him in the afterlife.

As Enkidu slept alone in his sickness, in bitterness of spirit he poured out his heart to his friend. "It was I who cut down the 1
cedar, I who leveled the forest, I who slew Humbaba and now see what has become of me. Listen, my friend, this is the dream I dreamed last night. The heavens roared, and earth rumbled back an answer; between them stood I before an awful being, the somber-faced man-bird; he had directed on me his purpose. His was a vampire face, his foot was a lion's foot, his hand was an eagle's talon. He fell on me and his claws were in my hair, he held me fast and I smothered; then he transformed me so that my arms became wings covered with feathers. He turned his stare towards me, and led me away to the palace of Irkalla, the Queen of Darkness, to the house from which none who enters ever returns, down the road from 2
which there is no coming back.

"There is the house whose people sit in darkness; dust is their food and clay their meat. They

Customizing Instruction

Less Proficient Readers

Focus Draw students' attention to the Focus direction at the top of the first column. Explain that these directions are included to help students pay attention to important aspects of the text as they read. Point out also that the three paragraphs that follow summarize what happens in the epic up to the point where their excerpt begins.

English Learners

1 Explain the meaning of "poured out his heart to his friend" *(told his friend all of the thoughts and feelings that were troubling him).*

2 Explain that "the house from which none who enters ever returns" and "the road from which there is no coming back" both refer to death.

Cross Curricular Link: Humanities

CYLINDER SEALS This image of Gilgamesh and Enkidu slaying Humbaba was made with a cylinder seal. The Sumerians made cylinder seals by carving pictures and designs on small stone cylinders. When the stones were rolled on wet clay, they would leave a raised image that would repeat continuously for as far as the stone was rolled. (Point out to students that the right edge of the picture above is identical to the left, showing the point where the seal begins to repeat the image.) The Sumerians and other Mesopotamian cultures after them used cylinder seals to make personal signatures or as a way of identifying ownership. They also bored holes through the cylinders lengthwise and wore them around their necks both to adorn themselves and to keep the seals handy. Cylinder seals have been used to identify bodies in ancient burial excavations (see page 38). Thousands of cylinder seals have been found in excavations throughout the Middle East and many are now in museums throughout the world.

Reading and Analyzing

Reading Skills and Strategies
CLARIFYING

A Students may find the scene and events described in Enkidu's dream confusing. Help them clarify this part of the story by inviting several students to retell it using their own words.

Reading Skills and Strategies
IDENTIFYING CULTURAL CHARACTERISTICS

B Students may wonder why Gilgamesh peels off his clothes after hearing Enkidu's dream. From the context, it seems clear that Gilgamesh is expressing his sense of awe, terror, and grief at what he hears.

Reading Skills and Strategies
MAKING INFERENCES

C Ask students why Enkidu believes his death will be a shameful one.
Possible Responses: Because Enkidu believes that the only way for a fighter to die honorably is in battle; because he has been cursed by the gods; because his sickness has made him weak and helpless; because he doesn't want his friend Gilgamesh to see that he has lost his strength.

Pause & Reflect
Possible Responses: a realm of darkness and desolation, with no hope of return or going to a better place; a frightening underworld kingdom with monstrous creatures and merciless gods; a place where all people, regardless of who they were on earth, experience the same fate

Active Reading CAUSE AND EFFECT

D Read aloud to students this statement of cause and effect. Then ask the following question: Why does Gilgamesh want to go in search of the immortal Utnapishtim?
Possible Responses: Gilgamesh hopes that Utnapishtim can share with him the secret of immortality; Gilgamesh hopes that Utnapishtim will be able to explain the mystery of life and death; Gilgamesh hopes that Utnapishtim will help him get into the good graces of the gods.

Reading Skills and Strategies
CLARIFYING

E Help students avoid confusion by explaining that Utnapishtim is like a father to Gilgamesh in the sense of being a person who is older and wiser and honored by the gods. As the primary survivor of flood, Utnapishtim may also be considered the ancestor of all people on earth.

"THE DREAM WAS MARVELOUS BUT THE TERROR WAS GREAT."

are clothed like birds with wings for covering, they see no light, they sit in darkness. I entered the house of dust and I saw the kings of the earth, their crowns put away for ever; rulers and princes, all those who once wore kingly crowns and ruled the world in the days of old. They who had stood in the place of the gods like Anu and Enlil, stood now like servants to fetch baked meats in the house of dust, to carry cooked meat and cold water from the water-skin. In the house of dust which I entered were high priests and acolytes[1], priests of the incantation and of ecstasy; there were servers of the temple, and there was Etana, that king of Kish whom the eagle carried to heaven in the days of old. I saw also Samuqan, god of cattle, and there was Ereshkigal the Queen of the Underworld; and Belit-Sheri squatted in front of her, she who is recorder of the gods and keeps the book of death. She held a tablet from which she read. She raised her head, she saw me and spoke: "Who has brought this one here?" Then I awoke like a man drained of
1 blood who wanders alone in a waste of rushes;
A like one whom the bailiff has seized and his heart pounds with terror."

Gilgamesh had peeled off his clothes, he listened to his words and wept quick tears, Gilgamesh listened and his tears flowed. He opened his mouth and spoke to Enkidu: "Who is there in strong-walled Uruk who has wisdom like this? Strange things have been spoken, why does your heart speak strangely? The dream was marvelous but the terror was great; we must treasure the dream whatever the terror; for the dream has shown that misery comes at last to the healthy man, the end of life is sorrow." And Gilgamesh lamented, "Now I will pray to the great gods, for my friend had an ominous dream." B

This day on which Enkidu dreamed came to an end and he lay stricken with sickness. One whole day he lay on his bed and his suffering increased. He said to Gilgamesh, the friend on whose account he had left the wilderness, "Once I ran for you, for the water of life, and I now have nothing." A second day he lay on his bed and Gilgamesh watched over him but the sickness increased. A third day he lay on his bed, he called out to Gilgamesh, rousing him up. Now he was weak and his eyes were blind with weeping. Ten days he lay and his suffering increased, eleven and twelve days he lay on his bed of pain. Then he called to Gilgamesh, "My friend, the great goddess cursed me and I must die in shame. I shall not die like a man fallen in battle; I feared to fall, but happy is the man who falls in the battle, for I must die in shame." And C
Gilgamesh wept over Enkidu. . . .

PAUSE & REFLECT How would you describe the afterlife depicted in Enkidu's dream?

1. **acolytes** (ăk′ə-līts′): assistants at religious services.

WORDS TO KNOW
incantation (ĭn′kăn-tā′shən) *n.* set of words chanted or sung as part of a religious ritual
lament (lə-mĕnt′) *v.* to express grief or sorrow
ominous (ŏm′ə-nəs) *adj.* threatening; signaling evil to come

Cross Curricular Link **Humanities**

VIEWS OF LIFE AFTER DEATH Sumerian views of the afterlife differ from those of most religions today in a number of ways. Instead of believing in different fates after death based on how one has lived life, the Sumerians believed that everyone would share the same fate. Their vision of this fate was mostly negative, as Enkidu's dream suggests. After death, all people—ordinary and great alike—go to the underworld, a place of darkness and sorrow. This view of the afterlife may seem bleak, but it helps to shed light on Gilgamesh's fear of death and on his sense that mortality calls into question the meaning of human existence.

However, the Sumerians did believe that some distinctions might be made after death. As in ancient Egypt, people of wealth and status would have their possessions buried along with them, most likely for use in the afterlife. For members of royalty this practice extended beyond material possessions to include the people in their lives: soldiers, servants, and even family members.

Another kind of distinction among the dead

FOCUS In this section, Gilgamesh goes in search of Utnapishtim. As you read, notice whom or what he meets on his journey, how these encounters help or hinder him, and what he must do each time in order to proceed.

THE SEARCH FOR EVERLASTING LIFE

Enkidu dies. For the first time, Gilgamesh is faced with a situation he cannot control. He also experiences for the first time the human emotions of grief and fear.

Bitterly Gilgamesh wept for his friend Enkidu; he wandered over the wilderness as a hunter, he roamed over the plains; in his bitterness he cried, "How can I rest, how can I be at peace? Despair is in my heart. What my brother is now, that shall I be when I am dead. Because I am afraid of death I will go as best I can to find Utnapishtim whom they call the Faraway, for he has entered the assembly of the gods." So Gilgamesh traveled over the wilderness, he wandered over the grasslands, a long journey, in search of Utnapishtim, whom the gods took after the deluge[2]; and they set him to live in the land of Dilmun, in the garden of the sun; and to him alone of men they gave everlasting life. D

At night when he came to the mountain passes Gilgamesh prayed: "In these mountain passes long ago I saw lions, I was afraid and I lifted my eyes to the moon; I prayed and my prayers went up to the gods, so now, O moon god Sin, protect me." When he had prayed he lay down to sleep, until he was woken from out of a dream. He saw the lions round him glorying in life; then he took his axe in his hand, he drew his sword from his belt, and he fell upon them like an arrow from the string, and struck and destroyed and scattered them.

So at length Gilgamesh came to Mashu, the great mountains about which he had heard many things, which guard the rising and the setting sun. Its twin peaks are as high as the wall of heaven and its paps reach down to the underworld. At its gate the Scorpions stand guard, half man and half dragon; their glory is terrifying, their stare strikes death into men, their shimmering halo sweeps the mountains that guard the rising sun. When Gilgamesh saw them he shielded his eyes for the length of a moment only; then he took courage and approached. When they saw him so undismayed the Man-Scorpion called to his mate, "This one who comes to us now is flesh of the gods." The mate of the Man-Scorpion answered, "Two thirds is god but one third is man."

Then he called to the man Gilgamesh, he called to the child of the gods: "Why have you come so great a journey; for what have you traveled so far, crossing the dangerous waters; tell me the reason for your coming?" Gilgamesh answered, "For Enkidu; I loved him dearly, together we endured all kinds of hardships; on his account I have come, for the common lot of man has taken him. I have wept for him day and night, I would not give up his body for burial, I thought my friend would come back because of my weeping. Since he went, my life is nothing; that is why I have traveled here in search of Utnapishtim my father; for men say he has entered the assembly of the gods, and has found everlasting life. I have a desire to question him concerning the living and the dead." The Man-Scorpion opened his mouth and said, speaking to Gilgamesh, "No man born of woman has done what you have asked, no mortal man has gone into the mountain; the length of it is twelve leagues[3] of darkness; in it there is no light, but E 2

2. **deluge** (dĕl'yo͞oj): an unusually heavy, destructive flood.

3. **twelve leagues:** roughly thirty-six miles.

can be found in another Sumerian tale, one in which Enkidu actually goes to the underworld but returns in spirit to tell Gilgamesh what happens to people in that place. The man with one son "sits by the wall and weeps," Enkidu reports, while the man with seven sons, "as if he were a companion of the gods . . . sits upon a throne and listens to music." The "famous warrior . . . who fell on the battlefield in glory" is tended by his grieving parents and wife, while of "the one who goes to the Nether World without leaving behind any to mourn for him" Enkidu says, "Garbage is what he eats in the Nether World. No dog would eat the food he has to eat."

The idea that a person's accomplishments in life or the people he or she has left behind would have an effect on the afterlife is one that more closely resembles many modern religious views.

Customizing Instruction

English Learners

1 Help students identify the correct meaning of *bailiff* here: a police officer with authority to enforce the law and arrest offenders.

Less Proficient Readers

Focus If students need help with the Focus directions at the beginning of this page, suggest they keep track of Gilgamesh's encounters by making a chart in their Reader's Notebooks like the one started below.

Encounter	Helps/Hinders/Both	What Gilgamesh Does
lions	hinder	prays to moon god for protection attacks and scatters the lions

English Learners

2 Make sure students understand that *no man born of woman* means no one who is a human being rather than a god.

Reading and Analyzing

Literary Analysis THE QUEST STORY

A During a quest story, the quest hero often encounters both helpers and hinderers. Often, both are combined into a single figure who tests the hero, helps if the hero passes the test, and hinders if the hero fails. Have students review the preceding two paragraphs and answer the following question: What test must Gilgamesh pass to get the help of the Man-Scorpions?

Possible Responses: He has to have enough courage to approach them despite their frightening appearance; he has to show that he is part god; he has to give a good answer to the question of why he has come there; he has to show that he is unafraid of the journey through the darkness of the mountain.

Pause & Reflect

Possible Responses: devotion to the gods, as when Gilgamesh prays when he comes to the mountain passes; courage and the ability to act swiftly, as when he scatters the lions; courage, as when he approaches the scorpion people; sincerity and truthfulness, as when he explains his purpose to the scorpion people; courage and perseverance, as when he walks 12 leagues through the darkness of the mountain; self-confidence and belief in himself, as when he responds to Shamash's discouraging remarks

Active Reading CAUSE AND EFFECT

B Have students complete the following cause-and-effect statements:

1. Siduri thinks Gilgamesh is a felon because . . .
(. . . he wears skins, has despair in his heart, and has the face of one who has made a long journey.)
2. Siduri bars the gate against Gilgamesh because . . .
(. . . she is afraid and suspicious.)
3. Gilgamesh looks desperate and weatherbeaten because . . .
(. . . he has travelled a long way and feels distraught over the death of Enkidu.)

Point out that the cause in #2 must be inferred and that the effect in #3 has multiple causes.

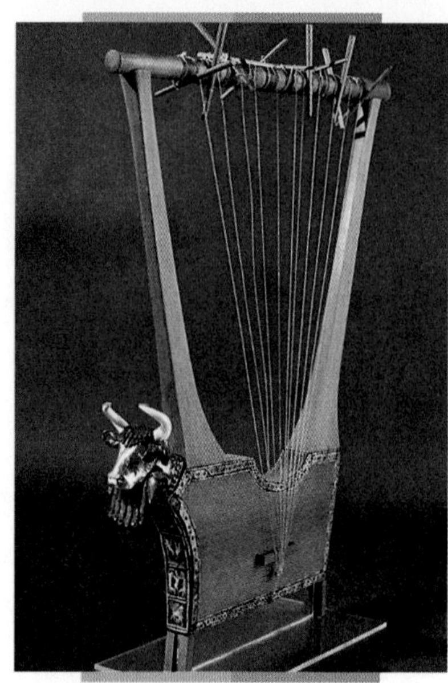

Sumerian bull-headed lyre. The British Museum, London.

the heart is oppressed with darkness. From the rising of the sun to the setting of the sun there is no light." Gilgamesh said, "Although I should go in sorrow and in pain, with sighing and with weeping, still I must go. Open the gate of the mountain." And the Man-Scorpion said, "Go, Gilgamesh, I permit you to pass through the mountain of Mashu and through the high ranges; may your feet carry you safely home.
A The gate of the mountain is open." . . .

Gilgamesh must walk 12 leagues in total darkness to pass through the mountain. But at last he reaches a wonderful world no mortal has seen.

1 There was the garden of the gods; all round him stood bushes bearing gems. Seeing it he went down at once, for there was fruit of carnelian[4] with the vine hanging from it, beautiful to look at; lapis lazuli leaves hung thick with fruit, sweet to see. For thorns and thistles there were haematite and rare stones, agate, and pearls from out of the sea. While Gilgamesh walked in the garden by the edge of the sea Shamash saw him, and he saw that he was dressed in the skins of animals and ate their flesh. He was distressed, and he spoke and said, "No mortal man has gone this way before, nor will, as long as the winds drive over the sea." And to Gilgamesh he said, "You will never find the life for which you are searching." Gilgamesh said to glorious Shamash, "Now that I have toiled and strayed so far over the wilderness, am I to sleep, and let the earth cover my head for ever? Let my eyes see the sun until they are dazzled with looking. Although I am no better than a dead man, still let me see the light of the sun."

PAUSE & REFLECT What quality or behavior do you think is most helpful to Gilgamesh in overcoming obstacles on his journey?

FOCUS As you read the next section, look for the paragraph in which Siduri offers advice to Gilgamesh. Then look for the paragraph in which Gilgamesh responds to this recommendation.

Beside the sea she lives, the woman of the vine, the maker of wine; Siduri sits in the garden at the edge of the sea, with the golden bowl and the golden vats that the gods gave her. She is covered with a veil; and where she sits she sees Gilgamesh coming towards her, wearing skins, the flesh of the gods in his body, but despair in his heart, and his face like the face of one who has made a long journey. She looked, and as she scanned the distance she said in her own heart, "Surely this is some felon; where is he going now?" And she

4. **carnelian** (kär-nēl′yən) **lapis lazuli** (lăp′ĭs lăz′ə-lē) **hematite** (hē′mə-tīt) **agate** (ăg′ĭt): gemstones of various colors. Carnelian is red or reddish-brown, lapis lazuli is deep blue, hematite is a dull metal shade, and agate is often multi-colored stripes.

Cross Curricular Link **Humanities**

TREASURES FROM THE ROYAL TOMBS OF UR The lyre shown above comes from the excavations of a burial site in the ancient Sumerian city of Ur. The excavation was carried out by British archaeologist Leonard Wooley in the 1920s. The site itself dates from 2600–2500 B.C., a period not long after the probable reign of King Gilgamesh (c. 2700 B.C.). Out of about 1,800 burials that Wooley uncovered, he classified 16 as "royal" based on the fact that along with the bodies were buried not only a wealth of material possessions, but also people, both servants and attendants of high rank.

The "bull-headed lyre" shown above comes from the tomb of a royal woman named Pu-abi, as indicated by an inscribed cylinder seal found at her breast. Pu-abi wore an elaborate headdress, strands of beads made from precious metals and semiprecious stone, a comb, necklaces, earrings, and a ring on each finger. A fillet, or diadem, of lapis lazuli and gold lay near her head. Other objects buried with Pu-abi include a

barred her gate against him with the cross-bar and shot home the bolt. But Gilgamesh, hearing the sound of the bolt, threw up his head and lodged his foot in the gate; he called to her, "Young woman, maker of wine, why do you bolt your door; what did you see that made you bar your gate? I will break in your door and burst in your gate, for I am Gilgamesh who seized and killed the Bull of Heaven, I killed the watchman of the cedar forest, I overthrew Humbaba who lived in the forest, and I killed the lions in the passes of the mountain."

Then Siduri said to him, "If you are that Gilgamesh who seized and killed the Bull of Heaven, who killed the watchman of the cedar forest, who overthrew Humbaba that lived in the forest, and killed the lions in the passes of the mountain, why are your cheeks so starved and why is your face so drawn? Why is despair in your heart and your face like the face of one who has made a long journey? Yes, why is your face burned from heat and cold, and why do you come here wandering over the pastures in search of the wind?"

Gilgamesh answered her, "And why should not my cheeks be starved and my face drawn? Despair is in my heart and my face is the face of one who has made a long journey, it was burned with heat and with cold. Why should I not wander over the pastures in search of the wind? My friend, my younger brother, he who hunted the wild ass of the wilderness and the panther of the plains, my friend, my younger brother who seized and killed the Bull of Heaven and overthrew Humbaba in the cedar forest, my friend who was very dear to me and who endured dangers beside me, Enkidu my brother, whom I loved, the end of mortality has overtaken him. I wept for him seven days and nights till the worm fastened on him. Because of my brother I am afraid of death, because of my brother I stray through the wilderness and cannot rest. But now, young woman, maker of wine, since I have seen your face do not let me see the face of death which I dread so much." B

She answered, "Gilgamesh, where are you hurrying to? You will never find that life for which you are looking. When the gods created man they allotted to him death, but life they retained in their own keeping. As for you, Gilgamesh, fill your belly with good things; day and night, night and day, dance and be merry, feast and rejoice. Let your clothes be fresh, bathe 2 yourself in water, cherish the little child that holds your hand, and make your wife happy in your embrace; for this too is the lot of man."

But Gilgamesh said to Siduri, the young woman, "How can I be silent, how can I rest, when Enkidu whom I love is dust, and I too shall die and be laid in the earth. You live by the seashore and look into the heart of it; young woman, tell me now, which is the way to Utnapishtim, the son of Ubara-Tutu? What directions are there for the passage; give me, oh, give me directions. I will

"NO MORTAL MAN HAS GONE THIS WAY BEFORE, NOR WILL, AS LONG AS THE WINDS DRIVE OVER THE SEA."

WORDS TO KNOW

allot (ə-lŏt') *v.* to give as a share or portion

Customizing Instruction

English Learners

1 English learners reading about a garden made out of stone may think they have misunderstood the text. Explain that this is "the garden of the gods" and is meant to be extraordinary.

Less Proficient Readers

Focus If students need help with the Focus directions, draw their attention to the following passages: Siduri offers her advice on page 39, second column, first full paragraph ("As for you, Gilgamesh, fill your belly . . . . for this too is the lot of man."). Gilgamesh responds in the next paragraph ("How can I be silent . . . I will wander still farther in the wilderness.")

Advanced Learners

2 Have students compare this statement with the one made by Gilgamesh on page 36: "misery comes at last to the healthy man, the end of life is sorrow." Then ask students whether they think Siduri's advice is good advice.

Possible Responses: Yes, because a person can't do anything about death and would be better off spending time enjoying life; no, because there's more to life than the pleasures of the moment and one's ultimate fate is worth thinking about.

wooden sledge, a pair of oxen, a chest of clothing, vessels of gold and silver, furniture, tools, and a board game. A total of 22 other people were buried with the princess, including 12 female attendants, one of whom—according to Wooley—was found with her fingers touching the strings of a lyre.

Reading and Analyzing

Literary Analysis THEME

A Point out to students that in the passage that follows Utnapishtim sets forth one of the great themes of literature, sometimes called the "mutability theme": the idea that all things, including human life, change and pass away. Stories, poems, and songs from many cultures and time periods have been written on this theme.

Pause & Reflect

Possible Responses: Gilgamesh is not easily discouraged; he is too overcome with grief and fear of death to give up on his quest; he believes he has a chance of gaining eternal life, despite Siduri's warning that he will not; Gilgamesh can't be satisfied with an ordinary human existence.

Literary Analysis THE QUEST STORY

B Point out to students that the story within the story—Utnapishtim's story of the flood—is itself a quest story. Utnapishtim does not travel from one place to another. Instead, he journeys through changes in the environment itself—from dry land to storm to sea and back again to dry land. Symbolically, he passes through the flood and arrives in safety on the other side.

Reading Skills and Strategies
MAKING INFERENCES

C Point out to students that this reference to Ea's oath is all we are told about why he saves Utnapishtim from the flood. Then ask students to infer the kind of oath that Ea made and why he might have made it.

Possible Responses: (kind of oath) He promised to protect Utnapishtim from harm; he promised to let Utnapishtim know about important decisions among the gods. (why Ea made the oath) Utnapishtim was an especially good man; Utnapishtim worshipped Ea loyally and Ea wanted to reward him; Ea owed Utnapishtim a favor.

cross the Ocean if it is possible; if it is not I will wander still farther in the wilderness." . . .

Siduri tells Gilgamesh that he must cross the ocean with the boatman Urshanabi. When she hints that Urshanabi might refuse to take him, Gilgamesh loses his temper. He smashes Urshanabi's sacred stones and the tackle and mast of his boat. Urshanabi explains that Gilgamesh has destroyed the very things that would protect them both from the waters of death. To make up for his actions, Gilgamesh must cut poles and push the boat himself. Eventually, he has to use his own body and clothing for a sail.

So Urshanabi the ferryman brought Gilgamesh to Utnapishtim, whom they call the Faraway, who lives in Dilmun at the place of the sun's transit, eastward of the mountain. To him alone of men the gods had given everlasting life.

Now Utnapishtim, where he lay at ease, looked into the distance and he said in his heart, musing to himself, "Why does the boat sail here without tackle and mast; why are the sacred stones destroyed, and why does the master not sail the boat? That man who comes is none of mine; where I look I see a man whose body is covered with skins of beasts. Who is this who walks up the shore behind Urshanabi, for surely he is no man of mine?" So Utnapishtim looked at him and said, "What is your name, you who come here wearing the skins of beasts, with your cheeks starved and your face drawn? Where are you hurrying to now? For what reason have you made this great journey, crossing the seas whose passage is difficult? Tell me the reason for your coming."

He replied, "Gilgamesh is my name. I am from Uruk, from the house of Anu." Then Utnapishtim said to him, "If you are Gilgamesh, why are your cheeks so starved and your face drawn? Why is despair in your heart and your face like the face of one who has made a long journey? Yes, why is your face burned with heat and cold; and why do you come here, wandering over the wilderness in search of the wind?" . . .

Gilgamesh explains that he is grieving over the death of his friend and afraid of dying himself. He has come to Utnapishtim to learn the secret of everlasting life.

Utnapishtim said, "There is no permanence. A Do we build a house to stand for ever, do we seal a contract to hold for all time? Do brothers divide an inheritance to keep for ever, does the flood-time of rivers endure? It is only the nymph of the dragon-fly who sheds her larva and sees the sun in his glory. From the days of old there is no permanence. The sleeping and the dead, how alike they are, they are like a painted death. What is there between the master and the servant when both have fulfilled their doom? When the Anunnaki, the judges, come together, and Mammetun the mother of destinies, together they decree the fates of men. Life and death they allot but the day of death they do not disclose."

Then Gilgamesh said to Utnapishtim the Faraway, "I look at you now, Utnapishtim, and your appearance is no different from mine; there is nothing strange in your features. I thought I should find you like a hero prepared for battle, but you lie here taking your ease on your back. Tell me truly, how was it that you came to enter the company of the gods and to possess everlasting life?" Utnapishtim said to Gilgamesh, "I will reveal to you a mystery, I will tell you a secret of the gods."

PAUSE & REFLECT Why doesn't Gilgamesh take Siduri's advice?

WORDS TO KNOW

transit (trăn′sĭt) *n.* passage

musing (myo͞o′zĭng) *adj.* thoughtfully questioning or meditating **muse** v.

FOCUS As you continue to read, look for passages that help you understand why the gods treat Utnapishtim as they do.

B

THE STORY OF THE THE FLOOD

1 You know the city Shurrupak, it stands on the banks of Euphrates? That city grew old and the gods that were in it were old. There was Anu, lord of the firmament,[5] their father, and warrior Enlil their counselor, Ninurta the helper, and Ennugi watcher over canals; and with them also was Ea. In those days the world teemed, the people multiplied, the world bellowed like a wild bull, and the great god was aroused by the clamor. Enlil heard the clamor and he said to the gods in council, 'The uproar of mankind is intolerable and sleep is no longer possible by reason of the babel.'[6] So the gods agreed to exterminate mankind. Enlil did this, but

C Ea because of his oath warned me in a dream. He whispered their words to my house of reeds, 'Reed-house, reed-house! Wall, O wall, hearken reed-house, wall reflect; O man of Shurrupak, son of Ubara-Tutu; tear down your house and build a boat, abandon possessions and look for life, despise worldly goods and save your soul alive. Tear down your house, I say, and build a boat. These are the measurements of the barque as you shall build her: let her beam[7] equal her length, let her deck be roofed like the vault that covers the abyss;[8] then take up into the boat the seed of all living creatures.'

"When I had understood I said to my lord, 'Behold, what you have commanded I will honor and perform, but how shall I answer the people, the city, the elders?' Then Ea opened his mouth and said to me, his servant, 'Tell them this: I have learned that Enlil is wrathful against me, I dare no longer walk in his land nor live in his city; I will go down to the Gulf to dwell with Ea my lord. But on you he will rain down abundance, rare fish and shy wild-fowl, a rich harvest-tide. In the evening the rider of the storm will bring you wheat in torrents.'

"In the first light of dawn all my household gathered round me, the children brought pitch and the men whatever was necessary. On the fifth day I laid the keel and the ribs, then I made fast the planking. The ground-space was one acre, each side of the deck measured one hundred and twenty cubits,[9] making a square. I built six decks below, seven in all, I divided them into nine sections with bulkheads between. I drove in wedges where needed, I saw to the punt-poles,[10] and laid in supplies. The carriers brought oil in baskets, I poured pitch into the furnace and asphalt and oil; more oil was consumed in caulking, and more again the master of the boat took into his stores. I slaughtered bullocks for the people and every day I killed sheep. I gave the shipwrights wine to drink as though it were river water, raw wine and red wine and oil and white wine. There was feasting then as there is at the time of the New Year's festival; I myself anointed my head. On the seventh day the boat was complete.

"Then was the launching full of difficulty; there was shifting of ballast[11] above and below till two thirds was submerged. I loaded into her all that I had of gold and of living things, my family, my kin, the beast of the field both wild

5. **firmament:** the vault of the heavens; the sky.
6. **babel:** loud, unpleasant noise.
7. **beam:** the widest part of a ship.
8. **vault that covers the abyss:** the sky as it stretches across the depths below.
9. **cubits:** ancient units of measure, originally equal to the length of the forearm from the elbow to the tip of the middle finger. Length ranges from 17 to 22 inches.
10. **punt-poles:** poles that propel a boat by pushing against the water's bottom.
11. **ballast** (băl'əst): heavy material placed into the bottom of a boat to enhance stability.

WORDS TO KNOW

teem (tēm) *v.* to be filled to overflowing

Customizing Instruction

Less Proficient Readers

Focus If students need help understanding the Focus statement, tell them to look for places where Utnapishtim does something that shows he is worthy of the gods' special favor.

Examples: (Page 41) Utnapishtim immediately agrees to do what Ea has commanded; Utnapishtim shows his cleverness when he anticipates that people will want to know why he is building a boat; he is generous with his workers. (Page 42) He faces the storm and the flood bravely; he is smart enough not to leave the boat until he has proof of dry land; he shows his compassion by weeping when he sees the destruction that has occurred. (Page 43) After leaving the boat, he sacrifices generously to the gods.

1 Make sure students understand that this section of the epic is narrated by Utnapishtim, who is telling his story to Gilgamesh.

Cross Curricular Link **Humanitites**

FLOOD STORIES The story Utnapishtim tells of a great flood that wipes out the entire human race (except for a chosen few) bears a remarkable resemblance to the Story of Noah and the Flood found in the Bible (see page 70). In both stories the flood comes about because of divine dissatisfaction with the human race, and in both stories a single exceptional individual survives the destruction with divine help and becomes the father of a new human race. While the Biblical story is much better known, the one in *The Epic of Gilgamesh* is at least 600 years older and may have been familiar to early Biblical authors. Some scholars believe that a real historical event underlies both stories. Flooding was a regular occurrence in the Tigris-Euphrates river valley, and the story Utnapishtim tells may hark back to an exceptionally large and destructive flood that occurred sometime around 3000 B.C. Like many other ancient civilizations, the Sumerians did not distinguish clearly between history and mythology. A semi-historical document known as the "Sumerian King-List" that dates from about 2000 B.C. lists Gilgamesh as the fifth king after the flood.

Reading and Analyzing

Reading Skills and Strategies
VISUALIZING

A Read the paragraph up to this point aloud. As you read, have students visualize the storm.

Reading Skills and Strategies
MAKING INFERENCES

B Ask students why Ishtar now regrets the decision she made with the other gods to destroy humanity.
Possible Responses: She realizes how awful the destruction is once she sees it with her own eyes; she feels guilty for betraying her people; it seems to her wrong that people should be treated no better than fish.

Active Reading CAUSE AND EFFECT

C Ask students to think of some possible causes for Enlil's decision to bless Utnapishtim and his wife, when a little earlier he was angry that any mortal had escaped destruction.
Possible Responses: Ea's words convince Enlil that he acted wrongly and he wants to make up for it; Enlil realizes that all the gods are against him now instead of supporting him, as they did before; Enlil realizes that Utnapishtim is a wise person deserving of special treatment.

Pause & Reflect
Possible Responses: Ea had made a promise to Utnapishtim; Utnapishtim obeys Ea without question; he is wise enough to be generous with his workers; he courageously faces a flood that terrifies even the gods; he sacrifices to all the gods after the flood subsides; as the only survivor, Utnapishtim is the logical recipient of Enlil's reparation.

"I DARE NO LONGER WALK IN HIS LAND NOR LIVE IN HIS CITY."

and tame, and all the craftsmen. I sent them on board, for the time that Shamash had ordained was already fulfilled when he said, 'In the
1 evening, when the rider of the storm sends down the destroying rain, enter the boat and batten her down.' The time was fulfilled, the evening came, the rider of the storm sent down the rain. I looked out at the weather and it was terrible, so I too boarded the boat and battened her down. All was now complete, the battening and the caulking; so I handed the tiller to Puzur-Amurri the steersman, with the navigation and the care of the whole boat.

"With the first light of dawn a black cloud came from the horizon; it thundered within where Adad, lord of the storm was riding. In front over hill and plain Shullat and Hanish, heralds of the storm, led on. Then the gods of the abyss rose up; Nergal pulled out the dams of the nether[12] waters, Ninurta the war-lord threw
A down the dikes, and the seven judges of hell, the Annunaki, raised their torches, lighting the land with their livid flame. A stupor of despair went up to heaven when the god of the storm turned daylight to darkness, when he smashed the land like a cup. One whole day the tempest raged, gathering fury as it went, it poured over the people like the tides of battle; a man could not see his brother nor the people be seen from heaven. Even the gods were terrified at the flood, they fled to the highest heaven, the firmament of Anu; they crouched against the walls, cowering like curs. Then Ishtar the sweet-voiced Queen of Heaven cried out like a woman in travail:[13] 'Alas the days of old are turned to dust because I commanded evil; why did I command this evil in the council of all the gods? I commanded wars to destroy the people, but are they not my people, for I brought them forth? Now like the spawn of fish they float in the ocean.' The great gods of heaven and of hell wept, they covered their mouths. B

"For six days and six nights the winds blew, torrent and tempest and flood overwhelmed the world, tempest and flood raged together like warring hosts. When the seventh day dawned the storm from the south subsided, the sea grew calm, the flood was stilled; I looked at the face of the world and there was silence, all mankind was turned to clay. The surface of the sea stretched as flat as a roof-top; I opened a hatch and the light fell on my face. Then I bowed low, I sat down and I wept, the tears streamed down my face, for on every side was the waste of water. I looked for land in vain, but fourteen leagues distant there appeared a mountain, and there the boat grounded; on the mountain of Nisir the boat held fast, she held fast and did not budge. One day she held, and a second day on the mountain of Nisir she held fast and did not budge. A third day, and a fourth day she held fast on the mountain and did not budge; a fifth day and a sixth day she held fast on the mountain. When the seventh day dawned I loosed a dove and let her go. She flew away, but finding no resting-place she returned. Then I loosed a swallow, and she flew away but finding no resting-place she returned. I loosed a raven, she saw that the waters had retreated, she ate, she flew 2

12. **nether:** lower.

13. **travail** (trə-vāl'): the pain of childbirth.

WORDS TO KNOW

ordain (ôr-dān') *v.* to establish by decree or law
stupor (stōō'pər) *n.* a dazed condition, almost without sense or feeling

Cross Curricular Link **Ecology**

THE FERTILE CRESCENT? The fertile crescent isn't what it used to be. Most of the flood plain that saw the birth of agriculture thousands of years ago has become desert. Even fresh water contains minute quantities of salt. Each time the region's rivers flood, the water eventually drains away or evaporates, but the salt remains. Very slowly, over many years, the salt level in some areas has rendered the soil unfit for raising crops. This process, occurring very slowly in nature, was speeded up by thousands of years of agricultural irrigation.

However, with greater technology comes a greater potential to affect the environment. Recent satellite images confirm that between 1973 and 2000 90% of the remaining permanent marshlands in the Tigris-Euphrates river valley disappeared. Scientists at the U.N. Environment Program (UNEP), analyzing images from NASA's Landsat satellites, discovered that most of this fertile area is now salt-encrusted desert. The researchers attribute this sudden change to two technological developments: extensive damming and drainage projects.

The environmental impact of this more recent change promises to be substantial. Some mammals found only in the affected area, such as the smooth-coated otter, are already considered extinct. In addition, about 40 species of waterfowl are endangered, and fisheries on the northern coast of the Arabian Gulf have seen their productivity plummet as a result of lost marshland spawning grounds. Perhaps the most disturbing result is the displacement of the Marsh Arabs, an indigenous people numbering about half a million who trace their origins to the ancient Babylonian and Sumerian cultures.

2 around, she cawed, and she did not come back. Then I threw everything open to the four winds, I made a sacrifice and poured out a libation[14] on the mountain top. Seven and again seven cauldrons I set up on their stands, I heaped up wood and cane and cedar and myrtle. When the gods smelled the sweet savor, they gathered like flies over the sacrifice. Then, at last, Ishtar also came, she lifted her necklace with the jewels of heaven that once Anu had made to please her. 'O you gods here present, by the lapis lazuli round my neck I shall remember these days as I remember the jewels of my throat; these last days I shall not forget. Let all the gods gather round the sacrifice, except Enlil. He shall not approach this offering, for without reflection he brought the flood; he consigned my people to destruction.'

"When Enlil had come, when he saw the boat, he was wroth and swelled with anger at the gods, the host of heaven, 'Has any of these mortals escaped? Not one was to have survived the destruction.' Then the god of the wells and canals Ninurta opened his mouth and said to the warrior Enlil, 'Who is there of the gods that can devise[15] without Ea? It is Ea alone who knows all things.' Then Ea opened his mouth and spoke to warrior Enlil, 'Wisest of gods, hero Enlil, how could you so senselessly bring down the flood?

Lay upon the sinner his sin,
Lay upon the transgressor[16] *his transgression,*
Punish him a little when he breaks loose,
Do not drive him too hard or he perishes;
Would that a lion had ravaged mankind
Rather than the flood,
Would that a wolf had ravaged mankind
Rather than the flood,
Would that famine had wasted the world
Rather than the flood,
Would that pestilence had wasted mankind
Rather than the flood.

It was not I that revealed the secret of the gods; the wise man learned it in a dream. Now take your counsel what shall be done with him.'

"Then Enlil went up into the boat, he took me by the hand and my wife and made us enter the boat and kneel down on either side, he standing between us. He touched our foreheads to bless us saying, 'In time past Utnapishtim was a mortal man; henceforth he and his wife shall live in the distance at the mouth of the rivers.' Thus it was that the gods took me and placed me here to live in the distance, at the mouth of the rivers." C

PAUSE & REFLECT What would you say is the main reason Utnapishtim is favored by the gods?

FOCUS As you read on, notice places in the text that show how Utnapishtim responds to the visit from Gilgamesh.

THE RETURN

Utnapishtim said, "As for you, Gilgamesh, who will assemble the gods for your sake, so that you may find that life for which you are searching? But if you wish, come and put it to the test: only prevail against sleep for six days and seven nights." But while Gilgamesh sat there resting on his haunches, a mist of sleep like soft wool teased from the fleece drifted over him, and Utnapishtim said to his wife, "Look at him now, the strong man who would have everlasting life, even now the mists of sleep are drifting over him." His wife replied, "Touch the man to wake him, so that he may return to his own land in peace, going back through the gate by which he came." Utnapishtim said to his wife, "All men are deceivers, even you he will attempt to deceive; 3 4 5

14. **libation:** liquid given as an offering to a god.
15. **devise** (dĭ-vīz): to plan or think things out.
16. **transgressor:** a person who breaks a command or law.

WORDS TO KNOW
prevail (prĭ-vāl') *v.* to hold out against; triumph over

Customizing Instruction

English Learners

1 Students may find the reference to "the rider of the storm" (along with similar references to the gods in the next paragraph) confusing. Explain that the ancient Mesopotamians thought of natural occurrences as actions of the gods. The references are poetic ways of talking about the storm itself. For example, "the rider of the storm sends down the destroying rain" is a poetic way of saying "a powerful rainstorm comes."

Less Proficient Readers

2 Make sure students understand that Utnapishtim releases the birds in order to find out if there is dry land anywhere. The dove and the swallow return, indicating that they did not find any. The raven does not come back because it finds a place where it can live.

Focus If students need help with the Focus directions, draw their attention to the following passages:

3 Utnapishtim suggests that no one will assemble the gods for Gilgamesh's sake.

4 Utnapishtim speaks scornfully of Gilgamesh's wish to become immortal.

5 Utnapishtim says that all men are deceivers.

(**Focus** continued at the top of page 45.)

MINI LESSON Grammar

DIAGNOSTIC: PARTS OF SPEECH

Instruction Words in English can be divided into eight categories, or parts of speech: nouns, pronouns, verbs, adjectives, adverbs, prepositions, conjunctions, and interjections. Articles *(a, an,* and *the)* are generally not included.

List the eight parts of speech on the board and display the sentences below.

The cheetah is one of the fastest land animals.

The space ship was able to land on the moon.

Mr. Jenkins bought a piece of land in Oregon.

Explain that the way a word is used in a sentence determines its part of speech. Have students explain what part of speech *land* is used as in each sentence.

Diagnostic Exercise Copy the sentences and label the part of speech of each word.

1. Gilgamesh lost his best friend.
2. Gilgamesh desperately feared death.
3. Yikes! The underworld sounded horrible.
4. He walked a great distance and pleaded for immortality.
5. In the end, he realized he was mortal.

(Sentence 1: noun-verb-pronoun-adjective-noun; Sentence 2: noun-adverb-verb-noun; Sentence 3: interjection-noun-verb-adjective; Sentence 4: pronoun-verb-adjective-noun-conjunction-verb-preposition-noun; Sentence 5: preposition-noun-pronoun-verb-pronoun-verb-adjective.)

For more instruction and practice in parts of speech, use McDougal Littell's ***Language Network:***

- Grade 10, Chapter 1, "The Parts of Speech"
- Grade 12, Review: Parts of Speech

Reading and Analyzing

Reading Skills and Strategies
CLARIFYING

A Ask students why Utnapishtim wants his wife to bake loaves of bread and put them beside Gilgamesh's head. *(Gilgamesh will see for himself the number of days he has slept by the degree to which the loaves have spoiled. With hard evidence before him, he won't be able to deny that he slept and failed the test.)*

Reading Skills and Strategies
MAKING INFERENCES

B Ask students why Utnapishtim banishes Urshanabi and forbids him ever again to cross the sea.

Possible Responses: It is forbidden for mortal men to enter the land of the gods, as Urshanabi helped Gilgamesh to do; by bringing him so close to eternal life, Urshanabi has made Gilgamesh's disappointment even greater.

Pause & Reflect

Possible Responses: Yes, because he gives Gilgamesh a test and Gilgamesh fails it; yes, because he gives Gilgamesh a gift in place of the immortality he cannot have; no—the sleep test is not fair, because Gilgamesh is exhausted; no, because Gilgamesh does as much to prove himself worthy of immortality as Utnapishtim.

HUMANITIES CONNECTION This relief carving of Gilgamesh, approximately 15 feet high, once adorned a wall in the palace of the eighth-century Assyrian king Sargon II.

MINI LESSON Viewing and Representing

Relief Carving of Gilgamesh

ART APPRECIATION

Instruction The Assyrian king Sargon II was a ruthless conqueror who took delight in displaying his power and success. He declared himself king of the world and built a new capital city at Khorsabad in northwest Mesopotamia. The new city had mud-brick walls over 75 feet thick, huge gateways with enormous stone statues, and a vast palace with walls covered with carvings in relief like the one shown above. The carvings depicted scenes from Sargon's military campaigns and other emblems of his greatness and might. At least two depict Gilgamesh.

Application Have students study the statue and the **Humanities Connection** on this page and then answer the following questions:

Why might King Sargon have chosen to decorate his palace with images of Gilgamesh?

Possible Responses: Gilgamesh was famous as a great king and a mighty warrior; he was superhuman—two thirds a god; even the gods respected Gilgamesh's courage and strength.

What are some characteristics of the way Gilgamesh is depicted that King Sargon might have liked?

Possible Responses: The figure is larger than life; carved out of stone, it appears very solid and strong; Gilgamesh has a fierce expression on his face; his arms and legs are thick and muscular; he is holding with one arm a lion that is smaller than he is; he is holding a club as if ready for battle.

therefore bake loaves of bread, each day one loaf, and put it beside his head; and make a mark on the wall to number the days he has slept."

So she baked loaves of bread, each day one loaf, and put it beside his head, and she marked on the wall the days that he slept; and there came a day when the first loaf was hard, the second loaf
A was like leather, the third was soggy, the crust of the fourth had mold, the fifth was mildewed, the sixth was fresh, and the seventh was still on the embers. Then Utnapishtim touched him and he woke. Gilgamesh said to Utnapishtim the Faraway, "I hardly slept when you touched and roused me." But Utnapishtim said, "Count these loaves and learn how many days you slept, for your first is hard, your second like leather, your third is soggy, the crust of your fourth has mold, your fifth is mildewed, your sixth is fresh and your seventh was still over the glowing embers when I touched and woke you." Gilgamesh said, "What shall I do, O Utnapishtim, where shall I go? Already the thief in the night has hold of my limbs, death inhabits my room; wherever my foot rests, there I find death."

1 Then Utnapishtim spoke to Urshanabi the ferryman: "Woe to you Urshanabi, now and for ever more you have become hateful to this harborage; it is not for you, nor for you are the crossings of this sea. Go now, banished from the
2 shore. But this man before whom you walked, bringing him here, whose body is covered with foulness and the grace of whose limbs has been spoiled by wild skins, take him to the washing-
3 place. There he shall wash his long hair clean as snow in the water, he shall throw off his skins and let the sea carry them away, and the beauty of his body shall be shown, the fillet[17] on his forehead shall be renewed, and he shall be given clothes to
cover his nakedness. Till he reaches his own city 3
and his journey is accomplished, these clothes will show no sign of age, they will wear like a new garment." So Urshanabi took Gilgamesh and led him to the washing-place, he washed his long hair as clean as snow in the water, he threw off his skins, which the sea carried away, and showed the beauty of his body. He renewed the fillet on his forehead, and to cover his nakedness gave him clothes which would show no sign of age, but would wear like a new garment till he reached his own city, and his journey was accomplished.

Then Gilgamesh and Urshanabi launched the boat on to the water and boarded it, and they made ready to sail away; but the wife of Utnapishtim the Faraway said to him, "Gilgamesh came here wearied out, he is worn out; what will you give him to carry him back to his own country?" So Utnapishtim spoke, and Gilgamesh took a pole and brought the boat in to the bank. "Gilgamesh, you came here a man wearied out, you have worn yourself out; what
shall I give you to carry you back to your own 4
country? Gilgamesh, I shall reveal a secret thing, it is a mystery of the gods that I am telling you. There is a plant that grows under the water, it has a prickle like a thorn, like a rose; it will wound your hands, but if you succeed in taking it, then your hands will hold that which restores his lost youth to a man."

PAUSE & REFLECT Do you think Utnapishtim treats Gilgamesh fairly?

17. **fillet** (fĭl′ĭt): narrow cloth or ribbon worn as a headband.

Customizing Instruction

Less Proficient Readers

1 Students may find the sudden reappearance of a character with a name similar to that of Utnapishtim confusing. Remind them that Urshanabi is the ferryman who brought Gilgamesh across the waters of death to the realm of the gods (see page 40).

Focus To continue helping students with the Focus directive on page 43, draw their attention to the following passages:

2 Utnapishtim banishes Urshanabi for bring Gilgamesh.

3 Utnapishtim commands Urshanabi to take Gilgamesh to the washing place and gives Gilgamesh clothes that show no sign of age.

4 Utnapishtim reveals to Gilgamesh, as a gift to carry home, a mystery of the gods.

MINI LESSON Grammar

CONCRETE AND ABSTRACT NOUNS

Instruction Explain that every noun is either concrete or abstract. A concrete noun names something that can be perceived with the senses—seen, heard, smelled, touched, or tasted. An abstract noun names an idea, quality, or characteristic. Display the following chart:

Concrete Nouns	shoe, scream, perfume
Abstract Nouns	beauty, truth, loyalty

Practice In the sentences below, identify the boldfaced nouns as either concrete or abstract.

1. Gilgamesh had **fears** about death. *(abstract)*
2. Utnapishtim told about a **flood.** *(concrete)*
3. Utnapishtim gained **immortality.** *(abstract)*
4. Gilgamesh gained **wisdom.** *(abstract)*
5. He engraved his story on **stone.** *(concrete)*

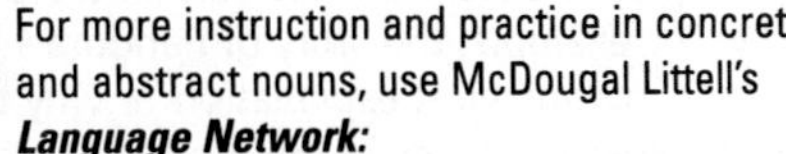

For more instruction and practice in concrete and abstract nouns, use McDougal Littell's ***Language Network:***

- Grade 10, Chapter 1, "The Parts of Speech"
- Grade 12, Review: Parts of Speech

Reading and Analyzing

Reading Skills and Strategies
MAKING INFERENCES

A Ask students what Gilgamesh is probably feeling as he speaks these words.

Possible Responses: Joy at finding the marvelous plant; pride in his ability to retrieve the plant from deep under the water; eager anticipation to give the plant to the old men of Uruk to eat and to eat it himself.

Reading Skills and Strategies
CLARIFYING

B Explain that, according to tradition, the "seven wise men" were master craftsmen who lived before the flood and taught humanity the crafts and technologies of civilization.

Reading Skills and Strategies
MAKING INFERENCES

C Ask students what Gilgamesh is probably feeling as he speaks these words.

Possible Responses: pride in his city; joy at being home again; relief to be among familiar surroundings where he is known and respected; warm friendship for Urshanabi, who helped him and has stayed with him

FOCUS As you read to the end, look for passages that show how Gilgamesh feels about the way his adventure concludes.

When Gilgamesh heard this he opened the sluices so that a sweet-water current might carry him out to the deepest channel; he tied heavy stones to his feet and they dragged him down to the water-bed. There he saw the plant growing; although it pricked him he took it in his hands; then he cut the heavy stones from his feet, and the sea carried him and threw him on to the shore. Gilgamesh said to Urshanabi the ferryman, "Come here, and see this marvelous plant. By its virtue a man may win back all his former strength. I will take it to Uruk of the strong walls; there I will give it to the old men to eat. Its name shall be 'The Old Men Are Young Again'; and at last I shall eat it myself and have back all my lost youth." So Gilgamesh returned by the gate through which he had come, Gilgamesh and Urshanabi went together. They traveled their twenty leagues and then they broke their fast; after thirty leagues they stopped for the night.

Gilgamesh saw a well of cool water and he went down and bathed; but deep in the pool there was lying a serpent, and the serpent sensed the sweetness of the flower. It rose out of the water and snatched it away, and immediately it sloughed[18] its skin and returned to the well. Then Gilgamesh sat down and wept, the tears ran down his face, and he took the hand of Urshanabi; "O Urshanabi, was it for this that I toiled with my hands, is it for this I have wrung out my heart's blood? For myself I have gained nothing; not I, but the beast of the earth has joy of it now. Already the stream has carried it twenty leagues back to the channels where I found it. I found a sign and now I have lost it. Let us leave the boat on the bank and go."

After twenty leagues they broke their fast, after thirty leagues they stopped for the night; in three days they had walked as much as a journey of a month and fifteen days. When the journey was accomplished they arrived at Uruk, the strong-walled city. Gilgamesh spoke to him, to Urshanabi the ferryman, "Urshanabi, climb up on to the wall of Uruk, inspect its foundation terrace, and examine well the brickwork; see if it is not of burnt bricks; and did not the seven wise men lay these foundations? One third of the whole is city, one third is garden, and one third is field, with the precinct of the goddess Ishtar. These parts and the precinct are all Uruk."

This too was the work of Gilgamesh, the king, who knew the countries of the world. He was wise, he saw mysteries and knew secret things, he brought us a tale of the days before the flood. He went a long journey, was weary, worn out with labor, and returning engraved on a stone the whole story. ❖

18. **sloughed** (slŭfd): cast off; shed.

Humanities

MYTHOLOGY One of the functions that myths have is to explain why the world is the way it is. Ancient cultures often accounted for natural phenomena with tales or legends that explained their origin. Such stories are sometimes called "pourquoi" stories, from the French word for *why*. For example, the story of Pandora's box gives a mythological explanation of why there are unpleasant things in the world.

In the story about the serpent stealing the flower that restores youth, we can see a pourquoi story that has been worked into *The Epic of Gilgamesh*. In the epic, the serpent sheds its skin when it steals the flower that restores youth, getting the benefit that Gilgamesh had hoped for. To explain the phenomenon of skin-shedding they had observed in snakes, the ancient Mesopotamians attributed to them a special power to remain youthful. In stories like the Gilgamesh epic, they gave an account of why snakes have this power and human beings do not.

Connect to the Literature

1. **What Do You Think?** How did you react when you learned the result of Gilgamesh's quest for immortality?

Comprehension Check
- Why does Gilgamesh want to find Utnapishtim?
- What story does Utnapishtim tell Gilgamesh?
- How does Utnapishtim become immortal?

Think Critically

2. What three adjectives would you use to describe Gilgamesh? Explain your choices.
3. Why can't Gilgamesh accept the fact that human beings die?

   THINK ABOUT
   - what Gilgamesh says when he decides to go in search of Utnapishtim
   - what Gilgamesh says to Shamash after passing through the mountain
   - what Gilgamesh tells Siduri when she asks him why his cheeks look starved and his face drawn
4. Why do you think the story ends with Gilgamesh proudly showing Urshanabi the city of Uruk?
5. **ACTIVE READING: ANALYZING CAUSE AND EFFECT** Look back in your READER'S NOTEBOOK at the examples of **cause-and-effect** relationships you recorded. What event in the story do you think had the strongest effect on Gilgamesh?

Extend Interpretations

6. **What If?** How do you think the story of Gilgamesh might continue? What kind of person—and king—will he be in the future?
7. **Connect to Life** In our world today, what are some different attitudes that people take toward death?

LITERARY ANALYSIS: THE QUEST STORY

A **quest story** is a story in which an individual known as the quest hero goes on a journey in order to achieve a goal. A quest hero may be part god or have friends (or enemies) who are gods. Because of this, he or she often has access to supernatural powers. However, quest heroes usually have ordinary human traits as well, both good and bad, that allow us to identify with them. Often, quest stories reflect the history, values, and beliefs of a particular culture.

Activity Analyze Gilgamesh as a quest hero by creating a diagram like the one started here.

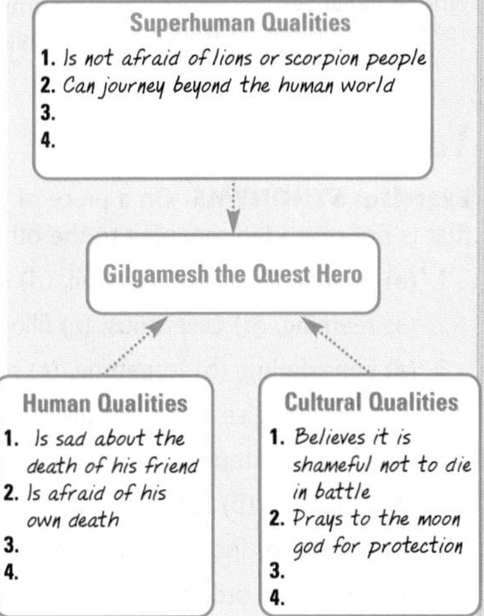

Connect to the Literature

1. **What Do You Think?**
   Some students may feel disappointment or sympathy because Gilgamesh failed to achieve his goal. Others may say it was wrong or arrogant of him to go against nature or human fate.

Comprehension Check

1. Gilgamesh wants to learn from Utnapishtim the secret of immortality.
2. Utnapishtim tells Gilgamesh the story of a great flood that destroyed almost all of humankind.
3. The gods give him immortality after he survives the flood.

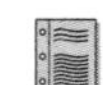
Use Selection Quiz in **Unit One Resource Book,** p. 8.

Think Critically

2. Answers will vary. Students may suggest adjectives that get at Gilgamesh's heroism, his arrogance, or his human weaknesses.
3. Answers will vary. Some students may point out that Enkidu's death makes Gilgamesh aware of and afraid of mortality. Others may say that Gilgamesh is like a spoiled child who can't accept what he doesn't like. Still others may see Gilgamesh's attempt to defy fate as heroic.
4. Students will probably say that Gilgamesh is glad to be back in his own land, but they may disagree about why. Some students will say that Gilgamesh has learned to accept his life as it is with its human limitations. Others may see his pride in the city as a sign that he has become less self-centered.
5. Answers will vary. Possible answers include the killing of Humbaba and the cutting down of the cedar forest, the death of Enkidu, Gilgamesh's failure to stay awake for seven days, and the loss of the plant that makes old men young. Have students give reasons for their answers.

Extend Interpretations

6. **What If?** Good responses will draw logical conclusions from the details and information given in the story. Some students will say that Gilgamesh will be a more modest, considerate person and a more benevolent king. Others may say that in his grief and defeat he will become even more self-centered and indifferent to his subjects.
7. **Connect to Life** Answers will vary. Possible Responses: belief in an afterlife; trying to postpone death through lifestyle and medical treatment, losing oneself in the pleasures of the moment to avoid thinking about it.

Literary Analysis

Activity You could make this a whole-class activity by having students suggest qualities and compiling them into a master list.

Use **Unit One Resource Book,** p. 6, for more practice.

Writing Options

1. **Definition of Heroism** Some students may define heroism in terms of physical strength and courage as shown by Gilgamesh before Enkidu's death. Others may define heroism in terms of inner strengths, such as dealing with grief or accepting defeat, strengths shown by Gilgamesh after Enkidu's death.
2. **Gilgamesh Adventure** Students might imagine Gilgamesh on his way to Utnapishtim, as in the story, or they might think up a new adventure for him, possibly based on how he has changed by the end of the story.

Activities & Explorations

1. **Gilgamesh Illustration** Encourage students to reread the part of the story that they are illustrating.
2. **City Plan** Encourage students to think about what it would be like to live in a city like Uruk. You may want to have students do this activity in conjunction with the Inquiry and Research assignment.

Inquiry & Research

Report on a Lost Civilization You may want to have students work in small groups to complete the research. Assign each group a particular aspect of Sumerian society to investigate, for example: social structure, religion, warfare, family life, technology, art. Have students include at least one nontextual medium when reporting on their research.

Vocabulary in Action

Synonyms

1. d
2. b
3. b
4. d
5. d
6. c
7. c
8. a
9. a
10. a

To assess skills and concepts taught in this selection, use **Formal Assessment Book,** p. 7.

Choices & CHALLENGES

Writing Options

1. Definition of Heroism How would you define heroism? Before writing, think about the kind of heroism Gilgamesh shows at different points in the story. Consider how your ideal hero would compare with Gilgamesh. Then write a paragraph giving your definition. Be sure to include some specific examples of heroic behavior.

2. Gilgamesh Adventure Write another episode of *The Epic of Gilgamesh* in which Gilgamesh has an encounter with a strange person or creature who either helps him or stands in his way.

Writing Handbook
See page R29: Narrative Writing.

Activities & Explorations

1. Gilgamesh Illustration Choose a memorable scene from *The Epic of Gilgamesh,* such as Enkidu's dream, Gilgamesh's encounter with the scorpion people, the garden of the gods, the flood, or the serpent stealing the flower that restores youth. Illustrate the scene as you envision it. ~ART

2. City Plan Using books or the Internet, find out what the ancient city of Uruk might have looked like. Then create a model or blueprint of the city, with labels indicating the most important structures and places. ~VIEWING AND REPRESENTING

Inquiry & Research

Report on a Lost Civilization The Sumerians are a mystery in the history of the ancient world. No one knows for sure where they came from, and their language was not related to that of any other people in the region. Yet their influence on future civilizations—even our own—was vast. Find out more about this lost civilization, and present your findings in an oral report.

Communication Handbook
See page R45: Finding Sources.

Vocabulary in Action

Exercise: SYNONYMS On a piece of paper, write the letter of the word in each set that is not related in meaning to the other words in the set.

1. (a) lament, (b) moan, (c) wail, (d) sing
2. (a) teeming, (b) cavernous, (c) filled, (d) crowded
3. (a) considering, (b) forgetting, (c) reflecting, (d) musing
4. (a) allot, (b) give, (c) distribute, (d) deny
5. (a) daze, (b) stupor, (c) spell, (d) sadness
6. (a) fortunate, (b) lucky, (c) ominous, (d) favored
7. (a) prayer, (b) incantation, (c) shrine, (d) chant
8. (a) forbid, (b) ordain, (c) decree, (d) establish
9. (a) refuse, (b) succeed, (c) prevail, (d) win
10. (a) transit, (b) roadblock, (c) obstruction, (d) barrier

Building Vocabulary
For a lesson on using a thesaurus to find synonyms, see page 558.

Connect to Today

The Quest to Find *Gilgamesh*

If Gilgamesh is "two-thirds a god and one-third a man," then fictional archaeologist Indiana Jones could be described as "two-thirds an adventurer and one-third a scholar." Most archaeology is not as hair-raising as the predicaments Indy gets into, but it too is often full of mystery and excitement.

One of the unsolved mysteries of contemporary archaeology is the text of the *Gilgamesh* epic itself. In the more than 150 years since the first fragments were discovered in the ruins of Nineveh, only about 80 percent of the story has been pieced together. The quest to find the rest continues today.

Piecing Together the Puzzle Recently the American scholar Theodore Kwasman found the long-lost opening lines of the epic—not seen by human eyes for 24 centuries. Kwasman made his discovery among the tablet fragments found at Nineveh in 1849, but he did his detective work at the British Museum in London, where the majority of the fragments are now housed.

Fragments connected by Theodore Kwasman. Tablet with opening lines of *Gilgamesh*. The British Museum, London.

To make his discovery, Kwasman not only had to read cuneiform; he also had to know the text of *Gilgamesh* well enough to connect a known passage to an unknown one.

What Happens Next? More work needs to be carried out by archaeologists. Their efforts to uncover ruins may someday give us a complete *Gilgamesh.* However, many obstacles remain, some of which would challenge Indiana Jones himself.

The region near Nineveh, now part of Iraq, has been torn by war in recent years, just as it was when Nineveh was destroyed in 612 B.C. Since the Gulf War in 1991, historical sites have been neglected—and even looted. Researchers from outside Iraq have been prevented from visiting the sites, and we have no way of knowing how much of this ancient treasure has been lost.

Small Group or Whole Class Discussion Many people feel that archaeological treasures removed from ancient Mesopotamian cities by Layard and others should be returned to Iraq. Other people, because of wars and political tension in the region, are glad that many artifacts are in places like the British Museum. What is your opinion? Who owns the treasures of the ancient world?

Connect to Today

The **Connect to Today** feature will help students relate the selection they have just read to contemporary events and issues affecting their own lives. Current archaeological research is directly involved in the reconstruction of the *Gilgamesh* epic and its mythological and historical contexts. In addition, recent events in the Middle East continue to have a strong impact on this research.

The Quest to Find Gilgamesh

Kwasman's discovery is a truly amazing piece of detective work. The two sets of fragments he connected are not from the same tablet, so he could not connect the fragments on the basis of their shape. Since the complete opening line had never been seen by modern eyes, he could not know what it said without joining the fragments. At the same time, he could not join the fragments without some idea of how they might logically fit together.

Andrew George, a University of London scholar and author of a new translation of the epic, claims that Kwasman's discovery has changed our understanding of the poem. According to George, the first line of the epic identifies Gilgamesh as "he who saw the watery deep, the country's foundation." Since Ea is the god of the waters and of the wisdom that underlies human society and government, George sees in the line a reference to Gilgamesh as a founder of civilization.

Small Group or Whole Class Discussion You might have individual students debate different positions on this question. The discussion could also be organized as a panel discussion between groups of like-minded students.

If you want to expand the discussion, you might have students investigate similar issues regarding native American burial sites.

Objectives

- appreciate different kinds of ancient Egyptian **poetry (Literary Analysis)**
- understand the role of the **speaker** in literature **(Literary Analysis)**
- learn to **identify cultural characteristics** of ancient Egyptian literature **(Active Reading)**

Thematic Link

These literary works all show the central role played by religion and **spiritual** concerns in Ancient Egyptian culture.

5-Minute Warm-Up

Daily Language SkillBuilder

Have students **proofread** the display sentences on page 15g and write them correctly.

PREPARING to *Read*

from the

BOOK OF THE DEAD

THE CHAPTER OF NOT LETTING THE BODY PERISH

ADORATION OF THE DISK

KING AKHENATEN and PRINCESS NEFERTITI

NEW KINGDOM POETRY

I'M GOING DOWNSTREAM ON KINGSWATER CANAL

WHENEVER I LEAVE YOU, I GO OUT OF BREATH

Build Background

Egyptian Culture The selections you are about to read reflect three important features of ancient Egyptian culture:

- concern about the afterlife
- worship of a sun god
- delight in everyday life

As different as these features might seem to be, they are interrelated. The Egyptians believed that in the afterlife people would have the same interests and experience the same pleasures as in earthly life. They saw the sun god as the giver of life to all of nature.

Book of the Dead The Book of the Dead is based upon the most important myth in Egyptian culture—the myth of Osiris. Osiris was a benevolent god who taught human beings agriculture and other arts of civilization. His younger brother Set became jealous and killed him for the throne. Isis, the sister of Osiris, found her brother's body and brought it back to life. Osiris then became lord of the otherworld.

Throughout their history, the Egyptians based many of their burial practices on this myth. In the Old Kingdom, they believed that when a pharaoh died, he rose, like Osiris, from the dead. In fact, they believed that the king became Osiris himself. To celebrate this event, the king's followers recited hymns and prayers based on the Osiris story and carved them permanently into the walls of the pyramids where the kings were buried. Such "pyramid texts" are the earliest works of Egyptian literature that have survived.

By the time of the Middle Kingdom, the privilege of becoming Osiris had been extended to all the nobility. This trend was taken a step further in the New Kingdom. They believed that a glorious afterlife as Osiris was available to anyone who had lived a good life and for whom the proper prayers were said. These prayers, based once again on the myth of Osiris, were written on papyrus scrolls and buried along with the dead. The Egyptians called these burial scrolls the Chapters of Coming Forth by Day, a name that shows their positive expectations for the afterlife.

The selection on pages 52–53 is taken from the burial papyrus of a man named Nu, who worked as a steward or property manager.

For a humanities activity, click on:

LESSON RESOURCES

UNIT ONE RESOURCE BOOK, pp. 9–10

ASSESSMENT RESOURCES
Formal Assessment, pp. 9–10
Teacher's Guide to Assessment and Portfolio Use
Test Generator

INTEGRATED TECHNOLOGY
Visit our Web site: classzone.com

ADDITIONAL RESOURCES
Lesson Planning Guide, pp. 3–4
Teacher's Sourcebook for Language Development

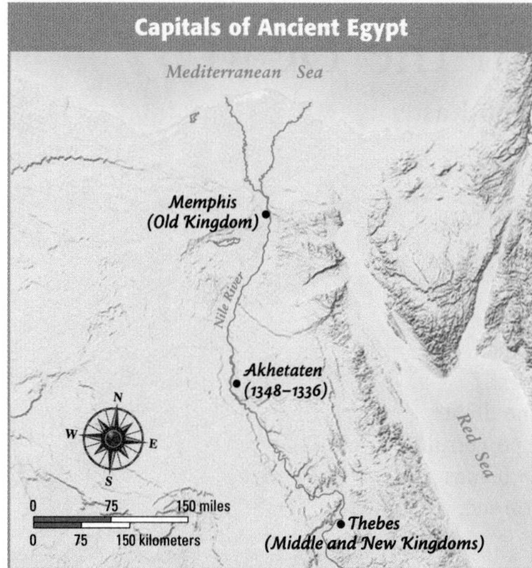

Adoration of the Disk The second example of ancient Egyptian literature was written by the pharaoh Akhenaten, who ruled Egypt about 1353–1336 B.C. Akhenaten rejected the traditional worship of many gods and goddesses. Instead, he declared that the sun god Aten was the only true god and built a new capital city in his honor. Akhenaten also wrote in Aten's honor the poem you will read on page 54.

New Kingdom Poetry The ancient Egyptians were obviously fascinated with death and the afterlife. This fact has led to a popular image of their culture as being as dried up and lifeless as one of their mummies. The truth is that the ancient Egyptians were a people who knew how to enjoy life immensely. This was especially true during the period of the New Kingdom, a time of unparalleled prosperity and cultural enrichment—the result of political expansion and international commerce.

The New Kingdom produced a body of excellent lyric poetry that reflects the Egyptians' joy in life. Like much poetry throughout the ages, many of these poems celebrate one of the great vital forces of human life—romantic love. On pages 57–58, you will find two examples of New Kingdom love poems.

Connect to Your Life

Each of these selections reveals something about what the ancient Egyptians valued. What do you think is most greatly valued in your own culture? Share your ideas with your classmates.

Focus Your Reading

LITERARY ANALYSIS: SPEAKER

In a work of literature, the **speaker** is the voice that speaks the ideas presented. The speaker is not necessarily the writer; he or she may be a creation of the writer, much like a character in a play. As you read these four works, try to form an impression of the person speaking based on what he or she says.

ACTIVE READING: IDENTIFYING CULTURAL CHARACTERISTICS

In order to understand a culture different from your own, you need to consider the culture's values, its philosophical and religious beliefs, the stories its people tell, and the images they use.

READER'S NOTEBOOK As you read these Egyptian selections, look for clues that help you identify **cultural characteristics** of the ancient Egyptians. Keep track of the clues you find by recording them in a chart like the one started here.

Selection	Clue	What It Reveals About the Egyptians
Book of the Dead	"Grant that I may descend into the Land of Eternity"	They wanted to live forever.

READING FOR INFORMATION
Reading Skills and Strategies
PREVIEWING

Help students with the **Build Background** essay by going over with them the four subheads and the information covered in each section. The first section deals with Egyptian culture in general and the following three introduce students to each of the three selections in the lesson.

READING THE MAP
Reading Skills and Strategies

Point out to students that the three capital cities shown on the map each correspond to a particular period in ancient Egyptian history: the Old Kingdom, the reign of King Akhenaten, and the Middle and New Kingdoms. Have students refer to page 20 to remind themselves of the dates of the three kingdoms. Akhenaten's dates are given just below the map under the heading **Adoration of the Disk.** Tell students that the location of Akhenaten's capital, like his worship of one god, was a major break with tradition and that Egypt soon returned to the old ways after his death.

Have students answer the following questions:

1. During which years was Memphis the capital of Egypt? *(approximately 2660–2180 B.C.)*
2. How long was Thebes the capital of Egypt? *(approximately 1,000 years; that is, from 2080–1075 B.C., minus the 12 years during which Akhetaten was the capital)*
3. During which Kingdom was Akhetaten the capital of Egypt? *(the New Kingdom)*
4. How long had Akhenaten been king when he moved the capital to Akhetaten? *(about five years)*

TIME MANAGEMENT

If your schedule requires that you cover the lesson objectives in a shorter time, use . . .

- Preparing to Read, p. 50
- Thinking Through the Literature, p. 59

If you want to take advantage of longer blocks of class time, use . . .

- TE Teaching Options: Speaking and Listening, pp. 52, 58; Viewing and Representing, pp. 53, 55, 56; Grammar, p. 57
- Choices & Challenges, p. 60
- The Translator at Work, p. 61.

Reading and Analyzing

Literary Analysis SPEAKER

The speaker in a literary work is usually the voice of a fictional character rather than that of the author. While Nu actually lived, his speech creates a strong impression of a character that can be analyzed by the reader without direct knowledge of the historical person. Students should pay particular attention to the speaker's **tone**.

Use **Unit One Resource Book,** p. 10, for more practice.

Literary Analysis DRAMATIC MONOLOGUE

A Point out that this line identifies the speaker of the lines that follow. Nu's speech is a dramatic monologue, a literary form in which the speaker addresses a silent or absent listener in a moment of high intensity or deep emotion, as if engaged in private conversation. In this case, the one addressed is the god Osiris. Prayers, hymns, and songs of praise—popular early forms of literature—often take the form of the dramatic monologue.

Active Reading

IDENTIFYING CULTURAL CHARACTERISTICS

B Explain that according to Egyptian religious beliefs, Nu both appeals to his "Divine Father Osiris" for help and himself becomes Osiris. The title *the Osiris Nu* in line 1 anticipates this transformation, as does the statement "I am Khepri" in paragraph 4 following "my divine father Khepri" in paragraph 2.

Use **Unit One Resource Book,** p. 9, for more practice.

from the Book of the Dead

Translated by Joseph Kaster

THE CHAPTER OF NOT LETTING THE BODY PERISH

A Words spoken by the Osiris Nu:

B Hail to thee, O my Divine Father Osiris! I came to heal thee! Do thou heal me, that I may be complete, and that I may be, indeed, like unto my divine father Khepri,[1] the divine
1 type of him who never corrupted. Come, then, make powerful my breath, O Lord of Breath, who exalts those divine beings who are like him! Come, make me endure, and fashion me, O thou Lord of the Sarcophagus![2]

Grant that I may descend into the Land of Eternity, according
2 as that which was done to thee together with thy father Atum[3], whose body did not see corruption, nor did he himself see decay.

I have never done that which thou hatest, but have acclaimed[4] thee among those who love thy Divine Essence. Let me not putrefy, as you do unto every god and every goddess, every animal and every reptile, when they perish, when their animating spirits go forth after their death.

Hail to thee, O my father Osiris! Thou livest with thy members. Thou didst not decay, thou didst not become worms, thou didst not wither, thou didst not putrefy. I am Khepri, and my limbs shall have eternity! I shall not decay, I shall not rot, I shall not putrefy, I shall not become worms, I shall not see corruption before the eye of Shu![5] I shall exist! I shall exist! I shall live! I shall live! I shall flourish! I shall flourish!

I shall wake up in contentment; I shall not putrefy; my intestines shall not perish; I shall not suffer injury. My eye

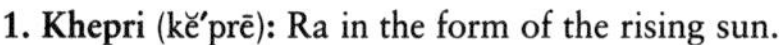

1. **Khepri** (kĕ′prē): Ra in the form of the rising sun.
2. **Sarcophagus** (sär-kŏf′ə-gəs): a stone coffin.
3. **Atum** (ä′təm): Ra in the form of the setting sun and creator of the world.
4. **acclaimed:** praised highly.
5. **Shu** (sho͞o): the god of the air.

MINI LESSON Speaking and Listening

DRAMATIC MONOLOGUE

Instruction Nu's monologue can be read in a number of different ways depending on how it is interpreted. The tone might be reverent, joyful, pleading, commanding, or even fearful. Each way of reading would suggest a different understanding of the purpose of the speech and Nu's attitude toward it.

Prepare Students can work either individually or in small groups. Have them reread Nu's monologue and think about how they imagine it to be spoken. Then have them make notes explaining how they think it should be read. Their notes should address not only tone, but also gestures, actions, volume, pauses, and musical accompaniment or sound effects.

Present Have individual students give dramatic readings of Nu's monologue. Then discuss the assumptions and interpretations that were reflected in each presentation.

This activity is particularly well suited to longer blocks of class time.

shall not decay; the form of my face shall not disappear; my ear shall not become deaf. My head shall not be separated from my neck. My tongue shall not be removed, my hair shall not be cut off. My eyebrows shall not be shaved away, and no evil defect shall befall me.

My body shall be enduring, it shall not perish. It shall not be destroyed, nor shall it be turned back whence it entered into this Land of Eternity!

Nakht scroll (18th Dynasty, 16th–14th centuries B.C.). Photograph copyright © Erich Lessing/Art Resource, New York.

HUMANITIES CONNECTION The Book of the Dead consists of papyrus scrolls that were found in the tombs of important individuals from the New Kingdom period. This scroll shows a nobleman and his wife making an offering to Osiris in order to win his blessing in the next world.

Customizing Instruction

English Learners

1 Explain that the word *type* means "model" or "example."

Less Proficient Readers

2 Students may need some help with this long sentence. Ask them to identify what "nor did he himself see decay" modifies. *(Atum)*

MINI LESSON Viewing and Representing

Nakht Funerary Papyrus Scroll

ART APPRECIATION The nobleman referred to in the **Humanities Connection,** whose name was Nakht, was a scribe and priest under the New Kingdom pharaoh Tuthmose IV.

Instruction Nakht and his wife are shown standing in the garden of their home. Behind them is their house, complete with trees in front and two roof vents used for cooling. In the background is a pool surrounded by trees. Many of the trees in the painting are shown bearing fruit. Standing behind Osiris is Isis, holding the *ankh*, the hieroglyphic symbol for life. Osiris holds the crook and flail, symbols of kingship and authority associated with him.

Application Ask students why scenes from Nakht's home and garden might have been included in his funeral papyrus.

Possible Responses: to show that Nakht has led an orderly life; to show his wealth and social status; to show that in the afterlife he will enjoy the same things he did in this life; to show hospitality toward Osiris and Isis

Reading and Analyzing

Reading Skills and Strategies
CLARIFYING

Explain that the "Disk" referred to in the title is Aten, or the sun-god in the physical form of the sun.

Literary Analysis SPEAKER

We don't meet the speaker of this poem directly until the final stanza. Before that, he is known to us by inference only from what he describes and how he seems to feel about it. Ask students what feelings the speaker expresses in the poem.

Possible Responses: love for the sun god; happiness at the coming of day; sadness at the thought of sunset and the night; joy in the vision of all the earth coming alive with the dawn; admiration for the scope and grandeur of all that lives under the sun; gratitude for all the sun's blessings; amazement at the variety and splendor of the god's creation; loyalty, respect, and affection for the sun god as a father

Reading Skills and Strategies
VISUALIZING

Much of the description and imagery in this poem is based on scenes of the sun shining on the earth and moving across the sky. If students keep the sun in mind as they read, they will find it easier to envision what happens in the poem.

Literary Analysis METAPHOR

(A) Ask students to explain the metaphors used in this line to describe the world after sunset. *(People are "blind" because they can't see in the dark and they "lie in death" because they are asleep; because the houses contain dead people, they are "tombs.")*

Adoration of the Disk

King Akhenaten and Princess Nefertiti

Translated by Robert Hillyer

Thy dawn, O Ra, opens the new horizon,
And every realm that thou hast made to live
Is conquered by thy love, as joyous Day
Follows thy footsteps in delightful peace.

And when thou settest, all the world is bleak;
(A) Houses are tombs where blind men lie in death;
Only the lion and the serpent move
Through the black oven of the sightless night.

Dawn in the East again! the lands awake,
And men leap from their slumber with a song;
They bathe their bodies, clothe them with fresh garments,
And lift their hands in happy adoration.

The cattle roam again across the fields;
Birds flutter in the marsh, and lift their wings
Also in adoration, and the flocks
Run with delight through all the pleasant meadows.

Both north and south along the dazzling river
Ships raise their sails and take their course before thee;
And in the ocean, all the deep-sea fish
Swim to the surface to drink in thy light.

For thou art all that lives, the seed of men,
The son within his mother's womb who knows
The comfort of thy presence near, the babe
To whom thou givest words and growing wisdom;

The chick within the egg, whose breath is thine,
Who runneth from its shell, chirping its joy,
And dancing on its small, unsteady legs
To greet the splendor of the rising sun.

Akhenaten offers a sacrifice to Aten, the sun god (1350 B.C., New Kingdom). Relief from Amarna, Egypt. Archaeological Museum, Cairo. Photograph copyright © Erich Lessing/Art Resource, New York.

HUMANITIES CONNECTION Here, Akhenaten, Nefertiti, and their eldest daughter worship the sun god Aten. The royal couple hold up libations, or ritual offerings of drink. The rays coming from the sun's disk end in hands for extending blessings and receiving the libations. This relief carving is from Akhenaten's palace.

Thy heart created all, this teeming earth,
Its people, herds, creatures that go afoot,
Creatures that fly in air, both land and sea,
Thou didst create them all within thy heart.

Men and their fates are thine, in all their stations,
Their many languages, their many colors,
1 All thine, and we who from the midst of peoples,
2 Thou madest different, Master of the Choice.

And lo, I find thee also in my heart,
I, Akhenaten, find thee and adore.
O thou, whose dawn is life, whose setting, death,
In the great dawn, then lift up me, thy son.

MINI LESSON Viewing and Representing

Relief carving of Akhenaten and his family

ART APPRECIATION The carving shown in the **Humanities Connection** above represents an actual worship ceremony that Akhenaten and his family performed daily.

Instruction Many such images were carved into the walls and balustrades of the royal palace at Akhetaten. Akhenaten, like other pharaohs, was considered to be a mediator between the human and the divine. For this reason, only members of the royal family were depicted worshipping Aten. Flowers and food were common offerings. In front of Akhenaten are two offering tables bearing bunches of lotus blossoms.

Application Ask students what other details of the art work they notice.

Possible Responses: two of the sun's hands hold out the ankh symbol, one above the king and one above the queen; Akhenaten is depicted much larger than Nefertiti, showing his importance; the members of the royal family are depicted with a lot of natural detail

Customizing Instruction

English Learners

Explain that the translator used some old forms of English words to make the text more poetic. Following is a list of modern English equivalents:

Thy (line 1): Your
thou (line 2): you
settest (line 5): set
thee (line 18)
art (line 21): are
givest (line 24): give
runneth (line 26): runs
didst (line 32): did
thine (line 35): yours
madest (line 36): made
lo (line 37): an exclamation used to attract attention or show surprise

1 Students learning English may think that *midst*, like *didst* in line 32, is an old verb form. Explain that *from the midst of* means "from among."

Less Proficient Readers

2 Students may need help understanding the phrase "we who from the midst of peoples, / Thou madest different" (lines 35–36). Ask them to restate the phrase more simply. *(we whom you made different from other people are yours also).*

Reading and Analyzing

Active Reading
IDENTIFYING CULTURAL CHARACTERISTICS

A Students may be confused by the reference to the "Sun Festival" and assume that they can't understand the poem without having more background information. Help students see how much information about the festival can be inferred from context. *(Line 1: the festival is held in honor of the sun; line 6: the festival takes place on a day holy to a god; lines 19-20: the god is Ra, the sun-god.)*

Reading Skills and Strategies
CLARIFYING

B The history of ancient Egypt dates from the unification of Upper and Lower Egypt (see page 20). For this reason, "Lord of Two Lands" was a traditional title for the Pharaoh. Here the title is given to the sun-god Ra.

Kat-Tep and his wife, Hetepheres (Fourth Dynasty, 2550 B.C.). Painted limestone statue. The British Museum, London. Photograph copyright © Michael Holford.

HUMANITIES CONNECTION This is a tomb sculpture of the high official Kat-Tep and his wife, Hetepheres. The depiction of them side by side and of equal height is unusual in Egyptian art. The difference in color between the two figures shows that Hetepheres' sphere of activity was indoors and Kat-Tep's outdoors.

MINI LESSON Viewing and Representing

Kat-Tep and His Wife, Hetepheres

ART APPRECIATION The sculpture shown in the **Humanities Connection** above was carved from limestone and painted to add more detail. It dates from the Fourth Dynasty of the Old Kingdom (about 2550 B.C.).

Instruction The depiction of the couple as of equal size and height suggests that they are equally important in the representation and that there was probably a good deal of equality in their relationship. (By contrast, in the carving on page 55, Akhenaten stands nearly twice as tall as Nefertiti.) The strength of their relationship is indicated in another way also: Hetepheres has her arm around her husband's waist.

Application Ask students why Kat-Tep and Hetepheres might have wanted themselves represented in this way in their tomb.

Possible Responses: because they wanted to be together in the afterlife; because their marriage was very important in their lives; because they wanted to show their mutual respect for one another; because they wanted to be remembered as a couple

I'm going downstream on Kingswater Canal

Translated by John L. Foster

A
I'm going downstream on Kingswater Canal,
with leave to attend Sun Festival;
I want to wander there where the tents
are pitched at the far end of Mertiu Lagoon.
I'll hurry along—I can hardly keep silent—
thinking of God's holy Day,
For maybe I'll see my truelove go by
bound for the Houses of Offering.

I'll stand there with you at the mouth of the Mertiu
(heart, are you with me or back in Ra's city?),
Then we'll turn back to Offeringhouse Orchard,
where I'll steal from the grove by the chapels
A branch for a festival fan.
There I can watch the whole celebration.

With my eyes upturned toward the holy garden,
and my arms full of flowering branches,
And my hair heavy with sweetsmelling unguents,
what a splendid Lady I'll be!—
Dressed fine like a princess, for Ra,
B
Lord of Two Lands, on His feast day.

Fine like a bride, love,
I'll stand there (waiting) beside you.

17 unguents (ŭng'gwənts): ointments.

Customizing Instruction

Less Proficient Readers

Students may think they are not understanding the poem because they do not understand all of the references to setting and action connected with the Sun Festival. Help students focus on the main thrust of the poem—the speaker's imagined encounter with her "truelove," which can be understood without knowing more specific details about the festival.

Advanced Learners

This poem is probably based on the ceremonial opening of the main canal at Heliopolis at the beginning of the inundation, or annual flooding of the Nile. Have students find out more about this event and the ceremonies surrounding it. They can then report back to the rest of the class any information that helps in the understanding of this poem.

MINI LESSON Grammar

COMMON AND PROPER NOUNS

Instruction Remind students that a common noun is a general name for a person, place, or thing. A proper noun is the name of a specific person, place, or thing. Common nouns are usually not capitalized; proper nouns are always capitalized. Display the following sentences, underlining the proper nouns, as shown:

Ra was an important god.
The Nile is a river in Egypt.
Ms. Sanchez has seen the pyramids.

Practice Have students copy the following sentences, capitalizing the proper nouns:

1. Omar rode his bike through egypt. *(Egypt)*
2. The capital of egypt is cairo. *(Egypt, Cairo)*
3. Arabic is the official language, but french and english are widely known. *(French, English)*
4. Mrs. carrick told about the pyramids. *(Carrick)*
5. Some pyramids are in the ancient city of giza, near the sahara desert. *(Giza, Sahara Desert)*

For more instruction and practice in common and proper nouns, use McDougal Littell's ***Language Network:***

- Grade 10, Chapter 1, "The Parts of Speech"
- Grade 12, Review: Parts of Speech

Reading and Analyzing

Literary Analysis METAPHOR

Point out that the basic metaphor of this poem is one that can be found in many contemporary love poems and songs. The presence of the beloved is metaphorically life itself—the very breath in the speaker's body. The metaphor is given a further poetic twist in lines 9–11 when the speaker imagines the beloved's kiss as a kind of romantic CPR (cardio-pulmonary resuscitation).

Reading Skills and Strategies CLARIFYING

A Make sure students understand that "my heart stands still inside me" is a figure of speech rather than a literal description of what happens to the speaker.

Whenever I leave you, I go out of breath

Translated by John L. Foster

Whenever I leave you, I go out of breath
(death must be lonely like I am);
I dream lying dreams of your love lost,
and my heart stands still inside me. **A**
I stare at my favorite datecakes—
they would be salt to me now—
And pomegranate wine (once sweet to our lips)
bitter, bitter as birdgall.

Touching noses with you, love, your kiss alone,
and my stuttering heart speaks clear:
Breathe me more of your breath, let me live!
Man meant for me,
God himself gave you as his holy gift,
my love to outlast forever.

8 **birdgall:** bitter substance derive[d] from the liver of a bird.

Relief from the tomb of Vizier Ramose (18th Dynasty). Thebes. Photograph copyright © Michael Holford.

MINI LESSON Speaking and Listening

ORAL INTERPRETATION

Instruction Point out that both this poem and the one on page 57 show a change in mood when the beloved comes on the scene. Have students pick one of the two poems to prepare for a dramatic reading.

Prepare Have students think about how the mood of their chosen poem changes from the beginning to the end and about how this change could be brought out in an oral reading through techniques such as tone, facial expression, and dramatic gestures.

Present Have several students give a dramatic reading of each poem. Then students can discuss which oral interpretations they thought were most successful and why.

Connect to the Literature

1. **What Do You Think?** Which of the four selections you just read seems most memorable to you? Why?

Think Critically

2. In the excerpt from the Book of the Dead, how would you describe the **tone,** or attitude, of Nu's speech? How does the tone relate to the situation described in the text?
3. In "Adoration of the Disk," why does the **speaker** think that Ra should be praised?
4. In "I'm going downstream . . .," why does the speaker delight in dreaming of herself standing like a bride beside her love?
5. **ACTIVE READING: IDENTIFYING CULTURAL CHARACTERISTICS** Look back at the list of **cultural characteristics** that you recorded in your READER'S NOTEBOOK. Get together with a few classmates and compare clues and interpretations for one selection. Then report your group's findings to the class as a whole.

Extend Interpretations

6. **Comparing Texts** Which of the selections gave you the strongest sense of the speaker as a person? Explain your answer.
7. **Comparing Texts** In both "I'm going downstream on Kingswater Canal" and "Whenever I leave you, I go out of breath," a female speaker addresses her absent beloved. What are some ways in which the poems differ?
8. **Connect to Life** Their literature and art show that the ancient Egyptians both appreciated everyday life and prepared extensively for death. How do their attitudes compare with those of your society?

LITERARY ANALYSIS: SPEAKER

The **speaker** in a work of literature is the voice that speaks the ideas presented. The speaker is not necessarily the writer, although in some cases he or she may be. The speaker relates ideas from his or her point of view. Sometimes, a writer will create a speaker with a distinct identity in order to achieve a certain effect.

Activity Choose one of the four selections, and jot down some notes describing your impression of the person speaking. Then, using your notes, read the selection aloud to the class in a way you think expresses the speaker's personality.

Connect to the Literature

1. **What Do You Think?** Accept all answers that reflect knowledge of the texts. Encourage students to provide supporting details.

Think Critically

2. Students will probably interpret Nu's tone as confident and energetic, showing his certainty about his place in the afterlife. Some students may perceive his voice as anxious and eager to win Osiris's favor, showing his concern about avoiding the fate of the dead.
3. Possible Responses: Ra is the creator of all of nature and the bringer of love and peace. Ra brings daylight and with it the many joyful activities of life. The speaker views Ra as his own father and protector.
4. Answers will vary. Students will probably say that the speaker is in love with someone she hopes one day to marry and that she is dreaming of this day. Some students may say that the speaker is imagining herself participating in the Sun Festival as a princess and the bride of Ra.
5. Possible Responses: (Book of the Dead) The Eyptians believe in life after death; they believe that Osiris can grant them immortality; they believe that prayers can have an important effect on one's fate after death. (Adoration of the Disk) The Egyptians believe that the Sun god gives life to all of nature; they value the life of all people and all creatures on the earth; they believe that the pharoah has a special relationship to god. (I'm going downstream, Whenever I leave you) The Egyptians value romantic love; they enjoy religious festivals; they enjoy dressing up and beautifying themselves; they understand the influence love has on a person's happiness.

Extend Interpretations

6. **Comparing Texts** Accept all answers that students can support with specific examples from the selection named. Ask students briefly to describe the speaker's personality.
7. **Comparing Texts** Possible Responses: In the first poem the speaker is hoping to meet her beloved, while in the second she is lamenting their separation; the first poem connects love to a religious festival and to marriage, and the second focuses more directly on the passionate side of love; the tone of the first poem is calm and confident, while that of the second poem mournful and passionate.
8. **Connect to Life** Possible Responses: Many people in contemporary society try to think about death as little as possible; many religions focus on preparation for the afterlife, but think of it as very different from this life; people today tend to focus on life on earth or life after death, but not both.

Literary Analysis

Activity Suggest that, to get started, students refer to their notes on the first Comparing Texts question. Then have them write down some ideas for expressing the personality of their speaker orally. You might have several students do each speaker. Then conclude the activity with a discussion of the differences between presentations.

Use **Unit One Resource Book,** p. 10, for more practice.

Writing Options

1. **Autobiographical Papyrus Scroll** You may want to have students brainstorm answers to the questions orally before beginning to write.
2. **Praise Poem** Help students get started by suggesting some topics for their poems such as their school, their town, their experience of nature, or the world of technology.

Activities & Explorations

Pyramid Cutaway You may want to have students do this project in small groups.

Inquiry & Research

Papyrus Demonstration You might expand this project by having students research the invention of other kinds of paper and early forms of the book, such as scrolls and tablets. Students might also compare the longevity of different writing media and its effect on our knowledge of ancient cultures.

To assess skills and concepts taught in these selections, use **Formal Assessment Book,** p. 9.

Writing Options

1. Autobiographical Papyrus Scroll What would you like people to find written about you when they open your tomb thousands of years from now? Would it be instructions for what to say in the next world, your deepest thoughts about life and death, or a description of your unique qualities as an individual? Use your answers to these questions to write your own Book of the Dead papyrus scroll. Place the scroll in your **Working Portfolio.**

2. Praise Poem In "Adoration of the Disk" the speaker praises all of creation. Make a list of some praiseworthy things in your own environment. Use the list to write a poem praising your surroundings.

Writing Handbook
See page R27: Descriptive Writing.

Activities & Explorations

Pyramid Cutaway Find out what the internal structure of one of the Egyptian pyramids was like and why it was designed that way. Then create a cutaway model, drawing, or blueprint to illustrate the structure to your classmates.
~ **VIEWING AND REPRESENTING**

Inquiry & Research

Papyrus Demonstration The Book of the Dead was written on scrolls of papyrus, a kind of paper made by the Egyptians from the stems of rushes. Find out how papyrus was made, and explain the method to your classmates, using drawings, photographs, or (if possible) real materials.

Section from *The Book of the Dead* of Nany. Ca. (1040–945 B.C.) Painted and inscribed papyrus. Western Thebes. Rogers Fund, 1930. (30.3.31). Image © The Metropolitan Museum of Art/Art Resource, New York.

Decoding Hieroglyphics

Pady-mahes (745–656 B.C.). Gray granite statue. Brooklyn (New York) Museum of Art, Charles Edwin Wilbour Fund.

The form of writing used by the ancient Egyptians is known as hieroglyphics. For more than 3,000 years these picture-signs were used not only to record words but also to decorate buildings, sacred monuments, and works of art. Hieroglyphic writing was often included in burials to give the deceased people speech in the afterlife.

The Rosetta Stone Thousands of examples of hieroglyphic texts survived the age of the pharaohs, but for almost 2,000 years no one could read them. Then, in 1799, after Napoleon's conquest of Egypt, French soldiers digging in the sand found a polished black stone covered in writing. The stone contained the same message in three different forms of writing: hieroglyphics, demotic (a simpler form of hieroglyphics), and Greek. Because ancient Greek was well known, it was possible to compare the texts and piece together the meaning of the hieroglyphics. By 1822 the French scholar Jean-François Champollion had broken the code.

How Hieroglyphics Work There's much more to reading hieroglyphics than knowing what each picture represents. Ancient Egyptian grammar was complex, and the hieroglyphics were used in several different ways. A hieroglyphic could represent an object, an idea related to the object, a letter, a syllable, or a grammatical relationship. For example, the hieroglyphic ~~~~, which represents a ripple of water, can stand for the word *ripple*, the idea of motion, the preposition *to,* or the sound *n.*

Below is the name *Akhenaten,* author of "Adoration of the Disk."

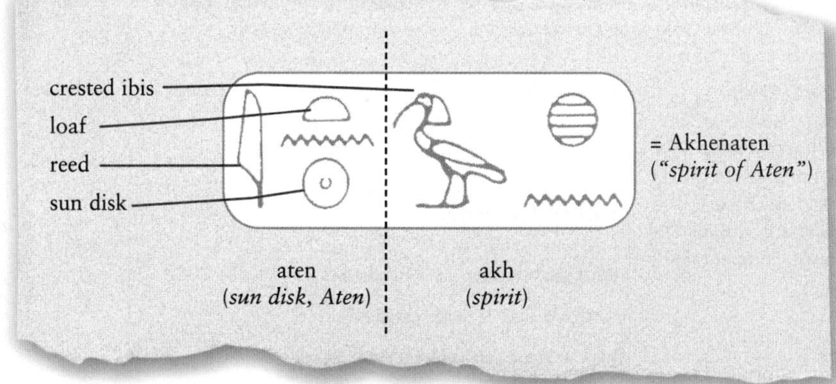

Activity Design picture-signs of your own for the following words: *family, education, happy.* Share your designs with your classmates, and discuss why you chose to represent the words in the way you did.

The Translator at Work

Activity Encourage students to think beyond just drawing the thing that they want to represent. The picture-signs should give some insight into what they signify and communicate this information in a clear, brief way. For example, a picture-sign for education might show an adult holding a small child by the hand. This image could suggest that education is like a stronger person helping a weaker one, that it is an expression of caring, or that it is a relationship based on trust.

THE TRANSLATOR AT WORK 61

This feature gives students an opportunity to compare, analyze, and form opinions about two creation narratives. The focus of this comparison is the similarities and differences across cultures of what it means to fulfill one's destiny as a human being. Used in conjunction with the **Standardized Test Practice** on page 87, the narratives will help students prepare for literature-based writing tests.

 Use **Unit One Resource Book,** p. 11, for more practice.

COMPARING LITERATURE ACROSS CULTURES

Creation Literature

OVERVIEW

Many cultures have stories about the creation of the world and of the human race. Such stories, even from unrelated cultures, can be remarkably similar, suggesting that the stories may reflect beliefs and values held by all people. However, the differences between creation stories are also revealing. Differences in particular details can reflect differences in the cultures from which the stories come.

In the pages that follow, you will be asked to compare and contrast the creation stories in the Hebrew Bible and the *Popol Vuh,* a work from the Mayan culture of Central America. You will explore what these two creation stories have in common and also reflect on their differences. On the basis of your comparison, you will decide what the stories reveal about the cultures from which they come.

Points of Comparison

The following list shows the basic plot of many creation stories. As you will later see, there are variations, but knowing this plot structure is a good place to start.

Creation Literature Plot Structure

- A creator creates people to inhabit the world.
- The creator has certain expectations of the people.
- The people do or do not meet these expectations.
- The creator punishes or rewards the people.

Analyzing Creation Literature Use a chart like the one shown to help you take notes about the stories. Add any other questions that you think will help you compare the two accounts.

Questions for Analysis	Genesis	*Popol Vuh*
What do the creators want the people they have created to do?		
How do the people meet or fail to meet the creators' expectations?		
What do the creators do in response?		
In the end, how do things get resolved?		
What do these details reveal about the culture?		

Standardized Test Practice: Comparison-and-Contrast Essay After you read both selections, you will have the opportunity to write a comparison-and-contrast essay. Your notes will help you plan and write the essay.

 Assessment **Standardized Test Practice**

COMPARISON-AND-CONTRAST ESSAY To provide practice to students in comparing two different pieces of literature, have them read both selections in this **Comparing Literature** feature, rather than treating each selection separately. Have them work with the chart shown on this page, filling it out as they finish reading each of the two selections. (Examples of how to fill out the chart are supplied on pages 75 and 86.) A sample assessment writing prompt and guidelines for responding to it in writing are on page 87.

FROM

Genesis

Build Background

The Hebrew Bible The Hebrew Bible is not just a literary work of the ancient Hebrews; it is the sum total of their literature. It contains histories, biographies, laws, genealogical records, census figures, songs, love poetry, stories, proverbs, and other kinds of writing. The Hebrews had a rich and diverse literary tradition, but they thought of it as all belonging together in a single sacred book, or Bible.

One reason for their way of thinking may be that, as a people, the ancient Hebrews were not as rooted in a particular geographical region as the peoples of Mesopotamia and Egypt. Not having a permanent homeland to define them, the Hebrews may have felt more keenly than others the value of literature as an expression of their culture's identity.

Another reason for the ancient Hebrews to view their entire literary tradition as sacred was that their religion was monotheistic. Unlike most other ancient peoples, the Hebrews believed in a single all-powerful deity, all-knowing and present everywhere. They also believed that they had a covenant with God—a special relationship in which God watched over them and guided their destiny. As a result, they wrote little that did not touch in some way on their religion.

The Bible as Literature Despite its close attachments to Hebrew history and culture, the Hebrew Bible contains many stories, images, and themes dealing with matters that are important to all people. It also contains many fine examples of various literary forms.

The Hebrew Bible has strong connections to our own culture for yet another reason. For hundreds of years, English-speaking writers have loved the Bible and have incorporated its stories, images, themes, and turns of phrase into literary works of their own. To know the English language and the English literary tradition is to be profoundly influenced by the Hebrew Bible.

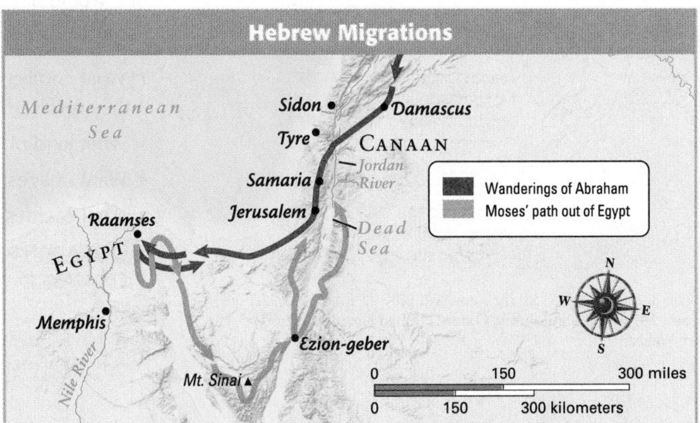

TIME MANAGEMENT

If you wish to cover only one of the selections, use . . .
- Preparing to Read, p. 63 or p. 76
- Thinking Through the Literature, p. 74 or p. 86

If you want to take advantage of longer blocks of class time, use . . .
- TE Teaching Options: Viewing and Representing, pp. 65, 69, 72, 77, 80, 83; Vocabulary Strategy, pp. 67, 81; Cross Curricular Link, pp. 66, 68, 70, 79; Grammar, pp. 71, 73, 78, 82
- Choices & Challenges, p. 75

Objectives
- appreciate **sacred literature (Literary Analysis, Active Reading)**
- recognize literary aspects of the **Bible**

Summary
Creation and the Fall God creates the world and all living things, including the first human beings. He gives them the Garden of Eden to live in and forbids them only one thing—to eat from the Tree of the Knowledge of Good and Evil. Adam and Eve disobey this command, and in punishment God casts them out of the garden.

Noah and the Flood Because of the wickedness of humanity, God decides to destroy all living things with a flood. He wants to spare Noah, however, because Noah is a righteous man. God tells Noah to build an ark, or boat, and to take his family and some of every kind of animal aboard. When this is done, God sends the flood. Afterward, Noah and his family remain on the ark until the water goes down and life returns to earth. Then they leave the ark, and God establishes a covenant, or special agreement, with them.

Use **Unit One Resource Book,** p. 12, for additional support.

Thematic Link
The **spiritual beginnings** of early literature are well-illustrated in the Book of Genesis, which tells the story of the divine origin of human beings and their relationship with God.

5-Minute Warm-Up
Daily Language SkillBuilder

Have students **proofread** the display sentences on page 15g and write them correctly.

Reading the Map
Remind students that Abraham migrated with his family and flocks from Ur in Mesopotamia along the fertile crescent northwest to Haran and then southwest to Canaan (see page 22). The map on this page shows in red the path of Abraham as he travelled further west to Egypt, then returned to Canaan to settle permanently, and of his descendants, who later returned to Egypt to escape a famine. The yellow line traces the path of Moses as he led the Hebrews out of captivity in Egypt through the desert back to Canaan.

READING FOR INFORMATION

Reading Skills and Strategies

SETTING A PURPOSE

Have students search for answers to the following questions as they read the **Build Background** essay.

Why was the Bible important to the ancient Hebrews? *(It contains the sum total of their literature; it helped express their cultural identity in the absence of strong geographical roots; it showed the religious connectedness of all of their writing.)*

What are some reasons the Hebrew Bible has been important in the English literary tradition? *(It deals with matters that are important to all people; it contains fine examples of literature; its stories, images, themes, and language have had a strong influence on writers in English.)*

When does the story of Noah take place in relation to other events told about in the Book of Genesis? *(after the creation of the world and the descendants of Adam and Eve have populated the world, but before the Hebrews migrate to Egypt)*

Reading and Analyzing

Literary Analysis SACRED LITERATURE

As they read pages 65–66, have students pay attention to God's own response to what he creates. Ask them what this response might suggest about Hebrew cultural values.

Possible Responses: God's judgment that what he has created is good shows that the Hebrews thought of the world as a good place; it shows that they thought of God as wanting good things for people.

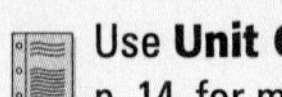
Use **Unit One Resource Book,** p. 14, for more practice.

Active Reading SACRED LITERATURE

Ask students to identify on pages 65 and 66 connections between this selection and other works of literature they have read.

Possible Responses: This is a narrative told in the third-person, omniscient, point of view; includes dialogue in God's words to the first man and woman; the story takes place in a particular setting; the story uses repetition as a technique for linking the sequence of events being described.

Use **Unit One Resource Book,** p. 13, for more practice.

The Book of Genesis The Book of Genesis is the first book in the Hebrew Bible. It tells the history of the Hebrew people from the creation of the world to their migration to Egypt because of a famine. In Egypt they became slaves, but they eventually fled that land under the leadership of Moses—events that are recounted in the Book of Exodus.

Genesis focuses on the interactions between God and particular human beings with whom he has a special relationship. The first of these are Adam and Eve, the first man and woman, whom God created after creating the heavens, the earth, plants, and animals. The story of Noah takes place at a later time, when the descendants of Adam and Eve have populated the world.

Jonah and the Whale from the Kennicott Bible (1 folio 305), Hebrew, Spain, 1476. Bodleian Library, Oxford, United Kingdom. Photo © The Art Archive.

Connect to Your Life

What comes to mind when you hear the names Adam and Eve? What do you know about the Garden of Eden or Noah and the Flood? With a group of classmates, share recollections of these biblical stories and discuss your impressions of them.

Focus Your Reading

LITERARY ANALYSIS: SACRED LITERATURE

Texts that convey the traditions, beliefs, and rituals of particular religions are often referred to as **sacred literature,** or **scriptures.** Although there is something to be learned from every good work of literature, sacred literature usually has as one of its main purposes the teaching of cultural values. As you read the two stories from Genesis, be alert for the teachings that they may contain.

ACTIVE READING: READING SACRED LITERATURE

Sacred literature usually has a higher status in a culture than ordinary literature, and it is often used in special ways. However, a work of sacred literature always has a literary form as well; it may be a story, a poem, a history, a biography, a song, a proverb. A good way to approach a work of sacred literature is to focus on the text itself. Read the words carefully, and ask the same questions you would of any other work of literature:

- What characters do I learn about?
- What conflicts are presented, and how are they resolved?
- What kind of language is used?
- What images or symbols are used?
- What themes does the work deal with?

READER'S NOTEBOOK As you read, look for answers to your questions and jot them down.

LESSON RESOURCES

UNIT ONE RESOURCE BOOK, pp. 11–19

ASSESSMENT RESOURCES
Formal Assessment, pp. 11–12
Teacher's Guide to Assessment and Portfolio Use
Test Generator

INTEGRATED TECHNOLOGY
Visit our Web site: classzone.com

ADDITIONAL RESOURCES
Lesson Planning Guide, pp. 5–6
Teacher's Sourcebook for Language Development

from Genesis

King James Bible

Creation AND THE Fall

1 In the beginning God created the heaven and the earth. And the earth was without form, and void; and darkness was upon the face of the deep. And the Spirit of God moved upon the face of the waters. And God said, "Let there be light": and there was light. And God saw the light, that it was good: and God divided the light from the darkness. And God called the light Day, and the darkness he called Night.

And the evening and the morning were the first day.

And God said, "Let there be a firmament in the midst of the waters, and let it divide the waters from the waters." And God made the firmament, and divided the waters which were under the firmament from the waters which were above the firmament: and it was so. And God called the firmament Heaven. 2

And the evening and the morning were the second day.

And God said, "Let the waters under the heaven be gathered together unto one place, and

The Creation of Adam, Michelangelo Buonarroti. Sistine Chapel, Vatican Palace, Vatican State. Scala/Art Resource, New York.

HUMANITIES CONNECTION In this detail from Michelangelo's paintings on the ceiling of the Sistine Chapel, God and Adam touch each other with extended hands. Through his act of creation, God is bridging the gap between heaven and earth. Adam also plays a role in creation: he must actively receive God's blessing.

Customizing Instruction

Less Proficient Readers

1 Explain that the first sentence is a summary of what we are going to be told about up through the second line on page 66.

English Learners

2 Students may find the reference to "the waters which were above the firmament" confusing. Explain that the waters here are waters of chaos—the formless void that exists before the earth or the oceans (see Cross Curricular Link on page 66).

Advanced Learners

While the King James version of the Bible is probably the best-known English translation, many other versions exist. Some emphasize accuracy of translation, some strive to be clear and understandable by general readers, and some have still other purposes. Have students compare at least two other versions of the Genesis story of Creation and the Fall. Students can present their findings in a report that explains the purpose of each version and includes examples of passages that illustrate this purpose. Encourage students to consider other aspects of the text also, such as illustrations, notes, and cross-references.

MINI LESSON Viewing and Representing

The Creation of Adam **by Michelangelo**

ART APPRECIATION Michelangelo used the nine central panels of the Sistine Chapel ceiling to portray scenes from the Book of Genesis: three show the creation of nature, three the story of Adam and Eve, and three the story of Noah. The painting shown on this page is the complete fourth panel—a depiction of the creation of Adam.

Have students study the painting and the **Humanities Connection.** Ask them why Michelangelo might have given Adam a role in creation, depicting him reaching toward God.

Possible Responses: to show that the relationship between people and God is reciprocal; to show that Adam was more than a body created from earth—he needed to receive life from God; to show that Adam understands he cannot live without God's help; to show that Adam instinctively loves God as his father

Reading and Analyzing

Reading Skills and Strategies
CLARIFYING

A Ask students what *the greater light* and *the lesser light* refer to. *(the sun and the moon)*

Reading Skills and Strategies
CONNECTING

B Ask students how God's actions on the seventh day of creation are commemorated in the modern world. *(As the Sabbath day, a day of rest and worship—Saturday in the Jewish tradition and Sunday in the Christian tradition)*

Literary Analysis MYTHOLOGY

C Point out that this sentence contains a mini "pourquoi" explanation of the marriage bond. (For a cross curricular link on "pourquoi" stories, see page 46.)

let the dry land appear": and it was so. And
God called the dry land Earth; and the gathering
together of the waters called he Seas: and God
saw that it was good. And God said, "Let the
earth bring forth grass, the herb yielding seed,
1 and the fruit tree yielding fruit after his kind,
whose seed is in itself, upon the earth": and it
was so. And the earth brought forth grass, and
herb yielding seed after his kind, and the tree
yielding fruit, whose seed was in itself, after his
kind: and God saw that it was good.

And the evening and the morning were the third day.

And God said, "Let there be lights in the firmament of the heaven to divide the day from the night; and let them be for signs, and for seasons, and for days, and years; and let them be for lights in the firmament of the heaven to give light upon the earth."

And it was so. And God made two great
A lights; the greater light to rule the day, and
the lesser light to rule the night: he made the
stars also. And God set them in the firmament of the heaven to give light upon the earth. And to rule over the day and over the night, and to divide the light from the darkness: and God saw that it was good.

And the evening and the morning were the fourth day.

And God said, "Let the waters bring forth
2 abundantly the moving creature that hath life,
and fowl that may fly above the earth in the
open firmament of heaven." And God created great whales, and every living creature that moveth, which the waters brought forth abundantly, after their kind, and every winged fowl after his kind: and God saw that it was good. And God blessed them, saying, "Be fruitful, and multiply, and fill the waters in the seas, and let fowl multiply in the earth."

And the evening and the morning were the fifth day.

And God said, "Let the earth bring forth the
living creature after his kind, cattle, and creeping
thing, and beast of the earth after his kind": and
it was so. And God made the beast of the earth
after his kind, and cattle after their kind, and
every thing that creepeth upon the earth after his 3
kind: and God saw that it was good.

God said, "Let us make man in our image, after our likeness: and let them have dominion[1] over the fish of the sea, and over the fowl of the air, and over the cattle, and over all the earth, and over every creeping thing that creepeth upon the earth." So God created man in his own image, in the image of God created he him; male and female created he them. And God blessed them, and God said unto them, "Be fruitful, and multiply, and replenish[2] the earth, and subdue it: and have dominion over the fish of the sea, and over the fowl of the air, and over every living thing that moveth upon the earth." And God said, "Behold, I have given you every herb bearing seed, which is upon the face of all the earth, and every tree, in the which is the fruit of a tree yielding seed; to you it shall be for meat. And to every beast of the earth, and to every fowl of the air, and to everything that creepeth upon the earth, wherein there is life, I have given every green herb for meat." And it was so. And God saw every thing that he had made, and, behold, it was very good.

And the evening and the morning were the sixth day.

Thus the heavens and the earth were finished, and all the host of them.

And on the seventh day God ended his work
which he had made; and he rested on the seventh
day from all his work which he had made. And B
God blessed the seventh day, and sanctified it:
because that in it he had rested from all his work
which God created and made.

1. **dominion:** authority; control.
2. **replenish:** fill up again.

Cross Curricular Link **Humanities**

THE FACE OF THE DEEP Possibly because of their origin as inland nomads, the Hebrews had a different symbolic relationship to water from that of the ancient river-dwelling Mesopotamians. The latter welcomed annual flooding and the irrigation it brought with it. Their hero Gilgamesh brings civilization from the watery deep. He crosses an ocean to learn wisdom from Utnapishtim in the realm of the gods and dives to the bottom of a channel to get the plant that makes old men young.

For the Hebrews, however, the watery deep is the chaos that precedes Creation and threatens civilization. When God divides the waters under the firmament from the waters above the firmament, we are to understand that the sky is holding back these waters, which completely surround God's Creation. God then divides the waters of chaos under the sky into dry land and waters or seas in the more usual sense. Later, when God brings the flood in the story of Noah, Hebrew readers would understand that he is actually undoing Creation, an act far more serious than causing bad weather.

4 In the day that the Lord God made the earth and the heavens, and every plant of the field before it was in the earth, and every herb of the field before it grew (for the Lord God had not caused it to rain upon the earth, and there was not a man to till the ground) there went up a mist from the earth, and watered the whole face of the ground. And the Lord God formed man of the dust of the ground, and breathed into his nostrils the breath of life; and man became a living soul.

> "Of every tree in the garden thou mayest freely eat: but of the tree of the **knowledge of good and evil,** thou shalt not eat of it: for in the day that thou eatest thereof thou shalt surely die."

And the Lord God planted a garden eastward in Eden; and there he put the man whom he had formed. And out of the ground made the Lord God to grow every tree that is pleasant to the sight, and good for food; the tree of life also in the midst of the garden, and the tree of knowledge of good and evil. And a river went out of Eden to water the garden; and from thence it was parted, and became into four heads. The name of the first is Pison:[3] that is it which compasseth the whole land of Havilah,[4] where there is gold; and the gold of that land is good: there is bdellium[5] and the onyx stone. And the name of the second river is Gihon:[6] the same is it that compasseth the whole land of Ethiopia. And the name of the third river is Hiddekel:[7] that is it which goeth toward the east of Assyria. And the fourth river is Euphrates.

And the Lord God took the man, and put him into the garden of Eden to dress it and to keep it. And the Lord God commanded the man, saying,
"Of every tree of the garden thou mayest freely
5 eat: but of the tree of the knowledge of good and evil, thou shalt not eat of it: for in the day that thou eatest thereof thou shalt surely die."

And the Lord God said,

"It is not good that the man should be alone; I will make him a help meet for him." And out of the ground the Lord God formed every beast of the field, and every fowl of the air; and brought them unto Adam to see what he would call them: and whatsoever Adam called every living creature, that was the name thereof. And Adam gave names to all cattle, and to the fowl of the air, and to every beast of the field; but for Adam
there was not found a help meet for him. 6

And the Lord God caused a deep sleep to fall upon Adam, and he slept: and he took one of his ribs, and closed up the flesh instead thereof; and the rib, which the Lord God had taken from man, made he a woman, and brought her unto the man.

And Adam said,

"This is now bone of my bones,
and flesh of my flesh:
She shall be called Woman,
because she was taken out of Man."

Therefore shall a man leave his father and his
mother, and shall cleave unto his wife: and they C
shall be one flesh. And they were both naked, the man and his wife, and were not ashamed.

Now the serpent was more subtle than any beast of the field which the Lord God had made.

And he said unto the woman,

---

3. **Pison** (pē-sōn′).
4. **Havilah** (hăv-ē-lä′).
5. **bdellium** (dĕl′ē-əm): a gum resin obtained from various shrubs and trees, used as a medicine.
6. **Gihon** (gē-hōn′).
7. **Hiddekel** (hĭ-dĕk′ĕl).

Customizing Instruction

English Learners

1 Explain that the King James Bible was translated at a time when the English language was spoken a little differently from the way it is now. Here, *his* means *its*.

2 Explain that in the older form of English used here, verbs are conjugated in a slightly different way. The third-person singular form, which is now made with *-s* or *-es (has)*, was made with *-th* or *-eth (hath)*.

3 Have students give the modern English form of *creepeth. (creeps)* Repeat the exercise with the following words on page 67: *compasseth (compasses), goeth (goes).*

Less Proficient Readers

4 Explain that a break in the chronology occurs here. The narrative backs up to the very beginning and condenses the entire creation story into one paragraph. In what follows, the story of the creation of the first man and the first woman is told in greater detail.

English Learners

5 Explain that in the older form of English used here, as in modern Spanish and other languages, the second-person singular has a polite form *(you)* and a familiar form *(thou)*. The *thou* form, which is not used in modern English, is made with *-st* or *-est (mayest, eatest)*. *Shalt* is irregular.

6 The phrase "a help meet for him" means "a helper suitable for him."

MINI LESSON Vocabulary

MULTIPLE MEANING WORDS Many words have more than one meaning. Context clues can help students figure out which meaning of the word applies in a particular sentence.

Instruction Display these meanings for the word *face*:

- the front of the head, including eyes, nose, and mouth
- to confront boldly or bravely
- to put another material on the surface of

Then display the following sentences and have students identify which meaning of the word *face* is used in each one:

- Bruce had a scratch on his *face*.
- Jane had to *face* her angry parents.

Practice Have students use a dictionary to find the correct definition for each italicized word.

1. The street *sign* was hidden by the trees. Please *sign* your name at the top of the test.
2. I turned on the *light* in my room. My dog is very *light*—only five pounds.
3. Tomato is my favorite *kind* of soup. Jane was *kind* to me when I was sick.

A lesson on words with multiple meanings appears on p. 156 in the Pupil's Edition.

Reading and Analyzing

Literary Analysis SACRED LITERATURE

Ask students what teachings they think the ancient Hebrews might have associated with God's reaction to Adam's and Eve's disobedience?

Possible Responses: People should obey the law of God; the more greedy you are, the less you will have; people are often responsible for the difficulty in their own lives; sometimes innocence is better than knowledge.

Active Reading READING SACRED LITERATURE

Ask students what they think is the effect of using dialogue to tell the part of the story in which God confronts Adam and Eve about their disobedience.

Possible Responses: The use of dialogue lets us see God discovering the disobedience and shows us what he is thinking about it; the dialogue creates suspense—we don't know how Adam and Eve will answer God's questions or how God will react to what they say.

Literary Analysis MYTHOLOGY

A Ask students to identify the "pourquoi" stories, or stories of how things came to be as they are, on this page. *(why people find nakedness shameful; why people wear clothes; why snakes crawl on their bellies; why childbirth is painful; why husbands have authority over their wives; why people have to work for a living; why people die)*

1 "Yea, hath God said, 'Ye shall not eat of every tree of the garden'?"

And the woman said unto the serpent,

"We may eat of the fruit of the trees of the garden; but of the fruit of the tree which is in the midst of the garden, God hath said, 'Ye shall not eat of it, neither shall ye touch it, lest ye die.'"

And the serpent said unto the woman,

"Ye shall not surely die: for God doth know that in the day ye eat thereof, then your eyes shall be opened, and ye shall be as gods, knowing good and evil."

And when the woman saw that the tree was good for food, and that it was pleasant to the eyes, and a tree to be desired to make one wise, she took of the fruit thereof, and did eat, and gave also unto her husband with her; and he did eat. And the eyes of them both were opened, and they knew that they were naked; and they sewed fig leaves together, and made themselves aprons.

And they heard the voice of the Lord God walking in the garden in the cool of the day: and Adam and his wife hid themselves from the presence of the Lord God amongst the trees of the garden.

And the Lord God called unto Adam, and said unto him,

"Where art thou?"

And he said,

"I heard thy voice in the garden, and I was
2 afraid, because I was naked; and I hid myself."

And he said,

"Who told thee that thou wast naked? Hast thou eaten of the tree, whereof I commanded thee that thou shouldest not eat?"

And the man said,

"The woman whom thou gavest to be with me, she gave me of the tree, and I did eat."

And the Lord God said unto the woman,

"What is this that thou hast done?"

And the woman said, "The serpent beguiled[8] me, and I did eat."

And the Lord God said unto the serpent,

"Because thou hast done this,
thou art cursed above all cattle,
and above every beast of the field;
upon thy belly shalt thou go,
and dust shalt thou eat 3
all the days of thy life:
And I will put enmity[9] between thee and the woman,
and between thy seed and her seed;
it shall bruise thy head,
and thou shalt bruise his heel."

Unto the woman he said,

"I will greatly multiply thy sorrow and thy conception;
in sorrow thou shalt bring forth children;
and thy desire shall be to thy husband,
and he shall rule over thee."

And unto Adam he said,

"Because thou hast hearkened unto the voice of thy wife, and hast eaten of the tree, of which I commanded thee, saying, 'Thou shalt not eat of it': 4

Cursed is the ground for thy sake;
in sorrow shalt thou eat of it all the days of thy life.
Thorns also and thistles shall it bring forth to thee;
and thou shalt eat the herb of the field;
in the sweat of thy face shalt thou eat bread,
till thou return unto the ground;
for out of it wast thou taken:
For dust thou art,
and unto dust shalt thou return." A

8. **beguiled** (bĭ-gīld'): deceived; tricked; misled.

9. **enmity:** hatred; hostility.

Cross Curricular Link **Humanities**

THE WORLD TREE The image of the tree appears frequently in literature and art. A symbol that occurs in many different cultures with very similar meanings is called an archetype (see page 31). The archetypal symbol of the tree is often called the "World Tree" or the "Cosmic Tree." Typically, the symbol will have one of two different but related meanings, one "vertical" and one "horizontal." Just as a real tree reaches down into the earth with its roots and up into the sky with its branches, so the archetypal tree can represent a bridge between earth and heaven—a place where mortal human beings can connect with the divine. This kind of tree is sometimes called the Tree of Knowledge, after the one in Genesis. The tree can also be understood horizontally as the center of the world and a source of life, just like the Tree of Life in the middle of the Garden of Eden. Although the Tree of Knowledge seems evil in the Genesis story, because it is forbidden and gets Adam and Eve in trouble, the story makes clear that both trees give access to god-like qualities.

The Judgement of Adam and Eve: "So Judged He Man" (1807), William Blake. The Huntington Library, Art Collections, and Botanical Gardens, San Marino, California/SuperStock.

And Adam called his wife's name Eve; because she was the mother of all living. Unto Adam also and to his wife did the Lord God make coats of skins, and clothed them.

And the Lord God said, "Behold, the man is become as one of us, to know good and evil: and now, lest he put forth his hand, and take also of the tree of life, and eat, and live for ever—" therefore the Lord God sent him forth from the garden of Eden, to till the ground from whence he was taken. So he drove out the man; and he placed at the east of the garden of Eden Cherubims,[10] and a flaming sword which turned every way, to keep the way of the tree of life.

10. **Cherubims** (chĕr′ə-bĭmz): angels second in power only to archangels.

Customizing Instruction

English Learners

1 *Yea* (respelling) is an older English form of "yes." *Ye* (respelling) is an older form of "you."

2 *Art* and *wast* are the present and past forms of the verb *to be* used with *thou*. *Where art thou?* Is the same as "Where are you?" and *thou wast* is the same as "you were."

3 *Thy*: your (possessive adjective formed from *thou*); *thee*: you (objective case of *thou*). Point out to students that *thou* changes in the same way as *my* and *me*.

Less Proficient Readers

4 Students may need help unraveling the structure of this sentence. Have one or more volunteers paraphrase the three lines before the colon, which are an adverb clause modifying *is* in line 4. *(Because you listened to your wife and ate from the tree I told you not to eat . . .)*

MINI LESSON Viewing and Representing

The Judgement of Adam and Eve **by William Blake**

ART APPRECIATION William Blake is usually considered one of the six major poets of English Romanticism (see page 870). He published his first major book, *Songs of Innocence,* nine years before Wordsworth and Coleridge brought out their Lyrical Ballads, which is considered to be the work that launched English Romanticism. However, Blake's genius did not become fully recognized until the 20th century.

In addition to being a poet, Blake was an artist and engraver. He illustrated not only his own poetry, but also many classical works of literature, including the Book of Genesis. Have students study the painting on this page and connect as many details as they can with the story of Adam and Eve.

Possible Responses: the painting represents a moment after the Fall, because Adam and Eve are wearing fig leaves; the trees of the Garden are in the background; God stands between Adam and Eve, telling them what their punishment will be; Adam is listening reverently to God; Eve is weeping with remorse; the serpent that tempts Eve is shown at the bottom

Reading and Analyzing

Reading Skills and Strategies
INFERRING

A Ask students why God tells Noah to take animals on board the ark in pairs of male and female. *(so that they can reproduce and not let the species die out)*

Reading Skills and Strategies
IDENTIFYING CULTURAL CHARACTERISTICS

B Ask for volunteers to explain why God commands Noah to take seven male-female pairs of every clean beast and only one male-female pair from among the unclean beasts. *(The ancient Hebrews regarded some animals, such as pigs, as unclean and therefore unfit to be eaten. Noah is to take more of the clean animals, because they will be needed for food as well as to replenish the earth.)*

Literary Analysis SYMBOLISM

C Point out to students that this passage is the origin of the symbol of the dove of peace, which is well-known from visual representations and expressions such as "to extend the olive branch." Ask students why the dove with an olive branch has come to symbolize peace.

Possible Response: because it shows Noah that God's destruction of the earth is over and new life has begun

Noah AND THE Flood

And it came to pass, when men began to multiply on the face of the earth, and daughters were born unto them, that the sons of God saw the daughters of men that they were fair; and they took them wives of all which they chose.

1 And the Lord said, "My spirit shall not always strive with man, for that he also is flesh; yet his days shall be a hundred and twenty years."

There were giants in the earth in those days; and also after that, when the sons of God came in unto the daughters of men, and they bore children to them, the same became mighty men which were of old, men of renown.[1] And God saw that the wickedness of man was great in the earth, and that every imagination of the thoughts of his heart was only evil continually. And it repented the Lord that he had made man on the earth, and it grieved him at his heart.

And the Lord said, "I will destroy man whom I have created from the face of the earth; both man, and beast, and the creeping thing, and the fowls of the air; for it repenteth me that I have made them."

But Noah found grace in the eyes of the Lord.

Noah was a just man and perfect in his generations, and Noah walked with God. And Noah begot three sons, Shem, Ham, and Japheth.[2]

And God said unto Noah, "The end of all flesh is come before me; for the earth is filled with violence through them; and, behold, I will destroy them with the earth. Make thee an ark of gopher wood; rooms shalt thou make in the ark, and shalt pitch it within and without with pitch. And this is the fashion which thou shalt make it of: the length of the ark shall be three hundred cubits, the breadth of it fifty cubits, and the height of it thirty cubits. A window shalt thou make to the ark, and in a cubit shalt thou finish it above; and the door of the ark shalt thou set in the side thereof; with lower, second, and third stories shalt thou make it. And, behold, I, even I, do bring a flood of waters upon the earth, to destroy all flesh, wherein is the breath of life, from under heaven; and everything that is in the earth shall die. But with thee will I establish my covenant;[3] and thou shalt come into the ark, thou, and thy sons, and thy wife, and thy sons' wives with thee. And of every living thing of all flesh, two of every sort shalt thou bring into the ark, to keep them alive with thee; they shall be male and female. A Of fowls after their kind, and of cattle after their kind, of every creeping thing of the earth after his kind, two of every sort shall come unto thee, to keep them alive. And take thou unto thee of all food that is eaten, and thou shalt gather it to thee; and it shall be for food for thee, and for them."

2 Thus did Noah; according to all that God commanded him, so did he. And the Lord said unto Noah, "Come thou and all thy house into the ark; for thee have I seen righteous before me in this generation. Of every clean beast thou shalt take to thee by sevens, the male and his female: and of beasts that are not clean by two, the male and his female. Of fowls also of the air by sevens, the male and the female; to keep seed alive upon the face of all the earth. B 3 For yet seven days, and I will cause it to rain upon the earth forty days and forty nights; and every living substance that I have made will I destroy from off the face of the earth."

And Noah did according unto all that the Lord commanded him. And Noah went in, and his sons, and his wife, and his sons' wives with him,

1. **renown:** fame based on good deeds.
2. **Japheth** (jā′fəth).
3. **covenant:** a formal agreement.

Cross Curricular Link Mathematics

COMPARING ARKS

Instruction Have students look over the specifications on this page for the building of the ark. Then have them look back at the dimensions and construction of Utnapishtim's boat (as well as the definition of the word *cubit*) on page 41.

Practice Ask students to compare Utnapishtim's boat with Noah's. Students might present their findings orally, in writing, or visually in the form of a chart, diagram, or scale drawing.

Possible Response: A cubit is 17–22 inches. At 120 cubits on a side, the top deck of Utnapishtim's boat would be 170–220 feet square, or 28,900–48,400 square feet, that is, from half the area of a football field to more than four fifths that area. Noah's ark is 300 by 50 cubits, or 425–550 feet by 71–92 feet, which is 30,175–50,600 square feet. Assuming a uniform cubit, Utnapishtim's boat and Noah's ark cover approximately the same area, though the boat is square and the ark is rectangular. Noah's ark is about 50 feet high, which would exactly hold the six lower decks of Utnapishtim's boat if each had a ceiling of eight feet, four inches.

Practice Utnapishtim says that his boat took up an acre (43,560 square feet) of ground space. If this is exactly correct, what was the size of his cubit? *(The square root of 43,560 is approximately 209. That number of feet on a side would be 2,508 inches. If that number of inches equals 120 cubits, then a cubit is 20.9 inches.)*

into the ark, because of the waters of the flood. Of clean beasts, and of beasts that are not clean, and of fowls, and of every thing that creepeth upon the earth, there went in two and two unto Noah into the ark, the male and the female, as God had commanded Noah. And it came to pass after seven days that the waters of the flood were upon the earth. In the six hundredth year of Noah's life, in the second month, the seventeenth day of the month, the same day were all the fountains of the great deep broken up, and the windows of heaven were opened. And the waters prevailed, and were increased greatly upon the earth; and the ark went upon the face of the waters. And the waters prevailed exceedingly upon the earth; and all the high hills, that were under the whole heaven, were covered. Fifteen cubits upward did the waters prevail; and the mountains were covered. And all flesh died that moved upon the earth, both of fowl, and of cattle, and of beast, and of every creeping thing that creepeth upon the earth, and every man. All in whose nostrils was the breath of life, of all that was in the dry land, died. And every living substance was destroyed which was upon the face of the ground, both man, and cattle, and the creeping things, and the fowl of the heaven; and they were destroyed from the earth: and Noah only remained alive, and they that were with him in the ark. And the waters prevailed upon the earth a hundred and fifty days.

And God remembered Noah, and every living thing, and all the cattle that was with him in the ark: and God made a wind to pass over the earth, and the waters assuaged.[4] The fountains also of the deep and the windows of heaven were stopped, and the rain from heaven was restrained; and the waters returned from off the earth continually: and after the end of the hundred and fifty days the waters were abated.[5] And the ark rested in the seventh month, on the seventeenth day of the month, upon the mountains of Ararat. And the waters decreased continually until the tenth month: in the tenth month, on the first day of the month, were the tops of the mountains seen.

And it came to pass at the end of forty days that Noah opened the window of the ark which he had made: and he sent forth a raven, which went forth to and fro, until the waters were dried up from off the earth. Also he sent forth a dove from him, to see if the waters were abated from off the face of the ground; but the dove found no rest for the sole of her foot, and she returned unto him into the ark, for the waters were on the face of the whole earth: then he put forth his hand, and took her, and pulled her in unto him into the ark. And he stayed yet other seven days; and again he sent forth the dove out of the ark; and the dove came in to him in the evening; and lo, in her mouth was an olive leaf plucked off: so Noah knew that the waters were abated from off the earth. And he stayed yet other seven days; and C

> And the waters prevailed upon the earth a hundred and fifty days.

sent forth the dove; which returned not again unto him any more. And it came to pass in the six hundredth and first year, in the first month, the first day of the month, the waters were dried up from off the earth: and Noah removed the covering of the ark, and looked, and, behold, the face of the ground was dry. And in the second month, on the seven and twentieth day of the month, was the earth dried.

And God spoke unto Noah, saying, "Go forth of the ark, thou, and thy wife, and thy sons, and

4. **assuaged** (ə-swājd′): became calm or smooth.

5. **abated:** reduced or removed altogether.

Customizing Instruction

Less Proficient Readers

1 Students may need help understanding the meaning of this sentence, which can be paraphrased as follows: "I can't be responsible for people indefinitely; they are only flesh. Let them live to be 120 years old."

English Learners

2 Students may have trouble following the sequence of events here. Explain that this paragraph repeats ideas stated in the previous one and does not represent any additional actions or passage of time.

Advanced Learners

3 Have students find out and report back to the class more about the dietary laws of the Hebrews. To help them get started, suggest they consult Leviticus, Chapter 11.

MINI LESSON Grammar

PLURAL AND POSSESSIVE NOUNS

Instruction Remind students that there are two rules for forming the possessive of a plural noun. Display the rules using the following chart:

Rule 1: If the noun ends in *s*, add an apostrophe after the *s*.	doctors-doctors' Hoffmans-Hoffmans' committees-committees'
Rule 2: If the noun does not end in *s*, add an apostrophe and *s*.	children-children's men-men's women-women's

Practice Have students write the possessive form of these plural nouns.

1. dentists *(dentists')*
2. watchmen *(watchmen's)*
3. people *(people's)*
4. birds *(birds')*
5. countries *(countries')*

For more instruction and practice in plural and possessive nouns, use McDougal Littell's ***Language Network:***

- Grade 10, Chapter 1, "The Parts of Speech"
- Grade 12, Review: Parts of Speech

Reading and Analyzing

Active Reading READING SACRED LITERATURE

A Ask students why some of God's words on this page are written in verse.

Possible Responses: because these points are especially important; so that people could remember them more easily; because these passages might have also existed as independent sayings or songs

Literary Analysis SACRED LITERATURE

B Ask students what might be some reasons that God gives this teaching about murder right after he has wiped out most of the human race with the flood?

Possible Responses: Because of Noah's goodness, God changes his mind about humanity and decides that they deserve to live; God forgives people for being evil, because it's their nature; after witnessing the flood, God doesn't want to see any more killing; now that God has made a covenant with people, killing someone would be especially bad; God has the right to take a human life, but people don't.

Literary Analysis MYTHOLOGY

C Ask students to identify the "pourquoi" story that occurs here. *(why a rainbow appears when there is a raincloud)*

The Building of the Ark (Gen. 6:13–17), the Flood (Gen. 8:6–11, Leaving the Ark (Gen. 8:18–19), the Sacrifice of Noah (Gen. 8:20–9:15) (c. 1250 A.D.). The Pierpont Morgan Library, New York.

HUMANITIES CONNECTION This manuscript illumination shows four scenes from the story of Noah and the Flood. Before the invention of the printing press, the Bible and other books had to be copied by hand. Individual copies often included illuminations—hand-painted illustrations and decorations—that made each volume unique.

MINI LESSON Viewing and Representing

Bible Illumination

ART APPRECIATION The four scenes pictured in this manuscript illumination of the story of Noah are (clockwise from upper left) the building of the ark, the flood, Noah leaving the ark, and Noah's sacrifice of thanksgiving to God. Ask students to study the illumination and the **Humanities Connection.** Then have them connect details from the artwork to the story.

Possible Responses: (The Building of the Ark) Noah listens to God speaking from a cloud about the flood to come; Noah cuts wood for the ark on a sawhorse with an axe while a plank leans up against the partially completed ark. (The Flood) The ark floats on the water after the storm is over; Noah releases a bird from the ark while his family watches and another bird flies toward the ark; the animals wait below deck; a bird feeds on a drowned horse floating in the water. (Noah Leaving the Ark) Noah and his family step across one gangplank while the animals cross another; birds fly away from the ark; trees can be seen, showing that the waters have subsided. (Noah's Sacrifice) Noah and his wife put pieces of meat on the fire; Noah's son hands him a piece of firewood; another son holds a lamb to be sacrificed; God, speaking from a cloud, promises never again to destroy the earth with a flood; the rainbow is represented as a scroll God holds on which are written the words of the covenant.

Ask students how this illumination might help readers better understand the text.

Possible Responses: by drawing the reader's attention to important events; by making the scenes easier to visualize; by supplying concrete details; by giving details not mentioned in the text, such as the carpenter's axe

thy sons' wives with thee. Bring forth with thee every living thing that is with thee, of all flesh, both of fowl, and of cattle, and of every creeping thing that creepeth upon the earth; that they may breed abundantly in the earth, and be fruitful, and multiply upon the earth."

And Noah went forth, and his sons, and his wife, and his sons' wives with him. Every beast, every creeping thing, and every fowl, and whatsoever creepeth upon the earth, after their kinds, went forth out of the ark.

1 And Noah builded an altar unto the Lord; and took of every clean beast, and of every clean fowl, and offered burnt offerings on the altar. And the Lord smelled a sweet savor; and the Lord said in his heart,

"I will not again curse the ground any more for man's sake; for the imagination of man's heart is evil from his youth; neither will I again smite[6] any more every thing living, as I have done.

A
While the earth remaineth,
seedtime and harvest, and cold and heat,
and summer and winter, and day and night
shall not cease."

And God blessed Noah and his sons, and said unto them, "Be fruitful, and multiply, and replenish the earth. And the fear of you and the dread of you shall be upon every beast of the earth, and upon every fowl of the air, upon all that moveth upon the earth, and upon all the
2 fishes of the sea; into your hand are they delivered. Every moving thing that liveth shall be meat for you; even as the green herb have I given you all things. But flesh with the life thereof, which is the blood thereof, shall ye not eat. And
3 surely your blood of your lives will I require; at the hand of every beast will I require it, and at the hand of man; at the hand of every man's brother will I require the life of man.

Whoso sheddeth man's blood,
by man shall his blood be shed;
for in the image of God
made he man." B

And God spoke unto Noah, and to his sons with him, saying,

"And I, behold, I establish my covenant with you, and with your seed after you; and with every living creature that is with you, of the fowl, of the cattle, and of every beast of the earth with you; from all that go out of the ark, to every beast of the earth. And I will establish my covenant with you; neither shall all flesh be cut off any more by the waters of a flood; neither shall there any more be a flood to destroy the earth."

And God said,

"This is the token of the covenant which I make between me and you and every living creature that is with you, for perpetual generations:

I do set my bow in the cloud,
and it shall be for a token of a covenant
between me and the earth.
And it shall come to pass,
when I bring a cloud over the earth,
that the bow shall be seen in the cloud

and I will remember my covenant, which is between me and you and every living creature of all flesh; and the waters shall no more become a flood to destroy all flesh. And the bow shall be
in the cloud; and I will look upon it, that I may C
remember the everlasting covenant between God and every living creature of all flesh that is upon the earth."

And God said unto Noah, "This is the token of the covenant, which I have established between me and all flesh that is upon the earth." ❖

---

6. **smite:** punish with a severe blow.

Customizing Instruction

English Learners

Help students connect the following older English forms on this page to their modern equivalents:

1 *builded* = "built"

2 *into your hand are they delivered* = "I am putting them in your power"

3 *require* = "demand an account of"

MINI LESSON Grammar

ACTION AND LINKING VERBS

Instruction Remind students that the two main types of verbs are action verbs and linking verbs. An action verb expresses an action. The action may be physical or mental. A linking verb describes how something is or looks. Linking verbs express a state of being. Some of the most common linking verbs are *become, seem, look, feel, sound, smell,* and forms of *be*. Display the following chart, underlining the verbs in the example sentences as shown:

Action Verbs	Joe started the car. The rain drenched us.
Linking Verbs	The sky looks gloomy. The clock is slow.

Some verbs can be either action or linking verbs. If you can substitute a form of *be* for the verb, then the verb is a linking verb. (Linking: The melon looked [is] ripe. Action: Ann looked at the melon.)

Practice Write the verb in each sentence and identify it as an action verb or a linking verb.

1. That tree looks beautiful. *(looks; linking)*
2. Don't take any fruit from it. *(do not take; action)*
3. The snake was deceptive. *(was; linking)*
4. Adam and Eve left the garden. *(left; action)*
5. They were ashamed. *(were; linking)*

For more instruction and practice in action and linking verbs, use McDougal Littell's ***Language Network:***

- Grade 10, Chapter 1, "The Parts of Speech"
- Grade 12, Review: Parts of Speech

Connect to the Literature

1. **What Do You Think?**
Some students may say that Adam and Eve get the punishment they deserve, because they know exactly what the rules are and because disobeying God is a serious offense. Other students may wonder why Adam and Eve shouldn't eat from the tree of the knowledge of good and evil and feel that their punishment is harsh.

Some students will say that the punishment of the flood is similar to the punishment given to Adam and Eve, because it is for disobedience and the punishment is death. Other students may point out that the flood kills "everything that is in the earth," even plants and animals, not just those who have displeased God, and so is a harsher punishment.

Comprehension Check

- The serpent tempts her, telling her she and Adam won't die and that they will become like gods.
- Eve is told she will have pain in childbirth and that she will be subservient to her husband; Adam is told that he will have to work hard for a living and that he will one day die.
- God regrets making human beings and feels they have filled the earth with violence.
- The dove he sends out returns with an olive leaf in her mouth.

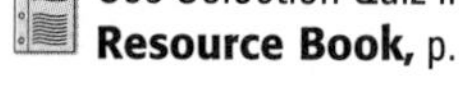
Use Selection Quiz in **Unit One Resource Book,** p. 15.

Think Critically

2. Possible Responses: God is loving and generous; he creates human beings and gives them all of creation. God is strict; he makes rules, expects people to follow them, and punishes disobedience. God is fair; he doesn't punish the righteous man Noah and his family. God is merciful and forgiving; he makes a promise never again to destroy the earth and its people with a flood.
3. Possible Responses: Human beings are easily tempted and disobedient; they blame others for their mistakes; some people can show exceptional goodness and faithfulness and follow God's commandments to the letter.
4. Answers will vary, but should show awareness of literary elements of the selection.

Connect to the Literature

1. **What Do You Think?**
How did you react to the punishment given to Adam and Eve? Did you react in the same way to the punishment of the Flood?

Comprehension Check
- Why does Eve eat the forbidden fruit?
- How are Adam and Eve punished for disobeying God?
- Why does God decide to destroy all living things with a flood?
- How does Noah know when dry land has reappeared?

Think Critically

2. In these stories, what qualities is God portrayed as having?

THINK ABOUT
- God's feelings about his creation, especially human beings
- his reaction after learning that Adam and Eve have disobeyed him
- his decision to destroy all living creatures with a flood
- the covenant he establishes with Noah and his descendants

3. What qualities of human beings are portrayed in these stories?
4. **ACTIVE READING: READING SACRED LITERATURE**
Review the questions on page 62 and the answers that you wrote in your READER'S NOTEBOOK. How did your observations about the literature help you to understand it?

Extend Interpretations

5. **What If?** What might have happened in the story of Adam and Eve if Eve had not listened to the serpent?
6. **Comparing Texts** *The Epic of Gilgamesh* and Genesis both contain stories of a flood that wipes out almost all living things. Compare these stories and their heroes, Utnapishtim and Noah. How might you account for the similarities between the two stories?
7. **Connect to Life** In the world today is goodness usually rewarded and evil usually punished? Give some examples to support your opinion.

LITERARY ANALYSIS: SACRED LITERATURE

A sacred text, or **scripture,** is a work of literature that has a special status in the culture from which it springs. It may be seen as divinely inspired and may be used in worship and viewed with reverence. It may also be a work of great beauty and artistry.

More than many other kinds of literature, sacred literature is likely to have teaching as one of its main purposes. What it teaches generally has to do with a culture's most important concerns: the basic principles of morality, the meaning of human existence, and the relationship between the human and the divine.

Cooperative Learning Activity With your classmates, create a list of the teachings to be found in the two stories from Genesis. Write the list on the board; then, next to each teaching, record the events or details that convey the teaching.

Genesis	
Teaching	What Conveys the Teaching
Don't blame others for your mistakes.	*dialogue between God and Adam after Adam ate the forbidden fruit*

Extend Interpretations

5. **What If?** Possible Responses: Adam and Eve would have lived forever with God in paradise; Adam and Eve would have sinned on some other occasion; Adam and Even would never have had children and become the ancestors of all humanity.
6. **Comparing Texts** In both stories, divine powers decide to destroy humanity with a flood, with the exception of one man and his family, who survive by building a boat. However, in Genesis, humanity is destroyed because of its sinfulness; in Gilgamesh, humanity is destroyed because it is bothering the gods. Noah and Utnapishtim are both exceptional people who receive divine help in avoiding the fate of the rest of the world. Whereas Noah is rewarded for his righteousness, however, Utnapishtim is spared because of his friendship with Ea. After the flood, Noah's reward—a covenant with God—extends to his descendants. Utnapishtim's reward after the flood is immortality for himself and his wife only. Accept all reasonable ideas students have about why the two stories are so similar.
7. **Connect to Life** Accept all reasonable responses.

Writing Options

Guide-for-Living Comparison According to the scholar Joseph Campbell, one purpose of religious and mythological stories is to guide people through the trials of living. How does the kind of guidance found in *The Epic of Gilgamesh* compare with that found in Genesis? Explore this question in an essay. Before writing, list some of the trials faced by Gilgamesh, Adam, Eve, and Noah. Next to each trial, jot down what the person did—or perhaps should have done—to deal with the situation. Use the list as a source of supporting examples as you write.

Writing Handbook
See page R31: Compare and Contrast.

Activities & Explorations

1. Bible Storyboard Choose a story from Genesis and make a storyboard showing how you would turn it into a movie. Include drawings, dialogue, director's tips, music ideas, and any other necessary information. Present your storyboard to the class. Be ready to explain why you think your movie would be effective. ~ **ART/VIEWING AND REPRESENTING**

2. Good vs. Evil Debate In the story of Noah and the Flood, God says that "the imagination of man's heart is evil from his youth." Do you think that people are more naturally inclined to do wrong or to do good? Debate the question with a classmate who has a different opinion. ~ **SPEAKING AND LISTENING**

Inquiry & Research

1. Bible Report Investigate the Hebrew Bible further by exploring a book other than Genesis. Find out what the book is about, what kind of writing it is, what significance it has in Jewish history and culture, and what influence it has had on other literature. Present your findings in the form of an oral report.

2. Genesis in the Arts Over the years, scenes from Genesis have been the subjects of many famous paintings. Use museum Web sites or art-history books to search for at least two such paintings. In a presentation to the class, display these works. Explain what scene each work depicts and which one you prefer.

Points of Comparison

Review the excerpt from Genesis and fill in the "Genesis" column of your comparison-and-contrast chart.

Paired Activity Compare your chart with that of a classmate and discuss the similarities and differences between them. On the basis of your discussion, decide whether you want to change any of your answers before going on to the next part of this lesson.

Questions for Analysis	Genesis	*Popol Vuh*
What do the creators want the people they have created to do?	*Live happily in the Garden of Eden, obey God's commands*	
How do the people meet or fail to meet the creators' expectations?		
What do the creators do in response?		
In the end, how do things get resolved?		
What do these details reveal about the culture?		

Points of Comparison

You may want to lead students in a discussion of the Questions for Analysis before having them fill out their charts, especially if you feel they need extra help in doing do.

Literary Analysis

Cooperative Learning Activity

Because students may legitimately disagree about both the teachings conveyed by the text and the textual details that support the teaching, you might use this activity to lead a lively classroom discussion.

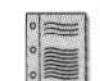
Use **Unit One Resource Book,** p. 14, for more practice.

Writing Options

Guide-for-Living Comparison Help students to avoid simply making a value judgment between the two works and instead to think about the kind of practical help each one offers in dealing with problems in everyday life.

Activities & Explorations

1. **Bible Storyboard** Help students consider different possibilities for presenting the story and their reasons for choosing one over another. You may want to invite some students to present a story from a part of Genesis not included in this book. If so, have students begin their presentations by summarizing the story for the rest of the class.
2. **Good vs. Evil Debate** Encourage students to support their views with specific examples and to offer thoughtful responses to the ideas and opinions of the person they are debating.

Inquiry & Research

1. **Bible Report** Be sure to tell students if you want them to avoid the Hebrew Bible selections that appear later in this book: Psalms 23 and 104 and the Book of Ruth. You may want to assign students specific parts to investigate. You could then use students' reports to help carry out a whole class project of creating a map of the Hebrew Bible.
2. **Genesis in the Arts** Encourage students to compare the different approaches to illustrating the scenes rather than the scenes themselves. You might want to suggest that students try to find two depictions of the same scene or event.

To assess skills and concepts taught in this selection, use **Formal Assessment Book,** p. 11.

Summary
The gods create the world out of chaos, then set about creating humanity. In contrast to the Genesis story of creation, the Mayan gods do not have a clear sense of what a human being is. They know only that they want their creature to speak, to recognize and praise their work, and to keep their days, that is, observe the sacred calendar (see mini-lesson on page 79). The gods' first attempt results in the animals, who fail to be human because they can't speak. The next two attempts result in the mud people, who cannot hold their shape, and the people of wood, who have empty hearts and minds. Finally the gods make creatures out of staple foods who succeed in being human. In fact, the people are too perfect—too much like the gods themselves—and so some of their knowledge is taken away.

Use **Unit One Resource Book,** pp. 16–17, for additional support and a glossary of proper names.

5-Minute Warm-Up

Daily Language SkillBuilder

Have students **proofread** the display sentences on page 15g and write them correctly.

Reading and Analyzing

Guide for Reading
The Guide for Reading notes in this selection are meant to help students read the text by dividing it into manageable sections. Each section begins with a **Focus** suggestion to help students read actively and with a purpose. Between sections, a **Pause & Reflect** question gives students an opportunity to stop and review what they have read and understood so far.

PREPARING to *Read*

Now that you have read one of the best-known creation stories, it's time to turn your attention to a less-familiar one, from a culture very different from the ancient Hebrews'. As you will see, the Mayan account of creation differs in many ways from that in Genesis. But there are also many surprising similarities between the accounts.

Build Background

Mayan Civilization The selection you are about to read is an excerpt from an important Mayan work—the *Popol Vuh.* The Maya were a Native American people who lived in what is now southern Mexico and Guatemala. They developed an advanced civilization that flourished from A.D. 250 to 900. Their cities were magnificent, with grand temples. Around 900, for reasons not completely understood, they abandoned the cities and migrated into the surrounding countryside. Spanish invaders entered their territory in the early 1500s, and by the middle of the century, most of the Maya had been conquered by the Spaniards.

The Maya excelled in painting and sculpture and developed advanced forms of mathematics and astronomy. Using paper prepared from fig-tree bark, they even made books. Other Mayan inventions include an accurate yearly calendar based on precise astronomical measurements and a complex system of hieroglyphic writing. Like the ancient Egyptians, the Maya used their written language to decorate as well as communicate.

In addition to their yearly calendar, the Maya created a sacred calendar of 260 days. Each day was associated with a particular god or goddess. Mayan priests used the calendar as a way of harmonizing their activities with divine forces. In the *Popol Vuh,* when the gods speak of "keeping days," they are referring to the use of the sacred calendar.

The *Popol Vuh,* or "book of the community," contains the Mayan story of the creation of the world. It was written not long after the Spanish conquest by an anonymous Mayan noble, who may have been trying to keep the work from becoming lost as a result of his people's defeat.

from

POPOL

VUH

Translated by Dennis Tedlock

GUIDE FOR READING

FOCUS In the opening section, you will learn about the very beginning of the world. As you read, notice how the gods think and talk about their creation.

This is the beginning of the Ancient Word, here in this place called Quiché.[1] Here we shall inscribe, we shall implant the Ancient Word, the potential and source for everything done in the citadel of Quiché, in the nation of Quiché people. . . .

This is the account, here it is:

Now it still ripples, now it still murmurs, ripples, it still sighs, still hums, and it is empty under the sky.

Here follow the first words, the first eloquence:

There is not yet one person, one animal, bird, fish, crab, tree, rock, hollow, canyon, meadow, forest. Only the sky alone is there; the face of the earth is not clear. Only the sea alone is pooled under all the sky; there is nothing whatever gathered together. It is at rest; not a single thing stirs. It is held back, kept at rest under the sky.

Whatever there is that might be is simply not there: only the pooled water, only the calm sea, only it alone is pooled.

Whatever might be is simply not there: only murmurs, ripples, in the dark, in the night. Only the Maker, Modeler alone, Sovereign Plumed Serpent, the Bearers, Begetters are in the water, a glittering light. They are there, they are enclosed in quetzal[2] feathers, in blue-green.

Thus the name, "Plumed Serpent." They are great knowers, great thinkers in their very being.

And of course there is the sky, and there is

Mayan cylindrical vessel decorated with mythological scene (seventh to eighth century). The Metropolitan Museum of Art (New York), The Michael C. Rockefeller Memorial Collection, Purchase, Nelson A. Rockefeller Gift, 1968.

also the Heart of Sky. This is the name of the god, as it is spoken.

And then came his word, he came here to the Sovereign Plumed Serpent, here in the blackness, 1
in the early dawn. He spoke with the Sovereign Plumed Serpent, and they talked, then they thought, then they worried. They agreed with each other, they joined their words, their thoughts. Then it was clear, then they reached accord[3] in the light, and then humanity was clear, when they conceived the growth, the generation of trees, of bushes, and the growth of life,

1. **Quiché** (kē-chā′).
2. **quetzal** (kĕt-säl′): Central American bird, with brilliantly covered plumage, often identified with the Sovereign Plumed Serpent.
3. **accord:** agreement.

Customizing Instruction

Less Proficient Readers

Focus Draw students' attention to the Focus at the top of the first column. Explain that these directions are included to help students pay attention to important aspects of the text as they read.

English Learners

Students not fluent in English may find the frequent repetition of the same concept in different words confusing. Make sure students understand that they are not necessarily missing something when they think a phrase means the same thing as one preceding it.

1 Make sure students understand that "Sovereign Plumed Serpent" here and "Heart of Sky" a few lines later are names. Suggest that students take note of the many names given in the text without trying to translate them literally word-for-word.

MINI LESSON Viewing and Representing

Mayan Deity

ART APPRECIATION At the height of their civilization, the Maya made many cylindrical ceramic vessels like the one shown here. Using the straight sides as a canvas, Mayan artists often decorated the vessels with elaborate mythological scenes. Here, the deity Chac-Xib-Chac, holding in his right hand a long-handled axe, dances and prepares to sacrifice on an altar a jaguar deity, whose left hind leg and tail are visible on the right.

These works of art have much in common with those of ancient civilizations in the other hemisphere. The Maya, like the Egyptians and Mesopotamians, favored mythological themes, showing the importance in their society of religious beliefs. Like the Egyptians, also, the Maya freely combined pictures with hieroglyphic writing, some of which can be seen in the upper right hand of the photograph.

Mayan art differs greatly from that of the ancient Middle East, however, in its realistic portrayal of action. Whereas Egyptian and Mesopotamian representations of scenes look posed, here the deity's sacrificial dance is full of motion, from the raised right leg to the upcast left hand. Even his bundle of long hair appears flipped over his head as if in a stop-action photograph.

Pause & Reflect (p. 78)
Possible Responses: hopeful that humans will praise their work; pleased; optimistic that their design will turn out well; worried about completing their work

Pause & Reflect (p. 79)
Possible Responses: They no longer expect the animals to talk and speak the gods' names; they want the animals to let themselves be eaten.

AND THEN THE EARTH AROSE BECAUSE OF THEM, IT WAS SIMPLY THEIR WORD THAT BROUGHT IT FORTH. FOR THE FORMING OF THE EARTH THEY SAID "EARTH."

of humankind, in the blackness, in the early dawn, all because of the Heart of Sky, named Hurricane. Thunderbolt Hurricane comes first, the second is Newborn Thunderbolt, and the third is Sudden Thunderbolt.

So there were three of them, as Heart of Sky, who came to the Sovereign Plumed Serpent, when the dawn of life was conceived:

"How should the sowing be, and the dawning? Who is to be the provider, nurturer?"

"Let it be this way, think about it: this water should be removed, emptied out for the formation of the earth's own plate and platform, then should come the sowing, the dawning of the sky-earth. But there will be no high days and no bright praise for our work, our design, until the rise of the human work, the human design," they said.

And then the earth arose because of them, it was simply their word that brought it forth. For the forming of the earth they said "Earth." It arose suddenly, just like a cloud, like a mist, now forming, unfolding. Then the mountains were separated from the water, all at once the great mountains came forth. By their genius alone, by their cutting edge alone they carried out the conception of the mountain-plain, whose face grew instant groves of cypress and pine.

And the Plumed Serpent was pleased with this:

"It was good that you came, Heart of Sky, Hurricane, and Newborn Thunderbolt, Sudden Thunderbolt. Our work, our design will turn out well," they said.

And the earth was formed first, the mountain-plain. The channels of water were separated; their branches wound their ways among the mountains. The waters were divided when the great mountains appeared.

Such was the formation of the earth when it was brought forth by the Heart of Sky, Heart of Earth, as they are called, since they were the first to think of it. The sky was set apart, and the earth was set apart in the midst of the waters.

Such was their plan when they thought, when they worried about the completion of their work.

PAUSE & REFLECT How do the gods seem to feel about their creation at this point?

FOCUS Now the gods will create the animals. As you read, notice what the gods expect of the animals and how they react to the animals' behavior.

Now they planned the animals of the mountains, all the guardians of the forests, creatures of the mountains: the deer, birds, pumas, jaguars, serpents, rattlesnakes, fer-de-lances[4], guardians of the bushes.

A Bearer, Begetter speaks:

"Why this pointless humming? Why should there merely be rustling beneath the trees and bushes?"

"Indeed—they had better have guardians," the others replied. As soon as they thought it and said it, deer and birds came forth.

4. **fer-de-lances** (fĕr′dl-ăn′səz): poisonous tropical snakes.

MINI LESSON Grammar

AUXILIARY VERBS

Instruction Remind students that auxiliary verbs, also called helping verbs, are combined with other verbs to create verb tenses or to show the passive voice.

Common auxiliary verbs include forms of *be*, forms of *do*, forms of *have*, and *could, should, would, may, might, must, can, shall,* and *will.*

Display the following example sentence:

Mara will visit Rome.

Point out the auxiliary verb *(will)* and discuss how it affects the main verb. *(It indicates that the verb* visit *is in the future tense.)*

Practice Identify the main verb (M) and the helping verb or verbs (H) in each sentence.

1. Two kids were swimming. *(M=swimming; H=were)*
2. Jan will run for president. *(M=run; H=will)*
3. Angus was still. *(M=still; H=was)*
4. Becky had been told. *(M=told; H=had, been)*
5. Harry and Kathy are going. *(M=going; H=are)*

For more instruction and practice in auxiliary verbs, use McDougal Littell's ***Language Network:***

- Grade 10, Chapter 1, "The Parts of Speech"
- Grade 12, Review: Parts of Speech

And then they gave out homes to the deer and birds:

"You, the deer: sleep along the rivers, in the canyons. Be here in the meadows, in the thickets, in the forests, multiply yourselves. You will stand and walk on all fours," they were told.

So then they established the nests of the birds, small and great:

"You, precious birds: your nests, your houses are in the trees, in the bushes. Multiply there, scatter there, in the branches of trees, the branches of bushes," the deer and birds were told.

When this deed had been done, all of them had received a place to sleep and a place to stay. So it is that the nests of the animals are on the earth, given by the Bearer, Begetter. Now the arrangement of the deer and birds was complete.

And then the deer and birds were told by the Maker, Modeler, Bearer, Begetter:

"Talk, speak out. Don't moan, don't cry out. Please talk, each to each, within each kind, within each group," they were told—the deer, birds, puma, jaguar, serpent.

"Name now our names, praise us. We are your mother, we are your father. Speak now:

'Hurricane,
Newborn Thunderbolt, Sudden Thunderbolt,
Heart of Sky, Heart of Earth,
Maker, Modeler,
Bearer, Begetter,'

1 Speak, pray to us, keep our days,"[5] they were told. But it didn't turn out that they spoke like people: they just squawked, they just chattered, they just howled. It wasn't apparent what language they spoke; each one gave a different cry. When the Maker, Modeler heard this:

"It hasn't turned out well, they haven't spoken," they said among themselves. "It hasn't turned out that our names have been named. Since we are their mason and sculptor, this will not do," the Bearers and Begetters said among themselves. So they told them:

"You will simply have to be transformed. Since it hasn't turned out well and you haven't spoken, we have changed our word:

"What you feed on, what you eat, the places where you sleep, the places where you stay, whatever is yours will remain in the canyons, the forests. Although it turned out that our days were not kept, nor did you pray to us, there may yet be strength in the keeper of days, the giver of praise whom we have yet to make. Just accept your service, just let your flesh be eaten.

"So be it, this must be your service," they were told when they were instructed—the animals, small and great, on the face of the earth.

And then they wanted to test their timing again, they wanted to experiment again, and they wanted to prepare for the keeping of days again. They had not heard their speech among the animals; it did not come to fruition and it was not complete.

And so their flesh was brought low: they served, they were eaten, they were killed—the animals on the face of the earth.

PAUSE & REFLECT How do the gods change their expectations of the animals?

FOCUS As you read the next section, notice what the gods say about their expectations and how they react to the mud person and the people of wood.

Again there comes an experiment with the human work, the human design, by the Maker, Modeler, Bearer, Begetter:

"It must simply be tried again. The time for the planting and dawning is nearing. For this we must make a provider and nurturer. How else 2

5. **keep our days:** pray to us according to the regular movements and rhythms of a calendar.

Customizing Instruction

Less Proficient Readers

Focus Help students to use the Focus on page 78 by pointing out that the animals in the section that follows are not doing anything unusual but just behaving like animals. Their behavior surprises the gods only because the gods expect something different.

Help students to use the Focus on page 79 by telling them that, in the section that follows, the Mayan gods have a clear idea of what they want people to do but not of how to make people.

Advanced Learners

1 Have students find out more about the Mayan calendar and its connection to Mayan ceremonies and activities such as sowing and harvesting. Students can then present this information to their classmates in order to help them better understand what the gods are looking for from their human creations.

English Learners

2 Students may be confused by the reference to planting. Explain that one use of the Mayan sacred calendar was to determine the proper time for sowing crops. The gods' goal, as the Maya conceive it, is to create people who will carry out all of the customs and rituals practiced by the Maya themselves.

Cross Curricular Link Humanities

THE MAYAN CALENDAR The 260 days of the Mayan sacred calendar were each assigned a designation based on a "week" in which the days were numbered 1–13 and 20 "months" named after things and concepts important to the Maya. The first day in this series would be 1-world, followed by 2-wind, 3-night-house, and 4-maize. After 13-reed, the numbering would start over with the 14th name: 1-jaguar, and so on up to the 20th name: 7-lord. Following this pattern, the designations do not repeat until all 260 combinations have occurred.

In addition to this sacred calendar, the Maya kept a yearly civil calendar of 365 days similar to the Gregorian calendar that we use. While they did not adjust this calendar with a leap year as we do, they estimated the exact length of a solar year slightly more accurately even than does the Gregorian calendar.

The Maya also maintained a third calendar known as the Long Count, an exact count of days from a zero point. According to this calendar, every day was represented with a number corresponding to the number of days since the start of the Mayan era, which they believed occurred in 3114 B.C.

Reading and Analyzing

Reading Skills and Strategies
CLARIFYING

A The entire following section will be unclear to students if they don't understand what happens in this paragraph. Sovereign Plumed Serpent and the other gods decide to call upon the divine grandparents, older than all the other gods, for help. The grandparents are to use a method of fortune-telling based on mathematics and the calendar to determine if the other gods should use wood to make people. Quiché shamans today still use coral-tree seeds to cast horoscopes.

B The "deception" referred to would be that of causing the divining process to result in a lie.

Reading Skills and Strategies
SUMMARIZING

C Have students summarize the preceding passage from the introduction of Xpiyacoc and Xmucane to here. *(The gods utter a prayer to Xpiyacoc and Xmucane asking for their help and listing many of their names. Xpiyacoc and Xmucane then use corn kernels and coral seeds to "count days" and divine the truth. Based on the results, Xpiyacoc and Xmucane tell the other gods to go ahead and make the wooden people.)*

can we be invoked[6] and remembered on the face of the earth? We have already made our first try at our work and design, but it turned out that they didn't keep our days, nor did they glorify us.

"So now let's try to make a giver of praise, giver of respect, provider, nurturer," they said.

So then comes the building and working with earth and mud. They made a body, but it didn't look good
1 to them. It was just separating, just crumbling, just loosening, just softening, just disintegrating, and just dissolving. Its head wouldn't turn, either. Its face was just lopsided, its face was just twisted. It couldn't look around. It talked at first, but senselessly. It was quickly dissolving in the water.

HUMANITIES CONNECTION This picture of Mayan warriors and their prisoners of war comes from Bonampak, a Mayan city that flourished 1,200 years ago. One building at Bonampak contains three rooms of murals, the most complete set of ancient paintings yet discovered in the New World.

"It won't last," the mason and sculptor said then. "It seems to be dwindling away, so let it just dwindle. It can't walk and it can't multiply, so let it be merely a thought," they said.

So then they dismantled, again they brought down their work and design. Again they talked:

"What is there for us to make that would turn out well, that would succeed in keeping our days and praying to us?" they said. Then they planned again:

A "We'll just tell Xpiyacoc,[7] Xmucane,[8] Hunahpu Possum, Hunahpu Coyote, to try a counting of days, a counting of lots," the mason and sculptor said to themselves. Then they invoked Xpiyacoc, Xmucane.

2 Then comes the naming of those who are the midmost seers: the "Grandmother of Day, Grandmother of Light," as the Maker, Modeler called them. These are names of Xpiyacoc and Xmucane.

When Hurricane had spoken with the Sovereign Plumed Serpent, they invoked the daykeepers, diviners, the midmost seers:

"There is yet to find, yet to discover how we are to model a person, construct a person again, a provider, nurturer, so that we are called upon and we are recognized: our recompense[9] is in words.

Midwife, matchmaker,
our grandmother, our grandfather,

---

6. **invoked:** prayed to.
7. **Xpiyacoc** (shpē′yä-kōk′).
8. **Xmucane** (shmo͞o′kä-nä′).
9. **recompense** (rĕk′əm-pĕns′): payment; reward.

MINI LESSON Viewing and Representing

Bonampak Mural

ART APPRECIATION The murals at Bonampak provide a good example of how technology can play an important role in the study of humanities and the arts. When the murals first gained worldwide attention, rain leaking through the limestone walls of the building containing the artworks had coated them with a thick white layer of calcite. The mineral had protected the images from deterioration but made them difficult to see. Artists wet the walls in order to view the images better and copied them as best they could.

In the mid-1980s Mexican archaeologists cleaned the calcite from the walls, but much of the detail of the paintings remained obscured, and they became vulnerable to further damage over time. In the early 1990s, researchers used color photographs of the cleaned walls, details revealed by direct observation, and features uncovered by infrared images to create computer reconstructions of the murals like the one shown in the **Humanities Connection**. The reconstructions not only show these works of art in a form close to the original for the first time in modern history; they also preserve the works in a form that will not suffer at the hands of time and the elements.

Xpiyacoc, Xmucane,
let there be planting, let there be the dawning
of our invocation, our sustenance, our
recognition
by the human work, the human design,
the human figure, the human form.
So be it, fulfill your names:
Hunahpu Possum, Hunahpu Coyote,
Bearer twice over, Begetter twice over,
Great Peccary, Great Coati,
lapidary, jeweler,
sawyer,[10] carpenter,
plate shaper, bowl shaper,
incense maker, master craftsman,
Grandmother of Day, Grandmother of Light.

You have been called upon because of our work, our design. Run your hands over the kernels of corn, over the seeds of the coral tree, just get it done, just let it come out whether we should carve and gouge a mouth, a face in wood," they told the daykeepers.

And then comes the borrowing, the counting of days; the hand is moved over the corn kernels, over the coral seeds, the days, the lots.

Then they spoke to them, one of them a grandmother, the other a grandfather.

This is the grandfather, this is the master of the coral seeds: Xpiyacoc is his name.

And this is the grandmother, the daykeeper, diviner who stands behind others: Xmucane is her name.

And they said, as they set out the days:

3 "Just let it be found, just let it be discovered,
say it, our ear is listening,
may you talk, may you speak,
just find the wood for the carving and
sculpting
by the builder, sculptor.
Is this to be the provider, the nurturer
when it comes to the planting, the dawning?
You corn kernels, you coral seeds,
you days, you lots:
may you succeed, may you be accurate,"

they said to the corn kernels, coral seeds, days, lots. "Have shame, you up there, Heart of Sky: attempt no deception before the mouth and face of Sovereign Plumed Serpent," they said. Then they spoke straight to the point: B

"It is well that there be your manikins, woodcarvings, talking, speaking, there on the face of the earth." C

"So be it," they replied. The moment they spoke it was done: the manikins, woodcarvings, human in looks and human in speech.

This was the peopling of the face of the earth:

They came into being, they multiplied, they had daughters, they had sons, these manikins, woodcarvings. But there was nothing in their hearts and nothing in their minds, no memory of their mason and builder. They just went and walked wherever they wanted. Now they did not remember the Heart of Sky.

And so they fell, just an experiment and just a cutout for humankind. They were talking at first but their faces were dry. They were not yet developed in the legs and arms. They had no blood, no lymph. They had no sweat, no fat. Their complexions were dry, their faces were

AND SO THEY FELL, JUST AN EXPERIMENT AND JUST A CUTOUT FOR HUMANKIND.

10. **lapidary . . . sawyer:** gemstone cutter . . . cutter of timber.

Customizing Instruction

English Learners

1 Make sure that students understand that the six verbs in this sentence all mean the same thing.

Less Proficient Readers

2 Make sure students understand that, in the paragraphs that follow, Xpiyacoc and Xmucane are called by many other names, but they are the only characters referred to.

3 Tell students that, in this indented quotation, Xpiyacoc and Xmucane are speaking to the kernels and seeds, asking them to reveal the truth accurately.

MINI LESSON Vocabulary Strategy

CONTEXT CLUES Remind students that sometimes they can understand the meaning of an unfamiliar word by examining the context in which the word is used. Often context clues are not in the same sentence. Students may need to look at the sentences that surround the word and infer, or draw conclusions about, the word's meaning.

Instruction Read aloud the paragraph on page 80 that begins, "So then comes the building and working with earth and mud." Tell students that they can use other words in this paragraph to figure out the meaning of the words *dissolving* and *disintegrating.* Point out these clues in the paragraph:

- the phrase "working with earth and mud"
- the words *separating, crumbling, loosening, softening*
- the phrase "dissolving in the water"

Also point out that the paragraph contains a string of words that all describe a single situation: how the mud humans fell apart. Tell students that because the words *dissolving* and *disintegrating* are part of this string of words, they probably have meanings similar to those words.

Practice Have students look up the words *dissolve* and *disintegrate* in the dictionary and check their definitions.

A lesson on context clues appears on p. 674 in the Pupil's Edition.

Reading Skills and Strategies
CONNECTING

(A) Ask students what other stories they have read in which gods destroy the people they have created with a flood. ("Creation and the Fall" *from Genesis;* "The Story of the Flood" *from The Epic of Gilgamesh*)

Pause & Reflect

Possible Responses: because the people of wood don't keep the gods' days or pray to them; because the gods tried especially hard when they made the people of wood and feel disappointed; because the people of wood look and speak like humans but have nothing in their hearts and minds

crusty. They flailed[11] their legs and arms, their bodies were deformed.

And so they accomplished nothing before the Maker, Modeler who gave them birth, gave them heart. They became the first numerous people here on the face of the earth.

A Again there comes a humiliation, destruction, and demolition. The manikins, woodcarvings were killed when the Heart of Sky devised a flood for them. A great flood was made; it came down on the heads of the manikins, woodcarvings.

The man's body was carved from the wood of the coral tree by the Maker, Modeler. And as for the woman, the Maker, Modeler needed the hearts of bulrushes for the woman's body. They were not competent, nor did they speak before the builder and sculptor who made them and brought them forth, and so they were killed, done in by a flood:

There came a rain of resin from the sky.

There came the one named Gouger of Faces: he gouged out their eyeballs.

1 There came Sudden Bloodletter: he snapped off their heads.

There came Crunching Jaguar: he ate their flesh.

There came Tearing Jaguar: he tore them open.

They were pounded down to the bones and tendons, smashed and pulverized even to the bones. Their faces were smashed because they were incompetent before their mother and their father, the Heart of Sky, named Hurricane. The earth was blackened because of this; the black rainstorm began, rain all day and rain all night. Into their houses came the animals, small and great. Their faces were crushed by things of wood and stone. Everything spoke: their water jars, their tortilla griddles, their plates, their cooking pots, their dogs, their grinding stones, each and every thing crushed their faces. Their dogs and turkeys told them:

"You caused us pain, you ate us, but now it is *you* whom *we* shall eat." And this is the grinding stone:

"We were undone because of you.

Every day, every day,
in the dark, in the dawn, forever,
r-r-rip, r-r-rip,
r-r-rub, r-r-rub,
right in our faces, because of you.

This was the service we gave you at first, when you were still people, but today you will learn of our power. We shall pound and we shall grind your flesh," their grinding stones told them.

And this is what their dogs said, when they spoke in their turn:

"Why is it you can't seem to give us our food? We just watch and you just keep us down, and you throw us around. You keep a stick ready when you eat, just so you can hit us. We don't talk, so we've received nothing from you. How could you not have known? You *did* know that we were wasting away there, behind you.

"So, this very day you will taste the teeth in our mouths. We shall eat you," their dogs told them, and their faces were crushed.

And then their tortilla griddles and cooking pots spoke to them in turn:

"Pain! That's all you've done for us. Our mouths are sooty, our faces are sooty. By setting us on the fire all the time, you burn us. Since *we* felt no pain, *you* try it. We shall burn you," all their cooking pots said, crushing their faces.

The stones, their hearthstones were shooting out, coming right out of the fire, going for their heads, causing them pain. Now they run for it, helter-skelter.

They want to climb up on the houses, but they fall as the houses collapse.

They want to climb the trees; they're thrown off by the trees.

---

11. **flailed:** thrashed; beat.

MINI LESSON Grammar

PRONOUN CASE

Instruction Pronouns take on different forms, depending on how they are used in sentences. These forms are called cases. Review the three cases of pronouns:

- **Nominative** form is used when a pronoun functions as the subject of a sentence. Example: I waited. (nominative pronoun forms: *I, you, he, she, it, we, they)*
- **Objective** form is used when the pronoun functions as a direct object, an indirect object, or an object of a preposition. Example: Mom watched me. (objective pronoun forms: *me, you, him, her, it, us, them*)
- **Possessive** form is used to show ownership. Example: My dog is lost. (possessive pronoun forms: *my, mine, your, yours, his, her, hers, its, our, ours, their, theirs*)

Practice Find each pronoun in the following sentences and identify its case:

1. What do we know about the Maya? *(we: nominative)*
2. Our teacher told us about them. *(our: possessive; us: objective; them: objective)*
3. They developed advanced forms of mathematics and astronomy. *(they: nominative)*
4. The Maya used their written language to decorate as well as to communicate. *(their: possessive)*
5. I studied the Mayan calendar in my math class. *(I: nominative; my: possessive)*

For more instruction and practice in pronoun use, use McDougal Littell's ***Language Network:***

- Grade 10, Chapter 8, "Using Pronouns"
- Grade 12, Chapter 6, "Using Pronouns"

Quetzlcoatl, the Plumed Serpent (center), fashioning a human being. *The Creation of Man,* Diego Rivera. Page from *Popol Vuh,* water color on paper. Copyright © 2001 Banco de México Diego Rivera & Frida Kahlo Museums Trust. Av. Cinco de Mayo No. 2, Col. Centro, Del. Cuauhtémoc 06059, México, D.F./Bridgeman Art Library.

They want to get inside caves, but the caves slam shut in their faces.

Such was the scattering of the human work, the human design. The people were ground down, overthrown. The mouths and faces of all of them were destroyed and crushed. And it used to be said that the monkeys in the forests today are a sign of this. They were left as a sign because wood alone was used for their flesh by the builder and sculptor.

So this is why monkeys look like people: they are a sign of a previous human work, human design—mere manikins, mere woodcarvings. . . .

PAUSE & REFLECT Why do you think the gods treat the people of wood so harshly?

FOCUS As you continue to read, notice what the first human beings are made of and how they behave.

And here is the beginning of the conception of humans, and of the search for the ingredients of the human body. So they spoke, the Bearer, Begetter, the Makers, Modelers named Sovereign Plumed Serpent:

"The dawn has approached, preparations have been made, and morning has come for the provider, nurturer, born in the light, begotten in the light. Morning has come for humankind, for the people of the face of the earth," they said. It all came together as they went on thinking in the darkness, in the night, as they searched and they sifted, they thought and they wondered.

And here their thoughts came out in clear light. They sought and discovered what was needed for human flesh. It was only a short while before the sun, moon, and stars were to appear above the Makers and Modelers. Split Place, Bitter Water Place[12] is the name: the yellow corn, white corn came from there.

And these are the names of the animals who brought the food: fox, coyote, parrot, crow. There were four animals who brought the news of the ears of yellow corn and white corn. They were coming from over there at Split Place, they showed the way to the split.

And this was when they found the staple[13] foods.

And these were the ingredients for the flesh of the human work, the human design, and the water was for the blood. It became human blood, and corn was also used by the Bearer, Begetter. 2

And so they were happy over the provisions of the good mountain, filled with sweet things, thick with yellow corn, white corn, and thick with pataxte and cacao, countless zapotes,

12. **Split Place, Bitter Water Place:** the site of a stronghold of the Quiché lords.

13. **staple:** principal; most basic.

Customizing Instruction

English Learners

1 Make sure students know these are not characters they are supposed to recognize. All we are told about them is their names, which are self-explanatory.

Less Proficient Readers

Focus To help students use the Focus, explain that in the section that follows the gods finally succeed at creating the kind of human beings they want.

Advanced Learners

2 Remind students that God in Genesis makes people out of earth or dust. In this story the people made from mud don't succeed, but the ones created from staple foods do. Ask students what this difference might reflect about the cultures.

Possible Responses: It might show that the Hebrews thought of people as receiving life directly from God, while the Maya saw people as dependent for life on their relationship with nature; it might show that agriculture was simply a practicality for the Hebrews, while for the Maya it was strongly connected to their religion.

MINI LESSON Viewing and Representing

The Creation of Man from Popol Vuh
by Diego Rivera

ART APPRECIATION Mexican artist Diego Rivera (1886–1957) is best-known for his large murals, or wall paintings, and for his fusion of three major influences on his work: his training in classical and modern painting techniques, his social and political concerns, and his interest in pre-Columbian history and mythology. The latter is particularly evident in his illustrations for the *Popol Vuh.*

Have students compare the illustration from the *Popol Vuh* above with the Mayan vase painting on page 77 and describe the similarities they find.

Possible Responses: The styles of the two paintings are much alike: Quetzcoatl and Chac-Xib-Chac wear similar dress, have similar facial expressions, and appear to move in the same way; the Rivera painting uses earth tones like the ones in the vase; in both paintings many figures are crowded into the available space in a way that suggests movement and busy activity.

Reading and Analyzing

Reading Skills and Strategies
CLARIFYING

A The first four true humans have "looks of the male kind" because they are all male. The *Popol Vuh* tells of the creation of women in a later part of the story (not included in this excerpt).

Pause & Reflect

Possible Responses: They look and act like human beings; they think as well as talk; they show a superhuman ability to see everything that exists.

anonas, jocotes, nances, matasanos,[14] sweets—the rich foods filling up the citadel named Split Place, Bitter Water Place. All the edible fruits were there: small staples, great staples, small plants, great plants. The way was shown by the animals.

And then the yellow corn and white corn were ground, and Xmucane did the grinding nine times. Food was used, along with the water she rinsed her hands with, for the creation of grease; it became human fat when it was worked by the Bearer, Begetter, Sovereign Plumed Serpent, as they are called.

After that, they put it into words:

the making, the modeling of our first mother-father,
with yellow corn, white corn alone for the flesh,
food alone for the human legs and arms,
for our first fathers, the four human works.

It was staples alone that made up their flesh.

These are the names of the first people who were made and modeled.

This is the first person: Jaguar Quitze.
And now the second: Jaguar Night.
1 And now the third: Not Right Now.
And the fourth: Dark Jaguar.

And these are the names of our first mother-fathers. They were simply made and modeled, it is said; they had no mother and no father. We have named the men by themselves. No woman gave birth to them, nor were they begotten by the builder, sculptor, Bearer, Begetter. By sacrifice alone, by genius alone they were made, they were modeled by the Maker, Modeler, Bearer, Begetter, Sovereign Plumed Serpent. And when they came to fruition, they came out human:

They talked and they made words.
They looked and they listened.
They walked, they worked.
They were good people, handsome, with looks of the male kind. Thoughts came into existence A
and they gazed; their vision came all at once.
Perfectly they saw, perfectly they knew every- 2
thing under the sky, whenever they looked. The moment they turned around and looked around in the sky, on the earth, everything was seen without any obstruction. They didn't have to walk around before they could see what was under the sky; they just stayed where they were.

As they looked, their knowledge became intense. Their sight passed through trees, through rocks, through lakes, through seas, through mountains, through plains. Jaguar Quitze, Jaguar Night, Not Right Now, and Dark Jaguar were truly gifted people.

PAUSE & REFLECT How do the first human beings behave?

FOCUS As you read to the end, notice what the gods do not like about the new kind of person and what they do about it.

And then they were asked by the builder and mason:

"What do you know about your being? Don't you look, don't you listen? Isn't your speech good, and your walk? So you must look, to see out under the sky. Don't you see the mountain-plain clearly? So try it," they were told.

And then they saw everything under the sky perfectly. After that, they thanked the Maker, Modeler:

"Truly now,
double thanks, triple thanks

14. **pataxte and cacao . . . matasanos:** Pataxte (pä′täsh-tā′) and cacao (kə-kou′) are two varieties of seeds from which chocolate is made. Zapotes (zə-pō′dēz), anonas (ə-nō′nəz), jocotes (hō-kō′tāz), and matasanos (măd′ə-sä′nōz) are kinds of tropical fruits.

that we've been formed, we've been given
our mouths, our faces,
we speak, we listen,
we wonder, we move,
our knowledge is good, we've understood
what is far and near,
and we've seen what is great and small
under the sky, on the earth.
Thanks to you we've been formed,
we've come to be made and modeled,
our grandmother, our grandfather,"

they said when they gave thanks for having been made and modeled. They understood everything perfectly, they sighted the four sides, the four corners in the sky, on the earth, and this didn't sound good to the builder and sculptor:

"What our works and designs have said is no good:

'We have understood everything, great and small,' they say." And so the Bearer, Begetter took back their knowledge:

"What should we do with them now? Their vision should at least reach nearby, they should see at least a small part of the face of the earth, but what they're saying isn't good. Aren't they
3 merely 'works' and 'designs' in their very names?
Yet they'll become as great as gods, unless they procreate, proliferate at the sowing, the dawning, unless they increase."

"Let it be this way: now we'll take them apart just a little, that's what we need. What we've found out isn't good. Their deeds would become equal to ours, just because their knowledge reaches so far. They see everything," so said

the Heart of Sky, Hurricane,
Newborn Thunderbolt, Sudden Thunderbolt,
Sovereign Plumed Serpent,
Bearer, Begetter,
Xpiyacoc, Xmucane,
Maker, Modeler,

as they are called. And when they changed the nature of their works, their designs, it was enough that the eyes be marred by the Heart of Sky. They were blinded as the face of a mirror is breathed upon. Their vision flickered. Now it was only from close up that they could see what was there with any clarity.

And such was the loss of the means of understanding, along with the means of knowing everything, by the four humans. The root was implanted.

And such was the making, modeling of our first grandfather, our father, by the Heart of Sky, Heart of Earth. ❖

Customizing Instruction

English Learners

1 In contrast to the names on page 82, these names do not reveal much that will help students understand what the characters are like. Suggest students just note that four people were created.

2 Make sure students understand that the verb *see* here is meant not only in the literal sense but also in the sense of understanding or having knowledge.

Less Proficient Readers

Focus Help students use the Focus on page 84 by telling them that the gods feel they have been too successful in their new creation.

Advanced Learners

3 Have students compare this statement with the similar concern expressed by God in Genesis (page 69) and discuss what cultural beliefs or values might lie behind this common theme.

Possible Responses: The theme might reflect the belief that people by nature are very close to being gods; it might show that being a good human means accepting one's limitations; it might serve to explain why human knowledge is imperfect.

COMPARING LITERATURE ACROSS CULTURES 85

Connect to the Literature

1. **What Do You Think?**
   Responses will vary. Follow up responses by asking students why they found a particular aspect of the selection surprising or what they had been expecting instead.

Comprehension Check

- The newly created people can see and understand everything, just as the gods can.
- The gods blind the people's eyes so that they can see only what is up close.

 Use Selection Quiz in **Unit One Resource Book,** p. 18.

Think Critically

2. Possible Responses: The gods are strict and unforgiving; they have specific expectations for the creatures they make; they don't seem to know how to make the kind of creature they want; they are afraid of making a creature that will know as much as they do.
3. Possible Responses: The people have to please the gods or be destroyed; the gods need the people to give them praise and count their days; the human beings feel grateful to the gods for creating them.
4. Possible Responses: Being alive is something to be thankful for; human existence has a purpose; people can't always see the "big picture;" it's good to live in an orderly way and to observe traditions; it's important to know your people's history.

Points of Comparison

Before having students complete their Points of Comparison charts, review the questions for analysis. You may want to help students get started by having them volunteer a couple of oral responses to one or two of the questions. This activity can also be conducted as a whole-class discussion, with students filling in their charts individually afterwards.

Connect to the Literature

1. **What Do You Think?** What surprised you the most as you read this excerpt from the *Popol Vuh?*

Comprehension Check

- What do the gods not like about the last kind of person they create?
- How do the gods correct this defect in their creatures?

Think Critically

2. How would you describe the gods in the *Popol Vuh?*
3. How would you describe the relationship between people and the gods?
4. What wisdom or values do you think this creation story conveys?

Points of Comparison

Paired Activity Now that you have read and studied both creation stories, work with a partner to compare and contrast them. First, review the answers about the Book of Genesis in your and your partner's comparison-and-contrast charts. Then, together, fill in answers under *Popol Vuh.*

Questions for Analysis	Genesis	*Popol Vuh*
What do the creators want the people they have created to do?	Live happily in the Garden of Eden; obey God's commands	Praise the gods and "keep their days"
How do the people meet or fail to meet the creators' expectations?		
What do the creators do in response?		
In the end, how do things get resolved?		
What do these details reveal about the culture?		

Standardized Test Practice

Writing About Literature

PART 1 Reading the Prompt

In writing assessments, you may be asked to compare and contrast works of literature that have similar topics or belong to the same type, such as the two creation stories that you have read. You are now going to practice writing an essay that involves this type of comparison.

Writing Prompt

Many cultures have creation stories that have been told for generations. Creation stories from different cultures often show remarkable similarities, reflecting beliefs and values common to all people. Such stories may, however, differ in significant ways that can reveal differences between cultures.

In a short essay, compare and contrast the creation accounts in the Book of Genesis and the *Popol Vuh*. Show what the two stories have in common; then look at differences between the two stories. Cite evidence from the texts to support your analysis. In your conclusion, summarize what the similarities and differences reveal about the two cultures. 1 2 3 4

STRATEGIES IN ACTION

1 I have to **compare and contrast** two creation stories.

2 I need to show **what the stories have in common** and **how they are different.**

3 I need to include **details, examples,** or **quotations** from the stories to support my ideas.

4 I need to develop a **conclusion** about what the similarities and differences reveal about the two cultures.

PART 2 Planning a Comparison-and-Contrast Essay

- Review the comparison-and-contrast chart that you filled out for Genesis and the *Popol Vuh.*
- In your chart, find examples of similarities and differences to point out in your essay.
- Create an outline to organize your ideas.

PART 3 Drafting Your Essay

Introduction Begin by introducing your topic. Identify the shared elements that make the stories comparable. Then explain briefly how you think they differ.

Body Discuss the similarities and differences in more detail. Use your comparison-and-contrast chart as a source of specific ideas and examples.

Conclusion Briefly summarize the major similarities and differences between the stories. Explain what you think they reveal about the cultures the stories came from.

Revision Check your use of signal words—such as *similarly, also, like, but, unlike,* and *while*—to make sure that your comparisons and contrasts are clear.

TEST PRACTICE

✓ Assessment **Standardized Test Practice**

RESPONDING TO A WRITING PROMPT Read aloud the writing prompt at the top of this page. Discuss the **Strategies in Action** by asking students to identify the words in the prompt that tell them what to do. Suggest that they mark up their comparison-and-contrast charts, identifying points to include in their essays. When students have finished drafting their essays, have them work with a partner to see if they have accomplished the tips given in Part 3 **Drafting Your Essay.**

PART 1 Reading the Prompt
Model the process:

- Read through the entire prompt.
- List key terms on the board ("compare and contrast," "evidence," "conclusion").
- Use the **Strategies in Action** to show how students can restate the prompt in their own words.

PART 2 Planning a Comparison-and-Contrast Essay

- Suggest students locate passages in the selections that relate to what they wrote in their charts.
- Suggest that students add other questions for analysis to the chart to bring out additional similarities and differences they have noticed.
- Suggest students look at the options for organizing a Comparison-and-Contrast essay given in the Writing Handbook (page R31).

PART 3 Drafting Your Essay

Introduction
Explain that the introduction should capture the reader's interest by presenting an intriguing problem or question. By setting up their essays as an attempt to answer the question or solve the problem, students can give them a clear and compelling purpose from the beginnning.

Body
Tell students that their essay will be more coherent, easier to follow, and more interesting if they refer back occasionally to the problem or question they began with and show how they are responding to it.

Conclusion
In their conclusion, students can present the findings of their investigation—the answer to the question or solution to the problem with which they began. The conclusion is also a good place to explain why the answer or solution matters, leaving the reader with a sense that something worthwhile has been accomplished.

Revision
You might want to suggest that students read each other's work and provide feedback on logic, clarity, tone, appropriate use of examples, correct use of grammar and punctuation, and other elements of good writing.

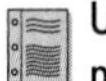
Use **Unit One Resource Book,** p. 19, for additional support.

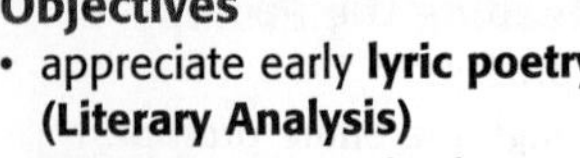

Objectives

- appreciate early **lyric poetry (Literary Analysis)**
- appreciate an early **short story (Literary Analysis)**
- understand the use of **description** in literature **(Literary Analysis)**
- understand the importance of **visualizing** in reading literature **(Active Reading)**

Thematic Link

The Psalms, songs of devotion written to or about God, show the strong **spiritual** connections of early Hebrew literature.

5-Minute Warm-Up

Daily Language SkillBuilder

Have students **proofread** the display sentences on page 15g and write them correctly.

Reading and Analyzing

Literary Analysis DESCRIPTION

Ask students to point to descriptive passages in the poem that they find especially vivid. Have them identify particular words and phrases that contribute to this vividness.

 Use **Unit One Resource Book,** p. 22, for more practice.

Active Reading VISUALIZING

Ask students which descriptive passages they found easy to visualize and which ones they found more challenging. *(Most students will find "paths of righteousness," "the valley of the shadow of death," and "the house of the Lord" harder to visualize, because they are more abstract than the other images used in the poem.)*

 Use **Unit One Resource Book,** p. 21, for more practice.

PSALM 23
PSALM 104
THE BOOK OF RUTH

Build Background

The Book of Psalms The Book of Psalms is the hymnal of ancient Israel. The word *psalm* (säm) comes from a Greek word meaning "to play the harp." Like many other lyric poems, psalms were originally intended to be sung. Most of the psalms were written to be used during worship in the temple. Many are attributed to King David, who ruled over Israel around 1000 B.C. Before becoming king, David was a shepherd. Shepherds spent long hours watching their flocks and often sang and played the harp to pass the time.

The Book of Psalms contains 150 songs on a wide variety of topics. Each describes a particular way God influences people or events in the world. Psalm 23 focuses on the relationship between God and a single individual. Psalm 104 describes God's connection to all of nature. Many of the psalms, like these, are songs of praise.

The Book of Ruth If the Book of Psalms presents us with some of the first lyric poems, the Book of Ruth gives us one of the first and most memorable short stories. Ruth is very different from earlier biblical heroes. When the story begins, she is not an important person at the center of Hebrew history. In fact, as a woman who is widowed, childless, and foreign, she is at the bottom of the social scale. Our interest in Ruth is in her story—in what motivates her as a character, in the conflict that she faces, and in how it gets resolved.

Connect to Your Life

The Book of Ruth is a story about a person who is completely dependent on the kindness of others. Think of a time when you had to depend on another person for something important. Did the person come through? What were your feelings throughout the experience? Discuss your experience with a classmate.

Focus Your Reading

LITERARY ANALYSIS: DESCRIPTION

Psalm 23, Psalm 104, and the Book of Ruth come alive through **description**—writing that helps readers picture **scenes, events,** and **characters.** Good description often involves the use of vivid language:

The trees of the Lord are full of sap,
the cedars of Lebanon, which he hath planted,
where the birds make their nests;
as for the stork,
the fir trees are her house.

As you read, think about the effects created by the descriptive details you encounter.

ACTIVE READING: VISUALIZING

When you **visualize,** you use your imagination to form pictures in your mind. The more precise the **details** a writer supplies, the better a reader is able to visualize a work's **setting, characters,** and **events.**

READER'S NOTEBOOK As you read these selections, write down details in the text where you can easily visualize what is being described.

LESSON RESOURCES

UNIT ONE RESOURCE BOOK, pp. 20–23

ASSESSMENT RESOURCES
Formal Assessment, pp. 13–14
Teacher's Guide to Assessment and Portfolio Use
Test Generator

INTEGRATED TECHNOLOGY
Visit our Web site: classzone.com

ADDITIONAL RESOURCES
Lesson Planning Guide, pp. 7–8
Teacher's Sourcebook for Language Development

Psalm 23

King James Bible

The Lord is my shepherd;
I shall not want.[1]
He maketh me to lie down in green pastures;
he leadeth me beside the still waters;
he restoreth my soul.
He leadeth me in the paths of righteousness
1 for his name's sake.
Yea, though I walk through the valley
of the shadow of death,
I will fear no evil: for thou art with me;
2 thy rod and thy staff they comfort me.
3 Thou preparest a table before me
4 in the presence of mine enemies:
Thou anointest my head with oil; my cup runneth over.[2]
Surely goodness and mercy shall follow me
all the days of my life,
and I will dwell in the house of the Lord forever.

1. **want:** be in need.
2. **Thou preparest . . . runneth over:** In this verse, the Lord is presented as a generous host who offers his guest food, oil for grooming, and an overflowing cup of wine. In ancient times, olive oil was used as a cleansing agent and was quite expensive.

David, the young shepherd, plays his pipe and a bell (I Samuel 16: 5–11). French manuscript illustration. The Granger Collection, New York.

Customizing Instruction

Less Proficient Readers

1 Explain that "for his name's sake" means "in keeping with his name," that is, with who the Lord is (God).

English Learners

2 The "rod" and the "staff" are two tools of the shepherd, probably the shepherd's crook (pictured in the illustration on this page), used to rescue an animal in a place difficult to reach, and a straight, heavy stick that could be used as a walking support or as a club in case of attack by a wild animal.

3 Make sure that students understand that *preparest a table* means to set a table with food.

4 Tell students that *mine* means *my*. You may want to review with students other peculiarities of Elizabethan English (see page 67).

Advanced Learners

Have students identify the two basic metaphors used in the poem. (*God as shepherd [lines 1–11]; God as generous host [lines 12–17]*)

Cross Curricular Link: Humanities

SHEPHERDS AND FLOCKS In a society that has to devote much of its energy to war, it's not surprising that herding animals would seem a peaceful and pleasant alternative. Shepherds often had to lead their flocks farther and farther away from settled areas in order to find unspoiled pasture land. Alone in a remote natural setting and often with little to do but watch gentle animals eat grass, shepherds could think, dream, pray, play musical instruments, and sing songs.

This, at least, is one romantic vision of the shepherd's life, one that underlies a whole tradition of "pastoral" poetry (from Latin *pastor:* "shepherd"). A pastoral poem frequently has a shepherd as its speaker, deals with the simple lives of country folk, and often has as its theme love or poetry itself.

In the story of the young David, which can be found in the Bible book of I Samuel, David appears to be the least likely of Jesse's sons to be chosen king because he is a shepherd rather than a warrior. It is David who has God's blessing, though, and the story strongly suggests that this is so in part because David has lived the solitary life of a shepherd and devoted more of his time to knowing God.

Reading and Analyzing

Literary Analysis DESCRIPTION

This poem consists almost entirely of description. It describes the natural world. But three things about the description give the poem its power.

- Everything in the world is described as an action of God. Instead of saying "it rains," the speaker of the poem says, "He watereth the hills from his chambers" (line 27).
- Because the description is so extensive and covers all of creation, it gives a sense of the greatness of God's achievement.
- The speaker's tone in describing creation gives a strong impression of his praiseful attitude and sense of awe at the grandeur of God.

Have students identify other examples of these three aspects of description in the poem.

Active Reading VISUALIZING

Ask students to imagine how they would capture the spirit of this poem in a visual representation.

Possible Responses: by having the visual representation be very large, with lots of individual scenes; by showing many different activities going on at the same time; by having different elements of the representation connect to make one magnificent "big picture"; by showing how everything in the representation is connected to a loving God

Reading Skills and Strategies
CONNECTING

[A] These lines are a direct reference to what God does to the waters of chaos in Genesis (see page 65 and the mini-lesson on page 66).

Psalm 104

King James Bible

***Bless** the Lord, O my soul.*
O Lord my God, thou art very great;
thou art clothed with honor and majesty.
Who coverest thyself with light as with a garment?
Who stretchest out the heavens like a curtain?
Who layeth the beams of his chambers in the waters?
Who maketh the clouds his chariot?
[1] Who walketh upon the wings of the wind?
Who maketh his angels spirits,
his ministers a flaming fire?
Who laid the foundations of the earth,
that it should not be removed for ever?
Thou coveredst it with the deep as with a garment;
the waters stood above the mountains.
At thy rebuke they fled;
at the voice of thy thunder they hastened away.
[A] They go up by the mountains,
they go down by the valleys
unto the place which thou hast founded for them.
Thou hast set a bound that they may not pass over,
that they turn not again to cover the earth.
[2] He sendeth the springs into the valleys,
which run among the hills.
They give drink to every beast of the field;
the wild asses quench their thirst.
[3] By them shall the fowls of the heaven have their habitation,
which sing among the branches.
He watereth the hills from his chambers:
The earth is satisfied with the fruit of thy works.
He causeth the grass to grow for the cattle,
and herb for the service of man:

Detail of *St. John the Baptist in the Wilderness*, Geertgen tot Sint Jans. 42 cm × 28 cm. Gemäldegalerie, Staatliche Museen zu Berlin. Photo © Bildarchiv Preussischer Kulturbesitz/Art Resource, New York.

That he may bring forth food out of the earth;
and wine that maketh glad the heart of man,
and oil to make his face to shine,
and bread which strengtheneth man's heart.
The trees of the Lord are full of sap,
the cedars of Lebanon, which he hath planted,
where the birds make their nests;
as for the stork,
the fir trees are her house.
The high hills are a refuge for the wild goats,
and the rocks for the conies.[1]
He appointed the moon for seasons;
the sun knoweth his going down.[2]

1. **conies:** animals similar to hares or rabbits.
2. **the sun knoweth his going down:** The sun knows when to set.

Customizing Instruction

Less Proficient Readers

1 Explain that these are rhetorical questions. The answer to each is the same and is meant to be obvious: the Lord. In some editions of the King James Bible these sentences are printed without question marks as relative clauses modifying *Lord my God* (line 1).

English Learners

2 Students may find the odd mixture of second and third person in referring to God confusing. Make sure they know that the speaker of the poem uses the two forms interchangeably, probably because the poem is written both to God and about God.

3 Tell students that *habitation* means "home" or "place to live."

MINI LESSON Vocabulary Strategy

WORD ORIGINS Explain that English contains many words derived from ancient languages, such as Latin and Greek. Learning a word's etymology, or origin, will help students remember the word's meaning and recognize related words.

Instruction Write the word *habitation* (p. 90) on the board and tell students that it comes from the Latin word *habitare,* which means "to dwell." Also explain that *habitation* means "natural environment" or "residence." Then display the following chart and read aloud the information in it:

Latin Word	Meaning	Words with This Root
habitare	to dwell	habitat, habitable, habitant, inhabitant

Practice In a dictionary, look up each of the words in the last column. Then write sentences, using each word correctly in a sentence.

A lesson in Greek and Latin roots appears on p. 340 in the Pupil's Edition.

PSALM 104 **91**

Summary: The Book of Ruth

Naomi is a Jewish widow living abroad in the country of Moab with her sons and their Moabite wives. One of the daughters-in-law is named Ruth. When Ruth's husband dies, instead of returning to her own people and gods, she declares her loyalty to Naomi, the Jewish people, and the Jewish God. Ruth returns with Naomi to her home town of Bethlehem, where, as childless widows, they are poor and without social status. However, because of her loyalty and other good qualities, Ruth finds a protector and husband in the wealthy landowner Boaz.

 Use **Unit One Resource Book,** p. 20, for additional support.

Thematic Link

In this story, Ruth is rewarded for her **spiritual** connection to her mother-in-law, the Jewish people, and God.

Historical Note

"In the days when the chieftains ruled" places the story sometime after the Exodus from Egypt but before the first king, that is, roughly around 1100 B.C. (see page 22). The date of composition is uncertain, but the reference to "Bethlehem in Judah" suggests that the story was written during the time of the Divided Kingdom.

Reading and Analyzing

Reading Skills and Strategies
CONNECTING

A Judah is the southernmost of the two divided kingdoms and the name from which we get the word *Jew*. Judah was one of the sons of Jacob (see page 22).

Reading Skills and Strategies
IDENTIFYING CULTURAL CHARACTERISTICS

B "Thus and more may the Lord do to me" is a traditional formula for the swearing of a solemn oath. The words would be accompanied by some sort of self-destructive gesture such as tearing clothing or hitting or scratching oneself. When Naomi sees this powerful gesture, she realizes how determined Ruth is.

Thou makest darkness, and it is night,
wherein all the beasts of the forest do creep forth.
The young lions roar after their prey,
and seek their meat from God.
The sun ariseth, they gather themselves together,
and lay them down in their dens.
Man goeth forth unto his work
and to his labor until the evening.
O Lord, how manifold are thy works!
In wisdom hast thou made them all;
the earth is full of thy riches.
So is this great and wide sea,
wherein are things creeping innumerable,
both small and great beasts.
There go the ships;
there is that leviathan,[3]
whom thou hast made to play therein.
These wait all upon thee,
that thou mayest give them their meat in due season.
That thou givest them they gather;
thou openest thine hand, they are filled with good.
Thou hidest thy face, they are troubled;
thou takest away their breath, they die,
and return to their dust.
Thou sendest forth thy spirit, they are created,
and thou renewest the face of the earth.
The glory of the Lord shall endure for ever;
the Lord shall rejoice in his works.
He looketh on the earth, and it trembleth;
he toucheth the hills, and they smoke.
I will sing unto the Lord as long as I live;
I will sing praise to my God while I have my being.
My meditation of him shall be sweet;
I will be glad in the Lord.
Let the sinners be consumed out of the earth,
and let the wicked be no more.
Bless thou the Lord, O my soul.
Praise ye the Lord.

3. **leviathan:** a monstrous sea creature sometimes identified with the whale.

The Book of Ruth

Jewish Publication Society of America

In the days when the chieftains ruled, there was a famine in the land; and a man of Bethlehem in Judah, with his wife and two sons, went to reside in the country of Moab.[1] The man's name was Elimelech,[2] his wife's name was Naomi,[3] and his two sons were named
Mahlon and Chilion—Ephrathites[4] of Bethlehem
A in Judah. They came to the country of Moab and
remained there.

Elimelech, Naomi's husband, died; and she
was left with her two sons. They married
Moabite women, one named Orpah and the
1 other Ruth, and they lived there about ten years.
Then those two—Mahlon and Chilion—also
died; so the woman was left without her two
sons and without her husband.

She started out with her daughters-in-law to
return from the country of Moab, for in the country of Moab she had heard that the Lord had
2 taken note of His people and given them food.
Accompanied by her two daughters-in-law, she
left the place where she had been living; and they
set out on the road back to the land of Judah.

But Naomi said to her two daughters-in-law, "Turn back, each of you to her mother's house. May the Lord deal kindly with you, as you have dealt with the dead and with me! May the Lord grant that each of you find security in the house of a husband!" And she kissed them farewell. They broke into weeping and said to her, "No, we will return with you to your people."

But Naomi replied, "Turn back, my daughters!
Why should you go with me? Have I any more
sons in my body who might be husbands for
3 you? Turn back, my daughters, for I am too old
to be married. Even if I thought there was hope
for me, even if I were married tonight and I also
bore sons, should you wait for them to grow up?
Should you on their account debar yourselves
from marriage? Oh no, my daughters! My lot is 3
far more bitter than yours, for the hand of the
Lord has struck out against me."

They broke into weeping again, and Orpah kissed her mother-in-law farewell. But Ruth clung to her. So she said, "See, your sister-in-law has returned to her people and her gods. Go follow your sister-in-law." But Ruth replied, "Do not urge me to leave you, to turn back and not follow you. For wherever you go, I will go; wherever you lodge, I will lodge; your people shall be my people, and your God my God.
Where you die, I will die, and there I will be
buried. Thus and more may the Lord do to me if B
anything but death parts me from you." When
[Naomi] saw how determined she was to go with her, she ceased to argue with her; and the two went on until they reached Bethlehem.

When they arrived in Bethlehem, the whole city buzzed with excitement over them. The women said, "Can this be Naomi?" "Do not call me Naomi," she replied. "Call me Mara,[5] for Shaddai[5] has made my lot very bitter. I went away full, and the Lord has brought me back empty. How can you call me Naomi, when the Lord has dealt harshly with me, when Shaddai has brought misfortune upon me!"

Thus Naomi returned from the country of Moab; she returned with her daughter-in-law Ruth the Moabite. They arrived in Bethlehem at

1. **Moab** (mō′ăb): an ancient kingdom east of the Dead Sea.
2. **Elimelech** (ĕl-ē-mĕl′ĕk).
3. **Naomi** (nā-ō′mē): a name meaning "pleasantness" in Hebrew.
4. **Ephrathites** (ĕ′frə-thīts′).
5. **Mara . . . Shaddai** (shə-dä′ē): *Mara* means "bitterness" in Hebrew; *Shaddai* is God.

Customizing Instruction

Less Proficient Readers

1 Make sure students understand the situation set up by the first two paragraphs: the three women have no male relatives, which means they have no one to provide for them.

English Learners

2 Explain that "The Lord had taken note of His people and given them food" is a way of saying that the famine in Judah—the reason Naomi and her husband came to Moab—has ended.

Less Proficient Readers

3 Help students understand Naomi's reasoning here. She is too old to marry, so cannot hope to provide a home for her daughters-in-law. They, however, can marry Moabite men. To do so would mean turning their backs on their Jewish family and traditions, but Naomi thinks they have little choice. In the next paragraph, Orpah takes this option, but Ruth refuses it.

Reading and Analyzing

Literary Analysis DESCRIPTION

Ask students to identify the different elements or scenes that make up the vivid description of the barley harvest.

Possible Responses: the reapers harvesting barley; Ruth gleaning in a field that has just been cut; Boaz speaking to his workers; Ruth bowing to the ground before Boaz; Ruth eating with Boaz and the reapers; the reapers pulling out stalks of grain to leave for Ruth; Ruth beating out her barley.

Active Reading VISUALIZING

Ask students to compare their visualizations of the barley harvest with the painting on this page and answer the following questions: What do you like about the way the painting represents the scene? What is missing from the painting?

Reading Skills and Strategies
MAKING INFERENCES ABOUT CHARACTER

A Ask students what these details tell us about Ruth. *(She is hard-working; she is anxious to provide for Naomi.)*

Literary Analysis THEME AND CULTURE

B Boaz recognizes Ruth's loyalty to Naomi as loyalty to the Jewish people and the God of Israel. The virtue of such loyalty, especially in a non-Jew, is a theme a Jewish audience of the time would recognize. But this scene contains another theme the audience would recognize: openness toward non-Jews rather than exclusivity.

Reading Skills and Strategies
IDENTIFYING CULTURAL CHARACTERISTICS

C In saying "Spread your robe over your handmaid," Ruth asks Boaz to marry her. This is not as presumptuous as it sounds, since Boaz could have many wives and would not be making an exclusive commitment. But in asking Boaz to marry her as a redeeming kinsman, Ruth is expressing strong loyalty to her deceased husband, because any children that come of her marriage to Boaz will be recognized as the former husband's heirs and inherit his property. This is the "latest deed of loyalty" that Boaz praises.

Summer, or Ruth and Boaz (1660), Nicolas Poussin. Musèe du Louvre, Paris/SuperStock.

the beginning of the barley harvest.

Now Naomi had a kinsman on her husband's side, a man of substance, of the family of Elimelech, whose name was Boaz.[6]

Ruth the Moabite said to Naomi, "I would
1 like to go to the fields and glean[7] among the ears of grain, behind someone who may show me kindness." "Yes, daughter, go," she replied; and off she went. She came and gleaned in a field, behind the reapers; and, as luck would have it, it was the piece of land belonging to Boaz, who was of Elimelech's family.

Presently Boaz arrived from Bethlehem. He greeted the reapers, "The Lord be with you!" And they responded, "The Lord bless you!" Boaz said to the servant who was in charge of the reapers, "Whose girl is that?" The servant in charge of the reapers replied, "She is a Moabite girl who came back with Naomi from the country of Moab. She said, 'Please let me glean and gather among the sheaves behind the reapers.'
A She has been on her feet ever since she came this morning. She has rested but little in the hut."

2 Boaz said to Ruth, "Listen to me, daughter. Don't go to glean in another field. Don't go elsewhere, but stay here close to my girls. Keep your eyes on the field they are reaping, and follow them. I have ordered the men not to molest you. And when you are thirsty, go to the jars and drink some of [the water] that the men have drawn."

She prostrated herself with her face to the ground, and said to him, "Why are you so kind as to single me out, when I am a foreigner?"

Boaz said in reply, "I have been told of all that you did for your mother-in-law after the death of your husband, how you left your father and mother and the land of your
birth and came to a people you had B
not known before. May the Lord reward your deeds. May you have a full recompense from the Lord, the God of Israel, under whose wings you have sought refuge!"

She answered, "You are most kind, my lord, 3
to comfort me and to speak gently to your maidservant—though I am not so much as one of your maidservants."

At mealtime, Boaz said to her, "Come over here and partake of the meal, and dip your morsel in the vinegar." So she sat down beside the reapers. He handed her roasted grain, and she ate her fill and had some left over.

When she got up again to glean, Boaz gave orders to his workers, "You are not only to let her glean among the sheaves, without interference, but you must also pull some [stalks] out of the heaps and leave them for her to glean, and not scold her."

She gleaned in the field until evening. Then she beat out what she had gleaned—it was about an *ephah*[8] of barley—and carried it back with

6. **Boaz** (bō′ăz).

7. **glean:** gather the remains after a crop has been harvested.

8. ***ephah*** (ē′fə): slightly more than a bushel.

MINI LESSON **Grammar**

ADJECTIVES AND ADVERBS

Instruction Remind students that adjectives and adverbs are both kinds of modifiers–that is, they describe or limit other words. Review adjective and adverb usage with students:

- An **adjective** modifies a noun or a pronoun. It answers the questions *what kind?, how many?,* or *which one?*. (*what kind:* comfortable seat, pink flowers; *how many:* ten tickets, most actors; *which one:* this seat, these friends)
- An **adverb** modifies a verb, an adjective, or another adverb. Many adverbs are formed by adding–ly to an adjective. An adverb answers the questions *how?, when?, where?,* or *to what extent?*. (*how:* quickly, slowly, well; *where:* here, there, outside; *when:* daily, soon, never; *to what extent:* almost, nearly)

Practice Choose the correct modifier in each sentence and identify it as an adjective or an adverb.

1. Naomi walked (slow, slowly) back to Bethlehem. *(slowly; adv.)*

her to the town. When her mother-in-law saw what she had gleaned, and when she also took out and gave her what she had left over after eating her fill, her mother-in-law asked her, "Where did you glean today? Where did you work? Blessed be he who took such generous notice of you!" So she told her mother-in-law whom she had worked with, saying, "The name of the man with whom I worked today is Boaz."

Naomi said to her daughter-in-law, "Blessed be he of the Lord, who has not failed in His kindness to the living or to the dead! For," Naomi explained to her daughter-in-law, "the man is related to us; he is one of our redeeming kinsmen."[9] Ruth the Moabite said, "He even told me, 'Stay close by my workers until all my harvest is finished.'" And Naomi answered her daughter-in-law Ruth, "It is best, daughter, that you go out with his girls, and not be annoyed in some other field." So she stayed close to the maidservants of Boaz, and gleaned until the barley harvest and the wheat harvest were finished. Then she stayed at home with her mother-in-law.

Naomi, her mother-in-law, said to her, "Daughter, I must seek a home for you, where you may be happy. Now there is our kinsman Boaz, whose girls you were close to. He will be winnowing[10] barley on the threshing floor tonight. So bathe, anoint yourself, dress up, and go down to the threshing floor. But do not disclose yourself to the man until he has finished eating and drinking. When he lies down, note the place where he lies down, and go over and uncover his feet and lie down. He will tell you what you are to do." She replied, "I will do everything you tell me."

She went down to the threshing floor and did just as her mother-in-law had instructed her. Boaz ate and drank, and in a cheerful mood went to lie down beside the grainpile. Then she went over stealthily and uncovered his feet and lay down. In the middle of the night, the man gave a start and pulled back—there was a woman lying at his feet!

"Who are you?" he asked. And she replied, "I am your handmaid Ruth. Spread your robe over your handmaid, for you are a redeeming kinsman." C

He exclaimed, "Be blessed of the Lord, daughter! Your latest deed of loyalty is greater than the first, in that you have not turned to younger men, whether poor or rich. And now, daughter, have no fear. I will do in your behalf whatever you ask, for all the elders of my town know what a fine woman you are. But while it is true I am a redeeming kinsman, there is another redeemer closer than I. Stay for the night. Then in the morning, if he will act as a redeemer, good! let him redeem. But if he does not want to act as redeemer for you, I will do so myself, as the Lord lives! Lie down until morning."

Naomi said to her daughter-in-law, "Blessed be he of the Lord, who has not failed in His kindness to the living or to the dead!

So she lay at his feet until dawn. She rose before one person could distinguish another, for he thought, "Let it not be known that the woman came to the threshing floor." And he said, "Hold out the shawl you are wearing." She held it while he measured out six measures of barley, and he put it on her back.

When she got back to the town, she came to her mother-in-law, who asked, "How is it with you, daughter?" She told her all that the man had done for her; and she added, "He gave me

9. **redeeming kinsmen:** According to Hebrew law, if a man died without a son, that man's brother or another male relative could take possession of the man's property and marry his widow.

10. **winnowing:** separating grain kernels from their tough outer covering.

Customizing Instruction

Less Proficient Readers

To aid in their understanding of this story, you may want to suggest that students make a chart showing the sequence of events from Ruth's arrival at the harvest field to Boaz's meeting with the elders (page 96).

1 Help students understand the meaning of *glean* by explaining that by Jewish law, the poor had the right to go in the fields after a harvest and pick up any stray grains that had fallen to the ground as the stalks were cut. How much grain they found would depend on the generosity of the owner. Naomi is too old to glean, so Ruth is volunteering to do so for both of them.

English Learners

2 Explain that Boaz uses the word *daughter* in a figurative sense as an older man and authority figure.

3 Tell students that *lord* is a term of respect. When capitalized, it refers to God.

2. Ruth was (certain, certainly) she wanted to go. *(certain; adj.)*
3. In Bethlehem, people thought Ruth looked (different, differently). *(different; adj.)*
4. Boaz (kind, kindly) helped Ruth. (kindly; adv.)
5. Ruth worked very (careful, carefully). *(carefully; adv.)*

For more instruction and practice in adjectives and adverbs, use McDougal Littell's ***Language Network:***

- Grade 10, Chapter 9, "Using Modifiers"
- Grade 12, Chapter 7, "Using Modifiers"

Reading Skills and Strategies
CLARIFYING

A As the closer relative to Ruth's deceased husband, "So-and-so" has the right to acquire his land. Boaz reminds the man that in acquiring the property he must also acquire the deceased relative's wife and that the property will be inherited by any children he has with the wife, who will be legally the descendants of the deceased. Once "So-and-so" realizes that he won't be gaining anything for his own descendants by the transaction, he loses interest.

Literary Analysis ALLUSION

B "Rachel and Leah" is an allusion to the Book of Genesis. Rachel and Leah were the wives of Jacob, or Israel, grandson of Abraham and father of the twelve sons who founded the twelve tribes of Israel.

Reading Skills and Strategies
CLARIFYING

C Boaz has just said that in marrying Ruth he is perpetuating the name of Mahlon, her deceased husband, not himself. When the elders say, "perpetuate your name in Bethlehem," they are simply wishing Boaz well. As an older man with other wives, Boaz would have plenty of descendants of his own to perpetuate his name, and indirectly his name will be perpetuated by this good deed.

D Literally speaking, the son is born to Ruth, not Naomi. But by the birth of a son who is the descendant of Naomi's son and husband and who is her own grandchild, Naomi's family is restored to her.

these six measures of barley, saying to me, 'Do not go back to your mother-in-law empty-handed.'" And Naomi said, "Stay here, daughter, till you learn how the matter turns out. For the man will not rest, but will settle the matter today."

Meanwhile, Boaz had gone to the gate and sat down there. And now the redeemer whom Boaz had mentioned passed by. He called, "Come over and sit down here, So-and-so!" And he came over and sat down. Then [Boaz] took ten elders of the town and said, "Be seated here"; and they sat down.

He said to the redeemer, "Naomi, now returned from the country of Moab, must sell the piece of land which belonged to our kinsman Elimelech. I thought I should disclose the matter to you and say: Acquire it in the presence of those seated here and in the presence of the elders of my people. If you are willing to redeem it, redeem! But if you will not redeem, tell me, that I may know. For there is no one to redeem but you, and I come after you." "I am willing to redeem it," he replied. Boaz continued, "When you acquire the property from Naomi and from Ruth the Moabite, you must also acquire the wife of the deceased, so as to perpetuate[11] the name of the deceased upon his estate." The redeemer replied, "Then I cannot redeem it for myself, lest I impair[12] my own estate. You take over my right of redemption, for I am unable to exercise it." A

Now this was formerly done in Israel in cases of redemption or exchange: to validate any transaction, one man would take off his sandal and hand it to the other. Such was the practice in Israel. So when the redeemer said to Boaz, "Acquire for yourself," he drew off his sandal. And Boaz said to the elders and to the rest of the people, "You are witnesses today that I am acquiring from Naomi all that belonged to Elimelech and all that belonged to Chilion and Mahlon. I am also acquiring Ruth the Moabite, the wife of Mahlon, as my wife, so as to perpetuate the name of the deceased upon his estate, that the name of the deceased may not disappear from among his kinsmen and from the gate of his home town. You are witnesses today."

All the people at the gate and the elders answered, "We are. May the Lord make the woman who is coming into your house like Rachel and Leah, both of whom built up the House of Israel! B Prosper in Ephrathah and perpetuate your name in Bethlehem! C And may your house be like the house of Perez whom Tamar bore to Judah[13]—through the offspring which the Lord will give you by this young woman."

So Boaz married Ruth; she became his wife, and he cohabited with her. The Lord let her conceive, and she bore a son. And the women said to Naomi, "Blessed be the Lord, who has not withheld a redeemer from you today! May his name be perpetuated in Israel! He will renew your life and sustain your old age; for he is born of your daughter-in-law, who loves you and is better to you than seven sons."

Naomi took the child and held it to her bosom. She became its foster mother, and the women neighbors gave him a name, saying, "A son is born to Naomi!" They named him Obed; D he was the father of Jesse, father of David.

This is the line of Perez: Perez begot Hezron, Hezron begot Ram, Ram begot Amminadab, Amminadab begot Nahshon, Nahshon begot Salmon, Salmon begot Boaz, Boaz begot Obed, Obed begot Jesse, and Jesse begot David.[14] ❖

11. **perpetuate:** cause to last or be remembered forever. If a redeeming kinsman marries Ruth, their son will be recognized as the heir of her first husband.
12. **impair:** weaken; damage.
13. **may your house be like . . . Judah:** Perez, the son of Judah, was an ancestor of Boaz. His mother, Tamar, had been a widow like Ruth.
14. **The line of Perez . . . David:** Through this lineage, Ruth is established as the ancestor of David, the most famous king of Israel.

Connect to the Literature

1. **What Do You Think?** Which scene in these three selections stands out most clearly in your mind? Describe the scene and discuss what interests you about it.

Comprehension Check

- In Psalm 23, what kind of relationship does the person speaking have with the Lord?
- How does Ruth react when Naomi decides to return to her homeland?
- What must Boaz do before he can marry Ruth?

Think Critically

2. In Psalm 23, why does the speaker expect goodness and mercy to follow him all the days of his life?
3. In Psalm 104, why does the speaker describe God's hiding his face and taking away his creatures' breath as well as all the good things he does?
4. In the Book of Ruth, why does Boaz marry Ruth?

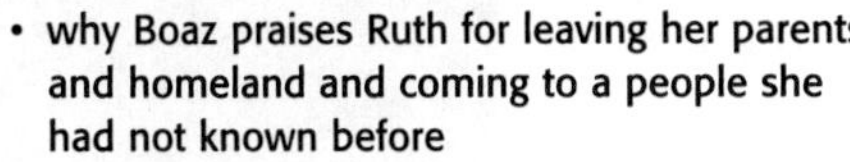

THINK ABOUT

- why Boaz praises Ruth for leaving her parents and homeland and coming to a people she had not known before
- why Naomi suggests that Ruth visit Boaz on the threshing floor
- why Boaz thinks that Ruth's coming to him shows more loyalty than staying with Naomi
- what it means to be a "redeeming kinsman"

5. **ACTIVE READING: VISUALIZING** Think about the visual details that you wrote down in your READER'S NOTEBOOK. How did visualizing help you understand and appreciate these selections?

Extend Interpretations

6. **What If?** How do you think the story of Ruth would have turned out if the other kinsman had agreed to marry her?
7. **Comparing Texts** How is Psalm 104 (pages 90–92) similar to and different from "Adoration of the Disk" (pages 54–55)? Support your response.
8. **Connect to Life** Can Ruth be a role model in our time, even though today's women are not completely dependent on or subservient to men?

LITERARY ANALYSIS: DESCRIPTION

Description is the process by which a writer creates a word picture of a **scene, event,** or **character.** Good descriptive writing appeals to the senses, helping the reader to see, hear, smell, taste, or feel the subject being described. It usually features vivid, precise language. Notice how descriptive details in the following passage bring to life Boaz's kindness to Ruth:

At mealtime, Boaz said to her, "Come over here and partake of the meal, and dip your morsel in the vinegar." So she sat down beside the reapers. He handed her roasted grain, and she ate her fill and had some left over.

Paired Activity With a partner, go through one of the selections and look for details that appeal to one or more of the senses. Create a chart like the one started below.

Detail	Senses				
	sight	sound	smell	taste	touch
"dip your morsel in the vinegar"	✓	✓	✓		

Connect to the Literature

1. **What Do You Think?** Responses will vary. Encourage students to identify specific passages in the text.

Comprehension Check

- The speaker has a close personal relationship with the Lord, from whom he receives special protection and care.
- Ruth insists on going with Naomi.
- He has to make sure Ruth's closer relative doesn't intend to marry her.

Use Selection Quiz in **Unit One Resource Book**, p. 23, for more practice.

Think Critically

2. Possible Responses: because the Lord has always taken care of him in the past; because he trusts the Lord and the strength of their relationship
3. Possible Responses: to show how much all living things depend on the power of God for their existence; to show what a difference God's presence makes in the world
4. Possible Responses: because he admires her loyalty to Naomi and to Mahlon; because Ruth is a good person who is in need of the help of a benefactor; because, by coming to Boaz for help rather than one of the younger men, Ruth shows that she appreciates his good qualities
5. Answers will vary. Encourage students to connect specific sensory details with their understanding and experience of the story.

Literary Analysis

Paired Activity Point out to students that they might have different sensory associations with the descriptive details in the story. For example, some students might say that the example given in the chart appeals to the senses of taste and touch, but not to sound.

Use **Unit One Resource Book**, p. 22, for more practice.

To assess skills and concepts taught in these selections, use **Formal Assessment Book,** p. 13.

Extend Interpretations

6. **What If?** Most students will say that Ruth and the other kinsman would not have had the same close, mutually respectful relationship as Ruth and Boaz. Some may say that "So-and-so" would treat Ruth badly, since his interest was in the property, not in her.
7. **Comparing Texts** Similarities: Both poems offer praise to a benevolent creator of the world and giver of life; both poems attempt to encompass all of nature in their praise; in both poems the speaker stresses a personal relationship with the creator. Differences: In "Adoration of the Disk," the creator is understood mainly in terms of the benefits that come from the sun as a natural force, while in Psalm 104 God is praised for the love and goodness that underlie creation; "Adoration" follows the structure of the movement of the sun, while Psalm 104 is more open, leaping from one aspect of nature to another; Ra is limited to the realm of the sun, while the Lord is maker of both night and day.
8. **Connect to Life** Some students will say that Ruth can be a role model because she is a good person with qualities that would shine forth in any situation. Other students may say that Ruth cannot be a good role model, because she is too passive and accepts her dependence on men without question.

ON YOUR OWN

Possible Objectives

This **On Your Own** featured selection may be used to achieve one or more of the following objectives:

- to give students the opportunity to read independently, either reading silently for a sustained period, reading and analyzing literature with a group, or using the Reader's Notebook to write in response to the literature
- to conduct a post-reading class discussion

Summary

A man has two sons. The younger one asks to receive his inheritance early, then leaves home and wastes everything living it up. When he falls on hard times, he returns home and his father forgives him unconditionally. The older brother resents his father's generosity, but the father defends his actions.

ON YOUR OWN

FROM THE NEW TESTAMENT KING JAMES BIBLE

The Parable of the PRODIGAL SON

The New Testament

In this part of Unit One, you have read several examples of sacred literature. In reflecting on some of them, you have thought about ways in which stories can be used to convey moral and spiritual truths. Now you will read a story from another sacred text—the New Testament.

The 27 books of the New Testament, together with the Hebrew Bible (Old Testament), make up the Christian Bible. The New Testament focuses on the teachings of Jesus of Nazareth and his apostles. Jesus often conveyed his teachings by telling a kind of story known as a ***parable.*** Parable *comes from a Greek word that means "to compare." Parables illustrate abstract truths using comparisons to familiar activities, such as farming, housekeeping, or family life.*

In the Gospel of Luke the parable of the Prodigal (wastefully extravagant) Son follows two other parables about finding lost things. Jesus tells these stories in response to a question about why he associates with sinners. As you read, ask yourself:

1. *Why does the father act as he does?*
2. *What does this story teach?*

The Return of the Prodigal Son (1773), Pompeo Baton. Oil on canvas, 173 cm × 122 cm. Kunsthistorisches Museum Gemäldegalerie, Vienna. Photograph copyright © Erich Lessing/Art Resource, New York.

"And the son said unto him, 'Father, I have sinned against heaven, and in thy sight, and am no more worthy to be called thy son.'"

And he[1] said, "A certain man had two sons: and the younger of them said to his father, 'Father, give me the portion of goods that falleth to me.' And he divided unto them his living. And not many days after the younger son gathered all together, and took his journey into a far country, and there wasted his substance with riotous living. And when he had spent all, there arose a mighty famine in that land; and he began to be in want. And he went and joined himself to a citizen of that country; and he sent him into his fields to feed swine. And he would fain[2] have filled his belly with the husks that the swine did eat: and no man gave unto him.

"And when he came to himself, he said, 'How many hired servants of my father's have bread enough and to spare, and I perish with hunger! I will arise and go to my father, and will say unto him, "Father, I have sinned against heaven, and before thee, and am no more worthy to be called thy son: make me as one of thy hired servants."'

"And he arose, and came to his father. But when he was yet a great way off, his father saw him, and had compassion, and ran, and fell on his neck, and kissed him. And the son said unto him, 'Father, I have sinned against heaven, and in thy sight, and am no more worthy to be called thy son.' But the father said to his servants, 'Bring forth the best robe, and put it on him; and put a ring on his hand, and shoes on his feet: and bring hither the fatted calf, and kill it; and let us eat, and be merry: for this my son was dead, and is alive again; he was lost, and is found.' And they began to be merry.

"Now his elder son was in the field: and as he came and drew nigh to the house, he heard music and dancing. And he called one of the servants, and asked what these things meant. And he said unto him, 'Thy brother is come; and thy father hath killed the fatted calf, because he hath received him safe and sound.' And he was angry, and would not go in: therefore came his father out, and intreated[3] him. And he answering said to his father, 'Lo, these many years do I serve thee, neither transgressed I at any time thy commandment: and yet thou never gavest me a kid,[4] that I might make merry with my friends: but as soon as this thy son was come, which hath devoured thy living with harlots, thou has killed for him the fatted calf.' And he said unto him, 'Son, thou art ever with me, and all that I have is thine. It was meet[5] that we should make merry, and be glad: for this thy brother was dead, and is alive again; and was lost, and is found.'"

---

1. **he:** Jesus.
2. **fain:** gladly.
3. **intreated:** entreated; urged.
4. **kid:** young goat.
5. **meet:** fitting; proper.

Discussion Questions

The introduction to this selection provides questions you might use for a post-reading class discussion.

1. Why does the father act as he does?
Possible Responses: The father loves his sons unconditionally; the father cares more about family than about property; the father understands that the younger son has learned a lesson.

2. What does this story teach?
Possible Responses: Love and compassion are more important than money; you should forgive people for their mistakes; exact fairness is not always the right thing.

Working Independently

You may want to set aside time each week for independent reading, without making an assignment related to the reading. Or once students have completed the reading, either alone or aloud in groups, you may ask them to work together on a project, such as a dramatization of the parable. If you choose to have students write responsively in their Reader's Notebook, suggest that they write about which character in the parable they most strongly identify with.

Objectives
- reflect on and assess student understanding of the unit part
- review important concepts from the reading
- assess and build portfolios
- set goals for future learning

Reflecting on the Literature
Help students get started by reviewing with them ways each of the selections in Unit One, Part 1, addresses what it means to be human and/or how best to live one's life.

Reviewing Literary Concepts
You might have students carry out the first part of the assignment—identifying heroes and their good qualities and explaining how the qualities help the heroes triumph—in writing and then answer the last two questions in a whole-class discussion.

Use **Unit One Resource Book,** p. 24, for additional support.

Building Your Portfolio
Students will use their Presentation Portfolios to file what they consider their highest quality work—the very best in their Working Portfolios.

For more information on using writing and assessing portfolios, see the **Teacher's Guide to Assessment and Portfolio Use,** p. 53–74.

Part Assessment
To assess skills and concepts taught in this unit part, use **Formal Assessment Book,** p. 15.

Reflect and Assess

What did you learn about ancient Mesopotamian, Egyptian, and Hebrew cultures from reading the selections in Unit One, Part 1? Did you discover anything unusual or unexpected? Use the following options to help you explore what you have learned.

The Flood (Gen. 8:6–11) (c.1250). The Pierpont Morgan Library, New York.

Reflecting on the Literature

Being Human In different ways, each of the selections in this part of the book explores what it means to be human and how best to live one's life. Think about the works you have read, and identify three pieces of wisdom that you think still apply today. In your own words, explain what the wisdom is and how it still applies.

Reviewing Literary Concepts

Kinds of Heroes A traditional hero has good qualities that help him or her triumph over a difficult opponent or situation. In this section you have encountered a wide range of heroes—from Gilgamesh, who is powerful enough to defy the gods, to Ruth, who has almost no power at all. Pick three heroes from the works you have read, and identify one or two good qualities each hero possesses. Then explain how these qualities help the heroes to triumph. Which hero impressed you the most? Why?

Building Your Portfolio

Writing Options Look back at the various Writing Options you completed for the lessons in this part of the book. Choose one that you think represents your best work. Write a cover note explaining the reasons for your choice and add the assignment to your **Presentation Portfolio.**

Self ASSESSMENT

READER'S NOTEBOOK

Below are some important names and terms that you learned in this part of the book. Explain what each one means and what significance it has in the study of early literature. If you have trouble with a term, look back at the place where it is introduced, or look it up in the **Glossary of Literary Terms** (page R91).

oral tradition
myth
quest story
Hebrew Bible
cuneiform
archetype
parable
The Book of the Dead
King Ashurbanipal's library
sacred literature
The Epic of Gilgamesh

Setting GOALS

What did you find to be the biggest challenge as you worked with the selections in Unit One, Part 1? Write down two strategies that you think will help you deal with this kind of challenge as you read other literature in this book.

Assessment Self Assessment

Students can look up the listed terms in the **Glossary of Literary Terms** on page R91 or they can find them introduced in context on the text pages indicated below.

oral tradition (pages 30, 32)
myth (page 30)
quest story (pages 31, 33)
Hebrew Bible (page 63)
cuneiform (pages 19, 24)
archetype (page 31)
parable (pages 30, 98)
The Book of the Dead (page 50)
King Ashurbanipal's library (pages 18, 25)
sacred literature (pages 30, 64)
The Epic of Gilgamesh (page 32)

Extend Your *Reading*

Conversations with Mummies

NEW LIGHT ON THE LIVES OF ANCIENT EGYPTIANS

ROSALIE DAVID AND RICK ARCHBOLD

This fascinating book describes how scientists use state-of-art technology, such as CAT scanners and electron microscopes, to study Egyptian mummies. Researchers have discovered what these ancient people ate, how they may have looked, what they died from, and more.

The Illustrated Hebrew Bible

75 SELECTED STORIES

ELLEN FRANKEL

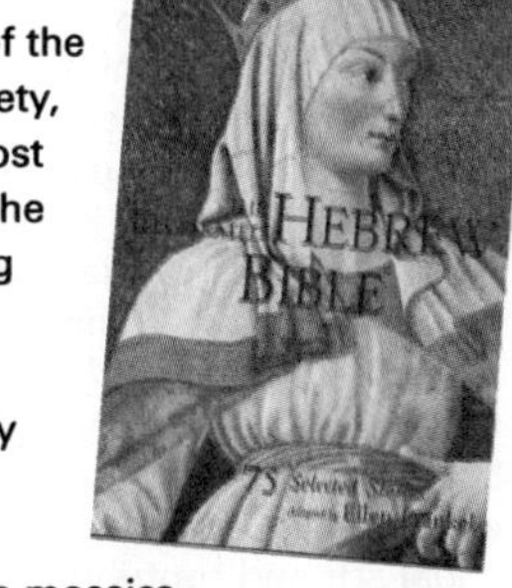

Frankel, editor-in-chief of the Jewish Publication Society, has chosen 75 of the most important stories from the Hebrew Bible, beginning with the Creation. They are retold in accessible language and beautifully illustrated with ancient artifacts, illuminated manuscripts, synagogue mosaics, and masterpieces by such artists as Rembrandt, Michelangelo, Titian, and Chagall.

And Even *More* . . .

Books

Echoes of Egyptian Voices JOHN L. FOSTER
These fresh translations of ancient Egyptian texts include "The Tale of the Shipwrecked Sailor," which may have inspired later stories of Sinbad the sailor.

Gilgamesh the King ROBERT SILVERBERG
This novel is an imaginative retelling of the epic by a noted science fiction writer.

A Dictionary of Creation Myths DAVID ADAMS LEEMING WITH MARGARET ADAMS LEEMING
This reference work retells creation myths from all over the world. Cross-references in entries guide readers to similar myths, and bibliographical sources are included.

Other Media

History Through Literature: Civilization and Writing
Part 1 of an acclaimed series traces the move from oral to written literature in ancient river valley civilizations. SVE & Churchill Media. (VIDEOCASSETTE AND CD-ROM)

Mysteries of Egypt
Using spectacular location shots and historical reenactments, Omar Sharif tells the story of ancient Egypt's rise and fall. National Geographic. (VIDEOCASSETTE AND DVD)

The Bible: A Literary Heritage
Shot in Israel, this film re-creates scenes from the Bible, showing the different genres of literature it contains. Learning Corporation of America. (VIDEOCASSETTE)

Genesis: World of Myths and Patriarchs

ADA FEYERICK

Drawing on archaeological discoveries, this book examines Mesopotamia, Canaan, and Egypt, and their influence on the book of Genesis. Included are helpful maps, photographs of artifacts and places, excerpts from ancient literature, and quotations from archaeologists who excavated important sites.

More Recommendations for Your Students

Difficulty Level: Easy

Pilbeam, Mavis and John Malam. *Mesopotamia and the Fertile Crescent, 10,000 to 539 B.C.* (Raintree Steck-Vaughn Publishers, 1999). In this addition to the Looking Back series (Volume 8), the authors trace the development of the Sumerians, the Babylonians, and the Assyrians from prehistoric societies to great civilizations. The book also provides a good introduction to the birth of writing and to the flood stories found in the Gilgamesh epic and the Bible.

Harris, Geraldine, Geraldine Hams, and Delia Pemberton. *Illustrated Encyclopedia of Ancient Egypt* (NTC Publishing Group, 2000). By providing students with 11 different "trails," each dealing with a particular aspect of ancient Egyptian life, this encyclopedia presents itself to students as a useful and fascinating chapter book.

Gilbert, Martin, ed. *The Illustrated Atlas of Jewish Civilization: 4,000 Years of Jewish History* (Macmillan, 1990). This book provides a beautiful blend of illustrations, maps, and text in a survey of Jewish history and culture from ancient times to the present.

Difficulty Level: Average

Brown, Dale, ed. Mesopotamia: *The Mighty Kings* (Time-Life, 1999). This beautifully illustrated book covers the two-thousand-year period of history of the "land between the rivers" from the rise of the Babylonian King Hammurabi to the conquest of the Persian King Cyrus the Great.

Seleem, Dr. Ramses. *The Illustrated Egyptian Book of the Dead* (Sterling Publishing Company, 2001). For students who would like to read more of the Book of the Dead, this volume provides a readable translation, powerful illustrations, and extensive commentary by a scholar who knows and loves the culture.

Meeks, Wayne A, et al. *The HarperCollins Study Bible* (Harpercollins, 1993). This Bible is designed for a wide audience. It uses a translation that is clear and readable, yet accurate. Annotated by the Society of Biblical Literature, it also includes the latest scholarship along with helpful information for student readers.

Difficulty Level: Challenging

Bottéro, Jean. *Everyday Life in Ancient Mesopotamia* (Baltimore: Johns Hopkins, 2001). Written by a person of enormous learning in the field, this book presents Mesopotamian history and culture from the perspective of daily life, including cookery, finance, medicine, women's rights, magic, and love.

McDowell, A. G. G. *Village Life in Ancient Egypt: Laundry Lists and Love Songs* (Oxford University Press, 1999). The title says it all. This book presents a unique perspective on the royal tombs in the Valley of the Kings by focusing on the life of the village in which the workers lived. Of special interest are many texts documenting everyday life of the time, such as letters, wills, purchase records, magical spells, and of course laundry lists and love songs.

In Unit One, Part 2, you will find examples of classic works from ancient India, translated from Sanskrit. These works are difficult to date precisely; each was probably composed or collected over a period of centuries, dating as far back as 1500 B.C.

World Art and Cultures Transparencies

AT6 Indian Mother Goddess

AT15 Subjugation of the Furious Elephant [detail]

You may use the listed transparencies to acquaint students with art from ancient India.

Pronunciations

Aryan (âr′ē-ən)

Magadha (mä′gə-də)

Ganges (găn′jēz′)

Asoka (ə-sō′kə)

Kapilavastu (kä′pĭ-lə-vŭs′to͞o)

Shiva (shē′və)

Madurai (mä′də-rī′)

Mohenjo-Daro (mō-hĕn′jō-där′ō)

Harappa (hə-răp′ə)

Hastinapura (hŭs′tĭ-nä′pə-rə)

Indraprastha (ĭn′drə-prŭs′tə)

Kosala (kō′sə-lə)

Ayodhya (ə-yōd′yə)

READING FOR INFORMATION

Reading Skills and Strategies

IDENTIFYING MAIN IDEAS

Have students read the text box labeled **Why It Matters.** Then ask: What are some important contributions of ancient India? *(the religions of Hinduism and Buddhism and their literature; folk tales; visual arts; contributions in math and science)* Tell students that they will learn more about these topics as they read the introduction.

Reading Skills and Strategies

SCANNING

Ask students to scan the boldfaced headings in the remaining text boxes to see what topics will be discussed. Also, point out that most of these boxes are keyed to the map by red numbers. Students should read a box, make a connection to the accompanying photograph, and then find the spot on the map that is referred to with the matching number.

PART 2 Sacred and Practical Teachings

Literature of Ancient India

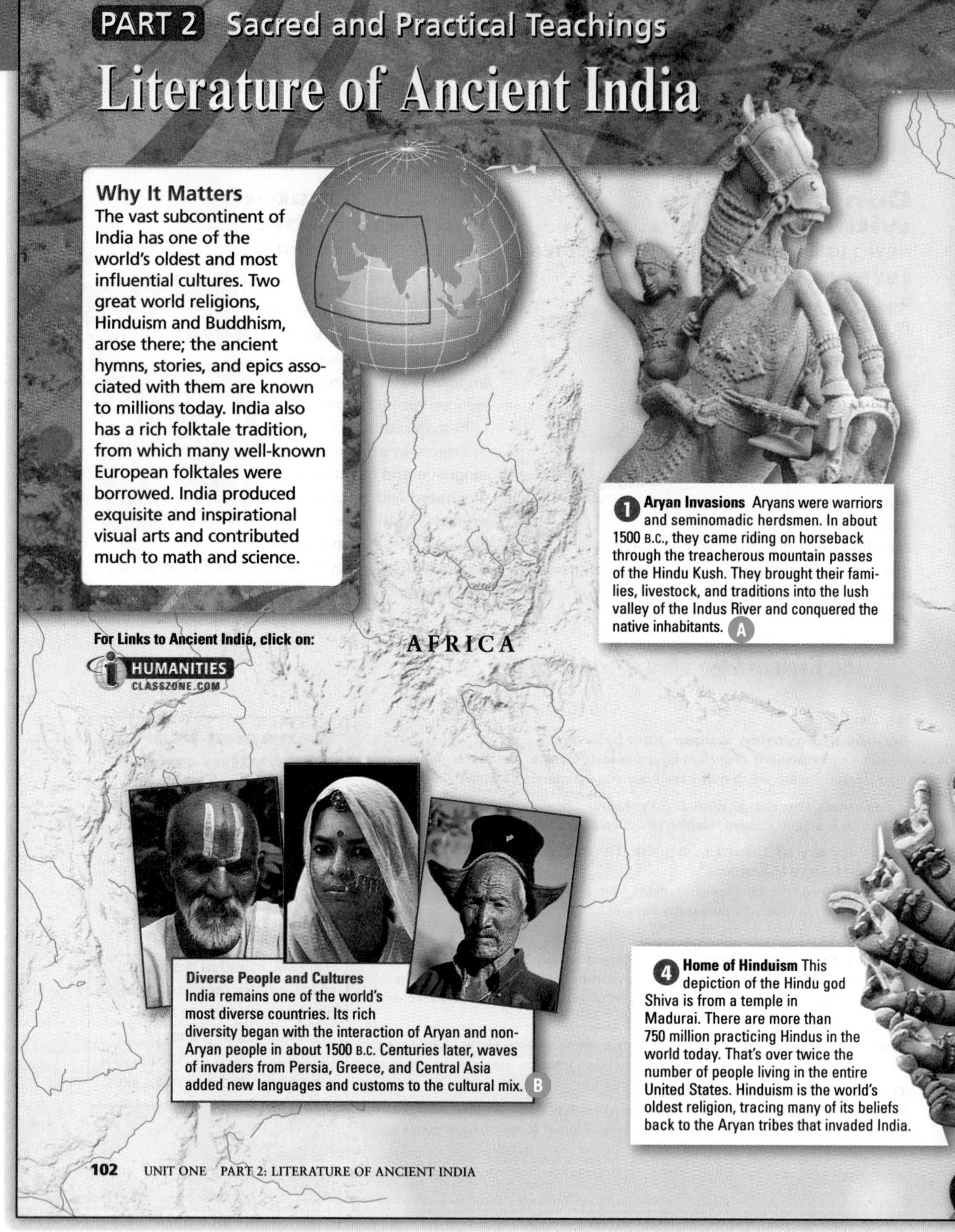

Why It Matters
The vast subcontinent of India has one of the world's oldest and most influential cultures. Two great world religions, Hinduism and Buddhism, arose there; the ancient hymns, stories, and epics associated with them are known to millions today. India also has a rich folktale tradition, from which many well-known European folktales were borrowed. India produced exquisite and inspirational visual arts and contributed much to math and science.

For Links to Ancient India, click on: HUMANITIES CLASSZONE.COM

1 Aryan Invasions Aryans were warriors and seminomadic herdsmen. In about 1500 B.C., they came riding on horseback through the treacherous mountain passes of the Hindu Kush. They brought their families, livestock, and traditions into the lush valley of the Indus River and conquered the native inhabitants. A

Diverse People and Cultures India remains one of the world's most diverse countries. Its rich diversity began with the interaction of Aryan and non-Aryan people in about 1500 B.C. Centuries later, waves of invaders from Persia, Greece, and Central Asia added new languages and customs to the cultural mix. B

4 Home of Hinduism This depiction of the Hindu god Shiva is from a temple in Madurai. There are more than 750 million practicing Hindus in the world today. That's over twice the number of people living in the entire United States. Hinduism is the world's oldest religion, tracing many of its beliefs back to the Aryan tribes that invaded India.

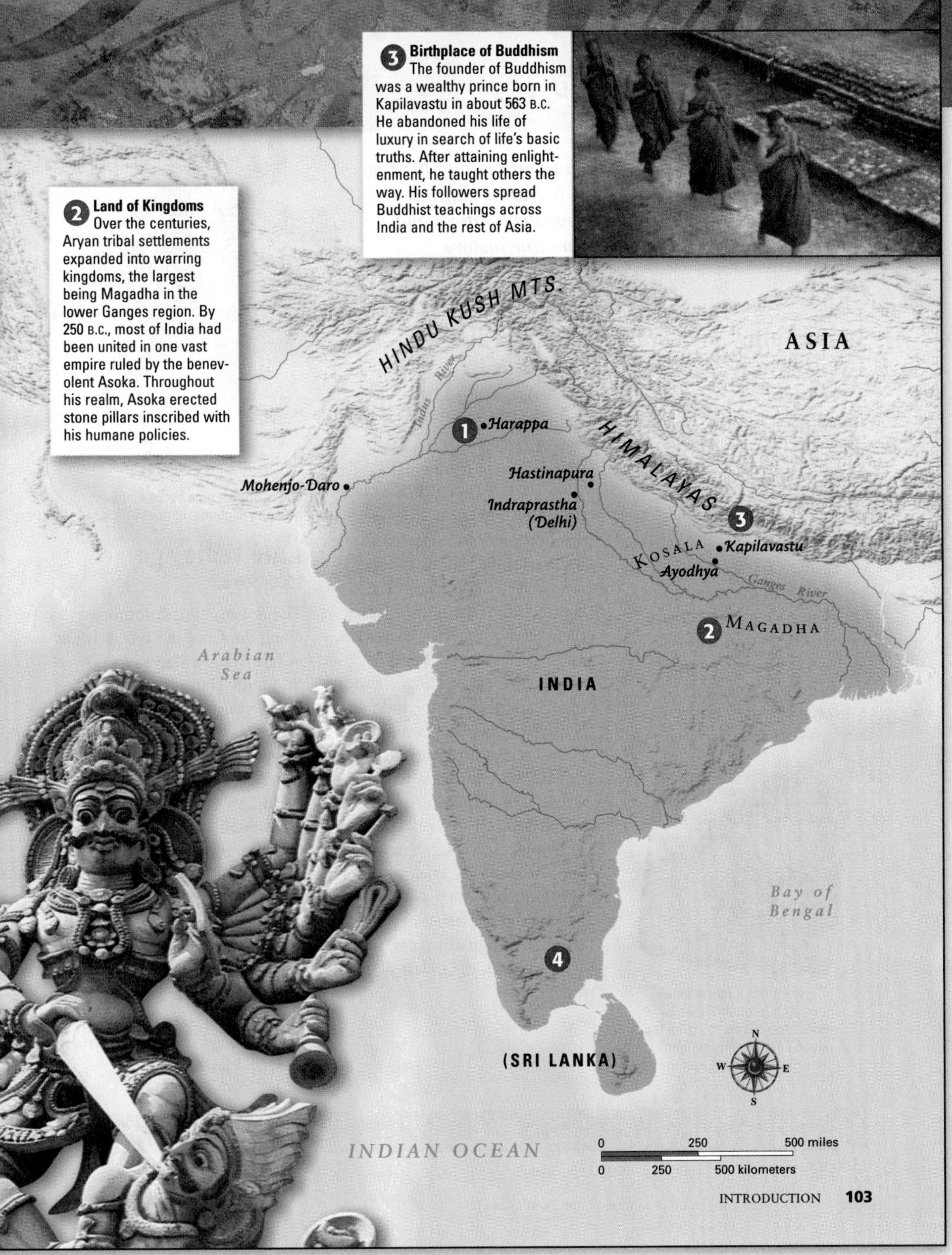

Historical Note

A Aryans and Nazism The original Aryans were not the blue-eyed blondes later idealized by the Nazis. Aryans were descendants of early Indo-Europeans who came from lands near the Caspian Sea and who later migrated southeast to Iran, then to India. Other groups of Indo-Europeans migrated west to various parts of Europe.

In the 19th century, scholars used *Aryan* to mean all early Indo-Europeans, not just those who migrated southeast. Certain scholars theorized that Aryans originated in northern Europe and that they were a separate race superior to Semites, including Jews. The Nazis embraced this false Aryan-race theory and used it to justify their killing of European Jews.

Geographical Note

B India's Diversity The number of ethnic groups in modern India is huge; people speak more than a thousand different languages and dialects. People also practice different religions: 82% of Indians are Hindu, 12% are Muslim, 2% are Christian, 2% are Sikh, and the rest belong to other faiths. Although Buddhism originated in India, few Buddhists live there today.

MINI LESSON Using the Map

Have students study the map on page 103 further, noticing the mountain ranges, rivers, cities, and kingdoms that appear on it. Ask the following questions:

- What mountain ranges border ancient India? *(the Hindu Kush, the Himalayas)*
- When Aryan groups migrated from the Indus River valley to the Ganges River valley, in what direction did they travel? *(southeast)*

Pronunciations
Vedas (vā′dəz)
Mahabharata (mə-hä-bä′rə-tə)
Ramayana (rä-mä′yə-nə)
Upanishads (o͞o-pă′nĭ-shädz′)
Jainism (jī′nĭz′əm)
Siddhartha Gautama (sĭd-där′tə gô′tə-mə)
Mahavira (mə-hä-vē′rə)
Chandragupta Maurya (chŭn′drə-goop′tə môr′yə)
Kautilya (kou-tĭl′yə)
Arthasastra (ŭr′tə-shäs′trə)
Bhagavad-Gita (bŭ′gə-vəd-gē′tä)

READING FOR INFORMATION

Reading Skills and Strategies

RECOGNIZING CHRONOLOGICAL ORDER

Tell students to read the heads for the five text columns on the spread and the colored dates below each of the heads. Five different historical periods are discussed, from earlier to later. The time line at the bottom of the spread summarizes the periods.

After students finish reading the columns, ask: What came before the early Vedic age? *(the Indus Valley civilization)*

Ask: What coincided, or overlapped, with the end of the late Vedic age? *(the rise of Buddhism and Jainism)*

Linguistic Note

A **Indo-European Languages** In the late 18th century, scholars noticed similarities among languages of Europe and Asia and theorized that they had a common ancestor. The Indo-European language family includes English, Sanskrit, Persian, Spanish, and German, among many other languages. Notice the resemblances among words in these languages.

English father
Sanskrit pitár
Persian puhdáhr
Spanish padre
German Vater

Historical Highlights

In ancient India, the link between literature and history was religion. From earliest times, literature expressed religious belief, which in turn drove the political and social forces that molded India's unique history.

Indus Valley Civilization

2500–1500 B.C.

About the time the Egyptians were building pyramids, people in the Indus Valley were creating complex cities. In the largest cities, Mohenjo-Daro and Harappa, brick public buildings and private homes stood on a grid of broad avenues and smaller cross-streets. Most houses had indoor bathrooms and sewer connections. After flourishing for centuries, however, this advanced civilization mysteriously declined.

Carved stone seals like this one were probably used by Indus merchants to stamp their goods. The writing on them has never been translated.

Early Vedic Age

1500–1000 B.C.

After the decline of the Indus civilization, Indo-European tribes invaded India from what is now Iran. They called themselves Aryans, "the ones of noble birth," and referred to the darker-skinned Indus people as *dasas,* "the dark ones." The conquering Aryans introduced their religion, their class system, and their language, Sanskrit, which is related to English and other languages in the Indo-European language family. This period of Indian history is called the Vedic age after the Aryan sacred literature known as the *Vedas,* four collections of hymns, prayers, magic spells, and rituals. Some basic concepts of Hinduism—such as the caste system and the belief in an afterlife—originally came from the *Rig Veda,* the oldest of the *Vedas.* A

Indra, shown on a battle elephant, was the mightiest of the Vedic gods.

Late Vedic Age

1000–500 B.C.

The Aryans spread southeast along the Ganges River, settling in farms and villages. As powerful family clans organized larger areas, violent conflicts arose over who should rule. Priests also grew more ambitious, causing concerns about their power.

India's great national epics, the *Mahabharata* and the *Ramayana,* describe political struggles of this period and also explain important social and religious concepts. The *Upanishads* interpreted Vedic hymns and introduced new spiritual principles of Hinduism—such as belief in one universal spirit, reincarnation, and karma.

INDUS VALLEY CIVILIZATION — 2500 B.C.

EARLY VEDIC AGE — 1500 B.C.

Rise of Buddhism and Jainism

560–321 B.C.

Buddhism and Jainism were new belief systems that attracted followers from all social classes.

Buddhism was founded by a young prince named Siddhartha Gautama. His religion was based on ethical behavior and nonviolence rather than worship of gods. Known as the Buddha, or "the Enlightened One," he preached throughout India for about 40 years.

Jainism also emphasized individual morality and nonviolence but was more strict. Its founder, Mahavira, believing that all living creatures had a soul, refused to harm even an insect.

The Buddha is shown with earlobes stretched long by the costly earrings he wore before giving up his wealth.

Age of Empires

321 B.C.–A.D. 500

India's first empire-builder, Chandragupta Maurya, succeeded in politically uniting the northern part of India for the first time. His advisor, Kautilya, wrote a "how-to" handbook for emperors, called the *Arthasastra*. Chandragupta's grandson, Asoka, further expanded the empire through war but promoted peace after he converted to Buddhism.

The Mauryan Empire began to break up soon after Asoka's death in 232 B.C., as waves of invaders poured into northern India. Stability returned about 500 years later during the Gupta Empire. The Gupta rulers presided over a golden age in which literature and the arts flourished.

Mauryan Empire, 250 B.C.

HINDU KUSH MTS.
HIMALAYAS
Indus River
Ganges River
Arabian Sea
Bay of Bengal
INDIAN OCEAN
N S W E
0 300 600 miles
0 300 600 kilometers

History to Literature

EVENT IN HISTORY	EVENT IN LITERATURE
Aryans invade the Indus Valley in about 1500 B.C.	The *Rig Veda* contains sacred hymns celebrating the Aryan way of life.
A civil war erupts over the large Bharata kingdom in about the tenth century B.C.	The *Mahabharata* describes a war between factions of the Bharata tribe: the Kauravas, ruling from their capital at Hastinapura, and the Pandavas, ruling from Indraprastha.
Aryan religious beliefs are questioned during the late Vedic Age and after the fall of the Mauryan Empire.	Holy men outline many principles of Hinduism in the *Upanishads;* later, the *Bhagavad-Gita* clarifies important Hindu concepts.
India enjoys a golden age during the Gupta Empire.	The great poet Kalidasa writes plays for Emperor Chandra Gupta II's court.

LATE VEDIC AGE | RISE OF BUDDHISM AND JAINISM | AGE OF EMPIRES

1000 B.C. | 560 B.C. | 321 B.C. | A.D. 500

Reading Skills and Strategies
USING THE MAP

Call attention to the map adjacent to **Age of Empires.** Point out that the purple shaded area is the area named by the red map title. Ask: What main idea does this map communicate? *(that the Mauryan Empire covered most of India in 250 B.C.)*

MINI LESSON Interpreting the Text

Call attention to the chart titled **History to Literature.** Tell students to look at the two column heads, Event in History and Event in Literature. Ask what they think the arrow means. *(that the historical events lead to the literary events; that the chart should be read across, not down)*

Then ask the following questions:

1. What literary work is linked to the Aryan invasion of the Indus valley? *(the* Rig Veda*)*
2. What historical event is linked to the *Mahabharata? (a civil war over the the Bharata kingdom)*

Pronunciations
Purusha (po͞o′rə-shə)
brahmans (brä′mənz)
kshatriyas (kə-shăt′rē-əz)
vaishyas (vī′shəz)
shudras(sho͞o′drəz)

READING FOR INFORMATION

Reading Skills and Strategies

CLASSIFYING

Have students read the italicized text at the top of the page, which introduces five social class divisions in India. Then tell them to read the rest of the page to find out what these classes are and how they differ. Encourage students to make notes for each column.

Ask: In the late Vedic age, which was the highest class? *(brahmans)* Which was the lowest class? *(outcastes or untouchables)*

Historical Note

Caste Reforms In modern times, there have been efforts to do away with the caste system. After India became independent of British rule in 1949, its new constitution outlawed caste distinctions. Later laws set penalties for discrimination against former untouchables, who are now called Scheduled Castes. A certain number of jobs, scholarships, and political seats are reserved for them, but most still face poverty and social prejudice.

People and Society

Perhaps the most durable Aryan tradition in India is the caste system, which still persists. According to the* Rig Veda, *four basic social classes emerged, in descending order, from the body of Purusha, the first man. These castes were based on occupation and skin color* (varna), *and separated Aryans from non-Aryans. In the late Vedic age, a fifth class division arose outside the caste system.

Brahmans

The **brahmans**, or priests, sprang from the mouth of Purusha. The Aryans devised their ranking system according to the purity and dignity they thought attached to an occupation. Since priests performed sacred rituals, they were considered the purest class and wore white clothes to distinguish themselves. Brahmans rose from being second in status in early Vedic times to being more powerful than kings in the late Vedic age.

Kshatriyas

Kshatriyas were warriors and rulers, who came from Purusha's arms. They wore red and commanded the most respect in early Vedic society.

A characteristic feature of the caste system is the concept of **dharma**, or roughly translated, "duty." Each class had sacred duties to perform to maintain the order of the universe. If you were born a warrior, you went to battle; you couldn't, for instance, sell vegetables in the market. As the god Krishna says in the *Bhagavad-Gita,* "It is better to do one's own duty badly than to do another's duty well."

Vaishyas

The vaishya caste consisted of farmers, merchants, and tradespeople such as carpenters and physicians. Most artisans, including poets and dancers, belonged to this caste. They emerged from Purusha's thighs and were assigned the color yellow.

The vaishyas, kshatriyas, and brahmans made up the three highest classes. During the late Vedic age, this social order hardened into a rigid hierarchy. Membership in a caste was strictly hereditary and usually not subject to change. One exception was that men in the top two castes could choose wives from a lower caste, although a lower-caste man could not marry up. That is, a priest could marry a farmer's daughter, but a farmer could not marry a priest's daughter.

Warriors were members of the kshatriya caste.

The British Library/The Art Archive.

Street-sweepers belonged to the category of outcastes.

Shudras

Shudras—servants and menial laborers—were the lowest of the four main castes. They came from Purusha's feet and wore the color black. This caste also included **dasas**, indigenous people conquered by Aryan tribes. Aryans gradually came to use the word *dasa* to mean "slave." Although a shudra's quality of life probably depended on his or her employer, it couldn't have been very satisfying. By the late Vedic age, it was legal to beat or even kill a shudra.

An interesting crack in the caste structure occurred during the shift from hereditary rule by tribal chiefs to the government of kingdoms by powerful monarchs. Although members of the kshatriya caste continued to rule local communities, most kings came from shudra families.

Outcastes

In later Vedic times, a new class division arose outside the caste system. **Outcastes,** also called **untouchables**, were thought to be so unclean, so polluted, that merely touching them endangered a person's purity. Generally, the nature of their work condemned outcastes: digging graves, for instance, or disposing of animal and human waste. Even butchers and leather workers fell into the category because they handled dead animals. Upper-caste Hindus went to extreme measures to avoid untouchables, requiring them to ring a bell as a warning of their presence.

Hindus believed that they could be born into a higher or lower caste in the next life, depending on their actions in their present life.

Women in Ancient India

Like most ancient people, the Aryans were patriarchal. In general, males ruled. Sons were favored over daughters, and women faced stricter moral standards than men. Warriors customarily had several wives. On the positive side, a woman usually chose the man she married, and widows could remarry. Girls attended school and could engage in religious activities when they grew up. Some of the hymns of the *Vedas* were composed by women.

Life got worse for women under Hinduism. Hindus considered women inferior, sinful, and a source of contamination.

Around the first century B.C., the *Laws of Manu* set down a detailed code of conduct for Hindus. Here are a few of the laws relating to women:

- Brides could be as young as eight.
- Warriors could abduct a bride and murder her family.
- Women were forbidden to own property or otherwise be independent.
- A wife couldn't displease her husband, even after he died.

Victoria & Albert Museum, London.

INTRODUCTION 107

Pronunciations
Panchatantra (pŭn′chə-tăn′trə)
Jataka (jä′tə-kə)
Tamil (tăm′əl)

READING FOR INFORMATION
Reading Skills and Strategies
USING TEXT ORGANIZERS

Have students look at the main head, **Arts and Culture,** on pages 108 and 109. Then have them scan the subheads to see which areas of arts and culture will be discussed. Call attention to the boldfaced run-in heads under the **Religion** section. Ask: What three religions will be described? *(Hinduism, Buddhism, Jainism)*

Point out the purple box around the sculpture of the god Shiva. Ask students what section of text they think the box goes with. *(Arts and Architecture)* Tell students to start in the upper right corner of the box and read the captions in a clockwise direction.

Arts and Culture

Perhaps the most important contribution of ancient India is its religious traditions. Hinduism and Buddhism share a reverence for the inner life and remind us of the riches to be found within ourselves. The literature, art, music, and dance that grew from these traditions are beautiful and moving, inspirational to people across the world.

Literature

The literature of ancient India remains a living tradition, tied to religion and moral instruction. Although Hinduism has changed significantly from the Aryan beliefs recorded in the *Vedas,* Hindus still chant hymns from the *Rig Veda* at weddings and funerals. The great epics, the *Mahabharata* and the *Ramayana,* contain exciting tales for children to enjoy as well as philosophical ideas for adults to ponder. The fables of the *Panchatantra* and the Jataka tales of the Buddha's past lives appeal to readers of all ages. The classic drama of the poet Kalidasa—known as the "Shakespeare of India"—is still performed on Indian stages.

A separate literary tradition developed in southern India among speakers of the Tamil language. Unlike Sanskrit, Tamil is not an Indo-European language. It is Dravidian.The earliest Tamil poetry dates from the first century A.D.

How Was Literature Presented?

The sacred *Vedas* were composed orally hundreds of years before they were written down. Priests kept the *Vedas* alive by memorizing them and teaching them to the next generation of priests. The hymns and rituals had to be recited perfectly to have the desired religious effect. This practice required extraordinary feats of memory. The *Rig Veda* alone contains more than 1,000 hymns.

The British Library/The Art Archive.

Text of the Sri Bhagavata Purana. Puranas explained Vedic concepts to ordinary people.

Religion

Hinduism began as a blending of Aryan and non-Aryan traditions and developed over a period of more than 2,500 years. Hindus basically believe in one god, Brahman. More an abstract spirit than a being, however, Brahman exists everywhere, both within all living things and in the surrounding cosmos. Below Brahman—and yet part of him—are three other gods: Brahma, the creator; Vishnu, the preserver; and Shiva, the destroyer. Vishnu is said to have come to earth in ten bodily forms, or *avatars.* The most important of these avatars are the mythical Krishna of the *Bhagavad-Gita,* the legendary king Rama of the *Ramayana,* and the historical Buddha.

Central to Hindu belief as well as to India's caste system is the concept of reincarnation. An individual soul *(atman)* evolves in a cycle of earthly existence by which it passes from one body at death to be reborn in another body. A person's quality of life depends on his or her actions, or *karma,* in a previous life. For example, an evil ruler might come back

MINI LESSON Interpreting the Text

These pages contain a lot of information, particularly the **Religion** section. Knowledge about Hinduism will help students as they read the literary selections.

As they read, encourage students to make two graphic organizers—one to show the relationships among Hindu gods and avatars, and another to illustrate the cycle of rebirth and its end. Students might begin the first graphic organizer like this:

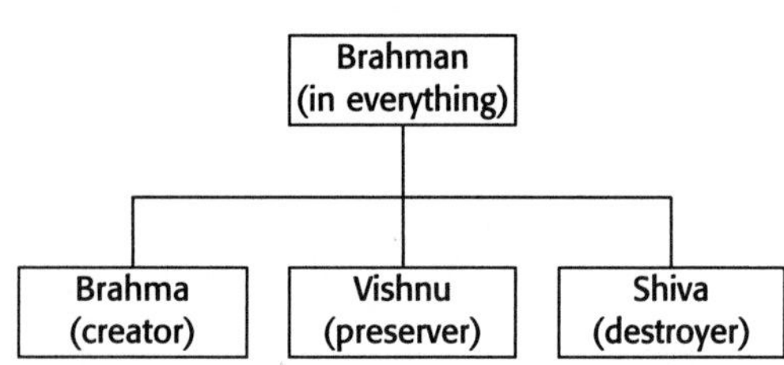

as an untouchable; a greedy merchant could return as a crow. The goal of existence is *moksha*—perfect understanding of the universe and, ultimately, a release from the cycle of rebirth and union with Brahman.

Buddhism arose as a reaction to Hinduism's complex rituals and the power of the Vedic priests. Buddhists accept the Hindu belief in reincarnation with the ultimate goal being enlightenment and union with the universal spirit *(nirvana)*. But Buddhists reject the caste system and don't worship Hindu gods. The way to salvation lies in moderation, specifically by following the Buddha's Middle Way, between desire and self-denial. Buddhists practice meditation, nonviolence, and religious toleration. After some of its ideas were absorbed by Hinduism, Buddhism eventually died out in India. It gained a stronger foothold in Sri Lanka, East Asia, and Southeast Asia.

Jainism, like Buddhism, arose in response to the power of the Vedic priests. Jains practice extreme forms of self-denial and nonviolence. The sect still exists in India today, but it never spread widely outside of India.

Arts and Architecture

Ancient Indian arts had a religious purpose. The classic Indian architectural form is the Hindu temple, made of stone blocks and carved with images of deities. Buddhist monuments, or *stupas,* were built in the shape of mounds, to symbolize the universe. Beautiful paintings line caves where Buddhist monks once worshiped, and some of the most famous Indian sculptures depict Hindu gods, such as Shiva.

Shiva the Destroyer

Shiva dancing. Courtesy of the Trustees of the Victoria & Albert Museum, London.

Students might begin the second graphic organizer like this:

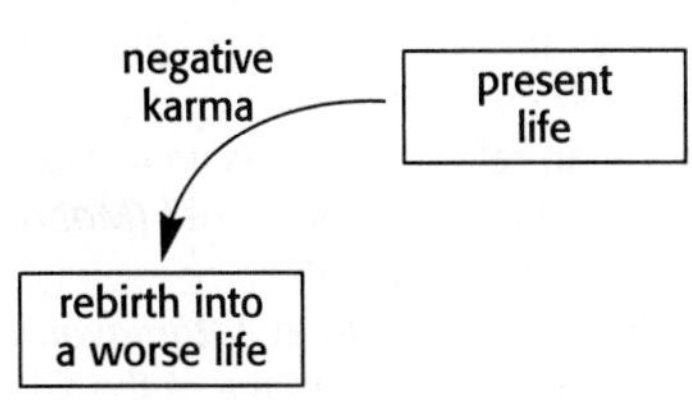

To check students' understanding of the section, ask:

1. What is an avatar? *(a bodily form of a god)*
2. Who are considered the most important avatars of Vishnu? *(Krishna, Rama, and the Buddha)*
3. What is the goal of existence in Hinduism? *(moksha)*

Time Line

ANCIENT INDIA (2500 B.C.–A.D. 500)

3000 B.C. A.D. 1 PRESENT

c. approximately
B.C. before Christ
A.D. after Christ

EVENTS IN INDIAN LITERATURE

2000 B.C. 1600 B.C. 1200 B.C.

1500–900 B.C. Hymns of the *Rig Veda* are composed

EVENTS IN INDIAN HISTORY

2000 B.C. 1600 B.C. 1200 B.C.

c. 2500–1700 B.C. Advanced civilization flourishes in the Indus River valley ➢

Sculpture of a priest-king from the Indus culture

c. 1500 B.C. Aryan tribes invade northwest India

c. 1100s B.C. Bharata tribe's victory in the Battle of the Ten Kings increases its power

1000–500 B.C. Aryan communities begin to appear in the Ganges River basin

900s B.C. Descendants of the Bharata kings fight for control of the kingdom

EVENTS IN WORLD HISTORY

2000 B.C. 1600 B.C. 1200 B.C.

2080–1640 B.C. Middle Kingdom in Egypt

c. 2000 B.C. Indo-European nomadic tribes begin migrating from what is now southern Russia, eventually spreading across Europe, Turkey, Iran, and India

1792–1750 B.C. Hammurabi reigns at the height of the Babylonian empire

c. 1400 B.C. Phoenicians develop an alphabet

1200–400 B.C. Olmec civilization thrives in southern Mexico

1050–221 B.C. Chou Dynasty rules in China

c. 1020 B.C. King Saul unites the Hebrews

MINI LESSON Using the Time Line

First, tell students to scan the small time line at the top of the page. Ask: How many years are covered in the period labeled Ancient India? *(3,000 years)*

Next, have students read across the large gold time line, **Events in Indian Literature,** noticing when literary works were written in relation to each other.

Have students skim across the other large time lines as well. Finally, tell them to read more carefully down the same period in all three time lines, to see which events happened during the same span of time. Ask the following questions to check understanding:

1. What civilizations were flourishing at the same time as the Indus River valley civilization? *(the Middle Kingdom of Egypt; the Babylonian Empire)*
2. What Indian religious figures were born in the same century as Confucius? *(Mahavira and Siddartha Gautama)*
3. Were the *Mahabharata* and *Ramayana* composed during the golden age of the Gupta Empire? *(No, they were composed earlier.)*

800 B.C.	400 B.C.	A.D. 1
750–550 B.C. Teachings of the *Upanishads* are written	**400–100 B.C.** *Mahabharata* and *Ramayana* are composed **c. 304 B.C.** Chandragupta Maurya's chief adviser writes the *Arthasastra* **c. 200 B.C.** Traditional fables are collected in the *Panchatantra* **c. 100 B.C.** *Bhagavad-Gita* is added to the *Mahabharata*	**A.D. 100s** Tamil poetry and drama flourish in southern India **A.D. 320–500** Under Gupta rulers, India experiences a golden age, with achievements in art, literature, religion, science, and mathematics **A.D. 400s** Kalidasa writes poetry and drama, including the famous play *Shakuntala*

800 B.C.	400 B.C.	A.D. 1
c. 599 B.C. Birth of Mahavira, founder of Jainism **c. 563 B.C.** Birth of Siddhartha Gautama, founder of Buddhism **500s B.C.** Aryan kingdom of Magadha expands by taking over smaller kingdoms	**326 B.C.** Alexander the Great invades the Indus Valley and temporarily brings it under Greek control **c. 321–301 B.C.** Chandragupta Maurya unites northern India in the Mauryan Empire **269–232 B.C.** Asoka brings Mauryan Empire to its height	**A.D. 320** Chandra Gupta I, from Magadha, begins building the Gupta Empire **A.D. 415** Death of Chandra Gupta II weakens Gupta Empire **A.D. 499** Aryabhata, an Indian mathematician, calculates the value of pi (π) and the number of days in a solar year **A.D. 500s** Huns and other Central Asian nomads overrun India

800 B.C.	400 B.C.	A.D. 1
551 B.C. Birth of Confucius in China **550–539 B.C.** Cyrus the Great builds the Persian Empire	**338 B.C.** Phillip II of Macedon conquers Greece **332–323 B.C.** Alexander the Great conquers Persia and spreads Greek culture throughout his empire **c. 200 B.C.** Emergence of Nazca culture in Peru **146 B.C.** Romans destroy Carthage in North Africa and expand their empire	**c. A.D. 29** Jesus is crucified **c. A.D. 65** First Buddhist monastery is built in China **c. A.D. 105** Chinese invent paper **c. A.D. 391** Christianity is declared the official religion of the Roman Empire **A.D. 449** Anglo-Saxons invade England

INTRODUCTION **111**

Pronunciations
ayurvedic (ī′yər-vā′dĭk)
chaturanga (chŭ′tər-ŭng′gä)
ahimsa (ə-hĭm′sä′)

READING FOR INFORMATION
Reading Skills and Strategies
CONNECTING

After students read the spread, have them share what more they know about the topics mentioned. Do any of the students practice yoga or meditation? Are any of them vegetarian or active in animal-rights causes? Whom have they heard described as a guru?

Connect to Today: The Legacy of Ancient India

Yoga and Meditation
Pre-Aryan artifacts show people sitting in the cross-legged positions associated with yoga. Yoga (Sanskrit for "union") is an ancient spiritual discipline involving special postures, controlled breathing, and meditation, or mental concentration. First introduced to the United States in 1893, yoga is practiced by more than 15 million Americans today.

Ancient "New Age" Ideas

Many other popular trends and practices of today originated in ancient India.

Vegetarianism was linked to the belief in nonviolence held by Jains, Buddhists and Hindus. Today, growing numbers of people have stopped eating meat, many for ethical and health reasons.

Animal rights also followed from nonviolence. Today, groups protest experimentation and product testing on animals.

Gurus, or personal spiritual teachers, taught Vedic wisdom to pupils who lived with them. Now the term is applied broadly to people who are experts in a particular area.

Ayurvedic medicine is gaining more practitioners in the West. This Indian system of healing, described in the ancient *Atharva Veda,* is based on body type.

Chess and Dice
The game of chess evolved from *chaturanga,* a four-player war game played in northwest India in ancient times. The pieces had different powers, and victory was based on exposing or capturing the king. Dice, too, came from India. Dice carved of nuts were found at the pre-Aryan site of Mohenjo-Daro.

Nonviolence
Nonviolence, or *ahimsa,* was one of the central beliefs of Jainism. It became part of Buddhism and Hinduism as well. The technique of passive resistance that 20th-century leader Mohandas Gandhi used in gaining Indian independence was based on *ahimsa.* Gandhi's strategy, in turn, influenced Martin Luther King, Jr.'s efforts in the U.S. civil rights movement.

Mathematics and Science
Some of the greatest achievements of ancient India were in math and science. Indians invented modern numerals, the concept of zero, and the decimal system—all of which we use today. Ancient Indian scientists figured out that the earth was round and that a solar year had 365 days.

Objectives
- understand and appreciate ancient Aryan **hymns (Literary Analysis)**
- recognize and discuss **paradox (Literary Analysis)**
- use strategies for **making inferences (Active Reading)**

Thematic Link
These two hymns come from the *Rig Veda*, an ancient Aryan book of **sacred teachings.**

5-Minute Warm-Up
Daily Language SkillBuilder

Have students **proofread** the display sentences on page 15g and write them correctly.

Reading and Analyzing

Literary Analysis PARADOX

A Invite students to identify more paradoxes in this passage.
Possible Responses: "There was neither death nor immortality," "There was no distinguishing sign of night or day," "That one breathed, windless."

Use **Unit One Resource Book,** p. 26, for additional support.

from the Rig Veda

Build Background

Book of Hymns The *Rig Veda* (rĭg-vä′də) is one of the sacred scriptures of the Aryans, who invaded India around 1500 B.C. The oldest of four *vedas,* or books of wisdom, it contains 1,028 hymns to Aryan gods. Ancient priests called *hotars* chanted these hymns at ritual sacrifices. The hymns were passed down orally for generations before finally being written down sometime around 600 B.C. Today in India they are still recited at weddings and other ceremonies, in exactly the same form.

Thirty-three gods are mentioned in the *Rig Veda.* Indra, a thunderbolt-hurling war god, is the most important. He is praised for conquering the *dasas,* the people who lived in northern India before the Aryans came. Other gods named are Agni, the fire god, who consumes the sacrifices, and Yama, the god of death.

Aryan Life The hymns in the *Rig Veda* are not merely songs in praise of the gods; they also reveal much about the daily concerns of the ancient Aryans. Some of these concerns seem surprisingly contemporary. One hymn, for example, describes how gambling destroys family life. "Let someone else fall into the trap of the brown dice," it urges. Another hymn encourages people to give charity to the poor, for "the riches of the man who gives fully do not run out."

The two hymns you will read are different in style and subject. The first, "Creation Hymn," speculates about how the world was created. "Burial Hymn" is essentially a funeral sermon.

Connect to Your Life

Have you ever heard or read a statement that seemed to contradict itself or express the impossible? "I know that I know nothing" is one such statement. Jot down some others and share them with a classmate.

Focus Your Reading

LITERARY ANALYSIS: PARADOX

Even the translator, Wendy Doniger O'Flaherty, admits that "Creation Hymn" is hard to understand. She writes, "It is meant to puzzle and challenge, to raise unanswerable questions, to pile up paradoxes." A **paradox** is a statement that seems contradictory or impossible yet suggests a truth. The line "There was neither death nor immortality" is a paradox. Look for others in the hymn, and try to take the translator's advice: "Be as open to the words as possible, letting them move [you] when they can."

ACTIVE READING: MAKING INFERENCES

To understand "Burial Hymn" you will have to **make inferences** about, or guess from clues, what is taking place during a funeral ritual. For example, reading the words "this wall" and "this hill," you might infer that the mourners are outdoors.

READER'S NOTEBOOK As you read, try to picture whom the priest is speaking to at different points in the ritual. Also imagine what actions he and the mourners are performing. Use a chart like the one below to organize your inferences.

Who is addressed?	What is happening?

LESSON RESOURCES

UNIT ONE RESOURCE BOOK, pp. 25–26

ASSESSMENT RESOURCES
Formal Assessment, pp. 17–18
Teacher's Guide to Assessment and Portfolio Use
Test Generator

INTEGRATED TECHNOLOGY
Visit our Web site: classzone.com

ADDITIONAL RESOURCES
Lesson Planning Guide, pp. 9–10
Teacher's Sourcebook for Language Development

from the Rig Veda

Translated by Wendy Doniger O'Flaherty

CREATION HYMN

1 There was neither non-existence nor existence then;
there was neither the realm of space nor the sky
which is beyond. What stirred? Where? In whose
protection? Was there water, bottomlessly deep?
2 There was neither death nor immortality then.
There was no distinguishing sign of night nor of
day. That one breathed, windless, by its own
impulse. Other than that there was nothing beyond.
3 Darkness was hidden by darkness in the beginning;
with no distinguishing sign, all this was water. The
life force that was covered with emptiness, that one
arose through the power of heat.
4 Desire came upon that one in the beginning; that
was the first seed of mind. Poets seeking in their
heart with wisdom found the bond of existence in
non-existence.
5 Their cord was extended across. Was there below?
Was there above? There were seed-placers; there
were powers. There was impulse beneath; there was
giving-forth above.
6 Who really knows? Who will here proclaim it?
Whence was it produced? Whence is this creation?
The gods came afterwards, with the creation of this
universe. Who then knows whence it has arisen?
7 Whence this creation has arisen—perhaps it formed
itself, or perhaps it did not—the one who looks
down on it, in the highest heaven, only he knows—
or perhaps he does not know.

2 That one: the unknown force that caused the creation of the world.

4 Desire . . . was the first seed of mind: Thought grew out of desire.

5 cord: something used as a boundary to separate the elements from one another.

6 The gods came afterwards: In other words, the gods are not the source of creation.

Customizing Instruction

Less Proficient Readers

- Explain the structure of "Creation Hymn." First, it speculates about what existed before the world was created; then, it describes what happened to create the world.
- Reassure students that they don't have to understand every line of the hymn. The hymn is full of unfamiliar ideas not easily translatable into English.
- Suggest that students mentally capitalize "that one" each time they read it and think of That One as a being or a principle.
- Explain that "heat" at the end of stanza 3 refers to *tapas*, a special kind of heat connected with spiritual activities such as fasting or enduring pain.

English Learners

If necessary, explain that a *hymn* is a song or poem that expresses religious feelings. Also explain the meaning of uncommon or archaic words such as *stirred* ("moved") and *whence* ("from where").

Advanced Learners

Ask students to consider the effect of the stately, archaic English used for the translation. Why do they think the translator chose such language?

Possible Responses: It may have corresponded to very formal Sanskrit; it may have suggested that a priest was speaking or that the occasion was ceremonial; it would sound "religious" to English-speaking readers, like the language of the King James Bible.

RIG VEDA **115**

Reading and Analyzing

Active Reading MAKING INFERENCES

(A) Have students read the first stanza of "Burial Hymn." Then ask them to infer how the speaker views death.

Possible Responses: as a being who can be addressed; as someone or something undesirable; as someone or something separate from the gods

(B) Have students read the second and third stanzas, noting that the speaker has gone from addressing death itself to addressing the mourners. Ask them to infer what is happening or has happened.

Possible Responses: The mourners have left one site and gone to another; they have been involved in a ritual inviting the gods to join them.

Use **Unit One Resource Book,** p. 25, for additional support.

Indra, King of Three Worlds from the Temple Car. Courtesy of the Trustees of the Victoria & Albert Museum, London.

HUMANITIES CONNECTION Indra, the greatest of the Vedic gods, is shown in this woodcarving from southern India. He holds his thunderbolt weapon, Vajra, as a scepter and sits on an elephant.

MINI LESSON Viewing and Representing

Indra, King of the Three Worlds, from the Temple Car

ART APPRECIATION Have students read the **Humanities Connection** caption and study the wood carving of Indra, the Vedic thunder god. About 250 hymns in the *Rig Veda* are dedicated to Indra—more than are dedicated to any other god. When not shown riding in his golden chariot, he is shown riding a great, white, four-tusked elephant named Airavata. Indra was worshipped for his many heroic deeds, particularly for slaying the dragon Vritra, who had stolen all the water in the world. After Indra split the dragon open, enabling the monsoons to come and crops to grow again, the gods elected him their king. After the Vedic religion developed into Hinduism, Indra was not worshiped as much. Other gods, Shiva and Vishnu, became more important.

Ask what features of this sculpture make Indra seem mighty and powerful.

Possible Responses: Indra's jewels and crown; his weapon/scepter; his size relative to the elephant; his serene smile

BURIAL HYMN

1 Go away, death, by another path that is your own,
different from the road of the gods. I say to you
who have eyes, who have ears: do not injure our
children or our men.

2 When you have gone, wiping away the footprint
of death, stretching farther your own lengthening
span of life, become pure and clean and worthy of
sacrifice, swollen with offspring and wealth.

3 These who are alive have now parted from those
who are dead. Our invitation to the gods has
become auspicious today. We have gone forward
to dance and laugh, stretching farther our own
lengthening span of life.

4 I set up this wall for the living, so that no one else
among them will reach this point. Let them live a
hundred full autumns and bury death in this hill.

5 As days follow days in regular succession, as
seasons come after seasons in proper order, in the
same way order their life-spans, O Arranger, so that
the young do not abandon the old.

6 Climb on to old age, choosing a long life-span, and
follow in regular succession, as many as you are.
May Tvastr who presides over good births be
persuaded to give you a long life-span to live.

7 These women who are not widows, who have good
husbands—let them take their places, using butter
1 to anoint their eyes. Without tears, without sickness, well dressed let them first climb into the
marriage bed.

2 you: the mourners at the burial.

3 auspicious (ô-spĭsh′əs): favorable; successful.

6 Tvastr (t′vä′shtər): creator of the gods and protector of all living things.

7 butter: Purified by ritual, the butter is to protect the women mourners' eyes; **let them . . . the marriage bed:** that is, before they are old or die.

Customizing Instruction

Less Proficient Readers

Advise students not to read "Burial Hymn" as one continuous poem. Call attention to the numbered stanzas and tell students to imagine that a priest is making separate statements at different points in a ceremony. As students read, they should identify directives, such as "Go away" or "become pure and clean," and should determine who is being spoken to.

English Learners

1 Explain that *anoint* means "to put oil on," often as part of a religious ceremony.

Reading and Analyzing

Literary Analysis FIGURATIVE LANGUAGE

A Ask students what the earth is being compared to in these stanzas. What do these comparisons suggest about the Aryans' view of death?

Possible Responses: The earth is compared to a protective mother and a soft, young girl. The comparisons suggest that the dead man will experience comfort after burial, as if he were a child again.

Active Reading MAKING INFERENCES

B Ask students what they infer the priest is doing at this point.

Possible Responses: burying the dead man; keeping the grave from collapsing on the dead man

Agni (God of Fire) (17th century). Panel from Temple Car. Tak. Madras. Inv:IM.15-1929. Photo © Victoria & Albert Museum, London/Art Resource, New York

HUMANITIES CONNECTION This 11th-century stone sculpture depicts Agni, the Vedic fire god. One of his roles was the purification of sacrifices.

8 Rise up, woman, into the world of the living. Come here; you are lying beside a man whose life's breath has gone. You were the wife of this man who took your hand and desired to have you.

9 I take the bow from the hand of the dead man, to be our supremacy and glory and power, and I say, "You are there; we are here. Let us as great heroes conquer all envious attacks."

10 Creep away to this broad, vast earth, the mother that is kind and gentle. She is a young girl, soft as wool to anyone who makes offerings; let her guard you from the lap of Destruction. **A**

11 Open up, earth; do not crush him. Be easy for him to enter and to burrow in. Earth, wrap him up as a mother wraps a son in the edge of her skirt.

12 Let the earth as she opens up stay firm, for a thousand pillars must be set up. Let them be houses dripping with butter for him, and let them be a refuge for him here for all his days.

13 I shore up the earth all around you; let me not injure you as I lay down this clod of earth. Let the fathers hold up this pillar for you; let Yama build a house for you here. **B**

14 On a day that will come, they will lay me in the earth, like the feather of an arrow. I hold back speech that goes against the grain, as one would restrain a horse with a bridle. ❖

8 Rise up, woman: The dead man's widow would have lain down beside his body.

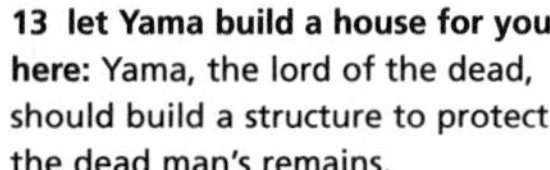

13 let Yama build a house for you here: Yama, the lord of the dead, should build a structure to protect the dead man's remains.

MINI LESSON Viewing and Representing

Stone Sculpture of Agni

ART APPRECIATION Have students read the **Humanities Connection** caption and study the sculpture of Agni, the Vedic fire god. About 200 hymns in the *Rig Veda* are addressed to Agni. He represents the fire of the sun and of lightning and of the sacrifice. The English word *ignite* is derived from his name. He is often pictured as red, with hair that stands on end like flames. Sometimes he is shown with two faces that are smeared with butter.

Butter had great religious importance to the Aryans, a cattle-raising people. They frequently offered clarified butter, called *ghee*, as a sacrifice to Agni, burning it in a fire. Modern Hindus still use butter as part of weddings, initiations, and other religious ceremonies.

Connect to the Literature

1. **What Do You Think?** What is the most interesting or puzzling idea you found in these hymns from the *Rig Veda?*

Comprehension Check
- Who knows how the universe was created, according to "Creation Hymn"?
- What does the priest ask of the earth in "Burial Hymn"?

Think Critically

2. What questions does "Creation Hymn" raise about how the universe was created? What answers does it give?
3. What are you told about "that one" who is mentioned in "Creation Hymn"?
4. **ACTIVE READING: MAKING INFERENCES** From the words of "Burial Hymn," what did you infer was happening during the funeral ritual? Refer to the chart you made in your READER'S NOTEBOOK.
5. Judging from "Burial Hymn," how would you say the ancient Aryans viewed death?

THINK ABOUT
- what they believe will happen to the dead man
- how desirable or frightening death seems

Extend Interpretations

6. **Comparing Texts** How would you compare the account of creation in "Creation Hymn" with the accounts from Genesis and the *Popol Vuh?*

THINK ABOUT
- what existed before creation
- the role played by the gods

7. **Connect to Life** How do the sentiments in "Burial Hymn" compare with those you've heard at modern funerals?

LITERARY ANALYSIS: PARADOX

A **paradox** is a statement that appears to be contradictory yet expresses a certain truth. "There was neither non-existence nor existence then" is a paradox and certainly hard to visualize, yet it helps the reader imagine a state before the most basic dimensions of our world were present. Religious and spiritual writings often contain paradoxes. Such paradoxes shake readers out of their normal ways of thinking and point them toward a higher level of understanding.

Cooperative Learning Activity With a small group of classmates, find other paradoxical statements in "Creation Hymn" and write them in a chart like the one below. Discuss each statement, exchanging ideas about what you think it means or what it makes you visualize. Choose one of the statements and summarize your discussion of it for the rest of the class.

Paradox	Interpretations
"There was neither non-existence nor existence then."	This was a time before all things or even the idea of things.

Connect to the Literature

1. **What Do You Think?** Answers will vary. Some students may be intrigued or puzzled by the idea of absolute nothingness, or the idea of "that one" who existed before all other things, or the idea that the world may have formed itself.

Comprehension Check
- Only the one who looks down on it knows, or perhaps no one at all knows (verse 7).
- He asks the earth not to crush the dead man (verse 11).

Think Critically

2. Possible Responses: The poem asks what there was before creation, what started creation, and who really knows how the universe was created. It suggests that before creation, there was only darkness, water, and a life force—"that one"—which began creation. The poem answers that no one really knows how the universe was created, except perhaps the one who looks down on it.
3. Possible Responses: Readers are told that "that one" caused itself to breathe, that it arose through the power of heat, and that desire came upon it and made it create the universe.
4. Possible Responses: Students may infer that the speaker is addressing mourners gathered outside, that he sets up a wall to keep death away, that the women in the group move to a special position, that the dead man's wife rises from beside him and rejoins the others, that the speaker takes the dead man's bow and then buries him in the ground.
5. Possible Responses: They view death as undesirable (since they want to keep death away) but not terrible (since they assume the dead man will be protected in a house in the earth).

Extend Interpretations

6. **Comparing Texts** All three accounts say that there was only darkness and water before creation. In Genesis and the *Popol Vuh,* the universe is created by one or more gods, while in "Creation Hymn" it is created by a life force existing even before gods.
7. **Connect to Life** Students may say that the appreciation of life, the recognition that the living and dead are separated, and the hope that the dead will be safe in the afterlife are sentiments similar to those expressed at modern funerals.

To assess skills and concepts taught in this selection, use **Formal Assessment Book,** pp. 17–18

Literary Analysis

Cooperative Learning Activity In their discussions, students might mention the difficulty of visualizing what is meant but feel the attempt brings them closer to something beyond the world as they know it.

Use **Unit One Resource Book,** p. 26, for more practice.

Objectives

- understand the following literary terms:
  - epic
  - epic hero
  - repetition
  - epithets
- recognize shared characteristics of cultures through reading
- recognize strategies for reading an epic

In Unit One, Part 2, students will be reading two ancient Indian epics. This lesson will give them some background on the epic as a literary form and on literary concepts related to the epic.

The Nature of an Epic
Reading Skills and Strategies
CONNECTING
Before students read the definition of an epic, you might ask them what kinds of movies or books they have heard described as "epic." Ask them to tell you what they think *epic* means.
Possible Responses: a long and very dramatic story; a story covering many years and involving many characters

Features of Epic Poetry
Reading Skills and Strategies
CONNECTING
To reinforce students' understanding of epithets, give examples of phrases that function as epithets in modern society—"lovely and talented" (usually applied to a starlet or beauty queen); "conservative Republican" (usually applied to a politician).

The Development of the Epic

In the Beginning Were Stories
Before written language and literature, there were stories. People told stories for entertainment, certainly. But they also created stories to define themselves as human beings and to explain their place in the universe. These stories, passed on orally from one generation to the next, became an early form of history.

The Nature of an Epic
These stories from the oral tradition provided the raw material for one of the oldest forms of literature, the epic. An **epic** is a long narrative poem that tells the deeds of a great person, an **epic hero.** In epics, myth and legend are woven into rich tapestries that express the core values and beliefs of particular cultures. Epics can also serve religious and nationalistic purposes. The *Mahabharata* and the *Ramayana,* two great epics of India, are as sacred to Hindus as the Bible is to Christians. The *Shah-nameh,* the national epic of Persia, glorifies Persia's past and justifies the rule of its kings.

Some of the translations of ancient epics you will encounter are in prose. Most likely, you've read an epic silently, alone. But all epics were originally composed as poetry for public performance. They were sung or recited by professional poets, known in different cultures as scops (Anglo-Saxon), bards (Celtic), sutas (Indian), and jalis (West African). Some epics existed for hundreds of years before being written down.

Rama. V&A Picture Library. Courtesy of the Trustees of the Victoria & Albert Museum, London.

Features of Epic Poetry
A feature of many epic poems is the **repetition** of particular words, phrases, and grammatical structures. In some cases, perhaps, such repetition served to help the poet with the difficult task of memorization. For example, when Gilgamesh stands at Siduri's gate, he identifies himself in this way:

> **. . . I am Gilgamesh who seized and killed the Bull of Heaven, I killed the watchman of the cedar forest, I overthrew Humbaba who lived in the forest, and I killed the lions in the passes of the mountain.**
> **—*The Epic of Gilgamesh***

Siduri replies by repeating what Gilgamesh just said: "If you are that Gilgamesh who seized and killed the Bull of Heaven, . . ." When epics were recited, repetitions also served as summaries of already presented actions, to help listeners remember what had happened before.

Another feature of many epics is the use of **epithets**—words or short phrases that highlight key qualities of characters or objects. For example, in the excerpt from the *Mahabharata,* the hero Arjuna is called "king of men" and "Terrifier."

A Larger-Than-Life Hero
An epic hero has to be larger than life—the strongest, the smartest, the bravest, the best—because such a hero represents a culture's ideal. Most epic heroes are part divine. Gilgamesh is "two-thirds a god." The Pandava brothers from the *Mahabharata* were fathered by gods. In the *Ramayana,* Prince Rama is actually an embodiment of the god Vishnu.

Even an epic hero who is semidivine, however, usually has very recognizable human traits. Gilgamesh may have superhuman strength and courage, but he suffers and dies like the rest of us mortals. He also makes mistakes, such as losing the magic plant that could have restored his youth. Arjuna, the "king of men" in the *Mahabharata,* seems perfect until Book 6 of the epic, when he loses his will to fight. In this episode, called separately the *Bhagavad-Gita*, the god Krishna has to convince Arjuna to do his duty (see page 128).

Characteristics of an Epic

Epics from different cultures can be very different. The Hindu epics are much more spiritual than the earthy *Epic of Gilgamesh,* for instance. However, most epics share these basic characteristics:

- The epic hero is usually male and holds a high position in society. He may be a king or a prince and is almost always an important historical or legendary figure.
- The hero's actions reflect the values of a culture; the hero's character embodies the culture's ideals.
- The epic setting is vast in scope, often involving the heavens and the underworld.
- The plot may be complicated by supernatural beings or events, and it may involve a dangerous journey.
- The tone of the epic is serious; characters often make long, formal speeches.
- The epic treats universal themes, such as good and evil—and expresses universal values, such as honor and courage.

The Epic Today

The epic is alive and well in the world today. Traditional and newly imagined epics offer writers and filmmakers a ready source of themes, action heroes, and special effects. A television version of the *Ramayana* captivated Indian viewers for 78 weeks in the late 1980s. Western audiences have never tired of the Greek *Odyssey*. Epic conflicts and heroes enliven much science fiction and fantasy, such as *Star Wars* and the *Dune* novels.

In the United States today, perhaps the closest equivalents of epic heroes can be found in the pages of comic books. Superman, Wonder Woman, and the X-Men all have supernatural powers and fight evil to save the world. Perhaps when you were young, you dreamed of being such a hero.

YOUR TURN What have you read or seen lately that contained elements of an epic? Who was the hero?

Strategies for Reading: The Epic

1. Notice which specific character traits help the epic hero to succeed.
2. Decide what values the epic hero reflects.
3. Determine whether these values are still valid today.
4. Keep a list or chart of supernatural events to see how important they are in the epic.
5. Reread passages that appear confusing.
6. Monitor your reading strategies, and modify them when your understanding breaks down. Remember to use the Strategies for Reading: **predict, visualize, connect, question, clarify,** and **evaluate.**

Characteristics of an Epic

Reading Skills and Strategies

SUMMARIZING

First, read through these characteristics aloud. Then have students summarize them. Students might summarize the first characteristic as "high-status hero," for example.

The Epic Today

YOUR TURN Accept any reasonable responses. Encourage students to name specific ways in which the work they name shows the epic characteristics listed on page 121.

LEARNING THE LANGUAGE OF LITERATURE 121

Objectives

- understand and appreciate an **epic (Literary Analysis)**
- analyze methods of **characterization in an epic (Literary Analysis)**
- **recognize contrasts** that help develop characters in an epic **(Active Reading)**

Summary

Drona, a martial arts master, devises a test for the Bharata princes he has been teaching. He places an artificial bird in a treetop and tells them to shoot the bird with an arrow when he finishes talking. One by one, he asks each prince if he can see the bird, the tree, Drona himself, and the other princes. When the princes say they can see everything, Drona scolds them and won't let them shoot. When he questions Arjuna, his best student, Arjuna says that he can see nothing but the bird's head. Drona is pleased, and Arjuna hits the target. Later, Arjuna shows his superiority again by killing a crocodile before the other princes can aim. As a reward, Drona gives Arjuna an invincible weapon.

 Use **Unit One Resource Book**, p. 27, for additional support.

Thematic Link

This excerpt from the sacred *Mahabharata* epic **teaches practical lessons** about excellence and mental focus.

 Use **Unit One Resource Book**, p. 30, for practice with Words to Know.

5-Minute Warm-Up

Daily Language SkillBuilder

Have students **proofread** the display sentences on page 15g and write them correctly.

PREPARING to *Read*

from the Mahabharata

Build Background

The World's Longest Epic The *Mahabharata* (mə-hä-bä'rə-tə) is the longest epic in the world. Composed of 100,000 Sanskrit couplets in 18 books, it is eight times the size of the *Iliad* and the *Odyssey* combined. It was recited by bards for generations before being written down sometime between 400 B.C. and A.D. 400. The author is said to be Vyasa (vyä'sə), a legendary sage who also appears in the story as the grandfather of the main characters.

The translator of the epic, J. A. B. van Buitenen, describes it as an encyclopedia of Brahmin-Indian civilization, containing "history, legend, edification; religion and art; drama and morality." Children in India today are taught the stories from the *Mahabharata,* and both ancient and modern writers have drawn on it for inspiration. The English director Peter Brook has produced Broadway and film versions of the epic for Western audiences.

The *Mahabharata* Story

Clashing Cousins *Mahabharata* means "great epic of the Bharata dynasty." The Bharatas were an ancient ruling family of India; in fact, the official name of the Republic of India is Bharat. The conflict in the story centers on two branches of the Bharata family: the Kauravas ("descendants of Kuru") and the Pandavas ("descendants of Pandu"). These cousins are rivals for a kingdom in north-central India.

The Kauravas are the 100 sons of the blind king Dhrtarastra (drĭ-tə-räsh'trə). They are demons in human form, born from pieces of flesh that were incubated in separate pots. The oldest is Duryodhana, a jealous plotter. The Pandavas are the five sons of Dhrtarastra's brother, Pandu. These sons—Yudhisthira, Bhima, Arjuna, and twins Nakula and Sahadeva—were actually fathered by gods. Yudhisthira, being the oldest of the cousins, is the rightful heir to the kingdom, but Duryodhana arranges to have the Pandavas exiled. He then burns down their house, but they escape.

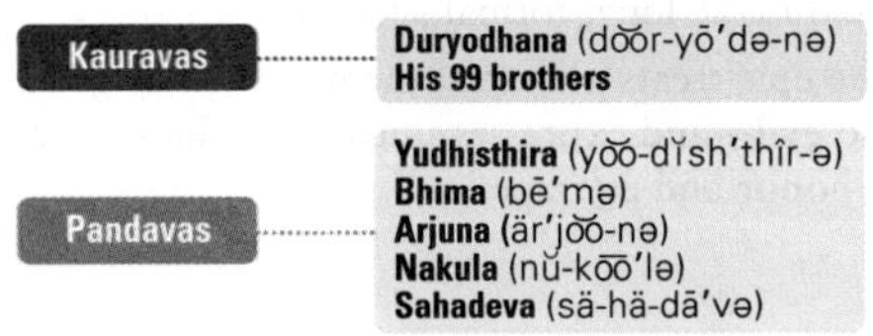

LESSON RESOURCES

UNIT ONE RESOURCE BOOK, pp. 27–31

ASSESSMENT RESOURCES
Formal Assessment, pp. 19–20
Teacher's Guide to Assessment and Portfolio Use
Test Generator

INTEGRATED TECHNOLOGY
Visit our Web site: classzone.com

ADDITIONAL RESOURCES
Lesson Planning Guide, pp. 11–12
Teacher's Sourcebook for Language Development

Connect to Your Life

You will read an excerpt from early in the epic, when the Pandavas and Kauravas (also called Kurus) are boys being raised together. Guided by the great teacher Drona, they are training to be warriors. Recall a time when you were part of a group learning a discipline, such as martial arts, music, or running. Perhaps there was a student who did better than others in the group. What set him or her apart?

Focus Your Reading

LITERARY ANALYSIS: CHARACTERIZATION IN AN EPIC

The word **characterization** refers to the techniques a writer uses to develop characters. In an epic, the hero is usually developed through his superhuman actions, his noble speeches, and the admiring or fearful reactions of other characters. **Epithets,** brief descriptive phrases such as "king of men," also point out a hero's greatness.

ACTIVE READING: SEEING CONTRASTS

Epics celebrate qualities that are admired in a culture. Arjuna's admirable qualities stand out when he is **contrasted** with, or shown as different from, others around him. For example, Arjuna is equally skillful with all weapons, whereas each of the other students excels with only one kind of weapon.

READER'S NOTEBOOK As you read this excerpt, make a list of the personal qualities Arjuna reveals. Also list qualities shown by the other students.

Arjuna	Other Students

WORDS TO KNOW **Vocabulary Preview**

esoteric honed invincible peer unvanquished

While the Pandavas are in exile, the great warrior Arjuna wins the hand of the princess Draupadi (drou'pə-dē) by stringing a bow that no one else can bend and hitting a target. When he gets home and tells his mother that he has won a prize, she tells him to share it with his brothers. Because he cannot disobey, all five brothers share Draupadi as a wife.

A Necessary War The Pandavas eventually return home. For a while, they and the Kauravas split the kingdom and rule different parts, but Duryodhana goads Yudhisthira into wagering his right to the kingdom in a dice game. When Yudhisthira loses, the Pandavas must go into exile again for 13 years. At the end of the 13 years, the Pandavas come back to claim the kingdom, but Duryodhana refuses to give it up. The cousins go to war.

One ally of the Pandavas is their cousin Krishna. Krishna serves as Arjuna's charioteer, but he is also a deity, an incarnation of the supreme god, Vishnu. He has descended to earth to restore *dharma* (law and righteousness). When Arjuna hesitates to fight against his kinsmen, Krishna lectures him on his duty. This moral lecture, the *Bhagavad-Gita*, is the most famous part of the *Mahabharata* (see page 128). After an 18-day battle, almost everyone is killed except the five Pandava brothers, and Yudhisthira is crowned king.

READING FOR INFORMATION

Reading Skills and Strategies

FINDING THE MAIN IDEA

As students read the boxed summary of the *Mahabharata* story, call attention to the two boldfaced subheads. The first is Clashing Cousins. Have students read this section to find out who the clashing cousins are *(the Kauravas and the Pandavas)*. The next subhead is A Necessary War. Have students read to find out why the war is necessary *(it will determine who rules the kingdom; it will restore dharma to earth).*

TIME MANAGEMENT

If your schedule requires that you cover the lesson objectives in a shorter time, use . . .

- Preparing to Read, pp. 122, 123
- Thinking Through the Literature, p. 126
- Vocabulary in Action, p. 127

If you want to take advantage of longer blocks of class time, use . . .

- TE Teaching Options: Vocabulary Strategy, p. 124; Viewing and Representing, p. 125
- Choices & Challenges: Writing Options, Activities & Explorations, Inquiry & Research, p. 127

Active Reading SEEING CONTRASTS

A Ask: How is Arjuna different from the other students? *(He is more expert with all weapons, he is more devoted to his guru.)*

Use **Unit One Resource Book,** p. 28, for more practice.

Reading Skills and Strategies
QUESTIONING

B Ask: Why do you think Drona scolds the students?
Possible Responses: He thinks they are too confident; he thinks they are lying to him; he thinks they should focus their attention.

Literary Analysis
CHARACTERIZATION IN AN EPIC

C Ask students what in this passage reveals to them that Arjuna is a hero.
Possible Responses: Drona's approving reaction to Arjuna; the epithet "bull-like warrior of the Pandavas"; Arjuna's calm, focused demeanor; Arjuna's success in hitting the target.

Use **Unit One Resource Book,** p. 29, for more practice.

Reading Skills and Strategies
DRAWING CONCLUSIONS

D Ask students to conclude what the test was. What made Arjuna succeed and the other students fail?
Possible Responses: Drona was testing the students' ability to focus completely on the target. Arjuna could exclude everything else from his awareness, but the other students were too distracted to hit the target.

from the Mahabharata

Translated by J. A. B. van Buitenen

ARJUNA, THE MIGHTY ARCHER

Of the Kurus who studied with Drona, Duryodhana and Bhima excelled in combat with clubs. Asvatthaman[1] surpassed all in all the esoteric arts. The twins were masters on the sword hilt, beyond all other men. Yudhisthira was the best on chariots. But Arjuna was the
1 best on every weapon. The Pandava, chief of the chiefs of warriors, was renowned on earth as far as the ocean for his insight, application, strength, and enterprise in all weapons. A Both in weaponry and devotion to his guru, the mighty Arjuna was distinguished by his excellence, even though the arms drills were the same for all; among all the princes he was the outstanding warrior. The evil-minded sons of Dhrtarastra could not stand the superior vigor of Bhimasena[2] and the expertness
2 of Arjuna, O king of men.

When all their studies were completed, Drona assembled them all to test their knowledge of weaponry, bull among men. He had craftsmen fashion an artificial bird and attach it to a treetop where it was hardly visible, and proceeded to point out the target to the princes.

Drona said:

Hurry, all of you! Quickly take your bows, put your arrow to the string, and take your position aiming at this bird. As soon as I give the word, shoot off its head. I shall order you one after the other, and you do it, boys!

Vaisampayana[3] *said:*

The great Angirasa[4] first turned to Yudhisthira. "Lay on the arrow, invincible prince," he said, "and as soon as I have ceased talking let go of it!" Yudhisthira then first took his loud-sounding bow and at his guru's command stood aiming at the bird. And while the Kuru prince stood there with his bow tensed, Drona said to him after a while, "Do you see the bird in the treetop, prince?" "I see it," Yudhisthira replied to his teacher. After a while Drona again said to him, "Now can you see the tree or me, or your brothers?" "Yes," he said to each question, "I see the tree, and yourself, and my brothers, as well as the bird." Then Drona said, dissatisfied, "Run off then!" and scolded him: "You won't be able to hit that target." Then the famous teacher questioned Duryodhana and the other sons of Dhrtarastra one after the other in the same way, to put them to the test; and also Bhima and the other pupils and the foreign kings. They all said that they could see everything, and were scolded. B

Thereupon Drona spoke smilingly to Arjuna, "Now you must shoot at the target. Listen. As soon as I give the word you must shoot the arrow. Now first stand there for a little while, son, and keep the bow taut." The left-handed archer C

1. **Asvatthaman** (əsh-və-tä'mən): Drona's son.
2. **Bhimasena** (bē'mə-sā'nə): Bhima.
3. ***Vaisampayana*** (vī'shəm-pä'yə-nə): one of the reciters of the epic. He learned it from his teacher Vyasa, the reputed author.
4. **Angirasa** (än-jĭr'ə-sə): title given to Drona, identifying him as a follower of the great teacher Angiras.

WORDS TO KNOW
esoteric (ĕs'ə-tĕr'ĭk) *adj.* understood by only a certain group
invincible (ĭn-vĭn'sə-bəl) *adj.* unable to be conquered

MINI LESSON Vocabulary Strategy

MULTISYLLABIC WORDS Remind students that a good way to approach unfamiliar word is to break them into their parts. Three important word parts are base words, prefixes, and suffixes. A **base word** is a word that can stand alone. A **prefix** is attached to the beginning of a base word, and a **suffix** is attached to the end of a base word.

Instruction Write the word *unvanquished* on the board. Ask a volunteer to identify the parts of this word. (prefix *un-*, base word *vanquish*, suffix *-ed*) Then explain that if students know the meaning of *vanquish* ("to defeat in battle"), they can figure out what *unvanquished* means. Share these steps with students:

- Strip away the affixes.
- Define the base word.
- Figure out the meanings of the affixes.
- Combine the meanings of the parts to determine the word's meaning.

Practice List the following words on the board and have students determine the meanings by breaking the words into parts.

1. premeditated
2. transcontinental
3. unqualified
4. unforeseen

A lesson on affixes appears on p. 864 of the Pupil's Edition.

Drona at the Well, Bhaktisiddhanta.

stretched the bow until it stood in a circle and kept aiming at the target as his guru had ordered. After a while Drona said to him in the same way, "Do you see this bird sitting there? And the tree? And me?" "I see the bird," Arjuna replied, "but I don't see the tree or you." Satisfied, the unvanquished

C Drona again waited a spell, then said to the bullike warrior of the Pandavas, "If you see the bird, describe it to me." "I see its head, not its body." At Arjuna's words Drona shuddered with pleasure. "Shoot!" he said, and the Partha[5] shot without hesitation, cut off the tree-perching bird's head with the honed blade of his arrow, and made the target tumble to the ground.

When Phalguna[6] had succeeded in the task,

D Drona embraced him and deemed Drupada and his party laid low in battle.[7]

A few days later the great Angirasa went with his pupils to the Ganges[8] to bathe, O bull among Bharatas. When Drona had plunged into the water, a powerful crocodile that lived in the river grabbed him by the shin, prompted by Time. Although he was quite able to save himself, he ordered his pupils, "Kill this crocodile and save me!" hurrying them on. He had not finished speaking before the Terrifier[9] with a burst of five arrows killed the crocodile under the water, while the others were still coming from everywhere in great confusion. And upon seeing the Pandava make such quick work of his task, Drona deemed him the best of all his students and was mightily pleased. The crocodile, cut to many pieces by the Partha's arrows, let go of the shin of the great-spirited Drona and returned to the five elements. Drona Bharadvaja then said to the great-spirited warrior, "Receive from me, strong-armed Arjuna, this outstanding invincible weapon that is named Brahma-Head, along with the instructions of how to release and return it. It should never be used against human beings, for if it is unleashed on one of little luster, it might burn up the world. This weapon, son, is said to be without its match in all three worlds.[10] Therefore you must hold it carefully; and listen to my word: should ever a superhuman foe oppress you, hero, use this weapon to kill him in battle."

The Terrifier gave his promise with folded hands and took that ultimate weapon. And the guru again said to him, "No man in the world shall be your peer as an archer!" ❖

5. **the Partha** (pär′tə): Arjuna. This title designates him as a son of Prtha-Kunti.
6. **Phalguna** (pəl-go͞o′nə): Arjuna.
7. **deemed Drupada** (dro͞o′pə-də) **. . . laid low in battle:** Drona agreed to teach the princes only if they would later attack King Drupada, Drona's former friend, who had snubbed him.
8. **Ganges** (găn′jēz′): a river in India, sacred to Hindus.
9. **the Terrifier:** title given to Arjuna.
10. **all three worlds:** the earth, the atmosphere, and the sky.

WORDS TO KNOW

unvanquished (ŭn′văng′kwĭsht) *adj.* undefeated
honed (hōnd) *adj.* finely sharpened **hone** *v.*
peer (pîr) *n.* equal

Customizing Instruction

Less Proficient Readers

Encourage students to look again at the chart on page 122 so that they know who the characters are.

1 Tell students that the same characters may be called by different names that indicate their ancestry or personal qualities. Arjuna is also called "the Pandava," "the Partha," "Phalguna," and "the Terrifier." Drona is also called "the great Angirasa."

 Use **Unit One Resource Book,** p. 27, for additional support.

English Learners

2 Call attention to epithets, such as "king of men," and "the left-handed archer," and make sure students know whom they describe. Point out that such epithets are not commonly used in modern literature. For fun, encourage students to come up with epithets that describe themselves.

Advanced Learners

Ask students if they think Drona's tests were good ones. After some discussion, invite students to name other tests passed by heroes in literature or film. Have them speculate about why heroes must undergo such tests.

Possible Responses: The tests distinguish the hero from all others; they prepare the hero for more crucial challenges later.

MINI LESSON Viewing and Representing

Drona at the Well by Bhaktisiddanta

ART APPRECIATION Bhaktisiddanta, an award-winning artist, was born Alfred J. Valerio in Corning, New York. He moved to Vrindavan, India, in 1977 after meeting his spiritual master, A. C. Bhaktivedanta Swami Prabhupada. The drawing *Drona at the Well* is a study for one of a series of high-relief panels depicting scenes from the *Mahabharata*. These panels are on permanent display in New Delhi.

In this scene, the young princes watch as Drona retrieves a ring he has dropped down the well. Reciting a special mantra, he shoots an arrow down the well, which returns with the ring on its end. After this feat, Drona is hired as the princes' teacher.

Ask: What traits do you see in Drona, based upon this drawing? How do the princes seem to be reacting to him?

Possible Responses: Students may see strength, serenity, or sternness in Drona. They may see fear and awe in the princes, except the one at front left (Duryodhana?), who seems insolent.

Connect to the Literature

1. **What Do You Think?** Answers will vary. Students should give reasons for their positive or negative opinion of Arjuna.

Comprehension Check

- He tests their skills by asking them to shoot a bird from a treetop.
- He is the only one who is focused on the bird's head and nothing else, and he kills a crocodile before the other students can even get ready.
- He gives Arjuna an invincible weapon, Brahma-Head.

Use Selection Quiz in **Unit One Resource Book,** p. 31.

Think Critically

2. Possible Responses: He is more skilled in all weapons; he is more devoted to his teacher; he is more focused on his target; and he can shoot more quickly.
3. Possible Responses: skill and versatility in weaponry; focus and patience; devotion to a master
4. Possible Responses: Students may admire Drona for testing his students so cleverly, or they may criticize him for so obviously favoring Arjuna or for not telling the students what he wants of them.
5. Possible Responses: Parents may tell this story to their children to encourage them to focus on a goal and not be distracted or to show them that excellence will be rewarded.

Extend Interpretations

6. **Comparing Texts** Drona may remind students of Obi-Wan Kenobi or Yoda from *Star Wars*, Mr. Miyagi from *The Karate Kid,* or other teacher figures.
7. **Connect to Life** Answers will vary. Students should be able to support their answers with an example from their own experiences.

Connect to the Literature

1. **What Do You Think?** What was your reaction to Arjuna?

Comprehension Check
- How does Drona test his students' skills in archery?
- How does Arjuna show that he is the best student?
- How does Drona reward Arjuna?

Think Critically

2. **ACTIVE READING: SEEING CONTRASTS** Review the two lists you made in your READER'S NOTEBOOK. In what ways is Arjuna different from the rest of the students?
3. Judging from your list of Arjuna's qualities, which traits do you think were admired in ancient India?
4. What is your opinion of Drona as a teacher?

- how he responds to Arjuna
- why he scolds the other students
- why he does not save himself from the crocodile

5. Why do you think Indian parents still tell this story to their children? What lessons does it contain?

Extend Interpretations

6. **Comparing Texts** Does Drona remind you of any other figure from literature, films, or comics? Explain.
7. **Connect to Life** Think about any lesson you found in the story. Based on your own experiences, do you think this lesson is true?

LITERARY ANALYSIS: CHARACTERIZATION IN AN EPIC

The word **characterization** refers to the techniques that a writer uses to develop a character. A writer may
- describe a character's physical appearance
- present the character's actions, words, thoughts, or feelings
- present other characters' reactions to the character
- make direct comments about the character

Epithets are a form of direct commentary often used in epics. They are brief descriptive phrases, such as "bull among men," that suggest a character's qualities.

Activity What alerts you that Arjuna is a hero? Go back through the selection and identify techniques used to characterize Arjuna.

Physical Description	Character's Actions/Words/Thoughts
Other Characters' Reactions	**Narrator's Direct Comments/Epithets**

Literary Analysis

Activity You might reproduce the chart on the board and write in evidence from each category as students identify it.

Use **Unit One Resource Book,** p. 29, for more practice.

Writing Options

1. Dramatic Monologue
Imagine that you are Duryodhana, the jealous cousin of Arjuna. How might you feel about Drona's archery tests? Write a monologue in which you express your feelings to your Kaurava brothers after the tests.

2. Remembering a Teacher
Recall the best teacher you ever had, in any subject. Think about his or her methods of getting you to excel. Was this teacher like or unlike Drona? Present your ideas in a brief reflective essay. Then place the essay in your **Working Portfolio.**

Writing Handbook
See page R31: Explanatory Writing.

3. Paragraph on Excellence
For the Connect to Your Life activity on page 123, you recalled a student who excelled in a particular discipline. What would you say is the most important quality needed to succeed in this discipline? Share your thoughts in a paragraph.

Activities & Explorations

1. Dramatic Reading Give a dramatic reading of this selection for younger students. You will need readers to take the parts of the narrator and the characters. Decide how much action you will show and whether you will use props or costumes. Simplify the text so that it can be easily spoken. Also present enough background for children to understand the story.
~ **PERFORMING**

2. Cover Illustration Imagine that this selection is being published as a children's book. Create an illustration that could be used on the cover. You might look at examples of Indian art for an appropriate style. ~ **ART**

Inquiry & Research

More *Mahabharata* Look in the library or on the Internet for other famous episodes from the *Mahabharata,* such as the stories of Shakuntala, Nala, and Savitri. Read these stories to the class.

Vocabulary in Action

EXERCISE: SYNONYMS AND ANTONYMS For each pair of words, write *S* if the words are synonyms or *A* if they are antonyms.

1. unvanquished–subdued
2. esoteric–secret
3. honed–dull
4. invincible–unbeatable
5. peer–superior

Building Vocabulary
Some of the Words to Know contain affixes. For an in-depth lesson on affixes, see page 864.

Writing Options

1. **Dramatic Monologue** Call attention to the line "The evil-minded sons of Dhrtarastra could not stand the superior vigor of Bhimasena and the expertness of Arjuna . . . ." Encourage students to recall feelings of jealousy they may have had toward a sibling or favored student.
2. **Remembering a Teacher** Tell students to make a comparison-contrast chart.
3. **Paragraph on Excellence** If students answered the Connect to Today question in writing, they can use their notes, or if they answered aloud, they can jot down qualities they mentioned. Then they can evaluate these qualities to see if one seems most important to success.

Activities & Explorations

1. **Dramatic Reading** Divide the class into several groups. One might be responsible for writing an introduction from information on the prereading pages. Another might turn the story into a script, pulling out lines of dialogue and simplifying narration. A third group might be the actual perfomers, and a fourth might be responsible for props and other aspects of staging.
2. **Cover Illustration** For ideas, students might look at the art from the *Ramayana* on following pages. There also may be children's books of Indian literature in the school or public library.

Inquiry & Research

One recent children's book is *Savitri: A Tale of Ancient India* by Aaron Shepard.

To assess skills and concepts taught in this selection, use **Formal Assessment Book,** p. 19–20.

Vocabulary in Action

1. A
2. S
3. A
4. S
5. A

The only religious scripture translated more often than the *Bhagavad-Gita* is the Bible. It is sacred to Hindus but also admired by others. Commentators believe it is so popular because it deals with universal questions—What is the right thing to do? How can one know God?—and offers comfort to those who are confused.

Additional Background

Most scholars believe the *Bhagavad-Gita* was originally a separate religious work, like the *Upanishads*, that was later placed into the *Mahabharata* epic. It contains ideas introduced in the *Upanishads* but presented in a simpler, more memorable way.

Perhaps the most important idea in the *Gita* is that of detached or desireless action as a path to salvation. The work also proposes personal devotion to God as another path to salvation. In the eleventh chapter, Krishna reveals himself to Arjuna as God. He appears in the most terrifying, infinite form, as the creator and destroyer of the universe. He tells Arjuna that all who rely on him and dedicate their actions to him will "reach the highest way." This doctrine of *bhakti yoga*, or "the discipline of devotion," has been embraced by Hindus ever since.

The *Bhagavad-Gita* has intrigued the West since the first European translations appeared in the 18th century. Henry David Thoreau took the book with him to Walden Pond and wrote that in comparison with it, "our modern world and its literature seem puny and trivial." The *Gita* influenced the transcendentalist philosophy of Thoreau and his friend Ralph Waldo Emerson, which held that there are higher truths than those recognized by society.

New English translations and commentaries on the *Gita* appear year after year. The popular film *The Legend of Bagger Vance* (2000), recast the work in an American setting, making its main figures a golf pro and his caddy.

Milestones in World Literature

Bhagavad-Gita

The *Bhagavad-Gita* (bŭ′gə-vəd-gē′tä)—literally, "song of the Lord"—is the most beloved and most widely translated religious work in India. Consisting of an 18-chapter episode in the *Mahabharata,* it begins on the eve of battle as the warrior-prince Arjuna sees his uncles, cousins, friends, and teachers lined up on the field against him. Overcome with grief, Arjuna suddenly refuses to fight. Mentioning his great-uncle and his teacher by name, he cries out in despair:

Krishna, how can I fight
against Bhishma and Drona
with arrows
when they deserve my worship?

It is better in this world
to beg for scraps of food
than to eat meals
smeared with the blood
of elders I killed.

Below: *Arjuna is led into battle by his charioteer, the god Krishna.*

Over the next 700 verses, the god Krishna explains to Arjuna the universal truth about existence and teaches him how to understand and act on that truth. Through a series of questions and answers, the *Gita* defines the basic ideas of Hindu philosophy.

One of these ideas is that of *dharma,* or sacred duty. Each of the four social classes—priests, warriors, tradespeople, and servants—has specific duties, which must be upheld to maintain the social and cosmic order. As a warrior, Arjuna has a sacred duty to fight—and to kill if necessary.

Another concept central to Hindu belief is that of reincarnation, or rebirth in another form. The cycle of death and rebirth depends on a person's actions, or *karma,* in each life. For example, by committing a crime, a person would generate negative karma that he or she would have to work through in the next life—say, by becoming the victim of another's crime. But as Arjuna's dilemma shows, following *dharma* (his duty as a soldier) can create negative *karma* (killing members of his own family). "Conflicting sacred duties confound my reason," Arjuna laments in the *Gita.* It also seems that one can never escape the cycle of death and rebirth or the suffering it involves.

But Krishna gives answers to Arjuna's dilemma. First, he reminds Arjuna that although the body dies, the spirit lives on eternally:

> **Our bodies are known to end,**
> **but the embodied self is enduring,**
> **indestructible, and immeasurable;**
> **therefore, Arjuna, fight the battle!**

Krishna then offers two ways to achieve *moksha,* or union with God and release from the cycle of reincarnation. The first way is to do one's duty without feeling attached to the results—to act without desire, in other words. For Arjuna, this means fighting the battle but taking no personal responsibility for its success or failure. Whatever happens will be God's will.

The other path to enlightenment is through meditation. Krishna tells Arjuna that by disciplining the mind to withdraw completely from the senses and fix itself on a single point, one can realize union with God. But even for the truly devout, this supreme goal may require many births to attain. Fortunately, there is the *Bhagavad-Gita* to show the way.

National Portrait Gallery, Smithsonian Institution, Washington, D.C.

The Bhagavad-Gita *influenced the 19th-century American writer Henry David Thoreau.*

Literary Chronology

c. 100 B.C.–A.D. 100 The *Bhagavad-Gita* is added to the *Mahabharata.*

c. A.D. 700s Sankara writes a famous commentary on the *Bhagavad-Gita.*

1785 Charles Wilkins publishes the first English translation of the *Gita.*

1845 Ralph Waldo Emerson and Henry David Thoreau read and praise the *Gita.*

1926 Mohandas Gandhi lectures on the *Gita,* which he has used to develop his concept of *satyagraha,* or nonviolent resistance.

1945 Viewing the first atomic bomb explosion, physicist J. Robert Oppenheimer quotes Krishna's words from the *Gita*: "I am become Death, shatterer of worlds."

1972 Hare Krishna founder A. C. Bhaktivedanta Swami Prabhupada publishes the *Bhagavad-Gita As It Is* for his followers.

1980 Philip Glass composes an opera, *Satyagraha,* whose libretto is Sanskrit excerpts from the *Gita.*

1986 Barbara Stoler Miller translates the *Gita.*

1995 Stephen Pressfield's novel, *The Legend of Bagger Vance* (later a movie), applies the *Gita* to the game of golf.

1999 An interactive CD-ROM version of the *Bhagavad-Gita* is produced.

2000 Stephen Mitchell publishes *The Bhagavad-Gita: A New Translation.*

2001 Jack Hawley publishes *The Bhagavad-Gita: A Walk-through for Westerners.*

This selection is included in the **World Literature InterActive Reader™.**

Objectives

- understand and appreciate an ancient **epic (Literary Analysis)**
- analyze **conflict in an epic (Literary Analysis)**
- improve comprehension by **classifying characters (Active Reading)**

Summary

Rama is waging a fierce battle against the ten-headed demon Ravana because Ravana has abducted Sita, Rama's wife. The gods send Rama a special chariot, and the battle takes to the sky. When Ravana is unable to destroy Rama with arrows and trickery, he unsuccessfully tries to enlist supernatural forces. Rama then cuts off Ravana's heads, but they all grow back. At last Rama kills Ravana with a special weapon, the Brahmasthra, aimed at his heart. As the demon lies dead, Rama praises what Ravana might have been, had he not been evil.

Use **Unit One Resource Book,** p. 32, for additional support.

Thematic Link

The epic *Ramayana* contains **spiritual teachings** about the nature of heroism, the powerful forces at work in the universe, and the results of true devotion to the gods.

Use **Unit One Resource Book,** p. 35, for practice with Words to Know.

5-Minute Warm-Up

Daily Language SkillBuilder

Have students **proofread** the display sentences on page 15g and write them correctly.

PREPARING to *Read*

FROM THE

RAMAYANA

Valmiki
c. 400 B.C.?

Wise Man of the Forest

The *Ramayana* (rä-mä'yə-nə), or "the journey of Rama," is India's second great epic and may be even more popular than the *Mahabharata.* Most of what is known about its author, Valmiki (väl-mē'kē), comes from the epic itself, for Valmiki is a character in the story.

According to the prologue, Valmiki was a wise man who lived deep in the forest. One day Narada, messenger to the gods, visited him and told him the story of Rama, the ideal man. Although very moved, Valmiki didn't feel capable of writing an epic worthy of so great a hero.

Inspired by Nature Later, as he was walking by the river, Valmiki spotted a pair of herons nesting in a tree. Suddenly, a hunter shot the male heron with an arrow. Valmiki was so affected by the female's grief for her mate that he cursed the hunter for causing such misery. He uttered this curse in a rhymed verse form that had never been heard before. He called it a *sloka* (shlō'kə), after *soka,* the Sanskrit word for grief. Valmiki realized that the *sloka* was the perfect medium to convey the story of Rama and his sorrowful separation from his wife, Sita.

India's First Poet The classical poets who came after Valmiki hailed him as the first true poet of India and praised his artistry. Later poets such as Kamban and Tulsidas used Valmiki's *Ramayana* as the basis of their own versions in the popular languages of India. The epic lives on in folksongs and dramatic performances, even in non-Hindu countries such as Thailand and Indonesia. As R. K. Narayan says in the introduction to his English translation, "Everyone knows the story but loves to listen to it again."

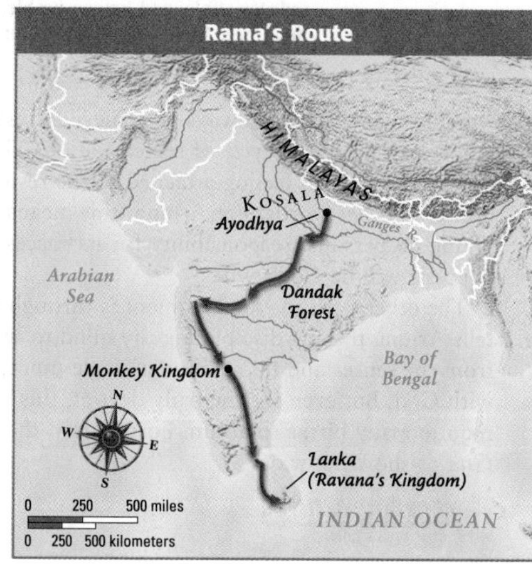

Above: Detail of illustration, Valmiki teaches the *Ramayana* in Dendaka Forest. Copyright © The British Museum, London.

LESSON RESOURCES

UNIT ONE RESOURCE BOOK, pp. 32–36

ASSESSMENT RESOURCES
Formal Assessment, pp. 21–22
Teacher's Guide to Assessment and Portfolio Use
Test Generator

INTEGRATED TECHNOLOGY
Visit our Web site: classzone.com

ADDITIONAL RESOURCES
Lesson Planning Guide, pp. 13–14
Teacher's Sourcebook for Language Development

Build Background

The Story of Rama

Hero in Exile Rama is the son of King Dasaratha (dä-shä-rä'tə), the ruler of Kosala. Exceptionally strong and brave, he wins the hand of the princess Sita by bending and stringing a bow that no other man could lift. King Dasaratha intends that Rama shall be his heir. However, the king's second wife—whom he had earlier promised to grant any two wishes—demands that her own son, Bharata, be given the throne and that Rama be exiled to the forest for 14 years. The king cannot break his promise, so Rama must leave. Sita and Lakshmana (lŭk'shmə-nə), Rama's loyal brother, go with him.

In the forest, Rama and Lakshmana kill demons who have been harassing holy men. Lakshmana cuts off the ears and nose of a female demon whose brother, Ravana (rä'və-nə), rules the island of Lanka. Ravana is immensely powerful, with 10 heads and 20 arms. He kidnaps Sita in revenge.

Monkeys Versus Demons Searching all of India for Sita, Rama makes an alliance with Sugreeva, the king of the monkeys. Hanuman, the monkey general, proves to be a particularly loyal and valuable ally. He leaps to the island of Lanka and finds the captive Sita. He watches as Ravana begs her to become his wife, whereupon Sita protests that she will have no other man but Rama. When they are alone, Hanuman offers to carry Sita back to Rama, but she refuses to be touched by any male but her husband. Hanuman returns to Rama, and they prepare to wage war on Ravana. The monkeys build a bridge across the sea to Lanka, and the battle begins.

Guide for Living In India, the *Ramayana* is not just an entertaining story, but a guide for living. Rama is viewed as the ideal man and ruler. He is worshiped as an incarnation of the god Vishnu. The devoted Sita is seen as the ideal wife; millions of Indian women are urged to be like her.

For a humanities activity, click on:

Connect to Your Life

Recall a grand battle between good and evil, perhaps presented in a movie, TV show, comic book or novel. Who was the hero and who was the villain? What was at stake? What powers or weapons were used? Who won? Make some notes for later comparison.

Focus Your Reading

LITERARY ANALYSIS: CONFLICT IN AN EPIC

A **conflict** is the struggle between opposing forces that moves a plot forward. In an epic, conflict is on a grand scale—supreme good versus monstrous evil, life versus death for thousands. In epic battles, the hero and his opponent often use supernatural powers and are aided by the gods. Look for such elements in the battle between Rama and Ravana.

ACTIVE READING: CLASSIFYING CHARACTERS

There are many characters in this battle, and their names are probably unfamiliar. It may help you to **classify,** or sort, these characters as allies of either Rama or Ravana. Vibishana, for example, is Ravana's brother, but he is on Rama's side.

READER'S NOTEBOOK As you read, put the characters in two groups according to their loyalty, either to Rama or to Ravana. Beside each name, write down something that will help you remember the character—such as a description of a physical or personality trait—and note the character's role in the battle.

WORDS TO KNOW **Vocabulary Preview**

benediction, dejectedly, formidable, impervious, incarnation, ineffectually, intermittently, parrying, primordial, pristine

READING FOR INFORMATION

Reading Skills and Strategies

RECOGNIZING CAUSE AND EFFECT

Before reading an excerpt of a literary work, it is helpful to know what caused the situation at the beginning of the excerpt. After students read the boxed summary, **The Story of Rama,** ask: Why is Rama waging war on Ravana? *(because Ravana has kidnapped Rama's wife, Sita)*

Using the Map

Have students study the map of Rama's route on page 130. Ask: Where does Rama start? *(Ayodhya)* How far does he go? *(to Lanka, Ravana's kingdom)*

TIME MANAGEMENT

If your schedule requires that you cover the lesson objectives in a shorter time, use . . .

- Preparing to Read, pp. 130, 131
- Thinking Through the Literature, p. 143
- Vocabulary in Action, p. 144

If you want to take advantage of longer class time, use . . .

- TE Teaching Options: Vocabulary Strategy, p. 132; Viewing and Representing, pp. 133, 137, 142; Speaking and Listening, p. 135; Grammar, p. 138; Cross-Curricular Link, p. 139; Informal Assessment, p. 140
- Choices & Challenges, p. 144
- Connect to Today, p. 145

Reading and Analyzing

Literary Analysis CONFLICT IN AN EPIC

Have students notice the scale of Rama and Ravana's conflict. It involves whole armies, their wives, courtiers, an entire city. Ask: What attitude does Ravana have toward Rama? *(rage mixed with admiration)*

 Use **Unit One Resource Book,** p. 34, for additional support.

from the Ramayana

Retold by R. K. Narayan

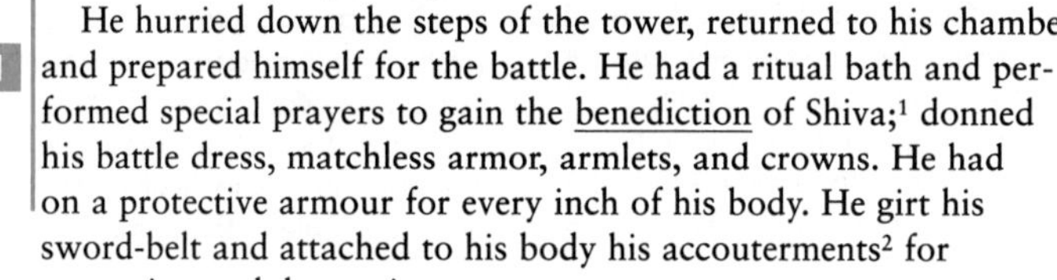

RAMA AND RAVANA IN BATTLE

Every moment, news came to Ravana of fresh disasters in his camp. One by one, most of his commanders were lost. No one who went forth with battle cries was heard of again. Cries and shouts and the wailings of the widows of warriors came over the chants and songs of triumph that his courtiers arranged to keep up at a loud pitch in his assembly hall. Ravana became restless and abruptly left the hall and went up on a tower, from which he could obtain a full view of the city. He surveyed the scene below but could not stand it. One who had spent a lifetime in destruction, now found the gory spectacle intolerable. Groans and wailings reached his ears with deadly clarity; and he noticed how the monkey hordes reveled in their bloody handiwork. This was too much for him. He felt a terrific rage rising within him, mixed with some admiration for Rama's valour. He told himself, "The time has come for me to act by myself again."

1 He hurried down the steps of the tower, returned to his chamber, and prepared himself for the battle. He had a ritual bath and performed special prayers to gain the benediction of Shiva;[1] donned his battle dress, matchless armor, armlets, and crowns. He had on a protective armour for every inch of his body. He girt his sword-belt and attached to his body his accouterments[2] for protection and decoration.

1. **Shiva** (shē′və): an important Hindu god.
2. **accouterments** (ə-kōō′tər-mənts): military equipment other than uniforms and weapons.

WORDS TO KNOW
benediction (bĕn′ĭ-dĭk′shən) *n.* blessing

MINI LESSON Vocabulary Strategy

ROOT WORDS Remind students that analyzing word parts is a good way to get an idea of a word's meaning. Word parts include **roots,** which are word parts that cannot stand alone; and **affixes** (prefixes and suffixes).

Instruction Display the following chart of common roots and their meanings:

Root	Meaning
bene	good, well
dic, dict	speak, say, tell
ject	throw, cast
mit	send, let go
carn	flesh

Explain that students can use word roots and their own knowledge of prefixes and suffixes to determine the meaning of difficult words. Write the word *dejectedly* on the board and ask a volunteer to find the root and its meaning in the chart. (*ject*: throw, hurl). Then ask volunteers to identify and give the meanings of the prefix (*de*: down) and the suffix (*ly*: in a way that is). Help students use the meaning of the word parts to figure out that *dejectedly* means "in a way that is cast down" or "in a low-spirited way."

Practice Have students use the chart above and their knowledge of affixes to write the meaning of each word below.

1. incarnate
2. benediction
3. intermittently

A lesson on Greek and Latin roots appears on p. 340 of the Pupil's Edition.

Rama fights Ravana. Courtesy of the Trustees of the Victoria & Albert Museum, London.

HUMANITIES CONNECTION Rama has dark blue skin because he is a form of the god Vishnu. Vishnu's blue skin represents endlessness or infinity.

Customizing Instruction

Less Proficient Readers

Point out that the hero, Rama, and his opponent, Ravana, have similar names. Students should take care to distinguish whose thoughts and actions are being described from paragraph to paragraph.

The first three paragraphs describe the battle from the viewpoint of the "bad guy," Ravana. After students read the first paragraph, ask: Who seems to be winning at this point? *(Rama)*

English Learners

1 Explain the meaning of *valour* (courage) and *armour* (protective clothing). Note their British spellings (kept at the original publisher's request). In American English, these words would normally be spelled *valor* and *armor*.

MINI LESSON Viewing and Representing

Rama fights Ravana

ART APPRECIATION Have students examine the painting and the **Humanities Connection** on page 132. Explain that Rama is an incarnation of Vishnu created expressly to kill the demon Ravana. Ravana had gained great powers from the gods through his worshipful activities but then terrorized the gods, even threatening to overthrow Indra. Brahma, the creator of the universe, had granted Ravana immunity from attack by gods, but Ravana had never asked for protection from human beings. Therefore, he could be killed only by a human. The frightened gods asked Vishnu, the preserver of the universe, to take human form. Vishnu descended to earth as Rama.

Ask students: What characters can you identify in the painting?

Possible Responses: Ravana, Rama, Lakshmana, Hanuman, the monkey army, the demon army, ladies of Ravana's court

Reading and Analyzing

Literary Analysis CONFLICT IN AN EPIC

A Call attention to this passage and ask students to restate Ravana's resolve in their own words.

Possible Response: He will either kill Rama or die trying.

Active Reading CLASSIFYING CHARACTERS

B Here many unfamiliar characters are introduced—all supporters of Rama. Encourage students to look for information in the text and footnotes that explains who these characters are.

Use **Unit One Resource Book,** p. 33, for additional support.

Literary Analysis CONFLICT IN AN EPIC

C Often in epics, the whole universe seems involved in the conflict. Frequently there are omens—signs from the natural world that hint at events to come. Ask: What do you think these ominous signs mean?

Possible Responses: that Ravana will lose; that the forces of the universe are against Ravana

Literary Analysis CHARACTERIZATION

D Ask why Rama destroys Ravana's armies. *(He hopes that Ravana will give up and that he can avoid killing Ravana.)* Discuss what Rama's motivation reveals about his character.

Possible Responses: Rama's desire to spare Ravana suggests that he is not vengeful and that he has respect and compassion for Ravana.

When he emerged from his chamber, his heroic appearance was breathtaking. He summoned his chariot, which could be drawn by horses or move on its own if the horses were hurt or killed. People stood aside when he came out of the palace and entered his chariot. "This is my resolve," he said to himself: "Either that woman Sita,[3] or my wife Mandodari,[4] will soon have cause to cry and roll in the dust in grief. Surely, before this day is done, one of them will be a widow." A

1 The gods in heaven noticed Ravana's determined move and felt that Rama would need all the support they could muster. They requested Indra[5] to send down his special chariot for Rama's use. When the chariot appeared at his camp, Rama was deeply impressed with the magnitude and brilliance of the vehicle. "How has this come to be here?" he asked.

"Sir," the charioteer answered, "my name is Matali.[6] I have the honor of being the charioteer of Indra. Brahma, the four-faced god and the creator of the Universe, and Shiva, whose power has emboldened Ravana now to challenge you, have commanded me to bring it here for your use. It can fly swifter than air over all obstacles, over any mountain, sea, or sky, and will help you to emerge victorious in this battle." B

Rama reflected aloud, "It may be that the rakshasas[7] have created this illusion for me. It may be a trap. I don't know how to view it." Whereupon Matali spoke convincingly to dispel the doubt in Rama's mind. Rama, still hesitant, though partially convinced, looked at Hanuman[8] and Lakshmana[9] and asked, "What do you think of it?" Both answered, "We feel no doubt that this chariot is Indra's; it is not an illusory creation."

Rama fastened his sword, slung two quivers full of rare arrows over his shoulders, and climbed into the chariot.

The beat of war drums, the challenging cries of soldiers, the trumpets, and the rolling chariots speeding along to confront each other, created a deafening mixture of noise. While Ravana had instructed his charioteer to speed ahead, Rama very gently ordered his chariot-driver, "Ravana is in a rage; let him perform all the antics he desires and exhaust himself. Until then be calm; we don't have to hurry forward. Move slowly and calmly, and you must strictly follow my instructions; I will tell you when to drive faster."

Ravana's assistant and one of his staunchest supporters, Mahodara[10]—the giant among giants in his physical appearance—begged Ravana, "Let me not be a mere spectator when you confront Rama. Let me have the honour of grappling with him. Permit me to attack Rama."

"Rama is my sole concern," Ravana replied. "If you wish to engage yourself in a fight, you may fight his brother Lakshmana."

Noticing Mahodara's purpose, Rama steered his chariot across his path in order to prevent Mahodara from reaching Lakshmana. Whereupon Mahodara ordered his chariot-driver, "Now dash straight ahead, directly into Rama's chariot."

The charioteer, more practical-minded, advised him, "I would not go near Rama. Let us keep away." But Mahodara, obstinate and intoxicated with war fever, made straight for Rama. He wanted to have the honour of a direct encounter with Rama himself in spite of Ravana's advice; and for this honour he paid a heavy price, as it was a moment's work for Rama to destroy him, and leave him lifeless and shapeless on the field. Noticing this, Ravana's anger mounted further. He commanded his driver, "You will not slacken now. Go." Many ominous signs were seen C

3. **Sita** (sē′tä): Rama's wife.
4. **Mandodari** (mən-dō′də-rē).
5. **Indra** (ĭn′drə): a warrior god, the lord of rain and thunder.
6. **Matali** (mä′tə-lē).
7. **rakshasas** (räk′shə-səz): demons.
8. **Hanuman** (hŭn′ŏŏ-mən): a monkey ally of Rama's.
9. **Lakshmana** (lŭk′shmə-nə): Rama's brother.
10. **Mahodara** (mə-hō′də-rə).

MINI LESSON Grammar

PREPOSITIONS

Instruction A **preposition** shows how one word is related to another word. Display these examples: *on, under, before, after, about, by.* Ask volunteers to write sentences using these prepositions. Next, display these sentences, underlining the prepositions: *The radio is on the red table. The movie was about a long journey.* Explain that a preposition is the first word in a **prepositional phrase.**

A prepositional phrase consists of a preposition, its object, and any modifiers of the object. Underline the prepositional phrase in the first sentence above and identify the object *(table)* and the modifier *(red)*. Then ask a volunteer to follow the same procedure with the second sentence.

Practice Write the prepositional phrases in these sentences. Circle the prepositions. There may be more than one prepositional phrase in a sentence.

1. The battle took place in the great sky and on the earth.
2. Ravana shot his arrows at mighty Rama.
3. Ravana's supernatural weapons flew at Rama but did not hit him.
4. From a great distance, the gods watched the battle.

For more instruction and practice in prepositions, use McDougal Littell's ***Language Network:***

- Grade 10, Chapter 1, "Prepositions"
- Grade 12, Review, "Prepositions"

Customizing Instruction

Less Proficient Readers

1 Point out that in the second paragraph, the scene shifts and the focus is now on Rama. Ask: Why do the gods give Rama a special chariot?
Possible Responses: They want Rama to defeat Ravana; they want the fighters to be more evenly matched.

English Learners

2 Call attention to the elevated language of this passage, which helps suggest the importance of the battle. Explain *of its own accord* (by itself), *agitating* (shaking), *commencement* (start), and *averted* (turned away).

Advanced Learners

3 Tell students it is understood that Rama is the hero of the *Ramayana*. Ask them to speculate about why the writer gives so much emphasis to Ravana's thoughts and feelings.
Possible Responses: to increase the tension of the story; to show that Ravana is a worthy adversary

C now—his bow-strings suddenly snapped; the mountains shook; thunders rumbled in the skies; tears flowed from the horses' eyes; elephants with decorated foreheads moved along dejectedly. Ravana, noticing them, hesitated only for a second, saying, "I don't care. This mere mortal Rama is of no account, and these omens do not concern me at all." Meanwhile, Rama paused for a moment to consider his next step; and suddenly turned towards the armies supporting Ravana, which stretched away to the horizon, and destroyed them. D He felt that this might be one way of saving Ravana. With his armies gone, it was possible that Ravana might have a change of heart. But it had only the effect of spurring Ravana on; he plunged forward and kept coming nearer Rama and his own doom.

When he emerged from his chamber, his heroic appearance was breathtaking. He summoned his chariot, which could be drawn by horses or move on its own if the horses were hurt or killed.

2 Rama's army cleared and made way for Ravana's chariot, unable to stand the force of his approach. Ravana blew his conch[11] and its shrill challenge reverberated through space. Following it another conch, called "Panchajanya,"[12] which belonged to Mahavishnu[13] (Rama's original form before his present incarnation), sounded of its own accord in answer to the challenge, agitating the universe with its vibrations. And then Matali picked up another conch, which was Indra's, and blew it. This was the signal indicating the commencement of the actual battle. Presently Ravana sent a shower of arrows on Rama; and Rama's followers, unable to bear the sight of his body being studded with arrows, averted their heads. Then the chariot horses of Ravana and Rama glared at each other in hostility, and the flags topping the chariots—Ravana's ensign of the Veena[14] and Rama's with the whole universe on it—clashed, and one heard the stringing and twanging of bow-strings on both sides, overpowering in volume all other sound. Then followed a shower of arrows from Rama's own bow. Ravana stood gazing at the chariot sent by Indra and swore, "These gods, instead of supporting me, have gone to the support of this petty human being. I will teach them a lesson. He is not fit to be killed with my arrows but I shall seize him and his chariot together and fling them into high heaven and dash them to destruction." 3 Despite his oath, he still strung his bow and sent a shower of arrows at Rama, raining in thousands, but they were all invariably shattered and neutralized by the arrows from Rama's bow, which met arrow for arrow. Ultimately Ravana, instead of using one bow, used ten with his twenty arms, multiplying his attack tenfold; but Rama stood unhurt.

Ravana suddenly realized that he should change his tactics and ordered his charioteer to fly the chariot up in the skies. From there he attacked and destroyed a great many of the

11. **conch** (kŏngk): a large spiral seashell, sometimes used as a trumpet.
12. **Panchajanya** (pän′chə-jŭn′yə).
13. **Mahavishnu** (mə-hä′vĭsh′no͞o): Hinduism's supreme god, who divides himself into the trinity of Brahma, Vishnu, and Shiva.
14. **ensign of the Veena** (vē′nə): a flag depicting a stringed musical instrument.

WORDS TO KNOW
dejectedly (dĭ-jĕk′tĭd-lē) *adv.* sadly; in a depressed way
incarnation (ĭn′kär-nā′shən) *n.* a bodily form taken on by a spirit

MINI LESSON Speaking and Listening

DRAMATIC READING

Prepare Explain that Rama and Ravana are very different in character. Their speeches, as well as their actions, clearly contrast them.

Assign one student to read Rama's speech at the top of the second column of page 134, beginning, "Ravana is in a rage . . . ." Ask another student to read Ravana's speech in the middle of the second column of page 135, beginning, "These gods, instead of supporting me . . . ." Tell students to use their tone of voice and gestures to suggest the characters' personalities and the differences between them.

Present After allowing practice time, have students deliver their speeches. Ask those students who are in the audience to discuss how hearing the speeches read aloud influences their understanding of the characters. Ask the performers what particular traits they were trying to communicate.

This activity is particularly well suited for longer blocks of class time.

Reading and Analyzing

Literary Analysis CONFLICT IN AN EPIC

A Make sure students notice the beyond-earth setting of the battle, the supernatural capabilities of the fighters, and the partisan involvement of the gods.

Active Reading CLASSIFYING CHARACTERS

B Point out that, amazingly, Matali is not dead, because Rama had the power to heal him. Ask: How does Matali help Rama here? *(He explains how Rama can conquer Ravana's illusions.)*

monkey army supporting Rama. Rama ordered Matali, "Go up in the air. Our young soldiers are being attacked from the sky. Follow Ravana, and don't slacken."

A There followed an aerial pursuit at dizzying speed across the dome of the sky and rim of the earth. Ravana's arrows came down like rain; he was bent upon destroying everything in the world. But Rama's arrows diverted, broke, or neutralized Ravana's. Terror-stricken, the gods watched this pursuit. Presently Ravana's arrows struck Rama's horses and pierced the heart of Matali himself. The charioteer fell. Rama paused for a while in grief, undecided as to his next step. Then he recovered and resumed his offensive. At that moment the divine eagle Garuda was seen perched on Rama's flagpost, and the gods who were watching felt that this could be an auspicious sign.

After circling the globe several times, the duelling chariots returned, and the fight continued over Lanka. It was impossible to be very clear about the location of the battleground as the fight occurred here, there, and everywhere. Rama's arrows pierced Ravana's armour and made him wince. Ravana was so insensible to pain and impervious to attack that for him to wince was a good sign, and the gods hoped that this was a turn for the better. But at this moment, Ravana suddenly changed his tactics. Instead of merely shooting his arrows, which were powerful in themselves, he also invoked several supernatural forces to
1 create strange effects: He was an adept in the use of various asthras[15] which could be made dynamic with special incantations. At this point, the fight became one of attack with supernatural powers, and parrying of such an attack with other supernatural powers. 1

Ravana suddenly realized that he should change his tactics and ordered his charioteer to fly the chariot up in the skies.

Ravana realized that the mere aiming of shafts with ten or twenty of his arms would be of no avail because the mortal whom he had so contemptuously thought of destroying with a slight effort was proving formidable, and his arrows were beginning to pierce and cause pain. Among the asthras sent by Ravana was one called "Danda," a special gift from Shiva, capable of pursuing and pulverizing its target. When it came flaming along, the gods were struck with fear. But Rama's arrow neutralized it.

Now Ravana said to himself, "These are all petty weapons. I should really get down to proper business." And he invoked the one called "Maya"—a weapon which created illusions and confused the enemy.

With proper incantations and worship, he sent off this weapon and it created an illusion of reviving all the armies and its leaders—Kumbakarna[16] and Indrajit[17] and the others—and bringing them back to the battlefield. Presently Rama found all those who, he thought, were no more, coming on with battle 2

15. **asthras** (ŭs′thrəz): arrows or other weapons powered by supernatural forces.
16. **Kumbakarna** (ko͝om′bə-kûr′nə): Ravana's brother.
17. **Indrajit** (ĭn′-drə-jĕt): Ravana's son.

WORDS TO KNOW

impervious (ĭm-pûr′vē-əs) *adj.* unable to be affected
parrying (păr′ē-ĭng) *n.* a warding off or turning aside **parry** *v.*
formidable (fôr′mĭ-də-bəl) *adj.* hard to overcome

Rama cuts off Ravana's heads. Copyright © The British Library, London.

HUMANITIES CONNECTION This painting is one of about 400 from a 17th-century *Ramayana* manuscript created for Jagat Singh I, ruler of Udaipur. It presents a sequence of events in Rama and Ravana's battle, so the same figures appear more than once.

cries and surrounding him. Every man in the
2 enemy's army was again up in arms. They seemed to fall on Rama with victorious cries. This was very confusing and Rama asked Matali, whom he had by now revived, "What is happening now? How are all these coming back? They were dead." Matali explained, "In
B your original identity you are the creator of illusions in this universe. Please know that Ravana has created phantoms to confuse you. If you make up your mind, you can dispel them immediately." Matali's explanation was a great help. Rama at once invoked a weapon called "Gnana"[18]—which means "wisdom" or "perception." This was a very rare weapon, and he sent it forth. And all the terrifying armies who seemed to have come on in such a great mass suddenly evaporated into thin air.

Ravana then shot an asthra called "Thama," whose nature was to create total darkness in all the worlds. The arrows came with heads exposing frightening eyes and fangs, and fiery tongues. End to end the earth was enveloped in total darkness and the whole of creation was paralyzed. This asthra also created a deluge of rain on one side, a rain of stones on the other, a hail-storm showering down intermittently, and a tornado sweeping the earth. Ravana was sure that this would arrest Rama's enterprise. But
Rama was able to meet it with what was named 1
"Shivasthra."[19] He understood the nature of the phenomenon and the cause of it and chose the appropriate asthra for counteracting it.

Ravana now shot off what he considered his deadliest weapon—a trident[20] endowed with extraordinary destructive power, once gifted to Ravana by the gods. When it started on its journey there was real panic all round. It came

18. **Gnana** (gnä'nə).

19. **Shivasthra** (shĭ-vŭs'thrə).

20. **trident** (trīd'nt): a spear with three prongs.

WORDS TO KNOW

intermittently (ĭn'tər-mĭt'nt-lē) *adv.* with stops and starts; on and off

Customizing Instruction

Less Proficient Readers

1 Clarify meaning: Ravana is skilled in using special supernatural weapons that become active when he recites spells or prayers. The battle rises to a new level.

Advanced Learners

2 Have students interpret the symbolic meaning of this episode. Ask: In the real world, how does "wisdom" or "perception" conquer "illusions"?

Possible Response: Sometimes people may be undermined by false ideas—the belief that others are against them, for example. But if they calm down and see things clearly, they may stop feeling threatened. Accept any other relevant example.

You might also talk about the Hindu concept of *maya*, meaning the illusory nature of the world we see around us. Ask students what they think of this idea and encourage them to find out more if they are interested.

English Learners

3 Simplify the phrases *arrest Rama's enterprise* (stop Rama's action) and *the nature of the phenomenon* (what the thing was).

MINI LESSON Viewing and Representing

Rama cuts off Ravana's heads

ART APPRECIATION Jagat Singh I ruled the western Indian kingdom of Mewar from 1628 to 1652. Its capital was Udaipur. Art flourished under his reign; he commissioned illustrated manuscripts for a new royal library. The greatest of these was a seven-volume illustrated *Ramayana*, overseen by the master painter Sahibdin. The more than 400 paintings in this work are distinguished by bold colors, stylized figures in profile, and multiple episodes depicted on a single page.

After students finish reading the selection, have them go back and identify the different events shown in the painting.

Possible Responses: Rama cuts off Ravana's heads; Ravana falls to the ground dead; Rama consoles Ravana's brother Vibishana; Rama and Hanuman congratulate each other on the victory.

Reading and Analyzing

Literary Analysis CONFLICT IN AN EPIC

A Ask: What does Ravana realize about his enemy, Rama?
Possible Response: that he is not a mere mortal but a divine being

Literary Analysis
CHARACTERIZATION

B Ask: What does Rama's decision not to finish off Ravana tell you about Rama?
Possible Response: that he is honorable and will not fight unfairly

Ask: What does Ravana's anger at his charioteer tell you about Ravana?
Possible Response: that he is hot-headed but has a sense of honor as well. He wants to be seen as brave and will not retreat.

Reading Skills and Strategies
EVALUATING

C Ask students how they feel about Ravana at this point.
Possible Responses: They may admire him; they may feel sorry that he is dead; they may be glad that he is now at peace.

on flaming toward Rama, its speed or course unaffected by the arrows he flung at it.

When Rama noticed his arrows falling down ineffectively while the trident sailed towards him, for a moment he lost heart. When it came quite near, he uttered a certain mantra[21] from the depth of his being and while he was breathing out that incantation, an esoteric syllable in perfect timing, the trident collapsed. Ravana, who had been so certain of vanquishing Rama with his trident, was astonished to see it fall down within an inch of him, and for a minute wondered if his adversary might not after all be a divine being although he looked like a mortal. Ravana thought to himself, "This is, perhaps, the highest God. Who could he be? Not Shiva, for Shiva is my supporter; he could not be Brahma, who is four faced; could not be Vishnu, because of my immunity from the weapons of the whole trinity. Perhaps this man is the primordial being, the cause behind the whole universe. But whoever he may be, I will not stop my fight until I defeat and crush him or at least take him prisoner." A

With this resolve, Ravana next sent a weapon which issued forth monstrous serpents vomiting fire and venom, with enormous fangs and red eyes. They came darting in from all directions.

Rama now selected an asthra called "Garuda" (which meant "eagle"). Very soon thousands of eagles were aloft, and they picked off the serpents with their claws and beaks and destroyed them. Seeing this also fail, Ravana's anger was roused to a mad pitch and he blindly emptied a quiver full of arrows in Rama's direction. Rama's arrows met them half way and turned them round so that they went back and their sharp points embedded themselves in Ravana's own chest.

Ravana was weakening in spirit. He realized that he was at the end of his resources. All his learning and equipment in weaponry were of no avail and he had practically come to the end of his special gifts of destruction. While he was going down thus, Rama's own spirit was soaring up. The combatants were now near enough to grapple with each other and Rama realized that this was the best moment to cut off Ravana's heads. He sent a crescent-shaped arrow which sliced off one of Ravana's heads and flung it far into the sea, and this process continued; but every time a head was cut off, Ravana had the benediction of having another one grown in its place. Rama's crescent-shaped weapon was continuously busy as Ravana's heads kept cropping up. Rama lopped off his arms but they grew again and every lopped-off arm hit Matali and the chariot and tried to cause destruction by itself, and the tongue in a new head wagged, uttered challenges, and cursed Rama. On the cast-off heads of Ravana, devils and minor demons, who had all along been in terror of Ravana and had obeyed and pleased him, executed a dance of death and feasted on the flesh.

Ravana was now desperate. Rama's arrows embedded themselves in a hundred places on his body and weakened him. Presently he collapsed in a faint on the floor of his chariot. Noticing his state, his charioteer pulled back and drew the chariot aside. Matali whispered to Rama, "This is the time to finish off that demon. He is in a faint. Go on. Go on."

But Rama put away his bow and said, "It is not fair warfare to attack a man who is in a faint. I will wait. Let him recover," and waited. B

When Ravana revived, he was angry with his charioteer for withdrawing, and took out his sword, crying, "You have disgraced me. Those who look on will think I have retreated." But his

21. **mantra** (măn′trə): a word, sound, or phrase used as a prayer or spell.

WORDS TO KNOW
primordial (prī-môr′dē-əl) *adj.* first-existing; original

MINI LESSON **Grammar**

INTERJECTIONS
Instruction Explain that an interjection is a word or phrase used to express emotion. Then display these examples: *Wow! Hooray! Yikes! Ugh! Hey!* A strong interjection is followed by an exclamation point. A mild interjection, such as *uh-oh* or *well,* is set off with commas. Display these example sentences: *Well, that was a good movie. Yikes! Did you see that spider?* Ask volunteers to make up sentences using the interjections you displayed. Make sure students use punctuation and capitalization correctly in their sentences.
Practice Rewrite the sentences below, underlining the interjections and adding the correct punctuation and capitalization.

1. Oh boy did you see that arrow fly?
2. Well I can tell you that I wouldn't want to be Ravana's enemy.
3. Whew that was a huge arrow!
4. Ouch Ravana just fell to the ground.
5. Hey I think Rama has won the battle.

For more instruction and practice in interjections, use McDougal Littell's ***Language Network:***

- Grade 10, Chapter 1, "Interjections"
- Grade 12, Review, "Conjunctions and Interjections"

B charioteer explained how Rama suspended the fight and forbore to attack when he was in a faint. Somehow, Ravana appreciated his explanation and patted his back and resumed his attacks. Having exhausted his special weapons, in desperation Ravana began to throw on Rama all sorts of things such as staves, cast-iron balls, heavy rocks, and oddments he could lay hands on. None of them touched Rama, but glanced off and fell ineffectually. Rama went on shooting his arrows. There seemed to be no end of this struggle in sight.

Now Rama had to pause to consider what final measure he should take to bring this campaign to an end. After much thought, he decided to use "Brahmasthra,"[22] a weapon specially designed by the Creator Brahma on a former occasion, when he had to provide one for Shiva to destroy Tripura,[23] the old monster who assumed the forms of flying mountains and settled down on habitations and cities, seeking to destroy the world. The Brahmasthra was a special gift to be used only when all other means had failed. Now Rama, with prayers and worship, invoked its fullest power and sent it in Ravana's direction,
1 aiming at his heart rather than his head; Ravana being vulnerable at heart. While he had prayed for indestructibility of his several heads and arms, he had forgotten to strengthen his heart, where the Brahmasthra entered and ended his career.

Rama watched him fall headlong from his chariot face down onto the earth, and that was the end of the great campaign. Now one noticed Ravana's face aglow with a new quality. Rama's arrows had burnt off the layers of dross,[24] the anger, conceit, cruelty, lust, and egotism which had encrusted his real self, and now his personality came through in its pristine form—of one who was devout and capable of tremendous attainments. His constant meditation on Rama, although as an adversary, now seemed to bear fruit, as his face shone with serenity and peace. 2 C Rama noticed it from his chariot above and commanded Matali, "Set me down on the ground." When the chariot descended and came to rest on its wheels, Rama got down and commanded Matali, "I am grateful for your services to me. You may now take the chariot back to Indra."

While he had prayed for indestructibility of his several heads and arms, he had forgotten to strengthen his heart.

Surrounded by his brother Lakshmana and Hanuman and all his other war chiefs, Rama approached Ravana's body, and stood gazing on it. He noted his crowns and jewelry scattered piecemeal on the ground. The decorations and the extraordinary workmanship of the armour on his chest were blood-covered. Rama sighed as if to say, "What might he not have achieved but for the evil stirring within him!"

At this moment, as they readjusted Ravana's blood-stained body, Rama noticed to his great shock a scar on Ravana's back and said with a smile, "Perhaps this is not an episode of glory for me as I seem to have killed an enemy who was turning his back and retreating. Perhaps I

---

22. **Brahmasthra** (brə-mŭs'thrə).
23. **Tripura** (trĭ-po͞o'rə).
24. **dross** (drŏs): waste matter; impurities.

WORDS TO KNOW

ineffectually (ĭn'ĭ-fĕk'cho͞o-əl-ē) *adv.* in a useless manner
pristine (prĭs'tēn') *adj.* pure; uncorrupted

Customizing Instruction

Less Proficient Readers

Have students make a chart summarizing the stages of the battle after Ravana launches the first asthra, "Danda." This chart might be set up like the one below:

	Ravana attacks with . . .	Rama defends or attacks with . . .
1	Danda—pursues and pulverizes	neutralizing arrow
2		
3		

Ask how Rama is finally able to kill Ravana. *(Rama shoots the Brahmasthra into Ravana's heart, which he forgot to strengthen.)*

Advanced Learners

1 Discuss what Ravana's vulnerability may symbolize.

Possible Response: It may suggest that it is more important for a person to develop spiritual strength than intellect or physical strength.

English Learners

2 Help students distinguish between *anger, conceit, cruelty, lust,* and *egotism*—five of Ravana's weaknesses. Encourage them to use a dictionary and discuss word meanings with an English-fluent partner.

Cross Curricular Link History

RAMA AND INDIAN POLITICS The *Ramayana* still influences modern politics in India, as shown by the Babri Masjid incident. The Babri Masjid was a Muslim mosque built in Ayodhya in 1528, during the time of the first Mughal ruler, Babur. Ayodhya is the reputed birthplace of Rama, and it is disputed whether Babur tore down a Hindu temple to Rama to build the mosque.

In the twentieth century, Hindu nationalists grew increasingly resentful of the mosque, seeing it as a symbol of past Muslim domination. Finally, in December 1992, Hindu demonstrators tore it down with sledgehammers and their bare hands. This act set off nationwide rioting between Hindus and Muslims that killed more than 1,000 people. Afterward, violence continued to occur on the anniversary of the act. The Hindu nationalist Bharatiya Janata Party, whom many held responsible for inciting the violence, gained power in government and announced plans to build a new temple to Rama on the site. So far, these plans have been unrealized.

Reading and Analyzing

Literary Analysis
CHARACTERIZATION

(A) Ask students what Rama's concern suggests to them about the heroic code of behavior.
Possible Response: It is shameful to attack a retreating enemy.

(B) Ask what Rama's instructions to Vibishana suggest about the heroic code.
Possible Response: that heroes should respect their enemies, even in defeat

Related Reading
Jonah Blank Jonah Blank became interested in Asia while he was an anthropology student at Yale. Since then he has edited the *Asahi Evening News* in Tokyo, covered Asia for *U.S. News and World Report,* and been an adviser on South Asian and Near East issues to the U.S. Senate Foreign Relations Committee. India is "a second homeland" to him, he has said. Blank's most recent book is *Mullahs on the Mainframe: Islam and Modernity among the Daudi Bohras.* This is a study of an Indian Muslim group who uses the Internet to connect believers around the world.

Discussion Questions

1. In Jonah Blank's view, how is Rama like Saint George?
   Possible Responses: They represent a world view in which good always conquers evil; their icons wear serene smiles.
2. According to Blank, why do people need such heroes?
   Possible Response: People want to be comforted by seeing evil defeated because in the real world, evil often wins.

Rama and Sita enthroned. Courtesy of the Trustees of the Victoria & Albert Museum, London.

A was wrong in shooting the Brahmasthra into him." He looked so concerned at this supposed lapse on his part that Vibishana,[25] Ravana's brother, came forward to explain. "What you have achieved is unique. I say so although it meant the death of my brother."

"But I have attacked a man who had turned his back," Rama said. "See that scar."

Vibishana explained, "It is an old scar. In ancient days, when he paraded his strength around the globe, once he tried to attack the divine elephants that guard the four directions.
When he tried to catch them, he was gored in
the back by one of the tuskers and that is the 1
scar you see now; it is not a fresh one though
fresh blood is flowing on it."

B Rama accepted the explanation. "Honour
him and cherish his memory so that his spirit
may go to heaven, where he has his place. And
now I will leave you to attend to his funeral
arrangements, befitting his grandeur." ❖ 2

25. **Vibishana** (vĭ-bē′ shə-nə).

Assessment Informal Assessment

STORY MAPS Review the elements of plot with students. Have them work in pairs or small groups to create story maps that include: Exposition; Rising Action; Climax; Falling Action.

RUBRIC

3 Full Accomplishment Story map is completely and accurately filled in. Sequence is correct.

2 Substantial Accomplishment Story map contains minor errors or inconsistencies. Sequence is correct.

1 Little or Partial Accomplishment Story map contains major errors or omissions. Sequence is not correct.

STORY MAP
Setting: Indian island of Lanka
Main Characters: Rama, a prince who is an incarnation of Vishnu; Ravana, a demon
Exposition: Ravana has kidnapped Rama's wife, Sita; Rama lays siege to Lanka.
Rising Action: Ravana vows to kill Rama; the gods send Rama a flying chariot; Ravana and Rama shoot arrows at each other; Ravana and Ravana launch asthras, or supernatural weapons, at each other.
Climax: Rama kills Ravana with the Brahmasthra.

from ARROW OF THE BLUE-SKINNED GOD: RETRACING THE RAMAYANA THROUGH INDIA

JONAH BLANK

In the 1980s, anthropologist and journalist Jonah Blank traveled through India, following the path Rama took in this famous epic. In his book Arrow of the Blue-Skinned God, *Blank relates the* Ramayana *to life in India today and tells what the epic means to him.*

Rama and the archer in a carriage attack Ravana. Copyright © The British Library, London.

When I was a boy, like most boys, I longed to become a knight in shining armor. My heroes were Sir Lancelot, King Richard the Lionheart, and . . . Saint George. I believed that there really had been a time when brave men devoted their lives to the cause of right. I would read Thomas Malory[1] entire afternoons and evenings, and desperately wish to slip back to those times. It always made me sad to put the book down and look out the window at the mundane[2] world, the world in which "Sir" was what a waiter called my father if he wanted a tip.

I did not bother to think that the Saracens[3] slain by valiant Crusaders were fighting a holy war of their own, knights just as righteous or unrighteous as the thundering chivalry of Europe. Nor did I think much about the women and children slaughtered by the Lionheart for the crime of being Muslim. My heroes had not yet been demythologized. . . .[4] But even then the knight with whom I most identified was Saint

1. **Thomas Malory:** author of *Le Morte d'Arthur,* a collection of tales about King Arthur and such knights as Sir Lancelot.
2. **mundane** (mŭn-dān′): ordinary; everyday.
3. **Saracens** (săr′ə-sənz): Muslims from the time of the Crusades, against whom Richard the Lionheart and others did battle.
4. **demythologized** (dē′mĭ-thŏl′ə-jīzd′): had the mythical or mysterious elements removed from.

Falling Action: Ravana is beautifully transformed in death; Rama orders a funeral honoring Ravana's former grandeur.

Customizing Instruction

Less Proficient Readers

1 Encourage students to use context clues to determine the meaning of *tuskers* (elephants)

English Learners

2 Explain that *befitting his grandeur* means "proper for his greatness."

George. Because he, more than any other, personified the triumph of good over evil. . . .

What Saint George represented, without my realizing it, was an entire world view in which good *always* beats evil, without even working up a sweat. When he kills the dragon, it is not a titanic clash between equally powerful enemies. For the knight, slaughtering a monster is no more difficult than swatting a mosquito. There is little drama, no chance that the dragon might actually win. Virtue *must* prevail—that is the natural order of the universe. It is an immensely comforting notion of life.

It is also the notion of life that underlies the Ramayana. I don't want to spoil the suspense (and I won't reveal the kicker), but in the end Rama wins. It was fated from the beginning. All the characters know it. Even the Demon King's counselors tell their master that he will lose, and only suicidal arrogance lets him ignore their warning. All Indians know how the epic turns out, yet they cluster around their televisions, radios, and school stages just the same.

Everyone, I think, longs for a world where good always trounces evil. When we go to the movies we know the hero will win out and the villain will be crushed, but we still grip the armrests in anticipation. What are action-thriller films if not morality plays? Does the sadistic[5] drug lord *ever* walk away unpunished? It is the same in most popular forms of fiction: right must defeat wrong, or else we'd feel cheated.

In real life, it is quite often evil that triumphs. In real life, rapists and murderers go free on judicial technicalities, slumlords and stock manipulators flourish as respected members of society. In real life, good, honest, hard-working people lose their livelihoods at the flick of a corporate raider's pen. Perhaps that is why we so desperately seek escape. We ache for a world where good always wins, because that is not the real world we inhabit. We long for Saint George. We long for Rama.

If you look at the icons of these two holy warriors, you notice that both faces wear the same untroubled expression. Both mouths are tinged with the same faint shadow of a placid smile. It is a smile of inner serenity, of divine self-confidence, of quiet contentment, a smile that comes from utter certainty that good is destined to prevail. ❖

5. **sadistic** (sə-dĭs′tĭk): loving or delighting in cruelty.

Saint George and the Dragon (17th century). Ivory. Cavalry Museum Pinerolo/The Art Archive/Dagli Orti.

MINI LESSON Viewing and Representing

Saint George and the Dragon (17th century)

ART APPRECIATION Jonah Blank compares the Hindu god Rama to Saint George. Explain that Saint George is the patron saint of England—a Christian knight who slew an evil dragon and saved a princess, legends claim. Blank notes that images of Saint George and Rama have the same expression.

Have students compare the image of Saint George on page 142 with the image of Rama on page 141. Is Blank correct—are the icons similar?

Possible Responses: Students may note that both icons wear blank expressions. Students may or may not detect a faint smile. They may see more exertion in Saint George's face.

Connect to the Literature

1. **What Do You Think?** What is your reaction to the battle between Rama and Ravana?

Comprehension Check
- What kinds of weapons do Rama and Ravana use against each other?
- How does Rama finally win the battle?
- How does Rama treat Ravana after killing him?

Think Critically

2. Ravana, with his 10 heads and 20 arms, would seem to have an advantage over Rama. Why do you think Rama is able to defeat him?

3. **ACTIVE READING: CLASSIFYING CHARACTERS** Review the chart of characters you classified in your READER'S NOTEBOOK. How much do Rama's and Ravana's allies affect the course of the battle?

4. How would you describe Rama's heroic code—that is, the set of rules that he, as a hero, must follow?

THINK ABOUT
- the chance he gives Ravana to recover
- his strategy and behavior in battle
- what he tells Ravana's brother after Ravana has been killed

5. Do you think that Ravana is heroic? Support your answer.

Extend Interpretations

6. **Critic's Corner** Barbara Powell writes of the *Ramayana,* "While it is alive with exciting action, intrigue, and profound emotions, it is sublimely spiritual as well." What spiritual or religious dimensions do you see in this excerpt?

7. **Comparing Texts** How would you compare Rama with Arjuna from the *Mahabharata?*

8. **Comparing Texts** In *Arrow of the Blue-Skinned God* (page 141), Jonah Blank compares Rama to Saint George. Name other heroes whom you would compare to Rama. Do you agree with Blank about why people need such heroes?

9. **Connect to Life** What similarities can you see between Rama and Ravana's struggle and the battle between good and evil that you recalled for the Connect to Your Life activity?

LITERARY ANALYSIS: CONFLICT IN AN EPIC

The **conflict,** or struggle, in an **epic** is large-scale. It involves great heroes, vast armies, and the fate of nations. Supernatural elements are common: the combatants have powers beyond those of ordinary humans, and the gods themselves may intervene on either side. The battle between Rama and Ravana is a perfect example of an epic conflict.

Cooperative Learning Activity With a group of classmates, discuss elements of the battle that make it an epic conflict, such as the flying chariot sent by Indra and the ominous signs that herald Ravana's attack. Keep a list during your discussion. Then choose a real-life conflict, such as a city-council election or a football game. Describe it as an epic conflict, adding elements similar to those on your list. Share your description with the rest of the class.

Connect to the Literature

1. **What Do You Think?** Students might describe the battle in terms of those they have seen in movies such as *Star Wars* or in superhero comic books.

Comprehension Check
- They use arrows, heavy projectiles, and supernatural asthras.
- He shoots a supernatural weapon, the Brahmasthra, into Ravana's vulnerable heart.
- He treats him with repect and wonders whether he killed him unfairly.

Use Selection Quiz in **Unit One Resource Book,** p. 36.

Think Critically

2. Possible Responses: Rama has divine support; he is a better strategist; he is cooler under pressure; his motives are pure and heroic.
3. Possible Responses: Rama's support from the gods, particularly their sending Indra's chariot and the charioteer Matali, helps Rama defeat Ravana. Ravana's allies, including the god Shiva, do not seem to help him much.
4. Possible Responses: Rama is brave, honest, fair, and magnanimous. He tries to end the conflict peacefully and refuses to fight Ravana while he is in a faint. He is concerned about possibly having wounded Ravana in the back.
5. Possible Responses: Some students may consider Ravana heroic because he is so determined to defeat Rama, even though he fears Rama may be divine. Other students may feel that Ravana's hotheadness, his reliance on illusion and trickery, and his kidnapping of Sita keep him from being heroic.

Extend Interpretations

6. **Critic's Corner** Students may mention these symbolic aspects of the battle: illusion is defeated by wisdom; a strong heart is more important than any other defense; great powers can be harnessed by prayer and meditation; people are capable of greatness but can be corrupted by human evils.
7. **Comparing Texts** Both Rama and Arjuna are calm, focused, expert archers. They are described as greater than all other men.
8. **Comparing Texts** Accept all reasonable, well-supported responses.
9. **Connect to Life** Accept all reasonable responses.

Literary Analysis

Cooperative Learning Activity
These descriptions are likely to be quite humorous. Students should refine them and look for publishing opportunities in their school paper or elsewhere.

Use **Unit One Resource Book,** p. 34, for more practice.

RAMAYANA 143

Writing Options

1. **Comparison Essay** Encourage students to use notes they may have taken for the **Connect to Your Life** activity or to expand on the answers they gave to question 9. They may choose to play up either similarities or differences in the struggles. They may want to make their main point in their first paragraph.
2. **Battle Lines** Tell students that the scene they choose doesn't have to be very long. Consider letting students collaborate.
3. **Definition Essay** If students need help, have them consult Definition Analysis in the **Writing Handbook**, p. R34.

Activities and Explorations

1. **Battle Scenes** If possible, involve an art teacher in this activity. You might also tell students to browse import shops for mask ideas.
2. **Comic Book** Have students bring in comic books for inspiration. Pages from the Amar Chitra Katha illustrated version of the *Ramayana* are available online. Students might compare their panels when they are done.

Inquiry and Research

The Epic Performed Go over the relevant section on research in the **Communication Handbook** at the back of this book. If you have a computer in class, suggest that students visit our Web site, classzone.com.

Vocabulary in Action

1. ineffectually
2. formidable
3. impervious
4. parrying
5. intermittently
6. primordial
7. benediction
8. incarnation
9. pristine
10. dejectedly

To assess skills and concepts taught in this selection, use **Formal Assessment Book**, p. 21–22.

Choices & CHALLENGES

Writing Options

1. Comparison Essay Compare the battle between Rama and Ravana with a struggle between good and evil in modern culture. You might see echoes of the *Ramayana* in *Star Wars,* or superhero comic books, for example.

2. Battle Lines Try to put the *Ramayana* back into its original form—poetry. Take a scene from this selection and rewrite it in rhymed or unrhymed verse suitable for reciting with music. Perform the poem.

3. Definition Essay What did it take to be a hero in ancient India? Write a definition based on the *Ramayana* and the *Mahabharata.* Use Rama, Arjuna, or any other characters from the epics as examples to support your ideas.

Activities & Explorations

1. Battle Scene In India, people frequently perform the *Ramayana* in folk plays. Write dialogue, then stage the battle between Rama and Ravana. Use masks or makeup to express the characters' larger-than-life qualities. Invent creative ways to suggest supernatural events that would be difficult to show onstage. ~ **PERFORMING**

2. Comic Book The *Ramayana* was once published as a comic book of more than 100 pages. Draw a few comic-book panels of your own to depict the battle scene. How do you envision the terrifying Ravana? ~ **ART**

Inquiry & Research

The Epic Performed Research a performance tradition based on the *Ramayana.* You might investigate *Ramlilas,* or annual drama festivals; *wayang kulit,* or Indonesian shadow-puppet plays; or *kathakali* or *bharatnatyam,* forms of Indian classical dance. Present your findings in an oral report that includes photographs or a videotape.

Communication Handbook
See page R45: Finding Sources.

Vocabulary in Action

EXERCISE: WORDS IN CONTEXT For each underlined word, write the Word to Know that could substitute for it in the context.

The two armies fought on aimlessly and (1) unproductively. Neither had realized how (2) overpowering the other's forces were; both had considered themselves (3) invulnerable to attack. But in truth they were evenly matched: the (4) avoidance of an attack by one brought on an equally clever move by the other. And so the battle went on (5) periodically for days.

The countries of the two armies were long-standing enemies, almost since the (6) earliest days of the world. Worshippers of different gods, both had gone into battle with a special (7) blessing from their priests to bring on victory. At a certain point one army thought they saw the (8) personification of their chief god floating high and (9) uncorrupted over the battlefield. But the image disappeared, and they went (10) sadly back into battle.

WORDS TO KNOW

benediction	impervious	intermittently	primordial
dejectedly	incarnation	parrying	pristine
formidable	ineffectually		

Building Vocabulary
For an in-depth lesson on using context clues, see page 674.

Modern Views of Rama and Sita

In Indian culture, Rama and his wife, Sita, embody such virtues as strength, leadership, devotion, and purity. However, some Indians question whether Rama and Sita are good role models in today's world. Their actions in the seventh book of the *Ramayana,* the *Uttara Kanda,* are particularly troubling to many people.

Unhappy Ending After Rama slays Ravana, he rejects Sita, saying he doubts she has remained pure during her captivity. She demands a trial by fire, and the god Agni, knowing she is innocent, saves her from the flames. Rama then states he had put Sita through the ordeal to prove her innocence before all his subjects. Months later, however, the people remain suspicious of Sita. For the good of the kingdom, Rama orders his brother Lakshmana to abandon Sita in the forest. There the pregnant Sita takes refuge with the poet Valmiki and gives birth to twin sons. These sons learn to recite the *Ramayana,* and eventually they perform it before Rama's court. When Rama realizes who they are, he invites Sita to return to him. He asks her to prove her purity once more, but she refuses and asks Mother Earth to swallow her up. Her wish is granted, and she disappears.

Are Rama and Sita Heroic? Given these events, modern Indians disagree about how to view Rama and Sita. Contemporary rural women sing folk songs calling Rama heartless and expressing sympathy for Sita. A 1998 exhibit, "Sita in the City," showed that South Asian immigrants in New York held wildly varying views of Sita. One mother saw Sita's chastity as something for teenage girls to emulate, but an activist against domestic violence called Sita "a lousy role model for women." Some people admiringly compared Sita to a modern single mother raising children alone. Some saw her fire test as a sign of virtue and strength, while others saw it as proof of women's oppression.

Group Discussion Who are some of the men and women—real or fictitious—held up as ideals in your own culture? Would you want to imitate them? Have they ever been challenged as proper role models? Explain.

Rama and Sita are seen as role models for modern Indian couples.

Connect to Today

Note Scholars believe that the seventh book of the *Ramayana*, the *Uttara Kanda,* is a later addition. For many people, the story ends when Rama is reunited with Sita and is crowned king of Ayodhya.

Group Discussion You might start the discussion by writing the names of the current president, a current movie star, and a popular sports figure on the chalkboard. Ask: Which person would you most want to be like? Why?

Possible Objectives

This **On Your Own** featured selection may be used to achieve one or more of the following objectives:

- to give students the opportunity to read independently, either reading silently for a sustained period, reading and analyzing literature with a group, or using the Reader's Notebook to write in response to the literature
- to conduct a post-reading class discussion
- to assess students' comprehension of the selection

Summary

In "Slow, the Weaver," a weaver is granted a wish by a fairy. His friend, the barber, tells him to wish for a kingdom. His wife tells him not to ask for a kingdom, as that would be too troublesome. On her advice, he asks for a second pair of arms and an extra head so that he can produce more cloth. When his wish is granted, people mistake him for a fiend and beat him to death.

In "The Brahman's Dream," a poor brahman imagines all the wealth that will come from his jar of barley-meal: livestock, gold, a great house, a wife with a dowry, a son. As he envisions kicking his wife to punish her, he accidentally kicks the jar and breaks it, covering himself with barley-meal and ruining his hopes.

ON YOUR OWN

FROM THE

PANCHATANTRA

Translated by ARTHUR W. RYDER

In this part of the book, you have read classic stories from ancient India and seen how they offer spiritual and practical lessons. Now you will read from another famous book of instructive stories from India. The Panchatantra *(pŭn′chə-tän′trə) is a collection of Sanskrit fables probably gathered around 200 B.C. Over the centuries it has been translated into more than 50 languages, including Arabic, Greek, and Hebrew, and its stories have spread all over the world. So many familiar tales can be traced back to the* Panchatantra *that it has been called the Mother of Folklore.*

Panchatantra *means "five books." The introduction explains that a king wanted to educate his three foolish sons. For this purpose he hired a Brahman, who proceeded to teach the principles of life by means of stories. These stories are arranged under five themes, or lessons. Often, stories are told within other stories, a technique repeated in such works as* The Thousand and One Nights.

The two stories you will read are taken from the fifth book. They deal with the theme of hasty action. A wheel bearer is telling the stories to his friend, a gold finder. As you read, consider the following questions:

1. *What lessons do the tales teach?*
2. *Do the tales seem familiar to you?*
3. *What similarities and differences can you find between the tales and other pieces of Indian literature you've read?*

SLOW, THE WEAVER

He who, lacking wit, does not
Harken to a friend,
Just like weaver Slow, inclines
To a fatal end. . . .

In a certain town lived a weaver named Slow. One day all the pegs in his loom broke. So he took an axe, and in his search for wood, came to the seashore. There he found a great sissoo[1] tree, and he thought: "This seems a good-sized tree. If I cut it down, I can make plenty of weaving-tools." He therefore lifted his axe upon it.

Now there was a fairy in the tree who said: "My friend, this tree is my home. Please spare it. For I live here in utter happiness, since my body is caressed by breezes cool from contact with ocean billows."

"But, sir," said the weaver, "what am I to do? While I lack apparatus made of wood, my family is pinched by hunger. Therefore, please move elsewhere, and quickly. I intend to cut it down."

"Sir," said the fairy, "I have taken a liking to you. Ask anything you like, but spare this tree."

"In that case," said the weaver, "I will go home and return after asking my friend and my wife." And when the fairy consented, the weaver started home. On entering the town, he encountered his particular friend, the barber, and said: "My friend, I have won the favor of a fairy. Tell me what to ask for."

And the barber said: "My dear fellow, if it is really so, ask for a kingdom. You can be king, and I will be prime minister. So we shall both taste the delights of this world before those of the world to come."

"Quite so, my friend," replied the weaver. "However, I shall ask my wife, too." "Don't," said the barber. "It is a mistake to consult women. As the saying goes:

Give a woman food and dresses
(Chiefly when her trouble presses);
Give her gems and all things nice;
Do not ask for her advice.

And again:

Where a woman, gambler, child,
As a guide is domiciled,[2]
Death advances, stage by stage—
So declares the ancient sage.

And once again:

Only while he does not hear
Woman's whisper in his ear,
May a man a leader be,
Keeping due humility.

Women seek for selfish treasures,
Think of nothing but their pleasures,
Even children by them reckoned
To their selfish comfort second."

And the weaver rejoined: "You may be right. Still, I shall ask her. She is a good wife."

So he made haste and said to her: "My dear wife, today we won the favor of a fairy. He offers anything we want. So I have come to ask you to tell me what to say to him. Here is my friend, the barber, who tells me to ask for a kingdom."

---

1. **sissoo** (sĭs′o͞o) **tree:** a kind of East Indian tree known for its strong, useful timber.
2. **domiciled** (dŏm′ĭ-sīld′): residing; making a home.

Working Independently

You may want to set aside time each week for independent reading, without making an assignment related to the reading. Or once students have completed the reading, either alone or aloud in groups, you may ask them to work together on a project, such as a dramatic performance of the stories. If you choose to have students write responsively in their Reader's Notebook, have them react to the lessons or messages they see in the stories.

Discussing the Selection

The last page of this selection provides questions you might use for a post-reading class discussion.

Using the Selection for Assessment

If you want to use this selection as the basis for assessment, see **Integrated Assessment Book,** pp. 1–6, for test questions.

"Dear husband," said she, "what sense have barbers? Do not take his advice. For the proverb says:

All advice you may discard
From a barber, child, or bard,
Monk or hermit or musician,
Or a man of base[3] condition.

"Besides, this king-business means a series of dreadful troubles and involves worry about peace, war, change of base, entrenchment, alliance, duplicity, and other matters. It never gives satisfaction. And even worse,

His very sons and brothers wish
The slaughter of a king;
As this is kingship's nature, who
Would not reject the thing?"

"Yes," said the weaver, "you are right. But tell me what to ask for." And she replied: "As it is, you turn out one piece of cloth a day, and this meets all our expenses. Now ask for a second pair of arms and an extra head, so that you may produce one piece of cloth in front and another behind. The price of one meets the household expenses, with the price of the other you may put on style and spend the time in honor among your peers."

On hearing this, he was delighted and said: "Splendid, my faithful wife! You have made a splendid suggestion. I am determined to follow it."

So the weaver went and laid his request before the fairy: "Well, sir, if you offer what I wish, pray give me a second pair of arms and an extra head." And in the act of speaking he became two-headed and four-armed.

But as he came home, delight in his heart, the people thought he was a fiend, and beat him with clubs and stones and things so that he died.

"And that is why I say:

He who, lacking wit, does not, . . .

and the rest of it."

Kanduri (1900), India. Cotton, 183" × 73". The Metropolitan Museum of Art, Purchase, Rogers Fund, Anonymous gift, in honor of W. G. and Mildred Archer, and Carolyn Kane Gift, 1986. (1986.53). Image © 2001 The Metropolitan Museum of Art.

Then the wheel-bearer continued: "Yes, any man becomes ridiculous when bitten by the demon of extravagant hope. There is sense in this:

Do not indulge in hopes
Extravagantly high:
Else, whitened like the sire
Of Moon-Lord, you will lie."

"How was that?" asked the gold-finder. And the other told the story of the Brahman's dream. ❖

3. **base:** low; inferior.

THE BRAHMAN'S DREAM

In a certain town lived a Brahman named Seedy, who got some barley-meal by begging, ate a portion, and filled a jar with the remainder. This jar he hung on a peg one night, placed his cot beneath it, and fixing his gaze on the jar, fell into a hypnotic reverie.[4]

"Well, here is a jar full of barley-meal," he thought. "Now if famine comes, a hundred rupees[5] will come out of it. With that sum I will get two she-goats. Every six months they will bear two more she-goats. After goats, cows. When the cows calve, I will sell the calves. After cows, buffaloes; after buffaloes, mares. From the mares I shall get plenty of horses. The sale of these will mean plenty of gold. The gold will buy a great house with an inner court. Then someone will come to my house and offer his lovely daughter with a dowry.[6] She will bear a son, whom I shall name Moon-Lord. When he is old enough to ride on my knee, I will take a book, sit on the stable roof, and think. Just then Moon-Lord will see me, will jump from his mother's lap in his eagerness to ride on my knee, and will go too near the horses. Then I shall get angry and tell my wife to take the boy. But she will be busy with her chores and will not pay attention to what I say. Then I will get up and kick her."

Being sunk in his hypnotic dream, he let fly such a kick that he smashed the jar. And the barley-meal which it contained turned him white all over.

"And that is why I say:

Do not indulge in hopes, . . .

and the rest of it." ❖

4. **reverie** (rĕv′ə-rē): a daydream.

5. **rupees** (ro͞o-pēz′): units of Indian money.

6. **dowry** (dou′rē): money or property given with a bride at marriage.

Discussion Questions

1. What lessons do the tales teach?
   Possible Responses: If you are not intelligent, listen to a wise friend. Don't take foolish advice. Don't get carried away by hopes.
2. Do the tales seem familiar to you?
   Possible Responses: "The Brahman's Dream" should remind students of Aesop's fable "The Milkmaid and Her Pail," which has the moral, "Don't count your chickens before they are hatched." "Slow, the Weaver" might remind students of other tales in which a granting of a wish leads to unexpected complications.
3. What similarities and differences can you find between the tales and other pieces of Indian literature you've read?
   Possible Responses: Students might say that the tales are similar to the epics in that they are concerned with teaching wise and proper behavior and they assume the existence of supernatural beings. Students might say the tales are different from the epics in that they are about regular people, not princes and gods, and they are more humorous.
4. What do these stories suggest about the way women were viewed in ancient India?
   Possible Responses: The stories suggest that women were viewed as stupid and selfish and that it was acceptable for them to be beaten by their husbands. But on the other hand, the men in the stories are also presented as stupid, so it may be hard to judge from the stories how women were viewed in real life.

Objectives

- write an Autobiographical Incident
- use a written text as a model for writing
- revise a draft to maintain a clear focus
- correct any run-on sentences

Introducing the Workshop

A Autobiographical Incident An autobiographical incident is a narrative about a writer's personal experience. In these accounts, writers tell of true experiences that reveal something important about themselves or their lives. This is something all people do, at least in conversation; the human urge to share stories is as old as civilization. Many people also choose to tell their own stories in writing, song, pictures, drama, or even film.

Ask students to name people whose autobiographical stories they have read or heard. Do these stories have anything in common? Point out that through writing an autobiographical incident, students will share one of their own life stories with readers.

Basics in a Box

B Using the Graphic
Like the divisions shown in the graphic, an autobiographical incident has a narrative structure with a beginning, middle, and end. As the graphic suggests, students can focus on each of these parts of their narrative and give special attention to the elements described in it.

C Presenting the Rubric
To better understand the assignment, students can refer to the Standards for Writing a Successful Autobiographical Incident. You may wish to discuss with them the complete rubric and student models in the Unit One Resource Book on pages 42–48.

For more instruction and practice in personal and reflective writing, use McDougal Littell's ***Language Network:***

- Grade 10, Chapter 18, "Autobiographical Incident"
- Grade 12, Chapter 17, "Application Essay"

Writing Workshop

Autobiographical Incident

For the memory books . . .

From Reading to Writing The excerpt from the *Ramayana* tells of Rama's fight to the death with Ravana. A full-scale battle always makes an exciting story. However, even a small-scale battle, such as a girl's internal struggle about changing her appearance, can make for good reading. An **autobiographical incident** is an event from a writer's own life. No matter how ordinary an event is, it can always be told with color and drama.

For Your Portfolio

WRITING PROMPT Write an essay about a memorable incident from your own life.

Purpose: To share and reflect upon a personal experience

Audience: Your classmates, friends, and family

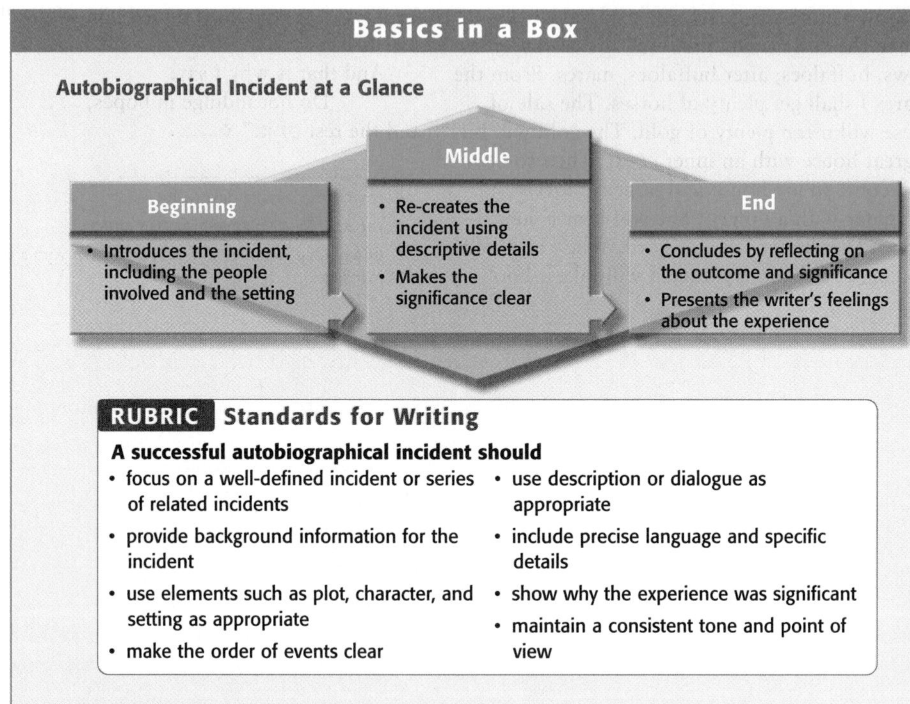

RUBRIC Standards for Writing

A successful autobiographical incident should

- focus on a well-defined incident or series of related incidents
- provide background information for the incident
- use elements such as plot, character, and setting as appropriate
- make the order of events clear
- use description or dialogue as appropriate
- include precise language and specific details
- show why the experience was significant
- maintain a consistent tone and point of view

LESSON RESOURCES

USING PRINT RESOURCES
Unit One Resource Book
- Prewriting, p. 37
- Drafting, p. 38
- Peer Response, pp. 39–40
- Revising, Editing, and Proofreading, p. 41
- Student Models, pp. 42–47
- Rubric, p. 48

USING MEDIA RESOURCES
Writing Coach CD-ROM
Visit our Web site: classzone.com

ADDITIONAL RESOURCES
For a complete view of Lesson Resources, see page 15f of this book.

Analyzing a Student Model

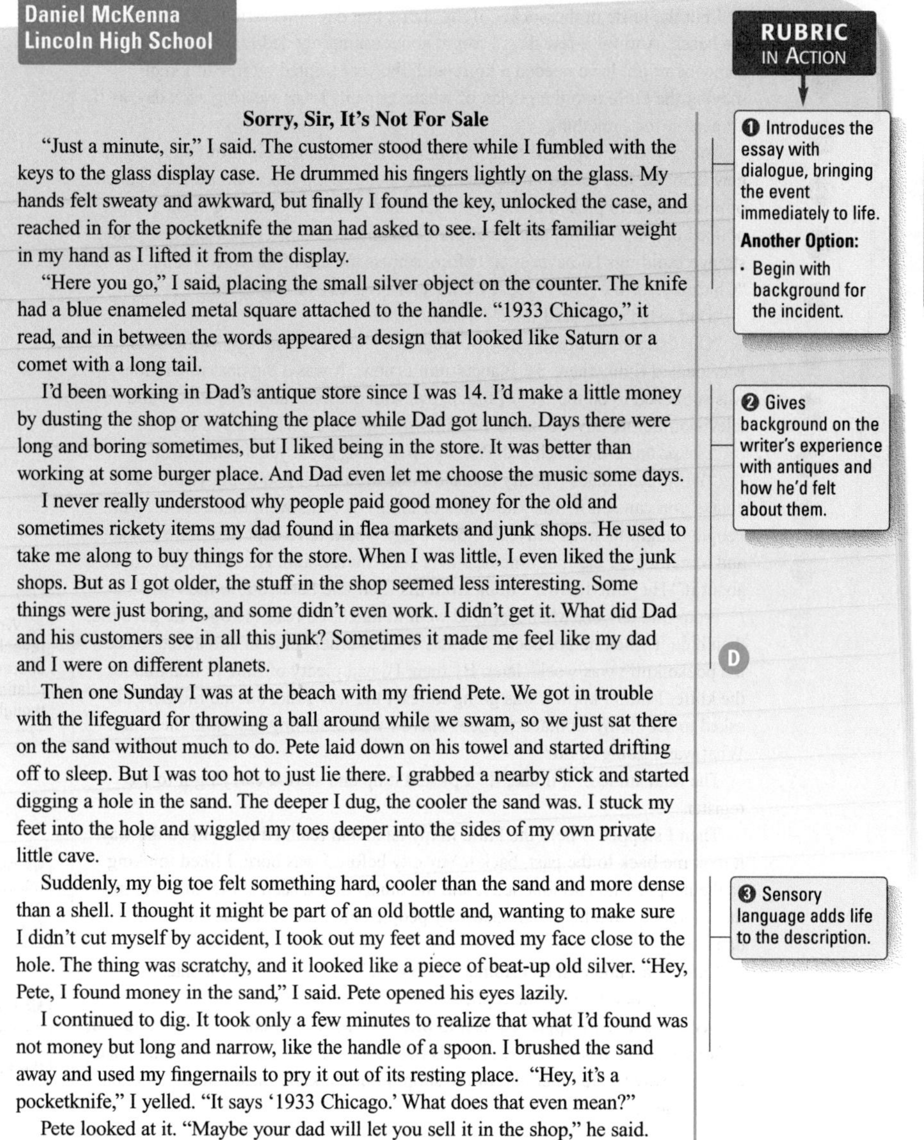

Daniel McKenna
Lincoln High School

RUBRIC IN ACTION

Sorry, Sir, It's Not For Sale

"Just a minute, sir," I said. The customer stood there while I fumbled with the keys to the glass display case. He drummed his fingers lightly on the glass. My hands felt sweaty and awkward, but finally I found the key, unlocked the case, and reached in for the pocketknife the man had asked to see. I felt its familiar weight in my hand as I lifted it from the display.

"Here you go," I said, placing the small silver object on the counter. The knife had a blue enameled metal square attached to the handle. "1933 Chicago," it read, and in between the words appeared a design that looked like Saturn or a comet with a long tail.

I'd been working in Dad's antique store since I was 14. I'd make a little money by dusting the shop or watching the place while Dad got lunch. Days there were long and boring sometimes, but I liked being in the store. It was better than working at some burger place. And Dad even let me choose the music some days.

I never really understood why people paid good money for the old and sometimes rickety items my dad found in flea markets and junk shops. He used to take me along to buy things for the store. When I was little, I even liked the junk shops. But as I got older, the stuff in the shop seemed less interesting. Some things were just boring, and some didn't even work. I didn't get it. What did Dad and his customers see in all this junk? Sometimes it made me feel like my dad and I were on different planets.

Then one Sunday I was at the beach with my friend Pete. We got in trouble with the lifeguard for throwing a ball around while we swam, so we just sat there on the sand without much to do. Pete laid down on his towel and started drifting off to sleep. But I was too hot to just lie there. I grabbed a nearby stick and started digging a hole in the sand. The deeper I dug, the cooler the sand was. I stuck my feet into the hole and wiggled my toes deeper into the sides of my own private little cave.

Suddenly, my big toe felt something hard, cooler than the sand and more dense than a shell. I thought it might be part of an old bottle and, wanting to make sure I didn't cut myself by accident, I took out my feet and moved my face close to the hole. The thing was scratchy, and it looked like a piece of beat-up old silver. "Hey, Pete, I found money in the sand," I said. Pete opened his eyes lazily.

I continued to dig. It took only a few minutes to realize that what I'd found was not money but long and narrow, like the handle of a spoon. I brushed the sand away and used my fingernails to pry it out of its resting place. "Hey, it's a pocketknife," I yelled. "It says '1933 Chicago.' What does that even mean?"

Pete looked at it. "Maybe your dad will let you sell it in the shop," he said. The idea started out there. Just take it to Dad, have him sell it, and get the cash. After all, it hadn't cost me anything to find it. Sell it and make a pure profit, right?

1 Introduces the essay with dialogue, bringing the event immediately to life.

Another Option:
- Begin with background for the incident.

2 Gives background on the writer's experience with antiques and how he'd felt about them.

D

3 Sensory language adds life to the description.

LANGUAGE SKILLS

Teaching the Lesson

Analyzing the Model

"Sorry, Sir, It's Not for Sale"

D The student model describes a turning point in the life of a boy who starts to sell an antique pocketknife but changes his mind when he realizes that he has begun to appreciate how collectibles connect him to the past.

Have students read the model. Then discuss the **Rubric in Action**. Point out key words and phrases in the student model that correspond to the elements mentioned in the **Rubric in Action.**

1. Have students suggest an alternate introduction based on the other option listed.
   Possible Response: The writer could explain the history of his feelings about antiques.
2. Ask students what they learn about the narrator from the explanation of why he thinks antiques are dull.
   Possible Response: His description of working with his dad and the time he has spent working around antiques shows that he has a strong relationship with his father but does not always understand why people might like buying old things.
3. Ask students to point out at least three examples of sensory language in the paragraph beginning with "Suddenly, my big toe . . ."
   Possible Responses: "cooler than the sand and more dense than a shell"; "The sand smelled like lake water"; "The thing was scratchy"; "it looked like a piece of beat-up old silver."
4. Point out that here, the narrator is characterizing himself using one of the four methods of characterization: 1) describing a character's physical appearance; 2) relating a character's own thoughts, feelings, or actions; 3) telling what other characters say or think about the character, or how they behave towards him or her; or 4) making direct comments about the character's nature.

MINI LESSON Patterns of Organization

Instruction An autobiographical incident has a structure that involves movement through time. Events can be presented in chronological order, using transitional words such as *then, next, later,* and *finally*. Within this structure, the incident builds towards a climax that usually takes place near the end of the narrative.

Activity Have students map the structure of the student model by marking changes in time, including any "flashback" moments that move from the present to recall an earlier moment.

Dan is waiting on a customer who wants to buy the pocketknife. → Background: Dan has grown up around antiques and finds them boring. → Flashback:
- Dan and Pete go to the beach, and Dan finds the pocketknife.
- Dan's dad teaches him about where the knife came from.
- Dan reads about the 1933 World's Fair.
- Dan puts the knife up for sale.

→ Dan realizes that he doesn't want to sell the knife after all. → Dan tells the customer that the knife isn't for sale and puts it back in his pocket.

5. Point out that these two paragraphs mark the turning point in the story, where the narrator describes his change of heart.
6. Ask students what the final paragraph reveals.
   Possible Responses: The father's sudden appearance shows a strong connection between the father and son; the knife resting in the boy's pocket reflects the way he has changed over the course of the experience.

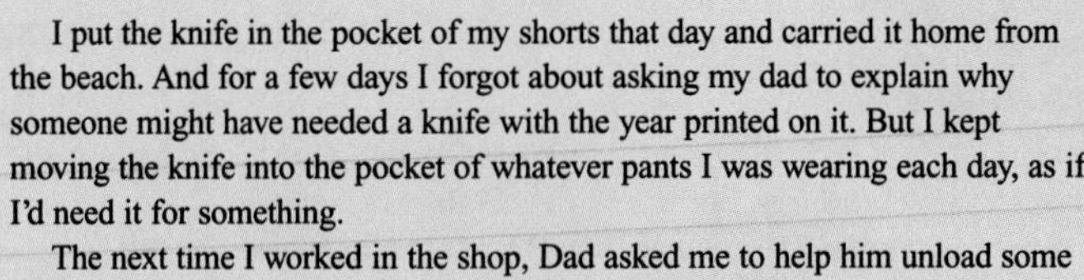

I put the knife in the pocket of my shorts that day and carried it home from the beach. And for a few days I forgot about asking my dad to explain why someone might have needed a knife with the year printed on it. But I kept moving the knife into the pocket of whatever pants I was wearing each day, as if I'd need it for something.

The next time I worked in the shop, Dad asked me to help him unload some new items he had stored in the backroom. Out of a big box, Dad pulled a bunch of postcards he'd picked up at a yard sale that weekend. Glancing at the pile, I noticed one card with a picture of the Chicago lakeshore. There were also some strange buildings I'd never seen before. Across the top of the card it said, "Chicago World's Fair, 1933, A Century of Progress" in big letters.

"Dad, what's this card for?" I asked.

"Oh, that's from the Century of Progress—the 1933 Chicago World's Fair. It was located right where the Planetarium is now. It was a big deal in its time. It was supposed to be the city of tomorrow, with demonstrations of robots and television before anyone had a TV at home," he said, "Why do you ask?"

"I found this at the beach with Pete. I keep meaning to ask you if I can sell it."

"Wow, Dan, that's a pretty unusual thing to find after so many years. Of course you can sell it. You know, lots of things like this were made for the fair. People bought them as souvenirs. Some guy would have kept this in his pocket and remembered the first time he'd ever seen a television. Here, I've got a book about it." He pulled down a book from his shelf and handed it to me.

From that day on, whenever Dad went to lunch, I'd read the book he gave me, then hide it when he got back. The day the customer came in and asked to see the pocketknife was weeks later. By then, I'd had plenty of time to think about the knife. I didn't know I was going to react the way I did, but the moment he asked to see it, my stomach flipped. There I was, watching him hold the knife. What was I going to do?

4 Writer reveals his own character by relating his thoughts.

The man smiled. "I'll take it." I picked it up and started carrying it to the register.

Then I stopped. I held the knife in my hand and realized that I liked the way it took me back to the past, back to my city before I was born. I liked thinking of the people who had touched it and the things they'd seen at the fair. And in that moment, I finally understood why people paid money for the "junk" in my dad's shop.

5 Reflects on the significance of his changing feelings.

I turned around to the customer. "Sorry, sir," I said. "It's not for sale."

"What? I don't get it," he replied.

My dad suddenly appeared next to me. "The seller just changed his mind. Sir, we've got some World's Fair postcards over here. Let me show you." And he led the man away to the other end of the shop. I put the knife back into my pocket. It's still there.

6 Uses dialogue and action to resolve the event.

Writing Your Autobiographical Incident

❶ Prewriting

Begin by choosing the incident you want to write about. You might choose to write about a major event that marked a turning point in your life, or perhaps you'll choose a smaller event that taught you a particular lesson.

Brainstorm a list of events from your life. To jog your memory, look through old photo albums and journals or diaries. Think about the first time you did certain things: your first day at a new school, or the first time you met your best friend. What stories do you like to tell your friends about yourself? After you choose an event, follow the steps below.

Planning Your Autobiographical Incident

1. **Test your topic.** Do you remember the incident well enough to write about it accurately? Is it a memory you can comfortably share with your class? What point will you make about this event?
2. **Think about your purpose and audience.** How will you show readers how and why the incident affected you?
3. **Sketch out ideas.** When and where did the incident take place? Was there something special about the setting? What were the key events? Who were the people involved? How did they look, act, and talk?

❷ Drafting

Start by writing down your memory of the incident as it comes to you. Don't worry about how it sounds or whether you've gotten it completely right; you can fix it later. Concentrate on getting the information from the beginning to the end, and don't worry about the details. As you draft, keep the following things in mind:

- Use elements of short story writing—**plot, character,** and **setting.** Include any background information your reader might need.
- Use **dialogue** when you can.
- Describe **sensory** details—sights, sounds, smells, tastes, and textures. This will make your writing more immediate.
- **Organize** your ideas. **Chronological order** is usually the clearest way to tell a story, but sometimes using **flashbacks** makes a great impact. Flashback is the technique of starting a story in the middle and then relating events from an earlier time.
- Write a **conclusion** that sums up your impression of the event or what you've learned from it.

After you finish your first draft, let it sit for a while. Then reread it. You might also want to ask your peer readers for their reactions.

Ask Your Peer Reader

- Why do you think this experience was important for me?
- Which part of the incident is described most vividly?
- What parts are unnecessary or need more explanation?

IDEABank

1. Your Working Portfolio

Build on the **Writing Options** you completed earlier in this unit:

- **Autobiographical Papyrus Scroll** p. 60
- **Remembering a Teacher** p. 127

2. Lifeline To jog your memory, create a time line of your life showing significant events from your life at school, at home, with your friends, and in your community. Choose one event to write about.

3. Family Resources Sometimes people in your family remember things that have escaped your memory. Ask a family member to recall significant events in your life. This may help you remember something you'd like to write about. Make a few notes on these events, and write about one of them.

Need help with your autobiographical incident?

See the **Writing Handbook** Narrative Writing, pp. R29–R30

LANGUAGE SKILLS

Guiding Student Writing

Prewriting

Choosing an Incident

If, after reading the **Idea Bank,** students are having difficulty choosing an incident, suggest they try the following:

- Look at old keepsakes—even look through a messy old drawer—as a way to jog your memory. Something as simple as a little picture, a program, or a birthday card can trigger memories of interesting or meaningful events.
- Make a list of events that have made you change your mind about something or someone. Did something happen that changed your impression of a friend or relative? Have you ever experienced a major shift in your thinking? Events with significant turning points often make good stories.

Planning the Autobiographical Incident

1. Have students freewrite about the event in question, recalling as much as they can about how the event was significant for them and how it might have changed them.
3. Have students create three lists to help them explore specific aspects of the event: Details of Setting, Key People, and Key Moments or Scenes.

Drafting

Organizing the Draft

When drafting an autobiographical incident, students will have to plan the way in which they want to tell the story. They might want to tell the story in chronological order, or perhaps incorporate a flashback. Encourage students to leave out details and events that distract from the main incident. The details in their narrative should lead toward the main point, and the events should lead up to the narrative's climax. Finally, the writer should conclude with a final reflection on the event's significance.

Revising

MAINTAINING A CLEAR FOCUS

Have students begin their revision by looking at their essay one paragraph at a time. For each paragraph, instruct students to identify the primary focus: is it narrating a particular part of the action? describing a character? making a point about the narrator's feeling? Then have them look through the paragraph and determine whether each sentence contributes to that focus. If they find elements that distract or do not contribute, they should consider deleting them or revising the paragraph for greater unity.

Editing and Proofreading

RUN-ON SENTENCES

Remind students that a run-on sentence is two or more independent clauses that have been run together, failing to show where one thought ends and another begins. Run-ons can be fixed by separating the two thoughts with the proper punctuation or a conjunction, or by showing the relationship between the two thoughts.

The most common type of run-on sentence is a comma splice, where two independent clauses are connected only by a comma:

> I decided to color my hair, my friends were doing the same thing.

There are several ways to correct this error.

Add a conjunction: I decided to color my hair, **and** my friends were doing the same thing.

Change the comma to a semicolon: I decided to color my hair**;** my friends were doing the same thing.

Replace the comma with an end mark, and start a new sentence: I decided to color my hair**.** **My** friends were doing the same thing.

Change one of the independent clauses into a subordinate clause: I decided to color my hair, **because** my friends were doing the same thing.

Reflecting

Ask students to consider their level of self-awareness, as reflected by this essay. In what ways do they feel that writing the essay enhanced their self-awareness? What specifics have they learned about themselves in the process? Have students add these self-evaluations to their working portfolios?

Need revising help?

Review the **Rubric,** p. 150

Consider **peer reader** comments

Check **Revision Guidelines,** p. R19

See the **Writing Handbook Elaboration,** p. R25

Need help with run-on sentences?

See the **Grammar Handbook,** p. R73

Publishing IDEAS

- Gather a group of classmates and read aloud your works to each other.
- Read your work to your family. Ask whether your recollection of the events matches theirs.

❸ Revising

The Law of Editing: For every vision, there is an equal and opposite revision.

TARGET SKILL ▶ MAINTAINING A CLEAR FOCUS Your writing will have a stronger impact if you include only the most important ideas and details. Extra details will distract your reader from the main point. When writing about your own life, it is sometimes tempting to include everything that comes to mind; however, leaving out irrelevant details can be as important as including the relevant ones.

> Much to my surprise, my moderately conservative mother was happy to let me dye my hair, although not permanently. ~~My mother is a very successful attorney.~~

❹ Editing and Proofreading

TARGET SKILL ▶ RUN-ON SENTENCES Even experienced writers can make the mistake of running two or more sentences together. Run-ons fail to show where one idea ends and another begins. This is incorrect and often confusing. To fix run-on sentences, use the correct punctuation or a conjunction to separate the two ideas.

> The fierce, warm wind of the blow dryer roared deafeningly in my ears, ^but^ all that I could hear was a powerful voice in my head declaring how beautiful my golden locks would be, glinting beneath the blazing summer sun by the side of a turquoise pool.

❺ Reflecting

FOR YOUR WORKING PORTFOLIO What did you learn or remember about your life as you wrote? Did it cause you to change your mind about the incident? How important does it seem now? Attach your reflections to your finished essay. Save your autobiographical incident in your **Working Portfolio.**

MINI LESSON Grammar

USING CORRECT PRONOUN CASE

Instruction Depending on their function in the sentence, pronouns take different cases: subject pronouns take the nominative case, while direct and indirect object pronouns, as well as the objects of prepositions, take the objective case. Many people confuse the nominative and objective cases, especially when the pronoun is part of a compound subject or object.

Practice Write the following sentences on the chalkboard.

> My mother read the Ramayana to my sister and me.
>
> My mother read the Ramayana to my sister and I.

Ask students which of the two sentences is correct, and why. *(The first sentence is correct, because* my sister and me *is the object of the preposition* to; me *is in the objective case, which is correct.* I *is in the nominative case, which is incorrect.)*

Standardized Test Practice Revising & Editing

Read this paragraph from the first draft of an autobiographical essay. The underlined sections may include the following kinds of errors:

- **run-on sentences**
- **fragments**
- **capitalization errors**
- **incorrect pronoun cases**

For each underlined section, choose the revision that most improves the writing.

I will never forget the first time I saw the ocean. I was eight years old, my family (1) got in the car and drove west. We lived in South Dakota, where the plains seemed to go on forever, but I could always see the other side of rivers and lakes. My brother and me were (2) very excited. Because we'd never taken such a long trip. (3) It took us two days to get to Oregon; we kept (4) pestering my parents, asking, "are we there yet?" (5) We drove across rushing rivers, through stunning deserts and mountain ranges. Finally we reached the Oregon coast; It was magnificent! (6) The waves crashed against the rocks, and the water seemed to extend forever. I wondered what was beyond the horizon. I knew that someday I would have to cross the ocean and find out for myself.

1. A. I was eight years old, because my family
   B. When I was eight years old, my family
   C. I was eight years old, but my family
   D. Correct as is

2. A. Me and my brother were
   B. My brother and myself were
   C. My brother and I were
   D. Correct as is

3. A. excited because we'd never taken such a long trip.
   B. excited, we'd never taken such a long trip.
   C. excited; Because we'd never taken such a long trip.
   D. Correct as is

4. A. Oregon, we kept
   B. Oregon: the whole time, we kept
   C. Oregon we kept
   D. Correct as is

5. A. asking: "are we there yet?"
   B. asking, "Are we there yet"
   C. asking, "Are we there yet?"
   D. Correct as is

6. A. reached the Oregon coast; it was magnificent!
   B. reached the Oregon coast, it was magnificent!
   C. reached the oregon coast. It was magnificent!
   D. Correct as is

Need extra help?

See the **Grammar Handbook**
Correcting Run-on Sentences, p. R73
Capitalization, p. R79
Correcting Sentence Fragments, p. R73
Pronoun Case, p. R57

TEST PRACTICE

Standardized Test Practice

Encourage students to review run-on sentences and sentence fragments in the Grammar Handbook, pp. R73–R74, before correcting the errors.

Answers:
1. B; **2.** C; **3.** A; **4.** D; **5.** C; **6.** A

To help students see the correct answer, cross out the phrase *my sister and* in both sentences. They will see that *My mother told me about the* Ramayana sounds right, while *My mother told I about the* Ramayana is clearly incorrect.

For more instruction and practice in pronoun case, use McDougal Littell's ***Language Network:***

- Grade 10, Chapter 8, "Using Pronouns"
- Grade 12, Chapter 6, "Using Pronouns"

Building Vocabulary

Objectives

- rely on context to determine the meanings of words with multiple meanings
- use reference materials such as a dictionary to determine precise word meanings

EXERCISE

Have students identify the word or words in the context that helped them determine the meaning of the unfamiliar word.

1. firmly decided or resolved
2. case for arrows
3. a position of attack
4. character
5. to appear unexpectedly

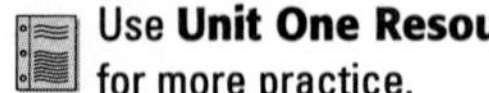

Use **Unit One Resource Book,** p. 49, for more practice.

Building Vocabulary

Words with Multiple Meanings

The English language changes constantly, gaining new words (such as *Internet*) and gaining new definitions for old words (such as *surf*). We are currently in a period of particularly rapid change. However, the language has been changing since it was first spoken. One result of this process is that many words have more than one meaning.

Words with multiple meanings can confuse readers, who may not always know which meaning the writer intended. And if the writer is using the word in a way the reader has never seen, it can be especially puzzling.

Look at the model below. The word mount can mean "get up on something, as a horse or bicycle" or "to increase in amount, extent, or intensity." Which of the two meanings do you think is correct here?

> **Noticing this, Ravana's anger mounted further.**
>
> —the *Ramayana*

Strategies for Building Vocabulary

As you read, keep an eye out for words that do not seem to mean what you expect them to mean. Then use the following strategies to determine the author's intended meaning.

❶ **Use Context Clues to Determine Meaning** When you encounter a word that is used in an unexpected way, look at the surrounding sentences for clues. Consider the word *surveyed* in the following example.

> **Ravana became restless and abruptly left the hall and went up on a tower, from which he could obtain a full view of the city. He surveyed the scene below but could not stand it.**
>
> —the *Ramayana*

One familiar meaning of *surveyed* is "conducted a statistical study on." However, it's clear from the context that Ravana did not pass around statistical questionnaires. On the other hand, you know that he climbed a tower to get a full view of the city. From this clue you can infer that in this context, *surveyed* means "examined or looked at fully."

❷ **Refer to the Dictionary** When context clues don't help, consult a dictionary. Remember, words with multiple meanings have multiple definitions, so be sure to consider each of the numbered definitions given. Which one makes the most sense in the sentence?

You can quickly eliminate definitions with the wrong part of speech. For example, the word *survey* can be a noun as well as a verb. However, the above sentence makes it clear that the word is used as a verb in this example.

In addition to definitions, many dictionary entries give sentences or phrases that show how a word is used. These examples can also help you determine which definition is the right one.

EXERCISE Use a dictionary or context clues to define each underlined word in these sentences from the *Ramayana.* Then choose a different definition for the same word and use it in your own sentence.

1. The gods in heaven noticed Ravana's determined move and felt that Rama would need all the support they could muster.
2. Rama fastened his sword, slung two quivers full of rare arrows over his shoulders, and climbed into the chariot.
3. Rama paused for a while in grief, undecided as to his next step. Then he recovered and resumed his offensive.
4. Ravana then shot an asthra called "Thama," whose nature was to create total darkness in all the worlds.
5. Rama's crescent-shaped weapon was continuously busy as Ravana's heads kept cropping up.

Sentence Crafting

Using Elements in a Series

Grammar from Literature Writers often link together a series of elements—nouns, verbs, modifiers, phrases, or clauses—in a single sentence. This technique makes ideas concise and often creates a pleasing rhythm, which can make a text easier to understand and remember.

A **series** includes three or more elements that have the same function in a sentence. For example, they might be parts of a compound subject, a compound object, or a series of similar phrases. The elements are separated by semicolons or commas with, usually, at least one coordinating conjunction. Notice the series in the examples below from the *Ramayana*.

series of direct objects
He had a ritual bath and performed special prayers to gain the benediction of Shiva; donned his battle dress, matchless armor, armlets, and crowns.

series of objects of a preposition
["]It can fly swifter than air over all obstacles, over any mountain, sea, or sky, **and will help you to emerge victorious in this battle."**

series of independent clauses
Many ominous signs were seen now—his bow-strings suddenly snapped; the mountains shook; thunders rumbled in the skies; tears flowed from the horses' eyes; elephants with decorated foreheads moved along dejectedly.

Using Series in Your Writing Look for places where listing elements will help you reduce unnecessary repetition and create rhythm. Notice how creating a series eliminates wordiness in the following examples.

WORDY
But Rama's arrows diverted **Ravana's. They also** broke **some of Ravana's arrows, and they** neutralized **some others.**

CONCISE
But Rama's arrows diverted, broke, **or** neutralized **Ravana's.**
—the *Ramayana*

Usage Tip In a series, items that are parallel in meaning should also be parallel in structure. In the sentence below, the last item in the series is not grammatically parallel with the other two items.

INCORRECT
adjective adjective independent clause
In battle, Rama is brave, strong, **and** the gods have blessed him with their gifts.

See page 483 for more instruction on parallel construction.

CORRECT
adjective adjective adjective
In battle, Rama is brave, strong, **and** blessed **with gifts from the gods.**

WRITING EXERCISE Combine each group of sentences below by creating a sentence containing a series.

1. Ravana heard cries of grief from his camp. He heard the wailing of widows. Groans of pain reached his ears.
2. In preparation for battle, Ravana bathed himself and prayed to the god Shiva. He also put on his suit of armor and emerged from his chamber.
3. Rama's chariot was large and brilliant. It was capable of flying over any obstacle.
4. Rama and Ravana both had great strength. They had powerful arms, too, and a desire to win.
5. Arrows flew, and people turned their heads in fear. However, the arrows did not meet their mark.

GRAMMAR EXERCISE Rewrite the sentences below, correcting any errors in parallelism.

1. Because of an illusion, Rama thought he saw Ravana's defeated army come back to life, rise up on the battlefield, and moving forward with battle cries.
2. Ravana shot an asthra that plunged the world into darkness, paralyzed creation, and whose purpose was to send storms down to the earth.
3. Rama's cleverness, his physical strength, and being magical allowed him to fight back.
4. Ravana's gifts of destruction—his knowledge and the special weaponry that was his—were running out.
5. Rama deflected Ravana's final asthra, which struck Ravana's heart, knocking him from his chariot and burning his face.

LANGUAGE SKILLS

Sentence Crafting

Objectives

- use elements in a series as a way to avoid wordiness
- use parallel sentence structure with serial elements that are parallel in meaning

WRITING EXERCISE

Answers may vary slightly, but student sentences should have a similar structure to these answers.

1. Ravana heard cries of grief, the wailing of widows, and groans of pain coming from his camp.
2. In preparation for battle, Ravana bathed himself, prayed to the god Shiva, put on his suit of armor, and emerged from his chamber.
3. Rama's chariot was large, brilliant, and capable of flying over any obstacle.
4. Rama and Ravana both had great strength, powerful arms, and a desire to win.
5. Arrows flew and people turned their heads in fear, but the arrows did not meet their mark.

GRAMMAR EXERCISE

1. Because of an illusion, Rama thought he saw Ravana's defeated army come back to life, rise up on the battlefield, and move forward with battle cries.
2. Ravana shot an asthra that plunged the word into darkness, paralyzed creation, and sent storms down to the earth.
3. Rama's cleverness, his physical strength, and his magic powers allowed him to fight back.
4. Ravana's gifts of destruction—his knowledge and special weaponry—were running out.
5. Rama deflected Ravana's final asthra, which struck Ravana's heart, knocked him from his chariot and burned his face.

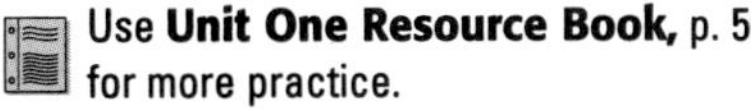
Use **Unit One Resource Book,** p. 50, for more practice.

Objectives
- reflect on and assess understanding of the unit part
- apply literary themes to life
- compare character development across texts
- assess and build portfolios

Reflecting on the Literature
A successful response will
- identify three lessons taught by the literature
- apply each lesson to modern life

Reviewing Literary Concepts
A successful response will
- name a descriptive trait for each of three characters from the selections
- identify the technique(s) of characterization that revealed this trait
- evaluate how effectively the characters were developed

Building Your Portfolio
For more information on using writing and assessing portfolios, see the **Teacher's Guide to Assessment and Portfolio Use,** pp. 53–74.

Part Assessment
To assess skills and concepts taught in this unit part, use **Formal Assessment Book,** pp. 23–24.

Literature of Ancient India

Reflect and Assess

What did you learn about ancient Indian literature from reading the selections in Unit One, Part 2? Did the literature surprise you in any way? Use the following options to help you explore what you have learned.

Detail of illustration, Rama fights Ravana. Courtesy of the Trustees of the Victoria & Albert Museum, London.

Reflecting on the Literature

Teaching Stories The ancient epics and folktales of India are still appreciated for the life lessons they present. Many people regard these stories as guides for behavior, even in the modern world. Think back over the selections you've read, and identify three lessons they teach. State each lesson in your own words, and discuss how a person might apply it today.

Reviewing Literary Concepts

Developing Characters In this part of the book, you learned about techniques of characterization, particularly in epics. Pick three characters from the Indian epics or folktales you've read, and come up with one descriptive trait for each. Then note how you learned of this trait—whether through the narrator's comments, through the character's actions, or through some other technique. Which of the three characters was developed most effectively, in your opinion?

Self ASSESSMENT

READER'S NOTEBOOK

Following are important terms that relate to this part of the book. Next to each term, write a sentence describing or defining it. If you are unclear about any term, go back through the unit or consult the **Glossary of Literary Terms** (page R91).

Aryans	characterization
Rig Veda	epithet
paradox	*Ramayana*
epic	conflict
Mahabharata	*Panchatantra*

Building Your Portfolio

Writing Workshop and Writing Options Look back at the autobiographical incident you wrote for the Writing Workshop and at the various writing options you completed. Which represents your best work? Add that assignment to your **Presentation Portfolio**, along with a cover note explaining why you are especially proud of it.

Setting GOALS

Would you like to read more of a particular work or of a certain type of literature featured in Unit One, Part 2? Ask your teacher or a librarian to help you locate works to read on your own.

Assessment Self Assessment

Students can look up the listed terms in the **Glossary of Literary Terms** on page R91 or they can find them introduced in context on the text pages indicated below.

Aryans (pp. 102, 114)
Rig Veda (p. 114)
paradox (p. 114)
epic (pp. 120, 121)
Mahabharata (pp. 122, 123)
characterization (pp. 123, 126)
epithet (pp. 123, 126)
Ramayana (pp. 130, 131)
conflict (pp. 131, 143)
Panchatantra (p. 146)

Extend Your *Reading*

Folktales from India

EDITED BY A. K. RAMANUJAN

Ramanujan, an award-winning translator and poet, gathers 110 tales translated from 22 Indian languages. He selected only tales told in households, by amateur storytellers. Excluded are myths, legends, and tales taken directly from Sanskrit literary texts. The works in the book are arranged in six broad categories: male-centered stories, female-centered stories, stories about families, humorous tales, animal fables, and stories about stories. The result is a delightfully varied and fresh collection, enhanced by Ramanujan's informative introduction.

The Eternal Cycle: Indian Myth

Part of Time-Life's *Myth and Mankind* series, this beautiful volume contains stories from Hindu, Buddhist, and Jain mythology, including examples from the *Rig Veda,* the *Mahabharata,* and the *Ramayana.* Lavishly illustrated with full-color photos of art and sacred sites, the book also contains mini-essays on such topics as the caste system, the Ganges River, and Indian festivals. A concluding section, "The Legacy of Indian Myth," examines how such mythology has influenced politics, popular entertainment, and the practices of Indian immigrants abroad.

And Even *More* . . .

Books

Theater of Memory BARBARA STOLER MILLER
Contemporary translations of Kalidasa's three surviving Sanskrit plays, including *Shakuntala and the Ring of Recollection.*

Indian Art: A Concise History ROY C. CRAVEN
A fascinating overview of Indian art, from early Indus Valley examples, through Hindu and Buddhist masterpieces, to Rajput miniature paintings.

Women Writing in India: 600 B.C. to the Present EDITED BY K. LALITA AND SUSIE J. THARU
An anthology of works by Indian women writers, including Atukuri Molla, who wrote her own *Ramayana,* and Mirabai, who wrote famous love lyrics to the god Krishna.

Other Media

Mahabharata
A three-hour film version of the epic, directed by Peter Brook and starring actors of many different nationalities. Parabola Video Library. (VIDEOCASSETTE)

India and the Infinite: The Soul of a People
This visually stunning documentary, narrated by Professor Huston Smith, examines India's major religions. Hartley Film Foundation. (VIDEOCASSETTE)

Snakes and Ladders

GITA MEHTA

Mehta is an Indian-born writer and documentary filmmaker who sees her homeland as "an extraordinary world spinning through an extraordinary time." Her short, entertaining personal essays examine life in India today, focusing on the nation's many contradictions.

More Recommendations for Your Students

Difficulty Level: Easy

Goodwin, William. *India (Modern Nations of the World)* (San Diego: Lucent, 2000). A survey of Indian history from ancient to modern times, written for a young adult audience.

Rothfarb, Ed. *In the Land of the Taj Mahal: The World of the Fabled Mughals* (NY: Henry Holt, 1997). This lively and well-researched history focuses on the accomplishments of India's Mughal period (1526–1724).

Staples, Suzanne Fisher. *Shiva's Fire* (NY: Farrar, Strous & Giroux, 2000). In this novel set in India, a talented girl faces spritual struggles as she becomes a *bharatnatyam* dancer.

Difficulty Level: Average

Powell, Barbara. *Windows into the Infinite: A Guide to the Hindu Scriptures* (Fremont, CA: Asian Humanities Press, 1996). This guide summarizes and comments on the Vedas, *Bhagavad-Gita,* Upanishads, Puranas and other scriptures.

Wolpert, Stanley. *A New History of India* (Oxford University Press, 1999). A popular, readable history, covering 4000 years in 544 pages.

Difficulty Level: Challenging

Tharoor, Shashi. *The Great Indian Novel* (Boston: Arcade, 1993). This fictional recasting of the *Mahabharata* epic satirizes 20th-century Indian politics.

Zimmer, Heinrich. *Myths and Symbols in Indian Art and Civilization* (Princeton University Press, 1972). This is a scholarly analysis of Indian mythology, illustrated with 70 plates of art.

The Classical Age of Greece and Rome
Together, the cultural achievements of ancient Greece and those of ancient Rome form the cornerstone of Western civilization.

Part 1
The Heroic Tradition: Literature of Ancient Greece In this part students will encounter some of the defining texts of Greek culture and thought. They will read some of the earliest models of Western literary genres such as the epic, lyric poetry, and drama, as well as works of history and philosophy.

Part 2
The Tradition Continues: Literature of Ancient Rome The selections in this part show how ancient Rome adopted and developed the traditions of Greece in the epic, lyric poetry, mythology, and history. A **Comparing Literature Across Cultures** feature gives students the opportunity to compare Roman perspectives on a well-known Homeric figure with those of American poets of the 19th and 20th centuries.

The Classical Age of Greece and Rome 800 B.C.–A.D. 200

Temple E at Selinus (now Selinunte), Italy. Photograph by Anne and Henri Stierlin.

UNIT TWO

". . . To the glory that was Greece
And the grandeur that was Rome."

—Edgar Allan Poe

Making Connections

Ask: What examples can you give of "the glory that was Greece" and "the grandeur that was Rome"?
Possible Response: Answers will vary. Encourage students to be specific in their responses and to work together, pooling their knowledge, to develop and refine them.

PART 1 SKILLS TRACE

Features and Selections	Literary Analysis	Reading and Critical Thinking	Writing Opportunities
The Classical Age of Greece and Rome 800 B.C. – A.D. 200			
The Heroic Tradition: Literature of Ancient Greece		Interpreting the Text, 165, 166, 169, 171 Using the Time Line, 172	
Learning the Language of Literature The Epics of Greece and Rome	The Epics of Greece and Rome, 176, 177	Strategies for Reading, 177	
EPIC POETRY *from the* Iliad *from* Books 1, 6, 22, 24	Epic Hero, 181, 223 Epic Similes and Epithets, 223 Epic Hero, 186, 190, 198, 206, 218	Evaluating, 181, 223 Evaluating, 186, 188, 198, 202, 208, 216 The Greek Gods, 183 Animal Sacrifice, 184 Prophecy and Divination, 185 War Prizes, 186 Tribal Society and the Greek Army, 187 Hector, 195 Troy, 197 Fate, 199 Hades, 204 Achilles' Armor, 208 Ransoms, 209 Burial Customs, 211 Life Expectancy in Ancient Greece, 213 Hospitality, 218	Ancient Values Essay, 224 Analysis of the Gods, 224 Homeric Argument, 224 Informal Assessment (Summarizing), 190, 206
The Translator at Work Homer and the Oral Tradition		Questions to Consider, 225 Comparing Translations, 225	
POETRY Poems by Sappho To an army wife He Is More Than a Hero To Aphrodite of the Flowers, at Knossos	Lyric Poetry, 227, 231 Lyric Poetry, 228	Clarifying, 227, 231 Clarifying, 228, 230 Lydia, 228 Aphrodite and the City of Knossos, 230	
NONFICTION *from* History of the Peloponnesian War Pericles' Funeral Oration	Author's Purpose, 233, 243 Author's Purpose, 234, 236, 240	Main Idea, 233, 243 Main Idea, 234, 236, 238, 240 Athens and Pericles, 234 Sparta, 237 Honor, 240	Extended Definition, 244 Analysis of Women's Role, 244 Informal Assessment (Outlining), 242
Connect to Today Nelson Mandela Celebrates a National Hero		Discussion, 245 Compare and Contrast, 245	
NONFICTION *from the* Apology	Speech, 247, 254 Speech, 248, 250, 252	Paraphrasing, 247, 254 Paraphrasing, 248, 250, 252 Socrates and His Legacy, 251 Standardized Test Practice (Identifying the Main Idea), 253	Dramatic Scene, 255 Newspaper Editorial, 255

LEGEND **Black type – Pupil Edition**
Green type – Teacher's Edition
DLS – Daily Language SkillBuilder

Speaking and Listening Viewing and Representing	Inquiry and Research	Grammar, Usage, and Mechanics	Vocabulary
Using the Map, 162			
Classic Illustration, 224 Using the Map, 180 Informal Assessment (Summarizing), 190 Art Appreciation, 193, 196, 214, 219 Performing a Dialogue, 203 Dramatizing a Conflict, 210 Delivering a Speech, 215	The Real Troy, 224	DLS, 178 Simple Subjects and Simple Predicates, 188 Complete Subjects and Complete Predicates, 200 Compound Subjects and Compound Predicates, 216	Context Clues, 224 Using a Dictionary to Find Precise Meaning, 182 Context Clues, 198
		DLS, 226	
Athens vs. Sparta Debate, 244 Delivering a Formal Speech, 236 Art Appreciation, 238 Discussion, 245	Legacy of Pericles, 244	DLS, 232	Meaning Clues, 244 Roots and Word Families, 235
Philosophical Dialogue, 255 Socrates in Caricature, 255 Art Appreciation, 249, 252	Philosopher in the Clouds, 255	DLS, 246	Word Meanings, 255 Context Clues, 248

LEGEND **Black type – Pupil Edition**
Green type – Teacher's Edition

DLS – Daily Language SkillBuilder

UNIT TWO
PART 1 SKILLS TRACE

Features and Selections	Literary Analysis	Reading and Critical Thinking	Writing Opportunities
DRAMA Oedipus the King	Tragic Hero, 261, 330 Dramatic Irony, 330 Tragic Hero, 262, 264, 268, 272, 276, 278, 284, 286, 288, 290, 294, 296, 300, 306, 310, 312, 314, 316, 318, 322, 324, 326	Strategies for Reading Greek Drama, 261, 330 Greek Theater, 260 Strategies for Reading Greek Drama, 262, 266, 268, 272, 274, 276, 278, 280, 282, 288, 290, 298, 306, 308, 310, 312, 316, 320, 324 Greek Religion, 262 The Plague, 264 The Oracle of Apollo at Delphi, 266 The Greek Chorus, 269 Exile, 274 Prophets, 275 Fate, 281 Oedipus as Tyrant, 287 Travel in Ancient Greece, 294 Oedipus and Pollution, 297 The Guilt and Innocence of Oedipus, 298 Standardized Test Practice (Identifying the Main Idea), 300 Culture of Shame, 315 Violence and Greek Staging, 316 Aristotle's Theory of Tragedy, 324 Oedipus: The Rest of the Story, 327	Personal Response, 331 Diary Entry, 331 Literary Analysis, 331 Informal Assessment (Summarizing), 282
Related Reading Myth		Discussion Questions, 329	
Communication Workshop Writing and Staging a Scene Standardized Test Practice Building Vocabulary Sentence Crafting		Analyzing a Student Model, 333–335	Writing and Staging Your Scene, 332, 336 Using Dialogue Effectively, 337 Choosing a Topic, 336 Planning a Script, 336
Reflect and Assess	Reflecting on the Literature (In Quest of Honor), 342 Reviewing Literary Concepts (Tragic Hero), 342		Building Your Portfolio, 342

UNIT TWO
PART 2 SKILLS TRACE

Features and Selections	Literary Analysis	Reading and Critical Thinking	Writing Opportunities
The Tradition Continues: Literature of Ancient Rome		Interpreting the Text, 347, 349 Using the Time Line, 353	
EPIC POETRY *from the* Aeneid The Fall of Troy	Culture Hero, 359, 380 Imagery, 380 Culture Hero, 360, 366, 376, 378	Predicting, 359, 380 Predicting, 360, 362, 370, 376 Mythology, 359, 365, 373 Sacrificial Rituals, 363	Interview with Aeneas, 381 Creusa's Story, 381 Compare-and-Contrast Essay, 381 Standardized Test Practice (Writing a Short Essay Answer), 379

LEGEND **Black type – Pupil Edition**
Green type – Teacher's Edition
DLS – Daily Language SkillBuilder

Speaking and Listening Viewing and Representing	Inquiry and Research	Grammar, Usage, and Mechanics	Vocabulary
View and Compare, 284, 328 **Theater Model, 331** **Role-Playing, 331** Choral Reading, 271 Speech, 273 Dramatizing Dialogue, 278 Informal Assessment (Summarizing), 282 Comparing Stagings of the Chorus, 284 Analyzing Setting, 290 Choral Reading, 313 Comparing Settings, 328	**Oedipus Complex, 331**	DLS, 259 Kinds of Sentences, 267	**Synonyms and Antonyms, 331** Using a Dictionary to Find Precise Meanings, 265 Antonyms, 272 Roots and Word Families, 307
Using Dialogue Effectively, 337 **Evaluating Your Interpretive Choices, 338**		**Possessives, 339** **Verb Tense, 339** **Commas, 339** **Using Participles, 341** Sentence Fragments, 337 Commas with Nonessential Phrases and Clauses, 339	**Homophones, 339** **Greek and Latin Roots, 340** **Strategies for Building Vocabulary, 340**
			Self Assessment, 342 Self Assessment, 342
Using the Map, 345			
Epic Storyboard, 381 **Oral Reading, 381** Using the Map, 357 Art Appreciation, 364, 371 Role-Playing, 372 Dramatic Reading, 378	**Roman Influences, 381**	DLS, 356 Direct Objects and Indirect Objects, 366–367 Subject Complements, 376, 377–378	**Word Meanings, 381** Context Clues, 362

LEGEND **Black type – Pupil Edition**
Green type – Teacher's Edition
DLS – Daily Language SkillBuilder

PART 2 SKILLS TRACE

Features and Selections	Literary Analysis	Reading and Critical Thinking	Writing Opportunities
Comparing Literature Across Cultures Perspectives on Helen of Troy	Speaker, 382	Compare and Contrast, 382, 387, 390	Standardized Test Practice (Comparison-and-Contrast Essay), 382
POETRY Helen of Troy	Speaker, 383, 387, 390	Making Inferences, 383, 387 Making Inferences, 384, 386	
POETRY To Helen	Speaker, 387, 390		
Comparing Literature Standardized Test Practice			Comparison-and-Contrast Essay, 391 Standardized Test Practice (Responding to a Writing Prompt), 391
POETRY Poems by Horace Seize the Day Better to live, Licinius, . . .	Theme, 393, 397 Theme, 394	Understanding Contrast, 393, 397 Contrast, 394, 396 Carpe Diem, 395	
POETRY *from* Metamorphoses The Story of Daedalus and Icarus **Related Reading** Landscape with the Fall of Icarus **Connect to Today** The Urge to Fly	Myth, 399, 404 Myth, 400, 402	Reading Narrative Poetry, 399, 404 Narrative Poetry, 400, 402 Ovid's *Metamorphoses*, 402	
Reflect and Assess	Reflecting on the Literature (Literature and Values), 410 Reviewing Literary Concepts (Appreciating Imagery), 410		Building Your Portfolio, 410
Standardized Test Practice		How to Read a Test Selection, 412 How to Answer Multiple-Choice Questions, 415	How to Respond in Writing, 416

LEGEND **Black type – Pupil Edition**
Green type – Teacher's Edition
DLS – Daily Language SkillBuilder

Speaking and Listening Viewing and Representing	Inquiry and Research	Grammar, Usage, and Mechanics	Vocabulary
Art Appreciation, 385 Poetry Reading Workshop, 386		DLS, 383	
Dramatic Reading, 389		DLS, 388	
Art Appreciation, 394		DLS, 392	
Art Appreciation, 403	Research Project, 405	DLS, 398 Parentheses and Dashes, 400	
			Self Assessment, 410 Self-Assessment, 410
		How to Revise and Edit Your Test Essay, 417	

LEGEND **Black type – Pupil Edition**
Green type – Teacher's Edition

DLS – Daily Language SkillBuilder

RESOURCE MANAGEMENT GUIDE
PART 1

	Unit Resource Book	Assessment	Integrated Technology and Media	Additional Support
The Heroic Tradition **Literature of Ancient Greece**			Humanities classzone.com	**World Art and Cultures Transparencies** • AT10 Greek painted oil flask • AT11 Greek marble sculptures
from the **Iliad** *from* **Book 1** *from* **Book 6** *from* **Book 22** *from* **Book 24** *pp. 178–225*	**Part 1** • Summary p. 4 • Glossary p. 5 **Book 1** • Active Reading p. 6 • Literary Analysis p. 7 • Selection Quiz p. 8 **Books 6 and 22** • Active Reading p. 9 • Literary Analysis p. 10 • Selection Quiz p. 11 **Books 1, 6, 22, and 24** • Active Reading p. 12 • Literary Analysis p. 13 • Words to Know p. 14 • Selection Quiz p. 15	• Selection Test, Formal Assessment pp. 25–30 • Teacher's Guide to Assessment and Portfolio Use Test Generator	Humanities Activity classzone.com Research Starter classzone.com	An excerpt from this selection is included in the *World Literature InterActive Reader*™. • RTC 50 Venn diagram • VTC 2 context clues, 35 figurative language, 59 using a dictionary • GTC 85 simple subjects and predicates, 84 complete subjects and predicates, 86 compound predicates • WTC 25 opinion statement
To an army wife **He Is More Than a Hero** **To Aphrodite of the Flowers, at Knossos** *pp. 226–231*	• Active Reading p. 16 • Literary Analysis p. 17	• Selection Test, Formal Assessment pp. 31–32 • Teacher's Guide to Assessment and Portfolio Use Test Generator		• RTC 7 making inferences
from **History of the Peloponnesian War** **Pericles' Funeral Oration** *pp. 232–245*	• Summary p. 18 • Active Reading p. 19 • Literary Analysis p. 20 • Words to Know p. 21 • Selection Quiz p. 22	• Selection Test, Formal Assessment pp. 33–34 • Teacher's Guide to Assessment and Portfolio Use Test Generator	Research Starter classzone.com	• RTC 12 main idea, 19 determining author's purpose • VTC 47 meaning of roots • WTC 36 compare and contrast
from the **Apology** *pp. 246–255*	• Summary p. 23 • Active Reading p. 24 • Literary Analysis p. 25 • Words to Know p. 26 • Selection Quiz p. 27	• Selection Test, Formal Assessment pp. 35–36 • Teacher's Guide to Assessment and Portfolio Use Test Generator	Research Starter classzone.com	• RTC 41 paraphrasing and summarizing • VTC 3 context clues • WTC 25 opinion statement
Milestones in World Literature **Greek Drama** *pp. 256–257*			Milestone Links classzone.com	
Oedipus the King *pp. 258–331*	• Summary p. 28 **Part 1** • Active Reading p. 29 • Literary Analysis p. 30 • Selection Quiz p. 31 **Part 2** • Active Reading p. 32 • Literary Analysis p. 33 • Selection Quiz p. 34 **Part 3** • Active Reading p. 35 • Literary Analysis p. 36 • Words to Know p. 37 • Selection Quiz p. 38	• Selection Test, Formal Assessment pp. 37–42 • Teacher's Guide to Assessment and Portfolio Use Test Generator	Humanities Activity classzone.com Research Starter classzone.com	An excerpt from this selection is included in the *World Literature InterActive Reader*™. • RTC 13 sequencing • LT 15 dramatic irony • VTC 59 using a dictionary, 15 synonyms and antonyms, 12 word origins–Anglo-Saxon • WTC 33 interpretive essay

UNIT TWO
RESOURCE MANAGEMENT GUIDE
PART 1

	Unit Resource Book	Assessment	Integrated Technology and Media	Additional Support
Communication Workshop: Writing and Staging a Scene *pp. 332–341*	**Unit Two Resource Book** • Prewriting p. 39 • Drafting and Elaboration p. 40 • Planning Your Scene p. 41 • Developing, Practicing, and Presenting p. 42 • Peer Response Guide pp. 43–44 • Revising and Refining Your Performance p. 45 • Student Models pp. 46–51 • Rubric and and Standards p. 52 Publishing Options classzone.com **Teacher's Guide to Assessment and Portfolio Use**	***Unit Assessment*** • Unit Two, Part 1 Test, Formal Assessment pp. 43-44 Test Generator	***Unit Technology*** classzone.com	

UNIT TWO
PART 2 RESOURCE MANAGEMENT GUIDE

	Unit Resource Book	Assessment	Integrated Technology and Media	Additional Support
The Tradition Continues **Literature of Ancient Rome**			Humanities classzone.com	**World Art and Cultures Transparencies** • AT12 The Forum • AT13 Roman painting • AT14 Trajan's Column [detail]
from the **Aeneid** **The Fall of Troy** *pp. 356–381*	• Summary p. 56 • Glossary p. 57 • Active Reading p. 58 • Literary Analysis p. 59 • Words to Know p. 60 • Selection Quiz p. 61	• Selection Test, Formal Assessment pp. 45–46 • Teacher's Guide to Assessment and Portfolio Use Test Generator	Humanities Activity classzone.com Research Starter classzone.com	This selection is included in the *World Literature InterActive Reader™*.
Helen of Troy *pp. 382–387* **To Helen** *pp. 388–391*	• Points of Comparison p. 62 • Active Reading p. 63 • Literary Analysis p. 64 • Compare/contrast Essay p. 65	• Selection Test, Formal Assessment pp. 47–48 • Teacher's Guide to Assessment and Portfolio Use Test Generator		
Seize the Day **Better to live, Licinius, . . .** *pp. 392–397*	• Active Reading p. 66 • Literary Analysis p. 67	• Selection Test, Formal Assessment pp. 49–50 • Teacher's Guide to Assessment and Portfolio Use Test Generator		
from **Metamorphoses** **The Story of Daedalus and Icarus** *pp. 398–405*	• Active Reading p. 68 • Literary Analysis p. 69	• Selection Test, Formal Assessment pp. 51–52 • Teacher's Guide to Assessment and Portfolio Use Test Generator	Research Starter classzone.com	
		Unit Assessment • Unit Two, Part 2 Test, Formal Assessment pp. 53–54 Test Generator • Unit Two, Integrated Assessment Test, Integrated Assessment pp. 7–12	***Unit Technology*** classzone.com	

DAILY LANGUAGE SKILLBUILDERS

Selection	SkillBuilder Sentences	Suggested Answers
from the Iliad	**1.** The Greek gods plays an important roll in the Iliad. **2.** "Who is the best fighter, Achilles or Hector: asked Mr Ramos.	**1.** The Greek gods play**ed** an important **role** in the <u>**Iliad**</u>. **2.** "Who is the **better** fighter, Achilles or Hector**?"** asked Mr**.** Ramos.
To an army wife He Is More Than a Hero To Aphrodite of the Flowers, at Knossos	**1.** Though we no very little about Sappho she is often considered the greatest woman poet of the ancient world. **2.** Sappho is famous for her short descriptive and intensely personal poetry.	**1.** Though we **know** very little about Sappho**,** she is often considered the greatest woman poet of the ancient world. **2.** Sappho is famous for her short**,** descriptive**,** and intensely personal poetry.
from History of the Peloponnesian War Pericles' Funeral Oration	**1.** Thucydides' wrote about the <u>Peloponnesian</u> war so that future generations could understand the events that occurred and understand their causes. **2.** He recreated a speech given by Pericles an athenian polititian to honor dead soldiers.	**1.** **Thucydides** wrote about the **Peloponnesian W**ar so that future generations could understand the events that occurred **and their causes.** (Students should remove the apostrophe from *Thucydides,* the underline from *Peloponnesian,* and the second instance of *understand.*) **2.** He recreated a speech given by Pericles**,** an **A**thenian **politician,** to honor dead soldiers.
from the Apology	**1.** 'If you take a philosophy class in college you'll learn about Plato and Socrates,' my Sister said. **2.** Neither my mom or dad know much about the greek philosophers.	**1.** **"**If you take a philosophy class in college**,** you'll learn about Plato and Socrates,**"** my **s**ister said. **2.** Neither my mom **nor** dad know**s** much about the **G**reek philosophers.
Oedipus the King	**1.** Oedipus did'nt realize he had killed his father and married his Mother. **2.** Antigone is another play by Sophocles it tells the tragic story of what happen to the children of Oedipus.	**1.** Oedipus did**n't** realize he had killed his father and married his **m**other. **2.** <u>**Antigone**</u> is another play by Sophocles**. I**t tells the tragic story of what happen**s** to the children of Oedipus.
from the Aeneid The Fall of Troy	**1.** Virgil was ask to write a National epic. To honor Rome. **2.** In this famous epic, Aeneas, the Trojan prince represents the ideal roman he is a faithful leader father and son.	**1.** Virgil was ask**ed** to write a **n**ational epic **t**o honor Rome. (Students should remove the period after *epic.*) **2.** In this famous epic, Aeneas, the Trojan prince**,** represents the ideal **R**oman**. H**e is a faithful leader**,** father**,** and son.
Helen of Troy To Helen	**1.** According to legend Helen was carryed off by Paris the Trojan kings son and thats what started the Trojan War. **2.** Which poem do you like best, Helen of Troy or To Helen?	**1.** According to legend**,** Helen was carr**ied** off by Paris**,** the Trojan king**'**s son, and that**'**s what started the Trojan War. **2.** Which poem do you like **better**, **"**Helen of Troy**"** or **"**To Helen**"**?
Seize the Day Better to live, Licinius, . . .	**1.** Seize the day remains a popular saying too this day. **2.** In your opinion, which of Horace's poem shown here give better advise?	**1.** **"**Seize the day**"** remains a popular saying **to** this day. **2.** In your opinion, which of Horace's poem**s** shown here give**s** better **advice**?
from Metamorphoses The Story of Daedalus and Icarus	**1.** Why did Icarus fly to close to the sun? ask Jeremy. **2.** I wonder why Ovid was banished from Rhome?	**1.** **"**Why did Icarus fly **too** close to the sun?**"** ask**ed** Jeremy. **2.** I wonder why Ovid was banished from **Rome.**

INTEGRATING GRAMMAR AND LITERATURE: GRAMMAR PLANNER

	Unit One	Unit Two	Unit Three	Unit Four	Unit Five	Unit Six	Unit Seven
Grammar Focus by Unit	Parts of Speech	The Sentence and Its Parts	Using Verbs	Using Modifiers	Using Phrases	Clauses and Sentence Structure	Clauses and Sentence Structure

The Language of Literature offers several options for integrating grammar instruction and literature.

- Each unit has a grammar focus. The Teacher's Edition includes Mini Lessons for the selections that help develop the grammar focus for the unit and spring from the content of the specific literature.
- The Pupil Edition includes several full-page lessons on Sentence Crafting. These lessons are related to both the literature and the grammar focus for a unit and help students use proper grammar in their own writing.
- Daily Language SkillBuilders in the Teacher's Edition provide students with ongoing proofreading practice and reinforce correct punctuation, spelling, grammar and usage, and capitalization.

Black type — Pupil Edition
Green type — Teacher's Edition

Part 1

The Sentence and Its Parts

Simple Subjects and Simple Predicates
from the *Iliad*, p. 188

Complete Subjects and Complete Predicates
from the *Iliad*, p. 200

Compound Subjects and Compound Predicates
from the *Iliad*, p. 216

Kinds of Sentences
Oedipus the King, p. 267

Sentence Fragments
Communication Workshop, p. 337

Using Participles
Sentence Crafting, p. 341

Punctuation

Commas with Nonessential Phrases and Clauses
Communication Workshop, p. 339
Standardized Test Practice, p. 339

Possessives
Standardized Test Practice, p. 339

Parts of Speech

Verb Tense
Standardized Test Practice, 339

Part 2

The Sentence and Its Parts

Direct Objects and Indirect Objects
from the *Aeneid*, pp. 366–367

Subject Complements
from the *Aeneid*, pp. 376–377

Punctuation

Parentheses and Dashes
from *Metamorphoses: The Story of Daedalus and Icarus*, p. 400

Unit Two, Part 1, introduces students to some of the defining works of ancient Greece. The works give students a representative sampling of Greek literature and thought.

World Art and Cultures Transparencies

AT10 Greek painted oil flask

AT11 Greek marble sculptures

You may use the listed transparencies to acquaint students with art from ancient Greece.

READING FOR INFORMATION

Reading Skills and Strategies

REVIEWING PRIOR KNOWLEDGE

Invite students to skim through the part opener, pages 162–175. Then ask them to share what they already know about ancient Greece, using questions such as the following as prompts:

- What do you know about the Greek gods?
- What other works of Greek literature have you read, if any? What were those works about?
- What names of people or places associated with ancient Greece can you recall?
- Have you ever seen Greek works of art or architecture? If so, describe what you saw.
- What else do you know about ancient Greece?

Then invite students to write down a few questions about ancient Greece that they would like answered by this introduction. As they read, have them record the answers.

Reading Skills and Strategies

READING A MAP

Tell students that this is a physical map, which shows the mountainous terrain of Greece and surrounding regions. The area shaded orange shows Greek territories. Explain that the red numbers link the boxed captions to specific places on the map. Students may find it helpful to compare this map to a contemporary one of the same region. Point out that ancient Greece extended much farther than Greece today.

PART 1 In the Name of Honor

Literature of Ancient Greece

Why It Matters

Greece is a small mountainous country, yet it gave birth to some of the most cherished ideas of Western civilization. The Greeks championed individual freedom, developed an early form of democracy, and demonstrated the power of rational thought. Greek ideals of beauty and justice have spread throughout the world. Greek literature, especially poetry and drama, continues to inspire writers today.

1 A Famous War Perhaps the most famous war ever described in literature was the **Trojan War,** in which a coalition of Greek states fought the inhabitants of Troy. This war is the subject of the ***Iliad,*** a long narrative poem by Homer that is still popular today. According to legend, Greek soldiers hid in a massive hollow statue of a horse and gained entrance to Troy.

For Links to Ancient Greece, click on:

HUMANITIES CLASSZONE.COM

A Seafaring People

Greece is surrounded by water and has little usable farmland. Thus, ancient Greeks set out in ships to trade with others. Shown here is a model of a 5th-century-B.C. Greek sailing ship.

162 UNIT TWO PART 1: LITERATURE OF ANCIENT GREECE

MINI LESSON Using the Map

Tell students to make use of the map and the map key to answer the following questions:

- Which sea did the Greek warriors have to cross in order to attack Troy? *(Aegean Sea)*
- What major city would the Spartan soldiers have to pass by in order to attack Athens? *(Corinth)*
- How far is Athens from Mt. Olympus? (a) less than 50 miles; (b) between 50 and 100 miles; (c) between 100 and 150 miles; (d) between 150 and 200 miles *(d)*
- When Oedipus traveled from Corinth to Thebes, in what direction did he head? *(northeast)*

2 A Mountainous Terrain Mountain ranges divide mainland Greece into various regions. The Greeks believed that their gods and goddesses lived at the top of the highest mountain in Greece—Mount Olympus (shown above). Greek **mythology** greatly influenced the literature of the Western world.

3 Cradle of Democracy The largest and most influential of the Greek city-states, **Athens** was the birthplace of democracy, drama, and philosophy. Athenian sculpture and architecture are still imitated today. Athens was named for Athena, the gray-eyed goddess of war and wisdom. A statue of Athena is shown here.

4 A Land of City-States The chains of mountains kept people isolated from one another and led to the creation of city-states—small independent areas centered around a single city. **Sparta** was a strong city-state known for its military way of life. Sparta and Athens were the main rivals in a war that lasted 27 years.

READING FOR INFORMATION

Reading Skills and Strategies

ANALYZING VISUAL IMAGES

Tell students that this introduction includes many visual images that represent the art and life of ancient Greece. Ask students what they can learn about the Greeks from the four main images on this page.

Possible Responses:

- Wooden replica of Trojan horse: This image, derived from legends of the Trojan War, suggests the cleverness and ingenuity of the Greeks.
- Photograph of Mt. Olympus: As we learn, the Greeks thought the gods lived on this mountain. The mountains must have inspired imagination and religious awe.
- Bronze statue of Athena: The realistic human form and intricate detail show that the Greeks must have been sophisticated in their art and in their ability to work with metal. Because Athena is a warrior-goddess, war may have been a common occurrence.
- Greek sailing ship: This ship looks very sophisticated in its design. The Greeks must have known a great deal about travelling the seas, as well as about shipbuilding.

Historical Note

A Trojan Horse Although Homer's *Iliad* is the most famous account of the Trojan War, the story of the Trojan horse is not mentioned there because Homer's epic does not address the war's end. A short version of the Trojan horse story appears in Book 8 of the *Odyssey*. Virgil's *Aeneid* provides a more complete version.

READING FOR INFORMATION
Reading Skills and Strategies
TEXT STRUCTURE
Explain to students that these two pages provide a brief outline of Greek history, ending with Rome's conquest of Greece in 146 B.C. Tell students to use the headings as a guide to content and to pay especially close attention to boldfaced terms. Tell students that the **History to Literature** feature shows connections between major historical events and literary works. Point out that the time line at the bottom provides a quick overview of the relative lengths of each time period.

Historical Note
Ⓐ **City-State** The term city-state is somewhat misleading because the territories of the city-states did not stop at urban borders. The major city-states, such as Sparta, Athens, and Corinth, controlled large amounts of territory, much of which was farmland.

Historical Highlights

Much of ancient Greek literature describes the heroes, villains, triumphs, and setbacks of Greek history. To understand the stories and ideas in the part ahead, it is vital to know something about the historical events that inspired many of them.

The Heroic Age

2000–1200 B.C.

The early Greeks are known as **Mycenaeans,** (mī′sə-nē′ənz) named after their leading city, Mycenae (mī-sē′ne). Mycenaeans were warriors and traders. They adapted an older writing system to the Greek language. Their kings gathered fortunes in gold and lived in palaces protected by stone walls. About 1250 B.C., Mycenaean warriors won a war against the wealthy city of **Troy** and may have burned the city to the ground.

The Decline

1200–800 B.C.

Not long after the defeat of Troy, Mycenaean civilization collapsed. A group of people from northern Greece—the Dorians—moved into the area the Mycenaeans had controlled. During the age that followed, knowledge of writing was lost. The Greeks kept their culture alive in songs and stories about the glories of their past, especially their heroes at Troy. **Homer** based his epic poems the ***Iliad*** and the ***Odyssey*** on these stories.

The Growth of City-States Ⓐ

800–500 B.C.

During this period, Greek tribal settlements grew into independent city-states. Because of the shortage of fertile land, numerous Greeks traveled great distances, from Southern Italy to Asia Minor, to found new city-states.

Each city-state had its own army, its own system of government, and its own way of life. For example, **Sparta** developed into a military state, while **Athens** became a major cultural center and thus a magnet for artistic talent from all over Greece. Around 500 B.C., the ruling aristocrats of Athens took a bold step. They extended power to all Athenian citizens (men aged 18 or older who were neither slaves nor foreigners). Athens became the world's first **democracy.**

The Greek hero Achilles bearing the corpse of his friend Patroclus

THE HEROIC AGE | THE DECLINE
2000 B.C. | 1200 B.C.

The Great Wars

500–400 B.C.

The Greek city-states often squabbled among themselves, but their biggest fear was an invasion by the Persians. When Persian forces landed on mainland Greece in 490 B.C., Athens defeated them. Later, the city-states joined together to fight their common enemy. The **Persian Wars** continued on and off for a number of years, with Greece ultimately the winner. At the end, Athens emerged more powerful than ever. B

Athens' supremacy was eventually challenged by its rival, Sparta. The **Peloponnesian War** between the two city-states lasted 27 years. It ended in 404 B.C. with Athens' complete surrender. C

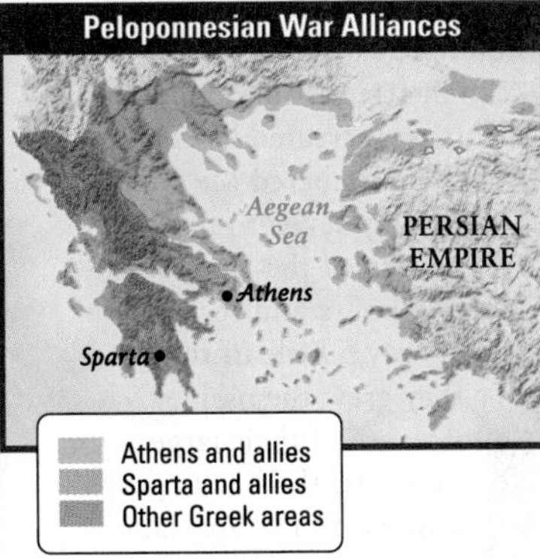

Macedonia and the Hellenistic Age

400–146 B.C.

With the fall of Athens, Greece had lost its center. Fighting between city-states continued, and the Greeks couldn't stop the army of **Philip II** of **Macedonia,** a kingdom north of Greece, from taking control of the country in 338 B.C. Philip's son, **Alexander the Great,** eventually united Greece, Persia, Egypt, and parts of India into one great empire.

Alexander died when he was only 33, and his empire fragmented shortly after his death. However, his conquests helped bring about a new culture, the **Hellenistic culture,** which blended Greek (Hellenic), Egyptian, Persian, and Indian influences. The influence of Greek culture continued even after the Romans conquered Greece in 146 B.C.

A scene from a burial tomb, showing a battle between the Macedonians and Persians

History to Literature

EVENT IN HISTORY	EVENT IN LITERATURE
Greek warriors defeat Trojans, about 1250 B.C.	Homer's *Iliad* and *Odyssey* celebrate heroes of the Trojan War.
Greeks defeat Persians, 479 B.C.	Greek playwright Aeschylus stages *Persians* in 472 B.C.
Athens becomes a major power, 5th century B.C.	Sophocles, who served as an Athenian general, explores issues of power and fate in his play *Oedipus the King,* performed in Athens c. 430 B.C.
War between Athens and Sparta, 431–404 B.C.	Greek historian Thucydides explains the events that led to the war in *History of the Peloponnesian War.*

THE GROWTH OF CITY-STATES	THE GREAT WARS	MACEDONIA AND THE HELLENISTIC AGE	
800 B.C.	500 B.C.	400 B.C.	146 B.C.

Historical Note

B Persian Wars When Persian forces landed on the Greek mainland in 490 B.C., only Athens and two small cities offered resistance. In the battle at Marathon, more than six thousand Persians were killed while fewer than two hundred Athenians died. The Persians returned nine years later with a force estimated at nearly 200,000 men and over 1,000 ships. The badly outnumbered Greeks decisively defeated the Persians at Plataea in 479 B.C. Intermittent battles continued until a peace treaty was signed in 449 B.C.

Historical Note

C Peloponnesian War The Peloponnesian War was actually a series of wars and rebellions. The first war took place between 431 B.C. and 421 B.C.; the second, between 414 B.C. and 404 B.C. During these years, various cities in each alliance revolted against Athens and Sparta, and a number of cities were torn apart by civil war. In the first war, the two great powers battled to a draw. Athenian power declined during the second war due to a disastrous attempt to expand its empire by attacking Syracuse in Sicily and the betrayal of one of its leaders, Alcibiades. The entrance of Persia into the war on the side of Sparta finally tipped the scale completely.

MINI LESSON Interpreting the Text

After students have read pages 164 and 165, ask the following questions to gauge understanding:

- The Mycenaean kings lived in palaces protected by stone walls. What does that suggest about Mycenaean culture? *(Warfare was probably common.)*
- After the knowledge of writing was lost, how did the Greeks keep their culture alive? *(through songs and stories about the past)*
- Greek tribal settlements evolved into city-states. What reason or reasons might be offered to explain why they did not unite into a single government? *(Accept all reasonable responses. Students may point out that the mountainous terrain would make it difficult to unify the city-states.)*
- What Greek city-state emerged as the most powerful after the defeat of Persia? *(Athens)*
- What was the Peloponnesian War? *(a war between Sparta and its allies and Athens and its allies)*
- How far did the empire of Alexander the Great extend? *(It included Greece, Persia, Egypt, and parts of India.)*

READING FOR INFORMATION
Reading Skills and Strategies
TEXT STRUCTURE

Make sure that students understand that the information on these pages provides an overview of two very different societies, Athens and Sparta, during the 400s B.C. Point out that five categories of people are described: aristocrats, common folk, slaves, warriors, and artists and writers. The role of women is addressed in **Women of Ancient Greece.** Ask students to note differences between Athens and Sparta as they read.

Historical Note

A **Military Sparta** In the eighth-century B.C., the Spartans conquered the fertile region of Messenia, forcing the Messenians to turn over one-half of their harvests. In the seventh-century B.C., the Messenians revolted and nearly defeated Sparta. In response to the revolt, Sparta turned itself into a military society. The state reduced the defeated Messenians to helots and turned their land over to Spartan warriors; each helot was assigned to work the land for an individual warrior. All aspects of Spartan life were organized to serve the needs of the military, and the state took complete control of education. Sparta even went so far as to ban the use of silver and gold, which further isolated the Spartans from the rest of Greece.

People and Society

In ancient Greece, the way you lived depended on your position in society. If you were one of the lucky few, you were born into wealth and power; the unlucky might face a life of slavery. Of course, your fate also depended on where and when you were born. Two different societies are described here—Athens and Sparta. During the 400s B.C., these two city-states were the most powerful and influential in Greece.

Aesop telling a fable

Aristocrats

An aristocrat is a member of the nobility, the ruling or privileged class in society. In Athens, the aristocrats were wealthy landowners. They inherited their land and positions in society. Owning land and having others work to support it gave the aristocrats time to devote themselves to politics, to the life of the mind, and to hunting. After an era of kings, the aristocrats ruled Athens, but eventually they shared their power with other citizens.

Sparta did not have a true aristocracy. Instead, a small group of rulers had authority over the society. Two kings headed the army, while 5 magistrates and a council of 28 elders and the kings governed the city. Only native Spartans, those whose ancestry could be traced to the city's original inhabitants, enjoyed the full rights of citizenship.

Common Folk

A large number of farmers, merchants, and resident foreigners made up the middle and lower classes in Athens. Farmers and merchants who were born in Athens enjoyed the full rights of citizenship. The foreigners were not citizens but were protected by law and had both privileges and duties. Some foreigners became powerful merchants and bankers.

In Sparta, the commoners were neither citizens nor slaves. They were people who could not trace their ancestry to Sparta. Constituting a fairly small class, the commoners lived as free people in Sparta and typically worked as merchants and farmers.

Scene from a Greek vase showing family life

Slaves

The elegant life and leisure of the Athenian aristocracy could not have been possible without the existence of slaves, who did most of the manual labor. **Aesop,** whose fables you probably read as a child, is thought to have been a slave. In Athens at the height of its glory, more than one-third of the population were slaves.

In Sparta, people called helots were treated like slaves. A They outnumbered the Spartans by seven to one. Helots farmed the land, working long hours and receiving in return only a little of the food they grew themselves. Because of their large numbers, the helots posed a threat to the Spartans. The Spartans routinely declared war on the helots so that they could kill any who seemed rebellious.

MINI LESSON Interpreting the Text

After students have read pages 166–167, ask them to come up with words and phrases to describe the different types of people living in Sparta and Athens.

Possible Responses:

Athens

- aristocrats were wealthy landowners
- diverse middle and lower classes, including farmers, merchants, resident foreigners; only people born in Athens were citizens
- large number of slaves
- all young men received military training; powerful navy
- many artists and writers
- women's lives not much better than slaves

Sparta

- small ruling class of warriors
- small class of commoners, people who could not trace ancestry to Sparta
- helots treated like slaves; worked the land; posed threat of rebellion
- entire society organized for war; young men trained by state to be warriors
- few artists or writers
- women had more freedom than those in Athens

Warriors

Because warfare was a fact of Greek life, all young Athenian men received training as soldiers. Athens, however, only assembled an army in times of war. Soldiers served in the military and then returned to more peaceful ways of life. Although the Athenians were reluctant warriors, their navy dominated the Greek world.

By contrast, the entire life of a Spartan man revolved around military service. At the age of 7, male children were sent to military schools, which taught toughness and discipline. At the age of 20, Spartans became soldiers and lived together in barracks. These young soldiers could marry but were not allowed to live at home with their families until they turned 30. Even then, however, men continued to serve in the military until the age of 60.

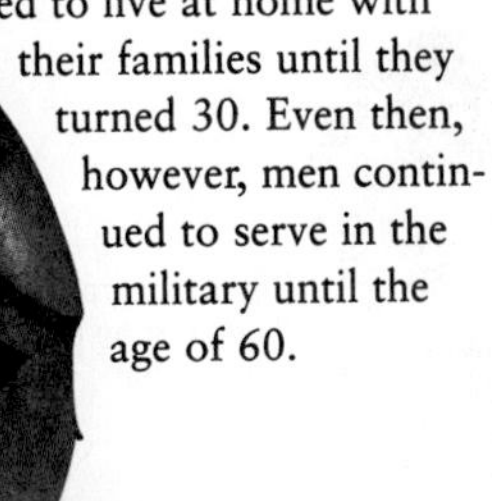

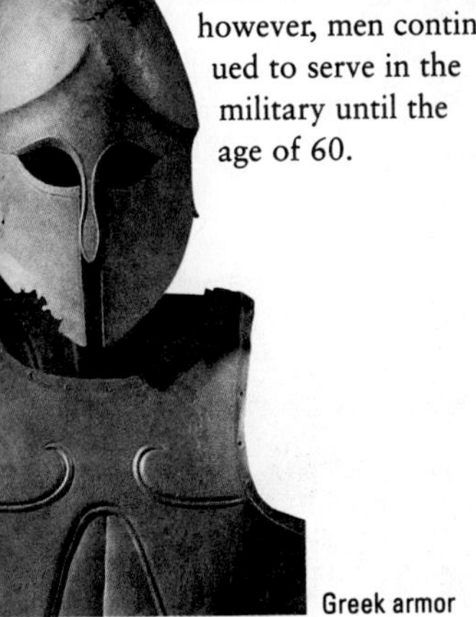

Greek armor

Detail from vase painting, showing a potter at work

Artists and Writers

Artists, including sculptors and potters, held an honorable position in Athenian society. Sculptors created the lifelike statues of gods that decorated the temples. Potters, who worked in a special quarter of the city, decorated their wares with scenes of gods and heroes as well as of everyday life. Many writers also enjoyed a special status in Athens. They were believed to have been inspired by the nine Muses, the goddesses of arts and sciences. Poets were often invited to read their latest works at banquets held in the homes of aristocrats. (B)

While Athens was the cultural center of the Greek world, Sparta did not value the arts. As a result, the city produced few artists or writers. Spartans learned to read and write, but they mainly read works that praised the heroics of soldiers at war.

Women of Ancient Greece

In general, an Athenian woman's life was not that much better than a slave's. Denied education and any hope of equality, women and girls were confined to the home, and their contact with men was severely limited. A girl married shortly after puberty, probably at 15, and most often to a man twice her age. The young wife then raised her children, separated from their father, in the women's quarters of the home. She was not even allowed to eat with her husband and his male friends.

Spartan women were allowed much more freedom than their Athenian counterparts. Although women did not receive military training, their physical education was similar to that accorded the men. Girls took part in athletics, and women engaged in business and owned land. Wives ran their own households since their husbands, after all, hardly ever lived at home.

167

Historical Note

(B) Another Side to Athens Athens has been celebrated throughout history as the birthplace of democracy and for its great achievements in poetry, drama, architecture, sculpture, and other arts. However, the Athenians were not particularly liked by their Greek neighbors. As a leader of the alliance against the Persians—the Delian League—the Athenians received annual payments from other city-states to build their navy. The Athenians used money left over to finance the construction of magnificent new buildings in Athens. Eventually, the Athenians treated other members of the Delian League as their subjects. Those who disagreed with Athenian policies often had their land confiscated and given to Athenian citizens. Athenian garrisons were established in each city and revolt of any kind was brutally punished.

READING FOR INFORMATION
Reading Skills and Strategies
CLARIFYING

Help students to understand that the term *culture* has a very broad meaning. Here, it refers to the beliefs, values, and patterns of behavior of the ancient Greeks. Point out that these four categories—**Religion, Political Life, Education and Philosophy,** and **Athletics**—represent areas in which the Greeks had great influence on the course of Western history.

Historical Note

A The Gods in Literature Much of what we know about the Greek gods comes from the literature of ancient Greece. The ancient Greek historian Herodotus credits the poets Homer and Hesiod with naming the gods and describing the proper rituals to honor the gods. In Homer's works, the twelve Olympians are characters who differ from humans only in their power and immortality. In Hesiod's *Theogony*, we learn the family trees of the Olympians and of many other Greek gods.

Historical Note

B Athenian Democracy Though Athens is credited as being the world's first democracy, a number of people living in the city had no say in its government. Only male citizens over the age of eighteen could participate in government. Women were excluded from government, as were all slaves and resident foreigners.

Culture

The culture of ancient Greece—its unique way of life—encouraged creativity and excellence in all pursuits. From fierce athletic competitions to boldly ambitious educational programs, the Greeks aimed for the best in all things. In such an atmosphere, literature flourished.

Religion A

Unlike the religions of the Jews, Christians, and Muslims, the religion of the ancient Greeks had no sacred writings (such as the Bible) and no commandments. Worship centered on an elite group of gods—the 12 Olympians, headed by Zeus and his wife, Hera.

The Greeks developed a rich set of **myths**, or traditional stories, about their gods. The gods quarreled and competed with each other and showed human qualities such as love, hate, and jealousy. Unlike humans, however, the gods lived forever. The gods held the ultimate power and served as a reminder of human limitations.

The 12 Olympians

Zeus
king of all divinities, god of thunder

Athena
goddess of war and wisdom

Ares
god of battle

Demeter
goddess of agriculture

Hera
queen of all divinities, goddess of marriage

Apollo
god of light, music, and poetry

Aphrodite
goddess of love and beauty

Hermes
messenger of the gods

Poseidon
god of the sea and earthquakes

Artemis
goddess of hunting

Hephaestus
god of fire and toolmaking

Hestia
goddess of home and family

Political Life

Many Greek city-states expected all citizens to become involved in politics. The most extensive **B** form of democracy in ancient Greece was found in Athens, where about one-fifth of the population could participate in government. A lawmaking body called the assembly passed laws and elected generals. Any citizen could be a part of the assembly and could submit a law for the assembly to debate. Each year, 500 citizens were chosen at random to serve on the Council of Five Hundred, which proposed laws and advised the assembly. Many positions were paid, so even poor citizens could hold office.

Detail of a bronze statue thought to be either Zeus or Poseidon

School of Athens, a Renaissance painting by the artist Raphael. In the center stand Plato and Aristotle.

Education and Philosophy

C The Greeks valued education because they believed that human beings could be perfected. Greek teachers—especially in Athens—taught their students to think for themselves, a privilege unique in the ancient world. Although such freedom caused conflict, it also produced some of the greatest minds of Western civilization.

Socrates dedicated himself to reason, truth, and virtue. He believed that true happiness depends on the goodness of one's soul.

Plato, Socrates' student and founder of the first school for higher education (the Academy), expanded Socrates' ideas into a wide-ranging philosophical system that examined the nature of reality.

Aristotle, Plato's student and tutor to Alexander the Great, emphasized scientific observation and studied plants, animals, the human body, language, literature, ethics, politics, and logic.

Athletics

Every four years, male athletes from all over the Greek world would stop what they were doing (even in times of war) and travel to the **Olympic Games.** Competitive events D included those still presented at the Olympics today—boxing, wrestling, the javelin and discus throws, and races of all kinds. The Greeks' love of games sometimes baffled their enemies. One Persian general reportedly exclaimed, "What kind of men have you brought us to fight against? It's not for money they compete, but for the mere achievement of excellence!"

Turning Points in Literature

The Alphabet

The alphabet we have today is the Roman version of the Greek alphabet, which the Greeks had developed from the Phoenician alphabet. Previous writing systems were extremely complicated and difficult to use, requiring years of training. The simplicity of using letters to represent all the sounds in the Greek language made widespread literacy a possibility for the first time in history.

Ancient and Modern Alphabets

Phoenician About 1000 B.C.	Greek About 1000 B.C.	Modern
𐤀	Α	A
𐤁	Β	B
𐤂	Γ	C

Historical Note

C **The First Teachers** The sophists were paid teachers who traveled from city to city in fifth-century Greece. They taught a range of subjects, such as mathematics, science, and geography, but their main purpose was to prepare young men for public life. Much of their instruction focused on the art of public speaking, especially argumentation, which was believed to be crucial for success in politics. Although Socrates did not receive payment for his teaching, he too can be considered a sophist.

Historical Note

D **Athletes and Money** Although the Greek athletes competed for the prize of a laurel wreath, money did play a role in Greek competition. Various city-states richly rewarded athletes for winning prizes; one prize might earn an athlete the equivalent of a wealthy man's income for a year. Also, city-states lured top athletes away from one another, often offering financial awards. The best athletes, in effect, were paid professionals, not unlike the athletes of today.

MINI LESSON Interpreting the Text

Have students read pages 168 and 169 and then answer the following questions:

- How is the religion of the ancient Greeks different from that of the Jews, Christians, and Muslims? *(The Greeks had no book of sacred writings, such as the Bible, and no commandments.)*
- How are the Olympian gods like human beings and how are they different? *(The Olympians exhibit human qualities and emotions. They are also immortal and more powerful than humans are.)*
- What are some features of Athenian democracy? *(Any citizen could join the assembly and submit laws for debate. Each year, 500 citizens were chosen at random to serve on the Council of Five Hundred, which would advise the assembly. Many positions were paid.)*
- Who are the three greatest thinkers of ancient Greece? *(Socrates, Plato, and Aristotle)*
- What were some of the events included in the Olympic Games? *(boxing, javelin and discus throws, and races)*
- What made the Greek language easy to use? *(The alphabet was simple; the letters represented all the sounds in the language.)*

READING FOR INFORMATION
Reading Skills and Strategies
SKIMMING
Explain to students that in reading nonfiction, it helps to skim material first before reading it more carefully. Point out that skimming is a cursory type of reading that will help students focus on the structure and main ideas of the text. Tell students to read only the introduction in its entirety. After that, they should read each of the subheadings and the first sentence of each paragraph, as well as the boldfaced terms. Students should also look quickly at the illustrations. Announce that you will give them 20 seconds to skim these two pages. After students have finished skimming, discuss what they learned. *(Accept all reasonable responses.)*

Historical Note
(A) Classical and Hellenistic Sculpture
The term *classical* is used to describe the sculpture, architecture, and art produced in fifth-century Greece. Phidias and other sculptors of this period produced figures marked by proportion, balance, and order. These figures presented an idealized and peaceful representation of human nature. Typically, the faces show only serenity.

Art produced after this period is known as *Hellenistic*. The statue of Demosthenes shown on this page represents that period. The face and torso are more realistically portrayed than in the classical period. The aging face and body of Demosthenes, for example, are clearly shown, in contrast to the youthful, athletic figures that dominate the classical period. Also, the expression on the face suggests thoughtfulness and care, in contrast to the serene expressions of the classical period.

Arts and Humanities

Greece forever influenced the art of the Western world. The ancient Greeks combined idealism—the quest for perfection—and realism to create works of great beauty. Even today, the influence of Greek architects, sculptors, and writers can be felt, from the design of many of our public buildings to the staging of the latest drama.

Sculpture

Greek sculptors were the first to portray the human body realistically. They created figures that were strong, graceful, and lifelike. Like Greek architects, Greek sculptors valued order, balance, and proportion in their work.

Many sculptors depicted the Greek gods and goddesses in idealized human form. One of the greatest sculptors, **Phidias,** created the statue of Athena that stood within the Parthenon. This statue no longer exists, but descriptions by Greek writers have enabled artists to create smaller copies of it. The original statue stood nearly 40 feet tall and was made of such precious materials as gold and ivory. (A)

Music and Dance

The Greeks greatly valued music. The ancient poems that we read today are essentially song lyrics whose melodies have been lost. The word *lyric* comes from the name of the lyre, a small harp used to accompany the poet-singer. Even drama developed from the songs of religious ritual.

Dance also played a vital role in Greek life. No religious ritual, victory celebration, or festival was complete without a dancing chorus or dancing flute players. The Olympic Games held elaborate dance competitions.

Literature

Greek literature begins with the **epics** the *Iliad* and the *Odyssey*, believed to have been composed by the blind poet **Homer.** Although the written forms of these long narrative poems date from the 700s B.C., oral versions existed much earlier. The Trojan War, which probably took place around 1250 B.C., forms the backdrop for the two epics.

During the 600s B.C., a new kind of poetry arose—the **lyric.** Possibly reaching its fullest expression on the island of Lesbos with such poets as **Alcaeus** and **Sappho,** the lyric was shorter and more personal than the epic. The lyric allowed poets to express their thoughts and feelings. Sappho, in particular, told of her loves and hates.

During the 400s B.C., drama became the most important literary form. The Greeks created the dramatic forms of **tragedy**—a serious drama about the downfall of a **tragic hero**—and **comedy.** The three greatest tragic dramatists were **Aeschylus, Sophocles,** and **Euripides.** The comedies of **Aristophanes** often poked fun at customs, politics, and respected Athenians.

A statue of Demosthenes, who was famous for his public speaking

The Parthenon, in Athens

A reconstruction of the Parthenon, which shows its original colors. The birth of Athena is depicted at the top.

Architecture

Many of the buildings of ancient Greece now lie in ruins, but among the structures remaining are astonishing examples of the Greek ideals of beauty, grace, and proportion. One of the best remaining examples is the **Parthenon**, a magnificent temple built to honor the goddess Athena. The temple, located on the **Acropolis**, the hill overlooking Athens, (B) demonstrates the classical Greek ideals. It is so harmonious with its site that it appears to grow out of the surrounding rock.

Greek architects also designed massive open-air theaters. The theater at Epidaurus, in the Peloponnesus, for example, could hold 14,000 spectators.

How Was Literature Presented?

Homer and poets like him probably sang their verses or recited them to music in the palaces of ruling warrior princes. Later, after the epics had been written down, they were memorized and recited by professional **rhapsodes** to large audiences at religious festivals. Lyric poetry was often sung—usually accompanied by the music of the lyre and sometimes by dancing—at small social gatherings, such as weddings and local festivals.

Dramatic festivals were such important public occasions that prisoners were released on bail to attend them. As many as 20,000 spectators could crowd into the Theater of Dionysus in Athens. Throughout the long Peloponnesian War, Athenian dramatic festivals continued uninterrupted behind the city walls.

Historical Note

(B) The Acropolis and Parthenon
Around 480 B.C., near the end of the Persian Wars, Persia destroyed the temples and statues on the Acropolis. The rebuilding of the Acropolis, under the leadership of Pericles, was the most ambitious project in the history of Greek architecture. The centerpiece of that project, the Parthenon, still dominates Athens today. The statue of Athena in the Parthenon, which stood nearly 40 feet tall, showed the goddess in full battle armor.

In Christian times, the Parthenon became a church, and the Virgin Mary replaced Athena. Later, under Turkish rule, the building became a mosque. At the beginning of the 1800s, Lord Elgin removed most of the sculpture from the Parthenon. The Elgin Marbles are now housed at the British Museum.

MINI LESSON Interpreting the Text

Have students read pages 170 and 171 and then answer the following questions:

- Which word does not describe the sculpture of ancient Greece? (a) idealistic (b) graceful (c) harmonious (d) chaotic *(d)*
- On what occasions did the Greeks dance? *(religious rituals, victory celebrations, festivals)*
- What form of literature is Homer associated with? *(epic)*
- How is a lyric poem different from an epic poem? *(The lyric poem is much shorter and more personal.)*
- Who were the four major dramatists of ancient Greece? *(Aeschylus, Sophocles, Euripides, and Aristophanes)*
- What are the Acropolis and the Parthenon? *(The Acropolis is the hill overlooking Athens. The Parthenon, the temple dedicated to Athena, was built there.)*
- What is a rhapsode? *(someone who recited poetry, usually epics, in public)*

READING FOR INFORMATION
Reading Skills and Strategies
SEQUENCING

Make sure that students realize the sequence of events shown on the time line. Model for them how to follow the order by reading aloud the first four entries listed under **Events in Greek Literature.** Point out that the three bands constitute parallel time lines, roughly covering the time from the founding of Greek city-states to Rome's conquest of Greece. Call attention to the key and point out that many dates are only approximate, requiring the use of *c.*, which stands for *circa*, meaning "about" or "in approximately."

Historical Note

(A) **The Persians** Almost all Greek tragedies are set in a remote past. Aeschylus' *Persians* is a notable exception. This play tells about the Greek naval victory over the Persians in the narrow waters of Salamis, which took place in 480 B.C. Interestingly, the play does not present events from the Greek point of view but from that of the Persians. Aeschylus himself may have participated in the battle of Salamis; he certainly took part in the great battle at Marathon (490 B.C.) in which the relatively small Athenian army defeated the much larger Persian forces.

Time Line

ANCIENT GREECE (800 B.C.–150 B.C.)

3000 B.C. — A.D. 1 — PRESENT

c. approximately
B.C. before Christ
A.D. after Christ

EVENTS IN GREEK LITERATURE

800 B.C. — 600 B.C.

c. 800–700 B.C. Homer composes the *Iliad* and the *Odyssey;* Greeks develop a letter alphabet

c. 625 B.C. Alcman, one of the few Spartan poets, composes choral songs for festivals

Greek vase (about 540 B.C.)

c. 600–580 B.C. Alcaeus and Sappho compose lyric poetry

534 B.C. First dramatic festival held in Athens honors the god Dionysus

486 B.C. Comedy presented at the dramatic festival in Athens

472 B.C. Aeschylus' tragedy *Persians* first staged in Athens (A)

c. 430 B.C. Sophocles' tragedy *Oedipus the King* performed in Athens

415 B.C. Euripides, called by Aristotle "the most tragic of poets," stages his tragedy *The Trojan Women*

EVENTS IN GREEK HISTORY

800 B.C. — 600 B.C.

800–750 B.C. Rise of Greek city-states

776 B.C. First recorded athletic games held in Olympia to honor the god Zeus

c. 750–700 B.C. Greeks begin establishing trade and settlements in Sicily and Italy

c. 735–715 B.C. Sparta conquers neighboring Messenia and enslaves its people

594 B.C. Solon reforms Athenian laws, making it illegal to enslave people who owe money

508 B.C. Political reforms make Athens a democracy

490–479 B.C. During the Persian Wars, the Greeks battle the Persians, eventually defeating them

461–429 B.C. Under the rule of Pericles, Athenian democracy reaches its height

431–404 B.C. The Peloponnesian War between Athens and Sparta ends with the fall of Athens

430 B.C. Plague strikes Athens during a siege by the Spartans

EVENTS IN WORLD HISTORY

800 B.C. — 600 B.C.

900–200 B.C. Assyrian Empire in Southwest Asia and North Africa

c. 800–400 B.C. Chavín civilization flourishes in Peru

753 B.C. Legendary date of the founding of Rome

750 B.C. Nubians unite the Nile Valley of Egypt

c. 700–500 B.C. Hindus write a series of philosophical works called the *Upanishads*

c. 563 B.C. Birth of Siddhartha Gautama, founder of Buddhism

550–539 B.C. Cyrus the Great of Persia builds an empire

538 B.C. Return of Hebrews to Jerusalem from Babylonian captivity

509 B.C. Founding of the Roman Republic

500 B.C. Speakers of the Bantu language begin migrating southward in Africa from what is now Nigeria

c. 500 B.C. Zapotec civilization flourishes in Mexico

479 B.C. Death of Confucius

MINI LESSON Using the Time Line

Have students refer to the time line to answer the following questions:

- Which came first, the Hindu *Upanishads* or *Persians* by Aeschylus? *(Upanishads)*
- In what century did the Greek tragedians—Aeschylus, Sophocles, and Euripides—write? *(5th-century B.C., or 400s B.C.)*
- What war was in progress around the time that *Oedipus the King* was first performed? *(the Peloponnesian War)*
- Who died first, Confucius or Socrates? *(Confucius)*
- Which famous Greek philosophers were alive when the Indian epic *Mahabharata* was first written down? *(Plato and Aristotle)*
- When the library was first built in Alexandria, Egypt, could it have contained books of pastoral poetry? *(No, pastoral poetry was developed in the 200s B.C.)*

400 B.C.

399 B.C. Socrates is tried and executed

387 B.C. Plato founds the Academy

367 B.C. Seventeen-year-old Aristotle becomes Plato's student

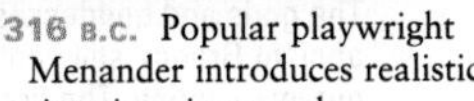

316 B.C. Popular playwright Menander introduces realistic situations in comedy

200 B.C.

200s B.C. Theocritus invents pastoral poetry—poems about nature and country life

200s B.C. Callimachus writes short poems about Greek mythology and history; later Roman poets imitate his style

200s B.C. Apollonius of Rhodes writes the *Argonautica,* a long romantic poem

400 B.C.

338 B.C. Philip II of Macedonia conquers Greece in the Battle of Chaeronea

334–323 B.C. Alexander the Great conquers Persia and spreads Greek culture throughout his empire (B)

323 B.C. Alexander dies; his empire eventually splits into a number of independent states

c. 300 B.C. Museum and library built in Alexandria, Egypt, as a center for poets, scholars, and scientists

200 B.C.

146–30 B.C. Romans gradually conquer the territory that once belonged to Alexander the Great's empire

400 B.C.

400–100 B.C. Indian epic *Mahabharata* first written down

321–301 B.C. Mauryan Empire unites northern India

c. 250 B.C. Kingdom of Meroë at its height in East Africa

c. 214-204 B.C. Construction of first Great Wall in China completed

200 B.C.

c. 200 B.C. Nazca culture arises in Peru

146 B.C. Rome destroys Carthage

44 B.C. Assassination of Julius Caesar

27 B.C. Roman Empire established, with Augustus as emperor

Historical Note

(B) Alexander the Great The greatest general of the ancient world, Alexander soared to power like a meteor. At the age of 18, he led a cavalry charge against an alliance of Greek cities in the Battle of Chaeronea. At the age of 20, after his father, King Philip II, had been killed, Alexander took power and immediately proclaimed himself king of Macedonia. When the Greek city of Thebes rebelled, he destroyed the city and sold the survivors into slavery.

Over the next 12 years, Alexander led his troops to great victories against the Persian empire of Darius III. Alexander's troops conquered Egypt, all of Asia Minor, and even part of India. His army traveled more than 11,000 miles under his leadership. Alexander modeled himself after the great Homeric heroes, and he even slept with his copy of the *Iliad* beneath his pillow. In his lifetime, he was widely praised as a divinity, the son of Zeus, which Alexander may have believed himself to be. He died of fever at the age of 32.

INTRODUCTION 173

READING FOR INFORMATION
Reading Skills and Strategies
CONNECTING
Have students study the images and captions to enhance their understanding of Greece's contributions to our world. Invite students to share what they know about the topics presented on these two pages.

Historical Note

(A) **The Modern Olympics** The modern Olympics were created by Baron Pierre de Coubertin, a French aristocrat interested in improving society through education. Baron de Coubertin formed the International Olympic Committee in 1894; two years later the first Olympics of the modern era were held in Athens, Greece.

Connect to Today: The Legacy of Ancient Greece

The Olympics (A)
The first documented Olympic Games were held in Greece in 776 B.C. Like our modern Olympics, the Greek games were held every four years and included foot races, wrestling, and the javelin throw. The Greeks' contests, however, chariot racing and trumpeting are no longer Olympic events!

Mythology
The gods and goddesses of ancient Greece still capture our imagination. The first humans to reach the moon did so in a spacecraft named for Apollo, the Greek god of light and truth.

Democracy
"Our constitution is called a democracy because power is in the hands not of a minority but of the whole people," the Athenian leader Pericles boasted in 431 B.C. Modern democracies, however, allow much larger segments of their populations to become citizens and voters than Athens did.

174 UNIT TWO

Comedy and Tragedy
Both of these forms of drama were invented in ancient Greece. Unlike today's plays, movies, and TV shows, Greek drama featured only male actors, who wore masks onstage. Many Greek plays, though, used special effects, including a crane that would let actors seem to descend from the sky.

The Legacy of Language

Words and Phrases

You may not know how to speak Greek, but many of the words you use have Greek origins. For example, the word **democracy** comes from the Greek root *demo,* meaning "people," and *crat,* meaning "rule." Here are just a few examples of English words that have Greek roots.

Root	Meaning	English Words
astra	star	astronaut, asterisk, astronomy
biblio	book	bibliography, Bible
log	word	dialogue, monologue, eulogy
polis	city, state	police, political, metropolis

Architecture
The marble columns and elegant lines of ancient Greek architecture are still admired and imitated today. The Lincoln Memorial, shown below, was designed on a plan similar to that of the Parthenon.

INTRODUCTION 175

Objectives

- understand the following literary terms:
  - epic
  - epithets
  - epic simile
  - epic hero
- recognize the importance of honor in Greek and Roman culture
- understand beliefs about the power of fate to determine individual destiny

Epic Conventions

In addition to the conventions described on page 176, the following epic conventions also apply to the *Iliad* and *Aeneid*:

- The hero is of great national or international significance.
- The setting is vast, covering large regions and both the natural and supernatural realms.
- The poem begins by calling upon a Muse for inspiration.
- The poem begins *in medias res,* in the middle of things. The reader is later told of earlier events through flashbacks.
- The poem in its original language follows a strict metrical pattern.

Literary Style

Point out that the *Iliad* may have first been told in oral form and later written down. The *Aeneid*, by contrast, is considered a **literary epic.** That is, it has no oral predecessors but was composed entirely by Virgil.

Experts have pointed out that the epithets in the *Iliad* give the poet–or reciter–a number of different ways to meet the metrical requirements of the line. The *Iliad* in its original Greek follows a dactylic hexameter pattern, which requires that every line have six stressed syllables and six unstressed syllables. For example, in one line Achilles may be described as "brilliant"; in another he may be the "swift runner." Those varying descriptions may have been simply a way of filling out the 12-syllable requirements of the line.

The Epics of Greece and Rome

In Unit One, you read excerpts from three Eastern epics: *The Epic of Gilgamesh* from Mesopotamia and the *Mahabharata* and *Ramayana* from India. As you may recall, an **epic** is a long narrative poem that deals with a hero's adventures and deeds. An epic hero—Gilgamesh or Rama, for example—reflects a culture's ideals, values, and beliefs.

Achilles Kills Hector (1630), Peter Paul Rubens.

In this unit, you will read excerpts from two epics of Western cultures: the *Iliad* from ancient Greece and the *Aeneid* from ancient Rome. Many scholars believe that these epics and the epics of Eastern civilizations derive from the same tradition. You may therefore notice some similarities between the Eastern and the Western epics. As you will see, however, the Greeks and Romans put their own unique stamps on the epic genre.

Epic Conventions

In the Greek and Roman epics, you will notice certain conventions, or devices, found in other epics. For example, both the *Iliad* and the *Aeneid* tell about events set in a distant and glorious past. The events are majestic in scale—heroic battles and dangerous quests. Like Gilgamesh and Rama, the Greek and Roman epic heroes are larger-than-life figures who perform great deeds. Both Achilles, the hero of the *Iliad,* and Aeneas, the hero of the *Aeneid,* are half divine: each has a goddess for a mother. Supernatural elements are found in these epics too. Gods, goddesses, and magical creatures appear, at times taking part in human affairs.

Literary Style

One of the distinctive qualities of Greek and Roman epics is their attribution to particular authors. Though these epics still show clear traces of the oral tradition, they also reveal the hands of individual writers shaping materials to create unified wholes. The Greek and Roman epics are also distinguished for the richness and power of their language. Two devices that contribute to the epics' dignified style are the epithet and the epic simile.

- Homer's style is marked by an extensive use of **epithets**—descriptive words and phrases that characterize persons and things. For example, the adjectives "brilliant" and "godlike" frequently appear before Achilles' name. He is also identified as "the swift runner," "the headstrong runner," and "the proud runner."
- As you know, a simile is a comparison that contains the word *like* or *as.* An **epic simile** is a simile that extends over several lines. Often, epic similes serve to increase the dramatic power of the passages in which they occur, as in Aeneas' description of Troy in flames:

> **"I knew the end then: Ilium was going down**
> **In fire, the Troy of Neptune going down,**
> **As in high mountains when the countrymen**
> **Have notched an ancient ash, then make their axes**
> **Ring with might and main, chopping away**
> **To fell the tree—ever on the point of falling,**
> **Shaken through all its foliage, and the treetop**
> **Nodding; bit by bit the strokes prevail**
> **Until it gives a final groan at last**
> **And crashes down in ruin from the height."**
>
> **—Virgil, *Aeneid***

The Importance of Honor

The Western epics reflect values that were important to Greek civilization and that later influenced ancient Rome. Honor was, certainly, one of these values. In the *Iliad,* heroes from all parts of Greece converge on Troy to fight for the honor of a betrayed king. Achilles, the greatest of these heroes, lives for honor. When his friend is slain in battle, Achilles fights with fury to avenge him and to reclaim his own honor. In the *Aeneid,* Aeneas is given a divine mission—to lead the Trojan refugees to Italy and to found the Roman people. Aeneas' sense of honor and duty ensures that he will remain true to his destiny.

The Power of Fate

The power of fate, or destiny, is a major theme in the epics of Greece and Rome. According to the Greeks, every person—hero or not—was given a distinct fate at birth. It was wise to accept one's fate; to attempt to avoid it was foolish. Such an attempt was a sign of pride, or hubris (hyo͞o′brĭs), and might lead to terrible consequences. For a long time, Achilles avoids his fate by refusing to take part in the fighting at Troy. As a result, many warriors are slain, and Achilles loses his best friend. Aeneas, on the other hand, accepts his fate and the sacrifices it demands. Again and again, he gives up his personal happiness—for example, the love of the queen of Carthage—to fulfill his destiny as the founder of Rome.

The Hero's Limitations

Like other epic heroes, Achilles and Aeneas are extraordinary but not perfect. They have human failings. Achilles, for example, sulks in his tent for a long time because he feels mistreated by his commander. Aeneas has lapses of judgment and moments of weakness. For example, as he carries his father from burning Troy he has a moment of panic:

> **"I took fright,**
> **And some unfriendly power, I know not what,**
> **Stole my addled wits. . . ."**
>
> **—Virgil, *Aeneid***

The *Iliad* and the *Aeneid* are masterpieces of Western civilization. Along with the great epics of Eastern civilizations, they show the tremendous vitality of the epic tradition in the ancient world.

Strategies for Reading: Greek and Roman Epics

1. Identify the epic hero's strengths and weaknesses.
2. Think about the values the epic hero represents.
3. Determine how the hero's actions affect his own life and the lives of other characters.
4. Consider the roles of fate and the gods in the events.
5. Look for epithets and epic similes, and consider what they add to the story.
6. Monitor your reading strategies, and modify them when your understanding breaks down. Remember to use the strategies for active reading: **predict, visualize, connect, question, clarify,** and **evaluate.**

The Importance of Honor

Remind students that honor often plays an important role in warrior societies. Ask them to consider why honor would matter in such societies.

Possible Response: When warriors share a belief in the importance of honor, they acknowledge their ties to one another. A warrior is duty-bound, for example, to help his fellow warriors in times of warfare. A warrior would also be obligated to help defend those whose honor has been violated. The values associated with honor, such as courage and loyalty, are useful for protecting warrior groups in times of conflict.

The Power of Fate

In ancient Greek and Roman literature, fate is sometimes referred to as three persons who controlled the birth, life, and death of everyone. Clotho spun the thread of destiny; Lachesis measured the thread of destiny; and Atropos cut the thread, which determined when death took place.

Strategies for Reading

Tell students that the *Iliad* and the *Aeneid* both have great plots and characters. While the poetic form of the language may put off many students, the works themselves are not as difficult to read as they may appear. Advise students that the more they read of these epics, the easier it will be to read them.

 An excerpt from this selection is included in the **World Literature InterActive Reader™.**

Objectives

- understand and appreciate excerpts from a Greek **epic (Literary Analysis)**
- recognize the characteristics of an **epic hero (Literary Analysis)**
- recognize and understand characteristics of **epic poetry,** such as **epithets** and **epic similes (Literary Analysis)**
- use strategies for **evaluating** characters and events **(Active Reading)**

Summary

In Book 1 Achilles and Agamemnon become involved in a bitter argument over the issue of war prizes. Agamemnon gets his way and takes Briseis away from Achilles, but Achilles announces that he will pull out of the war. In the excerpt from Book 6, the Trojan hero Hector says farewell to his wife and son. Book 22 describes the battle between Achilles and Hector, which ends in Hector's death. In Book 24, Hector's father, Priam, sneaks into Achilles' camp. The Trojan king begs Achilles to return the body of Hector, and Achilles does so.

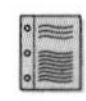 Use **Unit Two Resource Book,** p. 4, for additional support.

Thematic Link

Homer's epic explores the values of the warrior culture of ancient Greece, which places a premium on **glory and honor.**

 Use **Unit Two Resource Book,** p.15, for practice with Words to Know.

5-Minute Warm-Up

Daily Language SkillBuilder

Have students **proofread** the display sentences on page 161i and write them correctly.

PREPARING to *Read*

FROM THE ILIAD

HOMER

Homer
700s B.C.?

Author Mystery Homer has long been recognized as one of the world's greatest poets, but the man himself remains a mystery. Some scholars doubt that he ever actually existed, believing that the epics attributed to him are the work of many poets. Others agree with the ancient view that one great poet wrote both the *Iliad* and another famous epic, the *Odyssey.* If he existed, Homer was probably born somewhere in western Asia Minor (what is now Turkey). According to ancient tradition, Homer was blind. The story of his blindness, however, may have simply been a way of praising his wisdom, for Greek legends feature many stories of blind people with great insight.

Singers of the Trojan War It's likely that Homer heard singer-poets narrate tales about the Trojan War, a legendary ten-year war waged by Greeks against the wealthy city of Troy, or Ilium, in Asia Minor. Indeed, he may have himself been such a singer-poet, one who late in his life wrote down some of the stories he had told. Many scholars believe that the *Iliad* was created in the 700s B.C., though the circumstances of its composition remain unclear.

Homer as Teacher In later centuries, Homer's epics served as the centerpiece of Greek education. Children learned to read by studying his poems, and they memorized long passages. The epics kept alive the early Greeks' legends and myths and greatly influenced people's beliefs about the gods. Many read the poems not just for their exciting stories but because they believed that Homer had revealed important truths about human beings and their place in the universe.

Discovery of Troy In the late 19th century, archaeologists discovered the ruins of ancient Troy. The evidence they gathered has led many scholars to believe that Homer's tales about the Trojan War have some basis in fact. Greek armies probably did attack Troy sometime in the 1200s B.C., and they may have destroyed the city.

Ruins of ancient Troy

LESSON RESOURCES

UNIT TWO RESOURCE BOOK,
pp. 4–15

ASSESSMENT RESOURCES
Formal Assessment, pp. 25–30
Teacher's Guide to Assessment and Portfolio Use
Test Generator

INTEGRATED TECHNOLOGY
Visit our Web site: classzone.com

ADDITIONAL RESOURCES
Lesson Planning Guide, pp. 17–22
Teacher's Sourcebook for Language Development

The messenger god Hermes (left) has brought together Hera (top right), Athena (with shield), and Aphrodite, who is accompanied by her child, Eros. *The Judgment of Paris* (16th century), Giulio Romano. Ducal Palace, Mantua, Italy.

Build Background

Origins of the Trojan War According to legend, the Trojan War resulted from an argument among the gods. Eris, the goddess of strife, was angry because she had not been invited to the wedding of Peleus, a mortal king, and Thetis, a sea goddess. To get revenge, Eris threw a golden apple, labeled "for the fairest," into the midst of the wedding guests. A dispute arose when three goddesses—Hera, Athena, and Aphrodite—claimed the prize. Paris, the son of the Trojan king Priam, was chosen to decide which of the three was in fact the most beautiful. Each goddess offered Paris a bribe, but he awarded the apple to Aphrodite, who had promised him Helen, the most beautiful woman in the world.

Abduction of Helen Helen was already married to Menelaus, the king of Sparta, when Paris went to Sparta, where he stayed as a guest of the king. According to the customs of the time, a host and a guest had sacred obligations to each other. Paris, ignoring his duty to his host, took Helen back to Troy with him. Menelaus and his brother Agamemnon then gathered warriors from all over Greece to attack Troy and retrieve Helen.

Siege of Troy and the *Iliad* The Greek forces sailed to Troy and surrounded the city, besieging it for ten years. The events recounted in the *Iliad* take place during the final year of the war. The poem focuses on Achilles, the greatest Greek warrior. When he was an infant, his goddess mother had held him by the heel and dipped him into the river Styx in the realm of the dead. After that, Achilles could not be hurt in any part of his body, except for his heel. He does, however, have a fierce temper, which proves costly to the Greeks.

Bitter Feud Homer's story begins with a quarrel between Achilles and Agamemnon, the commander of the Greek forces. Achilles, filled with anger, withdraws from the war. As a result, the Trojans, led by the brave Hector, are able to drive the Greeks back to their ships. Achilles returns to combat only after his best friend, Patroclus, has been killed by Hector. With unstoppable energy, Achilles kills every Trojan in his path until he finally meets Hector in a man-to-man battle outside the city walls.

For a humanities activity, click on:

TIME MANAGEMENT

If your schedule requires that you cover the lesson objectives in a shorter time, use . . .

- Preparing to Read, pp. 178–181
- Thinking Through the Literature, p. 223
- Vocabulary in Action, p. 224

If you want to take advantage of longer class time, use . . .

- TE Teaching Options: Cross Curricular Link, pp. 183, 184, 185, 186, 187, 195, 197, 199, 204, 208, 209, 211, 213, 218; Viewing and Representing, pp. 193, 196, 214, 219; Speaking and Listening, pp. 203, 210, 215; Vocabulary Strategy, pp. 182, 198; Informal Assessment, pp. 190, 206; Grammar, pp. 188, 200, 216
- Choices & Challenges, p. 224

READING FOR INFORMATION

Reading Skills and Strategies
PREVIEWING

Have students preview the author and background information on these pages, noting the subheads, illustrations, and captions. Ask students what they expect to learn from reading these two pages of information. As they read, have them write down any questions that they have about the material. Remind students that previewing is an important strategy for reading nonfiction.

Historical Note

Reluctant Warriors Tell students that two of Greece's greatest warriors tried to get out of the war. Odysseus pretended to be insane so that he would not have to leave his farm and family. To protect her son, Thetis disguised Achilles as a young woman and sent him to live with other women. Both heroes were tricked into admitting their true nature and thus were obligated to serve with Agamemnon.

READING FOR INFORMATION
Reading Skills and Strategies
CLARIFYING
Invite volunteers to read aloud the names of each character in the **Cast of Characters.** Ask students to identify those characters that they already know something about and to discuss how they acquired their knowledge. Point out the family relations that link various characters.

 Use **Unit Two Resource Book,** p. 5, for a glossary.

Cast of Major Characters

Gods

Aphrodite (ăf′rə-dī′tē): the goddess of love and beauty; favors the Trojans

Apollo (ə-pŏl′ō): the god of healing, music, poetry, and prophecy; favors and protects the Trojans

Athena (ə-thē′nə): the goddess of wisdom and warfare; protects the Greeks

Hera (hîr′ə): the queen of the gods, sister and wife of Zeus; favors the Greeks

Hermes (hûr′mēz): the messenger of the gods

Thetis (thē′tĭs): a sea goddess, mother of Achilles

Zeus (zo͞os): the king of the gods, father of Aphrodite, Apollo, Athena, and Hermes; for the most part does not takes sides in the war

Greeks

Achilles (ə-kĭl′ēz): the mightiest Greek warrior, son of Thetis and the mortal king Peleus

Agamemnon (ăg′ə-mĕm′nŏn′): the king of Mycenae, brother of Menelaus and commander of all the Greek forces at Troy

Calchas (kăl′kəs): a priest and prophet

Helen (hĕl′ən): the wife of Menelaus, daughter of Zeus and the mortal woman Leda

Menelaus (mĕn′ə-lā′əs): the king of Sparta, whose wife, Helen, was carried off to Troy by Paris

Nestor (nĕs′tər): the king of Pylos, oldest and wisest of the Greek leaders

Odysseus (ō-dĭs′yo͞os′): the king of Ithaca, known for his craftiness.

Patroclus (pə-trō′kləs): a young Greek warrior, best friend of Achilles

Trojans

Andromache (ăn-drŏm′ə-kē): the wife of Hector

Astyanax (ə-stī′ə-năks′): the infant son of Hector and Andromache

Chryses (krī′sēz′): a priest of Apollo, whose daughter has been captured by the Greeks

Hector (hĕk′tər): the leader and greatest warrior of the Trojan army

Hecuba (hĕk′yə-bə): the queen of Troy, wife of Priam and mother of Hector and Paris

Paris (păr′ĭs): the Trojan prince whose abduction of Helen from Greece was the cause of the Trojan War

Priam (prī′əm): the king of Troy, father of Hector and Paris

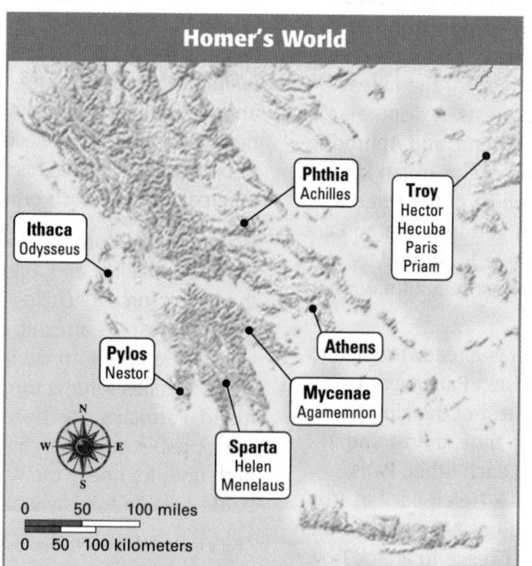

MINI LESSON Using the Map

Ask students the following questions as a means of studying the map:

- Which character lives at the farthest distance from Troy? *(Odysseus)*
- As the crow flies, how far is it between Sparta and Troy? *(approximately 300 miles or 480 kilometers)*
- For Achilles to travel from his home to Troy, which route would be shorter, land or sea? *(sea)*
- The Greeks sailed northeast on the Aegean Sea to travel to Troy. Which direction would they take to return to Greece? *(southwest)*
- Based on what you can observe in the map, why would it be difficult for Agamemnon to assemble an army from all parts of Greece?
  Possible Response: Greece is a mountainous terrain, so land travel would be difficult. Water also separates many of the cities and regions from one another.

Connect to Your Life

When people talk about Greek epics, the word *hero* often comes up. Review the following definitions of the word from the *American Heritage Dictionary.*

1. In mythology and legend, a man, often of divine ancestry, who is endowed with great courage and strength, celebrated for his bold exploits, and favored by the gods.
2. A person noted for feats of courage or nobility of purpose, especially one who has risked or sacrificed his or her life: *soldiers and nurses who were heroes in an unpopular war.*
3. A person noted for special achievement in a particular field: *the heroes of medicine.*

Which of these definitions most closely matches your own idea of a hero? In your judgment, what does a person need to be or to accomplish in order to be considered a true hero?

Focus Your Reading

LITERARY ANALYSIS: EPIC HERO

An epic hero is a larger-than-life figure whose actions are central to an epic poem. Epic heroes take part in dangerous adventures and accomplish great deeds that require courage and superhuman strength. In the *Iliad*, Hector describes his role in the following words:

> ***. . . To stand up bravely,***
> ***always to fight in the front ranks of Trojan soldiers,***
> ***winning my father great glory, glory for myself.***

Both Achilles and Hector may be considered epic heroes. As you will see, however, there are major differences between these two characters.

ACTIVE READING: EVALUATING

When you read, it is natural to form your own opinions about characters and events. In order to form reasonable opinions about those in the *Iliad,* keep the following points in mind:

- Try to examine why characters act the way they do, and look for the causes of major events.
- Remember that there's usually more than one perspective to consider. For example, in the quarrel between Achilles and Agamemnon, each man has a point.
- Look for evidence in the text to support your opinions.
- Be ready to change your mind if you gain new insights or find new evidence.

READER'S NOTEBOOK As you read, jot down your evaluations of key characters and events. The example shown here will help you get started.

Character or Event	Motive or Cause	My Evaluation
Agamemnon wants to take Briseis from Achilles.		*As a commander, he should be concerned about his troops, not his own desires.*

WORDS TO KNOW Vocabulary Preview

assent	gaunt	recoil	spurn
comply	lithe	recourse	waver
defile	pittance		

ILIAD 181

Reading and Analyzing

Guide for Reading

Explain that the most challenging selections in the textbook provide extra help for students. These selections are broken down into smaller, more manageable sections. Each section begins with a **Focus** that sets a purpose for reading and concludes with a **Pause & Reflect** question to check understanding. In the *Iliad*, previews of each section are also provided in italics. Some previews give a brief summary of previous events.

Reading Skills and Strategies
TEXT STRUCTURE

Before students begin reading, preview the structure of the textbook presentation of the *Iliad*. On page 182, draw attention to the title of Book 1, the Focus section, the preview, and the side notes. Also draw attention to the illustration on page 182, the first appearance of the Words to Know box on page 183, and the Pause & Reflect question on page 190. Point out that all of these elements aid student understanding.

Literary Analysis EPIC POETRY

A Tell students that the epic poems of ancient Greece begin with an invocation to one of the Muses. Here the poet calls upon the goddess of poetry and music to inspire him. The Muse *is* thought to be writing the poem through the poet.

Point out that the fight between Agamemnon and Achilles takes place long after the Trojan War has begun. Greek epics typically begin *in medias res,* which means "in the middle of the things."

Tell students that epic poetry is written in an elevated style, which relies on long sentences and formal diction. For that reason, students will need to be patient and deliberate in their reading.

from the

Iliad

Homer

Translated by Robert Fagles

GUIDE FOR READING

FOCUS In this excerpt from Book 1 of the *Iliad*, you will learn about the feud between Achilles and Agamemnon. As you read, evaluate the causes of the conflict between them and decide who is more to blame.

As the poem opens, the Greek army is suffering from a deadly **1** *plague. Apollo has sent the plague to punish the Greeks. The god is angry because Agamemnon, the Greek commander, has taken* **2** *the daughter of Chryses, Apollo's priest, as a war prize. When a prophet reveals the cause of Apollo's anger, Agamemnon reluctantly agrees to give her up. He insists, however, on being given Achilles' war prize as compensation. Achilles feels insulted and in his fury threatens to kill Agamemnon. The wise Nestor tries to make peace, with only partial success.*

Rage—Goddess, sing the rage of Peleus' son Achilles,
murderous, doomed, that cost the Achaeans countless losses,
hurling down to the House of Death so many sturdy souls,
A great fighters' souls, but made their bodies carrion,
feasts for the dogs and birds,
and the will of Zeus was moving toward its end.
Begin, Muse, when the two first broke and clashed,
Agamemnon lord of men and brilliant Achilles.

1 Goddess: a Muse (goddess of poetry and music) whom the poet calls upon for inspiration.

2 Achaeans (ə-kē'ənz): Greeks.

4 carrion: decaying flesh.

MINI LESSON Vocabulary Strategy

USING A DICTIONARY TO FIND PRECISE MEANING

Instruction Write the following on the board: "And a thick cloud of dust rose up/from the man [Hector] they [Greeks] dragged, his dark hair swirling round/that head so handsome once, . . . to be defiled in the land of his own fathers" (p. 211, lines 317–321).

Demonstrate for students how to use a dictionary to find the appropriate meaning of the verb *defiled*: "to destroy the purity, beauty, or honor of." Ask them why this meaning is more appropriate than others listed in the dictionary entries. *(This meaning of* defiled *precisely describes the corrupting of a person's being.)*

Practice Have students choose five of the remaining Words to Know. Ask students to write down the line(s) in which each word appears in the *Iliad*. Then ask them to reference each word in a dictionary and write the meaning that is most appropriate given the word's context.

Use **Unit Two Resource Book,** p. 15, for more practice.

A lesson on using reference tools appears on p. 558 in the Pupil's Edition.

Greek helmet and breast plate. Archaeological Museum, Sofia, Bulgaria.

What god drove them to fight with such a fury?
Apollo the son of Zeus and Leto. Incensed at the king
he swept a fatal plague through the army—men were dying
and all because Agamemnon <u>spurned</u> Apollo's priest.
Yes, Chryses approached the Achaeans' fast ships
3 to win his daughter back, bringing a priceless ransom
and bearing high in hand, wound on a golden staff,
the wreaths of the god, the distant deadly Archer.
He begged the whole Achaean army but most of all
the two supreme commanders, Atreus' two sons,
"Agamemnon, Menelaus—all Argives geared for war!
May the gods who hold the halls of Olympus give you
Priam's city to plunder, then safe passage home.
Just set my daughter free, my dear one . . . here,

10 Leto (lē′tō): a goddess; **incensed:** enraged.

16 Archer: Apollo, who was thought to be able to cause diseases by shooting people with his arrows.

18 Atreus' (ā′tro͞os′).

19 Argives (är′jīvz′): Greeks.

20 Olympus (ə-lĭm′pəs): the highest mountain in Greece, believed to be the home of the gods.

WORDS TO KNOW

spurn (spûrn) *v.* to reject in a scornful way

Customizing Instruction

Less Proficient Readers

Model the process of reading Homer and making use of the accompanying support material. Begin by reading the **Focus** aloud and modeling your thinking process. ("So, in Book 1, I'll need to look for the causes of the conflict between Agamemnon and Achilles.") Continue modeling the reading process through line 19 of the poem. Point out that various words are used to describe the Greeks and Trojans; for example, "Achaeans" and "Argives" both refer to the Greeks.

English Learners

Read aloud the proper names that appear on these pages, making use of the pronunciation key on page 180 if needed.

1 Point out that a "plague" is a deadly disease that can spread quickly.

2 Explain that a "war prize" is something that is given to a warrior as a reward for victory or in recognition of skill or courage.

3 Help students realize that a "ransom" is a payment made in exchange for the release of a captured person.

Cross Curricular Link **Humanities**

THE GREEK GODS The gods that Homer describes in the *Iliad* are very similar to human beings, but they are more powerful than humans, immortal, and ageless. A number of the major gods, known as the Twelve Olympians (see page 168 for more information), participate in the action of Homer's story. Because the gods can change their shapes and transport themselves at will, they often make unexpected appearances in the midst of battle. Apollo, Aphrodite, and Ares favor the Trojans and sometimes take action to protect their favorites. By contrast, Hera, Poseidon, and Athena favor the Greeks and similarly protect them. Zeus, the leader of the gods, also becomes involved in the action, though he generally maintains neutrality. At times, the gods even engage in the fighting. Ares kills a Greek soldier, and Aphrodite is wounded by another god.

The gods' interest in the Trojan War can be partially explained by their human offspring. For example, the Trojan hero Aeneas is the son of Aphrodite, while Helen of Troy is the daughter of Zeus. As portrayed by Homer, the gods possess the same vices and virtues exhibited by humans.

Literary Analysis CONFLICT

A Agamemnon refuses to listen to the advice of the other Greeks. He rejects the ransom offered by Chryses and insists that he will not give up his "girl." He even threatens harm to Chryses, which is an insult both to the priest and to Apollo.

Literary Analysis EPITHETS

B Call attention to Homer's use of short, descriptive phrases that point out a characteristic of a person or thing. Apollo is referred to here as the son of "sleek-haired Leto." Ask students to find another epithet on page 185.
Possible Response: In line 63, Hera is called "white-armed"; in line 99, Achilles is called a "matchless runner."

Reading Skills and Strategies
CAUSE AND EFFECT

Ask students to explain the cause-and-effect relationships that link these events: Agamemnon's rejection of Chryses' request for the return of Briseis, the plague, and Achilles' request to send for a prophet.
Possible Response: Because Chryses has been insulted and humiliated, he asks Apollo to pay back the Greeks. In response, Apollo sends a plague down, shooting the Greek animals and men with plague-infested arrows. After observing the effects of the plague, Achilles calls a meeting and suggests sending for a prophet to learn why Apollo is so angry.

accept these gifts, this ransom. Honor the god
who strikes from worlds away—the son of Zeus, Apollo!"

1 And all ranks of Achaeans cried out their <u>assent</u>:
"Respect the priest, accept the shining ransom!"
But it brought no joy to the heart of Agamemnon.
The king dismissed the priest with a brutal order
ringing in his ears: "Never again, old man,
let me catch sight of you by the hollow ships!
A Not loitering now, not slinking back tomorrow.
The staff and the wreaths of god will never save you then.
2 The girl—I won't give up the girl. Long before that,
old age will overtake her in *my* house, in Argos,
far from her fatherland, slaving back and forth
at the loom, forced to share my bed!
Now go,
don't tempt my wrath—and you may depart alive."

The old man was terrified. He obeyed the order,
turning, trailing away in silence down the shore
where the roaring battle lines of breakers crash and drag.
And moving off to a safe distance, over and over
B the old priest prayed to the son of sleek-haired Leto,
lord Apollo, "Hear me, Apollo! God of the silver bow
who strides the walls of Chryse and Cilla sacrosanct—
3 lord in power of Tenedos—Smintheus, god of the plague!
If I ever roofed a shrine to please your heart,
ever burned the long rich bones of bulls and goats
on your holy altar, now, now bring my prayer to pass.
Pay the Danaans back—your arrows for my tears!"

His prayer went up and Phoebus Apollo heard him.
Down he strode from Olympus' peaks, storming at heart
with his bow and hooded quiver slung across his shoulders.
The arrows clanged at his back as the god quaked with rage,
the god himself on the march and down he came like night.
Over against the ships he dropped to a knee, let fly a shaft
and a terrifying clash rang out from the great silver bow.
First he went for the mules and circling dogs but then,
launching a piercing shaft at the men themselves,
he cut them down in droves—
and the corpse-fires burned on, night and day, no end in sight.

36 loom: a device used for weaving cloth, a principal job of women in ancient Greek households.

44 Chryse (krī'sē): Chryses' hometown, site of a temple of Apollo; **Cilla** (sĭl'ə): another Trojan town.

45 Tenedos (tĕn'ə-dŏs): a small island off the Trojan coast; **Smintheus** (smĭn'thōōs): a title of Apollo.

49 Danaans (də-nā'ənz): Greeks.

50 Phoebus (fē'bəs): a title of Apollo in his role as god of the sun.

57 mules and circling dogs: the animals that are the first to be affected by the plague.

WORDS TO KNOW
assent (ə-sĕnt') *n.* agreement

Cross Curricular Link History

ANIMAL SACRIFICE Animal sacrifice played an important role in the religion of the ancient Greeks. Usually, domestic animals, such as cows, goats, or pigs, were sacrificed. The sacrifice often took place in front of a temple dedicated to a specific god, such as the famous temple of Apollo at Delphi. The choicest meat of the animal would be burned on an altar; then the rest of the meat would be eaten by the participants in the sacrifice. Such sacrifices were done for a variety of reasons: to please the gods, to purify those making the sacrifice, and to influence the course of future events. Those who ate the meat of the animal were thought to be given a share in the power of the god.

Nine days the arrows of god swept through the army.
On the tenth Achilles called all ranks to muster—
the impulse seized him, sent by white-armed Hera
grieving to see Achaean fighters drop and die.
Once they'd gathered, crowding the meeting grounds,
the swift runner Achilles rose and spoke among them:
"Son of Atreus, now we are beaten back, I fear,
the long campaign is lost. So home we sail . . .
if we can escape our death—if war and plague
are joining forces now to crush the Argives.
But wait: let us question a holy man,
4 a prophet, even a man skilled with dreams—
dreams as well can come our way from Zeus—
come, someone to tell us why Apollo rages so,
whether he blames us for a vow we failed, or sacrifice.
If only the god would share the smoky savor of lambs
and full-grown goats, Apollo might be willing, still,
somehow, to save us from this plague."
So he proposed
and down he sat again as Calchas rose among them,
Thestor's son, the clearest by far of all the seers
who scan the flight of birds. He knew all things that are,
all things that are past and all that are to come,
the seer who had led the Argive ships to Troy
with the second sight that god Apollo gave him.
For the armies' good the seer began to speak:
"Achilles, dear to Zeus . . .
you order me to explain Apollo's anger,
the distant deadly Archer? I will tell it all.
But strike a pact with me, swear you will defend me
with all your heart, with words and strength of hand.
For there is a man I will enrage—I see it now—
5 a powerful man who lords it over all the Argives,
one the Achaeans must obey . . . A mighty king,
raging against an inferior, is too strong.
Even if he can swallow down his wrath today,
still he will nurse the burning in his chest
until, sooner or later, he sends it bursting forth.
Consider it closely, Achilles. Will you save me?"

And the matchless runner reassured him: "Courage!
Out with it now, Calchas. Reveal the will of god,
whatever you may know. And I swear by Apollo

67 Son of Atreus: Agamemnon.

76–77 If only . . . full-grown goats: If Apollo would accept an animal sacrifice from the Greek forces.

80 seers: prophets.

81 scan the flight of birds: In ancient Greece, the behavior of birds was thought to provide signs of future events.

Customizing Instruction

Less Proficient Readers

Help students to identify the different speakers on these pages and to briefly summarize each speech.

1 All the Greek soldiers speak to Agamemnon. What do they want him to do? *(accept the ransom and return the girl)*

2 Agamemnon responds. What is his answer to Chryses? *(He refuses to give up the girl.)*

3 Chryses prays to Apollo. What does he want Apollo to do? *(punish the Greeks)*

4 Achilles suggests consulting a prophet. What does he want to learn? *(why Apollo is angry)*

5 Calchas, a prophet, stands up and asks Achilles for protection. Why is he afraid? *(He knows that his answer will anger a powerful Greek king.)*

English Learners

Explain the meaning of the following phrases:

Line 39: "where the roaring battle lines of breaks crash and drag" *(where the waves crash)*

Line 62: "to muster" *(to gather for a formal meeting)*

Line 84: "second sight" *(the gift of prophecy)*

Line 95: "swallow down his wrath" *(control his anger)*

Cross Curricular Link History

PROPHECY AND DIVINATION The ancient Greeks believed that the gods communicated with humans and that some people had special gifts that enabled them to interpret such communication and to foretell the future. The will of the gods could be expressed through dreams, through the flight patterns of birds, through figures created by the intestines of sacrificed animals, through divine possession, or other signs from human behavior or the natural world. When Calchas stands up in response to Achilles' suggestion that the Greeks question a prophet, he already knows the reason for Apollo's anger, thanks to his prophetic powers.

ILIAD 185

Reading and Analyzing

Literary Analysis EPIC HERO

A Point out that even in their heated argument, Achilles and Agamemnon seem aware of one another's stature. Here, Achilles refers sarcastically to his rival as "the best of the Achaeans." Later, Agamemnon says, "brave as you are, godlike Achilles" (line 154).

Use **Unit Two Resource Book,** p. 7, for more practice.

Reading Skills and Strategies
MAKING INFERENCES

B Ask students why Apollo has demanded 100 bulls in addition to the return of Chryseis. *(The bulls will be used in a sacrifice to Apollo.)*

Active Reading EVALUATING

C Ask students what Agamemnon's response to the news that he must return the girl reveals about his own character.

Possible Response: On one hand, Agamemnon seems to want the best for his people; on the other hand, he seems selfishly concerned about his own image and reputation.

Use **Unit Two Resource Book,** p. 6, for more practice.

Literary Analysis METAPHOR

D Ask students to explain the meaning of "armored in shamelessness." *(Agamemnon is so stubborn and proud that he feels no sense of shame.)*

dear to Zeus, the power you pray to, Calchas,
when you reveal god's will to the Argives—no one,
not while I am alive and see the light on earth, no one
1 will lay his heavy hands on you by the hollow ships.
None among all the armies. Not even if you mean
Agamemnon here who now claims to be, by far,
A the best of the Achaeans."
The seer took heart
and this time he spoke out, bravely: "Beware—
he casts no blame for a vow we failed, a sacrifice.
The god's enraged because Agamemnon spurned his priest,
he refused to free his daughter, he refused the ransom.
2 That's why the Archer sends us pains and he will
send us more
and never drive this shameful destruction from the Argives,
B not till we give back the girl with sparkling eyes
to her loving father—no price, no ransom paid—
and carry a sacred hundred bulls to Chryse town.
Then we can calm the god, and only then appease him."

118 appease: satisfy.

So he declared and sat down. But among them rose
the fighting son of Atreus, lord of the far-flung kingdoms,
Agamemnon—furious, his dark heart filled to the brim,
blazing with anger now, his eyes like searing fire.
With a sudden, killing look he wheeled on Calchas first:
"Seer of misery! Never a word that works to my advantage!
Always misery warms your heart, your prophecies—
never a word of profit said or brought to pass.
Now, again, you divine god's will for the armies,
bruit it out, as fact, why the deadly Archer
multiplies our pains: because I, I refused
that glittering price for the young girl Chryseis.
Indeed, I prefer *her* by far, the girl herself,
3 I want her mine in my own house! I rank her higher
than Clytemnestra, my wedded wife—she's nothing less
in build or breeding, in mind or works of hand.
But I am willing to give her back, even so,
if that is best for all. What I really want
is to keep my people safe, not see them dying.
C But fetch me another prize, and straight off too,
else I alone of the Argives go without my honor.
That would be a disgrace. You are all witness,
look—*my* prize is snatched away!"

128 bruit it out: report it.

130 Chryseis (krī-sē′ĭs): Chryses' daughter.

133 Clytemnestra (klī′təm-nĕs′trə).

Cross Curricular Link **History**

WAR PRIZES According to the customs of the time, victorious soldiers were expected to divide up the possessions of the losing side–including the women, who would become slaves and mistresses. The greatest prizes would be given to the most highly honored soldiers. Though Achilles promises to give Agamemnon even greater prizes in the future, Agamemnon feels disgraced by being asked to give up his prize.

But the swift runner
4 Achilles answered him at once, "Just how, Agamemnon,
great field marshal . . . most grasping man alive,
how can the generous Argives give you prizes now?
I know of no troves of treasure, piled, lying idle,
anywhere. Whatever we dragged from towns we plundered,
all's been portioned out. But collect it, call it back
from the rank and file? *That* would be the disgrace.
So return the girl to the god, at least for now.
We Achaeans will pay you back, three, four times over,
if Zeus will grant us the gift, somehow, someday,
to raze Troy's massive ramparts to the ground."

But King Agamemnon countered, "Not so quickly,
brave as you are, godlike Achilles—trying to cheat *me*.
Oh no, you won't get past me, take me in that way!
What do you want? To cling to your own prize
while I sit calmly by—empty-handed here?
5 Is that why you order me to give her back?
No—if our generous Argives *will* give me a prize,
a match for my desires, equal to what I've lost,
well and good. But if they give me nothing
I will take a prize myself—your own, or Ajax'
or Odysseus' prize—I'll commandeer her myself
and let that man I go to visit choke with rage!
Enough. We'll deal with all this later, in due time.
Now come, we haul a black ship down to the bright sea,
gather a decent number of oarsmen along her locks
and put aboard a sacrifice, and Chryseis herself,
in all her beauty . . . we embark her too.
Let one of the leading captains take command.
Ajax, Idomeneus, trusty Odysseus or you, Achilles,
you—the most violent man alive—so you can perform
the rites for us and calm the god yourself."
A dark glance
and the headstrong runner answered him in kind:
"Shameless—
D 6 armored in shamelessness—always shrewd with greed!
How could any Argive soldier obey your orders,
freely and gladly do your sailing for you
or fight your enemies, full force? Not I, no.
It wasn't Trojan spearmen who brought me here to fight.
The Trojans never did *me* damage, not in the least,

145 troves: collections.

152 raze: demolish; **ramparts:** defensive walls.

162 Ajax (ā′jăks′): the strongest Greek warrior next to Achilles—known as the Greater Ajax to distinguish him from another warrior of the same name.

163 commandeer (kŏm′ən-dîr′): seize by force.

171 Idomeneus (ī-dŏm′ə-no͞os′): the ruler of the island of Crete.

Customizing Instruction

Less Proficient Readers

Help students to recognize the various speakers on these pages and to briefly summarize each speaker's point.

1 What does Achilles promise to Calchas? *(that he will protect him from anyone who may take offense at his message)*

2 How does Calchas explain Apollo's anger? *(Apollo is angry because Agamemnon rejected the offer of a ransom and refused to return Chryseis to her father.)*

3 Why is Agamemnon so angry at Calchas? *(He feels insulted by being asked to give up the girl.)*

4 What offer does Achilles make to Agamemnon? *(If Agamemnon returns the girl, the Greeks will give him many more gifts when they conquer Troy.)*

5 The argument becomes more personal. What does Agamemnon say he will do? *(He will take another prize from someone else, but he will also release Chryseis.)*

6 Achilles becomes enraged by Agamemnon's attitude. What does Achilles mean by saying the Trojans never did him any damage? *(The Trojans stole Helen, Agamemnon's sister-in-law; Achilles has no quarrel with them.)*

English Learners

Explain the meaning of the following phrases:

Line 123: "wheeled on" *(turned against)*

Line 125: "misery warms your heart" *(bad news or the sorrows of others seems to make you glad)*

Line 147: "all's been portioned out" *(everything has already been divided and given out)*

Advanced Learners

How might the argument between Achilles and Agamemnon have been avoided?

Possible Response: Agamemnon would have to care less about his personal status and more about the needs of his entire force. Achilles would have to be less accusatory and more willing to negotiate. Both men would need to show more respect for one another.

Cross Curricular Link — Humanities

TRIBAL SOCIETY AND THE GREEK ARMY The Greek army depicted in the *Iliad* is a reflection of a society organized by tribes. At the request of Agamemnon, various tribal leaders, such as Achilles and Odysseus, agreed to join their forces together to retrieve Helen from Troy and restore her to her husband Menelaus, who is Agamemnon's brother. As a result, the unity of the army is fragile because the soldiers owe more loyalty to their tribal leaders than to the army's general, Agamemnon. By contrast, the Trojans are united under a single king, Priam, who is acknowledged as the hereditary leader of all the Trojans.

ILIAD 187

Literary Analysis CONFLICT

A Ask students why Achilles feels poorly treated by Agamemnon.

Possible Response: Achilles fights to exhaustion, but Agamemnon—who stays out of the battles—always gets a larger share of the war prizes.

Literary Analysis CHARACTERIZATION

B Draw attention to the number of times Agamemnon refers to himself in his verbal attack on Achilles. Ask students what character traits Agamemnon and Achilles have in common.

Possible Response: Both men have an enormous sense of pride; they seem quick to take offense if they are slighted in any way.

Active Reading EVALUATING

Ask students to consider whether Achilles and Agamemnon have good reasons for their anger.

Possible Response: Achilles makes a good point when he says that his prowess makes him deserving of as many prizes as Agamemnon. He makes a reasonable point when he says that Agamemnon should wait for prizes that can replace Chryseis. Achilles joined the war to restore honor to Agamemnon's family, so he may be justified in feeling that he deserves more respect than he has been shown. Agamemnon may have a valid point when he claims that he deserves the most honor because he is the general.

they never stole my cattle or my horses, never
in Phthia where the rich soil breeds strong men
did they lay waste my crops. How could they?
Look at the endless miles that lie between us . . .
shadowy mountain ranges, seas that surge and thunder.
No, you colossal, shameless—we all followed you,
to please you, to fight for you, to win your honor
back from the Trojans—Menelaus and you, you dog-face!
What do *you* care? Nothing. You don't look right or left.
And now you threaten to strip me of my prize in person—
the one I fought for long and hard, and sons of Achaea
handed her to me.
My honors never equal yours,
whenever we sack some wealthy Trojan stronghold—
my arms bear the brunt of the raw, savage fighting,
true, but when it comes to dividing up the plunder
the lion's share is yours, and back I go to my ships,
clutching some scrap, some pittance that I love,
when I have fought to exhaustion.
No more now—
back I go to Phthia. Better that way by far,
to journey home in the beaked ships of war.
I have no mind to linger here disgraced,
brimming your cup and piling up your plunder."

But the lord of men Agamemnon shot back,
"*Desert,* by all means—if the spirit drives you home!
I will never beg you to stay, not on *my* account.
Never—others will take my side and do me honor,
Zeus above all, whose wisdom rules the world.
You—I hate you most of all the warlords
loved by the gods. Always dear to your heart,
strife, yes, and battles, the bloody grind of war.
What if you are a great soldier? That's just a gift of god.
Go home with your ships and comrades, lord it over your
Myrmidons!
You *are* nothing to me—you and your overweening anger!
But let this be my warning on your way:
since Apollo insists on taking my Chryseis,
I'll send her back in my own ships with *my* crew.
But I, I will be there in person at your tents
to take Briseis in all her beauty, your own prize—

182 Phthia (fthī'ə): Achilles' homeland.

193 sack: capture and loot.

212 Myrmidons (mûr'mə-dŏnz'): Achilles' people.

213 overweening: arrogant.

218 Briseis (brī-sē'ĭs): a captive Trojan woman who was given to Achilles.

WORDS TO KNOW

pittance (pĭt'ns) *n.* a small reward; tiny amount

MINI LESSON **Grammar**

SIMPLE SUBJECTS AND SIMPLE PREDICATES

Instruction Remind students that the simple subject is the key word or words in the subject. It tells who or what performs the action in a sentence. The simple subject does not include modifiers. The simple predicate is the verb or verb phrase that tells something about the subject. Modifiers are not part of the verb phrase.

Model Write the following on the board:

Agamemnon held the daughter of Chryses as a war prize.

Have students identify the simple subject and simple predicate *(Agamemnon, simple subject; held, simple predicate).*

Practice Ask students to underline the simple subject once and the simple predicate twice.

1. Chryses pleaded strongly with Agamemnon for the return of his daughter.
2. Agamemnon brutally dismissed Chryses from the Greek palace.
3. The old priest prayed to the god Apollo for assistance.

For more instruction and practice, use McDougal Littell's ***Language Network:***

- Grade 10, Chapter 2, "The Sentence and Its Parts"
- Grade 12, Chapter 1, "The Parts of a Sentence"

Temple of Poseidon, Sounion, Greece.

Customizing Instruction

Less Proficient Readers
Make sure that students keep track of who is speaking and what the main points of dispute are.

1 What does Achilles threaten to do if Briseis is taken from him? *(return home with his men)*

2 Agamemnon responds by saying he does not care what Achilles does. What does Agamemnon say he will do? *(send Chryseis back and then go to Achilles' tents to take Briseis)*

English Learners
Explain the meaning of the following words and phrases:

Line 186: "colossal" *(giant or monster)*

Line 189: "You don't look right or left" *(You don't pay attention to anyone but yourself.)*

Line 194: "my arms bear the brunt" *(I do most of the work.)*

Line 196: "lion's share" *(the greatest or best part)*

Line 204: "Desert" *(leave or abandon—not a dry, sandy region)*

Advanced Learners
Both Achilles and Agamemnon seem to regard the dispute about war prizes as a test of manhood. Based on what you have read so far, how does a man in the society depicted by Homer prove his manhood?
Possible Response: A man can prove his manhood by demonstrating skill, bravery, or leadership in battle. Just as importantly, recognition from one's peers helps to confirm manhood. Both Achilles and Agamemnon are fighting to maintain their status among their peers.

Reading and Analyzing

Pause & Reflect

Possible Response: Agamemnon becomes enraged when he learns that Apollo is angry and demands that Chryseis be returned to her father. Achilles is angered by Agamemnon's demand that his lost prize be replaced immediately. In the course of argument, both men become even more enraged. Some students will blame Agamemnon more because he starts the argument; others may blame Achilles more because he threatens to take his men away from the battle.

Literary Analysis MYTHOLOGY

A Draw attention to Athena's direct intervention; she descends from the heavens and grabs Achilles by the hair to prevent him from hurting Agamemnon. The gods were believed to be capable of traveling great distances in an instant. Note that Athena makes herself visible to Achilles alone; she remains invisible to all others.

Literary Analysis EPIC HERO

B Ask students to describe Achilles' attitude toward the gods.

Possible Response: He instantly obeys Hera's order, which shows his respect for the gods and his humility before them.

Literary Analysis CULTURAL SETTING

C When Achilles swears his oath on the wooden scepter, he makes a sacred promise, so important that breaking it would be a sacrilege against the gods. Achilles swears that the Greeks will sorely miss him because nothing will bring him back.

so you can learn just how much greater I am than you
and the next man up may shrink from matching words
  with me,
from hoping to rival Agamemnon strength for strength!"

PAUSE & REFLECT The angry Achilles has threatened to take his men and return home. Why do Achilles and Agamemnon become so enraged at each other, and, in your judgment, who is more to blame?

FOCUS The anger of Achilles—"the most violent man alive"—is always dangerous. Read to find out how various characters, both human and divine, respond to his anger.

He broke off and anguish gripped Achilles.
The heart in his rugged chest was pounding, torn . . .
Should he draw the long sharp sword slung at his hip,
thrust through the ranks and kill Agamemnon now?—
or check his rage and beat his fury down?
As his racing spirit veered back and forth,
just as he drew his huge blade from its sheath,
down from the vaulting heavens swept Athena,
the white-armed goddess Hera sped her down:
1 Hera loved both men and cared for both alike.
Rearing behind him Pallas seized his fiery hair—
A only Achilles saw her, none of the other fighters—
struck with wonder he spun around, he knew her at once,
Pallas Athena! the terrible blazing of those eyes,
and his winged words went flying: "Why, why now?
Child of Zeus with the shield of thunder, why come now?
To witness the outrage Agamemnon just committed?
I tell you this, and so help me it's the truth—
he'll soon pay for his arrogance with his life!"

  Her gray eyes clear, the goddess Athena answered,
"Down from the skies I come to check your rage
if only you will yield.
The white-armed goddess Hera sped me down:
she loves you both, she cares for you both alike.
Stop this fighting, now. Don't lay hand to sword.
2 Lash him with threats of the price that he will face.
And I tell you this—and I *know* it is the truth—

232 Pallas (păl'əs): a title of Athena.

Assessment Informal Assessment

SUMMARIZING Ask students to work in pairs to prepare an oral summary of the dispute between Agamemnon and Achilles. One student should play the role of Achilles and present his side of the conflict. The other student can do the same for Agamemnon. Remind students that the best summaries of each character's viewpoint will be those that are the most accurate and complete.

RUBRIC

3 **Full Accomplishment** Student's account provides an accurate and thorough explanation.

2 **Substantial Achievement** Student's account is accurate, but some important information is missing.

1 **Little or Partial Achievement** Student's account is missing vital information, is inaccurate, or shows little understanding of the character.

one day glittering gifts will lie before you,
2 three times over to pay for all his outrage.
Hold back now. Obey us both."
So she urged
and the swift runner complied at once: "I must—
when the two of you hand down commands, Goddess,
B a man submits though his heart breaks with fury.
Better for him by far. If a man obeys the gods
3 they're quick to hear his prayers."
And with that
Achilles stayed his burly hand on the silver hilt
and slid the huge blade back in its sheath.
He would not fight the orders of Athena.
Soaring home to Olympus, she rejoined the gods
aloft in the halls of Zeus whose shield is thunder.

But Achilles rounded on Agamemnon once again,
lashing out at him, not relaxing his anger for a moment:
"Staggering drunk, with your dog's eyes, your fawn's heart!
Never once did you arm with the troops and go to battle
or risk an ambush packed with Achaea's picked men—
you lack the courage, you can see death coming.
Safer by far, you find, to foray all through camp,
commandeering the prize of any man who speaks against
you.
King who devours his people! Worthless husks, the men
you rule—
if not, Atrides, this outrage would have been your last.
I tell you this, and I swear a mighty oath upon it . . .
by this, this scepter, look,
that never again will put forth crown and branches,
now it's left its stump on the mountain ridge forever,
nor will it sprout new green again, now the brazen ax
C has stripped its bark and leaves, and now the sons of Achaea
pass it back and forth as they hand their judgments down,
upholding the honored customs whenever Zeus commands—
This scepter will be the mighty force behind my oath:
someday, I swear, a yearning for Achilles will strike
Achaea's sons and all your armies! But then, Atrides,
4 harrowed as you will be, *nothing* you do can save you—
not when your hordes of fighters drop and die,
cut down by the hands of man-killing Hector! Then—

262 rounded on: attacked with words.

268 foray: raid.

271 Atrides (ā-trī'dēz'): "son of Atreus"—that is, Agamemnon.

273 scepter: a rod symbolizing authority, handed in turn to each speaker in the warriors' assembly.

283 harrowed: distressed.

WORDS TO KNOW

comply (kəm-plī') *v.* to agree to a request or carry out an order; obey

Customizing Instruction

Less Proficient Readers

Focus Point out to students that Achilles is such an important leader and warrior that his anger cannot be ignored. Even the gods respond to his anger. Help students to keep track of who is speaking, what the character is talking about, and who is being spoken to. To help students visualize Athena's intervention, ask them to view the illustration on page 193.

1 How does Athena keep Achilles from attacking Agamemnon? *(She grabs him by the hair to stop him.)*

2 Athena says that she has been sent by Hera. What does she ask Achilles to do? *(hold back his anger)*

3 Why does Achilles say that a man should obey the gods? *(The gods are quick to respond to such a man's prayers.)*

4 Achilles swears that the Greeks will miss him in the future. What will save the Greeks from Hector? *(nothing)*

English Learners

Explain the following phrases to students:

Line 225: "thrust through the ranks" *(force his way through the soldiers)*

Line 227: "his racing spirit veered back and forth" *(In his excited anger, he could not make up his mind whether to attack.)*

Line 265: "arm with the troops" *(go to battle with the rest of the troops)*

Line 270: "Worthless husks" *(empty shells)*

Advanced Learners

Tell students that Athena was often depicted in Greek art as a warrior goddess. However, the women of Greek society did not participate in fighting wars. Ask students why the Greeks had such a powerful female goddess, even though Greek women had little power in their society.

Possible Responses: The Greek gods did not live by the same standards as human beings; in contrast to Homer's society, the gods are nearly equal with one another, so a warrior goddess is not a surprise. The female gods had great power primarily because they were divine, not because of their sex. By envisioning a powerful warrior goddess, the Greeks may have been recognizing female strength.

ILIAD 191

Reading Skills and Strategies
PREDICTING

A Ask students to predict how the two rivals will respond to Nestor's effort to end the conflict. *(Accept any reasonable response.)*

Literary Analysis EPIC POETRY

B Epic poems have a grand scope, often covering years of events and a vast geographical range. References to the heroes of the past contribute to such grandeur.

Reading Skills and Strategies
CLARIFYING

C Nestor advises Achilles to give in to Agamemnon. What reasons does Nestor give?
Possible Response: Agamemnon should be shown respect because he is a great king. He has more power than Achilles because he rules over more men; he rules over the entire army.

Reading Skills and Strategies
QUESTIONING

D Ask students why Agamemnon is so determined not to give in to Achilles.
Possible Response: Agamemnon feels that Achilles has shown him no respect. Because Achilles is such a powerful warrior, Agamemnon may feel threatened by him.

then you will tear your heart out, desperate, raging
that you disgraced the best of the Achaeans!"
Down on the ground
he dashed the scepter studded bright with golden nails,
then took his seat again. The son of Atreus smoldered,
glaring across at him, but Nestor rose between them,
the man of winning words, the clear speaker of Pylos . . .
Sweeter than honey from his tongue the voice flowed on
and on.
Two generations of mortal men he had seen go down by now,
those who were born and bred with him in the old days,
in Pylos' holy realm, and now he ruled the third.
He pleaded with both kings, with clear good will,
"No more—or enormous sorrow comes to all Achaea!
How they would exult, Priam and Priam's sons
and all the Trojans. Oh they'd leap for joy
to hear the two of you battling on this way,
you who excel us all, first in Achaean councils,
first in the ways of war.
Stop. Please.
Listen to Nestor. You are both younger than I,
and in my time I struck up with better men than you,
even you, but never once did they make light of me.
I've never seen such men, I never will again . . .
men like Pirithous, Dryas, that fine captain,
Caeneus and Exadius, and Polyphemus, royal prince,
and Theseus, Aegeus' boy, a match for the immortals.
They were the strongest mortals ever bred on earth,
the strongest, and they fought against the strongest too,
shaggy Centaurs, wild brutes of the mountains—
they hacked them down, terrible, deadly work.
And I was in their ranks, fresh out of Pylos,
far away from home—they enlisted me themselves
and I fought on my own, a free lance, single-handed.
And none of the men who walk the earth these days
could battle with those fighters, none, but they,
they took to heart my counsels, marked my words.
So now you listen too. Yielding is far better . . .
Don't seize the girl, Agamemnon, powerful as you are—
leave her, just as the sons of Achaea gave her,
his prize from the very first.
And you, Achilles, never hope to fight it out
with your king, pitting force against his force:

291 Pylos (pī'lŏs').

298 exult: rejoice.

307–309 Pirithous (pī-rith'ō-əs), **Dryas** (drī'əs) . . . **Caeneus** (sē'nōōs) **and Exadius** (ĭg-zăd'ē-əs) . . . **Polyphemus** (pŏl'ə-fē'məs) . . . **Theseus** (thē'syōōs), **Aegeus'** (ē'jōōs') **boy:** heroes of the legendary war fought by the Lapiths against the Centaurs (a monstrous race with bodies half human and half horse).

Detail of *Athena restrains Achilles from killing Agamemnon* (1757), Giambattista Tiepolo. Fresco. Villa Valmarana, Vicenza, Italy. Photo © Scala/Art Resource, New York.

no one can match the honors dealt a king, you know,
a sceptered king to whom great Zeus gives glory.
Strong as you are—a goddess was your mother—
he has more power because he rules more men.
C 4 Atrides, end your anger—look, it's Nestor!
I beg you, cool your fury against Achilles.
Here the man stands over all Achaea's armies,
our rugged bulwark braced for shocks of war."

But King Agamemnon answered him in haste,
"True, old man—all you say is fit and proper—
5 D but this soldier wants to tower over the armies,
he wants to rule over all, to lord it over all,
give out orders to every man in sight. Well,
there's one, I trust, who will never yield to him!
What if the everlasting gods have made a spearman of him?

HUMANITIES CONNECTION Athena intervenes in the argument between Achilles and Agamemnon. Note that Achilles is drawing his sword while Agamemnon has reacted defensively.

333 bulwark: defensive barrier.

Customizing Instruction

Less Proficient Readers

1 Point out that lines 290 to 331 focus on Nestor, who attempts to make peace. Explain that Nestor is old enough to be a grandfather to Achilles and to Agamemnon and that he has participated in many wars.

2 Ask students why Nestor thinks the Trojans would "leap for joy" to hear the argument between Achilles and Agamemnon. *(If the Greeks are divided, they'll be easier to beat in war.)*

3 Make sure that students understand that Nestor asks both men to yield. What does Nestor want Agamemnon to do? *(to let Achilles keep Briseis)*

4 What makes Agamemnon more powerful than Achilles? *(He's a king who rules more men.)*

5 According to Agamemnon, what does Achilles want to do? *(rule over everyone else)*

English Learners

Explain the meaning of the following words and phrases:

Line 285: "you will tear your heart out" *(You will be so desperate that you will feel like ripping out your heart.)*

Line 289: "smoldered" *(showed signs of anger)*

Line 292: "Sweeter than honey from his tongue" *(Words flowed smoothly and gracefully from Nestor)*

MINI LESSON Viewing and Representing

Athena restraining Achilles from killing Agamemnon **by Giambattista Tiepolo**

ART APPRECIATION Tiepolo (1696–1770) is considered one of the greatest Italian painters of the 18th century. His work is representative of the rococo style, a style of art that flourished in the 18th century, marked by elaborate ornamentation, bright colors, and theatrical depictions of subject matter.

Instruction Have students look at the painting and the **Humanities Connection** on this page. Explain that artists have many different techniques for suggesting motion. Draw attention to the ways in which Tiepolo's work suggests motion. Point out the lunging position of Achilles' torso and front leg, the bending of his arms, the backward tilt of his head, and the position of his cloak.

Application Have students find other aspects of the painting that suggest movement. Students may call attention to the folded left arm of Agamemnon; the bent arms of the most prominent soldiers in the background; the raised back leg of Athena and her outstretched hand clasping Achilles' hair; or other details. Then ask students to discuss whether the artist's depiction of the scene matches their own visualization of the events and characters.

Reading and Analyzing

Reading Skills and Strategies
CLARIFYING

(A) Ask students to explain what Achilles means by this statement. *(He will give up Briseis without a fight, but he refuses to give anything else to the Greeks.)*

Reading Skills and Strategies
CLARIFYING

(B) Point out that this preview of Book 6 also includes a brief summary of what happens in Books 2 through 5.

Thinking Through the Literature

1. Possible Response: The anger of Achilles fuels the anger of Agamemnon, who says that he will never yield to him; Athena descends to earth, grabs Achilles by the hair, and orders him to stop fighting; Nestor pleads with Achilles to stop his argument with Agamemnon.
2. Possible Response: Some students may blame Agamemnon more because he starts the argument by insisting on an immediate replacement for his lost prize. He also refuses to compromise and accept a prize later, and he insists on taking Briseis. Others may blame Achilles more because he refuses to give in to his general, threatens to take his soldiers away, and draws his sword.
3. Possible Response: Both characters are proud, quick to anger, concerned with their own public image, and intolerant of one another.
4. Possible Response: Athena becomes involved in the action when she grabs Achilles by the hair to stop him from attacking Agamemnon. She tells Achilles that she and Hera love both men, and she orders Achilles to stop. Her actions show that the gods become involved in human affairs.
5. Possible Response: Achilles' words foreshadow a time when the Greeks will want Achilles beside them in battle; without him, they will not be able to stop Hector.

Use Selection Quiz in **Unit Two Resource Book,** p. 8.

Have they entitled him to hurl abuse at *me*?"

"Yes!"—blazing Achilles broke in quickly—
"What a worthless, burnt-out coward I'd be called
if I would submit to you and all your orders,
whatever you blurt out. Fling them at others,
don't give me commands!
Never again, *I* trust, will Achilles yield to *you*.
And I tell you this—take it to heart, I warn you—
my hands will never do battle for that girl,
neither with you, King, nor any man alive.
You Achaeans gave her, now you've snatched her back.
But all the rest I possess beside my fast black ship—
not one bit of it can you seize against my will, Atrides.
Come, try it! So the men can see, that instant,
your black blood gush and spurt around my spear!"

Thinking Through the Literature

1. How do Athena, Agamemnon, and Nestor respond to the anger of Achilles?
2. Do you think Achilles or Agamemnon bears the greater share of the blame for their **conflict?** Explain your reasoning.
3. What do you learn about the **characters** of Agamemnon and Achilles in the excerpt from Book 1? Support your conclusions with details from the text.
4. Hera sends Athena to intervene in the conflict. Describe Athena's actions, and discuss what they suggest about the relationship between gods and mortals.
5. Review the oath that Achilles swears in lines 281–287. What future events might be **foreshadowed** by his words?

HECTOR RETURNS TO TROY

GUIDE FOR READING

FOCUS In the following scene, Hector's wife pleads with her husband to stay in the city with her. As you read, look for the reasons that she gives.

B *After Achilles withdraws from the war, the fighting between Trojans and Greeks begins again. Even without their best warrior, the Greeks do well on the battlefield. Hector, fearful that the Greeks are near victory, returns to Troy and tells the Trojans to ask the goddess Athena for help. He then visits his wife and child. Hector's wife, Andromache, pleads with him to stay in the city.*

At that, Hector spun and rushed from his house,
back by the same way down the wide, well-paved streets
throughout the city until he reached the Scaean Gates,
the last point he would pass to gain the field of battle.
There his warm, generous wife came running up to meet him,
Andromache the daughter of gallant-hearted Eetion
who had lived below Mount Placos rich with timber,
in Thebe below the peaks, and ruled Cilicia's people.
3 His daughter had married Hector helmed in bronze.
She joined him now, and following in her steps
a servant holding the boy against her breast,
in the first flush of life, only a baby,
Hector's son, the darling of his eyes
and radiant as a star . . .
Hector would always call the boy Scamandrius,
townsmen called him Astyanax, Lord of the City,
since Hector was the lone defense of Troy.
The great man of war breaking into a broad smile,
his gaze fixed on his son, in silence. Andromache,

3 Scaean (skē′ən) **Gates:** a gateway in Troy's wall, facing the Greek camp.

6 Eetion (ē-ĕt′ē-ŏn′).

8 Thebe (thē′bē): a town near Troy; **Cilicia's** (sĭ-lĭsh′əz) **people:** the inhabitants of the region surrounding Thebe.

15 Scamandrius (skə-măn′drē-əs).

Customizing Instruction

Less Proficient Readers

Focus Tell students that the following scene shows a completely different aspect of the Trojan War—its effect on family life.

1 Point out that Achilles does not want people to call him a coward for giving in to Agamemnon.

2 Make sure that students realize that Achilles agrees to give up Briseis only because he is disgusted by the other Greeks. She was given to him as a prize, but now she will be taken away, which is dishonorable in his eyes.

3 Help students to visualize this scene of family affection. Andromache has brought her infant son to Hector, just inside the gates of the city.

Cross Curricular Link Humanities

HECTOR Hector, the eldest son of Priam, king of Troy, is one of the greatest heroes of Greek and Roman literature. A loving son, loyal friend, devoted husband and father, Hector is portrayed in a positive light throughout the epic. Though Hector is regarded by all as the fiercest Trojan warrior, two Greeks are his superior in battle, Ajax and Achilles. In Book 7 of the *Iliad*, Ajax and Hector battle hand to hand, with inconclusive results. Later, in Book 22, Achilles and Hector meet face to face.

Hector stands apart from most military heroes in Western literature in one important respect: He fights for the side that opposes the author's own people. Many critics have praised Homer's uncommon ability to portray the enemy so sympathetically.

Reading and Analyzing

Literary Analysis CULTURAL SETTING

A Point out that Andromache believes that her life is controlled by "destiny" or fate. Explain that her belief in fate is typical of the ancient Greeks. Ask students what she believes will happen in the future. *(Hector will be killed and she will be left all alone.)*

Reading Skills and Strategies
CLARIFYING

B Ask students what Andromache means when she calls Hector her father, mother, and brother. *(He's the only family that she has left.)*

Reading Skills and Strategies
MAKING INFERENCES

C Why does Andromache want Hector to fight by the city walls? *(She does not want him to return to the open fields, where he will be more vulnerable to attack.)*

Pause & Reflect

Possible Response: Andromache believes that Hector is destined to die in battle. She wants to delay that moment as long as possible.

The departure of the warrior (about 500 B.C.), Nicoxenos Vasepainter. Red-figured amphora. Louvre, Paris. Photo © Erich Lessing/Art Resource, New York.

pressing close beside him and weeping freely now,
clung to his hand, urged him, called him: "Reckless one,
my Hector—your own fiery courage will destroy you!
A Have you no pity for him, our helpless son? Or me,
and the destiny that weighs me down, your widow,
now so soon. Yes, soon they will kill you off,
all the Achaean forces massed for assault, and then,
bereft of you, better for me to sink beneath the earth.
What other warmth, what comfort's left for me,
once you have met your doom? Nothing but torment!
I have lost my father. Mother's gone as well.
Father . . . the brilliant Achilles laid him low
when he stormed Cilicia's city filled with people,
Thebe with her towering gates. He killed Eetion,
not that he stripped his gear—he'd some respect at least—
for he burned his corpse in all his blazoned bronze,

27 bereft: deprived.

34 he'd some respect at least: Achilles showed respect for Eetion by not plundering his armor and by treating his corpse with appropriate ceremony. **1**

35 blazoned bronze: decorated armor.

then heaped a grave-mound high above the ashes
and nymphs of the mountain planted elms around it,
daughters of Zeus whose shield is storm and thunder.
And the seven brothers I had within our halls . . .
2 all in the same day went down to the House of Death,
the great godlike runner Achilles butchered them all,
tending their shambling oxen, shining flocks.
                                        And mother,
who ruled under the timberline of woody Placos once—
he no sooner haled her here with his other plunder
than he took a priceless ransom, set her free
and home she went to her father's royal halls
where Artemis, showering arrows, shot her down.
You, Hector—you are my father now, my noble mother,
B a brother too, and you are my husband, young and warm
    and strong!
Pity me, please! Take your stand on the rampart here,
before you orphan your son and make your wife a widow.
Draw your armies up where the wild fig tree stands,
there, where the city lies most open to assault,
C the walls lower, easily overrun. Three times
they have tried that point, hoping to storm Troy,
their best fighters led by the Great and Little Ajax,
3 famous Idomeneus, Atreus' sons, valiant Diomedes.
Perhaps a skilled prophet revealed the spot—
or their own fury whips them on to attack."

37 nymphs (nĭmfs): minor nature goddesses.

44 haled: dragged.

47 Artemis (är'tə-mĭs): goddess of the hunt and twin sister of Apollo.

56 Little Ajax: a Greek warrior known for his swiftness.

57 Diomedes (dī'ə-mē'dēz): another celebrated Greek warrior.

PAUSE & REFLECT Why is it so important to Andromache that Hector not return to the battlefield?

FOCUS Hector is determined to fight, even though he believes that Troy is doomed. As you read, pay attention to his reasons for fighting, as well as his worries about his wife's future.

And tall Hector nodded, his helmet flashing:
"All this weighs on my mind too, dear woman.
But I would die of shame to face the men of Troy
and the Trojan women trailing their long robes
if I would shrink from battle now, a coward.
Nor does the spirit urge me on that way.
I've learned it all too well. To stand up bravely,

Customizing Instruction

Less Proficient Readers

1 Make sure that students realize that Eetion is Andromache's father.

2 Ask students who killed all seven of Andromache's brothers. *(Achilles)*

3 Point out that Andromache is suggesting that Hector stay close to the city walls to do his fighting. She feels that he will be safer there.

Focus As students read about Hector's determination to fight, ask them to consider what they would do if they were in his situation.

English Learners

Point out the meanings of the followings words and phrases:

Line 34: "stripped his gear" *(removed his armor)*

Line 50: "rampart" *(a means of protection or defense)*

Advanced Learners

Ask students to describe Andromache's attitude toward Achilles. *(She shows some respect for Achilles, even though he killed her father and seven brothers. At the same time, she fears him, believing that her husband may be killed by him.)*

Cross Curricular Link History

TROY The city that is depicted in the *Iliad* probably bears some resemblance to the actual city. In 1870, Heinrich Schliemann began the excavation of the site of Troy in what is now northwest Turkey, some four miles from the Aegean Sea. The excavation eventually revealed that nine different cities had been built on the same site, each one built upon the ruins of the city that preceded it. The sixth city, which was probably destroyed by an earthquake around 1300 B.C., was fortified with a massive wall over 10 feet thick in places and more than 20 feet high. Scholars believe that the seventh city may have been the one written about in Greek literature. Evidence was found that the ancient Greeks attacked and burned that city of Troy around 1250 B.C.

Literary Analysis EPIC HERO

A Make sure that students realize that Hector is convinced the Trojans will lose. Ask students what impressions they have of Hector up to this point.
Possible Response: Hector seems to be a loving father and husband. His bravery and loyalty to Troy is remarkable, especially since he seems to know that Troy will be defeated.

Literary Analysis CULTURAL SETTING

B Point out that if the Trojans lose, Andromache is likely to be taken as a slave back to Greece. Ask why she would be "at another woman's beck and call." *(She would have to listen to the wife in charge of the household.)*

Active Reading EVALUATING

C Ask students to share their opinion of Hector's response to his wife.
Possible Response: Hector shows that he loves his wife dearly. They obviously have a close relationship, and Hector is responsive to his wife's feelings.

always to fight in the front ranks of Trojan soldiers,
winning my father great glory, glory for myself.
For in my heart and soul I also know this well:
A the day will come when sacred Troy must die,
Priam must die and all his people with him,
Priam who hurls the strong ash spear . . .
Even so,
it is less the pain of the Trojans still to come
that weighs me down, not even of Hecuba herself
or King Priam, or the thought that my own brothers
in all their numbers, all their gallant courage,
may tumble in the dust, crushed by enemies—
That is nothing, nothing beside your agony
when some brazen Argive hales you off in tears,
wrenching away your day of light and freedom!
Then far off in the land of Argos you must live,
laboring at a loom, at another woman's beck and call,
B fetching water at some spring, Messeis or Hyperia,
resisting it all the way—
the rough yoke of necessity at your neck.
And a man may say, who sees you streaming tears,
1 'There is the wife of Hector, the bravest fighter
they could field, those stallion-breaking Trojans,
long ago when the men fought for Troy.' So he will say
and the fresh grief will swell your heart once more,
widowed, robbed of the one man strong enough
to fight off your day of slavery.
No, no,
let the earth come piling over my dead body
before I hear your cries, I hear you dragged away!"

In the same breath, shining Hector reached down
for his son—but the boy recoiled,
cringing against his nurse's full breast,
2 screaming out at the sight of his own father,
terrified by the flashing bronze, the horsehair crest,
the great ridge of the helmet nodding, bristling terror—
so it struck his eyes. And his loving father laughed,
his mother laughed as well, and glorious Hector,
quickly lifting the helmet from his head,
set it down on the ground, fiery in the sunlight,
and raising his son he kissed him, tossed him in his arms,

83 Messeis (mə-sē′ĭs) . . . **Hyperia** (hī′pə-rī′ə): springs in Greece.

WORDS TO KNOW
recoil (rĭ-koil′) *v.* to pull back in fear or surprise

MINI LESSON **Vocabulary Strategy**

CONTEXT CLUES Call students' attention to the list of Words to Know. Remind them that often they can understand the meaning of an unfamiliar word by examining the context in which the word is used. Use the model sentences to demonstrate the strategy of using context clues.

Model Sentences

His father's great frame and shiny armor intimidated Hector's son. The boy quickly recoiled, away from the awesome warrior.

Instruction

- Write the model sentences on the chalkboard.
- Have students use the meaning of the sentences to infer meanings of the word *recoiled.*
- Ask a volunteer to use the word *recoiled* in a sentence.

Practice

Have students choose four other Words to Know in the selection, examine the context in which those words appear, and explain how context helps to explain the meaning of the word.

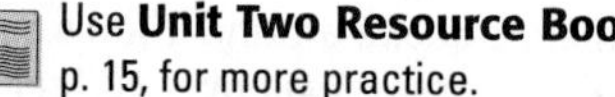

Use **Unit Two Resource Book,** p. 15, for more practice.

A lesson on context clues appears on p. 674 in the Pupil's Edition.

Greek bust of Zeus. Museo Nazionale, Naples Italy. Photograph copyright © Alinari-Viollet.

lifting a prayer to Zeus and the other deathless gods:
"Zeus, all you immortals! Grant this boy, my son,
may be like me, first in glory among the Trojans,
strong and brave like me, and rule all Troy in power
and one day let them say, 'He is a better man than his
father!'—
3 when he comes home from battle bearing the bloody gear
of the mortal enemy he has killed in war—
a joy to his mother's heart."
So Hector prayed
and placed his son in the arms of his loving wife.
Andromache pressed the child to her scented breast,
smiling through her tears. Her husband noticed,
C and filled with pity now, Hector stroked her gently,
trying to reassure her, repeating her name: "Andromache,
dear one, why so desperate? Why so much grief for me?
No man will hurl me down to Death, against my fate.

Customizing Instruction

Less Proficient Readers

1 Ask students what bothers Hector the most when he thinks about dying. *(that his wife will become a slave)*

2 Help students to visual the cause of the boy's terror. He sees his father in full armor and may not recognize him.

3 Ask students what Hector hopes for his son's future. *(He wants people to say that he's a better warrior than his father; his victories in battle will make his mother proud.)*

Cross Curricular Link Humanities

FATE In the *Iliad*, fate governs virtually everything that happens to a person, most importantly, the time of death. Characters often refer to fate as a goddess, the one who determines everyone's lot, or portion, in life. The other gods—even the great Zeus—are not supposed to interfere with the fate of mortals, for each person's fate cannot be changed. In some places in the *Iliad*, Homer personifies fate as three old women, the Fates. Clotho spins the thread of each person's destiny, Lachesis measures the length of each thread, and Atropos cuts the thread off, thus determining when death occurs. Each person's fate, therefore, is wrapped around his or her life like a thread. Both Hector and Achilles have been given knowledge of their fates, and both heroes know they are fated to die in the war.

Reading and Analyzing

Reading Skills and Strategies
CLARIFYING

(A) Make sure that students understand Hector's view of fate. He believes that no human being can escape his or her fate.

Literary Analysis EPITHET

(B) Point out that Hector is often referred to by the epithet "man-killing." Ask students whether that is a term of praise or criticism.
Possible Response: In the context of Greek culture, it is a term of praise because a warrior is judged by his success in battle. It's difficult for a modern audience, however, to regard such a term as positive.

Thinking Through the Literature

1. Hector keeps fighting because he feels that it would be cowardly to stop; he also wants to win glory for himself and his father.
2. Hector believes that his wife will be captured by the Greeks and turned into a slave.
3. Students may point out that Hector bravely accepts fate, even though he realizes that Troy will be defeated. Hector realizes that his actions cannot change or influence fate. Students may also note that Hector deeply grieves for his wife's future, though he calmly accepts the prospect of his own death.
4. Students are likely to call attention to Hector's positive qualities, such as his love for his wife and son, his courage, and his calm acceptance of his own death. Students may also notice his religious piety. Some students may view Hector as foolhardy for refusing to stay within the walls of Troy.
5. Some students may judge Achilles to be more heroic because he seems to be the most powerful of all the warriors. Others may find Hector to be more heroic because he continues to fight even though his side is doomed to defeat. Some students may also be drawn to Hector's humane qualities.

(A) And fate? No one alive has ever escaped it,
neither brave man nor coward, I tell you—
it's born with us the day that we are born.
So please go home and tend to your own tasks,
the distaff and the loom, and keep the women
working hard as well. As for the fighting,
men will see to that, all who were born in Troy
but I most of all."
Hector aflash in arms
took up his horsehair-crested helmet once again.
And his loving wife went home, turning, glancing
back again and again and weeping live warm tears.
She quickly reached the sturdy house of Hector,
(B) man-killing Hector,
and found her women gathered there inside
and stirred them all to a high pitch of mourning.
So in his house they raised the dirges for the dead,
(1) for Hector still alive, his people were so convinced
that never again would he come home from battle,
never escape the Argives' rage and bloody hands.

125 distaff (dĭs'tăf'): a device used in making wool or other fibers into thread.

136 dirges (dûr'jĭz): funeral songs.

Thinking Through the Literature

1. Why is Hector so determined to keep fighting?
2. What does Hector think the future holds for his wife?
3. Hector says that "no man alive has ever escaped" fate (line 121). How would you describe Hector's attitude toward fate? Use details from Hector's speech to his wife in lines 61–94 to support your judgment.
4. What do you learn about the **character** of Hector in the excerpt from Book 6? Consider his roles as husband, father, and warrior.
5. Review the description of an **epic hero** on page 181. In light of that description, who seems more heroic to you, Hector or Achilles? Use details from the poem to support your response.

MINI LESSON Grammar

COMPLETE SUBJECTS AND COMPLETE PREDICATES

Instruction Remind students that the complete subject includes the simple subject and all the words that modify it. The complete predicate includes the verb and all the words that modify it.

Model Write the following on the board: Young Andromache desperately feared Hector's death. Have students identify the simple subject and simple predicate *(Andromache, simple subject; feared, simple predicate).* Have students identify the complete subject and complete predicate *(Young Andromache, complete subject; desperately feared Hector's death, complete predicate).*

Practice Ask students to underline the complete subject once and the complete predicate twice.

1. The great warrior Hector comforted his wife.
2. Hector bravely returned to battle the Greeks.
3. The women of Hector's house expressed great sadness.

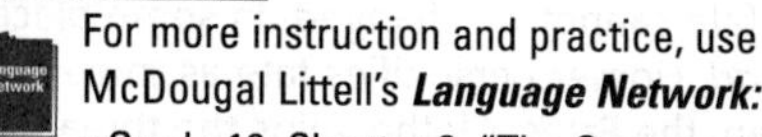

For more instruction and practice, use McDougal Littell's ***Language Network:***
- Grade 10, Chapter 2, "The Sentence and Its Parts"
- Grade 12, Chapter 1, "The Parts of a Sentence"

THE DEATH OF HECTOR

GUIDE FOR READING

FOCUS This excerpt from Book 22 describes a battle to the death between Achilles and Hector. As you read, evaluate Hector's chance of winning the battle.

2 *After Hector returns to battle, the Trojans gain the advantage. They drive the Greeks back to their ships and seem to have victory within reach. Greek leaders try to persuade Achilles to rejoin the fighting, offering many gifts. The proud Achilles still refuses to fight, though he does agree to keep his ships at Troy. After more fighting—and the fall of many Greek heroes—Achilles' best friend, Patroclus, appeals to him once more. Achilles refuses again, but he does agree to allow Patroclus to enter the battle. Wearing Achilles' armor and leading his troops, Patroclus succeeds in pushing the Trojans back. But Hector kills the brave Patroclus with the help of Apollo. He takes Achilles' armor from the corpse and wears it himself.*

Enraged and grief-stricken, Achilles decides to avenge the death of his friend. When Achilles tells his mother of his decision, she tearfully informs him that he is doomed to an early death, for once he kills Hector, his own death will follow. Achilles accepts his fate and enters the battle, wearing magnificent new armor made by the smith of the gods. In relentless pursuit of Hector, Achilles slaughters every Trojan in his path.

As Book 22 opens, the Trojan warriors have fled to the safety of the city—all except Hector. Achilles chases Hector around the walls of Troy until the gods decide to intervene.

So he wavered,
waiting there, but Achilles was closing on him now
like the god of war, the fighter's helmet flashing,
over his right shoulder shaking the Pelian ash spear,

4 Pelian (pē'lē-ən): made of wood from Mount Pelion in Greece.

WORDS TO KNOW

waver (wā'vər) *v.* to have difficulty in making a decision

Customizing Instruction

Less Proficient Readers

1 Make sure that students realize that the Trojan women are singing funeral songs because they believe that Hector will soon die.

Focus Point out that a great deal of Homer's text has been skipped over, which is summarized in the italicized text. Students need to realize that this battle is the climax of Homer's long story: the two greatest heroes fight.

2 You may find it helpful to read aloud all of the text in italics. Make sure that students understand that Achilles returns to battle only because Hector killed his best friend, Patroclus. As the scene opens, Achilles begins chasing Hector around the walled city of Troy.

English Learners

Explain the meaning of the following phrase:

Line 123: "it's born with us the day that we are born" *(Our fate is determined at the moment of our birth.)*

Advanced Learners

Suggest that students read the famous description of Achilles' new shield in Book 18 of the *Iliad.* They should be able to find a copy of the complete book at the library, or they can search for the specific chapter on the Internet. Ask students to give a brief description of his new shield. *(The shield shows peaceful activities, such as marriage ceremonies and harvest festivals; it also depicts violent scenes of the two armies at war.)*

Reading and Analyzing

Literary Analysis EPIC SIMILE

A This scene includes three famous epic similes. Point out the first one (lines 10–15) in which Achilles is compared to a hawk swooping down for the kill. Ask students to find one other epic simile on these two pages. *(Lines 39–44: The two rivals are compared to stallions racing against each other; lines 69–74: Achilles is compared to a dog hunting a fawn.)*

Reading Skills and Strategies VISUALIZING

Ask students to describe their mental images of the chase. *(Accept all reasonable responses.)*

Literary Analysis MYTHOLOGY

B Help students to appreciate Athena's shock at Zeus' suggestion that the gods might save Hector. Ask them how fate limits the power of the gods.

Possible Response: Though the gods have the power to save Hector, they should not do so because such action would be a violation of his fate. It seems that even the gods are prohibited from interfering with someone's fate.

Active Reading EVALUATING

C Ask students whether they believe that Hector's effort to run for safety is cowardly.

Possible Responses: Yes, because a hero should stand and fight. No, because Hector realizes Achilles is stronger and faster than he is.

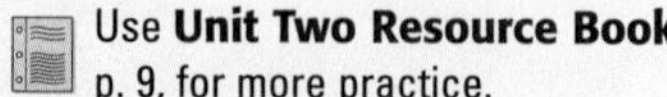
Use **Unit Two Resource Book,** p. 9, for more practice.

Pause & Reflect

Possible Response: Students are likely to believe that Hector has little chance of winning. The conversation between Zeus and Athena reveals that Hector is doomed.

that terror, and the bronze around his body flared
like a raging fire or the rising, blazing sun.
1 Hector looked up, saw him, started to tremble,
nerve gone, he could hold his ground no longer,
he left the gates behind and away he fled in fear—
and Achilles went for him, fast, sure of his speed
as the wild mountain hawk, the quickest thing on wings,
A launching smoothly, swooping down on a cringing dove
and the dove flits out from under, the hawk screaming
over the quarry, plunging over and over, his fury
driving him down to beak and tear his kill—
so Achilles flew at him, breakneck on in fury
with Hector fleeing along the walls of Troy,
fast as his legs would go. On and on they raced,
passing the lookout point, passing the wild fig tree
tossed by the wind, always out from under the ramparts
down the wagon trail they careered until they reached
the clear running springs where whirling Scamander
rises up from its double wellsprings bubbling strong—
and one runs hot and the steam goes up around it,
drifting thick as if fire burned at its core
but the other even in summer gushes cold
as hail or freezing snow or water chilled to ice . . .
And here, close to the springs, lie washing-pools
scooped out in the hollow rocks and broad and smooth
where the wives of Troy and all their lovely daughters
would wash their glistening robes in the old days,
the days of peace before the sons of Achaea came . . .
Past these they raced, one escaping, one in pursuit
and the one who fled was great but the one pursuing
greater, even greater—their pace mounting in speed
since both men strove, not for a sacrificial beast
or oxhide trophy, prizes runners fight for, no,
they raced for the life of Hector breaker of horses.
Like powerful stallions sweeping round the post for trophies,
galloping full stretch with some fine prize at stake,
a tripod, say, or woman offered up at funeral games
for some brave hero fallen—so the two of them
whirled three times around the city of Priam,
sprinting at top speed while all the gods gazed down,
and the father of men and gods broke forth among them
now:
"Unbearable—a man I love, hunted round his own city walls

21 careered: rushed.

22 Scamander (skə-măn′dər): the chief river of the plain below Troy.

41 tripod (trī′pŏd′): a three-legged cooking kettle. (Since all metal was very valuable in ancient Greece, tripods were often given as prizes in athletic contests.)

and right before my eyes. My heart grieves for Hector.
Hector who burned so many oxen in my honor, rich cuts,
now on the rugged crests of Ida, now on Ilium's heights.
But now, look, brilliant Achilles courses him round
2 the city of Priam in all his savage, lethal speed.
Come, you immortals, think this through. Decide.
Either we pluck the man from death and save his life
or strike him down at last, here at Achilles' hands—
for all his fighting heart."
But immortal Athena,
her gray eyes wide, protested strongly: "Father!
3 Lord of the lightning, king of the black cloud,
what are you saying? A man, a mere mortal,
B his doom sealed long ago? You'd set him free
from all the pains of death?
Do as you please—
but none of the deathless gods will ever praise you."

And Zeus who marshals the thunderheads replied,
"Courage, Athena, third-born of the gods, dear child.
Nothing I said was meant in earnest, trust me,
I mean you all the good will in the world. Go.
Do as your own impulse bids you. Hold back no more."

So he launched Athena already poised for action—
down the goddess swept from Olympus' craggy peaks.

PAUSE & REFLECT Zeus feels sorry for Hector and even wonders whether the gods should save him. Do you think Hector has a fair chance to win the battle?

FOCUS Athena is coming down to earth to help Achilles. As you read, notice how she assists Achilles.

And swift Achilles kept on coursing Hector, nonstop
as a hound in the mountains starts a fawn from its lair,
hunting him down the gorges, down the narrow glens
and the fawn goes to ground, hiding deep in brush
but the hound comes racing fast, nosing him out
until he lands his kill. So Hector could never throw
Achilles off his trail, the swift racer Achilles—
C time and again he'd make a dash for the Dardan Gates,
trying to rush beneath the rock-built ramparts, hoping

49 Ida (ī′də): a mountain range near Troy; **Ilium's** (ĭl′ē-əmz): Troy's.

50 courses: chases; hunts.

70 starts: frightens; **lair:** hiding place.

76 Dardan Gates: a gateway in Troy's wall.

Customizing Instruction

Less Proficient Readers

Make sure that all students realize that it is Achilles who is chasing Hector outside the walls of Troy. The chase lasts a long time because they run around the entire city three times.

1 Ask why Hector starts to run. *(He loses his nerve when he sees Achilles.)*

2 Ask students to notice details that help to explain why Zeus feels sorry for Hector and considers saving him. *(Hector "burned so many oxen" to honor Zeus; Zeus admits that Hector is "a man I love.")*

3 Make sure students understand that Athena is angry at Zeus. Hector is a mortal whose "doom [was] sealed long ago." He is fated to die, and the gods should not interfere.

Focus Remind students that the gods often take part in the action of the *Iliad.*

English Learners

Explain the meaning of the following words and phrases:

Lines 34–35: "the one who fled was great but the one pursuing greater, even greater" *(Hector was great but Achilles was even greater.)*

Line 38: "breaker of horses" *(a person who trains horses)*

Line 59: "doom sealed long ago" *(It was fated a long time ago that Hector should die.)*

Line 69: "coursing" *(chasing)*

MINI LESSON Speaking and Listening

PERFORMING A DIALOGUE Point out that the dialogue between Zeus and Athena in lines 46–66 shows the limited power of the gods. Though Zeus could rescue Hector from Achilles, he is not allowed to interfere in the fate of a mortal, a limit that Athena reminds him of.

Prepare Have students act out the dialogue between Athena and Zeus. You may find it helpful to have students first work in groups of four to study the lines. In each group, two students can work on Athena's lines, and two can work on those of Zeus. Students should plan both the verbal interpretation of the lines and nonverbal performance techniques, such as expressions, gestures, posture, and so on.

Present Ask each group to perform its interpretation. Two students may read each role in unison, or the group may choose one reader to play Zeus and one to play Athena.

This activity is particularly well suited for longer class periods.

ILIAD 203

Reading and Analyzing

Literary Analysis EPIC SIMILE

A Hector's inability to escape from Achilles is compared to a dream where two rivals take part in an endless chase. Ask students what the comparison suggests about Hector's state of mind. *(He feels hopeless.)*

Literary Analysis EPIC POETRY

B Point out that the gods once again become involved in the action. Zeus weighs the fates of the two rivals on a scale, which reveals that it is now Hector's time to die. Athena then descends to earth to help Achilles.

Reading Skills and Strategies CLARIFYING

C Ask students to explain how Athena is participating in the action. *(She has taken the form of Hector's brother, encouraging him to stand and fight Achilles.)*

men on the heights might save him, somehow, raining
spears
but time and again Achilles would intercept him quickly,
heading him off, forcing him out across the plain
and always sprinting along the city side himself—
endless as in a dream . . .
when a man can't catch another fleeing on ahead
and he can never escape nor his rival overtake him—
so the one could never run the other down in his speed
nor the other spring away. And how could Hector have fled
the fates of death so long? How unless one last time,
one final time Apollo had swept in close beside him,
driving strength in his legs and knees to race the wind?
And brilliant Achilles shook his head at the armies,
never letting them hurl their sharp spears at Hector—
someone might snatch the glory, Achilles come in second.
But once they reached the springs for the fourth time,
then Father Zeus held out his sacred golden scales:
in them he placed two fates of death that lays men low—
one for Achilles, one for Hector breaker of horses—
and gripping the beam mid-haft the Father raised it high
and down went Hector's day of doom, dragging him down
to the strong House of Death—and god Apollo left him.
Athena rushed to Achilles, her bright eyes gleaming,
standing shoulder-to-shoulder, winging orders now:
"At last our hopes run high, my brilliant Achilles—
Father Zeus must love you—
we'll sweep great glory back to Achaea's fleet,
we'll kill this Hector, mad as he is for battle!
No way for him to escape us now, no longer—
not even if Phoebus the distant deadly Archer
goes through torments, pleading for Hector's life,
groveling over and over before our storming Father Zeus.
But you, you hold your ground and catch your breath
while I run Hector down and persuade the man
to fight you face-to-face."
So Athena commanded
and he obeyed, rejoicing at heart—Achilles stopped,
leaning against his ashen spearshaft barbed in bronze.
And Athena left him there, caught up with Hector at once,
and taking the build and vibrant voice of Deiphobus
stood shoulder-to-shoulder with him, winging orders:
"Dear brother, how brutally swift Achilles hunts you—

94 sacred golden scales: the balance used by Zeus to decide people's fates.

97 mid-haft: by the handle in the middle.

109 groveling (grŏv'ə-lĭng): throwing himself to the ground.

116 Deiphobus (dē-ĭf'ə-bəs): a son of Priam.

Cross Curricular Link **Humanities**

HADES In Line 99, Hector is described as being dragged to the House of Death, more commonly known as Hades. The name Hades refers both to the god who is ruler of the dead and to his kingdom. In Homer's *Iliad*, the realm of the dead lies just beyond the Ocean, which was thought to encircle the earth. Those who have died (and who have been buried properly) are ferried across one of the rivers of Hades. There, they live a kind of shadow existence, knowing neither pain nor happiness. A fortunate few escape this dull and dreary afterlife and are taken to Elysium, a land of sun and happiness. Those who have made themselves enemies of the gods are taken to Tantarus, where they are punished.

Pallas de Velletri, attributed to Kresilas. Marble, 305 cm. Musée du Louvre, Paris. Photograph copyright © Herve Lewandowski. Réunion des Musées Nationaux/Art Resource, New York.

coursing you round the city of Priam in all his lethal speed!
Come, let us stand our ground together—beat him back."

"Deiphobus!"—Hector, his helmet flashing, called out to her—
"dearest of all my brothers, all these warring years,
of all the sons that Priam and Hecuba produced!
Now I'm determined to praise you all the more,
you who dared—seeing me in these straits—
to venture out from the walls, all for *my* sake,
while the others stay inside and cling to safety."

125 these straits: this distress.

C

The goddess answered quickly, her eyes blazing,
"True, dear brother—how your father and mother both
implored me, time and again, clutching my knees,
and the comrades round me begging me to stay!
Such was the fear that broke them, man for man,
but the heart within me broke with grief for you.
Now headlong on and fight! No letup, no lance spared!

Customizing Instruction

Less Proficient Readers

1 Remind students that the gods often take sides. Point out that Zeus is neutral. Ask students which god is on Hector's side *(Apollo)* and which god is on Achilles' side. *(Athena)* Explain that Apollo leaves Hector because it's Hector's time to die.

2 Make sure that students realize that the female god Athena has taken the shape of a male, namely, Hector's brother Deiphobus. By doing this, Athena is tricking Hector so that Achilles can kill him in battle.

English Learners

Explain the meaning of the following phrases:

Line 116: "taking the build and vibrant voice of Deiphobus" *(appearing as Deiphobus)*

Line 129: "clutching my knees" *(a gesture of begging)*

Advanced Learners

Explain that Homer's view of the gods is anthropomorphic, which means that the gods are given human characteristics. Ask students what human characteristics are exhibited by Athena in this scene.

Possible Response: Athena shows favoritism by intervening in the action to help Achilles. She deceives Hector by appearing under the disguise of Deiphobus, and lies to him to maintain her illusion.

ILIAD **205**

Reading and Analyzing

Literary Analysis EPIC HERO

A If Hector wins the fight, he will honor the corpse of Achilles. Ask students what this reveals about Hector.
Possible Response: He believes that warriors should follow rules of conduct; he has strong principles and a sense of honor.

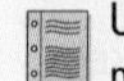
Use **Unit Two Resource Book,** p. 10, for more practice.

Reading Skills and Strategies
COMPARE AND CONTRAST

B Ask students to compare and contrast the two warriors in terms of how each one will treat the other after death. *(Hector has sworn to show respect to the corpse of Achilles and to return it to his people. Achilles refuses to make any such agreement.)*

Pause & Reflect
Possible Response: Athena comes down to earth and takes the form of Hector's brother, Deiphobus. She deceives Hector into thinking that he now has help, which leads him to stop running from Achilles.

Reading Skills and Strategies
QUESTIONING

C Ask students why Hector is so certain that he will die. *(He realizes that he is all alone and that by himself he is no match for Achilles.)*

So now, now we'll *see* if Achilles kills us both
and hauls our bloody armor back to the beaked ships
or he goes down in pain beneath your spear."

Athena luring him on with all her immortal cunning—
and now, at last, as the two came closing for the kill
it was tall Hector, helmet flashing, who led off:
"No more running from you in fear, Achilles!
Not as before. Three times I fled around
the great city of Priam—I lacked courage then
to stand your onslaught. Now my spirit stirs me
to meet you face-to-face. Now kill or be killed!
Come, we'll swear to the gods, the highest witnesses—
the gods will oversee our binding pacts. I swear
A I will never mutilate you—merciless as you are—
if Zeus allows me to last it out and tear your life away.
But once I've stripped your glorious armor, Achilles,
I will give your body back to your loyal comrades.
Swear you'll do the same."
A swift dark glance
and the headstrong runner answered, "Hector, stop!
B You unforgivable, you . . . don't talk to me of pacts.
There are no binding oaths between men and lions—
wolves and lambs can enjoy no meeting of the minds—
they are all bent on hating each other to the death.
So with you and me. No love between us. No truce
till one or the other falls and gluts with blood
Ares who hacks at men behind his rawhide shield.
Come, call up whatever courage you can muster.
Life or death—now prove yourself a spearman,
a daring man of war! No more escape for you—
Athena will kill you with my spear in just a moment.
Now you'll pay at a stroke for all my comrades' grief,
all you killed in the fury of your spear!"

PAUSE & REFLECT How does Athena help Achilles?

148 mutilate you: hack up your body.

159 gluts: satisfies.

160 Ares (âr'ēz): the god of war.

Assessment Informal Assessment

SUMMARIZING Ask students to write a one-paragraph summary of the fight between Achilles and Hector. Remind students that an effective summary will present the main events in chronological order and that summaries will be judged according to their accuracy and completeness.

RUBRIC

3 Full Accomplishment Student's account provides an accurate and thorough summary of the fight.

2 Substantial Achievement Student's account is accurate, but some important information is missing.

1 Little or Partial Achievement Student's account is missing vital information, is inaccurate, or shows little understanding of the conflict.

FOCUS Although Hector knows that he is doomed to die, he will stand and fight. As you read, look for the ways in which Achilles insults Hector, both with words and with actions.

With that,
shaft poised, he hurled and his spear's long shadow flew
but seeing it coming glorious Hector ducked away,
crouching down, watching the bronze tip fly past
1 and stab the earth—but Athena snatched it up
and passed it back to Achilles
and Hector the gallant captain never saw her.
He sounded out a challenge to Peleus' princely son:
"You missed, look—the great godlike Achilles!
So you knew nothing at all from Zeus about my death—
and yet how sure you were! All bluff, cunning with words,
that's all you are—trying to make me fear you,
lose my nerve, forget my fighting strength.
Well, you'll never plant your lance in my back
as I flee *you* in fear—plunge it through my chest
as I come charging in, if a god gives you the chance!
But now it's for you to dodge *my* brazen spear—
I wish you'd bury it in your body to the hilt.
How much lighter the war would be for Trojans then
if you, their greatest scourge, were dead and gone!"

Shaft poised, he hurled and his spear's long shadow flew
2 and it struck Achilles' shield—a dead-center hit—
but off and away it glanced and Hector seethed,
his hurtling spear, his whole arm's power poured
in a wasted shot. He stood there, cast down . . .
he had no spear in reserve. So Hector shouted out
to Deiphobus bearing his white shield—with a ringing shout
3 he called for a heavy lance—
but the man was nowhere near him,
vanished—
C yes and Hector knew the truth in his heart
and the fighter cried aloud, "My time has come!
At last the gods have called me down to death.
I thought he was at my side, the hero Deiphobus—
he's safe inside the walls, Athena's tricked me blind.
And now death, grim death is looming up beside me,
no longer far away. No way to escape it now. This,

185 scourge (skûrj): source of misery.

188 glanced: bounced.

Customizing Instruction

Less Proficient Readers

Focus Lead students to summarize the main events of these pages. Make sure that they understand that Hector promises to respect the corpse of Achilles, while Achilles does not.

1 By retrieving Achilles' spear, Athena gives him an unfair advantage.

2 Point out that Achilles' armor was handmade by a god. Ask students how that gives Achilles an advantage. *(When Hector throws his spear, it just bounces off, which shows the armor's strength.)*

3 Read aloud this passage so that students realize why Hector now expects to die.

English Learners

Line 159: "gluts with blood Ares" *(satisfies or fills up the god of war with blood)*

Line 183: "bury it in your body to the hilt." *(stick the spear in your body all the way to the handle)*

ILIAD 207

Reading and Analyzing

Active Reading EVALUATING

A Ask students what they think of Hector at this moment.

Possible Response: Hector shows himself to be a true hero; he knows that he will die but he is determined to die in glory.

Literary Analysis PLOT

B Remind students that Achilles had previously given his armor to Patroclus, which Hector took for his own after killing him. Achilles knows the one spot of Hector's body that is not protected—the lower part of his neck.

Literary Analysis CULTURAL SETTING

C A ransom, or payment, was the usual way of ensuring that the corpse of an important warrior would be returned to his family. Enemies in war were supposed to follow such customs as a matter of honor.

this was their pleasure after all, sealed long ago—
Zeus and the son of Zeus, the distant deadly Archer—
though often before now they rushed to my defense.
So now I meet my doom. Well let me die—
but not without struggle, not without glory, no,
in some great clash of arms that even men to come
will hear of down the years!"
And on that resolve
he drew the whetted sword that hung at his side,
tempered, massive, and gathering all his force
he swooped like a soaring eagle
launching down from the dark clouds to earth
to snatch some helpless lamb or trembling hare.
So Hector swooped now, swinging his whetted sword
and Achilles charged too, bursting with rage, barbaric,
guarding his chest with the well-wrought blazoned shield,
head tossing his gleaming helmet, four horns strong

208 whetted: sharpened.

209 tempered: hardened by heating.

215 well-wrought: skillfully made.

Greek soldiers arming themselves. Copyright © Peter Connolly.

Cross Curricular Link Humanities

ACHILLES' ARMOR The return of Achilles to battle was delayed while he awaited the delivery of new armor. Achilles' mother, the goddess Thetis, asked the god Hephaestus to make her son a new set of armor, even though she knew that once Achilles killed Hector he was fated to die thereafter. Hephaestus, the smith of the gods, made Achilles a shield of great strength and artistry. On the shield were painted scenes of the earth and skies, as well as detailed depictions of two contrasting cities. One city is marked by peaceful events, including marriages, festivals, and legal proceedings. The other city is threatened by two armies and characterized by acts of treachery and violence.

and the golden plumes shook that the god of fire
drove in bristling thick along its ridge.
Bright as that star amid the stars in the night sky,
star of the evening, brightest star that rides the heavens,
so fire flared from the sharp point of the spear Achilles
brandished high in his right hand, bent on Hector's death,
scanning his splendid body—where to pierce it best?
The rest of his flesh seemed all encased in armor,
burnished, brazen—*Achilles'* armor that Hector stripped
from strong Patroclus when he killed him—true,
but one spot lay exposed,
B where collarbones lift the neckbone off the shoulders,
the open throat, where the end of life comes quickest—
there
as Hector charged in fury brilliant Achilles drove his spear
1 and the point went stabbing clean through the tender neck
but the heavy bronze weapon failed to slash the windpipe—
Hector could still gasp out some words, some last reply . . .
he crashed in the dust—
godlike Achilles gloried over him:
"Hector—surely you thought when you stripped Patroclus' armor
that you, you would be safe! Never a fear of me—
far from the fighting as I was—you fool!
Left behind there, down by the beaked ships
his great avenger waited, a greater man by far—
that man was I, and I smashed your strength! And you—
2 the dogs and birds will maul you, shame your corpse
while Achaeans bury my dear friend in glory!"

Struggling for breath, Hector, his helmet flashing,
said, "I beg you, beg you by your life, your parents—
don't let the dogs devour me by the Argive ships!
Wait, take the princely ransom of bronze and gold,
C the gifts my father and noble mother will give you—
but give my body to friends to carry home again,
3 so Trojan men and Trojan women can do me honor
with fitting rites of fire once I am dead."

Staring grimly, the proud runner Achilles answered,
"Beg no more, you fawning dog—begging me by my parents!
4 Would to god my rage, my fury would drive me now
to hack your flesh away and eat you raw—

217 the god of fire: Hephaestus, who made Achilles' armor and shield.

222 brandished: waved.

241 maul: mangle.

252 fawning: cringing.

Customizing Instruction

Less Proficient Readers

Help students to understand the key moments in the battle and Hector's death scene.

1 How does Achilles deliver the mortal blow? *(He drives his spear through Hector's neck.)*

2 Make sure that students realize that Achilles will leave Hector's corpse out in the open air.

3 The dying Hector asks that his body be returned to his home, where it can be burned in a proper funeral service.

4 Make sure that students realize how angry Achilles becomes after hearing Hector's request.

English Learners

Line 213: "whetted sword" *(sharpened sword)*

Line 241: "maul you" *(tear you apart)*

Advanced Learners

Point out that some critics find evidence in this scene that suggests a glorification of war's violence, while others find evidence suggesting the repulsiveness of violence. Ask students to find words or phrases on these two pages to support each of these viewpoints.

Possible Response: On one hand, Achilles' triumph seems to be celebrated. His helmet is compared to the "brightest star that rides the heavens." The "godlike Achilles gloried over" Hector's corpse. On the other hand, Achilles' rage is "barbaric." His brutality to Hector in both word and action is excessive; Achilles seems barely human when he announces his wish "to hack your [Hector's] flesh away and eat you raw."

Cross Curricular Link History

RANSOMS In the culture of ancient Greece, ransoms were a common practice. In Book 1, Chryses offers Agamemnon a huge ransom for the return of his daughter; later, Hector's father will offer a ransom for the return of Hector's body. Such ransoms were a form of economic exchange. A ransom could be offered in exchange for a corpse, as payment for the release of a slave or prisoner, or in reparation for a crime. Homer describes incidents of Trojan soldiers who, when faced with death, offer their Greek attackers ransoms in exchange for their lives. The Greeks reject such offers, a sign of the war's savagery.

ILIAD **209**

Literary Analysis FORESHADOWING

Ⓐ Hector curses Achilles and says that he will be killed at the gates of Troy. Paris, Hector's brother, will kill Achilles by shooting an arrow at his only weak spot, his heel (which is where the phrase "Achilles' heel" comes from).

Literary Analysis CULTURAL SETTING

Ⓑ It was believed that the souls of the dead would descend to Hades, here referred to as the House of Death.

Literary Analysis CULTURAL SETTING

Ⓒ When Achilles and his men stab the corpse of Hector, they are violating religious customs, which required that a corpse be treated respectfully.

Reading Skills and Strategies
MAKING INFERENCES

Ⓓ Ask students why Achilles is so determined to shame the corpse of Hector. *(He is still enraged that Hector killed Patroclus; he also has no respect for the Trojans.)*

such agonies you have caused me! Ransom?
No man alive could keep the dog-packs off you,
not if they haul in ten, twenty times that ransom
and pile it here before me and promise fortunes more—
no, not even if Dardan Priam should offer to weigh out
your bulk in gold! Not even then will your noble mother
lay you on your deathbed, mourn the son she bore . . .
The dogs and birds will rend you—blood and bone!"

At the point of death, Hector, his helmet flashing,
said, "I know you well—I see my fate before me.
Never a chance that I could win you over . . .
Iron inside your chest, that heart of yours.
But now beware, or my curse will draw god's wrath
A upon your head, that day when Paris and lord Apollo—
for all your fighting heart—destroy you at the Scaean Gates!"

Death cut him short. The end closed in around him.
B Flying free of his limbs
his soul went winging down to the House of Death,
wailing his fate, leaving his manhood far behind,
his young and supple strength. But brilliant Achilles
1 taunted Hector's body, dead as he was, "Die, die!
For my own death, I'll meet it freely—whenever Zeus
and the other deathless gods would like to bring it on!"

With that he wrenched his bronze spear from the corpse,
laid it aside and ripped the bloody armor off the back.
And the other sons of Achaea, running up around him,
crowded closer, all of them gazing wonder-struck
at the build and marvelous, lithe beauty of Hector.
And not a man came forward who did not stab his body,
C glancing toward a comrade, laughing: "Ah, look here—
how much softer he is to handle now, this Hector,
than when he gutted our ships with roaring fire!"

Standing over him, so they'd gloat and stab his body.
But once he had stripped the corpse the proud runner Achilles
took his stand in the midst of all the Argive troops
and urged them on with a flight of winging orders:
"Friends—lords of the Argives, O my captains!
Now that the gods have let me kill this man

259 Dardan: descended from Dardanus, ancestor of the Trojan kings.

262 rend: tear apart.

WORDS TO KNOW

lithe (līth) *adj.* limber and graceful

MINI LESSON
Speaking and Listening

DRAMATIZING A CONFLICT Invite students to dramatize the final stage of the conflict between Achilles and Hector, beginning with line 235 on page 209 and ending with Achilles' words after Hector's death (lines 275–276). Tell students that they will need to study the motivation of each character and communicate each character's lines with appropriate emotion.

Prepare Have students work in groups of four to study the scene and prepare a dramatization. Two students in each group should be designated as "silent" actors; these two will pantomime the scene while the other two students read aloud the lines of Hector and Achilles. Each group should discuss what emotions should be expressed by the dialogue and how the "silent" actors can express those emotions.

Present Ask each group to perform its interpretation.Then ask the entire class to vote for the most effective dramatization. In an effective presentation, the lines will be clearly read with appropriate emotion, accompanied by movements, gestures, and expressions appropriate to the action.

This activity is particularly well suited for longer class periods.

who caused us agonies, loss on crushing loss—
more than the rest of all their men combined—
come, let us ring their walls in armor, test them,
see what recourse the Trojans still may have in mind.
Will they abandon the city heights with this man fallen?
Or brace for a last, dying stand though Hector's gone?
But wait—what am I saying? Why this deep debate?
Down by the ships a body lies unwept, unburied—
2 Patroclus . . . I will never forget him,
not as long as I'm still among the living
and my springing knees will lift and drive me on.
Though the dead forget their dead in the House of Death,
I will remember, even there, my dear companion.
Now,
come, you sons of Achaea, raise a song of triumph!
Down to the ships we march and bear this corpse on high—
we have won ourselves great glory. We have brought
magnificent Hector down, that man the Trojans
glorified in their city like a god!"
So he triumphed
D and now he was bent on outrage, on shaming noble Hector.
Piercing the tendons, ankle to heel behind both feet,
he knotted straps of rawhide through them both,
lashed them to his chariot, left the head to drag
and mounting the car, hoisting the famous arms aboard,
3 he whipped his team to a run and breakneck on they flew,
holding nothing back. And a thick cloud of dust rose up
from the man they dragged, his dark hair swirling round
that head so handsome once, all tumbled low in the dust—
since Zeus had given him over to his enemies now
to be defiled in the land of his own fathers.

So his whole head was dragged down in the dust.
And now his mother began to tear her hair . . .
she flung her shining veil to the ground and raised
4 a high, shattering scream, looking down at her son.
Pitifully his loving father groaned and round the king
his people cried with grief and wailing seized the city—
for all the world as if all Troy were torched and smoldering
down from the looming brows of the citadel to her roots.
Priam's people could hardly hold the old man back,
frantic, mad to go rushing out the Dardan Gates.

329 looming brows of the citadel (sĭt'ə-dəl): jutting battlements of the stronghold.

WORDS TO KNOW

recourse (rē'kôrs') *n.* something turned to for help or protection
defile (dĭ-fīl') *v.* to treat in a shameful way; destroy the beauty or honor of

Customizing Instruction

Less Proficient Readers

1 Remind students that Achilles knows he is fated to die before long. Ask students how Achilles feels about the prospect of his own death. *(He is a proud man who seems not to care about dying.)*

2 Remind students that Patroclus has yet to be buried. Achilles feels that it is more important to bury his friend than to attack Troy.

3 Ask students to describe this scene in their own words. *(Hector's body is tied to Achilles' chariot and dragged on the ground.)*

4 Ask students to visualize the positions of Hector's mother and father. *(They are probably standing on the walls of Troy, where they can see their son's corpse.)*

English Learners

Explain the meaning of the following phrases:

Line 266: "Iron inside your chest" *(You have no sympathy or feeling.)*

Line 286: "gutted our ships" *(destroyed our ships)*

Line 327: "wailing seized the city" *(The entire city wept and moaned in grief.)*

Cross Curricular Link: History

BURIAL CUSTOMS According to the customs of the age, the body of Hector should be returned to his family so that a proper burial can be performed. In such a ceremony, the corpse is placed on a pyre—a heap of inflammable materials—and burned in a public ceremony. The ashes and bones are then collected and buried. Such burial was required for the spirit of the departed person to be allowed into the underworld. By refusing to return Hector's corpse, Achilles is insulting the honor of Hector and his family and violating the will of the gods.

Reading and Analyzing

Literary Analysis CHARACTERIZATION

A Ask students what they learn about Priam.

Possible Response: He is overcome with grief, but determined to recover Hector's corpse. Hector was clearly his favorite son.

Literary Analysis CULTURAL SETTING

B Priam assumes the position of someone begging for a favor. He puts himself at the mercy of Achilles.

Literary Analysis EPIC SIMILE

C Ask student what this simile reveals about Achilles' response to Priam. *(He is amazed to see him.)*

Thinking Through the Literature

1. Possible Response: Achilles tells a dying Hector that his body will not be returned to his family. Then Achilles stabs Hector's corpse with his spear, and Achilles' comrades do the same. Finally, Achilles ties Hector's corpse to his chariot and drags it across the dirt.
2. Possible Response: Hector comes across as a vulnerable but courageous character. When Achilles chases him, Hector flees, which shows his fear of his enemy. However, he takes courage from the sight of his brother, Deiphobus, not realizing that he is being tricked by Athena. Believing that his brother stands behind him, Hector decides to stand and fight. When he realizes that he faces certain death, he attacks Achilles.
3. Possible Response: The gods play an active role in human life, as evidenced by Apollo helping Hector to outrun Achilles and Athena tricking Hector into stopping for battle. However, the power of the gods seems limited. Although Zeus wants to help Hector, he cannot alter Hector's fate. Such fate seems to have power even over the gods.
4. Possible Responses: Many students may feel that Achilles' actions are not justified, especially since Hector had promised to treat Achilles' corpse with respect. Other students may note that Achilles is deeply grieved over the loss of his friend Patroclus; his grief may provide some justification for his action.

He begged them all, groveling in the filth,
crying out to them, calling each man by name,
"Let go, my friends! Much as you care for me,
let me hurry out of the city, make my way,
all on my own, to Achaea's waiting ships!
I must implore that terrible, violent man . . .
Perhaps—who knows?—he may respect my age,
may pity an old man. He has a father too,
as old as I am—Peleus sired him once,
Peleus reared him to be the scourge of Troy
but most of all to me—he made my life a hell.
So many sons he slaughtered, just coming into bloom . . .
but grieving for all the rest, one breaks my heart the most
and stabbing grief for him will take me down to Death—
my Hector—would to god he had perished in my arms!
Then his mother who bore him—oh so doomed,
she and I could glut ourselves with grief."

Thinking Through the Literature

1. How does Achilles insult Hector with words and with actions?
2. What qualities of Hector's **character** stand out in the excerpt from Book 22?

- how Hector runs away from Achilles
- what persuades him to stand and fight
- how he faces his own certain death

3. Consider the roles played by Athena, Zeus, and Apollo in the excerpt from Book 22. To what extent do the gods seem to control human life? Support your conclusion with evidence from the text.

- the passage in which Zeus weighs the fates of Hector and Achilles (lines 93–99)
- Athena's words and actions
- Apollo's helping Hector to run away from Achilles (lines 86–89)

4. Do you think Achilles is justified in his treatment of Hector's corpse? Support your opinion with evidence from the text.
5. Review the reactions of Priam and Hecuba to Achilles' treatment of their son's corpse (lines 323–348). Why do you think Homer included a description of their grief?

5. Possible Responses: By showing the grief of Hector's parents, Homer gives the reader a vision of war's terrible effects. The scene of their grief also shows the depth of their love for their son.

Use Selection Quiz in **Unit Two Resource Book,** p. 11.

ACHILLES AND PRIAM

GUIDE FOR READING

FOCUS As you read about the meeting of Achilles and Priam, pay attention to Achilles' reasons for taking pity on his enemy.

1 *After Achilles kills Hector, the Greeks conduct funeral rites for Patroclus. In the following days, whenever Achilles is overcome by grief, he takes out his chariot and drags Hector's corpse around the grave of Patroclus. Apollo, still loyal to Hector, can do nothing to stop Achilles, but he does protect the corpse from all damage. Zeus, recognizing that Hector had always been faithful to the gods, sends a message to Achilles, telling him to give Hector's body to Priam in exchange for a ransom. Bowing to divine will, Achilles agrees. Zeus then sends a message to Priam, directing him to gather treasures and take them to Achilles. Aided by the god Hermes, Priam drives a wagonload of treasures to the enemy camp. Alone, he enters Achilles' hut to ask for the return of Hector's corpse.*

The majestic king of Troy slipped past the rest
B and kneeling down beside Achilles, clasped his knees
and kissed his hands, those terrible, man-killing hands
that had slaughtered Priam's many sons in battle.
Awesome—as when the grip of madness seizes one
who murders a man in his own fatherland and flees
C abroad to foreign shores, to a wealthy, noble host,
and a sense of marvel runs through all who see him—
so Achilles marveled, beholding majestic Priam.
His men marveled too, trading startled glances.
But Priam prayed his heart out to Achilles:
"Remember your own father, great godlike Achilles—
2 as old as *I* am, past the threshold of deadly old age!

Customizing Instruction

Less Proficient Readers

Read aloud the **Focus**, and ask students to look for phrases that help explain why Achilles takes pity on Priam.

1 Discuss the summary with students. Make sure that they realize that the god Hermes helped Priam to enter the enemy camp undetected; otherwise, he would have been killed or captured. Priam brings a load of treasures as a ransom for the body of Hector.

2 Point out that Priam is reminding Achilles of his own father, whom he hasn't seen for years and will never see again.

English Learners

Explain the meaning of the following words and phrases:

Line 332: "groveling" *(lying down in a begging position)*

Line 348: "glut ourselves with grief" *(fill ourselves with sadness)*

Line 13: "past the threshold of deadly old age" *(old enough to be approaching death)*

Cross Curricular Link History

LIFE EXPECTANCY IN ANCIENT GREECE Homer portrays Hector's father, Priam, as an old man. While it is difficult to gauge his age according to contemporary standards, we know that he is at least old enough to have fathered 50 sons and many daughters. In ancient Greece, life expectancy at birth was approximately 20 years. That estimated figure shows the precariousness of early life. Women often died in childbirth; children were subject to numerous life-threatening diseases; men, especially the young, were often killed in warfare. While some Greeks lived into their seventies and eighties—most notably, Sophocles and Plato—the majority died in youth, which adds a poignancy to the scene between Achilles and Priam.

Reading Skills and Strategies
CONNECTING

Ask students to discuss their feelings about Priam and Achilles as the scene unfolds. Do they feel sorry for either of the men? *(Accept any reasonable responses.)*

Reading Skills and Strategies
CLARIFYING

A Ask students why the two men are crying. *(Priam is grieving for Hector, while Achilles is grieving for Patroclus. The two enemies are united in sorrow.)*

B Ask students to explain the two different ways that Zeus distributes gifts from the "two great jars" of fate. *(For some men, Zeus distributes from both the jar of blessings and the jar of miseries. For other men, he distributes only from the jar of miseries.)*

HUMANITIES CONNECTION This detail from a Roman sarcophagus (stone coffin) sculpture shows the body of Hector tied to a chariot. Imagine how King Priam felt when he had to witness the dragging of his son's corpse.

No doubt the countrymen round about him plague him now,
with no one there to defend him, beat away disaster.
No one—but at least he hears you're still alive
and his old heart rejoices, hopes rising, day by day,
to see his beloved son come sailing home from Troy.
But I—dear god, my life so cursed by fate . . .
I fathered hero sons in the wide realm of Troy
and now not a single one is left, I tell you.
1 Fifty sons I had when the sons of Achaea came,
nineteen born to me from a single mother's womb
and the rest by other women in the palace. Many,
most of them violent Ares cut the knees from under.
But one, one was left me, to guard my walls, my people—
the one you killed the other day, defending his fatherland,
my Hector! It's all for him I've come to the ships now,
to win him back from you—I bring a priceless ransom.
Revere the gods, Achilles! Pity me in my own right,
remember your own father! I deserve more pity . . .

MINI LESSON Viewing and Representing

Detail of a sarcophagus sculpture

ART APPRECIATION Have students look at the illustration and the **Humanities Connection** on page 214. Explain to students that this detail is part of a larger scene that decorates the side of a Roman sarcophagus, or stone coffin. Greek myths and legends often served as the subject matter of Roman art. This sculpture illustrates a technique called high-relief. The sculptor carved the figures out of a slab of marble. In high relief, the figures are rounded and are nearly disengaged from the supporting background. Point out the details of the muscles in the horse and the human figures. Ask students whether this scupture presents a realistic or idealistic image of its subject matter.

Possible Responses: Realistic, because the human figures seem true to life in their proportions and level of detail. Idealistic, because Hector's body seems perfectly formed, as if he has no flaw.

I have endured what no one on earth has ever done before—
2 I put to my lips the hands of the man who killed my son."

Those words stirred within Achilles a deep desire
to grieve for his own father. Taking the old man's hand
A he gently moved him back. And overpowered by memory
both men gave way to grief. Priam wept freely
for man-killing Hector, throbbing, crouching
before Achilles' feet as Achilles wept himself,
now for his father, now for Patroclus once again,
and their sobbing rose and fell throughout the house.
Then, when brilliant Achilles had his fill of tears
and the longing for it had left his mind and body,
he rose from his seat, raised the old man by the hand
and filled with pity now for his gray head and gray beard,
he spoke out winging words, flying straight to the heart:
"Poor man, how much you've borne—pain to break the spirit!
What daring brought you down to the ships, all alone,
to face the glance of the man who killed your sons,
3 so many fine brave boys? You have a heart of iron.
Come, please, sit down on this chair here . . .
Let us put our griefs to rest in our own hearts,
rake them up no more, raw as we are with mourning.
What good's to be won from tears that chill the spirit?
So the immortals spun our lives that we, we wretched men
live on to bear such torments—the gods live free of sorrows.
There are two great jars that stand on the floor of Zeus's halls
B and hold his gifts, our miseries one, the other blessings.
When Zeus who loves the lightning mixes gifts for a man,
4 now he meets with misfortune, now good times in turn.
When Zeus dispenses gifts from the jar of sorrows only,
he makes a man an outcast—brutal, ravenous hunger
drives him down the face of the shining earth,
stalking far and wide, cursed by gods and men.
So with my father, Peleus. What glittering gifts
the gods rained down from the day that he was born!
He excelled all men in wealth and pride of place,
he lorded the Myrmidons, and mortal that he was,
they gave the man an immortal goddess for a wife.
Yes, but even on him the Father piled hardships,

55 the immortals spun our lives: the gods determined our fates.

62 ravenous (răv'ə-nəs): characterized by eager craving.

Customizing Instruction

Less Proficient Readers

1 Make sure that students realize Priam has lost all 50 of his sons. The fact that he has fathered so many sons does not shock anyone in his society.

2 Ask students what Priam is doing. *(He is kissing the hand of Achilles.)*

3 Point out that Achilles is giving Priam a compliment by praising his "heart of iron." He is praising his bravery for traveling all alone through the enemy camp.

4 Help students to realize that the "two great jars" are symbols for times of happiness and times of sorrow. According to Achilles, no human being can escape sorrow.

English Learners

Explain the meaning of the following phrases:

Line 14: "plague him now" *(bother him or cause him troubles)*

Line 23: "sons of Achaea" *(the young soldiers of Greece)*

Line 53: "rake them up no more" *(don't stir up the memories of what we have lost)*

Advanced Learners

There is a third possible way of distributing the gifts that Achilles does not mention: To some men, Zeus could give gifts only from the jar of blessings. Ask students why this possibility is not mentioned.

Possible Response: The Greeks did not believe that it was possible for anyone's life to be completely free of sorrows. Perhaps only the gods can receive unmixed blessings.

MINI LESSON Speaking and Listening

DELIVERING A SPEECH Explain that Priam's speech to Achilles is one of the most famous in the *Iliad*. Point out that Achilles has already been told by his mother, Thetis, that the gods are angry about his treatment of Hector's corpse. Also, Hermes suggested to Priam that he invoke Achilles' memory of his own father.

Prepare Have students work in pairs to prepare a presentation of the speech. Have them discuss the tone of voice that Priam would use in making his plea. Ask them to identify words and phrases that are likely to have a strong effect on Achilles; such words and phrases can be emphasized in the presentation. Each pair should decide how to divide the speech into two speaking parts.

Present Invite each pair to present their version of the speech. After each speech is finished, lead the class in identifying the strengths and weaknesses of the presentation.

This activity is particularly well suited for longer class periods.

ILIAD 215

Reading Skills and Strategies
COMPARE AND CONTRAST

A Ask students to compare and contrast the sorrows of Priam and Peleus.
Possible Response: Peleus only had one son and that son was doomed to an early death. There will be no one to care for Peleus or protect him in his old age. Priam lost a vast kingdom, as well as 50 sons.

Active Reading EVALUATING

B Ask students to judge the wisdom of Priam's decision to tell Achilles that he should quit the war and go home. *(Accept all reasonable responses.)*

Use **Unit Two Resource Book,** p. 12, for more practice.

Literary Analysis CULTURAL SETTING

C According to the customs of the time, Achilles had a sacred duty to be a good host to his guest. Zeus was the god who required such hospitality. Point out the irony that the Trojan War began with a violation of such laws: as Menelaus' house guest, Paris was obligated to respect his host's marriage to Helen. Instead, Paris took her away with him.

Pause & Reflect
Possible Response: Priam reminds Achilles of his own father; Achilles also feels sorry that Priam has lost all 50 of his sons to the war.

Literary Analysis CHARACTER

D The herald is an old servant of Priam's who had traveled with him to Achilles' camp.

no powerful race of princes born in his royal halls,
only a single son he fathered, doomed at birth,
cut off in the spring of life—
and I, I give the man no care as he grows old
since here I sit in Troy, far from my fatherland,
a grief to you, a grief to all your children.
And you too, old man, we hear you prospered once:
as far as Lesbos, Macar's kingdom, bounds to seaward,
Phrygia east and upland, the Hellespont vast and north—
that entire realm, they say, you lorded over once,
you excelled all men, old king, in sons and wealth.
But then the gods of heaven brought this agony on you—
ceaseless battles round your walls, your armies slaughtered.
You must bear up now. Enough of endless tears,
the pain that breaks the spirit.
Grief for your son will do no good at all.
You will never bring him back to life—
sooner you must suffer something worse."

But the old and noble Priam protested strongly:
"Don't make me sit on a chair, Achilles, Prince,
not while Hector lies uncared-for in your camp!
Give him back to me, now, no more delay—
I must see my son with my own eyes.
Accept the ransom I bring you, a king's ransom!
Enjoy it, all of it—return to your own native land,
safe and sound . . . since now you've spared my life."

A dark glance—and the headstrong runner answered,
"No more, old man, don't tempt my wrath, not now!
My own mind's made up to give you back your son.
A messenger brought me word from Zeus—my mother,
Thetis who bore me, the Old Man of the Sea's daughter.
And what's more, I can see through you, Priam—
no hiding the fact from me: one of the gods
has led you down to Achaea's fast ships.
No man alive, not even a rugged young fighter,
would dare to venture into our camp. Never—
how could he slip past the sentries unchallenged?
Or shoot back the bolt of my gates with so much ease?

78 Lesbos (lĕz′bŏs), **Macar's** (măk′ärz′) **kingdom:** an island off the coast of Asia Minor, south of Troy, whose first king was Macar.

79 Phrygia (frĭj′ē-ə): a region of northwestern Asia Minor; **Hellespont** (hĕl′ĭ-spŏnt′): a strait just north of Troy.

101 Old Man of the Sea's daughter: daughter of the sea god Nereus.

MINI LESSON **Grammar**

COMPOUND SUBJECTS AND COMPOUND PREDICATES

Instruction Remind students that a compound subject consists of two or more subjects that share the same verb and are joined by a conjunction.

Practice Write the following on the board:

Achilles and Priam exchanged respectful words.

Ask students to find the compound subject–the two persons, places, things, or ideas that the sentence is about *(Achilles, Priam).* Then ask them to identify the conjunction *(and).*

Tell students that the subject, the predicate, or both can be compound in a sentence. Write the following sentence on the board:

Achilles and Priam exchanged respectful words and mourned the losses of their loved ones.

Have students identify the compound subject and the compound predicate *(Achilles, Priam; exchanged, mourned).* Have students circle the conjunctions *(and, and).*

For more instruction and practice, use McDougal Littell's ***Language Network:***
- Grade 10, Chapter 2, "The Sentence and Its Parts"
- Grade 12, Chapter 1, "The Parts of a Sentence"

C

So don't anger me now. Don't stir my raging heart still more.
Or under my own roof I may not spare your life, old man—
suppliant that you are—may break the laws of Zeus!"

PAUSE & REFLECT For what reasons does Achilles take pity on Priam?

111 **suppliant:** one who humbly begs.

3

FOCUS Though Achilles has agreed to release Hector's body, the Greek hero still struggles to control his anger. As you read, think about whether Achilles acts as a good host to his royal visitor.

The old man was terrified. He obeyed the order.
But Achilles bounded out of doors like a lion—
not alone but flanked by his two aides-in-arms,
veteran Automedon and Alcimus, steady comrades,
Achilles' favorites next to the dead Patroclus.
D
They loosed from harness the horses and the mules,
they led the herald in, the old king's crier,
and sat him down on a bench. From the polished wagon
they lifted the priceless ransom brought for Hector's corpse
but they left behind two capes and a finely-woven shirt
to shroud the body well when Priam bore him home.
Then Achilles called the serving-women out:
"Bathe and anoint the body—
bear it aside first. Priam must not see his son."
4
He feared that, overwhelmed by the sight of Hector,
wild with grief, Priam might let his anger flare
and Achilles might fly into fresh rage himself,
cut the old man down and break the laws of Zeus.
So when the maids had bathed and anointed the body
sleek with olive oil and wrapped it round and round
in a braided battle-shirt and handsome battle-cape,
then Achilles lifted Hector up in his own arms
and laid him down on a bier, and comrades helped him
raise the bier and body onto the sturdy wagon . . .
Then with a groan he called his dear friend by name:
5
"Feel no anger at me, Patroclus, if you learn—
even there in the House of Death—I let his father
have Prince Hector back. He gave me worthy ransom
and you shall have your share from me, as always,
your fitting, lordly share."

114 **flanked:** accompanied on either side.

115 **Automedon** (ô-tŏm'ə-dŏn') . . . **Alcimus** (ăl'sĭ-məs).

122 **shroud:** wrap.

134 **bier** (bēr): a platform for laying out a corpse.

Customizing Instruction

Less Proficient Readers

1 Help students to realize that Achilles is trying to comfort Priam. He tells him that he should stop grieving because it won't do any good.

2 Point out that before Priam came to the camp, Achilles' mother, the goddess Thetis, had told her son that Zeus wanted him to accept the ransom for Hector's body.

Focus Ask students to predict how they think Achilles will treat Priam.

3 Before students begin this section, you might want to lead them in a discussion of what Achilles would be expected to do as a good host.

4 Ask students why Achilles does not allow Priam to see his son's corpse. *(If Priam goes wild with grief, Achilles may become enraged and hurt him.)*

5 Remind students that Patroclus is dead and that Achilles is speaking to his spirit. Ask students to paraphrase Achilles' meaning here. *(He's apologizing to Patroclus for giving Hector's body to Priam. He tells Patroclus that he will always be loyal to him.)*

English Learners

Explain the meaning of the following phrases:

Line 98: "don't tempt my wrath" *(don't speak in a way that will make me angry)*

Line 110: "I may not spare your life" *(I may kill you.)*

Line 124: "anoint the body" *(put special oils on the body)*

Reading and Analyzing

Literary Analysis MYTHOLOGY

A The following lines recount the story of Niobe. The mother of twelve boasted that she was superior to the goddess Leto, who only had two children. In response, Leto's children, Apollo and Artemis, killed all of Niobe's children. Niobe wept so much in her grief that she was turned into a column of stone.

Literary Analysis EPIC HERO

B Point out that epic heroes were physically beautiful. In this scene, both Achilles and Priam appreciate the beauty of their enemy.

Use **Unit Two Resource Book,** p. 13, for more practice.

So he vowed
and brilliant Achilles strode back to his shelter,
sat down on the well-carved chair that he had left,
at the far wall of the room, leaned toward Priam
and firmly spoke the words the king had come to hear:
1 "Your son is now set free, old man, as you requested.
Hector lies in state. With the first light of day
you will see for yourself as you convey him home.
Now, at last, let us turn our thoughts to supper.
A Even Niobe with her lustrous hair remembered food,
though she saw a dozen children killed in her own halls,
six daughters and six sons in the pride and prime of youth.
True, lord Apollo killed the sons with his silver bow
and Artemis showering arrows killed the daughters.
Both gods were enraged at Niobe. Time and again
she placed herself on a par with their own mother,
Leto in her immortal beauty—how she insulted Leto:
'All you have borne is two, but I have borne so many!'
So, two as they were, they slaughtered all her children.
Nine days they lay in their blood, no one to bury them—
Cronus' son had turned the people into stone . . .
then on the tenth the gods of heaven interred them.
And Niobe, gaunt, worn to the bone with weeping,
turned her thoughts to food. And now, somewhere,
lost on the crags, on the lonely mountain slopes,
on Sipylus where, they say, the nymphs who live forever,
dancing along the Achelous River run to beds of rest—
there, struck into stone, Niobe still broods
on the spate of griefs the gods poured out to her.

2 So come—we too, old king, must think of food.
Later you can mourn your beloved son once more,
when you bear him home to Troy, and you'll weep many
tears."

Never pausing, the swift runner sprang to his feet
and slaughtered a white sheep as comrades moved in
to skin the carcass quickly, dress the quarters well.
Expertly they cut the meat in pieces, pierced them with spits,
roasted them to a turn and pulled them off the fire.
Automedon brought the bread, set it out on the board
in ample wicker baskets. Achilles served the meat.

150 Niobe (nī′ə-bē).

161 Cronus' son: Zeus.

162 interred (ĭn-tûrd′): buried.

166 Sipylus (sĭp′ə-ləs): a mountain in western Asia Minor.

167 Achelous (ăk′ə-lō′əs).

169 spate: flood.

WORDS TO KNOW

gaunt (gônt) adj. thin and drawn

Cross Curricular Link History

HOSPITALITY To the ancient Greeks, hospitality meant far more than being pleasant to one's guest. Hospitality was a sacred duty that required both the host and guest to treat one another kindly and respectfully. A host who failed to meet the needs and wants of a guest would be subject to punishment for violating laws sacred to Zeus. Greek mythology has many stories of gods who appear disguised as strangers or travelers to test the hospitality of their hosts. Greek literature is filled with stories of hosts who offered lavish feasts to their guests, who gave them extravagant presents, or who made great sacrifices to satisfy their requests.

HUMANITIES CONNECTION
Here is another detail from a Roman sarcophagus sculpture, this one showing King Priam begging Achilles to return the body of his son, Hector.

They reached out for the good things that lay at hand
and when they had put aside desire for food and drink,
Priam the son of Dardanus gazed at Achilles, marveling
now at the man's beauty, his magnificent build—
face-to-face he seemed a deathless god . . .
and Achilles gazed and marveled at Dardan Priam,
beholding his noble looks, listening to his words.
But once they'd had their fill of gazing at each other,
the old majestic Priam broke the silence first:
"Put me to bed quickly, Achilles, Prince.
Time to rest, to enjoy the sweet relief of sleep.
Not once have my eyes closed shut beneath my lids
from the day my son went down beneath your hands . . .
day and night I groan, brooding over the countless griefs,
groveling in the dung that fills my walled-in court.
But now, at long last, I have tasted food again
and let some glistening wine go down my throat.
Before this hour I had tasted nothing."
He shook his head
as Achilles briskly told his men and serving-women

MINI LESSON Viewing and Representing

Detail of a sarcophagus sculpture

ART APPRECIATION Have students look at the illustration and the **Humanities Connection** on page 219. Explain that this is another detail from the same sarcophagus that is shown on page 214.

Instruction Demonstrate that both figures in this sculpture follow an S curve. The curve of Achilles is more pronounced and larger, which is appropriate for his position of power. Priam, as the supplicant, forms a smaller, less pronounced S. Tell students that artists often use S curves and C curves as a way of organizing their material and creating a pleasing effect.

Application Ask students to look for the use of S curves in other works of art. If possible, make art books available or encourage students to look online. Invite students to share examples of such curves.

Customizing Instruction

Less Proficient Readers

Ask students to identify the ways in which Achilles acts as host. *(He grants the request of his guest and prepares a feast for him.)*

1 The body of Hector is now ready to be returned to Troy.

2 Remind students that Priam has been so concerned with Hector that he has not eaten in days. Achilles has to persuade him to eat.

3 Point out that it has been days since Priam has slept. Achilles has held Hector's body for 12 days.

English Learners

Explain the meaning of the following terms:

Line 147: "lies in state" *(lies ready for a funeral)*

Line 187: "they'd had their fill" *(They had enough.)*

Advanced Learners

Ask students what Niobe and Priam have in common. *(They both lost many children; they both grieved deeply; they both were victims of the gods.)*

ILIAD 219

Reading Skills and Strategies
MAKING INFERENCES

A Ask students why they think Achilles is being so kind to Priam.
Possible Response: He feels sorry for Priam because he reminds Achilles of his own father. Perhaps he feels somewhat guilty for killing Priam's favorite son.

Literary Analysis PLOT

B Explain that Briseis—the cause of the conflict between Agamemnon and Achilles—was returned to Achilles after he rejoined the rest of the Greek army.

Pause & Reflect

Possible Response: Most students will probably agree that Achilles is a good host. He fulfills Priam's request for Hector's body; he shares a meal with his guest; and he arranges comfortable sleeping quarters for Priam. Some students may note that Achilles is still capable of killing Priam; he does not allow Priam to see Hector's body because Achilles is concerned that Priam might become angry, which would provoke his own anger.

Literary Analysis PLOT

C Explain that Hermes was sent by Zeus to transport Priam safely to and from the camp of Achilles. Hermes, the god of sleep and dreams, often communicated to sleeping people.

to make beds in the porch's shelter, to lay down
some heavy purple throws for the beds themselves
and over them spread blankets and thick woolly robes,
a warm covering laid on top. Torches held in hand,
they went from the hall and fell to work at once
and in no time two good beds were spread and made.
Then Achilles nodded to Priam, leading the king on
with brusque advice: "Sleep outside, old friend,
in case some Achaean captain comes to visit.
They keep on coming now, huddling beside me,
[1] making plans for battle—it's their duty.
But if one saw you here in the rushing dark night
he'd tell Agamemnon straightaway, our good commander.
Then you'd have real delay in ransoming the body.
One more point. Tell me, be precise about it—
[A] how many days do you need to bury Prince Hector?
I will hold back myself
and keep the Argive armies back that long."

And the old and noble Priam answered slowly,
"If you truly want me to give Prince Hector burial,
full, royal honors, you'd show me a great kindness,
Achilles, if you would do exactly as I say.
You know how crammed we are inside our city,
how far it is to the hills to haul in timber,
and our Trojans are afraid to make the journey.
Well, nine days we should mourn him in our halls,
on the tenth we'd bury Hector, hold the public feast,
on the eleventh build the barrow high above his body—
on the twelfth we'd fight again . . . if fight we must."

The swift runner Achilles reassured him quickly:
"All will be done, old Priam, as you command.
I will hold our attack as long as you require."

With that he clasped the old king by the wrist,
by the right hand, to free his heart from fear.
Then Priam and herald, minds set on the journey home,
bedded down for the night within the porch's shelter.
[B] And deep in his sturdy well-built lodge Achilles slept
with Briseis in all her beauty sleeping by his side.

PAUSE & REFLECT Is Achilles a good host to Priam? Give evidence from the text to support your evaluation.

206 brusque: blunt; curt.

226 barrow: a mound of stones or earth placed over a burial site.

232 by the right hand, to free his heart from fear: using his weapon hand, to show that he is not going to attack Priam.

233 herald: the aide who accompanied Priam to the Greek camp.

FOCUS Read to find out what happens when Priam brings Hector's corpse to the gates of Troy.

C

Now the great array of gods and chariot-driving men
slept all night long, overcome by gentle sleep.
But sleep could never hold the running Escort—
Hermes kept on turning it over in his mind . . .
how could he convoy Priam clear of the ships,
unseen by devoted guards who held the gates?
Hovering at his head the Escort rose and spoke:
"Not a care in the world, old man? Look at you,
how you sleep in the midst of men who'd kill you—
and just because Achilles spared your life. Now, yes,
you've ransomed your dear son—for a king's ransom.
But wouldn't the sons you left behind be forced
to pay three times as much for *you* alive?
What if Atrides Agamemnon learns you're here—
what if the whole Achaean army learns you're here?"

2

The old king woke in terror, roused the herald.
Hermes harnessed the mules and team for both men,
drove them fast through the camp and no one saw them.

Once they reached the ford where the river runs clear,
the strong, whirling Xanthus sprung of immortal Zeus,
Hermes went his way to the steep heights of Olympus
as Dawn flung out her golden robe across the earth,
and the two men, weeping, groaning, drove the team
toward Troy and the mules brought on the body.
No one saw them at first, neither man nor woman,
none before Cassandra, golden as goddess Aphrodite.
She had climbed to Pergamus heights and from that point
she saw her beloved father swaying tall in the chariot,
flanked by the herald, whose cry could rouse the city.
And Cassandra saw *him* too . . .
drawn by the mules and stretched out on his bier.
She screamed and her scream rang out through all Troy:
"Come, look down, you men of Troy, you Trojan women!
Behold Hector now—if you ever once rejoiced
to see him striding home, home alive from battle!
He was the greatest joy of Troy and all our people!"

3

239 Escort: Hermes.

256 Xanthus (zăn′thəs): another name for the river Scamander.

262 Cassandra (kə-săn′drə): a daughter of Priam.

263 Pergamus (pûr′gə-məs): the stronghold of Troy.

Customizing Instruction

Less Proficient Readers

Focus Before students read this last section of the *Iliad*, ask them to describe how the women of Troy reacted to Hector's return to battle at the end of Book 6 (page 200).

Possible Response: The women began lamenting his death because they were convinced he would die in battle. They clearly had strong feelings for him.

1 Make sure that students understand why Achilles tells Priam to sleep outside the tent. If Priam is seen by any of the soldiers who visit Achilles in his tent, then Agamemnon will be told of Priam's presence. The general would probably not allow Priam to take the body.

2 Explain that Hermes is afraid that Priam will be taken prisoner if the other Greeks discover him there. Agamemnon would demand a huge ransom for the release of such an important person.

3 Ask students what person Cassandra sees. *(Hector)*

English Learners

Explain the meaning of the following phrase:

Line 247: "king's ransom" *(a payment large enough to obtain the release of a king)*

Reading and Analyzing

Reading Skills and Strategies
VISUALIZING

A Ask students to describe the scene at the gates of Troy. *(A huge crowd goes outside the gates of Troy to see the corpse of Hector. There are so many people that Priam cannot drive the wagon through the gates.)*

Her cries plunged Troy into uncontrollable grief
and not a man or woman was left inside the walls.
They streamed out at the gates to meet Priam
bringing in the body of the dead. Hector—
his loving wife and noble mother were first
to fling themselves on the wagon rolling on,
the first to tear their hair, embrace his head
and a wailing throng of people milled around them.
And now, all day long till the setting sun went down
they would have wept for Hector there before the gates
if the old man, steering the car, had not commanded,
"Let me through with the mules! Soon, in a moment,
you can have your fill of tears—once I've brought him home.

Literary Analysis

Paired Activity Possible Responses:

Hector
- loving husband, devoted father
- strong sense of loyalty to his people
- honorable to his enemy

Achilles
- fierce anger
- devoted friend to Patroclus
- most powerful of all warriors
- savage in his treatment of the enemy

What They Have in Common
- physical strength and speed
- powerful and feared warriors
- loving sons

Examples of epithets
- "white-armed Hera" (p. 185, l. 63)
- "man-killing Hector" (p. 200, l. 133)
- "Hector breaker of horses" (p. 202, l. 38)

Examples of epic similes
- Hector and Achilles compared to stallions (p. 202, lines 39–44)
- Achilles' feelings about Priam kneeling before him compared to the sighting of a murderer who has fled to a foreign land (p. 213, lines 1–9)

Use **Unit Two Resource Book,** pp. 7, 10, 13, for more practice.

Connect to the Literature

1. **What Do You Think?** Has your opinion of Achilles changed as a result of his reception of Priam? Explain.

Comprehension Check

- When Priam asks for pity, what person does he ask Achilles to remember?
- Why do Priam and Achilles cry?
- How does Achilles show hospitality to Priam?
- Besides returning the body of Hector, what does Achilles agree to?

Think Critically

2. Which character in this episode do you feel more sympathetic toward, Achilles or Priam? Explain your response, using details from the poem.
3. In most of the *Iliad,* Achilles is defined by his anger. What other qualities of his **character** are revealed in the episode with Priam?

THINK ABOUT
- Achilles' feelings for his father
- his treatment of Priam and his concern that Priam not provoke his anger
- his words of advice to Priam

4. Review Achilles' statements about the two jars from which Zeus distributes his "gifts" to mortals (page 215, lines 57–64). What do his words suggest about the Greeks' view of fate?
5. **ACTIVE READING: EVALUATING** Review what you wrote in your READER'S NOTEBOOK. Did you change your opinion about characters as you read further and learned more about them? What influenced your judgments about the major events? Compare your evaluations with those of your classmates, and discuss any differences you note.

Extend Interpretations

6. **Critic's Corner** The French philosopher Simone Weil wrote, "The true hero, the true subject, the center of the *Iliad* is force. Force employed by man, force that enslaves man, force before which man's flesh shrinks away." Are there any aspects of human life that the epic presents as *not* being ruled by force?
7. **Connect to Life** The *Iliad* depicts a warrior society far different from our own society. Do you think the poem contains a **theme,** or message, that applies to life today? Give reasons to support your opinion.

LITERARY ANALYSIS: EPIC HERO

An **epic hero** is a larger-than-life figure whose adventures are the focus of an epic poem. Epic heroes take part in dangerous adventures that are often of historical or cultural importance. Their deeds usually reflect the ideas and values of a people. They possess great courage and extraordinary strength; many are assisted by supernatural beings.

Paired Activity Working with a partner, compare Hector and Achilles as epic heroes. Fill out a Venn diagram like the one shown, identifying what the two heroes have in common and what sets them apart. In your judgment, which character is more heroic?

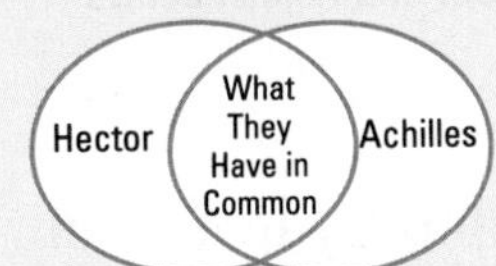

LITERARY ANALYSIS: EPIC SIMILES AND EPITHETS

Epic similes and epithets are descriptive devices frequently used by Homer. An **epithet** is an identifying word or phrase used with (or in place of) the name of a person or thing. For example, Achilles is often identified as "the swift runner."

An **epic simile** is one that stretches over a number of lines. One example can be found in Book 22, lines 10–15, where Achilles is compared to a wild mountain hawk. Find at least two other examples of epithets and two other examples of epic similes in the poem. Discuss how they contribute to your understanding of characters and events.

Connect to the Literature

1. **What Do You Think?** Accept all reasonable responses. Students should support their opinions with examples from the text.

Comprehension Check

- Priam asks Achilles to remember his father.
- Priam cries because he is grieving for Hector; Achilles cries in grief for his own father.
- Achilles shows his hospitality by serving Priam a meal and making sleeping arrangements for him.
- Achilles agrees to stop the war during Hector's funeral.

Use Selection Quiz in **Unit Two Resource Book,** p. 14.

Think Critically

2. Possible Responses: Priam is the more sympathetic character because he has lost so much during the war. Priam is a victim of the war's brutality. Achilles is the more sympathetic character because he is doomed to die after he kills Hector, yet he goes out of his way to be a good host to the father of his enemy.
3. Possible Response: Achilles shows love and pity for his father, realizing that they will never be reunited. He is a kind and sympathetic host to Priam, yet he also acts with foresight by keeping Priam away from the body of Hector. Achilles shows self-understanding by taking precautions to avoid anything that might provoke his anger.
4. Possible Responses: The two jars of fate suggest that human beings are not in control of their destiny. Whether one meets with "misfortune" or "good times" is a matter of fate or chance. The Greeks seem to have a pessimistic view of fate. Apparently, Zeus never takes all his "gifts" for an individual from the jar of "blessings."
5. Accept all reasonable responses. Students should identify what influenced their judgments of the characters and events. If their opinions of characters changed, they should explain the factors that influenced their opinions.

Extend Interpretations

6. **Critic's Corner** Some students may say that the relationship between Hector and his wife is not ruled by force because the couple demonstrates such a loving relationship. Others may disagree and point out that force still rules that relationship because Hector is fated to die. Some students might point to the scene between Achilles and Priam as an exception to the rule of force. The scene suggests that kindness and compassion can sometimes rule human encounters. Some might agree with Weil that in the end force rules everything.
7. **Connect to Life** Some students may discover a theme about violence in the *Iliad*, namely, that violence only serves to beget further violence. Others might identify a theme about fate, which suggests that human beings are not in control of their life. Others may focus on the text's celebration of honor. Such themes and others might be related to our contemporary society.

Writing Options

1. **Ancient Values Essay** Students may find it helpful to discuss their ideas with a partner. Encourage students to find quotations and supporting examples before they begin writing. Students may identify values such as honor, courage, obedience to the gods, loyalty, and the acceptance of fate.
2. **Analysis of the Gods** Students will probably draw attention to the human qualities of the gods, such as Apollo's anger toward Agamemnon, Zeus' pity for Hector, and Athena's loyalty to Achilles. They should point out that the gods are immortal and more powerful than humans. Humans should obey the will of the gods and accept their fate.
3. **Homeric Argument** Point out that both sides of this issue can be supported by evidence from the text. The best papers will be those that make the best arguments and refute the opposing viewpoint.

Activities & Explorations

Classic Illustration Before beginning their illustrations, students may find it helpful to look at illustrations of the *Iliad* available on the Internet.

Inquiry & Research

The Real Troy Students might begin their inquiry by reading entries about Troy in encyclopedias. Encourage students to find up-to-date information as they search the Internet.

Vocabulary in Action

1. comply
2. lithe
3. spurn
4. gaunt
5. waver
6. pittance
7. recoil
8. assent
9. recourse
10. defile

To assess skills and concepts taught in this selection, use **Formal Assessment Book**, pp. 25–30.

Choices & CHALLENGES

Writing Options

1. Ancient Values Essay From what you have read, what seem to have been the most important values of Homer's culture? First, review the text and identify passages that suggest cultural values, such as Agamemnon's statement that it would be a "disgrace" to "alone of the Argives go without my honor" (lines 138–140). Then choose two or three values to write about. Explain the importance of each value, and give quotations from the poem to illustrate each.

2. Analysis of the Gods What did the ancient Greeks believe about the gods? In what ways were gods and human beings alike, and in what ways were they different? How were people supposed to relate to the gods? Analyze the Greeks' religious beliefs, using examples from the poem to illustrate each point.

3. Homeric Argument Some critics have argued that Homer condemns the tragic waste of warfare. Others have claimed that Homer celebrates warfare and the values of the warrior. Take a position on this widely debated issue, and present examples from the poem to support your position.

Writing Handbook
See page R35: Persuasive Writing.

Activities & Explorations

Classic Illustration Choose a scene from the *Iliad* to illustrate. Carefully review the relevant passage, writing down visual details. Then create one illustration or a series of illustrations representing the scene. ~ ART

Inquiry & Research

The Real Troy Find out more about the discovery of the ruins of Troy. What do archaeologists now know about the ancient city? What connections do scholars see between the archaeological remains and the accounts in the *Iliad?*

Vocabulary in Action

EXERCISE: CONTEXT CLUES Write the word that best fills the blank in each sentence.

1. We saw the Trojan slave _______ with the order being barked at her; she dared not disobey.
2. As a young woman in Troy, she had been agile and _______ in her movements.
3. Then, she had not been afraid to _______ anyone who questioned or challenged her.
4. Now she is a _______ old woman living in Greece, so thin and weak she can barely walk.
5. Her weakened condition often makes her _______ when she should make a quick decision.
6. When she pleases her Greek master, she is given a mere _______ as a reward.
7. If an enemy approaches her, she will usually _______ fearfully.
8. She quickly nods in _______ when commanded to turn over her money.
9. What _______ does she have but to do as she is told?
10. Eventually, captivity will _______ even the strongest spirit.

WORDS TO KNOW

assent	gaunt	recoil	spurn
comply	lithe	recourse	waver
defile	pittance		

Building Vocabulary
For an in-depth lesson on Greek and Latin roots, see page 340.

Homer and the Oral Tradition

When Robert Fagles began translating Homer, he could often be heard "mumbling and muttering" to himself. Fagles went on to translate not only the *Iliad* but also the *Odyssey*—nearly 28,000 lines of poetry—and his muttering continued to the end.

Fagles's mumbling had a purpose—he was trying to capture the oral quality of Homer's language. Homer's poetry, Fagles says, was intended to be recited before spellbound listeners: "These poems weren't meant as literature or words on a page to be read, but as a song in the air." According to Fagles, the oral tradition that gave birth to Homer's epics helps to explain what the poet Matthew Arnold called the "speed, directness, and simplicity" of their language.

Another translator, Robert Fitzgerald, focused more on the literary aspects of Homer's poetry. Read the following translations of the passage about Hector's death to see the differences between the two versions.

Fagles

Death cut him short. The end closed in
around him.
Flying free of his limbs
his soul went winging down to the House
of Death,
wailing his fate, leaving his manhood far behind,
his young and supple strength.

Fagles begins with short sentences, which create emphasis when read aloud.

The line that begins "Flying free" is the start of one long sentence. Note how this sentence is broken into short phrases.

Fitzgerald

Even as he spoke, the end came, and death
hid him;
spirit from body fluttered to undergloom,
bewailing fate that made him leave his youth
and manhood in the world.

Fitzgerald uses one long sentence.

Notice the made-up word *undergloom*.

Questions to Consider

1. How would you describe the differences between the two translations?
2. Which translation do you think would be more effective when read aloud? Why?

The Translator at Work

READING FOR INFORMATION

Reading Skills and Strategies

COMPARING TRANSLATIONS

To help students recognize the differences between the two translators, bring in a copy of Fitzgerald's translation (available in many libraries). Invite students to read aloud excerpts from Fitzgerald's rendition of Homer's opening lines. Then have students read aloud from Fagles' rendition of the same part. By listening to longer excerpts, students may be better able to recognize the differences between translations.

To further highlight the differences, call attention to Fitzgerald's distinct spellings, which are an attempt to come closer to the the pronunciations of the ancient Greek. Print the following examples from Fitzgerald's translation on the board:

Akhilleus
Agamémnon
Kalchas
Khrysês
Menalaôs

Point out to students that the Greek language came before the invention of the Latin alphabet, which makes translating into a modern Latin-based language such as English even more challenging.

Questions to Consider

1. Possible Response: Fitzgerald's version is more formal and remote from contemporary English than Fagles' translation is. Fitzgerald uses words such as "fluttered," "undergloom," and "bewailing." Fagle's version seems easier to read aloud; the language comes closer to our own speech pattern.
2. Possible Response: Students are likely to believe that Fagles' translation is the more effective when read aloud because it makes use of shorter words and phrases, which makes it easier for the listener to follow.

Objectives

- understand and appreciate **lyric poetry (Literary Analysis)**
- make inferences about the **speaker** of a **lyric poem (Literary Analysis)**
- use strategies for **clarifying** difficult text **(Active Reading)**

Thematic Link

Sappho's lyrics express a personal vision, one that finds **glory and honor** in human relationships and in nature.

5-Minute Warm-Up

Daily Language SkillBuilder

Have students **proofread** the display sentences on page 161i and write them correctly.

PREPARING to *Read*

Sappho
c. 630–580 B.C.

Greatest Female Poet Sappho (săf'ō) is generally considered the greatest woman poet of the ancient world. Her image was stamped on coins and memorialized in statues and on vases. By the Middle Ages, however, all that survived of her work was quotations by other authors. Only two complete poems were preserved.

Celebrity of Her Era Most of what we know of Sappho's life comes through the writings of others. It is said that she was born into a wealthy family and was married to a prosperous businessman with whom she had had one daughter. While still in her youth, she became something of a celebrity, as much for her dynamic personality as for her poetry. It is likely that she was a central figure in a group of aristocratic women dedicated to the cultivation of poetry and the arts.

Freedom and Refinement Sappho lived more than a century after Homer, during a period of Greek culture marked by increased literacy, luxury, and leisure time. Prominent among the cultural centers of the time was the beautiful island of Lesbos, where Sappho spent most of her life. Located in the Aegean Sea off the coast of Asia Minor, Lesbos was unique in the ancient world for allowing women considerable freedom and social standing.

Personal Poetry Sappho often wrote about intensely personal subjects, such as her close friendships with other women and her relationship with her daughter. Because many of her poems appear to have been about love and several mention Aphrodite, the goddess of love, some people believe that she may have been the leader of a religious cult dedicated to Aphrodite. Others believe that she was simply following the poetic fashions of her time.

LESSON RESOURCES

UNIT TWO RESOURCE BOOK, pp. 16–17

ASSESSMENT RESOURCES
Formal Assessment, pp. 31–32
Teacher's Guide to Assessment and Portfolio Use
Test Generator

INTEGRATED TECHNOLOGY
Visit our Web site: classzone.com

ADDITIONAL RESOURCES
Lesson Planning Guide, pp. 23–24
Teacher's Sourcebook for Language Development

Connect to Your Life

The three poems you are about to read deal with forms of beauty, from the beauty of a beloved person to the beauty of nature. In the first poem, the speaker gives her opinion about "the finest sight on dark earth." In your judgment, what are some of the most beautiful sights in the world? What do your choices reveal about the kinds of things you value and appreciate?

Focus Your Reading

LITERARY ANALYSIS: LYRIC POETRY

A **lyric poem** is a short poem in which a speaker expresses personal thoughts and feelings. Sappho's lyrics are notable for their simple language and their expression of strong emotion, as in these lines:

. . . . If I meet
you suddenly, I can't
speak—my tongue is broken;

As you read the following poems, try to form an impression of the speaker of each poem and to identify the feelings expressed.

ACTIVE READING: CLARIFYING

When you are studying poetry, it's important to reread to **clarify** your understanding. During the process of rereading, your appreciation of a poem may change and develop.

READER'S NOTEBOOK As you read each poem, jot down what you learn about the speaker and the situation described. Also list any questions that come to mind. Then reread the poem to try to answer the questions and add to your understanding.

Build Background

Lyric Poetry By Sappho's time, the Homeric epic had given way to a shorter, more personal form of poetry called the lyric. Lyric poets customarily performed with musicians and dancers at festivals, weddings, and other gatherings. Although Sappho wasn't the first lyric poet, she raised the form to a high art.

The three poems you will read are typical of Sappho's poetry. "To an army wife, in Sardis" laments the absence of a woman named Anactoria, who may have been a close friend of Sappho's. "He Is More Than a Hero" may be addressed to another close female friend, though no name is given. "To Aphrodite of the Flowers, at Knossos" is addressed to the goddess of love.

Recovery of Sapphic Fragments Since around 1900, archaeological digs in Egypt have unearthed fragments of ancient manuscripts of Sappho's poems. Most of the manuscripts had been ripped into strips and used to wrap mummies. In general, these discoveries have yielded only disconnected bits of Sappho's poetry—groups of words that seem to celebrate love, beauty, nature, and the goddess Aphrodite. Still, they give us a fascinating glimpse into the mind of this highly regarded poet.

READING FOR INFORMATION

Reading Skills and Strategies

MAIN IDEA

Explain to students that subheadings can often help them identify the main idea of each section in a nonfiction text. Demonstrate this strategy by using the boldfaced subheading **Greatest Female Poet** on page 226 to identify the main idea of the first section of Sappho's biography. Point out that the entire paragraph focuses on Sappho's literary reputation.

Then ask students to explain how each subsequent subheading is related to the text that follows it.

Possible Response: The second section of Sappho's biography explains her celebrity status in her own society. The third section explains the freedom and refinement that characterized the society of Lesbos. The final section explains the intensely personal subjects of Sappho's poetry.

Tell students that the subheadings also serve as an outline of her biography, which is especially useful to remember when reviewing material for a test.

Reading Skills and Strategies

QUESTIONING

Explain that subheads can also be used as a prompt for active reading. For example, the subhead **Lyric Poetry** on page 227 can be turned into a question to guide reading: What is lyric poetry? Students can then read that section to find out the answer to that question. *(Lyric poetry is a shorter, more personal form of poetry than the epic.)* Ask students what questions might be prompted by the subhead **Recovery of Sapphic Fragments.** *(Accept all reasonable responses.)*

Reading and Analyzing

Literary Analysis LYRIC POETRY

Remind students that lyric poetry typically expresses personal feelings and thoughts. Point out that the speaker in this poem is addressing a woman named Anactoria.

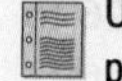 Use **Unit Two Resource Book,** p. 17, for more practice.

Active Reading CLARIFYING

A Point out that the poem begins with military references (cavalry corps, infantry, and a fleet of ships). The speaker says that some view these sights as wonderful, but she does not. Ask students what the speaker thinks is "the finest sight on dark earth." *("whatever one loves, is [finest].")*

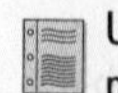 Use **Unit Two Resource Book,** p. 16, for more practice.

Literary Analysis ALLUSION

B The speaker alludes to Helen of Troy. According to Greek myths and legends, Helen was the most beautiful woman of the ancient world. She left her husband Menelaus and her daughter to run off with Paris, who took her to Troy and thus caused the Trojan War. As portrayed by Homer in the *Iliad*, Helen is a tragic figure. Aphrodite, the goddess of love, clouded Helen's judgment so that Paris could easily win her love.

Active Reading CLARIFYING

C Ask students how the speaker feels about the man described here. **Possible Response:** She's jealous of him because he is allowed to come close to the person being addressed. The man seems to have an intimate relationship with this person, who is presumably a woman.

To an army wife, in Sardis

Sappho

Translated by Mary Barnard

Relief with a dancing maenad (27 B.C. to 14 A.D.). Roman, Augustan. Pentelic marble, 56 3/16". The Metropolitan Museum of Art, New York.

A Some say a cavalry corps,
some infantry, some, again,
will maintain that the swift oars

of our fleet are the finest
sight on dark earth; but I say
that whatever one loves, is.

This is easily proved: did
not Helen—she who had scanned
the flower of the world's manhood—

B choose at first among men one
who laid Troy's honor in ruin?
warped to his will, forgetting

love due her own blood, her own
child, she wandered far with him.
So Anactoria, although you

being far away forget us,
1 the dear sound of your footstep
and light glancing in your eyes

would move me more than glitter
of Lydian horse or armored
tread of mainland infantry

15 Anactoria (ăn'ək-tôr'ē-ə): one of Sappho's friends, who had married and moved away.

20 Lydian (lĭd'ē-ən): from a kingdom on the mainland of Asia Minor near Lesbos.

Cross Curricular Link **History**

LYDIA During Sappho's lifetime, Lydia (located in Asia Minor in what is now Turkey) became the most powerful country in that region of the world. Lydia was a wealthy country, rich in natural resources, especially gold. The Greek cities along the Asian coast apparently enjoyed good relations with the Lydians, whom the Greeks respected for their sophisticated culture.

The well-financed Lydian army owed much of its success to its cavalry, which relied upon horse-drawn chariots. The Lydian Empire came to an end around 546 B.C. when the Persian forces of Cyrus the Great defeated the forces of Croesus, the last Lydian king. Croesus had been emboldened by the oracle's prophecy at the temple of Apollo at Delphi. When asked who would win a war between the Persians and Lydians, the oracle responded that a great power would fall. Croesus wrongly assumed that Persia would be that fallen power.

He Is More Than a Hero

Sappho

Translated by Mary Barnard

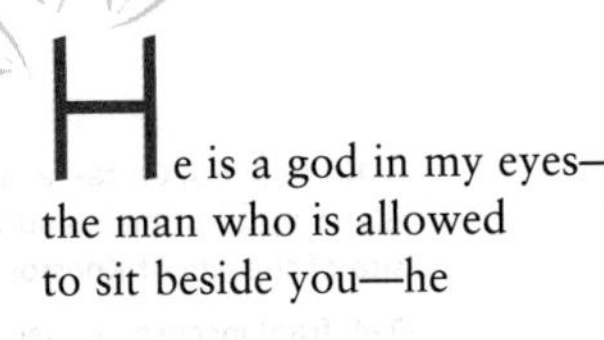

He is a god in my eyes—
the man who is allowed
C 2 to sit beside you—he

who listens intimately
to the sweet murmur of
your voice, the enticing

laughter that makes my own
heart beat fast. If I meet
you suddenly, I can't

speak—my tongue is broken;
a thin flame runs under
my skin; seeing nothing,

hearing only my own ears
3 drumming, I drip with sweat;
trembling shakes my body

and I turn paler than
dry grass. At such times
death isn't far from me

6 enticing: attractive; arousing desire.

Customizing Instruction

Less Proficient Readers

Explain to students that the entire poem, "To an army wife, in Sardis," is about the speaker's feelings for Anactoria, who is not named until line 15. Begin by explaining that the first sentence of the poem expresses the speaker's attitude toward love and beauty. Point out that the second sentence takes up the subject of Helen of Troy. Her life illustrates the power of love. (See annotation B on page 228, Literary Analysis: Allusion.)

1 How does the speaker seem to view Anactoria? *(The speaker views her as a special person and friend as revealed by "the dear sound of your footstep / and the light glancing in your eyes.")*

2 Point out that this poem is about three different people: the speaker, the speaker's friend (the "you" in line 3), and "the man who is allowed to sit beside" the friend. Ask why the man is a "god" in the speaker's eyes. *(He is privileged to be close to the speaker's friend.)*

3 Why does the speaker seem so overcome with emotion? *(The speaker seems be overwhelmed with passion for the absent friend.)*

English Learners

Explain the meaning of the following phrase:

Lines 10–12, p. 229: "my tongue is burning; a thin flame runs under my skin" *(My tongue feels as if it were on fire, as does my skin.)*

HE IS MORE THAN A HERO 229

Reading and Analyzing

Literary Analysis ALLUSION

A Make sure students realize that the speaker is addressing Aphrodite, the goddess of love and beauty. For an explanation of Knossos, see the mini-lesson below.

Literary Analysis SETTING

B Ask students to explain what kind of temple the speaker is describing. *(The "temple" is a scene of natural beauty, marked by apple trees, roses, and cold springs.)*

Active Reading CLARIFYING

C Point out that the entire poem can be read as a prayer to Aphrodite. What is the speaker praying for? *(The speaker wants Aphrodite to protect the beauty of this place and to make it fertile so that it can sustain itself.)*

A To Aphrodite of the Flowers, at Knossos

Sappho

Translated by Willis Barnstone

B
Leave Krete and come to this holy temple
where the graceful grove of apple trees
circles an altar smoking with frankincense.

Here roses leave shadow on the ground
and cold springs babble through apple branches
where shuddering leaves pour down profound sleep.

In our meadow where horses graze
and wild flowers of spring blossom,
anise shoots fill the air with a-
roma.

C
And here, Queen Aphrodite, pour
heavenly nectar into gold cups
and fill them gracefully with sudden joy.

1 Krete (krēt): Crete—a large island south of mainland Greece, site of the city of Knossos.

3–4 frankincense: a sweet-smelling tree resin burned as incense.

11 anise (ăn'ĭs): a fragrant herb.

Cross Curricular Link **History**

APHRODITE AND THE CITY OF KNOSSOS Knossos was the capital city of Crete, a large island south of Greece, and the center of the Minoan civilization, which flourished from about 2000 to 1400 B.C. The Palace of Knossos was one of the most famous buildings of the ancient world. It served both as a seat of government and a place of worship. The palace complex included a temple to Aphrodite, the goddess of sexual love, beauty, and fertility. The worship of Aphrodite had been associated with the island of Crete since prehistoric times.

When the speaker of Sappho's poem tells Aphrodite to "Leave Krete," she is urging the goddess to leave her home in the city to return to the beauties of nature.

Connect to the Literature

1. **What Do You Think?** Of the three poems, which do you think you understand best? Explain your reasons.

Think Critically

2. **ACTIVE READING: CLARIFYING** Look back at the comments and questions that you wrote in your  READER'S NOTEBOOK. Which questions were you able to answer? How? Discuss any unanswered questions with your classmates.

3. In each poem the **speaker** describes a person, situation, or **setting.** In your own words, explain what the speaker is describing in each case.

   THINK ABOUT
   - why thinking about Helen of Troy makes the speaker think of Anactoria's absence in "To an army wife, in Sardis"
   - how the speaker feels about the person spoken to in "He Is More Than a Hero"
   - the **setting** described in "To Aphrodite . . ."

4. On the basis of the three poems you have read, decide which two of the following statements best apply to Sappho. Use evidence from the poems to support your choices.

   She views life as a bitter struggle.

   She values intimate moments of friendship.

   She criticizes her culture's emphasis on beauty.

   She appreciates the beauty of nature.

Extend Interpretation

5. **Critic's Corner** The literary historian Peter Levi has described Sappho's poetry as "full of a pure, natural sweetness, and full of longing." Do you think his comment applies to any of these three poems? Explain why or why not.

6. **Connect to Life** If Sappho's poems were to be set to music today, what contemporary singer do you think would do them justice? Explain your choice.

LITERARY ANALYSIS: LYRIC POETRY

The ancient Greeks are credited with inventing lyric poetry. This form of poetry owes its name to the lyre (līr), a small harp that was used to accompany the recital or singing of poetry. Some lyrics, such as "He Is More Than a Hero," offer reflections on love and friendship. Others, such as "To Aphrodite of the Flowers, at Knossos," deal with reactions to nature. Today, any short poem in which a single speaker expresses his or her innermost thoughts and feelings is called a **lyric poem.**

Paired Activity Work with a partner to fill out a chart like the one shown. First, create a list of phrases or adjectives that describe the speaker of each poem. Then write phrases or sentences that tell what's important to the speaker.

Poem	Phrases That Describe Speaker	What Is Important to Speaker
"To an army wife"		
"He Is More Than a Hero"		
"To Aphrodite"		

Connect to the Literature

1. **What Do You Think?**
   Accept all reasonable responses.

Think Critically

2. Accept all reasonable responses. Invite students to help one another with any unanswered questions.
3. Possible Responses: In "To an army wife, in Sardis," the speaker, presumably a woman, is describing her feelings for an absent friend, Anactoria. The speaker draws upon the example of Helen of Troy to illustrate the strength of her longing for her friend. In "He Is More Than a Hero," the speaker, presumably a woman, is describing her envy of the man who is an intimate of her unnamed friend. In "To Aphrodite of the Flowers, at Knossos," the speaker is addressing Aphrodite and asking her to leave Crete. Aphrodite is invited to take up residence in a beautiful place in the countryside.
4. The two statements that best apply to Sappho's poems are:
   - She values intimate moments of friendship.
   - She appreciates the beauty of nature.

Extend Interpretations

5. **Critic's Corner** Some students may agree with Levi's judgment. They may find that the first two poems express longing. Some students may judge "To Aphrodite. . ." as a poem "full of a pure, natural sweetness" in its description of nature's beauty. Other students may find hints of such sweetness in the other two poems because the speaker has a strong affection for her friends.

   Those students who disagree with Levi may feel that the first two Sappho poems describe a passion beyond reason, control, or "a pure, natural sweetness."
6. **Connect to Life** Accept all reasonable responses.

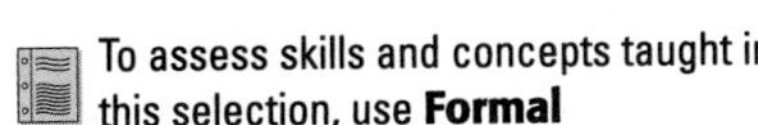
To assess skills and concepts taught in this selection, use **Formal Assessment Book,** pp. 31–32.

Literary Analysis

Paired Activity Possible Responses:

Words/Phrases That Describe Speaker

"To an army wife":
- intense
- romantic
- devoted friend
- sensitive

"He Is More Than a Hero":
- jealous of man
- overcome with passion
- misses friend

"To Aphrodite":
- appreciates beauty of nature
- seems devoted to Aphrodite

What Is Important to Speaker

"To an army wife":
- friendship
- appreciation of beauty
- romantic longing

"He Is More Than a Hero":
- close friendship
- passionate feelings

"To Aphrodite":
- a life at one with nature
- the worship of Aphrodite

Use **Unit Two Resource Book,** p. 17, for more practice.

Objectives

- understand and appreciate a **formal speech (Literary Analysis)**
- evaluate whether a speech achieves the **author's purpose (Literary Analysis)**
- use strategies for identifying **main idea (Active Reading)**

Summary

Pericles' speech was given at a public funeral for Athenian soldiers who died during the first year of the Peloponnesian War. After paying tribute to the Athenian ancestors, Pericles praises the city of Athens and its way of life. He calls attention to what sets Athens apart from other city-states: its democracy, its openness, its love of the beautiful, its commitment to public life, its generous relations with other people, and its adventurous spirit. After explaining the unique value of Athenian life, Pericles praises those soldiers who died in service to Athens. By the sacrifice of their lives, those soldiers "won prizes that never grow old," for their "glory remains eternal in men's minds."

 Use **Unit Two Resource Book,** p. 18, for additional support.

Thematic Link

Thucydides portrays a famous speech by Pericles in which the **glory and honor** of ancient Athens is explained.

 Use **Unit Two Resource Book,** p. 21, for practice with Words to Know.

5-Minute Warm-Up

Daily Language SkillBuilder

Have students **proofread** the display sentences on page 161i and write them correctly.

PREPARING to *Read*

from HISTORY OF THE PELOPONNESIAN WAR

PERICLES' FUNERAL ORATION

THUCYDIDES

Thucydides
c. 460–404 B.C.

A Citizen Disgraced One of the great historians of the ancient world, Thucydides (thōō-sĭd'ĭ-dēz') turned to writing only after he was disgraced in his native Athens. The great event of his lifetime was the bitter 27-year-long Peloponnesian War between Athens and Sparta. In 424 B.C., the citizens of Athens selected Thucydides as one of the ten *strategoi* (strə-tē'goi), or military leaders, of the city. Because of his rank and influence, he was given command of an Athenian fleet. However, when he failed to prevent the Spartans from capturing an important port city, he was recalled to Athens, put on trial, and exiled from his native city.

History for the Ages Thucydides turned his misfortune into an opportunity to work on the *History of the Peloponnesian War.* He wanted to provide a complete account of the war so that future generations could understand the events and their causes. To be as accurate and fair as possible, he traveled throughout the Peloponnesus (the peninsula forming the southern part of Greece), interviewing the Spartans and their allies.

In writing his history, Thucydides offered his own theories about how states interact with one another. For example, he argued that interactions between states are fundamentally immoral, no matter how just each state may be toward its own citizens: "The strong do what they have the power to do and the weak accept what they have to accept." His keen insights into the nature of international relations continue to influence scholars and political leaders today.

Mysterious Death Thucydides was allowed to return to Athens after the final defeat of the city in 404 B.C. He probably died only a few years later—perhaps violently during the political turmoil of the time. He left the *History of the Peloponnesian War* unfinished; its account abruptly stops about seven years before the war's end.

Athens	Sparta
Strong Navy. Located near the Aegean, Athens developed a powerful navy.	**Strong Army.** Land-locked and isolated by mountains, Sparta depended on its army.
Democracy. Citizens were encouraged to participate.	**Oligarchy.** Governed by a small group of rulers.
Education for Free Thinkers. Tutors and professional teachers educated male citizens.	**Military Training.** Males taken from home at age 7 and educated in strict military school.
Artistic. Great achievements in poetry, drama, history, painting, philosophy, architecture.	**Athletic.** Spartan athletes won many first prizes at the Olympic games.

LESSON RESOURCES

UNIT TWO RESOURCE BOOK, pp. 18–22

ASSESSMENT RESOURCES
Formal Assessment, pp. 33–34
Teacher's Guide to Assessment and Portfolio Use
Test Generator

INTEGRATED TECHNOLOGY
Visit our Web site: classzone.com

ADDITIONAL RESOURCES
Lesson Planning Guide, pp. 25–26
Teacher's Sourcebook for Language Development

Connect to Your Life

What comes to mind when you hear the word *patriotism*? Do you think that citizens should always try to feel love and devotion for their country? For five minutes, do some focused freewriting on what patriotism means to you.

Build Background

Who Was Pericles?

In writing his history, Thucydides recreated many important speeches. To do so, he relied on notes that he compiled from interviews as well as his own memory. Thucydides was probably in attendance early in 430 B.C. when Pericles (pĕr′ĭ-klēz′) gave his funeral **oration,** or formal speech, to honor the Athenian warriors who had been killed during the first year of the Peloponnesian War.

Like Thucydides, Pericles served as one of Athens' *strategoi.* More importantly, he was the greatest Athenian politician of his time, greatly respected for his wisdom, leadership, and virtue. So influential was he that historians have named the middle decades of the 400s the Age of Pericles. This period saw many of Athens' greatest achievements in art and culture, including the building of the Parthenon.

The Achievements of Pericles

- Enabled common people to hold any state office by having salaries paid to public officials
- Built up navy and expanded Athenian empire throughout the Mediterranean world
- Beautified Athens by spending city's fortune to build huge temples—including the Parthenon—and other public buildings
- Supported drama and other arts, personally financing a production by the playwright Aeschylus

Focus Your Reading

LITERARY ANALYSIS: AUTHOR'S PURPOSE

Authors and speakers communicate for various purposes: to inform, to express opinions, to entertain, to persuade. Near the beginning of his speech, Pericles announces his purposes:

> ***What I want to do is . . . to discuss the spirit in which we faced our trials and also our constitution and the way of life which has made us great. After that I shall speak in praise of the dead. . . .***

As you read, think about whether Pericles is convincing in his praise of Athens and of the soldiers who sacrificed their lives for their homeland.

ACTIVE READING: MAIN IDEA

To achieve his purposes, Pericles develops a number of ideas. Almost every paragraph sets forth a single main idea, which is then supported by details and examples. Sometimes, the main idea is clearly stated at the beginning of the paragraph, as in the second paragraph:

> ***I shall begin by speaking about our ancestors, since it is only right . . . to pay them the honor of recalling what they did.***

In other paragraphs, the main idea may not come until later.

READER'S NOTEBOOK As you read, look for the main ideas expressed about Athens and the soldiers who died. Starting with the sixth paragraph of the speech, on page 236, record the main idea of each paragraph.

WORDS TO KNOW **Vocabulary Preview**

abiding	incredulous	revelation	undeterred
culmination	relinquish	tangible	versatility
incompatibility	reproach		

READING FOR INFORMATION

Reading Skills and Strategies

CLARIFYING

Point out to students that *History of the Peloponnesian War* is a book-length study written by Thucydides, who lived during the same time as Pericles. One section of the book is devoted to Pericles' speech honoring the Athenian soldiers who had died. To help students keep track of the information about these two men on pages 232 and 233, write the names *Thucydides* and *Pericles* at the top of the board. Invite students to identify key facts about each person, which you can list in a column under each name. Discuss with students how they decided what facts were most important.

Possible Response:

Thucydides

- great historian of ancient world
- one of the *strategoi*, or military leaders
- banished from Athens
- began writing during exile
- interviewed people on both sides
- returned to Athens in 404 B.C.

Pericles

- also one of the *strategoi*
- greatest Athenian politician
- his rule called Age of Pericles
- enabled common people to hold office
- expanded empire
- built huge temples, such as Parthenon

Historical Note

Much of Thucydides' history is devoted to the speeches given by key participants in the war. Though Thucydides took notes of his interviews, he never claimed that his versions of the speeches duplicated the exact words of the originals. Rather, Thucydides composed the speeches based on his understanding of the issues and personalities involved.

TIME MANAGEMENT

If your schedule requires that you cover the lesson objectives in a shorter time, use . . .

- Preparing to Read, pp. 232–233
- Thinking Through the Literature, pp. 243-244
- Vocabulary in Action, p. 244

If you want to take advantage of longer blocks of class time, use . . .

- TE Teaching Options: Cross Curricular Link, pp. 234, 237, 240; Viewing and Representing, p. 238; Speaking and Listening, p. 236; Vocabulary Strategy, p. 235; Informal Assessment, p. 242
- Choices & Challenges, p. 244
- Connect to Today, p. 245

Reading and Analyzing

Literary Analysis CULTURAL SETTING

A Explain that Athens was divided into ten tribes. The tribes were not based on kinship but on areas of residence. In the 500s B.C., an Athenian statesman named Cleisthenes (respelling) divided the city into ten geographical regions; the people living in each region were assigned membership in the same tribe. Political representation in Athens was distributed equally among the tribes.

Active Reading MAIN IDEA

B Ask students to identify the main idea of this paragraph.

Possible Response: Pericles says that the soldiers who have fallen do not need his words of praise to prove their glory. Their actions brought glory, not his words.

Use **Unit Two Resource Book,** p. 19, for more practice.

Literary Analysis AUTHOR'S PURPOSE

C Read aloud the opening sentence in this paragraph. Explain that this type of statement provides a cue to the reader about how the speaker will organize his remarks, especially the phrase "I shall begin by speaking about our ancestors." Advise students to be on the lookout for other statements where the speaker discusses how he plans to proceed.

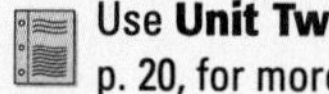

Use **Unit Two Resource Book,** p. 20, for more practice.

from History of the Peloponnesian War

Pericles' Funeral Oration

Thucydides

Translated by Rex Warner

In the same winter the Athenians, following their annual custom, gave a public funeral for those who had been the first to die in the war. These funerals are held in the following way: two days before the ceremony the bones of the fallen are brought and put in a tent which has been erected, and people make whatever offerings they wish to their own dead. Then there is a funeral procession in which coffins of cypress wood are carried on wagons. There is one coffin for each tribe, which contains the bones of members of that tribe. **A** One empty bier[1] is decorated and carried in the procession: this is for the missing, whose bodies could not be recovered. Everyone who wishes to, both citizens and foreigners, can join in the procession, and the women who are related to the dead are there to make their laments at the tomb. The bones are laid in the public burial-place, which is in the most beautiful quarter outside the city walls. Here the Athenians always bury those who have fallen in war. The only exception is those who died at Marathon,[2] who, because their achievement was considered absolutely outstanding, were buried on the battlefield itself.

When the bones have been laid in the earth, a man chosen by the city for his intellectual gifts and for his general reputation makes an appropriate speech in praise of the dead, and after the speech all depart. This is the procedure at these burials, and all through the war, when the time came to do so, the Athenians followed this ancient custom. Now, at the burial of those who were the first to fall in the war Pericles, the son of Xanthippus,[3] was chosen to make the speech. When the moment arrived, he came forward from the tomb and, standing on a high platform, so that he might be heard by as many people as possible in the crowd, he spoke as follows:

"Many of those who have spoken here in the past have praised the institution of this speech at the close of our ceremony. It seemed to them a mark of honor to our soldiers who have fallen in **B**

1. **bier** (bēr): a platform for laying out a corpse.
2. **Marathon:** the site of a famous Greek victory over the Persians in 490 B.C.
3. **Xanthippus** (zăn-thĭp'əs): a famous Athenian military commander.

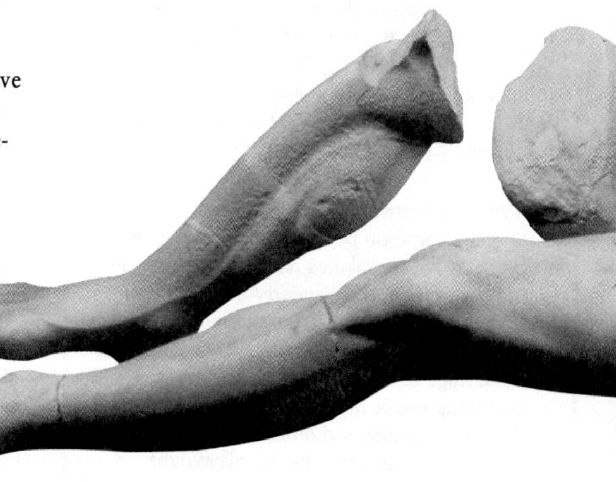

Cross Curricular Link History

ATHENS AND PERICLES During the years of Pericles' leadership, Athens reached the height of its political, economic, military, literary, and artistic glory. Athens was the leader of an alliance of 140 city-states, the Delian League, formed to protect Greece from the Persians. Using money from the League's treasury, Pericles built a 200-ship navy. The power of the navy helped fuel Athenian prosperity by assuring the safety of overseas trade, while enabling Athens to expand its empire. In Pericles' time, the Athenian empire controlled the entire Aegean Sea and its coastline.

Pericles used remaining funds from the Delian League to build the Parthenon and other buildings, filling the buildings with masterpieces of Greek sculpture. The Parthenon was such an ambitious project that it took 15 years (447–432 B.C.) to complete.

The theater also flourished under Pericles' leadership. The greatest Greek playwrights—Aeschylus, Sophocles, and Euripides—all wrote during those years.

war that a speech should be made over them. I do not agree. These men have shown themselves valiant in action, and it would be enough, I think, for their glories to be proclaimed in action, as you have just seen it done at this funeral organized by the state. Our belief in the courage and manliness of so many should not be hazarded on the goodness or badness of one man's speech. Then it is not easy to speak with a proper sense of balance, when a man's listeners find it difficult to believe in the truth of what one is saying. The man who knows the facts and loves the dead may well think that an oration tells less than what he knows and what he would like to hear: others who do not know so much may feel envy for the dead, and think the orator over-praises them, when he speaks of exploits that are beyond their own capacities. Praise of other people is tolerable only up to a certain point, the point where one still believes that one could do oneself some of the things one is hearing about. Once you get beyond this point, you will find people becoming jealous and incredulous. However, the fact is that this institution was set up and approved by our forefathers, and it is my duty to follow the tradition and do my best to meet the wishes and the expectations of every one of you.

"I shall begin by speaking about our ancestors, since it is only right and proper on such an occasion to pay them the honor of recalling what they did. In this land of ours there have always been the same people living from generation to generation up till now, and they, by their courage and their virtues, have handed it on

Fallen warrior. Glyptothek, Munich, Germany.

WORDS TO KNOW

incredulous (ĭn-krĕj'ə-ləs) *adj.* unwilling to believe; skeptical

Customizing Instruction

Less Proficient Readers

Ask students to describe the public funeral in their own words.

Possible Response: The bones of the dead are placed in a tent, where family members can pay their respects. The bones are then combined into a single coffin for each tribe. In a funeral procession, the coffins are carried by wagon to a public burial place outside of Athens.

1 Point out that Pericles contrasts an action—a state funeral for the soldiers—with words. Ask why an action is a better way of honoring the men than a speech. *(The men proved their bravery in action, so an action is a better tribute.)*

2 Tell students that Pericles is concerned about losing the good will of his audience. Ask them to identify phrases in this paragraph that identify what he is afraid of.

Possible Responses: Pericles is afraid that "some people may find it difficult to believe in the truth." Others "may feel envy for the dead" or become "incredulous" if the speaker goes too far in his praise.

English Learners

- Explain to students that "intellectual gifts" (p. 234) refer to qualities of the mind, such as good judgment and wisdom.
- Draw attention to the use of "hazarded" on page 235: "Our belief in the courage and manliness of so many should not be hazarded. . . ." Explain that *hazarded* in this context means "exposed to harm or danger."

MINI LESSON Vocabulary Strategy

ROOTS AND WORD FAMILIES

Instruction Words containing the same root are usually related in meaning. Knowing the root can help students understand other words in the same word family. For example, the word *versatility* contains the Latin root *vers-*, or *vert-* which means "turn" or "change." The idea of turning or changing can be seen in the definition of *versatility*— "an ability to do many things well; variability." The same idea is involved in the meanings of other words in the *vers-/vert-* family, such as *adversity* and *invert*.

Practice Have students work in small groups to compile a list of words that derive from the Latin root *vers-*, or *vert-* . Have them find at least five words (other than the ones discussed in class) stemming from this root. Some responses might include *adverse, adversary, avert, convert, conversion, inversion, verse, version, versus, vertebra, vertical, and vertigo.* Have students share their findings with the class, explaining how each word reflects the idea of turning or changing.

A lesson on recognizing word families appears on p. 1196 in the Pupil's Edition.

Literary Analysis CULTURAL SETTING

A Explain to students that Athens expanded its empire under Pericles. Athens gained virtually complete control of the Aegean Sea and eastern, northern, and western shores (see map on pages 162–163).

Literary Analysis AUTHOR'S PURPOSE

B Invite a student to read this sentence ("What I want. . .") aloud. Ask students why Pericles might have chosen to discuss the achievements of Athens before praising the dead.

Possible Response: The soldiers died to defend Athens and its way of life. Rather than praising the soldiers first, Pericles will explain what makes Athens worth fighting for.

Active Reading MAIN IDEA

C Point out that the beginning of a paragraph in nonfiction often sets a direction for the entire paragraph. Here, the two first sentences establish the controlling idea that Athens is a model to others. Ask students to identify key phrases in the paragraph that elaborate that idea.

Possible Responses:

- "every one is equal before the law"
- "No one . . . is kept in obscurity because of poverty."
- "We are free and tolerant in our private lives; but in public affairs we keep to the law."

Reading Skills and Strategies
COMPARE AND CONTRAST

D Tell students that Pericles contrasts Athens to its main enemy, Sparta. Ask students to give examples of key differences between the two cities.

Possible Response:

Athens

- no deportations
- no military training in childhood
- city-state fights its own wars
- soldiers meet danger "voluntarily"

Sparta

- deportations to protect secrets
- military training required for boys
- city-state fights wars with help of allies
- soldiers meet danger with "state-induced courage"

Our constitution is called a democracy because power is in the hands not of a minority but of the whole people.

to us, a free country. They certainly deserve our praise. Even more so do our fathers deserve it. For to the inheritance they had received they added all the empire we have now, and it was not without blood and toil that they handed it down to us of the present generation. And then we ourselves, assembled here today, who are mostly in the prime of life, have, in most directions, added to the power of our empire and have organized our State in such a way that it is perfectly well able to look after itself both in peace and in war. A

"I have no wish to make a long speech on subjects familiar to you all: so I shall say nothing about the warlike deeds by which we acquired our power or the battles in which we or our fathers gallantly resisted our enemies, Greek or foreign. What I want to do is, in the first place, to discuss the spirit in which we faced our trials and also our constitution and the way of life which has made us great. After that I shall speak in praise of the dead, believing that this kind of speech is not inappropriate to the present occasion, and that this whole assembly, of citizens and foreigners, may listen to it with advantage. B

"Let me say that our system of government does not copy the institutions of our neighbors. It is more the case of our being a model to others, than of our imitating anyone else. C Our constitution is called a democracy because power is in the hands not of a minority but of the whole people. When it is a question of settling private disputes, everyone is equal before the law; when it is a question of putting one person before another in positions of public responsibility, what counts is not membership of a particular class, but the actual ability which the man possesses. No one, so long as he has it in him to be of service to the state, is kept in political obscurity because of poverty. And, just as our political life is free and open, so is our day-to-day life in our relations with each other. We do not get into a state with our next-door neighbor if he enjoys himself in his own way, nor do we give him the kind of black looks which, though they do no real harm, still do hurt people's feelings. We are free and tolerant in our private lives; but in public affairs we keep to the law. This is because it commands our deep respect.

"We give our obedience to those whom we put in positions of authority, and we obey the laws themselves, especially those which are for the protection of the oppressed, and those unwritten laws[4] which it is an acknowledged shame to break.

"And here is another point. When our work is over, we are in a position to enjoy all kinds of recreation for our spirits. There are various kinds of contests and sacrifices regularly throughout the year; in our own homes we find a beauty and a good taste which delight us every day and which drive away our cares. Then the greatness of our city brings it about that all the good things from all over the world flow in to us, so that to us it seems just as natural to enjoy foreign goods as our own local products.

4. **unwritten laws:** customs.

MINI LESSON **Speaking and Listening**

DELIVERING A FORMAL SPEECH Have students prepare an oral delivery of an excerpt from the speech. They might, for example, begin at the part that starts with "I have no wish to make a long speech" and end with "it is an acknowledged shame to break." Alternatively, you might assign each student one paragraph from the speech, so that the entire speech will be delivered.

Prepare Allow time for students to rehearse their excerpts. Suggest that students divide long sentences into shorter phrases, based upon units of meaning. You may wish to model the presentation by reading aloud the first paragraph of Pericles' speech, beginning with "Many of those" on page 234.

Present If possible, set up a podium at the front of the room where students can present their excerpts. Ask the audience to give each speaker a ranking (with one the lowest and five the highest), using the following criteria:

- establishes eye contact with audience
- speaks clearly and slowly
- uses appropriate emphasis
- communicates the meaning of the passage

This activity is particularly well suited for longer class periods.

"Then there is a great difference between us and our opponents, in our attitude towards military security. Here are some examples: Our city is open to the world, and we have no periodical deportations[5] in order to prevent people observing or finding out secrets which might be of military advantage to the enemy. This is because we rely, not on secret weapons, but on our own real courage and loyalty. There is a difference, too, in our educational systems. The Spartans, from their earliest boyhood, are submitted to the most laborious training in courage; we pass our lives without all these restrictions, and yet are just as ready to face the same dangers as they are. Here is a proof of this: When the Spartans invade our land, they do not come by themselves, but bring all their allies with them; whereas we, when we launch an attack abroad, do the job by ourselves, and, though fighting on foreign soil, do not often fail to defeat opponents who are fighting for their own hearths and homes. As a matter of fact none of our enemies has ever yet been confronted with our total strength, because we have to divide our attention between our navy and the many missions on which our troops are sent on land. Yet, if our enemies engage a detachment[6] of our forces and defeat it, they give themselves credit for having thrown back our entire army; or, if they lose, they claim that they were beaten by us in full strength. There are certain advantages, I think, in our way of meeting danger voluntarily, with an easy mind, instead of with a laborious training, with natural rather than with state-induced courage. We do not have to spend our time practicing to meet sufferings which are still in the future; and when they are actually upon us we show ourselves just as brave as these others who are always in strict training. This is one point in which, I think, our city deserves to be admired. There are also others:

"Our love of what is beautiful does not lead to extravagance; our love of the things of the mind does not make us soft. We regard wealth as something to be properly used, rather than as something to boast about. As for poverty, no one need be ashamed to admit it: the real shame is in not taking practical measures to escape from it. Here each individual is interested not only in his own affairs but in the affairs of the state as well: even those who are mostly occupied with their own business are extremely well-informed on general politics—this is a peculiarity of ours: we

Bust of Pericles (c. 425 B.C.) Marble, 18⅞". Copyright © The British Museum.

5. **deportations:** expulsions of noncitizens.

6. **engage a detachment:** fight a single unit.

Customizing Instruction

Less Proficient Readers

Tell students that there are five complete paragraphs on pages 236–237, beginning with the paragraph that starts with "I have no wish." Model the process of identifying the most important sentence, or sentences, in a paragraph by reading the first complete paragraph aloud and commenting on the relative importance of each sentence. Then invite students to work in pairs to identify the most important sentences in the subsequent paragraphs.

Possible Responses:

Paragraph 2: "Let us say that our system of government does not copy the institutions of our neighbors. It is more the case of our being a model to others. . . ."

Paragraph 3: Only one sentence in paragraph

Paragraph 4: "When our work is over, we are in a position to enjoy all kinds of recreation for our spirits."

Paragraph 5: "Then there is a great difference between us and our opponent, in our attitude toward military security."

English Learners

Explain the meanings of the following phrases:

Page 236:

- "not without blood and toil" *(with great sacrifice and hard work)*
- "kept in political obscurity" *(prevented from holding public office)*
- "get into a state" *(become upset)*
- "those unwritten laws which it is an acknowledged shame to break" *(those rules of proper behavior that we would be ashamed to break)*

Page 237:

- "laborious training in courage" *(very difficult training to prepare young men for battle)*
- "their own hearths and homes" *(their own family life and homes)*

Cross Curricular Link — History

SPARTA Sparta during the era of Pericles can be best understood as a military state. The entire society was organized to support an efficient army that would protect the city and advance its interests. In the 700s B.C., Sparta had conquered its neighbor, Messenia. The conquest gave Sparta a large area of fertile land and a labor force—the Messenians, who became known as helots—to work the land. Each year, the helots had to give the Spartans half their crop. Around 600 B.C., the helots, who outnumbered the Spartans about 8 to 1, revolted. After the Spartans barely avoided defeat, they took measures to strengthen their state.

The state took complete responsibility for the education of boys, who were trained to become warriors. Spartan boys left home at age seven to move into army barracks. They were forced to sleep on the bare ground, were fed poorly, and were only lightly clothed. The boys were also encouraged to steal food and subjected to harsh physical punishment. Girls were trained to become mothers to future soldiers; infants who were sickly or physically deformed were abandoned and left to die. Despite the severity of Spartan life, some Athenians, most notably Plato, respected their discipline.

Reading and Analyzing

Reading Skills and Strategies
CLARIFYING

A Invite a student to read this entire sentence aloud. (It begins on page 237.) Then ask what this sentence reveals about the Athenians' attitude toward politics.

Possible Response: The Athenians believed that every individual should take an active interest in politics.

Active Reading MAIN IDEA

B This sentence states the main idea of the paragraph. Ask students to find examples in the remainder of the paragraph that support this statement.

Possible Response: According to Pericles, the Athenians treat others with kindness, "showing continued goodwill" to their friends. Even people who have been conquered by the Athenians have no complaint. The Athenians have left "memorials of good done to our friends."

Literary Analysis CULTURAL SETTING

C Ask students to explain what Pericles means when he says "each one of our citizens . . . is able to show himself the rightful lord and owner of his person. . . ."

Possible Response: The individual citizen in Athens has control over his own life because he is equal to other citizens before the law and he takes part in decisions that affect the city.

Partial view of the Parthenon, Athens, Greece

do not say that a man who takes no interest in
A politics is a man who minds his own business;
we say that he has no business here at all. We Athenians, in our own persons, take our decisions on policy or submit them to proper discussions: for we do not think that there is an
1 incompatibility between words and deeds; the worst thing is to rush into action before the consequences have been properly debated. And this is another point where we differ from other people. We are capable at the same time of taking risks and of estimating them beforehand. Others are brave out of ignorance; and, when they stop to think, they begin to fear. But the man who can most truly be accounted brave is he who best knows the meaning of what is sweet in life and of what is terrible, and then goes out undeterred to meet what is to come.

"Again, in questions of general good feeling there is a great contrast between us and most
other people. We make friends by doing good to B
others, not by receiving good from them. This 2
makes our friendship all the more reliable, since we want to keep alive the gratitude of those who are in our debt by showing continued goodwill to them: whereas the feelings of one who owes us something lack the same enthusiasm, since he knows that, when he repays our kindness, it will be more like paying back a debt than giving something spontaneously. We are

WORDS TO KNOW

incompatibility (ĭn′kəm-păt′ə-bĭl′ĭ-tē) *n.* a lack of harmony; conflict

undeterred (ŭn′dĭ-tûrd′) *adj.* not discouraged

238

MINI LESSON Viewing and Representing

The Parthenon, Athens, Greece

ART APPRECIATION Ask students to study the photograph of the Parthenon on page 171, as well as the contemporary painting on that page that shows its original colors. Explain that the Parthenon, a temple dedicated to Athena, was built by the architects Ictinus and Callicrates under the supervision of the sculptor Phidias, a friend of Pericles. The Parthenon originally housed a nearly 40-foot statue of Athena.

The temple reflects the Doric order of Greek architecture, which is distinguished by its fluted columns with square tops, or capitals. The design of the temple is based upon mathematical ratios, intended to create perfect order, proportion, and harmony. Eight columns are at each end of the temple, while 17 are along each side. To ensure that the columns look perfectly proportioned from a distance, the architects made slight adjustments. Ask students if they can notice the difference between the tops and bottoms of the columns shown on page 171. *(The bottoms of the columns have a slightly wider diameter than the tops.)* Point out that each column has a slight bulge in the middle.

unique in this. When we do kindnesses to others, we do not do them out of any calculations of profit or loss: we do them without afterthought, relying on our free liberality.[7] Taking everything together then, I declare that our city is an education to Greece, and I declare that in my opinion each single one of our citizens, in all the manifold aspects of life, is able to show himself the rightful lord and owner of his own person, and do this, moreover, with exceptional grace and exceptional versatility. And to show that this is no empty boasting for the present occasion, but real tangible fact, you have only to consider the power which our city possesses and which has been won by those very qualities which I have mentioned. Athens, alone of the states we know, comes to her testing time in a greatness that surpasses what was imagined of her. In her case, and in her case alone, no invading enemy is ashamed at being defeated, and no subject can complain of being governed by people unfit for their responsibilities. Mighty indeed are the marks and monuments of our empire which we have left. Future ages will wonder at us, as the present age wonders at us now. We do not need the praises of a Homer, or of anyone else whose words may delight us for the moment, but whose estimation of facts will fall short of what is really true. For our adven-
3 turous spirit has forced an entry into every sea
and into every land; and everywhere we have left behind us everlasting memorials of good done to our friends or suffering inflicted on our enemies.

Mighty indeed are the marks and monuments of our empire which we have left. Future ages will wonder at us, as the present age wonders at us now.

"This, then, is the kind of city for which these men, who could not bear the thought of losing her, nobly fought and nobly died. It is only natural that every one of us who survive them should be willing to undergo hardships in her service. And it was for this reason that I have spoken at such length about our city, because I wanted to make it clear that for us there is more at stake than there is for others who lack our advantages; also I wanted my words of praise for the dead to be set in the bright light of evidence. And now the most important of these words has been spoken. I have sung the praises of our city; but it was the courage and gallantry of these men, and of
people like them, which made her splendid. Nor 4
would you find it true in the case of many of the Greeks, as it is true of them, that no words can do more than justice to their deeds.

"To me it seems that the consummation[8] which has overtaken these men shows us the meaning of manliness in its first revelation and in its final proof. Some of them, no doubt, had their faults; but what we ought to remember first is their gallant conduct against the enemy in

7. **liberality:** generosity.

8. **consummation:** end

WORDS TO KNOW

versatility (vûr'sə-tĭl'ĭ-tē) *n.* an ability to do many things well
tangible (tăn'jə-bəl) *adj.* capable of being felt or perceived; concrete
revelation (rĕv'ə-lā'shən) *n.* a making known; exposure

Customizing Instruction

Less Proficient Readers

Help students to appreciate the main points that Pericles makes by asking the following questions:

1 The Athenians were famous for the length of their public discussions. Why is such discussion useful before taking action? *(The Athenians discuss possible risks before they take action, so they know what they are getting into.)*

2 How do the Athenians make friends? *(by doing good to others)*

3 During Pericles' rule, the Athenian empire expanded. According to Pericles, what trait of the Athenians played a key role in such expansion? *(their "adventurous spirit")*

4 What did the soldiers possess that made Athens "splendid"? *("courage and gallantry")*

English Learners

Explain the meaning of the following phrases:

Page 239:

- "forced an entry into every sea and every land" *(expanded Athenian power throughout the known world)*
- "shows us the meaning of manliness" *(shows us what it means to be truly a man)*

Advanced Learners

Invite students to read the Melian Dialogue in Thucydides' work. Students can read the text on the Internet and give an oral report about it. The dialogue is about negotiations that took place between Athens and Melos, an island friendly to Sparta. When the Melians refused to surrender, the Athenians attacked, killing all the men and selling the women and children into slavery.

Reading and Analyzing

Active Reading MAIN IDEA

A Ask students to restate this main idea in their own words.

Possible Response: The dead soldiers have done more good for our community than any evil they may have done during their lives: the good wipes out evil.

B Pericles tells his audience to imitate the departed soldiers. Ask students to identify examples in this paragraph of how the audience can do so.

Possible Response: The Athenians should "fix their eyes" . . . on the greatness of Athens . . . and fall in love with her." They should always show courage for the sake of Athens and do everything they can to protect their freedom. They should never relax their efforts in wartime.

Literary Analysis AUTHOR'S PURPOSE

C Pericles does not "commiserate with," or feel sorry for, the parents of the dead. Instead, he tries to comfort them. Ask students to look for evidence of the comfort that he gives.

Possible Response: The parents have the "good fortune" of knowing that their sons died with honor. Those who are capable of doing so should have more children, who can keep them from "brooding" about their lost ones. Those too old for any more children should remember the happiness of the past.

A 1 defense of their native land. They have blotted out evil with good, and done more service to the commonwealth than they ever did harm in their private lives. No one of these men weakened because he wanted to go on enjoying his wealth: no one put off the awful day in the hope that he might live to escape his poverty and grow rich. More to be desired than such things, they chose to check the enemy's pride. This, to them, was a risk most glorious, and they accepted it, willing to strike down the enemy and relinquish everything else. As for success or failure, they left that in the doubtful hands of Hope, and when the reality of battle was before their faces, they put their trust in their own selves. In the fighting, they thought it more honorable to stand their ground and suffer death than to give in and save their lives. So they fled from the reproaches of men, abiding with life and limb the brunt of battle; and, in a small moment of time, the climax of their lives, a culmination of glory, not of fear, were swept away from us.

B "So and such they were, these men—worthy of their city. We who remain behind may hope to be spared their fate, but must resolve to keep the same daring spirit against the foe. It is not simply a question of estimating the advantages in theory. I could tell you a long story (and you know it as well as I do) about what is to be gained by beating the enemy back. What I would 2 prefer is that you should fix your eyes every day on the greatness of Athens as she really is, and should fall in love with her. When you realize her greatness, then reflect that what made her great was men with a spirit of adventure, men who knew their duty, men who were ashamed to fall below a certain standard. If they ever failed in an enterprise, they made up their minds that at any rate the city should not find their courage lacking to her, and they gave to her the best

They have blotted out evil with good, and done more service to the commonwealth than they ever did harm in their private lives.

contribution that they could. They gave her their lives, to her and to all of us, and for their own selves they won praises that never grow old, the most splendid of sepulchers—not the sepulcher in which their bodies are laid, but where their glory remains eternal in men's minds, always there on the right occasion to stir others to speech or to action. For famous men have the whole earth as their memorial: it is not only the inscriptions on their graves in their own country that mark them out; no, in foreign lands also, not in any visible form but in people's hearts, their memory abides and grows. It is for you to try to be like them. Make up your minds that happiness depends on being free, and freedom 3 depends on being courageous. Let there be no relaxation in face of the perils of the war. The people who have most excuse for despising death are not the wretched and unfortunate, who have no hope of doing well for themselves, but those who run the risk of a complete reversal in their lives, and who would feel the difference most

WORDS TO KNOW

relinquish (rĭ-lĭng'kwĭsh) *v.* to give up; hand over
reproach (rĭ-prōch') *n.* blame; criticism
abiding (ə-bī'dĭng) *adj.* enduring **abide** *v.*
culmination (kŭl'mə-nā'shən) *n.* a high point or climax

Cross Curricular Link **Humanities**

HONOR Pericles presents a very different concept of honor than that presented in Homer's *Iliad.* In Homer's society, only the aristocrats can be said to possess honor because the aristocrats were recognized as naturally superior to the rest of society. The warriors, who were all aristocrats, were expected to act in honorable ways so that they would maintain their reputation among their peers. The virtues associated with honor—loyalty, courage, and excellence in battle—are all necessary for the success of the warrior band.

For Pericles, honor is a virtue available to all citizens, regardless of their position in society. Though the Athenian soldiers demonstrated the virtues of good warriors, what matters most is their motivation: they were acting to defend Athens and its ways of life. Their honor, to Pericles, must be viewed as the ultimate expression of a democratic society; they gave themselves freely for the sake of Athens.

At the feet of the goddess Athena, two Greek warriors draw lots (about 490 B.C.). Kunsthistorisches Museum, Vienna.

intensely, if things went wrong for them. Any intelligent man would find a humiliation caused by his own slackness more painful to bear than death, when death comes to him unperceived, in battle, and in the confidence of his patriotism.

C "For these reasons I shall not commiserate with those parents of the dead, who are present here. Instead I shall try to comfort them. They are well aware that they have grown up in a world where there are many changes and
4 chances. But this is good fortune—for men to end their lives with honor, as these have done, and for you honorably to lament them: their life was set to a measure where death and happiness went hand in hand. I know that it is difficult to convince you of this. When you see other people happy you will often be reminded of what used to make you happy too. One does not feel sad at not having some good thing which is outside one's experience: real grief is felt at the loss of something which one is used to. All the same, those of you who are of the right age must bear up and take comfort in the thought of having more children. In your own homes these new children will prevent you from brooding over those who are no more, and they will be a help to the city, too, both in filling the empty places, and in assuring her security. For it is impossible for a man to put forward fair and honest views about our affairs if he has not, like everyone else, children whose lives may be at stake. As for those of you who are now too old to have children, I would ask you to count as gain the greater part of your life, in which you have been happy, and remember that what remains is not long, and let your hearts be lifted up at the thought of the fair fame of the dead. One's sense of honor is the only thing that does not grow

Customizing Instruction

Less Proficient Readers

1 On the board, draw a balance, with the word *good* on one side and *evil* on the other. Ask students to think of examples of evil acts that the soldiers might have committed in their lives. List those acts above the word *evil* on the board. Ask students whether they agree with Pericles that an honorable death should count for more than previous deeds of evil. *(Accept all reasonable responses.)*

2 Ask students to imagine that they are in the audience listening to Pericles. Would they be moved by his words to love Athens? Why or why not? Encourage students to give examples from the essay to support their opinion. *(Accept all reasonable responses.)*

3 Ask students whether they agree with Pericles that "happiness depends on being free." *(Accept all reasonable responses.)*

4 Ask students to explain what they think Pericles means by "honor."
Possible Responses: For Pericles, honor means sacrificing your life for your community; showing courage in the face of danger; living—and dying—as a hero.

English Learners

Students may have difficulty with the following expressions:

Page 240:

- "So they fled from the reproaches of men" *(So they avoided the possibility of being criticized by other men)*
- "For famous men have the whole earth as their memorial" *(People who are famous will be remembered long after their death by people all over the world.)*

Page 241:

- "count as gain the greater part of your life" (consider most of your life—those years spent with your child—to be useful)

Advanced Learners

According to Aristotle, for a speech to be effective, the audience must respect the character of the speaker. Ask students what this speech reveals about the character of Pericles.
Possible Response: Pericles is a logical person, an eloquent speaker, and an ardent patriot who is committed to the principles represented by the Athenian democracy. He believes in freedom, appreciates beauty, promotes generosity, supports civic responsibility, and is willing to fight to protect what he loves.

Reading and Analyzing

Reading Skills and Strategies
EVALUATING

A Ask students what these comments reveal about Pericles' understanding of human nature.

Possible Response: He is a sharp judge of human nature because he realizes that the sons and brothers will face difficulties in their future. People will find them lacking in comparison to their dead fathers and brothers.

Literary Analysis CULTURAL SETTING

B Ask students what Pericles' comments reveal about the role of women in Athenian society.

Possible Response: Women clearly were not given the same respect or status as men. The women are advised to avoid drawing attention to themselves. Presumably, they should quietly fulfill their domestic duties, allowing men to run the state.

old, and the last pleasure, when one is worn out with age, is not, as the poet said, making money, but having the respect of one's fellow men.

"As for those of you here who are sons or brothers of the dead, I can see a hard struggle in front of you. Everyone always speaks well of the dead, and, even if you rise to the greatest heights of heroism, it will be a hard thing for you to get the reputation of having come near, let alone equaled, their standard. When one is alive, one is always liable to the jealousy of one's competitors, but when one is out of the way, the honor one receives is sincere and unchallenged. (A)

"Perhaps I should say a word or two on the duties of women to those among you who are now widowed. I can say all I have to say in a short word of advice. Your great glory is not to be inferior to what God has made you, and the greatest glory of a woman is to be least talked about by men, whether they are praising you or criticizing you. (B) I have now, as the law demanded, said what I had to say. For the time being our offerings to the dead have been made, and for the future their children will be supported at the public expense by the city, until they come of age. This is the crown and prize which she offers, both to the dead and to their children, for the ordeals which they have faced. Where the rewards of valor are the greatest, there you will find also the best and bravest spirits among the people. And now, when you have mourned for your dear ones, you must depart." ❖

MINI LESSON Informal Assessment

OUTLINING Have students work in pairs to create an outline of Pericles' speech. Refer them to the **Writing Handbook,** page R39, to see a model of an outline. Help students get started by demonstrating that the first three paragraphs constitute an introduction, beginning with the paragraph that starts on page 234 with "Many of those" and ending with the paragraph on page 236 that starts with "I have no wish." The first section of the outline might look like this:

I. Pericles' introduction
   A. Tells audience that a speech does not confer honor; actions do
   B. Recalls sacrifices of ancestors
   C. Sets purpose: to discuss the spirit of Athens and to praise the dead

RUBRIC

3 **Full Accomplishment** Student's outline provides a logical and complete presentation of major ideas.

2 **Substantial Accomplishment** Student's outline is generally effective, but may be missing a few key ideas or relationship between ideas may not be clear.

1 **Little or Partial Accomplishment** Student's outline is missing vital information or is not logically organized.

Connect to the Literature

1. **What Do You Think?** From your reading of the speech, what is your impression of Pericles? What details in the speech influenced your impression?

Comprehension Check
- According to Pericles, who has political power in Athens: a single person, a small group, or all the people?
- Who trains more rigorously for war, Athenians or Spartans?
- Which of these words describe the Athenians: thrifty, adventurous, generous, careless?

Think Critically

2. **ACTIVE READING: MAIN IDEA** Compare your  **READER'S NOTEBOOK** record of Pericles' main ideas with a partner's. What do you think are his most important ideas about Athens and the soldiers who died?

3. Pericles takes great pride in the democracy of Athens. Why is it important to him that all citizens participate in public life? Use details from the speech to support your conclusion.

4. Pericles says that Athens "deserves to be admired" for its approach to military security. Do you think he makes a convincing case? Explain why or why not.

THINK ABOUT
- his description of how the Spartans train for war
- his comment about the Spartans' use of allies
- the distinction he draws between "natural" and "state-induced" courage

5. Pericles asks his audience to "fix your eyes every day on the greatness of Athens" and to "fall in love with her." Why does Pericles think Athens is deserving of love? Use details from the text to support your response.

6. The soldiers who died, Pericles says, "won praises that never grow old." What do his comments reveal about the Athenians' view of honor?

Extend Interpretations

7. **Comparing Texts** Both Homer and Pericles celebrate military virtues, such as courage and honor. Discuss how Achilles' heroism compares with that of the Athenian soldiers memorialized by Pericles.

8. **Connect to Life** Do you think that Pericles' patriotism is still relevant today? Explain why or why not.

LITERARY ANALYSIS: AUTHOR'S PURPOSE

The most common purposes for writing or public speaking are to entertain, to inform or explain, to express an opinion, and to persuade. For example, a politician might give a speech to persuade people about an issue. A magazine writer might inform people about the same issue without taking a stand. Pericles announces his purposes on page 236, with the sentence that begins "What I want to do . . ."

Paired Activity Working with a partner, evaluate the success of Pericles' speech in fulfilling its purposes. Complete a chart like the one shown, giving a grade of 1 to 5 (with 1 being the lowest grade) for each purpose and explaining your reason.

Purpose	Success of Speech	
	Grade	Reason
To discuss the spirit of Athenians in facing trials		
To discuss Athens' constitution and the way of life that makes it great		
To speak in praise of the dead		

Connect to the Literature

1. **What Do You Think?** Accept all reasonable responses.

Comprehension Check
- all the people
- Spartans
- adventurous, generous

 Use Selection Quiz in **Unit Two Resource Book,** p. 22.

Think Critically

2. Possible Responses: Athens is a model to other cities because of its democracy; the Athenians know how to lead a balanced life, defending their city yet finding time for enjoyment; Athens is superior to Sparta in its free and open way of life; all Athenians take an active role in government; Athens wins friends through acts of kindness; the soldiers who died achieved glory; their fame should inspire the Athenians.
3. Possible Responses: According to Pericles, all citizens need to take an active interest in public life. In a democracy, power is in the hands of the "whole people," which requires that all citizens stay involved. Also, for the Athenians the well-being of the community is everyone's "business."
4. Possible Responses: Many students are likely to agree with Pericles. In his view, Sparta forces its male citizens to serve in the military, recruits allies to share in the fighting, and deports noncitizens to protect military secrets. By contrast, the Athenians fight their own battles; live without restrictions in their daily lives; and fight "voluntarily."
5. Possible Responses: Students may cite virtually any detail to support Pericles' claim that Athens is deserving of love, including the following: generations have made great sacrifices for Athens; the Athenian democracy is a model; the Athenians live balanced and productive lives; Athens is an open city that people serve freely; the Athenians love "what is beautiful" and know how to use wealth; all citizens take an interest in public life; the city is a good friend to its allies.
6. Possible Responses: The Athenians view honor as one of the highest virtues. Honor brings a kind of immortality because it preserves a person's reputation for generations to come.

Extend Interpretations

7. **Comparing Texts** For Achilles, honor is a way of celebrating individual greatness. Virtually everything that Achilles does is motivated by his desire to protect or enhance his own honor. He does not seem to care about the honor of his fellow Greeks, with the exception of Patroclus. By contrast, the Athenian soldiers did not act out of self-interest. Rather, their actions served the greater good of Athens. The soldiers gained honor because they sacrificed themselves for Athens.
8. **Connect to Life** Accept all reasonable responses.

Literary Analysis

Paired Activity Encourage each pair to discuss the speech first, based on the three purposes listed in the chart, before assigning grades. Explain that each grade will need to be supported by reasons based upon the text.

 Use **Unit Two Resource Book,** p. 20, for more practice.

Writing Options

1. **Extended Definition** Before students begin writing, discuss the various definitions of *patriotism* in the dictionary and their relevance to Pericles' speech. Make sure that students realize that an extended definition is longer and more elaborate than what is given in a dictionary.
2. **Analysis of Women's Role** You might want to give students the opportunity to expand their analysis by using other sources about the role of women in Athens, such as encyclopedias and online reference works. Also refer students to the information about Greek women on page 167. Make sure that students realize that most of Pericles' comments about Athens apply only to men.

Activities & Explorations

Athens vs. Sparta Debate Encourage students to review the information about Sparta and Athens on pages 166–167, as well as the section of Pericles' speech dealing with military security on page 237. You may wish to formulate a proposition for the debate, such as "Athens provides a better model than Sparta for the military security of the United States." One team could argue for the proposition; the other team could argue against it.

Inquiry & Research

Legacy of Pericles Encourage students to make use of multiple sources in their research. While encyclopedias provide a useful starting point, students should also look for essays and articles about Pericles. Plutarch's *Lives*, for example (available online), offers a not always flattering account of Pericles, which is both readable and brief.

Vocabulary in Action

1. a	6. a
2. b	7. b
3. a	8. c
4. b	9. b
5. c	10. c

To assess skills and concepts taught in this selection, use **Formal Assessment Book,** pp. 33–34.

Choices & CHALLENGES

Writing Options

1. Extended Definition Write an extended definition of patriotism based on Pericles' speech. First, find passages of the speech that show how he feels about Athens. Then arrange the passages into categories, like "Respect for Homeland's Ideals." Structure your writing by devoting a paragraph to each category.

2. Analysis of Women's Role Write an analysis of the role of women in Athenian society. First review the speech to find all of the references to women. Then draw conclusions about how women lived and what was expected of them. In your writing, use quotations from the speech.

Writing Handbook
See page R33: Analysis.

Activities & Explorations

Athens vs. Sparta Debate
With the class divided into two teams, debate the following question: Which city-state, Athens or Sparta, provides a better model for the way the United States should prepare for military conflict? Use examples from the speech to support your position. ~ **SPEAKING AND LISTENING**

Communication Handbook
See page R49: Critical Thinking.

Inquiry & Research

Find out more about the life and achievements of Pericles. In your judgment, was Pericles a true hero? Give an oral report in which you share the results of your research, along with your evaluation of the man's character.

Vocabulary in Action

EXERCISE: MEANING CLUES Choose the discussion topic in which each word would most likely be used.

1. **incredulous:** (a) a report that a spacecraft has landed downtown, (b) an apple tree flowering in the spring, (c) a family visiting relatives in another state
2. **abiding:** (a) a village marketplace, (b) a house where a family has lived for 50 years, (c) a car with a new paint job
3. **relinquish:** (a) a lost wallet handed over to the police, (b) a party attended by 30 guests, (c) an old-fashioned pocket watch found in an attic
4. **versatility:** (a) a beach crowded with swimmers, (b) a comedian who also sings and dances, (c) a left-handed person
5. **culmination:** (a) a collection of stamps, (b) a steep descent into a mountain valley, (c) a high-school graduation
6. **incompatibility:** (a) a married couple struggling to get along with one another, (b) a large, hard-to-service appliance, (c) a child afraid to sleep without a night light
7. **reproach:** (a) a cornfield buried in heavy snow, (b) a mother lecturing a disobedient child, (c) the building of a new road between towns
8. **revelation:** (a) a friend too busy to stay in touch, (b) a victory parade, (c) the reading of a long-lost relative's will
9. **tangible:** (a) light, puffy clouds, (b) firm evidence connecting a suspect to a crime, (c) four strong riders on a bicycle team
10. **undeterred:** (a) a driver sitting impatiently in rush-hour traffic, (b) a light breeze rustling through the trees, (c) a climber who reaches the top of a mountain

Building Vocabulary
A number of Words to Know in this lesson contain prefixes and suffixes. For an in-depth lesson on word parts, see page 340.

Nelson Mandela Celebrates a National Hero

Like Pericles, modern political leaders are sometimes called upon to honor those who have died for their country or ideals. In 1977 a famous political prisoner, Stephen Biko, died in a South African prison. Biko was a leader in the fight against apartheid, a government policy of racial segregation that discriminated against nonwhites. Later investigations revealed that Biko had been beaten to death by police officers.

In September 1997, Nelson Mandela, then the president of South Africa, gave a speech to pay tribute to Biko. As you read the following excerpts from his speech, look for similarities to Pericles' funeral oration.

Stephen Biko

"We are gathered here to pay homage to one of the greatest sons of our nation, Stephen Bantu Biko. His hope in life, and his life of hope, are captured by his resounding words: "In time, we shall be in a position to bestow on South Africa the greatest possible gift—a more human face." . . .

Today's occasion speaks of our resolve to preserve the memories of our heroes and heroines; to keep alive the flame of patriotism which burnt in the hearts and minds of the like of Steve Biko; to redeem the pledge to give a more human face to a society for centuries trampled upon by the jackboot of inhumanity. . . .

History called upon Steve Biko at a time when the political pulse of our people had been rendered faint by banning, imprisonment, exile, murder and banishment. . . .

It is the dictate of history to bring to the fore the kind of leaders who seize the moment, who cohere the wishes and aspirations of the oppressed. Such was Steve Biko, a fitting product of his time; a proud representative of the re-awakening of a people. . . .

In time, we must bestow on South Africa the greatest gift—a more humane society.

We are confident that by forging a new and prosperous nation, we are continuing the fight in which Steve Biko paid the supreme sacrifice."

Nelson Mandela (center) with Stephen Biko's sons

Discussion

1. What does Stephen Biko have in common with the Athenian soldiers praised by Pericles? Use quotations from both speeches to support your response.
2. Why was it important to Mandela to keep alive the memory of Biko? What did Mandela hope to accomplish for his country?

Connect to Today

Use this feature to show the relevance of world literature to students. The material relates the literature selection just read to a contemporary topic connected to students' lives today.

Historical Note

Stephen Biko was born on December 8, 1946. During the 1960s and 1970s, he was a leading activist in the struggle against South Africa's policy of apartheid. In 1969, he formed the South African Students' Organization and became its first president. Because of his political activities, Biko was "banned" in 1973, a government punishment that prohibited him from traveling, speaking in public, and writing for publication. Under the terms of his punishment, he could not meet with more than one nonfamily member at a time.

Biko was charged on multiple occasions for violations of South African law, but he was never convicted. In 1976, he was imprisoned for 101 days though charges were never filed. Biko was arrested again on August 18, 1977. Nearly a month later he died after having been severely beaten by police officers. Five officers confessed to the crime in 1997.

READING FOR INFORMATION

Reading Skills and Strategies

COMPARE AND CONTRAST

Draw a Venn diagram on the board, with one circle labeled *Biko* and the other labeled *Athenian soldiers.* Ask students what makes Biko different from the Athenian soldiers, and then fill in both circles with phrases from their responses.

Possible Responses: Biko was a social outcast because of his race; he was a victim of racism and injustice; he sacrificed his life trying to change his society for the better; he was a leader in the fight against oppression. The Athenian soldiers died trying to protect their existing way of life. Everyone in their society regarded them as heroes.

Discussion Questions

1. **Possible Response:** Both Biko and the soldiers sacrificed their life in service to a noble cause. The soldiers "gave her [Athens] their lives" and by doing so "won praises that never grow old." The example of their sacrifice will promote patriotism. Though the circumstances of Biko's death were much different, his sacrifice will also "keep alive the flame of patriotism." Biko's example will help future generations continue the fight for social justice.
2. **Possible Response:** Every nation needs heroes, and Stephen Biko seems a fitting hero for South Africa. By keeping alive the memory of Biko, Mandela may hope to inspire social activism and sacrifice to the common good. Biko's life may serve as a reminder of what was wrong with South Africa in the time of apartheid and as an inspiration for what South Africa might become, if citizens devote their lives to create a "more humane society."

Objectives

- understand and appreciate a **philosophical speech (Literary Analysis)**
- use strategies for **paraphrasing** text **(Active Reading)**

Summary

Socrates has been sentenced to death after being found guilty of neglecting the gods of Athens and corrupting the city's youth. In this speech, he explains to the jury why he has refused to defend himself or beg for mercy. He says that those who condemned him will in the end suffer more greatly than he will. As a way of consoling those who voted for his acquittal, Socrates explains that his conscience has led him to behave as he has. He considers his death as a blessing because it will either bring complete peace, like a dreamless sleep, or allow him to converse with the heroes of old. He closes by asking the jurors to guide his sons to put nothing ahead of goodness in their lives.

Use **Unit Two Resource Book,** p. 23, for additional support.

Thematic Link

Socrates achieves **glory and honor** not by heroism in battle but by adhering to moral principles, even at the price of death.

Use **Unit Two Resource Book,** p. 26, for practice with Words to Know.

5-Minute Warm-Up

Daily Language SkillBuilder

Have students **proofread** the display sentences on page 161i and write them correctly.

PREPARING to *Read*

from the

PLATO

Plato
c. 427–347 B.C.

Influential Philosopher Many regard Plato as the most influential philosopher in the history of the Western world. Most of what we know about Plato comes from his own writings. He was born, probably in Athens, to a high-ranking family. In his youth, he wrote poetry and reportedly was a champion wrestler. His life took an abrupt turn, however, when he became a devoted follower of Socrates.

Plato's Teacher, Socrates At this time, Socrates was an odd character—a poor old man who refused to wear shoes and who walked the streets of Athens in a shabby cloak. Socrates loved to engage people in philosophical conversations. Through a series of questions, he would lead people to examine their own thinking about concepts such as virtue, justice, and truth—a technique that became known as the Socratic method. Though Socrates was popular with the young, some Athenians viewed him as a threat to Athenian traditions and ideals. In 399 B.C., a group of citizens came together to prosecute him, charging him with neglecting the gods of Athens and corrupting its youth.

The Academy Socrates' conviction and execution for these "crimes" deeply affected Plato. He concluded that if humans were ever to rise above their narrow self-interests, they needed to be educated in philosophy. Around 387 B.C., Plato established a school, the Academy, where he invited only those individuals who were, in his words, "intoxicated to learn what was in their souls." The Academy—which some have called the first university of Europe—was actually a park, with groves of beautiful trees, running tracks, and shady walks, where students and teachers gathered to discuss ideas.

Plato's Legacy The Academy survived as a cultural institution for hundreds of years after Plato's death. In addition to influencing the development of mathematics, astronomy, philosophy, law, and political science, Plato's ideas have had a major impact on Jewish, Christian, and Islamic thought.

Other Works
Republic
Crito
Phaedo
Symposium

LESSON RESOURCES

UNIT TWO RESOURCE BOOK, pp. 23–27

ASSESSMENT RESOURCES
Formal Assessment, pp. 35–36
Teacher's Guide to Assessment and Portfolio Use
Test Generator

INTEGRATED TECHNOLOGY
Visit our Web site: classzone.com

ADDITIONAL RESOURCES
Lesson Planning Guide, pp. 27–28
Teacher's Sourcebook for Language Development

Connect to Your Life

In his speeches to the jury, Socrates refuses to compromise his principles, even though he knows his life is at stake. What is your attitude toward people who refuse to compromise their principles?

Focus Your Reading

LITERARY ANALYSIS: SPEECH

Most of Plato's works are **dialogues,** representations of conversations between two or more people. The *Apology,* however, consists of Socrates' speeches to the jury at his trial. You are about to read his concluding **speech,** or public talk, which takes place just after the jury has announced his death sentence. As you read, pay attention to how Socrates presents himself and to how he views the two sides of the jury—those who voted for his death and those who did not.

ACTIVE READING: PARAPHRASING

When you read a challenging work, such as this speech, it is often helpful to **paraphrase** passages, restating them in your own words. When you paraphrase, you try to express the author's meaning in a simpler way. The following passage is important for an understanding of Socrates' position:

> ***But I suggest, gentlemen, that the difficulty is not so much to escape death; the real difficulty is to escape from doing wrong, which is far more fleet of foot.***

This passage may be paraphrased as follows: "Our greatest challenge in life is not avoiding death, but avoiding evil, which comes upon us more quickly than death."

READER'S NOTEBOOK As you read, look for passages that you think are especially important or difficult. In your notebook, restate these passages in your own words.

WORDS TO KNOW **Vocabulary Preview**

annihilation disparage unscrupulous
culpable reconcile

Build Background

The Trial of Socrates

When Socrates was put on trial in 399 B.C., Athens was in a period of great turmoil. The city had been defeated by Sparta in 404 B.C. The Spartans forced Athens to install new rulers—a group known as the Thirty Tyrants—some of whom had been friends and followers of Socrates. These rulers, however, turned out to be corrupt and brutal. When democratic rule returned to Athens in 403 B.C., critics of Socrates blamed him for the abuses of the Thirty Tyrants, even though he had publicly disobeyed their orders.

Other citizens resented Socrates because he seemed to mock the traditions and values of Athens. Feelings of ill will intensified until Socrates, at age 70, was brought to trial. A jury of 500 male citizens heard the charges against him; then Socrates presented his own defense. Instead of trying to win the sympathy of the jury, Socrates refused to compromise. Even after he was found guilty, he might have escaped the death penalty by proposing a lesser penalty. But he proposed that the city reward him for his service to virtue and truth. Many jurors were insulted by his attitude, and, by a majority of votes, Socrates was sentenced to death. He was made to drink a potion containing hemlock, a deadly poison. Plato attended Socrates' trial and later based the *Apology* on his memory of what he had heard.

READING FOR INFORMATION

Reading Skills and Strategies

ACTIVATING PRIOR KNOWLEDGE

Encourage students to combine what they might already know about Socrates and Plato with the information presented here. Before students begin reading pages 246 and 247, write *Plato* and *Socrates* on the board, and then solicit information about both philosophers from students. Jot down phrases under each name to summarize what students already know. After students have read these two pages, discuss what new information was learned. Add phrases to each list on the board.

Then invite students to raise questions that might be answered in the selection. Write the questions on the board and encourage students to refer to them as they read the selection.

Historical Note

Socrates could have avoided the death penalty by taking either of two steps. He could have gone into voluntary exile before the verdict was announced, which was a typical course of action for citizens facing serious charges. Once the death penalty was invoked, he could have proposed his banishment as an alternative, which would have probably been acceptable to the jury. The sentencing vote to condemn Socrates to death actually passed by a wider margin than the trial vote that found him guilty in the first place. Socrates' unwillingness to compromise on the issue of his sentencing turned jurors against him.

TIME MANAGEMENT

If your schedule requires that you cover the lesson objectives in a shorter time, use . . .

- Preparing to Read, pp. 246–247
- Thinking Through the Literature, pp. 254–255
- Vocabulary in Action, p. 255

If you want to take advantage of longer blocks of class time, use . . .

- TE Teaching Options: Cross Curricular Link, p. 251; Viewing and Representing, pp. 249, 252; Vocabulary Strategy, p. 248; Standardized Test Practice, p. 253
- Choices & Challenges, p. 255

Literary Analysis ALLUSION

A Explain that Socrates was often referred to as a "wise man," though he did not claim such wisdom. A friend of Socrates once visited the oracle at Delphi and asked if any man was wiser than Socrates. The oracle replied that none were. Socrates interpreted this comment to mean that he was wise only because he admitted his own ignorance, in contrast to others who mistakenly claimed wisdom for themselves.

Active Reading PARAPHRASING

B Ask students to put this statement, beginning with "It is not" and ending with "other people," into their own words.

Possible Response: I wasn't condemned because I lacked convincing arguments for my case. You condemned me because I was not bold or shameless enough to flatter you. You would have liked to see me cry and express grief about my situation, which would be unworthy of me, though you are used to seeing such behavior in others.

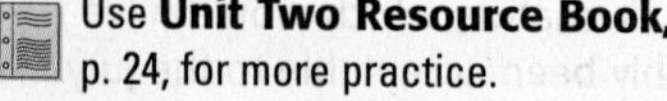
Use **Unit Two Resource Book,** p. 24, for more practice.

Literary Analysis SPEECH

C Point out that Socrates describes himself as a slow man who has been overtaken by death, which is swifter than he is. His accusers, however, though they are quick, have been overtaken by evil. Ask students why Socrates might have used the imagery of racing to describe himself and his accusers.

Possible Response: The imagery of a race would be familiar to Athenians because racing was a popular sport. He is making the point that it is only natural that death should be able to overtake an old man, but it is shocking and scandalous that his younger accusers gave in to evil.

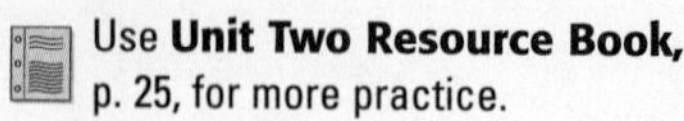
Use **Unit Two Resource Book,** p. 25, for more practice.

from the Apology

Plato

Translated by Hugh Tredennick

Well, gentlemen, for the sake of a very small gain in time you are going to earn the reputation—and the blame from those who wish to
A disparage our city—of having put Socrates to death, "that wise man"—because they will say I am wise even if I am not, these people who want to find fault with you.
1 If you had waited just a little while, you would have had your way in the course of nature. You can see that I am well on in life and near to death. I am saying this not to all of you but to those who voted for my execution, and I have something else to say to them as well.

No doubt you think, gentlemen, that I have been condemned for lack of the arguments which I could have used if I had thought it right to leave nothing unsaid or undone to secure my acquittal. But that is very far from the truth.
B It is not a lack of arguments that has caused my condemnation, but a lack of effrontery[1] and impudence, and the fact that I have refused to address you in the way which would give you most pleasure. You would have liked to hear me weep and wail, doing and saying all sorts of things which I regard as unworthy of myself, but which you are used to hearing from other people. But I did not think then that I ought to stoop to servility[2] because I was in danger, and I do not regret now the way in which I pleaded
2 my case. I would much rather die as the result of this defense than live as the result of the other sort. In a court of law, just as in warfare, neither I nor any other ought to use his wits to escape death by any means. In battle it is often obvious that you could escape being killed by giving up your arms and throwing yourself upon the mercy of your pursuers, and in every kind of danger there are plenty of devices for avoiding death if you are unscrupulous enough to stick at nothing. But I suggest, gentlemen, that the difficulty is not so much to escape death; the real difficulty is to escape from doing wrong, which is far more fleet of foot. 3
C In this present instance I, the slow old man, have been overtaken by the slower of the two, but my accusers, who are clever and quick, have been overtaken by the faster—by iniquity.[3] When I leave this court I shall go away condemned by you to death, but they will go away convicted by truth herself of depravity[4] and wickedness. And they accept their sentence even as I accept mine. No doubt it was bound to be so, and I think that the result is fair enough.

Having said so much, I feel moved to prophesy to you who have given your vote against me, for I am now at that point where the gift of prophecy comes most readily to men—at the point of death. I tell you, my executioners, that as soon as I am dead, vengeance shall fall upon you with a punishment far more painful than your killing of me. 4 You have brought about my death in the belief that through it you will be delivered from submitting your conduct to

1. **effrontery** (ĭ-frŭn′tə-rē): rude boldness.
2. **servility** (sər-vĭl′ĭ-tē): disgracefully humble behavior.
3. **iniquity** (ĭ-nĭk′wĭ-tē): wickedness.
4. **depravity** (dĭ-prăv′ĭ-tē): evil; corruption.

WORDS TO KNOW

disparage (dĭ-spăr′ĭj) *v.* to speak in a slighting way of; belittle

unscrupulous (ŭn-skrōō′pyə-ləs) *adj.* lacking a sense of right and wrong

248

MINI LESSON Vocabulary Strategy

CONTEXT CLUES

Instruction Students are expected to rely on context to determine the meaning of words. Have students read the first paragraph on page 248 of the *Apology*. Point out the idiomatic phrase "in the course of nature." Have students make inferences about the meaning of the phrase by examining the meaning of the words and sentences surrounding it. The phrases "well on in life" and "near death" indicate that *in the course of nature* means "in time" or "through the ordinary passage of time."

Practice Have students use context clues to infer the meaning of the following words or phrases, and explain how the context helped them.

1. "stoop to servility," second paragraph on page 248 *(lower oneself; act in an overly humble way,* as suggested by "weep and wail" and "things which I regard as unworthy of myself")
2. "amiss," first paragraph on page 250 *(wrong; faulty,* from its similarity to the common expression "faulty reasoning")

A lesson on using context clues appears on p. 674 in the Pupil's Edition.

Roman mosaic of the School of Plato. Museo Archeologico Nazionale, Naples, Italy. Alinari/Art Resource, New York.

HUMANITIES CONNECTION This Roman mosaic shows Plato at his Academy in Athens. Plato is holding a stick, which he may be using to draw a geometrical figure in the sand. The Acropolis is shown at top right.

Customizing Instruction

Less Proficient Readers

Many students may have difficulty with Plato's text because of the length and complexity of the sentences. Ask the following questions to help students recognize main ideas:

1 Socrates says that if his accusers would have "waited just a little while," they would have what they wanted. What do they want? *(his death)*

2 Socrates insists that he would rather die than have to defend himself in a different way. What would be so wrong if Socrates had defended himself in a different way?
Possible Response: He would be violating his own moral principles. Socrates does not believe that he has done anything wrong; he is not going to beg for mercy or humiliate himself.

3 Socrates says that evil is more of a threat to people than death. What do you think he means?
Possible Responses: Everyone will eventually die, but death is not an evil by itself. Evil is more of a threat than death, perhaps because it's so easy to do a wicked act.

4 Socrates says that his "executioners"—those who voted against him—will face vengeance after his death. Why might people blame the jury for his death? *(They will think that it was wrong to put a good man to death.)*

English Learners

Explain the meaning of the following phrases:

- "well on in life" *(old)*
- "leave nothing unsaid or undone" *(do everything possible)*
- "convicted by truth herself of depravity and wickedness" *(judged harshly for acts of evil)*
- "vengeance shall fall upon you" *(you will be punished for your evil)*

MINI LESSON Viewing and Representing

Roman mosaic of the School of Plato

ART APPRECIATION This wall panel, found in 1897 near Pompeii, Italy, depicts a meeting of seven philosophers. Point out other instruments of scientific and philosophic inquiry, such as the celestial sphere contained in the box on the ground and the sundial that stands behind the men. Ask students to study the mosaic and the **Humanities Connection** and to identify other means by which the artist suggested intellectual activity.

Possible Response: The facial expressions, postures, and arm positions of the subjects are all consistent with intellectual activity. For example, a man sits across from Plato, gazing intently at the philosopher with his chin resting on his hand. Next to that man, another man sits with upraised hand, as if seeking clarification or making a point. In the bottom left corner, two men seem to be having a separate conversation. Two of the men in the mosaic are holding what seem to be scrolls, another suggestion of the life of the mind.

Reading and Analyzing

Active Reading PARAPHRASING

A Ask students to paraphrase the passage that begins with "If you expect" and ends with "as you can."

Possible Response: If you think that you can avoid criticism of your evil life by having me put to death, you are mistaken. That way of escape is neither possible nor honorable. The best way to avoid criticism is to be a good man.

Literary Analysis SPEECH

B Explain that Socrates has up to this point been addressing those who condemned him. Now he turns his attention towards those who found him innocent. Ask students what Socrates means when he says that he will "reconcile" these jurors to "the result."

Possible Response: Socrates realizes that these jurors are upset by the verdict. He will help them accept it or come to terms with it.

Literary Analysis ALLUSION

C Explain that Socrates often mentioned this "prophetic voice." It was a kind of inner voice that had accompanied him since childhood. At times in his life, the voice warned him to turn back from actions. Because of this voice, which Socrates believed to come from the gods, Socrates did not take part in politics.

Literary Analysis SOCRATIC DIALOGUE

D This passage describes Socrates' way of searching for the truth. In his dialogues with individuals, he typically discovered that they were not as wise as they claimed to be.

THE BEST AND EASIEST WAY IS NOT TO STOP THE MOUTHS OF OTHERS, BUT TO MAKE YOURSELVES AS GOOD MEN AS YOU CAN.

criticism, but I say that the result will be just the opposite. You will have more critics, whom up till now I have restrained without your knowing it, and being younger they will be harsher to you and will cause you more annoyance. If you expect to stop denunciation[5] of your wrong way
A of life by putting people to death, there is some-
1 thing amiss[6] with your reasoning. This way of escape is neither possible nor creditable. The best and easiest way is not to stop the mouths of others, but to make yourselves as good men as you can. This is my last message to you who voted for my condemnation.

As for you who voted for my acquittal, I should very much like to say a few words to
B reconcile you to the result, while the officials are busy and I am not yet on my way to the place where I must die. I ask you, gentlemen, to spare me these few moments. There is no reason why we should not exchange fancies while the law permits. I look upon you as my friends, and I want you to understand the right way of regarding my present position.

Gentlemen of the jury—for *you* deserve to be so called—I have had a remarkable experience. In the past the prophetic voice[7] to which I have
become accustomed has always been my con- C
stant companion, opposing me even in quite trivial things if I was going to take the wrong course. Now something has happened to me, as you can see, which might be thought and is commonly considered to be a supreme calamity; yet neither when I left home this morning, nor when I was taking my place here in the court, nor at
any point in any part of my speech did the divine 2
sign oppose me. In other discussions it has often checked me in the middle of a sentence, but this time it has never opposed me in any part of this business in anything that I have said or done. What do I suppose to be the explanation? I will tell you. I suspect that this thing that has happened to me is a blessing, and we are quite mistaken in supposing death to be an evil. I have good grounds for thinking this, because my accustomed sign could not have failed to oppose me if what I was doing had not been sure to bring some good result.

We should reflect that there is much reason to hope for a good result on other grounds as well. Death is one of two things. Either it is annihilation, and the dead have no consciousness of anything, or, as we are told, it is really a change—a migration[8] of the soul from this place to another. Now if there is no consciousness but only a dreamless sleep, death must be a

5. **denunciation** (dĭ-nŭn′sē-ā′shən): disapproval; condemnation.
6. **amiss:** wrong; faulty.
7. **prophetic voice:** Socrates believed that at times he heard a divine voice warning him to avoid particular actions.
8. **migration** (mī-grā′shən): movement.

WORDS TO KNOW

reconcile (rĕk′ən-sīl′) *v.* to bring into agreement or harmony; cause to accept
annihilation (ə-nī′ə-lā′shən) *n.* a ceasing to exist; total destruction

marvelous gain. I suppose that if anyone were told to pick out the night on which he slept so soundly as not even to dream, and then to compare it with all the other nights and days of his life, and then were told to say, after due consideration, how many better and happier days and nights than this he had spent in the course of his life—well, I think that the Great King[9] himself, to say nothing of any private person, would find these days and nights easy to count in comparison with the rest. If death is like this, then, I call it gain, because the whole of time, if you look at it in this way, can be regarded as no more than one single night. If on the other hand death is a removal from here to some other place, and if
3 what we are told is true, that all the dead are there, what greater blessing could there be than this, gentlemen? If on arrival in the other world, beyond the reach of our so-called justice, one will find there the true judges who are said to preside in those courts, Minos and Rhadamanthus and Aeacus and Triptolemus[10] and all those other half-divinities who were upright in their earthly life, would that be an unrewarding journey? Put it in this way. How much would one of you give to meet Orpheus and Musaeus, Hesiod[11] and Homer? I am willing to die ten times over if this account is true. It would be a specially interesting experience for me to join them there, to meet Palamedes and Ajax, the son of Telamon,[12] and any other heroes of the old days who met their death through an unfair trial, and to compare my fortunes with theirs—it would be rather amusing, I think. And above all I should like to spend my
D time there, as here, in examining and searching people's minds, to find out who is really wise among them, and who only thinks that he is. What would one not give, gentlemen, to be able to question the leader of that great host against Troy, or Odysseus, or Sisyphus,[13] or the thousands of other men and women whom one could mention, to talk and mix and argue with whom would be unimaginable happiness? At any rate I presume that they do not put one to death there for such conduct, because apart from the other happiness in which their world surpasses ours, they are now immortal for the rest of time, if what we are told is true.

You too, gentlemen of the jury, must look forward to death with confidence, and fix your minds on this one belief, which is certain—that

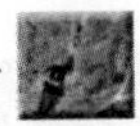

NOTHING CAN HARM A GOOD MAN EITHER IN LIFE OR AFTER DEATH, AND HIS FORTUNES ARE NOT A MATTER OF INDIFFERENCE TO THE GODS.

9. **the Great King:** Zeus.
10. **Minos** (mī′nəs) **and Rhadamanthus** (răd′ə-măn′thəs) **and Aeacus** (ē′ə-kəs) **and Triptolemus** (trĭp-tŏl′ə-məs): legendary rulers who were believed to serve as judges of the souls of the dead.
11. **Orpheus** (ôr′fyo͞os) **and Musaeus** (myo͞o-sē′əs), **Hesiod** (hē′sē-əd): like Homer, famous early Greek poets. (The first two are almost certainly mythical figures.)
12. **Palamedes** (păl′ə-mē′dēz) **and Ajax** (ā′jăks′), **son of Telamon** (tĕl′ə-mŏn′): two legendary participants in the Trojan War. Palamedes was unjustly executed for treason; Ajax, after being judged less worthy than Odysseus to receive Achilles' armor, killed himself in a fit of insanity.
13. **Sisyphus** (sĭs′ə-fəs): the legendary founder of the city of Corinth, famous for his cleverness.

Customizing Instruction

Less Proficient Readers

1 Explain that Socrates' way of living makes jurors uncomfortable because he points out flaws in their beliefs and actions. Ask students why putting Socrates to death won't make life any easier for these people. *(Others will still criticize them for doing wrong.)*

2 Explain that Socrates' "divine sign" acts as his conscience, telling him when to avoid evil. Socrates now interprets the silence of his divine sign, or prophetic voice, to mean that death is a blessing.

3 Remind students that the Greeks believed in an afterlife where the souls of the dead could converse with one another. Ask students why this kind of existence would be a blessing to Socrates. *(He loved to spend his time talking to people, questioning them about important issues.)*

English Learners

Explain the meanings of the following phrases on page 250:

- "not to stop the mouths of others" *(not to force people to be silent)*
- "exchange fancies" *(talk freely with one another)*
- "supreme calamity" *(ultimate disaster)*
- "dreamless sleep" *(completely peaceful sleep)*

Advanced Learners

Ask students to compare Socrates' view of his fellow Athenians with the view expressed by Pericles.

Possible Response: Socrates expresses a negative view of many citizens. The Athenians seem to have condemned him because he would not compromise his principles. Those who pressed charges against him acted wickedly. By contrast, Pericles expresses an idealistic view of the Athenians, whom he portrays as generous, principled, and self-sacrificing.

Cross Curricular Link History

SOCRATES AND HIS LEGACY Socrates lived in a city that equated physical beauty and grace with moral excellence, but he was an ugly man. In sharp contrast to the idealized human figures created by Athenian sculptors and painters, he had a snub nose, bulging eyes, a balding head, and protruding belly. His eyes were said to roll in a peculiar way when he conversed with others, a trait ridiculed by the playwright Aristophanes, who created a foolish and hopelessly unworldly philosopher named Socrates in *The Clouds.* In the wealthy city of Athens, Socrates refused to be paid for his teaching; he wore a ragged cloak; and he typically walked barefoot. Though he lived in a city in which women were expected to be quiet and submissive to their husbands, Socrates' wife was reputedly a shrew.

Yet many would argue that Socrates had a greater impact on the world than any other Athenian. His searching habits of thought influenced the entire course of Western philosophy. His moral teachings have been compared to those of Jesus, Buddha, and Confucius in their influence. People as diverse as Martin Luther King, Jr., Leo Tolstoy, and Henry David Thoreau have drawn inspiration from his life and philosophy.

APOLOGY 251

Reading and Analyzing

Active Reading PARAPHRASING

A Point out that "mechanically" here means by chance. Then ask students to paraphrase the passage beginning with "This present experience" and ending with "turned me back."

Possible Response: My being condemned to death did not happen by chance. I believe that the time has come for me to die so that I can be released from my troubles. That is why my divine sign never urged me to stop.

Literary Analysis SPEECH

B Make sure that students realize that Socrates is once again addressing those jurors who found him guilty. He is asking them to watch over his sons and to criticize them if they do wrong.

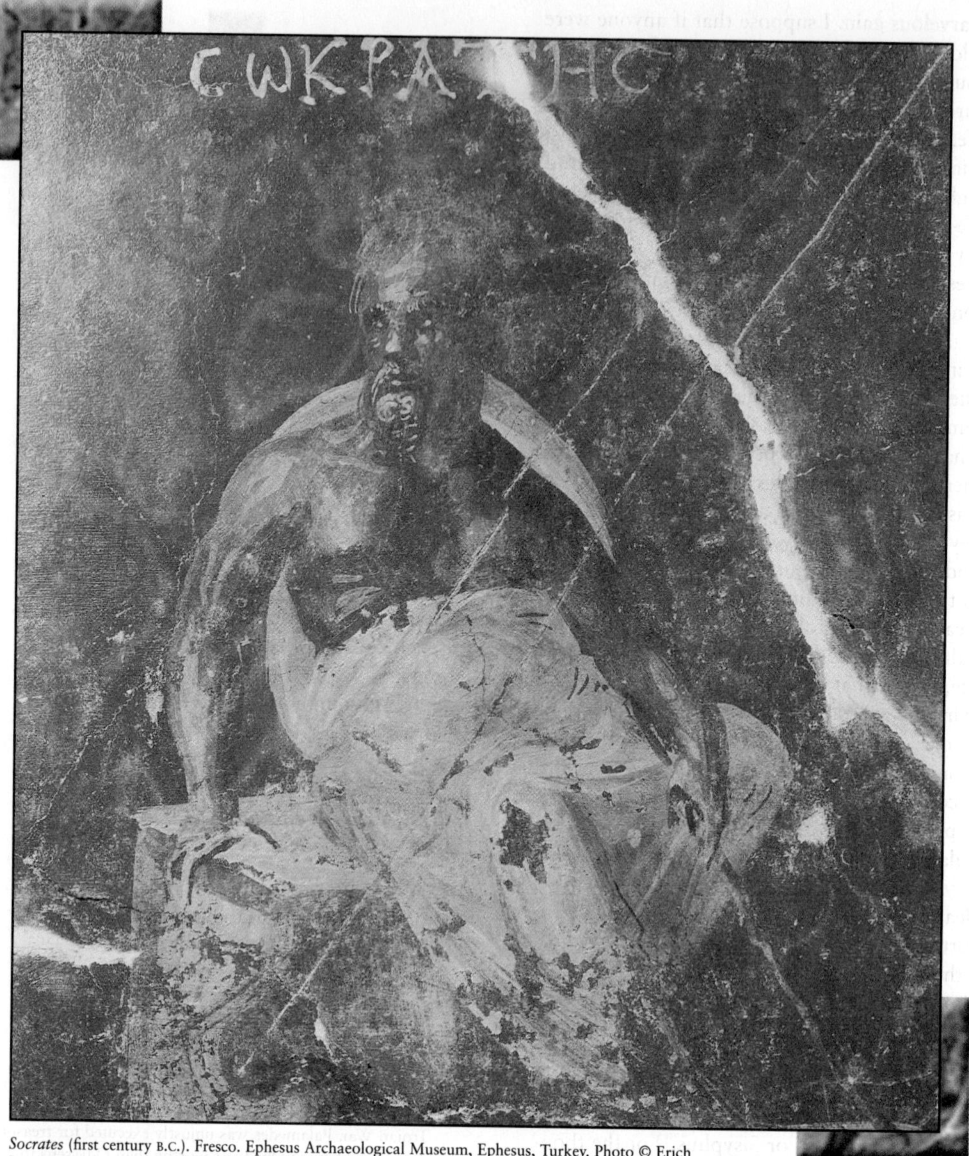

Socrates (first century B.C.). Fresco. Ephesus Archaeological Museum, Ephesus, Turkey. Photo © Erich Lessing/Art Resource, New York.

HUMANITIES CONNECTION This fresco—a painting done on fresh, moist wall plaster—depicting Socrates is from a Roman house at Ephesus (in what is now western Turkey).

MINI LESSON Viewing and Representing

Fresco of Socrates

ART APPRECIATION Have students study the illustration and the **Humanities Connection** on page 252. This fresco panel—one of only a few fresco portraits of Socrates in the world—was discovered in 1963 during the excavations of a private house located in Ephesus in present-day Turkey. The image of Socrates here bears a resemblance to earlier Greek statues of him, which portray a short, unattractive, pug-nosed man consistent with descriptions of Socrates in ancient texts. During the Roman Empire, private citizens often decorated their houses with images drawn from Greek history and mythology.

Ask students how this image of Socrates compares with their own mental image of the philosopher. *(Accept all reasonable responses.)*

nothing can harm a good man either in life or after death, and his fortunes are not a matter of indifference to the gods. This present experience of mine has not come about mechanically. I am quite clear that the time had come when it was better for me to die and be released from my distractions. That is why my sign never turned me back. For my own part I bear no grudge at all against those who condemned me and accused me, although it was not with this kind intention that they did so, but because they thought that they were hurting me; and that is culpable of them. However, I ask them to grant me one favor. When my sons grow up, gentlemen, if you think that they are putting money or anything else before goodness, take your revenge by plaguing them as I plagued you; and if they fancy themselves for no reason, you must scold them just as I scolded you, for neglecting the important things and thinking that they are good for something when they are good for nothing. If you do this, I shall have had justice at your hands, both I myself and my children.

Now it is time that we were going, I to die and you to live, but which of us has the happier prospect is unknown to anyone but God. ❖

WORDS TO KNOW

culpable (kŭl'pə-bəl) *adj.* deserving of blame

Customizing Instruction

Less Proficient Readers

Ask students to name three main ideas that are expressed on this page.

Possible Response:

1) Socrates says that this is the right time for him to die.
2) He does not resent those who condemned him even though they were wrong.
3) Socrates asks jurors to watch over his sons and to criticize them if they do wrong.

English Learners

Explain the meaning of the following phrases:

- "released from my distractions" *(released from my troubles)*
- "plaguing them"*(annoying or pestering them)*
- "which of us has the happier prospect is unknown to anyone but God" *(only God knows whether you or I will be happier in the future.)*

Advanced Learners

Invite students to read Xenophon's version of Socrates' *Apology*, which is available online. Ask students to contrast Socrates' view of his death in that work with the view expressed in Plato's version.

Possible Response: In Xenophon's version, Socrates looks forward to death as a way of avoiding the illnesses and weaknesses of old age. In Plato's version, Socrates never mentions those issues; rather, he looks forward to death because it will either give him complete peace or a chance to converse with great people from the past.

MINI LESSON Standardized Test Practice

IDENTIFYING THE MAIN IDEA Standardized tests often ask students to select the best main idea for a passage that they have read. Write the following question and answer choices on the board: Which statement best expresses Socrates' attitude towards death?

A. Because death will come to all of us, we should enjoy life while we can.

B. Death may bring about a dreamless sleep, which is a frightening prospect.

C. Death should not be feared because it is either peaceful or it will lead to another interesting world.

D. We will all have a chance to talk to the heroes of the past, so we should look forward to dying.

Lead students through the possible answers. Although many people may agree with the sentiments expressed in statement *A*, it does not represent Socrates' view. Statement *B* is partially correct–Socrates would agree with the first part–but the second part of the sentence does not reflect Socrates' view. Statement *D* is also partially correct, but it does consider the possibility that the dead "have no consciousness of anything" (p. 250). Statement *C* is the best choice because it offers the most complete and accurate account of Socrates' thought.

Connect to the Literature

1. **What Do You Think?** Accept all reasonable responses.

Comprehension Check

- He felt that telling the jury what it wanted to hear would compromise his principles.
- He received no message from his "prophetic voice" urging him to stop.
- He would like to be able to converse with the heroes of old.

Use Selection Quiz in **Unit Two Resource Book,** p. 27.

Think Critically

2. Students may pick any number of passages as being the most important or difficult. Allow time in class for students to work in pairs to edit their work.
3. Possible Responses: Socrates is cheerful because he is not afraid of what lies ahead. If death is "annihilation," he believes that it will be completely peaceful. If death is a "migration" to another world, he looks forward to meeting great people from the past. Socrates has a philosophic temperament, which enables him to face death without worry or dread. He is also courageous, so he does not allow himself to give in to fear or doubt.
4. Possible Responses: Socrates has devoted his life to virtue. It is more important for him to "escape from doing wrong" than to save his own life. He feels that moral principles should not be compromised, even at the risk of death. He is a religious man who listens to the "prophetic voice" within him whenever it opposes a course of action. Though Socrates considers the possibility that death is "annihilation," he seems to believe in an afterlife that would allow him to continue to be a philosopher in the next world. His statement about his sons shows that "goodness" comes before everything in his life.

Extend Interpretations

5. **Comparing Texts** Some students will find Pericles more heroic. They may be drawn to his idealistic vision of Athens and the way of life that it represents. Such students may note Pericles' contributions to democracy, to art, to the ideal of equality before the law, and to the glory of Athens. Other students may find Socrates more heroic because he stands apart from the crowd and sacrifices his own welfare and life for the sake of his principles. Such students may be drawn to Socrates' moral courage, his honesty, and his calm in the face of death. A few students may find both men equally heroic.
6. **Critic's Corner** Accept all reasonable responses. Encourage students to give reasons in support of their point of view.
7. **Connect to Today** Accept all reasonable responses.

Literary Analysis

Paired Activity Before students begin, have them identify which segments of the speech are directed toward those who voted to convict and which segments are directed toward those who voted for acquittal.

Use **Unit Two Resource Book,** p. 25, for more practice.

Connect to the Literature

1. **What Do You Think?** What are your impressions of Socrates as a person? Explain your judgment.

Comprehension Check

- Why didn't Socrates tell the jury what it wanted to hear?
- What does Socrates take as a sign that his death sentence is a "blessing"?
- What does Socrates say he would like about an afterlife?

Think Critically

2. **ACTIVE READING: PARAPHRASING** What do you think are the most important or difficult passages in this speech? Work with a partner to review and edit the paraphrases in your  READER'S NOTEBOOK. Then read aloud to your classmates one text passage and your paraphrase of it.
3. Socrates says that death is either "annihilation" or "a migration of the soul from this place to another." Why do you think Socrates is so cheerful in the face of death?
4. What values are most important to Socrates? Support your judgment with evidence from the text.

THINK ABOUT
- the way he chooses to defend himself
- the role that the "prophetic voice" plays in his life
- his final request about his sons

Extend Interpretations

5. **Comparing Texts** Socrates and Pericles represent two very different kinds of **heroes.** Pericles represented the Athenian ideal. He was a gifted leader and a wealthy aristocrat who was physically attractive and beloved by most citizens. Of these two men, which do you find more heroic? Use evidence from the *Apology* and *Pericles' Funeral Oration* to support your judgment.
6. **Critic's Corner** The scholar Gregory Vlastos has written that for Socrates "virtue matters more for your own happiness than does everything else put together." Do you think that Socrates was right? Give your reasons.
7. **Connect to Today** Earlier in the *Apology,* Socrates refers to himself as a "gadfly," an insect that annoys cattle. Socrates annoyed many Athenians because he made them think about their responsibility to be virtuous. Who are the gadflies of today? In what ways are they like Socrates?

LITERARY ANALYSIS: SPEECH

In ancient Greece, a **speech,** a formal talk in a public arena, was considered the most important form of communication. In fact, the Sophists (sŏf'ĭsts), Greek philosophers who were paid teachers, trained young men in the techniques of artful speaking. To be effective, a speech was supposed to express the character and authority of the speaker and appeal to the judgment and emotions of the audience.

Paired Activity With a partner, review Socrates' speech. Examine his description of his own character, as well as his attitudes toward the members of the jury who voted to convict him and toward those who voted to acquit him. Record your findings in a graphic organizer like the one shown.

How Socrates Describes His Character	Says that he will not do things "unworthy" of himself
Attitude Toward Those Who Voted to Convict	
Attitude Toward Those Who Voted to Acquit	

Writing Options

1. Dramatic Scene Imagine that Socrates meets with one of the prosecutors after his trial. Write a brief dramatic scene presenting the encounter. You may include other people in the scene, such as members of the jury and Socrates' friends. Drawing on what you have read about the trial, make up dialogue that you think would be believable. Place your writing in your **Working Portfolio.**

2. Newspaper Editorial The jury's decision in the trial of Socrates has been debated for centuries. Some people say that Socrates gave the jury no choice and brought about his own conviction. Others argue that the jury's decision was a great injustice. Read the rest of the *Apology* and decide whether the jury made the correct decision. Write a newspaper editorial that either praises or condemns the decision.

Writing Handbook
See page R35: Persuasive Writing.

Activities & Explorations

1. Philosophical Dialogue Socrates was famous for making people feel uncomfortable by asking them questions that challenged their whole way of thinking. With a partner, create an impromptu dialogue between Socrates and a prominent person in today's society. Socrates should ask a series of questions that challenge the values and beliefs of the other person. ~ **PERFORMING**

2. Socrates in Caricature Socrates often mocked his own physical appearance. Find physical descriptions of Socrates and draw a caricature of him—that is, a comic and exaggerated portrait. ~ **ART**

Inquiry & Research

Philosopher in the Clouds The comic playwright Aristophanes (ăr'ĭ-stŏf'ə-nēz) ridiculed Socrates in his play *The Clouds.* The play influenced public opinion and even played a role in Socrates' being brought to trial. Research how Aristophanes portrayed Socrates and decide whether it was a fair portrayal. Share your findings in an oral report.

Vocabulary in Action

EXERCISE: WORD MEANINGS Answer the questions below to show your understanding of the boldfaced words.

1. If Socrates wanted to disparage someone, would he say something bad or something good about that person?
2. If a member of the jury felt **culpable** for how he voted, would he feel guilty or relieved? Why?
3. Socrates says it is possible that death may bring **annihilation.** What does he mean?
4. If a member of the jury accepted a bribe, would that make him **unscrupulous?** Why?
5. Socrates asks the jurors who sided with him to **reconcile** themselves to the decision. What does he want them to do?

Building Vocabulary

The word *culpable* comes from the Latin word *culpa,* meaning "fault." For an in-depth lesson on Greek and Latin roots, see page 340.

Writing Options

1. **Dramatic Scene** Students who wish to write on this topic may find it helpful to discuss possible scenarios before they begin writing. Remind students that their scenes need to be consistent with what they know about Socrates and his accusers.
2. **Newspaper Editorial** Explain to students that newspaper editorials often judge the actions of prominent people, especially lawmakers and office holders. If time allows, ask students to bring in models of such editorials; then discuss the style of writing used for them.

Activities & Explorations

Philosophical Dialogue Before students write their dialogues, it might be helpful to first have them read one of the shorter dialogues of Plato, such as the *Ion*, in which Socrates interviews a rhapsode, or a poetry reciter, about the nature of inspiration. Even a few pages of reading might help.

Socrates in Caricature Students can find images of Socrates online.

Inquiry & Research

Philosopher in the Clouds Tell students that *The Clouds* is a short play and that it is much easier to read than a Greek tragedy. Students can scan the play and read only those parts that concern Socrates. Or, they can look online for information about how Socrates was presented in the play.

Vocabulary in Action

1. something bad
2. guilty; a person who voted innocent would not feel deserving of blame
3. Death would result in the complete destruction of the individual.
4. yes, because taking a bribe suggests that the person lacks a sense of right and wrong
5. He wants them to accept the decision.

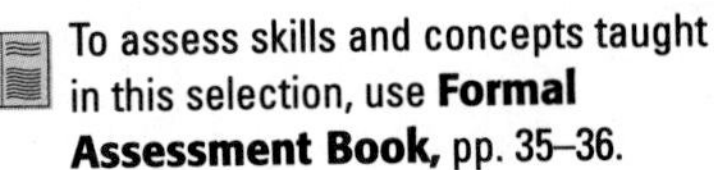
To assess skills and concepts taught in this selection, use **Formal Assessment Book,** pp. 35–36.

Additional Background

Aeschylus The earliest of the three great tragic dramatists, Aeschylus (c. 525–455 B.C.) was born of a noble family near Athens. He took part in the battle of Marathon and may also have been at Salamis, where the Greek navy defeated the Persians. He wrote between 80 and 90 plays, winning first prize at least 13 times in dramatic competitions.

Generally regarded as the founder of Greek tragedy, he diminished the role of the chorus and added a second actor, which made possible true dialogue and dramatic action.

Sophocles The son of a wealthy arms manufacturer, Sophocles (c. 496–406 B.C.) was a beloved and highly successful public figure. Born in Colonus, a suburb of Athens, he wrote 123 dramas, winning at least 24 first prizes and never finishing lower than second. He served Athens in many different roles, including that of treasurer and military commander. He is credited with introducing a third character to drama and increasing the number of chorus members.

Euripides The youngest of the three great tragic dramatists, Euripides (c. 484–406 B.C.) was the least appreciated and most controversial of the three. Though little is known about his life, he was considered eccentric by his contemporaries, and he did not participate in the public life of Athens. Although he wrote at least 88 plays, only four of them won first prize in his lifetime.

Euripides significantly reduced the role of the chorus. His dramas openly questioned traditional religious beliefs and brought an intense psychological realism to the stage.

Aristophanes Though he is considered the greatest of the comic dramatists, virtually nothing is known about the life of Aristophanes (c. 445–385 B.C.). In his plays, he made use of parody, exaggeration, and satire to mock prominent people and new ways of thought.

MILESTONES IN WORLD LITERATURE

GREEK DRAMA

Classical drama began long ago in ancient Greece—in the sixth century B.C. At that time, religious festivals took place in Athens each spring in honor of Dionysus (dī′ə-nī′səs), the god of wine and fertility, or new growth. At this festival, a chorus of masked dancers performed on a circular stage, singing hymns to this god. In 535 B.C. Thespis of Icaria, a Greek poet, introduced the first actor on stage. The word *thespian,* meaning "actor," comes from his name. The actor impersonated various characters by wearing different masks and costumes and took part in a dialogue with the leader of the chorus. With this occurrence, the first plays were born. Religious in nature, these plays explored deep questions such as the role of fate in human life or the relationship between mortals and the gods.

Throughout the sixth and fifth centuries B.C., Greek plays kept their religious purpose. The word *tragedy* reflects this purpose. It comes from the Greek word for *goat.* The goat was regarded as a sacred animal to Dionysus.

Ruins of Greek theater in Epidaurus

256 UNIT TWO PART 1: GREEK DRAMA

Modern production of Aeschylus' *Oresteia*

for prizes by staging plays before thousands of spectators at the festival of Dionysus in Athens. Hundreds of Greek tragedies were performed at these festivals. Sadly, fewer than 35 have survived.

The greatest writers of tragedy in ancient Greece were Aeschylus, Sophocles, and Euripides. Aeschylus (ĕs'kyə-ləs) added a second actor onstage, creating a dialogue between two characters. Sophocles (sŏf'ə-klēz') added a third actor, making plots more intriguing and complex. Euripides (yo͝o-rĭp'ĭ-dēz') created spectacular stage effects and portrayed characters in highly realistic ways. His play *Medea,* for example, explores the motives of a woman guilty of a horrid crime.

For the most part, these writers based their plays on familiar legends and myths. The audience knew the story behind the play, but the characters in the play, of course, did not. This contrast created an ironic perspective. Like the gods themselves, the audience looked on, knowing what would happen and yet caring deeply about the characters who suffered onstage.

Suffer they certainly did—bravely, passionately, and terribly. Consider Aeschylus' *Oresteia.* This set of three related plays tells the story of King Agamemnon's doomed family. This Greek commander sacrifices his daughter to the gods in return for a favorable wind so that his fleet can sail to Troy. When he returns home from the Trojan War, his wife murders him. Then Agamemnon's son, Orestes, kills his mother to avenge his father's murder and, to escape punishment, goes into exile. Another ill-fated family was that of Oedipus. Sophocles dramatized their sufferings in three masterful plays: *Oedipus the King* (page 258), *Antigone,* and *Oedipus at Colonus.*

Comedy was not as popular as tragedy among the ancient Greeks. The greatest writer of comedies was Aristophanes (ăr'ĭ-stŏf'ə-nēz). His satiric comedies poked fun at many well-known Athenians. *Lysistrata,* a domestic comedy, is still popular with audiences today. It shows clever and determined women banding together to stop their husbands from going to war.

Classical drama is a priceless legacy of ancient Greece. It includes several plays that rank as world masterpieces. These plays have inspired countless writers down through the centuries. In drama the Greeks developed a new literary form and showed its power. Even today Greek drama provides a way to ponder life's mysteries, to celebrate its glory, and to come to terms with its suffering.

Literary Highlights

Surviving Plays of Aeschylus

Oresteia, a trilogy of *Agamemnon, The Libation Bearers,* and *Eumenides*
Persians
Prometheus Bound
Seven Against Thebes
Suppliants

Surviving Plays of Sophocles

Ajax
Antigone
Electra
Oedipus the King
Oedipus at Colonus
Philoctetes
Trachinian Women

Major Plays of Euripides

Nineteen plays survive. The most notable are:
Bacchae
Electra
Hippolytus
Iphigenia at Aulis
Medea
Trojan Women

Major Plays of Aristophanes

Eleven plays survive. The most notable are:
Birds
Clouds
Lysistrata
Wasps

An excerpt from this selection is included in the **World Literature InterActive Reader™**.

Objectives

- understand and appreciate a Greek **drama (Literary Analysis)**
- recognize the characteristics of a **tragic hero (Literary Analysis)**
- recognize and understand **dramatic irony (Literary Analysis)**
- use **strategies for reading Greek drama (Active Reading)**

Summary

Oedipus, the beloved king of Thebes, sets out to save his subjects from a plague. He learns from the Delphic oracle that the plague is the result of an unpunished murder. The previous king, Laius, had been murdered while traveling to Delphi. To learn more, Oedipus calls upon the blind prophet Tiresias, who mysteriously accuses Oedipus of the crime.

Oedipus learns from his wife, Jocasta (the widow of Laius), that the king had been killed at a crossroads, similar to the place where Oedipus once killed an old man. That event occurred when Oedipus had been on his way to Thebes, after having left his home in Corinth to escape a prophecy that he would kill his father, King Polybus, and marry his mother, Merope.

When Oedipus had first arrived in Thebes, the city was being terrorized by the monstrous Sphinx, which killed all those who could not answer its riddle. Oedipus solved the riddle, and then as a reward was given rule over Thebes, as well as Jocasta for his wife.

A messenger arrives with news that King Polybus has died. The messenger reveals that a shepherd had given the infant Oedipus to Polybus and Merope. After hearing the shepherd's story, Oedipus realizes that he himself murdered Laius and that he is the child of Laius and Jocasta. To evade the same prophecy that Oedipus later heard, they had ordered a servant to abandon their son on a mountain, but the servant took pity and gave the boy to the shepherd. In disgrace, Jocasta kills herself; then Oedipus blinds himself and is exiled.

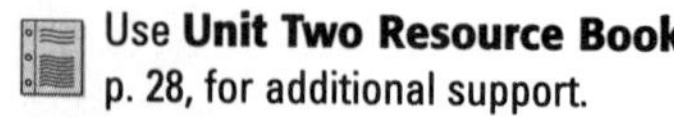

Thematic Link

Oedipus achieves the height of **glory and honor,** only to suffer a tragic fall.

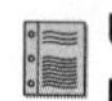

Use **Unit Two Resource Book,** p. 38, for practice with Words to Know.

PREPARING to *Read*

OEDIPUS *the* KING

— SOPHOCLES —

Sophocles
496?–406 B.C.

Public Figure Sophocles lived a long life and, by all accounts, a happy one. It spanned almost the entire fifth century B.C.—a century of great achievements in Athens, both in politics and art.

When he was young, Sophocles was a skillful wrestler, dancer, and musician. Later, he had a successful career in public life. As a military leader, he worked alongside Pericles, the great statesman who dominated Athenian politics for more than 30 years. Sophocles also served as an ambassador, as a public treasurer, and, in his 80s, as a member of a special commission appointed to guide Athens through a time of crisis. In addition, he seems to have helped in establishing the first Athenian public hospital. Handsome, charming, friendly, and well educated, Sophocles was highly regarded.

Great Dramatist As a writer, Sophocles' achievements were truly amazing. One of the greatest dramatists of the golden age of Greek drama, he composed more than 120 plays. Unfortunately, only 7 of them have survived intact. For about 30 years, he competed in the annual Dionysian dramatic festival, taking first prize at least 18 times. By contrast, Aeschylus received only 13 first prizes, and Euripides won only 4.

Sophocles was an innovator in drama. He enlarged the chorus from 12 to 15 members, introduced painted scenery, and added a third speaking actor. His plays are noted for their powerful language, superb artistry, and unforgettable characters. Sophocles never stopped writing plays, keeping his intellectual powers until the end of his life. He completed one of his greatest plays, *Oedipus at Colonus,* when he was about 90.

Tragic Vision It is ironic that Sophocles—gifted, admired, and successful as he was—had so dark a view of human life. He was deeply aware of life's pain and sorrow. His plays feature towering heroes who remind the audience of the vast potential of human beings. However, the very qualities that make these heroes great also lead to their ruin.

The Cities of Oedipus

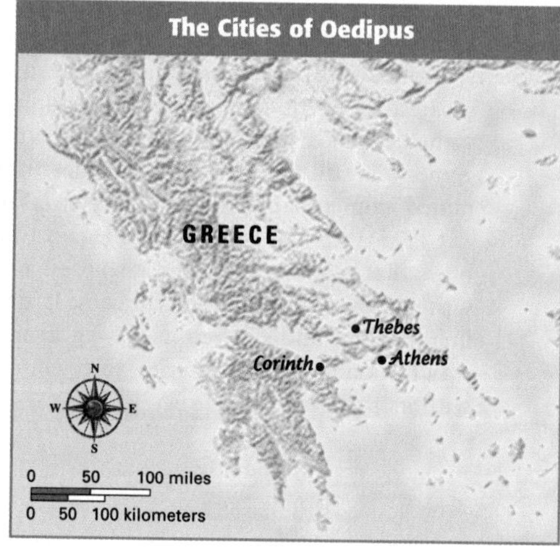

LESSON RESOURCES

UNIT TWO RESOURCE BOOK, pp. 28–38

ASSESSMENT RESOURCES
Formal Assessment, pp. 37–42
Teacher's Guide to Assessment and Portfolio Use
Test Generator

INTEGRATED TECHNOLOGY
Visit our Web site: classzone.com

ADDITIONAL RESOURCES
Lesson Planning Guide, pp. 29–34
Teacher's Sourcebook for Language Development

Build Background

Sophocles' Theban Plays Of all Sophocles' tragic characters, the one who has touched the hearts of audiences most deeply is Oedipus. Sophocles himself was fascinated with this king and his family. Two of his surviving tragedies—*Oedipus the King* and *Oedipus at Colonus*—are about Oedipus, and *Antigone* centers on one of his daughters. These three plays are sometimes called the Theban plays. Thebes, an ancient city in central Greece, was once among the most powerful of Greek city-states. The city is important in the legend of Oedipus and in all three plays.

Aristotle and Tragedy In the 300s B.C., the Greek philosopher Aristotle wrote an essay about drama, the *Poetics*. In this essay, Aristotle examined several works of Greek literature, describing their structures and effects. He praised *Oedipus the King* as the model of a perfectly made tragedy.

On the basis of his study of Sophocles' play, Aristotle characterized a **tragedy** as "an imitation of an action that is serious, complete, and of a certain magnitude." He also stated that a tragedy triggers two emotions in its audience: pity and terror.

The Legend of Oedipus

His Origins *Oedipus the King,* like nearly every other Greek tragedy, is based on a legend that was familiar to the ancient Greeks. According to this legend, Oedipus was the son of King Laius and Queen Jocasta of Thebes. An oracle told Laius that a son born to him and Jocasta would kill him. When Jocasta gave birth to a son, Laius ordered a servant to pin the baby's feet together and leave him exposed on a mountain to die. The servant took pity on the baby, however, and entrusted him to a shepherd. The shepherd gave the baby to the childless king and queen of Corinth—Polybus and Merope. They named the baby Oedipus, from words meaning "swollen foot," and raised him as their son.

A Fateful Night Oedipus grew to manhood believing that he was the son of Polybus and Merope. One night at a banquet, a drunkard blurted out to Oedipus that he was not his father's son. Oedipus then visited the oracle at Delphi to try to discover the truth about his parents. The oracle did not reveal Oedipus' true identity but did deliver a terrible prophecy—that Oedipus would kill his father and marry his mother.

Murder at a Crossroad Horrified at this disclosure, Oedipus fled from Corinth in an effort to prevent the prophecy from coming true. Making his way toward Thebes, he came upon King Laius and his servants at a crossroad. Oedipus quarreled with them about who had the right of way. Not realizing that Laius was his real father, Oedipus killed him in a fit of rage.

Riddle of the Sphinx When Oedipus reached Thebes, a monster was terrorizing it. Known as the Sphinx, the monster had the face of a woman, the body of a lion, and the wings of a bird. It sang an intriguing riddle: "What is it that walks on four legs in the morning, on two at midday, and on three in the evening?" Anyone who could not solve the riddle was devoured by the Sphinx. Oedipus, however, figured out the answer. He promptly replied, "Man, for he crawls as a baby, walks erect in maturity, and uses a staff in old age." On receiving this answer, the Sphinx destroyed itself, and Thebes was freed from the terror.

Oedipus, Ruler of Thebes As a reward for saving the city, Oedipus was given the throne of Thebes and the hand of Jocasta, the late king's widow. Not knowing that he was actually her son, Oedipus married her. For 20 years he ruled Thebes in peace with his wife and her brother Creon.

As the play begins, Thebes is in trouble once more. The city is reeling from a terrible plague. Naturally, the citizens go to Oedipus for help, remembering that he had saved the city from the Sphinx long ago. In his effort to bring the plague to an end, Oedipus discovers the secret of his birth and hurtles headlong into unspeakable suffering.

For a humanities activity, click on:

TIME MANAGEMENT

If your schedule requires that you cover the lesson objectives in a shorter time, use . . .

- Preparing to Read, pp. 258–261
- Thinking Through the Literature, p. 330
- Vocabulary in Action, p. 331

If you want to take advantage of longer class time, use . . .

- TE Teaching Options: Cross Curricular Link, pp. 260, 262, 264, 266, 269, 274, 275, 281, 287, 294, 297, 298, 315, 316, 324, 327; Viewing and Representing, pp. 284, 290, 328; Speaking and Listening, pp. 271, 273, 278, 313; Vocabulary Strategy, pp. 265, 272, 307; Standardized Test Practice, p. 300; Informal Assessment, p. 282; Grammar, pp. 267
- Choices & Challenges, p. 331

READING FOR INFORMATION
Reading Skills and Strategies
IDENTIFYING MAIN IDEAS AND DETAILS

After students have read these two pages, have them work in pairs to identify the main ideas and important details in each section of the text. One pair, for example, can work with the section labeled **Public Figure** in Sophocles' biography on page 258; another pair can work with the **Great Dramatist** section, and so on. For each section, students should identify one or two main ideas and identify four or five significant details. Each pair can give a brief oral report summarizing their findings.

Historical Note
What the Audience Knew Explain that Greek playwrights often wrote about legends and myths familiar to the audience. While Sophocles' audience would know the basic story of Oedipus—a man fated to kill his father and marry his mother—they might be surprised by some of the details in Sophocles' version. In Homer's account of Oedipus, which would be very familiar to Sophocles' audience, Oedipus continues to rule Thebes until his death. In Sophocles' version, Oedipus is exiled after he learns the terrible truth of his origins.

Most Greek dramas were set in a remote past, and *Oedipus the King* is no exception. However, it is possible that certain plot events may have had a special relevance to the audience. Some scholars believe the drama may have been first performed after Athens had suffered through a terrible plague, which began in 430 B.C.

Reading Skills and Strategies
USING THE MAP

Ask students to explain why the three cities on the map are labeled "The Cities of Oedipus."

Possible Response: Oedipus was born in Thebes and ruled there; he grew up in Corinth; his story was told by Sophocles in Athens.

5-Minute Warm-Up
Daily Language SkillBuilder

Have students **proofread** the display sentences on page 161i and write them correctly.

READING FOR INFORMATION

Reading Skills and Strategies

CLARIFYING

Invite volunteers to read aloud the names of each character in the **Cast of Characters.** Point out that the major characters are Oedipus, Creon, Tiresias, and Jocasta.

Reading Skills and Strategies

USING THE DIAGRAM

Refer students to the photograph of the ruins of a Greek theater on page 256 so that they can study both the photograph and diagram. Help students to visualize the size and spectacle of Greek theater. For purposes of comparison, point out that a large theater in the United States today might hold a few thousand people. Ask students what difficulties would be posed by having to stage a performance in the typical Greek theater.

Possible Response: It would be difficult to project the voices of the actors so that everyone in the audience could hear them. Also, because the theater itself is so large, many people in the audience might have trouble seeing the action on stage. Because two or three actors are playing all the roles, the actors need to be able to change costumes quickly.

To get the most out of your reading, try to imagine yourself attending a performance of *Oedipus the King* in fifth-century Athens. At dawn, you make your way to the Theater of Dionysus, built on the slope of a hill. As you enter the outdoor theater, you look up and see the gleaming white columns of the Parthenon—a temple dedicated to the goddess Athena—catching the morning sun. Then, with perhaps 17,000 other spectators, you settle down to watch as the events of the tragedy unfold.

Cast of Characters

Oedipus (ĕd′ə-pəs), king of Thebes

A **Priest** of Zeus

Creon (krē′ŏn′), brother of Jocasta

A **Chorus** of Theban citizens and their **Leader**

Tiresias (tī-rē′sē-əs), a blind prophet

Jocasta (jō-kăs′tə) the queen, wife of Oedipus

A **Messenger** from Corinth

A **Shepherd**

A **Messenger** from inside the palace

Antigone (ăn-tĭg′ə-nē) and **Ismene** (ĭs-mē′nē), daughters of Oedipus and Jocasta

Guards and attendants

Priests of Thebes

Typical Greek Theater

History

GREEK THEATER Greek tragedies were performed at the Greater Dionysia, a festival near the end of March. During this six-day festival, three playwrights, chosen by a city official, would each stage three tragedies and a satyr play. The tragedies would be either three separate plays linked by a shared theme or a trilogy on one theme. The satyr play, a bawdy burlesque that parodied a Greek myth, would comment on the theme of the tragedies. The satyr play took its name from its chorus, which always consisted of satyrs, mythical creatures that were half human, half beast. Each playwright would stage his plays over the course of one day. At the end of all the productions, ten judges, chosen by lot, would choose the winning playwright, who was awarded an ivy wreath.

The theater in ancient Athens was truly a communal affair. Virtually all citizens would attend the performances, as well as visitors. An admission fee was charged. Those citizens who could not afford to pay had their fees paid by the city. Because of the length of the performances, audiences brought food and drink with them. Athenian audiences could sometimes be rowdy, voicing their reactions with wild abandon.

Connect to Your Life

In this play, Sophocles tells the story of a king who learns to look at his past in a new way. Think about some events in your own past that you look at differently now that you are older. Why do you think your understanding of the events has changed?

Focus Your Reading

LITERARY ANALYSIS: TRAGIC HERO

The central character in a tragedy is called a **tragic hero.** Such a character, though noble, has a defect, or flaw. The flaw—which may be poor judgment, great pride, or weakness—helps to bring about his or her downfall. As you read this play, think about Oedipus' qualities. Also ask yourself whether or not he has a flaw.

ACTIVE READING: STRATEGIES FOR READING GREEK DRAMA

Use these strategies when reading this play:

- **Visualize** the characters and the events as you read.
- Keep in mind the sequence of events that make up the **plot.**
- Think about the hero's **motivations,** noble qualities, and any flaw, or defect, he may have.
- Consider how the words and actions of **minor characters** help you to understand the main characters.
- **Question** what happens in the play, and stop reading occasionally to **clarify** your understanding.

READER'S NOTEBOOK As you read this play, record your answers to the Pause & Reflect questions found at various points in the play. Apply the strategies listed above, and note any other thoughts or questions you may have.

WORDS TO KNOW **Vocabulary Preview**

appall	foreboding	mortify	revile
denounce	futile	oblivion	surmise
despondent	loathed	retract	swarthy
explicit	menace	reverberate	

OEDIPUS THE KING 261

Reading and Analyzing

Guide for Reading
Explain that the most challenging selections in the textbook provide extra help for students. These selections are broken down into smaller, more manageable sections. Each section begins with a **Focus** that sets a purpose for reading and concludes with a **Pause & Reflect** question to check understanding. In *Oedipus the King,* stage directions are also provided in italics. The stage directions are a part of the translator's version of the drama.

Reading Skills and Strategies
TEXT STRUCTURE
Before students begin reading, preview the structure of the textbook presentation of *Oedipus the King.* On page 262, draw attention to the Focus section, the stage directions, and the side notes. Also draw attention to the illustration on page 263, the first appearance of the Words to Know box on page 272, and the Pause & Reflect question on page 266. Point out that all of these elements aid student understanding.

Active Reading
STRATEGIES FOR READING GREEK DRAMA
A Refer students to the diagram of a Greek theater on pages 260–261. Point out that the skene serves as the "royal house of Thebes" for this scene and the rest of the play. Explain that Oedipus has been king for a long time and that he has earned the respect and admiration of his people. When he appears on stage, he is a commanding figure.

Use **Unit Two Resource Book,** p. 29, for more practice.

Literary Analysis TRAGIC HERO
B Oedipus insists on meeting personally with the priests. Ask students what his action suggests about him as a ruler.
Possible Response: He cares deeply for the welfare of his people.

Use **Unit Two Resource Book,** p. 30, for more practice.

Oedipus the King

Sophocles

Translated by Robert Fagles

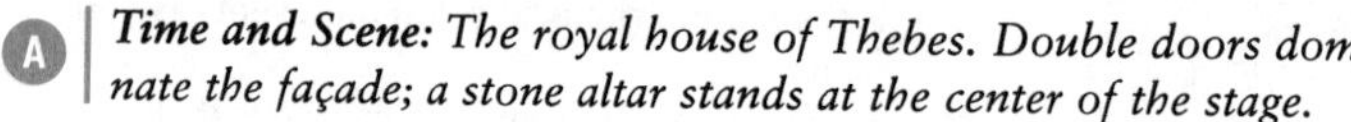

GUIDE FOR READING

FOCUS A terrible plague has struck the city of Thebes. Plants, animals, and people are dying in great numbers. The priests of the city seek help from Oedipus, their king. As you read, look for details that help you form impressions of Oedipus as a leader.

A *Time and Scene: The royal house of Thebes. Double doors dominate the façade; a stone altar stands at the center of the stage.*

Many years have passed since Oedipus *solved the riddle of the Sphinx and ascended the throne of Thebes, and now a plague has struck the city. A procession of priests enters; suppliants, broken and despondent, they carry branches wound in wool and lay them on the altar.*

The doors open. Guards assemble. Oedipus *comes forward, majestic but for a telltale limp, and slowly views the condition of his people.*

Oedipus. Oh my children, the new blood of ancient Thebes,
why are you here? Huddling at my altar,
praying before me, your branches wound in wool.
Our city reeks with the smoke of burning incense,
rings with cries for the Healer and wailing for the dead.
B I thought it wrong, my children, to hear the truth
from others, messengers. Here I am myself—
you all know me, the world knows my fame:
I am Oedipus.
(helping a Priest to his feet)

3 branches wound in wool: tokens placed on altars by people seeking favors from the gods.

5 the Healer: the god Apollo, who could both cause and cure plagues.

WORDS TO KNOW
despondent (dĭ-spŏn′dənt) *adj.* sad; depressed

Cross Curricular Link

Humanities

GREEK RELIGION At the beginning of the play, a procession of suppliants carry branches covered with wool and lay them on the altar. The suppliants come to the altar of Apollo because they believe that an angered god has caused the plague, and they are asking Apollo for help. The branches would be kept on the altar until the request has been granted.

Religious rituals in ancient Greece, which consisted of prayers and sacrifices, reflected the efforts of believers to demonstrate their belief in the gods and their piety. The Greeks believed that the gods took an active interest in human affairs. Typically, successes were viewed as the sign of divine favor while problems and failures were interpreted as the result of divine anger. The Greeks often asked for specific favors from the gods, but their requests were tempered by the realization that the gods did not always respond. Greek religious practices, in effect, served to placate the gods by reminding them that they were held in high esteem.

Although some intellectuals questioned beliefs about the gods in fifth-century Athens, most Athenians upheld traditional religious beliefs. Indeed, it was widely believed that one of the surest ways to incur the wrath of a god would be to deny his or her existence.

Christopher Plummer as Oedipus in a scene from the film *Oedipus the King* (1968).

HERE I
AM MYSELF—
YOU ALL KNOW ME,
THE WORLD KNOWS MY FAME:
I AM OEDIPUS.

Customizing Instruction

Less Proficient Readers

Model the process of reading a Greek drama and making use of the accompanying support material. Begin by reading the **Focus** aloud and modeling your thinking process. ("The people of Thebes must be desperate because so many are dying. I wonder what kind of leader Oedipus will show himself to be.") Continue modeling the reading process through line 15 of the poem. Help students to visualize the scene between Oedipus and the priests by acting out the gestures and movements of Oedipus.

English Learners

In addition to modeling the reading process (see above directions), make sure that students understand the following terms:

"suppliant" *(a person who is asking or begging for help)*

Line 1: "new blood of ancient Thebes" *(the latest generation of a long line of Theban people)*

Reading Skills and Strategies
CLARIFYING

A Make sure that students realize that the Priest is referring to the suppliants. They were chosen to represent a cross-section of Athenian age groups.

Literary Analysis METAPHOR

B Thebes is compared to a ship in danger of sinking. Point out that states have often been compared to ships. Ask students what the suppliants hope for. *(that Oedipus can take control of the "ship" and steer it toward safety)*

Literary Analysis TRAGIC HERO

C The suppliants say that Oedipus "cannot equal the gods," but they praise him as the "first of men." Ask students why they have such a high opinion of Oedipus.

Possible Response: The suppliants feel indebted to Oedipus because he freed Thebes from the Sphinx. He did so without any assistance, which suggests to the suppliants that Oedipus was helped by a god.

Literary Analysis DRAMATIC IRONY

D Point out the irony in the Priest's question. The entire play revolves around the issue of what Oedipus knows—and does not know.

Speak up, old man. Your years,
your dignity—you should speak for the others.
Why here and kneeling, what preys upon you so?
Some sudden fear? some strong desire?
You can trust me. I am ready to help,
I'll do anything. I would be blind to misery
not to pity my people kneeling at my feet.

Priest. Oh Oedipus, king of the land, our greatest power!
You see us before you now, men of all ages
clinging to your altars. Here are boys,
(A) still too weak to fly from the nest,
and here the old, bowed down with the years,
the holy ones—a priest of Zeus myself—and here
the picked, unmarried men, the young hope of Thebes.
And all the rest, your great family gathers now,
branches wreathed, massing in the squares,
kneeling before the two temples of queen Athena
or the river-shrine where the embers glow and die
and Apollo sees the future in the ashes.
Our city—
(B) look around you, see with your own eyes—
our ship pitches wildly, cannot lift her head
from the depths, the red waves of death . . .
Thebes is dying. A blight on the fresh crops
and the rich pastures, cattle sicken and die,
(1) and the women die in labor, children stillborn,
and the plague, the fiery god of fever hurls down
on the city, his lightning slashing through us—
raging plague in all its vengeance, devastating
the house of Cadmus! And black Death luxuriates
in the raw, wailing miseries of Thebes.

Now we pray to you. You cannot equal the gods,
your children know that, bending at your altar.
But we do rate you first of men,
both in the common crises of our lives
(2) and face-to-face encounters with the gods.
You freed us from the Sphinx, you came to Thebes
and cut us loose from the bloody tribute we had paid
(C) that harsh, brutal singer. We taught you nothing,
no skill, no extra knowledge, still you triumphed.
A god was with you, so they say, and we believe it—
you lifted up our lives.

26 river-shrine: a shrine of Apollo in Thebes, where priests foretold the future by interpreting the way offerings to the god burned.

31 blight: a disease that withers plants.

37 Cadmus (kăd′məs): the founder of Thebes; **luxuriates** (lŭg-zhŏŏr′ē-āts′): takes pleasure.

45 bloody tribute: the human lives taken by the Sphinx.

Science

THE PLAGUE Many people believe that the plague described by Sophocles is based upon the plague that afflicted Athens in 430 B.C., with a second outbreak occurring in 427 B.C. That plague, which killed at least a third of the population, including Pericles, has been called one of the great medical mysteries of history.

According to Thucydides, an eyewitness, the plague struck first in Ethiopia, traveled to Egypt and Libya, and then fell upon Athens. Its victims were "seized first with strong fevers, redness and burning of the eyes, . . . and expelled an unusually foul breath." Next came symptoms of "sneezing, hoarseness . . . a powerful cough . . . and every kind of bilious vomiting." The skin of victims was "reddish" and marked by "small blisters and ulcers." Victims were subject to unquenchable thirst; many even jumped into wells in desperation. Fevers were so high that sufferers insisted on being naked. Those who died typically did so between the seventh and ninth day of the disease.

Medical experts are still divided about the nature of the plague. Some find a striking similarity between the symptoms described by Thucydides and the Ebola virus. Others have concluded that the disease was most likely typhus fever.

So now again,
Oedipus, king, we bend to you, your power—
we implore you, all of us on our knees:
D find us strength, rescue! Perhaps you've heard
the voice of a god or something from other men,
Oedipus . . . what do you know?
The man of experience—you see it every day—
his plans will work in a crisis, his first of all.

Act now—we beg you, best of men, raise up our city!
Act, defend yourself, your former glory!
Your country calls you savior now
for your zeal, your action years ago.
Never let us remember of your reign:
you helped us stand, only to fall once more.
Oh raise up our city, set us on our feet.
The omens were good that day you brought us joy—
be the same man today!
Rule our land, you know you have the power,
3 but rule a land of the living, not a wasteland.
Ship and towered city are nothing, stripped of men
alive within it, living all as one.

Oedipus. My children,
I pity you. I see—how could I fail to see
what longings bring you here? Well I know
you are sick to death, all of you,
but sick as you are, not one is sick as I.
Your pain strikes each of you alone, each
in the confines of himself, no other. But my spirit
grieves for the city, for myself and all of you.
I wasn't asleep, dreaming. You haven't wakened me—
I have wept through the nights, you must know that,
groping, laboring over many paths of thought.
After a painful search I found one cure:
I acted at once. I sent Creon,
4 my wife's own brother, to Delphi—
Apollo the Prophet's oracle—to learn
what I might do or say to save our city.

Today's the day. When I count the days gone by
it torments me . . . what is he doing?
Strange, he's late, he's gone too long.

82 Delphi (děl'fī'): the site of a temple where prophecies were.

Customizing Instruction

Less Proficient Readers

Help students to understand the plague and Oedipus' role in the city by asking the following questions:

1 Describe the various effects of the plague. *(Crops die; cattle become sick and die; women die during childbirth; infants are born dead; and a deadly fever sweeps through the city.)*

2 The Priest remembers the time when Oedipus saved Thebes from the Sphinx. According to the people of Thebes, who helped Oedipus? *(a god)*

3 The Priest expresses the people's great need for Oedipus. Why does the priest tell Oedipus to "rule a land of the living, not a wasteland"? *(The priest wants Oedipus to save the people who are still alive. If Oedipus doesn't act soon, many more people will die.)*

4 Oedipus gives comfort by telling the Priest of his actions. What has Oedipus done? *(He sent Creon to the oracle at Delphi.)*

English Learners

Explain the meaning of the following phrases:

Line 22: "the picked, unmarried men" *(the young, single adult men who were chosen to be in the group that visits Oedipus)*

Line 33: "stillborn" *(dead at birth)*

Line 64: "omens" *(signs of what may happen in the future)*

Advanced Learners

Explain that *hubris* is a word of Greek origin that means "excessive pride" or "self-confidence." To avoid hubris, a person must acknowledge limits and not claim too much of himself or herself. The Priest shows an awareness of the dangers of hubris when he says to Oedipus, "You cannot equal the gods." A person who allowed himself to be treated as a god would clearly be guilty of hubris.

MINI LESSON Vocabulary Strategy

USING A DICTIONARY TO FIND PRECISE MEANINGS

Instruction Write the following lines on the chalkboard:

"Apollo was explicit: my son was doomed to kill my husband . . . my son, poor defenseless thing, he never had a chance to kill his father. They destroyed him first.
So much for prophecy. It's neither here nor there" (p. 299, lines 944–948).

Demonstrate for students how to use a dictionary to find the appropriate meaning of the adjective *explicit:* "fully and clearly expressed; leaving nothing implied." Ask them why this meaning is more appropriate than others listed in the dictionary entry.

Answer: This meaning of *explicit* describes the clarity and completeness of Apollo's prophecy.

Practice Have students choose five of the remaining Words to Know. Ask students to write down the lines(s) in which each word appears in *Oedipus the King*. Then ask them to look up each word in a dictionary and write the meaning that is most appropriate for the word's context. Have students discuss their choices.

A lesson on using reference tools appears on p. 558 in the Pupil's Edition.

Pause & Reflect
Possible Response: Oedipus is decisive, self-assured, and concerned for the welfare of his people.

Reading Skills and Strategies
MAKING INFERENCES
Ⓐ Creon's words and actions show that he is reluctant to share his information in front of the priests. Ask students what Creon is afraid of.
Possible Response: Creon seems worried that some people may be conspiring against Oedipus. Creon does not want to reveal information that could benefit the enemies of Oedipus.

Literary Analysis CULTURAL SETTING
Ⓑ The Greeks believed that certain acts, such as the murder of a king, offended the gods and corrupted, or polluted, the land. In some cases, ritual purification would be enough to pacify the gods and rid the land of pollution. In the case of Laius' murder, however, such purification cannot take place until those responsible have been brought to justice.

Active Reading
STRATEGIES FOR READING GREEK DRAMA
Ⓒ Ask students to summarize what Oedipus has learned from Creon.
Possible Response: The plague has been caused by the murder of Laius. Thebes can be freed from the plague only after the murderers have been punished.

Oedipus speaks to the chorus in Tyrone Guthrie film version of *Oedipus Rex* (1957).

But once he returns, then, then I'll be a traitor
if I do not do all the god makes clear.

Priest. Timely words. The men over there
are signaling—Creon's just arriving.

PAUSE & REFLECT What are your impressions of Oedipus as a leader?

FOCUS Creon is returning from Delphi with news from the god Apollo. Read to find out about the cause of the plague in Thebes.

Oedipus (*sighting* Creon, *then turning to the altar*).
Lord Apollo,
let him come with a lucky word of rescue,
shining like his eyes!

Priest. Welcome news, I think—he's crowned, look,
and the laurel wreath is bright with berries.

95 laurel wreath: a crown of leaves worn by those seeking the help of the oracle at Delphi.

Cross Curricular Link **History**

THE ORACLE OF APOLLO AT DELPHI The ancient Greeks believed that the temple of Apollo at Delphi marked the exact center of the world. The oracle at that temple was believed to speak for Apollo and thus communicate the will of Zeus (Apollo was the son of Zeus). The oracle's statements influenced public policies; heads of state, both Greek and non-Greek, asked for the oracle's consultation, as did private citizens. Two famous maxims were inscribed on the temple: "Know thyself" and "Nothing to excess."

Originally, the oracle was a young virgin; later, it was required that the oracle had to be a woman over fifty. This priestess, known as the Pythia, had to live apart from her husband and dress in a maiden's clothes. In response to a petitioner's request, the Pythia drank from a sacred spring and then entered the temple of Apollo. She probably descended into the underground part of the temple, accompanied by the petitioners and priests. In a room by herself, she would sit on a sacred tripod, chew laurel leaves (the tree sacred to Apollo), and proceed to speak the message of Apollo. According to some reports, the oracle would be in a frenzied trance and speak hysterically. Alhough the oracle could not be seen, her words were heard and recorded by the priests.

Oedipus. We'll soon see. He's close enough to hear—
(*Enter* Creon *from the side; his face is shaded with a wreath.*)
Creon, prince, my kinsman, what do you bring us?
What message from the god?

Creon. Good news.
I tell you even the hardest things to bear,
if they should turn out well, all would be well.

Oedipus. Of course, but what were the god's *words?* There's no hope
and nothing to fear in what you've said so far.

A **Creon.** If you want my report in the presence of these people . . .
(*pointing to the priests while drawing* Oedipus *toward the palace*)
I'm ready now, or we might go inside.

Oedipus. Speak out,
speak to us all. I grieve for these, my people,
far more than I fear for my own life.

Creon. Very well,
I will tell you what I heard from the god.
Apollo commands us—he was quite clear—
1 "Drive the corruption from the land,
don't harbor it any longer, past all cure,
B don't nurse it in your soil—root it out!"

Oedipus. How can we cleanse ourselves—what rites?
What's the source of the trouble?

2 **Creon.** Banish the man, or pay back blood with blood.
Murder sets the plague-storm on the city.

Oedipus. Whose murder?
Whose fate does Apollo bring to light?

Creon. Our leader,
3 my lord, was once a man named Laius,
before you came and put us straight on course.

Oedipus. I know—
or so I've heard. I never saw the man myself.

C **Creon.** Well, he was killed, and Apollo commands us now—
he could not be more clear,
4 "Pay the killers back—whoever is responsible."

117 Laius (lā'əs): the king of Thebes before Oedipus.

Customizing Instruction

Less Proficient Readers

Focus Before students begin reading this section, make sure they realize the importance of Creon's return to Thebes. Oedipus expects him to come back with an answer to the problems created by the plague.

To ensure that students understand the message that Creon brings back, ask the following questions:

1 What must be driven from the land and rooted out? *(the corruption)*

2 What caused "the plague-storm" that is corrupting the land and killing the people of Thebes? *(an act of murder)*

3 Who was murdered? *(Laius)*

4 What has Apollo commanded? *(The killers, or whoever is responsible, must pay for the murder.)*

English Learners

Explain the meaning of the following phrases:

Line 111: "don't nurse it in your soil" *(don't allow the corruption to stay in your land)*

Line 112: "cleanse ourselves" *(purify ourselves for religious purposes)*

Line 114: "pay back blood with blood" *(respond to a bloody act of murder by executing the murderer)*

MINI LESSON Grammar

KINDS OF SENTENCES

Instruction There are four kinds of sentences: declarative, interrogative, imperative, and exclamatory. A declarative sentence states a fact, wish, intent, or feeling. It ends with a period. An interrogative sentence asks a question and ends with a question mark. An imperative sentence gives a command, request, or direction and ends with either a period or an exclamation point. An exclamatory sentence expresses strong feeling or excitement and ends with an exclamation point.

Practice Write the following sentences from pp. 266–267 of *Oedipus the King* on the chalkboard:

"Lord Apollo, let him come with a lucky word or rescue, shining like his eyes!" *(exclamatory)*
"Creon, prince, my kinsman, what do you bring us?" *(interrogative)*
"There's no hope and nothing to fear in what you've said so far." *(declarative)*
"Speak out, speak to us all. " *(imperative)*

Have students identify each kind of sentence.

For more instruction and practice in using the four kinds of sentences, use McDougal Littell's ***Language Network:***

- Grade 10, Chapter 2, "The Sentence and Its Parts"
- Grade 12, Chapter 1, "The Parts of a Sentence"

Reading and Analyzing

Reading Skills and Strategies
CLARIFYING

A Ask students to describe Oedipus' response to the news that Thebes did nothing to track down the murderer. *(Oedipus seems outraged.)*

Literary Analysis TRAGIC HERO

B Ask students how Oedipus feels about his own abilities.

Possible Responses: Some students may note that Oedipus is supremely self-confident. He feels that he can solve the problem facing Thebes. Others may regard Oedipus as arrogant because he claims so much for himself, even saying that he is "Apollo's champion."

Pause & Reflect

Possible Response: King Laius, the ruler who preceded Oedipus, was killed while traveling to Delphi. His murder has gone unavenged.

Active Reading
STRATEGIES FOR READING GREEK DRAMA

C Help students to appreciate the dramatic role of the chorus. Remind students that the chorus consisted of a group of at least a dozen men who would sing or chant their lines. Here, the chorus speaks for the people of Thebes, who are desperate for an answer to their troubles. The chorus asks various gods for help.

Oedipus. Where on earth are they? Where to find it now,
the trail of the ancient guilt so hard to trace?

Creon. "Here in Thebes," he said.
Whatever is sought for can be caught, you know,
whatever is neglected slips away.

Oedipus. But where,
in the palace, the fields or foreign soil,
where did Laius meet his bloody death?

1 **Creon.** He went to consult an oracle, Apollo said,
and he set out and never came home again.

Oedipus. No messenger, no fellow-traveler saw what
happened?
Someone to cross-examine?

Creon. No,
they were all killed but one. He escaped,
terrified, he could tell us nothing clearly,
nothing of what he saw—just one thing.

Oedipus. What's that?
One thing could hold the key to it all,
a small beginning give us grounds for hope.

Creon. He said thieves attacked them—a whole band,
not single-handed, cut King Laius down.

2 **Oedipus.** A thief,
so daring, so wild, he'd kill a king? Impossible,
unless conspirators paid him off in Thebes.

Creon. We suspected as much. But with Laius dead
no leader appeared to help us in our troubles.

Oedipus. Trouble? Your *king* was murdered—royal blood!
A What stopped you from tracking down the killer
then and there?

Creon. The singing, riddling Sphinx.
She . . . persuaded us to let the mystery go
and concentrate on what lay at our feet.

Oedipus. No,
I'll start again—I'll bring it all to light myself!
Apollo is right, and so are you, Creon,
to turn our attention back to the murdered man.
Now you have *me* to fight for you, you'll see:
B I am the land's avenger by all rights,
and Apollo's champion too.

154 avenger: one who punishes wrongdoing.

3

But not to assist some distant kinsman, no,
for my own sake I'll rid us of this corruption.
Whoever killed the king may decide to kill me too,
with the same violent hand—by avenging Laius
I defend myself.

157 corruption: pollution; contamination.

(*to the priests*)

Quickly, my children.
Up from the steps, take up your branches now.

(*to the guards*)

One of you summon the city here before us,
tell them I'll do everything. God help us,
we will see our triumph—or our fall.

(Oedipus *and* Creon *enter the palace, followed by the guards.*)

Priest. Rise, my sons. The kindness we came for
Oedipus volunteers himself.
Apollo has sent his word, his oracle—
Come down, Apollo, save us, stop the plague.

(*The priests rise, remove their branches and exit to the side.*)

PAUSE & REFLECT What is the cause of the plague in Thebes?

FOCUS The chorus enters and chants a plea to the gods, describing the people's sufferings. As you read, look for details that help you visualize the sufferings of the people of Thebes.

(*Enter a* Chorus, *the citizens of Thebes, who have not heard the news that* Creon *brings. They march around the altar, chanting.*)

C

Chorus. Zeus!
Great welcome voice of Zeus, what do you bring?
What word from the gold vaults of Delphi
comes to brilliant Thebes? Racked with terror—
terror shakes my heart
and I cry your wild cries, Apollo, Healer of Delos
I worship you in dread . . . what now, what is your price?
some new sacrifice? some ancient rite from the past
come round again each spring?—

173 Delos (dē'lŏs'): the island where Apollo was born.

Customizing Instruction

Less Proficient Readers

Help students to synthesize what is revealed about the murder by asking the following questions:

1 Where was Laius killed? *(on the road to Delphi)*

2 Only one person survived the attack on King Laius' party. According to the survivor, what happened? *(A band of thieves attacked the king's party.)*

3 Oedipus seems confident that he will find the murderer. According to Oedipus, why is the search for the murderer a way of protecting himself? *(The person who murdered King Laius might also try to kill Oedipus.)*

Focus Review the diagram of the Greek theater on pages 260–261, and draw attention to the orchestra. Explain that chorus members danced to musical accompaniment while they sang or chanted their lines. Point out that the chorus represents the ordinary people of Thebes. They are terrified by the plague and beg the gods for help.

English Learners

Explain the meaning of the following words and phrases:

Line 149: "what lay at our feet" *(what is right before us)*

Line 171: "Racked with terror" *(Made to suffer with great fear)*

Cross Curricular Link — Humanities

THE GREEK CHORUS Greek theater had its origins in the choral performances given at festivals honoring Dionysus. A group of about 50 men would dance and sing hymns in praise of the god. According to legend, in the middle of the sixth century B.C. the poet Thespis engaged in dialogue with the choral leader. Thus, Thespis became the first actor, and drama was born. Aeschylus, 525–456 B.C., later reduced the chorus to twelve men and added a second actor. Sophocles is believed to have increased the chorus to fifteen and added a third actor to the stage.

In commenting upon the action, the chorus often expressed the fears and hopes of ordinary citizens and voiced judgments of the characters. The chorus sang and danced its lyrics accompanied by the flute, although little is known about the style of the music or dance. Unlike the actors, members of the chorus were not professionals, but talented amateurs. The playwright himself would supervise their training. For each production, a wealthy citizen was chosen as *choregus*, responsible for financing the cost of costumes and rehearsal. Sometimes the choregus would take the part of the choral leader who would engage in dialogue with the actors.

Reading and Analyzing

Reading Skills and Strategies
MAKING INFERENCES

As students read, ask them to look for evidence that reveals how the chorus feels about its chances of surviving the plague.

Possible Response: The chorus seems desperate and in despair. They ask the gods to provide a "shield against death" because they are convinced no human measures can save them ("no sword of thought"). The chorus is convinced that "Thebes is dying." Only the gods can help them now.

Literary Analysis SIMILE

A In this passage, the dying people of Thebes are compared to "seabirds winging west" at the end of day. The Greeks believed that the underworld was located in the west, where the sun set. Here, the phrase "the shores of Evening" refers to the underworld.

Reading Skills and Strategies
CLARIFYING

B Remind students that the Priest earlier described people swarming to the two temples dedicated to Athena and to the river-shrine of Apollo. Here, we learn that women from the countryside are also flocking to the altars of the gods. Ask students to describe the mood of the city. *(People are in a state of panic and hysterical despair.)*

Literary Analysis ALLUSION

C These lines refer to Ares, the god of war, who is blamed for causing the plague.

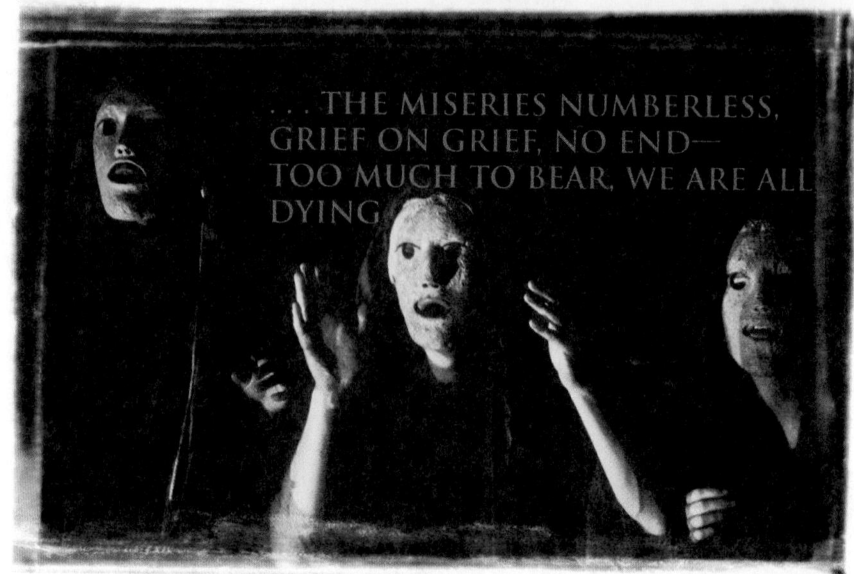

Masked members of the chorus, from a stage production of *Oedipus the King*, directed by Peter Hall (1996).

what will you bring to birth?
Tell me, child of golden Hope
warm voice that never dies!

You are the first I call, daughter of Zeus
deathless Athena—I call your sister Artemis,
heart of the market place enthroned in glory,
guardian of our earth—
I call Apollo, Archer astride the thunderheads of heaven—
O triple shield against death, shine before me now!
If ever, once in the past, you stopped some ruin
1 launched against our walls
you hurled the flame of pain
far, far from Thebes—you gods
come now, come down once more!

180–244 In this chant the chorus prays to various gods—Athena, Artemis, Apollo, Zeus, and Dionysus—for help and protection.

No, no
the miseries numberless, grief on grief, no end—
too much to bear, we are all dying
O my people . . .
Thebes like a great army dying

and there is no sword of thought to save us, no
and the fruits of our famous earth, they will not ripen
2 no and the women cannot scream their pangs to birth—
screams for the Healer, children dead in the womb
and life on life goes down
you can watch them go
A like seabirds winging west, outracing the day's fire
down the horizon, irresistibly
streaking on to the shores of Evening
Death
so many deaths, numberless deaths on deaths, no end—
Thebes is dying, look, her children
stripped of pity . . .
3 generations strewn on the ground
unburied, unwept, the dead spreading death
and the young wives and gray-haired mothers with them
B cling to the altars, trailing in from all over the city—
Thebes, city of death, one long cortege
and the suffering rises
wails for mercy rise
and the wild hymn for the Healer blazes out
clashing with our sobs our cries of mourning—
O golden daughter of god, send rescue
radiant as the kindness in your eyes!
Drive him back!—the fever, the god of death
4 that raging god of war
not armored in bronze, not shielded now, he burns me,
C battle cries in the onslaught burning on—
O rout him from our borders!
Sail him, blast him out to the Sea-queen's chamber
the black Atlantic gulfs
or the northern harbor, death to all
where the Thracian surf comes crashing.
Now what the night spares he comes by day and kills—
the god of death.

O lord of the stormcloud,
you who twirl the lightning, Zeus, Father,
thunder Death to nothing!

Apollo, lord of the light, I beg you—
whip your longbow's golden cord
showering arrows on our enemies—shafts of power

211 cortege (kôr-tĕzh'): funeral procession.

216 golden daughter of god: Athena.

223 Sea-queen's chamber: the ocean depths—home of Amphitrite, wife of the sea god Poseidon.

226 Thracian (thrā'shən) **surf:** the rough waters of the western Black Sea.

Customizing Instruction

Less Proficient Readers

1 Point out that the chorus has just asked three gods to help Thebes. These gods can form a "triple shield against Death." Ask students if the chorus seems confident of getting help. *(The chorus seems desperate, not confident.)*

2 Explain that Apollo is the Healer. Ask what needs to be healed in Thebes. *(Children are dying in the womb; the earth is not producing food; people everywhere are dying.)*

3 Point out that so many people are dying in Thebes that the corpses of the young and old are lying on the ground unburied.

4 Explain that the chorus is asking Athena and Apollo to drive out Ares, the god of war, who is blamed for the plague.

English Learners

Explain the meaning of the following phrases:

Line 195: "there is no sword of thought to save us" *(We cannot think of anything to save ourselves.)*

Line 207: "generations strewn on the ground" *(The corpses of children, adolescents, and all ages of adults lie on the ground.)*

Line 232: "whip your longbow's golden cord" *(pull the golden string of your archery bow)*

Advanced Learners

Tell students that some scholars believe this play was first performed during the Peloponnesian War near the time that Athens suffered through a plague. Ask students why Ares might be associated with the plague in the minds of Athenians. *(As the god of war, Ares is associated with destruction and death. The Athenians were facing death both on the outside of the city, from the Spartans, and within the city, from the plague.)*

OEDIPUS THE KING **271**

MINI LESSON Speaking and Listening

CHORAL READING Explain that the first choral song is known as a parados. It takes place as the chorus is entering the theater from two aisles that lead to the orchestra where the chorus will perform (see diagram on pages 260–261). The choral song is divided into two alternating sections, the strophe and the antistrophe

Prepare Divide the class into small groups, with each group responsible for one of the following sections:

- Strophe (lines 168–179)
- Antistrophe (lines 180–190, ending with "come down once more")
- Strophe (lines 190–203, ending with "Evening")
- Antistrophe (lines 203–217)
- Strophe (lines 218–230)
- Antistrophe (lines 231–243)

Give students time to study and rehearse their lines, allowing them to ask any questions about the meanings of lines. Explain to students that they need to read the lines clearly and in unison.

Present Have the entire class stand in place while each group reads its lines.

This activity is particularly well suited for longer class periods.

Literary Analysis GREEK MYTHOLOGY

A Explain that the god Dionysus was associated with wild excess. The followers of Dionysus, many of whom were women, would engage in frenzied rituals in remote mountain wilderness areas. The rituals involved drinking, dance, and music.

Pause and Reflect

Possible Response: Children die in the womb; fruits will not ripen; corpses litter the streets.

Literary Analysis DRAMATIC IRONY

B Point out that Sophocles' audience would have been aware of the irony here. Oedipus believes that he is a stranger to Thebes, though in actuality he was born there. Ask why he now counts himself a "native Theban."

Possible Response: Oedipus has lived in Thebes for a number of years and has ruled it. He considers himself a native now.

Active Reading

STRATEGIES FOR READING GREEK DRAMA

C Help students to realize the terms of Oedipus' proclamation. Anyone who knows the murderer must come forth; even if that person was an accomplice, his life will be spared. If anyone knows that the murderer was a foreigner, that person will be rewarded. Ask students to explain what type of punishment the murderer faces.

Possible Response: He will not be allowed in anyone's house; no one will be allowed to speak to him or pray for him. He will not be allowed to participate in religious rituals. He will be driven from Thebes.

Literary Analysis TRAGIC HERO

D Have students explain why Oedipus seems to identify with Laius. *(Both men served as king of Thebes; they were married to the same woman.)*

Help students to understand the reference to "blood-bonds." According to Oedipus, Laius might have conceived a child with Jocasta, which would have established a "blood bond" between the two men, but that was prevented by his murder.

champions strong before us rushing on!

Artemis, Huntress,
torches flaring over the eastern ridges—
ride Death down in pain!

A
God of the headdress gleaming gold, I cry to you—
your name and ours are one, Dionysus—
come with your face aflame with wine
your raving women's cries
your army on the march! Come with the lightning
come with torches blazing, eyes ablaze with glory!
Burn that god of death that all gods hate!

239 your name and ours are one, Dionysus (dī'ə-nī'səs): Dionysus, god of wine, was born of a Theban woman.

PAUSE & REFLECT What details helped you visualize Thebes as a city of death?

FOCUS Oedipus will now speak to his people. Read to find out what he intends to do to the killer or killers of Laius.

(Oedipus *enters from the palace to address the* Chorus, *as if addressing the entire city of Thebes.*)

Oedipus. You pray to the gods? Let me grant your prayers.
Come, listen to me—do what the plague demands:
you'll find relief and lift your head from the depths.

B
I will speak out now as a stranger to the story,
a stranger to the crime. If I'd been present then,
there would have been no mystery, no long hunt
without a clue in hand. So now, counted
a native Theban years after the murder,
to all of Thebes I make this proclamation:
if any one of you knows who murdered Laius,
the son of Labdacus, I order him to reveal
1
the whole truth to me. Nothing to fear,
even if he must denounce himself,
let him speak up
and so escape the brunt of the charge—
he will suffer no unbearable punishment,
nothing worse than exile, totally unharmed.

(Oedipus *pauses, waiting for a reply.*)

255 Labdacus (lăb'də-kəs).

WORDS TO KNOW

denounce (dĭ-nouns') *v.* to condemn publicly

272

MINI LESSON

Vocabulary Strategy

ANTONYMS

Instruction Words that have opposite or almost opposite meanings are antonyms. Antonyms in context can offer clues to meanings of unfamiliar words or terms.

Work with students to model the process of finding the meaning of a word by using its antonym.

Model Sentence

Oedipus sought to **denounce** Laius' killer, not to praise or to honor him in front of the masses.

Practice

- Write the model sentence on the chalkboard.
- Ask a volunteer to summarize the meaning of the sentence.
- Have students use the antonyms *praise* and *honor him in front of the masses* to guess the meaning of *denounce.*
- Ask a second volunteer to use the word *denounce* in a sentence.

Next,
if anyone knows the murderer is a stranger,
a man from alien soil, come, speak up.
I will give him a handsome reward, and lay up
gratitude in my heart for him besides.

(*silence again, no reply*)

But if you keep silent, if anyone panicking,
trying to shield himself or friend or kin,
rejects my offer, then hear what I will do.
I order you, every citizen of the state
C where I hold throne and power: banish this man—
whoever he may be—never shelter him, never
speak a word to him, never make him partner
to your prayers, your victims burned to the gods.
Never let the holy water touch his hands.
Drive him out, each of you, from every home.
2 *He* is the plague, the heart of our corruption,
as Apollo's oracle has just revealed to me.
So I honor my obligations:
I fight for the god and for the murdered man.

Now my curse on the murderer. Whoever he is,
a lone man unknown in his crime
or one among many, let that man drag out
3 his life in agony, step by painful step—
I curse myself as well . . . if by any chance
he proves to be an intimate of our house,
here at my hearth, with my full knowledge,
may the curse I just called down on him strike me!

These are your orders: perform them to the last.
I command you, for my sake, for Apollo's, for this country
blasted root and branch by the angry heavens.
Even if god had never urged you on to act,
how could you leave the crime uncleansed so long?
A man so noble—your king, brought down in blood—
you should have searched. But I am the king now,
I hold the throne that he held then, possess his bed
and a wife who shares our seed . . . why, our seed
D might be the same, children born of the same mother
might have created blood-bonds between us
if his hope of offspring had not met disaster—

274 holy water: water used for purification after a sacrifice to the gods.

285 intimate: friend.

Customizing Instruction

Less Proficient Readers

Focus Point out that Oedipus' speech is his first public announcement during the plague. Ask students to look for details that show Oedipus is trying to take control of a desperate situation.

1 Help students to understand that Oedipus is asking for two things. One, anyone who knows who murdered Laius must speak up. Two, the people of Thebes must treat the murderer as an outcast and drive him out of the city.

2 Help students to realize the severity of the punishment for the murderer. Unlike other exiles, the murderer can have no hope for a return to Thebes. He will be cut off from all contact with family or friends.

3 Point out that Oedipus' curse goes far beyond casting the murderer out of Thebes. Ask students what type of life the murderer will have. *(a life of agony)* Make sure that students understand that Oedipus includes himself in the curse. The curse will apply to him if he is hiding the murderer at his house.

English Learners

Explain the meaning of the following phrases:

Line 257: "even if he must denounce himself" *(even if the person must blame himself)*

Line 263: "a man from alien soil" *(a man from another country)*

Line 290: "blasted root and branch" *(torn completely apart by the plague)*

Line 292: "leave the crime uncleansed" *(allow the crime to go without punishment, which would purify the city)*

MINI LESSON Speaking and Listening

SPEECH Oedipus' speech (lines 245–314) is crucial because it presents his plan to bring the murderer to justice. Model for students how to present his speech dramatically by reading aloud lines 245–261. Demonstrate how to read lines expressively and coherently, using punctuation to divide words into meaningful groups. Then ask for four volunteers to read the rest of Oedipus' speech.

Prepare Divide the speech into the following sections: lines 261–279; lines 280–287; lines 288–306; lines 306–314. Give the volunteers time to prepare and rehearse their lines. Advise the students to read slowly and clearly, articulating beginning and ending consonants. Tell the students to express emotion that is appropriate to the words.

Present Invite the volunteers to recite their lines before the class. You may want to repeat your recitation of the lines that you modeled so that the class can hear the speech in its entirety. If possible, tape record the entire speech and replay it so that the performers can assess their own work.

This activity is particularly well suited for longer class periods.

Active Reading
STRATEGIES FOR READING GREEK DRAMA

A Point out that at various times in the drama, the leader of the chorus steps out from the chorus and participates in the dialogue.

Reading Skills and Strategies
CLARIFYING

B Ask students what it means for a blind person, such as Tiresias, to see "with the eyes of Apollo."

Possible Response: Tiresias has the gift of prophecy. He can reveal secrets that are known to the gods.

Pause & Reflect

Possible Response: The murderer will be forever banished from all houses and denied contact with all Thebans. He will be driven permanently from Thebes.

Literary Analysis CULTURAL SETTING

C Explain that prophets in ancient Greece were highly regarded because of their powers. See the mini-lesson on the bottom of the next page for more information.

but fate swooped at his head and cut him short.
So I will fight for him as if he were my father,
stop at nothing, search the world
to lay my hands on the man who shed his blood,
the son of Labdacus descended of Polydorus,
Cadmus of old and Agenor, founder of the line:
their power and mine are one.
Oh dear gods,
my curse on those who disobey these orders!
Let no crops grow out of the earth for them—
shrivel their women, kill their sons,
burn them to nothing in this plague
that hits us now, or something even worse.
But you, loyal men of Thebes who approve my actions,
may our champion, Justice, may all the gods
be with us, fight beside us to the end!

Leader. In the grip of your curse, my king, I swear
I'm not the murderer, I cannot point him out.
As for the search, Apollo pressed it on us—
he should name the killer.

Oedipus. Quite right,
but to force the gods to act against their will—
no man has the power.

Leader. Then if I might mention
the next best thing . . .

Oedipus. The third best too—
don't hold back, say it.

Leader. I still believe . . .
Lord Tiresias sees with the eyes of Lord Apollo.
Anyone searching for the truth, my king,
might learn it from the prophet, clear as day.

Oedipus. I've not been slow with that. On Creon's cue
I sent the escorts, twice, within the hour.
I'm surprised he isn't here.

Leader. We need him—
without him we have nothing but old, useless rumors.

Oedipus. Which rumors? I'll search out every word.

Leader. Laius was killed, they say, by certain travelers.

Oedipus. I know—but no one can find the murderer.

Leader. If the man has a trace of fear in him

304 Polydorus (pŏl'ə-dôr'əs).

305 Agenor (ə-jē'nôr'): Cadmus' father.

History

EXILE Exile was a standard punishment for unintentional murder in ancient Athens; it was sometimes imposed for treason as well. A citizen could also choose exile to escape the death penalty, an option that was available to Socrates, though he chose not to accept it. Exile could be accompanied by other penalties, such as the loss of property, the right to be buried in the territory of Athens, or the destruction of one's house. The punishment of exile was for life, unless the exiled person obtained pardon.

A different type of punishment, known as *ostracism*, also involved exile. A prominent but unpopular citizen might be banished from Athens for a period of ten years without loss of property. The ostracism was voted upon by the *ecclesia*, the governing assembly of Athens. The historian Thucydides was punished in this fashion for his military failures.

he won't stay silent long,
not with your curses ringing in his ears.

Oedipus. He didn't flinch at murder,
he'll never flinch at words.

PAUSE & REFLECT What curse does Oedipus put on the killer or killers of Laius?

FOCUS After the prophet Tiresias enters, he and Oedipus quarrel bitterly. In the heat of anger, Tiresias blurts out the identity of Laius' murderer. Read to find out whom Tiresias names.

(*Enter* Tiresias, *the blind prophet, led by a boy with escorts in attendance. He remains at a distance.*)

Leader. Here is the one who will convict him, look,
they bring him on at last, the seer, the man of god.
The truth lives inside him, him alone.

Oedipus. O Tiresias,
C master of all the mysteries of our life,
all you teach and all you dare not tell,
signs in the heavens, signs that walk the earth!
Blind as you are, you can feel all the more
what sickness haunts our city. You, my lord,
are the one shield, the one savior we can find.

We asked Apollo—perhaps the messengers
haven't told you—he sent his answer back:
"Relief from the plague can only come one way.
Uncover the murderers of Laius,
put them to death or drive them into exile."
So I beg you, grudge us nothing now, no voice,
no message plucked from the birds, the embers
or the other mantic ways within your grasp.
2 Rescue yourself, your city, rescue me—
rescue everything infected by the dead.
We are in your hands. For a man to help others
with all his gifts and native strength:
that is the noblest work.

Tiresias. How terrible—to see the truth
3 when the truth is only pain to him who sees!
I knew it well, but I put it from my mind,

354 mantic: prophetic.

Customizing Instruction

Less Proficient Readers

1 Ask student why Tiresias might be able to help Oedipus. *(He may know who the murderer is.)*

Focus Make sure that students realize that when Tiresias appears on stage, he already knows the name of the murderer. Tell students that Tiresias often speaks in riddles so it is not easy to understand his meaning.

2 Ask students how Tiresias can "rescue" the entire city. *(by naming the murderer)*

3 Help students realize that Tiresias is talking about the "truth" of the murder. He does not want to tell what he knows.

English Learners

Explain the meaning of the following words and phrases:

Line 315: "in the grip of your curse" *(held under the power of your curse)*

Line 352: "grudge us nothing" *(do not hold anything back from us)*

Cross Curricular Link History

PROPHETS Prophets, or seers, played a major role in Greek culture, but they were also subject to criticism and disbelief. Prophets, such as Calchas in Homer's *Iliad* and Tiresias in *Oedipus the King,* were thought to be capable of interpreting signs of what was to come. They might predict whether a man will meet death, disease, or lose property. In times of war, they might predict the outcome of battles; in times of trouble, they might recommend a course of action. The prophets often interpreted the will of the gods by explaining dreams, observing birds in flight, or examining the entrails of sacrificed animals. True prophets were believed to be divinely inspired, serving as instruments of the gods.

Unlike oracles, prophets had no ties to religious institutions; a person was a prophet if he claimed to be one. That meant, in practice, that a number of unscrupulous people made such claims. Some would target the rich and offer prophecy in exchange for money, even promising that they could deliver a client from evil. While many Greeks acknowledged the powers of prophecy, practicality required caution when dealing with those who made such claims.

Reading and Analyzing

Active Reading

STRATEGIES FOR READING GREEK DRAMA

A Help students to appreciate the dramatic impact of Tiresias' response. The prophet hints that he knows the truth of the murder, but he refuses to talk about it. Ask why Oedipus accuses Tiresias of acting "unlawfully."

Possible Response: Tiresias has violated Oedipus' order to tell what is known about the murderer. Also, the prophet refuses to cooperate in the midst of a deadly crisis that threatens all of Thebes.

Literary Analysis TRAGIC HERO

B Ask students why Oedipus becomes so enraged with Tiresias.

Possible Responses: Oedipus is used to having people obey his orders. He cannot understand why Tiresias won't share his information. He feels that Tiresias has no compassion for the suffering of Thebes.

Reading Skills and Strategies

MAKING INFERENCES

C Ask students why Oedipus is so quick to assume that Tiresias must be involved in the murder of Laius.

Possible Responses: Oedipus is so angry that he is not thinking clearly. From his viewpoint, there can be no other explanation for Tiresias' refusal to cooperate. Perhaps Oedipus feels insecure in his rule and is afraid that people may be plotting against him as well.

else I never would have come.

Oedipus. What's this? Why so grim, so dire?

Tiresias. Just send me home. You bear your burdens,
I'll bear mine. It's better that way,
please believe me.

[A] **Oedipus.** Strange response . . . unlawful,
unfriendly too to the state that bred and reared you—
you withhold the word of god.

Tiresias. I fail to see
that your own words are so well-timed.
I'd rather not have the same thing said of me . . .

Oedipus. For the love of god, don't turn away,
not if you know something. We beg you,
all of us on our knees.

[1] **Tiresias.** None of you knows—
and I will never reveal my dreadful secrets,
not to say your own.

Oedipus. What? You know and you won't tell?
You're bent on betraying us, destroying Thebes?

Tiresias. I'd rather not cause pain for you or me.
So why this . . . useless interrogation?
You'll get nothing from me.

379 interrogation (ĭn-tĕr′ə-gā′shən): questioning.

[2] [B] **Oedipus.** Nothing! You,
you scum of the earth, you'd enrage a heart of stone!
You won't talk? Nothing moves you?
Out with it, once and for all!

Tiresias. You criticize my temper . . . unaware
of the one *you* live with, you revile me.

Oedipus. Who could restrain his anger hearing you?
What outrage—you spurn the city!

Tiresias. What will come will come.
Even if I shroud it all in silence.

Oedipus. What will come? You're bound to *tell* me that.

Tiresias. I will say no more. Do as you like, build your
anger
to whatever pitch you please, rage your worst—

[C] [3] **Oedipus.** Oh I'll let loose, I have such fury in me—
now I see it all. You helped hatch the plot,
you did the work, yes, short of killing him

WORDS TO KNOW

revile (rĭ-vīl′) *v.* to abuse verbally; criticize harshly

YOU WON'T TALK? NOTHING MOVES YOU? OUT WITH IT, ONCE AND FOR ALL!

Oedipus accuses Tiresias in a London stage production of *Oedipus Rex*, with Laurence Olivier as Oedipus and Ralph Richardson as Tiresias (1945).

Customizing Instruction

Less Proficient Readers

1 Explain that Tiresias reveals that he knows "dreadful secrets" unknown to everyone else. He also says that these secrets involve Oedipus. Ask what these secrets are about. *(the murder of Laius)*

2 Ask for a volunteer to read these lines aloud in a way that communicates the anger of Oedipus.

3 Ask students if Oedipus is being logical in assuming that Tiresias must have been involved in the murder. *(Accept all reasonable responses.)*

English Learners

Explain the meaning of the following phrases:

Line 389: "shroud it all in silence" *(keep the truth hidden from view by being quiet)*

Line 394: "hatch the plot" *(come up with the plan to murder Laius)*

Advanced Learners

Ask students to look for clues on page 276 that relate to the secret of Oedipus' birth and his role in the murder of Laius.

Possible Response: In line 370, Tiresias hints that Oedipus has been unlawful in his actions: he is guilty of what he accuses Tiresias of. In line 375, Tiresias connects Oedipus to the "dreadful secrets" of the murder, which, as we will learn, involve his parentage. When Oedipus lashes out in anger, Tiresias responds that the king is "unaware of the one you live with" (line 385), which refers to Oedipus' marriage to his mother.

Reading and Analyzing

Active Reading
STRATEGIES FOR READING GREEK DRAMA

A Make sure that students understand the seriousness of Tiresias' accusation. Ask what it means that Oedipus is the "curse, the corruption of the land." *(He is the murderer.)*

Literary Analysis TRAGIC HERO

B Ask why Oedipus has such a hard time understanding Tiresias' accusation of murder.

Possible Responses: To Oedipus, it is simply unthinkable that he could be the murderer of Laius. Oedipus is a proud man, convinced of his abilities and judgment. He cannot even consider the possibility that he might be to blame for the plague.

Literary Analysis CONFLICT

C Point out the increasing bitterness of the argument. The king mocks the prophet for his blindness and ignorance. Ask what Tiresias means by his insult of Oedipus. *(Oedipus will one day be mocked for his blindness.)*

Reading Skills and Strategies
EVALUATING

D Point out that Oedipus accuses Creon of conspiring with Tiresias. Ask whether his accusation is fair.

Possible Responses: Some students will note that Oedipus has no evidence. He seems to be losing control of himself, acting rashly and irrationally. Therefore, his accusation is completely unfair. Others may excuse Oedipus' rash behavior as the result of the pressure he faces. Oedipus is desperately trying to make sense of a very strange situation.

Literary Analysis GREEK MYTH

E Oedipus compares the monstrous Sphinx—a winged creature with the head of a woman and the body of a lion—to the equally monstrous Furies. The Furies were hideous goddesses responsible for avenging murders within families.

with your own hands—and given eyes I'd say
you did the killing single-handed!

Tiresias. Is that so!
(A) I charge you, then, submit to that decree
you just laid down: from this day onward
speak to no one, not these citizens, not myself.
You are the curse, the corruption of the land!

Oedipus. You, shameless—
aren't you appalled to start up such a story?
You think you can get away with this?

Tiresias. I have already.
The truth with all its power lives inside me.

Oedipus. Who primed you for this? Not your prophet's
trade.

Tiresias. You did, you forced me, twisted it out of me.

Oedipus. What? Say it again—I'll understand it better.

Tiresias. Didn't you understand, just now?
Or are you tempting me to talk?

(B) **Oedipus.** No, I can't say I grasped your meaning.
Out with it, again!

Tiresias. I say you are the murderer you hunt.

Oedipus. That obscenity, twice—by god, you'll pay.

Tiresias. Shall I say more, so you can really rage?

Oedipus. Much as you want. Your words are nothing—
futile.

Tiresias. You cannot imagine . . . I tell you,
you and your loved ones live together in infamy,
you cannot see how far you've gone in guilt.

418 infamy (ĭn′fə-mē): disgrace.

Oedipus. You think you can keep this up and never suffer?

Tiresias. Indeed, if the truth has any power.

Oedipus. It does
but not for you, old man. You've lost your power,
stone-blind, stone-deaf—senses, eyes blind as stone!

(C) **Tiresias.** I pity you, flinging at me the very insults
each man here will fling at you so soon.

Oedipus. Blind,
lost in the night, endless night that nursed you!
You can't hurt me or anyone else who sees the light—

WORDS TO KNOW

appall (ə-pôl′) *v.* to horrify
futile (fyo͞ot′l) *adj.* useless

278

MINI LESSON Speaking and Listening

DRAMATIZING DIALOGUE To help students appreciate the dramatic tension of the dialogue between Oedipus and Tiresias, invite two volunteers to stage part of the scene, from lines 359–432.

Prepare As a prelude to the dramatization, have the entire class give performance suggestions to the volunteers. Use the following questions:

- What motivates each character in this scene?
- What range of emotions should be expressed by each character?
- How loudly should each character's lines be spoken?
- Where should the characters stand in relation to one another?
- What gestures and expressions would be appropriate to each character?

Present Allow the volunteers time to rehearse their lines, if possible, giving them at least a day. To simulate a Greek stage, have the entire class stand near the performers, as if the class were playing the role of the chorus and witnessing the dialogue.

This activity is particularly well suited for longer class periods.

you can never touch me.

Tiresias. True, it is not your fate
to fall at my hands. Apollo is quite enough,
and he will take some pains to work this out.

Oedipus. Creon! Is this conspiracy his or yours?

Tiresias. Creon is not your downfall, no, you are your own.

Oedipus. O power—
wealth and empire, skill outstripping skill
in the heady rivalries of life,
what envy lurks inside you! Just for this,
the crown the city gave me—I never sought it,
they laid it in my hands—for this alone, Creon,
the soul of trust, my loyal friend from the start
steals against me . . . so hungry to overthrow me
he sets this wizard on me, this scheming quack,
this fortune-teller peddling lies, eyes peeled
for his own profit—seer blind in his craft!

Come here, you pious fraud. Tell me,
when did you ever prove yourself a prophet?
When the Sphinx, that chanting Fury kept her death-watch here,
why silent then, not a word to set our people free?
There was a riddle, not for some passer-by to solve—
it cried out for a prophet. Where were you?
Did you rise to the crisis? Not a word,
you and your birds, your gods—nothing.
No, but I came by, Oedipus the ignorant,
I stopped the Sphinx! With no help from the birds,
the flight of my own intelligence hit the mark.

And this is the man you'd try to overthrow?
You think you'll stand by Creon when he's king?
You and the great mastermind—
you'll pay in tears, I promise you, for this,
this witch-hunt. If you didn't look so senile
the lash would teach you what your scheming means!

Leader. I would suggest his words were spoken in anger,
Oedipus . . . yours too, and it isn't what we need.
The best solution to the oracle, the riddle
posed by god—we should look for that.

434 heady: violent; passionate.

Customizing Instruction

Less Proficient Readers

As a way of making sure that students understand the conflict between Tiresias and Oedipus, write the names of both characters on the board. Lead students in a discussion of what each character is accused of. Tell them to find words and phrases on these pages that express those accusations and to write those phrases on the board under the appropriate character.

Possible Response

Oedipus

- "the curse, the corruption of the land"
- "you are the murderer you hunt"
- "you and your loved ones live together in infamy"

Tiresias

- "You've lost your power"
- "scheming quack"
- "fortune-teller peddling lies"
- "eyes peeled for his own profit"
- "you pious fraud"

English Learners

Explain the meaning of the following phrases:

Line 406: "Who primed you" *(who told you to do this)*

Line 428: "you can never touch me" *(you will never be able to hurt or disturb me)*

Line 458: "this witch-hunt" *(this attempt to find an innocent person to blame)*

OEDIPUS THE KING 279

Reading and Analyzing

Reading Skills and Strategies
PARAPHRASING

A Ask students to explain the meaning of Tiresias' accusations in their own words.

Possible Response: Though Oedipus has eyes to see, he is blind to the corruption of his life. Without knowing it, he has punished people in his own family, even those who have died. He is cursed by both his mother and his father. One day he will pay a terrible price and will be blinded.

Reading Skills and Strategies
CLARIFYING

B Remind students that Jocasta was given to Oedipus as a prize for defeating the Sphinx. Ask why Oedipus' marriage to Jocasta will lead to "the fatal harbor." *(Oedipus does not realize that Jocasta is his mother. He will suffer greatly when he finds out.)*

Literary Analysis PARADOX

C Explain that a paradox is a statement that seems to be contradictory. Though it may seem impossible for the birth of Oedipus to bring his destruction, that is indeed the case.

Literary Analysis TRAGEDY

D According to Aristotle, a tragedy can only occur if a good man falls from a great position in life. As Tiresias points out, the tragedy of Oedipus is tied to his "great good fortune" of becoming king.

Active Reading
STRATEGIES FOR READING GREEK DRAMA

E Point out that Tiresias is boldly direct. He says that Oedipus married his mother ("to his mother son and husband both") and killed his father ("spilled his father's blood"). Ask students why Oedipus does not respond. *(He has entered the palace and does not hear Tiresias.)*

Pause & Reflect
Possible Response: Oedipus

Tiresias. You are the king no doubt, but in one respect,
at least, I am your equal: the right to reply.
I claim that privilege too.
I am not your slave. I serve Apollo.
I don't need Creon to speak for me in public.
So,
you mock my blindness? Let me tell you this.
You with your precious eyes,
you're blind to the corruption of your life,
to the house you live in, those you live with—
who *are* your parents? Do you know? All unknowing
you are the scourge of your own flesh and blood,
A the dead below the earth and the living here above,
and the double lash of your mother and your father's
curse
will whip you from this land one day, their footfall
treading you down in terror, darkness shrouding
your eyes that now can see the light!
Soon, soon
you'll scream aloud—what haven won't reverberate?
What rock of Cithaeron won't scream back in echo?
That day you learn the truth about your marriage,
B the wedding-march that sang you into your halls,
the lusty voyage home to the fatal harbor!
And a crowd of other horrors you'd never dream
will level you with yourself and all your children.

There. Now smear us with insults—Creon, myself
and every word I've said. No man will ever
be rooted from the earth as brutally as you.

Oedipus. Enough! Such filth from him? Insufferable—
what, still alive? Get out—
faster, back where you came from—vanish!

Tiresias. I would never have come if you hadn't called me here.

Oedipus. If I thought you would blurt out such absurdities,
you'd have died waiting before I'd had you summoned.

Tiresias. Absurd, am I! To you, not to your parents:
the ones who bore you found me sane enough.

Oedipus. Parents—who? Wait . . . who is my father?

C **Tiresias.** This day will bring your birth and your destruction.

480 haven: place of safety.

481 Cithaeron (sĭ-thîr′ən): a mountain about 12 miles south of Thebes.

WORDS TO KNOW
reverberate (rĭ-vûr′bə-rāt′) *v.* to reflect a noise; resound

Oedipus. Riddles—all you can say are riddles, murk and darkness.

Tiresias. Ah, but aren't you the best man alive at solving riddles?

Oedipus. Mock me for that, go on, and you'll reveal my greatness.

Tiresias. Your great good fortune, true, it was your ruin.

Oedipus. Not if I saved the city—what do I care?

Tiresias. Well then, I'll be going.

(*to his attendant*)

Take me home, boy.

Oedipus. Yes, take him away. You're a nuisance here.
Out of the way, the irritation's gone.

(*turning his back on* Tiresias, *moving toward the palace*)

Tiresias. I will go,
once I have said what I came here to say.
I will never shrink from the anger in your eyes—
you can't destroy me. Listen to me closely:
the man you've sought so long, proclaiming,
cursing up and down, the murderer of Laius—
he is here. A stranger,
you may think, who lives among you,
he soon will be revealed a native Theban
but he will take no joy in the revelation.
Blind who now has eyes, beggar who now is rich,
he will grope his way toward a foreign soil,
a stick tapping before him step by step.

(Oedipus *enters the palace.*)

Revealed at last, brother and father both
to the children he embraces, to his mother
son and husband both—he sowed the loins
his father sowed, he spilled his father's blood!

Go in and reflect on that, solve that.
And if you find I've lied
from this day onward call the prophet blind.

(Tiresias *and the boy exit to the side.*)

PAUSE & REFLECT Whom does Tiresias name as the murderer of Laius?

Customizing Instruction

Less Proficient Readers

Read aloud lines 520–523. Explain that these comments are the most important in the scene because they reveal exactly what Tiresias knows. Then ask the following questions to make sure that students understand this information:

- How can Oedipus be both a "brother and father" to his children? *(He married his mother, which would make him a stepbrother to his own children.)*
- Why is Oedipus described as both a "son and husband" to Jocasta? *(She is both his mother and his wife.)*
- How did Oedipus spill his father's blood? *(He must have been the one who killed him.)*

English Learners

Explain the meaning of the following phrases:

Line 474: "the scourge of your own flesh and blood" *(the person who brings suffering to your own family)*

Line 476: "the double lash" *(the double punishment)*

Line 486: "level you with yourself and all your children" *(bring down you and your children)*

Line 489: "rooted from the earth" *(torn away from your homeland)*

Cross Curricular Link **Humanities**

FATE Tiresias tells Oedipus that he has been fated to be the murderer of his father and the husband of his mother. According to the Greeks, each person has a fate, or *moira*, assigned to him or her. While that fate cannot be changed, it is up to each person to bear that fate with grace and dignity. In a sense, one's fate marks the boundaries of one's life that cannot be crossed or altered. A person who seeks to overstep his or her fate would be guilty of *hubris*, or pride.

Homer speaks of Fate as a singular and impersonal power, sometimes treating it as a kind of god. Even the Olympian gods had no power to change fate. The poet Hesiod personified fate as three very old women who spin the threads of human destiny.

Reading and Analyzing

Active Reading

STRATEGIES FOR READING GREEK DRAMA

Explain to students that the chorus may have divided into two groups to perform this song. The first group would sing the first and third sections, each known as a strophe. The second group would sing the second and fourth sections, each known as an antistrophe. A letter marks the beginning of each of the four sections.

A Tell students that in this strophe the chorus imagines the murderer as an outcast on the run.

B This antistrophe continues the same line of thought. The fugitive, who is like a "wild mountain bull," cannot hope to escape the "dread voices" of Apollo and the Furies. Ask students if the chorus believes that Oedipus is the murderer. *(probably not, because they imagine the murderer being far away from Thebes)*

C In this strophe the chorus weighs the accusations of Tiresias and expresses its attitude toward Oedipus. Ask students to look for phrases that reveal whether the chorus believes Tiresias' charges.

Possible Response: The chorus is confused by the charges, which they "can't accept" and "can't deny." However, they still support Oedipus. They "know of nothing" that gives evidence of his guilt.

D In this antistrophe, the chorus expresses doubts about the prophetic powers of Tiresias. Ask students to explain the basis of their doubts. *(Tiresias is a "mere man." He may not be able to know what Zeus and Apollo know.)*

FOCUS The chorus describes the panic that the murderer of Laius must now feel and then reflects on Oedipus. As you read, look for details that suggest how the chorus feels about Oedipus at this point in the play.

A

Chorus. Who—
who is the man the voice of god denounces
resounding out of the rocky gorge of Delphi?
The horror too dark to tell,
whose ruthless bloody hands have done the work?
His time has come to fly
to outrace the stallions of the storm
his feet a streak of speed—
Cased in armor, Apollo son of the Father
lunges on him, lightning-bolts afire!
And the grim unerring Furies
closing for the kill.

B

Look,
the word of god has just come blazing
flashing off Parnassus' snowy heights!
That man who left no trace—
after him, hunt him down with all our strength!
Now under bristling timber
up through rocks and caves he stalks
like the wild mountain bull—
cut off from men, each step an agony, frenzied, racing
blind
but he cannot outrace the dread voices of Delphi
ringing out of the heart of Earth,
the dark wings beating around him shrieking doom
the doom that never dies, the terror—

C

The skilled prophet scans the birds and shatters me with
terror!
I can't accept him, can't deny him, don't know what to
say,
I'm lost, and the wings of dark foreboding beating—
I cannot see what's come, what's still to come . . .
and what could breed a blood feud between
Laius' house and the son of Polybus?
I know of nothing, not in the past and not now,
no charge to bring against our king, no cause

536 unerring: not turning aside; relentless; **Furies:** terrifying goddesses who pursue and punish criminals.

539 Parnassus' (pär-năs'əs) snowy heights: the peaks of the mountain that towers over Delphi.

555 the son of Polybus (pŏl'ə-bəs): Oedipus, who believes himself to be the son of Polybus, king of Corinth.

WORDS TO KNOW

foreboding (fôr-bō'dĭng) *n.* a sense of evil or danger to come

✓ Assessment Informal Assessment

SUMMARIZING Ask students to work in pairs to prepare an oral summary of what has happened to this point in the play. Tell students to explain the nature of the plague, Oedipus' response to the crisis, and the conflict between Oedipus and Tiresias. Students may present their summaries in the form of a newscast about this day in ancient Thebes.

RUBRIC

3 Full Accomplishment Student's account provides an accurate and thorough explanation of the events.

2 Substantial Achievement Student's account is accurate, but some important information is missing.

1 Little or Partial Achievement Student's account is missing vital information, is inaccurate, or shows little understanding of the events.

to attack his fame that rings throughout Thebes—
not without proof—not for the ghost of Laius,
not to avenge a murder gone without a trace.

Zeus and Apollo know, they know, the great masters
of all the dark and depth of human life.
But whether a mere man can know the truth,
whether a seer can fathom more than I—
there is no test, no certain proof
though matching skill for skill
a man can outstrip a rival. No, not till I see
these charges proved will I side with his accusers.
We saw him then, when the she-hawk swept against him,
saw with our own eyes his skill, his brilliant triumph—
there was the test—he was the joy of Thebes!
Never will I convict my king, never in my heart.

564 fathom: understand.

569 she-hawk: the Sphinx.

Thinking Through the Literature

1. Why does Oedipus send for Tiresias?
2. How does the chorus feel about Oedipus at this point in the play?
3. Why do you think Oedipus is so determined to discover the murderer of Laius?

THINK ABOUT
- how he feels about the people of Thebes
- how he once saved the city from the Sphinx
- why he might feel especially close to the murdered king

Customizing Instruction

Less Proficient Readers

Focus Many students may have difficulty understanding the chorus. Give an overview of each section, as provided by the lettered annotations on page 282. Then choose four pairs of students to recite each section of the song. In each pair, include one proficient reader and one who is less proficient.

Give each pair time to prepare their lines for presentation, and allow them to ask questions to clarify meaning. Tell students that each pair must recite the lines in unison.

English Learners

Explain the meaning of the following phrases:

Line 527: "the man the voice of god denounces" *(the man judged harshly by god)*

Line 533: "his feet a streak of speed" *(He is running fast.)*

Line 536: "unerring Furies" *(the Furies who never miss their target)*

Line 554: "blood feud" *(a battle between families)*

Advanced Learners

Remind students that there were a number of professional prophets in fifth-century Athens. Many were paid for their efforts; some were not honest. Ask students whether such information is relevant to their understanding of the various responses to Tiresias.

Possible Responses: Yes, because such information makes it easier to understand Oedipus' suspicions and his reluctance to accept Tiresias' prophesy. No, because Tiresias seems be respected by everyone except for Oedipus.

Thinking Through the Literature

1. Possible Response: Oedipus sends for Tiresias to find out more about the murder of Laius.
2. Possible Response: Although the chorus is disturbed by the accusations of Tiresias, they are still loyal to Oedipus. They saw him defeat the Sphinx with their own eyes and regard him as their hero.
3. Possible Responses: Oedipus is a determined leader. He knows that nothing can relieve Thebes of its suffering unless the murderer is uncovered. He also regards the discovery of the murderer as a personal challenge. He has not had such a test of his powers since his encounter with the Sphinx. Oedipus may feel vulnerable; the person who murdered Laius may one day pursue Oedipus. He wants justice for such a serious crime.

Use Selection Quiz in **Unit Two Resource Book,** p. 31.

OEDIPUS THE KING 283

Reading and Analyzing

Reading Skills and Strategies
PARAPHRASING

A Ask students to put this sentence into their own words.

Possible Response: If Oedipus thinks that I have done him an injury, I have no desire to live because my reputation will be ruined.

Literary Analysis TRAGIC HERO

B Ask students what they think of the way that Oedipus treats Creon.

Possible Response: While it is understandable that Oedipus is angry at the news of Tiresias' accusations, the king does not treat Creon fairly. Oedipus accuses him of plotting to kill him before giving Creon a chance to defend himself.

Use **Unit Two Resource Book,** p. 33, for more practice.

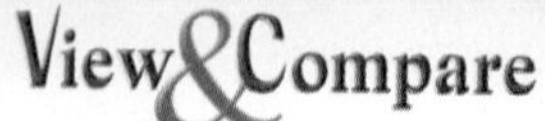

What do each of these images suggest about the chorus? Study the gestures, postures, costuming, and physical positions.

Tyrone Guthrie film version of *Oedipus Rex* (1957)

Peter Hall stage production of *Oedipus the King* (1996)

284

MINI LESSON Viewing and Representing

COMPARING STAGINGS OF THE CHORUS Tyrone Guthrie's film version of *Oedipus Rex,* based upon his stage production at the Stratford Festival Theatre in Canada, imitated ancient Greek theater. Actors wore elaborate masks and gowns. The masks covered three-quarters of the face, allowing the audience to see the mouth and jaw of the actor. From a distance, it looked as if the actor's mouth was actually part of the mask.

The Peter Hall production of *Oedipus the King* was first performed in the ancient theater at Epidaurus, Greece, before an audience of 10,000. All actors wore masks of either white-on-white or sand-against-blood colors. Hall had all performers speak directly to the audience instead of to one another.

View & Compare Possible Response: In the Guthrie image, students may note the elaborate costumes suggesting the robes of priests; the masks that give the performers an alien look; and the stately positions of the actors, who stand apart from one another. Such attributes suggest that the chorus has a ritual role. In the Hall production, the chorus is huddled together, as if in desperation. Their white masks against a background of painted white faces give performers a surreal look, one suggesting a nightmare.

FOCUS Creon defends himself against Oedipus' charge of treason. Read to find out how Oedipus treats Creon in this scene.

(*Enter* Creon *from the side.*)

Creon. My fellow-citizens, I hear King Oedipus
levels terrible charges at me. I had to come.
I resent it deeply. If, in the present crisis,
he thinks he suffers any abuse from me,
A anything I've done or said that offers him
the slightest injury, why, I've no desire
to linger out this life, my reputation in ruins.
The damage I'd face from such an accusation
is nothing simple. No, there's nothing worse:
1 branded a traitor in the city, a traitor
to all of you and my good friends.

Leader. True,
but a slur might have been forced out of him,
by anger perhaps, not any firm conviction.

Creon. The charge was made in public, wasn't it?
I put the prophet up to spreading lies?

Leader. Such things were said . . .
I don't know with what intent, if any.

Creon. Was his glance steady, his mind right
when the charge was brought against me?

Leader. I really couldn't say. I never look
to judge the ones in power.

(*The doors open.* Oedipus *enters.*)

Wait,
here's Oedipus now.

Oedipus. You—here? You have the gall
to show your face before the palace gates?
B You, plotting to kill me, kill the king—
I see it all, the marauding thief himself
scheming to steal my crown and power!
Tell me,
in god's name, what did you take me for,
2 coward or fool, when you spun out your plot?
Your treachery—you think I'd never detect it
creeping against me in the dark? Or sensing it,
not defend myself? Aren't you the fool,
you and your high adventure. Lacking numbers,

594 gall: rude boldness.

597 marauding: roaming in search of plunder.

Customizing Instruction

Less Proficient Readers

Focus Tell students that Oedipus believes that Creon is plotting against him.

1 Point out that Creon is badly shaken by what Oedipus has said about him. Still, he shows his loyalty to the city and its citizens.

2 Ask two students to act out this series of questions. One student should take the part of Oedipus and state the questions. The other should respond as Creon, showing his reaction with expressions, gestures, or words. Make sure that students realize that the wording of the questions gives Creon no way of defending his innocence.

English Learners

Explain the meaning of the following phrases:

Line 574: "levels terrible charges" *(accuses me of terrible things)*

Line 584: "slur" *(insult)*

Line 604: "your high adventure" *(your crazy plan)*

OEDIPUS THE KING 285

Reading and Analyzing

Literary Analysis TRAGIC HERO

A Explain that the Greeks greatly valued moderation, the ability to find a balance between extremes. Ask students whether they agree with Creon that Oedipus has lost his balance. *(Accept all reasonable responses.)*

Reading Skills and Strategies
SUMMARIZING

B In this speech, Creon defends himself by saying that he has no motive to conspire against Oedipus. Ask students to summarize the case that he makes for himself.

Possible Response: I have all the privileges of power but without the worries. I enjoy my current position in the state and people think highly of me. Why would I do anything to change that?

powerful friends, out for the big game of empire—
you need riches, armies to bring that quarry down!

Creon. Are you quite finished? It's your turn to listen
for just as long as you've . . . instructed me.
Hear me out, then judge me on the facts.

Oedipus. You've a wicked way with words, Creon,
but I'll be slow to learn—from you.
I find you a menace, a great burden to me.

Creon. Just one thing, hear me out in this.

Oedipus. Just one thing,
don't tell *me* you're not the enemy, the traitor.

Creon. Look, if you think crude, mindless stubbornness
such a gift, you've lost your sense of balance.

Oedipus. If you think you can abuse a kinsman,
then escape the penalty, you're insane.

Creon. Fair enough, I grant you. But this injury
you say I've done you, what is it?

Oedipus. Did you induce me, yes or no,
to send for that sanctimonious prophet?

Creon. I did. And I'd do the same again.

Oedipus. All right then, tell me, how long is it now
since Laius . . .

Creon. Laius—what did *he* do?

Oedipus. Vanished,
swept from sight, murdered in his tracks.

Creon. The count of the years would run you far back . . .

Oedipus. And that far back, was the prophet at his trade?

Creon. Skilled as he is today, and just as honored.

Oedipus. Did he ever refer to me then, at that time?

Creon. No,
never, at least, when I was in his presence.

Oedipus. But you did investigate the murder, didn't you?

Creon. We did our best, of course, discovered nothing.

Oedipus. But the great seer never accused me then—why
not?

Creon. I don't know. And when I don't, *I* keep quiet.

Oedipus. You do know this, you'd tell it too—
if you had a shred of decency.

606 quarry: the object of a hunt.

622 sanctimonious (săngk′tə-mō′nē-əs): making a show of being holy or pious.

WORDS TO KNOW
menace (mĕn′ĭs) *n.* a threat

Creon. What?
If I know, I won't hold back.

Oedipus. Simply this:
3 if the two of you had never put heads together,
we would never have heard about *my* killing Laius.

Creon. If that's what he says . . . well, you know best.
But now I have a right to learn from you
as you just learned from me.

Oedipus. Learn your fill,
you never will convict me of the murder.

Creon. Tell me, you're married to my sister, aren't you?

Oedipus. A genuine discovery—there's no denying that.

Creon. And you rule the land with her, with equal power?

4 **Oedipus.** She receives from me whatever she desires.

Creon. And I am the third, all of us are equals?

Oedipus. Yes, and it's there you show your stripes—
you betray a kinsman.

Creon. Not at all.
Not if you see things calmly, rationally,
as I do. Look at it this way first:
who in his right mind would rather rule
and live in anxiety than sleep in peace?
Particularly if he enjoys the same authority.
Not I, I'm not the man to yearn for kingship,
not with a king's power in my hands. Who would?
No one with any sense of self-control.
Now, as it is, you offer me all I need,
not a fear in the world. But if I wore the crown . . .
B there'd be many painful duties to perform,
5 hardly to my taste.
How could kingship
please me more than influence, power
without a qualm? I'm not that deluded yet,
to reach for anything but privilege outright,
profit free and clear.
Now all men sing my praises, all salute me,
now all who request your favors curry mine.
I am their best hope: success rests in me.
Why give up that, I ask you, and borrow trouble?
A man of sense, someone who sees things clearly

665 qualm: feeling of uneasiness or doubt.

669 curry: seek by flattery.

Customizing Instruction

Less Proficient Readers

Help students to keep track of the plot by asking the following questions:

1 Creon calmly responds to the angry Oedipus. How does Creon want to be judged? *(on the facts)*

2 Oedipus is making the point that Tiresias could have accused him years ago. Why is this important? *(Oedipus thinks that Creon persuaded Tiresias to make up such a charge.)*

3 Oedipus says that people would "never have heard" the accusation if Creon and Tiresias had not teamed up. What does he mean? *(The two men came up with a lie so that they could force Oedipus out of office.)*

4 Creon is making the point that he already has power. According to Creon, who are the three people who share the power to govern Thebes? *(Oedipus, Jocasta, and Creon)*

5 Ask students which of the following statements best sums up Creon's defense:

- I already have all the power I need, and I am happy in my position. *(correct choice)*
- I have no interest in public affairs, and I am happy to go unnoticed.

English Learners

Explain the meaning of the following phrases:

Line 605: "the big game of empire" *(the goal of winning control of Thebes)*

Line 627: "the count of the years would run you far back" *(It happened many years ago.)*

Line 639: "put heads together" *(come up with a plan together)*

Cross Curricular Link History

OEDIPUS AS TYRANT Though Oedipus is called a king in this translation, the Greek word used by Sophocles is *tyrannos*, which actually means tyrant. Today, the word tyrant has negative connotations, suggesting a harsh and cruel power wielded by an absolute ruler. For the Greeks, however, a tyrant was not necessarily a bad ruler. Rather, a tyrant was an ordinary citizen who became a supreme ruler without benefit of heredity. Oedipus is the ruler of Thebes not because of his birth but because of what he accomplished for the city. A number of tyrants ruled various city-states in Greece during the 500s B.C. Some were welcomed by citizens and helped to strengthen constitutional structures. Other tyrants, however, did become harsh and arbitrary rulers.

Creon, as a close associate and relative of Oedipus, shared in the status and benefits of the office, but Oedipus alone was the ruler.

Reading and Analyzing

Reading Skills and Strategies
MAKING INFERENCES

A Ask students to explain why Creon is so hurt by the accusations of Oedipus.
Possible Response: Oedipus is acting unreasonably. Even though he has no evidence, he has turned against his friend and relative.

Literary Analysis TRAGIC HERO

B Ask students to explain what this exchange reveals about Oedipus.
Possible Response: Oedipus is being stubborn, foolish, and unreasonable. He even violates his own proclamation by saying that he wants Creon dead, not merely banished. Oedipus refuses to listen to Creon, not allowing him a chance to defend himself.

Literary Analysis CULTURAL SETTING

C Help students to understand the strength of Creon's denial here. He is making an oath that he is innocent: "let me die and be damned if I've done you any wrong." Such an oath has a great moral and religious force.

Active Reading
STRATEGIES FOR READING GREEK DRAMA

D Explain that Sophocles wrote the dialogue between the chorus and Oedipus in a poetic form designed for singing. The singing emphasizes the dramatic tension. Most of the lines between this point and line 767 were meant to be sung.

Use **Unit Two Resource Book,** p.32, for more practice.

Reading Skills and Strategies
CLARIFYING

E Help students to realize the dilemma of Oedipus. If Creon is innocent, then Tiresias is telling the truth and Oedipus is guilty of the crime.

would never resort to treason.
No, I have no lust for conspiracy in me,
nor could I ever suffer one who does.

Do you want proof? Go to Delphi yourself,
examine the oracle and see if I've reported
the message word-for-word. This too:
1 if you detect that I and the clairvoyant
have plotted anything in common, arrest me,
execute me. Not on the strength of one vote,
two in this case, mine as well as yours.
But don't convict me on sheer unverified <u>surmise</u>.
How wrong it is to take the good for bad,
purely at random, or take the bad for good.
But reject a friend, a kinsman? I would as soon
A tear out the life within us, priceless life itself.
You'll learn this well, without fail, in time.
Time alone can bring the just man to light—
the criminal you can spot in one short day.

2 **Leader.** Good advice,
my lord, for anyone who wants to avoid disaster.
Those who jump to conclusions may go wrong.

Oedipus. When my enemy moves against me quickly,
plots in secret, I move quickly too, I must,
I plot and pay him back. Relax my guard a moment,
waiting his next move—he wins his objective,
I lose mine.

Creon. What do you want?
You want me banished?

Oedipus. No, I want you dead.

Creon. Just to show how ugly a grudge can . . .

Oedipus. So,
still stubborn? you don't think I'm serious?

B **Creon.** I think you're insane.

Oedipus. Quite sane—in my behalf.

Creon. Not just as much in mine?

Oedipus. You—my mortal enemy?

Creon. What if you're wholly wrong?

Oedipus. No matter—I must rule.

679 clairvoyant: person who can see the future—here, Tiresias.

683 unverified: not proved to be true.

WORDS TO KNOW

surmise (sər-mīz′) *n.* a conclusion based on little evidence; guess

Creon. Not if you rule unjustly.
Oedipus. Hear him, Thebes, my city!
Creon. My city too, not yours alone!
Leader. Please, my lords.
(*Enter* Jocasta *from the palace.*)
Look, Jocasta's coming,
and just in time too. With her help
you must put this fighting of yours to rest.

Jocasta. Have you no sense? Poor misguided men,
such shouting—why this public outburst?
3 Aren't you ashamed, with the land so sick,
to stir up private quarrels?
(*to* Oedipus)
Into the palace now. And Creon, you go home.
Why make such a furor over nothing?

Creon. My sister, it's dreadful . . . Oedipus, your husband,
he's bent on a choice of punishments for me,
banishment from the fatherland or death.

Oedipus. Precisely. I caught him in the act, Jocasta,
plotting, about to stab me in the back.

C **Creon.** Never—curse me, let me die and be damned
if I've done you any wrong you charge me with.

Jocasta. Oh god, believe it, Oedipus,
honor the solemn oath he swears to heaven.
Do it for me, for the sake of all your people.

D (*The* Chorus *begins to chant.*)

Chorus. Believe it, be sensible
give way, my king, I beg you!

Oedipus. What do you want from me, concessions?

727 concessions: favors.

Chorus. Respect him—he's been no fool in the past
and now he's strong with the oath he swears to god.

Oedipus. You know what you're asking?
4 **Chorus.** I do.
Oedipus. Then out with it!
E **Chorus.** The man's your friend, your kin, he's under oath—
don't cast him out, disgraced
branded with guilt on the strength of hearsay only.

Oedipus. Know full well, if that is what you want

Customizing Instruction

To help students understand the conflict between Oedipus and Creon, ask the following questions:

1 Creon challenges Oedipus to go to the oracle himself. If Creon is guilty, he wants to be executed. What does this suggest about him? *(He is innocent.)*

2 Whose side does the Leader take? *(Creon's)*

3 Why is Jocasta so upset? *(The men should not be arguing about private matters in public, especially in such a time of crisis.)*

4 Why does the chorus take the side of Creon? *(He has sworn an oath to his innocence; he has always been a reasonable person; he has been a good friend and family member.)*

Advanced Learners

Ask students which character is better qualified to be king, Oedipus or Creon. **Possible Responses:** Some students will choose Creon because he shows himself to be a loyal citizen, a reasonable man, and a person of moderation and integrity. Other students will choose Oedipus, despite his flaws. Oedipus welcomes the challenge of leadership and has proven himself in the past. Besides, Creon does not want to be king.

OEDIPUS THE KING 289

Reading and Analyzing

Active Reading

STRATEGIES FOR READING GREEK DRAMA

(A) Point out that the chorus is overwhelmed by emotion here. They swear their loyalty to Oedipus, yet they are sickened by the conflict between two beloved leaders.

Pause & Reflect

Possible Response: Oedipus believes that Creon has conspired with Tiresia, to make a false charge against the king. Oedipus believes that Creon wants to become the king.

Active Reading

STRATEGIES FOR READING GREEK DRAMA

(B) Explain that the dialogue between Jocasta and the chorus would have been sung in the original performance. Ask students to describe how the chorus feels about the conflict between Creon and Oedipus. *(The chorus is so disturbed that they do not even want to discuss what happened.)*

Literary Analysis **TRAGIC HERO**

(C) Point out that the chorus swears loyalty to Oedipus, even though he has just acted irresponsibly with Creon. Why does Oedipus have such a strong hold on their loyalty?

Possible Response: Oedipus saved the city from being destroyed by the Sphinx. That remarkable feat gives them hope that he can still lead Thebes out of its present crisis.

The Greek National Theater's performance of *Oedipus the King* in Rome's Colosseum (2000). Most of the figures shown here are statues, used to create a backdrop for the action.

1 you want me dead or banished from the land.

Chorus. Never—
no, by the blazing Sun, first god of the heavens!
(A) Stripped of the gods, stripped of loved ones,
let me die by inches if that ever crossed my mind.
But the heart inside me sickens, dies as the land dies
and now on top of the old griefs you pile this,
your fury—both of you!

Oedipus. Then let him go,
even if it does lead to my ruin, my death
or my disgrace, driven from Thebes for life.
2 It's you, not him I pity—your words move me.
He, wherever he goes, my hate goes with him.

Creon. Look at you, sullen in yielding, brutal in your rage—
you will go too far. It's perfect justice:
natures like yours are hardest on themselves.

MINI LESSON Viewing and Representing

ANALYZING SETTING In July of 2000 the National Theater of Greece staged a production of *Oedipus the King* in Rome's Colosseum, the first time in about 1,500 years that entertainment had been staged there. The performance took place at night under the light of an artificial moon. A recently restored wooden floor that spans the Colosseum like a bridge served as the stage. A number of white statues of human forms were used as part of the set.

Invite students to study the photographs on page 290 and page 292. Ask them how setting the play in the Colosseum amid so many statues might influence the audience's response.

Possible Response: The Colosseum might create a sense of grandeur, suggesting that the events have a monumental signficance and that the story of Oedipus achieves a kind of immortality. Or, the Colosseum might make it seem as if the human beings portrayed are small and weak, undercutting Oedipus' claims of greatness. The statues almost seem to be participants in the action. They create a ghostly effect, perhaps suggesting that human efforts are doomed to fail. In the photograph on page 292, the statues give a frozen quality to the scene, as if human beings are merely going through the motions.

Oedipus. Then leave me alone—get out!

Creon. I'm going.
You're wrong, so wrong. These men know I'm right.

(*Exit to the side.*)

PAUSE & REFLECT Why does Oedipus turn against Creon?

FOCUS As Creon leaves, Oedipus is still very angry. Jocasta tries to calm him down. Unintentionally, however, she awakens his deepest fears. Read to find out why he suddenly becomes afraid.

(*The* Chorus *turns to* Jocasta.)

Chorus. Why do you hesitate, my lady
why not help him in?

Jocasta. Tell me what's happened first.

Chorus. Loose, ignorant talk started dark suspicions
and a sense of injustice cut deeply too.

Jocasta. On both sides?

Chorus. Oh yes.

Jocasta. What did they say?

Chorus. Enough, please, enough! The land's so racked already
or so it seems to me . . .
End the trouble here, just where they left it.

Oedipus. You see what comes of your good intentions now?
And all because you tried to blunt my anger.

761 blunt: make less sharp.

Chorus. My king,
I've said it once, I'll say it time and again—
I'd be insane, you know it,
senseless, ever to turn my back on you.
You who set our beloved land—storm-tossed,
shattered—
straight on course. Now again, good helmsman,
steer us through the storm!

(*The* Chorus *draws away, leaving* Oedipus *and* Jocasta *side by side.*)

Jocasta. For the love of god,
Oedipus, tell me too, what is it?
Why this rage? You're so unbending.

Customizing Instruction

Less Proficient Readers

1 Make sure that students realize that Oedipus feels desperate. The chorus has chosen to support Creon. Ask why Oedipus believes that they want his death or banishment. *(If they believe Creon, then they must think that Oedipus is guilty.)*

2 Oedipus lets Creon go free because the king took pity on the chorus. Why would he feel sorry for them? *(He knows that they are loyal citizens, upset by the conflict between the two men; they believe in Creon's innocence yet remain loyal to Oedipus.)*

Focus Tell students that Oedipus will learn a disturbing piece of news from Jocasta.

3 The chorus compares Oedipus to a helmsman, or pilot, who once saved his ship from going down. How did Oedipus save Thebes in the past? *(He saved Thebes from the Sphinx.)* How can he save Thebes now? *(He must find a way to get rid of the plague.)*

English Learners

Explain the meaning of the following words and phrases:

Line 746: "sullen in yielding" *(giving in resentfully)*

Line 754: "Loose, ignorant talk": *(Careless and irresponsible talk)*

Line 765: "our beloved land–storm-tossed, shattered" *(our badly damaged homeland)*

Line 766: "helmsman" *(person who steers a ship)*

OEDIPUS THE KING **291**

Reading Skills and Strategies
MAKING INFERENCES

A Ask students to explain how Jocasta views prophets. *(She believes they have no power to predict the future; they are deceitful in their claims.)*

Literary Analysis PLOT

B Jocasta feels confident that she has proven an oracle wrong. Ask students to explain what was predicted and how Jocasta and her husband responded.
Possible Response: The oracle said that her son would kill her husband Laius. To keep that from happening, the parents abandoned their son on a mountain when he was only three days old.

Literary Analysis DRAMATIC IRONY

C Ask students to identify the irony of Jocasta's statement. *(She believes that Laius was not murdered by his son.)* Explain that there is a further irony here in the attitude that Jocasta expresses about Apollo. She claims, in effect, that she sidestepped the will of the god: "Apollo brought neither thing to pass." In her criticism of prophets, Jocasta seems to doubt all religious authorities.

Oedipus and Jocasta in the Greek National Theater's *Oedipus Rex*, staged in Rome's Colosseum (2000).

Oedipus. I will tell you. I respect you, Jocasta,
much more than these men here . . .
(*glancing at the* Chorus)
Creon's to blame, Creon schemes against me.

Jocasta. Tell me clearly, how did the quarrel start?

Oedipus. He says *I* murdered Laius—I am guilty.

Jocasta. How does he know? Some secret knowledge
or simple hearsay?

Oedipus. Oh, he sent his prophet in
to do his dirty work. You know Creon,
Creon keeps his own lips clean.

Jocasta. A prophet?
A Well then, free yourself of every charge!
Listen to me and learn some peace of mind:
1 no skill in the world,
nothing human can penetrate the future.
Here is proof, quick and to the point.

An oracle came to Laius one fine day
B (I won't say from Apollo himself
but his underlings, his priests) and it declared
2 that doom would strike him down at the hands of a son,
our son, to be born of our own flesh and blood. But Laius,
so the report goes at least, was killed by strangers,
thieves, at a place where three roads meet . . . my son—
he wasn't three days old and the boy's father
fastened his ankles, had a henchman fling him away
on a barren, trackless mountain.
There, you see?
C Apollo brought neither thing to pass. My baby
no more murdered his father than Laius suffered—
his wildest fear—death at his own son's hands.
That's how the seers and all their revelations
mapped out the future. Brush them from your mind.
3 Whatever the god needs and seeks
he'll bring to light himself, with ease.

Oedipus. Strange,
hearing you just now . . . my mind wandered,
my thoughts racing back and forth.

Jocasta. What do you mean? Why so anxious, startled?

792 henchman: trusted follower.

Customizing Instruction

Help students to realize that in this dialogue, Jocasta tries to comfort Oedipus by sharing her doubts about prophets and the influence of the gods. Ask the following questions to ensure understanding:

1 According to Jocasta, can any human being predict the future? *(no)*

2 Jocasta tells a story about her own son to convince Oedipus that prophecies can be wrong. What was her son supposed to do? *(kill his father, Laius)* What happened to her son? *(He was left to die on a mountain.)*

3 If no human being can know the will of a god, what value is there in priests and prophets? *(none)*

English Learners

Explain the meaning of the following phrases:

Line 778: "keeps his own lips clean" *(does not do bad deeds himself but has others do them)*

Line 787: "doom would strike him down" *(He would be killed.)*

Advanced Learners

Tell students that the Athenian philosopher Socrates was put to death after having been found guilty of impiety to the gods. How might the jury that found Socrates guilty view Jocasta?
Possible Response: The jury would probably be appalled by her statements about prophets and Apollo. Jocasta openly challenges beliefs that were sacred to the Athenians. Oedipus' remarks may be rash, but hers might be considered treasonous because they undermine the religion of the city-state.

OEDIPUS THE KING 293

Reading and Analyzing

Reading Skills and Strategies
CLARIFYING

A Make sure that students understand the timing of the events. Ask them why Oedipus is so upset at Jocasta's news? *(It means that Oedipus was traveling during the time that Laius was killed, which makes Oedipus a suspect.)*

Literary Analysis TRAGIC HERO

B Oedipus insists on pursuing his investigation, even though he suspects that he is the criminal. Ask students what that reveals about his character.
Possible Response: Oedipus shows courage. He insists on finding the complete truth although such truth might condemn him.

Oedipus. I thought I heard you say that Laius
was cut down at a place where three roads meet.

Jocasta. That was the story. It hasn't died out yet.

Oedipus. Where did this thing happen? Be precise.

Jocasta. A place called Phocis, where two branching roads,
one from Daulia, one from Delphi,
come together—a crossroads.

Oedipus. When? How long ago?

A
1
Jocasta. The heralds no sooner reported Laius dead
than you appeared and they hailed you king of Thebes.

Oedipus. My god, my god—what have you planned to do
to me?

Jocasta. What, Oedipus? What haunts you so?

Oedipus. Not yet.
Laius—how did he look? Describe him.
Had he reached his prime?

Jocasta. He was swarthy,
and the gray had just begun to streak his temples,
and his build . . . wasn't far from yours.

2
Oedipus. Oh no no,
I think I've just called down a dreadful curse
upon myself—I simply didn't know!

Jocasta. What are you saying? I shudder to look at you.

B
Oedipus. I have a terrible fear the blind seer can see.
I'll know in a moment. One thing more—

Jocasta. Anything,
afraid as I am—ask, I'll answer, all I can.

Oedipus. Did he go with a light or heavy escort,
several men-at-arms, like a lord, a king?

Jocasta. There were five in the party, a herald among them,
and a single wagon carrying Laius.

Oedipus. Ai—
now I can see it all, clear as day.
Who told you all this at the time, Jocasta?

3
Jocasta. A servant who reached home, the lone survivor.

Oedipus. So, could he still be in the palace—even now?

Jocasta. No indeed. Soon as he returned from the scene
and saw you on the throne with Laius dead and gone,

808 Phocis (fō'sĭs): a region of central Greece, between Delphi and Thebes.

809 Daulia (dô'lē-ə).

WORDS TO KNOW
swarthy (swôr'thē) *adj.* having a dark complexion

History

TRAVEL IN ANCIENT GREECE Travel in ancient Greece was rather primitive but commonly done. Roads probably consisted of nothing more than narrow beaten paths, which would explain why Oedipus and the party of Laius could not pass each other easily. Most people traveled by walking, even when great distances needed to be covered. While some people rode chariots or drove wagons, others viewed such means of transportation as a sign of softness or pride.

However primitive, the roads were considered sacred places protected by the gods. Even in times of war, people could often travel freely, especially if they were on their way to one of the many sacred shrines of Greece. The earliest treaties between city-states protected access to shrines. Even giving a traveler wrong directions was considered an offense against the gods. According to such customs, the behavior of both Oedipus and Laius in their roadside encounter violated standards of the courtesy that travelers might expect.

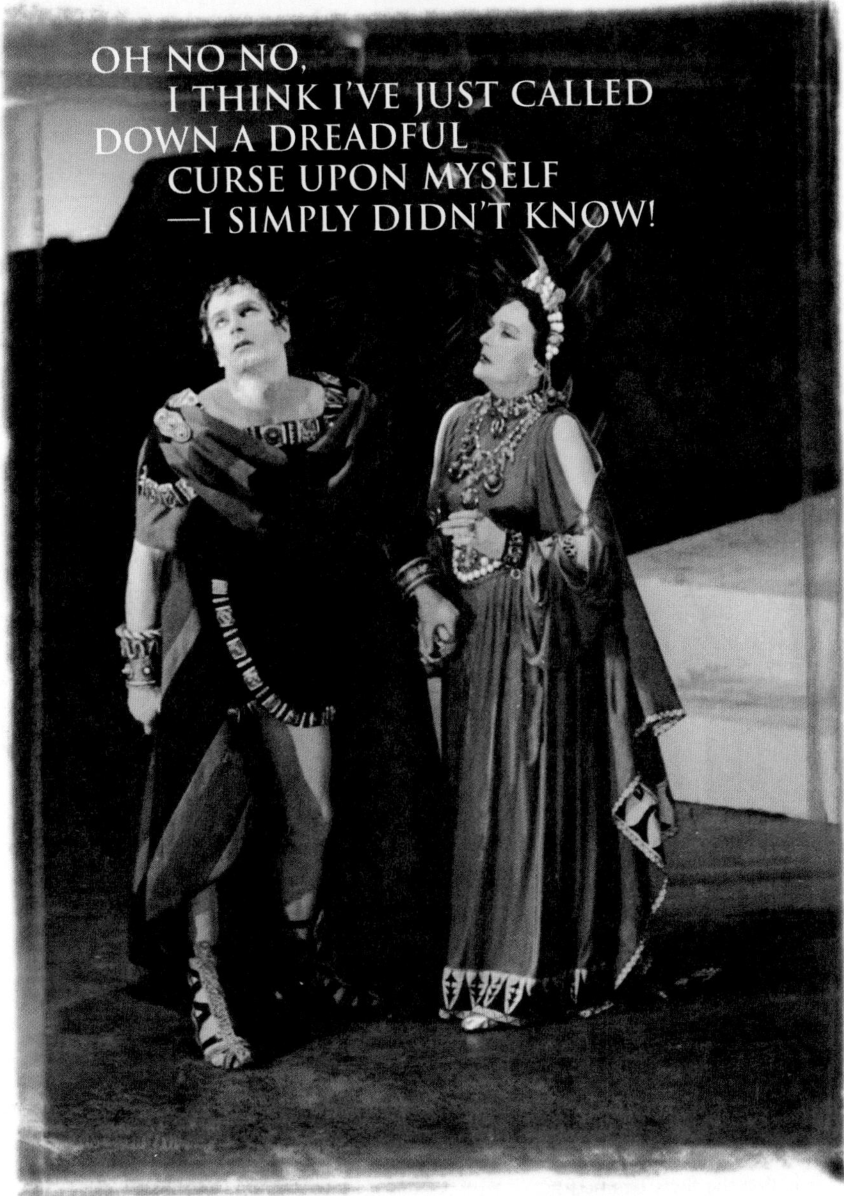

Laurence Olivier and Sybil Thorndike playing Oedipus and Jocasta in a production at the New Theatre in London (1945).

Customizing Instruction

Less Proficient Readers

Tell students that this part of the dialogue provides crucial clues about the murder of Laius. Ask the following questions to call attention to these clues:

1 Where was Oedipus when Laius was murdered? *(on his way to Thebes)*

2 After Jocasta gives a physical description of Laius, Oedipus fears that Tiresias was right. Why? *(He may have been the one who killed Laius.)*

3 Who told Jocasta about the murder? *(the lone survivor who returned to Thebes)*

English Learners

Explain the meaning of the following phrase:

Line 827: "men-at-arms" *(armed soldiers)*

Reading and Analyzing

Literary Analysis
CHARACTERIZATION

A Ask students what this passage reveals about Oedipus' feelings about his wife.

Possible Response: He feels very close to her and wants to confide in her. He seems to love her deeply.

Literary Analysis PLOT

B Ask students to restate the oracle's prophecy in their own words. *(Oedipus will marry his mother, produce children by her, and kill his father.)*

Reading Skills and Strategies
SUMMARIZING

C Tell students that Oedipus' account of this incident is crucial to the plot. Ask them to summarize what happened.

Possible Response: At a place where three roads meet, Oedipus encountered a wagon carrying an old man who resembled Jocasta's description of Laius. The old man and one of his attendants wanted to push Oedipus out of their way. When Oedipus responded in anger and hit the younger man, the old man struck Oedipus with his cattle prod. Oedipus made him pay by striking the old man with his staff and killing him. Then Oedipus killed the other members of the party.

Literary Analysis TRAGIC HERO

D Remind students of the curse that Oedipus placed upon the murderer at the beginning of the drama. That curse has the force of law: if Oedipus is guilty, he will be driven away from Thebes.

he knelt and clutched my hand, pleading with me
to send him into the hinterlands, to pasture,
far as possible, out of sight of Thebes.
I sent him away. Slave though he was,
he'd earned that favor—and much more.

Oedipus. Can we bring him back, quickly?

Jocasta. Easily. Why do you want him so?

Oedipus. I am afraid,
Jocasta, I have said too much already.
That man—I've got to see him.

Jocasta. Then he'll come.
But even I have a right, I'd like to think,
to know what's torturing you, my lord.

Oedipus. And so you shall—I can hold nothing back from
you,
now I've reached this pitch of dark foreboding.
Who means more to me than you? Tell me,
whom would I turn toward but you
as I go through all this?

My father was Polybus, king of Corinth.
My mother, a Dorian, Merope. And I was held
the prince of the realm among the people there,
till something struck me out of nowhere,
something strange . . . worth remarking perhaps,
hardly worth the anxiety I gave it.
Some man at a banquet who had drunk too much
shouted out—he was far gone, mind you—
that I am not my father's son. Fighting words!
I barely restrained myself that day
but early the next I went to mother and father,
questioned them closely, and they were enraged
at the accusation and the fool who let it fly.
So as for my parents I was satisfied,
but still this thing kept gnawing at me,
the slander spread—I had to make my move.
And so,
unknown to mother and father I set out for Delphi,
and the god Apollo spurned me, sent me away
denied the facts I came for,
but first he flashed before my eyes a future
great with pain, terror, disaster—I can hear him cry,

853 Dorian (dôr'ē-ən): descended from Dorus, the ancestor of one of the main divisions of the Greek people; **Merope** (mĕr'ə-pē').

866 gnawing at: biting at; tormenting.

867 slander: statements that unfairly harm a person's reputation.

869 spurned: rejected.

B

"You are fated to couple with your mother, you will
bring
a breed of children into the light no man can bear to
see—
you will kill your father, the one who gave you life!"
I heard all that and ran. I abandoned Corinth,
from that day on I gauged its landfall only
by the stars, running, always running
toward some place where I would never see
the shame of all those oracles come true.
And as I fled I reached that very spot
where the great king, you say, met his death.

C

Now, Jocasta, I will tell you all.
Making my way toward this triple crossroad
I began to see a herald, then a brace of colts
drawing a wagon, and mounted on the bench . . . a man,
just as you've described him, coming face-to-face,
and the one in the lead and the old man himself
were about to thrust me off the road—brute force—
and the one shouldering me aside, the driver,
I strike him in anger!—and the old man, watching me
coming up along his wheels—he brings down
his prod, two prongs straight at my head!
I paid him back with interest!
Short work, by god—with one blow of the staff
in this right hand I knock him out of his high seat,
roll him out of the wagon, sprawling headlong—
I killed them all—every mother's son!

Oh, but if there is any blood-tie
between Laius and this stranger . . .
what man alive more miserable than I?

D

More hated by the gods? *I* am the man
no alien, no citizen welcomes to his house,
law forbids it—not a word to me in public,
driven out of every hearth and home.
And all these curses I—no one but I
brought down these piling curses on myself!
And you, his wife, I've touched your body with these,
the hands that killed your husband cover you with
blood.

Customizing Instruction

Less Proficient Readers

Ask students to name important facts about the murder of Laius that are revealed on these pages.

Possible Response:

- When Oedipus was a young man, a drunk at a banquet shouted out that he was not his father's son.
- To learn the truth, Oedipus went to the oracle at Delphi, where he heard a prophecy that he would marry his mother and kill his father.
- Oedipus left Corinth to escape the prophecy.
- At a crossroads, Oedipus became involved in a roadside argument with an old man.
- In anger, Oedipus killed the man and his party.

English Learners

Explain the meaning of the following phrases:

Line 848: "this pitch of dark foreboding" *(this sense that something terrible will happen)*

Line 893: "prod" *(pointed object used to make animals move)*

Cross Curricular Link **History**

OEDIPUS AND POLLUTION Oedipus says that even Jocasta has been corrupted because she has been touched by the unclean hands of a murderer. Pollution, or *miasma*, was a very important religious concept to the Greeks. An unclean person, that is, someone who had offended the gods and who had not been ritually purified, could infect an entire community. The main causes of pollution were childbirth, death by natural causes, accidental homicide, and murder. Anyone contaminated by contact with participants in these events must undergo ritual purification before participating in any religious ceremonies.

An unpurified person gravely offended the gods, often incurring misfortune. A person who had committed murder, if left unpunished, could cause barrenness in women and cattle alike and blight crops—the very conditions that accompany the plague that afflicts Thebes.

To prevent pollution from infecting an entire community, elaborate rites of purification were performed on a daily basis.

Reading and Analyzing

Reading Skills and Strategies
MAKING INFERENCES

A At this point, Oedipus seems almost convinced that he did murder Laius. Ask students what Oedipus still does not realize. *(He still thinks that Polybus is his father; he does not realize that he is the son of Laius.)*

Literary Analysis
CHARACTERIZATION

B Jocasta is convinced that Oedipus could not have murdered Laius because the witness told her that a whole band of men killed him. Ask students how Jocasta feels about the prophecies that her son would kill Laius. *(She seems to hold them in contempt; she feels superior to the prophets and oracles.)*

Pause & Reflect

Possible Response: Oedipus remembers that he killed an old man at a triple crossroads.

Active Reading
STRATEGIES FOR READING GREEK DRAMA

C In this choral ode, the chorus expresses a very different attitude than they expressed earlier. They are shaken by the possibility that Oedipus might be guilty and are upset by Jocasta's contempt for religion. Ask students why they ask to be guided by "Destiny" in the opening strophe (lines 954–963). *(They want to live according to the will of the gods.)*

D In this antistrophe (lines 963–965), the chorus turns its attention to a proud tyrant. Who might they be referring to? *(Oedipus)*

Wasn't I born for torment? Look me in the eyes!
I am abomination—heart and soul!
A I must be exiled, and even in exile
never see my parents, never set foot
on native ground again. Else I am doomed
to couple with my mother and cut my father down . . .
Polybus who reared me, gave me life.
But why, why?
Wouldn't a man of judgment say—and wouldn't he be
right—
some savage power has brought this down upon my
head?

Oh no, not that, you pure and awesome gods,
never let me see that day! Let me slip
from the world of men, vanish without a trace
before I see myself stained with such corruption,
stained to the heart.

911 abomination (ə-bŏm′ə-nā′shən): a disgusting thing.

Leader. My lord, you fill our hearts with fear.
But at least until you question the witness,
do take hope.

1 **Oedipus.** Exactly. He is my last hope—
I am waiting for the shepherd. He is crucial.

Jocasta. And once he appears, what then? Why so urgent?

Oedipus. I will tell you. If it turns out that his story
matches yours, I've escaped the worst.

Jocasta. What did I say? What struck you so?

2 **Oedipus.** You said *thieves*—
he told you a whole band of them murdered Laius.
So, if he still holds to the same number,
I cannot be the killer. One can't equal many.
But if he refers to one man, one alone,
clearly the scales come down on me:
I am guilty.

3 **Jocasta.** Impossible. Trust me,
I told you precisely what he said,
and he can't retract it now;
the whole city heard it, not just I.
And even if he should vary his first report
by one man more or less, still, my lord,
he could never make the murder of Laius

WORDS TO KNOW

retract (rĭ-trăkt′) *v.* to take back; withdraw

Cross Curricular Link **History**

THE GUILT AND INNOCENCE OF OEDIPUS Modern audiences sometimes have difficulty understanding why Oedipus is so overwhelmed by a sense of guilt: "I am an abomination–heart and soul," he exclaims in line 911. After all, a modern reader may contend, Oedipus did not knowingly murder his father or wed his mother. In terms of Greek religious beliefs, however, his lack of intent or prior knowledge is irrelevant. Oedipus' actions violated the natural order and thus offended the gods–that alone is what matters. Oedipus, when viewed from the perspective of such beliefs, must be condemned for what he has done and what he is.

Ironically, Oedipus would probably have been found innocent of the murder of his father in a court of Athens. Athenian law took into account the intentions of the accused.

truly fit the prophecy. Apollo was explicit:
my son was doomed to kill my husband . . . my son,
poor defenseless thing, he never had a chance
to kill his father. They destroyed him first.

So much for prophecy. It's neither here nor there.
From this day on, I wouldn't look right or left.

Oedipus. True, true. Still, that shepherd,
someone fetch him—now!

Jocasta. I'll send at once. But do let's go inside.
I'd never displease you, least of all in this.

(Oedipus *and* Jocasta *enter the palace.*)

PAUSE & REFLECT Jocasta has told Oedipus that Laius was killed at "a place where three roads meet." Why does Oedipus become fearful when he hears this piece of information?

FOCUS The chorus now sings about the timeless laws that rule human life. Read to find out how the chorus feels about the old prophecies.

Chorus. Destiny guide me always
Destiny find me filled with reverence
pure in word and deed.
Great laws tower above us, reared on high
born for the brilliant vault of heaven—
Olympian Sky their only father,
nothing mortal, no man gave them birth,
their memory deathless, never lost in sleep:
within them lives a mighty god, the god does not
grow old.

Pride breeds the tyrant
violent pride, gorging, crammed to bursting
with all that is overripe and rich with ruin—
clawing up to the heights, headlong pride
crashes down the abyss—sheer doom!
No footing helps, all foothold lost and gone.
But the healthy strife that makes the city strong—
I pray that god will never end that wrestling:
god, my champion, I will never let you go.

969 strife: conflict.

WORDS TO KNOW

explicit (ĭk-splĭs'ĭt) *adj.* clear; definite

Customizing Instruction

Less Proficient Readers

Help students to understand crucial details related to the murder of Laius by asking the following questions:

1 Why does Oedipus regard the shepherd, who witnessed the murder, as his "last hope"? *(The shepherd will be able to tell the full story of the murder, which may prove Oedipus' innocence.)*

2 Why is Oedipus so concerned by the number of attackers. *(If a band of men attacked Laius, then Oedipus will know he is innocent.)*

3 Why is Jocasta so convinced that Oedipus is innocent? *(She was told that many men were involved in the murder.)*

Focus Tell students that in this ode the chorus defends the laws of the gods and criticizes Oedipus.

English Learners

Explain the meaning of the following phrases:

Line 936: "the scales come down on me" *(I will be found guilty according to the scales of justice.)*

Line 939: "can't retract it now" *(can't change his story now)*

Line 948: "It's neither here nor there." *(It does not matter to me any more.)*

Line 949: "I wouldn't look right or left." *(I will not pay any attention to the prophecies.)*

Advanced Learners

Ask students to think of a philosophic term that describes Jocasta's attitude toward the gods and to define that term in their own words.

Possible Response: Students may judge Jocasta to be a skeptic, that is, someone who doubts, questions, or disagrees with generally accepted truths. Accept other terms if reasonable.

OEDIPUS THE KING 299

Reading and Analyzing

Literary Analysis TRAGIC HERO

A Point out that many critics believe this strophe (lines 972–984) is about Oedipus. Ask students why the chorus seems to have turned against Oedipus.

Possible Responses: Evidence is mounting against Oedipus, pointing to him as the murderer. The chorus has been offended by his treatment of Creon, which shows Oedipus' pride and rashness. The chorus is scandalized by the way Jocasta dismisses prophecies. By going along with her, Oedipus is guilty of impiety.

B In this antistrophe (lines 985–997), the chorus declares its intent to remain faithful to Apollo and his prophecies. Ask students why the prophecies must "all come true." *(Only if the prophecies are fulfilled will faith in the gods be restored.)*

Reading Skills and Strategies
IDENTIFYING CAUSE AND EFFECT

C Tell students that Jocasta appears after a lapse of time. Remind them of her previous doubts about prophets and the gods. Ask why she is asking Apollo for help now.

Possible Response: Jocasta is upset by Oedipus' "terror," and she does not know what else to do.

Thinking Through the Literature

1. Possible Response: He killed an old man and his party.
2. Possible Response: He wanted to avoid the prophecy that he would kill his father and marry his mother.
3. Possible Response: Jocasta doubts that any prophet can foretell the future, so she does not believe in prophecies.
4. Possible Response: The chorus believes that prophecies must be believed or gods "will go down."

But if any man comes striding, high and mighty
   in all he says and does,
no fear of justice, no reverence
for the temples of the gods—
   let a rough doom tear him down,
repay his pride, breakneck, ruinous pride!
If he cannot reap his profits fairly
   cannot restrain himself from outrage—
mad, laying hands on the holy things untouchable!

   Can such a man, so desperate, still boast
   he can save his life from the flashing bolts of god?
If all such violence goes with honor now
   why join the sacred dance?

Never again will I go reverent to Delphi,
   the inviolate heart of Earth
   or Apollo's ancient oracle at Abae
   or Olympia of the fires—
   unless these prophecies all come true
   for all mankind to point toward in wonder.
   King of kings, if you deserve your titles
   Zeus, remember, never forget!
   You and your deathless, everlasting reign.

   They are dying, the old oracles sent to Laius,
   now our masters strike them off the rolls.
      Nowhere Apollo's golden glory now—
         the gods, the gods go down.

986 inviolate (ĭn-vī'ə-lĭt): pure.

987 Abae (ā'bē).

988 Olympia (ō-lĭm'pē-ə): the site of an oracle of Zeus.

Thinking Through the Literature

1. What did Oedipus do at "a place where three roads meet"?
2. Why did Oedipus run away from his home in Corinth?
3. How would you describe Jocasta's view of prophets and prophecies?
4. What is the chorus's attitude toward the old prophecies?

Assessment Standardized Test Practice

IDENTIFYING THE MAIN IDEA Tell students that some standardized tests may require them to identify the main idea of a passage they have read. Write the following question on the board or read it aloud.

Which statement best expresses the main idea expressed by Oedipus in lines 899–907 (p. 297)?

A. I killed Laius and must suffer.
B. Whoever killed Laius should be punished.
C. If I learn that I did kill Laius, then I must be exiled from Thebes.
D. Exile is the best punishment for murder.

Guide students through the process of selecting the best answer. *A* does not reflect Oedipus' uncertainty about whether he is the murderer. *B* is only partially correct; Oedipus is here concerned only about the possibility of his own guilt. *D* likewise is not specific enough to Oedipus. The best answer is *C*.

FOCUS Jocasta prays to the god Apollo, asking for help for her husband. Then a messenger arrives with startling news about Polybus, the king of Corinth. Read to find out what the news is.

(*Enter* Jocasta *from the palace, carrying a suppliant's branch wound in wool.*)

Jocasta. Lords of the realm, it occurred to me,
just now, to visit the temples of the gods,
so I have my branch in hand and incense too.

Oedipus is beside himself. Racked with anguish,
no longer a man of sense, he won't admit
the latest prophecies are hollow as the old—
he's at the mercy of every passing voice
if the voice tells of terror.
I urge him gently, nothing seems to help,
so I turn to you, Apollo, you are nearest.

(*placing her branch on the altar, while an old herdsman enters from the side, not the one just summoned by the king but an unexpected* Messenger *from Corinth*)

I come with prayers and offerings . . . I beg you,
cleanse us, set us free of defilement!
Look at us, passengers in the grip of fear,
watching the pilot of the vessel go to pieces.

1011 pilot of the vessel: Oedipus, who guides the "ship of state."

Messenger (*approaching* Jocasta *and the* Chorus).
Strangers, please, I wonder if you could lead us
to the palace of the king . . . I think it's Oedipus.
Better, the man himself—you know where he is?

Leader. This is his palace, stranger. He's inside.
But here is his queen, his wife and mother
of his children.

Messenger. Blessings on you, noble queen,
queen of Oedipus crowned with all your family—
blessings on you always!

Jocasta. And the same to you, stranger, you deserve it . . .
such a greeting. But what have you come for?
Have you brought us news?

Messenger. Wonderful news—
for the house, my lady, for your husband too.

Jocasta. Really, what? Who sent you?

Customizing Instruction

Less Proficient Readers

To help students realize that the chorus has turned against Oedipus, ask the following questions:

- How has Oedipus shown "no reverence for the temples of the gods"? *(He has treated Tiresias badly and goes along with Jocasta's doubts about the gods.)*
- What is an example of Oedipus' pride? *(the way he accuses Creon without allowing him to defend himself; the way he turns against Tiresias)*
- The chorus wants "these prophecies" to come true. What are they referring to? *(prophecies about Oedipus killing his father and marrying his mother)*

Focus Point out that Jocasta has been thoroughly upset by recent events. The woman who earlier dismissed the gods is now praying to Apollo for help.

English Learners

Explain the meaning of the following phrases:

Line 982: "the flashing bolts of god" *(punishment sent from the gods)*

Line 986: "the inviolate heart of earth" *(the pure center of the world)*

Line 995: "our masters strike them off the rolls" *(Our leaders take away the power of the oracles.)*

Line 1009: "set us free of defilement" *(free us from all impurity)*

Reading and Analyzing

Reading Skills And Strategies
MAKING INFERENCES

A Remind students that Jocasta has just made an offering to Apollo. Ask students to explain the relation between this statement and her recent action.
Possible Response: Jocasta still does not believe in the "prophecies of the gods." Only her desperation made her go through the motions of a religious offering to Apollo.

Literary Analysis TONE

B Ask for a volunteer to read this passage aloud in a manner that expresses Oedipus' sarcasm. How does Oedipus feel about the prophecies? *(He shares Jocasta's disbelief in them; he seems to view them with contempt.)*

Pause & Reflect
Possible Response: Polybus has died.

Reading Skills and Strategies
DRAWING CONCLUSIONS

C Ask students what this comment suggests about Jocasta's view of the gods.
Possible Response: By saying that "chance rules our lives," Jocasta seems to deny the existence of the gods, or at least she implies that they have no role in human life.

Reading Skills and Strategies
PARAPHRASING

D Invite students to put these two sentences into their own words.
Possible Response: Other men before you, Oedipus, have had nightmares about sleeping with their mother. Such things are only a product of fantasy; they don't mean anything. Oedipus, live carefree, without any worry of the future.

Messenger. Corinth.
I'll give you the message in a moment.
You'll be glad of it—how could you help it?—
though it costs a little sorrow in the bargain.

Jocasta. What can it be, with such a double edge?

Messenger. The people there, they want to make your Oedipus
king of Corinth, so they're saying now.

Jocasta. Why? Isn't old Polybus still in power?

Messenger. No more. Death has got him in the tomb.

Jocasta. What are you saying? Polybus, dead?—dead?

Messenger. If not,
if I'm not telling the truth, strike me dead too.

Jocasta (*to a servant*).
Quickly, go to your master, tell him this!

A
You prophecies of the gods, where are you now?
This is the man that Oedipus feared for years,
he fled him, not to kill him—and now he's dead,
quite by chance, a normal, natural death,
not murdered by his son.

Oedipus (*emerging from the palace*).
Dearest,
what now? Why call me from the palace?

Jocasta (*bringing the* Messenger *closer*).
Listen to *him*, see for yourself what all
those awful prophecies of god have come to.

Oedipus. And who is he? What can he have for me?

Jocasta. He's from Corinth, he's come to tell you
your father is no more—Polybus—he's dead!

Oedipus (*wheeling on the* Messenger).
What? Let me have it from your lips.

Messenger. Well,
if that's what you want first, then here it is:
make no mistake, Polybus is dead and gone.

Oedipus. How—murder? sickness?—what? what killed him?

Messenger. A light tip of the scales can put old bones to rest.

Oedipus. Sickness then—poor man, it wore him down.

1051 A light tip . . . to rest: A little disturbance can cause an old person to die.

Messenger. That,
and the long count of years he'd measured out.

Oedipus. So!
Jocasta, why, why look to the Prophet's hearth,
B the fires of the future? Why scan the birds
that scream above our heads? They winged me on
to the murder of my father, did they? That was my doom?
Well look, he's dead and buried, hidden under the earth,
and here I am in Thebes, I never put hand to sword—
unless some longing for me wasted him away,
then in a sense you'd say I caused his death.
But now, all those prophecies I feared—Polybus
packs them off to sleep with him in hell!
They're nothing, worthless.

PAUSE & REFLECT What does Oedipus learn about Polybus from the messenger?

FOCUS Read to find out how Oedipus happened to be raised as the son of Polybus.

Jocasta. There.
Didn't I tell you from the start?

Oedipus. So you did. I was lost in fear.

Jocasta. No more, sweep it from your mind forever.

Oedipus. But my mother's bed, surely I must fear—

Jocasta. Fear?
What should a man fear? It's all chance,
C chance rules our lives. Not a man on earth
can see a day ahead, groping through the dark.
Better to live at random, best we can.
And as for this marriage with your mother—
have no fear. Many a man before you,
in his dreams, has shared his mother's bed.
D Take such things for shadows, nothing at all—
Live, Oedipus,
as if there's no tomorrow!

Oedipus. Brave words,
1 and you'd persuade me if mother weren't alive.
But mother lives, so for all your reassurances
I live in fear, I must.

Customizing Instruction

Less Proficient Readers

Make sure that students realize why the death of Polybus is so important to Jocasta and Oedipus. Ask the following questions:

- What caused the death of Polybus? *(sickness and old age)*
- How do Oedipus and Jocasta feel about the prophecies now? *(They both feel that the prophecies were wrong.)*

Focus Tell students that Oedipus has a great surprise ahead of him.

1 Ask why Oedipus is still concerned about his mother being alive. *(The prophecy said he will marry his mother.)*

English Learners

Explain the meaning of the following phrases:

Line 1028: "such a double edge" *(The news is both happy and sad.)*

Line 1047: "wheeling on" *(turning toward)*

Line 1064: "packs them off to sleep with him to hell" *(The prophecies are as dead as Polybus; they have no power.)*

Advanced Learners

Point out that Sigmund Freud interpreted the dream mentioned by Jocasta as confirmation of his own theories of sexuality. According to Freud, "it is the fate of all of us to direct our first sexual impulse towards our mother. Our dreams convince us that this is true." The plot of *Oedipus the King*, Freud asserts, "merely shows us the fulfillment of our own childhood wishes." In Freud's view, that is why the legend of Oedipus must include "horror and self-punishment." Ask student to share their opinions of Freud's interpretations of the drama. *(Accept all reasonable responses.)*

OEDIPUS THE KING 303

Reading Skills and Strategies
CLARIFYING

A Make sure that students realize why the messenger came to Thebes. He came to tell Oedipus that the people of Corinth want him as their king.

Literary Analysis PLOT

B Point out that Oedipus' maimed ankles are crucial to the plot of the play. Ask students if they can recall earlier references in the drama to his ankles.

Possible Response: When Oedipus first appeared, he was walking with a "telltale limp." Later, Jocasta mentioned that her infant son's ankles were "fastened" by Laius before he was abandoned.

Jocasta. But your father's death,
that, at least, is a great blessing, joy to the eyes!

Oedipus. Great, I know . . . but I fear *her*—she's still alive.

Messenger. Wait, who is this woman, makes you so afraid?

Oedipus. Merope, old man. The wife of Polybus.

Messenger. The queen? What's there to fear in her?

Oedipus. A dreadful prophecy, stranger, sent by the gods.

Messenger. Tell me, could you? Unless it's forbidden
other ears to hear.

Oedipus. Not at all.
Apollo told me once—it is my fate—
I must make love with my own mother,
shed my father's blood with my own hands.
So for years I've given Corinth a wide berth,
and it's been my good fortune too. But still,
to see one's parents and look into their eyes
is the greatest joy I know.

1093 given Corinth a wide berth: stayed far away from Corinth.

Messenger. You're afraid of that?
That kept you out of Corinth?

Oedipus. My *father,* old man—
so I wouldn't kill my father.

Messenger. So that's it.
Well then, seeing I came with such good will, my king,
why don't I rid you of that old worry now?

Oedipus. What a rich reward you'd have for that!

A

Messenger. What do you think I came for, majesty?
So you'd come home and I'd be better off.

Oedipus. Never, I will never go near my parents.

Messenger. My boy, it's clear, you don't know what you're
doing.

Oedipus. What do you mean, old man? For god's sake,
explain.

Messenger. If you ran from *them,* always dodging home . . .

Oedipus. Always, terrified Apollo's oracle might come true—

Messenger. And you'd be covered with guilt, from both
your parents.

Oedipus. That's right, old man, that fear is always with me.

Messenger. Don't you know? You've really nothing to fear.

Oedipus. But why? If I'm their son—Merope, Polybus?
Messenger. Polybus was nothing to you, that's why, not in
blood.
Oedipus. What are you saying—Polybus was not my father?
Messenger. No more than I am. He and I are equals.
Oedipus. My father—
how can my father equal nothing? You're nothing to me!
Messenger. Neither was he, no more your father than I am.
Oedipus. Then why did he call me his son?
Messenger. You were a gift,
years ago—know for a fact he took you
from my hands.
Oedipus. No, from another's hands?
Then how could he love me so? He loved me, deeply . . .
Messenger. True, and his early years without a child
made him love you all the more.
Oedipus. And you, did you . . .
1 buy me? find me by accident?
Messenger. I stumbled on you,
down the woody flanks of Mount Cithaeron.
Oedipus. So close,
what were you doing here, just passing through?
Messenger. Watching over my flocks, grazing them on the
slopes.
Oedipus. A herdsman, were you? A vagabond, scraping for
wages?
Messenger. Your savior too, my son, in your worst hour.
Oedipus. Oh—
when you picked me up, was I in pain? What exactly?
Messenger. Your ankles . . . they tell the story. Look at them.
2 **Oedipus.** Why remind me of that, that old affliction?
B **Messenger.** Your ankles were pinned together. I set you free.
Oedipus. That dreadful mark—I've had it from the cradle.
Messenger. And you got your name from that misfortune
too,
the name's still with you.
Oedipus. Dear god, who did it?—
mother? father? Tell me.

1135 you got your name from that misfortune: Oedipus' name comes from Greek words meaning "swollen foot."

Customizing Instruction

Less Proficient Readers

Make sure that students understand the plot by asking the following questions:

1 How does the messenger know that Oedipus is not the son of Polybus? *(The messenger reports that Oedipus was found as an infant on the side of a mountain.)*

2 How were Oedipus' ankles damaged? *(They were pinned together when he was an infant.)*

English Learners

Explain the meaning of the following phrases:

Line 1125: "woody flanks" *(forests on the mountainside)*

Line 1128: "A vagabond, scraping for wages" *(a person who wanders from place to place, doing anything that pays a little money)*

Reading and Analyzing

Literary Analysis PLOT

A Draw attention to Jocasta's reaction to the news. Ask students to explain what might be going through her mind. *(She probably knows that Oedipus is the same infant whom she gave to a servant to abandon.)*

Reading Skills and Strategies
CLARIFYING

B Ask students why Jocasta wants Oedipus to forget about the shepherd. *(She knows that the shepherd will reveal that Oedipus is her son.)*

Active Reading
STRATEGIES FOR READING GREEK DRAMA

C Point out that dramatic tension is heightened because Oedipus and Jocasta have very different reactions to the news. Ask students what Jocasta realizes. *(that Oedipus is her son)* Then ask what Oedipus is thinking about here. *(He believes that he may not be of royal birth because he was abandoned in infancy.)*

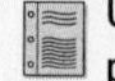
Use **Unit Two Resource Book,** p. 35, for more practice.

Pause & Reflect
Possible Response: Oedipus was found on a mountainside, then given to Polybus.

Literary Analysis TRAGIC HERO

D Remind students that Jocasta earlier referred to chance as the ruling principle of life: "chance rules our lives." Oedipus now turns that randomness into a goddess. Ask what this suggests about his state of mind.
Possible Response: He still feels that he is destined for great things. He will bravely and confidently face the future, regardless of what he learns.

Use **Unit Two Resource Book,** p. 36, for more practice.

Messenger. I don't know.
The one who gave you to me, he'd know more.
Oedipus. What? You took me from someone else?
You didn't find me yourself?
Messenger. No sir,
another shepherd passed you on to me.
Oedipus. Who? Do you know? Describe him.
Messenger. He called himself a servant of . . .
if I remember rightly—Laius.
(Jocasta *turns sharply.*)
Oedipus. The king of the land who ruled here long ago?
Messenger. That's the one. That herdsman was *his* man.
Oedipus. Is he still alive? Can I see him?
Messenger. They'd know best, the people of these parts.
(Oedipus *and the* Messenger *turn to the* Chorus.)
Oedipus. Does anyone know that herdsman,
the one he mentioned? Anyone seen him
in the fields, here in the city? Out with it!
The time has come to reveal this once for all.
Leader. I think he's the very shepherd you wanted to see,
a moment ago. But the queen, Jocasta,
she's the one to say.
Oedipus. Jocasta,
you remember the man we just sent for?
Is *that* the one he means?
Jocasta. That man . . .
why ask? Old shepherd, talk, empty nonsense,
don't give it another thought, don't even think—
Oedipus. What—give up now, with a clue like this?
Fail to solve the mystery of my birth?
Not for all the world!
Jocasta. Stop—in the name of god,
if you love your own life, call off this search!
My suffering is enough.
Oedipus. Courage!
Even if my mother turns out to be a slave,
and I a slave, three generations back,
you would not seem common.

Jocasta. Oh no,
listen to me, I beg you, don't do this.

Oedipus. Listen to you? No more. I must know it all,
must see the truth at last.

Jocasta. No, please—
for your sake—I want the best for you!

Oedipus. Your best is more than I can bear.

Jocasta. You're doomed—
may you never fathom who you are!

Oedipus. (*to a servant*).
Hurry, fetch me the herdsman, now!
Leave her to glory in her royal birth.

Jocasta. Aieeeeee—
man of agony—
2 that is the only name I have for you,
that, no other—ever, ever, ever!

(*Flinging through the palace doors. A long, tense silence follows.*)

PAUSE & REFLECT How did it come about that Oedipus was raised as Polybus' son?

FOCUS Oedipus wants to solve the mystery of his birth. What do you predict he will find out when he questions the herdsman?

Leader. Where's she gone, Oedipus?
Rushing off, such wild grief . . .
I'm afraid that from this silence
something monstrous may come bursting forth.

Oedipus. Let it burst! Whatever will, whatever must!
I must know my birth, no matter how common
it may be—I must see my origins face-to-face.
She perhaps, she with her woman's pride
may well be mortified by my birth,
but I, I count myself the son of Chance,
D the great goddess, giver of all good things—
I'll never see myself disgraced. She is my mother!
And the moons have marked me out, my blood-brothers,
one moon on the wane, the next moon great with power.

1192 on the wane: with its lighted part getting smaller day by day.

WORDS TO KNOW
mortify (môr'tə-fī') *v.* to embarrass or humiliate

Customizing Instruction

Less Proficient Readers

To make sure that students are following the plot, ask the following questions:

1 The messenger reveals that he received the infant that he later gave to Polybus from the shepherd. What do we already know about this shepherd? *(Jocasta and Laius gave him their baby to abandon.)*

2 Jocasta leaves the stage screaming in despair. Why? *(She knows that Oedipus is her son.)*

Focus Tell students that Oedipus seems to have regained his confidence, in contrast to the despair expressed by Jocasta. His search for truth will not be stopped.

English Learners

Explain the meaning of the following phrases:

Line 1173: "never fathom" *(never understand)*

Line 1187: "mortified by my birth" *(humiliated by learning who my parents are)* Explain that Oedipus thinks that Jocasta is upset because she may have married a commoner.

MINI LESSON Vocabulary Strategy

ROOTS AND WORD FAMILIES

Instruction Words containing the same root are usually related in meaning. Knowing the root can help students understand other words in the same word family. For example, the word *mortify* contains the Latin root *mors-*, or *mort-* which means "death." The idea of deadening or subduing can be seen in the definition of *mortify:* " to cause to experience shame, humiliation, or wounded pride." The same idea is involved in the meanings of other words in the *mors-/mort-* family, such as *mortal* and *mortuary*.

Practice Have students work in small groups to compile a list of words that derive from the Latin root *mors-*, or *mort-*. Have them find at least five words (other than the ones discussed in class) stemming from this root. Some responses might include *mortality, immortal, immortality, mortification, mortician,* and *postmortem.* Have students share their findings with the class, explaining how each word reflects the idea of death.

A lesson on using word families appears on p. 1198 in the Pupil's Edition.

Active Reading

STRATEGIES FOR READING GREEK DRAMA

(A) Explain that the chorus is strongly affected by the confidence expressed by Oedipus. In this song, they consider that he may prove to be the child of the gods. Ask students to describe the mood of the chorus.

Possible Response: The chorus is wildly enthusiastic and joyous; they seem to have forgotten all their previous dark thoughts about Oedipus.

Literary Analysis HISTORICAL SETTING

(B) The messenger is referring to a common practice of shepherds. During the spring and summer, shepherds would take their flocks to the mountains; they would return in September. According to the messenger, he and the shepherd worked as partners on the mountains over the course of three years.

That is my blood, my nature—I will never betray it,
never fail to search and learn my birth!

Chorus. Yes—if I am a true prophet
if I can grasp the truth,
by the boundless skies of Olympus,
at the full moon of tomorrow, Mount Cithaeron
you will know how Oedipus glories in you—
you, his birthplace, nurse, his mountain-mother!
And we will sing you, dancing out your praise—
you lift our monarch's heart!
Apollo, Apollo, god of the wild cry
may our dancing please you!
Oedipus—
(A) son, dear child, who bore you?
Who of the nymphs who seem to live forever
mated with Pan, the mountain-striding Father?
Who was your mother? who, some bride of Apollo
the god who loves the pastures spreading toward
the sun?
Or was it Hermes, king of the lightning ridges?
Or Dionysus, lord of frenzy, lord of the barren
peaks—
did he seize you in his hands, dearest of all his
lucky finds?—
found by the nymphs, their warm eyes dancing, gift
to the lord who loves them dancing out his joy!

1206 nymphs (nĭmfs): minor nature goddesses.

1207 Pan: the god of forests, pastures, and shepherds.

(Oedipus *strains to see a figure coming from the distance. Attended by palace guards, an old* Shepherd *enters slowly, reluctant to approach the king.*)

Oedipus. I never met the man, my friends . . . still,
if I had to guess, I'd say that's the shepherd,
the very one we've looked for all along.
Brothers in old age, two of a kind,
he and our guest here. At any rate
the ones who bring him in are my own men,
I recognize them.

(*turning to the* Leader)

But you know more than I,
you should, you've seen the man before.

Leader. I know him, definitely. One of Laius' men,
a trusty shepherd, if there ever was one.

Oedipus. You, I ask you first, stranger,
you from Corinth—is this the one you mean?

Messenger. You're looking at him. He's your man.

Oedipus. (*to the* Shepherd).
You, old man, come over here—
look at me. Answer all my questions.
Did you ever serve King Laius?

Shepherd. So I did . . .
a slave, not bought on the block though,
born and reared in the palace.

Oedipus. Your duties, your kind of work?

Shepherd. Herding the flocks, the better part of my life.

Oedipus. Where, mostly? Where did you do your grazing?

Shepherd. Well,
Cithaeron sometimes, or the foothills round about.

Oedipus. This man—you know him? ever see him there?

1 **Shepherd** (*confused, glancing from the* Messenger *to the King*).
Doing what?—what man do you mean?

Oedipus (*pointing to the* Messenger).
This one here—ever have dealings with him?

Shepherd. Not so I could say, but give me a chance,
my memory's bad . . .

Messenger. No wonder he doesn't know me, master.
But let me refresh his memory for him.
I'm sure he recalls old times we had
on the slopes of Mount Cithaeron;
he and I, grazing our flocks, he with two
B and I with one—we both struck up together,
three whole seasons, six months at a stretch
2 from spring to the rising of Arcturus in the fall,
then with winter coming on I'd drive my herds
to my own pens, and back he'd go with his
to Laius' folds.
(*to the* Shepherd)
Now that's how it was,
wasn't it—yes or no?

Shepherd. Yes, I suppose . . .
it's all so long ago.

Messenger. Come, tell me,

1249 Arcturus (ärk-to͝or′əs): a bright star. (For the Greeks, its rising just before the sun marked the beginning of autumn.)

Customizing Instruction

Less Proficient Readers

Ask the following questions to make sure that students understand the shepherd's role here:

1 Why does the shepherd seem confused?

Possible Response: He does not recognize the messenger, and he is afraid that he may be in trouble. He is overwhelmed by the experience of being taken to the king.

2 Why does the messenger know the shepherd? *(Years ago, they worked together as shepherds on the slopes of Mount Cithaeron.)*

English Learners

Explain the meaning of the following phrases:

Line 1218: "Brothers in old age" *(two men who are both old)*

Line 1231–1232: "a slave, not bought on the block though, born and reared in the palace" *(He did serve Laius as a slave, but he was not bought at an auction. He was born and raised in the palace of Laius.)*

OEDIPUS THE KING **309**

Reading and Analyzing

Active Reading
STRATEGIES FOR READING GREEK DRAMA

A Ask students why the shepherd is so reluctant to admit that he gave an infant to the messenger years ago.
Possible Response: The shepherd disobeyed the orders of the king and queen by saving the baby. He is terrified to admit what he did, for fear of all the trouble that will occur.

Literary Analysis **TRAGIC HERO**

B Ask students what they think of Oedipus in this scene.
Possible Responses: Many students will probably condemn his brutal treatment of the old shepherd. Oedipus seems willing to kill the man to get him to talk. Others may feel sympathy for Oedipus; he is driven to desperation in his search for his true identity.

Literary Analysis **PLOT**

C Invite two students to read aloud this exchange between the shepherd and Oedipus. Make sure that students realize the "horrible truth" that is revealed about Oedipus. *(He is the son of Laius and Jocasta.)*

The Shepherd in Peter Hall's stage production of *Oedipus the King* (1996).

you gave me a child back then, a boy, remember?
A little fellow to rear, my very own.

Shepherd. What? Why rake up that again?

Messenger. Look, here he is, my fine old friend—
the same man who was just a baby then.

Shepherd. Damn you, shut your mouth—quiet!

Oedipus. Don't lash out at him, old man—
you need lashing more than he does.

A **Shepherd.** Why,
master, majesty—what have I done wrong?

Oedipus. You won't answer his question about the boy.

Shepherd. He's talking nonsense, wasting his breath.

Oedipus. So, you won't talk willingly—
then you'll talk with pain.

(*The guards seize the* Shepherd.)

Shepherd. No, dear god, don't torture an old man!
Oedipus. Twist his arms back, quickly!
Shepherd. God help us, why?—
what more do you need to know?
Oedipus. Did you give him that child? He's asking.
Shepherd. I did . . . I wish to god I'd died that day.
Oedipus. You've got your wish if you don't tell the truth.
Shepherd. The more I tell, the worse the death I'll die.
Oedipus. Our friend here wants to stretch things out, does he?
(*motioning to his men for torture*)
Shepherd. No, no, I gave it to him—I just said so.
Oedipus. Where did you get it? Your house? Someone else's?
Shepherd. It wasn't mine, no, I got it from . . . someone.
Oedipus. Which one of them?
(*looking at the citizens*)
Whose house?
Shepherd. No—
god's sake, master, no more questions!
Oedipus. You're a dead man if I have to ask again.
Shepherd. Then—the child came from the house . . .
of Laius.
Oedipus. A slave? or born of his own blood?
Shepherd. Oh no,
I'm right at the edge, the horrible truth—I've got to say it!
Oedipus. And I'm at the edge of hearing horrors, yes, but I must hear!
Shepherd. All right! His son, they said it was—his son!
But the one inside, your wife,
she'd tell it best.
Oedipus. My wife—
she gave it to you?
Shepherd. Yes, yes, my king.
Oedipus. Why, what for?
Shepherd. To kill it.
Oedipus. Her own child,
how could she?

Customizing Instruction

Less Proficient Readers

Write *Oedipus* and *Shepherd* on the board. Then ask students to state what they learn about each character on these pages. You might wish to have students read aloud this scene to help make the meaning clearer.

Possible Response:

Oedipus
- tortures the old man to get him to speak
- keeps pressing for the truth, though he is "at the edge of hearing horrors"
- horrified that Jocasta could kill her own child

Shepherd
- afraid to admit what he knows
- after being tortured, admits that he received the infant from the house of Laius
- when pressed, also admits that Jocasta gave him the child and ordered him to kill it

English Learners

Explain the meaning of the following phrases:

Line 1259: "the same man who was just a baby then" *(Oedipus)*

Line 1286: "His son, they said it was—his son!" *(The shepherd is admitting that the baby was the son of Laius.)*

Advanced Learners

Aristotle describes two parts of a tragic plot, reversal and recognition. He defines reversal as "a change of one state of affairs to its exact opposite." He defines recognition as "a change from ignorance to knowledge." Ask students how this scene illustrate both parts.

Possible Response: Reversal is illustrated by the sudden change of Oedipus' fortune. He thought he was freed from the prophecy. Now, he realizes that he did kill his father and marry his mother. Recognition occurs when the shepherd tells Oedipus that Jocasta gave up her son to be killed; Oedipus finally knows his identity with absolute certainty.

OEDIPUS THE KING 311

Literary Analysis TRAGIC HERO

A Oedipus realizes the full horror of what he has done. Ask students what he plans to do.

Possible Response: Oedipus may be planning to kill himself and possibly Jocasta as well. He refers to "the lives" that I will "cut down."

Pause & Reflect

Possible Response: Oedipus has learned that he is the son of Laius and Jocasta.

Active Reading

STRATEGIES FOR READING GREEK DRAMA

B Help students to realize that the chorus is making a generalization about human life. Ask what lesson the chorus draws from the example of Oedipus' terrible fate.

Possible Response: The chorus concludes that happiness is "just a dream, a vision." The great "misery" of Oedipus illustrates the terrible truth that we can "count no man blest." True happiness and good fortune is not possible.

Literary Analysis ALLUSION

C Point out that these lines all refer to the Sphinx, described as "the virgin" with "claws hooked."

Monnett-Sully in the role of Oedipus in "Oedipe Roi" (1899), Leonetto Cappiello. Pastel and gouache, 56.5 × 47.1 cm. Photo by Gérard Blot. Musée d'Orsay, Paris. Photo © Réunion des Musées Nationaux/Art Resource, New York © 2007 Artists Rights Society (ARS), New York.

Shepherd. She was afraid—
  frightening prophecies.

Oedipus. What?

Shepherd. They said—
  he'd kill his parents.

Oedipus. But you gave him to this old man—why?

1 **Shepherd.** I pitied the little baby, master,
  hoped he'd take him off to his own country,

far away, but he saved him for this, this fate.
If you are the man he says you are, believe me,
you were born for pain.

Oedipus. O god—
all come true, all burst to light!
O light—now let me look my last on you!
I stand revealed at last—
cursed in my birth, cursed in marriage,
cursed in the lives I cut down with these hands!

(*Rushing through the doors with a great cry. The Corinthian* Messenger, *the* Shepherd *and attendants exit slowly to the side.*)

PAUSE & REFLECT What does Oedipus discover about his birth?

FOCUS The Chorus reacts to Oedipus' discovery of the truth of his birth. Read to find out what the Chorus thinks of him now.

Chorus. O the generations of men
the dying generations—adding the total
of all your lives I find they come to nothing . . .
does there exist, is there a man on earth
who seizes more joy than just a dream, a vision?
And the vision no sooner dawns than dies
blazing into <u>oblivion</u>.

You are my great example, you, your life
your destiny, Oedipus, man of misery—
I count no man blest.

You outranged all men!
Bending your bow to the breaking-point
you captured priceless glory, O dear god,
and the Sphinx came crashing down,
the virgin, claws hooked
like a bird of omen singing, shrieking death—
like a fortress reared in the face of death
you rose and saved our land.

WORDS TO KNOW
oblivion (ə-blĭv'ē-ən) *n.* a state of being forgotten

Customizing Instruction

Less Proficient Readers

1 Make sure that students understand that the shepherd gave the infant Oedipus to the messenger.

2 Ask students what Oedipus means when he says "all come true, all burst to light." *(Oedipus means that the prophecies that he would marry his mother and kill his father were true.)*

Focus Explain that the chorus offers a very gloomy view of human life. Remind students how much the chorus admired Oedipus before they learned the truth about his identity. He represented the best that a human being could achieve. His downfall makes them feel despair.

English Learners

Explain the meaning of the following phrases:

Lines 1311–1312: "O the generations of men / the dying generations" *(The chorus is speaking about the entire human race. All people belong to "dying generations" because everyone must die.)*

Line 1326: "like a fortress reared in the face of death" *(Oedipus suddenly appeared; for us, he was a mighty fort to protect us from the threat of death.)*

MINI LESSON Speaking and Listening

CHORAL READING Explain that Sophocles is famous for his choral songs and that this one is his most highly regarded.

Prepare Divide the class into four groups and assign each group one of the four sections:

- Strophe (lines 1311–1320)
- Antistrophe (lines 1321–1330)
- Strophe (lines 1331–1341)
- Antistrophe (lines 1341–1350)

To help students deliver their lines with the appropriate emotion, point out that for the chorus the story of Oedipus is a tragedy of the greatest possible magnitude. The chorus is expressing grief not merely for Oedipus but for the human condition. Allow each group time to rehearse their lines.

Present Have each group stand in a separate corner of the classroom to deliver their lines. To set the proper mood, you might call for fifteen seconds of complete silence and then give a hand signal for the first group to begin. Pause briefly at the end of each section to allow the words to resonate; then give a hand signal to the next group to begin.

This activity is particularly well suited for longer class periods.

Reading and Analyzing

Reading Skills and Strategies
PARAPHRASING

A Because this is a particularly difficult passage, lead the class in paraphrasing it. Begin by paraphrasing the first line yourself—O Oedipus, people will always remember your name. Then work with students to help them paraphrase the remaining lines.
Possible Response: You and your father were both served by the same harbor—you both slept with Jocasta. You and your father slept in the same wedding bed. How could the fields that your father plowed (his sexual union with Jocasta) which created you, remain silent for so long? How could the silence (about your true identity) last so long?

Literary Analysis TRAGIC HERO

B The chorus personifies time, giving it human attributes. It was inevitable that the "Time" would eventually reveal Oedipus' terrible secret. Ask students why the chorus says they wish they had never seen Oedipus. *(They are so horrified by what has happened to him that it would be better if they had never known him.)*

Literary Analysis ALLUSION

C The chorus refers to two great rivers. Even such rivers could not wash away the stain of Oedipus' corruption. Ask students what this allusion suggests about the extent of Oedipus' pollution. *(He has so corrupted the world that even the forces of nature cannot purify it.)*

Reading Skills and Strategies
PARAPHRASING

D Ask students to paraphrase this passage.
Possible Response: Once inside her bedroom, Jocasta cried for Laius, who died so long ago. She remembered how she gave birth to Oedipus; she gave life to the person who would murder Laius. After Oedipus was separated from his mother, he would return, making her the mother of his children.

From that day on we called you king
we crowned you with honors, Oedipus, towering over
all—
mighty king of the seven gates of Thebes.

1 But now to hear your story—is there a man more agonized?
More wed to pain and frenzy? Not a man on earth,
the joy of your life ground down to nothing
O Oedipus, name for the ages—
one and the same wide harbor served you
son and father both
A son and father came to rest in the same bridal chamber.
How, how could the furrows your father plowed
bear you, your agony, harrowing on
in silence O so long?

But now for all your power
B Time, all-seeing Time has dragged you to the light,
judged your marriage monstrous from the start—
2 the son and the father tangling, both one—
O child of Laius, would to god
I'd never seen you, never never!
Now I weep like a man who wails the dead
and the dirge comes pouring forth with all my heart!
I tell you the truth, you gave me life
my breath leapt up in you
and now you bring down night upon my eyes.

(*Enter a* Messenger *from the palace.*)

1347 dirge (dûrj): funeral song.

Thinking Through the Literature

1. What did the shepherd do with the baby he was ordered to kill?
2. At this point in the play, how does the Chorus regard Oedipus, the man who once saved Thebes?
3. How did Oedipus unknowingly bring about the thing he most tried to avoid?
4. What do you predict Oedipus will do now that he knows the truth about his birth?

Thinking Through the Literature

1. Possible Response: The shepherd gave the baby to the messenger.
2. Possible Response: The chorus is now horrified by the example of Oedipus. So terrible is his fate that they wish they had never seen him. He has made them feel that no one can be truly happy or blessed.
3. Possible Response: He left Corinth, so that he would not murder Polybus or marry Merope, the people whom he believed were his parents.
4. Accept all reasonable responses.

Use Selection Quiz in **Unit Two Resource Book,** p. 34.

FOCUS A messenger reveals the terrible events that have occurred offstage. Read to find out about these events.

Messenger. Men of Thebes, always first in honor,
what horrors you will hear, what you will see,
what a heavy weight of sorrow you will shoulder . . .
if you are true to your birth, if you still have
some feeling for the royal house of Thebes.
C I tell you neither the waters of the Danube
nor the Nile can wash this palace clean.
Such things it hides, it soon will bring to light—
terrible things, and none done blindly now,
all done with a will. The pains
we inflict upon ourselves hurt most of all.

Leader. God knows we have pains enough already.
What can you add to them?

Messenger. The queen is dead.

Leader. Poor lady—how?

3 **Messenger.** By her own hand. But you are spared the worst,
you never had to watch . . . I saw it all,
and with all the memory that's in me
you will learn what that poor woman suffered.

Once she'd broken in through the gates,
dashing past us, frantic, whipped to fury,
ripping her hair out with both hands—
straight to her rooms she rushed, flinging herself
across the bridal-bed, doors slamming behind her—
once inside, she wailed for Laius, dead so long,
remembering how she bore his child long ago,
D the life that rose up to destroy him, leaving
its mother to mother living creatures
with the very son she'd borne.
Oh how she wept, mourning the marriage-bed
where she let loose that double brood—monsters—

Cross Curricular Link History

CULTURE OF SHAME Jocasta's reaction to the news of Oedipus' true identity reflects the importance of shame in Greek culture. Jocasta has been ruined in the eyes of society. She and her entire family, both those living and those who have died, have lost their social standing by virtue of what Oedipus has done. She is frantic in rushing offstage because she realizes that her entire life has been disgraced and dishonored. In a society that so highly values public life, the life lived in community with others, Jocasta can never appear in public places again without calling forth the judgment of others. Her humiliation and despair is complete. She has internalized her society's judgment of her and so judges herself unfit to live.

Customizing Instruction

Less Proficient Readers

1 Help students to realize that the chorus feels as if their entire world has changed with the news of Oedipus' true identity. They feel sorry for Oedipus; no person on earth has to suffer such agony as he does.

2 Ask students to explain what it means that "Time has dragged you to the light." *(Oedipus could not escape the power of time, which made his secret known.)* Then ask who the chorus is referring to when they say "would to god / I'd never seen you." *(Oedipus)*

Focus Remind students that violent events in Greek dramas were typically reported and not portrayed onstage.

3 Ask students what has happened to Jocasta. *(She has killed herself.)*

English Learners

Explain the meaning of the following phrases:

Line 1332: "More wed to pain and frenzy?" *(Could any person be so thoroughly joined to pain and wild suffering?)* Explain to students that wed can mean "to unite closely" in addition to "to join in matrimony."

Line 1349: "my breath leapt in you" *(You were so important to my life that it seemed as if you gave me the power to breathe, as if you gave me life itself.)*

Line 1350: "you bring down night upon my eyes" *(You now bring a vision of death instead of life.)*

Line 1365: "By her own hand" *(She killed herself.)*

Reading and Analyzing

Reading Skills and Strategies
SUMMARIZING

A Tell students that the key actions all take place offstage and are reported (see cross curricular link below). Ask students to summarize what they learn about Oedipus' actions here.

Possible Response: After Oedipus learned the truth about his birth, he became enraged. He asked for a sword (presumably, to kill himself), then cried out, and threw himself against the locked doors of the bedroom, knocking the doors open. It seemed as if he had been under the direction of a "dark power."

Literary Analysis TRAGIC HERO

B Ask students how Oedipus responded to the sight of Jocasta's corpse.

Possible Response: Oedipus ripped the brooches from her robe and pierced his own eyes with them. He cried out that he would see no more pain with his eyes. He would be blind from "this hour on." Repeatedly, he drove the brooches into his eye sockets.

Active Reading
STRATEGIES FOR READING GREEK DRAMA

C Tell students that when Oedipus appears he is wearing a new mask, one that shows blood streaming from his eyes. The mask would help to communicate the horror of his situation to the audience. Point out that this exchange between Oedipus and the chorus—which continues through line 1496—is mostly sung. Ask students why the chorus asks Oedipus, "What madness swept over you?"

Possible Response: The chorus feels that Oedipus was mad to gouge his eyes out. He seems to be under the control of some "dark power," which they cannot understand.

husband by her husband, children by her child.
And then—
but how she died is more than I can say. Suddenly
Oedipus burst in, screaming, he stunned us so
we couldn't watch her agony to the end,
our eyes were fixed on him. Circling
like a maddened beast, stalking, here, there,
crying out to us—
Give him a sword! His wife,
no wife, his mother, where can he find the mother earth
that cropped two crops at once, himself and all his children?
A He was raging—one of the dark powers pointing the way,
none of us mortals crowding around him, no,
with a great shattering cry—someone, something leading him on—
he hurled at the twin doors and bending the bolts back
out of their sockets, crashed through the chamber.

1 And there we saw the woman hanging by the neck,
cradled high in a woven noose, spinning,
swinging back and forth. And when he saw her,
giving a low, wrenching sob that broke our hearts,
slipping the halter from her throat, he eased her down,
in a slow embrace he laid her down, poor thing . . .
then, what came next, what horror we beheld!

He rips off her brooches, the long gold pins
holding her robes—and lifting them high,
looking straight up into the points,
he digs them down the sockets of his eyes, crying, "You,
2 you'll see no more the pain I suffered, all the pain I caused!
B Too long you looked on the ones you never should have seen,
blind to the ones you longed to see, to know! Blind
from this hour on! Blind in the darkness—blind!"
His voice like a dirge, rising, over and over
raising the pins, raking them down his eyes.
And at each stroke blood spurts from the roots,

Cross Curricular Link Humanities

VIOLENCE AND GREEK STAGING In Greek theater most acts of extreme violence are reported to the audience rather than depicted onstage. For example, in Sophocles' *Antigone*, the title character hangs herself offstage; subsequently, her betrothed, Haemon, and his mother, Eurydice, also kill themselves in despair. In Aeschylus' *Agamemnon* the savage murder of Agamemnon and Cassandra are only reported by the chorus.

Practical reasons have been offered to explain such methods. Perhaps the most important is that only three actors—all performers were men—participated in any one production. The actor who played Jocasta might leave the stage in despair only to return later in the guise of another character. In Aeschylus' *Agamemnon*, the actor playing the title role apparently had to return after the murder to play the role of Agamemnon's enemy, Aegisthus. Also, violent action would be difficult to enact because the actors wore raised boots, masks, headdresses, and robes that limited physical movement. Dramatists may have preferred to show the spectacle of violence's aftermath—perhaps best represented by the bloody mask of Oedipus—rather than the violence itself.

splashing his beard, a swirl of it, nerves and clots—
black hail of blood pulsing, gushing down.

These are the griefs that burst upon them both,
coupling man and woman. The joy they had so lately,
the fortune of their old ancestral house
was deep joy indeed. Now, in this one day,
wailing, madness and doom, death, disgrace,
all the griefs in the world that you can name,
all are theirs forever.

Leader. Oh poor man, the misery—
has he any rest from pain now?

(*A voice within, in torment.*)

Messenger. He's shouting,
"Loose the bolts, someone, show me to all of Thebes!
My father's murderer, my mother's—"
No, I can't repeat it, it's unholy.
Now he'll tear himself from his native earth,
not linger, curse the house with his own curse.
But he needs strength, and a guide to lead him on.
This is sickness more than he can bear.

(*The palace doors open.*)

Look,
he'll show you himself. The great doors are opening—
you are about to see a sight, a horror
even his mortal enemy would pity.

3 (*Enter* Oedipus, *blinded, led by a boy. He stands at the palace steps, as if surveying his people once again.*)

Chorus. O the terror—
the suffering, for all the world to see,
the worst terror that ever met my eyes.
What madness swept over you? What god,
C what dark power leapt beyond all bounds,
beyond belief, to crush your wretched life?—
godforsaken, cursed by the gods!
I pity you but I can't bear to look.
I've much to ask, so much to learn,
so much fascinates my eyes,
but you . . . I shudder at the sight.

Customizing Instruction

Less Proficient Readers

To make sure that students are following the plot, ask the following questions:

1 What does Jocasta do in response to the news that she is the mother of Oedipus? *(She hangs herself.)*

2 Ask students what Oedipus did to blind himself *(He gouged his eyes out with Jocasta's brooches.)* Then ask students to tell what he said while he was blinding himself. *(He said that his eyes caused him too much pain. He chose to blind himself so that he would not have to look at the sights that gave him pain.)*

3 Ask students to explain what Oedipus looks like when he appears on stage. *(He is blind. The audience can see that his eyes are bleeding. He is a broken man.)*

English Learners

Explain the meaning of the following phrases:

Line 1386: "like a maddened beast, stalking, here, there" *(Oedipus is moving around like an angered animal; he does not know where to go.)*

Line 1399: "slipping the halter" *(taking the rope off)*

Line 1423: "Loose the bolts" *(unlock the door)*

Advanced Learners

The scholar E. R. Dodds makes the following point about the blinding of Oedipus:

> "*Oedipus Rex* is a play about the blindness of man and the desperate insecurity of the human condition: in a sense every man must grope in the dark as Oedipus gropes, not knowing who he is or what he has to suffer. . . . But surely the *Oedipus Rex* is also about human greatness. Oedipus is great . . . in virtue of his inner strength: strength to pursue truth at whatever personal cost, and strength to endure it when found."

Ask students if they agree that Oedipus is great. Tell them to give examples or quotations from the text to support their opinion. *(Accept all reasonable responses.)*

Reading and Analyzing

Literary Analysis METAPHOR

A Point out that Oedipus makes use of two metaphors. First, he compares his blindness to the act of drowning, for he feels as if he is being drowned by the horrors of his experience. Second, he compares the act of blinding himself to his memories, the "stab of memory" that is making him insane. Ask why he describes memory as a stab.

Possible Response: Each time Oedipus remembers his past it is as if he is being stabbed again. His memory brings sharp, piercing, and constant pain.

Reading Skills and Strategies
MAKING INFERENCES

B Make sure that students realize that Oedipus does not blame Apollo; he says simply that "Apollo ordained his agony." In other words, Apollo determined the fate of Oedipus. Ask students why Oedipus insists that he stabbed his eyes of his own free will.

Possible Responses: Oedipus is assuring the chorus that he acted voluntarily. No god, dark power, or evil force made him blind himself; he chose to do so as a way of punishing himself. Apollo may have chosen Oedipus' fate, but Oedipus has chosen how to respond to that fate.

Literary Analysis TRAGIC HERO

C Ask students whether they consider Oedipus to be heroic in his suffering. *(Accept all reasonable responses.)*

OH, OHH—
THE AGONY! I AM AGONY—

Laurence Olivier as Oedipus (1945).

Oedipus. Oh, Ohh—
the agony! I am agony—
where am I going? where on earth?
where does all this agony hurl me?
where's my voice?—
winging, swept away on a dark tide—
My destiny, my dark power, what a leap you made!

Chorus. To the depths of terror, too dark to hear, to see.

Oedipus. Dark, horror of darkness
my darkness, drowning, swirling around me
crashing wave on wave—unspeakable, irresistible
A headwind, fatal harbor! Oh again,
the misery, all at once, over and over
the stabbing daggers, stab of memory
raking me insane.

Chorus. No wonder you suffer
1 twice over, the pain of your wounds,
the lasting grief of pain.

Oedipus. Dear friend, still here?
Standing by me, still with a care for me,
the blind man? Such compassion,
loyal to the last. Oh it's you,
I know you're here, dark as it is
I'd know you anywhere, your voice—
it's yours, clearly yours.

Chorus. Dreadful, what you've done . . .
how could you bear it, gouging out your eyes?
What superhuman power drove you on?

Oedipus. Apollo, friends, Apollo—
2 he ordained my agonies—these, my pains on pains!
But the hand that struck my eyes was mine,
B mine alone—no one else—
I did it all myself!
What good were eyes to me?
Nothing I could see could bring me joy.

Chorus. No, no, exactly as you say.

Oedipus. What can I ever see?
C What love, what call of the heart
can touch my ears with joy? Nothing, friends.

1468 ordained: decreed; commanded.

Customizing Instruction

Less Proficient Readers

Students may have difficulty understanding why Oedipus puts himself through such suffering, even though he did not knowingly marry his mother and murder his father. Remind students that Oedipus' actions polluted Thebes, caused the plague, and in one way or another ruined the life of all his family members. Ask the following questions to help them understand the depth of Oedipus' pain:

1 Why does Oedipus suffer "twice over"? *(He suffers from the pain of his physical wounds and the pain of his grief about all the suffering he has caused.)*

2 Who determined the fate of Oedipus? *(Apollo)* Who is responsible for his blinding? *(Oedipus alone)*

OEDIPUS THE KING 319

Reading and Analyzing

Reading Skills and Strategies
CLARIFYING

A Explain that Oedipus now wishes that he had died in infancy. Ask students to identify the person whom Oedipus is referring to. *(the shepherd who decided to save Oedipus instead of abandoning him)*

Active Reading
STRATEGIES FOR READING GREEK DRAMA

B Ask students what seems to disturb Oedipus more, his marriage to his mother or his murder of his father.
Possible Response: In this passage, Oedipus seems more upset by the marriage to his mother. While he mentions the murder, he elaborates with considerable detail the horror of marrying his mother.

Literary Analysis PERSONIFICATION

C Tell students that personification is a figure of speech in which human qualities are attributed to an object, animal, or idea. Ask students to explain the personification here.
Possible Response: The intersection of the "triple roads," where the murder of Laius took place, is personified as drinking the blood of Laius. Because he is the father of Oedipus, the road is also described as having drunk the blood of Oedipus.

Reading Skills and Strategies
CLARIFYING

D Make sure that students understand the depth of Oedipus' horror. In ordinary circumstances, the marriage that produced Oedipus and the marriage that joined him to his wife should be two completely different events. But in his case the two marriages become blurred into one terrible marriage because the son married his mother, violating sacred human boundaries. In Oedipus' graphic account, the sperm that brought him into the world was brought "rising back" to the same woman who gave him birth, thus blurring all family distinctions ("fathers, brothers, sons—one murderous breed—brides, wives, mothers").

Take me away, far, far from Thebes,
quickly, cast me away, my friends—
this great murderous ruin, this man cursed to heaven,
the man the deathless gods hate most of all!

Chorus. Pitiful, you suffer so, you understand so much . . .
I wish you had never known.

Oedipus. Die, die—
whoever he was that day in the wilds
who cut my ankles free of the ruthless pins,
A he pulled me clear of death, he saved my life
for this, this kindness—
Curse him, kill him!
If I'd died then, I'd never have dragged myself,
my loved ones through such hell.

Chorus. Oh if only . . . would to god.

Oedipus. I'd never have come to this,
my father's murderer—never been branded
mother's husband, all men see me now! Now,
B loathed by the gods, son of the mother I defiled
coupling in my father's bed, spawning lives in the loins
that spawned my wretched life. What grief can crown this grief?
It's mine alone, my destiny—I am Oedipus!

Chorus. How can I say you've chosen for the best?
Better to die than be alive and blind.

Oedipus. What I did was best—don't lecture me,
no more advice. I, with *my* eyes,
1 how could I look my father in the eyes
when I go down to death? Or mother, so abused . . .
I have done such things to the two of them,
crimes too huge for hanging.
Worse yet,
the sight of my children, born as they were born,
how could I long to look into their eyes?
No, not with these eyes of mine, never.
Not this city either, her high towers,
the sacred glittering images of her gods—
I am misery! I, her best son, reared
as no other son of Thebes was ever reared,
I've stripped myself, I gave the command myself.

WORDS TO KNOW
loathed (lōthd) *adj.* intensely hated **loathe** *v.*

All men must cast away the great blasphemer,
the curse now brought to light by the gods,
the son of Laius—I, my father's son!

Now I've exposed my guilt, horrendous guilt,
could I train a level glance on you, my countrymen?
Impossible! No, if I could just block off my ears,
the springs of hearing, I would stop at nothing—
I'd wall up my loathsome body like a prison,
blind to the sound of life, not just the sight.
Oblivion—what a blessing . . .
for the mind to dwell a world away from pain.

O Cithaeron, why did you give me shelter?
Why didn't you take me, crush my life out on the spot?
I'd never have revealed my birth to all mankind.

O Polybus, Corinth, the old house of my fathers,
so I believed—what a handsome prince you raised—
under the skin, what sickness to the core.
Look at me! Born of outrage, outrage to the core.

O triple roads—it all comes back, the secret,
dark ravine, and the oaks closing in
where the three roads join . . .
C
You drank my father's blood, my own blood
spilled by my own hands—you still remember me?
What things you saw me do? Then I came here
and did them all once more!
D
Marriages! O marriage,
you gave me birth, and once you brought me into the
world
you brought my sperm rising back, springing to light
fathers, brothers, sons—one murderous breed—
brides, wives, mothers. The blackest things
a man can do, I have done them all!
No more—
2
it's wrong to name what's wrong to do. Quickly,
for the love of god, hide me somewhere,
kill me, hurl me into the sea
where you can never look on me again.

(beckoning to the Chorus *as they shrink away)*

1513 blasphemer (blăs-fē′mər): a person who shows disrespect for sacred things.

1517 train a level glance on you: look you straight in the eye.

1530 outrage: a horribly offensive act.

Customizing Instruction

Less Proficient Readers

Point out that in these pages Oedipus explains the depth of his horrors and his reasons for blinding himself. Ask students to look for words and phrases that identify the people who fill Oedipus with such guilt that he could never look at them again.

Possible Responses:

- "how could I look my father in the eyes when I go down to death"
- "Or mother"
- "the sight of my children . . . how could I long to look into their eyes?"
- "Not this city either"
- "could I train a level glance on you [the chorus], my beloved country-men?"

Ask the following questions to help students fully understand Oedipus' despair:

1 Oedipus explains that he chose not to kill himself. What was he afraid of in the afterlife? *(He would have seen Laius and Jocasta, and he could not have looked at them.)*

2 What does Oedipus ask the chorus to do? *(throw him into the sea)*

English Learners

Explain the meaning of the following phrases:

Line 1509: "the sacred glittering images of her gods": *(the holy statues of the gods)*

Line 1512: "I've stripped myself." *(I have made myself an outcast of Thebes, taking all my powers away.)*

Line 1522: "Oblivion–what a blessing" *(If I could cut myself off from all sights and sounds, that would be a blessing.)*

Line 1529: "under the skin, what sickness to the core" *(Beneath the surface, I was filled completely with sickness.)*

Reading and Analyzing

Pause & Reflect
Possible Response: Oedipus takes brooches from the robe of Jocasta's hanging corpse, and he gouges his eyes out with them.

Reading Skills and Strategies
DRAWING CONCLUSIONS
A Ask students why Creon is so concerned that Oedipus is standing in public view.
Possible Responses: Oedipus has been so thoroughly disgraced that it is not proper for him to be seen in public. He has polluted Thebes by his actions so even nature itself would not welcome his sight. Only family members should be allowed to see him.

Literary Analysis TRAGIC HERO
B Point out that Oedipus, though thoroughly humbled by his disgrace, still shows a kind of pride and courage. He submits to his destiny, convinced that "something great and terrible, something strange" will come his way. Ask students what he may be referring to. *(Accept all reasonable responses.)*

Reading Skills and Strategies
CONNECTING
C Ask students how they feel about Oedipus' request to see his daughters one more time. *(Accept all reasonable responses.)*

Closer,
it's all right. Touch the man of grief.
Do. Don't be afraid. My troubles are mine
and I am the only man alive who can sustain them.

1549 sustain: endure.

PAUSE & REFLECT How and why does Oedipus blind himself?

FOCUS Read to find out what happens to Oedipus at the end of the play.

(*Enter* Creon *from the palace, attended by palace guards.*)

Leader. Put your requests to Creon. Here he is,
just when we need him. He'll have a plan, he'll act.
Now that he's the sole defense of the country
in your place.

Oedipus. Oh no, what can I say to him?
How can I ever hope to win his trust?
I wronged him so, just now, in every way.
You must see that—I was so wrong, so wrong.

Creon. I haven't come to mock you, Oedipus,
or to criticize your former failings.

(*turning to the guards*)

You there,
have you lost all respect for human feelings?
At least revere the Sun, the holy fire
that keeps us all alive. Never expose a thing
A of guilt and holy dread so great it appalls
the earth, the rain from heaven, the light of day!
Get him into the halls—quickly as you can.
Piety demands no less. Kindred alone
should see a kinsman's shame. This is obscene.

1566 obscene: disgusting.

Oedipus. Please, in god's name . . . you wipe my fears away,
coming so generously to me, the worst of men.
Do one thing more, for your sake, not mine.

Creon. What do you want? Why so insistent?

1 **Oedipus.** Drive me out of the land at once, far from sight,
where I can never hear a human voice.

Creon. I'd have done that already, I promise you.
First I wanted the god to clarify my duties.

Oedipus. The god? His command was clear, every word:
death for the father-killer, the curse—
he said destroy me!

Creon. So he did. Still, in such a crisis
it's better to ask precisely what to do.

Oedipus. So miserable—
you would consult the god about a man like me?

Creon. By all means. And this time, I assume,
even you will obey the god's decrees.

Oedipus. I will,
I will. And you, I command you—I beg you . . .
the woman inside, bury her as you see fit.
It's the only decent thing,
to give your own the last rites. As for me,
never condemn the city of my fathers
to house my body, not while I'm alive, no,
let me live on the mountains, on Cithaeron,
my favorite haunt, I have made it famous.
2 Mother and father marked out that rock
to be my everlasting tomb—buried alive.
Let me die there, where they tried to kill me.

Oh but this I know: no sickness can destroy me,
B nothing can. I would never have been saved
from death—I have been saved
for something great and terrible, something strange.
Well let my destiny come and take me on its way!

About my children, Creon, the boys at least,
don't burden yourself. They're men,
wherever they go, they'll find the means to live.
But my two daughters, my poor helpless girls,
clustering at our table, never without me
C hovering near them . . . whatever I touched,
they always had their share. Take care of them,
3 I beg you. Wait, better—permit me, would you?
Just to touch them with my hands and take
our fill of tears. Please . . . my king.
Grant it, with all your noble heart.
If I could hold them, just once, I'd think

1604 hovering (hŭv′ər-ĭng): hanging about.

Customizing Instruction

Less Proficient Readers

Focus Ask students to exchange predictions with a classmate about what they think will happen to Oedipus. Help students to understand what Oedipus requests from Creon by asking the following questions:

1 What does Oedipus want Creon to do? *(to drive him out of Thebes to a place completely removed from human contact)*

2 Oedipus has no desire to live in Thebes because of what he has done to that city. Where does he want to go? *(Mount Cithaeron)* Why? *(It is the place where he was supposed to die as an infant; he wants to die there.)*

3 Whom does Oedipus want to take care of his daughters? *(Creon)* What final request does Oedipus make? *(He asks to see his daughters.)*

English Learners

Explain the meaning of the following phrases and lines:

Line 1552: "he's the sole defense of the country" *(Creon is now the only leader of Thebes, the person who must protect us.)*

Lines 1561–1563: "Never expose a thing . . . the light of day!" *(You should never allow the public to see a person who is guilty of such a terrible crime. The sight of him would horrify even nature–the earth, rain, and sunlight.)*

Lines 1566–1567: "Kindred alone should see a kinsman's shame." *(Only his family members should be allowed to see the shame of Oedipus.)*

Reading and Analyzing

Literary Analysis TRAGIC HERO

A Ask students how they view Oedipus now.

Possible Responses: He is a pathetic but noble figure. Even though his life is ruined, he insists on seeing his daughters one last time, which shows his concern for them. He has been humbled by his terrible fate.

Active Reading STRATEGIES FOR READING GREEK DRAMA

B Oedipus anticipates many great difficulties for his daughters. Explain to students that women without a family to protect them would be especially vulnerable. Ask students to summarize the problems that the two girls will face.

Possible Response: They won't be able to attend public gatherings. They won't have any family banquets where they can join in celebrations. When they are old enough to be married, no one will want to risk marriage to them because the entire family is cursed. They will forever be burdened by the shame of their father's actions and the scandal of having the same mother as their father does.

I had them with me, like the early days
when I could see their eyes.

(Antigone *and* Ismene, *two small children, are led in from the palace by a nurse.*)

What's that?
1 O god! Do I really hear you sobbing?—
my two children. Creon, you've pitied me?
Sent me my darling girls, my own flesh and blood!
Am I right?

Creon. Yes, it's my doing.
I know the joy they gave you all these years,
the joy you must feel now.

Oedipus. Bless you, Creon!
May god watch over you for this kindness,
better than he ever guarded me.
Children, where are you?
Here, come quickly—

(*groping for* Antigone *and* Ismene, *who approach their father cautiously, then embrace him.*)

Come to these hands of mine,
A your brother's hands, your own father's hands
that served his once bright eyes so well—
that made them blind. Seeing nothing, children,
knowing nothing, I became your father,
I fathered you in the soil that gave me life.

How I weep for you—I cannot see you now . . .
just thinking of all your days to come, the bitterness,
the life that rough mankind will thrust upon you.
Where are the public gatherings you can join,
the banquets of the clans? Home you'll come,
in tears, cut off from the sight of it all,
B the brilliant rites unfinished.
2 And when you reach perfection, ripe for marriage,
who will he be, my dear ones? Risking all
to shoulder the curse that weighs down my parents,
yes and you too—that wounds us all together.
What more misery could you want?
Your father killed his father, sowed his mother,
one, one and the selfsame womb sprang you—
he cropped the very roots of his existence.

Cross Curricular Link Humanities

ARISTOTLE'S THEORY OF TRAGEDY In the fourth-century B.C., the philosopher Aristotle offered a theory of tragedy in his *Poetics*. According to Aristotle, "tragedy is an imitation of an action that is serious, complete and of a certain magnitude." A tragedy should succeed in "arousing pity and fear in such a way as to accomplish a catharsis of such emotions." In Aristotle's view, the audience should feel pity for the hero because of his "unmerited misfortune," fear because the hero is someone "like ourselves."

Aristotle uses *Oedipus the King* as his example of a perfect tragedy. Indeed, a form of the word *catharsis* appears near the beginning of the play when Oedipus asks how the city can cleanse or purify itself. The word *catharsis,* meaning "purgation" or "purification," has both a medical and a religious meaning. By purging the powerful emotions of pity and fear, the audience is brought to virtuous end.

HOW I WEEP FOR YOU —I CANNOT SEE YOU NOW . . .

Oedipus speaks words of pity to his daughters, from the film *Oedipus the King* (1968), starring Christopher Plummer.

Customizing Instruction

Less Proficient Readers

Help students to appreciate the pathos of drama's conclusion by asking the following questions:

1 Why are the daughters of Oedipus crying? *(Although they are too young to understand events, they must know that something terrible has happened. They may also be afraid of the sight of their bloody father.)*

2 Ask students to look for phrases in this passage that suggest the difficult life ahead for the two girls.

Possible Response:

- "the bitterness, the life that rough mankind will thrust upon you."
- "Where are the public gatherings you can join, the banquets of the clans?"
- "Home you'll come, in tears, cut off from the sight of it all"
- "the curse that weighs down my parents, yes and you too—that wounds us all together."
- "What more misery could you want?"

English Learners

Explain the meaning of the following phrases and lines:

Line 1626: "I fathered you in the soil that gave me life." *(I became your father by the body of the same woman who gave birth to me.)*

Line 1641: "he cropped the very roots of his existence" *(Oedipus killed the source of his own life, his father.)*

Advanced Learners

Some critics have pointed out that the character of Oedipus may be interpreted as a symbol of fifth-century Athens. Like the city of Athens, Oedipus at the beginning of the drama is proud and supremely confident, a rationalist who believes that every problem has a solution. Ask students the following: If Oedipus is a symbol of Athens, what message is Sophocles communicating to his fellow citizens?

Possible Response Athens may need to learn humility and be subservient to the will of the gods, which cannot be understood or controlled by human intelligence. Athens, like Oedipus, must learn that it cannot master its own destiny.

Reading and Analyzing

Literary Analysis CULTURAL SETTING

A Point out that Sophocles is expressing a truth about his own society: the security and social status of women depended on marrying a man and having children. You might wish to point out the irony that in Athens, considered the birthplace of democracy and an open society, women were more subservient and powerless than those in Sparta.

Literary Analysis TRAGIC HERO

B Ask students to explain what Oedipus wants for his children.
Possible Response: He wants them to pray for a life that is better than his own. He hopes that they can find a place where they can live freely, in contrast to his own self-imposed imprisonment on Mount Cithaeron.

Literary Analysis THEME

C Creon here expresses a message of comfort. Ask students if this message may be considered one of the themes of the drama.
Possible Responses: Yes, because Creon is pointing out that even the worst agonies of human existence can be healed by the power of time. Time offers the possibility that one day even Oedipus can gain peace and an acceptance of his fate. No, because Oedipus can never recover his life. The damage done is so severe that it cannot be repaired or healed, even by a long duration of time.

Literary Analysis THEME

D Ask students what lesson the chorus draws from the life of Oedipus.
Possible Response: Oedipus' fall from the highest heights of human greatness illustrates that we cannot truly possess happiness. Pain and suffering may overtake any person, regardless of the person's knowledge, power, or reputation.

Such disgrace, and you must bear it all!
Who will marry you then? Not a man on earth.

Your doom is clear: you'll wither away to nothing,
single, without a child.

(*turning to* Creon)

Oh Creon,
you are the only father they have now . . .
we who brought them into the world
are gone, both gone at a stroke—
Don't let them go begging, abandoned,
women without men. Your own flesh and blood!
Never bring them down to the level of my pains.
Pity them. Look at them, so young, so vulnerable,
shorn of everything—you're their only hope.
Promise me, noble Creon, touch my hand!

(*reaching toward* Creon, *who draws back*)

You, little ones, if you were old enough
to understand, there is much I'd tell you.
Now, as it is, I'd have you say a prayer.
Pray for life, my children,
live where you are free to grow and season.
Pray god you find a better life than mine,
the father who begot you.

Creon. Enough.
You've wept enough. Into the palace now.

Oedipus. I must, but I find it very hard.

Creon. Time is the great healer, you will see.

Oedipus. I am going—you know on what condition?

Creon. Tell me. I'm listening.

Oedipus. Drive me out of Thebes, in exile.

Creon. Not I. Only the gods can give you that.

Oedipus. Surely the gods hate me so much—

Creon. You'll get your wish at once.

Oedipus. You consent?

Creon. I try to say what I mean; it's my habit.

Oedipus. Then take me away. It's time.

Creon. Come along, let go of the children.

Oedipus. No—
don't take them away from me, not now! No no no!

(clutching his daughters as the guards wrench them loose and take them through the palace doors)

2 **Creon.** Still the king, the master of all things?
No more: here your power ends.
None of your power follows you through life.

(Exit Oedipus *and* Creon *to the palace. The* Chorus *comes forward to address the audience directly.)*

D **Chorus.** People of Thebes, my countrymen, look on Oedipus.
He solved the famous riddle with his brilliance,
he rose to power, a man beyond all power.
Who could behold his greatness without envy?
Now what a black sea of terror has overwhelmed him.
Now as we keep our watch and wait the final day,
count no man happy till he dies, free of pain at last.

(Exit in procession.)

Customizing Instruction

Less Proficient Readers

1 Ask students why Oedipus describes the future life of his daughters to be "doom." *(No one will marry them; they will live single and childless as outcasts.)*

2 Make sure that students understand that Oedipus has no power in this situation. Creon is in charge, and he has ordered that Oedipus must be taken away, even though he does not want to leave his children.

English Learners

Explain the meaning of the following phrases:

Line 1653: "shorn of everything" *(They have lost everything in their lives.)*

Line 1684: "count no man happy till he dies" *(No man can be thought to be truly happy until he dies.)*

Humanities

OEDIPUS: THE REST OF THE STORY Sophocles returned to Oedipus in the last years of his life, writing *Oedipus at Colonus,* which was produced after Sophocles' death. As the play opens, Oedipus is an old man who has been wandering in exile with his daughters Antigone and Ismene. Oedipus and Antigone enter a sacred grove in Colonus outside Athens while awaiting the return of Ismene, who has gone to the oracle at Delphi.

When Ismene returns, she brings news that the welfare of Thebes depends on the presence of Oedipus, whether in life or death. She reports that Creon and the sons of Oedipus also know the prophecy. The two brothers, Eteocles and Polynices, are engaged in a bitter war for control of Thebes. Upon hearing that his sons will try to exploit their knowledge for their own advantage, Oedipus curses them and prays that their conflict will be fatal to them both.

Oedipus promises to become a protector of Athens if the Athenians and their king, Theseus, help him. After Oedipus rejects the offers of his two sons and Creon, Creon angrily orders Antigone and Ismene to be taken away, only to be stopped by Theseus. At the sound of thunder, Oedipus, aware that his time is near, takes Theseus to show him the place for Oedipus' grave, from which he will protect Athens.

OEDIPUS THE KING 327

The images below come from two different productions of* Oedipus the King. *One is a film version set amid the ruins of ancient Greece; the other is a theatrical production set in contemporary Africa. Study the images below. Which setting do you find more interesting? What are the advantages of a classical Greek setting? Why might a director choose a very different contemporary setting?

Oedipus stands apart from Creon and Jocasta. Hartford Stage's production of *Oedipus the King*, directed by Jonathan Wilson, produced in 2001.

Oedipus is helped by an elder of Thebes, after blinding himself. Hartford Stage's production of *Oedipus the King*.

Two images of Oedipus, played by Christopher Plummer, in a 1968 film version of *Oedipus the King*.

MINI LESSON Viewing and Representing

COMPARING SETTINGS The production of *Oedipus the King* by the Hartford Stage Company is set in contemporary Africa. This adaptation, written by Adrienne Kennedy, connects the plague of Thebes to the scourge of AIDS. The 1968 film version of *Oedipus the King*, starring Christopher Plummer, is set in the ruins of the ancient theater in Epidaurus, Greece.

View & Compare Possible Response: Some students may find the contemporary African setting more interesting because it departs so boldly from the original. By equating the Theban plague to AIDS, the production comments about a contemporary health crisis. The African setting may also be appropriate because Oedipus does seem like a tribal leader. As a tyrant, he has complete control of Thebes. The role of Tiresias, a spiritual medium, may work well in the context of African spiritualism. Finally, the African setting makes the point that *Oedipus the King* is universal.

Other students may find the classical Greek setting more interesting because it is truer to the spirit of the original. By using the ruins of a theater as a backdrop, the audience is more easily transported to the distant time of the original story.

MYTH

—MURIEL RUKEYSER—

Sphinx of Taharqa. Copyright © The British Museum, London.

Modern writers have often returned to the myths and legends of ancient Greece for their subjects. In this poem, a contemporary writer takes a humorous approach to Oedipus.

Long afterward, Oedipus, old and blinded, walked the
roads. He smelled a familiar smell. It was
the Sphinx. Oedipus said, "I want to ask one question.
Why didn't I recognize my mother?" "You gave the
wrong answer," said the Sphinx. "But that was what
made everything possible," said Oedipus. "No," she said.
"When I asked, What walks on four legs in the morning,
two at noon, and three in the evening, you answered,
Man. You didn't say anything about woman."
"When you say Man," said Oedipus, "you include women
too. Everyone knows that." She said, "That's what you think."

Related Reading

Muriel Rukeyser A poet, playwright, biographer, and social activist, Muriel Rukeyser (1913–1980) made her passionate and often outspoken views known to the world. Rukeyser attended Vassar College for two years in the early 1930s and later took classes at Columbia University in New York City, her hometown. As a reporter for Vassar's *Student Review,* she covered the famous 1932 Scottsboro trial in Alabama in which nine African-American youths were accused of raping two white girls. Rukeyser not only witnessed various major conflicts of the 20th century, she took sides, supporting the Spanish Loyalists in the Spanish Civil War, being jailed while protesting the Vietnam War, and travelling to South Korea in the 1970s to rally against the death sentence of a Korean writer. In her poetry and in other public comments, Rukeyser often spoke out against inequalities based on divisions of race, class, and gender.

Although Rukeyser's poetry strongly attacked many injustices, it also reflected an optimism that such injustices could be remedied. Critics compared the style of her poems to that of Walt Whitman. In the words of one critic, "like Whitman, Muriel Rukeyser has so much joy that it is not to be contained in regular verse but comes out in lines that are rugged and soaring."

Discussion Questions

1. Ask students to explain the joke of the poem.
   Possible Response: Oedipus has been punished because he gave the wrong answer to the Sphinx many years ago. The Sphinx, which in Rukeyser's revision of the Oedipus legend never died, informs Oedipus that he did not recognize his mother, Jocasta, because he had neglected to include women as well as men in his answer to the Sphinx's riddle.
2. Tell students that the poem reflects Rukeyser's feminist beliefs. Ask students to explain the message of the poem.
   Possible Response: People need to be sensitive to the role of women in their use of language. The Sphinx, which is part female, took offense at Oedipus' lack of inclusive language. He answered "Man" to the riddle, but should have answered "Man and Woman." While the poem is humorous, it is making an important point about our assumptions about language.

Connect to the Literature

1. **What Do You Think?** How did you react to the ending of this play? Discuss your impressions.

Comprehension Check
- Why does Jocasta hang herself?
- Whom does Oedipus hold in his arms before going into exile?
- Who becomes the ruler of Thebes at the end of the play?

Think Critically

2. **ACTIVE READING: STRATEGIES FOR READING GREEK DRAMA** Review what you recorded in your READER'S NOTEBOOK. What strategies helped you the most in reading this play? What questions do you still have about the play?

3. Oedipus blinds himself and is filled with self-hatred when he discovers the truth about his past. Does Oedipus deserve what happens to him, or is he a victim of fate? Cite lines from the play to support your opinion.

4. Tiresias, the prophet, is the agent of the god Apollo. How would you compare and contrast Oedipus and Tiresias?

- their physical condition
- their attitude toward the gods
- their insights into the truth

5. How would you describe the role of the chorus in this play? How does the chorus's attitude change as the play progresses?

Extend Interpretations

6. **The Writer's Style** The term **imagery** refers to words that appeal to the senses. One pattern of imagery in this play involves references to darkness and light, blindness and sight. Find some examples of such images in the play. Why do you think Sophocles used these images?

7. **Comparing Texts** Reread Muriel Rukeyser's poem "Myth" on page 329. What slant does the poet give to the story of Oedipus?

8. **Connect to Life** How much control do you think people actually have over their lives? Cite examples from your reading and your own experience as you explore this question.

LITERARY ANALYSIS: TRAGIC HERO

The term **tragic hero,** first used by Aristotle, refers to a dignified or noble character who is central to a drama. According to Aristotle, a tragic hero possesses a defect, or **tragic flaw,** that brings about or contributes to his or her downfall. This flaw may be poor judgment, pride, weakness, or an excess of an admirable quality. The tragic hero recognizes his or her own flaw but only after it is too late to change the course of events.

Paired Activity Determine to what extent Aristotle's definition of *tragic hero* applies to Oedipus. Consider whether the qualities that make him great also lead to his ruin.

LITERARY ANALYSIS: DRAMATIC IRONY

Irony is a contrast between what is expected and what actually exists or happens. **Dramatic irony** occurs when the reader or viewer of a play is aware of information that a character in the play is not aware of. For example, in line 119, Oedipus, speaking of King Laius, says that he "never saw the man." We readers realize—just as Sophocles' original audience did—that Oedipus has seen Laius. In fact, he killed him long ago. Reread a few scenes from the play, looking for examples of dramatic irony. Why do you think Sophocles used this technique?

Connect to the Literature

1. **What Do You Think?** Accept all reasonable responses.

Comprehension Check
- She is in despair now that Oedipus knows his identity.
- his two young daughters
- Creon

 Use Selection Quiz in **Unit Two Resource Book,** p. 37.

Think Critically

2. Accept all reasonable responses about which reading strategies proved most helpful. Allow the class as a whole to respond to any further questions that are raised.
3. Possible Response: Students who argue that Oedipus deserves his fate may point to his pride; his uncontrolled anger, which leads to the murder of Laius; and his choice of Jocasta as a marriage partner. He might have avoided marrying any woman old enough to be his mother. Students who argue that Oedipus is a victim of fate may point out that his fate could not have been escaped no matter what he did. The oracle made an unconditional prophecy. Also, Oedipus left his home in Corinth to avoid his fate. Make sure that students find quotes that support their interpretation.
4. Possible Response: Tiresias is old and blind; Oedipus is strong, healthy, and in possession of all of his faculties. Tiresias is a faithful servant of Apollo; he is humble before the gods. Oedipus demonstrates his belief in the gods when he sends to the oracle, but when he is challenged by Tiresias, he turns against the prophet and becomes skeptical about the gods. Tiresias knows the truth about Oedipus, but he dreads its consequences and is reluctant to speak. Oedipus seems much more confident that the truth cannot hurt him. But when he hears the truth, he cannot believe it and he turns against the prophet.
5. Possible Response: The chorus serves as the voice of the ordinary citizen. At first, it pledges its support of Oedipus, though it is shaken by the accusations of Tiresias. Later, as the truth begins to unfold, the chorus seems to turn against Oedipus, indirectly denouncing his pride and his challenge to the gods. In the end, the chorus is terror-stricken by the example of Oedipus.

Extend Interpretations

6. **The Writer's Style** Possible Response: The imagery of light and darkness, blindness and sight, is tied to issues of truth and the difficulty of discerning the reality beneath appearances. Tiresias is blind, but he sees the truth, while Oedipus, justly praised for his intelligence, fails to see the truth of his own identity. Oedipus tries to bring the light of truth to Thebes in order to cast away the darkness of the plague. He sets out to bring the murderer to light, only to discover the truth in the dark corners of his own past.
7. **Comparing Texts** Rukeyser takes a humorous approach. She uses Oedipus' encounter with the Sphinx to comment on the need for women to be treated as equals to men even in the choice of language.
8. **Connect to Life** Accept all reasonable responses.

Writing Options

1. Personal Response Aristotle explained that a tragedy stirs two emotions in its audience—pity and terror—directed toward the characters on stage. Write a personal-response essay, applying Aristotle's theory to your own reading of *Oedipus the King.* What events in the play evoked your deepest sympathy? What events in the play filled you with terror?

2. Diary Entry Choose an important character other than Oedipus in this play—such as Jocasta, Creon, Tiresias, or the messenger from Corinth. Then write a diary entry expressing that character's thoughts and feelings.

3. Literary Analysis The effect of the last scene would be different if the violent events—the death of Jocasta and the blinding of Oedipus—were dramatized onstage instead of being reported by a messenger. Write a brief essay explaining what a dramatist gains by making such events take place offstage rather than onstage.

Writing Handbook
See pages R31–R34: Explanatory Writing.

Activities & Explorations

1. Theater Model On the basis of the stage directions in the play, create a model of the stage for *Oedipus the King.* Then prepare an oral report or a multimedia presentation on the theater in ancient Greece. ~ **ART**

2. Role-Playing With a few classmates, choose one important scene from the play and act it out for the rest of the class. Then share with the class the insights you gained by playing a particular character.
~ **SPEAKING AND LISTENING**

Inquiry & Research

Oedipus Complex Sigmund Freud (1856–1939) is known as the father of psychoanalysis. He was intrigued by Sophocles' play and the myth of Oedipus. Freud coined the term *Oedipus complex* as a name for certain unconscious urges in the human mind. Find out about Freud's use of this term. Then prepare an oral report to share your findings.

RESEARCH STARTER
CLASSZONE.COM

Vocabulary in Action

EXERCISE: SYNONYMS AND ANTONYMS Identify each pair of words as synonyms or antonyms.

1. **denounce**—criticize
2. **swarthy**—pale
3. **retract**—promote
4. **despondent**—happy
5. **oblivion**—prominence
6. **appall**—delight
7. **reverberate**—echo
8. **foreboding**—warning
9. **surmise**—fact
10. **explicit**— implied
11. **loathed**—despised
12. **mortify**—shame
13. **menace**—threat
14. **futile**—effective
15. **revile**—praise

Building Vocabulary
The word *foreboding* has interesting connotations, suggesting fear and anxiety. For an in-depth lesson on denotation and connotation, see page 1090.

Literary Analysis

Tragic Hero Some students may decide that Oedipus is a perfect illustration of Aristotle's definition. Others may express reservations about Oedipus' tragic flaw, his pride, actually being the cause of his downfall. Such students may note that Oedipus would be doomed even if he had no flaws.

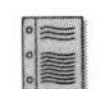
Use **Unit Two Resource Book,** pp. 30, 33, and 36, for more practice.

Dramatic Irony Students should be able to find numerous examples of such irony. They may note that such irony contributes to the dramatic tension of the play—the audience always knows more than Oedipus. They may also find that such irony underscores the theme that no person can fully understand their life.

Writing Options

1. **Personal Response** You may want to photocopy the short excerpt from Aristotle's *Poetics* that addresses pity and fear. In many editions, it is labeled by these words. Make sure that students realize that they need to explain fully why they feel sympathy and terror.
2. **Diary Entry** While students need to express the thoughts and feelings of their chosen character, they do not necessarily have to try to imitate the language used in the play. You may wish to encourage students to be creative in their use of language.
3. **Literary Analysis** It will help if you discuss this topic with the entire class before students begin writing.

Activities & Explorations

1. **Theater Model** Before students create a model, they should look at photographs and diagrams of the Greek stage, which are available online.
2. **Role-Playing** In the spirit of Greek theater, you might want to turn this activity into a contest, allowing the entire class to vote on the best presentation and follow-up discussion.

Inquiry & Research

Oedipus Complex Freud's interpretation of Oedipus can be found in his short book, *The Interpretation of Dreams,* which is widely available in bookstores and libraries. Be aware that the sexual nature and controversial assumptions of Freud's theory may be offensive to some students and parents.

Vocabulary in Action

1. synonym
2. antonym
3. antonym
4. antonym
5. antonym
6. antonym
7. synonym
8. synonym
9. antonym
10. antonym
11. synonym
12. synonym
13. synonym
14. antonym
15. antonym

To assess skills and concepts taught in this selection, use **Formal Assessment Book,** pp. 37–42.

Communication Workshop

Writing and Staging a Scene

Objectives

- write a Dramatic Scene
- use written text as a model for preparing the script
- practice and perform an interpretation of the scene
- revise a draft to use dialogue effectively
- refine the performance by evaluating interpretive choices

Introducing the Workshop

A Writing and Staging a Scene
Drama differs from other literary forms in that it is meant to be performed. In a play, the director, actors, and the crew all contribute their ideas and talents to the interpretation of the playwright's text. While the playwright is responsible for creating the text—without which there would be no play—he or she alone cannot bring a drama to life.

Like those in a novel or short story, characters in a drama are faced with a conflict. Typically, the action in a drama consists of the main character's struggle to resolve this conflict. Have students list engaging dramatic scenes from movies, television, or plays that involve sympathetic characters. What qualities do these scenes and characters have in common? Point out that in writing a dramatic scene, students will portray an interesting character struggling to resolve a conflict.

Basics in a Box
B Presenting the Rubric
To better understand the assignment, students can refer to the Standards for Writing and Staging a Scene. You may wish to discuss with them the complete rubric and student models in the Unit Two Resource Book on pages 46–52.

For more instruction and practice in narrative and literary writing, use McDougal Littell's ***Language Network:***

- Grade 10, Chapter 24, "Poetry"
- Grade 12, Chapter 23, "Dramatic Scene"

Communication Workshop

Writing and Staging a Scene

Literature through performance

From the Page to the Stage Although you'll find *Oedipus the King* printed in many books, Sophocles wrote it for the stage. Writing **drama** is different from writing prose, which the reader experiences alone, in his or her own mind. With a staged drama, the viewer's understanding of the play is influenced by the interpretation of the director and the performers. Many playwrights like to direct their own plays for this reason.

For Your Portfolio

WRITING PROMPT Write and stage a dramatic scene.

Purpose: To entertain

Audience: Your classmates and other interested students and adults

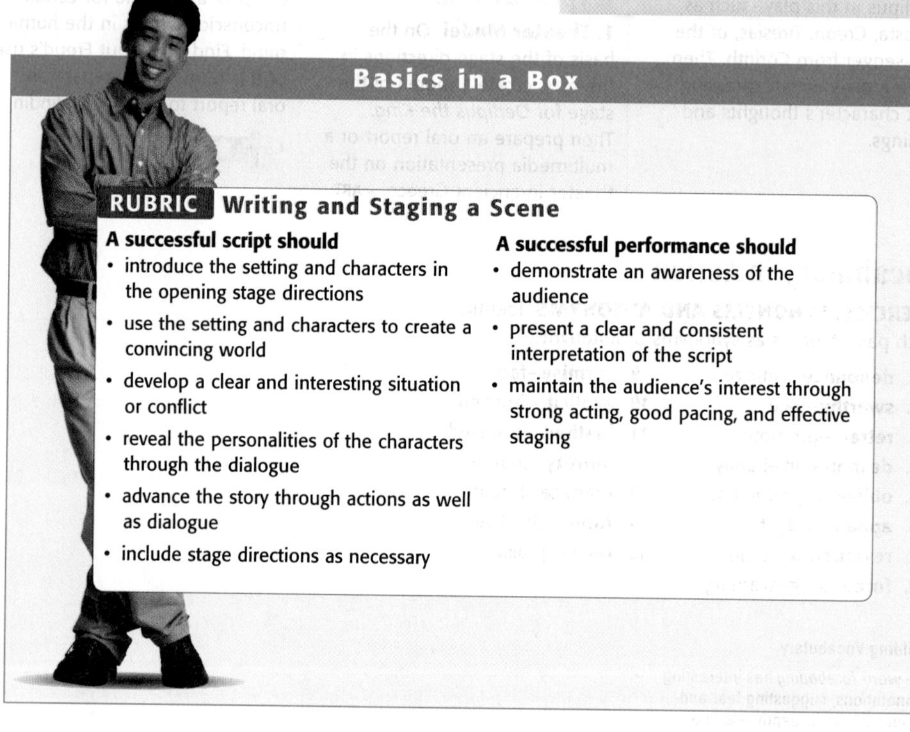

Basics in a Box

RUBRIC Writing and Staging a Scene

A successful script should

- introduce the setting and characters in the opening stage directions
- use the setting and characters to create a convincing world
- develop a clear and interesting situation or conflict
- reveal the personalities of the characters through the dialogue
- advance the story through actions as well as dialogue
- include stage directions as necessary

A successful performance should

- demonstrate an awareness of the audience
- present a clear and consistent interpretation of the script
- maintain the audience's interest through strong acting, good pacing, and effective staging

LESSON RESOURCES

USING PRINT RESOURCES
Unit Two Resource Book

- Prewriting, p. 39
- Drafting, p. 40
- Planning Your Scene, p. 41
- Developing, Practicing, and Presenting, p. 42
- Peer Response, pp. 43–44
- Revising and Refining Your Performance, p. 45
- Student Models, pp. 46–51
- Rubric and Standards, p. 52

USING MEDIA RESOURCES
Writing Coach CD-ROM
Visit our Web site: classzone.com

ADDITIONAL RESOURCES
For a complete view of Lesson Resources, see page 161h of this book.

Analyzing a Student Model

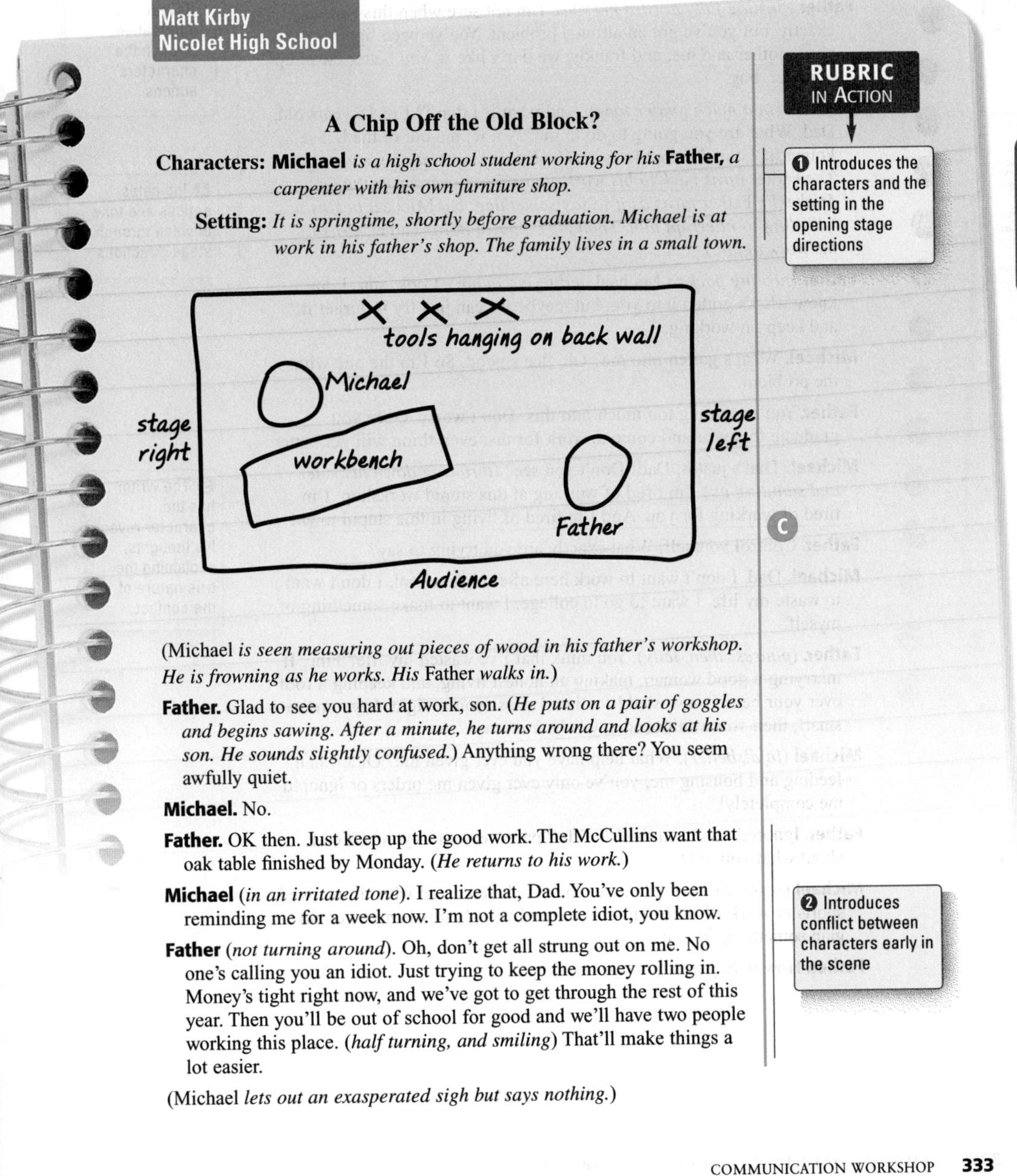

Matt Kirby
Nicolet High School

A Chip Off the Old Block?

Characters: Michael *is a high school student working for his* **Father,** *a carpenter with his own furniture shop.*

Setting: *It is springtime, shortly before graduation. Michael is at work in his father's shop. The family lives in a small town.*

(Michael *is seen measuring out pieces of wood in his father's workshop. He is frowning as he works. His* Father *walks in.)*

Father. Glad to see you hard at work, son. (*He puts on a pair of goggles and begins sawing. After a minute, he turns around and looks at his son. He sounds slightly confused.*) Anything wrong there? You seem awfully quiet.

Michael. No.

Father. OK then. Just keep up the good work. The McCullins want that oak table finished by Monday. (*He returns to his work.*)

Michael (*in an irritated tone*). I realize that, Dad. You've only been reminding me for a week now. I'm not a complete idiot, you know.

Father (*not turning around*). Oh, don't get all strung out on me. No one's calling you an idiot. Just trying to keep the money rolling in. Money's tight right now, and we've got to get through the rest of this year. Then you'll be out of school for good and we'll have two people working this place. (*half turning, and smiling*) That'll make things a lot easier.

(Michael *lets out an exasperated sigh but says nothing.*)

RUBRIC IN ACTION

❶ Introduces the characters and the setting in the opening stage directions

❷ Introduces conflict between characters early in the scene

LANGUAGE SKILLS

COMMUNICATION WORKSHOP 333

Teaching the Lesson

Analyzing the Model

"A Chip Off the Old Block?"

C The student model portrays a father and son who work together, but are not getting along very well. It becomes clear that the son does not want to continue working for his father, but wants to go to college. The father is unaware of his son's ambitions.

Have students read the model. Then discuss the Rubric in Action. Point out key words and phrases in the student model that correspond to the elements mentioned in the Rubric in Action.

1. Point out that the stage directions establish the setting and the relationship between the characters in a way that allows the reader to imagine something about the characters' values and situations in life. Ask students to predict what things might be important to each of the two characters.
   Possible Responses: The father cares about the success of his business; he wants his son's help in the shop; he is proud that his son is about to graduate from high school. The son likes working for his father; he doesn't like working for his father; he is eager to be done with school; he is worried about what he will do after he graduates.
2. Point out that by introducing the conflict early, the writer is establishing a certain kind of relationship between the father and son. Ask students to explain what this exchange indicates about the relationship between father and son.
   Possible Responses: It seems that Michael is irritated even before his father speaks, but his father does not realize this; Michael is sensitive to how his father treats him, and his father does not take him seriously.

MINI LESSON Viewing and Representing

REVIEW A PERFORMANCE

Dramatic Staging To extend the lesson, have students write a newspaper-style review of one or more student performances. Remind them to think of the Guidelines and Standards described on page 332 as they evaluate the performances.

To help students develop their reviews, have them use the following guidelines:

A well-written review
- identifies the subject at the beginning
- opens with a general opinion
- includes enough facts, examples, and specifics to support the general opinion
- displays logical organization
- quickly establishes a tone

Have students exchange reviews with other students who reviewed the same performance and compare them to their own responses.

3. Point out that a dramatist must rely on three things to reveal a character: 1) the character's actions; 2) the character's words; and 3) what other characters say about the character. Ask students which of these three techniques are being used here. Ask students to provide examples.
   Possible Responses: actions–father turns toward his son; character's words–father reveals his own anger; what the character says about other people–father talks about Michael's behavior
4. Point out to students that some playwrights make more extensive use of stage directions than others. Ask students how the level of detail in stage directions might affect a play's performance.
   Possible Responses: If the playwright does not include many stage directions, the director and actors have more freedom to interpret the script; extensive stage directions help the director and actors know what to do.
5. As in real life, characters in drama often say things other than what they're really thinking. This can be the source of dramatic tension. Point out to students that until this point in the script, Michael has not revealed what is really on his mind. This sudden revelation provides a turning point in the scene.

Father (*turning fully toward his son*). I'm not sure when this started exactly, but you've got an attitude problem. You've been lippin' off to your mother and me, and frankly, we don't like it. You better clean up your act, boy.

Michael (*in a much louder tone*). And what if I don't? I'm 18 years old, Dad. What are you going to do to me? Not let me out of the house? Forget it! I can do what I want. (*His* Father *stares at him, shocked. The* Father *turns back to his work, and silence overcomes the two.* *Michael's* Father *turns as if to say something, but* Michael *begins whistling to interrupt him. Thinking better of it, his* Father *turns to his work again.*)

Father (*turning back to* Michael *and trying again*). Look, son. I don't know what's gotten into you, but maybe we can just try to forget it and keep on working.

Michael. What's gotten into me? Oh, that's good. So I'm the one with the problem.

Father. You're reading too much into this. Don't worry. Once you graduate this year and come to work for me, everything will get better.

Michael. That's just it, Dad! Don't you see? (*throwing down his ruler and standing up*) I'm tired of working at this stupid workshop. I'm tired of working for you. And I'm tired of living in this stupid town!

Father. Control yourself. What exactly are you trying to say?

Michael. Dad, I don't want to work here after high school. I don't want to waste my life. I want to go to college. I want to make something of myself.

Father. (*pauses; then, icily*). You think that I've wasted my life? Fine. If marrying a good woman, making an honest living, and keeping a roof over your head is a wasted life, then I guess you're right. If you're so smart, then you won't need any help from me.

Michael (*in disbelief*). What help have you ever given me? Other than feeding and housing me, you've only ever given me orders or ignored me completely!

Father. Ignored you? You think I didn't pay attention to you? Or care about what you did?

Michael (*sarcastically*). Oh, sure, you cared. You cared when it involved sports or working in the shop. You cared what I did when you could gain something from it.

Father. How dare you talk to me that way!

❸ The writer has the father reveal information about himself and his son.

Another Option:
- Reveal information through the characters' actions.

❹ Indicates actions and tone of voice through stage directions

❺ The writer has the character reveal his thoughts, explaining the true nature of the conflict.

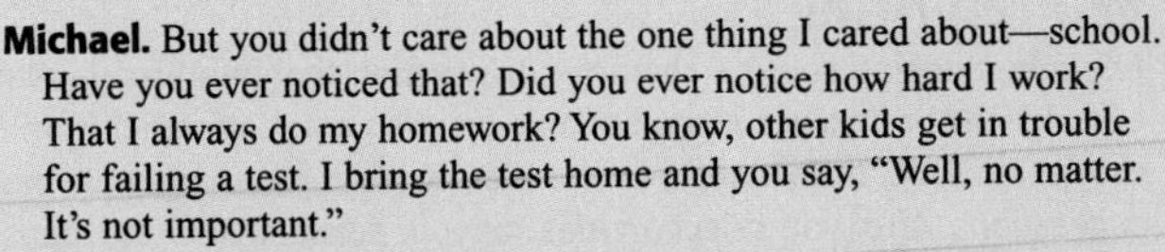

Michael. But you didn't care about the one thing I cared about—school. Have you ever noticed that? Did you ever notice how hard I work? That I always do my homework? You know, other kids get in trouble for failing a test. I bring the test home and you say, "Well, no matter. It's not important."

Father. So, I didn't yell at you! Are you going to be mad at me for that?

Michael (*almost in tears*). No, but it might have helped once in a while to notice and give me a little encouragement. Did you even know that in the last two years I've gone from a C-minus average to an A-minus? I have an *A-minus* in school, Dad. Does that mean anything to you?

Father (*distracted by* Michael's *emotion*). Son, don't cry. Men don't— (*stops, looks at* Michael *in astonishment*) You have an A-minus? (*visibly swelling with pride*) Well, I'll be. My boy, with an A-minus.

Michael (*looking up, wiping away a tear*). Dad?

Father. Imagine that. (*pauses*) I never knew you wanted to go to college. (Michael *nods.*) You know it costs a lot of money.

Michael (*with shy hopefulness*). Tuition at State isn't so bad. And they have scholarships . . .

Father (*thinking*). Can you work for me full time this summer? And over breaks? (Michael *nods, and his* Father *grins.*) Think you could stand it?

Michael (*grinning too*). I think I could manage.

Father. Well, let's see what we can do.

Michael (*smiling more broadly and standing up*). Do you mean that? We could really look into it?

Father. Sure we can. You know I want the best for you, Michael.

(*The two move together in an awkward embrace, and* Michael *is heard whispering a faint "Thank you."*)

❻ Uses stage directions and dialogue to present the resolution of the conflict

LANGUAGE SKILLS

6. Point out that while this scene ends with a neat resolution of the conflict—the characters make up from an argument—not all dramatic conclusions are so tidy. For example, a drama can end with a revelation, a death, a victory, or a departure. Ask students to recall the conclusions of films or plays they have seen.
Possible Response: Answers will vary. You may want to ask students to categorize their responses under the headings of "Revelations," "Deaths," "Victories," "Departures," or any other headings they find relevant.

Guiding Student Writing

Prewriting

Choosing a Topic

If, after reading the **Idea Bank,** students are having difficulty choosing a topic, suggest they try the following:

- Have students create three headings on a sheet of paper—*Character, Conflict, and Resolution*. Under each heading, have students list real and imagined examples of each, based on situations they know.
- Have students skim newspapers looking for interesting stories that might lead to the creation of a character and a scene.
- Have students begin by thinking of themes that express opposing ideas or conflicting emotions. Themes could include Nature vs. Technology, Hope vs. Despair, Remembering vs. Forgetting, and Tradition vs. Innovation. Then ask them to think of situations that might illustrate these themes.

Planning the Script

1. Point out to students that a setting can be suggestive of particular kinds of action; for example, a train station is the setting for events quite different than those that take place in a kitchen, a hospital, or a courtroom.
3. Encourage students to think of scenes from movies, television shows, and plays they have seen that depicted the same mood they would like to create. Ask them to list elements of those scenes that contributed to the mood.

Drafting

If students are having trouble getting started, suggest that they place their characters in a situation and imagine them talking to one another. The scene can grow out of what the characters say.

IDEABank

1. Your Working Portfolio
Build on the **Writing Option** you completed earlier in this unit:

- **Dramatic Scene,** p. 255

2. Fairy Tale Theater
Adapt a myth or fairy tale for the stage. You might want to consult a book of world folklore or mythology for ideas.

3. Conflict Chart
List conflicts that you have experienced, heard of, or read about. Build your scene around one of these conflicts.

Writing and Staging Your Scene

1 Prewriting

Begin by thinking about a character or situation that interests you and that experiences or involves a conflict. You can also adapt material from books, movies, ballads, or folklore. See the **Idea Bank** in the margin for more suggestions. After you select an idea for your scene, follow the steps below.

Planning Your Script

1. **Consider the basic elements of your scene.** Fill out a chart like the one below to help you identify the elements you need to include.

Characters	Setting	Plot	Stage Directions
Who are the characters? How do they interact?	When and where does the scene take place?	What events will happen? In what sequence will they occur?	How will the characters speak? What is the pace of the scene?

2. **Think about your audience.** Who will watch your scene? What language is appropriate for them? What background information will they need in order to understand the setting, characters, and action?
3. **Decide on a mood.** What general feeling do you want to convey? How can you use dialogue, setting, and action to create that mood?

2 Drafting

As you write your script, keep the following points in mind:

- Establish the **setting** and introduce the **characters** of your scene.
- Use **dialogue** to advance the plot and reveal details about the characters—personalities, interests, backgrounds, attitudes, and beliefs.
- Use **stage directions** to describe setting, costumes, lighting, sound effects, and props. Also use them to indicate gestures, tone of voice, and motion.

❸ Revising

TARGET SKILL ▶ USING DIALOGUE EFFECTIVELY Your characters' words should sound natural when spoken, so read your dialogue aloud. Use contractions and sentence fragments to mimic actual speech. Indicate tone of voice or emotion with precise stage directions. For example, you might instruct your actors through such directions as "whispers," "shouts," and "shivers."

Need help with dialogue?

See the **Writing Handbook**, p. R29.

> **Father.** *(thinking)* Can you work for me full-time this summer? ~~Can you work for me~~ *And* over breaks? ~~Do you~~ think you could stand it? *(Michael nods, and his Father grins.)*

❹ Planning Your Performance

With a group of classmates, choose a script from among the ones group members have written. After selecting a script, follow the steps below.

Steps for Planning Your Scene

1. **Assign acting roles.** You can hold auditions, draw straws, or assign roles by consensus.
2. **List and assign responsibilities.** Consider the following jobs. Which are necessary? Who will perform them?
   - director
   - prop manager
   - costumer
   - lighting manager
   - set designer
   - sound engineer
3. **Decide on an interpretation.** Discuss the scene and make collective decisions about the characters' motivations, actions, and emotions. What do you want the audience to think and feel after watching your scene?
4. **Create a "director's script."** Mark a copy of the script with notes on the staging, sets, action, and delivery. This script will serve as a record of the group's interpretive decisions. In creating the director's script, consider movement, gesture, tone of voice, pacing, and technical effects.
5. **Gather the props, costumes, and lighting materials you will need.** What materials will help to show the time and place of the scene and to establish the characters' personalities?

LANGUAGE SKILLS

Revising

USING DIALOGUE EFFECTIVELY

In the revised sample, point out that the writer makes changes in dialogue that reflect natural speaking habits.

Have students work in pairs to read their scripts aloud, revising for the rhythm and feel of spoken language. Have one student read a line of dialogue; then have the second student improvise an answer, without reading from the script. Compare the second student's response with the scripted response, making adjustments if necessary.

Planning the Performance

2. **Have students assess the facilities and equipment at their disposal and decide how elaborate a production to put on. Will they be performing in a theater or a classroom? Will they build a set, or simply arrange available furniture to suit their needs? What kind of costumes will they wear?**
3. **Some elements of a script are more open to interpretation than others. Have students identify the elements of character, setting, plot, or conflict that are particularly ambiguous. For example, if the setting is only slightly developed in the script, encourage students to brainstorm about any reasonable and interesting possibilities for their own interpretation of the setting.**

MINI LESSON **Grammar**

SENTENCE FRAGMENTS

Instruction While sentence fragments are technically incorrect in regular prose, many good writers use them to achieve a particular effect, especially in dialogue. Far from being incorrect, fragments in dialogue often reflect natural speech patterns.

Practice Write the following dialogue on the chalkboard. Ask students to point out sentences that would be better revised as fragments and to suggest revisions.

Meg: Did Mom tell you about Kirby?
Kyle: Did she tell me what about Kirby?
Meg: Well, it looks like he's going to stay with us while Aunt Cathy goes to see Grandma.
Kyle: How long is he going to stay?
Meg: I think he might stay for a whole month.

Possible Answers: In line 1: *Mom tell you about Kirby?*; in line 2: *What about Kirby?*; in line 5: *For how long?*; in line 6: *Maybe a whole month.*

For more instruction and practice in understanding and using sentence fragments, use McDougal Littell's ***Language Network:***
- Grade 10, Chapter 5, "Writing Complete Sentences"
- Grade 12, Chapter 16, "Style: Sound and Sense"

Practicing and Presenting

The first step in rehearsing a scene is blocking, or planning out the physical movements of characters. Students may want to break the scene into sections for this purpose. Once the entire scene has been blocked, they should practice it numerous times, allowing interruptions for direction or commentary. Finally, they should run through it several times without interruption, saving comments for afterward.

Once students have set the stage and are ready to incorporate costumes, props, lighting, and sound, suggest that students videotape a rehearsal so that the cast and crew can watch for areas to be improved before the performance.

Refining Your Performance

EVALUATING YOUR INTERPRETIVE CHOICES

Have students create a checklist. Include the standards listed here and on page 332, a way to indicate whether each standard has been met, and a space for comments.

Reflecting

Suggest that students also comment about what they learned about the dramatic arts in general. Was it more difficult to write and stage a scene than they thought it would be? What frustrations and rewards did they experience?

PRACTICING TIP

Make audio- or videotapes of the rehearsals so that you can listen for dialogue that needs to be louder or clearer, or watch for awkward stage movements.

Publishing IDEAS

- Choose several scenes from your class to perform for other classes.
- Videotape your scene to show to family and friends. Make a copy for your school library.

5 Practicing and Presenting

The entire cast should practice the scene several times before presenting it.

- **Read through the parts.** The actors should learn their lines. Then they should mark their scripts with the appropriate emotions and actions.
- **Walk through the action.** Actors should physically act out their parts, rehearsing their entrances, exits, and other motions. Do the actions make sense?
- **Do a complete run-through.** Finally, set up the stage and rehearse the scene with the costumes, props, and lighting that you have decided upon.

Ask Your Peer Reader

- What did you like best about the performance?
- Was there anything that didn't make sense to you? Explain.
- Which actions and emotions seemed most real to you? Which seemed awkward or unrealistic?
- Did you want to see more or less of anything? Explain.

After several rehearsals with just the cast, ask one or two other people to watch a rehearsal and offer feedback.

6 Refining Your Performance

TARGET SKILL ▶ EVALUATING YOUR INTERPRETIVE CHOICES Use these standards to evaluate the decisions you made in interpreting your scene.

- **Naturalness and clarity** Do the actors speak and interact in a realistic way? Do they move naturally? Does the scene make sense to the audience?
- **Communication of mood and character** Do the actors' voices, movements, and timing work together to show the emotions and values of the characters?
- **Consistency** Does each actor's performance fit the overall interpretation of the scene? Do the technical aspects all work together to support this interpretation?

7 Reflecting

FOR YOUR WORKING PORTFOLIO What did you you learn about writing and staging a scene? Attach your reflections to your marked-up script. Save your script in your Working Portfolio.

Standardized Test Practice Revising & Editing

Read this paragraph from the first draft of a drama review. The underlined sections may include the following kinds of errors:

- **incorrect possessives**
- **inconsistent verb tenses**
- **missing or misplaced commas**
- **misspelled homophones**

For each underlined section, choose the revision that most improves the writing.

> The Surprising Puppet Theaters (1) 11th annual Spring Pageant opened this passed weekend (2). True to form, the company put on a show worthy of everyones' time (3) and attention. The company choses (4) a theme for the pageant every year, and this year's theme is farming. It may not sound exciting, but the company's use of puppets, which range from ten inches to ten feet in height (5) brings new drama to the popular notions about farm life. In one scene, a potato does battle with a giant slug. In another scene, the farmer plays a haunting tune on his fiddle, encouraging his little sweet peas to grow. The farmer and his vegetables struggled (6) with drought, flood, pests, and storms, ending the show with a glorious, victorious harvest. Excellent performances and beautifully crafted puppets make this show a must-see!

1. **A.** The Surprising Puppet Theater's
   B. The Surprising Puppet Theaters'
   C. The Surprising Puppet's Theater
   D. Correct as is
2. **A.** this passt weekend
   B. this past weekend
   C. this paste weekend
   D. Correct as is
3. **A.** everyones time
   B. everybodys time
   C. everyone's time
   D. Correct as is
4. **A.** company chose
   B. company choosed
   C. company chooses
   D. Correct as is
5. **A.** puppets which range from ten inches to ten feet in height
   B. puppets, which range from ten inches to ten feet in height,
   C. puppets that range from ten inches to ten feet in height
   D. Correct as is
6. **A.** The farmer and his vegetables have struggled
   B. The farmer and his vegetables struggle
   C. The farmer and his vegetables struggles
   D. Correct as is

Need extra help?
See the **Grammar Handbook**
Quick Reference: Punctuation, p. R77
Verb Tense, p. R60

TEST PRACTICE

Standardized Test Practice

Have students read the entire passage before they correct the errors.

Answers:
1. A; **2.** B; **3.** C; **4.** C; **5.** B; **6.** B

MINI LESSON Grammar

COMMAS WITH NONESSENTIAL PHRASES AND CLAUSES

Instruction Point out to students that the error in #5 above has to do with nonessential and essential clauses and phrases. Essential clauses and phrases contain information that is necessary for the understanding of the word they modify: *The neighbors next door are angry.* Nonessential clauses and phrases contain information that is nice to have, but not necessary: *The neighbors, next door, are angry* (as opposed to the neighbors across the street). Nonessential clauses and phrases are set off by commas; essential clauses and phrases are not.

Practice Write the following sentences on the chalkboard. Ask students to identify the essential and nonessential phrases.

1. The blue jacket, hanging from the hook, is hers.
2. The blue jacket hanging from the hook is hers.

Answers: #1: nonessential; #2: essential

For more instruction and practice with using commas, use McDougal Littell's ***Language Network:***

- Grade 10, Chapter 11, "Punctuation"
- Grade 12, Chapter 9, "End Marks and Commas"

Objectives

- research word origins
- understand how to use knowledge of Greek and Latin roots to determine meanings
- use etymology as an aid to building word families
- use etymology as an aid to expanding vocabulary

EXERCISE

The form of roots may vary slightly; students may have a hard time separating the roots from affixes. Related words may also vary; sample responses follow.

Root	Meaning	English Words
1. *cen* (Latin)	to set on fire	incendiary, incense
2. *sacr* (Latin) OR *sanct* (Latin)	religious rite or ceremony holy	sacred, sacrilegious, sacristy sanctify; sanctum, sanctimonious
3. *coloss* (Latin or Greek)	huge	colossus
4. *cep* or *cap* (Latin)	to seize or capture	captive, perception, receptive
5. *mand* (Latin)	to entrust	mandate; command; mandatory; demand

Use **Unit Two Resource Book,** p. 53, for more practice.

Building Vocabulary

Analyzing Word Parts—Greek and Latin Roots

The History of English Many English words come from Anglo-Saxon, which is a Germanic language related to German, Dutch, and Swedish. However, a good number of English words have their roots in Latin, Greek, and French (which is descended from Latin). These words tend to be more difficult and specialized, as many of them were brought into English by scholars and priests to describe academic, religious, and political ideas. These words have changed over the years, but they still have recognizable word parts.

A **root** is the core part of a word, to which other roots or **affixes** (prefixes and suffixes) can be added to create new words. Consider the word *prophecies* in the example below. The Greek root *phetes* means "speaker," the prefix *pro-* means "before," and *-ies* is a common suffix for plural nouns. *Prophet* refers to one who predicts an event, or speaks of it before it happens, while *prophecies* refers to the predictions themselves.

> "Seer of misery! Never a word that works to my advantage!
>
> Always misery warms your heart, your prophecies—never a word of profit said or brought to pass."
>
> —Homer, the *Iliad*

Strategies for Building Vocabulary

Knowing how to break words into parts and to recognize common Greek and Latin roots can help you understand unfamiliar words.

❶ **Break a Word into Parts** When you first encounter an unfamiliar word, try to determine its root. For example, look at the word *appendage*. You might recognize the first and last syllables, *ap-* and *-age*, as a prefix and a suffix. That leaves the middle syllable, *pend*, as the most likely root.

❷ **Make an Educated Guess** Think about other words you know that have the same root. *Pendant* refers to something that hangs from a necklace, and *suspend* can mean "to hang." Perhaps *appendage* refers to something that hangs from something else.

❸ **Check Against the Dictionary** Look up the word in a dictionary and compare its definition with your guess. One definition of *appendage* is "a limb or organ joined to the trunk of a body"; an arm is an example of an appendage. To be joined to a body is almost the same as to be hanging from it. The earlier guess was close, if not exactly right.

❹ **Read the Etymology** At the end of many dictionary entries, you will find the word's etymology, or word history. This will give you insight about the word's root (or roots) and affixes. If the entry for *appendage* does not have an etymology, look at nearby entries for related words, such as *append*. You will likely find an etymology that applies. As expected, the etymology for *append* traces it to the Latin word *pendere*, which means "to hang." The following tables contain more Greek and Latin roots.

Greek Root	Meaning	English Words
cycl	circle	bicycle, recycle
graph	write	autograph, photograph, graphic
soph	wise	philosopher, sophisticated

Latin Root	Meaning	English Words
corp	body	corporation, corpse, corpulent
junct	join	juncture, junction, adjunct
pend	hang	pendulum, suspend, appendix

EXERCISE Use a dictionary to identify the meaning and root of each of these words from the *Iliad*. Use the information you find to create a chart like the ones above for the words' Greek and Latin roots. Be sure to indicate whether the roots are Greek or Latin.

1. incensed
2. sacrosanct
3. colossal
4. intercept
5. commandeer

Sentence Crafting Using Participles

Grammar from Literature A **participle** is a verb form used as an adjective. For example, in the passages below from Homer's *Iliad,* the word *terrifying* modifies *clash,* and *disgraced, brimming,* and *piling* modify *I.*

> **Over against the ships he dropped to a knee, let fly a shaft and a terrifying clash rang out from the great silver bow.**
>
> **"I have no mind to linger here disgraced, brimming your cup and piling your plunder."**

A **participial phrase** consists of a participle and any other words that modify or complete it. In the passages below from the *Iliad,* notice the participial phrases in blue. Then see the modified words in red.

> **The old man was terrified. He obeyed the order, turning, trailing away in silence down the shore**
>
> **. . . No way to escape it now. This, this was their pleasure after all, sealed long ago—**

Participial phrases allow you to describe two different actions in one sentence while bringing one of them into focus. Look at the following sentence and revision.

> DRAFT
> **The soldier cried out for revenge. He ran at his enemy.**
> REVISION
> **Crying out for revenge, the soldier ran at his enemy.**

Usage Tip As with other adjectives, it is important to place a participial phrase near the word it modifies. Many writers make the mistake of placing a participial phrase so far from the word it modifies that the meaning of the sentence is unclear or incorrect. This mistake is known as a **misplaced participle.** In the example below, it is the seer, not the war, who is looking into the future.

> MISPLACED PARTICIPLE
> **The seer predicted war looking into the future.**
> REVISED
> **Looking into the future, the seer predicted war.**

A **dangling participle** is one that does not clearly modify any noun or pronoun in a sentence. To fix a dangling participle, you can add a noun or pronoun to be modified by the phrase, or you can revise the sentence completely.

> DANGLING PARTICIPLE
> **Running from Achilles, it was a desperate race.**
> REVISED
> **Hector ran from Achilles in a desperate race.**

WRITING EXERCISE Rewrite each sentence, changing the underlined words to a participle or participial phrase.

1. Andromache begged him to stay close to home. <u>She feared that Hector would die in battle.</u>
2. <u>Hector imagined what would happen to her if he died.</u> He felt torn about what to do.
3. <u>He smiled at his baby son</u> and reached down to touch him.
4. <u>Hector's armor frightened his son.</u> The boy shrank from Hector's touch.
5. Hector prayed to Zeus. <u>He asked that his son grow up to be a great warrior.</u>

GRAMMAR EXERCISE The following paragraph contains one dangling and one misplaced participial phrase. Find and rewrite the incorrect sentences.

After winning a war, the Greek king Agamemnon kidnapped the daughter of Chryse, Apollo's priest. Chryse came to Agamemnon, begging for the return of his daughter, but the proud king refused. This made Apollo very angry. Sending a plague down on the Greek armies, both animals and men fell to the sickness. Burning day and night, Apollo watched the corpse-fires below. Achilles was the head of the Greek warriors. Wondering how they might appease Apollo, he called in Calchas, a prophet, to explain the god's anger.

LANGUAGE SKILLS

Sentence Crafting

Objectives

- understand participles and participial phrases
- understand the relationship between participles and the words they modify
- create participial phrases to combine sentences
- correct misplaced and dangling participles

WRITING EXERCISE

The wording of student responses may vary slightly; sample responses follow.

1. Andromache begged Hector to stay close to home, fearing that he would die in battle.
2. Imagining what would happen to her if he died, Hector felt torn about what to do.
3. Smiling at his baby son, he reached down to touch him.
4. Frightened by Hector's armor, the boy shrank from his touch.
5. Hector prayed to Zeus, asking that his son grow up to be a great warrior.

GRAMMAR EXERCISE

Dangling participial phrase: Sending a plague down on the Greek armies, <u>both animals and men fell to the sickness.</u>

Revised: Apollo sent a plague down on the Greek armies; both animals and men fell to the sickness.

Misplaced participial phrase: <u>Burning day and night</u>, Apollo watched the corpse-fires below.

Revised: Apollo watched the corpse-fires below burning day and night.

Use **Unit Two Resource Book,** p. 54, for more practice.

Objectives

- reflect on and assess understanding of the part
- compare and contrast different views of honor that are represented in the literature
- apply the term *tragic hero* to two characters or people
- show an understanding of literary and historical terms
- assess and build portfolios

Reflecting on the Literature

Suggest to students that they choose characters or people who embody different views of honor. Student responses should include quotes and examples that clearly illustrate each character's view of honor.

Reviewing Literary Concepts

A successful response will

- illustrate how the term *tragic hero* can be applied to each character or person
- show a mature understanding of the term and the chosen subjects
- include quotations and examples

Building Your Portfolio

Before students finalize their choice of writing to include in the Presentation Portfolio, you might want to have very brief conferences with them (one minute or so) to discuss their choices.

For more information on using writing and assessing portfolios, see the **Teacher's Guide to Assessment and Portfolio Use,** pp. 53–74.

Part Assessment

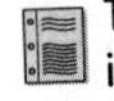
To assess skills and concepts taught in this unit part, use **Formal Assessment Book,** pp. 43–44.

Literature of Ancient Greece

Detail of fresco of Athena restraining Achilles from killing Agamemnon (1757), Giambattista Tiepolo. Villa Valmarana, Vicenza, Italy. Scala/Art Resource, New York.

Reflect and Assess

The selections in Unit Two, Part 1, introduced you to several masterpieces of ancient Greek literature. How has your understanding of ancient Greece been influenced by your readings? What are your strongest impressions of Greek thought and culture? Use the following options to review what you have learned.

Reflecting on the Literature

In Quest of Honor As you know, honor was very important to the ancient Greeks. Choose four characters or people from the selections, and discuss what honor means to each of them. Consider how each of your subjects can achieve honor and how honor can be lost. Do you think that the views of honor expressed in ancient Greece still have relevance today?

Reviewing Literary Concepts

Tragic Hero Review the meaning of **tragic hero,** as explained on pages 261 and 330. Then consider whether other historical figures or characters featured in the selections, besides Oedipus, might be considered as tragic heroes. Choose two characters or historical figures and discuss how the term **tragic hero** can be applied to each of them.

Building Your Portfolio

Communication Workshop and Writing Options Review the dramatic scene that you wrote for the Communication Workshop on page 000 and the various Writing Options you completed in this part of the book. In your judgment, which piece of writing is the most successful? Write a cover note explaining what you like about the work you chose, and add the assignment to your **Presentation Portfolio.**

Self ASSESSMENT

READER'S NOTEBOOK

The following list provides important names and terms from this part of Unit Two. Work with a partner to create a true-false or multiple-choice test that can be used to measure other students' understanding of these terms. For additional help, make use of the index or the **Glossary of Literary Terms** (beginning on page R91).

Homeric epic	Socrates
epic simile	Plato
Greek drama	Oedipus
Pericles	tragedy
Peloponnesian War	lyric

Setting GOALS

The literature of the ancient world is often quite challenging to read, as you have probably experienced for yourself. Make a list of your strengths and weaknesses as a reader of such literature. Then circle those weaknesses that you would like to work on in the months ahead.

Assessment Self Assessment

Students can look up the listed terms in the **Glossary of Literary Terms** or they can find them introduced in context on the text pages shown below.

Homeric epic (pp. 176–177)
epic simile (p. 176)
Greek drama (pp. 256–257)
Pericles (page 233)
Peloponnesian War (pp. 164 and 232)
Socrates (pp. 246–247)
Plato (p. 246)
Oedipus (p. 259)
tragedy (pp. 256–257 and 259)
lyric (pp. 170 and 227)

Extend Your *Reading*

The Greeks: Crucible of Civilization

PAUL CARTLEDGE

This book provides an introduction to the extraordinary achievements of ancient Greece by focusing on the lives of 15 men and women. The author, a professor of Greek history at Cambridge University, makes the past come alive through profiles of people such as the statesman Pericles, the poet Sappho, and the general Alexander.

The Ancient City: Life in Classical Athens and Rome

PETER CONNOLLY AND HAZEL DODGE

This unique and compelling work gives the reader a tour of daily life in ancient Athens and Rome. Through a combination of detailed drawings, fine art, and brief explanations, the reader is given a close-up picture of the economy, popular culture, government, architecture, fashion, religious ceremonies, and public festivals.

And Even *More* . . .

Books

Four Plays by Aristophanes WILLIAM ARROWSMITH, ED.
The Athenian playwright blended satire with broad comedy. His four most celebrated masterpieces are included: *The Clouds, The Birds, Lysistrata,* and *The Frogs.*

Mythology: Timeless Tales of Gods and Heroes EDITH HAMILTON
Hamilton has collected the most popular myths of ancient Greece. Her readable and authoritative retellings of the myths have been enjoyed by readers for decades.

The Wars of the Ancient Greeks VICTOR DAVIS HANSON
This richly illustrated book shows how the Greeks fought their wars, from the man-to-man combat described by Homer to the complex military campaigns of Alexander the Great.

Other Media

Great Cities of the Ancient World: Athens and Ancient Greece
Through special effects and full-motion video, the ruins of ancient Greece are restored to their original beauty. Reconstructions are shown of 25 structures in Athens and five other cities, including the Acropolis, the theater of Dionysus, and the Temple of Apollo at Delphi. 78 minutes. Zenger Media. (VIDEOCASSETTE)

The Road to Ancient Greece
This interactive program provides an introduction to the history and culture of ancient Greece. Zenger Media. (CD-ROM)

Inside the Walls of Troy: A Novel of the Women Who Lived the Trojan War

CLEMENCE MCLAREN

Two woman provide their own perspectives on the events of the Trojan War. The first narrator is the beautiful Helen; the second is Cassandra, a daughter of King Priam. Cassandra has a gift of prophecy, but it is her fate that no one believes her visions of the future.

More Recommendations for Your Students

Difficulty Level: Easy

Pearson, Anne. *Ancient Greece* (New York: Dorling Kindersley, 1992). A beautifully illustrated introduction to everyday life. Color photographs of armor, jewelry, temples, and more give an "eyewitness" view of Greek culture.

Sutcliff, Rosemary. *Black Ships Before Troy* (New York: Delacorte, 1993). In this illustrated retelling of Homer's *Iliad,* the author focuses on the major characters, events, and conflicts, from the war's beginning to its gripping conclusion.

Difficulty Level: Average

Kebric, Robert B. *Greek People* (Mountain View: Mayfield, 2001). Read about a fascinating assortment of Greek people, from the famous to the unknown. The author weaves together commentary with primary sources to introduce characters such as Ephialtes, who betrayed the Greeks to the Persians; women athletes; and criminals from the annals of Athenian courts.

Kerrigan, Michael. *Ancient Greece and the Mediterranean* (New York: DK Publishing, 2001). This richly illustrated book brings to life the story of the rise and fall of Greek civilization, from Minoan civilization to the Persian War, from the golden age of Athens to the triumphs of Alexander.

Difficulty Level: Challenging

Aeschylus. *The Oresteia,* trans. Ted Hughes (New York: Farrar, 1999). An influential contemporary poet translates the bloody and gripping tale of a family cursed by the gods. This set of three plays is the only surviving trilogy of Greek drama.

Herodotus. *The Histories* (New York: Penguin, 1972). From the heroic struggles of the Greeks against the Persians to the crocodile hunters of Egypt, Herodotus shares all that he learned in his far-flung travels in the ancient world.

Plato, *Last Days of Socrates,* trans. Hugh Tredennick (New York: Penguin, rpt. 1995). This short anthology of Plato's most famous works about the life of Socrates includes the *Euthyphro, Apology, Crito,* and *Phaedo.*

Unit Two, Part 2, provides students with an overview of Roman civilization followed by a rich sample of the literature created by Roman authors such as Virgil, Horace, Ovid, and Tacitus. In addition, the feature **Comparing Literature Across Cultures** includes poems by Sara Teasdale and Edgar Allan Poe that offer intriguing perspectives on the classical world.

World Art and Cultures Transparencies

AT12 The Forum
AT13 Roman painting
AT14 Trajan's Column [detail]

You may use the listed transparencies to acquaint students with art from ancient Rome.

READING FOR INFORMATION

Reading Skills and Strategies

PREVIEWING

Give students a few moments to look over this introduction. It provides background information about Roman civilization that creates a context for the literature in this part.

Reading Skills and Strategies

USING A KEY

Make sure students are aware of the types of information provided on pages 344 and 345: the map with its legend and distance scale, the images, and the captions. Point out that the purple area on the map shows the extent of the Roman Empire in A.D. 120. On the distance scale, 1 and 5/16 inches represents about 1,000 miles. The captions preceded by numbers in red circles tie the information to specific locations on the map.

PART 2 The Tradition Continues

Literature of Ancient Rome

Why It Matters

The Roman Empire was one of the largest and greatest empires of Western civilization. The Romans united the diverse peoples of the Mediterranean world under one political system. Moreover, the Romans maintained the longest period of peace that Western civilization has ever known. Their language, Latin, developed into such modern languages as Italian, French, and Spanish. The literary heritage of Rome reflects the values cherished by this civilization.

1 Creators of an Empire Rome evolved from a small community of shepherds and farmers nestled in the hills along the **Tiber River,** in what is now central Italy. Over the centuries, the Romans built a vast empire. At its height, it extended into three continents—Europe, Asia, and Africa.

For Links to Ancient Rome, click on: HUMANITIES CLASSZONE.COM

4 Pompeii Archaeologists have uncovered some of the splendors of ancient Roman life in the ruins of Pompeii, once a prosperous town in southern Italy. In A.D. 79, the volcano **Mount Vesuvius** erupted. It spewed gases that killed the people of Pompeii and volcanic ash that buried them, preserving forever the shape of their bodies as they died.

MINI LESSON Using the Map

Have students study the map on pages 344–345 and then answer questions such as the following:

- Which direction did Ovid go in traveling from Rome to the shores of the Black Sea? *(east)*
- Which city is closer to Rome—Athens or Constantinople? *(Athens)*
- Which sea did Virgil cross in traveling from Rome to Athens? *(Adriatic Sea)*
- Which city is closer to the Tigris River—Rome or Antioch? *(Antioch)*

READING FOR INFORMATION

Reading Skills and Strategies

CLARIFYING

Help students observe that the history of ancient Rome is divided into four periods, represented by different colors on the key at the bottom. This history, which spans more than 1,000 years, extends from 753 B.C., the traditional date for the founding of Rome, to A.D. 476, the traditional date for the fall of the Western Roman Empire. Tell students to use the headings as a guide to the content and to note the boldfaced terms. Point out the feature **History to Literature** and explain that it lists historical events on the left and corresponding literary events on the right. Finally, have students use the key at the bottom to identify which period of Roman history lasted the longest. *(the Roman Republic)*

Historical Note

(A) **Julius Caesar** In 44 B.C. on March 15 (known to Romans as the Ides of March), Caesar prepared to visit the Senate, unaware that a conspiracy of senators had targeted him for death. According to legend, Calpurnia, Caesar's wife, implored him to stay at home. She described to him her nightmare in which he lay bleeding to death from stab wounds. Disregarding his wife's pleas, Caesar proceeded to the Senate. Soon the conspirators encircled him and began stabbing him—again and again. They were led by Gaius Cassius and Marcus Brutus, who was Caesar's beloved friend and, according to some accounts, his illegitimate son. Caesar spoke his last words to Brutus: "Et tu, Brute?" ("And you, too, Brutus?")

Historical Highlights

Rome's long history was a spectacle of grand passion, heroic sacrifice, and some really bad behavior. It provided plenty of subject matter for Roman writers. Even in our own time, writers, playwrights, and filmmakers dip into Rome's history for stirring events and characters.

Legendary Beginnings

753 B.C.

The Romans gave themselves mythic origins. According to Virgil's *Aeneid*, their ancestor was the Trojan hero **Aeneas,** who fled from Troy and sailed to Italy. According to legend, Aeneas' descendants were the twins **Romulus** and **Remus,** who were nursed by a wolf. In 753 B.C., Romulus founded a settlement, naming it Rome after himself.

From about 616 to 509 B.C., the early Romans were ruled by the **Etruscans,** who had a more advanced civilization. Rome gradually evolved from a village into a city.

The Roman Republic

509–27 B.C.

The Romans ultimately revolted against the Etruscan kings and established a **republic.** It changed over the years as members of the upper class struggled with other citizens for power. Meanwhile, the Romans greatly expanded their territory. In the **Punic Wars,** the Romans defeated the Carthaginians of North Africa for control of the Mediterranean. By the 60s B.C., Rome ruled Greece, Macedonia, Asia Minor, Syria, and Judea. These conquests led to civil wars in Rome for the next 20 years. In 46 B.C., **Julius Caesar** seized control of the government; he ruled for about two years before he was assassinated. (A)

Romulus marks the site for the foundation of Rome.

Growth of the Roman Empire

27 B.C.–A.D. 200

Augustus Caesar

The first emperor of Rome renamed himself **Augustus,** which means "exalted one." Born Gaius Octavius, he was Julius Caesar's grandnephew and handpicked heir. He became emperor after defeating the forces of **Mark Antony** and **Cleopatra** in the Battle of Actium. Augustus brought peace to war-weary Romans, restoring law and order. He solidified the empire by strengthening the local administration of its provinces. His reign marked the beginning of a 200-year period of stability called the Pax Romana, Roman Peace. The peace and prosperity ushered in a golden age of art, architecture, and literature. No other period in Roman history ever matched the **Augustan Age** for artistic achievement. At the end of his long reign, Augustus

LEGENDARY BEGINNINGS

753 B.C.

THE ROMAN REPUBLIC

509 B.C.

boasted that he had found Rome a city of brick and left it a city of marble.

After Augustus' reign the empire grew only a little. In A.D. 43, the emperor **Claudius** invaded Britain, and later the emperor **Trajan** annexed parts of what is now Hungary and Romania.

However, the Augustan Age wasn't a golden age for everyone. Although the Pax Romana allowed **Christianity** to spread, Christians began to be persecuted in A.D. 64, when the emperor **Nero** blamed them for a fire that gutted Rome. Two **Jewish** rebellions against Roman rule met with swift and brutal retaliation. Those Jews who survived were exiled from their homeland for the next 1,800 years.

Decline and Fall of the Roman Empire

A.D. 200–476

One of the wisest of the Roman emperors was **Marcus Aurelius.** After he died in A.D. 180, Rome had a series of cruel and incompetent rulers. The empire also began to fray at the edges. Germanic tribes invaded from the north, disrupting trade and taxing the resources of the Roman army. Gradually, the structures of Roman society were overwhelmed. Economic problems weakened the empire as well. B

From a combination of external and internal forces, the Roman Empire in the west gradually declined and eventually fell. Even Christianity, which became the official religion of the empire in A.D. 391, couldn't save it. In the end, hordes of invaders overran the empire. Like the legendary city of Troy, Rome was plundered of its riches at last.

History to Literature

EVENT IN HISTORY	EVENT IN LITERATURE
Rome is founded in 753 B.C.	Virgil's epic *Aeneid* celebrates Aeneas as the ancestor of the Roman people.
Julius Caesar conquers Gaul from 58 to 50 B.C.	Caesar describes his adventures in *Commentaries on the Gallic War.*
Julius Caesar is assassinated in 44 B.C.	William Shakespeare's play *Julius Caesar,* written about 1600, dramatizes Caesar's death and the fate of the conspirators.
During Nero's reign, a devastating fire engulfs Rome.	In the *Annals,* the Roman historian Tacitus writes a revealing account of the fire and Nero's response to it.

GROWTH OF THE ROMAN EMPIRE — DECLINE AND FALL OF THE ROMAN EMPIRE

27 B.C. — A.D. 200 — A.D. 476

Historical Note

B **Barbarian Hordes** Two barbarians who struck terror in the hearts of Romans were Alaric and Attila. Alaric led the Visigoths, who stormed Rome in A.D. 410, plundering the city and setting it ablaze. Attila, the leader of the Huns, was known as the Scourge of God. After terrorizing the Eastern Roman Empire, Attila swept into the West. In A.D. 452, he and the Huns advanced against the gates of Rome. Pope Leo I, however, negotiated the withdrawal of the Huns and saved the city.

MINI LESSON Interpreting the Text

Have students read pages 346 and 347 and then answer questions such as the following:

- What did naming Aeneas the ancestor to Romulus and Remus accomplish? *(It gave the Romans the sense of extending back to mythic times.)*
- Whom did the Romans defeat in the Punic Wars? *(the Carthaginians)*
- What did Augustus accomplish as the first emperor of Rome? *(He restored law and order in Rome after years of civil war and then strengthened the empire.)*
- Which emperor was least sympathetic to the Christians? *(Nero)*
- Which emperor was known for his wisdom—Claudius, Trajan, Nero, or Marcus Aurelius? *(Marcus Aurelius)*

READING FOR INFORMATION
Reading Skills and Strategies
CLASSIFYING
Have students observe that the topic **People and Society** is divided into five categories, each one devoted to a social class: Patricians, Plebeians, the Urban Poor, the Army, and Slaves. The role of women is described in the feature **Women in Ancient Rome.** Tell students to pause after reading about each social class and to identify its distinctive features.

Historical Note
Ⓐ **Power Struggles** In the Roman Republic, two groups of citizens—the patricians and the plebeians—vied for power. The patricians were landowners who believed that their noble birth and inherited wealth entitled them to govern Rome. The plebeians had the right to vote as Roman citizens, but enjoyed little political influence. In 494 B.C., the senate allowed the plebeians to elect representatives called tribunes to protect their rights. These representatives were elected annually and had the power to veto the decrees of the senate. Over time, the plebeians attained political, but not social, equality with the patricians.

People and Society

Like the Greeks, the Romans were divided into classes. However, as the empire began to grow rapidly, money—more than class—became the great divider between people.

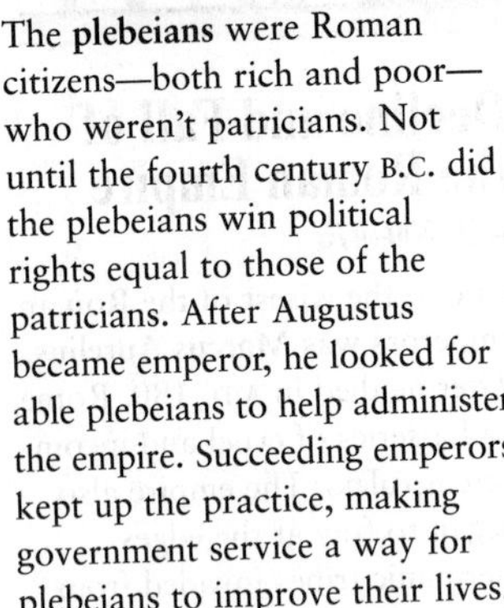

Patricians

Making up Rome's small but powerful upper class, the **patricians** were members of Rome's oldest and wealthiest families. Being a Roman patrician was more a matter of birth and bloodline than wealth.

Patricians exclusively ran the early republic, and their family organization became the model for Roman society. Basically, the father, or *paterfamilias,* was the head of the family. By law, he had absolute power over his property, his children, and his grandchildren until the day he died. He alone determined whether a newborn child was to be killed, sold into slavery, or welcomed into the family. He arranged his children's marriages, resolved family disputes, and could banish another family member at will.

Plebeians Ⓐ

The **plebeians** were Roman citizens—both rich and poor—who weren't patricians. Not until the fourth century B.C. did the plebeians win political rights equal to those of the patricians. After Augustus became emperor, he looked for able plebeians to help administer the empire. Succeeding emperors kept up the practice, making government service a way for plebeians to improve their lives.

In addition to government jobs, the empire generated a booming business in trade. Enterprising Romans made money as importers, exporters, shipbuilders, merchants, and in other business-related activities. As a result, Roman society had the largest, most comfortable **middle class** of all ancient societies.

The Urban Poor

For centuries, most Romans farmed small plots of land to make a living. When the empire expanded and farmers were required to serve in the army, they usually had to sell their farms to the big landowners. When the small farmers returned from military service, they found that slaves from the conquered territories now did most of the farm labor. The farmers had little choice but to follow the crowds flooding into Rome.

Of the 1 million people who lived in Rome in the Augustan Age, about three-fourths were unemployed and poor. The poor survived on free grain distributed by the government—one of the earliest known forms of welfare. They lived in some of the first **public housing** ever built: multistory, timber-frame tenement buildings. Overcrowded and hastily put up, these rickety structures were apt to collapse or catch fire, fatally trapping the inhabitants inside.

Roman bas-relief showing a middle-class family

348

Coin with the image of Julius Caesar

The Army

One way to escape grinding poverty was to join the army. From the time of Augustus, the Romans had a standing army of about 300,000 men. There were two classes of soldiers: **legionaries,** who were Roman citizens, and **auxiliaries,** noncitizens from the provinces.

A typical Roman soldier enlisted as a teenager and served for 25 years. His pay, although not high, was more than a laborer's, and he received excellent medical care. Discipline was harsh and training rigorous—the keys to the army's consistent success on the battlefield. During peacetime, Roman soldiers constructed the roads, bridges, and buildings of the empire. To relax, they could socialize in the towns that grew up around their camps. Upon being discharged, a legionary could expect a plot of land or a cash payment as a pension. An auxiliary was given Roman citizenship.

Slaves

Like the Greeks, the Romans captured people during wartime and used them as servants and laborers. But as slaves—some of them educated and highly skilled—poured into Rome from the conquered territories, they began to be used for more specialized jobs as tutors, bookkeepers, and clerks.

Conditions for slaves in the countryside were exceptionally harsh. In 73–71 B.C., an escaped gladiator named **Spartacus** led an uprising of more than 70,000 slaves. The Spartacus rebellion was brutally crushed. Rebels who were captured were crucified. The roads leading into Rome were lined with the crosses of executed slaves.

To their credit, though, the Romans were actually quite generous in freeing their slaves. The Roman dramatist Terence, for example, was a freed slave originally from Carthage.

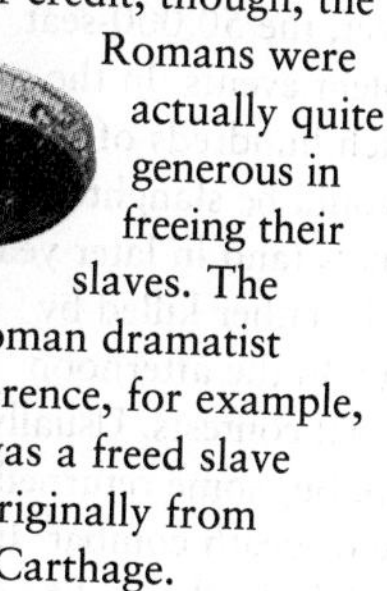

Women in Ancient Rome

Roman women enjoyed a much freer and more active life than did their counterparts in Greece. A Roman wife customarily ran the household, managing the money, organizing the work of the slaves, and taking care of the children. Although her marriage was arranged by her father, a woman could get divorced. Most Roman matrons took pride in their spinning and weaving. Girls received training in the textile arts from an early age. **B**

Although they weren't citizens, many Roman women owned property, controlled their own money, appeared openly in public, wore makeup, and got their hair done. They could attend some public performances, even though they often had to sit separately from the men. Women played female roles in the pantomime skits so popular among Roman audiences, but they were barred from acting in serious dramas. Still, Roman men were quite used to seeing educated women at dinner parties and priestesses in the temples. Under the emperor Domitian, women even appeared as gladiators in the Colosseum.

Historical Note

B **Roman Marriages** Both girls and boys in ancient Rome married at an early age—girls as young as 12 and boys slightly older. Marriages were arranged by the *paterfamilias*, the father of the family, to carry on the family name and protect its wealth. An important concern was the dowry, the money provided by the bride. The dowry remained her property throughout the marriage and was returned to her if her husband died or if the couple divorced. Since a woman married young, her odds of becoming a widow were high. She therefore needed her dowry in order to find a new husband. In ancient Rome, marriage was a legal, not a religious, bond. The union was not blessed by a religious ceremony. Engaged couples exchanged gifts, such as rings or pendants, as tokens of their devotion.

MINI LESSON Interpreting the Text

Have students read pages 348 and 349 and then answer questions such as the following:

- What powers did the *paterfamilias* have that heads of families don't have today? *(the power to determine what would happen to a newborn child in his family and to arrange his children's marriages)*
- Into which two classes did the citizens of Rome fall? *(patricians and plebeians)*
- What advantages were there to serving in the Roman army? *(decent pay, excellent medical care while in the service, and a pension or a plot of land upon retiring)*
- What is Spartacus known for? *(for leading a slave rebellion against Rome)*

READING FOR INFORMATION
Reading Skills and Strategies
MAIN IDEAS AND DETAILS

Tell students that some of the remarkable achievements of Roman civilization are described on pages 350 and 351. Have students use the heading of each section as a guide to its content. After reading each section, students might write brief summaries, listing the main idea and the key details.

Historical Note

A Colosseum Size mattered to the Romans. Large buildings and temples were regarded as better than smaller ones. The Colosseum, for example, was a magnificent feat of Roman engineering. The arena was vast, covering 3,500 square meters. Incredibly, it was built in only 10 years, begun by the Emperor Vespasian and completed by his sons, emperors Titus and Domitian. The word itself comes from the Latin word *colossus*, which means "gigantic."

Arts and Culture

Roman culture was a continuation of what the Greeks had started. To the Greek ideals of beauty, grace, and wisdom, the Romans added strength, integrity, and majesty. Greeks and Romans gave us the classical style, which we use today as a standard of comparison for all other Western art and literature.

Architecture and Engineering

It has been said that the true Roman artist was the engineer. The Romans basically adapted Greek architectural styles to suit their own purposes. What impressed the Romans was size rather than beauty. They invented **concrete** and perfected the **arch** as an architectural form so that they could build monumental structures worthy of a great empire—towering aqueducts and bridges, huge public baths, giant amphitheaters, and great domed rotundas. One of the Romans' greatest achievements was the network of **roads** that crisscrossed the empire—about 50,000 miles of paved highways and 200,000 miles of secondary roads. Some of them are still used today.

Public Entertainment

Roman emperors lavished free entertainments on their citizens, in part to pacify the poor. Chariot races were very popular. A huge U-shaped arena in Rome, the **Circus Maximus,** could accommodate 250,000 spectators. Just down the street, the 50,000-seat
A **Colosseum** showcased a variety of violent events. In the morning there might be organized hunts in which hundreds of tigers, leopards, bulls, lions, and elephants would be slaughtered. Next on the program, unarmed criminals (and in later years Christians) were led into the arena to be either killed by gladiators or eaten alive by wild beasts. In the afternoon
B came the star attraction—the gladiatorial contests. Usually, gladiators fought to win their freedom, but some returned to the arena for the sheer pleasure of life-or-death combat. In another spectacular event, the arena might be flooded to stage mock naval battles. One battle reportedly involved 24 ships and 19,000 men.

Law and Government

The Romans' most lasting contribution to the world was their system of law, which has influenced the legal systems of many nations—including the United States. These are the main principles of Roman law:

- All people have the right to equal treatment under the law.
- A person is considered innocent until proved guilty.
- The burden of proof rests with the accuser rather than the accused.

The governments of many nations, moreover, include a senate—in many ways similar to the legislative body of ancient Rome.

Colosseum

Art and Sculpture

Many Roman artists and sculptors imitated Greek models. But unlike the Greeks, who had idealized the human body, the Romans were sternly realistic. They excelled in painting. Large murals, called **frescoes,** decorated the walls of wealthy Romans' homes. Roman artists also contributed to two other art forms: the **bas-relief,** in which sculpted images stand out from a flat background, and the **mosaic,** in which small pieces of glass, stone, or tile are arranged to form designs or images on a flat surface.

Augustus Caesar

Religion

During the 300s B.C., the Romans adopted the major Greek gods, giving them Roman names. They singled out **Jupiter** (Zeus), **Juno** (Hera), and **Minerva** (Athena) as special favorites. Still, the earlier Roman household gods remained dear to Romans' hearts. Families regularly invoked **Vesta,** goddess of the hearth, to protect their homes. The temple of Vesta in Rome contained a sacred hearth, on which a fire was fed continually by "vestal virgins." Other popular deities included **Ceres,** goddess of the harvest, and **Janus,** the god who guarded doorways.

Literature

Roman writers borrowed freely from Greek literary models to create epic and lyric poems, comedies, and tragedies. But Roman literature, more than anything else, is about being Roman. From **Cicero's** philosophical essays to **Virgil's** poetry, **Horace's** odes, the histories of **Livy** and **Tacitus,** and the plays of **Plautus** and **Terence,** Roman literature illustrated the virtues of the Roman character—dignity, duty, integrity, and discipline—and inspired Romans to live up to their own ideals. Ovid narrated Roman as well as Greek myths in his *Metamorphoses* and accomplished for Roman literature what Augustus did for Rome: Ovid integrated the Greek and Roman cultures for the greater glory of Rome.

How Was Literature Presented?

When a Roman writer wanted an audience for his works, he had three options. He might hire a hall, invite some friends, and give a public recitation. This form of presentation was common because Romans had great respect for oratory and Roman literature was meant to be read aloud. Another way to publicize a literary work was to read it at a private party. Virgil, for example, recited his *Aeneid* at one of the emperor Augustus' dinner parties. Finally, a writer could buy writing materials and hire specially trained slave-copyists to produce a few books. The Roman version of a book was basically a rolled-up scroll of papyrus sheets.

Virgil reading from the *Aeneid*

Historical Note

B Gladiators A gladiatorial school was run by a *lanista*. He acquired gladiators in a number of ways: some were criminals sentenced by the state to serve three years in the arena; others were prisoners of war sold into slavery; still others were slaves whose masters wanted to dispose of them. Even free men, however, sometimes enlisted as gladiators to get out of debt or to vie for a chance at celebrity. Gladiators might win their freedom by earning enough prize money to purchase it or by winning the acclamation of the crowd. Some gladiators, however, chose to return to the arena after the emperor had awarded them the wooden sword—the token of their release from service. Women, too, sometimes fought in the arena.

INTRODUCTION 351

READING FOR INFORMATION
Reading Skills and Strategies
SEQUENCING
This time line shows major dates and events in Roman literature, Roman history, and world history from the founding of Rome to the end of the Pax Romana. The dates and events follow in sequence, moving down each column and from left to right. Help students understand that this period, which spans almost 1,000 years of human history, is characterized by the development of Rome from a village to an empire, the birth of important world religions, and the advent of new technologies. Also make sure students understand the abbreviations c., B.C., and A.D. Have students examine the key at the top, which visually represents the duration of the Roman Empire before and after A.D. 1.

Historical Note
A Hannibal To avenge Carthage's defeat at the hands of the Romans, Hannibal led a huge army of 50,000 infantry, 9,000 cavalry, and 60 elephants on a long trek from Spain across France and through the Alps. For more than a decade, Hannibal led his army up and down the Italian peninsula. He was finally defeated by the Romans at Zama near Carthage. Hannibal then took refuge among Rome's enemies. In 183 B.C., he committed suicide rather than submit to Rome.

Time Line

ANCIENT ROME (753 B.C.–A.D. 476)

2500 B.C. | A.D. 1 | PRESENT

c. approximately
B.C. before Christ's birth
A.D. after Christ's birth

EVENTS IN ROMAN LITERATURE

800 B.C. | 600 B.C. | 400 B.C.

240 B.C. Livius Andronicus' Latin version of a Greek play is performed before a Roman audience

c. 205 B.C. Comedy of Plautus first performed

EVENTS IN ROMAN HISTORY

800 B.C. | 600 B.C. | 400 B.C.

753 B.C. Legendary founding of Rome

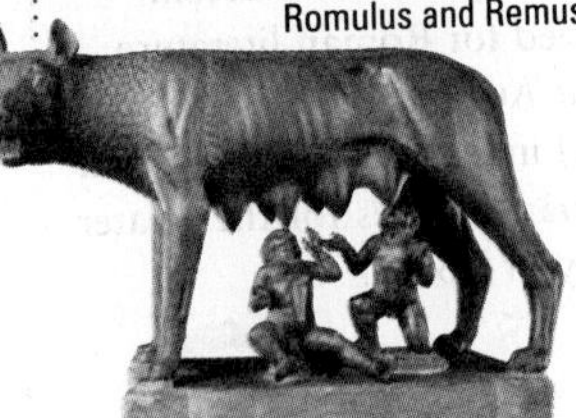
Romulus and Remus

509 B.C. Romans overthrow the Etruscans and establish a republic

450 B.C. First Roman law code, the Laws of the Twelve Tables, is posted in the forum

338–264 B.C. Romans conquer Italy

264 B.C. First gladiatorial contests held in Rome

264–241 B.C. First Punic War between Rome and Carthage

218–201 B.C. In the Second Punic War, the Carthaginian general Hannibal crosses the Alps to fight the Romans; he is eventually defeated **A**

EVENTS IN WORLD HISTORY

800 B.C. | 600 B.C. | 400 B.C.

c. 700s B.C. Homer composes the *Iliad* and the *Odyssey*

c. 563 B.C. Siddhartha Gautama, founder of Buddhism, born in India

c. 500 B.C. Nok culture in West Africa develops iron-making technology

c. 500 B.C. Zapotec civilization in Mexico builds Monte Albán, first city in the Americas

431–404 B.C. Peloponnesian War between Athens and Sparta

265–238 B.C. Asoka expands the Mauryan Empire in India

206 B.C. Beginning of Han Dynasty in China, which strengthens central government

200 B.C. — A.D. 1

166 B.C. Comedy of Terence first performed

149 B.C. Publication of Cato's history of Rome

51 B.C. Publication of Julius Caesar's *Commentaries on the Gallic War*

19 B.C. Publication of Virgil's *Aeneid* after his death

8 B.C. Death of Maecenas, patron of Virgil, Horace, and others

A.D. 8 Ovid exiled to the shore of the Black Sea

A.D. 54 Publication of Seneca's philosophical works

A.D. 98 Tacitus publishes *Germania*, a study of the Germanic tribes

A.D. 100 Juvenal creates his *Satires*

A.D. 174–180 Marcus Aurelius writes his *Meditations*

200 B.C. — A.D. 1

149–146 B.C. In the Third Punic War, the Romans destroy Carthage

73–71 B.C. Spartacus leads a slave uprising in southern Italy

58–50 B.C. Julius Caesar's army conquers Gaul

44 B.C. Julius Caesar is assassinated

31 B.C. Octavian defeats Mark Antony in the Battle of Actium

27 B.C. Octavian becomes the emperor Augustus

A.D. 14 Death of the emperor Augustus

C. A.D. 29 Crucifixion of Jesus of Nazareth

A.D. 64 Fire damages Rome

A.D. 70 Romans destroy the Temple in Jerusalem

A.D. 79 Eruption of Mount Vesuvius buries the Roman towns of Herculaneum and Pompeii (B)

A.D. 80 Completion of the Colosseum in Rome after ten years of work

A.D. 117 Roman Empire reaches its greatest extent under the emperor Trajan

A.D. 122–126 Hadrian's Wall is built across northern Britain (C)

A.D. 180 Death of Marcus Aurelius and the end of the Pax Romana

200 B.C. — A.D. 1

c. 200 B.C. Nazca culture arises in Peru

185 B.C. End of the Mauryan Empire

c. A.D. 65 First Buddhist monastery built in China

The Baiju monastery in Gyangze, China

c. A.D. 100 Zoskales becomes first king of Aksum in East Africa

A.D. 100–700 Moche culture flourishes in Peru

c. A.D. 105 Chinese invent paper

Historical Note

(B) Pompeii On 24 August A.D. 79, Mount Vesuvius erupted, covering Pompeii, a thriving port and market town, in a thick layer of ash. About 2,000 inhabitants were killed, some from the volcanic ash and others from the deadly fumes. For almost 1,700 years, Pompeii lay buried beneath the ash deposits, which preserved the shapes of the inhabitants' bodies. In 1748 the site was rediscovered and excavations began.

Historical Note

(C) Hadrian's Wall This structure extended for 74 miles along the northern edge of the Roman province in Britain. The wall served as a barrier to keep out invaders from the north. It was built mostly of stone, 8 to 10 feet thick and about 20 feet high. Deep ditches were dug in front and behind, and forts and watchtowers were strategically placed at intervals along the wall.

MINI LESSON Using the Time Line

SEQUENCE OF EVENTS Have students study the time line on pages 352 and 353 and then answer questions such as the following:

- Which literary work was written first, Caesar's *Commentaries on the Gallic War* or Marcus Aurelius' *Meditations*? *(Caesar's* Commentaries on the Gallic War*)*
- Could Julius Caesar have witnessed the eruption of Mount Vesuvius? *(no, he was assassinated before the eruption occurred)*
- Was paper invented before or after Julius Caesar's assassination? *(after)*
- Did Christianity arise before, during, or after the Pax Romana? *(during)*

READING FOR INFORMATION

Reading Skills and Strategies

CONNECTING

Have students study the images and read the captions to enhance their understanding of Rome's contributions to the modern world. Tell students that the poet Virgil in the *Aeneid* stated that government was Rome's most important contribution to civilization. Then ask: Which contribution do you consider most important, and why? How might the world be different if Rome had not existed? Help students imagine what the world might be like without representative governments, superhighways and stadia, and the many languages that derive from Latin.

Government at Work
The political system of the Romans strongly influenced modern governments. Like the senators of ancient Rome, the Congress of the United States carries on the business of government.

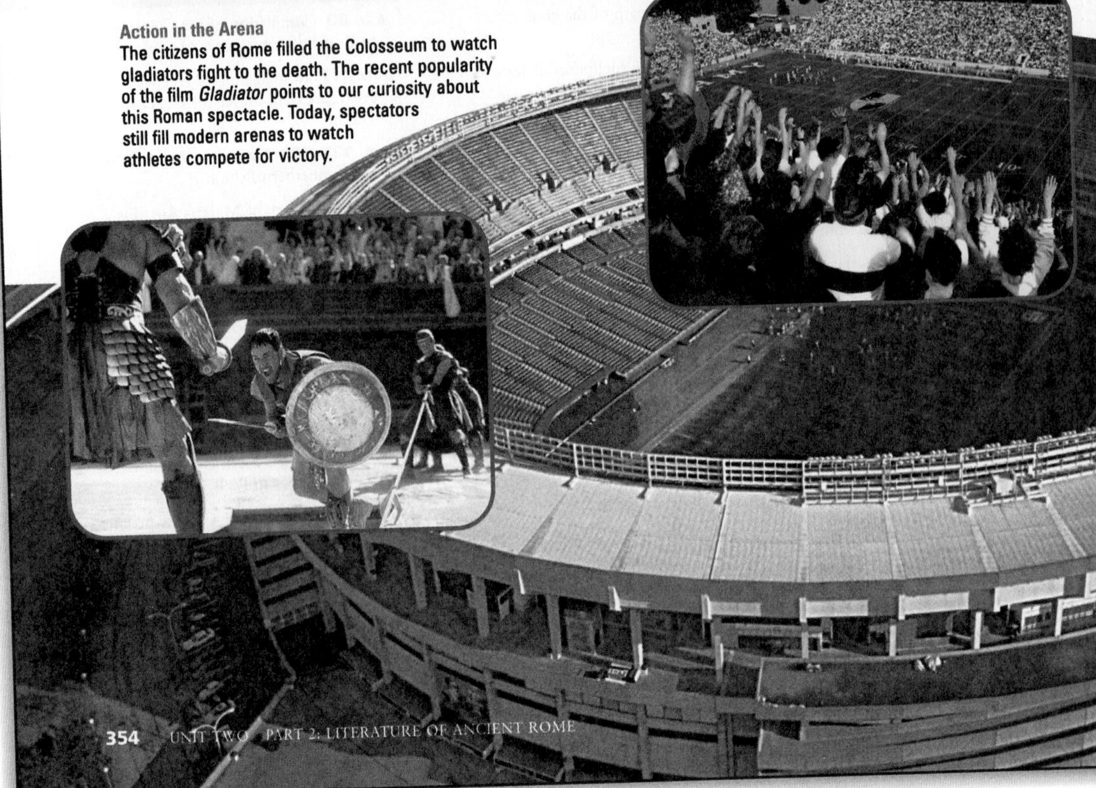

Action in the Arena
The citizens of Rome filled the Colosseum to watch gladiators fight to the death. The recent popularity of the film *Gladiator* points to our curiosity about this Roman spectacle. Today, spectators still fill modern arenas to watch athletes compete for victory.

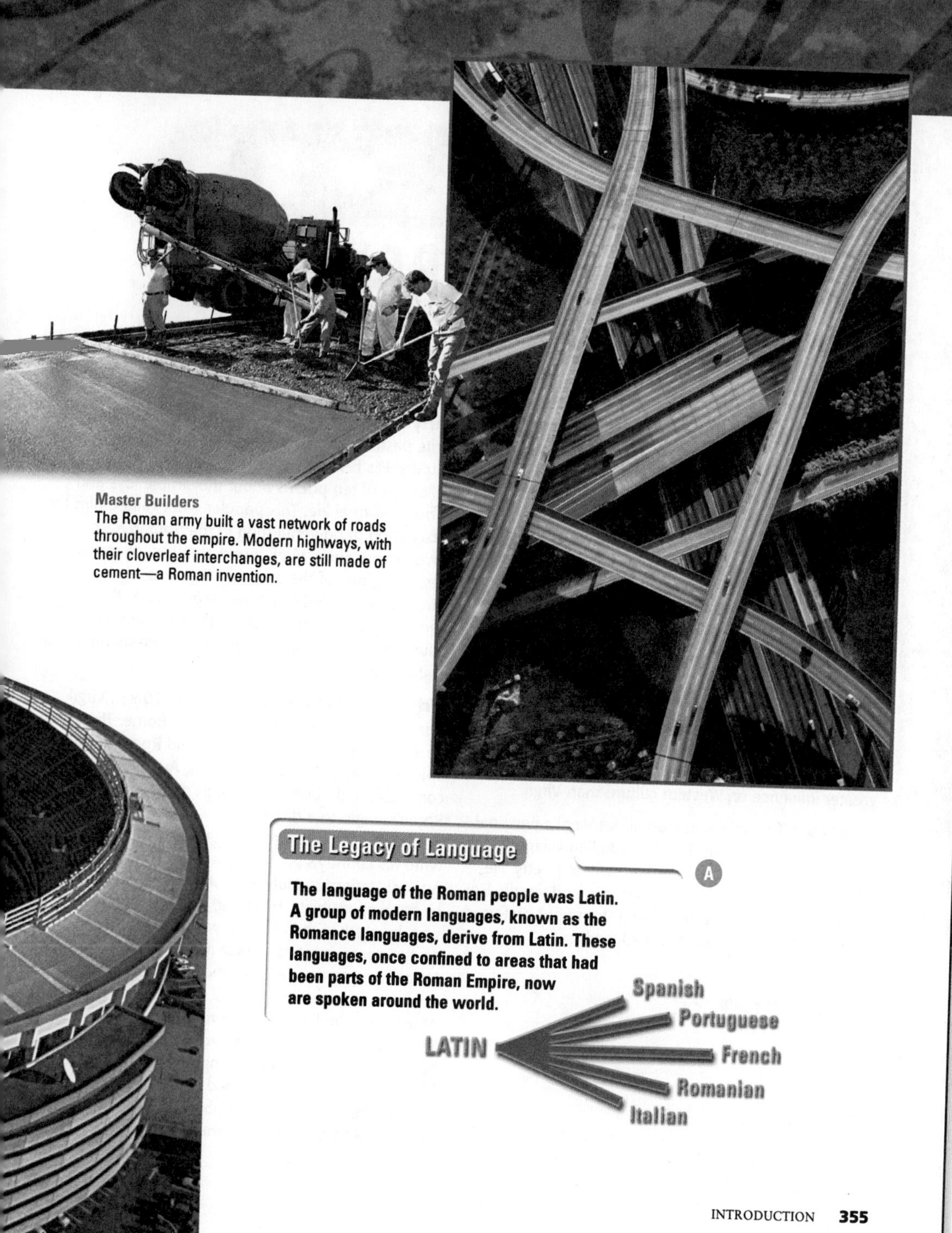

Master Builders
The Roman army built a vast network of roads throughout the empire. Modern highways, with their cloverleaf interchanges, are still made of cement—a Roman invention.

The Legacy of Language

The language of the Roman people was Latin. A group of modern languages, known as the Romance languages, derive from Latin. These languages, once confined to areas that had been parts of the Roman Empire, now are spoken around the world.

LATIN → Spanish, Portuguese, French, Romanian, Italian

Historical Note

A The Latin Language The Latin language has profoundly influenced Western culture. Long after the fall of Rome, Latin remained the language of the educated in Western Europe. Well into the 20th century, Latin was the liturgical language of the Roman Catholic Church. Not only do the Romance languages derive from Latin, so do countless words in English, including a host of legal and scientific terms.

This selection is included in the **World Literature InterActive Reader™.**

Objectives

- understand and appreciate a classic **epic poem (Literary Analysis)**
- identify the qualities of an ancient Roman **culture hero (Literary Analysis)**
- use the reading strategy of **predicting (Active Reading)**
- appreciate the author's use of imagery **(Literary Analysis)**

Summary

After many years of fighting, the Greeks appear to have sailed away from Troy, leaving behind a huge wooden horse as an offering to the gods. This horse, however, is filled with warriors in hiding. The Trojans do not know what to do with the wooden horse. Laocoön warns them to destroy it, but after he and his two sons are strangled by sea serpents, the Trojans bring the wooden horse inside the city. That night, a Greek spy lets out the hidden warriors, who open the city gates to their comrades. The Greeks set fire to Troy and slaughter its citizens. Pyrrhus, a Greek warrior, slays Priam, the king of Troy. Enraged at this murder, Aeneas considers killing Helen of Troy, whom he holds responsible for the war. His mother, the goddess Venus, stops him, however, and tells him to protect his own family. When Aeneas arrives home, his father at first refuses to flee from Troy, but omens induce him to change his mind. During the flight from Troy, Aeneas' wife, Creusa, becomes separated from the rest of the family. Aeneas searches in vain for her until he sees her ghost, who bids him farewell. He then rejoins his family and prepares to lead the Trojan refugees into exile.

Use **Unit Two Resource Book,** p. 56, for additional support.

Thematic Link

This epic poem tells of the Trojan **hero** Aeneas, who founds the settlement that will become Rome.

Use **Unit Two Resource Book,** p. 60, for practice with Words to Know.

5-Minute Warm-Up

Daily Language SkillBuilder

Have students **proofread** the display sentences on page 161i and write them correctly.

from the AENEID

THE FALL OF TROY • VIRGIL

Virgil
70–19 B.C.

Rome's Favorite Poet The ancient Romans considered Virgil their greatest poet. He was loved by all who knew him—from his friend and fellow poet Horace to the emperor Augustus himself. Long after Virgil's death, the monks of the Middle Ages kept copying his works, unlike some of the writings of other Roman authors. For more than 1,500 years, Virgil was the most honored poet of Europe. He even appears as Dante's guide through hell and purgatory in that poet's *Divine Comedy,* one of the greatest poems of the Middle Ages. Many believe that only the Bible has had a greater influence on Western culture than Virgil.

Personal Life Little is known about Virgil's personal life. A farmer's son born in a small Italian village, Virgil spent his early years studying and writing poetry. He never married and was considered shy and gentle. He studied philosophy and rhetoric in Rome but preferred to live in the countryside that he loved.

For a humanities activity, click on:

Early Works Virgil's love of rural life inspired him to write pastoral poetry—poems that celebrate life in the country. His first known work, the *Eclogues,* is a collection of ten poems about the simple joys and sorrows of rural life. This popular work gained him the recognition of powerful men in the Roman government. Soon, Virgil found a patron, or sponsor, in Maecenas, one of the emperor Augustus' chief ministers. Virgil dedicated his second work, the *Georgics,* to Maecenas. This work celebrates rural values—such as discipline and hard work—as the basis of the Roman character.

Writing the National Epic Around 30 B.C., Virgil was asked to write a poem to honor Rome. The poem he wrote, the *Aeneid,* would become Rome's national epic. According to some historians, Augustus commissioned Virgil to write it in order to trace Rome's origin to a divine plan.

Imagine the pressure on Virgil, commanded to write his country's great epic while his emperor waited! Understandably, he at times felt overwhelmed by the responsibility. However, good Roman that he was, he stuck with it. For ten years, he worked steadily on the poem, creating almost 10,000 lines of verse. He planned to devote three more years to revising the poem. Unfortunately, he fell ill on a journey from Athens and died shortly after returning to Italy. Supposedly, Virgil had left word with his friends to burn the manuscript if anything were to happen to him. Luckily, Augustus stepped in, overruling this request. He had the poem published in its unpolished form—for Rome and for all time.

LESSON RESOURCES

UNIT TWO RESOURCE BOOK, pp. 56–61

ASSESSMENT RESOURCES
Formal Assessment, pp. 45–46
Teacher's Guide to Assessment and Portfolio Use
Test Generator

INTEGRATED TECHNOLOGY
Visit our Web site: classzone.com

ADDITIONAL RESOURCES
Lesson Planning Guide, pp. 37–38
Teacher's Sourcebook for Language Development

Build Background

Written Epic Virgil's *Aeneid* is an example of a written epic. This form evolved from oral stories about legendary heroes whose brave deeds helped their people.

Written Epics from Different Cultures	
Babylon	***Epic of Gilgamesh*** (the oldest existing epic)
France	***Chanson de Roland***
Spain	***Cantar de mío Cid***
England	***Beowulf***
Germany	***Nibelungenlied***
Finland	***Kalevala***
India	***Mahabharata* and *Ramayana***

The *Aeneid* and the Augustan Age Written in the Latin language, the *Aeneid* is Virgil's masterpiece and the national epic of ancient Rome. Virgil imitated the Greek poet Homer by using many of the same elements found in Homer's epics. Virgil's hero is the Trojan prince Aeneas, who represents the ideal Roman. (The emperor considered himself a descendant of Aeneas.) The poem establishes the mythological roots of Rome, shows the nobility of its people, and foretells the coming of Augustus' glorious reign.

Virgil wrote the *Aeneid* between the years 30 and 19 B.C. In the year 31 B.C., the forces of Octavian (later to become the emperor Augustus) had defeated the fleets of Marc Antony and Cleopatra at the Battle of Actium. This battle marked the end of the Roman Republic and the beginning of the Roman Empire. Virgil felt that Augustus was ushering in a new era of peace, prosperity, and national pride after 20 years of bloody civil war.

Brimming with patriotism, Virgil set about to write an epic that would do for Roman civilization what Homer's *Iliad* and *Odyssey* had done for the people of Greece. Though based on these Greek epics, the *Aeneid* is Roman to its core, conveying Roman themes and emphasizing Roman values.

Aeneas as Epic Hero Throughout the epic, Virgil uses the Latin word *pius* to describe Aeneas. This term means "dutiful and loyal to family, to country, and to the gods." Aeneas is a good leader, a devoted father, and a loving son. No matter the cost, he always obeys the will of the gods. He endures terrible suffering but remains faithful to his mission. For example, he loses his wife before setting sail from Troy to Italy but still completes the journey. Through Aeneas' suffering, Virgil conveys a timeless truth about life: "at the heart of things there are tears."

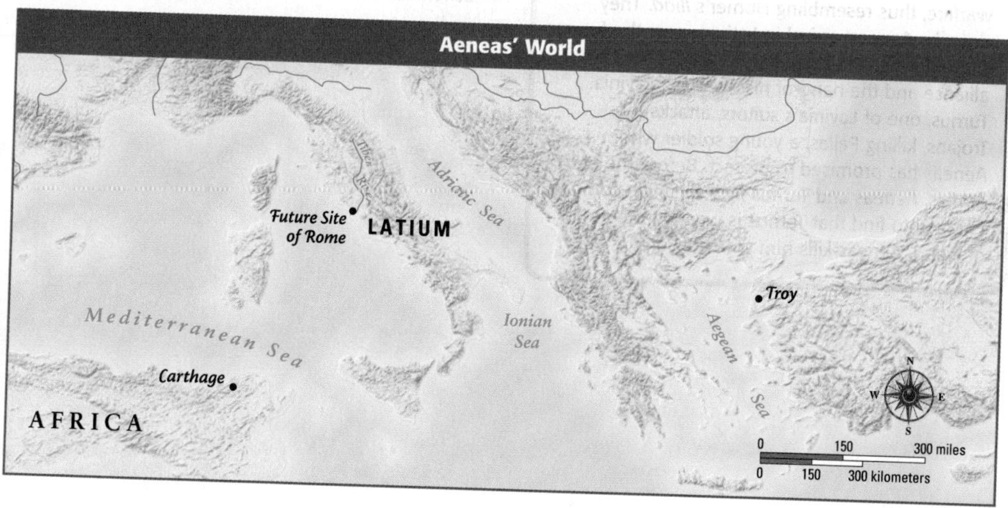

READING FOR INFORMATION

Reading Skills and Strategies

IDENTIFYING MAIN IDEAS

Point out the boldfaced headings in the text on pages 356 and 357, and tell students to use them as a guide to the main idea of each section. Students should read at a steady pace and then state the main idea of each section in their own words. Make sure students understand that Virgil wrote the *Aeneid* more than 2,000 years ago, shortly after Augustus Caesar had established the Roman Empire.

Biographical Note

Virgil was extremely shy and sensitive. After his *Eclogues* received great acclaim, crowds cheered when he appeared; this adulation troubled him, and he would often run away and hide. Later, Virgil was deeply hurt when some critics claimed that the *Aeneid* was unoriginal because some of it was derived from Homer's epics. Virgil intended to revise the epic in response to the criticism, but illness intervened.

Epic Poetry

Remind students that an epic is a long narrative poem on a serious subject presented in an elevated style. An epic describes the adventures of a hero whose deeds reflect the ideals and values of a group of people. For additional background, you may wish to have students study or review "The Epics of Greece and Rome" on pages 176 and 177 in the pupil edition.

MINI LESSON Using the Map

Have students study the map on this page and then answer questions such as the following:

- Which sea is farther east, the Adriatic Sea or the Aegean Sea? *(the Aegean Sea)*
- Which direction did Aeneas sail in traveling from Troy to Carthage? *(west)*
- Are Troy and Carthage more than or less than 900 miles apart? *(more than)*
- Is Rome north or south of Carthage? *(north)*

READING FOR INFORMATION

Reading Skills and Strategies

READING A SUMMARY

The Story of Aeneas Make sure that students grasp the key points of the summary:

- The Trojan hero Aeneas leads refugees from Troy after it falls to the Greeks.
- After a storm, he lands at Carthage, where he and the queen fall in love.
- He leaves her and sails to Italy.
- He establishes a settlement in Latium, defeating a local warrior in fierce combat.

Reading Skills and Strategies

UNDERSTANDING PHONETIC RESPELLING

Model for students how to use the phonetic respellings to pronounce the characters' names. Then have students read aloud each name in the list on page 359, using the phonetic respellings after each name.

Reading Skills and Strategies

TRACKING THE CHARACTERS IN THE *AENEID*

Students should notice that the characters in the *Aeneid* fall into one of three categories: Gods, Greeks, or Trojans. Tell students to note especially the following characters, who are most important in this excerpt: Venus among the Gods; Pyrrhus, or Neoptolemus, among the Greeks; and Aeneas, Laocoön, Creusa, and Priam among the Trojans.

Use **Unit Two Resource Book,** p. 57, for additional support.

The Story of Aeneas

The *Aeneid* is divided into 12 books. The first 6 resemble Homer's *Odyssey* in that they deal with the hero's wanderings. Shortly after the end of the Trojan War, Aeneas, his father, and his son, together with a band of refugees, leave Troy. They sail westward for Italy, as the ghost of Aeneas' wife has told him to do. Near Sicily, a storm separates Aeneas from his companions, and he lands on the African coast. There he meets Dido, the beautiful queen of Carthage. Strongly attracted to Aeneas, she gives a banquet in his honor. At the banquet, Aeneas relates his adventures, including the fall of Troy. Aeneas and Dido fall deeply and passionately in love. Aeneas, however, must leave her to fulfill his divine mission of finding a new home for the Trojans—the settlement that will become the city of Rome. Sailing from Carthage, he notices the flames of a funeral pyre. Dido, heartbroken over his departure, has taken her life.

Later, Aeneas visits a prophetess, the Cumaean Sibyl. With her, he descends to the underworld, where he meets his now-dead father, who shows him a vision. Aeneas sees the future generations of Romans who will descend from him. The line of descent culminates in the emperor Augustus.

The last 6 books of the *Aeneid* deal with warfare, thus resembling Homer's *Iliad.* They describe Aeneas' arrival in Latium, near the future site of Rome. The local king, Latinus, offers him alliance and the hand of his daughter Lavinia. Turnus, one of Lavinia's suitors, attacks the Trojans, killing Pallas, a young soldier whom Aeneas has promised to protect. Before the two armies, Aeneas and Turnus fight in single combat. Enraged to find that Turnus is wearing the armor of Pallas, Aeneas kills him with a sword.

Cast of Characters

Gods

Juno (jo͞o'nō): the queen of the gods

Mars (märz): the god of war

Neptune (nĕp'to͞on'): the god of the sea

Pallas (păl'əs): the goddess of wisdom; also known as **Minerva** (mĭ-nûr'və)

Venus (vē'nəs): the goddess of love and beauty, mother of Aeneas

Greeks

Menelaus (mĕn'ə-lā'əs): a leader of the expedition against Troy; husband of Helen

Neoptolemus (nē'ŏp-tŏl'ə-məs): a mighty warrior, son of the hero Achilles; also known as **Pyrrhus** (pĭr'əs)

Sinon (sī'nən): a warrior purposely left behind in Troy when the Greeks sailed away, pretending to give up the fighting

Ulysses (yo͝o-lĭs'ēz'): a leader known for his wily schemes

TIME MANAGEMENT

If your schedule requires that you cover the lesson objectives in a shorter time, use . . .

- Preparing to Read, pp. 356–359
- Thinking Through the Literature, p. 380
- Vocabulary in Action, p. 381

If you want to take advantage of longer blocks of class time, use . . .

- TE Teaching Options: Viewing and Representing, pp. 364, 371; Speaking and Listening, pp. 372, 378; Vocabulary Strategy, p 362; Cross-Curricular Link, pp. 359, 363, 365, 373; Grammar, pp. 366–367, 376–377; Standardized Test Practice, p. 379
- Choices & Challenges: p. 381

Connect to Your Life

At the end of this excerpt, Aeneas sets out to lead a band of refugees from Troy to Italy. Think of people from different walks of life whom you regard as good leaders. They may be politicians, teachers, military officers, or even characters from books or movies. What qualities do good leaders have? How do they respond to adversity and misfortune? Share your ideas with a small group of classmates.

Focus Your Reading

LITERARY ANALYSIS: CULTURE HERO

A **culture hero** is a larger-than-life figure who reflects the values of a people. A culture hero provides a noble image to inspire and guide the actions of all who share that culture. As you read, think about the character of Aeneas. Consider the qualities that make him heroic.

ACTIVE READING: PREDICTING

As a reading skill, **predicting** involves using clues in a story, along with prior knowledge and experience, to make reasonable guesses about what will happen later in the story. Good readers make and revise predictions almost unconsciously as they read.

READER'S NOTEBOOK As you read Aeneas' account of the fall of Troy, look for clues that seem to foreshadow future events. On a chart like the one below, jot down your predictions and the clues that led you to them. An example is shown.

Prediction	Clue
The wooden horse will bring about the destruction of Troy.	*". . . it cast a shadow / Over the city's heart." (lines 122–123)*

Editor's Note This selection was excerpted from a larger work. Material was deleted to shorten and focus the selection.

Trojans

Aeneas (ĭ-nē′əs): the hero of the epic and the son of the goddess Venus and Anchises, a mortal

Anchises (ăn-kī′sēz′): the father of Aeneas

Cassandra (kə-săn′drə): a daughter of Priam, whose prophecies always come true but are never believed

Creusa (krē-o͞o′zə): the wife of Aeneas

Hecuba (hĕk′yə-bə): the wife of Priam and queen of Troy

Helen (hĕl′ən): the wife of the Greek leader Menelaus, who betrayed him by running off with the Trojan prince Paris

Iulus (yo͞o′ləs): the young son of Aeneas and Creusa; also known as **Ascanius** (ăs-kā′nē-əs)

Laocoön (lā-ŏk′ō-ŏn′): a nobleman, brother of Anchises

Priam (prī′əm): the king of Troy

Politës (pə-lī′tēz′): a son of Priam

Cross Curricular Link **Humanities**

MYTHOLOGY Virgil's *Aeneid* is an epic poem that describes events during and after the Trojan War. According to legend, this war pitted the city-states of ancient Greece against the city of Troy in Asia Minor. The incident that led to the war occurred at the wedding feast of the mortal Peleus and the sea goddess Thetis. The goddess Eris, miffed because she was excluded from the feast, decided to cause trouble by sending a golden apple inscribed "For the most beautiful." The goddesses Hera (or Juno), Athena (or Minerva), and Aphrodite (or Venus) vied for the apple. Paris, the son of King Priam of Troy, was called upon to decide who should receive it. He awarded it to Aphrodite, who had promised him the beautiful Helen, the wife of King Menelaus of Sparta, in exchange. When Paris visited Sparta, Helen left her husband and ran off with Paris to Troy. Menelaus and his brother, King Agamemnon, then assembled a huge fleet to sail to Troy and recapture Helen. The war between Greece and Troy dragged on for ten years, with the Trojans led by Hector nearly victorious. Finally, Achilles, the champion of the Greeks, enraged at the death of his friend, Patroclus, entered the fray and killed Hector. Later, the Greeks used the stratagem of the wooden horse, described in this selection, to enter the city. They then burned Troy to the ground and reclaimed Helen.

AENEID 359

Reading and Analyzing

Reading Skills and Strategies
PREVIEWING
Give students a few minutes to skim, or glance through, the selection for clues about what might happen in it, using any evidence they can find, including pictures and captions in the text.

Guide for Reading
Tell students that this epic poem is broken into sections to help them understand it better and enjoy it more. At the beginning of each section, the **Focus** sets a purpose for reading. At the end of each section, the **Pause & Reflect** provides a question that checks student understanding.

Literary Analysis CULTURE HERO
Point out that the Trojan warrior Aeneas is the hero of this epic poem. He epitomizes the qualities of heart and mind honored in Roman society. Then ask students to recall some of these qualities from their reading of the background information on page 357.
Possible Response: devotion to family, to country, and to the gods

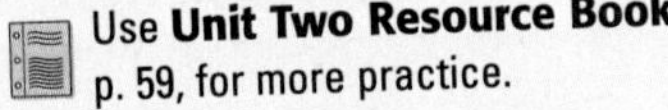
Use **Unit Two Resource Book,** p. 59, for more practice.

Active Reading PREDICTING
Remind students that they are expected to make predictions as they read and to support them with evidence from the text. The style of the epic includes providing several clues as to what will happen later. Tell students that they should be continually looking for these clues and making and revising predictions as they read. The **Focus** section in the **Guide for Reading** occasionally calls for a prediction.

Use **Unit Two Resource Book,** p. 58, for more practice.

from the Aeneid
The Fall of Troy
Virgil
Translated by Robert Fitzgerald

GUIDE FOR READING
FOCUS Aeneas is telling Queen Dido about the end of the Trojan War. After ten long years, the Greeks suddenly depart from Troy, leaving behind a huge wooden horse. Read to find out how the Trojans react to this parting gift.

1 "Knowing their strength broken in warfare, turned
Back by the fates, and years—so many years—
Already slipped away, the Danaan captains
By the divine handicraft of Pallas built
A horse of timber, tall as a hill,
And sheathed its ribs with planking of cut pine.
This they gave out to be an offering
2 For a safe return by sea, and the word went round.
But on the sly they shut inside a company
3 Chosen from their picked soldiery by lot,
Crowding the vaulted caverns in the dark—
The horse's belly—with men fully armed.

Offshore there's a long island, Tenedos,
Famous and rich while Priam's kingdom lasted,
A treacherous anchorage now, and nothing more.
They crossed to this and hid their ships behind it
On the bare shore beyond. We thought they'd gone,
Sailing home to Mycenae before the wind,
So Teucer's town is freed of her long anguish,
Gates thrown wide! And out we go in joy

3 Danaan (də-nā'ən): Greek.

6 sheathed: covered.

18 Mycenae (mī-sē'nē): the city ruled by the Greek commander, Agamemnon.

19 Teucer's (to͞o'sərz) **town:** Troy. (Teucer was the first Trojan king.)

Wooden horse inside the city of Troy, surrounded by Trojans; scene from *Helen of Troy* (1955).

To see the Dorian campsites, all deserted,
The beach they left behind. Here the Dolopians
Pitched their tents, here cruel Achilles lodged,
There lay the ships, and there, formed up in ranks,
They came inland to fight us. Of our men
One group stood marveling, <u>gaping</u> up to see
The dire gift of the cold unbedded goddess,
The sheer mass of the horse.
Thymoetes shouts
It should be hauled inside the walls and moored
High on the citadel—whether by treason
Or just because Troy's fate went that way now.
Capys opposed him; so did the wiser heads:
'Into the sea with it,' they said, 'or burn it,
Build up a bonfire under it,
This trick of the Greeks, a gift no one can trust,
Or cut it open, search the hollow belly!'

21 Dorian (dôr'ē-ən): Greek.

22 Dolopians (də-lō'pē-ənz): a group of Greek allies.

27 the cold unbedded goddess: Pallas, protector of the Greeks.

28 Thymoetes (thī-mē'tēz').

30 citadel (sĭt'ə-dəl): stronghold.

32 Capys (kăp'ĭs).

WORDS TO KNOW

gaping (gā'pĭng) *adj.* staring open-mouthed **gape** *v.*

Customizing Instruction

Less Proficient Readers

To add to their understanding of the story, tell students to try using the following tips:

- Read each section several times, and at least once aloud.
- Stop at the end of a line only when there is a punctuation mark—a comma, a period, a colon, a dash, or an exclamation mark.
- Use the sidenotes for help with difficult words and passages.
- After reading the first 12 lines, pause and summarize them. Then continue reading, pausing from time to time to summarize passages.

English Learners

1 The pronoun "their" in line 1 refers to the "Danaan captains" in line 3.

2 Explain the meaning of lines 7–8, "an offering for a safe return by sea." The Greeks trick the Trojans into believing that the wooden horse is an offering to the gods so that the Greek fleet can sail home safely.

3 In line 9 the word *company* means "a group of warriors." They were chosen "by lot" (line 10)—that is, by means of a random drawing.

Reading and Analyzing

Active Reading PREDICTING

A Ask students what they think might happen to Laocoön for hurling his spear against the wooden horse.

Possible Response: He might be punished by the goddess Pallas, or Minerva, who helped the Greeks build the wooden horse.

Literary Analysis EPIC

B Remind students that supernatural characters sometimes appear in epics, for example, the Cyclops in the *Odyssey*. Ask students to identify details that depict the serpents as supernatural.

Possible Responses: their enormous size, their swimming in unison, their ability to live on both water and land, their intentional attack, their red crests, and their fiery and bloody eyes

1

Contrary notions pulled the crowd apart.
Next thing we knew, in front of everyone,
Laocoön with a great company
Came furiously running from the Height,
And still far off cried out: 'O my poor people,
Men of Troy, what madness has come over you?
Can you believe the enemy truly gone?
A gift from the Danaans, and no ruse?
Is that Ulysses' way, as you have known him?
Achaeans must be hiding in this timber,
Or it was built to butt against our walls,
Peer over them into our houses, pelt
The city from the sky. Some crookedness
Is in this thing. Have no faith in the horse!
Whatever it is, even when Greeks bring gifts
I fear them, gifts and all.'
He broke off then
And rifled his big spear with all his might
Against the horse's flank, the curve of belly.
It stuck there trembling, and the rounded hull
Reverberated groaning at the blow.
If the gods' will had not been sinister,
If our own minds had not been crazed,
He would have made us foul that Argive den
With bloody steel, and Troy would stand today—
O citadel of Priam, towering still!

A

46 Achaeans (ə-kē'ənz): Greeks.

56 reverberated: echoed.

59 foul that Argive (är'jīv') **den:** slash the Greek hiding place.

2

But now look: hillmen, shepherds of Dardania,
Raising a shout, dragged in before the king
An unknown fellow with hands tied behind—
This all as he himself had planned,
Volunteering, letting them come across him,
So he could open Troy to the Achaeans.
Sure of himself this man was, braced for it
Either way, to work his trick or die.
From every quarter Trojans run to see him,
Ring the prisoner round, and make a game
Of jeering at him. Be instructed now
In Greek deceptive arts: one barefaced deed
Can tell you of them all. . . .

62 Dardania (där-dā'nē-ə): the region surrounding Troy.

73 deceptive arts: trickery.

WORDS TO KNOW

ruse (ro͞os) *n.* a trick

sinister (sĭn'ĭ-stər) *adj.* having an evil disposition or intent

MINI LESSON

Vocabulary Strategy

USING CONTEXT CLUES

Instruction Explain to students that they can often find the meanings of unfamiliar words by examining the word's context—the words, phrases, and sentences that surround the word. Point out the word *undulating* (page 363, line 87). This word is most likely unfamiliar to students, but they can probably figure out its meaning of "moving with a wavelike motion" from the context: a description of two attacking snakes. Also point out the word *suffused* (page 363, line 90). From the context, it is plain that suffused means "filled."

Practice Write the following sentences on the board. Ask students to use context clues to determine the meanings of the underlined words.

1. Laocoön believed that the Greek horse was a harmful ruse, not a helpful gift.
2. The snakes writhed around the limbs of Laocoön and his sons.
3. With hundreds of armed soldiers, the Greeks launched a prodigious attack.

Use **Unit Two Resource Book,** p. 60, for more practice.

A lesson on using context clues appears on p. 674 of the Pupil's Edition.

3 *The Greek spy, Sinon, tells a convincing lie about the Trojan horse. He explains that the Greeks built the wooden horse to win back the favor of the goddess Athena. He says that they were planning to sacrifice him to the goddess but he narrowly escaped. Sinon tells the Trojans to treat the statue with respect and to bring it within their city walls. If they do so, they will avoid doom and ensure that the Greeks will meet a terrible fate.*

And now another sign, more fearful still,
Broke on our blind miserable people,
Filling us all with dread. Laocoön,
Acting as Neptune's priest that day by lot,
Was on the point of putting to the knife
A massive bull before the appointed altar,
When ah—look there!
B From Tenedos, on the calm sea, twin snakes—
I shiver to recall it—endlessly
Coiling, uncoiling, swam abreast for shore,
Their underbellies showing as their crests
Reared red as blood above the swell; behind
They glided with great undulating backs.
Now came the sound of thrashed seawater foaming;
Now they were on dry land, and we could see
Their burning eyes, fiery and suffused with blood,
Their tongues a-flicker out of hissing maws.
We scattered, pale with fright. But straight ahead
They slid until they reached Laocoön.
Each snake enveloped one of his two boys,

91 maws: mouths.

94 boys: sons.

WORDS TO KNOW

undulating (ŭn'jə-lā'-tĭng) *adj.* moving with a wavelike motion **undulate** *v.*
suffused (sə-fyo͞ozd') *adj.* overspread; filled **suffuse** *v.*

Customizing Instruction

English Learners

1 Tell students that the sentence "Contrary notions pulled the crowd apart" means that the Trojans are torn by conflict. They disagree about what to do with the wooden horse. Some Trojans want to destroy it; others want to bring it inside the city.

2 The "unknown fellow" is Sinon, a Greek warrior. He has deliberately allowed himself to be captured by the shepherds in the hope of tricking the Trojans into bringing the wooden horse inside the city.

Less Proficient Readers

Use the following questions to guide students' understanding:

- What conflict divides the Trojans?

Possible Response: They cannot decide whether to destroy the wooden horse or bring it inside their city.

- What does Laocoön do to the wooden horse?

Possible Response: He hurls his spear against its flank.

3 Tell students to read the italicized passage carefully. It summarizes sections from the original that are not included in this excerpt. This passage will help students understand how Sinon deceives the Trojans.

Make sure that students realize that the two serpents are supernatural creatures, sent by the gods. Having swum from the island of Tenedos to Troy, the serpents slither along the ground, making their way toward the altar where Laocoön and his two sons are standing.

Cross Curricular Link History

SACRIFICIAL RITUALS Rituals, like the one Laocoön is performing, are found throughout history and in every culture. Rituals are ceremonial acts that occur in a sacred place and often mark a special time for the individual and the entire community–for example, the entry into a new stage of life or the start of a particular vocation. The goal of many rituals is to connect humans with a higher, sacred power. Rituals sometimes involve the sacrificial offerings of cattle or birds. Laocoön, for example, is about to sacrifice a bull.

Throughout the ancient world, the bull was regarded as a magnificent animal, the epitome of strength and vigor. The timeless fascination of this animal is reflected today in the ritual character of bullfighting in Spain and Mexico.

AENEID **363**

Reading and Analyzing

Reading Skills and Strategies
VISUALIZING

(A) Remind students that authors often use sensory details to appeal to a reader's five senses. Have students identify the words and phrases that helped them form mental pictures of Laocoön's death. How does Virgil make Laocoön's death seem dramatic?

Possible Response: Virgil describes in vivid detail the way the snakes coil around Laocoön, crushing and strangling him and his two sons. Laocoön's terrible shrieks as he tries desperately to free himself increase the dramatic force of the scene.

Reading Skills and Strategies
MAKING INFERENCES

(B) Ask students what they can infer about the Trojans from their reaction to Laocoön's death?

Possible Response: The Trojans are frightened and superstitious. They believe that they will offend the gods if they do not accept the wooden horse as a gift. They do not want to share the fate of Laocoön, who scorned the wooden horse.

Literary Analysis IRONY

(C) Dramatic irony occurs when the reader is aware of a reality of which one or more characters are not. Ask students to explain what is ironic about the Trojans' treatment of the wooden horse.

Possible Response: The Trojans sing hymns and touch the towrope for joy, not realizing they are escorting their mortal enemies into the city.

Sculpture of Laocoön (first century B.C.). Vatican Museums, Vatican State.

HUMANITIES CONNECTION This marble statue shows Laocoön and his two sons being crushed by sea serpents. Laocoön suffers for having warned his people about the Trojan horse. This statue was an original Hellenistic Greek work that may have been imported to Rome. Greek statues like this one met with great acclaim in the Roman world.

Twining about and feeding on the body.
Next they ensnared the man as he ran up
With weapons: coils like cables looped and bound him
Twice round the middle; twice about his throat
They whipped their back-scales, and their heads towered,
(A) While with both hands he fought to break the knots,
Drenched in slime, his head-bands black with venom,
Sending to heaven his appalling cries
Like a slashed bull escaping from an altar,
The fumbled axe shrugged off. The pair of snakes
Now flowed away and made for the highest shrines,
The citadel of pitiless Minerva,
Where coiling they took cover at her feet
Under the rondure of her shield. New terrors
(B) Ran in the shaken crowd: the word went round

102 appalling: horrifying.

108 rondure: circle.

MINI LESSON Viewing and Representing

Sculpture of Laocoön

ART APPRECIATION Have students read the **Humanities Connection** caption and study the image of the sculpture. Point out that this sculpture is admired for conveying a sense of frightful and desperate energy. Help students identify details in the sculpture that contribute to this effect.

Possible Responses: Laocoön, the priest of Apollo, and his two sons are hopelessly entangled in the coils of the snakes. The tendons and muscles in Laocoön's arms and legs are sharply defined. His torso is painfully twisted, and his face looks terrified as he realizes that he and his sons are doomed. Laocoön holds a snake by the neck as it bites him in the side.

Laocoön had paid, and rightfully,
For profanation of the sacred hulk
With his offending spear hurled at its flank.

B
'The offering must be hauled to its true home,'
They clamored. 'Votive prayers to the goddess
Must be said there!'
So we breached the walls
And laid the city open. Everyone
Pitched in to get the figure underpinned
With rollers, hempen lines around the neck.
Deadly, pregnant with enemies, the horse
Crawled upward to the breach. And boys and girls
Sang hymns around the towrope as for joy
They touched it. Rolling on, it cast a shadow
Over the city's heart. O Fatherland,
O Ilium, home of gods! Defensive wall
Renowned in war for Dardanus's people!
There on the very threshold of the breach
It jarred to a halt four times, four times the arms
1 In the belly thrown together made a sound—
Yet on we strove unmindful, deaf and blind,
To place the monster on our blessed height.
Then, even then, Cassandra's lips unsealed
C The doom to come: lips by a god's command
Never believed or heeded by the Trojans.
So pitiably we, for whom that day
Would be the last, made all our temples green
With leafy festal boughs throughout the city.

As heaven turned, Night from the Ocean stream
Came on, profound in gloom on earth and sky
And Myrmidons in hiding. In their homes
The Teucrians lay silent, wearied out,
And sleep enfolded them. The Argive fleet,
Drawn up in line abreast, left Tenedos
Through the aloof moon's friendly stillnesses
And made for the familiar shore. Flame signals
Shone from the command ship. Sinon, favored
2 By what the gods unjustly had decreed,
Stole out to tap the pine walls and set free

110–112 Laocoön had paid . . . its flank: Pallas had punished Laocoön for treating the wooden horse with disrespect by throwing his spear at it.

115 breached: broke through.

119 pregnant: filled.

124 Ilium (ĭl'ē-əm): another name for Troy.

139 Myrmidons (mûr'mə-dŏnz'): Greeks.

140 Teucrians (to͞o'krē-ənz): Trojans.

Cross Curricular Link — Humanities

MYTHOLOGY The beautiful Cassandra met a particularly frustrating and terrible fate. Though she always prophesied the truth, she was doomed never to be believed. The daughter of Priam, the King of Troy, and Hecuba, his queen, Cassandra was known for her beauty. So beautiful was she that the god Apollo fell in love with her and gave her a great power: the ability to foretell the future. When Cassandra spurned his love, Apollo punished her, ordaining that no one would ever believe her prophecies. In vain, Cassandra warned the Trojans to return Helen to the Greeks and not to bring the wooden horse inside the city. After Troy was sacked, King Agamemnon enslaved Cassandra and brought her to Mycenae. There she and Agamemnon were murdered by Agamemnon's wife, Clytemnestra, and her lover, Aegisthus.

Customizing Instruction

Less Proficient Readers

Review students' comprehension of lines 92–104 by asking the following questions:

- Whom do the serpents attack first? *(Laocoön's two sons)*
- What happens to Laocoön when he tries to rescue his sons? *(the serpents coil around him, strangling and crushing him)*
- Where do the serpents crawl after their attack? *(to the citadel of Minerva)*

1 Make sure students understand what happens in lines 126–130. Four times the wooden horse comes to a jarring halt on the threshold of the city, and the Trojans can even hear the clash of weapons of the warriors hiding inside.

2 Make sure students understand that in lines 145–148 Sinon, the Greek spy, approaches the wooden horse and lets out the warriors hiding inside it.

English Learners

Explain the meaning of the following phrases that might be difficult for students to understand:

- *Laocoön had paid* (line 110) means that he lost his life
- *deaf and blind* (line 129) means that the Trojans were out of their senses when they escorted the wooden horse inside their city

Advanced Learners

As students read, ask them to consider how important a role fate plays in the events of this epic poem.

Possible Response: Fate, or destiny, plays a crucial role in the events in the *Aeneid*. The goddess Minerva helps the Greeks construct the wooden horse, the instrument of Troy's downfall. Supernatural serpents kill Laocoön, the Trojan most strongly in favor of destroying the wooden horse. The Trojans are victims of a higher power that impels them to escort the wooden horse into the city, even though they hear the clash of arms from the warriors hidden inside.

AENEID 365

Pause & Reflect
Possible Response: The Trojans believe the trickery of Sinon and are terrified by the death of Laocoön.

Literary Analysis CULTURE HERO

A Remind students that a culture hero embodies the qualities revered by his or her society. Ask students what qualities Aeneas shows in this passage.
Possible Responses: devotion to his city, outstanding bravery, and an awareness of the power of fate

The Danaans in the belly. Opened wide,
The horse emitted men; gladly they dropped
Out of the cavern, captains first, Thessandrus,
Sthenelus and the man of iron, Ulysses;
Hand over hand upon the rope, Acamas, Thoas,
Neoptolemus and Prince Machaon,
Menelaus and then the master builder,
Epeos, who designed the horse decoy.
Into the darkened city, buried deep
In sleep and wine, they made their way,
Cut the few sentries down,
Let in their fellow soldiers at the gate,
And joined their combat companies as planned. . . .

150–155 Thessandrus (thə-săn'drəs) . . . **Sthenelus** (sthĕn'ə-ləs) . . . **Acamas** (ăk'ə-məs) . . . **Thoas** (thō'əs) . . . **Machaon** (mə-kā'ŏn') . . . **Epeos** (ĕ-pē'əs).

PAUSE & REFLECT Why do the Trojans bring the wooden horse inside their city?

FOCUS Terrible fighting rages outside the palace of Priam, the king of Troy. As you read, look for details that help you visualize this fighting.

1 2

The ghost of Hector visits Aeneas in his sleep, warning him about the Greek invasion. Hector tells Aeneas to flee the city so that one day he will be able to establish another great city—Rome. Aeneas awakens, puts on his armor, and goes out into the streets of the burning city. He and his comrades defeat a small band of Greek soldiers, take their armor, and put it on to disguise themselves. They continue to fight the invaders. Eventually, the Greeks see through the Trojans' disguise, and many of Aeneas' companions are killed.

MINI LESSON Grammar

DIRECT OBJECTS AND INDIRECT OBJECTS
Remind students that direct objects and indirect objects are complements. A complement is a word or group of words that completes the meaning of a verb. A direct object is the noun or pronoun that receives the action of a verb. It answers the question *what*? or *whom*? An indirect object is the noun or pronoun that tells *to whom* or *for whom* the action of the verb is being performed. In a sentence containing a direct object and an indirect object, the indirect object usually comes first.

Instruction Write the following sentences on the chalkboard:

We breached the walls.

The Greeks offered the Trojans an enormous wooden horse.

Ask students to identify the object(s) in each sentence (*walls*, DO; *horse*, DO; *Trojans*, IO).

Practice Have students identify the object(s) in each of the following sentences. Students should write DO for direct objects and IO for indirect objects.

The burning of Troy

A 3 Ashes of Ilium!
Flames that consumed my people! Here I swear
That in your downfall I did not avoid
One weapon, one exchange with the Danaans,
And if it had been fated, my own hand
Had earned my death. But we were torn away
From that place—Iphitus and Pelias too,
One slow with age, one wounded by Ulysses,
Called by a clamor at the hall of Priam.
Truly we found here a prodigious fight,
As though there were none elsewhere, not a death

167 Iphitus (ī′fĭ-təs) **and Pelias** (pĕl′ē-əs): Trojan soldiers.

WORDS TO KNOW

prodigious (prə-dĭj′əs) *adj.* impressively great; stupendous

Customizing Instruction

Less Proficient Readers

Focus Make sure students understand what they should look for while reading the next section: namely, details that help them imagine the fighting outside the King of Troy's palace.

1 Tell students to read the italicized passage, which summarizes lines not included in this excerpt. This passage will help students understand what happens after the Greeks set fire to the city.

2 Remind students that Hector is the dead son of Priam, King of Troy. The champion of the Trojans, Hector was killed by Achilles in single combat, and his body was dragged behind Achilles' chariot around the walls of Troy. Achilles later allowed Priam to bring back Hector's body to Troy for burial. The *Iliad* ends with Hector's funeral.

English Learners

3 Help students understand lines 161–166. Tell them that the phrases "Ashes of Ilium!/ Flames that consumed my people" refer to the fact that the city of Troy is burning to the ground. The phrase "my own hand/Had earned my death" means that Aeneas fought as many Greeks as he could. If the gods had wished it, Aeneas would have been slain, for he did not run away from the fighting.

Advanced Learners

Ask students to use Aeneas' actions to draw conclusions about the values that the Romans respected.

Possible Response: The Romans respected courage and intelligence in battle. Aeneas does not run away from the fighting, yet he disguises himself to gain an advantage against the Greeks.

1. Laocoön gave the Trojans good advice. (*advice*, DO; *Trojans*, IO)
2. Unfortunately, the Trojans ignored Laocoön's words. (*words*, DO)
3. The Trojans hauled the wooden horse into the city. (*horse*, DO).
4. The hollow statue hid hundreds of Greek soldiers. (*hundreds*, DO)
5. The Greeks brought the Trojans death and destruction. (*death*, DO; *destruction*, DO; *Trojans*, IO).

For more instruction and practice in direct and indirect objects, use McDougal Littell's ***Language Network:***

- Grade 10, Chapter 2, "The Sentence and Its Parts"
- Grade 12, Chapter 1, "The Parts of a Sentence"

Reading and Analyzing

Literary Analysis CONFLICT

A Remind students that in epic poetry the conflicts sometimes are grand in scope and are described in lofty language. Ask students to pick out details that suggest that this external conflict between the Greeks and the Trojans is a heroic struggle.

Possible Responses: Details such as "Mars gone berserk," "a tortoise shell of overlapping shields," and "The defenders wrenched out upperworks and rooftiles" all suggest a titanic struggle.

Literary Analysis EPIC SIMILE

B Remind students that a simile is a comparison between two things that uses the word *like* or *as*. Sometimes, Virgil develops a simile in great detail, going on for several lines. For example, in lines 206–213, Virgil develops a comparison between the warrior Pyrrhus and a snake. After students have read this epic simile, have them identify words and phrases that help them visualize a snake.

Possible Responses: "bronze and glittering," "hidden swollen underground," "writhes into the light," "on vile grass fed," "his old skin cast away," "glossy," "rolling slippery coils," "lifted underbelly," and "triple tongue a-flicker."

Pause & Reflect

Possible Responses: Students may mention several details that helped them picture the Greeks trying to scale the wall and the Trojans hurling missiles down on them.

In the whole city: Mars gone berserk, Danaans
In a rush to scale the roof; the gate besieged
By a tortoise shell of overlapping shields.
Ladders clung to the wall, and men strove upward
Before the very doorposts, on the rungs,
Left hand putting the shield up, and the right
Reaching for the cornice. The defenders
Wrenched out upperworks and rooftiles: these
For missiles, as they saw the end, preparing
To fight back even on the edge of death.
And gilded beams, ancestral ornaments,
They rolled down on the heads below. In hall
Others with swords drawn held the entrance way,
Packed there, waiting. Now we plucked up heart
To help the royal house, to give our men
A respite, and to add our strength to theirs,
Though all were beaten. And we had for entrance
A rear door, secret, giving on a passage
Between the palace halls; in other days
Andromachë, poor lady, often used it,
Going alone to see her husband's parents
Or taking Astyanax to his grandfather.
I climbed high on the roof, where hopeless men
Were picking up and throwing futile missiles.
Here was a tower like a promontory
Rising toward the stars above the roof:
All Troy, the Danaan ships, the Achaean camp,
Were visible from this. Now close beside it
With crowbars, where the flooring made loose joints,
We pried it from its bed and pushed it over.
Down with a rending crash in sudden ruin
Wide over the Danaan lines it fell;
But fresh troops moved up, and the rain of stones
With every kind of missile never ceased.

PAUSE & REFLECT What details helped you imagine the fighting outside Priam's palace?

172 berserk: recklessly violent.

178 cornice (kôr′nĭs): a molding at the top of a wall.

191 Andromachë (ăn-drŏm′ə-kē), **poor lady:** Andromachë's husband, the Trojan prince Hector, had been killed by Achilles earlier in the war.

193 Astyanax (ə-stī′ə-năks′): the son of Hector and Andromachë.

196 promontory (prŏm′ən-tôr′ē): a ridge of land extending into a body of water.

WORDS TO KNOW
respite (rĕs′pĭt) *n.* a rest

FOCUS What do you predict will happen when the Greek soldiers break into the palace?

Just at the outer doors of the vestibule
Sprang Pyrrhus, all in bronze and glittering,
As a serpent, hidden swollen underground
By a cold winter, writhes into the light,
On vile grass fed, his old skin cast away,
Renewed and glossy, rolling slippery coils,
With lifted underbelly rearing sunward
And triple tongue a-flicker. Close beside him
Giant Periphas and Automedon,
His armor-bearer, once Achilles' driver,
Besieged the place with all the young of Scyros,
Hurling their torches at the palace roof.
Pyrrhus shouldering forward with an axe
Broke down the stony threshold, forced apart
Hinges and brazen door-jambs, and chopped through
One panel of the door, splitting the oak,
To make a window, a great breach. And there
Before their eyes the inner halls lay open,
The courts of Priam and the ancient kings,
With men-at-arms ranked in the vestibule.
From the interior came sounds of weeping,
Pitiful commotion, wails of women
High-pitched, rising in the formal chambers
To ring against the silent golden stars;
And, through the palace, mothers wild with fright
Ran to and fro or clung to doors and kissed them.
Pyrrhus with his father's brawn stormed on,
No bolts or bars or men availed to stop him:
Under his battering the double doors
Were torn out of their sockets and fell inward.
Sheer force cleared the way: the Greeks broke through
Into the vestibule, cut down the guards,
And made the wide hall seethe with men-at-arms—
A tumult greater than when dikes are burst
And a foaming river, swirling out in flood,
Whelms every parapet and races on
Through fields and over all the lowland plains,
Bearing off pens and cattle. I myself
Saw Neoptolemus furious with blood

206 vestibule (vĕs'tə-byo͞ol'): entrance hall.

214 Periphas (pə-rī'fəs) . . . **Automedon** (ô-tŏm'ə-dŏn').

216 the young of Scyros (skī'rəs): the followers of Pyrrhus, who lived on the island of Scyros.

238 seethe: boil; surge.

241 whelms every parapet: overflows every protective wall.

WORDS TO KNOW

writhe (rīth) *v.* to twist about; squirm

Customizing Instruction

Less Proficient Readers

Focus Make sure that students base their predictions on information gleaned from their reading.

1 Point out that Aeneas uses a secret passage to gain entry into the palace. He then climbs onto the roof to help the defenders.

2 Help students understand the epic simile in lines 206–213 by asking basic questions after they have read the passage:

- Whose side is Pyrrhus on? *(the Greeks)*
- What is he compared to? *(a snake)*
- How do you think he will behave? *(in an evil way)*

Review students' understanding of lines 172–238 by asking the following questions:

- What is happening outside Priam's palace? *(The Greeks are attacking, trying to break down the door and climb onto the roof.)*
- What do Aeneas and his men do to the tower on the roof of the palace? *(They pry it up and push it over onto the Greeks attacking the palace.)*
- How do the Greek finally enter the palace? *(Pyrrhus batters the doors in and then rips them from their sockets.)*

3 Tell students that sometimes Pyrrhus is called Neoptolemus, as in line 244.

AENEID 369

Reading and Analyzing

Active Reading PREDICTING

A Have students predict what might happen to Priam as he prepares for battle against the Greeks.

Possible Response: Since Priam is old and very frail, he likely will be captured or killed by a Greek warrior.

Literary Analysis SIMILE

B Have students explain what the simile "like white doves blown down in a black storm" suggests about Hecuba and her daughters.

Possible Response: Hecuba and her daughters are battered, frail, and helpless against the assault ("a black storm") of the Greek warriors.

In the entrance way, and saw the two Atridae;
Hecuba I saw, and her hundred daughters,
Priam before the altars, with his blood
Drenching the fires that he himself had blessed.
Those fifty bridal chambers, hope of a line
So flourishing; those doorways high and proud,
Adorned with takings of barbaric gold,
Were all brought low: fire had them, or the Greeks.

1 A What was the fate of Priam, you may ask.
Seeing his city captive, seeing his own
Royal portals rent apart, his enemies
In the inner rooms, the old man uselessly
Put on his shoulders, shaking with old age,
Armor unused for years, belted a sword on,
And made for the massed enemy to die.
Under the open sky in a central court
Stood a big altar; near it, a laurel tree
Of great age, leaning over, in deep shade
Embowered the Penatës. At this altar
Hecuba and her daughters, like white doves
B Blown down in a black storm, clung together,
Enfolding holy images in their arms.
Now, seeing Priam in a young man's gear,
She called out:
'My poor husband, what mad thought
Drove you to buckle on these weapons?
Where are you trying to go? The time is past
For help like this, for this kind of defending,
Even if my own Hector could be here.
Come to me now: the altar will protect us,
Or else you'll die with us.'
She drew him close,
Heavy with years, and made a place for him
To rest on the consecrated stone.
Now see
Politës, one of Priam's sons, escaped
From Pyrrhus' butchery and on the run
Through enemies and spears, down colonnades,
Through empty courtyards, wounded. Close behind
Comes Pyrrhus burning for the death-stroke: has him,
Catches him now, and lunges with the spear.

245 the two Atridae (ā-trī'dē): Menelaus and his brother Agamemnon.

263 embowered the Penatës (pə-nā'tēz): sheltered the images of the household gods.

279 colonnades (kŏl'ə-nādz'): rows of columns.

The boy has reached his parents, and before them
Goes down, pouring out his life with blood.
Now Priam, in the very midst of death,
Would neither hold his peace nor spare his anger.
'For what you've done, for what you've dared,' he said,
'If there is care in heaven for atrocity,
May the gods render fitting thanks, reward you
As you deserve. You forced me to look on
At the destruction of my son: defiled
A father's eyes with death. That great Achilles
You claim to be the son of—and you lie—
Was not like you to Priam, his enemy;
2 To me who threw myself upon his mercy
He showed compunction, gave me back for burial
The bloodless corpse of Hector, and returned me
To my own realm.'
The old man threw his spear
With feeble impact; blocked by the ringing bronze,
It hung there harmless from the jutting boss.

288 atrocity (ə-trŏs'ĭ-tē): horrible cruelty.

291 defiled: stained; polluted.

296 compunction: pity.

299 feeble: weak.

300 jutting boss: the raised center of a shield.

HUMANITIES CONNECTION In this bas-relief sculpture, Pyrrhus prepares to kill Priam as his wife and daughters look on in horror.

The Death of Priam (1787–1792), Antonio Canova. Museo Correr, Venice, Italy.

MINI LESSON Viewing and Representing

The Death of Priam **by Antonio Canova**

ART APPRECIATION Have students read the **Humanities Connection** caption and study the image of the bas-relief sculpture. Tell students that the Italian sculptor Antonio Canova (1757–1822) was important in the Neoclassical movement, which emphasized balance and symmetry in works of art. Help students notice that Pyrrhus is the focus of this sculpture. He stands on the altar steps at the center, holding a knife in his right hand and the hair of Priam in his left. At either end of the sculpture, Trojan women turn away from the impending murder.

Customizing Instruction

Less Proficient Readers

1 Tell students that line 253 is a clue that the following passage will describe what ultimately happens to Priam, the king of Troy. Then check students' understanding of lines 253–274 by asking the following questions:

- What does Priam do to get ready for battle? *(He puts on his armor and ties a sword to his waist.)*
- Why does Hecuba try to prevent her husband from fighting the Greeks? *(She thinks that it is useless to try to fight and that her husband is too old for battle.)*

2 Help students understand lines 292–298. Point out that in these lines Priam, filled with anger, insults Pyrrhus by comparing him unfavorably with his father, Achilles. Priam reminds Pyrrhus that Achilles respected the sacredness of a father-son relationship. As proof, Achilles gave Priam the body of his slain son, Hector, to take back to Troy for burial. Priam states that Pyrrhus, who lacks his father's sense of mercy, is not Achilles' true son.

English Learners

Explain the meaning of the following phrases:

- *heavy with years* (line 275) means "very old"—a description of Priam
- *hold his peace* (line 286) means to say nothing
- *The old man* (line 298) refers to Priam

Advanced Learners

Ask students to think about ways to compare and contrast Aeneas and Pyrrhus.

Possible Response: Pyrrhus is filled with brute force. Aeneas, on the other hand, is not only courageous in battle but intelligent and compassionate. For example, he climbs onto the roof to help the desperate defenders of the royal palace.

AENEID 371

Reading Skills and Strategies
VISUALIZING

A Ask students to identify details that help them form mental pictures of the murder of Priam.

Possible Responses: details such as "he dragged him trembling," "Slipping in the pooled blood of his son," "The sword flashed in his right," "up to the hilt /He thrust it in his body" and "The vast trunk headless lies without a name"

Pause & Reflect
Possible Response: Pyrrhus murders Priam, first stabbing and then beheading him.

Literary Analysis INTERNAL CONFLICT

B Ask students to describe Aeneas' internal conflict.

Possible Response: Aeneas has just watched the murder of his king. He then notices Helen of Troy lurking about. He blames her for the terrible sufferings of his people. Filled with rage, he wants to avenge his fallen king and city by killing her. Still, he realizes that killing a woman is a dishonorable act.

Then Pyrrhus answered:
'You'll report the news
To Pelidës, my father; don't forget
My sad behavior, the degeneracy
Of Neoptolemus. Now die.'
With this,
To the altar step itself he dragged him trembling,
Slipping in the pooled blood of his son,
And took him by the hair with his left hand.
The sword flashed in his right; up to the hilt
He thrust it in his body.
A That was the end
Of Priam's age, the doom that took him off,
With Troy in flames before his eyes, his towers
Headlong fallen—he that in other days
Had ruled in pride so many lands and peoples,
The power of Asia.
On the distant shore
The vast trunk headless lies without a name.

302 Pelidës (pē-lī'dēz'): "son of Peleus"—that is, Achilles, who was killed earlier in the war.

303 degeneracy: decline into wickedness.

315 the vast trunk: Priam's huge body.

PAUSE & REFLECT What does Pyrrhus do to Priam, the king of Troy?

FOCUS Deeply moved by Priam's death, Aeneas notices Helen of Troy. He regards her as the cause of all the bloodshed. What do you predict he will do to Helen?

For the first time that night, inhuman shuddering
Took me, head to foot. I stood unmanned,
1 And my dear father's image came to mind
As our king, just his age, mortally wounded,
Gasped his life away before my eyes.
Creusa came to mind, too, left alone;
The house plundered; danger to little Iulus.
I looked around to take stock of my men,
But all had left me, utterly played out,
Giving their beaten bodies to the fire
Or plunging from the roof.
It came to this,
That I stood there alone. And then I saw
Lurking behind the doorsill of the Vesta,

328 the Vesta: the temple of Vesta, goddess of the hearth.

MINI LESSON Speaking and Listening

ROLE-PLAYING

Prepare Role-playing gives students the opportunity to explore literary characters and their conflicts more deeply by imagining themselves as those characters. Have students work in groups of four to prepare an interpretation of Priam's death-scene, lines 253–315. Assign parts for Aeneas (the narrator), Hecuba, Priam, and Pyrrhus. Encourage students to read aloud the lines of the text several times in order to "hear" the characters' voices and to discuss their interpretation with other members of the group.

Present Invite groups of four to role-play Aeneas, Hecuba, Priam, and Pyrrhus. They can present their interpretations for a variety of audiences, including their classmates, students from other classes, and teachers. Ask students in the audience to evaluate the performance and explain how it increased their understanding of the characters.

This activity is particularly well suited for longer blocks of class time.

In hiding, silent, in that place reserved,
The daughter of Tyndareus. Glare of fires
Lighted my steps this way and that, my eyes
Glancing over the whole scene, everywhere.
That woman, terrified of the Trojans' hate
For the city overthrown, terrified too
Of Danaan vengeance, her abandoned husband's
Anger after years—Helen, that Fury
Both to her own homeland and Troy, had gone
To earth, a hated thing, before the altars.
Now fires blazed up in my own spirit—
A passion to avenge my fallen town
And punish Helen's whorishness.
'Shall this one
Look untouched on Sparta and Mycenae
After her triumph, going like a queen,
And see her home and husband, kin and children,
With Trojan girls for escort, Phrygian slaves?
B Must Priam perish by the sword for this?
Troy burn, for this? Dardania's littoral
Be soaked in blood, so many times, for this?
Not by my leave. I know
No glory comes of punishing a woman,
The feat can bring no honor. Still, I'll be
Approved for snuffing out a monstrous life,
For a just sentence carried out. My heart
Will teem with joy in this avenging fire,
And the ashes of my kin will be appeased.'

So ran my thoughts. I turned wildly upon her,
But at that moment, clear, before my eyes—
2 Never before so clear—in a pure light
Stepping before me, radiant through the night,
My loving mother came: immortal, tall,
And lovely as the lords of heaven know her.
Catching me by the hand, she held me back,
Then with her rose-red mouth reproved me:
'Son,
Why let such suffering goad you on to fury
Past control? Where is your thoughtfulness
For me, for us? Will you not first revisit
The place you left your father, worn and old,

330 the daughter of Tyndareus (tĭn-dăr'ē-əs): Helen. (Tyndareus, although not actually Helen's father, was the husband of her mother, Leda.)

335–336 her abandoned husband's anger: the anger of Menelaus, the husband Helen deserted to run off with Paris.

342 Sparta (spär'tə): the city ruled by Menelaus.

345 Phrygian (frĭj'ē-ən): Trojan.

347 littoral (lĭt'ər-əl): seashore.

360 my loving mother: Venus.

364 goad: drive; urge.

WORDS TO KNOW

reprove (rĭ-pro͞ov') *v.* to scold

Customizing Instruction

Less Proficient Readers

Focus Make sure students consider Aeneas' feelings about Helen before making their predictions.

1 Help students understand lines 316–322. Standing on the roof of the palace, Aeneas has just witnessed the murder of Priam, his king. He shudders in horror and recalls his own father, who is in great danger of being killed by the Greeks. Not only his father but also his wife, Creusa, and his son, Iulus, are in imminent danger. His loved ones are unprotected.

2 Make sure students understand what is happening in lines 356–362. The pronoun *her* in line 356 refers to Helen. Aeneas turns wildly upon Helen and is ready to kill her. But at that moment Aeneas' mother, the goddess Venus, appears. Grabbing her son's hand, she prevents him from killing Helen. Tell students to keep in mind that Aeneas is half-human and half-divine. His father is human; his mother, a goddess.

Advanced Learners

Ask students what Virgil does to convey the tragedy of Priam's murder.

Possible Responses: Virgil takes the reader inside Priam's mind, showing what he sees in his final moments after Pyrrhus has run him through with a sword. Moreover, Virgil contrasts what Priam once was—a king who "had ruled in pride so many lands and peoples"—with what he now is—a headless corpse.

Cross Curricular Link Humanities

MYTHOLOGY A victim of her own wondrous beauty, Helen of Troy was mainly responsible for the Trojan War. She was the daughter of Zeus (or Jupiter), the king of the gods, and Leda, a mortal woman. In her youth, she was kidnapped by Theseus, an Athenian hero, and later rescued by Castor and Pollux, her brothers. Wooed by many Grecian heroes, she eventually married Menelaus, King of Sparta. When visiting Sparta, Paris, the son of King Priam and Queen Hecuba of Troy, persuaded Helen to run off to Troy with him. Menelaus' brother Agamemnon then raised a huge army from all the islands of Greece and sailed to Troy to force the Trojans to return Helen. A war ensued. After Paris was slain in this war, Helen married his brother Deiphobus. After Troy was sacked, Helen and Menelaus were reunited.

Reading and Analyzing

Literary Analysis EPIC

A Remind students that supernatural characters sometimes appear in epics. Have students identify the supernatural characters in this passage.

Possible Response: The gods Neptune, Juno, Pallas Tritonia, and Jupiter ("The Father") are all at work destroying the city of Troy.

Literary Analysis EPIC SIMILE

B Ask students to explain the comparison in lines 400–408.

Possible Response: Troy, which is slowly burning to the ground, is compared to an old ash tree that is being chopped down. Eventually, the repeated ax-strokes cause the tree to topple to the ground.

Pause & Reflect

Possible Response: Aeneas' mother Venus intervenes, telling him to spare Helen's life and to return to his family.

Or find out if your wife, Creusa, lives,
And the young boy, Ascanius—all these
Cut off by Greek troops foraging everywhere?
1 Had I not cared for them, fire would by now
Have taken them, their blood glutted the sword.
You must not hold the woman of Laconia,
That hated face, the cause of this, nor Paris.
The harsh will of the gods it is, the gods,
That overthrows the splendor of this place
And brings Troy from her height into the dust.
Look over there: I'll tear away the cloud
That curtains you, and films your mortal sight,
The fog around you.—Have no fear of doing
Your mother's will, or balk at obeying her.—
Look: where you see high masonry thrown down,
Stone torn from stone, with billowing smoke and dust,
Neptune is shaking from their beds the walls
That his great trident pried up, undermining,
Toppling the whole city down. And look:
Juno in all her savagery holds
A The Scaean Gates, and raging in steel armor
Calls her allied army from the ships.
Up on the citadel—turn, look—Pallas Tritonia
Couched in a stormcloud, lightening, with her Gorgon!
The Father himself empowers the Danaans,
Urges assaulting gods on the defenders.
Away, child; put an end to toiling so.
I shall be near, to see you safely home.'

She hid herself in the deep gloom of night,
And now the dire forms appeared to me
Of great immortals, enemies of Troy.
I knew the end then: Ilium was going down
In fire, the Troy of Neptune going down,
As in high mountains when the countrymen
Have notched an ancient ash, then make their axes
Ring with might and main, chopping away
B To fell the tree—ever on the point of falling,
Shaken through all its foliage, and the treetop
Nodding; bit by bit the strokes prevail
Until it gives a final groan at last
And crashes down in ruin from the height.

370 foraging: plundering.

373 the woman of Laconia (lə-kō'nē-ə): Helen.

385 undermining: digging under the foundations.

390 Tritonia (trī-tō'nē-ə): a title of Pallas.

391 Gorgon: the monstrous Medusa, whose head Pallas bears on her shield.

Now I descended where the goddess guided,
Clear of the flames, and clear of enemies,
For both retired; so gained my father's door,
My ancient home. I looked for him at once,
My first wish being to help him to the mountains;
But with Troy gone he set his face against it,
Not to prolong his life, or suffer exile. . . .

PAUSE & REFLECT Why does Aeneas decide to spare Helen's life?

FOCUS Aeneas will try to lead his father, his wife, and his son through the burning city. Read to find out what happens to Aeneas' wife.

Unmoved by the protests of his family, Aeneas' father refuses to leave his home. However, he is finally
2 *persuaded by two divine signs. First, a small flame appears on the head of Iulus, Aeneas' son, touching the boy but not burning him. After Aeneas and his wife put out the flame, there comes the second sign—a crack of thunder outside, followed by a falling star.*

Now indeed
My father, overcome, addressed the gods,
And rose in worship of the blessed star.

Customizing Instruction

Less Proficient Readers

1 Tell students that in lines 371–372, the goddess Venus tells her son, Aeneas, that she has protected his family from death during the attack on Troy. The goddess has kept Aeneas' son alive so that he can journey to Italy with his father and found a dynasty. Ask students the following questions to review their understanding of lines 373–395:

- According to Venus, who is responsible for the fall of Troy? *(the gods)*
- Whom does Venus tell Aeneas to be concerned about? *(his family)*
- Who guides Aeneas to his home? *(Venus)*

Focus If necessary, guide students to look ahead to lines 462–469. These lines reveal that Aeneas loses track of Creusa in his flight from the burning city. Later, her ghost returns to console him.

2 Make sure that students read the italicized summary and that they identify the heavenly signs that induce Aeneas' father to leave Troy: the flame on his grandson's head and the falling star.

English Learners

Explain the meaning of the following words and phrases:

- *The Father* (line 392) refers to Jupiter, the king of the gods
- *Ilium was going down in fire* (lines 399–400) means that the city of Troy was burning to the ground
- *retired* (line 411) means "to fall back, or retreat"

Advanced Learners

Ask students how they would describe the relationship between Aeneas and his mother.

Possible Responses: Aeneas stands in awe of his mother, the goddess of love. He accepts her reprimand without question, recognizes the wisdom of her counsel, and readily obeys her command to follow her to his home.

AENEID 375

Reading and Analyzing

Active Reading PREDICTING

A Ask students if they think Aeneas will be able to rescue his father, son, and wife from the burning city.

Possible Response: Chances are slim that Aeneas can rescue all three because a fire is raging in the city and Greek warriors are marauding in the streets.

Literary Analysis CULTURE HERO

B Ask students to identify qualities the Romans might admire in Aeneas.

Possible Responses: reverence for the household gods, loyalty to his aged father, and loving concern for his little son

'Now, now, no more delay. I'll follow you.
Where you conduct me, there I'll be.
Gods of my fathers,
(A) Preserve this house, preserve my grandson. Yours
This portent was. Troy's life is in your power.
I yield. I go as your companion, son.'
Then he was still. We heard the blazing town
Crackle more loudly, felt the scorching heat.

'Then come, dear father. Arms around my neck:
I'll take you on my shoulders, no great weight.
Whatever happens, both will face one danger,
Find one safety. Iulus will come with me,
My wife at a good interval behind.
Servants, give your attention to what I say.
At the gate inland there's a funeral mound
And an old shrine of Ceres the Bereft;
Near it an ancient cypress, kept alive
For many years by our fathers' piety.
By various routes we'll come to that one place.
Father, carry our hearthgods, our Penatës.
It would be wrong for me to handle them—
Just come from such hard fighting, bloody work—
Until I wash myself in running water.'

(B) When I had said this, over my breadth of shoulder
And bent neck, I spread out a lion skin
For tawny cloak and stooped to take his weight.
Then little Iulus put his hand in mine
And came with shorter steps beside his father.
My wife fell in behind. Through shadowed places
On we went, and I, lately unmoved
By any spears thrown, any squads of Greeks,
Felt terror now at every eddy of wind,
Alarm at every sound, alert and worried
Alike for my companion and my burden.
I had got near the gate, and now I thought
We had made it all the way, when suddenly
A noise of running feet came near at hand,
And peering through the gloom ahead, my father

422 portent: a sign of future events; omen.

433 Ceres the Bereft: the goddess of grain, whose daughter Proserpina was stolen away by Pluto, god of the underworld.

MINI LESSON Grammar

SUBJECT COMPLEMENTS Remind students that a subject complement follows a linking verb and describes or renames the subject. There are two kinds of subject complements: predicate adjectives and predicate nominatives. Predicate adjectives describe subjects by telling *which one, what kind, how much,* or *how many.* Predicate nominatives are nouns or pronouns that rename, identify, or define subjects.

Instruction Write the following sentences on the chalkboard:

The heat was scorching.

Aeneas was a great warrior and leader.

Ask students to identify the linking verb and subject complements in each sentence (*was*, LV, *scorching*, PA; *was*, LV, *warrior*, PN, *leader*, PN).

Practice Have students identify the linking verb and subject complement(s) in each sentence. Students should write LV for linking verb, PA for predicate adjective, and PN for predicate nominative.

1. Troy became a city in ruins following the Greek attack. (*became*, LV; *city*, PN)
2. The fire was unstoppable. (*was*, LV; *unstoppable*, PA)

Cried out:
'Run, boy; here they come; I see
Flame light on shields, bronze shining.'
I took fright,
And some unfriendly power, I know not what,
Stole all my addled wits—for as I turned
Aside from the known way, entering a maze
Of pathless places on the run—
Alas,
Creusa, taken from us by grim fate, did she
Linger, or stray, or sink in weariness?
There is no telling. Never would she be
Restored to us. Never did I look back
Or think to look for her, lost as she was,
Until we reached the funeral mound and shrine
Of venerable Ceres. Here at last
All came together, but she was not there;
She alone failed her friends, her child, her husband.
Out of my mind, whom did I not accuse,
1 What man or god? What crueler loss had I
Beheld, that night the city fell? Ascanius,
My father, and the Teucrian Penatës,
I left in my friends' charge, and hid them well
In a hollow valley.
I turned back alone
Into the city, cinching my bright harness.
Nothing for it but to run the risks
Again, go back again, comb all of Troy,
And put my life in danger as before:
First by the town wall, then the gate, all gloom,
Through which I had come out—and so on backward,
Tracing my own footsteps through the night;
And everywhere my heart misgave me: even
Stillness had its terror. Then to our house,
Thinking she might, just might, have wandered there.
Danaans had got in and filled the place,
And at that instant fire they had set,
Consuming it, went roofward in a blast;
Flames leaped and seethed in heat to the night sky.
I pressed on, to see Priam's hall and tower.
In the bare colonnades of Juno's shrine
Two chosen guards, Phoenix and hard Ulysses,
Kept watch over the plunder. Piled up here

459 addled wits: confused powers of mind.

477 cinching: fastening tightly.

484 my heart misgave me: I had feelings of dread.

3. Aeneas grew fearful for his family. (*grew*, LV; *fearful*, PA)
4. Aeneas' father appeared distraught. (*appeared*, LV; *distraught*, PA)
5. The strange vision was the ghost of Creusa, Aeneas' wife. (*was*, LV; *ghost*, PN)

For more instruction and practice in subject complements, use McDougal Littell's ***Language Network:***

- Grade 10, Chapter 2, "The Sentence and Its Parts"
- Grade 12, Chapter 1, "The Parts of a Sentence"

Customizing Instruction

Less Proficient Readers

To check students' understanding of lines 426–470, ask the following questions:

- How does Aeneas rescue his father from the burning city? *(by carrying his father on his shoulders)*
- How does Aeneas rescue his son? *(by leading him by the hand from the burning city)*
- Who gets lost during the flight from the city? *(Aeneas' wife, Creusa)*

1 To help students understand and relate to Aeneas' disturbed state of mind, ask them to describe how they might feel if they lost a loved one in a panic-stricken crowd.

English Learners

Explain the meaning of the following words and phrases:

- *interval* (line 430) means "distance"
- *my companion and my burden* (line 451) refer to Aeneas' son, Iules, and his father, Anchises
- *venerable* (line 468) means "highly respected"
- *failed* (line 470) is short for "failed to meet"

Literary Analysis CULTURE HERO

(A) Tell students that Aeneas' divine mission is to establish a settlement in Italy that will one day evolve into the city of Rome. Then ask students how Creusa's ghost helps strengthen him for this mission.

Possible Response: She tells him to accept the will of the gods and describes what the future will bring after he leaves Troy. She exhorts him to focus on his mission and get over his grief for her.

Reading Skills and Strategies
EVALUATING

(B) Ask students to share their impressions of Aeneas as he and his wife part forever.

Possible Response: Aeneas deeply loves his wife and is distraught at losing her. He wishes he could disclose all that is in his heart.

Were treasures of old Troy from every quarter,
Torn out of burning temples: altar tables,
Robes, and golden bowls. Drawn up around them,
Boys and frightened mothers stood in line.
I even dared to call out in the night;
I filled the streets with calling; in my grief
Time after time I groaned and called Creusa,
Frantic, in endless quest from door to door.
Then to my vision her sad wraith appeared—
Creusa's ghost, larger than life, before me.
Chilled to the marrow, I could feel the hair
On my head rise, the voice clot in my throat;
But she spoke out to ease me of my fear:

'What's to be gained by giving way to grief
So madly, my sweet husband? Nothing here
Has come to pass except as heaven willed.
You may not take Creusa with you now;
It was not so ordained, nor does the lord
Of high Olympus give you leave. For you
Long exile waits, and long sea miles to plow.
You shall make landfall on Hesperia
Where Lydian Tiber flows, with gentle pace,
Between rich farmlands, and the years will bear
Glad peace, a kingdom, and a queen for you.
Dismiss these tears for your beloved Creusa.
I shall not see the proud homelands of Myrmidons
Or of Dolopians, or go to serve
Greek ladies, Dardan lady that I am
And daughter-in-law of Venus the divine.
No: the great mother of the gods detains me
Here on these shores. Farewell now; cherish still
Your son and mine.'
With this she left me weeping,
Wishing that I could say so many things,
And faded on the tenuous air. Three times
I tried to put my arms around her neck,
Three times enfolded nothing, as the wraith
Slipped through my fingers, bodiless as wind,
Or like a flitting dream.
So in the end
As night waned I rejoined my company.
And there to my astonishment I found

503 wraith: ghost.

515 Hesperia (hĕ-spîr′ē-ə): "western land"—that is, Italy.

516 Lydian Tiber (lĭd′ē-ən tī′bər): the river beside which Rome would be built—called Lydian here because it flowed through the lands of the Etruscans, who originally came from Lydia in Asia Minor.

WORDS TO KNOW

tenuous (tĕn′yo͞o′əs) *adj.* thin or flimsy

MINI LESSON Speaking and Listening

DRAMATIC READING

Prepare Ask students to present to the class a dramatic reading of the passage containing Creusa's farewell to Aeneas, lines 508–526. Students can work in small groups to discuss Creusa's qualities (caring, determined, inspiring) and how those qualities will affect their choice of verbal and nonverbal performance techniques (tone, volume, gestures, and so on). Remind students that Creusa is speaking directly to her husband, Aeneas, in this passage.

Present Have students present their dramatic reading. Students should be able to justify their choice of verbal and nonverbal performance techniques by referring to lines in the text and to their interpretation of Creusa's character. Audience members should evaluate how the performance increases their understanding of both Creusa and Aeneas.

This activity is particularly well suited for longer blocks of class time.

Scene from *Helen of Troy* (1955).

New refugees in a great crowd: men and women
Gathered for exile, young—pitiful people
Coming from every quarter, minds made up,
With their belongings, for whatever lands
I'd lead them to by sea.
                                        The morning star
Now rose on Ida's ridges, bringing day.
Greeks had secured the city gates. No help
Or hope of help existed.
So I resigned myself, picked up my father,
And turned my face toward the mountain range."

540 Ida's ridges: the crests of a mountain range near Troy.

Customizing Instruction

Less Proficient Readers

1 Make sure students understand that Aeneas' wife, Creusa, has died. Her ghost or spirit appears to Aeneas, who is wild with grief. Aeneas reacts in horror upon seeing his wife's ghost. His hair rises, and he cannot speak.

2 Help students understand what Creusa's ghost says to her husband. Trying to console him, she tells him that unlike other Trojan women, she will not be captured and enslaved by the Greeks and forced to leave her beloved Troy. Her death has saved her from the terrible fate the living Trojan women must suffer.

Then ask students these questions to check their comprehension of lines 526–544:

- What happens to Creusa's ghost after the meeting with Aeneas? *(She vanishes into the air.)*
- What does Aeneas decide to do as the selection ends? *(to lead the crowd of refugees across the sea)*

English Learners

Explain these phrases to the students:

- *long sea miles to plow* (line 514) means that Aeneas must travel many miles by sea before finally arriving in Italy
- *the great mother of the gods detains me* (line 524) means that the goddess Juno prevents the dead Creusa from leaving Troy
- *resigned myself* (line 543) means that Aeneas accepts that he can do nothing more to save Troy

Advanced Learners

Ask students to compare Creusa's effect on Aeneas with Venus' effect on him.

Possible Response: They both help Aeneas to get control over his emotions. Venus calms his anger; Creusa soothes his grief.

AENEID **379**

✓ Assessment Standardized Test Practice

WRITING A SHORT ESSAY ANSWER Have students write a short essay response to the following question. Prompt: "Do you think that heroism comes easily to Aeneas? In your answer consider the obstacles he faces and how he responds to them."

RUBRIC

3 Full Accomplishment Students write a well-organized essay with evidence from the epic poem. They state an opinion about Aeneas and heroism and support it with details that show his response to obstacles, such as the murder of Priam, the danger to his family, and the loss of Creusa.

2 Substantial Accomplishment Students write a logical essay with some evidence from the epic poem. They state an opinion about Aeneas and heroism and support it somewhat. However, the opinion needs more support, or the writing may have distracting spelling, grammar, and usage errors.

1 Little or Partial Accomplishment Students do not develop an opinion about Aeneas and heroism. The essay lacks structure and supporting details and may be somewhat incoherent, with many spelling, grammar, and usage errors.

Connect to the Literature

1. **What Do You Think?** What was your reaction to Aeneas' loss of his wife?

Comprehension Check
- What trick do the Greeks use to conquer Troy?
- How do Laocoön and his two sons die?
- What does Aeneas do to help his old father reach safety?

Think Critically

2. **ACTIVE READING: PREDICTING** What predictions did you make in your  **READER'S NOTEBOOK** as you read this epic poem? Discuss with a classmate the clues that prompted your predictions.
3. How would you describe the relationship between Aeneas and his wife?
4. Two supernatural characters appear to Aeneas: his mother (the goddess Venus) and the ghost of his wife. How would you compare these characters?
5. Do you think Aeneas always acts the way a hero should? Explain your opinion.

   THINK ABOUT
   - his flight with his family from the burning city
   - his intent to kill Helen
   - his reaction to the killing of Priam
6. What role does fate, or destiny, play in Aeneas' life?

Extend Interpretations

7. **The Writer's Style** As you know, a **simile** is a comparison that uses the word *like* or *as.* Virgil introduces **epic similes**—similes that extend over several lines—in lines 206–213 and 399–408. What makes each effective?
8. **Critic's Corner** Joe Paterno, longtime football coach at Penn State University, found the *Aeneid* deeply moving when he read it in high school: "Aeneas, as Virgil created him, was a totally new kind of epic hero. . . . He lives his life not for 'me' and 'I,' but for 'us' and 'we.' Aeneas is the ultimate team man." Do you agree with Paterno's view of Aeneas? Cite lines from the poem to support your opinion.
9. **Connect to Life** How would you compare Aeneas' qualities with those of the leaders you discussed for the Connect to Your Life activity on page 359?

LITERARY ANALYSIS: CULTURE HERO

A **culture hero** is a larger-than-life figure who reflects the values of a people. Such a hero serves as a model of conduct for everyone in the culture. To the Romans in the time of Augustus, Aeneas was a culture hero. His values were the values that Romans felt they should strive to imitate. One way to identify Aeneas' values is to contrast him with a **foil,** or opposing character, in the epic poem. Pyrrhus is one possible foil.

Paired Activity
With a partner, create a Venn diagram like the one below. In the overlapping area, write the qualities that Aeneas and Pyrrhus have in common. In the other parts of the circles, write the qualities that are unique to each character. Then discuss how the two characters differ. From what you know about the ancient Romans, what qualities would they admire in Aeneas?

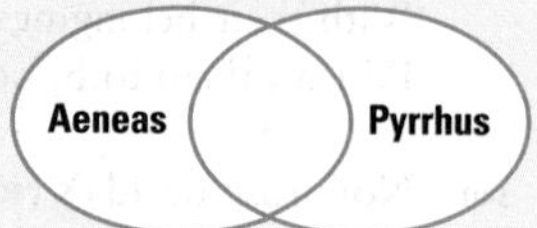

LITERARY ANALYSIS: IMAGERY

Imagery consists of descriptive words and phrases that re-create sensory experiences for the reader. Each image appeals to one or more of the five senses—sight, hearing, smell, taste, and touch. One of the most gripping episodes in the *Aeneid* is the description of the murder of Priam, the king of Troy, in lines 253–315. What images help you visualize the king's murder?

Connect to the Literature

1. **What Do You Think?** Most students will state that they were saddened by this loss and Aeneas' overwhelming grief.

Comprehension Check
- The Greeks construct a huge wooden horse and hide warriors inside it. When they are let out of the horse, these warriors open the city gates for their comrades to enter.
- They are strangled and crushed to death by sea serpents.
- Aeneas carries his father on his shoulders out of the burning city.

Use Selection Quiz in **Unit Two Resource Book,** p. 61.

Think Critically

2. Responses will vary. Students should cite specific lines in identifying the clues that support their predictions.
3. Possible Responses: They share a strong, loving relationship, based on mutual trust and concern. Aeneas nearly loses his mind when he discovers that his wife is lost. Creusa's spirit returns to comfort her husband and to help him resign himself to the will of the gods.
4. Possible Responses: Both characters intervene to calm Aeneas and to guide him to act with reason. Venus intervenes to prevent Aeneas from murdering Helen. Creusa intervenes to calm Aeneas, who is beside himself with grief over her loss.
5. Responses will vary. Some students may praise Aeneas, noting his great courage, his self-control, and his devotion to his family and city. He carries his father and holds his son by the hand to rescue them from the burning city. Other students may find his intent to kill Helen dishonorable, even though he is filled with grief and rage over the killing of Priam. These students may fault him for not challenging Pyrrhus, the murderer of Priam.
6. Possible Responses: Fate plays an important role in Aeneas' life. Were it not for fate, the Trojans would not have succumbed to the Greek trick of the wooden horse. The strangulation of Laocoön and his sons by sea serpents, however, fills the Trojans with dread, and they transport the wooden horse inside the city. Were it not for the omens he sees, Anchises might not have been persuaded to leave the city, and Aeneas and his family might have been slaughtered as a result.

Extend Interpretations

7. **The Writer's Style** Possible Response: Both epic similes create a vivid picture for the imagination. Students can picture Pyrrhus as an evil snake "all in bronze and glittering" and Troy itself as a huge ash tree crashing to the ground.
8. **Critic's Corner** Possible Response: Aeneas is the "ultimate team man" in that he comes to the aid of the defenders on the roof of Priam's palace. Rather than pursue private vengeance, he puts his family's safety first and rushes home to save his father, his wife, and his son. At the end of this excerpt, Aeneas joins the throng of comrades ready to follow him into exile.
9. **Connect to Life** In explaining their comparisons, students should note that Aeneas is a leader with great self-discipline. He puts the will of the gods first, not his personal desires.

Writing Options

1. Interview with Aeneas Write an interview for a newsmagazine, in which Aeneas discusses the role of fate, or destiny, in his life and his attitude toward the gods. Have Aeneas mention events that the gods controlled. Then have him explain how he felt about having little or no control over his future.

2. Creusa's Story What do you think happened to Creusa after she was separated from Aeneas during their flight from Troy? Write a dialogue in which Creusa's ghost tells more of her story to Aeneas.

3. Compare-and-Contrast Essay Whom do you admire more as a hero, Aeneas or Achilles, the hero of the *Iliad?* Why? Write a compare-and-contrast essay to explore your ideas.

Writing Handbook
See page R31: Compare and Contrast.

Activities & Explorations

1. Epic Storyboard Imagine that this excerpt from the *Aeneid* is to be made into part of a TV miniseries. You are planning a 30-second preview of the episode. With two or three classmates, prepare a storyboard—a series of sketches with captions—outlining the action of the preview. ~ **ART**

2. Oral Reading Imagine yourself as Aeneas, describing your adventures to Queen Dido at a banquet. Prepare an oral reading of a dramatic episode, such as the murder of Priam or your frantic search for Creusa. Practice reading with the appropriate tone of voice, pauses, and changes in pitch and volume. Then present your reading to the class. ~ **PERFORMING**

Inquiry & Research

Roman Influences The influence of Roman culture extends beyond literature. With a few classmates, find out more about Roman civilization and its effect upon later cultures of the world. Each group member may wish to do further research in one of the following categories, which are introduced on pages 350–351: Religion, Law and Government, Architecture and Engineering, Art and Sculpture.

Vocabulary in Action

EXERCISE: WORD MEANINGS For each sentence, write *T* if the statement is true or *F* if it is false.

1. Snakes are reptiles that **writhe,** or twist.
2. If you **reprove** your younger brother, you praise him.
3. A **tenuous** agreement is likely to be broken.
4. A **gaping** woman keeps her lips shut tight.
5. Some people seek a **respite** from their troubles by walking through the woods.
6. A **sinister** person is someone you can trust.
7. A **prodigious** weight is easy to lift.
8. Pretending to be ill can be a **ruse** to avoid work.
9. Fields of wheat blowing in the wind can be described as **undulating.**
10. Sometimes, the sky at sunset appears **suffused** with a rosy glow.

Building Vocabulary
For an in-depth lesson on using context clues, see page 674.

Writing Options

1. **Interview with Aeneas** To get students started on this assignment, have them recall the ideas they discussed for question 6 on page 380. Tell students to imagine themselves in Aeneas' situation and to consider how they might feel to be used as a tool of the gods.
2. **Creusa's Story** To make the assignment more challenging, have Creusa's ghost describe how she and Aeneas were separated. Both Creusa and Aeneas should remain true to character in the dialogue.
3. **Compare-and-Contrast Essay** To get students started on this assignment, have them make a Venn diagram similar to the one they used for the Literary Analysis activity. Tell students to consider which character is more courageous and successful in battle and which shows greater devotion to family and nation.

Activities & Explorations

1. **Epic Storyboard** Explain that a storyboard is a visual outline of a movie containing one drawing per camera shot. A storyboard should include instructions for camera angles, character positions, costumes, props, gestures, and backgrounds.
2. **Oral Reading** Encourage students to explain why they chose to emphasize certain words, phrases, and lines when reading the episode.

Inquiry & Research

Roman Influence Encourage students to use both print and electronic sources in their research. An excellent overview of Roman culture is found in Edith Hamilton's *The Roman Way* (W•W• Norton & Company, 1932).

Literary Analysis

Paired Activity Both Aeneas and Pyrrhus are brave and skilled in battle. Aeneas, however, is more sensitive and humane. Nothing ever restrains Pyrrhus. For example, he butchers Priam after killing the king's son before his father's eyes. Aeneas, however, turns away from killing Helen at his mother's request. The Romans would admire Aeneas' rationality, concern for his family, and obedience to the gods.

Use **Unit Two Resource Book,** p. 59, for more practice.

Imagery Students may mention several images, such as the following: "slipping in the pooled blood of his son," "took him by the hair with his left hand," "the sword flashed in his right," and "the vast trunk headless lies."

Vocabulary in Action

1. T	6. F
2. F	7. F
3. T	8. T
4. F	9. T
5. T	10. T

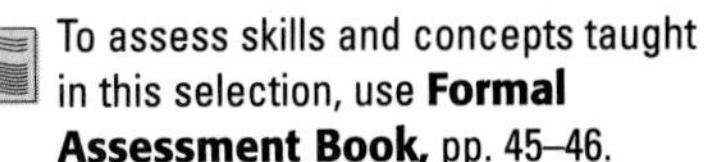

To assess skills and concepts taught in this selection, use **Formal Assessment Book,** pp. 45–46.

Assign both "Helen of Troy" by Sara Teasdale and "To Helen" by Edgar Allan Poe to prepare students for the sample writing assessment provided on page 391. Use the **Points of Comparison** chart to guide students in identifying the similarities and differences between the two selections.

 Use **Unit Two Resource Book,** p. 62, for more practice.

COMPARING LITERATURE ACROSS CULTURES

Perspectives on Helen of Troy

OVERVIEW

The epics, myths, and legends of ancient Greece and Rome have stirred the imagination of writers for centuries. When modern writers return to the classic stories and characters, they often bring fresh perspectives.

This lesson includes two well-known poems about Helen of Troy—one by the 20th-century American writer Sara Teasdale, the other by the 19th-century American writer Edgar Allan Poe. As you may recall, Virgil's Aeneas hated Helen because he blamed her for the destruction of Troy. These two poems provide a more sympathetic view of Helen. In the pages that follow, you will be asked to compare and contrast the treatments of Helen in these poems. Your comparisons should help you appreciate how modern writers can breathe new life into the classics.

Points of Comparison

Use a chart like the one shown to take notes about each poem. The questions in the chart should help you identify similarities and differences in the poems. If other questions come to mind, feel free to add them to your chart. You may also replace questions in the chart with ones of your own.

	"Helen of Troy," Sara Teasdale	"To Helen," Edgar Allan Poe
Who is the speaker of the poem? How would you describe the speaker?		
What emotions are expressed by the speaker? Which lines help you identify those emotions?		
In your opinion, which poem presents a more favorable view of Helen?		
In your opinion, which poem is more memorable? Why?		

Standardized Test Practice: Comparison-and-Contrast Essay After you finish reading the two poems, you will have the opportunity to write a comparison-and-contrast essay. Your notes will help you plan and write the essay.

 Assessment **Standardized Test Practice**

COMPARISON-AND-CONTRAST ESSAY To provide practice to students in comparing two different pieces of literature, have them read both selections in this **Comparing Literature** feature, rather than treating each selection separately. Have them work with the chart shown here on page 382, filling it out as they finish reading each of the two poems. (Examples of how to fill out the chart are supplied on pages 387 and 390.) A sample assessment writing prompt and guidelines for responding to it in writing are on page 391.

HELEN of TROY

~ Sara Teasdale ~

Sara Teasdale
1884–1933

A Popular and Honored Poet
Sara Teasdale was born and educated in St. Louis, Missouri. Her first volume of poetry, published in 1907, was praised for the delicate simplicity of the verse. In 1911 she published *Helen of Troy and Other Poems.* The first group of poems in this collection focuses on famous women of history, myth, and legend. In 1918 her book *Love Songs* won the Columbia University Poetry Society prize, the forerunner of the Pulitzer Prize in poetry. Although her works were widely read, her personal life was unhappy. Shy and withdrawn, she avoided public appearances and remained in semiseclusion after an unhappy marriage. She died at the age of 48, after a bout with pneumonia.

Build Background

"Helen of Troy" is set at daybreak, immediately after the Greek victory over the Trojans. As you may recall, the Greeks had built an enormous wooden horse, in which soldiers were hidden. The Trojans, tricked into believing that the horse was an offering to a goddess, had brought the horse into Troy. In the dark of night, the Greek soldiers emerged from the horse and attacked the city, killing many Trojans and setting fire to buildings. As the poem begins, Helen is looking at the flames of the burning city and reflecting on her life.

Connect to Your Life

According to legend, Helen of Troy was the most beautiful woman of the ancient world. Do you think that people gifted with physical beauty have an easier time in life than those who are ordinary in appearance? Are beautiful people and ordinary-looking ones treated differently? Use examples from your own experience to support your opinion.

Focus Your Reading

LITERARY ANALYSIS: SPEAKER

The **speaker** of a poem is the voice that "talks" in the poem, like the narrator in a story. In this poem, the poet has created a speaker far different from herself—the legendary Helen of Troy. By allowing Helen to speak for herself, the poet gives the reader a unique perspective on the events of the Trojan War.

ACTIVE READING: MAKING INFERENCES

As you read this poem, you will need to make **inferences,** or logical guesses, about its meaning. To make inferences about Helen, you will need to combine what you already know about her with what she states about herself. For example, she states that "I am she who loves all beauty—yet I wither it." You already know that Greeks battled the Trojans because of Helen. Her statement allows you to infer that she blames herself for the destruction of Troy.

READER'S NOTEBOOK As you read, record your inferences about Helen in your notebook.

Objectives

- understand and compare two **poems** about Helen of Troy **(Literary Analysis)**
- describe the **speaker** in each poem **(Literary Analysis)**
- **make inferences** about the speaker **(Active Reading)**

Thematic Link

These poems present different views of Helen of Troy, a classic figure from the **heroic tradition.**

5-Minute Warm-Up

Daily Language SkillBuilder

Have students **proofread** the display sentences on page 161i and write them correctly.

TIME MANAGEMENT

If you wish to cover only one of the selections, use . . .

- Preparing to Read, p. 383 or p. 388
- Thinking Through the Literature, p. 387 or p. 390

If you want to take advantage of longer blocks of class time, use . . .

- TE Teaching Options: Viewing and Representing, p. 385; Speaking and Listening, pp. 386, 389

Reading Skills and Strategies
PREVIEWING
Tell students to skim through the pages of this lesson and to note that it contains two poems by two different authors. These two poems concern Helen of Troy, whom students may recall from their reading of Homer's *Iliad* or Virgil's *Aeneid*. If students need additional background about Helen of Troy to understand these poems, share with them the information in the Cross Curricular Link on page 373.

Literary Analysis SPEAKER
Have students work with a partner to take turns reading the poem aloud and to brainstorm a list of questions about the speaker, Helen of Troy. Then as students reread the poem, have them look for answers to their questions.
Possible Questions: Why have the gods spared Helen's life? How does she feel about the evil she has caused? What might happen when she and her former husband meet again?

Use **Unit Two Resource Book,** p. 64, for more practice.

Active Reading MAKING INFERENCES
Remind students that writers often expect readers to make inferences, or to read between the lines. This is especially true when reading poetry. Readers must use details in the poem to infer what is suggested but not directly stated. To introduce this skill, read aloud the first five lines of the poem, and then call students' attention to details such as "the flames' red wings soar upward," "the funeral pyre," and "Troy is dead." From these details, students should infer that Troy is on fire and falling to ruin.

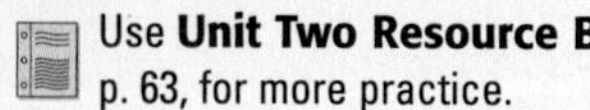
Use **Unit Two Resource Book,** p. 63, for more practice.

Helen of Troy

Sara Teasdale

1

Wild flight on flight against the fading dawn
The flames' red wings soar upward duskily.
This is the funeral pyre and Troy is dead
That sparkled so the day I saw it first,
And darkened slowly after. I am she
Who loves all beauty—yet I wither it.
Why have the high gods made me wreak their wrath—
Forever since my maidenhood to sow
Sorrow and blood about me? See, they keep
Their bitter care above me even now.
It was the gods who led me to this lair,
That though the burning winds should make me weak,
They should not snatch the life from out my lips.
Olympus let the other women die;
They shall be quiet when the day is done
And have no care to-morrow. Yet for me
There is no rest. The gods are not so kind
To her made half immortal like themselves.

It is to you I owe the cruel gift,
Leda, my mother, and the Swan, my sire,
To you the beauty and to you the bale;
For never woman born of man and maid
Had wrought such havoc on the earth as I,
Or troubled heaven with a sea of flame
That climbed to touch the silent whirling stars,
Blotting their brightness out before the dawn.
Have I not made the world to weep enough?
Give death to me.

3 pyre: a fire for burning a dead body.

6 wither it: cause it to fade.

7 wreak: inflict.

11 lair: hiding place.

18 half immortal: Helen was fathered by Jupiter, king of the gods, in the form of a swan; her mother, Leda, was human.

21 bale: evil.

LESSON RESOURCES

UNIT TWO RESOURCE BOOK, pp. 62–65

ASSESSMENT RESOURCES
Formal Assessment, pp. 47–48
Teacher's Guide to Assessment and Portfolio Use
Test Generator

INTEGRATED TECHNOLOGY
Visit our Web site: classzone.com

ADDITIONAL RESOURCES
Lesson Planning Guide, pp. 39–40
Teacher's Sourcebook for Language Development

Detail of *Helen of Troy* (1863), Dante Gabriel Rossetti. Oil on canvas, 38.2 cm × 27.7 cm. Inv. 2469. Hamburger Kunsthalle, Hamburg, Germany. Photo © Elke Walford/Bildarchiv Preussischer Kulturbesitz/Art Resource, New York.

HUMANITIES CONNECTION Dante Gabriel Rossetti, one of the most famous painters of the 1800s, was inspired by the theme of romantic love. The bright colors and sharp details in this painting of Helen of Troy are typical of his style.

2 Yet life is more than death;
How could I leave the sound of singing winds,
The strong clean scent that breathes from off the sea,
Or shut my eyes forever to the spring?
I will not give the grave my hands to hold,
My shining hair to light oblivion.
Have those who wander through the ways of death,
The still wan fields Elysian, any love
To lift their breasts with longing, any lips
To thirst against the quiver of a kiss?

33 oblivion (ə-blĭv'ē-ən): forgetfulness.

35 wan fields Elysian (ĭ-lĭzh'ən): pale land of the dead.

Customizing Instruction

Less Proficient Readers

- As with the *Aeneid*, tell students to read for complete sentences, pausing at the end of a line only if they come upon a mark of punctuation. Students should stop after each stanza to check their understanding, using the sidenotes to clarify difficult words and passages.
- Tell students that the poem falls into three sections: lines 1–28—Helen's reaction to the destruction of Troy; lines 28–63—Helen's desire to live and triumph, even if she is not loved for herself; lines 64–73—Helen's imagined meeting with her Greek husband, Menelaus

1 To get students started, tell them the speaker Helen has gone into hiding and is watching as Troy burns to the ground. She compares the thrust of the flames to the flight of birds.

English Learners

2 Call attention to the conjunction *yet* in line 28. Tell students that this word, like the word *but* or *however*, signals a contrast or a shift in thought. Explain the meaning of the following words and phrases:

- *snatch the life from out my lips* (line 13) means "cause me to die"
- *made the world to weep enough* (line 27) means "brought great suffering to the world"
- *sum* (line 51) means "the entire amount"

Advanced Learners

After students have read the poem, ask them to trace the pattern of light and dark imagery, beginning with "sparkled" in line 4 and "darkened" in line 5.

Possible Responses: "Blotting their brightness out before the dawn" (line 26), "My shining hair to light oblivion" (line 33), "the lands that lie beneath the sun" (line 48), "Till light turn darkness" (line 49), "Limned on the darkness like a shaft of light/ That glimmers and is gone" (lines 56–57), "lakes that glint beneath the stars/ Dark as sweet midnight" (lines 59–60), "hair aglow/ Like burnished gold" (lines 60–61), "the dusk of time" (line 62), and "to stain with blood/ That whiteness" (lines 69–70)

MINI LESSON Viewing and Representing

Helen of Troy **by Dante Gabriel Rossetti**

ART APPRECIATION Have students read the **Humanities Connection** caption and study the reproduction of the painting. Dante Gabriel Rossetti (1828–1882) was a British painter and poet. In 1848, he helped found an art movement known as the Pre-Raphaelite Brotherhood. It sought to imitate the simple, natural style of Italian painting in the early 1500s, before the time of Raphael. Tell students that Rossetti's paintings are known for their rich colors and striking details. Ask students to identify these qualities in *Helen of Troy.*

Possible Responses: Helen's cheeks and hands have a faint flush, and her lips are tinted red. Her eyes are prominent and arresting. Her gown is golden with red and white streaks. Her necklace is an intricate pattern of green and white. Helen's hair, a golden brown, has distinct strands and highlights.

Literary Analysis SPEAKER

A This passage is crucial to an understanding of Helen. Ask students what Helen believes men loved about her and what they failed to love.
Possible Response: Men loved her physical features and failed to love her spiritual depths.

Literary Analysis SIMILE

B Remind students that a simile is a figure of speech that makes a comparison, using the word *like* or *as*. Have students identify the similes in this passage.
Possible Responses: "hair like lakes that glint beneath the stars," "[lakes]dark as sweet midnight, " and "hair aglow like burnished gold."

Active Reading MAKING INFERENCES

C To understand the ending of the poem, students must infer what will happen when Menelaus and Helen meet again. Ask students why Menelaus will be unable to take revenge on Helen.
Possible Response: He will be enthralled by her beauty, powerless to stain his sword with her blood. Instead, he will embrace her.

I shall live on to conquer Greece again,
To make the people love, who hate me now.
My dreams are over, I have ceased to cry
Against the fate that made men love my mouth
And left their spirits all too deaf to hear
The songs that echoed always in my soul.

I have no anger now. The dreams are done;
Yet since the Greeks and Trojans would not see
Aught but my body's fairness, till the end,
In all the islands set in all the seas,
And all the lands that lie beneath the sun,
Till light turn darkness, and till time shall sleep,
Men's lives shall waste with longing after me,
For I shall be the sum of their desire,
The whole of beauty, never seen again.
And they shall stretch their arms and starting, wake,
With "Helen!" on their lips, and in their eyes
The vision of me. Always I shall be
Limned on the darkness like a shaft of light
That glimmers and is gone. They shall behold
Each one his dream that fashions me anew;—
With hair like lakes that glint beneath the stars
Dark as sweet midnight, or with hair aglow
Like burnished gold that still retains the fire.
I shall be haunting till the dusk of time
The heavy eyelids that are filled with dreams.

I wait for one who comes with sword to slay—
The king I wronged who searches for me now;
And yet he shall not slay me. I shall stand
With lifted head and look into his eyes,
Baring my breast to him and to the sun.
He shall not have the power to stain with blood
That whiteness—for the thirsty sword shall fall
And he shall cry and catch me in his arms.
I shall go back to Sparta on his breast.
I shall live on to conquer Greece again!

46 aught: anything.

56 limned (lĭmd)**:** painted.

61 burnished: polished.

65 The king I wronged: Menelaus, the husband Helen betrayed by running off with Paris to Troy.

MINI LESSON **Speaking and Listening**

POETRY READING WORKSHOP

Prepare Explain to students that the language of poetry is meant to be read and heard aloud. Organize students into pairs and have each pair practice reading excerpts from "Helen of Troy." As students practice reading their excerpts aloud, they should concentrate on hearing rhythms and on changing pace and pitch to match content.

Present Have students present oral interpretations of the poem. Students in each pair can take turns reading lines or passages. Discuss as a class the different interpretations. Students should show that they have used effective listening strategies.

This activity is particularly well suited for longer blocks of class time.

Connect to the Literature

1. **What Do You Think?** Do you admire the determination that Helen expresses in the last line of the poem? Explain.

Comprehension Check
- How does Helen feel about surviving Troy's destruction?
- Does Helen believe that her beauty will eventually fade?
- Does Helen think that her husband will forgive her?

Think Critically

2. **ACTIVE READING: MAKING INFERENCES** Review the inferences you recorded in your READER'S NOTEBOOK. On the basis of your inferences, how would you describe Helen's difficulties?
3. Helen's feelings change significantly over the course of the poem. Review the sections of the poem and identify the feelings expressed in each.
4. In your opinion, is Helen's beauty more a blessing or a curse to her? Use quotations from the poem to support your judgment.
5. Do you think Helen takes personal responsibility for the destruction of Troy? Use evidence from the poem to support your conclusion.

LITERARY ANALYSIS: SPEAKER

In a poem, the **speaker** is the voice imagined as speaking the poem's words. Sometimes the speaker can be identified with the poet; but in the case of "Helen of Troy," the speaker is clearly not Sara Teasdale. Helen speaks for herself, so that the reader sees the events of the war from her point of view.

Paired Activity With a partner, create two descriptions of Helen's character. The first should present Helen's view of herself, as conveyed by the poem. The second should present Helen from the point of view of another person—her husband, perhaps, or a Trojan woman whose husband has been killed in battle. Share the descriptions with your classmates, and discuss which one is closer to your own view of Helen.

Points of Comparison

Paired Activity With a partner, review "Helen of Troy," using the questions in your comparison-and-contrast chart to help you analyze the poem. Fill in your answers to the questions pertaining to "Helen of Troy." Don't forget that you can change or add to the questions.

	"Helen of Troy," Sara Teasdale	"To Helen," Edgar Allan Poe
Who is the speaker of the poem? How would you describe the speaker?		
What emotions are expressed by the speaker? Which lines help you identify those emotions?	bitterness (lines 7–10, lines 14–18)	
In your opinion, which poem presents a more favorable view of Helen?		
In your opinion, which poem is more memorable? Why?		

Connect to the Literature

1. **What Do You Think?** Answers will vary: Some students may admire Helen's determination as a sign of her strength of spirit in dire circumstances. Others may say that her determination reflects her ruthless streak.

Comprehension Check
- She wishes the gods had not spared her life.
- No, she believes that her beauty is immortal.
- Yes, because her husband will be unable to resist her beauty.

Think Critically

2. Possible Response: Helen's life is difficult because her godlike beauty causes men to love her appearance ("men love my mouth") and utterly miss what she is like inside ("their spirits all too deaf to hear/ The songs . . . in my soul").
3. Possible Response: section 1, remorse for having caused the destruction of Troy and bitterness at being spared by the gods; section 2, longing for death; section 3, joy in the pleasures of life and regret over not being loved for herself; section 4, pride in the realization that she will haunt men's dreams forever; section 5, joy and determination in her imagined victory over her husband.
4. Answers will vary. Students who think that Helen's beauty is primarily a blessing may state that her beauty will enable her to subdue her enraged husband (lines 64–73) and to reign as the ideal of beauty for all time (lines 50–55). Students who think that Helen's beauty is primarily a curse may state that Helen is deeply frustrated because she is sought after only for her physical attractiveness (lines 40–43). These students may also point out that Helen's beauty has caused terrible suffering (lines 3–6).
5. Possible Responses: Yes, because she admits that she "withers" all beauty and has brought great destruction into the world; no, because she sees herself as a mere tool of the gods, who ultimately control what happens (line 7, "Why have the high gods made me wreak their wrath—").

Literary Analysis

Paired Activity Students should conclude that Helen's view of herself is complex and paradoxical. She sees her beauty as a "cruel gift"—a godlike power that has caused great destruction. She also sees herself as doomed by the gods to inflict suffering on the world. Her husband's perspective of her—or that of a Trojan widow—probably would be one-sided and highly critical of Helen for precipitating the Trojan War.

Use **Unit Two Resource Book**, p. 64, for more practice.

Points of Comparison

Remind students that they don't have to have the same opinion as their partner does.

5-Minute Warm-Up

Daily Language SkillBuilder

Have students **proofread** the display sentences on page 161i and write them correctly.

PREPARING to *Read*

The poem by Sara Teasdale has given you one view of Helen—a portrait in her own words. Now you will see Helen from a very different perspective. Edgar Allan Poe's "To Helen" presents Helen from a male point of view.

Edgar Allan Poe
1809–1849

A Troubled Youth The son of traveling actors, Edgar Poe was orphaned at an early age and taken in by a wealthy Virginian couple. A moody adolescent, Poe began attending the University of Virginia. His heavy debts, however, led to a quarrel with his adoptive father, and he was forced to leave school. Later he was expelled from the U.S. Military Academy at West Point in 1831.

A Short Career Poe began his writing career by publishing a pamphlet of poems in 1827. He also worked as an editor and wrote stories and literary reviews, but money was scarce. For the most part, he was ignored until he won a literary prize in 1843. Illness, poverty, and the death of his beloved wife, Virginia, limited his literary production. Poe died at the age of 40 after being found sick and delirious on the streets of Baltimore.

An American Master Despite his troubled life, Poe was an originator of the modern short story and pioneered the detective mystery. His haunting poems are notable for their insistent sound effects, and his horror tales established him as a master of psychological terror.

Build Background

"To Helen" Poe seems to have been fascinated with the idea of Helen of Troy. Critics, however, are divided in their interpretations of "To Helen." Some believe that the poem is a tribute to the legendary Helen, a symbol of beauty. Others think that the poem was written about an actual woman, one whose beauty reminded Poe of the legendary Helen.

Detail of *Helen of Troy* (late 19th-early 20th century), Evelyn de Morgan. National Trust Photographic Library/From the De Morgan Foundation.

To Helen

Edgar Allan Poe

Helen, thy beauty is to me
Like those Nicean barks of yore,
That gently, o'er a perfumed sea,
The weary, way-worn wanderer bore
To his own native shore.

On desperate seas long wont to roam,
Thy hyacinth hair, thy classic face,
Thy Naiad airs have brought me home
To the glory that was Greece
And the grandeur that was Rome.

Lo! in yon brilliant window-niche
How statue-like I see thee stand!
The agate lamp within thy hand,
Ah! Psyche, from the regions which
Are Holy Land!

2 Nicean (nī-sē′ən) **barks:** ships of the ancient Mediterranean world.

6 wont: accustomed.

7 hyacinth (hī′ə-sĭnth): dark and curling.

8 Naiad (nā′əd): manner like that of a Greek goddess of streams.

13–14 The agate lamp . . . Psyche (sī′kē): In an ancient tale, the young woman Psyche used an oil lamp to view her sleeping husband—Venus' son Cupid—who had forbidden her to behold him.

Customizing Instruction

Less Proficient Readers

- Tell students they will enjoy this poem more and understand it better if they read it several times, pausing after each stanza to paraphrase the meaning.
- Tell students that when they come upon inverted word order, as in lines 3–5 and 11–12, they might try to put the words into the normal sequence. For example, the words in lines 3–5 might be rearranged as follows: "That gently bore the weary, way-worn wanderer o'er a perfumed sea to his own native shore."
- Explain that to the speaker "home" means experiencing Greek and Roman civilizations. Since Helen embodies the excellence of these civilizations, her beauty allows the speaker to experience the classical world.

English Learners

Students will have difficulty with Poe's diction, which is poetic and archaic. Explain to students the meaning of the following words and phrases:

- *thy* (line 1): your
- *barks* (line 2): ships
- *yore* (line 2): long ago
- *o'er* (line 3): over (the apostrophe replaces the letter *v*)
- *native shore* (line 5): place of birth
- *grandeur* (line 10): great size and beauty
- *yon* (line 11): that one

Advanced Learners

Have students research the myth of Cupid and Psyche and then use the information to explain in detail the allusion in line 14 of the poem.

MINI LESSON Speaking and Listening

DRAMATIC READING

Prepare This poem is particularly appropriate for a dramatic reading because of Poe's mastery of the techniques of sound—for example, alliteration, assonance, rhythm, and rhyme. Share with students these tips for dramatic reading:

- Identify with the feelings of the speaker.
- Read the poem several times so you know the language, rhyme, and rhythm.
- Read the poem naturally, emphasizing important words and phrases.
- Pause at the end of each complete thought, not necessarily at the ends of lines. Look for end punctuation to help you.
- Practice reading aloud, using a tape recorder if possible.

Present Have students work in groups of three to present a dramatic reading of "To Helen," with each student responsible for one stanza. Students should mark words to emphasize and places to pause. Audience members should assess how the performances enhance their understanding of the poem and the speaker.

This activity is particularly well suited for longer blocks of class time.

COMPARING LITERATURE ACROSS CULTURES 389

Connect to the Literature

1. **What Do You Think?**
Questions will vary. Some students may wonder about the allusion to Psyche at the end of the poem.

Comprehension Check
- "hyacinth hair" and "classic face"
- Helen standing in a window-niche, lamp in hand, calls to mind Psyche viewing her sleeping husband.

Think Critically

2. Possible Response: The speaker regards Helen as his inspiration and the guide to his spiritual home.
3. Possible Response: Helen's beauty epitomizes the ideals of classical perfection reflected in Greco-Roman civilization.
4. Responses will vary. The speaker addresses a supremely beautiful woman—if not the legendary Helen, then one whose beauty seems ideal and timeless.

Extend Interpretations

5. **The Writer's Style** Responses will vary. Students who think that Poe exaggerates the power of beauty may state that beauty is fleeting, subjective, and superficial. Students who think that Poe does not exaggerate the power of beauty may state that beauty has inspired countless writers and painters through the centuries.

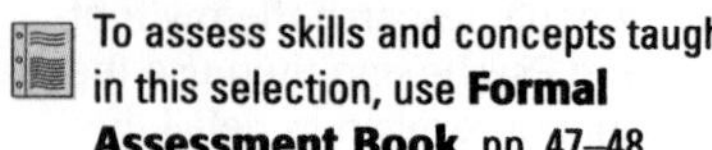
To assess skills and concepts taught in this selection, use **Formal Assessment Book,** pp. 47–48.

Points of Comparison

After students have completed their chart, initiate a class discussion on which poem is more memorable and why.

Connect to the Literature

1. **What Do You Think?**
Write down two questions that you have about the poem. Share them with your classmates, and see if anyone can answer them.

Comprehension Check
- List two details in the poem that describe Helen's beauty.
- What scene is described in the last stanza?

Think Critically

2. In the first stanza the speaker compares Helen to ancient ships that brought the "weary, way-worn wanderer" home. What does this comparison suggest about the speaker's attitude toward Helen?
3. In the second stanza the speaker refers to Greece and Rome in the past tense, which suggests that he is living in a different time. How might the beauty of Helen help to connect the speaker to "the glory that was Greece / And the grandeur that was Rome"?
4. Do you think the poem is about Helen of Troy, or is it about an actual woman who reminds the speaker of the legendary beauty? Can it be about both? Explain your reasoning.

Extend Interpretations

5. **The Writer's Style** Because of her beauty, Poe's Helen seems to possess a kind of godlike power. Do you think Poe exaggerates the power of beauty? Why or why not?

Points of Comparison

Paired Activity Now that you have read both poems about Helen, complete rows 1 and 2 of your comparison-and-contrast chart. Then work with a partner to discuss any remaining questions that you have and to complete the rest of the chart.

	Helen of Troy," Sara Teasdale	"To Helen," Edgar Allan Poe
Who is the speaker of the poem? How would you describe the speaker?		The speaker is an admirer of Helen.
What emotions are expressed by the speaker? Which lines help you identify those emotions?	bitterness (lines 7–10, lines 14–18)	
In your opinion, which poem presents a more favorable view of Helen?		
In your opinion, which poem is more memorable? Why?		

Writing About Literature

PART 1 Reading the Prompt

In writing assessments, you may be asked to compare and contrast works of literature with a common subject, such as the two poems about Helen of Troy that you have just read. You are now going to practice writing an essay that involves this type of comparison.

Writing Prompt

Helen of Troy has fascinated writers for centuries. Compare and contrast the two perspectives on Helen provided by Sara Teasdale and Edgar Allan Poe. (1) Consider what you learn about the two poems' speakers, and identify the emotions expressed in each poem. (2) In your opinion, which poem provides a more favorable view of Helen? Which is the more memorable poem? (3) Support your analysis with details and quotations from the poems. (4)

STRATEGIES IN ACTION

1. I have to **compare and contrast** two poems.
2. For each poem, I need to discuss the **speaker** and the emotions expressed.
3. I need to decide which poem is more favorable toward Helen and which is more memorable.
4. I need to include **details** and **quotations** from the poems to support my analysis.

PART 2 Planning a Comparison-and-Contrast Essay

- Review the comparison-and-contrast chart that you completed for the Points of Comparison features in this lesson.
- Using your chart, find examples of similarities and differences to point out in your essay. If necessary, review the poems again to find more evidence.
- Create an outline to organize your ideas.

PART 3 Drafting Your Essay

Introduction After introducing Helen of Troy to the reader, share your thoughts about why so much has been written about her. Then explain that you will be comparing two poems and identify the basis of your comparison. Describe what you found to be the most interesting similarity or difference in the poems.

Body You might use the questions in your comparison-and-contrast chart as a guide to the key points of your comparison. In one paragraph, for example, you might compare and contrast the speakers of the poems.

Conclusion Wrap up your essay with a summary of the poems' major differences and similarities.

Revision Check your use of signal words, such as *by contrast, similarly, also, both,* and *in the same way.* Make sure that the connections between your ideas are clear.

TEST PRACTICE

PART 1 Reading the Prompt
Model the process of reading a prompt.

- Read through the prompt in its entirely.
- List key words of the assignment on the board("Compare and contrast," "evidence").
- Define each key word using **Strategies in Action** to show how students can restate the prompts in their own words.

PART 2 Planning a Comparison-Contrast Essay
Model the process of planning a comparison-contrast essay.

- Read through the points listed in each row of the chart.
- Circle the similarities and underline the differences.
- Place a star next to the most important similarity or difference.
- Complete rows 3 and 4 of the chart.
- List the points to develop from least to most important.

PART 3 Drafting Your Essay
Introduction Tell students that the opening paragraph must introduce the comparison and attract the audience's attention. Opening with a question is an effective technique for attracting attention.
Body Tell students to try using feature-by-feature order, comparing and contrasting the characteristics of each poem, one characteristic at a time. Encourage students to use plenty of examples to bring their writing to life.
Conclusion Remind students that effective conclusions briefly restate the main points and leave the reader with something interesting to think about.
Revision Students should review their drafts to make sure that the organization is clear and that the language is direct and easy to understand.

Use **Unit Two Resource Book,** p. 65, for additional support.

Assessment Standardized Test Practice

RESPONDING TO A WRITING PROMPT Read aloud the writing prompt at the top of this page. Discuss the **Strategies in Action** by asking students to identify the words in the prompt that tell them what to do. Suggest that they mark up their comparison-and-contrast charts, identifying points to include in their essays. When students have finished drafting their essays, have them work with a partner to see if they have accomplished the tips given in Part 3 **Drafting Your Essay.**

Objectives

- understand and appreciate two **poems** by Horace **(Literary Analysis)**
- examine the **theme** of each of these poems **(Literary Analysis)**
- understand the use of **contrast** in these poems **(Active Reading)**

Thematic Link

These poems convey advice for living, reflecting **traditional** Roman values.

5-Minute Warm-Up

Daily Language SkillBuilder

Have students **proofread** the display sentences on page 161i and write them correctly.

POEMS BY HORACE

Horace
65–8 B.C.

Simple Pleasures If you lived in ancient Rome, you might have enjoyed spending time with the poet Horace. He was a friendly host who served fine foods and good wines. He was a good listener and companion—easygoing and humorous. His views on life, love, and just about everything else under the Roman sun were wise, witty, and down-to-earth.

Early Struggles Horace rose from humble beginnings. His father was a former slave who owned land in Italy's central highlands. He made sure that his son received an excellent education, first in Rome and later in Athens. This was at a time when education was a privilege usually reserved for the wealthy. While in Athens, Horace was swept up in the civil war that erupted in Rome in 44 B.C., after the murder of Julius Caesar. At the battle of Philippi in 42 B.C., Horace fought on Brutus' side—the losing side—against the forces of Marc Antony and Octavian (later the emperor Augustus). After Brutus' defeat, Horace returned to Rome, heartsick and penniless.

Rise to Fame Back in Rome, Horace managed to find a government job and began writing poems. His verse soon caught the eye of the poet Virgil, who introduced him to Maecenas (mē-sē'nəs), a rich patron of the arts. From then on, Horace's career as a poet was assured. Maecenas gave Horace a farm in the Sabine Hills, northeast of Rome. For the rest of his life, Horace lived on this farm, writing poetry and enjoying his role in the literary life of Rome.

Ever Popular Horace's poetry has made him the most quoted of all the Latin poets. He valued moderation, good sense, and living for the present moment. Horace coined the expression *Carpe diem*—"Seize the day"—which is still widely used. This sentiment is summed up best in Horace's words: "He is master of himself and happy who as the day ends can say, I have lived—tomorrow come cloud, come sunshine."

Other Works
Ars Poetica
Satires

LESSON RESOURCES

UNIT TWO RESOURCE BOOK, pp. 66–67

ASSESSMENT RESOURCES
Formal Assessment, pp. 49–50
Teacher's Guide to Assessment and Portfolio Use
Test Generator

INTEGRATED TECHNOLOGY
Visit our Web site: classzone.com

ADDITIONAL RESOURCES
Lesson Planning Guide, pp. 41–42
Teacher's Sourcebook for Language Development

Connect to Your Life

The poems you are about to read offer practical advice on how to live. What pieces of good advice have helped you the most during your high school years? Share one or two "nuggets of wisdom" with a small group of classmates.

Build Background

To Teach and Delight Horace once said, "Everyone has his own way of enjoying himself. Mine is to put words into meter." He put words into meter during the Augustan Age of Latin literature. This was the period when the emperor Augustus ruled Rome and established the Roman Empire. Augustus took a personal interest in the literary works created during his reign. Together with Virgil and Ovid, Horace was recognized as one of the great poets of the time.

Horace earned this reputation mainly because of his **odes.** These are short poems—almost like songs—written with grace, charm, and precision of language. Often addressed to a particular person, an ode expresses careful thoughts rather than deep emotions. Down through the centuries, Horace's odes have continued to offer readers wise and witty comments about life.

Horace had two purposes for writing: namely, to teach and delight. The Romans believed that all the arts should influence their audience in positive ways. As a Roman poet, therefore, Horace felt a responsibility to use his poetry to serve a didactic, or teaching, purpose. He felt that literature should teach moral values, help strengthen character, and show people how to live. The poems "Seize the Day" and "Better to live, Licinius, . . ." do all of these things.

Focus Your Reading

LITERARY ANALYSIS: THEME

A **theme** is a message or central idea that a writer shares with readers. A theme may be a lesson about life or about people and their actions. As you read each of these poems, think about the theme that Horace wants to convey.

ACTIVE READING: UNDERSTANDING CONTRAST

In each of these poems, the speaker uses contrasts to convey ideas. When two or more things are contrasted, the differences are emphasized. For example, in the poem "Seize the Day," the speaker contrasts two things the future may bring: either a number of years—"many a winter"—or maybe only one—"the last [winter]." As you read these poems, look for additional examples of contrast.

READER'S NOTEBOOK In your notebook, use a chart like the one shown below to record the contrasts you find in "Seize the Day." Then create a similar chart to record the contrasts you find in "Better to live, Licinius, . . ."

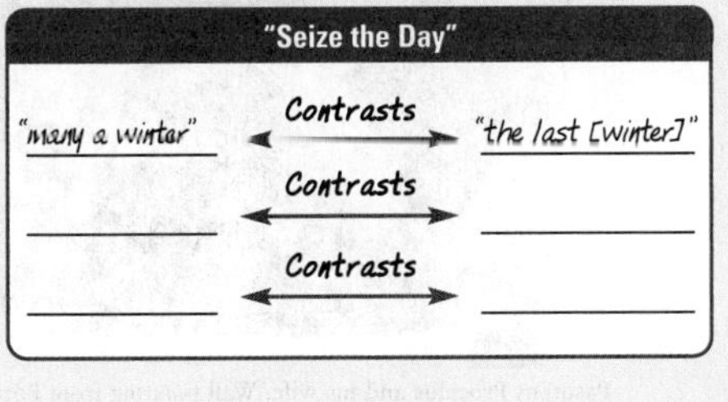

READING FOR INFORMATION

Reading Skills and Strategies

MAIN IDEA

Have students read the biographical sketch of Horace on page 392. Then ask them to list three key ideas that they learned about him. Students might mention ideas like the following:

- Horace rose from humble beginnings.
- His poetry was popular in Rome during the reign of Augustus Caesar.
- His poetry reinforces traditional Roman values—for example, moderation and good sense.

Reading Skills and Strategies

PREVIEWING

Point out that these poems offer advice in witty, concise, and imaginative language. Then have students think about the title of each poem. Students may be familiar with the phrase "Seize the Day," a plea to live in the present. Point out that the title of the second poem "Better to Live, Licinius," is a shortened version of "It is better to live, Licinius."

Literary Analysis THEME

A Tell students to think about the main message that the speaker in "Seize the Day" shares with the reader. This message is stated succinctly in line 8. Have students paraphrase this line to get at the theme of the poem.
Possible Response: Live for right now and don't rely on the future.

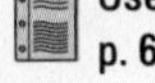 Use **Unit Two Resource Book,** p. 67, for more practice.

Active Reading

UNDERSTANDING CONTRAST

B Tell students that in each of the first two stanzas in "Better to Live, Licinius," the speaker contrasts two extremes. In the first stanza, the extremes are sailing in water that is too deep or too shallow. Ask students to identify the extremes in the second stanza.
Possible Response: "a run-down building" or "a palace"

 Use **Unit Two Resource Book,** p. 66, for more practice.

Seize the Day

Horace

Translated by David Mulroy

Ask not the forbidden question, the ends the gods
have assigned us, Leuconoe. Scorn Babylonian numbers.
Acceptance is better, whatever occurs—if Jove
has granted us many a winter or this is the last
that breaks the Etruscan sea against the rocks.
Be sensible, drink, and trim your hopes to fit
your limits. An envious age will have fled as we speak.
A Seize the day with little faith in tomorrow.

Pasquius Proculus and his wife. Wall painting from Pompeii. Museo Archeologico Nazionale, Naples, Italy.

HUMANITIES CONNECTION This portrait depicts a working-class man and woman. The woman holds writing implements, and the man holds a scroll. These objects suggest the couple's intellectual pursuits.

MINI LESSON Viewing and Representing

Pasquius Proculus and His Wife

ART APPRECIATION Have students read the **Humanities Connection** caption on page 394 and study the reproduction of the wall painting. Help students identify details in this painting. For example, the man wearing a toga holds a papyrus scroll with a red seal. The woman wearing a tunic and a mantle holds a stylus in her right hand and a wooden tablet in her left. Ask students what they might infer from this painting about the importance of literacy in Roman society.

Possible Response: The husband and wife in the painting express pride in their ability to read and write. Literacy, therefore, must have had a high value in Roman society.

Better to live, Licinius, . . .

Horace

Translated by Joseph P. Clancy

Pompeiian household shrine fresco. Ancient Art and Architecture Collection, Ltd.

Better to live, Licinius, not always
rushing into deep water, and not, when fear
of storms makes you shiver, pushing too close to
1 the dangerous coast.

2 A man who prizes golden moderation
stays safely clear of the filth of a run-down
building, stays prudently out of a palace
B others will envy.

5 moderation: avoidance of extremes.

7 prudently: in a manner showing good sense.

Cross Curricular Link **Humanities**

CARPE DIEM This Latin phrase, which means "seize the day," was coined by Horace. It expresses the theme that one should not put off living. This theme is found in many works of literature, especially English love poetry of the 16th and 17th centuries. Examples include many of Shakespeare's sonnets, Robert Herrick's "To the Virgins, To Make Much of Time," and Andrew Marvell's "To His Coy Mistress." In these poems, time is depicted as the inevitable destroyer of youth, beauty, and love, as in these well-known lines by Marvell:

But at my back I always hear
Time's winged chariot hurrying near;
And yonder all before us lie
Deserts of vast eternity.

Horace's "carpe diem" theme has never lost its appeal. Saul Bellow, the Nobel Prize-winning American novelist, even used the phrase as the title of a popular novella in 1956.

Customizing Instruction

Less Proficient Readers

1 Help students understand the comparison in the first stanza. The two dangers to avoid are sailing in deep water, too far from land, and sailing in shallow water, too close to shore. It is best to sail somewhere in the middle.

2 Tell students that the term *golden moderation* means a middle course between two extremes. For example, the middle course between fasting and overeating is to eat enough for good nutrition.

English Learners

- Help students with the third stanza of this poem by completing the following comparisons:

  "The giant pine is more often troubled by the wind" [than are shorter trees]

  "the tallest towers collapse with a heavier fall" [than do shorter towers]

  "bolts of lightning strike the tops of the mountains " [rather than the lower parts]

- Explain the meaning of the following words and phrases:

  –from "Seize the Day":

  breaks the Etruscan sea against the rocks (line 5)—makes the sea rough and choppy so that the waves slam against the rocks on shore

  trim your hopes (line 6)—set limits on what you expect the future to bring you

  an envious age will have fled (line 7)—a bitter time will have gone

  –from "Better to Live, Licinius . . ."

  the turn of the dice (line 15)—a sudden change

  take in sail (line 23)—shorten a sail so that the wind doesn't propel the boat too quickly

  Muse (line 19)—any one of the nine Greek goddesses of the arts and sciences

Advanced Learners

Ask students to imagine they are writing a modern essay or poem based on Horace's advice in "Better to Live, Licinius. . ." What contrasting images might convey the meaning of "golden moderation"?

Literary Analysis IMAGERY AND THEME

A Have students explain how the images in these lines connect to the theme of the poem.

Possible Response: The images "the giant pine," "the tallest towers," and "the tops of the mountains" describe huge things. Because of their extreme size, they are more vulnerable than things not so large.

Active Reading

UNDERSTANDING CONTRAST

B Ask students to point out the contrast in line 13 and to explain how it supports the idea of "golden moderation."

Possible Response: One who is aware of the reality of change controls his or her reaction in both good and bad times. This person is hopeful, instead of miserable, when things are going poorly and fearful, instead of jubilant, when things are going well.

Detail of Pompeiian household shrine fresco. Ancient Art and Architecture Collection, Ltd.

A
The giant pine is more often troubled by the
wind, and the tallest towers collapse with a
heavier fall, and bolts of lightning strike the
tops of the mountains.

B
Hopeful in the bad times, fearful in the good times,
that is the man who has readied his heart for
the turn of the dice. Jupiter brings back foul
winters; he also

takes them away. No, if things are bad now, they
will not remain that way: sometimes Apollo
wakes the silent Muse with his lyre and is not
always an archer.

When troubles come, show that you have a stout heart
and a stern face: but see that you have the good sense
to take in sail when it swells in a wind that's
a little too kind.

18 Apollo (ə-pŏl'ō): the god of both music and archery.

19 lyre (līr): a stringed instrument like a small harp.

21 stout: brave; determined.

Connect to the Literature

1. **What Do You Think?** How did you react to the advice given in each of these poems?

Think Critically

2. In "Seize the Day," why does the speaker advise Leuconoe to live for today?
3. In your own words, explain what you think the speaker of "Better to live, Licinius, . . ." means by "golden moderation."

THINK ABOUT
- the two types of residences to avoid (second stanza)
- what happens to the "giant pine" and the "tallest towers" (third stanza)
- the ways to react in bad and in good times (fourth stanza)

4. **ACTIVE READING: UNDERSTANDING CONTRAST** Review what you listed in your READER'S NOTEBOOK. For each poem, decide which contrast is most effective in conveying an idea.
5. To what extent do these poems both teach and delight? Support your answer with details from each poem.

Extend Interpretations

6. **The Writer's Style** Writers often use descriptive words and phrases to re-create sensory experiences for the reader. Such words and phrases are known as imagery. Each image appeals to one or more of the five senses. Cite examples of images in each of these poems. Which image do you find particularly effective?
7. **Comparing Texts** Which poem do you think offers better advice, and why?
8. **Connect to Life** In "Seize the Day," the speaker says that it is important to "trim your hopes to fit your limits" (lines 6–7). Do you agree? Use examples from your own experience to support your opinion.

LITERARY ANALYSIS: THEME

In a literary work, a **theme** is a message or central idea that the writer wants to share with readers. A theme may be a lesson about life or about people and their actions. Sometimes, writers state themes directly. Often, however, the reader must **infer** a central message by reading between the lines. Different readers may even discover different themes in the same work.

Activity Write a letter to a friend, in which you give advice about how to live. Include a discussion of the theme of one of Horace's poems.

Literary Analysis

Activity Students' letters should comment on the theme of one of the poems. The theme of "Seize the Day" is that it is better to live in the *here and now* and not defer enjoyment. The theme of "Better to live, Licinius, . . ." is that it is important to take a middle way, avoiding extremes of conduct and emotion.

Use **Unit Two Resource Book,** p. 67, for more practice.

Connect to the Literature

1. **What Do You Think?** Most students will say that the advice conveyed in these poems is sound, sensible, and down-to-earth.

Think Critically

2. Possible Responses: The speaker realizes that time is fleeting. Since death can occur at any time, it is better to enjoy the present moment.
3. Possible Responses: "Golden moderation" means avoiding extremes. For example, a person might choose a modest home, rejecting the extremes of "a run-down building" or a "palace." Things of extreme size—the "giant pine" and "the tallest towers"—are more vulnerable than smaller things. In good times, one should abate joy with fear because good times will pass; in bad times, one should moderate grief with hope because misfortunes will not last forever.
4. Responses will vary: For each contrast, students should identify the two extremes and explain the point of the contrast.
5. Possible Response: These poems teach and delight to a great degree. They convey practical advice in concise and memorable phrases, such as "seize the day."

Extend Interpretations

6. **The Writer's Style** Possible Response: Students may cite several images, such as "the last [winter] that breaks the Etruscan sea against the rocks," "the filth of a run-down palace," "the giant pine," "the tallest towers," and "bolts of lightning strike the tops of the mountains." Opinions as to which image is most effective will vary.
7. **Comparing Texts** Students should explain which approach to life is better—living in the present or avoiding extremes.
8. **Connect to Life** Students who agree may state that a sense of one's limitations precludes the taking of foolish risks. Students who disagree may state that it is important to dream big and strive for unattainable goals.

To assess skills and concepts taught in this selection, use **Formal Assessment Book,** pp. 49–50.

Objectives

- understand and appreciate a **myth** retold by Ovid **(Literary Analysis)**
- examine the concept of **myth (Literary Analysis)**
- understand the elements of **narrative poetry (Active Reading)**

Thematic Link

Drawing upon the heroic **tradition,** Ovid retells a Greek myth for a Roman audience.

5-Minute Warm-Up

Daily Language SkillBuilder

Have students **proofread** the display sentences on page 161i and write them correctly.

from
METAMORPHOSES
THE STORY OF DAEDALUS AND ICARUS
OVID

Ovid
43 B.C.–A.D. 18

A Poet's Poet Along with Horace and Virgil, Ovid was one of the great Roman poets during the reign of the emperor Augustus. His work had a lasting influence on later European literature, especially during the Middle Ages and the Renaissance. Both Geoffrey Chaucer (1340?–1400) and William Shakespeare (1564–1616) were greatly influenced by Ovid.

Early Years Ovid was born into a well-to-do family in 43 B.C.—one year after the murder of Julius Caesar. Educated in law and rhetoric, he held a few minor offices early in his working life and seemed destined for a career in public life. But against the wishes of his father, who urged him toward a career in law, Ovid began writing poems. His first work, the *Amores,* is a series of short and witty poems about a love affair. This work brought Ovid immediate success. Among his most popular works is the *Ars amatoria* [Art of love], published in 1 B.C. This handbook in verse offers lighthearted advice on ways to begin and maintain a romance.

Lasting Legacy Ovid's masterpiece is the *Metamorphoses.* This long narrative poem retells most of the important Greek and Roman legends and myths. Ovid, however, breathed new life into the old stories. He shaped them in imaginative ways, adding details and strengthening their structure. Ovid's retellings inspired European writers for centuries to come.

A Ruined Life Before Ovid was able to publish the *Metamorphoses,* he suffered a terrible misfortune. In A.D. 8, the emperor Augustus banished him from Rome. Ovid was exiled to Tomi, a remote fishing village on the Black Sea. The exact reason for this cruel punishment is not known. For Ovid, exile to the far reaches of the Roman Empire was a fate worse than death. He continued to write poems, however, and in some of them he pleaded to be allowed to return to Rome. These pleas fell on deaf ears, and Ovid died in exile in A.D 18.

LESSON RESOURCES

UNIT TWO RESOURCE BOOK, pp. 68–69

ASSESSMENT RESOURCES
Formal Assessment, pp. 51–52
Teacher's Guide to Assessment and Portfolio Use
Test Generator

INTEGRATED TECHNOLOGY
Visit our Web site: classzone.com

ADDITIONAL RESOURCES
Lesson Planning Guide, pp. 43–44
Teacher's Sourcebook for Language Development

Build Background

Stories About Magical Changes The *Metamorphoses* was Ovid's most ambitious work. It consists of nearly 12,000 lines of Latin verse. In it, some 250 stories, drawn mostly from Greek and Roman mythology, are retold. The poem begins with the creation of the world and ends with the transformation of the soul of Julius Caesar into a star in the sky. In most of the stories, a transformation, or metamorphosis, is important to the plot. For example, in one story, a maiden named Daphne, fleeing from the god Apollo, is transformed into a laurel tree.

In "The Story of Daedalus and Icarus," the main characters are living in exile—like Ovid himself in his later years. Daedalus and his son Icarus are prisoners on Crete, an island ruled by King Minos. Daedalus, whose name means "cunning craftsman," is a skillful architect, sculptor, and inventor. As the story begins, he is trying to find a way to escape from the island.

In this woodcut, M. C. Escher treats the idea of transformation, just as Ovid did in the *Metamorphoses. Sky and Water I* (1938), M. C. Escher http://www.mcescher.com.

Connect to Your Life

In this story, Daedalus devises a clever plan to escape from Crete. Think about books, movies, or television shows in which characters attempt to escape from captivity. Which attempts succeed? With a few classmates, retell some adventure stories whose plots feature escapes.

Focus Your Reading

LITERARY ANALYSIS: MYTH

"The Story of Daedalus and Icarus" is a retelling of a **myth.** A myth is a traditional story that usually features superhuman beings and unlikely events. As you read this myth, consider the wondrous events in it and their possible meanings.

ACTIVE READING: READING NARRATIVE POETRY

Ovid presents this myth in a **narrative poem**—one that tells a story. A narrative poem has **characters, setting,** a **plot,** and a **point of view,** all of which serve to develop a **theme.**

While reading this excerpt, ask yourself the following questions:

- What sequence of events makes up the plot?
- In what setting do the events occur?
- What characters take part in the events?
- From whose point of view is the story told?
- What theme emerges from the story?

READER'S NOTEBOOK Create a sequence chain like the one shown below. In the boxes, summarize key events in the order they occur.

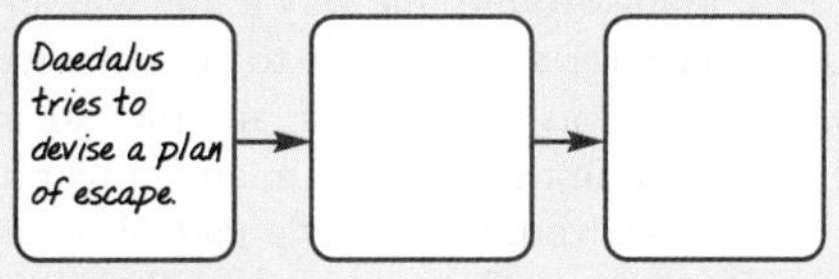

READING FOR INFORMATION

Reading Skills and Strategies

RECOGNIZING CONTRAST

Have students read the biographical sketch of Ovid on page 402. Make sure that students notice the contrast between Ovid's reputation while alive and then centuries later. While alive, he was disgraced by the emperor. Centuries later, he was idolized by the greatest poets of the Western world.

Reading Skills and Strategies
PREVIEWING
Have students examine the image on page 401 and then predict what this story might be about.

Literary Analysis MYTH
Remind students that myths are traditional stories, often concerning supernatural beings or events, that were told to explain natural processes or phenomena. For many ancient peoples, myths were both a kind of science and a religion, allowing humans to make sense of birth, death, and the origins of the universe.

 Use **Unit Two Resource Book,** p. 69, for more practice.

Active Reading
READING NARRATIVE POETRY
(A) Remind students that in narrative poems, as in short stories, plot is a key element. The plot of this narrative begins with Daedalus' decision to escape by air from the island of Crete. Ask students how lines 6–13 help develop the plot.
Possible Response: These lines show how Daedalus constructs the wings that will enable his son and himself to escape from Crete.

 Use **Unit Two Resource Book,** p. 68, for more practice.

from Metamorphoses
The Story of Daedalus and Icarus
Ovid
Translated by Rolfe Humphries

Homesick for homeland, Daedalus hated Crete
And his long exile there, but the sea held him.
"Though Minos blocks escape by land or water,"
Daedalus said, "surely the sky is open,
And that's the way we'll go. Minos' dominion
Does not include the air." He turned his thinking
Toward unknown arts, changing the laws of nature.
1 (A) He laid out feathers in order, first the smallest,
A little larger next it, and so continued,
The way that pan-pipes rise in gradual sequence.
He fastened them with twine and wax, at middle,
At bottom, so, and bent them, gently curving,
So that they looked like wings of birds, most surely.
And Icarus, his son, stood by and watched him,
Not knowing he was dealing with his downfall,
Stood by and watched, and raised his shiny face
To let a feather, light as down, fall on it,
Or stuck his thumb into the yellow wax,
Fooling around, the way a boy will, always,
Whenever a father tries to get some work done.
Still, it was done at last, and the father hovered,
Poised, in the moving air, and taught his son:
"I warn you, Icarus, fly a middle course:
Don't go too low, or water will weigh the wings down;
Don't go too high, or the sun's fire will burn them.
Keep to the middle way. And one more thing,
No fancy steering by star or constellation,

10 pan-pipes: a musical instrument made up of a series of hollow tubes of varying lengths.

17 down: the soft feathers of a baby bird.

21 hovered (hŭv′ərd): remained suspended in the air.

MINI LESSON **Grammar**

PARENTHESES AND DASHES Remind students that parentheses and dashes are used to set off information that interrupts the flow of sentences. Parentheses are used to set off nonessential explanatory material that is loosely related to the sentence. A dash is used to show an abrupt break in thought. If the thought continues after the break, a second dash is needed.

Instruction Write the following sentences on the chalkboard:

Daedulus kissed his son *Good-bye,* if he had known it.

Daedulus guides Icarus in flight O fatal art! and the wings move.

Ask students to rewrite each of the above sentences, adding parentheses or dashes wherever needed. *((Good-bye, if he had known it)), -O fatal art!-)*

Practice Have students rewrite the following sentences, adding parentheses or dashes wherever needed.

1. Although Daedulus longed to leave the island he had been there for years, he was trapped by the sea. *((he had been there for years))*

The Fall of Icarus (17th century), Jacob Peter Gowy. Oil on canvas, 195 cm × 180 cm. Museo del Prado, Madrid, Spain.

Customizing Instruction

Less Proficient Readers

- Tell students to read this poem as if it were a short story. At the beginning, the setting is Crete, an island of southeast Greece in the Mediterranean Sea. Have volunteers locate Crete on a globe or a world map.
- Read aloud to students lines 1–13 of the poem, modeling how to take in large chunks of meaning at a time. Tell students to pause at the end of a line only if they come upon a mark of punctuation.

English Learners

1 Point out that "unknown arts" refers to secret knowledge, such as magic.

Advanced Learners

Have students compare the theme of Ovid's poem with that of Horace's poem "Better to Live, Licinius . . . ."
Possible Response: Horace's poem teaches the importance of golden moderation, of avoiding extremes. If Icarus had followed Daedalus' advice—"Keep to the middle way"—and not soared toward "the vast heaven," he would not have lost his life.

2. Daedulus laid out birds' feathers from the smallest to the largest and fastened them with twine and wax. *((from the smallest to the largest))*
3. Daedulus created two sets of wings What wonderful inventions! to aid in his escape. *(-What wonderful inventions!-)*
4. Daedulus gave his son Icarus an impulsive boy the smaller of the two sets of wings. *((an impulsive boy))*
5. As Icarus flew closer to the sun, his wings weakened, and O terrible fortune! he fell into the sea. *(-O terrible fortune!-)*

For more instruction and practice in parentheses and dashes, use McDougal Littell's ***Language Network***:

- Grade 10, Chapter 11, "Punctuation"
- Grade 12, Chapter 10, "Other Punctuation Marks"

Reading and Analyzing

Literary Analysis FORESHADOWING

A Ask students to pick out details that foreshadow Icarus' death.

Possible Response: Daedalus' weeping and trembling and his fear as Icarus begins his flight foreshadow the catastrophe, as does the narrator's comment that Daedalus is unknowingly kissing his son goodbye forever.

Active Reading

READING NARRATIVE POETRY

B Have students recall the definition of climax. Then ask them to explain why this passage is the climax of this story.

Possible Responses: This passage marks the turning point of the story, the moment when the reader's interest and emotional intensity reach the highest pitch. Until this moment, the reader wonders what will happen as Icarus flies behind his father. Now the reader finds out. Icarus makes his fatal choice and falls headlong into the sea.

Literary Analysis MYTH

C Remind students that myths often explain aspects of the natural world. Ask students what this myth reveals about how the island of Ikaria got its name.

Possible Response: Ikaria was named after Icarus, who was buried on the island.

Related Reading

William Carlos Williams Tell students that William Carlos Williams (1883–1963) was an important American writer whose poetry is known for its clear, objective images. For more than 40 years, he was a medical doctor as well as an author. He wrote mostly at night or between visits from his patients, and at a typewriter hidden in his medical office desk.

Discussion Question

What specific words in the poem suggest that Icarus' death was not very important to the speaker?

Possible Response: *unsignificantly, unnoticed*

Follow my lead!" That was the flying lesson,
And now to fit the wings to the boy's shoulders.
Between the work and warning the father found
His cheeks were wet with tears, and his hands trembled.
A He kissed his son (*Good-bye,* if he had known it),
Rose on his wings, flew on ahead, as fearful
As any bird launching the little nestlings
Out of high nest into thin air. *Keep on,*
Keep on, he signals, *follow me!* He guides him
In flight—O fatal art!—and the wings move
And the father looks back to see the son's wings moving.
Far off, far down, some fisherman is watching
As the rod dips and trembles over the water,
Some shepherd rests his weight upon his crook,
Some ploughman on the handles of the ploughshare,
And all look up, in absolute amazement,
1 At those air-borne above. They must be gods!
They were over Samos, Juno's sacred island,
Delos and Paros toward the left, Lebinthus
Visible to the right, and another island,
Calymne, rich in honey. And the boy
Thought *This is wonderful!* and left his father,
Soared higher, higher, drawn to the vast heaven,
Nearer the sun, and the wax that held the wings
B Melted in that fierce heat, and the bare arms
Beat up and down in air, and lacking oarage
Took hold of nothing. *Father!* he cried, and *Father!*
Until the blue sea hushed him, the dark water
Men call the Icarian now. And Daedalus,
Father no more, called "Icarus, where are you!
Where are you, Icarus? Tell me where to find you!"
2 And saw the wings on the waves, and cursed his talents,
C Buried the body in a tomb, and the land
Was named for Icarus.

34 nestlings: young birds.

42 ploughshare: the cutting blade of a plow.

45–48 Samos (sā′mŏs′) . . . **Delos** (dē′lŏs′) . . . **Paros** (pâr′ŏs) . . . **Lebinthus** (lə-bĭn′thəs) . . . **Calymne** (kə-lĭm′nē): islands between mainland Greece and Asia Minor.

53 oarage: apparatus functioning as oars.

60–61 the land was named for Icarus: a reference to the island now named Ikaria.

Humanities

OVID'S *METAMORPHOSES* Ovid's *Metamorphoses* transmitted the riches of the Greek imagination to later generations, greatly influencing European art and literature, especially during the Middle Ages and the Renaissance. In the *Metamorphoses,* Ovid adapted and retold the classical myths. His powerful retellings of the myths—rich in fantasy, suspense, and narrative detail—became the standard versions that were passed down through the centuries.

In story after story, Ovid presents gods or humans who are seized by an uncontrollable passion and undergo a profound change. For example, the story of Niobe tells of a mother whose boasts about her lovely children anger the gods. She is forced to look on as her seven sons and seven daughters are slain by the arrows of Apollo and Artemis. Shocked and grief-stricken, Niobe is transformed into a stone from which water forever drips.

Other memorable Ovidian characters include Echo and Narcissus, Arachne, Hercules, Pygmalion and Galatea, Tereus and Philomela—and Pyramus and Thisbe, whose ill-starred rendezvous Shakespeare mocked in *A Midsummer Night's Dream.*

Landscape with the Fall of Icarus, Pieter Brueghel the Elder. Musée d'Art Ancien, Musées Royaux des Beaux-Arts, Brussels, Belgium. Photo © Scala/Art Resource, New York.

3 Landscape with the Fall of Icarus

WILLIAM CARLOS WILLIAMS

Ovid's story of Daedalus and Icarus has inspired many artists and writers. In the following poem, the speaker looks at a painting about the drowning of Icarus. As you read this poem, consider how the speaker views Icarus' death.

4

According to Brueghel
when Icarus fell
it was spring

a farmer was ploughing
his field
the whole pageantry

of the year was
awake tingling
near

the edge of the sea
concerned
with itself

sweating in the sun
that melted
the wings' wax

unsignificantly
off the coast
there was

a splash quite unnoticed
this was
Icarus drowning

1 Brueghel (broi'gəl): Pieter Brueghel the Elder (1525?–1569), who painted *Landscape with the Fall of Icarus.*

6 pageantry: colorful, showy display.

Customizing Instruction

Less Proficient Readers

1 Point out that the sentence "They must be gods" expresses the astonishment of the fisherman, the shepherd, and the plowman as they see Daedalus and Icarus flying like birds.

2 Make sure students understand why Daedalus "cursed his talents." He holds himself responsible for Icarus' death because he designed the wings that cost his son his life.

3 Explain that this poem comments on details in a famous painting that depicts Icarus' drowning. In the painting, only Icarus' legs are visible.

4 Have students notice that this poem has no punctuation marks. Tell students to read the poem aloud several times and to listen for the natural pauses that make the meaning clear.

English Learners

Explain the meaning of the following words and phrases:

- *follow my lead* (line 28) means "do what I do"
- *rod* (line 40) means "fishing pole"
- *the blue sea hushed him* (line 55) means that Icarus drowned

MINI LESSON Viewing and Representing

Landscape With the Fall of Icarus **by Peter Breughel the Elder**

ART APPRECIATION Have students study the reproduction of the painting by Brueghel (1525?–1569). This artist is known for his scenes of everyday life that suggest truths about human nature. In this painting, the landscape is seen from above, creating a perspective perhaps similar to Daedalus'. A peasant plows his field, preoccupied with his own concerns, and a ship sails along, ignoring a drowning boy whose legs are visible. Ask students to discuss why Brueghel places Icarus off to the side rather than at the center of the painting.

Possible Responses: By doing so, Brueghel suggests the insignificance of Icarus' drowning in the springtime setting.

Connect to the Literature

1. **What Do You Think?** What are your thoughts about what happens to Icarus?

Comprehension Check
- What does Daedalus use to make the wings for his son and himself?
- What warning does Daedalus give his son about flying?

Think Critically

2. **ACTIVE READING: READING NARRATIVE POETRY** Look back at the sequence chain you created in your READER'S NOTEBOOK. How would you summarize the plot of this myth?
3. To what extent is Daedalus responsible for his son's death? Cite reasons to support your answer.
4. Why do you think Icarus does not heed his father's warning?
5. How would you describe the relationship between Daedalus and Icarus?

THINK ABOUT
- Daedalus' feelings as he fits the wings on his son
- Icarus' last words
- Daedalus' reaction when he sees "the wings on the waves"

Extend Interpretations

6. **The Writer's Style** A writer may use **foreshadowing** to hint at the outcome of a story. For example, in lines 14 and 15, the narrator says, "And Icarus, his son, stood by and watched him, / Not knowing he was dealing with his downfall." These lines foreshadow Icarus' death. Find other passages that foreshadow the end of the story.
7. **Comparing Texts** Reread the poem "Landscape with the Fall of Icarus" on page 403. How does the speaker's description of Icarus' death differ from Ovid's?
8. **Connect to Life** What situations in modern life do the events in this myth call to mind?

LITERARY ANALYSIS: MYTH

A **myth** is a traditional story, usually concerning some superhuman being or unlikely event, that was once widely believed to be true. Myths were passed down from one generation to the next. Though the original authors are unknown, myths reflect particular cultures' values and beliefs. Ovid's retellings of the classical myths still captivate and inspire. These timeless tales also explore issues that are relevant today.

Cooperative Learning Activity Get together with a small group of classmates to discuss the following questions: What lessons does this myth teach about youth and age? about independence? about technology? about great talent? Record your responses, along with supporting examples, on a chart like the one shown below. Then share your chart with other groups.

Issues	Examples
youth and age	
independence	
technology	
great talent	

Connect to the Literature

1. **What Do You Think?** Possible Response: Students may say that what happens to Icarus is tragic but inevitable. He pays the price for his youthful daring.

Comprehension Check
- feathers, twine, and, wax
- fly a middle course

Think Critically

2. Possible Response: To escape from his island prison, Daedalus uses feathers to invent wings for his young son, Icarus, and himself, cautioning the boy to fly a middle course. Icarus, however, soars too close to the sun, which melts the wax holding the feathers of the wings together. As a result, Icarus plunges headlong into the sea and drowns.
3. Answers will vary. Some students may state that Daedalus is mainly responsible for his son's death. These students may point out that Daedalus was determined to find a way to escape from Crete. He studied "unknown arts," invented wings, gave his son flying instructions, and then launched him. Daedalus was aware that the risk was great and his son was adventurous. After Icarus drowned, Daedalus "cursed his talents" because his cleverness set in motion the events that led to his son's death. Other students may say that Daedalus is not to blame for his son's reckless act. If Icarus had heeded his father's advice, he would have arrived safely at his destination.
4. Possible Response: Icarus is a free spirit, young and fun-loving. Exhilarated by the wonder of flight, he cannot refrain from soaring higher and higher.
5. Possible Responses: The relationship is very warm and close. Daedalus weeps as he fits the wings on his son. Icarus calls to his father as he plunges to his death. When Daedalus sees his son's wings floating on the waves, he curses his own talent that cost his son his life.

Extend Interpretations

6. **The Writer's Style** Lines 18–20, which describe Icarus playing as his father works, foreshadow his playful conduct when airborne. Lines 30–35 depict Daedalus' foreboding as he prepares his son for flight. He weeps and his hands tremble as he kisses his son, not knowing that they are parting forever.
7. **Comparing Texts** The speaker describes Icarus' death as an event that goes unnoticed. In Ovid's description, on the other hand, Icarus' drowning is the central event, the climax of the narrative.
8. **Connect to Life** Responses will vary. Some students may compare Icarus in flight with an adolescent behind the wheel of a car.

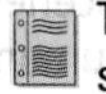
To assess skills and concepts taught in this selection, use **Formal Assessment Book,** pp. 51–52.

The Urge to Fly

For thousands of years, Ovid's story of Daedalus and Icarus has had a powerful hold on people's imagination. Perhaps the main reason for the story's appeal is that it deals with the fulfillment of one of mankind's oldest dreams—to fly like a bird. Have you ever pictured yourself flying like Icarus? What if you could soar through the air in a human-powered flying machine?

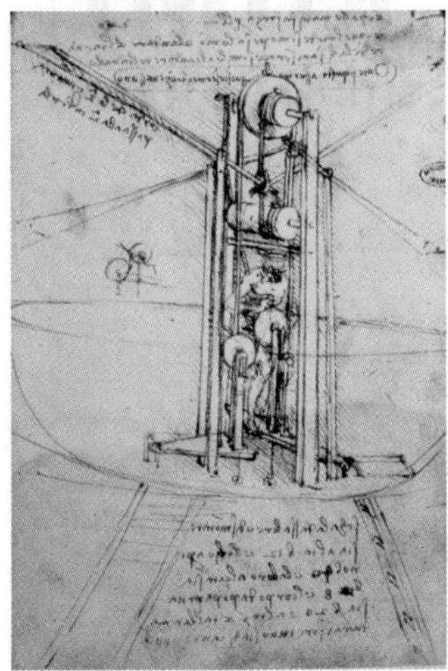

Leonardo da Vinci's drawing of a flying machine

In the 15th century, the Italian artist Leonardo da Vinci studied the flight of birds and drew sketches of flying machines. Thanks to recent advances in technology, this long-held dream is closer to reality. Take a look at the two photos of human-powered aircraft below.

A Modern Icarus At the time this book went to press, more than 100 human-powered flying machines had flown all over the world. The record for the longest distance flown in one of these machines was set in 1988 by Kanellos Kanellopoulos. Like Icarus, he flew from Crete. His destination was an island more than 70 miles away. Flying about 15 feet above the water, he stayed airborne for almost four hours. Only 35 feet short of the goal, his aircraft was damaged by a gust of wind and plunged into the sea. Unlike Icarus, however, Mr. Kanellopoulos was rescued.

Two human-powered flying machines: the *Gossamer Condor (top)* was the first machine capable of sustained flight; the *Monarch B (bottom)* completed a 1,500-meter flight in just three minutes in 1984.

Research Project Look up information about the latest advances in human-powered flight. Also find out who holds the current records for flying time and distance. Use the Internet as your main tool for research. (Be sure to check out the Raven Project site.) Present your findings to your classmates in a multimedia report.

Connect to Today

"The Urge to Fly" relates "The Story of Daedalus and Icarus" to the human dream of self-propelled flight. Students will read about the latest advances in the pursuit of the fulfillment of this dream.

Research Project Suggest that students work in pairs to do their research. Encourage students to predict, based on the data they find, what the future might be like for human-powered flight.

Literary Analysis

Cooperative Learning Activity Possible Responses: youth and age—young people are daring and older people are cautious; independence—an exhilarating but risky state; technology—a two-edged sword, beneficial but harmful if misused; great talent—a creative force that may have unforeseen consequences

Use **Unit Two Resource Book,** p. 69, for more practice.

Possible Objectives

This **On Your Own** featured selection may be used to achieve one or more of the following objectives:

- to give students an opportunity to read independently, either reading silently for a sustained period, reading and analyzing literature with a group, or using the Reader's Notebook to write in response to the literature
- to conduct a post-reading class discussion
- to assess students' comprehension of the selection

Summary

In this excerpt from the *Annals*, Tacitus describes the fire that destroyed most of ancient Rome in A.D. 64. He recounts the panic caused by the calamity, the Romans' chaotic efforts to escape, and the massive destruction of the city. Tacitus also describes Nero's relief efforts and the ostentatious way in which the emperor reconstructs his palace grounds in the aftermath of the fire. The historian also notes the persistent rumors that Nero himself had ordered that the fires be started. Finally, Tacitus describes Nero's attempts to dispel suspicion by blaming the Christians and publicly torturing them.

ON YOUR OWN

from **THE ANNALS**

THE BURNING OF ROME

TACITUS • *Translated by* **MICHAEL GRANT**

Tacitus
C. A.D. 56–120

Living in Turbulent Times Tacitus, one of the greatest historians of ancient Rome, lived in troubled times. Plague and fire frequently ravaged Rome. An eruption of Mount Vesuvius buried the splendors of Pompeii under tons of volcanic ash. Even though the Roman Empire expanded to its utmost limits, tyrants, rebellions, and wars left a bloody mark on the times. No wonder Tacitus felt the need to set the written record straight.

Writer of History Tacitus is known mainly for two historical works. Unfortunately, only portions of these works have survived. The first, called the *Histories,* covers the years A.D. 69–96, a period dominated by the reigns of the emperors Vespasian, Titus, and Domitian. Tacitus' second important work is the *Annals.* It deals with events from the death of Augustus in A.D. 14 to the death of Nero in A.D. 68.

In your study of ancient Rome, you have read poems by the three greatest poets of the Augustan Age—Virgil, Horace, and Ovid. Now you will read an account written by an ancient Roman historian. This account will help you imagine what life was like in Rome during a crisis.

In this excerpt Tacitus tells about a terrible fire that swept through Rome in A.D. 64. The fire began in the Circus Maximus, an arena in which chariot races were held, and raged out of control for several days. At the time, Nero was emperor. At first wise and serious, he had by this time become unpredictable and brutal. Many Romans even believed that Nero himself had secretly set fire to the city. As you read this excerpt, ask yourself these questions:

1. *What was Tacitus' purpose for writing?*
2. *What details are particularly interesting?*
3. *What does this account add to my understanding of ancient Rome?*

Now started the most terrible and destructive fire which Rome had ever experienced. It began in the Circus, where it adjoins the hills. Breaking out in shops selling inflammable[1] goods, and fanned by the wind, the conflagration instantly grew and swept the whole length of the Circus. There were no walled mansions or temples, or any other obstructions which could arrest it. First, the fire swept violently over the level spaces. Then it climbed the hills—but returned to ravage the lower ground again. It outstripped every countermeasure. The ancient city's narrow winding streets and irregular blocks encouraged its progress.

HUMANITIES CONNECTION This bust of a laurel-crowned ruler may depict the Emperor Nero. A moderate ruler at first, Nero later indulged in every kind of excess. Faced with plots against him, he took his own life.

Terrified, shrieking women, helpless old and young, people intent on their own safety, people unselfishly supporting invalids or waiting for them, fugitives and lingerers alike—all heightened the confusion. When people looked back, menacing flames sprang up before them or outflanked them. When they escaped to a neighboring quarter, the fire followed—even districts believed remote proved to be involved. Finally, with no idea where or what to flee, they crowded on to the country roads, or lay in the fields. Some who had lost everything—even their food for the day—could have escaped, but preferred to die. So did others, who had failed to rescue their loved ones. Nobody dared fight the flames. Attempts to do so were prevented by menacing gangs. Torches, too, were openly thrown in, by men crying that they acted under orders. Perhaps they had received orders. Or they may just have wanted to plunder unhampered.

Nero was at Antium.[2] He only returned to the city when the fire was approaching the mansion he had built to link the Gardens of Maecenas to

1. **inflammable:** able to burn.
2. **Antium** (ăn′tē-əm): a resort city on the Italian coast, about 30 miles south of Rome.

Working Independently

You may want to set aside time each week for independent reading, without making an assignment related to the reading. Or once students have completed the reading, either alone or aloud in groups, you may ask them to work together on a project, such as creating political cartoons that express the concerns of the Roman people about the fire, including their suspicions about its cause. If you choose to have students write responsively in their Reader's Notebook, suggest that they write about how Tacitus views his role as an interpreter of past events.

Discussing the Selection

The last page of this selection provides questions you might use for a post-reading class discussion.

Using the Selection for Assessment

If you want to use this selection as the basis for assessment, see **Integrated Assessment Book,** pp. 7–12, for test questions.

MINI LESSON Viewing and Representing

Bust of Emperor

ART APPRECIATION Have students study the image of the sculpture and the **Humanities Connection** on page 407. Remind students that Roman art, unlike Greek art, depicted subjects realistically. Have students identify the realistic details in the sculpture.

Possible Responses: the protruding lower lip, the prominent eyes, the laurel wreath, the aquiline nose, the cruel look, the broad shoulders

Then ask students to compare the sculpture with their impressions of Nero.

Possible Response: The ruler depicted in the sculpture looks haughty, imposing, and intimidating. These characteristics match those of Tacitus' Nero, a tyrant out to promote his own glory.

the Palatine.[3] The flames could not be prevented from overwhelming the whole of the Palatine, including his palace. Nevertheless, for the relief of the homeless, fugitive masses he threw open the Field of Mars, including Agrippa's public buildings, and even his own Gardens. Nero also constructed emergency accommodation for the destitute[4] multitude. Food was brought from Ostia and neighboring towns, and the price of corn was cut. Yet these measures, for all their popular character, earned no gratitude. For a rumor had spread that, while the city was burning, Nero had gone to his private stage and, comparing modern calamities with ancient, had sung of the destruction of Troy.

Nero had gone to his private stage and, comparing modern calamities with ancient, had sung of the destruction of Troy.

By the sixth day enormous demolitions had confronted the raging flames with bare ground and open sky, and the fire was finally stamped out. But before panic had subsided, or hope revived, flames broke out again in the more open regions of the city. Here there were fewer casualties; but the destruction of temples and pleasure arcades was even worse. This new conflagration caused additional ill-feeling because it started on Tigellinus' estate.[5] For people believed that Nero was ambitious to found a new city to be called after himself.

Of Rome's fourteen districts only four remained intact. Three were leveled to the ground. The other seven were reduced to a few scorched and mangled ruins. To count the mansions, blocks, and temples destroyed would be difficult. They included shrines of remote antiquity, the precious spoils of countless victories, Greek artistic masterpieces, and authentic records of old Roman genius. All the splendor of the rebuilt city did not prevent the older generation from remembering these irreplaceable objects. It was noted that the fire had started on July 19th, the day on which the Senonian Gauls[6] had captured and burnt the city.

But Nero profited by his country's ruin to build a new palace. Its wonders were not so much customary and commonplace luxuries like gold and jewels, but lawns and lakes and faked rusticity—woods here, open spaces and views there. With their cunning, impudent artificialities, Nero's architects and contractors outbid Nature.

They also fooled away an emperor's riches. For they promised to dig a navigable canal from Lake Avernus[7] to the Tiber estuary, over the stony shore and mountain barriers. The only water to feed the canal was in the Pontine marshes.[8] Elsewhere, all was

---

3. **Palatine** (păl′ə-tīn′): a hill on which many Roman emperors built their palaces.
4. **destitute:** without money or possessions.
5. **Tigellinus'** (tĭj′ə-lī′nəs) **estate:** the property of one of Nero's closest advisers.
6. **Senonian** (sə-nō′nē-ən) **Gauls:** a barbarian tribe that sacked Rome about 390 B.C.
7. **Lake Avernus** (ə-vûr′nəs): a lake near Naples, about 120 miles southeast of Rome.
8. **Pontine** (pŏn′tēn) **marshes:** a swampy region between Rome and Naples.

precipitous[9] or waterless. Moreover, even if a passage could have been forced, the labor would have been unendurable and unjustified. But Nero was eager to perform the incredible; so he attempted to excavate the hills adjoining Lake Avernus. Traces of his frustrated hopes are visible today.

In parts of Rome unfilled by Nero's palace, construction was not—as after the burning by the Gauls—without plan or demarcation.[10] Street-fronts were of regulated dimensions and alignment, streets were broad, and houses spacious. Their height was restricted, and their frontages protected by colonnades. Nero undertook to erect these at his own expense, and also to clear debris from building-sites before transferring them to their owners. He announced bonuses, in proportion to rank and resources, for the completion of houses and blocks before a given date. Rubbish was to be dumped in the Ostian marshes by corn-ships returning down the Tiber.

A fixed proportion of every building had to be massive, untimbered stone from Gabii or Alba (these stones being fireproof). Furthermore, guards were to ensure a more abundant and extensive public water-supply, hitherto diminished by irregular private enterprise. Householders were obliged to keep fire-fighting apparatus in an accessible place; and semi-detached houses were forbidden—they must have their own walls. These measures were welcomed for their practicality, and they beautified the new city. Some, however, believed that the old town's configuration had been healthier, since its narrow streets and high houses had provided protection against the burning sun, whereas now the shadowless open spaces radiated a fiercer heat.

So much for human precautions. Next came attempts to appease heaven. After consultation of the Sibylline books,[11] prayers were addressed to Vulcan, Ceres, and Proserpina. Juno, too, was propitiated. But neither human resources, nor imperial munificence,[12] nor appeasement of the gods, eliminated sinister suspicions that the fire had been instigated. To suppress this rumor, Nero fabricated[13] scapegoats—and punished with every refinement the notoriously depraved Christians (as they were popularly called). Their originator, Christ, had been executed in Tiberius' reign by the governor of Judaea, Pontius Pilatus. But in spite of this temporary setback the deadly superstition had broken out afresh, not only in Judaea (where the mischief had started) but even in Rome. All degraded and shameful practices collect and flourish in the capital.

First, Nero had self-acknowledged Christians arrested. Then, on their information, large numbers of others were condemned—not so much for incendiarism[14] as for their anti-social tendencies. Their deaths were made farcical.[15] Dressed in wild animals' skins, they were torn to pieces by dogs, or crucified, or made into torches to be ignited after dark as substitutes for daylight. Nero provided his Gardens for the spectacle, and exhibited displays in the Circus, at which he mingled with the crowd—or stood in a chariot, dressed as a charioteer. Despite their guilt as Christians, and the ruthless punishment it deserved, the victims were pitied. For it was felt that they were being sacrificed to one man's brutality rather than to the national interest. ❖

9. **precipitous** (prĭ-sĭp′ĭ-təs): very steep.
10. **demarcation:** marking of boundaries.
11. **Sibylline** (sĭb′ə-līn′) **books:** collections of prophecies, kept in a temple at Rome.
12. **munificence** (myo͞o-nĭf′ĭ-səns): generosity.
13. **fabricated:** dreamed up.
14. **incendiarism** (ĭn-sĕn′dē-ə-rĭz′əm): deliberate setting of fires.
15. **farcical** (fär′sĭ-kəl): ridiculous.

Answers to questions on page 406, pupil edition

1. **Possible Response:** to provide an objective, detached account of the burning of Rome
2. Responses will vary. Some students may state that the details about the people attempting to escape the fire are particularly interesting. Other students may state that the details describing Nero's conduct were most intriguing.
3. Responses will vary. Some students may mention that Tacitus' account helped them see the ancient Romans as similar to modern people. People today react to disasters much as the Romans reacted to the terrible fire–with confusion at the outset, then the spreading of rumors and the casting of blame.

Discussion Questions

1. What are your impressions of the Romans from Tacitus' account?
   Possible Response: Some students may state that they sympathize with the Romans who suffered from the horror of the fire. Others may state that they admire the Romans for rebuilding their city promptly and for enacting measures to safeguard it. Still others may state that they were repulsed by the plundering during the fire and the executions of the Christians afterwards.
2. Do you think the Romans were right to suspect Nero of causing the fire?
   Possible Responses: Students who think the Romans were right may say that Nero undoubtedly benefited from the fire that left the old city in ruins. This fire afforded him an opportunity to rebuild the city according to his own designs, constructing an elaborate woodland setting for his palace grounds. Moreover, his targeting the Christians seems like a ploy to divert suspicion from himself. Students who think the Romans were wrong may state that Nero responded promptly and even generously to the victims of the fire, opening his own gardens, erecting temporary housing, and importing food.

Objectives
- reflect on and assess understanding of Roman literature
- identify values reflected in Roman literature
- review imagery as a literary concept and identify examples of it
- understand important names and terms associated with Roman culture
- assess and build portfolios
- set a reading goal to increase understanding of Roman literature

Reflecting on the Literature
Literature and Values Students might mention that Virgil supports bravery, family loyalty, respect for the gods, compassion, and emotional control, as reflected in the conduct of Aeneas; Virgil condemns selfishness, violence, and cruelty, as reflected in the conduct of Pyrrhus; Horace supports moderation, good sense, and living in the present; Ovid supports self-discipline and the avoidance of extremes. Tacitus supports leadership that promotes the public good rather than personal glory.

Reviewing Literary Concepts
Appreciating Imagery If necessary, have students study or review the explanation of imagery on page 380. You may also wish to have students use the chart in the Unit Two Resource Book, page 70. Students should share their choices of images with a partner or in a small group.

Building Your Portfolio
Students will use their Presentation Portfolios to file what they consider their highest quality work in their Working Portfolios.

For more information on using writing and assessing portfolios, see the **Teacher's Guide to Assessment and Portfolio Use,** pp. 53–74.

Part Assessment

To assess skills and concepts taught in this unit part, use **Formal Assessment Book,** pp. 53–54.

Reflect and Assess

What did you learn about the literature of ancient Rome from reading the selections in Unit Two, Part 2? Why do you think it is important to learn about the ancient Romans and their literature? Use the following options to help you explore what you have learned.

Pasquis Proculus and his wife. Wall painting from Pompeii. Museo Archeologico Nazionale, Naples, Italy.

Reflecting on the Literature

Literature and Values The ancient Romans believed that literary works should serve a practical purpose—in Horace's words, "to teach and delight." In the selections in Part 2, the writers describe both conduct they favor and conduct they scorn. Think about the selections you've read, and identify the values each writer supports. Discuss whether these values are still important in today's world.

Reviewing Literary Concepts

Appreciating Imagery In this part of the book, you learned about a literary technique known as **imagery.** What images in the selections still stand out in your mind? List each image, and write the sense or senses that it appeals to. Which of these images do you think best supports the writer's message?

Building Your Portfolio

Writing Options Look back at the various Writing Options you completed for the lessons in this part of the book. Which piece of writing represents you at your creative best? Add that assignment to your **Presentation Portfolio**, along with a cover note explaining your choice.

Self ASSESSMENT

READER'S NOTEBOOK

You learned the following names and terms as you read the selections in this part. Write a sentence to describe or define each name or literary term. If you are unsure of a term, review its definition in Part 2 or check the **Glossary of Literary Terms** (page R91).

written epic	Emperor Augustus
epic similes	the Roman Empire
culture hero	*Metamorphoses*
Helen of Troy	narrative poem
"seize the day"	foreshadowing
odes	myth

Setting GOALS

The *Aeneid,* as you have learned, has had a profound influence on western culture and still stirs readers today. In this part, you read a lengthy excerpt from Book 2 of this epic poem. Why not read more of Virgil's masterpiece? Ask your teacher or a librarian to help you locate a modern translation to read on your own.

Assessment Self Assessment

If students need to review any of the key names or terms presented in Part 2, direct them to the pages indicated below:

written epics (page 357)
epic similes (page 380)
culture hero (pages 359 and 380)
Helen of Troy (pages 359 and 382)
"seize the day" (pages 392 and 394)
odes (page 393)
Emperor Augustus (pages 346, 347, 356, and 357)
the Roman Empire (pages 344 to 347)
Metamorphoses (pages 398 and 399)
narrative poem (page 399)
foreshadowing (page 404)
myth (pages 399 and 404)

Extend Your *Reading*

LITERATURE CONNECTIONS

Julius Caesar

WILLIAM SHAKESPEARE

This tragedy dramatizes the key events before and after Caesar's assassination. Shakespeare focuses on the conspirator Marcus Brutus, "the noblest Roman of them all." Loving Caesar yet fearing his growing power, Brutus decides to kill him for the good of Rome.

Here are just a few of the related readings that accompany *Julius Caesar:*

The Life of Caesar
BY SUETONIUS

Epitaph on a Tyrant
BY W. H. AUDEN

A Eulogy to Dr. Martin Luther King, Jr.
BY ROBERT F. KENNEDY

The Roman Way

EDITH HAMILTON

In this informal history, the author describes the Roman spirit as it is revealed in the works of the greatest authors of ancient Rome—including Virgil, Cicero, Caesar, and Horace. According to Hamilton, these authors were "Romans first, individual artists only second."

And Even *More* . . .

Books

Silver Pigs LINDSEY DAVIS
This mystery novel, set in A.D. 70, tells of the humorous adventures of Marcus Didius Falco, a dirt-poor detective. He shrewdly observes daily life in both Rome and Britain, giving the reader an inside view of political intrigue in the Roman Empire.

The Portable Roman Reader BASIL DAVENPORT, ED.
This anthology contains essential writings of many ancient Roman authors in fine English translations. Among the authors included are Terence, Plautus, Caesar, Cicero, Catullus, Virgil, Horace, Martial, Lucretius, Ovid, and Apuleius.

Other Media

Ancient Rome
Part of the History Through Art series, this video presents the story of Rome from the rule of the Etruscans through the decline of the Roman Empire. 40 minutes. Zenger Media. (VIDEOCASSETTE)

Spartacus
This film, directed by Stanley Kubrick, is based on the true story of a gladiator who led a slave revolt against the Roman Republic. Kirk Douglas, Laurence Olivier, and Jean Simmons star. 196 minutes. Zenger Media. (VIDEOCASSETTE)

Handbook to Life in Ancient Rome

LESLEY ADKINS AND ROY A. ADKINS

This handy reference, written by two professional archaeologists, contains a wealth of useful illustrations. The thematic chapters cover a variety of topics, including rulers, the legal system, and architectural feats.

More Recommendations for Your Students

Difficulty Level: Easy

Corbishley, Mike. *Ancient Rome* (Ny: Facts on File Inc., 1989). This introduction to the history of Rome covers such topics as the Etruscans, the beginning of Rome, and the rise of Julius Caesar.

Nardo, Don. *The Decline and Fall of the Roman Empire* (San Diego: Lucent Books, 1998). This study discusses Rome's rise to power and the complex reasons—especially military defeats and barbarian invasions—that led to its decline and fall.

Difficulty Level: Average

Dupont, Florence and Christopher Woodall (translator). *Daily Life in Ancient Rome* (Malden: Blackwell Publishers, 1994). This account draws heavily on primary sources to describe everyday life in Rome before Augustus Caesar's reign.

Tingay, G.I.F. and John Badcock. *These Were the Romans* (Chester Springs: Dufour Editions, Inc., 1990). This history, which includes quotations from several Roman speakers and writers, describes the growth of Roman civilization. One chapter, "Rome's Legacy," explores Rome's contributions to the modern world.

Difficulty Level: Challenging

Greenblatt, Miriam. *Augustus Caesar and Ancient Rome* (Tarrytown: Marshall Cavendish, Inc., 2000). This book describes the rise to power of young Octavian and his immensely popular reign as Rome's first emperor.

Shelton, Jo-Ann. *As the Romans Did: A Sourcebook in Roman Social History* (NY: Oxford University Press, Inc., 1997). This study explains the structure of Roman society, covering topics such as "Women in Roman Society," "Families," "Slaves," and "The Roman Army."

The **Reading and Writing for Assessment** feature provides practice in taking standardized tests. As students work through this lesson, they will learn strategies for reading comprehension questions, multiple-choice questions, and essay and short-answer questions. Boxed strategies located alongside the text will help guide students through the activities. These strategies model processes students can use as they take standardized tests.

This feature is based on and will help students prepare for state assessments as well as end-of-course assessments. It will also prepare students for the reading comprehension questions used on such college entrance examinations as the Scholastic Aptitude Test (SAT) and the American College Test (ACT).

Objectives

- understand and apply strategies for reading a test selection
- recognize literary and organizational techniques in a test selection
- understand and apply strategies for answering multiple-choice questions about a test selection
- respond to a writing prompt and present ideas in a logical order
- understand and apply strategies for revising and proofreading a test response

Standardized Test Practice

Reading & Writing for Assessment

Throughout high school, you will be tested on your ability to read and understand different kinds of reading selections. The tests will assess your basic understanding of ideas and knowledge of vocabulary. They will also assess your ability to analyze and evaluate the messages of the selections, along with the techniques the writers use in getting their messages across.

Some useful test-taking strategies are presented in this lesson. Practice applying the strategies by working through each of the models provided.

PART 1 How to Read a Test Selection

Sometimes a test requires you to read a passage and then answer multiple-choice questions about it. Applying these test-taking strategies, taking notes, and marking important passages as you read can help you focus on information.

STRATEGIES FOR READING A TEST SELECTION

- **Before you begin reading, skim the questions that follow the passage.** These can help focus your reading.
- **Think about the title.** What does it suggest about the overall message or theme of the selection?
- **Use active reading strategies, such as analyzing, predicting, and questioning.** Take notes in the margin or highlight important words and passages to help you focus your reading. (Do not do this, however, if the test directions forbid you to mark on the test.)
- **Look for main ideas.** You will often find them stated at the beginning or end of paragraphs. Sometimes they are implied rather than directly stated. After reading each paragraph, ask yourself, "What was this passage about?"
- **Note the literary elements and techniques used by the writer.** You might, for example, consider the writer's tone or use of comparison and contrast. Then ask yourself what effect is created by each element or technique.
- **Examine the sequence of ideas.** Are the ideas developed in chronological order, presented in order of importance, or organized in some other way—as causes and effects, for instance, or as problems and solutions?
- **Think about the writer's purpose and message.** What questions does the selection answer? What new questions does it raise? What generalizations can you make about the subject?

Reading Selection

❶ Ancient Greece Revived in Rome; Colosseum Reopens as Theater with Staging of *Oedipus Rex*

by Sarah Delaney

1 ❷ More than 15 centuries after its last gladiators saluted Caesar, the Roman Colosseum reopened tonight as a place of public entertainment, this time for a small, cultured audience rather than tens of thousands of plebeians screaming for blood. The draw for tonight's 500 people . . . was a Greek-language performance of the ancient Greek drama *Oedipus Rex.* As spotlights illuminated chambers and walls of the giant ruin, actors played out the classic story of love and incest.

2 Costas Galanakis, cast as the old blind seer, Tiresias, declared it "a great, emotional moment to perform here."

3 ❸ Concetta Notardonato, 47, a Roman and an avid theatergoer, said from her standing position on the third tier of the arena that "it's a great idea, and the setting is fantastic." But she felt ticket prices, about $25, were too high. And, she objected to the language. "We don't all know Greek," she lamented. "A unique performance like this should be more accessible to everybody; the Colosseum is a symbolic place for the people."

4 Opened in the year 80 as a venue for Rome's beloved spectacles, the grand stone structure closed and descended into ruin in the centuries after the fall of the empire. But this evening, courtesy of government agencies here, it reopened for a show ❹ that could not have been less like the mayhem of Ridley Scott's film *Gladiator.*

5 A large helium balloon floated in balmy summer air over the arena; the chorus, loosely clad in white, chanted and sang amid ghostly white plaster statues set up as part of the scenery. From the distance came the sounds of sirens and streetcars.

6 The stage was a newly built wooden platform. It partly re-created the arena's long-lost oak floor that covered walkways and cells where exotic beasts and armored fighters waited to come up and entertain Romans of every sort. The show, put on by the Greek National Theater, was the first of eight performances of Sophocles' *Oedipus* trilogy, including *Antigone* and an opera based on *Oedipus at Colonus. . . .*

STRATEGIES IN ACTION

❶ Look at the title.

ONE STUDENT'S THOUGHTS

"The title tells me that this article deals with ancient Greek culture and the Roman Colosseum."

❷ Look for main ideas. "This selection is about the reopening of the Roman Colosseum after more than 1,500 years."

YOUR TURN

Look at the end of the article for other stated main ideas.

❸ Evaluate sources of information. "The person being quoted lives in Rome and goes to the theater often. She probably knows what she's talking about, and maybe her views are shared by other theatergoers."

❹ Note the signal words indicating writer's use of contrast. "The writer tells me what this show is *not* like. Even if I've never seen the film *Gladiator*, I know that this show is not violent or rowdy."

YOUR TURN

Find other instances of comparison and contrast.

TEST PRACTICE

Teaching the Lesson

1 Begin by previewing the text. Note the title and identify the subject of the reading selection. Read through the questions and prompts at the end of the text. Ask students what they will need to look for as they read.

Possible Response: Students should look for information about the Colosseum and how it relates to Greek culture. They should also look for an explanation of the Colosseum's reopening and the reasons for this revival of Greek culture.

2 Students are more likely to be tested on the main ideas in the selection than on specific details. Ask students which ideas in this paragraph they think are important enough to be included on a test.

YOUR TURN Another main idea stated at the end of the article is that "the Colosseum by moonlight has enchanted visitors for centuries."

3 Reading comprehension tests often assess students' ability to recognize bias and evaluate sources of information.

4 Review with students other signal words or phrases that indicate contrast: *unlike, on the other hand, in contrast, contrary to, alternatively, rather than* and *as opposed to.*

YOUR TURN Other instances of comparison and contrast follow.

- In paragraph 1, the Colosseum's current audience ("a small, cultured audience") is contrasted with audiences of the past ("tens of thousands of plebeians screaming for blood").
- In paragraph 7, the Colosseum is compared in form to present-day sports facilities.
- In paragraph 12, the human spirit is compared to the sun and the moon; their task is contrasted with the tasks that they have in other places.

5 Some less proficient readers are inclined to take what they read at face value and not ask themselves questions about the text. Encourage students to let their minds go beyond the words at hand and to wonder about things that are curious or unclear to them. Use the following questions to guide students in formulating their own questions about the text.

- What questions do you have about the seating arrangements at the Colosseum in the old days?

Possible Responses: Why was social standing so important? Why did men and women have to sit separately?

- What would you like to know about the *venationes*?

Possible Responses: How did they get the wild animals from the wilderness to the Colosseum? Why did they keep the animals in the dark and without food? Why did people like to watch animals fight people? Why were the games abolished?

6 Use the following questions to help students unlock the meanings of unfamiliar words:

- Does the sentence or paragraph offer any clues to the word's meaning?
- Does the sentence restate or extend information provided earlier in the selection?

To save time on a test, students should first read the questions that follow the test selection. Then they can look for answers to the questions as they read. The beginning and end of a selection are often good places to look for information about a writer's purpose.

7 The Colosseum was begun by the emperor Vespasian. Built to hold 75,000 people, it has the same basic form as present-day sports facilities. ⑤ Even now, visitors can sense the awe that it commanded in its day.

8 A day at the Colosseum 20 centuries ago was a decidedly popular form of entertainment. Notices were placed around the city and entrance was free. Seating was determined by social standing and sex; the emperor and his family naturally got the best spot, near where today's politicians and selected guests were seated, at the east end of the elliptical arena.

9 Members of the ancient Roman Senate occupied the lowest section—the box seats—while choice places also went to priests, judges and ambassadors. Young men who had not yet reached adulthood had their own section, and their teachers were assigned places nearby. Women were ⑥ relegated to the top tiers. White cloth awnings around the top of the open-air bowl shielded spectators from the sun.

10 The *venationes,* or beast hunts, in the arena took place amid elaborate scenery evoking the exotic lands from which the tigers, lions, hippopotamuses or even giraffes were taken. Gladiators fought against or among the animals, which had often been held in the dark without food for long periods before being loosed into the arena.

11 Gladiatorial games were abolished in 438, the *venationes* in 523. In the centuries that followed, the structure was reduced to a quarry site from which marble and limestone were pilfered. An entire side of the structure disappeared.

12 Still, the Colosseum by moonlight has enchanted visitors for centuries, including the German poet Goethe, who wrote in his *Italian Journey* that "The Colosseum looked especially beautiful. . . . This is the kind of illumination by which to see the Pantheon, the Capitol, the square in front of St. Peter's. . . . Like the human spirit, the sun and the moon have a quite different task to perform here than they have in other places, for here their glance is returned by gigantic, solid masses."

STRATEGIES IN ACTION

⑤ Read actively by questioning.
"What was the Colosseum really like in 'its day'?"

⑥ Use context clues to unlock word meanings.
"Women were given the worst seats. *Relegated* must mean 'assigned to an undesirable place.'"

Skim the questions that follow the passage.
"I see there's a question about the writer's purpose. What is her purpose? She seems fairly enthusiastic, but is she really trying to persuade me? I think she is informing me."

Check Your Understanding

Have students use the following questions to test their own understanding of the selection before they answer the questions in their texts.

- What were the main ideas in the selection?
- How does the writer encourage readers to care about the information in the article?
- What structure does the writer use for the selection?
- Did the selection answer all your questions about the subject? If not, what questions remain unanswered?

PART 2 **How to Answer Multiple-Choice Questions**

Use the strategies in the box and the notes in the side column to help you answer the questions below and on the following pages.

On the basis of the selection you have just read, choose the best answer for each of the following questions.

1. After reading paragraph 1, what two things can you expect to find compared in this article?
   A. small audiences and large audiences
   B. ancient and modern entertainments in the Roman Colosseum
   C. life in the fifth century and life today
   D. people who are cultured and people who are bloodthirsty
2. According to one spectator, what is wrong with the performance of *Oedipus Rex?*
   A. The Colosseum is too crowded.
   B. The play is performed in Greek, which is unfamiliar to most of the Italian audience.
   C. The play is too old to be interesting.
   D. all of the above
3. Which of the following statements most closely paraphrases the quotation from Goethe?
   A. The Colosseum is like the human spirit.
   B. The Colosseum is the most beautiful building in Rome.
   C. The Colosseum and other Roman buildings are more massive than anything else lit by the sun and the moon.
   D. The Colosseum is so large that it blocks the light of the sun.
4. Which of the following statements best expresses the article's main idea?
   A. Greek plays are much better than beast hunts.
   B. Even after centuries of decay, the glory of the Colosseum lives on.
   C. The ancient Romans were unsophisticated.
   D. Everyone should see *Oedipus Rex.*
5. What was the writer's purpose for writing this article?
   A. to inform
   B. to persuade
   C. to entertain
   D. to remind

STRATEGIES FOR ANSWERING MULTIPLE-CHOICE QUESTIONS

- **Ask questions** that help you eliminate some of the choices.
- **Pay attention to choices** such as "all of the above" or "none of the above." To eliminate them, all you need to find is one answer that doesn't fit.
- **Skim your notes.** Details you noticed as you read may provide answers.

STRATEGIES IN ACTION

Pay attention to choices such as "all of the above."

ONE STUDENT'S THOUGHTS

"No one says anything at all about the Colosseum's being crowded, so I can eliminate choice A and, therefore, choice D as well."

YOUR TURN

Look at the quotations to see whether choice B or choice C makes more sense.

Skim your notes.

ONE STUDENT'S THOUGHTS

"I don't think a straightforward article like this is meant to entertain, and I really don't think the writer is trying to remind me of anything, so I can eliminate choices C and D."

YOUR TURN

What other choice can you eliminate?

TEST PRACTICE

Guiding Student Response

Multiple Choice Questions

1. B
2. B

YOUR TURN Choice **C** also does not make sense; nowhere in the article does anyone say anything about the play being too old or uninteresting. Theatergoer Concetta Notardonato does complain specifically about the play being performed in Greek, so choice **B** is correct.

3. C
4. B
5. A

YOUR TURN Choice **B** does not make sense; there is really nothing persuasive in the article. Rather than promote a particular side or point of view, it seems that it simply informs the reader by presenting an interesting story. Choice **A** makes the most sense.

Guiding Student Response

Short-Answer Question

The writer includes the quotation from Goethe in order to show that people across the centuries have been inspired and moved by the sight of the Colosseum.

YOUR TURN The first sentence in the last paragraph introduces Goethe as an example of the many visitors who have been so moved by the sight.

Essay Question

Possible Response to Prompt

According to this article, it seems that the ancient Romans enjoyed much rowdier, more violent forms of entertainment than the current Romans do. In ancient times, thousands of Romans crowded into the Colosseum to watch gladiators fight bloodthirsty wild animals. These games were open to the public at no charge and were attended by Romans of different social standing.

Today, on the other hand, a very different sort of show is taking place at the Colosseum. Sophocles' classic play *Oedipus Rex* is being produced in the original Greek language. This is a much more civilized event, and also a more exclusive one; audience members must pay about $25 for a ticket, and they'll have to know Greek if they're going to understand the play. It is not an event for the masses.

It is amazing that one theater should hold two such different productions, across so many centuries. The Colosseum, however, is such a grand and glorious place that audiences are enchanted by it, no matter what kind of show they see there.

PART 3 How to Respond in Writing

Sometimes, you may be asked to write answers to questions about a reading passage. **Short-answer questions** usually ask you to answer in a sentence or two. An **essay question** requires a fully developed piece of writing.

Short-Answer Question

STRATEGIES FOR RESPONDING TO SHORT-ANSWER QUESTIONS

- **Identify the key words** in the writing prompt that tell you the ideas to discuss. Make sure you know what is meant by each.
- **Make your response** direct and to the point.
- **Support your ideas** by using evidence from the selection.

Sample Question

Answer the following question in one or two sentences.

Why do you think the writer has included the quotation from Goethe at the end of the article?

STRATEGIES IN ACTION

Support your ideas by using evidence from the selection.

ONE STUDENT'S THOUGHTS

"I should look at the text leading up to the quotation. I'll probably find a clue there about why the writer used it."

YOUR TURN

Find the text that precedes the quotation from Goethe. How does the quotation fit into its context?

Essay Question

STRATEGIES FOR ANSWERING ESSAY QUESTIONS

- **Look for direction words** in the writing prompt—for example, *essay, analyze, describe,* or *compare and contrast*—that tell you how to respond.
- **List the points** you want to make before beginning to write.
- **Write an interesting introduction** that presents your main point.
- **Develop your ideas** by using evidence from the selection to support your statements.
- **Present the ideas** in a logical order.
- **Write a conclusion** that summarizes your points.
- **Check your work** for correct grammar.

Sample Prompt

From this article, what conclusions can you draw about the differences between entertainments in ancient Rome and in present-day Rome? Write a short essay in which you compare and contrast the forms of entertainment, using evidence from the text to support your conclusions.

Look for direction words.

ONE STUDENT'S THOUGHTS

"The prompt is asking me to *compare* and *contrast* the entertainment in ancient and contemporary Rome. I'll have to look for evidence about both kinds of entertainment, and explain how they are alike and how they are different."

YOUR TURN

Make a list of similarities and differences between ancient and contemporary Roman entertainment. You might want to organize your thoughts in a Venn diagram.

PART 4 How to Revise and Edit Your Test Essay

Here is part of a student's first draft in response to the writing prompt at the bottom of page 416. Read it and answer the multiple-choice questions that follow.

> Ancient and contemporary Romans chose very different kinds of public entertainment based on this article. First of all, the gladiator games and venationes were rowdy, violent spectacles open to all social classes. In contrast, the modern performance of *Oedipus Rex* was a much quieter, more civilized event. The cost of admission, and the fact that the performance was in Greek, limited the audience to educated people with some money to spend.
>
> It seems that ancient Romans were more concerned with showing everyone a noisy good time. Even if it involved bloodshed. Contemporary Romans have always appeared to have gentler tastes and to be more exclusive.

1. What is the BEST way to revise the first sentence of this essay?

A. According to this article, the writer shows great differences between entertainment in ancient and contemporary Rome.

B. Ancient and contemporary Romans are very different.

C. According to this article, ancient and contemporary Romans chose very different kinds of public entertainment.

D. There are two distinct differences between entertainment in ancient and contemporary Rome based on this article.

2. What is the BEST way to revise the beginning of the second paragraph?

A. It seems that ancient Romans are more concerned with showing everyone a noisy good time. Even if it involved bloodshed.

B. Ancient Romans were more concerned with showing everyone a noisy good time; even if it involved bloodshed.

C. It seems that ancient Romans were more concerned with showing everyone a noisy good time, even if it involved bloodshed.

D. Even if it involved bloodshed: it seems that ancient Romans were more concerned with showing everyone a noisy good time.

3. What is the BEST revision of the final sentence?

A. Contemporary Romans appear to have gentler tastes and to be more exclusive.

B. Contemporary Romans appeared to have gentler tastes and to be more exclusive.

C. Contemporary Romans are appearing to have gentler tastes and to be more exclusive.

D. Contemporary Romans will forever appear to have gentler tastes and to be more exclusive.

STRATEGIES FOR REVISING, EDITING, AND PROOFREADING

- **Read the passage carefully.**
- **Note the parts that are confusing** or don't make sense. What kinds of errors would such problems signal?
- **Look for errors** in grammar, usage, spelling, and capitalization. Common errors include:
  - run-on sentences
  - sentence fragments
  - faulty subject-verb agreement
  - unclear pronoun reference

Guiding Student Response

Answers

1. C
2. C
3. A

Check Your Understanding

Have students reread their own responses to the short-answer and essay questions. Then have students use the following questions to guide themselves as they revise and edit their own work.

- Have I responded directly to the direction words in the writing prompt?
- Have I supported my ideas with evidence from the selection?
- Have I presented my ideas in a logical order?
- Have I included an introduction and a conclusion?
- Have I used correct grammar?

Traditions in Chinese and Japanese Literature
In this unit, students will read classic literature from ancient China. They will also read later Japanese literature, which was influenced by Chinese traditions.

Part 1
From Observation to Insight: Literature of Ancient China This part introduces students to the teachings of Confucius and Lao-tzu, whose moral observations were the basis of the Confucian and Taoist philosophical systems, respectively. Part 1 also contains poems by Li Po and Tu Fu, the greatest poets of the T'ang dynasty, who intently observed nature to express insights about human life.

Part 2
Capturing the Moment: Literature of Japan The Japanese literature in this part often re-creates a single instant, experienced subjectively. Diary entries from *The Pillow Book,* for example, record the fleeting thoughts and feelings of a woman at the Heian court. Brief tanka and haiku poems present images from nature, capturing a moment, a season, an animal's movements, a mood. Students can compare traditional Japanese haiku with 20th-century haiku from the United States and Mexico in a **Comparing Literature Across Cultures** feature.

Traditions in Chinese and Japanese Literature 1600 B.C.–A.D. 1800

Moonlight on the River Sheba, Ando Hiroshige. Musée des Arts Asiatiques-Guimet, Paris. Photo © Bridgeman-Giraudon/Art Resource, New York.

"Everything has beauty but not everyone sees it."

—Confucius

Making Connections

Ask: Do you agree with Confucius that "Everything has beauty but not everyone sees it"? Why do you agree or disagree?

Possible Responses: Students who agree may note that certain people find beauty in things that most people fear, such as snakes or hurricanes. Students who disagree may believe there is no beauty to be found in such things as disease or murder.

PART 1 SKILLS TRACE

Features and Selections	Literary Analysis	Reading and Critical Thinking	Writing Opportunities	
Traditions in Chinese and Japanese Literature 1600 B. C. – A.D. 1800				
From Observation to Insight: Literature of Ancient China		Interpreting the Text, 424, 426 Using the Time Line, 429		
Learning the Language of Literature Moral Teaching Through Literature	Maxim, 432 Anecdote, 433 Parable, 433	Strategies for Reading, 433		
NONFICTION *from the* Analects	Maxim, 435, 439 Maxim, 436	Analyzing Maxims, 435, 439 Analyzing Maxims, 436, 438 Records of the Historian, 436		
NONFICTION *from the* Tao Te Ching **Related Reading** The Fish Rejoice	Paradox, 441, 445 Paradox, 442	Interpreting Paradoxes, 441, 445 Interpreting Paradoxes, 442 Tai Chi, 441		
POETRY *from the* Book of Odes Mulberry on the Lowland We Pick Ferns, We Pick Ferns	Repetition, 446, 451 Repetition. 446, 448, 450	Reading Poetry Aloud, 446, 451 Reading Poetry Aloud, 446, 450 Great Wall, 448 Standardized Test Practice (Evaluating and Making Judgments), 450		
POETRY The River-Merchant's Wife: A Letter Still Night Thoughts Gazing at the Lu Mountain Waterfall	Imagery, 453, 459 Imagery, 454, 456, 458	Visualizing, 453, 459 Visualizing, 454, 456, 458 Lu Mountain, 457	Mood Poem, 460 Notes for a Plot, 460 Descriptive Paragraph, 460	
The Translator at Work Translating Chinese Poetry		Comparing and Contrasting, 461	Activity (translating), 461	
POETRY Dreaming of Li Po Jade Flower Palace Song of P'eng-ya	Mood and Imagery, 463, 470 Mood and Imagery, 464, 466	Understanding and Appreciating Poetry, 463, 470 Understanding and Appreciating Poetry, 464, 466, 468 The Experience of Loss, 464 Dragons, 465	Informal Assessment (Prose Retelling), 468	
Related Reading Ozymandias				
Connect to Today The Refugees: People Without a Country			Research Project, 471	

LEGEND **Black type – Pupil Edition**
Green type – Teacher's Edition
DLS – Daily Language SkillBuilder

Speaking and Listening Viewing and Representing	Inquiry and Research	Grammar, Usage, and Mechanics	Vocabulary
Using the Map, 420			
Art Appreciation, 438		DLS, 434	
Art Appreciation, 443		DLS, 440	Suffixes, 442
Art Appreciation, 447 Choral Reading, 449		DLS, 446	
Film Score, 460 Landscape Painting, 460 Dramatic Reading, 460 Art Appreciation, 458	Cosmopolitan City, 460 Powerful Empress, 460	DLS, 452 Using Verbs: Principal Parts, 454	
Art Appreciation, 466, 469 Art Appreciation, 467	Research Project, 471	DLS, 462	

LEGEND **Black type – Pupil Edition**
Green type – Teacher's Edition
DLS – Daily Language SkillBuilder

UNIT THREE
PART 1 SKILLS TRACE

Features and Selections	Literary Analysis	Reading and Critical Thinking	Writing Opportunities
Writing Workshop Lyric Poetry Standardized Test Practice Building Vocabulary Sentence Crafting		Analyzing Student Models, 477, 478	Lyric Poetry, 476, 479 Using Sound Devices, 480 Using Parallelism for Effect, 483 Choosing a Topic, 479 Planning the Poem, 479
Reflect and Assess	Reflecting on the Literature (Thoughtful Observation), 484 Reviewing Literary Concepts (Lyric Poetry), 484		Building Your Portfolio, 484

UNIT THREE
PART 2 SKILLS TRACE

Features and Selections	Literary Analysis	Reading and Critical Thinking	Writing Opportunities
Capturing the Moment: Literature of Japan		Interpreting the Text, 488, 491 Using the Time Line, 495	
NONFICTION *from* The Pillow Book The Cat Who Lived in the Palace *from* Hateful Things *from* Graceful Things Embarrassing Things Letters Are Commonplace I Remember a Clear Morning	Diary, 499, 506 Diary, 500, 504	Examining Point of View, 499, 506 Examining Point of View, 500, 504 Women of the Heian Court, 504	Pillow Book, 507 List of Distressing Things, 507 Informal Assessment (Writing a Diary Entry), 503
NONFICTION Zen Teachings Zen Parables **Connect to Today** Zen – Alive and Well	Wisdom Literature, 511, 516 Wisdom Literature, 512, 514	Summarizing Main Ideas, 511, 516 Summarizing Main Ideas, 512 China's Influence, 514 Paired or Group Discussion, 517	Zen Solutions, 517
DRAMA The Deserted Crone	Setting and Characters, 519, 532 Setting and Characters, 522, 528, 530	Questioning, 519, 532 Questioning, 520, 522, 524, 526, 528 Moon Viewing in Japan, 521 Mountains of Japan, 522 Unit Conversions, 526 Amida Buddha, 530	Name and Legend, 533 Character Sketch, 533
POETRY Tanka Poetry	Diction, 535, 539 Diction, 536, 538	Comparing Moods, 535, 539 Comparing Moods, 536	

LEGEND **Black type – Pupil Edition**
Green type – Teacher's Edition
DLS – Daily Language SkillBuilder

Speaking and Listening Viewing and Representing	Inquiry and Research	Grammar, Usage, and Mechanics	Vocabulary
		Using Punctuation, 480 End Marks, 481 Comma Usage, 481 Quotation Marks, 481 Semicolons, 481 Using Parallelism for Effect, 483 End Punctuation, 480 Quotation Marks, 481 Commas in a Series, 483	Homophones, Homonyms, and Homographs, 482
			Self-Assessment, 484 Self-Assessment, 484
Using the Map, 486			
Scene Illustration, 507 Interview with Shōnagon, 507 Art Appreciation, 500, 502	Canine Communication, 507	DLS, 498 Simple Verb Tenses, 505	Analogies, 507 Context Clues, 501
Paired or Discussion Group, 517 Art Appreciation, 512, 515 Paired or Group Discussion, 517		DLS, 510	Context Clues, 513
Noh Performance, 533 Dramatic Presentation, 523 Choral Reading, 524 Art Appreciation, 527, 528	Shakespearean Noh Plays, 533	DLS, 518 Perfect Verb Tenses, 520 Passive and Active Voice, 529	Meaning Clues, 533 Etymology, 525
Art Appreciation, 538		DLS, 534	

LEGEND **Black type – Pupil Edition**
Green type – Teacher's Edition
DLS – Daily Language SkillBuilder

PART 2 SKILLS TRACE

Features and Selections	Literary Analysis	Reading and Critical Thinking	Writing Opportunities
Comparing Literature Across Cultures Haiku Across the Centuries		Compare and Contrast, 540, 546, 550	Standardized Test Practice (Comparison-and-Contrast Essay), 540
POETRY Japanese Haiku **Related Reading** *from* The Spring of My Life	Analyzing Imagery, 541, 546 Analyzing Imagery, 542, 544	Interpreting Details, 541, 546 Interpreting Details, 542 Traditional Clothing, 544	
POETRY Haiku in the 20th Century		Interpreting Details, 548 Civil Rights Movement, 549	
Comparing Literature Standardized Test Practice			Comparison-and-Contrast Essay, 551 Standardized Test Practice (Responding to a Writing Prompt), 551
Writing Workshop Problem-Solution Essay Standardized Test Practice Building Vocabulary Sentence Crafting		Analyzing a Student Model, 553–554	Problem-Solution Essay, 552, 555 Planning Your Problem-Solution Essay, 555 Elaborating with Facts and Statistics, 556 Patterns of Organization (Picturing Text Structure), 553 Choosing a Topic, 555 Planning the Problem-Solution Essay, 555
Reflect and Assess	Reflecting on the Literature (Recurring Topics), 560 Reviewing Literary Concepts (Identifying Imagery and Mood), 560		Building Your Portfolio, 560

LEGEND **Black type – Pupil Edition**
Green type – Teacher's Edition
DLS – Daily Language SkillBuilder

Speaking and Listening Viewing and Representing	Inquiry and Research	Grammar, Usage, and Mechanics	Vocabulary
		DLS, 541	
		DLS, 547	
		Incorrect Verb Forms, 556, 557 Passive Voice, 557 Double Negatives, 557 Capitalization Errors, 557 Creating Compound and Complex Sentences, 559 Incorrect Verb Forms, 556 Passive Voice, 557 Run-on Sentences, 559	Using Reference Tools, 558
			Self-Assessment, 560 Self-Assessment, 560

LEGEND **Black type – Pupil Edition**
Green type – Teacher's Edition **DLS – Daily Language SkillBuilder**

RESOURCE MANAGEMENT GUIDE PART 1

	Unit Resource Book	Assessment	Integrated Technology and Media	Additional Support
From Observation to Insight **Literature of Ancient China**			Humanities classzone.com	**World Art and Cultures Transparencies** • AT5 Chinese cooking vessel • AT9 Chinese army figures • AT16 Chinese tomb rubbing • AT25 *Court Ladies Preparing Newly Woven Silk* [detail] • AT60 Sorting of Cocoons
from the **Analects** *pp. 434–439*	• Active Reading p. 4 • Literary Analysis p. 5	• Selection Test, Formal Assessment pp. 55–56 • Teacher's Guide to Assessment and Portfolio Use Test Generator	Humanities Activity classzone.com	
from the **Tao Te Ching** *pp. 440–445*	• Active Reading p. 6 • Literary Analysis p. 7	• Selection Test, Formal Assessment pp. 57–58 • Teacher's Guide to Assessment and Portfolio Use Test Generator		
from the **Book of Odes** **Mulberry on the Lowland** **We Pick Ferns, We Pick Ferns** *pp. 446–451*	• Active Reading p. 8 • Literary Analysis p. 9	• Selection Test, Formal Assessment pp. 59–60 • Teacher's Guide to Assessment and Portfolio Use Test Generator		
The River-Merchant's Wife: A Letter **Still Night Thoughts** **Gazing at the Lu Mountain Waterfall** *pp. 452–461*	• Active Reading p. 10 • Literary Analysis p. 11	• Selection Test, Formal Assessment pp. 61–62 • Teacher's Guide to Assessment and Portfolio Use Test Generator	Research Starter classzone.com	
Dreaming of Li Po **Jade Flower Palace** **Song of P'eng-ya** *pp. 462–471*	• Active Reading p. 12 • Literary Analysis p. 13	• Selection Test, Formal Assessment pp. 63–64 • Teacher's Guide to Assessment and Portfolio Use Test Generator	Research Starter classzone.com	This selection is included in the *World Literature InterActive Reader™*.

Writing Workshop: Lyric Poetry *pp. 476–483*

Unit Three Resource Book
- Prewriting p. 14
- Drafting and Elaboration p. 15
- Peer Response Guide pp. 16–17
- Revising, Editing, and Proofreading p. 18
- Student Models pp. 19–24
- Rubric p. 25

Publishing Options classzone.com

Teacher's Guide to Assessment and Portfolio Use

Unit Assessment	*Unit Technology*
• Unit Three, Part 1 Test, Formal Assessment pp. 65–66 Test Generator • Unit Three Integrated Test, Integrated Assessment pp. 13–18	classzone.com

	Unit Resource Book	Assessment	Integrated Technology and Media	Additional Support
Capturing the Moment **Literature of Japan**			Humanities classzone.com	**World Art and Cultures Transparencies** • AT26 *The Descent of Amida and the 25 Bodhisattvas to Collect the Soul of the Deceased* • AT42 *Foreigners*
from **The Pillow Book** **The Cat Who Lived in the Palace** *from* **Hateful Things** *from* **Graceful Things** **Embarrassing Things** **Letters Are Commonplace** **I Remember a Clear Morning** *pp. 498–507*	• Summary p. 29 • Active Reading p. 30 • Literary Analysis p. 31 • Words to Know p. 32 • Selection Quiz p. 33	• Selection Test, Formal Assessment pp. 67–68 • Teacher's Guide to Assessment and Portfolio Use Test Generator	Research Starter classzone.com	
Milestones in World Literature **The Tale of the Genji** *pp. 508–509*			Milestone Links classzone.com	
Zen Teachings **Zen Parables** *pp. 510–517*	• Active Reading p. 34 • Literary Analysis p. 35	• Selection Test, Formal Assessment pp. 69–70 • Teacher's Guide to Assessment and Portfolio Use Test Generator		
The Deserted Crone *pp. 518–533*	• Summary p. 36 • Active Reading p. 37 • Literary Analysis p. 38 • Words to Know p. 39 • Selection Quiz p. 40	• Selection Test, Formal Assessment pp. 71–72 • Teacher's Guide to Assessment and Portfolio Use Test Generator	Research Starter classzone.com	
Tanka Poetry *pp. 534–539*	• Active Reading p. 41 • Literary Analysis p. 42	• Selection Test, Formal Assessment pp. 73–74 • Teacher's Guide to Assessment and Portfolio Use Test Generator		
Japanese Haiku *pp. 540–546* **Haiku in the 20th Century** *pp. 547–550*	• Points of Comparison p. 43 • Active Reading p. 44 • Literary Analysis p. 45 • Compare/contrast Essay p. 46	• Selection Test, Formal Assessment pp. 75–76 • Teacher's Guide to Assessment and Portfolio Use Test Generator		

Writing Workshop: Problem-Solution Essay *pp. 552–559*

Unit Three Resource Book
- Prewriting p. 47
- Drafting and Elaboration p. 48
- Peer Response Guide pp. 49–50
- Revising, Editing, and Proofreading p. 51
- Student Models pp. 52–57
- Rubric p. 58

Publishing Options classzone.com

Teacher's Guide to Assessment and Portfolio Use

Unit Assessment	*Unit Technology*
• Unit Three, Part 2 Test, Formal Assessment pp. 77–78 Test Generator	classzone.com

DAILY LANGUAGE SKILLBUILDERS

Selection	SkillBuilder Sentences	Suggested Answers
from the Analects	**1.** For 13 years confucius lived away from his home state of lu in china, advising rullers in other states. **2.** Why did confucius active in politics fail to gain any real political power in his lifetime	**1.** For 13 years **C**onfucius lived away from his home state of **L**u in **C**hina, advising **rulers** in other states. **2.** Why did **C**onfucius**,** active in politics**,** fail to gain any real political power in his lifetime**?**
from the Tao Te Ching	**1.** Did Lao-tzu wrote the Tao Te Ching the most important book of Taoist thought **2.** According too the tao said David people need to live close to nature.	**1.** Did Lao-tzu **write** the **Tao Te Ching,** the most important book of Taoist thought**?** **2.** **"**According **to** the **T**ao,**"** said David, **"**people need to live close to nature.**"**
from the Book of Odes Mulberry on the Lowland We Pick Ferns, We Pick Ferns	**1.** The people in the book of odes ranges from heroes to ordinary peeple. **2.** The various works, explained sara, were written as long ago as 1000 B.C."	1. The people in the **B**ook of **O**des range from heroes to ordinary **people**. [Students should delete the *s* from *ranges.*] **2.** **"**The various works,**"** explained **S**ara, **"**were written as long ago as 1000 B.C."
The River-Merchant's Wife: A Letter Still Night Thoughts Gazing at the Lu Mountain Waterfall	**1.** According to one legend Li Po drowned, when he tryed to embrace the moons reflection in the water **2.** When li po was twenty he began wander.	**1.** According to one legend**,** Li Po drowned when he **tried** to embrace the moon**'**s reflection in the water**.** [Students should delete the comma after *drowned.*] **2.** When **L**i **P**o was twenty**,** he began **to** wander.

DAILY LANGUAGE SKILLBUILDERS

Selection	SkillBuilder Sentences	Suggested Answers
Dreaming of Li Po Jade Flower Palace Song of P'eng-ya	**1.** Tu Fu who's poetry described the results of war were a poet-historian. **2.** Tu Fu greatly admired his frend and felow poet Li Po.	**1.** Tu Fu**,** **whose** poetry described the results of war**,** **was** a poet-historian. **2.** Tu Fu greatly admired his **friend** and **fellow** poet Li Po.
from the Pillow Book The Cat Who Lived in the Palace *from* Hateful Things *from* Graceful Things Embarrassing Things Letters Are Commonplace I Remember a Clear Morning	**1.** chinas greatest woman poet sufered great loss in his lifetime. **2.** She write six volumes of poetry of whom only 50 poems remain today.	**1.** **C**hina**'**s greatest woman poet **suffered** great loss in **her** lifetime. **2.** She **wrote** six volumes of poetry**,** of **which** only 50 poems remain today.
Zen Teachings Zen Parables	**1.** "Whose responsible for bringing Zen Buddhism to Japanese culture, asked the teacher" **2.** "Muso answered the students. His disciples were powerful military leaders."	**1.** "**Who's** responsible for bringing Zen Buddhism to Japanese culture**?"** asked the teacher. **2.** "Muso**,"** answered the students. **"**His disciples were powerful military leaders."
The Deserted Crone	**1.** Zeami and his Father both noh actors' in 14th century japan. **2.** Zeami was exiled in 1434. Zeami returned in 1441, but he dies only two years later.	**1.** Zeami and his **f**ather **were** both **N**oh **actors** in 14th century **J**apan. [Students should remove the apostrophe from *actors.*] **2.** Zeami was exiled in 1434 **and** returned in 1441, but he die**d** only two years later.

DAILY LANGUAGE SKILLBUILDERS

Selection	SkillBuilder Sentences	Suggested Answers
Tanka Poetry	**1.** how many facts do scholars knows about ono komachi one of the Six Immortals' of Poetry. **2.** Almost nothing is known about there lives.	**1.** **H**ow many facts do scholars **know** about **O**no **K**omachi**,** one of the Six **Immortals** of Poetry**?** [Students should remove the *s* from *knows* and the apostrophe from *Immortals'*.] **2.** Almost nothing is known about **their** lives.
Japanese Haiku	**1.** The haiku of basho, buson, and issa possess precision economy and delicacy. **2.** Issa who's life was filled with tragedy dies after his daughter was born.	**1.** The haiku of **B**asho, **B**uson, and **I**ssa possess precision**,** economy**,** and delicacy. **2.** Issa**, whose** life was filled with tragedy**,** die**d** after his daughter was born.
Haiku in the 20th Century	**1.** richard wright an established novelist created haiku near his lifes end. **2.** do richard wrights novels expose racism in america	**1.** **R**ichard **W**right**,** an established novelist**,** created haiku near his life**'**s end. **2.** **D**o **R**ichard **W**right**'**s novels expose racism in **A**merica**?**

	Unit One	Unit Two	Unit Three	Unit Four	Unit Five	Unit Six	Unit Seven
Grammar Focus by Unit	Parts of Speech	The Sentence and Its Parts	Using Verbs	Using Modifiers	Using Phrases	Clauses and Sentence Structure	Clauses and Sentence Structure

The Language of Literature offers several options for integrating grammar instruction and literature.

- Each unit has a grammar focus. The Teacher's Edition includes Mini Lessons for the selections that help develop the grammar focus for the unit and spring from the content of the specific literature.
- The Pupil Edition includes several full-page lessons on Sentence Crafting. These lessons are related to both the literature and the grammar focus for a unit and help students use proper grammar in their own writing.
- Daily Language SkillBuilders in the Teacher's Edition provide students with ongoing proofreading practice and reinforce correct punctuation, spelling, grammar and usage, and capitalization.

Black type — Pupil Edition
Green type — Teacher's Edition

Part 1

Using Verbs

Using Verbs: Principal Parts
"The River-Merchant's Wife: A Letter," p. 454

Sentence Structure

Using Parallelism for Effect
Sentence Crafting, p. 483

Punctuation

Using Punctuation
Writing Workshop, p. 480

End Marks
Standardized Test Practice, p. 481
End Punctuation, p. 480

Comma Usage
Standardized Test Practice, p. 481
Commas in a Series, p. 483

Quotation Marks
Standardized Test Practice, p. 481
Quotation Marks, p. 481

Semicolons
Standardized Test Practice, p. 481

Part 2

Using Verbs

Verb Tense

Simple Verb Tenses
from *The Pillow Book,* p. 505

Perfect Verb Tenses
The Deserted Crone, p. 520

Voice of a Verb

Passive and Active Voice
The Deserted Crone, p. 529

Passive Voice
Standardized Test Practice, p. 557
Standardized Test Practice, p. 557

Principal Parts of Verbs

Incorrect Verb Forms
Writing Workshop, p. 556
Standardized Test Practice, p. 557
Writing Workshop, p. 556

The Sentence and Its Parts

Creating Compound and Complex Sentences
Sentence Crafting, p. 559

Run-on Sentences
Sentence Crafting, p. 559

Using Modifiers

Double Negatives
Standardized Test Practice, p. 557

Capitalization

Capitalization Errors
Standardized Test Practice, p. 557

Unit Three, Part 1, introduces some of the important prose and poetry of ancient China. Both literary traditions influenced Chinese thought and literature for centuries.

World Art and Cultures Transparencies

AT5 Chinese cooking vessel
AT9 Chinese army figures
AT16 Chinese tomb rubbing
AT25 *Court Ladies Preparing Newly Woven Silk*
AT60 Sorting of Cocoons

You may use the listed transparencies to acquaint students with traditional Chinese art.

READING FOR INFORMATION

Reading Skills and Strategies

READING THE MAP

Tell students to use the key in the lower left-hand corner of page 420 to interpret the map. Point out that only the lavender area represents China as it was about 220 B.C. Have them look at the area of modern China shown on the inset map of the globe. Ask them how ancient China compares in size to China today. *(Ancient China was much smaller, perhaps one-fifth the size of modern China.)* Remind students that the numbers on the map correspond to the numbered captions and that the numbers should be read clockwise.

Language Note

Two systems of transliteration can be used to represent Chinese characters in English, the Wade-Giles system and the pinyin system. The Wade-Giles system has been used in most of the selections. Pinyin forms will be provided at point of use for important names and terms. NOTE: Some Wade-Giles and pinyin forms are identical. In such cases, a separate pinyin form will not be given.

Pronunciations

Anyang (än′yäng′)
Hao (hou)
Peking (pē′kĭng′); *pinyin* Beijing
Nanking (nän′kĭng′); *pinyin* Nanjing
Yangtze (yăng′dzŭ′); *pinyin* Chang
Ch′ang-an (chäng′än′); *pinyin* Xi′an
Lo-yang (lō′yäng′); *pinyin* Luoyang

PART 1 From Observation to Insight

Literature of Ancient China

Why It Matters
Everything about China is on a vast scale. It is the world's third-largest country in area and has the largest population. It also has the world's oldest continuing civilization, one that has been in existence for more than 3,500 years. The people of ancient China—philosophers, artists, writers, scientists—created a rich, brilliant culture. Their ideas, art, literature, and inventions command respect and wonder and still affect life today.

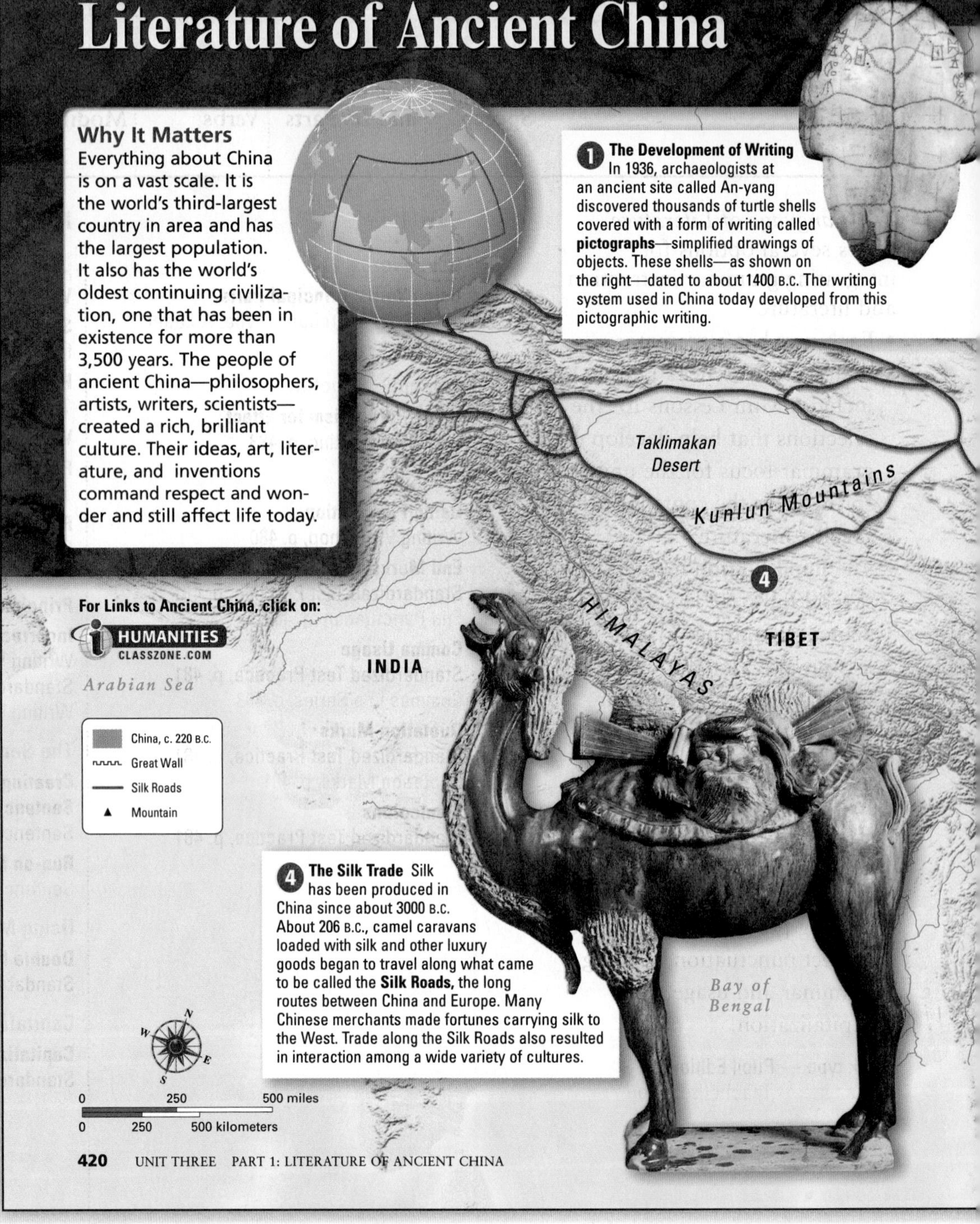

1 The Development of Writing In 1936, archaeologists at an ancient site called An-yang discovered thousands of turtle shells covered with a form of writing called **pictographs**—simplified drawings of objects. These shells—as shown on the right—dated to about 1400 B.C. The writing system used in China today developed from this pictographic writing.

For Links to Ancient China, click on: HUMANITIES CLASSZONE.COM

4 The Silk Trade Silk has been produced in China since about 3000 B.C. About 206 B.C., camel caravans loaded with silk and other luxury goods began to travel along what came to be called the **Silk Roads**, the long routes between China and Europe. Many Chinese merchants made fortunes carrying silk to the West. Trade along the Silk Roads also resulted in interaction among a wide variety of cultures.

420 UNIT THREE PART 1: LITERATURE OF ANCIENT CHINA

MINI LESSON Using the Map

Have students locate the Great Wall on the map. Was it continuous at the time this map represents? *(no)* Then ask them to find the Silk Roads. What kinds of terrain did the roads pass through? *(mountains and deserts)* Tell students that Ch'ang-an was an important city during much of the history of ancient China and was at times the capital of the empire. On what major river is the city situated? *(Yellow River)*

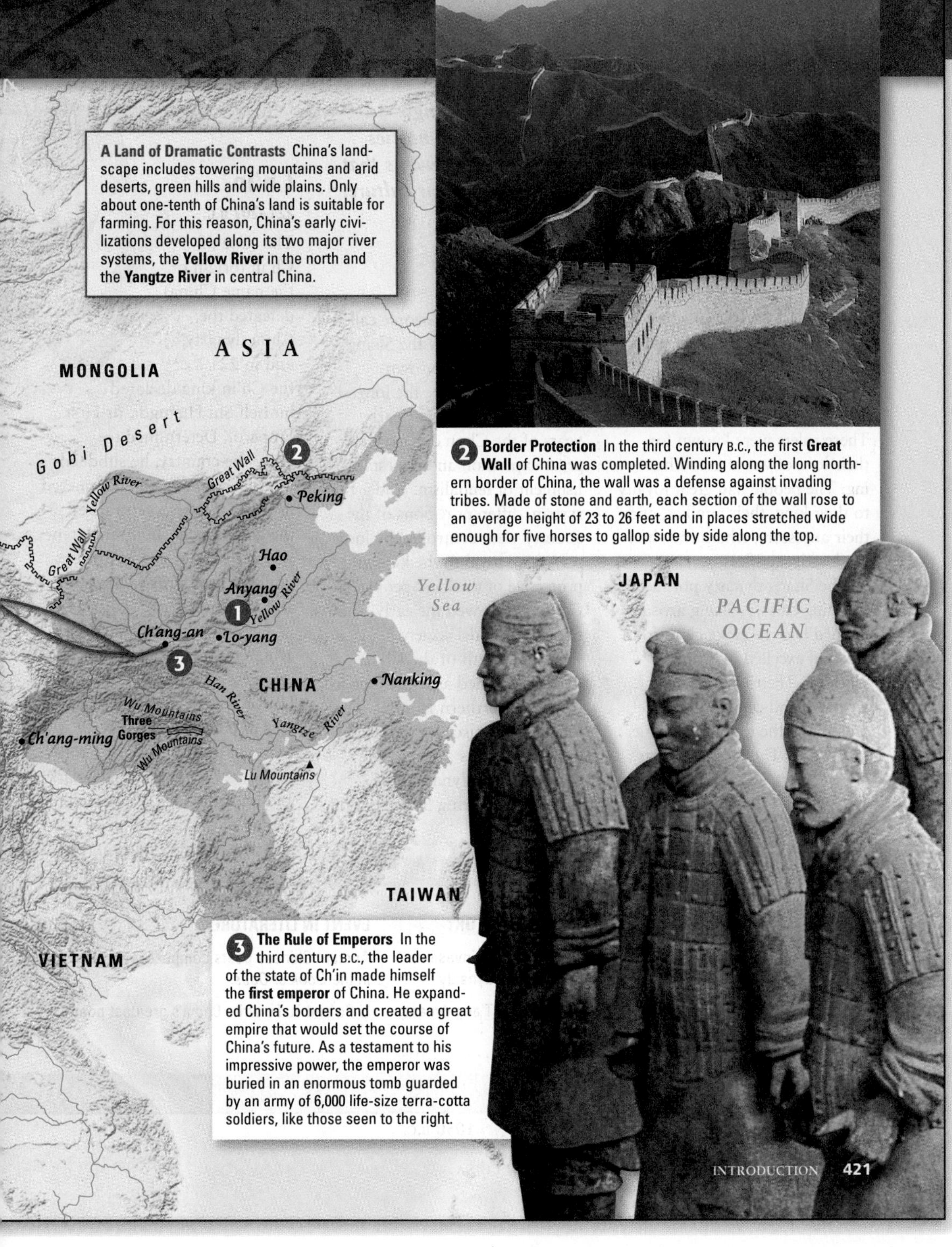

A Land of Dramatic Contrasts China's landscape includes towering mountains and arid deserts, green hills and wide plains. Only about one-tenth of China's land is suitable for farming. For this reason, China's early civilizations developed along its two major river systems, the **Yellow River** in the north and the **Yangtze River** in central China.

2 **Border Protection** In the third century B.C., the first **Great Wall** of China was completed. Winding along the long northern border of China, the wall was a defense against invading tribes. Made of stone and earth, each section of the wall rose to an average height of 23 to 26 feet and in places stretched wide enough for five horses to gallop side by side along the top.

3 **The Rule of Emperors** In the third century B.C., the leader of the state of Ch'in made himself the **first emperor** of China. He expanded China's borders and created a great empire that would set the course of China's future. As a testament to his impressive power, the emperor was buried in an enormous tomb guarded by an army of 6,000 life-size terra-cotta soldiers, like those seen to the right.

Art Note

Terra-cotta Soldiers The discovery of the terra-cotta soldiers came about by accident in March 1974. Peasants were digging a well in an area east of the First Emperor's tomb and came upon pieces of terra cotta in the ground. Archaeologists were called immediately, and they quickly realized that this was one of the greatest archaeological sites in China, and indeed in the world. Altogether there are four pits containing the more than 6,000 warriors in battle formation. The soldiers are individualized, with differences in facial features, hairstyle, height, posture, and weapons. Traces of color indicate that they had different color uniforms, which identified the unit of the army they belonged to. Most of the figures are infantryman, but some were officers, which is shown by headbands or headdresses that they wore. The soldiers also carried bronze weapons, and some had horses and chariots. The site continues to be excavated, and it has now become a museum, attracting millions of visitors from around the world every year.

Pronunciations
Shang (shäng)
Chou (jō); *pinyin* Zhou
Ch'in (chĭn); *pinyin* Qin
Shi Huangdi (shĭ' hwäng'dē')
Li Po (lē' pō'); *pinyin* Li Bo
Tu Fu (dōō' fōō'); *pinyin* Du Fu
Han (hän)
T'ang (täng); *pinyin* Tang
Sung (sŏŏng); *pinyin* Song

READING FOR INFORMATION
Reading Skills and Strategies
UNDERSTANDING CHRONOLOGICAL ORDER
Explain to students that the six dynasties discussed on pages 422 and 423 represent major periods in the history of ancient China. Have students look at the dates for each dynasty and the time line at the bottom of the page. Ask them to identify where there are large gaps of time between dynasties. *(There is a gap of almost 400 years between the Han and the T'ang dynasties and a gap of 53 years between the T'ang and the Sung dynasties.)* What was happening during these years? *(In both cases, the country became divided between rival factions and had no single ruler.)*

Historical Highlights

A dynasty consists of a series of rulers from a single family. Reading about some of the important dynasties in ancient China will help you understand the events that influenced and inspired Chinese writers and their culture.

Shang
c. 1600–1050 B.C.

Chinese history is marked by a succession of dynasties, beginning with the great Shang dynasty. The Shang were warrior-nobles headed by a king. These rulers were known for their love of warfare and hunting. The people had great loyalty to their king, their families, and their ancestors, whom they honored with sacrifices.

The Shang dynasty produced a stunning culture. Shang artisans learned how to make cloth from **silk** and excelled in **bronze-working.** Their beautiful weapons and ceremonial vessels are among the finest ever made. The Shang dynasty was also the first to leave written records

Bronze wine vessel

Chou
c. 1050–221 B.C.

About 1050 B.C., a people called the Chou overthrew the Shang and established their own dynasty. It was to be the longest in Chinese history. The early years of the Chou dynasty saw great expansion and the establishment of **feudalism.** Under this system, different regions of the country were controlled by lords who were loyal to the king and protective of the local people. Confucius viewed the early Chou reign as a model society.

The strength of the Chou dynasty lessened as tribes invaded from the northern frontier. The feudal lords also began to fight one another. As a result, the decline of the dynasty was called the **Warring States** period.

Terra-cotta soldier

Ch'in
221–207 B.C.

The state of Ch'in (origin of the name China) defeated the Chou dynasty, and in 221 B.C. the Ch'in king declared himself Shi Huangdi, or First Emperor. Determined to unify the country, he subdued internal conflicts and conquered invaders. He also centralized the **government,** built an extensive network of roads, and set uniform standards for weights and measures.

Although the First Emperor's achievements brought important changes, his methods were cruel. He forced vast numbers of peasants to build the **Great Wall.** Many of them died during construction. He murdered scholars and burned books. Revolt led to the fall of the dynasty three years after Shi Huangdi's death.

History to Literature

EVENT IN HISTORY	EVENT IN LITERATURE
Rebellions and invasions during Chou dynasty	Ancient Chinese poets compose war poems in the *Book of Odes.*
Prosperity in T'ang dynasty	Li Po and Tu Fu write China's greatest poetry.

SHANG	CHOU
1600 B.C.	1050 B.C.

Han

206 B.C.–A.D. 220

Following the downfall of the Ch'in dynasty, the Han dynasty came into power. This dynasty, which ruled China for more than 400 years, had lasting influence on China's government, education, culture, and commerce. The Han is divided into two periods, Former and Later. The Former Han was a glorious period of innovation and prosperity. Chinese commerce expanded, opening up the **Silk Roads** to most of Asia and, via India, all the way to Rome. Chinese agriculture, technology, arts, and literature also flourished. Nevertheless, social and political unrest ended the Former Han in about A.D. 9.

The Han were restored to power in A.D. 25, and the first decades of the Later Han were also prosperous. The religion of **Buddhism** spread from India to China, where it took root. Within a century, however, political, economic, and social problems began to weaken Han rule again. In A.D. 220, the last emperor abdicated, and the Later Han dynasty disintegrated into three rival kingdoms.

T'ang

A.D. 618–907

During the four centuries after the Han dynasty collapsed, many minor dynasties rose and fell before the T'ang dynasty came into power. The T'ang rulers again expanded the Chinese empire. They promoted foreign trade and improvements in agriculture, and they restored China's vast bureaucracy and civil service system.

T'ang China was a **golden age,** especially in poetry and painting. The capital city, **Ch'ang-an,** grew in wealth and population to become the most sophisticated city of its time. Scholarship thrived. The powerful Chinese woman emperor **Empress Wu** (A) ruled during this period.

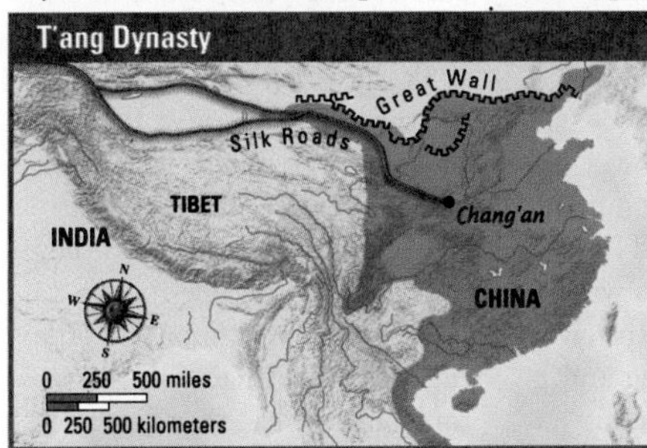

The T'ang empire became subject to rebel attacks under the rule of later, weaker emperors. In 907, it fell to rebel forces.

Sung

A.D. 960–1279

After the T'ang dynasty ended, rival warlords divided China into separate kingdoms. In 960, one general reunited China and established himself as the first Sung emperor. Although the Sung empire was smaller than the Han or T'ang, it produced a thriving culture.

Education spread. Literature, calligraphy, and painting flourished. The Chinese carefully studied human anatomy and made charts and models of the body. Among the most significant **inventions** of this era were movable type, paper money, and the use of the magnetic compass for sailing. The position of women declined during this era, however. Foreign trade—especially ocean trade—expanded under the Sung emperors. Chinese culture spread throughout Southeast Asia, and China became a major sea power. Yet despite economic prosperity and technological advances, the Sung dynasty fell to the Mongols in 1279.

CH'IN ▼ 221–207 B.C.

HAN	T'ANG	SUNG	
206 B.C.	A.D. 618	A.D. 960	A.D. 1279

READING FOR INFORMATION

Reading Skills and Strategies

USING THE MAP

Draw students' attention to the map on page 423. Encourage them to look at it carefully and then to look again at the map on pages 420 and 421. Ask them whether the Chinese empire covered more territory during the T'ang dynasty or in 220 B.C. (during the Ch'in dynasty). *(China was larger when it was ruled by the T'ang dynasty.)* Then have students compare the Great Wall on the two maps and ask them if there is any difference between them. *(The Great Wall is more fragmented in 220 B.C.)*

Historical Note

(A) **Empress Wu** The Empress Wu is considered one of the most remarkable women in all of Chinese history. She was a forceful and efficient leader who was also ruthlessly ambitious and cruel. In 655 she arranged to have the wife of the emperor murdered, and she then married him herself. She eliminated all who opposed her, often by executing them, even if they were members of her own family. The emperor was sickly, and for the last 23 years of his life, the empress was the real ruler of China. After he died, two of their sons ruled briefly, but in 690, when she was 65 years old, the empress usurped the throne, becoming the only woman sovereign in China's history. She ruled for the next 15 years and is credited with strengthening T'ang rule and greatly enriching cultural life. Chinese historians in the past have often overlooked her contributions, however, because of her extreme uses of power.

READING FOR INFORMATION
Reading Skills and Strategies
PREVIEWING AND CLASSIFYING

Have students read the italicized text at the top of page 424 and then look at the five main headings, which identify the social classes in ancient China. Suggest that they think about whether the division of the classes or their order of importance is unexpected in any way. Then tell them to read the descriptions of each class to learn what they are like and what differences there are between them. Ask students why peasants are next in importance to the ruling class. *(They produced food for the empire and so performed a vital function for the society.)* Then ask them to identify one aspect of class structure that indicates how rigid the society was.

Possible Responses: The lower classes were not allowed to take the civil service examinations and move into another class; the government controlled the resources artisans used and the goods merchants were allowed to sell.

Historical Note

A **Peasants** Peasants who were sent off to work on projects like the Great Wall or to fight in a war often never returned home. Soldiers who did not die in battle but were captured were often executed by the enemy or taken as slaves. Thousands of peasants died during the building of the Great Wall because of the harsh climate and conditions.

People and Society

Chinese society in ancient times had a strict class structure, with the emperor at the top and the lowliest workers at the bottom. Each of the four main social classes—the rulers, peasants, artisans, and merchants—was ranked according to its contribution to society.

Rulers

The **emperor** was the central figure of authority in ancient China. Powerful and wealthy, he presided over political, social, and religious rituals. Below the emperor were members of the royal family, nobles, and **scholar-officials** in the imperial civil service.

Emperor Wu, Chou dynasty

Chinese emperors often rewarded loyal followers with posts in the civil service. During the T'ang and Sung dynasties, however, a system of written examinations was developed to select officials. Applicants—primarily sons of wealthy landowners—studied and were tested on the Confucian classics. The successful scholar then joined the elite and privileged ranks of administrators and teachers.

Peasants

The mainstay of ancient Chinese society were the peasants, the **farmers** who raised the food for the empire. During the Chou dynasty, most peasants labored for wealthy feudal landowners, to whom they gave a large share of their harvest. As this system declined, peasants began to own their own land but still owed part of their yearly crops to the government.

Peasants ranked just below the ruling class because they performed an important role in Chinese society. However, they led difficult lives. Typically, they lived in a simple, one-room house with a dirt floor and little furniture. They had only a few tools. Every year, they faced devastating floods and droughts.

The peasants were often required to supply labor or military service to the government. **A** Emperors built roads and canals with this source of labor and filled the ranks of China's vast armies.

Rice farmers

Artisans

Artisans are craftspeople who work with their hands. Skilled artisans in ancient China made useful items such as tools for agriculture, weapons for war, furniture, and household goods. They also made luxury items—silk, porcelain, and carved jade—for the upper classes and for export. Artisans who produced the luxury items tended to be wealthy themselves, but those who produced everyday necessities were not.

Beginning in the Shang dynasty, Chinese emperors controlled the supply of raw materials that artisans used. Although some artisans worked independently, others labored in government-owned factories.

Artisans produced many of the works that were placed in the tombs of emperors and noblemen. These included eating utensils, jewelry, textiles, tools, and weapons. Archaeologists continue to discover rich treasures in ancient burial sites.

MINI LESSON **Interpreting the Text**

China's social classes were organized around a variety of functions and services the members of the class could carry out. Ask students how wealth was related to class structure. *(Being a member of one of the higher classes did not guarantee having more wealth. Most peasants were poor, and many merchants were rich.)* Then ask students whether they think the ranking of classes in ancient China was appropriate.

Possible Responses: Opinions will vary. Most students will say that the position of the ruling class at the top of the class structure is to be expected, but many may express surprise at peasants being next highest. Some students may think the position of the peasants is noteworthy, because it means they were valued more than in some societies. Others may point out, however, that the peasants were exploited, even though they were considered important. Some students will find the low ranking of merchants curiously modern, because they see it as a criticism of money and consumerism. Most students will find the lack of respect for servants and others in the lowest groups to be unacceptable.

Selling paper

Merchants

Merchants sold the goods that artisans made. Because they did not actually produce anything, they occupied a low place on China's social ladder. Strictly controlled by the government, merchants were allowed to sell only certain goods, such as silk, spices, tea, and porcelain. They were forced to pay heavy taxes but were prohibited from owning land. During Han times, a merchant even had to wear special clothing—a white turban bearing his name and trade and one white and one black shoe.

Although many merchants grew wealthy as a result of the growth of **trade** during the T'ang and Sung dynasties, they found it difficult to improve their social status. Traditionally, merchants were not allowed to take the civil service examination and so were excluded from government jobs. However, prosperous merchants sent their sons to schools that trained them for civil service jobs or arranged their daughters' marriages to civil servants.

Servants and Slaves

The people on the lowest rungs of Chinese society were not considered important or worthy enough to have a class of their own. Such people included servants, migrant laborers, professional soldiers, entertainers, butchers, and tanners. The Chinese also had slaves. During T'ang times, nomads from Mongolia and Central Asia who were captured in war were forced into slave labor. All these groups were regarded as inferior to the four main classes of society and thus were excluded from the civil service examination.

Women in Ancient China

Women were subservient to men in ancient Chinese society. Boys alone attended school and took the civil service exam. Few girls were educated unless their fathers taught them how to read and write. Marriages were arranged, and a girl as young as 14 might leave home to live with her husband's family.

In the Han and T'ang periods, some privileged women had a few more freedoms than in other dynasties. In T'ang times, women rode horses, hunted, played polo, and participated in politics. By the Sung period, however, the status of women had declined again, especially among the upper classes in cities. There a woman's work was deemed less important to the family's prosperity and prestige. B

One sign of women's changing status was the custom of binding the feet of upper-class girls to keep their feet from growing. The practice spread during the Sung period and continued into the 20th century. Women with bound feet could never walk normally. Their condition reflected the wealth and position of their families, since they were unsuited for manual labor.

Equestrienne on horse (725–750). Anonymous. T'ang dynasty (618–907). Chinese. Buff earthenware with polychrome pigments, 56.2 cm × 48.2 cm × dep.: 39.0 cm. The Art Institute of Chicago. Gift of Mrs. Pauline Palmer Wood, 970.1073. The Art Institute of Chicago. Photo © The Art Institute of Chicago. All rights reserved.

Historical Note

B Women in T'ang Times Although a few women had more independence during the T'ang period, the overall status of women and the attitudes toward them did not change. In a document called *Family Instructions of the Grandfather,* expectations for women were made clear: they should serve their husbands as they had served their fathers; their voices should not be heard; their bodies and even their shadows should not be seen; and they should not have conversations with their male in-laws.

Pronunciations
Taoism (dou'ĭz'əm): *pinyin* Daoism
Tao (dou); *pinyin* Dao

READING FOR INFORMATION
Reading Skills and Strategies
USING TEXT ORGANIZERS
Have students look at the headnote and the three main heads on pages 426 and 427 to see what areas of arts and culture will be presented. Then draw their attention to the three subheads in the section on **Philosophy and Religion.** Ask students what three sets of teachings will be discussed. *(Confucianism, Taoism, and Buddhism)* Tell students to scan the boldfaced terms in the text. Ask them what two poets are mentioned in the **Literature** section. *(Li Po and Tu Fu)* Finally, have them look over the boxed feature, **Turning Points in Literature.** Ask them what the subject of this feature is. *(invention of paper and printing)*

Arts and Culture

The ancient Chinese developed one of the most advanced civilizations of their time. Their art and literature are unsurpassed in beauty and craftsmanship, and their philosophical classics continue to be read for their wisdom and insight.

Philosophy and Religion

From the sixth century B.C. to the first century A.D., three main systems of thought took hold in ancient China—Confucianism, Taoism, and Buddhism. The teachings of Confucius and of Taoism emerged during the sixth century B.C.

Confucianism focused on the importance of family relationships and order in society. The teachings emphasized virtue in all interactions between people and valued learning, respect, and duty.

Taoism was based on following the Way, or Tao, a universal force underlying all of life. Taoists sought humility, simplicity, and harmony with nature.

Buddhism, based on the teachings of Siddhartha Gautama, originated in India and reached China about the first century A.D. More a religion than a philosophy, Buddhism emphasized detachment from earthly life in order to attain spiritual enlightenment.

From earliest times, the ancient Chinese also practiced religious devotion to their ancestors. They believed that the dead live on as spirits and are closely tied to the living. Ancestors were honored through offerings, prayers, and elaborate ceremonies.

These various philosophical and religious teachings existed together in ancient China. Sometimes they were in opposition, but in general there was tolerance and even a blending of beliefs and practices.

Confucius, major Chinese philosopher

Literature

China has one of the oldest continuing literary traditions in the world, dating back more than 3,000 years. It is a vast body of work, surpassing that of any other civilization. The earliest known major literary work is the *Book of Odes,* a collection of poems dating from the Shang and Chou dynasties. These poems have been revered, studied, and memorized throughout China's history.

In later dynasties, writing poetry was considered an essential accomplishment for scholars and gentlemen. The finest poems in all of China's literature were produced during the T'ang dynasty, when the lyric poets **Li Po** and **Tu Fu** were writing.

Prose was also a strong tradition. Important works include the *Analects* of Confucius, Taoist tales, philosophical essays, and *The Records of the Historian,* a main source of information about early China.

MINI LESSON Interpreting the Text

Although both Confucianism and Taoism were expanded into elaborate systems in later centuries, in their beginnings they were focused on simple collections of teachings. Neither was a religion. Ask students which of the two emphasizes relationships with people and which emphasizes the life of the individual. *(Confucianism emphasizes relationships and Taoism emphasizes the individual.)* Then ask students what connections are mentioned between the philosophical and religious teachings and the arts. *(Stone statues of the Buddha are found all over China, and Taoist thought influenced landscape painting.)*

The Arts

From Shang times, the ancient Chinese excelled in the arts. They distinguished themselves in the production of pottery, bronze work, sculpture, jade carvings, calligraphy, and painting. As early as 2000 B.C., Chinese artists used the potter's wheel to create beautiful vases and urns. They discovered how to make fine porcelain during later T'ang times. Chinese artists were known for their realistic sculpture. Examples of their skill include the lifelike terra-cotta figures buried in Shih Huang Ti's tomb and the thousands of stone Buddha statues carved into caves after Buddhism spread to China. Calligraphy, or "beautiful writing," was considered one of the fine arts. The best calligraphers became famous, and their work was much sought after.

Detail of *Nine Dragons* (c. 1244), Chen Rong. Hand scroll, ink and touches of red on paper, 18³⁄₁₆≤ ¥ 431¹¹⁄₁₆≤. Courtesy of the Museum of Fine Arts, Boston. Francis Gardner Curtis Fund, 1917.

During the Sung dynasty, Chinese painting reached its greatest glory. The focus shifted from the human figure to landscapes. Artists painted towering mountains, plunging waterfalls, and peaceful lakes. (A) This attention to landscape, which reflects the Taoist love of nature, influenced painting in China for the next thousand years. The paintings were done on silk or paper scrolls, and the artists often preferred black ink. Said one Sung artist, "Black is ten colors." During the Sung dynasty, the combination of the "three perfections"—calligraphy, poetry, and landscape painting—was regarded as the highest achievement of the arts.

Turning Points in Literature

During the Han dynasty, the invention of **paper** changed forever the way words were recorded in China. Chinese paper was made from mulberry bark, silk rags, hemp, bamboo, and fishing nets, which were mixed together and soaked in water. The mixture was then boiled, mashed, and pounded into pulp. A fine screen was dipped into the pulp to scoop up a thin layer of fibers. After the layer of pulp was pressed to remove the water, it was dried on a heated wall. The sheet of paper was then carefully peeled away.

The invention of paper led to the creation of books and spurred the Chinese inventions of **woodblock printing** and **movable type.** The first Chinese books, which were hand written by scholars, were made of paper rolled into long scrolls.

The use of paper also created new possibilities in the art of **calligraphy.** To produce the delicate strokes, calligraphers practiced for years to master the thousands of characters in the Chinese writing system.

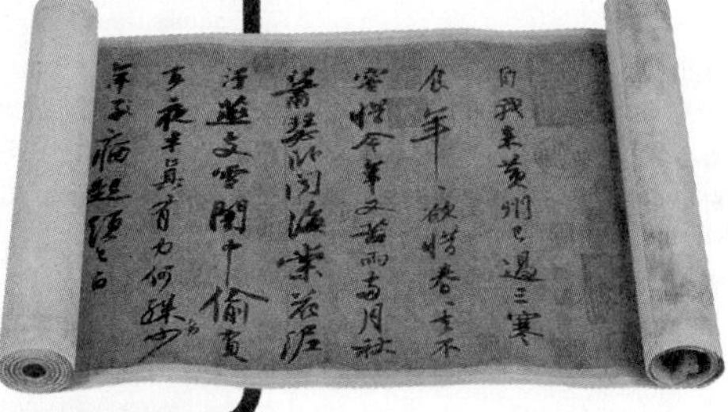

Cultural Note

(A) **Calligraphy** Calligraphy was a highly developed art, with many styles to express shades of thought and mood. An extremely pliable hair brush was used to make the delicate strokes, and beginners carefully copied the works of masters to learn the art. Each piece of calligraphy was considered to be a reflection of its creator's character. This was taken so seriously in the T'ang period that calligraphy became part of the evaluation of candidates for civil-service posts.

INTRODUCTION 427

Pronunciations

Lao-tzu (lou′dzŭ′); *pinyin* Laozi

Tao Te Ching (dou′ dĕ jĭng′); *pinyin* *Dao De Jing*

Shih Ching (shĭ′ jĭng′); pinyin Shi Jing

Chuang Tzu (jwäng′ dzŭ′); *pinyin* Zhuang Zi

Ssu-ma Ch'ien (sŏŏ′mä′ chē-ĕn′); *pinyin* Sima Qian

Siddhartha Gautama (sĭd-där′tə gô′tə-mə)

Nok (nŏk)

Pan Ku (bän′ gŏŏ′); *pinyin* Ban Gu

Pan Chao (bän′ jou′); *pinyin* Ban Zhou

T'ao Ch'ien (tou′ chē-ĕn′); *pinyin* Tao Qian

Wang Wei (wäng′ wā′)

tz'u (tsŭ); *pinyin* ci

Li Ch'ing-chao (lē′ chĭng′jou′); *pinyin* Li Qingzhao

Moche (mō′chā)

Time Line

ANCIENT CHINA (1600 B.C.–A.D. 1279)

3000 B.C. A.D. 1 PRESENT

c. approximately
B.C. before Christ
A.D. after Christ

EVENTS IN CHINESE LITERATURE

1200 B.C.

c. 1400–1100 B.C. Earliest evidence of Chinese writing is found on Shang oracle bones

c. 1000–600 B.C. Earliest known Chinese poems composed

800 B.C.

551–479 B.C. Confucius teaches about ethical values such as honesty, loyalty, and respect for elders; his disciples later record his teachings in *Analects*

c. 500s B.C. Lao-tzu, legendary founder of Taoism, develops teachings of *Tao Te Ching*

c. 500 B.C. The *Shih Ching (Book of Odes),* the first anthology of Chinese poetry, is compiled

400 B.C.

c. 330 B.C. Taoist philosopher Chuang Tzu writes the *Chuang Tzu*

c. 85 B.C. Ssu-ma Ch'ien writes *Records of the Historian,* a history of China through Emperor Wudi's reign

EVENTS IN CHINESE HISTORY

1200 B.C.

c. 1050 B.C. Chou dynasty is established and institutes feudalism

800 B.C.

771 B.C. Nomads from the north capture and plunder Hao, the Chou dynasty capital, and local warlords battle one another

c. 500s B.C. The Chinese begin to cast iron

475 B.C. Warring States period begins

400 B.C.

221 B.C. Shi Huangdi becomes emperor of China

c. 214 B.C. First Great Wall is begun

206 B.C.–A.D. 220 Silk routes opened up for trade during the Han dynasty

EVENTS IN WORLD HISTORY

1200 B.C.

c. 1200 B.C. The Trojan War is fought

c. 1020 B.C. The Hebrews establish the kingdom of Israel

1000–500 B.C. Aryan communities begin to appear in the Ganges River basin in India

800 B.C.

776 B.C. First recorded Olympic games, founded in Greece to honor the god Zeus

c. 563 B.C. Birth of Siddhartha Gautama, founder of Buddhism

509 B.C. Roman Republic is created

c. 500 B.C. Nok in West Africa develop ironmaking technology

400 B.C.

331–330 B.C. Alexander the Great conquers Syria, Mesopotamia, and Persia

218 B.C. Hannibal crosses the Alps

44 B.C. Julius Caesar is assassinated

30 B.C. Rome conquers Egypt

A.D. 1	A.D. 400	A.D. 800
A.D. 54 Pan Ku writes *History of the Former Han Dynasty* **c. A.D. 100** The first Chinese dictionary is compiled **A.D. 106** Pan Chao, a scholarly widow, sister of Pan Ku, and imperial historian after his death, writes *Lessons for Women* **A.D. 365** Birth of T'ao Ch'ien, important early lyric poet	**c. A.D. 690** Poetry writing is included in the civil service examination **A.D. 699** Birth of Wang Wei, painter and poet **A.D. 701** Birth of Li Po **A.D. 712** Birth of Tu Fu	**A.D. 868** *Diamond Sutra,* the first book with a printed date, is published **c. A.D. 900–1200** Song lyrics, or *tz'u,* sung by women entertainers become a major poetic form; Li Ch'ing-chao masters the genre

A.D. 1	A.D. 400	A.D. 800
A.D. 9 Period of the Former Han ends **A.D. 25** Period of Later Han begins under Kuang-wu ti **c. A.D. 65** Buddhism reaches China **c. A.D. 105** The Chinese invent paper	**A.D. 610** Grand Canal is completed, linking the Yangtze and the Yellow Rivers **A.D. 626–649** Civil service examination system is begun under T'ang emperor T'ai tsung **A.D. 690–705** Reign of Empress Wu **A.D. 756** An Lu-shan rebels capture T'ang capital city of Ch'ang-an	**c. A.D. 850** Gunpowder is invented **A.D. 907** Last T'ang emperor is deposed **A.D. 1126** Northern China falls to the Jin, invaders from the northeast **A.D. 1279** Sung dynasty falls to Mongols

A.D. 1	A.D. 400	A.D. 800
c. A.D. 29 Jesus is crucified **A.D. 100** Moche civilization develops in South America **c. A.D. 391** Christianity declared official religion of Roman Empire	**A.D. 449** Anglo-Saxon tribes invade England **A.D. 476** Fall of Roman Empire **c. A.D. 570** Birth of Muhammad **A.D. 750** Kingdom of ancient Ghana becomes an empire **A.D. 794** Beginning of Japan's Heian period	**A.D. 1054** The Christian church divides **A.D. 1066** Norman Conquest of England

READING FOR INFORMATION
Reading Skills and Strategies
READING A TIME LINE
Review with students the structure of the time line: the small time line at the top of the spread, the key to abbreviations on the left, and the three main time lines showing events in Chinese literature, in Chinese history, and in world history. Remind them that they can read across the time lines or down each period on all three time lines. Encourage them to do both.

MINI LESSON Using the Time Line

Have students refer to the time line to answer the following questions:

1. Approximately how long after Chinese writing developed was the first Chinese dictionary written? *(1,200 to 1,500 years later)*
2. What kingdom was being founded about the time the Chou dynasty was establishing feudalism? *(kingdom of Israel)*
3. Could Ssu-ma Ch'ien have written about the building of the Grand Canal? *(No, he lived in the first century B.C., and the canal was finished in A.D. 610)*
4. When did the T'ang dynasty end? *(A.D. 907)*

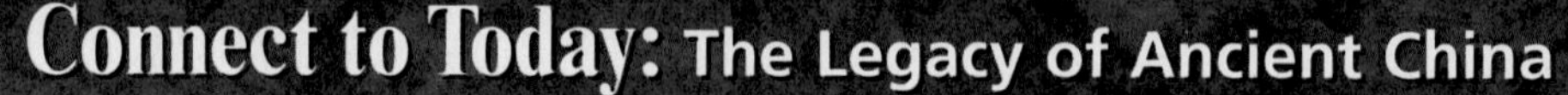

Connect to Today: The Legacy of Ancient China

READING FOR INFORMATION
Reading Skills and Strategies
CONNECTING
Have students read over the spread, looking at all the visuals as well. Then have them reread the question in the headnote and respond to it in a class discussion. Invite students to share any additional information they know about any of the five topics presented on the spread.

Cultural Note

A Yin-yang Symbols The familiar black-and-white yin-yang symbol shown on page 430 didn't become part of Taoist imagery until about the tenth century A.D. Before that time, the yin, or feminine, principle was symbolized by a tiger, and the yang, or male, principle was symbolized by a dragon. The tiger-dragon symbolism was reflected in the movie *Crouching Tiger, Hidden Dragon.*

The Chinese have made numerous contributions to art, science, medicine, technology, agriculture, philosophy, and mathematics. Many of the important inventions and ideas that first developed in ancient China still have an impact on life in the 21st century. How many of these Chinese innovations affect your daily life?

Philosophy
Although Lao-tzu's *Tao Te Ching* dates from about the 6th century B.C., his ideas still influence thought and literature around the world. Many contemporary authors have very loosely applied the teachings of the Tao to such unlikely subjects as how to train cats and dogs and how to practice effective leadership. The **yin-yang** diagram, a popular image today, symbolizes the unity of the Tao. A

Eating and Drinking
The art of making **porcelain** developed in China about 800. Made from a special clay and a mineral found only in China, this highly prized pottery became known as china. **Tea,** made from the leaves of the tea plant, was first popularized by the ancient Chinese.

Gingerroot

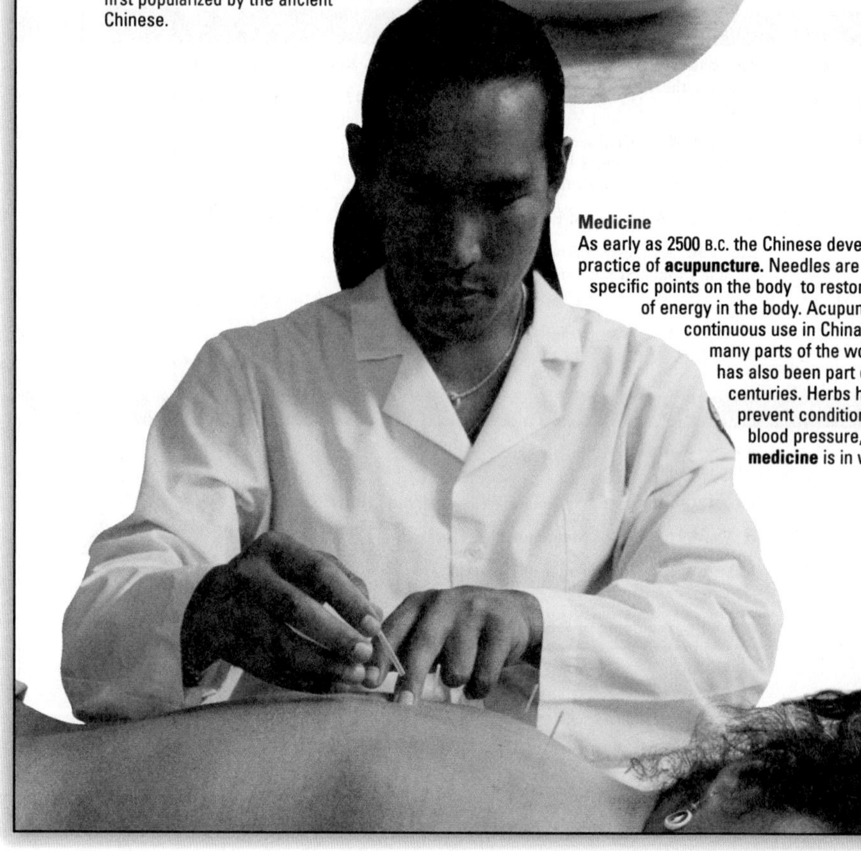

Medicine
As early as 2500 B.C. the Chinese developed the practice of **acupuncture.** Needles are inserted at specific points on the body to restore the balance of energy in the body. Acupuncture has been in continuous use in China and now is practiced in many parts of the world. Extensive use of herbs has also been part of Chinese medicine for centuries. Herbs have been used to treat and prevent conditions such as diabetes, high blood pressure, and lack of appetite. **Herbal medicine** is in wide use in the 21st century.

Entertainment
The Chinese invented the **kite** about 2,000 years ago. Kites were used for military purposes as well as for pleasure. The **yo-yo** and **playing cards** originated in China also. Gunpowder was invented by the Chinese about 850 and later was used to make **fireworks,** which were called fire trees, flame flowers, or peach blossoms.

Inventions
About the 1st century B.C., the Chinese invented the **wheelbarrow,** which they called the wooden ox. Other significant Chinese inventions include the **collar harness** for horses (3rd century B.C.); **paper** (2nd century A.D.); **matches** (6th century A.D.); the mechanical **clock** and movable **type** (11th century A.D.); and the magnetic **compass** (12th century A.D.).

INTRODUCTION 431

Objectives

- understand the different kinds of didactic literature:
  - maxim
  - anecdote
  - parable
- understand the purposes of didactic literature

Pronunciations

Lao-tzu (lou′dzŭ′)
Tao Te Ching (dou′ dĕ jĭng′)
Musō Soseki (mo͞o′sō sō-sĕk′ē)
Chuang Tzu (jwäng′ dzŭ′)

Maxim

Proverbs are closely related to maxims. They are most commonly old and well-known expressions, such as "The early bird catches the worm." Proverbs illustrate some general truth and are not usually attributable to a single author.

LEARNING the Language of Literature

Moral Teaching Through Literature

Practice Random Acts of Kindness

How would you convey an important message about right and wrong to your classmates? Would you print a slogan on a T-shirt? prepare a public-service announcement for radio or TV? design a button or a bumper sticker? In ancient civilizations around the world, such messages were often conveyed through **didactic literature**—literature that instructs its readers.

In didactic literature, writers teach lessons about how to live a moral life. They give their views about what is right and good, focusing on such qualities as honesty, courage, wisdom, and kindness. Sometimes they state their ideas directly, as in Horace's poem "Better to live, Licinius, . . ." At other times, they present their teachings by means of examples, as in the parable of the Prodigal Son in the New Testament.

Ancient Chinese and Japanese writers were among those who used literature to communicate their ideas about what they considered to be right and wrong. Philosophers and religious teachers in China and Japan recognized the power of literature to convey the moral ideals they followed and to persuade readers to act in certain ways. They and their followers expressed their teachings in various forms, including maxims, anecdotes, and parables.

Maxim

A **maxim** is a statement of a general truth about human behavior, perhaps offering some practical advice as well. Maxims vary in length from one or two brief sentences to a short paragraph. They are writers' attempts to put the spotlight on the right way to live—on what ideals to pursue and what actions and attitudes to avoid.

Some maxims are phrased in a particularly pointed and witty way. Because of their clever yet simple structure, such maxims—sometimes called **aphorisms**—are easy to recall and to memorize. An example is Confucius' statement "To study without thinking is futile. To think without studying is dangerous."

Zigong asked: "Is there any single word that could guide one's entire life?" The Master said: "Should it not be *reciprocity?* What you do not wish for yourself, do not do to others."

—Confucius, *Analects*

If you look to others for fulfillment,
you will never truly be fulfilled.
If your happiness depends on money,
you will never be happy with yourself.

—Lao-tzu, *Tao Te Ching*

If you make the acquisition and retention of goods or status your aim in life, this is a way to anxiety and sorrow.

—Musō Soseki, *Dream Conversations*

Anecdote

An **anecdote** is a brief story that focuses on a single interesting event, sometimes taken from the life of a real person. The event is meant to illustrate a particular truth or teaching. The Taoist philosopher Chuang Tzu used many delightful anecdotes to convey his ideas and reflections about the nature of the world.

> **Chuang Tzu said, "Once upon a time I dreamed myself a butterfly, floating like petals in the air, happy to be doing as I pleased, no longer aware of myself! But soon enough I awoke and then, frantically clutching myself, Chuang Tzu I was! I wonder: Was Chuang Tzu dreaming himself the butterfly, or was the butterfly dreaming itself Chuang Tzu? Of course, if you take Chuang Tzu and the butterfly together, then there's a difference between them. But that difference is only due to their changing material forms."**
>
> **—Chuang Tzu, *Chuang Tzu***

Parable

A **parable** is also a brief story, but its teaching is more pointed. Each plot detail is intended to illustrate an aspect of some moral truth. Early Japanese writers used parables to convey important concepts of Zen Buddhism.

> **"You are wise brothers," he told them. "You know what is right and what is not right. You may go somewhere else to study if you wish, but this poor brother does not even know right from wrong. Who will teach him if I do not? I am going to keep him here even if all the rest of you leave."**
>
> **A torrent of tears cleansed the face of the brother who had stolen. All desire to steal had vanished.**
>
> **—"Right and Wrong"**

YOUR TURN What are some other examples of literature that you have read in which morals are taught? What standards of behavior are encouraged? Did the writers include maxims, anecdotes, or parables?

Strategies for Reading: Didactic Literature

1. Notice the form of the work you are reading. Is it a maxim? an anecdote? a parable?
2. Identify the writer's message. Is it stated directly, or is it implied? Write a paraphrase of it.
3. Look for patterns of repetition, figurative language, and imagery. How does the writer help you remember the main point he or she is trying to communicate?
4. Monitor your reading strategies, and modify them when your understanding breaks down. Remember to use the Strategies for Active Reading: predict, visualize, connect, question, clarify, and evaluate.

Anecdote

Some anecdotes are humorous and make their point in an offhand way. Others may be compelling stories of human courage or ingenuity that make their point through poignancy and drama. You may want to invite students to share anecdotes they have heard or read that have made an impression on them.

Parable

Unlike anecdotes, parables are never stories about real people. They are sometimes almost little allegories that illustrate some truth point by point. Some students will be familiar with the parables from the Bible. Students from different cultures and religions might be able to recount parables they know from their traditions.

YOUR TURN Other types of literature that might include moral teaching are fables, folk tales, speeches, lectures, editorials, sermons, and religious scriptures. These different types of literature may address a wide range of behavior, from small, everyday matters to broad issues and concerns. Fables and folk tales often include a maxim, usually at the end. Speeches, lectures, editorials, sermons, and religious scriptures frequently include anecdotes or parables to illustrate a point.

Strategies for Reading

1. You might want to bring in additional examples of anecdotes and parables to help students understand the distinctions between them.
2. Students could keep two lists as they read, one of truths that are stated directly and one of those that are implied.
3. Remind students that a writer can use various elements of style to emphasize important ideas.
4. Tell students that the more they pay attention to what they do and don't understand as they read, the more they will gain from their reading experience.

Objectives
- understand and appreciate **didactic literature (Literary Analysis)**
- understand and appreciate **maxims (Literary Analysis)**
- use strategies for **analyzing maxims (Active Reading)**

Thematic Link
Confucius was a careful **observer** of human behavior and responded to what he saw with his teachings. The *Analects* contains Confucius' **insights** into how people should treat one another to create a good society.

5-Minute Warm-Up

Daily Language SkillBuilder

Have students **proofread** the display sentences on page 419i and write them correctly.

Language Note
The name *Confucius* is the Latinized form of *K'ung Fu-tzu* (ko͝ong' fo͞o'dzŭ'), "Master K'ung." The pinyin form is *Kong Fuzi.* Except for the name *Confucius,* this translation of the *Analects* uses pinyin names and terms.

Pronunciations
jen (zhŭn)
junzi (jo͝on'dzŭ')
li (lē)

PREPARING to *Read*

from the

ANALECTS

Confucius

Confucius
551–479 B.C.

Surprising Contrasts Confucius did not write a book, he failed to gain the political reforms he longed for, and at times he endured poverty and threats on his life. Yet his ideas became the foundation of Chinese thought and society for more than 2,000 years. Born to poor parents of noble ancestry, he showed a great love of learning from an early age, and he viewed himself as a scholar by the time he was 15. He sought out instruction in the Chinese classical arts and traditions, including music, archery, math, charioteering, calligraphy, poetry, and history.

Failed Ambitions Confucius was born at a time of crisis and violence in China. He had an abiding passion to restore the order and moral living of earlier times to his society. For many years he hoped to develop enough political power to put his ideas into practice. But although he was active in politics, he was never able to gain the power he sought. At one point he went into self-imposed exile from his home state of Lu for almost 12 years, advising rulers in other states and spreading his ideas on education and moral order.

Wise Teacher Despite Confucius' failure to change the political structure of his time, his reputation as a teacher grew. He broke new ground by offering his teaching not only to the aristocracy but also to people of other classes. He taught that the authority to rule should come from moral commitment, not from hereditary status. He eventually gained a large group of disciples, or followers, who revered him for his ideas on the importance of good character and the need for order and authority in all areas of life. It was his disciples who preserved his ideas and sayings, which were written down in the form known today as the *Analects.*

For a humanities activity, click on:

LESSON RESOURCES

UNIT THREE RESOURCE BOOK,
pp. 55–56

ASSESSMENT RESOURCES
Formal Assessment, pp. 55–56
Teacher's Guide to Assessment and Portfolio Use
Test Generator

INTEGRATED TECHNOLOGY
Visit our Web site: classzone.com

ADDITIONAL RESOURCES
Lesson Planning Guide, pp. 45–46
Teacher's Sourcebook for Language Development

Building Background

Lasting Legacy The *Analects* (*analect* means "a selection") is a collection of about 500 sayings, dialogues, and brief stories, which was put together over a period of many years following Confucius' death. The *Analects* presents Confucius' teachings on how people should live to create an orderly and just society. Over time, Confucian thought became the basis for the Chinese system of government and remained a part of Chinese life into the 20th century.

Confucius' view that true authority to rule comes from a commitment to moral living, not from an aristocratic birth, was revolutionary for his time. This view meant that rulers must have high standards for themselves and must care about what is best for their subjects. It also meant that all educated people had a responsibility to act with loyalty, courtesy, and respect. Three of the most important concepts in Confucius' teachings are humanity *(jen)*, gentleman *(junzi)*, and ritual *(li)*.

Key Confucian Concepts

- **Humanity** The concept of humanity represents the highest ideal for moral behavior in Confucian thought. Humanity is especially concerned with how a person behaves toward others. It is demonstrated in such attitudes as respect, truthfulness, generosity, and love. According to Confucius, humanity is the most important quality to have.
- **Gentleman** In Confucian thought, the word *gentleman* refers not to a man of aristocratic birth but to a person who is committed to an ethical life. An aristocrat could lose the right to be called a gentleman, and an ordinary person could become a gentleman. This shift in meaning reflects Confucius' teaching that the moral life is more important than social status.
- **Ritual** The term *ritual* covers all of what Confucius viewed as proper conduct. It includes everything from everyday manners to religious observances. Confucius thought that the observance of ritual was essential to a sense of order and respect in society.

Connect to Your Life

The *Analects* offers guidance about what is most important in life. What sources of wisdom and guidance are important to you in your life? family members? friends? books? teachers? Jot down three people or writings that you rely on, and note the reasons each one is important to you.

Focus Your Reading

LITERARY TERM: MAXIM

A **maxim** is a short, concise statement that expresses a general truth or rule of conduct. Maxims condense important ideas into memorable language that gets the reader's attention. The following section from the *Analects* is an example of a maxim:

> ***Don't worry if people don't recognize your merits; worry that you may not recognize theirs.***

As you read Confucius' thoughts and advice, look for statements that could be considered maxims.

ACTIVE READING: ANALYZING MAXIMS

When reading a maxim, you need to decide if it is true to life and how it relates to your own experiences.

READER'S NOTEBOOK As you read the *Analects,* write down the maxims you find in a chart like the following. In one column, list maxims that are primarily concerned with individual behavior. In the second, list those that involve relationships with others.

Individual Behavior	Relationships with Others
"To study without thinking . . ." (2.15)	

READING FOR INFORMATION

Reading Skills and Strategies

IDENTIFYING MAIN IDEAS

Tell students to scan pages 434 and 435 and ask them to find the section that highlights some of the main ideas in Confucius' writings. *(the box titled "Key Confucian Concepts")* Then ask them what ideas are listed. *(humanity, gentleman, and ritual)* Remind students to look for these ideas as they read the excerpts from the *Analects* and refer back to this feature to clarify their understanding.

Literary Analysis MAXIM

A maxim is usually short and expresses an observation or insight in language that is forceful and to the point. Ask students to identify one maxim in *Analects* 2.1 through 4.6.

Possible Response: The best example in this group is 2.15. Students may also cite one of the last three statements in 2.20, the statement in 3.26, or the second statement in 4.6 ("Whoever truly loves goodness . . .").

Use **Unit Three Resource Book,** p. 5, for more practice.

Active Reading ANALYZING MAXIMS

Ask two or three students to each read aloud one of the maxims on page 437. Have students discuss what makes each of the statements a maxim. Then ask them to paraphrase, or explain in their own words, what each maxim means. (Remind students that not all the teachings are written in the form of maxims.)

Possible Response: Students should note that the idea of each maxim is expressed directly and clearly in as few words as possible. They should also mention that each maxim addresses a specific attitude or behavior. Their paraphrases should reflect that they understand the intent of each maxim.

Use **Unit Three Resource Book,** p. 4, for more practice.

Literary Analysis PARALLELISM

In the *Analects,* Confucius often uses parallelism to emphasize the idea in a maxim. Explain to students that parallelism is the use of similar grammatical constructions to express ideas that are related or equal in importance. Have students find an example of parallelism in one of the maxims on page 437.

Possible Response: Parallelism is used in 1.16, 2.15, 2.20, 3.26, and 4.6.

from the

Analects

Confucius

Translated by Simon Leys

Confucious. © Luca Tettoni/Corbis.

Cross Curricular Link **History**

RECORDS OF THE HISTORIAN The main early source for biographical information about Confucius is the *Records of the Historian,* one of the most important historical works from ancient China. The author of this work was Ssu-ma Ch'ien (so͝o′mä′ chē-ĕn′), who lived approximately 145 B.C. to 90 B.C. In his monumental work, Ssu-ma Ch'ien attempted to put all of China's history, from the earliest times (c. 2700 B.C.) to his own time, in an organized form.

Ssu-ma Ch'ien had great respect for Confucius, and in his work he included a section called the "Hereditary House of Confucius," which was probably the first full-length biography written about the philosopher. Since Ssu-ma Ch'ien lived about four centuries after Confucius died, however, he had to rely on accounts that had been handed down over time. Although the biography includes incidents that would be considered questionable today, Ssu-ma Ch'ien is nevertheless respected as a skilled historian who chose his facts and anecdotes with care. His view of Confucius presents both faults of Confucius—his tendency to criticize people too bluntly, for example—as well as his great strengths as a thinker, teacher, and moral leader.

The Master[1] said: "Don't worry if people don't recognize your merits; worry that you may not recognize theirs." (1.16)

1 The Master said: "He who rules by virtue is like the polestar,[2] which remains unmoving in its mansion while all the other stars revolve respectfully around it." (2.1)

Ziyou[3] asked about filial piety.[4] The Master said: "Nowadays people think they are dutiful sons when they feed their parents. Yet they also feed their dogs and horses. Unless there is respect, where is the difference?" (2.7)

The Master said: "To study without thinking is futile.[5] To think without studying is dangerous." (2.15)

Lord Ji Kang[6] asked: "What should I do in order to make the people respectful, loyal, and zealous?"[7] The Master said: "Approach them with dignity and they will be respectful. Be yourself a good son and a kind father, and they will be loyal. Raise the good and train the incompetent, and they will be zealous." (2.20)

The Master said: "Authority without generosity, ceremony without reverence, mourning without grief—these, I cannot bear to contemplate."[8] (3.26)

The Master said: "I have never seen a man who truly loved goodness and hated evil. Whoever truly loves goodness would put nothing above it; whoever truly hates evil would practice goodness in such a way that no evil could enter him. Has anyone ever devoted all his strength to goodness just for one day? No one ever has, and yet it is not for want of strength—there may be people who do not have even the small amount of strength it takes, but I have never seen any." (4.6)

---

1. **Master:** Confucius.
2. **polestar:** the North Star, which, unlike other stars, appears to remain in the same place in the sky as the earth rotates.
3. **Ziyou** (dzŭ'yo͞o'): a younger disciple of Confucius, known for his literary talent.
4. **filial piety** (fĭl'ē-əl pī'ĭ-tē): respect and reverence for one's parents and ancestors—an important concept in Confucianism.
5. **futile** (fyo͞ot'l): useless.
6. **Lord Ji Kang** (jē' käng'): a powerful official in Confucius' home state of Lu.
7. **zealous** (zĕl'əs): enthusiastic.
8. **contemplate:** think about; consider.

Customizing Instruction

Less Proficient Readers

- Tell students that the *Analects* is a series of short, self-contained statements in which the Master, Confucius, presents individual teachings. Point out that the statements do not connect directly to what comes before or after them.
- Help students find the instances of parallelism and show them how to use this structural element to understand Confucius' ideas. Good examples are found in 1.16, 2.15, and 3.26.

1 Help students understand the analogy used in this section. Ask them to try paraphrasing the comparison. *(A person who rules with goodness and truth is like the North Star, which is dependable because it doesn't move. The people, like the stars that circle the North Star, trust and obey the virtuous ruler.)*

English Learners

- You may want to concentrate on two or three sections of the *Analects* with these students. Possible choices are 1.16 and 2.15. Paraphrase each section in simpler language.

Sample paraphrases:

1.16. Confucius said: "Don't be concerned if people don't recognize all your abilities. Instead, be concerned that you may be ignoring theirs."

2.15. Confucius said: "To learn a lot of information about a subject without giving any thought to what it means or whether it is true is a waste of time. On the other hand, to form opinions and judgments about a subject without having any knowledge about it can be disastrous."

- As necessary, make sure students understand the meaning of the following words: 1.16. merits *(good qualities)*; 2.7. respect *(an attitude of appreciation and honor)*; 2.20. train *(to teach how to do a task)*; incompetent *(not qualified or skilled for a task)*; 3.26. authority *(the power to be in charge)*; ceremony *(formal acts or rituals, such as a wedding)*; reverence *(an attitude of awe and honor)*.
- Explain that in 4.6, the phrase "not for want of strength" means "not because they don't have strength."

Advanced Learners

Have students work in pairs to prepare a debate on the ideas expressed in one section of the *Analects*, such as 2.15 or 4.6.

ANALECTS **437**

Reading and Analyzing

Literary Analysis IRONY

A Remind students that irony is the contrast between what is expected and what actually happens or exists. Ask students to reread 14.28 and explain why Zigong's statement, "Master, you have just drawn your own portrait," is ironic. Invite students to discuss what the irony reveals about Confucius and his followers.

Possible Response: Because Confucius had said that he was unable to follow the three principles he describes, Zigong's statement is a complete surprise. The contrast between the two statements shows Confucius' humility and the admiration of his followers.

Active Reading ANALYZING MAXIMS

B The final statement in 15.24, "What you do not wish for yourself, do not do to others," is a version of the golden rule, "Act toward others as you would have them act toward you." Have students consider whether the way this idea is stated in the *Analects* makes any difference in its meaning.

Possible Response: Students will likely point out that the statement of the idea in the *Analects* is in negative language and might seem less forceful than the positive statement in the more familiar version.

A Literary Gathering, Han Huang. Palace Museum, Beijing.

HUMANITIES CONNECTION This painting, done on silk, shows a group of scholars reading and writing. A mastery of literary skills was necessary for anyone wanting to hold a government position. The figure in the lower right is a servant grinding ink.

The Master said: "Do not worry if you are without a position; worry lest you do not deserve a position. Do not worry if you are not famous; worry lest you do not deserve to be famous." (4.14)

The Master said: "Set your heart upon the Way;[9] rely upon moral power; follow goodness; enjoy the arts." (7.6)

The Master said: "Without ritual,[10] courtesy is tiresome; without ritual, prudence[11] is timid; without ritual, bravery is quarrelsome; without ritual, frankness[12] is hurtful. When gentlemen treat their kin generously, common people are attracted to goodness; when old ties are not forgotten, common people are not fickle."[13] (8.2)

A The Master said: "A gentleman abides by three principles which I am unable to follow: his humanity[14] knows no anxiety; his wisdom knows no hesitation; his courage knows no fear." Zigong[15] said: "Master, you have just drawn your own portrait." (14.28)

B Zigong asked: "Is there any single word that could guide one's entire life?" The Master said: "Should it not be *reciprocity?* What you do not wish for yourself, do not do to others." (15.24)

9. **Way:** ideal pattern of behavior.
10. **ritual:** an important Confucian concept, as is "gentlemen" in the next sentence (see Building Background).
11. **prudence:** caution and forethought.
12. **frankness:** blunt, honest expression.
13. **fickle:** quick to change their mind or opinion.
14. **humanity:** virtuous behavior toward others (see Building Background).
15. **Zigong** (dzŭ'gŏŏng'): a diplomat and merchant who was one of Confucius' most dedicated disciples.

MINI LESSON Viewing and Representing

A Literary Gathering **by Han Huang**

ART APPRECIATION

Instruction During much of China's history, those in the upper classes were expected to be accomplished poets, and literary activities were viewed with great respect and admiration. This painting shows what would have been a common literary occasion. The artist Han Huang (hän'hwäng'), who lived from A.D. 723 to 789, was known for his paintings of people. He may have portrayed some of his close friends in this scene.

Application Ask students to describe what each of the five figures in the painting appears to be doing. Ask them also to note any differences they can find between the figures.

Possible Response: The two men on the bench are reading and possibly discussing a literary work, and the man leaning on the pine tree appears to be reflecting. The man on the far right seems to be thinking about the poem he will write. In contrast, the servant is busy preparing ink for the scholar to use. The portrayal of the servant, with part of her face hidden, her head bare, and her body bent over, seems to emphasize her lowly position in relation to the scholars.

Connect to the Literature

1. **What Do You Think?** Were the teachings in the *Analects* surprising in any way? Discuss your thoughts with a classmate.

Comprehension Check
- What kinds of behavior does Confucius talk about in the *Analects?*
- What does Confucius mean by the word *reciprocity?*

Think Critically

2. What kind of person does Confucius seem to be?

- the kinds of behavior he advises people to pursue
- his attitude toward the listener or reader
- how he views himself

3. Do you think Confucius views human nature in an optimistic or a pessimistic way? Explain your opinion.

4. **ACTIVE READING: ANALYZING MAXIMS** Look back at the chart you created in your READER'S NOTEBOOK. Does Confucius seem more concerned with individual behavior or with behavior toward others?

5. Do you agree with all of Confucius' teachings? Explain your opinion.

Extend Interpretations

6. **Critic's Corner** One critic suggests that reading the *Analects* is like being invited into a conversation with Confucius. Do you think this is a helpful way of approaching these excerpts? Explain your answer.

7. **Connect to Life** Choose one of Confucius' sayings that you think relates directly to life today. Explain your choice.

LITERARY ANALYSIS: MAXIM

A **maxim** offers insight into how life should be lived. Maxims can help you evaluate your own behavior and the values and goals of your society. They can be a gentle reminder of what is good, or they can be a sharp criticism of weakness or selfishness.

Paired Activity With a classmate, write three maxims about how you think people should live. Be as specific as you can. Try to make your maxims relate to attitudes and behavior in your family, school, and community. For example, try writing a maxim that relates to popular entertain-ment, to using the Internet, or to doing homework. Your maxims can be serious or humorous.

Connect to the Literature

1. **What Do You Think?** Possible Response: Students may express surprise that some of the ideas are so similar to those found in the teachings of other cultures and religions, especially the similarity of 15.24 to the golden rule.

Comprehension Check
- Possible Responses: He talks about how a person should view his or her own worth and how a person should relate to others. He emphasizes courtesy, respect, duty, kindness, and courage.
- *Reciprocity* means treating others as you would like them to treat you.

Think Critically

2. Possible Response: Confucius' aim is to live a moral and virtuous life and to teach others to live such a life. He looks for the most ethical, courteous, and generous way to respond to every situation. He is humble (especially clear in 14.28), but he is also firm in stating his views and ideas.
3. Possible Responses: Students who think Confucius' view is optimistic might say that he offers his teachings with the expectation that people can learn from them and will change their behavior. Those who think he is pessimistic might point out Confucius' criticism of children's attitudes toward parents in 2.7; his description of negative behavior in 2.15, 3.26, and 8.2; and his statement that he had "never seen a man who truly loved goodness" in 4.6.
4. Possible Response: Most students will say that Confucius seems most concerned with behavior toward others. The teachings in 2.15 and 4.14 are directly concerned with individual behavior; the rest of the teachings are concerned with behavior toward others or virtuous behavior in general.
5. Possible Responses: Most students will disagree with one or more of Confucius' teachings. Some may think there is too much emphasis on duty and authority. Others may offer examples of people who they think "truly loved goodness and hated evil." Some may not agree that *reciprocity* is the one word that could be a guide for life. Some students may say that they don't know whether or not they agree because some teachings need more explanation.

Extend Interpretations

6. **Critic's Corner** Possible Response: Students may say that thinking of the *Analects* in terms of a conversation helps them to think through the ideas and to form questions about parts they don't understand. A conversation is also less intimidating than a formal discussion or debate.
7. **Connect to Life** Answers will vary. Good responses will show a clear understanding of the Confucian teaching and an appropriate connection to contemporary life.

Literary Analysis

Paired Activity You might have students put together a class collection of maxims, organized according to the types of maxims that are created.

Use **Unit Three Resource Book,** p. 5, for more practice.

To assess skills and concepts taught in this selection, use **Formal Assessment Book,** pp. 55–56.

ANALECTS 439

Objectives

- understand and appreciate **didactic literature (Literary Analysis)**
- identify and understand **paradoxes (Literary Analysis)**
- use strategies for **interpreting paradoxes (Active Reading)**

Thematic Link

The wisdom of the *Tao Te Ching* moves from **observation** of the disharmony and struggles in the world to **insight** into how to create peace and simplicity in life.

5-Minute Warm-Up

Daily Language SkillBuilder

Have students **proofread** the display sentences on page 419i and write them correctly.

Pinyin Equivalents

- *Tao Te Ching: Dao De Jing*
- Lao-tzu: Laozi
- Ssu'ma Ch'ien: Sima Qian

from the Tao Te Ching

LAO-TZU

Lao-tzu
500s B.C.

Founder of Taoism Did Lao-tzu (lou'dzŭ') really exist? No one knows. Although a person named Lao-tzu is credited with being the first philosopher of Taoism (dou'ĭz'əm), the details of his life are a mystery. Legend claims that Lao-tzu (which means "Old Master" or "Old Philosopher") had a miraculous birth and lived to be 160.

The main source of information about his life is a biography written in about 100 B.C. by the Chinese historian Ssu-ma Ch'ien (sŏŏ'mä' chē-ĕn'). According to this work, Lao-tzu was the court archivist, or keeper of the sacred books, during the later years of the Chou dynasty. At one time he was supposedly visited by Confucius. The account says that Lao-tzu advised Confucius to get rid of his "air of pride and many desires." Confucius later told his students that Lao-tzu was like a dragon that "rides on the winds and clouds and ascends to heaven."

Tao Te Ching The biography describes Lao-tzu as a person who sought virtue and harmony with the universe rather than fame. When he realized that the Chou dynasty was on the decline, he set out for the western border of China. A border guard begged Lao-tzu to set down his teachings in a book. Lao-tzu then wrote the *Tao Te Ching* (dou' dĕ jĭng'), the main expression of Taoist thought. Nothing more was ever heard of him.

Lasting Influence Most scholars now think that the *Tao Te Ching* was written in the third or fourth century B.C., probably by more than one author. It will never be known if Lao-tzu had anything to do with the writings. Nevertheless, he has been a revered figure in China through many centuries, seen as a philosopher by some and as a saint and even a god by others. The teachings of Taoism have been a prominent force in Chinese civilization. The Taoist emphasis on virtue, simplicity, and harmony with nature has been valued for more than 2,000 years.

LESSON RESOURCES

UNIT THREE RESOURCE BOOK, pp. 6–7

ASSESSMENT RESOURCES
Formal Assessment, pp. 57–58
Teacher's Guide to Assessment and Portfolio Use
Test Generator

INTEGRATED TECHNOLOGY
Visit our Web site: classzone.com

ADDITIONAL RESOURCES
Lesson Planning Guide, pp. 47–48
Teacher's Sourcebook for Language Development

Build Background

Small but Powerful The *Tao Te Ching,* a short book of about 81 pages, is probably the best-known work in Chinese literature. After the Bible, it is the most translated book in history. The *Tao Te Ching* is concerned with teaching what is referred to as "the Way."

Confucian thought focuses on specific actions and emphasizes respect for authority and an orderly society. In contrast, Taoist thought focuses on the Way, or the Tao, a broad concept that refers to the source and purpose of all existence. The Tao gives birth to all living things, but it also becomes part of every living thing. It is a force that moves all things toward being in harmony with their true nature.

To live according to the Tao, a person needs to be close to nature and live in simplicity and joy. An important idea in the *Tao Te Ching* is what is called *wu-wei* (wo͞o'wā'), or nonaction. This concept means that instead of being competitive, ambitious, and active, a person should just let things happen. A simple life and freedom from desires are said to help people discover the Way.

Because of the nature of Taoist thought, contradictory statements run throughout the *Tao Te Ching* and challenge most readers. For example, here is a teaching from passage 22:

> ***If you want to be reborn,***
> ***let yourself die.***
> ***If you want to be given everything,***
> ***give everything up.***

Each reader is invited to ponder these mysterious sayings and decide what they might mean in his or her own life.

Woman practicing tai chi, a form of movement that expresses the principles of the *Tao Te Ching*

Connect to Your Life

It is important to most people to find some meaning in their lives. Think of a person who seems to have a strong sense of meaning in his or her life. What does this person value? How does this person act toward others? Describe the person to your classmates.

Focus Your Reading

LITERARY ANALYSIS: PARADOX

A **paradox** is a statement that seems contradictory but is actually true. The reader has to solve the puzzle of the apparent contradiction in order to understand what is being said. An example of a paradox is this statement from the New Testament:

> ***For whosoever will save his life shall lose it: . . . (Matthew 16:25)***

As you read the three excerpts from the *Tao Te Ching,* look for examples of paradox.

ACTIVE READING: INTERPRETING PARADOXES

When you come upon a paradox in your reading, you face the challenge of trying to figure out what it means. For example, in the biblical quotation above, the idea that if you save your life you will lose it doesn't seem to make sense. To understand the paradox, think about all the ways to interpret the words save and lose. In this case, save refers to being selfish. By not sharing your life with others, you lose meaning in life.

READER'S NOTEBOOK In a chart like the one below, write down any paradoxes that you identify as you read these excerpts. For each paradox, circle the words that seem contradictory. Then explain the paradox.

Paradox	Meaning

READING FOR INFORMATION
Reading Skills and Strategies
PREVIEWING

Have students look at the main divisions on these two pages. Tell them to scan the boldfaced heads on page 440 and in the **Build Background** section on page 441. Ask students what clues these heads give about the literature they will be reading. *(The heads "Lasting Influence" and "Small but Powerful" indicate that the* Tao Te Ching *is an important and impressive work.)* Then suggest that they look at the two colored heads under **Focus Your Reading** and read the four lines highlighted in the first column. Ask students what challenge they think this literature might present. *(Some of the statements may seem puzzling and will require some analysis to understand.)* Finally, encourage students to look at the photograph and caption on page 441. Ask them what connections are suggested. *(The modern practice of tai chi is related to an ancient Chinese literary work.)*

Cross Curricular Link **Humanities**

TAI CHI Tai chi is the abbreviated name of tai chi chuan (tī' chē' chwän'), which means "supreme ultimate force." It is a system of exercises intended to promote health and longevity, and it can be practiced as a martial art as well. An important concept related to tai chi is *chi*, which refers to the vital force that animates the body. One of the main purposes of tai chi is to foster the proper movement and balance of chi within the body so that a person can move toward harmony between the body, mind, and spirit.

Tai chi has its roots in Taoism, which sees the physical and spiritual dimensions of life as interconnected. From about the second century B.C., various groups of Taoists used health exercises, or movements, in their religious practice. Over the centuries, various styles of tai chi developed. Modern forms emerged in the early 19th century, and there are at least eight styles of tai chi now in use. Although these styles are no longer part of Taoist religious practices, the emphasis on harmony and balance reflects the ancient Taoist teachings.

Literary Analysis PARADOX

Point out to students that a paradox may be expressed in a brief, concise statement, as in the beginning of passage 37, or it may be developed through a more extended section, as in the middle of 37. Tell students to look for both short paradoxical statements and underlying paradoxical ideas as they read through the three excerpts.

Possible Responses: Brief statements include the last two lines of 44 and the first two lines of 68. Paradoxical ideas underlie the first and last sections of 44 and the second section of 68.

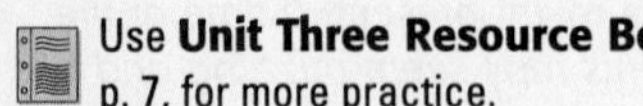
Use **Unit Three Resource Book,** p. 7, for more practice.

Active Reading
INTERPRETING PARADOXES

A Tell students that although a paradox expresses something true, it may be confusing at first. Help students to work through what the first two lines of passage 37 might mean.

Possible Response: Remind students that the Tao refers to an essential force, or way of being, in the universe. It is responsible for everything that exists. The difficulty in the statement in these two lines is that although the Tao is said to be the source of all life—through it "all things are done"—nevertheless it "never does anything." It works by not working—it allows life to unfold rather than making it happen. An analogy from everyday life might be letting a child develop at his or her own pace rather than trying to make the child perform certain tasks at a certain age.

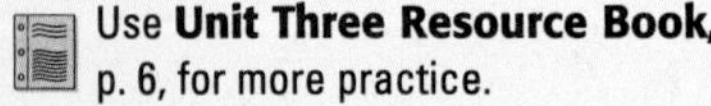
Use **Unit Three Resource Book,** p. 6, for more practice.

Literary Analysis DIDACTIC LITERATURE

Remind students that didactic literature is written to teach lessons about how to live a good and a moral life. Ask students to identify two lessons in these excerpts from the *Tao Te Ching.*

Possible Responses: Lessons include those found in the two statements in the middle section of 44, the first statement in the last section of 44, and the four statements in the first section of 68.

from the Tao Te Ching

Lao-tzu

Translated by Stephen Mitchell

A The Tao never does anything,
yet through it all things are done.

If powerful men and women
could center themselves in it,
1 the whole world would be transformed
by itself, in its natural rhythms.
People would be content
with their simple, everyday lives,
in harmony, and free of desire.

When there is no desire,
all things are at peace.

Detail of *Lady with Fan* (mid 19th century), Ju Qing. Album leaf, ink & color on silk, 27 cm × 36.5 cm. Collection of the Art Museum of the Chinese University of Hong Kong.

Fame or integrity:[1] which is more important?
2 Money or happiness: which is more valuable?
Success or failure: which is more destructive?

If you look to others for fulfillment,
you will never truly be fulfilled.
If your happiness depends on money,
you will never be happy with yourself.

Be content with what you have;
rejoice in the way things are.
3 When you realize there is nothing lacking,
the whole world belongs to you.

1. **integrity** (ĭn-tĕg′rĭ-tē): personal honesty and uprightness.

MINI LESSON **Vocabulary Strategy**

SUFFIXES

Instruction The suffixes *-ant, -able, -ive,* and *-ment* are examples of an affix, a word part attached to a base word to make a new word. These suffixes can indicate a state or quality.

Suffix	Meaning	Example
-ant	inclined to	important
-able	is, can be	valuable
-ive	inclined to	destructive
-ment	action or process	fulfillment

Practice Write the words *important, valuable, destructive,* and *fulfillment* on the board and have students identify the base words and suffixes. Have them explain the change in the word's function or meaning when the suffix is added.

Read each example word. Identify the suffix and its meaning. Identify the base word and its meaning. Explain what the example word means by using the definitions of the base word and suffix.

Base Word	Suffix
import	-ant
value	-able
destruct	-ive
fulfill	-ment

A lesson on affixes appears on p. 864 in the Pupil's Edition.

Lao-tzu riding his ox (1500s), Zhang Lu. Hanging scroll, ink and watercolor on silk. Collection of the National Palace Museum, Taipei, Taiwan, Republic of China. Photo © Bridgeman Art Library.

HUMANITIES CONNECTION This portrayal of Lao-tzu pictures the Taoist philosopher as a free spirit making a journey, following a fluttering butterfly. The scroll he is carrying represents the *Tao Te Ching*.

The best athlete
wants his opponent at his best.
The best general
enters the mind of his enemy.
The best businessman
serves the communal good.[2]
The best leader
follows the will of the people.

All of them embody
the virtue of non-competition.
Not that they don't love to compete,
but they do it in the spirit of play.
In this they are like children
and in harmony with the Tao.

2. **communal good:** welfare of the community.

MINI LESSON Viewing and Representing

Lao-tzu Riding an Ox by **Chang Lu**

ART APPRECIATION

Instruction The artist Chang Lu (jäng´ lo͞o´), who lived in the 16th century A.D., was known for his painting of wise men and godlike figures. A professional painter who was also a scholar, he created these portraits for rich patrons in northern China. There is no way of knowing what Lao-tzu looked like, of course—if in fact he did exist. But because he was revered through much of China's history, there have been various portraits of him painted by different artists. In most of the paintings still in existence, Lao-tzu is pictured riding in a cart pulled by a water buffalo. He is shown handing his manuscript to a guard as he heads west out of China. Chang Lu's painting is unusual in that Lao-tzu is pictured actually riding the animal. The work is one of the last examples of heroic paintings of important figures in Taoism.

Application Ask students what details of the painting might indicate that the figure is a wise and respected man.

Possible Responses: Details such as the age of the man; the serious expression on his face; the beautiful, flowing robe; and the scroll in his hand create an impression of dignity and respect.

Customizing Instruction

Less Proficient Readers

- Explain to students that they will be reading 3 of the 81 passages of the *Tao Te Ching*. Each passage is a separate teaching.
- Help students understand the nature of a paradox by giving one or two examples and discussing them: "The pen is mightier than the sword," "Haste makes waste," or "A soft answer turns away wrath."
- Suggest to students that one way to try to understand the statements in the *Tao Te Ching* is to think of the opposite of each one. For example, restate the fourth and fifth lines of passage 44 as "If you look to others for fulfillment, you will always be truly fulfilled." Ask students if this opposite statement is true. *(no)* Then have them discuss the meaning of the original statement.

English Learners

- You might want to focus on just one of the passages from the *Tao Te Ching* with these students, possibly 68. Tell the students to read each of the first four statements and think about why each one is true. *(The best athlete wants a challenge. The best general is interested in strategy. The best businessman wants to benefit his customers. The best leader serves the people.)*
- For the second section of 68, you might want to focus on key phrases and concepts: non-competition, competing in the spirit of play, and being like children. (These refer to competing without caring about winning. The competition is for the sake of enjoying the challenge.)

1 Explain that "transformed" means "to be greatly changed."

2 Make sure students understand that "valuable" refers not to the worth of money but to what has most meaning and importance in life.

3 Explain that the phrase "nothing lacking" means "nothing is missing."

Advanced Learners

There are many translations of the *Tao Te Ching* available. Have students find some of these and compare different versions of the three passages. Ask them to make a list of the most striking differences and briefly explain which translations they prefer.

Related Reading

Chuang Tzu Very little is known about the life of Chuang Tzu, but he is considered, along with Lao-tzu, as one of the founders of Taoism. The ancient historian Ssu-ma Ch'ien recorded that Chuang Tzu lived in the fourth century and was born in the state of Meng (mŭng), which is now Honan (hŭ'năn') province (pinyin *Henan*), south of the Yellow River.

Chuang Tzu was a minor official for a brief time but spent most of his life as a wandering Taoist philosopher. He preferred to live in freedom and solitude, allowing things to follow their own course according to the Tao. Stories written by his followers picture him as an eccentric who cared nothing about how he looked or what other people thought of him. He was not interested in the traditions and institutions of society, and he turned down offers of political office. He did not admire Confucianism and often poked fun at its teachings, though he valued his friendship with the Confucian scholar Hui Tzu.

Chuang Tzu's teachings are written in the book that bears his name, the *Chuang Tzu.* The present form of the book has about 30 chapters, but only the first 7 are considered to be Chuang Tzu's own work. Most of the material in the other chapters was probably written by his disciples.

The *Chuang Tzu* is admired for both its development of Taoist thought and its literary style. It has had a major influence on later Chinese writing, especially poetry. In his book, Chuang Tzu often used anecdotes, such as "The Fish Rejoice," to illustrate his points. These tales are imaginative, witty, and playful. In them, Chuang Tzu expresses his belief in the unity of the Tao and its presence in all parts of life.

Pinyin Equivalents

Chuang Tzu: Zhuang Zi
Hui Tzu: Hui Zi
Anhwei: Anhui

from CHUANG TZU

The Fish Rejoice

Chuang Tzu

Translated by Moss Roberts

The writer Chuang Tzu[1] believed that all living things are equal. In this tale, the human and animal worlds connect as Chuang Tzu rejoices with the fish.

Chuang Tzu and his close friend Hui Tzu[2] were enjoying each other's company on the shores of the Hao.[3] Chuang Tzu said, "The flashing fish are out enjoying each other, too, swimming gracefully this way and that. Such is the joy of fish!"

"You're no fish," said Hui Tzu. "How could you know their joy?"

"You're no Chuang Tzu," said Chuang Tzu. "How could you know I don't know the joy of fish?"

"If 'I am no Chuang Tzu,'" said Hui Tzu, "means 'I don't know Chuang Tzu,' then to be consistent, you don't know the joy of fish if you aren't a fish!"

"Let's go back to the beginning," said Chuang Tzu. "Your own question, 'How could you know the joy of fish?' already made an assumption about my knowing it! I don't have to jump in the water to know!"

1. **Chuang Tzu** (jwäng' dzŭ'): a Taoist philosopher of the fourth century B.C., author of a book (also called *Chuang Tzu*) that is one of the main works of Taoist literature.
2. **Hui Tzu** (hwē' dzŭ'): a Confucian scholar and senior minister at the royal court, with whom Chuang Tzu had a friendly rivalry.
3. **Hao** (hou): a river in the province of Anhwei in eastern China.

Ming dish (16th century). Porcelain with overglaze enamel decoration. Collection of the National Palace Museum, Taipei, Taiwan, Republic of China.

Discussion Questions

1. How would you describe Chuang Tzu and Hui Tzu?
   Possible Response: Chuang Tzu seems to be relaxed, humorous, ready to enjoy a lively discussion, and connected to nature. Hui Tzu seems serious, argumentative, and literal-minded.
2. Chuang Tzu says that when Hui Tzu asks the question "How could you know the joy of fish?" Hui Tzu is admitting that the fish are joyful and that Chuang Tzu knew this. Do you agree with Chuang Tzu's conclusion? Explain your opinion.
   Possible Responses: Hui Tzu hears about the joyful fish from Chuang Tzu. So when Hui Tzu refers to the joy of the fish himself, it could be said that he is admitting Chuang Tzu's knowledge of the fish. On the other hand, Hui Tzu could just be asking, "How could anyone know such a thing as the feelings of fish?" Some students may feel that the two friends are enjoying arguing for the sake of arguing and that neither one wins.

Connect to the Literature

1. **What Do You Think?** Which of the teachings do you most agree with? Explain your choice.

Comprehension Check
- Name one contrast that is presented in passage 37.
- What seems to be the Taoist attitude toward money as expressed in passage 44?
- What is identified as a virtue in passage 68?

Think Critically

2. In passage 37, the writer refers to "powerful men and women." What do you think is the Taoist attitude toward being a powerful person?

THINK ABOUT
- the Taoist emphasis on living a simple life in passage 37
- the warning in passage 44 that "if you look to others for fulfillment, you will never truly be fulfilled"
- the reference to competition in passage 68

3. According to your understanding of Taoist thought, what do you think are the correct answers to the questions posed in passage 44? Explain your ideas.
4. In passage 68, the writer speaks of competing in a "spirit of play." What do you think he means?
5. **ACTIVE READING: INTERPRETING PARADOXES** With a partner, compare the charts you created in your  READER'S NOTEBOOK. Discuss the paradoxes you identified and their meanings. How similar were your interpretations?

Extend Interpretations

6. **Comparing Texts** Reread "The Fish Rejoice" on page 444. Which of the excerpts from the *Tao Te Ching* do you think relates most closely to this tale? Support your ideas with details from the selections.
7. **Comparing Texts** Compare the passages you have read from the *Tao Te Ching* with the selections from the *Analects* on pages 437–438. How do the two schools of thought differ in their teachings about conduct in everyday life? How do they compare in their attitudes toward leadership and authority?
8. **Connect to Life** How would life in modern American society change if people lived according to Taoist teachings? Do you think the change would be for the better? Explain.

LITERARY ANALYSIS: PARADOX

The Tao Te Ching contains many **paradoxes**—statements that seem contradictory but nevertheless express truths. The use of paradox forces the reader to interpret the meaning of the passages. Understanding the paradox brings the reader closer to an understanding of the Tao. Consider the paradox in the following lines from passage 44:

When you realize there is nothing lacking,
the whole world belongs to you.

To understand the paradox, you must think about what "the whole world" probably means in Taoist thought. The paradox helps teach the Taoist principle of being content with a simple life.

Paired Activity Read the following lines from passage 33 of the *Tao Te Ching.*

If you realize that you have enough,
you are truly rich.
If you stay in the center
and embrace death with your whole heart,
you will endure forever.

With a partner, identify the paradoxes in the passage. Discuss possible interpretations of each paradox. Then write a brief paraphrase of each one.

Connect to the Literature

1. **What Do You Think?** Students should refer to specific passages and give reasons for their choices.

Comprehension Check
- The phrase "never does anything" contrasts with the phrase "all things are done."
- It can never make a person happy.
- an attitude of "non-competition"

Think Critically

2. Possible Response: The Taoist attitude does not seem to value being powerful or important. Trying to be a winner or trying to please others will not lead to peace and harmony.
3. Possible Response: A Taoist would say that integrity is more important than fame, happiness is more valuable than money, and success can be as destructive as failure. Achieving fame, money, and success never brings contentment.
4. Possible Response: To compete in the "spirit of play" seems to mean to participate for the sake of the game or the work itself, not for the sake of winning.
5. Possible Responses: Most students will identify paradoxes in the first two lines of passage 37, the last four lines of passage 44, and the first ten lines of passage 68. Other students may identify the middle section of 37 and the last two lines of 37 as paradoxical.

   Students may have lively disagreements about their different interpretations of the paradoxes. Ask them for explanations and support for their ideas.

Literary Analysis

Paired Activity After students have worked on the two paradoxes in this passage, they can compare their ideas in a class discussion.

 Use **Unit Three Resource Book,** p. 7, for more practice.

 To assess skills and concepts taught in this selection, use **Formal Assessment Book,** pp. 57–58.

Extend Interpretations

6. **Comparing Texts** Most students will say that passage 68 relates most closely to "The Fish Rejoice." The two friends are arguing in the "spirit of play." Each appreciates the sharpness of the other—"wants his opponent at his best."
7. **Comparing Texts** Possible Response: The teachings in the *Analects* promote an active life. The teachings in the *Tao Te Ching* focus on the individual being in harmony with the Tao and not seeking a busy, successful life. The Confucian teaching values authority. The teachings in the *Tao Te Ching* advise people to let go of power.
8. **Connect to Life** Accept all reasonable responses. Many students may feel that living according to Taoist teachings would make American life more peaceful and gentle. Others may feel that it would lead to a less productive and interesting society.

Objectives

- understand and appreciate **lyric poetry (Literary Analysis)**
- identify and analyze **repetition (Literary Analysis)**
- improve comprehension by **reading aloud (Active Reading)**

Thematic Link

The speakers in these two poems make detailed **observations** about love and about war and offer **insights** into the emotions they experience.

5-Minute Warm-Up

Daily Language SkillBuilder

Have students **proofread** the display sentences on page 419i and write them correctly.

Pinyin Equivalent

Shih Ching: Shi Jing

Reading and Analyzing

Literary Analysis REPETITION

Point out to students that repetition can involve one word or a whole line. Ask them to identify a word, a phrase, and a line that are repeated.

Possible Responses: Single words include *mulberry, lowland, graceful, leaves,* and *lord*. Phrases include "the mulberry on the lowland," "how graceful," "its leaves." Lines include lines 1, 5, and 9 and lines 3, 7, and 11.

Tell students that elements of structure can also be repeated. Ask them to give an example from the first three stanzas of the poem.

Possible Response: The first and third lines in each are exactly the same.

Use **Unit Three Resource Book,** p. 9, for more practice.

Active Reading

READING POETRY ALOUD

Remind students that this poem was first handed down orally. Tell them that when they read the poem aloud, they should be aware of how repeated words and rhythms might have helped people remember the poem when they were reciting it. Tell them also to listen for what the repeated elements emphasize in the poem.

Use **Unit Three Resource Book,** p. 8, for more practice.

from the BOOK OF ODES

Build Background

Ancient Masterpieces The *Book of Odes* is a group of 305 poems that are the most ancient works still in existence in Chinese literature. This collection was put together around the sixth century B.C., but some of the poems may date back to 1000 B.C. The poems were originally songs, set to music that has since been lost. The full history of how the poems first came to be and who collected them is not known. The glimpses they give of Chinese people in ancient times, however, make those people come to life.

The poems in the *Book of Odes* range from folk songs depicting everyday life to songs of court life and stately hymns. This is not a literature of heroes only. The voices of the common people, women as well as men, are heard. In the folk songs, they express their hopes and disappointments as they go about their daily tasks, as they search for love, and as they go to war. The court poems have many of the same subjects and concerns as the folk songs, but they reflect a more aristocratic lifestyle. The hymns, which include the oldest poems, were used in religious rituals.

In Chinese culture, the *Book of Odes* has been as important as national epics have been to the civilizations of Greece and Rome. The philosopher Confucius considered the poems an essential source of moral teaching. The *Book of Odes* has also been a model of poetic style in Chinese literature. The Chinese word for poetry, *shih* (shĭ), came from the original name of the work—*Shih Ching* ("Classic of Poetry"). These poems have, in fact, been so revered throughout the history of China that, until early in the 20th century, they had to be memorized in their entirety by all Chinese schoolchildren. Today the poems are appreciated for their beauty, freshness, and lyrical qualities.

Connect to Your Life

The two court poems that you are about to read express deep feelings about love and war. Think of a current popular song or type of music that conveys strong emotions. What features of the music appeal to the listener's experience and emotions? Compare your ideas with those of your classmates.

Focus Your Reading

LITERARY ANALYSIS: REPETITION

Poetry from an oral tradition that was sung usually uses **repetition**—sounds, words, and groups of words that are repeated for emphasis. As you read the poems, look for the repeated elements.

ACTIVE READING: READING POETRY ALOUD

Reading a poem aloud helps you hear the rhythms, repetition, and sound effects. Often, hearing the sounds of a poem allows you to better understand what it means.

READER'S NOTEBOOK After you have read these poems once or twice silently, read them aloud. Jot down one or two aspects of each poem that became clearer or more forceful to you. Use a chart like the one below to record your comments for each poem.

"Mulberry on the Lowland"	
Lines	**Comments on Reading Aloud**
4, 8, 12, and 16	*helps you feel the strength of the speaker's emotions*

LESSON RESOURCES

UNIT THREE RESOURCE BOOK, pp. 8–9

ASSESSMENT RESOURCES

Formal Assessment, pp. 59–60

Teacher's Guide to Assessment and Portfolio Use

Test Generator

INTEGRATED TECHNOLOGY

Visit our Web site: classzone.com

ADDITIONAL RESOURCES

Lesson Planning Guide, pp. 49–50

Teacher's Sourcebook for Language Development

from the Book of Odes

Mulberry on the Lowland

Translated by Arthur Waley

The mulberry on the lowland, how graceful!
Its leaves, how tender!
Now that I have seen my lord,
Ah, what delight!

The mulberry on the lowland, how graceful!
Its leaves, how glossy!
Now that I have seen my lord,
What joy indeed!

The mulberry on the lowland, how graceful,
Its leaves, how fresh!
Now I have seen my lord,
His high fame holds fast.

Love that is felt in the heart,
Why should it not be told in words?
To the core of my heart I treasure him,
Could not ever cease to love him.

1 **mulberry:** a tree valued in China because its leaves are the food of silkworms, the moth larvae that produce the fiber from which silk cloth is made.

Figure of sitting woman. Imperial Museum, Beijing. Robert Harding Picture Library, London.

HUMANITIES CONNECTION This figure of a woman was found in 1964 in a cotton field near the tomb of the first emperor of China. Rulers often had a variety of figures buried with them to help them in their afterlife. This piece would have represented an attendant or servant.

Customizing Instruction

Less Proficient Readers

- Make sure students understand that the speaker is a woman and that the word *lord* refers to the man she loves.
- Point out the basic structure of the poem: The speaker describes some appealing details of the mulberry tree, and this description of the beauty of the tree becomes a bridge to her expression of love toward her lord.

English Learners

- You might want to bring in a picture of a mulberry tree or describe the tree. (The mulberry tree has oval or heart-shaped toothed leaves and greenish-white flower clusters that hang from the branches. The fruits are white, red, or black. One variety of mulberry has drooping branches, which are particularly graceful.)
- Explain to students that *tender* (line 2) means "soft, young, and delicate," *glossy* (line 6) means "smooth and shiny," and *fresh* (line 10) means "new, pure, and undamaged."
- Explain that "holds fast" (line 12) means "stays the same" or "doesn't change."
- Explain that "core of my heart" (line 15) refers to the speaker's deepest feelings of love.

Advanced Learners

Have students work in pairs to analyze the relationship between the three words *tender, glossy,* and *fresh* and what the speaker says about her lord and her love for him. Suggest to students that they focus on different possible meanings and connotations of the three words. Have students compare their ideas in a class discussion.

MINI LESSON Viewing and Representing

Pottery Figure of a Seated Woman (page 447)
Bronze Figure of Horseman (page 448)

ART APPRECIATION

Instruction Beginning in the 1920s, archaeologists have been excavating vast tombs built by ancient Chinese rulers and noblemen. These tombs have yielded a staggering array of artifacts of great beauty and craftsmanship. The pottery figure of the woman on this page was individually created, not made from a mold, as some funeral figures were. The body is hollow, and the arms and head were made separately.

The horseman pictured on the next page is part of a set of small bronze figures—about 12 to 20 inches tall—that included 17 soldiers, 28 attendants, 39 horses, and 14 carriages. In life, the rank of an official was known from the number of chariots he had.

Application Have students look at the two figures and reread the **Humanities Connections** on pages 447 and 448. Ask them what emotions or mood each figure seems to show.

Possible Responses: The figure of the woman seems calm and quietly happy. The figure of the soldier seems ready for battle, and the horse looks spirited.

Reading and Analyzing

Reading Skills and Strategies
CLARIFYING
Explain to students that there are places where ferns grow in great numbers. Young ferns can be used for food and dried ferns can be used to make a rough mattress to sleep on. Point out that the descriptions of the ferns reveal the passage of time. Ask students to explain what the sequence of time is. *(The descriptions of the ferns seem to refer to three seasons of the year. The sprouting ferns appear in the spring, the tender ferns grow in the summer, and the tough ferns are found in the fall.)*

A What kinds of activities might be represented by kneeling and sitting down?
Possible Responses: praying, resting, eating, relaxing, talking, waiting

Literary Analysis REPETITION
Tell students that some scholars think that "We Pick Ferns, We Pick Ferns" was used as a marching song for foot soldiers. Ask students whether the rhythms of the English translation follow the rhythm of a march. *(no, because the rhythms are not regular)* Then ask them how the repeated words and lines might be appropriate to a marching song.
Possible Response: Repeated words and lines could have helped the soldiers stay together and march in unison. The repetition could also have provided a way to express some of the strongest emotions and experiences of being at war and so created a sense of solidarity between the soldiers.

Literary Analysis SYMBOL
Remind students that a symbol is a person, place, object, or activity that stands for something beyond itself. Ask students what they think the ferns might symbolize.
Possible Responses: Some students may say that the ferns symbolize ordinary life, which progresses through cycles to its natural end. This is in contrast to the dragging out of the war with no end in sight. Others may say that the ferns symbolize the hope of the soldiers, which gradually withers as the fighting continues with no letup and no victory.

Horseman (second century A.D.). Bronze. National Museum, Beijing. Photograph copyright © Erich Lessing/Art Resource, New York.

HUMANITIES CONNECTION This figure of an infantryman was one of three discovered in 1969 at the site of the tomb of a general. The figure is carrying a weapon called a halberd, which has both a blade and a spike.

Cross Curricular Link **History**

GREAT WALL The soldiers in "We Pick Ferns, We Pick Ferns" are fighting a fierce enemy called the Hsien-yün, one of many northern nomadic tribes that continually invaded China, carrying off crops and animals and causing great destruction. A main line of defense against these invaders was the Great Wall. The wall is the longest human-made structure in the world, and it was built entirely by hand of earth, stone, and brick. Today the main part of the wall measures about 1,500 miles in length, with additional sections adding another 2,250 miles. About 20 feet high and 12 feet across, the wall had 40-foot watchtowers every 100 to 200 yards. Soldiers sent signals from these towers when invaders were spotted. The first continuous wall was built about 214 B.C., and this wall was repaired, enlarged, and reworked by a series of emperors extending into the 12th century A.D. Each building and rebuilding of the wall required the work of hundreds of thousands—if not millions—of soldiers and peasants, many of whom died because of the long journey, the forbidding climate, and the cruel working conditions.

from the Book of Odes

We Pick Ferns, We Pick Ferns

Translated by Burton Watson

We pick ferns, we pick ferns,
for the ferns are sprouting now:
oh to go home, to go home
before the year is over!
No rooms, no houses for us,
all because of the Hsien-yün,
A no time to kneel or sit down,
all because of the Hsien-yün.

We pick ferns, we pick ferns,
the ferns now are tender:
oh to go home, to go home!
Our hearts are saddened,
our sad hearts smolder and burn.
We are hungry, we are thirsty,
1 no limit to our border duty,
no way to send home for news.

We pick ferns, we pick ferns,
now the ferns have grown tough:
oh to go home, to go home
in the closing months of the year!
The king's business allows no slacking,
no leisure to kneel or rest.
Our sad hearts are sick to death,
this journey of ours has no return!

6 Hsien-yün (shyŭn'yŭn'): fierce tribes who invaded China from the north and were finally driven back around 800 B.C.

Customizing Instruction

Less Proficient Readers

Explain to students that the speakers in this poem are soldiers who have been sent off to war far away from home. Ask students the following questions:

- What conditions do the soldiers face? *(no place to stay, hunger and thirst, constant fighting, no contact with family and friends)*
- What is their enemy like?

Possible Response: strong and determined

- What emotions do the soldiers express? *(homesickness, sorrow, loneliness, discouragement)*

English Learners

Make sure students know what ferns are. You might want to bring in some pictures.

1 Explain to students that "border duty" refers to soldiers keeping watch to spot enemy activity.

MINI LESSON Speaking and Listening

CHORAL READING

Prepare Remind students that a choral reading is a group recital of a poem or other piece of writing. Organize the class into groups of four and have the groups experiment with different ways of using four readers. One approach would be for one student to read the first two lines of each stanza, a second student to join on the second two lines, and so on. They could use this approach using single lines also. Another possibility would be to alternate individual readers instead of joining voices. Ask students to pay particular attention to repeated parts of the poem and to look for ways of introducing variety into the reading of the repeated words and phrases. Suggest to students that they work on building emotional intensity at appropriate points in each stanza.

Present Suggest to students that each of the four readers might want to stand in a different place in the classroom so that the reading builds from several directions. Have the audience comment on the effects created by each group.

This activity is particularly well suited for longer class periods.

Reading and Analyzing

Reading Skills and Strategies
CLARIFYING

Point out to students that there is a break or shift between the third and fourth stanzas. The poem no longer is following the time sequence set up in the earlier stanzas. Ask students what contrast is made in lines 25 to 27. *(The speakers ask a question, which sets up a contrast between the beauties of a spring landscape and the urgent demands of war.)*

Literary Analysis ALLITERATION AND ASSONANCE

Ask students to identify examples of alliteration in stanzas four and five and examples of assonance in stanza six. (Remind students that the same spelling may be used for different sounds.) (*Alliteration: the* sp *sound in* splendor, *the* ch *sound in* cherry *and* chariot, *and the* st *sound in* stallion, sturdy, strong, stop, *and* stalwart; *Assonance: the long* o *in* ago, snow, slow, sorrow, no, knows, *and* woe *and the* ou *sound in* out, now, *and* our)

Ask students to identify one effect of either the alliteration or the assonance in the poem.

Possible Responses: The *ch* sound in *cherry* and *chariot* emphasizes the contrast these two words suggest between a beautiful landscape and war. The *st* sound is forceful and emphasizes the strength of the war horses. The long *o* sound is sad and mournful.

Active Reading

READING POETRY ALOUD

Suggest to students that when they are reading these stanzas aloud, they should pay attention to the alliteration and assonance. Tell them to use these sounds to help express meaning.

Literary Analysis REPETITION

Point out that in these three stanzas, only words and phrases are repeated, not whole lines. Ask students how this change relates to what is being described in the stanzas.

Possible Response: These stanzas describe action and are less reflective in tone than the first three stanzas. The rhythms are also more varied. The repeated words and phrases occur in different places instead of being predictable.

Ink drawing. Collection of National Palace Museum, Taipei, Taiwan, Republic of China.

What splendor is here?
The splendor of cherry flowers.
What chariot is this?
The chariot of our lord.
The war chariot is yoked,
four stallions sturdy and strong.
How would we dare to stop and rest?
In one month, three engagements!

We yoke those four stallions,
four stallions stalwart and strong,
for our lord to ride behind,
for lesser men to shield.
Four stallions stately,
ivory bow-ends, fish-skin quivers:
could we drop our guard for a day?
The Hsien-yün are fearfully swift!

Long ago we set out
when willows were rich and green.
Now we come back
through thickly falling snow.
Slow slow our march,
we are thirsty, we are hungry,
our hearts worn with sorrow,
no one knows our woe.

38 quivers: cases for carrying arrows.

Assessment Standardized Test Practice

EVALUATING AND MAKING JUDGMENTS In some standardized tests, students are asked to analyze information in order to make inferences and generalizations. Display the following question for students.

Which statement best describes the attitude of the soldiers in "We Pick Ferns, We Pick Ferns"?

A. The soldiers are determined to keep on fighting until the enemy is defeated.

B. The soldiers make the most of their situation, appreciating the beauties of nature and expressing pride in their leader.

C. The soldiers do their duty, but they wish the fighting were over.

D. The soldiers try to avoid every battle that they can.

Lead students through the possible answers. A is incorrect because the soldiers fight many battles but they do not press on for victory. Although the soldiers do notice details of nature and do speak well of their lord, B is not correct because the soldiers do not in general have a positive frame of mind. D is not true because the soldiers do engage in many battles. C best reflects the soldiers' sense of duty combined with their discouragement and homesickness.

Connect to the Literature

1. **What Do You Think?** Which details from these poems were you able to visualize? Explain your response.

Comprehension Check
- What details about the mulberry tree does the speaker describe in "Mulberry on the Lowland"?
- How do the ferns change during the course of the poem "We Pick Ferns, We Pick Ferns"?

Think Critically

2. Do you think "Mulberry on the Lowland" tells more about the speaker or more about her lord? Explain your answer.

THINK ABOUT
- what she tells you about her lord
- what she tells you about her feelings

3. How successful is the military campaign in "We Pick Ferns, We Pick Ferns"?

THINK ABOUT
- how long the campaign seems to have lasted
- the conditions the soldiers face
- what the speaker says about the enemy

4. Why do you think the poet refers to ferns, cherry blossoms, and willows in a poem describing war?

5. **ACTIVE READING READING POETRY ALOUD** Look back at the notes you made in your **READER'S NOTEBOOK**. How was your understanding or appreciation of the poems helped by reading them aloud?

Extend Interpretations

6. **Critic's Corner** One critic has said that readers of the poems in the *Book of Odes* have found a "window into another person's heart, a person like themselves." Do you agree with this statement? Support your answer with details from the poems.

7. **Comparing Texts** These two poems portray different moods. Identify the mood in each poem, and list three words or phrases in each that help create this mood.

8. **Connect to Life** In "We Pick Ferns, We Pick Ferns," the speaker describes the loneliness and hardships of going to fight in a war. Do you think 21st-century soldiers face similar difficulties? Explain your answer.

LITERARY ANALYSIS: REPETITION

The **repetition** of various elements in a poem—sounds, words, phrases, or lines—helps to emphasize images or details, make connections between ideas, and create rhythmic patterns. Repetition can unify a poem by creating a clear structure.

Activity Find examples of repetition in "Mulberry on the Lowland" and "We Pick Ferns, We Pick Ferns," and record them in a chart like the one shown. For each example, explain what you think is the purpose of the repetition in the poem. Do you think repetition is more important in one of the poems than in the other? Discuss your conclusions with your classmates.

"Mulberry on the Lowland"

Examples	Purpose
"The mulberry on the lowland, how graceful!" (lines 1, 5, 9)	emphasizes the main image in the poem

Connect to the Literature

1. **What Do You Think?** Accept all reasonable responses, such as the mulberry tree, the details from nature, and the harsh conditions of war.

Comprehension Check
- The tree is on the lowland, is graceful, and has tender, fresh leaves.
- They are sprouting, then they are tender, and finally they become tough.

Think Critically

2. Possible Response: Most students will say that the poem tells more about the speaker. She says that her lord brings her delight and joy and that she will love him forever. The speaker does not describe her lord.
3. Possible Response: Most students will say that the military campaign does not seem to be very successful and may be a failure. It seems to drag on through almost a year, and the enemy is constantly attacking. The soldiers return sad and dejected in apparent defeat rather than in victory.
4. Possible Response: The ferns, cherry blossoms, and willows provide a contrast to the realities of war. This contrast emphasizes the harshness of the soldiers' circumstances.
5. Students' responses will vary but should be appropriate and specific. They may suggest that reading aloud helped them pay attention to details they may have missed otherwise or helped them visualize scenes in both poems.

Literary Analysis

Activity Repetition occurs in lines 1, 5, and 9; 2, 6, and 10; 3, 7, and 11, and 4 and 8 in "Mulberry on the Lowland." It occurs in lines 1–2, 9–11, and 17–19; 6 and 8; 25–29; and 30, 33, 34, and 37 in "We Pick Ferns, We Pick Ferns." Repetition establishes rhythms, reinforces meaning, creates emphasis, and helps provide structure. Answers will vary about whether repetition is more important in one of the poems.

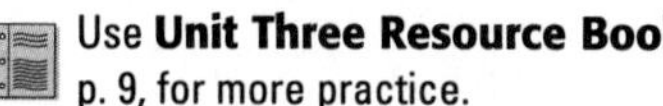
Use **Unit Three Resource Book,** p. 9, for more practice.

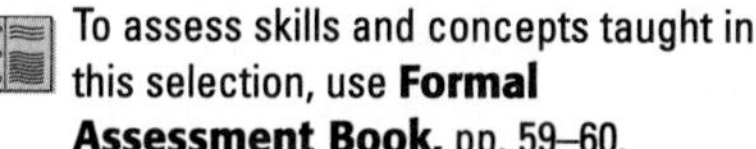
To assess skills and concepts taught in this selection, use **Formal Assessment Book,** pp. 59–60.

Extend Interpretations

6. **Critic's Corner** Many students will say that in both poems, the images, details, and feelings described did draw them into the experiences and emotions of the two speakers. In "Mulberry on the Lowland," the reader is drawn in to the speaker's pleasure in the tree and her feelings of joy and love. In "We Pick Ferns, We Pick Ferns," the reader is made aware of the discouragement of the soldiers through the images from nature and through the phrase "oh to go home."
7. **Comparing Texts** The mood of the first poem is happy ("delight," "joy," and "Love that is felt in the heart"). The mood of the second poem is sad ("no houses for us," "sick to death," and "worn with sorrow").
8. **Connect to Life** Soldiers today experience many of the same emotions as the soldiers in the poem: loneliness, fear, exhaustion, and discouragement. They also have to cope with danger, long hours, surprise attacks, poor food, and rough quarters. Communication is much better, however, so they are not as cut off from family and friends.

This selection is included in the **World Literature InterActive Reader™**.

Objectives

- understand and appreciate **lyric poetry (Literary Analysis)**
- identify and examine **imagery (Literary Analysis)**
- use **visualizing** to appreciate and enjoy the imagery in Li Po's poems **(Active Reading)**

Thematic Link

In these poems, Li Po moves **from observation to insight** as he portrays a relationship and explores moments of solitude.

5-Minute Warm-Up

Daily Language SkillBuilder

Have students **proofread** the display sentences on page 419i and write them correctly.

Pinyin Equivalent

Li Po: Li Bo

PREPARING to *Read*

Li Po
701–762

Famous Nonconformist Perhaps the best-known poet of China, Li Po (lē' pō') was a romantic nonconformist who spent most of his life traveling, writing poetry, and enjoying his friends. He was born in central Asia, where his ancestors had gone into exile. Although Li Po and his family returned to China when he was very young, he liked to emphasize his unusual beginnings and to appear as colorful a character as possible. He showed early literary talent, which might have led to a career in government. He never took the imperial civil-service examination, however. Instead, when he was about 19 years old, he began a series of journeys.

Wandering Poet It is hard to trace exactly the events of Li Po's life. He spent some years as a Taoist recluse in the mountains. He also married at least twice and had children. As he traveled, he became well-known as an intriguing personality, a notorious drinker, and a brilliant poet. He was welcomed wherever he went. In 742, Li Po arrived in the splendid T'ang capital of Ch'ang-an, where he was appointed a court poet. However, he was dismissed two years later, possibly because of his outrageous behavior. In 744, he met the poet Tu Fu, who greatly admired him and wrote several poems to and about him.

Turmoil and Change When rebellion broke out against the emperor in 755, Li Po became involved in political intrigue and suffered imprisonment and exile. He was later pardoned, but he had become sick, and political chaos was still erupting. He continued his travels, sometimes having to flee from rebel uprisings. He died from illness while visiting a relative in the winter of 762. A legend persists that Li Po drowned when he fell from a boat as he tried to embrace the moon's reflection. The whimsical quality of this story captures the hold that Li Po has had on the hearts and imagination of his readers through 13 centuries.

LESSON RESOURCES

UNIT THREE RESOURCE BOOK, pp. 10–11

ASSESSMENT RESOURCES
Formal Assessment, pp. 61–62
Teacher's Guide to Assessment and Portfolio Use
Test Generator

INTEGRATED TECHNOLOGY
Visit our Web site: classzone.com

ADDITIONAL RESOURCES
Lesson Planning Guide, pp. 51–52
Teacher's Sourcebook for Language Development

Build Background

Golden Age The T'ang dynasty, especially the years 713–765, saw a flourishing of poetry unequaled in all the history of China. This was brought about in part by the action of the Empress Wu, who made the writing of poetry part of the civil-service examinations. More than 2,200 poets were writing at the height of the T'ang period, and the nearly 49,000 poems that have survived are only a portion of their total work.

The two major poets of this period were Li Po and Tu Fu. While Tu Fu tended to be serious and formal in his poetry, Li Po was freewheeling and exuberant. He preferred poetic forms that allowed for variations in rhythm to those requiring strict, regular lines and patterns. He wrote about friendship, drinking, nature, solitude, love, and his yearnings for other times and places.

Three Poems by Li Po

"The River-Merchant's Wife: A Letter" (page 454) belongs to a tradition of Chinese poems that often portrayed a woman left alone by a lover. Although the speaker in many Chinese poems is the poet, in this work it is the young woman who has been left behind by her husband.

Probably Li Po's most famous poem is the brief **"Still Night Thoughts"** (page 456), written in his later years. The moon, which is central to this poem, occurs as an image in more than a third of Li Po's poems. For centuries, Chinese schoolchildren were taught to memorize "Still Night Thoughts."

"Gazing at the Lu Mountain Waterfall" (page 457) was written during Li Po's early travels and reflects the Taoist emphasis on living in harmony with nature. The poem provides a clear example of the force and energy that characterize Li Po's poems celebrating the beauty, wonder, and grandeur of the natural world.

Connect to Your Life

In two of the poems you are about to read, the speaker seems to long for those he or she loves, but in the third, the speaker seems to prefer solitude. Is it important to have some times of solitude? Is there a difference between solitude and loneliness? Write some of your thoughts about solitude in your journal.

Focus Your Reading

LITERARY ANALYSIS: IMAGERY

The term **imagery** refers to words and phrases that create vivid sensory experiences for the reader. Poets use imagery to make such details as sights and sounds clear and immediate. For example, in line 1 of "The River-Merchant's Wife: A Letter," the poet creates a picture of the speaker as a little girl through her words "my hair was still cut straight across my forehead." This description shows that she had a child's simple haircut, not a more elaborate style appropriate to a young woman.

As you read these poems, note the imagery that makes the descriptions and experiences sharp and memorable.

ACTIVE READING: VISUALIZING

Forming a mental picture from a written description is called **visualizing.** For example, vivid details in a description of a scene from nature help you see that scene in your imagination. In his poems, Li Po provides many details that allow you to visualize the times, places, and people he is writing about.

READER'S NOTEBOOK As you read, fill in a chart like the one below for each poem.

"Still Night Thoughts"	
Detail	**What I Visualize**
"Moonlight in front of my bed" (line 1)	bright moonlight streaming through a window

READING FOR INFORMATION

Reading Skills and Strategies

PREVIEWING

Point out to students that the boxed feature **Three Poems by Li Po** on page 453 introduces the poems they will be reading. Tell them that when they are preparing to read each poem, they should refer back to the information given in the appropriate paragraph. Suggest that they then skim through each poem once, looking for details and images that relate to the ideas explained on page 453. They might want to keep a list of these details and images so that they can see how the poem develops.

TIME MANAGEMENT

If your schedule requires that you cover the lesson objectives in a shorter time, use . . .

- Preparing to Read, pp. 452–453
- Thinking Through the Literature, p. 459

If you want to take advantage of longer blocks of class time, use . . .

- TE Teaching Options: Grammar, p. 454; Cross Curricular Link, p. 457; Viewing and Representing, p. 458
- Choices and Challenges, p. 460
- Translator at Work, p. 461

Literary Analysis IMAGERY

Remind students that imagery can relate to any of the five senses—sight, touch, hearing, taste, or smell.

Ask students what senses are appealed to in lines 1 to 4 and in lines 20 to 24.

Possible Responses: The images in lines 1 to 4 appeal to sight, touch, and hearing primarily. Some students may say that the flowers also appeal to smell and the plums to taste. The images in lines 20 to 24 appeal to sight, touch, and hearing.

Use **Unit Three Resource Book,** p. 11, for more practice.

Active Reading VISUALIZING

Ask students to describe the scene they visualize in lines 1 to 4.

Possible Responses: The description of the speaker's haircut and the boy playing horse on bamboo stilts indicates that they were very young children. The image of the speaker pulling flowers by the gate indicates that she was fairly quiet, while the boy playing horse and walking around her indicate that he was more active and perhaps noisy. "Playing with blue plums" also portrays a child who is constantly active, touching things, interacting with everything in the environment. Some students may say the little boy is showing off for the little girl and trying to get her attention.

Use **Unit Three Resource Book,** p. 10, for more practice.

Pinyin Equivalents

Chōkan : Changgan
Ku-tō-en : Qutang
Chō-fū-Sa : Zhangfeng Sha

The River-Merchant's Wife: A Letter

Li Po

Translated by Ezra Pound

While my hair was still cut straight across my forehead
I played about the front gate, pulling flowers.
You came by on bamboo stilts, playing horse,
You walked about my seat, playing with blue plums.
And we went on living in the village of Chōkan:
1 Two small people, without dislike or suspicion.

At fourteen I married My Lord you.
I never laughed, being bashful.
Lowering my head, I looked at the wall.
Called to, a thousand times, I never looked back.

At fifteen I stopped scowling,
I desired my dust to be mingled with yours
Forever and forever and forever.
Why should I climb the look out?

At sixteen you departed,
You went into far Ku-tō-en, by the river of swirling eddies,
And you have been gone five months.
The monkeys make sorrowful noise overhead.

5 Chōkan (chō'kăn): a town near Nanking in eastern China, located on the Yangtze River, China's longest.

14 Why . . . look out?: a reference to the story of a young wife who spent years in a tower, watching for the return of her departed husband.

16 Ku-tō-en (ko͞o'tō-ĕn'): a narrow, dangerous section of the Yangtze, far upriver from Chōkan; **eddies:** whirlpools.

MINI LESSON **Grammar**

USING VERBS: PRINCIPAL PARTS

Instruction Explain to students that verbs take different forms to show time of action and other kinds of information. Every verb has four basic forms called principal parts: the present, the past, and the present and past participles. The past and part participles of regular verbs, like *play*, are formed by adding *-ed* or *-d* to the present. The past and past participle of irregular verbs, like *grow*, are formed in some way other than adding *-ed* or *-d* to the present. Write the following forms of the verbs *play* and *grow* on the board.

Present	Past	Present Participle	Past Participle
play	played	is playing	have played
grow	grew	is growing	have grown

Practice Have students look up and write the principal parts of the following irregular verbs.

1. take *(take, took, taking, taken)*
2. rise *(rise, rose, rising, risen)*
3. break *(break, broke, breaking, broken)*
4. wear *(wear, wore, wearing, worn)*
5. cut *(cut, cut, cutting, cut)*

For more instruction and practice in learning the principal parts of verbs, use McDougal Littell's ***Language Network:***

- Grade 10, Chapter 6, "Using Verbs"
- Grade 12, Chapter 4, "Using Verbs"

Beauty Viewing Flowers (1800s), Gakutei Harunobu © Brooklyn Museum/Corbis.

You dragged your feet when you went out.
By the gate now, the moss is grown, the different mosses,
Too deep to clear them away!
The leaves fall early this autumn, in wind.
The paired butterflies are already yellow with August
Over the grass in the West garden;
2 They hurt me. I grow older.
If you are coming down through the narrows of the river
    Kiang,
Please let me know beforehand,
And I will come out to meet you
        As far as Chō-fū-Sa.

26 river Kiang (jyäng): that is, the Yangtze.

29 Chō-fū-Sa (chō'fōō-sä'): "Long Wind Beach," several hundred miles upriver from Chōkan.

Customizing Instruction

Less Proficient Readers

- Remind students that the poem is meant to be a letter that the speaker is writing to her husband.
- Make sure students are aware of the time sequence in the poem and the basic story line. *(The speaker begins with her childhood, when she and her husband first knew each other. Then she moves to age 14, when she married; 15, when her love awakened; and 16, when her husband left on his journey. Then she expresses her feelings about his absence.)*

1 Make sure students understand that the phrase "without dislike or suspicion" describes a kind of neutral relationship between the two children. They didn't mind being together and they trusted each other, but they weren't best friends either.

2 Ask students what the speaker means when she says that the butterflies ("they") hurt her.
Possible Responses: They may hurt her for two reasons. The butterflies flying in pairs are a painful reminder that her mate is far away. The image of the butterflies "already yellow with August/Over the grass in the West garden" conveys a feeling of sadness, of something coming to an end.

English Learners

- Explain that stilts are poles with footrests on them that enable a person to walk high off the ground. Try to bring in a picture of stilts.
- Tell students that "small people" (line 6) refers to the speaker and her husband when they were children.
- Make sure students know the meaning of the following words: line 8, bashful (*shy*); line 11, scowling (*frowning*).

Advanced Learners

Have students explain why the speaker asks the question in line 14.
Possible Response: She is so in love with her husband that she is sure he will never go away, leaving her to watch and wait for him.
Then ask students to explain how this line becomes ironic in the poem.
Possible Response: The speaker's husband does go on a journey, and after five months, she has apparently not heard from him and is desperately missing him. She is now in the position of the woman in the tower. She doesn't know where, when, or even if he will return.

THE RIVER-MERCHANT'S WIFE: A LETTER 455

Literary Analysis IMAGERY

Point out to students that in the brief poem "Still Night Thoughts," the central image of the moon is developed through vivid details. Ask them to identify two of these details.

Possible Responses: The details include the moonlight on the floor in front of the speaker's bed, the reference to frost on the ground, and the bright moon in the sky.

Active Reading VISUALIZING

A Ask students to briefly describe the scene they visualize as they read this passage from "Gazing at the Lu Mountain Waterfall."

Possible Response: A high waterfall, arching like a rainbow, plunges down mountainsides and foams through canyons. It is so wide the speaker thinks at first it is the Milky Way falling to earth. The waterfall creates strong winds and a billowing mist. It bursts and thunders, overcoming everything in its path.

Literary Analysis HYPERBOLE

B Tell students that the figure of speech called hyperbole exaggerates the truth for emphasis. Ask students to identify the two examples of hyperbole in these lines. *(Describing the waterfall as being" three thousand feet high" and flowing "dozens of miles" through canyons are examples.)*

Ask students why the poet might have used hyperbole.

Possible Response: The exaggerations convey how awe-inspiring and overwhelming the waterfall is to the poet.

Reading Skills and Strategies MAKING INFERENCES

C Ask students what they learn about the speaker through the phrase "white rainbow of mystery."

Possible Response: To the speaker, the waterfall is not just a beautiful scene to enjoy but a source of wonder that can give meaning to life.

Literary Analysis METAPHOR

D Ask students to explain the metaphor in line 15. *(The drops of water splashing into the air as the waterfall hits the rocks look like pearls.)*

Pinyin Equivalent

Kiangsi: Jiangxi

Still Night Thoughts

Li Po

Translated by Burton Watson

1
Moonlight in front of my bed—
I took it for frost on the ground!
I lift my head, gaze at the bright moon,
lower it and dream of home.

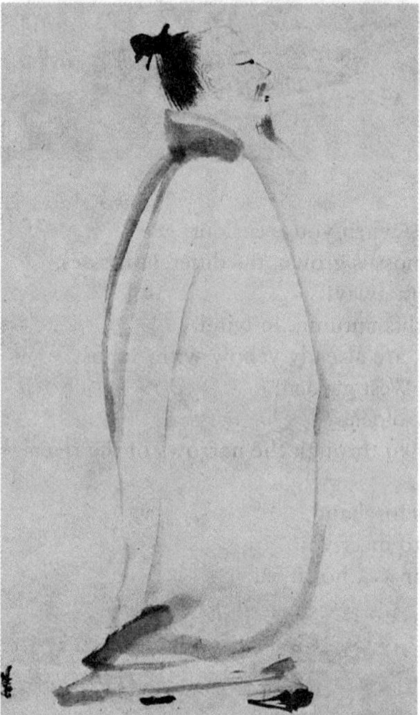

Li Po (Southern Song Dynasty), Liang Kai. Hanging Scroll, ink on paper, 31 2/3″ × 12 1/8″ (80.4cm × 30.7 cm). Tokyo National Museum.

Gazing at the Lu Mountain Waterfall

Li Po

Translated by David Hinton

1

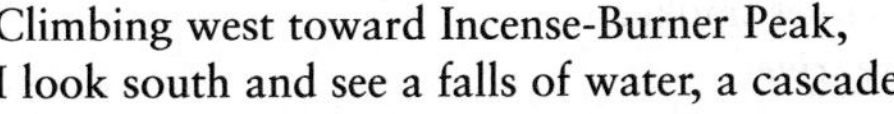

Climbing west toward Incense-Burner Peak,
A I look south and see a falls of water, a cascade

B hanging there, three thousand feet high,
then seething dozens of miles down canyons.

Sudden as lightning breaking into flight,
C its white rainbow of mystery appears. Afraid

at first the celestial Star River is falling,
splitting and dissolving into cloud heavens,

I look up into force churning in strength,
all power, the very workings of Creation.

It keeps ocean winds blowing ceaselessly,
shines a mountain moon back into empty space,

empty space it tumbles and sprays through,
rinsing green cliffs clean on both sides,

D sending pearls in flight scattering into mist
and whitewater seething down towering rock.

Here, after wandering among these renowned
mountains, the heart grows rich with repose.

Why talk of cleansing elixirs of immortality?
Here, the world's dust rinsed from my face,

I'll stay close to what I've always loved,
content to leave that peopled world forever.

1 Incense-Burner Peak: a peak of Lu Mountain in China's Kiangsi province. Seeking to escape a war in his home region, Li Po moved to a town near Lu Mountain for a time.

7 celestial Star River: the Milky Way.

18 repose: rest; calm.

19 elixirs of immortality: magic potions with the power to make people live forever.

Customizing Instruction

Less Proficient Readers

1 Make sure that students understand that the speaker is looking at the moonlight falling on the floor in a room. It is so bright and white that he compares it to frost outside.

English Learners

- You might want to ask students to describe a big waterfall they have seen to give them a context for reading "Gazing at the Lu Mountain Waterfall."
- Make sure students understand the following terms: cascade *(waterfall)*; seething *(moving violently as though boiling)*; churning *(moving and shaking)*; renowned *(famous)*.
- Explain to students that in lines 5 and 6, the "lightning" and "white rainbow of mystery" are not literal descriptions but are images used in comparisons to show how impressive and amazing the waterfall is.

Advanced Learners

Explain that the relationship to nature described in "Gazing at the Lu Mountain Waterfall" has similarities to views of nature expressed in the poems of William Wordsworth. Have students read one or two of Wordsworth's poems, such as "My Heart Leaps Up" (p. 901), "The Tables Turned," or "I Wandered Lonely As a Cloud," and look for similarities between his views of nature and Li Po's. Ask them to write a short paper discussing the similarities they find.

Possible Response: The main similarity is that nature is a source of meaning for Li Po and for Wordsworth. It connects to what is eternal, true, and sacred. Communing with nature brings joy and peace.

NOTE: You may also want to have students look at Wordsworth's sonnet "The World Is Too Much with Us" on p. 900 to see his ideas about being cut off from nature.

Cross Curricular Link **Geography**

LU MOUNTAIN Lu Mountain, called by the Chinese "the most beautiful mountain under heaven," is part of a spectacular scenic area in China known today as Lu Shan. It is located in Kiangsi (kyäng′ shē′) province, northwest of P'o-yang Lake. Lu Mountain was viewed as a holy place for centuries and is considered one of the spiritual centers of Chinese civilization. Both Taoism and Buddhism have long associations with the mountain, and until World War II, the area had about 300 Buddhist temples and Taoist shrines.

One of the most stunning features of Lu Shan is its waterfalls. Descriptions speak of them roaring like thunder and surging like sea waves, wrapping the valleys and peaks in mist. A waterfall known as the three-cascades, or the three-step, waterfall—the "first wonder" of Lu Shan—falls in three stages and has a drop of about 500 feet.

The area also has abundant plant life—about 3,000 species—and hundreds of thousands of migrating birds, including one of the largest groups of cranes in the world. Lu Shan is now listed in the Chronology of Recognition of World Heritages in China.

Active Reading VISUALIZING

As you imagine the scene in this section of the poem, in what ways is it different from the scene in the first section? *(In this section, the speaker is describing the waterfall from a distance instead of close up. It is majestic but less immediate and overwhelming.)*

Literary Analysis IMAGERY

A The speaker again refers to the waterfall as the Milky Way ("Star River") and says it is falling through "nine heavens." Ask students to explain the effect of this imagery.

Possible Response: This description gives a sense of both the grandeur and the mystery of the waterfall. The references to the Milky Way and nine heavens place this wonder of nature beyond ordinary experience, and so make a fitting closing to the poem.

2

Sunlight on Incense-Burner kindles violet smoke.
Watching the distant falls hang there, river

headwaters plummeting three thousand feet in flight,
A I see Star River falling through nine heavens.

Early Spring, Kuo Hsi. Collection of the National Palace Museum, Taiwan, Republic of China.

HUMANITIES CONNECTION Landscape painting flourished in the 11th and 12th centuries and is considered the finest of all Chinese painting. Its forms and styles continue to influence traditional painting in China to this day.

MINI LESSON Viewing and Representing

Early Spring **by Kuo Hsi**

ART APPRECIATION

Instruction In the 11th century in China, artists shifted from painting people to painting landscapes. These landscapes usually depict towering mountains and wide valleys, often with rivers or plunging waterfalls. Human figures are insignificant. This style of painting reflects the ancient view of mountains as sacred places, and the overall effect is one of immeasurable distance and mystery.

Early Spring is a hanging scroll, painted in ink and color on silk. There are tiny human figures in the lower left-hand part of the picture and a cluster of buildings almost hidden to the left of the center.

Application Have students examine the painting and look again at the **Humanities Connection** on page 458. Ask them how the painting reflects the view of nature expressed in "Gazing at the Lu Mountain Waterfall."

Possible Response: The sense of grandeur and enormous space created in the painting matches the speaker's responses of wonder and awe at seeing the Lu Mountain waterfall.

Connect to the Literature

1. **What Do You Think?** Which of these poems appealed to you the most?

Comprehension Check

- In "The River-Merchant's Wife: A Letter," why is the wife writing a letter?
- In "Still Night Thoughts," what does the speaker say the moonlight looks like?
- What kind of scene does the poet describe in "Gazing at the Lu Mountain Waterfall"?

Think Critically

2. How would you describe the relationship between the speaker of "The River-Merchant's Wife: A Letter" and her husband?

- how long they have known each other
- the description in line 19 of her husband's attitude when he left home
- how she feels about his absence

3. What do you think are the speaker's feelings in "Still Night Thoughts"?
4. In "Gazing at the Lu Mountain Waterfall," what effect does seeing the waterfall have on the speaker?

- his description of the waterfall in line 6
- what he means by "the heart grows rich with repose" (line 18)
- his conclusion in lines 21 and 22

5. **ACTIVE READING: VISUALIZING** Look back at the charts you completed in your **READER'S NOTEBOOK**. How did visualizing the scenes in these poems help you understand the experiences being described?

Extend Interpretations

6. **Comparing Texts** Look again at "Mulberry on the Lowland" (page 447) from the *Book of Odes.* What similarities and differences are there between the feelings of the speaker in that poem and those of the speaker in "The River-Merchant's Wife: A Letter"?
7. **Connect to Life** In much of Li Po's poetry, nature is a source of renewal and serenity. How do people in today's world view nature?

LITERARY ANALYSIS: IMAGERY

One of the most important elements of any poem is its **imagery,** the words and phrases that create vivid sensory experiences for the reader. Most images are visual, but imagery may also appeal to the other four senses: hearing, smell, taste, and touch. In the following lines from "Gazing at the Lu Mountain Waterfall," the imagery appeals to sight, hearing, and touch:

empty space it tumbles and sprays through,
rinsing green cliffs clean on both sides,

Paired Activity With a classmate, list examples of imagery from Li Po's poems in a chart like the one below. Then discuss how the imagery helps convey particular emotions, scenes, and ideas.

Image	Poem/Line(s)	Sense(s) Appealed To
"empty space . . . on both sides"	"Gazing at the . . .", lines 13–14	sight, hearing, touch

Connect to the Literature

1. **What Do You Think?** Accept all reasonable responses. Students should support their choices with details from the poems.

Comprehension Check

- Her husband has gone away on a long trip.
- He says the moonlight looks like "frost on the ground."
- He describes a huge waterfall in a mountainous area.

Think Critically

2. Possible Response: The speaker seems to be deeply in love with her husband, but it isn't clear how responsive he is. The poem reveals more about the speaker's feelings than those of her husband. They played together as children but apparently were not close friends, since the speaker describes their relationship as only "without dislike or suspicion." When they married at 14, the speaker was shy and reserved, but by 15 she had fallen in love with her husband. She indicates that he also loves her by saying that he dragged his feet when he left on his journey. She experiences great loneliness and sadness while he is gone, and she longs to hear from him. The reader is left wondering when she will hear from him and if he will return.
3. Possible Response: The speaker seems to be both enjoying the moonlight and longing for home. He first is spellbound by the beauty and peacefulness of the moon, but then it makes him think of seeing the moon at home, and he dreams of being there.
4. Possible Response: The speaker seems to have an almost overwhelming sense of wonder as he looks at the waterfall. He is awed by its size, beauty, and power, and he even compares it to the Milky Way. The experience seems to have a religious or mystical meaning for him, so that he speaks finally of remaining in the mountains near the waterfall to live a life of reflection and peace.
5. Responses will vary. Students should support their answers with details from the poems.

Extend Interpretations

6. **Comparing Texts** Possible Response: In each poem, the speaker expresses deep love. In "Mulberry on the Lowland," the speaker is happy because she has seen her lord. In "The River-Merchant's Wife: A Letter," however, the speaker has been separated from her husband for five months and is full of sadness. Her love is causing her great pain instead of great joy.
7. **Connect to Life** Possible Responses: People today have varying views of nature. Many find outdoor activities important to their sense of well-being. Some find religious meaning in being alone with nature. Environmentalists respect all parts of nature as essential to life on earth. People are also aware of nature as a potentially destructive force. Finally, some see nature primarily as an economic resource.

Literary Analysis

Paired Activity Students should identify a variety of images appealing to the senses of sight, hearing, and touch. You might have a class discussion in which you ask students to choose an example of imagery that they think is especially effective and explain their choice to the class.

Use **Unit Three Resource Book,** p. 11, for additional practice.

Writing Options

1. Mood Poem Using "Still Night Thoughts" as a model, write a four-line poem that expresses a mood. Choose a central image that helps create that mood. Aim for simplicity. Place the poem in your **Working Portfolio.**

2. Notes for a Plot Think of "The River-Merchant's Wife: A Letter" as the beginning of a short story. Write notes describing how the story might develop. Keep in mind the elements of character, setting, and conflict as you imagine possible details.

3. Descriptive Paragraph Imagine that you are preparing a travel guidebook for the Lu Mountain area. For your guidebook, write a prose description of the scene Li Po portrays in "Gazing at the Lu Mountain Waterfall." Try to make your description appealing but accurate.

Writing Handbook
See page R27: Descriptive Writing.

Activities & Explorations

1. Film Score Suppose you have been asked to provide music for a short film based on "The River-Merchant's Wife: A Letter." Look for recordings of pieces of music that you think would help convey the events and emotions described in the poem. Play them in a sequence that matches them to the developments in the wife's story. ~ **MUSIC**

2. Landscape Painting Create a painting or drawing based on some detail of nature described in one of the poems. The subject of the painting can be a small detail or a wide view. ~ **ART**

3. Dramatic Reading Prepare a dramatic reading of one of the two long poems. You may want to do this with one or more other students. Consider using costumes or props to enhance your presentation. ~ **SPEAKING AND LISTENING**

Inquiry & Research

1. Cosmopolitan City Ch'ang-an, the capital of the T'ang empire, was the largest, richest, and most sophisticated city of its day. It had a population of 2 million, and it was a center of learning, art, trade, religion, and government. Investigate what life in this city was like at its height in the T'ang period.

2. Powerful Empress Investigate the rule of the Empress Wu, the only Chinese woman to reign in her own right. Find out how she came to power and what kind of leader she was.

Writing Options

1. **Mood Poem** Students' poems should focus on a single image that clearly relates to a particular mood. Have students review the images they listed in their chart for the Imagery Paired Activity on page 459 to get ideas.
2. **Notes for a Plot** Suggest to students that they begin by reviewing what the poem does and does not reveal about the speaker and her husband. Encourage them to think about different possible directions the story might take and what new elements or surprising turns they might introduce.
3. **Descriptive Paragraph** You might suggest that students look at some travel books to get a feel for how they are written. Mention to them that exaggeration is not appropriate in travel writing. Remind them that their paragraphs should be detailed, convincing, and inviting.

Activities & Explorations

1. **Film Score** Students might want to work in pairs on this activity. Students who have some experience making tapes could help those who need some instruction. If possible, provide time for the class to listen to the tapes created and compare the choices the students have made.
2. **Landscape Painting** Encourage students to think about using a distinct style to convey a particular mood in their landscape. You might suggest that they look again at the painting *Early Spring* on page 458 and note the mood it conveys. The mood they express in their painting can be light or serious, depending on the detail they choose.
3. **Dramatic Reading** Suggest to students that they could use simple gestures or sound effects as part of their interpretations.

Inquiry & Research

1. **Cosmopolitan City** An especially good presentation of the T'ang city of Ch'ang-an can be found in *Ancient China* (Time-Life Great Ages of Man series), by Edward Schafer. Students can also look for information in encyclopedias and in *The Cambridge Illustrated History of China,* by Patricia Ebrey; *The Land and Peoples of China,* by John S. Major; and *The Companion to Chinese History,* by Hugh B. O'Neill. Students might want to focus on one aspect of life in Ch'ang-an, such as the arts or court life.
2. **Powerful Empress** The Empress Wu was a ruthless but extremely effective ruler—a fascinating figure and one of the most capable women in Chinese history. Students can find excellent biographies of her and discussions of her reign in encyclopedias and on the Internet.

To assess skills and concepts taught in this selection, use **Formal Assessment Book,** pp. 61–62.

Translating Chinese Poetry

Translators of poetry want to convey the meaning of the original poem as closely as possible. They also, however, wish to produce the most finely crafted poem possible, which may require them to take some liberties with the original. Translators of Chinese poetry have additional challenges. Unlike English, Chinese does not have an alphabet. Instead, it has about 40,000 characters—symbols that represent words or parts of words. To read Chinese, a person must have memorized thousands of characters.

A further challenge in translating Chinese poetry involves the verbal structure of the poems. There are few conjunctions or pronouns. Verbs do not have tenses. Nouns do not show number. The subject of a sentence may be omitted. Not surprisingly, translators sometimes differ in how they interpret the same sequences of words.

The following are lines 25 and 26 of "The River-Merchant's Wife: A Letter." Under the Chinese characters is a character-by-character translation by Wai-lim Yip.

In his verse translation below, Wai-lim Yip adds connecting words, replaces several words, and develops complete sentences to express his interpretation of the lines. (*These* refers to the butterflies described in the previous lines.)

These smite my heart.
I sit down worrying and youth passes away.

Now compare two more translations of the same lines.

They hurt me. I grow older.
—Ezra Pound

And, because of all this, my heart is breaking
And I fear for my bright cheeks, lest they fade.
—Witter Bynner

You can see that each translator makes different decisions about words and structure to convey the meaning of the original and to create a distinctive style.

Activity Look again at the character-by-character translation of the two lines from Li Po's poem, and reread the three verse translations. Then try writing your own translation of the lines. You can choose different words or combine words or phrases that the other translators have used.

The Translator at Work

Pronunciations

Wai-lim Yip (wī′lĭm′ yĭp′)
Witter Bynner (wĭt′ər bĭn′ər)

READING FOR INFORMATION

Reading Skills and Strategies

COMPARING AND CONTRASTING

Point out to students that they will be comparing and contrasting three different translations of two lines of Li Po's poem. Suggest that they write down the three translations of line 25 on one piece of paper and then the three translations of line 26 on another. Have them list words and phrases in each set of translations that are expressing the same idea or image. Then ask them to think about which translation seems closest to the character-by-character translation and which one they prefer.

Activity Encourage students to experiment with different possibilities. Variations could include creating different rhythms, using rhyme, elaborating on the basic images, or condensing the language. Some may want to write two or three versions. It also may help some students to write a prose paraphrase of the lines before translating them into verse. Students' translations should reflect careful attention to the character-by-character translation and should show some attempt at style and originality.

Objectives
- understand and appreciate **lyric poetry (Literary Analysis)**
- understand how **imagery** contributes to creating **mood (Literary Analysis)**
- use strategies to **understand and appreciate poetry (Active Reading)**

Thematic Link
In his poems, Tu Fu writes about private life as well as about political events taking place in his society. He moves **from observation to insight** concerning the relationship between personal experience and public events.

5-Minute Warm-Up
Daily Language SkillBuilder

Have students **proofread** the display sentences on page 419j and write them correctly.

Pinyin Equivalents
Tu Fu: Du Fu
Fu-chou: Fuzhou
P'eng-ya: Pengya
Feng-hsien: Fengxian
Ch'ang-an: Xi'an
Lo-yang: Luoyang

SELECTED POEMS
Tu Fu

Tu Fu
712–770

Failed Political Career Tu Fu is considered by many readers and critics to be the greatest of all Chinese poets. Unfortunately, his poetic genius was not generally recognized during his own lifetime. He was also unlucky in his political career. Born into a poor scholarly family, Tu Fu received a classical education. Yet as a young man he repeatedly failed the examinations in prose and poetry that would have earned him a high position in the imperial government. Although he eventually held a series of minor posts, Tu Fu endured a life of poverty and uncertainty.

Witness to War In 755, Tu Fu was granted a position in the imperial court, in the capital city of Ch'ang-an. Before he could begin serving, however, the city was attacked by rebel forces. Fearful for his family's safety, Tu Fu moved his wife and children from their home in Feng-hsien, about 80 miles northeast of Ch'ang-an, to Fu-chou. He describes this journey in "Song of P'eng-ya" (page 468). The war and its aftermath continued to affect Tu Fu for many years. Constantly searching for government work, the poet wandered from place to place. He was often forced to hide from the rebels or flee before their advancing armies. Illnesses, including asthma and malaria, also began to plague Tu Fu during this time.

Productive Final Years By the end of 759, Tu Fu had become disillusioned with public life. Although the decision brought financial hardship on his family, Tu Fu chose to retire and concentrate on his poetry. As a result, the last 11 years of his life were very productive ones. His output as well as the quality and complexity of his work increased greatly. This accomplishment is particularly remarkable in light of the revolts and unrest that continued to afflict the region. It was, in fact, while fleeing by boat before a Tibetan invasion that Tu Fu died.

The Land of Tu Fu

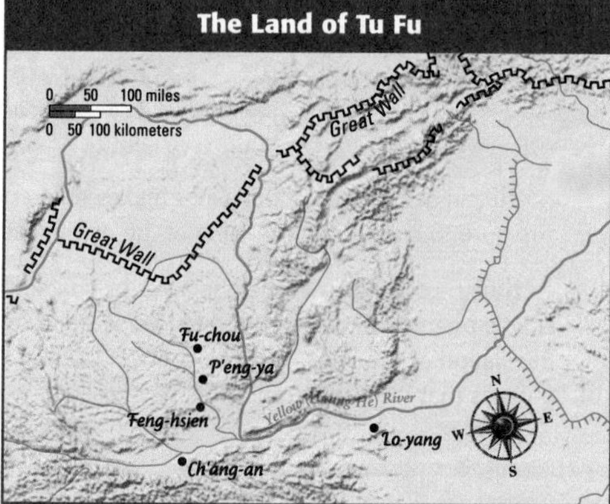

LESSON RESOURCES

UNIT THREE RESOURCE BOOK,
pp. 12–13

ASSESSMENT RESOURCES
Formal Assessment, pp. 63–64
Teacher's Guide to Assessment and Portfolio Use
Test Generator

INTEGRATED TECHNOLOGY
Visit our Web site: classzone.com

ADDITIONAL RESOURCES
Lesson Planning Guide, pp. 53–54
Teacher's Sourcebook for Language Development

Build Background

Poet-Historian Much of Tu Fu's poetry reflects the events of his time. Deeply affected by the political upheaval of the High T'ang period, Tu Fu wrote about the devastation of war, the decay of Chinese society, and the suffering of the common people. In later centuries, his accounts earned him a reputation as a poet-historian.

The major political event of Tu Fu's time was the An Lu-shan Rebellion of 755–757. An Lu-shan was a very powerful military governor whose armies stormed and captured the capital of Ch'ang-an. Tu Fu himself was held prisoner by the rebels for a time. As a result of his experiences, the poet wrote compassionately about the lives of those most affected by war—the poor.

Private Perspectives Tu Fu often wrote about public events. But he wrote about these events in terms of his own private experiences of them. In "Song of P'eng-ya," for example, a poem about the rebellion, Tu Fu wrote lovingly about his children. The intimate family details make the event personal and touching. Such scenes of domestic life are not found in Chinese poetry before Tu Fu but became more common after him.

Fellow Artists Tu Fu is most often compared to his friend and contemporary Li Po. However, the two poets couldn't have been more different. Li Po was a Taoist romantic whose style was original and bold. Tu Fu was a Confucian moralist who longed to be useful to society and wrote carefully crafted poems. It is said that Li Po is the people's poet, while Tu Fu is the poets' poet.

Tu Fu and Li Po met and traveled together briefly. Although they saw each other only once more after that early encounter, Tu Fu continued to admire Li Po. He wrote more than a dozen poems about his friend, including "Dreaming of Li Po." Li Po, on the other hand, is said to have made fun of Tu Fu for his painstaking approach to writing. In a poem addressed to Tu Fu, he gently teased his fellow-poet:

How is it you've gotten so thin since we parted?
Must be all those poems you've been suffering over.

Connect to Your Life

Think about a recent public event that had an impact on you. You might consider a natural disaster or a political incident. Get together with a partner to discuss the event. What private insight or perspective could you provide about the event that wouldn't appear in a newspaper account of it?

Focus Your Reading

LITERARY ANALYSIS: MOOD AND IMAGERY

Mood is the feeling or atmosphere that a writer creates for the reader. One element that contributes to the mood of a poem is **imagery**—the words and phrases that create sensory experiences. Notice the mood evoked in the following lines from "Jade Flower Palace":

The stream swirls. The wind moans in
The pines.

As you read the poems by Tu Fu, consider how words and images contribute to the mood.

ACTIVE READING: UNDERSTANDING AND APPRECIATING POETRY

A poem is made up of many elements working together. Rhythms, sounds, word choice, and imagery all contribute to the final form and meaning of a poem. It will help you to fully appreciate a poem if you read the poem several times. It will also help if you read the poem aloud. With each reading, you will discover new connections and insights that you missed earlier.

READER'S NOTEBOOK Read each of Tu Fu's poems three times, including once aloud. After each reading, use a chart like the one below to record your impressions and insights.

"Dreaming of Li Po"
First Reading
Second Reading
Third Reading

READING FOR INFORMATION

Reading Skills and Strategies

READING A MAP

Tell students that locating cities and towns on a map can help them visualize references to those places. The poem "Song of P'eng-ya" describes the Pe'ng-ya Road that Tu Fu and his family have to travel to get from one town to another. The map on page 462 shows the location of P'eng-ya in relation to the capital of Ch'ang-an and the two towns where Tu Fu's family lived. Ask students to identify two features on the map that help establish the general area of China where the towns are located. *(the Great Wall to the north and the Yellow River to the east and south)*

TIME MANAGEMENT

If your schedule requires that you cover the lesson objectives in a shorter time, use . . .

- Preparing to Read, pp. 462–463
- Thinking Through the Literature, p. 470

If you want to take advantage of longer blocks of class time, use . . .

- TE Teaching Options: Cross Curricular Link, pp. 464 and 465; Viewing and Representing, pp. 466, 467, and 469; Informal Assessment, p. 468
- Related Reading, p. 467
- Connect to Today, p. 471

Literary Analysis MOOD AND IMAGERY

A Remind students that mood is the feeling, or atmosphere, that a writer creates for the reader. Have students look at lines 5 to 10, in which the speaker describes his dream about Li Po. Ask students what mood is conveyed in these lines.

Possible Response: The mood is one of longing and sadness.

Then ask students how the imagery in the lines contributes to creating the mood.

Possible Responses: Images that help create the mood include the old friend entering the speaker's dreams, the speaker pining, the friend looking different, the long road, the friend in the dream coming from lush green forests and then going back, the speaker left in "borderland blackness."

Use **Unit Three Resource Book,** p. 13, for more practice.

Active Reading

UNDERSTANDING AND APPRECIATING POETRY

Tell students that as they read and reread the poem, they should be aware of how new impressions and insights change their interpretation of the poem. Suggest that they try to identify the words or details that they think are most important to understanding the poem.

Use **Unit Three Resource Book,** p. 12, for more practice.

Reading Skills and Strategies
CLARIFYING

B Ask students whom "you're" refers to. *("You're" refers to Li Po.)*

Ask students to explain why they think Tu Fu switched from referring to Li Po in the third person (he) to addressing him directly (you).

Possible Response: In the first 10 lines of the poem, Tu Fu feels far away from his friend, and the use of the third-person pronoun reinforces the sense of separation and loss. When he speaks directly to Li Po in line 11, his friend seems closer and Tu Fu seems to feel less sad.

Pinyin Equivalent

Yangtze: Chang

Dreaming of Li Po

Tu Fu

Translated by Burton Watson

1 Parting from the dead, I've stifled my sobs,
but this parting from the living brings me constant pain.
South of the Yangtze is a land of plague and fever;
no word comes from the exile.
Yet my old friend has entered my dreams,
proof of how long I've pined for him.
A He didn't look the way he used to,
the road so far—farther than I can guess.
His spirit came from where the maple groves are green,
then went back, leaving me in borderland blackness.
B Now you're caught in the meshes of the law—
how could you have wings to fly with?
The sinking moon floods the rafters of my room
and still I seem to see it lighting your face.
Where you go, waters are deep, the waves so wide—
don't let the dragons, the horned dragons harm you!

3–4 South of the Yangtze (yäng'dzŭ') . . . **exile:** Li Po had been sent into exile in southwest China for his involvement with a prince who led a minor rebellion.

Cross Curricular Link **Psychology**

THE EXPERIENCE OF LOSS In the first two lines of "Dreaming of Li Po," Tu Fu compares the pain of being separated from Li Po to mourning someone who has died. Today it is recognized that there are many different kinds of loss in addition to loss through death and that these experiences may involve a significant grief process. Examples of other kinds of loss include such things as the ending of an important relationship, loss of health, permanent injury resulting from an accident, loss of a job, having to give up career or education plans, loss of a home through fire or flood, being the victim of a crime, moving away from home, immigrating to a new country, and so on. Psychologists stress the need to acknowledge these losses and seek help through such means as professional counseling, support groups, reading, writing in a journal, exercise, religious practices, or talking with family members or a friend. Psychologists also emphasize that major losses take time to heal but that the experience of such a loss can bring personal growth and increased self-understanding.

Ceramic jar with dragon (1426–1435).
The Metropolitan Museum of Art, New York.

Cross Curricular Link **Humanities**

DRAGONS Dragons have been part of many cultures from earliest times. They take different forms, which always combine characteristics of several creatures, such as bird, fish, deer, snake, lion, tiger, crocodile, and horse. In China, the dragon has been an important image and symbol for thousands of years. It is pictured having the body of a snake, the scales of a fish, the head of a horse, the beard of a goat, the antlers of a deer, and the claws of an eagle. Unlike the dragons in many cultures, the dragon in China is not an evil creature but a benevolent one. The first symbol of the yang principle was, in fact, the dragon—and recent excavations indicate that this representation may have been in existence as early as 3000 B.C. Because the yang principle includes the male element, the dragon later became a symbol of the emperor and was part of the Chinese flag until 1911. Chinese dragons were thought to control rain, rivers, and lakes. Although they usually brought prosperity, they could be angered and become destructive. In "Dreaming of Li Po," Tu Fu alludes to this aspect of dragons in using them as metaphors for Li Po's enemies.

Customizing Instruction

Less Proficient Readers

1 Make sure students understand that the speaker is talking about missing his friend, who is still alive, and not grieving for someone who has died.

Explain to students that in lines 5–10, the speaker, Tu Fu, is describing dreaming about his friend Li Po.

Point out the shift from the third person to the second person in line 11. Make sure students understand that in lines 11–16, the speaker is addressing Li Po directly.

English Learners

- Explain the following words and terms: plague *(a highly infectious disease affecting a large number of people)*; exile *(a person forced by legal means to live away from his or her native land)*; pined *(had intense longing for)*
- Explain the following metaphors: "meshes of the law" *(The law is compared to a net, or mesh, in which things get caught)*; "horned dragons" *(The political leaders who exiled Li Po, and so are his enemies, are compared to dangerous creatures.)*

Advanced Learners

Ask students to analyze the structure of this poem. Ask them to identify the main sections of the poem and to explain what happens in each section.

Possible Response: This poem can be broken down into three sections: lines 1–4, 5–10, and 11–16. In the first section, the speaker expresses his deep feelings of loss because of being separated from his friend. He also explains that his friend has been exiled to a distant place full of disease, and his friend has not sent him any word.

In the second section, the speaker tells about dreaming of his friend. In describing his dream, the speaker draws the reader into his feelings of loss and sorrow. The details are poignant—"he didn't look the way he used to"—and the last phrase, "borderland blackness," conveys the feeling of emptiness and bleakness that can come at the end of a sad or disturbing dream. The word *borderland* especially gives the sense of a kind of no-man's land, desolate and lonely.

In the third section, when the speaker addresses his friend directly, the poem becomes more energetic. The speaker seems to be feeling more connected to his friend, and less sad. In the last two lines he encourages his friend and seems more hopeful.

Reading and Analyzing

Literary Analysis MOOD AND IMAGERY

Have students identify what they think is the mood of "Jade Flower Palace."

Possible Responses: bleakness, desolation, hopelessness

Then ask them to identify three examples of the imagery that help create this mood.

Possible Responses: Examples of imagery include wind moaning in the pines, rats scurrying over broken tiles, palace in ruins, ghost fires, black rooms, shattered pavements, organ pipes whistling and roaring, storm scattering leaves, and solitary stone horse.

Active Reading

UNDERSTANDING AND APPRECIATING POETRY

Point out to students that this poem has many run-on lines—one line runs into the next without any grammatical break or punctuation. Suggest to students that they read the poem paying particular attention to the run-on lines. Ask them to explain the effect of these lines.

Possible Response: The run-on lines create a sense of unpredictability. The reader doesn't know when a thought will start or stop. Because the lines do not have a regular structure, they reinforce the idea of things being out of control.

Reading Skills and Strategies
ANALYZING

Point out to students that in lines 3–5, the speaker asks a question, "What prince, long ago,/Built this palace, standing in/Ruins beside the cliffs?" Ask students why they think the poet included this question at this point in the poem.

Possible Response: The question connects the palace ruins to a person who built them and lived in them. This connection, along with the references to "his" dancing girls, courtiers, and chariots, makes the poem personal and tragic. The speaker is not just looking at interesting ruins but reflecting on a human story.

Pinyin Equivalent

T'ai-tsung: Taizong

Jade Flower Palace

Tu Fu

Translated by Kenneth Rexroth

The stream swirls. The wind moans in
The pines. Grey rats scurry over
Broken tiles. What prince, long ago,
Built this palace, standing in
Ruins beside the cliffs? There are
Green ghost fires in the black rooms.
The shattered pavements are all
Washed away. Ten thousand organ
Pipes whistle and roar. The storm
Scatters the red autumn leaves.
His dancing girls are yellow dust.
Their painted cheeks have crumbled
Away. His gold chariots
And courtiers are gone. Only
A stone horse is left of his
Glory. I sit on the grass and
Start a poem, but the pathos of
It overcomes me. The future
Slips imperceptibly away.
Who can say what the years will bring?

3–4 What prince . . . built this palace: The palace had been the summer home of T'ai-tsung, emperor of China from A.D. 626 to 649.

17 pathos (pā'thŏs'): sorrow.

19 imperceptibly (ĭm'pər-sĕp'tə-blē): in a barely noticeable way.

Running horse (Han Dynasty). Bronze. Imperial Museum, Beijing. Robert Harding Picture Library, London.

HUMANITIES CONNECTION This piece of sculpture depicts a so-called celestial horse, one of a tall breed of horses introduced into China in the first century B.C. This is the only known ancient Chinese sculpture of a galloping horse.

MINI LESSON Viewing and Representing

Bronze Figure of a Flying Horse

ART APPRECIATION

Instruction This piece of sculpture is about 9½ inches tall. Although the position of the legs is not a completely accurate reflection of a horse in a gallop, the rendering is far more realistic than other attempts of the time. The rear hoof is balanced on a sparrow with its wings spread, a detail possibly connected to the lady Chao, the wife of the first-century emperor Ch'eng Ti. She was called the flying swallow because of her skill in dancing.

Application Have students look at the figure of the horse and reread the **Humanities Connection** on page 466. Then have them reread lines 15–17 of the poem. Ask them what it might be like to come upon such a piece of sculpture in the midst of empty ruins.

Possible Response: Answers will vary, but many students will probably say that the figure of this vigorous, beautiful animal would be a sharp reminder of the kind of life that had once been lived in the ruins. There would also be a feeling of loneliness in seeing this single figure remaining, with no one left to enjoy it.

OZYMANDIAS

Percy Bysshe Shelley

2 trunkless legs: legs separated from the rest of the body.

4 visage (vĭz'ĭj): face.

6 those passions: that is, Ozymandias' passions.

8 This line may be paraphrased as "The sculptor's hand, which mocked the passions of the king, and the king's heart, which fed those passions."

10 Ozymandias (ŏz'ĭ-măn'dēəs): title of the Egyptian pharaoh Rameses II, who reigned from 1304 to 1237 B.C.

I met a traveler from an antique land,
Who said—"Two vast and trunkless legs of stone
Stand in the desert. . . . Near them, on the sand,
Half sunk a shattered visage lies, whose frown,
And wrinkled lip, and sneer of cold command,
Tell that its sculptor well those passions read
Which yet survive, stamped on these lifeless things,
The hand that mocked them, and the heart that fed;
And on the pedestal, these words appear:
My name is Ozymandias, King of Kings,
Look on my Works, ye Mighty, and despair!
Nothing beside remains. Round the decay
Of that colossal Wreck, boundless and bare
The lone and level sands stretch far away."

HUMANITIES CONNECTION This stone head is part of a massive set of sculptures at the burial site in Turkey of King Antiochus I, who ruled about 50 B.C. Few people know anything about him or his kingdom of Commagene now, despite the magnificent memorial he created for himself.

Related Reading

Percy Bysshe Shelley, 1792–1822

The poet Shelley, an idealist and a rebel, led an unconventional life that ended tragically at the age of 29. Born into an aristocratic and wealthy family, he was sent away to boarding school at the age of ten. The bullying and teasing he experienced there created in him a hatred of injustice. As an adolescent, Shelley adopted radical views of the institutions of society and religion, and many of these opinions remained with him throughout his life.

Shelley's domestic affairs were much criticized by his contemporaries. He eloped with a 16-year-old girl, Harriet Westbrook, when he was 18. The marriage did not go well, despite the birth of two children, whom Shelley loved. He abandoned Harriet and ran away with Mary Wollstonecraft Godwin, whom he married after Harriet committed suicide. Shelley and Mary had three children eventually, but he was denied custody of his two children by Harriet. Shunned by some and unable to publish much of his work in England, Shelley felt himself increasingly an outcast and moved to Italy. There, although in the midst of great anguish at the deaths of two of his children, Shelley wrote some of his best works, including "Ode to the West Wind" and "To A Skylark." He was working on a major poem, *The Triumph of Life,* when he was suddenly drowned in a boating accident.

In spite of his personal failings, Shelley was seen by his friends as both loving and unselfish. He was intelligent, extremely well read, and passionate in his writing. His lyrics are some of the most dazzling in English literature. His other works include philosophical and political poems, essays, literary criticism, satires, and dramas. Shelley's masterpiece is *Promotheus Unbound,* a complex verse drama in four acts that combines myth and political allegory. His sonnet "Ozymandias" was written in 1818, shortly before he went to Italy.

Discussion Questions

1. How would you describe the personality of Ozymandias?
   Possible Response: He was proud, arrogant, and self-centered.
2. What is ironic about the words inscribed on the pedestal, quoted in lines 10–11?
   Possible Response: The words are ironic because the works of Ozymandias are in ruins.

MINI LESSON Viewing and Representing

Stone Head of Antiochus I at Nemrut Dag (Mt. Nimrod)

ART APPRECIATION

Instruction Antiochus I was the ruler of a tiny kingdom. His monument is on a desolate mountain peak, where it lay forgotten for almost 2,000 years until it was discovered in 1881. It includes a rock mound 164 feet high, 30-foot statues of gods, and stone relief carvings. On his throne the king had inscribed," I, Antiochus, caused this monument to be erected in commemoration of my own glory and of that of the gods." The monument is one of Turkey's most important archaeological sites. The statues and carvings have suffered serious erosion and breakage over time, and the area is now listed as a World Heritage Site by UNESCO.

Application Tell students to look again at the stone head and reread the **Humanities Connection** on page 467. Then ask them how King Antiochus's monument reflects the themes in "Ozymandias."

Possible Response: Antiochus' monument was intended to immortalize him, but it fell into ruin, and he and his kingdom became an obscure memory. The broken statues and eroded carvings reflect the theme that nothing escapes the ravages of time.

Literary Analysis NARRATIVE POEM

Tell students that "Song of P'eng-ya" is a narrative poem—it tells a story. Ask students to identify or explain the characters, setting, and plot.

Possible Response: Characters: the speaker, his wife (assumed in the reference to "whole family"), his two children, and his friend, Sun Tsai. **Setting:** the P'eng-ya Road, which is a muddy trail going through rough mountain terrain. **Plot:** the speaker and his family are refugees, fleeing from enemy forces. They have left everything behind and they are making slow progress, begging food from strangers, eating wild fruits, and sleeping outdoors. After ten days, they meet an old friend who takes them in, gives them food and shelter, and treats them with great care and kindness.

Active Reading

UNDERSTANDING AND APPRECIATING POETRY

Ask students what impression they have of the speaker after reading the poem several times.

Possible Response: The speaker seems like a dignified and courageous person who has deep feelings. He is tender with his children and grateful for the kindness and loyalty of his friend, whom he loves and admires.

Literary Analysis IMAGERY

Suggest to students that the detailed imagery in the poem helps to draw the reader into the experience being described. Ask students to identify several images that seem especially direct and forceful.

Possible Responses: Examples could include "whole family endlessly trudging" (l. 5), "baby girl in her hunger bit me" (l. 9), "she squirmed and wailed" (l. 12), "importantly he searched for sour plums" (l. 14), "through mud and slime we pulled each other on" (l. 16), "trails slick, clothes wet and clammy" (l. 18), "as dusk turned to darkness" (l. 29), "their tears fell in streams" (l. 34), and "My little chicks had gone sound to sleep" (l. 35).

Pinyin Equivalents

T'ung-chia: Tongjia
Lu-tzu: Luzi
Sun Tsai: Sun Zai

Song of P'eng-ya

Tu Fu

Translated by Burton Watson

I remember when we first fled the rebels,
hurrying north over dangerous trails;
night deepened on P'eng-ya Road,
the moon shone over White-water Hills.
A whole family endlessly trudging,
begging without shame from the people we met:
valley birds sang, a jangle of soft voices;
we didn't see a single traveler returning.
The baby girl in her hunger bit me;
fearful that tigers or wolves would hear her cries,
I hugged her to my chest, muffling her mouth,
but she squirmed and wailed louder than before.
The little boy pretended he knew what was happening;
importantly he searched for sour plums to eat.
Ten days, half in rain and thunder,
through mud and slime we pulled each other on.
There was no escaping from the rain,
trails slick, clothes wet and clammy;
getting past the hardest places,
a whole day advanced us no more than three or four li.
Mountain fruits served for rations,
low-hung branches were our rafter and roof.
Mornings we traveled by rock-bedded streams,
evenings camped in mists that closed in the sky.
We stopped a little while at the marsh of T'ung-chia,
thinking to go out by Lu-tzu Pass;
an old friend there, Sun Tsai,
ideals higher than the piled-up clouds;
he came out to meet us as dusk turned to darkness,

1 rebels: troops led by the traitorous general An Lu-shan, who attacked and captured the Chinese capital of Ch'ang-an in A.D. 756.

3 P'eng-ya (pŭng'yä') Road: a road to the town of P'eng-ya, about 130 miles north of Ch'ang-an. Tu Fu and his family passed through P'eng-ya as they sought safety from the rebel forces.

20 three or four li: less than a mile and a half.

25 T'ung-chia (tŏŏng'jyä').

26 Lu-tzu (lōō'dzŭ').

27 Sun Tsai (sōōn' dzī').

Assessment Informal Assessment

PROSE RETELLING Ask students to write one or two paragraphs retelling the events described in lines 1 to 29 of "Song of P'eng-ya." Tell them to think of their retelling as the beginning of a short story. Remind them that they should pay attention to characters, setting, and action.

RUBRIC

3 Full Accomplishment The retelling gives a clear and detailed picture of the characters and setting and describes events in an accurate and interesting way.

2 Substantial Accomplishment The retelling gives a general sense of the characters and setting and describes events in correct order.

1 Little or Partial Accomplishment The retelling does not reflect the characters, setting, or events as they are presented in the poem.

Circular box with garden scene, Yung Lo. Collection of the National Palace Museum, Taipei, Taiwan, Republic of China.

HUMANITIES CONNECTION Lacquer is made from the sap of the lac tree, which is native to China. To create a piece of solid lacquer thick enough for carving this type of box, as many as 40 applications of thin lacquer had to be layered, a process that took many days.

called for torches, opening gate after gate,
heated water to wash our feet,
cut strips of paper to call back our souls.
Then his wife and children came;
seeing us, their tears fell in streams.
My little chicks had gone sound to sleep;
he called them to wake up and eat from his plate,
said he would make a vow with me,
the two of us to be brothers forever.
At last he cleared the room where we sat,
wished us goodnight, all he had at our command.
Who is willing, in the hard, bleak times,
to break open, lay bare his innermost heart?
Parting from you, a year of months has rounded,
Tartar tribes still plotting evil,
and I think how it would be to have strong wings
that would carry me away, set me down before you.

32 cut strips of paper to call back our souls: It was believed that the soul could leave the body when a person was frightened. The ritual referred to here was intended to restore the souls of the frightened travelers.

44 Tartar tribes: the forces of An Lu-shan.

MINI LESSON Viewing and Representing

Carved Lacquer Box with Garden Scene

ART APPRECIATION

Instruction Although lacquer itself is not a precious substance—such as jade is, for example—luxury objects made of lacquer have been produced in China since the 5th century B.C. The red box is an example of carved lacquer, which was introduced in the 12th century. The box has two styles of carving. The garden scene on the top is in high relief on a background of three patterns representing earth, water, and air. The decoration around the side shows flowers of the four seasons—peony, pomegranate, chrysanthemum, and camellia. In the garden scene, two men are playing chess while a third person is watching, leaning on a staff with a bundle of firewood next to him. A servant is on the far left.

Application Have students look carefully at the box and reread the **Humanities Connection** on page 469. Ask students how the scene on the box reflects the mood in lines 27–40 of the poem.

Possible Response: In the scene on the box, it appears that one of the men is entertaining his friend. The surroundings are comfortable and beautiful. This scene conveys the sense of hospitality and generosity that Tu Fu's friend Sun Tsai extends to him and his family.

Customizing Instruction

Less Proficient Readers

To help students follow the events in the poem, ask them the following questions:

- What are the speaker and his family doing? *(fleeing from rebel troops)*
- How many children are in the family *(two, an infant girl and a little boy)*
- What conditions does the family have to deal with? *(lack of food, danger of attack, bad weather, difficult trails)*
- What happens in lines 27–29? *(They meet an old friend.)*

Set a Purpose Have students read to find out what the friend does.

English Learners

Explain that many of the sentences in the poem consist of a series of long phrases and clauses. Sometimes transition words are not used, so it is necessary to read carefully to find the connections between the phrases and clauses. Help students first find the sentences in the poem and then figure out how the phrases and clauses in each sentence fit together. Perhaps you could work through lines 1–4 together, and then the students could work in pairs on some of the other sentences. You might mention that some sentences are just two lines long, but one is actually eight lines long (lines 25–32)!

Advanced Learners

Point out to students that although this poem is telling a story, the poet provides almost no transition words to signal the sequence of events. The narrative is told instead through clusters of images. Ask students to describe the effects of this style.

Possible Response: This style creates a series of scenes that convey with convincing detail the experiences of the speaker and his family. The absence of transition words creates an intensity and urgency that reflect the feelings and dire circumstances of the speaker and his family. This style also gives a sense of spareness, which reflects the refugees' need to focus on only the essentials in order to survive.

Connect to the Literature

1. **What Do You Think?** Responses will vary, but students should give examples.

Comprehension Check

- Li Po has been exiled to a remote area by his political enemies.
- The prince died long ago, and the palace he built is in ruins.
- His friend gives food, shelter, and protection to Tu Fu and his family.

Think Critically

2. Possible Responses: "land of plague and fever" refers to the part of southern China where Li Po had been exiled; "wings to fly with" is a metaphoric reference to Li Po escaping the control of the authorities; "waters" is a metaphoric reference to Li Po's dangerous political position; "horned dragons" is a metaphoric reference to Li Po's political enemies.
3. Possible Response: The once beautiful palace is now in ruins. Theme: All of life is subject to change and decay, and not even the rich and powerful can escape this fate.
4. Possible Responses: Details would include the family's poverty (lines 5–6), the plight of the children (lines 9–14), and the physical hardships the family suffers (lines 15–24).
5. Responses will vary. Students should give specific examples of how their understanding of the poems grew with repeated readings.

Literary Analysis

Paired Activity Students may identify the following moods:

- "Dreaming of Li Po": loss (and possibly hope in lines 11–16)
- "Jade Flower Palace": desolation
- "Song of P'eng-ya": heartsickness (and possibly relief or comfort in lines 27–40)

The images they choose should clearly contribute to creating the moods they identify. You might want to have a class discussion in which students can explain their idea about the moods in the poems.

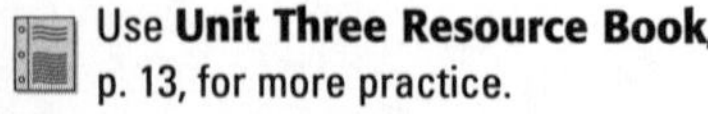
Use **Unit Three Resource Book,** p. 13, for more practice.

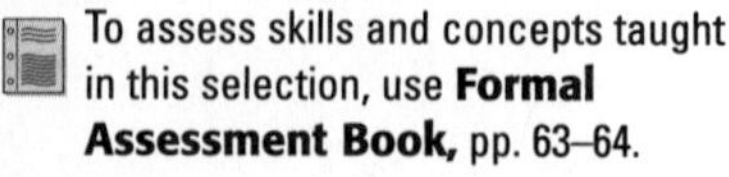
To assess skills and concepts taught in this selection, use **Formal Assessment Book,** pp. 63–64.

Connect to the Literature

1. **What Do You Think?** Which poem do you think has the most vivid images? Explain why.

Comprehension Check

- In "Dreaming of Li Po," why is Tu Fu so worried about Li Po?
- What has apparently happened to the prince and the palace in "Jade Flower Palace"?
- In "Song of P'eng-ya," what act of kindness does Tu Fu's friend perform?

Think Critically

2. In "Dreaming of Li Po," what might each of the following refer to: "land of plague and fever," "wings to fly with," "waters," "horned dragons"?
3. How would you summarize the theme, or message, of "Jade Flower Palace"?

   THINK ABOUT
   - the details used to describe the palace
   - what is left of the palace
   - what life was probably like in the palace

4. In "Song of P'eng-ya," what details does Tu Fu provide about a family fleeing from a rebel army that wouldn't appear in a factual historical account?
5. **ACTIVE READING: UNDERSTANDING AND APPRECIATING POETRY** Look back at the charts you created in your  READER'S NOTEBOOK. Did your impressions and reactions change after the second and third readings of the poems? Did you discover new connections or insights? Discuss your experience with a classmate.

Extend Interpretations

6. **Comparing Texts** Compare "Jade Flower Palace" with "Ozymandias" (pages 466–467). How do the narrators differ in their attitude toward their subject? What similar atmosphere and message do the poems convey?
7. **Critic's Corner** One critic has said that Tu Fu's appeal may be due to "the way he documents his life, from the smallest details to the biggest dimensions of social context." Do the poems you have read support this statement? Explain your answer.
8. **Connect to Life** Although Tu Fu wrote in the eighth century, his poems are still enjoyed today. In what ways are his poems relevant to the modern world?

LITERARY ANALYSIS: MOOD AND IMAGERY

The **mood** of a poem is the feeling or atmosphere the writer creates for the reader. Many elements can contribute to the mood, including word choice, descriptive details, and even rhythm. One of the most important elements is **imagery,** words and phrases that create sensory experiences. Remember that imagery can appeal to any of the five senses—sight, smell, hearing, taste, and touch.

Paired Activity With a partner, come up with a word or phrase that captures the mood of each one of Tu Fu's poems. Write it in the center circle of a word web like the one below. Then, in the surrounding circles, add images from the poem that contribute to the overall mood. Share your word webs with the rest of the class.

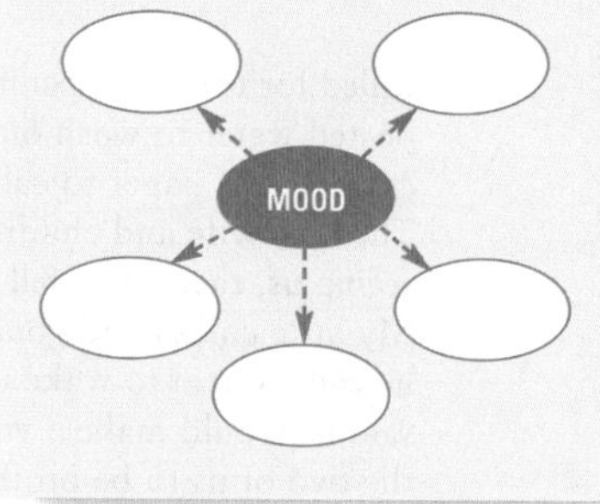

Extend Interpretations

6. **Comparing Texts** The narrator of "Jade Flower Palace" feels sorrow, but the narrator of "Ozymandias" is ironic and detached. Both poems describe an atmosphere of ruin and convey the message that nothing is permanent and that attempts to achieve immortality are doomed.
7. **Critic's Corner** Most students will agree. For example, in "Dreaming of Li Po," Tu Fu reveals both feelings of personal friendship and an awareness of the political dangers of his time.
8. **Connect to Life** Most students will recognize that these poems touch on topics that are of great interest and concern today: friendship, grief and loss, questions about the meaning of life, the uncertainty of the future, the inevitable realities of change and death, the threat of war and upheaval, and the plight of refugees.

The Refugees: People Without a Country

Tu Fu and his family fled rebel armies in 756, but the anguish of the refugee was not new then, and continues even today, in every country. In fact, one estimate places the number of refugees in the world today at over 12 million. But what causes thousands of people to suddenly leave their homes, livelihoods, and everything they know, only to live in overcrowded refugee camps, or worse?

What Makes a Refugee? Sometimes a country is torn by war or politics, the stronger faction terrorizing and forcing out its "enemies." Sometimes religious and ethnic differences cause one group to be persecuted by another, to the point where the victimized group has to flee. And sometimes a whole population of refugees can be created by the failure of the economy, or by a sudden environmental disaster.

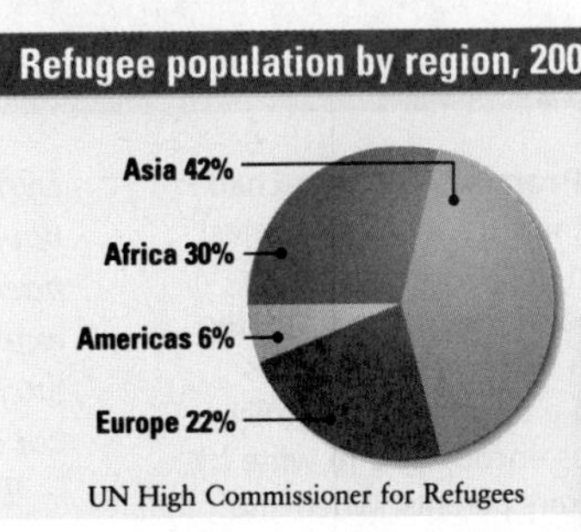

How many of the following refugee situations sound familiar to you, either because you've heard about it, or because you or someone in your family lived through it?

- Russian political and religious refugees
- conflict in Bosnia-Herzegovina
- Ethiopian famine
- the flight of the Vietnamese boat people
- the Palestinian situation
- ethnic cleansing in Kosovo
- the Irish famine
- the Chinese invasion of Tibet

Research Project It's one thing to hear about these situations. It's another to truly understand them—or to do something to help. Do some research on one of the above situations. Create a report or multimedia presentation that will help others understand it as well, and that might even encourage someone to get involved. Your presentation may include information about:

- the problem or conflict that caused the situation
- the number of refugees displaced
- lives of the refugees in exile
- relief efforts
- a resolution of the crisis, or recent developments
- the future

Connect to Today

Use this feature to show the relevance of world literature to students. The material relates the literature selection just read to a contemporary topic connected to students' lives.

READING FOR INFORMATION

Reading Skills and Strategies

READING A PIE CHART

Have students look at the pie chart showing refugee population by region in 2000. Point out to them that the colored sections of the chart give a quick visual interpretation of the percentages listed with each region. Ask them to consider what the impact of the information would be if it were included only in the text and not shown in the chart.

Research Project You may want to have students work in pairs or small groups on this project. Suggest that they read current newspapers and newsmagazines to learn about recent refugee problems. Their presentation could include an outside speaker, if there is a local agency or organization working with the particular refugee situation they are researching.

Opportunities for Extension Students may want to organize a campaign in their grade or in the entire school to help with relief efforts for refugees. This could be done in conjunction with a local agency or with a national group.

Possible Objectives

This **On Your Own** featured selection may be used to achieve one or more of the following objectives:

- give students the opportunity to read independently, either reading silently for a sustained period, reading and analyzing literature with a group, or using the **Reader's Notebook** to write in response to the literature
- conduct a postreading class discussion
- assess students' comprehension of the selection

Pinyin Equivalent

Li Ch'ing-chao: Li Qingzhao

ON YOUR OWN

Poems of Li Ch'ing-chao

TRANSLATED BY Kenneth Rexroth

Li Ch'ing-chao
1084?–1151?

Early Promise Li Ch'ing-chao (lē' chĭng'jou'), China's greatest woman poet, was one of the most accomplished and spirited women of her time. She was born to a distinguished family and was encouraged to write by her literary parents. When she was 18, Li Ch'ing-chao married a student in the Imperial Academy. Deeply happy in their marriage, the couple shared a passion for literature, art, and antiquities. Together they collected a vast number of paintings, sculptures, and manuscripts—enough to fill ten huge rooms.

Tragic Loss Calamity struck in 1126 when the Jin from Manchuria invaded China. In the chaos that followed, Li Ch'ing-chao was separated from her husband for many months. She eventually reached him, but in the meantime the Jin burned the couple's house, and much of their precious artwork went up in flames. A far worse tragedy occurred in 1129, when Li Ch'ing-chao's husband fell ill and died.

Enduring Legacy In the years that followed, Li Ch'ing-chao was often in flight from the Jin invaders. Despite the upheaval and loneliness, she continued to write. By the end of her life, she had written six volumes of poetry and seven of essays. Unfortunately, all of her work was lost except for about 50 poems. Little is known about her last years, but her poetry is a rare treasure that the world has held in high esteem for more than 800 years.

Lyric Poetry In this part of the book, you have read a number of lyric poems. ***Lyric poems*** *are poems in which the speakers express personal thoughts and feelings. Such poems can have a variety of forms and cover a wide range of subjects and emotions.*

The poetry of Li Ch'ing-chao is also in the lyric tradition. Her poems are known for the depth of feeling they express, from the joys of young love to the despair of grief. In addition, her work is praised for its clear imagery. Li Ch'ing-chao's poems were originally set to music, and she is considered a master of the song lyric of her time.

The two poems you are about to read are from two different periods of her life. The first was written when she was a young woman, probably in the early days of her marriage. The second poem was written after her husband had died. As you read the poems, ask yourself these questions:

1. *What images reflect the speakers' feelings most effectively?*
2. *Both poems are set in spring. What are the differences between them?*
3. *Are there any similarities, in theme or imagery, between these poems and the other ancient Chinese poems in this part of Unit Three?*

TWO SPRINGS

Spring has come to the women's quarter.
Once more the new grass is kingfisher green.
The cracked red buds of plum blossoms
Are still unopened little balls.
Blue-green clouds carve jade dragons.
The jade powder becomes fine dust.
I try to hold on to my morning dream.
I have already drained and broken
The cup of Spring.
Flower shadows lie heavy
On the garden gate.
In the orange twilight
Pale moonlight spreads
On the translucent curtain.
Three times in two years
My lord has gone away to the East.
Today he returns,
And my joy is already
Greater than the Spring.

1 women's quarter: In Li Ch'ing-chao's time, living spaces for men and women were generally separate.

2 kingfisher: a bright-colored crested bird.

14 translucent (trăns-lo͞o'sənt): letting light shine through.

Spring Morning in the Han Palace. Qui Ying. Collection of the National Palace Museum, Taipei, Taiwan, Republic of China.

HUMANITIES CONNECTION This scene from a silk scroll painting gives glimpses into the restricted inner sections of the palace. The artist may have painted himself in the figure of the portrait painter in the center.

Working Independently

You may want to set aside time each week for independent reading, without making an assignment related to the reading. Or once students have completed the reading, either alone or aloud in groups, you may ask them to work together on a project, such as working in pairs to prepare a reading of the two poems. If you choose to have students write responsively in their Reader's Notebook, suggest that they write about the different senses appealed to in the images in the poems.

Using the Selection for Assessment

If you want to use this selection as the basis for assessment, see **Integrated Assessment Book,** pp. 13–18, for test questions.

MINI LESSON Viewing and Representing

Spring Morning in the Han Palace **by Qui Ying**

ART APPRECIATION

Instruction This scene is part of a silk scroll that is 12 inches high and 226⅛ inches long. Such scrolls were viewed by unrolling them a little at a time on a table. This example, which was one of the most well-known paintings of its time, gives the viewer a glimpse of the elegant areas of the palace where the women lived. The settings are luxurious, and the women are engaged in a variety of pleasant activities. This particular scene is near the end of the scroll.

Application Have students spend some time looking carefully at the details in the painting and rereading the **Humanities Connection** on page 473. Ask them to describe as many activities as they can identify in the painting.

Possible Responses: One woman is having her portrait painted. A servant is fanning her. Another woman is peeping out from behind a pillar to watch the painter. Some of the women are walking, and others are talking. The woman on the lower left seems to be swatting something or trying to catch something.

Ask students how they would describe the mood in this scene.

Possible Response: Everything seems to be beautifully ordered and unhurried.

ON PLUM BLOSSOMS

This morning I woke
In a bamboo bed with paper curtains.
I have no words for my weary sorrow,
No fine poetic thoughts.
The sandalwood incense smoke is stale,
The jade burner is cold.
I feel as though I were filled with quivering water.
To accompany my feelings
Someone plays three times on a flute
"Plum Blossoms Are Falling
in a Village by the River."
How bitter this Spring is.
Small wind, fine rain, *hsiao, hsiao,*
Falls like a thousand lines of tears.
The flute player is gone.
The jade tower is empty.
Broken hearted—we had relied on each other.
I pick a plum branch,
But my man has gone beyond the sky,
And there is no one to give it to.

13 *hsiao, hsiao* (shyou): words mimicking the sad sound of the rainfall.

Humanities

PLUM BLOSSOMS The flowers of the plum tree have been an enduring image in Chinese culture for thousands of years. Loved for their delicate beauty and sweet but faint scent, the blossoms are also seen as a symbol of the strength and perseverance of the Chinese people. The fact that the plum tree often begins to bloom while it is still winter and snow is on the ground is taken as a sign of hope and courage. The flowers emerge on branches that grow from what a contemporary painter of plum blossoms, Wang Chengxi (wäng′ chŭng′shē′), calls "dragon-like" trunks. The contrast between the fragile blossoms and the rough, gnarled trunks is seen as an image of the triumph of the human spirit over harshness and difficulty. Chinese poets and artists have taken the image of the plum blossom as their subject from ancient times until the present century, portraying with care and detail this tender yet eternal beauty.

Detail of *The Old Plum* (1647), attributed to Kano Sansetsu. The Metropolitan Museum of Art (New York).

Discussion Questions

You might want to use the questions on page 472 for a postreading class discussion.

1. **Possible Responses:** For "Two Springs," students may say that the speaker's feelings of joyful love are reflected most clearly in the images "new grass is kingfisher green" (l. 2), "cracked red buds . . . little balls" (ll. 3–4), and "Blue-green clouds carve jade dragons" (l. 5). Students may note that the speaker's longing for her lord is reflected in the images "Flower shadows . . . garden gate" (ll. 10–11) and "In the orange twilight . . . translucent curtain" (ll. 12–14).
   For "On Plum Blossoms," students may say that the speaker's deep grief is reflected in the images "The sandalwood incense . . . quivering water" (ll. 5–7), "Someone . . . 'by the river'" (ll. 9–11), "Small wind . . . lines of tears" (ll. 13–14), "The flute player . . . tower is empty" (ll. 15–16), and "I pick. . . give it to" (ll. 18–20).
2. **Possible Reponses:** The moods and subjects in the two poems are opposite. In "Two Springs," the mood is one of joyful anticipation and love. Not even the joys of spring can compare with the speaker's happiness as she waits for her lord's return. In "On Plum Blossoms," the mood is one of deep and intense grief. The speaker is full of loneliness and desolation. Spring is bitter instead of joyful because its beauties remind the speaker of all she has lost.
3. **Possible Reponses** are as follows:
   Similarities in theme:
   - "Two Springs": In "Mulberry on the Lowlands," the speaker expresses the joys of love and her happy anticipation of seeing her lord. In "The River-Merchant's Wife: A Letter," the speaker expresses her deep love for her husband, but the mood is one of sad longing rather than joy.
   - "On Plum Blossoms": In "The River-Merchant's Wife: A Letter," the speaker is full of loneliness and longing for her absent husband. In "Dreaming of Li Po," the speaker is grieving because he has been separated form his friend. In "Song of P'eng-ya," the speaker expresses the pain of having to flee from his homeland and become a refugee.

Similarities in imagery:
Students should note that in all of the ancient Chinese poems they have read there is imagery from nature.

- Two Springs": In "Mulberry on the Lowland," images from nature reflect the love and joy of the speaker.
- "On Plum Blossoms": In "We Pick Ferns, We Pick Ferns," beautiful images from nature contrast with the painful feelings and circumstances of the speakers. In "The River-Merchant's Wife: A Letter" and "Jade Flower Palace," images from nature reflect the sadness of the poems. In "Song of P'eng-ya," imagery fron nature is used to give a vivid sense of the speaker's difficult experiences.

Objectives

- write a Lyric Poem
- use a written text as a model for writing
- revise a draft to add sound devices
- use punctuation correctly

Introducing the Workshop

A Lyric Poetry Remind students that modern poetry is different from poetry written prior to the twentieth century, and in particular, very different from the nursery rhymes and other poetry that many children learn early in life. Much of modern poetry does not follow the standard conventions of rhyme and meter, although it frequently uses sound devices such as alliteration, assonance, rhyme, and repetition to create a sense of rhythm and emphasis.

Ask students to name their favorite poets and poems. Read aloud in class some examples of both the traditional styles of rhyming poetry and the modern style of unrhymed poetry. Ask students to identify, compare, and contrast elements of the different styles. Point out that the lyrics of many pop songs have a more traditional rhyme and meter than much contemporary poetry.

Point out that writing a poem gives students the opportunity to express their ideas and feelings in a more concentrated and lyrical way than other types of writing do. Many people find poetry a powerful outlet for their feelings and a way to share those feelings with others.

Basics in a Box

B Presenting the Graphic Like the colors on a painter's palette, the details in a poem are blended and intensified to create an overall meaning. The graphic suggests elements that students can use to draft a successful poem.

C Presenting the Rubric To better understand the assignment, students can refer to the Standards for Writing a Successful Poem. You may wish to discuss with them the complete rubric and student models in the Unit Three Resource Book on pages 19–25.

For more instruction and practice in narrative and literary writing, use McDougal Littell's ***Language Network:***

- Grade 10, Chapter 24, "Poetry"
- Grade 12, Chapter 23, "Dramatic Scene"

Writing Workshop Lyric Poetry

Painting with Words . . .

From Reading to Writing Not everyone can explain what poetry is, but most people know it when they see it. **Poetry** is a form of creative writing that emphasizes language and imagery. In poetry, the sound of the (A) words and their arrangement on the page work together with the meaning to create a strong impact—one of beauty, excitement, sadness, or even fear. Some poems, such as Li Ch'ing-chao's "Two Springs," express personal thoughts and feelings. Such poems are known as **lyric poems.** Often, a lyric poem will describe a single image or moment rather than tell a story.

For Your Portfolio

WRITING PROMPT Write a poem that describes an experience, an idea, a place, a person, or a feeling.

Purpose: To express yourself in an original way

Audience: Your classmates, friends, or family

Basics in a Box

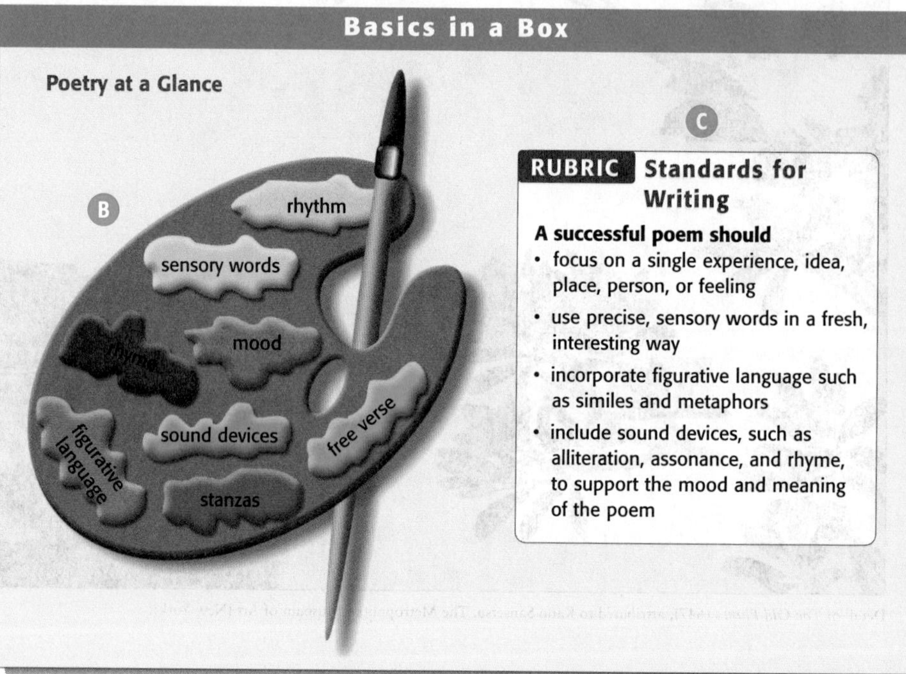

RUBRIC Standards for Writing

A successful poem should

- focus on a single experience, idea, place, person, or feeling
- use precise, sensory words in a fresh, interesting way
- incorporate figurative language such as similes and metaphors
- include sound devices, such as alliteration, assonance, and rhyme, to support the mood and meaning of the poem

LESSON RESOURCES

USING PRINT RESOURCES
Unit Three Resource Book

- Prewriting, p. 14
- Drafting, p. 15
- Peer Response, pp. 16–17
- Revising, Editing, and Proofreading, p. 18
- Student Models, pp. 19–24
- Rubric, p. 25

USING MEDIA RESOURCES
Writing Coach CD-ROM
Visit our Web site: classzone.com

ADDITIONAL RESOURCES
For a complete view of Lesson Resources, see page 419g of this book.

Analyzing Student Models

Shakira Hightower
Dover High School

Harlemite Easter

I take Daryl uptown to see the parade
marching on the Avenue

I watch his eyes
watching
little girls with Vaselined legs
white socks/gloves
hats atop ringlets and ribbons
pinks, yellows
dresses that rise when they spin and
feet that go tippity-tap in Sunday
patent leather

I follow him
following
smoothly shaven heads
of little boys and men
collars being tugged at
but under the mindful eyes of

Women
wearing flowers and pumps
that match
purses
that match
hats

I look at him
looking at them filing
into the churches along the corners
of the Avenue
on Easter

D

RUBRIC IN ACTION

1. Focuses on an experience
2. Repetition creates rhythm and emphasis.
3. Uses alliteration and assonance to create rhythm
4. Repetition here is similar to repetition at number 2.
5. Alliteration, repetition, and assonance combine with a vivid description of the women's appearance.
6. Repetition similar to that at numbers 2 and 4
7. Line breaks emphasize *Avenue* and *Easter.*

Teaching the Lesson

Analyzing the Model
"Harlemite Easter"; "Revolution"; "Yellow"

D Three student models present three examples of poems with strong imagery and sensory language. Each poem presents a vivid depiction of a scene or an image. Students can take turns reading aloud the poems and the **Rubric in Action.** Point out key words and phrases in the student models that correspond to the elements mentioned in the **Rubric in Action.**

"Harlemite Easter"

1. Point out to students that the first two lines of the poem introduce a scene to the reader, framing it like a camera.

2, 4, and 6. Point out to students that the writer uses repetition within the word pairs *watch* and *watching, follow* and *following,* and *look* and *looking.* Ask them to identify how else the writer uses repetition in those three places. *(The writer uses three word pairs with parallel structure, another form of repetition.)*

3. Ask students how the words *ringlets* and *ribbons* match in content as well as form.
Possible Response: *Ringlets* and *ribbons* both describe the hairstyles of the little girls.

5. Ask students to identify the alliteration and assonance in this example. (W *in* women wearing; a *in* that, match, *and* hats.)

7. Point out to students that the beginning and the end of a line are two places where a word will often get special attention or emphasis.

LANGUAGE SKILLS

"Revolution"

1. Ask students how this poem would be different without sensory description.
   Possible Responses: The poem would not be as interesting; the poem would be less vivid; the poem would be shorter.
2. Ask students to point out the words and phrases that signal personification in this poem.
   Possible Responses: *whispers urgently; shyly it shows me; pulse; hair; behind the ears; breathe tired thanks; erupt in revolution*

"Blue"

1. Ask students to jot down a few more images that come to mind when they think of the color blue.
   Possible Responses: a blue crayon; ink; police uniforms; stripes on the flag; flowers such as hydrangeas and forget-me-nots; the blue part of flame, or any personal belongings that happen to be blue.

2, 3. Point out to students that this type of poem, sometimes called a list poem, by its nature uses similes and metaphors to compare and connect the subject (the color blue) with multiple objects. Ask students why they think a list poem is effective.
Possible Response: List poems allow the poet to combine images that typically are not thought of together. The possibilities are seemingly endless and can create a rich experience for readers.

Susan Gray
Solomon Schechter High School

Revolution

When I water the plants I like to watch
the soil sponges darken in welcome,
feel the wet dirt yield to my finger.
I sniff the soft earth
as water dribbles out the bottom.
The violet whispers urgently from its
plastic pot.
Shyly it shows me the veins under the
leaves.
I take its pulse. I smooth its hair.
I scratch it behind the ears.
The old yellow leaves breathe tired
thanks,
while the young ones at center bristle
green
as they erupt in revolution.

RUBRIC IN ACTION

❶ The sensory description involves sight, touch, and smell.

❷ The poet uses personification, characterizing the violet as a shy, whispering person.

Vanessa Jones
Middleton High School

Blue

Blue—

the sky as clouds break
into floating white islands;

the jay darting from tree to tree,
its feathers glistening in the sun;

the stone in my ring,
as deep a blue as the ocean current;

your eyes catching the light
of a summer afternoon.

❶ The entire poem springs from a single idea—the color blue.

❷ A simile helps convey the intensity of the blue stone by comparing it to the ocean.

❸ After naming various things in life that are objectively blue, the poet turns to the personal ("your eyes"), suggesting a relationship of some kind.

Writing Your Poem

❶ Prewriting

Many poets start with a single phrase, image, or feeling. Find a quiet place to work and then reflect about moments, places, people, or ideas that strike you in some way. Jot down your thoughts and any interesting words that come to mind, especially those describing sensory experiences. See the **Idea Bank** in the margin for more suggestions. After choosing a topic, follow the steps below.

Planning Your Poem

1. **Write freely about your topic.** Review the notes you made while searching for a topic. Circle any interesting words, images, and details. Then make a concept web to explore ideas related to those items.
2. **Identify the mood you want to express.** Does your topic make you feel happy, sad, curious, angry? Think about images and details that will create or reinforce that mood.
3. **Choose a focus.** Which word, line, or image seems to lead to other good images and ideas? Look for one powerful phrase to begin your poem.

❷ Drafting

Writing freely, compose your poem, playing with ideas and language. Choose words for their meaning and their sound. Read your writing aloud and listen for its rhythm, or cadence. Consider using some of the following poetic devices.

DEVICE	EXAMPLE
Sound Devices	
alliteration assonance rhyme repetition	yelping and yammering howling loudly bags of rags into the cold, cold night
Figures of Speech	
simile	The park was as quiet as midnight.
metaphor	Winter was a blanket that covered the city.
personification	The clock tower guarded the citizens as they slept.

In general, use descriptive language that appeals to the five senses. Also experiment with stanzas, line breaks, and indented lines. When you're done with your draft, read it aloud and listen to the language. Think about how you might add shape to your poem by changing words, line breaks, and punctuation.

IDEABank

1. Your Working Portfolio
Build on the **Writing Option** you completed earlier in this unit:

- **Mood Poem,** p. 460

2. Personality Poem
Think about the most unusual person you know. How would you describe this person? What is unusual about him or her? Write a poem characterizing the person.

3. Found Photo
Look through newspapers, magazines, or books to find a photograph that suggests strong emotion or an unusual situation. Write a poem about what you see in the photo.

LANGUAGE SKILLS

Guiding Student Writing

Prewriting

Choosing a Topic

If, after reading the **Idea Bank,** students are having difficulty choosing an incident, suggest they try the following:

- Observe objects in nature, such as flowers, plants, insects, clouds, or the moon. Use the details of your observation as the basis for your poem.
- Sit in a park, playground, shopping center, or some other public place and watch the people passing by. Focus on specific movements and interactions. Use your observations as the basis for your poem.
- Throughout the day, listen carefully to people talking. Choose a line of dialogue as the basis for your poem.

Planning the Poem

2. Encourage students to look for actions and objects that best express the emotions they wish to convey. They may begin by naming the mood, then describing the object or action that best expresses that mood.
3. Have students write each image on the top of a page and then respond to it by letting language freely follow in response. After developing several images, they can choose the one that has the most potential as a starting point.

Drafting

Since poetry is meant to be heard as much as read, encourage students to read aloud as they compose their poems, constantly listening to the sounds of words and revising for sound as well as content. Students can also read their poems aloud to a partner. Have partners give thoughtful comments about the images and sounds in the poem.

Revising

USING SOUND DEVICES

In an exercise to develop the ear, have students review their drafts and underline or circle as many repeated or rhyming sounds as they can find. Ask them to consider which of these repetitions creates an interesting rhythm or pleasing sound. Where in the poem might they add more of these sound devices?

Finally, ask students to select a few key words in their poems, such as words with interesting sounds or words that create a prominent image. For each of these words, have students make a list of at least ten words that rhyme, that share initial vowels or consonants (alliteration) or that share an internal vowel or consonant (assonance or consonance). Have students refer to these lists when revising their poems.

Editing and Proofreading

USING PUNCTUATION

Ask a volunteer to read the example aloud as it was originally punctuated. Discuss the problems with this type of reading. Then have the same person read the poem again with the new punctuation added. Explain that punctuation—commas, periods, exclamation points, and dashes—indicate pauses and inflection for the reader. Punctuation can also clarify the meaning of the poem.

Have students choose partners and read their poems aloud to one another. Both partners should listen for places where punctuation is needed. Students might also experiment with different types of punctuation and then read the different versions aloud.

Remind students that even though some poetry uses unusual punctuation, they should consider their own punctuation carefully and strive for an error-free final draft of their poems.

Reflecting

Ask students to express what they discovered about their feelings and subject matter. Have students add these self-evaluations to their working portfolios.

IDEABank

Sound confusing?

For definitions of *alliteration, assonance, repetition, rhyme,* and *meter,* look in the **Glossary of Literary Terms,** p. R91

Need revising help?

Review the **Rubric,** p. 476

Consider **peer reader** comments

Check **Revision Guidelines,** p. R19

Puzzled by punctuation?

See the **Grammar Handbook,** pp. R77–R78

Publishing IDEAS

- Submit your poem to your school's literary magazine.
- Publish your poem in your own chapbook, or booklet.
- Read your poem aloud at a class poetry circle. Record the readings on videotape or audiotape.

3 Revising

TARGET SKILL ▶ USING SOUND DEVICES Sound and rhythm are important features of poetry. Add features such as alliteration, assonance, repetition, rhyme, or meter to your poem in order to create rhythm and emphasis.

Ask Your Peer Reader

- How does this poem make you feel?
- Which images are the strongest or most vivid?
- What is the most interesting aspect of the poem?

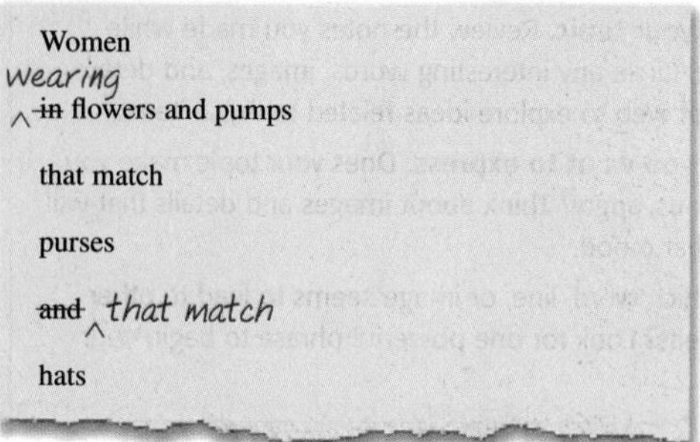
Women
wearing
~~in~~ flowers and pumps
that match
purses
~~and~~ that match
hats

4 Editing and Proofreading

TARGET SKILL ▶ USING PUNCTUATION When you write poetry, you are freed from certain prose conventions. Nonetheless, punctuation marks have the same meaning in poetry as they do in prose. In general, use standard rules for punctuating your poetry. Punctuation will clarify your ideas, helping you communicate your meaning.

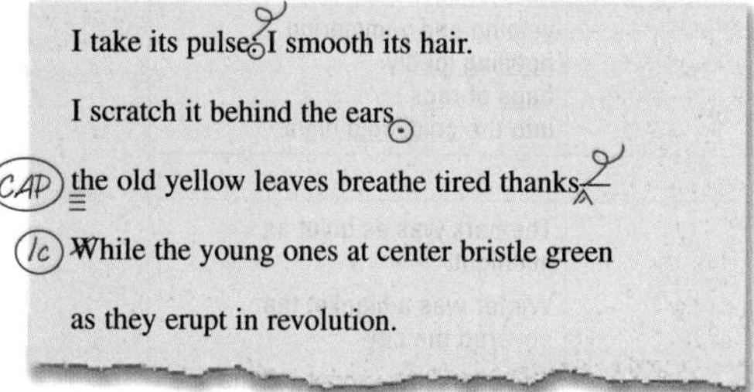
I take its pulse, I smooth its hair.
I scratch it behind the ears.
(CAP) the old yellow leaves breathe tired thanks,
(lc) While the young ones at center bristle green
as they erupt in revolution.

5 Reflecting

FOR YOUR WORKING PORTFOLIO In writing your poem, what did you learn about your topic and about yourself? Did you come up with any surprising descriptions? What techniques would you like to try in your next poem? Attach your answers to your finished work. Save your poem in your **Working Portfolio.**

MINI LESSON Grammar

END PUNCTUATION

Instruction Explain to students that end punctuation includes periods (used at the end of declarative sentences and most imperative sentences), question marks (used at the end of interrogative sentences), and exclamation points (used at the end of exclamatory sentences or after some imperative sentences). Write the following sentences on the board.

She found a delightful garden to visit.
Where is the garden?
There are so many unusual flowers!

Discuss with students the tone or emotion suggested by the end punctuation below.

Practice Ask students to read the sentences below and add the end marks that match the tone designated in parentheses.

1. Did you see the first leaves fall? (curious)
2. The trees will soon be bare. (melancholy)
3. Get out and rake those leaves! (angry)

For more instruction and practice with end marks, use McDougal Littell's ***Language Network:***

- Grade 10, Chapter 11, "Punctuation"
- Grade 12, Chapter 9, "End Marks and Commas"

Standardized Test Practice Revising & Editing

Read this paragraph from the first draft of an essay. The underlined sections may include the following kinds of errors:

- **incorrect end marks**
- **errors in comma usage**
- **incorrect quotation marks**
- **incorrect use of semicolons**

For each underlined section, choose the revision that most improves the writing.

Every year I go to a great summer camp. It's a poetry workshop; students from around the city come together to express themselves (1) in writing. The Young Poets as the students are called work in classes of ten. (2) We spend every morning writing, every afternoon we share our work. (3) Our counselor calls out, 'Who wants to give us a poem?' (4) Every Friday afternoon is the Grand Jamboree, where we all read recite, rap, or sing (5) our poems from the week. What part do I enjoy the most. (6) I like meeting new people and hearing so many different voices.

1. **A.** It's a poetry workshop, students from around the city come together to express themselves
   B. It's a poetry workshop, students from around the city come together; to express themselves
   C. It's a poetry workshop; students from around the city, come together to express themselves
   D. Correct as is
2. **A.** The Young Poets, as the students are called, work in classes of ten.
   B. The Young Poets, as the students are called work in classes of ten.
   C. The Young Poets as the students are called, work in classes of ten.
   D. Correct as is
3. **A.** We spend every morning writing: every afternoon we share our work.
   B. We spend every morning writing, every afternoon, we share our work.
   C. We spend every morning writing; every afternoon we share our work.
   D. Correct as is
4. **A.** calls out, "Who wants to give us a poem?"
   B. calls out: 'Who wants to give us a poem?'
   C. calls out—"Who wants to give us a poem?"
   D. Correct as is
5. **A.** read, recite rap or sing
   B. read recite rap or sing
   C. read, recite, rap, or sing
   D. Correct as is
6. **A.** What part do I enjoy the most!
   B. What part do I enjoy the most?
   C. What part do I enjoy the most.
   D. Correct as is

Need extra help?

See the **Grammar Handbook**
Correcting Run-On Sentences, p. R73
Capitalization, p. R79
Correcting Fragments, p. R73
Quick Reference: Punctuation, p. R77

Standardized Test Practice

Encourage students to read the complete paragraph before they answer the questions. Then demonstrate how students can eliminate incorrect choices for the first question.

A. This choice is incorrect because it joins two complete sentences with a comma, making it a run-on sentence.

B. This choice is incorrect because the phrase following the semicolon is a fragment, and a semicolon can only be used to join two complete independent clauses.

C. This choice is incorrect because there is no reason to put a comma after *city*.

D. This choice is correct because a semicolon is joining two independent clauses.

Answers:
1. D; **2.** A; **3.** C; **4.** A; **5.** C; **6.** B

TEST PRACTICE

MINI LESSON Grammar

QUOTATION MARKS

Instruction Tell students that double quotation marks (") set off direct quotations and some titles. Single quotation marks (') are used to enclose a quotation within a quotation. Write the following example on the board:

Bill wrote, "Everyone loves it here. One tourist said, 'This is paradise!'"

Underline the quotation marks and note how the double and single quotation marks are used.

Practice Have students punctuate the following sentences with the correct quotation marks.

1. The sign on the wall read, Prices Reduced.
2. The store clerk said, I overheard a customer say This is too expensive.
3. Are you kidding? asked the clerk.
4. These shoes are expensive said the customer.

For more instruction and practice with using quotation marks, use McDougal Littell's ***Language Network:***

- Grade 10, Chapter 11, "Punctuation"
- Grade 12, Chapter 10, "Other Punctuation"

Objectives

- research word origins as an aid to understanding meanings and derivations
- use a dictionary to determine precise usage and pronunciation
- practice classifying homophones, homonyms, and homographs

Building Vocabulary

Homophones, Homonyms, and Homographs

Words with Similar Sounds and Spellings The English language contains many unrelated words that happen to have the same spelling and/or pronunciation. Many of these words have entirely different origins; the resemblance is only a coincidence. However, their similarity often confuses readers and writers. Read the excerpt on the right. If you didn't know that the verb *pine* means "to long for," you might think it had something to do with an evergreen tree.

Pine and *pine* are **homonyms**–words that have the same pronunciation and spelling but different meanings. One word comes from the Latin *pīnus,* meaning "pine tree," and the other comes from the Greek *poinē,* meaning "penalty."

> **Parting from the dead, I've stifled my sobs, . . .**
> **Yet my old friend has entered my dreams, proof of how long I've pined for him.**
> —"Dreaming of Li Po" by Tu Fu

Strategies for Building Vocabulary

In addition to homonyms, **homophones** and **homographs** may confuse readers and writers. Use the information below to help you distinguish these words from their confusing partners.

❶ **Homophones** The term *homophone* comes from two Greek words: *homos* ("same"), and *phōnē* ("sound"). Homophones are words that sound the same but are spelled differently and have different meanings. Practice will help you remember the different spellings and meanings of words like *foreword* and *forward, sight* and *site*, and *principal* and *principle.*

Homophones

Alike in	Different in	Example
pronunciation	spelling and meaning	*holy* and *wholly*

❷ **Homonyms** The term *homonym* comes from the Greek words *homos* ("same") and *onumos* ("name"). Although homonyms have the same spelling and pronunciation, they are actually different words with different derivations. The fact that they are spelled and pronounced alike is a coincidence. These words have separate entries in the dictionary. *Tire* ("to grow weary") and *tire* ("a wheel covering") are homonyms.

Homonyms

Alike in	Different in	Example
pronunciation and spelling	meaning	*loaf* ("a mass of bread") and *loaf* ("to be idle")

❸ **Homographs** The term *homograph* comes from the Greek words *homos* ("same") and *graphē* ("writing"). Homographs are spelled the same but have different meanings and pronunciations. *Content* (kŏn'tĕnt'), meaning "subject matter" and *content* (kən-tĕnt'), meaning "satisfied" are two examples. Like homonyms, homographs have separate dictionary entries.

Homographs

Alike in	Different in	Example
spelling	meaning and pronunciation	*invalid* ("not valid; faulty") and *invalid* ("one completely disabled by illness")

EXERCISE Look up each pair of nouns in a dictionary. Pronounce each noun and identify its meanings and origins. Then classify the two words as homophones, homonyms, or homographs, and use each word in a sentence.

1. *mail* and *mail*
2. *compound* and *compound*
3. *wet* and *whet*
4. *bear* and *bear*
5. *miner* and *minor*

EXERCISE

Students' definitions and etymologies may vary, depending on the dictionaries they use. However, they should still find comparable versions of the homonyms, homophones, and homographs listed below. Sample responses are given.

1. **mail** (māl) materials, such as letters, handled in the postal system (Middle English *male*, bag, from Old French, of German origin)
   mail (māl) flexible armor made of overlapping metal rings, loops of chain, or scales (Middle English, from Old French *maile*, from Latin *macula*, blemish, mesh)
   (Homonyms)
   My paycheck was lost in the mail.
   The knight wore a suit of chain mail.
2. **compound** (kŏm pound′) to add to; increase (alteration of Middle English *compounen*, from Latin *compōnere)*
   compound (kŏm′ pound) a building or buildings set off and closed in by a barrier (alteration of Malay *kampong*, village)
   (Homographs)
   Harry was trying to help, but he only compounded the error.
   There were soldiers posted all around the compound.
3. **wet** (wĕt) covered or soaked with a liquid (Middle English, from Old English *waet*)
   whet (hwĕt *or* wĕt) to sharpen or to make more keen (Middle English *whetten*, from Old English *hwettan*)
   (Homophones *or* Homographs)
   (Since *whet* has two different pronunciations, it might be considered to have the same or a different pronunciation from *wet.*)
   After being left in the rain, the book was all wet.
   The smell of dinner cooking will really whet your appetite.
4. **bear** (bâr) to hold up or support (Middle English *beren*, from Old English *beran*)
   bear (bâr) a large omnivorous mammal of the family Ursidae (Middle English *bere*, from Old English *bera*)
   (Homonyms)
   Those beams can bear a lot of weight.
   A huge bear came out of the woods.
5. **miner** (mī′ nər) one who works to extract ore or minerals from the earth (Middle English, from Old French, from Vulgar Latin *mīna*, probably of Celtic origin)
   minor (mī′ nər) lesser or smaller (Middle English, from Latin)
   (Homophones)
   The miner was covered with coal dust.
   She has a minor part in the play.

Use **Unit Three Resource Book,** p. 26, for more practice.

Sentence Crafting — Using Parallelism for Effect

Grammar from Literature When writers want to say something powerful or memorable, they sometimes use **parallelism** to create emphasis. Parallelism is the expression of related concepts using similar grammatical structures. You learned on page 157 that parallel construction is grammatically necessary when listing elements in a series. It is also a graceful and effective way to group similar ideas and to show contrast between opposing or greatly different ideas. Look at the following model.

> **Lord Ji Kang asked: "What should I do in order to make the people respectful, loyal, and zealous?" The Master said: "Approach them with dignity** and they will be respectful. **Be yourself a good son and a kind father,** and they will be loyal. **Raise the good and train the incompetent,** and they will be zealous."
>
> —Confucius, *Analects*

In each of the three sentences, the Master says, **"Do** (something) **and they will be** (something)." The repetition of this structure creates a strong rhythmic pattern, which is both graceful and memorable.

Notice how the parallel construction highlights the contrast in this second passage from Confucius' *Analects.*

> **The Master said: "To study without thinking is** futile. **To think without studying is** dangerous."

What if the Master had said, "To study without thinking is futile. The other way around is dangerous"? The statement would have had the same meaning, but it would not have had the same effect.

GRAMMAR EXERCISE You will find parallelism in the writings and speeches of many authors and orators. For each of the following quotations, write down the groups of words that have parallel form.

1. "The Master said: 'Authority without generosity, ceremony without reverence, mourning without grief—these, I cannot bear to contemplate.'" (*Analects*)
   (*Sample answer: authority without generosity, ceremony without reverence,* and *mourning without grief*)
2. "Truthful words do not flatter.
   Flattering words are not true." (*Tao Te Ching,* 81)
3. "A president's hardest task is not to *do* what is right, but to *know* what is right." (Lyndon B. Johnson, State of the Union Address, January 4, 1965)
4. "She handled her brushes with a certain ease and freedom which came, not from long and close acquaintance with them, but from a natural aptitude." (Kate Chopin, *The Awakening*)

WRITING EXERCISE Choose three of the six passages quoted on this page, including those in the Grammar Exercise. Then write three of your own passages, imitating the structure of the passages you chose. For example, if you chose to imitate the first quotation in the Grammar Exercise, you might write: "The baker said: 'Bread without yeast, cake without sugar, doughnuts without holes—these, I will not sell in my shop.'"

Sentence Crafting

Objectives

- recognize the use of grammatical parallelism as a stylistic device that creates rhythm and emphasis
- practice writing sentences with parallel structure

GRAMMAR EXERCISE

2. *Truthful words do not flatter* and *flattering words are not true*
3. *not to do what is right* but *to know what is right*
4. *not from long and close acquaintance with them,* but *from a natural aptitude*

WRITING EXERCISE

Student responses will vary. Sample responses follow.

1. Matilda asked: "What should I do in order to make my house clean, orderly, and fragrant?" Her father said: "Use plenty of hot water, and it will be clean. Put away your belongings, and it will be orderly. Bake sweet-smelling foods, and it will be fragrant."
2. A student's hardest job is not to *know* the right answer, but to *say* the right answer.
3. She answered the questions with a certain bluntness that came not from her desire to offend, but from her interest in telling the truth.

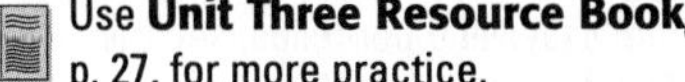
Use **Unit Three Resource Book,** p. 27, for more practice.

MINI LESSON Grammar

COMMAS IN A SERIES

Instruction Tell students that in a sentence that lists a series of three or more items, a comma is used after every item except the last one. Write the following examples on the board.

The air was dusty, harsh, and gray.

The weather will be pleasant today, raw tomorrow, and tropical next week.

Practice Ask students to punctuate the following sentences with commas.

1. The best gifts come in small packages big ideas or simple moments (Insert commas after *packages* and *ideas.*)
2. Does art represent truth fantasy or madness? (Insert commas after *truth* and *fantasy.*)
3. In poetry you can find birds that speak trees that weep and people who transform. (Insert commas after *speak* and *weep.*)

For more instruction and practice with commas, use McDougal Littell's ***Language Network:***

- Grade 10, Chapter 11, "Punctuation"
- Grade 12, Chapter 9, "End Marks and Commas"

BUILDING VOCABULARY AND SENTENCE CRAFTING 483

Objectives
- reflect on and assess understanding of the unit
- compare and summarize themes across texts
- analyze two examples of lyric poetry
- assess and build portfolios

Reflecting on the Literature
Suggest that students list details and ideas that strike them as they review the selections. Tell them to include some of them as examples in their summary.

Reviewing Literary Concepts
A successful response will
- choose two lyric poems
- identify the speaker, the experience described in the poem, and the main emotion
- include an explanation of how the poem affects the student

 Use **Unit Three Resource Book,** p. 28, for additional support.

Building Your Portfolio
Students will use their Presentation Portfolios to file what they consider their highest quality work—the very best projects and activities from their Working Portfolios.

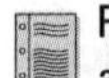 For more information on using writing and assessing portfolios, see the **Teacher's Guide to Assessment and Portfolio Use,** pp. 53–74.

Part Assessment
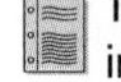 To assess skills and concepts taught in this unit part, use **Formal Assessment Book,** pp. 65–66.

Reflect and Assess

What impressions of the people of ancient China did you have after reading the selections in this part of Unit Three? What joys, sorrows, and concerns did you discover in the literature? Use the activities below to help you think further about what you have read.

Detail of *Spring Morning in the Han Palace.* Qui Ying. Collection of the National Palace Museum, Taiwan, Republic of China.

Reflecting on the Literature

Thoughtful Observation Ancient Chinese literature touches on many aspects of life, from details of everyday experience to larger questions about the right way to live. The writers are careful observers of both beauty and human relationships. Think back over the selections you have read, and call to mind details that delighted you and thoughts that stirred you. Briefly summarize the view of life that you find in this literature.

Reviewing Literary Concepts

Lyric Poetry You have read lyric poems by several poets in this part of the book. These poems present a variety of emotions and situations. Which two poems especially appealed to you? For each one, identify the speaker and the experience the poem deals with. Then note the main emotion the speaker expresses. What makes each poem particularly moving to you?

Self ASSESSMENT

READER'S NOTEBOOK

The names and terms below are important in this part of the book. On a piece of paper, list the words. Then write a sentence or two explaining each one. If you are not certain about a term, review the lessons or check the **Glossary of Literary Terms** (page R91).

didactic literature
Analects
maxim
Tao Te Ching
paradox
Taoism
Book of Odes
lyric poetry
imagery
mood

Building Your Portfolio

Writing Workshop and Writing Options Look back at the lyric poem you wrote for the Writing Workshop on page 476 and your work for the Writing Options on page 460. Which piece are you most pleased with? Put that piece in your **Presentation Portfolio**, along with a note explaining why you think it works well.

Setting GOALS

Think about the works you have read in this part of Unit Three. Which author or selection would you like to investigate further? Look at the suggestions in Extend Your Reading, or ask your teacher or a librarian to help you find additional works or different translations.

Assessment Self Assessment

Students can look up the listed terms in the **Glossary of Literary Terms** on page R91 or they can find them introduced in context on the text pages indicated below.

didactic literature (p. 432)
Analects (pp. 434–435)
maxim (p. 435)
Tao Te Ching (pp. 440–441)
paradox (p. 441)
Taoism (pp. 440–441)
Book of Odes (p. 446)
lyric poetry (p. 472)
imagery (p. 453)
mood (p. 463)

Extend Your *Reading*

A Floating Life: The Adventures of Li Po

SIMON ELEGANT

This historical novel conveys Li Po's genius as a poet as well as his appetite for adventure. The novel presents the poet's life in the form of a memoir told by Li Po to a young boy, who copies it down as a writing exercise. Li Po's spirit comes to life in a series of tales dealing with his experiences at the emperor's court and in exile. Based on historical accounts, Elegant's fiction captures the essence of Li Po while faithfully portraying life in eighth-century China.

In the Land of the Dragon: Imperial China, A.D. 960–1368

This volume of Time-Life's *What Life Was Like* series traces the history of China from the beginning of the Sung dynasty through the rise and fall of the Mongol Empire. During much of this period, art and culture flourished and important inventions helped transform the world. Prosperity gave way to great upheaval, however, when the Mongols overran and conquered China. This tumultuous time is vividly brought to life through the book's engaging text and beautiful illustrations.

And Even *More* . . .

Books

The Essential Confucius THOMAS CLEARY, TRANS.
In this edition, the teachings of Confucius are grouped by subject to make them easier to understand. The format is easy to follow and helps make Confucian thought clear and direct.

The Terracotta Army of the First Emperor of China
WILLIAM LINDESAY AND GUO BAOFU
Photographs, diagrams, and informative text tell the story behind the incredible life-size pottery warriors discovered in China in 1974.

Other Media

The Tao of Pooh
Benjamin Hoff reads his best-selling book, in which he uses the beloved bear Winnie-the-Pooh and his friends to explain basic Taoist beliefs. Harper Audio. (AUDIOCASSETTE)

China: Dynasties of Power
This film in the Lost Civilizations series examines the glory and might of ancient China's greatest rulers and re-creates the building of the Great Wall. Time-Life Video. (VIDEOCASSETTE)

Chuang Tsu: Inner Chapters

JANE ENGLISH AND GIA-FU FENG, TRANS.

The wisdom and humor of the Taoist philosopher Chuang Tzu are evident in these fables and anecdotes. English's black-and-white photographs of nature enhance the text and help draw the reader into the spiritual world of Taoism.

More Recommendations for Your Students

Difficulty Level: Easy

Hall, Eleanor J. *Ancient Chinese Dynasties* (San Diego: Lucent Books, 2000). Hall gives a clear and accurate introduction to the early Chinese dynasties. She begins with a time line and goes on to present details of everyday life as well as culture and customs of the various dynasties.

Kerven, Rosalind. *In the Court of the Jade Emperor: Stories from Old China* (Cambridge, England: Cambridge U. P., 1994). This collection includes 15 myths, legends, and folk tales that have been carefully researched. The stories give a vivid glimpse into the civilization of ancient China.

Ross, Frank, and Michael Goodman, ill. *Oracle Bones, Stars and Wheelbarrows: Ancient Chinese Science and Technology* (Boston: Houghton Mifflin, 1990). This work of nonfiction covers a fascinating array of inventions and discoveries.

Difficulty Level: Average

Rexroth, Kenneth, ed. and trans. *One Hundred Poems from the Chinese* (NY: New Directions, 1956). This collection of lyric poetry contains works by nine poets of ancient China. The poems explore friendship, the beauties of nature, and both the richness and the inevitable changes life brings.

Tsai, Chih Chung, and Brian Bruya, trans. *Confucius Speaks* (NY: Anchor Books, 1996). An introduction to the life and thought of Confucius through sophisticated and witty cartoons by Tsai Chih Chung, a famous cartoonist from East Asia.

Whitfield, Susan. *Life Along the Silk Road* (Berkeley, CA: U. of California P., 2001). In this work of nonfiction, the author brings alive the world of the Silk Road about 800 to 1000 A.D. through narratives about various individuals who traveled the road—a merchant, a soldier, and so on.

Difficulty Level: Challenging

Debaine-Francfort, Corinne. *The Search for Ancient China* (NY: Abrams, 1999). This small but detailed nonfiction account tells the fascinating stories of archaeologists' discoveries of treasures from ancient China. Many superb illustrations.

Mallory, J. P., and Victor H. Mair. *The Tarim Mummies: Ancient China and the Mystery of the Earliest Peoples from the West* (NY: Thames and Hudson, 2000). This stunning nonfiction account describes the surprising discovery in western China of the best-preserved mummies in the world.

Watson, Burton, ed. and trans. *The Columbia Book of Chinese Poetry* (NY: Columbia U. P., 1986). This is a highly respected and accessible anthology spanning 23 centuries of ancient Chinese poetry.

Unit Three, Part 2, provides an overview of traditional Japanese literature, spanning about 800 years, that introduces students to the literature's forms and themes.

World Art and Cultures Transparencies

AT26 *The Descent of Amida and the 25 Bodhisattvas to Collect the Soul of the Deceased*

AT42 *Foreigners*

You may use the listed transparencies to acquaint students with traditional Japanese art.

Pronunciation Guide

Honshu (hŏn′sho͞o)
Hokkaido (hô′kī-dō′)
Kyushu (kyo͞o′sho͞o)
Shikoku (shē′kô-ko͞o′)
Edo (ā′dō)
Heian (hā′än)
Kyoto (kyō′tō)

READING FOR INFORMATION

Reading Skills and Strategies

READING THE MAP

Point out that the numbers on the map correspond to the numbered visuals. Encourage students to read the captions in a clockwise manner, noting the appropriate numbered location on the map. Students should also notice that Japanese cities on the map are in boldfaced type. The names in parentheses following Edo and Heian are those cities' present-day names. Names of Japan's four major islands are in italic type.

PART 2 Capturing the Moment

Literature of Japan

Why It Matters

Simplicity. Discipline. Nature. These three words reflect the major themes of the literature selections that you will read in this part. The words also reflect the foundations of modern Japanese culture. As a result, the best way to understand Japan as it is today may be to study its history and traditional literature and art. You may even find interesting similarities between Japanese culture and your own.

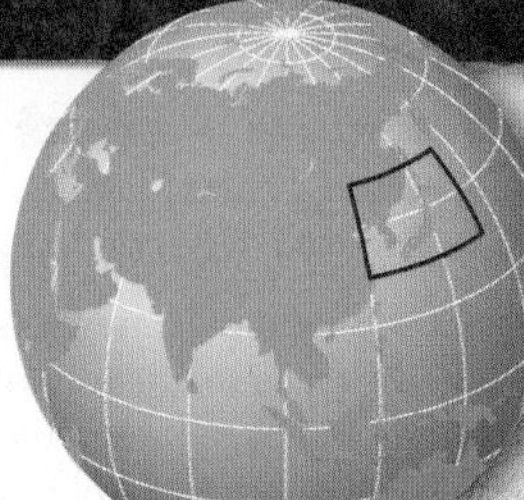

ASIA

CHINA

KOREA

Yellow Sea

Religious Traditions A large red gate usually marks the entrance to a Shinto shrine. **Shinto** and **Buddhism,** the two main religions of Japan, are based on a respect for nature.

For Links to Japan, click on: HUMANITIES CLASSZONE.COM

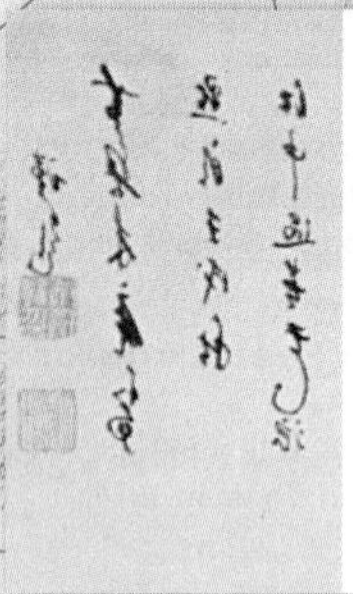

4 The Influence of China Around A.D. 500, Chinese ideas and customs began to influence the Japanese. Important influences included Buddhism and the Chinese system of writing.

3 An Island Culture There are about 4,000 islands in the Japanese island group. Most Japanese live on the four largest islands—**Honshu, Hokkaido, Kyushu,** and **Shikoku.** Many people depend on the sea for food and industry.

486 UNIT THREE PART 2: LITERATURE OF JAPAN

MINI LESSON **Using the Map**

Have students look at the map and identify the two countries closest to Japan. *(Korea, China)* What body of water did visitors from these two countries have to cross to reach Japan? *(Sea of Japan)* Then ask students to think about the advantages and disadvantages of being an island nation. During its early history, how might the country have benefited from its relative isolation in times of war? *(Japan was naturally protected from outside attack.)* What drawbacks might the Japanese have endured in the exchange of goods and ideas? *(Ideas and imported goods would have taken a long time to reach them.)*

1 A Mountainous Terrain About 70 percent of Japan is covered by mountains and hills. **Mount Fuji,** the country's highest and most famous mountain, is considered sacred. More than 100,000 people climb it each year.

2 The Way of the Warrior Beginning in the 12th century and continuing until 1867, Japan was controlled by powerful warlords, called **shoguns,** and their loyal warriors, called **samurai.** The first shoguns established their center of power in **Kamakura.**

Cultural Note

Religion Tell students that Shinto worshipers believe in *kami*, divine spirits that dwell in nature. Any unusual or especially beautiful tree, waterfall, rock, or mountain is considered the home of a kami. The red gates (called *torii*) that stand before Shinto shrines are set in areas of natural beauty. The gates serve as symbolic entrances to the supernatural world of the kami.

Geographical Note

Mt. Fuji Tell students that the early Japanese believed that Mount Fuji, similar to Mount Olympus in Greek mythology, was the home of Shinto gods and goddesses.

Pronunciation Guide
Taira (tī′rä)
daimyo (dīm′yō′)
Go-Daigo (gō′dī′gō)
Ashikaga Takauji (ä′shē-kä′gä tä-kou′jē)
Oda Nobunaga (ō′dä nō′bo͞o-nä′gä)
Toyotomi Hideyoshi (tō′yō-tō′mē hē′dĕ-yō′shē)
Tokugawa Ieyasu (tō′ko͞o-gä′wä ē′ĕ-yä′so͞o)
Sekigahara (sĕ′kē-gä-hä′rä)
Sei Shōnagon (sā′ shō′nä-gōn′)
Murasaki Shikibu (mo͞o′rä-sä′kē shē′kē-bo͞o′)
Genji (gĕn′jē)
Heike (hā′kĕ)

READING FOR INFORMATION
Reading Skills and Strategies
CREATING A TIME LINE
Have students create a time line, similar to the one at the bottom of pages 488 and 489, and label the historical periods and dates. As students read each section of the **Historical Highlights,** they should add important dates to the time line. Keeping their own time lines will help students better understand the flow of events in early Japanese history.

Historical Note
(A) Heian Period Tell students that, during the Heian period, the Japanese nobles looked down on the common people, who could not share in the arts and elegant culture enjoyed at court. These aristocrats lived so far above the common people that they were called "dwellers among the clouds."

Historical Highlights

Until the 7th century, Japan was ruled by strong local clans, or families. In the 700s, however, the Japanese established a centralized imperial government.

Heian Period (A)

794–1185

The Heian period marked the high point of imperial rule in Japan. The imperial court and many noble families moved from the old capital, **Nara,** to the new one, **Heian** (now Kyoto), where a highly cultured court society arose. Gentlemen and ladies of the court filled their days with poetry writing, painting, and elaborate ritual.

During most of the Heian period, Japan's central government was controlled by the rich Fujiwara family. By the middle of the 11th century, however, their power began to be challenged by private landowners, who hired samurai to protect their land. In time, large military clans controlled armies of samurai. This marked the beginning of a **feudal system** of localized rule in Japan.

Kamakura Period

1185–1333

Japan's two most powerful clans—the Taira and the Minamoto—fought for power during the late 1100s. After almost 30 years of war, the Minamoto clan emerged victorious. In 1192, Minamoto Yoritomo became Japan's first shogun, or "great general." Though the emperor reigned from **Kyoto,** which had been built on the ruins of war-torn Heian, the real center of power was at Yoritomo's military headquarters in Kamakura.

Over time, the Kamakura shoguns strengthened their control by assigning **daimyo,** or military governors, to oversee particular regions. The daimyo also oversaw the samurai. By the late 1200s, victories over the Mongols had drained the shoguns' treasury. Loyal samurai became angry when the government could no longer pay them. As a result, the samurai attached themselves more closely to their daimyo.

Ashikaga Period

1338–1467

By the early 14th century, the political and social stability of Japan had weakened. In 1333, the Kamakura shogunate was overthrown by Emperor Go-Daigo, who sought to restore imperial authority. In 1336, Go-Daigo was himself ousted by a powerful military leader, **Ashikaga Takauji.** Go-Daigo set up court in Yoshino, and Takauji established a new military and imperial government in Kyoto in 1338. For the next 54 years, the two imperial courts were constantly at war.

In the early 15th century, the rival courts were briefly brought together when Ashikaga Yoshimitsu, the third Ashikaga shogun, established peace and gained control. However, conditions began to deteriorate once again as the central government's control of the noble landowners under its command gradually lessened. The bitter conflict and political unrest that had marked the Ashikaga period continued as nobles struggled for land and power.

HEIAN PERIOD
794

KAMAKURA PERIOD
1185

MINI LESSON Interpreting the Text

Between the Heian period and the Tokugawa period, what characterized much of Japan's history? *(war)* Why did the shoguns have trouble maintaining a centralized government?
Possible Response: Regional daimyo became very powerful and didn't want to give up their authority.

Warring States Period

1467–1568

In 1467, civil war threw Japan into chaos. Daimyo in hundreds of separate regions took power away from the shogun, seizing control of old feudal estates and offering peasants and others protection in return for their loyalty. They also built fortified castles and created small armies of samurai. These warrior-chieftains became lords in a new kind of Japanese feudalism.

A number of ambitious daimyo sought to take control of the entire country. One of them, the ruthless **Oda Nobunaga,** defeated his rivals and seized the imperial capital of Kyoto in 1568. However, Nobunaga was not able to unify all of Japan.

After Nobunaga's death in 1582, one of his generals, **Toyotomi Hideyoshi,** attempted to complete the fallen leader's mission. By 1590, Hideyoshi controlled most of the country. His later efforts to extend his power by conquering Korea ended in failure.

Samurai sword

Detail of statue of Tokugawa Ieyasu at Toshogu Shrine in Nikko

Tokugawa Period

1603–1867

After Hideyoshi's death in 1598, **Tokugawa Ieyasu** completed the unification of Japan. In 1600, he defeated his rival daimyo at the Battle of Sekigahara. Three years later, Ieyasu became Japan's ruling shogun. He moved Japan's capital to **Edo,** a small fishing village that would later become the city of **Tokyo.**

Under the Tokugawa shogunate, Japan enjoyed relative stability and prosperity. Japanese culture, which began to reflect the tastes of a sophisticated urban population, also flourished. However, in an attempt to control foreign influence, Japan instituted a "closed country policy" for more than 200 years. The policy ended in 1854 when Japan established trade with the United States. B

History to Literature

EVENT IN HISTORY	EVENT IN LITERATURE
Kana, a Japanese writing system based on Chinese characters, is introduced during the Heian period.	Sei Shōnagon *(The Pillow Book)* and Murasaki Shikibu *(The Tale of Genji),* ladies in waiting in the Heian court, write detailed accounts of court life in Japanese.
The Taira and Minamoto clans clash during the late 1100s.	An anonymous nobleman writes *The Tale of the Heike,* a war epic that chronicles the rise and fall of the Taira family.

ASHIKAGA PERIOD	WARRING STATES PERIOD	TOKUGAWA PERIOD	
1338	1467	1603	1867

READING FOR INFORMATION

Reading Skills and Strategies

READING THE HISTORY TO LITERATURE CHART

Make sure students understand that each **Event in History** corresponds to the **Event in Literature** immediately to its right. Point out that each pair of events can be linked in a single sentence that shows their relationship. For example: "Because the kana system of writing was introduced during the Heian period, Sei Shōnagon and Murasaki Shikibu were able to write detailed accounts of court life in Japanese." Then have students link the second pair of events in a sentence.

Possible Response: After the Taira and Minamoto clans clashed during the late 1100s, an anonymous nobleman wrote *The Tale of the Heike,* chronicling the rise and fall of the Taira family.

Historical Note

B **Closed Country Policy** Tell students that Japan sealed its borders largely as a reaction to the rapid spread of Christianity throughout the country. Western missionaries had succeeded in converting hundreds of thousands of Japanese to Christianity. The Tokugawa shoguns feared that the Christian converts, with the support of Christian foreigners, would start another civil war. As a result, the shoguns crushed Christianity and persecuted Christians. They closed the country to foreigners, only allowing trade with a small group of Protestant Dutch.

Pronunciation Guide
Bushido (bo͞o'shĭ-dō')

READING FOR INFORMATION
Reading Skills and Strategies
CLARIFYING
Be sure students understand that the sections on pages 490 and 491 describe life for groups of people during the Tokugawa period. Point out that the groups are organized in the order of their position on the social scale, with rulers at the top and artisans and merchants on the bottom. The **Women in Early Japan** feature summarizes what life was like for women throughout Japan's early history.

Historical Note
Ⓐ **Shogun's Power** Explain that the shogun forced the daimyo's families to remain in the capital when the daimyo returned to their lands. The families would be held hostage only if the daimyo tried to rebel.

Cultural Note
Ⓑ **Samurai** Tell students that even the samurai were divided into an upper and lower class. The two classes enjoyed very different privileges. While upper-class samurai could ride horses and hunt and fish, lower-class samurai could not enjoy these pleasures. In addition, the lower-class samurai received much less pay, forcing them to earn extra money by making handicrafts—a humiliating thing for a samurai to have to do.

People and Society

During the Tokugawa period, Japanese society became rigidly ordered. The rulers were at the top of the social scale, followed by samurai, peasants, artisans, and merchants. Since a person's position was determined by birth, it was nearly impossible for Japanese to improve their social status.

Rulers

The emperor, who was believed to be descended from the Shinto sun goddess, held the highest rank in Japanese society. He lived in a vast palace with his family and other nobles and was never seen by the common people. He held no political power.

Real control of the country was in the hands of the shogun. Ⓐ The shogun acted as a military dictator and ruled in the emperor's name. He oversaw the daimyo who governed at the local level. To keep the daimyo from rebelling, the shogun required that they spend every other year in the capital. When the daimyo returned to their lands, they had to leave their families behind, in Edo, as hostages.

Ⓑ Samurai

Samurai were an elite class of warriors who were loyal to the daimyo. They fought for their lords in exchange for pay and lived according to a demanding code of behavior called **Bushido,** or "the way of the warrior." A samurai warrior was expected to show reckless courage, reverence for the gods, fairness, and generosity toward those weaker than himself. Many samurai practiced **Zen Buddhism,** which stresses self-discipline and living in harmony with nature.

In battle, samurai wore elaborate armor made of metal and wood. The warriors carried richly crafted swords with fine steel blades. The blades of new swords were usually tested on iron sheets, but they were sometimes tested on condemned criminals. Only samurai were allowed to carry swords. More than just a weapon, the sword was symbolic of the samurai's courage and loyalty; in fact, it represented his soul. A true samurai would have died before giving up his sword.

During the Tokugawa period, special schools were established to instruct the sons of samurai. There boys learned such skills as sword fighting, martial arts, archery, and horsemanship. The schools also provided instruction in literature. For, in addition to being accomplished soldiers, samurai were expected to be well versed in the Confucian classics. Many samurai also wrote poetry.

490

Swordsmiths crafting samurai swords

Peasants

In Tokugawa Japan, peasant farmers made up about 80 percent of the population. In theory, these farmers were valued because, according to Confucian teaching, the ideal society depended on agriculture. In reality, however, the farmers bore a heavy tax burden—paying as much as half of their harvests. In order to pay their taxes, some peasants were forced to sell their family members into slavery.

The peasants' daily lives were also harshly regulated by the ruling class. They were not allowed to carry swords or use their family names. They were even told what crops to produce, when to work, what to eat, and what to wear. Fed up with their miserable lives, some peasants took part in uprisings against the ruling class. Others abandoned their farms and fled to the cities. There they mixed freely with samurai, artisans, and merchants.

Artisans and Merchants

Artisans played an important role in Japanese society because they produced the goods necessary for everyday life. In the 17th century, some of the most successful artisans in Japan were roofers, carpenters, and stonemasons. Swordsmiths who crafted samurai swords sometimes became close personal friends of the samurai.

Merchants held the lowest status in Tokugawa society because they did not produce anything. Nonetheless, many merchants enjoyed great prosperity. They sold rice, salt, paper, straw mats, noodles, and other goods. They also acted as bankers, lending money to nobles and samurai. Wealthy businessmen lived in lavish homes in the cities and patronized the arts. As urban areas grew, Japan's merchant class gradually became more powerful and respected.

Women in Early Japan

In the Heian period, aristocratic women produced the greatest literature of the time. **Sei Shōnagon** wrote *The Pillow Book,* a witty and revealing diary of court life, and **Murasaki Shikibu** wrote *The Tale of Genji,* considered by many to be the first novel ever written.

During the Kamakura period, samurai wives managed households alone if their husbands died or went to war. Some of these women even engaged in warfare.

By the Tokugawa period, however, the role of most women had become severely restricted. The supreme duty of a woman was to honor the men in her life. Although the rise of large commercial centers had increased employment opportunities for women by the mid-1700s, the typical Japanese woman was a peasant wife who led a sheltered and restricted life. She carried out her duties at home and in the fields and obeyed her husband without question.

READING FOR INFORMATION

Reading Skills and Strategies

CLASSIFYING

Have students draw a five-level pyramid that reflects the classes in Tokugawa society. Students should place rulers at the top level of the pyramid and merchants at the bottom. Within each level, have students jot down notes about the class's duties, privileges, and place in society.

Cultural Note

C Confucian Teaching Remind students that Confucius was a major Chinese philosopher who was born in the 6th century B.C. Tokugawa society was based on Confucian ideas about classes. According to these ideas, virtue and service to the state were greatly valued, while business and financial matters were despised. As a result, merchants were placed lower than the peasants because they were involved in moneymaking.

MINI LESSON Interpreting the Text

Ask students what words they would use to characterize Tokugawa society.

Possible Responses: highly structured, disciplined, unbending, unfair

Which level of society seemed to have had the most freedom? Why?

Possible Response: The merchants had more freedom because they were able to change their fortune, create their own wealth, and (to a certain extent) reinvent their position in society.

Pronunciation Guide
Kanami Kiyotsugu (kă-nä′mē kē′yō-tso͞o′go͞o)
Zeami Motokiyo (ză-ä′mē mō′tō-kē′yō)
bunraku (bo͝on′rä′ko͞o)
Matsuo Bashō (mä-tso͞o′ō bä′shō)
Andō Hiroshige (än′dō hē′rō-shē′gĕ)
Katsushika Hokusai (kä′tso͞o-shē′kä hō′ko͞o-sī′)

READING FOR INFORMATION
Reading Skills and Strategies
PREVIEWING
Have students preview pages 492 and 493. Ask them to read the introductory information beneath the **Arts and Culture** title and scan the four headings and boldfaced terms on the pages. Then have them study the visuals and their captions. Before students begin reading the sections, encourage them to discuss what they expect to learn about arts and culture in Japan.

Cultural Note
A **Kabuki** Tell students that an edict passed in 1629 banned women from the stage in kabuki drama. Young male actors assumed the women's roles. Later, in 1649, a further edict was issued, declaring that female roles would be played only by older men.

Art Note
B **Woodblock Prints** Tell students that early woodblock prints illustrated beautiful women and kabuki actors. In the 19th century, the Japanese artists Andō Hiroshige and Katsushika Hokusai raised woodblock printing to a more serious art form by creating dramatic landscape prints. With their unusual treatment of light and color, the two artists also influenced 19th century French impressionists.

Arts and Culture

Although Chinese cultural influence remained strong in Japan, distinctive styles of Japanese drama, art, literature, and architecture began to emerge.

Theater

Three very different drama traditions developed in Japan, and all three forms remain alive today. **Noh,** the oldest form, developed in 14th-century Japan as religious drama. Noh was perfected in the late 14th and early 15th centuries by **Kanami Kiyotsugu** and his son **Zeami Motokiyo.** Influenced by the simplicity and discipline of Zen Buddhism, Noh features actors who wear masks and use formal language, mime, and stylized gestures to convey the relation between the real and supernatural worlds.

A Two other forms of drama—**kabuki** and **bunraku**— developed in the 17th century. Townspeople flocked to kabuki performances in which troupes of actors in colorful costumes acted out dramas about historical events or contemporary urban life. Unlike Noh theater, kabuki features elaborate sets, special effects such as trap doors and revolving stages, and melodramatic plots.

During the Tokugawa period, bunraku, or puppet theater, rivaled kabuki in popularity. In bunraku, two or three puppeteers manipulate a single puppet that is four feet tall. The puppets are made to move in accompaniment to music and the tale told by a narrator. During the performance, the puppeteers, musician, and narrator are all visible to the audience.

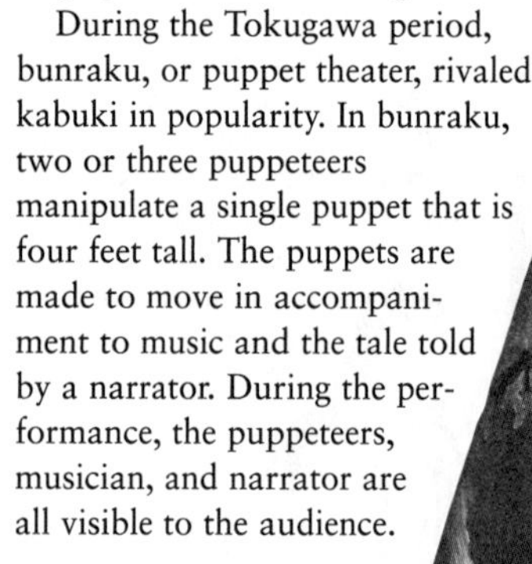
Masked Noh actor

Painting

Japanese art has always been characterized by an appreciation of beauty and tradition. Artists of the Heian period painted scrolls that combined images and calligraphy. During the Kamakura period, many artists used a series of pictures on long scrolls to tell historical tales.

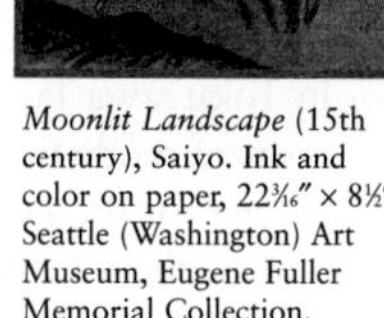
Moonlit Landscape (15th century), Saiyo. Ink and color on paper, 22¹³⁄₁₆″ × 8½″. Seattle (Washington) Art Museum, Eugene Fuller Memorial Collection.

In the 14th century, ink painting began to flourish. Inspired by the art of Sung China, Japanese artists developed their own style of painting with black ink. The works of these artists, who captured scenes of nature with skillful brushwork, reflected the Zen Buddhist values of simplicity and beauty.

During the Tokugawa period, artists captured the sophisticated atmosphere of city life in colorful woodblock prints. The technique of woodblock printing allowed artists to produce many copies of popular pictures and sell them at reasonable prices. B

Literature

Early Japanese writers excelled in poetry. The first Japanese poetry anthology was compiled in about 759. The collection contains more than 4,500 poems. Most of the poems are **tanka,** 31-syllable lyrical poems that deal mostly with nature and love. From the 700s until the 1500s, tanka was the most common form of poetry in Japan.

Literature—poetry and prose—flourished during the Heian period. Most writers at that time were members of the nobility. Two of the finest writers were Sei Shōnagon and Murasaki Shikibu, both of whom depicted Heian court life in their prose.

Toward the end of the Heian period, Japanese poets began to divide tanka into smaller parts. From this practice, Japanese poets created the **haiku,** a 17-syllable poem that presents images of nature. Great haiku masters, among them Matsuo Bashō, wrote their verse during the Tokugawa period.

C Religion and Architecture

Shinto, meaning "way of the gods," was Japan's earliest—and only native—religion. Based on a reverence for nature, Shinto has no complex rituals or philosophy. Buddhism, which was introduced into Japan in the 6th century, is more complex. Buddhists believe that they can achieve peace by eliminating any attachment to material things. A form of Buddhism called Zen came to Japan in the 12th century. Zen followers try to achieve a state of spiritual enlightenment through both self-discipline and meditation.

Statue of the Great Buddha in Kamakura

Many architectural monuments in Japan are religious buildings. Buddhist temples are distinguished by their gracefully curved tile roofs. Shinto shrines are simple wooden structures designed to fit in with their natural surroundings. These temples and shrines and the modern buildings they have inspired reflect the Japanese desire to remain in harmony with nature.

The Golden Pavilion, a Buddhist temple in Kyoto

493

READING FOR INFORMATION
Reading Skills and Strategies
COMPARING

After students finish reading the sections on these pages, have them discuss the attributes of Japanese arts and culture. Ask them what qualities Japanese drama, art, literature, religion, and architecture have in common.

Possible Responses: simplicity, delicacy, love of nature

Cultural Note

C **Religion** Tell students that when Buddhism was introduced into Japan, the Japanese did not give up their Shinto beliefs. In time, Shintoists adopted some Buddhist rituals, and some Shinto gods and goddesses were worshiped in Buddhist temples.

Pronunciation Guide

Todaiji (tō-dī′jē)
Anasazi (ä′nə-sä′zē)
Ki Tsurayuki (kē′ tso͞o′rä-yo͞o′kē)
Yoshida Kenkō (yō-shē′dä kĕn′kō)
Tenochtitlán (tĕ-nōch′tē-tlän′)
Asai Ryōi (ä′sī rē-ō′ē)
Ueda Akinari (o͞o-ĕd′ä ä′kē-nä′rē)

READING FOR INFORMATION

Reading Skills and Strategies

READING A TIME LINE

Have students scan the time line. First, have them read the abbreviations in the legend and find examples of their use. Then explain that the small time line at the top of page 494 represents the span of years covered in this book and indicates the years spanned by Unit Three, Part 2. Finally, point out that the large time line is divided into three sections: **Events in Japanese Literature, Events in Japanese History,** and **Events in World History.** The time line describes some of the major events that occurred during the years covered by this part and is divided into 200-year increments.

Historical Note

A Anasazi Civilization Tell students that the Anasazi lived where the present-day states of Utah, Arizona, Colorado, and New Mexico meet. The Anasazi built impressive cliff dwellings in the sheer walls of deep canyons. By the 900s, the Anasazi were living in pueblos, villages of large, apartment-style compounds made of stone and sun-baked clay. One of the largest, Pueblo Bonito, housed about 1,000 people and contained more than 600 rooms.

Historical Note

B Magna Carta Tell students that the Magna Carta (Great Charter) is the most celebrated document in English history. King John was forced to sign the document, which limited his powers and eventually guaranteed basic political rights to all English citizens. The Magna Carta became a model when other countries, including the United States, created their government.

Time Line

JAPAN (700–1870)

3000 B.C. | A.D. 1 | PRESENT

c. approximately
B.C. before Christ
A.D. after Christ

EVENTS IN JAPANESE LITERATURE

700

712 *Records of Ancient Matters,* a history and one of the oldest surviving Japanese books, is completed

c. 759 *Collection of Ten Thousand Leaves,* an anthology of more than 4,500 poems, is compiled

900

900s *Tale of the Bamboo Cutter,* the first work of Japanese fiction, is written

905 Ki Tsurayuki and others compile the first of 20 imperial poetry anthologies

c. 1000 Sei Shōnagon writes *The Pillow Book*

c. 1010 Murasaki Shikibu writes *The Tale of Genji*

1100

c. 1220 *The Tale of the Heike,* a chronicle of the rise and fall of Japan's Taira (Heike) family, is written

Detail of Japanese screen. Asian Art Museum of San Francisco. The Avery Brundage Collection, Chong-Moon Lee Center for Asian Art and Culture.

EVENTS IN JAPANESE HISTORY

700

752 The Great Buddha, a bronze statue standing more than 50 feet tall, is dedicated at Todaiji Temple in Nara

794 A new capital, Heian (site of present-day Kyoto), is established

800s Kana, a system for writing Japanese, is developed

838 The last Japanese mission to T'ang China is made

900

1100

1185 The Kamakura period begins as the Minamoto clan crushes the Taira clan

1191 A sect of Zen Buddhism is introduced from China

1192 Minamoto Yoritomo becomes the first shogun and rules from military headquarters in Kamakura

1274 & 1281 The Mongols attack Japan

EVENTS IN WORLD HISTORY

700

800 Charlemagne, who unites much of Europe, is crowned emperor of the Holy Roman Empire

900

A **900s** Anasazi civilization in North America enters classic Pueblo period

1095 Pope Urban II issues call for First Crusade

1100

1215 England's King John signs the Magna Carta B

1235 Sundiata founds the Mali Empire in Africa

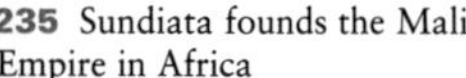

1279 Kublai Khan conquers the Sung Dynasty and establishes Mongol rule in China

1300	1500	1700
c. 1330 Buddhist priest Yoshida Kenkō writes *Essays in Idleness* **1439** The last imperial poetry anthology appears **1443** Zeami Motokiyo, who was instrumental in the development of Noh drama, dies	**c. 1661** Asai Ryōi, a samurai and the first professional writer in Japan, publishes the novel *Tales of the Floating World* **1694** Haiku poet Matsuo Bashō writes *The Narrow Road to the Deep North,* a travel account interspersed with haiku	**1776** Ueda Akinari writes *Tales of Moonlight and Rain,* a collection of supernatural tales

1300	1500	1700
1338 The Ashikaga period begins; two imperial courts are established, one at Kyoto and one at Yoshino **1467** The Warring States period begins	**1543** The Portuguese arrive in Japan and introduce firearms **1549** St. Francis Xavier introduces Christianity in Japan **1603** Tokugawa Ieyasu unites Japan and moves the capital to Edo **1614** Christianity is banned in Japan **1630s** The shogun bans Japanese travel abroad; most ports are closed to foreigners	**1707** Mt. Fuji erupts **1853** American commodore Matthew C. Perry arrives in Edo Bay **1854** The Treaty of Kanagawa is signed, granting the United States access to two Japanese ports **1868** After the Tokugawa shogunate is overthrown, a new imperial government is established, with its capital in Edo **D**

1300	1500	1700
C **1325** Aztecs build the city of Tenochtitlán **1347** Bubonic plague spreads to Europe, eventually killing millions **1368** Chinese rebels overthrow the Mongols **1455** The Gutenberg Bible is produced on a printing press in Germany **1492** Christopher Columbus sails across the Atlantic Ocean	**1607** Jamestown becomes the first permanent North American colony **1631** Shah Jahan orders the building of the Taj Mahal in India 	**1776** The American colonies declare their independence from Britain **1789** The French Revolution begins **1804** Haiti gains independence from France **1830** Greece gains independence from the Ottoman Turks

Historical Note

C **Aztecs** Tell students that, according to legend, the Aztecs were guided to Tenochtitlán by their sun god, who told them to look for a place where an eagle perched on a cactus, holding a snake in its mouth. Today such an eagle appears on the national flag of Mexico.

Historical Note

D **Meiji Era** Tell students that after the Tokugawa shogunate was overthrown, Emperor Mutsuhito established a new government. He chose the name *Meiji* for his reign, which means "enlightened rule." The Meiji government, which lasted until 1912, embraced modern Western ways and began building its empire. Japan became a powerful imperialistic nation, successfully defeating Russia in a war over Korea in 1905.

MINI LESSON Using the Time Line

Have students use the time line to answer the following questions:

1. What event in Japanese history occurred in 838? *(The last Japanese mission to T'ang China was made.)*
2. For what period in Japanese history are there no entries recorded? *(900–1100)*
3. What year did the last imperial poetry anthology appear? *(1439)*
4. How many years did the Ashikaga period last? *(129)*
5. What characterized the events in world history between 1700 and 1870? *(struggles for independence)*

Pronunciation Guide
Issey Miyake (ēs′sā mē-yä′kĕ)
Rei Kawakubo (rā′ kä′wä-ko͞o′bō)

READING FOR INFORMATION
Reading Skills and Strategies
SUMMARIZING
Have students study the visuals and read the captions on pages 496 and 497. Then ask volunteers to summarize the information in each caption in a single sentence.

Cultural Note
Ⓐ **Food** Point out that the items in containers on the sushi tray are used as a dressing. The round bowl contains soy sauce, and the square plate contains pink slices of pickled ginger and the spicy green horseradish known as wasabi.

Art Note
Ⓑ **Origami** Tell students that origami originated in A.D. first-century China with the invention of paper. The Chinese used the folded paper to make such practical objects as vases, bowls, and boxes.

Connect to Today: The Legacy of Japan

Ⓐ **Food**
Traditional Japanese foods have become a part of the American diet. Sashimi (shown above) consists of thin slices of raw fish. Sushi (shown below) consists of cold cooked rice dressed with vinegar and wrapped in seaweed along with slices of raw or cooked fish, vegetables, or egg.

Zen
Japanese tea gardens, such as this one in San Francisco's Golden Gate Park, are popular attractions in many American cities. The Zen-inspired setting offers an oasis of peace and tranquillity to ease the stress of modern life.

Ⓑ **Art**
Origami, or the art of paper folding, originated in China but is traditionally associated with Japanese culture. Both simple and intricate designs can be created by folding a single sheet of paper. One of the most popular origami shapes is the crane, which symbolizes long life and happiness to the Japanese. Origami associations around the world attest to the art's continuing popularity.

Nature
Bonsai, the art of growing miniature trees or plants in pots, originated in China but was perfected in Japan. For the Japanese, bonsai represents the harmony among people, nature, and the divine. Today the miniature trees are cultivated worldwide.

Fashion
In recent decades, many Japanese designers have rocked the fashion world. They have combined Western materials and styles with the traditional Japanese principles of beauty and simplicity to create an innovative look.

497

Cultural Note

C Bonsai Tell students that a bonsai tree is sometimes referred to as "heaven and earth in one container" because it is complete in itself and yet part of nature. Tradition dictates that a bonsai should always be placed in an off-center position in its container. The center point is symbolically where heaven and earth meet, and nothing should occupy that spot.

Objectives

- understand and appreciate a **diary** that provides insight into early Japanese culture **(Literary Analysis)**
- use **point of view** to draw conclusions about the author **(Active Reading)**

Summary

In the entry entitled "The Cat Who Lived in the Palace," Shōnagon tells the story of a pampered palace dog named Okinamaro who falls from favor after frightening a palace cat. The dog is banished from the palace and, apparently, beaten to death. Okinamaro survives, however, and returns to the palace where he is welcomed and granted an imperial pardon. In the other entries, Shōnagon shares her opinions and observations about people's behavior, simple pleasures, and the wonder of nature.

 Use **Unit Three Resource Book,** p. 29, for additional support.

Thematic Link

In these diary entries, Shōnagon vividly **captures a moment** of everyday Heian court life.

 Use **Unit Three Resource Book,** p. 32, for practice with Words to Know.

5-Minute Warm-Up

Daily Language SkillBuilder

Have students **proofread** the display sentences on page 419j and write them correctly.

from

THE PILLOW BOOK

Sei Shōnagon

Sei Shōnagon
965?–1013?

Woman of Mystery Very little is known about the Japanese writer Sei Shōnagon (sā' shō'nä-gōn'). She is widely believed to have been the daughter of Motosuke (mō'tō-so͞o'kĕ), a well-known scholar and poet. However, whether Shōnagon was Motosuke's natural or adopted daughter is uncertain. Even the writer's real name is unknown. *Shōnagon,* a name given her at the imperial court where she served, means "minor counselor"; *Sei* refers to her family name.

A Sharp Wit Most of what we do know about Shōnagon comes from *The Pillow Book,* a sort of diary she kept while serving as lady in waiting to Empress Sadako (sä-dä'kō) during the last decade of the 900s. *The Pillow Book* is a collection of character sketches, lists, anecdotes, and poems that provides a vivid glimpse into the lives of the Japanese nobility during the Heian (hā'ən) period (794–1185). During this period, the capital was moved from Nara to Heian, the present-day city of Kyoto, and a highly refined court society arose among the upper class. The book also reveals Shōnagon as an intelligent woman who enjoyed conversing and matching wits with men as an equal.

Literary Rivals Shōnagon worried about how her book would be received. She probably knew that it would not find favor with Murasaki Shikibu (mo͞o'rä-sä'kē shē'kē-bo͞o'), the author of *The Tale of Genji* (see page 508). Murasaki, a lady in waiting for another empress at the Heian court, had a reputation for finding fault with her contemporaries. In her diary, Murasaki predicted that Shōnagon's unconventional behavior would have terrible consequences: "Someone who makes such an effort to be different from others is bound to fall in people's esteem, and I can only think that her future will be a hard one." Actually, nothing is known of Shōnagon's life after she left the palace. The traditional belief is that she died alone and in poverty. However, that bleak end may have been imagined by those who, like Murasaki, believed that was what Shōnagon deserved.

LESSON RESOURCES

UNIT THREE RESOURCE BOOK,
pp. 29–33

ASSESSMENT RESOURCES
Formal Assessment, pp. 67–68
Teacher's Guide to Assessment and Portfolio Use
Test Generator

INTEGRATED TECHNOLOGY
Visit our Web site: classzone.com

ADDITIONAL RESOURCES
Lesson Planning Guide, pp. 57–58
Teacher's Sourcebook for Language Development

Build Background

Random Notes *The Pillow Book* is the first and best example of a Japanese genre known as *zuihitsu* (zo͞o'ē-hē'tso͞o), which means "random notes" or "occasional writings." In addition to lists, character sketches, and notes, Sei Shōnagon's collection includes brief essays ranging from observations of nature to witty comments on her experiences at the imperial court. Scholar and translator Arthur Waley has called the collection of observations and anecdotes of Heian court life "the most important document of the period that we possess."

In an anecdote appearing in the book's epilogue, Shōnagon claims that she began writing her accounts when a court official brought Empress Sadako a bundle of notebooks.

> *"Let me make them into a pillow," I said.*
>
> *"Very well," said Her Majesty. "You may have them."*

Pillow refers to an informal book of notes written by noblemen and noblewomen at night, in the privacy of their bedrooms. The books may have been tucked away in the drawers of the wooden pillows on which the nobility rested their heads while they slept.

The Pillow Book was not actually printed until the 1600s. It was read, however, well before then. At some point in the process—perhaps after the first draft was completed in about 996—the book apparently was circulated around the court. According to Shōnagon, it was well received. She wrote: "[S]trange as it may seem, people who have read it say such things as, 'You put us all in the shade!'" Shōnagon's wit and the beauty of her language continue to be admired and have inspired Japanese writers for more than a thousand years.

Connect to Your Life

In these writings, you will read lists of things that Shōnagon finds hateful, graceful, and embarrassing. List some of the items you would record under these categories. Then get together with a partner and share your lists.

Focus Your Reading

LITERARY ANALYSIS: DIARY

A **diary** is a writer's personal day-by-day account of his or her experiences and impressions. As you read the excerpts from Sei Shōnagon's diary, think about some of the differences between her account of the period in which she lived and what you might find in a traditional history text.

ACTIVE READING: EXAMINING POINT OF VIEW

Point of view refers to the method of narrating used in a piece of writing. Shōnagon's diary—like any diary—is written from the first-person point of view. That is, the author is an active participant in the events and situations she describes and comments on. While you learn about everyday court life, you also learn about Shōnagon. When you read the judgments she makes about others, you can draw conclusions about her personality.

READER'S NOTEBOOK As you read the diary excerpts, create three different charts and list the things Shōnagon finds hateful, embarrassing, and graceful. After you list an item, write down what the observation reveals about the author.

WORDS TO KNOW **Vocabulary Preview**

ablution, basking, ignoramus, banish, clandestine

READING FOR INFORMATION

Reading Skills and Strategies

USING AN ANECDOTE

Direct students' attention to the second paragraph in **Build Background.** Read aloud the boxed dialogue. Tell students that the "I" in the dialogue refers to Sei Shōnagon. The dialogue is part of an anecdote that explains how Shōnagon came to write *The Pillow Book.* Then read aloud the rest of the paragraph, which explains what a *pillow* was. Ask students to discuss the similarities between writing in a pillow book and keeping a journal or diary today.

Possible Response: Both are written in private, often at night, and kept hidden from others.

TIME MANAGEMENT

If your schedule requires that you cover the lesson objectives in a shorter time, use . . .

- Preparing to Read, pp. 498–499
- Thinking Through the Literature, p. 506
- Vocabulary in Action, p. 507

If you want to take advantage of longer blocks of class time, use . . .

- TE Teaching Options: Viewing and Representing, pp. 500 and 502; Vocabulary Strategy, p. 501; Informal Assessment, p. 503; Cross Curricular Link, p. 504; Grammar, p. 505
- Choices & Challenges, p. 507

Reading Skills and Strategies
PREVIEWING
Have students preview the diary entries by reading the entry titles. Explain that the titles appear in the text in colored bars. Remind students that the entries are randomly ordered. Unlike most diaries, *The Pillow Book* is not a record of its author's daily life. Students should not look for the chronological ordering of entries they would find in most diaries.

Literary Analysis DIARY
Point out that diary writers may include whatever they like, in whatever style they like, in their diary. Sei Shōnagon chose to present an incident that occurred in the palace in the form of a story. As students read the selection, encourage them to look for details that provide information about Heian court life.

 Use **Unit Three Resource Book,** p. 31, for more practice.

Active Reading
EXAMINING POINT OF VIEW
Tell students that Shōnagon plays an active role in "The Cat Who Lived in the Palace." After reading the first page of the story, discuss with students what they have learned about Shōnagon's character.
Possible Responses: She is fond of animals and has an emotional nature. She is not afraid to take action or use her influence.

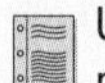 Use **Unit Three Resource Book,** p. 30, for more practice.

Literary Analysis DESCRIPTION
A Point out the description of Okinamaro decorated with flowers. Remind students that description is writing that helps a reader picture events and characters. Ask students what picture the description helps them form about the dog before his banishment. *(a happy, pampered dog)* As students continue reading, have them contrast that picture with later descriptions of the animal.

from The Pillow Book

Sei Shōnagon

Translated by Ivan Morris

Woman and a Cat. Utagawa Kunimasa. Tokyo National Museum.

HUMANITIES CONNECTION The cat in this painting is perched on top of a foot warmer. In the extravagant Heian period, aristocrats were accustomed to luxury.

MINI LESSON Viewing and Representing

Woman and a Cat **by Utagawa Kunimasa**

ART APPRECIATION This woodblock print of a young woman teasing a white kitten is a type of Japanese print called *ukiyo-e,* meaning "pictures of the floating world." These prints most often portrayed scenes from everyday life or from popular entertainment. The "floating world" refers to the Buddhist belief in the fleeting nature of life.

The *ukiyo-e* artists used brilliant designs and bold colors in their works. Invite students to study the **Humanities Connection** on page 500 and to discuss the colors and designs in *Woman and a Cat.* Point out that artists use colors, design, and other details to convey a particular mood in their work. Then ask students to describe the mood created by the artist in this print. What details in the picture contribute to its mood?

Possible Responses: The artist creates a lively, playful, intimate mood. The painting's warm yellow background, the cheerful design in the foot warmer and in the woman's clothing, the expression on the woman's face, the stance of the kitten, and the bows in the cat's and in the woman's hair contribute to the picture's mood.

THE CAT WHO LIVED IN THE PALACE

The cat who lived in the Palace had been awarded the headdress of nobility and was called Lady Myōbu.[1] She was a very pretty cat, and His Majesty saw to it that she was treated with the greatest care.

One day she wandered on to the veranda, and Lady Uma, the nurse in charge of her, called out, "Oh, you naughty thing! Please come inside at once." But the cat paid no attention and went on basking sleepily in the sun. Intending to give her a scare, the nurse called for the dog, Okinamaro.[2]

"Okinamaro, where are you?" she cried. "Come here and bite Lady Myōbu!" The foolish Okinamaro, believing that the nurse was in earnest, rushed at the cat, who, startled and terrified, ran behind the blind in the Imperial Dining Room, where the Emperor happened to be sitting. Greatly surprised, His Majesty picked up the cat and held her in his arms. He summoned his gentlemen-in-waiting. When Tadataka, the Chamberlain,[3] appeared, His Majesty ordered that Okinamaro be chastised and banished to Dog Island. The attendants all started to chase the dog amid great confusion. His Majesty also reproached Lady Uma. "We shall have to find a new nurse for our cat," he told her. "I no longer feel I can count on you to look after her." Lady Uma bowed; thereafter she no longer appeared in the Emperor's presence.

The Imperial Guards quickly succeeded in catching Okinamaro and drove him out of the Palace grounds. Poor dog! He used to swagger about so happily. Recently, on the third day of the Third Month,[4] when the Controller First Secretary paraded him through the Palace grounds, Okinamaro was adorned with garlands of willow leaves, peach blossoms on his head, and cherry blossoms round his body. How could the dog have imagined that this would be his fate? We all felt sorry for him. "When Her Majesty was having her meals," recalled one of the ladies-in-waiting, "Okinamaro always used to be in attendance and sit opposite us. How I miss him!"

It was about noon, a few days after Okinamaro's banishment, that we heard a dog howling fearfully. How could any dog possibly cry so long? All the other dogs rushed out in excitement to see what was happening. Meanwhile a woman who served as a cleaner in the Palace latrines ran up to us. "It's terrible," she said. "Two of the Chamberlains are flogging a dog. They'll surely kill him. He's being punished for having come back after he was banished. It's Tadataka and Sanefusa[5] who are beating him." Obviously the victim was Okinamaro. I was absolutely wretched and sent a servant to ask the men to stop; but just then the howling finally ceased. "He's dead," one of

1. **Lady Myōbu** (myō'bo͞o): a name formed from titles given to a high-ranking lady in waiting.
2. **Okinamaro** (ō-kē'nä-mä'rō).
3. **Tadataka** (tä'dä-tä'kä), **the Chamberlain:** one of the officials in the emperor's private office.
4. **third day of the Third Month:** the day of the annual Peach Festival, when palace dogs were often decorated with flowers and leaves.
5. **Sanefusa** (sä'nĕ-fo͞o'sä).

WORDS TO KNOW
basking (băs'kĭng) *n.* warming oneself pleasantly **bask** *v.*
banish (băn'ĭsh) *v.* to force to leave a place or country

Customizing Instruction

Less Proficient Readers

Explain the following terms used in "The Cat Who Lived in the Palace":

- lady-in-waiting: an upper-class woman appointed to serve the Empress
- gentleman-in-waiting: an upper-class man appointed to serve the Emperor
- Her Majesty: title used to address or refer to the Empress
- His Majesty: title used to address or refer to the Emperor

Set a Purpose As students read the story, have them identify and record its narrative elements (characters, setting, conflict, and plot) in a chart. Also, encourage them to pay particular attention to the actions of Tadataka, the Empress, and Okinamaro. Doing so will help students keep track of what's going on in the story.

English Learners

Students may be confused by Shōnagon's practice of attributing human actions, thoughts, and feelings to Okinamaro. Point out, for example, that the word *swagger*, which is usually used to describe a person's proud way of walking, is used to describe the dog's behavior. The dog also seems to understand the nurse when she tells him to bite the cat. Ask students to look for other examples of human emotions attributed to the dog as they read.

Advanced Learners

Point out that the men in the story treat Okinamaro harshly while the women seem to feel sorry for the dog and want to help him. Then ask students what this apparent conflict suggests about life in the Heian court.
Possible Response: The women lived in close contact at the court and tended to align themselves against the men.

MINI LESSON Vocabulary Strategy

CONTEXT CLUES

Instruction Call students' attention to the list of **Words to Know** on page 499. Tell students that sometimes they will need to infer the meaning of an unfamiliar word by examining all the information in the sentence or paragraph around it. Then read the following excerpt from page 501 aloud: "But the cat paid no attention and went on basking sleepily in the sun."

- Write the model sentence on the chalkboard.
- Ask a volunteer to paraphrase the sentence.
- Have students use the meaning of the sentence to suggest meanings for the word *basking*.
- Ask a volunteer to use the word *basking* in a sentence.

Practice Read the following sentences. Ask students to use context clues to determine the meanings of the italicized terms.

1. The king *banished* the jester from the court.
2. They didn't want anyone to know what they were planning, so they had *clandestine* meetings after school.
3. I looked like an *ignoramus* when I tripped over my own shoelace.

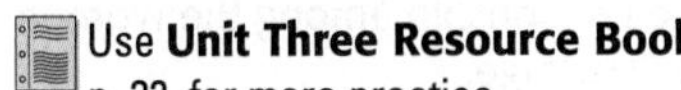
Use **Unit Three Resource Book,** p. 32, for more practice.

A lesson on using context clues appears on p. 674 in the Pupil's Edition.

Literary Analysis DIALOGUE

Tell students that writers often use dialogue to advance the plot of a narrative. Ask them to summarize what they learn from the dialogue on this page. *(The women don't believe that the dog who has entered the palace is Okinamaro.)* Then ask students how the narrative would have been affected if Shōnagon had summarized action throughout the story instead of using dialogue.

Possible Responses: The story wouldn't be as lively and engaging. The reader wouldn't feel as close to the action.

Reading Skills and Strategies PREDICTING

Have students pause in their reading after they finish page 502. Then ask them to predict whether they think the dog will turn out to be Okinamaro. Whatever its identity, what do they think will happen to the dog?

Possible Responses: Students may disagree about the dog's identity. Regardless of its identity, some students will think the dog will be thrown out of the palace or killed. Others will think the dog will be allowed to stay.

Three Women Reading a Letter, Katsukawa Terushige. Tokyo National Museum.

the servants informed me. "They've thrown his body outside the gate."

That evening, while we were sitting in the Palace bemoaning Okinamaro's fate, a wretched-looking dog walked in; he was trembling all over, and his body was fearfully swollen.

"Oh dear," said one of the ladies-in-waiting. "Can this be Okinamaro? We haven't seen any other dog like him recently, have we?"

We called to him by name, but the dog did not respond. Some of us insisted that it was Okinamaro, others that it was not. "Please send for Lady Ukon,"[6] said the Empress, hearing our discussion. "She will certainly be able to tell." We immediately went to Ukon's room and told her she was wanted on an urgent matter.

"Is this Okinamaro?" the Empress asked her, pointing to the dog.

"Well," said Ukon, "it certainly looks like him, but I cannot believe that this loathsome creature is really our Okinamaro. When I called Okinamaro, he always used to come to me, wagging his tail. But this dog does not react at all. No, it cannot be the same one. And besides, wasn't Okinamaro beaten to death and his body thrown away? How could any dog be alive after being flogged by two strong men?" Hearing this, Her Majesty was very unhappy.

6. **Ukon** (o͞o′kōn).

MINI LESSON Viewing and Representing

Three Women Reading a Letter **by Katsukawa Terushige**

ART APPRECIATION Tell students that a work of art can provide a glimpse into the lives of the people it depicts. A picture can show relationships among people and reflect aspects of the society. Clues in a picture can help the viewer draw conclusions about the people and society. Then ask students what conclusions they can draw about the relationship among the women in the print by Terushige.

Possible Response: The two women kneeling and holding the scroll appear to be the servants of the woman who is seated and reading a letter.

What might be the purpose of the screen?

Possible Responses: to separate the women from the men; to provide privacy; to provide an area of peace and tranquillity

When it got dark, we gave the dog something to eat; but he refused it, and we finally decided that this could not be Okinamaro.

On the following morning I went to attend the Empress while her hair was being dressed and she was performing her ablutions. I was holding up the mirror for her when the dog we had seen on the previous evening slunk into the room and crouched next to one of the pillars. "Poor Okinamaro!" I said. "He had such a dreadful beating yesterday. How sad to think he is dead! I wonder what body he has been born into this time.[7] Oh, how he must have suffered!"

At that moment the dog lying by the pillar started to shake and tremble, and shed a flood of tears. It was astounding. So this really was Okinamaro! On the previous night it was to avoid betraying himself that he had refused to answer to his name. We were immensely moved and pleased. "Well, well, Okinamaro!" I said, putting down the mirror. The dog stretched himself flat on the floor and yelped loudly, so that the Empress beamed with delight. All the ladies gathered round, and Her Majesty summoned Lady Ukon. When the Empress explained what had happened, everyone talked and laughed with great excitement.

The news reached His Majesty, and he too came to the Empress's room. "It's amazing," he said with a smile. "To think that even a dog has such deep feelings!" When the Emperor's ladies-in-waiting heard the story, they too came along in a great crowd. "Okinamaro!" we called, and this time the dog rose and limped about the room with his swollen face. "He must have a meal prepared for him," I said. "Yes," said the Empress, laughing happily, "now that Okinamaro has finally told us who he is."

The Chamberlain, Tadataka, was informed, and he hurried along from the Table Room. "Is it really true?" he asked. "Please let me see for myself." I sent a maid to him with the following reply: "Alas, I am afraid that this is not the same dog after all." "Well," answered Tadataka, "whatever you say, I shall sooner or later have occasion to see the animal. You won't be able to hide him from me indefinitely."

Before long, Okinamaro was granted an Imperial pardon and returned to his former happy state. Yet even now, when I remember how he whimpered and trembled in response to our sympathy, it strikes me as a strange and moving scene; when people talk to me about it, I start crying myself.

from HATEFUL THINGS 1

One is in a hurry to leave, but one's visitor keeps chattering away. If it is someone of no importance, one can get rid of him by saying, "You must tell me all about it next time"; but, should it be the sort of visitor whose presence commands one's best behavior, the situation is hateful indeed. . . .

A man who has nothing in particular to recommend him discusses all sorts of subjects at random as though he knew everything. . . .

To envy others and to complain about one's own lot; to speak badly about people; to be inquisitive about the most trivial matters and to resent and abuse people for not telling one, or, if
one does manage to worm out some facts, to 2
inform everyone in the most detailed fashion as if one had known all from the beginning—oh, how hateful!

7. **what body he has been born into this time:** Buddhism teaches that after death the soul or spirit is reborn in a new body.

WORDS TO KNOW

ablution (ə-blo͞o'shən) *n.* a washing or cleansing of the body

Customizing Instruction

Less Proficient Readers

Have students summarize the story using the charts they were instructed to begin on page 501.

Possible Response: Sei Shōnagon and other women at the Heian court are saddened when a dog named Okinamaro is banished from court. When Okinamaro reappears, the women hide him until the dog receives an imperial pardon.

1 Remind students that in addition to stories and anecdotes, Shōnagon's diary contains lists and brief essays. Point out that three lists and two essays follow "The Cat Who Lived in the Palace." The first list begins on this page with the heading "from Hateful Things."

English Learners

2 Point out the idiom *to worm out.* Explain that the expression means "to find out information by questioning someone in a clever and dishonest manner." Tell students that the expression is based on the curved crawling motion of a worm.

Informal Assessment

WRITING A DIARY ENTRY Have students rewrite "The Cat Who Lived in the Palace" as a traditional diary entry. In one or two paragraphs, students should summarize the main events in the story. They should also maintain Sei Shōnagon's point of view and style.

RUBRIC

3 **Full Accomplishment** Student's diary entry shows a thorough understanding of the events in the story and reflects the author's style.

2 **Substantial Accomplishment** Student's diary entry shows a general understanding of the story and a basic grasp of the author's style.

1 **Little or Partial Accomplishment** Student's diary entry shows little understanding of the story or the author's style.

Reading and Analyzing

Literary Analysis DIARY

A Discuss the descriptions of the upper-class people in "from Graceful Things." Ask students how the details Shōnagon provides about the upper class differ from information they might find in a traditional history text.
Possible Responses: Shōnagon provides precise details about their clothing, appearance, and pastimes.

Literary Analysis FIGURATIVE LANGUAGE

B Tell students that figurative language is language that communicates meanings beyond the literal meanings of the words. Explain that types of figurative language include the simile, which compares two unlike things using the words *like* or *as*, and personification, in which human qualities are attributed to objects or animals. Point out the simile in the first paragraph of "I Remember a Clear Morning": "the raindrops hung on [the threads of the spider web] like strings of white pearls." Then have students identify an example of personification in the second paragraph. *("the branches began to stir, then suddenly sprang up of their own accord")*

Active Reading

EXAMINING POINT OF VIEW

Discuss with students the glimpses into Shōnagon's private life as revealed by the lists and essays on these pages. Based on these entries, what do they conclude is important to her?
Possible Responses: appearances, her own comfort, her status, beauty, nature, good writing

1 One is just about to be told some interesting piece of news when a baby starts crying.

A flight of crows circle about with loud caws.

An admirer has come on a clandestine visit, but a dog catches sight of him and starts barking. One feels like killing the beast. . . .

One has gone to bed and is about to doze off when a mosquito appears, announcing himself in a reedy voice. One can actually feel the wind made by his wings and, slight though it is, one finds it hateful in the extreme.

A carriage passes with a nasty, creaking noise. Annoying to think that the passengers may not even be aware of this! If I am traveling in someone's carriage and I hear it creaking, I dislike not only the noise but also the owner of the carriage.

One is in the middle of a story when someone butts in and tries to show that he is the only clever person in the room. Such a person is hateful, and so, indeed, is anyone, child or adult, who tries to push himself forward.

One is telling a story about old times when someone breaks in with a little detail that he happens to know, implying that one's own version is inaccurate—disgusting behavior! . . .

A newcomer pushes ahead of the other members in a group; with a knowing look, this person starts laying down the law and forcing advice upon everyone—most hateful.

A *from* GRACEFUL THINGS

A slim, handsome young nobleman in a Court cloak.

A pretty girl casually dressed in a trouser-skirt, over which she wears only a loosely sewn coat. Some herbal balls are attached to her sleeve by a long cord, and she is seated by the balustrade,[8] her face hidden behind a fan.

An attractive young woman raises the lower part of a white curtain of state[9] and attaches it to the cross-bar on top. Over her unlined robe of white damask she wears a coat of violet gauze. She is engaged in writing practice, and the fine, smooth sheets of her notebook are elegantly bound by threads of uneven shading.

A letter written on fine green paper is attached to a budding willow branch.

A bearded basket,[10] beautifully dyed, is attached to a five-needled pine branch.

A fan with three ribs. Five-ribbed fans are too thick and they look ugly in the middle.

An attractively designed cypress box.

Thin white braid.

A cypress-thatched roof, neither too new nor too old, is beautifully covered with iris.

Below a green bamboo blind one catches sight of a curtain of state whose bright, glossy material is decorated with a pattern of decaying wood. It is pretty too when the ornamental curtain-cord is allowed to flutter in the breeze.

One day by the balustrade before a set of thin head-blinds I saw a pretty cat with a red collar and a white name-tag. He looked very elegant as he walked along, pulling his anchor cord[11] and biting it.

EMBARRASSING THINGS

While entertaining a visitor, one hears some servants chatting without any restraint in one of the back rooms. It is embarrassing to know that one's visitor can overhear. But how to stop them?

8. **balustrade** (băl′ə-strād′): a railing supported by short posts or columns.
9. **curtain of state:** a portable frame hung with cloth strips, used to screen women from the view of men and strangers.
10. **bearded basket:** a bamboo basket with the loose ends of the bamboo wrapped around the outside, giving the basket a shaggy appearance.
11. **anchor cord:** a tether used to keep a cat from straying too far.

WORDS TO KNOW

clandestine (klăn-dĕs′tĭn) *adj.* secret

Humanities

WOMEN OF THE HEIAN COURT Heian women of the upper classes were sheltered from public view by screens and curtains and their ladies in waiting. As a result, eavesdropping and spying were widely practiced at court. However, a woman could find other ways to allow herself to be identified. For instance, she could allow the sleeve of her gowns—and she might wear as many as 12 at one time—to trail beneath her screen or from her carriage door. A woman might also perfume her gowns with a distinctive incense or fragrance that most residents of the court could easily recognize.

Since a woman was sometimes viewed from the back, her hair was another means by which she could be identified. A woman's hair was usually at least as long as she was tall. The long, flowing black tresses created a mysterious effect and were celebrated in both poetry and art.

A man whom one loves gets drunk and keeps repeating himself.

To have spoken about someone not knowing that he could overhear. This is embarrassing even if it be a servant or some other completely insignificant person.

To hear one's servants making merry. This is equally annoying if one is on a journey and staying in cramped quarters or at home and hears the servants in a neighboring room.

Parents, convinced that their ugly child is adorable, pet him and repeat the things he has said, imitating his voice.

An ignoramus who in the presence of some learned person puts on a knowing air and converses about men of old.

A man recites his own poems (not especially good ones) and tells one about the praise they have received—most embarrassing.

Lying awake at night, one says something to one's companion, who simply goes on sleeping.

In the presence of a skilled musician, someone plays a zither[12] just for his own pleasure and without tuning it.

An adopted son-in-law who has long since stopped visiting his wife runs into his father-in-law in a public place.

LETTERS ARE COMMONPLACE

Letters are commonplace enough, yet what splendid things they are! When someone is in a distant province and one is worried about him, and then a letter suddenly arrives, one feels as though one were seeing him face to face. Again, it is a great comfort to have expressed one's feelings in a letter even though one knows it cannot yet have arrived. If letters did not exist, what dark depressions would come over one! When one has been worrying about something and wants to tell a certain person about it, what a relief it is to put it all down in a letter! Still greater is one's joy when a reply arrives. At that moment a letter really seems like an elixir of life.

I REMEMBER A CLEAR MORNING

I remember a clear morning in the Ninth Month[13] when it had been raining all night. Despite the bright sun, dew was still dripping from the chrysanthemums in the garden. On the bamboo fences and criss-cross hedges I saw tatters of spider webs; and where the threads were broken the raindrops hung on them like strings of white pearls. I was greatly moved and delighted. B

As it became sunnier, the dew gradually vanished from the clover and the other plants where it had lain so heavily; the branches began to stir, then suddenly sprang up of their own accord. Later I described to people how beautiful it all was. What most impressed me was that they were not at all impressed. ❖

Detail of *Five Beautiful Women* (early 19th century), Katsushika Hokusai. Ink and color on silk. Margaret E. Fuller Purchase Fund, Seattle Art Museum, Seattle, Washington. Photograph by Susan Dirk. Photo © Seattle Art Museum.

12. **zither:** the koto, a Japanese instrument played by plucking its 13 strings.
13. **Ninth Month:** the autumn month in which the Chrysanthemum Festival was held.

WORDS TO KNOW

ignoramus (ĭg′nə-rā′məs) *n.* a foolish or ignorant person

Customizing Instruction

Less Proficient Readers
Encourage students to use a cluster diagram to keep track of the items in each of Shōnagon's lists. Have students include at least five items in each cluster diagram.

English Learners
1 Explain the multiple meanings of the word *one*. Tell students that *one* can describe a number, and it can also serve as a pronoun meaning "a person." Tell students that the pronoun *you* is often used instead of *one*, particularly in informal speech. Shōnagon uses both meanings of the word in *The Pillow Book*. To help students figure out which meaning of the word is being used, point out that *one* used as a pronoun is usually followed by a verb, while *one* used as a number is usually followed by a noun.

Advanced Learners
Have students read other selections from *The Pillow Book*. Ask them to compare what they already know about Shōnagon with what they learn about her from reading the other selections. Did they gain any new insights into Shōnagon's character? Have students share their findings with the class.

MINI LESSON Grammar

SIMPLE VERB TENSES

Instruction A verb tense is the form taken by a verb to show the time of an action or condition. There are six verb tenses: three simple tenses and three perfect tenses. The three simple tenses are past, present, and future. Remind students that the present tense can also show an action or condition that occurs regularly or is generally true.

Shōnagon recorded her observations.
She writes eloquently.
Her insights will ring true for many.

Underline the verbs as shown, and have students identify the tenses. Explain what each tense tells about the time of the action.

Practice Have students identify the verb tense in the following sentences.

1. *The Pillow Book* will withstand the test of time. *(future)*
2. Shōnagon admires graceful things. *(present)*
3. Her life was interesting. *(past)*

For more instruction and practice in verb tenses, use McDougal Littell's ***Language Network:***
- Grade 10, Chapter 6, "Using Verbs"
- Grade 12, Chapter 4, "Using Verbs"

Connect to the Literature

1. What Do You Think?
Some students may think that Okinamaro's story was the most interesting. Others may prefer the list of embarrassing things.

Comprehension Check
- Okinamaro is afraid he will be beaten again if he betrays his identity.
- Some of the hateful things include a visitor who chatters incessantly, a buzzing mosquito when you're trying to sleep, and a creaking carriage.
- Letters are splendid things because receiving one brings the writer near. Shōnagon also believes that expressing feelings in a letter is a comfort.

Use Selection Quiz in **Unit Three Resource Book,** p. 33.

Think Critically

2. Shōnagon and the other ladies of the court are pleased to have Okinamaro back. They are afraid that Tadataka will try to kill the dog again.
3. Possible Responses: Students might describe Shōnagon as proud, arrogant, sensitive, artistic.
4. Possible Response: Shōnagon couldn't understand how others could be so insensitive to the beauty of nature.

Extend Interpretations

5. **Critic's Corner** Most students will agree, citing Shōnagon's evident appreciation of her own tastes and talents and her contempt for those she considers beneath her.
6. **Connect to Life** Students should note that since people still find many of the same things hateful, graceful, and embarrassing, human nature has remained essentially the same.

Connect to the Literature

1. What Do You Think?
Which part of *The Pillow Book* did you think was the most interesting? Explain.

Comprehension Check
- Why doesn't Okinamaro answer to his name after his banishment from the court?
- What are some of the hateful things that Shōnagon lists?
- Why does Shōnagon consider letters "splendid things"?

Think Critically

2. After the ladies recognize the dog as Okinamaro, why do you think Shōnagon sends word to Tadataka that "this is not the same dog after all"?

THINK ABOUT
- what Tadataka does to Okinamaro when the dog is banished
- how the Empress and the ladies welcome Okinamaro back

3. **ACTIVE READING: EXAMINING POINT OF VIEW**
Review the charts that you created in your  READER'S NOTEBOOK. How would you describe the author, based on the things she finds hateful, graceful, and embarrassing?

4. Shōnagon says that when she described a beautiful morning to people, what most impressed her was "that they were not at all impressed." What do you think she means?

Extend Interpretations

5. **Critic's Corner** Murasaki Shikibu, the author of *The Tale of Genji* and a contemporary of Shōnagon's, wrote that Shōnagon had "the most extraordinary air of self-satisfaction." Based on what you have read of *The Pillow Book,* do you agree or disagree? Explain your answer.

6. **Connect to Life** Review the lists of hateful, graceful, and embarrassing things you created for the Connect to Your Life on page 499. Are any of the items you listed similar to those Shōnagon mentions? Which of her observations do you agree with? Considering that *The Pillow Book* was written over a thousand years ago, what generalizations can you make about human nature?

LITERARY ANALYSIS: DIARY

A **diary** contains a writer's personal day-by-day account of his or her experiences and impressions. In many ways, *The Pillow Book* isn't a typical diary. While most diaries are written in chronological order, Sei Shōnagon's book is randomly arranged. Also, diaries are usually not intended to be read by others. However, Shōnagon carefully crafted her writing with an eye to its eventual publication. Nonetheless, like other diaries, *The Pillow Book* provides an intimate glimpse into the life of its author. In the following passage, for example, notice the details that reveal Shōnagon's duties as a lady in waiting.

On the following morning I went to attend the Empress while her hair was being dressed and she was performing her ablutions. I was holding up the mirror for her when the dog we had seen on the previous evening slunk into the room and crouched next to one of the pillars.

Paired Activity Review the section titled "The Cat Who Lived in the Palace." From the descriptions and dialogue Shōnagon provides, what insights do you gain into life at the Heian court and the author's relationships with the people there? With a partner, list what you learned. Then think about the different kinds of details you might find in a more historical text on Heian court life. What are the advantages and disadvantages of each type of account?

Literary Analysis

Paired Activity The reader gains insight into the roles of the many people who live at court as well as of the status of the court animals. Shōnagon appears to enjoy a privileged position and authority at court.
Advantages of a diary: intimate details provided by a first-hand account
Disadvantages of a diary: lack of objectivity

Use **Unit Three Resource Book,** p. 31, for more practice.

Writing Options

1. Pillow Book Create a "pillow book" of your own. Record anecdotes about school events, and write down your impressions and observations about the students and teachers in your classes. Like Shōnagon, create a title for each group of notes. If you like, you can share some of your notes with the class. However, since a pillow book is meant to be a type of diary, you may choose to keep the contents to yourself.

Writing Handbook
See pages R27–R28: Descriptive Writing.

2. List of Distressing Things Elsewhere in *The Pillow Book,* Shōnagon makes a list of "surprising and distressing things." Think about events that you find both unexpected and upsetting and compose your own list.

Activities & Explorations

1. Scene Illustration Create a drawing or painting that illustrates a description or scene from the selection. Share your work with classmates. ~ **ART**

2. Interview with Shōnagon With a partner, take turns playing the role of Sei Shōnagon and conduct an interview about court life. Write a list of questions to prepare for the interview. For instance, you might ask Shōnagon's opinion of people in the court, including the Empress and the servants. You might also ask about Shōnagon's likes and dislikes. ~ **SPEAKING AND LISTENING**

Communications Handbook
See page R52: Conducting Interviews.

Inquiry & Research

Canine Communication In "The Cat Who Lived in the Palace," Okinamaro seems to express deep emotion when the ladies recognize him. Do you think dogs are really capable of expressing emotion, or do they just communicate their basic needs? Find out what researchers have discovered about how and what dogs communicate. Then share your findings with the rest of the class.

Vocabulary in Action

EXERCISE: ANALOGIES On your paper, write the word that best completes each analogy.

1. nervous : tense :: hidden : ________________
2. brilliant : genius :: foolish : ________________
3. lake : swimming :: sun : ________________
4. liberate : enslave :: invite : ________________
5. overweight : diet :: unclean : ________________

WORDS TO KNOW

ablution basking ignoramus
banish clandestine

Building Vocabulary
For an in-depth study of analogies, see page 768.

Writing Options

1. **Pillow Book** Tell students that they should write freely in their pillow books and not worry about grammar, spelling, and punctuation. Remind them that they will not have to show their diaries to anyone.
2. **List of Distressing Things** Encourage students to use freewriting to get their ideas flowing.

Activities & Explorations

1. **Scene Illustration** Suggest that students try to visualize the description or scene they select before they illustrate it. They can consider shapes, colors, arrangements of objects, and so on.
2. **Interview with Shōnagon** Although students should prepare a list of questions, they should be ready to pursue any new line of questions that might be triggered by the interviewee's answers. When acting the part of Shōnagon, students should try to be consistent with the character of the writer revealed in *The Pillow Book.*

Inquiry & Research

Canine Communication Students may be able to find print material in journals on dogs, animal behavior, or nature. On the Internet, students might begin searching under the key words "canine communication."

Vocabulary in Action

1. clandestine
2. ignoramus
3. basking
4. banish
5. ablution

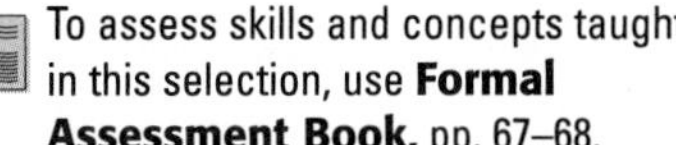

To assess skills and concepts taught in this selection, use **Formal Assessment Book,** pp. 67–68.

The Tale of Genji is generally considered to be the greatest work of Japanese fiction. Although some traditional Buddhists disdained the narrative and condemned Murasaki Shikibu for having described people who never actually lived, this reaction was unusual. For centuries *The Tale of Genji* has influenced Japanese literature and art and its power continues to be felt.

Additional Background

The original text of *The Tale of Genji* in Murasaki Shikibu's own hand no longer exists. The narrative that we have now was derived from the many copies made of the work after it was written. In fact, copies of portions of *The Tale of Genji* were made and circulated around the Heian court before Murasaki had finished the whole work. As the copies multiplied, the text was probably altered somewhat and the chapters were rearranged.

Illustration of the text probably began almost as soon as the copying did. Early readers began illustrating scenes from *The Tale of Genji* for their own pleasure and to enhance the experience of other readers. This practice is recorded in the tale itself. Murasaki describes aristocratic women copying and illustrating romantic narratives or listening to others read them aloud. Reading *The Tale of Genji* was, thus, very likely a multimedia experience.

While women were primarily involved in copying and circulating *Genji*, men eventually became the work's curators. They preserved, collected, and collated the text into its present form. However, whether the 54-chapter work is as its author intended it to be will never be known.

Lady Murasaki Shikibu

The Tale of Genji

Yasunari Kawabata, a Japanese writer who won the Nobel Prize in literature in 1968, has called *The Tale of Genji* (gĕn′jē) "the highest pinnacle of Japanese literature." However, this 11th-century masterpiece, which is considered the world's first novel, was almost totally unfamiliar to Western readers until English translations of the work were published in the 20th century. To this day, little is known about the author of the work, Murasaki Shikibu.

Born around 978, Murasaki was the daughter of a provincial governor who was also a scholar of Chinese and a renowned poet. As a child, Murasaki eavesdropped on her brother's lessons and learned Chinese more quickly than he did. Murasaki's brilliance led her father to regret that she had not been born a boy. In 998, she married a middle-aged man with whom she had a daughter in the following year. Four years after her husband's death in 1001, Murasaki was appointed a lady in waiting to Empress Akiko. Many believe that she penned *The Tale of Genji* while she was in service at the imperial court.

Written at the height of the highly cultured Heian period, *The Tale of Genji* relates the many romances of its hero, Prince Genji, the handsome son of an emperor. Known as the Shining Prince, Genji embodies the high-

Phoenix Hall, built during the Heian period by the noble Fujiwara family

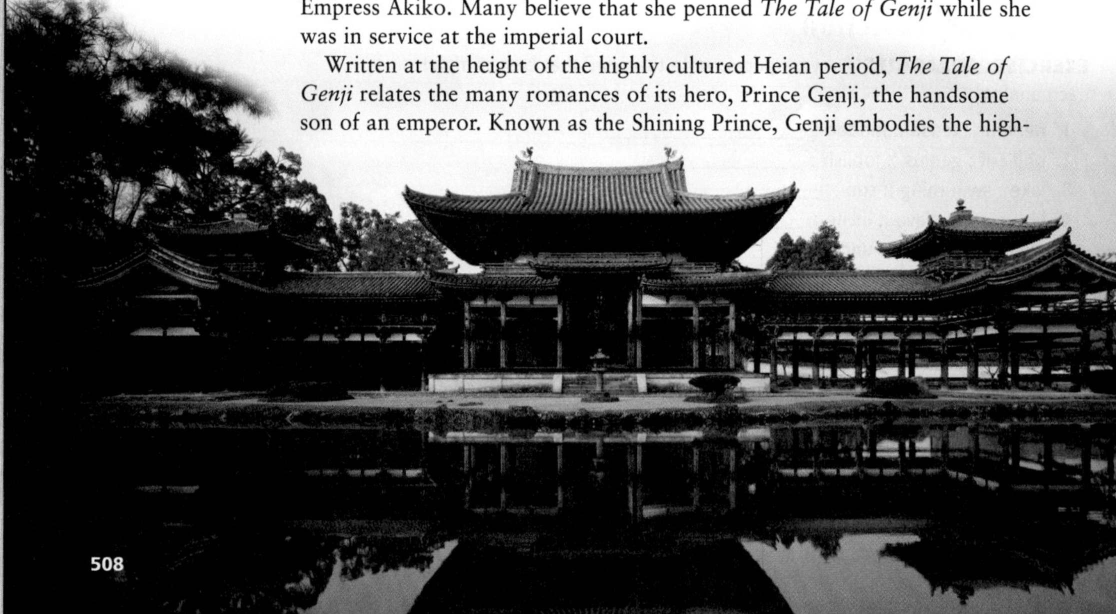

Fan Painting (court lady) (c.1650–1700), Honolulu (Hawaii) Academy of Arts, Gift of John Gregg Allerton, 1984.

Fan showing Murasaki Shikibu at her desk

highest ideals of Heian society—courtliness and sensitivity to nature. During the course of the novel, Genji marries three times and romances numerous women. Following his death, the tone of the novel grows more serious as it follows the next two generations of the prince's family.

The Tale of Genji offers a unique glimpse into Heian court society. The reader learns, for example, that aristocratic women blackened their teeth, covered their faces with white powder, shaved their eyebrows, and then painted brows high on their foreheads. Men used distinctive perfumes as a mark of identification. Both men and women were expected to be accomplished poets. To begin a romance, a man or woman composed a short poem that demonstrated his or her fine taste and artistry. The other person replied in kind. An error in poetic style could end the romance.

The novel does more than provide an account of Heian court life. It also reveals keen insight into the human heart because Murasaki created characters with emotional depth. Strikingly modern in its three-dimensional portrayal of characters, *The Tale of Genji* is often hailed as the first psychological novel.

With its compelling characters and dramatic events, *The Tale of Genji* has influenced Japanese culture for centuries. The novel has inspired painters and poets; its passages have been incorporated in many Japanese Noh plays (see page 518). Japanese readers value the novel for its treatment of such traditional Japanese themes as nature, simplicity, and the impermanence of life. Yet, with its universal themes of love, loyalty, friendship, and family ties, the novel also has appeal for readers around the world.

Prince Genji with his Lover in a Boat Admiring the Snow in the Garden, wood-block print by Utagawa Hiroshige. Copyright © Bass Museum of Art/Corbis.

Literary Chronology

c. 1010 Murasaki Shikibu writes *The Tale of Genji.*

1009–1059 Lady Sarashina pens *The Sarashina Diary* (called *As I Crossed a Bridge of Dreams* in the English translation), which describes the author's obsession with *The Tale of Genji.*

12th Century *The Tale of Genji* is one of the main subjects of Yamato-e, a narrative style of Japanese painting.

14th–15th Centuries Many stories of the Noh drama, including those by Zeami Motokiyo, are drawn from *The Tale of Genji.*

1925–1933 The first complete English translation of *The Tale of Genji*—written by Arthur Waley—is published in six volumes.

1976 Edward G. Seidensticker publishes a new English translation of *The Tale of Genji.*

1987 An animated film version of *The Tale of Genji* is deemed by Japan's Ministry of Education one of the most significant movies ever produced in Japan.

MILESTONES IN WORLD LITERATURE **509**

Objectives

- identify the contradiction and moral in **Zen parables (Literary Analysis)**
- understand and appreciate Japanese **wisdom literature (Literary Analysis)**
- **summarize the main ideas** in Zen teachings **(Active Reading)**

Thematic Link

Zen teachings and parables provide rules for living and convey scholarly learning. They also help the reader understand the spirit of Zen, which emphasizes the importance of living in the present and **capturing the moment.**

5-Minute Warm-Up

Daily Language SkillBuilder

Have students **proofread** the display sentences on page 419j and write them correctly.

ZEN Teachings and Parables

Musō Soseki (1275–1351)

Pupil and Teacher From the time he was a young boy, Musō Soseki (mo͞o'sō sō-sĕk'ē) studied Shingon Buddhism. Soon after his teacher died, however, Musō converted to Zen Buddhism. He received instruction in Zen from both Chinese and Japanese masters but could not find the enlightenment he sought. Enlightenment is a state of spiritual awakening in which the individual rises above the desire for such earthly things as success and possessions. Musō's awakening finally occurred one day when he started to lean against a wall but lost his balance and fell. According to Musō's own account of the incident, his "wall of darkness" disappeared when he fell. In time, Musō himself became an influential Zen teacher with more than 50 disciples, an unusually high number.

Powerful Disciples In the 1330s, a powerful clan by the name of Ashikaga (ä'shē-kä'gä) established a new military government, with its capital at Kyoto. Members of this clan served as shoguns, or military leaders, of Japan. Two of Musō's most powerful disciples were Ashikaga shoguns. Influenced by Musō's Zen teachings, these shoguns instituted new policies affecting commerce, religion, and culture. In this way, Zen teachings helped further the development of Japanese civilization. In addition to teaching the shoguns, Musō also instructed the emperor, from whom he received the title Kokushi (kō-ko͞o'shē), or National Teacher.

Lasting Legacy Under Musō's influence, Zen received official recognition from the imperial court and spread throughout Japan. Musō also helped shape monasteries into serious centers for Zen study. He served at several of these and supervised the building of new temples. Some time before his death, Musō left the following verse to his disciples. The lines reflect the Zen belief that we are merely transient, or temporary, and that our earthly life is a vehicle to a richer afterlife.

> ***With one stroke I erase my delay in the transient world.***
> ***What does this mean? Yasa!***

LESSON RESOURCES

UNIT THREE RESOURCE BOOK, pp. 34–35

ASSESSMENT RESOURCES
Formal Assessment, pp. 69–70
Teacher's Guide to Assessment and Portfolio Use
Test Generator

INTEGRATED TECHNOLOGY
Visit our Web site: classzone.com

ADDITIONAL RESOURCES
Lesson Planning Guide, pp. 59–60
Teacher's Sourcebook for Language Development

Build Background

Path to Enlightenment Zen is a form of Buddhism that originated in China, where it is called Ch'an. According to legend, Zen was first taught by a Buddhist monk named Bodhidharma (bō-dĭ-dür'mə), who came to China from India in the A.D. 500s. By the 1100s, Zen had spread to Japan, where it quickly became a powerful religious and cultural force. During the 13th century, the samurai were drawn to Zen because of the importance it placed on discipline and simplicity. Zen also influenced the arts, inspiring the stylized structure of Noh drama and the conciseness of haiku.

Zen masters and their disciples aspire to achieve a state of spiritual enlightenment called satori (sä-tôr'ē). They believe that satori can be attained through meditation and by living a life of self-discipline and simplicity. Bodhidharma himself is said to have achieved satori only after gazing at a wall for nine years. Zen followers try to open their mind to new ways of thinking. They also try to control their ego.

The selections you are about to read include three Zen teachings and two Zen parables. The teachings are taken from a collection of Musō Soseki's replies to questions posed by one of the Ashikaga shoguns. The parables appear in a collection of stories drawn from a 13th-century book called the *Shaseki-shu* (shä-sĕk'ē-sho͞o') and from anecdotes of Zen monks. Both the teachings and the parables are intended to help others understand the spirit of Zen, which has been described as a door opening to insight.

Connect to Your Life

How would you sum up your own philosophy of life? Do you try to live by a certain set of rules, or do you have a more relaxed approach to life? Get together in a small group and take turns discussing your philosophy.

Focus Your Reading

LITERARY ANALYSIS: WISDOM LITERATURE

Wisdom literature is writing that teaches rules for living and conveys scholarly learning. Wisdom literature often takes the form of **parables,** brief stories that are meant to teach a lesson or illustrate a moral truth. The parables you are about to read contain paradoxes, or contradictions, designed to make the reader question conventional logic. As you read the parables, think about the contradiction each one contains.

ACTIVE READING: SUMMARIZING MAIN IDEAS

When you summarize the **main idea** of a piece of writing, you identify its main point. Sometimes the main point is clearly stated. Other times, however, you must "read between the lines" to figure out what point the writer is trying to get across.

READER'S NOTEBOOK Keeping track of important details can help you identify and summarize a main idea. As you read the Zen teachings, record the details of each in a web diagram like the one below.

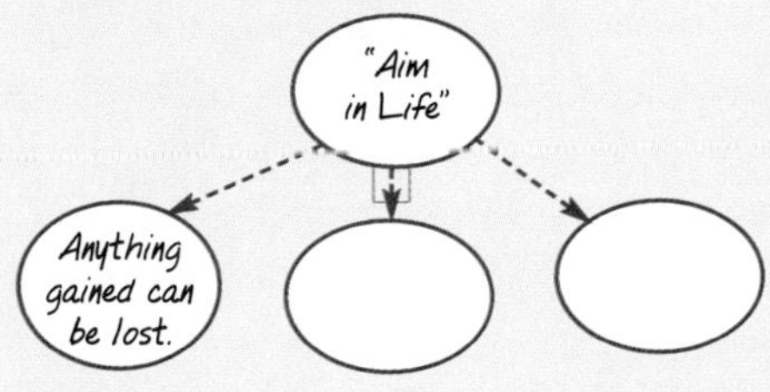

READING FOR INFORMATION

Reading Skills and Strategies

CLARIFYING

Students may have trouble understanding the concept of enlightenment, which is discussed in the biography of Musō Soseki and in **Build Background.** Read aloud and discuss the manner of Soseki's spiritual awakening, or satori. Ask students to recall a time when they were confused by a particular problem and then suddenly experienced a moment of clarity or understanding. How did they feel before the moment of clarity? How did they feel immediately after? Explain that what they experienced was a kind of enlightenment.

TIME MANAGEMENT

If your schedule requires that you cover the lesson objectives in a shorter time, use . . .

- Preparing to Read, pp. 510–511
- Thinking Through the Literature, p. 516

If you want to take advantage of longer blocks of class time, use . . .

- TE Teaching Options: Viewing and Representing, pp. 512 and 515; Vocabulary Strategy, p. 513; Cross Curricular Link, p. 514
- Choices & Challenges, p. 517
- Connect to Today, p. 517

Literary Analysis
WISDOM LITERATURE

Tell students that tone reflects a writer's attitude toward a subject and diction is a writer's choice of words. Then, before students begin reading the teachings and parables, ask them to think about what kind of tone and diction they might expect to find in writing that teaches rules for living.
Possible Responses: The tone would be serious; the diction would be formal.
As students read the selections, ask them to notice the tone and diction.

Use **Unit Three Resource Book,** p. 35, for more practice.

Active Reading
SUMMARIZING MAIN IDEAS

Remind students that the main idea in a piece of writing is its most important point. Provide these tips for identifying and summarizing a main idea:

- Look for the main idea in the first sentence in a paragraph, which is where it often appears.
- Note that all the other sentences in the paragraph should be related to the main idea.
- Summarize the main idea by putting it into your own words.

Use **Unit Three Resource Book,** p. 34, for more practice.

Reading Skills and Strategies
CLARIFYING

Encourage students to reread the Zen teachings and parables and then to stop and review their understanding. Point out that although the teachings and parables are short, the diction and contradictions in the selections make them difficult to absorb in only one reading. To further enhance students' understanding, explain that contradiction is at the heart of Zen, which teaches two seemingly conflicting goals: understanding your own nature and disregarding your own individuality. Have students discuss this apparent contradiction. Ask them to think about how achieving the first goal might lead to the second.

Zen Teachings

Musō Soseki

Translated by Thomas Cleary

Aim in Life

Read to find out what Zen followers think about earthly goods.

There is ultimately no means of safeguarding anything in this world; anything you gain can be lost, destroyed, or taken away. For this reason, if you make the acquisition and retention of goods or status your aim in life, this is a way to anxiety and sorrow.

HUMANITIES CONNECTION Every day the monks at Daisen-in, a famous Zen garden in Kyoto, rake the sand into furrows representing a calm ocean. Three mounds of sand are formed but only two are ever visible at one time, demonstrating that the world cannot be perceived in its entirety.

MINI LESSON Viewing and Representing

Zen Garden at Daisen-in

ART APPRECIATION The Zen, or dry, garden at Daisen-in represents a scene of mountains, islands, and water using only stones and sand. In this miniature landscape, a waterfall flows over cliffs to a river where it passes several islands before reaching the ocean. The garden expresses the idea that a limitless world can be found in a small space. Have students study the **Humanities Connection** on page 512. Ask students what the miniature world in a Zen garden might represent.

Possible Responses: the natural world, life or longevity, paradise

What might be the purpose of viewing a Zen garden?

Possible Responses: meditation, achieving a sense of inner peace, contemplation, appreciating simplicity

Contamination of Virtue

What should be the motivation for doing a good deed?

Doing good seeking rewards is contaminated virtue. Doing good without thought of reward, dedicating it to enlightenment, is uncontaminated virtue. Contamination and noncontamination refer to the state of mind of the doer, not to the good deed itself.

Hypocritical Scholars

Note the author's wisdom about teachers.

Many Buddhist scholars do not actually aspire to enlightenment but really study to enhance their own reputation and prestige and to feed their personal pride. When they get some knowledge, they set themselves up as teachers and fool the ignorant. They tell people their bit of knowledge and interpretation and give formal approval to any scholars whose views correspond with their own. This is a big mistake.

Customizing Instruction

Less Proficient Readers

Help students understand that wisdom literature is literature that instructs human beings about wise and moral behavior. Explain that this type of writing can be found in the literature of most cultures. Point out that the proverbs, or memorable sayings, in the Bible are a form of wisdom literature. The parables in the New Testament are other examples. As students read the Zen teachings and parables, have them think about the messages the selections convey.

English Learners

Students may have difficulty with some of the concepts in the Zen teachings. You might explain the following:

- "contaminated virtue": goodness that has been corrupted, or spoiled, in some way. A good deed performed to impress someone is an example of contaminated virtue.
- "uncontaminated virtue": goodness that is pure. A good deed performed to help others is an example of uncontaminated virtue.
- "hypocritical": something that is dishonest or insincere. A hypocritical scholar, for example, studies not to gain knowledge but to be able to boast about his or her learning.

Advanced Learners

Have students work with a partner to identify similar teachings in other cultures. Ask students to list the teachings they find and share them with the rest of the class.

MINI LESSON Vocabulary Strategy

CONTEXT CLUES

Instruction Sometimes writers suggest the meanings of words with one or two examples. Point out the following sentence in "Aim in Life" on page 512: "There is ultimately no means of safeguarding anything in this world; anything you gain can be lost, destroyed, or taken away." Tell students that they can determine the meaning of *safeguarding* by noting that "no means of safeguarding" is later explained in the sentence with the phrase, "anything you gain can be lost, destroyed, or taken away." Ask students to explain the meaning of *safeguarding* in that context *(to secure or protect something).*

Practice Have students determine the meaning of the underlined words in the following sentences, using context clues.

1. Patience and kindness are virtues to be admired.
2. The groundwater was undrinkable because of contamination, such as bacterial parasites, chemical agents, and animal waste.
3. Retention of documents can be accomplished through several methods: saving files on disks, storing paper documents in a filing system, or binding documents in books.

A lesson on using context clues appears on p. 674 in the Pupil's Edition.

Reading and Analyzing

Literary Analysis
WISDOM LITERATURE

Explain that parables usually have the following characteristics:

- They teach a moral lesson in a short and focused format.
- They are a type of allegory, a work in which the characters and events stand for abstract ideas and principles.

Ask students to identify these characteristics in the parable "Publishing the Sutras."

Possible Responses: The parable teaches that the acts of putting religious doctrine into practice and helping others are more important than writing or publishing the doctrines; Tetsugen symbolizes the spread of enlightenment through Zen Buddhism.

Reading Skills and Strategies
EVALUATING

After students read "Right & Wrong," ask them to identify some of the characteristics of a wise Zen master.

Possible Responses: merciful, forgiving, compassionate, generous, patient

Zen Parables

Translated by Nyogen Senzaki and Paul Reps

Publishing the Sutras

Why does Tetsugen give away the money he collects for his books?

Tetsugen,[1] a devotee of Zen in Japan, decided to publish the sutras,[2] which at that time were available only in Chinese. The books were to be printed with wood blocks in an edition of seven thousand copies, a tremendous undertaking.

Tetsugen began by traveling and collecting donations for this purpose. A few sympathizers would give him a hundred pieces of gold, but most of the time he received only small coins. He thanked each donor with equal gratitude. After ten years Tetsugen had enough money to begin his task.

It happened that at that time the Uji River[3] overflowed. Famine followed. Tetsugen took the funds he had collected for the books and spent them to save others from starvation. Then he began again his work of collecting.

Several years afterwards an epidemic spread over the country. Tetsugen again gave away what he had collected, to help his people.

For a third time he started his work, and after twenty years his wish was fulfilled. The printing blocks which produced the first edition of sutras can be seen today in the Obaku[4] monastery in Kyoto.[5]

The Japanese tell their children that Tetsugen made three sets of sutras, and that the first two invisible sets surpass even the last.

1. **Tetsugen** (tĕt-so͞o′gĕn).
2. **sutras** (so͞o′trəz): scriptures setting forth Buddhist doctrines.
3. **Uji** (o͞o′jē).
4. **Obaku** (ō′bä-ko͞o′).
5. **Kyoto** (kyō′tō): Japan's imperial capital from A.D. 794 to 1869.

History

CHINA'S INFLUENCE Among the Chinese influences brought to Japan were Buddhism, landscape painting, cooking, gardening, drinking tea, and hairdressing. For a time, the Japanese even modeled their government on China's. Many of these ideas first reached Japan through the Koreans, beginning around the 500s.

The Japanese also adopted the Chinese system of writing. Unfortunately, Chinese, with its complex characters and monosyllabic words, was ill-suited to Japanese, with its polysyllabic, highly inflected words. Eventually, a system of Japanese characters, called kana, was developed. However, the new script was considered suitable to be used only by Japanese women. Monks, diplomats, and scientists continued to write in Chinese.

Right & Wrong

Read to find out why students are best taught by example.

When Bankei[6] held his seclusion-weeks of meditation, pupils from many parts of Japan came to attend. During one of these gatherings a pupil was caught stealing. The matter was reported to Bankei with the request that the culprit be expelled. Bankei ignored the case.

Later the pupil was caught in a similar act, and again Bankei disregarded the matter. This angered the other pupils, who drew up a petition asking for the dismissal of the thief, stating that
1 otherwise they would leave in a body.

When Bankei had read the petition he called everyone before him. "You are wise brothers," he told them. "You know what is right and what is not right. You may go somewhere else to study if you wish, but this poor brother does not even know right from wrong. Who will teach him if I do not? I am going to keep him here even if all the rest of you leave."

A torrent of tears cleansed the face of the brother who had stolen. All desire to steal had vanished.

●

Carving of Zen Priest Hotto Kokushi. Cleveland Museum of Art, Ohio/Superstock.

HUMANITIES CONNECTION During the Kamakura period, respected artists began creating realistic sculpted portraits of leading Zen priests. These sculptures were traditionally displayed only on special occasions. In this sculpture, the Zen master's hands are positioned in a characteristic meditative pose.

6. **Bankei** (bän′kā): a Zen master known as a realistic, down-to-earth teacher.

Customizing Instruction

Less Proficient Readers

Explain that a paradox is a statement that seems to contradict itself but, in fact, reveals some element of truth. For instance, ask students why the statement "standing is more tiring than walking" is a paradox. *(Because, although walking would seem to require more energy, standing still is generally more exhausting.)* Because a paradox is often surprising, it draws the reader's attention to what is being said. To help students identify the paradoxes in the Zen parables, have them look for the most surprising statement in each one.

Have students use the italicized focus statement that appears with each parable to help them understand the parable's main point.

- For "Publishing the Sutras," have them answer the question.

Possible Response: Tetsugen gives away the money to help people.

- For "Right & Wrong," recast the focus statement to form a question: What example does Bankei set? Have them answer this question.

Possible Response: Bankei sets an example as a responsible, caring teacher.

English Learners

1 Explain that the expression *leave in a body* means "to leave together at the same time." Then ask students what the expression *to move in a body* might mean. *(to move or act together)*

MINI LESSON Viewing and Representing

Carving of Zen priest Hoto Kokushi

ART APPRECIATION The sculpted portraits of leading Zen masters created during the Kamakura period rank among the greatest works of realism in Japan. The sculptures show an expressive likeness of the subjects by emphasizing the individuality of their features. Have students study Kokushi's face in the sculpture and the **Humanities Connection** on page 515. Then ask them to identify the realistic features in the sculpture.

Possible Responses: large ears, thin face, small mouth, large skull

Why do you think the sculptors chose to create such realistic portraits? What effect do these artists achieve?

Possible Responses: The subjects are identifiable as individuals; the portraits bring the Zen priests to life.

Connect to the Literature

1. **What Do You Think?** Be sure that students give reasons for their opinions.

Comprehension Check

- A person who cares only about possessions and status will know only anxiety and sorrow because these things can easily be lost or destroyed.
- Twice Tetsugen collected enough money to publish the sutras, but each time he gave the funds to people in need.
- The students drew up a petition calling for the dismissal of a pupil caught stealing.

Think Critically

2. Possible Responses: Students who agree might say that the positive results of a good deed are independent of the doer. Students who disagree might say that a good deed done for the wrong reasons is tainted in some way.
3. Hypocritical Buddhist scholars might be considered "contaminated" because they seek reward rather than aspire to enlightenment.
4. Possible Response: The parable suggests that putting one's beliefs into practice is more important than merely publishing those beliefs.
5. Possible Response: The thief is moved by Bankei's determination to help him.
6. Possible Summaries: "Aim in Life"—You will be unhappy if you dedicate your life to the attainment of material goods; "Contamination of Virtue"—Those who wish to be rewarded for a good deed taint the intention of the deed but not the deed itself; "Hypocritical Scholars"—Buddhist scholars who study and teach only to enhance their reputation are hypocrites and fool only the ignorant.

Connect to the Literature

1. **What Do You Think?** Which teaching or parable did you like the best? Why?

Comprehension Check

- According to Muso- Soseki, what will happen to a person who cares only about possessions and status?
- Why did Tetsugen take 20 years to publish the sutras?
- Why did Bankei's pupils become angry and draw up a petition?

Think Critically

2. According to Musō Soseki, a good deed cannot be spoiled by the selfish intentions of the doer. Do you agree? Explain your answer.
3. Why might the state of mind of a hypocritical Buddhist scholar be considered "contaminated"?
4. What does the parable "Publishing the Sutras" suggest about what is important to Zen followers?
5. In the parable "Right & Wrong," the thief cries and loses his desire to steal after Bankei refuses to dismiss him. Why do you think Bankei's decision has such a powerful effect on the thief?
6. **ACTIVE READING: SUMMARIZING MAIN IDEAS** Compare the web diagram that you created in your **READER'S NOTEBOOK** with those of some of your classmates. Based on the details you recorded, how would you summarize the **main idea** in each Zen teaching?

Extend Interpretations

7. **Comparing Texts** Compare the Zen teachings and stories you have read with the teachings from the *Tao Te Ching* (page 440). What do both philosophies teach about worldly possessions? Which philosophy do you think would be more difficult to follow? Explain your answer.
8. **Connect to Life** Bankei refuses to give up trying to teach his student right from wrong. Think of a time when someone showed a great deal of patience while trying to teach you something. What did you learn? How did you feel toward your teacher? Do you think patience is a necessary characteristic of a teacher?

LITERARY ANALYSIS: WISDOM LITERATURE

Writing that teaches rules for living and conveys scholarly learning is called **wisdom literature.** One form of wisdom literature is the **parable**—a story that teaches a moral or lesson about life. The story told in a Zen parable often appears simple, but it contains a deep underlying message. A Zen parable may also contain a paradox, or contradiction. For example, consider the contradiction in the following lines from "Publishing the Sutras":

The Japanese tell their children that Tetsugen made three sets of sutras, and that the first two invisible sets surpass even the last.

Thinking about the contradiction presented in a story can help you infer the story's message, or moral.

Cooperative Learning Activity With a group of classmates, analyze the two Zen parables you have read. Identify the contradiction in each parable. Then use your understanding of the contradiction to help you decide the parable's moral. Write down your ideas in a chart like the one shown below. Share your conclusions with the rest of the class.

Parable	Contradiction	Moral
"Publishing the Sutras"		
"Right & Wrong"		

Extend Interpretations

7. **Comparing Texts** Both Zen and Taoism teach the unimportance of worldly possessions. Many students will think Zen would be more difficult to follow because, unlike Taoism, the philosophy provides few guidelines and precepts for behavior.
8. **Connect to Life** Students should recall a teacher whose patience enabled them to learn something they had difficulty comprehending. Most will appreciate the teacher's effort and think that patience is a necessary characteristic of a teacher.

Literary Analysis

Cooperative Learning Activity Possible Responses: "Publishing the Sutras"—Contradiction: The first two sets of invisible sutras surpass the third real set; Moral: Actions are more valuable than words.
"Right & Wrong"—Contradiction: Bankei will allow the thieving pupil to stay even if all the other pupils leave; Moral: An amoral pupil is in need of more instruction than those who know right from wrong.

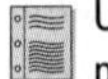
Use **Unit Three Resource Book,** p. 35, for more practice.

Writing Options

Zen Solutions Suppose someone in your class constantly cheats on tests. Imagine that this person copies others' answers and secretly uses detailed notes during tests. As a result of this cheating, the person receives high grades. Think about how you would apply what you have learned from the Zen teachings and parables to deal with this problem. Then write a paragraph explaining how you would handle the matter. Place the paragraph in your **Working Portfolio.**

Connect to Today

Zen—Alive and Well

When Zen was introduced in the West in the 20th century, people found new ways to express and interpret its spirit. In the 1950s, for example, the Beats—a group of young, unconventional writers—interpreted Zen as a philosophy of living without restrictions or inhibitions. Beat writers such as Jack Kerouac and Allen Ginsberg tried to express their Zen spirit by producing works that were spontaneous, free of literary devices, and unrestricted by formal grammar.

Here are some other ways that the Zen spirit survives today.

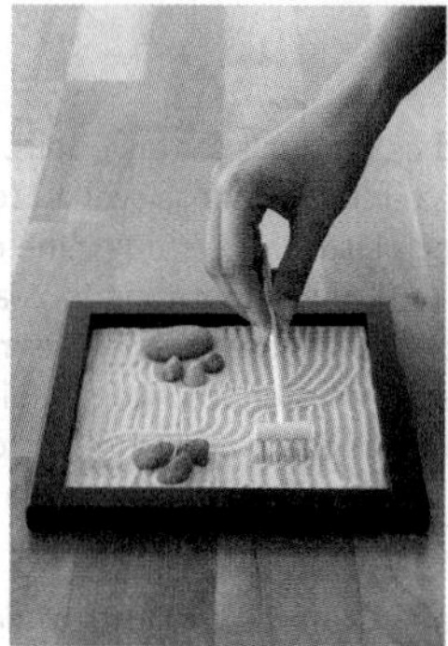

Today, certain companies manufacture miniature desktop "gardens" that mimic the type of traditional Zen garden discussed on page 512. Considered a workplace "toy," these miniature gardens are quite popular.

To reduce the stress of daily modern life and find meaning in a world dominated by possessions and status, many people have turned to Zen meditation.

In karate, a traditional Japanese martial art, students practice a sort of meditation in action. They are expected to perform all movements with an intense, Zenlike focus on the present.

Paired or Group Discussion Do you think Zen can be a part of everyday life as we live it today? If true Zen lies in being fully present in the here and now, how can you adapt Zen to taking a test? playing computer games? standing in line at the grocery store?

Writing Options

Zen Solutions In their essays, students should clearly state the problem and explain how they would solve it. A Zen solution to the problem would probably involve an effort to work with the student and explain why this behavior is wrong.

To assess skills and concepts taught in this selection, use **Formal Assessment Book,** pp. 69–70.

Connect to Today

Use this feature to show the relevance of world literature to students. The material relates the literature selection just read to a contemporary topic connected to students' lives today.

Paired or Group Discussion Possible Responses: Zen might help students achieve a sense of calm during a test, remove their competitive edge while playing a computer game, and instill them with patience while standing in line at the grocery store.

Objectives

- understand and appreciate a Japanese **Noh drama (Literary Analysis)**
- identify and examine the relationship between **setting and characters (Literary Analysis)**
- use a **questioning** strategy to understand the setting, characters, and action in a challenging play **(Active Reading)**

Summary

A traveler and two companions journey to Mount Obasute in mid-autumn to view the full moon. There the traveler meets an old woman and, later, a villager. The villager tells the traveler the story of Mount Obasute: Long ago, a man abandoned his aunt on the mountain and she turned to stone. The old woman's spirit still clings to the world and returns to Mount Obasute at the time of the full moon. The traveler realizes that the woman's spirit spoke to him through the old woman he met earlier. That night the ghost of the old woman appears before the traveler. She dances and tells him of her longing for the world and her unsuccessful attempts to leave it behind.

Use **Unit Three Resource Book,** p. 36, for additional support.

Thematic Link

In *The Deserted Crone,* Zeami Motokiyo tells the sad tale of an old woman who is unable to leave the material world behind. The woman's inability to **capture the moment** and set her spirit free dooms her to constantly relive the past.

Use **Unit Three Resource Book,** p. 39, for practice with Words to Know.

5-Minute Warm-Up

Daily Language SkillBuilder

Have students **proofread** the display sentences on page 419j and write them correctly.

THE DESERTED CRONE

Zeami Motokiyo

Father and Son Born in 1363, Zeami Motokiyo (zä-ä'mē mō'tō-kē'yō) is known as the leading playwright of Japanese Noh (nō) drama. Noh began in 14th-century Japan as religious drama. Zeami, along with his father, Kanami Kiyotsugu (kän-ä'mē kē'yō-tso͞o'go͞o), developed Noh into one of the world's great dramatic forms. In 1374, when Zeami was only 11 years old, he and his father, both Noh actors, performed before the shogun Ashikaga Yoshimitsu (ä'shē-kä'gä yō'shē-mē'tso͞o). The military leader was so impressed with the two actors that he offered their troupe his patronage. After Kanami died, Zeami took over the Noh acting school that his father had started. Zeami also began writing sophisticated new plays for his aristocratic audience. In 1422, Zeami became a Zen monk, and his son Motomasa (mō'tō-mä'sä) took his place as the leading figure in Noh theater.

Writer and Critic Zeami was the most prolific and talented of the Noh playwrights. In addition to plays, Zeami also wrote critical works on the Noh. His treatises were intended as manuals for his pupils, who began their training as children. In these works, Zeami identified the main principles of Noh acting. One of these he called *yūgen* (yo͞o'gĕn). According to Zeami, *yūgen* was "true beauty and gentleness." The term was also used to name the mysterious, indefinable quality underlying the text of the play and the actors' gestures. Zeami's own performances were said to convey this mysterious quality.

Exile and Death Zeami's charmed existence ended in 1429 when another member of the Ashikaga clan became shogun. The new military leader refused to allow Zeami's son Motomasa to perform at the imperial court in Kyoto. Motomasa died in 1432, and Zeami was exiled in 1434. He was allowed to return to Kyoto after the shogun's death in 1441. Zeami died just two years later. According to legend, the greatest playwright of Noh drama died alone in a Buddhist temple near Kyoto in 1443.

LESSON RESOURCES

UNIT THREE RESOURCE BOOK, pp. 36–40

ASSESSMENT RESOURCES
Formal Assessment, pp. 71–72
Teacher's Guide to Assessment and Portfolio Use
Test Generator

INTEGRATED TECHNOLOGY
Visit our Web site: classzone.com

ADDITIONAL RESOURCES
Lesson Planning Guide, pp. 61–62
Teacher's Sourcebook for Language Development

Build Background

The Magic of Noh Theater The curtain opens on a square stage with little scenery. A single note from a flute is played, and several characters appear in stylized masks and costumes. As the Noh play unfolds, the main character is revealed to be a ghost who is reluctant to leave the world. A long dance concludes the play.

Noh theater developed from dances performed at Shinto and Buddhist temples and shrines during harvest festivals and other celebrations. The dramatic form developed by Zeami retained its religious roots and appealed to Zen Buddhists because the plays were said to lead to spiritual enlightenment.

Every Noh play features certain principal roles. Here are the roles in *The Deserted Crone*.

shite (shē'tĕ): the main character, who performs the central dance

mae-jite (mī'jē'tĕ): the shite of the first part of the play

nochi-jite (nō'chē-jē'tĕ): the shite of the second part of the play

waki (wä'kē): a secondary character, who asks questions or introduces the story

wakizure (wä'kē-zo͞o'rĕ): a companion of the waki

kyōgen (kyō'gĕn): a peasant or villager from the area in which the play is set

Noh and Greek Drama

In some ways, Noh is similar to Greek drama. In both forms, all the roles are performed by male actors who wear masks to convey character and emotion. Like a Greek tragedy, Noh drama is accompanied by dance, music, and a chorus. Plays in the two forms are often based on historical and legendary traditions.

Unlike a Greek tragedy, however, a Noh play involves little actual drama. The lines are spoken slowly, and Noh actors use gestures and movements to suggest meaning. Although a typical Noh play is only as long as a single act in a Greek play, the performance usually takes about an hour. The time is absorbed by the slow recitation of the lines and the concluding dance.

Connect to Your Life

Get together with a partner or small group and discuss a play you have seen performed recently, either live or on a movie or television screen. How does watching a play differ from watching a movie? What do you enjoy most about seeing a play? What do you like least? Jot down your thoughts.

Focus Your Reading

LITERARY ANALYSIS: SETTING AND CHARACTERS

The **setting** of a play is the time and place of the action. In Noh drama, often the only scenery on stage is a pine tree at the back. Thus, setting must be suggested by the play's dialogue and action. **Characters** are the people who participate in the action. Noh characters appear flat and one-dimensional. However, the words they speak help convey **mood,** or feeling. As you read the play, think about the relationship between the setting and the characters.

ACTIVE READING: QUESTIONING

When you read a challenging piece of writing, it is often helpful to stop occasionally and question what is happening. Searching for reasons behind events and characters' feelings can help you understand what you are reading.

READER'S NOTEBOOK As you read *The Deserted Crone,* write down any questions you have about the characters, setting, and action. Write down the answers, too, if you can figure them out from the text.

WORDS TO KNOW **Vocabulary Preview**

delusion inhospitable unimpeded
fleeting solace

READING FOR INFORMATION
Reading Skills and Strategies
COMPARING AND CONTRASTING

Discuss the comparison of Noh and Greek drama that appears on page 519. To help students visualize the similarities and differences between the two types of drama, draw a Venn diagram on the board. Fill in the diagram during the class discussion. You might want to leave the diagram on the board. After students finish reading the play, encourage them to come up with new characteristics to add to the diagram.

TIME MANAGEMENT

If your schedule requires that you cover the lesson objectives in a shorter time, use . . .

- Preparing to Read, pp. 518–519
- Thinking Through the Literature, p. 532
- Vocabulary in Action, p. 533

If you want to take advantage of longer blocks of class time, use . . .

- TE Teaching Options: Grammar, pp. 520 and 529; Cross Curricular Link, pp. 521, 522, 526, and 530; Speaking and Listening, pp. 523 and 524; Vocabulary Strategy, p. 525; Viewing and Representing, pp. 527 and 528;
- Choices & Challenges, p. 533

Reading Skills and Strategies
PREVIEWING
Encourage students to scan the Noh play before they begin reading it. Have them read the **Focus** statement and study the diagram of the Noh stage on page 520. Also, have students look at the art and read the captions. The masks in particular may help students visualize the stylized nature of a Noh play.

Guide for Reading
Direct students' attention to the **Guide for Reading** and **Focus** headings on this page. Explain that the information under the Focus heading is intended to help them understand the play and concentrate on its main ideas. Tell students that at two points during the play, two **Pause & Reflect** questions will ask them to stop and think about what they have read.

Literary Analysis DICTION
A Tell students that the diction, or word choice, in *The Deserted Crone* is formal and abstract. Point out that the diction suits the form and theme of the Noh drama. Then have students explain the meaning of the phrase "bestirred myself." *(urged myself to take action)* As students read, encourage them to list formal and abstract words and phrases from the play and then write a synonym for each word listed.

Active Reading QUESTIONING
Tell students that the words in a Noh play are often used to symbolize action. Then ask students what action is represented by lines 9–13. *(The traveler and his companions are journeying to Sarashina.)*

Use **Unit Three Resource Book,** p. 37, for more practice.

The Deserted Crone

Zeami Motokiyo

Translated by Stanleigh H. Jones, Jr.

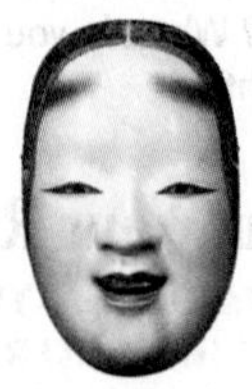
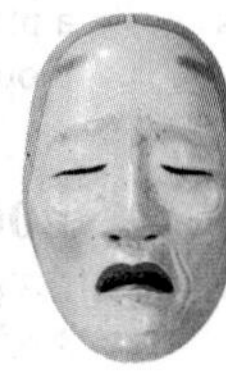
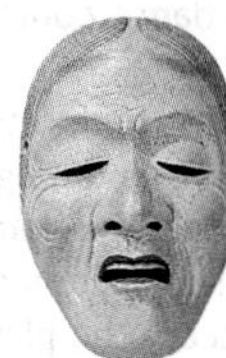

GUIDE FOR READING

FOCUS In this play, a traveler journeys to Mount Obasute to view the full moon at the height of autumn. Read to find out whom he encounters at Obasute and what he learns there.

PERSONS A Traveler from the Capital (*waki*)
Two Companions to the traveler (*wakizure*)
An Old Woman (*mae-jite*)
The Ghost of the old woman (*nochi-jite*)
A Villager (*kyōgen*)

PLACE Mount Obasute (ō'bä-sōō'tĕ) in Shinano Province

TIME The fifteenth night of the eighth month (midpoint of autumn, when the moon is full)

THE NOH STAGE

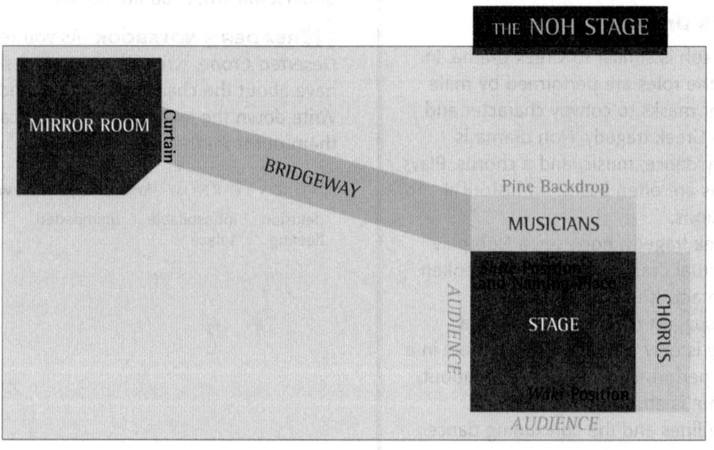

MINI LESSON **Grammar**

PERFECT VERB TENSES

Instruction Remind students that there are six verb tenses. The three simple verb tenses are past, present, future. The three perfect tenses are past perfect, present perfect, and future perfect. Explain the tenses and write their examples on the board as follows.

Present perfect tense places an action or condition in a stretch of time leading up to the present:

The traveler has reached the mountain.

Past perfect tense places a past action or condition before another past action or condition:

The old woman had lived near the mountain before she was abandoned.

Future perfect tense shows that an action or a condition in the future will precede another future action or condition:

By the time the moon rises, the ghost will have appeared.

Practice Have students identify the perfect verb tenses in the following sentences.

1. Half of autumn will have passed. *(future perfect)*
2. That aged figure has come again. *(present perfect)*
3. There's a gentleman I have never seen before. *(present perfect)*

For more instruction, and practice in verb tenses, use McDougal Littell's ***Language Network:***
- Grade 10, Chapter 6, "Using Verbs"
- Grade 12, Chapter 4, "Using Verbs"

Scene from a Noh play

(*A* Traveler *and two* Companions *from the Capital* [Kyoto] *enter and face each other at stage center. They wear short swords and conical* kasa *hats made of reeds.*)

Together. Autumn's height,
The full moon's night is near,
Soon the full moon's glory.
Let us go and visit Mount Obasute.

(*The* Traveler *removes his hat and faces front.*)

Traveler. I am a man of the Capital. I have yet to see the moon of Sarashina and this autumn I have bestirred
A myself at last. I hurry now to Obasute Mountain.

(*He puts his hat back on and faces his* Companions.)

Together. On our journey—
1 Fleeting are the dreams at inns along the way,
Fleeting are the dreams at inns along the way,
And once again we take our leave;
Nights and days in lonely hostels
Bring us here to famed Sarashina,

(*The* Traveler *faces front and takes a few steps forward, then returns to his place.*)

6 **Sarashina** (sä'rä-shē'nä): a locale in the mountains of central Japan—a popular place for viewing the moon.

WORDS TO KNOW

fleeting (flē'tĭng) *adj.* happening or passing swiftly

Customizing Instruction

Less Proficient Readers

Tell students that *crone* is an impolite word used to refer to an old woman. Then ask them to explain what "deserted crone" means. *(abandoned old woman)*

Point out that throughout the drama, lines of verse are indented while lines of prose dialogue are not. Ask students to identify lines of verse and dialogue on page 521.

English Learners

1 Point out that the repeated lines spoken by the traveler and his companions are not a mistake. Explain that repetition is often used in poetry. In this case, the lines are repeated for emphasis and to create rhythm.

Advanced Learners

Ask students to think about the author's purpose for creating the traveler. Whose point of view does he represent?

Possible Response: The traveler represents the reader's or audience's point of view.

Cross Curricular Link **Humanities**

MOON VIEWING IN JAPAN On September 15th, a traditional moon-viewing ceremony, called Otsuki-mi, is held in Japan. The night of the 15th is considered the best time to view the full moon because the sky is particularly clear at that time of year. Across the country, the Japanese celebrate by offering autumn foods, such as chestnuts, watermelons, and rice dumplings, to the full moon. They place these foods on tables placed outdoors or on windowsills. Unfortunately, this traditional moon-viewing ceremony is not observed as frequently as it once was because of the smog and high-rise buildings in cities.

Reading and Analyzing

Literary Analysis SETTING AND CHARACTERS

Remind students that the setting of a play is the time and place of the action. Characters are the people who take part in the action. Have students identify the setting of *The Deserted Crone* and name the characters they have encountered so far. *(setting: Obasute Mountain; characters: traveler, companions, old woman)* What words would students use to describe the setting?

Possible Responses: remote, lonely, beautiful

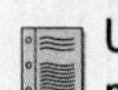

Use **Unit Three Resource Book,** p. 38, for more practice.

Active Reading QUESTIONING

A Why does the old woman call the traveler's question "thoughtless"?

Possible Responses: She knew the woman who was abandoned there; she is old herself and identifies with the abandoned woman's fate.

Literary Analysis PERSONIFICATION

B Tell students that personification is a figure of speech in which human qualities are attributed to things or animals. Ask students to explain why "The lonely heart of autumn" is an example of personification. *(because a heart and feelings of loneliness are attributed to the season)* Encourage students to look for other examples of personification as they read the play.

Literary Analysis CHORUS

Point out the use of a chorus in the drama. Tell students that a chorus is a group of people who speak or sing in unison during a drama. In Noh plays, the chorus consists of eight to ten men who sit alongside the stage. The chorus often speaks for the characters; it may also narrate or explain what is happening in the play. The chorus is accompanied by the orchestra, which consists of a flute player and several drummers. As students read the play, have them note the role of the chorus.

Together. We have reached Obasute Mountain, Reached Obasute Mountain.

(*His return indicates that he has arrived. He takes off his hat and faces front.*)

Traveler. We have traveled so swiftly that we are here already at Mount Obasute.

Companion. Indeed, that is so.

(*The* Companions *move to the* waki-*position. The* Traveler *goes to stage center.*)

Traveler. Now that I am here at Mount Obasute I see that all is just as I imagined it—the level crest, the infinite sky, the unimpeded thousands of leagues of night flooded by the moon so clear. Yes, here I will rest and tonight gaze upon the moon.

(*The* Old Woman, *wearing the* fukai *mask, slowly starts down the bridgeway. The* Traveler *moves to the* waki-*position.*)

Old Woman. You there, traveler, what is it you were saying?

(Traveler, *standing, goes downstage left.*)

Traveler. I have come from the Capital, and this is my first visit here. But tell me, where do you live?

Old Woman. In this village, Sarashina. Tonight is that mid-autumn night for which all have waited.

The moon has hurried the dusk of day,
And now the high plain of heaven
Glows in mounting brilliance—
In all directions, the crystalline night.
How wonderful the moon this evening!

Traveler. Oh, are you from Sarashina? Can you tell me then the spot where in ancient days the old woman was left to die?

(*The* Old Woman *has reached the* shite-*position.*)

A **Old Woman.** You ask of the fate of the old woman of Obasute?—a thoughtless question. But if you mean the remains of the woman who sang:

"No solace for my heart at Sarashina
When I see the moon
Shining down on Mount Obasute,"

[Stage Direction] ***fukai*** (fo͝o′kī) **mask:** a mask representing the face of a middle-aged woman.

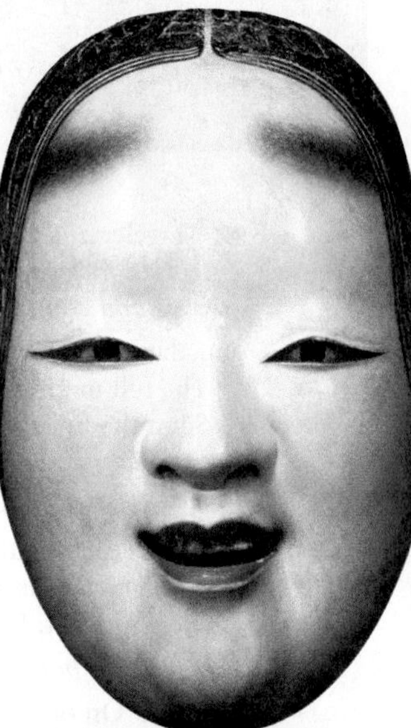

Noh mask, Momoyama period (1573–1615).

WORDS TO KNOW

unimpeded (ŭn′ĭm-pē′dĭd) *adj.* not held back or obstructed

solace (sŏl′ĭs) *n.* comfort in sorrow or distress

522

Cross Curricular Link **Geography**

MOUNTAINS OF JAPAN About 70 percent of Japan is covered by mountains and hills. Many of the mountains were formed by volcanic action. Mount Fuji, Japan's highest peak, is part of a chain of volcanoes on the island of Honshu. In fact, there are more than 150 volcanoes on the Japanese islands, 60 of which are active. This high number of volcanoes creates instability under the islands, making Japan subject to frequent earthquakes. Fortunately, most of these do not result in serious damage.

On the positive side, the volcanoes have created a land of great beauty. Thousands of people visit Japan every year to climb its mountains and enjoy the spectacular scenery.

They are here in the shadow of the little laurel tree—the remains of an old woman long ago abandoned.

Traveler. Then here beneath this tree lie the woman's remains, the woman who was deserted?

Old Woman. Yes, deep in the loam,
Buried in obscure grasses
Cut by the reaper.
Short-lived, they say, as is this world,
And already now . . .

Traveler. It is an ancient tale,
Yet perhaps attachments still remain.

Old Woman. Yes, even after death . . . somehow . . .

Traveler. The dismal loneliness of this moor,

Old Woman. The penetrating wind,

B **Traveler.** The lonely heart of autumn.

Chorus (*for the* Old Woman). Even now,
"No solace for my heart at Sarashina,
No solace for my heart at Sarashina."
At dusk of day on Mount Obasute
The green lingers in the trees,
The intermingled pines and laurels,
The autumn leaves so quickly tinged.
Thin mists drift over One-Fold Mountain—
Folds of faintly dyed cloth;
In a cloudless sky a doleful wind.
Lonely mountain vista,
Remote and friendless landscape.

68 doleful: very sad; full of grief.

Old Woman. Traveler, from where have you come?

Traveler. I am from the Capital, as I told you, but I have long heard of the beauties of the moon at Sarashina, and I come here now for the first time.

Old Woman. Are you indeed from the Capital? If that is so, then I will show myself with the moon tonight and entertain you here.

Traveler. Who are you that you should entertain me tonight?

Old Woman. In truth, I am from Sarashina . . .

Traveler. But where do you live now?

Old Woman. Where do I live? On this mountain . . .

Traveler. This famous mountain that bears the name . . .

MINI LESSON Speaking and Listening

DRAMATIC PRESENTATION

Prepare Have students work in groups to prepare a dramatic reading of lines 60–70 to convey the sad mood of the speech. Encourage performers to use the following techniques to convey mood:

- changes in volume, or loudness, of speech
- changes in speed of delivery
- changes in tone of voice
- facial expressions
- gestures or other body language

Present Have each group present its dramatic reading to the class. Encourage students in the audience to take notes during each reading, jotting down the techniques the performers use to convey mood. After the presentations, invite students to discuss what they learned about the play's mood.

This activity is particularly well suited for longer class periods.

Customizing Instruction

Less Proficient Readers

Call students' attention to the stage directions in the play. Tell students that in most plays, stage directions direct performers to position themselves to the right, left, front, or back of the stage. In Noh plays, however, the stage directions often direct performers to specific places on the stage (the *waki*-position, for instance) that represent their importance in the drama. Encourage students to refer to the diagram on page 520 to help them visualize the characters' movements.

Students may have difficulty understanding what is going on in the play. Have them track the actions and speeches of the two main characters in separate charts. Students should add to their charts after reading each page, summarizing in their own words what has happened to that point.

Sample Chart:

Traveler	Old Woman
Travels to Mount Obasute and meets an old woman	Talks about the old woman of Obasute; promises to return with the full moon and entertain the traveler

English Learners

Tell students that a Noh play is set in a specific month and season. The setting and mood of the play convey the feeling of that time. Point out that *The Deserted Crone* takes place in autumn. Direct students' attention to the following words and clues that suggest the play's autumn setting:

- "the lonely heart of autumn": Explain that "lonely heart" may refer to the midpoint of autumn or to the old woman's sadness and loneliness.
- "green lingers in the trees": Explain that this phrase refers to the changing color of leaves in autumn.
- "a doleful wind": Explain that *doleful* means "sad or sorrowful" and is a mood associated with autumn.

Pause & Reflect

Possible Response: Most students will conclude that the old woman is the deserted crone. Their conclusion should be based on the words of the chorus and of the old woman herself.

Literary Analysis ANECDOTE

A Remind students that an anecdote is a brief story that focuses on a single revealing event. Point out that an anecdote has all the elements of a longer narrative, including characters, setting, conflict, and plot. Have students read the story the villager tells of Mount Obasute and identify its narrative elements. *(characters: Wada no Hikonaga, his wife, and his aunt; setting: Mount Obasute; conflict: the wife hates the aunt; plot: complying with his wife's demands, Hikonaga abandons his aunt on Mount Obasute, where she turns to stone)*

Active Reading QUESTIONING

After students read the anecdote, ask them why they think the old woman's attachment to the world turned her to stone. What might the stone symbolize?

Possible Responses: The old woman turned to stone because her longing for the world prevented her from ascending to the spirit world. The stone may represent the weight of her longing.

Old Woman. Obasute Mountain of the Deserted Crone.

1 **Chorus** (*for the* Old Woman). Even to pronounce the name—
How shameful!
Long ago I was abandoned here.
Alone on this mountainside
I dwell, and every year
In the bright and full mid-autumn moon
I try to clear away
The dark confusion of my heart's attachment.
That is why tonight I have come before you.

Chorus (*narrating*). Beneath the tree,
In the evening shadows,
She vanished like a phantom,
Like an apparition . . . disappeared . . .

(*She exits.*)

91–92 I try . . . heart's attachment: Following Buddhist teachings, the woman tries to free herself from worldly desires in order to achieve enlightenment and final rest.

PAUSE & REFLECT What conclusion can you draw about the old woman's identity? What evidence supports your conclusion?

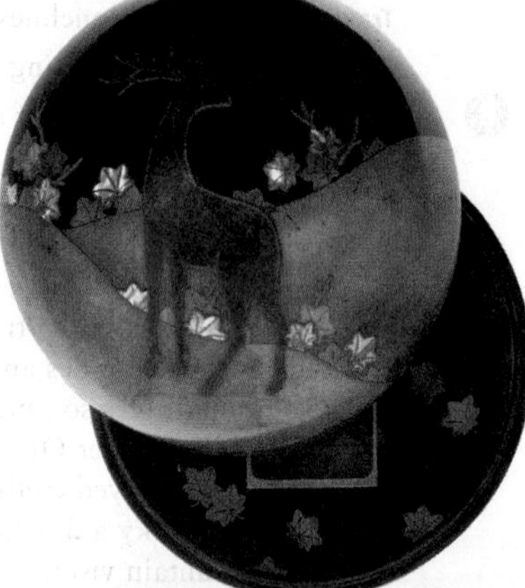

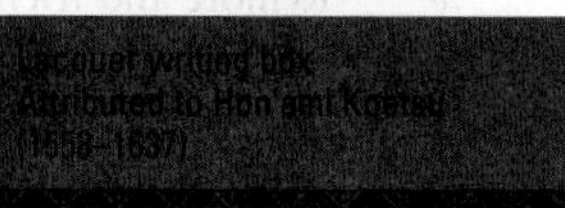

Lacquer writing box
Attributed to Hon'ami Koetsu
(1558–1637)

FOCUS Read to find out more about the old woman and how she came to Mount Obasute.

(*The* Villager *enters and stands at the naming-place. He wears a short sword.*)

Villager. I live at the foot of this mountain.
Tonight the moon is full, and I think I will climb the mountain and gaze at the moon.

(*He sees the* Traveler.)

Ah! There's a gentleman I have never seen before. You sir, standing there in the moonlight, where are you from and where are you bound?

Traveler. I am from the Capital. I suppose you live in this neighborhood?

Villager. Yes indeed, I do.

Traveler. Then come a bit closer. I have something to ask you.

Villager. Certainly.

(*He kneels at stage center.*)

MINI LESSON Speaking and Listening

CHORAL READING

Prepare Have students choose lines of verse spoken by the chorus and work in groups to plan a choral reading of the lines. Tell students that a choral reading is a group presentation, but one in which every student does not necessarily read every line. Share the following guidelines for choral reading:

- Keep in mind that some lines sound better with a light tone of voice while others sound better with a heavy tone of voice.
- Have some lines read by a few voices or only one, and have other lines read by the whole group.
- Avoid a singsong effect.
- Plan the reading, keeping in mind the verse's rhythm, tone, and mood.

Present After the groups practice, have them present their reading to the class. Then invite students to discuss the role of the chorus in the play.

This activity is particularly well suited for longer class periods.

Villager. You said you had something to ask. What might it be?

Traveler. You may be somewhat surprised at what I have to ask, but would you tell me anything you may know about the pleasures of moonviewing at Sarashina and the story of Obasute Mountain?

Villager. That is indeed a surprising request. I do live in this vicinity, it is true, but I have no detailed knowledge of such matters. Yet, would it not appear inhospitable if, the very first time we meet, I should say I know nothing of these things you ask? I will tell you, then, what in general I have heard.

Traveler. That is most kind of you.

Villager. Well then, here is the story of Mount Obasute: Long ago there lived at this place a man named Wada no Hikonaga. When he was still a child his parents died and he grew up under the care of an aunt. From the day of his marriage his wife hated his aunt and made many accusations against her. But Hikonaga would not listen to her. At length, however, his wife spoke out so strongly that he forgot his aunt's many years of kindness and bowing to his wife's demands, he said one day to the old woman: "Not far from this mountain is a holy image of the Buddha. Let us go there and make our offerings and prayers." A So he brought her to this mountain and in a certain place he abandoned her. Later he looked back at the mountain where now the moon was bright and clear. He wanted to go back and fetch his aunt, but his wife was a crafty woman and she detained him until it was too late. The old woman died and her heart's attachment to this world turned her to stone. Hikonaga later went in search of her, and when he saw the stone he realized the dreadful thing he had done. He became a priest they say. Ever since then the mountain has been called Mount Obasute—Mountain of the Deserted Old Woman. Long ago it seems that the mountain was known as Sarashina Mountain. Well, that is what I know of the story. But why do you ask? It seems such an unusual request.

124–125 Wada no Hikonaga (wä'dä nō hē'kō-nä'gä).

Traveler. How kind of you to tell me this story! I asked you for this reason: As I said a little while ago, I am from the Capital, but I had heard about Sarashina and so I made a special journey here to view the moon. A short while

WORDS TO KNOW

inhospitable (ĭn-hŏs'pĭ-tə-bəl) *adj.* unfriendly or unwelcoming to a guest

Customizing Instruction

Less Proficient Readers

1 Point out that lines 85–93 summarize the core of the play. Have students read the lines a couple of times and then rephrase the lines in their own words.

Help students connect the villager's story to the rest of the drama. Ask: Who is Hikonaga's aunt? Who is she in the drama? *(the old woman)*

English Learners

Students may be confused by the references on these pages to the old woman and her "heart's attachment" to the natural world. Explain that the heart is often used to represent love or the soul. The old woman loves the natural world so much that she doesn't want to leave it.

MINI LESSON Vocabulary Strategy

ETYMOLOGY

Instruction Explain that learning a word's etymology—its history and origin—can help students make sense of words they do not know and recognize word families, or words that share a common root. To find out a word's etymology, they may use information found in its dictionary entry.

For example, write the word *inhospitable* and the etymology of the word *hospitable* on the board:

inhospitable, from Latin *hospitare*, to put up as a guest, from hospes, *hospit-*, guest or host

Explain that *in-* and *-able* are affixes, and the root word is *hospit-*. Ask students to talk about the word's meaning based on the etymology. Have them list other words that contain the same root word. *(hospital, hospice, hostel, hostage)*

Practice Have students discuss the etymology of the following words and use the dictionary to research the Latin root meaning. Then have them create a list of words that have the same root.

1. unimpeded, from Latin *impedire*. See *ped- (pedestrian, pedal, centipede)*
2. delusion, from Latin *delusio, delusion-*, from *delusus*, past participle of *deludere*, to delude. See delude. delude, from Latin *deludere: de + ludere*, to play *(illusion, allude, elusive)*

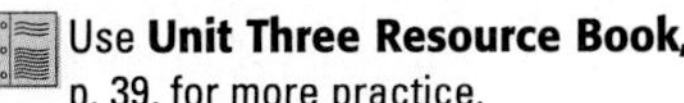

Use **Unit Three Resource Book,** p. 39, for more practice.

A lesson on Greek and Latin roots appears on p. 340 in the Pupil's Edition.

Pause & Reflect
Possible Reponse: Wada no Hikonaga brought the old woman to Mount Obasute to abandon her there. Soon after she turned to stone.

Literary Analysis SUPERNATURAL ELEMENTS
Tell students that supernatural elements are beings, powers, or events that are unexplainable by the laws of nature. Ask students to identify the supernatural element that has been introduced into the play. *(The ghost of the old woman has appeared.)* Then ask them what effect the appearance of the ghost has on their impression of the old woman and her story.
Possible Responses: The ghost makes the old woman's story seem more poignant. The ghost makes the old woman seem more strange and frightening.

Active Reading QUESTIONING
Ask students why the ghost of the old woman appears with the full moon. What is the connection between the old woman and the moon?
Possible Response: The moon, for the old woman, represents the beauty and inconstancy of the natural world.

ago, as I was waiting for the moon to rise, an old woman appeared to me from nowhere and recited to me the poem about Obasute Mountain. She promised to entertain me this night of the full moon, and I asked her who she was. Long ago, she told me, her home was in Sarashina, but now she dwelled on Mount Obasute. She had come here this night in order to dispel the dark confusion of her heart's attachment. No sooner had she spoken than here, in the shadows of this tree, she vanished.

Villager. Oh! Amazing! It must be the old woman's spirit, still clinging to this world, who appeared and spoke with you. If so, then stay awhile; recite the holy scriptures and kindly pray for her soul's repose. I believe you will see this strange apparition again.

Traveler. I think so too. I will gaze at the moon and cleanse my heart. For somehow I feel certain I shall see this mysterious figure again.

Villager. If you have any further need of me, please call.

Traveler. I will.

Villager. I am at your service.

(*He exits.*)

PAUSE & REFLECT Why did Wada no Hikonaga bring the old woman to Mount Obasute? What happened to her there?

FOCUS As you continue reading, think about why the old woman is drawn to Obasute and the real world.

Traveler and Companions. Evening twilight deepens,
And quickens on the moon which sheds
Its first light-shadows of the night.
How lovely:
Ten thousand miles of sky, every corner clear—
Autumn is everywhere the same.
Serene my heart, this night I shall spend in poetry.
"The color of the moon new-risen—
Remembrances of old friends
Two thousand leagues away."

Math

UNIT CONVERSIONS Explain that a league is a unit used to measure length. The measurement dates back to the time of the ancient Roman Empire, when the Gauls used a league equal to 1,500 Roman paces.

In the United States, a league equals 3 miles; a mile equals 5,280 feet. In *The Deserted Crone,* the traveler composes lines of poetry in which he recalls his old friends "two thousand leagues away." Have students use these equivalencies to convert 2,000 leagues into miles *(6,000)* and then into feet *(31,680,000)*.

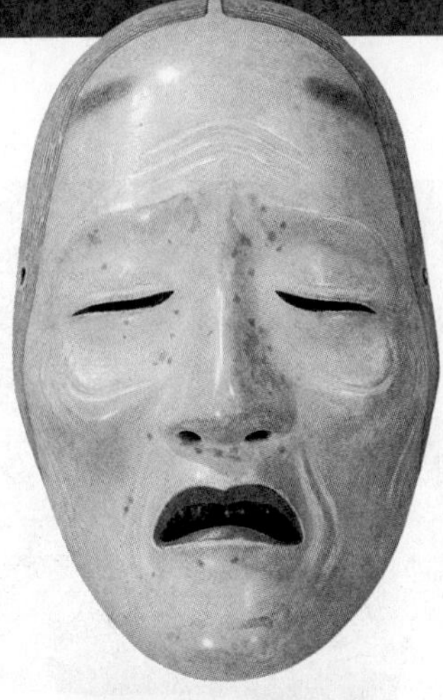

HUMANITIES CONNECTION The *uba* mask was originally used in a play in which an old woman and an old man represent the spirits of two pine trees. It has since come to be used as well for the roles of ordinary old women.

(*The* Ghost *of the old woman enters, wearing the* uba *mask. She stands at the* shite-*position.*)

Ghost. How strange and wonderful this moment,
Superb yet strange this moment out of time—
Is my sadness only for the moon tonight?
With the dawn
Half of autumn will have passed,
And waiting for it seemed so long.
The brilliant autumn moon of Mount Obasute,
So matchless, flawless I cannot think
I have ever looked upon the moon before;
Unbearably beautiful—
Surely this is not the moon of long ago.

Traveler. Strange,
In this moonlit night already grown so late
A woman robed in white appears—
Do I dream?—Is it reality?

Ghost. Why do you speak of dreams?
That aged figure who came to you by twilight
In shame has come again.

Traveler. What need have you for apologies?

[Stage Direction] ***uba*** (o͞o'bä) **mask:** a mask representing the face of an old woman who has once been beautiful.

Customizing Instruction

Less Proficient Readers

Help students understand that the sight of the moon triggers memories and feelings for both the traveler and the old woman. Point out that the traveler feels calm as he gazes at the moon and begins composing poetry about his far-away friends. Then ask students how the ghost of the old woman reacts to the sight of the moon.

Possible Response: The old woman is saddened by the sight. She can only think about how long she has waited the moon and how quickly it will pass.

English Learners

Make sure students understand that the old woman and the ghost are the same character. She apparently has the ability to appear in either guise. Explain that the ghost of the old woman only appears on this day in mid-autumn to see the full moon of Mount Obasute. The old woman is drawn to the moon and the mountain by its beauty and her memories. Then ask students what they would miss in the real world. What place would they haunt?

Advanced Learners

Point out that upon seeing the ghost of the old woman, the traveler wonders whether he is dreaming or whether the apparition is real. Ask students to consider the relationship between dream and reality in the play. What does this relationship suggest about the connection between the real world and the spirit world?

Possible Response: The real world exerts such a strong fascination that people may confuse it with—or even prefer it to—the spirit world.

MINI LESSON Viewing and Representing

Uba Mask

ART APPRECIATION Noh masks are used to represent beautiful women, young princes, warriors, drunkards, demons, and gods. The masks are usually worn by the *shite*, or leading character. In the middle of the play—as in *The Deserted Crone*—the shite often changes masks. The second mask reveals the character's true being. Details in the masks also convey the characters' qualities. For instance, the mask of a young woman represents her plump face, clear eyes, and smiling expression. Ask students to identify the details in the *uba* mask that suggest the features of an old woman.

Possible Responses: deep wrinkles; thin, drawn face; thinning, gray hair

How does the expression on the mask reflect the old woman's emotional state?

Possible Response: The sad, bereft expression on the mask reflects the old woman's emotional state.

Literary Analysis SETTING AND CHARACTERS

Tell students that setting often plays an important role in what happens and why in a narrative. Setting can even serve as a source of conflict. Ask students to describe the role setting plays in the old woman's conflict.

Possible Response: The old woman is so drawn to the mountain that she cannot leave the real world.

Literary Analysis SIMILE AND METAPHOR

Remind students that both a simile and a metaphor make a comparison between two things that are basically unlike. A simile uses the words *like* or *as* to make the comparison; a metaphor does not. You might provide the following examples:

simile: She was as eager as a puppy.

metaphor: She was a volcano, ready to erupt.

Then have students identify a simile and a metaphor in lines 215–226. *(simile: "Like the lady-flower nipped by time . . . I wither in robes of grass"; metaphor: "this world is all a dream")*

Active Reading QUESTIONING

Ask students what lines 227–228 mean.

Possible Response: The ghost of the old woman appears once a year to see the full moon. When the moon viewing is over, the old woman's remains will return to the earth.

Kariginu, Noh costume. The Newark Museum, Newark, New Jersey.

HUMANITIES CONNECTION The *kariginu* (hunting robe) is considered the most important outer garment for male actors in Noh plays. Originally worn by Heian aristocrats, such robes were later adopted by elite samurai as their most formal garment.

MINI LESSON Viewing and Representing

Kariginu

ART APPRECIATION Costumes in Noh drama reveal the type of character being portrayed and are worn according to well-established conventions. All characters, no matter who or what they represent, wear beautiful costumes. The costumes create an elegant effect but also rather bulky figures since the actors wear at least five layers of clothing. No garment ever conceals the one beneath it. The outer garment is always a richly embroidered piece, such as the kariginu pictured above. The costumes are so elaborate and difficult to put on that two or three costumers are needed to dress a single actor. Have students study the **Humanities Connection** on page 528. Ask students which character in *The Deserted Crone* would probably wear the kariginu.

Possible Response: the traveler

What might the kariginu shown on this page suggest about the personality of the character who wears it?

Possible Responses: The kariginu might suggest that the character is serious, normal, down to earth.

This place, as everybody knows is called . . .
Obasute—

Ghost. Mountain where an old hag dwells.

Traveler. The past returns,
An autumn night . . .

Ghost. Friends had gathered
To share the moon together . . .
Grass on the ground was our cushion . . .

Traveler. Waking, sleeping, among flowers,
The dew clinging to our sleeves.

Together. So many varied friends
Reveling in the moonlight . . .
When did we first come together?
Unreal—like a dream.

Chorus (for the Ghost). Like the lady-flower nipped
by time,
The lady-flower past its season,
I wither in robes of grass;
Trying to forget that long ago
I was cast aside, abandoned,
I have come again to Mount Obasute.
How it shames me now to show my face
In Sarashina's moonlight, where all can see!
Ah, well, this world is all a dream—
Best I speak not, think not,
But in these grasses of remembrance
Delight in flowers, steep my heart in the moon.

(*She gazes upward, then advances a few steps during the following passage.*)

Chorus (*for the* Ghost). "When pleasure moved me,
I came;
The pleasure ended, I returned."
Then, as now tonight, what beauty in the sky!

Ghost. Though many are the famous places
Where one may gaze upon the moon,
Transcending all—Sarashina.

Chorus (*for the* Ghost). A pure full disk of light,
Round, round, leaves the coastal range,
Cloudless over Mount Obasute.

Ghost. Even though the vows of the many Buddhas

227–228 "When pleasure . . . I returned": An allusion to the words of a nobleman in ancient China, who journeyed to see a friend but turned back as soon as he reached the friend's gate. When asked the reason for his action, the nobleman said, "Moved by pleasure, I came; the pleasure ended, I returned."

Customizing Instruction

Less Proficient Readers

Explain that the traveler is speaking for the ghost at this point in the drama, both when he speaks lines alone and when he speaks together with the ghost. Ask students what effect this sudden change in the role of the traveler has on the play.

Possible Response: It adds to the dreamlike quality of the play.

English Learners

Help students understand the verse in lines 215–226 by rearranging the phrases in the sentences into a simpler order. For example, the first three lines of the verse could be rearranged to read: "I wither in robes of grass like the lady-flower nipped by time, the lady-flower past its season." Explain that *nipped* means "decayed or wasted." Then help students rearrange the phrases in the next three lines.

MINI LESSON Grammar

PASSIVE AND ACTIVE VOICE

Instruction Tell students that the voice of an action verb indicates whether the subject performs or receives the action. The verb is in the active voice when the verb's subject performs the action expressed by the verb. The verb is in the passive voice when the verb's subject receives the action of the verb. Write the following sentences on the board:

Her heart's attachment turned her to stone.
She was turned to stone by her heart's attachment.

Underline the verbs as shown. Have students identify the subject of the verbs. Point out that in the first sentence, the subject performs the action, and in the second, the subject receives the action.

Practice Have students copy the following sentences. Ask them to identify them as being in the active or passive voice.

1. I wither in robes of grass. *(active)*
2. Long ago she was abandoned here. *(passive)*
3. He brought her to this mountain. *(active)*
4. The moon is dimly seen. *(passive)*

For more intruction and practice in passive and active voice, use McDougal Littell's ***Language Network:***

- Grade 10, Chapter 6, "Using Verbs"
- Grade 12, Chapter 4, "Using Verbs"

Literary Analysis
SETTING AND CHARACTERS

Point out that the description of the setting in these pages conveys the theme of the temporary nature of the earthbound world. Have students identify words and phrases that reveal this theme.

Possible Responses: "the inconstancy of this world"; "all is perpetual change"; "moments, brief as dew"

What words and phrases suggest that the old woman is still bound to the earth?

Possible Responses: "a butterfly at play"; "my heart is bound by memories"; "ache with longing for the past"

Literary Analysis CONFLICT

A Ask students what internal conflict is revealed in lines 285–292. *(The old woman cannot resign herself to leaving the natural world.)* What phrases reveal her knowledge of the world's inconstancy?

Possible Responses: "unshakeable delusions"; "bitter world"

Reading Skills and Strategies
INFERRING

After students finish reading the play, ask what they can infer about the fate of the old woman. Where will she go after the traveler leaves the mountain? When will the ghost likely reappear?

Possible Responses: The old woman will vanish beneath the earth; her ghost will continue to reappear on the mountain on the night of the mid-autumn moon.

Chorus. Cannot be ranked in terms of high or low,
None can match the light of Amida's Vow,
Supreme and all-pervading in its mercy.

(*She dances.*)

And so it is, they say,
The westward movement of the sun, the moon, and stars
Serves but to guide all living things
Unto the Paradise of the West.
The moon, that guardian who stands on Amida's right,
Leads those with special bonds to Buddha:
Great Seishi, "Power Supreme," he is called,
For he holds the highest power to lighten heavy crimes.
Within his heavenly crown a flower shines,
1 And its jeweled calyx reveals with countless leaves
The pure lands of all the other worlds.
The sounds of the wind in the jeweled tower,
Tones of string and flute,
Variously bewitch the heart.
Trees by the Pond of Treasures,
Where the lotus blooms red and white,
Scatter flowers along their avenues;
On the water's little waves—
A riot of sweet fragrances.

Ghost. The incomparable voices of the birds of paradise—

Chorus (*for the* Ghost). Peacocks and parrots call their notes
In harmonies of imitation.
Throughout that realm—unimpeded, all-pervading—
The radiance that gives his name—"Light without limit."
But here the moon through its rift of clouds,
Now full and bright, now dimly seen,
Reveals the inconstancy of this world
Where all is perpetual change.

Ghost. My sleeves move again in dances
Of sweet remembered nights of long ago.

(*She continues to dance, her song alternating back and forth between herself and the* Chorus.)

238 Amida's Vow: the promise made by the Buddha Amida to establish a paradise—known as the Western Paradise or Pure Land—into which the faithful would be reborn after death.

239 all-pervading: spreading throughout all things.

246 Seishi (sä'shē): one of Amida's two attendants, who offers wisdom to human beings.

249 calyx (kā'lĭks): a cuplike structure enclosing the base of a flower.

250 other worlds: the infinite Buddha paradises in the universe.

254 Pond of Treasures: a pool in the Western Paradise.

263 "Light without limit": another name for Seishi.

Tosa fan. Private collection.

Cross Curricular Link **Humanities**

AMIDA BUDDHA Amidism, a Buddhist sect, began in India and reached Japan around the 9th century. Worshipers of Amida believe that the buddha established the Western Paradise or Pure Land, where the dying would be welcomed. There they would remain until the time of their final enlightenment. Amidism gained popularity in Japan, due in part perhaps to the fact that entering the paradise did not require the performance of good works. Salvation was guaranteed to those who invoked Amida Buddha's name a single time, particularly at the hour of their death.

The Pure Land is described in Buddhist scriptures as a beautiful place, filled with birds, flowers, and precious gems. Immediately after people die, it is said that they enter into lotus buds. These open up after their occupants have become purified.

Chorus. "No solace for my heart at Sarashina
When I see the moon
Shining down on Mount Obasute"
When I see the shimmering moon.

Ghost. No stranger to the moon,
I dally among the flowers
For these moments, brief as dew on autumn grasses . . .

Chorus. Fleeting as the dew indeed . . .
Why should I have come here?
A butterfly at play . . .

Ghost. Fluttering . . .
Dancing sleeves . . .

Chorus. Over and return, over and . . .

Ghost. . . . Return, return
Autumn of long ago.

Chorus. My heart is bound by memories,
Unshakable delusions.
In this piercing autumn wind tonight
I ache with longing for the past,
Hunger after the world I knew—
Bitter world,
Autumn,
Friends.
But even as I speak,
See how the night already pales,
And daylight whitens into morning.
I shall vanish,
The traveler will return.

(*The* Traveler *exits.*)

Ghost. Now, alone,
Deserted,
A moss-grown wintry hag.

(*She watches the* Traveler *depart, and weeps.*)

Chorus. Abandoned again as long ago.
And once again all that remains—
Desolate, forsaken crag,
Mountain of the Deserted Crone.

(She spreads her arms and remains immobile at the shite-*position.)*

WORDS TO KNOW
delusion (dĭ-lo͞o′zhən) *n.* a false idea or belief

Customizing Instruction

Less Proficient Readers

1 Help students understand that lines 240–258 describe a Buddhist paradise. Read the lines aloud, using the sidenotes to explain difficult terms and concepts. Then have students compare the paradise with Sarashina. Which would they prefer to inhabit?

English Learners

Help students understand the following phrases:

- "brief as dew": very brief; The phrase refers to morning dew drying quickly in the early morning sun.
- "unshakeable delusions": falseness; The old woman realizes that her memories are false but cannot let them go.
- "hunger after the world": long for the world; The old woman wants to live again in the natural world.

Advanced Learners

Ask students why the old woman isn't drawn to the Western Paradise.
Possible Responses: Her memories aren't bound there. She may fear the unknown.

THE DESERTED CRONE 531

Connect to the Literature

1. **What Do You Think?** Students will probably pity the old woman.

Comprehension Check

- Wada no Hikonaga's wife hated the old woman and persuaded her husband to abandon her on Mount Obasute.
- The old woman returns because she cannot sever her ties with the material world.

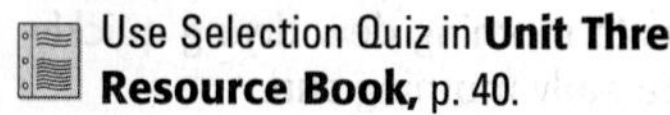
Use Selection Quiz in **Unit Three Resource Book,** p. 40.

Think Critically

2. Have groups share their strategies with the class. Write the strategies on the board, and discuss how each one can be used to answer questions about *The Deserted Crone.*
3. Possible Responses: The old woman may feel that she was torn from life before she was ready. Her lonely death may make her long for companionship. The beauty of nature may also help the old woman forget the ugliness of her death.
4. Possible Responses: The moon of Mount Obasute seems to represent the ever-changing world of the living. The light cast by the moon holds people to the earth, while that shed by Amida leads the dead to paradise.
5. Possible Response: The play creates a melancholy mood.
6. Possible Responses: The play suggests that life and the physical world are fleeting, cruel, beautiful.

Extend Interpretations

7. **Comparing Texts** Possible Responses: The chorus in *The Deserted Crone* often speaks for the old woman or for her spirit. Both choruses help advance plot and reveal traits of characters.
8. **Connect to Life** Possible Responses: The descriptions suggest that old women were considered worthless, expendable, pathetic. Some students may say that old women are viewed differently today because women have more freedom and a greater role in society. Others may contend that elderly women are still undervalued today.

Connect to the Literature

1. **What Do You Think?** What is your reaction to the plight of the old woman in this play?

Comprehension Check

- Why was the woman abandoned on Mount Obasute?
- Why does the ghost of the old woman return every year to dance in the full mid-autumn moon?

Think Critically

2. **ACTIVE READING: QUESTIONING** Get together in a small group and discuss the questions that you wrote in your **READER'S NOTEBOOK**. If you still have unanswered questions, see if others in the group can answer them. Then discuss the strategies you used to answer your questions, such as rereading or using a dictionary to define unfamiliar words. Which strategies were most helpful?
3. Why do you think the spirit of the old woman still clings to the real world?

- the manner of her death
- her memories of viewing the moon with friends
- her appreciation of the beauty of nature

4. What does the moon that shines on Mount Obasute seem to represent? How does the light cast by the moon compare with the light shed by Amida and other Buddhist deities?
5. How would you describe the **mood,** or feeling, created by the play?
6. What does the play seem to suggest about the nature of life and the physical world?

Extend Interpretations

7. **Comparing Texts** In Sophocles' *Oedipus the King,* the chorus plays an active role, occasionally advising the main characters and voicing opinions. What different role does the chorus play in *The Deserted Crone?* In what way, if any, are the roles of the two choruses similar?
8. **Connect to Life** The old woman in the play is described as a crone, a wintry hag, and a withered flower. What do these descriptions suggest about how elderly women were regarded in Zeami's time? Do you think old women are viewed differently today? Explain your answer.

LITERARY ANALYSIS: SETTING AND CHARACTERS

In a play, **setting** is the time and place in which the action occurs. **Characters** are the people who participate in the action. In *The Deserted Crone,* the setting and the main character are closely related. The play takes place on Mount Obasute, which has been named for the old woman. At the end of the play, the mountain seems to become further identified with the old woman when it is described as a "desolate, forsaken crag."

Cooperative Learning Activity With a small group of classmates, go back through the play and look for other instances in which similarities between the old woman and the setting are made.

Literary Analysis

Cooperative Learning Activity Possible Responses: "obscure grasses cut by the reaper," "dismal loneliness of this moor," "the lady-flower past its season," "a moss-grown wintry hag"

Use **Unit Three Resource Book,** p. 38, for more practice.

Writing Options

1. Name and Legend Think of a place, one that is famous or one that exists not far from your home. Create a new name for it, and then write a legend that explains how the place got its name. For example, you might rename a park in your community "Park of the Lazy Student" and write a story based on that name. You can write a humorous story or a sad one, similar to the legend of Mount Obasute.

2. Character Sketch Write a character sketch of the old woman in *The Deserted Crone.* Use figurative language and sensory details to describe the woman's appearance and how she feels when she sees the moon at mid-autumn. Also, explain how she came to be abandoned on the mountain and tell why she clings to the real world. In your character sketch, try to create the melancholy mood that is conveyed in the play when the woman is described.

Writing Handbook
See pages R27–R28: Descriptive Writing.

Activities & Explorations

Noh Performance Work with a small group of classmates to perform *The Deserted Crone.* Assign roles and use the stage directions and diagram on page 520 to help you put on the play. Use understated gestures and actions to depict character. Also choose music to evoke the proper mood. If possible, design and create paper Noh masks for the actors to wear. After you have rehearsed the play, perform it for the rest of the class.
~ **PERFORMING**

Inquiry & Research

Shakespearean Noh Plays
Kuniyoshi Munakata Ueda, a Japanese scholar who has devoted his life to poetry, has written several Shakespearean plays for the Noh stage. Some of the plays he has written, staged, and directed are *Hamlet, Macbeth,* and *King Lear.* Munakata Ueda, who has performed the *shite* role in many productions, worked for six years before he felt fully capable of chanting English in the Noh style. Find out more about Munakata Ueda and his Noh Shakespeare Group or about other modern Noh theater companies. If possible, bring pictures or a video of a performance to share with the class.

Vocabulary in Action

EXERCISE: MEANING CLUES On your paper, write the word that is described by each clue.

1. A member of the clergy might offer this to console grieving relatives at a funeral.
2. This describes the progress of a car that does not have to stop at red lights.
3. A person who does not offer food or drink to a guest might be called this.
4. If you believe that the Queen of England lives in your closet, you are probably laboring under this.
5. When time goes by quickly, it is often described in this way.

WORDS TO KNOW
delusion inhospitable unimpeded
fleeting solace

Building Vocabulary
For an in-depth study of context clues, see page 674.

Writing Options

1. **Name and Legend** Have students share their legends with the class.
2. **Character Sketch** Before students begin their character sketches, encourage them to use a web diagram to list the old woman's character traits and describe her appearance and emotions.

Activities & Explorations

Noh Performance Remind students to use the stage directions and diagram to determine where they should position themselves as they perform the drama. Encourage them, too, to use slow, subtle movements to convey emotion.

Inquiry & Research

Shakespearean Noh Plays Tell students that they can begin their search on the Internet by entering the key words "Noh Shakespeare."

Vocabulary in Action

1. solace
2. unimpeded
3. inhospitable
4. delusion
5. fleeting

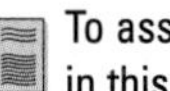
To assess skills and concepts taught in this selection, use **Formal Assessment Book,** pp. 71–72.

Objectives

- understand and appreciate **tanka** poems **(Literary Analysis)**
- identify and evaluate **diction** in poetry **(Literary Analysis)**
- describe and **compare moods** in tanka poems **(Active Reading)**

Thematic Link

Tanka poets use imagery to **capture a moment** and convey a specific emotion, insight, or observation.

5-Minute Warm-Up

Daily Language SkillBuilder

Have students **proofread** the display sentences on page 419k and write them correctly.

tanka poetry

Tanka Poets

Ono Komachi (circa mid-800s) Because she is named in the preface to an important anthology of Japanese verse, Ono Komachi (ō'nō kō-mä'chē) is revered as one of the Six Immortals of Poetry. However, almost nothing is known about the poet's life. In fact, historical facts about Komachi have become obscured by the legends created about her. Perhaps because she wrote passionate love poetry, she is said to have been a matchless beauty who conquered many men's hearts. Other legends describe the poet's cruel treatment of her lovers and—perhaps as revenge—her loss of beauty in old age. As a result of these legends, Komachi became the subject of a series of Noh plays.

Lady Ise (875?–939) Born into a family of prominent scholars and poets, Lady Ise (ē'sĕ) served as a lady in waiting at the Heian court during the reigns of Emperors Uda (o͞o'dä) and Daigo (dī'gō). Like Ono Komachi, Ise wrote passionate poetry. A woman of immense talent and reportedly a great beauty, Ise received much attention from men all her life. Some of these men tried to take advantage of her position at court, but she is said to have used her literary ability to outsmart them.

Ki Tsurayuki (868?–946?) Ki Tsurayuki (kē' tso͞o'rä-yo͞o'kē) was the most influential poet of his age. Many of his poems were combined with painting on Japanese screens. These screen poems were composed at the request of the emperor or another high official and publicly displayed. The poems were often technically brilliant, but they lacked depth of feeling. Tsurayuki's later work, however, revealed more personal feeling and demonstrated his considerable poetic gifts. He also pioneered the travel-diary form in his *Tosa Diary.* Written from the point of view of a fictional woman, the diary describes Tsurayuki's journey from Japan's Tosa province to Kyoto.

Saigyō (1118–1190) Saigyō (sī'gyō) is one of the three most beloved poets in Japanese literature. At the age of 23, he abandoned a promising military career to become a Buddhist monk. While living as a hermit, he composed poems about nature and the impermanence of life, a basic Buddhist belief. He also helped develop the meditative travel diary, a form later perfected by poet Matsuo Bashō (mä-tso͞o'ō bä'shō).

Ono Komachi

LESSON RESOURCES

UNIT THREE RESOURCE BOOK, pp. 41–42

ASSESSMENT RESOURCES
Formal Assessment, pp. 73–74
Teacher's Guide to Assessment and Portfolio Use
Test Generator

INTEGRATED TECHNOLOGY
Visit our Web site: classzone.com

ADDITIONAL RESOURCES
Lesson Planning Guide, pp. 63–64
Teacher's Sourcebook for Language Development

Connect to Your Life

What's your favorite way to capture a moment in time? Would you prefer to write about the moment, draw a picture of it, photograph it, or talk about it? Get together with a partner and take turns recalling a special moment that occurred recently in each of your lives. Discuss how you tried to hold on to the moment.

Build Background

Short Songs Tanka (täng'kə) are Japanese lyrical poems that express a single thought or tell a brief story. Tanka means "short songs," and a traditional tanka poem consists of just 31 syllables divided among five lines. The first and third lines contain 5 syllables each; the remaining lines contain 7 syllables each. This rigid construction is usually not retained in English translations of the poems. Instead, translators try to preserve the mood and imagery of the poetry.

Tanka was the dominant form of Japanese verse from the 700s until the 1500s. It emerged shortly after Japan developed a system for writing Japanese. At this time, Japanese writers began to write in Japanese instead of Chinese. The earliest examples of tanka appeared in a collection of poetry written in the 700s. By the early 900s, tanka was thriving as a uniquely Japanese form. During the Heian period, aristocrats routinely composed and exchanged tanka with their loved ones.

Not surprisingly, love is a common theme in tanka. The beauty of nature and the passage of time are other frequent subjects. Tanka poets attempt to capture a moment and evoke a certain response through the use of imagery. Much of what the poets say, however, is implied rather than directly stated. The reader must read between the lines to understand the insight expressed.

Eventually, tanka inspired the more concise verse form known as haiku (hī'ko͞o), a three-line poem of 17 syllables. In time, haiku surpassed tanka as the major Japanese poetic form. Nonetheless, Japanese poets continue to write tanka today. Many take part in a tanka-writing contest held at the beginning of each year by the emperor of Japan.

Focus Your Reading

LITERARY ANALYSIS: DICTION

Diction refers to a writer's choice of words. Diction includes both the words used and the way the writer arranges them. In the tanka poems you are about to read, the diction is **figurative** rather than **literal.** The words imply meaning; they don't state it directly. As you read the poems, be aware of the diction used by the poets.

ACTIVE READING: COMPARING MOODS

Mood is the feeling or atmosphere that a writer creates for the reader. The use of imagery can help set the mood. **Imagery** refers to words and phrases that create vivid sensory experiences for the reader by appealing to one of more of the senses of sight, smell, hearing, taste, and touch.

READER'S NOTEBOOK As you read each tanka poem, list in a chart the words or phrases that contribute to the poem's feeling or atmosphere.

Poem	Words and Phrases
"I've gone to him"	
"Spring rains"	
"In this world"	
"As I look"	

READING FOR INFORMATION

Reading Skills and Strategies

CLASSIFYING CHARACTERISTICS

Help students understand the characteristics of tanka poetry listed in **Build Background.** In class, create a chart that classifies these characteristics. Organize the information under the following headings: Form, Themes, Use of Imagery, Poetic Style. When discussing form, you might point out that the traditional syllable pattern of tanka poetry is not always strictly adhered to in English translations. In fact, the poems they are about to read do not conform to the traditional pattern.

TANKA POETRY 535

Reading Skills and Strategies
VISUALIZING
Before students read the tanka, tell them that the poems evoke strong images. Encourage students to try to visualize as they read and pay attention to the images that form in their mind. You might have students use a cluster diagram to record the images each poem brings to mind.

Literary Analysis DICTION
Remind students that the poets represented on these pages use figurative diction. Meaning is implied, or suggested, rather than stated directly. Then ask students what meaning is suggested by the phrase "my feet never resting" in the tanka by Ono Komachi.
Possible Response: The narrator never stops thinking about the "him" of the poem.

Use **Unit Three Resource Book,** p. 42, for more practice.

Active Reading COMPARING MOODS
Ask students to describe the mood evoked by the poems on pages 536 and 537.
Possible Responses: "I've gone to him"–dreamlike, melancholy; "Spring rains weaving"–joyful, playful; "In this world"–sad, yearning.
Then ask students which tanka create a similar mood.
Possible Response: "I've gone to him" and "In this world"

Use **Unit Three Resource Book,** p. 41, for more practice.

Literary Analysis IMAGERY
Ask students to note the imagery in Lady Ise's poem. Remind students that imagery refers to words and phrases that create images in the reader's mind by appealing to the senses. Point out that the majority of these images are visual. For example, the phrase "spring rains weaving eccentric brocades" appeals to the sense of sight. Ask students to describe the images created by this phrase.
Possible Response: rain splashing, creating a zigzag pattern on the street

Tanka Poetry

Translated by Burton Watson

I've gone to him
by dream paths,
my feet never resting—
but it can never match
one glimpse of him in real life

—Ono Komachi

Spring rains weaving
eccentric brocades
across the face of the water—
will they dye all the hills green?

—Lady Ise

Japanese writing box and tools

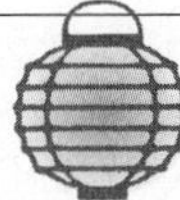

In this world
there are many kinds of longing,
but no longing to match
the longing for one's child

—Ki Tsurayuki

Man and Boy Walking, Edo Period Egoyomi, Brooklyn Museum, Brooklyn, New York. Photo © Brooklyn Museum/Corbis.

Customizing Instruction

Less Proficient Readers
Help students understand the tanka by providing the following tips:

- Read each poem several times—aloud, if possible.
- Identify the images that linger in your mind. Name the sense or senses each image appeals to.
- Think about mood. Ask yourself: How do I feel as I read the poem?
- Summarize the poem's topic or theme in one sentence.

English Learners
Help students understand the following phrases from the tanka:

- "dream paths": places gone to in a dream; The narrator has seen him in her dreams.
- "spring rains weaving eccentric brocades": the pattern made by rain; Explain that *eccentric* means "unusual," and *brocade* is a heavy fabric with a complicated design.
- "dye all the hills green": make the grass on the hills turn green; The rain will cause the grass to grow so that it will appear to have been dyed green.
- "many kinds of longing": strong desires; A longing suggests a desire that cannot be fulfilled.

Literary Analysis DICTION

Have students think about the diction used in Saigyō's poem. Then ask them what meaning is implied by the phrase "my mind goes roaming."

Possible Response: I think about things that happened in the past.

How would students reword the phrase "till I live again"?

Possible Response: until I vividly recall my memories

Reading Skills and Strategies
MAKING INFERENCES

Tell students that inferences are logical guesses based on clues in the text and on the reader's own knowledge. Then ask them what they can infer about the effect of the moon on the narrator.

Possible Response: The moon triggers memories of autumns from the narrator's youth.

What feelings do these memories seem to inspire?

Possible Responses: happiness, sadness, melancholy

As I look at the moon
my mind goes roaming,
till I live again
the autumns that I
knew long ago.

—Saigyō

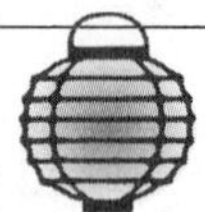

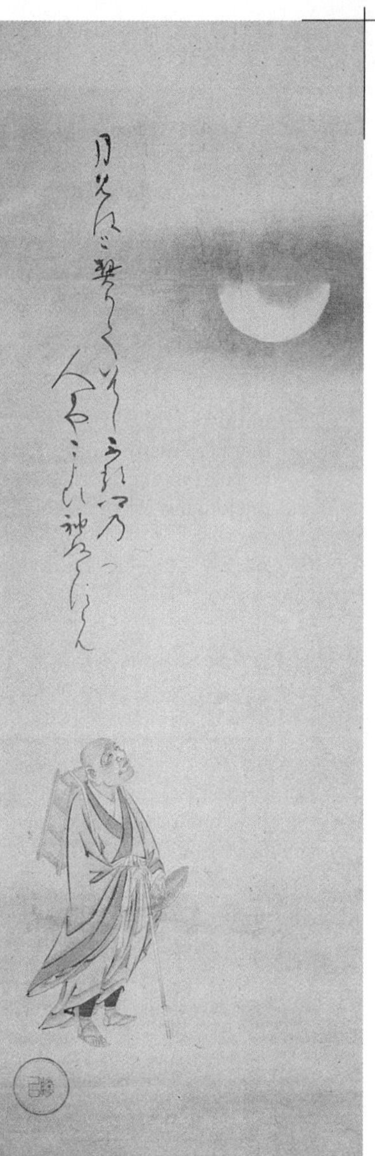

Poet Saigyō Viewing the Moon (c.1637), Iwasa Katsumochi. Gunma Prefectural Museum of Modern Art, Gunma Prefecture, Japan.

HUMANITIES CONNECTION
The inscription on this scroll transcribes a poem by Saigyō, in which he wrote: "I wonder if the sleeves of those I left at home / are wet with tears tonight."

MINI LESSON Viewing and Representing

Poet Saigyō Viewing the Moon **by Iwasa Katsumochi**

ART APPRECIATION This painting shows the poet Saigyō, dressed in a monk's cassock and with a book box on his back, looking up at the moon. Saigyō traveled extensively after he became a monk and lived as a hermit. Have students study the painting and the **Humanities Connection** on page 538. Point out that the poem inscribed on the scroll painting begins "'When we see the moon . . .' were our / parting words." Ask students to describe the mood of the painting. What details in the painting help create this mood?

Possible Responses: The mood of the painting is one of sadness and longing. The mood is created by the poem, by the moon half hidden by a cloud, and by the expression on Saigyō's face.

How does the mood of the painting compare with the mood of the poem on this page?

Possible Responses: Both are sad, reflective, full of longing for the past.

Connect to the Literature

1. **What Do You Think?** Which of these tanka did you enjoy the most? Discuss with the class the reasons for your choice.

Think Critically

2. What impressions of nature do the tanka by Lady Ise and Saigyō convey?
3. In the tanka by Komachi and Tsurayuki, what can you infer about the subjects?
4. What do these poems suggest about time and change?

- the glimpse of spring in Lady Ise's poem
- the longing expressed by Tsurayuki
- Saigyō's reflection on autumn

5. **ACTIVE READING: COMPARING MOODS** Review the chart that you created in your READER'S NOTEBOOK. How would you describe the mood in each one of the poems? Compare your ideas with a classmate. Decide if any of the tanka have similar moods.

Extend Interpretations

6. **What If?** If Lady Ise's poem were about winter rather than spring, what images might be used?
7. **Comparing Texts** Which of the tanka have a dreamlike or otherworldly quality? According to Buddhist teaching, the soul lives on after death. How do some of the tanka reflect the Buddhist belief in an afterlife?
8. **Connect to Life** Although the tanka you have read were written hundreds of years ago, the emotions and insights they convey are still fresh today. Select one of the tanka and identify modern images that might evoke the same response.

LITERARY ANALYSIS: DICTION

Diction refers to a writer's choice of words. Diction includes both the vocabulary used by a writer and the way in which the chosen words are arranged. Diction can be described as **formal** or **informal,** and as **literal** or **figurative.** The figurative diction in the four tanka fits the poems' mood and meaning. Consider the diction in these lines by Ono Komachi:

I've gone to him
by <u>dream paths,</u>
<u>my feet never resting</u>—

"Dream paths" implies a sleeping or unconscious state, while "my feet never resting" suggests that the speaker is unceasing in her desire to reach the "him" of the poem. The lines convey a yearning, dreamlike state.

Paired Activity Reread the following tanka by Lady Ise, paying particular attention to the underlined phrases. Then rewrite the phrases, using literal diction.

<u>Spring rains weaving</u>
<u>eccentric brocades</u>
across the face of the water—
<u>will they dye all the hills green?</u>

Get together with a partner and share your new versions. Discuss the differences between the literal and figurative versions.

Connect to the Literature

1. **What Do You Think?** Students should support their opinions by citing specific images or language from the tanka.

Think Critically

2. Possible Response: The poems convey the beauty and evocative power of nature.
3. Possible Response: Students might infer that the subjects have died or gone away.
4. Possible Response: The poems suggest that time and life are fleeting and ever-changing.
5. Possible Responses: Komachi creates a mood of melancholy longing. Lady Ise creates a joyful mood. Tsurayuki creates a sad mood. Saigyō creates a nostalgic mood. Students should note that the moods created by Komachi and Tsurayuki are similar.

Extend Interpretations

6. **What If?** Possible Responses: Winter images might include falling snowflakes, sparkling ice, hills covered in white.
7. **Comparing Texts** Possible Responses: The tanka by Komachi has a dreamlike quality. The poem suggests that the subject is dead but that the narrator has visited him—if only in her dreams—in the afterlife.
8. **Connect to Life** Possible Response: In the tanka by Saigyō, an image of falling leaves might evoke the same nostalgic response.

Literary Analysis

Paired Activity Possible Responses: Spring rains falling, making intricate patterns on the water, will the rain make the grass on the hills turn green? Students should note that the literal version is less interesting because it does not convey the images created by the figurative version.

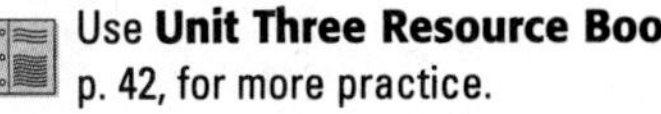

Use **Unit Three Resource Book**, p. 42, for more practice.

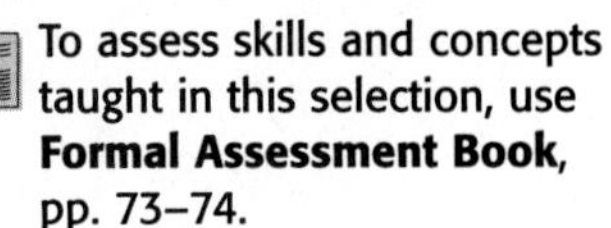

To assess skills and concepts taught in this selection, use **Formal Assessment Book**, pp. 73–74.

Assign the haiku in both **Japanese Haiku** and **Haiku in the 20th Century** to prepare students for the sample writing assessment provided on page 551. Use the Points of Comparison chart to guide students in identifying the similarities and differences between traditional and 20th-century haiku.

 Use **Unit Three Resource Book,** p. 43, for more practice.

COMPARING LITERATURE ACROSS CULTURES

Haiku Across the Centuries

OVERVIEW

One of the most popular forms of poetry is the haiku. This type of poetry originated in Japan hundreds of years ago. It's a form that has many rules, but they are relatively easy to follow.

This lesson contains haiku of three great Japanese masters. Also included are haiku of two famous 20th-century writers, one Mexican and one American, to show how poets continue to play with the form. In the pages that follow, you will be asked to compare and contrast various haiku. Comparing traditional haiku with haiku written in the 20th century will help you see which elements of the poems have changed and which have remained the same.

Points of Comparison

The following poem illustrates the basic rules of haiku. As you will later see, poets don't always follow these rules, but knowing the rules is a good way to start.

Traditional Haiku

Spun in high, dark clouds,
Snow forms vast webs of white flakes
And drifts lightly down.

One word or phrase suggests season.
- First line has 5 syllables.
- Second line has 7 syllables.
- Third line has 5 syllables.

Poem presents an image from nature—here, an image of snow falling.

Analyze the Poems Use a chart like the one shown to help you take notes about the poems. You will first choose two traditional haiku, each by a different Japanese poet, to analyze in depth. Later, you will choose a 20th-century haiku to compare with the other two.

	Traditional	Traditional	20th-Century
Author			
First line of poem			
Traditional form (5/7/5 syllables)? (yes/no)			
Season/season word (if present)			
Image(s)			
Mood suggested			

Standardized Test Practice: Comparison-and-Contrast Essay After you have finished reading all the poems, you will have the option of writing a comparison-and-contrast essay. Your notes will help you plan and write the essay.

Assessment **Standardized Test Practice**

COMPARISON-AND-CONTRAST ESSAY To provide practice to students in comparing literature from different times and cultures, have them read both sections in this Comparing Literature feature—**Japanese Haiku** and **Haiku in the 20th Century**—rather than treating each section separately. Have them work with the chart shown here on page 540, filling it out as they finish reading each section. (Examples of how to fill out the chart are supplied on pages 546 and 550.) A sample assessment writing prompt and guidelines for responding to it in writing are on page 551.

Japanese Haiku

Objectives

- understand and appreciate **haiku (Literary Analysis)**
- identify and **analyze imagery** in poetry **(Literary Analysis)**
- **interpret details** to understand a poem's mood **(Active Reading)**

Thematic Link

Haiku poets use vivid images to **capture a moment** in a particular season and make an observation about nature.

5-Minute Warm-Up

Daily Language SkillBuilder

Have students **proofread** the display sentences on page 419k and write them correctly.

Japanese Haiku Poets

Matsuo Bashō (1644–1694) (mä-tso͞o'ō bä'shō) is considered the greatest master of the haiku. Bashō led a contemplative life, seeking a deeper understanding of the world through his solitary travels and in the writing of haiku. In 1684, he began the first of many journeys that provided inspiration for much of his poetry and travel journals. By the time of his death, Bashō had more than 2,000 students.

Yosa Buson (1716–1784) Recognized as the second-greatest master of haiku, Yosa Buson (yō'sä bo͞o'sōn) moved to the Japanese capital of Edo at the age of 20 to study painting and poetry. Although he made his living as a painter, Buson also wrote poetry full of vivid images.

Kobayashi Issa (1763–1828) Kobayashi Issa (kō'bä-yä'shē ēs'sä) dealt with tragedy all his life. His first four children died in infancy, and his wife died shortly after giving birth to the fourth child. Issa remarried, and a healthy daughter was born after his death. Issa's poetry often reflects the pain of his personal suffering.

Build Background

Precision, Economy, and Delicacy Haiku possesses three qualities greatly valued in Japanese art: precision, economy, and delicacy. In just 17 syllables, a haiku must create a couple of vivid images that convey an emotion or an observation about nature.

Haiku poets also frequently use a seasonal word or image, called a kigo (kē'gō), to bring a certain time of year to mind. For instance, "cherry blossoms" carries the suggestion of spring; "snowfall" indicates a wintry scene.

For a humanities activity, click on:

Connect to Your Life

Many of the poems you are about to read convey images of the seasons. With a partner, list images and emotions that come to mind when you think about each season. You might refer to these notes as you read the haiku.

Focus Your Reading

LITERARY ANALYSIS: ANALYZING IMAGERY

Imagery consists of words and phrases that appeal to the senses of a reader. These words help bring a piece of writing to life by creating vivid images in the reader's mind. A haiku usually contains two main images. For example, the poem on page 540 presents an image of dark clouds and one of vast webs of white flakes. Readers must draw a connection between the images to understand the poem's meaning. As you read the haiku, think about the images being compared in each one.

ACTIVE READING: INTERPRETING DETAILS

In order to fully appreciate haiku, you should read each poem slowly. Allow a mental picture to form, based on the details provided. Then read the poem a second time, stopping to think about the mood or emotion created by the details.

READER'S NOTEBOOK As you read the haiku by Bashō, Buson, and Issa, jot down the details from each poem in a chart. Try to picture the images suggested by the details, and think about how they make you feel. Then record your emotional response to the poem.

TIME MANAGEMENT

If you wish to cover only one of the selections, use . . .

- Preparing to Read, p. 541 or p. 547
- Thinking Through the Literature, p. 546 or p. 550

If you want to take advantage of longer blocks of class time, use . . .

- TE Teaching Options: Cross Curricular Link, pp. 544 and 549
- Related Reading, p. 545

Literary Analysis

ANALYZING IMAGERY

A Have students identify the two main images in this haiku by Matsuo Bashō. *(withered winter grass and waves of warm spring air)* Which senses do the images appeal to? *(sight, touch)* How do the images differ? *(They are contrasting: one evokes an image of winter, the other, of spring.)* Then ask students to describe the connection between the images.

Possible Response: The haiku suggests the coming of spring, with the winter grass fading before the approaching warmer air.

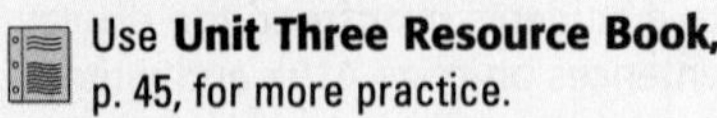

Use **Unit Three Resource Book,** p. 45, for more practice.

Active Reading

INTERPRETING DETAILS

B Have students discuss the mental picture that forms when they read *Bashō's Death Poem*. What details help them form this picture? What mood or emotion is created by the details?

Possible Responses: The details that might help students form a picture include "sick on my journey" and "desolate moors." The mood created by these details is sad, defeated, and bleak.

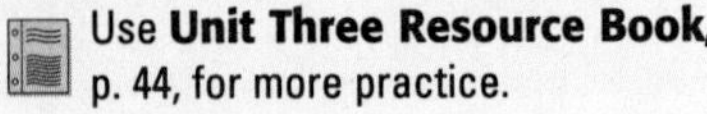

Use **Unit Three Resource Book,** p. 44, for more practice.

Literary Analysis THEME

Tell students that theme is a perception or message about life or human nature in a work of literature. In poetry, imagery and figurative language help convey theme. Then discuss some of the themes compressed into these haiku.

Possible Responses: These haiku express themes of pure sensation; passage of time; harmony with nature; serenity; death.

Haiku Poets

Matsuo Bashō

Translated by Sam Hamill

Pitifully—under
a great soldier's empty helmet,
a cricket sings

A

Withered winter grass—
waves of warm spring air
shimmering just above

After morning snow
onion shoots rise in the garden
like little signposts

B

Sick on my journey,
only my dreams will wander
these desolate moors

LESSON RESOURCES

UNIT THREE RESOURCE BOOK, pp. 43–46

ASSESSMENT RESOURCES
Formal Assessment, pp. 75–76
Teacher's Guide to Assessment and Portfolio Use
Test Generator

INTEGRATED TECHNOLOGY
Visit our Web site: classzone.com

ADDITIONAL RESOURCES
Lesson Planning Guide, pp. 65–66
Teacher's Sourcebook for Language Development

Yosa Buson

Translated by Robert Hass

Coolness—
the sound of the bell
as it leaves the bell.

White blossoms of the pear
and a woman in moonlight
reading a letter.

1 The old man
cutting barley—
bent like a sickle.

It cried three times,
the deer,
then silence.

Customizing Instruction

Less Proficient Readers

Have students read the poems aloud with a partner and then discuss their impressions.

English Learners

1 To help with the elliptical nature of haiku, have students try to supply missing words to turn the poems into sentences. For instance, the haiku by Buson might be recast as follows: "The old man who is cutting barley is bent like a sickle."

Advanced Learners

Have students write a paragraph stating what similar and differing views of the world the haiku reflect. Remind them to include examples to support their ideas.

Possible Response: Students may say that some haiku express the harshness of nature and humanity, while others rejoice in their beauty.

Literary Analysis
ANALYZING IMAGERY

Have students discuss the images in the haiku by Issa. Ask students what mood is conveyed by the images in each poem.

Possible Responses: "A huge frog and I"—a playful mood; "Asked how old he was—a happy mood; "In a dream"—a dreamlike mood; "The pheasant cries"—a mood of wonder

Literary Analysis HAIKU

Point out that the pattern of five, seven, and five syllables within three lines works well in Japanese, in which no syllable has a marked stress, and the typical syllable is short and uniform. In English, with its marked stresses and long syllables, this pattern does not achieve the same effect. Thus, although Bashō, Buson, and Issa followed the strict requirements of the haiku form when they wrote their poetry, the exact number and pattern of syllables in their poems cannot usually be reproduced in English translations.

Kobayashi Issa

Translated by Robert Hass

A huge frog and I,
staring at each other,
neither of us moves.

Asked how old he was,
the boy in the new kimono
stretched out all five fingers.

In a dream
my daughter lifts a melon
to her soft cheek.

The pheasant cries
as if it just noticed
the mountain.

Cross Curricular Link **Humanities**

TRADITIONAL CLOTHING The kimono is the traditional clothing of Japan. The garment, a long, wide-sleeved robe fastened around the middle with a belt, or obi, has been worn in Japan since its earliest history. As climate and customs changed and weaving and dyeing skills developed, the style of the kimono evolved over the centuries. Today, the emperor and his family wear kimonos from the Heian period on formal occasions.

Ordinary Japanese citizens also wear kimonos for special events but dress in a more modern version of the garment. Men generally wear a dark, conservatively styled kimono. Women wear much more colorful robes. The color, sleeve length, and details concerning how the obi is tied depend on the season and the wearer's age, social position, and marital status. Children also dress in colorful kimonos for special festivals and holidays. For instance, on November 15, called "7-5-3 Day," boys who are three or five years old and girls who are three or seven dress in kimonos and pay special visits to local temples.

from
The Spring of My Life

KOBAYASHI ISSA

This excerpt from Kobayashi Issa's diary captures the love and delight he felt for his infant daughter. Though prose, this delicate portrait reflects the art of the great haiku master.

Last summer, around the day for bamboo planting, a daughter was born to us in this world so full of sad events. Though she may have been born stupid, we hoped she would grow up to be a clever girl, and decided to call her Sato.[1] This year, from around the day we celebrated her birthday, she began to laugh if we clapped our hands, and to nod her head if we patted it lightly.

Once, when she saw a child her age with what is called a pinwheel, she wanted it for herself badly and fussed so much that we hurriedly got one for her. But soon she was chewing on it noisily and then she threw it away. Without showing a drop of regret, she turned her attention to something else, and began breaking the bowls that happened to be at hand. Soon bored with that too, she started tearing the thin paper off the sliding door. We said, "Well done! well done!" as though praising her. She thought we meant it and, cackling, went on tearing away intently. Not a speck of dust in her heart, she seemed as bright and pure as the full moon of autumn. As if witnessing a superb actor, I felt the wrinkles being smoothed out of my heart.

Again, when someone came along and said to her, "Where's the bow-wow?" she'd point at a dog, and when asked, "Where's the caw-caw?" she'd point at a crow. From her mouth to the tips of her fingers she brimmed with charm and lovableness, and I thought she was gentler than the butterflies that play around the first spring herbs. 1

The child must have been protected by the buddhas. On the evening before the anniversary of someone's death, as soon as I lit a candle and tinkled the bell at our family altar, wherever she might be, she would busily crawl up beside me, press together the hands that were as small as sprouting ferns, and recite "Nammu, Nammu"[2]—her voice touching, elegant, stirring, admirable.

—*Translated by* Hiroaki Sato

1. Sato (sä'tō): a name related to the Japanese word *satoshi*, meaning "clever" or "bright."
2. "Nammu, Nammu": a child's imitation of the phrase *Namu Amida Butsu*, "Praise to Amida Buddha."

Customizing Instruction

Less Proficient Readers
Some students may have difficulty understanding the figurative language Issa uses in the diary excerpt. Encourage them to try to visualize the images Issa creates with his language. For instance, the simile "she seemed as bright and pure as the full moon of autumn" might bring to mind images of a full moon on a clear night. Students should also think about how the images make them feel. A full moon, for example, may make them feel happy.

English Learners
1 In Issa's diary excerpt, point out the phrases "Where's the bow-wow?" and "Where's the caw-caw?" Explain that, in English, "bow-wow" represents the sound made by a dog, and "caw-caw" represents the sound made by a crow. You might share these other typical animal sounds:
- meow: cat
- moo: cow
- baa: sheep
- cock-a-doodle-do: rooster

Then ask students what words represent these animal sounds in their first languages.

Related Reading
More About Kobayashi Issa Issa often wrote about animals, especially small creatures. His haiku teem with frogs, fleas, and crickets. Issa also wrote fondly about children. His love of children is apparent in this diary excerpt, in which Issa writes with great tenderness about his daughter, Sato. Tragically, the child died of smallpox shortly after her first birthday.

Discussion Questions
1. What images and figurative language in the diary excerpt recall the imagery in Issa's haiku?
   Possible Responses: "she seemed as bright and pure as the full moon of autumn"; "I felt the wrinkles being smoothed out of my heart"; "hands that were as small as sprouting ferns"
2. Critics have said that the Japanese haiku poets capture "the eternal and the momentary" in their work. In what way is Issa's description of his daughter both timeless and fleeting?
   Possible Responses: The description captures the nature of a child from any time or culture, yet it is also personal, bringing Sato to vivid life.

Connect to the Literature

1. **What Do You Think?**
   Be sure students support their opinions using specific details from the haiku.

Think Critically

2. Possible Response: The poets all find beauty in the small, simple details of nature. They see in nature the resurgence and continuation of human life.
3. Possible Responses: Emotional responses to Bashō's haiku might include hopefulness and melancholy. Emotional responses to Buson's haiku might include peacefulness and inspiration. Emotional responses to Issa's haiku might include joyfulness and tenderness.

Literary Analysis

Cooperative Learning Activity Make a chart on the board, listing four or five of the haiku. Then have groups share the images and meanings they identified in the poems. Compile their ideas in the chart.

Use **Unit Three Resource Book,** p. 45, for more practice.

Points of Comparison

Point out that partners should share their charts and make changes to them only if they are persuaded that the change is a better response. Partners' charts should not be identical.

Connect to the Literature

1. **What Do You Think?**
   Which of these haiku do you think is the most powerful? Explain.

Think Critically

2. What impressions of nature do the three haiku poets seem to share?
3. **ACTIVE READING: INTERPRETING DETAILS**
   Compare the charts that you recorded in your READER'S NOTEBOOK with those of a classmate. Were your emotional responses to the haiku similar? Discuss.

LITERARY ANALYSIS: ANALYZING IMAGERY

Imagery consists of words and phrases that appeal to the senses and create vivid images for the reader. In most haiku, two images are presented and compared. For example, the Bashō poem beginning "Pitifully . . ." contrasts a great soldier with a singing cricket. The connection seems to be that both of them have worn the helmet. Since the helmet is now empty, the soldier may represent death. Because the cricket is singing, it may represent continuing life.

Cooperative Learning Activity
With a group of classmates, analyze the images in the other haiku. Identify the images being compared, and determine what they might represent. Then discuss the meaning of each poem.

Points of Comparison

Review the haiku, and fill in your comparison-and-contrast chart. Focus on the two haiku you decided to analyze. The following questions may help focus your attention:

- Does the haiku follow the traditional syllable form?
- Is there a specific season suggested by a word or phrase?
- Is there one main image or two? What are the images describing?
- What mood is suggested by each image? That is, what thoughts or feelings are expressed by each image?

Paired Activity Share your chart with a classmate, and discuss the similarities and differences between the two haiku. Use your discussion to help you fill in your charts.

	Traditional	Traditional	20th-Century
Author	Bashō	Buson	
First line of poem	"Pitifully under"		
Traditional form (5/7/5 syllables)? (yes/no)	no		
Season/season word (if present)	summer/ "cricket"		
Image(s)			
Mood suggested			

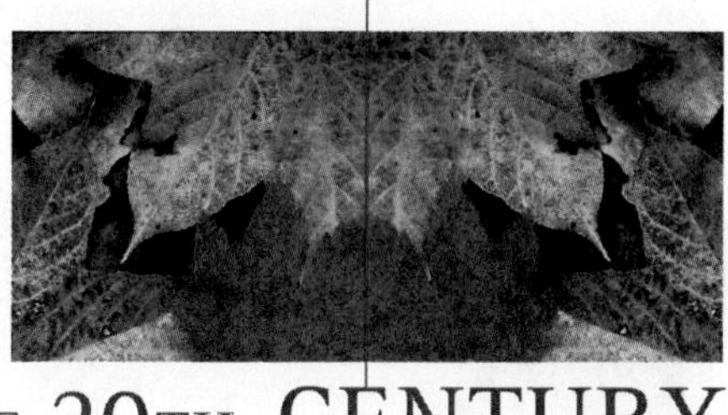

HAIKU IN THE 20TH CENTURY

Now that you have read several examples of traditional Japanese haiku, it's time to turn your attention to modern haiku by authors far removed from Japan. Western writers have been interested in studying and writing haiku since early in the 20th century. As you will see, these 20th-century poems have much in common with traditional Japanese haiku, but they also differ in interesting ways.

José Juan Tablada
1871–1945

A Restless Spirit Born in Mexico City, José Juan Tablada (hô-sā' hwän' tä-blä'dä) was a respected journalist, poet, and art critic. Tablada had a restless spirit and a questioning mind. As a young man, he broke away from modernism, a literary movement that stressed innovation and the rejection of traditional forms. Instead, Tablada wrote in a lively, playful style about Mexico's ancient religions and heritage. After a trip to Japan in 1900, he also introduced the haiku form into the Spanish language. In 1914, during the Mexican Revolution, Tablada was forced to leave his country for political reasons. He fled to New York, where he lived in exile for four years. In 1918 the new president of Mexico pardoned Tablada and appointed him to a diplomatic position in South America, but the poet resigned after two years because of health problems. He returned to New York, where he remained until his death.

Richard Wright
1908–1960

A Social Commentator Richard Wright, the son of a poor sharecropper, was born in Mississippi. His childhood was marked by hunger, beatings, and a struggle against the religious and racial restrictions imposed on him by his family and his culture. He wrote later that it was only through books that he managed to stay alive, books that he got by borrowing a white man's library card. As a young man, Wright escaped to Chicago, where he embarked on his writing career. In 1940, he gained international fame for his novel *Native Son.* In his fiction and in his autobiographies, *Black Boy* and *American Hunger,* Wright exposed the brutal racism in American life. During the last 18 months of his life, however, the writer began constructing delicate, vivid images of nature in haiku. Ill and living in Paris, Wright worked intensely on these poems. Before his death he collected 817 of his haiku into a manuscript, but he did not live to witness its publication.

5-Minute Warm-Up

Daily Language SkillBuilder

Have students **proofread** the display sentences on page 419k and write them correctly.

Reading and Analyzing

Literary Analysis METAPHOR

Remind students that a metaphor is a figure of speech that makes a comparison between two things that are basically unlike, yet have something in common. Unlike a simile, a metaphor does not contain the word *like* or *as*. Have students read Tablada's haiku "Watermelon" and ask what two things are being compared. *(summer and a slice of watermelon)* Then have students explain the comparison's effect.

Possible Response: The comparison creates a joyful, exuberant effect.

Active Reading

INTERPRETING DETAILS

Ask students to notice the details in Tablada's "Flying Fish." What image is suggested by the "sun's gold"? What do students see when they read "the pane of the sea bursts into splinters"? Why do they think the poem is called "Flying Fish"?

Possible Responses: The "sun's gold" suggests the sun's rays. The "splinters" represent light glinting off the water, or "pane of the sea." Flying fish may refer to the light dancing and sparkling across the surface of the sea.

Reading Skills and Strategies
DRAWING CONCLUSIONS

Tell students that readers must often draw their own conclusions about what they read. To do so, readers infer, or figure out, ideas that are not stated and combine these inferences with stated facts. In Wright's haiku about summer, what do students infer about the "siren cutting through / The hot summer air"?

Possible Response: The siren is a police car.

Considering that Richard Wright wrote about racism in his prose work, what conclusions can students draw about where the siren is blaring and what it represents?

Possible Responses: The siren is blaring through a city's ghetto. The siren represents the oppressive authority of white society.

Haiku

José Juan Tablada

MEXICO

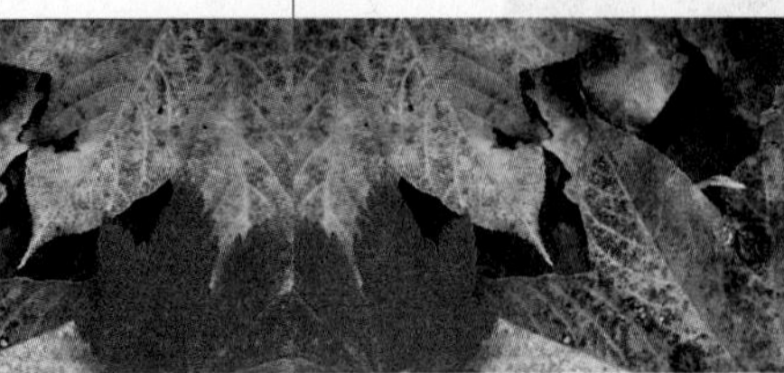

DRY LEAVES

The garden is full of dry leaves.
I never saw that many leaves
on the trees, when they were green, in the spring.

–TRANSLATED BY W. S. Merwin

FLYING FISH

Struck by the sun's gold
the pane of the sea bursts into splinters.

–TRANSLATED BY W. S. Merwin

WATERMELON

Red cold
guffaw of summer,
slice
of watermelon!

–TRANSLATED BY Samuel Beckett

Haiku

Richard Wright

UNITED STATES

A soft wind at dawn
Lifts one dry leaf and lays it
Upon another.

The metallic taste
Of a siren cutting through
The hot summer air.

Just enough of snow
To make you look carefully
At familiar streets.

The Rhythm of a Corner (1957). Photo by W. Eugene Smith.

Customizing Instruction

Less Proficient Readers
Have students compare images in Tablada's and Wright's haiku. Ask them to identify haiku that use the same images *("Dry Leaves" and "A soft wind at dawn")* Which season do the poems probably represent? *(autumn)* What different images do the two poets use to represent summer? *(Tablada uses a watermelon; Wright uses a siren.)*

Advanced Learners
Point out that Tablada's haiku have titles, while Wright's are untitled. Have students work with a partner to come up with titles for Wright's haiku. Explain that the titles should convey the haiku's mood or meaning.

Cross Curricular Link **History**

CIVIL RIGHTS MOVEMENT In the 1950s, most of American society was segregated. African Americans were forced to use separate schools, streetcars, and public restrooms. The facilities in these establishments were always inferior to those reserved for white people. Around the middle of the decade, however, African Americans began to demand equal rights. In 1954, *Brown v. Board of Education* struck down segregation in schools, declaring it unconstitutional. In 1955, Rosa Parks's refusal to sit in the "colored" section of a Montgomery, Alabama, bus prompted a boycott of the buses. The boycott, which resulted in the Supreme Court's outlawing bus segregation, was led by a young pastor named Dr. Martin Luther King, Jr.

In spite of this progress, segregation and hatred remained a fact of life for African Americans. Police sirens, such as the one suggested in Richard Wright's haiku, were a repressive and frightening reminder of white authority. Nonetheless, the civil rights movement continued to grow. In the 1960s, African Americans kept fighting for, and winning, greater equality.

Connect to the Literature

1. **What Do You Think?** Students should identify images that appeal to their senses.

Think Critically

2. Possible Response: The mood of the haiku seems to be cheerful and wondering.
3. Possible Responses: In the haiku about fall and winter, the speakers react to the seasonal changes in nature. In the haiku about summer, the season triggers an image of urban unrest.
4. Possible Responses: To Tablada, summer represents a time of happiness and relaxation. To Wright, summer represents a time of fear and danger.

Points of Comparison

After students have completed their charts, initiate a class discussion about their entries. Encourage students to tell which haiku or poet they liked best and to explain why.

To assess skills and concepts taught in this selection, use **Formal Assessment Book,** pp. 75–76

Connect to the Literature

1. **What Do You Think?**
Which image in these haiku did you find most striking? Why?

Think Critically

2. In general, what seems to be the mood of Tablada's haiku?
3. Fall, summer, and winter are represented in the three haiku by Wright. What do these poems suggest about the speakers' reactions to the seasons?
4. Compare Tablada's "Watermelon" with Wright's haiku about summer. Based on these poems, what do you think summer represents to each poet?

THINK ABOUT
- the mood and tone of each poem
- the sensory details used
- the images each poet uses to depict summer

Points of Comparison

Paired Activity Now that you have read and studied all of the poems, work with a partner to compare and contrast the haiku you already analyzed with one by a 20th-century author. Together, respond to the Points of Comparison questions on page 546. Use your discussion to help you complete the comparison-and-contrast chart.

	Traditional	Traditional	20th-Century
Author	Bashō	Buson	Wright
First line of poem	"Pitifully under"	"The old man"	"Just enough of snow"
Traditional form (5/7/5 syllables)? (yes/no)	no	no	yes
Season/season word (if present)	summer/ "cricket"		
Image(s)			
Mood suggested			

Standardized Test Practice

Writing About Literature

PART 1 Reading the Prompt

In writing assessments, you may be asked to compare and contrast works of literature that share a similar form, such as the haiku that you have analyzed. You are now going to practice writing an essay that involves this type of comparison.

Writing Prompt

Traditional Japanese haiku and haiku written in the 20th century have interesting similarities and differences. Choose three haiku—two by different Japanese poets and one by a 20th-century poet—and compare and contrast them. (1) For each haiku, discuss the form (the pattern of syllables), the season (if known), the images, and the thoughts and feelings expressed by those images. (2) Point out differences and similarities among the haiku. Give evidence from the poems to support your analysis. (3)

STRATEGIES IN ACTION

(1) I have to **compare and contrast** three haiku.

(2) For each poem, I need to discuss the **form, season, images,** and **thoughts and feelings** expressed.

(3) I need to include **details, examples,** or **quotations** from the poems to support my opinion.

PART 2 Planning a Comparison-and-Contrast Essay

- Review the comparison-and-contrast chart that you began and completed on pages 540, 546, and 550.
- Using your chart, find examples of similarities and differences to point out in your essay.
- Create an outline to help organize your ideas.

PART 3 Drafting Your Essay

Introduction Begin by introducing your topic and identifying the basis of comparison. Briefly express your opinion about what the three haiku have in common. Then explain what you see as major differences.

Body You may wish to devote one paragraph to each poem. Within your paragraphs, you will need to discuss how each poem is different from the others and how it is similar. Pay the most attention to the feelings and ideas expressed by each poem. Use your comparison-and-contrast chart to help you identify details and examples.

Conclusion Wrap up your essay with a summary of the major differences and similarities.

Revision Check the use of signal words, such as *similarly, also, like, but, unlike,* and *while,* to show the relationship between comparisons and contrasts.

TEST PRACTICE

PART 1 Reading the Prompt
Model the process of reading a prompt:

- Read through the entire prompt.
- List key words of the assignment on the board ("compare and contrast," "evidence").
- Define each key word using Strategies in Action to show how students can restate the prompts in their own words.

PART 2 Planning a Comparison-Contrast Essay

- Students can use the chart they have been filling out for the traditional and 20th-century haiku (referenced on pages 540, 546, and 550).
- Encourage students to pay particular attention to similarities and differences in images and mood among the haiku. The form and season words used should be discussed as secondary points.
- In organizing their outlines, students may use a subject-by-subject order, listing all of the features in one poem at a time, or a feature-by-feature order, comparing a single feature in all of the poems at a time.

PART 3 Drafting Your Essay
Introduction Tell students that opening their essay with a quotation from one of the poems can be an effective way to introduce their opinion. Using a quotation can grab and engage a reader's attention.
Body Remind students that each paragraph in the body of their essay should support their thesis and flow logically from one to another. Students should also make sure that each paragraph supports a single main idea.
Conclusion Suggest that students conclude by summarizing their ideas and emphasizing their main points. However, they should be careful not to introduce new ideas in their conclusions.
Revision In addition to signal words, students may want to use word chains that refer to something that came before. Common word chains include pronouns and repeated or reworded key words.

Use **Unit Three Resource Book,** p. 46, for additional support.

Assessment Standardized Test Practice

RESPONDING TO A WRITING PROMPT Read aloud the writing prompt at the top of this page. Discuss the **Strategies in Action** by asking students to identify the words in the prompt that tell them what to do. Suggest that they mark up their comparison-and-contrast charts, identifying points to include in their essays. When students have finished drafting their essays, have them work with a partner to see if they have accomplished the tips given in Part 3 **Drafting Your Essay.**

Objectives

- write a Problem-Solution Essay
- use a written text as a model for writing
- revise a draft to elaborate with facts and statistics
- correct errors in verb forms

Introducing the Workshop

A Problem-Solution Essay Explain to students that in a problem-solution essay, the writer proposes a detailed solution to an existing problem. Identifying and solving problems are practical skills with many applications in business, school, and the community. Ask students to describe instances in their lives when they have encountered a problem and proposed a solution. Ask them to comment on how successful they were in convincing others to support the changes they proposed.

Discuss some of the general features of a convincing solution to a problem. Point out that by writing a problem-solution essay, students will be presenting a solution to an existing problem.

Basics in a Box

B Using the Graphic As suggested by the graphic, the introduction states and analyzes an existing problem. The "light bulb," or body of the essay, provides readers with an enlightened solution to the problem. The conclusion restates the problem and explains the benefits of the solution.

C Presenting the Rubric To better understand the assignment, students can refer to the Standards for Writing a Successful Problem-Solution Essay. You may wish to discuss with them the complete rubric and student models in the Unit Three Resource Book on pages 52–58.

For more instruction and practice in informative exposition, use McDougal Littell's ***Language Network:***

- Grade 10, Chapter 23, "Problem-Solution Essay"
- Grade 12, Chapter 22, "Proposal"

Writing Workshop

Problem-Solution Essay

Writing to Solve Problems

A **From Reading to Writing** In his *Zen Teachings,* Musō Soseki tells a number of short morality tales. These tales are meant to serve as examples for readers, offering advice about how to handle life's troubles and problems. A good deal of nonfiction writing throughout history has contained some sort of advice or solution to problems. Even today, many people—such as journalists, business people, or concerned citizens—write **problem-solution essays** as a way of exploring an issue and proposing a solution.

For Your Portfolio

WRITING PROMPT Write a problem-solution essay examining a problem that deeply interests you.

Purpose: To inform and to persuade

Audience: Anyone interested in the problem you are addressing

Basics in a Box

B

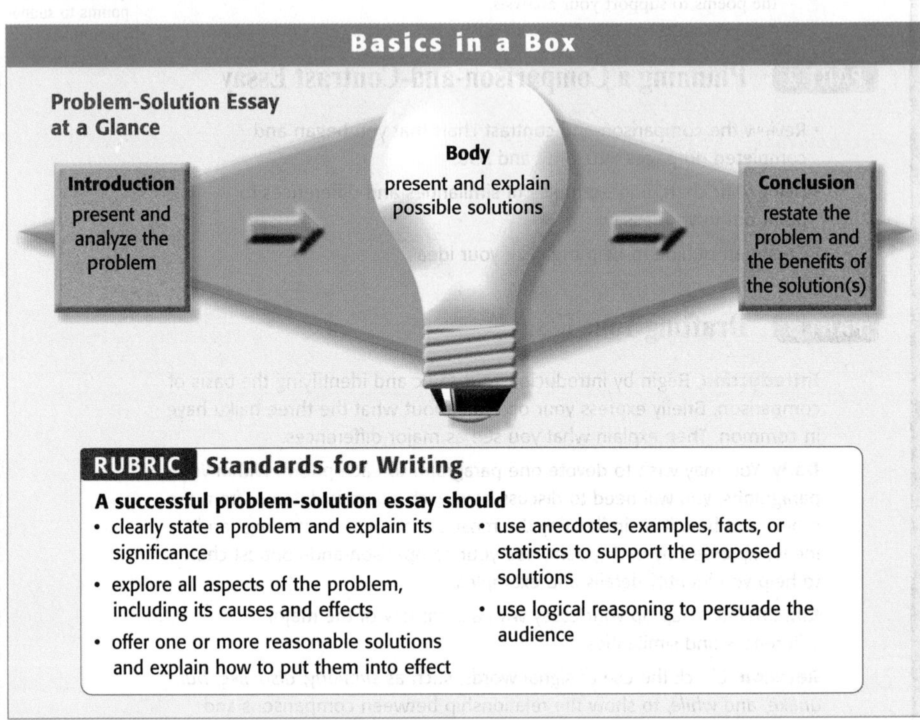

C

RUBRIC Standards for Writing

A successful problem-solution essay should

- clearly state a problem and explain its significance
- explore all aspects of the problem, including its causes and effects
- offer one or more reasonable solutions and explain how to put them into effect
- use anecdotes, examples, facts, or statistics to support the proposed solutions
- use logical reasoning to persuade the audience

LESSON RESOURCES

USING PRINT RESOURCES
Unit Three Resource Book

- Prewriting, p. 47
- Drafting, p. 48
- Peer Response, pp. 49–50
- Revising, Editing, and Proofreading, p. 51
- Student Models, pp. 52–57
- Rubric, p. 58

USING MEDIA RESOURCES
Writing Coach CD-ROM
Visit our Web site: classzone.com

ADDITIONAL RESOURCES
For a complete view of Lesson Resources, see page 419h of this book.

Analyzing a Student Model

by Lucy Kinnear
Burr Oak High School

RUBRIC IN ACTION

The Need for Elder Care

Last week there was a fire in our apartment. My mom, my little brother, and I were standing outside when Mom suddenly shouted, "I smell smoke!" She turned and ran inside, just in time to put out a fire that started after my grandmother accidentally placed a newspaper on the lit stove. Grandma was sitting in the living room, reading a magazine and oblivious to the fire. If a similar fire had happened while Grandma was alone, she might not have been able to put out the flames before they spread.

> ❶ Introduces problem with an anecdote
>
> **Other Option:**
> - Begin with a direct explanation of the problem

My grandmother is a relatively strong, healthy woman. She moved in with us last year after my grandfather died. Since then she has become depressed, and six months ago she suffered a small stroke, which caused her to become forgetful and distracted. We love having her at home, but I do worry about her. Both of my parents work, and my grandmother is left alone every day until I get home from school. I fear that one day an accident will happen and we'll arrive too late. (D)

This isn't just one family's problem; it's a problem faced by every American family with elderly members. Even active, healthy people in their 70s or 80s may need someone around the house. Otherwise, they may not be able to get help if they are injured, and they may not receive proper nutrition. In addition, the boredom and loneliness suffered by the elderly can cause mental and physical health problems.

> ❷ Describes the problem on a societal level

Ironically, people who are too healthy and independent to enter nursing homes are the ones most likely to suffer from this problem. Most of them can't afford—or don't want—a full-time companion. For many independent elderly people, the last thing they want is to have some stranger come in and take charge of their lives.

Elder care has changed greatly over the centuries. For one thing, we now have more elderly people in our population. The life expectancy of Americans has almost doubled in the past two hundred years, rising from age 35 to age 75. Since 1990, the number of elderly people in the United States has grown quickly, and people age 85 and older are the fastest-growing group of elderly people. The U.S. Census Bureau predicts that by the year 2050, as many as 20 percent of Americans could be elderly, up from 12 percent in 1997.

> ❸ Identifies one cause of the problem and elaborates with statistics

LANGUAGE SKILLS

Teaching the Lesson

Analyzing the Model
"The Need for Elder Care"

(D) The writer addresses a family problem, which is also a societal problem. After analyzing the problem's causes and effects, she suggests a solution that larger communities might want to adopt.

After students read the model, they can take turns reading aloud the **Rubric in Action.** Point out key words and phrases in the student model that correspond to the elements mentioned in the **Rubric in Action.**

1. Point out to students that introducing an essay with an anecdote is an effective way to quickly gain readers' attention, interest, and sympathy. However, writers should be careful to avoid anecdotes that are stereotypical or melodramatic.
2. Point out that the topic sentence of the third paragraph acts as a transition between the introduction and the rest of the essay.
3. Have students label the specific aspect of the problem that this paragraph addresses. *(The number of elderly people in our population has risen significantly in the past 200 years, and they are now the fastest-growing segment of the population.)*

MINI LESSON Patterns of Organization

PICTURING TEXT STRUCTURE

Instruction Stating the problem and offering clear solutions is an important part of writing a problem-solution essay. Good writers signal their readers to let them know which sections define the problem and which propose solutions.

Activity Have students analyze the text structure of the student model by working in pairs to discuss what the writer accomplished in each paragraph of the essay.

I. Introduces the problem: lack of care for the elderly

II. Explains the problem
  A. Nationwide problem
  B. Growing elderly population
  C. Breakdown of extended family
  D. Traditional caregivers no longer at home

III. Proposes solution: day-care centers for senior citizens
  A. Professionally staffed
  B. Tailored to serve emotional, physical, and intellectual needs

IV. Summarizes reasons to adopt solutions

4. Point out that the writer uses three quarters of the essay to explain the problem, devoting only the final fourth to the proposal of a solution. A writer decides how much room to devote to the problem and the solution, depending on the topic and the audience. Ask students why they think this writer chose to focus primarily on the problem rather than the solution.
   Possible Response: Establishing the seriousness of the problem is the first step in solving it. If the readers do not recognize the problem or take it seriously, they are unlikely to support any solution.
5. Ask students to identify the details used to make this proposal sound appealing.
   Possible Response: The writer discusses elderly people in respectful and compassionate terms; she describes the centers as professionally run institutions; the proposed centers are warm and friendly places that offer companionship; they would offer food and places to rest; they would offer intellectual stimulation in the form of books and classes.
6. Discuss with students the tactic of considering and countering an opposing viewpoint. Ask them why this writer and so many other writers use this technique.
   Possible Response: By anticipating any objections a reader might have, a writer can relieve the reader's concerns; by showing that she has thought of possible objections, the writer shows herself to be thoughtful and aware of more than one point of view, which makes her more credible.
7. Ask students whether they find the proposal convincing, and why. If it is not convincing, what could the writer have done differently?
   Possible Responses: Yes, the writer did a good job of explaining the issue and proposing a thorough, detailed solution; No, the writer did not convince me that these centers would actually be nice places—she should have gone into more detail about how they would be planned; No, she did not convince me that she knows enough about elderly people to propose a good solution; she should have cited expert opinions on the topic.

However, even as they increase in number, fewer elderly people are living in nursing homes. Between 1985 and 1995, the number of nursing home residents age 85 and older decreased by 10 percent. More and more people are spending their later years at home, and many of them live alone.

In generations past, older people have lived with their grown children. However, most Americans no longer live with their extended families. Today, the elderly still rely on their children or other relatives, but they most often live apart from them—sometimes even in a different state. While more people are relying on younger relatives for their care, there are fewer people with time to care for them.

Women have traditionally cared for the elderly, and women still make up the majority of caregivers. However, the majority of these women now hold paying jobs in addition to their family responsibilities. People in almost one-fourth of U.S. households provide some form of care to elderly relatives or friends. It's easy to see the financial, emotional, and physical strain that can result from these conditions.

❹ Explores other causes of the problem

We need day-care centers for senior citizens who live alone or who are home alone during the day. This is not to say that the elderly should be treated like children. They are adults with a lifetime of experience and individual needs. However, structured companionship and care can go a long way in meeting these needs. These centers should be warm, friendly, and professionally staffed. People would find companionship among their peers. There would be classes to take, books to read, food to eat, and a place to nap. No one would go hungry because he or she forgot to eat or felt too tired to prepare a meal.

❺ Proposes a solution to the problem, offering some detail about how it should work

Some object that such a center wouldn't really be all that happy, cheerful, or homey—that it would end up as a place to tuck away unwanted seniors. This must not happen. These centers must make it a priority to maintain an energetic and nurturing atmosphere, giving attention to individual needs. A caring staff and a wide range of activities could make the center comfortable for all.

❻ Anticipates and counters a possible objection to this solution

It always takes people a while to adapt to new ideas, and day care for the elderly must be introduced in a caring and respectful manner. Its primary goal should be to provide services with dignity and compassion. With this goal in mind and community resources behind it, elder day care can fill a gap that we cannot afford to ignore.

❼ Concludes by summing up the goals of the proposed solution and arguing for its necessity

Writing your Problem-Solution Essay

❶ Prewriting

Begin by thinking of a meaningful problem that exists in a local, national, or international community. Brainstorm a list of problems that affect you directly or indirectly, or problems you've read about. Try to focus on problems that are specific enough to be reasonably addressed; for example, world hunger is a lot harder to tackle than hunger in your own community. See the **Idea Bank** in the margin for more suggestions. After you have selected a problem in need of a solution, follow the steps below.

Planning Your Problem-Solution Essay

1. **Think about the problem.** Why do you think this is a serious problem? Whom does it affect and how? What are its causes?
2. **Brainstorm possible solutions.** How might this problem be solved? Draw a cluster map to display possible solutions.
3. **Consider each solution and eliminate impractical ones.** Does one solution stand out as the best? Would people support it? What kind of political and economic backing might it draw? What kind of opposition might it attract?
4. **Identify your audience.** Who will read your essay? What do your readers already know and think about the problem? How can you address their concerns?
5. **Research necessary supporting facts.** What kinds of data will help support the solution to the problem? Do you need to do research, consult experts, or examine your own thoughts?

❷ Drafting

At first, just write the essay from beginning to end, getting your thoughts on paper. Don't worry yet about form or completeness; that will come later. Consider using the following structure:

- **Identify** the problem and explain why it's important.
- **Explain** the problem's causes and effects, giving facts, statistics, examples, or quotations to support your points.
- **Explain** and support the proposed solution or solutions. Address any concerns or objections you anticipate from your audience.
- **Conclude** by summarizing your solution and describing how to achieve it.

IDEABank

1. Your Working Portfolio
Build on the **Writing Option** you completed earlier in this unit:
Zen Solutions, p. 517.

2. Talk of the Town
Read the front section of your local newspaper. What issues are causing problems? What solutions can you offer?

3. Community Beat
As you walk, bicycle, or otherwise travel through your community, make a mental note of any problems you see, such as a dangerous empty lot or unplowed streets. Think about what solutions you might propose.

LANGUAGE SKILLS

Guiding Student Writing

Prewriting

Choosing a Topic

If after reading the **Idea Bank** students are having difficulty choosing a problem, suggest they try the following:

- List problems you face in your job.
- Focus on social problems in your community, such as unemployment, after-school programs, crime, or ethnic conflicts.
- Focus on problems faced by teenagers.
- Think about problems for which teenagers could be part of the solution, such as tutoring younger children or working with elderly people.

Planning the Problem-Solution Essay

1. Having identified a problem's causes and effects, students should think about whether the causes can be eliminated or the effects can be altered.

4, 5. Encourage students to anticipate any objections to their solution and look for facts and statistics that will help them counter those objections.

Drafting

Some students will prefer to draft freely and see where their ideas take them. Others might prefer working from an outline based on the four headings suggested in the text.

Some students might prefer an in-between approach, where they do not write a formal outline but write down their thoughts, quickly sketching out the paragraphs and planning briefly what they will say in each one.

Encourage students not to be slowed by their "internal editor," but to write down as much as they can, saving all improvements for later.

Revising

ELABORATING WITH FACTS AND STATISTICS

"Since 1990" is more accurate and factual than "In the last few years." By identifying people of age 85 and older as the fastest-growing group, the writer is elaborating on the sentence by making it more specific.

Editing and Proofreading

INCORRECT VERB FORMS

If students need help with correct verb forms, use the Grammar Mini-Lesson at the bottom of this page.

The sentence is written in the present tense, as indicated by "I do." The correct form of *love* in the present tense is *loved*.

Reflecting

Have students write brief notes addressing the question in the text. Then have them clip their responses to their essays and place both in their working portfolios.

Need revising help?

Review the **Rubric,** p. 552

Consider **peer reader** comments

Check **Revision Guidelines,** p. R19

Review the **Elaboration Guidelines,** p. R25

Need help with verb forms?

See the **Grammar Handbook,** p. R59

Publishing IDEAS

- Send your essay as a letter to the editor of your local or school newspaper.
- Post your essay to a chat room or electronic bulletin board on the topic.

3 Revising

TARGET SKILL ▶ ELABORATING WITH FACTS AND STATISTICS As you revise your essay, look for places where you can elaborate on your ideas by adding facts and statistics. A fact is a statement that can be proved or disproved by the use of reference materials or by firsthand observation. Statistics are facts expressed in numbers.

Ask Your Peer Reader

- How would you define the problem I've described?
- Which information did you find most convincing? Which was the least convincing?
- What questions do you still have about the problem or the solution?
- What parts are unclear?

~~In the last few years~~ *Since 1990*, the number of elderly people in the United States has grown quickly, *and people age 85 and older are the fastest-growing group of elderly people.*

4 Editing and Proofreading

TARGET SKILL ▶ INCORRECT VERB FORMS Verbs take different forms to show tense, mood, and voice. The use of incorrect verb forms can confuse your reader and make a bad impression in situations where standard English is expected, such as school essays. Read your work carefully and check for errors in verb forms. If you aren't sure whether a verb form is correct, check a grammar book that lists the principal parts of verbs.

We loved having her at home, but I do worry about her.

5 Reflecting

FOR YOUR WORKING PORTFOLIO How did writing your essay help you find a solution to the problem? Attach your answer to your finished work. Save your problem-solution essay in your **Working Portfolio.**

MINI LESSON Grammar

INCORRECT VERB FORMS

Instruction Review the four principal parts of a verb: present (*walk*), present participle (*is walking*), past (*walked*), and past participle (*have walked*). Also review the difference between regular verbs (where *-ed* or *-d* is added to the present to form the past or past participle) and irregular verbs.

Practice Write the following paragraph on the chalkboard and underline the verbs in boldface. Have students correctly write the verb forms.

Our family **took** a vacation next month. *(is taking/will take)* This year, we **will be agreeing** to do things differently. *(have agreed/agree)* Instead of taking a trip somewhere, we **were going** to stay in town. *(are going)* We **plan** five or six day-long activities. *(have planned/planned)* We **gone** to museums and to the beach. *(will go)* We **are visiting** my grandparents, and probably have a picnic or two. *(will visit/are going to visit)*

For more instruction and practice in verb forms, use McDougal Littell's ***Language Network:***

- Grade 10, Chapter 6, "Using Verbs"
- Grade 12, Chapter 4, "Using Verbs"

Read this paragraph from the first draft of a letter to the editor. The underlined phrases may include the following kinds of errors:

- **incorrect verb forms**
- **weak use of the passive voice**
- **double negatives**
- **capitalization errors**

For each underlined phrase, choose the revision that most improves the writing.

Winter has come, and it has brung a foot of snow. (1) Last Monday's blizzard turned the streets of hoagland falls into a disaster area. (2) Although the snowplows came out early Monday morning, only a few major streets were plowed by them. (3) People spent hours on Monday and Tuesday shoveling out their cars on side streets, only to have them plown under (4) when the city finally sent out the plows again without telling no one they were coming. (5) Why doesn't the city plow alternate sides of the streets on alternate days? If people know what to expect, their cars can be moved (6) in time to make room for the plows and to save their own cars from being plowed in.

1. **A.** it has broughten a foot of snow.
   B. it has brought a foot of snow.
   C. it brang a foot of snow.
   D. Correct as is
2. **A.** Hoagland Falls into a disaster area.
   B. Hoagland Falls into a Disaster Area.
   C. Hoagland falls into a disaster area.
   D. Correct as is
3. **A.** only a few major streets were plowed.
   B. they plowed only a few major streets.
   C. plowing only a few major streets.
   D. Correct as is
4. **A.** plowed under
   B. plow under
   C. being plowed under
   D. Correct as is
5. **A.** without telling nobody they were coming.
   B. without telling.
   C. without telling anyone they were coming.
   D. Correct as is
6. **A.** their cars can always be moved
   B. they can move their cars
   C. their cars can be moved by them
   D. Correct as is

Need extra help?

See the **Grammar Handbook**
Verbs, pp. R59–R61
Voice, p. R61
Double Negatives, p. R64
Quick Reference: Capitalization, p. R79

TEST PRACTICE

Standardized Test Practice

Before students begin the exercise, you may wish to review briefly the types of errors that the passage may contain. Encourage students to read all the choices carefully before they select the correct answer to each question.

Answers:
1. B; **2.** A; **3.** B; **4.** A; **5.** C; **6.** B

MINI LESSON Grammar

PASSIVE VOICE

Instruction Explain to students that voice refers to the relationship of a verb to its subject. If a verb is in the active voice, its subject performs an action. When a verb is in the passive voice, the subject receives the action. Write the following sentences on the chalkboard:

Active voice: We ate the salad.

Passive voice: The salad was eaten by us.

Overuse of the passive voice can be awkward or unclear. Encourage students to use the active voice whenever they can.

Practice Have students rewrite the following sentences, changing verbs from the passive to the active voice.

1. The flower garden has been ruined by the rabbits.
2. I was given a passing grade by Mr. Spokes.
3. A beautiful toast was given by the bride's sister.

For more instruction and practice in using the active voice, use McDougal Littell's ***Language Network:***

- Grade 10, Chapter 6, "Using Verbs"
- Grade 12, Chapter 4, "Using Verbs"

Objectives

- expand vocabulary through the use of dictionaries and thesauruses
- review strategies for using a dictionary and a thesaurus
- become familiar with the kinds of information found in a dictionary, including the definition, sample usage, etymology, and related words
- practice using a dictionary to understand words
- practice using a thesaurus to find appropriate synonyms

EXERCISE

You may need to point out to students that the etymology is not always given for every single form of a word. If they do not find the etymology in the first entry they look up, they should look in entries of related words.

Student responses may vary slightly in the number of definitions or extent of the etymology given, depending upon their dictionaries. Student sentences will vary; sample responses are given.

1. **earnest** *adj.* (1) showing deep sincerity or seriousness; (2) of a serious nature (ME *ernest*, from Old English *eornoste*) **earnestly, earnestness**
   Gabriel made an earnest plea to her parents for a later curfew. (solemn)
2. **adornment** *n.* (1) the act of adorning; (2) something that beautifies; an ornament (from ME *adornen*, from Old French *adourner*, from Latin *ad+ōrnāre*, to decorate) **adorn, adorner**
   The queen wore a headdress, earrings, and several other adornments. (ornaments)
3. **loath** *adj.* unwilling (ME *loth*, displeasing, loath, from Old English *lāth*, hateful, loathsome) **loath, loathsome**
   I am loath to do much cooking in this heat. (reluctant)
4. **acquisition** *n.* something gained (ME *adquisicioun*, attainment, from Latin *acquisitiōn-*, from *acquīrere*, to acquire.) **acquire, acquisitive**
   The museum's latest acquisition is a painting by Picasso. (addition)
5. **contaminate** *v.* to make pure or unclean by contact (ME *contaminat-en*, from Latin *contāmināre*) **contaminator, contaminant**
   The diseased meat will contaminate the rest of the meat if we are not careful. (taint)

Use **Unit Three Resource Book,** p. 59, for more practice.

Building Vocabulary

Using Reference Tools

In an age of information, when we have hundreds of reference tools to choose from, the dictionary and the thesaurus remain two of the most valuable and reliable. The following strategies can help you make the most of these trusty, familiar books.

Strategies for Building Vocabulary

❶ **Dictionary** A dictionary entry has many parts. By taking a few extra moments to study the entire entry, you can strengthen your understanding of that word and of related words.

> **ar•dor** (är'dər) *n.* Ⓐ 1. Fiery intensity of feeling. Ⓑ *He began to write songs with renewed ardor.* 2. Strong enthusiasm or devotion; zeal. 3. Intense heat or glow, as of fire. Ⓒ [ME *ardour,* from OF, from L *ārdor,* from ārdēre, to burn. Ⓓ see **ARSON**]

Ⓐ **Numbered Definitions** Read every definition to be sure you've found the one you're looking for, and to get a more complete sense of the word.

Ⓑ **Sample Usage** Seeing a word used in context is often the fastest and easiest way to understand it.

Ⓒ **Etymology** This brief history shows the succession of a word's "ancestors" in other languages, starting with the most recent. Many dictionaries use standard abbreviations here, such as *ME* for Middle English, *OF* for Old French, and *L* for Latin. You can find a key to these abbreviations in the front of your dictionary. You can see here that *ardor* is descended from the Latin word *ārdēre,* which means "to burn."

Ⓓ **Related Words** Knowing other English words with the same root can shed light on a word's meaning.

All of this information should help you remember that *ardor* describes a fiery passion or heat, and it is descended from the Latin word for *burn.* The next time you see this word or related words in print, or have reason to use them, you'll be on much stronger ground.

❷ **Thesaurus** Imagine that you want to think of another word for *stubborn* in this sentence: "Yoshi tried to convince his cousin to change his mind, but Hiro remained stubborn." Then look at the following thesaurus entry for *stubborn.*

> **stubborn** *adjective* Firmly, often unreasonably resolved or determined: adamant, implacable, incompliant, obstinate.

Look at the synonyms listed. Each of the synonyms has a different **connotation,** or shade of meaning. For example, *adamant* means "stubbornly inflexible," while *implacable* means "impossible to pacify or satisfy." When you're unsure of a word's exact meaning, check the dictionary.

In this case, *adamant* is probably the best substitute for *stubborn.* Remember, though, that a fancy word is not necessarily better than a plain one, and sometimes you may wish to stick with your first choice. Nonetheless, a look in the thesaurus will always show you the range of words available to you.

EXERCISE For each of the words below, use a dictionary to find their definitions and etymologies, and any related words. Write down this information, choose one definition (if the word has more than one), and then use the word in a sentence. Finally, look up the word in a thesaurus and find a synonym to replace the word in your sentence.

1. earnest **2.** adornment **3.** loath
4. acquisition **5.** contaminate

Sentence Crafting

Creating Compound and Complex Sentences

Grammar from Literature Skilled writers know how to construct sentences that express ideas concisely and effectively. Using a variety of sentence structures can strengthen your writing and add shape to your paragraphs.

A **simple sentence** contains a single independent clause, which can stand alone. A **compound sentence** consists of two independent clauses connected by a semicolon, or by a comma and a coordinating conjunction, such as *and, but,* or *or.*

independent clause
He summoned his gentlemen-in-waiting.

independent clause — coordinating conjunction — independent clause
All the ladies gathered round, and Her Majesty summoned Lady Ukon.

—Sei Shōnagon, *The Pillow Book*

A **complex sentence** consists of one independent clause and at least one subordinate clause, which does not express a complete thought and cannot stand alone as a sentence. Subordinate clauses are introduced by subordinating conjunctions, such as *when, if, before,* or *where.*

subordinate clause
When the Empress explained what had happened,
independent clause
everyone talked and laughed with great excitement.

—*The Pillow Book*

Showing connections between ideas is an important feature of good writing. Look through your writing for related ideas and consider combining them in compound or complex sentences.

RELATED IDEAS
Lady Uma didn't like dogs. She found this one charming.

COMPOUND SENTENCE — coordinating conjunction
Lady Uma didn't like dogs, but she found this one charming.

COMPLEX SENTENCE
subordinating conjunction
Although Lady Uma didn't like dogs, she found this one charming.

Usage Tip A subordinate clause that stands alone is called a **fragment.** Complete sentence fragments by combining them with independent clauses or rewriting them as independent clauses.

FRAGMENT
When Lady Uma picked up the dog. He started to growl.
CORRECT
When Lady Uma picked up the dog, he started to growl.

If you use a comma between the two independent clauses in a compound sentence, you must also include a coordinating conjunction. Leaving out the coordinating conjunction results in a type of run-on sentence known as a comma splice.

COMMA SPLICE
The dog snapped at her, she let him drop.
CORRECT
The dog snapped at her, so she let him drop.

WRITING EXERCISE Combine the following pairs of sentences using the conjunction given in parentheses. Identify the new sentence as compound or complex.

1. The Emperor was given a cat. He was very fond of her. (semicolon)
2. She was only a cat. He awarded her a title of nobility. (although)
3. Okinamaro, one of the dogs at court, harassed the cat. He was banished to Dog Island. (when)
4. A dog from the island was beaten severely. He had tried to return to court. (because)
5. The people at court didn't recognize the dog at first. They finally realized it was Okinamaro. (but)

GRAMMAR EXERCISE Rewrite the following sentences, correcting any sentence fragments and comma splices.

1. Lady Myōbu was a very lovely cat. Who had the best of everything.
2. She ate the finest treats, she slept on a silken pillow.
3. Lady Uma fed the cat. Whenever she was hungry.
4. As long as she lived. The cat wanted for nothing.
5. The Empress loved her, the Emperor thought she could do no wrong.

LANGUAGE SKILLS

Objectives

- use varied sentence structure to express meanings and achieve desired effect
- revise drafts by rethinking content, organization, and style, to better accomplish the task

WRITING EXERCISE

1. The Emperor was given a cat; he was very fond of her.
2. Although she was only a cat, he awarded her a title of nobility.
3. When Okinamaro, one of the dogs at court, harassed the cat, he was banished to Dog Island.
4. A dog from the island was beaten severely because he had tried to return to court.
5. The people at court didn't recognize the dog at first, but they finally realized it was Okinamaro.

GRAMMAR EXERCISE

1. Lady Myōbu was a very lovely cat who had the best of everything.
2. She ate the finest treats and slept on a silken pillow.
3. Lady Uma fed the cat whenever she was hungry.
4. As long as she lived, the cat wanted for nothing.
5. The Empress loved her, and the Emperor thought she could do no wrong.

Use **Unit Three Resource Book,** p. 60, for more practice.

MINI LESSON Grammar

RUN-ON SENTENCES

Remind students that a run-on sentence is made up of two or more sentences that are written as though they were one sentence. Write the following sentence on the board:

I forgot to move the car, I got a parking ticket.

Explain to students that a run-on sentence can be repaired in any one of four ways:

Add a conjunction: I forgot to move the car, and I got a parking ticket.

Change the comma to a semicolon: I forgot to move the car; I got a parking ticket.

Form two sentences: I forgot to move the car. I got a parking ticket.

Change one sentence into a subordinate clause: Because I forgot to move the car, I got a parking ticket.

For more instruction and practice in correcting run-on sentences, use McDougal Littell's ***Language Network:***

- Grade 10, Chapter 4, "Clauses and Sentence Structure"
- Grade 12, Chapter 3, "Using Clauses"

Objectives
- reflect on and assess understanding of Japanese culture and values
- evaluate theme in traditional Japanese literature
- identify imagery and mood in traditional Japanese literature
- assess and build portfolios

Reflecting on the Literature
You might have students work in groups of three to identify the topics and their messages. Each student in a group should work on one topic.
Possible Responses: Nature—In Matsuo Bashō's haiku "Withered winter grass," the poet's observation of the succession of the seasons seems to suggest a hopeful message of rebirth and renewal; Time—In Zeami Motokiyo's *The Deserted Crone,* the old woman suffers because she cannot let go of the physical world, which suggests the futility of trying to live in the past; Duty—In the Zen parable "Right & Wrong," Bankei is willing to sacrifice all of his honest pupils in order to save one who doesn't know right from wrong, suggesting that a teacher's duty is to teach those who need him most.

 Use **Unit Three Resource Book,** p. 61, for additional support.

Reviewing Literary Concepts
Encourage students to work with a partner to list or chart the sensory details used to create each word picture. Have pairs study their lists of sensory details and take turns reading the selection aloud to help identify its mood. Tell students that they should listen for changes in the reader's voice that might indicate the selection's mood.

Building Your Portfolio
Students will use their Presentation Portfolios to file what they consider their highest quality work—the very best projects and activities from their Working Portfolios.

 For more information on using writing and assessing portfolios, see the **Teacher's Guide to Assessment and Portfolio Use,** pp. 53–74.

Part Assessment
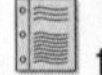 To assess skills and concepts taught in this unit part, use **Formal Assessment Book,** pp. 77–78.

Reflect and Assess

What did you learn about Japanese culture from reading the selections in Unit Three, Part Two? Did the literature give you a better understanding of traditional Japanese values? Use the following options to help you explore what you have learned.

Detail of *Five Beautiful Women* (early 19th century), Katsushika Hokusai. Ink and color on silk. Margaret E. Fuller Purchase Fund, Seattle Art Museum, Seattle, Washington. Photograph by Susan Dirk. Photo © Seattle Art Museum.

Reflecting on the Literature

Recurring Topics Nature, time, and duty are recurring topics in traditional Japanese literature. Think about the literature you have read in this part of the book. Then choose three selections: one that makes an observation about nature, one that deals with time, and one that comments on duty. In your own words, state the writer's message about each topic.

Reviewing Literary Concepts

Identifying Imagery and Mood Most of the selections in this part of the book use vivid images to help bring a character, a setting, or an object to life. Select three images found in the literature that you think are especially striking. What sensory details did the writer use to create each word picture? Then think about the mood the image conveys. In your opinion, which image most powerfully conveys a particular mood?

Self ASSESSMENT

READER'S NOTEBOOK
The following list contains terms that you encountered as you learned about traditional Japanese literature. Copy the list on a piece of paper. Then work with a partner to write a sentence describing or defining each word or concept. If you don't remember the meaning of a term, review the lesson in which it appeared or consult the **Glossary of Literary Terms** (page R91).

haiku	simplicity
Noh drama	Zen
The Pillow Book	imagery
tanka	parable

 Building Your Portfolio

Writing Workshop and Writing Options Review the problem-and-solution essay you wrote for the Writing Workshop on page 552 and the various Writing Options you completed for the lessons in this part of the book. Which piece would you consider sharing with others? Add the assignment to your **Presentation Portfolio**, along with a cover note telling what obstacles you overcame to write it.

Setting GOALS

Try your hand at writing some of the traditional Japanese literary forms you have learned about. You might write delicate haiku or tanka about nature, or you might keep a *Pillow Book*-style journal in which you record your observations and philosophy of life. If you prefer working in a group, collaborate with your classmates on writing a modern Noh play.

Key Standard for Grade 12
R3.2 Analyze the way in which the theme of a selection represents a view of life; use evidence from the text to support the claim.
***Other Standards* R3.3, R3.4, R3.7, R3.9**

Assessment **Self Assessment**

Students can look up the listed terms in the **Glossary of Literary Terms** on page R91 or they can find them introduced in context on the text pages indicated below.
haiku (p. 541)
Noh drama (p. 519)
The Pillow Book (p. 499)
tanka (p. 535)
simplicity (p. 486)
Zen (p. 511)
imagery (p. 541)
parable (p. 511)

Extend Your *Reading*

As I Crossed a Bridge of Dreams

LADY SARASHINA; IVAN MORRIS, TRANS.

Enchanted by *The Tale of Genji,* Lady Sarashina spent her youth longing to go to Kyoto and visit the novel's setting. When she finally traveled to the capital, however, she spent most of her time reading. Her own "Prince Genji" appeared, but their love ended, and Lady Sarashina returned to her former quiet existence. As the author looks back over her life, a delicate portrait emerges of a woman who was not a scholar, like Murasaki Shikibu, or an amusing storyteller, like Sei Shōnagon, but a deeply sensitive writer who preferred fiction to real life.

Legends of the Samurai

HIROAKI SATO

In this collection of stories about the samurai, Hiroaki Sato presents legends ranging in origin from ancient times to the early 18th century. Through translations of original tales, laws, and eyewitness reports, the author traces the samurai's beginnings and rise to political power. The result is an authentic picture of the samurai warrior, who was as celebrated for his skill in battle as for his devotion to a code of duty, discipline, and artistry.

And Even *More* . . .

Books

The Spring of My Life and Selected Haiku
KOBAYASHI ISSA; SAM HAMILL, TRANS.
Issa's diary and poems to his daughter are moving and reveal his deep appreciation of nature and simplicity.

Essays in Idleness
YOSHIDA KENKŌ; DONALD KEENE, TRANS.
Similar to *The Pillow Book,* this collection of insights and observations by a 14th-century Buddhist priest reflects the culture and values of medieval Japan.

Other Media

Seven Samurai
Set in the 16th century, this classic film by the Japanese director Akira Kurosawa tells the story of a band of samurai hired to protect a small Japanese village. Home Vision Cinema. (VIDEOCASSETTE, DVD)

Sanctuary: Music from a Zen Garden
Gentle duets for Japanese versions of the flute and zither still the mind and soothe the spirit. EMD/Narada. (AUDIO CD)

Five Modern Nō Plays

YUKIO MISHIMA; DONALD KEENE, TRANS.

Yukio Mishima adapted traditional Noh plays, using contemporary settings and characters. While preserving the spirit and themes of the original works, Mishima has presented the plays in a form that can be easily understood by Western audiences.

More Recommendations for Your Students

Difficulty Level: Easy

Hall, Eleanor J. *Life Among the Samurai* (San Diego: Lucent Books, 1998). This nonfiction work provides an account of life in the warrior class during Japan's medieval period.

Macdonald, Fiona. *Step Into Ancient Japan* (NY: Anness Publishing, 1999). Readers can explore Japan's early civilization and culture in this illustrated historical text.

Difficulty Level: Average

Hass, Robert, ed. *The Essential Haiku: Versions of Bashō, Buson, and Issa* (NY: Ecco Press, 1995). A collection of the finest works of the foremost Japanese haiku masters.

Haugaard, Erik Christian. *The Samurai's Tale* (Boston: Houghton Mifflin Company, 1990). In this novel about 16th-century Japan, a young boy dreams of becoming a samurai.

Difficulty Level: Challenging

Akutagawa, Ryunosuke. *Rashomon and Other Stories* (NY: Liveright, 1999). The short stories in this collection are characterized by the Zen-inspired paradox between dream and reality.

Suzuki, Daisetz Teitaro. *Essays in Zen Buddhism* (NY: Grove Press, 1986). These essays provide clear insight into the teachings and practices of Zen Buddhism.

Literature of the Middle East and Africa
The selections in Unit Four come from societies that prize literature highly as a tool of teaching and enlightenment. The works presented here all show how cultures with strong traditions use stories, songs, sacred writings, poems, and proverbs to pass on knowledge, beliefs, and values.

Part 1
Mysticism, Morals, Magic: Persian and Arabic Literature This part will expose students to the variety of texts produced in Persian and Arabic during the rise and dominance of the Islamic Empire. These texts include overtly moralistic works such as The Koran, magical tales of pre-Islamic times such as those found in *The Thousand and One Nights,* and poetry and wisdom of the Sufi mystics.

Part 2
Giving Guidance, Praising Greatness: West African Oral Literature The selections in this part will give students an experience of the variety of oral literature from West Africa, from the guiding wisdom of myths and folk tales to praise songs honoring gods, kings, and other important figures. A **Comparing Literature Across Cultures** feature gives students the opportunity to compare African trickster tales with similar stories found in a Native American tradition.

Literature of the Middle East and Africa A.D. 300–1900

Gnawa musicians, descendants of West Africans enslaved in Morocco, play a form of Islamic religious music.

"Knowledge enables its possessor to distinguish right from wrong; it lights the way to Heaven; it is our friend in the desert, our society in solitude, our companion when friendless."

—Muhammad

Making Connections

Ask: How can knowledge be a friend in times of loneliness or isolation?

Possible Responses: Knowledge can be an advisor—it can help a person deal with problems or find ways to become successful and happy; knowledge is the wisdom of those who have lived before, so to have knowledge is to have their companionship.

UNIT FOUR
PART 1 SKILLS TRACE

Features and Selections	Literary Analysis	Reading and Critical Thinking	Writing Opportunities
Literature of the Middle East and Africa: A.D. 300–1900			
Mysticism, Morals, Magic: Persian and Arabic Literature		Interpreting the Text, 567, 571 Using the Time Line, 573	
SCRIPTURE *from* The Koran *the* Exordium Faith in God Night Daylight	Parallelism, 577, 581 Parallelism, 578, 580	Questioning, 577, 581 Questioning, 578, 580 The Koran, 578	
TALE *from* The Thousand and One Nights The Second Voyage of Sindbad the Sailor **Connect to Today** Sindbad Yesterday, Today, and Tomorrow	Plot, 583, 589 Plot, 584, 586, 588	Analyzing Problems and Solutions, 583, 589 Analyzing Problems and Solutions, 584, 586 The Thousand and One Nights, 584	Sindbad Adventure, 590 Persuasive Essay, 590
POETRY *from the* Rubáiyát of Omar Khayyám **The Translator at Work** FitzGerald's Rubáiyát	Metaphor and Theme, 594, 598 Metaphor and Theme, 594, 596	Drawing Conclusions About Tone, 594, 598 Drawing Conclusions about Tone, 594, 596 Questions to Consider, 599	
POETRY Poems by Rumi Birdsong from Inside the Egg The Grasses	Imagery and Tone, 601, 605 Imagery and Tone, 602, 604	Reading Difficult Poetry, 601, 605 Reading Difficult Poetry, 602, 604 Mysticism and Literature, 602	
Reflect and Assess	Reflecting on the Literature (Human Fate), 610 Reviewing Literary Concepts (Reflecting on Theme), 610		Building Your Portfolio, 610

UNIT FOUR
PART 2 SKILLS TRACE

Features and Selections	Literary Analysis	Reading and Critical Thinking	Writing Opportunities
Giving Guidance, Praising Greatness: West African Oral Literature		Interpreting the Text, 617 Using the Time Line, 620	
MYTH How the World Was Created from a Drop of Milk	Myth, 624, 627 Myth, 624, 626	Analyzing Relationships, 624, 627 Analyzing Relationships, 624, 626 Chemical Elements, 626	
LEGEND The First Bard Among the Soninke	Legend, 628, 631 Legend, 628, 630	Identifying Cultural Values, 628, 631 Identifying Cultural Values, 628, 630	

LEGEND **Black type – Pupil Edition**
Green type – Teacher's Edition
DLS – Daily Language SkillBuilder

Speaking and Listening Viewing and Representing	Inquiry and Research	Grammar, Usage, and Mechanics	Vocabulary
Using the Map, 564			
Art Appreciation, 580		DLS, 576	
Art Discussion, 590 Sindbad Illustration, 590 Dramatic Presentation, 586 Art Appreciation, 587	"Sindbad's World" Report, 590	DLS, 582 Adjectives and Adverbs, 588	Context Clues, 590 Context Clues, 585
Group Discussion, 591			
Art Appreciation, 596		DLS, 594 Problems with Modifiers, 597	
Using the Map, 601 Art Appreciation, 603		DLS, 600	
			Self Assessment, 610 Self Assessment, 610
Using the Map, 613			
Dramatic Reading, 625		DLS, 624	
Art Appreciation 629		DLS, 628	Context Clues: Definition, 630

LEGEND **Black type – Pupil Edition**
Green type – Teacher's Edition
DLS – Daily Language SkillBuilder

PART 2 SKILLS TRACE

Features and Selections	Literary Analysis	Reading and Critical Thinking	Writing Opportunities
EPIC *from* Sundiata: An Epic of Old Mali Childhood The Lion's Awakening	Conflict, 633, 640 Conflict, 634, 636, 638	Predicting, 633, 640 Predicting, 634, 636, 638 Informal Assessment, 636 The Sosso-Bala, 638	Character Analysis, 641 Evaluation of Themes, 641 Biographical Article, 641
SONGS Praise Songs for Orishas Obatala: God of Creation Shango: God of Thunder Oshun: River Goddess **Connect to Today** Orishas in the Americas	Characterization, 643, 648 Characterization, 644, 646	Synthesizing, 643, 648 Synthesizing, 644, 646 The Oshun River, 647	Research Project, 649
Comparing Literature Across Cultures Trickster Tales	Analyzing Trickster Tales, 650, 657, 662	Compare-and-Contrast, 650	Standardized Test Practice (Comparison-and-Contrast Essay), 650
TALES Tales of Anansi the Spider All Stories Are Anansi's Anansi Plays Dead	Trickster Tale, 651 Trickster Tale, 652, 654	Interpreting Themes, 651, 657 Interpreting Themes, 652, 656 African Rock Python, 653 The Tar-Baby Motif, 656	
TALES Tales of Iktomi the Spider Iktomi and the Wild Ducks Iktomi Takes Back a Gift	Trickster Tale, 658, 660	Interpreting Themes, 660 The Trickster Archetype, 658 Tricksters in Daily Life, 659 Lakota Cosmology, 661	
Comparing Literature Standardized Test Practice		Reading the Prompt, 663	Comparison-and-Contrast Essay, 663 Standardized Test Practice (Responding to a Writing Prompt), 663
Writing Workshop Personality Profile Standardized Test Practice Building Vocabulary Sentence Crafting		Analyzing a Student Model, 669–670 Patterns of Organization (Picturing Text Structure), 669	Personality Profile, 671 Adding Detail, 672
Reflect and Assess	Reflecting on the Literature (Cultural Values), 676 Reviewing Literary Concepts (Oral Genres), 676		Building Your Portfolio, 676
Standardized Test Practice		How to Read a Test Selection, 678 How to Answer Multiple-Choice Questions, 681	How to Respond in Writing, 682 How to Revise and Edit a Test Selection, 683

LEGEND **Black type – Pupil Edition**
Green type – Teacher's Edition
DLS – Daily Language SkillBuilder

Speaking and Listening Viewing and Representing	Inquiry and Research	Grammar, Usage, and Mechanics	Vocabulary
Griot's Performance, 641 Movie Review, 641 Art Appreciation, 635, 639	Modern Griots, 641 Ancient Mali, 641	DLS, 632 Modifiers in Comparisons, 637	Related Words, 641 Prefixes and Suffixes, 634
Choral Reading, 644 Art Appreciation, 646		DLS, 642 Problems with Comparisons, 645	
Art Appreciation, 655		DLS, 651	Context Clues: Comparison and Contrast, 654
		DLS, 658	
		Errors in Subject-Verb Agreement, 672, 673 Plurals, 673 Pronoun Agreement, 673 Use of who and whom, 673 Adverbs and Adverb Phrases, 675 Agreement Problems with Indefinite Pronouns as Subjects, 673 Agreement Problems with Phrases Between Subject and Verb, 675	Context Clues, 674
			Self Assessment, 676 Self Assessment, 676

LEGEND **Black type – Pupil Edition**
Green type – Teacher's Edition

DLS – Daily Language SkillBuilder

RESOURCE MANAGEMENT GUIDE PART 1

	Unit Resource Book	Assessment	Integrated Technology and Media	Additional Support
Mysticism, Morals, Magic **Persian and Arabic Literature**			Humanities classzone.com	**World Art and Cultures Transparencies** • AT21 Muslim Koran from Egypt • AT22 Great Mosque of Cordoba • AT24 Camp of a Prince • AT39 Military Campaign of Suleiman • AT66 *Persian Musicians*
from **The Koran** *the* **Exordium** **Faith in God** **Night** **Daylight** ***pp. 576–581***	• Active Reading p. 4 • Literary Analysis p. 5	• Selection Test, Formal Assessment pp. 79–80 • Teacher's Guide to Assessment and Portfolio Use Test Generator	Humanities Activity classzone.com	
from **The Thousand and One Nights** **The Second Voyage of Sindbad the Sailor** ***pp. 582–591***	• Summary p. 6 • Active Reading p. 7 • Literary Analysis p. 8 • Words to Know p. 9 • Selection Quiz p.10	• Selection Test, Formal Assessment pp. 81–82 • Teacher's Guide to Assessment and Portfolio Use Test Generator	Research Starter classzone.com	
Milestones in World Literature **The Shahnameh – Epic of Persia** ***pp. 592–593***			Milestone Links classzone.com	
from the **Rubáiyát of Omar Khayyám** ***pp. 594–599***	• Active Reading p. 11 • Literary Analysis p. 12	• Selection Test, Formal Assessment pp. 83–84 • Teacher's Guide to Assessment and Portfolio Use Test Generator		
Birdsong from Inside the Egg **The Grasses** ***pp. 600–605***	• Active Reading p. 13 • Literary Analysis p. 14	• Selection Test, Formal Assessment pp. 85–86 • Teacher's Guide to Assessment and Portfolio Use Test Generator		
		Unit Assessment	***Unit Technology***	
		• Unit Four, Part 1 Test, Formal Assessment pp. 87–88 Test Generator • Unit Four Integrated Test, Integrated Assessment pp. 19–24	classzone.com	

	Unit Resource Book	Assessment	Integrated Technology and Media	Additional Support
Giving Guidance, Praising Greatness **West African Oral Literature**			Humanities classzone.com	**World Art and Cultures Transparencies** • AT17 Nok sculpture • AT32 Ghana commemorative funerary head • AT33 Benin plaque [detail] • AT44 *Slaves Below the Deck of the* Albenez • AT77 Multiple-Mask Headdress
How the World Was Created from a Drop of Milk ***pp. 624–627***	• Active Reading p. 16 • Literary Analysis p. 17	• Selection Test, Formal Assessment pp. 89–90 • Teacher's Guide to Assessment and Portfolio Use Test Generator		
The First Bard Among the Soninke ***pp. 628–631***	• Summary p. 18 • Active Reading p. 19 • Literary Analysis p. 20 • Selection Quiz p. 21	• Selection Test, Formal Assessment pp. 91–92 • Teacher's Guide to Assessment and Portfolio Use Test Generator		
from* Sundiata: An Epic of Old Mali** **Childhood** **The Lion's Awakening** ***pp. 632–641	• Summary p. 22 • Active Reading p. 24 • Literary Analysis p. 25 • Words to Know p. 26 • Selection Quiz p. 27	• Selection Test, Formal Assessment pp. 93–94 • Teacher's Guide to Assessment and Portfolio Use Test Generator	Humanities Activity classzone.com Research Starter classzone.com	This selection is included in the *World Literature InterActive Reader*™.
Praise Songs for Orishas **Obatala** **Shango** **Oshun** ***pp. 642–649***	• Active Reading p. 28 • Literary Analysis p. 29	• Selection Test, Formal Assessment pp. 95–96 • Teacher's Guide to Assessment and Portfolio Use Test Generator	Research Starter classzone.com	
Tales of Anansi the Spider **All Stories Are Anansi's** **Anansi Plays Dead** ***pp. 650–657*** **Tales of Iktomi the Spider** **Iktomi and the Wild Ducks** **Iktomi Takes Back a Gift** ***pp. 658–663***	• Comparison Chart p. 30 • Summary p. 31 • Active Reading p. 32 • Literary Analysis p. 33 • Selection Quiz p. 34 • Summary p. 35 • Selection Quiz p. 36 • Compare/contrast Essay p. 37		• Selection Test, Formal Assessment pp. 97–98 • Teacher's Guide to Assessment and Portfolio Use Test Generator	

Writing Workshop: Personality Profile *pp. 668–675*

Writing Workshop		Unit Assessment	Unit Technology
Unit Four Resource Book • Prewriting p. 38 • Drafting and Elaboration p. 39 • Peer Response Guide pp. 40–41 • Revising, Editing, and Proofreading p. 42 • Student Models pp. 43–45 • Rubric p. 46	Publishing Options classzone.com **Teacher's Guide to Assessment and Portfolio Use**	• Unit Four, Part 2 Test, Formal Assessment pp. 99–100 Test Generator	classzone.com

DAILY LANGUAGE SKILLBUILDERS

Selection	SkillBuilder Sentences	Suggested Answers
from The Koran *the* Exordium Faith in God Night Daylight	**1.** One important act of worship is to give charity to the poor in the Islamic faith. **2.** My father made a pilgrimage proclaiming the goodness of the Lord to the holy city of Mecca.	**1.** One important act of worship **in the Islamic faith** is **to give charity to the poor.** **2.** My father made a pilgrimage to **the holy city of Mecca, proclaiming the goodness of the Lord.**
from The Thousand and One Nights The Second Voyage of Sindbad the Sailor	**1.** In The Thousand and One Nights, the two main characters sindbad and aladdin tell stories about their adventures. **2.** Sindbad recounts his adventures in two cities baghdad and basrah which are both located in Iraq.	**1.** In The Thousand and One Nights, the two main characters**, S**indbad and **A**laddin**,** tell stories about their adventures. **2.** Sindbad recounts his adventures in two cities**, B**aghdad and **B**asrah**,** which are both located in Iraq.
from the Rubáiyát of Omar Khayyám	**1.** Professor Banthia said tomorrow we will talk about different prospectives and themes in Khayyám's poems. **2.** I'm not sure what the versus in the book stands for.	**1.** Professor Banthia said**, "T**omorrow we will talk about different **perspectives** and themes in Khayyám's poems.**"** **2.** I'm not sure what the **verses** in the book **stand** for. [Students should remove the *s* from *stands.*]

DAILY LANGUAGE SKILLBUILDERS

Selection	SkillBuilder Sentences	Suggested Answers
Birdsong from Inside the Egg The Grasses	**1.** Rumi was a Sufi mystic that believed in having a spiritual connection with God. **2.** Them poems speak about our awareness of God within all person.	**1.** Rumi was a Sufi mystic **who** believed in having a spiritual connection with God. **2.** **The** poems speak about our awareness of God within **each** person.
How the World Was Created from a Drop of Milk	**1.** "Many civilizations have there own creation stories, said Marianne, this Fulani myth explains how death came into the world," she added. **2.** Did you ever see the movie planet of the apes? asked Steve. it shows how other planets besides earth can exist.	**1.** "Many civilizations have **their** own creation stories," said Marianne. **"**This Fulani myth explains how death came into the world," she added. **2.** "Did you ever see the movie **<u>Planet of the Apes</u>**?" asked Steve. **"I**t shows how other planets besides **E**arth can exist."
The First Bard Among the Soninke	**1.** The older brother killed his younger brother an animal. **2.** Founded nearly two thousand years ago, the Soninke people built the ancient empire of Ghana, which became an important trading center.	**1.** The older brother killed **an animal for his younger brother.** **2.** Founded nearly two thousand years ago, **the ancient empire of Ghana became an important trading center for** the Soninke people.
from Sundiata: An Epic of Old Mali Childhood The Lion's Awakening	**1.** Sogolon's son is most valorous than Sassouma's son. **2.** Sogolon thought that the day her son walked for the first time was the most finest day she had ever lived.	**1.** Sogolon's son is **more** valorous than Sassouma's son. **2.** Sogolon thought that the day her son walked for the first time was the **finest** day she had ever lived.

DAILY LANGUAGE SKILLBUILDERS

Selection	SkillBuilder Sentences	Suggested Answers
Praise Songs for Orishas Obatala: God of Creation Shango: God of Thunder Oshun: River Goddess	**1.** Praise songs typically describe their subjects' deeds' and qualities'. **2.** Which of the three praise songs do you preferred?	**1.** Praise songs typically describe their subjects' **deeds** and **qualities.** [Students should remove the apostrophe from *deeds'* and *qualities'*.] **2.** Which of the three praise songs do you **prefer**?
Tales of Anansi the Spider All Stories Are Anansi's Anansi Plays Dead	**1.** Anansi plans a scheme to fool everyone, but little does he know that it will turn against him and became his ultimate downfall. **2.** Imagine that you were writing a book called tricksters and storytellers which famous tricksters would you write about?	**1.** Anansi plans a scheme to fool everyone, but little does he know that **his scheme** will turn against him and **become** his ultimate downfall. **2.** Imagine that you **are** writing a book called **<u>Tricksters and Storytellers</u>. W**hich famous tricksters would you write about?
Tales of Iktomi the Spider Iktomi and the Wild Ducks Iktomi Takes Back a Gift	**1.** According to the Lakota Iktomi is a culture hero who created time and space, invented language and foretold the coming of the European settlers. **2.** Iktomi the tricky spider-man pretends to be friendly until he gets his way and fools you.	**1.** According to the Lakota, Iktomi is a culture hero who created time and space, invented language, and foretold the coming of the European settlers. **2.** Iktomi, the tricky spider-man, pretends to be friendly until he gets his way and fools you.

INTEGRATING GRAMMAR AND LITERATURE: GRAMMAR PLANNER

	Unit One	Unit Two	Unit Three	Unit Four	Unit Five	Unit Six	Unit Seven
Grammar Focus by Unit	Parts of Speech	The Sentence and Its Parts	Using Verbs	Using Modifiers	Using Phrases	Clauses and Sentence Structure	Clauses and Sentence Structure

The Language of Literature offers several options for integrating grammar instruction and literature.

- Each unit has a grammar focus. The Teacher's Edition includes Mini Lessons for the selections that help develop the grammar focus for the unit and spring from the content of the specific literature.
- The Pupil Edition includes several full-page lessons on Sentence Crafting. These lessons are related to both the literature and the grammar focus for a unit and help students use proper grammar in their own writing.
- Daily Language SkillBuilders in the Teacher's Edition provide students with ongoing proofreading practice and reinforce correct punctuation, spelling, grammar and usage, and capitalization.

Black type — Pupil Edition
Green type — Teacher's Edition

Part 1

Using Modifiers

Adjectives and Adverbs
"The Second Voyage of Sindbad the Sailor," from *The Thousand and One Nights*, p. 588

Problems with Modifiers
from the *Rubáiyát of Omar Khayyám*, p. 597

Part 2

Using Modifiers

Modifiers in Comparisons
from *Sundiata: An Epic of Old Mali*, p. 637

Problems with Comparisons
Praise Songs for Orishas: "Shango: God of Thunder," p. 645

Using Adverbs and Adverb Phrases
Sentence Crafting, p. 675

Subject-Verb Agreement

Errors in Subject-Verb Agreement
Writing Workshop, p. 672
Standardized Test Practice, p. 673
Standardized Test Practice, p. 673
Sentence Crafting, p. 675

Nouns

Plurals
Standardized Test Practice, p. 673

Using Pronouns

Pronoun Agreement
Standardized Test Practice, p. 673

Use of *Who* and *Whom*
Standardized Test Practice, p. 673

PART 1

In Unit Four, Part 1, you will find that despite the separate and very different traditions of Persia and Arabia, the rise of Islam brought the two cultures together. It also launched a period of artistic and intellectual fervor that transformed both cultures and helped bring about many of their finest achievements. The works in this part were written between about A.D. 650 and 1500 during the growth and establishment of the Muslim world.

World Art and Cultures Transparencies

AT21 Muslim Koran from Egypt
AT22 Great Mosque of Cordoba
AT24 Camp of a Prince
AT39 Military Campaign of Suleiman
AT66 *Persian Musicians*

You may use the listed transparencies to acquaint students with art from the Islamic Empire.

Pronunciations

Ferdowsi (fər-dou′sē)
Omar Khayyám (ō′mär kī-yäm′)
Rumi (ro͞o′mē)
Sadi (sä-dē′)
Ctesiphon (tĕs′ə-fôn′)

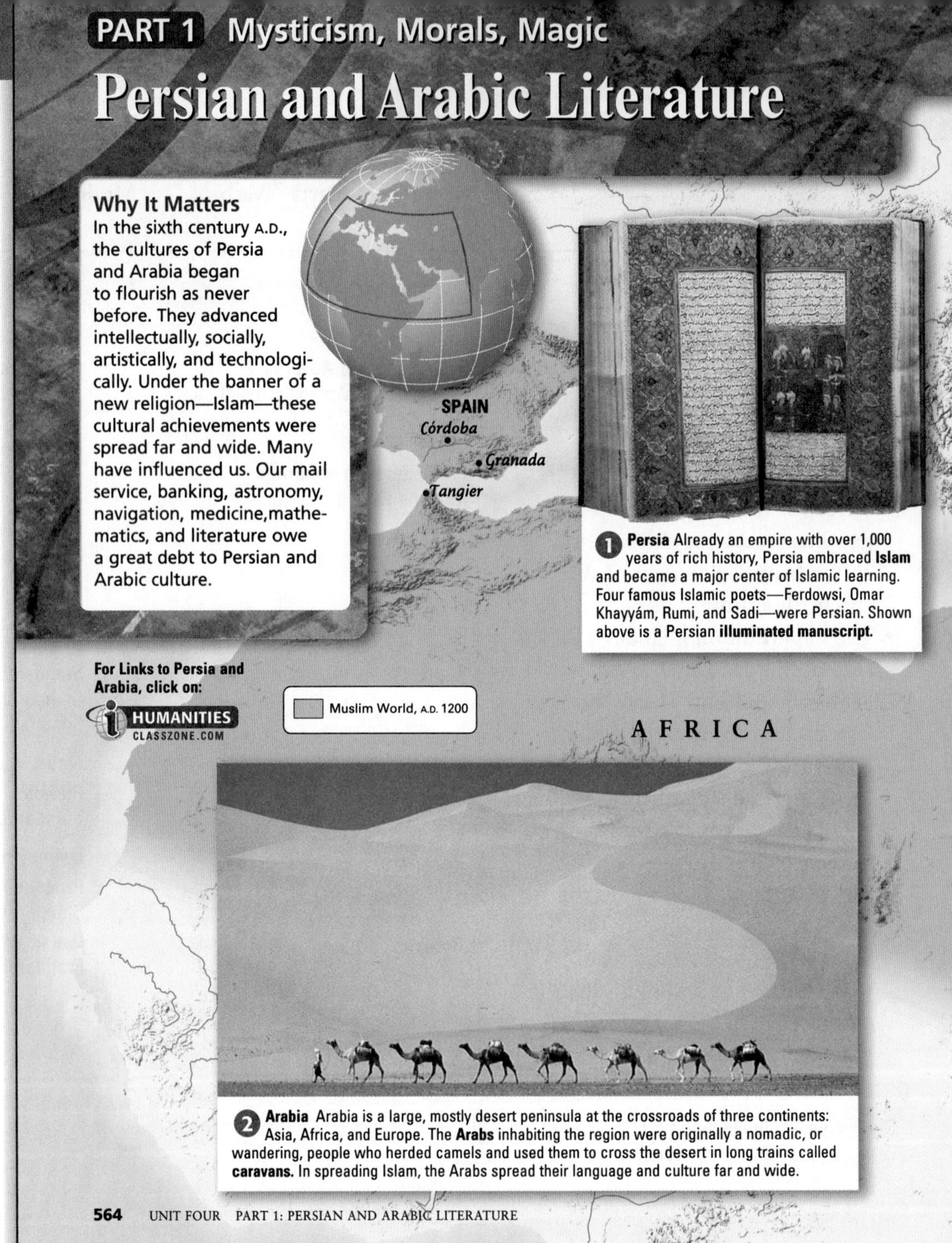

1 Persia Already an empire with over 1,000 years of rich history, Persia embraced **Islam** and became a major center of Islamic learning. Four famous Islamic poets—Ferdowsi, Omar Khayyám, Rumi, and Sadi—were Persian. Shown above is a Persian **illuminated manuscript.**

2 Arabia Arabia is a large, mostly desert peninsula at the crossroads of three continents: Asia, Africa, and Europe. The **Arabs** inhabiting the region were originally a nomadic, or wandering, people who herded camels and used them to cross the desert in long trains called **caravans.** In spreading Islam, the Arabs spread their language and culture far and wide.

564 UNIT FOUR PART 1: PERSIAN AND ARABIC LITERATURE

MINI LESSON Using the Map

Have students answer the following questions, referring to the map on pages 564–565:

1. Where on this map is the "Fertile Crescent," the geographic region shown on the map on pages 16–17? *(The earlier map concentrates on the area shown on page 565 that includes the upper Nile, the upper half of the Arabian peninsula, and the Tigris-Euphrates river valley.)*
2. How much of the Fertile Crescent belongs to the Muslim world? *(all of it)*
3. How much time has elapsed on this map since the establishment of the Persian empire in the sixth century, B.C.? *(about 1,700 years)*
4. How many continents does the Muslim World include? *(three: Asia, Africa, and Europe)*
5. Sudan today occupies the middle third of the western coast of the Red Sea. Based on this map, what would you expect to be Sudan's main religion? *(Islam)*
6. Judging from this map, would you be likely today to find Islamic architecture in Spain? *(yes)*

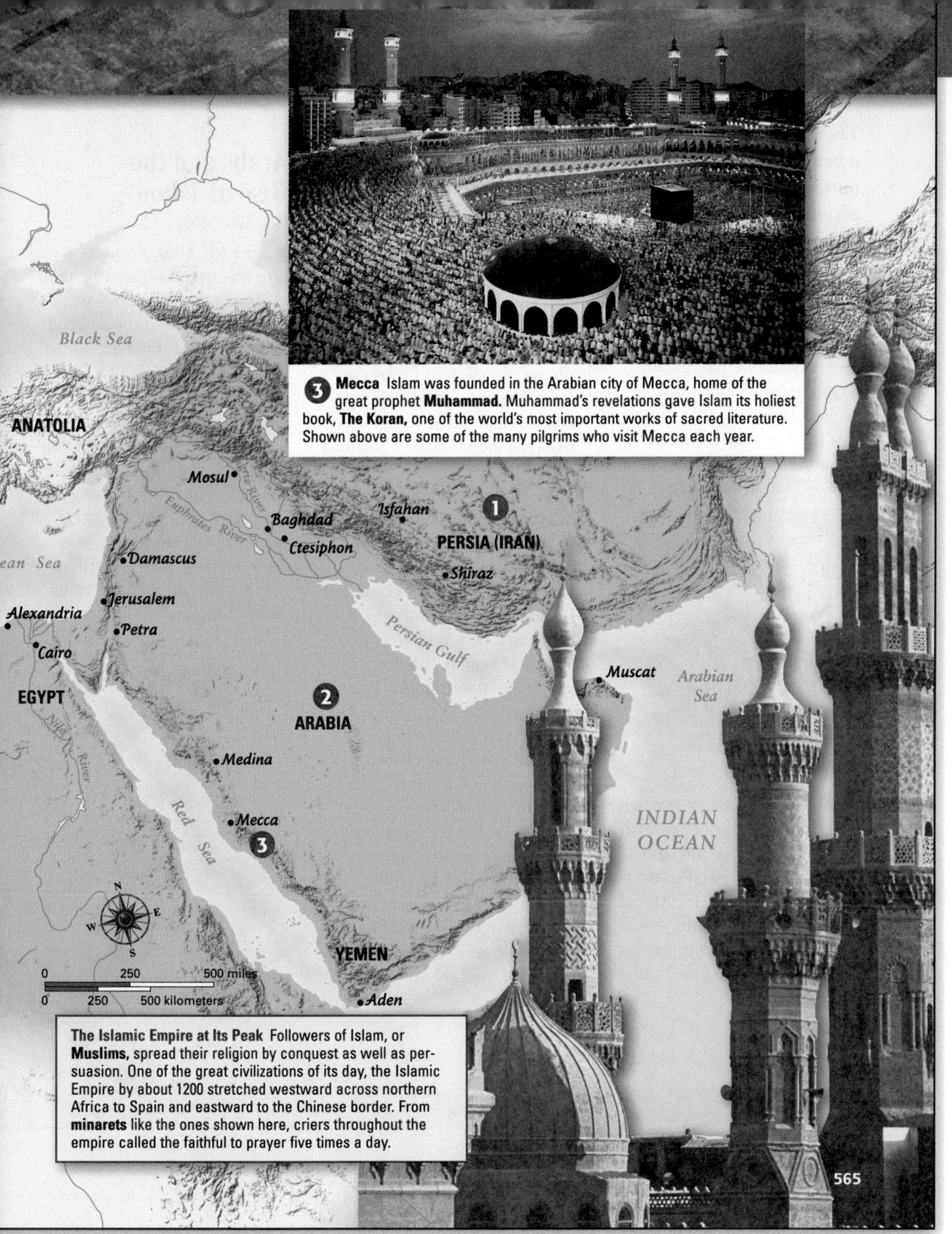

3 **Mecca** Islam was founded in the Arabian city of Mecca, home of the great prophet **Muhammad.** Muhammad's revelations gave Islam its holiest book, **The Koran,** one of the world's most important works of sacred literature. Shown above are some of the many pilgrims who visit Mecca each year.

The Islamic Empire at Its Peak Followers of Islam, or **Muslims,** spread their religion by conquest as well as persuasion. One of the great civilizations of its day, the Islamic Empire by about 1200 stretched westward across northern Africa to Spain and eastward to the Chinese border. From **minarets** like the ones shown here, criers throughout the empire called the faithful to prayer five times a day.

READING FOR INFORMATION

Reading Skills and Strategies

ESTABLISHING SEQUENCE OF EVENTS

Have students use the information in the text boxes on pages 564–565 to establish a sequence for the following events: the spread of Islam from Arabia, the establishment of the Persian empire, Persia's acceptance of Islam, the birth of Muhammad, the peak of growth of the Islamic Empire, the creation of The Koran, and Persian influence on modern mail service. *(1. the establishment of the Persian empire, 2. the birth of Muhammad, 3. the revelation of The Koran, 4. the spread of Islam from Arabia, 5. Persia's acceptance of Islam, 6. the peak of growth of the Islamic Empire, and 7. Persian influence on modern mail service)*

Historical Note

Persia Students may recall that the Persian empire played an important role in the history and culture of the ancient world set forth in Unit One, Part 1. In 539 B.C., the Persian king Cyrus the Great conquered the second Babylonian empire, making Mesopotamia part of the Persian empire and freeing the Jews to return to Palestine. In Unit Four, Part 1, we are concerned with the Persian empire as it existed more than ten centuries later.

Geographical Note

The Middle East Many of the political issues and conflicts that characterized the region during the rise of Islam still exist today and are often in the news. You may want to have students compare this map with a current political map of the Middle East in order to establish connections to modern nations such as Israel, Iraq, and Iran.

Pronunciations
Darius (də-rī′əs)
Xerxes (zûrk′sēz)
Zoroaster (zôr′ō-ăs′tər)
Cambyses (kăm-bī′sēz)
Sassanids (sə-sä′nĭdz)
caliphs (kā′lĭfs)
Abbasid (ə-băs′ĭd′)
Samanids (sə-mä′nĭdz)
Bukhara (bo͞o-kär′ə)
Seljuks (sĕl′jo͞oks′)
Malik (mă-lĭk′)
Shahnameh (shä′nä′mə)
Sufism (so͞o′fĭz′əm)

READING FOR INFORMATION
Reading Skills and Strategies
SETTING A PURPOSE
Read aloud to students the introduction in italics to **Historical Highlights** on this page. Suggest that, as they read, students look for characteristics and developments in each culture that might have helped it to benefit the other.
Possible Responses: (Persia) Zoroastrianism, a religion with a strong moral vision; military prowess; respect for other cultures; improvements in travel and commerce; a well-established presence in the region (Arabia); a shared historical tradition with the Hebrews; familiarity with other cultures along trade routes; the leadership of Muhammad; the Islamic faith; military prowess

Historical Highlights

The Persian empire had existed for almost 1,200 years when it embraced the new religion, Islam, spreading outward from Arabia. The encounter between the two peoples was one that benefited both and led to major cultural advances.

Pre-Islamic Persia

(1000 B.C.–A.D. 642)

The Persians were originally **Aryan** nomads. Some time around 1000 B.C., they settled in a plateau west of India that became known as Persia, or **Iran**—"land of the Aryans."

Darius receiving his son Xerxes

Around 600 B.C., a prophet and religious reformer named **Zoroaster** founded a religion that would influence Persian culture for the next 1,200 years. Zoroastrianism saw the world and human morality in terms of a struggle between good and evil divinities.

Like other peoples of the region, the Persians evolved into a military power in order to survive. In 550 B.C., **Cyrus the Great** began to establish a Persian empire that would stretch from the Indus River to Anatolia (now Turkey). Unlike other conquerors, Cyrus did not loot and destroy conquered lands; instead, he treated the people mercifully, respecting their customs and beliefs. His successors **Cambyses II** and **Darius I** extended Cyrus's conquests. Darius built a system of roads to tie the empire together and introduced coinage and standardized weights and measures to promote trade. Eventually he was defeated by the Greeks at the Battle of Marathon in 490 B.C. In 331 B.C., **Alexander the Great** conquered the Persian Empire, making it part of his own. Then, in 224 B.C., a native Persian dynasty, the Sassanids, regained control of the region and ruled until the coming of Islam in A.D. 642.

Arabs and the Rise of Islam

(A.D. 570–1258)

In the early 600s, Persian culture was overshadowed by that of Arabia. Arabic tradition teaches that the Arabs descend from **Abraham,** the ancestor of the Hebrews. Originally desert nomads, some Arabs became farmers and traders. Towns arose at oases—desert watering holes—or along the coast, often near main trade routes. One such town was **Mecca,** where the prophet **Muhammad** was born in about 570. According to tradition, the Angel Gabriel visited Muhammad and

PRE-ISLAMIC PERSIA

1000 B.C. A.D. 1

revealed to him the will of God, or Allah. Muhammad began to preach **Islam,** or "submission to Allah's will." The new faith alarmed the citizens of Mecca, who forced the prophet and his followers to flee to Medina. There they launched successful military campaigns against the enemies of Islam. By 631, most of Arabia had sworn allegiance to the new faith, and by 640, so had Persia. After Muhammad's death, a series of **caliphs,** or successors, ruled the expanding Empire. From 762 to 1258, the Abbasid dynasty ruled from the great capital **Baghdad.** By 1200, the empire had reached its greatest expansion. In 1258, the rise of independent Muslim states began to break it apart.

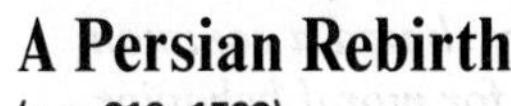

A Persian Rebirth

(A.D. 819–1502)

In the ninth century, a Persian dynasty called the **Samanids** gained power in the northeastern part of the Islamic Empire, spearheading a renaissance, or rebirth, of Persian culture. The Persian city of **Bukhara** soon rivaled the Islamic capital of Baghdad as a center of learning, and in 945 the Persians took control of Baghdad itself. Although educated Persians then spoke and wrote Arabic, the language of Islamic ritual, now they began also writing in Persian. Persian culture continued to flourish even when the Persians lost political power to Turkish-speaking peoples from central Asia like the **Seljuks,** who captured Baghdad in 1055. Great admirers of Persian learning, the Seljuk sultans, or shahs (Persian for "kings"), moved the capital to **Isfahan** in Persia and appointed Persians as prime ministers. The famous Seljuk sultan Malik Shah was a great patron of the arts and sciences as well as a powerful political leader. Persia remained under Turkish rule until 1502.

The great mosque commissioned by Malik Shah in Isfahan, Persia

Islam spread by conquest as well as by persuasion.

History to Literature

EVENT IN HISTORY	EVENT IN LITERATURE
Muhammad becomes the prophet of Islam.	Allah's revelations to Muhammad are gathered in The Koran.
Trade and navigation flourish in the region.	*The Thousand and One Nights* tells the adventures of a sailor named Sindbad.
The Samanids support a revival of Persian culture.	The Samanids commission a Persian epic called the *Shahnameh.*
A mystical form of Islam called Sufism arises.	Rumi gives poetic expression to the ideas of Sufism.

ARABS AND THE RISE OF ISLAM — PERSIAN REBIRTH

A.D. 570 A.D. 819 A.D. 1258 A.D. 1502

READING FOR INFORMATION
Reading Skills and Strategies
CLARIFYING

Students may be confused by the apparently conflicting facts that the Abbasid caliphate ruled from 762 until 1258 and that Baghdad fell under control of the Persians in 945 and the Turks in 1055. Explain that the caliphate—the office held by the official successors of Muhammad—was allowed to rule in name, at least over religious matters, even when other dynasties held the actual reins of power. In part, this was good politics in a passionately Islamic empire; in part, it simply reflects the fact that the conflicts and changes of power took place among groups of people who shared a single faith.

MINI LESSON Interpreting the Text

Tell students that ethnic, national, or other political groups sometimes seem to have a personality that affects their interactions with other groups. After students have read these two pages, have them describe the personalities of the main political groups discussed.

Possible Responses: (pre-Islamic Persians) inclined to see the world in terms of good and evil; merciful to people they conquered; tolerant of other customs and beliefs; innovative in developing the country
(Islamic Arabs) faithful; determined to fight for their religion; persistent
(Islamic Persians) interested in their own culture; interested in learning and the arts
(Turkish Seljuks) appreciative of other cultures, appreciative of the arts and sciences

Pronunciations
Bedouins (bĕd′o͞o-ĭnz)
emirs (ĭ-mîrz′)
viziers (vĭ-zîrz′)
al-Ma′mun (ăl-mă-mo͞on′)
dervishes (dûr′vĭsh-ĭz)
fakirs (fə-kîrz′)

READING FOR INFORMATION
Reading Skills and Strategies
SETTING A PURPOSE
Have students read the introduction in italics on this page. Suggest that, as they read, students look for ways different groups of people were connected by their common religion and examples of how Islam created or affected new social groups.

Possible Responses: (how people were connected by religion) Nomads made up the core of the Islamic armies; Islam meant better treatment for the poor, for slaves, and for women; religion affected how people were taxed; the religious ruler al-Ma′mun brought together people of different cultures in the House of Wisdom. (how Islam created new groups) Religious leaders became the new ruling class; non-Muslims made up a new lower class; Islamic support of learning created a new class of scholars; mystical Islam created a new social group—dervishes, or monks.

People and Society

In one way, the groups of people who made up the Islamic empire were very similar. They shared a common faith and a common set of guidelines for moral behavior. In other ways, they were quite different. Because of its size, the empire included a wide variety of cultural backgrounds. The spread of Islam also helped create new social roles and class distinctions.

Nomads

The Islamic empire included many Arabs who remained desert nomads, or wanderers, like their ancestors. Known as **Bedouins,** they were organized into tightly knit clans that were further grouped into tribes. The Bedouins prided themselves on their ability to survive in the rough desert terrain. They were also excellent warriors and made up the core of the Islamic armies.

Nomads in the desert

The Ruling Class

The Islamic empire was initially a **theocracy,** or government by religious authority. Religious leaders held the political reins. However, by the 10th century, these leaders had become puppet rulers. Political power was held instead by military dictators or hereditary aristocrats such as **emirs** ("princes"), **sultans** ("rulers"), and **shahs** ("kings"), who often governed with the help of chief ministers known as **viziers.** Members of the ruling class were often strong supporters of learning and the arts.

The Lower Classes

Muhammad's moral perspective was influenced at least in part by the plight of the poor in Mecca. The lives of those in poverty was greatly improved under Islam, which stressed the importance of helping the needy and giving charity to the poor. Islamic teaching also encouraged the freeing of slaves.

Breadmaker pounding grain to make flour

As the Islamic empire expanded, it welcomed conquered peoples into its fold and allowed them to enter Muslim society. However, society did make some distinctions between those who were born Muslim, those who converted, and those who practiced other religions. Converts to Islam paid higher taxes than born Muslims, and nonbelievers paid a still higher tax. Nevertheless, if they paid their tax and did not promote their religions, non-Muslims were treated reasonably well.

Scholars in the House of Wisdom

Merchants and Traders

Many Arabs grew wealthy as merchants and traders. Local merchants sold their wares in outdoor town and city markets, called **bazaars;** other traders traveled land and sea to obtain and sell their goods. Arabia and Persia were connected to the major ocean and land trade routes of the time, and many merchants and traders from other lands passed through these regions. Their presence, together with Arabs' and Persians' own travels abroad, made commerce not only a source of great wealth and abundance of goods, but also one of information and ideas.

The Learned Class

Scholars, scientists, writers, and artists were valued members of Islamic society. They often received financial support from powerful rulers who saw scientific and cultural achievements as an important part of their legacy. In the early 800s, Caliph al-Ma'mun dreamed that he spoke with the Greek philosopher Aristotle. Inspired by this dream, the caliph opened a combination academy and library in Baghdad called the **House of Wisdom.** There, scholars of different cultures and beliefs worked side by side translating texts from Greece, India, Persia, and elsewhere.

Islamic Mystics

Respect also went to religious leaders and **dervishes**—mystic monks who sought a close personal relationship with Allah. Many mystics were associated with **Sufism,** an Islamic movement that flourished in the 12th and 13th centuries. Sufi dervishes belonged to brotherhoods like those of European monks and often lived in schools or communities similar to monasteries. Traveling dervishes, called fakirs, lived by begging and were given charity in accordance with the teachings of Islam.

Sufi dervishes today continue to practice sacred dance as a form of worship.

Women in the Islamic World

The lives of women improved under Islam, which granted them important rights concerning marriage, family, and property. As believers in Islam, women were considered equal to men in the eyes of Allah, though over time they were forced to live increasingly secluded lives.

READING FOR INFORMATION

Reading Skills and Strategies

CONNECTING

Draw students' attention to the following visual details on pages 568–569. Invite students to supply information from their personal experience or knowledge about each detail and to explain its relevance to the accompanying text.

- the camel in the photograph of the nomads *(adapted for life in the desert, camels can store water in their humps)*
- the mode of dress of the nomads *(offers protection from desert heat, wind, and sand)*
- the hawk in the painting under **The Ruling Class** *(used to hunt small animals, called "hawking," associated with the upper class)*
- the square held by the second man from the right in the painting of the House of Wisdom *(measurement tool used in drawing, measuring, building, illustrating mathematical principles; could be used in studying geometry, architecture, or navigation)*
- the activity of the woman in the illustration for **Women in the Islamic World** *(she is writing, an activity that shows she is educated; representation of a woman writing shows that the activity was common)*

Historical Note

In 661, 29 years after the death of Muhammad, a family known as the Umayyads came to power. They abandoned the simple life of previous caliphs and surrounded themselves with the wealth and ceremony common among non-Muslim rulers. In response, a Muslim minority arose called Shiah (shē′ə), who believed that the caliph should be a descendant of Muhammad. The Sufis represented another response. They shunned the luxurious life of the Umayyads and pursued a life of poverty and spiritual devotion.

Pronunciations
muezzin (myo͞o-ĕz′ĭn)
Alhambra (ăl-hăm′brə)
Umayyad (o͞o-mī′ăd)
Averroës (ə-vĕr′ō-ēz′)
Maimon (mī-mōn′)
Maimonides (mī-mŏn′ĭ-dēz′)
arabesques (ăr′ə-bĕsks′)
calligraphy (kə-lĭg′rə-fē)

Historical Note

A The Dome of the Rock was constructed at the command of Caliph Abd al-Malik in 687. It was built on the site where the Temple of Solomon once stood and where today the Temple ruins known as the "Wailing Wall" can be found. The site is sacred alike to Jews, Christians, and Muslims, and members of all three faiths worship there side by side. (For additional information about the site, see the historical note on page 23.)

Arts and Culture

Because of Muslim tolerance of conquered peoples and the emphasis on learning, the Islamic Empire blended a rich variety of cultures and traditions. At a time when Europe was in its Middle Ages, the Muslim world displayed great intellectual and artistic liveliness, producing many works of scholarship and art.

Islamic Architecture

The Islamic Empire is renowned for magnificent architecture, both religious and secular. Islamic houses of worship, called **mosques**, are typically domed, with beautiful arched or vaulted walkways. Often they are decorated with carved lacelike patterns called arabesques. Next to the central portion of the mosque is a graceful high tower, called a **minaret** (from the Arabic for "beacon"), from which a crier known as a **muezzin** calls the faithful to pray five times a day. Palaces, too, are domed and vaulted. One of the most splendid Muslim palaces is the Alhambra in Granada, Spain; perhaps the most famous of the scores of classical mosques is the Great Mosque of Damascus, sometimes called the Umayyad Mosque because it was built in the era of the Umayyad caliphs. Shown below is the "Dome of the A Rock," built on the Temple Mount, site of Solomon's Temple in Jerusalem.

Astrolabe

Scholarship and Science

A spirit of inquiry thrived in the Islamic world, spurred by Muhammad's own emphasis on study and learning as well as by the many new cultural contacts Muslims made as their empire expanded. Muslim cities from Spain to central Asia flourished as centers of learning; great universities encouraged the study of religion, philosophy, law, and Arabic grammar. At the Baghdad academy and research library known as the House of Wisdom, major translations were undertaken and many new works of scholarship were written. In Muslim Spain, Averroës reconciled Islamic thinking with the ideas of the Greek philosopher Aristotle. In Egypt, the Spanish Jew Moses Ben Maimon (Maimonides) reconciled philosophy and Jewish law in a noted philosophical work, *Guide for the Perplexed.* Alhazen's book *Optics* aided in the development of the telescopic lens and led to advances in astronomy that benefited mapmaking and navigation.

Literature

Arabic Literature In pre-Islamic times, Arabic literature was composed mainly in the oral tradition. Elaborate odes, called *qasida,* were memorized and recited to celebrate important occasions; short lyrics expressed strong emotions such as love or grief. With the advent of Islam, such poetic traditions continued and were often put into writing. Also written down was the official text of Islam's sacred book, the Koran, in about 653. A century later, Arabic literature entered a golden age that saw the production of many types of literature, including works of history, philosophy, science, and biography.

Persian Literature Persia produced great literature before the advent of Islam, including the *Avesta,* the sacred text of the Zoroastrian religion. But afterward came a long period when virtually all literary and scholarly writing was in Arabic. Then, in the ninth century, the native Samanids gained power, fostering a cultural revival that produced major literary works in Persian. The blending of the Persian poetic tradition with the mystical brand of Islam known as Sufism resulted in some of the great lyric poetry of the world.

Decorative Arts

From elegantly carved swords of Damascus to the beautiful ceramic tiles and exquisitely woven carpets of Persia, the Islamic world produced a vast array of decorative art. Much of it was abstract, for although the representation of living creatures is not expressly banned in the Koran, Islamic thought condemned such images on the grounds that only Allah could create life. Buildings, walls, furniture, fabrics, pottery, metalwork, and other creations often displayed abstract designs called arabesques, in which interlaced lines formed a delicate symmetrical pattern. The prayer rug shown above includes an image of a mosque prayer niche. Like the niche itself, the image must point toward Mecca during prayer.

One type of Islamic art that was not abstract, Persian miniature paintings depicted people and animals in recognizable, often urban, scenes. Sometimes they were painted onto silk, but most often they were used as manuscript illustrations.

How Was Literature Presented ?

Because of the Islamic ban on the artistic representation of people and animals, words took on artistic importance, and a rich tradition of Islamic calligraphy—writing used as a form of visual art—developed. Using reed pens, Islamic calligraphers produced exquisite writing in the graceful vertical letters of the Arabic alphabet. Calligraphy was also an integral part of illuminated manuscripts, which were often decorated with gold and silver, brilliant colors, and intricate designs. Islamic rulers commissioned the creation of ornately bound illuminated manuscripts of treasured works like the Persian national epic the *Shahnameh* and, later, *The Thousand and One Nights.*

READING FOR INFORMATION
Reading Skills and Strategies
MAKING INFERENCES

As students read pages 570–571, have them list ways these artistic and cultural achievements or their effects might be visible in our world today.

Possible Responses: Many mosques and palaces are still standing today; Muslim art and architecture exist in places that were once part of the Islamic empire, such as Spain; advances in navigation helped bring European people and culture to the Western Hemisphere; the results of research in fields such as optics can be seen in modern technological breakthroughs such as the Hubble telescope; many literary works, including The Koran, are available today because they were written down during the time of the Islamic empire; Islamic decorative styles can still be seen in buildings, furnishings, and other modern creations.

Historical Note

Decorative art had special meaning in the preparation of copies of The Koran, such as the one shown here. Artists regarded the work as an act of religious devotion. Although they avoided using pictures to illuminate the text, they created designs that still had meaning. The geometric perfection and endlessly repeating patterns of the decorations illustrate the infinite quality of Allah.

MINI LESSON Interpreting the Text

Tell students that in some ways religion strongly supported the arts, while in others it discouraged them. Have students review these two pages and make a list of examples of each of these two kinds of influence. After discussing their examples, you may want to extend this activity by leading students in a discussion of the following question: What role does art have to play in important social institutions such as religion and politics?

Possible Responses: (Supported) encouraged the building of beautiful houses of worship; encouraged an interest in the products of other cultures; inspired the writing of the *Avesta* and The Koran; Sufism produced great poetry; the avoidance of creating images of living creatures led to the development of abstract art forms and calligraphy (Discouraged) the emphasis on religion may have discouraged other artistic themes; Persian literature received less attention when Arabic became the main language; representational art was discouraged as too much like idolatry

Pronunciations

ghazals (găz′əlz)
Uthman (o͝oth-män′)
Abu-Bakr (ä′bo͞o-bä′kər)
Ibn Ishaq (ĭb′ən ē-shäk′)
Abu Nuwas (ə-bo͞o′ no͞o-wäs′)
Khamriyyat (käm′rē-yät′)
al-Khwarizmi (ăl-kwär′ĭz-mē)
Ibn Hazm (ĭb′ən KHăz′əm)
Ghaznevid (gœz′nə-vĭd′)
Farid-ad-Din Attar (fär-ē′də-dēn′ ə-tär′)
Ibn Khaldun (ĭb′ən kăl-do͞on′)
Muqaddimah (mo͞o′kä-dē′mə)
Osman (ŏz′mən)
Safavid (sə-fä′vĭd)

READING FOR INFORMATION

Reading Skills and Strategies
CONNECTING

It may help students to get a better sense of the time period covered in this part if they compare the bar at the top of this page with that of time lines in other parts of the book they have studied so far.

Time Line

PERSIA AND ARABIA (A.D. 500–1500)

2500 B.C. | A.D. 1 | PRESENT

c. approximately
B.C. before Christ
A.D. after Christ

EVENTS IN LITERATURE

A.D. 500

- **c. 500** Pre-Islamic oral poetry flourishes in Arabic; translated Sanskrit tales, in Persia
- **610** Beginning of revelations to Prophet Muhammad that become the Koran
- **c.622** First *ghazals*, or love lyrics, composed in Arabic
- **c. 653** Uthman, third caliph, authorizes the official text of The Koran

A.D. 700

- **c. 750** Golden age of Arabic literature begins; Ibn Ishaq composes definitive biography of Muhammad
- **c. 800** Arabic poet Abu Nuwas creates his famous poetry collection the *Khamriyyat*
- **c. 800** Tales later collected in *The Thousand and One Nights* start appearing in Arabic

A.D. 900

- **c. 920** Rudaki initiates revival of Persian-language poetry
- **1010** Ferdowsi completes his version of the Persian epic the *Shahnameh*
- **c. 1050** Arabic mystic Ibn Hazm composes his philosophical work *The Ring of the Dove*
- **c. 1075** Malik Shah becomes the patron of astronomer and poet Omar Khayyám

EVENTS IN THE MIDDLE EAST

A.D. 500

- **c. 570** Birth of Muhammad
- **622** Muhammad's flight to Medina
- **632** Death of Muhammad; Abu-Bakr becomes first caliph
- **637-641** Arabs conquer Jerusalem, Alexandria, and Persia
- **661** Umayyad Dynasty comes to power and makes Damascus the new Islamic capital

A.D. 700

- **786-809** Caliph Harun al-Rashid makes Baghdad the center of Arabic culture
- **c. 819-900** Samanid Dynasty wields power in Persia and spurs a cultural revival
- **830** Caliph al-Ma'mun builds the House of Wisdom in Baghdad
- **c. 850** Al-Khwarizmi outlines the principles of algebra

A.D. 900

- **998** Mahmud, a Ghaznevid Turk, becomes sultan of the Persian province of Khurasan
- **1064** Seljuk Turks come to power in much of Islamic Empire
- **1099** Crusaders capture Jerusalem and massacre Muslims and Jews

EVENTS IN WORLD HISTORY

A.D. 500

- **c. 250** Rise of Mayan civilization in Mexico
- **527** Justinian I becomes Byzantine emperor
- **618** Beginning of China's T'ang Dynasty

A.D. 700

- **732** Battle of Tours in France stops Muslim incursions in Europe
- **794** Beginning of Japan's Heian period, known for its elegant imperial court life
- **800** Charlemagne crowned first Holy Roman Emperor, uniting western Europe
- **c. 850** Empire of Ghana flourishes in western Africa

A.D. 900

- **c. 900** Anasazi civilization in North America enters classic Pueblo period
- **1054** Christianity splits into Eastern Orthodox and Roman Catholic
- **1066** Normans under William I invade and conquer England
- **1095** Pope Urban II begins the Crusade to wrest the Holy Land from the Muslims

A.D. 1100	A.D. 1300	A.D. 1500
c. 1177 Persian mystic Farid-ad-Din Attar completes allegoric poem *The Conference of the Birds* **1244** Rumi meets Shams ad-Din, inspiration for the poems in *Divan-e Shams* **1257-1258** Sadi composes his *Bustan* and *Gulistan*	**c. 1360** Persian poet Hafiz composes his *Divan* **c. 1370** Persian poetry begins to decline **1375-1379** Ibn Khaldun writes the *Muqaddimah*, a monumental history of world civilization	**c. 1500** *The Thousand and One Nights* is recorded in its present form

A.D. 1100	A.D. 1300	A.D. 1500
1187 Muslims under the Kurdish leader Saladin recapture Jerusalem **1218** Mongols under Genghis Khan invade Persia	**c. 1300** Turkish chieftain Osman I founds the Ottoman state in present-day Turkey **1383–1385** Mongol rebel Timur the Lame (Tamerlane) briefly holds power in Persia **1453** Byzantine capital, Constantinople, falls to the Ottoman Turks	**1502** Safavid Dynasty comes to power in Persia **1520** Suleiman the Magnificent rules the Ottoman Empire

A.D. 1100	A.D. 1300	A.D. 1500
c. 1150 Angkor Wat, magnificent temple compound in present-day Cambodia, completed **1209** Genghis Khan begins Mongol conquests in Asia **1279** Mongol ruler Kublai Khan conquers China **1235** Sundiata founds Mali Empire in Africa	**c. 1300** Western Europe's Renaissance begins in Italy **c. 1450** Aztecs flourish in Mexico; Incas in Peru **c. 1455** German printer Johannes Gutenberg prints landmark Bible on his new press **1492** Muslims driven from Spain; Columbus makes voyage of discovery to the New World	**1517** Martin Luther begins Reformation **1521** Cortés conquers Aztecs

MINI LESSON Using the Time Line

Have students answer the following questions based on the time line:

1. How long before the collection of tales in *The Thousand and One Nights* was recorded in its present form did the first of its tales begin to appear in Arabic? *(about 700 years)*
2. Was algebra used in the construction of the House of Wisdom? *(no, because Al-Khwarizmi did not outline the principles of algebra until about twenty years later)*
3. Was Jerusalem in Islamic or Christian hands when Charlemagne was crowned first Holy Roman Emperor? *(Islamic)*
4. For how many years did The Koran have to be copied by hand? *(at least 800 years—Uthman authorized the text in 653, whereas the printing press was not in use until 1455)*
5. To what ethnic group would you expect Omar Khayyám's patron, the ruler Malik Shah, to belong? *(the Seljuk Turks, since they came to power in much of the Islamic empire in 1064, 11 years before Malik Shah became Omar's patron)*

INTRODUCTION 573

Pronunciation
sakk (säk)

READING FOR INFORMATION
Reading Skills and Strategies
EVALUATING
After they have read pages 574–575, ask students which of these contributions they think they would find it easiest to live without. Have them give reasons for their responses.

Connect to Today: The Legacy of Persia and Arabia

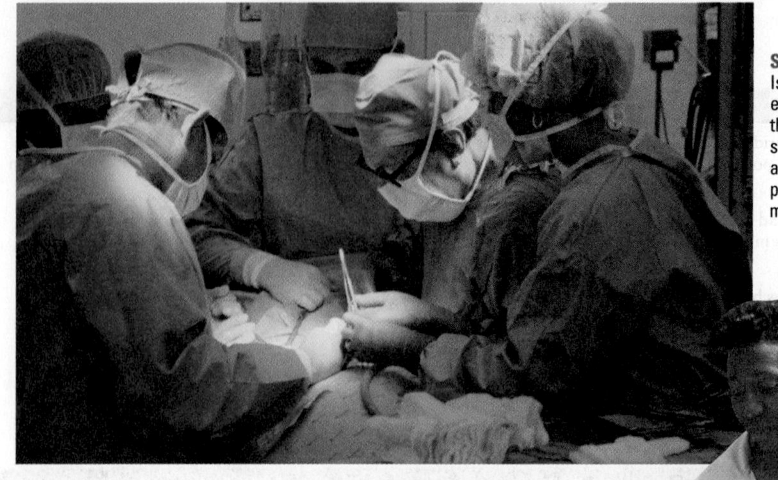

Surgery
Islamic physicians pioneered eye surgery and developed the use of anesthetics during surgery. Their experiments and careful records helped pave the way for today's medical breakthroughs.

Modern Banking
To make it easier to conduct business, money handlers established banks throughout the Islamic Empire. Using a letter of credit from a bank in one city, a merchant could get cash from a bank in another. The Arabic word for such a letter was *sakk,* from which we get the word *check.*

The Mail System
Did you ever hear the famous postal service slogan, "Neither snow, nor rain, nor heat, nor gloom of night stays these couriers from the swift completion of their appointed rounds"? The statement was first applied not to the U.S. mail but to the relay system of royal messengers that Darius I established in the ancient Persian Empire.

574

0 1 2 3 4 5
6 7 8 9

Mathematics
Though devised in India, our number system comes to us through the efforts of Arabic mathematicians—which is why we call *1, 2, 3,* and so on, "Arabic numbers." Probably the most famous Arabic mathematician was al-Khwarizmi, who laid out most of the principles of algebra that we still use today. In fact, the mathematical term *algorithm* comes from the Latin pronunciation of al-Khwarizmi's name.

$12x^2-3y^2$

Word Origins

Algebra and **algorithm** are just two of many words that come to English from Arabic or Persian. Here are some others. Notice that several start with *al-*, Arabic for *the.*

admiral	cipher	sofa
alcohol	coffee	syrup
alcove	cotton	tariff
alfalfa	henna	zenith
arsenal	magazine	zero
bazaar	monsoon	

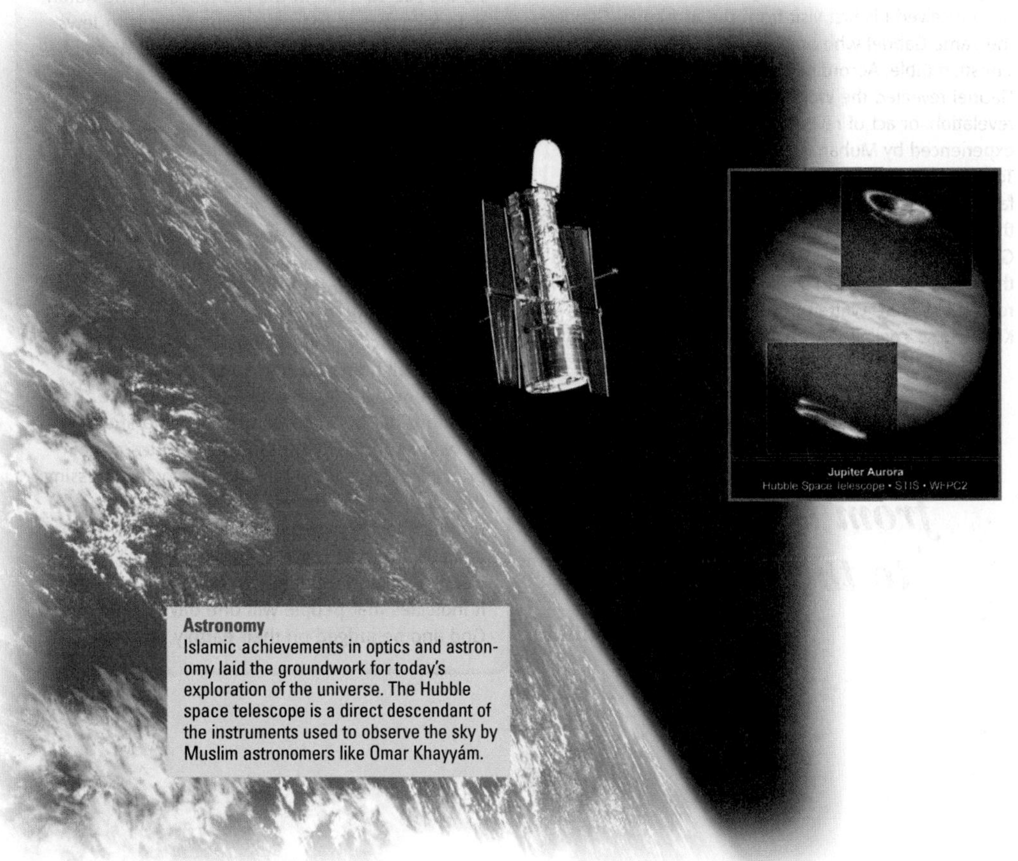

Astronomy
Islamic achievements in optics and astronomy laid the groundwork for today's exploration of the universe. The Hubble space telescope is a direct descendant of the instruments used to observe the sky by Muslim astronomers like Omar Khayyám.

INTRODUCTION 575

Objectives

- appreciate one of the world's great **sacred texts (Literary Analysis)**
- understand the use of **parallelism** in literature **(Literary Analysis)**
- learn to use **questioning** as a reading strategy **(Active Reading)**

Thematic Link

The Koran presents the **moral** vision underlying Islam and much of the literature of Persia and Arabia.

5-Minute Warm-Up

Daily Language SkillBuilder

Have students **proofread** the display sentences on page 563g and write them correctly.

PREPARING to *Read*

from THE

Build Background

The Birth of Islam In about A.D. 610, when the prophet Muhammad was 40 years old, he is said to have received his first visit from the archangel Gabriel—the same Gabriel who appears in the Jewish and Christian Bible. According to tradition, during this visit Gabriel revealed the Word of God to Muhammad. This revelation, or act of revealing, was the first of many experienced by Muhammad throughout his life. Together, these revelations formed the basis of the faith called Islam, which literally means "surrender to the will of Allah," or God. At first Muhammad reported God's revelations orally, and his followers memorized them and recited them in ritual prayers. Later the revelations were written down in a book called The Koran (also spelled Qur'an), which means "recitation."

"Seek knowledge from the cradle to the grave."

—Muhammad

What Is The Koran?

As the sacred book of the Islamic faith, The Koran is to followers of Islam what the Bible is to Jews and Christians. It is considered the true Word of God as revealed to Muhammad. In fact, followers of Islam—called Muslims—believe that The Koran they read is simply a copy of an eternal book found in heaven. To Muslims, The Koran is the world's most important book, the chief authority in all matters of Islamic life. It is a continuing source of inspiration to those who read or recite it.

The most important idea in The Koran is the principle of **monotheism,** the concept that there is only one God. God is the creator of the universe. Though merciful and compassionate, he still requires all human beings to submit to his will. Human beings are seen as the greatest of God's creations but also as creatures capable of evil as well as good. The Koran clearly states moral principles that should be followed in life, stressing the value of daily prayer, faith, work, charity, brotherly love, respect for elders, kindness to animals, honesty, humility, bravery, justice, cleanliness, and moderation, among other things. It indicates that people will one day stand before God and be judged on their earthly behavior.

LESSON RESOURCES

UNIT FOUR RESOURCE BOOK, pp. 4–5

ASSESSMENT RESOURCES
Formal Assessment, pp. 79–80
Teacher's Guide to Assessment and Portfolio Use
Test Generator

INTEGRATED TECHNOLOGY
Visit our Web site: classzone.com

ADDITIONAL RESOURCES
Lesson Planning Guide, pp. 69–70
Teacher's Sourcebook for Language Development

Connect to Your Life

Each *sura* of The Koran opens with the same line: "In the name of God, the Compassionate, the Merciful." What do the words *compassionate* and *merciful* mean to you? Discuss your definitions of these words, along with some examples of merciful and compassionate behavior.

Focus Your Reading

LITERARY ANALYSIS: PARALLELISM

The use of similar grammatical constructions to express ideas that are related or equal in importance is called **parallelism.**

If not us, who?	*If not now, when?*
FIRST IDEA	SECOND IDEA

Parallelism can also be used to contrast ideas.

Some soar like eagles.	*Some crawl like bugs.*
FIRST IDEA	SECOND IDEA

As you read the selection from The Koran, look for examples of parallelism.

ACTIVE READING: QUESTIONING

In reading a challenging text, it can be helpful to keep track of questions as they come up and to actively look for answers.

READER'S NOTEBOOK As you read this selection, jot down any questions you have. These might concern who or what is being talked about, the meanings of particular words or phrases, or the connection between parts of sentences, for example. If you think you might know the answer, write that down too, even if you are not sure. Use a chart like the one shown to record your questions and answers. Write in pencil so that you can make revisions later on.

My Questions About The Koran

Questions	Answers
Who is speaking?	

Worship and The Koran In addition to following the moral principles expressed in The Koran, Muslims are expected to perform five formal acts of worship, called the Five Pillars of Islam:

1. professing their faith
2. praying five times a day
3. giving charity to the poor
4. fasting from sunrise to sundown during the holy month of *Ramadan,* the ninth month of the Islamic calendar
5. making a pilgrimage to the holy city of Mecca, birthplace of Muhammad.

In praying, Muslims recite passages from The Koran, including a short opening *sura,* or chapter, that is usually translated as "The Exordium," or "Introduction." (See page 578.)

Muslim women and children observe *Ramadan.*

For a humanities activity, click on:

READING FOR INFORMATION

Reading Skills and Strategies

PREVIEWING

Help students with the **Build Background** essay by going over with them the three subheads and the information covered in each section. The first section ("The Birth of Islam") explains the origin of The Koran. The second section ("What Is The Koran?") talks about the role of The Koran in Islam and sets forth some of the sacred book's teachings. The third section ("Worship and The Koran") explains how Muslims practice their faith and how they use The Koran in doing so.

Literary Analysis PARALLELISM

Help students understand the concept of parallelism by pointing out the following pairs of parallel elements in "Faith in God":

heavens	earth
life	death
First	Last
Visible	Unseen

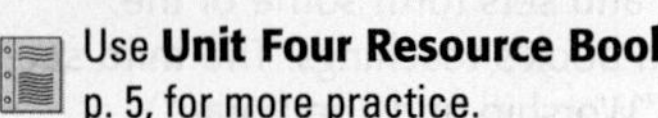
Use **Unit Four Resource Book,** p. 5, for more practice.

Active Reading QUESTIONING

A After they have finished reading "Faith in God," ask students what they think might be the purpose of the first five paragaphs in this section.

Possible Response: to give reasons why a person should have faith in God

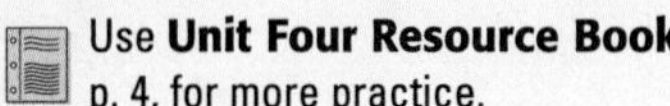
Use **Unit Four Resource Book,** p. 4, for more practice.

from The Koran

Translated by N. J. Dawood

the Exordium

IN THE NAME OF GOD
THE COMPASSIONATE
THE MERCIFUL

Praise be to God, Lord of the Universe,
The Compassionate, the Merciful,
Sovereign of the Day of Judgment!
You alone we worship, and to You alone
we turn for help.
Guide us to the straight path,
The path of those whom You have favored,
Not of those who have incurred[1] Your wrath,
Nor of those who have gone astray.

Faith in God

In the Name of God, the Compassionate, the Merciful

All that is in the heavens and the earth gives glory to God. He is the Mighty, the Wise One.

A It is He that has sovereignty[2] over the heavens and the earth. He ordains life and death, and has power over all things.

He is the First and the Last, the Visible and the Unseen. He has knowledge of all things.

1. **incurred:** brought upon oneself.
2. **sovereignty** (sŏv′ər-ĭn-tē): supremacy of authority or rule.

Humanities

THE KORAN The word *Koran*, or *Qur'an,* means "recitation" or "reading." While the Bible represents a wide variety of literary forms, genres, and authors, all spanning a period of more than a thousand years, The Koran has a uniform structure, represents a single literary form, and has a single author. Each *sura,* or chapter, of The Koran is a direct statement of instruction to the faithful by Allah through Muhammad. As such, The Koran is both a recitation of God's word to Muhammad and a collection of religious wisdom suitable for reading and recitation by believing Muslims.

Like the New Testament, The Koran is a book that takes for granted the existence of the sacred scriptures of the Hebrews, especially the Torah (see Unit One, Part 1), and that sees itself as commenting upon and perfecting a tradition to which it itself belongs. These assumptions can be seen in the following excerpt:

It is We [Allah]
who sent the Torah,
in it guidance and light . . . .
And We caused to follow after them
Jesus son of Mary,
confirming the truth
of the Torah before him;
and we gave him the Gospel,
in it guidance and light . . . .
And we sent the Book [Koran] to you
with truth, confirming
the scripture before it
and safeguarding it.
The Essential Koran (pages 44–45)

It was He who created the heavens and the earth in six days, and then mounted the throne. He knows all that goes into the earth and all that emerges from it, all that comes down from heaven and all that ascends to it. He is with you
A wherever you are. God is cognizant[3] of all your actions.

He has sovereignty over the heavens and the earth. To God shall all things return. He causes the night to pass into the day, and causes the day to pass into the night. He has knowledge of the inmost thoughts of men.

Have faith in God and His Apostle[4] and give in alms[5] of that which He has made your inheritance; for whoever of you believes and gives in alms shall be richly rewarded.

And what cause have you not to believe in God, when the Apostle calls on you to have faith in your Lord, who has made a covenant with you, if you are true believers?

Night

In the Name of God, the Compassionate, the Merciful

By the night, when she lets fall her darkness, and by the radiant day! By Him that created the male and the female,
your endeavors have varied ends! 1

For him that gives in charity and guards himself against
evil and believes in goodness, We[6] shall smooth the path of 2
salvation; but for him that neither gives nor takes and dis-
believes in goodness, We shall smooth the path of affliction. 3
When he breathes his last, his riches will not avail him.

It is for Us to give guidance. Ours is the life to come, Ours the life of this world. I warn you, then, of the blazing fire, in which none shall burn save the hardened sinner, who denies the Truth and gives no heed. But the good man who purifies himself by almsgiving shall keep away from it: and so shall he that does good works for the sake of the Most High only,
seeking no recompense. Such men shall be content. 4

---

3. **cognizant:** aware.
4. **Apostle:** Muhammed.
5. **alms:** money or goods given as charity to the poor.
6. **We:** God.

Customizing Instruction

Less Proficient Readers

1 Tell students that *your endeavors have varied ends* means "different kinds of behavior have different consequences." This statement is explained in the next two paragraphs.

English Learners

2 Explain to students that the use of the first-person plural forms *We, Us,* and *Ours* doesn't indicate more than one person but rather honors the special status of God.

3 Explain that *affliction* is a condition of pain, suffering, or distress. Point out that in common usage the verb *afflict* appears most often in its past participle form, *afflicted,* as in the expression *she was afflicted with an illness.*

Less Proficient Readers

4 Students will probably not know the word *recompense* but probably will know the related words *compensate* and *compensation.* Ask them to define these words, look at the context of *recompense,* and then guess at its meaning. *(repayment or reward)*

THE KORAN 579

Literary Analysis PARALLELISM

A Ask students to think about why this *sura* and the previous one both begin with parallel statements about day and night.
Possible Responses: Referring to both day and night suggests that God's influence extends over everything; the references are a reminder that God has created both night and day; the distinction between night and day parallels the distinction God makes between the "hardened sinner" and the "good man."

Active Reading QUESTIONING

B Ask students why the speaker might think the listener needs this reassurance.
Possible Reponses: because life can sometimes be hard, making it seem as though God isn't there; because the generosity of God won't be evident until the life to come

HUMANITIES CONNECTION Islamic belief discourages the use of images to represent living things. As a result, illuminations of The Koran, like the one here, often rely on the use of abstract designs and decorative lettering to achieve striking effects.

Daylight

In the Name of God, the Compassionate, the Merciful

By the light of day, and by the dark of night, your Lord has not forsaken you,[7] nor does He abhor[8] you.

The life to come holds a richer prize for you than this present life. You shall be gratified with what your Lord will give you.

Did He not find you an orphan and give you shelter?
Did He not find you in error and guide you?
Did He not find you poor and enrich you?
Therefore do not wrong the orphan, nor chide[9] away the beggar. But proclaim the goodness of your Lord.

7. **you:** Muhammad, Allah's prophet.
8. **abhor:** to strongly reject; hate violently.
9. **chide:** to scold mildly; reprimand.

MINI LESSON **Viewing and Representing**

Illuminated Page of The Koran

ART APPRECIATION Have students study the illuminated page shown in the **Humanities Connection** and identify decorative elements used by the artist. *(bold calligraphy, the interlocking motif above the text, the ornate box enclosing the text, the two gold-leaf medallions)*

Tell students that the avoidance of representing living creatures goes back to the second of the Ten Commandments—the prohibition against idolatry ("Thou shalt not make unto thee any graven image"). However, this rule was not always adhered to with perfect consistency, especially in parts of the Islamic Empire with strong pre-Islamic traditions of representational painting, such as Persia, Turkey, and India. It is from these lands that we get what portraits we have of the historical and literary figures of the Islamic Empire.

Because of his unique status in Islam and the great reverence in which he was held, representations of Muhammad were avoided with special care. For the very same reasons, he was a figure of great interest, and there are exceptions to this rule as well. However, even in paintings that freely portray his form among those of other people, the Prophet's face is usually left blank or covered with a veil out of respect.

Sometimes calligraphy itself was used cleverly to create texts in the shape of people or animals. Perhaps because the texts often have a religious significance and merely outline images without realistically portraying them, they do not seem to violate the prohibition.

Connect to the Literature

1. **What Do You Think?** What image or images did you find most memorable in these excerpts? Explain your response.

Think Critically

2. **ACTIVE READING: QUESTIONING** With a small group of classmates, discuss the questions that you wrote in your  READER'S NOTEBOOK. Together try to come up with answers to all of the questions. Make a note of any unanswered questions to bring up with the class as a whole.
3. According to The Koran, what qualities and actions make a person righteous?
4. How do the excerpts you read support the idea of "God, the Compassionate, the Merciful"?

   THINK ABOUT
   - the kind of behavior God wants from people
   - how God punishes sin
   - how God rewards goodness

Extend Interpretations

5. **Different Perspectives** How might the words of The Koran be applied not just to individuals but also to governments or social groups?
6. **The Writer's Style** Based on their tone, word choice, imagery, and other literary qualities, how do you think these excerpts from The Koran should be read aloud in order best to convey their meaning?
7. **Connect to Life** What kind of rules or guidelines for behavior do you think a person should follow in life? How do these compare with those set forth in The Koran?

LITERARY ANALYSIS: PARALLELISM

Parallelism is the use of similar grammatical forms or sentence structures to express ideas that are related or of equal importance.

Did He not find you in error and guide you?

Did He not find you poor and enrich you?

In some cases parallel constructions bring ideas together in a way that suggests they are opposites. This is sometimes referred to as **antithesis.**

For him that gives in charity . . . We shall smooth the path of salvation; but for him that neither gives nor takes . . . We shall smooth the path of affliction.

Parallelism gives writers a way to emphasize relationships and ideas while adding a kind of rhythm to their words.

Cooperative Learning Activity
With a group of classmates, find other examples of parallelism and antithesis in the selection from The Koran. Then discuss which example of parallelism or antithesis is the most powerful.

Literary Analysis

Cooperative Learning Activity You might extend this activity by having students look for familiar examples of parallelism and antithesis in songs, speeches, ads, slogans, etc.

 Use **Unit Four Resource Book,** p. 5, for more practice.

Connect to the Literature

1. **What Do You Think?**
   Accept all reasonable responses. Encourage students to identify passages with which their memorable images are connected.

Think Critically

2. As an alternative to discussing each group's unanswered questions with the whole class, you might have each group answer another group's questions in discussion and then present them to the class.
3. Possible Responses: Believing in God, being mindful of what God has done for people, practicing charity and goodness, avoiding evil, doing good works for God's sake only, trusting in God's care, proclaiming God's goodness, and warning nonbelievers of the consequences of turning from God
4. Possible Responses: God has created the world for people to live in; God tries to help the sinner by warning of the consequences of sin; God lavishly rewards goodness; God reserves the fire of punishment only for the "hardened sinner"; God wants people to take care of the beggars and orphans; God promises a better life after death.

Extend Interpretations

5. **Different Perspectives** Possible Responses: Countries might practice charity towards poorer or less fortunate nations; governments might incorporate principles of religion into their laws; businesses might care more about practicing charity and kindness than making profits.
6. **The Writer's Style** Answers will vary. Have students cite specific examples of tone, word choice, imagery, and other literary qualities in their answers. Students can demonstrate their opinions by reading particular passages aloud.
7. **Connect to Life** Answers will vary. Encourage students to be specific in describing their rules or guidelines for behavior and to base their comparisons and contrasts on specific passages in The Koran.

 To assess skills and concepts taught in this selection, use **Formal Assessment Book,** p. 79

Objectives

- understand and appreciate a **tale (Literary Analysis)**
- know the elements of **plot** in fiction **(Literary Analysis)**
- **analyze problems and solutions** in a story **(Active Reading)**

Summary

Following his desire for travel and adventure, Sindbad embarks on a commercial sea voyage. While exploring an island, he falls asleep and his ship leaves him. Soon he discovers that the island is the home of a giant bird called a roc. By hitching a ride tied to one of the roc's talons, Sindbad escapes from the island, only to find himself in a mountain-locked valley filled with precious stones and giant snakes. Taking advantage of an ingenious method used to retrieve gems from the valley, Sindbad ties himself to a sheep's carcass and is airlifted once again by a giant bird, this time to safety. On his way home, Sindbad visits another island where he witnesses more marvels.

 Use **Unit Four Resource Book,** p. 6, for additional support.

Thematic Link

The Thousand and One Nights reveals the strong element of the **magical** in Persian and Arabic literature. Gathered from far and wide, the stories and folk tales in this collection include fantasy, legend, and supernatural characters and events.

 Use **Unit Four Resource Book,** p. 9, for practice with Words to Know.

5-Minute Warm-Up

Daily Language SkillBuilder

Have students **proofread** the display sentences on page 563g and write them correctly.

from **THE THOUSAND AND ONE NIGHTS**

Build Background

A Famous Collection Have you ever heard of Aladdin and the Magical Lamp, Sindbad the Sailor, or Ali Baba and the Forty Thieves? All are characters from *The Thousand and One Nights,* one of the world's best-known story collections. Written in Arabic and sometimes called *The Arabian Nights,* this famous collection dates in its present form to about the 15th century A.D. The stories themselves, however, had been floating around the Middle East for many centuries before that.

A Thousand and One Nights of Storytelling The title *The Thousand and One Nights* refers to the loose framework, called a **frame story,** that joins all the stories together in one long narrative. This frame story tells of Shahryar (shă-ryär'), the powerful ruler of a central Asian kingdom, who has come to hate all women after having been betrayed by one. Each day Shahryar weds a new wife, only to have her executed the next day, before he weds another. Finally Scheherezade (shə-hĕr'ə-zäd'), the clever daughter of the king's vizier, or prime minister, concocts a plan to put an end to the violence. She agrees to marry the king, and on their wedding night she begins a gripping story but leaves it unfinished. Fascinated by the tale, the king spares her life so that she can complete the story the next night. She does so but then moves on to another story that she does not finish. Again he spares her life the next day so that she can finish that night, and again she leaves a new story unfinished. This continues for a thousand and one nights, until finally the king realizes that he loves Scheherezade and does not want her killed.

Origins of the Tales The tradition of using a frame story to hold together a collection of loosely related stories seems to go back at least as far as ancient India. The *Panchatantra* (see page 146), which is about 1,000 years older than the Arabic collection, is organized in this way, and many of the tales told by Scheherezade can be found there in one version or another. Other tales very likely come from other traditions, some even older. Some scholars believe that the basic plot of the Sindbad tales may go back to an ancient Egyptian story called "The Tale of the Shipwrecked Sailor," which predates *The Thousand and One Nights* by more than 3,500 years.

LESSON RESOURCES

UNIT FOUR RESOURCE BOOK, pp. 6–10

ASSESSMENT RESOURCES
Formal Assessment, pp. 81–82
Teacher's Guide to Assessment and Portfolio Use
Test Generator

INTEGRATED TECHNOLOGY
Visit our Web site: classzone.com

ADDITIONAL RESOURCES
Lesson Planning Guide, pp. 71–72
Teacher's Sourcebook for Language Development

Connect to Your Life

Recall an important project or trip that you undertook and the reasons you had for doing so. What did you hope to gain? What were some of the problems that you faced? What did you do to overcome them?

Focus Your Reading

LITERARY ANALYSIS: PLOT

The **plot** of a story is the chain of related events that take place in the story. Usually, the events of a plot progress because of a **conflict,** or struggle between a character and another person, nature, circumstances, or even him or herself. For example, in the following selection the main character gets left behind by his ship while he is visiting a strange island. As a story progresses, new conflicts, or **complications,** arise. As you read "The Second Voyage of Sindbad the Sailor," take note of the complications that Sindbad must face.

ACTIVE READING: ANALYZING PROBLEMS AND SOLUTIONS

From the point of view of a character, a conflict is a problem that he or she must try to solve. A character's attempts to solve a problem may succeed, or they may fail. Either way, the attempted solution may lead to new complications.

READER'S NOTEBOOK As you read about Sindbad's second voyage, look for the problems he faces, the solutions he comes up with, and the results that follow. Keep track of the problems and solutions on a chart like the one below.

Problem	Sindbad's Solution	Result
Sindbad has no shelter for the night.	Sindbad finds a cave to sleep in.	

WORDS TO KNOW **Vocabulary Preview**

confounded oblivious tumult
jubilant sumptuous

The Sindbad Tales

The excerpt you are about to read is one of several tales about a man named Sindbad (often spelled *Sinbad*). His story begins in Baghdad (in present-day Iraq) during its heyday as the commercial and cultural capital of the Islamic empire. At the beginning of the story, we are introduced to a poor Baghdad porter, or baggage carrier, who sits outside a palace and wonders why the rich man inside deserves such wealth. That rich man, Sindbad the Sailor, invites the porter in and proceeds to tell his story. Sindbad explains that as a merchant in the reign of Harun al-Rashid (A.D. 786–809), he made seven voyages to strange and distant lands, each voyage fraught with peril but leaving him wealthier than before. In the end, the porter agrees that Sindbad deserves his riches, and Sindbad shares some of them with the porter.

READING FOR INFORMATION

Reading Skills and Strategies

PREVIEWING

Help students actively read the **Build Background** essay by having them prepare to explain each of the following terms and its connection to the selection:

- *The Thousand and One Nights*
- frame story
- Scheherazade
- *Panchatantra*
- "The Tale of the Shipwrecked Sailor"
- Sindbad

TIME MANAGEMENT

If your schedule requires that you cover the lesson objectives in a shorter time, use . . .

- Preparing to Read, pp. 582–583
- Thinking Through the Literature, p. 589
- Vocabulary in Action, p. 590

If you want to take advantage of longer blocks of class time, use . . .

- TE Teaching Options: Viewing and Representing, p. 587; Vocabulary Strategy, p. 585; Cross Curricular Link, p. 584; Grammar, p. 588; Speaking and Listening, p. 586
- Choices & Challenges, p. 590
- Connect to Today, p. 591

Reading and Analyzing

Literary Analysis PLOT

A Ask students to identify the conflict described in this paragraph. *(Sindbad's ship has sailed without him, so he is now stranded on the island.)*

Use **Unit Four Resource Book,** p. 8, for more practice.

Reading Skills and Strategies
ANALOGIES

B Point out that Sindbad here quotes a proverb, a short pithy saying that expresses a basic truth or piece of practical wisdom. Like many proverbs, this one is based on an analogy, a comparison that uses a known or familiar thing to explain something else. Have students identify what two things are being compared and what Sindbad means when he quotes the proverb. *(Sindbad compares risking his life a second time on a dangerous voyage to dropping a jar for the second time. His point is that he probably won't be as lucky this time.)*

Active Reading
ANALYZING PROBLEMS AND SOLUTIONS

C Have students identify the steps Sindbad takes to solve his problem in this paragraph. *(He climbs a tree to get a better idea of where he is; he investigates a mysterious white object that might help him in some unknown way; he looks for a door to the "dome," thinking he might find shelter or another person.)*

Use **Unit Four Resource Book,** p. 7, for more practice.

Literary Analysis PLOT

D Ask students to identify the complication described in this paragraph. *(Not only is Sindbad trapped on an island, but the island is inhabited by a dangerous monster.)*

Reading Skills and Strategies
CLARIFYING

E Ask students to whom this sentence refers. *(Allah)*

from The Thousand and One Nights

The Second Voyage of Sindbad the Sailor

Translated by N. J. Dawood

1 For some time after my return to Baghdad I continued to lead a joyful and carefree life, but it was not long before I felt an irresistible longing to travel again about the world and to visit distant cities and islands in quest of profit and adventure. So I bought a great store of merchandise and, after making preparations for departure, sailed down the Tigris to Basrah.[1] There I embarked, together with a band of merchants, in a fine new vessel, well-equipped and manned by a sturdy crew, which set sail the same day.

Aided by a favorable wind, we voyaged for many days and nights from port to port and from island to island, selling and bartering our goods, and haggling with merchants and officials
2 wherever we cast anchor. At length Destiny carried our ship to the shores of an uninhabited island, rich in fruit and flowers, and jubilant with the singing of birds and the murmur of crystal streams.

Here passengers and crew went ashore, and we all set off to enjoy the delights of the island. I strolled through the green meadows, leaving my companions far behind, and sat down in a shady thicket to eat a simple meal by a spring of water. Lulled by the soft and fragrant breeze which blew around me, I lay upon the grass and presently fell asleep.

A I cannot tell how long I slept, but when I awoke I saw none of my fellow-travelers, and soon realized that the ship had sailed away without anyone noticing my absence. I ran in frantic haste towards the sea, and on reaching the shore saw the vessel, a white speck upon the vast blue ocean, dissolving into the far horizon. 3

Broken with terror and despair, I threw myself upon the sand, wailing: "Now your end has come, Sindbad! The jar that drops a second time is sure to break!" B I cursed the day I bade farewell to the joys of a contented life and bitterly repented my folly in venturing again upon 4 the hazards and hardships of the sea, after having so narrowly escaped death in my first voyage.

At length, resigning myself to my doom, I rose and, after wandering about aimlessly for some time, climbed into a tall tree. From its top I gazed long in all directions, but could see nothing save the sky, the trees, the birds, the sands, and the boundless ocean. As I scanned the interior of the island more closely, however, I gradually became aware of some white object looming in the distance. C At once I climbed down the tree and made my way towards it. Drawing nearer, I found to my astonishment that it was a white dome of extraordinary dimensions. I walked all round it, but could find no door or entrance of any kind; and so smooth and slippery was its surface that any attempt to climb it would have been fruitless. I walked round it again, and, making a mark in the sand near its base, found that its circumference measured more than fifty paces.

Whilst I was thus engaged the sun was suddenly

1. **sailed down the Tigris to Basrah** (bäs′rə): The Tigris River runs south through present-day Iraq to the port city of Basrah.

WORDS TO KNOW
jubilant (jo͞o′bə-lənt) *adj.* extremely joyful

Cross Curricular Link **Humanities**

THE THOUSAND AND ONE NIGHTS *The Thousand and One Nights* took shape during the expansion of the Islamic Empire. As Arabic culture spread to new lands, works from a wide variety of literary traditions were translated into Arabic and incorporated into Islamic culture. While the book might seem like just one literary work among others, in fact it is one of the first great anthologies of world literature.

The influence of this collection on later literature has been enormous. Sindbad, Ali Baba, Aladdin, and even Scheherezade herself are familiar to many people from countless books and movies, and the tales have supplied material for authors from Boccaccio and Chaucer to H.G. Wells, C.S. Lewis, John Barth, and Naguib Mahfouz.

A poignant example of this influence appears in the well-known story by Charles Dickens, *A Christmas Carol.* Revisiting his childhood in the company of the Ghost of Christmas Past, Scrooge vividly recalls his first experience of reading the tales during a Christmas holiday when he had been left at school:

> "Why, it's Ali Baba!" Scrooge exclaimed in ecstasy. "It's dear old honest Ali Baba! Yes, yes, I know! One Christmas time, when yonder solitary child was left here all alone, he did come, for the first time, just like that."

hidden from my view as by a great cloud and the world grew dark around me. I lifted up my eyes
D towards the sky, and was <u>confounded</u> to see a gigantic bird with enormous wings which, as it flew through the air, screened the sun and hid it from the island.

The sight of this prodigy[2] instantly called to my mind a story I had heard in my youth from pilgrims and adventurers—how in a far island dwelt a bird of monstrous size called the roc, which fed its young on elephants; and at once I realized that the white dome was none other than a roc's egg. In a twinkling the bird alighted upon the egg, covering it completely with its wings and stretching out its legs behind it on the ground. And in this posture it went to sleep.
E (Glory to Him who never sleeps!)

Rising swiftly, I unwound my turban from my head, then doubled it and twisted it into a rope with which I securely bound myself by the waist to one of the great talons of the monster. "Perchance this bird," I thought, "will carry me away to a civilized land; wherever I am set down, it will surely be better than a solitary island."

I lay awake all night, fearing to close my eyes lest the bird should fly away with me while I slept. At daybreak the roc rose from the egg, and,
5 spreading its wings, took to the air with a terrible cry. I clung fast to its talon as it winged its way through the void and soared higher and higher until it almost touched the heavens. After some time it began to drop, and sailing swiftly downwards came to earth on the brow of a steep hill.

Trembling with fear, I hastened to untie my turban before the roc became aware of my presence. Scarcely had I released myself when the monster darted off towards a great black object lying near and, clutching it in its fearful claws, took wing again. As it rose in the air I was astonished to see that this was a serpent of immeasurable length; and with its prey the bird vanished from sight.

"NO SOONER DO I ESCAPE FROM ONE PERIL THAN I FIND MYSELF IN ANOTHER MORE GRIEVOUS."

Looking around, I found myself on a precipitous hillside overlooking an exceedingly deep and vast valley. On all sides towered craggy mountains whose beetling[3] summits no man could ever scale. I was stricken with fear and repented my rashness. "Would that I had remained in that island!" I thought to myself. "There at least I lacked neither fruit nor water, while these barren steeps offer nothing to eat or drink. No sooner do I escape from one peril than I find myself in another more grievous. There is no strength or help save in Allah!"

When I had made my way down the hill I marveled to see the ground thickly covered with the rarest diamonds, so that the entire valley blazed with a glorious light. Here and there among the glittering stones, however, coiled deadly snakes and vipers, dread keepers of the fabulous treasure. Thicker and longer than giant palm-trees, they could have swallowed whole elephants at one gulp. They were crawling back into their sunless dens, for by day they hid themselves from their enemies the rocs and the eagles and moved about only at night.

Overwhelmed with horror, and <u>oblivious</u> of hunger and fatigue, I roamed the valley all day searching with infinite caution for a shelter where I might pass the night. At dusk I came

2. **prodigy:** a rare or extraordinary event.

3. **beetling:** overhanging.

WORDS TO KNOW

confounded (kən-foun′dĭd) *adj.* confused; befuddled
oblivious (ə-blĭv′ē-əs) *adj.* not aware; unmindful

Customizing Instruction

Less Proficient Readers

1 Help students understand this long and complicated sentence by having them restate it in their own words.
Possible Response: After I returned home, I was happy for a while, but soon I wanted to go travelling again to have fun and make money.

English Learners

2 Explain that Destiny and (in the next column) doom both mean "fate." Also, students may have learned the rule that in English adjectives precede the nouns they modify. Point out that occasionally, as in this sentence, long adjective phrases follow the nouns they modify. The phrases *rich in fruits and flowers* and *jubilant with the singing of birds and the murmur of crystal streams* both modify *island.*

Advanced Learners

3 Sindbad assumes his ship will not return for him. Ask students to infer possible reasons for this assumption.
Possible Responses: By the time his absence is noticed, the ship might not be able to find its way back to the island; Sindbad's men might take advantage of the opportunity to steal his ship and his merchandise; Sindbad's absence might not be noticed for such a long time that no one will know when he left the ship.

Less Proficient Readers

4 Help students understand this long and complicated sentence by having them identify the simple subject and predicate. *(I cursed and repented.)*

5 Have students explain in their own words the steps Sindbad follows in getting off the island. *(He twists his turban into a rope, ties himself to one of the bird's claws, holds on as the bird flies away, and unties himself once the bird lands.)*

MINI LESSON Vocabulary Strategy

CONTEXT CLUES Remind students that sometimes they can understand the meaning of an unfamiliar word by examining the context in which the word is used.

Instruction Read aloud the last full sentence on page 585 that begins, "Overwhelmed with horror." Tell students they can use other words in this sentence to figure out the meaning of the word *oblivious*.

- Ask a volunteer to summarize the meaning of the sentence.
- Have students use the meaning of the sentence to infer meanings for *oblivious*.
- Ask another volunteer to use *oblivious* in a sentence.

Practice Have students use context clues to infer the meanings of the italicized Words to Know in the sentences below.

1. The *jubilant* contest-winner jumped up and down and clapped her hands.
2. Jen was *confounded* by the first test question, but she quickly answered the rest of the questions.
3. Myra kept her *sumptuous* diamond necklace in the vault.
4. The farmer's children caused a *tumult* in order to scare the crows from the corn.

Use **Unit Four Resource Book,** p. 9, for additional support.

A lesson on using context clues appears on p. 674 in the Pupil's Edition

Active Reading

ANALYZING PROBLEMS AND SOLUTIONS

A Ask students why Sindbad doesn't roll back the stone and leave the cave until daybreak. *(It's safe for Sindbad to leave the cave at dawn, because the serpents only leave their caves at night. During the night it is safer for Sindbad to stay still, because he might attract the snake's attention and the snake could leave the cave to chase him.)* Point out to students that the evidence for the first answer can be found on page 585, but the second answer must be inferred.

B Ask students the following questions: What kinds of problems might Sindbad have with the man? How does Sindbad prevent these problems from occurring? *(Problems: the man might think Sindbad is a thief, an evil spirit, or a vagabond, and refuse to help him; the man might demand that Sindbad give him all of his jewels, since Sindbad took the man's bait and put it to another use. Solutions: Sindbad explains that he is not an evil spirit, but an honest merchant, like the man himself; Sindbad promises that he has a good story to tell; he gives the man some of the jewels.)*

Literary Analysis PLOT

Ask students where on this page they think the moment of greatest suspense comes—the moment they felt the most curious to see how a particular conflict would be resolved.

Possible Responses: when Sindbad spends the night in the cave with the enormous serpent; when Sindbad is perplexed by the appearance of the sheep carcass; when Sindbad is lifted into the air by the giant vulture; when the vulture lands and Sindbad frees himself; when the merchant acts suspicious toward Sindbad

upon a narrow-mouthed cave, into which I crawled, blocking its entrance from within by a great stone. I thought to myself: "Here I shall be
1 safe tonight. When tomorrow comes, let Destiny do its worst."

Scarcely had I advanced a few steps, when I saw at the far end of the cave an enormous serpent coiled in a great knot round its eggs. My
2 hair stood on end and I was transfixed with terror. Seeing no way of escape, however, I put my trust in Allah and kept vigil all night. At day break I rolled back the stone and staggered out
A of the cave, reeling like a drunken man.

As I thus stumbled along I noticed a great joint of flesh come tumbling down into the valley from rock to rock. Upon closer inspection I found this to be a whole sheep, skinned and drawn. I was deeply perplexed at the mystery, for there was not a soul in sight; but at that very moment there flashed across my mind the memory of a story I had once heard from travelers who had visited the Diamond Mountains—how men obtained the diamonds from this treacherous and inaccessible
3 valley by a strange device. Before sunrise they would throw whole carcasses of sheep from the top of the mountains, so that the gems on which they fell penetrated the soft flesh and became embedded in it. At midday rocs and mighty vultures would swoop down upon the mutton and carry it away in their talons to their nests in the mountain heights. With a great clamor the merchants would then rush at the birds and force them to drop the meat and fly away, after which it would only remain to look through the carcasses and pick out the diamonds.

As I recalled this story a plan of escape formed in my mind. I selected a great quantity of priceless stones and hid them all about me, filling my pockets with them and pressing them into the folds of my belt and garments. Then I unrolled my turban, stuffed it with more diamonds, twisted it into a rope as I had done before, and, lying down below the carcass, bound it firmly to my chest. I had not remained long in that position when I suddenly felt myself lifted from the ground by the talons of a huge vulture which had tightly closed upon the meat. The bird climbed higher and higher and finally alighted upon the top of a mountain. As soon as it began to tear at the flesh there arose from behind the neighboring rocks a great tumult, at which the bird took fright and flew away. At once I freed myself and sprang to my feet, with face and clothes all bloody.

I saw a man come running to the spot and stop in alarm as he saw me. Without uttering a word he cautiously bent over the carcass to examine it, eyeing me suspiciously all the while; but finding no diamonds, he wrung his hands and lifted up his arms, crying: "O heavy loss! Allah, in whom alone dwell all power and majesty, defend us
from the wiles of the Evil One!" 4

Before I could explain my presence the man, shaking with fear, turned to me and asked: "Who are you, and how came you here?"

"Do not be alarmed, sir," I replied, "I am no evil spirit, but an honest man, a merchant by profession. My story is an extraordinary one, and the adventure which has brought me to these mountains surpasses in wonder all the marvels that men have seen or heard of. But first pray
accept some of these diamonds, which I myself B
gathered in the fearful valley below."

I took some splendid jewels from my pocket and offered them to him, saying: "These will bring you all the riches you can desire."

The owner of the bait was overjoyed at the unexpected gift; he warmly thanked me and called down blessings upon me. Whilst we were thus talking, several other merchants came up from the mountain-side. They crowded round us, listening in amazement to my story, and congratulated me, saying: "By Allah, your escape was a miracle; for no man has ever set foot in that valley and returned alive. Allah alone be praised for
your salvation." 5

WORDS TO KNOW

tumult (to͞o′mŭlt′) *n.* a disorderly noisiness or disturbance

MINI LESSON Speaking and Listening

DRAMATIC PRESENTATION

Instruction Help students prepare a dramatic interpretation of the section of the story on this page beginning, "As soon as it began to tear at the flesh," and continuing to the end of the page. Explain that how the characters act and speak their lines in this scene would depend on what each one is thinking and feeling at different points in the action.

Prepare Have one group of students work with Sindbad as a character and another with the owner of the sheep carcass. Each group should discuss its character's thoughts and feelings in this scene, come up with at least two different interpretations of them, and make notes explaining how each interpretation should be conveyed in action and speech.

Present Ask each group to select one person to portray one interpretation of its character, and have the two students act out the scene. Then ask each group to select another person to portray the other interpretation and act out the scene again. If time allows, the two groups can discuss their respective interpretations.

This activity is particularly well suited to longer blocks of class time.

Illustration by Edmund Dulac.

HUMANITIES CONNECTION Edmund Dulac (1882–1953) was one of the most successful and best-loved book illustrators of all time. His works were among the first to be reproduced using the process of color separation, which yields colors faithful to the original.

Customizing Instruction

English Learners

1 Students may need help with the expression *let Destiny do its worst.* Help them paraphrase the last two sentences of this paragraph. *(I'll be safe tonight, whatever may happen tomorrow.)*

2 Explain that the expression *my hair stood on end* means "I was very frightened." Ask students if they have a similar expression in their first language. Explain that *transfixed* means pinned and held motionless like a butterfly in a collection. Make sure students understand that *kept vigil* here means "stayed awake and watched."

3 Students may find the word *device* confusing. Explain that here the word refers to a way or method of doing something, not to a machine.

4 Students may not understand the reference to the "Evil One." *(Satan, or the Devil)*

Advanced Learners

5 Draw students' attention to the merchants' explanation for Sindbad's escape. Have students review the story up to this point, noting Sindbad's and others' explanations of why things happen as they do. Then read aloud Sindbad's exclamation at the beginning of this page, "When tomorrow comes, let Destiny do its worst," and have students answer the following question: What controls destiny in this story?

Possible Responses: Allah, because the story takes place in an Islamic setting; blind luck, because there's no way to predict what happens; Sindbad's own ingenuity, because most of what happens results from his choices and actions

MINI LESSON Viewing and Representing

Illustration of Sindbad Hanging from the Roc's Talon **by Edmund Dulac**

ART APPRECIATION Have students study the illustration and answer the following questions:

1. What passage from the story does the illustration depict? *(Sindbad's flight with the roc from the island on which he was left behind to the valley of the diamonds, p. 585)*
2. How do we know that the illustration doesn't show Sindbad's escape from the valley on page 586? *(there's no sheep's carcass in the picture)*
3. What other details from the story are shown in the illustration? *(the valley with its steep sides, the diamonds lying on the ground, the barrenness of the valley)*
4. How does the illustration reflect the time of day that the action takes place? *(the flight takes place at daybreak, which is shown in the bright golds and reds of the roc and Sindbad and in the fact that most of the valley is still in darkness)*
5. What important detail from the description of the scene in the story is not included in the illustration? *(the giant snakes)*

Literary Analysis PLOT

Ask students what major complications in the plot of this story are described on this page. *(none)*

Reading Skills and Strategies
CLARIFYING

A Make sure students understand that *karkadan* is defined in the paragraph that follows.

Reading Skills and Strategies
CONNECTING

Have students reread **Merchants and Traders** on page 569 and answer the following question: What aspects of Sindbad's life might have seemed familiar or plausible to readers living during this historical period?

Possible Responses: Sindbad's love of travel and adventure; his wealth from his profession of merchant and trader; his interest in hearing and telling travel stories; his interest in new ideas, customs, and marvels; his tendency to mix fact and fantasy, as in the descriptions of the camphor tree and the karkadan

Literary Analysis FRAME STORY

B Have students compare the last three paragraphs of the selection with the first sentence on page 584 and answer the following question about the frame story: Based on what these passages reveal about Sindbad, what do you think might be one reason he goes on his third adventure?

Possible Responses: He becomes bored with his carefree life and longs to travel again; he forgets the perils and hardships of his previous voyage; he wants to be able to astound his friends with another good story; he needs more money after spending it all on sumptuous living.

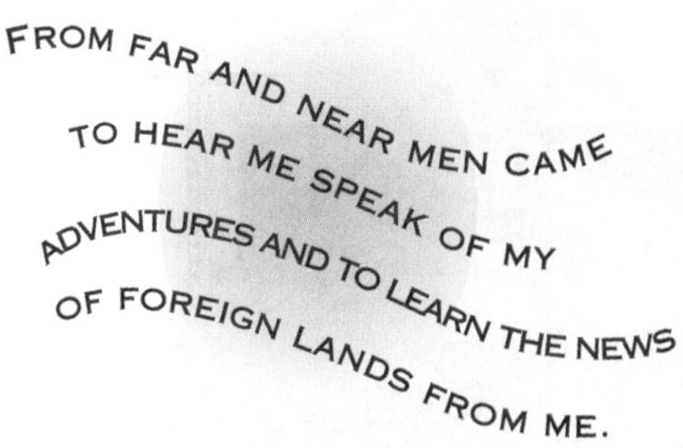

The merchants then led me to their tent. They gave me food and drink and there I slept soundly for many hours. Early next day we set out from our tent and, after journeying over a vast range of mountains, came at length to the seashore. After a short voyage we arrived in a pleasant, densely wooded island, covered with trees so huge that beneath one of them a hundred men could shelter from the sun. It is from these trees that the aromatic substance known as camphor is extracted. The trunks are hollowed out, and the sap oozes drop by drop into vessels which are placed beneath, soon curdling into a crystal gum.

A In that island I saw a gigantic beast called the karkadan,[4] or rhinoceros, which grazes in the fields like a cow or buffalo. Taller than a camel, it has a single horn in the middle of its forehead, and upon this horn Nature has carved the likeness of a man. The karkadan attacks the elephant and, impaling it upon its horn, carries it aloft from place to place until its victim dies. Before long, however, the elephant's fat melts in the heat of the sun and, dripping down into the karkadan's eyes, puts out its sight, so that the beast blunders helplessly along and finally drops dead. Then the roc swoops down upon both animals and carries them off to its nest in the high mountains. I also saw many strange breeds of buffalo in that island.

I sold a part of my diamonds for a large sum and exchanged more for a vast quantity of merchandise. Then we set sail and, trading from port to port and from island to island, at length arrived safely in Basrah. After a few days' sojourn[5] there I set out upstream to Baghdad, the City of Peace.

Loaded with precious goods and the finest of my diamonds, I hastened to my old street and, entering my own house, rejoiced to see my friends and kinsfolk. I gave them gold and presents, and distributed alms among the poor of the city.

I soon forgot the perils and hardships of my travels and took again to sumptuous living. I ate well, dressed well, and kept open house for innumerable gallants and boon companions.[6]

From far and near men came to hear me speak of my adventures and to learn the news of foreign lands from me. All were astounded at the dangers I had escaped and wished me joy of my return. Such was my second voyage. B

Tomorrow, my friends, if Allah wills, I shall relate to you the extraordinary tale of my third voyage. ❖

4. **karkadan** (kär′kə-dăn′).
5. **sojourn:** a brief stay or visit.
6. **gallants** (gə-lănts′) **and boon companions:** fashionably dressed men and pleasant, merry companions.

WORDS TO KNOW
sumptuous (sŭmp′cho͞o-əs) *adj.* costly; magnificent

MINI LESSON **Grammar**

ADJECTIVES AND ADVERBS

Instruction Remind students that adjectives and adverbs are both modifiers—that is, they describe or limit other words. Review adjective and adverb usage with students.

- An **adjective** modifies a noun or a pronoun. It answers the question what kind, how many, or which one. (what kind: sharp teeth, scenic highway; *how many:* five desks, some students, several states; *which one:* this game, these players)
- An **adverb** modifies a verb, an adjective, or another adverb. Many adverbs are formed by adding *–ly* to an adjective. An adverb answers the question *how, when, where,* or *to what extent.* (*how:* quickly, slowly, well; *where:* here, there, outside; *when:* daily, soon, never; *to what extent:* almost, nearly)

Practice For each sentence, write the correct choice of modifier and identify it as an adjective or an adverb.

1. Sindbad arrived *(safe, safely)* in Baghdad. *(safely; adv.)*
2. The (aromatic, aromatically) substance is called camphor. (*aromatic; adj.)*
3. The merchants collected the (precious, preciously) gems. *(precious; adj.)*
4. The giant beast fumbled (helpless, helplessly) on the beach. *(helplessly; adv.)*
5. A karkadan is (vast, vastly) different from an elephant. *(vastly; adv.)*

For more instruction and practice, use McDougal Littell's ***Language Network:***

- Grade 10, Chapter 9, "Using Modifiers"
- Grade 12, Chapter 7, "Using Modifiers"

Connect to the Literature

1. **What Do You Think?** Based on this story, do you think Sindbad deserves his wealth? Explain your response.

Comprehension Check
- How does Sindbad escape the island?
- How does Sindbad escape the mountain?

Think Critically

2. **ACTIVE READING: ANALYZING PROBLEMS AND SOLUTIONS** With a classmate, go over the problems, solutions, and results you each recorded in your READER'S NOTEBOOK. Based on your discussion, do you see Sindbad as a good problem solver?

3. Does Sindbad succeed more because he is lucky or because he is clever? Support your opinion with examples.

4. Judging from the story, do you think Sindbad deserves to be called a heroic character?

- his motives in making the voyage
- how he responds to danger and defeat
- how he treats others

Extend Interpretations

5. **Different Perspectives** How do you think King Shahryar might respond to Scheherezade's story about Sindbad the Sailor?

6. **Connect to Life** In your opinion, does the greatest success belong to those who, like Sindbad, take the biggest risks? Explain.

LITERARY ANALYSIS: PLOT

The **plot** is the chain of related events that take place in a story. In most plots events are set in motion by **conflicts**—struggles between a character and external or internal forces. Most plots include the following stages:

Exposition This stage provides groundwork for the plot. Characters are introduced, the setting is described, and conflicts are identified.

Rising Action As the story progresses, complications usually arise, causing difficulties for the main characters.

Climax This is the turning point of the story, the moment when interest and intensity reach their peak. Usually, an important discovery or decision is made.

Falling Action This stage consists of events that occur after the climax. Often, the conflict is resolved.

Cooperative Learning Activity With a group of classmates, identify the four elements of a plot in "The Second Voyage of Sindbad the Sailor." Create a diagram like the one below to illustrate your findings.

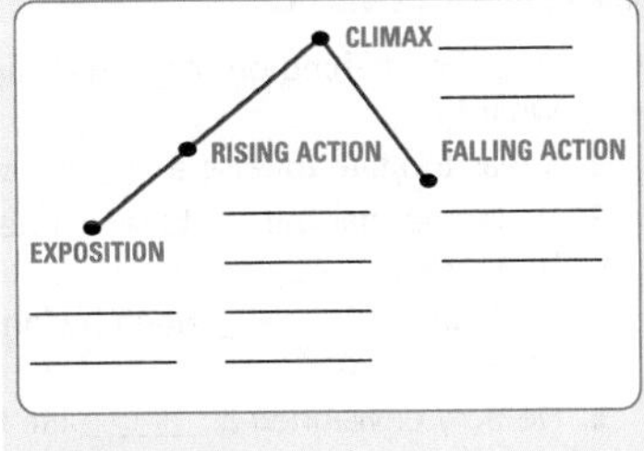

Literary Analysis

Cooperative Learning Activity Have each group create its chart on the board or on newsprint. You can then have students compare charts one element at a time as a whole-class activity. Make sure students understand that their analyses don't all have to be the same to be valid.

Use **Unit Four Resource Book,** p. 8, for more practice.

Connect to the Literature

1. **What Do You Think?** Accept all reasonable responses based on Sindbad's character as depicted in the story.

Comprehension Check
- He ties himself to one of the roc's talons with his turban and escapes when the roc flies away.
- He ties himself to one of the sheep carcasses used by gem hunters and is carried away by a giant vulture.

Use Selection Quiz in **Unit Four Resource Book,** p. 10.

Think Critically

2. Accept all reasonable responses. Encourage students to respond to Sindbad's abilities as presented in the story rather than judging his solutions by a real-world standard.
3. Some students may say that Sindbad succeeds because of the protection of Allah. To bring them back to the question of Sindbad's character, ask them whether they think Sindbad earns this protection or not.
4. Students' opinions will vary but should be based on details from the story. Most students will find Sindbad bold, resourceful, and adventurous; others may see him more as a victim of bad luck and his own poor judgment or as someone tempted by greed.

Extend Interpretations

5. **Different Perspectives** (If students need a reminder about Sharyar, Scheherazade, and the overarching frame story of *The Thousand and One Nights,* have them reread **A Thousand and One Nights of Storytelling** on page 582.) Possible Responses: He would be fascinated and eager to hear about the next voyage; he would identify with Sindbad's daring; he would value Scheherazade for her ability to tell such a good story; he would be reminded by Sindbad's near tragedy of his own threat to Scheherazade and feel sympathy for her.
6. **Connect to Life** Accept all responses that students can support with real-life examples and logical reasoning.

Writing Options

1. **Sindbad Adventure** You might conduct the brainstorming session as a small group discussion. Students can then build on the ideas generated in their groups in individual narratives.
2. **Persuasive Essay** If students need help getting started, you can give them some examples of people who might work harder than it seems for their wealth: a star athlete, a popular musician, a super model, an actor, or a writer.

Activities and Explorations

1. **Art Discussion** This activity and the one following are closely related. This activity calls for students to interpret the selection, choose an aspect of the story that would benefit from visual representation, and defend that choice logically. The activity that follows calls for students to create illustrations based on their choices. Make sure students understand that they might choose something described in the story but could also choose something not described that they think would help the reader understand the story. For example, one could illustrate Sindbad with a spirit at each ear, one representing security and enjoyment of the good life and the other representing excitement and adventure.
2. **Sindbad Illustration** Suggest that students use their captions as a way to express succinctly their reasons for choosing their illustrations. For instance, in the example given above, the caption might read *Sindbad's Divided Heart.*

Inquiry and Research

"Sindbad's World" Report Make sure students understand that their research need not cover the entire history of the Islamic Empire. They can present their findings in the form of a "slice of life" from a particular moment in that history focusing on a particular trade route, trader, or kind of expedition.

Writing Options

1. Sindbad Adventure
Imagine that Sindbad made eight voyages instead of seven. Write a story about his eighth voyage. Before you write, brainstorm answers to these questions:

- Where does Sindbad go?
- What difficulties does he encounter?
- How does he deal with them?
- What does he bring back from his journey?

Writing Handbook
See page R29: Narrative Writing.

2. Persuasive Essay To a person who knew nothing of Sindbad's adventures, his wealth might seem undeserved. Think of a successful person you know who might appear simply lucky but who has earned his or her success in ways that are not apparent. Write a persuasive essay arguing that this person deserves his or her success.

Activities & Explorations

1. Art Discussion Imagine that "The Second Voyage of Sindbad the Sailor" could have only one illustration. Decide what this should be. Then, with two or three classmates who have different ideas, stage a panel discussion in which you all present the reasons for your choices. ~ SPEAKING AND LISTENING

2. Sindbad Illustration Decide what one illustration the story should have, as in the assignment above. Then create the illustration, adding a short quotation from the story as a caption. ~ ART, VIEWING AND REPRESENTING

Inquiry & Research

"Sindbad's World" Report
Sindbad's story unfolds against the backdrop of an Islamic empire that was at the center of major world-trade routes. Many people made or lost a fortune—or even their life—on voyages to acquire or trade goods. Find out more about these expeditions—the destinations they had, the routes they followed, the treasures they sought, the dangers they faced. Present your findings in an oral report that includes at least one visual aid, such as a map, a chart, or an illustration.

RESEARCH STARTER
CLASSZONE.COM

Vocabulary in Action

EXERCISE: CONTEXT CLUES Write the Word to Know that would best fill in the blank in each sentence.

1. When left behind on the island, Sindbad was at first ______; he did not know what to do.
2. It was too late to raise a ______ on the shore, for the boat was long gone.
3. He feared that the roc to which he tied himself would notice him, but the huge bird was ______.
4. Sindbad was ______ when he landed in the field of diamonds, for he could not believe his good luck.
5. He now envisioned a ______ life filled with every luxury.

WORDS TO KNOW
confounded oblivious tumult
jubilant sumptuous

Building Vocabulary
For an in-depth lesson on understanding context clues, see page 674.

Vocabulary in Action

Context Clues
1. confounded
2. tumult
3. oblivious
4. jubilant
5. sumptuous

To assess skills and concepts taught in this selection, use **Formal Assessment Book,** p. 81.

Sindbad Yesterday, Today, and Tomorrow

A Perennial Favorite People don't seem to get tired of Sindbad (or Sinbad) the Sailor. Since 1935, this character and his exploits have been the subject of at least nineteen movies, three television series, and numerous books, plays, musicals, and video games.

Some of these productions are based on the actual Sindbad stories in *The Thousand and One Nights.* Others just borrow the main character and create entirely new adventures for him. Even when the names are unfamiliar, some influence may be perceived. The book *Robinson Crusoe* (1719) owes something to Sindbad, as does Jules Verne's *Mysterious Island* (1874).

In science fiction of the last century, outer space has replaced the sea as the passageway to the unknown. Such space travelers as Captain Kirk and Captain Picard of the *Star Trek* series can be thought of as modern-day versions of Sindbad.

Group Discussion Why do you think Sindbad and Sindbad-like stories continue to hold such fascination for us? Support your response to this question with examples from your own experience with books, movies, and television.

One of the earliest Sindbad films, *Sinbad the Sailor* (1947), starred Douglas Fairbanks, Jr., and Maureen O'Hara.

Jules Verne's *Mysterious Island* featured a giant bird much like Sindbad's roc. Here is a scene from the movie based on Verne's novel.

Connect to Today

Sindbad Yesterday, Today, and Tomorrow Use this feature to show the relevance of world literature to students. The material relates the literature selection just read to a contemporary topic connected to students' lives today.

Group Discussion If students have trouble thinking of examples, or if you want to broaden the discussion, point out that the word *trek* in the title *Star Trek* means "journey" or "voyage." Help students connect the idea of a voyage, as undertaken by Sindbad or Sindbad-like figures, with the concept of a quest (explained on page 31). In a quest, the voyage may be real or it may be metaphorical, for example, a voyage of learning or self-discovery.

CONNECT TO TODAY 591

Additional Background

Ferdowsi During the ninth and tenth centuries, a native Persian dynasty called the Samanids wrested control of Persia, modern-day Iran, from Arabic hands. As part of their effort to revive the ancient Persian culture and language, Samanid rulers commissioned a court poet named Dakiki to create a national epic recounting Persia's heroic history. After composing just a thousand lines, however, Dakiki was murdered, a victim of the violent political infighting of the day. The task was then taken up by a local landowner named Abu ol-Kasem Mansur—now known as Ferdowsi, or "Heavenly One"—who hoped the project would pay for his daughter's dowry.

By the time Ferdowsi completed *The Shahnameh* 35 years later, the Samanids had been overthrown by the Turkish sultan Mahmud, who is said to have been dissatisfied with the Persian nationalism of the final product. According to legend, Mahmud had initially offered Ferdowsi a gold coin for every line but ultimately paid him only a silver one. Ferdowsi was so furious with Mahmud's stingy payment that he tossed the money to a bath attendant and street vendor just outside Mahmud's palace and brought the manuscript to a neighboring prince instead. The prince diplomatically paid Ferdowsi the full amount for his work on the condition that he keep the dedication to Mahmud.

MILESTONES IN WORLD LITERATURE

Ferdowsi

The Shahnameh

—Epic of Persia

The *Shahnameh,* or *Book of Kings,* is the national epic of Persia. It tells the story of the Persian people from the creation of the world to the Arab conquest. A long poem of some 60,000 couplets, or pairs of rhymed lines, the *Shahnameh* recounts the stories not only of kings but also of other great Persian heroes, real and mythical, from ancient times up through the 7th century.

The *Shahnameh* had special significance in 11th-century Persia. By that time, Persia had embraced Islam and become integrated into the Islamic empire. But the Persian historical and cultural tradition, which

Leaf from First Small *Shahnameh.* The Metropolitan Museum of Art, New York.

Leaf from Iranian manuscript of The Shahnameh [Book of Kings], Ferdowsi. The Metropolitan Museum of Art, New York.

extended back over 1,400 years, was becoming lost. Because Arabic was the official tongue of religion, law, and education, even the Persian language had begun to lose its identity.

In an effort to revive Persian culture and language, members of the ruling Samanid dynasty of the 9th and 10th centuries commissioned a national epic. Eventually this ambitious project was taken up by a man now known as Ferdowsi, or "Heavenly One." For Ferdowsi, the *Shahnameh* was a labor of love, and he kept at it for 35 years, finally completing the work in 1010.

The history, mythology, and legends that make up the Shahnameh had existed in oral and written versions long before Ferdowsi began his project. But he incorporated them all into a single great work of extraordinary artistry and beauty. Like those of Greece and Rome, Persia's national epic not only embodies a culture but also represents a great poetic achievement.

The *Shahnameh*

Ferdowsi incorporated Dakiki's verses, which focused on the pre-Islamic Persian religious prophet Zoroaster (see page 566). Beginning with the creation of the world, the epic presents the early history of Persia in terms of a Zoroastrian struggle between the first kings, good men and champions of civilization, and the forces of evil.

After a thousand years of this struggle, one of the kings, Faridun, divides his kingdom among his three sons. One of the sons is given the land of Persia, another that of Turan, a land traditionally identified with that of the Turks. The son who rules over Persia is murdered by his brothers, resulting in enmity and war between Persian and Turan. This portrayal of conflict between Persia and the Turkish Sultanate in a way favoring Persia probably contributed to Mahmud's dissatisfaction with Ferdowsi's work.

MILESTONES IN WORLD LITERATURE 593

Objectives

- appreciate a form of lyric poetry called the **rubai (Literary Analysis)**
- explore the relationship between **metaphor and theme** in poetry **(Literary Analysis)**
- learn to **draw conclusions about tone** in poetry **(Active Reading)**

Thematic Link

The *Rubáiyát of Omar Khayyám* develops an unusual and compelling **moral** perspective based on observations about human existence.

5-Minute Warm-Up

Daily Language SkillBuilder

Have students **proofread** the display sentences on page 563g and write them correctly.

Reading and Analyzing

Reading Skills and Strategies

CLARIFYING

Make sure students understand that although the stanzas are numbered, they are not strictly sequential. Each rubai is a poem unto itself, yet fits thematically into the group as a whole.

Literary Analysis

METAPHOR AND THEME

A Help students prepare to see the relationship between metaphor and theme in these poems by analyzing this metaphor in stanza 7. Use a chart like the one shown.

What poem is talking about	What this thing is compared to (metaphor)	What the comparison means (theme)
a human lifetime	a bird making a short flight	life is short (so enjoy it)

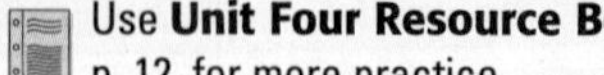
Use **Unit Four Resource Book,** p. 12, for more practice.

Active Reading

DRAWING CONCLUSIONS ABOUT TONE

Ask students to describe the tone used in stanza 7. Tell them that they may detect more than one kind of tone.

Possible Responses: (lines 5–6) warm and inviting; carefree; encouraging; (lines 7–8) wistful; foreboding; warning

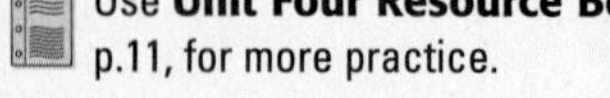
Use **Unit Four Resource Book,** p.11, for more practice.

FROM THE Rubáiyát of Omar Khayyám

Translated by Edward FitzGerald

Omar Khayyám
1048–1131

The Early Years Omar Khayyám attended a good local school in his native city of Nishapur. There he received firm grounding in the sciences and philosophies of the day. He went on to study in Balkh and Samarkand, important Islamic cultural centers in central Asia.

The Ironies of Fame In Samarkand, Omar Khayyám published an important book on algebra, which brought him to the attention of the powerful sultan Malik Shah. So impressed was the sultan that he asked Omar to help develop a new calendar and to build an astronomical observatory.

Though Omar Khayyám wrote important works on astronomy, mathematics, medicine, and philosophy, he is today best known for his poetry. Yet during his lifetime and for centuries after his death, his achievements in science and mathematics overshadowed his literary accomplishments.

Build Background

Edward FitzGerald The British poet Edward FitzGerald (1809–1883) deserves credit for bringing Omar Khayyám's work to public attention. FitzGerald translated Omar's poems and published them in 1859. The *Rubáiyát* quickly captured the imagination of the English-speaking world, and it remains one of our best-known and most beloved works.

The *Rubáiyát* In Omar Khayyám's day, Persian poets expressed insights about life in four-line poems in which the first, second, and fourth lines rhymed. The Arabic word for such a poem is *rubái* (ro͞o'bī), and the plural *rubáiyát* (ro͞o'bī-yät').

Connect to Your Life

What is your philosophy of life? Try to answer this question in a single sentence that you would offer as advice to others.

Focus Your Reading

LITERARY ANALYSIS: METAPHOR AND THEME

A **metaphor** is a comparison that does not contain the word *like* or *as.* Such a comparison may be stated directly, as in "Life is a broken-winged bird," or it may be implied, as in "the Bird of Time." In literature, metaphors can be an effective means of conveying **theme**—a message or insight about life or human nature that the writer wishes to communicate.

As you read these poems from the *Rubáiyát,* look for metaphors that are used to express theme.

ACTIVE READING: DRAWING CONCLUSIONS ABOUT TONE

Tone is an expression of the attitude—the thoughts or feelings—that a writer has about a subject. In speaking, tone can be communicated through the voice. A writer, however, establishes tone through choice of words and details.

READER'S NOTEBOOK Jot down at least one thought or feeling that each poem seems to express. Then think of one or two adjectives that describe the tone.

Poem	Writer's Attitude	Tone
1	Thought: Don't waste the day sleeping! Feelings: excitement, eagerness	Excited, optimistic

LESSON RESOURCES

UNIT FOUR RESOURCE BOOK, pp. 11–12

ASSESSMENT RESOURCES
Formal Assessment, pp. 83–84
Teacher's Guide to Assessment and Portfolio Use
Test Generator

INTEGRATED TECHNOLOGY
Visit our Web site: classzone.com

ADDITIONAL RESOURCES
Lesson Planning Guide, pp. 73–74
Teacher's Sourcebook for Language Development

1

Wake! For the Sun, who scatter'd into flight
The Stars before him from the Field of Night,
Drives Night along with them from Heav'n, and strikes
The Sultan's Turret with a Shaft of Light.

7

[1] Come, fill the Cup, and in the fire of Spring
Your Winter-garment of Repentance fling:
[A] The Bird of Time has but a little way
To flutter—and the Bird is on the Wing.

12

A Book of Verses underneath the Bough,
A Jug of Wine, a Loaf of Bread—and Thou
Beside me singing in the Wilderness—
Oh, Wilderness were Paradise enow!

13

Some for the Glories of This World; and some
Sigh for the Prophet's Paradise to come;
Ah, take the Cash, and let the Credit go,
Nor heed the rumble of a distant Drum!

27

Myself when young did eagerly frequent
[2] Doctor and Saint, and heard great argument
About it and about: but evermore
[3] Came out by the same door where in I went.

28

[4] With them the seed of Wisdom did I sow,
And with mine own hand wrought to make it grow;
And this was all the Harvest that I reap'd—
"I came like Water, and like Wind I go."

4 Sultan's (so͞ol-tănz') **turret:** a tower in the palace of a Muslim ruler.

6 repentance: sorrow for having done wrong.

9 bough: branch of a tree.

12 enow: enough.

14 the Prophet's Paradise: the Paradise promised by Muhammad.

Customizing Instruction

Less Proficient Readers
If you would like to focus on a small number of the more accessible stanzas, have students read 7, 12, 13, 63, and 64.

1 Help students understand this complex metaphor. Time, represented by the movement of the sun, is compared to a warrior on the attack. Light striking the turret means a new day, time to wake and get out of bed, but it also means that time is passing and should not be wasted. The attack on a Sultan shows that not even kings are immune to the passage of time.

English Learners

2 Explain that *Doctor* here does not refer to a medical doctor but rather to a very learned person or scholar such as a Doctor of Philosophy.

3 Help students interpret this action metaphorically rather than literally: the speaker suggests he left knowing as little as when he arrived.

4 The antecedent of the pronoun *them* is "Doctor and Saint" in the previous stanza.

TIME MANAGEMENT

If your schedule requires that you cover the lesson objectives in a shorter time, use . . .
- Preparing to Read, p. 594
- Thinking Through the Literature, p. 598

If you want to take advantage of longer blocks of class time, use . . .
- TE Teaching Options: Viewing and Representing, p. 596; Grammar, p. 597
- The Translator at Work, p. 599

Detail of *Fête champêtre* [Picnic on the grass] (c. 1610–1615). Riza. The Keir Collection, England.

HUMANITIES CONNECTION Persian art is noted for its beautiful and detailed miniatures. Many of them were created as book illuminations, which had to be painted by hand and needed to be small.

29

Into this Universe, and *Why* not knowing
1 Nor *Whence,* like Water willy-nilly flowing;
  And out of it, as Wind along the Waste,
I know not *Whither,* willy-nilly blowing.

46

And fear not lest Existence closing your
Account, and mine, should know the like no more;
  The Eternal Sákí from that Bowl has pour'd
Millions of Bubbles like us, and will pour.

26 whence: from where; from what place.

28 whither: to what place or condition.

31 the Eternal Sákí (sä'khē): the form of God who intoxicates the soul through the pouring of the wine of love.

Reading and Analyzing

Active Reading

DRAWING CONCLUSIONS ABOUT TONE

A Ask students which of the three following words best describes the tone of this stanza: *bitter, resigned, carefree.* Have them give reasons for their choices.

Possible Responses: *(bitter)* The speaker is deeply disappointed that we are mortal and there is no life after death. *(resigned)* The speaker suggests that this life is all there is and that we should accept that idea rather than chasing illusions; the speaker takes comfort in knowing the truth. *(carefree)* The speaker suggests that this life is all there is and so we should enjoy it.

Literary Analysis

METAPHOR AND THEME

B Help students understand this extended metaphor, also called a conceit, using a diagram like the one shown.

"Magic Shadow-shapes"	IS TO	"We"
AS "Master of the Show"	IS TO	______ *(God or fate)*

Then ask students what theme or themes might be suggested by the comparison of God or fate to the "Master of the Show."

Possible Responses: God or fate doesn't care about people or have a plan for them, but only manipulates them for amusement; God or fate doesn't ask more of us than our immediate existence, so why should we?

Reading Skills and Strategies

CLARIFYING

C Stanza 98, which explains the "Him" of line 57, reads as follows:

Would but some wingéd Angel ere too late
Arrest the yet unfolded Roll of Fate,
  And make the stern Recorder otherwise
Enregister, or quite obliterate.

MINI LESSON Viewing and Representing

Fête Champêtre [Picnic on the Grass]

ART APPRECIATION It is easy to forget that a "copy" of a book meant something very different in the time before the invention of printing technology. When books had to be transcribed and bound by hand, each copy was an individual work of art.

This is especially true of book illuminations, or illustrations, like the one shown in the **Humanities Connection** above. The amount of detail alone is an indication of how long the artist had to work to create the painting: sometimes an entire year. A book containing many such miniature paintings, each unique in itself, would be among the owner's most treasured and valuable possessions.

Only the rich and powerful could commission an illuminated manuscript. Artists were highly sought after and lavishly rewarded. To support their work, a benefactor often had not only to pay them well, but also to maintain studios where they could live, train apprentices, get the assistance they needed, and work on long-term projects. Supplies could be very costly also: many illuminations required gold and silver leaf as well as other expensive pigments and carefully prepared papers.

63

A Oh threats of Hell and Hopes of Paradise!
One thing at least is certain—*This* Life flies;
One thing is certain and the rest is Lies;
The Flower that once has blown for ever dies.

64

Strange, is it not? that of the myriads who
Before us pass'd the door of Darkness through,
Not one returns to tell us of the Road,
Which to discover we must travel too.

68

B We are no other than a moving row
Of Magic Shadow-shapes that come and go
Round with the Sun-illumined Lantern held
In Midnight by the Master of the Show;

69

But helpless Pieces of the Game He plays
Upon this Checker-board of Nights and Days;
Hither and thither moves, and checks, and slays,
And one by one back in the Closet lays.

71

The Moving Finger writes; and, having writ,
2 Moves on: nor all your Piety nor Wit
3 Shall lure it back to cancel half a Line,
Nor all your Tears wash out a Word of it.

96

Yet Ah, that Spring should vanish with the Rose!
That Youth's sweet-scented manuscript should close!
The Nightingale that in the branches sang,
Ah whence, and whither flown again, who knows!

99

C Ah Love! could you and I with Him conspire
To grasp this sorry Scheme of Things entire,
Would not we shatter it to bits—and then
Re-mold it nearer to the Heart's Desire!

37 myriads (mĭr'ē-ədz): countless numbers (of people).

42 Magic Shadow-shapes: shapes that appear on the inside of a magic lantern, a device that once was used to project enlarged images of pictures.

47 hither and thither: here and there.

49 the Moving Finger: fate.

57 with Him conspire: plot together with the Recorder of everyone's fate (mentioned in stanza 98).

Customizing Instruction

English Learners

1 Explain that *willy-nilly* can mean both "whether it wants to or not" and "haphazardly."

Less Proficient Readers

2 Have students explain the metaphor in stanza 71. *(The writing of the finger is the history of what happens in our lives, which is constantly unfolding and leaving the past behind, but which cannot ever be changed, no matter what we do.)*

Advanced Learners

3 Have students research the literary allusion in stanza 71 by reading Chapter 5 of the Book of Daniel in the Bible. Students can then report their findings to the class.

Possible Response: The Moving Finger is an allusion to the story of Belshazzar's feast. Belshazzar was king of Babylon during the time the Hebrews were enslaved there. Belshazzar had taken sacred vessels from the Temple and used them to eat, drink, and be merry. A hand appears and writes a message on the wall, which the prophet Daniel interprets as foretelling Belshazzar's defeat by the Persians. From this story we get the expression "to see the writing on the wall," which means to see an indication of bad fortune to come. By alluding to this story, the poem makes the hand of fate seem more threatening and awesome.

MINI LESSON Grammar

PROBLEMS WITH MODIFIERS

Instruction The words *this, that, these,* and *those* are demonstrative pronouns that can be used as adjectives. There are three rules you need to remember when using these words as adjectives.

- They must agree in number with the words they modify.
  This dog is barking at me. *These* shoes are too tight.
- Never use *here* or *there* with one of these words.
  This ~~here~~ map will help us get home.
- Never use the pronoun *them* as an adjective in place of *these* or *those*.
  ~~Them~~ These apples were picked this morning.

Practice Rewrite the sentences below to correct errors in modifier use. If a sentence is correct, write "Correct."

1. Although Omar Khayyám wrote books about science and mathematics, them books are not what he is best known for today. *(those books or these books)*
2. This here poet's work was translated by Edward FitzGerald, a British poet. *(This poet's)*
3. Do you like these kind of poetry or do you prefer less philosophical poetry? *(this kind)*
4. I read them poems last night, but I didn't understand them. *(these poems or those poems)*
5. I've been meaning to read that there book all summer. *(that book)*

For more instruction and practice in using modifiers, use McDougal Littell's ***Language Network:***

- Grade 10, Chapter 9, "Using Modifiers"
- Grade 12, Chapter 7, "Using Modifiers"

Connect to the Literature

1. **What Do You Think?** Accept all reasonable responses. Encourage students to identify the stanza in which their image occurs and to explain why it interests them.

Think Critically

2. Students may need help seeing beyond the speaker's pessimism to his strong affirmation of life and its pleasures. Possible Responses: Life is short, so enjoy it while you can; don't waste time pondering religious or philosophical questions, because these are things we can't be sure of; pay attention to the things that matter—good company, love, food, drink, poetry; remember that we all share the same fate and that this brings us closer to each other.
3. Make sure that students understand that the speaker's tone may sometimes be at variance with the apparently cynical content of his comments. The speaker's tone is sometimes sad or resigned, but it is also often enthusiastic, tender, confident, wise, reassuring, and even darkly humorous. These more positive expressions of tone support the themes of enjoyment of life in the present and appreciation for the connectedness to others that comes from shared joys and sorrows.
4. From stanzas 12 and 99 we can infer that the speaker is addressing his beloved. From other stanzas we can infer that the speaker is talking to someone, possibly younger, who might be wondering about the meaning of life or trying to decide what is important. The person being addressed is probably someone who appreciates the speaker's wisdom and affection.

Connect to the Literature

1. **What Do You Think?** What did you find to be the most interesting image in these poems? Explain.

Think Critically

2. How would you describe the philosophy of life expressed by the **speaker?**

THINK ABOUT
- what he compares time to in poems 7 and 71
- the actions he advocates in poems 1, 7, 12, and 13
- the importance of the individual in poems 28, 29, and 46
- his view of death in poems 63, 64, 68, 69, and 96

3. **ACTIVE READING: DRAWING CONCLUSIONS ABOUT TONE** Look back over the chart you created in your READER'S NOTEBOOK. What generalizations can you make about the overall tone of the *Rubáiyát?* How does the tone support the theme or themes of these poems?
4. What do we learn from these poems about the person they are addressed to?

Extend Interpretations

5. **Critic's Corner** Scholar and translator Peter Avery points out that Omar Khayyám lived in unstable times in northeastern Persia, "when there was occasion for pessimism and little room for a sense of security." In what way might the poems of the *Rubáiyát* be seen as a response to this?
6. **Comparing Texts** Compare these poems from the *Rubáiyát* with Horace's famous ode "Seize the Day" (page 392). How are the themes similar and how are they different?
7. **Connect to Life** The speaker suggests that happiness can be achieved very simply, with "A Book of Verses . . . , / A Jug of Wine, a Loaf of Bread—and Thou." Do you think most people can be satisfied with such simple pleasures? Give reasons for your opinion.

LITERARY ANALYSIS: METAPHOR AND THEME

In poetry, **metaphors**—comparisons made without the word *like* or *as*—often help convey **themes,** or insights that the writer wishes to communicate. For example, in poem 7, time is compared to a bird that has already completed part of a short journey. This comparison helps convey the theme that time is limited and passes quickly.

Paired Activity With a partner, identify at least five other metaphors in these poems. Explain what two things are compared in each metaphor, and determine what theme or themes the metaphor helps convey. Create a chart like the one started below to record your findings.

Poem	Metaphor	Theme(s)
1	The sun is compared to a warrior on the attack	
7		

Extend Interpretations

5. **Critic's Corner** The pessimism of these poems could be a reflection of Omar Khayyám's own sense of the lack of stability and security in life. On the other hand, another person in this situation might have turned to religion and philosophy for consolation, and Omar Khayyám does not do this. Instead, he advocates letting go of the struggle for certainty of any kind and focusing on the pleasures of the moment.
6. **Comparing Texts** Both poems develop the *carpe diem* ("seize the day") theme against the background of uncertainty about either the future of this life or the ultimate intentions of the gods. The poems are strikingly different in tone, however. Horace's poem is somber and practical. Omar Khayyám's, on the other hand, is alternately melancholy, rousing, and ironic.
7. **Connect to Life** Students may need help focusing their attention away from the trivial question—what things and activities give the most pleasure—to the important one: whether a person can be happy without giving much thought to the large questions of religion, philosophy, or morality.

Literary Analysis

Paired Activity If students need help connecting metaphors with themes, tell them that by comparing the sun to a warrior on the attack, the poem suggests that the passage of time is threatening because it brings us closer to death. This idea—and the related one of living in the moment—are major themes of the *Rubáiyát.*

Use **Unit Four Resource Book,** p. 12, for more practice.

To assess skills and concepts taught in this selection, use **Formal Assessment Book,** p. 83.

FitzGerald's *Rubáiyát*

Many English-speaking readers know the work of Omar Khayyám only through the translations of Edward FitzGerald, a 19th-century British poet. FitzGerald's rendition of the *Rubáiyát* is admired by many as a literary treasure and has been reprinted in hundreds of editions since it was first published in 1859.

FitzGerald admitted that his versions were not absolutely faithful to Omar Khayyám's original poems. He translated only some of them, and these he arranged in a different order, to flow as one man's thoughts during a single day. Sometimes, to achieve the effect he wanted, FitzGerald "mashed" two verses into one, introduced new ideas, or left out unfamiliar references to Persian history. Critics view the result as a collaboration—the product of the hybrid poet "Omar-FitzGerald," in the words of Louis Untermeyer.

Edward FitzGerald
1809–1883

Because FitzGerald took so many liberties with the poems, other translators have attempted more faithful versions. They hoped to strip away FitzGerald's 19th-century quirks, such as overly romanticized language, and reveal to readers what Omar Khayyám actually said. Compare one of the best-known quatrains translated by FitzGerald to a more literal translation:

Edward FitzGerald

A Book of Verses underneath the Bough,
A Jug of Wine, a Loaf of Bread—and Thou
Beside me singing in the Wilderness—
Oh, Wilderness were Paradise enow!

FitzGerald keeps the *aaba* rhyme scheme of the original, but chooses archaic words to fit this pattern.

FitzGerald introduces ideas not present in the original poem.

Robert Graves and Omar Ali-Shah

A gourd of red wine and a sheaf of poems—
A bare subsistence, half a loaf, not more—
Supplied us two alone in the free desert:
What Sultan could we envy on his throne?

This is an unrhymed translation. Notice that the language is simpler and more direct.

This line keeps the original comparison to a sultan's life.

Questions to Consider

1. What other differences do you notice in the translations? How much do they affect meaning?
2. Which translation do you prefer, and why?

The Translator at Work

Questions to Consider

1. **Possible Responses:** In the second translation, a "bare subsistence" is enough, while the first seems to describe something more like a feast; FitzGerald adds music to the mix by adding "Thou / Beside me singing . . . "; FitzGerald compares the scene to heavenly joy—"Paradise", while the second translation compares the scene to earthly wealth and power—a "Sultan . . . on his throne"; the first poem ends with an exclamation, while the second ends with a rhetorical question; the last line of FitzGerald's translation seems like a burst of emotion, while the ending of the second poem seems more of a logical conclusion.
2. Before getting students' responses to this question, you might want to have them take turns reading the stanzas aloud. You can then help students get started by asking which stanza seemed to read better.

   As they give reasons for their responses to question 2, encourage students to extend their thinking to literary translations in general by asking questions such as the following:
   - Which is more important, translating the words of a poem exactly or preserving its form?
   - Is it okay for the translator to change a poem if he or she makes it a better poem?

Objectives
- appreciate **lyric poetry (Literary Analysis)**
- understand the connection between **imagery and tone (Literary Analysis)**
- build strategies for **reading difficult poetry (Active Reading)**

Thematic Link
In his poetry Rumi expresses insights gained from the form of Islamic **mysticism** called Sufism.

5-Minute Warm-Up
Daily Language SkillBuilder

Have students **proofread** the display sentences on page 563h and write them correctly.

Rumi
1207–1273

The Road to Konya The poet Jalal ad-Din, known as Rumi (ro͞o'mē), was born in the Persian city of Balkh, now part of Afghanistan. His father was a famous Muslim religious scholar, and Rumi was educated to follow in his footsteps. Fleeing from a Mongol attack on Balkh, the family eventually settled in Konya, capital of the Turkish region of Anatolia. The name Rumi reflects the poet's ties to this region, for Anatolia was also called Rum (ro͞om).

An Important Encounter Like his father, Rumi was a Muslim mystic, believing that spiritual awareness comes in flashes brought on by deep contemplation. The most influential event in his spiritual life occurred in 1244, when he met another mystic, Shams ad-Din, on the streets of Konya. The two became very close, devoting virtually all their time to mystical contemplation, until one day Shams disappeared—killed, it was proved much later, by one of Rumi's jealous followers. To ease his sense of loss, Rumi composed his *Divan-e-Shams,* a collection of poems in Shams's honor. He signed the poems with Shams's name instead of his own to show that he and Shams were spiritually one.

Lasting Fame The mystical form of Islam that Rumi and Shams practiced is known as **Sufism.** Rumi was one of Sufism's greatest thinkers, producing several volumes of prose explaining the Sufi philosophy. His most famous work, however, is a volume of poetry called the *Masnavi* (mäs-nä'vē). An epic of 26,000 couplets, or rhymed pairs of lines, the Masnavi offers guidance on how to live, behave, and practice Sufism. So important was the *Masnavi* to Persian-speaking people that it has been called the Persian Koran.

Persia and Anatolia

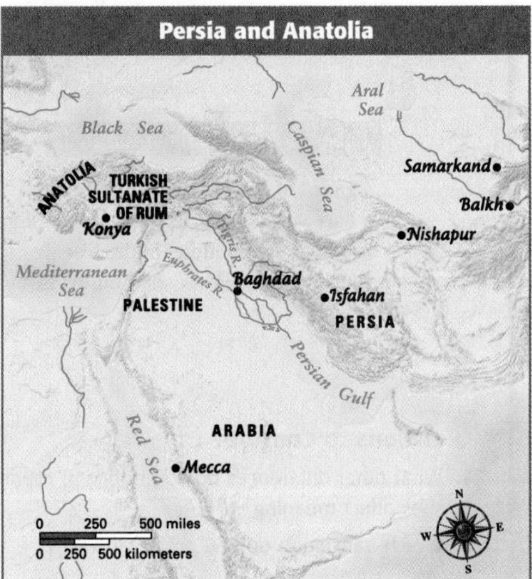

LESSON RESOURCES

UNIT FOUR RESOURCE BOOK, pp. 13–14

ASSESSMENT RESOURCES
Formal Assessment, pp. 85–86
Teacher's Guide to Assessment and Portfolio Use
Test Generator

INTEGRATED TECHNOLOGY
Visit our Web site: classzone.com

ADDITIONAL RESOURCES
Lesson Planning Guide, pp. 75–76
Teacher's Sourcebook for Language Development

Build Background

What Is Sufism? Sufism is a mystical form of Islam in which Muslims seek spiritual love and wisdom through direct personal experience with God. An early form of Sufism arose in the 7th century as a reaction to the materialism of the Islamic world. However, the real flowering of Sufism took place in the 12th and 13th centuries, when Sufi brotherhoods were established in special communities, or schools. Like the monks of medieval Europe, Sufi mystics tried to avoid what they considered the lures and traps of the material world. In fact, they are often called *dervishes,* from the Persian word for a monk who lives in poverty. Rumi founded an order of Sufi mystics that embraced sacred dance as a form of worship. Because of this practice, these mystics acquired the nickname "whirling dervishes."

Prayer in the Mosque (19th century), Jean-Léon Gérôme. The Metropolitan Museum of Art, New York.

The Poetry of Love From the viewpoint of literature, Sufism is of great importance, for it inspired some of the finest mystical love poetry in the world. Most of that poetry was written in Arabic, Persian, Turkish, and Urdu (the chief language of Indian Muslims and today's Pakistan). Rumi, who wrote in Persian, is often named as the greatest of the Sufi poets.

Connect to Your Life

In these poems Rumi tries to convey experiences that are hard to put into words. What experiences or feelings might you find difficult to express? Why might this be difficult for you?

Focus Your Reading

LITERARY ANALYSIS: IMAGERY AND TONE

When writers use words and phrases to create vivid sensory experiences for the reader, they are making use of **imagery.** Although most imagery appeals to the sense of sight, imagery may also appeal to the senses of smell, hearing, taste, or touch. The title "Birdsong from Inside the Egg," for example, appeals to the senses of both sight and hearing. Often, a writer uses imagery to convey his or her **tone,** or attitude, toward a subject. The image of a bird's song coming from inside an egg expresses an attitude of amazement and joy. As you read Rumi's poems, notice the images that he uses and think about the kind of tone they convey.

ACTIVE READING: READING DIFFICULT POETRY

Rumi's poetry presents difficulties for many readers because of its use of unusual images to convey abstract ideas. Even an experienced reader depends on strategies such as these:

- Read each poem slowly and deliberately.
- Read each poem several times. Read first to get an overall sense of the poem's meaning. Then focus on understanding individual parts.
- Write down notes about the stanzas and images that you think you understand.
- If you are still confused by certain sections of a poem, don't be too concerned. Use the parts of the poem that you do understand to help make sense of the ones that may still be unclear.

READER'S NOTEBOOK As you read each poem several times, jot down notes about specific stanzas or images that you think you understand. Allow yourself to make guesses at times about the ideas Rumi is expressing.

READING FOR INFORMATION

Reading Skills and Strategies

SETTING A PURPOSE FOR READING

Help students set a purpose for reading the **Build Background** essay by having them look for answers to the following questions:

1. Why did Rumi's family move to Konya? *(to escape a Mongol attack on Balkh)*
2. What was the most important event in Rumi's spiritual life? *(his meeting with Shams-ad-Din)*
3. What is the "Persian Koran"? *(Rumi's book of poetry the Masnavi, which offers guidance on Sufism)*
4. What is a "whirling dervish"? *(Sufi mystics who worship by dancing)*
5. How did Sufism influence literature? *(it inspired some of the world's finest poetry)*
6. In the painting on this page, *Prayer in the Mosque,* identify the following:
   - the prayer rug *(lower middle, underneath the man in the foreground wearing red and gold)*
   - the prayer niche *(far left, just above the heads of the worshippers)*
   - the Sufi mystic *(the man with uncut hair wearing only a loincloth in keeping with the Sufi commitment to simplicity and poverty)*

MINI LESSON Using the Map

Point out to students that the map on page 600 is similar to that on pages 564–565, but does not show northern Africa and Spain and includes more of the eastern reaches of Persia. Have students use the map to answer the following questions:

1. How far and in what direction did Rumi's family travel in their move from Balkh to Konya? *(about 1,500 miles west)*
2. What kind of scenery would have been most familiar to Rumi—desert, mountains, or seacoast? *(mountains)*

Have students reread "The Early Years" on page 594 and continue using the map to answer questions 3 and 4.

3. How was the region of Rumi's birth different a century and a half earlier when Omar Khayyám lived there? *(The region was more politically stable, because Omar Khayyám was able to study in the cities of Nishapur, Balkh, and Samarkand.)*
4. Who would have been more likely to travel by river en route to the Islamic capital of Isfahan, Rumi in Konya or Omar Khayyám in Samarkand? *(Rumi)*

Active Reading

READING DIFFICULT POETRY

Remind students that they will need to read these poems several times in order to understand them. They will also have to read actively, working to make sense of what the poet is saying, but their efforts will be rewarded. Go over the specific reading strategies listed on page 601 and encourage students to apply them to each poem.

Use **Unit Four Resource Book,** p. 13, for more practice.

Literary Analysis **IMAGERY AND TONE**

A The strong connection between imagery and tone in this poem is apparent even in the title. Have students take a moment to imagine what the title describes and to consider the thoughts and feelings it evokes. Then have students think of adjectives to describe the tone.

Possible Responses: (Thoughts and Feelings) The contents of an egg are too undeveloped to sing like a bird; the idea of a song coming from an egg seems comical; the sound of birdsong coming from an egg would be amazing, wonderful, or even miraculous. (Tone) comical; wonder-filled

Use **Unit Four Resource Book,** p. 14, for more practice.

Reading Skills and Strategies
VISUALIZING

B Have students visualize the actions of the chicken and the rabbit. Then ask what the two images have in common. *(Both images are of small, weak animals deliberately but ignorantly getting close to one so powerful that it could destroy them.)*

Active Reading

READING DIFFICULT POETRY

C After students finish the poem, have them go back to the title and think about what it means.

Possible Responses: A person who is only just beginning to understand God is like an egg—unformed as yet, but with the potential one day to sing; the poem is like the song of an egg because it is imperfect—the poet is attempting to do something way beyond his abilities: describe the presence of God; the poem is like birdsong from an egg because it is wise and beautiful—though the speaker's knowledge of God is limited, it inspires him to sing.

A

Birdsong from Inside the Egg

Rumi

Translated by Coleman Barks

Sometimes a lover of God may faint
1 in the presence. Then the beloved bends
and whispers in his ear, "Beggar, spread out
your robe. I'll fill it with gold.

I've come to protect your consciousness.
Where has it gone? Come back into awareness!"

This fainting is because
lovers want *so much.*

A chicken invites a camel into her henhouse,
and the whole structure is demolished.

B
A rabbit nestles down
with its eyes closed
in the arms of a lion.

There is an *excess*
in spiritual searching
that is profound ignorance.

Let that ignorance be our teacher!
The Friend breathes into one
2 who has no breath.

A deep silence revives the listening
and the speaking of those two
who meet on the riverbank.

18 the Friend: the form of God who functions as a playful, happy acquaintance.

20 revives: gives new spirit to; renews in the mind.

Humanities

MYSTICISM AND LITERATURE Mysticism is a form of religion that aims at knowledge of divine reality outside the more usual channels of logic, learning, faith, or forms of worship. The mystic understands God to be transcendent, or beyond the limits of ordinary experience, yet seeks to know God directly.

Mysticism does not exist only in Islam. Many Eastern religions, such as Hinduism and Buddhism, are mystical by their very nature. In the West, both Judaism and Christianity have strong mystical traditions existing alongside their more orthodox forms.

One way used by many mystics to go beyond ordinary experience is literary expression. Religious texts make up a substantial part of the world's literature, which includes myths, sacred scripture, wisdom stories, songs, prayers, theological writings, sermons, and meditations. Even more than other religious writers, mystics use the tools of poetry to communicate their experience: symbols, metaphors, figures of speech, unusual images, and playful turns of phrase. In their effort to go beyond ordinary thoughts and ideas, mystics create language that is fresh, original, and often very beautiful.

Topkapi Saray Museum, Istanbul, Turkey.

HUMANITIES CONNECTION This detail from a 16th-century Turkish manuscript illustrates a miraculous story in which a cow bows down before Rumi.

3 Like the ground turning green in a spring wind.
Like birdsong beginning inside the egg.

Like this universe coming into existence,
the lover wakes, and whirls
in a dancing joy,

then kneels down
C in praise.

Customizing Instruction

Less Proficient Readers

It may help students understand this poem if you have them imagine that the speaker is talking to them directly in an attempt to explain what it is like to experience God.

English Learners

1 Explain that the "presence" referred to is the presence of God. The "beloved" refers to God also.

2 Students may confuse the noun *breath* and the verb *breathe*. Draw students' attention to the difference in spelling and pronunciation between the two words.

3 Tell students that "to turn green" here means to become covered with new plant growth.

MINI LESSON Viewing and Representing

Detail from a 16th-century Turkish Manuscript

ART APPRECIATION As with many saintly religious figures, legends have grown up around the life of Rumi. Like St. Francis of Assissi, Rumi is reputed to have had a special relationship with the natural world as God's creation. Animals and trees are supposed to have bowed before him, like the cow in the painting shown above in the **Humanities Connection.** According to another story, one of Rumi's disciples was shocked one day to see him carrying a tray heaped with delicacies, because Rumi was known to live the plain and simple life of a Sufi monk. Thinking that his master might be a hypocrite, the disciple followed him and discovered that he was taking the food to a dog that had just given birth to six puppies. When Rumi saw the disciple, the holy man said, "You know your heart is awake when you can hear a mother dog's soft cries for help from miles away."

Reading and Analyzing

Literary Analysis IMAGERY AND TONE

A Have students visualize the images of the axe, the flame, and the butcher. Then ask the following questions:

How do these analogies support the statement in line 5?

Possible Response: Each of the analogies shows how being strong does not protect something from destruction.

How would you describe the tone conveyed by these images?

Possible Responses: The absurdity of the images—the axe worrying about the branch, the flame considering the size of the woodpile, and the butcher running from a flock of sheep—gives the analogies a humorous tone but also makes them seem more threatening.

Active Reading

READING DIFFICULT POETRY

B Have students explain the reference in line 29 in light of the statement in lines 1–2. *(Instead of being uprooted by the wind, the grasses are enlivened and made even more beautiful by its blowing. To do with the straws "as the wind does with the grasses" is to subject them to a powerful force that is energizing rather than destructive.)*

The Grasses

Rumi

Translated by Coleman Barks

The same wind that uproots trees
makes the grasses shine.

The lordly wind loves the weakness
and the lowness of grasses.
Never brag of being strong.

The axe doesn't worry how thick the branches are.
It cuts them to pieces. But not the leaves.
A It leaves the leaves alone.

A flame doesn't consider the size of the woodpile.
A butcher doesn't run from a flock of sheep.

What is form in the presence of reality?
Very feeble. Reality keeps the sky turned over
like a cup above us, revolving. Who turns
the sky wheel? The universal intelligence.

And the motion of the body comes
from the spirit like a waterwheel
that's held in a stream.

The inhaling-exhaling is from spirit,
now angry, now peaceful.
Wind destroys, and wind protects.

There is no reality but God,
says the completely surrendered sheikh,
who is an ocean for all beings.

The levels of creation are straws in that ocean.
The movement of the straws comes from an agitation
in the water. When the ocean wants the straws calm,
it sends them close to shore. When it wants them
back in the deep surge, it does with them
B as the wind does with the grasses.
This never ends.

22 sheikh (shēk): a spiritual master in the Islamic tradition.

Connect to the Literature

1. **What Do You Think?** Which image in these two poems did you find most memorable? Explain your choice.

Think Critically

2. **ACTIVE READING: READING DIFFICULT POETRY** Look back at the notes you made in your READER'S NOTEBOOK. Are there any portions of the poems that you still find confusing? With a group of classmates, work at clarifying the overall meaning of each poem.

3. In "Birdsong from Inside the Egg," what advice does Rumi have for the lover of God?

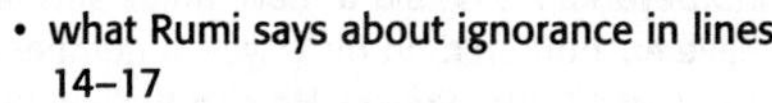

THINK ABOUT
- God's response to the fainted lover
- the explanation of why the fainting occurs
- what Rumi says about ignorance in lines 14–17
- the comparisons in lines 23–29

4. In "The Grasses," what is being compared to the grasses? What message is the poet trying to communicate with this comparison?

5. Is the relationship described between a person and God different in the two poems? Support your response with examples from the poems.

LITERARY ANALYSIS: IMAGERY AND TONE

The use of words and phrases to create sensory experiences for readers is called **imagery.** Images not only bring a poem to life; they can also help a writer convey his or her **tone,** or attitude, toward a subject. Rumi's images are often unusual or surprising and frequently express a strong attitude.

Cooperative Learning Activity With a group of classmates, identify images in these two poems that you think convey a particular tone. Then discuss how you think each poem's tone supports the meaning of the poem. Create charts like the one shown here to prepare for your discussion.

Image	Line(s)	Tone
Birdsong a camel going into a henhouse	9-10	

Extend Interpretations

6. **Critic's Corner** According to scholar Dick Davis, Rumi's work has the "reputation of being simultaneously both very simple and very difficult to understand properly." Do you agree? Cite examples from the poems to illustrate your opinion.

7. **Comparing Texts** Compare Rumi's poetry with the Zen teachings of Musō Soseki (page 512). What do the two selections have in common? Which do you find easier to comprehend, and why?

8. **Connect to Life** In your opinion, how relevant is Rumi's advice for people living in today's world?

Connect to the Literature

1. **What Do You Think?** Accept all reasonable responses. You might want to have students identify and read aloud the lines in which their image appears.

Think Critically

2. After the groups have had a chance to discuss the poems, you might have them present their findings to each other, perhaps in the form of a paraphrase.
3. Possible Responses: to stay conscious and receptive to God's gifts; to understand that in seeking God we may be asking for more than we can handle; to accept that God is beyond our understanding and to learn from that; to approach God through silence; to accept that we have only the barest beginning of a knowledge of God, like the first green of spring or the song of a bird still inside the egg; to be open to the joy and admiration that comes from knowing God
4. Possible Responses: The poem uses grasses that are beautified rather than destroyed by the wind as an analogy for how people should understand their relationship to God. By accepting God's power over them and the sometimes violent and unpredictable nature of human existence, people can live in harmony with the divine.
5. Possible Responses: (Similar) God's power seems overwhelming yet also can transform human existence into something beautiful. (Different) "Birdsong" is addressed to someone who actively seeks God, while "The Grasses" seems to describe how God affects all people, even if they aren't aware of it; in "Birdsong," God is like a lover or a friend, while in "The Grasses" God seems more like a force of nature.

Extend Interpretations

6. **Critic's Corner** Students may want to begin by formulating their own evaluations of Rumi's poetry and the experience of reading it. They can then compare their opinions to that of Davis more specifically.
7. **Comparing Texts** Possible Responses: Both authors seek in their writing to teach spiritual wisdom; both distinguish between true and false ways of practicing religion. Most students will say that Soseki's writing is easier to comprehend. Follow up by asking which kind of writing is more effective. Some students may say that Rumi's concrete images and imaginative metaphors have more impact on the reader than Soseki's simple statements of fact.
8. **Connect to Life** Answers will vary. If students need help getting started, you might follow up with one or more of these questions: Is religion important in modern society? What is the role of mysticism in religion? Is truth simple and easy to understand or something you have to work at?

To assess skills and concepts taught in this selection, use **Formal Assessment Book,** p. 85.

Literary Analysis

Cooperative Learning Activity To extend this activity, you might have students look in magazines or on the Internet for examples of images that express a strong tone. After sharing the examples they find, students can create an illustration for one of the poems that captures its tone.

Use **Unit Four Resource Book,** p. 14, for more practice.

Possible Objectives

This **On Your Own** featured selection may be used to achieve one or more of the following objectives:

- to give students the opportunity to read independently, either reading silently for a sustained period, reading and analyzing literature with a group, or using the Reader's Notebook to write in response to the literature
- to conduct a post-reading class discussion
- to assess students' comprehension of the selection

Summary

This excerpt contains four tales. In the first, a condemned man is saved by the kindly lie of a minister. The second is about a high official who loses his job and—when he gets it back—no longer wants it. In the third tale, a wrestling instructor defeats his boastful star pupil. In the fourth, a man sentenced to death finds the words that will save his life.

ON YOUR OWN

from the Gulistan

SADI

Translated by Omar Ali-Shah

Sadi
1213–1292

A Sufi and a Wandering Dervish Like Rumi, Sadi (sä-dē') was a member of the mystical Sufi sect. As a Sufi, he had neither possessions nor a home, choosing instead to devote his life to wandering, study, meditation, and writing. During a long period of exile from his native Persia, Sadi traveled throughout the Middle East and beyond. He is said to have made several pilgrimages to Mecca and to have encountered on his travels a number of famous Sufi mystics, including perhaps Rumi himself. He eventually returned to Persia and in his later years wrote the works he is best known for, including the *Gulistan.*

The Gulistan, *or "Rose Garden," includes stories, poems, witty sayings, and personal anecdotes. Most of the stories are simple fables that attempt to teach something about life. Sadi brought to his writing not only his religious outlook but also his extensive experience of the world. The* Gulistan *is filled with the Sufi spririt, but it is also noted for its humor, worldly wisdom, and profound understanding of human nature.*

Like several other works of literature you have read, Sadi's Gulistan *contains short, simple stories intended to teach wisdom. Mixed in with these stories are* ***proverbs,*** *brief sayings that express general truths or give practical advice. The proverbs are meant to help the reader make sense of the stories. In each of the tales that follow, someone does something unusual or surprising. As you read, ask yourself,*

1. *Why do the characters behave as they do?*
2. *How do the proverbs connect to the stories?*
3. *What wisdom does each story teach?*

Tale 1

They tell of a king who gave the command that a captive should be executed. The unfortunate victim, in a state of despair, began to abuse the king with vile language, for it is said that he who washes his hands of life speaks all that he has in his heart.

> The tongue of a desperate man sheds
> its curb as the cornered cat springs
> at the dog.
> At the instant of necessity when
> flight is impossible the bare hand
> will grasp the keen blade of the sword.

The king asked: "What does he say?" One of his ministers, a man of kindly disposition, replied: "My Lord, he says: 'And those who restrain anger and pardon men, and Allah loves the doer of good,' a verse from the Holy Koran." The king was touched with pity and pardoned him, but another minister of contradictory character said: "It is not meet for those of our standing to speak aught but the truth in the presence of kings. The man abused His Majesty."

The king's face clouded at these words and he said: "That falsehood of his is more acceptable to me than the truth you have spoken, for it was a well-intentioned lie, whereas your truth was malicious. Have not the wise said: 'The well-intentioned lie is better than the truth which causes mischief'?"

> Whosoever advises the king as to his
> actions does ill if he advises aught
> but good.
> Over the vault of Feridun[1] was
> inscribed:
> "The world, O brother, remains with
> no one, attach your heart to the
> world's Creator—Enough!
> Lean not nor rely upon the world's
> promises for many have been reared
> by it and perished.
> When it is time for the pure soul
> to leave
> what matter if from a throne
> or from the naked earth?"

Tale 15

A Vizier,[2] who had been dismissed from office, entered a Sufi fraternity.[3] The blessing of their meditations communicated itself to him and gave him peace of mind. His former master became well-disposed to him again and bade him return to court. The Vizier demurred[4] and said: "Being out of office and close to wisdom is better than any occupation."

> Those who seat themselves in a
> safe corner
> are safe from the teeth of dogs
> and the tongues of men.
> They tear up the paper and
> break the pen and escape the
> hands and tongues of cavilers.[5]

---

1. **the vault of Feridun** (fĕr′ĭ-do͞on′): the tomb of a legendary Persian hero and ruler.
2. **vizier** (vĭ-zîr′): a high officer in a Muslim government.
3. **Sufi fraternity:** a group of members of a Muslim sect that values love of and devotion to God above all else.
4. **demurred** (dĭ-mûrd′): refused; objected.
5. **cavilers** (kăv′ə-lərz): individuals who find fault with others, especially about small things.

Working Independently

You may want to set aside time each week for independent reading, without making a related assignment. Or once students have completed the reading, you may ask them to work together on a project, such as reading other selections from the *Gulistan* or reporting on Hafiz's life and times. If you choose to have students write responsively in their Reader's Notebook, suggest that they write about times in their lives when they have experienced situations similar to the ones written about in these tales.

Using the Selection for Assessment

If you want to use this selection as the basis for assessment, see Integrated Assessment Book, pp. 19–24, for test questions.

Said the king: "I need a man of wisdom to advise me on the government of the realm."

Replied the Vizier: "The sign of wisdom is not to engage in such activities: the *Huma* is superior to all other birds in that it eats bones and does not trouble any other bird."

They asked a lynx: "How was it that you became a servant of the lion?" He replied: "I eat the remains of his prey and live, safe from any enemies under the shadow of his authority."

They questioned: "Now that you have the protection of his might and have acknowledged your debt to him, why do you not approach nearer and enter the inner circle of his special servants and fellows?" The lynx replied: "However, at the same time I am not inapprehensive of[6] his strength."

> If a Zoroastrian feeds his fire[7] for
> a hundred years
> he has only to fall in once to
> be consumed.

Sometimes a courtier may be rewarded by gold, sometimes by the loss of his head.

As the sages say, it is as well to be on guard against the fickleness of monarchs, for they may take umbrage[8] at a salute or give a robe of honor in reply to abuse.

> Surely it is true when they say that
> great wit is a merit in a courtier but
> a fault in the wise.
> Conduct yourself with dignity;
> leave jesting to courtiers.

Tale 27

A certain man was skilled in the art of wrestling and had mastered three hundred and sixty excellent throws and sleights[9] and developed new stratagems every day. He had a favorite pupil to whom he taught three hundred and fifty-nine of these maneuvers, postponing the instruction of the last secret. Soon the youth reached such a standard of proficiency that no one could stand against him.

One day, in the presence of the king, the stripling[10] declared himself equal to his master in strength and skill. The king was displeased at such boastfulness and commanded that they should wrestle before him. A spacious place was chosen and the audience was composed of the lords and ladies of the realm and athletes from all over the world.

In the contest the young man charged, like a mad elephant, with such force that a mountain of iron would have been uprooted by the impact. The master, knowing his pupil to be stronger and as skilled as he himself, used the secret hold, overcame the youth and flung him to the ground. A great shout arose from the audience and the king bestowed a robe of honor and money on the winner.

---

6. **not inapprehensive of:** somewhat fearful of.
7. **Zoroastrian** (zôr′ō-ăs′trē-ən) **feeds his fire:** In the temples of Zoroastrianism (a religion founded by the Persian Prophet Zoroaster), a fire was kept burning constantly.
8. **umbrage** (ŭm′brĭj)**:** offense.
9. **sleights** (slīts)**:** tricks.
10. **stripling:** young man.

608 UNIT FOUR PART 1

Sadi in conversation with a rich, adventurous merchant (1207–1292). Persian miniature. Bibliotheque Nationale, Paris. Photo © Visioars/akg-images, London.

Rebuking the loser, the king said: "You presumed to overcome your teacher yet failed in your presumption." The youth replied: "My lord, my master withheld from me one hold and used it today, thus he triumphed not by strength."

Said the master: "This hold I reserved for such a day, for have the wise not said: 'Do not give a friend so much power that should he wish to harm you, he will be able to do so'? Have you not heard of the teacher who suffered wrong from his pupil:

'Every day I instructed him in archery
until the day when his arm waxed strong,
and he shot me.
Perhaps fidelity[11] was a stranger
in the world or no one practiced
it in days of yore.
No one who has learned archery from me
has failed to make me his target!'"

Tale 30

A king ordered the execution of an innocent man. The condemned said: "O King, do not injure yourself on account of the anger that you feel for me." "What do you mean?" said the king. He replied: "My punishment will be over in a moment but the guilt of it will be with you forever.

As the wind sweeps over the desert
so does the term of life.
The suffering, the joy, the ugly and
the beautiful have passed away.
The tyrant thought to punish
yet that punishment I escaped
is now fixed on him."

This admonition impressed the king, who gave up the idea of shedding his blood. ❖

11. **fidelity:** faithfulness; loyalty.

Discussion Questions

The introduction to this selection provides questions you might use for a post-reading class discussion.

1. Why do the characters behave as they do?
   Possible Responses: (Tale 1) The kindly minister may want to protect the king from abuse, or he may feel pity for the condemned man. The unkind minister may want the condemned man to pay for his abuse, he may want the king to feel insulted, or he may want to get the other minister into trouble for lying. (Tale 15) The Vizier may refuse to accept his old position because he realizes that the king's approval is as fickle as his disapproval; he may also realize that closeness to power brings with it danger as well as privilege. (Tale 27) The master may withhold the last maneuver because he knows the student has talent, but he doesn't know whether the student has wisdom; he may also know that success often brings with it arrogance and ingratitude and want to protect himself from those things. (Tale 30) The condemned man may just want to save his own life, or he may want to help the king avoid a mistake. The king may spare the man because he realizes it was wrong to condemn an innocent person in anger, or he may be grateful to the man for his concern and honesty.
2. How do the proverbs connect to the stories?
   Possible Responses: The proverbs reinforce each story by stating its themes directly, elaborating on them, or illustrating them with further examples and analogies.
3. What wisdom does each story teach?
   Possible Responses: (Tale 1) Intention is more important than truthfulness; one should act out of love of God rather than a sense of responsibility. (Tale 15) What appears a loss at first may be an opportunity; power and influence bring risks as well as rewards. (Tale 27) Don't presume to think you know more than your teacher; don't give away all your power, because you never know how it will be used. (Tale 30) The moral or spiritual consequences of an action matter more than its physical result; violence hurts the perpetrator more than the victim.

GULISTAN 609

Objectives

- reflect on and assess student understanding of the unit part
- review important concepts from the reading
- assess and build portfolios
- set goals for future learning

Reflecting on the Literature

Help students get started by discussing with them the definition of fate that applies to each of the selections in Unit Four, Part 1: The Koran *(God's will)*, "The Second Voyage of Sindbad the Sailor *(luck, reward or punishment for actions, divine will)*, the *Rubáiyát (the human condition, the whimsy of the gods)*, poems by Rumi *(the encounter with the divine presence as ultimate reality)*.

Reviewing Literary Concepts

Make sure students understand that when they explain in their own words the "truths" presented in the selections, they are talking about themes developed in the text and not necessarily ideas they agree with. Have students support their statements of theme with examples from the selections. Students should save their personal opinions for answering the final question and support them with examples and logical reasoning.

 Use **Unit Four Resource Book,** p. 15, for additional support.

Building Your Portfolio

Students will use their Presentation Portfolios to file what they consider their highest quality work–the very best in their Working Portfolios. If students feel that the writing assignment they completed for *The Thousand and One Nights* is not strong enough, have them revise it until they are ready to include it in their Presentation Portfolios.

 For more information on using writing and assessing portfolios, see the **Teacher's Guide to Assessment and Portfolio Use,** pp. 53–74.

Part Assessment

 To assess skills and concepts taught in this unit part, use **Formal Assessment Book,** p. 87.

Reflect and Assess

What has reading the selections in Unit Four, Part 1, contributed to your understanding and appreciation of Persian and Arabic literature? What new discoveries did you make? Use the following activities to help you explore what you have learned.

Detail of *Fête Champêtre* [Picnic on the grass] (c. 1610-1615, Riza). The Keir Collection, England.

Reflecting on the Literature

Human Fate Each of the selections in this part of the book explores how human beings are affected by fate. Fate might be understood as luck, as divine will, or simply as part of the general human condition. Fate might or might not be affected by human action or inaction. Think about the works you have read, and identify three different views of fate. Describe each view in your own words. Then choose the one you feel best applies to the world we live in, and explain why.

Reviewing Literary Concepts

Reflecting on Theme In different ways, the selections in this part of the book offer truths to live by. Choose three of these truths, each one from a different selection, and explain each briefly in your own words. For each truth, include at least one example of how a person might live by it. Which of the three do you think is most relevant to your own life? Explain your answer.

Building Your Portfolio

Writing Options Look back at the written assignment that you chose to complete for *The Thousand and One Nights.* If you feel that it is good enough, write a cover note explaining its strong points and add the piece to your **Presentation Portfolio.**

Self ASSESSMENT

READER'S NOTEBOOK

Below are some important names and terms that you encountered in this part of the book. Go through the list and explain the meaning or significance of each one. If you have trouble with a term, go back to the place where it was first introduced and try to determine its meaning or significance in context, or look it up in the **Glossary of Literary Terms** (page R91).

Islam	Sindbad
antithesis	conflict
rubâi	imagery
metaphor	Sufism
Scheherezade	frame story

Setting GOALS

Of the selections you read in this part of the book, of which would you like to read more? Write a paragraph explaining your choice, and make arrangements to carry out this reading some time over the next month.

Assessment Self Assessment

Students can look up the listed terms in the **Glossary of Literary Terms** on page R91 or they can find them introduced in context on the text pages indicated below.

Islam (pages 566–567, 576–577)
antithesis (pages 577, 581)
rubâi (page 594)
metaphor (pages 594–598)
Scheherazade (page 582)
Sindbad (page 583)
conflict (pages 583, 589)
imagery (pages 601, 605)
Sufism (pages 569, 601)
frame story (page 582)

Extend Your *Reading*

Night & Horses & the Desert

An Anthology of Classical Arabic Literature

ROBERT IRWIN, ED.

This anthology will help you delve more deeply into the Arabic literary tradition while still focusing on its highlights. Organized by historical period, the collection includes literature not only from the great age of Arabic literature, but also from pre-Islamic times.

The Essential Rumi

COLEMAN BARKS, TRANS.

That the work of a 13th-century Persian mystic should resonate so strongly with modern readers and make him one of the most widely read poets in America is an amazing tribute to the power of literature to bridge the gap between cultures. This collection contains some of Rumi's finest work in a translation that sparkles.

And Even *More* . . .

Books

The Gift: Poems by Hafiz, the Great Sufi Master
DANIEL LADINSKY, TRANS.
Hafiz is the other great Sufi mystic and poet, with a style uniquely his own.

Rumi Speaks Through Sufi Tales KRISH KHOSLA
This collection shows that Rumi excelled as a storyteller as well as a poet.

Other Media

Islam: 600–1200
This video focuses on the history, culture, and religion of the Islamic world during its golden age. Zenger Media. (VIDEOCASSETTE)

Rumi: Poet of the Heart
This documentary, featuring Coleman Barks, Robert Bly, and Deepak Chopra and narrated by Debra Winger, focuses on Rumi's life and work and their relevance in our own time. Magnolia Films. (VIDEOCASSETTE)

Scheherezade
In this symphonic tone poem, the 19th-century Russian composer Nikolai Rimski-Korsakov celebrates and brings to musical life several of the tales from *The Thousand and One Nights.* Nonesuch. (AUDIO CD)

Arabian Nights and Days

NAGUIB MAHFOUZ

In this spellbinding work, the renowned Nobel Prize–winning novelist Naguib Mahfouz retells many of the tales from *The Arabian Nights.* Set in medieval times but with a distinctly modern flavor, these versions bring new life to the classic stories.

More Recommendations for Your Students

Difficulty Level: Easy

Yeoman, John, reteller. *The Seven Voyages of Sinbad the Sailor* (New York: Simon and Schuster, 1997). In this accessible, illustrated retelling students can read the entire history of the world's most famous man of the sea.

Lattimore, Deborah Nourse, reteller and illustrator. *Arabian Nights: Three Tales* (New York: HarperCollins, 1995). This beautiful retelling of three of the classic stories from the collection has a manageable vocabulary and lots of illustrations to aid in comprehension.

Alden, Carella. *Royal Persia: Tales and Art of Iran* (New York: Parents Magazine Press, 1972). This book gracefully recaps the history of Persia through its art with a vocabulary molded for less advanced readers.

Difficulty Level: Average

Cleary, Thomas, translator and editor. *The Essential Koran: The Heart of Islam* (New York: HarperCollins, 1993). This volume contains an introductory selection of readings from The Koran in a very accessible translation. Extensive notes on the text are provided that will help students with comprehension.

Fletcher, Susan. *Shadow Spinner* (New York: Simon and Schuster, 1998). This is a gripping retelling of the story of Scheherazade, well researched historically and rich in cultural detail.

The Arabian Nights and The Rubáiyát of Omar Khayyám. Excellent online versions of these classics, presented by the Electronic Literature Foundation, can be found at **www.arabiannights.org.**

Difficulty Level: Challenging

Hourani, Albert. *A History of the Arab Peoples* (Cambridge: Harvard University Press, 1998). Divided into five chronological periods, this work chronicles the history of the Arab peoples from the rise of Islam to the present.

Holt, P.M. et al., editors. *The Cambridge History of Islam* (Cambridge, England: Cambridge University Press, 1996). This volume contains a comprehensive history of Islamic countries in the form of separate essays written by outstanding scholars in the various fields.

In Unit Four, Part 2, you will find examples of oral literature from West Africa—myth, legend, epic, praise songs, trickster tales, and proverbs. Most of the literature was collected in the 20th century but it is assumed to be older, predating European colonization. It is recognized that North, East, Central, and Southern Africa also have rich literary traditions, but focusing on West Africa allows for the acknowledgment of continuities between West African and American cultural forms that resulted from the Atlantic slave trade. Furthermore, it is recognized that West Africa has a very old tradition of written literature, mostly in Arabic. However, space limitations required narrowing the focus to oral literature.

World Art and Cultures Transparencies

AT17 Nok sculpture

AT32 Ghana commemorative funerary head

AT33 Benin plaque [detail]

AT44 *Slaves Below the Deck of the* Albenez

AT77 Multiple-Mask Headdress

You may use the listed transparencies to acquaint students with art from West Africa.

Pronunciations

Timbuktu (tĭm′bŭk-to͞o′)

Mali (mä′lē)

Djenné-Djeno (jĕ-nā′jĕ-nō′)

Ghana (gä′nə)

Benin (bə-nĭn′)

Soninke (sō-nĭng′kā)

Fulani (fo͞o-lä′nē)

Yoruba (yôr′ə-bə)

PART 2 Giving Guidance, Praising Greatness

West African Oral Literature

Why It Matters
West Africa has a rich cultural tradition, full of wisdom, grandeur, and humor. Much of the art, music, and oral literature of the area recalls the glories of its ancient kingdoms. These cultural forms traveled with West Africans when millions of them were brought to the Americas during the Atlantic slave trade. Today, distinctive parts of U.S., Latin American, and Caribbean culture show West African influence.

1 Traditional and Islamic Beliefs Traditional African religions coexisted with **Islam** after North African traders brought it to West Africa in the 800s. **Timbuktu,** a successful trade center in Mali, became a focus of Islamic learning, attracting scholars to its university and the mosque of Sankore, shown in the picture above.

For Links to West Africa, click on:
HUMANITIES CLASSZONE.COM

SOUTH AMERICA

2 Wealthy Cities and Empires Ancient cities such as Djenné-Djeno prospered through trade. North African caravans laden with blocks of salt and other goods would cross the Sahara desert to trade for gold, ivory, and other precious resources of West Africa. Centers of the **gold trade** expanded into the great empires of **Ghana** and **Mali**.

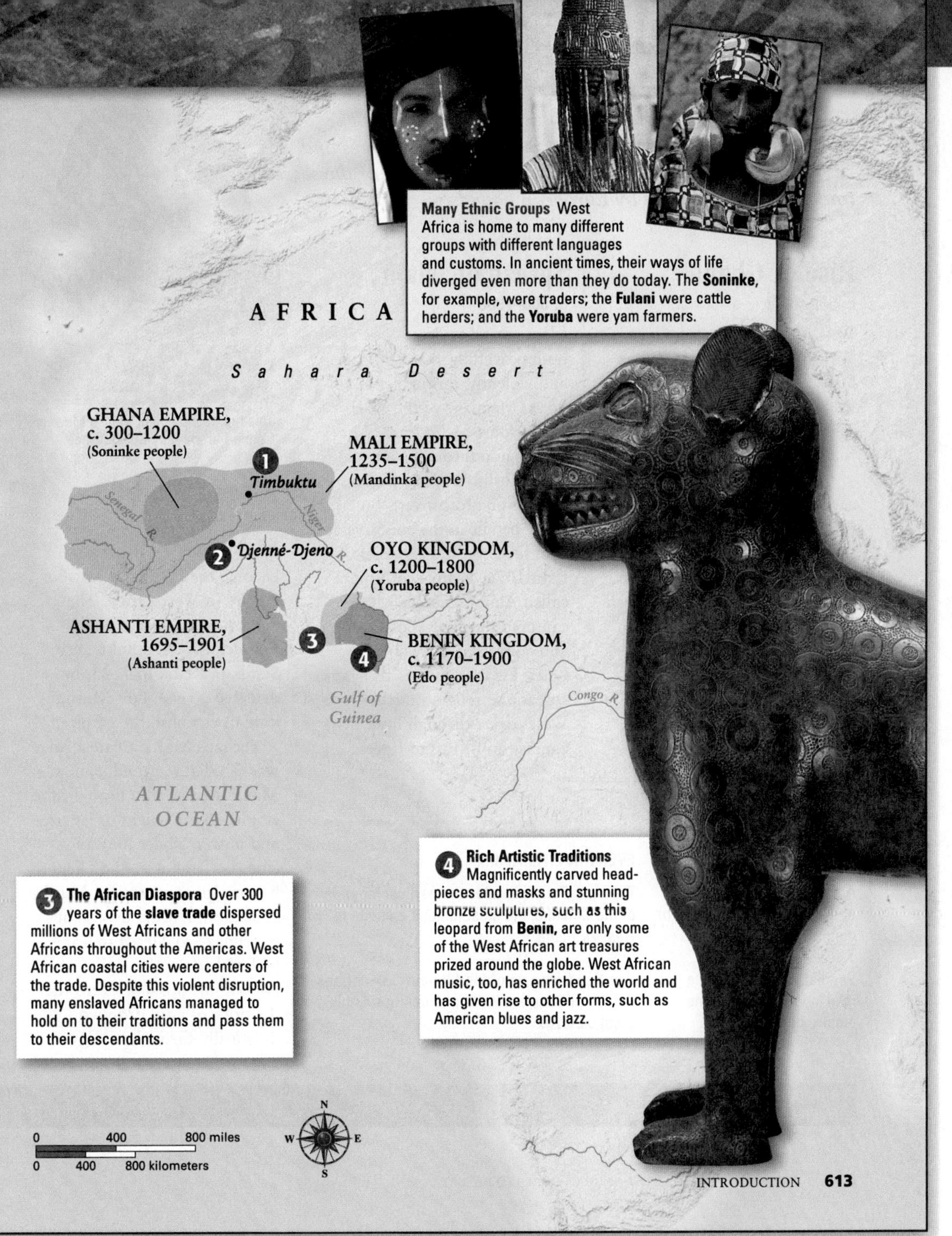

Many Ethnic Groups West Africa is home to many different groups with different languages and customs. In ancient times, their ways of life diverged even more than they do today. The **Soninke**, for example, were traders; the **Fulani** were cattle herders; and the **Yoruba** were yam farmers.

3 The African Diaspora Over 300 years of the **slave trade** dispersed millions of West Africans and other Africans throughout the Americas. West African coastal cities were centers of the trade. Despite this violent disruption, many enslaved Africans managed to hold on to their traditions and pass them to their descendants.

4 Rich Artistic Traditions Magnificently carved headpieces and masks and stunning bronze sculptures, such as this leopard from **Benin,** are only some of the West African art treasures prized around the globe. West African music, too, has enriched the world and has given rise to other forms, such as American blues and jazz.

INTRODUCTION 613

READING FOR INFORMATION

Reading Skills and Strategies

IDENTIFYING CAUSE AND EFFECT

Have students read the text box labeled **Why It Matters.** Then ask: Why do parts of U.S., Latin American, and Caribbean culture show West African influence? *(because West Africans transplanted their cultural forms when they were brought to the Americas during the Atlantic slave trade)*

Reading Skills and Strategies

SCANNING

Ask students to scan the boldfaced headings in the remaining text boxes to preview important facts about West Africa. Point out the red numbers that are keyed to spots on the map.

Geographical Note

The map on page 613 shows some (but not all) important kingdoms and empires of precolonial West Africa. These do not correspond to modern West African countries with the same names. The present-day country of Ghana is southwest of the ancient Ghana empire, along the coast in the same area where the Ashanti (Asante) empire was. The modern country of Mali does not have the same borders as the ancient Mali empire. The modern country of Benin was formerly called Dahomey. It is east of the ancient kingdom of Benin, which lies in present-day Nigeria. It might be useful to show a current map of Africa for comparison.

MINI LESSON Using the Map

Direct students to study the map on page 613, which shows five empires or kingdoms of precolonial West Africa, their dates, and (in parentheses) the ethnic groups that founded them. Ask the following questions:

- Which of these was the earliest kingdom or empire founded? *(Ghana)*
- Which was the latest founded? *(the Ashanti Empire)*
- Which was the largest? *(Mali)*
- What people founded the kingdom of Oyo? *(the Yoruba)*

Pronunciations
Almoravids (ăl′mə-rä′vĭdz)
Mandinka (măn-dĭng′kə)
Sundiata Keita (so͝on-jä′tä kē′tä)
Mansa Musa (män′sä mo͞o-sä′)
oba (ō′bä)
alafin (ä′lä-fēn′)
Ife (ē′fā)
Oyo (ō′yō)
Edo (ĕd′ō)
Ashanti (ə-shăn′tē)
Asante (ə-sän′tē)

READING FOR INFORMATION
Reading Skills and Strategies
UNDERSTANDING CHRONOLOGICAL ORDER
Tell students to read the heads for the six text columns on the spread and the colored dates below each of the heads. Six significant events are discussed, some of which overlap in time. The time line at the bottom of the spread places kingdoms and empires in time relation to one another.

After students finish reading the columns, ask the following questions:

- Did the spread of Islam to West Africa begin before or after the rise of the Mali empire? *(before)*
- Which occurred earlier, the Atlantic slave trade, or European colonization of Africa? *(the Atlantic slave trade)*

Language Note
The names of African language and ethnic groups can be difficult to keep straight. A language group, such as the Akan, may include several different ethnic groups with variant names—for example, the Ashanti (also called the Asante), the Fante, and the Baule. The Mande language group includes the following ethnic groups: Soninke, Mandinka (also called Malinke), Bambara, Dyula, and Mende.

Historical Highlights

The history of West Africa is both exciting and tragic. The region was shaped by the rise and fall of mighty empires and city-states, the spread of a new religion, the wounds of the slave trade, and colonization by European powers.

This representation of Mansa Musa is from a 14th-century Spanish map.

Rise of Ghana
c. 300–1200

West Africa's first empire was ancient **Ghana**, founded by the **Soninke** people, merchants who lived just south of the Sahara. They named their state after their ruler, or *ghana* ("war chief").

Called "the land of gold" by early travelers, Ghana ironically produced no gold itself. Instead, the Soninke kings took advantage of their strategic location between northern and southern trade routes. The gold that draped these kings in splendor came from taxing traders. Eventually, Ghana was weakened by Islamic invasions.

Spread of Islam
c. 800–1900

Islam spread to West Africa both peacefully, through trade, and violently, through conquest. Members of the local ruling courts, who learned of the religion through contact with Muslim traders, were usually the first to convert. But many people in the countryside kept their traditional beliefs.

In 1076, Islamic reformers called **Almoravids** (or Moors) captured the capital of Ghana and converted its people. Later, **Fulani** converts to Islam spread the religion farther into West Africa through holy wars against non-Muslim rulers.

History to Literature

EVENT IN HISTORY	EVENT IN LITERATURE
Ancient Ghana, the empire of the Soninke, flourishes for hundreds of years.	The epic *Dausi* includes the earliest legends of the Soninke; the most famous episode is *Gassire's Lute.*
Sundiata Keita defeats a rival king and founds the empire of Mali.	The *Sundiata* epic of the Mandinka describes the life of Sundiata Keita and celebrates his great victory.

Rise of Mali
1235–1500

Mali succeeded Ghana to become the first great Muslim empire in West Africa. The *Sundiata* epic tells of Mali's founder, the **Mandinka** hero **Sundiata Keita.** In 1235, he defeated a rival, non-Muslim king to establish the empire.

Perhaps Mali's greatest ruler was Sundiata's grandnephew, **Mansa Musa,** who brought the empire to the height of its size and power. Under him, the cities of Timbuktu and Djenné became great centers of Muslim education. During his famous pilgrimage to Mecca in 1324, he lavished so many gifts of gold on his hosts in Cairo that the price of gold dropped drastically throughout Egypt.

GHANA EMPIRE
300

Forest Kingdoms Prosper

c. 1170–1900

While Mali was at its height, smaller forest kingdoms to the south were prospering as well. One forest group was the **Yoruba,** a deeply religious people who composed eloquent praise songs to their gods. The Yoruba had a government of ruling families, each headed by a strong king called an *oba* or *alafin,* who was considered divine. One of the achievements of the Yoruba was the creation of city-states. The two biggest, **Ife** and **Oyo,** supported large populations of traders, craftspeople, and artists.

The **Edo** people of **Benin,** southwest of Ife near the coast, had a government and trading system similar to those of the Yoruba. Benin has become world-famous for the fine quality of its royal sculpture. Gleaming brass plaques commemorating the king's achievements adorned the palace walls, and elegantly cast bronze heads immortalized the royal family. In the 1470s, the first Portuguese trading ships sailed into Benin's port, making a contact that would open up West Africa to the **Atlantic slave trade.**

This painting depicts the tragedy of the Atlantic slave trade. Millions of Africans were captured, enslaved, and shipped to the Americas.

Atlantic Slave Trade

1518–1870

Traditionally, slavery in West Africa was small-scale. Africans regularly enslaved prisoners of war or minor criminals. The large-scale business of trading slaves first began with the Muslims in West Africa and continued with the Portuguese. Then, after 1625, Europeans increased their demand for slaves to work their mines and plantations in the Americas and the Caribbean islands. In exchange for slaves, Europeans offered guns. This led to local wars and raids designed to bring in prisoners, who would be sold as slaves for more guns. Even African kings who resisted the thriving trade couldn't stop it. As a result, West Africa lost between 10 and 15 million of its people.

Ashanti Empire

1695–1901

The **Ashanti** (or Asante) were one group involved in the slave trade. Originally small farmers, they banded together in 1695 to form a strong union. The symbol of their unity was the Golden Stool, which they believed was brought from heaven for their ruler to sit on.

The empire prospered until the 1870s, when it began a series of wars with the British that led to its **colonization.** The Ashanti experience was repeated throughout Africa during the period known as the "Scramble for Africa" (1880–1900). With superior weapons, the European powers colonized 90 percent of the African continent, imposing new governments, languages, and faiths.

FOREST KINGDOMS				
MALI EMPIRE			ASHANTI EMPIRE	
1170	1235	1500	1695	1901

Historical Note

The slave trade existed over a larger region of Africa than that represented by the selections in this book. Other slave trading centers were farther south, near the Congo River and Angola. (Many Africans enslaved from this region were sent to the Portuguese colony of Brazil.) There were also some trading centers along the southeast coast of the continent.

Language Note

Much of West Africa was colonized by France, which is why a good deal of literature and commentary from the region is in the French language. The version of the *Sundiata* epic that appears in this anthology was first rendered in French, and then the French version was translated to English. The modern countries of Ghana and Nigeria were former British colonies; Akan and Yoruba literature from these regions often appears in English translation.

READING FOR INFORMATION
Reading Skills and Strategies
CLASSIFYING

The columns on this spread distinguish among different social groups in pre-colonial West Africa. After students read, ask the following questions:

- What is a diviner? *(a religious figure who communicates with the spirit world and helps or heals people)*
- What is a queen mother? *(the mother or widow of a king, who has some political power of her own)*

People and Society

With the rise of kingdoms and empires in West Africa came a division of society into different classes. But the class system was generally not as rigid as those found in Europe and India. Changing circumstances allowed for some movement up and down the social ladder.

Rulers

At the top of the social ladder in West Africa were the **kings**, nobles, and **chiefs**. These members of high-ranking families controlled the government and the wealth. Rulers were also spiritual leaders of their people. Sometimes, groups of rulers shared power among themselves.

Since none of the early West African civilizations used money, rulers accumulated their wealth in goods and services. For example, traders paid taxes in gold, and fishermen gave a portion of their catch. In return, the people received the protection of the king's army.

Priests

Religion in West Africa touched all aspects of people's lives. **Priests** of traditional religions presided over shrines and directed sacrifices and other ceremonies, while Islamic teachers instructed from the Koran. When people needed help with personal problems, they went to the local diviner. **Diviners** were special religious figures who were thought to understand messages from the spirit world. After tracing the cause of a person's problem, they would recommend a solution. Diviners also acted as healers, treating people's physical problems with herbal medicines.

Brass head from the court of Benin

Craftspeople

The class of craftspeople included a variety of professional men and women: musicians, singers, poets, dancers, storytellers, weavers, potters, leatherworkers, metalworkers, woodworkers, even hairdressers and tattoo artists. These people often worked directly for the king and lived in or near his court. Such royal patronage usually required artists to celebrate the ruler in their art. This was especially true in the forest kingdoms. The Yoruba established one of the greatest schools of sculpture in the world at Ife. The Edo people of Benin developed their famous style of **royal sculpture** after learning from Ife artists.

Used to measure gold, this weight from Ghana depicts a farming family.

Freeborn People

The classification of freeborn generally applied to the great mass of ordinary people who weren't slaves. Rich merchants, traders, and landowners as well as humble farmers, fishermen, and miners were all considered freeborn. As time went on and kingdoms grew larger, there also emerged a group of appointed officials, usually freeborn, who helped run the government.

Still, *free* was a relative term in West Africa. Everyone owed something to the rulers—either a product or a service. Craftspeople, although technically free, lived under a variety of restrictions, depending on what king they worked for. And in wartime, a free man or woman could be captured and turned into a slave overnight.

Slaves

Slavery among early West Africans was looser than what later developed in the Americas. Enslaved war captives and lawbreakers often shared the same jobs as the freeborn, working on farms, in mines, and in homes. Unlike Greek and Roman rulers, who never trusted their slaves to fight for them, West African kings frequently used slaves as professional soldiers. Still, slaves had fewer rights than the freeborn, and they could be sold anytime.

Some slaves managed to gain their freedom through loyal service, hard work, or marriage into their owner's family. Those lucky enough to be court slaves working directly for the king often enjoyed greater power and privilege than the freeborn. In a few instances, freed slaves even became chiefs and kings.

Women in West Africa

According to an Ashanti proverb, "It's a woman who gave birth to a man; it's a woman who gave birth to a chief." This saying indicates the high status that women, especially mothers, enjoyed in West Africa. Most husbands and wives worked as equal economic partners. Women usually didn't hold political office, although a few warrior-queens existed. A more typical leadership role for a woman was that of queen mother. Often the mother or widow of a former king, a **queen mother** had to give consent before another man could be king. As advisor to the king, she attended political meetings and had veto power over the king's laws. Queen mothers sometimes acted as judges and even rode into battle on occasion.

MINI LESSON Interpreting the Text

The fifth column on this spread describes slavery in early West Africa and distinguishes it from slavery in other parts of the world. As students read, tell them to notice comparisons and contrasts. Ask the following questions to check understanding:

- Who was enslaved? *(war captives and lawbreakers)*
- How were the lives of enslaved and freeborn people similar? *(They had similar jobs.)*
- How were their lives different? *(The enslaved had fewer rights; they could be sold.)*
- Judging from your own knowledge of slavery in the Americas, how was early West African slavery different? *(It was not race-based and hereditary; it allowed slaves to fight as soldiers; it could be escaped by marriage into a master's family; it provided privileges to court slaves.)*

Pronunciations
orishas (ō-rē′shäz)
jalis (jä′lēz) (*Jali* also can be spelled as *jeli* , *dieli,* or *dyeli.*)
griots (grē-ōz′)
kora (kō′rä)
xalam (hä′läm)

READING FOR INFORMATION
Reading Skills and Strategies
IDENTIFYING MAIN IDEAS
Direct students to read the text chunks on this page very carefully. You might write the following questions on the board to guide their reading. Then discuss the answers in class.

- What are some functions of West African oral literature? *(It entertains, educates, and culturally unites people.)*
- What elements do traditional West African religions share? *(the idea of one creator god; worship of lesser gods and spirits; belief in the influence of ancestral spirits; belief in witches and sorcerers; belief in diviners)*
- What is distinctive about West African music and dance? *(Music is social, melodic rather than harmonic, improvisational, varied in instrumentation, and rhythmically sophisticated. Dance is also rhythmic, energetic, and social.)*
- What is distinctive about West African art? *(It is used to evoke spiritual power and is expressionistic rather than realistic.)*

Arts and Culture

West African culture has always been tied to the life of the community. Literature, religion, music, and art—like eating and drinking—are part of people's daily existence. For this reason, many of West Africa's cultural traditions remain as vital today as they were hundreds of years ago.

Literature

West Africa has an extremely rich and varied **oral tradition,** encompassing grand epics and humble proverbs; solemn praise poems and funny trickster tales; stories about people, animals, and supernatural forces; origin myths and riddles. In earlier times, as now, oral literature entertained the community and helped educate the young in the history and values of a people. Literary performance customarily brought people together, not only in the smallest villages but also in the biggest cities and at the king's palace. It culturally united large empires and gave the people cause for pride and celebration. All the ethnic groups of Mali could rejoice in the glorious life of their first empire builder, Sundiata. The Yoruba in the cities and the countryside alike could sing praises to the same ***orishas,*** or family of gods.

How Was Literature Presented?

The grand epics of the Soninke, Mandinka, and other groups were not read from books but were performed by professional bards called *dielis,* or griots. Griots recount the histories of prominent families, compose praise songs, play instruments, advise rulers, and perform many other functions. Griots belong to their own special caste and pass their knowledge to their children.

Religion

Traditional West African religions, although varied, shared common elements:

- the idea of one god who withdrew from human affairs after the creation
- worship of lesser gods and spirits who were more active in human affairs
- faith in the ability of **ancestral spirits** to influence the lives of living family members
- belief in witches and sorcerers who caused misfortune
- faith in the ability of diviners to solve problems both supernatural and natural

Fundamental to all these beliefs is the idea of a connection between the spirit world and the natural world. Rulers had the responsibility of maintaining harmony between these two worlds to ensure rain, good crops, and other life-sustaining conditions.

With the introduction of Islam, many of the old beliefs and practices died out. But some old ways persisted. For example, West African Muslim women often shocked Arab Muslim visitors by mixing freely with men in public and leaving their face unveiled—two things Arab women were forbidden to do.

618

Music and Dance

In West Africa, music is generally a social activity—part of games, ceremonies, festivals, and work. African musicians favor melody over harmony, and **improvisation** over strict rules. They use the distinctive qualities of musical instruments and human voices to maximum effect. Xylophones, flutes, horns, and whistles combine with different stringed instruments, such as the *kora,* the 21-string harp, and the *xalam,* the ancestor of the banjo. And driving all the music is the rhythm of the drums. The sheer variety of African percussion instruments is mind-boggling, including drums, bells, and rattles of all shapes, sizes, and materials. In rhythmical sophistication African music is unsurpassed.

African dance is as rhythmic and energetic as the music. Dancing—in solo or group performances—accompanies the music at most social and religious functions. Like the music, it serves to reinforce the vitality of the community.

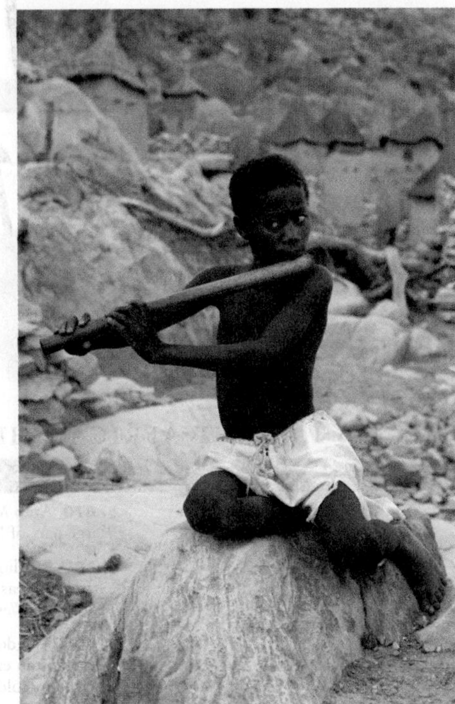

In West Africa, musicianship is highly regarded, and children are encouraged to become skilled at a young age.

Art

West African art includes exquisite jewelry, pottery, and sculpture made from such materials as wood, clay, ivory, and metal. In ancient times, most art was religious and used to evoke spiritual power. For example, someone might carve a beautiful figurine to entice an ancestral or nature spirit to inhabit it. In a similar way, individuals wore elaborate masks and headpieces to attract different spirits. Typically, African ritual art aims to express a spirit's essence—its power to make crops grow, for example—rather than its outward appearance. The idea that art need not represent a thing realistically in order to express its essence is the founding principle of modern art. The **expressionistic** design of African ritual objects influenced a number of modern artists, notably the 20th-century Spanish artist Pablo Picasso.

Time Line

WEST AFRICAN ORAL LITERATURE
(A.D. 300–1900)

2500 B.C. A.D. 1 PRESENT

c. approximately
B.C. before Christ
A.D. after Christ

EVENTS IN LITERATURE

300

c. 300–1100 Soninke epic poets compose the *Dausi,* which has survived only in fragments ➢

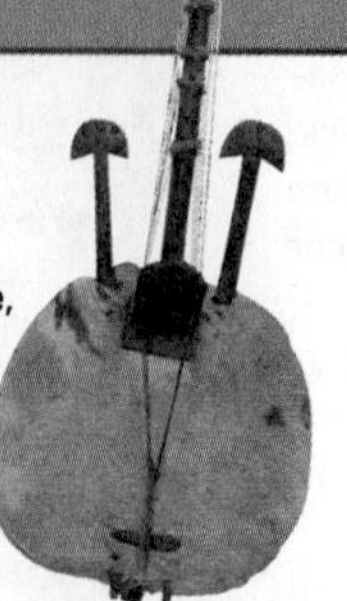

The kora, or lute, accompanies performances of epics.

900

1068 Muslim scholar Abu Ubayd al-Bakri completes first written history of West Africa

EVENTS IN WEST AFRICAN HISTORY

300

c. 300 Kingdom of ancient Ghana founded by the Soninke people, according to legend

600

c. 670 Arab Muslims rule Egypt and large part of North African coast

c. 800 Muslim traders from North Africa increase travel across the Sahara to West Africa

c. 800 Kingdom of ancient Ghana develops an empire from wealth gained in gold-salt trade

900

1050s Muslim Almoravids move from the western Sahara to conquer Morocco

1076 Almoravids overrun Ghana empire

c. 1100–1600 ➢ Walled city of Ife is center of most powerful Yoruba kingdom

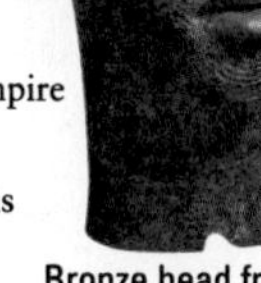

Bronze head from Ife depicting a king or god

EVENTS IN WORLD HISTORY

300

500–1500 Middle Ages in Europe

c. 570 Birth of Muhammad, prophet of Islam

600

618–907 T'ang Dynasty expands Chinese Empire

622 Beginning of the Muslim era

750 Muslim Empire extends from Atlantic Ocean to Indus River

771–814 Charlemagne builds empire that includes all of France and parts of Spain, Italy, and Germany

850 Chinese invent gunpowder

900

900s Anasazi civilization in North America enters classic Pueblo period

939 Vietnam gains independence from China

1054 Christian Church divides into Roman Catholic and Eastern Orthodox

1095 Beginning of the Crusades, a 200-year struggle between Christians and Muslims over the Holy Land

MINI LESSON Using the Time Line

First, tell students to notice the span of years (300–1900) covered by the time lines.

Next, have students read across the large gold time line, **Events in Literature,** noting in particular when Mali's *Sundiata* epic was composed.

Have students read across the red time line, **Events in West African History,** to see what contributed to the rise and fall of different empires.

Finally, tell them to read down the same period in all three time lines, to see which events happened during the same span of time. Ask the following questions to check understanding:

- What other world empires were founded in the same century as the Mali empire? *(the Aztec empire, the Mongol empire)*
- Was it possible that Ibn Battuta met Sundiata Keita on his trip to Mali? *(No)*
- Did the Ashanti empire exist before the beginning of the Atlantic slave trade? *(No)*

1200	1500	1800
c. 1250–1400 Mandinka poets compose Mali's epic, *Sundiata* **1352** North African historian Ibn Battuta visits Mali, later writes of his travels	**1650** African scholar Abd al-Rahman as-Sadi writes a history of ancient Ghana and Mali **1789** Olaudah Equiano, a freed slave originally from Benin, publishes his autobiography, *The Interesting Narrative of the Life of Olaudah Equiano*	

1200	1500	1800
1203–1235 Fulani people control former Ghana trade routes **1235** Sundiata Keita defeats Fulani army and founds Mali empire **1324–1325** Mali king Mansa Musa goes on pilgrimage to Mecca and brings back Arab architect to build mosques in Timbuktu and Gao **c. 1400s** Mali declines **1480s** Kingdom of Benin begins trading with Portuguese	**1518** Spanish carry first cargo of enslaved Africans directly from West Africa to Caribbean islands **1625** Atlantic slave trade expands **c. 1650–1789** City-state of Oyo replaces Ife as center of Yoruba power **1695–1717** Founding of Ashanti empire **mid-1700s** British exchange more than 100,000 guns a year for enslaved Africans	**c. 1800** Most West African kingdoms involved in Atlantic slave trade **1807–1826** Ashanti battle British over control of coast **1874** British burn Ashanti capital during Ashanti-British war **1884–1885** European powers divide Africa among themselves at Berlin Conference **1901** Ashanti empire becomes British colony

1200	1500	1800
1200–1521 Aztecs build empire in Mexico **1206–1227** Genghis Khan builds Mongol Empire **1345–1347** Epidemic of ➢ bubonic plague devastates large areas of China, the Middle East, and Europe **1492** Christopher Columbus reaches the Caribbean	**1507** Spain conquers territory in the Caribbean and Central America	**c. 1800** Africans make up half the populations of Brazil and Venezuela **1804** Napoleon becomes emperor of France **1804** Haiti gains independence from France **1821** Mexico declares independence from Spain **1861–1865** Civil War ends slavery in the United States

Plague victims in 14th-century Europe

INTRODUCTION 621

Pronunciations
merengue (mə-rĕng′gā)
mambo (mäm′bō)
samba (săm′bə)
dashiki (də-shē′kē)
djellaba (jə-lä′bə)
kente (kĕn′tā)
santería (sän-tĕ-rē′ä)
Anansi (ä-nän′sē)
Fon (fŏn)
son (sôn)

READING FOR INFORMATION
Reading Skills and Strategies
CONNECTING

After students read the spread, have them show examples of African or African-influenced cultural forms familiar to them. They might play recordings of the styles of music listed in the chart. They might model African hair and clothing styles, bring in examples of cloth or jewelry, or demonstrate dance steps.

Connect to Today: The Legacy of West Africa

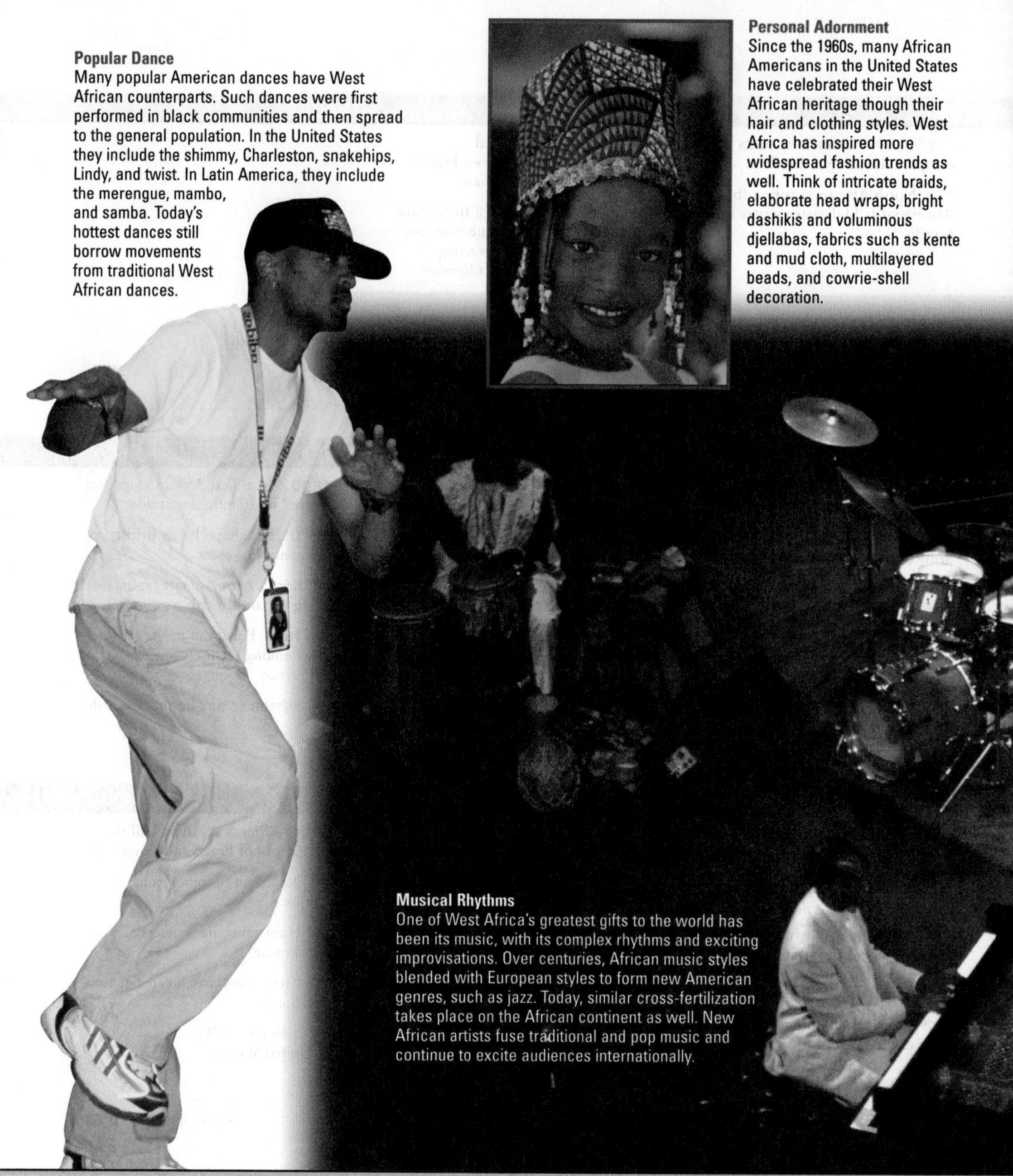

Popular Dance
Many popular American dances have West African counterparts. Such dances were first performed in black communities and then spread to the general population. In the United States they include the shimmy, Charleston, snakehips, Lindy, and twist. In Latin America, they include the merengue, mambo, and samba. Today's hottest dances still borrow movements from traditional West African dances.

Personal Adornment
Since the 1960s, many African Americans in the United States have celebrated their West African heritage though their hair and clothing styles. West Africa has inspired more widespread fashion trends as well. Think of intricate braids, elaborate head wraps, bright dashikis and voluminous djellabas, fabrics such as kente and mud cloth, multilayered beads, and cowrie-shell decoration.

Musical Rhythms
One of West Africa's greatest gifts to the world has been its music, with its complex rhythms and exciting improvisations. Over centuries, African music styles blended with European styles to form new American genres, such as jazz. Today, similar cross-fertilization takes place on the African continent as well. New African artists fuse traditional and pop music and continue to excite audiences internationally.

Worship Styles
Traditional influences can be seen in the modern religious practices of many Americans descended from Africans. The call-and-response pattern of African-American church sermons is characteristically West African, as are emotional, animated expressions of devotion. Ancient African gods are still worshiped in the Americas—for example, by those Cubans who practice the religion known as *santería*.

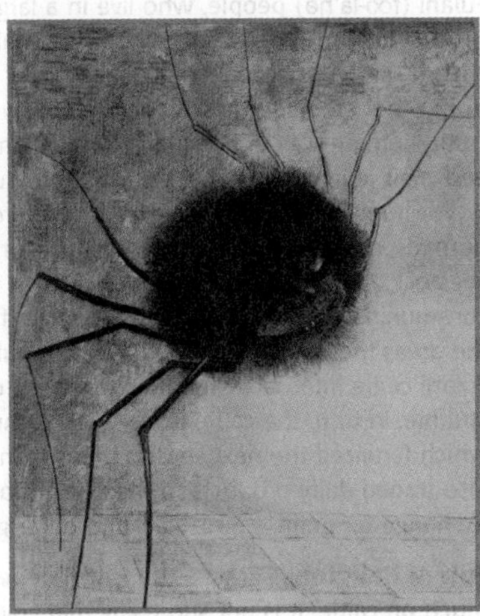

Storytelling
Familiar folktales told about Brer Rabbit and Anansi the spider are versions of traditional West African trickster tales.

African-Based Music

Many styles of popular music show West African or other African influences.

Blues is similar to the music played and sung by West African griots.

Jazz, like African music, has syncopated, or shifting, rhythms and is improvised by musicians who respond to one another's signals.

Calypso, from Trinidad, uses rhythms from Yoruba and Fon religious music.

Salsa comes from the Cuban *son,* which has a syncopated beat and is played on African instruments.

Samba, played at Carnival in Brazil, is based on Angolan rhythms and is named for a navel-touching dance step.

INTRODUCTION 623

Objectives

- understand and appreciate a Fulani **myth (Literary Analysis)**
- use strategies for **analyzing relationships (Active Reading)**

Thematic Link

This myth explains how the world was created and **gives guidance** about the danger of pride.

5-Minute Warm-Up

Daily Language SkillBuilder

Have students **proofread** the display sentences on page 563h and write them correctly.

Reading and Analyzing

Literary Analysis MYTH

A Point out that the phrase "In the beginning" signals that this is a creation story. Ask what existed at the beginning of creation. *(a huge drop of milk)*

Note that not everything is explained. For example, it is not stated where the drop of milk or the god Doondari came from.

Use **Unit Four Resource Book,** p. 17, for more practice.

Active Reading

ANALYZING RELATIONSHIPS

Ask students what would be the fourth and fifth events they would add to the diagram begun on page 624. *(fire created water; water created air)*

Note that many ancient cultures believed the universe was composed of four or five elements. In ancient Greece, these were earth, air, fire, and water. In ancient China, these were earth, wood, metal, fire, and water.

Have students discuss the five elements mentioned in the Fulani myth. Ask them to speculate about why these elements were important enough to be created first.

Possible Responses: Water, air, and the sun's heat (fire) are necessary for life; iron makes useful tools; much of the earth is stone.

Also ask students about relationships they see among the elements, particularly connections between an element and the one it creates.

Possible Responses: Iron is found within stone; fire is needed to smelt and work iron.

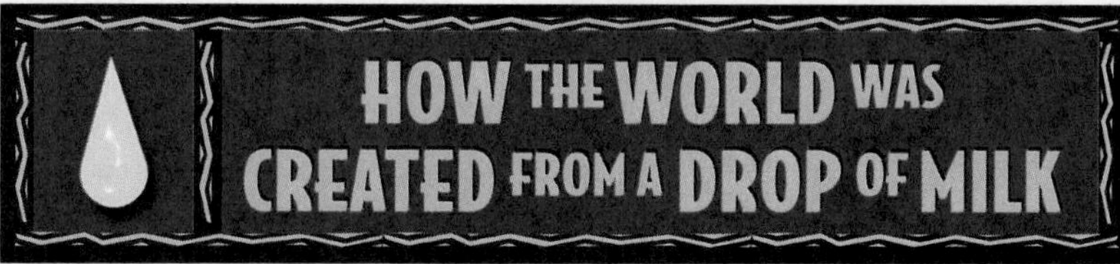

HOW THE WORLD WAS CREATED FROM A DROP OF MILK

Build Background

Cattle-Herding People "How the World Was Created from a Drop of Milk" is a myth from the Fulani (fo͞o-lä'nē) people, who live in a large territory that includes Senegal, Guinea, Mali, Niger, Nigeria, and Cameroon. The Fulani are set apart from other ethnic groups of West Africa by their cattle-herding way of life, their Fulfulde language, and their relatively fair skin and sharp features.

For hundreds of years, many Fulani were nomads, migrating in search of pasture for their livestock. Although they lived in their own isolated communities, they often cooperated with farmers in the areas they moved to. The farmers would allow Fulani cattle into harvested fields to graze on stubble. In turn, the cattle left behind manure, which fertilized the next season's crops. The Fulani also traded dairy products to their neighbors in exchange for grain, vegetables, and other goods.

Fulani Religion Because the Fulani depended so much on cattle, it is not surprising that cow and dairy images appear in many Fulani myths. The Fulani traditionally worshiped a supreme, all-powerful god, whom they called Gueno (gwā'nō), as well as lesser gods. Doondari (do͞on-dä'rē), a creator god, is one of the forms Gueno takes. These gods are mentioned in the myth you are about to read, which dates from the Fulani's pre-Islamic past. Since the 18th century, most Fulani have adopted Islam as their religion and have played a major role in spreading Islam throughout West Africa.

Connect to Your Life

This myth explains, among other things, how death came into the world. What explanations have you heard for the existence of death?

Focus Your Reading

LITERARY ANALYSIS: MYTH

A **myth** is a traditional story that explains why the world is the way it is. A creation story is a particular kind of myth that tells how the earth and human beings were created. Note what this Fulani creation story explains about the world.

ACTIVE READING: ANALYZING RELATIONSHIPS

To understand the set of beliefs about the world presented in a myth, you must pay attention to the relationships in the story. Here are some important types of relationships to look for.

Chronological—X happened before Y happened.

Cause-and-effect—X caused Y to happen.

Hierarchical—X ranks above Y.

Constituent—X is made up of Y and Z.

READER'S NOTEBOOK As you read this myth, notice the relationships among the beings and elements mentioned. Draw diagrams to show a few of these relationships. For example, a diagram putting one set of events in chronological order is shown below.

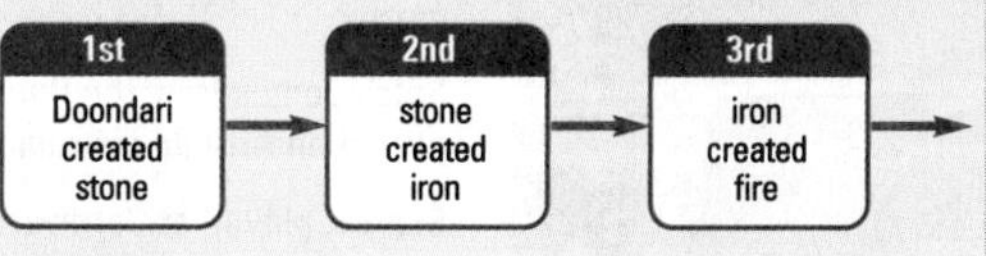

LESSON RESOURCES

UNIT FOUR RESOURCE BOOK, pp. 16–17

ASSESSMENT RESOURCES

Formal Assessment, pp. 89–90

Teacher's Guide to Assessment and Portfolio Use

Test Generator

INTEGRATED TECHNOLOGY

Visit our Web site: classzone.com

ADDITIONAL RESOURCES

Lesson Planning Guide, pp. 77–78

Teacher's Sourcebook for Language Development

Fulani woman making butter. Chad. Copyright © Jacques Jangoux/Tony Stone Images.

At the beginning there was a huge drop of milk. (A)
Then Doondari came and he created the stone.
Then the stone created iron;
And iron created fire;
And fire created water;
And water created air.
Then Doondari descended the second time. And he
took the five elements

Customizing Instruction

Less Proficient Readers

- Give more examples of the different kinds of relationships students will look for in the poem. To demonstrate hierarchical relationships, for example, you might ask them to rank a superindentent, a sophomore, a teacher, and a principal according to power they hold in a school. To demonstrate constituent relationships, you might ask them what an apple pie is made of.
- Instead of having students work independently, you might work together as a class to draw diagrams showing the relationships in the myth.

English Learners

There are few difficult words in this myth; however, it is essential that students understand the meaning of *descended* ("came down") and *eternal* ("without beginning or end"; "never dying").

Advanced Learners

Have students read the famous poem "Death Be Not Proud (Holy Sonnet 10)" by the 17th-century English poet John Donne. Ask them to compare the ideas about death and eternity in the works.

Possible Responses: In both works, death is described as "proud" but is proven inferior to an eternal force. In the Fulani myth, the eternal God conquers death, but in Donne's poem, humans conquer it too, with eternal life in heaven.

MINI LESSON Speaking and Listening

DRAMATIC READING

Instruction This myth and the other selections in Unit 4, Part 2, were originally passed down orally, not read from a book.

Prepare Ask a volunteer to present this myth aloud, as if it were a sermon to the class. Assign a small group to help with suggestions for gestures, facial expressions, and vocal techniques that would enhance the presentation.

Present Have the rest of the class listen carefully as the performer speaks. Discuss whether the myth is more meaningful or interesting when spoken aloud. Talk about the overall mood, or emotional feeling, of the myth.

HOW THE WORLD WAS CREATED FROM A DROP OF MILK 625

Literary Analysis MYTH

Tell students that creation myths explain how human beings came to exist. Ask: In this myth, how was the first human created? *(Doondari created him from stone, iron, fire, water, and air.)*

Active Reading

ANALYZING RELATIONSHIPS

A Ask: According to the myth, what caused blindness to exist?

Possible Response: Doondari created blindness because he wanted to weaken man, who acted too proud.

Ask: According to the myth, what is more powerful than blindness? *(sleep)*

B Ask: According to the myth, what caused death to exist?

Possible Response: Doondari created death in order to conquer worry.

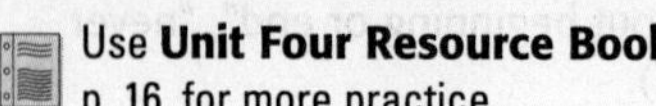

Use **Unit Four Resource Book,** p. 16, for more practice.

And he shaped them into man.
But man was proud.
A Then Doondari created blindness and blindness defeated
man.
But when blindness became too proud,
Doondari created sleep, and sleep defeated blindness;
But when sleep became too proud,
Doondari created worry, and worry defeated sleep;
B But when worry became too proud,
Doondari created death, and death defeated worry.
But when death became too proud,
Doondari descended for the third time,
And he came as Gueno, the eternal one,
And Gueno defeated death.

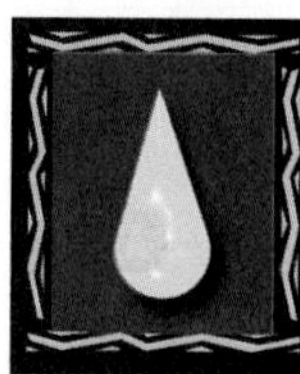

Cross Curricular Link **Science**

CHEMICAL ELEMENTS Today, when scientists use the term *element*, they usually mean a chemical element. A chemical element is a substance that cannot be broken down into simpler substances through ordinary chemical processes such as burning or electrolysis. Water, for example, is *not* an element because it can be broken down into hydrogen and oxygen.

There are 112 known elements. Those most abundant in the earth's crust are oxygen, silicon, aluminum, iron, and calcium. Air is composed mostly of the elements nitrogen and hydrogen. Ninety-five percent of the human body consists of oxygen, carbon, hydrogen, and nitrogen. Tiny amounts of iron and other trace elements are present as well.

Connect to the Literature

1. **What Do You Think?** What questions do you have about events in this myth?

Think Critically

2. How was the world created, according to the first part of the myth? Summarize events in your own words.
3. **ACTIVE READING: ANALYZING RELATIONSHIPS** Look over the diagrams you created in your READER'S NOTEBOOK. What relationships do you see presented in the myth?
4. How do you interpret the series of defeats in the myth? In what sense does blindness defeat man, sleep defeat blindness, and so on?
5. Why do you think Doondari returns as Gueno to defeat death?
6. What truths about human nature or life do you find in this myth?

Extend Interpretations

7. **What If?** If man had not been proud, how might the world have turned out?
8. **Comparing Texts** How would you compare this Fulani creation story with the creation stories from the Hebrew Bible (page 62) and *Popol Vuh* (page 76)? THINK ABOUT
   - what exists in the beginning
   - how humans are created
   - whether the creators are satisfied with their creations
   - what the creators do in the end
9. **Connect to Life** How satisfying do you find this Fulani myth's explanation of why death exists?

LITERARY ANALYSIS: MYTH

A **myth** is a traditional story, passed down through generations, that explains why the world is the way it is. Myths are essentially religious, and in them, events usually result from the actions of gods. Myths have the following functions:

- **To explain features of the natural world.** For example, the Mayan *Popol Vuh* (page 77) explains that monkeys look like people because they are an earlier, failed version of human beings.
- **To support social customs.** Recall that according to a myth in the *Rig Veda* (page 115), the four social classes of India were created from the mouth, arms, thighs, and feet of Purusha, the first man.
- **To guide people through life.** Even today, the ancient Greek myth of Icarus, who died after flying too close to the sun, warns people not to overreach.

Cooperative Learning Activity Think about these functions of myths as you reread "How the World Was Created from a Drop of Milk." Working in small groups, write down all that this myth explains about the natural world. When you have finished, discuss how the myth might also offer guidance for living.

Connect to the Literature

1. **What Do You Think?** Responses will vary.

Think Critically

2. Possible Responses: The first thing that existed was a huge drop of milk. Then the god Doondari created the stone, which created iron, which created fire, which created water, which created air. Then Doondari created man from these five elements.
3. Possible Responses: Students may see chronological relationships—stone was created before air, for example. They may see constituent relationships—man is made of the five elements. They may see hierarchical relationships—worry is stronger than sleep. They may see cause and effect relationships—Doondari created blindness because man was too proud. Accept any reasonable responses.
4. Possible Responses: Physical blindness defeats man in that it makes it more difficult for people to work and protect themselves. Or the myth may refer to humans' inability to see the complete truth, which limits them. Sleep may defeat blindness in that it handicaps all people equally or in that it sends insightful dreams.
5. Possible Responses: because Doondari wanted nothing to be more powerful than he; because a world ruled only by death would be miserable
6. Possible Responses: that humans are prideful; that people who worry cannot sleep; that death ends all worries

Extend Interpretations

7. **What If?** Possible Responses: The world would have been perfect; the world would have been bland; there would have been no death.
8. **Comparing Texts** Possible Responses: The creation stories are similar: little or nothing exists in the beginning; one or more gods create humans from other elements; the creators are dissatisfied with humans, so they make existence harder for humans and let them suffer death.
9. **Connect to Life** Some students may find the myth's explanation of death satisfying; they may be comforted by the idea of death as an end of worry. Other students may find the explanation unsatisfying and prefer alternatives.

To assess skills and concepts taught in this selection, use **Formal Assessment Book,** pp. 89–90.

Literary Analysis

Cooperative Learning Activity
Possible Responses: The myth explains how stone, iron, fire, and water were created; how humans were created; and why there are blindness, sleep, worry, and death. The myth might offer guidance for living in that it warns against becoming too proud or shows that even the most troublesome forces in life can be countered.

Use **Unit Four Resource Book,** p. 17, for more practice.

The FIRST BARD AMONG the SONINKE

Retold by Ousmane Sako and Harold Courlander

Objectives
- understand and appreciate a Soninke **legend (Literary Analysis)**
- identify **cultural values (Active Reading)**

Summary
Long ago, two brothers became lost while hunting. The younger brother was about to die from hunger, but the older brother saved his life by cutting a piece of flesh from his own thigh, cooking it, and giving it to the younger brother to eat. The younger brother figured out what the older had done when he saw his brother's bloody thigh as they were walking toward a distant village. Out of gratitude, he became the older brother's dieli, or bard. He promised that he and his descendants would forever praise and serve the older brother and the brother's descendants. Since then, noble families have had bards.

Use **Unit Four Resource Book,** p. 18, for additional support.

Thematic Link
This legend explains the origin of dieli, who **praise the greatness** of heroes.

5-Minute Warm-Up
Daily Language SkillBuilder

Have students **proofread** the display sentences on page 563h and write them correctly.

Build Background
Soninke Society The Soninke people founded the ancient Ghana empire nearly two thousand years ago. This empire, located in present-day Mali and Mauritania, flourished as a center of trade across the Sahara Desert. Soninke society was divided into several classes. At the bottom were slaves. At the top were ruling families and Islamic officials. Just below the nobility, enjoying high prestige and power, were bards.

The Role of the Bard In many traditional African societies, bards are responsible for preserving the history of their people. They are also storytellers, musicians, praise singers, advisers, and genealogists. The Soninke word for bard, *dieli* (jä' lē), means "singer of family history." In the world of the ancient Soninke, this function was especially important, since people were judged by the prestige of their ancestors as well as by their own accomplishments. Another meaning of dieli is "blood." Read this legend about the origin of the dieli to find out why.

Connect to Your Life
In this story, one person helps another. Think of a time when someone helped you. What would you have done if that person had been hurt in helping you?

Focus Your Reading
LITERARY ANALYSIS: LEGEND

A **legend** is a story that has been handed down from the past and that is popularly believed to be based on historical fact. Legends differ from myths in that they claim to tell about real people and are often set in a particular time and place. Like some myths, however, certain legends explain the origin of social customs and institutions. As you read this legend, note what it explains about Soninke society.

ACTIVE READING: IDENTIFYING CULTURAL VALUES

Legends can reveal much about the cultural values of an ethnic group or nation. For example, the legends of King Arthur and his knights show that bravery, chivalry, and loyalty were admired in medieval England.

READER'S NOTEBOOK As you read the story, jot down actions or practices that are presented as good. Be prepared to infer from them what is valued in Soninke culture.

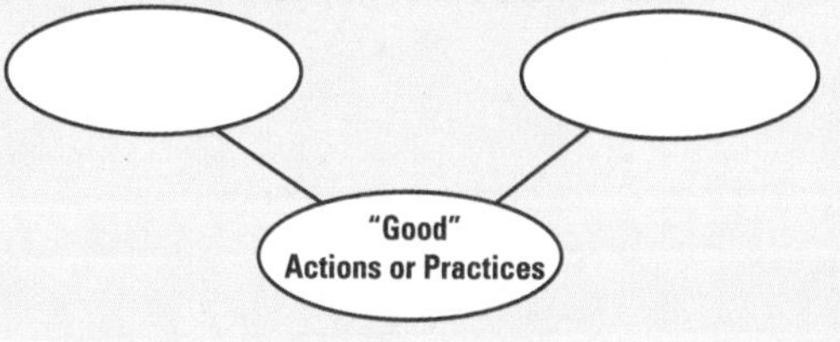

Reading and Analyzing
Literary Analysis LEGEND

A Ask: When and where does this story take place? How realistic do the characters and situation seem?

Possible Responses: The story takes place in the West African bush, in ancient times. The characters seem like ordinary men in a plausible situation.

Use **Unit Four Resource Book,** p. 20, for more practice.

Active Reading
IDENTIFYING CULTURAL VALUES

B Ask: What kind of person does the older brother seem to be?

Possible Responses: caring, patient, responsible, determined, self-sacrificing

Use **Unit Four Resource Book,** p. 19, for more practice.

LESSON RESOURCES
UNIT FOUR RESOURCE BOOK, pp. 18–21

ASSESSMENT RESOURCES
Formal Assessment, pp. 91–92
Teacher's Guide to Assessment and Portfolio Use
Test Generator

INTEGRATED TECHNOLOGY
Visit our Web site: classzone.com

ADDITIONAL RESOURCES
Lesson Planning Guide, pp. 79–80
Teacher's Sourcebook for Language Development

In ancient times there were two brothers who went hunting for game in the bush. They traveled far, but they did not find any game to kill. One, two, three days they were in the bush, hunting, hunting. They did not find anything. They became lost. They did not know how to return to their village. Hunger overtook them. Because it was the dry season, there was no fruit for them to eat. Because they could not find game, they had no meat to eat.

On the fourth day the younger brother said to the older: "My brother, I cannot go any farther. I am too hungry. I have no strength to go on. If I am to die, I will die here."

The older brother answered: "Yes, rest here. You are my younger brother and I do not want you to die. I will go on ahead and try to find a small animal of some kind. Then you will have something to eat. Wait for me. I will come back."

The older brother left the younger and went ahead. He did not find anything. There was no game of any kind. At last he took out his knife and cut a piece of meat from his thigh, and after that he returned to where his younger brother was waiting. He said: "Oh yes! I found a small animal and killed it. I will make a fire. I will cook the meat for you. When you have eaten it, you will feel strong again." He made a fire and cooked the meat. When it was ready, he gave it to the younger brother. The younger brother ate, and his strength returned.

After a while the older brother saw smoke in the distance and knew there must be a village out there. He said: "Oh younger brother, don't

Five terracotta horseback riders. Courtesy of Bernard de Grunne.

HUMANITIES CONNECTION These ancient terracotta horsemen have Soninke scarification marks on their temples. The Soninke and other groups traditionally adorned their bodies with patterns of raised scars.

Customizing Instruction

Less Proficient Readers

Give students a preview of the story's structure. It is a tale of two brothers and how they act toward one another. The brothers are not named, so students should stay aware of which brother is which and think about why they treat each other as they do.

English Learners

Students may not be familiar with the term *bard*. Make sure English learners understand what bards do. (Review the explanation in **Build Background,** if necessary.) You might ask for equivalent words for *bard* in the students' first languages.

Advanced Learners

Talk about modern situations in which someone offers part of his or her body to save another's life. Examples would be blood, kidney, or bone marrow donation. Discuss whether such acts are considered noble in our society.

MINI LESSON Viewing and Representing

Five terracotta horseback riders

ART APPRECIATION Ask students to look at the art and read the **Humanities Connection** on page 629. Thousands of terracotta or bronze sculptures have been found in the Inland Niger Delta region of West Africa, in what is now the modern country of Mali. Many are thought to date from the 10th through 14th centuries, the period when the Ghana empire was declining and the Mali empire was rising.

A large group of terracotta statues portray men on horseback. Often, they are bearded, with decorative scarring on their faces. Daggers are sheathed on their arms and quivers strapped across their backs. The figures were originally painted in bright colors that have worn off over time. Little is known about who made these statues and what they were used for.

Ask students: What guesses would you make about the society that produced these statues?

Possible Responses: It may have been a wealthy society, or at least had a wealthy segment. The weapons indicate that they fought. They valued their horses and liked adorning themselves.

Active Reading
IDENTIFYING CULTURAL VALUES

A Call attention to the sentence, "To give someone your own flesh and blood is the greatest expression of love." Note that this is a direct statement of a Soninke cultural value: self-sacrifice is considered good in this society.
Ask: What other cultural values can you infer from the younger brother's speech?
Possible Responses: It is considered good to show gratitude; to celebrate greatness; to serve others; and to honor and follow the will of one's ancestors.

Literary Analysis LEGEND

B Note that the legend explains a present custom: why bards are called dieli. Ask a student to repeat the explanation. *(Bards are called dieli, or "blood," because they are descended from the brother whose life was saved with a gift of blood.)*
Ask what other present customs are explained by the legend.
Possible Responses: The legend also explains why dieli serve noble families, why they sing and play songs about great deeds of the past, and why the sons of dieli also become dieli.

Henceforth I will be your dieli—
the bard who sings of your great deeds and of
the history of your family.

you see the smoke in the distance? There is a village at that place. Now we will be saved from starvation. I will go ahead to make certain, then I will come back for you."

The younger brother answered: "No, now I feel strong again. I will go with you."

So they started out. They traveled toward the place where the smoke was rising. The older brother kept his bloody thigh covered as best he could, but blood stained his clothing. When the younger brother saw that, he asked: "What is it? What happened to you?" He uncovered the older brother's wound. He touched it. Then he understood everything.

He said: "Yes, my older brother! Now I understand what you have done for me. You saved my life with flesh taken from your thigh. A To give someone your own flesh and blood is the greatest expression of love. Henceforth I will be your dieli—the bard who sings of your great deeds and of the history of your family. Whatever you ask of me, I will do it. I will follow you and serve you. My family will follow your family. My grandson will follow your grandson. My descendants will follow your descendants forever. We will be as slaves to your people until the end of time and sing praises of your noble character."

The younger brother became the slave and bard of the older brother. His descendants became slaves and bards of the older brother's descendants. They were called dieli, meaning blood, because of the older brother's blood gift that had saved the younger brother's life. Because they wished to please their masters, the dieli became accomplished singers and musicians, and they sang stories of times that had passed, of great events and ancestor heroes. To this day the bards pass their knowledge and their songs on to their sons, and the sons become the bards and historians of the family descended from the older brother. B

Of the two brothers who went hunting together in the bush, the younger brother became the first dieli, and ever since that day it has been the custom for noble families to have bards to recall the happenings of ancient days. ❖

MINI LESSON **Vocabulary Strategy**

CONTEXT CLUES: DEFINITION Tell students that definition clues are one type of context clue. Explain that sometimes a writer directly defines a word, especially if the word is likely to be unfamiliar to readers. Definition clues are often signaled by commas or dashes. They may also be signaled by key words and phrases, such as "that is," "in other words," "or," and "also called."

Instruction On the board, copy this model sentence from the story: "They were called dieli, meaning blood, because of the older brother's gift of blood that had saved the younger brother's life."

Ask a volunteer to find the definition clue in this sentence that gives the meaning of the word *dieli.* (clue: "meaning blood") Then point out that the phrase "meaning blood" is set apart from the sentence using commas.

Practice In each sentence below, use the definition clue to write the meaning of the italicized word.

1. The scientists studying air pollution measured the concentration of *particulates,* that is, solid or liquid particles suspended in the air.
2. The settlers reached the *piedmont,* a gently rolling foothill area between a plain and mountains.
3. The house was designed in the form of a *hexagon*—a shape having six angles and six sides—and built on stilts.

A lesson on using context clues appears on p. 674 of the Pupil's Edition.

Connect to the Literature

1. **What Do You Think?** How did you react to the older brother's sacrifice?

Comprehension Check
- What does the older brother do to feed the younger brother?
- How does the younger brother learn where the food came from?
- How does the younger brother reward the older brother?

Think Critically

2. Do you think that the younger brother responds appropriately after he learns how he was saved? Explain.
3. **ACTIVE READING: IDENTIFYING CULTURAL VALUES** Look over the notes you made in your READER'S NOTEBOOK. What can you infer about Soninke values from the things presented as good in this legend?
4. Imagine the storyteller and describe his **tone,** or attitude toward the events he relates.

Extend Interpretations

5. **Comparing Texts** Both "How the World Was Created from a Drop of Milk" and "The First Bard Among the Soninke" tell about origins, or beginnings. Compare the views of human nature in these selections.
6. **Connect to Life** In modern American culture, how might someone who saved a life be rewarded? Would the reward be comparable to the one in this legend?

LITERARY ANALYSIS: LEGEND

A **legend** is a story that has been handed down from the past and that is popularly believed to be based on historical events. Unlike myths, legends claim to tell of real human beings and are often set in a particular time and place. Still, events in legends may be exaggerated; legendary heroes are often larger than life. The stories of King Arthur and Robin Hood are examples of legends.

Some legends explain a tradition or social custom. What does "The First Bard Among the Soninke" explain about the profession of the bard?

Cooperative Learning Activity Working in small groups, create a legend to explain a custom practiced at your school or in society. For example, you might explain why your school honors its particular mascot.

Connect to the Literature

1. **What Do You Think?** Some students may find it noble; others may find it gruesome.

Comprehension Check
- He slices a piece of flesh from his own thigh and cooks it.
- He sees the blood staining his brother's clothing as they travel.
- He becomes the older brother's dieli, or bard, promising that he and his descendants will forever sing praises to his brother and his brother's descendants.

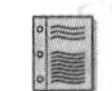
Use Selection Quiz in **Unit Four Resource Book,** p. 21

Think Critically

2. Possible Responses: Some students may think becoming the older brother's dieli is the right thing to do; others may think it is wrong to predetermine how the brothers' descendants will relate to each other.
3. Possible Responses: Students might infer that the Soninke value self-sacrifice, gratitude, nobility, history, music, and lineage.
4. Possible Responses: The speaker's tone is serious and admiring. He speaks as though he is narrating events that actually happened.

Literary Analysis

Possible Response: The legend explains that bardic families and noble families are related, descended from brothers. Bards sing praises to noble families because their ancestor was saved by his brother, an ancestor of the nobles. The sons of bards also become bards because their ancestor promised that his descendants would serve the descendants of the noble brother.

Use **Unit Four Resource Book,** p. 20, for more practice.

Cooperative Learning Activity Remind students that their legends must explain a custom. The explanation does not have to be very plausible, however. Read groups' legends aloud.

Extend Interpretations

5. **Comparing Texts** Possible Responses: The Fulani myth paints humans as too proud, while the Soninke legend paints humans as honorable and self-sacrificing.
6. **Connect to Life** Possible Response: In modern American culture, someone who saved a life might get a medal or monetary payment or might be praised in newspapers or on television. Such a reward might be considered comparable to the one in the Soninke legend because it ensures fame. It might not be considered comparable because it does not require lifelong service from the person saved and his descendants.

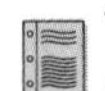
To assess skills and concepts taught in this selection, use **Formal Assessment Book,** pp. 91–92.

This selection is included in the **World Literature InterActive Reader™**.

Objectives

- understand and appreciate a Mandinka **epic (Literary Analysis)**
- recognize and discuss **internal and external conflict (Literary Analysis)**
- use strategies for **predicting (Active Reading)**
- analyze qualities of an **epic hero (Literary Analysis)**

Summary

Sogolon Djata (also called Sundiata), the son of king Nare Maghan, has not learned to walk as other children his age have. It seems unlikely that he will become great, as was foretold. He and his mother, Sogolon Kedjou, are constantly mocked by the king's first wife, Sassouma. After the king dies, Sassouma banishes them to the back yard and installs her own son on the throne. One day, Sassouma insults Sogolon Kedjou when she asks to have some baobab leaves for cooking. In response to his mother's rage, Sogolon Djata decides that he will walk that day and will bring his mother a whole baobab tree. He does so as a crowd watches, and thereafter becomes popular and respected.

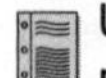
Use **Unit Four Resource Book,** p. 22, for additional support.

Thematic Link

This epic **praises the greatness** of Sundiata Keita, founder of the Mali empire.

Use **Unit Four Resource Book,** p. 26, for practice with Words to Know.

5-Minute Warm-Up

Daily Language SkillBuilder

Have students **proofread** the display sentences on page 563h and write them correctly.

from Sundiata

An Epic of Old Mali

Build Background

Mali's Lion King *Sundiata* is the most famous African epic. It tells the story of Sundiata Keita (so͞on-jä'tä kē'tä), who founded the Mali empire in the 13th century. Although loosely based on historical events, the epic transforms its hero into a legendary figure with extraordinary powers. Like the *Iliad* of Greece and the *Ramayana* of India, *Sundiata* played an important role in shaping a national identity.

The historical Sundiata was also known as Sogolon Djata, Mari Djata, and the Lion of Mali. He came from the royal family of the Mandinka (also called Malinké or Mandingo), who live in the western Sudan region. He rose to power in about 1235, after defeating Soumaoro Kante (kän'tā), king of Sosso. Sundiata created a strong, centralized monarchy with a standing army, which allowed him to expand Mali's territory westward into large gold fields. The empire's capital was at Niani, in present-day Guinea. Mali became the most powerful state in the Sudan, renowned for its prosperity and stable society.

Told by Griots There is no single author of this oral epic, nor is there any fixed version. Trained storytellers known as **griots** (grē-ōz') have adapted it to suit different audiences and occasions. Even today, *Sundiata* is performed frequently in West African villages. The version you will read is a prose adaptation by D. T. Niane, who based his work on the performances of Mamoudou Kouyaté (mä-mo͞o'do͞o ko͞o-yä'-tā), a griot from Guinea. In this version, Niane attempts to capture some of the flavor of the griot's performance.

Recited with Music A performance of *Sundiata* has three components. In addition to reciting the narrative sections of the epic, the griot chants praise poems describing the greatness of the characters. He or she also sings songs to the accompaniment of the *kora* or *balafon* (instruments resembling a harp and a xylophone). Griots must be highly trained to memorize and perform a work as complex as the *Sundiata* epic. In Mandinka society they are greatly respected for their vital role in linking past and present. Mamoudou Kouyaté described griots as "the memory of mankind."

Mali, 13th Century

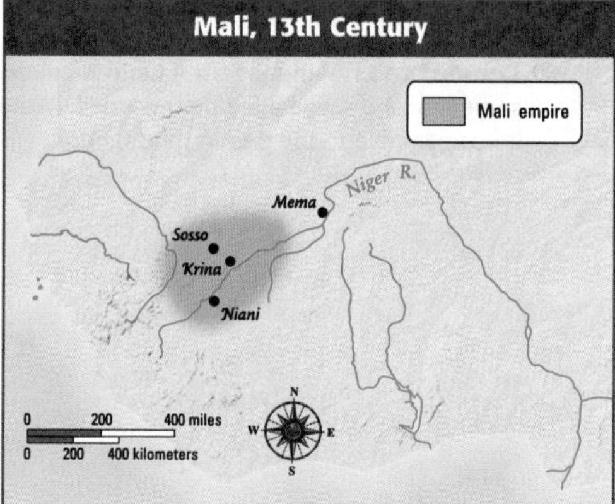

LESSON RESOURCES

UNIT FOUR RESOURCE BOOK, pp. 22–27

ASSESSMENT RESOURCES
Formal Assessment, pp. 93–94
Teacher's Guide to Assessment and Portfolio Use
Test Generator

INTEGRATED TECHNOLOGY
Visit our Web site: classzone.com

ADDITIONAL RESOURCES
Lesson Planning Guide, pp. 81–82
Teacher's Sourcebook for Language Development

The Story of Sundiata

Late-Blooming Hero As a literary character, Sundiata has much in common with other epic heroes. He is the son of King Naré Maghan. His mother is Sogolon Kedjou, the king's second wife. Sogolon is an ugly, hunchbacked "buffalo-woman" whom the king married because of a prophecy that she would give birth to a great ruler. Despite the prophecy, the child Sundiata lags far behind other children and seems destined for failure.

Sassouma Bérété is the king's first wife. She is an ambitious woman who wants to ensure that her own son, Dankaran, inherits the throne. After the king dies, she persuades Dankaran to send Sundiata and his mother into exile. Sundiata travels to various kingdoms and becomes a mighty warrior and adviser to the king of Mema.

Return from Exile After learning that the evil sorcerer Soumaoro Kante has conquered Mali and other kingdoms in the region, Sundiata returns home. He makes alliances with other rulers and attacks Soumaoro on the battlefield at Krina. He kills Soumaoro with a magic arrow tipped with the spur of a white rooster. He then unites the region's kingdoms into a powerful empire, which he rules wisely and justly.

In the following excerpt, you will read about a famous incident from Sundiata's youth involving a baobab tree.

For a humanities activity, click on:

Connect to Your Life

Have you ever had to prove you could do something when others thought you couldn't? What made you prove yourself? How did others respond to you afterward? Share your story with classmates.

Focus Your Reading

LITERARY ANALYSIS: CONFLICT

Conflict is the struggle between opposing forces. An **external conflict** pits a character against some outside force, such as a storm or an enemy soldier. An **internal conflict** occurs within a character. For example, a character may desire something but be afraid to pursue it. As you read, be aware of the conflicts in Sundiata and note which ones are external and which are internal.

ACTIVE READING: PREDICTING

A **prediction** is a guess about what will happen next in a story. When making predictions, take the following things into account:

- details about characters, setting, and events
- **foreshadowing**, or hints about what is going to happen
- your own experience and your knowledge of human behavior

READER'S NOTEBOOK As you read *Sundiata,* create a chart like this one to record your predictions, together with the information or knowledge that led you to make them.

I Predict . . .	Because . . .

WORDS TO KNOW **Vocabulary Preview**

affront, blandly, condiment, derisively, heedless, imperceptibly, innuendo, intrigue, malicious, taciturn

READING FOR INFORMATION

Reading Skills and Strategies
FINDING THE MAIN IDEA

Tell students that the information on the prereading pages answers three main questions:

- Who was the historical Sundiata?
- How is the *Sundiata* epic traditionally performed?
- What is the plot of the epic?

Students should pay attention to the boldfaced subheads, which will help them see which topic is being discussed.

Reading Skills and Strategies
READING A MAP

Direct students to look at the map of the Mali empire on page 632 and note the locations of Niani and other cities mentioned in **Build Background.** Ask: What river runs through the middle of the empire? *(the Niger River)*

TIME MANAGEMENT

If your schedule requires that you cover the lesson objectives in a shorter time, use . . .

- Preparing to Read, pp. 632, 633
- Thinking Through the Literature, p. 640
- Vocabulary in Action, p. 641

If you want to take advantage of longer blocks of class time, use . . .

- TE Teaching Options: Vocabulary Strategy, p. 634; Viewing and Representing, pp. 635, 639; Informal Assessment, p. 636; Grammar, p. 637; Cross-Curricular Link, p. 638
- Choices & Challenges, p. 641

Literary Analysis ORAL EPIC

A Point out that the griot is speaking directly to the people around him, perhaps pointing to different individuals as he speaks.

Literary Analysis CONFLICT

B Ask: What conflicts, or problems, do you see in the story so far?

Possible Responses: Sogolon Djata cannot walk, although he is old enough, and the other children do not like him. Sassouma takes pleasure in goading Sogolon Kedjou about her son's weakness. Both Sogolon and the king want their son to walk, but it seems hopeless.

Use **Unit Four Resource Book,** p. 25, for more practice.

Active Reading PREDICTING

C Ask: What do you predict? Why?

Possible Response: Students will probably predict that Manding Boukari will help his brother Sundiata, who will become a mighty king. Students may reason that in epics, soothsayers' prophecies usually come true.

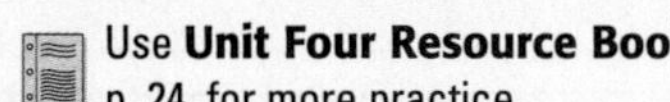

Use **Unit Four Resource Book,** p. 24, for more practice.

from Sundiata: An Epic of Old Mali

Recorded by D. T. Niane

Translated by G. D. Pickett

Childhood

A God has his mysteries which none can fathom. You, perhaps, will be a king. You can do nothing about it. You, on the other hand, will be unlucky, but you can do nothing about that either. Each man finds his way already marked out for him and he can change nothing of it.

1 Sogolon's son[1] had a slow and difficult childhood. At the age of three he still crawled along on all-fours while children of the same age were already walking. He had nothing of the great beauty of his father Naré Maghan.[2] He had a head so big that he seemed unable to support it; he also had large eyes which would open wide whenever anyone entered his mother's house. He was taciturn and used to spend the whole day just sitting in the middle of the house. Whenever his mother went out he would crawl on all-fours to rummage about in the calabashes[3] in search of food, for he was very greedy.

Malicious tongues began to blab. What three-year-old has not yet taken his first steps? What three-year-old is not the despair of his parents through his whims and shifts of mood? What three-year-old is not the joy of his circle through his backwardness in talking? Sogolon Djata[4] (for it was thus that they called him, prefixing his mother's name to his), Sogolon Djata, then, was very different from others of his own age. He spoke little and his severe face never relaxed into a smile. You would have thought that he was already thinking, and what amused children of his age bored him. Often Sogolon would make some of them come to him to keep him company. These children were already walking and she hoped that Djata, seeing his companions walking, would be tempted to do likewise. But nothing came of it. Besides, Sogolon Djata would brain the poor little things with his already strong arms and none of them would come near him any more.

The king's first wife[5] was the first to rejoice 2
at Sogolon Djata's infirmity. Her own son, Dankaran Touman,[6] was already eleven. He was a fine and lively boy, who spent the day running about the village with those of his own age. He had even begun his initiation in the bush.[7] The king had had a bow made for him and he used to go behind the town to practice archery with his companions. Sassouma was quite happy and snapped her fingers at Sogolon, whose child was still crawling on the ground. Whenever the latter happened to pass by her house, she would say, "Come, my son, walk, jump, leap about. The

1. **Sogolon's son:** Sundiata. Sogolon is his mother.
2. **Naré Maghan** (nä-rā′ mä′gäɴ): king of a large territory in Mali.
3. **calabashes** (kăl′ə-bă′shəz): fruits whose dried shells are used to make dishes, bottles, rattles, pipes, and drums.
4. **Sogolon Djata** (sō′gō-lôn′ jä′tä): This, as well as Mari Djata, is an alternate name of Sundiata.
5. **the king's first wife:** Sassouma Bérété (sä′so͞o-mä bā′rā-tā).
6. **Dankaran Touman** (dän-kä′räɴ to͞o′mäɴ).
7. **initiation in the bush:** preparation, through learning tribal history, for becoming a full-fledged member of the tribe.

WORDS TO KNOW

taciturn (tăs′ĭ-tûrn′) *adj.* not talkative
malicious (mə-lĭsh′əs) *adj.* evil; wicked

634

MINI LESSON **Vocabulary Strategy**

PREFIXES AND SUFFIXES Remind students that they can often determine the meaning of unfamiliar words by breaking them down into parts. Three main parts of words are **prefixes**—added to the beginning of words; **suffixes**—added to the end of words; and **base words**—words that can stand alone. Common prefixes include *in-*, *im-*, *pro-*, *pre-*, and *re-*. Common suffixes include *-age*, *-ant*, *-ure*, and *-tion.*

Instruction Show students how to understand the word *imperceptibly,* from the list of Words to Know. Explain that *im-* is a prefix that means "not", *-ly* is a suffix that means "in a (specified) way," and *perceptible* is a base word that means "able to be perceived by the senses or the mind." Have students use the meanings of the word parts to write a definition of *imperceptibly* (in a way that cannot be perceived by the senses or the mind). Point out that the spelling of a base word sometimes changes when a word part is added.

Practice Write the base word and affixes for each word in the list. You may wish to check the spellings of the base words in a dictionary.

1. invisibly *(in-, visible, -ly)*
2. unhelpful *(un-, help, -ful)*
3. movement *(move, -ment)*
4. unimaginable *(un-, imagine, -able)*
5. heedless *(heed, -less)*

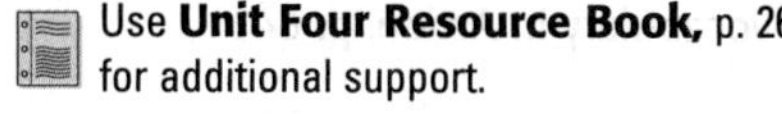

Use **Unit Four Resource Book,** p. 26, for additional support.

A lesson on affixes appears on p. 864 of the Pupil's Edition.

jinn[8] didn't promise you anything out of the ordinary, but I prefer a son who walks on his two legs to a lion that crawls on the ground." She spoke thus whenever Sogolon went by her door. The innuendo would go straight home and then she would burst into laughter, that diabolical laughter which a jealous woman knows how to use so well.

Her son's infirmity weighed heavily upon Sogolon Kedjou; she had resorted to all her
B talent as a sorceress to give strength to her son's legs, but the rarest herbs had been useless. The king himself lost hope.

How impatient man is! Naré Maghan became imperceptibly estranged[9] but Gnankouman Doua never ceased reminding him of the hunter's words.[10] Sogolon became pregnant again. The king hoped for a son, but it was a daughter called Kolonkan. She resembled her mother and had nothing of her father's beauty. The disheartened king debarred Sogolon from his house and she lived in semi-disgrace for a while. Naré Maghan married the daughter of one of his allies, the king of the Kamaras.[11] She was called Namandjé[12] and her beauty was legendary. A year later she brought a boy into the world. When the king consulted soothsayers on the destiny of this son he received the reply that Namandjé's child would be the right hand of some mighty king. The king gave the newly-born
C the name of Boukari. He was to be called Manding Boukari or Manding Bory later on.

Naré Maghan was very perplexed. Could it be that the stiff-jointed son of Sogolon was the one the hunter soothsayer had foretold?

"The Almighty has his mysteries," Gnankouman Doua would say and, taking up
3 the hunter's words, added, "The silk-cotton tree emerges from a tiny seed."

One day Naré Maghan came along to the house of Nounfaïri,[13] the blacksmith seer of Niani. He was an old, blind man. He received the king in the anteroom which served as his workshop. To the king's question he replied, "When the seed germinates growth is not always easy; great trees grow slowly but they plunge their roots deep into the ground." 3

"But has the seed really germinated?" said the king.

"Of course," replied the blind seer. "Only the growth is not as quick as you would like it; how impatient man is."

Terracotta seated figure. The Metropolitan Museum of Art, New York.

HUMANITIES CONNECTION Many sitting, kneeling, or sleeping figures have been found at ancient sites in Mali. Scholars think they might represent prisoners.

8. **jinn:** spirits that have supernatural influence over people.
9. **estranged:** unsympathetic or indifferent.
10. **Gnankouman Doua** (nyän′ko͞o-män do͞o′ä) . . . **the hunter's words:** Gnankouman Doua is the king's griot and chief counselor. A hunter had foretold that the king must marry the ugly Sogolon, who would bear him a great son.
11. **Kamaras** (kä′mä-räs): a clan related to that of Naré Maghan.
12. **Namandjé** (nä-män′jā).
13. **Nounfaïri** (no͞o-fä′rē).

WORDS TO KNOW

innuendo (ĭn′yo͞o-ĕn′dō) *n.* an indirect hint or reference, usually negative
imperceptibly (ĭm′pər-sĕp′tə-blē) *adv.* in a barely noticeable way

Customizing Instruction

Less Proficient Readers

1 Explain that the main character, Sundiata, is called by several different names: Sogolon's son, son of Sogolon, Sogolon Djata, Mari Djata, and Djata.

2 Clarify that the king, Nare Maghan, has two wives. His first wife is Sassouma Berete, whose son is Dankaran Touman. The king's second wife is Sogolon Kedjou, whose son is Sogolon Djata.

Use the Glossary in **Unit Four Resource Book,** p. 23, for additional support.

3 Help students relate the proverbs to the characters' situation. Explain that the silk-cotton tree is a huge tree that can grow to be 200 feet high. Discuss the idea expressed by the proverb—that something small can grow to be great. You might repeat the similar English proverb, "Mighty oaks from little acorns grow."

Ask: Who is like a tiny seed? *(Sogolon Djata)*

Ask: What is Nounfaïri really trying to tell the king? *(that Sogolon Djata will grow up to be great, but it will take time)*

English Learners

Ask students if they can guess from context the meaning of *infirmity* ("weakness") and *soothsayers* ("people who predict the future").

Advanced Learners

If students have read *Oedipus the King* in Unit 2, have them compare Nounfaïri with Teiresias, the blind soothsayer from the play.

MINI LESSON Viewing and Representing

Terracotta seated figure

ART APPRECIATION Have students look at the sculpture and read the **Humanities Connection** on page 635. Scholar Bernard de Grunne has proposed another theory about these terracotta figures. He spoke to people still living in the area where the terracottas were found, and they told him that the figures represented ancestor gods and ancient kings to which people prayed and made sacrifices. As they prayed to a figure, people were supposed to copy its posture and gestures. A certain position might mean a request for children; another might mean a request to harm an enemy, for example.

Another scholar, Roderick J. McIntosh, warns that it is almost impossible to learn what the statues meant to people living many centuries ago simply by asking people who are alive today. He complains that because most of the statues were looted from sites and not scientifically excavated, useful information about their age, location, and context has been lost.

Ask students to come up with other theories about what this statue represents or what it was used for.

Reading and Analyzing

Reading Skills and Strategies
MAKING INFERENCES

A Ask: Why do you think the king and Doua are so confident?
Possible Response: because the young Sundiata acts mature and kingly

Literary Analysis CONFLICT

B Ask: What conflicts are made clear in this passage?
Possible Responses: The king intended for Mari Djata to have the throne, but Sassouma Berete has taken power. Mari Djata has a great destiny but may be kept from fulfilling it. Sassouma is persecuting Sogolon.

Literary Analysis
CHARACTERIZATION

C Ask students how they would explain Sassouma's behavior.
Possible Responses: She is jealous of Sogolon; she wants to make sure she stays in power; she is just plain mean.

Active Reading PREDICTING

D Ask: What do you predict Mari Djata will do? Why?
Possible Responses: He will walk and will bring his mother a whole baobab tree. It seems likely that he will do this because he declares it matter-of-factly, not boastfully.

1 This interview and Doua's confidence gave the king some assurance. To the great displeasure of Sassouma Bérété the king restored Sogolon to favor and soon another daughter was born to her. She was given the name of Djamarou.[14]

However, all Niani talked of nothing else but the stiff-legged son of Sogolon. He was now seven and he still crawled to get about. In spite of all the king's affection, Sogolon was in despair. Naré Maghan aged and he felt his time coming to an end. Dankaran Touman, the son of Sassouma Bérété, was now a fine youth.

One day Naré Maghan made Mari Djata come to him and he spoke to the child as one speaks to an adult. "Mari Djata, I am growing old and soon I shall be no more among you, but before death takes me off I am going to give you the present each king gives his successor. In Mali every prince has his own griot.[15] Doua's father was my father's griot, Doua is mine and the son of Doua, Balla Fasséké[16] here, will be your griot. Be inseparable friends from this day forward. From his mouth you will hear the history of your ancestors, you will learn the art of governing Mali according to the principles which our ancestors have bequeathed to us. I have served my term and done my duty too. I have done everything which a king of Mali ought to do. I am handing an enlarged kingdom over to you and I leave you sure allies. May your destiny be accomplished, but never forget that Niani is your capital and Mali the cradle of your ancestors."

The child, as if he had understood the whole meaning of the king's words, beckoned Balla Fasséké to approach. He made room for him on the hide he was sitting on and then said, "Balla, you will be my griot."

"Yes, son of Sogolon, if it pleases God," replied Balla Fasséké.

The king and Doua exchanged glances that radiated confidence. **A**

The Lion's Awakening

A short while after this interview between Naré Maghan and his son the king died. Sogolon's son was no more than seven years old. The council of elders met in the king's palace. It was no use Doua's defending the king's will which reserved the throne for Mari Djata, for the council took no account of Naré Maghan's wish. With the help of Sassouma Bérété's intrigues, Dankaran Touman was proclaimed king and a regency council[17] was formed in which the queen mother was all-powerful. A short time after, Doua died.

As men have short memories, Sogolon's son was spoken of with nothing but irony and scorn. People had seen one-eyed kings, one-armed kings, and lame kings, but a stiff-legged king had never been heard tell of. No matter how great the destiny promised for Mari Djata might be, the throne could not be given to someone who had no power in his legs; if the jinn loved him, let them begin by giving him the use of his legs. Such were the remarks that Sogolon heard every day. The queen mother, Sassouma Bérété, was the source of all this gossip.

Having become all-powerful, Sassouma Bérété persecuted Sogolon because the late Naré Maghan had preferred her. She banished Sogolon and her son to a back yard of the palace. Mari Djata's mother now occupied an old hut which had served as a lumber-room of Sassouma's.

The wicked queen mother allowed free passage to all those inquisitive people who wanted to see the child that still crawled at the age of

14. **Djamarou** (jä'-mä-ro͞o).
15. **griot** (grē-ō'): an advisor, oral historian, and praise-singer.
16. **Balla Fasséké** (bä'lä fä-sā-kā').
17. **regency council:** group chosen to rule in place of a monarch who is too young to assume control.

WORDS TO KNOW
intrigue (ĭn'trēg') *n.* secret scheme; plot

Assessment Informal Assessment

Stop students after they finish the first section, "Childhood." Ask them to imagine that *Sundiata* is being shown as a miniseries, with a recap before each new episode. ("Last week, on *Sundiata* . . .") What three scenes would they show from this episode to summarize what has happened before showing the next episode, "The Lion's Awakening"?

After discussion of their choices, have students come up with three important questions raised in this episode that they think will be answered later in the story.

seven. Nearly all the inhabitants of Niani filed into the palace and the poor Sogolon wept to see herself thus given over to public ridicule. Mari Djata took on a ferocious look in front of the crowd of sightseers. Sogolon found a little consolation only in the love of her eldest daughter, Kolonkan. She was four and she could walk. She seemed to understand all her mother's miseries and already she helped her with the housework. Sometimes, when Sogolon was attending to the chores, it was she who stayed beside her sister Djamarou, quite small as yet.

Sogolon Kedjou and her children lived on the queen mother's left-overs, but she kept a little garden in the open ground behind the village. It was there that she passed her brightest moments looking after her onions and gnougous. One day she happened to be short of condiments and went to the queen mother to beg a little baobab leaf.[18]

"Look you," said the malicious Sassouma, "I have a calabash full. Help yourself, you poor woman. As for me, my son knew how to walk at seven and it was he who went and picked these baobab leaves. Take them then, since your son is unequal to mine." Then she laughed derisively with that fierce laughter which cuts through your flesh and penetrates right to the bone.

Sogolon Kedjou was dumbfounded. She had never imagined that hate could be so strong in a human being. With a lump in her throat she left Sassouma's. Outside her hut Mari Djata, sitting on his useless legs, was blandly eating out of a calabash. Unable to contain herself any longer, Sogolon burst into sobs and seizing a piece of wood, hit her son.

"Oh son of misfortune, will you never walk? Through your fault I have just suffered the greatest affront of my life! What have I done, God, for you to punish me in this way?"

Mari Djata seized the piece of wood and, looking at his mother, said, "Mother, what's the matter?"

"Shut up, nothing can ever wash me clean of this insult."

"But what then?"

"Sassouma has just humiliated me over a matter of a baobab leaf. At your age her own son could walk and used to bring his mother baobab leaves."

"Cheer up, Mother, cheer up."

"No. It's too much. I can't."

"Very well then, I am going to walk today," said Mari Djata. "Go and tell my father's smiths to make me the heaviest possible iron rod. Mother, do you want just the leaves of the baobab or would you rather I brought you the whole tree?"

"Ah, my son, to wipe out this insult I want the tree and its roots at my feet outside my hut."

Balla Fasséké, who was present, ran to the master smith, Farakourou,[19] to order an iron rod.

Sogolon had sat down in front of her hut. She was weeping softly and holding her head between her two hands. Mari Djata went calmly back to his calabash of rice and began eating again as if nothing had happened. From time to time he looked up discreetly at his mother who was murmuring in a low voice, "I want the whole tree, in front of my hut, the whole tree."

All of a sudden a voice burst into laughter behind the hut. It was the wicked Sassouma telling one of her serving women about the scene of humiliation and she was laughing loudly so that Sogolon could hear. Sogolon fled into the hut

18. **gnougous** (nyōō′gōōz) . . . **baobab** (bā′ō-băb) **leaf:** Gnougous are African food plants. The baobab is a tree whose leaves are used for seasoning.

19. **Farakourou** (fä-rä-kōō′rōō).

WORDS TO KNOW

condiment (kŏn′də-mənt) *n.* a spice or other substance used as a seasoning
derisively (dĭ-rī′sĭv-lē) *adv.* in a mocking or jeering manner
blandly (blănd′lē) *adv.* in an easygoing, unconcerned way
affront (ə-frŭnt′) *n.* an open insult

Customizing Instruction

English Learners

1 Students may associate the term *interview* with questioning by employers or reporters. Explain that an interview can also be any formal, face-to-face meeting.

Less Proficient Readers

2 Clarify that although the king meant for Mari Djata to take the throne, it is given to Dankaran instead. Dankaran's mother, Sassouma, will rule until Dankaran is old enough.

Advanced Learners

3 Discuss why the people will not allow someone who cannot walk to be king. Ask students if they think someone who cannot walk could be elected president of the United States.

MINI LESSON Grammar

MODIFIERS IN COMPARISONS

Instruction Adjectives and adverbs can be used to compare two or more things. There are three degrees of comparison: positive, comparative, and superlative.

Positive The king is tall.

Comparative The king is taller than the prince.

Superlative The king is the tallest person in the kingdom.

Regular and Irregular Comparisons Most modifiers change in regular ways to show comparison. *–Er* and *–est* (as in *tall, taller, tallest*) are the most common endings. However, sometimes *more* and *most* are used, particularly with words of more than two syllables and with words that end in *ly.* (*more* expensive, *most* kindly) Some modifiers have irregular comparative and superlative forms. Common examples include *good, better, best; much, more, most; bad, worse, worst.*

Practice For each sentence, write the correct comparative or superlative form.

1. This prince is the (brighter, brightest) of the three students. *(brightest)*
2. Mari Djata turned out to be (stronger, strongest) than his rival. *(stronger)*
3. The baobob tree is the (more important, most important) tree in the kingdom. *(most important)*
4. Sogolon was (angrier, more angry) than ever before. *(angrier)*

For more instruction and practice in using modifiers, use McDougal Littell's ***Language Network:***

- Grade 10, Chapter 9, "Using Modifiers"
- Grade 12, Chapter 7, "Using Modifiers"

Active Reading PREDICTING

A Ask: What do you think Mari Djata will do with the iron bar?

Possible Responses: He will lift it; he will use it as a walking stick; he will threaten Sassouma with it.

Literary Analysis GRIOT

B Have students notice the role of Sundiata's griot, Balla Fasséké. He encourages the prince and sings praise songs celebrating his actions before the crowd. Later, he will do the same thing when Sundiata fights Soumaoro at the battle of Krina.

Literary Analysis CONFLICT

C Ask: Why did the queen mother have no more peace of mind after Sogolon Djata walked?

Possible Responses: She may have feared that Sogolon Djata would take the throne and end her power; she may have feared that he would punish her for insulting his mother.

and hid her face under the blankets so as not to have before her eyes this heedless boy, who was more preoccupied with eating than with anything else. With her head buried in the bed-clothes Sogolon wept and her body shook violently. Her daughter, Sogolon Djamarou, had come and sat down beside her and she said, "Mother, Mother, don't cry. Why are you crying?"

Mari Djata had finished eating and, dragging himself along on his legs, he came and sat under the wall of the hut for the sun was scorching. What was he thinking about? He alone knew.

1 The royal forges were situated outside the walls and over a hundred smiths worked there. The bows, spears, arrows and shields of Niani's warriors came from there. When Balla Fasséké came to order the iron rod, Farakourou said to him, "The great day has arrived then?"

A "Yes. Today is a day like any other, but it will see what no other day has seen."

The master of the forges, Farakourou, was the son of the old Nounfaïri, and he was a soothsayer like his father. In his workshops there was an enormous iron bar wrought by his father Nounfaïri. Everybody wondered what this bar was destined to be used for. Farakourou called six of his apprentices and told them to carry the iron bar to Sogolon's house.

When the smiths put the gigantic iron bar down in front of the hut the noise was so frightening that Sogolon, who was lying down, jumped up with a start. Then Balla Fasséké, son of Gnankouman Doua, spoke.

"Here is the great day, Mari Djata. I am speaking to you, Maghan,[20] son of Sogolon. The waters of the Niger can efface[21] the stain from the body, but they cannot wipe out an insult. Arise, young lion, roar, and may the bush know that from henceforth it has a master."

The apprentice smiths were still there, Sogolon had come out and everyone was watching Mari Djata. He crept on all-fours and came to the iron bar. Supporting himself on his knees and one hand, with the other hand he picked up the iron bar without any effort and stood it up vertically. Now he was resting on nothing but his knees and held the bar with both his hands. A deathly silence had gripped all those present. Sogolon Djata closed his eyes, held tight, the muscles in his arms tensed. With a violent jerk he threw his weight on to it and his knees left the ground. Sogolon Kedjou was all eyes and watched her son's legs which were trembling as though from an electric shock. Djata was sweating and the sweat ran from his brow. In a great effort he straightened up and was on his feet at one go—but the great bar of iron was twisted and had taken the form of a bow!

Then Balla Fasséké sang out the "Hymn to the Bow," striking up with his powerful voice: B

"Take your bow, Simbon,[22]
Take your bow and let us go.
Take your bow, Sogolon Djata."

When Sogolon saw her son standing she stood dumb for a moment, then suddenly she sang these words of thanks to God who had given her son the use of his legs:

"Oh day, what a beautiful day,
Oh day, day of joy;
Allah Almighty, you never created a finer day.
So my son is going to walk!"

Standing in the position of a soldier at ease, Sogolon Djata, supported by his enormous rod, was sweating great beads of sweat. Balla Fasséké's song had alerted the whole palace and people came running from all over to see what had happened, and each stood bewildered before

20. **Maghan:** name relating Sundiata to his father.

21. **efface** (ĭ-fās′): to rub out; erase.

22. **Simbon:** a title used for a great hunter.

WORDS TO KNOW

heedless (hēd′lĭs) *adj.* thoughtless; unmindful

Music

THE SOSSO-BALA The Sosso-Bala is a balafon (an instrument like a xylophone) believed to have been owned by Soumaoro Kante, the Sosso king that Sundiata defeated in 1235. According to legend, Soumaoro stole Sundiata's griot, Balla Fasséké, and made him praise Soumaoro on this instrument. Sundiata claimed it as a war trophy after his victory.

The instrument still exists and is considered a sacred symbol of the Mande people. Kept in the village of Niagassola, in present-day Guinea, it is cared for by descendants of Balla Fasséké and played only on special occasions. It left the country for the first time in 1996, to be played in Paris for the 90th birthday of Senegalese president Leopold Sedar Senghor (see page 1182). In May 2001, UNESCO declared "the cultural space of the Sosso-Bala" to be one of 19 "masterpieces of the oral and intangible heritage of humanity." Other cultural forms on its list included Georgian polyphonic singing and Japanese Nogaku theatre.

Sogolon's son. The queen mother had rushed there and when she saw Mari Djata standing up she trembled from head to foot. After recovering his breath Sogolon's son dropped the bar and the crowd stood to one side. His first steps were those of a giant. Balla Fasséké fell into step and pointing his finger at Djata, he cried:

"Room, room, make room!
The lion has walked;
Hide antelopes,
Get out of his way."

Behind Niani there was a young baobab tree and it was there that the children of the town came to pick leaves for their mothers. With all his might the son of Sogolon tore up the tree and
2 put it on his shoulders and went back to his mother. He threw the tree in front of the hut and said, "Mother, here are some baobab leaves for you. From henceforth it will be outside your hut that the women of Niani will come to stock up."

C Sogolon Djata walked. From that day forward the queen mother had no more peace of mind. But
3 what can one do against destiny? Nothing. Man, under the influence of certain illusions, thinks he can alter the course which God has mapped out, but everything he does falls into a higher order which he barely understands. That is why Sassouma's efforts were vain against Sogolon's son, everything she did lay in the child's destiny. Scorned the day before and the object of public ridicule, now Sogolon's son was as popular as he
4 had been despised. The multitude loves and fears strength. All Niani talked of nothing but Djata; the mothers urged their sons to become hunting companions of Djata and to share his games, as if they wanted their offspring to profit from the nascent glory of the buffalo-woman's son.[23] The words of Doua on the name-giving day[24] came back to men's minds and Sogolon was now surrounded with much respect; in conversation people were fond of contrasting Sogolon's modesty with the pride and malice of Sassouma Bérété. It was because the former had been an exemplary wife and mother that God had granted strength to her son's legs for, it was said, the more a wife loves and respects her husband and the more she suffers for her child, the more valorous will the child be one day. Each is the child of his mother; the child is worth no more than the mother is worth. It was not astonishing that the king Dankaran Touman was so colorless, for his mother had never shown the slightest respect to her husband and never, in the presence of the late king, did she show that humility which every wife should show before her husband. People recalled her scenes of jealousy and the spiteful remarks she circulated about her co-wife and her child. And people would conclude gravely, "Nobody knows God's mystery. The snake has no legs yet it is as swift as any other animal that has four." ❖

HUMANITIES CONNECTION Many ancient terracotta figures from Mali depict proud horsemen—whether mythical ancestors or conquering warlords, no one is sure.

Terracotta horse and rider. Werner Forman Archive. Courtesy Entwistle Gallery, London.

23. **nascent** (năs′ənt) . . . **the buffalo-woman's son:** Sogolon, Sundiata's mother, had a buffalo for a totem. A totem is a family emblem and protector. Nascent means "emerging."

24. **the words of Doua on the name-giving day:** Gnankouman Doua had stated that Sundiata would be the first of a great line of kings.

Customizing Instruction

English Learners

1 Explain that a *forge* is a workshop where metal tools are made, a smith is a metalworker, and *apprentices* are people who are learning skills.

Less Proficient Readers

2 Ask: What does it mean that Sundiata bends the iron bar into a bow and that he brings a baobab tree to his mother's hut? *(It means that he is exceptionally strong.)*

3 Call attention to the line "But what can one do against destiny? Nothing." Remind students that at the beginning of the excerpt it was stated, "Each man finds his way already marked out for him and he can change nothing of it." Ask students to restate this idea in their own words. Then ask what in the story supports this idea.
Possible Responses: It was predicted that Sundiata would be great; even though he could not walk and was scorned by others, he proved himself great eventually.

Advanced Learners

4 Point out the line, "The multitude loves and fears strength." Have a volunteer explain this statement in his or her own words. Discuss whether this is true of people, asking students to support their opinions with examples.

MINI LESSON Viewing and Representing

Terracotta horse and rider

ART APPRECIATION Have the class study the art and read the **Humanities Connection** on page 639. Tell students that many family names in Mali are related to horses. Cissé means "horseman"; Kalé means "spotless horse"; Souwaré means "dappled horse."

Ask: How is this terracotta horseman different in style from the terracotta figure on page 635? What might account for the differences? How well do the figures work as illustrations for the story?

Possible Responses: The horseman's bodily features are sharper and more detailed; he is more decorated; he looks more proud. The figures may differ because they were made at different times, by different ethnic groups, or for different purposes. To some students, the figures may work well as illustrations because they suggest a dejected person who cannot walk (which Sundiata once was) and a proud warrior (which is what he became). To other students, the figures may not work well as illustrations because they are not specific enough to the story.

Connect to the Literature

1. **What Do You Think?** Were you surprised by Sundiata's actions after his mother is insulted? Why or why not?

Comprehension Check
- Why is Sundiata scorned as a young boy?
- How does Sassouma treat Sundiata and his mother after the king's death?
- How does Sundiata change the people's opinion of him?

Think Critically

2. **ACTIVE READING: PREDICTING** How accurate were the predictions you made in your READER'S NOTEBOOK? Discuss with classmates the details that either helped or misled you.
3. Describe how Sundiata changes from the beginning of the selection to the end. What do you think makes him change?
4. How would you compare Sogolon Kedjou and Sassouma?

- their relationship with the king
- their treatment of others
- the narrator's comments about them

5. Based on what you have read in *Sundiata,* which qualities do you think were most admired in traditional Mandinka society? Support your answer with details from the story.

Extend Interpretations

6. **The Writer's Style** How well does the recorder, D. T. Niane, convey the sense that a griot is performing the epic for an audience? Discuss what an actual griot would be able to do that the written text cannot do.
7. **Connect to Life** Do you agree with the ideas about life expressed in this epic? For example, do you agree that a person cannot change his or her fate, or that a child is worth no more than its mother?

LITERARY ANALYSIS: CONFLICT

Conflict is the struggle between opposing forces. **External conflict** occurs when a character is pitted against an outside force, such as another character, a physical obstacle, or an aspect of nature or society. **Internal conflict** occurs when the struggle takes place within a character. In this excerpt from *Sundiata,* for example, Naré Maghan is torn between his wish to believe the prophecies about Sundiata's future greatness and doubts raised by Sundiata's appearance and behavior. The selection also has numerous examples of external conflict, such as the rivalry between Sogolon Kedjou and Sassouma.

Paired Activity With a classmate, review external and internal conflicts in the selection. Fill in a chart like the one below, indicating which opposing forces are involved in each conflict and how the conflict is resolved, if it is.

Conflict	External or Internal?	Resolution

REVIEW: EPIC HERO

An **epic hero** is usually someone of high social status who performs courageous and sometimes even superhuman deeds. Epic heroes generally reflect the ideals and values of their culture. With a small group of classmates, discuss Sundiata's heroic qualities. Compare his experiences and deeds with those of other epic heroes, such as Rama, Arjuna, and Aeneas. Refer to the background on page 633.

Connect to the Literature

1. **What Do You Think?** Responses will vary. Make sure students explain their reactions.

Comprehension Check
- Sundiata is scorned because he cannot walk, is unattractive, and does not speak or smile.
- Sassouma banishes Sundiata and his mother to an old hut, ridicules them, and allows others to do the same.
- Sundiata changes the people's opinion of him by walking and then pulling up a baobab tree.

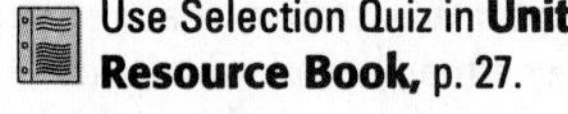
Use Selection Quiz in **Unit Four Resource Book,** p. 27.

Think Critically

2. Responses will vary. Students might point to the blacksmith's proverb about the silk-cotton tree, the section title "The Lion's Awakening," and Sundiata's asking his mother whether she wants the whole baobab tree as signs that Sundiata will show greatness.
3. Possible Responses: Sundiata changes from the slow, awkward butt of jokes to a strong, commanding, popular leader. Students may say that he changes because it is his destiny or because he wants to end his mother's humiliation.
4. Possible Responses: Sogolon is modest, respectful to her husband, and vulnerable to humiliation, while Sassouma is hateful, scheming, and disrespectful to her husband.
5. Possible Responses: The Mandinka appear to have admired modesty, beauty, strength, acceptance of fate, respect for authority, and devotion to children.

Extend Interpretations

6. **The Writer's Style** Students may think that the text gives the sense of performance by including direct comments to an audience, such as "You, perhaps, will be a king," and by including songs such as "Hymn to the Bow" and proverbs that relate the story to daily life. Students may note that an actual griot could provide music, mimic actions and voices, and adjust the story to the people around him.
7. **Connect to Life** Some students may disagree that people cannot change their fate or that a wife's respect for her husband determines a child's worth. They may find it easier to agree that human beings are impatient, that no one can understand God's mysteries, or that people love and fear strength.

Literary Analysis

Paired Activity One external conflict Sogolon faces is Sassouma's repeated humiliation. An external conflict Sundiata faces is his mother's anger at his inability to walk. These conflicts are resolved when Sundiata walks and shows his true strength. Sassouma faces an external conflict after Sundiata walks and becomes popular with the people. Her power to rule is threatened. This conflict is unresolved at the end of the excerpt.

Use **Unit Four Resource Book,** p. 25, for more practice.

Epic Hero Possible Responses: Sundiata is like other epic heroes in that he is unfairly banished and deprived of his kingdom; he is wise and calm with superhuman strength; he defeats an evil opponent; he rules or establishes a great kingdom; he fulfills the destiny that has been foretold for him.

Writing Options

1. Character Analysis How can you tell, just from this brief excerpt, that Sundiata will grow up to be a great hero? In a short essay, describe the heroic characteristics that he shows. Place the essay in your **Working Portfolio.**

Writing Handbook
See page R33: Analysis.

2. Evaluation of Themes The griot Mamoudou Kouyaté stated, "I teach kings the history of the ancestors so that the lives of the ancients might serve them as an example." Write a few paragraphs explaining how this episode from *Sundiata* does or does not offer good lessons for modern people.

3. Biographical Article Perhaps Sundiata reminds you of someone else who proved his or her worth after being ridiculed. If so, write a biographical article recounting this person's triumph. Place the paper in your **Working Portfolio.**

Activities & Explorations

1. Griot's Performance Perform part of this selection as you think a griot might have performed it. Add appropriate music and gestures. Encourage your audience to respond with comments such as "That's true" and "Indeed." Look back at page 618 to see how griots look, and, if you like, dress the part.
~ SPEAKING AND LISTENING

2. Movie Review If possible, view *Keita: Heritage of the Griot,* a film by West African director Dani Kouyaté that dramatizes the *Sundiata* epic. Afterward, discuss how closely the film conforms to what you imagined and how it presents the griot's role.
~ VIEWING AND REPRESENTING

Inquiry & Research

1. Modern Griots Do research on contemporary musicians from West Africa who perform in the griot tradition, such as Foday Musa Suso, Salif Keita, and Boubacar Traoré. Bring in recordings of their music to share with the class.

2. Ancient Mali Work in a small group to find out more about the ancient Mali empire. Give oral reports on various topics related to the empire—for example, the pilgrimage of ruler Mansa Musa or the description of Mali given by Berber traveler Ibn Battuta.

Vocabulary in Action

EXERCISE: RELATED WORDS Write the letter of the word in each set that is not related in meaning to the other words in the set.

1. (a) plot, (b) intrigue, (c) gathering, (d) scheme
2. (a) wicked, (b) confused, (c) malicious, (d) harmful
3. (a) salt, (b) potato, (c) ketchup, (d) condiment
4. (a) hurriedly, (b) blandly, (c) unworriedly, (d) casually
5. (a) compliment, (b) praise, (c) honor, (d) affront
6. (a) derisively, (b) mockingly, (c) simply, (d) sarcastically
7. (a) impossibly, (b) unnoticeably, (c) scarcely, (d) imperceptibly
8. (a) heedless, (b) unconcerned, (c) blameless, (d) unaware
9. (a) enthusiastic, (b) quiet, (c) taciturn, (d) withdrawn
10. (a) insinuation, (b) innuendo, (c) implication, (d) incompetence

Building Vocabulary
For an in-depth lesson on word connotation and denotation, see page 1090.

Vocabulary in Action

1. c	6. c
2. b	7. a
3. b	8. c
4. a	9. a
5. d	10. d

To assess skills and concepts taught in this selection, use **Formal Assessment Book,** pp. 93–94.

Writing Options

1. **Character Analysis** Encourage students to meet in pairs to discuss Sundiata's heroic characteristics before they begin to write. As well as Sundiata's own actions, they should consider others' reactions to him.
2. **Evaluation of Themes** First, hold a brief class discussion. Ask: Is there anything from this story that you would apply to your own life, or is the world of the story too foreign? After about ten minutes, cut students off and have them start writing.
3. **Biographical Article** You might bring in models of such articles from *People* or other magazines. Allow time for students to interview their subjects to get quotes that will bring the story to life.

Activities & Explorations

1. **Griot's Performance** Perhaps you might invite a drama teacher or a professional storyteller to speak to students about bringing stories to life.
2. **Movie Review** *Keita: Heritage of the Griot* is available from
California Newsreel
149 Ninth Street
San Francisco, CA 94103
(415) 621-6196

Inquiry and Research

1. **Modern Griots** Students might start their research with *The Rough Guide to World Music: Africa, Europe, and the Middle East* by Simon Broughton. Or they might browse the African music section in a large record store, looking specifically for performers from Mali and Guinea.
2. **Ancient Mali** Encyclopedias that might be helpful include *Africana*, edited by Kwame Appiah and Henry Louis Gates, and *Africa South of the Sahara,* by Europa Publications. Translations of Ibn Battuta's travelogue include *The Adventures of Ibn Battuta* by Ross E. Dunn and *Ibn Battuta in Black Africa*, edited by Said Hamdun and Noël King.

Objectives

- appreciate Yoruba **praise songs (Literary Analysis)**
- recognize techniques of **characterization** in praise songs **(Literary Analysis)**
- **synthesize** information to develop an overall impression **(Active Reading)**

Thematic Link

These praise songs **praise the greatness** of orishas, or Yoruba gods.

5-Minute Warm-Up

Daily Language SkillBuilder

Have students **proofread** the display sentences on page 563i and write them correctly.

Build Background

Songs That Celebrate Praise songs are one of the most common forms of poetry in West Africa. Bards or griots perform them in public to honor gods, kings, and other important figures. Often the songs are composed spontaneously. Praise songs usually describe their subjects' deeds and qualities in glowing terms. The praise may be mixed with criticism, however, if the singer wants to challenge leaders to live up to their responsibilities. In the Yoruba (yôr'ə-bə) language, praise songs are called *oriki* (ō-rē'kē). Most Yoruba have a personal praise song, which on formal occasions is used to announce their arrival. The most poetic and complex oriki are those dedicated to the *orishas* (ō-rē'shäz), or gods.

Yoruba Religion Although many Yoruba are Christian or Muslim, the traditional Yoruba religion is still widely practiced. In the traditional Yoruba religion, Olorun (ō-lō-ro͝on') or Olodumare (ō-lō'do͞o-mä-rā') is the supreme being. Yet no shrines are dedicated to him, nor is he honored with offerings and other rituals. Because he is such a remote and incomprehensible figure, worshipers turn to the orishas, a group of lesser gods.

Yoruba myths about orishas vary. Some orishas are thought of as notable humans who were given divine status after death. The orishas personify forces of nature. Each one is associated with particular colors and materials. According to tradition, there are 401 orishas. Many are local gods; others are worshiped throughout Yoruba lands. Following are some of the principal orishas.

Orisha	Qualities
Obatala (ō-bä'tä-lä)	Creator god who formed the earth and human beings. People with hunchbacks and other deformities are sacred to him, because he made them while drunk.
Shango (shän'gō)	God of thunder. Quick-tempered, but generous to his followers.
Oshun (ō-so͞on')	Beautiful river goddess and healer. Kind, gentle, and motherly, she can make women fertile.
Ogun (ō-go͞on')	God of iron and war. Personifies creative and destructive forces.
Eshu (ā-so͞o')	Trickster god. Carries messages between the gods and humankind.

LESSON RESOURCES

UNIT FOUR RESOURCE BOOK, pp. 28–29

ASSESSMENT RESOURCES
Formal Assessment, pp. 95–96
Teacher's Guide to Assessment and Portfolio Use
Test Generator

INTEGRATED TECHNOLOGY
Visit our Web site: classzone.com

ADDITIONAL RESOURCES
Lesson Planning Guide, pp. 83–84
Teacher's Sourcebook for Language Development

Connect to Your Life

In these songs, the speakers praise Yoruba gods. Think of poems, prayers, or songs from your own culture that praise God or great leaders. What qualities are glorified in these poems or songs?

Focus Your Reading

LITERARY ANALYSIS: CHARACTERIZATION

The term **characterization** refers to the techniques that writers use to develop characters. Characters may be portrayed through

- physical description
- their speech, thoughts, feelings, and actions
- other characters' reactions to them
- direct comments by the narrator or speaker

As you read each praise song, imagine that it is being recited aloud, about a character. Look for images in the song that give you a sense of the orisha's personality.

ACTIVE READING: SYNTHESIZING

When you put together ideas and information to reach a conclusion or achieve some kind of insight, you are **synthesizing.** For example, you might look for patterns in a literary work or connect something in the work with background information already learned. Synthesizing is necessary for you to truly understand what you read.

READER'S NOTEBOOK As you read each praise song, create a word web for the orisha it describes. Fill in the web with words or phrases from the song that offer clues to the orisha's character. Also include information from the Build Background section or the sidenotes that adds to your understanding of the orisha.

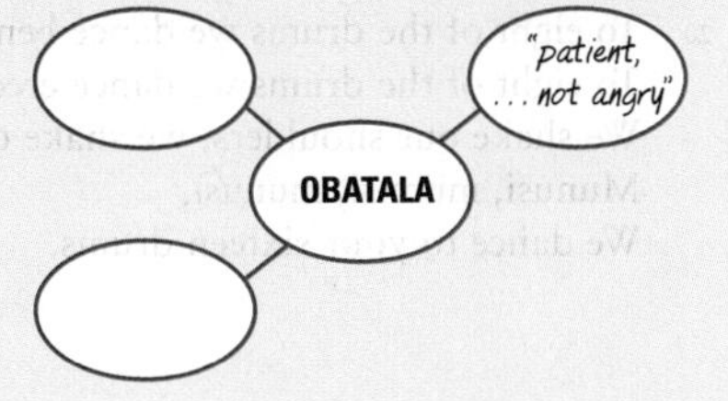

Methods of Worship Orishas are honored in different ways. They can be worshiped daily at shrines or temples dedicated to them. People can seek their advice through reading the pattern of palm nuts or cowrie shells tossed on a sacred tray. Through initiation, people can become priests or priestesses of a particular orisha, who "claims" them. At special ceremonies involving dance and sacred drumming, orishas are believed to come to earth and possess these followers, who wear clothing in the orishas' special colors and carry objects associated with them, such as Shango's double-headed ax. At these ceremonies, oriki are sung.

Shango priest

READING FOR INFORMATION

Reading Skills and Strategies

READING A CHART

Call attention to the chart in the second column of page 642. Students will be reading praise songs to the first three orishas in the chart. Information in the chart will help students distinguish the orishas from one another. Direct students to read an orisha's name, pronounce it silently, and then read across to learn important qualities of that orisha.

Reading Skills and Strategies

STUDYING A PHOTOGRAPH

Have students look at the photo of the Shango priest on page 643. Note that he is wearing red and white—Shango's colors. He holds a red parrot feather in his mouth and a rattle and a double-headed ax in his hands. These are symbols of Shango's power.

TIME MANAGEMENT

If your schedule requires that you cover the lesson objectives in a shorter time, use . . .

- Preparing to Read, pp. 642, 643
- Thinking Through the Literature, p. 648

If you want to take advantage of longer blocks of class time, use . . .

- TE Teaching Options: Speaking and Listening, page 644; Grammar, p. 645; Viewing and Representing, p. 646; Cross-Curricular Link, p. 647
- Connect to Today, p. 649

Literary Analysis CHARACTERIZATION

A Ask: What has the speaker directly told you about Obatala? *(He is patient; he is not angry; he silently passes judgment; he watches people.)*

B Obatala is described physically: "His eye is full of joy, / He rests in the sky like a swarm of bees." Ask: What does this physical description suggest to you about his character?

Possible Responses: He is happy, proud, and serene in his power.

 Use **Unit Four Resource Book,** p. 29, for more practice.

Active Reading SYNTHESIZING

Have students come up with a single sentence or phrase that describes Obatala, based on the first four stanzas.

Possible Response: He is a watchful, caring father.

 Use **Unit Four Resource Book,** p. 28, for more practice.

Literary Analysis ANALOGY

C Point out that the ideas in this praise song to Shango are developed through analogy, or comparison. In the first stanza, as animals must pay respect to the lord of the forest in order to avoid harm, so too must the speaker pay respect to Shango. Have students look for other analogies that show the speaker's relationship to Shango.

Praise Songs for Orishas

He is patient, he is not angry.
He sits in silence to pass judgment.
He sees you even when he is not looking.
He stays in a far place—but his eyes are on the town.

The granary of heaven can never be full.
The old man full of life force.

He kills the novice.
And wakens him to let him hear his words.
We leave the world to the owner of the world.
Death acts playfully till he carries away the child.
He rides on the hunchback.
He stretches out his right hand.
He stretches out his left hand.

He stands by his children and lets them succeed.
He causes them to laugh—and they laugh.
Ohoho—the father of laughter.
His eye is full of joy,
He rests in the sky like a swarm of bees.

We dance to our sixteen drums that sound jingin, jingin,
To eight of the drums we dance bending down,
To eight of the drums we dance erect.
We shake our shoulders, we shake our hips.
Munusi, munusi, munusi,
We dance to your sixteen drums.

5 granary: a place for storing grain.

7 He kills the novice: Persons being initiated into most orisha groups go through a ritual of symbolic death and resurrection.

11 He rides on the hunchback: Hunchbacks are sacred to Obatala.

15 He causes them to laugh: He gives them the breath of life after creating them.

MINI LESSON Speaking and Listening

CHORAL READING

Prepare Assign groups of students to perform a choral reading of each of these praise songs. They must decide which lines should be spoken by a single voice, and which should be spoken by the group. They also should consider whether female or male voices seem better for particular lines. They should plan gestures and movements that are suggested by the words. If they choose to have drum accompaniment to the songs, what rhythms would they associate with each orisha?

Present Have each group perform its reading before the other groups. Ask the class to evaluate which performance most fully evokes the character of an orisha.

Those who are rich owe their property to him.
Those who are poor, owe their property to him.
He takes from the rich and gives to the poor.
Whenever you take from the rich—come and give it to me!

Obatala—who turns blood into children.
I have only one cloth to dye with blue indigo.
I have only one headtie to dye with red camwood.
But I know that you keep twenty or thirty children for me
Whom I shall bear.

30–31 indigo . . . camwood: plant sources of blue and red dye.

When the elephant wakes up in the morning
He must pay his respects to his new wife.
When the guinea fowl wakes up in the morning
It must prostrate to the lord of the forest.
If it fails to greet him thus,
It will be killed by the hunter.
He will carry it home on his back.
He will sell it in the market
And use the money to make charms.
If the antelope wakes in the morning
And does not bow to the lord of the forest
The hunter will come and eat its head with pounded yam.
Shango, I prostrate to you every morning,
Before I set out to do anything.

The dog stays in the house of its master
But it does not know his intentions.
The sheep does not know the intentions
Of the man who feeds it.
We ourselves follow Shango
Although we do not know his intentions.
It is not easy to live in Shango's company.
Crabs' feet are confusion.
The parrot's feet are crooked.

3 guinea fowl: a pheasantlike bird of Africa.

4 prostrate: to lie face down in worship.

Customizing Instruction

Less Proficient Readers

Tell students that these praise songs are full of ideas that do not translate well. As they read, they should try to form a general impression of each orisha, not try to figure out the precise meaning of each line. Using the side notes will be essential, but they still won't understand everything.

Allow students to work together instead of independently to synthesize an impression of each orisha. They might jointly fill in a word web.

English Learners

1 Explain that *Ohoho, jingin,* and *munusi* are not English words. They may be onomatopoeic words that imitate the sounds of laughter and drumming.

MINI LESSON Grammar

PROBLEMS WITH COMPARISONS

Instruction Review comparisons with students. Most modifiers change in regular ways to show comparison. *–Er* and *–est* (as in *tall, taller, tallest*) are the most common endings. However, sometimes *more* and *most* are used, particularly with words of more than two syllables and with words that end in *ly.* (more expensive, most kindly) Some modifiers have irregular comparative and superlative forms. Common examples include *good, better, best; much, more, most; bad, worse, worst.*

Avoiding Comparison Problems When using modifiers to compare two or more items, writers often make the mistake of creating double comparisons. To avoid creating double comparisons, don't use both ways of forming comparisons or superlatives at the same time. Using *more* and *–er* or *most* and *–est* together results in a double comparison.

Wrong: I can run the <u>most fastest</u>.
Correct: I can run the <u>fastest</u>.

Practice Rewrite the sentences below to correct any comparison problems. If a sentence is correct, write "Correct."

1. Of the three orishas, Shango is the *more unpredictable* one. *(most unpredictable)*
2. Oshun seems to be the *most happiest* orisha. *(happiest)*
3. People feel *more safer* when Obatala is watching. *(safer)*
4. Does one orisha seem *more good* than the others? *(better)*
5. Oshun is mysterious, but Shango is even *more mysterious. (Correct)*

For more instruction and practice in using modifiers, use McDougal Littell's ***Language Network:***

- Grade 10, Chapter 9, "Using Modifiers"
- Grade 12, Chapter 7, "Using Modifiers"

Literary Analysis
CHARACTERIZATION

A **What impression do you get of Shango from his action of riding fire like a horse?**

Possible Response: Shango is someone who is mighty and in control of dangerous elements.

Active Reading **SYNTHESIZING**

Ask students to come up with three adjectives that describe Shango.

Possible Responses: powerful; dangerous; confusing

When the crab leaves its hole
We do not know which direction it is taking.
Shango went to Ibadan and arrived at Ilorin.

Rain beats the Egungun mask, because he cannot find shelter.
He cries: "Help me, dead people in heaven, help me!"
But the rain cannot beat Shango.
They say that fire kills water.
A He rides fire like a horse.
Lightning—with what kind of cloth do you cover your body?
With the cloth of death.
1 Shango is the death that drips to, to, to,
Like indigo dye dripping from a cloth. . . .

26 Ibadan (ē-bäd'n) **. . . Ilorin** (ē'lə-rēn'): Ibadan is a city in southwestern Nigeria. Ilorin is about 95 miles northeast of it.

27 Rain beats the Egungun (ā-gōōn'gōōn) **mask:** Egungun festivals, involving dancers wearing elaborate masks, are held to honor dead ancestors. If the dancers are not on good terms with Shango, the god of thunder, rain may spoil their ceremony.

Shango, God of Thunder. Dahomey (now Benin), Africa. Photo © Gianni Dagli Orti/Musée des Arts Africains et Océaniens/The Art Archive.

RIVER GODDESS

We call her and she replies with wisdom.
She can cure those whom the doctor has failed.
She cures the sick with cold water.
When she cures the child, she does not charge the father.
We can remain in the world without fear.
Iyalode who cures children—help me to have my own child.
Her medicines are free—she feeds honey to the children.
She is rich and her words are sweet.
Large forest with plenty of food.
Let a child embrace my body.
The touch of a child's hand is sweet.

2 Owner of brass.
Owner of parrots' feathers.
Owner of money.

My mother, you are beautiful, very beautiful.
Your eyes sparkle like brass.
Your skin is soft and smooth,
You are black like velvet.

Everybody greets you when you descend on the world.
Everybody sings your praises.

6 Iyalode (ē-yä'lō-dā): a title given to a woman chief in Yoruba communities, here used in reference to Oshun.

Customizing Instruction

Less Proficient Readers

1 Explain that "to, to, to," is meant to suggest dripping. Ask what mental picture of Shango is created by these lines.

2 Explain that in this sense, "owner of" means that Oshun rules over these aspects of the world and that her worshippers may wear or ask for these things.

Cross Curricular Link Geography

THE OSHUN RIVER There actually is an Oshun River in western Nigeria. On it lies the city of Oshogbo (pop. 465,000), which has an annual festival in August dedicated to the goddess Oshun. According to legend, the city was founded in the 17th century, when a princess from Oyo moved there. With the help of the goddess Oshun, she became pregnant and delivered a baby boy on the river bank. This child became the first Ataoja, or king, of Oshogbo.

On the last day of the festival, thousands walk in procession to the river, to the shrine of Oshun. A young virgin starts from the palace of the Ataoja, carrying on her head a sacred calabash filled with relics of the goddess. At the river, the chief priestess of Oshun throws sanctified food to the fish, Oshun's special messengers. Women make sacrifices and pray for fertility. Mothers thank Oshun for their children. Finally, the whole crowd throws its caps and headwraps into the air and shouts, "Oshogbo!" Then they bathe in the sacred water.

PRAISE SONGS FOR ORISHAS **647**

Connect to the Literature

1. **What Do You Think?** Responses will vary. Students may be surprised by the informal tone of the songs, unexpected comparisons, and references to things that are not explained.

Think Critically

2. Possible Responses: Obatala—patient, supportive, giving father
   Shango—strong, dangerous, demanding master
   Oshun—kind, beautiful, healing mother
3. Possible Response: Humans respect, praise, and fear the gods; and in turn, the gods grant them life, success, and children.
4. Possible Responses: The tone seems respectful but familiar, not distantly reverential. Sometimes it is joking ("when you take from the rich, come and give to me") or accepting ("It is not easy to live in Shango's company.")
5. Responses will vary. Some students may prefer Obatala's patience; others may prefer Shango's fierceness; others may prefer Oshun's gentleness.

Extend Interpretations

6. **Critic's Corner** Some students may feel that the fragmentary, allusive quality of the songs makes them difficult to understand; others may feel that this quality makes them exciting to try to figure out.
7. **Connect to Life** Students may say that these songs, like other hymns, express familiar sentiments: awe, appreciation, fear, and love of a deity.

Connect to the Literature

1. **What Do You Think?** What did you find most surprising or unusual in these praise songs?

Think Critically

2. **ACTIVE READING: SYNTHESIZING** Look over the word webs you created in your **READER'S NOTEBOOK.** What overall impression do you get of each orisha?
3. Describe the relationship between humans and gods found in the praise songs.
4. What seems to be the tone, or attitude, of the speakers in the praise songs?
5. Which of the orishas do you find most appealing? Explain why.

   THINK ABOUT
   - what role each orisha plays in human affairs
   - each orisha's personality traits

Extend Interpretations

6. **Critic's Corner** The Yoruba praise song has been described as "a collage of verbal images." A collage is an artwork made of different fragments joined together. Commentators also note that praise songs contain **allusions,** or references, to longer stories familiar in the culture. How do these characteristics of praise songs affect your reading of the songs?
7. **Connect to Life** Which ideas in the praise songs remind you of views expressed in other religious works familiar to you? Explain.

LITERARY ANALYSIS: CHARACTERIZATION

The composers of these praise songs rely on the same techniques of **characterization** that fiction writers use to develop characters. Following are the four basic means of characterization:

- description of the character's physical appearance
- presentation of the character's speech, thoughts, feelings, and actions
- presentation of other characters' reactions to the character
- the speaker's or narrator's direct comments about the character

Cooperative Learning Activity
With classmates, look again at the word webs you made in your **READER'S NOTEBOOK** for Obatala, Shango, and Oshun. Identify words from the songs that help create your impressions of these orishas. Which methods of characterization do these words represent? Use these same methods of characterization to write a praise song about your teacher or a classmate.

Literary Analysis

Cooperative Learning Activity Possible Responses: "He is patient"—speaker's direct comments; "I prostrate to you every morning"—presentation of others' reactions to the character; "He rides fire like a horse"—presentation of character's actions; "Your eyes sparkle like brass"—physical description.

Ask students to use all four techniques of characterization in their own praise songs.

Use **Unit Four Resource Book,** p. 29, for more practice.

To assess skills and concepts taught in this selection, use **Formal Assessment Book,** pp. 95–96.

Orishas in the Americas

If you are a fan of Latin music, the names of Shango, Obatala, and other orishas may already be familiar to you. Artists as diverse as Mongo Santamaria, Celia Cruz, Carlos Santana, and Desi Arnaz have recorded songs related to the Yoruba gods. "Babalu," which you may have heard Arnaz sing on *I Love Lucy*, is addressed to the orisha Babalu Ayé, who gives smallpox to those who anger him. Many aspects of Latin American culture show the influence of Yoruba religion.

How Did the Yoruba Religion Spread? Yoruba who were captured during the Atlantic slave trade (1518–1870) brought their religion to Latin America and the Caribbean. In Cuba, the religion is practiced as *santería* (sän-tĕ-rē'ä) or *lucumí* (lo͞o-ko͞o-mē'). In Brazil, it is known as *candomblé* (kän-dōm-blā'), while in Trinidad, it is called *shangó*. The rituals remain very similar but have taken on new forms in a new setting. Because the religion was repressed by Christian slaveholders, enslaved Yoruba disguised their faith by identifying their orishas with Catholic saints. The orisha Shango, for example, became identified with Saint Barbara.

As Latin American and Caribbean immigrants have come to the United States, they have brought the Yoruba religion to this country, where it has gained more followers. According to a *Boston Globe* newspaper article, more than 100,000 people in the United States today practice some form of Yoruba-based religion.

Research Project Find out more about the Yoruba religion as it is practiced in the Americas or as it has influenced U.S. or Latin American culture. You might investigate and report on one of the following topics (or another of your choice):

- Sacred *bata* rhythms in Afro-Cuban music
- Yoruba-influenced visual artists, such as the Brazilian sculptor Mestre Didi
- Oyotunji Village in South Carolina, an African-American re-creation of a traditional Yoruba village
- The 1993 Supreme Court decision upholding religious freedom in *Church of the Lukumi Babalu Aye* v. *City of Hialeah*

Actor in spirit costume, South Carolina

Connect to Today

Use this feature to show the relevance of world literature to students. The material relates the literature selection just read to contemporary music and other topics that may be of interest to students.

Research Project Our Web site, classzone.com, contains links to other Web sites with information about the suggested topics.

The following books might also be useful for those wanting a general overview of the Yoruba religion.

Altar of My Soul, by Marta Moreno Vega

Santeria: African Spirits in the Americas, by Joseph M. Murphy

Trickster Tales
Assign both "Tales of Anansi the Spider" and "Tales of Iktomi the Spider" to prepare students for the sample writing assessment provided on page 663. Use the **Points of Comparison** chart to guide students in identifying the similarities and differences between the selections.

 Use **Unit Four Resource Book,** p. 30, for more practice.

Trickster Tales

OVERVIEW

The **trickster tale** is a genre of literature found in West Africa and all over the world. It is a humorous folktale in which an animal or person creates mischief by trying to outwit others. Usually a culture will have a whole cycle of stories about the same trickster character. Famous tricksters include the Native American Coyote, the African-American Brer Rabbit (who descended from a West African trickster hare), and even the cartoon character Bugs Bunny.

In the pages that follow, you will read trickster tales from West African and Native American cultures. You will compare and contrast Anansi the spider, a West African trickster, and the Native American spider known as Iktomi, and you will decide how well each character displays the qualities of a trickster. Through this comparison, you will decide if the two tricksters are basically the same character.

Points of Comparison

The trickster is a complex character with both admirable and terrible qualities. He can be a **culture hero** who brings good things to people and teaches them to live properly. He can be a **clever deceiver** who uses trickery to capture or humiliate others. He can also be a **fool** whose greed or arrogance leads to his own downfall. The chart below lists some common characteristics of tricksters.

Analyzing Trickster Tales
As you read the Anansi stories, keep track of the trickster characteristics you see in Anansi on a chart similar to this one. Later you will do the same for Iktomi.

Trickster Characteristics	Anansi (West African)	Iktomi (Native American)
clever		
heroic		
supernaturally powerful		
greedy, selfish		
lying, deceitful		
proud, self-important		
foolish		

Standardized Test Practice: Comparison-and-Contrast Essay After you have finished reading all the stories, you will have the information you need to write a comparison-and-contrast essay. Your notes will help you include details and examples from the stories.

Assessment **Standardized Test Practice**

COMPARISON-AND-CONTRAST ESSAY To provide practice to students in comparing different pieces of literature, have them read both pairs of stories in this **Comparing Literature** feature, rather than treating each selection separately. Have them work with the chart shown here on page 650, filling it out as they finish reading each of the four stories. (Examples of how to fill out the chart are supplied on pages 657 and 662.) A sample assessment writing prompt and guidelines for responding to it in writing are on page 663.

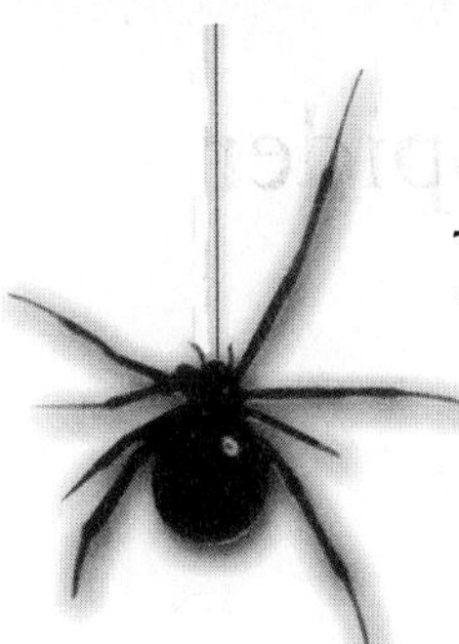

Tales of Anansi the Spider

Connect to Your Life

How would you get someone to do what you wanted him or her to do, without that person's realizing what you were up to? Share a strategy that worked for you.

Build Background

West African Tricksters There are several tricksters in African folklore. In east, central, and southern Africa and the western Sudan, the trickster is the hare. Among the Yoruba, Edo, and Ibo of Nigeria, the trickster is the tortoise. Anansi the spider is the famous trickster of the Ashanti people, who live in Ghana. All Ashanti folktales are referred to as *anansesem,* or "spider tales," whether Anansi appears in them or not.

Hundreds of stories have been told about Anansi; his wife, Aso; and his sons, Kweku Tsin and Intikuma. Traditionally, the stories are told only after dark. Anansi is a culture hero to the Ashanti, responsible for scattering wisdom throughout the world and otherwise making things as they are today. He is also a model for bad behavior, however. Through Anansi stories, the Ashanti make fun of human faults.

Anansi Abroad Anansi stories were brought to the Americas as a result of the slave trade. Many Ashanti were enslaved in Jamaica, and Anansi stories are told there as Anancy or Aunt Nancy stories. Stories told in Jamaica are almost identical to the original West African stories, although modern writers such as Andrew Salkey have invented new Anansi stories to comment on today's world.

Focus Your Reading

LITERARY ANALYSIS: TRICKSTER TALE

A **trickster tale** involves a human or animal character who engages in clever deceit, physical harm, or magic to try to get what he or she desires. Sometimes the trickster fools others; sometimes he or she is fooled. Trickster tales are usually humorous, and often they explain how some feature of the world or society came to be. Look for these qualities in the Anansi tales you are about to read.

ACTIVE READING: INTERPRETING THEMES

Often, the beginning or end of a trickster tale will state outright what feature of the world the story explains. The first story, for example, tells you:

"In this way Anansi . . . became the owner of all stories."

The more important theme of a trickster tale is usually unstated, however. Frequently it is a moral lesson that can be inferred from what is rewarded or punished in the story. One unstated theme of the first story might be "If you let yourself be flattered, you might suffer."

READER'S NOTEBOOK. As you read each Anansi tale, take notes following the model below.

__________ is rewarded for __________.

__________ is punished for __________.

Lesson: __________.

Objectives

- understand and appreciate **trickster tales (Literary Analysis)**
- **interpret themes** in trickster tales **(Active Reading)**

Summary

In "All Stories are Anansi's," the trickster spider Anansi wants to become owner of all stories. To do this he must bring three things to the Sky God Nyame: Mmoboro, the hornets; Onini, the python; and Osebo, the leopard. Anansi captures the hornets by tricking them into flying into an empty gourd. He captures the python by persuading him to be tied to a pole. He captures the leopard by trapping him in a pit, tying his tail to a rope, and killing him.

In "Anansi Plays Dead," the spider hatches a plan to keep food for himself during a famine. He pretends he is dying and asks to be buried next to the yam patch on his farm. His family follows his wishes, but during the night Anansi steals food from the fields. Hoping to catch the culprit, Anansi's family sets up a figure made of sticky gum in the fields. Anansi tries to beat up the figure and is caught fast. When his family finds him the next morning, he is humiliated.

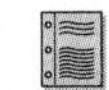
Use **Unit Four Resource Book,** p. 31, for additional support.

Thematic Link

These Anansi stories **give guidance** about human traits and the proper way to behave in society.

5-Minute Warm-Up

Daily Language SkillBuilder

Have students **proofread** the display sentences on page 563i and write them correctly.

TIME MANAGEMENT

If you wish to cover only one of the selections, use . . .

- Preparing to Read, p. 651 or p. 658
- Thinking Through the Literature, p. 657 or p. 662

If you want to take advantage of longer blocks of class time, use . . .

- TE Teaching Options: Cross-Curricular Links, pp. 653, 656, 658, 659, 661; Vocabulary Strategy, p. 654; Viewing and Representing, p. 655

Reading and Analyzing

Active Reading

INTERPRETING THEMES

A Ask: What makes Anansi able to trick the hornets?

Possible Responses: They are trusting; they don't ask questions; they act in a swarm.

Use **Unit Four Resource Book,** p. 32, for more practice.

Literary Analysis **TRICKSTER TALE**

B Note that trickster tales often explain some feature of society or the natural world. Ask: What does this passage explain? *(why Anansi is considered the owner of all stories)*

Use **Unit Four Resource Book,** p. 33, for more practice.

Active Reading

INTERPRETING THEMES

C Ask students whether they think Anansi deserves to own the stories. Have them defend their opinions.

Possible Responses: He deserves the stories because he did what the Sky God asked of him, which no one else had been able to do. He deserves the stories because he embodies what people want in stories—cleverness and entertainment. He does not deserve the stories because he is not a good person.

Tales of Anansi the Spider

Retold by Harold Courlander

All Stories Are Anansi's

In the beginning, all tales and stories belonged to Nyame, the Sky God. But Kwaku Anansi,[1] the spider, yearned to be the owner of all the stories known in the world, and he went to Nyame and offered to buy them.

The Sky God said: "I am willing to sell the stories, but the price is high. Many people have come to me offering to buy, but the price was too high for them. Rich and powerful families have not been able to pay. Do you think you can do it?"

Anansi replied to the Sky God: "I can do it. What is the price?"

"My price is three things," the Sky God said.
1 "I must first have Mmoboro, the hornets. I must then have Onini, the great python. I must then have Osebo,[2] the leopard. For these things I will sell you the right to tell all stories."

Anansi said: "I will bring them."

A He went home and made his plans. He first cut a gourd from a vine and made a small hole in it. He took a large calabash and filled it with water. He went to the tree where the hornets lived. He poured some of the water over himself, so that he was dripping. He threw some water over the hornets, so that they too were dripping. Then he put the calabash on his head, as though to protect himself from a storm, and called out to the hornets: "Are you foolish people? Why do you stay in the rain that is falling?"

The hornets answered: "Where shall we go?"

"Go here, in this dry gourd," Anansi told them. The hornets thanked him and flew into the gourd through the small hole. When the last of them had entered, Anansi plugged the hole with a ball of grass, saying: "Oh, yes, but you are really foolish people!" A

He took his gourd full of hornets to Nyame, the Sky God. The Sky God accepted them. He said: "There are two more things."

Anansi returned to the forest and cut a long bamboo pole and some strong vines. Then he walked toward the house of Onini, the python, talking to himself. He said: "My wife is stupid. I say he is longer and stronger. My wife says he is shorter and weaker. I give him more respect. She gives him less respect. Is she right or am I right? I am right, he is longer. I am right, he is stronger."

When Onini, the python, heard Anansi talking to himself, he said: "Why are you arguing this way with yourself?"

The spider replied: "Ah, I have had a dispute with my wife. She says you are shorter and weaker than this bamboo pole. I say you are longer and stronger."

Onini said: "It's useless and silly to argue when you can find out the truth. Bring the pole and we will measure."

So Anansi laid the pole on the ground, and the python came and stretched himself out beside it.

---

1. **Nyame** (nyä′mĕ′) . . . **Kwaku Anansi** (kwā′ ko͞o ä-nän′sē). *Kwaku* means "Wednesday-born."
2. **Mmoboro** (mō-bō′rō) . . . **Onini** (ō-nē′nē) . . . **Osebo** (ō-sĕ-bô′).

LESSON RESOURCES

UNIT FOUR RESOURCE BOOK, pp. 30–37

ASSESSMENT RESOURCES
Formal Assessment, pp. 97–98
Teacher's Guide to Assessment and Portfolio Use
Test Generator

INTEGRATED TECHNOLOGY
Visit our Web site: classzone.com

ADDITIONAL RESOURCES
Lesson Planning Guide, pp. 85–86
Teacher's Sourcebook for Language Development

"You seem a little short," Anansi said.

The python stretched further.

"A little more," Anansi said.

"I can stretch no more," Onini said.

"When you stretch at one end, you get shorter at the other end," Anansi said. "Let me tie you at the front so you don't slip."

"Whenever a man tells a story, he must acknowledge that it is Anansi's tale."

He tied Onini's head to the pole. Then he went to the other end and tied the tail to the pole. He wrapped the vine all around Onini, until the python couldn't move.

"Onini," Anansi said, "it turns out that my wife was right and I was wrong. You are shorter than the pole and weaker. My opinion wasn't as good as my wife's. But you were even more foolish than I, and you are now my prisoner."

Anansi carried the python to Nyame, the Sky God, who said: "There is one thing more."

Osebo, the leopard, was next. Anansi went into the forest and dug a deep pit where the leopard was accustomed to walk. He covered it with small branches and leaves and put dust on it, so that it was impossible to tell where the pit was. Anansi went away and hid. When Osebo came prowling in the black of night, he stepped into the trap Anansi had prepared and fell to the bottom. Anansi heard the sound of the leopard falling, and he said: "Ah, Osebo, you are half-foolish!"

When morning came, Anansi went to the pit and saw the leopard there.

"Osebo," he asked, "what are you doing in this hole?"

"I have fallen into a trap," Osebo said. "Help me out."

"I would gladly help you," Anansi said. "But I'm sure that if I bring you out, I will have no thanks for it. You will get hungry, and later on you will be wanting to eat me and my children."

"I swear it won't happen!" Osebo said.

"Very well. Since you swear it, I will take you out," Anansi said.

He bent a tall green tree toward the ground, so that its top was over the pit, and he tied it that way. Then he tied a rope to the top of the tree and dropped the other end of it into the pit.

"Tie this to your tail," he said.

Osebo tied the rope to his tail.

"Is it well tied?" Anansi asked.

"Yes, it is well tied," the leopard said.

"In that case," Anansi said, "you are not merely half-foolish, you are all-foolish."

And he took his knife and cut the other rope, the one that held the tree bowed to the ground. The tree straightened up with a snap, pulling Osebo out of the hole. He hung in the air head downward, twisting and turning. And while he hung this way, Anansi killed him with his weapons.

Then he took the body of the leopard and carried it to Nyame, the Sky God, saying: "Here is the third thing. Now I have paid the price."

Nyame said to him: "Kwaku Anansi, great warriors and chiefs have tried, but they have been unable to do it. You have done it. Therefore, I will give you the stories. From this day onward, all stories belong to you. Whenever a man tells a story, he must acknowledge that it is Anansi's tale." B

In this way Anansi, the spider, became the owner of all stories that are told. To Anansi all these tales belong. C

Customizing Instruction

Less Proficient Readers

Point out that the animals in these stories are not entirely animals but have characteristics of people. They talk, and they have human relationships and human frailties.

English Learners

1 You might show photos of hornets, a python, and a leopard to students who may be unfamiliar with English names for these animals.

Advanced Learners

Tell students to notice what Anansi uses against each animal; the hornets' tendency to act as a swarm, the python's pride in its length, and the leopard's habit of prowling at night. Ask: How might Anansi catch some other animal—an elephant or a crocodile, for example? Have students write a new episode to be added to the tale.

Cross Curricular Link Science

AFRICAN ROCK PYTHON Onini is the African rock python *(Python sebae)*, the largest snake species in Africa. It is found in grasslands south of the Sahara, from the western coast to central southern Africa. The longest one ever seen was 30 feet, but most are between 15 and 20 feet and weigh between 100 and 200 pounds. The rock python has no fangs; it is a constrictor which squeezes its prey to death. It eats birds, monkeys, pigs, deer, even crocodiles, but when swollen with food, it is sluggish and vulnerable to predators of its own.

Literary Analysis TRICKSTER TALE

A Ask: What new trait of Anansi's is revealed here?

Possible Responses: greed, selfishness

Literary Analysis IRONY

B Ask: What's ironic about the request of Anansi's family?

Possible Response: They ask Anansi to protect the crops, but do not know (as readers do) that Anansi is the one stealing them.

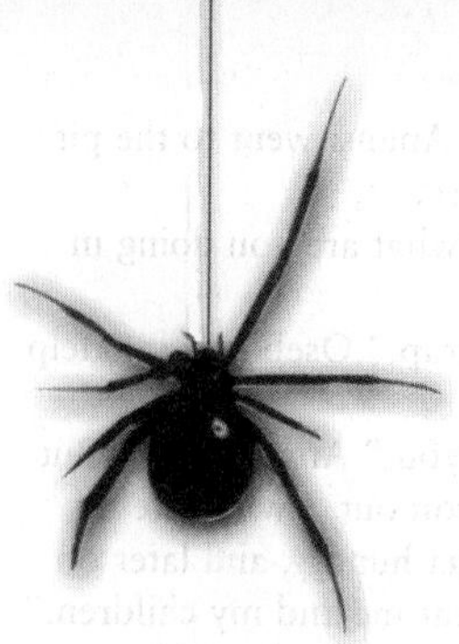

Anansi Plays Dead

One year there was a famine in the land. But Anansi and his wife Aso[1] and his sons had a farm, and there was food enough for all of them. Still the thought of famine throughout the country made Anansi hungry. He began to plot how **A** he could have the best part of the crops for himself. He devised a clever scheme.

One day he told his wife that he was not feel-**1** ing well and that he was going to see a sorcerer. He went away and didn't return until night. Then he announced that he had received very bad news. The sorcerer had informed him, he said, that he was about to die. Also, Anansi said, the sorcerer had prescribed that he was to be buried at the far end of the farm, next to the yam patch. When they heard this news, Aso, Kwaku Tsin, and Intikuma[2] were very sad. But Anansi had more instructions. Aso was to place in his coffin a pestle and mortar,[3] dishes, spoons, and cooking pots, so that Anansi could take care of himself in the Other World.

The sorcerer had informed him, he said, that he was about to die.

In a few days, Anansi lay on his sleeping mat as though he were sick, and in a short time he pretended to be dead. So Aso had him buried at the far end of the farm, next to the yam patch, and they put in his coffin all of the cooking pots **2** and other things he had asked for.

But Anansi stayed in the grave only while the sun shone. As soon as it grew dark, he came out of the coffin and dug up some yams and cooked them. He ate until he was stuffed. Then he returned to his place in the coffin. Every night he came out to select the best part of the crops and eat them, and during the day he hid in his grave.

Aso and her sons began to observe that their best yams and corn and cassava[4] were being stolen from the fields. So they went to Anansi's grave and held a special service there. They asked **B** Anansi's soul to protect the farm from thieves.

That night Anansi again came out, and once more he took the best crops and ate them. When Aso and her sons found out that Anansi's soul

1. Aso (ä′sō′).
2. Kwaku Tsin (kwā′ko͞o chĭn) . . . Intikuma (ĭn′tĭ-ko͞o′mə).
3. pestle and mortar: a small, club-shaped tool for grinding substances, and the container in which the grinding is done.
4. cassava (kə-sä′və): a large, starchy plant root eaten as a food.

MINI LESSON **Vocabulary Strategy**

CONTEXT CLUES: COMPARISON AND CONTRAST Two types of context clues are comparison clues and contrast clues. When **comparison** is used, an unfamiliar word is compared to other, more familiar words. Signal words for comparisons include *like, as, in the same way,* and *similar to.* When **contrast** is used, an unfamiliar word is contrasted with more familiar words that have opposite meanings. A contrast clue is often signaled by the words *but, although, unlike,* and *however.*

Instruction

- Write the first two sentences of page 654 on the board, underlining *famine*.
- Circle the clue word *but* at the beginning of the second sentence and ask whether it signals a contrast or a comparison. *(contrast)*
- Ask a volunteer to summarize the meaning of the contrast.
- Have students use clues in the second sentence to figure out the meaning of the word *famine.*

Follow the same procedure with this model sentence: The peccary, like other members of the hog family, searches for food with its snout.

Practice Use context clues to determine the meaning of the italicized words in the sentence below.

1. I expected my new plant to *thrive,* but it withered and died in only a week.
2. June's *astute* answer was as clever as the teacher's question.

A lesson on using context clues appears on p. 674 of the Pupil's Edition.

Customizing Instruction

English Learners

1 Explain that a *sorcerer* is the same as a *diviner*, a term students learned earlier. This is a person who communicates with the spirit world and can foretell the future. People ask him for help with illnesses and problems.

Less Proficient Readers

2 Ask: What was Anansi's clever scheme? *(to pretend to be dead so that he could be buried near the crops and steal food at night without people knowing)*

Detail of Wrapper (1900s), Fantes peoples. Mill-woven wool, embroidery thread, 304.2" × 198.7". Photo © Franko Khoury/National Museum of African Art, Smithsonian Institution, Washington, D.C.

HUMANITIES CONNECTION Important chiefs in Ghana wear embroidered *akunitam* cloth, or "cloth of the great." Some symbols on the cloth represent characters from folk tales. Anansi the spider is in the upper left corner.

MINI LESSON Viewing and Representing

Akunitam cloth

ART APPRECIATION Have students study the cloth and read the **Humanities Connection** on page 655. *Akunitam* is a relatively recent art form but is greatly admired, as are other Ghanaian fabric arts. Examples are in major museum collections, including the Smithsonian and the Art Institute of Chicago. The designs on akunitam are embroidered by machine on woolen blanket fabric. According to Herbert M. Cole and Doran H. Ross, authors of *Arts of Ghana,* each cloth is a set of allusions, or references, to a chief's power and responsibility. Ask: What symbols do you see on this cloth?
Possible Responses: guns, swords, a chief's umbrella, a ceremonial stool, a crown, a shield, a crescent moon and stars, animals

Literary Analysis HUMOR

A Ask: What is humorous or ironic about these exchanges?

Possible Responses: Readers know, but Anansi does not, that the gum-man is not alive and is not responding to him. Readers also know that the more Anansi attacks the gum-man, the worse off he will be.

Active Reading INTERPRETING THEME

B Note that in trickster tales, the trickster doesn't always win; sometimes he is punished. Ask what Anansi is punished for.

Possible Responses: for trying to fool people; for being greedy during a famine

Literary Analysis TRICKSTER TALE

C Have a volunteer restate what this passage explains. *(why spiders hide in dark corners)*

was not protecting them, they devised a plan to catch the person who was stealing their food. They made a figure out of sticky gum. It looked like a man. They set it up in the yam patch.

That night Anansi crawled out of his coffin to eat. He saw the figure standing there in the moonlight.

"Why are you standing in my fields?" Anansi said.

The gum-man didn't answer.

"If you don't get out of my fields, I will give you a thrashing," Anansi said.

The gum-man was silent.

"If you don't go quickly, I will have to beat you," Anansi said.

There was no reply. The gum-man just stood there. Anansi lost his temper. He gave the gum-man a hard blow with his right hand. It stuck fast to the gum-man. Anansi couldn't take it away.

"Let go of my right hand," Anansi said. "You are making me angry!"

But the gum-man didn't let go.

"Perhaps you don't know my strength," Anansi said fiercely. "There is more power in my left hand than in my right. Do you want to try it?"

As there was no response from the gum-man, Anansi struck him with his left hand. Now both his hands were stuck. A

"You miserable creature," Anansi said, "so you don't listen to me! Let go at once and get out of my fields or I will really give you something to remember! Have you ever heard of my right foot?"

There was no sound from the gum-man, so Anansi gave him a kick with his right foot. It, too, stuck.

"Oh, you like it, do you?" Anansi shouted. "Then try this one, too!"

He gave a tremendous kick with his left foot, and now he was stuck by both hands and both feet.

"Oh, are you the stubborn kind?" Anansi cried. "Have you ever heard of my head?"

And he butted the gum-man with his head, and that stuck as well.

"I'm giving you your last chance now," Anansi said sternly. "If you leave quietly, I won't complain to the chief. If you don't, I'll give you a squeeze you will remember!"

The gum-man was still silent. So Anansi took a deep breath and gave a mighty squeeze. Now he was completely stuck. He couldn't move this way or that. He couldn't move at all.

In the morning when Aso, Kweku Tsin, and Intikuma came out to the fields, they found Anansi stuck helplessly to the gum-man. They understood everything. They took him off the gum-man and led him toward the village to be judged by the chief. People came to the edge of the trail and saw Anansi all stuck up with gum. They laughed and jeered and sang songs about him. He was deeply shamed, and covered his face with his headcloth. And when Aso, Kweku Tsin, and Intikuma stopped at a spring to drink, Anansi broke away and fled. He ran into the nearest house, crawled into the rafters, and hid in the darkest corner he could find. B

From that day until now, Anansi has not wanted to face people because of their scoffing and jeering, and that is why he is often found hiding in dark corners. ❖ C

Humanities

THE TAR-BABY MOTIF Students may find "Anansi Plays Dead" very similar to the African-American story of Bre'r Rabbit and the Tar Baby. Tar baby stories are widespread in the world, especially in Africa. They are tale type K741, according to the Stith Thompson system of classifying folk tales by motifs, or recurring elements.

Among the Navajo, for example, it is Skunk who is captured by a pine-gum man when he has been stealing corn. In a story from ancient India, a raja's son fights a hairy demon and is stuck fast with every blow.

The tar baby tale is well known but controversial in the United States. In the 1880s, it was retold in African-American dialect by white Southern writer Joel Chandler Harris. Harris created a narrator called Uncle Remus, an elderly former slave who tells tales to the young son of a plantation owner. African Americans objected strongly to the use of dialect and to the characterization of Uncle Remus as a loyal and faithful servant with fond memories of slavery.

Uncle Remus remains a problematic figure, but in recent years, there has been a renewed appreciation of the tales themselves and of Harris's role in preserving them. African-American author Julius Lester has published four collections of Uncle Remus stories for children, removing the dialect and the plantation setting. He does not want these universal stories to be forgotten: "Whether we are black or white, slave or free, child or adult, Bre'r Rabbit is us."

Connect to the Literature

1. **What Do You Think?** What was your opinion of Anansi after reading the first story? Did it change after you read the second story?

Comprehension Check
- In the first tale, how did Anansi meet the three demands of the Sky God?
- In the second tale, why did Anansi pretend he was dead?
- How did Anansi's family find out that he was not really dead?

Think Critically

2. **ACTIVE READING: INTERPRETING THEMES** Look at the notes you took in your READER'S NOTEBOOK. Tell what these two stories explain about the natural world or society. What other, unstated lessons do they teach?

3. What do you think was the best example of trickery in these stories? Why?

4. What did you learn from these stories about the culture of the Ashanti people?

THINK ABOUT
- their source of food
- their natural surroundings
- their social groups
- their values and beliefs

Points of Comparison

Review the two Anansi stories and fill in the "Anansi" column of your comparison-and-contrast chart.

Paired Activity Compare your chart with that of a classmate and discuss the similarities and differences between them. On the basis of your discussion, decide whether you want to change any of your answers before going on to the next part of this lesson. An example is given for you.

Trickster Characteristics	Anansi (West African)	Iktomi (Native American)
clever	Traps hornets by persuading them to fly into a gourd	
heroic		
supernaturally powerful		
greedy, selfish		
lying, deceitful		
proud, self-important		
foolish		

Points of Comparison

Remind students that they can change their answers if they are convinced by their partner, but they can keep their original answer if they are satisfied with it.

Connect to the Literature

1. **What Do You Think?** After reading the first story, students may have admired Anansi's cleverness, but after reading the second, they may have been appalled by his greed and bad temper.

Comprehension Check
- Anansi captures the hornets by persuading them to fly into an empty gourd, captures the python by persuading him to be tied to a pole, and captures the leopard by trapping him in a pit and then persuading him to let his tail be tied to a rope.
- He pretended to be dead so that he could eat food from the farm without anyone suspecting him.
- They set out a gum-man to trap the food thief and Anansi got stuck to it.

 Use Selection Quiz in **Unit Four Resource Book,** p. 34.

Think Critically

2. Possible Responses: They explain why stories are considered to belong to Anansi and why spiders hide in dark corners. They also teach that it is possible for the weak to defeat the strong through trickery, that people should beware of flatterers and those who pretend to do favors, and that thieves will eventually be caught.
3. Possible Responses: Some may believe that Anansi's catching the python through flattery was the most effective example; others may choose different examples.
4. Possible Responses: Students may say they learned that the Ashanti farmed yams, corn, and cassava; that they sometimes faced famine; that they lived in an environment with hornets, pythons, and leopards; that they lived in villages; that they were judged by chiefs and treated by sorcerers; and that they buried their dead, prayed to them, and believed in another world after death.

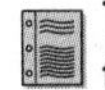 To assess skills and concepts taught in this selection, use **Formal Assessment Book,** pp. 97–98.

Summary

In "Iktomi and the Wild Ducks," the spider Iktomi catches some ducks to eat by telling them that he will teach them to dance. He says that if they do not close their eyes to concentrate, they will be turned into ugly mud hens. As they sway around him with their eyes closed, he clubs them dead. One suspicious duck opens his eye, sees what Iktomi is doing, and warns the others. This duck is turned into a mud hen, and the narrator explains that this is why mud hens swim alone, warily.

In "Iktomi Takes Back a Gift," the starving Iktomi prays to Inyan, the Rock, for food and gives his blanket as a gift. Soon afterward, Iktomi finds a freshly killed deer. As he prepares to cook the deer, the weather grows cold, and Iktomi wants his blanket back. He talks himself into believing that Inyan did not help him and that a rock doesn't need a blanket anyway. He goes to get his blanket, but when he returns to where the deer was, there is only a heap of dry bones. Iktomi regrets only not eating first, then taking back the blanket.

 Use **Unit Four Resource Book,** p. 35, for additional support.

Thematic Link

The Lakota use these trickster tales to **give guidance** about proper and wise behavior.

5-Minute Warm-Up

Daily Language SkillBuilder

Have students **proofread** the display sentences on page 563i and write them correctly.

Reading and Analyzing

Literary Analysis TRICKSTER TALE

A Point out that often the trickster is motivated by hunger. He is usually plotting to eat other animals or steal food from them.

PREPARING to *Read*

Now that you have read two stories about Anansi, the Ashanti trickster, you will read two stories about Iktomi, a Native American trickster. Judge how similar the tales are.

Build Background

The Lakota The spider-man Iktomi is the trickster of the Lakota people, also known as the Teton Sioux. Originally from the woodlands of Minnesota, the Lakota migrated to the Great Plains in the late 1700s and dominated the area that is now South Dakota, North Dakota, and Nebraska. There they maintained a nomadic way of life, hunting buffalo on horseback. The Lakota were forced onto reservations with the coming of white settlers and the destruction of buffalo herds at the end of the 19th century. The following two stories were recorded on the Rosebud Sioux Reservation in South Dakota.

Iktomi the Spider Iktomi is a culture hero who, according to the Lakota, created time and space, invented language, named the animals, and foretold the coming of the white man. He is so sacred to the Lakota that they avoid squashing spiders. But even though Iktomi is sacred, he is not completely good. He has been called "the grandfather of lies" and "the imp of mischief whose delight is to make others ridiculous."

Retold by **Richard Erdoes and Alfonso Ortiz**

Cross Curricular Link **Humanities**

THE TRICKSTER ARCHETYPE Why are trickster tales common to so many cultures? The stories are widespread not simply because they have traveled, scholars believe, but because the trickster is archetypal, or universal in human experience. Scholars see the trickster's function as allowing people to imagine breaking rules without actually breaking them and as allowing them to acknowledge that disorder, as well as order, is present in the real world.

 Iktomi and the Wild Ducks 

One day, Iktomi,[1] the spider fellow, was taking a walk to see what he could see. Tiptoeing through the woods, he saw water sparkling through the leaves. "I am coming to a lake," Iktomi said to himself. "There might be some fat ducks there. I shall creep up to this lake very carefully so that I cannot be seen. Maybe I shall catch something."

Iktomi crept up to the water's edge on all fours, hiding himself behind some bushes. Sure enough, the lake was full of nice, plump ducks. At the sight of them Iktomi's mouth began to water. But how was he to catch the birds? He had neither a net nor his bow and arrows. But he had a stick. He suddenly popped up from behind the bushes, capering[2] and dancing.

"Ho, cousins, come here and learn to dance. I have eight legs and I am the best dancer in the world."

All the ducks swam to the shore and lined up in a row, spellbound[3] by Iktomi's fancy dancing. 2 After a while Iktomi stopped. "Cousins, come closer still," he cried. "I am the gentle, generous Spider-Man, the friend of all the birds, cousin to all fliers, and I shall teach you the duck song.

1. **Iktomi** (ēk′tō-mē).
2. **capering:** leaping and jumping playfully.
3. **spellbound:** fascinated; as if in a trance.

Customizing Instruction

Less Proficient Readers

1 Again, remind students that Iktomi is both a spider and a man. He has eight legs like a spider, but he is large enough to want to eat ducks.

English Learners

2 English learners, and other students as well, may never have seen Native American fancy dancing. As part of building background, you might show students a video or still photos of powwow dancing.

Cross Curricular Link Humanities

TRICKSTERS IN DAILY LIFE You might have students discuss this quote from writer Julius Lester:

Teachers and parents know Trickster well, because there is one in every classroom and every large family. Trickster is the class clown, the child who seems to have a genius for walking a thin line between fun and trouble, the child who is always "up to something," but you can never punish him or her because what he or she does is disruptive but never rebellious or serious enough to merit severe punishment. And it is always entertaining because Trickster is charming and likeable, surrounded as he or she is by an aura of innocence and vulnerability.

Reading and Analyzing

Literary Analysis TRICKSTER TALE

A Call attention to the trickster's supernatural powers—he actually was able to change the duck into a mud hen for disobeying.

B Also, ask what this story explains about the natural world. *(why mud hens swim alone and not with ducks; why they dive under the water when they hear someone approach)* You might show students photos of ducks and mud hens for illustration.

Active Reading

INTERPRETING THEME

C Ask students to tell you what they believe the last line means. Ask if they have heard similar sayings. You could repeat the lines from Ecclesiastes, "a living dog is better than a dead lion."

Literary Analysis TRICKSTER TALE

D Ask what human frailties Iktomi shows in this passage.

Possible Responses: ingratitude; excuse-making; selfishness

I don't quite trust that fellow with the eight legs. I'll risk one eye. One red eye isn't so bad.

Now, when I start singing, you must all close your eyes in order to concentrate better. Do not peek while I sing, or you will be turned into ugly mud hens with red eyes. You don't want this to happen, do you? You have, no doubt, noticed my stick. It is a drumstick with which I will beat out the rhythm. Are you ready? then close your eyes."

Iktomi started to sing and the foolish ducks crowded around him, doing as he had told them, flapping their wings delightedly and swaying to and fro. And with his stick Iktomi began to club them dead—one after another.

Among the ducks was one young, smart one. "I better check on what's happening," this duck said to himself. "I don't quite trust that fellow with the eight legs. I'll risk one eye. One red eye isn't so bad." He opened his left eye and in a flash saw what Iktomi was up to. "Take off! Take off!" he cried to the other ducks. "Or we'll all wind up in this man's cooking pot!"

The ducks opened their eyes and flew away, quacking loudly.

Still, Iktomi had a fine breakfast of roast duck. The Spider-Man's power turned the smart young duck into a mud hen.

This is why, to this day, mud hens swim alone, away from other ducks, always on the lookout, diving beneath the water as soon as they see or hear anyone approaching, thinking it might be wicked Iktomi with a new bag of tricks. Better a live, ugly mud hen than a pretty, dead duck.

Iktomi Takes Back a Gift

Tunka, Inyan, the Rock, is the oldest divinity in the Lakota cosmology.[1] *Everything dies; only the Rock is forever.*

Iktomi, the tricky Spider-Man, was starving. There had been no game for a long time. Iktomi was just skin and bones. His empty stomach growled. He was desperate. Then it occurred to him to go for help to Inyan, the Rock, who has great powers, and who might answer his prayers.

Iktomi wrapped himself in his blanket, because it was late in the year and cold. Then he went to a place where a large upright rock was
2 standing. This rock was *lila wakan,*[2] very sacred. Sometimes people came to pray to it.

When Iktomi arrived at that place he lifted up his hands to Inyan: *"Tunkashila, onshimalaye,*[3] grandfather, have pity on me. I am hungry. If you do not help me, I will starve to death. I need meat, grandfather."

Iktomi took his blanket from his shoulder and draped it around Inyan. "Here, grandfather, *tunkashila,* accept this gift. It is the only thing I have to give. It will keep you warm. Please let me find something good to eat."

After praying to Inyan for a long time, Iktomi went off to search for food. He had a feeling Inyan would answer his prayers, and he was right. Iktomi had not gone very far when he came upon a freshly killed deer. It had an arrow piercing its neck, the feathered nock sticking out on one side of the neck and the arrowhead on the other.

"Ohan,"[4] said Iktomi, "the deer has been able to run for a distance after being hit and the hunter has lost it. Inyan has arranged it that way. Well, that is only fair. Did I not give him my blanket? Well, anyhow, *pilamaya,*[5] *tunkashila*—thank you, grandfather!"

Iktomi took his sharp knife out of its beaded knife sheath and began to skin and dress the deer. Then he gathered wood and, with his strike-a-light and tinder, made a fire. There was not much wood and it was wet. It wasn't much of a fire. And it had grown very cold. Iktomi was shivering. His teeth were chattering. He was saying to himself: "What good is my blanket to Inyan? He is just a rock. He does not feel either
cold or heat. He does not need it. And, anyway, D
I don't think Inyan had anything to do with my finding this deer. I am smart. I saw certain tracks. I smelled the deer. So there, I did it all by myself. I did not have to give Inyan anything. I shall take my blanket back!"

Iktomi went back to the sacred rock. He took the blanket off him. *"Tunkashila,"* he said, "this blanket is mine. I am freezing. You don't need this blanket; I do."

Iktomi wrapped the blanket tightly around his body. "Ah, that feels good," he said. "Imagine, giving a blanket to a rock!"

When Iktomi came back to the place where he had left the deer, he discovered that it had disappeared—vanished, gone! Only a heap of dry bones was left. There were no tracks or any signs that somebody had dragged the deer away. It had been transformed into dry bones by a powerful magic.

"How mean of Inyan," said Iktomi, "and how stupid of me. I should have eaten first and then
taken the blanket back." ❖ 3

1. **cosmology:** a concept of the universe and all its parts and laws.
2. *lila wakan* (lē'lä wä-käɴ').
3. *tunkashila, onshimalaye* (to͞oɴ'kä-shē-lä, o͞oɴ'shē-mä-lä-yeh).
4. *ohan* (ō-hŭɴ'): OK; all right.
5. *pilamaya* (pē-lä'mä-yä).

Customizing Instruction

English Learners

1 Explain the idioms *take off* ("run away"), *on the lookout* (watching for danger), and *bag of tricks* (clever schemes).

Less Proficient Readers

2 Explain that the unfamiliar Lakota words are followed by an English translation. For example, *lila wakan* means "very sacred." The pronunciations are given in the footnotes.

Advanced Learners

3 Encourage students to examine their feelings about Iktomi. Are they appalled? amused? admiring? Invite them to talk about their reactions to other tricksters they may be familiar with, such as Bugs Bunny or the Native American trickster Coyote.

Cross Curricular Link — Humanities

LAKOTA COSMOLOGY The Lakota have an interesting creation story, worth comparing to some of the others in this anthology.

Inyan, the Rock, was the first of the gods. He was not created but always existed, and had no physical form. At the beginning, the only other thing that existed was Han, or shapeless darkness. Inyan, wishing to create something, made a huge disk, Maka, from his own blood. This was the Earth. The blue blood from Inyan's veins became the waters of the Earth. The power of Inyan's blood separated from the waters and became Skan, or the Sky. Inyan, then drained of power, became the rocks of the Earth. These gods created other gods in turn, including Wi (the Sun), and Aap (Light).

Inyan later had two sons. One was Ksa, the god of wisdom, who, after playing a nasty trick on other gods, became known as Iktomi, the imp of mischief.

Connect to the Literature

1. **What Do You Think?** Students' answers will vary. Some may prefer Iktomi's clever plan to catch the ducks while others prefer the humor of Iktomi's punishment for taking back the gift.

Comprehension Check

- He catches the ducks by telling them he will teach them to dance if they close their eyes, then clubbing them to death while they cannot see.
- He loses the deer because he takes back the blanket he gave to the god Inyan, who sent the deer to him.

Use Selection Quiz in **Unit Four Resource Book**, p. 36.

Think Critically

2. The story explains how mud hens came to be, why they swim alone and away from ducks, and why they frequently dive beneath the water.
3. Possible Responses: It shows that Iktomi is not sorry for his bad behavior; it shows that he blames others and does not recognize his own faults.
4. Possible Responses: Iktomi breaks many social rules. He lies; he gains others' trust in order to harm them; he takes back gifts, he is ungrateful; he flatters himself; he is not ashamed when punished. Children might learn from these stories not to blindly trust others and to be grateful for gifts.
5. Possible Responses: Students might say they learned that the Lakota value dancing, music, and cleverness; that they enjoy roast duck; that they consider rocks divine; that they pray to the gods for better circumstances and consider it wrong not to show gratitude.

Connect to the Literature

1. **What Do You Think?** Which one of these stories did you enjoy more? Explain your choice.

Comprehension Check

- How does Iktomi catch the wild ducks?
- Why does Iktomi lose the deer he has found?

Think Critically

2. What feature of the natural world is explained by "Iktomi and the Wild Ducks"?
3. What do you think of Iktomi's statement at the end of "Iktomi Takes Back a Gift"?
4. What social rules does Iktomi violate in the two stories? Discuss the lessons the stories might present to children.
5. What do you learn about Lakota culture from these stories?

Points of Comparison

Paired Activity Now that you have read the last two stories, work with a partner to evaluate Iktomi as a trickster. Fill in the "Iktomi" column of your chart. Then compare and contrast Anansi and Iktomi. What characteristics of the trickster do they share?

Trickster Characteristics	Anansi (West African)	Iktomi (Native American)
clever	Traps hornets by persuading them to fly into a gourd	Catches ducks by saying he will teach them to dance
heroic		
supernaturally powerful		
greedy, selfish		
lying, deceitful		
proud, self-important		
foolish		

Points of Comparison

After students have completed their charts, initiate a class discussion about the characteristics of tricksters. Encourage students to tell whether they prefer Anansi or Iktomi and to explain why.

Writing About Literature

PART 1 Reading the Prompt

In writing assessments, you may be asked to compare and contrast characters. You are now going to practice writing an essay that involves this type of comparison.

Writing Prompt

The West African character Anansi and the Native American character Iktomi are two famous tricksters in world literature. Compare Anansi and Iktomi, discussing how well they show the characteristics of the trickster. Would you say that they are essentially the same character, or do they have important differences? Give evidence from the four stories you read to support your analysis. 1 2 3 4

STRATEGIES IN ACTION

1 I have to **compare** two **characters.**

2 I have to evaluate how well each shows **characteristics of the trickster.**

3 I have to conclude whether they are **more alike** or **more different.**

4 I need to include **details, examples,** or **quotations** from the stories to support my opinion.

PART 2 Planning a Comparison-and-Contrast Essay

- Review the comparison-and-contrast chart that you filled out for the West African and Native American trickster tales.
- In your chart, look for examples of similarities and differences to point out in your essay.
- Create an outline to help organize your ideas.

PART 3 Drafting your Essay

Introduction Begin by introducing your topic, the trickster, and identifying the typical trickster's characteristics. Briefly state who Anansi and Iktomi are, and identify the cultures they come from.

Body You can organize in two ways. 1) You can discuss Anansi first, showing how he has characteristics of the trickster. Then discuss Iktomi. 2) Alternatively, you can organize by characteristic, discussing how Anansi and Iktomi are clever. Then discuss how they are heroic. Use your comparison-and-contrast chart for details and examples.

Conclusion Wrap up your essay by drawing a conclusion about whether Anansi and Iktomi are alike enough to be thought of as basically the same character.

Revision Make sure that you have used signal words, such as *similarly, also, but, unlike,* and *while,* to make your comparisons and contrasts clear.

TEST PRACTICE

Assessment Standardized Test Practice

RESPONDING TO A WRITING PROMPT Read aloud the writing prompt at the top of this page. Discuss the **Strategies in Action** by asking students to identify the words in the prompt that tell them what to do. Suggest that they mark up their comparison-and-contrast charts, identifying points to include in their essays. When students have finished drafting their essays, have them work with a partner to see if they have accomplished the tips given in Part 3 **Drafting Your Essay.**

Part 1 Reading the Prompt
Model the process of reading a prompt.

- Read through the whole prompt.
- List key words of the assignment on the board ("Compare," "evidence").
- Define each key word using **Strategies in Action** to show how students can restate the prompts in their own words.

Part 2 Planning a Comparison-and-Contrast Essay

- Students can use the chart they have been filling out (referenced on pages 650, 657, and 662).
- Tell students that they may use information from the introductions to the stories as well as information within the stories to write their essays.
- Suggest that students expand their charts with more rows for other similarities or differences they see.
- By going back through their charts and coding similarities one way and differences another, they can judge whether Anansi and Iktomi are the same character.

Part 3 Drafting Your Essay

Introduction Suggest that students condense information from the Overview page (p. 650) to define the trickster. They should stress that the trickster has many sides.

Body Remind students to strive for parallelism in their organization. If students discuss Anansi's characteristics in the first half, then in the second half, they should discuss these same characteristics, in the same order, as they apply to Iktomi. Alternatively, they might discuss each characteristic of the trickster in turn. They could begin with the characteristics that Anansi and Iktomi share and then discuss the characteristics they do not share.

Conclusion If students do not think the differences between Anansi and Iktomi are meaningful, they might conclude that they are basically the same character. If students see an important distinction between the two tricksters, they might write, "Although Anansi and Iktomi are similar in several ways, . . ." and then present their conclusion.

Revision Suggest that students leave time for revising their essays.

Use **Unit Four Resource Book,** p. 37, for additional support.

This **On Your Own** featured selection may be used to achieve one or more of the following objectives:

- To give students the opportunity to read independently, that is, reading silently for a sustained period, reading and analyzing literature with a group, or using the Reader's Notebook to write in response to the literature.
- To conduct a post-reading class discussion

ON YOUR OWN

West African oral literature is particularly rich in **proverbs**—*short, well-known sayings that express widely held beliefs. Proverbs are used in every culture; some proverbs that may be familiar to you are "Look before you leap," and "The early bird catches the worm." Such sayings are not really about leaping or catching worms, of course; they are simple ways of making a point. The first statement warns a listener not to act too hastily, and the second encourages taking initiative.*

Proverbs have the same function in West Africa that they do all over the world. They warn, encourage, and console people. West Africans are especially proud of their proverbs, regarding their use as necessary for good conversation. As the Nigerian writer Chinua Achebe has said, "Proverbs are the palm oil with which words are eaten."

Look at the symbols on these pages. They are found stamped on Ghanaian adinkra cloth, a fabric traditionally worn at funerals and other important rituals. Many of the adinkra symbols have proverbs associated with them. For example, the ram's horn symbol ꕥ suggests the saying, "It is the heart and not the horns that leads a ram to charge." The symbol is linked to the idea of strength.

The West African proverbs you will read are from a collection which identifies some by ethnic group and some only by nation. As you read each proverb, consider the following questions:

- *What does the proverb mean? You may want to restate it in your own words.*
- *What visual images does the proverb bring to mind?*
- *To what kinds of situations might the proverb apply?*

One camel does not make fun of another camel's hump. **Guinea**

It takes a whole village to raise one child. **Yoruba**

Only when you have crossed the river, can you say the crocodile has a lump on his snout. **Ashanti**

A wise man who knows proverbs reconciles difficulties. **Yoruba**

To spend the night in anger is better than to spend it repenting. **Senegal**

Ashes will always blow back into the face of the thrower. **Yoruba**

Working Independently
You may want to set aside time each week for independent reading, without making an assignment related to the reading. Or, once students have completed the reading, either alone or aloud in groups, you may ask them to work together on a project, such as a set of flash cards with a proverb on the front and its explanation on the back. If you choose to have students write responsively in their Reader's Notebook, suggest that they choose a proverb that appeals to them, explain what it means, and follow up with an anecdote illustrating its truth.

Discussing the Selection
The last page of this selection provides questions you might use for a post-reading class discussion.

Art Note
Read in pairs, and downward, the adinkra symbols on this page signify "congratulations" and "wisdom"; "goodbye" and "have courage"; "strength" and "faithfulness."

Art Note
The symbols on this page signify "enjoy yourself" and "royalty"; "good fortune" and "give me your heart"; "forgiveness" and "faith."

Don't look where you fell, but where you slipped. **Liberia**

If familiarity were useful, water wouldn't cook fish. **Fulani**

If something that was going to chop off your head only knocked off your cap, you should be grateful. **Yoruba**

If you are in hiding, don't light a fire. **Ashanti**

No one can leave his character behind him when he goes on a journey. **Yoruba**

Love does not hear advice. **Ghana**

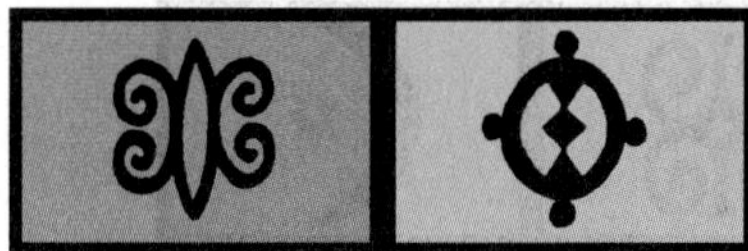

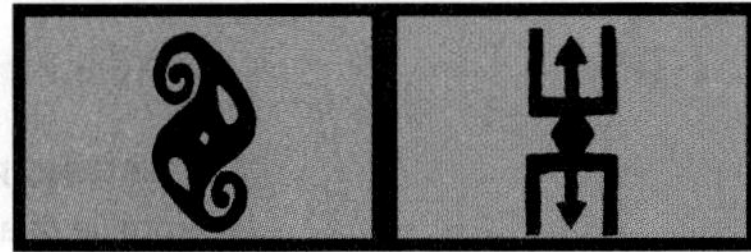

Money is sharper than a sword. **Ashanti**

When you get older you keep warm with the wood you gathered as a youth. **Bambara**

The one who is carried does not realize how far away the town is. **Nigeria**

Lying will get you a wife, but it won't keep her. **Fulani**

The wisdom of this year is the folly of the next. **Yoruba**

Art Note

The symbols on this page signify "I shall meet you again" and "understanding"; "two good friends" and "you have changed"; "house of peace" and "the king sees all."

Discussion Questions

1. What do these proverbs mean?
   Possible Responses: "One camel does not make fun of another camel's hump" means that people should not ridicule others' traits because they may share the same traits.
   "It takes a whole village to raise one child," means that the entire community, not just the parents, shapes and provides for a child as he or she grows up.
   "Only when you have crossed the river, can you say that the crocodile has a lump on its snout" means that if you want to criticize someone, it is best to make sure that he or she is not in a position to harm you.
   Accept all reasonable interpretations of the other proverbs.
2. What visual images do these proverbs bring to mind?
   Possible Responses: Responses will vary but probably will correspond to the actual words of the proverbs—a camel pointing and laughing at another camel, for example.
3. To what kinds of situations might these proverbs apply?
   Possible Responses: "One camel does not make fun of another camel's hump" might be said to a child who is teasing another or to a candidate who is criticizing his or her opponent, for example. Accept all reasonable responses.
4. Which proverbs do you find particularly true or appealing? Explain.
   Accept all responses.

Objectives
- write a Personality Profile
- use a written text as a model for writing
- revise a draft to add details
- edit to correct any errors in subject-verb agreement

Introducing the Workshop

A Personality Profile Many forms of news media, such as television and film documentaries, newspapers, and magazines, contain personality profiles. A profile might describe a celebrity, such as an athlete or a movie star, or it might describe an ordinary person who has had an interesting experience or remarkable achievement. Have students name a few people they have read about or seen in profiles. Point out that through writing a personality profile, students will also be able to introduce their readers to interesting people that they might never otherwise meet.

Ask students to discuss what makes one person fascinating to another. Some will be interested in celebrities or people with extraordinary lives or talents. Others will be more interested in reading about a relative or close friend with unique qualities.

Basics in a Box

B Using the Graphic Like the tiles in a mosaic, the items in a personality profile work together to create an overall impression. The graphic offers suggestions for pieces that students can use to draft an effective essay.

C Presenting the Rubric To better understand the assignment, students can refer to the Standards for Writing a Successful Personality Profile. You may wish to discuss with them the complete rubric and student models in the Unit Four Resource Book on pages 43–46.

For more instruction and practice in descriptive writing, use McDougal Littell's ***Language Network:***
- Grade 10, Chapter 19, "Focused Description."
- Grade 12, Chapter 18, "Personality Profile."

Writing Workshop — Personality Profile

Describing an interesting individual . . .

From Reading to Writing The excerpt from D. T. Niane's version of the epic *Sundiata,* on page 634, contains a number of characters who repeatedly hurt, frustrate, and anger one another. Niane makes these characters seem real and believable by describing their actions, their words, and their physical appearance. Writers use the same techniques (A) in creating the **personality profiles** that appear in newspapers and magazines. In a personality profile, compelling information and lively writing are used to present a detailed portrait of a real person.

For Your Portfolio

WRITING PROMPT Write a personality profile of a person you know or admire.

Purpose: To acquaint the reader with the person described

Audience: Your peers, family, or general readers

Basics in a Box

Personality Profile at a Glance

(B)

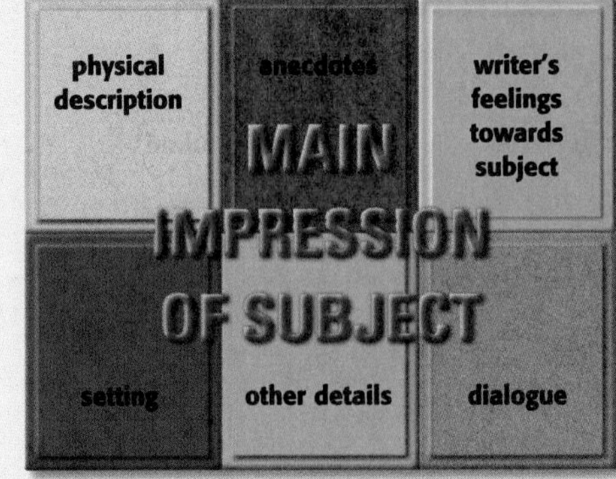

RUBRIC Standards for Writing

A successful personality profile should
- create a vivid impression of a person with lively description, details, anecdotes, and/or dialogue
- put the person in a context that reveals aspects of his or her personality
- make it clear why the person is important to the writer
- be a word portrait that shows the person's character
- have a unified tone and create a unified impression
- capture the reader's interest at the beginning and convey a sense of completeness at the end

LESSON RESOURCES

USING PRINT RESOURCES

Unit Four Resource Book
- Prewriting, p. 38
- Drafting, p. 39
- Peer Response, pp. 40–41
- Revising, Editing, and Proofreading, p. 42
- Student Models, pp. 43–45
- Rubric, p. 46

USING MEDIA RESOURCES

Writing Coach CD-ROM

Visit our Web site: classzone.com

ADDITIONAL RESOURCES

For a complete view of Lesson Resources, see page 563f of this book.

Analyzing a Student Model

José Flores
Oak Park and River Forest
High School

RUBRIC IN ACTION

Model Teacher, Model Person

She could not be a more normal-looking person. No taller than five feet, hair always tidy and pulled back in a ponytail, she is the very essence of normal—until she begins to talk. Her choice of words, her gestures, and the emotion with which she speaks make up a personality that is anything but ordinary. Respected by her peers, loved by her students, and confident in herself and her methods, she personifies her profession and sets an example for others who wish to do what she does.

❶ Captures reader's interest by contrasting the person's ordinary physical appearance with her unusual speaking manner; creates suspense by not immediately identifying her

At first glance the classroom, like the teacher, looks normal. Upon closer inspection, however, it becomes clear that very little is usual here. Visible immediately are two wooden shelves overflowing with tissue boxes, as well as books that could fill the history section of a library. There are pictures drawn by past students and a monstrous red structure just poking out from under a purple drop cloth. Students sit, somewhat frightened by now, waiting for her to speak, preparing to bolt out of their desks and run if necessary.

❷ Places her in the context of her own classroom, which helps to reveal her personality

D

"Write down something that you want me to ask you about. If you don't, you may be sorry." With this warning she lets the class write and stands above them, like a hawk examining its prey. Eventually, she comes to the unfortunate victim she was looking for, the one with a blank sheet of paper.

❸ Bit of dialogue shows how she relates to her students.

"Justify your existence in this universe!" she tells him. The hapless student desperately searches his mind, looking for something satisfactory, wondering at the same time if she is serious. She eventually moves on, smiling as everyone who has blank paper scrambles to write. As the day begins, her system has already begun to work.

Day after day, students walk into the room to be introduced to something new. Bit by bit, they pick up information about what makes Mrs. Belle unique and what makes the room uniquely hers. The protruding object under the drop cloth turns out to be a *Fallbeil*, or miniature guillotine, painted deep red and fully workable. As she unveils it, the students gasp in disbelief. She calmly takes a pencil, sticks it in the hole, and drops the wooden blade. The blade falls with a sickening crack, and flying pencil shrapnel clears to reveal two halves of a pencil—the splintered remains of Mrs. Belle's latest victim. The lesson begins, and everyone's gaze is fixed on the short woman with the pencil shavings on her shirt.

❹ Anecdote helps to reveal Mrs. Belle's methods of capturing her students' attention.

LANGUAGE SKILLS

Teaching the Lesson

Analyzing the Model

"Model Teacher, Model Person"

D The student model is a profile of the writer's history teacher. Have students read the model and analyze its effectiveness. Then discuss the Rubric in Action. Point out key words and phrases in the student model that correspond to the elements mentioned in the Rubric in Action.

2. Ask students to consider what the classroom setting reveals about the teacher.
   Possible Responses: The tissue boxes show that she is a nurturing teacher; the books show that she is well-read; the student pictures on the wall show that she is proud of her students.
3. Point out that the writer is continuing to create suspense here. He is introducing Mrs. Belle to the reader in such a way that the reader shares the experience of a new student just getting to know her.
4. Ask students to explain why this paragraph is so effective.
   Possible Responses: The paragraph contains a little story, and narrative is always more interesting than description; the miniature guillotine is a dramatic object; the teacher momentarily takes on the role of an executioner, which is in strong contrast to what one would expect.

MINI LESSON Patterns of Organization

Instruction Word choice and ideas are important parts of effective writing. However, the structure of a text—the way in which the words and ideas are organized—also adds to the effectiveness of a written piece.

Activity Have students analyze the text structure of the student model by constructing an image such as a graphic organizer. While the graphic organizer on page 668 shows the basic features of a personality profile, students' graphic should reflect how the student writer has organized his piece. Students might first write a note about each paragraph to see how the paragraphs relate to one another and to the whole graphic.

5. Ask students to read the entire first paragraph on this page and point out all of the things named by the writer that are unique about Mrs. Belle.

   Possible Responses: She takes students on restaurant field trips; she makes jokes; she keeps odd items in her classroom
6. Point out that the writer's feelings towards a subject are an important component of a personality profile. In other kinds of writing, the writer's feelings are less important.
7. Point out that the writer concludes by making a larger statement about educators and how they should be. This extra insight adds to the significance of the essay and emphasizes the point that Mrs. Belle is an extraordinary person.

Mrs. Belle hands out papers, which turn out to be permission slips. She is doing what so few high school teachers do: a real-world field trip. Her field trips take the students to restaurants, and they happen after school. Three times a year, caravans of people unite in a migration that is so full of fun and laughter that it actually seems preferable to the various European adventures that she has talked about. At this point it becomes clear that through the field trips, the jokes, and the odd items in her room, she makes every moment in class keenly memorable. And as they remember the class, her students remember history. By being personal and unique, she has earned the trust of her students, and she can be sure that they know and appreciate the history that she is teaching.

5 Creates a strong impression of Mrs. Belle as a unique, creative individual

Mrs. Belle is a woman who has realized that fun and teaching go together, and in that order. She is strict, one of the strictest teachers about homework, and she won't take excuses. Here, however, in sharp contrast to other classes, students feel that they *must* do their work, not for fear of a bad grade but for fear of disappointing her—a fear equal to that of diving off the ten-meter platform for the first time. Students know for certain that she will not disappoint, and they feel comforted by what she says whenever she assigns a report: "I won't let anything bad happen to you." As the class warms up, the lesson plan expands to include toy soldiers, paper clips, pencils, whiteout, and other things that ordinarily have nothing to do with history but here make perfect sense.

6 Shows why she is important to the writer (who is presumably one of her students) as well as how other students feel about her

Mrs. Belle's room is always filled with kids; this is the risk she takes by making it clear that her door is always open for any kind of help. Her former and current students have a certain kinship, a sense that they have known one of the best that the educational system has to offer. They cherish the time they have spent in her class and wait like children in line at an ice-cream truck for the opportunity to be taught by her again. Her students love history, they love her class (if not the rest of school), and they treat their fellow students with courtesy and respect. She teaches not only that which her curriculum dictates but also that which her experience and morals dictate, that which life necessitates, making her the kind of teacher all educators should strive to be and the kind of person all people should try to emulate.

7 Sums up her excellence as a teacher and a person

Writing Your Personality Profile

❶ Prewriting

Whom do you want to describe? With a few classmates, discuss what kinds of people you find interesting and what is remarkable about them. Consider the people you know—neighbors, relatives, teachers, friends, community leaders. Who strikes you as particularly interesting or admirable? What comes to mind when you think about that person? See the **Idea Bank** in the margin for more suggestions. After you select a subject, follow the steps below.

Planning Your Personality Profile

1. **Explore your attitude toward the subject.** Why is the person important to you? What details or incidents can you present to show his or her importance to you?
2. **Set your goal for writing.** What impression of the person do you want to create in the reader's mind? Analyze your subject to find an angle—a dominant impression or theme that conveys the essence of the person.
3. **Consider the traits you would like to depict.** What stands out about the person? Use a chart like this one to record details.

Personality Characteristics			
How Person Looks	What Person Says	How Person Behaves	How Others React

4. **Plan your organizational structure.** There are several ways to organize a personality profile:
   - **In Chronological Order** Narrate events in the order in which they occurred. You might want to focus on a series of events that reveals something special about the person, or on a day in his or her life.
   - **By Category** One at a time, analyze different aspects of your subject's personality, such as interests, behaviors, or opinions.
   - **In Order of Importance** Many writers place the most important event or detail at the very beginning or the very end of their piece.

Ask Your Peer Reader

- What dominant impression did you get of my subject?
- How would you describe my attitude toward the person?
- What details were particularly vivid or memorable?
- What details, if any, distracted you from the picture I was trying to present?
- What more would you like to know about the person?

❷ Drafting

Start by simply getting your ideas down on paper. Keep your goal in mind as you try to get into the flow of your writing. Roughly following your organizational plan, get down everything you want to say. Later, you can cut unnecessary details or add things you've forgotten.

IDEABank

1. Your Working Portfolio
Build on one of the Writing Options you completed earlier in this unit:
- **Character Analysis,** p. 641
- **Biographical Article,** p. 641

2. Personal Heroes
Who are your role models? Think about people you admire—ones known to you personally and ones in public life. What traits of theirs do you wish to emulate?

3. And the Winner Is . . .
Imagine that you're going to give an award to the person who best exemplifies a certain trait—kindness, originality, honesty, or humor, for example. Whom would you honor, and why?

Have a Question?

See the **Writing Handbook**
Introductions, p. R22
Descriptive Writing, pp. R27–R28

LANGUAGE SKILLS

Guiding Student Writing

Prewriting

Choosing a Subject

If, after reading the **Idea Bank,** students are having difficulty choosing their subjects, suggest they try the following:

- Collect feature articles about personalities from newspapers, sports magazines, or TV and movie reviews.
- Watch a home video of friends, teammates, or family at an event at school or home. Describe one of the people during that event.
- Look through photographs of friends and relatives. Freewrite about one that is particularly compelling. Consider the following questions: What is the person doing? What is the setting of the picture? Why did someone choose to take this picture?

Planning the Personality Profile

1. Have students work in pairs to clarify their feelings about the subject. One student should describe his or her feelings about the subject. The listener should then ask questions to clarify the speaker's ideas. After ten minutes, tell students to switch roles and begin the process again.
2. Visually-oriented students may find it helpful to sketch out their subject in his or her surroundings.
3. From the characteristics in their table, have students choose 3 or 4 major ideas they'd like to share about their subjects.
4. Remind students that the student model represents only one approach to writing a personality profile. They may wish to begin their own writing by outlining their draft or drawing a graphic organizer that helps them visualize how details may be grouped.

Drafting

Beginnings and Endings

If students want to write an engaging beginning, have them write two or three possible beginnings and read them to their writing partners. They can use their partners' responses to help them decide which opening will be most compelling.

Revising

ADDING DETAIL

You might do a simple activity to guide students through the process of adding detail. Ask a volunteer to create a very simple sentence (subject, predicate, and adjective or direct object) describing your classroom. Then have students suggest additional modifiers, phrases, or precise verbs that create a more detailed description. Have students compare the initial simple sentence with the final product.

Editing and Proofreading

ERRORS IN SUBJECT-VERB AGREEMENT

The subject of the sentence is compound: *choice, gestures,* and *emotion.* Compound subjects joined by *and* are plural, so the verb, *make,* must also be plural.

Reflecting

Encourage students to recognize and evaluate the way in which they approached the writing assignment. Which prewriting strategies were most helpful? How did the praise or suggestions of their peer readers help them improve their personality profiles? Have them add these self-evaluations to their working portfolios.

Need revising help?

Review the **Rubric,** p. 668.

Consider **peer reader** comments.

Check **Revision Guidelines,** p. R19.

Confused by subject-verb agreement?

See the **Grammar Handbook,** pp. R74–R76.

Publishing IDEAS

- Collect the class's profiles in a booklet titled *People to Know.* Distribute the booklet in your school or to local libraries, churches, or community centers.
- Submit your profile to a student-writing Web site.

❸ Revising

TARGET SKILL ▶ ADDING DETAIL In descriptive writing, concrete details and examples help the reader envision a scene. With them, you can show a person's traits in action instead of just naming them. Remember, however, to select details carefully, so that they build a coherent impression.

> ^ and flying pencil shrapnel clears to reveal two halves of a pencil—
> The blade falls with a sickening crack ~~and the pencil breaks in two~~, the splintered remains of Mrs. Belle's latest victim. The lesson begins, and everyone's gaze is fixed on ~~her.~~ the short woman with the pencil shavings on her shirt.

❹ Editing and Proofreading

TARGET SKILL ▶ ERRORS IN SUBJECT-VERB AGREEMENT A verb must agree with its subject in person and number. Sometimes it can be difficult to determine whether a verb's subject is singular or plural.

> Her choice of words, her gestures, and the emotion with which she speaks make~~s~~ up a personality that is anything but ordinary.

When reading the model above, you might think that the verb *makes* agrees with the subject *emotion.* However, the true subject is compound: *choice, gestures,* and *emotion*. A compound subject whose parts are joined by *and* takes a plural verb form, so *make* is correct. Review your writing for any errors in subject-verb agreement.

❺ Reflecting

FOR YOUR WORKING PORTFOLIO What did you discover about your subject while writing the personality profile? What did you learn about yourself or about life? Attach your answers to these questions to your finished personality profile. Save your personality profile in your **Working Portfolio.**

Options

Managing the Paper Load

Have students choose one major question they would like you to address as you review their first drafts. Ask them to write this question on the top of their draft. Some students may want help with organization while others might have questions about grammar. This can help you focus your first review.

Read this paragraph from the first draft of a personality profile. The underlined sections may include the following kinds of errors:

- **errors in subject-verb agreement**
- **errors in pronoun agreement**
- **incorrect plurals**
- **errors in the use of *who* and *whom***

For each underlined section, choose the revision that most improves the writing.

I walk into a neighborhood café and see an elderly man standing next to the piano, singing his heart out. He sings with great passion, and the crowd love him (1). After a couple of songs, he asks, "Whom in the audience can sing (2) the harmony for 'This Land Is Your Land'?" I raise my hand, and he invites me up to join him for a song. I've never had so much fun singing with anyone! After our duet, he sings a few more solos (3) and then takes a bow. At the end of the show, everyone in the house has a smile on their face (4) and are clapping wildly (5). Afterwards, over a cup of coffee, Leo asks me if I'd like to sing with him again. Who knew (6) that I'd meet such a great person just by walking into a café?

1. A. the crowd loves him
B. the crowd loved him
C. the crowds love him
D. Correct as is

2. A. Whomever in the audience can sing
B. Who's in the audience can sing
C. Who in the audience can sing
D. Correct as is

3. A. soloes
B. solo's
C. soloe's
D. Correct as is

4. A. everyone in the house has a smile on the face
B. everyone in the house has a smile on his or her face
C. everyone in the house has a smile on their faces
D. Correct as is

5. A. was clapping wildly
B. were clapping wildly
C. is clapping wildly
D. Correct as is

6. A. Whom knew
B. Whomever knew
C. Who's
D. Correct as is

Need extra help?

Review the **Grammar Handbook**

Subject-verb agreement, p. R74

Pronoun agreement, p. R57

Interrogative Pronouns, p. R58

Answers:
1. A; **2.** C; **3.** D; **4.** B; **5.** C; **6.** D

MINI LESSON Grammar

AGREEMENT PROBLEMS WITH INDEFINITE PRONOUNS AS SUBJECTS

Instruction Remind students that subject-verb agreement can be particularly confusing when the subject is an indefinite pronoun. When used as subjects, some indefinite pronouns are always plural *(both, few, many, and several)* and some can be either singular or plural, depending on how they're used *(all, more, none, any, most, and some)*. The rest of the indefinite pronouns (including *everyone, anybody,* and *nobody*) are always singular.

Practice Write the following sentences on the chalkboard:

Everyone likes to go to the movies.

Everyone like to go to the movies.

Ask students which of the two sentences is correct and why. *(The first sentence is correct because* everybody *is a singular indefinite pronoun and takes a singular verb,* likes.*)*

For more instruction and practice in subject-verb agreement, use McDougal Littell's ***Language Network:***

- Grade 10, Chapter 7, "Subject-Verb Agreement"
- Grade 12, Chapter 5, "Subject-Verb Agreement."

Objectives

- use context clues as a strategy for building vocabulary
- recognize and apply a variety of context clues for determining the meaning of a word
- create sentences with context clues to indicate a word's meaning

EXERCISE

1. silent; contrast clue; the word *although* signals contrast with *encouraged her son to speak.*
2. skill and quickness; contrast clue; the words *while* and *only* signal contrast with *crawl.*
3. mean-spirited; example clue; *people said he was an ugly, stupid cripple* is an example of *malicious talk.*
4. confused; restatement clue; *he couldn't understand* is a restatement of the king's feelings.
5. insulted; inference clue; one can infer that Sogolon would feel insulted after Sassouma laughed in her face.

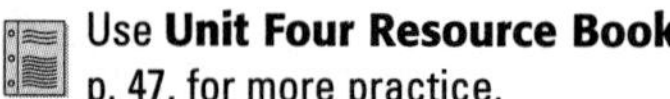
Use **Unit Four Resource Book,** p. 47, for more practice.

Building Vocabulary — Using Context Clues

Reading is one of the best ways to improve vocabulary—better than studying word lists or dictionaries. Whenever you read, you are likely to encounter unfamiliar words. Often, you can infer the meanings of such words from clues in the surrounding passages—that is, from the words' **context.** For example, in the following sentence about *Sundiata*, the word *enigma* is immediately followed by a definition.

> **In the end, the condition of Mari Djata remains an enigma—a deep and confounding mystery.**

Being alert to context clues will help you absorb unfamiliar words as you read.

Strategies for Building Vocabulary

Here are a few types of context clues.

❶ Definition or Restatement Clues The model above shows that a writer sometimes provides a clue to a word's meaning by restating the meaning. In the example above, the restatement is in the form of an **appositive**—a phrase that explains a word or idea. An appositive follows the word it explains, separated from it by a comma or dash. Other restatements are signaled by such words as *that is, or, in other words,* and *also called.*

❷ Example Clues Sometimes an unfamiliar word is followed by one or more examples that illustrate its meaning. In the passage below, a king is talking to his son, and he gives examples of kings and their successors. These examples can help you determine that *successor* means "one who takes the place of another."

> **". . . before death takes me off I am going to give you the present each king gives his successor. In Mali every prince has his own griot. Doua's father was my father's griot, Doua is mine and the son of Doua, Balla Fasséké here, will be your griot."**
>
> —*Sundiata*

❸ Comparison and Contrast Clues You may be able to infer a word's meaning if a writer compares or contrasts it with a more familiar idea. Comparisons are often signaled by words such as *like, as, similar to,* and *also.* Contrasts are signaled by words such as *although, but, unlike, rather than,* and *however.* For example, in the sentence "Far from being a kind friend to Sogolon, Sassouma was horribly **vindictive,**" the words *far from* signal a contrast between *vindictive* and *kind.*

❹ Inference Clues The meaning of a word is often suggested by the general sense of the words and sentences that surround it.

Sogolon is troubled by her son's infirmity and has been unable to "give strength to her son's legs." *Infirmity* must refer to the legs' lack of strength. One can infer from the context that an infirmity is a physical weakness or illness.

> **Her son's infirmity weighed heavily upon Sogolon Kedjou; she had resorted to all her talent as a sorceress to give strength to her son's legs, but the rarest herbs had been useless.**
>
> —*Sundiata*

EXERCISE Explain the meaning of the boldfaced word in each sentence. Then identify the type of context clue and the details that helped you to define it.

1. Although Sogolon encouraged her son to speak, he remained **taciturn.**
2. While the other children walked with **agility,** Mari Djata could only crawl.
3. She overheard the **malicious** talk about her son; people said he was an ugly, stupid cripple.
4. The king was **perplexed**; he couldn't understand why his son had turned out this way.
5. Sassouma insulted Sogolon and laughed in her face. Sogolon had never been so **affronted.**

Sentence Crafting — Using Adverbs and Adverb Phrases

Grammar from Literature Look at the sentences from "Anansi Plays Dead" below. Notice the information that the highlighted adverbs and adverb phrases add to the sentences. (One-word adverbs appear in red type; adverb phrases appear in blue type.)

when — how
One day he told his wife that he was not feeling well and
where — where
that he was going to see a sorcerer. He went away and
how — when
didn't [not] return until night.

how
Anansi struck him with his left hand.

when — to what extent — how
Now he was completely stuck. He couldn't [not] move
where — how — to what extent
this way or that. He couldn't [not] move at all.

As you can see, adverbs and adverb phrases answer the questions *how, where, when, for what purpose,* and *to what extent.* They modify verbs, adjectives, and other adverbs.

Types of Adverb Phrases Prepositional phrases can function as adverb phrases. The following sentence contains a prepositional phrase modifying the verb *covered*, answering the question *how.*

> **He was deeply shamed, and covered his face with his headcloth.**
> —"Anansi Plays Dead"

Infinitive phrases can also function as adverb phrases. In the sentence below, the highlighted infinitive phrase modifies the verb *came*, answering the question *for what purpose.*

> **Every night he came out to select the best part of the crops and eat them, and during the day he hid in his grave.**
> —"Anansi Plays Dead"

Using Adverbs in Your Writing When you revise a piece of writing, examine the verbs and modifiers you have used. Would the addition of adverbs and adverb phrases telling *how, when, where, for what purpose,* and *to what extent* make your writing more precise or accurate? Notice how crucial the adverbs are in this synopsis of part of "Anansi Plays Dead."

> **Every night, Anansi emerged silently from his grave to steal the best crops from the field and cook them for himself. He did this for days. Finally, his wife and son made a figure out of sticky gum and set it in the fields. Anansi confronted the gum-man angrily and attacked him with great confidence. He soon found himself stuck by every limb to the gum-man.**
> —"Anansi Plays Dead"

Try rereading the passage, mentally deleting all of the adverbs and adverb phrases. Without these modifiers, the passage makes little sense. Which of the adverbs and adverb phrases are essential to the expression of complete thoughts? Which are not essential but add useful or interesting information? In your own writing, look for places to include adverbs and adverb phrases that provide interesting details.

WRITING EXERCISE Rewrite the following sentences, adding adverbs and adverb phrases that modify the underlined words. Follow the instructions in parentheses, using your imagination to come up with suitable modifiers.

1. Anansi <u>visited</u> the hornets. (Tell where and when he visited the hornets.)
2. He <u>captured</u> them. (Tell how and where he captured them.)
3. Although the hornets <u>complained</u>, he <u>refused</u> to let them go. (Tell how and where they complained and to what extent he refused.)
4. He <u>presented</u> the gourd full of hornets to Nyame, the Sky God. (Tell when and how he presented the gourd.)
5. The Sky God <u>accepted</u> them. (Tell how the Sky God accepted them.)

LANGUAGE SKILLS

Sentence Crafting

Objectives

- use adverbs to add rhythm to writing and to create exact descriptions
- recognize how prepositional phrases and infinitive phrases can function as adverbs
- revise drafts by examining verbs and modifiers to make writing more precise and accurate
- use adverbs to modify adjectives and other adverbs

EXERCISE

Student responses will vary. Sample responses follow; adverbs and adverb phrases are underlined.

1. Anansi visited the hornets <u>at their nest</u> <u>every day</u>.
2. He captured them <u>with a gourd under the tree</u>.
3. Although the hornets complained <u>loudly</u> <u>from inside the gourd</u>, he <u>stubbornly</u> refused to let them go.
4. <u>The next day</u> he <u>proudly</u> presented the gourd full of hornets to Nyame, the Sky God.
5. The Sky God <u>graciously</u> accepted them.

Use **Unit Four Resource Book,** p. 48, for more practice.

MINI LESSON Grammar

AGREEMENT PROBLEMS WITH PHRASES BETWEEN SUBJECT AND VERB

Instruction Point out to students that many people make errors in subject-verb agreement when a prepositional phrase appears between the subject and the verb in a sentence. They sometimes make the verb agree with the object of the preposition rather than the subject. Write the following sentence on the chalkboard.

> The best of all books are the one that tells a good story.

Point out that *are* agrees with *books,* which is not the true subject. Draw a line through *of all books* and explain that the true subject is *best* and *of all books* is a prepositional phrase modifying *best.* Cross out *are* and write in *is*, explaining that *is* agrees with *best,* which is a singular subject. Encourage students to mentally screen out intervening prepositional phrases when trying to determine correct subject-verb agreement.

For more instruction and practice in subject-verb agreement, use McDougal Littell's ***Language Network:***

- Grade 10, Chapter 7, "Subject-Verb Agreement"
- Grade 12, Chapter 5, "Subject-Verb Agreement."

Objectives
- reflect on and assess understanding of the part
- generalize about West African cultural values
- distinguish genres of oral literature
- assess and build portfolios

Reflecting on the Literature
A successful response will
- identify one or two cultural values expressed in each selection
- explain what in the selection supports the cultural value
- make one or more generalizations about West African cultural values

Reviewing Literary Concepts
A successful response will
- identify distinguishing characteristics of myth, legend, oral epic, praise song, trickster tale, and proverb
- state which genres lose the most in written translation
- offer reasons for this choice of genres

Building Your Portfolio

For more information on using writing and assessing portfolios, see the **Teacher's Guide to Assessment and Portfolio Use,** pp. 53–74.

Part Assessment
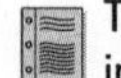
To assess skills and concepts taught in this unit part, use **Formal Assessment Book,** pp. 99–100.

Mid-Year Test

For mid-year assessment of skills and concepts taught in the preceding units, use **Formal Assessment Book,** pp. 101–108.

Reflect and Assess

Did you gain a better appreciation of oral literature after reading the West African selections in Unit 4, Part 2? What did you discover about West African societies? Use the following activities to pull together what you've learned.

Five terracotta horseback riders. Courtesy of Bernard de Grunne.

Reflecting on the Literature

Cultural Values One important function of oral literature is to instill values. For each selection you have read in Part 2, identify one or two cultural values that you think are taught or supported. You might phrase these as Do's or Don'ts—for example, "Don't be too proud." Explain why you believe the selection expresses that particular value. After considering all the selections, try to make some generalizations about West African cultural values.

Reviewing Literary Concepts

Oral Genres In this part of the book, you were introduced to several genres of oral literature: myth, legend, oral epic, praise-song, trickster tale, and proverb. Tell what makes them different from one another. Which genres do you think lose the most in written translation?

Building Your Portfolio

Writing Workshop and Writing Options Look again at the character profile you wrote for the Writing Workshop and at any writing options you completed. Which was your most effective piece of writing? Add that assignment to your **Presentation Portfolio**, along with a note identifying your favorite passage and what you were trying to accomplish in it.

Self ASSESSMENT

READER'S NOTEBOOK

Following are important terms from this part of the book. Create groups of two or more related terms, then explain how they are connected. Different groupings are possible. If you are unclear about any term, go back through the unit or consult the **Glossary of Literary Terms** (page R91).

Sundiata	Mali
internal conflict	trickster tale
Yoruba	griot
orishas	praise song
Anansi	external conflict

Setting GOALS

Look back through your assignments and notebook to identify writing or critical thinking skills that you would like to strengthen.

Assessment Self Assessment

Students can look up the listed terms in the **Glossary of Literary Terms** on page R91 or they can find them introduced in context on the text pages indicated below.

Sundiata (pp. 614, 632)
internal conflict (pp. 633, 640)
Yoruba (pp. 615, 642)
orishas (p. 642)
Anansi (p. 651)
Mali (pp. 614, 632)
trickster tale (p. 650)
griot (pp. 618, 632)
praise song (p. 642)
external conflict (pp. 633, 640)

Extend Your *Reading*

The Hero with an African Face

CLYDE W. FORD

Ford, a psychotherapist, explores "the mythic wisdom of traditional Africa." He retells and interprets myths and epics from different parts of the continent, finding such universal themes as death and resurrection, the master animal, and the sacred circle. An especially interesting chapter covers the *Mwindo Epic,* from the Congo.

Jali Kunda

This book and companion music CD introduce the West African tradition of the jali (dieli), or griot. At the heart of the book is a memoir by the Mandinka griot Foday Musa Suso, who now lives and records in the United States. Many full-page color photographs of musicians are included, along with commentary on griots by the poet Amiri Baraka and the music critic Robert Palmer. The CD offers two different performances of *Sundiata.*

And Even *More* . . .

Books

Voices of the Ancestors: African Myth
Another impressive book in Time-Life's Myth and Mankind series, containing creation stories and other narratives illustrated with masterworks of African art.

Leaf and Bone: African Praise-Poems JUDITH GLEASON
Praise poems from all over Africa, addressed to orishas, rulers, common people, animals—even trains and bicycles.

West African Trickster Tales MARTIN BENNETT
More tales of Anansi the spider, as well as tales about the trickster hare and trickster tortoise.

Other Media

The Roots of African Civilization
This 25-minute film uses location footage, expert commentary, and photographs of art to introduce viewers to precolonial West Africa. Knowledge Unlimited. (VIDEOCASSETTE)

Encarta Africana
An absorbing multimedia encyclopedia of African and African-American cultures containing thousands of essays and photos, along with virtual tours, interactive maps, and music. Microsoft. (CD-ROM)

West Africa Before the Colonial Era

BASIL DAVIDSON

An easy-to-read survey of West African history before 1850. Among its topics are ancient Ghana and Mali, Yoruba kingdoms, the economy, religion, social groups, and the slave trade.

More Recommendations for Your Students

Difficulty Level: Easy

Abrahams, Roger D. *African-American Folktales.* (NY: Pantheon, 1999). Stories from the U.S. South and the Caribbean Islands, including many trickster tales.

Abrahams, Roger D. *African Folktales.* (NY: Pantheon, 1983). *Gassire's Lute* and the *Mwindo Epic* appear in this collection of 95 stories from all regions of Africa.

Koslow, Philip. *The Kingdoms of Africa series.* (Philadelphia: Chelsea House, 1995). Volumes include *Ancient Ghana: Land of Gold; Mali: Crossroads of Africa; Yorubaland: The Flowering of Genius;* and *Asante: The Gold Coast.*

Difficulty Level: Average

Dadié, Bernard Binlin. *The Black Cloth: A Collection of African Folktales.* (Amherst: University of Massachusetts Press, 1987). Tales of the trickster spider retold by a writer from the Ivory Coast.

Murray, Jocelyn, ed. *Cultural Atlas of Africa.* (NY: Facts on File, 1998). A one-volume survey covering geography, history, culture, and political states.

Suso, Bamba, and Banna Kanute. *Sunjata.* (London: Penguin, 1999). Translations of live performances of the *Sundiata* epic by two Gambian griots.

Difficulty Level: Challenging

Condé, Maryse. *Segu.* (NY: Penguin, 1998). This historical novel follows the fortunes of the Traore family, who live in the West African Segu kingdom at the beginning of the 19th century.

Finnegan, Ruth. *Oral Literature in Africa.* (London: Oxford University Press, 1970). One of the best-known scholarly works on the subject.

The **Reading and Writing for Assessment** feature provides practice in taking standardized tests. As students work through this lesson, they will learn strategies for answering reading comprehension questions, multiple-choice questions, and essay and short-answer questions. Boxed strategies located alongside the text will help guide students through the activities. These strategies model processes students can use as they take standardized tests.

This feature is based on and will help students prepare for state assessments as well as end-of-course assessments. It will also prepare students for the reading comprehension questions used on such college entrance examinations as the Scholastic Aptitude Test (SAT) and the American College Test (ACT).

Objectives

- understand and apply strategies for reading a test selection
- recognize literary and organizational techniques in a test selection
- understand and apply strategies for answering multiple-choice questions about a test selection
- respond to a writing prompt and present ideas in a logical order
- understand and apply strategies for revising and proofreading a test response

Standardized Test Practice

Reading & Writing for Assessment

When you studied strategies for reading a test selection on pages 412–417, you practiced techniques for success on reading and writing assessments. These kinds of tests are often important end-of-course examinations.

The following pages will give you more test-taking strategies. You will have a chance to apply them in the practice activities that follow the selection.

PART 1 How to Read a Test Selection

In many tests, you will read a selection and then answer multiple-choice questions about it. Applying the basic strategies that follow can help you focus on the information you will need to know.

STRATEGIES FOR READING A TEST SELECTION

- **Before you begin reading, skim the questions that follow the selection.** These can help focus your reading.
- **Use your Strategies for Reading, such as clarifying, evaluating, and questioning.** As you read, make notes in the margin or underline key words and passages, as long as the test directions allow you to do so.
- **Think about the title.** What does it suggest about the overall message or theme of the selection?
- **Look for main ideas.** You will often find a main idea stated at the beginning or end of a paragraph. Sometimes it is implied, not stated. After reading each paragraph, ask yourself, "What was this paragraph about?"
- **Note the literary elements and techniques used by the writer.** Look out for such elements as descriptive language and the use of quotations. Then ask yourself what effect the writer achieves with each one.
- **Examine the sequence of ideas.** Are the ideas developed in chronological order, presented in order of importance, or organized in some other way? What does the sequence of ideas suggest about the writer's message?
- **Unlock word meanings.** Use context clues and word parts to help you unlock the meaning of unfamiliar words.
- **Think about the message or theme.** What larger lesson can you draw from the selection? That is, can you infer anything or make generalizations about other similar situations, human beings, or life in general?

Reading Selection

❶ Edison's Curse
by Stanley Coren

1 ❷ "Most people overeat 100 percent, and oversleep 100 percent, because they like it. That extra 100 percent makes them unhealthy and inefficient. The person who sleeps eight or ten hours a night is never fully asleep and never fully awake—they have only different degrees of doze through the twenty-four hours."

2 The man who wrote these words in his diary was not a psychologist, psychiatrist, or medical researcher. It was Thomas Alva Edison, the man who changed the world by creating over 1,300 inventions, including the phonograph, the electric typewriter, the first practical motion picture camera and projector, and the carbon microphone (which made the telephone possible). ❸ Yet it is not Edison the inventor who captures our interest at the moment, but Edison the social engineer who profoundly changed the psychology of the modern world. It was his desire to be known as the man who finally eradicated the waste of human potential represented by all those hours spent in "unproductive sleep."

3 Edison's reasoning was really quite simple: If sleep could be eliminated, it would add additional hours to the work day. This would improve productivity, bring prosperity to all of society, and hasten the progress of civilization. "Anything which tends to slow work down is a waste," he explained. "We are always hearing people talk about 'loss of sleep' as a calamity. They better call it loss of time, vitality, and opportunities."

4 His plan was fairly straightforward and involved an invention that he had worked on for many years—the electric lightbulb. This great boon to society would banish the darkness and thus make it possible for people to work continuously through the night hours. Edison believed, from personal experience, that sleep was merely a bad habit and could be done away with quite easily. "For myself I never found need of more than four or five hours sleep in the twenty-four," he claimed. His personal experience also convinced him that sleep was ❹ deleterious to health and made people lazy and stupid. "When by chance I have taken more [hours of sleep than usual]," he wrote, "I wake dull and indolent." Edison was later able to confirm his personal experiences with sleep and with the beneficial effects of the lightbulb using other observations: "When I went through Switzerland in a motor-car, so that I could visit little towns and villages, I noted the effect of artificial light on the inhabitants. Where water power and electric light had been developed, everyone seemed normally

STRATEGIES IN ACTION

❶ Think about the title; read actively by questioning.

ONE STUDENT'S THOUGHTS

"Is this about Thomas Edison, inventor of the light bulb? What kind of curse could this be?"

❷ Note the writer's technique of using a quotation for the introduction.

"That's a pretty extreme statement. I wonder if this quotation reflects the writer's point of view."

❸ Notice the article's main idea.

"Now I see that this essay is going to be about Edison and how he influenced our sleep patterns."

❹ Use context clues to determine word meanings.

"Here, the writer is discussing the negative effects that Edison attributed to sleep. *Deleterious* must mean 'harmful.'"

YOUR TURN

Use context clues to determine the meaning of other words in the selection.

Strategies in Action

1. Begin by previewing the text. Note the title and identify the subject of the reading selection. Read through the questions and prompts at the end of the text. Ask students what they will need to look for as they read.

   Possible Response: Students should look for information about Edison and what kind of curse he might have caused or received.
2. Remind students to read the quotation critically; the fact that someone has been quoted to say that most people sleep too much does not mean the statement is necessarily true.
3. Students are more likely to be tested on the main ideas in the selection than on specific details. Ask students which ideas in this paragraph they think are important enough to be included on a test.
4. Use the following questions to help students unlock the meanings of unfamiliar words:

- Does the sentence or paragraph offer any clues to the word's meaning?
- Does the sentence restate or extend information provided earlier in the selection?

YOUR TURN Earlier in the paragraph the writer uses the word *banish.* He says that "this great boon to society [by which he means the light bulb] would *banish* the darkness." When I think about what the light bulb does to darkness, I know that it makes the darkness disappear. I can infer, then, that to banish something is to make it disappear.

TEST PRACTICE

5. Some less proficient readers are inclined to take what they read at face value and not evaluate the validity or the source of what they read. Remind students that writers often include quotations not to make the point that the quoted statement is true, but rather to demonstrate something about the speaker. In this case, the writer is demonstrating that Edison was scornful of people who did not have electric power or electric light. What he perceives as a lack of intelligence is probably a simplicity that he finds among rural people who may be uneducated and unfamiliar with technology.
6. Suggest that students draw a graphic organizer to illustrate the cause-and-effect relationships in this paragraph. Their graphic organizer might look something like this:

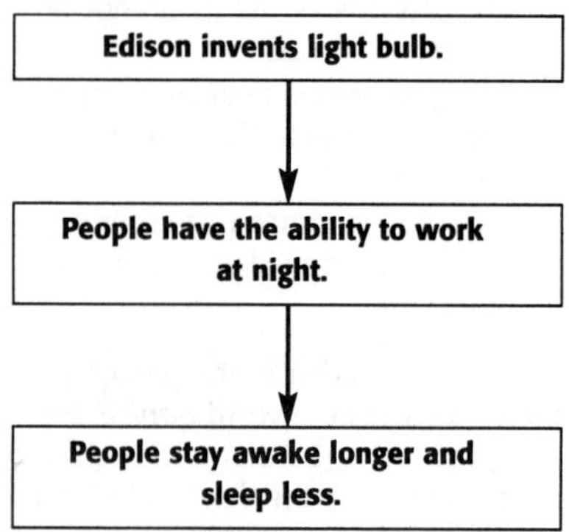

Have students note that the human need for sleep is *not* affected by these changes.

7. Students having trouble with sequence may find it helpful to plot each paragraph on a time line that starts four million years ago and ends in the present. They need not worry about exact dates, although you might want to let them know that Edison invented the first incandescent light bulb in 1879.
8. To save time on a test, students should first read the questions that follow the test selection. Then they can look for answers to the questions as they read. The beginning and end of a selection are often good places to look for information about a writer's purpose.

intelligent. ❺ Where these appliances did not exist, and the natives went to bed with the chickens, staying there till daylight, they were far less intelligent.". . .

5 Did Edison have any effect on human sleep patterns as a result of his invention? I think he would be gratified to learn that ❻ people regularly sleep less now than before the lightbulb was invented and that he is, at least partly, responsible for that. . . .

6 When Edison introduced the lightbulb, he was opening the door to a new technological era that had the potential to allow us to abandon sleep and work around the clock. However, the intended user of this new technology is a biological machine with a very long history of adaptive evolution. Technology has evolved at a speed that has far outstripped the rate of biological evolution. Our physiology cannot change with a flick of the switch. Human beings today are making demands on their bodies and their minds that are in conflict with their biological nature. . . .

7 ❼ For some 4 million years man was basically a hunter and a gatherer. Gathering such foods as nuts, berries, and roots required light and could not be efficiently done in the dark. Hunting also required light. The end result was that man slept through the dark hours because it was too inefficient and too dangerous to do anything else. After all, if there were saber-toothed tigers out there in the dark, it was safer to be asleep in a nice, well-hidden cave. Given the average light cycles in the regions of the world where man is believed to have originally developed, human beings were probably dealing with up to 14 hours of darkness, or relative darkness, each day. Presumably, much of this time was spent sleeping. . .

8 Unfortunately, we still have the physiology of the hunter-gatherer. . . . Evolution has not yet responded to the needs of the night shift worker or the hard-driving, ambitious stock manager monitoring the Tokyo exchange prices from his New York apartment in the middle of the night. No matter how wasteful sleep may seem to us today, it has probably evolved for a purpose.

9 Just how much flexibility do we have in terms of our sleep requirements? Is sleep really a worthless time-out period that merely squanders one-third of our lives? If so, can we find some way to go without it or at least reduce its wasteful impact? If not, are there any long-term or serious consequences of our modern proclivity to do without sleep or at least to cheat as much as possible on our sleep time? ❽ The answers to these questions are becoming more important because it is beginning to look like many current problems may have more to do with too little sleep rather than with time wasted sleeping. It seems that we have not evolved fast enough to keep pace with our present technological world.

STRATEGIES IN ACTION

❺ Read actively by evaluating.
"This can't be true. Perhaps Edison was noticing that people with electric lights were more cultured or sophisticated, which he mistook for intelligence."

❻ Note cause-and-effect relationships.
"Edison's invention of the light bulb gave people the opportunity to work through the night and thus give up sleep."

❼ Note the sequence of ideas.
"The writer has chosen to present his information not in chronological order but in another logical order. He begins with Edison's time and then takes us back in time in order to provide background about human sleep patterns."

❽ Skim the questions that follow the selection.
"I see there's a question about the writer's perspective. I think he believes we should question the belief that we can sacrifice sleep for work without negative consequences."

680

Check Your Understanding

Have students use the following questions to test their own understanding of the selection before they answer the questions in their texts.

- What were the main ideas in the selection?
- How does the writer encourage readers to care about the information in the article?
- What structure does the writer use for the selection?
- Did the selection answer all your questions about the subject? If not, what questions remain unanswered?

PART 2 How to Answer Multiple-Choice Questions

Use the strategies in the box at the right and the notes below them to help you answer the questions below.

Choose the best answer for each of the following questions about the selection you have just read.

1. What is "Edison's curse"?
   A. a tendency to overeat
   B. the modern tendency to sacrifice sleep for work
   C. lower levels of intelligence
   D. all of the above
2. Which of the following best describes Thomas Edison as presented in this essay?
   A. an innovator
   B. a social critic
   C. a hard worker
   D. all of the above
3. According to the writer, how did the introduction of the light bulb affect people's sleep habits?
   A. Electric light made it possible for people to work and be active after dark, and as a result, they slept less.
   B. Exposure to electric light changed the chemistry of the human brain in such a way that people required less sleep.
   C. The light bulb made people more intelligent and thus aware of the wastefulness of too much sleep.
   D. People were so excited by the light bulb that they simply could not sleep.
4. Human physiology hasn't changed much since humans were engaged in which of the following lifestyles?
   A. farming
   B. factory work
   C. hunting and gathering
   D. office work
5. Which statement best expresses the writer's point of view?
   A. It is time for human evolution to catch up with technology.
   B. People should better respect the biological need for sleep.
   C. Thomas Edison was ahead of his time.
   D. none of the above

STRATEGIES FOR ANSWERING MULTIPLE-CHOICE QUESTIONS

- **Ask questions** that help you eliminate some of the choices.
- **Pay attention to choices** such as "all of the above" or "none of the above." To eliminate them, all you need to find is one answer that doesn't fit.
- **Skim your notes and the text you've underlined.** Details you noticed as you read may provide answers.

STRATEGIES IN ACTION

Pay attention to choices such as "all of the above."

ONE STUDENT'S THOUGHTS

"Can I eliminate any of the first three choices? Actually, the essay depicts Edison as both an innovator and a social critic, and I don't have the option to choose only two answers: it's either all or one. When I think about it, the essay also conveys that he was a hard worker. The answer must be D."

Skim your notes.

ONE STUDENT'S THOUGHTS

"The writer makes it quite clear that human physiology (and therefore, human brain chemistry) has not changed to accommodate current lifestyles, so I can eliminate choice B."

YOUR TURN

What other choice can you eliminate?

TEST PRACTICE

Guiding Student Response

Multiple Choice Questions

1. B
2. D

YOUR TURN Choice D does not apply because the writer never mentions anything about how people felt about the light bulb when it was invented. Choice C is incorrect; the writer makes it clear that sleep has to do not with intelligence but with biological need.

3. A
4. C
5. B

Short-Answer Question

By quoting Edison about his own sleep habits and his observations of the Swiss villages, the writer shows that Edison believed that sleep was a waste of time and that he believed electric light made people more intelligent and, therefore, less needful of sleep.

YOUR TURN In paragraph 4, the writer quotes Edison as saying that too much sleep makes him dull. He also quotes Edison's description of his trip through Switzerland.

Essay Question

Possible Response to Prompt

The development of technology has caused a significant change in human sleep patterns. For millions of years, human beings were hunter-gatherers who rose with the sun every morning and went to bed as the sun set every evening. This means that people were sleeping as much as fourteen hours a night.

When Thomas Edison invented the light bulb, all of that changed. The light bulb allowed people to stay up and work after dark. With other things to do besides sleep, people began to sleep less. We all know that the average person sleeps far less than fourteen hours a night!

Technology has both tempted and allowed people to sleep less. The light bulb has been a significant cause of this change in human behavior.

PART 3 How to Respond in Writing

Sometimes you will be asked to write answers to questions about a reading selection. **Short-answer questions** usually ask you to answer in a sentence or two. **Essay questions** require a fully developed piece of writing.

Short-Answer Question

- **Identify the key words** in the writing prompt—the words that tell you what ideas to discuss. Make sure you know what each word means.
- **Make your response** direct and to the point.
- **Support your ideas** with evidence from the selection.
- **Use correct grammar.**

Sample Prompt

Answer the following question in one or two sentences.

How does the writer's use of quotations help to characterize Edison?

STRATEGIES IN ACTION

Identify the key words in the writing prompt.

ONE STUDENT'S THOUGHTS

"The key words are *quotations* and *characterize.* I will have to find examples of quotations in the selection and then explain how the writer uses them to characterize Edison. Maybe I can find one quotation in particular to use as an example."

YOUR TURN

Go back to the selection and find a quotation that reveals something about Edison.

Essay Question

STRATEGIES FOR ANSWERING ESSAY QUESTIONS

- **Look for direction words** in the writing prompt—words such as *essay, analyze, describe,* or *compare and contrast* that tell you how to respond directly to the prompt.
- **List the points** you want to make before beginning to write.
- **Write an interesting introduction** that presents your main point.
- **Develop your ideas** by using evidence from the selection that supports the statements you make.
- **Present your ideas** in a logical order.
- **Write a conclusion** that summarizes your points.
- **Check your work** for correct grammar.

Sample Prompt

How has the development of technology caused a change in human sleep patterns? Write an essay in which you analyze this cause-and-effect relationship as it is presented in the selection.

Look for direction words.

ONE STUDENT'S THOUGHTS

"The prompt is asking me to write an *essay* in which I *analyze* the *cause-and-effect relationship* between technology and sleep habits as presented in the selection. I'll have to look through the selection for statements about this relationship and write about the different parts of that relationship."

YOUR TURN

Make a list of statements from the selection that connect technology and sleep in some way. What are the different aspects of the relationship between the two?

PART 4 **How to Revise and Edit a Test Selection**

Here is part of a student's first draft in response to the writing prompt at the bottom of page 682. Read the draft and then answer the multiple-choice questions that follow.

The writer of this essay makes it clear that the sleep habits in our society have been strongly affected by developments in technology—by the introduction of the electric light bulb. Before electric light was available, humans had little reason to stay up late, as they couldn't do much in the dark. When the light bulb was introduced. People suddenly had the ability to work late into the night. Since the invention of the lightbulb people sleep less, although their physical need for sleep had not changed. This loss of sleep will surely have a great effect on our society.

1. What is the BEST modifier to add to the phrase following the dash in the first sentence?

A. specifically,

B. mostly,

C. partly,

D. also,

2. What is the BEST change, if any, to make to the sentences in lines 5–7 ("When the light bulb . . . late into the night.")?

A. When the light bulb was introduced; people suddenly had the ability to work late into the night.

B. When the light bulb was introduced, people suddenly had the ability to work late into the night.

C. People suddenly had the ability to work late into the night when the light bulb was introduced.

D. Make no change.

3. What is the BEST change, if any, to make to the sentence in lines 7–8 ("Since the invention . . . had not changed.")?

A. Since the invention of the light bulb people sleep less, although their physical need for sleep did not change.

B. Since the invention of the light bulb people sleep less, although their physical need for sleep has not changed.

C. Since the invention of the light bulb people sleep less, although their physical need for sleep is not changed.

D. Make no change.

STRATEGIES FOR REVISING, EDITING, AND PROOFREADING

- **Read the text carefully.**
- **Note the parts that are confusing** or don't make sense. What kinds of errors would such problems signal?
- **Look for errors** in grammar, usage, spelling, and capitalization. Common errors include:
  - run-on sentences
  - sentence fragments
  - lack of subject-verb agreement
  - unclear pronoun reference
  - lack of transition words

Guiding Student Response

Answers

1. A
2. B
3. B

Check Your Understanding

Have students re-read their own responses to the short-answer and essay questions. Then have students use the following questions to guide themselves as they revise and edit their own work.

- Have I responded directly to the direction words in the writing prompt?
- Have I supported my ideas with evidence from the selection?
- Have I presented my ideas in a logical order?
- Have I included an introduction and a conclusion?
- Have I used correct grammar?

READING AND WRITING FOR ASSESSMENT 683

Europe in Transition
In this unit, students will read European literature from the Middle Ages, Renaissance, and Enlightenment, a span of centuries marked by great political and spiritual change.

Part 1
Heroic Quests: Literature of the Middle Ages This part includes excerpts from *The Song of Roland,* in which a hero dies defending the Christian faith, and *Perceval*, in which a pure-hearted knight goes in quest of the Holy Grail. An **Author Study** feature examines the work of Dante Aligheri. It focuses on his *Inferno*, in which the narrator is guided on a journey through Hell.

Part 2
Human Possibility: Literature of the Renaissance and Enlightenment
The literature in Part 2 is more secular, concerned with human possibilities in the physical world. For example, in *Utopia*, Thomas More attempts to describe the perfect society. In *Don Quixote* and *Candide*, Cervantes and Voltaire mock idealists who seek glory and a perfect world. In their artful sonnets, Petrarch and Shakespeare elevate earthly love between men and women. A feature, **Comparing Literature Across Cultures,** allows students to compare two other sonnets by female poets of the time.

Europe in Transition
400–1789

Primavera [Spring] (c. 1481), Sandro Botticelli. Uffizi, Florence, Italy. Photograph copyright © Scala/Art Resource, New York.

"We are such stuff as dreams are made on. . . ."

—William Shakespeare

Making Connections

Explain that the quotation on page 685, from Shakespeare's play *The Tempest,* comments on the insubstantial and impermanent nature of human life.

Ask: How important are dreams, and why? Is it good or bad to have one's life compared to a dream?

Possible Responses: Dreams are important because they inspire art and lead people to achieve what they imagine. Dreams are unimportant because they do not last and often do not make much sense. A life resembling a dream is good because it is full of beauty and surprise. A life resembling a dream is bad because it is brief and inconsequential.

PART 1 SKILLS TRACE

Features and Selections	Literary Analysis	Reading and Critical Thinking	Writing Opportunities
Europe in Transition 400–1789			
Heroic Quests: Literature of the Middle Ages		Interpreting the Text, 689, 691 Using the Time Line, 693	
EPIC *from* The Song of Roland	Epic Hero, 697, 707 Epic Hero, 698, 700, 702, 706	Questioning, 697, 707 Questioning, 698, 704, 706 Christians and Muslims in the Middle Ages, 699 The Code of Chivalry, 702 Relics, 705 What Follows in *The Song of Roland,* 706	
ROMANCE *from* Perceval: The Story of the Grail	Romance, 709, 722 Romance, 710, 716, 720	Strategies for Reading a Romance, 709, 722 Strategies for Reading a Romance, 710, 712, 714, 716, 718 Arthurian Literature: The Holy Grail, 710 What Follows in *Perceval: The Story of the Grail,* 720 Wagner's *Parsifal,* 721	
Connect to Today The Arthurian Legend in Film and Story		Group Discussion, 723	
AUTHOR STUDY **Dante Alighieri**		Using the Time Line, 733	
EPIC POETRY *from the* Inferno Canto 1 Canto 3 Canto 5 *from* Canto 34	Allegory, 736, 759 Allegory, 738, 740, 748	Clarifying Meaning, 736, 759 Clarifying Meaning, 738, 740, 742, 746, 750, 754, 756 Virgil, 740 Hierarchy of Evil, 742 The Rivers of the Underworld, 745 Courtly Lovers, 751 What Follows in *The Divine Comedy,* 756	Subject Analysis, 761
from La Vita Nuova The First Sight of Beatrice The Effects of Love		Clarifying Meaning, 758 Paradiso, 757	
The Author's Style Author Study Project	Analysis of Style, 760		Changing Style, 760 Imitation of Style, 760
Writing Workshop Subject Analysis Standardized Test Practice Building Vocabulary Sentence Crafting		Analyzing a Student Model, 763–764 Patterns of Organization (Analyzing Text Structure), 763	Subject Analysis, 762, 765 Subject Analysis, 762 Choosing a Subject, 765 Planning the Analysis, 765 Drafting, 765
Reflect and Assess	Reflecting on the Literature (The Literature of Honor), 770 Reviewing Literary Concepts (Romance), 770		Building Your Portfolio, 770

LEGEND **Black type – Pupil Edition**
Green type – Teacher's Edition
DLS – Daily Language SkillBuilder

Speaking and Listening Viewing and Representing	Inquiry and Research	Grammar, Usage, and Mechanics	Vocabulary
Using the Map, 687			
Art Appreciation, 701, 704		DLS, 696 Adverb Phrases, 703	Specialized Vocabulary, 698
Art Appreciation, 713, 715 Dramatic Reading, 719 Group Discussion, 723		DLS, 708 Adjective Phrases, 717	Homonyms, 711
Dramatic Reading, 761 Art Appreciation, 738, 746, 754 Dramatic Presentation, 753	Character Profile, 761	DLS, 736 Dashes, 755	Analogies, 761 Context Clues, 739 Using Synonyms, 744
Speaking and Listening, 760	Mapping Dante's Exile (Biographical Sources, Historical Sources), 761 Biographical Sources, 761		
		Using the Active Voice, 766 Avoiding Redundancy, 766, 767 Verb Tenses (inconsistent), 767 Parallelism, 767 Misplaced Modifiers, 767 Changing Word Order for Sentence Variety, 769 Misplaced Modifiers, 767 Using Commas, 769	Understanding Analogies, 768
			Self Assessment, 770 Self Assessment, 770

LEGEND **Black type – Pupil Edition**
Green type – Teacher's Edition
DLS – Daily Language SkillBuilder

PART 2 SKILLS TRACE

Features and Selections	Literary Analysis	Reading and Critical Thinking	Writing Opportunities
Human Possibility: Literature of the Renaissance and Enlightenment		Interpreting the Text, 776, 779 Using the Time Line, 780	
FICTION *from* The Decameron Federigo's Falcon Related Reading *from* The Art of Courtly Love	Situational Irony, 785, 792 Situational Irony, 786, 788, 790	Predicting, 785, 792 Predicting, 786, 788 Jousts and Tournaments, 786 Rules of Courtly Love, 788 Falconry, 789 Discussion Question, 791	Dramatic Scene, 793 Comparing Portrayals of Love, 793
ROMANCE *from* Utopia The Land and Its People Occupations The Commonwealth Outside Utopia Connect to Today Searching for Utopia	Author's Purpose, 795, 802 Author's Purpose, 796, 798	Drawing Conclusions, 795, 802 Drawing Conclusions, 796, 798 More, the Reformer, 796 More's Trial and Execution, 800 Group Activity, 803 Group Activity, 803	Informal Assessment (Summarizing), 799
Learning the Language of Literature The Sonnet	The Sonnet, 804, 805	Strategies for Reading, 805	
POETRY The Sonnet Poets Sonnet 3 To Hélène The Translator at Work Dealing with the Sonnet	Extended Metaphor, 806, 810 Extended Metaphor, 806	Comparing and Contrasting Speakers, 806, 810 Comparing and Contrasting Speakers, 808 Women in Sonnets, 808 Ronsard's Influence, 809 Paired Activity (Compare and Contrast), 811	
POETRY Shakespeare Sonnets Sonnet 29 Sonnet 30 Sonnet 64	Meter, 813, 817 Meter, 814	Clarifying Meaning in Sonnets, 813, 817 Clarifying Meaning in Sonnets, 814, 816 Phrases from Shakespeare, 814	
Comparing Literature Across Cultures Sonnets by Women		Compare and Contrast, 820, 823, 826	Comparison-and-Contrast Essay, 820 Standardized Test Practice (Comparison-and-Contrast Essay), 820
POETRY Sonnet 23	Tone, 821, 823 Tone, 822	Analyzing Diction, 821, 823 Analyzing Diction, 822	
POETRY Sonnet 165		Analyzing Diction, 824 Sor Juana's Life as a Nun, 824	
Comparing Literature Standardized Test Practice			Comparison-and-Contrast Essay, 827 Standardized Test Practice (Responding to a Writing Prompt), 827

LEGEND **Black type – Pupil Edition**
Green type – Teacher's Edition
DLS – Daily Language SkillBuilder

Speaking and Listening Viewing and Representing	Inquiry and Research	Grammar, Usage, and Mechanics	Vocabulary
Using the Map, 772			
Storytelling Festival, 793 Booklet of Quotations, 793 Discussion Question, 791	Report on Courtly Love, 793	DLS, 784 Participles and Participial Phrases, 790	Context Clues, 793 Related Words, 787
Group Activity, 803 Group Activity, 803		DLS, 794 Gerunds, 801	Antonyms, 803 Word Families, 798
Analyzing Visual Images, 807		DLS, 806	
Reading Poetry Aloud, 816		DLS, 812	
		DLS, 821	
Oral Interpretation of Poetry, 825		DLS, 824	

LEGEND **Black type – Pupil Edition**
Green type – Teacher's Edition
DLS – Daily Language SkillBuilder

Features and Selections	Literary Analysis	Reading and Critical Thinking	Writing Opportunities
FICTION *from* Don Quixote Chapter 1, Part 1 Chapter 7, Part 1 Chapter 8, Part 1 **Related Reading** A Soldier of Urbina	Characterization, 829, 844 Characterization, 830, 832, 834, 836, 838, 840	Analyzing Exposition, 829, 844 Analyzing Exposition, 830, 832, 834 International Popularity of *Don Quixote,* 830 Knights-Errant and Romances, 832 Standardized Test Practice (Identifying Cause and Effect), 836 Sancho Panza, 838 Don Quixote: The Rest of the Story, 842 Discussion Questions, 843	Speech about Chivalry, 845 Letter from Sancho, 845
FICTION *from* Candide Chapter I Chapter II	Satire and Humor, 849, 856 Satire and Humor, 850, 852, 854	Making Judgments, 849, 856 Making Judgments, 850, 852, 854 Liebniz and the Best of All Possible Worlds, 851 The Prussian Army, 853	Satirical Writing, 857 War Diary, 857
Communication Workshop Persuasive Speech Standardized Test Practice Building Vocabulary Sentence Crafting		Analyzing a Student Model, 859–860 Patterns of Organization (Picturing Text Structure), 860	Writing and Delivering Your Persuasive Speech, 861 Steps for Planning Your Speech, 861
Reflect and Assess	Reflecting on the Literature (In Pursuit of an Ideal), 866 Reviewing Literary Concepts (Sonnet), 866		Building Your Portfolio, 866

LEGEND **Black type – Pupil Edition**
Green type – Teacher's Edition
DLS – Daily Language SkillBuilder

Speaking and Listening Viewing and Representing	Inquiry and Research	Grammar, Usage, and Mechanics	Vocabulary
Quixote Improv, 845 Art Appreciation, 833, 839	Chivalrous Knights, 845 Fantasy and Reality, 845	DLS, 828	Context Clues, 845 Using a Dictionary to Find Precise Meaning, 831
Discussion Questions, 843		Infinitive Phrases, 843	
Candide's Song, 857 Voltaire News, 857 Art Appreciation, 855	The Lisbon Earthquake, 857 Voltaire's World, 857	DLS, 848 Placement of Participial Phrases, 854	Synonyms, 857 Context Clues, 852
Writing and Delivering Your Persuasive Speech, 861 Steps for Delivering Your Speech, 862 Responding to Audience Feedback, 862 Steps for Delivering the Speech, 862		Pronoun Case, 863 Combining Sentences, 863 Pronoun-Antecedent Agreement, 863 Subject-Verb Agreement, 863 Using Noun Clauses, 865 Subject-Verb Agreement, with Indefinite Pronouns as Subjects, 863 Using *Who* and *Whom*, 865	Affixes, 864
			Self Assessment, 866 Self Assessment, 866

LEGEND **Black type – Pupil Edition**
Green type – Teacher's Edition
DLS – Daily Language SkillBuilder

RESOURCE MANAGEMENT GUIDE PART 1

	Unit Resource Book	Assessment	Integrated Technology and Media	Additional Support
Heroic Quests **Literature of the Middle Ages**			Humanities classzone.com	**World Art and Cultures Transparencies** • AT28 Tomb of Charlemagne [detail] • AT30 Notre Dame de Paris • AT31 *Entry of the Crusaders into Constantinople, 12 April 1204*
from **The Song of Roland** *pp. 696–707*	• Summary p. 4 • Active Reading p. 5 • Literary Analysis p. 6 • Selection Quiz p. 7	• Selection Test, Formal Assessment pp. 109–110 • Teacher's Guide to Assessment and Portfolio Use Test Generator	Humanities Activity classzone.com	
from **Perceval: The Story of the Grail** *pp. 708–723*	• Summary p. 8 • Active Reading p. 9 • Literary Analysis p. 10 • Selection Quiz p. 11	• Selection Test, Formal Assessment pp. 111–112 • Teacher's Guide to Assessment and Portfolio Use Test Generator		
Author Study **Dante Alighieri** *pp. 732–735*			Author Link classzone.com NetActivities	
from the **Inferno** **Canto 1** **Canto 3** **Canto 5** *from* **Canto 34** *pp. 736–756* *from* **La Vita Nuova** **The First Sight of Beatrice** **The Effects of Love** *pp. 757–761*	• Summary p. 12 • Active Reading p. 13 • Literary Analysis p. 14 • Words to Know p. 15 • Selection Quiz p. 16	• Selection Test, Formal Assessment pp. 113–114 • Teacher's Guide to Assessment and Portfolio Use Test Generator	Research Starter classzone.com	An excerpt from this selection is included in the *World Literature InterActive Reader*™.

Writing Workshop: Subject Analysis *pp. 762—769*

Unit Five Resource Book
- Prewriting p. 17
- Drafting and Elaboration p. 18
- Peer Response Guide pp. 19–20
- Revising, Editing, and Proofreading p. 21
- Student Models pp. 22–26
- Rubric p. 27

Publishing Options classzone.com

Teacher's Guide to Assessment and Portfolio Use

Unit Assessment	Unit Technology
• Unit Five, Part 1 Test, Formal Assessment pp. 115–116 Test Generator • Unit Five Integrated Test, Integrated Assessment pp. 25–30	classzone.com NetActivities

	Unit Resource Book	Assessment	Integrated Technology and Media	Additional Support
Human Possibility **Literature of the Renaissance and Enlightenment**			Humanities classzone.com	**World Art and Cultures Transparencies** • AT36 *The Last Supper* • AT37 *Mona Lisa* • AT38 *Wedding Portrait* • AT41 The Tower of Belem • AT43 *Meeting of Cortes and Montezuma* • AT45 *Banquet of the Officers of Haarlem's Civic Guard, Saint George Company* • AT48 *The Astronomer* • AT49 *The Pottery-Mender* • AT50 *Portrait of Marie Antoinette with Her Children*
from **The Decameron** **Federigo's Falcon** *pp. 784–793*	• Summary p. 31 • Active Reading p. 32 • Literary Analysis p. 33 • Words to Know p. 34 • Selection Quiz p. 35	• Selection Test, Formal Assessment pp. 117–118 • Teacher's Guide to Assessment and Portfolio Use Test Generator	Research Starter classzone.com	
from **Utopia** **The Land and Its People** **Occupations** **The Commonwealth Outside Utopia** *pp. 794–803*	• Summary p. 36 • Active Reading p. 37 • Literary Analysis p. 38 • Words to Know p. 39 • Selection Quiz p. 40	• Selection Test, Formal Assessment pp. 119–120 • Teacher's Guide to Assessment and Portfolio Use Test Generator	Research Starter classzone.com	
Sonnet 3 **To Hélène** *pp. 806–811*	• Active Reading p. 41 • Literary Analysis p. 42	• Selection Test, Formal Assessment pp. 121–122 • Teacher's Guide to Assessment and Portfolio Use Test Generator		
Sonnet 29 **Sonnet 30** **Sonnet 64** *pp. 812–817*	• Active Reading p. 43 • Literary Analysis p. 44	• Selection Test, Formal Assessment pp. 123–124 • Teacher's Guide to Assessment and Portfolio Use Test Generator		
Milestones in World Literature **The Plays of Shakespeare** *pp. 818–819*			Milestone Links classzone.com	
Sonnet 23 *pp. 820–823* **Sonnet 165** *pp. 824–827*	• Points of Comparison p. 45 • Active Reading p. 46 • Literary Analysis p. 47 • Compare/contrast Essay p. 48	• Selection Test, Formal Assessment pp. 125–126 • Teacher's Guide to Assessment and Portfolio Use Test Generator	Humanities Activity classzone.com	

	Unit Resource Book	Assessment	Integrated Technology and Media	Additional Support
from **Don Quixote** **Chapter 1, Part 1** **Chapter 7, Part 1** **Chapter 8, Part 1** ***pp. 828–845***	• Summary p. 49 • Active Reading p. 50 • Literary Analysis p. 51 • Words to Know p. 52 • Selection Quiz p. 53	• Selection Test, Formal Assessment pp. 127–128 • Teacher's Guide to Assessment and Portfolio Use Test Generator	Research Starter classzone.com	This selection is included in the *World Literature InterActive Reader™*.
Milestones in World Literature **The Plays of Molière** ***pp. 846–847***			Milestone Links classzone.com	
from **Candide** **Chapter I** **Chapter II** ***pp. 848–857***	• Summary p. 54 • Active Reading p. 55 • Literary Analysis p. 56 • Words to Know p. 57 • Selection Quiz p. 58	• Selection Test, Formal Assessment pp. 129–130 • Teacher's Guide to Assessment and Portfolio Use Test Generator	Research Starter classzone.com	

Communication Workshop: Persuasive Speech *pp. 858–865*

Unit Five Resource Book
- Planning and Drafting p. 59
- Practicing and Delivering p. 60
- Peer Response Guide pp. 61–62
- Refining Your Delivery p. 63
- Student Models pp. 64–68
- Rubric and Standards p. 69

Publishing Options classzone.com

Teacher's Guide to Assessment and Portfolio Use

Unit Assessment	Unit Technology
• Unit Five, Part 2 Test, Formal Assessment pp. 131–132 Test Generator	classzone.com

Selection	SkillBuilder Sentences	Suggested Answers
from The Song of Roland	**1.** Roland the count rode his horse through the spanish passes. **2.** Grabbing their swords, the horses are mounted by the soldiers.	**1.** Roland the **C**ount rode his horse through the **S**panish passes. **2.** Grabbing their swords, **the soldiers mounted the horses.**
from Perceval: The Story of the Grail	**1.** The boy restrain his self from asking about the white lance. **2.** Although they are centuries old. The legends about king Arthur still entertain modern audiences.	**1.** The boy **restrains himself** from asking about the white lance. **2.** Although they are centuries old**, t**he legends about **K**ing Arthur still entertain modern audiences.
from the Inferno Canto 1 Canto 3 Canto 5 *from* Canto 34	**1.** He set out, and I followed where he lead. **2.** There's words over the door that I can't understand.	**1.** He set out, and I followed where he **led**. **2.** **There are** words over the door that I can't understand.
from La Vita Nuova The First Sight of Beatrice The Effects of Love	**1.** The sight of Beatrice effected Dante strangely. **2.** Dante been teased by friends who wanted to know why was he acting so strange.	**1.** The sight of Beatrice **affected** Dante strangely. **2.** Dante **had** been teased by friends who wanted to know why he **was** acting so strange.
from The Decameron Federigo's Falcon	**1.** Who do Federigo finally marry? **2.** In Medieval times, love was a kind of suffering.	**1.** **Whom does** Federigo finally marry? **2.** In **m**edieval times, love was a kind of suffering.
from Utopia The Land and Its People Occupations The Commonwealth Outside Utopia	**1.** In the book "Utopia," a mysterious traveler visits a faraway island. **2.** Thomas More an English author became a member of parliament.	**1.** In the book **<u>Utopia</u>**, a mysterious traveler visits a faraway island. **2.** Thomas More**,** an English author**,** became a member of **P**arliament.

DAILY LANGUAGE SKILLBUILDERS

Selection	SkillBuilder Sentences	Suggested Answers
Sonnet 3 To Hélène	1. A sonnet is suppose to have fourteen lines. 2. Petrarch loved Laura, but she does not love him.	1. A sonnet is **supposed** to have fourteen lines. 2. Petrarch loved Laura, but she **did** not love him.
Sonnet 29 Sonnet 30 Sonnet 64	1. His love, because the young man thought of her, made him feel much better. 2. Shakespeare was one of London's most successful playwrights he wrote more than 35 plays.	1. **Because he thought of his love,** the young man **felt** much better. 2. Shakespeare was one of London's most successful playwrights**. He** wrote more than 35 plays.
Sonnet 23	1. Louise Labé's father could neither read nor write, however; he worked to give her an education. 2. The man in the poem promised always to love her, unfortunately; he gone away.	1. Louise Labé's father could neither read nor write**;** however**,** he worked to give her an education. 2. The man in the poem promised always to love her**. Unfortunately,** he **went** away.
Sonnet 165	1. Sor Juana's letter, it criticized a well-known priest. 2. Although, you are not here with me. You will be in my thoughts for ever.	1. Sor Juana's letter **criticized** a well-known priest. [Students should remove the comma and *it*.] 2. Although you are not here with me**, you** will be in my thoughts **forever**. [Students should remove the comma after *Although*.]
from Don Quixote Chapter 1, Part 1 Chapter 7, Part 1 Chapter 8, Part 1	1. Don Quixote polished each piece of armor and adjusted them to fit his body. 2. The priest and the barber tried to cure they're friend's sickness by hiding his books.	1. Don Quixote polished each piece of armor and adjusted **it** to fit his body. 2. The priest and the barber tried to cure **their** friend's sickness by hiding his books.
from Candide Chapter I Chapter II	1. Twice Voltaire insulted important people and were imprisoned both times. 2. Neither the shooting nor the beatings was a desirable punishment for Candide.	1. Twice Voltaire insulted important people and **was** imprisoned both times. 2. Neither the shooting nor the beatings **were** a desirable punishment for Candide.

INTEGRATING GRAMMAR AND LITERATURE: GRAMMAR PLANNER

Grammar Focus by Unit	Unit One	Unit Two	Unit Three	Unit Four	Unit Five	Unit Six	Unit Seven
	Parts of Speech	The Sentence and Its Parts	Using Verbs	Using Modifiers	Using Phrases	Clauses and Sentence Structure	Clauses and Sentence Structure

The Language of Literature offers several options for integrating grammar instruction and literature.

- Each unit has a grammar focus. The Teacher's Edition includes Mini Lessons for the selections that help develop the grammar focus for the unit and spring from the content of the specific literature.
- The Pupil Edition includes several full-page lessons on Sentence Crafting. These lessons are related to both the literature and the grammar focus for a unit and help students use proper grammar in their own writing.
- Daily Language SkillBuilders in the Teacher's Edition provide students with ongoing proofreading practice and reinforce correct punctuation, spelling, grammar and usage, and capitalization.

Black type — Pupil Edition
Green type — Teacher's Edition

Part 1

Using Phrases

Prepositional Phrase as Adverb
from *The Song of Roland,* p. 703

Prepositional Phrase as Adjective
from *Perceval: The Story of the Grail,* p. 717

Punctuation

Dashes
from the *Inferno,* p. 755

Comma Uses
Sentence Crafting, p. 769

Using Verbs

Voice of a Verb
Writing Workshop, p. 766

Shifts in Tense
Standardized Test Practice, p. 767

Style

Redundancy
Writing Workshop, p. 766
Standardized Test Practice, p. 767

Parallelism
Standardized Test Practice, p. 767

Changing Word Order for Sentence Variety
Sentence Crafting, p. 769

Using Modifiers

Misplaced Modifiers
Standardized Test Practice, p. 767
Standardized Test Practice, p. 767

Part 2

Using Phrases

Verbals: Participles
"Federigo's Falcon," from *The Decameron,* p. 790

Verbals: Gerunds
"The Commonwealth Outside Utopia," from *Utopia,* p. 801

Verbals: Infinitives
"A Soldier of Urbina," p. 843

Placement of Participial Phrases
Chapter II, from *Candide,* p. 854

Subject-Verb Agreement

Lack of Subject-Verb Agreement
Standardized Test Practice, p. 863

Agreement with Indefinite Pronouns as Subjects
Standardized Test Practice, p. 863

Using Pronouns

Cases
Standardized Test Practice, p. 863

Pronoun-Antecedent Agreement
Standardized Test Practice, p. 863

Who* and *Whom
Sentence Crafting, p. 865

Clauses and Sentence Structure

Noun Clauses
Sentence Crafting, p. 865

The Sentence and Its Parts

Combining Sentences
Standardized Test Practice, p. 863

Unit Five, Part 1, provides an overview of the Middle Ages and a rich sample of medieval literature, including excerpts from *Song of Roland,* Chrétien de Troyes' "Perceval: The Story of the Grail," and Marie de France's "The Lay of the Were-Wolf." In addition, the **Dante Alighieri Author Study** offers students an opportunity to focus on a major work by one of the greatest poets of all time.

World Art and Cultures Transparencies

AT28 Tomb of Charlemagne [detail]

AT30 Notre Dame de Paris

AT31 *Entry of the Crusaders into Constantinople, 12 April 1204*

You may use the listed transparencies to acquaint students with art from the Middle Ages.

READING FOR INFORMATION

Reading Skills and Strategies

PREVIEWING

Give students a few moments to look over this introduction. It provides background information about the Middle Ages, providing students with a context for the literature they will read in this unit part.

Reading Skills and Strategies

USING A KEY

Make sure students are aware of the types of information provided on pages 686 and 687: the map with its distance scale, the images of medieval life, and the captions. On the distance scale, 1 and $\frac{11}{16}$ inches represents 500 miles. Point out that the numbers in red circles preceding the captions relate their information to specific locations on the map.

PART 1 Heroic Quests

Literature of the Middle Ages

Why It Matters

Valiant knights, elegant damsels, towering cathedrals, moated castles—such associations have helped establish the Middle Ages as an era of magical romance and adventure. Learning about that fascinating time will help you explore its mysteries and understand its magnificent literature.

For Links to the Middle Ages, click on: HUMANITIES CLASSZONE.COM

To the Manor Born In the social and economic system called **feudalism,** lords granted land in exchange for loyalty and military service. A lord's estate, called a manor, was a self-sufficient small community that included workshops and a church as well as houses and farmland. Peasants called **serfs** worked the land belonging to the manor.

3 **Towns and Cities** As farming improved and the population grew, small communities gradually evolved into towns and cities, where **guilds** —organizations of skilled workers—gained great influence. Cities like Paris and London became important trading centers; Italian ports like Venice and Naples prospered from trade with the East.

686 UNIT FIVE PART 1: LITERATURE OF THE MIDDLE AGES

1 Age of Faith During the Middle Ages, the church was a civilizing force in an otherwise unstable world. The church guided human conduct, and its ceremonies and sacraments were important to community life. As an expression of faith, people built huge **cathedrals** like the one at Chartres, France, pictured above, and made pilgrimages to sacred sites.

2 Age of Warfare Castles were built for protection in an era of almost constant warfare. Over time, pagan warriors gave way to Christian knights who followed (at least in theory) a code of conduct known as **chivalry.** Knights also took part in the **Crusades,** wars to free Jerusalem from Muslim rule.

MINI LESSON Using the Map

Have students study the map on pages 686 and 687 and then answer questions such as the following:

- Which direction did the Crusaders from France take to reach Jerusalem? *(southeast)*
- How many miles lie between Paris and Jerusalem? *(about 2,000 miles)*
- Which city is closer to Rome—Florence or Paris? *(Florence)*
- Which body of water separates England and France? *(the English Channel)*

READING FOR INFORMATION
Reading Skills and Strategies
CLARIFYING

Tell students that the history of the Middle Ages is divided into four periods, each represented by a different color on the key at the bottom of these pages. The Middle Ages extend from 476, the traditional date for the fall of the Western Roman Empire, to 1500, a time shortly after Gutenberg's invention of the printing press and Columbus's voyage to the New World. Tell students to use the column headings as a guide to the content and to note the boldfaced terms. Point out that the feature **History to Literature** lists historical events on the left and corresponding literary events on the right. Finally, have students use the color key at the bottom to identify the year that divides the Early Middle Ages and the High Middle Ages. *(A.D. 1000)*

Historical Note

A **Monasticism** The church built monasteries, or religious communities for men. Their members, known as monks, gave up all their possessions, devoting their lives to prayer and self-discipline. Similarly, women with a religious vocation joined convents and became nuns. Around 520, Benedict of Nursia, an Italian monk, drew up a rule for monastic life that set aside time each day for prayer, study, and work. Monasteries in Western Europe soon became centers of learning. Monks opened schools, set up libraries, and copied by hand works of classical antiquity, thus preserving them for future generations.

Historical Highlights

The fall of the Western Roman Empire ushered in a period of European history known as the Middle Ages. A new social order gradually emerged in this period, which lasted from 476 until about 1500.

The Beginnings

476–700

The European Middle Ages, or medieval period, began in A.D. 476, when the Western Roman Empire finally collapsed. Western Europe became a collection of tribal kingdoms, each with its own laws and customs. Trade and communications declined, roads deteriorated, and many cities died out. Learning also declined, except for what was preserved in the one major institution that survived the collapse—the **Roman Catholic Church.** After a time, religious communities sprang up in the countryside—monasteries for men and convents for women. Gradually, many of the Germanic tribes began to adopt Christianity, starting with the Franks (who occupied what is now France). The church itself began to wield political influence under **Gregory I,** who became pope in 590.

The Early Middle Ages

700–1000

In the early 700s, Charles Martel came to power among the Franks, establishing a dynasty. His grandson **Charlemagne,** or Charles the Great, expanded the kingdom, uniting most of western Europe in an empire that was the forerunner of the Holy Roman Empire. After his death in 814, however, his heirs split the empire. In these violent times, there arose a system now called **feudalism,** in which landowners, or **lords,** gave out parcels of land, called **fiefs,** in exchange for military service. A person receiving a fief was known as a **vassal.** It was possible for one lord to have several vassals, some of whom might even live in a different country.

Charlemagne

The High Middle Ages

1000–1300

As invasions subsided and farming improved, western Europe entered a period of prosperity often called the High Middle Ages. Feudalism dominated continental Europe and was introduced into Britain when **William of Normandy** invaded England in 1066. During this period trade resumed, towns again sprang up, and occupations became more diversified. Merchants and skilled workers banded together in organizations called **guilds.** They held trade fairs and traveled the roads, exchanging not only goods but new ideas. The spread of ideas led to the founding of new centers of learning—the first **universities.**

Throughout the feudal age, the church was a powerful force that bound the people of Europe together. Saint Dominic

THE BEGINNINGS 476 | THE EARLY MIDDLE AGES 700

and Saint Francis of Assisi founded new orders of traveling preachers who proclaimed the gospel and helped the needy. The new wealth in this age of faith found an outlet in the building of great cathedrals and the making of **pilgrimages,** or journeys to holy sites.

In 1095, Pope Urban II issued a call for a holy war, or **crusade,** to take Jerusalem from Muslim control. Over the next two centuries, several expeditions of knights set out on the Crusades. Though the effort ultimately failed, contact with Byzantine and Muslim cultures contributed to the rebirth of prosperity and learning in western Europe.

The Late Middle Ages

1300–1500

About 1300, medieval Europe entered a period of great change. The growth of banking was transforming the old economy into one based on trade and commerce. Since a strong central government was better for trade, city merchants began to support a strong monarchy. Towns grew into cities, offering a life free of feudal restrictions but also one in which crowded conditions helped spread fires and deadly diseases. Between 1347 and 1352, a terrible plague known as the **Black Death** devastated Europe. B

It was a time of conflict within the church and between nations. In England, John Wycliffe began to question church authority. The French monarchy, too, came into conflict with the church during the Great Schism, in which rival popes ruled in Rome and France.

France's great rival of this period, however, was England, with its hereditary claims to French lands. In the **Hundred Years' War** (1337–1453) England gave up those claims but not before executing **Joan of Arc,** a girl who had rallied the French. Spain also saw much fighting until Ferdinand and Isabella succeeded in expelling the Muslims in 1492—the year in which Isabella agreed to finance Columbus's voyage across the Atlantic Ocean.

History to Literature

EVENT IN HISTORY	EVENT IN LITERATURE
Charlemagne's army is attacked in Spain.	The *Song of Roland* celebrates a hero who was killed in that attack.
Thomas à Becket is murdered at Canterbury Cathedral, which becomes a place of pilgrimage.	Geoffrey Chaucer's *Canterbury Tales* vividly portrays people from different walks of life on a pilgrimage to this cathedral.
Political feuds in the Italian city of Florence cause Dante to be banished.	While in exile, Dante is inspired to compose his masterpiece, *The Divine Comedy.*

The Wife of Bath from *The Canterbury Tales*

THE HIGH MIDDLE AGES — THE LATE MIDDLE AGES

1000 — 1300 — 1500

Historical Note

B The Black Death The bubonic plague, known as the Black Death, terrorized Europe. Deriving its name from the dark spots it produced on the skin, the plague was spread by infected fleas carried by rats. The Black Death began in Asia, traveled along the trade routes to Europe, and then swept first through Italy and later through France, Germany, England, and other countries. By 1400, the Black Death had claimed about 40 million lives in Europe alone.

MINI LESSON Interpreting the Text

Have students read pages 688 and 689 and then answer questions such as the following:

- Which institution grew stronger even after the fall of the Western Roman Empire? *(the Church)*
- How were Charles Martel and Charlemagne related? *(Charlemagne was Charles Martel's grandson.)*
- Feudalism was a system of land holding in western Europe during the Middle Ages. What obligation did a vassal owe his lord in return for the land he received? *(military service)*
- How did it happen that William of Normandy had vassals in two countries, France and England? *(As the duke of Normandy, he had vassals in France. After invading England, he acquired vassals in that country too.)*
- What armies fought each other in the Crusades? *(knights from Europe and Muslim forces)*

READING FOR INFORMATION
Reading Skills and Strategies
CLASSIFYING
Have students observe that the topic **People and Society** on page 690 is divided into four categories, each of which describes a social group in the Middle Ages: The Ruling Class, The Clergy, Serfs, and Merchants and Artisans. The feature **Women in the Middle Ages** focuses on the role of women in that period. Tell students to pause after reading about each social class and to think about its distinctive features.

Historical Note
(A) **Serfs** Under the feudal system, people belonged to one of three groups, defined by their function in society: those who fought (nobles and knights), those who prayed (women and men of the church) and those who worked (the peasants). Most peasants were serfs, or people who by law could not leave the manor, or the lord's estate. In return for strips of farmland, serfs tended the lord's lands, cared for his animals, and did other needed tasks. Women worked alongside their husbands, tilling the fields and doing chores. Serfs lived in small, dirt-floor cottages and subsisted on simple foods—vegetables, brown bread, grain, and soup.

People and Society

The Ruling Class

Under feudalism, the ruling class included kings, lords, ladies, and their families—all making up a hereditary nobility. Almost every noble was a vassal of someone above and a lord over those below. Though a king was an acknowledged leader, his real power extended only over his own land. Lords called **barons,** who had received land from a king, wielded great power. They, in turn, had the allegiance of lesser lords and knights.

The knights were expected to follow a code of conduct known as **chivalry.** This code stressed loyalty—to God, to one's feudal lord, and to one's chosen lady.

The Clergy

The church had its own hierarchy, at the top of which was the pope. The church owned much land, and those in charge of church lands—for example, bishops at cathedrals and abbots at monasteries—were often as powerful as feudal lords.

In monasteries and convents, monks and nuns devoted much of their time to study and prayer. Friars did not live in monasteries. Instead, they lived in the outside world, traveling and preaching. Priests serving lords might live comfortably, but many priests were poor and came from the peasant class.

Serfs

Many people in the Middle Ages were **serfs,** peasants who (A) were bound to the land and not permitted to leave the manors where they were born. They farmed the land and did outdoor tasks. In exchange for their labor, their lords were expected to house and protect them.

Merchants and Artisans

After a time, towns and cities offered a more varied life outside the feudal structure. Skilled workers belonged to **guilds,** which regulated particular trades—baking, weaving, tailoring, carpentry, and so on. An apprentice worked for a master craftsman without pay for five to nine years. After learning the craft, he was promoted to journeyman and was paid for his work. To rise to master craftsman, a journeyman had to produce a "master piece" that met guild standards.

Women in the Middle Ages

In early feudal times, the wife of a lord could inherit his property and was even expected to defend the manor when her husband was away. Some women even dressed in armor and mounted warhorses. Other women had positions of authority in convents and abbeys. Most women, however, were still poor and powerless. They spent their lives bearing children, raising their families, and doing household tasks.

Arts and Culture

Religion and Medieval Culture

During the Middle Ages, the cultural life of western Europe centered on religion. Writers and artists expressed their faith in a variety of art forms. Scholars explored it in philosophical writings and at the new universities. Most people, though, could not read. For them, the arts served as teaching tools. From paintings, sculptures, stained-glass windows, and dramatic presentations of Bible stories, medieval people learned the truths of their faith.

Literature and Manuscripts

During the Middle Ages, scholarly works were written in **Latin**, which was regarded as the language of the educated in Europe. The Celtic and Germanic cultures, however, had oral traditions in which traveling poet-musicians sang in their native languages about heroic deeds and human joys and sorrows. In the 1100s, epics like the French *Song of Roland* and the Spanish *Song of My Cid* celebrated national heroes, and Celtic legends of a king named Arthur were retold in popular romances. Poet-musicians like the Provençal **troubadours** and the German **minnesingers** entertained at noble courts, singing of love and honor. Medieval monks working as scribes wrote down some of these oral compositions; they also copied the Bible and other works in beautiful **illuminated manuscripts**—decorated with gold, silver, and colorful designs and illustrations.

Scholarship and Universities

Medieval scholarship fell mainly to the clergy; in fact, many lords and ladies never even learned to read and write. At first, monasteries and cathedral schools were the centers of learning, but after the 11th century scholars founded important universities in Paris, Bologna, Oxford, and many other cities. The course of study included religion, philosophy, law, medicine, geometry, astronomy, music, grammar, and logic. Instruction was conducted in Latin.

Arts and Architecture

Medieval works of art were intended to glorify God. Nowhere was this religious purpose more evident than in the awe-inspiring **cathedrals,** which often took generations of devoted effort to complete. Until about 1100, most cathedrals were built in the **Romanesque** style, with small windows and thick walls and columns. Then in the 1100s, the **Gothic** style replaced the Romanesque. Gothic cathedrals thrust upward as if reaching toward heaven. They had tall spires, vaulted ceilings, and huge stained-glass windows that let in light. Paintings, sculptures, and woodcarvings enhanced their interiors. Gothic cathedrals were magnificent temples of the human spirit.

READING FOR INFORMATION
Reading Skills and Strategies
SUMMARIZING

Tell students that the **Arts and Culture** page describes some of the remarkable achievements of the Middle Ages. Have students use the heading of each section as a clue to its content. After students have read a section, have them briefly summarize it, listing the key points.

Historical Note

B **Thomas Aquinas** The scholar Thomas Aquinas (1225–1274) was an Italian Dominican friar. He became the most influential thinker of the Middle Ages. In 1256, he was named professor of theology at the University of Paris. Aquinas, who saw no conflict between faith and reason, taught that the truths of Christianity could be proven by logical argument. Between 1266 and 1273, he wrote his greatest work, *Summa Theologiae,* which combined Aristotle's ideas with Christian beliefs. Aquinas and other scholars at the universities were called Scholastics, and their philosophy was known as Scholasticism. Their ideas about law and government greatly influenced European thought.

MINI LESSON **Interpreting the Text**

Have students read pages 690 and 691 and then answer questions such as the following:

- Under the feudal system, who had the greatest power? *(the lord with the most land and the most vassals)*
- How did friars differ from monks? *(Friars were preachers who traveled about instead of living in monasteries.)*
- What practical use did the fine arts serve in the Middle Ages? *(They taught the illiterate religious stories and truths.)*
- What features distinguished the Gothic style of architecture from the Romanesque? *(tall spires, vaulted ceilings, and huge windows)*

READING FOR INFORMATION
Reading Skills and Strategies
SEQUENCING

This time line shows major dates and events in medieval literature, events in Europe, and events in world history. The dates and events follow in sequence, moving down each column and from left to right. Help students understand that the Middle Ages are often viewed as a transition between Roman times and the Renaissance, the revival of classical learning in Western Europe. Also make sure students understand the abbreviations *c.*, which means "approximately," and A.D., which means "after Christ was born." Have students examine the color key at the top, which visually represents the duration of the Middle Ages.

Historical Note

A Crusades The Crusades led to much cultural exchange between Western Europe and the Muslim world. For example, in the 1100s, Christian scholars visited Muslim libraries in Spain, and Jewish scholars translated Arabic versions of works by Aristotle and other classical Greek writers into Latin. Thus, new resources for knowledge in such disciplines as science, philosophy, law, and mathematics were opened to Western Europe.

Time Line

MEDIEVAL EUROPE (476–1500)

A.D. 1 — PRESENT

c. approximately
B.C. before Christ
A.D. after Christ's birth

EVENTS IN LITERATURE

A.D. 400

427 St. Augustine of Hippo completes his monumental Latin work *The City of God*

524 Roman scholar Boethius writes *The Consolation of Philosophy*

c. 550 Welsh poets Taliesin and Aneirin compose and sing oral verse

597 Irish poet Dallán Forgaill composes *Elegy of St. Columba*

600

c. 650 *Heldenlieder*, early oral Germanic verse in praise of heroes

731 The Venerable Bede completes his Latin history of the English people

c. 750 Earliest versions of Old English epic *Beowulf*

800

c. 850 Scandinavian skalds compose oral verse

c. 950 Beginnings of drama medieval in Europe

c. 950 Oldest surviving Provençal verse

EVENTS IN EUROPE

A.D. 400

449 Traditional date of Britain's invasion by Angles, Saxons, and Jutes

476 Collapse of the Western Roman Empire

520 St. Benedict begins writing rules for monasteries

527 Justinian I becomes Byzantine emperor

600

711 Muslim forces take control of Spain

732 Charles Martel triumphs in Battle of Tours, stopping further Muslim advances in Europe

771 Charlemagne becomes king of the Franks

790–795 Danes (Vikings) attack Britain and Ireland

800

800 Charlemagne is crowned emperor

c. 860 Vikings under Prince Rurik found a Russian state

912 Abd ar-Rahman III takes power in Muslim Spain, making it a center of learning

962 Otto I, a German king, is crowned Holy Roman Emperor

EVENTS IN WORLD HISTORY

A.D. 400

400 Nazca civilization flourishing in Peru; Zapotec civilization, in Mexico

500 Empire of Aksum dominates northeastern Africa

c. 500 Indian mathematicians calculate the value of pi

c. 560 Buddhism is introduced in Japan

600

c. 610 Muhammad begins preaching the faith of Islam

618 Beginning of China's T'ang Dynasty

650 Mayan ➢ civilization flourishing in Mexico

794 Beginning of Japan's Heian period

800

850 Empire of Ghana flourishing in western Africa

c. 900 Anasazi civilization in North America enters classic Pueblo period

935 Korea's Koryo Dynasty begins

939 Vietnamese win independence from China

1000	1200	1400
c. 1100 "Kilhwch and Olwen," Welsh tale that makes early mention of King Arthur **c. 1100** *Song of Roland,* French epic **c. 1140** *Song of My Cid,* Spanish epic **c. 1160** Marie de France and Chrétien de Troyes write narrative verse	**c. 1200** *Nibelungenlied,* German epic by an anonymous Austrian poet **c. 1225** Snorri Sturluson preserves Norse (Scandinavian) mythology in his *Prose Edda* **1321** Italian poet Dante Alighieri completes his allegorical epic *The Divine Comedy* **1386** England's Geoffrey Chaucer begins writing *The Canterbury Tales*	**c. 1450** Medieval morality plays grow popular **1461** French poet François Villon writes his *Testament* **1485** Pioneer English printer William Caxton prints Sir Thomas Malory's famed retelling of Arthurian romances, *Le Morte d'Arthur*

1000	1200	1400
1054 Final split between Eastern Orthodox and Roman Catholic churches **1066** Norman conquest of England **1095** Pope Urban II initiates the Crusades to take the Holy Land from the Muslims (A) **1152** Eleanor of Aquitaine marries Henry II of England	**1260** Chartres Cathedral consecrated in France (B) **1337** Start of Hundred Years' War between France and England **1347** Bubonic plague called the Black Death begins to sweep across Europe	**1431** Joan of Arc is burned at the stake (C) **1453** Byzantine capital of Constantinople falls to the Ottoman Turks **1455** German printer Johann Gutenberg prints landmark Bible on his new press **1492** Muslims ousted from Spain; Columbus begins first voyage to the New World

1000	1200	1400
c. 1000 Viking explorer Leif Eriksson lands in North America **1055** Seljuk Turks come to power in eastern Islamic Empire **1099** Knights of the First Crusade capture Jerusalem **1187** Muslims under Saladin retake Jerusalem from Christian crusaders	**1206** Genghis Khan begins Mongol conquests in Asia **1235** Sundiata founds western Africa's Mali Empire **1368** Chinese overthrow Mongols and establish Ming Dynasty **1398** Timur the Lame (Tamerlane), central Asian invader, devastates India	**1420** Mutota begins Mutapa Empire in southern Africa **1438** Pachacutec becomes ruler of Incas **1502** Montezuma II becomes ruler of Aztecs **1502** First enslaved Africans taken to the Americas

Historical Note

(B) **Chartres Cathedral** A masterpiece of Gothic architecture, Chartres Cathedral is filled with light and rich in beauty. Its 176 stained-glass windows illustrate Bible stories, as do the stone carvings that frame every door. The main part of the cathedral was built in the mid-13th century. According to art historian Kenneth Clark, Chartres Cathedral is "a masterpiece of harmonious proportion."

Historical Note

(C) **Joan of Arc** In 1429, Joan of Arc, a teenaged peasant girl, claimed to hear the voices of saints, who gave her the mission of driving the English from France. She led the French army to victory at Orléans and then had Charles VII crowned King of France at Rheims Cathedral. She was later captured by the Burgundians, who handed her over to the English. They, in turn, gave her to the church authorities to stand trial. Convicted of witchcraft and heresy, she was burned to death at the stake. Though many centuries have passed since her death, the French still honor Joan of Arc as their greatest patriot.

MINI LESSON Using the Time Line

SEQUENCE OF EVENTS Have students study the time line on pages 692 and 693 and then answer questions such as the following:

- Which literary work was composed first, *Beowulf* or the *Nibelungenlied? (Beowulf)*
- Could Joan of Arc have visited Chartres Cathedral? *(Yes, the cathedral was completed about 171 years before her execution.)*
- Did Genghis Khan live before or after Charlemagne? *(after)*
- Was Buddhism introduced to Japan before, during, or after the First Crusade? *(before)*

READING FOR INFORMATION
Reading Skills and Strategies
CONNECTING

Have students study the images and read the captions to increase their understanding of the legacy of the Middle Ages. Then ask students to identify other examples of medieval influence in modern times. You might point out that novels and films about the Old West derive from medieval romances. Cowboy heroes like the Lone Ranger ride on horseback, righting wrongs and defeating villains, as did the knights in Arthurian romances. In addition, the gargoyles that protrude from medieval cathedrals sometimes "decorate" modern buildings as well.

Connect to Today: The Legacy of the Middle Ages

Medieval Festivals
The age of chivalry lives again at medieval fairs. Modern audiences enjoy the pageantry and excitement of a joust as two "knights" on horseback charge at each other.

Courtly Love
The notion of love as a passionate relationship based on personal choice derives from the "courtly love" tradition of the Middle Ages. In this tradition, a lover was required to make sacrifices to prove himself worthy of his beloved. This tradition influences dating and courtship rituals today.

Knights (A)
The Middle Ages continue to stir the imagination. With his skill in battle, his valor, and his moral code of behavior, what is a Jedi knight in *Star Wars* but an updated version of a medieval knight?

Monarchy
Prince William of Great Britain, the grandson of Elizabeth II, helped design his own coat of arms (shown above) to mark his 18th birthday. The design incorporates Elizabeth's coat of arms with the addition of a white label of three points with a red escallop shell on the central point. This shell is derived from the Spencer coat of arms, used by Prince William's mother—the late Diana, princess of Wales.

Historical Note

(A) **Knights** The sons of nobles began their training for knighthood at an early age. At the age of seven, a boy left his family to become a page in a lord's castle, serving his lord and lady, learning courtly manners and the fine points of chivalry, and receiving training in sword fighting. At 14, a page became a squire, or a servant to a knight. His duties included accompanying the knight and taking care of the knight's weapons and horse. Around the age of 21, a squire was dubbed a knight. For a year or two, he might travel with other young knights, sometimes fighting in local wars. Mock battles called tournaments also tested and honed a knight's fighting skills. To the blaring of trumpets, the waving of banners, and the cheering of lords and ladies, knights on horseback charged at each other, trying to unseat their opponent.

Objectives

- understand and appreciate a medieval French **epic poem (Literary Analysis)**
- examine the concept of the **epic hero (Literary Analysis)**
- use the reading strategy of **questioning (Active Reading)**

Summary

Oliver, who is Roland's companion in arms, climbs a hill to scout the enemy, observing a countless number of Saracens. Returning to the Franks, he advises Roland to summon King Charles for reinforcements by blowing an oliphant, or horn. Roland refuses, fearing a loss of reputation if he were to call for help. During the terrible battle, Roland, Oliver, Archbishop Turpin, and the other French nobles fight valiantly, killing thousands of Saracens. Still, the Saracens eventually prevail. Urged by the Archbishop, Roland prepares to blow the oliphant, this time to summon King Charles to avenge the slain French. Roland blows with superhuman force, bursting his blood vessels, and then falls into a faint. A Saracen then tries to steal Roland's sword. Roland revives, kills the thief, and tries to smash his sword, but it will not break. Lying on his sword and oliphant, Roland dies. His soul ascends to heaven.

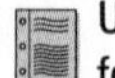

Use **Unit Five Resource Book,** p. 4, for additional support.

Thematic Link

In this medieval French poem, a **heroic** knight lives and dies by the chivalric code.

5-Minute Warm-Up

Daily Language SkillBuilder

Have students **proofread** the display sentences on page 685j and write them correctly.

Build Background

The National Epic of France *The Song of Roland* is the earliest surviving French epic poem. It is a masterpiece of a form of medieval French poetry known as *chanson de geste,* or "song of deeds." These poems—mixing fiction with fact—retell the legends of King Charlemagne (shär'lə-mān') and his court. This particular poem focuses primarily on the noble deeds of Count Roland, the nephew of Charlemagne.

Charlemagne ruled the Franks (an early Germanic tribe) from 768 to 814. In 800, he was crowned emperor by Pope Leo III. A civilized king, he helped spread Christianity, art, and learning throughout western Europe. During the Middle Ages, he was regarded as the ideal of a Christian ruler.

The Song of Roland is loosely based on an incident that occurred during one of Charlemagne's wars. In 778, the king led a siege on the Spanish city of Saragossa. Unable to take the city, he retreated across the Pyrenees, the mountain range that divides Spain and France. In the narrow valley of Roncesvalles (rŏn'sə-vălz'), his rear guard was attacked and destroyed by local Basque (băsk) warriors. Among those slain was Roland, a leader of the rear guard.

In *The Song of Roland,* the skirmish against the Basques is changed to a battle against the Muslims—referred to as "Saracens" or "pagans." This change had deep meaning for Christians in the 12th century. Fresh in their minds were memories of the First Crusade. This "holy war" had been fought from 1096 to 1099 in an attempt to recover the Holy Land from the Muslims. By fighting the Muslims, Roland is thus depicted as a kind of crusader—a Christian warrior who fights to the death against the enemies of Christ.

Unknown Authorship With its stirring descriptions of battle, *The Song of Roland* was very popular during the Middle Ages. The earliest manuscript of the poem dates from the decades after 1100. No one knows who composed the poem or whether it was the work of a single author. Some scholars believe that the poem is the product of several oral poets, each of whom added something to the retelling before passing it down to the next generation. The poem was most likely performed as an entertainment at court by French poets, called *trouvères* (tro͞o-vĕr'), who recited or sang such poems before French lords and ladies.

LESSON RESOURCES

UNIT FIVE RESOURCE BOOK, pp. 4–7

ASSESSMENT RESOURCES
Formal Assessment, pp. 109–110
Teacher's Guide to Assessment and Portfolio Use
Test Generator

INTEGRATED TECHNOLOGY
Visit our Web site: classzone.com

ADDITIONAL RESOURCES
Lesson Planning Guide, pp. 89–90
Teacher's Sourcebook for Language Development

The Story of Roland

As the poem begins, Charlemagne has fought against the Saracens in Spain for seven years. He is supported by his vassals, or those knights who have sworn loyalty to him—including Roland, Oliver, and Archbishop Turpin. The Saracen leader, Marsilion, agrees to accept Charlemagne's demands if the Franks will leave Spain and return to France. Though Roland suspects foul play, he offers to deliver Charlemagne's reply to the Saracens. Charlemagne, however, refuses to send Roland or any of the other volunteers on this risky mission. Roland then nominates his stepfather, Ganelon (gän-lôn'), to serve as envoy to the Saracens. Angry with his stepson for endangering him, Ganelon stoops to treachery. He encourages the Saracens to attack Charlemagne's rear guard on the return to France. He then persuades Charlemagne to give Roland the command of this unit.

As this excerpt begins, Roland and his troops are trapped in a mountain pass in the Pyrenees, greatly outnumbered by the Saracens. Roland's companion Oliver has gone to scout the enemy.

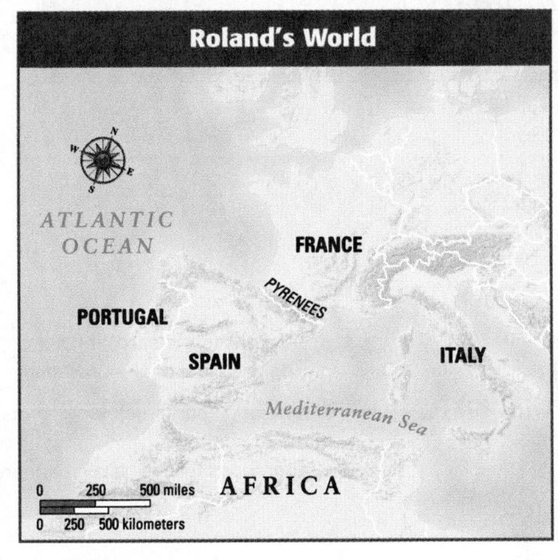

For a humanities activity, click on:

Connect to Your Life

In this poem, Roland finds himself in a difficult situation. He must decide whether to fight the Saracens with only his own troops or to summon his king for reinforcements. How do you react when you find yourself in difficult situations? Do you usually rely on yourself, or do you seek help from someone you trust? Share your views with a small group of classmates.

Focus Your Reading

LITERARY ANALYSIS: EPIC HERO

In an epic poem, as you recall, the main character is the **epic hero,** a larger-than-life figure. In the Middle Ages, poets adapted the concept of the epic hero to reflect the values important to their culture. As you read this excerpt from *The Song of Roland,* consider Roland's decisions and actions. What do they reveal about his values?

ACTIVE READING: QUESTIONING

To understand Roland's function as the **epic hero,** ask yourself questions as you read. Try using the following tips:

- Pay attention to all questions that come to mind.
- Search for reasons behind events. Ask yourself why the characters act as they do.
- Be aware of your own response to what you read. Note any points that cause surprise, confusion, or other emotions.
- Jot down your questions, and supply the answers if and when you find them.

READER'S NOTEBOOK As you read, record any questions that come to mind about the events or characters in the poem. Jot down the answers to your questions as they become clear.

Why does Roland decide to fight the Saracens on his own?

READING FOR INFORMATION

Reading Skills and Strategies

READING A SUMMARY

The Story of Roland Make sure that students grasp the key points of the summary:

- Charlemagne and the French are at war with the Saracens.
- Ganelon goes on a diplomatic mission to the Saracens.
- Ganelon turns traitor and induces the Saracens to attack Charlemagne's rear guard.
- Ganelon then arranges to have Roland lead the rear guard.
- Roland's rear guard is trapped while crossing the Pyrenees.

Reading Skills and Strategies

USING THE MAP

Have students study the map on this page and then answer questions such as the following:

- Which mountains separate France and Spain? *(Pyrenees)*
- Which body of water do Spain, France, and Italy border? *(the Mediterranean Sea)*
- Is Italy closer to France or to Portugal? *(France)*
- Which two bodies of water does France border? *(the Atlantic Ocean and the Mediterranean Sea)*

TIME MANAGEMENT

If your schedule requires that you cover the lesson objectives in a shorter time, use . . .

- Preparing to Read, pp. 696–697
- Thinking Through the Literature, p. 707

If you want to take advantage of longer blocks of class time, use . . .

TE Teaching Options: Viewing and Representing, pp. 701, 704; Vocabulary Strategy, p 698; Cross-Curricular Link, pp. 699, 702, 705, 706; Grammar, p. 703

Reading and Analyzing

Editor's Note This selection was excerpted from a larger work. Material was deleted to shorten and focus the selection.

Reading Skills and Strategies
PREVIEWING
Give students a few minutes to skim, or glance through, the selection for clues about what might happen in it, using any evidence they can find, including pictures and captions in the text.

Literary Analysis EPIC HERO

A Tell students that Roland, the hero of this poem, stands for values that belong to the chivalric code. Have students read lines 12–19 and then ask them what values are important to Roland.

Possible Responses: Personal honor, or reputation, is important to Roland. Though his troops are badly outnumbered, he refuses to call for reinforcements for fear that he appear cowardly.

 Use **Unit Five Resource Book,** p. 6, for more practice.

Active Reading QUESTIONING

B Remind students that they should ask questions about what happens while they read. Searching for reasons behind events can help them be more involved with what they are reading. To model the strategy, pose the following question for students: Why does Oliver say to Roland that no man in the rear-guard will ever be in another?

Possible Response: Oliver believes that the entire rear-guard will be slain.

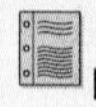 Use **Unit Five Resource Book,** p. 5, for more practice.

from The Song of Roland

Translated by Frederick Goldin

Illustration of Charlemagne's army setting off for Spain. Photograph by Dagli Orti/Biblioteca Nazionale Marciana, Venice/The Art Archive.

81

Oliver has gone up upon a hill,
sees clearly now: the kingdom of Spain,
and the Saracens assembled in such numbers:
helmets blazing, bedecked with gems in gold,
those shields of theirs, those hauberks sewn with brass,
and all their spears, the gonfanons affixed;
cannot begin to count their battle corps,
there are too many, he cannot take their number.
And he is deeply troubled by what he sees.
He made his way quickly down from the hill,
came to the French, told them all he had seen. . . .

3 Saracens (săr′ə-sənz): Muslims during the time of the Crusades.

5 hauberks (hô′bərks): long tunics made of chain mail.

6 gonfanons (găn′fə-nänz′): banners.

MINI LESSON Vocabulary Stategy

SPECIALIZED VOCABULARY

Instruction Have students read pages 698–699 of *The Song of Roland.* Point out the specialized vocabulary word *gonfanons* (page 698, line 6). Have students determine its meaning by using information found in the side column. Next, point out the specialized word *vassals* (page 699, line 23). Have students make inferences about its meaning by examining its context. The phrases "Roland is good, and Oliver is wise" and "men of amazing courage" suggest that vassals are brave and honorable knights.

Practice Have students use side column information and/or context clues to determine the meaning of the following specialized words. Have students explain which method(s) they used in their work.

1. "hauberks," page 698, line 5 *(side note and/or context clues; "sewn with brass" suggests that hauberks are garments made of metal)*
2. "olifant," page 699, line 30 *(side note and/or context clues; "Charles is far away" and "to sound" suggest that an olifant is a horn that can be heard across long distances)*
3. "lance," page 699, line 42 *(context clues; "He bears his arms" and "hefting it, working it, now swings the iron point up toward the sky" suggest that a lance is a long weapon with a metal head)*

83

[1] Said Oliver: "The pagan force is great;
from what I see, our French here are too few.
[2] Roland, my companion, sound your horn then,
[A] Charles will hear it, the army will come back."
Roland replies: "I'd be a fool to do it.
I would lose my good name all through sweet France.
I will strike now, I'll strike with Durendal,
the blade will be bloody to the gold from striking!
These pagan traitors came to these passes doomed!
I promise you, they are marked men, they'll die." . . .

87

Roland is good, and Oliver is wise,
both these vassals men of amazing courage:
once they are armed and mounted on their horses,
they will not run, though they die for it, from battle.
Good men, these Counts, and their words full of spirit.
Traitor pagans are riding up in fury.
Said Oliver: "Roland, look—the first ones,
on top of us—and Charles is far away.
You did not think it right to sound your olifant:
if the King were here, we'd come out without losses.
Now look up there, toward the passes of Aspre—
you can see the rear-guard: it will suffer.
[B] No man in that detail will be in another."
Roland replies: "Don't speak such foolishness—
shame on the heart gone coward in the chest.
We'll hold our ground, we'll stand firm—we're the ones!
We'll fight with spears, we'll fight them hand to hand!" . . .

91

Roland went forth into the Spanish passes
on Veillantif, his good swift-running horse.
He bears his arms—how they become this man!—
[3] grips his lance now, hefting it, working it,
now swings the iron point up toward the sky,
the gonfanon all white laced on above—
the golden streamers beat down upon his hands:
a noble's body, the face aglow and smiling.
Close behind him his good companion follows;
the men of France hail him: their protector!

18 Durendal (dü-rən-däl′): the name of Roland's sword, said to be the same sword formerly used by the Trojan hero Hector.

30 olifant (äl′ə-fənt): Roland's horn.

32 the passes of Aspre (äs′prə): passages through the Pyrenees.

40 Veillantif (vā-yən-tēf′).

Customizing Instruction

Less Proficient Readers

- Tell students to pause after reading each section of this poem and then to summarize it in a single sentence. Model how to use this strategy for the first section, which might be summarized as follows: *Scouting the enemy troops, Oliver discovers that they greatly outnumber the French.*
- Clarify for students the key characters in this epic: Oliver (mentioned in line 1) is Roland's friend, his companion in arms. Both Oliver and Roland are vassals, or loyal knights, to King Charles, or Charlemagne (mentioned in line 15), their feudal lord. Oliver and Roland are the leaders of the French rear-guard, whom the Saracens are preparing to attack. The Saracens are led by Marsilion (mentioned in line 114). The French warrior Ganelon (mentioned in line 145) has turned traitor and has incited the Saracens to attack the French.

1 Tell students that the main external conflict, or struggle, involves the French and the Saracens. The Saracens are sometimes referred to as pagans—those opposed to Christ.

English Learners

Explain the meaning of the following words and phrases:

- *bedecked* (line 4) means "decorated"
- *affixed* (line 6) means "attached"
- *good name* (line 17) means "reputation"
- *vassals* (line 23) means "loyal knights"
- *detail* (line 34) means "a small group of soldiers chosen for a special task"
- *hefting* (line 42) means "lifting"

2 Share with students the origin of the word *companion*. It comes from the Latin words for "with" and "bread." To the ancient Romans, a companion was someone that you would eat bread with—therefore, a close friend.

3 Read these lines aloud to students, helping them visualize the details in this description of Roland. You might ask students to recall images of knights from movies or books. Encourage students to mention and describe heroes honored in their native cultures.

THE SONG OF ROLAND 699

Cross Curricular Link History

CHRISTIANS AND MUSLIMS IN THE MIDDLE AGES

In *The Song of Roland,* the French forces fight the Muslims, sometimes called "Saracens" or "pagans" in the poem. Throughout the Middle Ages, Christians generally had a hostile attitude toward the Muslims, the followers of Islam, the religion based on the teachings of Muhammad (570?–632). Christians regarded Islam as a heresy and Muhammad as a false prophet. In the *Inferno*, for example, Dante depicts Muhammad deep in Hell, continually split in two for having caused religious disunity.

This view of Muhammad and Islam helped bring about the Crusades. These so-called "holy wars" were fought against the Muslim Turks to gain control of Jerusalem and the Holy Land, where Jesus had lived and preached. In 1096, heeding the call of Pope Urban II, more than 50,000 knights—many of whom were French—marched eastward on the First Crusade. Less than one-fourth of the original army reached Jerusalem, capturing the city on July 15, 1099. The Crusaders then set up feudal states in the Holy Land, which were vulnerable to Muslim attack. A number of other military expeditions to the Holy Land, therefore, followed in the 12th and 13th centuries.

In Spain, however, Jewish scholars in the 12th century sometimes enjoyed peaceful contact with Muslim scholars, who helped transmit much of Greek culture to Western Europe.

Literary Analysis EPIC HERO

A Ask students to evaluate Roland as a warrior.

Possible Response: Roland seems superhuman, a peerless fighter who, sword in hand, slays countless pagans. He and his horse are drenched with the enemy's blood, and slain pagans litter the ground.

Reading Skills and Strategies
VISUALIZING

B Point out to students that authors often use sensory details to appeal to a reader's five senses and to make a description come alive. Have students identify the details that helped them form mental pictures of the storm. What mood, or feeling, do these details help create?

Possible Responses: Details such as "tempests of wind and thunder," "bolts of lightning hurtling and hurtling down," and "a great darkness at noon falls on the land" help create an ominous, or threatening, mood—a sense that something terrible will happen.

He looks wildly toward the Saracens,
and humbly and gently to the men of France;
and spoke a word to them, in all courtesy:
"Barons, my lords, easy now, keep at a walk.
These pagans are searching for martyrdom.
We'll get good spoils before this day is over,
no king of France ever got such treasure!"
And with these words, the hosts are at each other. . . .

105

Roland the Count comes riding through the field,
holds Durendal, that sword! it carves its way!
and brings terrible slaughter down on the pagans.
To have seen him cast one man dead on another,
the bright red blood pouring out on the ground,
his hauberk, his two arms, running with blood,
his good horse—neck and shoulders running with blood!
And Oliver does not linger, he strikes!
and the Twelve Peers, no man could reproach them;
and the brave French, they fight with lance and sword.
The pagans die, some simply faint away!
Said the Archbishop: "Bless our band of brave men!"
Munjoie! he shouts—the war cry of King Charles. . . .

110

The battle is fearful and full of grief.
Oliver and Roland strike like good men,
the Archbishop, more than a thousand blows,
and the Twelve Peers do not hang back, they strike!
the French fight side by side, all as one man.
The pagans die by hundreds, by thousands:
whoever does not flee finds no refuge from death,
like it or not, there he ends all his days.
And there the men of France lose their greatest arms;
they will not see their fathers, their kin again,
or Charlemagne, who looks for them in the passes.
Tremendous torment now comes forth in France,
a mighty whirlwind, tempests of wind and thunder,
rains and hailstones, great and immeasurable,
bolts of lightning hurtling and hurtling down:
it is, in truth, a trembling of the earth.
From Saint Michael-in-Peril to the Saints,

54 spoils: the goods or property seized by the victors after a battle.

65 the Twelve Peers: Charlemagne's chief vassals.

68 the Archbishop: Archbishop Turpin, one of the Twelve Peers.

69 munjoie (mŭn-zhwä'): a medieval war cry of the Franks, meaning "mount joy."

HUMANITIES CONNECTION Some of the finest art in the Middle Ages is found in the illuminations that decorate the pages of manuscripts. This one, which dates from about the year 1250, shows attacking knights being driven back from a well-defended town.

from Besançon to the port of Wissant,
there is no house whose veil of walls does not crumble.
A great darkness at noon falls on the land,
there is no light but when the heavens crack.
No man sees this who is not terrified,
and many say: "The Last Day! Judgment Day!
The end! The end of the world is upon us!"
They do not know, they do not speak the truth:
it is the worldwide grief for the death of Roland. . . .

130

And Roland says: "We are in a rough battle.
I'll sound the olifant, Charles will hear it."
Said Oliver: "No good vassal would do it.
When I urged it, friend, you did not think it right.
If Charles were here, we'd come out with no losses.
Those men down there—no blame can fall on them."
Oliver said: "Now by this beard of mine,
If I can see my noble sister, Aude,
once more, you will never lie in her arms!"

86–87 From Saint Michael-in-Peril . . . Wissant: Saint-Michael-in-Peril is a monastery on an island off the coast of France called Mont Saint Michel. Besançon (bĭ-zäɴ-sôn') is a city of eastern France; Wissant (vē-säɴ') is a port town in the northwest tip of France. The lines mean "throughout all of France."

103 Aude (ō'də) **. . . never lie in her arms:** Roland was to marry Oliver's sister, Aude.

MINI LESSON Viewing and Representing

Illuminated French manuscript

ART APPRECIATION Have students read the **Humanities Connection** caption and study the reproduction of the illumination from a medieval French manuscript. Illuminated manuscripts, which were produced mainly during the Middle Ages and the Renaissance, were written and decorated by hand with bright colors and metals. One of the world's most beautiful books is *The Book of Kells,* an illuminated manuscript that dates from the late 8th or early 9th century.

Ask students to describe their impressions of medieval warfare based on the illumination on page 701.

Possible Responses: Medieval warfare was chaotic, fought with simple weapons such as swords, javelins, and bows and arrows. It involved bloody hand-to-hand combat. Fallen warriors were liable to be trampled in the mad whirl of battle.

Customizing Instruction

Less Proficient Readers

You can check students' comprehension of lines 1–104 by asking the following questions:

- What does Oliver observe from the top of a hill? *(a mighty Saracen army)*
- What does Oliver ask Roland to do? *(to sound his horn to summon King Charles)*
- Why does Roland refuse Oliver's request? *(He wants to keep his reputation as a fearless fighter.)*
- What does Roland do with his sword Durendal? *(kills many of the enemy)*
- What event in nature suggests that Roland will die in the battle? *(a terrible storm in France)*

1 Make sure that students notice the contrast conveyed by the adverb *wildly* and the adverbial phrase *humbly and gently.* Roland is full of savage fury toward the enemy, but the model of courtesy, or polite behavior, toward his own troops.

English Learners

Explain the meaning of the following words and phrases:

- *martyrdom* (line 53) means "death for one's beliefs"
- *hosts* (line 56) means "armies"
- *running* (line 62) means "dripping"
- *reproach* (line 65) means "find fault with"
- *greatest arms* (line 78) refers to the best warriors in France
- *torment* (line 81) means "great suffering of body or mind"
- *tempests* (line 82) means "storms"
- *The Last Day! Judgment Day* (line 92) refers to the end of the world when all will be judged according to their deeds.

Advanced Learners

As students read, ask them to compare and contrast Roland and Oliver.

Possible Response: Both Roland and Oliver are courageous warriors. Oliver, who is prudent and cautious, tries to avoid unnecessary risks. Roland, who is bold and daring, is willing to face death for the sake of honor.

Literary Analysis CONFLICT

A Remind students that they are expected to identify basic conflicts, or struggles. One conflict in this poem involves the French and the pagans. Another conflict involves Roland and his friend Oliver. Ask students why Oliver is angry at Roland.

Possible Response: Oliver believes that Roland has acted foolishly, throwing away his own life and the lives of his soldiers, instead of asking for reinforcements in time.

Literary Analysis EPIC HERO

B Discuss how lines 147–151 illustrate the heroic qualities of Roland.

Possible Response: Roland suffers terrible pain and gives up his life for the French troops. Though his blood vessels are bursting, he still succeeds in blowing the horn loudly enough to summon King Charles.

131

And Roland said: "Why are you angry at me?"
Oliver answers: "Companion, it is your doing.
I will tell you what makes a vassal good:
it is judgment, it is never madness;
1 restraint is worth more than the raw nerve of a fool.
Frenchmen are dead because of your wildness.
A And what service will Charles ever have from us?
If you had trusted me, my lord would be here,
we would have fought this battle through to the end,
Marsilion would be dead, or our prisoner.
Roland, your prowess—had we never seen it!
And now, dear friend, we've seen the last of it.
No more aid from us now for Charlemagne,
a man without equal till Judgment Day,
you will die here, and your death will shame France.
We kept faith, you and I, we were companions;
and everything we were will end today.
We part before evening, and it will be hard."

112 If you had trusted . . . be here: Oliver earlier had asked Roland to blow his horn, but Roland had refused.

115 prowess (prou'ĭs): skill; ability.

132

Turpin the Archbishop hears their bitter words,
digs hard into his horse with golden spurs
and rides to them; begins to set them right:
"You, Lord Roland, and you, Lord Oliver,
I beg you in God's name do not quarrel.
To sound the horn could not help us now, true,
but still it is far better that you do it:
let the King come, he can avenge us then—
these men of Spain must not go home exulting!
Our French will come, they'll get down on their feet,
and find us here—we'll be dead, cut to pieces.
They will lift us into coffins on the backs of mules,
2 and weep for us, in rage and pain and grief,
and bury us in the courts of churches;
and we will not be eaten by wolves or pigs or dogs."
Roland replies, "Lord, you have spoken well."

131 exulting: rejoicing.

133

Roland has put the olifant to his mouth,
he sets it well, sounds it with all his strength.

Cross Curricular Link **History**

THE CODE OF CHIVALRY In *The Song of Roland,* Roland is portrayed as a Christian knight who lives by the code of chivalry. The word *chivalry* derives from the Old French word *chevalerie,* which means "horse soldiery." The code of chivalry refers to the system of values and ideals of conduct held by knights—or those on horseback—in medieval Europe. According to this code, a knight was devoted to three masters: his earthly feudal lord, his heavenly Lord, and his chosen lady. True knights, like Roland and Oliver, had deep faith and were willing to die for the Christian religion. They loved their native land, gave generously to all, and championed the weak. They fought for the right and never fled from the enemy.

Chivalric values inspired the songs and poems created by minstrels who entertained French lords and ladies at court. Sadly, the conduct of some knights in real life sometimes fell far short of the ideals expressed in literary works like *The Song of Roland.*

The hills are high, and that voice ranges far,
they heard it echo thirty great leagues away.
King Charles heard it, and all his faithful men.
And the King says: "Our men are in a battle."
3 And Ganelon disputed him and said:
"Had someone else said that, I'd call him liar!"

145 **disputed:** disagreed with.

134

B And now the mighty effort of Roland the Count:
he sounds his olifant; his pain is great,
and from his mouth the bright blood comes leaping out,
and the temple bursts in his forehead.
That horn, in Roland's hands, has a mighty voice:
King Charles hears it drawing through the passes.
Naimon heard it, the Franks listen to it.
And the King said: "I hear Count Roland's horn;
he'd never sound it unless he had a battle."
Says Ganelon: "Now no more talk of battles!
You are old now, your hair is white as snow,
the things you say make you sound like a child.
You know Roland and that wild pride of his—
what a wonder God has suffered it so long!
Remember? he took Noples without your command:
the Saracens rode out, to break the siege;
they fought with him, the great vassal Roland.
Afterwards he used the streams to wash the blood
from the meadows: so that nothing would show.
He blasts his horn all day to catch a rabbit,
he's strutting now before his peers and bragging—
who under heaven would dare meet him on the field?
So now: ride on! Why do you keep on stopping?
The Land of Fathers lies far ahead of us." . . .

153 **Naimon** (nā-môɴ'): an advisor to Charlemagne.

161 **Noples** (nô'plə): a city in Spain.

170 **the Land of Fathers:** France.

168

4 Now Roland feels that death is very near.
His brain comes spilling out through his two ears;
prays to God for his peers: let them be called;
and for himself, to the angel Gabriel;
took the olifant: there must be no reproach!
took Durendal his sword in his other hand,
and farther than a crossbow's farthest shot
he walks toward Spain, into a fallow land,

174 **the angel Gabriel:** an archangel, or higher class of angel, who often serves as God's messenger.

178 **fallow:** plowed but left unseeded; unused.

Customizing Instruction

Less Proficient Readers

1 This proverb sums up Oliver's views and explains his anger toward Roland. Ask students to paraphrase this line. If necessary, provide the following model: *It is better to hold your emotions in check than to act wildly without thinking.*

2 Explain that it was considered a terrible dishonor to a knight if his corpse lay unburied for animals to eat. The Archbishop knows that all of the French forces will be killed by the Saracens. If Charles does not arrive, their rotting bodies will be food for animals. That is why the Archbishop implores Roland to sound his horn.

3 Remind students that Ganelon has betrayed Roland and the rear-guard to the Saracens. He now tries to convince King Charles that the rear-guard is not under attack.

4 Make sure that students understand that Roland has mortally injured himself by blowing his horn with such force.

English Learners

Explain the meaning of the following words and phrases:

- *my lord* (line 112) refers to King Charles
- *had we never seen it* (line 115) means "I wish that we had never seen it"
- *part* (line 122) means "die"
- *that voice* (line 141) refers to the sound made when Roland blows the horn
- *league* (line 142) refers to a distance of about three miles
- *strutting* (line 167) means "walking in a proud way"
- *peers* (line 173) refers to the nobles with King Charles

Advanced Learners

Ask students to compare Ganelon with other notorious villains in books and movies.

Possible Responses: Answers will vary. Students who have read Shakespeare's play *Othello* may mention that Ganelon reminds them of Iago in his malice, treachery, and verbal skills.

MINI LESSON Grammar

ADVERB PHRASES

Instruction An adverb phrase is a prepositional phrase that modifies a verb, an adjective, or an adverb, telling when, where, how, why, or to what extent something is done.

Model Sentence

A mighty sound erupted from Roland's horn.

In the above model sentence, have students identify the adverb phrase *(from Roland's horn)* and the word the adverb phrase modifies. *(The verb "erupted")*

Practice Have students underline the adverb phrase and identify the word the phrase modifies.

1. The horn blast echoed through the mountain passes. *(echoed)*
2. Bright blood leapt out of Roland's mouth. *(out)*
3. The brave knight lay dead from the great effort. *(dead)*

For more instruction and practice in adverb phrases, use McDougal Littell's ***Language Network:***

- Grade 10, Chapter 3, "Using Phrases"
- Grade 12, Chapter 2, "Using Phrases"

Reading Skills and Strategies
PREDICTING

(A) Have students predict what the dying Roland will do to the Saracen trying to steal his sword.

Possible Response: Since Roland values his sword highly, he will probably fight the thief with his last ounce of strength.

Reading Skills and Strategies
VISUALIZING

(B) Ask students to identify details that help them form mental pictures of Roland's killing of the Saracen.

Possible Response: details such as "strikes on the helm," "shatters the steel, and the head, and the bones," and "sent his two eyes flying out of his head"

Active Reading QUESTIONING

(C) Ask students why Roland strikes his sword against a rock.

Possible Response: to break it so that it will not fall into enemy hands

HUMANITIES CONNECTION Warfare in the Middle Ages was violent and chaotic, as this illumination from a French manuscript shows. Notice the armed knights on horseback and the people trampled underfoot.

and climbs a hill: there beneath two fine trees
stand four great blocks of stone, all are of marble;
and he fell back, to earth, on the green grass,
has fainted there, for death is very near.

169

High are the hills, and high, high are the trees;
there stand four blocks of stone, gleaming of marble.
Count Roland falls fainting on the green grass,
and is watched, all this time, by a Saracen:
who has feigned death and lies now with the others,
has smeared blood on his face and on his body;
and quickly now gets to his feet and runs—
a handsome man, strong, brave, and so crazed with pride
that he does something mad and dies for it:
laid hands on Roland, and on the arms of Roland,
and cried: "Conquered! Charles's nephew conquered!
I'll carry this sword home to Arabia!"
(A) As he draws it, the Count begins to come round.

170

Now Roland feels: *someone taking his sword!*
opened his eyes, and had one word for him:
"I don't know you, you aren't one of ours";

187 feigned (fānd): pretended.

MINI LESSON Viewing and Representing

Illuminated French manuscript

ART APPRECIATION Have students read the **Humanities Connection** caption and study the reproduction of the illumination which, like the one shown on page 704, is from a medieval French manuscript. Then ask students to use this illumination to draw additional conclusions about medieval warfare.

Possible Responses: Horses were important in medieval wars, bearing knights into battle. Archers defended fortified places by shooting arrows at attacking troops. Before the invention of cannon and gunpowder, catapults were used to hurl large stones against enemy fortifications.

grasps that olifant that he will never lose,
strikes on the helm beset with gems in gold,
shatters the steel, and the head, and the bones,
sent his two eyes flying out of his head,
dumped him over stretched out at his feet dead;
and said: "You nobody! how could you dare
lay hands on me—rightly or wrongly: how?
Who'll hear of this and not call you a fool?
Ah! the bell-mouth of the olifant is smashed,
the crystal and the gold fallen away."

207 bell-mouth: the rounded end of a horn through which the sound is emitted.

171

Now Roland the Count feels: his sight is gone;
gets on his feet, draws on his final strength,
the color on his face lost now for good.
Before him stands a rock; and on that dark rock
in rage and bitterness he strikes ten blows:
the steel blade grates, it will not break, it stands unmarked.
"Ah!" said the Count, "Blessed Mary, your help!
Ah Durendal, good sword, your unlucky day,
for I am lost and cannot keep you in my care.
The battles I have won, fighting with you,
the mighty lands that holding you I conquered,
that Charles rules now, our King, whose beard is white!
Now you fall to another: it must not be
a man who'd run before another man!
For a long while a good vassal held you:
there'll never be the like in France's holy land." . . .

214 grates: makes a rasping noise.

173

Roland the Count strikes down on a dark rock,
and the rock breaks, breaks more than I can tell,
1 and the blade grates, but Durendal will not break,
the sword leaped up, rebounded toward the sky.
The Count, when he sees that sword will not be broken,
softly, in his own presence, speaks the lament:
"Ah Durendal, beautiful, and most sacred,
the holy relics in this golden pommel!
Saint Peter's tooth and blood of Saint Basile,
a lock of hair of my lord Saint Denis,
and a fragment of blessed Mary's robe:
your power must not fall to the pagans,

232 pommel: the knob on the handle of a sword.

233–234 Saint Peter's . . . Saint Denis: Saint Peter was one of the twelve Apostles of Christ; St. Basile was an early church leader; Saint Denis was the patron saint of France.

Customizing Instruction

Less Proficient Readers

You can check students' comprehension of lines 105–236 by asking the following questions:

- Why does Oliver quarrel with Roland during the battle? *(Oliver is angry because Roland's refusal to summon King Charles has cost the lives of many French troops.)*
- Why does Archbishop Turpin urge Roland to blow his horn even though the battle is lost? *(Archbishop Turpin wants Charles to avenge their deaths and to bury their bodies.)*
- What happens to Roland when he blows his horn? *(His great effort causes blood to spurt from his mouth.)*
- What does Roland do to the Saracen trying to steal his sword? *(smashes him with his horn, killing him)*

1 Point out to students that Roland's sword is magical and holy—somewhat like King Arthur's sword *Excalibur*. In its handle are relics, or sacred things.

English Learners

Explain the meaning of the following words and phrases:

- *arms* (line 192) refers to Roland's weapons
- *come round* (line 195) means "wake up"
- *beset* (line 200) means "decorated"
- *lament* (line 230) means "words of sorrow "
- *Blessed Mary's robe* (line 235) refers to the gown worn by Mary, the mother of Jesus Christ

Cross Curricular Link: History

RELICS In lines 233–235 of *The Song of Roland,* Roland mentions relics carried in the pommel of his sword—for example, Saint Peter's tooth and the blood of Saint Basile. Relics are the mortal remains of a holy person or objects associated with him or her. Relics are venerated among followers of Christianity and Buddhism. By venerating relics, the faithful believe that they give honor to a holy person.

The practice dates back to the early years of Christianity, when, according to tradition, handkerchiefs from Saint Paul's body were used to heal the sick. In the Middle Ages, it was believed that in the presence of certain relics, miracles might occur.

Two of the most venerated relics were the True Cross, the wood on which Jesus Christ was crucified, and the Holy Sepulchre, Christ's tomb in Jerusalem. The desire to protect these relics from the Muslims inspired the Crusades, the military campaigns to the Holy Land in the Middle Ages.

THE SONG OF ROLAND 705

Literary Analysis EPIC HERO

A Ask students what Roland's death reveals about his character.

Possible Responses: Roland values his good name and his soul. He tries to prevent the Saracens from stealing his sword and his oliphant. He turns his face toward the enemy so that the French will say he died with honor. He also asks God to pardon his sins.

Active Reading QUESTIONING

B Ask students why the author introduces supernatural characters in this epic poem.

Possible Responses: Supernatural characters are part of the epic tradition, appearing in such epics as the *Iliad* and the *Aeneid*. Instead of gods and goddesses, the author of *The Song of Roland* describes angels participating in the action. Through this heavenly escort, the author conveys the message that worthy Christian knights like Roland will receive an eternal reward.

you must be served by Christian warriors.
May no coward ever come to hold you!
It was with you I conquered those great lands
that Charles has in his keeping, whose beard is white,
the Emperor's lands, that make him rich and strong."

174

Now Roland feels: death coming over him,
death descending from his temples to his heart.
He came running underneath a pine tree
and there stretched out, face down, on the green grass,
lays beneath him his sword and the olifant.
He turned his head toward the Saracen hosts,
and this is why: with all his heart he wants
King Charles the Great and all his men to say,
he died, that noble Count, a conqueror;
makes confession, beats his breast often, so feebly,
offers his glove, for all his sins, to God. . . .

252 offers his glove: a sign of submission to a lord.

176

Count Roland lay stretched out beneath a pine;
he turned his face toward the land of Spain,
began to remember many things now:
how many lands, brave man, he had conquered;
and he remembered: sweet France, the men of his line,
remembered Charles, his lord, who fostered him:
cannot keep, remembering, from weeping, sighing;
but would not be unmindful of himself:
he confesses his sins, prays God for mercy:
"Loyal Father, you who never failed us,
who resurrected Saint Lazarus from the dead,
and saved your servant Daniel from the lions:
now save the soul of me from every peril
for the sins I committed while I still lived."
Then he held out his right glove to his Lord:
Saint Gabriel took the glove from his hand.
He held his head bowed down upon his arm,
he is gone, his two hands joined, to his end.
Then God sent him his angel Cherubin
and Saint Michael, angel of the sea's Peril;
and with these two there came Saint Gabriel:
they bear Count Roland's soul to Paradise.

263–264 who resurrected . . . from the lions: In the New Testament, Jesus raised Lazarus from the dead. In the Old Testament, God tamed the lions into whose cage the prophet Daniel had been thrown.

271–272 his angel Cherubin and Saint Michael: *Cherubim* is a class of angels, but the word is used here to refer to one specific angel. Saint Michael is an archangel, known for his skill in battle.

Cross Curricular Link — Humanities

WHAT FOLLOWS IN *THE SONG OF ROLAND* This excerpt from *The Song of Roland* ends with Roland's glorious death. Later, King Charles and the Franks respond to the blast of Roland's oliphant. They reach the battlefield and find it littered with the French dead. The Franks then drive the Saracens into the river Ebro, where they all drown. Later, Baligant, the emir of Babylon, attacks King Charles's troops who are burying their death at Roncevalles. King Charles kills Baligant, the pagan army flees, and the Franks eventually capture the city of Saragossa in Spain.

After the Franks return to France, Ganelon is put on trial. He is found guilty of treason and sentenced to a painful death. Galloping horses tear him limb from limb.

Connect to the Literature

1. **What Do You Think?** How did you react to Roland's death?

Comprehension Check
- Why do Roland and his companion Oliver quarrel before the battle?
- What happens to Roland when he sounds the horn?

Think Critically

2. **ACTIVE READING: QUESTIONING** Review the questions you listed in your READER'S NOTEBOOK. Discuss with a classmate any questions you still have about this poem.

3. If you were in Roland's position, would you have summoned Charlemagne before the battle or not? Support your answer with details from the poem.

4. How would you evaluate Count Roland as a vassal, or loyal knight, to Charlemagne?

- his attitude toward Charlemagne
- his deeds in battle
- his sense of honor
- Oliver's view of Roland's key decision

Extend Interpretations

5. **What If?** While blowing his horn, Roland spits blood and bursts his temples. Eventually, he dies from his superhuman efforts. Imagine, instead, that he had died in battle, slain by a Saracen. How do you think your reaction to the poem might be different?

6. **The Writer's Style** Words and phrases that appeal to one or more of the five senses are called **imagery.** Reread one of your favorite passages in this poem, perhaps the description of Roland advancing toward the enemy (lines 39–46) or of the storm darkening France (lines 81–93). What images make the passage come alive for you?

7. **Connect to Life** Explain the meaning of the following **aphorism,** or wise saying, and discuss how it might apply to students today: "Restraint is worth more than the raw nerve of a fool." (line 108)

LITERARY ANALYSIS: EPIC HERO

The **hero,** or **protagonist,** is the central character in a literary work. A hero's good qualities help him or her to triumph over an enemy. **Epic heroes** are larger-than-life figures who do amazing deeds and display great courage. They provide examples of noble behavior that inspire and guide other members of their culture. Count Roland lives by certain values that were important in medieval society. Taken together, these noble values were referred to as a code of honor, or code of chivalry.

Cooperative Learning Activity With a small group of classmates, identify several contrasts between Roland, the hero, and Ganelon, the villain. On a chart like the one shown below, jot down your conclusions. Then use your chart as a starting point to discuss the values that make up Roland's code of chivalry.

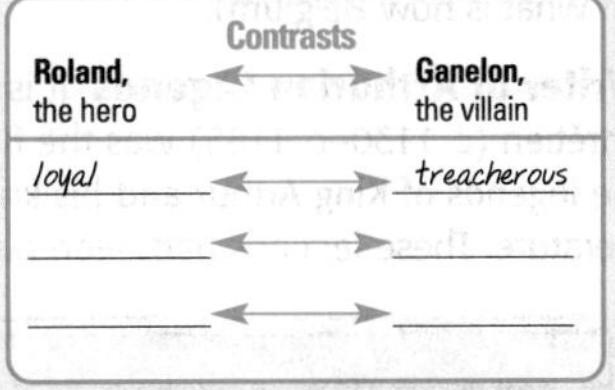

Connect to the Literature

1. **What Do You Think?** Possible Response: Students may say that Roland's death was heroic and sublime.

Comprehension Check
- Oliver wants Roland to summon King Charles, but Roland believes this would be cowardly.
- He bursts his blood vessels and dies from the exertion.

Use Selection Quiz in **Unit Five Resource Book,** p. 7.

Think Critically

2. Answers will vary. Some students may wonder what happens to Oliver in the battle. Other students may ask whether Charles ever discovers Ganelon's treachery.
3. Answers will vary. Some students might state that they would not have summoned King Charles because they think they can win the battle without his help. Other students might state that they would have summoned him because not to do so is foolhardy, preferring glory over the lives of his troops.
4. Answers will vary. Students who think that Roland is an ideal knight may state that he is a skilled warrior who has defeated many of King Charles's enemies. Students who think that Roland is less than ideal may state that he takes unnecessary risks to gain glory.

Extend Interpretations

5. **What If?** Possible Response: If Roland had been slain in battle by a Saracen, his heroic stature would diminish. Another warrior would have triumphed over him. By having Roland die from superhuman exertion, the poet suggests that Roland remains unconquered.
6. **The Writer's Style** Answers will vary. Among the vivid images are the following: "now swings the iron point up toward the sky" (line 43), "the golden streamers beat down upon his hands" (line 45), "tempest of wind and thunder" (line 82), "bolts of lightning hurtling and hurtling down" (line 84).
7. **Connect to Life** Responses will vary. Some students may state that students need restraint, or self-discipline, to resist peer pressure and to avoid rash acts.

Literary Analysis

Cooperative Learning Activity Possible Responses: Roland is respectful toward Charles; Ganelon is disrespectful toward him. Roland is honorable; Ganelon is unscrupulous. Roland is courageous; Ganelon is cowardly. Roland is religious; Ganelon is irreligious. Students should conclude that Roland's chivalric code endorses such values as loyalty and respect for one's liege lord, personal honor, courage in battle, and faith in God.

Use **Unit Five Resource Book,** p. 6, for more practice.

To assess skills and concepts taught in this selection, use **Formal Assessment Book,** p. 109–110.

Objectives
- identify the qualities of a medieval **romance (Literary Analysis)**
- use **strategies for reading a romance (Active Reading)**

Summary
The boy, later identified as Perceval, rides in search of his mother. Suddenly, he comes upon a river and notices two men in a boat, one fishing and the other rowing. The one fishing offers him lodgings for the night and tells him how to find his castle. Arriving at the castle, the boy enters the hall and meets the lord, who sits in a bed and is unable to stand. He treats the boy with great courtesy, giving him a wondrous sword and holding a banquet in his honor. At the banquet, the boy notices two marvelous objects: a lance with a drop of blood flowing from its tip and a golden grail carried from chamber to chamber. Though the boy longs to ask about the lance and the grail, he remains silent for fear of seeming foolish. Next morning, the boy awakes to find the castle deserted. He rides off into the forest and comes upon a maiden weeping over a slain knight. She tells the boy that by not asking about the lance and the grail, he has failed to heal the Fisher King and prevent great evils. She also informs him of his mother's death and renames him "Perceval the Wretched."

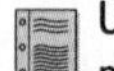
Use **Unit Five Resource Book,** p. 8, for additional support.

Thematic Link
This medieval romance tells of the **heroic quest** of Perceval, one of King Arthur's knights.

5-Minute Warm-Up
Daily Language SkillBuilder

Have students **proofread** the display sentences on page 685j and write them correctly.

FROM Perceval: THE STORY OF THE GRAIL

Chrétien de Troyes

Medieval Poet Chrétien de Troyes (krā-tyăɴ' də trwä') was the author of five narrative poems, or **romances,** about King Arthur's knights. Little else is known of this poet's life. His name suggests a connection with Troyes, a city in northeastern France. His excellent education is reflected in his poems. From the dedication of one of them, it can be inferred that he served at the court of Marie, the Countess of Champagne. Chrétien also may have served as a court poet to Philip, Count of Flanders (in what is now Belgium).

Writer of Arthurian Legends It is believed that Chrétien (c. 1130–c. 1185) was the first to introduce the legends of King Arthur and his knights into French literature. These legends had been passed down orally from one generation to the next in Wales and in Brittany, a region in northwestern France. In composing his works, Chrétien adapted the legends to suit the times in which he lived. His characters are noble heroes inspired by love, honor, and loyalty to their king.

Down through the centuries, Chrétien's Arthurian romances have inspired many authors in different countries, including Sir Thomas Malory, who retold the Arthurian legends in English in *Le Morte d'Arthur* ("The Death of Arthur"), a work completed around 1470. It is from Malory's writings that most of the English-speaking world has come to know King Arthur.

Other Works
Cligés; Yvain; Lancelot

Illustration from medieval manuscript of Perceval at the castle of the wounded Fisher King. Bibliothèque Nationale de France, Paris.

LESSON RESOURCES

UNIT FIVE RESOURCE BOOK, pp. 8–11

ASSESSMENT RESOURCES
Formal Assessment, pp. 111–112
Teacher's Guide to Assessment and Portfolio Use
Test Generator

INTEGRATED TECHNOLOGY
Visit our Web site: classzone.com

ADDITIONAL RESOURCES
Lesson Planning Guide, pp. 91–92
Teacher's Sourcebook for Language Development

Build Background

The Code of Chivalry Chrétien depicts Arthur as a great king who holds a magnificent court at Camelot. To this court flock the bravest warriors in the land, including Gawain and Lancelot. They form a special fellowship, the Knights of the Round Table. Arthur's knights live by the code of chivalry. This code stresses the highest standards—courage, loyalty, honor, and protection of the weak. One of the knights inspired by this code is Perceval, the hero of Chrétien's poem *Perceval: The Story of the Grail.*

The Holy Grail This poem introduced one of the most important elements of Arthurian literature: the quest for the Holy Grail. After Chrétien, other writers imagined the grail as the cup Jesus drank from at the Last Supper. This cup was also said to hold drops of Jesus' blood shed at the crucifixion. Supposedly, the grail lay hidden in a magic castle, and only a truly pure knight could find it. Many of Arthur's knights searched in vain for the Holy Grail. Perceval, however, was one of the few knights privileged to see it.

Perceval the Knight

When Perceval was a boy, his mother tried to shelter him from knightly adventures. She feared that he would be killed, as were her two other sons and her husband. However, after Perceval encountered several knights, his mother changed her mind. She realized that her son must be free to follow his destiny. She then sent him to King Arthur's court. As he rode off, Perceval saw his mother faint from grief. Nevertheless, he continued on his way. Later, filled with remorse, he tried to find her again. The excerpt you are about to read begins at this point in the story.

Connect to Your Life

In many popular movies, the main character goes on a **quest,** a journey to attain a particular goal. This quest involves a series of adventures that serve as tests or trials. Consider Dorothy in *The Wizard of Oz.* In order to return home to Kansas, she first must overcome many obstacles. Working with a small group, list books or other movies that feature quests. What tests or trials do the main characters face?

Focus Your Reading

LITERARY ANALYSIS: ROMANCE

A **romance** is an imaginative story that describes the deeds of noble heroes. The main character usually goes on a quest in which he faces difficult tests and trials. On this quest, magical or even supernatural events sometimes occur.

ACTIVE READING: STRATEGIES FOR READING A ROMANCE

Romances contain elements found in other narratives—for example, **setting, characters,** and **plot.** In romances, however, these elements create a sense of mystery and wonder. Read a romance the way you might read a fairy tale or a fantasy. Open your mind to the strange and the unusual. Try to visualize the wondrous characters and scenes. Step into the world of chivalry—a world of brave knights, glorious ladies, magical castles, and mysterious events.

READER'S NOTEBOOK This romance is composed of different episodes involving the hero Perceval, or, as he is called, "the boy." As you read, keep track of what happens to him. Create a flow chart like the one below. In each box describe an event and Perceval's reaction to it.

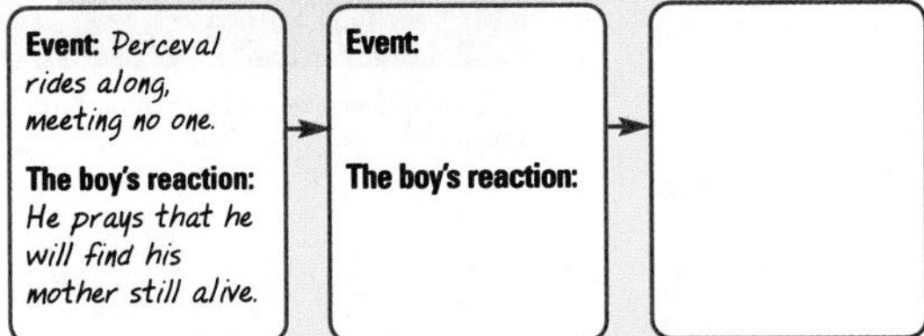

READING FOR INFORMATION

Reading Skills and Strategies

MONITORING READING STRATEGIES

Tell students to adjust their reading strategies to suit the kind of material they are reading. As they read the biographical sketch, they should look for one or two key ideas about the author. When reading the sections **The Code of Chivalry** and **The Holy Grail,** students should look for details about each topic. Finally, as students read **Perceval the Knight,** they should keep track of the sequence of events.

TIME MANAGEMENT

If your schedule requires that you cover the lesson objectives in a shorter time, use . . .

- Preparing to Read, pp. 708–709
- Thinking Through the Literature, p. 722

If you want to take advantage of longer blocks of class time, use . . .

- TE Teaching Options: Viewing and Representing, pp. 713, 715; Speaking and Listening, p. 719; Vocabulary Strategy, p. 711; Cross-Curricular Link, pp. 710, 720, 721; Grammar, p. 717
- Connect to Today, p. 723

Editor's Note This selection was excerpted from a larger work. Material was deleted to shorten and focus the selection.

Reading Skills and Strategies
PREVIEWING
Discuss with students what they know about Arthurian legends. Then have students look at the images throughout the selection for clues about the content.

Guide for Reading
Tell students that this selection is broken into sections to help them understand it better and enjoy it more. At the beginning of each section, the **Focus** sets a purpose for reading. At the end of each section, the **Pause & Reflect** provides a question that checks student understanding.

Literary Analysis ROMANCE

A Point out that the hero of this romance is the boy, later identified as Perceval. He rides alone on horseback, hoping to find his mother whom he left behind when he set out for King Arthur's court. Then ask students to identify the first trial or test the boy encounters.

Possible Response: a river that cannot be crossed

 Use **Unit Five Resource Book,** p. 10, for more practice.

Active Reading
STRATEGIES FOR READING A ROMANCE
Remind students that they are expected to make judgments about the characters in a romance. Ask students to describe their impressions of the lord fishing from a boat.

Possible Response: The lord seems kindly disposed to the boy, offering him a night's rest at his castle.

 Use **Unit Five Resource Book,** p. 9, for more practice.

from Perceval: The Story of the Grail

Chrétien de Troyes

Translated by Nigel Bryant

Perceval in Quest of the Holy Grail, Ferdinand Leeke. Photograph copyright © Christie's Images, New York.

Cross Curricular Link **Humanities**

ARTHURIAN LITERATURE: THE HOLY GRAIL The earliest tales of King Arthur and his knights come from Welsh literature of the 6th through 12th centuries. Geoffrey of Monmouth's *The History of the Kings of Britain,* written in Latin between 1135 and 1139, depicted Arthur as a glorious king, a world conqueror who defeats the Roman army. Drawing upon Celtic legends, Chrétien de Troyes in the late 12th century portrayed Arthur as the ruler of a host of knights. It was Chrétien who combined the religious theme of the Holy Grail with the marvelous adventures of Arthurian romance.

According to legend, the grail was brought to Britain by Joseph of Arimathea. It was lodged in a mysterious castle and guarded by the Fisher King, who suffered from a grievous wound. Many of King Arthur's knights searched for the grail in vain. Perceval, however, discovered the castle where the grail lay hidden, but failed to ask the key question that would have cured the Fisher King. Lancelot was not allowed to enter the castle because he had sinned with Guinevere. Finally, Galahad, Lancelot's son and a knight pure of heart, entered the Grail Chapel and beheld the sacred cup. He was then taken up to heaven.

Manuscript illumination of Galahad, Boort, Perceval, and his sister arriving at an island, from *The Romance of Saint Graal* (Fifteenth century).

GUIDE FOR READING

FOCUS Searching for his mother, the boy finds his way blocked by a river. He calls to a stranger whom he sees fishing from a boat. Read to find out how this stranger treats him.

All day long he rode on, meeting no earthly being, neither Christian man nor Christian woman, who could guide him on his way. He constantly prayed to God the sovereign father to grant that he might find his mother full of life and health, if it were His will. He was still praying when he caught sight of a river flowing down a hill. He saw that the water was swift and deep and he did not dare to ride in; and he said:

"Oh! almighty Lord, if only I could cross this river I think I'd find my mother on the other side, if she's still alive."

He rode along the bank until he came near a rock, and the river washed all round it so that he could go no further. But suddenly he noticed a boat with two men on board, sailing downstream. He stopped and waited, thinking that they would sail on down to him. But they stopped and stayed dead still in midstream, most securely anchored. The one at the front was fishing with a line, baiting his hook with a little fish slightly bigger than a minnow. The boy, not knowing what to do or where to find a crossing, greeted them and asked them:

"Tell me, my lords, is there a bridge across this river?"

And the one who was fishing replied:

"No indeed, brother, by my faith; nor is there any boat, I think, bigger than the one we're in, which wouldn't carry five men. You can't cross on horseback for twenty leagues upstream or 4
down, for there's no ferry or bridge or ford." 5

"Then tell me, in God's name," he said, "where I could find lodging."

And the man replied:

"You've need of that and more besides, I think. I will give you lodging tonight. Ride up through the cleft[1] in that rock, and when you come to the top you'll see a house in a valley ahead of you where I live, near the river and the woods."

So he climbed up on to the rock; but when he reached the top he looked all around him and

1. **cleft:** an opening made by a crack or break.

Customizing Instruction

Less Proficient Readers

Tell students to use the image on page 710 to help them visualize the main character, referred to as "the boy." Then point out that this story describes the boy's adventures. Like other romances, this story consists of related episodes, each of which has a different setting:

- Episode 1, set along a riverbank, describes the boy's meeting with a stranger fishing from a boat.
- Episode 2, set inside the Fisher King's castle, describes a glorious banquet and the boy's two wondrous visions.
- Episode 3, set in the forest, describes the boy's meeting with a maiden, who turns out to be his cousin.

Focus If necessary, guide students to look ahead to the dialogue in the second column on page 711. It provides clues about how the stranger treats the boy.

1 Point out to students that the boy is deeply religious, praying to God as he rides along.

2 Make sure students realize the boy's situation. Hungry and tired from having ridden many miles on horseback, he must find food and lodging for the night. To do so, he thinks he must find a way to cross the river.

English Learners

Explain the meaning of the following words:

3 *bank:* the land along the sides of a river

4 *league:* about three miles

5 *ford:* a shallow place in a river where one can walk across

MINI LESSON Vocabulary Strategy

HOMONYMS

Instruction Homonyms are two or more words with the same pronunciation and often the same spelling, but with different meanings and origins.

Examples:

die: to cease living

die: a device used for cutting, forming, and stamping material

Practice Have a volunteer locate the word *leagues* (page 711) in a dictionary. Discuss how the reader knows which definition is the correct one in this context *(The word is used to indicate units of measure, not groups or organizations.)* Have students locate other examples of homonyms on this page and, using context, determine which meaning of each word is applicable *(Other homonyms: "will," "bank," and "bridge")*

Active Reading

STRATEGIES FOR READING A ROMANCE

A Remind students that strange or unusual events often occur in a romance. Then ask students to predict what might happen to the boy after he meets the lord of the castle.

Possible Responses: The lord might treat the boy courteously and give him a precious object to take with him on his quest; the lord might imprison the boy in the castle, thus preventing him from continuing his quest.

Reading Skills and Strategies

VISUALIZING

B Remind students that authors often use sensory details to appeal to a reader's five senses. Have students identify the phrases that help them form mental pictures of the lord.

Possible Responses: "sitting in a bed," "a most handsome nobleman with graying hair," "a hat of sable, dark as mulberry," and "leaning on his elbow"

saw nothing but sky and earth; and he said:

"What did I come up here to find? Foolishness and nonsense! God bring disgrace on the one who sent me here! What fine guidance he gave

BUT JUST THEN, in a valley nearby, the top of a tower caught his eye. From here to Beirut you would not have found a more handsome one or one more finely placed.

me, telling me I'd find a house when I reached the top! Fisherman who told me so, you did a most unworthy deed, if you said it to do me harm."

But just then, in a valley nearby, the top of a
1 tower caught his eye. From here to Beirut you would not have found a more handsome one or one more finely placed. It was square and built of gray rock, flanked by two smaller towers. The hall stood before the tower, and lodges before the hall. The boy rode down towards it, saying that the one who had sent him there had guided him well, and he praised the fisherman, no longer calling him treacherous or dishonest or untruthful, now that he had found a place to lodge. He headed towards the gate; and before
2 the gate he found a drawbridge, and it was lowered. He rode in over the bridge, and four boys came to meet him; two of them disarmed him, while the third led away his horse and gave it hay and oats; the fourth dressed him in a fresh and brand new mantle[2] of scarlet cloth. Then they led him to the lodges; and I tell you, a man
A could have searched as far as Limoges[3] without finding or seeing any so handsome. The boy stayed in the lodges until he was summoned to go to the lord, who sent two servants to him. He returned with them to the hall, which was square, being as long as it was wide. In the middle of the hall he saw, sitting in a bed, a most
handsome nobleman with graying hair; on his 3
head he wore a hat of sable, dark as mulberry,
covered in a deep rich cloth on top, and his B
whole gown was the same. He was leaning on his elbow, and before him was a huge fire of dry logs, blazing brightly, surrounded by four columns. Four hundred men could easily have sat around that fire and each would have had an excellent place. The columns were very strong, supporting a tall, wide chimney of heavy bronze. The two servants who were escorting the boy, one on each side of him, came before their lord. When the lord saw him coming he greeted him at once, and said:

"My friend, don't be upset if I don't get up to meet you, for I'm unable to."

"In God's name, sir," said the boy, "say no more about it; may God give me joy and health, it doesn't upset me at all."

But the worthy man so exerted himself for the boy's sake that he struggled up as much as he could; then he said:

"Come here, my friend. Don't be afraid of me: sit down here beside me, you're quite safe. I command you."

The boy sat down at his side, and the nobleman asked him:

"Where have you come from today, my friend?"

"Sir," he said, "I rode this morning from Beaurepaire[4]—that was its name."

"God help me," said the nobleman, "you've traveled a very long way today. You must have

2. mantle: a long, sleeveless coat or cloak.

3. Limoges (lē-mōzh'): a city in west-central France.

4. Beaurepaire (bō'rə-pâr'): a fortified town that the boy has just rescued from attackers.

HUMANITIES CONNECTION This illustration from a 13th-century manuscript depicts a medieval banquet like the one Perceval attends at the Fisher King's castle. The guests share goblets and dishes and eat with their fingers.

Customizing Instruction

Less Proficient Readers

To make sure students understand the plot of the romance so far, ask the following questions:

- What does the boy do as he rides along? *(prays to God that he might find his mother still alive)*
- What is the stranger in the boat doing? *(fishing)*
- How does the stranger help the boy? *(offers him lodgings for the night)*
- Where is the nobleman sitting when the boy first sees him? *(in a bed)*

1 Point out that the castle magically appears. At first, the boy saw "nothing but sky and earth."

2 This story is very descriptive. As students read, they must be able to form mental pictures of the details pertaining to medieval life, such as "gate" and "drawbridge. " You might read descriptive passages aloud to students, pausing occasionally to allow students to visualize the scene.

3 Make sure students infer that the "handsome nobleman" is the fisherman whom the boy saw in the boat. The nobleman is too ill even to stand up. Later, the boy will learn that the nobleman suffers from a terrible wound received in battle.

English Learners

Have three volunteers read aloud this passage, one taking the part of the boy, another taking the part of the nobleman, and a third reading the narrator's words.

MINI LESSON Viewing and Representing

Illustrated manuscript

ART APPRECIATION Have students read the **Humanities Connection** caption and study the reproduction of the illustration of a banquet in progress. Banquets, which celebrated key events in the lives of the nobles and the community, were important social activities for knights. While the food was served, music and other forms of entertainment were often provided. Each guest used a trencher, or a plate made from a slice of old brown bread. The main courses consisted of roasted meats, poultry, or fish. Dried fruit and wine would follow. Ask students what they think they might like or dislike about medieval banquets.

Possible Responses: Eating without utensils would be challenging. Sharing goblets and dishes would seem unusual, at least at first.

Reading Skills and Strategies

CONNECTING

A Ask students how they think they would feel if they were given a priceless sword.

Possible Responses: honored, grateful, humbled

Pause & Reflect

Possible Response: The lord of the castle recognizes that the boy's noble nature entitles him to have the sword.

Active Reading

STRATEGIES FOR READING A ROMANCE

B Tell students that marvelous events often occur in romances. Ask students to compare the lance with the sword given to the boy.

Possible Response: The sword, though splendid and beautiful, is not magical or supernatural. The lance, however, with the drop of blood flowing from its tip, is more than natural.

THE SWORD'S POMMEL was made of the finest gold of Arabia or Greece, and the scabbard was of golden thread from Venice.

left before the watch blew the dawn signal this morning."

"No indeed," said the boy. "The first hour[5] had already been sounded, I promise you."

While they were talking thus, a boy came in through the door; he was carrying a sword hung round his neck, and presented it to the nobleman.
1 He drew it half out of its scabbard, and saw clearly where it was made, for it was written on the sword. And he also learned from the writing that it was of such fine steel that there was only one way it could ever be broken, which no-one
2 3 knew except the one who had forged and tempered it. The boy who had brought it to him said:

"Sir, the beautiful fair-haired girl, your niece, has sent you this present; you never saw a finer sword as long and as broad as this. You may give it to whoever you like, but my lady would be most happy if it were put to good use where it's bestowed.[6] The one who forged the sword has only ever made three, and he's about to die, so this is the last he'll ever make."

4 And straight away the lord girded his guest with the sword by its straps, which themselves
5 were worth a fortune. The sword's pommel was made of the finest gold of Arabia or Greece, and the scabbard was of golden thread from Venice. With all its rich decoration, the lord presented it to the boy and said:

"Good brother, this sword was intended and destined for you, and I very much want you to have it; come, gird it on and draw it."

The boy thanked him, and girded it on so that it was not restricting, and then drew it, naked, from the scabbard; and after gazing at it for a while, he slid it back into the sheath. And truly, it lay splendidly at his side, and even better in his hand, and it seemed indeed that in time of need he would wield it like a man of valor. Behind him he saw some boys standing around the brightly burning fire; he noticed the one who was looking after his arms, and he entrusted the sword to him, and he kept it for him. Then he sat down again beside the lord, who treated him with the greatest honor. And no house lit by candles could ever provide a brighter light than there was in that hall.

PAUSE & REFLECT The stranger turns out to be the lord of the castle. Why do you think he gives the boy the wondrous sword?

FOCUS The boy observes two marvelous objects carried from room to room in the castle. As you read, look for details that tell you about these objects.

While they were talking of one thing and another, a boy came from a chamber clutching a white lance[7] by the middle of the shaft, and passed between the fire and the two who were sitting on the bed. Everyone in the hall saw the white lance with its white head; and a drop of blood issued from the tip of the lance's head, and right down to the boy's hand this red drop ran. The lord's guest gazed at this marvel that had appeared there that night, but restrained himself from asking how it came to be, because he remembered the advice of

5. **the first hour:** six o'clock in the morning.

6. **bestowed** (bĭ-stōd'): presented as a gift or honor.

7. **lance:** a weapon with a long wooden handle and a sharp metal point.

Detail of *Mystery of the Holy Grail,* W. Hauschild. Neuschwanstein Castle, Germany. Photograph by Dagli Orti/The Art Archive.

HUMANITIES CONNECTION This painting depicts the maiden as she carries the Holy Grail. Notice the unearthly quality that the artist conveys through the maiden's look of reverence and the light radiating from the chalice.

Customizing Instruction

Less Proficient Readers

Focus To provide additional direction, identify the marvelous objects—the white lance (mentioned in the last paragraph on page 714) and the grail (mentioned in the continuing paragraph on page 715). Point out that both objects have religious meanings. According to the gospels, a lance pierced Jesus' side after his death on the cross. Jesus drank from a grail—a chalice or a cup—at the Last Supper on the night before his death.

English Learners

Explain the meaning of the following terms:

1 *scabbard:* a case to hold the blade of a sword

2 *forged:* shaped by heating and pounding

3 *tempered:* brought to the right condition

4 *girded:* fastened with a belt or band

5 *pommel:* a round knob at the end of the handle of a sword

6 *sheath:* a case to hold the blade of a sword

7 *head:* top part

Advanced Learners

Ask students to compare the sword given to the boy with Durendal, Roland's sword in *The Song of Roland.*

Possible Response: Both swords are splendid and priceless objects, fit to be used by the greatest warriors to do noble deeds. The boy's sword has yet to be tested in battle. Roland's sword, however, has helped him defeat many enemies of King Charles. The pommel of Roland's sword also contains relics.

MINI LESSON Viewing and Representing

Mystery of the Holy Grail

ART APPRECIATION Have students read the **Humanities Connection** caption and study the reproduction of the painting on page 715. Ask students how they would describe the maiden's expression in this painting.

Possible Responses: The maiden looks serene and otherworldly. She seems to be having a deeply spiritual experience.

Reading Skills and Strategies
VISUALIZING

A Ask students to identify details that help them form mental pictures of the grail procession.

Possible Responses: details such as "candlesticks of the finest gold, inlaid with black enamel," "a girl . . . fair and comely and beautifully adorned," "so brilliant a light appeared that the candles lost their brightness," "the grail. . . was made of fine, pure gold," and "in it were set precious stones of many kinds"

Active Reading
STRATEGIES FOR READING A ROMANCE

B Ask students to predict whether the boy's silence will bring him good or ill.

Possible Response: It may bring him ill. In a romance the hero faces difficult tests or trials. Perhaps the boy's test is to overcome his lack of confidence and ask about the grail. Something bad may happen to him for failing this test.

Literary Analysis
INTERNAL CONFLICT

C Remind students that an internal conflict is a struggle between opposing forces within a character. Then ask students to describe the boy's internal conflict.

Possible Response: Though he wants to ask the lord about the marvels he has witnessed, he remains silent, fearing that the lord and the other nobles might scorn him if he speaks.

Literary Analysis ROMANCE

D Ask students to identify events in this passage that help create a mood of mystery and wonder.

Possible Response: the empty castle the morning after the sumptuous banquet, the boy's horse saddled and his lance and shield ready for him, the raising of the drawbridge after the boy rides out

the nobleman who had made him a knight,[8] who had taught and instructed him to beware of talking too much; he feared it would be considered base[9] of him if he asked, so he did not. Just then two other boys appeared, and in their hands they held candlesticks of the finest gold, inlaid with black enamel. The boys who carried the candlesticks were handsome indeed. In each candlestick burned ten candles at the very least. A girl who came in with the boys, fair and comely[10] and beautifully adorned, was holding a grail between
A her hands. When she entered holding the grail, so brilliant a light appeared that the candles lost
1 their brightness like the stars or the moon when the sun rises. After her came another girl, holding a silver trencher.[11] The grail, which went ahead, was made of fine, pure gold; and in it were set precious stones of many kinds, the richest and most precious in the earth or the sea: those in the grail surpassed all other jewels, without a doubt. They passed before the bed as the lance had done, and disappeared into anoth-
2 er chamber. The boy saw them pass, but did not dare to ask who was served from the grail, for he had taken the words of the wise nobleman to heart. I fear he may suffer for doing so, for I have heard it said that in time of need a man can talk too little as well as too much. I don't know
B whether it will bring him good or ill, but he asked nothing.

The lord commanded the boys to bring them water and to lay the cloths. Those whose job it usually was did as they were bidden, and the lord and the boy washed their hands in warm water. Two boys brought in a wide table of ivory—according to my source-book it was all one solid piece—and they held it for a moment in front of their lord and the boy until two other boys
3 came with two trestles. The wood of which the trestles were made had two fine qualities: they would last forever, for they were made of ebony, a wood which need never be expected to rot or burn—it is proof against both. The table was set upon these trestles and the cloth was laid. And what should I say about the cloth? No legate[12] or cardinal or pope ever dined at one so white. The first dish was a haunch of venison,[13] seasoned with hot pepper and cooked in fat. There was no shortage of clear, delicious wine to drink, from golden cups. Before them a boy carved pieces from the peppered haunch of venison, drawing the haunch

WHEN SHE ENTERED holding the grail, so brilliant a light appeared that the candles lost their brightness like the stars or the moon when the sun rises.

to him with the silver trencher, and presented the pieces to them on a slice of perfectly baked bread. And meanwhile the grail passed before them again, but the boy did not ask who was served from it: he
refrained because of the nobleman's well-meaning 4
warning not to talk too much—he had taken it to 5
heart and remembered it constantly. But he held
his tongue more than he should have done, for as 6
each dish was served he saw the grail pass before him, right before his eyes, and he did not know who was served from it and he longed to know. But he said to himself that before he left he would

8. **the nobleman . . . a knight:** a noble knight had taught the boy the duties and responsibilities of knighthood. He advised the boy not to say too much because his speech would reveal his lack of education.

9. **base:** beneath his dignity.

10. **comely** (kŭm′lē): attractive.

11. **trencher:** a platter on which food is carved or served.

12. **legate** (lĕg′ĭt): an official messenger, often from the pope.

13. **venison:** meat from a deer.

certainly ask one of the boys of the court, but he would wait till the morning when he took his leave of the lord and the rest of the household. And so he put it off till a later time, and concentrated on eating and drinking.

They were not mean[14] with the wines and dishes, and they were delicious and most agreeable. The food was fine and good: the worthy man and the boy were served that night with all the dishes befitting a king or a count or an emperor. And after they had dined they stayed up together and talked, while the boys prepared the beds and provided fruit to eat—and there was fruit of the dearest kind: dates, figs and nutmegs, and cloves and pomegranates, and to finish there were electuaries and ginger from Alexandria, then pliris archonticum and digestive stomaticum.[15] Then there were many different drinks to taste: sweet, aromatic wine, made with neither honey nor pepper, and old mulberry wine and clear syrup. The boy, who had no knowledge of these, was filled with wonder. Then the nobleman said:

"Good friend, it's time to take to our beds for the night. I'll go now, if you don't mind, and sleep there in my chambers, and whenever you wish you can go to sleep in here. I have no strength in my body: I shall have to be carried."

Then four servants, strong and hearty, came from the chamber, and taking hold of the four corners of the blanket that was spread across the bed on which the nobleman was sitting, they carried him where they were told. Other boys stayed with his guest and served him and fulfilled his every need: when he wished they took off his shoes and clothes and bedded him in sheets of fine white linen.

7 He slept until the morning when day had broken and the household had risen; but he could see no-one as he looked about him, and he had to get up alone whether he liked it or not. Seeing that he had no choice he did the best he could, and put on his shoes without waiting for help;
then he went to don his arms again, finding that 8
they had been brought and left at the head of a table. When he had fully armed his limbs he headed for the doors of the chambers which he had seen open the night before; but the move was fruitless,[16] for he found them shut tight. He called and beat and barged a good deal. Nobody opened up for him or said a word. After calling out for quite a while he turned back to the door of the hall. He found it open, and went down the steps to find his horse saddled, and saw his lance and shield leaning against a wall. He mounted and went looking everywhere, but did not find a living soul and could not see a squire or boy. So he came straight to the gate and found the drawbridge lowered: it had been left like that so that, D
at whatever time he came to leave, nothing should stop him passing straight across. Seeing that the bridge was down he thought the boys must all have gone into the woods to check their traps and snares. He had no wish to stay any longer, and decided to go after them to see if any of them would tell him why the lance bled, if perhaps there were something wrong, and where the grail was carried. And so he rode out through the gate; but before he had got across the bridge, he felt his horse's hooves rise high into the air. The horse made a great leap; and if he had not jumped so well both horse and rider would have been in a sorry plight. The boy looked back to see what had happened, and saw that the bridge had been raised. He called out, but no-one replied.

"Hey!" he cried. "Whoever raised the bridge, talk to me! Where are you? I can't see you.

---

14. **mean:** stingy.

15. **electuaries** (ĭ-lĕk′cho͞o-ĕr′-ēz) . . . **pliris archonticum** (plē′rĭs är-kôn′tĭ-ko͝om) **and digestive stomaticum:** Electuaries were medicines mixed with sweet liquid into a pasty mass. Pliris archonticum and digestive stomaticum were digestive aids.

16. **fruitless** (fro͞ot′lĭs): unsuccessful.

Customizing Instruction

Less Proficient Readers

Review students' comprehension of pages 714–717 by asking the following questions:

- What does the lord of the castle give the boy? *(a splendid sword)*
- What is unusual about the white lance? *(a drop of blood runs down from its tip)*
- Who carries the grail from room to room? *(a beautiful girl)*
- Why doesn't the boy ask about the white lance and the grail? *(He is afraid of sounding stupid.)*

1 Make sure that students can explain the simile, or comparison, in this passage. Just as the brightness of the rising sun blots out other heavenly lights, so the radiance of the grail makes the candles seem dim.

English Learners

Explain the meaning of the following words and phrases:

2 *chamber:* room

3 *trestles:* frameworks used to support a table

4 *refrained:* kept from doing something

5 *taken it to heart:* believed deeply

6 *held his tongue:* did not speak

7 *day had broken:* dawn had come

8 *don his arms:* put on his armor

Advanced Learners

Ask students to draw conclusions about the relationship between the nobleman and the boy.

Possible Response: The nobleman is the host, and the boy is his guest. The nobleman opens his house to the boy to make him feel honored and welcome. The nobleman recognizes the boy's goodness and heroic potential, giving him a splendid sword, preparing a banquet in his honor, and allowing him to see the grail procession. The boy appreciates his host's generosity and courtesy, but is too self-conscious and shy to ask questions.

MINI LESSON Grammar

ADJECTIVE PHRASES

Instruction An adjective phrase is a prepositional phrase that modifies a noun or a pronoun. An adjective phrase tells which one or what kind.

Model Sentence

The banquet featured food of the finest quality.

In the above model sentence, have students identify the adjective phrase *(of the finest quality)* and the word the adjective phrase modifies. *(The noun "food")*

Practice Ask students to underline the adjective phrase and to identify the word the phrase modifies.

1. Perceval was an honored guest <u>of the Fisher King</u>. *(guest)*
2. The grail <u>of pure gold</u> captured the knight's interest. *(grail)*
3. Perceval had never seen anything <u>of such brilliance and rarity</u>. *(anything)*

For more instruction and practice in adjective phrases, use McDougal Littell's ***Language Network:***

- Grade 10, Chapter 3, "Using Phrases"
- Grade 12, Chapter 2, "Using Phrases"

PERCEVAL: THE STORY OF THE GRAIL 717

Pause & Reflect
Possible Response: The bleeding lance and the radiant grail represent holy objects, closely associated with Jesus Christ. The lance pierced Jesus' side at the crucifixion. The grail was the cup used at the Last Supper.

Active Reading
STRATEGIES FOR READING A ROMANCE

A Remind students that when reading a romance they should note sudden changes in setting. Then ask them to contrast the setting of this episode with the setting of the previous one.
Possible Response: This episode is set in a forest; the previous episode was set in a castle, where a sumptuous banquet was served. The scene has shifted from the civilized world to the world of nature.

Reading Skills and Strategies
EVALUATE

B Ask students to share their impressions of the girl in the forest.
Possible Responses: The girl seems to love the slain knight deeply and feels that her life has lost its meaning. She expresses her grief in an exaggerated, dramatic way.

Come out and let me look at you: there's something I want to ask you."

But he was wasting his time calling out like this, for nobody would answer him.

PAUSE & REFLECT What do you think the bleeding lance and the radiant grail might represent?

FOCUS The boy leaves the castle in a troubled state of mind. In the forest, he comes upon a weeping maiden. Read to find out what she tells him about the lord of the castle.

He headed towards the forest, and came upon a path where he found fresh tracks where horses had passed.

A "I think," he said, "that the ones I'm looking for went this way."

So he went galloping through the wood as far as the tracks led him, until he chanced to see a girl beneath an oak tree weeping and crying and lamenting, filled with sorrow and misery.

"Alas!" she cried. "How unfortunate I am! I
B was born in an evil hour! Cursed be the hour I was conceived and the hour when I was born!
1 Nothing has caused me such anguish before. Would to God my love were not dead in my arms: it would have been better by far if he had lived and I had died. Why did Death, who has brought me such grief, take his soul rather than mine? What's my life worth when I see the one I loved most lying dead? Truly, with him gone I care nothing for my life or my body. Come, Death, and take my soul! Let it be the chambermaid and companion of his, if he'll accept it."

Such was the girl's lament for a knight she was holding, whose head had been cut off. The boy rode straight up to her when he saw her, and as he came near he greeted her, and she greeted him, her head bowed, never ceasing to lament. And the boy asked her:

"Young lady, who killed this knight who is lying in your lap?"

"Good sir," she replied, "a knight killed him, this very morning. But there's something that quite amazes me: God save me, you could ride, so they say, forty leagues the way you've come, and you wouldn't find any good or honest or wholesome lodging, yet your horse is well fed and his coat smooth. If he'd been washed and groomed and given a manger of oats and hay he
wouldn't have had a fuller belly or a sleeker 2
coat. And it seems to me that you yourself had a comfortable and restful night."

"Truly, dear girl," he said, "I had all the comfort possible last night, and if it shows it's with good reason. But if you shouted loudly from where we are now, it would be heard quite clearly where I lodged last night. You don't know this country very well, and haven't explored it at all, for without a doubt I had the finest lodging I've ever had."

"Oh, sir! then you lodged at the house of the rich Fisher King!"

AND THE BOY ASKED HER:
"Young lady, who killed this knight who is lying in your lap?"

"By the Savior, girl, I don't know if he's a fisherman or a king, but he's very wise and
courteous. I can't tell you anything more, except 3
that I came across two men in a boat very late yesterday, sailing gently along. One of them was rowing, the other was fishing with a hook, and he told me the way to his house last night, and gave me lodging."

And the girl said:

"Good sir, he *is* a king, I can assure you. But he was wounded in a battle and completely crippled, so that he's helpless now, for he was

The Forest Crossed by Perceval to Liberate Amfortas at the Castle of the Grail, Christian Jank. Neuschwanstein Castle, Germany. Photograph by Dagli Orti/The Art Archive.

struck by a javelin through both his thighs; and he still suffers from it so much that he can't mount a horse. But when he wants to engage in some pleasure and sport he has himself placed in a boat and goes fishing with a hook; that's why he's called the Fisher King. And he finds his enjoyment that way because he couldn't manage or cope with any other sport: he can't hunt in the woods or along the riverbanks and marshes. But he has men to hunt the wildfowl, and huntsmen and archers who go shooting with their bows in the forests. That's why he likes to live in this house just here; for in all the world he could
4 never find a retreat so suited to his needs, and he's had a house built befitting a rich king."

"By my faith, young lady, it's true what you say, and I wondered at it when I came before him last night. I stood a little way from him, and he told me to come and sit beside him, and not
to take it for haughtiness if he didn't get up to 5
greet me, for he didn't have the strength or power; so I went and sat at his side."

"Truly, he did you a great honor when he seated you beside him. And tell me now: when you sat down at his side, did you see the lance whose point bleeds, though it has neither flesh nor veins?"

"Did I see it? Yes, in faith!"

"And did you ask why it bled?"

"God help me, I didn't say word."

"Then I tell you, you've done great wrong. And did you see the grail?"

Customizing Instruction

Less Proficient Readers

Focus Point out to students that the weeping maiden will explain to the boy the meaning of his experiences in the castle. As students learn about the lord of the castle, make sure they understand why he was unable to rise from his bed.

English Learners

Explain the meaning of the following words:

1 *anguish:* grief
2 *sleeker:* smoother
3 *courteous:* polite and kind
4 *retreat:* safe, quiet place
5 *haughtiness:* pride

Advanced Learners

Have students compare the weeping maiden with the girl who carries the grail.

Possible Response: The girl who carries the grail is silent, poised, and serene—far removed from ordinary human emotions. She carries a holy object, the source of eternal life and salvation. The weeping maiden, on the other hand, vents her grief in a verbal torrent and is very emotional. She holds a dead man in her arms and scolds the boy for his failure in the castle.

MINI LESSON Speaking and Listening

DRAMATIC READING

Prepare Role-playing allows students to explore literary characters deeply and to experience their conflicts and emotions. Have students prepare a dramatic reading of the boy's dialogue with the maiden in the forest, beginning with the girl's words "Good sir, he *is* a king . . ." at the bottom of page 718 and continuing until the end of the excerpt. Students should work in groups of three, with one student reading the boy's part, another reading the maiden's part, and a third reading the narrator's paragraph on page 720.

Remind students that much of the dialogue between the boy and the maiden is charged with emotion and that they should read their parts aloud several times to discover these emotions and how to convey them.

Present Invite groups of three to play the roles of Perceval, the maiden, and the narrator. Ask students in the audience to evaluate the performance and explain how it increased their understanding of the characters.

This activity is particularly well suited for longer blocks of class time.

Reading Skills and Strategies
CONNECTING

A Ask students to imagine themselves in the boy's place. Then ask them how they might feel if they found out that they had missed an opportunity to work a miracle.

Possible Responses: amazed, regretful, determined to make up for the lost opportunity

Literary Analysis ROMANCE

B Ask students to describe what is unusual about the hero's tests in this romance.

Possible Response: The hero is tested not in battle but at a banquet without any forewarning. He realizes that he has been tested only after his cousin informs him of his failure.

"I saw it clearly."
"Who was holding it?"
"A girl."
"Where did she come from?"
"From a chamber."
"And where did she go?"
"She went into another chamber."
"Did anyone go ahead of the grail?'
"Yes."
"Who?"
"Two boys, that's all."
"What were they holding in their hands?"
"Candlesticks full of candles."
"And who came after the grail?"
"Another girl."
"What was she holding?"
"A small silver trencher."
"Did you ask them where they were going?"
"Not a word crossed my lips."

"God help me, so much the worse. What's your name, friend?"

And the boy, who did not know his name, guessed and said that his name was Perceval the Welshman, not knowing if it were true or not. But it was true, though he did not know it. And when the girl heard this she stood up before him and said angrily:

"Your name is changed, good friend."

"To what?"

"Perceval the wretched! Oh, luckless Perceval! 1
How unfortunate you are to have failed to ask
all this! You would have healed the good king
who is crippled, and he would have regained the A
use of his limbs and the rule of his land—and
you would have profited greatly! But know this
now: many ills will befall both you and others. 2
And know this, too: this has come upon you
because of the sin against your mother,[17] for she
has died of grief on your account. I know you
better than you know me; you don't know who I
am, but I was brought up with you at your
mother's house for a very long time: I'm your
cousin and you are mine. And I grieve no less for
your misfortune in not learning what was done
with the grail or where it's taken, than for your
mother who has died, or for this knight whom I
loved and adored because he called me his dear
love and loved me like a noble, loyal knight."

"Oh, cousin!" cried Perceval. "If what you've told me is true, tell me how you know."

"I know it to be true," said the girl, "for I saw
her laid in the earth." ❖ 3

17. **the sin against your mother:** Perceval had left his mother to become a knight.

Humanities

WHAT FOLLOWS IN *PERCEVAL: THE STORY OF THE GRAIL* Perceval vanquishes the knight who killed his cousin's lover, sending him as a prisoner to King Arthur's court. Later, when Perceval arrives at Camelot, he is warmly received. At Caerleon, in the presence of King Arthur and Queen Guinivere, an ugly maiden rides up on a mule. She rebukes Perceval for his failure to cure the Fisher King's wound and for the misfortunes to come. Perceval then sets off in search of the Holy Grail.

As years go by, Perceval continues his quest, defeating other knights and sending them as prisoners to Camelot. Finally, having learned of Christ's saving mercy, Perceval seeks out a hermit to confess his sins. The hermit reveals that the Fisher King is actually Perceval's uncle and that Perceval failed his test in the castle because he unknowingly had committed a great sin: namely, leaving his mother and breaking her heart. As he prays with the hermit, Perceval rekindles his Christian faith. (Chrétien's unfinished romance ends at this point.)

Lancelot and Guinevere: The Dawn of Love (1867), after Gustave Doré. Steel engraving. The Granger Collection, New York.

Customizing Instruction

Less Proficient Readers

Review students' comprehension of pages 718–721 by asking the following questions:

- What does the weeping maiden hold in her arms? *(a beheaded knight)*
- Why is the Fisher King now helpless? *(He suffers from a javelin wound through his thighs.)*
- What should the boy have done in the castle? *(He should have asked the Fisher King about the lance and the grail.)*
- What name does the weeping maiden give the boy? *(Perceval the Wretched)*

English Learners

Explain the meaning of the following words and phrases:

1 *wretched:* grief

2 *ills:* evils

3 *laid in the earth:* buried

Advanced Learners

Ask students what they think it would have been like to live in the world depicted in this medieval romance.

Possible Responses: It would have been unsettling to live in a world where strange and unpredictable events occur; it would have been uplifting to live in a world where chivalric ideals motivate knightly actions.

Cross Curricular Link **Music**

WAGNER'S *PARSIFAL* The legend of the Holy Grail, which Chrétien introduced into Arthurian literature, has inspired many creative people down through the centuries. One of them was the German composer Richard Wagner (1813–1883). He treated the grail legend in his final opera, *Parsifal*, produced in 1882. Rich in Christian symbols and ethical themes, the opera portrays the knights of the grail. Their ruler Amfortas, like the Fisher King in Chrétien's romance, suffers from a terrible wound. He can be cured only by a "pure fool" with a sacred spear. Parsifal is that long-awaited pure fool. He resists worldly temptations and retrieves the sacred spear from an evil magician. With a touch of that spear, Parsifal heals Amfortas, redeeming the knights of the grail.

Connect to the Literature

1. **What Do You Think?** Students may state that the boy's missed opportunities made them feel frustrated. If he were less self-conscious, he could have done much good.

Comprehension Check

- A drop of blood flows from the lance's tip.
- "Perceval the Wretched" because he failed to heal the Fisher King

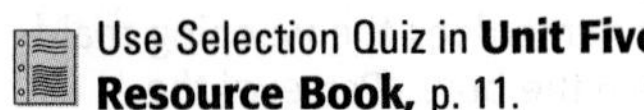
Use Selection Quiz in **Unit Five Resource Book,** p. 11.

Think Critically

2. Possible Responses: Perceval learns that he must trust himself and not feel self-conscious in courtly settings.
3. Answers will vary. Students should cite evidence in the romance to support their predictions. Some students may state that Perceval will set off in quest of the Holy Grail. (You may choose to share with students the information about Perceval provided in the mini-lesson at the bottom of page 720.)
4. Responses will vary. Some students may say that Perceval is completely responsible for not asking about the lance and the grail. These students may state that the Fisher King treats Perceval courteously and would not have laughed at him for asking questions. These students may add that Perceval shows poor judgment in taking the nobleman's advice to heart. Students who say that Perceval is not to blame may state that the boy was trying to be polite and did not foresee the consequences of his silence.

Extend Interpretations

5. **Comparing Texts** Possible Responses: Roland faces a military crisis; Perceval, a social dilemma. Roland acts impulsively, defying death for the sake of honor. Perceval is self-conscious and unsure of himself. Roland trusts himself and his own judgment. Perceval trusts others instead.

Connect to the Literature

1. **What Do You Think?** What was your reaction to the boy's missed opportunities?

Comprehension Check

- What is strange about the lance that is carried in the castle?
- What name does the boy's cousin give him in the forest? Why?

Think Critically

2. **ACTIVE READING: STRATEGIES FOR READING A ROMANCE** Review the flow chart you made in your READER'S NOTEBOOK. What do you think is the most important lesson that the boy learns from his adventures?
3. What do you **predict** the boy will do now that his cousin has told him about his mistake and its consequences?
4. To what extent is the boy to blame for not asking about the lance and the grail? Explain your answer.

THINK ABOUT
- the way the lord of the castle has treated him
- the boy's reason for keeping silent

Extend Interpretations

5. **Comparing Texts** How does Perceval differ from Roland, the epic hero of *The Song of Roland?*
6. **Connect to Life** Perceval finds out from his cousin that he should have asked the Fisher King about the lance and the grail. Based on your own experience, when is it important to speak up? When is it important to remain silent?

LITERARY ANALYSIS: ROMANCE

A **romance** is an imaginative story that includes such elements as noble heroes, chivalric codes of honor, passionate love, and daring deeds. Popular in the Middle Ages, romances still appeal to readers today. One reason is that they transport readers from everyday life to a make-believe world. In this world, marvelous events—even supernatural ones—happen as a matter of course:

While they were talking of one thing and another, a boy came from a chamber clutching a white lance by the middle of the shaft. . . . Everyone in the hall saw the white lance with its white head; and a drop of blood issued from the tip of the lance's head, and right down to the boy's hand this red drop ran.

Moreover, the heroes of romances are suited to this make-believe world. Writers of romances tend to idealize their heroes, depicting them as larger-than-life.

Cooperative Learning Activity With a small group of classmates, imagine that Perceval has been transported from the make-believe world of medieval romance to the everyday world of a modern high school. How might he handle real-life situations? Brainstorm a list of situations, and then improvise a skit in which Perceval deals with one or two of them. Perform your skit for other groups.

6. **Connect to Life** Responses will vary. Some students may state that it is important to speak up to defend a principle or prevent an injustice. Other students may state that at times it is important to remain silent to spare someone else's feelings.

Literary Analysis

Cooperative Learning Activity As students plan their skits, tell them that Perceval must remain true to his character in the medieval romance—very noble, somewhat foolish, and painfully self-conscious.

Use **Unit Five Resource Book,** p. 10, for more practice.

To assess skills and concepts taught in this selection, use **Formal Assessment Book,** pp. 111–112.

The Arthurian Legend in Film and Story

In 12th-century France, the legends about King Arthur and his knights inspired Chrétien de Troyes to write romances. Down through the centuries, these same legends have cast their spell on countless other authors. Today, they continue to entertain and thrill modern audiences and readers. Arthur and his knights still brandish sword and lance in books, movies, Broadway shows, comic strips, Web sites, and computer and video games. "Knights," clad in armor, gallop and joust at medieval fairs and restaurants.

Moreover, the ideals represented by King Arthur and his knights still exert their magical power. People still go on quests, embrace noble causes, and try to make the world a better place.

Ioan Gruffudd, Keira Knightley, and Clive Owen in the 2004 film *King Arthur*

Books

T. H. White, *The Once and Future King* (1958)

John Steinbeck, *The Acts of King Arthur and His Noble Knights* (1976)

Mary Stewart, *The Last Enchantment* (1979)

Rosemary Sutcliff, *The Road to Camlann* (1982)

Marion Zimmer Bradley, *The Mists of Avalon* (1982)

Deepak Chopra, *The Return of Merlin* (1995)

Movies and Television

Camelot (1967)

Monty Python and the Holy Grail (1975)

Excalibur (1981)

Indiana Jones and the Last Crusade (1989)

First Knight (1995)

The TV miniseries *Merlin* (1998)

King Arthur (2004)

Computer and Video Games

The Quest: Interactive Game

Zelda

Warcraft

Group Discussion Where have you come upon traces of the Arthurian legend in the modern world? Why do you think people today still retell and enjoy stories about a legendary medieval king and his knights? Share your views with a small group of classmates.

Connect to Today

"The Arthurian Legend in Film and Story" relates the excerpt from "Perceval: the Legend of the Grail" to examples of the Arthurian legend in modern culture. These examples attest to the timeless appeal of King Arthur and his knights.

Group Discussion As a starting point for the discussion, students might ask themselves what aspect of the Arthurian legends appeals the most to them—for example, the mysterious settings, the quests for adventure, or the chivalric ideals.

Possible Objectives

This **On Your Own** featured selection may be used to achieve one or more of the following objectives:

- to give students an opportunity to read independently, either reading silently for a sustained period, reading and analyzing literature with a group, or using the Reader's Notebook to write in response to the literature
- to conduct a post-reading class discussion
- to assess students' comprehension of the selection

Summary

In "The Lay of the Were-Wolf," a noble and his wife are happily married except for the fact that he leaves her each week for three days. Out of love, he reveals to her his dark secret: namely, that during those three days he roams the forest as Bisclavaret—a were-wolf. He also tells her where he hides his clothes in the forest when he changes into a wolf. Without these clothes, he cannot resume his human shape. The wife soon betrays her husband to a knight, who steals the clothes in the forest and marries her. One day, the king, hunting in the forest, comes upon a wolf (the noble in his changed state), whom he adopts as a pet. At a banquet, the wolf, usually playful and friendly, suddenly attacks the knight who stole his clothes. Later, at a country lodge, the wolf furiously bites his former wife. When questioned, the lady reveals her betrayal of her first husband. The king obtains the stolen clothes and leaves them with the wolf in a secret room. When the king returns, he finds the missing noble in the wolf's place.

THE LAY OF THE WERE-WOLF

MARIE de FRANCE

Translated by Eugene Mason

Marie de France
(c. 1140–c. 1190)

Her Life Marie de France is the earliest known French woman poet. As with Chrétien de Troyes, little is known about her. In fact, she is known as Marie de France only because the epilogue to her *fables* states, *"Marie ai nun, si sui de France"* ("Marie is my name, I come from France"). The dialect of Norman French in which she wrote suggests that she grew up in Brittany, a region in northwestern France just south of Normandy. She seems to have been well educated and to have spent time in England at the court of Eleanor of Aquitaine. Under Eleanor's influence, this court became a center of learning and literary activity.

Her Poetry Marie de France earned a place in literary history for a particular type of poem known as the *lai* (lā). A **lai** (or *lay*) is a brief narrative poem about love and adventure. In writing her lais, Marie de France mostly drew on Celtic legends from Brittany. She composed her lais to entertain an aristocratic audience, probably performing them to music. Like the romances of Chrétien de Troyes, her lais reflect 12th-century views about chivalry and courtly love. In all, she wrote twelve lais.

The lais of Marie de France often explore the problems faced by noble women and men who are in love. In "The Lay of the Were-Wolf," for example, the main character is a noble who suffers from a horrid affliction. Periodically, he flees to the woods where he changes from a human into a wolf. Out of his great love for his wife, he reveals this dark secret to her. You are about to read a prose translation of Marie de France's narrative poem. As you read, ask yourself these questions:

1. *How is the depiction of courtly life in this story similar to that in the excerpt from* Perceval: The Story of the Grail?
2. *How does the main character in this story compare with werewolves depicted in horror movies?*

Amongst the tales I tell you once again, I would not forget the Lay of the Were-Wolf. Such beasts as he are known in every land. Bisclavaret[1] he is named in Brittany; whilst the Norman[2] calls him Garwal.

It is a certain thing, and within the knowledge of all, that many a christened man has suffered this change, and ran wild in woods, as a Were-Wolf. The Were-Wolf is a fearsome beast. He lurks within the thick forest, mad and horrible to see. All the evil that he may, he does. He goeth to and fro, about the solitary place, seeking man, in order to devour him. Hearken, now, to the adventure of the Were-Wolf, that I have to tell.

1. **Bisclavaret** (bēs-klä-və-rā′).
2. **Brittany . . . the Norman:** Brittany is a region of northwestern France. Normans are people from Normandy, the region just to the northeast of Brittany.

Working Independently

You may want to set aside time each week for independent reading, without making an assignment related to the reading. Or once students have completed the reading, either alone or aloud in groups, you may ask them to work together on a project, such as improvising a dramatic skit based on this story. If you choose to have students write responsively in their Reader's Notebook, suggest that they contrast Bisclavaret's relationship with his wife and his relationship with the king.

Discussing the Selection

The two questions on page 725 of the pupil edition are suitable for a post-reading class discussion. See the side column on page 731 for possible responses to these questions.

Using the Selection for Assessment

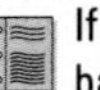

If you want to use this selection as the basis for assessment, see **Integrated Assessment Book,** pp. 25–30, for test questions.

In Brittany there dwelt a baron who was marvelously esteemed of all his fellows. He was a stout knight, and a comely, and a man of office and repute. Right private was he to the mind of his lord, and dear to the counsel of his neighbors. This baron was wedded to a very worthy dame, right fair to see, and sweet of semblance.[3] All his love was set on her, and all her love was given again to him. One only grief had this lady. For three whole days in every week her lord was absent from her side. She knew not where he went, nor on what errand. Neither did any of his house know the business which called him forth.

On a day when this lord was come again to his house, altogether joyous and content, the lady took him to task, right sweetly, in this fashion,

"Husband," said she, "and fair, sweet friend, I have a certain thing to pray of you. Right willingly would I receive this gift, but I fear to anger you in the asking. It is better for me to have an empty hand, than to gain hard words."

When the lord heard this matter, he took the lady in his arms, very tenderly, and kissed her.

"Wife," he answered, "ask what you will. What would you have, for it is yours already?"

"By my faith," said the lady, "soon shall I be whole. Husband, right long and wearisome are the days that you spend away from your home. I rise from my bed in the morning, sick at heart, I know not why. So fearful am I, lest you do aught to your loss, that I may not find any comfort. Very quickly shall I die for reason of my dread. Tell me now, where you go, and on what business! How may the knowledge of one who loves so closely, bring you to harm?"

"Wife," made answer the lord, "nothing but evil can come if I tell you this secret. For the mercy of God do not require it of me. If you but knew, you would withdraw yourself from my love, and I should be lost indeed."

When the lady heard this, she was persuaded that her baron sought to put her by with jesting words.[4] Therefore she prayed and required him the more urgently, with tender looks and speech, till he was overborne, and told her all the story, hiding naught.

"Wife, I become Bisclavaret. I enter in the forest, and live on prey and roots, within the thickest of the wood."

After she had learned his secret, she prayed and entreated the more as to whether he ran in his raiment, or went spoiled of vesture.[5]

"NOTHING BUT EVIL CAN COME IF I TELL YOU THIS SECRET."

"Wife," said he, "I go naked as a beast."

"Tell me, for hope of grace, what you do with your clothing?"

"Fair wife, that will I never. If I should lose my raiment, or even be marked as I quit my vesture, then a Were-Wolf I must go for all the days of my life. Never again should I become man, save in that hour my clothing were given back to me. For this reason never will I show my lair."[6]

"Husband," replied the lady to him, "I love you better than all the world. The less cause have you for doubting my faith, or hiding any tittle[7] from me. What savor is here of friendship? How have I made forfeit of your love; for what sin do you mistrust my honor? Open now your heart, and tell what is good to be known."

3. **semblance:** outward appearance.
4. **put her by with jesting words:** put her off or distract her by joking with her.
5. **raiment . . . vesture:** Both words are old-fashioned terms for clothing.
6. **lair:** an animal's den.
7. **tittle:** very small bit or portion.

726 UNIT FIVE PART 1

The Werewolf of Eschenbach, Germany (1685). Line engraving. The Granger Collection, New York.

So at the end, outwearied and overborne by her importunity,[8] he could no longer refrain, but told her all.

"Wife," said he, "within this wood, a little from the path, there is a hidden way, and at the end thereof an ancient chapel, where oftentimes I have bewailed my lot. Near by is a great hollow stone, concealed by a bush, and there is the secret place where I hide my raiment, till I would return to my own home."

On hearing this marvel the lady became sanguine[9] of visage, because of her exceeding fear. She dared no longer to lie at his side, and turned over in her mind, this way and that, how best she could get her from him. Now there was a certain knight of those parts, who, for a great while, had sought and required this lady for her love. This knight had spent long years in her service, but little enough had he got thereby, not even fair words, or a promise. To him the dame wrote a letter, and meeting, made her purpose plain.

"Fair friend," said she, "be happy. That which you have coveted so long a time, I will grant without delay. Never again will I deny your suit. My heart, and all I have to give, are yours, so take me now as love and dame."

Right sweetly the knight thanked her for her grace, and pledged her faith and fealty.[10] When she had confirmed him by an oath, then she told him all this business of her lord—why he went, and what he became, and of his ravening[11] within the wood. So she showed him of the chapel, and of the hollow stone, and of how to spoil the

8. **importunity** (ĭm′pôr-to͞o′nĭ-tē′): persistence in asking.

9. **sanguine** (săng′gwĭn) **of visage:** red in the face.

10. **fealty:** loyalty; allegiance.

11. **ravening:** seeking prey or plunder.

THE LAY OF THE WERE-WOLF 727

Were-Wolf of his vesture. Thus, by the kiss of his wife, was Bisclavaret betrayed. Often enough had he ravished[12] his prey in desolate places, but from this journey he never returned. His kinsfolk and acquaintance came together to ask of his tidings, when this absence was noised abroad. Many a man, on many a day, searched the woodland, but none might find him, nor learn where Bisclavaret was gone.

The lady was wedded to the knight who had cherished her for so long a space. More than a year had passed since Bisclavaret disappeared. Then it chanced that the King would hunt in that self-same wood where the Were-Wolf lurked. When the hounds were unleashed they ran this way and that, and swiftly came upon his scent. At the view the huntsman winded on his horn, and the whole pack were at his heels. They followed him from morn to eve, till he was torn and bleeding, and was all adread lest they should pull him down. Now the King was very close to the quarry, and when Bisclavaret looked upon his master, he ran to him for pity and for grace. He took the stirrup within his paws, and fawned upon the prince's foot. The King was very fearful at this sight, but presently he called his courtiers to his aid.

"Lords," cried he, "hasten hither, and see this marvelous thing. Here is a beast who has the sense of man. He abases[13] himself before his foe, and cries for mercy, although he cannot speak. Beat off the hounds, and let no man do him harm. We will hunt no more to-day, but return to our own place, with the wonderful quarry we have taken."

The King turned him about, and rode to his hall, Bisclavaret following at his side. Very near to his master the Were-Wolf went, like any dog, and had no care to seek again the wood. When the King had brought him safely to his own castle, he rejoiced greatly, for the beast was fair and strong, no mightier had any man seen. Much pride had the King in his marvelous beast. He held him so dear, that he bade all those who wished for his love, to cross the Wolf in naught, neither to strike him with a rod, but ever to see that he was richly fed and kenneled warm. This commandment the Court observed willingly. So all the day the Wolf sported with the lords, and at night he lay within the chamber of the King. There was not a man who

12. **ravished:** seized and carried away by force.

13. **abases:** lowers or degrades oneself.

did not make much of the beast, so frank was he and debonair.[14] None had reason to do him wrong, for ever was he about his master, and for his part did evil to none. Every day were these two companions together, and all perceived that the King loved him as his friend.

Hearken now to that which chanced.

The King held a high Court, and bade his great vassals and barons, and all the lords of his venery[15] to the feast. Never was there a goodlier feast, nor one set forth with sweeter show and pomp. Amongst those who were bidden, came that same knight who had the wife of Bisclavaret for dame. He came to the castle, richly gowned, with a fair company, but little he deemed whom he would find so near. Bisclavaret marked his foe the moment he stood within the hall. He ran towards him, and seized him with his fangs, in the King's very presence, and to the view of all. Doubtless he would have done him much mischief, had not the King called and chidden him, and threatened him with a rod. Once, and twice, again, the Wolf set upon the knight in the very light of day. All men marveled at his malice, for sweet and serviceable was the beast, and to that hour had shown hatred of none. With one consent the household deemed that this deed was done with full reason, and that the Wolf had suffered at the knight's hand some bitter wrong. Right wary of his foe was the knight until the feast had ended, and all the barons had taken farewell of their lord, and departed, each to his own house. With these, amongst the very first, went that lord whom Bisclavaret so fiercely had assailed.[16] Small was the wonder that he was glad to go.

> NEITHER MAN NOR LEASH MIGHT RESTRAIN THE FURY OF THE WOLF.

No long while after this adventure it came to pass that the courteous King would hunt in that forest where Bisclavaret was found. With the prince came his wolf, and a fair company. Now at nightfall the King abode within a certain lodge of that country, and this was known of that dame who before was the wife of Bisclavaret. In the morning the lady clothed her in her most dainty apparel, and hastened to the lodge, since she desired to speak with the King, and to offer him a rich present. When the lady entered in the chamber, neither man nor leash might restrain the fury of the Wolf. He became as a mad dog in his hatred and malice. Breaking from his bonds he sprang at the lady's face, and bit the nose from her visage. From every side men ran to the succor[17] of the dame. They beat off the wolf from his prey, and for a little would have cut him in pieces with their swords. But a certain wise counselor said to the King, "Sire, hearken now to me. This beast is always with you, and there is not one of us all who has not known him for long. He goes in and out amongst us, nor has molested any man, neither done wrong or felony to any, save only to this dame, one only time as we have seen. He has done evil to this lady, and to that knight, who is now the husband of the dame. Sire, she was once the wife of that lord who was so close and private to your heart, but who went, and none might find where he had gone. Now, therefore, put the dame in a sure place, and question her straitly, so that she may tell—if perchance she knows thereof—for what reason this Beast holds her in such mortal hate. For many a strange deed has chanced, as well we know, in this marvelous land of Brittany."

14. **debonair** (dĕb′ə-nâr′): pleasant; carefree and cheerful.

15. **venery** (vĕn′ə-rē): the huntsmen of the king.

16. **assailed:** attacked repeatedly and violently.

17. **succor:** help; aid.

THE LAY OF THE WERE-WOLF **729**

HUMANITIES CONNECTION This 15th-century woodcut from Germany shows a werewolf attacking its victim while a stunned companion looks on. The artist captures the fury of the werewolf, who has lost his humanity and descended to the level of a beast. Notice the contrast between the woods, where the beast dwells, and the house, where humans live.

MINI LESSON Viewing and Representing

Woodcut of werewolf

ART APPRECIATION Have students read the **Humanities Connection** caption and study the reproduction of the woodcut. To make a woodcut, an artist cuts away at the surface of a block of wood, using chisels, knives, or gouges. The uncut or raised portion of the wood thus forms an image, which is painted with ink. A sheet of paper is then placed over the block of wood. By rubbing the paper against the block of wood, the artist transfers the image to the paper. The woodcut reproduced in the pupil edition depicts a werewolf, a figure common in European folklore. Ask students to identify details in the woodcut that convey the beast's savagery.

Possible Responses: Standing on its hind limbs, the werewolf uses its front paws to seize the victim and hold him securely. The werewolf's large tongue, snarling lips, and huge pointed teeth can be seen.

The King listened to these words, and deemed the counsel good. He laid hands upon the knight, and put the dame in surety[18] in another place. He caused them to be questioned right straitly, so that their torment was very grievous. At the end, partly because of her distress, and partly by reason of her exceeding fear, the lady's lips were loosed, and she told her tale. She showed them of the betrayal of her lord, and how his raiment was stolen from the hollow stone. Since then she knew not where he went, nor what had befallen him, for he had never come again to his own land. Only, in her heart, well she deemed and was persuaded, that Bisclavaret was he.

Straightway the King demanded the vesture of his baron, whether this were to the wish of the lady, or whether it were against her wish. When the raiment was brought him, he caused it to be spread before Bisclavaret, but the Wolf made as though he had not seen. Then that cunning and crafty counselor took the King apart, that he might give him a fresh rede.[19]

"Sire," said he, "you do not wisely, nor well, to set this raiment before Bisclavaret, in the sight of all. In shame and much tribulation must he lay aside the beast, and again become man. Carry your wolf within your most secret chamber, and put his vestment therein. Then close the door upon him, and leave him alone for a space. So we shall see presently whether the ravening beast may indeed return to human shape."

"SO WE SHALL SEE PRESENTLY WHETHER THE RAVENING BEAST MAY INDEED RETURN TO HUMAN SHAPE."

The King carried the Wolf to his chamber, and shut the doors upon him fast. He delayed for a brief while, and taking two lords of his fellowship with him, came again to the room. Entering therein, all three, softly together, they found the knight sleeping in the King's bed, like a little child. The King ran swiftly to the bed and taking his friend in his arms, embraced and kissed him fondly, above a hundred times. When the man's speech returned once more, he told him of his adventure. Then the King restored to his friend the fief[20] that was stolen from him, and gave such rich gifts, moreover, as I cannot tell. As for the wife who had betrayed Bisclavaret, he bade her avoid his country, and chased her from the realm. So she went forth, she and her second lord together, to seek a more abiding city, and were no more seen.

The adventure that you have heard is no vain fable. Verily and indeed it chanced as I have said. The Lay of the Were-Wolf, truly, was written that it should ever be borne in mind. ❖

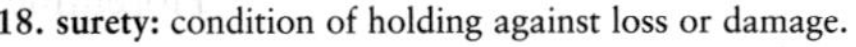

18. **surety:** condition of holding against loss or damage.

19. **rede** (rēd): piece of advice or counsel.

20. **fief** (fēf): piece of land; estate.

You might use the questions on page 725 for a post-reading class discussion.

Discussion Questions

1. How is the depiction of courtly life in this story similar to that in the excerpt from *Perceval: The Story of the Grail?*
   Possible Response: In both literary works, courtly life is contrasted with life in nature. The court is depicted as an oasis of civilization, set apart from a violent world. The court is where people are free to express noble thoughts and feelings. For example, inside the castle the Fisher King extends kindness, hospitality, and generosity to Perceval. At court, the king tenderly nurtures a wolf, who plays with the lords, eventually resuming his human shape. At court, the banquet is the central event—a communal feast of sharing.
2. How does the main character in this story compare with werewolves depicted in horror movies?
   Possible Response: In most horror movies, the audience sees the werewolf violently killing its victims. In this story, on the other hand, the werewolf kills no one, though he does attack his two betrayers. Horror movies usually explain what causes the main character to change into a werewolf. In this story, the reader never discovers what causes the main character's affliction. The ending of this story is unusual too: the main character is not killed but rewarded. Presumably, he will change into a wolf again, but even then the king and the nobles will not harm him. The main character in this story seems more sympathetic than do werewolves portrayed in horror movies.

THE LAY OF THE WERE-WOLF **731**

Objectives

- appreciate the work of a great world poet
- understand the connection between an author's works and his philosophies and beliefs
- learn about medieval life and culture

Presenting the Author

The **Author Study** offers students the opportunity to concentrate on a masterpiece by Dante Alighieri, one of the greatest writers in the Middle Ages. Students can also learn about Dante's life and get to know the man behind the masterpiece.

READING FOR INFORMATION
Reading Skills and Strategies
MONITORING READING STRATEGIES

Encourage students to monitor and modify their reading strategies as they read the **Life and Times** section. For example, students might summarize information in the running text and pay attention to the sequence of events in the time line.

Dante's Youth and Education

A Dante grew up when the Middle Ages were ending and the Renaissance was just beginning. In an age of intense mental activity, Dante spent his youth developing his intellect. He probably attended schools taught by the Franciscans or the Dominicans. Dante also studied under the renowned Florentine teacher, Bruno Latini—a jurist, a politician, and the author of an encyclopedia. Instruction, conducted in Latin, was based on courses in the liberal arts, divided into the Trivium and the Quadrivium. The Trivium included grammar, logic, and rhetoric; the Quadrivium included arithmetic, music, geometry, and astronomy.

AUTHOR STUDY

Dante Alighieri

OVERVIEW

"More can be learned about how to write poetry from Dante than from any English poet."

—T. S. Eliot

Italy's Poetic Genius

Dante Alighieri (dän′tā ä′lē-gyĕ′rē) *is widely regarded as the world's greatest poet of ideas. He was not only a learned man but also a keen observer of everyday life. His poem,* The Divine Comedy, *is a monumental work—vast in scope, rich in meaning, and timeless in appeal. Like a medieval cathedral, it is a marvel of construction and detail. In this poem, Dante turned Christian ideas into great literature. One of Dante's countless admirers, the Irish poet William Butler Yeats, once called him "the chief imagination of Christendom."*

1265–1321

A SCHOLAR AND PUBLIC SERVANT Dante was born in the city of Florence, in the west-central Italian region of Tuscany. His father provided him with a fine education in both classical and Christian literature. One of his teachers was Brunetto Latini, a Florentine scholar who stressed not only scholarship but the importance of participating in community life. By the age of 18, Dante had taught himself how to write verse. The Florentine poet Guido Cavalcanti, with whom Dante became

HIS LIFE

1265 Is born in Florence, Italy

1274 Meets Beatrice for the first time

1245 1250 1255 1260 1265 1270

HIS TIMES

1248 King Louis IX of France (Saint Louis) leads the Seventh Crusade.

1260 Ghibellines defeat Guelphs, killing or exiling many of their leaders.

1273 St. Thomas Aquinas completes his Christian philosophical work *Summa theologiae.*

TIME MANAGEMENT: Teaching Options

If you want to present this lesson as an author study, use all the materials listed under Overview on page 732 in the pupil edition.

If you want to teach only the *Inferno,* use "Preparing to Read" on page 736 and then select one or more of the cantos:

- Canto 1, pp. 737–741
- Canto 3, pp. 742–747
- Canto 5, pp. 748–752
- Canto 34, pp. 753–756

close friends, encouraged Dante's poetic efforts. Yet, true to Latini's teachings, Dante made writing and scholarship secondary to public service. After serving in the army, he pursued a career in politics and diplomacy.

FLORENCE AND ITS POLITICS By the time Dante (B) was born, Florence had evolved into a largely independent city-state. Like many other Italian city-states, it had prospered greatly from trade with the Middle East and Asia and the equipping of soldiers for the Crusades. Moreover, Florence had become the banking center of a growing commercial economy that was replacing feudalism in western Europe.

As a city-state, Florence was basically self-governing and created its own foreign policy. Nevertheless, it suffered from political conflict that had arisen years earlier in the Holy Roman Empire. The conflict was between the Guelphs (gwĕlfs), or those who supported the authority of the pope in Rome, and the Ghibellines (gĭb′ə-lēnz′), or those who supported the authority of the emperor, usually a German-speaking monarch.

LITERARY *Contributions*

Works in Italian By showing the literary power of the Italian language, Dante inspired writers throughout western Europe to write in their native tongues instead of in Latin. Dante's Italian works include

- ***La Vita Nuova*** **[The New Life]**
- ***Il Convivio*** **[The Banquet]**
- ***La Divina Commedia*** **[The Divine Comedy], an epic poem in three parts:**
  - ***Inferno*** **[Hell]**
  - ***Purgatorio*** **[Purgatory]**
  - ***Paradiso*** **[Paradise]**

Works in Latin Like most other educated writers of his day, Dante also wrote in Latin, the language of Church scholarship. His Latin works include

- ***De Vulgari Eloquentia*** **[Concerning Vernacular Eloquence]**
- ***De Monarchia*** **[On Monarchy]**
- ***Eclogae Latinae*** **(poetry)**

Medieval Florence

1277 Is betrothed to Gemma Donati

1289 Fights against the Ghibellines in the Battle of Campaldino

1290 Mourns Beatrice

c. 1293 Writes *La Vita Nuova*

1302 Is exiled from Florence

1275 1280 1285 1290 1295 1300 1305

1274 Edward I of England is crowned at Westminster Abbey.

1279 Kublai Khan conquers China's Sung Dynasty.

1291 Crusades end with Muslims maintaining control of Jerusalem.

1295 Italian traveler Marco Polo returns to Venice from China.

c. 1301 The artist Cimabue creates his *St. John the Evangelist.*

Florence

(B) Few cities can rival Florence, Italy, in importance to western civilization. Florence was the birthplace of the Renaissance, a period of astonishing artistic and intellectual activity. Some of the world's most creative people lived and worked in Florence: writers such as Dante, Boccaccio and Petrarch; painters and sculptors, such as Leonardo da Vinci, Michelangelo, Giotto, and Fra Angelico; the political thinker Machiavelli; and the great astronomer Galileo. In the early 1400s, the Medici family came to power in the city. Under the rule of its most famous member, Lorenzo the Magnificent, Florence reached its pinnacle of glory in the late 15th century.

MINI LESSON Using the Time Line

Have students study the time line on pages 732–734 and then answer questions such as the following:

- Could Aquinas's *Summa Theologiae* have influenced *The Divine Comedy? (Yes, Aquinas completed that work about 35 years before Dante began writing* The Divine Comedy.)
- Approximately how old was Dante when he began writing *The Divine Comedy? (43)*
- Did Dante write *La Vita Nuova* before or after Edward I of England's coronation? *(after)*
- Which event came first—the end of the Crusades or Dante's exile from Florence? *(the end of the Crusades)*

Dante's Banishment

(A) It is difficult for modern readers to appreciate how dreadful a punishment exile was in the Middle Ages. A fate almost as grim as death, exile cut the victim off from family and city, removing all means of support. Dante suffered this punishment as a result of party politics. He was a member of the White Guelphs, the party that opposed the Pope and was led by a powerful family, the Cerchi. The rival party, the Black Guelphs, supported the Pope and was led by another powerful family, the Donati. In May of 1300, the two families and their followers fought in the streets of Florence. When the rioting spread, Pope Boniface VIII excommunicated the White Guelph leaders. Dante was one of three ambassadors selected by the White Guelphs to go to Rome on a diplomatic mission to the Pope. While Dante was away from Florence, the Black Guelphs seized control of the city. On January 27, 1302, Dante was tried *in absentia* and found guilty of defying the Pope. He lost all his property and was banished from Florence. According to a contemporary account, Dante learned of his banishment when he reached Siena on his journey home to Florence. He fled for his life and never saw his native city again.

Dante, who supported the Guelphs, fought the Ghibellines in the Battle of Campaldino in 1289.

POLITICAL LIFE AND EXILE In 1295, Dante joined Florence's medical guild, which was open to all scholars, and used his membership as a springboard to public office. He rose from city councilman to prior, a high-ranking position, and also served as an occasional ambassador to other Italian city-states. Unfortunately, Florence was again in turmoil. The Guelphs had split into two factions—the Whites and the Blacks. Dante, a White Guelph, sided against the Pope, instead of with him. In 1301, while
(A) Dante was away on a diplomatic mission, the Black Guelphs gained control of Florence. They banished Dante from the city. He spent the rest of his life in exile, mostly at the courts of those sympathetic to the White Guelphs.

DANTE'S INSPIRATION Most of Dante's early verse is courtly love poetry, in which the speaker expresses love for an ideal lady out of his reach. Though Dante married Gemma Donati, a woman to whom he had been betrothed when he was a boy, the object of his poetic devotions was a woman named Beatrice—probably Beatrice Portinari, daughter of a Florentine nobleman. According to *La vita nuova*—a collection of his early love poems to Beatrice and his accounts of how he came to write them—Dante met Beatrice only twice: once when he was nine and again nine years later. Yet in her he saw all that was virtuous, and her untimely death at age 24 broke his heart.

THE DIVINE COMEDY Dante wrote his (B) masterpiece, the epic poem *The Divine Comedy,* during his exile. He began the poem around 1308 and finished it shortly before his death in 1321. It consists of three sections: *Inferno, Purgatorio,* and *Paradiso.* Each section is divided into parts called *cantos* (the Italian word *canto* comes from a Latin word meaning "song"). The cantos, 100 in all, are written in three-line stanzas in a verse form known as *terza rima,* which Dante himself created. To Dante, the number three had deep spiritual meaning. It suggested the divine mystery of the three persons in one God, which is central to Christian belief.

c. 1308
Begins *The Divine Comedy*

1319
Moves to the court of Guido Novello da Polenta in Ravenna

1321
Completes *The Divine Comedy;* dies in Ravenna

1310 1315 1320 1325

1312
Henry VII is crowned Holy Roman Emperor but dies a year later.

c. 1320
The artist Giotto paints frescoes in Florence's Santa Croce chapels.

1325
The Aztecs found their capital, Tenochtitlán, on the site of present-day Mexico City.

734 UNIT FIVE PART 1

Dante and His Poem (1465), Domenico di Michelino. Duomo, Florence, Italy.

The Divine Comedy: Dante's Dream Vision

This painting by a 15th-century Italian artist was inspired by Dante's masterpiece, *The Divine Comedy.* In the center of the painting, Dante holds a book of his poetry. To his left is the city of Florence, with its domed cathedral. The other scenes show the places Dante visits in the three sections of *The Divine Comedy:* On his right, sinners descend into the terrible pit that is Hell. In the back, sinners try to climb the mountain of Purgatory, which leads to Paradise.

In *The Divine Comedy,* Dante himself is the main character, a traveler who stands for all of humanity. He first journeys down into the Inferno, or Hell, a hideous realm where sinners receive fitting eternal punishments. He then travels to Purgatory, a place of temporary punishment, and finally to Paradise, where he stands before the throne of God. On his journey, Dante encounters characters from mythology, from history, and from his own time—including some of his friends and enemies. The poem, therefore, is not only an imaginative vision of the afterlife but also a rich portrait of medieval times.

When Dante wrote his poem, he gave it the title *Commedia* [Comedy] because it ends happily. In time, it became known as *The Divine Comedy* because of its deeply spiritual content. To many readers, the poem suggests the soul's odyssey from the darkness of sin to a glimpse of eternal glory, beauty, and truth.

One of the greatest works in all of literature, Dante's poem was very popular in his own lifetime. According to one commentator, children ran after Dante in the streets to touch the garment of the man who had visited Hell. Down through the centuries, the poem has inspired a host of writers, artists, and musicians. C

The Divine Comedy

B Dante's poem is widely regarded as a masterpiece of medieval literature. It is a dream vision that describes Dante's supernatural journey through Hell, Purgatory, and Heaven. His guides on this journey are first Virgil, who represents human reason, and then Beatrice, who represents faith or divine knowledge. The poem is distinguished by its vast learning, its analysis of social problems in medieval Italy, its imaginative power, its spiritual depth, and its magnificent language. Dante wrote this poem in Italian, rather than Latin. Together with Boccaccio and Petrarch, Dante helped to establish Italian as a literary language.

Literary Influence

C Dante influenced countless writers. *The Divine Comedy* and *On Eloquence in the Vernacular* influenced Geoffrey Chaucer when he wrote *The Canterbury Tales* (1386–1400). John Milton's *Paradise Lost* (1667) owed much to Dante. Nineteenth-and twentieth-century writers as diverse as Henry Wadsworth Longfellow, Ralph Waldo Emerson, Percy Bysshe Shelley, Lord Byron, Alfred Tennyson, Victor Hugo, Friedrich von Schlegel, Ezra Pound, T. S. Eliot, and Seamus Heaney acknowledged their debt to Dante.

This selection is included in the **World Literature InterActive Reader™**.

Objectives
- understand and appreciate four cantos from a **medieval allegorical poem (Literary Analysis)**
- identify the characteristics of a medieval **allegory (Literary Analysis)**
- use the reading strategy of **clarifying meaning (Active Reading)**

Summary
In Canto 1, Dante in midlife finds himself trapped in a dark forest. He is threatened by a leopard, a lion, and a she-wolf—all representing the forces of evil. Then he meets the ghost of Virgil, who offers to guide him through a place of eternal punishment. In Canto 3, Dante and Virgil enter the Vestibule of Hell, where reside the souls of those who did neither good nor evil in the world. They next see Charon, gathering a crowd of souls to ferry across the river Acheron. In Canto 5, Dante and Virgil come upon Minos, who assigns each soul to a level in Hell according to his or her earthly sins. As they continue their descent, Dante and Virgil see spirits blown about in mighty winds. Among them are the lovers, Paolo and Francesca. She relates to Dante how she and Paolo first fell in love. In Canto 34, Dante and Virgil reach the lowest level of hell, reserved for betrayers, who are covered in ice. Dis, the ruler of this realm, is a three-faced giant who holds a sinner in each of his mouths.

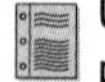
Use **Unit Five Resource Book,** p. 12, for additional support.

Thematic Link
This medieval allegory tells of a spiritual **quest** through an eternal place where the wicked are punished for their evil deeds on earth.

Use **Unit Five Resource Book,** p. 15, for practice with Words to Know.

Editor's Note This selecton was excerpted from the acclaimed translation of Dante's *Inferno* by poet Robert Pinsky.

5-Minute Warm-Up

Daily Language SkillBuilder

Have students **proofread** the display sentences on page 685j and write them correctly.

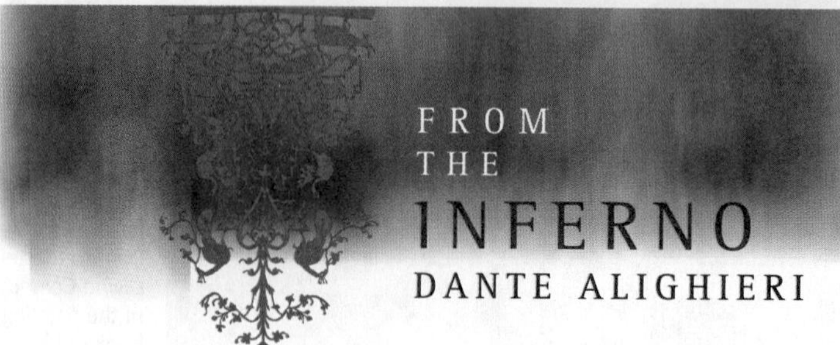

FROM THE INFERNO
DANTE ALIGHIERI

Build Background

The *Inferno* is the first of the three sections of *The Divine Comedy.* Here, Dante describes the first stage of his journey through the afterlife. He and his guide, the Roman poet Virgil, travel through the different circles, or levels, of Hell.

Dante envisions Hell as a pit within the earth where sinners are punished in the afterlife for their evil deeds. This pit is shaped like a cone that funnels downward. It has nine levels: the lower the level, the worse the sinner—and the more terrible the punishment.

Connect to Your Life

With a classmate, list several acts that you consider wrong—for example, forgery, theft, and murder. Debate the seriousness of the actions and rank them from least to most serious. What did you rank as the greatest wrong?

Focus Your Reading

LITERARY ANALYSIS: ALLEGORY
The Divine Comedy can be read as an **allegory,** a work with two layers of meaning. In an allegory, most of the characters, places, objects, and events stand for abstract ideas or qualities. For example, in the *Inferno*, a physical place—such as the "dark woods"—stands for Dante's spiritual condition.

ACTIVE READING: CLARIFYING MEANING
To explore meaning in this allegory, use these tips:
- Refer to the Guide for Reading, the Preview paragraphs, and the sidenotes for help in understanding difficult words and passages.
- Reread difficult passages slowly and carefully. Try to **paraphrase** them—that is, restate them in your own words.
- Ask yourself what the characters, places, objects, and events might represent.

READER'S NOTEBOOK As you read, take notes about the characters and events. Write down the Pause & Reflect questions you encounter and provide an answer for each.

WORDS TO KNOW **Vocabulary Preview**

abject	discourse	hapless
avail	disdain	imbued
compulsion	fortitude	protrude
discern		

LESSON RESOURCES

UNIT FIVE RESOURCE BOOK,
pp. 12–16

ASSESSMENT RESOURCES
Formal Assessment, pp. 113–114
Teacher's Guide to Assessment and Portfolio Use
Test Generator

INTEGRATED TECHNOLOGY
NetActivities
Visit our Web site: classzone.com

ADDITIONAL RESOURCES
Lesson Planning Guide, pp. 93–94
Teacher's Sourcebook for Language Development

from the Inferno

Dante Alighieri

Translated by Robert Pinsky

GUIDE FOR READING

FOCUS Dante finds himself trapped in a dark forest. As you read, try to decide what the path, the woods, and the three beasts might represent.

Preview *Halfway through life, Dante wanders off the right path and into dark, frightening woods. As he tries to climb a hill, he finds his way blocked by three beasts—a leopard, a lion, and a she-wolf. He later meets the spirit of the poet Virgil, who tells him he must take another path. Virgil offers to guide Dante on a journey through Hell and Purgatory.*

CANTO 1

Midway on our life's journey, I found myself
In dark woods, the right road lost. To tell
About those woods is hard—so tangled and rough

And savage that thinking of it now, I feel
The old fear stirring: death is hardly more bitter.
And yet, to treat the good I found there as well

I'll tell what I saw, though how I came to enter
I cannot well say, being so full of sleep
Whatever moment it was I began to blunder

Off the true path. But when I came to stop
Below a hill that marked one end of the valley
That had pierced my heart with terror, I looked up

Customizing Instruction

Less Proficient Readers

- Give students a few minutes to skim, or glance through, the selection for clues about the content. Tell students to look over the Previews, the images, and the captions in the text.
- Explain that this poem describes a spiritual journey. Dante, who goes on this journey, represents all humans. The journey begins in a dark forest and then proceeds into Hell, a place of eternal punishment.
- Tell students to read for complete sentences, moving from line to line and stanza to stanza, stopping only when they come upon a period.
- Point out that students should use the sidenotes for help with difficult words and passages and should read several passages aloud to clarify meaning.
- Explain that it is important for students to read the italicized Previews carefully. They summarize the canto to come and will help students keep their reading on track.
- This selection is especially challenging because of the "poetic" diction, the inverted word order, and the long sentences. Work with students to help them paraphrase difficult sentences.

Guide for Reading

Tell students that this poem is broken into sections to help them understand it better and enjoy it more. At the beginning of each section, the **Focus** sets a purpose for reading. At the end of each section, the **Pause & Reflect** provides a question to check student understanding.

TIME MANAGEMENT

If your schedule requires that you cover the lesson objectives in a shorter time, use . . .

- Preparing to Read, p. 736
- Thinking Through the Literature, pp. 741, 747, 752, and 759
- Vocabulary in Action, p. 761

If you want to take advantage of longer blocks of class time, use . . .

- TE Teaching Options: Viewing and Representing, pp. 738, 746, 754; Speaking and Listening, p. 753; Vocabulary Strategy, pp. 739, 744; Cross-Curricular Link, pp. 740, 742, 745, 751, 756; Grammar, p. 755
- Choices & Challenges, p. 761

INFERNO 737

Literary Analysis ALLEGORY

A Point out that the *Inferno* is an allegory, or a literary work filled with symbols. Then ask students to think about the phrase "that grim defile/ That never left any alive who stayed in it." Ask students what "that grim defile"—a physical place—suggests about Dante's spiritual condition.

Possible Response: Dante's spiritual condition is alarming. A prisoner of sin, he is in danger of losing his soul.

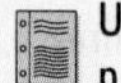
Use **Unit Five Resource Book,** p. 14, for more practice.

Active Reading CLARIFYING MEANING

B Remind students to try paraphrasing difficult passages to help clarify their meaning. Then ask students to restate lines 40–45 in their own words.

Possible Response: The she-wolf made me depressed so that I gave up hope of trying to reach the top of the mountain. I felt defeated when that animal came running toward me, forcing me to go back down to the dark woods.

Use **Unit Five Resource Book,** p. 13, for more practice.

Pause & Reflect

Possible Response: The she-wolf terrifies Dante, filling him with such despair that he cannot ascend the mountain.

The Granger Collection, New York.

HUMANITIES CONNECTION This illumination, from a 15th-century Italian manuscript, shows Virgil rescuing Dante from the three beasts. Leaving the dark woods, the two poets embark on their journey.

Toward the crest and saw its shoulders already
 Mantled in rays of that bright planet that shows
 The road to everyone, whatever our journey.

Then I could feel the terror begin to ease
 That churned in my heart's lake all through the night.
 As one still panting, ashore from dangerous seas,

Looks back at the deep he has escaped, my thought
A Returned, still fleeing, to regard that grim defile
 That never left any alive who stayed in it.

After I had rested my weary body awhile
 I started again across the wilderness,
 My left foot always lower on the hill,

And suddenly—a leopard, near the place
 The way grew steep: lithe, spotted, quick of foot.
 Blocking the path, she stayed before my face

13 crest: the top of the hill.

14 that bright planet: the sun, which in Dante's time was believed to be a planet that moved around the earth.

17 my heart's lake: This detail reflects the medieval belief that the heart was a reservoir for blood.

20 defile: a steep, narrow valley.

25–38 a leopard . . . a lion . . . a grim she-wolf: These three animals are generally believed to stand for lust, pride, and greed, the three general categories of sin treated in the poem.

MINI LESSON **Viewing and Representing**

Illuminated Italian manuscript

ART APPRECIATION Have students read the **Humanities Connection** caption on page 738 and study the reproduction of the illumination. Help students identify details in this illumination. The three beasts block the path leading up the mountain. The sun's rays illumine the sky behind the trees of the dark forest. Virgil is dressed in blue and Dante in crimson. Ask students what they might infer about the relationship between these two figures.

Possible Response: Virgil is the teacher, the guide, and the advisor. He raises his hands to warn his pupil to go no farther along the path blocked by the three beasts. Virgil protects Dante, preventing him from making a fatal mistake.

And more than once she made me turn about
To go back down. It was early morning still,
The fair sun rising with the stars attending it

As when Divine Love set those beautiful
Lights into motion at creation's dawn,
And the time of day and season combined to fill

My heart with hope of that beast with festive skin—
But not so much that the next sight wasn't fearful:
A lion came at me, his head high as he ran,

Roaring with hunger so the air appeared to tremble.
Then, a grim she-wolf—whose leanness seemed to compress
All the world's cravings, that had made miserable

Such multitudes; she put such heaviness
Into my spirit, I lost hope of the crest.
B Like someone eager to win, who tested by loss

Surrenders to gloom and weeps, so did that beast
Make me feel, as harrying toward me at a lope
She forced me back toward where the sun is lost.

34 that beast with festive skin: the leopard, whose coat is gaily colored.

38–39 whose leanness . . . cravings: whose thinness seemed to squeeze together all the desires of the world.

44 harrying: moving threateningly.

PAUSE & REFLECT How does Dante react to the she-wolf?

FOCUS Driven back into the dark woods, Dante meets the spirit of Virgil. Read to find out why Virgil is a good guide for the lost poet.

While I was ruining myself back down to the deep,
Someone appeared—one who seemed nearly to fade
As though from long silence. I cried to his human shape

In that great wasteland: "Living man or shade,
Have pity and help me, whichever you may be!"
1 "No living man, though once I was," he replied.

"My parents both were Mantuans from Lombardy,
And I was born *sub Julio,* the latter end.
I lived in good Augustus's Rome, in the day

46 ruining: falling into ruin or disaster.

49 shade: a spirit of a dead person.

52 Mantuans from Lombardy: Lombardy, a region in northern Italy, is where the city of Mantua is located.

53 *sub Julio*: during the reign of Julius Caesar.

54 Augustus's Rome: Rome under its first emperor, Augustus, grandnephew of Julius Caesar.

Customizing Instruction

Less Proficient Readers

Make sure that students can summarize what happens in the first 21 lines of the poem. Dante says that when he had reached middle age, he realized that he had lost his way in life and was trapped in a dark forest that filled him with dread. Trying to find a way out of the forest, he stops beneath a hill whose top reflects the sunlight.

Focus If necessary, guide students to look ahead to lines 70–72 and 88–90. In these lines, Virgil offers to help Dante escape from the dark forest.

Use the following questions to check students' comprehension of lines 22–45:

- What does Dante try to do to escape from the dark forest? *(climbs a hill)*
- What three animals block his path? *(a leopard, a lion, and a she-wolf)*
- Which of the three animals forces Dante to go back down to the dark woods? *(the she-wolf)*

1 Point out that these lines are spoken by the spirit of Virgil, who gives clues about his identity. He tells Dante that he lived in Rome during Augustus Caesar's reign and that he wrote the *Aeneid*.

English Learners

Explain the meaning of the following words that might be difficult for students to understand:

- *mantled* (line 14) means "dressed"
- *grim* (line 20) means "frightening"
- *lithe* (line 26) means "bending easily"
- *multitudes* (line 40) means "great numbers"
- *heaviness* (line 40) means "sadness"
- *the deep* (line 46) refers to the dark woods

MINI LESSON Vocabulary Strategy

CONTEXT CLUES Call students' attention to the list of Words to Know on p. 736.

Demonstrate the strategy of using context clues using the following model:

The <u>hapless</u> cyclist was taken directly to the hospital after his terrible fall.

Instruction

- Write the model sentence on the chalkboard.
- Ask a volunteer to paraphrase the meaning of the sentence.
- Have students use the meaning of the sentence to suggest meanings for the word *hapless*.
- Ask a volunteer to use the word *hapless* in a sentence.

Practice Write the following sentences on the chalkboard. Ask students to use context clues to determine the meanings of the underlined words.

1. Cliff divers, mountain climbers, and ski jumpers all demonstrate great <u>fortitude</u>. *(fortitude means courage)*
2. The art collector was able to <u>discern</u> easily between the masterpiece and an imitation. *(discern means to perceive through the eyes or intellect)*
3. Tracy felt a <u>compulsion</u> to dance when she heard the salsa band playing. *(a compulsion is an irresistible impulse)*

A lesson on using context clues appears on p. 674 of the Pupil's Edition.

Reading and Analyzing

Literary Analysis ALLEGORY

A Tell students to review the sidenote for lines 25–38 (on page 738), which explains what the she-wolf might represent. Then ask students to identify details in this passage that suggest that the she-wolf represents greed.
Possible Response: "she cannot appease her voracity" and "feeding makes her hungrier"

Active Reading CLARIFYING MEANING

B Remind students that the speaker of this passage is Virgil, who lived for a time in a great city, Rome, and knew the emperor, Augustus Caesar. Then tell students that in this passage Virgil uses the terms "Emperor" and "city" in a figurative sense. Ask students to identify "the Emperor" and "His city."
Possible Response: The Emperor is God; his city is heaven.

1 Of the false gods who lied. A poet, I hymned
Anchises' noble son, who came from Troy
When superb Ilium in its pride was burned.

But you—why go back down to such misery?
Why not ascend the delightful mountain, source
And principle that causes every joy?"

"Then are you Virgil? Are you the font that pours
So overwhelming a river of human speech?"
I answered, shamefaced. "The glory and light are yours,

That poets follow—may the love that made me search
Your book in patient study avail me, Master!
2 You are my guide and author, whose verses teach

The graceful style whose model has done me honor.
See this beast driving me backward—help me resist,
For she makes all my veins and pulses shudder."

"A different path from this one would be best
For you to find your way from this feral place,"
He answered, seeing how I wept. "This beast,

The cause of your complaint, lets no one pass
A Her way—but harries all to death. Her nature
Is so malign and vicious she cannot appease

Her voracity, for feeding makes her hungrier.
Many are the beasts she mates: there will be more,
Until the Hound comes who will give this creature

A painful death. Not nourished by earthly fare,
He will be fed by wisdom, goodness and love.
Born between Feltro and Feltro, he shall restore

Low Italy, as Nisus fought to achieve.
And Turnus, Euryalus, Camilla the maiden—
All dead from wounds in war. He will remove

56 Anchises' (ăn-kī'sēz') noble son: Aeneas (ĭ-nē'əs), who fled from Troy (Ilium) when it was burned and eventually founded Rome. His story is told in Virgil's *Aeneid* (see pages 356–381).

71 feral: wild; savage.

75–76 appease her voracity: satisfy her hunger.

78–81 the Hound . . . Feltro and Feltro: The Hound may be Cangrande della Scala, who supported Dante in exile and who was born in Verona, between the cities of Feltre and Montefeltro.

82–83 Nisus . . . Turnus, Euryalus (yo͝o-rī'ə-ləs), Camilla the maiden: These are characters in Virgil's *Aeneid* who die in the war between the Trojans and the Latins.

WORDS TO KNOW
avail (ə-vāl') *v.* to be of use to; help

Cross Curricular Link **Humanities**

VIRGIL The Roman poet Virgil (70–19 B.C.) profoundly influenced Dante. Virgil's epic poem the *Aeneid*, which describes a journey through the underworld, served as a model for *The Divine Comedy*. To Dante, Virgil was the supreme pagan poet—a philospher, an artist, and a link to Homer. In *The Divine Comedy,* Virgil appears as a central character. Though a pagan in Limbo, he undertakes a divine mission: namely, to rescue Dante from the dark forest and lead him through Hell and Purgatory to Beatrice, who will then escort him to Heaven. Virgil serves as Dante's guide and mentor, making key decisions and protecting him as they descend through Hell. (See pages 356–359 of the pupil edition for more information about Virgil and the *Aeneid*.)

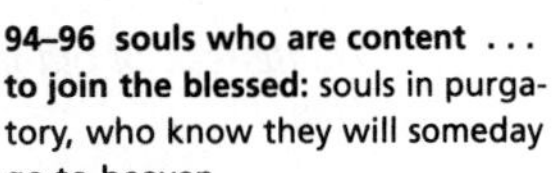

This lean wolf, hunting her through every region
Till he has thrust her back to Hell's abyss
Where Envy first dispatched her on her mission.

Therefore I judge it best that you should choose
To follow me, and I will be your guide
Away from here and through an eternal place:

To hear the cries of despair, and to behold
Ancient tormented spirits as they lament
3 In chorus the second death they must abide.

Then you shall see those souls who are content
To dwell in fire because they hope some day
To join the blessed: toward whom, if your ascent

Continues, your guide will be one worthier than I—
When I must leave you, you will be with her.
For the Emperor who governs from on high

B Wills I not enter His city, where none may appear
Who lived like me in rebellion to His law.
His empire is everything and everywhere,

But that is His kingdom, His city, His seat of awe.
Happy is the soul He chooses for that place!"
I: "Poet, please—by the God you did not know—

Help me escape this evil that I face,
And worse. Lead me to witness what you have said,
4 Saint Peter's gate, and the multitude of woes—"

Then he set out, and I followed where he led.

94–96 souls who are content . . . to join the blessed: souls in purgatory, who know they will someday go to heaven.

97 one worthier than I: Beatrice.

100–101 where none may appear . . . His law: Virgil, a pagan Roman, did not worship God and thus cannot enter Heaven.

Thinking Through the Literature

1. How does Dante feel about himself at the beginning of the story?
2. What is Dante's attitude toward Virgil?
3. What do you **predict** might happen to Dante on his journey through Hell?

Customizing Instruction

Less Proficient Readers

1 Tell students that "the false gods who lied" refers to the pagan gods worshipped by the Romans. Virgil lived before Jesus Christ, whom Dante regards as the true god, was born.

2 Explain lines 65–67. Dante has studied Virgil's works, especially the *Aeneid*, and has modeled his own poetic style upon Virgil's.

3 Point out that the phrase "the second death" refers to the suffering of the wicked in Hell.

4 Tell students that "Saint Peter's gate" was in Purgatory, where the souls who will someday enter Heaven are "purged," or cleansed of their sins. Dante is asking Virgil to accompany him as far as he can.

English Learners

Explain the meaning of the following words that might be difficult for students to understand:

- *font* (line 61) means "fountain"
- *shudder* (line 69) means "to shake or tremble"
- *feral* (line 71) means "wild or savage"
- *malign* (line 75) means "evil"
- *fare* (line 79) means "food"
- *dispatched* (line 87) means "sent"

Advanced Learners

As students read, tell them to look for details that will help them draw conclusions about Dante's relationship with Virgil. For example, in Canto 1, Dante calls Virgil "master" and extols his verse as "a river of human speech." These details suggest that Dante reveres Virgil as a teacher.

Thinking Through the Literature

1. Possible Responses: Dante feels lost, confused, and depressed at the beginning of the story. He can find no way out of the confusion caused by sin.
2. Possible Responses: Dante admires Virgil, whose poems have inspired his own writing. Dante regards himself as a student and Virgil as a renowned teacher and spiritual guide.
3. Possible Responses: Dante will meet spirits in terrible torment. They may be the spirits of people he once knew, who might motivate him to amend his life.

Active Reading CLARIFYING MEANING

A Ask students to paraphrase this inscription above the doorway to Hell.
Possible Response: Give up all hope [of ever being happy again], you who pass through this doorway.

Literary Analysis IMAGERY

B Remind students that imagery refers to words and phrases that create vivid sensory experiences for the reader. Point out that this passage is rich in images that appeal to the senses of hearing, sight, or touch. Then have students identify these images.
Possible Response: hearing: "sighs, groans, and laments . . . Resounding," "strange languages," "horrible screams," "cries as of troubled sleep," "tortured shrillness," "a coil of tumult," and "noises like the slap of beating hands"; sight: "starless air," "a ceaseless flail," "dark and timeless air," "sand in a whirlwind"; touch: "the slap of beating hands" and "sand in a whirlwind"

GUIDE FOR READING

FOCUS The two poets arrive at the gate of Hell and read the inscription above it. They then enter the vestibule and notice the souls confined there. Read to find out about these souls.

Preview *In Canto 2, Virgil explains that Beatrice, the woman Dante had idealized and loved from afar when she was alive, descended from Heaven in order to ask him to guide Dante on his journey. In Canto 3, Virgil takes Dante through the gate of Hell into a dark, starless vestibule. They notice the souls of the unsure, those who chose neither good nor evil in life. When the two poets arrive at the shore of the river Acheron, Dante sees an old man gathering sinners to ferry across the river into Hell.*

CANTO 3

THROUGH ME YOU ENTER INTO THE CITY OF WOES,
THROUGH ME YOU ENTER INTO ETERNAL PAIN,
THROUGH ME YOU ENTER THE POPULATION OF LOSS.

JUSTICE MOVED MY HIGH MAKER, IN POWER DIVINE,
WISDOM SUPREME, LOVE PRIMAL. NO THINGS WERE
BEFORE ME NOT ETERNAL; ETERNAL I REMAIN.

A ABANDON ALL HOPE, YOU WHO ENTER HERE.
These words I saw inscribed in some dark color
Over a portal. "Master," I said, "make clear

Their meaning, which I find too hard to gather."
Then he, as one who understands: "All fear
Must be left here, and cowardice die. Together,

1 We have arrived where I have told you: here
You will behold the wretched souls who've lost
The good of intellect." Then, with good cheer

In his expression to encourage me, he placed
His hand on mine: so, trusting to my guide,
I followed him among things undisclosed.

5 primal: original; most important.

9 portal: doorway.

14–15 souls . . . intellect: those who have lost sight of God.

Cross Curricular Link **Humanities**

HIERARCHY OF EVIL In the *Inferno*, Virgil and Dante visit Hell, a place of eternal punishment. As they descend from one level to the next, they come upon even worse sinners who endure even greater punishments. To medieval Christian theology, all sins were considered evil, but some sins more so than others. Sins against the spirit, such as betrayal, were regarded as worse than sins against the flesh, such as illicit love. Moreover, certain sins were designated as "deadly" because they were not only evil in themselves but led to other sins. Among the seven deadly sins were pride, covetousness, lust, envy, gluttony, wrath, and sloth. Saint Thomas Aquinas (1225–1274) discussed the types of sin in *Summa Theologiae*, a work that deeply influenced Dante.

Inscription over the Gate (1824–1827), William Blake. Illustration to Hell, Canto 3, of Dante's *The Divine Comedy*. Watercolor, 52.7 x 37.4 cm. Tate Gallery, London/Art Resource, New York.

The sighs, groans and laments at first were so loud,
Resounding through starless air, I began to weep:
Strange languages, horrible screams, words <u>imbued</u>

B With rage or despair, cries as of troubled sleep
Or of a tortured shrillness—they rose in a coil
Of tumult, along with noises like the slap

Of beating hands, all fused in a ceaseless flail
That churns and frenzies that dark and timeless air
Like sand in a whirlwind. And I, my head in a swirl

Of error, cried: "Master, what is this I hear?
What people are these, whom pain has overcome?"
2 He: "This is the sorrowful state of souls unsure,

Whose lives earned neither honor nor bad fame.
And they are mingled with angels of that base sort
Who, neither rebellious to God nor faithful to Him,

30–37 souls unsure, . . . glory over them: those souls who in life acted neither for good nor evil but only for themselves. They are unfit for Heaven and not allowed in Hell proper.

WORDS TO KNOW
imbued (ĭm-byōōd') *adj.* filled or inspired **imbue** *v.*

Customizing Instruction

Less Proficient Readers

Focus Make sure that students understand that this canto is set in the vestibule, or entrance hall, to Hell. As Virgil and Dante continue on their way, they notice a river that sinners cross to reach Hell itself.

Again, make sure that students read the italicized Preview, which summarizes what happens in this canto.

Tell students that the word *he* followed by the colon is a different way of writing "he said."

1 This is a key passage in this canto. It indicates that the wicked in Hell are doomed never to enjoy the sight of God and, thus, never to know happiness. As students continue reading, tell them to look for details that describe the suffering of these souls.

2 Help students understand that Dante hears the cries of "the souls unsure." In life, these souls refused to take a stand, either for good or for evil. Thus, in the afterlife, they go neither to Heaven nor to Hell but suffer on its outskirts.

English Learners

Explain the meaning of the following words that might be difficult for students to understand:

- *abandon* (line 7) means "to give up"
- *gather* (line 10) means "to understand"
- *undisclosed* (line 18) means "not told or revealed"
- *laments* (line 19) means "weeping and crying"
- *tumult* (line 24) means "loud noise"
- *fame* (line 31) means "reputation"
- *base* (line 32) means "low in value"

Reading and Analyzing

Literary Analysis IRONY

A You might point out that the punishments described by Dante fit the crimes committed by the sinners. Those who in life never took a stand either for good or for evil—the "hapless ones never alive"—never cease moving in the vestibule of Hell. Never aroused by anything in life, they are endlessly stung by wasps and flies.

Reading Skills and Strategies VISUALIZING

B Ask students to identify details that help them form mental pictures of Charon.

Possible Responses: details such as "an old man in a boat," "white-haired," "grizzled jaws," "gray ferryman," and "red wheels of flame about his eyes"

Pause & Reflect

Possible Response: They must forever run behind a whirling banner and be bitten by insects, with insect larvae under their feet.

Chose neither side, but kept themselves apart—
Now Heaven expels them, not to mar its splendor,
And Hell rejects them, lest the wicked of heart

Take glory over them." And then I: "Master,
What agony is it, that makes them keen their grief
With so much force?" He: "I will make brief answer:

They have no hope of death, but a blind life
So abject, they envy any other fate.
To all memory of them, the world is deaf.

Mercy and justice disdain them. Let us not
Speak of them: look and pass on." I looked again:
A whirling banner sped at such a rate

It seemed it might never stop; behind it a train
Of souls, so long that I would not have thought
Death had undone so many. When more than one

I recognized had passed, I beheld the shade
Of him who made the Great Refusal, impelled
By cowardice: so at once I understood

A

Beyond all doubt that this was the dreary guild
Repellent both to God and His enemies—
Hapless ones never alive, their bare skin galled

By wasps and flies, blood trickling down the face,
Mingling with tears for harvest underfoot
By writhing maggots. Then, when I turned my eyes

Farther along our course, I could make out
People upon the shore of some great river.
"Master," I said, "it seems by this dim light

That all of these are eager to cross over—
Can you tell me by what law, and who they are?"
He answered, "Those are things you will discover

38 keen: to wail with sadness.

49–51 the shade of him . . . by cowardice: probably a reference to Pope Celestine V, who gave up his title after only five months due to political pressures on him.

52–53 the dreary guild repellent . . . enemies: the unhappy group offensive to both God and demons.

54 galled: broken; made sore.

57 maggots: the larva of flies, often found in decaying matter.

WORDS TO KNOW

abject (ăb'jĕkt') *adj.* very low or miserable in condition
disdain (dĭs-dān') *v.* to look down on or treat with contempt
hapless (hăp'lĭs) *adj.* unfortunate

MINI LESSON **Vocabulary Strategy**

USING SYNONYMS Call students' attention to the list of Words to Know on p. 736. Remind them that supplying familiar synonyms in connection with new words often helps people learn new words.

Practice Write the following words on the chalkboard and have the students copy them in a single column on their papers: (v.) *help, filled, miserable, scorn, unlucky, determine, urge, conversation, courage,* (v.) *project.*

As students proceed through the selection, have them enter the appropriate Word to Know next to the correct synonym. Have students interpret the connotative difference.

Monitor students' work periodically, perhaps by calling upon students to share their entries with the class. Encourage more capable students to supply additional synonyms for words such as *abject, hapless,* and *fortitude. (help–avail, filled–imbued, miserable–abject, scorn–disdain, unlucky–hapless, determine–discern, urge–compulsion, courage–fortitude, project–protrude)*

When we have paused at Acheron's dismal shore."
I walked on with my head down after that,
Fearful I had displeased him, and spoke no more.

PAUSE & REFLECT How are the souls of the unsure punished in the afterlife?

64 Acheron's (ăk'ə-rŏnz') **dismal shore:** Acheron is the first river Dante comes upon in Hell. This river will flow downward to form the frozen lake at the lowest level of Hell.

FOCUS Dante notices an old man in a boat. Read to find out who he is and what he does.

Then, at the river—an old man in a boat:
White-haired, as he drew closer shouting at us,
"Woe to you, wicked souls! Give up the thought

1 Of Heaven! I come to ferry you across
Into eternal dark on the opposite side,
Into fire and ice! And you there—leave this place,

You living soul, stand clear of these who are dead!"
B And then, when he saw that I did not obey:
"By other ports, in a lighter boat," he said,

"You will be brought to shore by another way."
My master spoke then, "Charon, do not rage:
Thus is it willed where everything may be

Simply if it is willed. Therefore, oblige,
And ask no more." That silenced the grizzled jaws
Of the gray ferryman of the livid marsh,

Who had red wheels of flame about his eyes.
But at his words the forlorn and naked souls
Were changing color, cursing the human race,

God and their parents. Teeth chattering in their skulls,
They called curses on the seed, the place, the hour
2 Of their own begetting and their birth. With wails

And tears they gathered on the evil shore
That waits for all who don't fear God. There demon
3 Charon beckons them, with his eyes of fire;

67–68 an old man . . . white-haired: Charon (kâr'ən), who, in classical mythology, ferries souls of the dead across the river of death.

83–85 the forlorn and naked souls . . . their parents: The souls of the damned are without divine grace and are not permitted to repent; they can only curse.

Customizing Instruction

Less Proficient Readers

Focus If necessary, direct students to the details about Charon in lines 89–92. From these details, students should conclude that Charon is a demon who gathers the sinners waiting on the riverbank and transports them to Hell.

1 Make sure that students understand this passage. In lines 69–72, Charon mocks the sinners waiting near the river and gloats over their future punishment. With the words "And you there," he speaks only to Dante, ordering him to stand apart from the dead souls, whom he wishes to ferry across the river.

2 Point out to students that the wicked who did not fear God when they were alive are now paralyzed with fear as they anticipate their punishment in Hell.

3 Explain that the antecedent of the pronoun *them* is "all who don't fear God."

English Learners

Point out to students that the word *lest* in line 36 is a conjunction that means "for fear that" and that lines 36 and 37 may be paraphrased as follows: "And Hell refuses to admit the souls unsure for fear that the sinners in Hell might feel a sense of pride in comparing themselves to these souls." Then explain the meaning of the following words:

- *disdain* (line 43) means "to reject"
- *train* (line 46) means "group"
- *maggots* (line 57) means "insects in an early stage when they look like worms"
- *woe* (line 69) means "great sorrow"
- *oblige* (line 79) means "to do a favor for"
- *livid* (line 81) means "pale or red"
- *forlorn* (line 83) means "sad or unhappy"
- *begetting* (line 87) means "coming into being"

Cross Curricular Link: Mythology

THE RIVERS OF THE UNDERWORLD Charon ferries the souls of the wicked across the river Acheron into the interior of Hell. Acheron is one of the four rivers of the underworld described in the *Inferno*. The others are the Styx, a muddy river; Phlegethon, a river of blood; and Cocytus, a river of ice at the very bottom of Hell. In Canto 14 of the *Inferno*, Virgil explains to Dante the source of these rivers. On the island of Crete is a statue of an old man, made of metals such as gold, silver, iron, and brass. Tears drop from this statue into a cavern, forcing their way to the underworld where they form the Acheron, the Styx, and the Phlegethon. These rivers, in turn, flow down to form the Cocytus. All of these rivers as well as the ferryman Charon appear in the *Aeneid*.

Literary Analysis SIMILE

A Remind students that a simile is a comparison between two things that uses the word *like* or *as*. Ask students to explain the two comparisons in this passage.

Possible Response: The souls swept away ("Adam's evil seed") are compared to leaves—dead and rotten—falling from a tree. These souls respond to Charon's call as readily as trained falcons obey the call of a hunter.

Active Reading CLARIFYING MEANING

B Have students read this passage slowly and carefully. Remind them that Virgil is speaking to Dante. Then ask them what Virgil implies about Dante's soul.

Possible Response: Virgil implies that Dante's soul does not belong among the wicked in Hell. That is why Charon objects to Dante's presence at the riverbank.

Wood engraving after Gustave Doré. The Granger Collection, New York.

HUMANITIES CONNECTION This woodcut depicts Virgil and Dante observing the eternal punishment of greedy sinners who bought or sold religious offices. The sinners are set, heads down, in a perforated rock. Their protruding feet are scorched by flames.

MINI LESSON Viewing and Representing

Woodcut of Virgil and Dante

ART APPRECIATION Have students read the **Humanities Connection** caption and study the reproduction of the wood engraving. Point out that the sinners at this level of Hell are guilty of simony—the buying or selling of spiritual goods, such as indulgences, or positions in the church. Remind students that at each level of Hell, the punishment fits the crime. Then ask students to explain why the punishment of these sinners is fitting.

Possible Response: The sinners spend eternity in an inverted position with the soles of their feet scorched by flames. In life, these sinners inverted the proper order of things in that they regarded material goods—namely, money—as more important than spiritual goods. "Burning" greed motivated them.

Crowded in a herd, they obey if he should summon,
  And he strikes at any laggards with his oar.
  As leaves in quick succession sail down in autumn

Until the bough beholds its entire store
  Fallen to the earth, so Adam's evil seed
  Swoop from the bank when each is called, as sure

As a trained falcon, to cross to the other side
  Of the dark water; and before one throng can land
  On the far shore, on this side new souls crowd.

"My son," said the gentle master, "here are joined
  The souls of all who die in the wrath of God,
  From every country, all of them eager to find

Their way across the water—for the goad
  Of Divine Justice spurs them so, their fear
  Is transmuted to desire. Souls who are good

Never pass this way; therefore, if you hear
  Charon complaining at your presence, consider
  What that means." Then, the earth of that grim shore

Began to shake: so violently, I shudder
  And sweat recalling it now. A wind burst up
  From the tear-soaked ground to erupt red light and batter

My senses—and so I fell, as though seized by sleep.

92 laggards: individuals who lag behind.

95 seed: descendants.

103 goad: something that prods.

104–105 their fear . . . desire: In life the sinners hardened their hearts against grace. They are now required by Divine Justice to wish for Hell.

Thinking Through the Literature

1. What are your impressions of Charon, the demon boatman?
2. Why does Charon complain about Dante's presence at the river?
3. In lines 93–96, the souls at the river are compared to leaves falling from a tree. Why is this simile effective?

Customizing Instruction

Less Proficient Readers

Point out that the pronoun *they* in line 91 refers to the condemned sinners, "all who don't fear God" in line 89. Then use the following questions to guide students' understanding of Canto 3:

- According to the words above the gate of Hell, what must the wicked abandon, or give up? *(hope)*
- Which spirits eternally follow a whirling banner? *(the souls unsure)*
- What does Charon do at the River Acheron? *(gathers the souls of the wicked and ferries them across the river to Hell)*
- At the end of this canto, the ground shakes and a mighty wind arises. What happens to Dante as a result? *(he faints)*

English Learners

Explain the meaning of the following words:

- *summon* (line 91) means "to call or send for"
- *store* (line 94) means "great amount"
- *bank* (line 96) means "the land along the side of a river"
- *throng* (line 98) means "crowd"
- *wrath* (line 101) means "anger"
- *batter* (line 111) means "beat"

Advanced Learners

Have students identify images of darkness used by Dante to describe Hell in this canto.

Possible Response: "dark color" (line 8), "dark and timeless air" (line 26), "blind life" (line 40), "dim light" (line 60), "dismal shore" (line 64), "eternal dark" (line 71), "grim shore" (line 108)

Thinking Through the Literature

1. Possible Response: Charon is a grisly figure, old and ill-tempered, with fiery circles around his eyes. He taunts and abuses the souls waiting to cross the river.
2. Possible Response: Charon complains because Dante, who is alive and good, does not belong with the dead and wicked.
3. Possible Response: This simile suggests the incredible number, the moral decay, and the frailty of the souls at the river.

Reading and Analyzing

Literary Analysis ALLEGORY

A Remind students that when reading an allegory, they should look for symbols. In this passage, the "hurricane of Hell" stands for passion or desire. Ask students to explain the connection between the wind and passion.

Possible Response: They both are strong forces that can rage out of control, destroying all in their path.

Literary Analysis SIMILE

B Have students explain what the simile "As winter starlings riding on their wings/ Form crowded flocks" suggests about the sinners in the violent wind.

Possible Response: The sinners in the "hurricane of Hell" are weak, helpless, and at the mercy of the wind. Crowding together, they are battered and blown about.

Pause & Reflect

Possible Response: Minos curls his tail around his body. The number of coils indicates the sinner's level in Hell.

GUIDE FOR READING

FOCUS Dante and Virgil enter the second level of Hell. At its gate, sinners are judged by Minos. As you read, look for details that describe this character and how he passes judgment.

Preview *Minos judges each sinner to determine his or her proper place in Hell. This level, dark and stormy, is home to the souls of Cleopatra, Helen of Troy, and other illicit lovers. Dante speaks with one of them, Francesca of Ravenna, who tells him how she and her brother-in-law Paolo fell in love. Their torment fills Dante with pity, causing him to faint.*

CANTO 5

1

So I descended from first to second circle—
Which girdles a smaller space and greater pain,
Which spurs more lamentation. Minos the dreadful

Snarls at the gate. He examines each one's sin,
Judging and disposing as he curls his tail:
That is, when an ill-begotten soul comes down,

2

It comes before him, and confesses all;
Minos, great connoisseur of sin, discerns
For every spirit its proper place in Hell,

And wraps himself in his tail with as many turns
As levels down that shade will have to dwell.
A crowd is always waiting: here each one learns

His judgment and is assigned a place in Hell.
They tell; they hear—and down they all are cast.
"You, who have come to sorrow's hospice, think well,"

Said Minos, who at the sight of me had paused
To interrupt his solemn task mid-deed:
"Beware how you come in and whom you trust,

Don't be deceived because the gate is wide."
My leader answered, "Must you too scold this way?
His destined path is not for you to impede:

3 Minos: In classical mythology, Minos was a wise king of Crete who, after his death, became a judge of the dead in the underworld. Here, Minos is a monster that assigns each soul its proper depth in Hell.

8 connoisseur: someone with great knowledge and discriminating taste.

15 hospice: shelter for travelers.

WORDS TO KNOW

discern (dĭ-sûrn') *v.* to perceive with the eyes or intellect

Thus is it willed where every thing may be
  Because it has been willed. So ask no more."
  And now I can hear the notes of agony

In sad crescendo beginning to reach my ear;
  Now I am where the noise of lamentation
  Comes at me in blasts of sorrow. I am where

All light is mute, with a bellowing like the ocean
A Turbulent in a storm of warring winds,
  The hurricane of Hell in perpetual motion

3 Sweeping the ravaged spirits as it rends,
  Twists, and torments them. Driven as if to land,
  They reach the ruin: groaning, tears, laments,

And cursing of the power of Heaven. I learned
  They suffer here who sinned in carnal things—
  Their reason mastered by desire, suborned.

PAUSE & REFLECT How does Minos indicate each sinner's place in Hell?

FOCUS Dante and Virgil look at the spirits of the great lovers. As you read about Francesca and Paolo, try to picture the moment they fall in love.

As winter starlings riding on their wings
  Form crowded flocks, so spirits dip and veer
  Foundering in the wind's rough buffetings,

B

Upward or downward, driven here and there
  With never ease from pain nor hope of rest.
  As chanting cranes will form a line in air,

So I saw souls come uttering cries—wind-tossed,
  And lofted by the storm. "Master," I cried,
4 "Who are these people, by black air oppressed?"

"First among these you wish to know," he said,
  "Was empress of many tongues—she so embraced
  Lechery that she decreed it justified

25 crescendo: a gradual but steady increase in sound.

28 mute: dim.

35 carnal: having to do with the flesh.

36 suborned: led to commit evil acts.

Customizing Instruction

Less Proficient Readers

Tell students to make sure they read the **Preview,** which provides a summary of what happens in the canto, and the two **Focus** sections. Students should look for details about Minos in the first part of the canto and details about the two lovers in the second part.

1 Make sure students understand that as Dante descends from one level to the next, the area get smaller and the souls suffer more.

2 Help students understand lines 6–13. Condemned sinners come before a judge, Minos, and confess their evil deeds. He sentences each sinner to a particular level in Hell based on his or her deeds—the greater the evil, the lower the level in Hell. Minos wraps his tail around his body, using the number of turns of his tail to indicate that level.

3 To help students imagine what this suffering might be like, ask them to describe violent windstorms they have experienced or read about. Have students tell what it feels like to be at the mercy of the wind.

4 Tell students to notice lines 44–45. Dante addresses a question to Virgil, whom he calls "Master." To answer this question, Virgil will point to a number of people in the following lines, all of whom are blown about by the violent wind.

English Learners

Explain the meaning of the following words:

- *girdles* (line 2) means "surrounds"
- *lamentation* (line 3) means "great grief"
- *cast* (line 14) means "thrown"
- *impede* (line 21) means "block"
- *turbulent* (line 29) means "wild"
- *ravaged* (line 31) means "ruined"
- *rends* (line 31) means "rips"
- *carnal* (line 35) means "bodily"
- *veer* (line 38) means "turn"
- *foundering* (line 39) means "sinking"

Reading and Analyzing

Active Reading CLARIFYING MEANING

A Tell students to refer to the sidenotes to learn about the sinners mentioned in this passage. After students have reviewed the sidenotes, ask them what the sinners have in common.

Possible Response: They let their passions, rather than reason, control their actions.

Literary Analysis SPEAKER

B Ask students what they can infer about Dante from his reaction to the souls blown about in the wind.

Possible Response: Dante is sensitive and compassionate. The suffering of the lovers touches his heart.

Literary Analysis CHARACTERIZATION

C Ask students to tell what these lines reveal about the lovers.

Possible Response: In life, Francesca and her lover were seized by intense passion that filled them with rapture. This passion, which cost them their lives, also transcended death. Even in Hell, these lovers still cling to each other.

Legally, to evade the scandal of her lust:
  She is that Semiramis of whom we read,
  Successor and wife of Ninus, she possessed

The lands the Sultan rules. Next, she who died
  By her own hand for love, and broke her vow
  To Sychaeus's ashes. After her comes lewd

And wanton Cleopatra. See Helen, too,
  Who caused a cycle of many evil years;
  And great Achilles, the hero whom love slew

In his last battle. Paris and Tristan are here—"
  He pointed out by name a thousand souls
  Whom love had parted from our life, or more.

When I had heard my teacher tell the rolls
  Of knights and ladies of antiquity,
  Pity overwhelmed me. Half-lost in its coils,

"Poet," I told him, "I would willingly
  Speak with those two who move along together,
  And seem so light upon the wind." And he:

"When they drift closer—then entreat them hither,
  In the name of love that leads them: they will respond."
  Soon their course shifted, and the merciless weather

Battered them toward us. I called against the wind,
  "O wearied souls! If Another does not forbid,
  Come speak with us." As doves whom desire has
    summoned,

With raised wings steady against the current, glide
  Guided by will to the sweetness of their nest,
  So leaving the flock where Dido was, the two sped

Through the malignant air till they had crossed
  To where we stood—so strong was the compulsion
  Of my loving call. They spoke across the blast:

50–51 Semiramis (sə-mĭr'ə-mĭs') . . . **Ninus** (nī'nəs): Semiramis , an Assyrian queen known widely for her sexual excesses, took control after the death of her husband, Ninus.

52–54 she who died . . . Sychaeus's (sĭ-kē'ə-sĭz) **ashes:** Dido, the queen of Carthage who, according to the *Aeneid,* vowed to remain faithful to the memory of her dead husband, Sychaeus, but fell in love with Aeneas. When Aeneas left for Italy, the abandoned Dido committed suicide.

55–56 Cleopatra . . . Helen . . . evil years: Cleopatra was queen of Egypt and a mistress to Julius Caesar and Mark Antony. Helen, according to Greek mythology, was the most beautiful of women. She left her husband, Menelaus (mĕn'ə-lā'əs) to run off with Paris, a prince of Troy. This action set off the Trojan War.

57 Achilles: the hero of the Trojan War who, according to one legend, deserted the Greeks when he fell in love with Polyxena (pə-lĭk'sĕ-nə), daughter of King Priam of Troy. On his way to meet her in a temple, he was slain by Paris.

58 Paris and Tristan: Paris' love for Helen caused the Trojan War. Tristan, a hero from medieval romances, had a love affair with his uncle's bride.

71 Another: God.

WORDS TO KNOW

compulsion (kəm-pŭl'shən) *n.* an irresistible impulse to act

Dante's Dream (1871), Dante Gabriel Rossetti. Board of Trustees of the National Museums and Galleries on Merseyside, Walker Art Gallery, Liverpool, England.

"O living soul, who with courtesy and compassion
Voyage through black air visiting us who stained
The world with blood: if heaven's King bore affection

For such as we are, suffering in this wind,
Then we would pray to Him to grant you peace
For pitying us in this, our evil end.

Now we will speak and hear as you may please
To speak and hear, while the wind, for our discourse,
Is still. My birthplace is a city that lies

Where the Po finds peace with all its followers.
Love, which in gentle hearts is quickly born,
Seized him for my fair body—which, in a fierce

Manner that still torments my soul, was torn
2 Untimely away from me. Love, which absolves
C None who are loved from loving, made my heart burn

With joy so strong that as you see it cleaves
Still to him, here. Love gave us both one death.
Caina awaits the one who took our lives."

These words were borne across from them to us.
When I had heard those afflicted souls, I lowered
My head, and held it so till I heard the voice

Of the poet ask, "What are you thinking?" I answered,
"Alas—that sweet conceptions and passion so deep
Should bring them here!" Then, looking up toward

87–88 My birthplace . . . all its followers: The speaker is Francesca Malatesta (frän-chäs'kä mä'lä-tĕs'tä)—a real-life contemporary of Dante's—whose home was Ravenna, a city on the Po River. She was married to Giovanni Malatesta in 1275 but fell in love with his younger brother, Paolo (pä'ō-lō). The affair continued for several years until Giovanni happened upon them and killed them both.

94 cleaves: clings.

96 Caina . . . our lives: Caina, part of the lowest circle of Hell, holds the spirits of those who betrayed their kin. Francesca expects that it will be her husband's fate to go there. When Dante wrote the *Inferno,* Giovanni Malatesta was still alive.

WORDS TO KNOW

discourse (dĭs'kôrs') *n.* talk; conversation

Customizing Instruction

Less Proficient Readers

1 Help students understand what happens in lines 66–78. Virgil tells Dante to ask the two lovers to come over and speak to them. When the wind drives the two lovers closer, Dante calls out to them. They leave the other lovers ("the flock where Dido was") and come to Dante and Virgil.

2 Help students use the sidenotes to understand these difficult lines. Francesca tells Dante that noble ones ("gentle hearts") may spontaneously fall in love. Paolo looked at Francesca's beauty ("my fair body") and was seized by love. Francesca lost her life in a violent way (she was murdered by her husband), and the memory of her violent death still troubles her soul. Those who are loved are obliged to return that love. Francesca's heart was filled with joy because of Paolo's love, and their hearts still cling together.

English Learners

Explain the meaning of the following words:

- *vow* (line 53) means "sacred promise"
- *wanton* (line 55) means "without restraint"
- *antiquity* (line 62) means "the distant past"
- *hither* (line 67) means "here"
- *malignant* (line 76) means "evil"
- *absolves* (line 92) means "to free someone from a duty"
- *afflicted* (line 98) means "injured"
- *conceptions* (line 101) means "thoughts"

Advanced Learners

Ask students how Dante, the poet who wrote the *Inferno*, and Dante, the main character in the work, differ in their attitudes toward Francesca and Paolo.

Possible Response: As a poet, Dante follows Christian beliefs, consigning the lovers to Hell for their illicit love and describing their suffering. As a character, he feels pity for the lovers, whose sweet passion led to their ruin.

Cross Curricular Link Humanities

COURTLY LOVERS The noble lovers Francesca and Paolo spend eternity in the second level of Hell, where fierce winds punish the lustful. In the Middle Ages, lust was regarded as one of the seven deadly sins. (See the Cross Curricular Link on page 742 for information about the seven deadly sins.) Dante portrays Francesca and Paolo as courtly lovers. The tradition of courtly love developed in southern France in the late 12th century and influenced the works of Chrétien de Troyes and Marie de France. In literary works in this tradition, a noble lady, beautiful and intelligent, is loved passionately by a courageous knight. The lady, alas, is unattainable because she is already married—to someone she doesn't really love. In the Middle Ages, aristocratic marriages were arranged, based on financial or family interests, not on romantic love. Unlike some storybook lovers, Francesca and Paolo consummate their love. Their lust leads to their murder and the loss of their immortal souls.

INFERNO 751

Reading and Analyzing

Literary Analysis FLASHBACK

A Remind students that a flashback is an account of what happens before the main events in a story. In this flashback, Francesca recalls how she and Paolo fell in love. Ask students to summarize what happens.

Possible Response: Francesca and Paolo were reading a romance about Lancelot's forbidden love for Guinevere, King Arthur's wife. As they read, they repeatedly glanced from the book into each other's eyes. Finally, when they read about Lancelot's kissing Guinevere, the two lovers also kissed for the first time.

Reading Skills and Strategies VISUALIZING

B Remind students that authors often use sensory details to appeal to a reader's five senses. Have students identify the words and phrases that help them form mental pictures of the setting—the lowest level of Hell. How does Dante create a mood of mystery?

Possible Response: The air is dark and foggy. Dante thinks he perceives something in the distance, perhaps the blades of a windmill. He notices spirits covered in ice. These details create a mood of mystery, making the reader eager to find out what will happen next.

The lovers: "Francesca, your suffering makes me weep
  For sorrow and pity—but tell me, in the hours
  Of sweetest sighing, how and in what shape

Or manner did Love first show you those desires
  So hemmed by doubt?" And she to me: "No sadness
  Is greater than in misery to rehearse

Memories of joy, as your teacher well can witness.
  But if you have so great a craving to measure
  Our love's first root, I'll tell it, with the fitness

Of one who weeps and tells. One day, for pleasure,
  We read of Lancelot, by love constrained:
  Alone, suspecting nothing, at our leisure.

Sometimes at what we read our glances joined,
  Looking from the book each to the other's eyes,
  And then the color in our faces drained.

But one particular moment alone it was
  Defeated us: *the longed-for smile,* it said,
  Was kissed by that most noble lover: at this,

This one, who now will never leave my side,
  Kissed my mouth, trembling. A Galeotto, that book!
  And so was he who wrote it; that day we read

No further." All the while the one shade spoke,
  The other at her side was weeping; my pity
  Overwhelmed me and I felt myself go slack:

Swooning as in death, I fell like a dying body.

113 Lancelot, by love constrained: In the Arthurian legends, Lancelot was King Arthur's noblest knight. He could not resist falling in love with the king's wife, Guinevere.

122 Galeotto (gä'lĕ-ō'tō): the go-between who passed messages from Lancelot to Guinevere.

126 go slack: lose muscle tension or become unconscious.

Thinking Through the Literature

1. What was your reaction to Francesca and Paolo?
2. In his book *The Power of Myth,* the writer and scholar Joseph Campbell states that the lines describing how Francesca and Paolo fell in love are "the most famous lines in Dante." Why do you think these lines appeal to many readers?
3. All the lovers in this level of Hell are buffeted by strong, dark winds. What do you think the winds might represent?

Thinking Through the Literature

1. Responses will vary. Many students will say that like Dante they too felt sorry that such passionate lovers should suffer so terribly in the afterlife.
2. Possible Response: These lines describe how two people are caught up in the moment and suddenly fall in love, much to their own surprise. The lines suggest that love is an overwhelming emotional experience that just happens to people.
3. Possible Response: The winds are dark and uncontrollable. They represent the passion or desire that seized the lovers in life.

GUIDE FOR READING

FOCUS Dante and Virgil have reached the lowest level of Hell. As you read, look for details that help you visualize it.

Preview *In Cantos 6–33, Dante and Virgil travel down through the successive levels of Hell. In Canto 34, they enter the final level, home to Dis, the ruler of Hell. The shades dwelling there are frozen in ice. Dis is a three-faced giant. His upper body protrudes from the ice of the river Cocytus. Each of his bloody mouths holds a sinner guilty of a terrible betrayal—Judas Iscariot, Brutus, and Cassius.*

FROM

CANTO 34

"And now, *Vexilla regis prodeunt*
Inferni—therefore, look," my master said
As we continued on the long descent,

"And see if you can make him out, ahead."
As though, in the exhalation of heavy mist
Or while night darkened our hemisphere, one spied

2

A mill—blades turning in the wind, half-lost
Off in the distance—some structure of that kind
I seemed to make out now. But at a gust

B

Of wind, there being no other shelter at hand,
I drew behind my leader's back again.
By now (and putting it in verse I find

Fear in myself still) I had journeyed down
To where the shades were covered wholly by ice,
Showing like straw in glass—some lying prone,

And some erect, some with the head toward us,
And others with the bottoms of the feet;
Another like a bow, bent feet to face.

1–2 *Vexilla regis prodeunt Inferni* (vĕk-sĭl'ə rĕg'ĭs prō'dĕ-ŏŏnt ĭn-fĕr'nē): a Latin phrase meaning "The banners of the king of Hell advance" (an alteration of the first line of a famous Christian hymn).

15 prone: face downward.

Customizing Instruction

Less Proficient Readers

1 Make sure students understand that in these lines Dante asks Francesca to describe the moment when she and Paolo first fell in love. Francesca retells her experience in the flashback that follows.

Then ask students the following questions to check their comprehension of Canto 5:

- Who judges the sinners, determining their level in Hell? *(Minos)*
- What punishment do Francesca and Paolo suffer? *(being blown about by strong winds)*
- What characters were Francesca and Paolo reading about when they fell in love? *(Lancelot and Guinevere)*

Focus Make sure students understand that they should look for details that help them form mental pictures of the lowest level of Hell. If necessary, direct students to lines 14–15, which describe souls at this level encased in ice.

Tell students to read the **Preview,** which summarizes what happens in this canto.

2 Point out that in these lines Dante describes his impressions of what it was like to enter the lowest level of Hell. He compares his experiences to that of trying to identify a large object like a windmill at night.

English Learners

Explain the meaning of the following words:

- *hemmed* (line 107) means "surrounded"
- *drained* (line 117) means "flowed away or disappeared"
- *longed-for* (line 119) means "desired"
- *swooning* (line 127) means "fainting"
- *descent* (line 3) means "moving down to a lower place"
- *exhalation* (line 5) means "giving off"
- *prone* (line 15) means "lying face downward"

MINI LESSON Speaking and Listening

DRAMATIC PRESENTATION

Prepare Ask students to prepare a dramatic presentation of the dialogue between Dante and Francesca in lines 103–124 on page 752. Students can work in pairs, with one student taking Dante's part and the other student Francesca's. Tell students that performers use an array of techniques to stress ideas and convey emotions:

- changes in volume, or loudness
- changes in speed of delivery
- changes in tone of voice
- facial expressions
- gestures or other body language

Present Have pairs of students give their dramatic presentations. Audience members should practice their listening skills while their classmates perform, noting some of the techniques used to stress ideas and convey emotions. After the presentations, invite both performers and audience members to share new insights about Francesca's character.

This activity is particularly well suited for longer blocks of class time.

INFERNO 753

Reading Skills and Strategies
CONNECTING

A Ask students how they feel as they imagine themselves accompanying Dante to the lowest depths of Hell.
Possible Response: anxious, curious, frightened

Active Reading CLARIFYING MEANING

B Remind students that they should reread difficult passages and then try to restate them in their own words. Then have students reread and paraphrase lines 33–35.
Possible Response: Dis, or Lucifer, is so huge that the difference in size between his arm and a giant is greater than the difference between a giant's height and mine.

Pause & Reflect
Possible Response: The shades are covered in ice.

Dante and Virgil in the Ninth Circle of the Inferno, Gustave Doré. Photograph copyright © Christie's Images.

HUMANITIES CONNECTION This painting by the French artist Gustave Doré (1832–1883) depicts Virgil and Dante in the ninth circle of the Inferno, where betrayers are fixed in ice. The poets notice two heads in the same hole. One of the heads gnaws on the nape of the other's neck.

MINI LESSON Viewing and Representing

Dante and Virgil in the Ninth Circle of the Inferno **by Gustave Doré**

ART APPRECIATION Have students read the **Humanities Connection** caption and study the reproduction of the detail from the engraving. Tell students that Gustave Doré (1832–1883) was acclaimed for his illustrations of literary works. The artist Vincent van Gogh called Doré "an artist of the people" because his illustrations had enormous popular appeal. Doré made 76 full-page folio engravings for Dante's *Inferno*. It has been said that the genre of horror stories derives from Edgar Allan Poe's writings and Dore's engravings for the *Inferno*. Ask students to identify details in this engraving that help to create a mood of horror.

Possible Response: the murky atmosphere, the blood flowing from the mouth of the sinner chewing on the neck of another sinner, the heads and twisted torsos protruding from the ice

When we had traveled forward to the spot
From which it pleased my master to have me see
That creature whose beauty once had been so great,

He made me stop, and moved from in front of me.
"Look: here is Dis," he said, "and here is the place
Where you must arm yourself with the quality

Of fortitude." How chilled and faint I was
On hearing that, you must not ask me, reader—
I do not write it; words would not suffice:

A

I neither died, nor kept alive—consider
1 With your own wits what I, alike denuded
Of death and life, became as I heard my leader.

21–23 That creature whose beauty . . . Dis: Dis, or Lucifer, was the most beautiful of the angels until he rebelled against God and was cast from Heaven.

27 suffice: be enough; be sufficient.

29 denuded: stripped bare.

PAUSE & REFLECT What covers the shades in the lowest level of Hell?

FOCUS At last, Dante views Dis, or Lucifer, the ruler of Hell. Look for details that describe this character.

The emperor of the realm of grief protruded
From mid-breast up above the surrounding ice.
A giant's height, and mine, would have provided

B

Closer comparison than would the size
Of his arm and a giant. Envision the whole
That is proportionate to parts like these.

If he was truly once as beautiful
As he is ugly now, and raised his brows
2 Against his Maker—then all sorrow may well

Come out of him. How great a marvel it was
For me to see three faces on his head:
In front there was a red one; joined to this,

Each over the midpoint of a shoulder, he had
Two others—all three joining at the crown.
That on the right appeared to be a shade

WORDS TO KNOW

fortitude (fôr'tĭ-to͞od') *n.* courage

protrude (prō-tro͞od') *v.* to jut out; project

Customizing Instruction

Less Proficient Readers

Focus Make sure students understand that Dante's supernatural journey is nearing its end. Only one more wicked creature remains to be seen: namely, Dis—the fallen angel who now rules Hell.

1 Help students imagine Dante's mental state just before he looks upon Dis. He is so terrified that he feels like a zombie, neither dead nor alive.

2 Tell students that it is important that they understand the contrast between what Dis once was and what he now is. He once was the most beautiful creature; he now is the ugliest one. His awareness of this change causes him endless grief.

English Learners

Explain to students that "the emperor of the realm of grief" in line 31 refers to Dis, or Lucifer. He is huge and sticks out of the ice from the chest upwards. Then explain the meaning of the following words and phrases:

- *his Maker* (line 39) refers to God
- *marvel* (line 40) means "wonder"
- *crown* (line 44) means "the top of the head"

MINI LESSON Grammar

DASHES

Instruction Remind students that dashes are used to set off explanatory or parenthetical material in sentences. Have students read page 755 of *The Inferno*. Point out Dante's use of a dash in lines 25-27: "How chilled and faint I was/On hearing that, you must not ask me, reader—/I do not write it; . . . " Have students identify the information that is set off by the dash *("I do not write it)*. Next, have students identify two other examples from page 755 in which dashes are used to set off explanatory or parenthetical statements *(examples are found in lines 37-40 and lines 40-44).*

Practice Ask students to rewrite each sentence below, adding dashes where needed and underlining the parenthetical or explanatory information that is set off.

1. Dante is guided through Hell by the spirit of Virgil(—) a famous poet.
2. Charon (—) the white-haired demon, (—) tells Dante to leave the Acheron river.
3. Dante and Virgil(—) poets and travelers on a supernatural journey, (—) quickly depart from the "evil shore."

For more instruction and practice in using dashes, use McDougal Littell's ***Language Network:***

- Grade 10, Chapter 11, "Punctuation"
- Grade 12, Chapter 10, "Other Punctuation Marks"

INFERNO 755

Literary Analysis
IMAGERY AND MOOD

A Ask students to identify the mood that images such as the six weeping eyes and the tears mixed with "bloody foam" help to create.
Possible Response: a mood of horror and disgust

Active Reading CLARIFYING MEANING

B Tell students to read the sidenote for information about Judas Iscariot. Remind them that the *Inferno* was written in the Middle Ages, when the Church was a major force in Western Europe. Then ask why Dante places Judas in the mouth of Dis.
Possible Response: Judas committed the worst sin in betraying Jesus, whom Dante regards as the savior of the world. Judas's proper place is in the mouth of Dis, the arch-betrayer who rebelled against God.

1

Of whitish yellow; the third had such a mien
　As those who come from where the Nile descends.
　Two wings spread forth from under each face's chin,

Strong, and befitting such a bird, immense—
　I have never seen at sea so broad a sail—
　Unfeathered, batlike, and issuing three winds

That went forth as he beat them, to freeze the whole
　Realm of Cocytus that surrounded him.
　He wept with all six eyes, and the tears fell

A

Over his three chins mingled with bloody foam.
　The teeth of each mouth held a sinner, kept
　As by a flax rake: thus he held three of them

In agony. For the one the front mouth gripped,
　The teeth were as nothing to the claws, which sliced
　And tore the skin until his back was stripped.

B

"That soul," my master said, "who suffers most,
　Is Judas Iscariot; head locked inside,
　He flails his legs. Of the other two, who twist

With their heads down, the black mouth holds the shade
　Of Brutus: writhing, but not a word will he scream;
　Cassius is the sinewy one on the other side.

But night is rising again, and it is time
　That we depart, for we have seen the whole."
　As he requested, I put my arms round him . . .

46 mien (mĕn): appearance.

53 Cocytus (kō-kī'təs): a river of Hell.

57 flax rake: a rake for combing seeds out of a flax plant so that cloth can be woven.

62 Judas Iscariot (jŏŏ'dəs ĭ-skăr'ē-ət): the betrayer of Jesus Christ.

65–66 Brutus . . . Cassius (kăsh'əs): betrayers of Julius Caesar. In Dante's time, Caesar's assassination was considered to be a setback to the development of the Roman Empire.

66 sinewy: lean and muscular.

Humanities

WHAT FOLLOWS IN *THE DIVINE COMEDY* The *Inferno,* which is the first of the three major sections of *The Divine Comedy,* is followed by *Purgatorio* (Purgatory) and then *Paradiso* (Heaven). In *Purgatorio*, Virgil and Dante, emerging in the Southern Hemisphere, come upon the Mountain of Purgatory. It is divided into seven terraces, on each of which the souls of repentant sinners are cleansed of a deadly sin. At the top of the mountain, the two poets find an earthly paradise. Beatrice appears, replacing Virgil as Dante's guide.

In *Paradiso*, Beatrice and Dante ascend through several spheres, in each of which the souls of the saved—for example, great teachers, saints, and angels—enjoy a particular stage of happiness. In the final sphere, Dante, with the help of the mystic St. Bernard, has a vision of God. The poem ends with Dante's experience of spiritual bliss.

FROM

LA VITA NUOVA

TRANSLATED BY MARK MUSA

PREPARING to *Read*

Build Background *La Vita Nuova* [The New Life], a short work by Dante, contains sonnets and a prose narrative about his love for Beatrice. In this excerpt from the work (page 758), Dante tells of the moment he fell in love with her. His love for Beatrice—powerful and passionate—may remind you of the love between Francesca and Paolo, immortalized in Canto 5 of the *Inferno.*

Beata Beatrix (1864–1870), Dante Gabriel Rossetti. Oil on canvas, 86.4 cm × 66 cm. Tate Gallery. Photo © Tate, London/Art Resource, New York.

Customizing Instruction

Less Proficient Readers

1 Make sure students are able to visualize Dis. This giant has three faces, which are joined at the top of his head. The face in front is red, the face on the right is whitish yellow, and the face on the left is black. Beneath each face is a pair of huge wings. These beating wings freeze the air and the river.

English Learners

To help students understand line 47, ask for a volunteer to point out the location of the Nile River on a globe or a world map. Then explain the meaning of the following words:

- *immense* (line 49) means "very large"
- *unfeathered* (line 51) means "without feathers"
- *issuing* (line 51) means "causing"
- *flails* (line 63) means "waving the arms about"
- *writhing* (line 65) means "twisting"

Advanced Learners

Remind students of the Christian doctrine of the Holy Trinity: namely, that in God there are three divine persons—the Father, the Son, and the Holy Spirit. Then ask students how this doctrine might have influenced Dante's depiction of Dis.

Possible Response: Instead of being a divinity that includes three persons, Dis is a hideous giant with three faces. He is a grotesque inversion of the divine.

MINI LESSON More From the Author

PARADISO While writing *The Divine Comedy,* Dante lived in exile from his beloved city of Florence. He endured this dreadful punishment for many years, from 1302 until his death in 1321. In *Paradiso,* he describes his sufferings as an exile. Among the souls of the blessed is Cacciaguida, Dante's great-great-grandfather. Cacciaguida informs Dante that he will be banished from Florence and suffer great adversity:

"All that you held most dear you will put by
and leave behind you; and this is the arrow
the longbow of your exile first lets fly.

You will come to learn how bitter as salt and stone
is the bread of others, how hard the way that goes
up and down stairs that never are your own.

And what will press down on your shoulders most
will be the foul and foolish company
you will fall into on that barren coast."
(Canto 17, lines 55–63)

—Translated by John Ciardi

Reading Skills and Strategies
CONNECTING

A Ask students whether they believe in love at first sight. Then ask them whether they think a boy of nine could have such strong feelings upon seeing a girl for the first time.

Possible Response: Answers will vary. Some students may state that first impressions can be very intense at any age. These students may add that Dante was very sensitive—sensitive enough to fall in love at a young age. Other students may state that love develops over time and does not happen at first sight, especially to a boy of nine.

Active Reading CLARIFYING MEANING

B Tell students that a summary is a short restatement of a writer's main ideas. Then have a volunteer model the strategy by summarizing the information in this passage.

Possible Response: After looking upon Beatrice, Dante fell in love with her and spent most of his time thinking about her. As a result, he seemed to lose physical strength. When questioned, he admitted he was in love but would not reveal whom he loved.

THE FIRST SIGHT OF BEATRICE

Nine times already since my birth the heaven of light had circled back to almost the same point, when there appeared before my eyes the now glorious lady of my mind, who was called Beatrice even by those who did not know what her name was. She had been in this life long enough for the heaven of the fixed stars to be able to move a twelfth of a degree to the East in her time; that is, she appeared to me at about the beginning of her ninth year, and I first saw her near the end of my ninth year. She appeared dressed in the most patrician[1] of colors, a subdued and decorous crimson, her robe bound round and adorned in a style suitable to her years. At that very moment, and I speak the truth, the vital spirit, the one that dwells in the most secret chamber of the heart, began to tremble so violently that even the most minute veins of my body were strangely affected; and trembling, it spoke these words: *Ecce deus fortior me, qui veniens dominabitur michi.*[2]

THE EFFECTS OF LOVE

After that vision my natural spirit was interfered with in its functioning, because my soul had become wholly absorbed in thinking about this most gracious lady; and in a short time I became so weak and frail that many of my friends were worried about the way I looked; others, full of malicious curiosity, were doing their best to discover things about me, which, above all, I wished to keep secret from everyone. I was aware of the maliciousness of their questioning and, guided by Love who commanded me according to the counsel of reason, I would answer that it was Love who had conquered me. I said that it was Love because there were so many of his signs clearly marked on my face that they were impossible to conceal. And when people would ask: "Who is the person for whom you are so destroyed by Love?" I would look at them and smile and say nothing.

1. **patrician:** noble.
2. ***Ecce deus . . . michi:*** "Here is a god stronger than I who comes to rule over me."

Connect to the Literature

1. **What Do You Think?** What was your reaction to Dante's vision of Hell?

Comprehension Check
- What type of sinner is found in the lowest level in Hell?
- Of all the sinners in Hell, who suffers the most?

Think Critically

2. **ACTIVE READING: CLARIFYING MEANING** Using your READER'S NOTEBOOK, work with a partner and compare your answers to the Pause & Reflect questions. Also try to clarify any points of confusion that either of you might still have about what happens in this excerpt.
3. Think about Dante's portrayal of himself. What are his main qualities?
4. How would you describe the relationship between Dante and Virgil?
5. Are the punishments that Dante describes fair or not? Explain your opinion.

   THINK ABOUT
   - the punishment of the souls of the unsure
   - the fact that illicit lovers are punished less severely than other sinners
   - the fact that betrayers receive the most severe punishment of all
   - the fact that all these punishments are eternal

Extend Interpretations

6. **What If?** At the lowest level of Hell, Virgil and Dante come upon Dis, who is said to be weeping. Imagine that Dis were portrayed in some other way—for example, as grinning or gloating. How do you think your reaction might differ?
7. **Critic's Corner** One famous admirer of Dante's work was Ralph Waldo Emerson, a 19th-century American poet and essayist. Emerson praised *The Divine Comedy* as "the best textbook" for teaching the art of writing. In the excerpt you read, identify three or more qualities of good writing—for example, the use of vivid details—that an aspiring writer should take notice of.
8. **Connect to Life** Based on what you have read in this excerpt, to what extent do you think the *Inferno* is relevant to readers today? Explain.

LITERARY ANALYSIS: ALLEGORY

A **symbol** is a person, place, or object that has a concrete meaning in itself and stands for something beyond itself. For example, the American flag is a symbol of the United States. An **allegory** is a literary work filled with symbols. Dante's *Divine Comedy* can be read as an allegory. Here are some important points to keep in mind:

- It has two levels of meaning—a literal one and a symbolic one.
- To explore the symbolic meaning, pay attention to details about the characters, objects, events, and settings. For example, details describing the she-wolf in Canto 1 of the *Inferno* suggest that this animal represents greed:

Her nature
Is so malign and vicious she
cannot appease
Her voracity, for feeding makes
her hungrier. (lines 74–76)

Paired Activity The chart below lists several details from the *Inferno*. Go back through the poem, and then write down what you think each detail might mean on a symbolic level. Compare your interpretations with a partner's.

Person, Object, Place, Event	Possible Meaning
The dark woods	The confusion and misery caused by sin
A whirling banner followed by many souls	
The character of Virgil	
The dark wind that tortures the lovers	
The ice at the lowest level of Hell	

Connect to the Literature

1. **What Do You Think?** Many students may be left with a feeling of awe. Other students may express feelings of horror or disgust. Some students may be concerned about the seemingly unfair punishment of sinners such as Paolo and Francesca.

Comprehension Check
- betrayers
- Judas, the betrayer of Jesus

Use Selection Quiz in **Unit Five Resource Book,** p. 16.

Think Critically

2. Responses will vary. Students should identify points of confusion and then tell the strategies they used to help clarify meaning.
3. Possible Response: Dante seems devout, sensitive, self-conscious at times, well-educated, poetic, and sympathetic to others' suffering.
4. Possible Response: Dante reveres Virgil, regarding him as a supreme master or teacher, worthy of devotion and trust. Dante has studied Virgil's works, particularly the *Aeneid*, and has derived from them inspiration for his own poetry. Having followed Virgil as a model for poetry, Dante now trusts him as his spiritual guide.
5. Answers will vary. Some students may state that the punishments are fair, based on medieval ideas, and suit the crimes. For example, the souls of the unsure follow a banner whirling from side to side. Moreover, those who commit the worst sins—betraying one's leader—are punished most severely. Other students may state that the punishments are unfair. These students may point out that extenuating circumstances are not taken into account. For example, Paolo and Francesca fell in love in an unguarded moment. These students may add that "forever" is too long for punishments to last.

Extend Interpretations

6. **What If?** Possible Response: By depicting Dis as weeping, Dante suggests that the arch-betrayer suffers the most.
7. **Critic's Corner** Students might mention these qualities of good writing: creating a sympathetic speaker or narrator; bringing characters to life in dramatic scenes through vivid details and dialogue; describing settings precisely; using the imagination to create new experiences for readers.
8. **Connect to Life** Answers will vary. Some students may state that the evils depicted in Dante's poem still plague humans today. Other students may state that the opening scene especially portrays the difficulty of staying on the right path—a difficulty that humans struggle with today.

Literary Analysis

Paired Activity Possible Responses: a whirling banner followed by many souls—indecision, infirmity, irresolution; the character of Virgil—reason, light, and literary achievement; the dark wind that tortures the lovers—uncontrollable emotion; the ice at the lowest level of Hell—the lifelessness and inhumanity of the greatest evil

Use **Unit Five Resource Book,** p. 14, for more practice.

Analysis of Style

A First Activity
Possible Responses:
vivid details and images: "I found myself in dark woods" from Canto 1; "the tears fell/ Over his three chins mingled with bloody foam" from Canto 34
figurative language: "As leaves in quick succession . . . so Adam's evil seed / Swoop from the bank when each is called," from Canto 3
allusions: "See Helen, too, . . . And great Achilles, . . . Paris and Tristan are here—" from Canto 5
diction: "Adam's evil seed" from Canto 3; "Who caused a cycle of many evil years" and "the hero whom love slew" from Canto 5

B Second Activity
Answers will vary. Vivid details and images are found in many lines, including lines 54–55 in Canto 3 ("their bare skin galled/ By wasps and flies, blood trickling down the face"). As an example of figurative language, students may mention the simile in lines 18–21 in Canto 1 ("As one still panting . . . in it"); as an example of allusion, "good Augustus's Rome" in line 54 in Canto 1; and as an example of precise words, "that dark and timeless air" in line 26 in Canto 3.

C Third Activity
Choices of passages will vary. Some students may mention lines 37–44 in Canto 5 ("As winter starlings . . . lofted by the storm"). These lines contain vivid details and images ("wind-tossed,/ And lofted by the storm"), precise word choices ("dip and veer," "foundering," "buffetings," "never ease from pain nor hope of rest"), and similes that compare the tormented spirits to winter starlings and cranes flying in the wind.

Dante's Poetic Language

The **style** of a work of literature is the particular way in which it is written. A writer's style reflects his or her unique way of communicating with the reader. In the *Inferno,* for example, Dante used poetic language to convey his imaginative vision of eternal punishments in the afterlife.

Key Aspects of Dante's Style

- vivid details and images that convey ideas and feelings
- figurative language, including similes like those found in classical epics
- allusions to legendary or historical figures
- precise and sometimes lofty words

Analysis of Style

At the right are brief passages from the *Inferno.* Study the list of stylistic elements above, and read each excerpt carefully. Then complete the following activities:

- A Find examples of each aspect of Dante's style in the excerpts.
- B Find additional examples of each aspect in other passages from the *Inferno.*
- C Find a passage from the *Inferno* that you think is especially moving. With a partner, discuss the stylistic techniques Dante used.

Applications

1. **Changing Style** Choose a passage from the *Inferno* that contains figurative language. Then write a **paraphrase** of the passage, expressing the same ideas in everyday prose. Read your paraphrase and Dante's original to a partner. Discuss what Dante has conveyed through his use of poetic language.
2. **Imitation of Style** Try imitating Dante's style as you write a few three-line stanzas about a fitting punishment for a notorious evildoer of the 20th century—for example, Hitler or Stalin.
3. **Speaking and Listening** Present an oral reading of one of the four passages to the right. Choose appropriate phrasings, pitches, and gestures to convey the emotion of the passage.

from the **Inferno, Canto 1**

Midway on our life's journey, I found myself
In dark woods, the right road lost. To tell
About those woods is hard—so tangled and rough
And savage that thinking of it now, I feel
The old fear stirring: death is hardly more bitter.

from the **Inferno, Canto 3**

As leaves in quick succession sail down in autumn
Until the bough beholds its entire store
Fallen to the earth, so Adam's evil seed
Swoop from the bank when each is called,

from the **Inferno, Canto 5**

See Helen, too,
Who caused a cycle of many evil years;
And great Achilles, the hero whom love slew
In his last battle. Paris and Tristan are here—"

from the **Inferno, Canto 34**

He wept with all six eyes, and the tears fell
Over his three chins mingled with bloody foam.

Applications

1. **Changing Style** Students might select the passage from Canto 3 found on this page or another of their own choice. In comparing their prose paraphrase with Dante's original, students should conclude that Dante's poetic language creates vivid pictures for the imagination and suggests a rich array of meanings.
2. **Imitation of Style** Have students work in small groups to look up information about the evildoer's crime. In writing their stanzas, students should describe a punishment commensurate with the crime.
3. **Speaking and Listening** Students might work in pairs to rehearse the passage they select, reading it over and over again until they are familiar with the structure and the language. Tell students to read naturally, not theatrically, and at a slower pace than in normal conversation. Remind them that every word conveys meaning in a passage of poetry and that the audience needs time to absorb the ideas and images.

Writing Option

Subject Analysis Write a brief essay in response to this prompt: Does Dante make his journey through Hell believable to the reader? Support your opinion with details from the poem. Place your analysis in your **Working Portfolio.**

Writing Handbook
See page R35: Persuasive Writing.

Activities & Explorations

Dramatic Reading With three or four classmates, rehearse and perform a dramatic reading of one of the cantos in the *Inferno.* Add background music or sound effects to accompany your performance.
~ **SPEAKING AND LISTENING**

Inquiry & Research

Character Profile Research one of the legendary or historical figures who appear in the *Inferno*—for example, Virgil, Charon, Cleopatra, Dido, Tristan, Francesca Malatesta, Brutus, or Judas Iscariot. Report your findings in a written profile.

Vocabulary in Action

EXERCISE: ANALOGIES Choose a word from the list of Words to Know to complete each analogy.

1. enjoyable : unpleasant :: lucky : _____
2. observe : detect :: examine : _____
3. speech : individual :: _____ : partners
4. notice : observe :: assist : _____
5. sports : strength :: crisis : _____
6. poor : _____ :: hungry : starving
7. created : made :: inspired : _____
8. _____ : outward :: withdraw : inward
9. shower : thunderstorm :: habit : _____
10. applause : enjoy :: ridicule : _____

WORDS TO KNOW

abject	discern	fortitude	protrude
avail	discourse	hapless	
compulsion	disdain	imbued	

Building Vocabulary
For an in-depth lesson on analogies, see page 768.

Where did Dante live after he was banished from Florence? What might his life have been like during those dark years? Working with a small group of classmates, research Dante's life during his exile from Florence. Then create an interactive map that shows Italy in Dante's time. On the map, identify several sites he visited during his exile. Each group member should choose one of these sites and look up information about Dante's connection with it. Then record the information so that users of the map can listen to it.

Biographical Sources Supplement the information on Dante provided on pages 732–735 with information from reference books, literary biographies, and reliable online sources. These sources might include Web sites maintained by university literature departments and reputable literary societies (including Dante societies).

Historical Sources Use reference books, historical atlases, and books or other sources on Italian history to help you map the Italian city-states in Dante's day. Again, consider reliable online Web sites, such as those maintained by Italian cities and by reputable historical or medieval societies.

Choices & Challenges

Writing Option

Subject Analysis As a prewriting activity, students might work in pairs to list several details from Dante's poem and then decide whether they ring true or not. You might tell students that *The Divine Comedy* is a dream vision and that the *Inferno* may be compared to a nightmare.

Activities & Explorations

Dramatic Reading The encounters with characters such as Charon (Canto 3), Minos (Canto 5), and Francesca (Canto 5) are richly dramatic. Students should experiment with different interpretations and portrayals.

Inquiry & Research

Character Profile Students should consult standard reference works as well as online encyclopedias to do the research for their written profiles. Students familiar with Shakespeare's play *The Tragedy of Julius Caesar* might compare Shakespeare's view of Brutus with Dante's.

Vocabulary in Action

1. hapless
2. discern
3. discourse
4. avail
5. fortitude
6. abject
7. imbued
8. protrude
9. compulsion
10. disdain

Author Study Project

Mapping Dante's Exile Students should include on their maps Dante's native city of Florence and the following places he visited during his exile: Verona, Lunigiana, Poppi, Lucca, and Ravenna. Students might provide facts about each place (for example, location, size, and places of interest) as well as specific information about its importance to Dante during his exile.

Biographical Sources Tell students to check modern translations of *The Divine Comedy* for information about Dante in the introduction, notes, and essays. For example, Allen Mandelbaum's verse translation of the *Inferno* contains his essay "Dante in his Age" that tells about Dante's years in exile. R. W. B. Lewis's brief biography of Dante, published in 2001, is also a good resource.

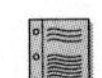
To assess skills and concepts taught in this selection, use **Formal Assessment Book,** p. 113–114.

Objectives
- write a Subject Analysis
- use a written text as a model for writing
- revise a draft to change any awkward use of passive voice to active voice
- edit for redundancy

Introducing the Workshop

A Subject Analysis Point out that a subject analysis is a common form of writing, often found in textbooks, newspapers, and magazines. Even television or film documentaries often take the form of a subject analysis. Their purpose is to present an overview of the subject, then go into a detailed presentation of the parts, showing how these parts contribute to the whole.

Have students name examples of in-depth analyses of any topic that they have seen or read. List them on the board. Ask students whether they can identify patterns in the kinds of subjects analyzed or in the approaches to analysis. Point out that writing a subject analysis will allow students to gain an in-depth view of a subject and help them better understand it.

Basics in a Box

B Using the Graphic Like the pieces shown in the pie chart, the sections of a subject analysis focus individually on the parts that make up a whole. This graphic suggests that students move from the overall subject to its component parts and then back to the overall subject.

C Presenting the Rubric To better understand the assignment, students can refer to the Standards for Writing a Successful Subject Analysis. You may wish to discuss with them the complete rubric and student models in the Unit Five Resource Book on pages 22–27.

For more instruction and practice in expository writing, use McDougal Littell's ***Language Network:***
- Grade 10, Chapter 23, "Problem-Solution Essay"
- Grade 12, Chapter 20, "Subject Analysis"

Writing Workshop — Subject Analysis

Examining the parts of a subject . . .

A **From Reading to Writing** In this unit you've read selections on topics ranging from werewolves to chivalry to the Holy Grail. You can explore such topics further by analyzing them in writing. In a **subject analysis,** a writer breaks a topic into parts and examines each one. For example, an analysis of werewolves might treat the history of werewolf folklore, the characteristics of werewolves, and the parts of the world where tales of these creatures are told. Analysis can be applied to a wide variety of topics. In the essay on the following page, the writer analyzes different aspects of school athletics.

For Your Portfolio

WRITING PROMPT Write an essay in which you present an analysis of a subject of your choice.

Purpose: To explain the parts of a subject and examine how they relate to one another

Audience: Readers interested in understanding the subject in depth

Basics in a Box

Subject Analysis at a Glance

B

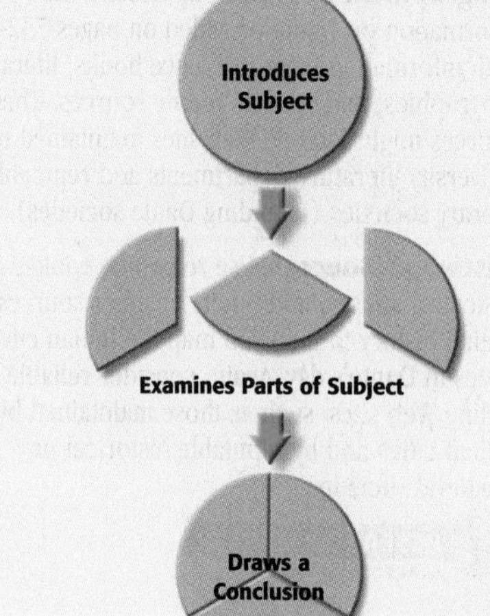

RUBRIC Standards for Writing

A successful subject analysis should
- introduce the subject in an interesting, informative manner
- identify the subject's principal parts
- examine each part thoroughly
- present information in a logical order
- show how the parts relate to the whole subject and how the discussion of them supports the analysis's main idea, or thesis
- include an effective conclusion

C

LESSON RESOURCES

USING PRINT RESOURCES
Unit Five Resource Book
- Prewriting, p. 17
- Drafting, p. 18
- Peer Response, pp. 19–20
- Revising, Editing, and Proofreading, p. 21
- Student Models, pp. 22–26
- Rubric, p. 27

USING MEDIA RESOURCES
Writing Coach CD-ROM
Visit our Web site: classzone.com

ADDITIONAL RESOURCES
For a complete view of Lesson Resources, see page 685g in this book.

Analyzing a Student Model

Bryan Dobkin
Buffalo Grove High School

Going the Distance

What comes to mind when you hear the term *student athlete?* Perhaps you think of a swimmer getting up to practice at 5 A.M. every day or of football players performing drills like recruits at boot camp. On the other hand, maybe you think of exclusive social cliques or of jocks flunking their classes. Whatever mental picture you have of student athletes, one thing is true: school sports—from lacrosse to gymnastics to basketball—play a major part in the lives of many young people. Before becoming involved yourself, it's helpful to think about the many aspects of athletics in the school community.

First of all, being part of a team is a great gift for any kid to have. The team atmosphere can make a student feel safe and secure in what is sometimes a very scary environment. When a student enters high school and is surrounded by hundreds of new faces, joining a sports team is a great way to meet people with similar interests. A team can provide an athlete with a very close circle of friends to rely on and look to for guidance. Teammates often feel great respect for and pride in one another. Being on a sports team can also provide a student with a sense of self-worth, the positive feeling that comes from being part of the team.

Second, playing on a sports team teaches students many skills that are of great use in school and in life. Having a coach is a great way to learn respect and obedience. Many teachers have commented that students who are involved in sports have a greater respect for them and are much easier to teach. Sports also teach kids self-discipline, holding them back from dangerous or self-destructive behavior. By engaging in illegal activities, such as drinking or doing drugs, a student athlete jeopardizes not only his or her health and school career but also his or her spot on a team. This is a strong incentive to avoid such activities. Participating in a sport also increases an athlete's awareness of bodily health, so the athlete is likely to think twice before putting his or her health at risk.

RUBRIC IN ACTION

1. Writer introduces the subject by asking the reader a question and giving a reason for the analysis.
   Other Options:
   - Tell an interesting anecdote.
   - Present a surprising fact.
2. States the main idea
3. Identifies and examines one positive element—athletic camaraderie
4. Identifies other positive elements—respect and self-discipline—and gives supporting examples

LANGUAGE SKILLS

Teaching the Lesson

Analyzing the Model

"Going the Distance"

D The essay analyzes the role of school sports in the lives of teenagers. Have students read the model and then discuss the Rubric in Action. Point out key words and phrases in the student model that correspond to the elements mentioned in the Rubric in Action.

1. Have students suggest alternate openings based on the other options listed.
   Possible Reponses: "I live across the street from school, and at five o'clock every Saturday morning I am awakened by the swim team, boarding the bus for their weekly meet."
3. Ask students to identify the topic sentence of this paragraph. *(First of all, being part of a team is a great gift for any kid to have.)* Then have them identify the supporting details of that statement.
   Possible Responses: Team atmosphere provides security for students; sports is a good way to meet people; teammates support one another; playing sports provides a sense of self-worth.
4. Ask students what conclusion can be drawn from this paragraph.
   Possible Responses: Discipline learned in one area of life can be brought into other areas.

MINI LESSON Patterns of Organization

ANALYZING TEXT STRUCTURE

Instruction Explain that logical structure is crucial to the success and effectiveness of a written text.

Activity Have students analyze the text structure of the student model by constructing an image such as a graphic organizer. Students' graphic should reflect how the writer has organized her piece. Students might first write a note about each paragraph to see how the paragraphs relate to one another and to the whole topic.

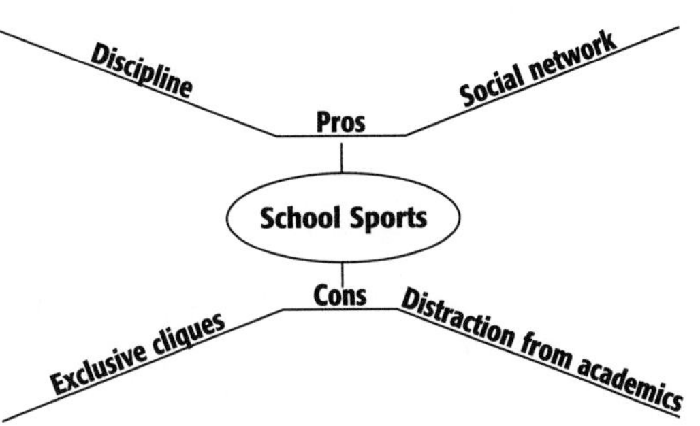

5, 6. Point out to students that this writer is discussing the pros and cons of school sports, which is a very common format for subject analysis.

7. Until this point, the writer has been analyzing the effects of sports on student athletes; now, he is broadening his analysis to look at sports and how it affects the entire school community.

8. Have students suggest an alternate ending based on one of the other options. Compare its effect with the strategy used in the model. **Possible Responses:** Will sports improve or worsen with time? *or* We would be much worse off without them.

School sports are not without their problems, however. Some student athletes do not have enough time to thoroughly concentrate on their schoolwork. Most high school coaches require athletes to practice every school day and on many weekends and holidays. The athletic contests usually take place on the weekends, sometimes every week. After a full day of school, an athlete must attend practice, which in most cases does not end until the middle of the evening. He or she then has to return home, only to spend the rest of the evening on schoolwork. After such a physically and mentally tiring day, many students do not have the energy or the drive to complete their schoolwork. They sometimes end up with grades that do not fully reflect their abilities. Poor grades can be damaging to the future of any student, especially the college-bound. Even for those who intend to play sports in college, a strong academic record remains the most important factor in college admissions.

❺ Uses a transition to turn to negative aspects of school sports

❻ Examines one negative element—distraction from schoolwork

Another negative aspect of school sports is the effect they have on non-athletes. I mentioned that sports teams provide student athletes with circles of friends. Sometimes, however, these social circles can turn into exclusive cliques, creating an unpleasant or even threatening environment for other students. The members of a football team, for example, may feel a need to act macho and put down people that aren't like them. Many people feel that they are excluded or looked down upon by such a group because they do not participate in the same activity. The social atmosphere created by a strong sports culture may actually affect students' confidence and inhibit the learning process. How can students be expected to concentrate in class when they are being ridiculed outside of class?

❼ Examines another negative element—sports' effect on a school's social environment

School sports are obviously a strong force in shaping the lives of both student athletes and nonathletes. They bring kids together socially while teaching them things like discipline and respect. On the other hand, sports may take time away from more important academic work, and they may create an environment that makes it hard for some students to learn. No matter what view you take on the subject, sports in school will be with us for a long time. Being aware of sports' various influences will help us ensure that they remain a positive experience for everyone.

❽ Concludes by showing how the reader can use the information in the analysis

Other Options:

- Leave the reader with a question to consider.
- Draw a general conclusion from specific information presented.

Writing Your Subject Analysis

❶ Prewriting

Begin your search for a topic by listing issues or problems that you would like to understand better. You might consider matters of local or national importance, such as school security or high-tech innovations. See the **Idea Bank** for more suggestions. After you have chosen your topic, follow the steps below.

Planning Your Analysis

1. **Explore the topic.** What do you already know about the topic? What do you want to know? Draft a list of questions on the subject. Consider what sources will be likely to provide you with answers to your questions—books, magazines, reference materials, experts, or on-line sources.
2. **Think about your purpose and audience.** Do you simply want to inform your readers, or do you want your analysis to persuade them to accept a conclusion? What will they already know about the subject? What background information will they require? What terms will you need to define? What tone will be most appropriate?
3. **Write a thesis statement.** What is the main point that you'd like to communicate? Write this idea in one or two sentences.
4. **Break the subject into parts.** Analysis is the breakdown of a subject into its parts. Will your analysis involve steps in a process, stages of development, elements of a problem, pros and cons, or other characteristics?

Now think about how to **organize** your analysis. Although every topic will require a slightly different approach, the steps below can help you develop a solid structure.

- Provide a **provocative introduction** to quickly attract readers' interest.
- **Identify your subject** and the purpose of your analysis in a sentence or short paragraph.
- **Describe the parts** that make up your subject.
- **Examine each part** in relationship to other parts or to the subject as a whole.

Incorporate these features into an **outline** for your essay.

❷ Drafting

Using your outline as a guide, write your first draft. Try to write freely, without worrying about details or mistakes. You can take care of those things later. As you get your ideas down on paper, you may find that you want to change your thesis statement, or you may decide to rearrange your ideas.

Ask Your Peer Reader

- What are the key points of my analysis? Which terms, if any, should I define?
- Describe the structure of my analysis.
- What could I change or add to make my analysis clearer?

IDEABank

1. Your Working Portfolio
Build on the **Writing Options** you completed earlier in this unit:
- **Subject Analysis,** p. 761

2. Periodical Search
Read through several magazines and newspapers to find a topic that interests you. Take notes on any interesting articles, jotting down ideas for your analysis.

3. Web Hunt
Look through reputable Web sites for news and information on political, scientific, artistic, or social topics that appeal to you. You might start with general Web sites, then pursue links to more-specific sites that look interesting.

Guiding Student Writing

Prewriting

Choosing a Subject

If, after reading the Idea Bank, students are having difficulty choosing their topics, suggest they try the following:

- Explore a museum site on the Internet. Choose a topic to analyze based on your online visit.
- Create a chart with headings that focus on various issues: Neighborhood, School, City, State, and National.
- Look through the local television guide for documentary or news shows on scientific or social topics of interest. Watch one of these shows and jot down ideas for an analysis.

Planning the Analysis

1. Have students brainstorm about a topic by using the "cubing" technique. Instruct them to picture their subject as a cube with each of the six sides representing a different activity: *describe, compare, associate, analyze, apply,* and *argue for or against.* Any side can lead to a topic suggestion.
3. Have students work in pairs to articulate their thesis statements. As they explain their main ideas to their partners, the listener should ask questions to help clarify the speaker's intentions.
4. Remind students that dividing a topic into subparts for analysis helps make the task manageable. The divisions should be consistent—parts based on the same principle of division—and complete—no important parts should be omitted.

Drafting

The model represents one approach to writing a subject analysis. Remind students that introductions need not be exactly this length nor take this approach. The heart of a subject analysis is the breakdown of the topic into its parts. Once they choose the parts of their analysis, students may find it useful to create an outline from which to work. By identifying their subtopics on a topic outline, they can systematically focus their paragraphs.

Revising

USING THE ACTIVE VOICE

In the second sentence, before revision, the verb, *has been commented,* is in the passive voice. The subject, *it,* is the receiver of the action. In the revised sentence the verb, *have commented,* is in the active voice; the subject is *teachers,* who are the performers of the action.

In the third sentence, before revision, the subject, *students,* is the receiver of the verb, *are taught,* which is in the passive voice. The performer of the action, *sports,* is the object of the preposition *by*. In the revision, *sports* is the subject, *teach* is the verb (in the active voice) and *kids,* the receiver of the action, is the direct object.

Editing and Proofreading

AVOIDING REDUNDANCY

Point out that in the revised sentence, *properly* means basically the same thing as *thoroughly*. The two words are redundant. Remind students to read their own work carefully for similarly redundant words or phrases when revising.

Reflecting

As students write their reflections, have them consider how breaking their subject into its parts gave them a more complete understanding of their topic. Have them review their conclusions and draw relevant questions for further study. Have them discuss how they might pursue their current topic further for other projects in other forms.

Option

Managing the Paper Load

Instead of commenting in writing on each student draft before final revisions are turned in, have students meet in groups of four to discuss one another's papers. Ask groups to formulate a brief written response for each paper. When a group has finished, join its discussion, using its written response as a touchstone for your response to each paper. Have students use this feedback and discussion to complete final revisions.

Need revising help?

Review the **Rubric,** p. 762

Consider **peer reader** comments

Check **Revision Guidelines,** p. R19

Confused by active and passive voice?

See the **Grammar Handbook,** p. R61

Publishing IDEAS

- Submit your work to your school or community newspaper.
- If you know of a local organization that is concerned with your topic, send it a copy of your analysis.

❸ Revising

TARGET SKILL ▶ USING THE ACTIVE VOICE Writing sentences in the active voice can help you create a lively and engaging style. While the passive voice is sometimes necessary, its overuse can make your writing clumsy and dull.

> Having a coach is a great way to learn respect and obedience. ~~It has been commented upon by many teachers~~ [Many teachers have commented] that students who are involved in sports have a greater respect for them and are much easier to teach. ~~Students are also taught self-discipline by sports and are held back~~ [Sports also teach kids self-discipline, holding them back] from dangerous or self-destructive behavior.

❹ Editing and Proofreading

TARGET SKILL ▶ AVOIDING REDUNDANCY Needless repetition will weaken your writing. When reviewing your work, keep an eye out for redundant words or phrases. These can easily slip into your work, especially during revision, when you might add a new word but forget to take out the word it was meant to replace.

> School sports are not without their problems, however. Some student athletes do not have enough time to thoroughly concentrate on their schoolwork ~~properly~~.

❺ Reflecting

FOR YOUR WORKING PORTFOLIO How did writing your analysis affect your thinking about your topic? How might you pursue the topic further? Attach your answers to your finished work. Save your analysis in your **Working Portfolio.**

Teaching Tip

When students are proofreading a draft for punctuation errors, encourage them to begin with the last sentence and work backwards through the paper. This enables them to focus strictly on the grammatical correctness of each sentence without becoming distracted by the content.

Standardized Test Practice **Revising & Editing**

Read this paragraph from the first draft of a subject analysis. The underlined sections may include the following kinds of errors:

- **inconsistent use of verb tenses**
- **redundant wording**
- **errors in parallelism**
- **misplaced modifiers**

For each underlined section, choose the revision that most improves the writing.

The werewolf appears in folklore around the world, in tales most prominently from Europe (1). The term *werewolf* comes from the Old English *werwulf*, which means "man-wolf." This creature is a person who turns into a wolf, usually at night and he often does this under a full moon (2). The tales vary; some werewolves have chosen their condition of being a werewolf (3), whereas others are bitten (4) by werewolves or transformed by magic spells. A werewolf usually preys on people. These people sometimes try to protect themselves (5) by bringing the werewolf back to human form or by injuring him (the injury will appear on the werewolf's human form, allowing others to identify him or her). In 16th-century France there were many reports of werewolves. People suspected of being werewolves, or *loups-garous*, were convicted and executed for being *loups-garous* (6).

1. A. in tales from most prominently Europe
   B. most prominently in tales from Europe
   C. in most prominently tales from Europe
   D. Correct as is
2. A. usually doing this at night and he often does it under a full moon
   B. usually at night and often doing this under a full moon
   C. usually at night and often under a full moon
   D. Correct as is
3. A. have chosen their condition of being a werewolf
   B. werewolves have chosen their werewolf-condition
   C. werewolves have chosen their condition
   D. Correct as is
4. A. whereas others were bitten
   B. whereas others have been bitten
   C. whereas others will be bitten
   D. Correct as is
5. A. tried to protect themselves
   B. have tried to protect themselves
   C. will try to protect themselves
   D. Correct as is
6. A. or *loups-garous,* were convicted and executed
   B. or *loups-garous,* were convicted and executed for being werewolves
   C. or *loups-garous,* were convicted and executed for this crime
   D. Correct as is

Standardized Test Practice

Suggest that students read the passage completely before they begin to correct the errors. Then demonstrate how students can eliminate incorrect choices for the first question.

A. This is not the best choice because it is awkward; *from* should not be separated from *Europe; most prominently* should be nearer to *appears,* which it modifies.

B. This is the best choice. *Most prominently* is closest to the independent clause, because it modifies the main verb, *appears.* It is correctly followed by *in tales,* which is modified by *from Europe.*

C. This is not the best choice; *most prominently* appears to modify *tales,* which is incorrect.

D. This is not the best choice. *Most prominently* is an adverb phrase modifying *appears;* its current location suggests that it modifies *in tales,* which is incorrect.

Answers:
1. B; **2.** C; **3.** C; **4.** B; **5.** D; **6.** A

TEST PRACTICE

MINI LESSON Grammar

MISPLACED MODIFIERS

Instruction Remind students that a misplaced modifier is a word or phrase that is placed so far away from the word it modifies that the meaning of the sentence is unclear or incorrect. Write the following sentence on the chalkboard:

Jo caught her skirt on a nail leaning out the window.

Point out that this sentence makes it unclear whether Jo or the nail is leaning out the window. Write this revision on the board.

Leaning out the window, Jo caught her skirt on a nail.

Now the modifier, *leaning out the window,* is next to *Jo,* the word it modifies.

Practice Have students correct the misplaced modifiers in the following sentences:

1. The customer sued the company angered by the fraud. *(Angered by the fraud, the customer sued the company.)*
2. Max sent a box to Carrie full of dishes. *(Max sent a box full of dishes to Carrie.)*

For more instruction and practice in modifier placement, use McDougal Littell's ***Language Network:***

- Grade 10, Chapter 9, "Using Modifiers"
- Grade 12, Chapter 7, "Using Modifiers"

Objectives
- read and understand analogies
- understand how analogies are used in literary language
- solve analogy problems that appear on standardized tests
- analyze the relationships between words to complete analogies

EXERCISE
Answers will vary; possible responses follow.
1. tree (classification)
2. cookbook (part to whole/location)
3. obnoxious (antonyms)
4. starvation (cause to effect)
5. judge (description)

Use **Unit Five Resource Book,** p. 28, for more practice.

Building Vocabulary

Understanding Analogies

Recognizing Relationships Good writers often help us notice connections between things, people, and experiences. Frequently, they do so by making comparisons. One type of comparison is called an **analogy**. In the following excerpt from Dante's *Inferno*, for example, the narrator asks a stranger whether he is the Roman poet Virgil.

> **"Then are you Virgil? Are you the font that pours So overwhelming a river of human speech?"**

In his inquiry, the narrator compares Virgil and his speech to a font (spring) and the water flowing from it.

As you can see, the analogy involves two pairs of things that are related to each other in the same way. A spring pours forth water, and a poet pours forth human speech.

Strategies for Building Vocabulary

Analogies are at the heart of literary metaphors, but they can also be used to test your ability to make logical connections. When used for this purpose, they are often presented as formulas. The analogy discussed above, for example, could be expressed as follows:

FONT : WATER :: poet : speech

To read this, you would say, "A font is to water as a poet is to speech."

❶ Determine Word Relationships The first step in analyzing an analogy is to determine the relationship between the first pair of words in it. What do you think is the relationship between these two words?

DOZE : SLEEP

When trying to complete an analogy, it's often helpful to formulate a sentence that expresses the relationship between the first pair of words. In this case you could say, "To doze is to sleep lightly." Now try to fit the following word pairs into the sentence "To x is to y lightly." Which pair makes the best sense?

(A) whisper : talk
(B) scorch : heat
(C) rotate : revolve
(D) sing : shout

Although the words in each pair are related in some way, pair A best parallels the relationship between *doze* and *sleep*: "To whisper is to talk lightly."

❷ Distinguish Different Types of Analogies Many standardized tests require you to complete analogies. This chart will help you to become familiar with some of the more common types of analogies.

Common Relationships in Analogies

Type	Example	Relationship
Degree of intensity	WHISPER : SHOUT	x is a less (or more) intense form of y.
Synonyms	MIRTH : HUMOR	x is the same as y.
Antonyms	RIDICULOUS : SERIOUS	x is the opposite of y.
Classification	GRASS : PLANT	x is a type of y.
Description	FUNNY : COMEDIAN	x is a characteristic of y.
Part to whole	ERASER : PENCIL	x is a part of y.
Cause to effect	POVERTY : HUNGER	x leads to y.
Worker to creation	CARPENTER : HOUSE	x is one who makes y.
Location	FLOWERS : GARDEN	x is found in y.

EXERCISE Complete each analogy, identifying the relationship that the word pairs exemplify.

1. SPANIARD : EUROPEAN :: oak : ________
2. DEFINITION : DICTIONARY :: recipe : ________
3. AMIABLE : HOSTILE :: charming : ________
4. FEAR : HESITATION :: hunger : ________
5. CREATIVE : MUSICIAN :: strict : ________

Grammar from Literature In both poetry and prose, writers vary the structure of their sentences. They do this for a number of reasons:

- to emphasize certain ideas
- to create poetic effects
- to add variety to paragraphs

One way to change a sentence's structure is to invert, or reverse the order of, the subject and the verb. In an inverted sentence, the verb precedes the subject.

INVERTED (verb: are; subject: the days)
"Husband, right long and wearisome are the days that you spend away from your home."
—Marie de France, "The Lay of the Were-Wolf"

SUBJECT FIRST (subject: the days; verb: are)
"Husband, the days that you spend away from your home are right long and wearisome."

Besides inverting the subject and the verb, you can also place other sentence parts in unusual places.

(adverbs: Right sweetly; subject: the knight; verb: thanked)
Right sweetly the knight thanked her for her grace, and pledged her faith and fealty.
—Marie de France, "The Lay of the Were-Wolf"

(prepositional phrase: from his mouth; subject: blood; verb: comes)
and from his mouth the bright blood comes leaping out,
—*The Song of Roland*

(direct object: guidance; subject: he; verb: gave)
What fine guidance he gave me, . . .
—Chrétien de Troyes, *Perceval*

As you look at your own writing, ask yourself these questions to see whether you should consider using unusual word orders:

- Are my sentences too similar in structure or length?
- Do I want to emphasize certain words or ideas?
- Would changing the order of sentence elements create an interesting rhythm?

Usage Tip When you place a verb before its subject, make sure you use a verb form that agrees with the subject. Plural subjects need plural verbs; singular subjects need singular verbs. This issue also arises in sentences beginning with *here* or *there*. In such sentences, the introductory word does not function as a subject.

INCORRECT
Deep in the woods lurk a great beast.

CORRECT
Deep in the woods lurks a great beast.

Punctuation Tip When you move more than one prepositional phrase to the beginning of a sentence, remember to put a comma after the last of the prepositional phrases.

(prep. phrase, prep. phrase)
On the last day of the festival, the werewolf died.

(prep. phrase, prep. phrase)
After all of their hard work, the farm still failed.

WRITING EXERCISE Change the structure of each sentence by moving the underlined words to a different position. (You may have to make other adjustments to the wording.) Remember to punctuate the revised sentence correctly.

1. A baron lived in Brittany <u>long ago.</u>
2. He had <u>a beautiful young wife.</u>
3. He left her alone <u>for three days out of every week.</u>
4. He wandered the countryside as a werewolf <u>when he was away from her.</u>
5. His young wife was <u>so curious</u> about his secret that she begged him to tell her where he went.

PROOFREADING EXERCISE Rewrite the sentences below, correcting any errors in punctuation or usage.

1. "There come a time each week when I must leave home and go into the woods," he told his wife.
2. "During this part of the week I run about as a werewolf."
3. "In that form I hunt for my food just as a wolf does."
4. "Beneath this hollow rock lie my clothing."
5. "There has been many times I have wished my life could be different."

LANGUAGE SKILLS

Sentence Crafting

Objectives

- vary sentence structure to express meanings and achieve desired effect
- revise drafts by rethinking content organization and style

WRITING EXERCISE

1. Long ago there lived a baron in Brittany.
2. A beautiful young wife had he.
3. For three days out of every week he left her alone.
4. When he was away from her, he wandered the countryside as a werewolf.
5. So curious about his secret was his young wife that she begged him to tell her where he went.

PROOFREADING EXERCISE

1. "There comes a time each week when I must leave home and go into the woods," he told his wife.
2. "During this part of the week, I run about as a werewolf."
3. "In that form I hunt for my food just as a wolf does." OR "In that form I hunt for my food, just as a wolf does."
4. "Beneath this hollow rock lies my clothing."
5. "There have been many times I have wished my life could be different."

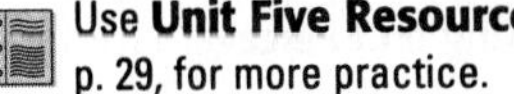

Use **Unit Five Resource Book,** p. 29, for more practice.

MINI LESSON **Grammar**

USING COMMAS

Instruction Commas serve many functions. Among other things, they should be used

- to set off a personal title or business abbreviation;
- when writing a date, between the day of the month and the year (and after the year in a date within a sentence); and
- to set off a direct quotation from the rest of a sentence.

Practice Have students add commas where appropriate to the following sentences:

1. I said "We have too much work to do." (*after* said)
2. Chris Lagos president of the company decided to hire four new employees. (*after* Lagos *and* company)
3. "That's a good idea" I said. (*after* idea)
4. The new people will start on August 5 2004 at the building on Main Street. (*after* 5 *and* 2004)
5. Octavio Cruz the director of personnel will welcome them. (*after* Cruz *and* personnel)

For more instruction and practice with using commas, use McDougal Littell's ***Language Network:***

- Grade 10, Chapter 11, "Punctuation"
- Grade 12, Chapter 9, "End Marks and Commas"

Objectives
- reflect on and assess understanding of medieval literature
- identify the values of the main characters in the selections
- review romance as a literary genre and identify mysterious events in romantic plots
- understand important names and terms associated with medieval culture
- assess and build portfolios
- set a reading goal to increase understanding of medieval literature

Reflecting on the Literature
The Literature of Honor Students may state that Roland values honor and courage; Perceval, the chivalric code; the main character in "The Lay of the Were-Wolf," love and justice; Dante in the excerpts from the *Inferno*, guidance and compassion.

Reviewing Literary Concepts
Romance If necessary, have students study the explanation of romance on pages 709 and 722. Students may cite the following events:

–from "Perceval":
- the sudden appearance of the Fisher King's castle
- the carrying of the lance and the grail from chamber to chamber in the castle
- Perceval's cousin's revelations about the Fisher King and Perceval's mistake

–from "The Lay of the Were-Wolf":
- the nobleman's transformation into a were-wolf
- the were-wolf's attacks on his former wife and her new husband
- the were-wolf's transformation into human form after putting on his former clothes

These events are essential to the plot.

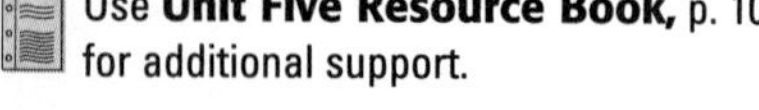
Use **Unit Five Resource Book,** p. 10, for additional support.

Building Your Portfolio
Students will use their Presentation Portfolios to file what they consider their highest quality work in their Working Portfolios.

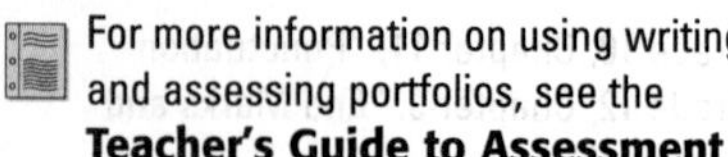
For more information on using writing and assessing portfolios, see the **Teacher's Guide to Assessment and Portfolio Use,** pp. 53–74.

Part Assessment
To assess skills and concepts taught in this unit part, use **Formal Assessment Book,** pp. 115–116.

Reflect and Assess

What did you learn about the Middle Ages from reading the selections in Unit Five, Part 1? Why do you think medieval literature is still valued and enjoyed? Use the following options to help you explore what you have learned.

Detail of French manuscript illustration of warfare in the Middle Ages—the siege of a fortified town (1250). The Granger Collection, New York.

Reflecting on the Literature

The Literature of Honor The literature of the Middle Ages often paints idealized portraits of aristocratic society. In many of the tales, the main characters are noble figures, inspired by the highest motives. Think about the selections you've read, and identify the main character in each one. What values does each character hold dear?

Reviewing Literary Concepts

Romance In this part of the book, you learned about a type of imaginative story known as a **romance.** In a romance, some of the events described are far removed from those of ordinary life. Recall the plots of the excerpt from *Perceval: The Story of the Grail* and "The Lay of the Were-Wolf." What mysterious events in these stories impressed you the most? How important are these events to the plot of the story?

Self ASSESSMENT

READER'S NOTEBOOK
In this part you learned the following names and terms as you read the selections. Write a sentence to describe or define each one. If you have trouble recalling a name or a term, review the lesson where it is introduced.

Charlemagne	courtly love
epic hero	lais
the Crusades	allegory
feudalism	*Divine Comedy*
romances	quests
Arthurian legend	Holy Grail
chivalry	

Building Your Portfolio

Writing Workshop and Writing Options Look back at the subject analysis you wrote for the Writing Workshop on page 762 and at the writing options you completed for the Author Study on Dante Alighieri. Which writing assignment did you find most challenging? Add that assignment to your **Presentation Portfolio**, along with a cover note explaining your choice.

Setting GOALS

The stories of King Arthur and his knights have greatly influenced western culture and are still popular today. Look back at the titles of books about King Arthur listed in the Connect to Today on page 723. Choose one of these books to read.

Assessment Self Assessment

If students need to review any of the key names or terms presented in Part 1, direct them to the pages indicated below:

Charlemagne (pages 688, 689, 692, 696, 697, and 707)
epic hero (pages 697 and 707)
the Crusades (pages 686, 688, 693, 696, and 733)
feudalism (pages 686 and 690)
romances (pages 690, 708, 709, 722, and 724)
Arthurian legend (pages 693, 708, and 723)
chivalry (pages 686, 694, and 709)
courtly love (page 694)
lais (page 724)
allegory (pages 736 and 759)
quests (pages 709 and 723)
Holy Grail (pages 709, 715, and 722)

Extend Your *Reading*

LITERATURE CONNECTIONS

The Canterbury Tales: Selected Works

GEOFFREY CHAUCER

People from different classes and walks of life set forth on a pilgrimage to the shrine of Thomas à Becket in Canterbury, England. Along the way, they tell tales—tales that vividly portray life in the Middle Ages. This rich sample contains the complete Prologue and seven of the tales.

Here are just a few of the related readings that accompany *The Canterbury Tales:*

***from* The Life and Times of Chaucer**
BY JOHN GARDNER

Laüstic (The Nightingale)
BY MARIE DE FRANCE

***from* The Autobiography of Malcolm X**
BY MALCOLM X

A Distant Mirror: The Calamitous 14th Century

BARBARA W. TUCHMAN

In this acclaimed work, the author explores the stark contrasts of life in the 14th century. It was a splendid era of castles, cathedrals, and chivalry. It was also a tortured century racked with war and plague. Through these pages gallops the knight, a figure of bravery and folly.

And Even *More* . . .

Books

Joan of Arc MARY GORDON
In this brief biography, the author, a best-selling novelist, draws upon her understanding of character and eye for detail. She probes the mystery of the peasant girl who led the armies of France to glory, only to die a terrible death at the stake.

The Medieval Reader NORMAN F. CANTOR, ED.
This rich collection of almost 100 first-hand accounts of medieval life includes letters, essays, and documents as well as excerpts from literary works. Among the writers represented are prominent women such as Christine de Pisan and Hildegard von Bingen.

Other Media

Becket
This film traces the friendship and later the feud between Henry II of England and Thomas à Becket, the Archbishop of Canterbury. Richard Burton, Peter O'Toole, and Sir John Gielgud star. 151 minutes. Zenger Media. (VIDEOCASSETTE)

The Medieval World

PHILIP STEELE

This account, easy-to-read and richly illustrated, provides a good introduction to the age of chivalry. It gives the reader an inside look at castle life, providing details about topics such as food and drink, and hunting and hawking.

More Recommendations for Your Students

Difficulty Level: Easy

Harper, James. *Revelations: The Medieval World* (NY: Holt, 1995). This history covers four aspects of medieval life: castles, commerce, cathedrals, and warfare.

Skurzynski, Gloria. *Spider's Voice* (NY: Atheneum, 1999). The main character of this novel becomes involved in the ill-fated love affair between Eloise and Abelard in 12th-century France.

Sutcliffe, Rosemary. *The Shining Company* (NY: Farrar, Straus and Giroux, 1990). Written by the foremost writer of historical fiction for young adults, this novel is based on *The Gododdin,* the earliest surviving poem from present-day Scotland.

Difficulty Level: Average

Hanawalt, Barbara. *The Middle Ages: An Illustrated History* (NY: Oxford University Press, 1998). In this study, an acclaimed historian explores the history and culture of the European Middle Ages.

Morris, Gerald. *The Squire, His Knight, and His Lady* (Boston: Houghton Mifflin, 1998). This novel is an imaginative retelling of the medieval poem "Sir Gawain and the Green Knight."

Willis, Connie. *Doomsday Book* (NY: Bantam Books, 1992). The heroine of this science fiction novel visits Oxford, England, in 1348, as the Black Death ravages the country.

Difficulty Level: Challenging

Cahill, Thomas. *How the Irish Saved Civilization: The Untold Story of Ireland's Heroic Role from the Fall of Rome to the Rise of Medieval Europe* (NY: Doubleday, 1995). This popular history tells of the Irish monks and scribes who copied by hand the manuscripts of classical Greek and Roman writers, preserving their works and keeping learning alive during the Dark Ages.

Hugo, Victor. *The Hunchback of Notre Dame* (NY: Dodd Mead, 1928). In this classic novel set in medieval Paris, a deformed hunchback falls hopelessly in love with a beautiful gypsy girl.

Unit Five, Part 2, provides an overview of the Renaissance and Enlightenment and a rich sample of literature from these periods, including stories and poems by Boccaccio, Petrarch, and Shakespeare, and excerpts from longer works by Cervantes and Voltaire. The selections focus on the literature of Western Europe. Although there were thriving literary traditions in other regions of the world, European nations shared a common culture that had its roots in the classical heritage of Ancient Greece and Rome.

World Art and Cultures Transparencies

AT36 *The Last Supper*
AT37 *Mona Lisa*
AT38 *Wedding Portrait*
AT41 *The Tower of Belem*
AT43 *Meeting of Cortes and Montezuma*
AT45 *Banquet of the Officers of Haarlem's Civic Guard, Saint George Company*
AT48 *The Astronomer*
AT49 *The Pottery-Mender*
AT50 *Portrait of Marie Antoinette with Her Children*

You may use the listed transparencies to acquaint students with European art from the Renaissance and Enlightenment.

PART 2 Human Possibility

Literature of the Renaissance and Enlightenment

Why It Matters

The era between 1300 and 1798 produced a revolution in thought. The Renaissance, which means "rebirth" in French, ushered in a return to the classical learning of ancient Greece and Rome and a flowering of the arts. Its focus on human potential led to the Enlightenment, or Age of Reason. New ideas about government, science, and the arts paved the way for the modern world.

For Links to the Renaissance and Enlightenment, click on:

HUMANITIES
CLASSZONE.COM

Europe in 1648

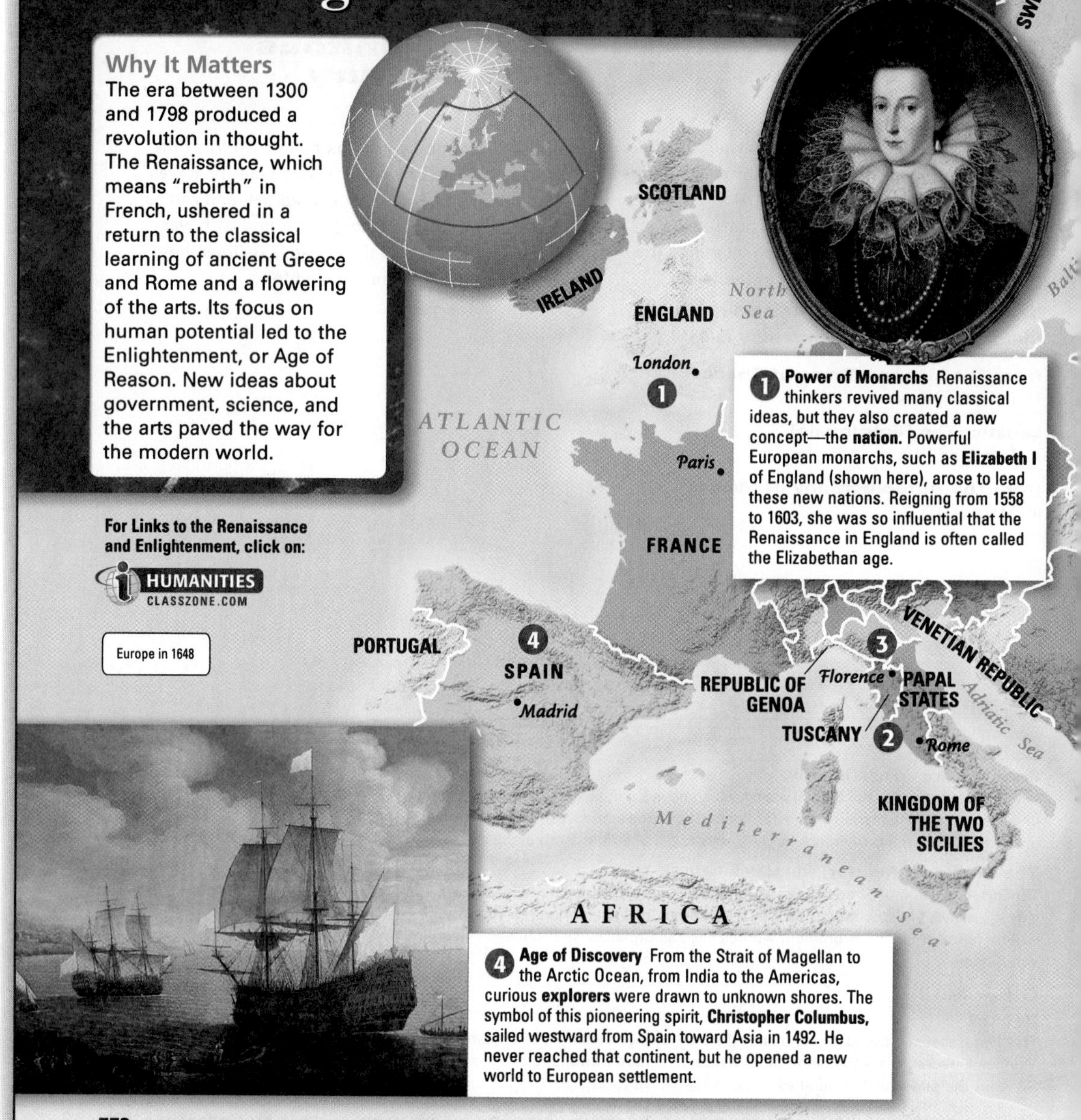

1 Power of Monarchs Renaissance thinkers revived many classical ideas, but they also created a new concept—the **nation.** Powerful European monarchs, such as **Elizabeth I** of England (shown here), arose to lead these new nations. Reigning from 1558 to 1603, she was so influential that the Renaissance in England is often called the Elizabethan age.

4 Age of Discovery From the Strait of Magellan to the Arctic Ocean, from India to the Americas, curious **explorers** were drawn to unknown shores. The symbol of this pioneering spirit, **Christopher Columbus,** sailed westward from Spain toward Asia in 1492. He never reached that continent, but he opened a new world to European settlement.

772 UNIT FIVE PART 2: LITERATURE OF THE RENAISSANCE AND ENLIGHTENMENT

MINI LESSON Using the Map

Have students study the map on pages 772–773 and then answer questions such as the following:

- In which direction did the Spanish fleet sail when it tried to invade England? *(north)*
- Which city is closer to Paris—London or Florence? *(London)*
- Which body of water separates Europe from Africa? *(the Mediterranean)*
- Which two European countries are located on the same island? *(England and Scotland)*

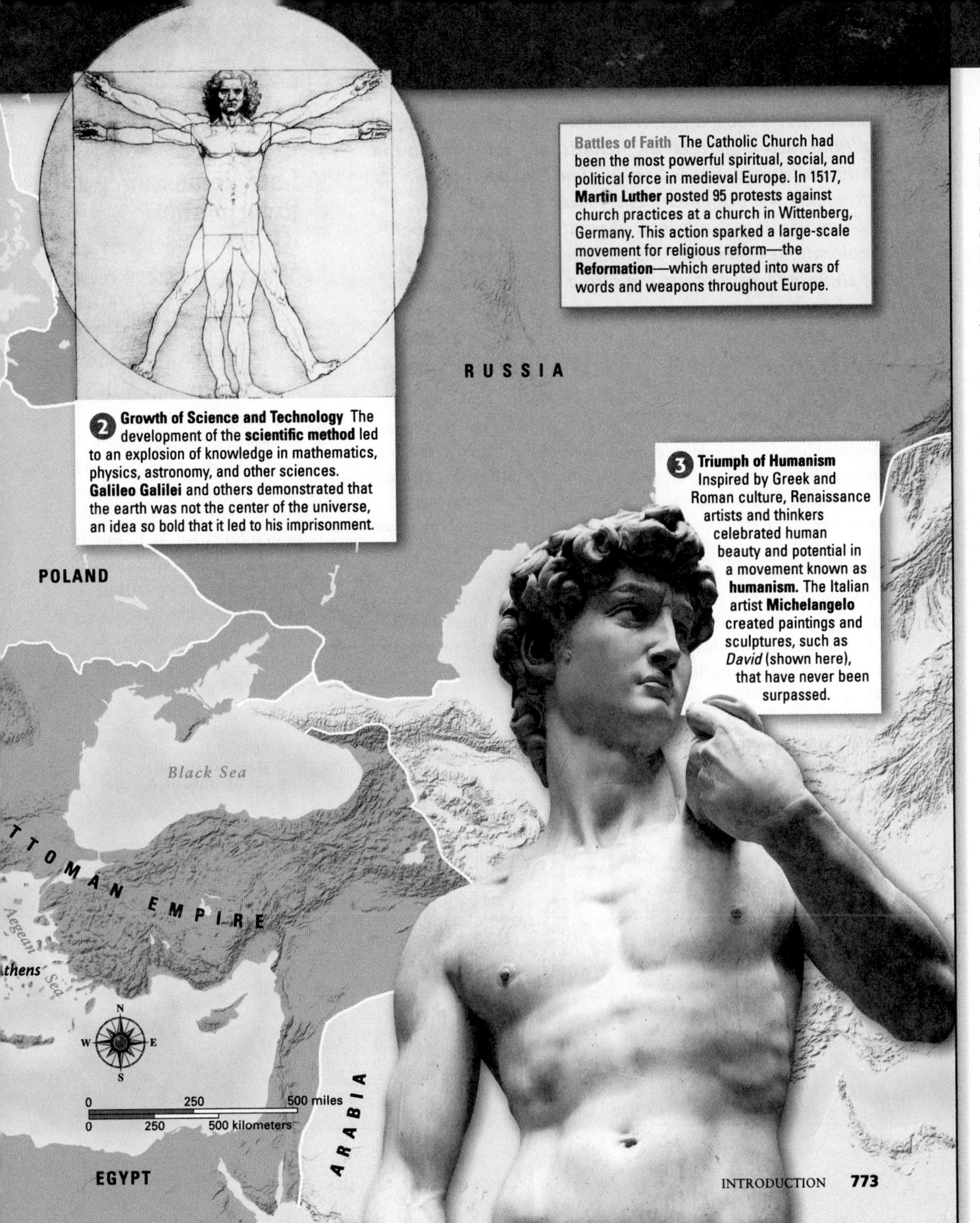

Battles of Faith The Catholic Church had been the most powerful spiritual, social, and political force in medieval Europe. In 1517, **Martin Luther** posted 95 protests against church practices at a church in Wittenberg, Germany. This action sparked a large-scale movement for religious reform—the **Reformation**—which erupted into wars of words and weapons throughout Europe.

2 **Growth of Science and Technology** The development of the **scientific method** led to an explosion of knowledge in mathematics, physics, astronomy, and other sciences. **Galileo Galilei** and others demonstrated that the earth was not the center of the universe, an idea so bold that it led to his imprisonment.

3 **Triumph of Humanism** Inspired by Greek and Roman culture, Renaissance artists and thinkers celebrated human beauty and potential in a movement known as **humanism.** The Italian artist **Michelangelo** created paintings and sculptures, such as *David* (shown here), that have never been surpassed.

READING FOR INFORMATION

Reading Skills and Strategies
PREVIEWING

Give students a few moments to look over this introduction. It provides background information about the Renaissance and Enlightenment, giving students a context for the literature they will read in this part.

Reading Skills and Strategies
USING A KEY

Make sure students are aware of the types of visual information provided on pages 772 and 773: the map with its distance scale, the images, and the captions. On the distance scale, 1 and 11/16 inches represents 500 miles. Point out that the outlined area in the globe near the upper-left corner shows the extent of the territory represented on the map. Tell students that some of the European countries' boundaries and political names have changed over the centuries. The numbers in red circles that precede the picture captions tie their information to specific locations on the map.

READING FOR INFORMATION
Reading Skills and Strategies
CLARIFYING

Tell students that the Renaissance is divided into three periods, each represented by a different color on the key at the bottom. Explain that these divisions mainly apply to Italy; the Renaissance developed later in other European nations. Point out that the Late Renaissance and the Reformation are overlapping periods. Tell students to use the text headings as a guide to the content and to note the boldfaced terms. Point out that the feature **History to Literature** lists historical events on the left and corresponding literary events on the right.

Biographical Note

A **Martin Luther** Martin Luther (1483–1546) was one of the most influential figures in the history of religion. His study of the Bible and his observation of corruption when he visited Rome led him to reject some traditional beliefs and practices of the Roman Catholic Church. In 1517, he expressed his opposition in 95 theses, which he posted on the door of a church in the German town of Wittenberg. Copies of the document soon spread throughout Europe. Church officials fiercely criticized Luther, but many clergy and laymen were attracted to his ideas. When he was excommunicated in 1521 because he refused to recant, Luther gained the protection of German princes. In addition to founding the denomination known as Lutheranism, Martin Luther laid the groundwork for other Protestant denominations.

Historical Highlights

In the early 1300s, a powerful mix of social, political, and cultural factors sparked the Renaissance, which began in Italy and spread across Europe. The Renaissance and its aftermath, the Enlightenment, touched all aspects of human life. It was a period of great progress, from bold explorations of the heavens and the earth to the creation of stunning works of art, yet also a time of violence and poverty for many.

Early Renaissance

1300–1495

Several conditions in early-14th-century Italy made it fertile ground for a cultural revolution: (1) Cities grew and became powerful. (2) Extensive trade promoted a lively exchange of ideas. (3) A successful merchant class had the time and money to support art and literature. (4) The heritage of ancient Greece and Rome inspired artists and thinkers.

Philosophers and scholars who knew the ancient Latin and Greek masters often challenged traditional ways of thinking. New ideas spread like wildfire from city to city.

Along with the factors that encouraged change, there was a powerful force opposing it—the Catholic Church. The church expected its members to be more concerned with heavenly than with worldly matters.

High Renaissance

1495–1530

When the Renaissance was at its height in Italy, citizens of Florence and Rome viewed their cities as rivals of ancient Athens. Princes, church leaders, and men of fortune dominated politics. These men sponsored artists such as **Michelangelo, Leonardo da Vinci,** and **Raphael,** who gave people new ways of looking at themselves.

Late Renaissance and Reformation

1530–1600

As the printing press was helping to spread literacy and new ideas, impatience with church corruption was triggering a movement for religious reform—the **Reformation.** Beginning with the public protest of a German monk named **Martin Luther** in 1517, the movement spread across Europe. For decades, **Protestants**—led by Luther in Germany, **John Calvin** in France, and **Henry VIII** in England—fought Catholics. As the pope's power declined, nations such as England and Spain took center stage. A

Pope Julius II restored Rome to its old splendor. Michelangelo helped to design St. Peter's Basilica.

EARLY RENAISSANCE | HIGH RENAISSANCE

1300 | 1495 | 1520

This painting of France's King Louis XIV shows his splendor and pride.

Age of Kings

1600–1700

Convinced that they had a divine right to rule, monarchs sought and achieved absolute power. **Philip II** of Spain created a wealthy empire that stretched from Africa to the New World. **Louis XIV** made France the most powerful nation in Europe, but his lavish lifestyle and continual wars led to great suffering among his people. In Russia, **Peter the Great** turned what had been an isolated territory into a power competitive with other European nations.

In England, the government, after a bloodless revolution, limited the power of the monarch. England created a **constitutional monarchy,** a form of government still used today.

Age of Enlightenment

1700–1789

During the Enlightenment, human concerns, from government to personal happiness, became subjects of wide-reaching philosophical thought. One English political thinker, **Thomas Hobbes,** concluded that a strong government was needed to control people's basically evil nature. His countryman **John Locke,** on the other hand, found people to be essentially good and able to govern themselves. **Mary Wollstonecraft** argued that women had as much potential as men. In France, thinkers such as **Voltaire, Jean Jacques Rousseau,** and **Baron de Montesquieu** challenged long-held assumptions about the privileges of the upper class, the divine right of kings, and the authority of the church. Toward the end of the era, a new belief in the rights of the individual inspired revolutions in America and France and helped change the course of Western civilization.

History to Literature

EVENT IN HISTORY	EVENT IN LITERATURE
Exploration around the world expands Europe's horizons during the 1400s and 1500s.	In 1516, Thomas More publishes *Utopia,* a fictional account of a perfect society in the New World.
Puritan religious reformers seek power and influence in England in the late 1500s.	Shakespeare satirizes Puritans around 1600 in *Twelfth Night.*
In 1749, Voltaire serves as adviser to the Prussian king Frederick the Great, an ambitious reformer.	In 1578, Voltaire satirizes people who seek to create a perfect society in *Candide.*

LATE RENAISSANCE AND REFORMATION	AGE OF KINGS	AGE OF ENLIGHTENMENT	
	1600	1700	1800

Historical Note

B Divine Right In some European countries, the power of the monarch was traditionally limited by nobles. The pope also played an important political role in countries where Roman Catholicism was the established religion. During the 17th century, some kings claimed that they received the right to rule directly from God and therefore should have no limitations on their authority. This doctrine of divine right was especially controversial in England, where the rights of nobles had been established since the signing of the Magna Carta in 1215.

READING FOR INFORMATION
Reading Skills and Strategies
CLASSIFYING

Point out to students that the section **People and Society** is divided into five categories, each of which describes a social group in the Renaissance and Enlightenment: Aristocrats, Clergy, Soldiers, the Middle Class, and Peasants and Farmers. Make sure students understand that during these periods, the majority of people fell into the last category. The feature **Women in the Renaissance and Enlightenment** describes the conditions that most women faced and identifies several women who led exceptional lives. Tell students to pause after reading about each social group and to think about the group's distinctive features.

Historical Note

A **The Medici** For much of the Renaissance, Florence was under the control of the Medici, a family of bankers and merchants. At first they governed Florence by determining who held political office. Eventually they became hereditary rulers. The Medici were great patrons of the arts and letters. They commissioned works from some of the most famous Renaissance artists, including Sandro Botticelli, Leonardo da Vinci, and Michelangelo. Two of the Medici became popes and were able to extend the family tradition of artistic patronage at the Vatican.

People and Society

The revolution in ways of thinking about the world that took place in the Renaissance and Enlightenment eventually produced revolutionary changes in people's day-to-day lives. The rigid class distinctions of feudalism gradually gave way to new roles, rights, and responsibilities.

Lorenzo de Medici (1449–1492) was a ruler of Florence.

Aristocrats

Membership in the aristocracy in this period was not simply a matter of birth. Merchants who made their own fortunes could be awarded titles and enjoy all the accompanying power. Many bankers and merchants, like the A powerful **Medici** family of Florence, used their riches to promote culture rather than just their own welfare. Without their influence, the great artist **Michelangelo** might have remained a poor stonecutter.

Clergy

Although the clergy had wielded much power during the Middle Ages, their role began to change as the winds of reform gathered force. Some clergymen, such as **Martin Luther** in Germany, brought about social change as they broke from the church. Others, such as the Dutch scholar **Desiderius Erasmus,** criticized the church from within. Still others, such as **Cardinal Richelieu** in France, aligned themselves with the established powers. All, however, were forced to reexamine their roles in a changing world.

Martin Luther in 1533

Soldiers

The life of a soldier in the Renaissance and Enlightenment, as in other periods of history, was hard and often short. Although the Republic of Venice was employing 30,000 soldiers by 1509, the occupation was no longer a passport to wealth and influence, as it had been in the Middle Ages. The growth of professional armies—groups of soldiers who would work for the highest bidder—made the work less prestigious. As power shifted from the battlefield to the marketplace and the bank vault, making war became just another dangerous job.

The Middle Class

A business boom in the 16th century created not only a merchant aristocracy but also a thriving middle class of people who made their livings in a variety of occupations. Crafts, shopkeeping, manufacturing, banking, and trade offered ways for people to earn more money with less backbreaking effort than working the land. For the first time, even art and literature could provide their practitioners a living wage.

MINI LESSON Interpreting the Text

Have students read pages 776 and 777 and then answer questions such as the following:

- What were two ways one could become part of the aristocracy? *(One could be born into it or acquire titles through great wealth.)*
- How did the professionalization of warfare affect soldiers? *(Soldiers generally lost prestige and power.)*
- What social class would a shopkeeper have belonged to? *(the middle class)*
- Which social class had the greatest number of people? *(peasants and farmers)*
- Why were Elizabeth I and Catherine the Great highly unusual for women of their time? *(They ruled nations at a time when few women had any voice in politics.)*

Peasants and Farmers

Despite the social and economic changes during the Renaissance and Enlightenment, four out of every five people were still farmers. These peasants labored long hours on land they didn't own for the privilege of paying taxes to their lords. Even death was no release, since half their money often went to their masters when they died. Although some peasants became tenant farmers, laborers, or artisans, they seldom could escape the cycle of hard work and hardship that kept them in poverty.

Women in the Renaissance and Enlightenment

While powerful monarchs such as England's **Elizabeth I** and Russia's **Catherine the Great** were shaping history and Spain's **Teresa of Avila** was helping to reform the Catholic Church, the majority of women led less remarkable lives. Often working in the fields, women seldom had any voice in their own lives, let alone in religion, philosophy, or politics. B

One notable woman who devoted her life to the advancement of equality between the sexes was **Mary Wollstonecraft** (1759–1797). A self-taught British citizen, Wollstonecraft argued that the rights of man must be extended to include the rights of women. She urged that women be educated in the same manner as men to achieve their full potential.

Mary Wollstonecraft

This painting by an unknown 16th-century artist shows a marketplace in Antwerp, a city in what is now Belgium.

Biographical Note

B Elizabeth I Queen Elizabeth I (1533–1603) ruled England from 1558 to 1603. Only 25 when she ascended the throne, she guided England in its rise as a major European power and skillfully handled the country's religious, political, and economic problems. Elizabeth never married, probably because she did not want to give up her authority to a husband. She became known as the Virgin Queen (the colony of Virginia was named in her honor). Although there was a widespread belief that women were unfit to rule, Elizabeth overcame her subjects' doubts through hard work, intelligence, and brilliant rhetoric. The queen projected a public image that combined strength with femininity. On the eve of an attempted Spanish invasion, she said to her troops: "I know I have the body of a weak and feeble woman, but I have the heart and stomach of a king; and a King of England too." Elizabeth's devotion to politics did not keep her from enjoying the many pleasures available at court. She was especially fond of music, dancing, theater, and poetry. English literature and art flourished during her reign.

READING FOR INFORMATION
Reading Skills and Strategies
SUMMARIZING
Tell students that the **Arts and Culture** section describes some of the remarkable achievements of the Renaissance and Enlightenment. Have students use the heading of each section as a clue to its content. After students have read a section, tell them to briefly summarize it, listing the key points.

Biographical Note
A **Galileo Galilei** Galileo Galilei (1564–1642) was an Italian astronomer and mathematician. Early in his career, he did pioneering research on motion. One of his experiments reportedly involved dropping objects from the Leaning Tower of Pisa. In 1609, Galileo became the first person to use the newly invented telescope for astronomical observation. His discoveries led him to accept Copernicus's theory that the planets in our solar system revolve around the sun. This theory was highly controversial because it conflicted with the Bible's description of a stationary Earth. After Galileo published a book about planetary motion in 1632, the Catholic Church condemned him for heresy and banned his books. He spent the rest of his years living under house arrest. However, Galileo continued to perform scientific research, and his books were published outside Italy, where they had a great influence on scholars. The Catholic Church waited until 1992 before it formally cleared Galileo of wrongdoing.

Arts and Culture

The period of renewed interest in classical ideas and culture was also marked by a spirit of exploration and expansion of human horizons. This rebirth led to radically new approaches and achievements in almost every artistic and cultural activity.

Sir Isaac Newton

Philosophy and Science

The development of the scientific method led to a totally new way of thinking about the natural world. The Polish scientist Nicolaus Copernicus challenged perhaps the most basic idea about the universe—that the earth was at its center. His sun-centered model was later proved true by the German astronomer Johannes Kepler. The Italian Galileo Galilei made observations of A the planets that also supported Copernicus's theory. In the global spirit of the Renaissance, the English scientist Isaac Newton later combined these discoveries into a unified set of laws describing motion. During the Enlightenment, also known as the Age of Reason, philosophers shone the light of reason on everything from individual rights to government and social responsibilities.

Enlightenment Thinkers at a Glance

Person	Idea	Impact
Jean Jacques Rousseau (1712–1778)	"Man is born free and everywhere he is in chains."	Democratic governments worldwide are based on the consent of the governed.
Baron de Montesquieu (1689–1755)	"Power should be a check to power."	Constitutions in France, the United States, and Latin America guarantee separation of powers.
Voltaire (1694–1778)	"Each individual [has] his natural rights. . . ."	Bills of rights in England, France, and the United States guarantee individual freedoms.

Literature

Writers increasingly relied on their native languages, such as English, Spanish, and Italian, instead of the Latin favored by the Middle Ages to express their ideas. A spirit of experimentation greatly influenced the literature of the era.

Tales written by the Italian Giovanni Boccaccio in the 14th century paved the way for the new genre of the **novel.** This literary form was refined by the 16th-century French writer François Rabelais, the 17th-century Spaniard Miguel de Cervantes, and the 18th-century Englishmen Daniel Defoe and Henry Fielding.

Another genre, **lyric poetry,** was practiced by writers throughout Europe, from Francesco Petrarch in Italy to Pierre de Ronsard in France to William Shakespeare in England.

Dramatists such as Shakespeare and Oliver Goldsmith in England, Molière and Jean Racine in France, and Lope de Vega in Spain provided popular entertainment to an increasingly literate public.

The literature of the late 17th and 18th centuries is sometimes called **neoclassical** because it reflects the order and restraint that marked the literature of ancient Rome.

In this painting, the Dutch artist Jan Vermeer (1632–1675) shows himself at work.

Painting, Sculpture, and Architecture

The new way of looking at the world that developed in the Renaissance drastically affected the way visual artists portrayed it. They devised new techniques based on classical Greek and Roman ideals of proportion. Leonardo da Vinci and Michelangelo did anatomical studies that helped artists create realistic figures. The use of perspective, a technique in which lines converge at a vanishing point, gave an illusion of depth and distance in the paintings of the Italians Raphael and Titian, the Dutchman Rembrandt, and the German Albrecht Dürer. As sculptors and architects, da Vinci, Donatello, and Michelangelo brought technical mastery of proportion to near perfection.

B

Music

Music also experienced a rebirth in three distinct periods—Renaissance, baroque, and classical. In the **Renaissance** period (1450–1600), sacred music was joined by new forms reflecting national tastes. New types of instrumental music also developed, often for the lute.

Baroque music (1600–1750) showed experimentation, complex melodies, and dance rhythms. Prominent composers included Johann Sebastian Bach and Antonio Vivaldi. Drama and music were blended in **opera,** a new form.

In the **classical** period (1750–1825), composers made use of tightly structured rhythms and melodies. Franz Joseph Haydn and Wolfgang Amadeus Mozart were two of the leading composers; the leading instrument was the piano.

Turning Points in Literature

The Printing Press

Although the Chinese had invented movable type around 1045, it didn't come into common use until Johann Gutenberg (1400?–1468?) recreated it in Germany four centuries later. With this invention, hundreds of identical copies could be produced quickly and cheaply; works no longer had to be copied by hand, as scribes had done for centuries. Mass-produced books, newspapers, and magazines dealt with both religious and secular topics.

Biographical Note

B **Leonardo da Vinci** Leonardo da Vinci (1452–1519) was the quintessential Renaissance man, an extraordinary artist who became deeply involved in many fields of science. He is best known for two of his masterpieces, *The Last Supper* and the *Mona Lisa.* The latter is probably the most famous painting in the world. When he wasn't creating artworks for patrons, Leonardo did research in anatomy, biology, mathematics, physics, and geology. In addition, he was a superb engineer who foresaw the possibility of mechanical flight. Leonardo recorded his investigations in notebooks using a right-to-left script that can be read with a mirror. The beautiful drawings in these notebooks reveal that for Leonardo, science and art were not separate endeavors but complementary ways of exploring the world.

MINI LESSON Interpreting the Text

Have students read pages 778 and 779 and then answer questions such as the following:

- What did Copernicus conclude about the relationship between the earth and the sun. *(The earth revolves around the sun.)*
- What development made a writer's nationality more important to his or her work? *(Writers increasingly wrote in their native languages instead of Latin.)*
- What scientific practice helped visual artists create realistic portrayals of the human body? *(They studied anatomy.)*
- What musical form was most influenced by literature? *(opera)*
- Why did the printing press increase literacy in Europe? *(More people had access to books because they were cheaper and more plentiful.)*

READING FOR INFORMATION

Reading Skills and Strategies

SEQUENCING

This time line shows major dates and events in European literature, European history, and world history from the Renaissance through the Enlightenment. The dates and events follow in sequence, moving down each column and from left to right. Help students understand that during the 500 years covered on the time line, Europe grew in power due to technological, scientific, and economic innovation as well as military conquest. Make sure students realize that China, the Ottoman Empire, and other great powers were also flourishing during this time span, and that Europe was enriched by contact with different cultures. Also make sure students understand the abbreviations *c.* and A.D. Have them examine the key at the top, which visually depicts the duration of the Renaissance and Enlightenment.

Historical Note

A Bubonic Plague Bubonic plague, or "the Black Death," struck Europe in 1347. Over the next few years, it killed about a third of Europe's population. In *The Decameron,* Boccaccio gives a sense of how the plague devastated Florence: "when all the graves were full, huge trenches were dug in all of the cemeteries of the churches and into them the new arrivals were dumped by the hundreds." Bubonic plague is spread by fleas that have bitten infected rodents. In humans, it causes high fever, vomiting, delirium, and other severe symptoms. As the disease spreads, the body's lymph nodes swell and become very painful. Unless treated, bubonic plague kills most of its victims within a few days.

EVENTS IN EUROPEAN LITERATURE

1300

1307 Dante Alighieri begins composing *The Divine Comedy* in Italy

1341 Francesco Petrarch is crowned poet laureate in Rome

1348 Boccaccio begins writing *The Decameron*

1375 Robin Hood appears in popular English literature

1400

1455 Gutenberg Bible is produced on a printing press in Germany

1477 Chaucer's *Canterbury Tales* is printed in England

1498 Comedies of the ancient Greek playwright Aristophanes are published in Venice

1500

1523 Hans Sachs writes a poetic allegory honoring Martin Luther

1532 French writer François Rabelais publishes the first book of *Gargantua and Pantagruel*

1543 Polish scientist Nicolaus Copernicus publishes his work on the solar system

A pilgrim in Chaucer's *Canterbury Tales*

EVENTS IN EUROPEAN HISTORY

1300

1337 Hundred Years' War between England and France begins

A **1347–1350** Bubonic plague kills a third of Europe's population

1389 Truce signed by England, Scotland, and France

1400

1428 Joan of Arc leads a French army against the English

1497 Italian Leonardo da Vinci paints *The Last Supper*

1500

1508 Michelangelo begins painting the ceiling of the Sistine Chapel in Rome

1517 Martin Luther posts protests of church practices on a church door in Wittenberg, Germany, starting the Reformation

1522 Magellan's expedition sails around the world C

1534 Henry VIII of England breaks with the Catholic Church

EVENTS IN WORLD HISTORY

1300

1300 Osman establishes the Ottoman Empire in Anatolia

1325 Aztecs build their capital, Tenochtitlán, in Mexico

1325 Noh drama develops in Japan

1368 Hung-wu founds the Ming Dynasty in China

1400

1400 Iroquois League is formed in North America

1438 Pachacutec becomes ruler of the Incas in Peru

B **1453** Ottomans conquer Constantinople

1464 Sunni Ali founds the Songhai Empire in West Africa

1492 Christopher Columbus reaches Hispaniola in North America

1500

1501 Ismail I founds the Safavid Dynasty and establishes Islam as the state religion in Persia

1502 First enslaved Africans exported to North America

1521 Cortés conquers the Aztecs in Mexico

1532 Pizarro conquers the Incas in Peru

MINI LESSON Using the Time Line

SEQUENCE OF EVENTS Have students study the time line on pages 780 and 781 and then answer questions such as the following:

- Which literary work was written first, *Utopia* or *Don Quixote? (Utopia)*
- Could Michel de Montaigne have written about the exploration of North America? *(yes, Columbus reached North America 88 years before Montaigne published his first essays)*
- Which group arrived in North America first, the English or enslaved Africans? *(enslaved Africans)*
- Did the French Revolution occur before or after the American Revolution? *(after)*

1500	1600	1700
1551 Thomas More's *Utopia* translated into English from Latin 1580 Michel Eyquem de Montaigne publishes his first essays	1601 William Shakespeare completes *Hamlet* 1605 Miguel de Cervantes publishes the first part of *Don Quixote* 1667 John Milton publishes the first version of *Paradise Lost* 1670 Molière writes the ballet-comedy *Le Bourgeois Gentilhomme*	1726 Jonathan Swift publishes *Gulliver's Travels* 1759 Voltaire publishes *Candide* 1773 Johann Wolfgang von Goethe writes the earliest version of *Faust* 1781 Jean Jacques Rousseau publishes *Confessions*

1550	1600	1700
1558 Elizabeth I is crowned queen of England **1588** Spanish Armada is defeated by England	**1640** Portugal gains independence **1649** England declared a commonwealth **1669** Venice loses its last colony, Crete, to the Turks **1697** France attempts to colonize West Africa	**1707** England and Scotland unite as Great Britain **1793** King Louis XVI executed in French Revolution **1796** Spain declares war on England **1798** France captures Rome and occupies Egypt

1550	1600	1700
	1603 Tokugawa regime begins in Japan 1607 English settle Jamestown in North America 1631 Shah Jahan builds the Taj Mahal in India 1636 Chinese Manchus conquer Korea 1689 Peter the Great becomes czar of Russia	1713 Peace of Adrianople signed by Russia and Turkey 1763 Treaty of Paris recognizes British control of India 1765 Chinese forces invade Burma 1776 American colonists declare their independence from England 1789 George Washington inaugurated as first president of the United States

INTRODUCTION 781

Historical Note

B Fall of Constantinople

Constantinople, the capital of the Byzantine Empire, fell to Turkish forces in 1453 after a 40-day siege. Once the greatest city of the Christian world, it became the new capital of the Ottoman Empire. Europeans felt threatened by the rise of this powerful Muslim state. However, the fall of Constantinople ultimately benefited Europe in unexpected ways. Many Greek scholars fled to Italy, bringing with them important knowledge of classical culture. In addition, the loss of traditional routes to the East spurred European nations to undertake new exploration. The Ottoman Empire reached its height during the 16th century, when it included Asia Minor, the Balkans, and parts of North Africa and the Middle East. Although Islam was the official state religion, the Ottoman rulers were relatively tolerant of their non-Muslim subjects.

Historical Note

C Magellan's Expedition In 1522, the *Victoria* sailed into Spain with 17 Europeans and four East Indians aboard. These survivors of Magellan's expedition were the first people to circumnavigate the world. Magellan, a Portuguese captain working for Spain, began the expedition in 1519 with a crew of about 250 men aboard five ships. He was hoping to find a westward route to the Spice Islands. Early on, the expedition was plagued by mutinies and the freezing weather of the southern Atlantic. About a year into the voyage, the explorers sailed south of South America into the Pacific (this passage has since been named the Strait of Magellan). Magellan and his crew were the first Europeans to explore the Pacific, which was much larger than they had expected. Sailing for months without reaching land, they suffered from disease and malnutrition. Magellan died in 1521 while participating in a battle between two local groups in the Philippines.

READING FOR INFORMATION
Reading Skills and Strategies
CONNECTING

Have students study the images and read the captions to help them understand the legacy of the Renaissance and Enlightenment. Then challenge them to think of other ways in which these periods influenced modern times. You might remind students that the societies of North and South America were created as a result of the exploration and colonialist activities of European nations during the Renaissance and Enlightenment. You might also point out that economic innovations during these periods laid the groundwork for modern systems of global trade and free markets.

Connect to Today: The Legacy of the Renaissance and Enlightenment

Mass Communication
The beginnings of the communication explosion in our contemporary world can be traced to the Renaissance and Enlightenment. The printing press made books affordable, and the resulting increase in literacy helped to usher in mass communication. Magazines and newspapers informed the masses and helped shape public opinion.

Human Rights
The term *human rights* originated in the 20th century, but the concept has roots in the Renaissance and Enlightenment. Bills of rights in England (1689), France (1789), and the United States (1791) were intended to protect individual rights and freedoms. These important documents influence today's activists who seek to protect the safety and liberty of peoples around the world.

Congreſs OF THE United States
begun and held at the City of New-York, on
Wednesday the Fourth of March, one thousand seven hundred and eighty nine

Can those who denied Human Rights now provide Human Rights?

Science and Medicine
Modern science and medicine owe a great deal to the scientific discoveries of the Renaissance and Enlightenment. In the 17th century, for example, the British physician William Harvey discovered the secrets of the circulation of blood.

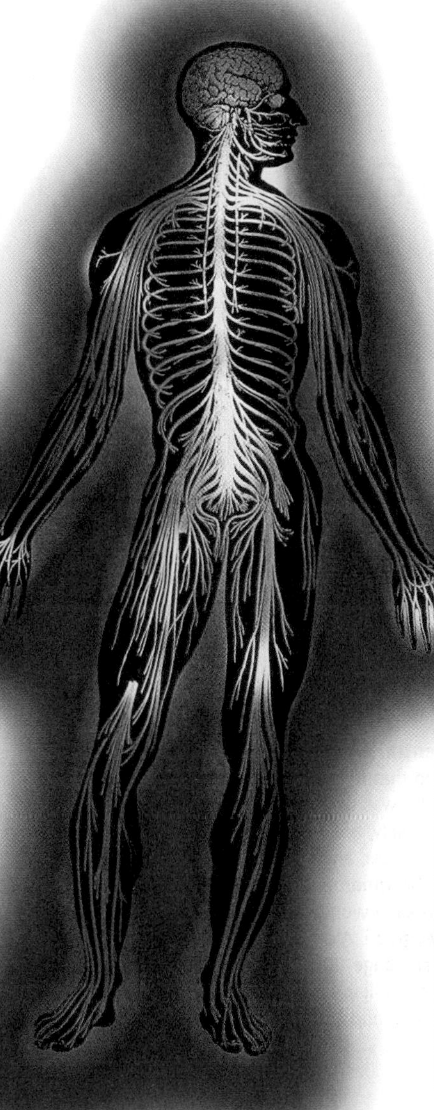

Mathematics and Engineering
The electronic world that we know today, with its graphing calculators, DVDs, computers, and the Internet, has its origins in the Renaissance and Enlightenment. The French philosopher and mathematician Blaise Pascal created a calculating machine in 1642.

The Legacy of Language

Words and phrases from the Renaissance and Enlightenment still influence our language today. Here's just a sample of expressions that have their origins in this time period.

Renaissance Man An educated man in the Renaissance was expected to develop knowledge and skills in many areas. The term was first applied to Leon Battista Alberti, an Italian writer, musician, mathematician, and artist. Today, the term is applied to any person notable for a broad range of achievements and interests.

Utopian This word comes from Utopia, the name of an imaginary island where life is nearly perfect—the subject of a book by the English scholar and statesman Thomas More. Now, the term *utopian* means "based on hopelessly impractical ideals."

Quixotic This word also comes from a literary work, the comic novel *Don Quixote* by the Spanish writer Miguel de Cervantes. Its hero, Don Quixote, is a dreamer who pursues his ideals without regard to their practicality. The word *quixotic* now describes any idealistic effort that has little chance of success.

"Liberty! Equality! Fraternity!" This phrase helped to start the French Revolution in 1789. It became not only a declaration of rights for all people but also a call to arms. Echoes of this phrase still spur people to political action.

Historical Note

A The Scientific Revolution Modern science had its origins in the 17th and 18th centuries. This period is often referred to as the Scientific Revolution. The contributions of various scientific pioneers, especially in the fields of astronomy, physics, and biology, led to a new way of looking at the natural world. Some of these scientists emphasized the use of abstract reasoning to deduce general laws that describe how the universe works. Others emphasized the importance of observation and experimentation. Often their discoveries placed them in conflict with church teachings and with theories that originated in ancient Greece. For example, the English physician William Harvey (1578–1657) discovered how blood circulates through the body by experimenting with mammals. He tied off arteries and noticed that they bulged with blood on the heart side; the opposite occurred with veins. Based on these and other observations, he proposed that blood is pumped from the heart through arteries and that it flows back toward the heart through veins. When Harvey published his theory, it aroused a great deal of controversy because it refuted the teachings of Galen, a Greek writer who probably never even dissected a human body. Galen's explanation of blood movement had been accepted for over 1,400 years.

Objectives
- understand and appreciate an Italian **story (Literary Analysis)**
- identify examples of **situational irony (Literary Analysis)**
- use strategies for **predicting (Active Reading)**

Summary
In Florence, a young man named Federigo falls in love with Monna Giovanna, a beautiful and wealthy married woman. He spends lavishly in order to impress her, but she ignores him. After he exhausts his fortune, he retires to a small farm with his magnificent hunting falcon. In the meantime, Monna Giovanna's husband dies. She spends the summer at an estate near Federigo's farm, and her son grows friendly with Federigo. When the boy becomes ill, he tells his mother that he would get better if he had Federigo's falcon. She reluctantly goes to the farm and says that she would like to dine with Federigo. Having no food or money in the house, Federigo kills his falcon to provide her with a meal. When they have finished eating, Monna Giovanna reveals her purpose for visiting him. Federigo breaks down in tears and reveals why he cannot give her the falcon. Her son dies soon afterward. When her brothers urge her to remarry, Monna Giovanna chooses Federigo because he behaved so nobly toward her.

Use **Unit Five Resource Book,** p. 31, for additional support.

Thematic Link
In this story, Boccaccio explores the **human possibility** for noble sacrifice.

Use **Unit Five Resource Book,** p. 34, for practice with Words to Know.

5-Minute Warm-Up
Daily Language SkillBuilder

Have students **proofread** the display sentences on page 685j and write them correctly.

from THE DECAMERON

federigo's falcon

GIOVANNI BOCCACCIO

Giovanni Boccaccio
1313–1375

An Overbearing Father Giovanni Boccaccio (jō-vän'nē bō-kä'chē-ō') began writing poetry as a youth, but his early talent was not rewarded. Instead, his father, a merchant from Florence, demanded that Boccaccio forget about writing and learn business. While still a teenager, Boccaccio was sent from his home in Florence to Naples, where he was apprenticed to a banker for 6 years. He disliked commerce, so his father arranged for him to study religious law, a pursuit he also found disagreeable. After about 12 years in Naples, Boccaccio was recalled home to seek other employment. Although he later held several government and diplomatic positions, none of his jobs were very satisfactory, and he often lived on the brink of poverty.

A Source of Inspiration Fortunately, despite his father's objections, Boccaccio had continued to write. In Naples, he produced an abundance of prose and poetry. It was also in Naples that he may have met his beloved "Fiammetta," a young woman who became the subject of much of his early writing and who appears as a narrator in *The Decameron.* The real identity of this woman, who probably died in the plague of 1348, has never been proven.

An Influential Poet and Scholar Boccaccio complained that because his father "strove to bend" his talent, he was unable to become "a distinguished poet." Eventually, however, he did achieve greatness as a poet, storyteller, and scholar. He completed his long work, *The Decameron,* in 1353. He then turned to writing scholarly works in Latin, including a biography of Dante Alighieri. Along with his lifelong friend Petrarch (see page 806), Boccaccio helped to set new directions for Italian literature and for the study of classical Greek and Latin texts.

LESSON RESOURCES

UNIT FIVE RESOURCE BOOK, pp. 31–35

ASSESSMENT RESOURCES
Formal Assessment, pp. 117–118
Teacher's Guide to Assessment and Portfolio Use
Test Generator

INTEGRATED TECHNOLOGY
Visit our Web site: classzone.com

ADDITIONAL RESOURCES
Lesson Planning Guide, pp. 97–98
Teacher's Sourcebook for Language Development

Build Background

Boccaccio's Classic Tales

The Decameron is the first great work of prose fiction in Italian. Its 100 tales are set within a **frame story,** or outer story, about ten young friends who leave Florence to escape the plague. While passing time in the countryside, they amuse themselves by telling stories over a period of ten days (the word *decameron* means "work of ten days"). Each day a different "king" or "queen" is appointed to direct the entertainment of the group. Fiammetta, the queen of the fifth day, asks everyone to provide tales about rocky love affairs that end happily.

Fiammetta's own story, "Federigo's Falcon," involves a frustrated lover whose most precious possession is a falcon. During the Middle Ages, many noblemen in western Europe practiced the sport of falconry. Trainers would catch falcons, other types of hawks, or eagles and teach them to hunt prey.

Love, however, not hunting, is the subject of "Federigo's Falcon." Federigo will do anything to gain the affection of a married noblewoman with whom he has fallen in love. His dilemma is a typical one in the literature of **courtly love.** This philosophy of love takes its name from the royal courts of the Middle Ages. Under the rules of courtly love, a man had to dedicate his life to his lady, whom he idealized in word and deed. During this time in Europe, most upper-class marriages were arranged for reasons of wealth or family reputation, so writers did not consider marriage fertile ground for such romance. Many tales of courtly love tell about the love between one man and the wife of another, an arrangement that was permitted as long as the passion remained idealized.

Connect to Your Life

In this story, a man sacrifices everything for the woman he loves. Share examples of sacrifices for love that you have heard of or read about. What were the results of these sacrifices?

Focus Your Reading

LITERARY ANALYSIS: SITUATIONAL IRONY

Irony is a contrast between expectation and reality. **Situational irony** occurs when a character or the reader expects one thing to happen but something entirely different happens. A famous story by O. Henry illustrates such irony: a young married man buys his wife combs for her beautiful hair, only to learn that she has cut her hair and sold it to pay for a present for him. As you read Boccaccio's story, look for examples of situational irony.

ACTIVE READING: PREDICTING

A **prediction** is an attempt to determine what will happen next in a story. When you predict, you combine information from the text with your own prior knowledge to make guesses about how the **plot** will advance. As you read further, you will often come across new information that may cause you to adjust your prediction.

READER'S NOTEBOOK After reading the first five paragraphs of "Federigo's Falcon," make a prediction about what will happen. Then adjust your prediction or make new predictions every time you encounter important new information. Record your predictions and adjustments.

WORDS TO KNOW **Vocabulary Preview**

anguish	discretion	inevitably
commend	donor	meagerly
compel	illustrious	presumption
diminish		

READING FOR INFORMATION

Reading Skills and Strategies

RECOGNIZING IMPORTANT DETAILS

Tell students to identify important details in the **Preparing to Read** pages. As they read the biographical sketch, they should look for one or two experiences that had a major influence on Boccaccio's writing. When reading the **Build Background** section, they should look for details about customs and beliefs portrayed in the story and about the structure of *The Decameron.*

TIME MANAGEMENT

If your schedule requires that you cover the lesson objectives in a shorter time, use . . .

- Preparing to Read, pp. 784-785
- Thinking Through the Literature, p. 792
- Vocabulary in Action, p. 793

If you want to take advantage of longer blocks of class time, use . . .

- TE Teaching Options: Cross Curricular Link, pp. 786, 788, 789; Vocabulary Strategy, p. 787; Grammar, p. 790
- Choices and Challenges, p. 793

Reading and Analyzing

Literary Analysis SITUATIONAL IRONY

After students have read the third paragraph, ask them to explain what is ironic about Federigo's attempts to win Monna Giovanna's love.

Possible Response: Federigo tries to impress Monna Giovanna by spending lavishly, but he only ends up impoverishing himself.

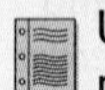

Use **Unit Five Resource Book,** p. 33, for more practice.

Active Reading PREDICTING

Ask students to predict what will happen when Monna Giovanna and her son spend the summer at an estate near Federigo's farm.

Possible Response: The boy's wish to have the falcon will somehow bring Federigo and Monna Giovanna together.

Use **Unit Five Resource Book,** p. 32, for more practice.

Literary Analysis THEME

Point out to students that in the second paragraph, the narrator says that one of her purposes in telling the story is to show the power of beauty. Encourage students to note incidents and descriptions in the story that support this theme.

from The Decameron

Federigo's Falcon

Giovanni Boccaccio

Translated by Mark Musa and Peter Bondanella

Filomena had already finished speaking, and when the Queen saw there was no one left to speak except for Dioneo,[1] who was exempted because of his special privilege, she herself with a cheerful face said:

It is now my turn to tell a story and, dearest ladies, I shall do so most willingly with a tale similar in some respects to the preceding one, its purpose being not only to show you how much
1 power your beauty has over the gentle heart, but
also so that you yourselves may learn, whenever it
2 is fitting, to be the donors of your favors instead
of always leaving this act to the whim of Fortune,[2] who, as it happens, on most occasions bestows such favors with more abundance than discretion.

You should know, then, that Coppo di Borghese Domenichi,[3] who once lived in our city and perhaps still does, a man of great and respected authority in our times, one most illustrious and worthy of eternal fame both for his way of life and his ability much more than for the nobility of his blood, often took delight, when he was an old man, in discussing things from the past with his neighbors and with others. He knew how to do this well, for he was more logical and had a better memory and a more eloquent style of speaking than any other man. Among the many beautiful tales he told, there was one he would often tell about a young man who once lived in Florence named Federigo, the son of Messer Filippo Alberighi,[4] renowned
above all other men in Tuscany for his prowess 3
in arms and for his courtliness.[5]

As often happens to most men of gentle breeding, he fell in love, with a noble lady named Monna Giovanna,[6] in her day considered to be one of the most beautiful and most charming ladies that ever there was in Florence; and in order to win her love, he participated in jousts[7] and tournaments, organized and gave banquets, spending his money without restraint; but she, no less virtuous than beautiful, cared little for these things he did on her behalf, nor did she care for the one who did them. Now, as Federigo was spending far beyond his means and getting nowhere, as can easily happen, he lost his wealth and was reduced to poverty, and was left with nothing to his name but his little farm (from whose revenues he lived very meagerly) and one falcon, which was among the finest of its kind in the world.

---

1. **Dioneo . . . privilege:** Dioneo (dē′ô-nā′ō) had been given permission always to tell the last story of the day.
2. **Fortune:** the power, personified, that supposedly distributes good and bad luck to people.
3. **Coppo di Borghese Domenichi** (kôp′pō dē bōr-gā′zĕ dō-mĕ′nē-kē).
4. **Messer Filippo Alberighi** (măs′sĕr fē-lēp′pō äl-bĕ-rē′gē).
5. **courtliness:** elegance and refinement.
6. **Monna Giovanna** (mä′nä gē-ō-vä′nä).
7. **jousts:** combats between two men on horseback.

WORDS TO KNOW

donor (dō′nər) *n.* person who gives or contributes something
discretion (dĭ-skrĕsh′ən) *n.* a sense of carefulness and restraint in one's actions or words
illustrious (ĭ-lŭs′trē-əs) *adj.* well known and respected
meagerly (mē′gər-lē) *adv.* poorly; scantily

786

Cross Curricular Link **History**

JOUSTS AND TOURNAMENTS During the Middle Ages, tournaments developed as a means of training knights in combat. Eventually they became a form of public entertainment. Groups of mounted knights charged at each other with lances and swords. A knight would win the armor and horse of any opponent he knocked to the ground. He could also expect to be rewarded by his designated lady, who was usually married to another gentleman. The church disapproved of tournaments because they promoted adultery and often ended in bloodshed. By the 14th century, rules of combat were established that made tournaments less dangerous. The group battles were replaced by a series of jousts between individual knights who would win points for landing blows or unseating the opponent. The knights generally fought with blunted weapons and wore heavy armor to minimize injury. Tournaments began to lose their popularity in the 16th century, when the introduction of gunpowder eliminated the military role of horse-mounted lancers.

Monna Giovanna was now a widow, and every summer, as our women usually do, she would go to the country with her son to one of their estates very close by to Federigo's farm.

La Pia de Tolommei (1868-1880), Dante Gabriel Rossetti. Oil on canvas, 104.8 cm × 120.6 cm. Spencer Museum of Art, University of Kansas.

More in love than ever, but knowing that he would never be able to live the way he wished to in the city, he went to live at Campi, where his farm was. There he passed his time hawking whenever he could, imposing on no one, and enduring his poverty patiently. Now one day, during the time that Federigo was reduced to these extremes, it happened that the husband of Monna Giovanna fell ill, and realizing death was near, he made his last will: he was very rich, and he left everything to his son, who was just growing up, and since he had also loved Monna Giovanna very much, he made her his heir should his son die without any legitimate[8] children; and then he died.

Monna Giovanna was now a widow, and every summer, as our women usually do, she would go to the country with her son to one of their estates very close by to Federigo's farm. Now this young boy of hers happened to become more and more friendly with Federigo and he began to enjoy birds and dogs; and after seeing Federigo's falcon fly many times, it made him so happy that he very much wished it were his own, but he did not dare to ask for it, for he could see how precious it was to Federigo. During this time, it happened that the young boy took ill, and his mother was much grieved, for he was her only child and she loved him dearly; she would spend the entire day by his side, never ceasing to comfort him, asking him time and again if there was anything he wished, begging him to tell her what it might be, for if it was possible to obtain

8. **legitimate** (lə-jĭt′ə-mĭt): born of parents who are legally married to each other.

Customizing Instruction

Less Proficient Readers

Make sure that students understand the concept of a frame story. "Federigo's Falcon" is narrated by Fiammetta, one of ten young Italians who take turns telling stories in the countryside as they wait for the plague to end. Point out that Fiammetta, the "queen" of the fifth day's entertainment, tells a love story that she heard from an old man in Florence.

English Learners

1 Explain that the word *gentle* means "noble," "chivalrous," or "refined."

2 Explain that the word *favors* means "friendly regard" or "consent to intimacy."

3 Explain that the phrase "prowess in arms" means "exceptional skill in combat or use of weaponry."

Advanced Learners

Point out to students that the idea of courtly love plays an important role in this story. As they read, suggest that they note examples of Federigo's courtly behavior.

MINI LESSON Vocabulary Strategy

RELATED WORDS

Instruction Tell students that they can often figure out the meaning of a word by thinking of a related word. Point out that the word *discretion* (page 786, paragraph 2) is related to the word *discreet.* Write the following sentences on the board: Federigo did not show discretion in his courtship efforts. His friends urged him to be more discreet. The adjective *discreet,* which means "showing prudence," will help students figure out the meaning of *discretion.* Point out that the word *presumption* (page 789, paragraph 3) is related to the word *presume.* Write down the following sentences: The lady feared that she was guilty of presumption. She hated to presume on his good nature. The word *presume,* which means "to take advantage of someone or go beyond proper limits," will help students figure out the meaning of *presumption.*

Practice Have students examine other related words. For each pair below, write down the first word and have students predict the definition of the second word.

exclamation/exclaim
solitude/solitary
solemnity/ solemn
plenitude/plenty

Reading and Analyzing

Literary Analysis SITUATIONAL IRONY

Ask students what is ironic about Monna Giovanna's visit to Federigo's farm.

Possible Response: She expects that Federigo will give her the falcon after she dines with him, but her visit causes him to kill the bird to provide her with a meal.

Active Reading PREDICTING

Ask students to predict how Federigo will respond to Monna Giovanna's request for the falcon.

Possible Responses: He might be tormented by the realization that he is unable to help her when she finally needs him; he might be angry at himself for having killed the bird.

Reading Skills and Strategies
DRAWING CONCLUSIONS

Ask students why they think Monna Giovanna is so reluctant to ask Federigo for the falcon. What does her reaction suggest about her feelings for him?

Possible Responses: She may be reluctant because she still feels nothing for him and doesn't want to put herself in his debt; she may regret that her rejection has caused him so much grief and may feel that such a request would hurt him again.

She knew that Federigo had been in love with her for some time now. . . .

it, she would certainly do everything in her power to get it. After the young boy had heard her make this offer many times, he said:

"Mother, if you can arrange for me to have Federigo's falcon, I think I would get well quickly."

1 When the lady heard this, she was taken aback for a moment, and then she began thinking what she could do about it. She knew that Federigo had been in love with her for some time now, but she had never deigned[9] to give him a second look; so, she said to herself:

"How can I go to him, or even send someone, and ask for this falcon of his, which is, as I have
2 heard tell, the finest that ever flew, and furthermore, his only means of support? And how can I be so insensitive as to wish to take away from this nobleman the only pleasure which is left to him?"

And involved in these thoughts, knowing that she was certain to have the bird if she asked for it, but not knowing what to say to her son, she stood there without answering him. Finally the love she bore her son persuaded her that she should make him happy, and no matter what the consequences might be, she would not send for the bird, but rather go herself to fetch it and bring it back to him; so she answered her son:

"My son, cheer up and think only of getting well, for I promise you that first thing tomorrow morning I shall go and fetch it for you."

The child was so happy that he showed some improvement that very day. The following morning, the lady, accompanied by another woman, as if they were out for a stroll, went to Federigo's modest little house and asked for him. Since the weather for the past few days had not been right for hawking, Federigo happened to be in his orchard attending to certain tasks, and when he heard that Monna Giovanna was asking for him at the door, he was so surprised and happy that he rushed there; as she saw him coming, she rose to greet him with womanly grace, and once Federigo had welcomed her most courteously, she said:

"How do you do, Federigo?" Then she continued, "I have come to make amends[10] for the harm you have suffered on my account by loving
me more than you should have, and in token of 3
this, I intend to have a simple meal with you and this companion of mine this very day."

To this Federigo humbly replied: "Madonna,[11] I have no recollection of ever suffering any harm because of you; on the contrary: so much good have I received from you that if ever I was worth anything, it was because of your worth and the love I bore for you; and your generous visit is certainly so very dear to me that I would spend all over again all that I spent in the past, but you have come to a poor host."

And having said this, he humbly led her through the house and into his garden, and because he had no one there to keep her company, he said:

"My lady, since there is no one else, this good woman, who is the wife of the farmer here, will keep you company while I see to the table."

Though he was very poor, Federigo until now had never realized to what extent he had wasted his wealth; but this morning, the fact that he had nothing in the house with which he could
honor the lady for the love of whom he had in 4
the past entertained countless people, gave him cause to reflect: in great anguish, he cursed himself and his fortune, and like someone out of his senses he started running here and there through-

9. **deigned** (dānd): considered worthy of one's dignity.

10. **make amends:** make payment of some sort for a loss or injury.

11. **Madonna:** Italian for "my lady," a polite way to address a married woman. "Monna" is a contraction of this term.

WORDS TO KNOW
anguish (ăng'gwĭsh) *n.* agony

Cross Curricular Link **History**

RULES OF COURTLY LOVE Federigo's devotion to Monna Giovanna conforms to the ideals of courtly love. This romantic code of behavior first appeared in the poetry of French troubadours in the early 12th century. The most common type of courtly lover is a young knight or nobleman who falls in love with an unobtainable lady, usually the wife of his lord. Pledging to serve her faithfully, he offers to prove his worthiness through a test of his bravery. If she accepts and he is successful, she must reward his service, perhaps by kissing or caressing him. A courtly lover was supposed to have the self-discipline to resist consummating his love. Since privacy was scarce in aristocratic courts, he was also supposed to be discreet. Courtly love developed as a literary convention, not as a realistic description of aristocratic life. However, it did influence people's behavior, especially the courtship rituals leading up to marriage.

out the house, but unable to find either money or anything he might be able to pawn,[12] and since it was getting late and he was still very much set on serving this noble lady some sort of meal, but unwilling to turn for help to even his own farmer (not to mention anyone else), he set his eyes upon his good falcon, which was sitting on its perch in a small room, and since he had nowhere else to turn, he took the bird, and finding it
4 plump, he decided that it would be a worthy food for such a lady. So, without giving the matter a second thought, he wrung its neck and quickly gave it to his servant girl to pluck, prepare, and place on a spit to be roasted with care; and when he had set the table with the whitest of tablecloths (a few of which he still had left), he returned, with a cheerful face, to the lady in his garden and announced that the meal, such as he was able to prepare, was ready.

The lady and her companion rose and went to the table together with Federigo, who waited
5 upon them with the greatest devotion, and they ate the good falcon without knowing what it was they were eating. Then, having left the table and spent some time in pleasant conversation, the lady thought it time now to say what she had come to say, and so she spoke these kind words to Federigo:

"Federigo, if you recall your former way of life and my virtue, which you perhaps mistook for harshness and cruelty, I have no doubt at all that you will be amazed by my presumption when you hear what my main reason for coming here is; but if you had children, through whom you might have experienced the power of parental love, I feel certain that you would, at least in part, forgive me. But, just as you have no child, I do have one, and I cannot escape the laws common to all mothers; the force of such laws compels me to follow them, against my own will and against good manners and duty, and to ask of you a gift which I know is most

Peregrine Falcon (1796). Raia Serfagee of Tanjore Collection. Photo © British Library/The Art Archive.

precious to you; and it is naturally so, since your extreme condition has left you no other delight, no other pleasure, no other consolation; and this gift is your falcon, which my son is so taken by that if I do not bring it to him, I fear his sickness will grow so much worse that I may lose him. And therefore I beg you, not because of the love that you bear for me, which does not oblige you in the least, but because of your own nobleness, which you have shown to be greater than that of all others in practicing courtliness, that you be pleased to give it to me, so that I may say that I have saved the life of my son by means of this gift, and because of it I have placed him in your debt forever."

12. **pawn:** borrow money against.

WORDS TO KNOW

presumption (prĭ-zŭmp'shən) *n.* bold or outrageous behavior
compel (kəm-pĕl') *v.* to force or pressure

Customizing Instruction

Less Proficient Readers

Have students create a chain-of-events chart to show which incidents have led Federigo to kill his falcon.

Use the following questions to make sure that students understand the plot of the story so far:

- How does Federigo try to win Monna Giovanna's love? *(He spends lavishly.)*
- How does she respond to his efforts? *(She ignores him.)*
- Why must Federigo live on a farm? *(He has wasted his fortune.)*
- Why does Monna Giovanna want Federigo's falcon? *(She thinks it will help her ill son get better.)*
- Why does Federigo kill the falcon? *(He wants to provide her with a good meal.)*

English Learners

1 Explain that the phrase *taken aback* means "surprised."

2 Explain that the phrase *heard tell* means "heard said."

3 Explain that the phrase *in token of* means "as an indication of."

5 Explain that the phrase *waited upon them* means "served them."

Advanced Learners

4 Have students reread the paragraph on pages 788–789 that describes Federigo's killing of the falcon. Ask them to analyze the methods of characterization that Boccaccio used in this paragraph.
*(**Federigo's physical appearance:** he returns to the table with a cheerful face; **his thoughts, feelings, and actions:** anguished and desperate; kills the bird without giving it a second thought; **narrator's direct comments:** Federigo had never before realized the extent to which he had wasted his wealth.)*

Cross Curricular Link History

FALCONRY Falconry is the sport of hunting with falcons or other birds of prey. It originated in Asia several thousand years ago. During the Middle Ages and Renaissance, falconry was highly popular among European aristocrats. On a hunt, the falconer walks through fields with the bird perched on the falconer's arm, which is protected by a heavy glove. The falcon's head is covered with a hood to keep it quiet. When small prey such as a rabbit or another bird is spotted, the hood is lifted and the bird is released. The falcon then flies off to kill or capture the prey. Falcons must be extensively trained because they are naturally afraid of humans.

FEDERIGO'S FALCON 789

Reading and Analyzing

Literary Analysis SITUATIONAL IRONY

Ask students to explain why the outcome of this story is ironic.

Possible Responses: Federigo thinks that his worst misfortune was to have killed the bird, but this action allows him to marry the woman he loves; Monna Giovanna had ignored Federigo when he was wealthy, but after he loses his money, she insists that he is the only man she will marry.

Literary Analysis
INTERNAL CONFLICT

Ask students what internal conflict Monna Giovanna experiences after Federigo explains his killing of the falcon.

Possible Response: She admires the greatness of his spirit, but she also grieves because she now has little hope of saving her son.

Reading Skills and Strategies
QUESTIONING

Ask students why Monna Giovanna might feel that Federigo's actions have demonstrated "the greatness of his spirit."

Possible Response: Although Federigo is now poor, he continues to serve her proudly, even though it means destroying his most precious possession.

When he heard what the lady requested and knew that he could not oblige her because he had given her the falcon to eat, Federigo began to weep in her presence, for he could not utter a word in reply. The lady at first thought his tears were caused more by the sorrow of having to part with the good falcon than by anything else, and she was on the verge of telling him she no longer wished it, but she held back and waited for Federigo's reply once he stopped weeping. And he said:

"My lady, ever since it pleased God for me to place my love in you, I have felt that Fortune has been hostile to me in many ways, and I have complained of her, but all this is nothing compared to what she has just done to me, and I shall never be at peace with her again, when I think how you have come here to my poor home, where, when it was rich, you never deigned to come, and how you requested but a small gift, and Fortune worked to make it impossible for me to give it to you; and why this is so I shall tell you in a few words. When I heard that you, out of your kindness, wished to dine with me, I considered it only fitting and proper, taking into account your excellence and your worthiness, that I should honor you, according to my possibilities, with a more precious food than that which I usually serve to other people. So I thought of the falcon for which you have just asked me and of its value and I judged it a food worthy of you, and this very day I had it roasted and served to you as best I could. But seeing now that you desired it another way, my sorrow in not being able to serve you is so great that never shall I be able to console myself again."

And after he had said this, he laid the feathers, the feet, and the beak of the bird before her as proof. When the lady heard and saw this, she first reproached him for having killed a falcon such as this to serve as a meal to a woman. But then to herself she commended the greatness of his spirit, which no poverty was able, or would be able, to diminish; then, having lost all hope of getting the falcon and thus, perhaps, of improving the health of her son, she thanked Federigo both for the honor paid to her and for his good intentions, and then left in grief to return to her son. To his mother's extreme sorrow, whether in disappointment in not having the falcon or because his illness inevitably led to it, the boy passed from this life only a few days later.

After the period of her mourning and her bitterness had passed, the lady was repeatedly urged by her brothers to remarry, since she was very rich and still young; and although she did not wish to do so, they became so insistent that remembering the worthiness of Federigo and his last act of generosity—that is, to have killed such a falcon to do her honor—she said to her brothers:

"I would prefer to remain a widow, if only that would be pleasing to you, but since you wish me to take a husband, you may be sure that I shall take no man other than Federigo degli Alberighi."

In answer to this, her brothers, making fun of her, replied:

"You foolish woman, what are you saying? How can you want him? He hasn't a penny to his name."

To this she replied: "My brothers, I am well aware of what you say, but I would much rather have a man who lacks money than money that lacks a man."

Her brothers, seeing that she was determined and knowing Federigo to be of noble birth, no matter how poor he was, accepted her wishes and gave her with all her riches in marriage to him; when he found himself the husband of such a great lady, whom he had loved so much and who was so wealthy besides, he managed his financial affairs with more prudence than in the past and lived with her happily the rest of his days. ❖

WORDS TO KNOW

commend (kə-mĕnd') *v.* to express approval of; praise
diminish (dĭ-mĭn'ĭsh) *v.* to lessen
inevitably (ĭn-ĕv'ĭ-tə-blē) *adv.* unavoidably

MINI LESSON **Grammar**

PARTICIPLES AND PARTICIPIAL PHRASES

Instruction Participles and participial phrases are verb forms that function as adjectives. They modify nouns or pronouns. A participial phrase consists of a participle and its modifiers and complements. Participles are either in the present or past tense. Present participles end in *-ing.* Most past participles end with *-d, -ed, -t,* or *-n.*

Activity Write these examples on the board.

The agonized Federigo told Monna Giovanna the source of their meal.

Losing all hope of getting the falcon, she thanked Federigo and left.

The underlined word in the first sentence is a past participle ending in *-ed.* It modifies the noun *Federigo.* The underlined part of the second sentence is a present participial phrase that modifies the pronoun *she.*

Practice Ask students to underline each participle or participial phrase and to tell whether the participle is past or present.

1. Caring little for tournaments, Monna Giovanna ignored Federigo. *(present)*
2. Frustrated, Federigo continued to spend money. *(past)*
3. Depleted of his wealth, Federigo retired to a farm. *(past)*
4. Lacking a father, the boy grew close to Federigo. *(present)*

For more instruction and practice in participles and participial phrases, see McDougal Littell's ***Language Network:***

- Grade 10, Chapter 3, "Using Phrases"
- Grade 12, Chapter 2, "Using Phrases"

FROM

the art of *courtly* love

ANDREAS CAPELLANUS

Translated by John Jay Parry

Andreas Capellanus lived in the 1100s and is thought to have been a chaplain at a French court. Around 1185, he wrote The Art of Courtly Love, which established a set of rules for love among the nobility. The following excerpt comes from the beginning of his work, where he defines love as a type of suffering.

Love is a certain inborn suffering derived from the sight of and excessive meditation upon the beauty of the opposite sex, which causes each one to wish above all things the embraces of the other and by common desire to carry out all of love's precepts[1] in the other's embrace.

That love is suffering is easy to see, for before the love becomes equally balanced on both sides there is no torment greater, since the lover is always in fear that his love may not gain its desire and that he is wasting his efforts. He fears, too, that rumors of it may get abroad, and he fears everything that might harm it in any way, for before things are perfected a slight disturbance often spoils them. If he is a poor man, he also fears that the woman may scorn his poverty; if he is ugly, he fears that she may despise his lack of beauty or may give her love to a more handsome man; if he is rich, he fears that his parsimony[2] in the past may stand in his way. To tell the truth, no one can number the fears of one single lover. This kind of love, then, is a suffering which is felt by only one of the persons and may be called "single love." But even after both are in love the fears that arise are just as great, for each of the lovers fears that what he has acquired with so much effort may be lost through the effort of someone else, which is certainly much worse for a man than if, having no hope, he sees that his efforts are accomplishing nothing, for it is worse to lose the things you are seeking than to be deprived of a gain you merely hope for. The lover fears, too, that he may offend his loved one in some way; indeed he fears so many things that it would be difficult to tell them.

1. **precepts:** rules that dictate a particular course of conduct.
2. **parsimony:** extreme stinginess.

Andreas Capellanus *The Art of Courtly Love*, written by Andreas Capellanus, had an enormous influence on the love literature of the Middle Ages. After it was translated from Latin into French, the handbook became so popular that the bishop of Paris condemned it. Capellanus seems to have based his ideas on two verse books about love by the Roman poet Ovid. He may have served in the court of Countess Marie de Champagne, a great patron of medieval love poetry.

Discussion Question

Ask students whether they agree with Capellanus that all lovers are afflicted with the fears he describes.

Possible Response: Although all lovers experience uncertainty at some point in their romantic affairs, the torment and constant fear he describes are typical only of immature or highly passionate lovers.

Connect to the Literature

1. **What Do You Think?**
Possible Responses: Some students may respond that the story's opening and the light tone of the narration led them to expect a happy ending. Others may respond that although the happy ending didn't surprise them, they didn't anticipate the events that make it possible.

Comprehension Check

- He spends it trying to impress Monna Giovanna.
- She hopes it can help her son to recover.
- He cooks the falcon so that he can provide an appropriate meal for her.

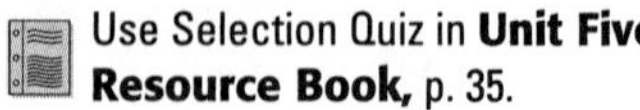
Use Selection Quiz in **Unit Five Resource Book,** p. 35.

Think Critically

2. Students may have adjusted their predictions after Federigo decides to kill the falcon or after the boy dies because these events make a happy ending seem less likely.
3. Some students will say that his actions illustrate the foolishness of love because Federigo only fulfills his happiness through an unlikely turn of events. Others might argue that there is beauty in Federigo's constant love for Monna Giovanna, despite the pain it has caused him, and that love makes him a better person.
4. Most students will consider her to be a sensitive and virtuous person, but some might fault her for not doing more to prevent Federigo's lavish spending.
5. Possible Responses: Chance can play an important role in determining our fates; one is more likely to win someone's affection through simple acts of devotion than through lavish spending.

Extend Interpretations

6. **What If?** Some students will feel that she still might have been grateful for his willingness to part with the falcon; others will argue that only the death of her son allowed her to inherit the money and choose Federigo as her husband.
7. **Comparing Texts** Federigo does lose his wealth because of love, and he feels anguished when he cannot provide Monna Giovanna with an appropriate meal. However, he seems generally content even while impoverished. The story's conclusion does not indicate any suffering after their marriage, although Capellanus suggests that the suffering never ceases.
8. **Connect to Life** Possible Response: People today might be pressured by religious or social conventions or because they want to enjoy practical benefits that come from marriage, but these pressures are not as strong as the ones a woman faced in the Middle Ages, when defying the wishes of family members could have grave consequences.

Literary Analysis

Paired Activity Students might respond that the irony suggests how misunderstanding often affects the course of love. Possible chart entries:

- Monna Giovanna expects that it would be a great sacrifice for Federigo to part with the falcon. He only grieves because he cannot fulfill her request.
- Federigo expects to please Monna Giovanna by cooking the falcon. His action destroys the hope that brought her to him.

Use **Unit Five Resource Book,** p. 33, for more practice.

Connect to the Literature

1. **What Do You Think?** Were you surprised by the turn of events in this story? Why or why not?

Comprehension Check
- How does Federigo lose his wealth?
- Why does Monna Giovanna want Federigo's falcon?
- What happens when she goes to visit him?

Think Critically

2. **ACTIVE READING: PREDICTING** Look again at the initial prediction you recorded in your READER'S NOTEBOOK. How accurate was it? What adjustments or new predictions did you make as you read the story?
3. Do you think the actions of Federigo illustrate the beauty of love or the foolishness of love? Explain your reasoning.
4. What is your opinion of Monna Giovanna?

THINK ABOUT
- her response to Federigo's lavish spending
- the promise she makes to her son
- her behavior at Federigo's house
- her decision to marry Federigo

5. Fiammetta explains that her story shows females the power that their beauty has "over the gentle heart." What other lessons does the story offer? Explain.

Extend Interpretations

6. **What If?** Suppose that Monna Giovanna had explained the purpose of her visit before Federigo killed the falcon. Do you think she still would have married him? Why or why not?
7. **Comparing Texts** In *The Art of Courtly Love,* Andreas Capellanus suggests that love always involves suffering. Compare his view of love with the way Boccaccio portrays love in "Federigo's Falcon."
8. **Connect to Life** Monna Giovanna's decision to remarry is influenced by her brothers. What sort of pressures today influence a person's decision to marry? Are these pressures as strong as the ones that Monna Giovanna faced?

LITERARY ANALYSIS: SITUATIONAL IRONY

Irony is a contrast between what is expected and what actually exists or happens. **Situational irony** occurs when a character or the reader expects one thing to happen but something entirely different happens. For example, in Boccaccio's tale, Federigo spends lavishly in the hope of winning Monna Giovanna's favor, but she visits him only after he is impoverished.

Paired Activity With a partner, create a chart like the one below and list the ironic situations that occur in the story. Then discuss what the irony suggests about the nature of love.

What's Expected	What Actually Happens
Federigo expects to impress his lady with his wealth.	*She finally visits him when he is too poor to feed her.*

REVIEW: PLOT As you know, the **plot** of a story usually includes the following stages: **exposition, rising action, climax,** and **falling action.** Create a diagram in which you identify these stages in "Federigo's Falcon." (See page 000 for an example of such a diagram.)

Writing Options

1. Dramatic Scene Write a dialogue in which Monna Giovanna explains to her brothers why Federigo is the only man she would ever marry. Start by reviewing the last few paragraphs of the story.

2. Comparing Portrayals of Love Write a brief essay comparing how love is portrayed in Boccaccio's story and in another work you have read, such as a poem by Sappho. Include specific examples from both works.

Writing Handbook
See page R31: Compare and Contrast.

Activities & Explorations

1. Storytelling Festival With a small group of classmates, create some stories about great sacrifices made for love. The stories can be original creations or retellings of well-known stories. Rehearse your stories, and then present them orally to the rest of the class.
~SPEAKING AND LISTENING

2. Booklet of Quotations With a group of classmates, prepare a booklet of famous quotations about love. Illustrate your booklet with drawings, photographs, or copies of art. ~ ART

Inquiry & Research

Report on Courtly Love
Prepare an oral report on the history of courtly love. When did courtly love begin? How were gentlemen supposed to woo ladies, and how were the ladies supposed to respond?

Vocabulary in Action

EXERCISE: CONTEXT CLUES Write the vocabulary word that is closest in meaning to the italicized word or phrase in each sentence.

1. Nothing could *reduce* Federigo's love for Monna Giovanna.
2. Federigo did not show *good judgment* when he spent all his money trying to impress her.
3. Federigo's overspending led in an inescapable manner to the loss of his fortune.
4. Only a request from her sick son could *irresistibly drive* Monna Giovanna to ask a favor.
5. Because Federigo lived *with a lack of abundant resources,* Monna Giovanna was reluctant to ask for his last precious possession.
6. After Monna Giovanna apologized for her *daring and insulting request,* Federigo wept.
7. Federigo thought Monna Giovanna would *speak highly of* the excellent meal.
8. The boy wanted Federigo to be a *patron or supporter* by making a gift of his falcon.
9. After the meal, Federigo could not disguise his *suffering* over having served the bird.
10. Perhaps Federigo eventually became *noted* for his faithfulness in love.

WORDS TO KNOW

anguish, commend, compel, diminish, discretion, donor, illustrious, inevitably, meagerly, presumption

Building Vocabulary
For an in-depth lesson on denotation and connotation, see page 1098.

Plot Students may note that the rising action begins when Monna Giovanna goes to the country every summer, and her son becomes friendly with Federigo. They may identify the climax as the moment when Monna asks Federigo to make a gift of his falcon.

Writing Options

1. **Dramatic Scene** Tell students that Monna Giovanna's speaking style in their scenes should be consistent with her dialogue in the story.
2. **Comparing Portrayals of Love** Remind students that their essays should have a clear thesis statement. Before they begin writing, they should decide whether to use a subject-by-subject order or feature-by-feature order for the comparison.

Activities & Explorations

1. **Storytelling Festival** Tell students that they should choose stories that are fairly brief. Encourage them to use gestures and voice inflection to make their storytelling more lively.
2. **Booklet of Quotations** Suggest that students consult collections of quotations, such as *Bartlett's Familiar Quotations,* as well as studies on the nature and history of love.

Inquiry & Research

Report on Courtly Love You might wish to have students work in pairs or small groups to prepare oral presentations. Encourage them to incorporate visual media, such as maps and illustrations, in their reports. Students might consult the following works:

- "Introduction," *The Art of Courtly Love,* trans. John Jay Parry
- *The Courtly Love Tradition,* by Bernard O'Donoghue
- *Love in the Western World,* by Denis de Rougemont

Vocabulary in Action

1. diminish
2. discretion
3. inevitably
4. compel
5. meagerly
6. presumption
7. commend
8. donor
9. anguish
10. illustrious

To assess skills and concepts taught in this selection use **Formal Assessment Book,** p. 117–118.

PREPARING to Read

Objectives

- understand and appreciate a **philosophical romance (Literary Analysis)**
- understand the **author's purpose (Literary Analysis)**
- use strategies for **drawing conclusions (Active Reading)**

Summary

The island of Utopia has 54 nearly identical city-states. Once a year, three elders from each city go to a central location to discuss common concerns. All citizens must work for two-year periods on farms. When they are not engaged in agriculture, citizens must practice a particular craft. Everyone works for six hours a day. Spare time is devoted to some occupation, usually intellectual pursuits. Many citizens attend daily public lectures before daybreak. Although the work day is relatively brief, no one lacks for necessities. This is possible because everyone works at a useful trade, unlike in other nations. By abolishing the use of money and private property, the Utopians have eliminated greed and crime from their commonwealth. No one is rich or poor; all are taken care of. By contrast, the laborers in other nations work like beasts of burden and live in poverty.

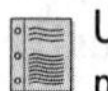 Use **Unit Five Resource Book,** p. 36, for additional support.

Thematic Link

This romance suggests how a rationally organized society can unleash **human possibility.**

 Use **Unit Five Resource Book,** p. 39, for practice with Words to Know.

5-Minute Warm-Up

Daily Language SkillBuilder

Have students **proofread** the display sentences on page 685j and write them correctly.

Sir Thomas More

Utopia

Sir Thomas More
1477–1535

A Privileged Childhood Born in London, Thomas More was the son of a prominent English lawyer and judge. As a boy, he attended a prestigious school and served as a page in the home of the Archbishop of Canterbury. The archbishop took an interest in the boy, whom he said would grow to be a "marvellous man," and later supported More's attendance at Oxford University. While studying at Oxford, More became friends with some of England's most influential humanist scholars (see page 773 for a discussion of Renaissance humanism).

Brilliant Lawyer, Statesman, and Scholar A devoutly religious man, More seriously considered becoming a monk but instead pursued a career in law and politics. In 1504, around the time of his first marriage, he became a member of Parliament. With exacting self-discipline, More also continued his literary and scholarly pursuits. His household became famous for its hospitality to scholars. While More was serving on a diplomatic mission, he began to write his famous book *Utopia,* an account of an ideal society. More coined the name *Utopia* by combining two Greek words that together mean "no place." In 1518, the highly respected More was appointed by King Henry VIII to act as an ambassador. More was knighted in 1521 and eight years later became lord chancellor—the highest position next to the king in the English monarchy.

A Violent Death In 1532, More resigned as lord chancellor because he opposed Henry VIII's plan to divorce the queen and marry Anne Boleyn in defiance of the Roman Catholic Church. In 1534, after the king had broken away from the church and married Boleyn, More refused to take the Oath of Supremacy, which recognized Henry as the head of the English church. As a result, More was imprisoned in the Tower of London. At his trial for treason, he was found guilty and sentenced to die. Before his beheading, More uttered the conviction that he was "the king's good servant, but God's first." Because he put his religious beliefs ahead of his duties to the government, More was eventually made a saint. Widely admired for his intelligence and his devotion to his faith, More inspired the play *A Man for All Seasons* (1960), by Robert Bolt.

LESSON RESOURCES

UNIT FIVE RESOURCE BOOK,
pp. 36–40

ASSESSMENT RESOURCES
Formal Assessment, pp. 119–120
Teacher's Guide to Assessment and Portfolio Use
Test Generator

INTEGRATED TECHNOLOGY
Visit our Web site: classzone.com

ADDITIONAL RESOURCES
Lesson Planning Guide, pp. 99–100
Teacher's Sourcebook for Language Development

Build Background

Utopia: An Ideal Society

Criticism of English Society Thomas More's *Utopia* is a **philosophical romance,** a work of fiction devoted to the exploration of ideas. At the center of the book is a mysterious traveler named Raphael Hythloday (hĭth'lə-dā'). As a sailor, Hythloday has seen much of the newly discovered world. The book, which consists of two parts, begins with a conversation in a garden in Antwerp, Belgium, between Hythloday, More (as a character in his own book), and other humanist thinkers. Hythloday criticizes the evils of the poverty and the luxury that he has seen in England. In 1516, when *Utopia* was published, English society was marked by great extremes in wealth, education, and status. Though merchants, bankers, lawyers, and nobles lived very well, most citizens lived in poverty, disease, and ignorance.

The Island of Utopia In the second part of the book, Hythloday describes his visit to a faraway land called Utopia, a large, crescent-shaped island that does not have the inequalities and injustices of England. Utopian society is governed according to principles of reason. As a result, everyone has work and everyone is educated. Since private property has been abolished there, the citizens have no need for money. Instead, all that is produced is shared equally. In one of the book's many whimsical passages, we learn that the Utopians fashion their chamber pots from gold and silver so that these metals will not be overvalued by citizens. Curiously, even in this model society there are some serfs who perform tasks considered unfit for citizens.

WORDS TO KNOW **Vocabulary Preview**

benevolent, compulsory, grave, hinder, incessantly, indigent, insatiable, novice, prevalent, superfluous

Connect to Your Life

What comes to mind when you hear the word *utopia?* Do you have your own mental image of a perfect society, or do you recall books or films that deal with the effort to create a perfect world? With a small group of classmates, discuss your ideas and images of utopia.

Focus Your Reading

LITERARY ANALYSIS: AUTHOR'S PURPOSE

Authors typically write for one or more of the following purposes: to entertain, to inform, to express opinions, or to persuade. As you read the excerpt from *Utopia,* consider what purpose or purposes More might have had when he wrote the book.

ACTIVE READING: DRAWING CONCLUSIONS

To identify More's purpose for writing, you will need to draw conclusions based upon the text. A conclusion is a logical statement that combines what you already know with what you learn from your reading. Consider the following passage from More's text:

> ***Agriculture is the one pursuit which is common to all, both men and women, without exception.***

You know that in most societies only some people are farmers. You might conclude from this passage that More believes that farming is so important that everyone should share in the work.

READER'S NOTEBOOK Make a chart, like the one shown below, to keep track of how Utopia differs from other countries as described in the excerpt. The differences will help you to draw conclusions about More's values and purpose for writing.

	In Utopia	In Other Countries
Farming		
Other Occupations		
Money		

READING FOR INFORMATION
Reading Skills and Strategies
MONITORING READING STRATEGIES

Tell students to adjust their reading strategies to suit the kind of material they are reading. As they read the biographical sketch, they should look for one or two key ideas about the author. When reading **Build Background,** they should look for information that helps explain why More wrote *Utopia* as well as details that describe the nature and structure of the book. Finally, as students read the selection, they should pay attention to the contrasts that the narrator draws between Utopia and the outside world.

Editor's Note

This selection was excerpted from a larger work. Material was deleted to shorten and focus the selection.

TIME MANAGEMENT

If your schedule requires that you cover the lesson objectives in a shorter time, use . . .

- Preparing to Read, pp. 794-795
- Thinking Through the Literature, p. 802
- Vocabulary in Action, p. 803

If you want to take advantage of longer blocks of class time, use . . .

- TE Teaching Options: Cross Curricular Link, pp. 796, 800; Vocabulary Strategy, p. 798; Informal Assessment, p. 799; Grammar, p. 801
- Connect to Today, p. 803

Literary Analysis AUTHOR'S PURPOSE

A Ask students to identify the author's purpose from the first two paragraphs after they have read them.

Possible Response: to inform readers about the physical layout of Utopia.

Use **Unit Five Resource Book,** p. 38, for more practice.

Active Reading

DRAWING CONCLUSIONS

Point out that the selection describes some of the work requirements in Utopia. Ask students what conclusions they can draw about Utopian society from the description of agricultural practices.

Possible Responses: People are treated as equally as possible; the government plays a large role in structuring people's lives.

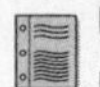

Use **Unit Five Resource Book,** p. 37, for more practice.

Literary Analysis TONE

Ask students to describe the narrative tone used so far in the selection. Then have them discuss the effect of this tone on the reader.

Possible Responses: The tone is matter-of-fact or journalistic; it encourages the reader to believe that the narrator is describing a real place.

from Utopia

Sir Thomas More

Translated by G. C. Richards

The Land and Its People

The island contains fifty-four city-states, all spacious and magnificent, identical in language, traditions, customs, and laws. They are similar also in layout and everywhere, as far as the nature of the ground permits, similar even in appearance. None of them is separated by less than twenty-four miles from the nearest, but none is so isolated that a person cannot go from it to another in a day's journey on foot. From
1 each city three old and experienced citizens meet to discuss the affairs of common interest to the
A island once a year at Amaurotum,[1] for this city, being in the very center of the country, is situated most conveniently for the representatives of all sections. It is considered the chief as well as the capital city.

The lands are so well assigned to the cities that each has at least twelve miles of country on every side, and on some sides even much more, to wit, the side on which the cities are farther apart. No city has any desire to extend its territory, for they consider themselves the tenants rather than the masters of what they hold.

Everywhere in the rural districts they have, at suitable distances from one another, farmhouses well equipped with agricultural implements. They are inhabited by citizens who come in succession[2] to live there. No rural household numbers less than forty men and women, besides two serfs attached to the soil. Over them are set a master and a mistress, serious in mind and ripe in years. Over every group of thirty households rules a phylarch.[3]

Twenty from each household return every year to the city, namely, those having completed two years in the country. As substitutes in their place, the same number are sent from the city. They are to be trained by those who have been there a year and who therefore are more expert in farming; they themselves will teach others in the following years. There is thus no danger of anything going wrong with the annual food supply through want of skill, as might happen if all at one time were newcomers and novices at farming. Though this system of changing farmers is the rule, to prevent any individual's being forced against his will to continue too long in a life of rather hard work, yet many men who take a natural pleasure in agricultural pursuits obtain leave 2
to stay several years.

The occupation of the farmers is to cultivate the soil, to feed the animals, and to get wood and convey it to the city either by land or by water, whichever way is more convenient. They breed a vast quantity of poultry by a wonderful contrivance. The hens do not brood over the eggs, but the farmers, by keeping a great number of them at a uniform heat, bring them to life and hatch them.[4] As soon as they come out of the shell, the chicks follow and acknowledge humans as their mothers! . . .

1. **Amaurotum** (ä-mô-rō'to͝om).
2. **in succession:** by turns; one after another.
3. **phylarch** (fī'lärk): officer in charge of 30 rural households.
4. **the farmers . . . hatch them:** The device described is similar to the incubators used today for hatching eggs.

WORDS TO KNOW

novice (nŏv'ĭs) *n.* a beginner in a job or activity

Cross Curricular Link **History**

MORE, THE REFORMER Thomas More vigorously opposed the Reformation even when his life was at stake. However, he was certainly not against reform. Along with many of his fellow humanists, More criticized corruption, greed, and hypocrisy in the church as well as in secular institutions. The well-born More gained firsthand knowledge of social problems when he served as an undersheriff of London, which required him to preside over court cases. Contemporaries described him as an impartial judge who showed great compassion for the poor.

More felt that education was an important means of improving society. In *Utopia*, he describes how the citizens on the imaginary island devote much of their spare time to intellectual pursuits. More's interest in education led him to set up an excellent school in his household. Most of the students under his supervision were girls.

How Utopians breed chickens by incubation, Francois Van Bleyswyck. Bibliothèque Nationale de France, Paris.

Customizing Instruction

Less Proficient Readers

Make sure that students understand the structure of *Utopia*. This excerpt is narrated by a fictional traveler named Raphael Hythloday, who claims to have visited the island. He is describing the island to More and other humanist thinkers.

Use the following questions to make sure that students understand the main points on the first page:

- How is Utopia organized? *(It has 54 city-states surrounded by rural land.)*
- Who does the farmwork? *(Everyone takes turns working on farms for two-year periods.)*

English Learners

1 Explain that the term *city-state* describes a self-governing state that consists of an independent city and surrounding territory.

2 Explain that the word *pursuits* means "activities."

Advanced Learners

Ask students to consider whether the requirement that everyone take turns doing farm work is fair. Encourage them to think of situations in which this requirement would create hardship for some citizens.

Active Reading

DRAWING CONCLUSIONS

A Ask students why the Utopians might all wear clothes cut from the same pattern. Have students identify similar practices in our own society.

Possible Responses: It is more practical for them to wear the same clothes; the uniform clothing emphasizes that they are all equal; a similar practice in our society is the requirement of school uniforms.

Literary Analysis AUTHOR'S PURPOSE

B Point out that narrator digresses from his description of Utopian occupations to explain how the Utopians can supply all of their needs by working only six hours each day. Ask students why the author might have chosen to include this digression.

Possible Response: The digression is an opportunity to express an opinion about idleness and luxury in European society.

Reading Skills and Strategies
SUMMARIZING

Ask students to summarize the description of how the Utopians occupy their time.

Possible Response: When not engaged in agriculture, they must work at a particular craft for six hours a day. Most devote their free time to intellectual pursuits, such as attending lectures, but they can also spend it practicing their trade.

Occupations

Agriculture is the one pursuit which is common to all, both men and women, without exception. They are all instructed in it from childhood, partly by principles taught in school, partly by field trips to the farms closer to the city as if for recreation. Here they do not merely look on, but, as opportunity arises for bodily exercise, they do the actual work.

Besides agriculture (which is, as I said, common to all), each is taught one particular craft as his own. This is generally either wool-working or linen-making or masonry[5] or metal-working or carpentry. There is no other pursuit which occupies any number worth mentioning. As for clothes, these are of one and the same pattern throughout the island and down the centuries, though there is a distinction between the sexes and between the single and married. The garments are comely to the eye, convenient for bodily movement, and fit for wear in heat and cold. Each family, I say, does its own tailoring. A

Of the other crafts, one is learned by each person, and not the men only, but the women too. The latter as the weaker sex have the lighter occupations and generally work wool and flax. To the men are committed the remaining more laborious crafts. For the most part, each is brought up in his father's craft, for which most have a natural inclination. But if anyone is attracted to another occupation, he is transferred by adoption to a family pursuing that craft for which he has a liking. Care is taken not only by his father but by the authorities, too, that he will be assigned to a grave and honorable householder. Moreover, if anyone after being thoroughly taught one craft desires another also, the same permission is given. Having acquired both, he practices his choice unless the city has more need of the one than of the other.

The chief and almost the only function of the syphogrants[6] is to manage and provide that no one sit idle, but that each apply himself industriously to his trade, and yet that he be not wearied like a beast of burden with constant toil from early morning till late at night. Such wretchedness is worse than the lot of slaves, and yet it is almost everywhere the life of workingmen—except for the Utopians. The latter divide the day and night into twenty-four equal hours and assign only six to work. There are three before noon, after which they go to dinner. After dinner, when they have rested for two hours in the afternoon, they again give three to work and finish up with supper. Counting one o'clock as beginning from midday, they go to bed about eight o'clock, and sleep claims eight hours.

The intervals between the hours of work, sleep, and food are left to every man's discretion, not to waste in revelry[7] or idleness, but to devote the time free from work to some other occupation according to taste. These periods are commonly devoted to intellectual pursuits. For it is their custom that public lectures are daily delivered in the hours before daybreak. Attendance is compulsory only for those who have been specially chosen to devote themselves to learning. A great number of all classes, however, both males and females, flock to hear the lectures, some to one and some to another, according to their natural inclination. But if anyone should prefer to devote this time to his trade, as is the case with many minds which do not reach the level for any of the higher intellectual disciplines, he is not hindered; in fact, he is even praised as useful to the commonwealth. . . .[8]

But here, lest you be mistaken, there is one B

5. **masonry:** stonework or brickwork.
6. **syphogrant** (sĭf′ō-grănt): another word for phylarch.
7. **revelry** (rĕv′əl-rē): loud partying or merrymaking.
8. **commonwealth:** nation or state governed by its people.

WORDS TO KNOW

grave (grāv) *adj.* serious
compulsory (kəm-pŭl′sə-rē) *adj.* required
hinder (hĭn′dər) *v.* to keep from doing something

MINI LESSON **Vocabulary Strategy**

WORD FAMILIES

Instruction Many words in English have a Latin root, or base word. Knowing the Latin root can help students understand other words in the same word family because they are usually related in meaning. Tell students that the word *benevolent* (page 801, paragraph 1) is in the same family as *benediction, benefactor, benefic,* and *benefit*. They share the Latin root *bene*, which means "well." By looking at context clues and thinking about other words in the same family, students can figure out the meaning of *benevolent*. Tell students that the word *prevalent* (page 800, paragraph 4) is in the same family as *valiant, valor, value, evaluate, prevail,* and *invalid*. These words come from the Latin word *valére*, which means "to be strong." Point out to students that strong things are more likely to be "widely or commonly occurring," which is the meaning of *prevalent*.

Practice Have students try to write definitions of other words in the same family as *benevolent* and in the same family as *prevalent*. After they have checked their definitions with a dictionary, have them write each word in a sentence.

A lesson on word families appears on p. 1198 in the Pupil's Edition.

How the island of Utopia is shaped like a crescent, Francois Van Bleyswyck. Bibliothèque Nationale de France, Paris.

point you must examine more closely. Since they devote but six hours to work, you might possibly think the consequence to be some scarcity of
1 necessities. But so far is this from being the case that the aforesaid[9] time is not only enough but more than enough for a supply of all that is requisite[10] for either the necessity or the convenience of living. This phenomenon you too will understand if you consider how large a part of the population in other countries exists without working. First, there are almost all the women, who constitute half the whole; or, where the women are busy, there as a rule the men are snoring in their stead.[11] Besides, how great and
2 how lazy is the crowd of priests and so-called religious! Add to them all the rich, especially the masters of estates, who are commonly termed gentlemen and noblemen. Reckon with them their retainers[12]—I mean, that whole rabble of good-for-nothing swashbucklers.[13] Finally, join in the lusty[14] and sturdy beggars who make some disease an excuse for idleness. You will certainly find far less numerous than you had supposed those whose labor produces all the articles that mortals require for daily use.

Now estimate how few of those who do work are occupied in essential trades. For, in a society where we make money the standard of everything, it is necessary to practice many crafts which are quite vain and superfluous, ministering only to luxury and licentiousness.[15] Suppose the host of those who now toil were distributed over only as few crafts as the few needs and conveniences demanded by nature. In the great abundance of commodities which must then arise, the prices set on them would be too low for the craftsmen to earn their livelihood by their work. But suppose all those fellows who are now busied with unprofitable crafts, as well as all the lazy and idle throng, any one of whom now consumes as much of the fruits of other men's labors 3
as any two of the workingmen, were all set to work and indeed to useful work. You can easily see how small an allowance of time would be enough and to spare for the production of all that is required by necessity or comfort (or even pleasure, provided it be genuine and natural). . . .

---

9. **aforesaid:** spoken of earlier.
10. **requisite** (rĕk′wĭ-zĭt): required; essential.
11. **stead:** place or position generally occupied by someone else.
12. **retainers:** servants or attendants of people with money or high rank.
13. **swashbucklers:** adventurers; in this case, probably a reference to those who seek personal gain.
14. **lusty:** strong; vigorous.
15. **licentiousness** (lī-sĕn′shəs-nĭs): immoral behavior, especially of a sexual nature.

WORDS TO KNOW

superfluous (so͞o-pûr′flo͞o-əs) *adj.* more than is needed; unnecessary

Customizing Instruction

Less Proficient Readers

1 Help students understand the point that the narrator is making when he addresses the reader directly. Point out that in More's time, most laborers worked considerably longer than six hours a day. Discuss with students the reasons given to explain how the Utopians can satisfy their needs with a short work day.

Advanced Learners

2 Remind students that More himself was a devout man who became a saint because he died for his religious beliefs. Call their attention to the narrator's negative remark about priests and religious people. Ask students to discuss what this remark might suggest about the relationship between the author and the narrator.

English Learners

3 Explain to students that the word *fruits* means "results" or "products" in the phrase "the fruits of other men's labors."

✓ Assessment Informal Assessment

SUMMARIZING Ask students to write a one-paragraph summary of the narrator's description of occupations in Utopia. Remind students that summaries will be judged according to their accuracy and completeness.

RUBRIC

3 Full Accomplishment Student's account provides an accurate and thorough summary of the information in the section and the narrator's explanation of why six-hour work days are sufficient.

2 Substantial Accomplishment Student's account is accurate, but some important information is missing.

1 Little or Partial Accomplishment Student's account is missing vital information, is incomplete, or shows little understanding of the narrator's explanation.

Literary Analysis PERSUASION

Point out that writers often appeal to our emotions as well as our intellect in order to persuade us. Ask students to identify statements in this section that make an emotional appeal.

Possible Responses: The description of elderly people afflicted with illness and poverty after working hard all their lives; the suggestion that there is a "conspiracy of the rich"; the description of the rich as "evil men with insatiable greed."

Reading Skills and Strategies
EVALUATING IDEAS

After students finish reading the selection, discuss the main points raised in this last section with them. Ask them whether they think that Hythloday's criticism of societies outside of Utopia is still valid today. Then ask them whether the economic system of Utopia could really work.

Possible Responses: Although many countries have developed social safety nets, much of the world's population remains impoverished; the experience of Communist nations suggests that the economic system of Utopia could not work on a large scale.

Reading Skills and Strategies
ANALYZING STYLE

Point out to students that in this section, the narrator asks many questions without expecting any answer. Ask them why More might have chosen to use such rhetorical questions instead of direct statements.

Possible Responses: The questions give a sense that the narrator is trying to convince people in his presence; they are an effective way to convince readers because the readers supply the answers.

The Commonwealth Outside Utopia

1 Now I have described to you, as exactly as I could, the structure of that commonwealth which I judge not merely the best but the only one which can rightly claim the name of a commonwealth. Outside Utopia, to be sure, men talk freely of the public welfare—but look after their private interests only. In Utopia, where nothing is private, they seriously concern themselves with public affairs. Assuredly in both cases they act reasonably. For, outside Utopia, how many are there who do not realize that, unless they make some separate provision for themselves, however flourishing the commonwealth, they will themselves starve? For this reason, necessity compels them to hold that they must take account of themselves rather than of the people, that is, of others.

On the other hand, in Utopia, where everything belongs to everybody, no one doubts, provided only that the public granaries[16] are well filled, that the individual will lack nothing for his private use. The reason is that the distribution of goods is not niggardly.[17] In Utopia there is no poor man and no beggar. Though no man has anything, yet all are rich.

For what can be greater riches for a man than to live with a joyful and peaceful mind, free of all worries—not troubled about his food or harassed by the querulous[18] demands of his wife or fearing poverty for his son or worrying about his daughter's dowry, but feeling secure about the livelihood
2 and happiness of himself and his family: wife, sons, grandsons, great-grandsons, great-great-grandsons, and all the long line of their descendants that gentlefolk anticipate? Then take into account the fact that there is no less provision for those who are now helpless but once worked than for those who are still working.

At this point I should like anyone to be so bold as to compare this fairness with the so-called justice prevalent in other nations, among which, upon my soul, I cannot discover the slightest trace of justice and fairness. What brand of justice is it that any nobleman whatsoever or goldsmith-banker or moneylender or, in fact, anyone else from among those who either do no work at all or whose work is of a kind not very essential to the commonwealth, should attain a life of luxury and grandeur on the basis of his idleness or his nonessential work? In the meantime, the common laborer, the carter, the carpenter, and the farmer perform work so hard and continuous that beasts of burden could scarcely endure it and work so essential that no commonwealth could last even one year without it. Yet they earn such scanty fare and lead such a miserable life that the condition of beasts of burden might seem far preferable. The latter do not have to work so incessantly nor is their food much worse (in fact, sweeter to their taste) nor do they entertain any fear for the future. The workmen, on the other hand, not only have to toil and suffer without return or profit in the present but agonize over the thought of an indigent old age. Their daily wage is too scanty to suffice even for the day: much less is there an excess and surplus that daily can be laid by for their needs in old age.

Now is not this an unjust and ungrateful commonwealth? It lavishes great rewards on so-called gentlefolk and banking goldsmiths and the rest of that kind, who are either idle or mere

16. **granaries** (grăn′ə-rēz): storage houses for grain.

17. **niggardly:** stingy.

18. **querulous** (kwĕr′ə-ləs): complaining; grumbling.

WORDS TO KNOW

prevalent (prĕv′ə-lənt) *adj.* widely or commonly occurring
incessantly (ĭn-sĕs′ənt-lē) *adv.* continually; without stopping
indigent (ĭn′dĭ-jənt) *adj.* without money; very poor

Cross Curricular Link **History**

MORE'S TRIAL AND EXECUTION Thomas More was imprisoned in the Tower of London in 1534 for refusing to recognize Henry VIII as the head of the Church of England. More had avoided openly declaring his opposition to the king, and at his trial he vigorously defended himself against the charge of treason. Nevertheless, the jury unanimously declared him guilty. Now that his fate was sealed, More finally spoke his mind, saying that he could not accept any act that would divide the church from Rome or place it under the authority of a layman. He was sentenced to be drawn, hanged, and quartered—the traditional punishment for a traitor. However, the king changed the punishment to beheading. More displayed great dignity and even humor throughout his trial and imprisonment, right up to the moment of his execution.

parasites[19] and purveyors[20] of empty pleasures. On the contrary, it makes no benevolent provi-
3 sion for farmers, colliers, common laborers, carters, and carpenters without whom there would be no commonwealth at all. After it has misused the labor of their prime[21] and after they are weighed down with age and disease and are in utter want, it forgets all their sleepless nights and all the great benefits received at their hands and most ungratefully requites them[22] with a most miserable death.

What is worse, the rich every day extort a part of their daily allowance from the poor not only by private fraud but by public law. Even before they did so it seemed unjust that persons deserving best of the commonwealth should have the worst return. Now they have further distorted and debased the right[23] and, finally, by making laws, have palmed it off as justice. Consequently, when I consider and turn over in my mind the state of all commonwealths flourishing anywhere today, so help me God, I can see nothing else than a kind of conspiracy of the rich, who are aiming at their own interests under the name and title of the commonwealth. They invent and devise all ways and means by which, first, they may keep without fear of loss all that they have amassed by evil practices and, secondly, they may then purchase as cheaply as possible and abuse the toil and labor of all the poor. These devices become law as soon as the rich have once decreed their observance in the name of the public—that is, of the poor also!

Yet when these evil men with insatiable greed have divided up among themselves all the goods which would have been enough for all the people, how far they are from the happiness of the Utopian commonwealth! In Utopia all greed for money was entirely removed with the use of money. What a mass of troubles was then cut away! What a crop of crimes was then pulled up by the roots! Who does not know that fraud, theft, rapine,[24] quarrels, disorders, brawls, seditions, murders, treasons, poisonings, which are avenged rather than restrained by daily executions, die out with the destruction of money? Who does not know that fear, anxiety, worries, toils, and sleepless nights will also perish at the same time as money? What is more, poverty, which alone money seemed to make poor, forthwith[25] would itself dwindle and disappear if money were entirely done away with everywhere. ❖

19. **parasites:** people who live off the generosity of others.
20. **purveyors:** suppliers.
21. **prime:** a period or phase of peak condition.
22. **requites them:** pays them back.
23. **debased the right:** corrupted what is right, lowering its value.
24. **rapine:** forcible seizure of another's property.
25. **forthwith:** immediately.

WORDS TO KNOW

benevolent (bə-nĕv′ə-lənt) *adj.* intended to promote the happiness of others; kindly
insatiable (ĭn-sā′shə-bəl) *adj.* impossible to satisfy

Customizing Instruction

Less Proficient Readers

Use the following questions to make sure that students understand the narrator's main points about societies outside of Utopia:

- Why, according to the narrator, must people outside Utopia concern themselves mainly with their private interests? *(They will starve unless they take care of themselves.)*
- What is unjust about the way laborers are treated outside of Utopia? *(Although they perform the most essential work, they are paid the least.)*

English Learners

1 Tell students that *commonwealth* refers to a state, or nation. Point out that this term is derived from the words *common* and *weal* ("good"), which suggests that the state is founded for the public good. The narrator plays off this meaning when he says that only Utopia can rightly claim the name of commonwealth.

2 Tell students that a *dowry* is money or property that a bride's family gives to her husband or his family at marriage.

3 Tell students that the word *colliers* means "coal miners."

MINI LESSON Grammar

GERUNDS

Instruction A gerund is a verb form that ends in *-ing* and functions as a noun. Gerunds can be used in sentences in almost every way that nouns can be used. A gerund phrase consists of a gerund and its modifiers and complements.

Practice Write the following examples on the board:

Farming is done by all citizens.

Saving money for retirement is unnecessary.

The underlined word in the first sentence is a gerund. The underlined section of the second sentence is a gerund phrase. The gerund *saving* is modified by the direct object *money* and the prepositional phrase *for retirement.* Make sure that students do not confuse gerunds with present participles, which also end in *-ing.*

For more instruction and practice in gerunds and gerund phrases, see McDougal Littell's ***Language Network:***
- Grade 10, Chapter 3, "Using Phrases"
- Grade 12, Chapter 2, "Using Phrases"

Connect to the Literature

1. **What Do You Think?** Possible Responses: Some students might say they would like to live in Utopia because all citizens are treated equally; others might say that they would dislike living there because its laws discourage personal initiative and creativity.

Comprehension Check
- 40
- Everyone works, and only useful trades are practiced.
- All clothes are cut to the same pattern.

Use Selection Quiz in **Unit Five Resource Book,** p. 40.

Think Critically

2. Possible benefits: everyone has a place in society; no one is overworked. Possible drawbacks: takes away incentive for people to work hard; discourages innovation; people might lack the freedom to develop their talents.
3. The Utopians think that money causes greed and crime. Some students might agree that money must be eliminated to achieve social justice; others might argue that money is necessary to develop a complex society.
4. In Utopia everyone shares in the farm work; people only work six hours a day; there is no money; everyone's future is secure; everyone lives in the same manner. In other countries only farmers do agricultural work; work hours vary widely, with laborers putting in long hours; one must save up for one's old age; some people live in great splendor while most endure poverty.
5. Some students might feel that Utopia is an ideal society because everyone's basic needs are taken care of and there is no inequality or crime. Others might respond that it isn't ideal because these benefits come at the expense of personal freedom and privacy.

Connect to the Literature

1. **What Do You Think?** Do you think that you would like to live in Utopia? Cite details in the text to support your response.

Comprehension Check
- About how many people live in a rural household: 5, 10, or 40?
- Why don't Utopians have to work long hours?
- How would you describe Utopian fashions?

Think Critically

2. Most Utopian men learn their father's craft, and most workers follow the same daily schedule. What are the benefits of such a system, and what are the drawbacks? Support your opinion with details from the text.
3. Why have the Utopians done away with money? What do you think of this idea?
4. **ACTIVE READING: DRAWING CONCLUSIONS** Get together with a classmate and compare the charts you made in your  **READER'S NOTEBOOK**. What are the main differences between Utopia and other countries? What conclusions can you draw about those differences?
5. All aspects of life in Utopia are meant to promote "the public welfare." Do you think that Utopia is truly an ideal society?

THINK ABOUT
- how Utopians achieve equality
- the duties that Utopian individuals have to society
- the amount of personal freedom in Utopian society

Extend Interpretations

6. **Critic's Corner** The writer Anatole France made the following comment about the human desire for a perfect society: "Without the Utopias of other times, men would still live in caves, miserable and naked. . . . Utopia is the principle of all progress." What do you think France meant? Explain.
7. **Connect to Life** Suppose that Raphael Hythloday were transported to the present time. Do you think he would consider our economy "a kind of conspiracy of the rich"?

LITERARY ANALYSIS: AUTHOR'S PURPOSE

Authors write for any of the following purposes:
- to entertain (for example, a comical sketch)
- to inform (for example, a news article)
- to express opinions (for example, an editorial)
- to persuade (for example, a political speech)

An author may fulfill more than one purpose in a particular piece of writing. For example, newspaper editorial writers often try to persuade readers as well as express opinions.

Cooperative Learning Activity Make a list, like the one shown below, of More's possible purposes for writing *Utopia.* Feel free to add other ideas that come to mind. Then put a check next to the statement that, in your judgment, best describes More's purpose. Compare your choice with those of your classmates, and explain your reasoning.

Possible Purposes
- To persuade people that Utopia should be imitated in real life
- To express opinions about the failings of English society
- To entertain readers with a thought-provoking work

Extend Interpretations

6. **Critic's Corner** Possible Response: Humans have become more advanced because some people have imagined ideal societies and have made efforts to achieve them.
7. **Connect to Life** Students might respond that Hythloday would still see great inequalities in modern capitalism. Other students might argue that he would have a better view of our economy if he learned about the history of Communist states.

Literary Analysis

Cooperative Learning Activity Students should list plausible purposes and should justify their choice of the best one with sound reasoning.

Use **Unit Five Resource Book,** p. 38, for more practice.

Vocabulary in Action

EXERCISE: ANTONYMS Match each word in the first column with the word in the second column that is most nearly opposite in meaning. Use each word only once.

1. novice	a. cruel
2. prevalent	b. encourage
3. indigent	c. optional
4. compulsory	d. carefree
5. insatiable	e. satisfiable
6. superfluous	f. master
7. benevolent	g. wealthy
8. hinder	h. occasionally
9. incessantly	i. unusual
10. grave	j. essential

Building Vocabulary

For an in-depth lesson on using a dictionary and a thesaurus, see page 558.

Connect to Today

Searching for Utopia

The longing for an ideal society began long before Thomas More's day, and people have never stopped imagining such a place. Plato described an ideal state in his *Republic,* and Jonathan Swift portrayed a rational and "humane" world of intelligent horses in *Gulliver's Travels.* In modern times, some political leaders have tried to create utopias in their countries, often with disastrous results. To enforce the equal sharing of property, for example, various communist governments have treated citizens with shocking brutality. Books and movies like *The Giver, Brave New World,* and *Animal Farm* show how the "perfect" society can go horribly wrong.

Group Activity With a small group of classmates, devise your own ideal community. Give it a name. Where will it be? Who can live there? Decide on the government, the housing, the community's work ethic, and its social rules. Then give an oral or written report describing your ideal place.

Illustration showing Sir Thomas More's island of Utopia

Vocabulary in Action

1. f	6. j
2. i	7. a
3. g	8. b
4. c	9. h
5. e	10. d

To assess skills and concepts taught in this selection, use **Formal Assessment Book,** pp. 119–120.

Connect to Today

"Searching for Utopia" relates the excerpt from *Utopia* to the history of human efforts to imagine and create an ideal society. It also mentions the genre of dystopian literature, which depicts the dangers of such efforts.

Group Activity Before they begin planning their ideal community, students might list the social problems that they most want to eliminate.

Objectives
- learn about the history of the sonnet
- understand why the sonnet became so popular
- become familiar with the structure of the sonnet

The Ever-Popular Sonnet
The term *sonnet* comes from an Italian word that means "little song." Sonnets were first composed by 13th century Sicilian poets. Over the next three centuries, the form spread throughout Europe. Except for a period of neglect in the 18th century, the sonnet has continued to thrive. Rilke, W. H. Auden, and Dylan Thomas are some of the most distinguished modern sonnet writers.

What Is a Sonnet?
Fewer words rhyme in English than in Italian. To overcome this handicap, English poets developed a rhyme scheme that is less difficult to work with than that of the Petrarchan sonnet. Poets have continued to experiment with the sonnet structure, varying the rhyme scheme and the number of lines. Some poets have even written unrhymed sonnets. The adaptability of the sonnet is one reason why it has remained so popular over the centuries.

The Sonnet

The Ever-Popular Sonnet

The sonnet became one of the most popular literary forms of the Renaissance, and its popularity continues today. Because Renaissance sonnets so often deal with love, they appealed especially to the young. As a new art form, the sonnet represented a break with the past because Renaissance poets typically wrote sonnets in their own language instead of in Latin, the literary language of the Middle Ages.

Reasons for Popularity The sonnet became popular because it caught the spirit of the age. Poets used the sonnet to express deeply personal feelings about love and life. Readers enjoyed the sonnet partly because they found their own thoughts and feelings reflected there. The sonnet also provided a feast for the ears because poets created beautiful sound patterns that made the poems a pleasure to read aloud.

The Sonnet Through the Ages

1300s	Francesco Petrarch *1304–1374*	ITALY
1500s	Pierre de Ronsard *1524–1585* William Shakespeare *1564–1616*	FRANCE ENGLAND
1600s	Sor Juana Inés de la Cruz *1651?–1695*	MEXICO
1800s	William Wordsworth *1770–1850*	ENGLAND
1900s	Jorge Luis Borges *1899–1986* Gwendolyn Brooks *1917–2000*	ARGENTINA UNITED STATES

Sonnet Structure A sonnet is a highly structured form of poetry. Renaissance writers and readers knew the "rules" of that structure. Knowing the basic elements of sonnet structure will help you become a better reader of sonnets.

What Is a Sonnet?

Length A sonnet is 14 lines long.

Rhyme Scheme A sonnet typically follows a **rhyme scheme,** or pattern of end rhyme, which makes the poem pleasing to the ear and easier to memorize. To identify a poem's rhyme scheme, you assign a letter of the alphabet to each line according to the rhymed sound at the end of the line, as illustrated by the example on the next page.

The Petrarchan Sonnet One type of sonnet, the Petrarchan sonnet, takes its name from Petrarch, the Italian poet who perfected the form. Petrarchan sonnets are often divided into two major sections. The first section, called an **octave,** is eight lines, and the second, a **sestet,** is six lines.

The Shakespearean Sonnet When the sonnet form reached England, poets modified its form somewhat. Shakespeare became such a master of the English form that eventually it took his name: the Shakespearean sonnet. Study his "Sonnet 73" on the next page.

A Sonnet Analyzed

The following poem illustrates the structure of the Shakespearean sonnet. Note that the poem consists of three groups of four rhymed lines, called **quatrains,** and a rhymed pair of lines, called a **couplet.**

Generally, the first quatrain introduces a situation or problem. Here, the speaker asks someone ("thou") to notice how he is in decline, like the autumn.

That time of year thou mayst in me behold *a*
When yellow leaves, or none, or few, do hang *b*
Upon those boughs which shake against the cold, *a*
Bare ruined choirs, where late the sweet birds sang. *b*
In me thou see'st the twilight of such day *c*
As after sunset fadeth in the west; *d*
Which by and by black night doth take away, *c*
Death's second self, that seals up all in rest. *d*
In me thou see'st the glowing of such fire, *e*
That on the ashes of his youth doth lie, *f*
As the deathbed whereon it must expire, *e*
Consumed with that which it was nourished by. *f*
This thou perceiv'st, which makes thy love more strong, *g*
To love that well which thou must leave ere long. *g*

—Shakespeare, *Sonnet 73*

The rhyme pattern, *abab,* marks this group of four lines as a quatrain.

In this quatrain, the speaker compares himself to the day fading at twilight.

Here, the speaker compares himself to a fire, which must die out.

Often, a turn, or shift in thought, occurs in the third quatrain or in the couplet. Here, the couplet provides a new twist on the subject developed in the previous quatrains: Because everything in life is subject to decline and death, we must love while we can.

Strategies for Reading: The Sonnet

1. Read the sonnet several times, at least once aloud.
2. Use letters to label like-sounding words or syllables at the ends of lines. The labeling will allow you to identify the **rhyme scheme**. Then use the rhyme scheme and end punctuation marks to identify major units of thought or feeling.
3. In your own words, describe the situation introduced in the first part of the sonnet. Continue through each of the major units of thought, stating in your own words the ideas or feelings expressed by the speaker.
4. Look for a **turn,** if there is one.
5. Study the **imagery** and **figurative language** for clues to the emotions expressed.

Strategies for Reading

Tell students that Shakespearean sonnets are written in iambic pentameter, the most common meter in English poetry. Each line can be divided into five metrical units that consist of an unstressed syllable followed by a stressed syllable. Point out instances where Shakespeare varies from this pattern. For example, he creates a dramatic effect by opening the final couplet with a stressed syllable.

LEARNING THE LANGUAGE OF LITERATURE 805

Objectives

- understand and appreciate **sonnets (Literary Analysis)**
- identify **extended metaphors (Literary Analysis)**
- use strategies for **comparing and contrasting speakers (Active Reading)**

Thematic Link

These sonnets demonstrate the **possibility** of immortal love through literature.

5-Minute Warm-Up

Daily Language SkillBuilder

Have students **proofread** the display sentences on page 685k and write them correctly.

Reading and Analyzing

Literary Analysis

EXTENDED METAPHOR

Remind students that in an extended metaphor, two things are compared at length and in various ways. Tell them that as they read this poem, they should pay attention to images that are related to each other in some way. For example, the word *strokes* in line 6 means "hits" or "blows," which describes the action of the arrow imagery that appears later in the poem.

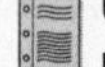

Use **Unit Five Resource Book,** p. 42, for more practice.

Francesco Petrarch
1304–1374

Renaissance Man Francesco Petrarch's life reflects the spirit of the Renaissance. As a scholar, Petrarch (pē'trärk') promoted interest in the literature of ancient Greece and Rome, even helping to recover lost texts. As a poet writing in his native Italian, he perfected the sonnet form. Because of his influence, the sonnet spread to all corners of Europe. He also had a deep interest in religious studies, which led him to join the clergy. In 1340, Petrarch received invitations from both Paris and Rome to become poet laureate. He chose Rome and in 1341 was honored for being that city's first poet laureate since ancient times.

Build Background

The Mysterious Laura Like his friend Giovanni Boccaccio, Petrarch was inspired by a mysterious woman who probably died in the plague of 1348. Most of the 366 sonnets and odes in the Canzoniere (Book of Songs), Petrarch's poetic masterpiece, are about his love for this woman, known as Laura. Most of what we know about Laura comes from the poems. "Sonnet 3" describes the first time Petrarch sees Laura, reportedly in a church during Good Friday services on April 6, 1327. Although Laura did not return his love, Petrarch remained devoted to her, and his poems explore the conflicting emotions she aroused in him.

Connect to Your Life

In the two sonnets that follow, the speakers address women whom they love but who do not return their love. Discuss examples of books and films featuring characters who try to get someone to fall in love with them. What tactics do they use? Which of the tactics are most effective?

Focus Your Reading

LITERARY ANALYSIS: EXTENDED METAPHOR

A **metaphor** is a comparison between two things that are basically unlike but have something in common. In an **extended metaphor**, two things are compared at length and in various ways. As you read the sonnets, look for metaphors that make simple comparisons and for extended metaphors.

ACTIVE READING: COMPARING AND CONTRASTING SPEAKERS

As you will see, the speakers in the following two poems express very different ideas about love. These different ideas may reflect the personalities of the poets.

READER'S NOTEBOOK As you read each sonnet, pay close attention to the feelings and attitudes of the speaker. Look for evidence of each speaker's "personality" in clues provided in the poems. Record your findings in your notebook.

LESSON RESOURCES

UNIT FIVE RESOURCE BOOK,
pp. 41–42

ASSESSMENT RESOURCES
Formal Assessment, pp. 121–122
Teacher's Guide to Assessment and Portfolio Use
Test Generator

INTEGRATED TECHNOLOGY
Visit our Web site: classzone.com

ADDITIONAL RESOURCES
Lesson Planning Guide, pp. 101–102
Teacher's Sourcebook for Language Development

Sonnet 3

Francesco Petrarch

Translated by Joseph Auslander

HUMANITIES CONNECTION This late-19th-century painting illustrates Petrarch's first sight of Laura. The young Petrarch, shown in red, is staring at Laura, whose attention is focused elsewhere.

It was the morning of that blessèd day
Whereon the Sun in pity veiled his glare
For the Lord's agony, that, unaware,
I fell a captive, Lady, to the sway
Of your swift eyes: that seemed no time to stay
The strokes of Love: I stepped into the snare
Secure, with no suspicion: then and there
I found my cue in man's most tragic play.
Love caught me naked to his shaft, his sheaf,
The entrance for his ambush and surprise
Against the heart wide open through the eyes,
The constant gate and fountain of my grief:
How craven so to strike me stricken so,
Yet from you fully armed conceal his bow!

4 sway: influence; control.

5 stay: to hold back; stop.

8 man's most tragic play: the crucifixion of Christ, celebrated on Good Friday.

9 Love . . . his sheaf: Love is often personified by a young boy shooting an arrow (shaft). A sheaf is a case for carrying arrows.

13 craven: cowardly.

Customizing Instruction

Less Proficient Readers

Make sure that students have a clear idea of the time and place in which this poem is set. Ask them to identify details that provide clues to the setting. *(the morning of that blessèd day . . . the Lord's agony)*

Ask students to describe the speaker's feelings in their own words.

Possible Response: He is frustrated because he has fallen deeply in love with a woman who doesn't share his feelings.

English Learners

Break this poem up into manageable segments for students. Lines 1–5 describe the poem's setting. Lines 5–12 describe in figurative language the act of falling in love at first sight. Lines 13–14 describe the speaker's feelings about this event.

Advanced Learners

Point out that an exchange of glances is the only action described in this poem. Have students discuss the importance of eye contact in courtship. Ask them why the speaker would describe his eyes as the "constant gate and fountain of my grief."

Possible Response: They are a gate because love must pass through them to reach his heart; they are a fountain because tears flow from them.

MINI LESSON Viewing and Representing

Petrarch's First Sight of Laura **by William Cave Thomas**

ANALYZING VISUAL IMAGES Have students look at the illustration and the **Humanities Connection** on page 807. Ask students what details in this painting illustrate the event described in "Sonnet 3."

Possible Responses: The boy taking communion at the altar and the architecture in the background are clues that the people are in church; Petrarch's gaze and gestures suggest that he is agitated or strongly affected by the sight of Laura; Laura's posture and her staring off to the side suggest that she isn't interested in him, or at least she does not notice him.

Literary Analysis IMAGERY

Remind students that imagery is words and phrases that appeal to the senses. Have students identify the senses that are appealed to by the images in "To Hélène." Ask them what sort of mood these images help create in the poem.

Possible Responses: The poem includes visual ("at evening candle-lit") and auditory ("murmur") imagery. The image of Hélène sitting by the fire might also appeal to the sense of touch since it suggests warmth. These images help create a somber mood.

Active Reading

COMPARING AND CONTRASTING SPEAKERS

Tell students that as one reads a poem, the speaker takes on a distinct personality. Remind them to look for evidence of the speaker's thoughts and feelings as they read each sonnet.

 Use **Unit Five Resource Book,** p. 41, for more practice.

Pierre de Ronsard
1524–1585

Early Years Pierre de Ronsard (rôN-sär') was born in a French castle. His father, a soldier, planned for Ronsard to pursue a military and diplomatic career. As a youth, Ronsard served as a page and a squire at the French court, but his career abruptly ended after a serious illness left him partially deaf. He then devoted himself to a classical education and studied Greek and Latin poets.

Prince of Poets In the 1550s, Ronsard published a number of poetry collections, which established his reputation. Ambitious and often arrogant, he claimed to be the first French lyrical poet and set out to prove himself as the literary equal of Horace and Petrarch. As a result of his success, Ronsard was called "the Prince of French Poets" and was honored in 1558 by being named the official court poet by King Henry II.

Years of Obscurity Toward the end of his life, however, Ronsard experienced another serious illness as well as the failure of *La Franciade* (1572), his sprawling epic about France. He also lost favor with the French king, Henry III, who preferred another poet. During this time, he wrote a series of sonnets about Hélène de Surgères, a young lady-in-waiting at the French court. These sonnets reflect the sufferings and disappointments of an aging poet. Ronsard was largely ignored for two centuries after his death in 1585.

Old Woman Reading (1665), Harmenz van Rijn Rembrandt. Private collection/The Bridgeman Art Library, London.

Cross Curricular Link **Humanities**

WOMEN IN SONNETS Petrarch owed much to the courtly love tradition. Like the knights of medieval poetry, his speaker has fallen passionately in love with a beautiful but unobtainable lady. However, Laura has no husband; it is her aloofness, not social convention, that keeps her from returning the speaker's love. In one of his books, Petrarch makes clear that marriage and motherhood were incompatible with the sort of idealized love he wished to celebrate in his sonnets: "Let those have wives who take delight in endless company with women, nightly embraces and wranglings, the wailing of babies and sleepless nights. . . . We, if it may be, will propagate our name not by marriage but by talent, not by children but by books, not by the aid of a woman but of virtue." Petrarch's attitudes toward women and love are echoed in the sonnets of Ronsard and many other sonnet writers in the Renaissance.

TO HÉLÈNE

PIERRE DE RONSARD

Translated by Humbert Wolfe

When you are old, at evening candle-lit
beside the fire bending to your wool,
1 read out my verse and murmur, "Ronsard writ
this praise for me when I was beautiful."
And not a maid but, at the sound of it,
though nodding at the stitch on broidered stool,
will start awake, and bless love's benefit
2 whose long fidelities bring Time to school.
I shall be thin and ghost beneath the earth
by myrtle shade in quiet after pain,
but you, a crone, will crouch beside the hearth
mourning my love and all your proud disdain.
And since what comes to-morrow who can say?
Live, pluck the roses of the world to-day.

6 broidered: embroidered.

10 by myrtle shade: under the shade of a myrtle tree.

11 crone: old woman.

Customizing Instruction

Less Proficient Readers

Point out that the poem's opening phrase indicates that the speaker is discussing something that will happen in the future. Make sure students understand that although the speaker describes Hélène as an old woman, he is addressing his beloved in her youth.

English Learners

1 Explain that the word *writ* is used as the past tense for *write*.

2 Explain that the phrase "bring to school" can mean "discipline" or "reprimand" (Ronsard is suggesting in line 8 that ideal love brings immortality).

Cross Curricular Link Humanities

RONSARD'S INFLUENCE In one of his early collections of verse, the Irish poet William Butler Yeats included a poem that was based on Ronsard's "To Hélène":

When You Are Old

When you are old and grey and full of sleep,
And nodding by the fire, take down this book,
And slowly read, and dream of the soft look
Your eyes had once, and of their shadows deep;

How many loved your moments of glad truce,
And loved your beauty with love false or true,
But one man loved the pilgrim soul in you,
And loved the sorrows of your changing face;

And bending down beside the glowing bars,
Murmur, a little sadly, how Love fled
And paced upon the mountains overhead
And hid his face amid a crowd of stars.

Connect to the Literature

1. **What Do You Think?** Which images remain in your mind after reading these sonnets?

Comprehension Check
- In "Sonnet 3," who has been struck by the arrows of love?
- What future event is imagined in "Sonnet to Hélène"?

Think Critically

2. What do you learn about the speaker in "Sonnet 3" and about the woman he loves?
3. Review the closing **couplet,** the last two lines, of "Sonnet to Hélène." What do these lines reveal about what the speaker desires?
4. In your judgment, why does each poem include references to death?

THINK ABOUT
- why the speaker in "Sonnet 3" takes his "cue" from the Crucifixion
- how the speaker in "Sonnet to Hélène" imagines his own death

5. **ACTIVE READING: COMPARING AND CONTRASTING SPEAKERS** Look over the information you recorded in your READER'S NOTEBOOK. What similarities and differences do you see between the speaker in Petrarch's "Sonnet 3" and the speaker in Ronsard's "Sonnet to Hélène"?

Extend Interpretations

6. **The Writer's Style** The term **tone** refers to a writer's attitude toward his or her subject. How would you describe the **tone** of each sonnet? How does the tone help convey each sonnet's meaning?
7. **Connect to Life** Which of these poems offers a more realistic portrayal of love? Explain your reasoning.

LITERARY ANALYSIS: EXTENDED METAPHOR

A **metaphor** is figurative language that makes a comparison between two essentially different things that have something in common. Unlike a simile, a metaphor does not contain the word *like* or *as.* At the end of Ronsard's "Sonnet to Hélène," the phrase "pluck the roses of the world to-day" is a metaphor in which the enjoyment of love is compared to picking roses while they are in bloom.

In an **extended metaphor,** two things are compared at length and in various ways. Petrarch's "Sonnet 3" contains a central, extended metaphor in which falling in love is compared to being trapped and then struck by an arrow. This metaphor is interwoven throughout most of the poem.

Paired Activity With a partner, make a list of each word and phrase used to extend the central metaphor in "Sonnet 3." Then write your interpretation of the metaphor.

Connect to the Literature

1. **What Do You Think?** Possible Responses: love striking the speaker of "Sonnet 3" with his arrow; the image of Hélène beside the fire.

Comprehension Check
- the speaker
- Hélène will read the speaker's verse when she is old and regret rejecting him.

Think Critically

2. The speaker has fallen in love with a woman who does not love him; he resents that love didn't strike her as well.
3. He wants her to love him and stop rejecting his love for her.
4. "Sonnet 3" compares falling in love to being hunted and suggests that the speaker is a martyr to love. In "To Hélène," the speaker suggests that our mortality makes it important for us to experience love while we can.
5. Possible Responses: Both are in love with women who do not love them. The speaker of "Sonnet 3" offers no details that describe himself or his beloved, he portrays his beloved in idealistic terms, and he seems fatalistic about his experience of love; the speaker of "To Hélène" indicates that he is older than his beloved, he describes her "proud disdain," and he seems to harbor some hope that she may yet love him.

Extend Interpretations

6. **The Writer's Style** Possible Responses: "Sonnet 3" is written in a passionate tone that helps express the idea that unrequited love is a kind of martyrdom. The restrained tone of "To Hélène" gives us a sense of the speaker's maturity and is well suited to the rational argument he addresses to his beloved.
7. **Connect to Life** Students will probably respond that Ronsard's poem offers a more realistic portrayal because the speaker criticizes Hélène and describes how old age will affect her. Some students might respond that "Sonnet 3" offers a more realistic expression of a spurned lover's feelings.

Literary Analysis

Paired Activity Words and phrases: "fell a captive"; "strokes of Love"; "stepped into the snare"; "Love caught me naked to his shaft, his sheaf"; "ambush and surprise"; "fully armed"; "his bow." Possible interpretation: Love has shot an arrow into the speaker but has not struck the woman he loves.

Use **Unit Five Resource Book,** p. 42, for more practice.

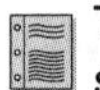

To assess skills and concepts taught in these selections, use **Formal Assessment Book,** pp. 121–122.

Dealing with the Sonnet

As you might imagine, translating a sonnet from one language to another is no easy task. To translate a sonnet by Petrarch, for example, a translator must decide whether to try to follow the Italian rhyme scheme in English. The translator also must work hard to find English words and phrases that suggest the meaning of the original Italian. At the same time, the English itself has to sound like a poem.

The following examples, using the first four lines of Petrarch's "Sonnet 3," illustrate some of the choices that translators make.

Petrarch's Original Italian

Era il giorno ch'al sol si scoloraro
Per la pietá del suo fattore i rai,
Quando i' fui preso, e non me ne guardai,
Ché i be' vostr'ochhi, donna, mi legaro.

Note that each line ends with a vowel, forming an *abba* rhyming pattern. As you can see, many Italian words end in vowels, which makes rhyming easy.

Translation by Joseph Auslander

It was the morning of that blessèd day
Whereon the Sun in pity veiled his glare
For the Lord's agony, that, unaware,
I fell a captive, Lady, to the sway

Auslander followed Petrarch's *abba* rhyme pattern. To find a rhyme for "day," however, Auslander chose "sway," which meant that he could not complete the sentence at the end of line 4.

Auslander established rhythm by using iambic pentameter. Each line has ten syllables, which follow a regular pattern of emphasis. See page 817 for more information about meter.

Auslander took some liberties. He made his reference to the Good Friday setting more obvious than Petrarch's: Auslander's translation refers directly to "the Lord's agony," while Petrarch's reference is more subtle.

Paired Activity With a partner, study the following translation of the same four lines from Petrarch's sonnet. Compare and contrast this version with Auslander's version. Which one do you prefer? Explain.

Translation by Mark Musa

It was the day the sun's ray had turned pale
with pity for the suffering of his Maker
when I was caught, and I put up no fight,
my lady, for your lovely eyes had bound me.

The Translator at Work

Literary Note Point out to students that the excerpt discussed on this page consists only of the first four lines of Petrarch's poem. The complete rhyme scheme of a Petrarchan sonnet is as follows:

Octave: *abbaabba*

Sestet: *cdecde* or *cdcdcd*

Explain to students that it is more difficult to come up with rhymes for a Petrarchan sonnet than for a Shakespearean sonnet because there are fewer choices for line endings.

Paired Activity Most students will probably prefer Musa's translation because it is more direct and doesn't have archaic constructions. Some might prefer the formal elegance of Auslander's translation.

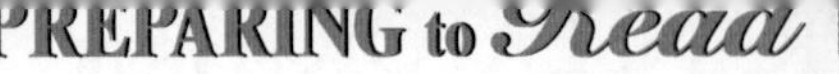

Objectives
- understand and appreciate **sonnets (Literary Analysis)**
- analyze **meter (Literary Analysis)**
- use strategies for **clarifying meaning in sonnets (Active Reading)**

Thematic Link
The psychological complexity of these sonnets gives a sense of the richness of **human possibility.**

5-Minute Warm-Up
Daily Language SkillBuilder

Have students **proofread** the display sentences on page 685k and write them correctly.

William Shakespeare
1564–1616

Ordinary Beginnings William Shakespeare, considered by many to be the greatest writer of the Western world, was the son of a merchant of Stratford-upon-Avon, England. Little is known about his youth. Although never educated at a university, he most likely attended his local grammar school, where he would have studied Latin and classical literature. In 1582, at the age of 18, he married Anne Hathaway, with whom he had two daughters and a son. Probably during the 1580s, he moved to London, where he launched his career as an actor and playwright for the Lord Chamberlain's Men (later known as the King's Men), London's leading theater company.

Popular Bard Shakespeare quickly became one of London's most prominent and successful playwrights. During his lifetime, he composed more than 35 plays, as well as 154 sonnets and two narrative poems. No other playwright of the period could match his range, and audiences responded strongly to his memorable and recognizably human characters. Shakespeare's plays appealed to everyone, from refined aristocrats to uneducated laborers.

Lasting Fame Shakespeare's success as a writer made him a wealthy, important citizen. He was one of seven shareholders who financed the construction of the Globe Theater in 1599. His plays were performed before Queen Elizabeth I and King James I. He was a welcome visitor in the homes of some of the finest families in London, a respected figure in the literary establishment, a loyal friend to fellow actors, and apparently a shrewd investor, because he was able to live in comfortable retirement after he left the theater. Today, Shakespeare's plays are performed more frequently, and in more countries, than the works of any other playwright.

LESSON RESOURCES

UNIT FIVE RESOURCE BOOK, pp. 43–44

ASSESSMENT RESOURCES
Formal Assessment, pp. 123–124
Teacher's Guide to Assessment and Portfolio Use
Test Generator

INTEGRATED TECHNOLOGY
Visit our Web site: classzone.com

ADDITIONAL RESOURCES
Lesson Planning Guide, pp. 103–104
Teacher's Sourcebook for Language Development

Build Background

Shakespeare's Sonnets Though Shakespeare is best known as a playwright, his sonnets alone would have made him an important author. In 1609, a collection of the sonnets appeared in print. He probably wrote most of them in the 1590s, when it was fashionable for English poets to create sonnet sequences—groups of sonnets arranged to form a narrative. As the chart below illustrates, Shakespeare's sonnets go beyond the conventions of the typical sonnet sequence.

Typical Sonnet Sequence	Shakespeare's Sonnets
Addressed to Beautiful, unattainable woman	• Some written to a handsome young man, a friend of the speaker • Some written to a mysterious "dark lady" • Some not addressed to anyone in particular
Subject Matter • The lady's coldness and beauty • The speaker's contradictory feelings • The immortality of poetry	The typical subjects, plus a broader range of issues, such as • friendship • fame • moral responsibility • the inevitability of death

WORDS TO KNOW **Vocabulary Preview**

anguish, commend, compel, deign, discretion, legitimate, meagerly, oblige, presumption, reproach

Connect to Your Life

With a classmate, share examples of songs about love. Do your examples show that love makes people feel more secure, or do they portray people who are made anxious by love? Why do you think love can have both of these effects?

Focus Your Reading

LITERARY ANALYSIS: METER

One of the distinctive characteristics of a sonnet is the **meter,** or predictable **rhythm.** The meter of a poem is like the beat of a song. The **Shakespearean sonnet** relies on the most commonly used type of meter in English poetry—**iambic pentameter.** In simple terms, that means that each ten-syllable line has five major stresses, following a pattern of unstressed and stressed syllables, a "da DUM, da DUM" rhythm. Note the five stresses in these lines from "Sonnet 29":

When in disgrace with Fortune and men's eyes
I all alone beweep my outcast state

When you read the sonnets that follow, try reading them aloud so that you can catch the beat.

ACTIVE READING: CLARIFYING MEANING IN SONNETS

Shakespeare's sonnets may be difficult to understand because he arranged words to fit the meter and rhyme scheme of the sonnet form. You can often clarify the meaning of a line or lines by following these two steps:

1. Rearrange the word order. Rearrange a line so that the subject comes closer to the verb: "When [I am] in disgrace."
2. **Paraphrase** certain lines by putting them in your own words. For example, the lines displayed above might be paraphrased as follows: "In those times when I have fallen out of favor because of misfortune or other people's bad opinion of me, I feel so completely alone that I cry."

READER'S NOTEBOOK As you read the sonnets, try paraphrasing some of their lines in your notebook.

READING FOR INFORMATION
Reading Skills and Strategies
ACTIVATING PRIOR KNOWLEDGE
Encourage students to share what they already know about Shakespeare and his works. Record such information on the board. After students have read pages 812 and 813, discuss what new information was learned. Add information to the list on the board.

Reading and Analyzing

Active Reading
CLARIFYING MEANING IN SONNETS

A Point out that the subject of the first sentence in "Sonnet 29" does not appear until the beginning of the second line. Have students rearrange the order of the first two lines to clarify their meaning. Then have them paraphrase the lines.

Possible Responses: when I, in disgrace with Fortune and men's eyes, beweep all alone my outcast state; when I, lacking good luck and the respect of others, lament my sad condition.

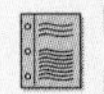
Use **Unit Five Resource Book,** p. 43, for more practice.

Literary Analysis METER

B Tell students that when they read the sonnets aloud, they should not rigidly follow the iambic pattern when it makes words sound unnatural. Shakespeare sometimes departs from the strict meter for emphasis or to add variety. For example, line 5 begins with a stressed syllable followed by an unstressed syllable: "Wishing me like to one more rich in hope."

Use **Unit Five Resource Book,** p. 44, for more practice.

Literary Analysis ALLITERATION

C Explain to students that alliteration is the repetition of initial consonant sounds. For example, the initial *s* sound is repeated three times in the first line of "Sonnet 30." Tell students that poets often use alliteration to emphasize certain words, to create mood, to underscore meaning, and to enhance rhythm. Encourage them to look for other examples of alliteration as they read the sonnets.

Sonnet 29

William Shakespeare

When in disgrace with Fortune and men's eyes
I all alone beweep my outcast state,
And trouble deaf heaven with my bootless cries,
And look upon myself and curse my fate,
Wishing me like to one more rich in hope,
Featur'd like him, like him with friends possess'd,
Desiring this man's art, and that man's scope,
With what I most enjoy contented least;
Yet in these thoughts myself almost despising,
Haply I think on thee, and then my state
(Like to the lark at break of day arising
From sullen earth) sings hymns at heaven's gate,
For thy sweet love rememb'red such wealth brings,
That then I scorn to change my state with kings.

2 state: condition.

3 bootless: useless.

6 featured like him, . . . possess'd: attractive-looking like one man, having friends like another.

7 scope: knowledge or intellectual powers.

10 haply: by chance or accident; **state:** mood.

12 sullen: dark; gloomy.

Love Among the Ruins (1894), Sir Edward Burne-Jones. Oil on canvas. Wightwick Manor, Staffordshire, United Kingdom. Photo © The Bridgeman Art Library.

Cross Curricular Link **Humanities**

PHRASES FROM SHAKESPEARE Many common phrases and familiar expressions in the English language first appeared in Shakespeare's works. Listed below are some examples and the plays they appear in:

- "an eye-sore" *(The Taming of the Shrew)*
- "bated breath" *(The Merchant of Venice)*
- "devil incarnate" *(Henry V)*
- "eaten me out of house and home" *(Henry IV, Part 2)*
- "good riddance" *(Troilus and Cressida)*
- "in my heart of hearts" *(Hamlet)*
- "into thin air" *(The Tempest)*
- "one fell swoop" *(Macbeth)*
- "pomp and circumstance" *(Othello)*
- "salad days" *(Antony and Cleopatra)*
- "strange bedfellows" *(The Tempest)*
- "The better part of valour is discretion." *(Henry IV, Part 1)*
- "The course of true love never did run smooth." *(A Midsummer Night's Dream)*
- "We have seen better days." *(As You Like It)*
- "wear my heart on my sleeve" *(Othello)*

Sonnet 30

William Shakespeare

Sir Henry Percy, Nicolas Hilliard. Rijksmuseum, Amsterdam, The Netherlands.

When to the sessions of sweet silent thought
I summon up remembrance of things past,
I sigh the lack of many a thing I sought,
And with old woes new wail my dear time's waste;
Then can I drown an eye (unus'd to flow)
For precious friends hid in death's dateless night,
And weep afresh love's long since cancell'd woe,
And moan th' expense of many a vanish'd sight;
Then can I grieve at grievances foregone,
And heavily from woe to woe tell o'er
The sad account of fore-bemoaned moan,
Which I new pay as if not paid before:
  But if the while I think on thee, dear friend,
  All losses are restor'd, and sorrows end.

3 sigh: sigh for.

4 new . . . waste: express new sorrow for the waste of precious time.

6 dateless: never-ending.

7 cancell'd: paid in full with sadness.

8 expense: loss.

9 foregone: past.

10 heavily: sadly; **tell:** count.

11 sad . . . moan: the upsetting total of previously expressed sorrows.

Customizing Instruction

Less Proficient Readers

Use the following questions to check student's comprehension of the sonnets:

- What causes the speaker of "Sonnet 30" to grieve on occasion? *(his lack of good fortune and his personal deficiencies)*
- What things from the past does the speaker of "Sonnet 30" remember? *(things that he failed to acquire or achieve; friends who are now dead; old love affairs; the sight of things that are now gone; old grievances)*

English Learners

Point out to students that missing letters in some of the words in these poems are indicated with an apostrophe. For example, the apostrophe in *vanish'd* (line 8 of "Sonnet 30") indicates that the letter *e* is missing.

Advanced Learners

"Sonnet 29" and "Sonnet 30" both discuss how thinking about love or friendship can brighten one's mood. Have students discuss the differences between these two poems.

Possible Response: In "Sonnet 29," the speaker discusses being depressed about his present state of affairs, while in "Sonnet 30," the speaker's sadness is brought on by his contemplation of what he has lost or suffered in the past.

SONNET 30 **815**

Literary Analysis PERSONIFICATION

A Personification is a figure of speech in which human qualities are attributed to an object, animal, or idea. For example, in lines 1–2 of "Sonnet 64," Shakespeare describes monuments defaced by the cruel hand of time. Ask students to find other examples of personification in the poem.

Possible Responses: brass is a slave to decay; the ocean is hungry; the shore has a kingdom.

Active Reading

CLARIFYING MEANING IN SONNETS

Point out that the actions described in the first eight lines of "Sonnet 64" are summed up in the phrases "state itself confounded to decay" and "interchange of state." Have students paraphrase lines 9–12 to clarify their meaning.

Possible Response: When I have seen instances of things changing condition or falling into decay, such ruin has made me realize that time will come and take my love away.

Sonnet 64

William Shakespeare

A
When I have seen by Time's fell hand defaced
The rich proud cost of outworn buried age;
When sometime lofty towers I see down rased,
And brass eternal slave to mortal rage;
When I have seen the hungry ocean gain
Advantage on the kingdom of the shore,
And the firm soil win of the wat'ry main,
Increasing store with loss, and loss with store;
When I have seen such interchange of state,
Or state itself confounded to decay,
Ruin hath taught me thus to ruminate,
That Time will come and take my love away.
  This thought is as a death, which cannot choose
  But weep to have that which it fears to lose.

1 fell: cruel.

2 The rich . . . age: The monuments of old that were produced by great wealth and pride.

3 sometime: formerly.

4 brass . . . rage: long-lasting brass damaged by the destructive power of decay.

7 win of: gain at the expense of.

8 Increasing store . . . store: One gaining as the other loses, and vice versa.

9 state: condition.

10 state itself confounded: greatness itself reduced.

11 ruminate: to think about for a long time.

MINI LESSON **Speaking and Listening**

READING POETRY ALOUD Share the following strategies with students to help them read poetry aloud:

- Read through the poem carefully, noting down any unfamiliar words. Look up the meaning and pronunciation of these words in a dictionary.
- Pay attention to the feelings that the poem stirs up in you. Think about how you can convey those feelings to your listeners.
- Notice the meter or rhythm of the poem and any sound devices, such as rhyme or alliteration. Consider how you can use these elements to make your reading more enjoyable.
- When you read the poem aloud, you should not stop at the end of a line unless it coincides with the completion of a thought. You can usually tell where a thought is completed by looking for punctuation such as a period, question mark, or semicolon. You might also occasionally add brief pauses to emphasize certain words or create suspense.

Connect to the Literature

1. **What Do You Think?** Which sonnet made the most sense to you? Which sonnet left you with the most questions? Share your initial reactions with a classmate.

Comprehension Check
- What changes the speaker's mood in "Sonnet 29"?
- In "Sonnet 30," how does the speaker feel about the past?
- Which word best describes time in "Sonnet 64": *destructive, creative, powerless?*

Think Critically

2. The last six lines of "Sonnet 29" express a very different mood from the first eight lines. Such a shift in thought is called a **turn.** Describe both moods and explain what causes them.

THINK ABOUT
- why the speaker compares himself with others
- how the speaker views himself
- how the speaker feels about his "sweet love"

3. In "Sonnet 30," what does the speaker feel that he has lost, and how can such losses be "restored" (line 14)?

4. In "Sonnet 64," what are the powers of time, and how does the speaker feel about such powers?

5. **ACTIVE READING: CLARIFYING MEANING IN SONNETS** Get together with a classmate and compare what you each recorded in your READER'S NOTEBOOK. Then choose a particularly challenging passage (two to four lines) and restate that passage in your own words. Explain how the passage contributes to your understanding of the poem.

Extend Interpretations

6. **Critic's Corner** The critic Edward Dowden says that Shakespeare's sonnets "tell more of Shakespeare's sensitiveness than of Shakespeare's strength." Based on your readings, do you agree with this statement? Why or why not?

7. **Comparing Texts** Compare and contrast the speakers in two of the sonnets. What are the similarities and differences in their attitudes toward love?

8. **Connect to Life** Which of the three sonnets comes closest to your own views of love? Explain.

LITERARY ANALYSIS: METER

Meter is the rhythmical pattern of poetry. Like the beat of a song, meter establishes a predictable emphasis on certain syllables in the poem. A technique called **scanning** will enable you to determine the meter of a poem. To scan a poem, you need to mark the stressed and unstressed syllables, as shown by this example:

When I | have seen | by Time's | fell hand | defaced
The rich | proud cost | of out | worn bur | ied age;

When reading these lines aloud, you stress the syllables marked by the slanted lines. The syllables are grouped in units called **feet,** marked off by vertical lines. The pattern illustrated above—the basic pattern of Shakespeare's poetry—is called **iambic pentameter.** *Pentameter* means that there are five feet in each line. An **iamb** is a foot that consists of an unstressed syllable followed by a stressed one.

Paired Activity Work with a partner to scan one of the three sonnets. Be aware that Shakespeare sometimes varies the pattern by adding an extra syllable to a foot or by using a foot that is not an iamb. For example, some critics believe that line 2 of "Sonnet 29" begins with two accented syllables:

I all alone.

Literary Analysis

Paired Activity You might want to have one partner read the poem aloud while the other reads against the scanned poem to help them make sure that they have caught all variations in the meter.

Use **Unit Five Resource Book,** p. 44, for more practice.

To assess skills and concepts taught in these selections, use **Formal Assessment Book,** p. 123–124.

Connect to the Literature

1. **What Do You Think?** Answers will vary. Many students will find "Sonnet 64" the most challenging because of the complexity of its ideas.

Comprehension Check
- Thinking of his beloved's sweet love makes him realize that he is fortunate.
- He is saddened by it.
- destructive

Think Critically

2. In the first eight lines, the speaker is depressed over his lack of accomplishment; in the next six lines, thinking about his love makes him happy with his life.
3. "Losses" refers not only to friends who have died and old loves that have faded, but also to the pains and frustrations of his past. Thinking about his dear friend restores these losses, presumably by making him forget them.
4. Time causes things to alter in form or fall into ruin. These powers frighten the speaker because he knows that his beloved will be affected by them.
5. Answers will vary.

Extend Interpretations

6. **Critic's Corner** Students who agree might respond that the speakers of these sonnets are morbidly concerned with their own misfortunes and with fears about mortality. Students who disagree might respond that the speakers of "Sonnet 29" and "Sonnet 30" show strength in overcoming their despair with the help of love.
7. **Comparing Texts** Possible Response: The speakers of "Sonnet 29" and "Sonnet 64" are both strongly affected by love. The speaker of "Sonnet 29" becomes joyous and gains self-esteem when he thinks about his beloved. By contrast, love makes the speaker of "Sonnet 64" more insecure because he broods upon his lover's inevitable death.
8. **Connect to Life** Answers will vary.

SHAKESPEARE SONNETS 817

The Publication of Shakespeare's Works

Shakespeare's sonnets were published in one volume in 1609, when he was 45 and at the height of his fame as a playwright. However, only 18 of his plays appeared in print during his lifetime. Elizabethan playwrights generally sold plays to theater companies and did not receive money for publication. (Shakespeare owned a share of his theater company's profits, which provided the bulk of his income.) The theater companies were reluctant to allow their plays to be published because they wanted to prevent rival companies from performing them. Those plays that did get published appeared in cheap quarto editions, which were often based on the playwright's rough drafts or on the memories of actors who performed in them. Shakespeare isn't even listed as the author on about half of his quartos. Seven years after his death, two of Shakespeare's close associates collected nearly all of his plays and published them in a handsome bound volume. This 1623 edition, known as the First Folio, played a crucial role in preserving Shakespeare's work for posterity.

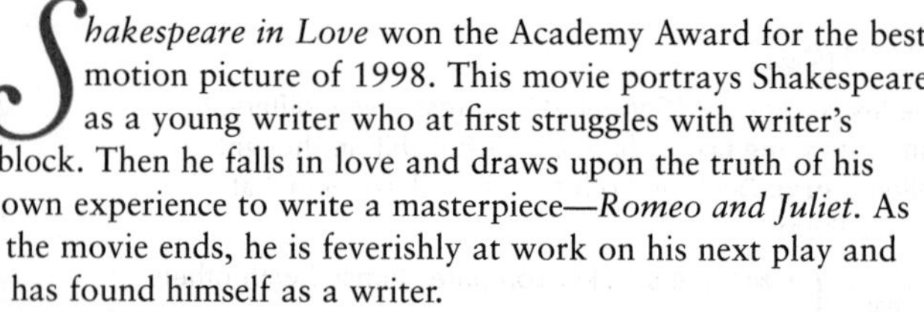

Shakespeare in Love won the Academy Award for the best motion picture of 1998. This movie portrays Shakespeare as a young writer who at first struggles with writer's block. Then he falls in love and draws upon the truth of his own experience to write a masterpiece—*Romeo and Juliet.* As the movie ends, he is feverishly at work on his next play and has found himself as a writer.

Although audiences loved this movie, it is based more on fiction than fact. Most of the details of Shakespeare's life are unknown. What is certain is that he became one of the greatest dramatists who ever lived. From about 1590 to 1613, he wrote approximately 37 plays. Most of them were very popular in his time. Today, almost 400 years after his death, his plays still are widely read and performed all over the world. Their timeless appeal supports what Ben Jonson—a rival playwright—wrote of Shakespeare: "He was not of an age, but for all time."

Selected Plays by William Shakespeare

Histories	*Richard II, Richard III, Henry IV (Parts 1 and 2), Henry V*
Comedies	*The Comedy of Errors, The Taming of the Shrew, A Midsummer Night's Dream, The Merchant of Venice, As You Like It, Much Ado about Nothing, Twelfth Night*
Tragedies	*Romeo and Juliet, Julius Caesar, Hamlet, Othello, King Lear, Macbeth, Antony and Cleopatra*
Romances	*The Winter's Tale, The Tempest*

Most of these plays were first performed at the Globe Theater in London, England. This open-air theater could hold about 3,000 spectators. Its stage jutted out into a courtyard, allowing the actors to perform very close to the audience.

Like people today, this audience went to the theater to be entertained. Shakespeare gave them what they wanted—powerful speeches, sword fights, humor, and supernatural events. But Shakespeare did much more than write crowd pleasers. He also created characters who lived and breathed—characters as complex as real people —and put them in thrilling scenes. As the audience looked on, Romeo and Juliet expressed their doomed love, Hamlet held up a skull and looked death in the face, Mark Antony in *Julius Caesar* turned the citizens of Rome into a raging mob, and Macbeth met three witches who recognized his guilty soul.

Above:
An illustration of the Globe Theater

These characters and many others spoke some of the most beautiful language ever written for the theater. Shakespeare's language is marked by vivid imagery, an incredibly rich vocabulary, and subtle rhythms. Shakespeare used words in new ways to forge fresh comparisons and convey profound insights. For example, consider the following metaphorin *As You Like It:*

> **All the world's a stage,**
> **And all the men and women merely players;**
> **They have their exits and their entrances,**
> **And one man in his time plays many parts,**
> **His acts being seven ages.**

Notice the insight about human life that the following lines from *The Tempest* convey:

> **We are such stuff**
> **As dreams are made on, and our little life**
> **Is rounded with a sleep.**

Shakespeare's plays are treasures of the English language. They continue to stir the imagination, expand the mind, and engage the feelings. They invite readers and audiences to experience what it means to be human.

Shakespeare's Rivals

Shakespeare was the greatest playwright of his age and perhaps of any age. However, he did have rivals (some of whom made appearances in the film *Shakespeare in Love*). Here are a few other notable Elizabethan playwrights:

Christopher Marlowe Marlowe's plays, written in stirring blank verse, feature tragic heroes who are driven by excessive ambition. His great tragedy *Doctor Faustus* is about a scholar who sells his soul to the devil in exchange for knowledge and power.

Ben Jonson Many of Jonson's plays are comedies that expose human folly. Although he sometimes criticized Shakespeare's writing, Jonson wrote a beautiful poem for the First Folio that paid tribute to his genius.

John Webster Webster's two great tragedies, both set in Italy, portray a world of violence and decadence. In *The Duchess of Malfi,* Webster created one of the most complex and sympathetic heroines in Elizabethan drama.

MILESTONES IN WORLD LITERATURE **819**

Assign both "Sonnet 23" by Louise Labé and "Sonnet 165" by Sor Juana Inés de la Cruz to prepare students for the sample writing assessment provided on page 827. Use the **Points of Comparison** chart to guide students in identifying the similarities and differences between the two selections.

Use **Unit Five Resource Book,** p. 45, for a copy of the chart.

COMPARING LITERATURE ACROSS CULTURES

Sonnets by Women

OVERVIEW

As you know, the sonnet became popular in many different countries during the Renaissance. This lesson includes sonnets by two extraordinary women of the Renaissance, the French writer Louise Labé and the Mexican writer Sor Juana Inés de la Cruz. In order to write, both women had to break down barriers created by prejudice and social custom, for women were not expected to become authors.

In the pages that follow, you will be asked to compare and contrast two sonnets, both of which are about women who have been badly treated in love. Your comparisons should help you to appreciate the sonnet form and the perspective of two fascinating Renaissance writers.

Points of Comparison

Because the great majority of writers in the Renaissance period were male, most sonnets about love expressed a man's point of view. In this lesson, you will see love expressed from another perspective—a woman's. As you will see, both sonnets express various complaints about the man's role in love.

Analyzing Love Sonnets As you read the two sonnets, use a chart like the one shown to make notes about each sonnet.

	Sonnet 23 Louise Labé	Sonnet 165 Sor Juana Inés de la Cruz
What do you learn about the speaker's past relationship with the man being addressed?		
How does the speaker now feel about the man? What is the speaker's tone, or attitude, toward the subject of love?		
Does the speaker take any pleasure in her memories of love?		
How would you describe the personality of the speaker?		

Standardized Test Practice: Comparison-and-Contrast Essay After you finish reading the two sonnets, you will have the opportunity to write a comparison-and-contrast essay. Your notes will help you plan and write the essay.

Assessment Standardized Test Practice

COMPARISON-AND-CONTRAST ESSAY To give students practice in comparing two different pieces of literature, have them read both selections in this **Comparing Literature** feature, rather than treating each selection separately. Tell them to create a chart like the one shown here on page 820, and have them fill it out as they finish reading each of the two poems. (Examples of how to fill out the chart are supplied on pages 823 and 826.) A sample assessment writing prompt and guidelines for responding to it in writing are on page 827.

SONNET 23

Louise Labé

Objectives
- understand and compare two sonnets about women's experience in love **(Literary Analysis)**
- describe the **tone** expressed by the speaker in each poem **(Literary Analysis)**
- analyze the **diction** in each poem **(Active Reading)**

Thematic Link
These sonnets each present a woman's view of love in an era when the claims made for love seemed to expand **human possibility.**

5-Minute Warm-Up

Daily Language SkillBuilder

Have students **proofread** the display sentences on page 685k and write them correctly.

Louise Labé
1524?–1566

A Courtly Education Louise Labé (lä-bā') was born in Lyon, France. Her father was a prosperous ropemaker who could neither read nor write, yet he prepared his daughter for entrance into polite society by giving her an education. She studied Latin, Italian, music, and horsemanship, becoming an accomplished lute player, singer, and rider. In about 1543, she married a much older widower who was a successful ropemaker like her father. Before her husband's death in 1560, Labé fell in love with the poet Olivier de Magny, the subject of many of her love poems.

Literary Success In 1555, Labé published her only book, *Works*, which included 24 love sonnets and a prose "debate" between Folly and Love. In the book's preface, Labé called on women to set aside their chores and frivolous pastimes to pursue literature and other cultural activities.

Build Background

As you will see, the man who is addressed in "Sonnet 23" was well schooled in the ways of courtly love. According to the "rules" of such love, the male was supposed to be extravagant in his praise of the woman's beauty, comparing her physical qualities to the wonders of the natural world and swearing an eternal love.

Connect to Your Life

People in love often make it seem as if they have no power to resist. Think of phrases drawn from poetry, popular music, or your own experience that suggest love's power. Is it healthy or wise to think of love in such terms?

Focus Your Reading

LITERARY ANALYSIS: TONE

In oral communication, tone is usually easy to identify because the speaker's voice expresses the speaker's attitude and emotion. In writing, the tone is often more difficult to identify because the reader must make inferences about the writer's attitude. As you read "Sonnet 23," try to identify the tone, or attitude, expressed by the speaker about the man being described.

ACTIVE READING: ANALYZING DICTION

In poetry, the writer's **diction,** or word choice, often provides clues to the tone. In the first eight lines of "Sonnet 23," we learn how the man once described the speaker and his love for her. Beginning with line 9 the speaker expresses her own feelings about their relationship.

READER'S NOTEBOOK As you read, jot down key phrases from lines 1–8 and lines 9–14. You will analyze these phrases later.

TIME MANAGEMENT

If you wish to cover only one of the selections, use . . .
- Preparing to Read, p. 821 or p. 824
- Thinking Through the Literature, p. 823 or p. 826

If you want to take advantage of longer blocks of class time, use . . .
- TE Teaching Options: Cross-Curricular Link, p. 824; Speaking and Listening, p. 825

Reading and Analyzing

Literary Analysis SONNET

Point out that this poem follows the form of the Petrarchan or Italian sonnet. The first eight lines, or the octave, describe the speaker's problem. The next six lines, or the sestet, show the speaker's response to that problem. The poem is written in iambic pentameter.

Reading Skills and Strategies
PARAPHRASING

A Point out that the speaker begins by asking the man being addressed four questions about their past relationship. Ask students to rephrase the questions in simpler language.
Possible Responses: 1) What did I gain from all the times you praised my beauty? 2) What happened to all those tears that you shed for me? 3) Did you die, like you promised you would if you broke your word to me? 4) What happened to your promises to be faithful?

Literary Analysis TONE

Ask students how the speaker now feels about the man.
Possible Response: The speaker seems angry and bitter about the way the man failed to live up to his promises of love.

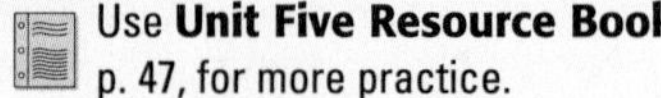
Use **Unit Five Resource Book,** p. 47, for more practice.

Active Reading DICTION

B Point out the speaker's use of the word "friend" in line 11. Ask students why the poet might have chosen this particular word.
Possible Response: The speaker is being sarcastic. The man can not be considered her friend because he did not prove constant in his love.

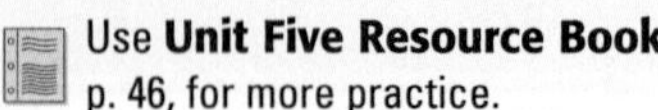
Use **Unit Five Resource Book,** p. 46, for more practice.

Sonnet 23

Louise Labé

Translated by
Willis Barnstone

Lady with Unicorn, Raphael. Galleria Borghese, Rome. Photo © Scala/Art Resource, New York.

What good is it to me if long ago
you eloquently praised my golden hair,
A compared my eyes and beauty to the flare
of two suns where, you say, love bent the bow,
sending the darts that needled you with grief?
Where are your tears that faded in the ground?
Your death? by which your constant love is bound
in oaths and honor now beyond belief?
Your brutal goal was to make *me* a slave
beneath the ruse of being served by you.
B Pardon me, friend, and for once hear me through:
I am outraged with anger and I rave.
Yet I am sure, wherever you have gone,
your martyrdom is hard as my black dawn.

2 eloquently: with powerful, persuasive words.

5 needled: pierced.

12 rave: speak wildly.

14 martyrdom: great suffering or death for one's beliefs.

LESSON RESOURCES

UNIT FIVE RESOURCE BOOK, pp. 45–48

ASSESSMENT RESOURCES
Formal Assessment, pp. 125–126
Teacher's Guide to Assessment and Portfolio Use
Test Generator

INTEGRATED TECHNOLOGY
Visit our Web site: classzone.com

ADDITIONAL RESOURCES
Lesson Planning Guide, pp. 105–106
Teacher's Sourcebook for Language Development

Connect to the Literature

1. **What Do You Think?** Based on your reading of the poem, what is your first impression of the speaker? Explain.

Think Critically

2. What do the first eight lines of the poem reveal about the past relationship between the speaker and the man being addressed?

- the language that he used to praise her beauty
- the promises that he made
- why the speaker says, "What good is it to me"

3. **ACTIVE READING: ANALYZING DICTION** Working with a partner, review the key phrases that you recorded in your **READER'S NOTEBOOK**. What do these phrases tell you about the speaker's attitude toward the man?
4. Why do you think the speaker accuses the man of wanting to make her "a slave / beneath the ruse of being served by you" (lines 9–10)?
5. The couplet at the end of the poem is puzzling to many readers. What do you think the speaker means by referring to the man's "martyrdom"? Explain.

LITERARY ANALYSIS: TONE

The **tone** of a literary work is the attitude that the writer takes toward his or her subject. To identify the tone of a poem, you may find it helpful to read the work aloud, as if giving a dramatic reading before an audience. You should try different ways of reading the poem, expressing a different emotion each time, to see which interpretation works best. For example, in one oral reading of "Sonnet 23" you might express the speaker's anger, while in another you might express her indifference.

Paired Activity With a partner, choose one phrase or line in "Sonnet 23" that best conveys the speaker's feelings toward the man. Then practice reading the poem aloud so that every line expresses the speaker's feelings. You may divide the poem into groups of lines so that you and your partner can take turns reading. Then recite the poem to the class.

Points of Comparison

Activity Review "Sonnet 23" and answer the questions in your comparison-and-contrast chart that pertain to it. An example has been done for you.

	Sonnet 23 Louise Labé	Sonnet 165 Sor Juana Inés de la Cruz
What do you learn about the speaker's past relationship with the man being addressed?	*The man promised to love her always.*	
How does the speaker now feel about the man? What is the speaker's tone, or attitude, toward the subject of love?		
Does the speaker take any pleasure in her memories of love?		
How would you describe the personality of the speaker?		

Connect to the Literature

1. **What Do You Think?** Answers will vary.

Think Critically

2. Possible Response: The man apparently was in love with the speaker. He praised her beauty; cried tears to show his feeling; and swore that he would be constant in his love to her. The speaker apparently believed his declarations of love and responded in kind.
3. Possible Response: Phrases such as "what good is it to me," "Where are your tears," "Your brutal goal," "outraged with anger," and "hard as my black dawn" suggest the speaker's anger and bitterness toward the man. She feels that her own love for the man was betrayed.
4. Possible Response: The man claimed to idealize the woman and presented himself as her servant. In actuality, that was a pose of love that gave him control over her.
5. Possible Response: The speaker may be ironic here. Perhaps she believes that she has been the only one to suffer, while the man presumably moved on to other conquests.

Literary Analysis

Paired Activity Most students will probably detect the anger expressed by the speaker, though some pairs may name other feelings or attitudes, such as bitterness, scorn, contempt, or even indifference. Advise pairs to practice their oral readings before reciting to the class.

Use **Unit Five Resource Book,** p. 47, for more practice.

Points of Comparison

Students should be able to fill in the first three boxes of the chart for "Sonnet 23" based upon their answers to the **Think Critically** questions on this page. You may wish to lead a class discussion of the last question in the chart about the speaker's personality. Students may note the speaker's pride and her intense passion.

To assess skills and concepts taught in these selections, use **Formal Assessment Book,** p. 125–126.

5-Minute Warm-Up

Daily Language SkillBuilder

Have students **proofread** the display sentences on page 685k and write them correctly.

Reading and Analyzing

Literary Analysis
SONNET STRUCTURE

Tell students that the sonnet structure can help them divide the poem into major units of thought. Help students realize that the speaker is talking about a man whom she once loved, but she seems to be speaking to her mental image or memory of the man, not the real person. In lines 1–4, the speaker tells that image or memory to "Stay." In lines 5–8, the speaker asks a question of that image or memory of the man. In lines 9–14 she comes to a conclusion about her own power over the man who caused her so much pain.

Active Reading DICTION

Point out that this poem makes use of abstract and sophisticated diction, which makes it a challenging poem to read. The speaker uses terms associated with magic and enchantment ("illusion of enchantment"), science ("like steel to magnet"), and criminal behavior ("fugitive" and "prisoner") to communicate her complex feelings about love.

PREPARING to *Read*

The Louise Labé poem has given you one woman's perspective on love gone wrong. The following poem offers another woman's perspective on this topic, though the feelings expressed are different.

Noble Beginnings Juana Inés de la Cruz (hwän'ä ē-nās dä lä kro͞os) was born into a noble Mexican family. By the time she was 6 years old, she was able to read every book in her grandfather's library. At about the age of 15, she became a lady-in-waiting to the Marquise of Mancera, the wife of Mexico's governor. For several years, she lived in the palace where she wrote, studied, and served the Marquise.

A Religious Calling When she was about 19, Juana Inés became a nun. This decision gave her an opportunity to pursue her writing and education. While living in a convent, she accumulated thousands of books, acquired scientific instruments, and corresponded with friends in Spain and the United States. Because she was not burdened with household responsibilities, she had time to write songs, poetry, and plays. However, in 1690, Sor Juana faced a crisis when she published a highly critical letter about the ideas of a well-known Jesuit priest. Persecuted by the Archbishop of Mexico as a result of writing this letter, she was forced to stop writing altogether and had to turn over her books and scientific equipment to charity. After Sor Juana died in an epidemic in 1695, the Archbishop's representatives confiscated her remaining possessions—except one carefully hidden poem.

Build Background

Some scholars believe that her sonnets are about previous relationships in her life. Others believe that the sonnets are not biographical but simply a product of her rich imagination. In "Sonnet 165," the speaker addresses a man who seems to have broken off his romantic relationship with her.

Sor Juana Inés de la Cruz, 1648?–1695
Sister Juana Inés de la Cruz (1750), Miguel Cabrera. Museo National de Historia, Castillo de Chapultepec, Mexico City, D.F., Mexico. Photograph copyright © Schalkwijk/Art Resource, New York.

Cross Curricular Link **Humanities**

SOR JUANA'S LIFE AS A NUN In the 17th century, many young women in Roman Catholic countries, such as Mexico and Spain, became nuns. Usually, that meant that they took vows committing their lives to Jesus Christ in obedience to the teachings of the Roman Catholic Church. Such vows typically required poverty, chastity, obedience to Church superiors, and separation from society by living in an enclosed convent. So complete was their dedication that they were known as "brides of Christ."

Many women who became nuns were strongly motivated to become more perfect in their faith. Their daily lives were strictly controlled, dedicated to prayer and other devotional practices, rigorous self-discipline, and communal service. Sor Juana Inés de la Cruz, however, even after having lived in a convent for 22 years, admitted that her reasons for joining had been quite different from the norm. She sought "freedom and quiet" so she could pursue her "studious endeavors." In 1693, just two years before her death, Sor Juana underwent a mysterious religious crisis after which she became humble, pious, and intensely committed to spiritual perfection.

SONNET 165

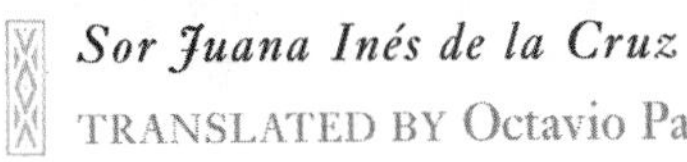

Sor Juana Inés de la Cruz
TRANSLATED BY Octavio Paz

[1] Stay, shadow of contentment too short-lived,
illusion of enchantment I most prize,
fair image for whom happily I die,
sweet fiction for whom painfully I live.
[2] If to your charms attracted I submit,
obedient, like steel to magnet fly,
by what logic do you flatter and entice,
only to flee, a taunting fugitive?
'Tis no triumph that you so smugly boast
[3] that I fell victim to your tyranny;
though from encircling bonds that held you fast
your elusive form too readily slipped free,
and though to my arms you are forever lost,
you are a prisoner in my fantasy.

2 illusion: something that misleads because it is not real.

7 entice: to attract by arousing hopes; tempt.

8 a taunting fugitive: one who runs away, mocking or making fun as he goes.

12 elusive: hard to catch or pin down.

Customizing Instruction

Less Proficient Readers

[1] Tell students that the speaker probably had a romantic relationship with the man addressed in the poem. She's talking to the man as he exists in her mind. Ask students to pick out words or phrases that suggest pleasurable experiences recalled by the speaker. *("contentment," "prize," "enchantment," "fair image," "sweet fiction")*

[2] Point out that in these lines the speaker admits that she was attracted to the man, but he is the one who left. Ask students to pick out words that describe the man's actions *("flatter," "entice," "flee")*

[3] Tell students that the man must have boasted about his relationship with the speaker. Ask students what word describes the power that he had over her. *(tyranny)*

English Learners

Explain the meaning of the following words and phrases:

Line 1: "shadow of contentment" *(happiness that is not real)*

Line 4: "sweet fiction" *(a pleasurable lie or deception)*

Line 6: "like steel to magnet" *(like metal that is being drawn to a powerful magnet)*

Line 11: "encircling bonds" *(the hugging arms of two people in love)*

Line 14: "fantasy" *(thoughts or imagination)*

Advanced Learners

Ask students to consider whether the speaker in the poem expresses personality characteristics that are also expressed in the painting of the author on page 824.

Possible Response: The speaker is learned, sophisticated, and aloof—all of those characteristics are expressed by the portrait, which shows an extensive library and a proud, confident, and somewhat aloof subject.

MINI LESSON Speaking and Listening

ORAL INTERPRETATION OF POETRY

Prepare Explain to students that all poems, even those in translation, are meant to be read and heard aloud. Organize students into pairs and have each pair practice one section of "Sonnet 165" (lines 1–4, 5–8, and 9–14). Before students begin, they should discuss the emotions that are expressed in their section. Have students practice reading their sections aloud to express those emotions.

Present Have students present oral interpretations of their sections of the poem. Students in each pair can take turns reading the lines or divide their reading in another way. Have all pairs that were assigned lines 1–4 read first, then discuss as a class the different interpretations expressed by the various pairs. Proceed in this manner until all pairs have presented and the entire poem has been discussed.

This activity is particularly well suited for longer blocks of class time.

COMPARING LITERATURE ACROSS CULTURES 825

Connect to the Literature

1. **What Do You Think?** Some students may note that the speaker expresses anger and disappointment about the man. Others may note that the speaker and the man were in a romantic relationship.

Think Critically

2. Possible Response: These phrases show both an attraction toward the man and a rejection of him. While the speaker's involvement with the man must have given her happiness, she now judges those times as illusory and deceptive, suggesting that the man was not sincere in his affection.
3. Possible Response: The man seems to have flirted with the speaker and led her on, only to "flee" when she showed affection in response.
4. Possible Response: The man seems to be the one who left the relationship. Perhaps when he found that his flirting worked, he became reluctant to make a commitment. He also boasted about his relationship afterwards, which still angers the speaker.
5. Possible Response: Although the man left the speaker in misery, she now has some control over him because she can keep alive her illusions of what their love might have been. She can think whatever she wants about him because he cannot control her thoughts.

Extend Interpretations

6. **Connect to Life** Possible Response: People have such strong desire for romantic love that their wishes often take the place of reality. Dreams of what love should be often cloud people's actual experience of love. Also, people describe love in such idealized terms that it is perhaps inevitable that fantasy becomes blurred with reality.

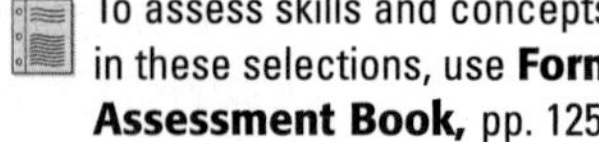
To assess skills and concepts taught in these selections, use **Formal Assessment Book,** pp. 125–126.

Connect to the Literature

1. **What Do You Think?** In analyzing poetry, it helps to begin by focusing on what you understand. With a partner, write down two statements about this poem that you believe are true. Compare your statements with those of your classmates.

Think Critically

2. In the poem's first four lines, the speaker refers to the man being addressed as a "shadow of contentment," an "illusion of enchantment," and "sweet fiction." What does such language suggest about the speaker's feelings toward the man?
3. In lines 5–6, the speaker admits to her romantic attraction to the man. According to lines 7–8, how does the man respond to her attraction?
4. Based on lines 9–14, what do you think happened to the relationship between the speaker and the man?
5. What might the speaker mean when she concludes, "you are a prisoner in my fantasy" (line 14)?

Extend Interpretations

6. **Connect to Life** Why do you think reality and fantasy so often become blended in the experience of romantic love?

Points of Comparison

Activity Now that you have read both poems, complete the rest of your comparison-and-contrast chart. If you are still uncertain about the meanings of certain lines, discuss them with your classmates. An additional example has been filled in.

	Sonnet 23 Louise Labé	Sonnet 165 Sor Juana Inés de la Cruz
What do you learn about the speaker's past relationship with the man being addressed?	The man promised to love her always.	He left her.
How does the speaker now feel about the man? What is the speaker's tone, or attitude, toward the subject of love?		
Does the speaker take any pleasure in her memories of love?		
How would you describe the personality of the speaker?		

Points of Comparison

After students have completed their charts, discuss their entries with the entire class. Encourage students to support their judgments with examples from the poems. After the discussion, some students may wish to change their charts, which should be allowed.

Standardized Test Practice

PART 1 Reading the Prompt

In writing assessments, you may be asked to compare and contrast works of literature with a common subject, such as the two poems that you have just read. You are now going to write an essay that involves this type of comparison.

Writing Prompt

Throughout the centuries, poets have praised the experience of love. Yet love can also go wrong. Compare and contrast the two poems by Louise Labé and Sor Juana Inés de la Cruz. (1) How do the speakers in these poems view their romantic relationships? Consider what you (2) learn about the men involved and each speaker's tone, or attitude, toward love. In your opinion, which speaker seems to have the healthier or more sensible attitude about the loss of love? (3) Support your analysis with details and quotations from the poems. (4)

STRATEGIES IN ACTION

1. I have to **compare and contrast** two poems.
2. For each poem, I have to discuss the speaker's view of the romance and the speaker's tone.
3. I have to decide which speaker has a healthier attitude about the loss of love.
4. I have to include **details and quotations** from the poems to support my analysis.

PART 2 Planning a Comparison-and-Contrast Essay

- Review the comparison-and-contrast chart that you completed for "Sonnet 23" and "Sonnet 165."
- Using your chart, find examples of similarities and differences to point out in your essay. If necessary, review the poems again to find more evidence.
- Create an outline to organize your ideas.

PART 3 Drafting Your Essay

Introduction You might begin by offering your own thoughts about why poets write about the loss of love. Introduce the two poems and briefly explain what they have in common. Describe interesting differences between the poems.

Body The questions in your comparison-and-contrast chart may help you identify the key points you want to make. In one paragraph, for example, you might explain the romantic relationship described in one of the sonnets. Use examples and details.

Conclusion Wrap up your essay with a summary of the poems' major similarities and differences.

Revision Look for places where you may not have explained your ideas fully. Also, see if more examples or quotes are needed.

PART 1 Reading the Prompt

Model the process of reading a prompt.

- Read through the prompt in its entirety.
- List key words of the assignment on the board ("Compare and contrast," "details and quotations").
- Define each key word and use **Strategies in Action** to show how students can restate the prompts in their own words.

PART 2 Planning a Comparison-and-Contrast Essay

- Have students review their completed charts, and invite them to add information or revise entries, if needed.
- Tell students to circle entries in their chart that reveal similarities between the two poems. Have them underline entries that reveal differences.
- Tell students that they can follow one of two organizational patterns: subject-by-subject or feature-by-feature (refer them to page R32 in the **Writing Handbook**).

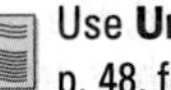
Use **Unit Five Resource Book,** p. 48, for more support.

PART 3 Drafting Your Essay

Introduction Tell students that the opening paragraph must introduce the comparison and attract the audience's attention. Opening with an interesting quotation from one of the poems may be an effective strategy.

Body Those students who use a feature-by-feature order should compare and contrast the features of each poem, one at a time. Those who use a subject-by-subject order should discuss each poem in its entirety.

Conclusion Remind students that effective conclusions briefly restate main points and leave the reader with something interesting to think about.

Revision Students should review their drafts to make sure that the organization is clear and that the language is direct and easy to understand.

Assessment Standardized Test Practice

RESPONDING TO A WRITING PROMPT

Read aloud the writing prompt at the top of this page. Discuss the **Strategies in Action** by asking students to identify the words in the prompt that tell them what to do. Suggest that they mark up their comparison-and-contrast charts, identifying points to include in their essays. When students have finished drafting their essays, have them work with a partner to see if they have accomplished the tips given in Part 3 **Drafting Your Essay.**

 This selection is included in the **World Literature InterActive Reader™.**

Objectives
- understand and appreciate an excerpt from a comic **novel (Literary Analysis)**
- recognize techniques of **characterization (Literary Analysis)**
- **analyze exposition (Active Reading)**

Summary
A gentleman farmer in the village of La Mancha devotes his life to reading books of chivalry. He becomes so involved in such stories that he loses his wits and decides to become a knight errant. He names his horse Rocinante and calls himself Don Quixote de la Mancha, dedicating his noble deeds to a peasant woman whom he names Dulcinea del Toboso. After his first adventures end badly, Don Quixote sets out for a second time accompanied by his peasant neighbor Sancho Panza, who agrees to serve as his squire. When the two men come upon windmills in a field, the would-be knight swears that they are giants and attacks them. As a result, both horse and rider are knocked to the ground. Don Quixote, steadfast in his imagination, insists that a magician has tricked him by turning giants into windmills.

 Use **Unit Five Resource Book,** p. 49, for additional support.

Thematic Link
Don Quixote lives in a world of his own imagination, which seems to offer unlimited **human possibility.**

 Use **Unit Five Resource Book,** p. 52, for practice with Words to Know.

5-Minute Warm-Up
Daily Language SkillBuilder

Have students **proofread** the display sentences on page 685k and write them correctly.

Miguel de Cervantes
1547–1616

From Soldier to Slave Little is known about the early years of Spanish writer Miguel de Cervantes. The son of a barber-surgeon—in those days, barbers set bones and performed other medical duties—he was born in a small town near Madrid. As a young man, he enlisted as a soldier and, in 1571, fought against the Turks in the Battle of Lepanto, where he was severely wounded. Cervantes proved to be a worthy soldier, showing great courage in battle and advancing to the rank of captain. On his return voyage to Spain in 1575, he was captured by pirates and taken to Algiers as a slave. Despite his repeated efforts to escape, he remained in captivity for five years, until he was freed following the payment of a ransom.

Disappointment and Failure In the next 25 years after his return to Spain, Cervantes suffered a series of disappointments. He expected to be rewarded with an important position but instead struggled to earn a living in various jobs, including royal messenger, tax collector, and commissary for the navy. Cervantes also tried his hand at writing fiction, drama, and poetry. Though he met with some success, he could not support himself by writing. Twice he was imprisoned over monetary matters. By his own account, he came up with the idea for *Don Quixote* while in prison.

Success and Acclaim In 1605, Cervantes published the first part of *Don Quixote*, the novel that turned his life around. This satire about the adventures of an elderly, idealistic knight was an immediate success, bringing Cervantes international fame and at least some financial stability. In 1615, he published a second part to the novel, which became another great success.

LESSON RESOURCES

UNIT FIVE RESOURCE BOOK, pp. 49–53

ASSESSMENT RESOURCES
Formal Assessment, pp. 127–128
Teacher's Guide to Assessment and Portfolio Use
Test Generator

INTEGRATED TECHNOLOGY
Visit our Web site: classzone.com

ADDITIONAL RESOURCES
Lesson Planning Guide, pp. 107–108
Teacher's Sourcebook for Language Development

Build Background

The Tale of *Don Quixote*

First Modern Novel *Don Quixote* is generally considered the first modern novel. Its hero, Don Quixote, is a poor, elderly gentleman who loses his mind from reading too many tales about the daring deeds of heroic knights. Don Quixote decides to win fame as a knight, assisted by a peasant "squire" named Sancho Panza. Cervantes devoted over a 100 chapters to their comically ill-fated adventures.

A Parody of Romances In the novel's prologue, Cervantes declares that his intention is to parody romances, the most popular form of literature in Spain for much of the 16th century. A **parody** imitates or mocks another work or type of literature. There was certainly plenty to mock in the romance genre. These rambling narratives told of knights who performed incredible deeds of valor without ever feeling any fear or doubt. Cervantes exposed the absurdity of romances by placing his hero in a realistic setting. Instead of encountering brave knights and evil sorcerers, Don Quixote attempts to fulfill chivalric ideals in a world of barbers, innkeepers, and farmers. He mistakes windmills for giants and country inns for castles.

A Quixotic Hero Cervantes achieved something more than parody in *Don Quixote.* The novel is a fascinating exploration of the relationship between fantasy and reality. Although Don Quixote is clearly mad, he does achieve a kind of nobility through his idealism and persistence. From his name comes the term *quixotic,* which describes an impractical idealist, someone who gallantly tries to pursue unreachable goals.

For a humanities activity, click on:

Connect to Your Life

Don Quixote mistakes his fantasies for reality. What is your attitude toward fantasy and imagination? Do you think that such activities should be left to children, or do they serve a useful purpose for adult life? Give examples.

Focus Your Reading

LITERARY ANALYSIS: CHARACTERIZATION

Characterization refers to the techniques used to develop characters. Writers can portray a character through a combination of physical description; the speech, thoughts, feelings, or actions of the character; what other characters do, say, or think in response to that character; and direct commentary by the narrator. The following quote illustrates direct commentary by the narrator:

> ***This gentleman of ours was close on to fifty, of a robust constitution but with little flesh on his bones and a face that was lean and gaunt.***

As you read notice how the various techniques are used to develop the main character.

ACTIVE READING: ANALYZING EXPOSITION

Exposition is the stage of the plot that provides background information. The first chapter of *Don Quixote* serves as an exposition that introduces the main character.

READER'S NOTEBOOK As you read the first chapter, record information about Don Quixote, using a chart like the one shown.

Don Quixote	
What He Reads	Image of Himself
Imaginative Way of Seeing	
sees cardboard, imagines a helmet's visor	

WORDS TO KNOW **Vocabulary Preview**

affable
conjecture
haughty
incongruous
indolent
infatuation
ingenuity
interminable
lucid
scrutinizing

READING FOR INFORMATION
Reading Skills and Strategies
SUMMARIZING

Tell students that a summary presents a shortened version of information. Invite students to work in pairs to summarize each section of the Cervantes biography on page 828 and **The Tale of Don Quixote** on page 829. Each pair should create a one-to-two sentence summary of the section. To model the skill of summarizing, share with students the following summary of **From Soldier to Slave:** *Miguel de Cervantes, the son of a barber-surgeon, was born near Madrid. After achieving honor in the army, he was captured by pirates and held for ransom.*

Historical Note

A **romance** as a literary genre is derived from the Old French word *romans*, which means written in French. A romance refers to any imaginative story concerned with noble heroes, chivalry, passionate love, daring deeds, and supernatural events. As a literary form, the romance began in France during the Middle Ages. The genre quickly gained popularity and spread throughout Europe.

The modern meaning of a romance as a deep emotional attachment has its origins in the tales of knights, such as Lancelot, who swore devotion to their ladies.

TIME MANAGEMENT

If your schedule requires that you cover the lesson objectives in a shorter time, use . . .
- Preparing to Read, pp. 828–829
- Thinking Through the Literature, p. 844
- Vocabulary in Action, p. 845

If you want to take advantage of longer class time, use . . .
- TE Teaching Options: Cross Curricular Link, pp. 830, 832, 838, 842; Viewing and Representing, pp. 833, 839; Vocabulary Strategy, p. 831; Standardized Test Practice, p. 836; Grammar, p. 843
- Choices & Challenges, p. 845

Reading and Analyzing

Literary Analysis CHARACTERIZATION

Point out that these two pages of *Don Quixote* combine physical description with direct commentary by the narrator. Ask students to summarize what they learn about Don Quixote's character.

Possible Response: Don Quixote is a gentleman, but he does not have much money, probably because he spends all his time reading books of chivalry. He has sold off parts of his farm so that he can buy more books. He seems lost in a dream world of fantastic stories.

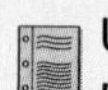
Use **Unit Five Resource Book,** p. 51, for more practice.

Active Reading

ANALYZING EXPOSITION

Explain that authors often use description to help readers form a mental image of their characters. Ask students to identify the passage on page 831 that describes Don Quixote's appearance.

Possible Response: He "was close on fifty, of a robust constitution but with little flesh on his bones and a face that was lean and gaunt."

Use **Unit Five Resource Book,** p. 50, for more practice.

Literary Analysis NARRATOR

Remind students that the narrator is the character or voice from whose point of view events are told. Ask students to pick out details that give hints about the narrator's attitude towards his subject. Have them explain what those details reveal.

Possible Response: Students may notice details such as "the name of which I have no desire to recall," This gentleman of ours," "They will try to tell you that." The narrator seems amused by his own tale; he is informal, irreverent, and playful.

from Don Quixote

Miguel de Cervantes

Translated by Samuel Putnam

In a village of La Mancha[1] the name of which I have no desire to recall, there lived not so long ago one of those gentlemen who always have a lance in the rack, an ancient buckler,[2] a skinny nag, and a greyhound for the chase. A stew with more beef than mutton in it, chopped meat for
1 his evening meal, scraps for a Saturday, lentils on Friday, and a young pigeon as a special delicacy for Sunday, went to account for three-quarters of his income.

1. **La Mancha:** a high, flat, barren region in central Spain.
2. **buckler:** a small, round shield carried or worn on the arm.

Cross Curricular Link **History**

INTERNATIONAL POPULARITY OF *DON QUIXOTE*

Next to the Bible, *Don Quixote* may be the most widely read book in the world. The novel was an immediate success, going through six editions in 1605 when Part One of the novel was published. Within the next ten years, English and French translations became available, and the fame of *Don Quixote* spread. Records show that figures of Don Quixote, Sancho Panza, and the horse Rosinante appeared in festive parades from Peru to Germany between 1605 and 1617. A Spanish writer tried to capitalize on the novel's appeal by publishing his own sequel to the tale, one year before Cervantes released Part Two in 1615.

The novel's popularity continued through the following centuries. The English novelist Henry Fielding (1707–1754) announced that his *Joseph Andrews* was "written in imitation of . . . Cervantes." The poet William Wordsworth found reason in the madness of Don Quixote. In France, the philosopher Voltaire (1694–1778) called himself a Don Quixote; fans of the novel included Napoleon Bonaparte (1769–1821), the writer Gustave Flaubert (1821–1880), and the painter Eugene Delacroix (1798–1863). The German writer Goethe (1749–1832) called Cervantes his "life-jacket," while the philosophers Hegel (1770–1831) and Schopenhauer (1788–1860) drew lessons from the knight and the squire.

Today, the novel can be read in Chinese, Bulgarian, and more than 50 other languages.

The rest of it he laid out on a broadcloth greatcoat[3] and velvet stockings for feast days, with slippers to match, while the other days of the week he cut a figure in a suit of the finest homespun. Living with him were a housekeeper in her forties, a niece who
2 was not yet twenty, and a lad of the field and market place who saddled his horse for him and wielded the pruning knife.

This gentleman of ours was close on to fifty, of a robust constitution[4] but with little flesh on his bones and a face that was lean and gaunt. He was noted for his early rising, being very fond of the hunt. They will try to tell you that his surname was Quijada or Quesada[5]—there is some difference of opinion among those who have written on the subject—but according to the most likely conjectures we are to understand that it was really Quejana.[6] But all this means very little so far as our story is concerned, providing that in the telling of it we do not depart one iota from the truth.

You may know, then, that the aforesaid gentleman, on those occasions when he was at leisure, which was most of the year around, was in the habit of reading books of chivalry with such pleasure and devotion as to lead him almost
3 wholly to forget the life of a hunter and even the administration of his estate. So great was his curiosity and infatuation in this regard that he even sold many acres of tillable land in order to be able to buy and read the books that he loved, and he would carry home with him as many of them as he could obtain.

Don Quixote on Horseback (1870), Honoré Daumier. Neue Pinakothek, Munich, Germany. Photo © Scala/Art Resource, New York.

Of all those that he thus devoured none pleased him so well as the ones that had been composed by the famous Feliciano de Silva,[7] whose lucid prose style and involved conceits[8] were as precious to him as pearls; especially when he came to read those tales of love and amorous challenges that are to be met with in many places, such a
passage as the 4
following, for example: "The reason of the unreason that afflicts my reason, in such a manner weakens my reason that I with reason lament me of your comeliness." And he was similarly affected when his eyes fell upon such lines as these: ". . . the high Heaven of your divinity divinely fortifies you with the stars and renders you deserving of that desert your greatness doth deserve."

3. **broadcloth greatcoat:** heavy wool overcoat.
4. **robust constitution:** vigorous, healthy physical nature.
5. **Quijada** (kē-hä′dä) **or Quesada** (kĕ-sä′dä): last names mistakenly given to the main character.
6. **Quejana** (kĕ-hä′nä).
7. **Feliciano de Silva** (fĕ-lē-syä′nô dĕ sĕl′vä): a Spanish author of fictional books about knights.
8. **conceits:** lengthy, exaggerated comparisons.

WORDS TO KNOW

conjecture (kən-jĕk′chər) *n.* a conclusion based on guesswork
infatuation (ĭn-făch′o͞o-ā′shən) *n.* a foolish, unreasonable attraction
lucid (lo͞o′sĭd) *adj.* clear; easily understood

Customizing Instruction

Less Proficient Readers

1 Explain to students that Don Quixote is introduced in the first paragraph as a "gentleman," which means that he belongs to the upper class of society. Ask students what details suggest that Quixote is not a wealthy man. **Possible Response:** He has to spend most of his money on food, but he can only afford "chopped meat for his evening meal, scraps for a Saturday, lentils on Friday."

2 Ask students who lives with Quixote. *(a housekeeper, a niece, and a servant boy)*

3 Point out that Don Quixote spends most of his time reading "books of chivalry," which are about the adventures of knights. Ask students how his habit of constant reading contributes to his poverty. *(He neglects his farm and even sold off parts of it so he could afford to buy more books.)*

4 Help students to realize that Don Quixote reads books about the adventures that knights undertake for love. Read aloud the quoted passage in a humorous way to illustrate that it really makes no sense.

English Learners

Explain the meaning of the following words and phrases:

- "a lance in the rack" *(a spear-like weapon kept in a stand)*
- "lentils" *(a type of bean)*
- "nag" *(an old or worn-out horse)*
- "a suit of the finest homespun" *(a suit made of cloth produced in the home)*
- "we do not depart one iota from the truth" *(we tell the complete truth)*

MINI LESSON Vocabulary Strategy

USING A DICTIONARY TO FIND PRECISE MEANING

Instruction Write the following lines on the chalkboard: "Of all those that he [Don Quixote] devoured none pleased him so well as the ones that had been composed by the famous Feliciano de Silva, whose lucid prose style and involved conceits were as precious to him as pearls" (p. 831).

Demonstrate for students how to use a dictionary to find the appropriate meaning of the adjective *lucid:* "easily understood; intelligible." Ask them why this meaning is more appropriate than others listed in the dictionary entry. *(This meaning of* lucid *precisely describes the clarity of de Silva's writing style. The other meanings do not apply.)*

Practice Have students choose five of the remaining Words to Know. Ask students to write down the lines(s) in which each word appears in *Don Quixote.* Then ask them to reference each word in a dictionary and write the meaning that is most appropriate given the word's context within the selection. Have students discuss their choices.

A lesson on using a dictionary appears on p. 558 in the Pupils' Edition

Reading and Analyzing

Literary Analysis ROMANCE

A Point out that romances, or tales about the adventures of knights, were often unrealistic. The knights were nearly always in battle, suffering countless serious injuries, and even losing limbs that were typically restored by magic potions. See the **Cross Curricular Link** below for more information.

Literary Analysis CHARACTERIZATION

B The village priest and barber play major roles in the novel. They even join Don Quixote for some of his adventures, all the while trying to trick him into returning home. Ask students what Don Quixote's conversations with the barber and the priest suggest about their relationship to him and about the popularity of romances.

Possible Response: The priest and barber enjoy talking to Don Quixote about books of chivalry, which shows that he is well liked. Clearly, many people besides Don Quixote enjoyed reading and discussing romances.

Active Reading

ANALYZING EXPOSITION

C Ask students why Don Quixote might have been so attracted to stories about knights. What needs did such stories fulfill?

Possible Response: Don Quixote probably loved such stories because of their adventure, romance, and heroic quests. He may have lacked such things in his own life.

The poor fellow used to lie awake nights in an effort to disentangle the meaning and make sense out of passages such as these, although Aristotle[9] himself would not have been able to understand them, even if he had been resurrected for that sole purpose. He was not at ease in his mind over those wounds that Don Belianís[10] gave
A and received; for no matter how great the surgeons who treated him, the poor fellow must have been left with his face and his entire body covered with marks and scars. Nevertheless, he was grateful to the author for closing the book with the promise of an interminable adventure to come; many a time he was tempted to take up his pen and literally finish the tale as had been promised, and he undoubtedly would have done so, and would have succeeded at it very well, if his thoughts had not been constantly occupied with other things of greater moment.

He often talked it over with the village curate,[11] who was a learned man, a graduate of Sigüenza,[12] and they would hold long discussions as to who had been the better knight, Palmerin of England or Amadis of Gaul;[13] but Master
B Nicholas, the barber of the same village, was in the habit of saying that no one could come up to
1 the Knight of Phoebus,[14] and that if anyone *could* compare with him it was Don Galaor,[15] brother of Amadis of Gaul, for Galaor was ready for anything—he was none of your finical[16] knights, who went around whimpering as his brother did, and in point of valor he did not lag behind him.

In short, our gentleman became so immersed in his reading that he spent whole nights from sundown to sunup and his days from dawn to dusk in poring over his books, until, finally, from 2
so little sleeping and so much reading, his brain dried up and he went completely out of his mind. He had filled his imagination with everything that he had read, with enchantments, knightly encounters, battles, challenges, wounds, with tales of love and its torments, and all sorts of impossible things, and as a result had come to C
believe that all these fictitious happenings were true; they were more real to him than anything else in the world. He would remark that the Cid Ruy Díaz[17] had been a very good knight, but there was no comparison between him and the Knight of the Flaming Sword,[18] who with a sin- 3
gle backward stroke had cut in half two fierce and monstrous giants. He preferred Bernardo del

9. **Aristotle:** Greek philosopher (384-322 B.C.) widely known for his wisdom.
10. **Don Belianís** (dôn bĕ-lyä-nēs'): hero of a knighthood romance.
11. **curate** (kyŏŏr'ĭt): priest in charge of a parish.
12. **Sigüenza** (sē-gwĕn'sä): a "minor" university of Spain, whose graduates were often mocked.
13. **Palmerin of England or Amadis** (ä'mə-dĭs) **of Gaul:** two legendary knights known for bravery and unbelievably heroic deeds.
14. **Knight of Phoebus** (fē'bəs): hero of a romance called *Knight of the Sun, Mirror of Princes and Knights.*
15. **Galaor** (gä-lä-ôr').
16. **finical:** finicky; picky.
17. **Cid Ruy Díaz** (sēd rwē dē'äs): Rodrigo Díaz, known as the Cid, was an actual Spanish military leader and national hero about whom an epic poem was written.
18. **Knight of the Flaming Sword:** Amadis of Greece, a hero of romances who had a red sword stamped on his shield.

WORDS TO KNOW
interminable (ĭn-tûr'mə-nə-bəl) *adj.* unending

Cross Curricular Link **History**

KNIGHTS-ERRANT AND ROMANCES Don Quixote was not alone in his love of romance. The books that "dried up" Quixote's brain also served as the most popular form of reading in the 16th century. Throughout Europe, from the northern countries of Scandinavia to Italy in the south, people loved to read fantasic stories about knights who wandered the known world in search of adventure. Such books typically made use of stock characters and situations: lords and ladies, knights and their squires, dwarfs and giants, powerful magicians and enchantments, and, of course, damsels in trouble. Knights would pursue the Holy Grail (the cup or plate that, according to legend, Jesus used during the Last Supper), fight their enemies, kill evil ogres, participate in tournaments, become trapped by enchantments, lose their limbs with startling frequency, and prove their virtue.

Many such stories were based upon England's King Arthur and the Knights of the Round Table and France's Charlemagne and his Twelve Peers.

In short, our gentleman became so immersed in his reading that he spent whole nights . . . and his days from dawn to dusk in poring over his books. . . .

Don Quixote in His Library (about 1868), Gustave Doré. Engraving by Heliodore Joseph Pisan. Private collection. Photo © Bridgeman Art Library.

HUMANITIES CONNECTION For centuries, artists have been drawn to the story of *Don Quixote*. This woodcut provides a humorous portrayal of Don Quixote's crowded imagination. Note the many knights, the dragon, and the damsels in distress.

Customizing Instruction

Less Proficient Readers

Ask students the following questions to make sure that they are following the plot:

1 What does Don Quixote discuss with the barber and village priest? *(They discuss books about the adventures of knights.)*

2 What activity "dries up" Don Quixote's brain and makes him lose his mind? *(his constant reading about knights)*

3 Don Quixote compares real heroes to literary characters as if they were the same. What does this reveal about his mind? *(He cannot tell the difference between real life and stories.)*

English Learners

Explain the meaning of the following phrases:

- "immersed in his reading" *(lost in his reading)*
- "these fictitious happenings" *(these made-up events)*

Advanced Learners

Point out that a number of great literary works, such as Gustave Flaubert's *Madame Bovary* and Fyodor Dostoyevsky's *Crime and Punishment*, have focused on main characters whose reading habits lead to trouble. Ask students to consider why authors, whose livelihood depends on having readers, might write about the dangers of reading.

Possible Response: Reading, like any other activity, can be carried too far, especially when reading leads one to lose touch with ordinary reality. Authors themselves probably read more than other people, which may make them sensitive to the risks of spending too much time lost in books.

MINI LESSON Viewing and Representing

Don Quixote in his library **by Gustave Doré**

ART APPRECIATION The French artist Gustave Doré (1832–1883) is best known for his dramatic illustrations of literary masterpieces, such as *Don Quixote*, Milton's *Paradise Lost*, and Dante's *Divine Comedy*. His most famous works often depict dreamlike scenes and give evidence of his love of the grotesque and bizarre. Have students look at the illustration and **Humanities Connection** on page 833. Point out such outlandish details as the two miniature knights jousting on mice and the oversized head at the bottom of the illustration. Ask students to find other evidence of the grotesque or fantastic in the illustration.

Possible Response: A dragon-like creature is slithering beneath Don Quixote's chair; an ogre-like figure is chaining a woman to a book at the bottom right; thoughout the right-side of the illustration, figures seem to blur into one another, so that horses, dragons, knights, and their weapons seems nearly indistinguishable; many of the figures violate rules of proportion: the horses are smaller than Quixote's chair; the books are bigger than some of the people; and the lance near the top of the chair seems longer than the dragon at top right.

Reading and Analyzing

Literary Analysis ALLUSION

A The Christian Spaniards generally regarded Muslims as enemies, in part because the Muslims had battled Christians for centuries in Spain. The reference to the Muslim prophet Mohammed, the founder of Islam, reflects the prejudices and ignorance of the Christians. Muslim religion actually prohits the creation of such images.

Literary Analysis CHARACTERIZATION

B Read aloud this passage, which explains the purpose of all of Don Quixote's adventures. Ask students what he hopes to achieve.

Possible Response: Don Quixote wants to win honor for himself by righting wrongs and facing great danger.

Reading Skills and Strategies VISUALIZING

C Explain that a morion is a type of helmet worn in the 16th century that does not provide any protection for the face. Don Quixote wants a traditional knight's helmet to cover his face completely. Point out that wearing a morion with "old pieces of armor" will make Don Quixote look very foolish.

Active Reading ANALYZING EXPOSITION

D The naming of his horse is the first of many such naming events in the novel. Don Quixote is constantly renaming the ordinary people and places that he encounters so that they can live up to his romantic ideals.

Literary Analysis CHARACTERIZATION

E Tell students that Don Quixote places such importance on his own invented name so that he can live up to his model, Amadis of Gaul. Ask students what this reveals about Don Quixote.

Possible Response: Don Quixote believes that if he imitates his heroes he will become a great knight himself. He tries to set a high standard for his own life.

Carpio,[19] who at Roncesvalles had slain Roland despite the charm the latter bore, availing himself of the stratagem which Hercules employed when he strangled Antaeus, the son of Earth, in his arms.

He had much good to say for Morgante[20] who, though he belonged to the haughty, overbearing race of giants, was of an affable disposition and well brought up. But, above all, he cherished an admiration for Rinaldo of Montalbán,[21] especially as he beheld him sallying forth from his castle to rob all those that crossed his path, or when he thought of him overseas (A) stealing the image of Mohammed which, so the story has it, was all of gold. And he would have liked very well to have had his fill of kicking that (1) traitor Galalón,[22] a privilege for which he would have given his housekeeper with his niece thrown into the bargain.

> AT LAST, WHEN HIS WITS WERE GONE BEYOND REPAIR, HE CAME TO CONCEIVE THE STRANGEST IDEA THAT EVER OCCURRED TO ANY MADMAN IN THIS WORLD.

At last, when his wits were gone beyond repair, he came to conceive the strangest idea that ever occurred to any madman in this world. It now appeared to him fitting and necessary, in order to win a greater amount of honor for himself and serve his country at the same time, to become a knight-errant[23] and roam the world on (2) horseback, in a suit of armor; he would go in quest of adventures, by way of putting into prac- (B) tice all that he had read in his books; he would right every manner of wrong, placing himself in situations of the greatest peril such as would redound[24] to the eternal glory of his name. As a reward for his valor and the might of his arm, the poor fellow could already see himself crowned Emperor of Trebizond[25] at the very least; and so, carried away by the strange pleasure that he found in such thoughts as these, he at once set about putting his plan into effect.

The first thing he did was to burnish up some old pieces of armor, left him by his great-grandfather, which for ages had lain in a corner, moldering and forgotten. He polished and adjusted them as best he could, and then he noticed that one very important thing was lacking: there was no closed helmet, but only a (C) morion, or visorless headpiece, with turned up brim of the kind foot soldiers wore. His ingenuity, however, enabled him to remedy this, and he proceeded to fashion out of cardboard a kind of half-helmet, which, when attached to the morion, gave the appearance of a whole one. True, when he went to see if it was strong enough to withstand a good slashing blow, he was somewhat disappointed; for when he drew his sword and gave it a couple of thrusts, he succeeded

19. **Bernardo del Carpio** was another subject of Spanish epic poetry. The story referred to here puts him at the battle portrayed in the French epic *The Song of Roland* and claims he killed Roland by lifting him up into the air until Roland was dead, as Hercules did to the giant Antaeus.
20. **Morgante** (môr-gän'tĕ): ferocious giant in an Italian romantic poem who later became sweet and loving.
21. **Rinaldo of Montalbán** (môn-täl-bän'): hero of a series of French epic poems.
22. **Galalón** (gä-lä-lôn'): Ganelon, the stepfather and betrayer of Roland, the French epic hero.
23. **knight-errant:** knight who wanders the countryside in search of adventure to prove his chivalry.
24. **redound:** to have an effect.
25. **Trebizond:** a former Greek empire, often referred to in stories of knighthood.

WORDS TO KNOW

haughty (hô'tē) *adj.* overly proud; tending to look down on others
affable (ăf'ə-bəl) *adj.* pleasant; agreeable
ingenuity (ĭn'jə-no͞o'ĭ-tē) *n.* cleverness

only in undoing a whole week's labor. The ease with which he had hewed it to bits disturbed him no little, and he decided to make it over. This time he placed a few strips of iron on the inside, and then, convinced that it was strong enough, refrained from putting it to any further test; instead, he adopted it then and there as the finest helmet ever made.

After this, he went out to have a look at his nag; and although the animal had more *cuartos,* or cracks, in its hoof than there are quarters in a
B real,[26] and more blemishes than Gonela's steed[27] which *tantum pellis et ossa fuit,*[28] it nonetheless looked to its master like a far better horse than Alexander's Bucephalus or the Babieca of the Cid.[29] He spent all of four days in trying to think up a name for his mount; for—so he told himself—seeing that it belonged to so famous and worthy a knight, there was no reason why it should not have a name of equal renown. The kind of name he wanted was one that would at once indicate what the nag had been before it came to belong to a knight-errant and what its present status was; for it stood to reason that, when the master's worldly condition changed, his
D horse also ought to have a famous, high-sounding appellation, one suited to the new order of things and the new profession that it was to follow.

After he in his memory and imagination had made up, struck out, and discarded many names, now adding to and now subtracting from the list, he finally hit upon "Rocinante,"[30] a name that impressed him as being sonorous[31] and at the same time indicative of what the steed had been when it was but a hack, whereas now it was nothing other than the first and foremost of all the hacks[32] in the world.

Having found a name for his horse that pleased his fancy, he then desired to do as much for himself, and this required another week, and by the end of that period he had made up his mind that he was henceforth to be known as Don Quixote,[33] which, as has been stated, has led the authors of this veracious[34] history to assume that his real name must undoubtedly have been Quijada, and not Quesada as others would have it. But remembering that the valiant Amadis was not content to call himself that and nothing more, but added the name of his kingdom and fatherland that he might make it famous also, and thus came to take the name

> ... AND BY THE END OF THAT PERIOD HE HAD MADE UP HIS MIND THAT HE WAS HENCEFORTH TO BE KNOWN AS DON QUIXOTE. ...

Amadis of Gaul, so our good knight chose to add his place of origin and become "Don Quixote de la Mancha"; for by this means, as he E
saw it, he was making very plain his lineage and 4
was conferring honor upon his country by taking its name as his own.

---

26. **quarters in a real** (rā-äl′)**:** a real was a coin worth about five cents.
27. **Gonela's steed:** the horse of the Italian court comedian Pietro Gonela which was famous for having gas.
28. ***tantum pellis et ossa fuit:*** Latin phrase meaning "He was only skin and bones."
29. **Alexander's Bucephalus** (byo͞o-sĕf′ə-ləs) **or the Babieca** (bä-byĕ′kä) **of the Cid:** famous horses. Alexander is Alexander the Great, the early conqueror of Asia.
30. **Rocinante** (rô-sē-nän′tĕ).
31. **sonorous** (sŏn′ər-əs)**:** having a full, rich sound.
32. **foremost of all the hacks:** *Rocin* means "nag" or "hack" in Spanish; *ante* means "before" or "first." So the name Rocinante indicates that it is the first, or premier, nag.
33. **Quixote** (kē-hō′tĕ)**:** the literal meaning is a piece of armor that protects the thigh.
34. **veracious:** truthful.

Customizing Instruction

Less Proficient Readers

Ask students the following questions to make sure that they are following the plot:

1 Don Quixote wishes that he could kick a villain in a literary work. How does this wish illustrate his madness? ***(Don Quixote can't tell the difference between real life and stories.)***

2 What does Don Quixote decide to do? ***(He plans to become a knight and travel around the world in search of adventure.)***

3 Don Quixote is convinced that he has a great horse. What is his horse really like? ***(It's old and has many flaws.)***

4 How did Don Quixote de la Mancha choose the last part of his name? ***(He came from the area of Spain known as La Mancha.)***

English Learners

Explain the meaning of the following phrases:

- **"sallying forth"** ***(rushing out to do battle)***
- **"burnish up"** ***(shine)***
- **"equal renown"** ***(similar fame)***

Literary Analysis ROMANCE

A Read aloud this paragraph to illustrate the humorous extremes of Don Quixote's language. His manner of speech, with its elaborate twists and turns and its elevated diction, imitates the speech of heroes of romance. According to the conventions of such literature, a victorious knight would send his defeated foe to the knight's lady to serve her.

Literary Analysis CHARACTERIZATION

B Don Quixote apparently was interested in the girl, but "she never knew or suspected it." Ask students what this statement reveals about Don Quixote.

Possible Response: He is generally a passive person who does not take action to fulfill his wishes and desires.

Literary Analysis PLOT

C Explain to students that in Chapter 6 the village priest and barber began the process of evaluating Don Quixote's books. Most were thrown in a pile for burning, but some were saved for their literary merit. The two men eventually grew tired of the long task, so in the end they decided to burn all remaining books. As the narrator points out, some worthy books were probably burned.

Reading Skills and Strategies
MAKING INFERERNCES

D Point out that characters throughout the novel talk to Don Quixote by using language and ideas drawn from the books of romance. Ask students to explain why.

Possible Response: Don Quixote is so entranced by the language and ideas of such books that he cannot understand anything else. To communicate to him, other characters have to enter the world of his imagination.

And so, having polished up his armor and made the morion over into a closed helmet, and having given himself and his horse a name, he naturally found but one thing lacking still: he must seek out a lady of whom he could become enamored; for a knight-errant without a ladylove was like a tree without leaves or fruit, a body without a soul.

"If," he said to himself, "as a punishment for my sins or by a stroke of fortune I should come upon some giant hereabouts, a thing that very commonly happens to knights-errant, and if I should slay him in a hand-to-hand encounter or perhaps cut him in two, or, finally, if I should vanquish and subdue him, would it not be well to have someone to whom I may send him as a
A present, in order that he, if he is living, may
1 come in, fall upon his knees in front of my sweet lady, and say in a humble and submissive tone of voice, 'I, lady, am the giant Caraculiambro,[35] lord of the island Malindrania, who has been overcome in single combat by that knight who never can be praised enough, Don Quixote de la Mancha, the same who sent me to present myself before your Grace that your Highness may dispose of me as you see fit'?"

Oh, how our good knight reveled in this speech, and more than ever when he came to think of the name that he should give his lady! As the story goes, there was a very good-looking
farm girl who lived near by, with whom he had B
once been smitten,[36] although it is generally believed that she never knew or suspected it. Her name was Aldonza Lorenzo,[37] and it seemed to him that she was the one upon whom he should bestow the title of mistress of his thoughts. For her he wished a name that should not be incongruous with his own and that would convey the 2
suggestion of a princess or a great lady; and, accordingly, he resolved to call her "Dulcinea del Toboso,"[38] she being a native of that place. A musical name to his ears, out of the ordinary and significant, like the others he had chosen for himself and his appurtenances.[39]

35. **Caraculiambro** (kä-rä-kōō-lyäm′brô).
36. **smitten:** entranced with; in love with.
37. **Aldonza Lorenzo** (äl-dôn′sä lô-rĕn′sô).
38. **Dulcinea del Toboso** (dōōl-sē-nĕ′ä dĕl tô-bô′sô).
39. **appurtenances:** additions to something; accessories.

WORDS TO KNOW

incongruous (ĭn-kông′grōō-əs) *adj.* not appropriate; out of place

Assessment Standardized Test Practice

IDENTIFYING CAUSE AND EFFECT In some standardized tests, students are asked to identify cause and effect relationships. Write the following question on the board:

Why does Don Quixote change the name of his horse?

A. Because he had lost his wits, he had forgotten the horse's name.
B. The horse's old name reminded Don Quixote of an evil knight.
C. According to the books he had read, a knight's horse needed an impressive name.
D. He wanted to honor his niece.

Guide students through the process of choosing the correct answer. While it is true that Don Quixote lost his wits, nothing in the text suggests that he forgot the horse's previous name, which makes *A* incorrect. Likewise there is no mention of an evil knight at this point in the text, nor is there any mention of the horse's previous name, which makes *B* incorrect. *C* is correct because the text shows that the idea for naming the horse came from books that Don Quixote read. *D* is incorrect because the niece is not mentioned as a reason for renaming the horse.

After completing his preparations, Don Quixote sets off on his first adventure. During his three days of travel, he persuades an innkeeper to dub him a knight. Then he "rescues" a servant boy from his master's beating, but as soon as "our knight" leaves, the master beats the boy even harder. Don Quixote next mistakes a traveling group of merchants for hostile knights. After insulting the merchants for failing to swear to the beauty of Dulcinea del Toboso, he is badly beaten. A neighbor finds him on the road and carries him home, to the great relief of his family and friends. They blame Don Quixote's mad behavior on his reading habits, so for his own good they decide to burn his books.

. . . That night the housekeeper burned 3 all the books there were in the stable yard and in C all the house; and there must have been some that went up in smoke which should have been preserved in everlasting archives,[40] if the one who did the scrutinizing had not been so indolent. Thus we see the truth of the old saying, to the effect that the innocent must sometimes pay for the sins of the guilty.

One of the things that the curate and the barber advised as a remedy for their friend's sickness was to wall up the room where the books had been, so that, when he arose, he would not find them missing—it might be that the cause being removed, the effect would cease—and they could D tell him that a magician had made away with them, room and all. This they proceeded to do as quickly as possible. Two days later, when Don Quixote rose from his bed, the first thing he did was to go have a look at his library, and, not finding it where he had left it, he went from one part of the house to another searching for it. Going up to where the door had been, he ran his hands over the wall and rolled his eyes in every direction without saying a word; but after some little while he asked the housekeeper where his study was with all his books.

She had been well instructed in what to answer him. "Whatever study is your Grace talking about?" she said. "There is no study, and no books, in this house; the devil took them all away."

"No," said the niece, "it was not the devil but an enchanter who came upon a cloud one night, the day after your Grace left here; dismounting from a serpent that he rode, he entered your study, and I don't know what all he did there, 4 but after a bit he went flying off through the roof, leaving the house full of smoke; and when we went to see what he had done, there was no study and not a book in sight. There is one thing, though, that the housekeeper and I remember very well: at the time that wicked old fellow left, he cried out in a loud voice that it was all on account of a secret enmity that he bore the owner of those books and that study,

40. **archives:** places where records and other documents are stored.

WORDS TO KNOW

scrutinizing (skro͞ot'n-īz-ĭng) *n.* observing or inspecting with great care **scrutinize** *v.*
indolent (ĭn'də-lənt) *adj.* lazy

Customizing Instruction

Less Proficient Readers

Make sure that students are following the plot by asking the following questions:

1 Why does Don Quixote need a lady to serve? *(If he defeats a giant in battle, he wants to send the giant to serve the lady.)*

2 Why does Don Quixote give the farm girl Aldonza Lorenzo the name of Dulcinea del Toboso? *(In his imagination, she is not a farm girl but a beautiful lady, worthy of a knight.)*

3 What happens to Don Quixote's books? *(They are burned.)*

4 How does Don Quixote's niece explain the disappearance of his study and all his books. *(She says an enchanter came at night, making everything disappear.)*

English Learners

Explain the meaning of the following words and phrases:

- "vanquish and subdue" *(defeat and bring under control)*
- "reveled in this speech" *(felt great joy when speaking this way)*
- "secret enmity" *(secret hatred)*

Advanced Learners

Ask students to describe the style of language used in romances based upon their reading of *Don Quixote* to this point.

Possible Response: Romances relied upon long sentences with elevated and formal diction. The language presented the subject in an idealized manner. The characters and even their horses were given romantic and exotic names.

Reading and Analyzing

Literary Analysis HUMOR

A Make sure that students realize that the niece's farfetched story about an evil magician imitates romances. Don Quixote believes her without question, only correcting the name that his niece supplies for the enchanter. Ask students what's funny about his correction.

Possible Response: His niece has made up her story entirely, but Don Quixote offers a correction to make her fantastic tale more accurate. He is so out of touch with reality that he "corrects" it according to the books that he has read.

Literary Analysis CHARACTERIZATION

B Tell students that Sancho Panza plays a key role in the novel (see **Cross Curricular Link** below). Ask students what they learn about him here.

Possible Response: Sancho is a poor, uneducated farmer, a neighbor of Don Quixote who is persuaded to become his squire. Don Quixote promises Sancho Panza adventure and rewards, which may include being named governor of an island.

Literary Analysis ROMANCE

C Point out that Don Quixote measures all of his actions according to what he has read about in books. He is troubled by having Sancho ride an ass because romances do not include such an ordinary form of transportation. Ask students how Don Quixote plans to obtain a horse for his squire.

Possible Response: Don Quixote will do battle with the first knight who is not polite to him. After winning the fight, Don Quixote will take the knight's horse and give it to Sancho.

and that was why he had done the mischief in this house which we would discover. He also said that he was called Muñatón[41] the Magician."

A "Frestón, he should have said," remarked Don Quixote.

"I can't say as to that," replied the housekeeper, "whether he was called Frestón or Fritón;[42] all I know is that his name ended in a *tón.*"

1 "So it does," said Don Quixote. "He is a wise enchanter, a great enemy of mine, who has a grudge against me because he knows by his arts and learning that in the course of time I am to fight in single combat with a knight whom he favors, and that I am to be the victor and he can do nothing to prevent it. For this reason he seeks to cause me all the trouble that he can, but I am warning him that it will be hard to gainsay or shun that which Heaven has ordained." . . .

B 2 In the meanwhile Don Quixote was bringing his powers of persuasion to bear upon a farmer who lived near by, a good man—if this title may be applied to one who is poor—but with very few wits in his head. The short of it is, by pleas and promises, he got the hapless rustic to agree to ride forth with him and serve him as his squire. Among other things, Don Quixote told him that he ought to be more than willing to go, because no telling what adventure might occur which would win them an island, and then he (the farmer) would be left to be the governor of it. As a result of these and other similar assurances, Sancho Panza forsook his wife and children and consented to take upon himself the duties of squire to his neighbor.

> THE SHORT OF IT IS, BY PLEAS AND PROMISES, HE GOT THE HAPLESS RUSTIC TO AGREE TO RIDE FORTH WITH HIM AND SERVE HIM AS HIS SQUIRE.

Next, Don Quixote set out to raise some money, and by selling this thing and pawning that and getting the worst of the bargain always, he finally scraped together a reasonable amount. He also asked a friend of his for the loan of a buckler and patched up his broken helmet as well as he could. He advised his squire, Sancho, of the day and hour when they were to take the road and told him to see to laying in a supply of those things that were most necessary, and, above all, not to forget the saddlebags. Sancho replied that he would see to all this and added that he was also thinking of taking along with him a very good ass that he had, as he was not much used to going on foot. 3

C With regard to the ass, Don Quixote had to do a little thinking, trying to recall if any knight-errant had ever had a squire thus asininely[43] mounted. He could not think of any, but nevertheless he decided to take Sancho with the intention of providing him with a nobler steed as soon as occasion offered; he had but to appropriate the horse of the first discourteous knight he met. Having furnished himself with shirts and all the other things that the innkeeper had recommended, he and Panza rode forth one night unseen by anyone and without taking leave of wife and children, housekeeper or niece. They went so far that by the time morning came they were safe from discovery had a hunt been started for them. . . .

41. **Muñatón** (mo͞o-nyä-tôn′).

42. **Frestón** (frĕs-tôn′) **or Fritón** (frē-tôn′): Frestón, a magician, was thought to be the author of *History of Belianís of Greece.*

43. **asininely:** foolishly; ridiculously. The word is derived from the name of the animal.

Cross Curricular Link Humanities

SANCHO PANZA The character of Sancho Panza is one of the most beloved in Western literature. An illiterate and comical peasant, the squat and earthy Sancho serves as a perfect foil to the lanky and dreamy Don Quixote. While his master imagines that he is a knight fighting magicians, giants, and even entire armies, Sancho remains grounded in ordinary reality, for he realizes that life is often exactly as it appears to be. Sancho joins Don Quixote because he wants to be governor of an island. Don Quixote also suggests that other rewards, such as being named a count and having his wife and children ennobled, may be given him for his faithful service.

As their adventures continue, the two men develop a genuine affection for each other, and they even learn from one another. Sancho from time to time believes in the same illusions as his master, especially when Don Quixote explains that they are both victims of enchantment. Don Quixote on occasion listens to Sancho's practical advice, making concessions that would not be expected of a knight. Upon his return home, Sancho proclaims, "there's nothing better in the world than to be the honored squire of a knight errant who's out looking for adventures."

Detail of *Don Quixote and the Dead Mule* (1867), Honoré Daumier. Musée d'Orsay, Paris. Photograph copyright © Erich Lessing/Art Resource, New York.

Customizing Instruction

Less Proficient Readers

Make sure that students are following the plot by asking the following questions:

1 Don Quixote believes his niece's story that his books and study have been destroyed by a magician. Why does Quixote so quickly blame the magician Frestón? *(He believes that Frestón is his great enemy.)*

2 How does Don Quixote convince Sancho Panza to join him? *(He tells him that he may be given an island to govern.)*

3 Why does Sancho insist on taking his ass? *(He doesn't want to walk.)*

English Learners

Explain the meaning of the following words and phrases:

- "enchanter" *(magician or one who casts spells)*
- "hapless rustic" *(unfortunate or unlucky country person)*
- "buckler" *(a small round shield carried or worn on the arm)*
- "laying in a supply" *(assemble a supply)*

Advanced Learners

Don Quixote promises Sancho Panza that he will "appropriate the horse of the first discourteous knight" that he meets. Ask students why courtesy is such an important part of the code of chivalry.

Possible Response: A knight is expected to follow certain rules of language and behavior that govern his relations to other people. Such rules establish reciprocal duties: for example, knights were expected to treat other knights with appropriate respect because all knights belonged to the same elite class. An act of discourtesy was a serious breech of social rules that could get one killed.

MINI LESSON Viewing and Representing

Detail of *Don Quixote and the Dead Mule* by Honoré Daumier

ART APPRECIATION The French artist Honoré Daumier (1808–1879) created numerous works about the adventures of Don Quixote. This detail from a larger drawing illlustrates an episode in the novel. The critic H. W. Janson notes that for Daumier Cervantes's work embodies a "tragic conflict within human nature that forever pits the soul against the body, ideal aspirations against harsh reality." Point out that the dark mass of Sancho's body in this drawing might suggest that "harsh reality," while the vertical lines of the Don Quixote figure might suggest those "ideal aspirations." Ask students to note other ways in which the artist highlights the differences between Don Quixote and Sancho Panza.

Possible Response: Don Quixote's lance points upward and seems to merge with the clouds, suggesting his otherworldly character. Quixote's body seems to cast no shadow and is defined by lightly shaded masses, suggesting Don Quixote's spiritual hopes and romantic dreams. Most of the lines depicting Quixote's horse are vertical, as if both horse and rider are united in an idealistic mission. The mountain opposite Quixote is grand and lofty, perhaps a symbol of his quest.

By contrast, Sancho Panza and his ass seem joined to the earth. The ass is looking downward and burdened by the weight of Sancho and the bags. The darkness of Sancho's figure seems at one with the shadows on the ground, as if Sancho represents everything that pulls the human spirit downward. The mountain opposite Sancho seems squat and limited, perhaps symbolic of Sancho himself.

Reading and Analyzing

Literary Analysis CHARACTERIZATION

A This scene, in which Don Quixote imagines that windmills are actually giants, marks the beginning of the most famous episode in the novel. Ask students what Don Quixote's comments here reveal about his frame of mind.

Possible Response: Don Quixote interprets everything that he sees in terms of the books that he has read. He looks upon the windmills as "lawless giants" and feels compelled to attack them. Don Quixote feels that his actions are noble because in his eyes he is fighting for the sake of good.

Reading Skills and Strategies
COMPARE AND CONTRAST

B Explain to students that these windmills are used to grind grain. Ask students to describe the difference between Sancho's perception of the windmills and Don Quixote's perception.

Possible Response: Don Quixote is a romantic idealist; he imagines the windmills to be fierce enemies that he must battle. Sancho is a practical realist; he sees the windmills for what they are.

Literary Analysis ROMANCE

C Point out that Don Quixote follows a prescribed formula for preparing for battle, one that he has learned from his reading. He calls upon his "lady Dulcinea" before starting battle, both as a sign of his loyal service to her and as a call for her protection. Ask students to suggest what activity the real "Dulcinea" (the peasant girl Aldonza Lorenzo) might be engaged in while Don Quixote is calling her name.

Possible Response: She may be working in the fields or tending to farm animals.

FROM
CHAPTER 8
Part 1

At this point they caught sight of thirty or forty windmills which were standing on the plain there, and no sooner had Don Quixote laid eyes upon them than he turned to his squire and said,
A "Fortune is guiding our affairs better than we could have wished; for you see there before you,
1 friend Sancho Panza, some thirty or more lawless giants with whom I mean to do battle. I shall deprive them of their lives, and with the spoils from this encounter we shall begin to enrich ourselves; for this is righteous warfare, and it is a great service to God to remove so accursed a breed from the face of the earth."

"What giants?" said Sancho Panza.

"Those that you see there," replied his master, "those with the long arms some of which are as much as two leagues in length."

"But look, your Grace, those are not giants
B but windmills, and what appear to be arms are
2 their wings which, when whirled in the breeze, cause the millstone to go."

"It is plain to be seen," said Don Quixote, "that you have had little experience in this matter of adventures. If you are afraid, go off to one side and say your prayers while I am engaging them in fierce, unequal combat."

Saying this, he gave spurs to his steed Rocinante, without paying any heed to Sancho's warning that these were truly windmills and not giants that he was riding forth to attack. Nor even when he was close upon them did he perceive what they really were, but shouted at the top of his lungs, "Do not seek to flee, cowards and vile creatures that you are, for it is but a single knight with whom you have to deal!"

At that moment a little wind came up and the big wings began turning.

"Though you flourish as many arms as did the giant Briareus,"[44] said Don Quixote when he perceived this, "you still shall have to answer to me."

He thereupon commended himself with all his
heart to his lady Dulcinea, beseeching her to suc- C
cor[45] him in this peril; and, being well covered with his shield and with his lance at rest, he bore down upon them at a full gallop and fell upon
the first mill that stood in his way, giving a 3
thrust at the wing, which was whirling at such a speed that his lance was broken into bits and

44. **Briareus** (brē-âr′yo͞os): a mythological giant with 100 arms.

45. **succor:** to provide aid; help.

Don Quixote and the Windmill, after Gustave Doré. Engraving by Heliodore Joseph Pisan. Bibliothèque Nationale de France, Paris. Giraudon/Art Resource, New York.

Customizing Instruction

Less Proficient Readers

Ask students the following questions to make sure that they are following the plot:

1 What does Don Quixote imagine that he sees when he and Sancho come across a field full of windmills? *(evil giants)*

2 Does Sancho Panza agree with Don Quixote's interpretation of the scene? *(No, Sancho only sees the actual windmills.)*

3 What happens when Quixote attacks the first windmill? *(The wings of the windmill break Don Quixote's lance, knocking down Don Quixote and his horse.)*

English Learners

Explain the meaning of the following words and phrases:

- "laid eyes upon them" *(saw them)*
- "spoils" *(things taken from a person who has been defeated in battle)*
- "any heed" *(any attention)*
- "commended himself" *(dedicating himself)*
- "beseeching" *(asking)*

DON QUIXOTE **841**

Reading Skills and Strategies
DRAWING CONCLUSIONS

After Don Quixote falls to the ground, he does realize that the windmills are not giants. Ask students what his explanation about "that magician Frestón" reveals about Don Quixote's state of mind.

Possible Response: Though Don Quixote at times can plainly recognize reality, he still insists upon theories of magic to explain any mistakes he has made. His mind is so thoroughly filled with stories that he cannot recognize his own failings or mistakes.

Literary Analysis PLOT

Point out that the encounter with the windmill is typical of many of the adventures that Don Quixote and Sancho Panza undertake. The adventure begins with one of Don Quixote's romantic visions; one or both of the main characters is hurt as a result of the disparity between idealistic vision and brute reality; and both characters gladly resume their travels, retelling stories of past adventures and predicting future adventures along the way.

both horse and horseman went rolling over the plain, very much battered indeed. Sancho upon his donkey came hurrying to his master's assistance as fast as he could, but when he reached the spot, the knight was unable to move, so great was the shock with which he and Rocinante had hit the ground.

"God help us!" exclaimed Sancho, "did I not tell your Grace to look well, that those were nothing but windmills, a fact which no one could fail to see unless he had other mills of the same sort in his head?"

"Be quiet, friend Sancho," said Don Quixote. "Such are the fortunes of war, which more than any other are subject to constant change. What is more, when I come to think of it, I am sure that this must be the work of that magician Frestón, the one who robbed me of my study and my books, and who has thus changed the giants into windmills in order to deprive me of the glory of overcoming them, so great is the enmity that he bears me; but in the end his evil arts shall not prevail against this trusty sword of mine."

"May God's will be done," was Sancho Panza's response. And with the aid of his squire the knight was once more mounted on Rocinante, who stood there with one shoulder half out of joint. And so, speaking of the adventure that had just befallen them, they continued along the Puerto Lápice highway[46]; for there, Don Quixote said, they could not fail to find many and varied adventures, this being a much traveled thoroughfare. . . . ❖

46. **Puerto Lápice** (pwĕr'tô lä'pē-sĕ).

Cross Curricular Link **Humanities**

DON QUIXOTE: THE REST OF THE STORY Don Quixote and Sancho Panza continue their comically adventurous travels. At one point, they encounter two flocks of sheep, which Don Quixote imagines to be two armies in battle. Quick to act, he charges—or rather, trots—into battle. In his mind, he proves himself a great warrior, but the sheep pay a costly price. Another time, Don Quixote frees an entire chain gang of prisoners. Though he commands the men to serve Dulcinea, they only become angry and stone him. Sancho Panza, for his loyal service, is repeatedly beaten up. His ass is mysteriously stolen from him, though he insists he was sitting on it at the time. As a punishment for not paying his bill at an inn, mistaken as a castle by Don Quixote, Sancho suffers the indignity of being tossed in a blanket before an amused crowd. Part One concludes with the priest and barber tricking Don Quixote into returning home.

In Part Two, a student named Sampson Carrasco convinces Don Quixote and Sancho Panza to once again seek adventure. This time, they encounter many people who have already heard about them because they have read the novel. The student twice disguises himself as a knight and challenges Don Quixote, defeating him the second time. Don Quixote returns home dejected, catches a fever, and awakens cured of his madness. To the great sadness of those who know him, he dies a few days later.

A SOLDIER OF URBINA[1]

Jorge Luis Borges

Translated by ALASTAIR REID

Beginning to fear his own unworthiness
for campaigns like the last he fought, at sea,
this soldier, resigning himself to minor duty,
wandered unknown in Spain, his own harsh country.

To get rid of or to mitigate[2] the cruel
weight of reality, he hid his head in dream.
The magic past of Roland and the cycles
of Ancient Britain[3] warmed him, made him welcome.

Sprawled in the sun, he would gaze on the widening
plain, its coppery glow going on and on;
he felt himself at the end, poor and alone,

unaware of the music he was hiding;
plunging deep in a dream of his own,
he came on Sancho and Don Quixote, riding.

1. **Urbina:** Cervantes served as a soldier under Captain Diego Urbina.
2. **mitigate:** to moderate; lessen in intensity.
3. **cycles of Ancient Britain:** stories and poems about King Arthur and knights of his era.

Jorge Luis Borges (1899–1986) was a powerful literary voice from Buenos Aires, Argentina. A private and learned man who eventually went blind, Borges achieved international fame for his imaginative, ingenious short stories. His stories portray a puzzling, mysterious world, where boundaries between dream and reality, past and present, fact and fantasy are often blurred.

Borges, who also wrote critically acclaimed poetry and essays, acknowledged his own indebtedness to Cervantes' great novel. Another important Latin American writer, Carlos Fuentes, once described Borges as a child of La Mancha because his works so clearly show the influence of Cervantes.

Discussion Questions

1. In the first stanza, the speaker describes the life of Cervantes. What do we learn about the life of "this soldier."
   Possible Response: Though Cervantes had proven himself a good soldier in battles at sea, when he returned to Spain he was forced to wander "unknown," taking unimportant jobs.
2. According to the speaker, what did Cervantes do to escape "the cruel weight of reality"?
   Possible Response: He lost himself in tales of knights' adventures; "he hid his head in dream."
3. According to the speaker, how did Cervantes come up with the idea of Sancho and Don Quixote?
   Possible Response: These characters came to Cervantes while he was "deep in a dream of his own."

MINI LESSON Grammar

INFINITIVE PHRASES

Instruction Remind students that an infinitive is a verb form that usually begins with the word *to* and acts as a noun, an adjective, or an adverb. An infinitive phrase consists of an infinitive plus its modifiers and complements. An infinitive phrase can function as a noun, adjective, or adverb.

Model Sentence

To live as a knight-errant was Don Quixote's greatest wish.

Write the above model sentence on the chalkboard. Have students identify the infinitive phrase *(To live as a knight-errant)* and its function within the sentence *(noun/subject).*

Practice Ask students to underline the infinitive phrase and to identify its function in each sentence.

1. His first task was to polish some old pieces of armor. *(noun)*
2. Afterwards, Don Quixote sought to give his horse a special name. *(adverb)*
3. In the end, he was one to leave home for unknown places and adventures. *(adjective)*

For more instruction and practice in infinitive phrases, use McDougal Littell's ***Language Network:***

- Grade 10, Chapter 3, "Using Phrases"
- Grade 12, Chapter 2, "Using Phrases"

Thinking Through the Literature

1. **What Do You Think?** Responses will vary.

Comprehension Check

- Don Quixote spends so much time reading about knights that he loses his mind.
- Don Quixote tells Sancho that he may be named governor of an island.
- Don Quixote believes that the windmills are actually giants.

Use Selection Quiz in **Unit Five Resouce Book,** p. 53.

Think Critically

2. Possible Response: Students may draw attention to any number of details, including the following: Don Quixote spends so much time reading that he forgets "the life of a hunter and even the administration of his estate"; he lies awake nights trying to understand meaningless passages from books; he cannot tell the difference between events in books and events in real life.
3. Possible Response: Some students may be amused by the contrast between Don Quixote's code of chivalry and his actual life; others may be saddened. All students should note that in every detail Don Quixote's actual life falls comically short of his heroic ideal. His horse is old and weak; his "lady" is a farm girl who doesn't even know him; his great adventures are an exercise in folly.
4. Possible Response: Sancho Panza is a poor, illiterate peasant, so he does not have his master's grand and romantic self-image. Sancho is practical, realistic, and guided by self-interest, in sharp contrast to the literary-minded, otherworldly, idealistic, and self-sacrificing Don Quixote.
5. Possible Response: The windmill attack illustrates Don Quixote's separation from reality. He attacks inanimate objects, believing them to be evil giants. Yet the attack also illustrates his persistence. Once Don Quixote recognizes the windmills, he creates another interpretation based upon an evil magician to explain his deception. Despite his failure, he immediately goes off in search of another adventure.
6. Accept all reasonable responses.

Thinking Through the Literature

1. **What Do You Think?** Do you like the character of Don Quixote? Explain why or why not.

Comprehension Check
- What causes Don Quixote's madness?
- Why does Sancho Panza agree to become Don Quixote's squire?
- Why does Don Quixote attack the windmill?

Think Critically

2. **ACTIVE READING: ANALYZING EXPOSITION** Look over the chart you made in your READER'S NOTEBOOK. What details in the exposition help you understand why Don Quixote "went completely out of his mind"?
3. The knights' code of honor, or **chivalry,** idealizes qualities such as bravery, courtesy, and gallantry toward women. Contrast the ideal image of a knight with Don Quixote's actual life. Do you find the contrast amusing or sad? Explain.

- Don Quixote's fragile helmet and his "skinny nag" Rocinante
- his "great lady," the farm girl Dulcinea del Toboso
- his quest for heroic adventures

4. A **foil** is a character who provides a striking contrast to another character. How does Sancho Panza serve as a foil to Don Quixote? Give examples to support your opinion.
5. What does Don Quixote's encounter with the windmill illustrate about his character?
6. Do you predict that Don Quixote's fantasies will turn out to be dangerous to himself and others? Why or why not?

Extend Interpretations

7. **Compare Texts** In "A Soldier of Urbina" on page 843, the poet imagines how Cervantes came to create his major characters. According to the poem, what do Cervantes and Don Quixote have in common?
8. **Connect to Life** Don Quixote's fantasies lead him into ridiculous situations and sometimes even cause injury. Is fantasy in adults always harmful? Or are there times when it can be healthy and useful? Explain.

LITERARY ANALYSIS: CHARACTERIZATION

Characterization refers to the techniques that writers use to develop characters. There are four basic methods of characterization:
1. A writer may describe the physical appearance of the character. For example, Cervantes tells us that Don Quixote "has little flesh on his bones."
2. A character's nature may be revealed through his or her own speech, thoughts, feelings, or actions. Don Quixote's sale of land to pay for books reveals his lack of practicality.
3. The speech, thoughts, feelings, and actions of other characters may be used to develop a character. Sancho Panza's willingness to go along on the journey suggests that Don Quixote is persuasive.
4. The narrator may make direct comments about the character's nature. In this excerpt, the narrator tells us that Don Quixote's "wits were gone beyond repair."

Paired Activity With a partner, identify five short passages in this excerpt that help create a strong impression of either Don Quixote or Sancho Panza. Use a chart like the one shown to record your findings.

Don Quixote		
Passage	Method of Characterization	Qualities Revealed
"his wits were gone beyond repair"	4	

Extend Interpretations

7. **Compare Texts** Possible Response: Both are dreamers who lose themselves in books. Their romantic dreams seem to make up for the deficiencies of their lives.
8. **Connect to Life** Accept all reasonable responses.

Literary Analysis

Paired Activity Before students begin their charts, review the four types of characterization with them. Make sure that students understand what is distinct about each type. When students have completed their charts, solicit examples from the students. Have the entire class judge each example to determine whether the example clearly illustrates one of the four types of characterization.

Use **Unit Five Resource Book,** p. 51, for more practice.

Writing Options

1. Speech about Chivalry Does the concept of chivalry have any value in the modern world? Write a persuasive speech on the topic. Before you begin, review the information about chivalry on pages 690 and 709. Begin the speech with a clear statement of your opinion. Then present your supporting points clearly and logically. Finish up with a summation of your argument. Place the speech in your **Working Portfolio.**

2. Letter from Sancho Pretend you are Sancho Panza and write a letter to your wife after the windmill incident. Describe what happened to Don Quixote and reveal your thoughts about him. Explain whether the incident raised any doubts in your mind about the journey.

Writing Handbook
See page R27: Descriptive Writing.

Activities & Explorations

Quixote Improv With a small group, create an improvised dramatization in which Don Quixote and Sancho Panza take part in an adventure in your community. Imagine, for example, how Don Quixote might respond to a football game or a car wash.
~SPEAKING AND LISTENING

Inquiry & Research

1. Chivalrous Knights Find out more about one of the famous knights mentioned in *Don Quixote.* Which romance does the knight appear in? What adventures does he have? Is this character based on a real person or is he entirely fictional? Report your findings to the class.

2. Fantasy and Reality Theories of mental health have changed considerably since Cervantes' time. With a partner, research mental disorders that involve mistaking fantasy for reality. How might a psychologist diagnose Don Quixote? Do you think Don Quixote would be happier if his disorder were brought under control?

Vocabulary in Action

EXERCISE: CONTEXT CLUES On your paper, complete each of the following sentences.

1. A(n) _________ story about a knight's adventure would not confuse its readers.
2. Some romances were _________ tales that piled one adventure on another.
3. In coming up with Rocinante's unusual name, Don Quixote showed considerable _________.
4. Don Quixote's _________ with books about knights kept him reading and reading.
5. As a landowner, Don Quixote was _________ and impractical because all he did was read.
6. Sancho Panza was a(n) _________ fellow who got along easily with his master.
7. Some knights could be _________ in their treatment of their inferiors.
8. After _________ the windmills, Sancho Panza realized that they were not giants after all.
9. The _________ scene of an old man fighting the windmills is a famous one.
10. Readers might _________ that Don Quixote will someday become an honored knight.

WORDS TO KNOW

affable, conjecture, haughty, incongruous, indolent, infatuation, ingenuity, interminable, lucid, scrutinizing

Building Vocabulary
For a more in-depth lesson on affixes, see page 864.

Vocabulary in Action

1. lucid
2. interminable
3. ingenuity
4. infatuation
5. indolent
6. affable
7. haughty
8. scrutinizing
9. incongruous
10. conjecture

To assess skills and concepts taught in this selection, use **Formal Assessment Book,** pp. 127–128.

Writing Options

1. **Speech about Chivalry** Those students who write about this topic may find it helpful to meet in a small group to discuss the issues before writing. Advise students to consider opposing points of view as a means of sharpening their own argument. For example, those who argue that chivalry has lost its value should consider how they would respond to the best arguments to the contrary.
2. **Letter from Sancho** Before students write, they should review the introduction to Sancho on page 838. Remind students that Sancho speaks in a manner that is very different from Don Quixote's bookish and flowery language.

Activities & Explorations

Quixote Improv Make sure that all groups realize that their dramatizations should reflect the differences between Don Quixote and Sancho Panza. Though each group can choose its own "adventure," all should aim to create recognizable versions of the two main characters.

Inquiry & Research

1. **Chivalrous Knights** Students should be able to learn about literary characters such as Amadis of Gaul, Palmerin of England, and Roland by using the indexes of encyclopedias or by searching the Internet. Information about historical and legendary figures such as the Cid and Alexander can also be found in that manner.
2. **Fantasy and Reality** If you are aware of any students who have experienced serious mental or emotional disorders, you may wish to guide them to another topic. This topic is relevant to the literature, but it should be handled in a manner that is respectful of people with such disorders.

Additional Background

- Molière's father was a successful furniture merchant in Paris and upholsterer to the king.
- As a youth, Molière was a promising scholar of Greek and Latin; he studied law and received a law degree in 1641.
- Molière's first venture in theater was a failure; the theater group that he founded in 1643 struggled for a few years and then went bankrupt.
- For the next twelve years, Molière traveled throughout France with an itinerant company. He learned a great deal about comedy from Italian *commedia dell'arte* companies, which blended farcical subjects, improvised dialogue, and slapstick physical movements.
- When Molière's theater company returned to Paris in 1658, they gave a performance before King Louis XIV. The king became Molière's patron.
- Besides writing, Molière was also considered the greatest comic actor of his era. His wealth of facial expressions, range of voice, and mastery of physical movement earned praise even from his enemies.
- As a theatrical manager, Molière produced not only his own plays but also those by other leading playwrights, such as Corneille and Racine.
- Ironically, Molière died after being seized by a coughing fit while performing the lead role in *The Imaginary Invalid,* a play about a hypochondriac.

The Plays of Molière

Molière (mōl-yâr) is considered by many to be the greatest French playwright of all time. Today, more than three centuries after his death, his comedies are still popular in France. In translation, they still delight and instruct people throughout the world. Several of his works rank as masterpieces of world literature.

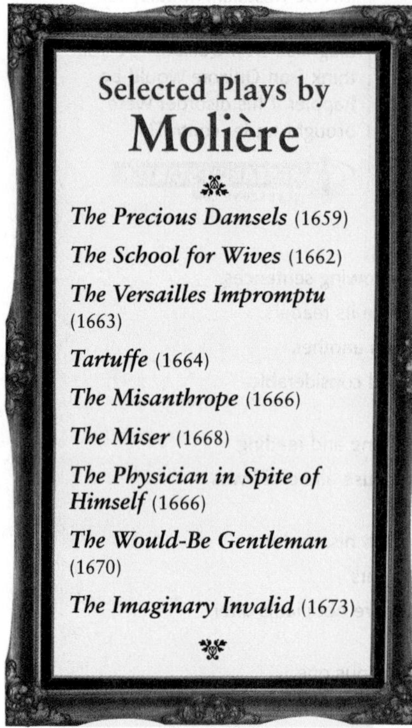

Selected Plays by Molière

The Precious Damsels (1659)
The School for Wives (1662)
The Versailles Impromptu (1663)
Tartuffe (1664)
The Misanthrope (1666)
The Miser (1668)
The Physician in Spite of Himself (1666)
The Would-Be Gentleman (1670)
The Imaginary Invalid (1673)

Molière was the stage name of Jean Baptiste Poquelin (zhän băh-tēst' pôk-lăn). Molière, whose lifelong love of the theater made him excel at his craft, began his career as an actor and a director. Later, he would perform the lead role in several of his own plays. He kept both the stage and his audience in mind when he wrote his comedies—about 32 in all.

To Molière, the main function of comedy was to "correct men's vices." Often he would base a play on a particular vice or failing and then exaggerate his selected trait in one of the characters. These characters are universal types—fanatics and flirts, quacks and misers, hypocrites and hypochondriacs. Molière pokes fun at their extreme conduct, which is contrary to moderation and good sense. Like other writers of the Enlightenment, he believed that the universe is ruled by reason. His comedies teach that human life should be rational too.

Molière's first great comedy was *The School for Wives* (1662). The main character is a middle-aged man who wants to marry his ward, a young lady. He is convinced that he has reared her to be the ideal wife by limiting her education. She, however, chooses to follow

Above:
Scene from The Imaginary Invalid. *18th century French painting.*

her own heart and rejects him. Love conquers all—even the best-laid schemes of the controlling protagonist. This play, like many others by Molière, triggered heated protests.

By far, the bitterest attacks were directed at Molière's play *Tartuffe* (tär-to͝of'). In this play, the title character pretends to be pious in order to deceive the gullible and fill his own pockets. He tricks a religious fanatic and nearly ruins the man's family. The play shows the folly of too much trust and too little sense. It was perceived, however, as an attack on religion, and banned for several years.

The Misanthrope is generally considered Molière's greatest play. The title, which means "hater of humankind," applies to its main character, Alceste. He takes sincerity to ridiculous extremes, scornful of telling even a white lie. Though Alceste is an idealist with some admirable traits, his extreme reactions make him comic. Still, at the end of this play, the audience is left to ponder the need for more truth in everyday life.

Molière's comedies target human folly. They make audiences and readers laugh and think—and look within. One translator of Molière's plays describes their effect this way: "Again and again he leads us from the enjoyable but shallow reaction of laughing at a fool to recognizing in that fool others whom we know, and ultimately ourselves." Perhaps this is why his plays are still enjoyed today.

Below:
A print of Molière in the lead role in his play The School for Husbands

Literary Chronology
In addition to the plays listed on page 846, here are other notable plays by Molière:
The School for Husbands (1661)
Don Juan (1665)
Amphitryon (1668)
George Dandin (1668)
Scapin (1671)
The Learned Ladies (1672)

MILESTONES IN WORLD LITERATURE 847

Objectives

- understand and appreciate an excerpt from a **philosophical tale (Literary Analysis)**
- recognize techniques of **satire and humor (Literary Analysis)**
- **make judgments (Active Reading)**

Summary

The innocent young Candide grows up in a baron's household, where he is tutored by the always optimistic Dr. Pangloss. The tutor teaches his student that they live in the "best of all possible worlds," a maxim that Dr. Pangloss takes to ridiculous extremes. One day Candide is caught kissing the baron's daughter, Cunegonde. The angry baron expels Candide from his household. The forlorn and lovesick Candide wanders to a neighboring town, where he is apparently befriended by two soldiers. The soldiers trick Candide into drinking to the health of the King of Bulgarians, a gesture interpreted as Candide's consent to serve in the king's army. Against his will, Candide is forced to train as a soldier. After a failed escape, he is brutally beaten by his regiment, only to be saved from death by the intercession of the King of the Bulgarians. The king hopes to generate favorable publicity by his act of mercy.

Use **Unit Five Resource Book,** p. 54, for additional support.

Thematic Link

The innocent Candide naively believes that he lives in an earthly paradise, mistaking **human possibility** for perfection.

Use **Unit Five Resource Book,** p. 57, for practice with Words to Know.

5-Minute Warm-Up

Daily Language SkillBuilder

Have students **proofread** the display sentences on page 685k and write them correctly.

FROM *Candide*

VOLTAIRE

Voltaire
1694–1778

Early Success Philosopher, poet, playwright, historian, and rebel—Voltaire (vōl-târ′) was all of these. Born François-Marie Arouet, he was imprisoned early in his literary career for insulting the regent, or acting ruler, of the French monarchy. Shortly after his release from prison in 1718, his first major play, *Oedipe* (œ-dĕp′), achieved international success, and he chose the pen name Voltaire. Other successes quickly followed. By his early 30s, Voltaire became independently wealthy through wise investments and enjoyed the status of an honored celebrity at the court of King Louis XV.

English Influence Circumstances changed abruptly when Voltaire insulted a young nobleman in 1726. Given the option of imprisonment or exile, Voltaire chose exile in England, where he befriended many writers and political leaders. After Voltaire returned to Paris in 1729, he wrote a book praising England's political liberties and traditions of tolerance. However, the book was thought to be critical of the French government. In 1734, fearing another unpleasant jail term, Voltaire was forced to flee Paris again.

Exile and Return For the next four decades, Voltaire spent most of the time away from Paris, living as far away as Berlin and Geneva. He produced a steady flow of essays, books, plays, poems, pamphlets, and letters. Many of his works criticized religious intolerance and persecution and advocated the use of reason. His most famous work, *Candide* (1759), used satire to attack optimism and simple-minded idealism. Although Voltaire enjoyed a triumphant return to Paris at age 83, the excitement of his return proved too much for him, and he died shortly thereafter. Always a controversial figure in his lifetime, Voltaire was later regarded as a kind of "saint of reason." During the French Revolution, his remains were removed to the Panthéon in Paris, where many of France's most famous citizens are buried.

LESSON RESOURCES

UNIT FIVE RESOURCE BOOK, pp. 54–58

ASSESSMENT RESOURCES
Formal Assessment, pp. 129–130
Teacher's Guide to Assessment and Portfolio Use
Test Generator

INTEGRATED TECHNOLOGY
Visit our Web site: classzone.com

ADDITIONAL RESOURCES
Lesson Planning Guide, pp. 109–110
Teacher's Sourcebook for Language Development

Build Background

A Comic Masterpiece

Candide is Voltaire's most widely read work of fiction. This philosophical tale tells about the comic misadventures of an innocent young man who has grown up in the household of a powerful baron. From his tutor, Dr. Pangloss, Candide learns that all is for the best in "this best of all possible worlds." After he is cast out of this "paradise," Candide travels the world in an effort to reunite with his beloved Cunegonde (kun-gônd'), the Baron's daughter. He wanders through Europe and the Americas, occasionally meeting up with members of his former household, who also endure great misfortune. At each turn, Candide learns more about the flaws of humanity, realizing that all is not for the best. Although the novel ends on a relatively happy note, Candide realizes that the world is not the paradise he once imagined.

The Best of All Possible Worlds Voltaire wrote *Candide* in reaction to a way of looking at the world known as **optimism.** An optimist is a person who looks for the best in every situation and person. According to the philosopher associated with optimism, Gottfried Wilhelm Leibniz (līp'-nĭts), our world is "the best of all possible worlds." The English poet Alexander Pope put it another way, "Whatever is, is right." Voltaire was attracted to such ideas in his youth. However, he came to reject such optimism because he felt it did not do justice to the tragedies and suffering of human life. Also, he feared that optimism discouraged people from trying to remedy injustices and social problems.

Connect to Your Life

For some people, the glass is always half full; others see it as half empty. Do you prefer to be in the company of optimists or their opposites, the pessimists? What are the advantages and disadvantages of each of these outlooks on life?

Focus Your Reading

LITERARY ANALYSIS: SATIRE AND HUMOR

Satire is a literary technique in which ideas, customs, behaviors, or institutions are ridiculed for the purpose of improving society. In satire, **humor** and exaggeration are used as weapons of mockery, intended to provoke the reader's laughter and thought. For example, the Baron is "one of the most powerful lords" in his kingdom because "his castle possessed a door and windows."

ACTIVE READING: MAKING JUDGMENTS

To appreciate the intended meaning of a satirical work, readers must make judgments about the characters. For example, readers might begin judging Pangloss when Voltaire introduces him as a teacher of "metaphysico-theologo-cosmolonigology." By exaggerating Pangloss's area of study, Voltaire encourages us to be skeptical of his ideas.

READER'S NOTEBOOK As you read this excerpt from *Candide,* record key information about the main characters in a chart like the one shown.

Character	Trait(s)
Dr. Pangloss	*Pretentious, spends his time studying ridiculous subjects*
The Baron	
Candide	
Cunegonde	

WORDS TO KNOW **Vocabulary Preview**

candor, docile, pensive, reiterated, vivacity

READING FOR INFORMATION

Reading Skills and Strategies
CHRONOLOGICAL ORDER

Working with the entire class, compose a time line based upon Voltaire's biography on page 848. Record years and events on the board or on an overhead transparency. Point out that time lines can be a useful study aid for literature and history.

Reading Skills and Strategies
SCANNING

Explain to students that scanning is a type of quick reading to look for specific information. Scanning is used when people flip through phone books to locate a number and when they review a book index to find a specific topic or name. Demonstrate scanning by having the entire class quickly look for information in **A Comic Masterpiece** that identifies Dr. Pangloss *(the tutor to Candide).* In this case, one looks for the name first, then quickly looks for surrounding information that identifies who Dr. Pangloss is. Have students practice this skill by finding answers to the following questions, which can be written on an overhead transparency so that you can deal with one question at a time:

- Who is Cunegonde *(the girl Candide loves)*
- Where does Candide travel to? *(throughout Europe and the Americas)*
- What lesson does Candide learn? *(the world is not a paradise)*

Historical Note

Voltaire's antagonism towards optimism was influenced by the responses to a tragic earthquake in Lisbon, Portugal, in 1755, which took the lives of thousands. Some people, notably the philosopher Jean-Jacques Rousseau, claimed that even such a terrible event would eventually lead to good. Voltaire was outraged because he felt such a view ignored the suffering caused by the tragedy.

TIME MANAGEMENT

If your schedule requires that you cover the lesson objectives in a shorter time, use . . .

- Preparing to Read, pp. 848-849
- Thinking Through the Literature, p. 856
- Vocabulary in Action, p. 857

If you want to take advantage of longer class time, use . . .

- TE Teaching Options: Cross Curricular Links, pp. 851, 853; Viewing and Representing, p. 855; Vocabulary Strategy, p. 852; Grammar, p. 854
- Choices & Challenges, p. 857

Active Reading MAKING JUDGMENTS

A Make sure that students realize that Candide is an illegitimate child; he was probably taken into the Baron's household to avoid scandal. The Baron's sister would not marry the "decent honest gentleman," who is probably Candide's father, simply because he was not a member of the nobility.

Ask students to judge what this reveals about her values.

Possible Response: The Baron's sister judges people according to the status of their birth, not the quality of their character.

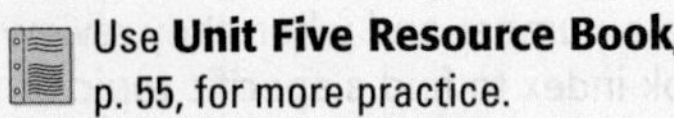

Use **Unit Five Resource Book,** p. 55, for more practice.

Literary Analysis CULTURAL SETTING

B Explain that standards of beauty in the 18th century were different than those of today. Thinness in a woman was viewed as a sign of poverty rather than of beauty. Cunegonde's "plump" figure was an integral part of her appeal.

Literary Analysis SATIRE AND HUMOR

C Help students to appreciate the absurdity of Pangloss's teaching. He is backwards in his reasoning: spectacles were made to fit the human nose; breeches were tailored to fit the leg, and so on. Ask students to come up with other humorous examples that might be used to continue Pangloss's train of thought.

Possible Response: Heads were created for hats; hands were created so that gloves could be worn.

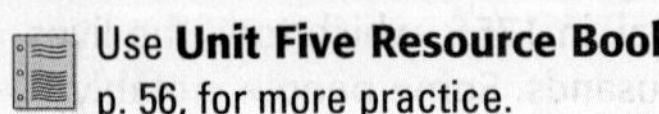

Use **Unit Five Resource Book,** p. 56, for more practice.

from Candide

Voltaire

Translated by Richard Aldington

Uniforms of imperial cavalry (18th century). Watercolor. Heeresgeschichtliches Museum, Vienna, Austria. Photograph copyright © Erich Lessing/Art Resource, New York.

Chapter I

How Candide was brought up in a noble castle, and how he was expelled from the same

In the castle of Baron Thunder-ten-tronckh in Westphalia[1] there lived a youth, endowed by Nature with the most gentle character. His face was the expression of his soul. His judgment was quite honest and he was extremely simple-minded; and this was the reason, I think, that he was named Candide.[2] Old servants in the house suspected that he was the son of the Baron's sister and a decent honest gentleman of the neighborhood, whom this young lady would never marry because he could only prove seventy-one quarterings,[3] and the rest of his genealogical tree[4] was lost, owing to the injuries of time.

The Baron was one of the most powerful lords in Westphalia, for his castle possessed a door and windows. His Great Hall was even decorated with a piece of tapestry. The dogs in his stable-yards formed a pack of hounds when necessary; his grooms were his huntsmen; the village curate was his Grand Almoner.[5] They all called him "My Lord," and laughed heartily at his stories.

The Baroness weighed about three hundred and fifty pounds, was therefore greatly respected, and did the honors of the house with a dignity which rendered her still more respectable. Her
B
daughter Cunegonde,[6] aged seventeen, was rosy-cheeked, fresh, plump and tempting. The Baron's son appeared in every respect worthy of his father. The tutor Pangloss[7] was the oracle of the house, and little Candide followed his lessons with all the candor of his age and character. 2

Pangloss taught metaphysico-theologo-cosmolonigology.[8] He proved admirably that there is no effect without a cause and that in this best of all possible worlds, My Lord the Baron's castle was the best of castles and his wife the best of all possible Baronesses. 3

"'Tis demonstrated," said he, "that things cannot be otherwise; for, since everything is made for an end, everything is necessarily for the best end. Observe that noses were made to wear spectacles; and so we have spectacles. Legs were visibly instituted to be breeched, and we have breeches. Stones were formed to be quarried and to build castles; and My Lord has a very noble castle; the greatest Baron in the province should have the best house; and as pigs were made to be C

1. **Baron Thunder-ten-tronckh** (thŭn′dər-tĕn-trônk′) **in Westphalia** (wĕst-fāl′yə): Westphalia is a region of west-central Germany.
2. **Candide** (kän-dēd′): a French word meaning "innocent" or "without sophistication."
3. **seventy-one quarterings:** quarterings are divisions in coats of arms that indicate connections with other noble families; 71 of these is a ridiculous number.
4. **genealogical tree:** a diagram showing ancestry in a family.
5. **Grand Almoner:** a person in charge of distributing charity, or alms, to the poor.
6. **Cunegonde** (kun-gônd′).
7. **Pangloss:** a combination of Greek words meaning "all" and "tongue."
8. **metaphysico-theologo-cosmolonigology** (mĕt′ə-fĭz′ĭ-kō-thē-ŏl′-ə-gō-kŏz-mŏl′ə-nĭ-gŏl′ə-jē): a made-up field of study. The ending *-nigology* comes from a French word meaning "foolish."

WORDS TO KNOW

candor (kan′dər) *n.* frankness; openness

Customizing Instruction

Less Proficient Readers

To make sure that students are following the plot, ask the following questions:

1 According to the old servants in the Baron's household, who are Candide's parents? *(the Baron's sister and an "honest gentleman of the neighborhood")*

2 Who is Candide's tutor? *(Pangloss)*

3 Which of the following phrases expresses the meaning of "best of all possible worlds"?
- No other world could possibly be better than ours. (correct choice)
- People always try their best, even if things don't work out.

English Learners

Explain the meaning of the following words and phrases:
- "pack of hounds" *(pack of hunting dogs)*
- "grooms" *(servants who take care of horses)*
- "oracle" *(a wise person)*
- "spectacles" *(eyeglasses)*
- "breeches" *(pants)*

Cross Curricular Link Humanities

LEIBNIZ AND THE BEST OF ALL POSSIBLE WORLDS The German philosopher Gottfried Wilhelm von Leibniz (1646–1716) based his views of the world upon his understanding of God. According to Leibniz, because God is all-good, all-knowing, and all-powerful, it must logically follow that our world is the best of all possible worlds. As a result of God's perfection, the entire universe and all the events in that universe are linked in a complex chain of cause and effect. While an event, such as a tragic earthquake killing thousands, may seem to be evil when viewed from a limited perspective, ultimately that event—like everything else in the universe—will contribute to the greater good and the harmony of the universe.

Voltaire's *Candide* provides a humorous attack on such views. After Candide and Pangloss witness the famous Lisbon earthquake, Pangloss attempts to console the inhabitants: "For, said he, all this is for the best, since if there is a volcano at Lisbon, it cannot be somewhere else." Near the end of the tale, when Pangloss is dying of syphilis, Candide asks him if the disease is the work of the Devil. Pangloss clings to his optimism and insists that his disease is further evidence that ours is the best of all possible worlds. Pangloss points out that the disease was brought to Europe from the New World, which also gave Europe chocolate and cochineal (a popular red dye). Those two goods provide benefits to Europe that far outweigh the negative effects of the disease.

Literary Analysis
CHARACTERIZATION

A Point out that Candide explains his view of happiness as if he were describing a kind of heaven that offers different levels of perfection. Ask students what this passage reveals about him.

Possible Response: Candide is a simple-minded, naive, and foolish young man. He admires the Baron, loves Cunegonde, wants to see her every day, and believes Dr. Pangloss to be the greatest teacher in the world.

Reading Skills and Strategies
MAKING INFERENCES

B Help students to appreciate the tongue-in-cheek humor of this scene. Ask students what Pangloss is doing with the "very pretty" maid. *(The two are engaged in sexual activity.)* Have students describe Cunegonde's reaction to the scene she observes.

Possible Response: Cunegonde becomes excited while watching the activities. Although the narrator uses the language of scholarship to convey her response, it is clear that she is yearning for a physical relationship with Candide.

Literary Analysis SATIRE AND HUMOR

C Explain to students that this scene playfully presents the stereotypical romantic meeting. It begins with a secret rendezvous, is moved forward by a dropped handkerchief, continues with an innocent physical gesture, and ends with wild passion. Ask students to explain what makes this a funny scene.

Possible Responses: The romance moves so quickly from a polite and discreet meeting to passion. The narrator adds to the humor by adding playful details such as "their hands wandered," "observing this cause and effect," and "kicking him in the backside frequently and hard."

Active Reading MAKING JUDGMENTS

D Draw attention to the ridiculousness of the soldiers' explanation. They tell Candide that he never has to pay for his meals because he is so short. Indeed, he will never "be short of money." Ask students what Candide's response reveals about him.

Possible Response: Candide is laughably ignorant and easily duped. They men are clearly lying, but he insists that "everything is for the best."

The Stolen Kiss (late 1780s), Jean-Honoré Fragonard. Oil on canvas, 45 cm × 55 cm. The Hermitage, St. Petersburg, Russia.

eaten, we eat pork all the year round; consequently, those who have asserted that all is well talk nonsense; they ought to have said that all is for the best."

A Candide listened attentively and believed innocently; for he thought Mademoiselle Cunegonde extremely beautiful, although he was never bold enough to tell her so. He decided that after the happiness of being born Baron of Thunder-ten-tronckh, the second degree of happiness was to be Mademoiselle Cunegonde; the third, to see her every day; and the fourth to listen to Doctor Pangloss, the greatest philosopher of the province and therefore of the whole world.

B One day when Cunegonde was walking near the castle, in a little wood which was called The Park, she observed Doctor Pangloss in the bushes, giving a lesson in experimental physics to her mother's waiting-maid, a very pretty and docile brunette. Mademoiselle Cunegonde had a great inclination for science and watched breathlessly 1 the reiterated experiments she witnessed; she observed clearly the Doctor's sufficient reason, the effects and the causes, and returned home very much excited, pensive, filled with the desire of learning, reflecting that she might be the sufficient reason of young Candide and that he might be hers.

C On her way back to the castle she met Candide and blushed; Candide also blushed. She bade him good-morning in a hesitating voice; Candide replied without knowing what he was saying. Next day, when they left the table after dinner, Cunegonde and Candide found themselves behind a screen; Cunegonde dropped her handkerchief, Candide picked it up; she innocently held his hand; 2 the young man innocently kissed the young lady's hand with remarkable vivacity, tenderness and grace; their lips met,

WORDS TO KNOW

docile (dŏs′əl) *adj.* obedient; easily led or managed
reiterated (rē-ĭt′ə-rāt′əd) *adj.* repeated **reiterate** *v.*
pensive (pĕn′sĭv) *adj.* thoughtful; moody
vivacity (vĭ-văs′ĭ-tē) *n.* liveliness

852

MINI LESSON Vocabulary Strategy

CONTEXT CLUES

Instruction Call students' attention to the list of Words to Know. Demonstrate the strategy of using context clues using the following model:

Martha did not discipline her young nephew because he was already *docile*.

- Write the model sentence on the chalkboard.
- Ask a volunteer to paraphrase its meaning.
- Have students use the meaning of the sentence to suggest meanings for *docile*.
- Ask a volunteer to use *docile* in a sentence.

Practice Write the following sentences on the board. Ask students to use context clues to determine the meanings of the underlined words.

1. Aunt Jean became pensive after looking at photographs of long-forgotten friends. *(pensive means thoughtful; moody)*
2. The emcee spoke with such vivacity that she charmed even reluctant audience members and viewers. *(vivacity means liveliness).*

A lesson on using context clues appears on page 674 in the Pupil's Edition.

their eyes sparkled, their knees trembled, their hands wandered. Baron Thunder-ten-tronckh passed near the screen, and, observing this cause and effect, expelled Candide from the castle by kicking him in the backside frequently and hard. Cunegonde swooned;[9] when she recovered her senses, the Baroness slapped her in the face; and all was in consternation[10] in the noblest and most agreeable of all possible castles.

. . . FOR HE THOUGHT *Mademoiselle Cunegonde* EXTREMELY BEAUTIFUL, ALTHOUGH HE WAS NEVER BOLD ENOUGH TO TELL HER SO.

Chapter II

What happened to Candide among the Bulgarians

Candide, expelled from the earthly paradise, wandered for a long time without knowing where he was going, turning up his eyes to Heaven, gazing back frequently at the noblest of castles which held the most beautiful of young Baronesses; he lay down to sleep supperless between two furrows in the open fields; it snowed heavily in large flakes. The next morning the shivering Candide, penniless, dying of cold and exhaustion, dragged himself towards the neighboring town, which was called Waldberghofftrarbk-dikdorff. He halted sadly at the door of an inn. Two men dressed in blue noticed him.

"Comrade," said one, "there's a well-built young man of the right height."

They went up to Candide and very civilly invited him to dinner.

"Gentlemen," said Candide with charming modesty, "you do me a great honor, but I have no money to pay my share."

"Ah, sir," said one of the men in blue, "persons of your figure and merit never pay anything; are you not five feet five tall?"

"Yes, gentlemen," said he, bowing, "that is my height."

"Ah, sir, come to table; we will not only pay your expenses, we will never allow a man like you to be short of money; men were only made to help each other."

"You are in the right," said Candide, "that is what Doctor Pangloss was always telling me, and I see that everything is for the best."

They begged him to accept a few crowns, he took them and wished to give them an IOU; they refused to take it and all sat down to table.

"Do you not love tenderly . . ."

"Oh, yes," said he. "I love Mademoiselle Cunegonde tenderly."

"No," said one of the gentlemen. "We were asking if you do not tenderly love the King of the Bulgarians."

9. **swooned:** fainted.

10. **consternation:** condition of being greatly upset.

Customizing Instruction

Less Proficient Readers

Ask students the following questions to make sure that they are following the plot:

1 After Cunegonde observes the passion of Pangloss and a maid in the garden, what does she want? *(She wants Candide.)*

2 What happens when Candide and Cunegonde are discovered kissing? *(The Baron kicks Candide out of the castle—and kicks his backside, too)*

3 What do the two soldiers offer to do for Candide? *(They offer to buy him dinner and to pay all his expenses, making sure he is never short of money.)*

English Learners

Explain the meaning of the following phrases:

- "experimental physics" *(the science of matter and energy, but here a humorous reference to sex)*
- "bade him good morning" *(wished him good morning)*
- "supperless" *(having gone without an evening meal)*
- "furrows" *(a long and narrow ditch)*

Advanced Learners

Ask students how Candide and Don Quixote can both be considered idealists.

Possible Response: Both characters are idealists because they see the world as filtered through their ideals, which often leads them to mistaken judgments. Don Quixote, influenced by his reading of romances, sees giants when he looks at a windmill. Candide, influenced by the optimism of Dr. Pangloss, mistakes the conniving soldiers for compassionate friends. In both narratives, the main characters sustain their naive illusions even after those illusions have been shown to be false. Both characters yearn for an idealized world that cannot exist.

Cross Curricular Link History

THE PRUSSIAN ARMY Candide's encounter with the soldiers who were recruiting for the King of the Bulgarians is based upon real-life practices. In Voltaire's lifetime, the Prussian army under Frederick I and Frederick II, known as Frederick the Great, relied upon the recruitment of foreign men to swell its ranks. Prussian officers traveled throughout Europe, offering potential recruits money and the promise of good meals in the king's army. The recruiters often sought out tall men, who were especially valued as soldiers. One historian notes that "No traveler six feet tall or over was safe on Prussian soil and not much safer in neighboring countries. Tall men would be drugged, knocked on the head, tied up" and forcefully enrolled in the army. Deserters could be sentenced to hanging, beheading, burning, or other forms of torture.

The Prussian army was famous for its strict discipline and frequent punishments. As one officer reported, "Every accident was punished as if it were a crime. A slip in the manual exercises, an improperly polished button on the uniform . . . would draw down a severe paining." For more serious offenses, soldiers were made to run the gauntlet, a punishment faced by Candide on page 854.

Reading and Analyzing

Reading Skills and Strategies
CLARIFY

A Ask students to explain how the soldiers justify their kidnapping of Candide.

Possible Response: The soldiers interpret Candide's drinking to the king's health as a sign of his intent to become the king's soldier. They have been looking for an excuse to take him by force to the army.

Reading Skills and Strategies
MAKING INFERENCES

B Have students explain why Candide is punished for taking a walk.

Possible Response: The other men believe he is trying to desert the army, which may be his intent.

Literary Analysis SATIRE AND HUMOR

C Ask students to explain the humor of the judges' question.

Possible Response: Candide has no freedom so he has no real choice: he can either be beaten to death by the regiment or shot in the head.

Active Reading MAKING JUDGMENTS

D Explain to students that Voltaire served as an advisor to Frederick the Great, so this portrayal of a king may have been based upon his own experience. Ask students to judge the king's character and abilities.

Possible Response: The king seems to be vain and only concerned about his own public image. He pardons Candide for the sake of favorable publicity. Also, the narrator is being ironic by referring to his "vast genius." That statement only reflects the king's opinion of himself.

"YOU ARE NOW THE SUPPORT, THE AID, THE DEFENDER, *the hero of the Bulgarians;* YOUR FORTUNE IS MADE AND YOUR GLORY ASSURED."

"Not a bit," said he, "for I have never seen him."

"What! He is the most charming of Kings, and you must drink his health."

A "Oh, gladly, gentlemen." And he drank.

"That is sufficient," he was told. "You are now the support, the aid, the defender, the hero of the Bulgarians; your fortune is made and your glory assured."

They immediately put irons[11] on his legs and took him to a regiment. He was made to turn to the right and left, to raise the ramrod[12] and return the ramrod, to take aim, to fire, to double
1 up, and he was given thirty strokes with a stick; the next day he drilled not quite so badly, and received only twenty strokes; the day after, he only had ten and was looked on as a prodigy[13] by his comrades.

Candide was completely mystified and could not make out how he was a hero. One fine spring day he thought he would take a walk, going straight
B ahead, in the belief that to use his legs as he
2 pleased was a privilege of the human species as well as of animals. He had not gone two leagues when four other heroes, each six feet tall, fell upon him, bound him and dragged him back to a cell.

He was asked by his judges whether he would rather be thrashed thirty-six times by the C
whole regiment or receive a dozen lead bullets at once in his brain. Although he protested that men's wills are free and that he wanted neither one nor the other, he had to make a choice; by virtue of that gift of God which is called *liberty,* he determined to run the gauntlet[14] thirty-six times and actually did so twice. There were two thousand men in the regiment. That made four thousand strokes which laid bare the muscles and nerves from his neck to his backside. 3
As they were about to proceed to a third turn, Candide, utterly exhausted, begged as a favor that they would be so kind as to smash his head; he obtained this favor; they bound his eyes and he was made to kneel down. At that moment the
King of the Bulgarians came by and inquired the D
victim's crime; and as this King was possessed of a

11. Voltaire is mocking the military recruiting practices of Frederick the Great, the Prussian king whom Voltaire served for three years.

12. **ramrod:** a rod used to ram gunpowder and bullets into a musket.

13. **prodigy:** person of remarkable skill or intelligence.

14. **run the gauntlet:** military punishment in which a person is forced to run between two lines of soldiers who beat the person as he passes.

MINI LESSON **Grammar**

PLACEMENT OF PARTICIPIAL PHRASES

Instruction A participle is a verb form that functions as an adjective. A participial phrase consists of a participle plus any modifiers and complements. Remind students to place a participial phrase as near as possible to the noun or pronoun it modifies.

Sentence with a Misplaced Modifier

Waddling on the shore and plunging into the water, zoologists study flocks of penguins. Write the above sentence on the chalkboard. Have students identify the participial phrases *(waddling on the shore and plunging into the water)* and the word they modify *(the noun "zoologists")*. Next, ask students to rewrite the sentence so that the participial phrases are closer to the word they modify *(Zoologists study flocks of penguins waddling on the shore and plunging into the water)*.

Practice Ask students to rewrite the following sentences, placing the participial phrases closer to the nouns or pronouns they modify.

1. Cheering wildly in the stands, the star basketball player waved at the fans. *(The star basketball player waved at the fans cheering wildly in the stands.)*
2. Launched late at night, the spectators were amazed by the brilliant fireworks. *(The spectators were amazed by the brilliant fireworks launched late at night).*

For more instruction and practice in using participial phrases, use McDougal Littell's ***Language Network:***

- Grade 10, Chapter 25: "Using Phrases"
- Grade 12, Chapter 24, "Using Phrases"

Assassination of Albrecht Wallenstein, Duke of Friedland (18th century). Watercolor. Heeresgeschichtliches Museum, Vienna, Austria. Photograph © Erich Lessing/Art Resource, New York.

HUMANITIES CONNECTION This 18th-century watercolor painting shows soldiers in the midst of carrying out an assassination. Note the bright colors and elegant tailoring of the uniforms.

vast genius, he perceived from what he learned about Candide that he was a young metaphysician[15] very ignorant in worldly matters, and therefore pardoned him with a clemency[16] which will be praised in all newspapers and all ages. An honest surgeon healed Candide in three weeks with the ointments recommended by Dioscorides.[17] He had already regained a little skin and could walk when the King of the Bulgarians went to war with the King of the Abares. ❖

15. **metaphysician** (mĕt′ə-fĭ-zĭsh′-ən): philosopher who studies the nature of reality.
16. **clemency:** mercy.
17. **Dioscorides** (dī′əs-kôr′ĭ-dēz′): a Greek physician of the first century A.D.

Customizing Instruction

Less Proficient Readers
Ask students the following questions to make sure that they are following the plot:

1 What happens to Candide when he is kidnapped and taken to the army? *(He is forced to spend his time in military drills, and he is beaten each day.)*

2 Why is Candide taken to prison? *(He tried to walk out of the army.)*

3 Why can't Candide go through the gauntlet for a third time? *(He is so badly beaten that his entire back is an open wound.)*

4 Why does the King of the Bulgarians pardon Candide? *(He wants good publicity.)*

English Learners
Explain the meaning of the following phrases:

- "given thirty strokes with a stick" *(beaten thirty times with a stick)*
- "mystified" *(confused)*
- "vast genius" *(great intelligence—the narrator is being sarcastic)*

MINI LESSON Viewing and Representing

Assassination of Albrecht Wallenstein, Duke of Friedland

ART APPRECIATION Have students look at the illustration and the **Humanities Connection** on this page. Explain that this 18th-century watercolor painting depicts a historical event. Albrecht Wallenstein (1583–1634) was the leader of the armies that served Ferdinand II, the Holy Roman Emperor, during the early years of Thirty Years War (1618–1648). Emperor Ferdinand suspected Wallenstein of plotting with the enemy; eventually, Wallenstein fled with a few of his officers. This painting, by an unknown artist, shows the assassination of Wallenstein and his officers at the hands of their fellow officers, who remained loyal to the emperor. The painting might be the creation of a folk artist. Draw attention to the use of strong colors, the lack of perspective, and the crooked lines in the windows—all signs of an unschooled artist. Ask students if they can pick out the victims of the assassination.

Possible Response: The victims seem to the man in the red jacket leaning against the table, the man sprawled on the floor, the man crossing the doorway, and the man standing behind the same door in the yellow jacket.

Connect to the Literature

1. **What Do You Think?** What mental image of Candide did you form as you were reading? What details in the text contribute to that image?

Comprehension Check
- Why does the Baron expel Candide from his castle?
- Why does the Bulgarian army give Candide a beating?

Think Critically

2. **ACTIVE READING: MAKING JUDGMENTS** With a classmate, compare the charts you created in your READER'S NOTEBOOK. What judgments can you make about the main characters based on the information you recorded?

3. What types of behaviors or institutions does Voltaire ridicule in this selection?

THINK ABOUT
- why the Baron's sister "would never marry" the honest gentleman
- the Baron's reason for expelling Candide from his castle
- Pangloss' teaching methods, both in the castle and in the woods
- Candide's treatment in the Bulgarian army

4. Why do you think the Baron approves of Pangloss' philosophy? Do you think the people who are the Baron's subjects would have the same opinion? Explain.

5. Much of the humor in *Candide* comes from the **narrator.** How would you describe the narrator's attitude? Read aloud passages from the selection in a way that expresses his attitude.

Extend Interpretations

6. **Compare Texts** Compare Candide's experiences with those of Don Quixote. What similarities and differences do you see between them?

7. **Different Perspectives** How would this selection be different if it were narrated by Candide? Why might Voltaire have decided against using a first-person narrator?

8. **Connect to Life** If Voltaire were writing today, what philosophies or ways of thinking do you think he would mock? Give reasons to support your opinion.

LITERARY ANALYSIS: SATIRE AND HUMOR

Humor is always an important element in satire, which uses mockery as a tool for the purpose of improving society. The three basic types of humor all involve exaggeration and/or irony. (For a definition of irony, see page R98.)

- **Humor of situation** usually involves exaggerated events. For example, Candide innocently expects to be helped by the men dressed in blue, but they end up forcing him into the army.
- **Humor of character** often involves exaggerated personality traits or characters who fail to recognize their own flaws. Pangloss's exaggerated self-satisfaction is an example of this type of humor.
- **Humor of language** may include sarcasm, exaggeration, word play, or absurdity. The name *Pangloss,* which means "all tongue" or "all words" in Greek, is an example of this type of humor.

Cooperative Learning Activity With a small group, find six more examples of Voltaire's humor in the selection. For each example, decide which type of humor it is and what is being mocked. Use a chart like the one shown to record your findings.

Passage	Type of Humor	What Is Mocked
"They all called him 'my Lord' and laughed heartily at his stories."	humor of situation	People laugh at the Baron's stories only because of his power.

Connect to the Literature

1. **What Do You Think?** Responses will vary. Students may note that Candide is described by the soldiers as only five feet tall.

Comprehension Check
- The Baron catches Candide kissing Cunegonde.
- Candide was caught trying to desert.

 Use Selection Quiz in **Unit Five Resource Book,** p. 58.

Think Critically

2. Possible Responses: Candide is a foolish young man so influenced by Pangloss that he is ill-equipped to live in the world. Candide's optimism leads him to believe whatever people tell him. Cunegonde is nearly equal to Candide in her simplicity, though she does seem to give freer expression to her physical desires. Pangloss spouts idiotic maxims: he is either a simpleton or, more likely, a hypocrite who tells people what they want to hear.
3. Possible Response: Voltaire pokes fun at class snobbery and hypocrisy of the nobility. In Pangloss, he mocks abstract philosophy that blurs good judgment and proves an obstacle to life. He ridicules the empty discipline, deceptive recruiting practices, and inhumane brutality of the military.
4. Possible Response: The message that this is the best of all possible worlds only serves to support the baron's power and place in society. Pangloss's philosophy, in effect, says that the Baron deserves everything that he has. If this is the best of all possible worlds, then the Baron is one of the best people in that world.
5. Possible Response: Students may choose virtually any passage to illustrate the narrator's tone, or attitude towards his subject. The narrator exhibits an attitude that may be interpreted as playful, satiric, mocking, bemused, or indignant.

Extend Interpretations

6. **Compare Texts** Possible Response: Both Don Quixote and Candide are obsessed by a certain way of looking at the world. Don Quixote views his life through the filter of his reading of romances, which leads to ridiculous mistakes in his perception. Candide views his life in terms of Pangloss's philosophy. He sees reality—unlike Quixote—but he does not understand it.
7. **Different Perspectives** Possible Response: As a narrator, Candide would probably interpret everything that happens to him in an optimistic way. He would always remind the reader of Dr. Pangloss's teachings, which would try the reader's patience. Voltaire likely knew that readers would prefer the perspective of a narrator who is brighter and more sophisticated than Candide.
8. **Connect to Life** Possible Response: Accept all reasonable responses.

Literary Analysis

Cooperative Learning Activity Before students begin their charts, review the three types of humor with them. Make sure that students understand what is distinctive about each type. When students have completed their charts, solicit examples from the students. Have the entire class judge each example to determine whether the example clearly illustrates one of the three types of humor.

 Use **Unit Five Resource Book,** p. 56, for more practice.

Writing Options

1. Satirical Writing Write a brief satirical tale. First, choose a behavior or institution that you want to ridicule in order to improve society. Then imagine characters and a plot that will convey your message. In your satire, use exaggeration and irony to create humor.
Writing Handbook
See page R29: Narrative Writing.

2. War Diary At the end of the selection, Candide has barely survived his punishment. Pretend you are Candide and write a diary entry in which you express your thoughts and feelings about the army's treatment of you.

Activities and Explorations

1. Candide's Song With a partner, create song lyrics based on Candide's experiences or philosophy of life. If you are bold enough, put your lyrics to music and perform it before your classmates. ~**MUSIC**

2. Voltaire News Working with a small group, create a television news report in the mocking style of Voltaire. First, find news items that are worthy of ridicule. Then write your news report in a way that shows your mockery of the events or people involved. Present your report to the class. ~ **SPEAKING AND LISTENING**

Inquiry & Research

1. The Lisbon Earthquake In 1755, a terrible earthquake struck Lisbon, Portugal. Find out more about this earthquake and the effect it had on Voltaire. If possible, also review Voltaire's poem, *The Lisbon Disaster.* Give an oral report on your findings.
Communication Handbook
See page R47: Skimming and Scanning.

2. Voltaire's World With a small group of students, do research to find out what daily life was like for the average European during the 18th century. Each student should focus on a particular aspect of daily life, such as work or nutrition. After you report your findings to the group, discuss whether this information contradicts or supports Leibniz's view that this is "the best of all possible worlds."

EXERCISE: SYNONYMS Write on your paper the letter of the word that is the best synonym for the boldfaced word.

1. Voltaire's outraged **candor** about the failings of French leaders frequently got him into trouble.
   (a) unfairness (b) honesty (c) ignorance (d) forgetfulness
2. The outspoken French philosopher was never known as a **docile** personality.
   (a) bold (b) aggressive (c) mild (d) irritating
3. His prose style is famous for its wit, sarcasm, and **vivacity.**
   (a) vitality (b) viciousness (c) vanity (d) vagueness
4. He frequently **reiterated** his strong criticisms of authorities.
   (a) rejected (b) restated (c) softened (d) regretted
5. Despite his bold and daring humor, Voltaire also had his quietly **pensive** moments.
   (a) carefree (b) angry (c) cheerful (d) reflective

Building Vocabulary
For an in-depth lesson on context clues, see page 674.

Writing Options

1. **Satirical Writing** Discuss with students examples of satirical tales that they know about, whether in books or movies. Make sure that students realize that effective satire portrays its subject in a way that elicits critical judgment as well as laughter.
2. **War Diary** Remind students that their diary entries should reflect the personality and beliefs of Candide. Students should consider how Pangloss might interpret Candide's experience, since it is likely that Candide's diary would reflect Pangloss's teachings.

Activities & Explorations

1. **Candide's Song** Point out to students that the story of Candide has been turned into a Broadway musical. Students may find it helpful to review the text to find quotes about Candide or other characters that may be incorporated into their lyrics.
2. **Voltaire News** Discuss examples of satirical news reports that have been on television, ranging from the *Weekend Review* feature on *Saturday Night Live* to the *Jon Stewart Show.*

Inquiry & Research

1. **The Lisbon Earthquake** Students should be able to find out about this earthquake in reference sources about Voltaire's life as well as via online search engines. You may also wish to direct students to the entire text of *Candide*, which includes an episode in which Pangloss and Candide travel to Lisbon around the time of the earthquake.
2. **Voltaire's World** Make sure that students realize that they are to investigate the lives of average people, not the lives of the wealthy and privileged. Students may find it helpful to use topics such as 18th century workers, 18th century public health, and so on when searching for information.

Vocabulary in Action

1. b
2. c
3. a
4. b
5. d

To assess skills and concepts taught in this selection, use **Formal Assessment Book,** pp. 129–130.

Objectives
- write and deliver a Persuasive Speech
- use a written text as a model for speaking
- revise a draft in response to audience feedback

Introducing the Workshop

A Persuasive Speech Ask students to identify occasions when people deliver persuasive speeches *(campaign rallies, fund-raising events, student council debates, and sermons)*. Discuss what makes a persuasive speech effective. Identify and list techniques used by good speakers. Also consider what issues make compelling material. Some students may be interested in government politics while others may be drawn to issues of health, technology, the environment, education, or, as with the student writer, media.

Basics in a Box

B Representing the Rubric To better understand the assignment, students can refer to the Standards for Writing and Delivering a Successful Persuasive Speech. You may wish to discuss with them the complete rubric and student models in the Unit Five Resource Book on pages 63–68.

For more instruction and practice in persuasive writing, use McDougal Littell's ***Language Network:***
- Grade 10, Chapter 22, "Persuasive Essay"
- Grade 12, Chapter 22, "Proposal"

Communication Workshop — Persuasive Speech

Speaking Your Mind . . .

From Reading to Writing In *Utopia,* Sir Thomas More wrote persuasively about the benefits of life in his imaginary society. While More presented his ideas in a book, many people choose to persuade others
A through speech. In a **persuasive speech,** a speaker tries to convince his or her audience to adopt a certain point of view or take a certain action. Whether addressing a student council meeting or an international peace summit, a speaker uses certain basic strategies to persuade his or her audience.

For Your Portfolio

WRITING PROMPT Write and deliver a persuasive speech about an issue that is important to you.

Purpose: To convince others to agree with you

Audience: Anyone who can help you achieve your goal or whose views you want to change

Basics in a Box

B

RUBRIC Writing and Delivering Your Speech

Content

A successful persuasive speech should
- open with an example, anecdote, or thesis statement
- clearly state the issue and your position on it
- be geared to the audience you're trying to persuade
- provide facts, examples, statistics, and reasons to support your position
- answer opposing views
- show clear reasoning
- include strategies, such as frequent summaries, to help listeners remember your message and the reasons for your position
- end with a strong restatement of your position or a call to action

Delivery

An effective speaker should
- convey enthusiasm and confidence
- stand with straight, relaxed posture and make eye contact with the audience
- include gestures and body language to enhance the presentation
- incorporate visual aids effectively

LESSON RESOURCES

USING PRINT RESOURCES
Unit Five Resource Book
- Planning and Drafting, p. 59
- Practicing and Delivering, p. 60
- Peer Response, pp. 61–62
- Refining Your Delivery, p. 63
- Student Models, pp. 64–68
- Standards for Evaluation, p. 69

USING MEDIA RESOURCES
Writing Coach CD-ROM
Visit our Web site: classzone.com

ADDITIONAL RESOURCES
For a complete view of Lesson Resources, see page 685i in this book.

Analyzing a Student Model

Leahruth Jemilo
Walter Payton High School

RUBRIC IN ACTION

Do You Buy It?

I was watching TV when an eye-catching commercial came on. A pretty woman got her cute boyfriend to buy her something in a store, apparently because her silky, smooth hair was irresistible to him; the ad was promoting a shampoo. But really—if I used this shampoo, would it help me attract cute guys and get them to run errands for me? I think not. The ad appealed to me, though, because I wanted to be as beautiful as the woman in it, and I wanted boys to react to me in the same way. So I bought the shampoo. Why was I so strongly influenced by advertising? We teenagers must resist these tempting but false advertisements. They do not portray the real world, and they make us feel bad about ourselves.

Americans experience a daily onslaught of advertising images. According to one estimate, the average adult is exposed to more than 250 ads every day on television and radio and in magazines and newspapers. This constant exposure to ads can't help but affect the way we view the world and the way we see ourselves. I know it affects me. I remember seeing another TV commercial, one for tight leather pants. The girl modeling the pants was very thin and attractive. As I sat on my couch wishing that I had her pants and could look as good in them as she, I suddenly regretted the food that I was nibbling on. How did this commercial have the power to make me regret what I ate and how I looked? This experience is widespread. In a Canadian study of female university students, subjects in an experimental group became depressed and hostile when asked about their mood, body satisfaction, and eating patterns after viewing magazine ads featuring female fashion models.

The fact is, fashion models serve as role models for us. As teenagers, we are still developing our own identities, constantly looking for examples and ideas of how to look or act or think. Unfortunately, the look we admire is not a healthy one. You don't have to look very far to see that most teen fashion models fit the same mold—thin, with a few variations in hair length or skin color. Many magazines, newspapers, and responsible adults tell us that these skinny girls are unattractive and not good role models for growing teenage girls. Yet, the advertisements

1. Opens with a personal anecdote
2. Clearly states the issue
3. Gestures can add emphasis to a personal anecdote.
4. Cites university study as supporting evidence
5. Connects with audience
6. Visual aids can provide examples of skinny fashion models.

C

LANGUAGE SKILLS

Teaching the Lesson

Analyzing the Model

"Do You Buy It"

C The student model presents an argument that teenagers should look critically at advertisements delivering unhealthy messages. Specifically, she speaks of advertisements with unrealistic or unhealthy depictions of teenagers and their effect on teen self-esteem. Suggest that students read the model and ask a volunteer to deliver the model speech. Point out key words and phrases in the student model that correspond to the numbered Rubric in Action.

1. Ask students how else this speaker might introduce her speech.
   Possible Reponses: She could begin by stating the issue; she could begin by urging teenagers to resist the influence of advertising.
2. Remind students not to leave out this important statement, and not to wait too long to include it.
3. Encourage student speakers to relay anecdotes with the same enthusiasm or expression they would use when talking to a friend or family member, even if they are using more formal language.
4. Explain to students that evidence from academic studies lends credibility to a speaker.
5. Point out to students the speaker's use of the pronoun *we* as a means of establishing a connection with her audience.
6. Ask students how the visual aid might help the speaker and her audience.
   Possible Response: It reinforces the speaker's point by helping the audience visualize the extremely thin women depicted in advertisements.

7. Point out that facts and statistics can be a very important part of a speaker's supporting evidence. Also remind students, however, that statistics can be used to distort the truth, and they should take care to use such numbers responsibly and place them in a larger context.
8. Ask students why presenting and answering an opposing view is an effective persuasive technique.
   Possible Response: Listeners who might disagree with the speaker will begin to develop opposing arguments in their heads as they listen to the speaker. By anticipating these arguments, the speaker can answer the concerns of these listeners and allow them to be open to new ideas.
9. Point out to students that a persuasive speech frequently ends with a call to action of some sort. Here, the speaker calls on her listeners to look at advertisements more critically. Ask students what else a speaker might call upon listeners to do.
   Possible Responses: vote for a certain candidate; participate in activism; give money to a particular cause; buy a particular product

continue to showcase only skinny models. These ads affect how teens feel about themselves and contribute to the forces that push teens toward unhealthy diets, depression, and eating disorders.

Eating disorders affect more than 5 million Americans—men and women—each year. Of those 5 million people, 95 percent are women between the ages of 12 and 25. About a thousand women die every year from anorexia nervosa, an eating disorder marked by severe weight loss and a persistent unwillingness to eat, partly in response to a distorted body image. It is also estimated that 15 percent of young women have substantially disordered eating attitudes and behavior, which can lead to actual eating disorders.

❼ Gives statistics as supporting evidence

Can we really blame the advertisers? After all, they're just trying to sell their products. Of course they are going to portray their products in an attractive light. What else would they do? If teenagers have self-image problems, they just have to toughen up a little. You won't get very far in life if you're going to be pushed around by a TV commercial!

❽ Presents and answers opposing viewpoint

This is all true, of course. Advertisers are not in the business of making us feel better about ourselves or expanding our narrow notions of beauty, and we're not likely to change that. What we can change is the way we perceive advertising messages. Teens must be able to distinguish between healthy fitness and the unusually perfect and uniform images of teen models in the media.

So whenever you read a magazine, watch TV, or drive by a billboard, remember that the people in the ads are models. They were hired because they look a certain way. Ads are designed to make you feel that you are missing something, that you need something. If you suddenly feel too fat or too plain or too boring, the advertisers have done their job. And if you suddenly begin to think that a PRODUCT is your key to feeling thin or glamorous or exciting, remember that personal transformations don't come in snazzy, colorful packages. You can't buy happiness, no matter how many people claim to sell it.

❾ Ends by calling on audience to think critically about advertisements

MINI LESSON Patterns of Organization

PICTURING TEXT STRUCTURE

Instruction Though the content of an argument is critical to an effective persuasive speech, a clear and logical structure may be equally important. The arrangement of ideas and supporting details can make a persuasive speech particularly effective.

Activity Have students draw a graphic organizer representing the structure of the student model. Ask them to begin by identifying the purpose of each paragraph in the speech. A possible graphic organizer is shown.

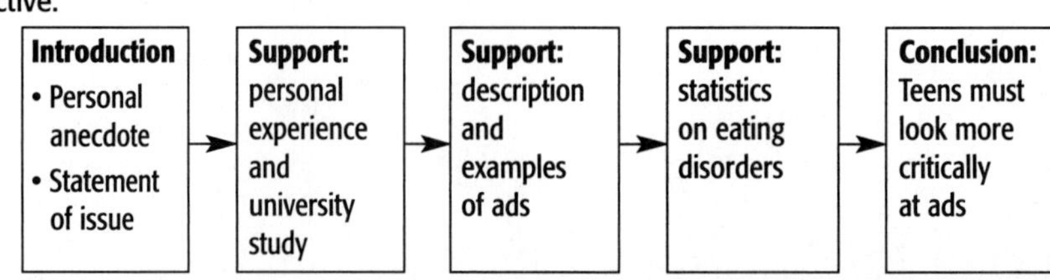

Writing and Delivering Your Persuasive Speech

❶ Planning and Drafting

To find a topic for your speech, make a list of issues you feel strongly about. Also, with your classmates, **brainstorm** a list of any issues you like to debate. See the **Idea Bank** in the margin for more suggestions. After you've chosen a topic that you'd like to cover in a speech, follow the steps below.

Steps for Planning Your Speech

1. **Clarify your position.** How do you feel about the issue, and why?
2. **Find support for your position.** What research will you have to do to back up your case? Where can you find that information? Which evidence will help you make your point most effectively?
3. **Identify your audience.** What do your listeners already know about the issue? What is their position on it?
4. **Consider how to grab your listeners' attention.** What startling statistic, amusing anecdote, or intriguing question can you use to hook your audience at the beginning of your speech?
5. **Decide how to present your arguments.** How can you organize your arguments so they have the greatest impact? Do you want to begin with the argument your audience will probably agree with and then move to more controversial points? Would it be better to put your strongest argument at the beginning or the end?

Think about how to present your speech. Would your listeners respond best to a straightforward, scholarly approach, or would humor be more effective? Might they respond to a dramatic presentation, or is it best to be low-key? What verbal and nonverbal techniques will work best to capture and hold your audience's interest and attention?

When you have finished planning, draft your speech. As you are writing and revising, you might want to read parts of it out loud. If something is hard to say, it probably sounds awkward, and you should think of another way to say it.

❷ Practicing and Delivering

The best way to practice your speech is to present it aloud over and over again. Try speaking in front of a mirror or videotaping your speech so that you can evaluate and improve your posture, gestures, eye contact, and use of visual aids. You might tape-record a practice session so you can critique your voice quality and effectiveness.

IDEABank

1. Your Working Portfolio

Look for ideas in the **Writing Option** you completed earlier in this unit:

- **Speech About Chivalry,** p. 845

2. Media Watch

Keep your eyes and ears open for discussions in the media of topics you feel strongly about.

3. Community Concerns

Make a list of problems or needs in your community. What can be done about them? Choose one of these issues to write your speech about.

LANGUAGE SKILLS

Guiding Student Writing

Planning and Drafting

If after reading the Idea Bank students are having a hard time choosing their subjects, suggest they try the following:

- Scan the editorial pages of a newspaper for a week to look for current issues.
- Attend a city council or school board meeting to find out what community problems are being addressed.

Steps for Planning the Speech

2. Suggest that students use print resources, such as the *Reader's Guide to Periodical Literature* and a world almanac, as well as online search engines and directories. For information on local issues, students can go to the town or city hall or check their local library for records.
4. Urge students to keep an eye out for interesting details or anecdotes as they conduct their research. In some sources, these items may appear in sidebars, charts, or footnotes.
5. Remind students that there are many effective ways to organize persuasive arguments. For example, the writer of the student model begins by describing her personal experience, then moves on to give facts and statistics on the matter. Not until the end does she present and answer opposing viewpoints.

Practicing and Delivering

Have students work in pairs to practice their speeches. If students use tape-recordings, partners can listen to these together and suggest improvements.

Steps for Delivering the Speech

1. Students who are very anxious about public speaking should take special note that taking deep breaths before beginning their speech can be a very effective tool for calming the nerves. Also remind students to be sure and keep breathing while they speak; some speakers actually forget to breathe when they are nervous.
2. If possible, have students practice their speeches in the room where they'll be delivering them. This will help them understand how well or poorly their voices carry.
4. Remind students to keep their gestures and facial expressions natural. Overly dramatic behavior can seem forced or unprofessional.
5. Caution students to keep their visual aids clear and simple. Complicated charts, graphs, or maps will be hard for an audience to see and comprehend.

Refining the Delivery

RESPONDING TO AUDIENCE FEEDBACK

Ask for one or two volunteers to deliver drafts of their own speeches so that classmates can offer a sample peer review. Facilitate this review by helping reviewers offer constructive feedback and helping the speakers interpret and respond to the comments.

Reflecting

Encourage students to consider how writing a persuasive speech differed from other writing tasks. Did they approach the process differently because the final product was to be delivered orally? How, if at all, did the presence of a live audience affect the final product?

Need revising help?

Review the **Rubric,** p. 858

Consider **peer reviewer** comments

Check **Revision Guidelines,** p. R19

Publishing IDEAS

- Record the delivery of your speech on videotape or audiotape.
- Set up a soapbox event with several other classmates, delivering your speeches in turn.
- If there is a community organization concerned with your topic, write the organization and offer to speak at one of its meetings.
- Deliver your speech to your family.

Steps for Delivering Your Speech

1. **Breathe deeply.** Deep, steady breaths will help you remain calm and collected. Good deep breathing is also very important to good speaking; it helps you speak loudly enough to be heard and avoid tiring your voice.
2. **Use your voice effectively.** Speak out and be sure to enunciate clearly. If your audience can't easily hear and understand what you're saying, all of your hard work will be lost. Speak more loudly and clearly than you would in conversation, but try to maintain a natural tone of voice.
3. **Maintain eye contact.** Look directly at different members of the audience while you speak.
4. **Incorporate gestures and facial expressions.** Remember, your listeners are more likely to be interested in your topic if they can see that you are interested.
5. **Use visual aids.** Organize your information in charts, graphs, or drawings that will reinforce your message. Make sure your materials are large enough and clear enough that everyone in the audience can read them.

❸ Refining Your Delivery

TARGET SKILL ▶ RESPONDING TO AUDIENCE FEEDBACK A persuasive speech is successful only if it convinces your audience. Here are some comments your peer reviewers might make, along with ways you can change your speech or delivery in response to the comments.

- **I couldn't hear/understand you.** This is a common complaint. Speak loudly and pronounce your words carefully. Remember that most people speak too fast, so watch your speed too.
- **It seemed as if you were reading your speech rather than saying it.** Learn your speech well enough that you don't have to keep your eyes glued to the paper. Then you will have the freedom to look around and speak naturally.
- **I didn't always know what you were talking about.** As you make a transition, include a summary, such as the following: "I've just explained that *X* is true for these reasons. Now let's think for a moment about *Y*."
- **Your evidence didn't convince me.** Anticipate arguments from your listeners with opposing views and gather additional expert opinions, facts, statistics, and examples.

Ask Your Peer Reviewer

- What part of my argument was most convincing?
- Which points do you disagree with, and why?
- What aspects of my delivery were most effective? Which could use improvement?

❹ Reflecting

FOR YOUR WORKING PORTFOLIO What did you learn about your topic from writing and delivering your speech? Write your response and attach it to your speech. Save your speech in your **Working Portfolio.**

Option

Managing the Paper Load

Have students submit their outlines, graphic organizers, or drafts for your quick review. This will enable you to evaluate the main argument and supporting material early in the planning phase.

Read this paragraph from the first draft of a persuasive speech. The underlined sections may include the following kinds of errors:

- **incorrect pronoun case**
- **lack of pronoun-antecedent agreement**
- **correctly written sentences that should be combined**
- **lack of subject-verb agreement**

For each underlined section, choose the revision that most improves the writing.

There is a proposal before the school board that would require students to wear school uniforms. Although many students want the right to wear his or her own clothing (1) to school every day, there is great advantages (2) to school uniforms. Many students are obsessed with appearances. They pay great attention to clothing, hair, jewelry, and makeup (3). Some students are very critical of others who don't dress as well as them, (4) and students that can't afford designer clothing (5) are branded as outcasts. Besides easing these problems, school uniforms create a sense of order and discipline in a school. Some of the schools that have instituted the wearing of uniforms has noticed (6) improved student behavior.

1. **A.** every student wants the right to wear their own clothing
   B. many students want the right to wear their own clothing
   C. many students want the right to wear one's own clothing
   D. Correct as is

2. **A.** there are great advantages
   B. there is great advantage
   C. there is great advantages
   D. Correct as is

3. **A.** appearances. They really pay great attention to clothing, hair, jewelry, and makeup.
   B. appearances, paying great attention to clothing, hair, jewelry, and makeup.
   C. appearances, they pay great attention to clothing, hair, jewelry, and makeup.
   D. Correct as is

4. **A.** who don't dress as well as they do
   B. who don't dress as well as they should
   C. who don't dress as well as they're peers
   D. Correct as is

5. **A.** students what can't afford designer clothing
   B. students whom can't afford designer clothing
   C. students who can't afford designer clothing
   D. Correct as is

6. **A.** Some of the schools that has instituted the wearing of uniforms have noticed
   B. Some of the schools that has instituted the wearing of uniforms has noticed
   C. Some of the schools that have instituted the wearing of uniforms have noticed
   D. Correct as is

Need extra help?

See the **Grammar Handbook**
Pronoun Case, p. R57
Pronoun Agreement, p. R57
Subject-Verb Agreement, p. R74

Standardized Test Practice

As students read through the sample passage and try to determine correct subject-verb agreement, remind them to first identify the subject of a sentence and, if necessary, mentally screen out any words or phrases that appear between the subject and the verb. As they try to determine correct pronoun-antecedent agreement, remind them to first identify the pronoun and its antecedent.

Answers:
1. B; **2.** A; **3.** D; **4.** A; **5.** C; **6.** C

MINI LESSON Grammar

SUBJECT-VERB AGREEMENT WITH INDEFINITE PRONOUNS AS SUBJECTS

Instruction When used as a subject, some indefinite pronouns *(all, more, none, any, most,* and *some)* are either singular or plural, depending on how they're used. Such a pronoun takes the number of its antecedent. If the antecedent is singular, then the pronoun is singular; if the antecedent is plural, then the pronoun is plural. Write the following sentences on the board:

Some of my friends are from Michigan.
Some of my lunch is missing.

In the first sentence, *some* refers to *friends,* which is plural. Therefore, the verb, *are,* is plural. In the second sentence, *some* refers to the singular *lunch*, so the verb is also singular. In the third sentence, *some* refers to the plural *pets*, so the verb is plural.

Practice Have students choose the correct form of the verb for the following sentences. The correct form is underscored.

1. None of my siblings (likes, <u>like</u>) to play soccer.
2. Most of the movie (<u>takes</u>, take) place in Mexico.
3. All of the answers (is, <u>are</u>) correct.
4. There are six pies. All (is, <u>are</u>) made with sugar.
5. Some of the juice (<u>tastes</u>, taste) like strawberries.

For more instruction and practice in subject-verb agreement, use McDougal Littell's ***Language Network:***

- Grade 10, Chapter 7, "Subject-Verb Agreement"
- Grade 12, Chapter 5, "Subject-Verb Agreement."

Building Vocabulary

Objectives

- identify the two kinds of word parts: roots and affixes
- identify the two kinds of affixes: prefixes and suffixes
- recognize word parts in order to decode unfamiliar words
- apply meanings of word roots and affixes in order to comprehend
- new words use word parts and word roots to build vocabulary
- use reference material such as a dictionary to determine precise meaning and usage

EXERCISE

Students' sentences will vary. Sample sentences are provided.

1. *signify* (to mean): *sign-* (to mean) + *-ify* (to cause to become)
   The rows of flags signify patriotism.
2. *expatriate* (to move from one's native land): *ex-* (out of) + *patri-* (native land) + *-ate* (to act upon)
   During the war, the professor did not feel safe in his homeland and decided to expatriate.
3. *aviary* (a place for holding birds): *aviar-* (bird) + *-y* (place for activity)
   The aviary contains five different kinds of parrots.
4. *implode* (to violently collapse inward): *im-* (toward the inside) + *-plode* (from *explode,* derived from Latin *explodere,* to drive out by clapping)
   The dynamite caused the building to implode.
5. *disquieting* (troubling): *dis-* (not) + *quiet* (peace) + *-ing* (ending used to form adjectives)
   I just received the disquieting news of Margie's illness.

Use **Unit Five Resource Book,** p. 69, for more practice.

Building Vocabulary — Analyzing Word Parts—Affixes

What's in a Word? One way to determine the meaning of an unfamiliar word is to break it down into parts. There are three kinds of word parts: **base words,** which by themselves are complete words; **roots,** which are the core parts of words; and **affixes,** which can be added (or affixed) to roots or base words. Look at the words in the passage on the right. Which words seem to consist of more than one part?

Two examples are the nouns *curiosity* and *infatuation.* The first consists of the Latin root *curios* and the affix *-ity;* the second consists of the Latin root *fatu* and the affixes *in-* and *-ation.* Another word in the passage, the adjective *tillable,* consists of the base word *till* and the affix *-able.*

> **So great was his curiosity and infatuation in this regard that he even sold many acres of tillable land in order to be able to buy and read the books that he loved, and he would carry home with him as many of them as he could obtain.**
>
> —Miguel de Cervantes, *Don Quixote*

Strategies for Building Vocabulary

Affixes can be added to the beginnings or ends of roots or base words. Affixes added to the beginning of words and roots are called **prefixes;** affixes added to the end are called **suffixes.** The word *infatuation,* for example, consists of a prefix, a root, and a suffix.

Prefix		Root		Suffix
in-	+	*fatu*	+	*-ation*
"in"		"foolish"		"condition"

The parts come together to mean, literally, "in a foolish condition." This is very close to the proper definition, "a foolish passion or attraction."
The following strategies can help you recognize common affixes.

1 Look for Prefixes The prefix *in-* is part of many words. For example, the word *ingrate,* meaning "a person who is not thankful," is formed by adding the prefix *in-,* here meaning "not," to the Latin root *grat,* meaning "pleasing" or "thankful." Some prefixes have more than one meaning—for example, the prefix *in-* can also mean "in" or "into." The table on the right shows the meanings of several common prefixes.

2 Identify Suffixes Adding or changing a suffix often changes a word from one part of speech to another. For example, the suffix *-tion* changes the verb *illustrate* into the noun *illustration.* You can find more examples of suffixes in the following table. Note that some suffixes have more than one meaning.

Prefix	Meaning	Words
auto-	self	autobiography, autonomy
dis-	not, opposite of	disgust, displeasure
ex-	former *or* out of	ex-husband *or* expel
hyper-	excessive, excessively	hyperactive, hyperconscious
im-	not *or* into	imbalance *or* immigrate
pan-	all	panorama, pan-American

Suffix	Meaning	Words
-arium, -ary	a place for	aquarium, mortuary
-tion	action, process, state, quality of	caution, hesitation
-fy, -ify, -efy	cause to become, make	quantify, purify, liquefy
-ment	action, process *or* result of action or process	development *or* amazement
-ous	full of, characterized by	porous, fabulous, envious
-tude	state or condition	gratitude, servitude

EXERCISE Identify the word parts that make up each word below. Use the meanings of the word parts to help define the word. Check the definition of the word in a dictionary, and then use the word in a sentence.

1. signify **2.** expatriate **3.** aviary **4.** implode **5.** disquieting

Sentence Crafting Using Noun Clauses

Grammar from Literature A noun clause is a subordinate clause that is used as a noun in a sentence. It can serve any of the functions of a single-word noun, including subject, direct object, or object of a preposition. Notice the noun clauses, printed in blue, in the following passages from *Don Quixote.*

> **"But look, your Grace, those are not giants but windmills, and** what appear to be arms (noun clause as subject) **are** (verb) **their wings which, when whirled in the breeze, cause the millstone to go."**
>
> **". . . I don't know** (verb) what all he did there, (noun clause as direct object) **but after a bit he went flying off through the roof, leaving the house full of smoke. . . ."**
>
> **Going up to** (preposition) where the door had been, (noun clause as object of preposition) **he ran his hands over the wall and rolled his eyes in every direction without saying a word. . . .**

A noun clause can be introduced by a pronoun (such as *what, whatever, who, whoever, whom,* or *whomever*) or by a subordinating conjunction (such as *how, that, when, where, whether,* or *why*). One common type of noun clause begins with *that* and follows a verb such as *tell, say, see,* or *know.*

> **Among other things, Don Quixote told him** that he ought to be more than willing to go, **because no telling what adventure might occur which would win them an island. . . .** —*Don Quixote*

In this type of clause, it is common for *that* to be understood rather than stated directly: "Don Quixote told him (that) he ought to be more than willing to go."

Using Noun Clauses in Your Writing Noun clauses allow you to express ideas efficiently and gracefully. Most people use noun clauses without even knowing what they are. Imagine how you might rewrite the following sentence without a noun clause.

> WITH NOUN CLAUSE
> **Candide was completely mystified and could not make out** how he was a hero. —*Candide*

Usage Tip People are often puzzled about whether to use *who* or *whom* in a noun clause. The choice depends on how the pronoun functions within the clause. Use *who* (or *whoever*) when the word functions as a subject or a predicate nominative. Use *whom* (or *whomever*) when it functions as a direct object, an indirect object, or the object of a preposition.

> **I don't know** whom you mean.
> (*YOU* IS THE SUBJECT OF THE CLAUSE, AND *WHOM* IS THE DIRECT OBJECT OF *MEAN.*)
>
> **Feel free to invite** whomever you like.
> (*YOU* IS THE SUBJECT OF THE CLAUSE, AND *WHOMEVER* IS THE DIRECT OBJECT OF *LIKE.*)
>
> Whoever wants to come **is welcome.**
> (*WHOEVER* IS THE SUBJECT OF THE CLAUSE.)

WRITING EXERCISE Rewrite each sentence or pair of sentences, changing the underlined words to a noun clause. Add introductory words or switch the order of sentence elements if necessary. Eliminate the words in italics.

1. Don Quixote loved to read *books.* He read any books he could get his hands on.
2. Books on chivalry were *something that* he really loved.
3. *Somehow* he decided to become a knight. *It* was a mystery.
4. Would he be a good knight? He did not worry about *that.*
5. You never know *the kinds of things* people will decide to do.

GRAMMAR EXERCISE Rewrite the sentences below, correcting errors in pronoun usage. If a sentence contains no error, write *Correct.*

1. Don Quixote wondered who he should love and honor.
2. He also had to decide whom to choose as a trusted companion.
3. In his search for foes, Don Quixote would fight whoever came along.
4. It's hard to imagine whom would be afraid of such a silly knight.
5. Whoever had the slightest strength or skill could surely beat him.

Sentence Crafting

LANGUAGE SKILLS

Objectives
- recognize that subordinate clauses can function as nouns in a sentence
- use noun clauses to improve sentence variety
- revise drafts by using subordinate clauses to clarify the relationships among ideas
- practice creating complex sentences by linking noun clauses with an independent clause
- use *who* and *whom* correctly in a noun clause

WRITING EXERCISE
1. Don Quixote loved to read whatever he could get his hands on.
2. Books on chivalry were what he really loved.
3. How he decided to become a knight was a mystery.
4. He did not worry about whether he would be a good knight.
5. You never know what people will decide to do.

GRAMMAR EXERCISE
1. Don Quixote wondered whom he should love and honor.
2. Correct
3. In his search for foes, Don Quixote would fight whomever came along.
4. It's hard to imagine who would be afraid of such a silly knight.
5. Correct

Use **Unit Five Resource Book,** p. 70, for more practice.

MINI LESSON Grammar

USING *WHO* AND *WHOM*

Instruction Point out to students that many people have trouble using *who* and *whom*, not only in noun clauses but also in questions. Remind them that the case of the pronoun *who* is determined by the pronoun's function in a sentence. *Who* is the nominative form, and *whom* is the objective form. Write the following sentences on the board:

Who wrote that book? The author is who?
Whom did you see?

Ask students to identify the function of *who* or *whom* in each of the sentences. (In the first sentence, *who* is the subject; in the second sentence, *who* is a predicate nominative; in the third sentence, *whom* is the direct object of *see.*)

Practice Have students choose the correct version of *who* or *whom* in the following sentences. The correct answer is underscored.

1. (Who, <u>Whom</u>) do you love?
2. You can write to (whoever, <u>whomever</u>) you like.
3. (<u>Whoever,</u> whomever) would do such a thing?
4. Her brother is (<u>who,</u> whom)?
5. (<u>Who,</u> Whom) is your best friend?

For more instruction and practice with who and whom, use McDougal Littell's ***Language Network:***
- Grade 10, Chapter 8, "Using Pronouns"
- Grade 12, Chapter 6, "Using Pronouns"

Objectives
- reflect on and assess understanding of the part
- analyze three different ideals presented in the literature
- compare and contrast a modern sonnet to one in the past
- show an understanding of literary and historical terms
- assess and build portfolios

Reflecting on the Literature
Students may find it helpful to review all the selections in a class discussion, focusing on the various ideals expressed in the literature. Don Quixote, for example, seeks to achieve the ideals of knighthood while Candide insists that ours is the best of all possible worlds.

Reviewing Literary Concepts
Make sure that students understand what a discussion of sonnet form requires. They should study the logical structure of each sonnet, the rhyme scheme, and, if applicable, the metrical pattern. Refer students to Compare and Contrast in the **Writing Handbook,** pages R31–R33.

Building Your Portfolio
Before students finalize their choice of writing to include in the Presentation Portfolio, you might want to have very brief conferences with them (one minute or so) to discuss their choices.

For more information on using writing and assessing portfolios, see the **Teacher's Guide to Assessment and Portfolio Use,** pp. 53–74.

Part Assessment

To assess skills and concepts taught in this unit part, use **Formal Assessment Book,** pp. 131–132.

Reflect and Assess

What have you learned about the Renaissance and Enlightenment as a result of your readings? What are you likely to remember about this literature and the ways of thinking it represents? Use the following options to review what you have learned.

Lady with Unicorn, Raphael. Galleria Borghese, Rome. Photo © Scala/Art Resource, New York

Reflecting on the Literature

In Pursuit of an Ideal In the Renaissance and Enlightenment, many people pursued ideals, from a perfect romance to a just society. Review the selections in this part, and identify three different types of ideals that are presented in them. Explain each ideal in your own words and discuss whether it is an ideal that can be reached by human beings. Do you think that these ideals continue to influence people's beliefs and behavior today?

Reviewing Literary Concepts

Sonnet Review the explanation of the sonnet form on pages 804 and 805. Then find a modern poem, one written after 1900, that is a sonnet. Write a brief essay that compares and contrasts your modern sonnet with one of the sonnets in Unit Five, Part 2. Pay attention to both the form and the content of the poems.

Building Your Portfolio

Communication Workshop and Writing Options Review the persuasive speech that you wrote for the Communication Workshop on page 858 and the various Writing Options you completed in this part of the book. What do these pieces reveal about your strengths and weaknesses as a writer? On a piece of paper, make one list that identifies your strengths as a writer and one list that identifies your weaknesses. Attach the paper to the assignment that best illustrates your strengths, and add them both to your **Presentation Portfolio.**

Self ASSESSMENT

READER'S NOTEBOOK

The following list consists of important names and terms from this part of Unit Five. Copy the terms in your notebook. Next to each term, jot down a brief explanation of what it means. For additional help, make use of the index or the **Glossary of Literary Terms** (on page R91).

Renaissance	courtly love
situational irony	*Utopia*
extended metaphor	tone
Petrarchan sonnet	satire
Enlightenment	
Shakespearean sonnet	

Setting GOALS

Are you a good reader of poetry? Make a list of your strengths and weaknesses as a reader of poetry. Then circle those weaknesses that you would like to work on. In Unit Six, Part 1, you will have many opportunities to work on your poetry skills.

Assessment Self Assessment

Students can look up the listed terms in the **Glossary of Literary Terms** or they can find them introduced in context on the text pages shown below.

Renaissance (pp. 772 and 774)
situational irony (pp. 785 and 792)
extended metaphor (pp. 806 and 810)
Petrarchan sonnet (p. 804)
Enlightenment (pp. 772 and 775)
Shakespearean sonnet (pp. 804 and 805)
courtly love (p. 785)
Utopia (p. 795)
tone (pp. 821 and 823)
satire (pp. 849 and 856)

Extend Your *Reading*

LITERATURE CONNECTIONS

The Tempest

WILLIAM SHAKESPEARE

For 12 years, Prospero, the former duke of Milan, Italy, has lived on a remote island with his daughter, Miranda. His life changes abruptly when survivors of a recent shipwreck arrive—including his hated brother, Antonio, the man who stole Prospero's throne. Prospero's magical powers are put to the test as he battles with his brother and contends with his daughter's new love, his enemy's son.

Here are just a few of the related readings that accompany *The Tempest:*

Rappaccini's Daughter
BY NATHANIEL HAWTHORNE

Caliban
BY NORRIE EPSTEIN

LITERATURE CONNECTIONS

Macbeth

WILLIAM SHAKESPEARE

On a bloody battlefield, Macbeth, a young Scottish nobleman, wins a great victory. After meeting three witches who hail him as king of Scotland, Macbeth's ambitions are stirred. Only the good king Duncan stands between Macbeth and the throne of Scotland. How far will Macbeth go to achieve his ambition? And, once the crimes begin, where will they end?

Here are just a few of the related readings that accompany *Macbeth:*

Insomniac
BY OCTAVIO PAZ

Like a Bad Dream
BY HEINRICH BÖLL

How Many Children Had Lady Macbeth?
BY DON NIGRO

And Even *More* . . .

Books

The House of Medici: Its Rise and Fall CHRISTOPHER HIBBERT
The Medicis were perhaps the richest family of the European Renaissance. They were patrons of great artists and scientists, including Leonardo da Vinci and Galileo, yet they also committed great crimes.

Renaissance Lives: Portraits of an Age THEODORE K. RABB
The author tells the story of the Renaissance through short biographies of writers, scientists, merchants, artists, and saints.

Other Media

History Through Literature: Renaissance and Reformation
This half-hour video makes history come alive through dramatic readings and insightful commentary by America's poet laureate Robert Pinsky. Clearvue. (VIDEO)

Molière: The Misanthrope
An acclaimed production of one of Molière's most popular plays. Films for the Humanities & Sciences. (VIDEO)

Age of Exuberance
DONALD JOHNSON GREENE

In this spirited and humorous account of life in 18th-century England, Greene examines some of the stereotypes about Enlightenment culture. As the author shows, life had much more to offer than the calm pursuit of rational pleasures.

More Recommendations for Your Students

Difficulty Level: Easy

Hunter, Mollie. *You Never Knew Her as I Did* (New York: Harper, 1981). This swift-paced story tells about the last years of Mary, Queen of Scots, from the perspective of a 17-year-old who enters into a conspiracy to set her free from her island prison.

Stevenson, Robert Louis. *The Black Arrow* (New York: Dodd, 1949). Adventures of a young man in Britain during the War of the Roses, 1455–1485.

Difficulty Level: Average

Chartier, Roger, ed. *A History of Private Life*, vol. 3, *Passions of the Renaissance* (Cambridge: Belknap, 1989). This richly illustrated collection of essays explores various aspects of private life in the Renaissance and Enlightenment. Topics include manners, intimacy, private religious devotion, and family life.

Voltaire, Francois-Marie Arouet. *Candide* (New York: Penguin, 1990). Is this the best of all possible worlds? Candide learns the answer to that question through a series of painfully amusing adventures, including war, religious persecution, and natural disasters. A satiric masterpiece.

Difficulty Level: Advanced

Krennick, Isaac, ed. *Portable Enlightenment Reader* (New York: Viking-Penguin, 1996). More than 100 selections represent the defining ideas of the Enlightenment. Authors include Kant, Voltaire, Rousseau, Newton, Locke, and Madison.

Cervantes, Miguel de. *Don Quijote*, trans. Burton Raffel (New York: Norton, 2000). The full story of the would-be knight and his faithful companion, from the first adventure to the deathbed scene. Fifteen essays are included, as well as source materials and maps.

19th-Century European Literature
Unit Six covers the two most important literary movements of 19th-century Europe: Romanticism (together with its later development Symbolism) and realism. Both movements influenced literature in other parts of the world, including the Americas.

Part 1
Expressions of the Heart: The Age of Romanticism In this part students will read some of the best known authors of Romanticism, including Goethe, Wordsworth, Heine, Hugo, and Baudelaire. A **Comparing Literature Across Cultures** feature allows students to compare works of the English Romantic poet William Wordsworth with works by Cuban poet José Martí and Inuk (Eskimo) writer Uvavnuk.

Part 2
Life's Lessons: The Emergence of Realism The selections in this part represent some of the best-known writers of the realist movement: Maupassant, Tolstoy, Chekhov, and Ibsen. This part includes an **Author Study** feature that gives students a chance to study the great writer Tolstoy in more depth. A **Comparing Literature Across Cultures** feature gives students the opportunity to compare stories by the Russian realist Chekhov and the Indian author Tagore.

19th-Century European Literature
1798–1899

Dance at the Moulin de la Galette, Montmartre (1876), Auguste Renoir. Oil on canvas, 131 cm × 175 cm. Musée d'Orsay, Paris. Réunion des Musées Nationaux/Art Resource, New York.

Making Connections

Ask: Do you think the heart or the mind should rule in human affairs?

Possible Responses: The heart, because without love and compassion, human endeavors would be meaningless; the mind, because only logical reasoning and experience can lead to understanding and fairness.

PART 1 SKILLS TRACE

Features and Selections	Literary Analysis	Reading and Critical Thinking	Writing Opportunities
19th-Century European Literature 1798–1899			
Expressions of the Heart The Age of Romanticism		Interpreting the Text, 872, 875 Using the Time Line, 877	
Learning the Language of Literature Romanticism	Romanticism, 878, 879	Strategies for Reading, 879	
VERSE DRAMA *from* Faust Prologue in Heaven Faust's Study **Related Reading** *from* Letter to His Friends	Dialogue, 881, 896 Dialogue, 882, 886, 890	Clarifying Meaning, 881, 896 Clarifying Meaning, 882, 884, 888, 892 Hierarchy of Devils, 882 Alchemy, 888 Early Faust Tales, 892 What Happens Next in *Faust*, 894 Discussion Questions, 894	Divine Dialogue, 897 Story of Ambition, 897 Informal Assessment (Casting Notes), 886
Comparing Literature Across Cultures Romantic Poetry		Compare and Contrast, 898, 904, 908	Comparison-and-Contrast Essay, 898 Standardized Test Practice (Comparison-and-Contrast Essay), 898
POETRY Poems by William Wordsworth The World Is Too Much With Us My Heart Leaps Up **Related Reading** *from the* Grasmere Journals	Figurative Language, 899, 903 Figurative Language, 900	Drawing Conclusions About Meaning, 899, 903 Drawing Conclusions About Meaning, 900 Discussion Questions, 902 Life at Dove Cottage, 902	Nature Poem, 904 Cause-and-Effect Paragraph, 904
POETRY Romantic Poetry from Other Cultures *from* Simple Verses Shaman Song	Figurative Language, 906	Drawing Conclusions About Meaning, 906 Xenophon, 906	
Comparing Literature Standardized Test Practice			Comparison-and-Contrast Essay, 909 Standardized Test Practice (Responding to a Writing Prompt), 909
POETRY The Lorelei	Literary Ballad, 910, 913 Literary Ballad, 910, 912	Interpreting Symbols, 910, 913 Interpreting Symbols, 912 "The Lorelei" as Folk Song, 912	
POETRY *from* The Expiation Russia 1812 **Connect to Today** Victor Hugo on Stage and Screen	Setting in Narrative Poetry, 915, 920 Setting in Narrative Poetry, 916, 918	Visualizing Setting, 915, 920 Visualizing Setting, 916, 918 Attila the Hun, 916 Paired Discussion, 921	
POETRY Poems by Charles Baudelaire Invitation to the Voyage The Albatross	Sound Devices, 923, 927 Sound Devices, 924	Interpreting Sensory Details, 923, 927 Interpreting Sensory Details, 924, 926 Albatross, 926	
Reflect and Assess	Reflecting on the Literature (Romantic Subjects), 932 Reviewing Literary Concepts (Figurative Language), 932		Building Your Portfolio, 932

LEGEND **Black type – Pupil Edition**
Green type – Teacher's Edition
DLS – Daily Language SkillBuilder

Speaking and Listening Viewing and Representing	Inquiry and Research	Grammar, Usage, and Mechanics	Vocabulary
Using the Map, 870			
Character Portrait, 897 **Dramatic Reading, 897** Art Appreciation, 883, 891 Dramatic Reading, 885, 890 Interview, 889	**Who Was Faust?, 897**	DLS, 880 Independent and Subordinate Clauses, 895	**Context Clues, 897** Using a Dictionary to Determine Precise Meanings, 884
Poem Illustration, 904 Art Appreciation, 901	**Failed Friendship, 904**	DLS, 899	
		DLS, 905	
		DLS, 910	
Art Appreciation, 917, 918		DLS, 914 Adjective Clauses, 919	
Art Appreciation, 924		DLS, 922	Synonyms, 925
			Self Assessment, 932 Self Assessment, 932

LEGEND **Black type – Pupil Edition**
Green type – Teacher's Edition
DLS – Daily Language SkillBuilder

PART 2 SKILLS TRACE

Features and Selections	Literary Analysis	Reading and Critical Thinking	Writing Opportunities
Life's Lessons The Emergence of Realism		Interpreting the Text, 936 Using the Time Line, 940	
Learning the Language of Literature Realism	Realism, 942, 943	Strategies for Reading, 943	
FICTION A Piece of String	Characterization in Realism, 945, 952 Characterization in Realism, 946, 948, 950	Interpreting Details, 945, 952 Interpreting Details, 946, 948 Peasant Life, 946 Village Notary, 948 Development of Psychology, 950	Speech for the Defense, 953 Cause-and-Effect Essay, 953
AUTHOR STUDY **Leo Tolstoy**		Using the Time Line, 955	
FICTION How Much Land Does a Man Need?	Theme in Fiction, 958, 972 Theme in Fiction, 960, 966, 968, 970	Drawing Conclusions, 958, 972 Drawing Conclusions, 960, 962, 966 Tolstoy's *Anna Karenina,* 961 Measuring Area, 967	News Coverage, 973 Family Letter, 973 Children's Version, 973
LETTER Letter from Leo Tolstoy to N. A. Nekrasov		Identifying Loaded Language, 975	
FICTION What Men Live By	Foreshadowing, 976, 995 Foreshadowing, 978, 984, 990, 992	Predicting, 976, 995 Predicting, 978, 986, 990 Religion and Society, 980 Folk Tales, 982 Nineteenth-Century Russia, 984	Standardized Test Practice (Responding to a Writing Prompt), 988–989 Standardized Test Practice (Writing a Short Essay Answer), 990
DIARY *from* Sonya Tolstoy's Diary		Reading a Diary, 994	
The Author's Style Author Study Project	Analysis of Styles, 996		Changing Styles, 996 Folk Tale, 997 Maxims for Living, 997 Explanatory Essay, 997
Comparing Literature Across Cultures Realism in Fiction		Compare and Contrast, 998, 1007, 1014	Comparison-and-Contrast Essay, 998 Standardized Test Practice (Comparison-and-Contrast Essay), 998
FICTION A Problem	Irony, 999, 1006 Irony, 1000, 1002, 1004	Understanding Characters' Values, 999, 1006 Understanding Characters' Values, 1000, 1002, 1004 Siberia, 1003	
FICTION The Artist		Understanding Characters' Values, 1010, 1012 Calcutta, 1009 Women in India, 1010 Indian Art, 1013	
Comparing Literature Standardized Test Practice			Comparison-and-Contrast Essay, 1015 Standardized Test Practice (Responding to a Writing Prompt), 1015

LEGEND **Black type – Pupil Edition**
Green type – Teacher's Edition
DLS – Daily Language SkillBuilder

Speaking and Listening Viewing and Representing	Inquiry and Research	Grammar, Usage, and Mechanics	Vocabulary
Using the Map, 934			
Character Interviews, 953 Town Banner, 953 Art Appreciation, 949 Re-creating a Scene, 951	Peasant Life, 953	DLS, 944	Related Words, 953 Prefixes, 947
Imaginary Dialogue, 973 Pakhom on Trial, 973 Art Appreciation, 960, 969 Dramatization, 962 Land of the Bashkirs (Geography), 964	Peasant Communes, 973 Tolstoy and Gandhi, 973	DLS, 958 Subordinate Clauses: Adverb Clauses, 970–971	Compound Words, 963 Using Context Clues, 966
Art Appreciation, 987, 991		DLS, 976 If/Then Complex Sentences, 992–993	Idioms, 981 Analogies, 986
Speaking and Listening, 996 News Display, 997 Story Dramatization, 997	Biography, 997 Creating a Photo Biography, 997 Primary Print Sources, 997 Secondary Print Sources, 997 Computer Resources, 997 Multimedia Project, 997		
Art Appreciation, 1001		DLS, 999 Capitalization, 1005	Context Clues, 1007 Context Clues, 1004
Art Appreciation, 1011		DLS, 1008	

LEGEND **Black type – Pupil Edition**
Green type – Teacher's Edition
DLS – Daily Language SkillBuilder

Features and Selections	Literary Analysis	Reading and Critical Thinking	Writing Opportunities
DRAMA A Doll's House Act One Act Two Act Three	Realistic Drama, 1019 Characters in Realistic Drama, 1043 Setting in Realistic Drama, 1062 Theme in Realistic Drama, 1081 Realistic Drama (Characters), 1020, 1024, 1026, 1028, 1030, 1032, 1034, 1036, 1038, 1040, 1044, 1048, 1052, 1058, 1060, 1068, 1074, 1076 Realistic Drama (Setting), 1034, 1038, 1044, 1048, 1050 Realistic Drama (Theme), 1064, 1066, 1078	Strategies for Reading Realistic Drama, 1019, 1043, 1062, 1081 Realistic Drama (Dialogue), 1020, 1022, 1040, 1046, 1056, 1064, 1070 Realistic Drama (Stage Directions), 1020, 1026, 1030, 1034, 1044, 1046, 1050, 1056, 1060, 1064 Realistic Drama (Cast of Characters), 1020 Realistic Drama (Visualizing), 1050, 1060, 1072 Middle-Class Life in the 19th Century, 1020 Norway, 1025 Medicine in the 19th Century, 1026 Women's Rights, 1028–1029 Blackmail, 1038 Christmas in Norway, 1044 Working Women in the 19th Century, 1046 Calling Cards, 1052 Tarantella, 1060 Standardized Test Practice (Arranging Events in Sequential Order), 1061 Hysteria, 1065 Divorce in the 19th Century, 1075 Initial Reaction to *A Doll's House*, 1078	Torvald's Response, 1082 Nora's Diary, 1082 Cause Analysis, 1082 Informal Assessment (Writing a Response), 1079
The Translator at Work Translating Drama			
Connect to Today Women in Society		Paired or Group Discussion, 1083	
Writing Workshop Cause-and-Effect Essay Standardized Test Practice Building Vocabulary Sentence Crafting		Analyzing a Student Model, 1085–1086	Cause-and-Effect Essay, 1087 Choosing a Subject, 1087 Planning the Cause-and-Effect Essay, 1087
Reflect and Assess	Reflecting on the Literature (Exploring Realism), 1092 Reviewing Literary Concepts (Interpreting Irony), 1092		Building Your Portfolio, 1092

LEGEND **Black type – Pupil Edition**
Green type – Teacher's Edition DLS – Daily Language SkillBuilder

Speaking and Listening Viewing and Representing	Inquiry and Research	Grammar, Usage, and Mechanics	Vocabulary
View & Compare, 1042 Ibsen Improvisation, 1082 Set Design, 1082 Art Appreciation, 1023, 1036, 1072 Dramatic Presentation, 1024, 1048 Dramatic Interpretation, 1035 Informal Assessment (Using a Graphic), 1041 Comparing Portrayals of Character, 1042 Portraying a Relationship, 1054 Staging a Scene, 1059 Dramatic Reading, 1064 Analyzing Meaning, 1077 Comparing Scenes, 1080	Seeking Equality, 1082	DLS, 1018 Noun Clause, 1066–1067	Word Meanings, 1082 Context Clues, 1040 Suffixes, 1057
Activity (compare translations), 1063			
Paired or Group Discussion, 1083			
		Using Transitional Words and Phrases, 1088 Sentence Fragments, 1089 Run-on Sentences, 1089 Comma Errors, 1089 Using Adverb Clauses, 1091 Adverb Clauses, 1091	Misspelled Homophones, 1088, 1089 Recognizing Denotations and Connotations, 1090 Homophones, 1089
			Self Assessment, 1092 Self Assessment, 1092

LEGEND **Black type – Pupil Edition**
Green type – Teacher's Edition
DLS – Daily Language SkillBuilder

RESOURCE MANAGEMENT GUIDE PART 1

	Unit Resource Book	Assessment	Integrated Technology and Media	Additional Support
Expressions of the Heart **The Age of Romanticism**			Humanities classzone.com	**World Art and Cultures Transparencies** • AT51 *Napoleon Crossing the St. Bernard Pass* • AT56 *The Lady of Shalott*
from **Faust** **Prologue in Heaven** **Faust's Study** *pp. 880–897*	• Summary p. 4 • Active Reading p. 5 • Literary Analysis p. 6 • Words to Know p. 7 • Selection Quiz p. 8	• Selection Test, Formal Assessment pp. 133–134 • Teacher's Guide to Assessment and Portfolio Use Test Generator	Humanities Activity classzone.com	This selection is included in the *World Literature InterActive Reader™*.
The World Is Too Much With Us **My Heart Leaps Up** *pp. 898–904* *from* **Simple Verses** **Shaman Song** *pp. 905–909*	• Points of Comparison p. 9 • Active Reading p. 10 • Literary Analysis p. 11 • Compare/contrast Essay p. 12	• Selection Test, Formal Assessment pp. 135–136 • Teacher's Guide to Assessment and Portfolio Use Test Generator	Research Starter classzone.com	
The Lorelei *pp. 910–913*	• Active Reading p. 13 • Literary Analysis p. 14	• Selection Test, Formal Assessment pp. 137–138 • Teacher's Guide to Assessment and Portfolio Use Test Generator		
from **The Expiation** **Russia 1812** *pp. 914–921*	• Active Reading p. 15 • Literary Analysis p. 16	• Selection Test, Formal Assessment pp. 139–140 • Teacher's Guide to Assessment and Portfolio Use Test Generator		
Invitation to the Voyage **The Albatross** *pp. 922–927*	• Active Reading p. 17 • Literary Analysis p. 18	• Selection Test, Formal Assessment pp. 141–142 • Teacher's Guide to Assessment and Portfolio Use Test Generator		
		Unit Assessment	***Unit Technology***	
		• Unit Six, Part 1 Test, Formal Assessment pp. 143–144 Test Generator • Unit Six Integrated Test, Integrated Assessment pp. 31–36		

	Unit Resource Book	Assessment	Integrated Technology and Media	Additional Support
Life's Lessons **The Emergence of Realism**			Humanities classzone.com	**World Art and Cultures Transparencies** • AT53 *Couturiere* • AT55 *Arrival of the Normandy Train*
A Piece of String *pp. 944–953*	• Summary p. 20 • Active Reading p. 21 • Literary Analysis p. 22 • Words to Know p. 23 • Selection Quiz p. 24	• Selection Test, Formal Assessment pp. 145–146 • Teacher's Guide to Assessment and Portfolio Use Test Generator		
Author Study **Leo Tolstoy** *pp. 954–957*			Author Link classzone.com NetActivities	
How Much Land Does a Man Need? *pp. 958–973*	• Summary p. 25 • Active Reading p. 26 • Literary Analysis p. 27 • Selection Quiz p. 28	• Selection Test, Formal Assessment pp. 147–148 • Teacher's Guide to Assessment and Portfolio Use Test Generator	Research Starter classzone.com	
What Men Live By *pp. 976–997*	• Summary p. 29 • Active Reading p. 30 • Literary Analysis p. 31 • Selection Quiz p. 32	• Selection Test, Formal Assessment pp. 149–150 • Teacher's Guide to Assessment and Portfolio Use Test Generator	Research Starter classzone.com	This selection is included in the *World Literature InterActive Reader™*.
A Problem *pp. 998–1007* **The Artist** *pp. 1008–1015*	• Summaries pp. 33, 40 • Points of Comparison p. 34 • Active Reading p. 35 • Literary Analysis p. 36 • Words to Know p. 37 • Selection Quizzes pp. 38, 41 • Planning an Essay p. 39	• Selection Test, Formal Assessment pp. 151–152 • Teacher's Guide to Assessment and Portfolio Use Test Generator		
Milestones in World Literature **The Novels of Dostoyevsky** *pp. 1016–1017*		Milestone Links classzone.com		
A Doll's House *pp. 1018-1083*	**Act One** • Summary p 42 • Active Reading p. 43 • Literary Analysis p. 44 • Selection Quiz p. 45 **Act Two** • Summary p. 46 • Active Reading p. 47 • Literary Analysis p. 48 • Selection Quiz p. 49 **Act Three** • Summary p. 50 • Active Reading p. 51 • Literary Analysis p. 52 • Words to Know p. 53 • Selection Quiz p. 54	• Selection Test, Formal Assessment pp. 153–158 • Teacher's Guide to Assessment and Portfolio Use Test Generator	Research Starter classzone.com	

Writing Workshop: Cause-and-Effect Essay *pp. 1084–1091*		*Unit Assessment*	*Unit Technology*
Unit Six Resource Book • Prewriting p. 55 • Drafting p. 56 • Peer Response pp. 57–58 • Revising, Editing, and Proofreading p. 59	• Student Models pp. 60–62 • Rubric p. 63 Publishing Options classzone.com **Teacher's Guide to Assessment and Portfolio Use**	• Unit Six, Part 2 Test, Formal Assessment pp. 159–160 Test Generator	classzone.com NetActivities

DAILY LANGUAGE SKILLBUILDERS

Selection	SkillBuilder Sentences	Suggested Answers
from Faust Prologue in Heaven Faust's Study	**1.** The author Johann Wolfgang von Goethe who inspired literary movements was also a scientist and a statesman. **2.** Goethe told a friend that he didn't think the second part of the play Faust would loose any of the first part's spark.	**1.** The author Johann Wolfgang von Goethe**,** who inspired literary movements**,** was also a scientist and a statesman. **2.** Goethe told a friend that he didn't think the second part of the play **Faust** would **lose** any of the first part's spark.
The World Is Too Much With Us My Heart Leaps Up	**1.** The friendship of the two poet's led to the publication of a book of poetry. **2.** The writers observations about himself and nature inspired many beautiful poems.	**1.** The friendship of the two **poets** led to the publication of a book of poetry. **2.** The **writer's** observations about himself and nature inspired many beautiful poems.
from Simple Verses Shaman Song	**1.** José Martí traveled a lot and then moves to New York City. **2.** Uvavnuk a 19th century Inuk woman is the subject of many legends, in one of them she was hit by lightning and filled with spiritual enlightenment.	**1.** José Martí traveled a lot and then **moved** to New York City. **2.** Uvavnuk**,** a 19th century Inuk woman**,** is the subject of many legends**;** in one of them**,** she was hit by lightning and filled with spiritual enlightenment.
The Lorelei	**1.** The author Heinrich Heine wrote Essays against the goverments of France and Germany. **2.** A Maiden sung a strange song that lured sailors to their deaths.	**1.** The author Heinrich Heine wrote **e**ssays against the **governments** of France and Germany. **2.** A **m**aiden **sang** a strange song that lured sailors to their deaths.

DAILY LANGUAGE SKILLBUILDERS

Selection	SkillBuilder Sentences	Suggested Answers
from The Expiation Russia 1812	**1.** "Did you know asked Randy, that Victor Hugo was driven into exile when Napoleon III came into power?" **2.** It must of been difficult for napoleon's soldiers to travel through the snow and cold.	**1.** "Did you know," asked Randy, "that Victor Hugo was driven into exile when Napoleon III came into power?" **2.** It must **have** been difficult for **N**apoleon's soldiers to travel through the snow and cold.
Invitation to the Voyage The Albatross	**1.** I was surprised to find out that Charles Baudelaire translated some of the works of Edgar Allan Poe said Moira. **2.** "Yes," said Justin. He was also found guilty of a crime when he published <u>The Flowers of Evil</u>.	**1.** "I was surprised to find out that Charles Baudelaire translated some of the works of Edgar Allan Poe," said Moira. **2.** "Yes," said Justin. "He was also found guilty of a crime when he published <u>The Flowers of Evil</u>."
A Piece of String	**1.** The old man couldn't never prove his innocence cause he always had been stingy. **2.** Its to bad no body believed that he didn't steal the pocketbook.	**1.** The old man **could** never prove his innocence **because** he always had been stingy. **2.** **It's too** bad **nobody** believed that he didn't steal the pocketbook.
How Much Land Does a Man Need?	**1.** The number of acres he owned were important to Pakhom. **2.** The peasants, feeling anger toward Pakhom, strays onto his land on purpose.	**1.** The number of acres he owned **was** important to Pakhom. **2.** The peasants, feeling anger toward Pakhom, **stray** onto his land on purpose.

DAILY LANGUAGE SKILLBUILDERS

Selection	SkillBuilder Sentences	Suggested Answers
What Men Live By	**1.** Leo Tolstoy, who retold many russian stories, experienced a Spiritual Crisis in 1878. **2.** Simon believed that god had sent the helpless man to him.	**1.** Leo Tolstoy, who retold many **R**ussian stories, experienced a **s**piritual **c**risis in 1878. **2.** Simon believed that **G**od had sent the helpless man to him.
A Problem	**1.** Each family member had their opinion about Sasha's crime. **2.** Neither Ivan nor Sasha's paternal uncles wanted his nephew's case to go to trial.	**1.** Each family member had **his or her** opinion about Sasha's crime. **2.** Neither Ivan nor Sasha's paternal uncles wanted **their** nephew's case to go to trial.
The Artist	**1.** If anyone criticized the wife's artwork, they were scolded. **2.** Some of the art was destroyed so that they would remain secret.	**1.** If anyone criticized the wife's artwork, **he or she was** scolded. **2.** Some of the art was destroyed so that **it** would remain secret.
A Doll's House	**1.** Nora often asked her husband for money, and quickly spent it. **2.** Dr Rank knowing he would die soon told Nora how he really felt about her.	**1.** Nora often asked her husband for money and quickly spent it. [Students should remove the comma after *money.*] **2.** Dr. Rank, knowing he would die soon, told Nora how he really felt about her.

Grammar Focus by Unit	Unit One	Unit Two	Unit Three	Unit Four	Unit Five	Unit Six	Unit Seven
	Parts of Speech	The Sentence and Its Parts	Using Verbs	Using Modifiers	Using Phrases	Clauses and Sentence Structure	Clauses and Sentence Structure

The Language of Literature offers several options for integrating grammar instruction and literature.

- Each unit has a grammar focus. The Teacher's Edition includes Mini Lessons for the selections that help develop the grammar focus for the unit and spring from the content of the specific literature.
- The Pupil Edition includes several full-page lessons on Sentence Crafting. These lessons are related to both the literature and the grammar focus for a unit and help students use proper grammar in their own writing.
- Daily Language SkillBuilders in the Teacher's Edition provide students with ongoing proofreading practice and reinforce correct punctuation, spelling, grammar and usage, and capitalization.

Black type — Pupil Edition
Green type — Teacher's Edition

Part 1

Clauses and Sentence Structure

Independent Clauses, Dependent Clauses
from "Letter to His Friends," p. 895

Adjective Clauses
"Russia 1812," from "The Expiation," p. 919

Part 2

Clauses and Sentence Structure

Kinds of Clauses: Dependent
"How Much Land Does a Man Need?" pp. 970–971

Complex Sentences: If/Then
"What Men Live By," pp. 992–993

Noun Clauses
Act Three, *A Doll's House,* pp. 1066–1067

Adverb Clauses
Sentence Crafting, p. 1091
Sentence Crafting, p. 1091

The Sentence and Its Parts

Sentence Fragments
Standardized Test Practice, p. 1089

Run-on Sentences
Standardized Test Practice, p. 1089

Capitalization

Titles and Family Names
"A Problem," p. 1005

Punctuation

Comma Errors
Standardized Test Practice, p. 1089

Phrases

Transitional Words and Phrases
Writing Workshop, p. 1088

Unit Six, Part 1, concentrates on some of the major Romantic poets in Europe because Romanticism was primarily a European movement. The selections in the part convey the imagination and emotion of Romanticism. Students will discover that these selections echo qualities that are still evident today in contemporary culture.

World Art and Cultures Transparencies

AT51 *Napoleon Crossing the St. Bernard Pass*

AT56 *The Lady of Shalott*

You may use the listed transparencies to acquaint students with art from the Romantic period.

READING FOR INFORMATION

Reading Skills and Strategies

READING A MAP

Tell students that the map shows Europe's boundaries in 1810. Point out that the French Empire was at its height at this time. The French Empire comprised all of the territory shown in green on the map, including the Illyrian Provinces, Rome, and Corsica—Napoleon's birthplace.

PART 1 Expressions of the Heart

The Age of Romanticism

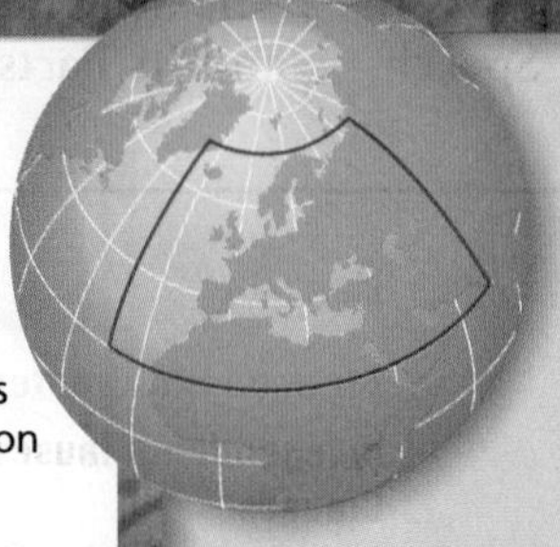

Why It Matters

At the end of the 18th century, a movement called **Romanticism** began to influence the social and political life of Europe. The Romantics rejected science and reason and instead embraced nature, emotion, and individual experience. These rebellious ideas inspired the Romantics to champion the rights of the common people. Eventually, Romanticism's revolutionary spirit inspired a desperate struggle for freedom and reform.

1 Enlightened Ideas France was the birthplace of Romanticism's spiritual father, **Jean Jacques Rousseau** (shown here). His ideas echoed those expressed earlier by England's **John Locke,** who declared that all humans are created equal.

A Time of Upheaval
The Romantic period was a time of rebellion and revolution. As many Europeans tried to bring about political and social changes, the boundaries of countries were torn apart and redrawn.

KINGDOM OF DENMARK AND NORWAY
UNITED KINGDOM OF GREAT BRITAIN AND IRELAND
London
Berlin
CONFEDERATION OF THE RHINE
Rhine R.
Paris
Seine R.
Danube
FRENCH EMPIRE
SWITZERLAND
ITALY
ILLYRIAN
ATLANTIC OCEAN
PORTUGAL
Madrid
SPAIN
CORSICA
Rome
SARDINIA
Mediterranean Sea
SICILY
AFRICA

For Links to Romanticism, click on:
HUMANITIES CLASSZONE.COM

4 Idealized Nature Romantic artist **John Constable** drew inspiration for many of his paintings from his homeland, the countryside of southeastern England. Like many other Romantic artists, Constable idealized nature, creating landscapes that glorified its tranquillity and beauty.

A

870 UNIT SIX PART 1: THE AGE OF ROMANTICISM

MINI LESSON **Using the Map**

Tell students that by 1810, Napoleon controlled many supposedly independent lands as well as those that were formally part of the French Empire. The only major European countries free from Napoleon's control were Great Britain, the Ottoman Empire, Portugal, and Sweden. Ask students what physical factor might have helped these countries escape French rule. *(The countries are far from France, separated by land or sea.)*

Revolutionary Fervor Defending equality and human rights, the **French Revolution** inspired revolutions across Europe. The French Revolution began in Paris in 1789, after peasants stormed the Bastille, a prison and a hated symbol of royal oppression.

The Spread of Nationalism Feelings of **nationalism**—devotion to one's nation rather than to a ruler—were stirred throughout Europe when **Napoleon Bonaparte** attempted to impose French rule on the continent. Eventually this nationalistic spirit inspired the people of Greece to wage a successful struggle for their independence.

Geographical Note

European Boundaries Point out that Europe's boundaries are very different today. You might display a current map of Europe in class so that students can make their own comparisons.

Art Note

A John Constable Tell students that, like other Romantics, Constable embraced emotion saying, "Painting is but another word for feeling." The artist also expressed his deep reverence for nature when he declared: "The landscape painter must walk in the fields with a humble mind. No arrogant man was ever permitted to see Nature in all her beauty."

Historical Highlights

READING FOR INFORMATION
Reading Skills and Strategies
CREATING A TIME LINE
Have students use the information on pages 872 and 873 to create a time line representing the key events of the Romantic age. Students should begin their time lines in the 1600s with John Locke's theories and end in the mid-1800s with the emergence of realism. Encourage students to add dates and notes to their time lines as they read each section.

Historical Note
A The Bastille Tell students that the Bastille was a political prison. Its inmates had broken no laws but were sent there by order of the king, often only because they were suspected of disloyalty. The Bastille was a huge fortress, with walls ten feet thick. Although people told terrifying stories about the Bastille's deep dungeons and the cruel treatment of its prisoners, conditions in the Bastille were actually better than in many other Parisian prisons. Nonetheless, the people of Paris did not storm the Bastille on July 14, 1789, to free its prisoners. Earlier that day, they had forced their way into a public hospital for wounded soldiers and taken more than twenty thousand muskets. However, they had found very little gunpowder. This, they were told, they would have to seize at the Bastille.

To understand the enormous impact of Romanticism on the social and political life of Europe, it is important to know about the events that led up to and occurred during the movement.

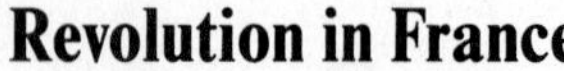

Roots in the Enlightenment

Romanticism is rooted in the **Enlightenment,** a movement of the 17th and 18th centuries that championed science and reason. Enlightenment philosophers believed that the power to reason was equal in all people and defended human dignity and worth. The 17th-century English philosopher John Locke even declared that people had rights to life, liberty, and happiness.

In the 18th century, Locke's ideas were echoed by Jean Jacques Rousseau. The French philosopher believed that laws and government should reflect the people's will. Rousseau's ideas influenced the leaders of the French Revolution. With his belief in people's natural goodness and in the value of the individual, Rousseau also foreshadowed Romanticism.

Revolution in France

Although Rousseau's ideas helped inspire the French Revolution, outrage at the social and economic conditions in France in the second half of the 1700s actually ignited the conflict. In 1788, taxes on the poor were raised just when wages dropped and food supplies were scarce. Tensions finally exploded on July 14, 1789, when a mob of Parisians A seized the Bastille. The French Revolution had begun.

At first, the revolution brought about positive change. Feudalism in France was ended, the country was declared a republic, and a new constitution was drafted. Tragically, the revolution also produced the **Reign of Terror,** led by a group of revolutionaries. From 1793 to 1794, this group executed anyone judged to be an enemy of the new French republic. Tens of thousands of people were executed by guillotine.

Rise and Fall of Napoleon

Beginning in 1792, the new republic engaged in a series of wars to defend and spread the ideas of the French Revolution. With all citizens involved in the war effort, a sense of nationalism arose throughout the French republic. Leading the battles was the young, heroic general Napoleon Bonaparte, who would crown himself emperor of France in 1804.

In time, it became clear that Napoleon's ambitions extended well beyond the borders of France. He wanted to conquer all of Europe. To prevent French domination, European allies mobilized forces against Napoleon. Fearful that Russia would join the alliance, Napoleon invaded that country in 1812. The decision proved disastrous. Napoleon lost more than 500,000 men. His losses encouraged his enemies to attack. In 1815, Napoleon suffered a decisive defeat at the **Battle of Waterloo** in Belgium.

872

MINI LESSON Interpreting the Text

Ask students the following questions about the information on pages 872 and 873:
How did Napoleon's ambitions betray the principles of the French Revolution?
Possible Response: His desire to conquer other lands was in contrast with the ideals of freedom and government by the people.
How did Napoleon's desire for French domination ironically advance these principles?
Possible Response: He inspired those he tried to dominate to fight for their own independence.

Napoleon's army retreats from Russia.

Struggles for Independence

Inspired first by the French Revolution's ideals of freedom and later by opposition to the Napoleonic invasions, national movements gained momentum in 19th-century Europe. These movements often led to revolutions for independence.

Greece waged the first successful revolution in 1830. That same year, Belgium also gained its independence. Not all of the bids for freedom were successful, however. When a group of young Russian aristocrats called the Decembrists led a rebellion against Czar Nicholas I in December 1825, the uprising was quickly crushed.

Revolutionary fervor was rekindled in 1848, when France once again rose up against its king. Soon, ethnic uprisings had swept across Europe, sparking revolts in Austria, Hungary, and Germany. Although these uprisings were suppressed by the ruling powers, people's dreams of freedom were not crushed.

Revolution in Industry

While political and social revolutions erupted in France and swept across Europe, rebellion was repressed in Great Britain. Those in power had moved decisively to keep Britain from falling victim to the violence and anarchy they saw in France. Instead, Great Britain was involved in a different kind of revolution that had begun in the 1700s—an industrial revolution, which changed the economy from one mainly centered on agriculture to one driven by industry.

Industrialization would eventually greatly improve people's standards of living and opportunities. In the early 1800s, however, the rapid pace of industrialization caused many serious problems, including unsafe working conditions, child labor, and unhealthy urban living conditions. Reformers sought to correct the labor and social problems caused by industrialization, but their efforts were often equated with revolution and crushed. Largely as a result of these reformist efforts, Romanticism faded in England, and a new movement called **realism** began to emerge. Realists focused on everyday life, often bringing social problems to public attention.

History to Literature

Events that occurred during the Romantic age inspired writers of the time as well as writers throughout the 19th century.

EVENT IN HISTORY	EVENT IN LITERATURE
French Revolution	English novelist Charles Dickens uses the French Revolution as the background of his 1859 novel *A Tale of Two Cities,* which is set in London and Paris.
Napoleon's invasion of Russia	In a narrative poem called "The Expiation," about the career of Napoleon Bonaparte, French writer Victor Hugo vividly describes the French army's retreat from Moscow.

Historical Note

B Greek Independence Tell students that when Greece fought for its independence against the Ottoman Empire, many Europeans and Americans were strongly sympathetic. Some even joined in the struggle. One such was the British Romantic poet, Lord Byron, who volunteered to serve as a soldier for the Greek cause in 1823. Byron led a group of Greek soldiers but, unfortunately, died of a fever in 1824. Byron is still regarded as a national hero in Greece—not for his poetry but for his dedication to the country's revolution.

Historical Note

C Child Labor Tell students that before laws were passed restricting child labor, children as young as six years old worked in British factories. The children often began their workday at 5 A.M. and labored until 9 P.M. During the 16-hour shift, the children were typically allowed only a 40-minute break for lunch. To keep the young workers awake and alert during the afternoon and evening hours, adult overseers sometimes whipped the children.

READING FOR INFORMATION
Reading Skills and Strategies
TAKING NOTES
On pages 874 and 875, students will learn about European philosophers, artists, writers, and composers. To help students process and recall the information, encourage them to take notes as they read. For instance, as they read the **Painting** section, students might record the artists' names, their countries of origin, and brief notes about their works' subject matter and style.

Arts and Culture

Romanticism dominated European intellectual and artistic life in the first half of the 19th century. The Romantics created a new movement of individual freedom and self-expression in literature, art, and music.

Philosophy

Before the Romantic movement, most philosophers emphasized intellect and reason over instincts and emotion. This philosophical tradition began to change with Jean Jacques Rousseau, whose ideas about the individual and the power of the imagination inspired Romantic philosophers in the 19th century.

One of these was the German philosopher **Arthur Schopenhauer,** who rejected the idea that reason could be used to explain the world. Instead, he believed that people experience the world through their senses. As a result, Schopenhauer claimed, people experience the world not as it is, but as their senses perceive it. Such ideas inspired Romantic artists, writers, and composers to use their senses and emotions to describe the world and to convey a poetic wonder about nature and life.

In this painting, Delacroix represents a Moroccan chief greeting members of his tribe.

Painting

Romantic artists broke with conventional subject matter to paint subjects that were dramatic and imaginative. These artists were united by their desire to express their individual feelings and beliefs.

Many Romantic artists painted landscapes to convey their feelings about nature. The two most important English landscape artists were John Constable and **J. M. W. Turner.** Constable expressed his love for the English countryside by portraying its beauty and harmony. Turner, on the other hand, emphasized the energy and destructive force of the natural world. **Caspar David Friedrich,** considered the greatest German Romantic painter, also focused on the power of nature. The otherworldly quality of Friedrich's work inspires the viewer with a sense of mystery and awe. (See page 878 for an example of Friedrich's work.)

The greatest French Romantic painter, **Eugène Delacroix,** broke away from the landscape artists to depict more exotic subject matter. Many of his paintings reflect his fascination with the people and history of other cultures. Delacroix created a sense of mood and mystery in these works through the use of rich color and deep shadow.

Turner used color and indistinct shapes to convey the power and energy of nature.

Literature

Romanticism deeply influenced the literature of England, France, and Germany. While the Romantic movement and literature of each country had unique features, they also shared many defining characteristics, such as an emphasis on emotion, imagination, the individual, and nature.

In England, critics traditionally mark the beginning of the Romantic movement with the publication in 1798 of the poetry collection *Lyrical Ballads* by **William Wordsworth** and **Samuel Taylor Coleridge.** In France, Romanticism began around the time of the French Revolution. **Victor Hugo** eventually emerged as the leading Romantic writer in France. One of the leaders of the early Romantic movement in Germany was **Johann Wolfgang von Goethe.** In their poetry, all of these Romantic writers explored the intricate workings of their own minds and the complexities of their emotions.

You can learn more about Romantic literature in *Learning the Language of Literature* on pages 878–879.

Music

In the early years of the 19th century, composers began to experiment with classical musical forms, adding intense personal feeling. Their music reflected the Romantic emphasis on originality, individuality, and emotion. German composer **Ludwig van Beethoven** helped bridge the classical and Romantic periods in music. Although his formal musical techniques were classical, the passion and dramatic expressiveness of his music made it a model for Romantic composers.

Strongly sympathetic to the ideals of the French Revolution, Beethoven composed his Symphony No. 3, the *Eroica* ("Heroic"), and dedicated it to Napoleon with these words: "a grand symphony dedicated to Bonaparte." However, after hearing that Napoleon had declared himself emperor, Beethoven tore up the original inscription and replaced it with the words "composed to celebrate the memory of a great man."

Ludwig van Beethoven

Cultural Note

A ***Lyrical Ballads*** Tell students that, in his preface to *Lyrical Ballads,* Wordsworth sought to explain what he was trying to accomplish with his poetry. Wordsworth wrote that his principal object was to choose "incidents and situations from common life" and to describe them with language "really used by men." Above all, he hoped to make these incidents and situations interesting by conveying the "elementary feelings" associated with them.

Cultural Note

B **Beethoven** Tell students that Beethoven's disenchantment with Napoleon was revealed in a later work. In 1813, Beethoven composed the *Battle Symphony,* later titled *Wellington's Victory,* to commemorate the British general's victory over Napoleon in Spain in June of that year. Some critics maintain that it is the worst music Beethoven ever wrote.

MINI LESSON Interpreting the Text

Have students answer the following questions: How did Beethoven feel about Napoleon and his role in the French Revolution?

Possible Response: Beethoven felt that Napoleon was a hero.

How did Beethoven feel about Napoleon after he declared himself emperor? Why?

Possible Response: Beethoven was disappointed because he felt that Napoleon had been seduced by power.

READING FOR INFORMATION
Reading Skills and Strategies
READING A TIME LINE
Have students scan the time line. Point out that the time line is divided into ten-year increments and three main sections. The first section details the cultural events that occurred in Europe during the Romantic age. The second section describes the historical events that occurred in Europe during the period, while the third section tells what was going on in the rest of the world. Encourage students to read one section at a time. Doing so will help students understand the sequence of cultural and historical events.

Historical Note
(A) **Reign of Terror** Tell students that the Reign of Terror was the name given the rule of Maximilien Robespierre, who governed France as a dictator for nearly one year. Robespierre set out to eliminate "enemies of the republic." However, some of the people sent to the guillotine were fellow revolutionaries who challenged Robespierre's leadership. Many others were sent to death on flimsy charges. For example, one tavern keeper was executed because he sold sour wine "to the defenders of the country." Approximately 3,000 people were executed during the Reign of Terror. About 85 percent of those killed belonged to the poor or middle classes—people for whose benefit the Revolution had supposedly been carried out.

Historical Note
(B) **Cotton Gin** Tell students that the cotton gin was a highly efficient machine for cleaning the seeds from cotton. Armed with the gin, wealthy planters bought huge areas of land, and then put an enormous slave labor force to work cultivating cotton. By 1820, this plantation system of farming had transformed much of the South into a "cotton kingdom." In this way, the cotton gin accelerated the expansion of slavery.

Time Line

ROMANTICISM (1790–1850)

A.D. 1 — PRESENT

EVENTS IN EUROPEAN ROMANTICISM

1790	1800	1810
1793 French painter Jacques Louis David paints *The Murder of Marat* **1794** William Blake publishes *Songs of Experience* **1797** Samuel Taylor Coleridge writes "Kubla Khan" (published in 1816) **1798** William Wordsworth and Samuel Taylor Coleridge publish *Lyrical Ballads*	**1800** Dorothy Wordsworth begins keeping her *Grasmere Journals* **1804** Ludwig van Beethoven completes Symphony no. 3, *Eroica* **1805** J. M. W. Turner paints *The Shipwreck* **1808** Goethe publishes *Faust, Part 1*	**1818** Mary Shelley's *Frankenstein* published anonymously **1819** Percy Bysshe Shelley writes "Ode to the West Wind"; John Keats writes "Ode on a Grecian Urn"

EVENTS IN EUROPEAN HISTORY

1790	1800	1810
1792 France declared a republic (A) **1793** Mass executions carried out in France as the Reign of Terror begins; French king Louis XVI executed by guillotine **1796** Spain declares war on Britain **1799** Coup d'état establishes Napoleon as dictator of France	**1800** Act of Union passed, creating United Kingdom of Great Britain and Ireland **1804** Napoleon crowns himself emperor of France **1805** Napoleon begins conquering most of Europe **1807** British slave trade abolished	**1812** Napoleon invades Russia; Britain fights United States in War of 1812 **1814** Congress of Vienna opens, seeking to remake Europe after Napoleon's downfall **1815** Allied armies under British leader Wellington defeat Napoleon at Waterloo; Napoleon banished to St. Helena

EVENTS IN WORLD HISTORY

1790	1800	1810
1790 Philadelphia becomes capital of the United States (B) **1794** Eli Whitney patents cotton gin, paving the way for increasing slavery by making it more profitable **1799** George Washington dies	**1801** Thomas Jefferson becomes president of the United States **1803** United States buys Louisiana Territory from France; Robert Fulton powers boat by steam **1804** Haiti gains independence from France	**1810** Revolts in New Granada, Rio de la Plata, and Mexico **c. 1816** Zulu chief Shaka begins rule over large kingdom in southeastern Africa

1820	1830	1840
1820 Blake illustrates the Book of Job **1821** Keats, age 25, dies of tuberculosis **1822** Shelley, age 32, drowns off coast of Italy **1824** Lord Byron, age 38, dies of fever **1827** Heine publishes *The Book of Songs*; Beethoven dies; Blake dies	**1832** Goethe publishes *Faust, Part 2;* Goethe dies; French writer George Sand publishes *Indiana* **1833** Russian poet and novelist, Aleksandr Pushkin, publishes *Eugene Onegin* **1834** Victor Hugo's novel *The Hunchback of Notre Dame* becomes a bestseller; Coleridge dies	**1843** William Wordsworth appointed poet laureate of England **1844** French writer Alexandre Dumas publishes best-selling novel *The Count of Monte Cristo* **1845** Hugo begins writing *Les Misérables* (published in 1862)

1820	1830	1840
1821 Greeks begin war for independence ➢ **1825** Decembrist revolt in Russia crushed	**1830** Greece wins full independence from Ottoman Turks; Belgium declares independence from the Netherlands; Charles X of France is removed from power by revolution and is succeeded by Louis Philippe (C) **1834** Spanish Inquisition finally suppressed after six centuries **1837** Victoria becomes queen of Great Britain	**1842** Riots and strikes break out in the industrial regions of England **1843** Military revolt in Spain **1848** Revolution in France leads to the establishment of Second Republic; Louis Napoleon elected president of France; revolutions sweep across Europe (C)

1820	1830	1840
1821 Spain's Latin American empire begins to collapse as Mexico, several Central American states, and Venezuela win independence **1823** U.S. president Monroe issues Monroe Doctrine to keep Europe out of Latin America **1824** Simón Bolívar liberates last Spanish colonies in Latin America	**1831** Nat Turner leads Virginia slave revolt **1836** Texas gains independence from Mexico and becomes a republic **1839** First Opium War between Britain and China begins	**1842** First Opium War between Britain and China ends **1847** Liberia becomes independent republic (D) **1848** First U.S. women's rights convention meets in Seneca Falls, New York; ➢ gold discovered in California

A WOMAN'S DECLARATION

Historical Note

(C) Revolutions in France Students may be confused by the fact that revolutions occurred in France in 1830 and again in 1848. Tell them that the revolution begun in 1798 was not ultimately successful. In 1815, the monarchy was restored to power. In 1830, revolution removed the ruling king, Charles X, and established King Louis Philippe. By 1848, however, Louis Philippe had fallen from favor. The monarchy was overturned, and a new republic was established. Louis Napoleon, the nephew of Napoleon Bonaparte, won the presidential election in 1848. Four years later, though, he took the title of Emperor Napoleon III and became a strong ruler. It was not until 1875 that France finally set up a democratic republic.

Historical Note

(D) Liberia Tell students that, beginning in 1815, colonies in Liberia were established for free African Americans. After Liberia gained its independence, the Liberians charged the United States with injustices that forced them to seek a new life in Africa. Liberia was not recognized by the United States until 1862, during the Civil War.

MINI LESSON Using the Time Line

Have students use the time line to answer the following questions:

1. What event in European history occurred in 1837? *(Victoria became queen of Great Britain.)*
2. During what decade did many important British Romantic poets die? *(1820s)*
3. In what year did Haiti gain independence from France? *(1804)*
4. How long did the First Opium War between Britain and China last? *(3 years)*
5. What events in European and world history characterized much of the period between 1790 and 1850? *(wars and struggles for independence)*

Objectives

- identify the characteristics of Romantic writing
- compare the values of Romantic writers with those of neoclassical writers
- understand the history of Romanticism in Germany, England, and France, and identify major Romantic writers in these countries

Revolt Against Neoclassicism
Explain to students that neoclassical writers modeled their works on those of ancient Greece and Rome, which they believed contained universal truths and rules of form important in writing. Neoclassicists stressed balance, order, logic, sophisticated wit, and emotional restraint, focusing on society and the human intellect and avoiding personal feelings. Some of the major neoclassical writers included Alexander Pope, Jonathan Swift, Samuel Johnson, and Voltaire.

Romanticism

Have you ever been surprised by the power of emotions expressed in a literary work? Maybe you've tried to convey your own feelings in a poem or story. Writing that emphasizes the expression of intense emotion is called **Romantic.** Romantic writing is also marked by an intense interest in nature, individual experience, and the imagination.

Romanticism was an artistic and intellectual movement that began in Europe in the late 18th century and continued well into the mid-19th century. The movement revolutionized ideas regarding artistic creation and forms of expression in Germany, England, and France. In fact, many of the intensely emotional and imaginative qualities of Romantic writing are evident in literature today.

Romanticism often emphasized the individual's experience with nature. *The Wanderer Above the Sea of Clouds.* (1818). Caspar David Friedrich. Hamburg Kunsthalle, Germany. The Bridgeman Art Library.

Revolt Against Neoclassicism

Romantic writers rebelled against the neoclassical ideals of the 18th century. While the neoclassicists valued reason, form, and order, the Romantics celebrated spontaneous feeling and freedom from rules and conventions. While the neoclassicists wrote tightly controlled poetry in the classical mold and witty satiric essays, the Romantics wrote serious lyric poems about their own experiences. The chart below identifies some of the differences between neoclassical and Romantic writers.

Neoclassical Writers	Romantic Writers
▶ Stressed reason and intellect	▶ Stressed emotions and imagination
▶ Wrote about objective issues that concerned society as a whole, such as politics and religion	▶ Wrote about subjective experiences of the individual, such as desires, hopes, and dreams
▶ Respected the man-made institutions of church and state	▶ Appreciated nature in all its creative and destructive forces
▶ Believed in order in all things	▶ Believed in spontaneity in thought and action
▶ Maintained traditional standards	▶ Believed in experimentation
▶ Focused on adult concerns, primarily those of the ruling class	▶ Reflected on the experiences of childhood, unsophisticated societies, and common people
▶ Controlled emotion, which was often expressed in the form of wit	▶ Celebrated intense passion and vision
▶ Followed formal rules and diction in poetry	▶ Sought a more natural poetic form and diction

Romantic Movements Across Europe

German Romanticism Romanticism in Germany developed as a series of separate movements. Some of the defining characteristics of German Romanticism first appeared in the late-18th-century movement called *Sturm und Drang* (shtŏŏrm′ ŏŏnt dräng′), meaning "Storm and Stress." Among the leading figures in this movement, which glorified nature, emotion, and originality, was the writer Johann Wolfgang von Goethe. The handsome, brooding main character of Goethe's popular first novel, *The Sorrows of Young Werther* (1774), came to represent the model young **Romantic hero.** Later movements in German Romanticism emphasized an interest in folklore and an exploration of the supernatural.

YOUR TURN Why do you think many Romantics were attracted to the supernatural?

English Romanticism Critics often mark the beginning of the English Romantic age with the publication of the poetry collection *Lyrical Ballads* by William Wordsworth and Samuel Taylor Coleridge in 1798. In his famous preface to *Lyrical Ballads,* Wordsworth defined Romantic poetry as "the spontaneous overflow of powerful feelings."

In addition to Wordsworth and Coleridge, poets William Blake, Lord Byron, Percy Bysshe Shelley, and John Keats dominated the English Romantic movement. These poets deliberately chose language and subjects taken from common life instead of upper-class life. They also turned to nature to stimulate their own thinking and reflect on the relationship between the real and the ideal.

YOUR TURN Why do you think the Romantics found such strong inspiration in the natural world?

French Romanticism The Romantic movement did not emerge in France until 1820. Profoundly influenced by the events and ideas of the French Revolution, the French people called for "a new society, a new literature." They found a literary leader in Victor Hugo, whose highly personal and emotional poetry, novels, and dramas reflected Romanticism's independence from the rules of neoclassicism. Among his best-known works are *The Hunchback of Notre Dame* (1831) and *Les Misérables* (1862), both of which reveal Hugo's interest in the suffering of common people. Other major French Romantics were the novelists George Sand and Stendhal.

Strategies for Reading: Romantic Literature

1. Notice how the Romantic writers freely embraced such subjects as life, death, love, and nature.
2. Read each poem aloud several times and identify its sound devices. Think about what mood these devices help create.
3. Pay attention to the extensive use of imagery and figurative language and try to visualize the images and comparisons being made.
4. Watch for elements of the exotic and supernatural and think about what these might represent.
5. **Monitor** your reading strategies and modify them when your understanding breaks down. Remember to use your strategies for Active Reading: **predict, visualize, connect, question, clarify,** and **evaluate.**

Romantic Movements Across Europe

German Romanticism You may want to further explain the concept of the Romantic hero. Tell students that Romantic heroes are rebellious, moody figures of great passion and strong will. In Goethe's novel, Werther is hopelessly in love and ultimately destroyed by his great passion.

YOUR TURN

Possible Response: The supernatural allowed Romantic writers to freely use their imaginations.

English Romanticism Tell students that the poems in *Lyrical Ballads,* with their simple language and subject matter drawn largely from nature and common life, represented a sharp departure from the more formally crafted poetry of the day. Though now considered a cornerstone of England's Romantic movement, *Lyrical Ballads* was praised by only a handful of critics when it was first published in 1798.

YOUR TURN

Possible Response: The natural world brought the Romantics closer to God and the ideal.

French Romanticism Tell students that Victor Hugo felt that a poet should lead the people, and his writing became overtly political toward the end of his life.

Strategies for Reading

Tell students that although Romantic poetry may seem old-fashioned, Romanticism emphasized the expression of individual thoughts and feelings, a trend that continues to dominate contemporary poetry, fiction, art, and song lyrics. As students read the selections in this part, ask them to compare the topics and themes they encounter with those found in contemporary culture.

 This selection is included in the **World Literature InterActive Reader™.**

Objectives

- understand and appreciate a **drama** that expresses the passion and individuality of the Romantic age **(Literary Analysis)**
- examine how **dialogue** reveals characters' personalities **(Literary Analysis)**
- determine what a **soliloquy** reveals about a character's thoughts **(Literary Analysis)**
- use strategies to **clarify meaning** in a challenging literary work **(Active Reading)**

Summary

When the excerpt from *Faust* begins, Mephisto is in heaven, speaking with the Lord. The devil wishes to make a deal with Faust, who has lately been expressing deep dissatisfaction with his life. Confident that Faust will ultimately choose the right path, the Lord allows Mephisto to make his pact. Accordingly, Mephisto soon appears in Faust's study, where the devil states his proposition. Faust, who is disgusted with the academic knowledge he has accumulated, agrees to sell his soul to the devil in exchange for attaining a Godlike knowledge of the world. If Faust ever becomes satisfied with what he learns, he claims that he will gladly die and the devil can take his soul. Mephisto eagerly assents and has Faust sign the pact in blood.

 Use **Unit Six Resource Book,** p. 4, for additional support.

Thematic Link

In Goethe's drama, Faust denies reason and listens to the passionate **expressions of his heart.** He makes a pact with the devil in order to attain Godlike knowledge.

 Use **Unit Six Resource Book,** p. 7, for practice with Words to Know.

5-Minute Warm-Up

Daily Language SkillBuilder

Have students **proofread** the display sentences on page 869i and write them correctly.

PREPARING to *Read*

FROM

Faust

Johann Wolfgang von Goethe

Johann Wolfgang von Goethe
1749–1832

Literary Giant Considered one of the giants of world literature, the German poet, playwright, and novelist Johann Wolfgang von Goethe (yō'hän vôlf'gäng vôn gœ'tə) inspired literary movements and influenced the novel form. He was also a scientist and a statesman. Born in Frankfurt am Main, Goethe was groomed by his father to study law. The young man, however, had other ideas. At the University of Leipzig and later at the university in Strasbourg, Goethe neglected his law courses to study music, art, and architecture and to write poetry and plays. During a long recovery from an illness, he pursued an interest in magic and the occult. All of these early interests are evident in Goethe's important works. One of his first, the novel *The Sorrows of Young Werther* (1774), achieved great success and helped initiate the *Sturm und Drang* literary movement, the forerunner of the Romantic movement in Germany.

Years at Weimar Goethe's fame brought him to the attention of Duke Charles Augustus, who in 1775 invited the writer to move to his court at Weimar. Goethe accepted the invitation, and Weimar became his home for the rest of his life. During his first ten years there, Goethe largely abandoned his literary aspirations. Made a minister of state, he dedicated himself to his duties. In 1786, however, Goethe embarked on a two-year trip to Italy, and it was during this period that he "found himself again as an artist." His subsequent friendship with the German poet and playwright Friedrich von Schiller strengthened his resolve to return to literature.

The Writing of *Faust* In particular, Goethe resumed his work in dramatizing the Faust (foust) legend. The poet's fascination with Faust had begun in his boyhood, when he saw a puppet show about the legendary magician. In the 1770s, he had started to write a verse drama about Faust. In 1790, a fragment of the work was published. By 1797, Goethe had begun working in earnest on the drama and decided to present the story in two parts. *Faust, Part 1,* published in 1808, was well received. Goethe did not return to work on the second part until 1824. It was finally completed in 1832, shortly before his death.

LESSON RESOURCES

UNIT SIX RESOURCE BOOK,
pp. 4-8

ASSESSMENT RESOURCES
Formal Assessment, pp. 133–134
Teacher's Guide to Assessment and Portfolio Use
Test Generator

INTEGRATED TECHNOLOGY
Visit our Web site: classzone.com

ADDITIONAL RESOURCES
Lesson Planning Guide, pp. 113–114
Teacher's Sourcebook for Language Development

Build Background

The Faust Legend The Faust legend was based on a real person named Johann Faust, who died around 1540. The real Faust was a German astrologer and magician. Legend has it that he performed such magical feats as producing wine from thin air. People also said that he had sold his soul to the devil to gain knowledge. In 1587, an anonymous collection of legends about Faust appeared in print, and it was widely read. The story of Faust was retold over the next two centuries in German popular dramas and puppet shows.

All of these works portrayed Faust as a sinner who deserved damnation. Goethe, however, portrayed him as a much more sympathetic character. He chose to present Faust as a Romantic hero, emphasizing his tormented emotions and his restless search for knowledge. Although Goethe called his drama a **tragedy,** it ends with Faust's salvation.

Drama, Epic, or Poetry? It is difficult to determine what **genre,** or literary form, Goethe's *Faust* belongs to. With its dialogue and stage directions, *Faust* is certainly a drama. However, because of its great length and many scene changes, it is rarely performed on stage. The work contains elements of an **epic,** but epics are narratives, not dramas. Even the poetry Goethe wrote for the two-part *Faust* is difficult to categorize, since he used such a wide variety of poetic styles. All in all, *Faust* might be said to transcend genre.

The Story of *Faust*

Have you ever heard the phrases "to make a deal with the devil" or "to sell your soul to the devil"? These phrases originated with the Faust legend. In Goethe's version, Doctor Faust, a university professor, is dissatisfied with his own academic studies. He makes a deal with the devil Mephisto (mə-fĭs′tō), who promises to help Faust discover real knowledge. They agree that if Faust ever becomes contented, the devil will seize his soul.

For a humanities activity, click on:

Connect to Your Life

In this excerpt, Faust is willing to give up his soul to attain a god-like knowledge and experience of the world. What would you give up to achieve your dream? Health? Love? Your soul? The respect of others? Share your thoughts with a classmate.

Focus Your Reading

LITERARY ANALYSIS: DIALOGUE

Written conversation between two or more people, in either fiction or nonfiction, is called dialogue. In fiction, **dialogue** is used to bring characters to life and to give readers insights into the characters' personalities. As you read this excerpt from *Faust,* think about how the dialogue reveals the characters' personalities.

ACTIVE READING: CLARIFYING MEANING

The elevated language and the way in which words are arranged in Goethe's *Faust* can pose real challenges for readers. Here are some suggestions for **clarifying meaning** as you read:

- **Read Sidenotes and Words to Know** Use the notes in the margins and the Words to Know at the bottom of the pages to learn the meaning of unfamiliar words.
- **Reorder Words** Unusual word order is often used in poetry to maintain **meter** or a **rhyme scheme.** Reorder the words so that they sound more natural and make sense to you.
- **Paraphrase** Restate difficult lines and speeches in your own words.
- **Summarize** Clarify the speeches in *Faust* by summarizing the most important idea or ideas being expressed.

READER'S NOTEBOOK As you read the excerpt, write down particularly difficult passages and use the strategies listed above to clarify meaning.

WORDS TO KNOW **Vocabulary Preview**

abate	genial	resolute	waive
connive	humanely	sloth	
despair	repose	stature	

READING FOR INFORMATION

Reading Skills and Strategies

REVIEWING GENRE

You may want to review some of the boldfaced terms that refer to genre in **Build Background.**

- **Tragedy:** A tragedy is a dramatic work that presents the downfall of a dignified character who is involved in historically or socially significant events.
- **Drama:** Drama is literature in the form of a play.
- **Epic:** An epic is a long narrative poem on a serious subject, presented in an elevated or formal style.
- **Poetry:** Poetry is language arranged in lines that attempts to re-create emotions and experiences and suggest meanings beyond the literal meanings of the words.

After students finish reading the excerpt from Faust, have them discuss what elements of these genres are contained in the work.

TIME MANAGEMENT

If your schedule requires that you cover the lesson objectives in a shorter time, use . . .

- Preparing to Read, pp. 880–881
- Thinking Through the Literature, p. 896
- Vocabulary in Action, p. 897

If you want to take advantage of longer blocks of class time, use . . .

- TE Teaching Options: Cross-Curricular Link, pp. 882, 888, 892, and 894; Viewing and Representing, pp. 883 and 891; Vocabulary Strategy, p. 884; Speaking and Listening, pp. 885, 889, and 890; Informal Assessment, p. 886; Grammar, p. 895
- Related Reading, p. 895
- Choices & Challenges, p. 897

Guide for Reading

Direct students' attention to the **Guide for Reading** and **Focus** headings on this page. Explain that the information under the Focus heading is intended to help them understand the drama and concentrate on its main ideas. Tell students that at two points during the play, a **Pause & Reflect** question will ask them to stop and think about what they have read.

Literary Analysis DIALOGUE

Point out that the dialogue between Mephisto and the Lord provides insight into the characters' personalities—particularly the devil's. Have students reread Mephisto's speech in lines 1–22. Then ask them what words they would use to describe the devil.

Possible Responses: sarcastic, disrespectful, funny, scornful, persuasive

Use **Unit Six Resource Book,** p. 6, for more practice.

Active Reading CLARIFYING MEANING

A Have students use the sidenotes to figure out who Mephisto refers to as "the small god of the world." *(humankind)* Then ask them to summarize Mephisto's opinion of humankind.

Possible Responses: Mephisto views humankind as unhappy, loathsome, and stupid.

Use **Unit Six Resource Book,** p. 5, for more practice.

Literary Analysis RHYME SCHEME

Tell students that a rhyme scheme is the pattern of end rhyme in a poem. A rhyme scheme is charted by assigning a letter of the alphabet, beginning with *a*, to each line. Then point out that the rhyme scheme in *Faust* is irregular. The rhyme scheme in the first eight lines is *abab.* However, the rhyme scheme changes in lines 9–16. Ask students to identify the rhyme scheme in those lines. *(aabb)*

from Faust

Johann Wolfgang von Goethe

Translated by Walter Kaufmann

GUIDE FOR READING

FOCUS In this verse drama, the devil Mephisto proposes a bet to win Faust's soul. Read to find out what the Lord thinks of the devil's bet.

The "Prologue in Heaven" introduces the devil Mephisto, one of the drama's main characters. In Heaven, surrounded by the archangels Raphael, Gabriel, and Michael, the Lord allows Mephisto to appear before him. After the three archangels praise God's glorious works on Earth, Mephisto addresses the Lord.

Prologue in Heaven

Mephisto:

Since you, oh Lord, have once again drawn near,
And ask how we have been, and are so genial,
And since you used to like to see me here,
You see me, too, as if I were a menial.
I cannot speak as nobly as your staff,
Though by this circle here I shall be spurned:
My pathos would be sure to make you laugh,
Were laughing not a habit you've unlearned.
Of suns and worlds I know nothing to say;
I only see how men live in dismay.
The small god of the world will never change his ways
And is as whimsical—as on the first of days.
His life might be a bit more fun,
Had you not given him that spark of heaven's sun;
He calls it reason and employs it, resolute
To be more brutish than is any brute.

4 menial (mē′nē-əl): servant.

7 pathos (pā′thŏs): quality or situation that arouses pity or sadness.

11 The small god of the world: humankind.

WORDS TO KNOW

genial (jēn′yəl) *adj.* pleasant; agreeable
resolute (rĕz′ə-lo͞ot′) *adj.* resolved; determined

882

Cross Curricular Link Humanities

HIERARCHY OF DEVILS In the hierarchy of devils, Mephisto—or Mephistopheles, as he is also known—is a minor figure. In fact, Mephisto is mentioned only in literature connected with the Faust legend. Goethe elevates Mephisto somewhat, placing the devil in heaven and conversing freely with God.

However, the chief devil is Satan, whose story is told in the Old Testament. Before humans were created, Satan was known as Lucifer, the Prince of Angels. When Lucifer led a revolt against God, he and his army were cast from heaven. As a devil, or "fallen angel," Satan vowed to corrupt humanity. This he accomplished in the Garden of Eden, where Satan assumed the form of a snake to entice Adam and Eve and cause their downfall.

HUMANITIES CONNECTION Several operas have been based on Goethe's *Faust*. In *Mefistofele*, by Italian composer Arrigo Boito, the devil is the central character. Samuel Ramey, pictured here, has received worldwide accolades for his performance of this role.

He seems to me, if you don't mind, Your Grace,
Like a cicada of the long-legged race,
That always flies, and, flying, springs,
And in the grass the same old ditty sings;
If only it were grass he could repose in!
There is no trash he will not poke his nose in.

The Lord:

Can you not speak but to abuse?
Do you come only to accuse?
Does nothing on the earth seem to you right?

Mephisto:

No, Lord. I find it still a rather sorry sight.
Man moves me to compassion, so wretched is his plight.
I have no wish to cause him further woe.

WORDS TO KNOW

repose (rĭ-pōz') *v.* to rest

Customizing Instruction

Less Proficient Readers

Tell students that the excerpt is divided into two scenes. In the first, called "Prologue in Heaven," Mephisto is addressing God, or the Lord. The devil proposes a bet with the Lord to gain Faust's soul, and the Lord agrees to it. In the second scene, called "Faust's Study," Mephisto confronts Faust and presents his deal. In exchange for showing Faust all the world has to offer, Mephisto will win the man's soul. Faust accepts this pact with the devil.

English Learners

Help students understand the following phrases:

- "that spark of heaven's sun" (line 14): reason; Mephisto is referring to the fact that humans are the only creatures who can reason.
- "like a cicada of the long-legged race" (line 18): Cicadas are large, winged insects; the male of the species makes a characteristic droning sound. Mephisto is comparing the behavior of humans to that of these insects.
- "the same old ditty sings" (line 20): A ditty is a simple song or tune. Mephisto claims that people repeatedly make the same mistakes.

Advanced Learners

Point out that Mephisto's conversation with the Lord contains several examples of verbal irony. Remind students that verbal irony occurs when a character says one thing but means another. Then ask students to identify instances of verbal irony in Mephisto's speeches.
Possible Responses: "Were laughing not a habit you've unlearned"; "I have no wish to cause him further woe"

MINI LESSON Viewing and Representing

Photo of Samuel Ramey

ART APPRECIATION Tell students that in Boito's opera, Mefistofele—or Mephisto—is a cool, sarcastic character. Much like Goethe's devil, he is a fascinating character whose plots and dishonesty trap Faust. Have students study the photo and the **Humanities Connection** on page 883. Then ask them what details in the devil's appearance suggest his fiendish purpose.
Possible Responses: his red jacket; pointed ears; fierce, determined expression; clenched fist

What do the devil's expression and posture suggest about what he has in mind for Faust?
Possible Response: He wants to get Faust in his clutches and seize the man's soul.

Literary Analysis METAPHOR

Remind students that a metaphor is a figure of speech that compares two things that are basically unlike but have something in common. Unlike a simile, a metaphor does not contain the words *like* or *as*. Then ask students to identify the metaphor in lines 40 and 41. Who is the gardener? Who is the tree? What do the bloom and fruit represent?

Possible Responses: The gardener is the Lord. The tree is a human being—in this case, Faust. The bloom and fruit represent the person's faith and goodness.

Active Reading CLARIFYING MEANING

A Have students reorder some of the words in lines 30–37 to help them clarify the meaning of Mephisto's speech. For example, they might reorder the wording in line 31 to read: "The poor fool's meat and drink are not earthly." Then ask students to use this technique and the sidenote to help them summarize the lines.

Possible Response: Faust is not satisfied with anything on earth, and his dissatisfaction gives him no peace.

Literary Analysis SOLILOQUY

B Tell students that a soliloquy is a speech that a character makes while alone on stage. Direct students' attention to the soliloquy on page 885. Then ask them what the speech reveals about Mephisto's attitude toward the Lord. What words and phrases in the speech support their ideas?

Possible Responses: Mephisto is disrespectful of the Lord and refers to him ironically. The phrases "Old Man" and "noble squire" support this idea.

Pause & Reflect

Possible Response: The Lord believes that Faust is a good man and will choose the "right road."

The Lord:
Do you know Faust?

Mephisto:
The doctor?

The Lord:
Aye, my servant.

Mephisto:
Lo!
He serves you most peculiarly, I think.
Not earthly are the poor fool's meat and drink.
His spirit's ferment drives him far,
And he half knows how foolish is his quest:
From heaven he demands the fairest star,
And from the earth all joys that he thinks best;
And all that's near and all that's far
Cannot soothe the upheaval in his breast.

The Lord:
Though now he serves me but confusedly,
I shall soon lead him where the vapor clears.
The gardener knows, however small the tree,
That bloom and fruit adorn its later years.

Mephisto:
What will you bet? You'll lose him yet to me,
If you will graciously connive
That I may lead him carefully.

The Lord:
As long as he may be alive,
So long you shall not be prevented.
Man errs as long as he will strive.

Mephisto:
Be thanked for that; I've never been contented
To waste my time upon the dead.
I far prefer full cheeks, a youthful curly-head.
When corpses come, I have just left the house—
I feel as does the cat about the mouse.

The Lord:
Enough—I grant that you may try to clasp him,
Withdraw this spirit from his primal source
And lead him down, if you can grasp him,

31–32 Not earthly . . . drives him far: Faust is not interested in food and drink; he is driven by the agitation in his soul.

39 I shall soon . . . where the vapor clears: The Lord will help Faust think clearly.

54 his primal source: God, or the desire for good.

WORDS TO KNOW

connive (kə-nīv') *v.* to fail to take action; secretly cooperate

MINI LESSON **Vocabulary Strategy**

USING A DICTIONARY TO DETERMINE PRECISE MEANINGS

Instruction In a dictionary, more than one sense, or meaning, is listed for most words. Meanings are usually numbered and listed from most common to least common, showing subtle but often important differences.

Practice Have students use a dictionary to look up the underlined word in each of the following sentences and write down the definition that is most appropriate for the word. In addition, as students encounter the Words to Know in their reading, have them check those definitions in the dictionary.

1. "And all that's near and all that's far / Cannot soothe the upheaval in his breast." (lines 36–37) *(a disruption or upset)*
2. "A good man . . . / Remembers the right road throughout his quest." (lines 58–59) *(a course or path)*
3. "Yet that is surely not to say / That you should join the herd you hate." (lines 88–89) *(a large number of people)*

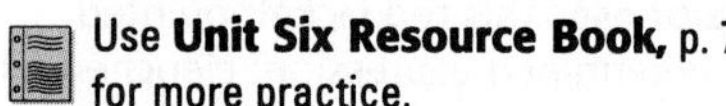

Use **Unit Six Resource Book,** p. 7, for more practice.

A lesson on using reference tools appears on p. 558 of the Pupil's Edition.

Upon your own abysmal course—
And stand abashed when you have to attest:
A good man in his darkling aspiration
Remembers the right road throughout his quest.

Mephisto:
Enough—he will soon reach his station;
About my bet I have no hesitation,
And when I win, concede your stake
And let me triumph with a swelling breast:
Dust he shall eat, and that with zest,
As my relation does, the famous snake.

The Lord:
Appear quite free on that day, too;
I never hated those who were like you:
Of all the spirits that negate,
The knavish jester gives me least to do.
For man's activity can easily abate,
He soon prefers uninterrupted rest;
To give him this companion hence seems best
Who roils and must as Devil help create.
But you, God's rightful sons, give voice
To all the beauty in which you rejoice;
And that which ever works and lives and grows
Enfold you with fair bonds that love has wrought,
And what in wavering apparition flows
That fortify with everlasting thought.
(*The heavens close, the Archangels disperse.*)

Mephisto (*alone*):

B

I like to see the Old Man now and then
And try to be not too uncivil.
It's charming in a noble squire when
He speaks humanely with the very Devil.

PAUSE & REFLECT Why does the Lord allow Mephisto to strive for Faust's soul?

57 And stand . . . attest: and be ashamed when you must admit.

58 darkling: dim; confused.

65 the famous snake: Satan, who, disguised as a serpent, tempted Eve in the Garden of Eden.

69 knavish jester: foolish joker.

71–72 He soon . . . seems best: People need a challenge to keep them from becoming lazy and complacent.

73 roils (roilz): disturbs; vexes.

74 But you, God's rightful sons: The Lord is now addressing the archangels.

WORDS TO KNOW

abate (ə-bāt') *v.* to lessen in intensity

humanely (hyo͞o-măn'lē) *adv.* in a compassionate or sympathetic way

Customizing Instruction

Less Proficient Readers

1 Tell students that Mephisto proposes his bet in lines 42–44. Have students reread the lines and restate the bet in their own words.

Possible Response: Mephisto bets that he can win Faust's soul if the Lord will let him try.

Then ask students why Mephisto chooses Faust. How does Faust's nature suggest that he may be willing to sell his soul?

Possible Response: Faust's dissatisfaction with life on earth and his desire to attain all that heaven has to offer suggest that he may be willing to sell his soul.

2 Discuss lines 51–52. Then ask students to describe how a cat feels about a mouse.

Possible Responses: A cat likes to hunt and trap a mouse. Then the cat often plays with the mouse before killing and eating it.

Point out that this is how Mephisto feels about Faust.

English Learners

Define the following words and phrases:

- "graciously connive": kindly allow
- "your own abysmal course": Mephisto's path, which leads to ruin and damnation
- "darkling aspiration": confused desires and goals
- "quest": a person's search for the path to goodness

MINI LESSON Speaking and Listening

DRAMATIC READING

Prepare Have students work in pairs to present a dramatic reading of lines 42 through 65. Point out that the personalities of the two characters speaking these lines are very different. Mephisto is sarcastic and mocking; the Lord is dignified and formal. Encourage students to use tone of voice, gestures, and facial expressions to convey the characters' personalities and underscore the differences between them.

Present Have student pairs present their readings to the class. Ask students in the audience to use the readings to describe the two characters' personalities. Then ask them to discuss how hearing the lines read aloud influenced their understanding of the characters. Finally, have students discuss which character's voice has a stronger presence and why.

This activity is particularly well suited for longer class periods.

Literary Analysis DIALOGUE

Have students compare the dialogue between Mephisto and Faust with the exchanges between Mephisto and the Lord. Then ask students what similarities they notice in the way Mephisto speaks to both characters. In what way does Mephisto treat them differently?

Possible Responses: Mephisto is sarcastic and mocking toward both. However, Mephisto shows some deference to the Lord; with Faust, the devil shows little respect.

Literary Analysis ROMANTIC HERO

Review the characteristics of a Romantic hero. Tell students that Romantic heroes are rebellious, moody figures, tormented by their emotions and frustrated with their human limits. Then ask students how these characteristics are displayed by Faust.

Possible Response: Faust is in despair and willing to sell his soul to the devil for the chance to advance his knowledge.

As students continue to read the drama, have them look for qualities that characterize Faust as a Romantic hero.

Reading Skills and Strategies
DRAWING CONCLUSIONS

Have students reread lines 100–104. Then ask them what conclusions they can draw about Faust's opinion of Mephisto.

Possible Response: Faust distrusts Mephisto and believes that the devil wants something in return for his services.

FOCUS Read to find out what happens when Mephisto presents his proposition to Faust.

Frustrated by the limits of human knowledge, Faust employs magic to summon the Spirit of the Earth. The Spirit, however, is too powerful for Faust and vanishes. Desperate to escape his earthbound life, Faust is about to take poison when he hears a choir of angels. Their song momentarily recalls him to life, but his dissatisfaction quickly resurfaces. Faust seeks to lift his spirits by walking in the countryside. There he sees a strange poodle. The dog follows Faust to his study, where the animal reveals himself to be Mephisto. Faust tries to hold the devil but in vain. Mephisto soon returns, however, and offers a remedy for Faust's unhappiness.

Faust's Study

Mephisto:

Stop playing with your melancholy
That, like a vulture, ravages your breast;
The worst of company still cures this folly,
For you are human with the rest.
Yet that is surely not to say
That you should join the herd you hate.
I'm not one of the great,
But if you want to make your way
Through the world with me united,
I should surely be delighted
To be yours, as of now,
Your companion, if you allow;
And if you like the way I behave,
I shall be your servant, or your slave.

Faust:

And in return, what do you hope to take?

Mephisto:

There's so much time—so why insist?

Faust:

No, no! The Devil is an egoist
And would not just for heaven's sake

 Assessment **Informal Assessment**

CASTING NOTES To assess students' understanding of the three main characters in *Faust*, suggest the following scenario: *You are the casting director for a dramatization of this selection. Create a casting note for the main characters (the Lord, Mephisto, and Faust) that will help the actors play their roles. Describe each character's personality traits, motives or desires, and relationship to the other characters.*

RUBRIC

3 Full Accomplishment Students accurately and concisely describe each character's personality, motives or desires, and relationship to others.

2 Substantial Accomplishment Students accurately describe characters' personalities, motives, and relationships, but descriptions are not concise.

1 Little or Partial Accomplishment Students have difficulty describing the characters and their motives, omitting or misrepresenting important details.

Christian Nickel as Faust in 2000 stage production of Goethe's *Faust*. Staged in Berlin by Peter Stein. Photograph copyright © Ruth Walz.

Turn into a philanthropist.
Make your conditions very clear;
Where such a servant lives, danger is near.

Mephisto:

1
Here you shall be the master, I be bond,
And at your nod I'll work incessantly;
But when we meet again *beyond,*
Then you shall do the same for me.

Faust:

Of the beyond I have no thought;
When you reduce this world to nought,
The other one may have its turn.
My joys come from this earth, and there,
That sun has burnt on my despair:

102 philanthropist (fĭ-lăn'thrə-pĭst): person who promotes human well-being through charitable donations or activities.

105 bond: servant or slave.

110 nought: nothing.

WORDS TO KNOW

despair (dĭ-spâr') *n.* complete loss of hope

Customizing Instruction

Less Proficient Readers

Focus Explain that the setting has changed: the scene is now set in Faust's study and Faust and Mephisto are speaking together.

Set a Purpose Tell students that Mephisto and Faust are the main characters in the drama. Have students keep track of the characters by summarizing their speeches and actions in a chart like the one below.

Characters	Speeches	Actions
Mephisto	Mephisto offers to be Faust's slave.	
Faust	Faust asks what Mephisto wants in return.	

1 Point out that in lines 105–108, Mephisto clearly states his terms. Ask students to explain what Mephisto means by *here* and *beyond.* (Here *refers to earth;* beyond *refers to the afterlife.*)

English Learners

Help students understand some of the following words and phrases in Faust's speech in lines 109–113:

- "this world": the earthly life
- "The other one": the spiritual world, or afterlife
- "That sun has burnt on my despair": The sun, a symbol of enlightenment and knowledge, has mocked Faust's desires and increased his hopelessness.

Active Reading CLARIFYING MEANING

A Ask students to paraphrase lines 141–146. To help students understand the lines, encourage them to reorder the words so that they sound more natural. They should also refer to the sidenotes and Words to Know to learn the meaning of unfamiliar words and phrases.

Possible Response: If I ever grow lazy, you may kill me. If your flattery should make me become too pleased with myself or if I become attracted by pleasure, then you may seize my soul.

Literary Analysis SARCASM

B Tell students that sarcasm refers to a type of verbal irony in which a remark's literal meaning is complimentary but the actual meaning is critical. Then ask students to explain why the remark in lines 179 through 182 is an example of sarcasm.

Possible Response: Faust seems to be politely indicating that the choice of writing instruments is up to Mephisto, but he is really ridiculing the devil for his pettiness.

Reading Skills and Strategies
COMPARE AND CONTRAST CHARACTERS

Have students compare and contrast Faust and Mephisto. Ask students what qualities the two characters have in common. How do they differ?

Possible Responses: Both are intelligent, careful, and sarcastic. However, while Faust is intensely emotional, Mephisto is flippant and controlled.

Once I have left those, I don't care:
What happens is of no concern.
I do not even wish to hear
Whether beyond they hate and love,
And whether in that other sphere
One realm's below and one above.

Mephisto:
So minded, dare it cheerfully.
Commit yourself and you shall see
My arts with joy. I'll give you more
Than any man has seen before.

Faust:
What would you, wretched Devil, offer?
Was ever a man's spirit in its noble striving
Grasped by your like, devilish scoffer?
But have you food that is not satisfying,
Red gold that rolls off without rest,
Quicksilver-like, over your skin—
A game in which no man can win—
A girl who, lying at my breast,
Ogles already to entice my neighbor,
And honor—that perhaps seems best—
Though like a comet it will turn to vapor?
Show me fruit that, before we pluck them, rot,
And trees whose foliage every day makes new!

Mephisto:
Such a commission scares me not,
With such things I can wait on you.
But, worthy friend, the time comes when we would
Recline in peace and feast on something good.

Faust:
If ever I recline, calmed, on a bed of sloth,
You may destroy me then and there.
If ever flattering you should wile me
That in myself I find delight,
If with enjoyment you beguile me,
Then break on me, eternal night!
This bet I offer.

Mephisto:
I accept it.

126 grasped: understood.

144 That in myself I find delight: I become too pleased with myself.

WORDS TO KNOW
sloth (slôth) *n.* laziness

ALCHEMY Alchemy was a mystical philosophy that flourished in medieval Europe. Alchemists aimed to transform base metals into gold. They believed that a substance called the philosopher's stone could be used in this transformation process. The stone, which alchemists thought existed in the form of a powder, could also be used to cure illnesses, prolong life, and perfect the human soul.

Eventually, alchemy became closely associated with astrology. Alchemists believed that each heavenly body represented a certain metal. For example, the sun was supposed to represent gold and Mercury was said to represent the metal mercury, also called quicksilver. Quicksilver was considered magical because it was not wet, yet was impossible to pick up. Faust refers to these properties in lines 128–129. Although alchemists failed to find the philosopher's stone, their work on chemical substances helped develop the modern science of chemistry.

Faust:

Right.
If to the moment I should say:
Abide, you are so fair—
Put me in fetters on that day,
I *wish* to perish then, I swear.
Then let the death bell ever toll,
Your service done, you shall be free,
The clock may stop, the hand may fall,
As time comes to an end for me.

Mephisto:

Consider it, for we shall not forget it.

Faust:

That is a right you need not waive.
I did not boast, and I shall not regret it.
As I grow stagnant I shall be a slave,
Whether or not to anyone indebted.

Mephisto:

At the doctor's banquet tonight I shall do
My duties as a servant without fail.
But for life's sake, or death's—just one detail:
Could you give me a line or two?

Faust:

You pedant need it black on white?
Are man and a man's word indeed new to your sight?
Is not my spoken word sufficient warrant
When it commits my life eternally?
Does not the world rush on in every torrent,
And a mere promise should hold me?
Yet this illusion our heart inherits,
And who would want to shirk his debt?
Blessed who counts loyalty among his merits.
No sacrifice will he regret.
And yet a parchment, signed and sealed, is an abhorrent
Specter that haunts us, and it makes us fret.
The word dies when we seize the pen,
And wax and leather lord it then.
What, evil spirit, do you ask?
Paper or parchment, stone or brass?
Should I use chisel, style, or quill?
It is completely up to you.

159 As I grow stagnant: if I stay as I am now.

161 the doctor's banquet: an awards dinner for professors that Faust would be attending.

165 You pedant . . . white?: Are you so narrow-minded that you need it in writing?

175–176 abhorrent (ăb-hôr′ənt) **specter:** hateful ghost or spirit.

181 style: slender, pointed writing instrument once used on wax tablets.

WORDS TO KNOW

waive (wāv) *v.* to voluntarily give up; abandon

Customizing Instruction

Less Proficient Readers

1 Read aloud lines 127–136. Explain that Faust is describing sights and experiences that are contrary to nature. For instance, Faust challenges Mephisto to produce food that does not satisfy hunger and fruit that rots before it can be picked. Discuss some of the other negative situations Faust imagines. Then help students understand that Faust wants to see these things because they are beyond the limits of human knowledge.

English Learners

Have students work with native English-speaking partners to summarize the characters' speeches. You might have half the class summarize Mephisto's speeches and the other half summarize Faust's speeches. Students can then share their summaries with the entire class.

Advanced Learners

Point out line 177: "The word dies when we seize the pen." Then invite students to explain what particular meaning this line might have for poets—particularly Romantic poets.
Possible Response: The "word," which recalls the biblical "word of God," represents pure thought. When poets try to translate pure thought into words, the thought becomes corrupted and loses its true meaning. The line suggests the desire of Romantic poets to become Godlike in their writing.

MINI LESSON Speaking and Listening

INTERVIEW

Prepare Have pairs of students role-play an interview with either Mephisto or Faust. Encourage interviewers to ask questions that examine the characters' motives, desires, and opinions. Interviewees should make sure their answers are consistent with what they know about the characters' personalities. Share with students the following guidelines for conducting an interview:

- Interviewers should prepare their questions ahead of time.
- Interviewers should avoid asking "yes-or-no" questions.
- Interviewers should be prepared to revise questions or follow the interviewee's line of thinking if it is interesting or relevant.
- Interviewees should gather their thoughts before responding.
- Interviewees' answers should be appropriate to the questions asked.

Present Have several student pairs conduct their interviews before the class. At the end of each interview, ask students what they have learned about the character. You might also invite the audience to pose their own questions.

This activity is particularly well suited for longer class periods.

Pause & Reflect

Possible Responses: Faust will lose his soul if he ever becomes lazy or complacent. The devil might think that signing in blood symbolizes the seriousness of the pact and creates a strong bond between them.

Literary Analysis DIALOGUE

After students read pages 890 and 891, ask them what the dialogue reveals about Mephisto's opinion of Faust. What does the devil seem to think Faust wants? Does Mephisto understand Faust?

Possible Responses: Mephisto thinks that Faust wants to experience all the world's pleasures, but Faust has no desire to feel joy and happiness.

Literary Analysis HYPERBOLE

A Tell students that hyperbole is a figure of speech in which the truth is exaggerated for emphasis. Have students read lines 220–224. Then ask them to identify an example of hyperbole in these lines. (*"contain / Within my spirit summit and abyss"*) What does the hyperbole emphasize about Faust's state of mind?

Possible Response: The hyperbole emphasizes Faust's deep desire to learn everything within heaven and earth; it suggests that he would be willing to do anything to gain this knowledge.

Reading Skills and Strategies EVALUATING

Ask students to discuss their opinion of Faust.

Possible Responses: Some students may think Faust is sympathetic and understand his frustration with life. Others may think he is too proud and believe he should be satisified with life.

Do students think Faust should have signed the pact with Mephisto? Why or why not?

Possible Responses: Some students will think that Faust should not have signed the pact because he can't win. Others will think Faust was right to sign because the deal will give him a chance at experiences not possible for most humans.

Mephisto:

Why get so hot and overdo
Your rhetoric? Why must you shrill?
Use any sheet, it is the same;
And with a drop of blood you sign your name.

Faust:

If you are sure you like this game,
Let it be done to humor you.

Mephisto:

Blood is a very special juice.

PAUSE & REFLECT According to Faust's own terms, under what conditions will he lose his soul? Why do you suppose the devil wants to sign the pact in blood?

FOCUS As you continue reading, think about what types of knowledge and experience Faust hopes to gain from the bargain with Mephisto.

Faust:

You need not fear that someday I retract.
That all my striving I unloose
Is the whole purpose of the pact.
Oh, I was puffed up all too boldly,
At your rank only is my place.
The lofty spirit spurned me coldly,
And nature hides from me her face.
Torn is the subtle thread of thought,
I loathe the knowledge I once sought.
In sensuality's abysmal land
Let our passions drink their fill!
In magic veils, not pierced by skill,
Let every wonder be at hand!
Plunge into time's whirl that dazes my sense,
Into the torrent of events!
And let enjoyment, distress,
Annoyance and success
Succeed each other as best they can;
For restless activity proves a man.

191 unloose: unleash; give free rein to.

194 At your rank . . . place: Faust suggests that his pride places him on a level with the devil.

Mephisto:

You are not bound by goal or measure.
If you would nibble everything

MINI LESSON **Speaking and Listening**

DRAMATIC READING

Prepare Invite a volunteer to prepare a dramatic reading of lines 190–208, in which Faust describes himself and what he expects from the bargain with Mephisto. Before the performance, explain to listening students that the volunteer will do two readings of the lines.

Present During the first reading, have listeners close their eyes and listen for meaning and mood. Then, during the second reading, have listeners jot down any repeated sounds or rhymes they hear and any particularly striking images. After both readings, discuss students' reactions and impressions. Ask them what the lines suggest about Faust's state of mind.

This activity is particularly well suited for longer class periods.

Bruno Ganz as Faust and Adam Oest as Mephisto in 2000 stage production of Goethe's *Faust*. Staged in Berlin by Peter Stein. Photograph copyright © Ruth Walz.

HUMANITIES CONNECTION This photograph is of a rare live production of both parts of *Faust*, staged in Berlin. The marathon presentation of the drama took 21 hours—15 for the performance itself, 6 for intermissions.

Or snatch up something on the wing,
You're welcome to what gives you pleasure.
But help yourself and don't be coy!

213 coy: shy in a false way.

Faust:

Do you not hear, I have no thought of joy!
The reeling whirl I seek, the most painful excess,
Enamored hate and quickening distress.
Cured from the craving to know all, my mind
Shall not henceforth be closed to any pain,
1 And what is portioned out to all mankind,
I shall enjoy deep in my self, contain
Within my spirit summit and abyss,
Pile on my breast their agony and bliss,
And thus let my own self grow into theirs, unfettered,
Till as they are, at last I, too, am shattered.

Customizing Instruction

Less Proficient Readers

1 Explain that in lines 214–224, Faust tells what he hopes to gain from his deal with the devil. Tell students that Faust wishes to learn everything and feel everything—even experiences that cause pain or distress. Then ask students what they would give anything to learn, experience, or acquire.

English Learners

Students may be confused by Faust's assertion in line 208 that "restless activity proves a man." Tell students the line means that constant action is necessary for success. Explain that Faust wants to be so busy that he has no time to think.

Advanced Learners

Have students identify examples of paradox in Faust's speech in lines 214–224. *(enamored hate, quickening distress)* Then ask students to describe the effect of these paradoxes.

Possible Response: The paradoxes underscore Faust's confused emotional state of mind as well as his desire to achieve seemingly contradictory goals.

MINI LESSON Viewing and Representing

Photo of Stage Production of *Faust*

ART APPRECIATION Tell students that the director of the stage production of *Faust* followed Goethe's stage directions as closely as possible. He also had his actors recite every one of the 12,111 lines in the two-part drama. Have students study the photo and the **Humanities Connection** on page 891. Point out that Faust and Mephisto seem to be discussing the terms of the bet. Then ask them what details in the photo suggest the setting of the scene they are reading.

Possible Responses: the books and papers, Faust's chair

What details of appearance and behavior distinguish the characters?

Possible Responses: Faust is dressed in his professor's gown and seems to be intent on making a point. Mephisto is dressed in a red cape and seems to be listening closely but skeptically.

Reading and Analyzing

Literary Analysis IRONY

Tell students that verbal irony occurs when a character says one thing but means another. Point out that Mephisto's reference to Faust's "worthy head" is an example of verbal irony because the devil has nothing but contempt for Faust. Ask students what effect this type of irony has on the reader.

Possible Responses: The irony makes the reader more suspicious of Mephisto; it also encourages the reader to be more critical.

Active Reading CLARIFYING MEANING

A Have students clarify lines 242–245 by asking them to summarize each line in a single word. For example, the word *courage* might summarize line 242, "The lion's daring."

Possible Response: "The swiftness of the hind"—speediness; "The northerner's forbearing"— caution; "And the Italian's fiery mind"—creativity

Reading Skills and Strategies
MAKING INFERENCES

B Have students read lines 255–258. Then ask them what they can infer about Mephisto's opinion of Faust's aspirations.

Possible Response: Mephisto doesn't take them seriously. He doesn't think it's possible for Faust to achieve his goals.

What can you infer about Mephisto's repeated use of the pronoun *we* when talking to Faust?

Possible Response: Mephisto's trying to suggest that he and Faust are on the same side and, by extension, that he has Faust's interests at heart.

Mephisto:
Believe me who for many a thousand year
Has chewed this cud and never rested,
That from the cradle to the bier
The ancient leaven cannot be digested.
Trust one like me, this whole array
Is for a God—there's no contender:
He dwells in his eternal splendor,
To darkness we had to surrender,
And you need night as well as day.

Faust:
And yet it is my will.

Mephisto:
It does sound bold.
But I'm afraid, though you are clever,
Time is too brief, though art's forever.
Perhaps you're willing to be told.
Why don't you find yourself a poet,
And let the gentleman ransack his dreams:
And when he finds a noble trait, let him bestow it
Upon your worthy head in reams and reams:
A
The lion's daring,
The swiftness of the hind,
The northerner's forbearing
And the Italian's fiery mind,
Let him resolve the mystery
How craft can be combined with magnanimity,
Or how a passion-crazed young man
Might fall in love after a plan.
If there were such a man, I'd like to meet him,
As Mr. Microcosm I would greet him.

Faust:
Alas, what am I, if I can
Not reach for mankind's crown which merely mocks
Our senses' craving like a star?

Mephisto:
B
You're in the end—just what you are!
Put wigs on with a million locks
And put your foot on ell-high socks,
You still remain just what you are.

228 The ancient leaven: all the experience and sensation that the world has to offer.

241 reams and reams: very large amounts.

247 How craft . . . magnanimity (măg'nə-nĭm'ĭ-tē): how cunning can be combined with a noble heart.

251 Mr. Microcosm (mī'krə-kŏz'əm): a person who would embody all the qualities that Mephisto has named.

257 ell-high socks: An ell is a measurement 45 inches long.

Cross Curricular Link **Humanities**

EARLY FAUST TALES In 1587, a collection of tales about Faust called the *Faustbuch (Faust Book)* was published anonymously. Many of the tales were based on the exploits of such magicians and alchemists as Merlin and Roger Bacon but were attributed to Faust. The tales were crudely written and filled with broad humor directed at those whom Faust tricked. However, the descriptions of Mephisto and hell were designed to frighten the reader and serve as a warning to would-be sinners.

Nonetheless, magic manuals with Faust's name on them became very popular after the publication of the *Faustbuch.* In addition to other spells, the manuals contained detailed instructions on how to avoid or break a deal made with the devil.

Faust:

I feel, I gathered up and piled up high
In vain the treasures of the human mind:
When I sit down at last, I cannot find
New strength within—it is all dry.
My stature has not grown a whit,
No closer to the Infinite.

Mephisto:

Well, my good sir, to put it crudely,
You see matters just as they lie;
We have to look at them more shrewdly,
Or all life's pleasures pass us by.
Your hands and feet—indeed that's trite—
And head and seat are yours alone;
Yet all in which I find delight,
Should they be less my own?

271–272 Yet all . . . less my own?: Shouldn't I possess all the things that give me pleasure?

WORDS TO KNOW

stature (stăch'ər) *n.* status or importance gained by growth or achievement

Customizing Instruction

Less Proficient Readers

Explain the concept of "Mr. Microcosm." Tell students that a microcosm is a small system or world that contains all the elements—and contradictions—of a much larger system. Mephisto suggests that Faust, who is frustrated with his earthbound limitations, would like to embody all of the characteristics and opposing forces of the universe.

English Learners

Explain the meaning of the following lines:

- "That from the cradle to the bier" (line 227): The "cradle" represents birth; the "bier," or coffin, represents death. Thus, the line means "in a person's entire lifetime."
- "The ancient leaven cannot be digested" (line 228): Humans cannot understand, or digest, all the experience and sensation that the world has to offer.
- "Time is too brief, though art's forever" (line 236): Mephisto is referring to the idea that, while life is fleeting, a work of art lives on forever.
- "My stature has not grown a whit" (line 263): Faust says that the knowledge he has accumulated has not increased his standing at all.
- "No closer to the Infinite" (line 264): The "Infinite" refers to God. Faust is lamenting the fact that he has not achieved a Godlike understanding of the world.

FAUST 893

Literary Analysis SOLILOQUY

A Have a volunteer read aloud Mephisto's soliloquy on page 894. Then ask students to explain what Mephisto plans to do to Faust. (*tempt him with all life has to offer but without satisfying any of his real desires*) What does the soliloquy reveal about Mephisto's true attitude toward Faust?
Possible Response: Mephisto has nothing but contempt for Faust.

How does this attitude contrast with Mephisto's manner when he made the deal with Faust?
Possible Response: When Mephisto made the deal with Faust, the devil was friendlier and more sympathetic.

Reading Skills and Strategies PREDICTING

Point out that the dialogue between Mephisto and the student is not included in this excerpt. Ask students to predict what Mephisto will say to the young man. Do they think that the devil will speak seriously—as Faust would—to the student? Or might Mephisto try to corrupt the young man?
Possible Response: Answers will vary, but most students will suppose that Mephisto will try to corrupt the student. You might read aloud the deleted lines in class so that students can find out whether their predictions were correct.

Suppose I buy myself six steeds:
I buy their strength; while I recline
I dash along at whirlwind speeds,
For their two dozen legs are mine.
Come on! Let your reflections rest
And plunge into the world with zest!
I say, the man that speculates
Is like a beast that in the sand,
Led by an evil spirit, round and round gyrates,
And all about lies gorgeous pasture land.

279 the man that speculates: someone who thinks too much.

281 gyrates (jī'rāts'): spins.

Faust:
How shall we set about it?

Mephisto:
Simply leave. . . .

A student appears outside Faust's study. When Faust exclaims that he doesn't want to see the student, Mephisto dons the doctor's cap and gown. After the soliloquy that appears here, Mephisto will pretend to be Faust while the doctor prepares for their trip.

Some fifteen minutes should be all I need;
Meanwhile get ready for our trip, and speed!
(Faust *exit.*)

Mephisto (*in* Faust's *long robe*):
Have but contempt for reason and for science,
Man's noblest force spurn with defiance,
Subscribe to magic and illusion,
The Lord of Lies aids your confusion,
And, pact or no, I hold you tight.—
The spirit which he has received from fate
Sweeps ever onward with unbridled might,
Its hasty striving is so great
It leaps over the earth's delights.
Through life I'll drag him at a rate,
Through shallow triviality,
That he shall writhe and suffocate;
And his insatiability,
With greedy lips, shall see the choicest plate
And ask in vain for all that he would cherish—
And were he not the Devil's mate
And had not signed, he still must perish.

A

289 The Lord of Lies: the devil.

296 shallow triviality: all that is of no importance or consequence.

Humanities

WHAT HAPPENS NEXT IN *FAUST* Soon after Mephisto and Faust set off on their adventures, they encounter Gretchen, with whom Faust falls in love. Eager to seduce the young woman, he persuades her to give her mother a sleeping potion, which proves fatal. The situation becomes more desperate after Gretchen discovers she is pregnant and Faust kills the young woman's brother in a street fight. Mephisto tries to erase Gretchen from Faust's memory, but the woman draws Faust back to her. He finds her in prison, where she has been wrongly condemned to death for killing her baby. *Part 1* ends with Gretchen's refusal to escape with Faust and her subsequent redemption.

While *Part 1* deals with the world of private emotion, *Part 2* deals with the world of public affairs. Faust uses magic to aid an emperor and conjure up the spirit of Helen of Troy. At the end of the drama, an aged Faust realizes a dream by developing a large piece of land and making it prosper. When he expresses his satisfaction, Faust falls down dead. Mephisto steps in to claim the man's soul, but heavenly spirits, led by Gretchen, drive the devil away. The play ends as Faust's soul is carried off to heaven.

FROM

Letter to His Friends

Johann Wolfgang von Goethe

Johann Wolfgang von Goethe (1828), J. K. Stieler. Oil on canvas. The Granger Collection, New York.

Goethe wrote this letter to a friend near the end of his two-year stay in Italy. The letter reveals his eagerness to resume writing as well as his reawakened interest in the Faust legend.

March 1, 1788

It has been a week of rich experience for me, and seems like a month in my memory. First I drew up a plan for "Faust,"[1] and I trust it will be a successful one. To write this play now is, of course, a very different thing from what it was fifteen years ago. I think it will lose nothing by its long suspension, especially as I now believe I have recovered the thread. Also in respect to the tone in general I feel content. I have already written out a new scene, and if I fumigate[2] the paper, nobody, I should think, would recognize it from the old.

—Translated by Berthold Biermann

1. **drew up a plan for "Faust":** At this time, Goethe was revising his first version of the play, which would be published as *Faust, Ein Fragment* in 1790.
2. **fumigate:** use smoke or fumes to disinfect. Goethe is saying that he could use smoke to make the new paper appear old.

Customizing Instruction

Less Proficient Readers
Make sure students understand why Mephisto puts on Faust's robe. Explain that the devil is preparing to talk to one of Faust's students while Faust himself prepares for his journey.

Have students complete the charts that they began on page 887. Ask students to use their charts to summarize the scene in Faust's study.
Possible Response: Mephisto appears before Faust and offers to make a deal with him. In exchange for Faust's soul, Mephisto will be his slave on earth. Faust accepts the bargain. Mephisto may seize Faust's soul only when the latter expresses contentment.

Related Reading
More About Johann Wolfgang von Goethe Goethe undertook his trip to Italy in great secrecy. Determined to escape his duties at Weimar, which he had come to regard as a "terrible disease," Goethe set out on his travels, disguised as a merchant. Seeking to renew himself, the poet cut himself off from his cultural past and embraced the classical forms he admired in Italy. Resolving to "occupy myself only with lasting conditions," Goethe revised and completed several works he had begun previously.

Discussion Questions

1. In his letter, Goethe refers to the tone of his play. How would you describe the tone of the letter?
   Possible Responses: hopeful, positive, humorous
2. What does the letter reveal about Goethe's attempts to write a play about Faust?
   Possible Response: The drama is difficult to write, but Goethe is determined to finish it.

MINI LESSON **Grammar**

INDEPENDENT AND SUBORDINATE CLAUSES
Instruction Remind students that there are two kinds of clauses: independent and subordinate. An independent clause, or main clause, can stand alone as a complete sentence. However, a subordinate clause cannot stand alone; it depends on an independent clause to form a complete sentence. Subordinate clauses often begin with subordinating conjunctions such as *after, because, since, that, when,* and *which* and relative pronouns such as *who, whom, whose, which,* and *that.*

Practice Have students copy the following sentences. Ask them to identify the underlined clauses as independent or subordinate.

1. "When I sit down at last, I cannot find / New strength within—it is all dry." (lines 261–262) *(subordinate)*
2. "Stop playing with your melancholy / That, like a vulture, ravages your breast" (lines 84–85) *(independent)*
3. "Where such a servant lives, danger is near." (line 104) *(independent)*

For more instruction and practice in independent and subordinate clauses, use McDougal Littell's ***Language Network:***
- Grade 10, Chapter 4, "Clauses and Sentence Structure"
- Grade 12, Chapter 3, "Using Clauses"

Connect to the Literature

1. **What Do You Think?** Students will probably be horrified by the deal and believe that Faust has placed himself in grave danger.

Comprehension Check

- Among other things, Faust challenges Mephisto to show him food that isn't satisfying, fruit that rots before it's picked, and trees whose foliage renews every day.
- Faust claims that his knowledge hasn't made him equal to God, which is his ambition.

 Use Selection Quiz in **Unit Six Resource Book,** p. 8.

Think Critically

2. On earth, Mephisto will work hard for Faust. After Faust dies, however, he will be enslaved to the devil.
3. Possible Responses: Faust doesn't seem to think that Mephisto can be trusted. The devil seems to underestimate Faust and think that he is primarily interested in seeking pleasure.
4. Possible Responses: Faust is melancholy and brooding; he wants to experience and feel everything intensely; he feels that he has unlimited potential.
5. Possible Response: Some people are never satisfied; they always want more.

Extend Interpretations

6. **What If?** Possible Responses: Some students will think that Mephisto would have pursued his plan because it is the devil's nature to challenge authority. Others will claim that Mephisto would not have been able to approach Faust without the Lord's approval.
7. **Critic's Corner** Possible Responses: Students may cite Mephisto's wit and sarcasm in his dealings with the Lord and Faust.
8. **Connect to Life** Possible Responses: Some students will say that constant action is necessary in today's world to keep up with the competition. Others will say that success is meaningless without taking time for reflection and relaxation.

Connect to the Literature

1. **What Do You Think?** What is your reaction to the deal Faust makes with Mephisto? Share your response in a classroom discussion.

Comprehension Check

- What are some of the things Faust challenges Mephisto to show him?
- Why is Faust dissatisfied with the knowledge he has gained from his academic studies?

Think Critically

2. **ACTIVE READING: CLARIFYING MEANING** Get together with a classmate and discuss the passages you recorded in your  READER'S NOTEBOOK. Work together to clarify the meaning of any passages that still confuse you. Then use paraphrasing to restate lines 105–108 in your own words.
3. What seems to be Faust's opinion of Mephisto? What does the devil think of Faust? Provide details that support your answer.
4. Based on what you have learned about the Romantic hero, what characteristics of this type of hero does Faust display?

   THINK ABOUT
   - Mephisto's remark to Faust, "Stop playing with your melancholy" (line 84)
   - the desire Faust expresses when he says, "I shall enjoy deep in my self, contain / Within my spirit summit and abyss" (lines 220–221)
   - Faust's lament, "Alas, what am I, if I can / Not reach for mankind's crown" (lines 252–253)
5. What do you think is the most important **theme,** or message about human nature, conveyed by this selection?

Extend Interpretations

6. **What If?** Suppose that the Lord had not allowed Mephisto to strike his bargain with Faust. Do you think that the devil would have pursued his plan anyway and challenged Faust? Why or why not?
7. **Critic's Corner** According to critic Irmgard Wagner, "against Faust's emotional and spiritual nature," Mephisto is "cool intelligence." What evidence in the excerpt you've read supports this characterization of the devil?
8. **Connect to Life** Faust claims that "restless activity proves a man." In today's world, do you think this is true? Is constant action necessary to achieve success? Explain your answer.

LITERARY ANALYSIS: DIALOGUE

Dialogue—the written conversation between two or more people—helps bring characters in a drama to life by providing insight into their personalities. It also reveals the relationships between the characters. Read the following lines of dialogue between the Lord and Mephisto:

The Lord: Can you not speak but to abuse? / Do you come only to accuse? / Does nothing on the earth seem to you right?

Mephisto: No, Lord. I find it still a rather sorry sight. / Man moves me to compassion, so wretched is his plight. / I have no wish to cause him further woe.

The conversation reveals Mephisto's ironic wit and his teasing relationship with the Lord.

Cooperative Learning Activity With a small group of classmates, choose two or three examples of dialogue from the excerpt. Then use a chart like the one below to list the personality traits revealed by the dialogue. Also, indicate what the dialogue suggests about the relationships between the characters.

Dialogue	Traits Revealed	Relationships Revealed

SOLILOQUY A **soliloquy** is a speech in a dramatic work that a character makes while alone on stage. In the speech, the character reveals his or her thoughts to the audience. Reread Mephisto's soliloquy at the end of the excerpt from *Faust.* What does the speech reveal about Mephisto's motives?

Literary Analysis

Cooperative Learning Activity Write the chart on the board and have groups take turns adding their data. Discuss the entries in class.

 Use **Unit Six Resource Book,** p. 6, for more practice.

Soliloquy Possible Response: The soliloquy reveals Mephisto's intention to confound Faust and destroy him.

Writing Options

1. Divine Dialogue Write a dialogue between Faust and the Lord after Faust signs his pact with Mephisto. Have Faust explain what he hopes to gain from the bargain, and have the Lord offer some advice. Make sure the dialogue reveals each character's personality.

2. Story of Ambition A "Faustian bargain" is a decision to betray one's values in order to gain power, wealth, or some other advantage. Write a story about someone who makes a Faustian bargain. First, decide what your main character wishes to gain and what values he or she will betray. Then plan other story elements, including setting, plot, and additional characters. You might want to create an events chart to help you organize the story's action.

Writing Handbook
See page R29: Narrative Writing.

Activities & Explorations

1. Character Portrait Draw a picture of what you think Faust or Mephisto might look like. Your portrait should convey the character's personality as it is revealed by the dialogue in the excerpt you just read. ~ **ART**

2. Dramatic Reading With a classmate, prepare a dramatic reading of one of the scenes in *Faust.* First, rehearse your lines and discuss what tones and gestures you should use in delivering them. Then present the scene to the class. If you like, play background music during the performance that reflects the mood of the scene. ~ **PERFORMING**

Inquiry & Research

Who Was Faust? Find out more about the real Faust and share your discoveries with the class.

Vocabulary in Action

EXERCISE: CONTEXT CLUES Write the word that best completes each sentence.

1. Mephisto seemed a _______ fellow, pleasant and agreeable to talk to.
2. Yet his mind was firmly made up: he was _______ in his desire to ensnare Faust.
3. Mephisto thought that to succeed, he needed the Lord to plot, or _______, with him.
4. Though he spoke to Faust _______, Mephisto would show him no kindness.
5. He simply wanted to win over someone of Faust's importance and _______.
6. Faust knew the shortcomings of the world: hate instead of love, _______ rather than hard work.
7. Still, his desire to experience the world did not _______; instead, it increased in intensity.
8. He was willing to _______ all chance for salvation to get what he wanted.
9. Would Faust ever regret his decision and feel _______ over his terrible bargain?
10. When his life was over, would he not want to cease his activity and _______ with the Lord?

WORDS TO KNOW

abate	genial	resolute	waive
connive	humanely	sloth	
despair	repose	stature	

Building Vocabulary
For an in-depth study of context clues, see page 674.

Writing Options

1. **Divine Dialogue** You might make this a paired activity and have partners work together to write the dialogue. Invite volunteers to read their dialogue to the class.
2. **Story of Ambition** Compile the stories into one volume that the class can share.

Activities & Explorations

1. **Character Portrait** Before students begin drawing their character portraits, have them identify lines of dialogue that reveal the character's personality.
2. **Dramatic Reading** Encourage students to choose a scene in which the conflict between the two characters is evident or a central theme is discussed.

Inquiry & Research

Who Was Faust? Discuss the legends in class. Ask students to identify ways in which the character in the legends is similar to the character in Goethe's *Faust.*

Vocabulary in Action

1. genial
2. resolute
3. connive
4. humanely
5. stature
6. sloth
7. abate
8. waive
9. despair
10. repose

To assess skills and concepts taught in this selection, use **Formal Assessment Book,** pp. 133–134.

FAUST 897

Assign the poems by William Wordsworth and the Romantic poetry by José Martí and Uvavnuk to prepare students for the sample writing assessment provided on page 909. Use the **Points of Comparison** chart to guide students in identifying the similarities and differences between the Wordsworth poems and those by Martí and Uvavnuk.

Use **Unit Six Resource Book,** p. 9, for more practice.

Romantic Poetry

OVERVIEW

Poets of the Romantic period celebrated strong emotions, the imagination, and above all, nature. In fact, Romantic poetry is often called nature poetry. However, Romantic poets did not merely describe the natural world they saw around them. They looked to nature for inspiration and spiritual comfort.

In this lesson you will read two poems by the well-known British Romantic poet William Wordsworth. You will also read a poem by the Cuban poet José Martí and one by the Inuk (Eskimo) poet Uvavnuk. Martí and Uvavnuk composed their poems after the Romantic period had ended in Europe. Although Wordsworth, Martí, and Uvavnuk lived in different times and places, they are connected by their love of nature. In the pages that follow, you will be asked to compare and contrast the works of all three poets. Comparing poems of the Romantic period with two written outside of the period will help you identify similarities and differences in Romantic poetry across cultures.

Points of Comparison

Analyzing the Poem Create a chart like the one shown to help you take notes about the poems. First you will analyze the two Wordsworth poems in depth. Later you will compare them with the poems by Martí and Uvavnuk.

	"The World Is Too Much With Us" (Wordsworth)	"My Heart Leaps Up" (Wordsworth)	from *Simple Verses* (Martí)	"Shaman Song" (Uvavnuk)
Speaker's Point of View				
Images of Nature				
Mood Suggested by the Images				
Poet's Tone				
Comparisons Made				
Poet's View of Nature				

Standardized Test Practice: Comparison-and-Contrast Essay After you have finished reading all the poems, you will be asked to write a comparison-and-contrast essay. Your notes will help you plan and write the essay.

Assessment Standardized Test Practice

COMPARISON-AND-CONTRAST ESSAY To provide practice to students in comparing literature from different times and cultures, have them read both sections in this **Comparing Literature** feature—Poems by William Wordsworth and Romantic Poetry from Other Cultures—rather than treating each section separately. Have them work with the chart shown here on page 898, filling it out as they finish reading each section. (Examples of how to fill out the chart are supplied on pages 904 and 908.) A sample assessment writing prompt and guidelines for responding to it in writing are on page 909.

POEMS BY

WILLIAM WORDSWORTH

William Wordsworth 1770–1850

A Romantic Legend William Wordsworth is considered one of the great English poets. Powerfully imaginative and inspired by the beauty of nature, he became a leader of the Romantic movement in England. He was born in the beautiful Lake District of northern England. There he stored up images and emotions that would later find their way into his writing. In 1795, Wordsworth and his sister, Dorothy, settled in the county of Dorset, not far from where the poet Samuel Taylor Coleridge was living. The remarkable friendship that developed between the poets eventually led to the publication of *Lyrical Ballads* (1798), Wordsworth and Coleridge's famous collection of poetry, which signaled the beginning of Romanticism in England. Wordsworth was named Britain's poet laureate in 1843.

Build Background

The Importance of Nature Wordsworth claimed that people could understand their own feelings only by living a simple life, one close to nature. Drawing on images from nature and common experience and allowing his imagination free play, he made fresh observations about life and the world around him. In "The World Is Too Much With Us," for instance, the sea inspires the poet to think about mighty Greek gods.

Connect to Your Life

Think about a favorite natural setting, such as a prairie, a beach, or a mountain cliff. With a partner, discuss the setting and the images and feelings it inspires.

Focus Your Reading

LITERARY ANALYSIS: FIGURATIVE LANGUAGE

Language that communicates meaning beyond the literal meaning of the words is called **figurative language.** Similes, metaphors, and personification are types of figurative language. A **simile** uses the word *like* or *as* to make a comparison. A **metaphor** makes a comparison without using *like* or *as.* In **personification,** human qualities are attributed to an object, animal, or idea. As you read the following poems by Wordsworth, look for examples of these types of figurative language.

ACTIVE READING: DRAWING CONCLUSIONS ABOUT MEANING

When you **draw conclusions** about the meaning of a text, you make logical judgments based on information you already know and details in the work. For instance, in Wordsworth's "The World Is Too Much With Us," details such as "Getting and spending" might lead you to conclude that "the world" refers to the world of money and possessions.

READER'S NOTEBOOK As you read Wordsworth's poems, use details and your own knowledge to record the conclusions you draw about meaning.

Objectives

- understand and appreciate **Romantic poetry (Literary Analysis)**
- identify types of **figurative language** in poetry **(Literary Analysis)**
- use imagery to identify **theme** in poetry **(Literary Analysis)**
- use details to **draw conclusions** about meaning in poetry **(Active Reading)**

Thematic Link

Like other Romantic poets, William Wordsworth listened to the **expressions of his heart** to make fresh observations about nature and the world around him.

5-Minute Warm-Up

Daily Language SkillBuilder

Have students **proofread** the display sentences on page 869i and write them correctly.

TIME MANAGEMENT

If you wish to cover only one of the selections, use . . .

- Preparing to Read, p. 899 or p. 905
- Thinking Through the Literature, p. 903 or p. 908

If you want to take advantage of longer blocks of class time, use . . .

- TE Teaching Options: Viewing and Representing, p. 901; Cross Curricular Link, pp. 902 and 906
- Related Reading, p. 902
- Choices & Challenges, p. 904

Literary Analysis
FIGURATIVE LANGUAGE

Point out that both of the Wordsworth poems use the human heart as a metaphor. Ask students what the heart represents in both poems.
Possible Responses: the human spirit, human nature, emotions, ability to feel

Use **Unit Six Resource Book,** p. 11, for more practice.

Literary Analysis THEME

Tell students that theme is a perception or message about life or human nature in a work of literature. In poetry, imagery and figurative language help convey theme. Then ask students what the two poems suggest about life.
Possible Response: The poems suggest that life is greatly enhanced by a close relationship with nature.

Active Reading
DRAWING CONCLUSIONS ABOUT MEANING

Have students reread these lines from "The World Is Too Much With Us": "For this, for every thing, we are out of tune; / It moves us not." Ask students what "this" refers to. *(the beauty and majesty of nature)* Then ask them what conclusions they can draw about the meaning of the lines.
Possible Responses: People are unaware of or disconnected from nature; it does not stir our emotions.

Use **Unit Six Resource Book,** p. 10, for more practice.

The World Is Too Much With Us

William Wordsworth

The world is too much with us; late and soon,
Getting and spending, we lay waste our powers:
Little we see in Nature that is ours;
We have given our hearts away, a sordid boon!
This Sea that bares her bosom to the moon;
The winds that will be howling at all hours,
And are up-gathered now like sleeping flowers;
For this, for every thing, we are out of tune;
It moves us not.—Great God! I'd rather be
A Pagan suckled in a creed outworn;
So might I, standing on this pleasant lea,
Have glimpses that would make me less forlorn;
Have sight of Proteus rising from the sea;
Or hear old Triton blow his wreathèd horn.

4 sordid boon: degrading gift.

10 a Pagan: a non-Christian (in this case, a worshiper of the gods of ancient Greece).

11 lea (lē): meadow.

13–14 Proteus (prō'tē-əs) . . . **Triton** (trīt'n): sea gods of Greek mythology.

British Iron Company's Works at Corngraves, near Halesowen, West Midlands, c. 1835. Oxford Science Archive, Oxford, Great Britain. Photo © HIP/Art Resource, NY.

HUMANITIES CONNECTION This painting reflects the development of the Industrial Revolution. Wordsworth believed that industrialization would destroy communities and the countryside. The poet particularly criticized child labor, which he felt would deny children an education through nature.

LESSON RESOURCES

UNIT SIX RESOURCE BOOK,
pp. 9–12

ASSESSMENT RESOURCES
Formal Assessment, pp. 135–136
Teacher's Guide to Assessment and Portfolio Use
Test Generator

INTEGRATED TECHNOLOGY
Visit our Web Site: classzone.com

ADDITIONAL RESOURCES
Lesson Planning Guide, pp. 115–116
Teacher's Sourcebook for Language Development

My Heart Leaps Up

William Wordsworth

The Passing Shower (1868), George Inness. Courtesy of the Canajoharie Library and Art Gallery, Canajoharie, New York.

My heart leaps up when I behold
    A rainbow in the sky:
So was it when my life began;
So is it now I am a man;
So be it when I shall grow old,
    Or let me die!
The Child is father of the Man;
And I could wish my days to be
Bound each to each by natural piety.

9 piety (pī′ĭ-tē): religious feeling and devotion.

Customizing Instruction

Less Proficient Readers

Tell students that reading poetry aloud can help them identify mood. Encourage them to get together with a partner and take turns reading the Wordsworth poems aloud. While one student reads, the other should listen for images and tone of voice that suggest mood. After students have finished reading the poems, ask them to discuss the mood in each poem.

Possible Responses: "The World Is Too Much With Us": sad, yearning, angry; "My Heart Leaps Up": happy, hopeful, pious

English Learners

Pair English learners with native English speakers. Have the pairs work together to paraphrase the two poems, sentence by sentence.

Help students understand some of the difficult words and phrases in the two poems:

- "suckled": brought up on; taught at an early age
- "a creed outworn": an old system of belief
- "forlorn": sad, alone
- "The Child is father of the Man": A child's impressions and experiences determine who he or she will be as an adult.

Advanced Learners

Encourage students to read Wordsworth's Preface to *Lyrical Ballads.* This essay-like introduction will give them insight not only into Wordsworth and his poetry, but into much of Romantic poetry.

MINI LESSON Viewing and Representing

British Iron Company's Works at Congraves

ART APPRECIATION Have students study the painting and the **Humanities Connection** on page 900. Then ask them to compare it with the one by George Inness on page 901. What different images do the two paintings present of the relationship between humans and nature?

Possible Responses: The painting on page 900 presents an image of nature that has been destroyed by humans; the Inness painting presents an image in which humans live in harmony with nature.

How do the images in each painting help convey the mood of the poem with which it appears?

Possible Responses: The images of nature destroyed by industry in the painting on page 900 convey the mood of despair in "The World Is Too Much With Us." The images of the rainbow and bucolic landscape in the Inness painting convey the peaceful, joyful mood of "My Heart Leaps Up."

COMPARING LITERATURE ACROSS CULTURES 901

Related Reading

Dorothy Wordsworth (1771–1855), the only girl of five children, was separated from her brothers after their mother died in 1778. However, she and her brother William had a strong bond. At age 24, she went to keep house for him, and the two became inseparable. It was then that they met Samuel Taylor Coleridge (1772–1834), and the three developed a close friendship. In 1829, she suffered from a severe illness, and she spent the last 20 years of her life both mentally and physically disabled.

Although Dorothy privately circulated her manuscripts and allowed William to publish portions as part of his own prose, she had no real desire to publish her work. Her complete journals did not appear until four decades after her death.

Discussion Questions

1. Dorothy Wordsworth uses detailed description to bring a country scene to life. Which images and examples of figurative language reveal Dorothy Wordsworth's poetic nature?
   Possible Responses: "fairy valleys in the vale"; "travelling not in a bustle but not slowly to the lake"; "pile wort that shone like stars of gold in the sun"; "the simplicity of the mountains"; "glittering lively lake"
2. What mood is evoked by the journal entry? Which of the two William Wordsworth poems has a similar mood?
   Possible Responses: The journal entry has a joyous and peaceful mood. "My Heart Leaps Up" has a similar mood.

from the

GRASMERE JOURNALS

Dorothy Wordsworth

FRIDAY 16 APRIL, 1802 (GOOD FRIDAY)

When I undrew my curtains in the morning, I was much affected by the beauty of the prospect and the change. The sun shone, the wind had passed away, the hills looked cheerful, the river was very bright as it flowed into the lake. The church rises up behind a little knot of rocks, the steeple not so high as an ordinary three storey house. Trees, in a row in the garden under the wall. After Wm had shaved we set forward. The valley is at first broken by little rocky woody knolls that make retiring places, fairy valleys in the vale, the river winds along under these hills travelling not in a bustle but not slowly to the lake. . . . As we go on the vale opens out more into one vale with somewhat of a cradle bed. Cottages with groups of trees on the side of the hills. We passed a pair of twin children two years old sat on the next bridge which we crossed a single arch. We rested again upon the turf and looked at the same bridge. We observed arches in the water occasioned by the large stones sending it down in two streams. . . . Primroses by the roadside, pile wort that shone like stars of gold in the sun, violets, strawberries, retired and half buried among the grass. When we came to the foot of Brothers Water I left William sitting on the bridge and went along the path on the right side of the lake through the wood. I was delighted with what I saw. The water under the boughs of the bare old trees, the simplicity of the mountains and the exquisite beauty of the path. There was one grey cottage. . . . I hung over the gate, and thought I could have stayed for ever. When I returned I found William writing a poem descriptive of the sights and sounds we saw and heard. There was the gentle flowing of the stream, the glittering lively lake, green fields without a living creature to be seen on them. . . .

Cross Curricular Link Humanities

LIFE AT DOVE COTTAGE While much of the Grasmere Journals contains Dorothy Wordsworth's lyrical descriptions of the countryside, many of the entries also provide glimpses into everyday life at Dove Cottage. We learn about the Wordsworths' friends, neighbors, and daily activities. The reader also reads much about the state of their health. Colds, headaches, and other illnesses frequently afflicted the Wordsworths. On February 6, 1802, for instance, Dorothy writes: "I was stopped in my writing, and made ill by the letters. William a bad headache; he made up a bed on the floor, but could not sleep." Some of their discomfort may have been due to the weather, which Dorothy often describes as cold, rainy, and windy.

She also writes about such household chores as gardening, baking, and cleaning. In this, Dorothy and her brother were helped by a neighbor, Molly Fisher, who was taken on as a servant. Although they paid Molly relatively generous wages, the Wordsworths were not particularly well off. They were able to regularly buy tea and newspapers—luxuries that many of their neighbors could not afford. However, they rarely bought clothes or ate meat and gratefully accepted the occasional barrel of flour sent by a relative.

Connect to the Literature

1. **What Do You Think?** What images remain in your mind after reading "The World Is Too Much With Us" and "My Heart Leaps Up"?

Think Critically

2. In "The World Is Too Much With Us," what does the speaker think we have lost? How?
3. In "My Heart Leaps Up," what is the speaker hoping for in line 5?
4. What do you think the speaker means by "The Child is father of the Man" (line 7)? How does this belief reflect Romantic ideals?
5. **ACTIVE READING: DRAWING CONCLUSIONS ABOUT MEANING** Get together with a partner and compare the notes you recorded in your READER'S NOTEBOOK. Did you draw similar conclusions about meaning in the poems?
6. Determine Wordsworth's **tone,** or attitude toward the subject, in each poem, and then compare and contrast the tones. Cite examples in your response.

Extend Interpretations

7. **Comparing Texts** How does Dorothy Wordsworth's response to nature compare with her brother's? What similarities do you see in the imagery and the feelings expressed?
8. **Critic's Corner** Samuel Taylor Coleridge praised Wordsworth for capturing "the perfect truth of nature in his images and descriptions." Do you agree with this assessment of Wordsworth's writing? Support your answer with examples from the two poems.
9. **Connect to Life** If Wordsworth were alive today, what do you think he would say about the state of the environment and our relationship to nature? Explain.

LITERARY ANALYSIS: FIGURATIVE LANGUAGE

Figurative language is language that conveys meaning beyond the literal meanings of the words. Writers use figurative language to create effects, to emphasize ideas, and to evoke emotions. Types of figurative language include **simile, metaphor,** and **personification.** Notice the metaphor in the fourth line of "The World Is Too Much With Us":

We have given our hearts away, a sordid boon!

In this metaphor, hearts given away are compared to "a sordid boon," or an undesirable gift. This comparison emphasizes the idea that our inability to appreciate nature has made us worthless.

Paired Activity Reread "The World Is Too Much With Us" with a partner, and work together to find an example of a simile and one of personification. Then discuss the effect created by this figurative language.

REVIEW: THEME

Theme in a work of literature is a message or idea about life or human nature. In poetry, **imagery**—words and phrases that create vivid sensory experiences for the reader—often conveys theme. Use the nature imagery in the Wordsworth poems to help you identify the theme of each one.

Connect to the Literature

1. **What Do You Think?** Students should identify images that appeal to one or more of the senses.

Think Critically

2. Possible Response: The speaker thinks we have lost touch with the natural world as a result of our preoccupation with the world of business.
3. Possible Response: The speaker hopes that he will always be inspired by the beauties of nature.
4. Possible Responses: A child's impressions and experiences inspire or affect those he or she will have as an adult. Romanticism stresses the importance of childhood experiences and feelings.
5. Initiate a class discussion about the meaning of the two poems. Point out that readers can draw many different conclusions about poetry.
6. Possible Response: The tone in "The World Is Too Much With Us" is weary, while that in "My Heart Leaps Up" is more hopeful.

Extend Interpretations

7. **Comparing Texts** Possible Responses: Like her brother, Dorothy reveals an almost reverential love and appreciation of nature. Both writers use figurative language and sensory details that appeal to sight and sound to describe scenes in nature. Both express feelings of joy and delight.
8. **Critic's Corner** Students who agree might cite Wordsworth's images of the sea beneath the moon and the howling winds in "The World Is Too Much With Us" and the rainbow in "My Heart Leaps Up."
9. **Connect to Life** Possible Response: Wordsworth would say that people are more alienated than ever from nature and that their actions are destroying it.

Literary Analysis

Paired Activity The simile in the poem is the comparison between the upgathered winds and sleeping flowers. An example of personification is the sea baring her bosom to the moon. Students should understand that this figurative language creates vivid images for the reader.

Use **Unit Six Resource Book,** p. 11, for more practice.

Theme Possible Responses: A theme of "The World Is Too Much With Us" is that being out of touch with nature diminishes life and one's own worth. A theme of "My Heart Leaps Up" is that revering nature brings humans closer to God and to the natural stages in their own life.

Writing Options

1. **Nature Poem** Encourage students to visualize their setting and freewrite about the thoughts and feelings it inspires.
2. **Cause-and-Effect Paragraph** Some of the causes include the stresses and demands of everyday life, our reliance on cars, and the fact that most people live in cities. Some of the results include a decreased appreciation for life and diminished concern for the environment.

Activities & Explorations

Poem Illustration Have students who choose to create a collage or mural work within small groups. Display all of the finished artwork and then discuss how the illustrations evoke the poetry's language and themes.

Inquiry & Research

Failed Friendship Students should discover that Coleridge's drug addiction and dissipation caused the rift between the two poets.

Points of Comparison

You might write the chart on the board and have the class discuss and fill in the first column. Then have students work on their own to fill in entries for the second column.

Writing Options

1. Nature Poem Write a poem about the natural setting you discussed for the Connect to Your Life activity on page 899. Describe the setting and your thoughts and feelings about it.

2. Cause-and-Effect Paragraph In "The World Is Too Much With Us," Wordsworth expresses sorrow over the fact that people have lost touch with nature. Think about what may cause people today to become alienated from the natural world. What do you think are the results of such alienation? Organize your thoughts in a cause-and-effect paragraph and place it in your **Working Portfolio.**

Writing Handbook
See page R32: Cause and Effect.

Activities & Explorations

Poem Illustration Illustrate a scene from one of Wordsworth's poems. Use the poet's descriptive imagery to help you capture the scene in a drawing, a collage, or even a large mural to decorate your classroom. ~ **ART**

Inquiry & Research

Failed Friendship Wordsworth and Coleridge collaborated on *Lyrical Ballads,* which heralded the beginning of the Romantic movement in Britain. The close friends also lived for a time as neighbors. However, by 1810 their friendship had soured. For the rest of their lives, the two famous poets rarely met or spoke to each other. Do research to find out what caused the rift between Wordsworth and Coleridge. Share your findings in an oral report.

Points of Comparison

Review the poems, and fill in the first two columns of your comparison-and-contrast chart. The following questions may help you focus your ideas:

- What is the speaker's point of view (first-person, second-person, or third-person)?
- What images of nature does the poem contain?
- What mood, or feeling, is created by these images?
- How would you describe the poet's tone?
- To whom or what is the subject compared?
- How do you think the poet views nature?

Cooperative Learning Activity Share your chart with a small group of classmates, and discuss the similarities and differences between the two Wordsworth poems.

	"The World Is Too Much With Us" (Wordsworth)	"My Heart Leaps Up" (Wordsworth)	from *Simple Verses* (Martí)	"Shaman Song" (Uvavnuk)
Speaker's Point of View	first-person			
Images of Nature	sea beneath the moon			
Mood Suggested by the Images				
Poet's Tone				
Comparisons Made				
Poet's View of Nature				

Romantic Poetry from Other Cultures

Romantic literature is not limited to a particular time in Europe. Themes dealing with individual experience, strong emotions, and nature appear in works from other cultures and times as well. As you read the poems by José Martí and Uvavnuk, compare the poets' impressions of nature with those of the Romantic poet William Wordsworth.

José Martí
1853–1895

Writer and Revolutionary Born in Havana, Cuba, José Martí (hō-sā' mär-tē') was a political activist, journalist, and leader in the Modernist movement in Spanish literature. He began his political career at the age of 16, when he first spoke out for Cuban independence. In 1871 Martí was deported to Spain and sentenced to hard labor for his activities, but he was released after six months. Once freed, Martí remained in Spain, where he received his university education. Over the next several years, Martí traveled a great deal, finally moving to New York City in 1881. There he worked as a journalist and as a poet, writing his most influential collection, *Simple Verses.*

Though an exile, Martí never abandoned the struggle for Cuban independence. In 1892 he helped form the Cuban Revolutionary Party; three years later, he arrived in Cuba with a small army of supporters. Martí died in the first battle he fought, but the seeds of revolution had been sown. Cuba eventually gained its independence, and Martí became celebrated as a great revolutionary hero.

Joyous Shaman Details about Uvavnuk (o͞o-vav'no͝ok), an Inuk (Eskimo) woman who probably lived in the 19th century, come largely from legends that were retold to Danish explorer Knud Rasmussen in the early 20th century. Rasmussen recorded the stories and published them in 1927. According to his reports, Uvavnuk, an ordinary woman, was suddenly struck by a ball of light from either a meteor or a bolt of lightning. The strike filled her with spiritual enlightenment. From that day on, she was a shaman—a medium between the physical world and the spirit world. Uvavnuk began to receive messages and songs from the spirit world. It was said that everyone who heard her sing the "Shaman Song" was filled with joy and cleansed of evil. As legend has it, because of Uvavnuk's enlightenment her people enjoyed many years of great happiness and good fortune.

Eskimo shaman figure

5-Minute Warm-Up

Daily Language SkillBuilder

Have students **proofread** the display sentences on page 869i and write them correctly.

Literary Analysis
FIGURATIVE LANGUAGE

Have students identify the simile in "Shaman Song." *("The great sea / frees me, moves me, / as a strong river carries a weed.")* Then ask them what is being compared in the simile. *(The sea is compared to a strong river; the speaker is compared to a weed.)*

Literary Analysis REPETITION

Tell students that repetition is a technique in which a sound, word, phrase, or line is repeated for emphasis or unity. Ask students to identify the repeated phrase in the Martí poem. *(I know)* Have students discuss the effect of the repeated phrase.
Possible Responses: The repeated phrase helps create rhythm, unifies the stanzas, emphasizes the speaker's viewpoint.

Active Reading
DRAWING CONCLUSIONS ABOUT MEANING

Point out that in the first three stanzas of the Martí poem, the speaker emphasizes his point of view by repeatedly using the pronoun *I.* In the fourth stanza, however, the speaker refers to "a heart weary-worn" without specifying whose heart, or spirit, is worn out. What conclusions can students draw about whose heart is weary?
Possible Response: The speaker's heart is weary.

What conclusion can you draw about the relationship between the frightened fawn in the poem and the speaker?
Possible Responses: Both are tired, ready to give up, ready to die.

from Simple Verses

José Martí

Cuba

Translated by Manuel A. Tellechea

I know of Egypt and Niger,
Of Persia and Xenophon, no less,
But more than these I prefer
The fresh mountain air's caress.

I know the ancient histories
Of man and his struggles for power,
But I prefer the buzzing bees
That hover round the bellflower.

I know the sound the wind made
When through the boughs it was flying:
Let no one tell me I'm lying,
There is no song as well played.

I know of a frightened fawn
That seeks the fold to expire,
And of a heart weary-worn
That dies hidden without ire.

1 Egypt and Niger: The African countries of Egypt and Niger were sites of important ancient civilizations.

2 Persia and Xenophon (zĕn′ə-fən): Persia is the former name of Iran; Xenophon was a Greek commander who led a troop of soldiers in the service of a Persian prince.

14 seeks the fold to expire: returns home to die.

16 ire: anger.

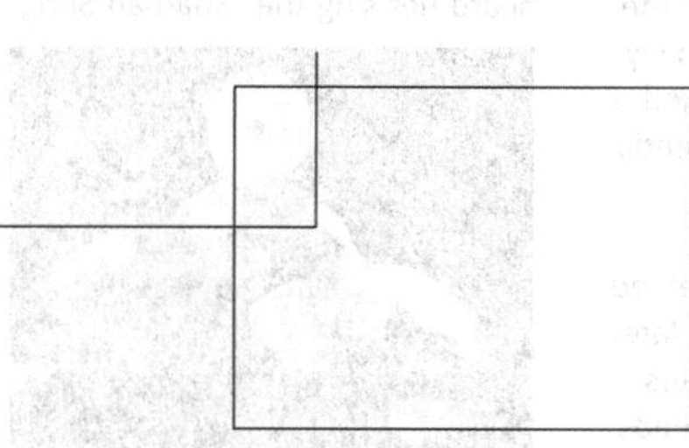

Cross Curricular Link **History**

XENOPHON Xenophon was born in Athens around 430 B.C. He studied under Socrates but was more interested in becoming a soldier than in becoming a philosopher. After he left Athens, Xenophon joined the Greek troops, called the Ten Thousand, that served Prince Cyrus the Younger of Persia.

In 401 B.C., in an effort to seize the Persian throne from Cyrus's brother, the Greek troops fought in Persia in the Battle of Cunaxa. When Cyrus was killed, the Ten Thousand were forced to flee or surrender and the Greek generals were slaughtered. Stranded in a foreign land without a commander, the remaining Greeks chose Xenophon to lead their retreat. He undertook the 1,500-mile march and led the troops on their perilous journey.

Shaman Song

Uvavnuk

Inuk (Eskimo)

Translated by Jane Hirshfield

The great sea
frees me, moves me,
as a strong river carries a weed.
Earth and her strong winds
move me, take me away,
and my soul is swept up in joy.

Sunset at Sea (1906), Thomas Moran. Brooklyn Museum, Brooklyn, New York. Photo © Brooklyn Museum/Corbis.

Customizing Instruction

Less Proficient Readers

Draw the following chart on the board and have the class work together to specify what the speaker in the first three stanzas of Martí's poem prefers to human achievement.

Stanzas	What Speaker Prefers to Human Achievement
First	*(prefers fresh mountain air to important ancient civilizations)*
Second	*(prefers buzzing bees to man's struggles for power)*
Third	*(prefers the sound the wind makes to a song)*

English Learners

Explain the multiple meanings of the following verbs and phrases in "Shaman Song":

- "moves me": The verb *move* can mean "to change position." It can also mean "to stir emotions." In the poem, the verb may have both meanings.
- "swept up in joy": "Sweep up" often refers to the act of cleaning with a broom or brush. In "Shaman Song," however, the phrase "swept up in joy" means "greatly excited by emotion."

Connect to the Literature

1. **What Do You Think?** Students should support their choices by identifying specific images, moods, or sensory details in the poems.

Think Critically

2. Possible Response: The speaker feels a close and joyful connection to the natural world.
3. Possible Responses: In the first three stanzas, the speaker compares the sights and sounds of nature with human achievement. In the fourth stanza, the speaker compares a dying animal to his own weary, resigned state.
4. Possible Responses: In the Martí poem, details describing mountain air, buzzing bees, blowing winds, and a frightened fawn convey the idea that even the smallest events in nature surpass people's greatest accomplishments. In Uvavnuk's poem, details describing the sea, river, and winds convey the idea of the power and grandeur of nature.

Points of Comparison

After students have completed their charts, initiate a class discussion about their entries. Encourage students to tell which poem they liked best and to explain why.

To assess skills and concepts taught in this selection, use **Formal Assessment Book,** pp. 135–136.

Connect to the Literature

1. **What Do You Think?** Which poem do you prefer? Give reasons for your choice.

Think Critically

2. In "Shaman Song," how would you describe the speaker's relationship to nature?
3. Compare the first three stanzas of Martí's poem with the last stanza. How does the content of this stanza differ from the others?
4. Review the poems and note the **sensory details** that each contains. What ideas about nature do these details convey?

THINK ABOUT
- Martí's comparison of nature with human achievements
- Uvavnuk's images of a strong river and strong winds
- the **moods** these images convey

Points *of* Comparison

Cooperative Learning Activity Now work with a small group of students to compare and contrast the Wordsworth poems you have already analyzed with those by Martí and Uvavnuk. Respond to the Points of Comparison questions on page 904. Use your answers to help you complete your chart.

	"The World Is Too Much With Us" (Wordsworth)	"My Heart Leaps Up" (Wordsworth)	from *Simple Verses* (Martí)	"Shaman Song" (Uvavnuk)
Speaker's Point of View	*first-person*		*first-person*	
Images of Nature	*sea beneath the moon*		*fresh mountain air's caress*	
Mood Suggested by the Images				
Poet's Tone				
Comparisons Made				
Poet's View of Nature				

Writing About Literature

PART 1 Reading the Prompt

In writing assessments you may be asked to compare and contrast works of literature that, like the poems you have analyzed, share a similar theme. You are now going to practice writing an essay that involves this type of comparison.

Writing Prompt

Poetry from different cultures and time periods can have interesting thematic similarities and differences. You will compare and contrast four Romantic poems—two by William Wordsworth, one by José Martí, and one by Uvavnuk. (1) For each poem, discuss the point of view, (2) nature images, mood, tone, comparisons made, and view of nature expressed. Point out differences and similarities among the poems. Be sure to provide evidence from the poems to support your analysis. (3)

STRATEGIES IN ACTION

(1) I have to **compare and contrast** four Romantic poems that deal with nature.

(2) For each poem, I need to discuss the **point of view, nature images, mood, tone, comparisons made,** and **view of nature expressed.**

(3) I need to include **details, examples,** or **quotations** from the poems to support my opinion.

PART 2 Planning a Comparison-and-Contrast Essay

- Review the comparison-and-contrast chart that you completed for all four poems.
- Using your chart, find examples of similarities and differences to point out in your essay.
- Create an outline to help organize your ideas.

PART 3 Drafting Your Essay

Introduction Begin by introducing your topic and identifying the basis of comparison. Briefly express your opinion about what the four poems have in common. Then explain what you see as major differences.

Body You may wish to devote one paragraph to each poem. Within your paragraphs, you will need to discuss how each poem is different from the others and how it is similar. Pay the most attention to the images and mood conveyed in each poem. Use your comparison-and-contrast chart to identify details and examples.

Conclusion Wrap up your essay with a summary of the major differences and similarities.

Revision Check that you have used signal words, such as *similarly, also, like, but, unlike,* and *while,* to show the relationships between your comparisons and contrasts.

PART 1 Reading the Prompt
Model the process of reading a prompt:

- Read through the entire prompt.
- List key words of the assignment on the board ("compare and contrast," "evidence").
- Define each key word using **Strategies in Action** to show how students can restate the prompts in their own words.

PART 2 Planning a Comparison-and-Contrast Essay

- Students can use the chart they have been filling out for the four Romantic poems (referenced on pages 898, 904, and 908).
- Encourage students to pay particular attention to similarities and differences in the poets' view of nature. The images of nature and mood suggested by the images can be used to support students' ideas.
- In organizing their outlines, students may wish to group together poets whose view of nature is similar.

PART 3 Drafting Your Essay
Introduction Tell students that opening their essay with a quotation from one of the poems can be an effective way to introduce their opinion. Opening with a quotation can engage a reader's attention and also lend authority to the essay.
Body Remind students that each paragraph in the body of their essay should be unified, supporting a single main idea. The paragraphs should support the students' thesis and flow logically from one to another.
Conclusion Suggest that students conclude by summarizing their ideas and emphasizing their main points. However, they should be careful not to introduce new ideas in their conclusion.
Revision In addition to using signal words, students should also energize their writing by replacing dull words with lively ones, and by making general language specific.

Use **Unit Six Resource Book,** p. 12, for additional support.

Assessment Standardized Test Practice

RESPONDING TO A WRITING PROMPT Read aloud the writing prompt at the top of this page. Discuss the **Strategies in Action** by asking students to identify the words in the prompt that tell them what to do. Suggest that they mark up their comparison-and-contrast charts, identifying points to include in their essays. When students have finished drafting their essays, have them work with a partner to see if they have accomplished the tips given in Part 3 **Drafting Your Essay.**

Objectives

- understand and appreciate a **Romantic literary ballad (Literary Analysis)**
- identify and evaluate **imagery** in poetry **(Literary Analysis)**
- **interpret symbols** to gain a deeper understanding of a literary work **(Active Reading)**

Thematic Link

In "The Lorelei," Heinrich Heine tells the legend of a maiden who lures boatmen to their death with her song. Heine reveals that **expressions of the heart** can also disclose the destructive power of love.

5-Minute Warm-Up

Daily Language SkillBuilder

Have students **proofread** the display sentences on page 869i and write them correctly.

Reading and Analyzing

Literary Analysis LITERARY BALLAD

Tell students that a literary ballad often recounts a tragic incident. Have students read the first two stanzas of "The Lorelei." Then ask them to identify words and phrases in the poem that suggest that the narrator is about to tell a sad story.

Possible Responses: "the sadness / That's fallen on my breast"; "will not let me rest"

Use **Unit Six Resource Book,** p. 14, for more practice.

Reading Skills and Strategies
VISUALIZING SETTING

Read aloud the second stanza. Ask students to identify sensory details in the lines that help them visualize the setting.

Possible Responses: "air grows cool in the twilight"; "softly the Rhine flows on"; "peak of a mountain sparkles"; "the setting sun"

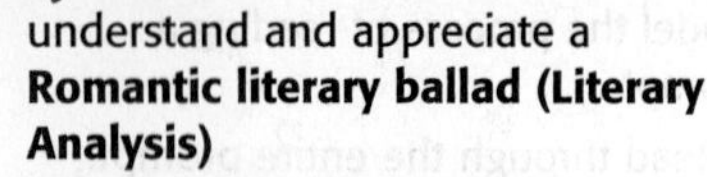

THE Lorelei

HEINRICH HEINE *Translated by* Aaron Kramer

Heinrich Heine
1797–1856

A Controversial Figure Born in Düsseldorf, Germany (then Prussia), to Jewish parents, Heinrich Heine (hīn'rĭкн hī'nə) was a controversial figure in his homeland. Heine converted to Protestantism because government positions were not open to Jews at the time. His conversion was in vain, however, for he was never offered any of the jobs he desired. Instead, Heine turned to writing. His reputation as a poet was established with *The Book of Songs,* published in 1827. Besides poems, Heine's writings also included expressions of his political views. After settling in Paris in 1831, he wrote essays against the governments of both France and Germany. As a result, the German government eventually banned all of his works. In 1848, a serious illness permanently confined the poet to what he called his "mattress grave." Although in tremendous pain, Heine continued to write until his death.

Build Background

Legend of the Lorelei The Lorelei is the name of a cliff overlooking the Rhine River. The echo heard at the cliff inspired a legend about a maiden who drowned herself after a lover betrayed her. According to the legend, the spirit of the maiden sits upon a rock, combing her hair in the moonlight and singing a haunting song that lures boatmen to their death. Heine had his own Lorelei, a cousin who rejected him and married another man. Her rejection was the inspiration for the poem you are about to read and for many of Heine's other folk ballads.

Connect to Your Life

With a classmate, discuss stories you have read about love or an attraction that dooms the lover. What do you think accounts for people's interest in such stories?

Focus Your Reading

LITERARY ANALYSIS: LITERARY BALLAD

A **folk ballad** is a narrative poem that was originally intended to be sung. Traditional folk ballads were composed by unknown authors and passed down orally. A **literary ballad** is written by a single author in conscious imitation of the folk-ballad style. Literary ballads became popular during the Romantic period. As you read "The Lorelei," listen for its musical qualities.

ACTIVE READING: INTERPRETING SYMBOLS

A **symbol** is a person, place, object, or activity that stands for something beyond itself. When you interpret symbols in a literary work, you look beyond the work's literal meaning to gain a deeper understanding.

READER'S NOTEBOOK As you read "The Lorelei," write down your interpretation of the symbols in the poem.

LESSON RESOURCES

UNIT SIX RESOURCE BOOK,
pp. 13–14

ASSESSMENT RESOURCES
Formal Assessment, pp. 137–138
Teacher's Guide to Assessment and Portfolio Use
Test Generator

INTEGRATED TECHNOLOGY
Visit our Web Site: classzone.com

ADDITIONAL RESOURCES
Lesson Planning Guide, pp. 117–118
Teacher's Sourcebook for Language Development

Loreley (1864), Eduard Jakob von Steinle. 213.5 cm × 135.4 cm. Schack-Galerie, Munich, Germany/Bayer & Mitko/Artothek.

1 I cannot explain the sadness
That's fallen on my breast.
An old, old fable haunts me,
And will not let me rest.

The air grows cool in the twilight,
And softly the Rhine flows on;
The peak of a mountain sparkles
Beneath the setting sun.

Customizing Instruction

Less Proficient Readers

Tell students that the narrator is recalling an old fable, or brief story. Point out that the fable contains all the elements of a narrative, including setting, characters, conflict, and plot. As students read Heine's poem, encourage them to record these elements in a chart like the one below. Doing so will help students keep track of what's going on in the poem.

Setting	Characters	Conflict	Plot
(mountain peak overlooking Rhine)			

Encourage students to read the poem aloud, stopping after each stanza to think about its images and mood.

English Learners

1 Help students understand the lines "the sadness / That's fallen on my breast." Explain that the speaker is describing a feeling of sadness so strong that it seems like a weight pressing against his heart or chest. As students read the poem, encourage them to note any other words or phrases that they do not understand. After students finish reading, have pairs get together to discuss any words and phrases listed.

Advanced Learners

Ask students to read another of Heine's literary ballads from his collection called *Songs of Love & Grief.* Have them compare the imagery and symbols used in the poem with those in "The Lorelei." Encourage students to share the similarities and differences they note with the class.

THE LORELEI 911

Reading and Analyzing

Literary Analysis LITERARY BALLAD

Invite a volunteer to read lines 9–16 of the poem aloud. Then ask students to discuss what contributes to the poem's musical qualities.
Possible Responses: rhyme scheme, repetition, dreamy mood

Have students explain how the repetition of the words *gold* and *golden* contributes to the mood of the lines.
Possible Response: The repetition gives the poem a timeless, fairy-tale quality.

Literary Analysis IMAGERY

Ask students to note the imagery in "The Lorelei." Remind students that imagery refers to words and phrases that create images in the reader's mind by appealing to the senses. Ask students what senses are appealed to by the images in lines 13–16.
Possible Responses: "comb of gold"—sight; "sings an evensong"—sight, sound; "wonderful melody reaches a boat as it sails along"—sound, sight

Active Reading
INTERPRETING SYMBOLS

Point out that the boatman is helpless before the Lorelei. Then ask students what the Lorelei might symbolize.
Possible Responses: all women, fate, love, death

What might the boatman represent?
Possible Responses: all men, human beings

Use **Unit Six Resource Book,** p. 13, for more practice.

More lovely than a vision,
A girl sits high up there;
Her golden jewelry glistens,
She combs her golden hair.

With a comb of gold she combs it,
And sings an evensong;
The wonderful melody reaches
A boat, as it sails along.

The boatman hears, with an anguish
More wild than was ever known;
He's blind to the rocks around him;
His eyes are for her alone.

—At last the waves devoured
The boat, and the boatman's cry;
And this she did with her singing,
The golden Lorelei.

Cross Curricular Link **Music**

"THE LORELEI" AS FOLK SONG The lines of music on pages 911 and 912 are from the melody that Friedrich Silcher composed for Heine's "The Lorelei." Silcher used a simple, sentimental tune when he set the poem to music. The folk song became so beloved that it became part of German heritage.

During the 1930s and 1940s, however, the folk song was in danger of disappearing from German songbooks. Hitler and the Nazis had tried to erase the names of Heine and other Jewish authors from German history. They destroyed Heine's grave and banned his works. When they tried to ban "The Lorelei," though, there was a public outcry. As a result, the Nazis were forced to leave the popular poem in songbooks but attributed it to "author unknown."

Connect to the Literature

1. **What Do You Think?** Which image in this poem did you find most striking? Explain.

Comprehension Check
- What vision does the speaker recall?
- What effect does the girl's singing have on the boatman?

Think Critically

2. **ACTIVE READING: INTERPRETING SYMBOLS** With a classmate, discuss the interpretation of **symbols** you wrote down in your  READER'S NOTEBOOK. What do you think the Lorelei represents? Her song? The destroyed boat?

3. What does this poem suggest about the nature of love?

THINK ABOUT
- how the speaker feels as he recalls the "old, old fable" (line 3)
- the description of the girl
- the fate of the boatman

4. How would you describe the **mood** of "The Lorelei"? How does the mood reflect the Romantic spirit?

Extend Interpretations

5. **The Writer's Style** There are four images involving gold in "The Lorelei." What effect does this repeated image have on the portrayal of the girl?

6. **Comparing Texts** In what way is the representation of the sea in Wordsworth's "The World Is Too Much With Us" similar to that of the Rhine in "The Lorelei"? How do the images differ?

7. **Connect to Life** "The Lorelei" depicts a man who is overwhelmed by a song. Think of a time when you have had a strong emotional response to a song. Why do you think music has such a powerful effect on people?

LITERARY ANALYSIS: LITERARY BALLAD

"The Lorelei" is an example of a **literary ballad,** a poem that the writer has composed in the style of anonymous folk ballads. Typically, a **folk ballad**
- is a brief narrative poem originally intended to be sung
- is made up of four-line stanzas
- contains repetitions of lines or stanzas, sometimes with the wording slightly varied
- recounts a single dramatic, often tragic, episode
- contains supernatural elements
- includes dialogue
- implies more than it actually tells

Cooperative Learning Activity With a group of classmates, determine which typical characteristics of a folk ballad are contained in "The Lorelei." Refer to the list above for help. Compare your findings with those of other groups.

REVIEW: IMAGERY The term **imagery** refers to words and phrases that create vivid sensory experiences for the reader. Reread "The Lorelei" and identify several examples of imagery. To which sense or senses does each image appeal?

Connect to the Literature

1. **What Do You Think?** Images might include the girl combing her hair, the boatman's anguish, or the boat's sinking.

Comprehension Check
- The speaker recalls a vision of a lovely girl singing as a boat sails by.
- The girl's singing causes the boatman to become blind to all but her.

Think Critically

2. Possible Responses: The Lorelei represents women, particularly beautiful women. Her song represents a woman's love or seductive powers. The destroyed boat represents the destructive force of a woman's love.
3. Possible Response: The poem suggests that love makes men go mad and ultimately destroys them.
4. Possible Responses: The poem's mood may be described as sad, ominous, threatening. The mood reflects the brooding, anguished nature of the Romantic spirit.

Extend Interpretations

5. **The Writer's Style** Possible Response: The images of gold make the girl seem unattainable and removed.
6. **Comparing Texts** Possible Responses: In both poems, the bodies of water are described as beautiful and peaceful. At the end of "The Lorelei," however, the river reveals its destructive power.
7. **Connect to Life** Possible Response: Students might point out the power of music to evoke memories and set moods.

Literary Analysis

Cooperative Learning Activity
Students should note that the poem contains all of the listed characteristics except dialogue.

Use **Unit Six Resource Book,** p. 14, for more practice.

Imagery You might have pairs of students get together to discuss the imagery in the poem.

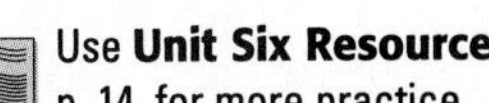

To assess skills and concepts taught in this selection, use **Formal Assessment Book,** pp. 137–138.

Objectives

- understand and appreciate a Romantic **narrative poem (Literary Analysis)**
- examine the role of **setting in narrative poetry (Literary Analysis)**
- use details from a literary work to **visualize setting (Active Reading)**

Thematic Link

In "Russia 1812," Victor Hugo describes the terrible suffering of Napoleon's army as it retreated from Moscow. Hugo gives voice to the **expressions of his heart** as he details the destructive power of nature and Napoleon's defeat.

5-Minute Warm-Up

Daily Language SkillBuilder

Have students **proofread** the display sentences on page 869j and write them correctly.

Victor Hugo
1802–1885

Early Years Victor Hugo was a poet, novelist, and dramatist whose talent was only matched by his larger-than-life personality. His early years were unsettled. The son of a general who served under Napoleon Bonaparte, Hugo spent much of his childhood traveling with his father to Italy and Spain during the Napoleonic Wars.

Artistic Success Hugo achieved early success as a writer, and he tackled his work with great energy. In 1826, he began an intense, 17-year period of writing and publishing plays, poems, and novels. In 1827, he established himself as the leader of the Romantic movement in France with the preface to his epic play *Cromwell.* In the preface Hugo spoke out against the restrictions of classical literature and called for writing that explored emotions and personal experience. He gained wider fame with the publication in 1831 of the Romantic historical novel *The Hunchback of Notre Dame.* Hugo's creative activity temporarily came to a halt in 1843, following the death of his daughter Léopoldine. Overwhelmed by grief, he published nothing during the next 10 years.

A Hero's Goodbye Eventually Hugo turned to politics, accepting an important post in the French government in 1845. However, six years later he was driven into exile when Louis Napoleon—later Napoleon III—seized power. While in exile, Hugo resumed writing and completed the protest novel *Les Misérables.* Published in 1862, the novel was a huge success in France and abroad. Soon after Napoleon III fell from power in 1870, Hugo returned to France. He resumed his political career for a time, but illness soon forced him to retire. Upon his death, Hugo was given a hero's funeral. European leaders, cavalry regiments, and as many as three million other people wound through the streets of Paris to honor him.

Hugo's funeral procession

LESSON RESOURCES

UNIT SIX RESOURCE BOOK, pp. 15–16

ASSESSMENT RESOURCES
Formal Assessment, pp. 139–140
Teacher's Guide to Assessment and Portfolio Use
Test Generator

INTEGRATED TECHNOLOGY
Visit our Web Site: classzone.com

ADDITIONAL RESOURCES
Lesson Planning Guide, pp. 119–120
Teacher's Sourcebook for Language Development

Build Background

Napoleon's Crime and Punishment Victor Hugo wrote "The Expiation" while living in exile. The epic poem appeared in a collection of satiric poetry directed at Napoleon's nephew Louis Napoleon. Hugo detested Louis Napoleon, whom he referred to as "Napoleon the Dwarf."

"The Expiation" recounts the rise and fall of Napoleon Bonaparte. The first part of the poem describes the early days of his reign. It introduces the crime that must be expiated, or made amends for: Napoleon's seizure of power in France in 1799. The second part of "The Expiation" deals with the Battle of Waterloo, where Napoleon was decisively defeated in 1815. The third part portrays Napoleon's subsequent exile on the island of Saint Helena.

The poem you are about to read, "Russia 1812," appears in the first section. It describes the result of Napoleon's disastrous invasion of Russia. The emperor set out in June 1812 with about 600,000 soldiers from all over his empire. By the time the troops reached Moscow in September, the Russians had abandoned and set fire to the city. With no place to spend the winter, Napoleon ordered his army to withdraw. As the troops trudged westward, a cold, early winter set in. The temperature fell as low as 22 degrees below zero. The soldiers were also plagued by attacks from Russian Cossacks. By the time the troops reached Poland, only about 10,000 men remained.

In "The Expiation," after each major defeat suffered by Napoleon, the emperor asks whether this is the penance, or punishment, he must pay for his crime. Each time a voice replies, "No." Finally the punishment becomes clear: Thirty years after Napoleon's death, the emperor in his tomb hears the voice of Napoleon III. The disgrace that the nephew has brought on the name of Napoleon is his uncle's punishment.

Political cartoon, 1803

Connect to Your Life

Think about a hero of yours who has suffered some kind of defeat. The hero may be a political or community leader, an artist, or an athlete. How did you feel about your hero after the loss? Did you still support him or her? Did your attitude toward your hero change in any way? Share your experiences with a classmate.

Focus Your Reading

LITERARY ANALYSIS: SETTING IN NARRATIVE POETRY

A **narrative poem** is a poem that tells a story. Thus it contains many of the basic elements of a story, including characters, plot, and setting. The **setting** is the time and place of the action. Setting may play an important role in what happens. As you read "Russia 1812," think about how the setting affects the poem's plot, characters, and theme.

ACTIVE READING: VISUALIZING SETTING

When you read you probably **visualize,** or form mental pictures using details from the piece. Visualizing setting will help you understand what's happening. For example, by visualizing the setting of "Russia 1812" from the details that Hugo provides, you can gain insight into what Napoleon and his soldiers endured as they marched through Russia.

READER'S NOTEBOOK As you read the poem, use a chart like the one below to record the images that help you visualize the setting. Jot down specific lines from the poem and descriptions of the pictures they bring to mind.

Lines	Images of Setting

READING FOR INFORMATION

Reading Skills and Strategies

CLARIFYING

Students may have trouble understanding the concept of expiation, which is briefly defined in **Build Background.** Tell them that expiation is the act of making amends, or atoning, for something. For example, a criminal may make amends for a crime by serving a jail sentence. Point out that the word frequently has religious or spiritual connotations. In religious terms, a sinner may expiate a wrongdoing through confession. As students read "Russia 1812," have them note the religious overtones of Napoleon's expiation.

TIME MANAGEMENT

If your schedule requires that you cover the lesson objectives in a shorter time, use . . .
- Preparing to Read, pp. 914–915
- Thinking Through the Literature, p. 920

If you want to take advantage of longer blocks of class time, use . . .
- TE Teaching Options: Cross Curricular Link, p. 916; Viewing and Representing, pp. 917 and 918; Grammar, p. 919;
- Connect to Today, p. 921

Literary Analysis
SETTING IN NARRATIVE POETRY

Point out that the speaker describes the setting in great detail on these pages. Ask students how the setting affects Napoleon's soldiers.

Possible Responses: The soldiers are freezing and dying in the snow. The snow has become their greatest enemy.

 Use **Unit Six Resource Book,** p. 16, for more practice.

Active Reading VISUALIZING SETTING

A Read aloud lines 5–9. Ask students to close their eyes and visualize the setting described. What images do the lines bring to mind?

Possible Responses: blinding snow; a vast, white landscape; people covered in snow

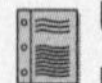 Use **Unit Six Resource Book,** p. 15, for more practice.

Literary Analysis MOOD

B Have students read lines 22–28. Then ask them to describe the mood created by the lines.

Possible Responses: somber, mournful, funereal

What details help convey this mood?

Possible Responses: "no longer living men"; "mourners parading under the black sky"; "mute avenger"; "buried the huge army in a huge shroud"

Reading Skills and Strategies
MAKING INFERENCES

In line 40, the speaker states: "They went to sleep ten thousand, woke up four." What do students infer happened to the other six thousand soldiers? *(They died in their sleep.)*

Russia 1812

from The Expiation

Victor Hugo

Translated by Robert Lowell

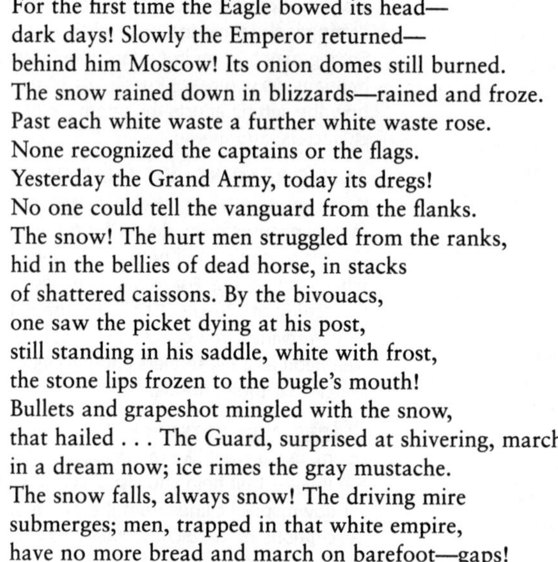

The snow fell, and its power was multiplied.
For the first time the Eagle bowed its head—
dark days! Slowly the Emperor returned—
behind him Moscow! Its onion domes still burned.
The snow rained down in blizzards—rained and froze.
Past each white waste a further white waste rose.
A None recognized the captains or the flags.
Yesterday the Grand Army, today its dregs!
No one could tell the vanguard from the flanks.
The snow! The hurt men struggled from the ranks,
hid in the bellies of dead horse, in stacks
of shattered caissons. By the bivouacs,
one saw the picket dying at his post,
still standing in his saddle, white with frost,
the stone lips frozen to the bugle's mouth!
Bullets and grapeshot mingled with the snow,
that hailed . . . The Guard, surprised at shivering, march
in a dream now; ice rimes the gray mustache.
The snow falls, always snow! The driving mire
submerges; men, trapped in that white empire,
have no more bread and march on barefoot—gaps!
They were no longer living men and troops,
but a dream drifting in a fog, a mystery,
mourners parading under the black sky.
B The solitude, vast, terrible to the eye,
was like a mute avenger everywhere,
as snowfall, floating through the quiet air,
buried the huge army in a huge shroud.
Could anyone leave this kingdom? A crowd—

2 the Eagle: Napoleon; also, the standard on his coat of arms.

4 onion domes: The domes on Russian Orthodox churches are traditionally onion shaped.

9 the vanguard . . . the flanks: The vanguard is the troops leading an army; the flanks are those troops composing the sides of a military formation.

12 caissons (kā'sŏnz') . . . **bivouacs** (bĭv'o͞o-ăks'): Caissons are vehicles used to carry ammunition; bivouacs are temporary encampments.

13 picket: soldier on the alert to warn of an enemy's approach.

16 grapeshot: a cluster of small iron balls shot from a cannon.

18 rimes: covers with frost.

19 mire: deep, heavy mud or slush.

26 mute: silent; unable to speak.

Cross Curricular Link History

ATTILA THE HUN Attila was a king who united the Huns and greatly extended the Hunnish kingdom. When Attila ascended with his brother to the throne in A.D. 434, the kingdom was centered around present-day Hungary. He greatly extended the empire by conquering surrounding territories.

Attila earned a reputation for being cruel and merciless. Much of this reputation was deserved. Attila killed his brother in 445 so that he could rule alone. In 450, he demanded the sister of Roman emperor Valentinian III as his bride. When the emperor refused, Attila invaded Gaul (now mainly France). Attila stormed through Gaul, devastating everything in his path and forcing those he conquered to join his army. His conquest was halted in 451, however, after the bloody Battle of Châlons. Even Attila was moved by the sight of so much carnage.

On the March from Moscow (19th century), John Laslett Pott.
Forbes Magazine Collection, New York/The Bridgeman Art Library, London.

HUMANITIES CONNECTION Hunger was another hardship faced by Napoleon's soldiers. Thousands of horses died during the homeward march, and the hungry soldiers fought over the animals.

each man, obsessed with dying, was alone.
Men slept—and died! The beaten mob sludged on,
ditching the guns to burn their carriages.
Two foes. The North, the Czar. The North was worse.
In hollows where the snow was piling up,
one saw whole regiments fallen asleep.
Attila's dawn, Cannaes of Hannibal!
The army marching to its funeral!
Litters, wounded, the dead, deserters—swarm,
crushing the bridges down to cross a stream.
They went to sleep ten thousand, woke up four.
Ney, bringing up the former army's rear,

36 Attila's . . . Hannibal: In A.D. 451 Attila, king of the Huns, engaged in the fierce and bloody Battle of Châlons but withdrew his troops once dawn revealed tens of thousands of soldiers on both sides lying dead. In 216 B.C. the Carthaginian general Hannibal defeated a Roman army larger than his own at Cannae (kăn'ē), by drawing the Romans into a trap.

41 Ney: Michel Ney (1769–1815), one of Napoleon's most famous commanders, was in charge of the troops defending the rear of the retreating French army.

Customizing Instruction

Less Proficient Readers

Explain the paradox in lines 29–30: "A crowd– / each man, obsessed with dying, was alone." Tell students that the men feel alone in a crowd because they are thinking about their own death. Fear makes them feel alone.

1 Students may be confused by the references to Attila and Hannibal in line 36. Direct students' attention to the sidenote that explains the line. You might also share with them the information in the Cross Curricular Link on page 916.

English Learners

Help students understand who the "two foes" are in line 33.

- "The North"—cold, frozen Russia
- "the Czar"—the emperor of Russia, Czar Alexander I

Then ask students to explain why the speaker claims that the North was worse.

Possible Response: The North was worse because the snow was a more deadly enemy.

MINI LESSON Viewing and Representing

On the March from Moscow **by John Laslett Pott**

ART APPRECIATION After Napoleon reached Moscow, he remained there for five weeks while he attempted to negotiate with Czar Alexander I. The Czar, however, did not respond. Finally, Napoleon ordered his troops to withdraw; three weeks later, it began to snow. As temperatures fell below zero, one soldier wrote, "Our nostrils froze. We seemed to be marching in a world of ice." Have students study the painting and the **Humanities Connection** on page 917. Ask them to identify details in the painting that suggest the terrible cold.

Possible Responses: The soldiers are wearing heavy clothing; snow is on the ground; the soldiers are blowing on their hands and pulling their cloaks around their shoulders to keep themselves warm.

What details indicate that the soldiers are ill-prepared and suffering in the cold?

Possible Responses: the desperate look in their eyes; their red, raw hands and faces; the makeshift bindings on their feet; the lack of gloves and warm hats; the fact that the drummer boy can apparently no longer walk on his own

Literary Analysis IMAGERY

A Have students identify the simile and the things being compared in lines 45–48. *("terrible squadrons . . . rush sabering through the camp like dervishes")* Ask students to describe the images created by the simile.
Possible Responses: chaos; swords slashing everywhere; soldiers running through the camp, dealing out death

What senses to these images appeal to?
Possible Responses: sight, touch, sound

Literary Analysis
SETTING IN NARRATIVE POETRY

B Have students read lines 49–52. Make sure students understand that these lines describe Napoleon as he witnesses the destruction of his once mighty army. Then ask students what theme, or message, might be derived from Napoleon's downfall.
Possible Response: Pride comes before a fall.

How does setting affect the poem's theme?
Possible Response: The setting brings about Napoleon's downfall.

Active Reading VISUALIZING SETTING

C Point out that Napoleon is placed in a slightly different setting in lines 55–57. Ask students to identify the setting.
Possible Response: During the watch, Napoleon is in a lighted tent, pacing back and forth.

What does the setting and Napoleon's behavior suggest about the Emperor's state of mind?
Possible Responses: Napoleon is upset and can't sleep; he's trying to figure out how to save his men.

Napoleon Bonaparte During Campaign in France, 1814 (1864), Jean-Louis-Ernest Meissonier. Musée d'Orsay, Paris.

HUMANITIES CONNECTION
To ensure that he would not be captured alive by the enemy during the Russian campaign, Napoleon wore a vial of poison around his neck in a small leather bag.

hacked his horse loose from three disputing Cossacks . . .
All night, the *qui vive?* The alert! Attacks;
retreats! White ghosts would wrench away our guns,
or we would see dim, terrible squadrons,
circles of steel, whirlpools of savages,
rush sabering through the camp like dervishes.
And in this way, whole armies died at night.

The Emperor was there, standing—he saw.
This oak already trembling from the axe,
watched his glories drop from him branch by branch:
chiefs, soldiers. Each one had his turn and chance—
they died! Some lived. These still believed his star,
and kept their watch. They loved the man of war,
this small man with his hands behind his back,
whose shadow, moving to and fro, was black
behind the lighted tent. Still believing, they
accused their destiny of *lèse-majesté.*
His misfortune had mounted on their back.
The man of glory shook. Cold stupefied
him, then suddenly he felt terrified.
Being without belief, he turned to God:
"God of armies, is this the end?" he cried.

42 Cossacks: mounted Russian soldiers.

43 *qui vive?* (kē vēv'): a French phrase (meaning literally "Who lives?") used by sentries to determine the allegiance of those entering a military camp. It is equivalent to "Who goes there?"

47 dervishes: members of a Muslim religious sect whose devotions involve whirling dances.

58 *lèse-majesté* (lĕz'mä-zhĕs-tā'): a crime committed against a ruler.

60–61 stupefied him: dulled his senses.

MINI LESSON Viewing and Representing

Campaign in France, 1814 **by Ernest Meissonier**

ART APPRECIATION Napoleon's campaign in France in 1814 was his last. Great Britain, Austria, and Prussia had formed an alliance with Russia after the Russian invasion of 1812. In 1814, the allied armies marched into France, forcing Napoleon to retreat to Paris. In March of that year, Paris was captured by the allies, and Napoleon abdicated on April 11. Have students study the painting and the **Humanities Connection** on page 918. Tell them that the painting shows Napoleon leading his troops in retreat. Ask students to study the painting and suggest adjectives that describe Napoleon's expression and bearing.
Possible Responses: grim, determined, proud, alone

How would they describe the mood of the painting?
Possible Responses: somber, subdued, defeated

And then at last the expiation came,
as he heard some one call him by his name,
some one half-lost in shadow, who said, "No,
Napoleon." Napoleon understood,
restless, bareheaded, leaden, as he stood
before his butchered legions in the snow.

64 expiation: atonement, or amends for a wrong.

The alert! Attacks; retreats! White ghosts would wrench away our guns . . .

Customizing Instruction

Less Proficient Readers

1 Help students understand that God is speaking to Napoleon at the end of the poem. Tell them that Napoleon asks whether the disastrous campaign in Russia is his final punishment. When God says no, Napoleon stands alone in the snow, weighed down by his guilt.

English Learners

Help students understand the following lines and phrases:

- "white ghosts": the Cossacks; In the snow, their forms appear white and ghostly.
- "circles of steel": the Cossacks' swords; The swords are slightly curved, making them appear to be circles of steel as they slash through the air.
- "whirlpools of savages": A whirlpool is a rapidly rotating current of water; The Cossacks, or "savages," encircle the camp and move through it like whirlpools.
- "rush sabering through the camp like dervishes": Sabers are swords; The Cossacks run through the camp, turning this way and that as they attack with their swords so that they appear to be whirling.

Advanced Learners

Have students compare the first stanza of the poem (lines 1–48) with the second (lines 49–69). How do the mood and tone change in the second stanza?

Possible Responses: The mood in the second stanza is quieter, more thoughtful and reflective. The tone is less forgiving.

What impact do these changes have on the reader?

Possible Response: The reader is left thinking more about Napoleon and his role in the disaster than in the fate of his men.

MINI LESSON Grammar

ADJECTIVE CLAUSES

Instruction A subordinate clause used as an adjective is called an adjective clause. An adjective clause is used to modify a noun or pronoun. Adjective clauses are often introduced by a relative pronoun such as *who, whom, which,* or *that.* They may also begin with *whose, where,* or *when.* Write the following sentence on the board:

> "They loved the man of war, / this small man with his hands behind his back, / whose shadow, moving to and fro, was black / behind the lighted tent." (lines 54–57)

Underline the adjective clause as shown. Have students identify the noun that the adjective clause modifies. *(man)*

Practice Have students copy the following sentences. Ask them to underline the adjective clauses and identify the nouns or pronouns they modify.

1. Victor Hugo was the French writer who led the Romantic movement in France. *(who led the Romantic movement in France/writer)*
2. The foul weather that froze the soldiers was a fierce enemy. *(that froze the soldiers/weather)*
3. Napoleon Bonaparte, who was a proud and determined leader, wondered if this was the end. *(who was a proud and determined leader/Napoleon Bonaparte)*
4. A leader's greatness depends on the wisdom that guides him. *(that guides him/wisdom)*

For more instruction and practice in adjective clauses, use McDougal Littell's ***Language Network:***

- Grade 10, Chapter 4, "Clauses and Sentence Structure"
- Grade 12, Chapter 3, "Using Clauses"

Connect to the Literature

1. **What Do You Think?** Students will probably express feelings of sadness, horror, or pity.

Comprehension Check

- The army faces the intense cold of the Russian winter as well as attack by Russian soldiers.
- Napoleon feels responsible for his soldiers' deaths. He also fears that he himself is about to die.

Think Critically

2. Discuss in class the images that helped students visualize the poem's setting. Ask them to describe the setting based on these images.
3. The picket is supposed to warn of an enemy's approach, but he himself was taken by surprise by another enemy: the cold. Other examples of irony might include the description of a crowd being alone and the description of regiments falling asleep.
4. The metaphor is contained in lines 50–51. Napoleon is the oak; the branches represent his soldiers.
5. Possible Response: The speaker views Napoleon as a fallen hero, one who was once great but who has now been brought down by pride.

Extend Interpretations

6. **The Writer's Style** Possible Response: The repetition helps readers visualize the snow and understand its inescapability.
7. **Comparing Texts** Possible Responses: Both poems convey the destructive power of nature. The Romantics celebrated both the beauty and the destructive force of nature.
8. **Connect to Life** Possible Response: Climate and terrain played a major factor in the outcome of the Vietnam War. The jungle conditions in many of the war zones greatly aided the Vietcong.

Connect to the Literature

1. **What Do You Think?** What is your reaction to the description in this poem of the suffering endured by Napoleon's army?

Comprehension Check

- What dangers does the army face as it retreats from Moscow?
- How does Napoleon feel as he watches his army die?

Think Critically

2. **ACTIVE READING: VISUALIZING SETTING** With a partner, discuss the chart you each created in your  READER'S NOTEBOOK. Choose three images that contributed the most to your visualizing of the setting.
3. **Irony** is a surprising contrast between expectation and reality. What is ironic about the description of the picket in lines 13–15? What other examples of irony can you find in the poem?
4. Identify the metaphor in the beginning of the poem's second stanza. Who is the oak? What do the branches represent?
5. What do you think is the speaker's attitude toward Napoleon?

THINK ABOUT
- the way in which Napoleon is described
- how the soldiers feel about him
- how Napoleon reacts after turning to God

Extend Interpretations

6. **The Writer's Style** Notice the repetition of the word *snow* in the first 19 lines of "Russia 1812." Why do you think Hugo chose to repeat this word? How does the repetition affect your reading of the poem?
7. **Comparing Texts** Compare the depiction of nature in "Russia 1812" with that in Heine's "The Lorelei." What similar view of nature is presented in these poems? How does this view correspond with the Romantic idea of nature?
8. **Connect to Life** How has climate or terrain affected soldiers or battles in modern wars you've heard or read about? In what wars have physical conditions helped determine the outcome?

LITERARY ANALYSIS: SETTING IN NARRATIVE POETRY

Like all literary works that tell a story, a **narrative poem** has characters, a plot, and a setting. **Setting,** the time and place of the action, often plays an important role in helping the reader understand the story's plot and characters. Setting can also support or enhance a story's theme. In the following lines from "Russia 1812," notice what the frozen setting suggests about Napoleon, the "Eagle" of the second line:

The snow fell, and its power was multiplied.
For the first time the Eagle bowed its head—dark days!

Paired Activity With a classmate, complete a diagram like the one shown below. Briefly describe the setting of "Russia 1812." Then note ways in which the setting connects to the plot, characters, and theme of the narrative.

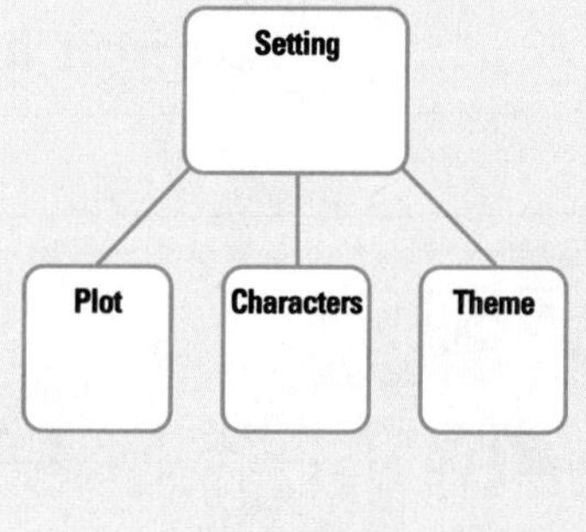

Literary Analysis

Paired Activity Draw the diagram on the board and fill it in with students' ideas. Students should note that the setting determines the plot's main conflict of person against nature; the characters are only seen in relation to the setting; the setting is a direct cause of Napoleon's downfall and so helps establish the theme of pride coming before a fall.

 Use **Unit Six Resource Book,** p. 16, for more practice.

 To assess skills and concepts taught in this selection, use **Formal Assessment Book,** pp. 139–140.

Victor Hugo on Stage and Screen

An individual's struggle against a cruel society, hopeless love, grand passions—such Romantic elements appeal to modern audiences. So it's probably not too surprising that many of Victor Hugo's best-known novels and plays have been translated to the stage and screen. Taking his subjects from common life, Hugo wrote about the hopes and dreams of ordinary people. Audiences identify with these characters, whose emotions and struggles reflect their own.

It's not every day that a 19th-century French novel is turned into a long-running Broadway play. During performances of *Les Misérables,* the musical adaptation of Hugo's novel, audiences cheered as Jean Valjean repeatedly escaped the clutches of the relentless policeman Javert.

Hugo's novel *The Hunchback of Notre Dame* tells the story of Quasimodo, the deformed bell ringer who loves the beautiful gypsy Esmeralda. The many films based on the novel capture the sadness and even the nobility of Quasimodo's situation.

Giuseppe Verdi's opera *Rigoletto* is based on Hugo's play *The King Has Fun.* Rigoletto, a hunchbacked jester, tries to protect his daughter from the powerful Duke—with tragic consequences. The characters' intense feelings are well suited to opera.

Paired Discussion Discuss the Romantic elements in movies and other productions you have seen. You might recall dramas featuring dashing heroes, acts of individual courage, or strong emotions.

Connect to Today

Use this feature to show the relevance of world literature to students. The material relates the literature selection just read to a contemporary topic connected to students' lives today.

Paired Discussion Before students get together with their partners, you might ask the class to name some dramas that contain Romantic elements. For example, students might identify such movies as *Titanic, Braveheart,* and *Robin Hood.* List the titles on the board so that pairs can use them as a springboard for their own discussions.

Objectives
- understand and appreciate poetry that contains elements of both **Romanticism** and **Symbolism (Literary Analysis)**
- identify and evaluate **sound devices** in poetry **(Literary Analysis)**
- determine what **symbols** might represent in poetry **(Literary Analysis)**
- **interpret sensory details** in poetry **(Active Reading)**

Thematic Link
Like most Romantics, Charles Baudelaire wrote passionate poetry. Instead of writing about the beauties of nature, however, Baudelaire used the **expressions of his heart** to describe the treachery of love and the cruelty of life.

5-Minute Warm-Up

Daily Language SkillBuilder

Have students **proofread** the display sentences on page 869j and write them correctly.

POEMS BY Charles BAUDELAIRE

Charles Baudelaire
1821–1867

Wild Youth Charles Baudelaire (bōd-lâr'), possibly the most influential French poet of the 19th century, is almost as well-known for his extravagant lifestyle as for his writing. His stepfather, a strict disciplinarian, tried to tame the young Baudelaire by sending him to a military boarding school. Later, the boy was sent to a high school in Paris from which he was expelled for his outrageous behavior. Baudelaire further displeased his family when he announced his intention to become a writer. He enrolled in law school but rarely attended. Instead, he fell in with a radical crowd and began leading an unconventional existence. Alarmed, Baudelaire's stepfather sent the young man on a voyage to India in 1841. Although Baudelaire returned to France before completing the trip, the voyage had a powerful influence on his writing.

Rich Man, Poor Man Shortly after his return, Baudelaire received his inheritance and began living a life of leisure. However, within two years he had spent nearly half of the money. His family consequently took control of his finances, and Baudelaire was forced to earn a living as an art critic. From 1852 to 1865, he also translated the works of American writer Edgar Allan Poe. Baudelaire's translations established Poe's reputation in France. They also helped Baudelaire clarify his own ideas about poetry.

Last Years Baudelaire's fame grew as a result of his translations, and some of his own poetry began to appear in print. In 1857 he published *The Flowers of Evil,* a collection of poems about love and the role of the artist. The collection caused a scandal. Baudelaire and his publisher were both charged with and found guilty of obscenity and blasphemy. Six of the poems were banned. Although Baudelaire continued to write, he never recovered from the failure of *The Flowers of Evil.* During an unsuccessful lecture tour in Belgium, Baudelaire became severely ill. In 1866 he returned to Paris, where he died the next year in his mother's arms, at the age of 46. At his funeral, already calling themselves his followers, were the writers who would become the leaders of the Symbolist movement.

The Absinthe Drinker (about 1876), Edgar Degas. Oil on canvas, 36¼" × 26¾". Musée d'Orsay, Paris.

LESSON RESOURCES

UNIT SIX RESOURCE BOOK,
pp. 17–18

ASSESSMENT RESOURCES
Formal Assessment, pp. 141–142
Teacher's Guide to Assessment and Portfolio Use
Test Generator

INTEGRATED TECHNOLOGY
Visit our Web Site: classzone.com

ADDITIONAL RESOURCES
Lesson Planning Guide, pp. 121–122
Teacher's Sourcebook for Language Development

Build Background

Beauty in Evil Although Baudelaire's poetry contains elements of Romanticism, his themes helped pave the way for the **Symbolists,** poets who used symbols to suggest meaning and mood. Like the Romantics, Baudelaire wrote with great passion. Unlike the Romantics, however, he was passionate about depicting what he saw as the ugliness of city life and the cruelty of existence.

In *The Flowers of Evil,* Baudelaire described the human condition. According to the poet, good and evil existed side by side within people. Left to their own devices, Baudelaire believed, people would be inclined toward evil. They could only be saved through art.

"The Albatross" and "Invitation to the Voyage" both appear in the first section of *The Flowers of Evil.* "The Albatross" is based on an incident Baudelaire witnessed during his uncompleted voyage to India. Some sailors on the ship had captured an albatross and were amusing themselves by watching its futile efforts to escape. Albatross are large sea birds whose long, narrow wings allow them to glide gracefully over water but hamper them from taking flight except from the open sea. "Invitation to the Voyage" is one of several poems that Baudelaire wrote for Marie Daubrun, an actress he fell in love with.

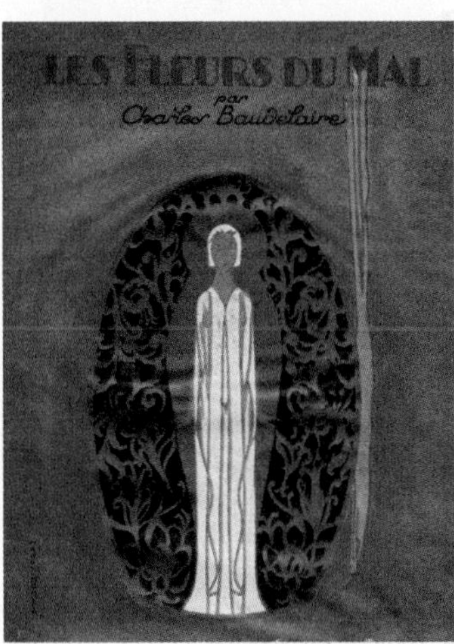

Cover of French edition of *Les Fleurs du Mal* [The flowers of evil]. New York University Libraries.

Connect to Your Life

In "Invitation to the Voyage," the speaker describes an ideal land where he and his love would be happy together. Describe a place—real or imaginary—where you think you would be perfectly happy. Compare descriptions with a small group of students.

Focus Your Reading

LITERARY ANALYSIS: SOUND DEVICES

Poets use a variety of **sound devices** to produce special qualities of sound. These include the following:

- **repetition**—repeated words and phrases
- **alliteration**—the repetition of consonant sounds at the beginnings of words
- **rhyme scheme**—the pattern of rhyme at the ends of lines

As you read the poems, be aware of the sound devices used by Baudelaire.

ACTIVE READING: INTERPRETING SENSORY DETAILS

Sensory details are words and phrases that appeal to the reader's sense of sight, hearing, touch, smell, and taste. The images created by sensory details help bring a piece of writing to life. Notice how the following sensory details from "Invitation to the Voyage" appeal to the sense of smell:

Flowers of rarest bloom
Proffering their perfume
Mixed with the vague fragrances of amber;

READER'S NOTEBOOK As you read the poems by Baudelaire, use a chart like the one below to record sensory details. Then indicate which sense or senses each detail appeals to.

Poem	Sensory Details	Sense(s) Appealed To
"Invitation to the Voyage"		
"The Albatross"		

READING FOR INFORMATION
Reading Skills and Strategies
EVALUATING

Read aloud the second paragraph in **Build Background** on page 923. Ask students whether they agree with Baudelaire's opinion that good and evil exist side by side within people. Do they believe that people are more inclined toward evil than good? Baudelaire claimed that art saved people from following their evil nature. Do students agree? If not, what do they think prevents people from behaving badly?

Literary Analysis SOUND DEVICES

A Read aloud lines 24–26. Ask students to identify the alliteration in these lines. (*the letter* s *in the words* should, soul's, speaking, sweet, *and* secret) Explain that poets often use alliteration to emphasize certain words or images, to heighten mood, and to establish a musical effect. Then ask students what word, mood, or idea is emphasized by the alliteration in these lines.

Possible Responses: The alliteration emphasizes the words *sweet* and *secret.* It also creates a mood of mystery.

 Use **Unit Six Resource Book,** p. 18, for more practice.

Active Reading
INTERPRETING SENSORY DETAILS

B Have students identify the senses appealed to in lines 35–38. *(sight, touch)* Then ask them what images are created by the sensory details in these lines.

Possible Responses: the sight and warmth of a warm setting sun; the sight of a landscape slowly becoming bathed in a warm light

 Use **Unit Six Resource Book,** p. 17, for more practice.

Invitation to the Voyage

Charles Baudelaire

Translated by Richard Wilbur

My child, my sister,
dream
How sweet all things would seem
Were we in that kind land to live together,
And there love slow and long,
There love and die among
Those scenes that image you, that sumptuous weather.
Drowned suns that glimmer there
Through cloud-disheveled air
Move me with such a mystery as appears
Within those other skies
Of your treacherous eyes
When I behold them shining through their tears.

There, there is nothing else but grace and measure,
Richness, quietness, and pleasure.

8 cloud-disheveled (dĭ-shĕv'əld) **air:** sky streaked with clouds.

13 grace and measure: beauty and a sense of proportion.

On Board a Sailing Ship (1818–1819), Caspar David Friedrich. Oil on canvas, 71 cm × 56 cm. The Hermitage, St. Petersburg, Russia/Giraudon/Art Resource, New York.

MINI LESSON Viewing and Representing

On Board a Sailing Ship **by Caspar David Friedrich**

ART APPRECIATION The German Romantic artist Caspar David Friedrich frequently used symbols to convey meaning in his paintings. Friedrich's work is often filled with a mystical, other worldly quality that reflects his deep religious beliefs. Have students study the painting on page 924. Then ask them what the couple, the ship, the sea, and the distant land might represent.

Possible Responses: The couple symbolizes lovers, all people, hope. The ship symbolizes the earthly life, time. The sea symbolizes the world, change, isolation. The distant land represents heaven, hope, death.

In what way is the mood of the painting similar to the mood of the poem?

Possible Responses: Both are dreamy, mystical, ambiguous.

Furniture that wears
The luster of the years
Softly would glow within our glowing chamber,
Flowers of rarest bloom
Proffering their perfume
Mixed with the vague fragrances of amber;
Gold ceilings would there be,
Mirrors deep as the sea,
The walls all in an Eastern splendor hung—
Nothing but should address
The soul's loneliness,
Speaking her sweet and secret native tongue.

There, there is nothing else but grace and measure,
Richness, quietness, and pleasure.

See, sheltered from the swells
There in the still canals
Those drowsy ships that dream of sailing forth;
It is to satisfy
Your least desire, they ply
Hither through all the waters of the earth.
The sun at close of day
Clothes the fields of hay,
Then the canals, at last the town entire
In hyacinth and gold:
Slowly the land is rolled
Sleepward under a sea of gentle fire.

There, there is nothing else but grace and measure,
Richness, quietness, and pleasure.

19 proffering: offering.

23 in an Eastern splendor hung: covered with rich cloths and wall hangings from the Orient.

29 swells: large waves.

33 ply: travel a course regularly.

Customizing Instruction

Less Proficient Readers

Point out that each stanza of the poem describes a different aspect of "that kind land" where the speaker would like to live. Read aloud each stanza, and have students identify details that describe the place.

Possible Responses: 1st stanza—"sumptuous weather," "Drowned suns"; 2nd stanza—"Furniture that wears / The luster of the years," "Gold ceilings," "Mirrors deep as the sea," "The walls all in an Eastern splendor hung"; 3rd stanza—"still canals," "drowsy ships," "a sea of gentle fire"

Point out, too, that each stanza represents one of the qualities repeated in the refrain: richness, quietness, or pleasure. As students read the poem, encourage them to look for details that suggest these qualities. As an example, you might ask them what "still canals" in the third stanza might suggest. *(quietness)*

English Learners

Help students understand the following difficult passages in the poem:

- lines 7–12: The speaker is comparing the suns that exist in the land and that shine through clouds and rain to his beloved's eyes when they fill with tears.
- lines 24–26: The speaker suggests that the place would ease loneliness.
- lines 39–40: "A sea of gentle fire" is a metaphor for the color of the setting sun. As the sun sets, it covers the land with its glow.

Advanced Learners

Point out the paradox of the speaker's reference to his beloved's "treacherous eyes." Then have students identify and discuss other paradoxes in the poem.

Possible Responses: "her sweet and secret native tongue"; "a sea of gentle fire"

MINI LESSON Vocabulary Strategy

SYNONYMS Remind students that synonyms are words with the same or nearly the same meanings. Synonyms can be found by looking in a thesaurus. Write the following sentence on the board:

"Drowned suns that glimmer there / Through cloud-disheveled air" (lines 7–8)

Have students use a thesaurus to find a synonym for the underlined word. *(flash, flicker, shimmer)*

Practice Have students find a synonym for the underlined words in the following lines from "Invitation to the Voyage." Encourage students to read the surrounding lines to derive meaning from the context.

1. "Mixed with the vague fragrances of amber" (line 20) *(aroma, scent, pleasing odor)*
2. "The walls all in an Eastern splendor hung—" (line 23) *(glory, greatness, grandeur)*
3. "Those drowsy ships that dream of sailing forth" (line 31) *(sleepy, nodding, slumbery)*

A lesson on using reference tools appears on p. 558 of the Pupil's Edition.

Literary Analysis SYMBOL

Ask students what the sailors might represent.

Possible Responses: society, cruelty, prejudice, ignorance

Active Reading

INTERPRETING SENSORY DETAILS

A Have students identify sensory details in the poem's last stanza. What senses do these details appeal to?

Possible Responses: "a stormy day"—sight, sound; "the hooting crowds"—sight, sound; "his wings are in the way"—sight, touch

What feelings does this description of the Poet/albatross inspire in the reader?

Possible Responses: feelings of sadness, admiration, pity, love

Reading Skills and Strategies

DRAWING CONCLUSIONS

Ask students what conclusions they can draw about the speaker's sympathies. How does the speaker feel about the sailors? about the albatross?

Possible Responses: The speaker thinks the sailors are contemptible and mean-spirited. The speaker thinks the albatross is noble and ill-used.

The Albatross

Charles Baudelaire

Translated by James McGowan

The Great Family (La grande famille) (1963), René Magritte. Oil on canvas. Private collection. Photo © SuperStock. Art © 2007 C. Herscovici, Brussels/Artists Rights Society (ARS), New York.

Often, when bored, the sailors of the crew
Trap albatross, the great birds of the seas,
Mild travelers escorting in the blue
Ships gliding on the ocean's mysteries.

And when the sailors have them on the planks,
Hurt and distraught, these kings of all outdoors
Piteously let trail along their flanks
Their great white wings, dragging like useless oars.

This voyager, how comical and weak!
Once handsome, how unseemly and inept!
One sailor pokes a pipe into his beak,
Another mocks the flier's hobbled step.

The Poet is a kinsman in the clouds
Who scoffs at archers, loves a stormy day;
But on the ground, among the hooting crowds,
He cannot walk, his wings are in the way.

6 distraught: confused and upset.

10 unseemly and inept: inappropriate and clumsy.

Cross Curricular Link **Science**

ALBATROSS Sailors have long considered the albatross to be a good omen. They believe that an albatross following their ship meant that land was near. Actually, the birds are only interested in the scraps of food thrown from the ship. The albatross is an open-ocean bird that does not touch land for up to five years at a time. The birds only return to land to breed. A pair of albatross stays just long enough to hatch and raise a single chick.

Albatross spend most of their time in the air. They fly for miles, gliding gracefully on the wind. The birds follow the air currents above the ocean's waves so well that they may not have to flap their wings for days. Albatross can even sleep while flying. Although the birds sometimes rest on the open sea, they rarely sleep on the water. Doing so makes them easy targets for killer whales and human hunters.

Connect to the Literature

1. **What Do You Think?** Which of these poems do you prefer? Explain why.

Think Critically

2. **ACTIVE READING: INTERPRETING SENSORY DETAILS** The stanzas in "Invitation to the Voyage" represent richness, quietness, and pleasure—the three qualities repeated in the **refrain.** Get together with a partner and review the sensory-detail chart you created in your READER'S NOTEBOOK. Use the chart to determine which stanza represents which quality in the poem. What sensory details helped you make your determinations?

3. What does "Invitation to the Voyage" suggest about love?

THINK ABOUT
- the speaker's reference to his beloved's "treacherous eyes" in the first stanza
- the speaker's reference to the "soul's loneliness" in the second stanza

4. In "The Albatross," the speaker compares the bird to the poet in society. Through this comparison, what do you think Baudelaire is expressing about both poetry and society?

5. How would you describe the **mood** of each poem?

Extend Interpretations

6. **Comparing Texts** Compare the view of women and love in "Invitation to the Voyage" with that presented in Heine's "The Lorelei." What words do you think the speakers of these poems would use to describe the characters of the women they love?

7. **Critic's Corner** Some critics maintain that the poems in *The Flowers of Evil* contain both Romantic and classical elements. Refer to the chart on page 878 in Learning the Language of Literature, then identify some of these elements in the two poems you've read.

8. **Connect to Life** Think again about your answer to question 4. Do you think poets and artists are seen or treated differently today? Explain your opinion.

LITERARY ANALYSIS: SOUND DEVICES

Like many poets, Baudelaire used **sound devices** to help emphasize certain words, create a mood, and unify his work. Such devices include **repetition** (repeated words and phrases), **alliteration** (the repetition of consonant sounds at the beginnings of words), and **rhyme scheme** (the pattern of rhyme at the ends of lines). Notice the use of repetition (*how*), alliteration (*p*), and rhyme scheme (*weak/beak* and *inept/step*) in the following lines from "The Albatross":

This voyager, how comical and weak!
Once handsome, how unseemly and inept!
One sailor pokes a pipe into his beak,
Another mocks the flier's hobbled step.

Paired Activity With a partner, identify at least one example of repetition, alliteration, and rhyme scheme in each of the poems. Then discuss how the sound devices affect the mood and meaning of the poems.

SYMBOL A **symbol** is a person, a place, an object, or an activity that stands for something beyond itself. In "The Albatross," for example, the sea bird is used as a symbol representing the poet. Several other symbols are named in the last stanza of the poem, including "archers," "stormy day," "hooting crowds," and "wings." Reread the poem and then discuss with a group of classmates what these symbols might represent.

Literary Analysis

Paired Activity Have several sets of partners get together to discuss and compare their charts. Students should understand that the sound devices reinforce mood and convey meaning in the poems.

Use **Unit Six Resource Book,** p. 18, for more practice.

Symbol Possible Responses: The archers might represent critics and others who wish to attack poets. A stormy day might represent the controversy created by a poet's work. Hooting crowds might represent society. The bird's wings might represent the poet's soaring imagination.

To assess skills and concepts taught in this selection, use **Formal Assessment Book,** pp. 141–142.

Connect to the Literature

1. **What Do You Think?** Students should support their preferences with specific details from the poems.

Think Critically

2. Details such as "love slow and long" and "sumptuous weather" suggest that the first stanza represents pleasure. Details such as "gold ceilings" and "walls all in an Eastern splendor hung" suggest that the second represents richness. Details such as "drowsy ships" and "Sleepward under a sea of gentle fire" suggest that the third represents quietness.
3. Possible Response: The poem suggests that love is fraught with betrayal and loneliness.
4. Possible Response: Baudelaire is saying that poetry is misunderstood and society is resistant to new ideas.
5. Possible Responses: The mood in "The Albatross" may be described as sad or tragic. The mood in "Invitation to the Voyage" might be described as drowsy or dreamlike.

Extend Interpretations

6. **Comparing Texts** Possible Responses: The speakers might use words such as treacherous, beautiful, mysterious, irresistible.
7. **Critic's Corner** Possible Responses: Classical elements include an adherence to formal rules and diction and a focus on adult concerns. Romantic elements include an emphasis on emotions and imagination and a celebration of passion and vision.
8. **Connect to Life** Possible Responses: Some students may claim that poets and artists are still misunderstood. Others may say that poets and artists today have much more freedom than those in Baudelaire's time.

Possible Objectives

The poems in this **On Your Own** feature may be used to achieve one or more of the following objectives:

- to give students the opportunity to read independently, either reading silently for a sustained period, reading and analyzing literature with a group, or using the Reader's Notebook to write in responses to the literature
- to conduct a post-reading class discussion
- to assess students' comprehension of the poems

ON YOUR OWN

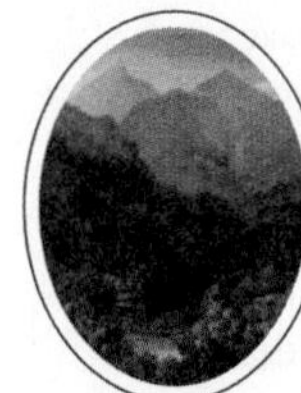

ARTHUR RIMBAUD

The SLEEPER in the VALLEY

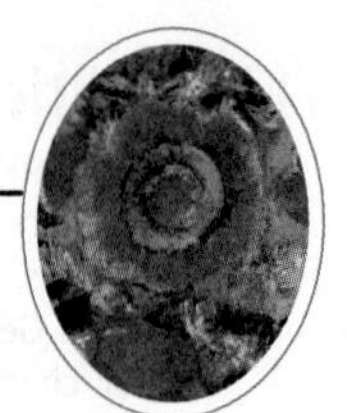

AUTUMN SONG

PAUL VERLAINE

Paul Verlaine
1844–1896
Arthur Rimbaud
1854–1891

Baudelaire's Followers Arthur Rimbaud (răm-bō′) and Paul Verlaine (vĕr-lān′) belonged to the Symbolist movement in France. The Symbolists were a group of writers and artists who used symbols to evoke ideas and emotions. The leaders of the Symbolist movement were chiefly inspired by Charles Baudelaire, whose exploration of controversial subject matter contrasted with Romanticism's emphasis on nature and emotion.

A Troubled Friendship When Rimbaud and Verlaine met in 1871, the two poets began an intense friendship. After a couple of years, however, the pair had a violent falling-out. Verlaine shot his friend, wounding him in the wrist. As a result, Verlaine was given a two-year jail sentence.

After their split, Rimbaud published a collection of poetry called *A Season in Hell.* Unfortunately, the book was not well received. Deeply hurt and disillusioned with literature, Rimbaud apparently never wrote another poem. He was only 19 years old.

Verlaine, on the other hand, achieved some success with the publication of *Wisdom* in 1880. He also published Rimbaud's *Illuminations* in 1886, which made its author famous.

Although Rimbaud and Verlaine sought to break away from the emotion and self-indulgence (as they regarded it) of Romantic poetry, their work is not entirely free of Romantic elements. The view of nature expressed in the poems you are about to read, for example, has much in common with the Romantic view. As you read the poems, ask yourself:

1. *How do the images of nature in the poems compare with those you've observed in Romantic poetry?*
2. *What other Romantic elements do the poems contain?*
3. *What symbols can you identify? Whom or what do they represent?*

The Sleeper in the Valley

Arthur Rimbaud

Translated by William Jay Smith

This is the green wherein a river chants
Whose waters on the grasses wildly toss
Its silver tatters, where proud sunlight slants
Within a valley thick with beams like moss.

A youthful soldier, mouth agape, head bare,
And nape where fresh blue water cresses drain
Sleeps stretched in grass, beneath the cloud, where
On abundant green the light descends like rain.

His feet on iris roots, smiling perhaps
As would some tiny sickly child, he naps.
O nature, he is cold: make warm his bed.

This quiver of perfume will not break his rest;
In sun he sleeps, his hand on quiet breast.
Upon one side there are two spots of red.

5 agape: wide open.

6 nape: the back of the neck.

Working Independently

You may want to set aside time each week for independent reading, without making an assignment related to the reading. Or once students have completed the reading, either alone or aloud in groups, you may ask them to work together on a project, such as presenting a dramatic reading of one of the poems. If you choose to have students write responsively in their Reader's Notebook, suggest that they write about the images and sounds that a favorite season inspires.

Using the Selections for Assessment

If you want to use these selections as the basis for assessment, see **Integrated Assessment Book,** pp. 31–36, for test questions.

THE SLEEPER IN THE VALLEY **929**

Autumn Song

Paul Verlaine

Translated by Louis Simpson

Violins complain
Of autumn again,
        They sob and moan.
And my heartstrings ache
Like the song they make,
        A monotone.

Suffocating, drowned,
And hollowly, sound
        The midnight chimes.
Then the days return
I knew, and I mourn
        For bygone times.

And I fall and drift
With the winds that lift
        My heavy grief.
Here and there they blow,
And I rise and go
        Like a dead leaf.

6 monotone: sound or song with one note.

930 UNIT SIX PART 1

Two Girls Among the Flowers (about 1905), Odilon Redon. Oil on canvas. Museum of Fine Arts, Houston, Texas. © SuperStock.

HUMANITIES CONNECTION Odilon Redon was one of the greatest French Symbolist artists. Like the writers of the Symbolist movement, Redon tried to give form to his thoughts, emotions, and dreams.

Discussion Questions

You might use the questions on page 928 for a post-reading class discussion.

1. How do the images of nature in the poems compare with those you've observed in Romantic poetry?
Possible Responses: Similarities—Nature is portrayed as beautiful, mysterious, destructive; nature inspires reflection and observations about life. Differences—In "The Sleeper in the Valley" and "Autumn Song," nature is connected with death; many of the reflections nature inspires are negative.
2. What other Romantic elements do the poems contain?
Possible Responses: "The Sleeper in the Valley" is imaginative and uses natural diction. "Autumn Song" is experimental in form and stresses emotion.
3. What symbols can you identify? Whom or what do they represent?
Possible Responses: In "The Sleeper in the Valley," the sleeper may represent death, war, disappointment; the valley may represent life, earth, eternity. In "Autumn Song," autumn may represent death, the passage of time, age; the winds may represent change, time, life.

MINI LESSON

Viewing and Representing

Two Heads Among Flowers **by Odilon Redon**

ART APPRECIATION For much of his artistic career, Odilon Redon produced black and white drawings of dark, mysterious subjects. It wasn't until the 1890s that Redon turned to painting and created pictures with flowers and bright colors. Like his earlier work, his more cheerful paintings were inspired by his dreams. Have students study the painting and the **Humanities Connection** on page 931. What emotions does the artist convey with the painting?
Possible Responses: happiness, hope, love

What does the painting suggest about the relationship between people and nature?
Possible Responses: The painting suggests a close relationship; the young girls seem to be merging with the garden; their heads are like the flowers in the painting.

Objectives

- reflect on and assess understanding of European Romanticism
- evaluate Romantic subjects and themes
- identify figurative language and its effect in Romantic poetry
- assess and build portfolios

Reflecting on the Literature

You might have students work in groups of four to identify the subjects and evaluate their messages. Each student in a group should work on one subject.

Possible Responses: Life—In Victor Hugo's "Russia 1812," the narrator indicates that success is short-lived and can be quickly replaced by failure; Death—In Johann Wolfgang von Goethe's *Faust*, the title character suggests that death is preferable to living a life of complacency and contentment; Love—Heinrich Heine's "The Lorelei" reveals the treachery and destructive power of love; Nature—In William Wordsworth's "My Heart Leaps Up," the speaker claims that nature can inspire and enhance life.

Reviewing Literary Concepts

After students identify examples of figurative language in the literature, have them get together in small groups to share their ideas.

Possible Responses: Simile—In *Faust*, Mephisto compares melancholy to a vulture that "ravages your breast" (lines 84–85). The comparison identifies Faust's state of mind and emphasizes his suffering; Metaphor—In "Russia 1812," Napoleon is compared to an oak "already trembling from the axe" (lines 49–51). The metaphor underscores Napoleon's former strength and power and how much he has lost; Personification—In Charles Baudelaire's "Invitation to the Voyage," drowsy ships are said to "dream of sailing forth" (line 31). The personification emphasizes the fantastical nature of the place in the poem.

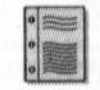
Use **Unit Six Resource Book,** p. 19, for additional support.

Building Your Portfolio

Invite volunteers to select a piece from their Presentation Portfolio to share with the class. Students should read the piece aloud, using an appropriate tone and delivery.

For more information on using writing and assessing portfolios, see the **Teaching Guide to Assessment and Portfolio Use,** pp. 53–74.

Reflect and Assess

What did you learn about Romanticism from reading the selections in Unit Six, Part 1? Did the literature stimulate your own imagination and feelings? Use the following options to help you explore what you have learned.

Detail of *On Board a Sailing Ship* (1818–1819), Caspar David Friedrich. Oil on canvas, 71 cm × 56 cm. The Hermitage, St. Petersburg, Russia/Giraudon/Art Resource, New York.

Reflecting on the Literature

Romantic Subjects Life, death, love, and nature are favorite subjects of Romantic writers. Think about how the literature in this part of the book deals with these subjects. Then choose four selections: one that reveals a perception about life, one that comments on death, one that makes an observation about love, and one that conveys an impression of nature. State what the selection suggests about the subject, and indicate whether you agree with the writer's ideas.

Reviewing Literary Concepts

Figurative Language Romantic poets used figurative language, such as similes, metaphors, and personification, to create effects, emphasize ideas, and evoke emotions. Look back over the literature in this part of the book and choose an example of a simile, a metaphor, and personification. Identify the type of figurative language used, and explain its effect.

Building Your Portfolio

Writing Options Review the various Writing Options you completed for the lessons in this part of the book. Which piece would you consider reading aloud to your classmates? Add the assignment to your **Presentation Portfolio**, and include a note with ideas on the speaking rate, tone, facial expressions, and gestures you might use for an effective delivery.

Self ASSESSMENT

READER'S NOTEBOOK

The following list contains concepts and terms that you encountered as you learned about European Romantic writers. Copy the list on a separate piece of paper. Then work with a small group of classmates to write a sentence describing or defining each word or term. If you don't remember the meaning of a term, review the lesson in which it appeared or consult the **Glossary of Literary Terms** (page R91).

the natural world
Faust
setting
literary ballad
imagery
"Russia 1812"
sound devices
Symbolists

Setting GOALS

Look over the list of books in **Extend Your Reading** on the following page. Select one of the books and read it. After you finish reading, write a paragraph or two identifying some of the Romantic elements in the book.

Assessment Self Assessment

Students can look up the listed terms in the **Glossary of Literary Terms** on page R91 or they can find them introduced in context on the text pages indicated below.

the natural world (p. 898)
Faust (p. 880)
setting (p. 915)
literary ballad (p. 910)
imagery (p. 913)
"Russia 1812" (p. 914)
sound devices (p. 923)
Symbolists (p. 928)

Part Assessment

To assess skills and concepts taught in this unit part, use **Formal Assessment Book,** pp. 143–144.

Extend Your *Reading*

Les Misérables

VICTOR HUGO; LEE FAHNESTOCK, TRANS.

Set in Paris during the political upheaval of the 1820s and 1830s, Hugo's romantic epic tells the story of the outcast Jean Valjean. After being unjustly imprisoned, Valjean struggles to make a new life for himself. His dreams of a normal life, however, are threatened by the police inspector Javert, who is bent on tracking down Valjean and returning him to prison. This sweeping tale is at once a suspenseful thriller and a perceptive study of human nature. Hugo brings his characters to vibrant life as they fight—and die—for their personal and political freedom.

The Sorrows of Young Werther

JOHANN WOLFGANG VON GOETHE; MICHAEL HULSE, TRANS.

This novella created such a stir when it was published that it became fashionable for young German men to imitate Werther's manner of dress, as well as his most desperate acts. The young hero's hopeless passion for the unattainable Charlotte is described largely through letters written to a friend. In the best Romantic tradition, Werther meditates on beauty, art, and nature as he longs for his beloved. With its tragic ending, the story paints a heart-rending portrait of those who become obsessed with love.

And Even *More* . . .

Books

Songs of Love & Grief HEINRICH HEINE; WALTER W. ARNDT, TRANS.
Full of anguish and irony, the German songs in this collection convey the Romantic spirit through Heine's use of mood and imagery.

The Grasmere Journals DOROTHY WORDSWORTH; PAMELA WOOF, ED.
Observations on walks, weather, friends, and poetry provide an intimate glimpse into life at Dove Cottage for Dorothy Wordsworth and her famous brother.

Other Media

Napoleon
From his humble upbringing in Corsica to his glorious days as emperor, Napoleon's life holds the viewer spellbound in this dramatic four-hour documentary. PBS Home Video. (VIDEOCASSETTE)

The Hunchback of Notre Dame
In this 1939 film—widely considered the best screen adaptation of Hugo's classic novel—Charles Laughton creates a touching portrait of the hunchback Quasimodo. Turner Home Video. (VIDEOCASSETTE, DVD)

Frankenstein

MARY WOLLSTONECRAFT SHELLEY

This gothic novel about the monster created by Dr. Frankenstein has little in common with the popular horror films of the same name. The monster of Shelley's masterpiece is a tragic hero whose very human search for love and companionship contrasts with the actions of the scientist who has overthrown the laws of nature.

More Recommendations for Your Students

Difficulty Level: Easy

Halliwell, Sarah (Ed.). *The Romantics: Artists, Writers, and Composers* (Orlando, FL: Raintree/Steck Vaughn, 1998). This work provides a basic introduction to the major figures of European Romanticism.

Symonds, Jimmy. *Eyewitness Classics: The Hunchback of Notre Dame* (NY: DK Publishing, 1997). Using illustrations, photographs, and maps, this retelling of Victor Hugo's classic novel allows readers to enter the world of the original story.

Difficulty Level: Average

Hibbert, Christopher. *The Days of the French Revolution* (NY: Quill, 1999). This historical narrative presents a highly readable account of the events and characters of the French Revolution.

Wordsworth, Jonathan. *William Wordsworth and the Age of English Romanticism* (New Brunswick, NJ: Rutgers University Press, 1987). Illustrated with paintings by artists of the period, this volume explores the contributions of Wordsworth and other British poets to the Romantic movement.

Difficulty Level: Challenging

Goethe, Johann Wolfgang von (W.H. Auden and Elizabeth Mayer, Trans.). *Italian Journey* (East Rutherford, NJ: Penguin USA, 1992). Goethe reveals much about himself as he describes the people and places he encounters during his life-changing sojourn in Italy.

Owen, W.J.B. *Wordsworth and Coleridge: Lyrical Ballads,* 1798 (NY: Oxford University Press, 1969). This collaborative work signaled the beginning of Romanticism in England.

Unit Six, Part 2, presents several works of realism, the literary movement that emerged following romanticism. The first realist writers were from Europe, but the movement eventually influenced the development of literature throughout the world.

World Art and Cultures Transparencies

AT53 *Couturier*

AT55 *Arrival of the Normandy Train, Gare Saint-Lazare*

You may use the listed transparencies to acquaint students with examples of European art from the second half of the 19th century.

READING FOR INFORMATION

Reading Skills and Strategies

PREVIEWING

Have students look at the labels of the five boxed annotations located on the map. Ask them what seem to be some of the major developments or beliefs of this period. *(scientific discoveries and inventions, sharply divided economic classes, injustices needing reform, belief in progress, importance of railroads)* Then have them look at the visuals. Ask them what invention created in the 19th century is still in widespread use today. *(camera)* Finally, ask what working conditions were like in a 19th-century factory. *(difficult and dangerous)*

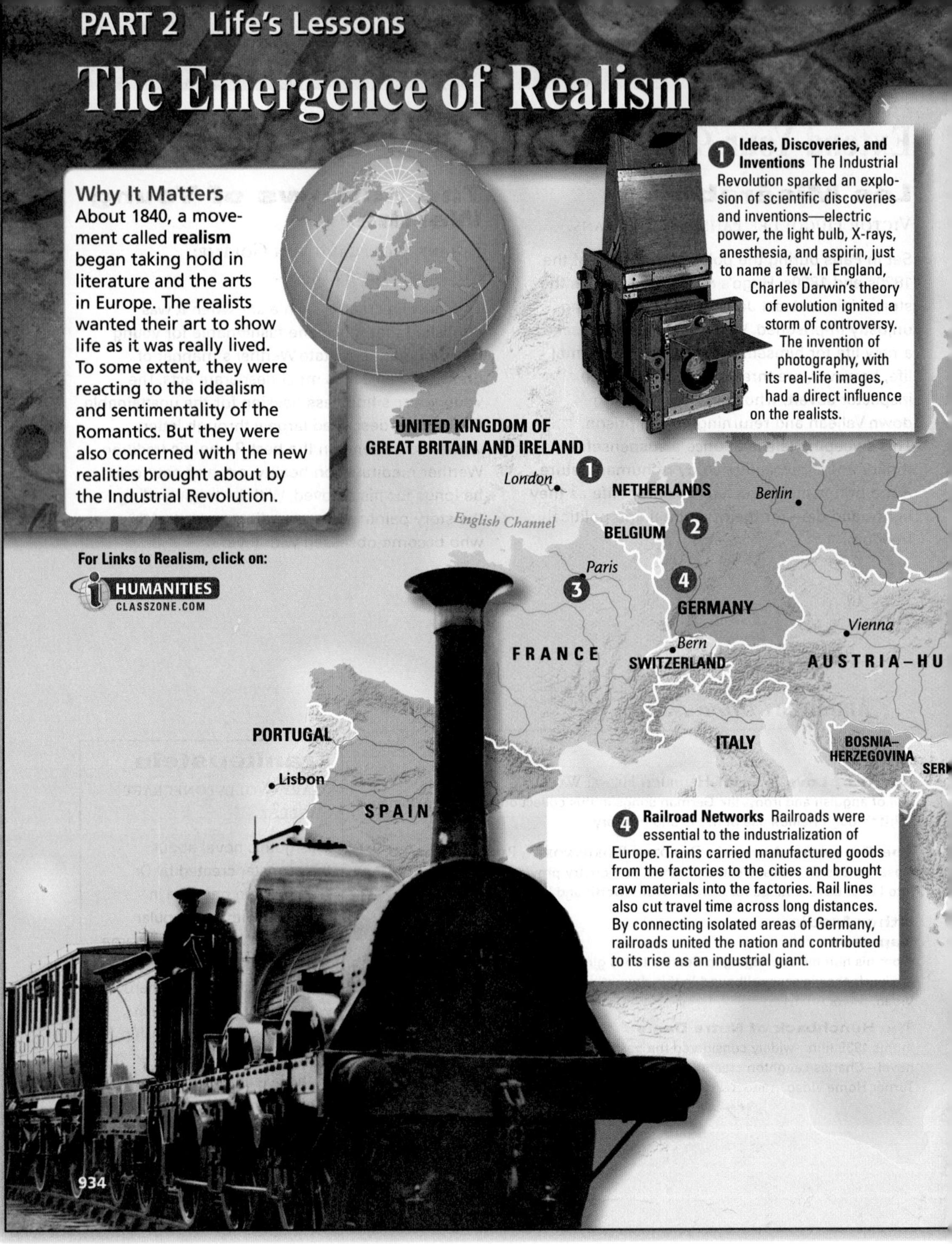

PART 2 Life's Lessons

The Emergence of Realism

Why It Matters

About 1840, a movement called **realism** began taking hold in literature and the arts in Europe. The realists wanted their art to show life as it was really lived. To some extent, they were reacting to the idealism and sentimentality of the Romantics. But they were also concerned with the new realities brought about by the Industrial Revolution.

1 Ideas, Discoveries, and Inventions The Industrial Revolution sparked an explosion of scientific discoveries and inventions—electric power, the light bulb, X-rays, anesthesia, and aspirin, just to name a few. In England, Charles Darwin's theory of evolution ignited a storm of controversy. The invention of photography, with its real-life images, had a direct influence on the realists.

4 Railroad Networks Railroads were essential to the industrialization of Europe. Trains carried manufactured goods from the factories to the cities and brought raw materials into the factories. Rail lines also cut travel time across long distances. By connecting isolated areas of Germany, railroads united the nation and contributed to its rise as an industrial giant.

For Links to Realism, click on: HUMANITIES CLASSZONE.COM

934

MINI LESSON Using the Map

Have students locate Paris and London on the map. Tell them to use the scale given on page 935 to measure the approximate distance between the two cities. *(London is about 200 miles from Paris.)* Ask students to identify the largest and the smallest countries on the map. *(Russia and Montenegro)*

2 Rich and Poor The Industrial Revolution brought great advances but had a dark side as well. **Middle-class** businessmen profited from the growth of **factories.** But those in the **working class,** which included women and children as well as men, were overworked and underpaid. They toiled 12 to 14 hours a day, sometimes under dangerous conditions, as shown in this 1875 painting of a German steel factory.

Attempts at Reform Injustice and harsh conditions in the 19th century prompted calls for reform. Some of the resulting efforts met with success. **Suffrage,** or the right to vote, was extended to men outside the aristocracy in Britain, France, and Germany. The British abolished slavery throughout their empire in 1833, and the French freed the slaves in their colonies in 1848. Russian serfs—peasants who labored in the fields under conditions very similar to those of slavery—gained their freedom in 1861.

3 Monument to Progress The French government had the Eiffel Tower built to celebrate the 100th anniversary of the French Revolution and to symbolize industrial progress. Though light and airy in appearance, the 984-foot iron tower is extremely strong. Considered an engineering marvel when it opened in 1889, the Eiffel Tower still amazes tourists visiting Paris.

Historical Note

Railway Boom In the mid-1840s, railway lines began to be built all over England. By 1850 trains were traveling 30 to 50 miles an hour (a great advance over the first trains, which traveled at about 14 miles an hour), and they quickly became an essential and economical means of transporting manufactured goods. Other European countries followed Britain's lead, and railroads became an important British export.

Cultural Note

Eiffel Tower In addition to commemorating the 100th anniversary of the French Revolution, the Eiffel Tower was built as the gateway to the International Exposition of 1889. When the French government sponsored a contest for designs for the monument, over 100 entries were submitted. The winning design was by Gustave Eiffel, a bridge engineer. Eiffel, who wanted to show how iron and steel could be used in new ways, financed the project himself. Although many people criticized the design initially, about 2 million visitors came the first year, fascinated by what was at the time the tallest structure in the world. Today the Eiffel Tower is the most famous sight in Paris.

Pronunciations
Louis Pasteur (lwē′ päs-tœr′)
Guy de Maupassant (gē′ də mō-pă-säN′)

READING FOR INFORMATION

Reading Skills and Strategies

IDENTIFYING MAIN IDEAS AND DETAILS

Tell students that some of the main developments of the second half of the 19th century are described on pages 936 and 937. Have them read the italicized paragraph on page 936 and then read each of the five sections, noting each head first. Ask them to state the main idea of each section and to give one supporting detail for each. *(ethnic groups broke away from empires and became nations—Germany and Italy; imperialist nations took over colonies—Africa; machines and factories made possible the production of inexpensive goods—textiles and pottery; working class suffered and reforms were set in motion—child labor laws; scientific discoveries changed the quality of life—pasteurization)*

Historical Note

A German and Italian Flags The 1848 German flag, shown on this page, is known as the German Tricolor. The three-band design was used only briefly in the 19th century and once more for a period of about 14 years in the early 20th century. Other designs were used in the intervening years until the German Tricolor was adopted for a third time on May 8, 1949. It remains the official flag of the Federal Republic of Germany today.

Green, white, and red stripes were first used in Italian flags in the late 18th century. The colors were discontinued after the Napoleonic period but reinstated in 1848. The arms in the center of the 1848 flag represent the Kingdom of Sardinia, or Savoy, under which the states of Italy were united. The arms of Savoy were removed in 1946, and the flag with three plain stripes has been in use since then.

Historical Highlights

The second half of the 19th century in Europe has been called the Second Industrial Revolution, the Age of Imperialism, and the Age of Reform. Regardless of the title, the events of this time period had a global impact and far-reaching consequences. We are still feeling the effects today.

Children living in poverty in London, about 1860

Development of Nations

One of the ideas unleashed by the French Revolution was **nationalism,** the belief that people who share a common culture and history make up a nation. After Napoleon's defeat at Waterloo in 1815, three major empires remained on the European continent: the Austrian Empire, the Russian Empire, and the Ottoman Empire. In the mid-1800s, ethnic groups within these empires demanded nationhood and democratic reforms in an outburst of revolts. During this same period, independent German and Italian states also unified into two nations. But the eventual cost of German unification was dictatorship and two world wars. Though tattered, the Russian Empire remained intact until the communist revolution of 1917.

A

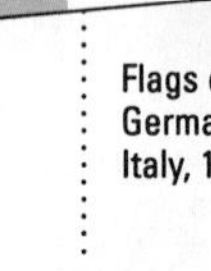

Flags of Germany and Italy, 1848

Imperialism

To improve their economies, the industrialized nations of Europe began to look for new sources of raw materials. The Europeans descended on resource-rich Africa and expanded their holdings in Asia. By the turn of the century, they had carved up Africa into colonies, with Britain and France having the largest share. In addition, the British controlled India and joined the French, Dutch, and Americans in dividing Southeast Asia. This process of taking over and then dominating another country is called **imperialism.** Its effect in the 19th century, for the most part, was to increase the wealth of the imperialist nations at the expense of the colonies.

Queen Victoria

Mass Production

The Industrial Revolution changed the nature of work. What used to be made by hand could now be produced faster and cheaper by machines. The operation of the machines was divided among the factory workers, who each specialized in some function of the production process. Mass production of textiles and pottery made inexpensive clothes and dishes available for the first time.

Mass production, and industrialization in general, benefited people of the middle class more than anyone else. Many factory owners, merchants, and bankers got rich. The standard of living also rose for shop owners, accountants, factory managers, architects, office workers, and carpenters.

936

MINI LESSON Interpreting the Text

Have students review the five main sections. Ask them to list three positive and three negative developments in the late 19th-century Europe.

Possible Responses: positive: forming of independent nations, better standard of living for the middle class, vaccines for diseases; negative: exploitation of colonies in Africa and Asia, poverty of working class, women refused the right to vote

Then have them discuss the consequences of one or two of these developments in the 21st century.

Need for Reform

The working class lived and worked under terrible conditions. Children as young as five often had to work. The British Parliament did pass some laws restricting the age of child laborers and limiting the workday in factories to ten hours for women and children. Workers also formed unions to negotiate for improved working conditions. One successful reform effort was the spread of **free public education** in most European nations by the late 1800s.

As more men won voting rights, women started organizing to get the vote as well, especially in Britain. Despite women's protests, however, no European countries gave women the vote at this time.

Scientific Breakthroughs

The amazing scientific and technological achievements of the 19th century would eventually revolutionize people's lives. Experiments with electricity introduced a new kind of power and made electric inventions such as the light bulb possible. The full impact of such inventions as the telephone and the automobile wouldn't be felt until the next century, but discoveries in the field of biology had more immediate effects. Working in the mid-1800s, French chemist **Louis Pasteur** discovered that bacteria caused disease. This discovery led not only to the development of pasteurization, a process for killing harmful bacteria in milk and other foods, but also to the use of germ-killing antiseptics in hospitals. New vaccines for many serious diseases, such as typhoid fever were also developed during this time.

Louis Pasteur

History to Literature

EVENT IN HISTORY	EVENT IN LITERATURE
Czar Alexander II frees Russian serfs.	Novelist Leo Tolstoy portrays peasant life in *Anna Karenina*.
The Industrial Revolution causes changes among the social classes.	Short-story writer Guy de Maupassant examines moral conflicts of the French middle class and peasants.

Historical Note

B Child Labor in Victorian England
The Industrial Revolution brought with it horrendous abuses, especially of children. Most poor families could not survive without the children working, and going to school was out of the question. In the worst situations, young children worked 16-hour days, often under dangerous conditions. Laws passed in 1833 did limit the workday to 12 hours and prohibited children nine and younger from working, but this legislation applied only to the textile industry. Other industries, such as mining, ship-building, and construction, still employed children as young as five. The laws limiting the workday to 10 hours for women and children were passed in 1847. Unfortunately, however, as late as 1860 half of England's children still had no access to even the barest minimum of education.

Pronunciations

Gustave Courbet (gōō-stäv′ kōōr-bĕ′)
Honoré Daumier (ô-nô-rā′ dōm-yā′)
Camille Corot (kä-mē′yə kô-rō′)
Auguste Rodin (ô-güst′ rô-dăN′)
Honoré de Balzac (ô-nô-rā′ də bäl-zäk′)
Gustave Flaubert (gōō-stäv′ flō-bâr′)
Émile Zola (ā-mēl′ zō-lä′)
Fyodor Dostoyevsky (fyôd′ər dŏs′tə-yĕf′skē)
Anton Chekhov (ən-tôn′ chĕk′ôf)
August Strindberg (ou′gəst strĭn′bûrg′)
Henrik Ibsen (hĕn′rĕk ĭb′sən)
Friedrich Engels (frē′drĭKH ĕng′əls)
Gregor Mendel (grā′gōr′ mĕn′dəl)

READING FOR INFORMATION

Reading Skills and Strategies

CLASSIFYING

Tell students that the second half of the 19th century saw radical shifts in thought and expression. Direct them to the four sections on pages 938 and 939, which highlight some of these shifts. Suggest that they take note of the four areas identified in the heads and then read each section. Next have them read the **Connect to Today** feature. Lead them in a discussion of other effects and consequences of the shifts and changes presented in the four categories.

Cultural Note

(A) **Rodin's Sculptures** Auguste Rodin is considered by some critics to be the greatest portraitist in the history of sculpture. The realism of his work was so striking to his contemporaries that they once accused him of creating a bronze figure from a mold formed on a real person. The great project of Rodin's career was a commission he was given to create an enormous bronze door for a new museum of the decorative arts (Musée des Arts Décoratifs). The themes for the door were taken from Dante's *Inferno,* and the door itself came to be known as *The Gates of Hell (La Porte de L'Enfer)*. Two of the figures originally made for the door are among Rodin's most famous works. *The Thinker (Le Penseur)* was intended as a seated figure of Dante for the upper part of the door, and *The Kiss (Le Baiser)*, was meant to represent the lovers Paolo and Francesca, from Canto V of the *Inferno.*

Arts and Culture

With people crowding into industrial cities and more voices calling for reform, troubling social and political realities became impossible to ignore. Artists and intellectuals faced the issues directly. Scientists, meanwhile, tried to better understand the physical world.

Visual Arts

When a 19th-century French painter examined early photographs, he boldly declared: "From today painting is dead." He was wrong. The camera's factual accuracy actually inspired realist art.

Realism began in France with the work of three painters: Gustave Courbet, Honoré Daumier, and Camille Corot. Courbet headed the movement away from idealized Romantic painting and toward an accurate record of contemporary life. One of his greatest works, *The Stone Breakers,* shows two men laboring in a stark rural landscape. The raw honesty of Courbet's painting shocked the French art world, who expected to see pictures of smiling peasants in clean clothes. Daumier, a painter and sculptor, also drew cartoons. These cartoons ruthlessly satirized French politicians, businessmen, lawyers, and other rising middle-class professionals who took themselves too seriously. Corot was a landscape painter whose small, naturalistic sketches captured the basic truth the realists aimed for.

(A) The French sculptor Auguste Rodin can be considered a realist, although he wasn't officially part of the movement. His portrayals of the human figure were so lifelike they caused scandals.

Rodin's *The Thinker*

Literature

Realist writers also rebelled against Romanticism as too emotional and idealistic. Influenced by the real-world emphasis of photography and science, they took a hard look at the people around them—such as peasants, coal miners, clerks, middle-class wives, orphans, and thieves.

Novels were particularly well suited to examining contemporary life because they could show development over time and extensive interaction among characters. Many great novelists were writing during this period: Honoré de Balzac, Gustave Flaubert, and Émile Zola in France; George Eliot in Britain; and Leo Tolstoy and Fyodor Dostoyevsky in Russia. Guy de Maupassant and Anton Chekhov mastered the **short story** form to capture brief but meaningful glimpses into characters' everyday lives. (B)

Drama also underwent drastic changes. Scandinavian playwrights August Strindberg and Henrik Ibsen produced brutally insightful plays about class conflict, women's roles, and middle-class hypocrisy. Such issues unsettled middle-class audiences, who were used to happy endings in the theater.

Karl Marx

Political Thought

One response to the economic inequities and harsh working conditions of the 19th century was *The Communist Manifesto,* a pamphlet published in 1848 by **Karl Marx** and his friend **Friedrich Engels.** In it, Marx argued that the workers, whom he called the proletariat, should overthrow the greedy business owners, or capitalists, and take control of the industries. The ultimate goal Marx set was the establishment of justice and equality in a classless society with no private property and no government. Marx's ideas led to major revolutions in the 20th century before declining in influence late in the century.

Scientific Theories

The development of science and scientific theory, with its focus on the physical world, was one of the important influences on realism in the 19th century. One of the most controversial scientific ideas was proposed in 1859 by **Charles Darwin** in his book *On the Origin of Species.* Darwin theorized that the great diversity of species on earth resulted from what he called natural selection: As members of a species compete for food, only those whose traits give them an advantage will survive long enough to reproduce. These survivors in turn pass the traits on to their offspring. Darwin's theory came to be known as the theory of evolution.

During the same period, an Austrian botanist, **Gregor Mendel,** (C) was exploring the question of how physical traits are passed on from one generation to another. In his work, Mendel studied the differences in pea plants. He theorized that similar traits passed from the parent plants to their descendants occurred on paired hereditary units, now called **genes.** Mendel's experiments established the laws of heredity and began the science of genetics.

Connect to Today

In the 21st century, we are still living with ideas and perspectives generated in the latter half of the 19th century.

- Realism has had a direct influence on film. This influence is seen in the use of realistic settings and true-to-life portrayals of people and situations.
- Although weakened, communism is still a revolutionary force in parts of Latin America, Africa, and Southeast Asia.
- Refinements of Mendel's original discoveries have made further genetic research possible. Breakthroughs are leading to new treatments for diseases such as cancer.

Literary Note

(B) Charles Dickens Both Leo Tolstoy and Fyodor Dostoyevsky read and greatly admired the works of Charles Dickens, perhaps the greatest English novelist of the 19th century. Though Dickens was not part of the realist movement, his novels included elements of realism, such as his depictions of working-class poverty, the abuses of children by greedy and cruel adults, the criminal world, and the hypocrisy of the wealthy and the powerful. He differed from the realists in his use of complicated plots, inventive and original characterizations, and humor.

Science Note

(C) Gregor Mendel The botanist Gregor Mendel was an Augustinian monk who had a lifelong interest in science. Spurred by observations he made in his father's orchards, he pursued scientific reading on his own and later studied physics, chemistry, mathematics, zoology, and botany at the University of Vienna. He taught natural science in a technical high school near the monastery but, ironically, never passed the examination for a teacher's license. He did, however, have access to important scientific books in both the school and the monastery libraries, and he helped form the Natural Science Society with some of his colleagues from the high school.

Mendel carried out his famous experiments with pea plants in the monastery garden. By crossing plants with different characteristics, such as presence or absence of color, seed shape, and tallness or shortness, he was able to formulate the basic laws of heredity. When Mendel presented his work in two scientific papers, however, other biologists did not grasp the importance of what he had discovered. It was not until 14 years after his death—and 34 years after he published his papers—that several botanists performing similar experiments realized that Mendel had already reached the very conclusions they were pursuing.

Pronunciations

Karl Benz (kärl′ bĕnts′)
Guglielmo Marconi (gōō-yĕl′mō mär-kō′nē)
Marie (mä-rē′) and Pierre (pyĕr′) Curie (kü-rē′)
Benito Juárez (bĕ-nē′tô hwä′rĕs)
Ashanti (ə-shăn′tē)
Laos (lous)
Boers (bōrz)

READING FOR INFORMATION

Reading Skills and Strategies

READING A TIME LINE

Review with students the three-part structure of the time line, which shows events in European realism, European history, and world history. Draw their attention to the small time line at the top of the page. Ask them to compare it with the small time lines given for the early parts in the books, for example those on pages 110 and 428. Ask them what the main difference is. *(The section of the time line representing realism is much shorter in relation to the whole time line than are the sections representing ancient India and ancient China on the earlier time lines.)*

Time Line

REALISM (1840–1899)

A.D. 1 — PRESENT

EVENTS IN EUROPEAN REALISM

1840

1829–1847 Honoré de Balzac writes *The Human Comedy,* a collection of novels and short stories about French society

1848 Karl Marx and Friedrich Engels publish *The Communist Manifesto*

1849 French painter Gustave Courbet ushers in the realist movement in art

1850

1857 Publication in France of Gustave Flaubert's realistic novel *Madame Bovary*

1859 Charles Darwin publishes *On the Origin of Species by Means of Natural Selection*

1860

1860 George Eliot's novel *The Mill on the Floss* analyzes the impact of mechanization on a rural family

1865–1869 Publication of Leo Tolstoy's great novel *War and Peace,* set during the Napoleonic Wars

1866 Fyodor Dostoyevsky publishes *Crime and Punishment,* a novel about the moral and psychological consequences of a murder

EVENTS IN EUROPEAN HISTORY

1840

1842 Ether is first used as an anesthesia in surgery

1847 British Parliament passes a law limiting the workday to ten hours for women and children

1848 Revolutions erupt in France, Italy, Austrian Empire, and Germany

1850

1850s Early development of modern photography

1852 Napoleon III proclaims himself emperor of France

1858 Completion of the first successful trans-Atlantic telegraph cable

1860

1860 In London, Florence Nightingale opens the first school to train nurses

1860s French chemist Louis Pasteur discovers the germ origin of disease and invents the process of pasteurization

1860s Liberal reforms in Britain and France extend voting rights and allow more freedom of the press

1861 Alexander II frees Russia's 20 million serfs

EVENTS IN WORLD HISTORY

1840

1842 Hong Kong given to Britain after the Chinese are defeated in the First Opium War (1839–1842)

1844 Samuel Morse sends first long-distance telegraph message between Baltimore and Washington, D.C.

1850

1853 Commodore Matthew Perry opens U.S. relations with Japan

Susan B. Anthony dollar

1860

1867 The last Japanese shogun steps down, ending over 700 years of military rule

1867 Mexican reformer Benito Juárez reelected president after defeating the French

1869 Elizabeth Cady Stanton and Susan B. Anthony found the National Woman Suffrage Association

940 UNIT SIX PART 2: THE EMERGENCE OF REALISM

MINI LESSON Using the Time Line

Have students refer to the time line to answer the following questions:

1. How long after the freeing of the Russian serfs did Leo Tolstoy write *Anna Karenina?* *(14–16 years)*
2. Could *A Doll's House* have influenced Elizabeth Cady Stanton and Susan B. Anthony's decision to form the National Woman Suffrage Association? *(no, because the play wasn't produced until ten years later)*
3. What was invented the same year that Émile Zola published his novel *Germinal? (the first car with an internal combustion engine)*
4. Which was used first in medicine—ether or X-rays? *(ether)*

1870	1880	1890
1875–1877 Tolstoy's novel *Anna Karenina* examines romantic love and family life **1879** Henrik Ibsen produces *A Doll's House,* which shocks audiences with its uncompromising portrayal of a middle-class marriage	**1880** French sculptor Auguste Rodin casts the bronze statue *The Thinker* **1880–1890** Guy de Maupassant writes most of his famous short stories **1885** Émile Zola uses an extreme form of realism called naturalism in his novel *Germinal,* about a coal miners' strike	**1892–1898** Anton Chekhov writes short stories about Russian peasants, intellectuals, and factory owners **1896** Chekhov's play *The Seagull* is performed in St. Petersburg

1870	1880	1890
1871 Otto von Bismarck completes the unification of the German Empire, making it one of the most powerful European nations **1871** Trade-Union Act of 1871 makes British labor unions legal	**1884** Invention of the automatic machine gun **1885** German engineer Karl Benz invents the first automobile with an internal combustion engine	**1895** Discovery of X-rays **1895** Guglielmo Marconi invents wireless telegraphy, or radio **1898** French physicists Marie and Pierre Curie discover radium **1899** The medicinal value of aspirin is recognized

1870	1880	1890
1873–1874 The Ashanti of West Africa fight a war with the British **1876** Alexander Graham Bell patents the telephone **1877** Thomas A. Edison invents the phonograph **1879** Edison invents the light bulb	**1884** Congo Basin in Africa falls under control of King Leopold II of Belgium **1883** Brooklyn Bridge completed in New York **1887** Land of Zulus in southern Africa falls under British control **1888** Easy-to-use Kodak box camera first produced	**1893** Laos becomes part of French Indochina, which already included Vietnam and Cambodia **1894–1895** Japan and China fight over Korea in the Sino-Japanese War **1898** With help from the United States, Cuba gains independence from Spain **1899–1902** Boers—descendants of Dutch and German settlers in southern Africa—rebel against British rule

Historical Note

A **Aspirin** Aspirin, one of the most widely used medicines in the world, belongs to a group of chemical compounds known as salicylates. For centuries, people used the bark of the willow tree to relieve pain and fever. The effective ingredient in the bark was a chemical that the body converts to a salicylate. In 1853, a French chemist, Charles Gerhardt, produced the aspirin compound in a laboratory, but its use as a pain reliever—similar to that of the willow bark—was not immediately recognized. It took until the end of the century for a German scientist, Heinrich Dreser (hīn′rĭKH drā′zər), to explain and publicize the medicinal value of aspirin.

Objectives
- understand the development and characteristics of realism
- understand the differences between romanticism, realism, and naturalism

Pronunciations
Honoré de Balzac (ô-nô-rā′ də bäl-zäk′)
Gustave Flaubert (go͞o-stäv′ flō-bâr′)
Henrik Ibsen (hĕn′rĕk ĭb′sən)
Guy de Maupassant (gē′ də mō-pă-säɴ′)
Anton Chekhov (ən-tôn′ chĕk′ôf)
Victor Hugo (vēk′tôr ü-gō′)
Émile Zola (ā-mēl′ zō-lä′)

Characteristics of Realism
The realist writers' focus on everyday occurrences often involved a focus on seemingly trivial behavior. For them, all aspects of a character's attitudes and actions were legitimate subjects for literature. Exploring the most insignificant details of a personality or a relationship could reveal important complexities, contradictions, and ironies.

Realism

Realism refers to the accurate—or realistic—portrayal of life in literature and the arts. In fiction and drama, the term is often used to describe works that deal with the daily struggles and disappointments of ordinary people.

Realism was a product of the new realities that took hold in Europe in the 19th century. These included the ups and downs of democratic reform, the social and economic changes brought about by the Industrial Revolution, and new methods of observation opened up by science and photography.

Characteristics of Realism

Realist writers were a varied group, but they shared certain ideas about their writing.

A New Kind of Subject Matter Romantic writers of the early 19th century had glorified the individual. Realists weren't looking for glory or grandeur or heroism, however; they were looking for an understanding of their time. And understanding for them lay in the facts of an individual's life. Therefore, the characters they wrote about were often peasants, businessmen, and housewives. Upper-class characters were portrayed with faults rather than idealized. Instead of creating elaborate plots, the realists focused on everyday occurrences. The result was a closer examination of character, especially as it related to moral behavior.

A New View The realistic writers took the view that life doesn't always work out for the best. As a result, their works often did not have happy endings.

A Change in Method The writing of the Romantics tended to be emotional and highly imaginative. The realists, however, adopted the scientific method of detached observation and recording of facts to describe their characters. Much of their writing has the clarity and precision of a black-and-white photograph. To better understand how these two methods differ, compare the following descriptions:

Major Writers of Realism

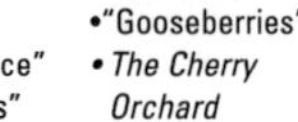

Honoré de Balzac	George Eliot	Gustave Flaubert	Leo Tolstoy	Henrik Ibsen	Guy de Maupassant	Anton Chekhov
1799–1850	1819–1880	1821–1880	1828–1910	1828–1906	1850–1893	1860–1904
• *Old Goriot* • *Cousin Bette*	• *Adam Bede* • *The Mill on the Floss*	• *Madame Bovary* • *Sentimental Education*	• *War and Peace* • *Anna Karenina*	• *An Enemy of the People* • *The Wild Duck*	• "The Necklace" • "Two Friends"	• "Gooseberries" • *The Cherry Orchard*

They were no longer living men and troops,
but a dream drifting in a fog, a mystery,
mourners parading under the black sky.
—*Victor Hugo, "Russia 1812"*

Then a wagon passed at the jerky trot of a nag, shaking strangely, two men seated side by side and a woman in the bottom of the vehicle, the latter holding on to the sides to lessen the hard jolts.
—*Guy de Maupassant, "A Piece of String"*

YOUR TURN Which passage is more emotional and which is more informational? Describe the kinds of details each writer uses to achieve such opposite effects.

Realism in Drama

There was little serious drama being written in the mid-19th century. Most productions were light entertainment—melodrama and farce. When realism burst upon the stage with Ibsen's *A Doll's House* in 1879, it brought back energy and creativity to the theater. Although attacked by critics and the public alike, Ibsen had opened the door to a new era in drama.

Beyond Realism to Naturalism

Naturalism developed out of realism and was more concerned with plot than character. Coming later in the century and heavily influenced by new scientific theories, naturalists portrayed human life as determined by outside forces of heredity and environment. In the works of French novelist Émile Zola, the foremost writer of the naturalistic movement, the characters are trapped in a world they can't control; only the strong survive.

Three Ways of Looking at a Sparrow

To understand the different points of view of a Romantic, a realist, and a naturalist, consider how each might write about a sparrow.

Romantic Point of View:

Behold the lowly sparrow—
So small, so innocent!
Such gifts that nature brings
Make me glad to see
tomorrow.

Realist Point of View:
The sparrow searches for food. He hops around, looking under leaves, picking at twigs, cocking his head to listen for danger.

Naturalist Point of View:
The sparrow is quick, but not quick enough. The hawk swoops, capturing its prey in its strong talons.

Strategies for Reading: Realistic Literature

1. Pay attention to concrete details for information about characters and setting.
2. Notice the values of the characters and whether any characters have conflicting values.
3. Determine what causes a character's downfall.
4. Look for truths about ordinary life.
5. **Monitor** your reading strategies and modify them when your understanding breaks down. Remember to use your Strategies for Active Reading: **predict, visualize, connect, question, clarify,** and **evaluate.**

YOUR TURN The passage from "Russia 1812" is more emotional than the passage from "A Piece of String." The words and phrases that appeal to the emotions include "no longer living men," "a dream drifting in a fog," "a mystery," and "mourners . . . under a black sky." The factual details in the passage from "A Piece of String" include "jerky trot of a nag," "two men seated side by side," "a woman in the bottom of the vehicle," and "holding on to the sides to lessen the hard jolts." Students may note that while Hugo creates a mood, Maupassant creates a sharp and vivid picture.

Beyond Realism to Naturalism

The naturalists tended to focus on the negative aspects of a character, relationship, or situation. Because of the importance they placed on the influence of heredity and environment, they described settings and characters in almost clinical detail. One critic described Zola's fiction as an "autopsy on life." The naturalists, particularly Zola, influenced many realist writers, including Maupassant, Chekhov, and Ibsen.

Three Ways of Looking at a Sparrow

You might want to have students create their own sets of comparisons. Tell them to choose another subject from nature, such as a plant, animal, or rock, and write descriptions of it from the romantic, realist, and naturalist points of view.

Strategies for Reading

1. Students might want to keep two lists of particularly striking details, one for characters and one for setting. They could compare their choices when they have finished reading all the selections.
2. Tell students that they should look for negative values as well as positive ones. Suggest that they look also for whether any characters change their values during the course of a selection.
3. Suggest to students that they think about characters' motivations, inconsistencies, and preoccupations.
4. Tell students to especially consider what the writers reveal about people's self-understanding.
5. Remind students that the more they pay attention to what they do and don't understand as they read, the more they will gain from their reading experience.

Objectives

- understand and appreciate a **short story** in the **realist tradition (Literary Analysis)**
- recognize and understand techniques of **characterization in realism (Literary Analysis)**
- **interpret details** to draw conclusions about characters and themes **(Active Reading)**

Summary

As Maître Hauchcome, a practical, shrewd, and self-conscious businessman, enters Goderville on market day, he pauses to pick up a piece of string and notices that he is being watched by an enemy, Maître Malandain. Later that day, a public crier announces that a black leather pocketbook full of money was lost along the road that morning. Hauchecome's enemy accuses him of stealing it. Although the pocketbook with its money is soon returned to its owner, the townspeople continue to believe that the crafty Hauchecome is guilty—that he set up the return of the pocketbook—and they continue to laugh at him and reproach him for the crime. Hauchecome becomes obsessed with vindicating himself, especially since he knows that although he did not do what he was accused of, he would have been capable of it. His obsession with proving his innocence consumes him, driving him to illness and, finally, to his death.

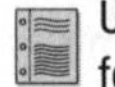 Use **Unit Six Resource Book,** p. 20, for additional support.

Thematic Link

In this story, Maupassant portrays an incident in which a character suffers the consequences of not learning some of **life's lessons.**

 Use **Unit Six Resource Book,** p. 23, for practice with Words to Know.

A Piece of STRING

Guy de Maupassant

Guy de Maupassant
1850–1893

The Well-Crafted Story
Guy de Maupassant (gē'də mō-pă-sän') is considered by many to be the greatest French short story writer and an inspiration to generations of European and American writers. He always presented his characters objectively—not by judging them but by simply recording their actions. And with remarkable precision, he focused on the exact gesture, feeling, or word that defined each character's personality. The effect was to make his perfectly crafted stories seem, in his words, "to be pieces of human existence torn from reality."

Unremarkable Beginnings Maupassant was born to upper-middle-class parents in the French province of Normandy. After high school, he served in the French army and studied law in Paris. In his early 20s, he took a clerical position with the French government, a job he disliked but apparently succeeded at.

Becoming a Writer When he was a young writer, Maupassant's inspiration and guide was Gustave Flaubert (gōō-stäv' flō-bâr'), the author of *Madame Bovary* (1857) and other realistic works. Flaubert was a friend of Maupassant's mother and invited the young Maupassant regularly to his house in Paris for lunch and conversation. At these lunches, Flaubert discussed writing style and technique, and he critiqued pieces that Maupassant had written. Flaubert also introduced the young writer to leading literary figures, such as the naturalistic writer Émile Zola (ā-mēl' zō-lä'). Though Maupassant disliked being labeled, he did develop a naturalistic tone in his own work.

Rich and Famous Maupassant's first short story, "Ball of Fat," appeared in 1880 in an anthology compiled by Émile Zola. This story, considered to be one of his best, made Maupassant famous. Over the next 10 years, he produced an enormous amount of work: more than 300 short stories, six novels, three travel books, and one book of poetry. He sold his stories to magazines and newspapers, published them in collections, and eventually grew quite rich. Maupassant only enjoyed his success a short time before his deteriorating health overcame him. He died in an asylum from complications of an incurable disease a month before his 43rd birthday.

Other Works
"The Necklace"
"The Jewelry"
"The Umbrella"
A Life
Good Friend

5-Minute Warm-Up

Daily Language SkillBuilder

Have students **proofread** the display sentences on page 869j and write them correctly.

LESSON RESOURCES

UNIT SIX RESOURCE BOOK,
pp. 20–24

ASSESSMENT RESOURCES
Formal Assessment, pp. 145–146
Teacher's Guide to Assessment and Portfolio Use
Test Generator

INTEGRATED TECHNOLOGY
Visit our Web site: classzone.com

ADDITIONAL RESOURCES
Lesson Planning Guide, pp. 123–124
Teacher's Sourcebook for Language Development

Build Background

Maupassant's Norman Roots "A Piece of String" is set in Normandy, a farming region of northern France. A beautiful area of low hills, fields, and hedges, Normandy is famous for its butter, cheeses, and apple cider. When Maupassant was a boy, he had many opportunities to observe Norman peasants. These small-scale farmers generally led difficult lives. Peasant families consumed most of what they raised and sold the rest in open-air markets. Some traditional Norman markets are still in existence today.

Maupassant once wrote of Normandy:

> *I love this land, and I love to live in it because my roots are here, those deep and delicate roots that attach a man to the land where his fathers were born and died, attach him to the thoughts men think, the food they eat, the words they use, their peasant drawl; to the odors that rise from the soil and the villages and linger in the very air itself.*

Despite this deep attachment, he avoided sentimentality in his Norman stories. The peasants he portrays are sometimes stingy, coarse, and cruel. Maupassant wanted his fiction to be true to life, even if that life was unpleasant. Like other realist writers associated with naturalism, he was especially interested in how people's social circumstances and natural drives can determine their fates.

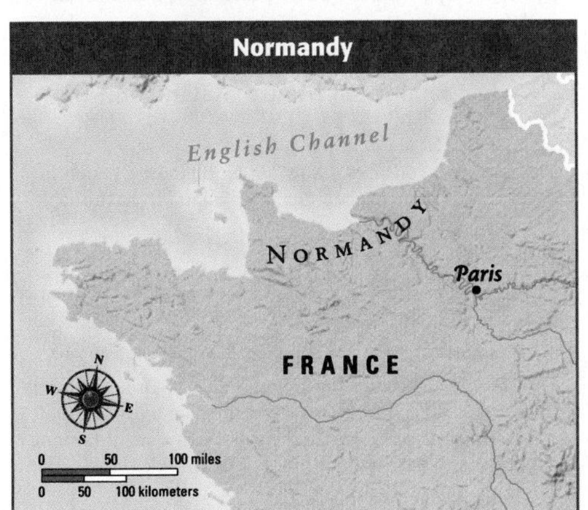

Connect to Your Life

How do you think you would feel if you were falsely accused of wrongdoing? How might such an experience affect the way you interact with people? Share your thoughts with the class.

Focus Your Reading

LITERARY ANALYSIS: CHARACTERIZATION IN REALISM

Characterization refers to the techniques used to develop characters. Writers can portray characters through physical description of the character, a character's words and actions, the words and actions of other characters, and direct commentary by the narrator.

Because realist writers are concerned with examination of character, characterization is an important element in their works. As you read this story, notice which techniques Maupassant uses.

ACTIVE READING: INTERPRETING DETAILS

"A Piece of String" is filled with **details** that help create a realistic impression of the people and way of life described in the story. Interpreting these details will help you draw conclusions about Maupassant's characters and themes.

READER'S NOTEBOOK As you read the story, create cluster diagrams like the one below to help you organize descriptive details. Create one diagram for the setting; another for the main character, Maître Hauchecome; and a third for the peasants in general.

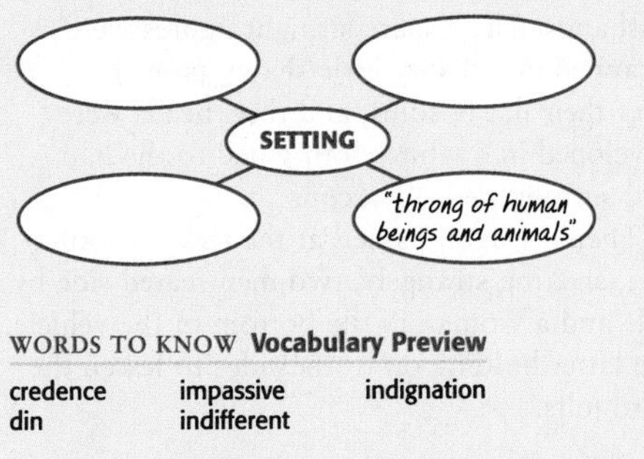

WORDS TO KNOW **Vocabulary Preview**

credence
din
impassive
indifferent
indignation

READING FOR INFORMATION

Reading Skills and Strategies

USING TEXT ORGANIZERS

Tell students that in addition to the main heads, a variety of formats is used on pages 944 and 945 to convey different kinds of information. Point out the list of **Other Works** on page 944. Ask students how many short stories and how many novels are included in the list. *(three short stories and two novels)* Then draw their attention to the call-out quote, map, and cluster diagram on page 945. Ask them the following questions:

- Who wrote the quotation and what is the subject? *(Maupassant wrote it; the subject is his attachment to the region of Normandy, in France.)*
- According to the map, where is Normandy in relation to Paris? *(northwest)*
- What can a cluster diagram help you organize? *(details about a main topic, which is named in the center circle)*

TIME MANAGEMENT

If your schedule requires that you cover the lesson objectives in a shorter time, use . . .

- Preparing to Read, pp. 944–945
- Thinking Through the Literature, p. 952
- Vocabulary in Action, p. 953

If you want to take advantage of longer blocks of class time, use . . .

- TE Teaching Options: Cross Curricular Link, pp. 946, 948, 950; Vocabulary Strategy, p. 947; Viewing and Representing, p. 949; Speaking and Listening, p. 951
- Choices & Challenges, p. 953

Literary Analysis CHARACTERIZATION IN REALISM

Remind students of the four methods of characterization. Ask them to identify two different methods used to develop the character of Maître Hauchecome on these pages and to give examples of each.

Possible Responses: physical description—he has pain when he bends over (p. 946, col. 2); **action of the character himself**—he hides the string under his blouse (p. 947, col. 1); **action of another character**—Maître Malandain watches him when he is picking up the string; **commentary by the narrator**—he describes Hauchecome and Malandain as "good haters" (p. 947, col. 1).

Then ask whether the details given in their examples idealize the character or make him seem ordinary.

Possible Response: Most students will say that Hauchecome seems ordinary and perhaps not very appealing.

Use **Unit Six Resource Book,** p. 22, for additional support.

Active Reading INTERPRETING DETAILS

Point out to students that the descriptions on these pages give many details about the setting and the peasants who come to town on market day. Ask them to identify three details describing the setting and three describing the peasants.

Possible Responses: Details about the setting include the roads full of people (p. 946, col. 1), the shouting and noise in the public square (p. 946, col. 2), the smells and sounds of animals, (p. 946, col. 2), and the jumble of carts and wagons parked in the court of Jourdain's inn (p. 947, col. 2). Details about the peasants include the men walking slowly and bent over (p. 946, col. 1), the women carrying baskets with chickens and ducks in them (p. 946, col. 1), the full-cut starched blue blouses that the men wear (p. 946, col. 1), and the bargaining at the market (p. 947, col 1).

Use **Unit Six Resource Book,** p. 21, for additional support.

A Piece of String

Guy de Maupassant

Along all the roads around Goderville[1] the peasants and their wives were coming toward the burgh[2] because it was market day. The men were proceeding with slow steps, the whole body bent forward at each movement of their long twisted legs, deformed by their hard work, by the weight on the plow which, at the same time, raised the left shoulder and swerved the figure, by the reaping of the wheat which made the knees spread to make a firm "purchase,"[3] by all the slow and painful labors of the country. Their blouses, blue, "stiff-starched," shining as if varnished, ornamented with a little design in white at the neck and wrists, puffed about their bony bodies, seemed like balloons ready to carry them off. From each of them a head, two arms, and two feet protruded.

Some led a cow or a calf by a cord, and their wives, walking behind the animal, whipped its haunches with a leafy branch to hasten its progress. They carried large baskets on their arms from which, in some cases, chickens and, in others, ducks thrust out their heads. And they walked with a quicker, livelier step than their husbands. Their spare straight figures were wrapped in a scanty little shawl, pinned over their flat bosoms, and their heads were enveloped in a white cloth glued to the hair and surmounted[4] by a cap.

Then a wagon passed at the jerky trot of a nag, shaking strangely, two men seated side by side and a woman in the bottom of the vehicle, the latter holding on to the sides to lessen the hard jolts.

In the public square of Goderville there was a crowd, a throng of human beings and animals mixed together. The horns of the cattle, the tall hats with long nap of the rich peasant, and the headgear of the peasant women rose above the surface of the assembly. And the clamorous, shrill, screaming voices made a continuous and savage din which sometimes was dominated by the robust lungs of some countryman's laugh, or the long lowing of a cow tied to the wall of a house.

All that smacked of the stable, the dairy and the dirt heap, hay and sweat, giving forth that unpleasant odor, human and animal, peculiar to the people of the field.

Maître Hauchecome, of Breaute,[5] had just arrived at Goderville, and he was directing his steps toward the public square, when he perceived upon the ground a little piece of string. Maître Hauchecome, economical like a true Norman, thought that everything useful ought to be picked up, and he bent painfully, for he suffered from rheumatism. He took the bit of thin cord from the ground and began to roll it carefully when he noticed Maître Malandain,[6] the

1. **Goderville** (gôd-ər-vēl′): town in Normandy, a region in northwest France, about ten miles inland from the English Channel.
2. **burgh** (bûrg): town.
3. **purchase:** position of the body necessary in order to move a large weight.
4. **surmounted** (sər-mount′ĭd): placed above or on top of.
5. **Maître Hauchecome** (mĕ′trə ōsh-côm′), **of Breaute** (brōt): *Maître* is French for *master.* Breaute, like most of the other places mentioned in the story, was a small farming community within a few miles of Goderville.
6. **Maître Malandain** (mä-län-dăN′).

WORDS TO KNOW

din (dĭn) *n.* loud, confused noise

Cross Curricular Link **History**

PEASANT LIFE Nineteenth-century French peasants lived a hard but self-sufficient life that was not greatly different from that of peasants in earlier centuries. Though some peasants had wealth, many faced the constant threat of poverty. A bad harvest, damaging weather, or some piece of personal bad luck could be disastrous. There was little flow of cash, peasants being much more comfortable bartering with their neighbors at market. Many families fed and clothed themselves almost entirely on what they could produce on their own. Often, the only items that had to be bought were iron and salt, and accounts were settled sometimes only once a year. Peasants continued to use ancient tools, such as wooden plows, and were not interested in the new farm machinery that was becoming available in other countries.

Peasants did not venture far from their local area. Many spoke dialects or even other languages than French, and they had distinctive customs and dress. They did not think of themselves primarily as French citizens but as belonging to the land and village of their birth.

"... they were on bad terms, being both good haters. Maître Hauchecome was seized with a sort of shame to be seen thus by his enemy, picking a bit of string out of the dirt."

harness-maker, on the threshold of his door, looking at him. They had heretofore had business together on the subject of a halter,[7] and they were on bad terms, being both good haters. Maître Hauchecome was seized with a sort of shame to be seen thus by his enemy, picking a bit of string out of the dirt. He concealed his "find" quickly under his blouse, then in his trousers' pocket; then he pretended to be still looking on the ground for something which he did not find, and he went toward the market, his head forward, bent double by his pains.

1

He was soon lost in the noisy and slowly moving crowd, which was busy with interminable bargainings. The peasants milked, went and came, perplexed, always in fear of being cheated, not daring to decide, watching the vender's eye, ever trying to find the trick in the man and the flaw in the beast.

The women, having placed their great baskets at their feet, had taken out the poultry which lay upon the ground, tied together by the feet, with terrified eyes and scarlet crests.

They heard offers, stated their prices with a dry air and impassive face, or perhaps, suddenly deciding on some proposed reduction, shouted to the customer who was slowly going away: "All right, Maître Authirne,[8] I'll give it to you for that."

Then little by little the square was deserted, and the Angelus[9] ringing at noon, those who had stayed too long, scattered to their shops.

At Jourdain's[10] the great room was full of people eating, as the big court was full of vehicles of all kinds, carts, gigs, wagons, dump carts, yellow with dirt, mended and patched, raising their shafts to the sky like two arms, or perhaps with their shafts in the ground and their backs in the air.

Just opposite the diners seated at the table, the immense fireplace, filled with bright flames, cast a lively heat on the backs of the row on the right. Three spits were turning on which were chickens, pigeons, and legs of mutton; and an appetizing odor of roast beef and gravy dripping over the nicely browned skin rose from the hearth, increased the jovialness,[11] and made everybody's mouth water.

All the aristocracy of the plow[12] ate there, at Maître Jourdain's, tavern keeper and horse dealer, a rascal who had money.

The dishes were passed and emptied, as were the jugs of yellow cider. Everyone told his affairs, his purchases, and sales. They discussed the crops. The weather was favorable for the green things but not for the wheat.

7. **halter:** strap with a noose by which horses are tied or led.
8. **Maître Authirne** (ō-tîrn').
9. **Angelus** (ăn'jə-ləs): the church bells that ring to announce the Angelus prayer, which is recited at morning, noon, and evening.
10. **Jourdain's** (zhōōr-dănz').
11. **jovialness:** state of heartiness and good cheer.
12. **aristocracy of the plow:** humorous way of referring to farmers.

WORDS TO KNOW

impassive (ĭm-păs'ĭv) *adj.* revealing no emotion; expressionless

Customizing Instruction

Less Proficient Readers

Students may have difficulty with the long sentences in this story. Help them work through one or two examples: "The men were proceeding . . ." (p. 946, col. 1); "Then a wagon . . ." (p. 946, col. 1); "They heard offers . . ." (p. 947, col 1); "At Jourdain's . . ." (p. 947, cols. 1–2).

1 Make sure students understand that after Hauchecome realizes that Malandain is watching him, he hides the string and pretends he is still looking for something. Ask why he keeps on looking. *(so Malandain won't think he is a stingy person who would bother with a worthless piece of string)*

To help students keep track of the many descriptive details on these pages, have them make a chart with five columns for the five senses (sight, hearing, taste, touch, and smell). Tell them to list details in the story in the appropriate column.

English Learners

- Make sure students understand the following terms: p. 946, col. 1, "jerky trot of a nag" *(uneven walking of an old horse)*; p. 946, col. 2, "tall hats with long nap of the rich peasant" *(high black hats made of a thick, furry material)*; p. 946, col. 2, "savage din" *(loud, wild, confusing combination of noises)*; p. 946, col. 2, "economical" *(careful about money)*; p. 947, col. 1, "good haters" *(The two men completely dislike and despise each other.)*
- Help students make their way through the story by identifying transition words and phrases. Examples include "Along all the roads" (p. 946, col. 1), "Then a wagon" (p. 946, col. 1), "In the public square" (p. 946, col. 2), "They had heretofore" (p. 947, col. 1), "He was soon" (p. 947, col. 1), and "Just opposite" (p. 947, col. 2).

Advanced Learners

Maupassant uses three similes in these pages. Have students identify them and comment on their effect.

Possible Response: On page 946, col.1, the shiny finish of the peasants' blouses is compared to varnish, and the blouses are compared to balloons. On page 947, col. 2, the shafts of the dump carts sticking up in the air are compared to two arms. All three similes create clear, vivid images.

MINI LESSON

Vocabulary Strategy

PREFIXES

Instruction Point out to students that words like *indirect* and *impossible* begin with prefixes. The prefix *in-* means "not," and the prefix *im-* is a variation of *in-*, also meaning "not" in this case. *Indirect*, therefore, means "not direct," or "roundabout." *Impossible* means "not possible." The addition of the prefix changes the meaning of the word to its opposite.

Practice Have students work in pairs to find the meaning of each word below.

incorrect (*not correct; in + correct*)
inconsiderate (*not considerate; in + considerate*)
impatient (*not patient; im + patient*)
immovable (*not movable; im + movable*)

A lesson containing prefixes appears on p. 864 of the Pupil's Edition.

Reading and Analyzing

Literary Analysis
CHARACTERIZATION IN REALISM

Ask students to identify an example of the following three kinds of characterization used to portray Maître Hauchecome on this page: description by the narrator, words or actions of the character, and words and actions of other characters.

Possible Responses: **description**—"surprised and disturbed," "more bent than in the morning" (p. 948, col. 1), "astounded" and "terrified," "flushed with anger," and "furious" (p. 948, col. 2); **words or actions of the character**—numerous examples of dialogue, rummaging in his pocket and pulling out the piece of string, and spitting to enforce his words (p. 948, col. 2); **words and actions of other characters**—the accusations and responses of the mayor and the mayor's shaking his head in disbelief (p. 948, col. 2).

Active Reading INTERPRETING DETAILS

Ask students to name three details that give a realistic impression of the scenes described on this page.

Possible Responses: Details include everyone in the inn running to the door with their mouths full and napkins in their hands, the public crier speaking in a "jerky voice" with irregular phrases, and the diners finishing their coffee (p. 948, col. 1).

Literary Analysis PLOT AND CONFLICT

Remind students that one of the elements of plot is conflict. Ask them to describe the conflict that develops in this part of the story.

Possible Responses: Maître Hauchecome is falsely accused of stealing a pocketbook by Maître Malandain, who saw him pick up the piece of string.

Reading Skills and Strategies
CLARIFYING

A Ask students what the old man remembers and understands. *(He remembers that Malandain watched him picking up the string and hiding it and realizes that the harness-maker is trying to make it look like he was stealing the pocketbook.)*

Suddenly the drum beat in the court, before the house. Everybody rose except a few indifferent persons, and ran to the door, or to the windows, their mouths still full and napkins in their hands.

After the public crier had ceased his drum-beating, he called out in a jerky voice, speaking his phrases irregularly:

"It is hereby made known to the inhabitants
1 of Goderville, and in general to all persons
present at the market, that there was lost this
morning, on the road to Benzeville,[13] between
2 nine and ten o'clock, a black leather pocketbook
containing five hundred francs[14] and some business papers. The finder is requested to return same with all haste to the mayor's office or to Maître Fortune Houlbreque of Manneville,[15] there will be twenty francs reward."

Then the man went away. The heavy roll of the drum and the crier's voice were again heard at a distance.

Then they began to talk of this event, discussing the chances that Maître Houlbreque had of finding or not finding his pocketbook.

And the meal concluded. They were finishing their coffee when a chief of the gendarmes[16] appeared upon the threshold.

He inquired:

"Is Maître Hauchecome, of Breaute, here?"

Maître Hauchecome, seated at the other end of the table, replied:

"Here I am."

And the officer resumed:

"Maître Hauchecome, will you have the goodness to accompany me to the mayor's office? The mayor would like to talk to you."

The peasant, surprised and disturbed, swallowed at a draft his tiny glass of brandy, rose, and, even more bent than in the morning, for the first steps after each rest were specially difficult, set out, repeating: "Here I am, here I am."

The mayor was awaiting him, seated on an armchair. He was the notary[17] of the vicinity, a stout, serious man, with pompous[18] phrases.

"Maître Hauchecome," said he, "you were seen this morning to pick up, on the road to Benzeville, the pocketbook lost by Maître Houlbreque, of Manneville."

The countryman, astounded, looked at the mayor, already terrified, by this suspicion resting on him without his knowing why.

"Me? Me? Me pick up the pocketbook?"

"Yes, you, yourself."

"Word of honor, I never heard of it." 3

"But you were seen."

"I was seen, me? Who says he saw me?"

"Monsieur Malandain, the harness-maker."

The old man remembered, understood, and A
flushed with anger.

"Ah, he saw me, the clodhopper, he saw me pick up this string, here, M'sieu',[19] the Mayor." And rummaging in his pocket he drew out the little piece of string.

But the mayor, incredulous, shook his head.

"You will not make me believe, Maître Hauchecome, that Monsieur Malandain, who is a man worthy of credence, mistook this cord for a pocketbook."

The peasant, furious, lifted his hand, spat at one side to attest[20] his honor, repeating:

"It is nevertheless the truth of the good God, the sacred truth, M'sieu' the Mayor. I repeat it

13. **Benzeville** (băNz-vēl′).
14. **francs:** A franc is the basic monetary unit of France.
15. **Maître Fortune Houlbreque of Manneville** (fôr-tün′ o͞ol-brĕk′, män-vēl′).
16. **gendarmes** (zhän′därmz′): armed police.
17. **notary:** a person with the legal authority to witness and certify documents.
18. **pompous** (pŏm′pəs): full of self-importance.
19. **M'sieu** (mə-syœ′): shortened form of *monsieur,* French for *mister* or *sir.*
20. **attest** (ə-tĕst′): to testify to; to affirm.

WORDS TO KNOW

indifferent (ĭn-dĭf′ər-ənt) *adj.* having no particular interest or concern
credence (krēd′ns) *n.* belief; trust

948

Cross Curricular Link **History**

VILLAGE NOTARY In the small towns and villages of 19th-century France, one of the most influential figures was the notary. The notary held a key position in the society because he had control of a variety of legal and financial affairs and functioned as both a lawyer and a tax collector. He was involved in virtually every aspect of people's lives and knew the business of everyone in the village. He took care of marriage contracts, title searches, bank loans, and wills. He drew up deeds to property and functioned as a real estate agent. Notaries sometimes worked on Sundays, doing business with the peasants coming in to church from the countryside. Some had stalls in the markets and actually had peasants sign blank pieces of paper that they filled in later. Often, the notary was also the mayor, as is the case in "A Piece of String." Today, village notaries have much less power but still handle some functions, including real estate transactions, in provincial France.

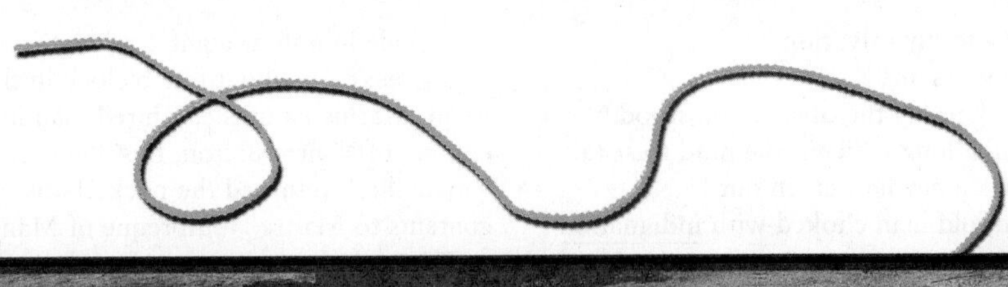

The Peasants of Flagey Returning from the Fair (1855), Gustave Courbet. Oil on canvas, 208.5 cm × 275 cm. Musée des Beaux-Arts, Besançon, France. Photo © Erich Lessing/Art Resource, New York.

HUMANITIES CONNECTION This painting caused a stir in the Paris art world of the 1850s because it showed peasants as they really were rather than in some romanticized, sentimental way. The critics did not think that Courbet's realistic portrayal of such people was fitting in a work of art.

Customizing Instruction

Less Proficient Readers

- Make sure that students understand what Hauchecome is accused of and why. Ask them the following questions: What is the relationship between Hauchecome and Malandain? *(They have had bad business dealings, and they hate each other.)* What is Hauchecome accused of? *(stealing a pocketbook with 500 francs in it)* What is the basis of the accusation? *(Malandain saw Hauchecome picking up the string, hiding it, and pretending to look for something else.)*
- Suggest to students that as they read page 948, they list the names of the characters and the sequence of events. *(characters: the public crier, Maître Fortune Houlbreque [owner of the lost pocketbook], a police officer, Hauchecome, the mayor, Malandain; sequence of events: public crier makes announcement, peasants at the inn discuss matter, an officer calls Hauchecome, Hauchecome goes to see the mayor, the mayor makes the accusation, Hauchecome denies it.)*

English Learners

1 Make sure students understand the announcement made in the third paragraph on page 948. Explain what a public crier is, and work through the paragraph with students.

2 Explain that the word *pocketbook* refers to a man's wallet, not a woman's purse.

3 Have students work in pairs to read the passages of dialogue aloud. Explain words and phrases that they do not understand.
Continue to draw students' attention to transition words, such as *suddenly, after, then,* and *but.*

Advanced Learners

Remind students that dramatic irony exists when the reader knows something that a character does not. Ask them to identify two examples of dramatic irony in this part of the story. *(When the officer tells Hauchecome that someone saw him picking up the pocketbook, the reader knows that it was Malandain, but Hauchecome does not. When Hauchecome says he didn't take the pocketbook, the reader knows that Hauchecome is telling the truth, but the mayor does not.)*

MINI LESSON Viewing and Representing

The Peasants of Flagey Returning from the Fair, Ornans **by Gustave Courbet**

ART APPRECIATION

Instruction In the mid-19th century, the art world was accustomed to seeing peasants portrayed as young and attractive, happily working in the fields. Gustave Courbet's (go͞o-stäv′ ko͞or-bĕ′) portrayal of the real farmers of Flagey (flä-zhā′) returning from the fair at Ornans (ôr-näɴ′) with their animals, baskets, and peddler's packs was considered to be in bad taste.

In addition to criticizing the realistic depiction of the peasants, the art world did not like the stiffness of the figures. Courbet was, however, incorporating a qualilty of folk art in his work. He felt that this quality was closer to the realities of rural life than was the graceful style of conventional painters.

Application Tell students to look carefully at the painting and to reread the **Humanities Connection** on page 949. Ask them what details of the painting reflect the setting and characters of the story.

Possible Response: Details could include the predominance of the farm animals, many people on the road together, the woman with a basket on her head, the women and one man walking on foot, the tall black hat, the women's shawls and head coverings, and the man carrying a sack of goods.

Literary Analysis
CHARACTERIZATION IN REALISM

Point out that Maupassant uses all four methods of characterization to portray Hauchecome at the end of the story. Ask students the following questions:

What do we learn about Hauchecome?
Possible Response: Hauchecome cannot stop cornering people and trying to make them believe him. His increasingly complicated explanations emphasize his inability to ignore the situation and go on with his life.

How well does Hauchecome understand himself?
Possible Response: He seems to have little self-understanding, because he doesn't seem to realize that his behavior is out of proportion to the situation. He is unable to just laugh and forget the whole thing. Instead, he is so consumed by the misunderstanding that he gets sick.

Why is it so important to him to make people believe him?
Possible Response: Although he is more than capable of lying and using trickery himself, his insistence on telling his story reveals that he cannot stand to be misunderstood.

Literary Analysis REALISM
Remind students that works of realism portray the everyday difficulties and disappointments of ordinary people. Ask them to suggest how this part of the story shows characteristics of realism.
Possible Responses: Hauchecome's inability to drop the subject of his innocence reflects the human tendency to overreact to something unimportant. Other people's gossiping and making fun of him reflects the way real people react to someone else's mistakes and foolishness.

on my soul and my salvation."

The mayor resumed:

"After picking up the object, you stood like a stilt, looking a long while in the mud to see if any piece of money had fallen out."

The good, old man choked with indignation and fear.

"How anyone can tell—how anyone can tell—such lies to take away an honest man's reputation! How can anyone—"

There was no use in his protesting, nobody believed him. He was confronted with Monsieur Malandain, who repeated and maintained his affirmation.[21] They abused each other for an hour. At his own request, Maître Hauchecome was searched, nothing was found on him.

Finally the mayor, very much perplexed, discharged him with the warning that he would consult the public prosecutor and ask for further orders.

The news had spread. As he left the mayor's office, the old man was surrounded and questioned with a serious or bantering[22] curiosity, in which there was no indignation. He began to tell the story of the string. No one believed him. They laughed at him.

He went along, stopping his friends, beginning endlessly his statement and his protestations, showing his pockets turned inside out, to prove that he had nothing.

They said:

"Old rascal, get out!"

And he grew angry, becoming exasperated, hot, and distressed at not being believed, not knowing what to do and always repeating himself.

Night came. He must depart. He started on his way with three neighbors to whom he pointed out the place where he had picked up the bit of string; and all along the road he spoke of his adventure.

In the evening he took a turn in the village of Breaute, in order to tell it to everybody. He only met with incredulity.[23]

It made him ill at night.

The next day about one o'clock in the afternoon, Marius Paumelle, a hired man in the employ of Maître Breton, husbandman at Ymanville,[24] returned the pocketbook and its contents to Maître Houlbreque of Manneville.

This man claimed to have found the object in the road; but not knowing how to read, he had carried it to the house and given it to his employer.

The news spread through the neighborhood. Maître Hauchecome was informed of it. He immediately went the circuit and began to recount his story completed by the happy climax. He was in triumph.

"What grieved me so much was not the thing itself, as the lying. There is nothing so shameful as to be placed under a cloud on account of a lie."

He talked of his adventure all day long, he told it on the highway to people who were passing by, in the wineshop to people who were drinking there, and to persons coming out of church the following Sunday. He stopped strangers to tell them about it. He was calm now, and yet something disturbed him without his knowing exactly what it was. People had the air of joking while they listened. They did not seem convinced. He seemed to feel that remarks were being made behind his back.

On Tuesday of the next week he went to the market at Goderville, urged solely by the necessity he felt of discussing the case.

Malandain, standing at his door, began to laugh on seeing him pass. Why?

21. **affirmation:** something declared to be true.
22. **bantering:** spoken in a teasing or playful way.
23. **incredulity** (ĭn'krĭ-do͞o'lĭ-tē): unwillingness or inability to believe; doubt.
24. **Marius Paumelle** (pō-mĕl') . . . **Maître Breton** (brĕ-tôɴ'), **husbandman at Ymanville** (ü-män-vēl'): *Husbandman* is an archaic word meaning "farmer."

WORDS TO KNOW
indignation (ĭn'dĭg-nā'shən) *n.* anger caused by something mean or unjust

Cross Curricular Link **History**

DEVELOPMENT OF PSYCHOLOGY In "A Piece of String," Maupassant focuses on the extreme reactions of Hauchecome to an ordinary and even trivial incident. This focus on human behavior and emotions was a characteristic of realism and coincided with the beginnings of what was to become modern psychology. In the 19th century, philosophers and scientific thinkers in Scotland, Germany, and the United States discovered new ways of exploring the connections between the body and the mind. They used experiments to measure sensory perceptions, probed the emotions through introspection, and analyzed mental processes. They published their findings in ground-breaking works that established some of the foundations for the great methods and insights of psychology that were to come in the 20th century.

"A piece of string, a piece of string—look—here it is, M'sieu' the Mayor."

He approached a farmer from Crequetot,[25] who did not let him finish, and giving him a thump in the stomach said to his face:

"You big rascal."

Then he turned his back on him.

Maître Hauchecome was confused, why was he called a big rascal?

When he was seated at the table, in Jourdain's tavern he commenced to explain "the affair."

A horse dealer from Monvilliers[26] called to him:

"Come, come, old sharper, that's an old trick; I know all about your piece of string!"

Hauchecome stammered:

"But since the pocketbook was found."

But the other man replied:

"Shut up, papa, there is one that finds, and there is one that reports. At any rate you are mixed with it."

The peasant stood choking. He understood. They accused him of having had the pocketbook returned by a confederate, by an accomplice.

He tried to protest. All the table began to laugh.

He could not finish his dinner and went away, in the midst of jeers.

He went home ashamed and indignant, choking with anger and confusion, the more dejected that he was capable with his Norman cunning of doing what they had accused him of, and even boasting of it as of a good turn. His innocence to him, in a confused way, was impossible to prove, as his sharpness was known. And he was stricken to the heart by the injustice of the suspicion.

Then he began to recount the adventures again, prolonging his history every day, adding each time, new reasons, more energetic protestations, more solemn oaths which he imagined and prepared in his hours of solitude, his whole mind given up to the story of the string. He was believed so much the less as his defense was more complicated and his arguing more subtle.

"Those are lying excuses," they said behind his back.

He felt it, consumed his heart over it, and wore himself out with useless efforts. He wasted away before their very eyes.

The wags[27] now made him tell about the string to amuse them, as they make a soldier who has been on a campaign tell about his battles. His mind, touched to the depth, began to weaken.

Toward the end of December he took to his bed.

He died in the first days of January, and in the delirium of his death struggles he kept claiming his innocence, reiterating:

"A piece of string, a piece of string—look—here it is, M'sieu' the Mayor."❖

25. **Crequetot** (krĕk-tō').

26. **Monvilliers** (môN-vē-yĕr'). Also spelled *Montivilliers.*

27. **wags:** people who like to make jokes.

MINI LESSON

Speaking and Listening

RE-CREATING A SCENE

Instruction Point out to students that on pages 950 and 951 the narrator describes several of Hauchecome's attempts to tell his story. Occasionally, actual lines of dialogue are included, but for the most part description is used to give a vivid sense of Hauchecome's interactions with his neighbors.

Prepare Have students work in groups of three or four and ask each group to develop a scene with dialogue based on one of the descriptions of Hauchecome's conversations (typically 15 to 20 lines of the story). After choosing a section, the students should make notes on how they see the scene unfolding. They may want to write out lines of dialogue at this point, unless some members of the group want to improvise their lines. If a scene involves a number of characters, the group may want to bring in some extras. The group should practice their scene, acting out the attitudes and emotions of the characters involved.

Present When presenting their scenes, the groups can use props or costumes if they wish.

This activity is particularly well suited for longer class periods.

Customizing Instruction

Less Proficient Readers

- Make sure students understand what actually happened to the pocketbook, how Hauchecome responds, and what people think. *(The pocketbook is returned to its owner by a hired man, who says he found it in the road. Hauchecome thinks everyone will now acknowledge his innocence, but people assume the hired man was an accomplice and continue to think Hauchecome is guilty.)*
- Help students understand what the narrator reveals about Hauchecome when he describes his "Norman cunning" (p. 951, cols. 1–2). *(The narrator reveals that Hauchecome was known for being shrewd and crafty and in the past had carried out acts like the one he is now wrongly accused of.)*

English Learners

- Help students understand that Hauchecome is caught in a cycle. The more he tells people his story in the hope of being believed, the more they don't believe him.
- Make sure students understand what is referred to by the two statements that the "news had spread" (p. 950, cols. 1, 2). *(The first statement refers to the news that Hauchecome has been accused of stealing the pocketbook. The second statement refers to the news that the pocketbook has been found.)*
- Make sure students understand the following terms and phrases: p. 950, col. 1, "stood like a stilt" *(stood stiff and still, like a pillar or post)*; p. 950, col. 2, "happy climax" *(the fact that the pocketbook has been found)*; p. 951, col. 1, "confederate . . . accomplice" *(a partner or helper in carrying out the crime)*; p. 951, col. 2, "energetic protestations" *(excited explanations)*; p. 951, col. 2, "solemn oaths" *(phases, such as "in the name of God" or "by my honor," that are meant to emphasize the seriousness and truthfulness of the speaker).*

Advanced Learners

Note that the title of the story is taken from Hauchecome's last words. Have students locate other places in the story where the string is mentioned, and ask them to analyze Maupassant's use of the detail in the story. Suggest that they consider how it functions as a detail in a work of realism and how it is ironic.

Connect to the Literature

1. **What Do You Think?** Accept all reasonable responses. Students should support their ideas with details from the story.

Comprehension Check

- His enemy, Monsieur Malandain, sees him picking up a piece of string but tells the mayor that he saw Maître Hauchecome taking the pocketbook.
- Everyone still believes that Hauchecome is guilty.

Use Selection Quiz in **Unit Six Resource Book,** p. 24.

Think Critically

2. Possible Response: They disapprove of him, but they seem more amused than angry. They thump his chest, laugh at him, and teasingly call him "big rascal" and "old sharper."
3. Possible Response: He is to blame because he has feuded with Malandain; he tries to hide his miserliness from Malandain; he has been deceptive and crafty in the past; his attempts to explain his behavior are increasingly insistent.
4. Possible Responses: Because Hauchecome has often been dishonest in the past, being innocent is a kind of achievement that he cannot bear to lose.
5. Hauchecome's attempts to control his situation completely backfire. Maupassant seems to be saying that control is an illusion.

Literary Analysis

Cooperative Learning Activity

Possible responses: (1) Hauchecome is bent over with rheumatism; description of physical appearance; he is not young; (2) he hides the string and pretends to be looking for something; character's own actions; he tries to cover up his actions because he doesn't want to be caught looking miserly; (3) others say that his explanations are "lying excuses"; words of other characters; no one believes his story; (4) "he was capable with his Norman cunning of doing what they had accused him of"; narrator's direct comment; tells that he was known for his craftiness.

Use **Unit Six Resource Book,** p. 22, for more practice.

Connect to the Literature

1. **What Do You Think?** What were your thoughts about Maître Hauchecome as you finished reading this story?

Comprehension Check

- Why is Maître Hauchecome accused of taking the pocketbook?
- What happens after the pocketbook is returned by someone else?

Think Critically

2. **ACTIVE READING: INTERPRETING DETAILS** Get together with a classmate and compare the cluster diagrams you created in your READER'S NOTEBOOK. How would you describe the attitude of the other peasants toward Maître Hauchecome's suspected misbehavior? What details give you this impression?
3. In your opinion, to what extent is Maître Hauchecome responsible for his downfall?

THINK ABOUT
- his relationship with Maître Malandain
- his dealings with people in the past
- his behavior when no one believes him innocent

4. Why do you think Maître Hauchecome tries so hard to persuade others of his innocence?
5. Maître Hauchecome tries to camouflage his stinginess when he takes the piece of string, but ironically his action leads to a much more serious misunderstanding. What message does Maupassant seem to be giving about how much control human beings have over their lives?

Extend Interpretations

6. **What If?** Suppose that Maître Hauchecome had not kept insisting that he was innocent. How might the story have turned out differently?
7. **Critic's Corner** The great Russian novelist Leo Tolstoy wrote that Maupassant had the "gift of seeing what others have not seen." Based on your reading of "A Piece of String," do you agree with Tolstoy? Why or why not?
8. **Connect to Life** The peasants of Goderville made assumptions about Maître Hauchecome based on their experience with him. Their assumptions led to the wrong conclusion, however. What does this story have to say about making judgments concerning other people's behavior?

LITERARY ANALYSIS: CHARACTERIZATION IN REALISM

Characterization refers to the techniques that writers use to develop characters. There are four basic methods of characterization:

- A writer may describe the physical appearance of the character.
- A character's nature may be revealed through his or her own speech, thoughts, feelings, or actions.
- The speech, thoughts, feelings, or actions of other characters in response to a character can be used to develop that character.
- The narrator can make direct comments about the character's nature.

Most realistic writers use the fourth method sparingly, preferring to let readers form their own judgments of characters. However, sometimes the best way to convey information is through direct comments. For example, Maupassant's narrator tells us that Maître Hauchecome is "economical like a true Norman."

Cooperative Learning Activity With a group of classmates, identify four details in the story that reveal aspects of Maître Hauchecome's character. For each detail, identify the characterization method that Maupassant used and what the detail reveals about the character. Fill in a chart such as the one below.

Detail	Characterization Method	What It Reveals
peasants' bent backs	description of physical appearance	the difficulty of their lives

Extend Interpretations

6. **What If?** Possible Responses: The other peasants might have been more willing to believe him or would have forgotten about the incident; if he wasn't so obsessed about his innocence, his health probably wouldn't have failed him.
7. **Critic's Corner** Possible Response: Most students will agree with Tolstoy, saying that Maupassant is able to reveal characters' true motivations, reactions, and emotions exactly and convincingly.
8. **Connect to Life** Possible Response: Most students will say that it is important to look at all the evidence carefully before making a judgment about someone's behavior. They might note that being misjudged can cause a person to feel isolated and distrusted. Two lessons this story seems to teach are that it is important to give people the benefit of the doubt and that laughter can be destructive.

Writing Options

1. Speech for the Defense
Suppose that Maître Hauchecome does go to trial for theft. Imagine that you are a provincial official assigned to defend him at the trial. Write your opening speech in which you explain how Maître Hauchecome himself is the victim in this situation.

2. Cause-and-Effect Essay
Write a brief essay in which you discuss the chain of events that leads to Maître Hauchecome's death. Before you begin, create a diagram showing how events are related. In your essay, present causes and effects in a logical order. Keep in mind that an action can have more than one effect and an outcome can have several causes. Place your draft in your **Working Portfolio.**

Writing Handbook
See pages R32–R33: Cause and Effect.

Activities & Explorations

1. Character Interviews With two other classmates, stage interviews with Maître Hauchecome and Monsieur Malandain, first with one and then with the other. Ask each to explain his relationship with the other person and the reasons for his own behavior. Then bring the two together and have the rest of the class offer brief opinions about how they might have changed their behavior.
~ **SPEAKING AND LISTENING**

Communications Handbook
See page R52: Conducting Interviews.

2. Town Banner Create a design for a banner to be displayed in the public square of Goderville. The design should reflect some interesting aspect of town life, such as wares for sale at the market or a lively gathering at the Jourdain tavern. Base your design on specific details in the story. ~ **ART**

Inquiry & Research

Peasant Life Find out more about the lives of the peasants in 19th-century France. Explore such topics as whether they were educated, what kinds of work they did, whether they owned land, what their family structure was like, and what their celebrations and festivals were. Summarize what you learn in a written report.

Vocabulary in Action

EXERCISE: RELATED WORDS Write the letter of the word in each set that has a meaning different from the other words in the set.

1. (a) laughter, (b) fun, (c) amusement, (d) indignation
2. (a) impassive, (b) handicapped, (c) expressionless, (d) emotionless
3. (a) din, (b) den, (c) noise, (d) blare
4. (a) contrasting, (b) unmatching, (c) unalike, (d) indifferent
5. (a) faith, (b) credence, (c) belief, (d) church

Vocabulary in Action

1. d
2. b
3. b
4. d
5. d

To assess skills and concepts taught in this selection, use **Formal Assessment Book,** pp. 145–146.

Writing Options

1. **Speech for the Defense** Suggest to students that they draw up two lists, one of evidence against Hauchecome and one of evidence in his favor. Then they should develop their speech taking both lists into account and showing how certain details have been manipulated to frame him.
2. **Cause-and-Effect Essay** Suggest to students that they could begin their essay by stating the effect—the death of Hauchecome—and then showing the chain of events that leads up to it. Remind them to use clear transitions and to give details and examples to illustrate the causes and effects they discuss.

Activities & Explorations

1. **Character Interviews** Tell students to spend some time creating clear and focused questions to ask in the interviews. Tell them also to remember to take careful notes during each interview so that they can ask appropriate follow-up questions. After the class has witnessed three or four sets of interviews, have them compare and contrast what they have heard.
2. **Town Banner** Students may want to work in pairs on this assignment. Students skilled in art might team up with those less skilled. Encourage students to be as creative as they like. Possibilities to consider are a collage, a set of panels or squares showing a variety of details, or one strong single image that conveys the atmosphere of market day.

Inquiry & Research

Peasant Life Students can research the Internet, encyclopedias, and books on 19th-century France. Books that would give interesting views of French village life include *Celestine: Voices from a French Village,* by Gillian Tindall, a detailed account of life in rural France in the late 19th and early 20th centuries; *A Village in France,* by Louis Clergeau and Jean-Mary Couderc, a photographic portrait of a French village in the early 20th century; and *The Horse of Pride,* by Pierre-Jakez Hélias, an account of a traditional village in Brittany. Advanced students may want to look at *France 1848–1945,* Vol. I, by Theodore Zeldin.

Author Study

Objectives

- appreciate the style and ideas of one of the world's greatest novelists
- learn about 19th-century Russian literature and culture
- better understand the connection between an author's writing and his or her beliefs and values

Presenting the Author

The **Author Study** offers a unique opportunity for students to focus on the work of a major writer. In addition, students can gather information about the life of Leo Tolstoy, gaining insight into the real person behind his famous works.

READING FOR INFORMATION

Reading Skills and Strategies

PREVIEWING

Have students preview the **Life and Times** section, noting the basic text organizers: title, subheads, captions, and time line. Ask students to describe the information they would expect to find in each section. Have students use the subheads to create a graphic organizer. As they read, have them categorize information from the article under the appropriate heading. Remind students that when they do independent research, they should use text organizers to locate and organize information.

Life and Times

Childhood

A Tolstoy's mother died when he was only two years old, and his father died when he was nine. Yet critic John Bayley writes that Tolstoy's childhood was "happier than that of any other great writer." The person who was in great part responsible for this was his cousin Tatiana, whom he called Aunt Tatiana. She was devoted to him, and he to her, throughout his life. He wrote her heartfelt letters when he was a young man, telling his news and expressing his affection: "My memory of you is so vivid that after having written this, I left off writing for a few minutes and tried to picture to myself the happy moment when I would see you again, when you would weep with joy at seeing me and I too would weep like a child as I kiss your hands."

AUTHOR STUDY

Leo Tolstoy

OVERVIEW

1828–1910

The Great Novelist and Moralist

Leo Tolstoy has been hailed not only as one of the world's greatest novelists but also as a great thinker and reformer. The author of the epic novel* War and Peace *was a man of contradictions, however. Tolstoy was a wealthy aristocrat who dressed as a peasant, a famous novelist who later condemned his great works, and a stern moralist who ultimately failed to live up to his own high standards.

"The hero of my tale . . . is Truth."

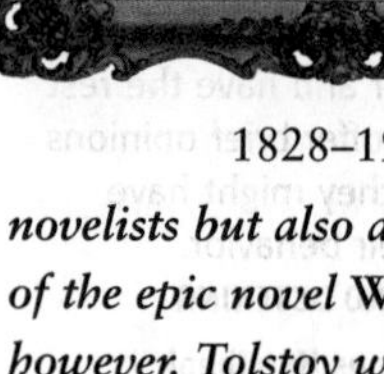

Leo Tolstoy

A HAPPY CHILDHOOD Tolstoy did not have the easiest childhood, but he remembered it as being a happy time. Both of his parents died before he was 10 years old, and in the next few years he lost his grandmother and an aunt, both of whom had cared for him. The love and care of another aunt and in particular a favorite cousin gave him abundant security and affection, however. As a boy, he was like a ray of light, said his sister, full of passion and charm.

Tolstoy was educated at home by private tutors and then attended a university for a few years without obtaining a degree.

HIS LIFE

1828 Born August 28 at his family's estate

1844 Enters Kazan University

1825 1830 1835 1840

HIS TIMES

1825 Decembrist uprising crushed by czar's troops

1837 Victoria becomes Queen of the United Kingdom of Great Britain and Ireland

B At age 19, he inherited his family's 2,000-acre estate, Yasnaya Polyana, about 130 miles from Moscow. His weakness for gambling and late-night parties never seemed to hurt the handsome young count, for he always had plenty of money. C In 1851, Tolstoy joined his brother in the army and later was wounded and almost killed by an exploding bomb.

THE MAKING OF A WRITER Tolstoy's writing began with his diary, which he started when he was 18 and continued, with interruptions, throughout his long life. His first published work, *Childhood*, was a short fictionalized account of his "blissful" early life and won him instant success. Over the next years, he published several stories based on his experiences in the army.

In his early fiction, Tolstoy refined his considerable talent by experimenting with narrative techniques and characterization. As a realist, he was careful to portray authentic characters and situations. And although he made radical changes in his life, Tolstoy never abandoned his realist principles. "An artist is an artist because he sees things not as he wishes to see them but as they really are," he declared in 1894. Truth was always his hero.

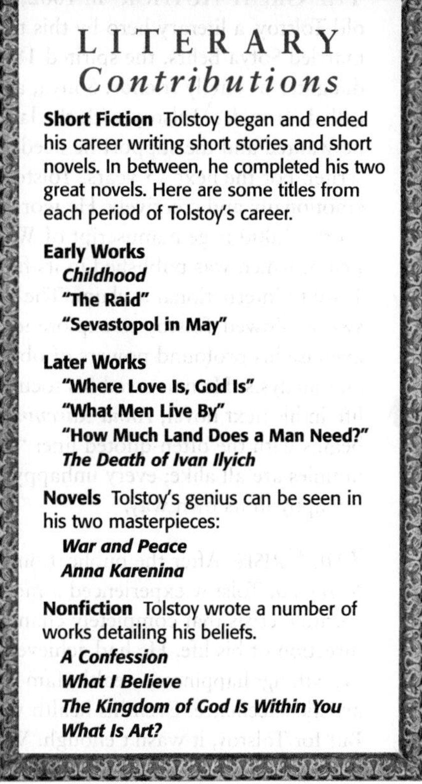

LITERARY *Contributions*

Short Fiction Tolstoy began and ended his career writing short stories and short novels. In between, he completed his two great novels. Here are some titles from each period of Tolstoy's career.

Early Works
- ***Childhood***
- **"The Raid"**
- **"Sevastopol in May"**

Later Works
- **"Where Love Is, God Is"**
- **"What Men Live By"**
- **"How Much Land Does a Man Need?"**
- ***The Death of Ivan Ilyich***

Novels Tolstoy's genius can be seen in his two masterpieces:
- ***War and Peace***
- ***Anna Karenina***

Nonfiction Tolstoy wrote a number of works detailing his beliefs.
- ***A Confession***
- ***What I Believe***
- ***The Kingdom of God Is Within You***
- ***What Is Art?***

Tolstoy wearing the uniform of an artillery officer

Time line (1845–1875)

- **1851** Fights in the Caucasus with Russian army
- **1852** *Childhood* first published
- **1853–1856** Russia loses to France, England, and Turkey in Crimean War; Sevastopol under siege for 11 months
- **1859** Starts school for children of serfs on his family estate
- **1861** Czar Alexander II frees Russian serfs, who can now own land
- **1862** Marries Sofya Behrs
- **1863** Abraham Lincoln issues the Emancipation Proclamation
- **1866** Publication of Fyodor Dostoyevsky's *Crime and Punishment*
- **1869** Publishes *War and Peace*
- **1872** Karl Marx's *Das Kapital* translated into Russian
- **1875–1877** Publishes *Anna Karenina*
- **1878** Spiritual Crisis

1845 · 1850 · 1855 · 1860 · 1865 · 1870 · 1875

Family Estate

B Yasnaya Polyana, which means "sunlit meadows," was acquired by Tolstoy's maternal great-grandfather, C. F. Volkonsky, in 1763. Tolstoy was born on the estate and lived most of his life there. (In 19th-century Russia, the youngest son inherited the family home.) When Tolstoy was a child, his older brother, Nikolay, told him and his other brothers and his sister that the secret of happiness was written on a mysterious green stick buried near a gorge on the estate. When Tolstoy died, he left instructions that he wanted to be buried near the spot where the green stick was supposed to be. Today thousands of visitors make the pilgrimage to Tolstoy's grave every year.

Military Service

C When Tolstoy first joined the army, he was stationed in the Caucasus, where the fighting involved only intermittent skirmishes with local Chechen tribesmen. Army life was not rigorous and left time for writing and socializing. Tolstoy looked back at those years as one of the happiest times of his life. In 1854, however, he joined action in the Crimean War, where the fighting was fierce and badly managed. Tolstoy's first encounter with cannon fire terrified him, and the destruction and loss of life horrified him. His experiences in the Caucasus and in the Crimean War are reflected in several of his early works as well as in *War and Peace*.

MINI LESSON Using the Time Line

Sequence of Events Have students study the time line on pages 954–956 and answer questions such as the following:

- How old was Tolstoy when he fought in the Caucasus? *(23)*
- Did Tolstoy publish *War and Peace* before or after Abraham Lincoln issued the Emancipation Proclamation? *(six years after)*
- Could Karl Marx's *Das Kapital* have influenced *Anna Karenina? (yes,* Das Kapital *was translated into Russian three years earlier)*
- Did Tolstoy live to see World War I? *(no, he died four years before it began)*

Ask students what possible connections they might infer between Tolstoy's life and events in Russia or in the world of his time.

Possible Response: Tolstoy started a school for children of serfs two years before the czar freed Russian serfs and four years before Abraham Lincoln issued the Emancipation Proclamation. Therefore, there was probably widespread interest around this time in improving the lives of the lower classes.

TOLSTOY AUTHOR STUDY 955

Anna Karenina

A One of the main characters in *Anna Karenina* is Konstantin Levin, a young estate owner. The character of Levin is based on Tolstoy himself. Such details as how he proposes marriage to Kitty, the death of a dissolute brother from consumption, and Levin's involvement with the life and work of the peasants on his estate are virtually autobiographical incidents.

Famine

B In 1891 a terrible famine broke out in Russia. Tolstoy, Sonya, and their children organized relief efforts and worked tirelessly for two years. By July 1892 Tolstoy had set up 246 soup kitchens, which fed 13,000 people daily. Another 124 children's kitchens fed 3,000 daily. The family organized care for village children and distribution of medical supplies. Tolstoy also raised sizable donations of money through international appeals.

Censorship

C Ironically, government banning of some of Tolstoy's works and his excommunication by the church actually increased his popularity and made him something of a hero. In order to keep Tolstoy's works in circulation, Sonya dedicated herself to publishing a full edition of all of his works, including the religious nonfiction. She worked out of a converted shed near their Moscow home, and she consulted Dostoyevsky's widow, Anna, for advice on how to carry out her plans.

THE GREAT AUTHOR In 1862, the 34-year-old Tolstoy, a literary hero by this time, married Sofya Behrs, the spirited 18-year-old daughter of family friends. Sonya, as she was called, provided Tolstoy with the large family he wanted and the support he needed as a writer. For the next 15 years, Tolstoy prospered emotionally and creatively. He worked steadily on the 3,000-page manuscript of *War and Peace,* which was published in its final form in 1869 to international acclaim. The novel's epic sweep allowed Tolstoy to explore ideas and to exercise his profound powers of observation and analysis. He narrowed his focus to family life in his next novel, *Anna Karenina,* which begins with the often-quoted line: "Happy families are all alike; every unhappy family is unhappy in its own way." **A**

THE CRISIS After the publication of *Anna Karenina,* Tolstoy experienced a moral and spiritual crisis that completely changed the direction of his life. He had achieved everything: happiness, wealth, fame, and artistic excellence. Even his health was good. But for Tolstoy, it wasn't enough. What's the point of all this success, he asked himself, if I'm just going to die anyway? At first, he turned to the Russian Orthodox Church to find an answer to the meaning of life. However, he soon rejected the church and all institutions as corrupt and gradually developed a personal faith based on the teachings of Jesus. Tolstoy analyzed his crisis in *A Confession* and explained his newfound purpose in life: to locate the goodness within and promote that goodness in the world.

Tolstoy tried to practice what he preached. He worked among the poor, helped with famine relief, and simplified his life so as not to participate in what he considered an evil social, economic, and political system. He also became a pacifist, a vegetarian, and a strong supporter of nonviolent civil disobedience. **B**

To continue promoting his vision of the kingdom of God, Tolstoy wrote essays and religious tracts explaining his ideas. These writings disturbed many people. The government considered him a dangerous threat, and most of his nonfiction was banned in Russia. Tolstoy's most controversial work was his last novel, *Resurrection,* in which he attacked both the church and the state. The church responded by excommunicating him. **C**

1882 Completes *A Confession,* which is banned in Russia; publishes "What Men Live By"

1886 Publishes *The Death of Ivan Ilyich* and "How Much Land Does a Man Need?"

1891–1892 Organizes famine relief

1901 Excommunicated from Russian Orthodox Church; meets Anton Chekhov

1910 Dies at Astapovo railway station

1880 1885 1890 1895 1900 1905 1910

1881 Terrorist group assassinates Alexander II

1898 Anton Chekhov's *The Seagull* performed in Moscow

1899 Sigmund Freud publishes *The Interpretation of Dreams*

1905–1906 Revolutionary strikes, peasant uprisings, mutinies, and violent clashes disrupt Russian Empire

1914 Beginning of World War I

956

A CHANGE IN STYLE In the fiction Tolstoy wrote after 1880, his style as well as his purpose for writing had changed. He dismissed his two great novels as frivolous and appealing only to the upper classes. Art for him now had to be simple and direct; it had to be accessible to the common people; and it had to have a clear moral. Tolstoy's new style and purpose drove all of his later fiction, including "How Much Land Does a Man Need?" (page 958) and "What Men Live By" (page 976).

Tolstoy writing

UNHAPPY ENDING Although Tolstoy attracted devoted followers after his conversion, he alienated most of his family. His son Ilya wrote: "From the fun-loving, lively head of our family he was transformed before our eyes into a stern, accusatory prophet." Tolstoy became increasingly disturbed by the gap between his strict moral values and his comfortable aristocratic life, which his wife wanted to maintain for their children's future. D

In a desperate effort to escape the complications of his life, Tolstoy fled his ancestral home in secret on October 28, 1910. A few days later, he lay dying of pneumonia in the stationmaster's house at a railway station. Just a few feet away was a crush of photographers and reporters eager to record the great man's last moments. Surrounded by his closest followers and several of his children, Tolstoy whispered his final words, "To seek, always to seek . . ."

 NetActivities: **Author Exploration**

What's So Great About *War and Peace*?

War and Peace is acclaimed by many modern writers as the world's greatest novel. Set in the years 1805 to 1820, it tells the stories of five aristocratic families during the time of Napoleon's war against Russia. With its vast scope and hundreds of characters, *War and Peace* has everything—heroism and villainy, history and philosophy, innocence and maturity, battle scenes and love stories. And all is woven together in Tolstoy's flawless narrative style—as though life were writing itself, according to one critic.

Copyrights

D **As part of trying to rid himself of his property and possessions, Tolstoy wanted to put his copyrights in the public domain. He had told Sonya in 1883 and confirmed again in 1891 that the copyrights to works published before 1881—which included *War and Peace* and *Anna Karenina*—belonged to her. A few months before he died, however, he made a secret will that stated that all his works would be in the public domain. This meant that Sonya would have no control over his literary estate and could no longer derive income from publishing them.**

TOLSTOY AUTHOR STUDY **957**

Objectives

- understand and appreciate a Russian **short story (Literary Analysis)**
- identify **theme in fiction (Literary Analysis)**
- use strategies for **drawing conclusions (Active Reading)**

Summary

After listening to a conversation between his wife and her sister, the peasant Pakhom declares, "If I had plenty of land, I shouldn't fear the Devil himself!" The Devil, who hears Pakhom's boast, decides to let Pakhom have all the land he desires in order to get him in his power. Pakhom begins to purchase land, but as he obtains more and more, he becomes less and less satisfied. Eventually he seeks land from the Bashkirs, a people who live a long distance away. He strikes a deal with their chief: he will pay a thousand rubles for as much land as he can encompass on foot in one day. But he must return to his starting point by sunset or lose all his money. Because of his greed, Pakhom walks too far. As the sun begins to set, he runs to reach his starting point, taxing his physical endurance. This effort costs him his life.

 Use **Unit Six Resource Book,** p. 25, for additional support.

Thematic Link

One of Tolstoy's aims in his moral tales was to teach important **life lessons.** In this tale, Tolstoy shows what happens when need turns into greed.

5-Minute Warm-Up

Daily Language SkillBuilder

Have students **proofread** the display sentences on page 869j and write them correctly.

How Much Land Does a Man Need?

Leo Tolstoy

Translated by Louise and Aylmer Maude

Build Background

Searching for Solutions As a social reformer, Tolstoy strongly supported the freeing of the serfs in 1861. Before that time, Russian serfs were like slaves in that they were considered the property of large landowners such as Tolstoy himself. After gaining their freedom, some serfs bought land and even grew wealthy, but most remained dirt poor.

Tolstoy felt a deep affection for humble peasants, whose work on the land he thought gave them a deep understanding of life's meaning. He frequently labored alongside the serfs of his own estate and tried to improve their lot through education. But the longer Tolstoy worked among the poor, the more he believed that material solutions—money or land, for instance—were not the answer to society's basic problems, which he considered to be moral rather than economic. One of Tolstoy's most popular and compelling stories, "How Much Land Does a Man Need?" dramatizes these ideas.

Connect to Your Life

"If only I had . . . " Sound familiar? Name one thing you really want and one thing you absolutely need. Discuss with your classmates the difference between the two. Then think about how your life might change if you could get exactly what you want.

Focus Your Reading

LITERARY ANALYSIS: THEME IN FICTION

The theme of a short story is its central idea, insight, or observation. Most themes in fiction are not stated directly but must be interpreted and inferred from the story. For example, the theme of Maupassant's "A Piece of String" might be stated this way: Once a man is accused, people automatically think he's guilty, even if he's later proven innocent.

The title of Tolstoy's story gives a clue to its theme. As you read, think about Tolstoy's answer to the question of need.

ACTIVE READING: DRAWING CONCLUSIONS

Drawing conclusions from details in the story can help you determine the **theme.** In Tolstoy's story, watch for small things—scraps of dialogue, brief thoughts, and descriptions—that subtly build up to a big revelation at the end.

READER'S NOTEBOOK This story is divided into nine sections. As you read, stop at the end of each section and jot down notes about important details. For example, you might note the dialogue between the two sisters in section I.

LESSON RESOURCES

UNIT SIX RESOURCE BOOK,
pp. 25–28

ASSESSMENT RESOURCES
Formal Assessment, pp. 147–148
Teacher's Guide to Assessment and Portfolio Use
Test Generator

INTEGRATED TECHNOLOGY
NetActivities
Visit our Web site: classzone.com

ADDITIONAL RESOURCES
Lesson Planning Guide, pp. 125–126
Teacher's Sourcebook for Language Development

I

An elder sister came to visit her younger sister in the country. The elder was married to a tradesman in town, the younger to a peasant in the village. As the sisters sat over their tea talking, the elder began to boast of the advantages of town life: saying how comfortably they lived there, how well they dressed, what fine clothes her children wore, what good things they ate and drank, and how she went to the theater, promenades, and entertainments.

The younger sister was piqued,[1] and in turn disparaged[2] the life of a tradesman, and stood up for that of a peasant.

"I would not change my way of life for yours," said she. "We may live roughly, but at least we are free from anxiety. You live in better style than we do, but though you often earn more than you need, you are very likely to lose
1 all you have. You know the proverb, 'Loss and gain are brothers twain.'[3] It often happens that people who are wealthy one day are begging
2 their bread the next. Our way is safer. Though a peasant's life is not a fat one, it is a long one. We shall never grow rich, but we shall always have enough to eat."

The elder sister said sneeringly:

"Enough? Yes, if you like to share with the pigs and the calves! What do you know of elegance or manners! However much your goodman
3 may slave, you will die as you are living—on a dung heap—and your children the same."

"Well, what of that?" replied the younger. "Of course our work is rough and coarse. But, on the other hand, it is sure, and we need not bow to any one. But you, in your towns, are surrounded by temptations; today all may be right, but
4 tomorrow the Evil One may tempt your husband with cards, wine, or women, and all will go to ruin. Don't such things happen often enough?"

Pakhom, the master of the house, was lying on the top of the stove[4] and he listened to the women's chatter.

"It is perfectly true," thought he. "Busy as we are from childhood tilling[5] mother earth, we  5
peasants have no time to let any nonsense settle in our heads. Our only trouble is that we haven't land enough. If I had plenty of land, I shouldn't fear the Devil himself!"

The women finished their tea, chatted a while about dress, and then cleared away the tea-things and lay down to sleep.

But the Devil had been sitting behind the stove, and had heard all that was said. He was pleased that the peasant's wife had led her husband into boasting, and that he had said that if he had plenty of land he would not fear the Devil himself.

"All right," thought the Devil. "We will have a tussle. I'll give you land enough; and by means of that land I will get you into my power."

II

Close to the village there lived a lady, a small landowner who had an estate of about three hundred acres. She had always lived on good terms with the peasants until she engaged as her steward[6] an old soldier, who took to burdening

1. **piqued** (pēkt): irritated; angry.
2. **disparaged** (dĭ-spăr'ĭjd): belittled; put down.
3. **twain:** two.
4. **Pakhom** (pä'KHōm) . . . **lying on top of the stove:** The stoves and ovens in Russian peasant homes had large tops that were often used for sleeping because they provided extra warmth.
5. **tilling:** ploughing land to prepare it for planting.
6. **steward:** person in charge of the household affairs of a large estate.

TIME MANAGEMENT

If your schedule requires that you cover the lesson objectives in a shorter time, use . . .
- Preparing to Read, p. 958
- Thinking Through the Literature, p. 972

If you want to take advantage of longer blocks of class time, use . . .
- TE Teaching Options: Viewing and Representing, pp. 960, 969; More from the Author, p. 961; Speaking and Listening, p. 962; Vocabulary Strategy, pp. 963, 966; Cross-Curricular Link, pp. 964, 967; Grammar, pp. 970–971
- The Author's Style, p. 996
- Choices & Challenges, p. 973
- Letter from Leo Tolstoy to N. A. Nekrasov, pp. 974–975
- Author Study Project, p. 997

Customizing Instruction

Less Proficient Readers

Make sure that students understand the debate between the two sisters: the elder sister claims that town life is better, while the younger sister insists that farm life is. You might want to have pairs of students read the dialogue and then ask other students to list the main points each sister makes.

Use the following questions to discuss with students the connection between the sisters' conversation, Pakhom's thoughts, and the Devil's response:
- Which sister does Pakhom agree with? *(his wife)*
- What does Pakhom think he needs? *(plenty of land)*
- What does Pakhom say about the Devil? *(He wouldn't fear even the Devil if he had enough land.)*
- What is the Devil's response? *(He will give Pakhom the land he wants in order to get control over him.)*

English Learners

1 Explain that "Loss and gain are brothers twain" (paragraph 3) is a proverb—a short saying that expresses a basic truth or gives practical advice. Point out that the younger sister explains the meaning of the proverb in the very next sentence. Ask students to share any proverbs they know from their own cultures.

2 Explain that "though a peasant's life is not a fat one, it is a long one" means that though a peasant's life is not luxurious, it is a strong and enduring one.

3 Help students use context clues to understand the comment the elder sister is making about the younger sister's life.

4 Explain that "Evil One" is a name for the Devil.

5 Make sure that students understand that "mother earth" is a reference to the land.

Advanced Learners

Point out to students that irony and foreshadowing are important in this story. Tell them to watch for both elements as they read. As they progress through the story, have them review earlier passages that contribute to either irony or foreshadowing. Suggest that they make notes about connections between irony and foreshadowing and possible themes in the story.

Literary Analysis THEME IN FICTION

Paying attention to what happens to the main character in a short story can help the reader figure out the theme of the story. Tell students to keep track of the themes that emerge as the character of Pakhom is developed in the story.

 Use **Unit Six Resource Book,** p. 27, for more practice.

Active Reading

DRAWING CONCLUSIONS

Point out to students that the story has already revealed some details about Pakhom's goals in life and his reactions to his circumstances. Ask students what conclusions they can draw about Pakhom by the end of section II.

Possible Responses: Pakhom thinks owning a lot of land would solve his problems. He isn't a patient person, he doesn't like to spend money, and he takes out his frustrations on his family. He is also a hard worker, a smart businessman, and a good farmer.

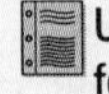 Use **Unit Six Resource Book,** p. 26, for additional support.

Literary Analysis FOLK TALE

A Explain to students that Tolstoy often based his later moral tales on folk tales. Remind them that folk tales are usually intended to teach a lesson. They also often have an element of the supernatural, such as the presence of the devil, or "Evil One." Have students look for these characteristics of a folk tale as they read.

Tolstoy in the Field of Labour (1889), after Ilya Yefimovich Repin. Photograph copyright © Gianni Dagli Orti/Corbis.

HUMANITIES CONNECTION Tolstoy came to believe that the peasants' way of life had more truth and value than the aristocracy's. Tolstoy dressed like the peasants and joined them in their work. This painting shows Tolstoy plowing on one of his estates.

the people with fines. However careful Pakhom tried to be, it happened again and again that now a horse of his got among the lady's oats, now a cow strayed into her garden, now his calves found their way into her meadows—and he always had to pay a fine.

Pakhom paid up, but grumbled, and going home in a temper, was rough with his family. All through that summer, Pakhom had much trouble because of this steward, and he was even glad when winter came and the cattle had to be stabled. Though he grudged the fodder[7] when they could no longer graze on the pasture-land, at least he was free from anxiety about them.

In the winter the news got about that the lady was going to sell her land and that the keeper of the inn on the high road was bargaining for it. When the peasants heard this they were very much alarmed.

"Well," thought they, "if the innkeeper gets the land, he will worry us with fines worse than the

7. **fodder:** food for livestock, such as hay or straw.

MINI LESSON Viewing and Representing

Tolstoy in the Field of Labour **after Ilya Yefimovich Repin**

ART APPRECIATION

Instruction This painting is a reproduction of one made by the Russian artist Repin, who is best known for his painting of historical subjects.

Application Have students study the painting and the **Humanities Connection** on page 960. Ask them what evidence they see in the story of Tolstoy's first-hand knowledge of farming and farm life. Then ask them what they think Tolstoy valued most in the peasants' way of life.

Possible Responses: The story includes details of farm work (sowing, plowing, making hay), descriptions of problems farmers face (horses getting into the oats), and an accurate picture of farmers' concerns about good soil, good weather, and having enough land.

Tolstoy seems to value the closeness to the land, the satisfying hard physical work, and the simplicity of peasant life.

lady's steward. We all depend on that estate."

So the peasants went on behalf of their commune,[8] and asked the lady not to sell the land to the innkeeper, offering her a better price for it themselves. The lady agreed to let them have it. Then the peasants tried to arrange for the commune to buy the whole estate, so that it might be
1 A held by them all in common. They met twice to discuss it, but could not settle the matter; the Evil One sowed discord among them and they could not agree. So they decided to buy the land individually, each according to his means; and the lady agreed to this plan as she had to the other.

Presently Pakhom heard that a neighbor of his was buying fifty acres, and that the lady had consented to accept one half in cash and to wait a year for the other half. Pakhom felt envious.

"Look at that," thought he, "the land is all being sold, and I shall get none of it." So he spoke to his wife.

"Other people are buying," said he, "and we must also buy twenty acres or so. Life is becoming impossible. That steward is simply crushing us with his fines."

2 So they put their heads together and considered how they could manage to buy it. They had one hundred rubles[9] laid by. They sold a colt and one half of their bees, hired out one of their sons as a laborer and took his wages in advance; borrowed the rest from a brother-in-law, and so scraped together half the purchase money.

Having done this, Pakhom chose out a farm of forty acres, some of it wooded, and went to the lady to bargain for it. They came to an agreement, and he shook hands with her upon it and paid her a deposit in advance. Then they went to town and signed the deeds; he paying half the price down, and undertaking to pay the remainder within two years.

So now Pakhom had land of his own. He borrowed seed, and sowed it on the land he had bought. The harvest was a good one, and within a year he had managed to pay off his debts both to the lady and to his brother-in-law. So he became a landowner, plowing and sowing his own land, making hay on his own land, cutting his own trees, and feeding his cattle on his own pasture. When he went out to plow his fields, or to look at his growing corn, or at his grass-meadows, his heart would fill with joy. The grass that grew and the flowers that bloomed there 3
seemed to him unlike any that grew elsewhere. Formerly, when he had passed by that land, it had appeared the same as any other land, but now it seemed quite different.

So Pakhom was well-contented, and everything would have been right if the neighboring peasants would only not have trespassed on his corn-fields and meadows. He appealed to them most civilly, but they still went on: now the communal herdsmen would let the village cows stray into his meadows, then horses from the night pasture would get among his corn. Pakhom turned them out again and again, and forgave their owners, and for a long time he forbore to prosecute any one. But at last he lost patience and complained to the district court. He knew it was the peasants' want of land, and no evil intent on their part, that caused the trouble, but he thought:

"I cannot go on overlooking it or they will destroy all I have. They must be taught a lesson."

So he had them up, gave them one lesson, and

8. **commune:** in late 19th-century Russia, a local organization of peasants that held land in common for its members. A peasant could also own land individually while still belonging to the commune.

9. **rubles:** The ruble is the basic monetary unit of Russia.

Customizing Instruction

English Learners

1 Make sure that students understand why the plan for the commune to buy the whole estate fails.

- Ask students to use context clues to figure out what they think the word *discord* means. *(setting people against one another)*
- Remind students who *the Evil One* is in the story. Review with them the plan the Devil announces in section I.

2 Explain that "put their heads together" is an expression that means that Pakhom and his wife talked together to figure out a way to raise money to buy land.

Less Proficient Readers

3 Ask students to explain in their own words how Pakhom is feeling. *(happy, contented, proud, satisfied)*

Set a Purpose Ask students to read to find out what Pakhom does next.

Advanced Learners

Have students discuss Pakhom's strengths and weaknesses up to this point in the story. Have them also cite any contradictions between Pakhom's behavior and his feelings. *(strengths: he is hard-working, ambitious, thoughtful about the future, enjoys farm life; weaknesses: he worries a lot, gets mad easily and takes it out on his family, acts selfishly; contradictions: believes peasants are free from temptations, but falls into the Devil's trap; resents landowners but wants to become one himself, worries about fines but goes into debt to buy land)*

MINI LESSON More from the Author

TOLSTOY'S *ANNA KARENINA* Tolstoy expressed some of his own feelings about his land through the experiences of the young Konstantin Levin in his novel *Anna Karenina.* In the following passage, Levin is looking over his estate and the farming preparations being made in early spring:

> *And at the brisk amble of the good, too-long-inactive little horse, who snorted over the puddles and tugged at the reins, Levin rode across the mud of the yard, out of the gate and into the fields.*
>
> *If Levin felt happy in the cattle- and farm-yards, he felt still happier in the fields. Swaying rhythmically to the amble of his good little mount, drinking in the warm yet fresh smell of the snow and the air as he went through the forest over the granular, subsiding snow that still remained here and there with tracks spreading in it, he rejoiced at each of his trees with moss reviving on its bark and buds swelling. When he rode out of the forest, green wheat spread before him in a smooth, velvety carpet over a huge space, with not a single bare or marshy patch, and only spotted here and there in the hollows with the remains of the melting snow.*
>
> —Translated by Richard Pevear and Larissa Volokhonsky

Literary Analysis IRONY

A After students have read these two lines, have them reread the first four paragraphs in section II. Ask them to explain why the reference to "fines" in section III is ironic.

Possible Response: This is an example of situational irony, which occurs when a character or the reader expects one thing to happen but something entirely different occurs. In section II, Pakhom's animals get into the neighboring landowner's fields and he hates having to pay fines. When he becomes a landowner himself, he gets irritated with the peasants' animals getting on his land, takes the peasants to court, and gets some of them fined.

Literary Analysis CHARACTERIZATION

B One method of characterization is through a character's thoughts, actions, and words. Ask students what aspects of Pakhom's character are revealed in this passage.

Possible Response: His thoughts, words, and actions reveal that he is angry and vengeful. He no longer has a sense of connection with his peasant neighbors and is at odds with everyone.

Active Reading

DRAWING CONCLUSIONS

C Ask students what conclusion they can make about Pakhom's physical condition.

Possible Response: He is strong and has great stamina and endurance.

Reading Skills and Strategies
CONNECTING

D Ask students how they think Pakhom's family members might feel about moving again, especially to a distant place. Invite students to share from their own experiences if they wish. *(unhappy because their lives are so unsettled; frustrated because Pakhom never seems to ask them before making a decision)*

[A] then another, and two or three of the peasants were fined. After a time Pakhom's neighbors began to bear him a grudge for this, and would now and then let their cattle on to his land on [1] purpose. One peasant even got into Pakhom's wood at night and cut down five young lime [2] trees for their bark. Pakhom passing through the wood one day noticed something white. He came nearer and saw the stripped trunks lying on the ground, and close by stood the stumps where the trees had been. Pakhom was furious.

"If he had only cut one here and there it would have been bad enough," thought Pakhom, "but the rascal has actually cut down a whole clump. If I could only find out who did this, I would pay him out."[10]

He racked his brains as to who it could be. Finally he decided: "It must be Simon—no one else could have done it." So he went to Simon's [B] homestead to have a look round, but he found nothing, and only had an angry scene. However, he now felt more certain than ever that Simon had done it, and he lodged a complaint. Simon was summoned. The case was tried, and retried, [3] and at the end of it all Simon was acquitted, there being no evidence against him. Pakhom felt still more aggrieved, and let his anger loose upon the elder and the judges.

"You let thieves grease your palms,"[11] said he. "If you were honest folk yourselves you would not let a thief go free."

So Pakhom quarreled with the judges and with his neighbors. Threats to burn his building began to be uttered. So though Pakhom had [4] more land, his place in the commune was much worse than before.

About this time a rumor got about that many people were moving to new parts.

"There's no need for me to leave my land," thought Pakhom. "But some of the others might leave our village and then there would be more room for us. I would take over their land myself and make my estate a bit bigger. I could then live more at ease. As it is, I am still too cramped to be comfortable."

"I WOULD TAKE OVER THEIR LAND MYSELF AND MAKE MY ESTATE A BIT BIGGER."

One day Pakhom was sitting at home when a peasant, passing through the village, happened to call in. He was allowed to stay the night, and supper was given him. Pakhom had a talk with this peasant and asked him where he came from. The stranger answered that he came from beyond the Volga[12] where he had been working. One word led to another, and the man went on to say that many people were settling in those parts. He told how some people from his village had settled there. They had joined the commune, and had had twenty-five acres per man granted them. The land was so good, he said, that the rye sown on it grew as high as a horse, and so thick that five cuts of a sickle made a sheaf. One peasant, he said, had brought nothing with him but his bare hands, and now he had six horses and two cows of his own.

10. **pay him out:** get even with him.

11. **grease your palms:** bribe you.

12. **the Volga:** the longest river in Russia, the Volga flows from north of Moscow to the Caspian Sea.

MINI LESSON Speaking and Listening

DRAMATIZATION

Prepare Help students prepare a dramatization of Pakhom's transformation from peasant to landowner. Have students reread section II, paragraphs 1–2, and section III, paragraphs 1–4. Point out that Pakhom treats the peasants who trespass on his land in the same way that the steward earlier had treated him. Ask students to think about Pakhom's reasoning in each situation and to make a list of arguments—based on the story and on their own experience—he might use to justify his position.

Present Have pairs of students stage two dialogues, one between the steward and Pakhom, and one between Pakhom and a peasant who trespasses on his land. In each dialogue, Pakhom should try to win the other character over to his point of view. You may want to have several pairs stage each dialogue. Then invite students to discuss what they learned from the performances about Pakhom's character.

This activity is particularly well suited to longer blocks of class time.

Pakhom's heart kindled with desire. He thought: "Why should I suffer in this narrow hole, if one can live so well elsewhere? I will sell my land and my homestead here, and with the money I will start afresh over there and get everything new. In this crowded place one is always having trouble. But I must first go and find out all about it myself."

Towards summer he got ready and started. He went down the Volga on a steamer to Samara,[13] then walked another three hundred miles on foot, and at last reached the place. It was just as the stranger had said. The peasants had plenty of land: every man had twenty-five acres of communal land given him for his use and any one who had money could buy, besides, at two shillings an acre as much good freehold[14] land as he wanted.

Having found out all he wished to know, Pakhom returned home as autumn came on, and began selling off his belongings. He sold his land at a profit, sold his homestead and all his cattle, and withdrew from membership of the commune. He only waited till the spring, and then started with his family for the new settlement.

As soon as Pakhom and his family reached their new abode, he applied for admission into the commune of a large village. He stood treat[15] to the elders and obtained the necessary documents. Five shares of communal land were given him for his own and his sons' use: that is to say—125 acres (not all together, but in different fields) besides the use of the communal pasture. Pakhom put up the buildings he needed, and bought cattle. Of the communal land alone he had three times as much as at his former home, and the land was good corn-land. He was ten times better off than he had been. He had plenty of arable[16] land and pasturage, and could keep as many head of cattle as he liked.

At first, in the bustle of building and settling down, Pakhom was pleased with it all, but when he got used to it he began to think that even here he had not enough land. The first year, he sowed wheat on his share of the communal land and had a good crop. He wanted to go on sowing wheat, but had not enough communal land for the purpose, and what he had already used was not available; for in those parts wheat is only sown on virgin soil or on fallow[17] land. It is sown for one or two years, and then the land lies fallow till it is again overgrown with prairie grass. There were many who wanted such land and there was not enough for all; so that people quarreled about it. Those who were better off wanted it for growing wheat, and those who were poor wanted it to let to dealers, so that they might raise money to pay their taxes. Pakhom wanted to sow more wheat, so he rented land from a dealer for a year. He sowed much wheat and had a fine crop, but the land was too far from the village—the wheat had to be carted more than ten miles. After a time Pakhom noticed that some peasant-dealers were living on separate farms and were growing wealthy; and he thought:

"If I were to buy some freehold land and have a homestead on it, it would be a different thing altogether. Then it would all be nice and compact."

The question of buying freehold land recurred to him again and again.

13. **Samara** (sə-mâr′ə): city in southeastern Russia, on the Volga River.

14. **freehold:** land held for life with the right to pass it along to one's heirs.

15. **stood treat:** paid for the cost of drinks or entertainment.

16. **arable** (ăr′ə-bəl): fit for plowing and planting.

17. **fallow:** ploughed but left unplanted during a growing season.

Customizing Instruction

Less Proficient Readers

Make sure students understand the different forms of property ownership mentioned in the story:

- *Communal land* belonged to a commune (footnote 8) and could be used by a farmer who was part of the commune.
- *Freehold land* (footnote 14) was held for life and might be inherited by a person's descendants. The word *homestead* refers to the house and other buildings a farmer put on his land.
- *Rented land* could be communal or freehold land used temporarily in exchange for a fee.

English Learners

1 Explain that to do something "on purpose" means to intend, or mean, to do it, not to do it accidentally.

2 Tell students that lime trees are linden trees, graceful shade trees that are valued for their light wood. You might want to bring in a photo of a linden tree to show students.

3 Help students understand the legal terms and process being described. Ask students what they think each of the following terms or phrases might mean:

- lodged a complaint *(filed a formal, legal accusation)*
- summoned *(called to appear in court)*
- tried, and retried *(the case was heard in court two times)*
- acquitted *(declared innocent)*

Advanced Learners

4 Invite students to comment on the statement the narrator makes about Pakhom in these lines. Ask if they think that Pakhom would agree with the narrator's view of how his life is going. Have them consider what Pakhom's values and motivations are.

MINI LESSON Vocabulary Strategy

COMPOUND WORDS

Instruction Remind students that they can often figure out the meaning of unfamiliar words by breaking them down into parts: base words, roots, prefixes, and suffixes. Base words can stand alone. For example, the word *reread* is made up of the prefix *re-* and the base word *read.* Sometimes an unfamiliar word will be made of two or more familiar base words that provide clues to its meaning. Such words are called **compound words.** For example, in the story the word *freehold* (page 963, paragraph 2), which refers to land that is privately owned, is made of the familiar words *free* and *hold.* "Freehold land" is land that one holds free from any conditions or limitations, in contrast to communal land, which one must share.

Practice Have students work in pairs to create a list of compound words in the story. Ask them to write a definition for each one, then to explain how the base words' meanings relate to that of the compound word. Then have students check their definitions in a dictionary. (other examples: *tradesman, goodman,* and *landowner,* p. 959; *innkeeper,* p. 960; *undertaking* and *overlooking,* p. 961)

Reading and Analyzing

Reading Skills and Strategies
EVALUATING

A Ask students whether they agree with Pakhom's assumption that owning property makes a person more independent.

Possible Responses: Yes, because you have more control over what belongs to you; you get to be in charge. No, because ownership brings with it responsibility; if anything goes wrong, it's the owner's loss.

Literary Analysis TONE

B Ask students to identify the tone used from here to the end of this paragraph to describe the Bashkirs. Then discuss with them the effect of the tone on the reader.

Possible Responses: The tone is direct and objective. The narrator makes no judgment about the way of life of the Bashkirs and so gives readers the opportunity to make judgments for themselves.

He went on in the same way for three years, renting land and sowing wheat. The seasons turned out well and the crops were good, so that he began to lay money by. He might have gone on living contentedly, but he grew tired of having to rent other people's land every year, and having to scramble for it. Wherever there was good land to be had, the peasants would rush for it and it was taken up at once, so that unless you were sharp about it you got none. It happened in the third year that he and a dealer together rented a piece of pasture land from some peasants; and they had already plowed it up, when there was some dispute and the peasants went to law about it, and things fell out so that the labor was all lost.

"If it were my own land," thought Pakhom, A "I should be independent, and there would not be all this unpleasantness."

So Pakhom began looking out for land which he could buy; and he came across a peasant who had bought thirteen hundred acres, but having got into difficulties was willing to sell again cheap. Pakhom bargained and haggled with him, and at last they settled the price at 1,500 rubles, 1 part in cash and part to be paid later. They had all but clinched the matter when a passing dealer happened to stop at Pakhom's one day to get a feed for his horses. He drank tea with Pakhom and they had a talk. The dealer said that he was just returning from the land of the Bashkirs,[18] far away, where he had bought thirteen thousand acres of land, all for 1,000 rubles. Pakhom questioned him further, and the tradesman said:

"All one need do is to make friends with the chiefs. I gave away about one hundred rubles worth of silk robes and carpets, besides a case of tea, and I gave wine to those who would drink it; and I got the land for less than a penny an acre." And he showed Pakhom the title-deeds, saying:

"The land lies near a river, and the whole prairie is virgin soil."

Pakhom plied him with questions, and the 2 tradesman said:

"There is more land there than you could cover if you walked a year, and it all belongs to the Bashkirs. They are as simple as sheep, and land can be got almost for nothing."

"There now," thought Pakhom, "with my one thousand rubles, why should I get only thirteen hundred acres, and saddle myself with a debt besides? If I take it out there, I can get more than ten times as much for the money."

Pakhom inquired how to get to the place, and as soon as the tradesman had left him, he prepared to go there himself. He left his wife to look after the homestead, and started on his journey taking his man with him. They stopped at a town on their way and bought a case of tea, some wine, and other presents, as the tradesman had advised. On and on they went until they had gone more than three hundred miles, and on the seventh day they came to a place where the Bashkirs had pitched their tents. It was all just as the tradesman had said. The people lived on the B steppes,[19] by a river, in felt-covered tents. They neither tilled the ground, nor ate bread. Their cattle and horses grazed in herds on the steppe. The colts were tethered[20] behind the tents, and the mares were driven to them twice a day. The mares were milked, and from the milk kumiss[21] was made. It was the women who prepared kumiss, and they also made cheese. As far as the

18. **Bashkirs** (băsh-kîrz′): group of people of Asiatic origin who lived in southwest Russia.

19. **steppes** (stĕps): vast semidry, grass-covered plains.

20. **tethered** (tĕth′ərd): tied up with a rope or chain.

21. **kumiss** (ko͞o-mĭs′): an intoxicating beverage made from mare's or camel's milk.

Cross Curricular Link Geography

LAND OF THE BASHKIRS Using a map of Russia, locate the city of Samara, about 500 miles southeast of Moscow. Then locate the Ural Mountains on the west and the Volga River on the east, near Samara. This is the area settled by the Bashkirs, a Turkish people, in the 13th through the 15th centuries. The Bashkirs were originally nomadic, traveling from place to place with their animals and living in their felt tents. They were divided into tribes and carried out all their affairs through these tribes. Tolstoy loved what he viewed as the romantic life of the Bashkirs and bought an estate in the region. His wife, Sonya, wrote in her diary that he was excited to meet peasants on the move on their way to settle in remote areas.

The Harvest, Paul Serusier. Musée des Beaux-Arts, Nantes, France.

Customizing Instruction

Less Proficient Readers

1 Help students understand the implications of these figures. Pakhom is about to make a deal in which he would pay 1,500 rubles for 1300 acres. The traveler to whom he talks got 13,000 acres for 1,000 rubles. So Pakhom learns he could get ten times the land for two-thirds the cost.

Advanced Learners

2 Suggest to students that they keep this paragraph in mind as they read to the end of the story. Have them review the passage when they have finished reading, and ask them to point out how it foreshadows what happens and how it is ironic.

Literary Analysis THEME IN FICTION

A Ask students how Tolstoy portrays the Bashkirs and what relationship their attitude toward life might have to the theme of the story.
Possible Response: The Bashkirs have all they need, don't do much work, have few worries, are good-natured, and enjoy life. Through them, the author shows that you can have enough and live happily without constantly trying to acquire more wealth.

Active Reading
DRAWING CONCLUSIONS

B Ask students how the Bashkirs' attitude toward the land is different from the attitude of Pakhom.
Possible Response: The Bashkirs do not seem to care very much about how much land they own, and they give it away easily. Pakhom is constantly thinking about how much land he owns and how he can get more.

Literary Analysis FOLK TALE

C Tell students that in folk tales, characters often must agree to fulfill some condition or requirement in order to get what they want. Ask them to explain Pakhom's bargain with the Bashkirs.
Possible Response: For 1,000 rubles, Pakhom can have as much land as he can walk around in a day as long as he returns to the spot where he started before sundown.

Reading Skills and Strategies
PREDICTING

D Ask students what they think will happen the next day.
Possible Responses: Pakhom may fulfill the bargain and get a lot of land but still be dissatisfied; Pakhom will be too greedy and will not get the land.

"HOW CAN I TAKE AS MUCH AS I LIKE?" THOUGHT PAKHOM.

men were concerned, drinking kumiss and tea, eating mutton, and playing on their pipes, was A all they cared about. They were all stout and merry, and all the summer long they never thought of doing any work. They were quite ignorant, and knew no Russian, but were good-natured enough.

As soon as they saw Pakhom, they came out of their tents and gathered round their visitor. An interpreter was found, and Pakhom told them he had come about some land. The Bashkirs seemed very glad; they took Pakhom and led him into one of the best tents, where they made him sit on some down cushions placed on a carpet, while they sat round him. They gave him some tea and kumiss, and had a sheep killed, and gave him mutton to eat. Pakhom took presents out of his cart and distributed them among the Bashkirs, and divided the tea amongst them. The Bashkirs were delighted. They talked a great deal among themselves, and then told the interpreter to translate.

"They wish to tell you," said the interpreter, "that they like you, and that it is our custom to do all we can to please a guest and to repay him for his gifts. You have given us presents, now tell us which of the things we possess please you best, that we may present them to you."

"What pleases me best here," answered Pakhom, "is your land. Our land is crowded and the soil is exhausted; but you have plenty of land and it is good land. I never saw the like of it." 1

The interpreter translated. The Bashkirs talked among themselves for a while. Pakhom could not understand what they were saying, but saw that they were much amused and that they shouted and laughed. Then they were silent and looked at Pakhom while the interpreter said:

"They wish me to tell you that in return for your presents they will gladly give you as much land as you want. You have only to point it out with your hand and it is yours."

The Bashkirs talked again for a while and began to dispute. Pakhom asked what they were disputing about, and the interpreter told him that some of them thought they ought to ask their chief about the land and not act in his absence, while others thought there was no need to wait for his return.

While the Bashkirs were disputing, a man in a large fox-fur cap appeared on the scene. They all became silent and rose to their feet. The interpreter said, "This is our chief himself."

Pakhom immediately fetched the best dressing-gown and five pounds of tea, and offered these to the chief. The chief accepted them, and seated himself in the place of honor. The Bashkirs at once began telling him something. The chief listened for a while, then made a sign with his head for them to be silent, and addressing himself to Pakhom, said in Russian:

MINI LESSON **Vocabulary Strategy**

USING CONTEXT CLUES

Instruction Remind students that they can often find the meanings of strange words or words used in unfamiliar ways by examining **context clues**—the surrounding words, phrases, and sentences. Point out the word *tract* (page 967, paragraph 14). Students may not know this word, but they can probably figure out its meaning of "area" from the context: a discussion of measuring land. Also point out the word *sealed* (page 967, paragraph 7). From the context, it is plain that this word has a meaning different from the one with which they are probably familiar. The meaning here is "recorded legally" or "made official."

Practice Have students make a chart with three columns headed *Word, My Definition,* and *Dictionary Definition.* Have students enter the following words in column 1:

mutton (page 966, paragraph 1)
dispute (page 966, paragraph 7)
whence (page 967, paragraph 16)
turf (page 967, paragraph 18)
circuit (page 967, paragraph 18)
dispersed (page 967, paragraph 19)

Ask students to find each word in the story and to fill in column 2 based on each word's context. Then have students fill in column 3 using a dictionary and compare these definitions with their own.

A lesson on using context clues appears on p. 674 of the Pupil's Edition.

"Well, let it be so. Choose whatever piece of land you like; we have plenty of it."

B "How can I take as much as I like?" thought Pakhom. "I must get a deed to make it secure, or else they may say, 'It is yours,' and afterwards may take it away again."

"Thank you for your kind words," he said aloud. "You have much land, and I only want a little. But I should like to be sure which bit is mine. Could it not be measured and made over to me? Life and death are in God's hands. You good people give it to me, but your children might wish to take it away again."

"You are quite right," said the chief. "We will make it over to you."

"I heard that a dealer had been here," continued Pakhom, "and that you gave him a little land, too, and signed title-deeds to that effect. I should like to have it done in the same way."

The chief understood.

"Yes," replied he, "that can be done quite easily. We have a scribe, and we will go to town with you and have the deed properly sealed."

"And what will be the price?" asked Pakhom.

"Our price is always the same: one thousand rubles a day."

Pakhom did not understand.

"A day? What measure is that? How many acres would that be?"

"We do not know how to reckon it out," said the chief. "We sell it by the day. As much as you can go round on your feet in a day is yours, and the price is one thousand rubles a day."

Pakhom was surprised.

"But in a day you can get round a large tract of land," he said.

The chief laughed.

"It will all be yours!" said he. "But there is one condition: If you don't return on the same day to the spot whence you started, your money is lost."

"But how am I to mark the way that I have gone?"

"Why, we shall go to any spot you like, and stay there. You must start from that spot and make your round, taking a spade with you. Wherever you think necessary, make a mark. At every turning, dig a hole and pile up the turf; then afterwards we will go round with a plow from hole to hole. You may make as large a circuit as you please, but before the sun sets you must return to the place you started from. All the land you cover will be yours." C

Pakhom was delighted. It was decided to start early next morning. They talked a while, and after drinking some more kumiss and eating some more mutton, they had tea again, and then the night came on. They gave Pakhom a feather-bed to sleep on, and the Bashkirs dispersed for the night, promising to assemble the next morning at day-break and ride out before sunrise to the appointed spot. D

VII

Pakhom lay on the feather-bed, but could not sleep. He kept thinking about the land.

"What a large tract I will mark off!" thought he. "I can easily do thirty-five miles in a day. The days are long now, and within a circuit of thirty-five miles what a lot of land there will be! I will sell the poorer land, or let it to peasants, but I'll pick out the best and farm it. I will buy two ox-teams, and hire two more laborers. About a hundred and fifty acres shall be plow-land, and I will pasture cattle on the rest."

Pakhom lay awake all night, and dozed off only just before dawn. Hardly were his eyes closed when he had a dream. He thought he was lying in that same tent and heard somebody chuckling outside. He wondered who it could be,

Customizing Instruction

Less Proficient Readers
Make sure students understand the Bashkirs' method of buying and selling land: Pakhom will pay 1,000 rubles for as much land as he can walk around in a day instead of paying a set amount of money per acre of land. Remind students that Pakhom will get a great deal more land by the Bashkir's method than he would ordinarily.

Set a Purpose Have students think about why the Bashkirs might use this method as they read through the rest of the story.

English Learners

1 Explain to students that the expression *I never saw the like of it* means "I never saw any land as good as this land is."

Cross Curricular Link **Mathematics**

MEASURING AREA Tell students to assume that Pakhom could, as he boasted, walk 35 miles in one day. Then challenge them to use mathematical formulas to figure out which of the following approaches would secure him the most land:

- walking around a circle whose circumference is 35 miles
- walking around a square, each side of which is 8.75 miles long
- walking around a rectangle, two sides of which are 5 miles long and the other two, 12.5 miles

(The circle would secure the most land, since the areas are as follows: circle–approximately 97.5 square miles; square–approximately 76.6 square miles; rectangle–62.5 square miles.)

Students could also make calculations to determine how many acres each area would be. Have them compare these figures with the number of acres Pakhom was expecting to buy from the peasant in section IV, page 964.

(One square mile equals 309,760 square yards. One acre equals 4,840 square yards. Division of 309,760 by 4,840 equals 640 acres. Multiplication of 640 times 97.5 square miles equals 62,400 acres; 640 times 76.6 square miles equals 49,024 acres; 640 times 62.5 square miles equals 40,000 acres.)

Literary Analysis THEME IN FICTION

A Ask students what relationship they think Pakhom's dream and his response to it might have to the theme of the story.

Possible Responses: The dream seems to be a warning that Pakhom's desire for more and more land is foolish or evil and might end in disaster for him. The dream might also show that Pakhom is aware at some level that his ambition is leading him astray.

Reading Skills and Strategies SUMMARIZING

B Ask students to summarize the sequence of events in section VIII as Pakhom begins to walk.

Possible Response: Pakhom goes to the top of a small hill with the Bashkirs, and the chief puts down his hat to mark the starting spot. Pakhom lays down his money and gets ready with bread, water, and his spade. He decides to walk toward the east and begins, stopping to dig holes to mark where he has walked. The day grows warm, he takes off his boots, and he figures out what direction he will take next.

Literary Analysis SIMILE

C Ask students why Tolstoy might have used similes to describe the land.

Possible Response: The similes are vivid and help to convey the excitement Pakhom feels as he looks at the good land.

and rose and went out, and he saw the Bashkir chief sitting in front of the tent holding his sides and rolling about with laughter. Going nearer to the chief, Pakhom asked: "What are you laughing at?" But he saw that it was no longer the chief, but the dealer who had recently stopped at his house and had told him about the land. Just as Pakhom was going to ask, "Have you been here long?" he saw that it was not the dealer, but the peasant who had come up from the Volga, long ago, to Pakhom's old home. Then he saw that it was not the peasant either, but the Devil himself with hoofs and horns, sitting there and chuckling, and before him lay a man barefoot, prostrate on the ground, with only trousers and a shirt on. And Pakhom dreamt that he looked more attentively to see what sort of man it was that was lying there, and he saw that the man was dead, and that it was himself! He awoke A horror-struck.

"What things one does dream," thought he.

Looking round he saw through the open door that the dawn was breaking.

"It's time to wake them up," thought he. "We ought to be starting."

He got up, roused his man (who was sleeping in his cart), bade him harness; and went to call the Bashkirs.

"It's time to go to the steppe to measure the land," he said.

The Bashkirs rose and assembled, and the chief came too. Then they began drinking kumiss again, and offered Pakhom some tea, but he would not wait.

"If we are to go, let us go. It is high time," said he.

VIII

The Bashkirs got ready and they all started: B some mounted on horses, and some in carts. Pakhom drove in his own small cart with his servant and took a spade with him. When they reached the steppe, the morning red was beginning to kindle. 1 They ascended a hillock (called by the Bashkirs a *shikhan*[22]) and dismounting from their carts and their horses, gathered in one spot. The chief came up to Pakhom and stretching out his arm toward the plain:

"See," said he, "all this, as far as your eye can reach, is ours. You may have any part of it you like."

Pakhom's eyes glistened: it was all virgin soil, as flat as the palm of your hand, as black as the seed of a poppy, and in the hollows different kinds of grasses grew breast high. C

The chief took off his fox-fur cap, placed it on the ground and said:

"This will be the mark. Start from here, and return here again. All the land you go round shall be yours."

Pakhom took out his money and put it on the cap. Then he took off his outer coat, remaining in his sleeveless under-coat. He unfastened his girdle[23] and tied it tight below his stomach, put a little bag of bread into the breast of his coat, and tying a flask of water to his girdle, he drew up the tops of his boots, took the spade from his man, and stood ready to start. He considered for some moments which way he had better go—it was tempting everywhere.

"No matter," he concluded, "I will go towards the rising sun."

He turned his face to the east, stretched himself, and waited for the sun to appear above the rim.

"I must lose no time," he thought, "and it is

22. ***shikhan*** (shē′KHän).

23. **girdle:** a belt or sash that fastens around the waist.

Vladimirka, a Street in Siberia (about 1890), Isaac Levitan. Tretyakov Gallery, Moscow, Russia. Photo © Scala/Art Resource, New York.

easier walking while it is still cool."

The sun's rays had hardly flashed above the horizon, before Pakhom, carrying the spade over his shoulder, went down into the steppe.

Pakhom started walking neither slowly nor quickly. After having gone a thousand yards he stopped, dug a hole, and placed pieces of turf one on another to make it more visible. Then he went on; and now that he had walked off his stiffness he quickened his pace. After a while he dug another hole.

Pakhom looked back. The hillock could be distinctly seen in the sunlight, with the people on it, and the glittering tires of the cart-wheels. At a rough guess Pakhom concluded that he had walked three miles. It was growing warmer; he took off his under-coat, flung it across his shoulder, and went on again. It had grown quite warm now; he looked at the sun, it was time to think of breakfast.

"The first shift is done, but there are four in a day, and it is too soon yet to turn. But I will just take off my boots," said he to himself.

He sat down, took off his boots, stuck them into his girdle, and went on. It was easy walking now.

"I will go on for another three miles," thought he, "and then turn to the left. This spot is so fine, that it would be a pity to lose it. The fur-

Customizing Instruction

English Learners

1 Explain that "the morning red was beginning to kindle" means that the sun was beginning to rise and color the sky red.

Less Proficient Readers

2 Help students understand what the two similes in these lines tell about the land. Explain that "flat as the palm of your hand" means that the land was smooth and even and so would be easy to plow, unlike hilly or rocky land. "Black as the seed of a poppy" means that the dirt was very rich and dark and so would be excellent soil for farming.

Advanced Learners

Have students look back at the end of section I and review what the Devil was planning to do. Then have them reread the description of Pakhom's dream. Ask them to consider what relationship they think the Devil does or does not have to the chief, the dealer, and the peasant. Then tell them to review the dream after they have finished the story and see whether or not their interpretation has changed.

MINI LESSON Viewing and Representing

Motherland **by A. M. Vasnetsov**

ART APPRECIATION

Instruction The Russian artist A. M. Vasnetsov is known for his vivid depictions of nature in central Russia. In this landscape, he sets small details in a wide expanse of land and sky.

Application Ask students to identify as many details in the painting as they can. *(Details include rows of various plants; flowering weeds and broken plow in the foreground; man plowing with a team of horses; birds; roofs; trees; a tower; and lakes in the distance.)* Then ask students to describe the effect produced by the wide perspective combined with the small details.

Possible Responses: The wide perspective gives a sense of vastness and space, as though the land and sky go on forever. The details portray human life as small and insignificant in comparison to nature. The painting shows how the "motherland" surrounds and protects her children.

Reading Skills and Strategies
VISUALIZING

A Have students visualize Pakhom as he tries to make it back to the starting point. Ask them to list details that convey his physical condition.

Reading Skills and Strategies
QUESTIONING

B Ask students why Pakhom couldn't stop running, even though he was afraid he was going to die from the strain.

Possible Response: Even in the face of death, he couldn't give up the possibility of getting more land.

Literary Analysis IRONY

C Point out that Pakhom remembers his dream twice as he tries to reach the hill. Ask students to explain the irony in his remembering the dream at this point in the story.

Possible Response: If Pakhom had paid attention to the dream when he first awoke, he might have been more careful and not gotten himself in trouble. When he remembers it at the end of the story, he realizes too late what the dream meant and the price he has to pay—he has lost the chance to save himself.

Literary Analysis THEME IN FICTION

D Ask: What answer does the last sentence give to the question in the title of the story? What theme does it suggest?

Possible Response: The last sentence says that Pakhom needed only six feet of earth for a grave. This is an ironic comment on Pakhom's constant desire for more land and suggests the theme that being greedy may result in loss rather than gain.

ther one goes, the better the land seems."

He went straight on for a while, and when he looked round, the hillock was scarcely visible and the people on it looked like black ants, and he could just see something glistening there in the sun.

"Ah," thought Pakhom, "I have gone far enough in this direction, it is time to turn. Besides I am in a regular sweat, and very thirsty."

He stopped, dug a large hole, and heaped up pieces of turf. Next he untied his flask, had a drink, and then turned sharply to the left. He went on and on; the grass was high, and it was very hot.

Pakhom began to grow tired: he looked at the sun and saw that it was noon.

"Well," he thought, "I must have a rest."

He sat down, and ate some bread and drank some water; but he did not lie down, thinking that if he did he might fall asleep. After sitting a little while, he went on again. At first he walked easily: the food had strengthened him; but it had become terribly hot and he felt sleepy, still he
1 went on, thinking: "An hour to suffer, a life-time to live."

He went a long way in this direction also, and was about to turn to the left again, when he perceived a damp hollow: "It would be a pity to leave that out," he thought. "Flax[24] would do well there." So he went on past the hollow, and dug a hole on the other side of it before he turned the corner. Pakhom looked towards the hillock. The heat made the air hazy: it seemed to be quivering, and through the haze the people on the hillock could scarcely be seen.

"Ah!" thought Pakhom, "I have made the sides too long; I must make this one shorter." And he went along the third side, stepping faster. He looked at the sun: it was nearly half-way to the horizon, and he had not yet done two miles of the third side of the square. He was still ten miles from the goal.

"No," he thought, "though it will make my
land lop-sided, I must hurry back in a straight 2
line now. I might go too far, and as it is I have a great deal of land."

So Pakhom hurriedly dug a hole, and turned straight towards the hillock.

"IT WOULD BE A PITY TO LEAVE THAT OUT," HE THOUGHT.

Pakhom went straight towards the hillock, but A
he now walked with difficulty. He was done up
with the heat, his bare feet were cut and bruised, 3
and his legs began to fail. He longed to rest, but it was impossible if he meant to get back before sunset. The sun waits for no man, and it was sinking lower and lower.

"Oh dear," he thought, "if only I have not blundered trying for too much! What if I am too late?"

He looked towards the hillock and at the sun. He was still far from his goal, and the sun was already near the rim.

24. **flax:** a plant grown for its seed and for its fine fibers.

MINI LESSON **Grammar**

SUBORDINATE CLAUSES: ADVERB CLAUSES

Instruction A clause is a group of words with a subject and a predicate that may or may not be a sentence. If the words can stand independently they are a sentence. However, if the clause begins with a subordinating conjunction—such as *since, when, where, wherever, because, although, so that,* or *as if*—then it is subordinate, or dependent. Often a subordinate clause adds adverbial information. Because a subordinate clause does not express a complete thought, it must be attached to an independent clause in order to make sense. Subordinating conjunctions show the relationship of a subordinate clause to an independent clause. Such a relationship may be one of time, place, cause, condition, purpose, or manner. The following is an example from "How Much Land Does a Man Need?"

Model Write the following example on the chalkboard:

"If I had plenty of land, I shouldn't fear the Devil himself!"

The underlined part of the sentence is a subordinate clause used as an adverb. Its relationship to the independent clause is one of condition; it tells under what conditions Pakhom would not

Pakhom walked on and on; it was very hard walking but he went quicker and quicker. He pressed on, but was still far from the place. He began running, threw away his coat, his boots, his flask, and his cap, and kept only the spade which he used as a support.

"What shall I do?" he thought again, "I have grasped too much and ruined the whole affair. I can't get there before the sun sets."

And this fear made him still more breathless. Pakhom went on running, his soaking shirt and trousers stuck to him and his mouth was parched. His breast was working like a blacksmith's bellows, his heart was beating like a hammer, and his legs were giving way as if they did not belong to him. Pakhom was seized with terror lest he should die of the strain.

B Though afraid of death, he could not stop. "After having run all that way they will call me a fool if I stop now," thought he. And he ran on and on, and drew near and heard the Bashkirs yelling and shouting to him, and their cries inflamed his heart still more. He gathered his last strength and ran on.

The sun was close to the rim, and cloaked in mist looked large, and red as blood. Now, yes now, it was about to set! The sun was quite low, but he was also quite near his aim. Pakhom could already see the people on the hillock waving their arms to hurry him up. He could see the fox-fur cap on the ground and the money on it, and the chief sitting on the ground holding his sides. And Pakhom remembered his dream.

"There is plenty of land," thought he, "but will God let me live on it? I have lost my life, I have lost my life! I shall never reach that spot!"

Pakhom looked at the sun, which had reached the earth: one side of it had already disappeared. With all his remaining strength he rushed on, bending his body forward so that his legs could hardly follow fast enough to keep him from falling. Just as he reached the hillock it suddenly grew dark. He looked up—the sun had already set! He gave a cry: "All my labor has been in vain," thought he, and was about to stop, but he heard the Bashkirs still shouting, and remembered that though to him, from below, the sun seemed to have set, they on the hillock could still see it. He took a long breath and ran up the hillock. It was still light there. He reached the top and saw the cap. Before it sat the chief laughing and holding his sides. Again Pakhom remembered his dream, and he uttered a cry: his legs gave way beneath him, he fell forward and reached the cap with his hands. C

"Ah, that's a fine fellow!" exclaimed the chief. "He has gained much land!"

Pakhom's servant came running up and tried to raise him, but he saw that blood was flowing from his mouth. Pakhom was dead!

The Bashkirs clicked their tongues to show their pity.

His servant picked up the spade and dug a grave long enough for Pakhom to lie in, and buried him in it. Six feet from his head to his heels was all he needed. ❖ D

fear the devil. (You may wish to remind students that in current American style, a comma always follows a subordinate clause at the beginning of a sentence.)

Practice Ask students to underline each subordinate clause and to tell whether its relationship to the main clause is one of time, place, cause, condition, purpose, or manner.

1. The peasants wanted to buy the whole estate so that they could all hold it in common. *(purpose)*
2. When Pakhom went out to plow his fields, his heart would fill with joy. *(time)*
3. Wherever you think necessary, make a mark in the ground with your spade. *(place)*
4. Pakhom's legs were giving way as if they did not belong to him. *(manner)*
5. Although he was afraid of death, he could not stop running. *(condition)*

For more instruction and practice in adverb clauses, use McDougal Littell's ***Language Network:***

- Grade 10, Chapter 4, "Clauses and Sentence Structure"
- Grade 12, Chapter 3, "Using Clauses"

Customizing Instruction

Less Proficient Readers
Help students follow Pakhom's thoughts and actions. Have them note whether or not his actions change as a result of his thoughts.

Advanced Learners
1 After students have finished reading the story, have them reread Pakhom's thoughts on page 970. Ask them to explain how Pakhom's comment is an ironic foreshadowing. Then have them work in pairs to discuss the use of irony and foreshadowing throughout the story, using the notes they were directed to make on page 959.

English Learners
2 Explain that *lop-sided* means "larger on one side than the other." The shape of Pakhom's piece of land will be uneven because he cannot take the time to walk the same length around all sides.

3 Explain that "done up with the heat" means that Pakhom was completely exhausted by it.

Connect to the Literature

1. **What Do You Think?** Possible responses: Some students may feel sorry for Pakhom because he worked so hard and was so close to getting what he wanted. Others may not feel sorry for him and may think that he brought death on himself because of his greediness and selfishness.

Comprehension Check

- He has conflicts with the peasants for trespassing and cutting his trees. When he takes them to court, he angers his neighbors and the judges.
- He can get ten times more land for his money from the Bashkirs.
- Pakhom dies just as he reaches the point of winning the land.

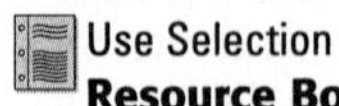
Use Selection Quiz in **Unit Six Resource Book,** p. 28.

Think Critically

2. Possible Responses: Many students will say that Pakhom causes his own downfall because he is never satisfied with the land he has. He has turned his wants into his needs. Others may say that the Devil influences Pakhom's thoughts and controls what happens to him.
3. Possible Responses: Students who say that Pakhom's fate is inevitable may cite his growing desire for more land and his inability to be content. They also may cite the Devil's threat and say Pakhom was doomed from that moment. Students who disagree may say that at any point he could have chosen to make the best of what he already had. He could also have paid attention to his dream and either returned to his home or chosen to walk around a smaller piece of the Bashkirs' land.
4. Possible Responses: Pakhom's wife tells her sister that the city is full of temptation, but Pakhom is tempted in the country. Pakhom plans what he will do with all the land he will buy, but he gets only enough for his grave.
5. Possible Response: The Bashkirs are carefree, good-natured, and generous. Pakhom and the other peasants work all the time, are not content, and try to acquire more land and money. Most students will say that Tolstoy admires the Bashkirs more. Their way of life is peaceful and wise, but Pakhom's way ends in death.

Connect to the Literature

1. **What Do You Think?** Did you feel sorry for Pakhom at the end of the story? Why or why not?

Comprehension Check
- After buying his first farm, what conflicts does Pakhom have?
- Why does he want to buy land from the Bashkirs?
- What happens at the end of the story?

Think Critically

2. What causes Pakhom's downfall?

THINK ABOUT
- how his motivation for wanting land changes in the story
- what part the Devil plays
- what the last line implies about wants and needs

3. **ACTIVE READING: DRAWING CONCLUSIONS** Look back at the details you recorded in your READER'S NOTEBOOK. Do you think Pakhom's fate is inevitable? If so, why? If not, at what point could he have avoided what happened?
4. This story is full of **ironies,** surprising twists and reversals that are the opposite of what you'd expect. Name one or two ironies that you found.
5. Contrast the Bashkirs and their way of life with Pakhom and the other peasants. Which group, if any, do you think Tolstoy admires more? Explain your answer.

Extend Interpretations

6. **What if?** What if Pakhom had succeeded in getting back to the hilltop alive and received his land? Would he have been satisfied? Explain why or why not.
7. **Connect to Life** How is Tolstoy's 19th-century story about a Russian peasant's drive for land relevant to people living in the United States in the 21st century?

LITERARY ANALYSIS: THEME IN FICTION

In a story, **theme** is the main idea about life or human nature inferred from the characters and events. Clues to theme can sometimes be found in the story's title and also in what a reader may already know about the author's life or beliefs.

Cooperative Learning Activity Get together with a small group of classmates to determine the theme of Tolstoy's story. In your discussion, consider these points:
- what you know about Tolstoy's moral principles
- Pakhom's motivation and behavior
- how the opening dialogue between the sisters relates to Pakhom's fate
- what central issue the title of the story points to
- what is considered wrong or evil in the story

Then write a statement of the theme as your group understands it. Compare your thematic statement with those of other groups.

Extend Interpretations

6. **What If?** Many students will say that Pakhom might have been content with a huge amount of land for a while but would have wanted more eventually because of his greed. Some students may say that his dream and his near brush with death would have changed him, and he would have settled down.
7. **Connect to Life** Students may say that many people in the United States are overly concerned with accumulating wealth and possessions. The story of Pakhom illustrates the possibility that acquiring possessions may bring undesirable consequences: ill health, broken relationships, unhappiness, or even death.

Literary Analysis

Cooperative Learning Activity Possible statements of theme could include the following:
- Wealth and material possessions do not bring happiness.
- Greed destroys peace of mind.
- Contentment and love are more important than success.
- Ruthless ambition leads to destruction.

You might want to have each group write its statement of theme on the chalkboard or on a poster board.

Use **Unit Six Resource Book,** p. 27, for additional support.

Writing Options

1. News Coverage Write a news item reporting on Pakhom's death. Try to imitate Tolstoy's own unbiased tone in relating events.

Writing Handbook
See page R29: Narrative Writing.

2. Family Letter Suppose you are Pakhom's wife. Write a letter to your sister after you learn of Pakhom's death telling her what your life has been like since your earlier conversation. Take into account the difference of opinion that existed between you and your sister at that time.

3. Children's Version Rewrite this story as a tale for kindergarten children. Be sure to simplify the plot and the language and to state the moral clearly at the end.

Activities & Explorations

1. Imaginary Dialogue Imagine that Tolstoy was a character in his story. What might he tell Pakhom to help him, and how might Pakhom respond? Working with a partner, create a dialogue between Tolstoy and Pakhom and perform it for the class. ~ **PERFORMING**

2. Pakhom on Trial In a court of law, Pakhom could not be charged with doing anything illegal. But what about in Tolstoy's moral court? With a group of classmates, create a trial in which Pakhom can be judged morally. Divide your group into a prosecution team and a defense team. The prosecution team comes up with at least one charge of wrongdoing. The defense team pleads guilty or not guilty to the charge. The two teams should present their cases in front of the rest of the class, who serves as the jury. After the cases have been presented, the jury discusses the merits of the cases and decides on the verdict and the sentence. ~ **SPEAKING AND LISTENING**

Communications Handbook
See page R49: Critical Thinking.

Inquiry & Research

1. Peasant Communes
Research peasant communes in Russia before and after serfdom was abolished in 1861. What was the purpose of the communes, and how were they organized? Was the communal system economically efficient? Report your findings to the class.

2. Tolstoy and Gandhi
Following his spiritual crisis, Tolstoy explored many new ideas and eventually became a pacifist. His views on nonviolence were an important influence on the Indian leader Mohandas Gandhi. Research biographies of Tolstoy as well as his diaries and letters to learn more about his views and his relationship to Gandhi. Write a brief summary of what you learn.

Writing Options

1. **News Coverage** Remind students that newspaper articles should be as objective as possible. In their articles, they should recount clearly and simply who Pakhom was, what he was doing, and what happened to him.
2. **Family Letter** You might want to have students get together in small groups to discuss how Pakhom's wife might be feeling about Pakhom's ambitions, the many moves she has had to make, and the circumstances of Pakhom's death. They can also discuss what her attitude toward her sister might be at this point. Tell students that the letter should reflect her strongest feelings and should sound personal and convincing.
3. **Children's Version** You might have students work in pairs to brainstorm about how they would create a simple tale out of this story. Remind them that the vocabulary must be very easy, and each sentence should contain only a few words. You could bring in some kindergarten-level books from the library for them to look at.

Activities & Explorations

1. **Imaginary Dialogue** The student playing Pakhom should reread the story carefully and make a list of the thoughts, motivations, and actions of Pakhom. The student playing Tolstoy should reread the biographical material in this **Author Study** and then reread the story to look for further clues about Tolstoy's viewpoint. The students should practice their dialogue to make it as natural as possible.
2. **Pakhom on Trial** The prosecution team may come up with more than one charge. It should also produce evidence to support each charge, and it should present a method of punishment. The defense team must prepare a defense and propose either that the charge(s) be dropped or that the punishment be lessened. You can act as the judge to ensure fairness and proper procedures. If the jury consists of more than 12 people, a two-thirds majority can rule.

Inquiry & Research

1. **Peasant Communes** Two history books that might be useful are *The Russian Peasantry 1600–1930: The World the Peasants Made* by David Moon and *A History of Russia, the Soviet Union, and Beyond* by David Mackenzie. Interested students might want to read *Anna Karenina,* in which Tolstoy describes many scenes from peasant life. Tell students that in doing their research, they can also look under the Russian word for a peasant commune: *obshchina*.
2. **Tolstoy and Gandhi** Two detailed biographies are those by Henri Troyat and A. N. Wilson. Some of Tolstoy's letters to Gandhi are included in *Tolstoy's Letters,* Volume II, translated by R. F. Christian. Students could also look at Tolstoy's later diaries as well as his own writings on nonviolence, especially his works *What I Believe* and *The Kingdom of God Is Within You.* Students who want to do further research could consult *Tolstoy and Gandhi, Men of Peace,* by Martin Green. When students have finished their summaries, you may want to have them share their impressions of Tolstoy.

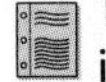
To assess skills and concepts taught in this selection, use **Formal Assessment Book,** pp. 147–148.

Biographical Note

When Tolstoy sent his manuscript for *Childhood* to the editor N. A. Nekrasov, he was aiming as high as he could go in Russian literary circles of the 1850s. *The Contemporary,* the journal that Nekrasov edited, was read and respected by the most important writers of that time. Nekrasov's publication of *Childhood* did, in fact, launch Tolstoy's reputation. Such writers as Turgenev and Dostoyevsky gave Tolstoy's work high praise. One reviewer said the new writer "L. N." was a "new and remarkable talent."

Because *The Contemporary* was progressive and intellectual, it was a target for government censorship. When Tolstoy wrote this letter complaining about all the changes that had been made in his work, he blamed Nekrasov. In fact, some of the alterations were made by the censors.

Although Tolstoy never sent this letter to Nekrasov, he did send it to Nikolay Tolstoy, his brother. In the second letter that he wrote—and sent—to Nekrasov, he was more conciliatory and kept the way open to send him other manuscripts. In response, Nekrasov wrote back that although he did not pay for a new author's first work, he would pay well for anything Tolstoy offered him in the future. Tolstoy did in fact publish several other works in *The Contemporary.*

Letter from Leo Tolstoy to N. A. Nekrasov

Translated by R. F. Christian

PREPARING to *Read*

Build Background

When Nikolay Nekrasov, editor of the Russian journal *The Contemporary*, accepted Tolstoy's novel *Childhood* for publication, Tolstoy admitted in his diary that it "made me absurdly happy." This was Tolstoy's first published work, so naturally he was nervous about the public's reaction to it. At first, he didn't even sign his name, only the initials L. N. (for Lev Nikolayevich, his first and middle names). But when he read the piece as it was first printed, Tolstoy was furious at the changes made to the original. In a fit of anger, he dashed off the following letter. He never sent it, however, and later, when he had calmed down, he wrote a milder version.

Starogladovskaya, 18 November 1852

Dear Sir,

I was extremely displeased to read in *The Contemporary,* No. IX, a *story* entitled *A History of My Childhood,* and to recognize it as the *novel Childhood* which I sent to you. I made it the first condition of publication that you should *first evaluate the manuscript and send me what you think it is worth.* This condition has not been fulfilled. The second condition was that nothing should be altered in it. Still less has that condition been fulfilled: you have altered everything, starting with the title. Having read this pathetic, mutilated story with the saddest of feelings, I tried to discover the reasons which prompted the editors to behave so ruthlessly towards it. Either the editors set themselves the task of mutilating this novel as much as possible, or else they entrusted the proof-reading, without any checking, to a completely illiterate employee. The title *Childhood* and the few words of the introduction explained the idea of the work; but the title *A History of My Childhood* contradicts the idea of the work. Who is interested in the history of *my* childhood? . . . It is not possible or necessary to list all the alterations of this sort; but not to speak of the innumerable scraps of meaningless phrases, the misprints, the incorrectly transposed punctuation marks, the bad spelling or the unfortunate word alterations such as *to breathe* for *to pant* (of dogs), or *dropped to the ground in tears* for *fell* (cattle drop), which prove ignorance of the language, I would mention one alteration which is incomprehensible to me. Why has the whole story of Natalya Savishna's love been omitted, a story which depicted her and the old way of life and which imparted significance and humanity to the character? . . . It's incomprehensible. I will only say that when I read the work in print I experienced the unpleasant feeling which a father experiences at the sight of his beloved son whose hair has been cut in an ugly and uneven way by a self-taught hairdresser. "Where did those bare patches and forelocks come from, when he was a fine-looking boy before?" My child was not very handsome to start with, but to make matters worse he has been cropped and mutilated. I can only console myself with the fact that I have the opportunity to publish the whole novel separately under my own name, and to renounce completely the story of *A History of My Childhood,* which by rights belongs not to me, but to an unknown employee of your editorial staff.

I have the honor to be, Sir,
Your most obedient servant,
L.N.

READING FOR INFORMATION
Reading Skills and Strategies
IDENTIFYING LOADED LANGUAGE

Point out to students that Tolstoy was displeased about actual changes that had been made in his manuscript. In this letter, he does not express his opinions calmly, however, but with strong emotions. Have students identify words, phrases, and statements that are examples of emotionally charged, or loaded, language. Ask students to evaluate how this language affects the force of the points Tolstoy wants to make. Have them discuss how Nekrasov might have reacted if he had received the letter.

Possible Responses: Examples of loaded language include "you have altered everything," "pathetic, mutilated," "completely illiterate employee," "innumerable scraps of meaningless phrases," "ignorance of the language," and "renounce completely." The strong language actually weakens Tolstoy's points, because the reader tends not to take such language seriously and to dismiss the ideas as exaggerated. Nekrasov would no doubt have reacted in a similar way and been alienated toward Tolstoy. Thus Tolstoy would have produced exactly the opposite effect of what he wanted—namely, to be published and respected.

This selection is included in the **World Literature InterActive Reader™**.

Objectives

- understand and appreciate a Russian **short story (Literary Analysis)**
- recognize and appreciate **foreshadowing (Literary Analysis)**
- **predict** events in a plot **(Active Reading)**

Summary

A poor shoemaker named Simon meets a naked, freezing man who will say only that his name is Michael and that God is punishing him. Simon takes the man home and teaches him his trade. One day a gentleman arrives and demands boots that will last a year. Michael makes slippers instead, and soon a messenger delivers the news that the man has died and needs slippers to be buried in. Several years later, a woman orders shoes for her twin girls. She tells how she adopted the girls after their mother died and describes them as the joy of her life. After the woman and the girls leave, Simon and his wife notice light streaming from Michael. He explains that he has been a disobedient angel. When he refused to take the soul of the girls' mother, God sent him to earth to learn what dwells in man, what is not given to man, and what men live by.

Use **Unit Six Resource Book**, p. 29, for additional support.

Thematic Link

In this folk tale, Tolstoy explores the **lessons to be learned** from relationships with God and with others.

5-Minute Warm-Up

Daily Language SkillBuilder

Have students **proofread** the display sentences on page 869k and write them correctly.

What Men Live By

Leo Tolstoy

Translated by Louise and Aylmer Maude

Build Background

A Tale Retold In his later years, Tolstoy was very attracted to folk literature because of its wide appeal and the deep truths it expresses. He felt that this literature spoke to the most basic feelings and yearnings shared by all people. He chose a number of tales and legends from the Russian tradition to retell, using them as a way of conveying his beliefs about the meaning of life. In an article called "On Truth in Art, which was published in 1887, Tolstoy wrote:

> ***. . . there are fairy tales, parables, fables, legends, in which marvelous things are described which never happened or ever could happen, and these legends, fairy tales, and fables are true, because they show wherein the will of God has always been, and is, and will be.***

Based on a folk tale Tolstoy heard from a traveling storyteller, "What Men Live By" tells what happens when a poor peasant encounters a stranger in need. In retelling the tale, Tolstoy wanted to retain the simplicity and moral force of the original, while at the same time creating a good short story. As you read it, you can decide whether he succeeded.

Connect to Your Life

Would you give your last dollar to your friend? to a stranger? Discuss the idea of giving with your classmates. Then create a few moral guidelines that people could use when making decisions about giving.

Focus Your Reading

LITERARY ANALYSIS: FORESHADOWING

Foreshadowing is a writer's use of hints or clues to suggest what will happen later. For example, in "How Much Land Does a Man Need?" Pakhom's dream in section VII foreshadows his fate at the end. As you read, look for clues that foreshadow what's to come.

ACTIVE READING: PREDICTING

Predicting what will happen next in a story can alert you to foreshadowing. Keep in mind what you know about Tolstoy, and always use your own ability to figure things out in making your predictions.

READER'S NOTEBOOK "What Men Live By" has many strange events that are not explained until the end of the story. As you come across each event in your reading, write a question about it and then a brief **prediction** that might answer the question. Use a chart like this one to keep track of your predictions.

Question	Prediction
1. *Who's the stranger that appears in section I?*	1.

LESSON RESOURCES

UNIT SIX RESOURCE BOOK, pp. 29–32

ASSESSMENT RESOURCES

Formal Assessment, pp. 149–150

Teacher's Guide to Assessment and Portfolio Use

Test Generator

INTEGRATED TECHNOLOGY

NetActivities

Visit our Web site: classzone.com

ADDITIONAL RESOURCES

Lesson Planning Guide, pp. 127–128

Teacher's Sourcebook for Language Development

I

A shoemaker named Simon, who had neither house nor land of his own, lived with his wife and children in a peasant's hut and earned his living by his work. Work was cheap but bread was dear, and what he earned he spent for food. The man and his wife had but one sheep-skin coat between them for winter wear, and even that was worn to tatters, and this was the second year he had been wanting to buy sheep-skins for a new coat. Before winter Simon saved up a little money: a three-ruble note lay hidden in his wife's box, and five rubles and twenty kopeks[1] were owed him by customers in the village.

So one morning he prepared to go to the village to buy the sheep-skins. He put on over his shirt his wife's wadded nankeen[2] jacket, and over that he put his own cloth coat. He took the three-ruble note in his pocket, cut himself a stick to serve as a staff, and started off after breakfast. "I'll collect the five rubles that are due to me," thought he, "add the three I have got, and that will be enough to buy sheep-skins for the winter coat."

He came to the village and called at a peasant's hut, but the man was not at home. The peasant's wife promised that the money should be paid next week, but she would not pay it herself. Then Simon called on another peasant, but this one swore he had no money, and would only pay twenty kopeks which he owed for a pair of boots Simon had mended. Simon then tried to buy the sheep-skins on credit, but the dealer would not trust him.

"Bring your money," said he, "then you may have your pick of the skins. We know what debt-collecting is like."

So all the business the shoemaker did was to get the twenty kopeks for boots he had mended and to take a pair of felt boots a peasant gave him to sole with leather.

Simon felt downhearted. He spent the twenty kopeks on vodka and started homewards without having bought any skins. In the morning he had felt the frost; but now, after drinking the vodka, he felt warm even without a sheep-skin coat. He trudged along, striking his stick on the frozen earth with one hand, swinging the felt boots with the other, and talking to himself.

"I'm quite warm," said he, "though I have no sheep-skin coat. I've had a drop and it runs through my veins. I need no sheep-skins. I go along and don't worry about anything. That's the sort of man I am! What do I care? I can live without sheep-skins. I don't need them. My wife will fret, to be sure. And, true enough, it *is* a shame; one works all day long and then does not get paid. Stop a bit! If you don't bring that money along, sure enough I'll skin you, blessed if I don't. How's that? He pays twenty kopeks at a time! What can I do with twenty kopeks? Drink it—that's all one can do! Hard up, he says he is! So he may be—but what about me? You have house, and cattle, and everything; I've only what I stand up in! You have corn of your own growing, I have to buy every grain. Do what I will, I must spend three rubles every week for bread alone. I come home and find the bread all used up and I have to work out another ruble and a half. So just you pay up what you owe, and no nonsense about it!"

By this time he had nearly reached the shrine[3] at the bend of the road. Looking up, he saw something whitish behind the shrine. The daylight was fading, and the shoemaker peered at the thing without being able to make out what it was. "There was no white stone here before. Can it be an ox? It's not like an ox. It has a head like a man, but it's too white; and what could a man be doing there?"

1. **kopeks** (kō′pĕks): A kopek is one hundredth of a ruble.
2. **nankeen:** a sturdy cotton cloth.
3. **shrine:** a place at which devotion is paid to God or a holy person.

Customizing Instruction

Less Proficient Readers

Have students describe the living conditions of the poor peasant, Simon. Elicit that his family has little to eat, has few clothes, and cannot depend on other peasants to pay for Simon's work, since they are just as poor. Tell students that the first two sections of the story concern Simon's attempts to collect what is owed him. Have students read to find out what happens.

English Learners

You may want to review some of the concepts in the story that may be unfamiliar to students. Ask students what they know about the craft of shoemaking and Russian history. Make sure they understand the information in **Build Background** on page 976.

Explain the meaning of idioms such as "Work was cheap but bread was dear" *(wages were low, but food was expensive)*; "to buy . . . on credit" *(to buy something that will be paid for at a later time)*; "take my measure" *(measure someone for clothes or shoes)*; "the thought they spend on their own welfare" *(thinking about their own well-being)*.

Make sure that students understand that in paragraphs 7–13 Simon is thinking out loud rather than talking to someone.

Advanced Learners

Ask students to consider how each character in the story is rewarded or punished for his or her behavior. How do these consequences support the story's theme?

TIME MANAGEMENT

If your schedule requires that you cover the lesson objectives in a shorter time, use . . .

- Preparing to Read, p. 976
- Thinking Through the Literature, p. 995

If you want to take advantage of longer blocks of class time, use . . .

- TE Teaching Options: Cross-Curricular Link, pp. 980, 982, 984; Vocabulary Strategy, pp. 981, 986; Viewing and Representing, pp. 987, 991; Standardized Test Practice, pp. 988–989, 990; Grammar, p. 992
- *from* Sonya Tolstoy's Diary, pp. 993–994
- The Author's Style, p. 996
- Choices & Challenges, p. 997
- Author Study Project, p. 997

Active Reading PREDICTING

Predicting the events of a story is like using clues to solve a puzzle. Have students use the "clues" in the title and the first five paragraphs on this page to predict what might happen in the lives of Simon and his wife Matrëna.

Possible Responses: Students might think that Simon and Matrëna will find some way to end their poverty or that they will continue to have financial problems. Some students might think the couple will learn the importance of other things besides money.

 Use **Unit Six Resource Book,** p. 30, for more practice.

Literary Analysis FORESHADOWING

Foreshadowing provides hints or clues to future events in a story. Tolstoy uses foreshadowing to add suspense and prepare the reader for events to come. Suggest that students keep a running list of clues provided through foreshadowing that help them confirm or contradict their predictions.

 Use **Unit Six Resource Book,** p. 31, for more practice.

Literary Analysis THEME

Have students think about the theme of this story as they read. Explain that the theme is the central message or idea in a work of literature. It should not be confused with the subject of the work; rather, it is a perception about life or human nature. Have students consider what this story reveals about life and human nature.

Active Reading PREDICTING

A Ask students to predict how Simon's wife will react to the stranger.

Possible Response: Simon knows his wife is going to be unhappy that he is returning without the sheepskins. He says that she won't be pleased that he is bringing along a naked man. Therefore, she probably won't want the young man in her house.

The Grey House (1917), Marc Chagall. Fundacion Coleccion Thyssen-Bornemisza, Madrid. Photo © Nimatallah/Art Resource, New York © 2007 Artists Rights Society (ARS), New York/ADAGP, Paris.

He came closer, so that it was clearly visible. To his surprise it really was a man, alive or dead, sitting naked, leaning motionless against the shrine. Terror seized the shoemaker, and he thought, "Some one has killed him, stripped him, and left him here. If I meddle I shall surely get into trouble."

So the shoemaker went on. He passed in front of the shrine so that he could not see the man. When he had gone some way he looked back, and saw that the man was no longer leaning against the shrine but was moving as if looking towards him. The shoemaker felt more frightened than before, and thought, "Shall I go back to him or shall I go on? If I go near him something dreadful may happen. Who knows who the fellow is? He has not come here for any good. If I go near him he may jump up and throttle me, and there will be no getting away. Or if not, he'd still be a burden on one's hands. What could I do with a naked man? I couldn't give him my last clothes. Heaven only help me to get away!"

So the shoemaker hurried on, leaving the shrine behind him—when suddenly his conscience smote him and he stopped in the road. 1

"What are you doing, Simon?" said he to

himself. "The man may be dying of want, and you slip past afraid. Have you grown so rich as to be afraid of robbers? Ah, Simon, shame on you!"

2 So he turned back and went up to the man.

II

3 Simon approached the stranger, looked at him and saw that he was a young man, fit, with no bruises on his body, but evidently freezing and frightened, and he sat there leaning back without looking up at Simon, as if too faint to lift his eyes. Simon went close to him and then the man seemed to wake up. Turning his head, he opened his eyes and looked into Simon's face. That one look was enough to make Simon fond of the man. He threw the felt boots on the ground, undid his sash, laid it on the boots, and took off his cloth coat.

"It's not a time for talking," said he. "Come, put this coat on at once!" And Simon took the man by the elbows and helped him to rise. As he stood there, Simon saw that his body was clean and in good condition, his hands and feet shapely, and his face good and kind. He threw his coat over the man's shoulders, but the latter could not find the sleeves. Simon guided his arms into them, and drawing the coat on well, wrapped it closely about him, tying the sash round the man's waist.

Simon even took off his cap to put it on the man's head, but then his own head felt cold and he thought: "I'm quite bald, while he has long curly hair." So he put his cap on his own head again. "It will be better to give him something for his feet," thought he; and he made the man sit down and helped him to put on the felt boots, saying, "There, friend, now move about and warm yourself. Other matters can be settled later on. Can you walk?"

The man stood up and looked kindly at Simon but could not say a word.

"Why don't you speak?" said Simon. "It's too cold to stay here, we must be getting home. There now, take my stick, and if you're feeling weak lean on that. Now step out!"

The man started walking and moved easily, not lagging behind.

As they went along, Simon asked him, "And where do you belong to?"

"I'm not from these parts."

"I thought as much. I know the folks hereabouts. But how did you come to be there by the shrine?"

"I cannot tell."

"Has some one been ill-treating you?" 4

"No one has ill-treated me. God has punished me."

"Of course God rules all. Still, you'll have to find food and shelter somewhere. Where do you want to go to?"

"It is all the same to me."

Simon was amazed. The man did not look like a rogue, and he spoke gently, but yet he gave no 5 account of himself. Still Simon thought, "Who knows what may have happened?" And he said to the stranger: "Well then, come home with me and at least warm yourself awhile."

So Simon walked towards his home, and the stranger kept up with him, walking at his side. The wind had risen and Simon felt it cold under his shirt. He was getting over his tipsiness by now and began to feel the frost. He went along sniffling and wrapping his wife's coat round him, and he thought to himself: "There now—talk about sheep-skins! I went out for sheep-skins and come home without even a coat to my back, and what is more, I'm bringing a naked man along with me. Matrëna[4] won't be pleased!" And A when he thought of his wife he felt sad, but when he looked at the stranger and remembered

4. **Matrëna** (mä-trō′nä).

Customizing Instruction

English Learners

1 Tell students that a *conscience* is what makes a person feel responsible for doing what is right or good. Ask students why Simon's conscience bothers him at this point.
Possible Responses: Simon feels guilty because he has been thinking only of himself; he believes it is wrong to ignore someone in need.

Less Proficient Readers

2 Ask students why Simon turns back and goes up to the stranger.
Possible Responses: Simon realizes that he is being selfish; he knows it is his Christian duty to show charity; he recognizes that the man's needs may be greater than his own; Simon realizes that it is unlikely the man would want to rob a poor person.

3 Tell students that as they read this section and the next section, they should pay close attention to Simon's thoughts regarding the naked man. Have students use a chart, such as a flow-chart, to keep track of how Simon's opinion of the naked man changes.

English Learners

4 Make sure students understand that the man's answers are meant to be unclear because he is not telling Simon the whole truth.

5 Tell students that a rogue is a scoundrel, or an unprincipled person. Ask students why Simon at first thinks the man might be a rogue.
Possible Response: By offering so little information about himself, the man appears to have something to hide.

TOLSTOY AUTHOR STUDY 979

Literary Analysis IRONY

A This passage at the beginning of section III is a good example of dramatic irony because the reader knows what Matrëna does not know: Despite her planning, Matrëna cannot make the bread last until Friday because Simon is bringing home someone else to feed. The dramatic irony at the beginning of section III continues throughout the section as Matrëna makes false assumptions about what her husband has been up to. Ask students how this irony contributes to our understanding of Matrëna's personality and our feelings toward her.

Possible Response: Some students may see this section as showing that Matrëna is harsh and unfair and unable to recognize the goodness in her husband. Other students may see her reaction as a natural one, given the circumstances, and sympathize with her concerns.

Reading Skills and Strategies QUESTIONING

After students have read section III, discuss with them the questions raised so far. The overarching question concerns the identity of the naked man. Have students work in pairs or small groups to create a list of specific questions that have been raised in the story so far.

Possible Responses: Why can't the man tell how he came to the shrine? Why was he naked and freezing? How will Simon and Matrëna survive the winter without a new coat and with no money?

how he had looked up at him at the shrine, his heart was glad.

III

Simon's wife had everything ready early that day. She had cut wood, brought water, fed the children, eaten her own meal, and now she sat thinking. She wondered when she ought to make bread: now or tomorrow? There was still a large piece left.

A "If Simon has had some dinner in town," thought she, "and does not eat much for supper, the bread will last out another day."

She weighed the piece of bread in her hand again and again and thought: "I won't make any more today. We have only enough flour left to bake one batch. We can manage to make this last out till Friday."

So Matrëna put away the bread and sat down at the table to patch her husband's shirt. While she worked she thought how her husband was buying skins for a winter coat.

"If only the dealer does not cheat him. My good man is much too simple; he cheats nobody, but any child can take him in. Eight rubles is a lot of money—he should get a good coat at that price. Not tanned skins, but still a proper winter coat. How difficult it was last winter to get on without a warm coat. I could neither get down to the river nor go out anywhere. When he went out he put on all we had, and there was nothing left for me. He did not start very early today, but still it's time he was back. I only hope he has not gone on the spree!"[5]

Hardly had Matrëna thought this than steps were heard on the threshold and some one entered. Matrëna stuck her needle into her work and went out into the passage. There she saw two men: Simon, and with him a man without a hat and wearing felt boots.

Matrëna noticed at once that her husband smelt of spirits. "There now, he has been drinking," thought she. And when she saw that he was coatless, had only her jacket on, brought no parcel, stood there silent, and seemed ashamed, her heart was ready to break with disappointment. "He has drunk the money," thought she, "and has been on the spree with some good-for-nothing fellow whom he has brought home with him."

Matrëna let them pass into the hut, followed them in, and saw that the stranger was a young, slight man, wearing her husband's coat. There was no shirt to be seen under it, and he had no hat. Having entered, he stood neither moving nor raising his eyes, and Matrëna thought: "He must be a bad man—he's afraid."

Matrëna frowned, and stood beside the stove looking to see what they would do.

Simon took off his cap and sat down on the bench as if things were all right.

"Come, Matrëna; if supper is ready, let us have some."

Matrëna muttered something to herself and did not move but stayed where she was, by the stove. She looked first at the one and then at the other of them and only shook her head. Simon saw that his wife was annoyed, but tried to pass it off. Pretending not to notice anything, he took the stranger by the arm.

"Sit down, friend," said he, "and let us have some supper."

The stranger sat down on the bench.

"Haven't you cooked anything for us?" said Simon.

Matrëna's anger boiled over. "I've cooked, but not for you. It seems to me you have drunk your wits away. You went to buy a sheep-skin coat but come home without so much as the coat you had on and bring a naked vagabond home with

5. **on the spree:** on a wild or carefree outing.

Cross Curricular Link History

RELIGION AND SOCIETY Explain that in the 19th century Russia had Christianity as an official religion (like many other nations) and the Russian Orthodox Church as the official form of Christianity. As a result, almost everyone shared the same faith and forms of worship, regardless of degree of wealth or social standing. Ask students what role strong religious faith might play in the lives of poor peasants like Simon and Matrëna.

Possible Responses: Poor people might cling strongly to their faith and try harder to be generous; people with very little might find it harder to live up to the ideal of charity toward all.

"HE HAS DRUNK THE MONEY," THOUGHT SHE, "AND HAS BEEN ON THE SPREE WITH SOME GOOD-FOR-NOTHING FELLOW WHOM HE HAS BROUGHT HOME WITH HIM."

you. I have no supper for drunkards like you."

1 "That's enough, Matrëna. Don't wag your tongue without reason! You had better ask what sort of man—"

"And you tell me what you've done with the money?"

Simon found the pocket of the jacket, drew out the three-ruble note, and unfolded it.

"Here is the money. Trifonov did not pay, but promises to pay soon."

Matrëna got still more angry; he had bought no sheep-skins but had put his only coat on some naked fellow and had even brought him to their house.

She snatched up the note from the table, took it to put away in safety, and said: "I have no supper for you. We can't feed all the naked drunkards in the world."

"There now, Matrëna, hold your tongue a bit. First hear what a man has to say—!"

"Much wisdom I shall hear from a drunken fool. I was right in not wanting to marry you—a drunkard. The linen my mother gave me you drank; and now you've been to buy a coat—and have drunk it too!"

Simon tried to explain to his wife that he had only spent twenty kopeks; tried to tell how he had found the man—but Matrëna would not let him get a word in. She talked nineteen to the dozen[6] and dragged in things that had happened ten years before. 2

Matrëna talked and talked, and at last she flew at Simon and seized him by the sleeve.

"Give me my jacket. It is the only one I have, and you must needs take it from me and wear it yourself. Give it here, you mangy dog, and may the devil take you."

Simon began to pull off the jacket, and turned a sleeve of it inside out; Matrëna seized the jacket and it burst its seams. She snatched it up, threw it over her head, and went to the door. She meant to go out, but stopped undecided—she wanted to work off her anger, but she also wanted to learn what sort of a man the stranger was.

IV

Matrëna stopped and said: "If he were a good man he would not be naked. Why, he hasn't even a shirt on him. If he were all right, you would say where you came across the fellow."

"That's just what I am trying to tell you," said Simon. "As I came to the shrine I saw him sitting all naked and frozen. It isn't quite the weather to sit about naked! God sent me to him or he would have perished. What was I to do? How do we know what may have happened to him? So I took him, clothed him, and brought him along. Don't be so angry, Matrëna. It is a sin. Remember, we must all die one day."

Angry words rose to Matrëna's lips, but she looked at the stranger and was silent. He sat on the edge of the bench, motionless, his hands folded on his knees, his head drooping on his breast, his eyes closed, and his brows knit as if in

6. **nineteen to the dozen:** quickly and excessively.

Customizing Instruction

Less Proficient Readers

Before students continue reading, discuss the first two sections of the story in class. Ask these questions:

- Why can't Simon buy sheepskins to make a winter coat? *(The people who owe him money cannot pay him.)*
- Whom does Simon see by the shrine? *(a stranger)*
- What does Simon decide to do about the man? *(After walking past the man, Simon decides to go back and take the stranger home.)*

English Learners

1 Point out the idiom *wag your tongue.* Tell students that the expression means "to talk without stopping." Explain that *hold your tongue* means the opposite of *wag your tongue.* Then ask them what *hold your tongue* means. *("to say nothing at all")*

2 Direct students to the footnote for the meaning of the idiom *nineteen to the dozen.* This phrase suggests that she is talking so fast that she gets in an extra seven words for every twelve she says.

Advanced Learners

In section III, Tolstoy explores the contrast between what one expects or believes and what is actually the case. For example, Matrëna thinks that because Simon is late he might have been drinking, when actually he is late for other reasons. Have students construct a chart to show the contrasts between Matrëna's expectations and reality.

MINI LESSON Vocabulary Strategy

IDIOMS

Instruction Every language is made up of idioms—that is, phrases which are not meant to be taken literally, but whose meaning is understood by speakers of that language. For example, one speaker may say she "caught a cold." Another might say that something "caught his eye." Usages like these develop over the years and defy logic.

Practice Have students look for idioms in this story, especially in section III in the conversation between Matrëna and Simon. Ask students to refer to the context to determine what such idioms might mean. One example is given below.

1. "He has drunk the money." (p. 980) Context: Just before Matrëna thought this, she noticed that her husband smelled of spirits, or liquor. She also noticed that he had no parcel, which meant he had not bought the sheepskins. She assumed that he had collected the money and bought liquor with it—thus the idiom "He has drunk the money."
2. "Don't wag your tongue." (p. 981)
3. "She talked nineteen to the dozen." (p. 981)

Reading and Analyzing

Literary Analysis RUSSIAN SHORT STORY

A Ask students what Simon's anguished question to Matrëna suggests about the couple.

Possible Responses: They are religious; they believe that love of God is synonymous with love of their fellow man; they normally try to do the right thing; they believe that God will reward or punish them according to their actions.

Reading Skills and Strategies QUESTIONING

B Ask students why they think Matrëna's attitude toward the stranger has changed.

Possible Responses: Simon reminds her of God's role in their lives; she feels genuinely sorry for the stranger; she is curious about his situation; she recognizes he is neither a drunk nor likely to harm them.

Literary Analysis THEME

Simon is able to get Matrëna to put aside her righteous anger by invoking her love of God. Ask students how this points to the theme of the story.

Possible Response: Simon has reminded Matrëna of her love of God, and this will be Michael's first lesson—that love dwells in people.

pain. Matrëna was silent, and Simon said:
A "Matrëna, have you no love of God?"

Matrëna heard these words, and as she looked at the stranger, suddenly her heart softened towards him. She came back from the door, and going to the stove she got out the supper. Setting a cup on the table, she poured out some kvas.[7] Then she brought out the last piece of bread and set out a knife and spoons.

"Eat, if you want to," said she.

Simon drew the stranger to the table.

"Take your place, young man," said he.

Simon cut the bread, crumbled it into the broth, and they began to eat. Matrëna sat at the corner of the table, resting her head on her hand and looking at the stranger.

1 And Matrëna was touched with pity for the stranger and began to feel fond of him. And at once the stranger's face lit up; his brows were no longer bent, he raised his eyes and smiled at
2 Matrëna.

When they had finished supper, the woman cleared away the things and began questioning the stranger. "Where are you from?" said she.

"I am not from these parts."

"But how did you come to be on the road?"

"I may not tell."

"Did some one rob you?"

"God punished me."

"And you were lying there naked?"

"Yes, naked and freezing. Simon saw me and had pity on me. He took off his coat, put it on me, and brought me here. And you have fed me, given me drink, and shown pity on me. God will reward you!"

Matrëna rose, took from the window Simon's old shirt she had been patching, and gave it to the stranger. She also brought out a pair of trousers for him.

"There," said she, "I see you have no shirt. Put this on, and lie down where you please, in the loft or on the stove." B

The stranger took off the coat, put on the shirt, and lay down in the loft. Matrëna put out the candle, took the coat, and climbed to where her husband lay on the stove.

Matrëna drew the skirts of the coat over her and lay down but could not sleep; she could not get the stranger out of her mind.

When she remembered that he had eaten their last piece of bread and that there was none for tomorrow and thought of the shirt and trousers she had given away, she felt grieved; but when she remembered how he had smiled, her heart was glad.

Long did Matrëna lie awake, and she noticed that Simon also was awake—he drew the coat towards him.

"Simon!"

"Well?"

"You have had the last of the bread and I have not put any to rise. I don't know what we shall do tomorrow. Perhaps I can borrow some of the neighbor Martha."

"If we're alive we shall find something to eat."

The woman lay still awhile, and then said, "He seems a good man, but why does he not tell us who he his?"

"I suppose he has his reasons."

"Simon!"

"Well?"

"We give; but why does nobody give us anything?"

Simon did not know what to say; so he only said, "Let us stop talking" and turned over and went to sleep.

---

7. **kvas** (kväs): a Russian drink, similar to beer, made from fermented grains.

Cross Curricular Link **Humanities**

FOLK TALES Cultures all over the world tell folk tales or their variants, the myth and the fable. In many folk tales the characters are animals, as they are in the African trickster tales. The hare plays the part of trickster in Bantu and western Sudan tales. In West Africa, the spider or the tortoise is the trickster. Sometimes the trickster is a human being, as in Benin and Tanzania and among the Zulu. The spider trickster, Anansi, made his way into Jamaican folk tales as Anancy.

In one folk tale told by the Yoruba of Africa, the tortoise steals a gourd from the gods that contains all the wisdom of the world. He hangs the gourd around his neck, but when he gets to a tree trunk lying in the road, he is unable to climb over it because the gourd gets in his way. The tortoise is so anxious to get home he does not think to put the gourd across his back. Frustrated, the tortoise smashes the gourd. And, so the tale goes, that is why today wisdom is scattered all over the world in tiny pieces.

Still-Life with Lamp (1910), Marc Chagall. Oil on canvas, 70 cm × 45 cm. Private collection. Courtesy Galerie Rosengart, Lucerne, Switzerland © 2007 Artists Rights Society (ARS), New York/ADAGP, Paris.

V

In the morning Simon awoke. The children were still asleep; his wife had gone to the neighbor's to borrow some bread. The stranger alone was sitting on the bench, dressed in the old shirt and trousers, and looking upwards. His face was brighter than it had been the day before.

Simon said to him, "Well, friend; the belly wants bread and the naked body clothes. One has to work for a living. What work do you know?"

"I do not know any."

This surprised Simon, but he said, "Men who want to learn can learn anything."

"Men work and I will work also."

"What is your name?"

"Michael."

"Well, Michael, if you don't wish to talk about yourself, that is your own affair; but you'll have to earn a living for yourself. If you will work as I tell you, I will give you food and shelter."

"May God reward you! I will learn. Show me what to do."

Customizing Instruction

English Learners

1 Point out that the word *touched* has a different meaning from the one students are probably used to. Here, it means "affected emotionally" or "made to have feelings." Ask students how the stranger is touched by Matrëna in the sentence following.

Less Proficient Readers

2 Ask students what happens when Matrëna meets the stranger.

- How does Matrëna react to the stranger at first? *(She is rude and does not want him in her house.)*
- What causes Matrëna to have a change of heart? *(Simon appeals to her love of God.)*
- What does the stranger do when Matrëna's heart softens toward him? *(He smiles at her.)*

English Learners

3 Point out the difference in meaning between the word *want* here ("to need") and four lines later: "Men who want to learn can learn anything."

Literary Analysis FOLK TALE

Folk tales often incorporate magical features. What aspects of Michael's behavior so far have seemed magical?

Possible Response: Students may point out his ability to learn a craft when he previously knew nothing about work.

Literary Analysis RUSSIAN SHORT STORY

Mythic tales often involve a challenge to the hero by forces that seem overpowering. Ask students to describe the challenge of making boots that will last a year. Why does this task seem intimidating?

Possible Response: Students may comment that the gentleman seems so large and rough that probably nothing he owns can survive a year of use.

Literary Analysis IRONY

A After students have read the next section of the story, have them return to the gentleman's words. Ask students what kind of irony is used here. *(situational)*

Literary Analysis FORESHADOWING

B After students have read the next section of the story, have them return to this point. Ask them what function Matrëna's words serve. *(They foreshadow the gentleman's death.)*

1 Simon took yarn, put it round his thumb and began to twist it.

"It is easy enough—see!"

2 Michael watched him, put some yarn round his own thumb in the same way, caught the knack[8], and twisted the yarn also.

Then Simon showed him how to wax the thread. This also Michael mastered. Next Simon showed him how to twist the bristle in, and how to sew, and this, too, Michael learned at once.

Whatever Simon showed him he understood at once, and after three days he worked as if he had sewn boots all his life. He worked without stopping and ate little. When work was over he sat silently, looking upwards. He hardly went into the street, spoke only when necessary, and neither joked nor laughed. They never saw him smile, except that first evening when Matrëna gave him supper.

VI

Day by day and week by week the year went round. Michael lived and worked with Simon. His fame spread till people said that no one sewed boots so neatly and strongly as Simon's workman, Michael; from all the district round people came to Simon for their boots, and he began to be well off.

One winter day, as Simon and Michael sat working, a carriage on sledge-runners, with three horses and with bells, drove up to the hut. They looked out of the window; the carriage stopped at their door; a fine servant jumped down from the box and opened the door. A gentleman in a fur coat got out and walked up to Simon's hut. Up jumped Matrëna and opened the door wide. The gentleman stooped to enter the hut, and when he drew himself up again his head nearly reached the ceiling and he seemed quite to fill his end of the room.

Simon rose, bowed, and looked at the gentleman with astonishment. He had never seen any one like him. Simon himself was lean, Michael was thin, and Matrëna was dry as a bone, but this man was like some one from another world: red-faced, burly, with a neck like a bull's, and looking altogether as if he were cast in iron.

The gentleman puffed, threw off his fur coat, sat down on the bench, and said, "Which of you is the master bootmaker?"

"I am, your Excellency," said Simon, coming forward.

Then the gentleman shouted to his lad, "Hey, Fédka,[9] bring the leather!"

The servant ran in, bringing a parcel. The gentleman took the parcel and put it on the table.

"Untie it," said he. The lad untied it.

The gentleman pointed to the leather.

"Look here, shoemaker," said he, "do you see this leather?"

"Yes, your honor."

"But do you know what sort of leather it is?"

Simon felt the leather and said, "It is good leather."

"Good, indeed! Why, you fool, you never saw such leather before in your life. It's German and cost twenty rubles."

Simon was frightened and said, "Where should I ever see leather like that?"

"Just so! Now, can you make it into boots for me?"

"Yes, your Excellency, I can."

Then the gentleman shouted at him: "You *can*, can you? Well, remember whom you are to make them for, and what the leather is. You must make me boots that will wear for a year, neither losing shape nor coming unsewn. If you can do it, take the leather and cut it up; but if you can't, say so. I warn you now, if your boots come

8. **knack:** the exact way of doing something.

9. **Fédka** (fyĕd′kă).

Cross Curricular Link History

NINETEENTH-CENTURY RUSSIA The continuation of a peasant class into the 19th century is one of the distinctive elements of Russian history and culture. The peasant class in Russia was essentially a class of serfs. These people, although not technically slaves, led very slavelike lives.

For centuries in Russia, it was customary for peasants to renegotiate their status with the landowners after the gathering of the harvest, on or about St. George's Day (November 24). Toward the end of the 16th century, however, the power of the nobles and the church over the peasant class was so great that it became nearly impossible for serfs to pay any debts they might owe and leave the land. Their condition degenerated until it began to interfere with the economic development of Russia itself. The Emancipation of 1861 transferred to each serf a portion of the land the serf's family had been cultivating and arranged for the former landowners to be compensated over a period of years.

A unsewn or lose shape within a year I will have you put in prison. If they don't burst or lose shape for a year, I will pay you ten rubles for your work."

Simon was frightened and did not know what to say. He glanced at Michael and nudging him with his elbow, whispered: "Shall I take the work?"

Michael nodded his head as if to say, "Yes, take it."

Simon did as Michael advised and undertook to make boots that would not lose shape or split for a whole year.

Calling his servant, the gentleman told him to pull the boot off his left leg, which he stretched out.

"Take my measure!" said he.

Simon stitched a paper measure seventeen inches long, smoothed it out, knelt down, wiped his hands well on his apron so as not to soil the gentleman's sock, and began to measure. He measured the sole, and round the instep, and began to measure the calf of the leg, but the paper was too short. The calf of the leg was as thick as a beam.

"Mind you don't make it too tight in the leg."

Simon stitched on another strip of paper. The gentleman twitched his toes about in his sock looking round at those in the hut, and as he did so he noticed Michael.

"Whom have you there?" asked he.

"That is my workman. He will sew the boots."

"Mind," said the gentleman to Michael, "remember to make them so that they will last me a year."

Simon also looked at Michael and saw that Michael was not looking at the gentleman, but was gazing into the corner behind the gentleman, as if he saw some one there. Michael looked and looked, and suddenly he smiled, and his face became brighter.

"What are you grinning at, you fool?" thundered the gentleman. "You had better look to it that the boots are ready in time."

"They shall be ready in good time," said Michael.

"Mind it is so," said the gentleman, and he put on his boots and his fur coat, wrapped the latter round him, and went to the door. But he forgot to stoop, and struck his head against the lintel.[10]

He swore and rubbed his head. Then he took his seat in the carriage and drove away.

When he had gone, Simon said: "There's a figure of a man for you! You could not kill him with a mallet. He almost knocked out the lintel, but little harm it did him."

And Matrëna said: "Living as he does, how should he not have grown strong? Death itself can't touch such a rock as that." B

VII

Then Simon said to Michael: "Well, we have taken the work, but we must see we don't get into trouble over it. The leather is dear, and the gentleman hot-tempered. We must make no mistakes. Come, your eye is truer and your hands have become nimbler than mine, so you take this measure and cut out the boots. I will finish off the sewing of the vamps."[11] 3

Michael did as he was told. He took the leather, spread it out on the table, folded it in two, took a knife and began to cut out.

Matrëna came and watched him cutting and was surprised to see how he was doing it. Matrëna was accustomed to seeing boots made, and she looked and saw that Michael was not cutting the leather for boots, but was cutting it round.

She wished to say something, but she thought to herself: "Perhaps I do not understand how

10. **lintel:** horizontal beam at the top of a door frame.

11. **vamps:** upper parts of shoes or boots, covering the instep or the instep and the toes.

Customizing Instruction

English Learners

1 Be sure students understand that this sentence and the following passages describe Simon's efforts to teach Michael the shoemaking trade.

2 *Caught the knack* may suggest to English learners either that Michael became ill or that he developed skill in catching things thrown to him. Help students use context clues to determine the correct meaning of this idiomatic expression: "figured out how to do it."

3 Students might not understand the expression *your eye is truer.* Explain that Michael is younger than Simon and can see more accurately to measure, cut straight lines, and do the close work required to make perfect boots. Then have students use context clues to determine the meaning of *nimbler.* Point out that the ending *-er* indicates a comparative form meaning "more nimble." Students should be able to infer from Simon's statement that "nimble hands" are more capable, since he is asking Michael to do a difficult and important task. Students may not be able to determine the exact meaning of *nimble (agile or graceful)* from context clues, so direct them to a dictionary if necessary.

Active Reading PREDICTING

A Ask students to stop at this point and predict what will happen as a result of Michael making slippers rather than boots.

Possible Responses: Many students will assume that Michael's apparent mistake will cause Simon and Matrëna to get into trouble for ruining the expensive leather and possibly to become poor again; other students may pick up on Michael's tendency to do excellent work and assume that he has some good reason for not following instructions.

Reading Skills and Strategies
SUMMARIZING

B Ask students to summarize in a sentence or two what happens in sections VI and VII of this story.

Possible Responses: Michael does good work and Simon's business prospers; Michael makes slippers for a gentleman who orders boots–Michael seems to know in advance that the gentleman will die and not need boots but rather slippers for his corpse.

Literary Analysis SYMBOL

Ask students to describe the light that has come from Michael on three occasions. Ask what the light represents.

Possible Responses: purity; knowledge.

Ask students how Tolstoy's use of this symbol contributes to the meaning of the story.

Possible Response: Students may argue that it is not clear yet how the symbol is being used.

Reading Skills and Strategies
SUMMARIZING

Summarizing is a way of pointing out the most important information in a text. For example, in section VIII, a summary would not include the detail of Matrëna putting away iron pots, but it would emphasize Michael's reaction upon hearing of the woman and the two girls. Have students work in pairs to write a summary of the section. Then have each pair share its summary with the class and receive feedback.

gentlemen's boots should be made. I suppose Michael knows more about it—and I won't interfere."

When Michael had cut up the leather he took a thread and began to sew not with two ends, as boots are sewn, but with a single end, as for soft slippers.

Again Matrëna wondered, but again she did not interfere. Michael sewed on steadily till noon. Then Simon rose for dinner, looked around, and saw that Michael had made slippers out of the gentleman's leather.

"Ah!" groaned Simon, and he thought, "How is it that Michael, who has been with me a whole year and never made a mistake before, should do such a dreadful thing? The gentleman ordered high boots, welted,[12] with whole fronts, and Michael has made soft slippers with single soles and has wasted the leather. What am I to say to the gentleman? I can never replace leather such as this."

And he said to Michael, "What are you doing, friend? You have ruined me! You know the gentleman ordered high boots, but see what you have made!" A

Hardly had he begun to rebuke[13] Michael, when "rat-tat" went the iron ring hung at the door. Some one was knocking. They looked out of the window; a man had come on horseback and was fastening his horse. They opened the door, and the servant who had been with the gentleman came in.

"Good day," said he.

"Good day," replied Simon. "What can we do for you?"

"My mistress has sent me about the boots."

"What about the boots?"

"Why, my master no longer needs them. He is dead."

"Is it possible?"

"He did not live to get home after leaving you but died in the carriage. When we reached home and the servants came to help him alight, he rolled over like a sack. He was dead already, and so stiff that he could hardly be got out of the carriage. My mistress sent me here, saying: 'Tell the bootmaker that the gentleman who ordered boots of him and left the leather for them no longer needs the boots, but that he must quickly make soft slippers for the corpse. Wait till they are ready and bring them back with you.' That is why I have come."

Michael gathered up the remnants of the leather; rolled them up, took the soft slippers he had made, slapped them together, wiped them down with his apron, and handed them and the roll of leather to the servant, who took them and said: "Good-bye, masters, and good day to you!" B

VIII

Another year passed, and another, and Michael was now living his sixth year with Simon. He lived as before. He went nowhere, only spoke when necessary, and had only smiled twice in all those years—one when Matrëna gave him food, and a second time when the gentleman was in their hut. Simon was more than pleased with his workman. He never now asked him where he came from and only feared lest Michael should go away.

They were all at home one day. Matrëna was putting iron pots in the oven; the children were running along the benches and looking out of the window; Simon was sewing at one window and Michael was fastening on a heel at the other.

One of the boys ran along the bench to Michael, leant on his shoulder, and looked out of the window.

"Look, Uncle Michael! There is a lady with

12. **welted:** made with a leather strip stitched between the shoe sole and the vamp.

13. **rebuke:** to criticize; express disapproval of.

MINI LESSON **Vocabulary Strategy**

ANALOGIES

Instruction Review with students the meaning of the term *analogy,* focusing on word analogies. Remind students that a word **analogy** consists of two pairs of words that have the same type of relationship in each pair. The relationship may be cause and effect, part and whole, item to category, characteristic quality, function, synonym, or antonym.

Model Write the following word analogy on the board and then read it aloud:

sycamore : tree :: robin : bird

(Sycamore *is to* tree *as* robin *is to* bird.)

Then elicit from students the relationship between each pair of words. *(A sycamore is a type of tree as a robin is a type of bird.)*

Practice Have students complete the following analogy: shoemaker : shoes ::

A. newspaper : printer
B. architecture : buildings
C. athlete : sports
D. carpenter : cabinets

(A shoemaker makes shoes as a carpenter makes cabinets.)

A lesson on working with analogies appears on p. 768 of the Pupil's Edition.

The Harvest, Natalia Goncharova. Russian State Museum, St. Petersburg, Russia. Photo © Scala/Art Resource, New York © 2007 Artists Rights Society (ARS), New York/ADAGP, Paris.

little girls! She seems to be coming here. And one of the girls is lame."

When the boy said that, Michael dropped his work, turned to the window, and looked out into the street.

Simon was surprised. Michael never used to look out into the street, but now he pressed against the window, staring at something. Simon also looked out and saw that a well-dressed woman was really coming to his hut, leading by the hand two little girls in fur coats and woolen shawls. The girls could hardly be told one from the other, except that one of them was crippled in her left leg and walked with a limp.

The woman stepped into the porch and entered the passage. Feeling about for the entrance she found the latch, which she lifted and opened the door. She let the two girls go in first, and followed them into the hut.

"Good day, good folk!"

"Pray come in," said Simon. "What can we do for you?" 1

Customizing Instruction

Less Proficient Readers

Ask students the following questions about Michael:

- Why does Simon come to be well off after Michael moves in? *(Michael becomes an expert shoemaker whose work is valued in the district.)*
- What does Michael do after the gentleman orders the boots? *(He uses the leather to make soft slippers.)*
- Why doesn't Michael suffer any consequences for his decision? *(The man dies; slippers are needed for his corpse.)*
- What do you think is the importance to the story of Michael's foreknowledge?

Possible Response: Students may recognize that Tolstoy is withholding information that would enable the reader to understand fully.

English Learners

1 Point out the use of the word *pray.* Tell students that they can use cause and effect to determine the meaning of the word. After Simon speaks to the woman, she comes inside and sits down by the table. Also, students can infer from the situation and Simon's tone what sort of word *pray* is: The woman is a customer and Simon politely asks, "What can we do for you?" This implies that *pray* is a word used as part of courtesy. In this context, *pray* means "please."

MINI LESSON Viewing and Representing

Grain Harvest **by Natalya Sergeyevna Goncharova**

ART APPRECIATION This 1908 painting shows many of the characteristics of Goncharova's folk art. During summers, she studied the peasants at work at her family's Cotton Factory estate. Their lives became a favorite theme of hers.

Application Have students look at the home in the picture. How do the colors and textures affect the meaning of the painting?

Possible Responses: The lumpy, rather stark textures emphasize the hard work of the peasants. The bold, natural colors bring out the peasants' close association with nature.

Why would you characterize this work as an example of folk art?

Possible Responses: Its subject is the harvest, a central event in the lives of peasants, or common folk; it appears to have been painted by an untrained artist.

Then, ask students to compare the home in the painting with their image of Simon and Matrëna's home. How do they think the homes are different? How might they be similar?

Possible Responses: This home is painted and has a nice green lawn around it, but Simon and Matrëna's home is probably in worse condition. This home appears to be small, and Simon and Matrëna's home is probably also small.

Literary Analysis CHARACTER

A Have students analyze the character of the woman in section IX based on the story she tells.

Possible Responses: She is kind, compassionate, generous, appreciative of kindness in others, devout in her faith, willing to take on added responsibility, practical, full of gratitude; she loves the two girls without regard for the fact that they are not her own children or that one of them is lame.

Reading Skills and Strategies CLARIFYING

B Ask students how the twins were able to survive after their mother's death. *(A neighbor woman, who had just had her own baby, took care of them.)*

Literary Analysis SYMBOL

C Point out that this is the third time in the story that Michael has smiled. Ask students why this instance might be particularly meaningful.

Possible Response: This time the whole hut lights up, and Michael is gazing toward heaven.

THEY ALL LOOKED TOWARDS HIM AND SAW HIM SITTING, HIS HANDS FOLDED ON HIS KNEES, GAZING UPWARDS AND SMILING.

The woman sat down by the table. The two little girls pressed close to her knees, afraid of the people in the hut.

"I want leather shoes made for these two little girls, for spring."

"We can do that. We never have made such small shoes, but we can make them; either welted or turnover shoes,[14] linen lined. My man, Michael, is a master at the work."

Simon glanced at Michael and saw that he had left his work and was sitting with his eyes fixed on the little girls. Simon was surprised. It was true the girls were pretty, with black eyes, plump, and rosy-cheeked, and they wore nice kerchiefs and fur coats, but still Simon could not understand why Michael should look at them like that—just as if he had known them before. He was puzzled but went on talking with the woman and arranging the price. Having fixed it, he prepared the measure. The woman lifted the lame girl on to her lap and said: "Take two measures from this little girl. Make one shoe for the
1 lame foot and three for the sound one. They
both have the same-sized feet. They are twins."

Simon took the measure and, speaking of the lame girl, said: "How did it happen to her? She is such a pretty girl. Was she born so?"

"No, her mother crushed her leg."

Then Matrëna joined in. She wondered who this woman was and whose the children were, so she said: "Are not you their mother, then?"

"No, my good woman; I am neither their mother nor any relation to them. They were quite strangers to me, but I adopted them."

"They are not your children and yet you are so fond of them?"

"How can I help being fond of them? I fed them both at my own breasts. I had a child of
my own, but God took him. I was not so fond of 2
him as I now am of these."

"Then whose children are they?"

IX

The woman, having begun talking, told them the whole story.

"It is about six years since their parents died, A
both in one week: their father was buried on the Tuesday, and their mother died on the Friday. These orphans were born three days after their father's death, and their mother did not live another day. My husband and I were then living as peasants in the village. We were neighbors of theirs, our yard being next to theirs. Their father was a lonely man, a wood-cutter in the forest. When felling trees one day they let one fall on him. It fell across his body and crushed his bowels out. They hardly got him home before his soul went to
God; and that same week his wife gave birth to 3
twins—these little girls. She was poor and alone; she had no one, young or old, with her. Alone she gave them birth, and alone she met her death.

14. **turnover shoes:** shoes made with a piece of leather folded over.

Assessment Standardized Test Practice

RESPONDING TO A WRITING PROMPT Have students write an essay in response to the following prompt: "Compare and contrast Matrëna and Mary, the woman with the twins. Consider the effect of charity on the women's lives, their maternal feelings, and their views of God." Remind students to support their answers with evidence from the story.

RUBRIC

3 Full Accomplishment Students write well-supported essays that both compare and contrast two women. Students demonstrate thorough understanding of the women's character development and discuss the effects of charity on their lives, maternal feelings, and views of God. Students may recognize that, in this story, charitable behavior leads to financial prosperity.

"The next morning I went to see her, but when I entered the hut, she, poor thing, was already stark and cold. In dying she had rolled on to this child and crushed her leg. The village folk came to the hut, washed the body, laid her out, made a coffin, and buried her. They were good folk. The babies were left alone. What was to be done with them? I was the only woman there who had a baby at the time. I was nursing my first-born—eight weeks old. So I took them for a time. The peasants came together, and thought and thought what to do with them; and at last they said to me: 'For the present, Mary, you had better keep the girls, and later on we will arrange what to do
4 for them.' So I nursed the sound one at my breast, but at first I did not feed this crippled one. I did not suppose she would live. But then I thought to myself, why should the poor innocent suffer? I pitied her and began to feed her. And so I fed my own boy and these two—the three of them—at my own breast. I was young and strong and had good food, and God gave me so much milk that at times it even overflowed. I used sometimes to feed two at a time, while the third was waiting. When one had had enough I nursed the third. And God so ordered it that these grew up, while my own was buried before he was two years old. And I had no more children, though we prospered. Now my husband is working for the corn merchant at the mill. The pay is good and we are well off. But I have no children of my own, and how lonely I should be without these little girls! How can I help loving them! They are
B the joy of my life!"

She pressed the lame little girl to her with one hand, while with the other she wiped the tears from her cheeks.

And Matrëna sighed, and said: "The proverb is true that says, 'One may live without father or mother, but one cannot live without God.'"

So they talked together, when suddenly the whole hut was lighted up as though by summer lightning from the corner where Michael sat. They all looked towards him and saw him sitting, his hands folded on his knees, gazing upwards and smiling. C

X

The woman went away with the girls. Michael rose from the bench, put down his work, and took off his apron. Then, bowing low to Simon and his wife, he said: "Farewell, masters. God has forgiven me. I ask your forgiveness, too, for anything done amiss."

And they saw that a light shone from Michael. And Simon rose, bowed down to Michael, and said: "I see, Michael, that you are no common man, and I can neither keep you nor question you. Only tell me this: how is it that when I found you and brought you home, you were gloomy, and when my wife gave you food you smiled at her and became brighter? Then when the gentleman came to order the boots, you smiled again and became brighter still? And now, when this woman brought the little girls, you smiled a third time and have become as bright as day? Tell me, Michael, why does your face shine so, and why did you smile those three times?"

And Michael answered: "Light shines from me because I have been punished, but now God has pardoned me. And I smiled three times, because God sent me to learn three truths, and I have learnt them. One I learnt when your wife pitied me, and that is why I smiled the first time. The second I learnt when the rich man ordered the boots, and then I smiled again. And now, when I saw those little girls, I learnt the third and last, and I smiled the third time."

And Simon said: "Tell me, Michael, what did God punish you for? and what were the three truths? that I, too, may know them."

And Michael answered: "God punished me for

Customizing Instruction

English Learners

1 4 Ask students to determine the multiple meanings of *sound* in the woman's instructions to "make one shoe for the lame foot and three for the sound one" and in the description, "I nursed the sound one at my breast, but at first I did not feed this crippled one."

In this case, the context clue students should focus on is the contrast drawn between *lame* and *sound,* and *crippled* and *sound.* Help students understand that *sound* means "well" or "whole" in this context.

2 3 Point out to students that *God took him* and *his soul went to God* both mean that he died.

2 Substantial Accomplishment Students support answers with evidence from the text but may only compare or contrast Matrëna and Mary. Students demonstrate basic understanding of the women's character development and discuss at least two of following: the effects of charity on the women's lives, maternal feelings, and views of God.

1 Little or Partial Accomplishment Students fail to support answers with logical evidence from the text. Students do not understand the women's character development and may touch on only one of the following: the effects of charity on the women's lives, maternal feelings, and views of God.

Active Reading PREDICTING

A Have students stop at this point and make a prediction about why God punished Michael. Urge students to look back at the three times that Michael smiled before they consider their predictions.

Possible Responses: for disobeying God; for doubting God's wisdom and purpose

Reading Skills and Strategies CLARIFYING

B Ask students what Michael was punished for.

Possible Responses: for disobeying God; for acting as if he knew more than God

Literary Analysis FORESHADOWING

C Point out to students that Michael tells both Simon (page 979) and Matrëna (page 982) that God has punished him. Ask students why Simon and Matrëna miss these clues.

Possible Responses: They think Michael is using a common expression to say that he is down on his luck; they are looking for ordinary explanations, not miraculous ones.

Reading Skills and Strategies MAKING INFERENCES

D Ask students what Michael means when he says that if Matrëna drove him out into the cold, *she* would die.

Possible Responses: that she would have crushed the spirit of love within herself; that her soul would have perished; that she would have condemned herself to eternal damnation because of her sin

disobeying him. I was an angel in heaven and (A) disobeyed God. God sent me to fetch a woman's soul. I flew to earth and saw a sick woman lying alone who had just given birth to twin girls. They moved feebly at their mother's side but she could not lift them to her breast. When she saw me, she understood that God had sent me for her soul, and she wept and said: 'Angel of God! My husband has just been buried, killed by a falling tree. I have neither sister, nor aunt, nor mother: no one to care for my orphans. Do not take my soul! Let me nurse my babes, feed them, and set them on their feet before I die. Children cannot live without father or mother.' And I hearkened[15] to her. I placed one child at her breast and gave the other into her arms, and returned to the Lord in heaven. I flew to the Lord, and said: 'I could not take the soul of the mother. Her husband was killed by a tree; the woman has twins and prays that her soul may not be taken. She says: "Let me nurse and feed my children, and set them on their feet. Children cannot live without (B) father or mother." I have not taken her soul.' And God said: 'Go—take the mother's soul, and learn three truths: Learn *What dwells in man, What is not given to man,* and *What men live by.* When thou hast learnt these things, thou shalt return to heaven'. So I flew again to earth and took the mother's soul. The babes dropped from her breasts. Her body rolled over on the bed and crushed one babe, twisting its leg. I rose above the village, wishing to take her soul to God, but a wind seized me and my wings drooped and dropped off. Her soul rose alone to God, while I (C) fell to earth by the roadside."

XI

And Simon and Matrëna understood who it was that had lived with them and whom they had clothed and fed. And they wept with awe and with joy. And the angel said: "I was alone in the field, naked. I had never known human needs, cold and hunger, till I became a man. I was famished, frozen, and did not know what to do. I saw, near the field I was in, a shrine built for God, and I went to it hoping to find shelter. But the shrine was locked and I could not enter. So I sat down behind the shrine to shelter myself at least from the wind. Evening drew on, I was hungry, frozen, and in pain. Suddenly I heard a man coming along the road. He carried a pair of boots and was talking to himself. For the first time since I became a man I saw the mortal face of a man, and his face seemed terrible to me and I turned from it. And I heard the man talking to himself of how to cover his body from the cold in winter, and how to feed his wife and children. And I thought: 'I am perishing of cold and hunger and here is a man thinking only of how to clothe himself and his wife, and how to get bread for themselves. He cannot help me.' When the man saw me he frowned and became still more terrible and passed me by on the other side. I despaired; but suddenly I heard him coming back. I looked up and did not recognize the same man: before, I had seen death in his face; but now he was alive and I recognized in him the presence of God. He came up to me, clothed me, took me with him, and brought me to his home. I entered the house; a woman came to meet us and began to speak. The woman was still more terrible than the man had been; the spirit of death came from her mouth; I could not breathe for the stench[16] of

15. **hearkened:** paid attention to; listened.

16. **stench:** foul smell.

Assessment Standardized Test Practice

WRITING A SHORT ESSAY ANSWER Have students write a short essay in response to the following question. Remind them to support their answer with evidence from the story. Prompt: Why does Tolstoy tell the story from Simon and Matrëna's viewpoint, never giving the reader insight into Michael's thoughts?

RUBRIC

3 Full Accomplishment Students write well-organized essay with evidence from story. They recognize that Tolstoy restricts the viewpoint to Simon and Matrëna in order to make Michael a mysterious figure.

2 Substantial Accomplishment Students write logical essay with some evidence from story. They recognize that Tolstoy restricts the viewpoint to Simon and Matrëna in order to make Michael a mysterious figure. However, essay may only touch on this point briefly, or it may have distracting spelling, grammar, and usage errors.

1 Little or Partial Accomplishment Students do not recognize that Tolstoy restricts viewpoint to Simon and Matrëna in order to make Michael a mysterious figure. Essay is disorganized and may be somewhat incoherent with many spelling, grammar, and usage errors.

The Dream (1939), Marc Chagall. Gouache on paper, 20⁹⁄₁₆" × 26¾". Acquired 1942. The Phillips Collection, Washington, D.C. © 2007 Artists Rights Society (ARS), New York/ADAGP, Paris.

HUMANITIES CONNECTION The word *dream* occurs in the titles of a number of Marc Chagall's works, and many of his paintings have a magical, unreal quality. People, animals, and buildings appear to float in the air, and details are combined in such unexpected ways that it seems possible for anything to happen.

death that spread around her. She wished to drive me out into the cold, and I knew that if she did so she would die. Suddenly her husband spoke to her of God, and the woman changed at once. And when she brought me food and looked at me, I glanced at her and saw that death no longer dwelt in her; she had become alive, and in her too I saw God.

"Then I remembered the first lesson God had set me: *'Learn what dwells in man.'* And I understood that in man dwells Love! I was glad that God had already begun to show me what He had promised, and I smiled for the first time. But I had not yet learnt all. I did not yet know *What is not given to man,* and *What men live by.*

"I lived with you and a year passed. A man came to order boots that should wear for a year without losing shape or cracking. I looked at him, and suddenly, behind his shoulder, I saw my comrade—the angel of death. None but me saw that angel; but I knew him, and knew that before the sun set he would take the rich man's soul. And I thought to myself, 'The man is making preparation for a year and does not know that he will die before evening.' And I remembered God's second saying, *'Learn what is not given to man.'*

Customizing Instruction

Less Proficient Readers

1 As students read section XI, have them complete a chart that lists the three lessons, under what circumstances Michael learns each lesson, and the students' rephrasing of each lesson.

MINI LESSON Viewing and Representing

***The Dream* by Marc Chagall**

ART APPRECIATION

Application Have students read the **Humanities Connection** caption and study the painting by Chagall. Point out that Tolstoy's story and the painting both combine details that are dreamlike with details that are realistic. Have students identify details of each kind in the painting and in the story. Then ask students how the combination of realistic and dreamlike details affects their reaction to the two works of art.

Possible Responses: The realistic details make the supernatural details of each work more convincing; the dreamlike details help bring out the symbolic or poetic qualities of the painting and the story.

Literary Analysis FORESHADOWING

A Have students look back at the proverb Matrëna quotes on page 989: "One may live without father or mother, but one cannot live without God." Ask students to explain the meaning of this proverb in light of this paragraph.
Possible Responses: God's help is more dependable than that of people; even when things seem hopeless, God can find an answer; only certain people can be someone's parents, but God's love can operate through anyone.

Reading Skills and Strategies
SUMMARIZING TEXT

B Have students work in pairs to summarize the lessons that Michael learns. Then discuss whether these lessons are useful to us today.

Literary Analysis FOLK TALE

C Often in folk tales things return to "normal" at the end, and it is true of this story. Discuss with students the importance of things returning to "normal" at the end.
Possible Responses: Having everything return to normal at the end of the story is a way of showing that the conflict has been resolved; the return to normal speaks to the idea that life goes on.

"What dwells in man I already knew. Now I learnt what is not given him. It is not given to man to know his own needs. And I smiled for the second time. I was glad to have seen my comrade angel—glad also that God had revealed to me the second saying.

"But I still did not know all. I did not know *What men live by.* And I lived on, waiting till God should reveal to me the last lesson. In the sixth year came the girl-twins with the woman; and I recognized the girls and heard how they had been kept alive. Having heard the story, I thought, 'Their mother besought[17] me for the children's sake, and I believed her when she said **A** that children cannot live without father or mother; but a stranger has nursed them and has brought them up.' And when the woman showed her love for the children that were not her own and wept over them, I saw in her the living God, and understood *What men live by.* And I knew that God had revealed to me the last lesson and had forgiven my sin. And then I smiled for the **B** third time."

XII

And the angel's body was bared, and he was clothed in light so that eye could not look on him; and his voice grew louder, as though it came not from him but from heaven above. And the angel said: "I have learnt that all men live not by care for themselves, but by love.

"It was not given to the mother to know what her children needed for their life. Nor was it given to the rich man to know what he himself needed. Nor is it given to any man to know whether, when evening comes, he will need boots for his body or slippers for his corpse.

"I remained alive when I was a man, not by care of myself but because love was present in a passer-by and because he and his wife pitied and loved me. The orphans remained alive not because of their mother's care, but because there was love in the heart of a woman, a stranger to them, who pitied and loved them. And all men live not by the thought they spend on their own welfare, but because love exists in man.

"I knew before that God gave life to men and desires that they should live; now I understood more than that.

"I understood that God does not wish men to live apart, and therefore he does not reveal to them what each one needs for himself; but he wishes them to live united, and therefore reveals to each of them what is necessary for all.

"I have now understood that though it seems to men that they live by care for themselves, in truth it is love alone by which they live. He who has love, is in God, and God is in him, for God is love."

And the angel sang praise to God, so that the hut trembled at his voice. The roof opened, and a column of fire rose from earth to heaven. Simon and his wife and children fell to the ground. Wings appeared upon the angel's shoulders and he rose into the heavens.

And when Simon came to himself the hut stood as before, and there was no one in it but his own family. ❖ **C**

17. **besought:** begged.

MINI LESSON **Grammar**

IF/THEN COMPLEX SENTENCES

Instruction An "if/then" complex sentence consists of a subordinate clause that begins with *if* and an independent clause that begins with *then.* There is a clear cause-and-effect relationship between the two clauses. If the clauses were separate sentences, the cause-and-effect relationship might still be recognized, but it would not be as clear.

Model Write the following sentences on the chalkboard:

Simon thought the stranger was in need.
Simon felt that he should help him.

Ask students if the two sentences have a cause-and-effect relationship. *(Yes. The stranger seeming to be in need triggers Simon's feeling that he should help.)* How could the ideas be combined in one "if/then" complex sentence? *(If the stranger were in need, then Simon would help him.)* Point out that the compound sentence shows the cause-and-effect relationship more clearly and reads more smoothly.

Practice Have students combine the following sentences into "if/then" complex sentences.

1. Simon's conscience stopped him. Otherwise, he would have ignored the downtrodden

from Sonya Tolstoy's Diary

Translated by Alexander Werth

PREPARING to *Read*

Build Background

Sonya Tolstoy, Tolstoy's dutiful wife for 48 years, was a competent, independent woman with extraordinary mental and physical stamina. Not only did she give birth to 13 children and manage Tolstoy's large estate, but she also read, copied, and commented on all of his manuscripts. Sonya was an able and intelligent critic, and Tolstoy took her observations and insights seriously. Their son Ilya recalled her diligence: "Leaning over the manuscript and trying to decipher my Father's scrawl with her short-sighted eyes, she used to spend whole evenings at work, and often stayed up late at night after everyone else had gone to bed." Her contributions were indispensable to Tolstoy's work.

Like her famous husband, Sonya Tolstoy kept a diary when she could find the time. The first entry printed here (in which she refers to Tolstoy by his nickname, Lyova) concerns the novel *War and Peace*, which Sonya eventually copied seven times. The second entry is about *Anna Karenina*. Read these excerpts for insights into both husband and wife.

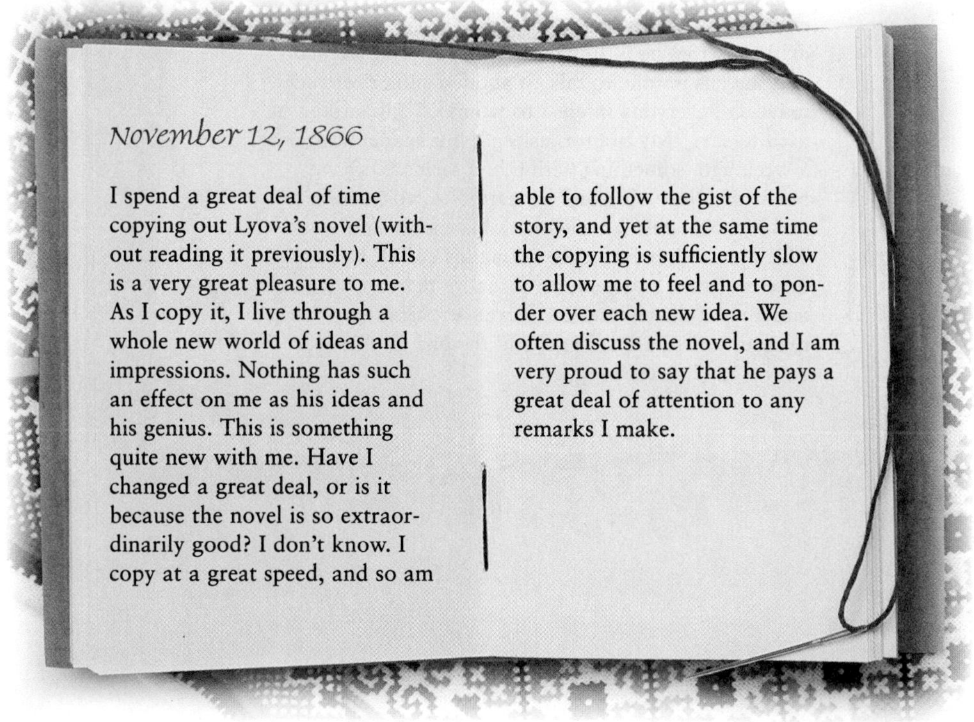

November 12, 1866

I spend a great deal of time copying out Lyova's novel (without reading it previously). This is a very great pleasure to me. As I copy it, I live through a whole new world of ideas and impressions. Nothing has such an effect on me as his ideas and his genius. This is something quite new with me. Have I changed a great deal, or is it because the novel is so extraordinarily good? I don't know. I copy at a great speed, and so am able to follow the gist of the story, and yet at the same time the copying is sufficiently slow to allow me to feel and to ponder over each new idea. We often discuss the novel, and I am very proud to say that he pays a great deal of attention to any remarks I make.

Biographical Note

Sonya Tolstoy began writing a diary in 1855 when she was 11. With some interruptions, she continued keeping one until her death in 1919. Leo Tolstoy also kept a diary for most of his life. The two diaries together provide an intimate portrayal of their marriage.

Sonya Tolstoy was a good writer, read widely, and was passionately committed to supporting and promoting Tolstoy's literary career. Copying his works was a staggering task. In addition to the sheer quantity of material, the pages were so hard to read that she sometimes had to use a magnifying glass to decipher them. They were full of crossed-out lines, notes in the margins, abbreviations, corrections, and scribbles that only she could read. She wrote the pages out in a clear script, only to get some of them back the next night with more changes.

In 1870 Sonya began another kind of diary, a notebook in which she set out to describe Tolstoy the writer. In her first entry on February 14, 1870, she wrote: "It occurred to me that I might render a service to posterity by recording, not so much Lyova's everyday life, as his mental activities, so far as I was able to watch them." The diary entry from November 20, 1876, is from this notebook, referred to as "Various Entries for Future Reference." Sonya's recording of Tolstoy's observations about embroidery and Anna Karenina give an unusual glimpse into Tolstoy's methods as a realist.

stranger. *(If Simon's conscience hadn't stopped him, then he would have ignored the downtrodden stranger.)*

2. Matrëna almost left the cottage without hearing her husband's explanation. She almost didn't help the stranger. *(If Matrëna had left the cottage without hearing her husband's explanation, then she wouldn't have helped the stranger.)*
3. The peasant woman might not have sheltered the orphaned twins. The girls would likely have died without shelter. *(If the peasant woman hadn't sheltered the orphaned twins, then the girls would likely have died.)*
4. Michael had to learn three truths while living on earth. God would not return him to heaven unless he did. *(If Michael failed to learn three truths while living on earth, then God would not return him to heaven.)*

For more instruction and practice in complex sentences, use McDougal Littell's ***Language Network:***

- Grade 10, Chapter 4, "Clauses and Sentence Structure"
- Grade 12, Chapter 3, "Using Clauses"

TOLSTOY AUTHOR STUDY 993

READING FOR INFORMATION

Reading Skills and Strategies

READING A DIARY

Remind students that a diary is a writer's personal account of his or her experiences and thoughts. Point out that when reading a diary, a person has to keep in mind the motivation and objectivity of the writer in order to evaluate the writer's reliability. Discuss with students any information they learn or impressions they gather about Sonya and Leo Tolstoy from these two diary entries. Ask them to comment on how reliable they think the entries might be.

Possible Responses: The first diary entry shows Sonya's great admiration for Tolstoy and her involvement with his work. She seems to be in awe of him in an almost childlike way. The second entry shows Tolstoy's sharp observation of human behavior and his use of it in his writing. The end of the entry suggests that Tolstoy was erratic in his work habits and wrote in spurts. Although Sonya's admiration for Tolstoy is evident, her descriptions in these two entries seem fairly objective. She herself is a sharp observer and clear writer.

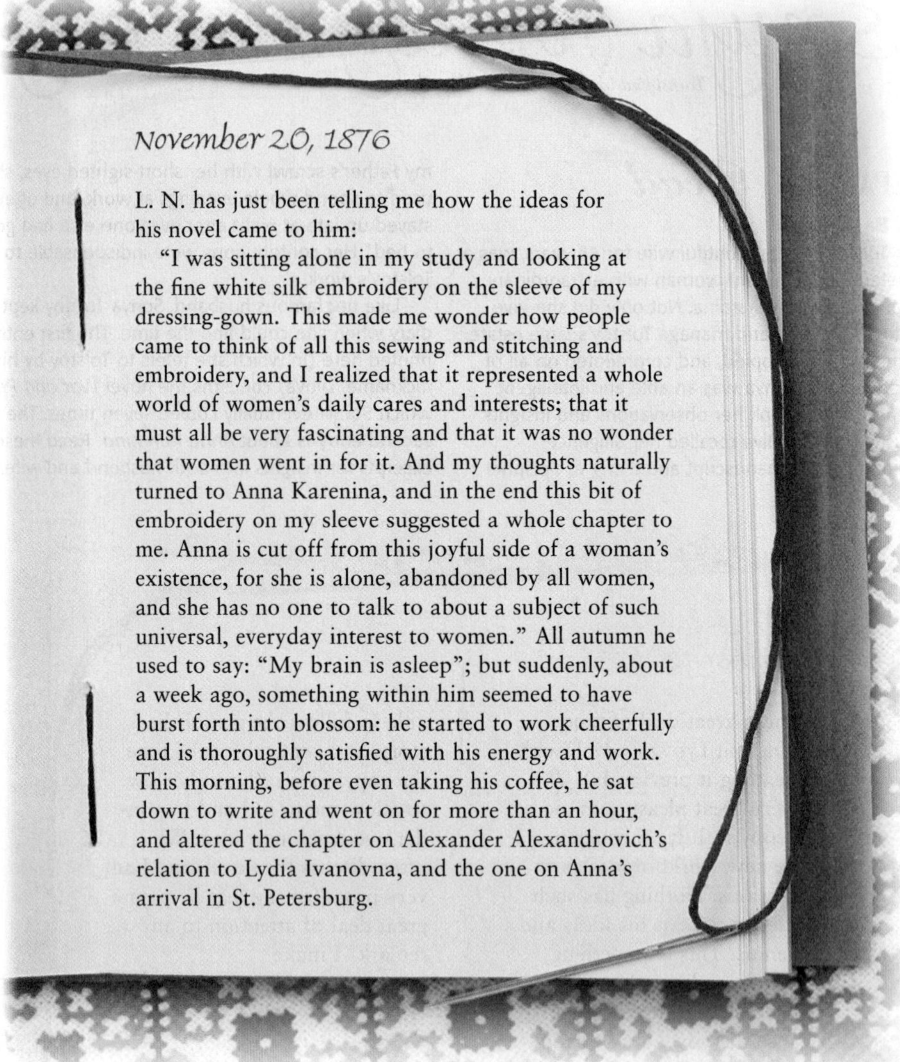

November 20, 1876

L. N. has just been telling me how the ideas for his novel came to him:

"I was sitting alone in my study and looking at the fine white silk embroidery on the sleeve of my dressing-gown. This made me wonder how people came to think of all this sewing and stitching and embroidery, and I realized that it represented a whole world of women's daily cares and interests; that it must all be very fascinating and that it was no wonder that women went in for it. And my thoughts naturally turned to Anna Karenina, and in the end this bit of embroidery on my sleeve suggested a whole chapter to me. Anna is cut off from this joyful side of a woman's existence, for she is alone, abandoned by all women, and she has no one to talk to about a subject of such universal, everyday interest to women." All autumn he used to say: "My brain is asleep"; but suddenly, about a week ago, something within him seemed to have burst forth into blossom: he started to work cheerfully and is thoroughly satisfied with his energy and work. This morning, before even taking his coffee, he sat down to write and went on for more than an hour, and altered the chapter on Alexander Alexandrovich's relation to Lydia Ivanovna, and the one on Anna's arrival in St. Petersburg.

Connect to the Literature

1. **What Do You Think?** What is your reaction to Michael's explanation of what men live by?

Comprehension Check
- Why does Simon take the stranger home?
- What happens to the man who ordered the boots?
- How did the twin babies survive after their mother's death?

Think Critically

2. **ACTIVE READING: PREDICTING** Review the chart you made in your READER'S NOTEBOOK. How accurate were your predictions? Which explanation of a mystery took you most by surprise? Discuss your responses with your classmates.
3. In your own words, explain what the three lessons are that Michael learns and how they are related.
4. Besides love, what are some other virtues illustrated by the characters in this story? Support your answer with evidence from the story.

- why Simon and Matrëna each change from their initial reaction to Michael
- how Michael acts during his punishment
- what the woman says about caring for the twins

5. Do you think Michael deserved to be punished by God? Give reasons for your opinion.

Extend Interpretations

6. **Different Perspectives** Suppose you lived in the same village as Simon and Matrëna. How do you think you would view the events that occur in their household?
7. **Connect to Life** Taking in a stranger can be dangerous in our society today. What do you think would happen if Michael appeared in your neighborhood in need of food, clothing, and shelter? Do you think it would be possible for him to learn the same lessons? Give reasons for your answers.

LITERARY ANALYSIS: FORESHADOWING

In a story, hints or clues about what will happen later is called **foreshadowing.** In this story, Tolstoy uses this technique not only to suggest later events but also to point toward fuller understanding of events. For example, when Simon takes in Michael, the reader doesn't know the true significance of this act until Michael's identity is revealed. Still, clues that Michael is an angel come in Section I when Simon first sees "something whitish behind the shrine." As a master storyteller, Tolstoy uses foreshadowing selectively, giving just enough hints to keep his readers guessing.

Paired Activity Working with a partner, go back through the story to look for four other clues that lead to the moment when Michael reveals his identity. Use a chart like the one below to list the clues and to briefly explain the significance of each one in foreshadowing Michael's revelation that he is an angel.

Event: Michael Reveals His Identity	
Clue	**Significance of Clue**
1. Simon sees "something whitish behind the shrine"	1. suggests something out of the ordinary is going on
2.	
3.	
4.	

Connect to the Literature

1. **What Do You Think?** Student reactions should be grounded in the text and in their own experience. Students should provide examples to support their opinions.

Comprehension Check
- It is cold, and the stranger has no clothes and no place to go.
- He dies in his carriage on the way home.
- A neighbor woman took them in, fed them, and raised them as her own.

Use Selection Quiz in **Unit Six Resource Book,** p. 32.

Think Critically

2. Possible Response: Mysteries might include Michael not revealing his identity, each of his smiles, his making the slippers instead of boots, his looking at the little girls as though he had seen them before, and the hut filling with light.
3. Possible Response: The first lesson ("Learn what dwells in man") is that people have love for others within them that can overcome feelings of anger or dislike. The second lesson ("What is not given to man") is that no one knows what might happen next in his life. The third lesson ("What men live by") is that what makes life worth living is to love and care for others instead of caring only about yourself. They are related in this way: If each person expresses the love that God has given him or her, then people will live together in harmony and look out for each other's needs, and they will be united in God.
4. Possible Responses: Other virtues include courage, compassion, a sense of duty, hard work, and patience.
5. Possible Responses: Yes, because he should have trusted that God knew more than he did. No, because he was responding in a loving way to the mother's natural love of her children. To deny her request to live would have been cruel.

Extend Interpretations

6. **Different Perspectives** Possible responses include being suspicious of the stranger, being jealous of Simon and Matrëna's good fortune, or believing that the stranger has special powers.
7. **Connect to Life** Students may say that if such a person appeared in their neighborhood, residents might call the police. The stranger might end up in a homeless shelter. There he might receive help, but it would be hard for him to learn the lessons. Other students may say that some people in the neighborhood would try to talk to the stranger and help him. He might be able to learn the lessons from these people.

Literary Analysis

Paired Activity Additional clues: the first time the stranger looks at Simon, Simon becomes fond of him; the stranger is clean, healthy, kindly; the stranger won't tell anything about himself; when Simon and Matrëna remember the stranger's look, it makes their hearts glad; he "worked as if he had sewn boots all his life"; he foresees the death of the rich man; a light shines from Michael.

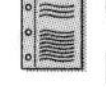
Use **Unit Six Resource Book,** p. 31, for more practice.

Analysis of Styles

A First activity

For excerpt from *War and Peace*:

tone: Tolstoy describes Rostov's thoughts and actions without making any comments about them.

characterization: The description of Rostov shows his naive expectations of what a battle would be like, then beginning recognition of the realities of war, and finally the full impact of the shock and terror of his situation.

details: Sharp descriptive details include the rattling sound of the bullets; the river, sky, and sun in the landscape; the sun going behind a cloud; and the stretchers. Details describing emotions and thoughts include Rostov picturing himself slashing at someone with a sword and the combination of the shooting and the sudden cloudiness making him feel "one sensation of sickening fear."

narration: Tolstoy portrays the transition of Rostov from an inexperienced soldier to one fully aware of the danger of war in a natural flow of thoughts and actions that seem true to life.

For "What Men Live By" excerpt:

theme: Matrëna's behavior conveys the message that it is good to show compassion toward others.

word choice: The excerpt is written with easy one- and two-syllable words—*cut, eat, table, touched, face*—used in short phrases and clauses.

characters and **plot:** The descriptions of Simon, Matrëna, and the stranger and their actions are direct and easy to understand.

B Second activity

Possible Responses:

- In the first excerpt, the narrator describes many thoughts and feelings of Rostov; in the second excerpt, the narrator primarily describes simple actions of the three characters.
- Many of the sentences in the first excerpt are long and complex. The sentences in the second excerpt are relatively short and easy to follow.
- The actions described in the first excerpt are fast-paced and reflect the confusion of a battle scene. The actions in the second excerpt are unhurried and orderly.

Tolstoy's Contrasting Styles

The style of Tolstoy's early fiction and his great novels has been called saturated realism because these works so fully absorb the reality of life. In his later fiction, however, he was concerned primarily with conveying a clear and simple moral message.

Key Aspects of Tolstoy's Styles

Realism
- An impartial, or unbiased, **tone** that carries no judgment
- Vivid **characterization** that reveals complex emotions
- Carefully selected **details** to render a scene, reveal an emotion, or express a thought with absolute clarity
- A smooth **narration** that seems to flow naturally

Moral Tales
- Clear messages, or **themes,** that convey moral truth
- Simple, direct **word choice** that all can understand
- Uncomplicated **characters** and **plot** that appeal to a wide range of readers

Analysis of Styles

The first excerpt on the right details a young man's first combat experience, and the second portrays Matrëna and the stranger. After studying the aspects of Tolstoy's two styles above, read the excerpts. Then complete these activities:

- A Find an example of each aspect of Tolstoy's realist style in the first excerpt. Do the same for the moral tales style in the second excerpt.
- B Identify two differences in style between the two excerpts.
- C Look for any aspects of realism that are present in the excerpt from "What Men Live By."

Applications

1. **Changing Styles** Try rewriting a brief passage from "How Much Land Does a Man Need?" or "What Men Live By" in the realist style of the excerpt from *War and Peace.*
2. **Speaking and Listening** In their later years, how do you suppose Simon and Matrëna would describe their life with Michael? Pretend to be one of them and tell your story, using the style of the original tale or a more realistic style.

from **War and Peace**

Rostov . . . stepped on the bridge, not knowing what he had to do. There was no one to slash at with his sword (that was how he always pictured a battle to himself). . . . He stood and looked about him, when suddenly there was a rattle on the bridge, like a lot of nuts being scattered, and one of the hussars, the one standing nearest him, fell with a groan on the railing. Rostov ran up to him with the others. Again some one shouted. "Stretchers!" Four men took hold of the hussar and began lifting him up. . . . Nikolay Rostov turned away, and began staring into the distance, at the waters of the Danube, at the sky, at the sun, as though he were searching for something. . . . "Here is *it, it,* death hanging over me, all round me. . . . One instant, and I shall never see that sunshine, that water, that mountain gorge again. . . ." At that moment the sun went behind the clouds; more stretchers came into view ahead of Rostov. And the terror of death and of the stretchers, and the loss of the sunshine and life, all blended into one sensation of sickening fear.

from **"What Men Live By"**

Simon cut the bread, crumbled it into the broth, and they began to eat. Matrëna sat at the corner of the table, resting her head on her hand and looking at the stranger.

And Matrëna was touched with pity for the stranger and began to feel fond of him. And at once the stranger's face lit up; his brows were no longer bent, he raised his eyes and smiled at Matrëna.

C Third activity

Aspects of realism in the second excerpt include description of ordinary activities, such as cutting bread and crumbling it in the broth, and the portrayal of ordinary people—the peasants Simon and Matrëna.

Applications

1. **Changing Styles** Students might look for a passage which could be rewritten to include a character's thoughts or to include a description of some complex action.
2. **Speaking and Listening** Students should
   - support a valid interpretation of how the character might tell the story
   - establish mood and convey meaning using voice, movement, gestures, and facial expressions.

Writing Options

1. Folk Tale Rewrite "What Men Live By" as the folk tale that you imagine Tolstoy first heard. What details would you omit to shorten and simplify the tale?

2. Maxims for Living Write three maxims, or rules of conduct, that could help people lead more meaningful and rewarding lives. You can use the guidelines for giving that you created in the Connect to Your Life activity on page 976.

3. Explanatory Essay Draw conclusions about Tolstoy's values from "How Much Land Does a Man Need?" and "What Men Live By." First, go back through the stories, listing virtues and vices and citing examples that illustrate them. Then write your conclusions, using selective examples as your support. Use a chart like the one below to organize your ideas.

Virtues	Vices
Generosity: Simon gives Michael his coat.	Envy: Pakhom envies a neighbor who buys land.

Writing Handbook
See page R25: Elaboration.

Activities & Explorations

1. News Display With your classmates, create a display of newspaper and magazine articles and photos that illustrate the theme of "What Men Live By." ~ VIEWING AND REPRESENTING

2. Story Dramatization With a small group of classmates, choose an excerpt from "What Men Live By" to dramatize in front of the class. ~ PERFORMING

Inquiry & Research

Biography Find out more about Sonya Tolstoy. A fascinating account of her relationship with her husband can be found in the second chapter of *The Hidden Writer: Diaries and the Creative Life* (1997) by Alexandra Johnson.

Tolstoy's long, interesting life is well documented in both words and photographs. Work with a small group of classmates to create a photo biography of Tolstoy that highlights important stages in his life and shows the changes he went through. Use photos of Tolstoy to focus your research and guide you to the information to be included in the captions. For example, an image of Tolstoy as a young army cadet could lead you to information on his war experience and his writing about that experience. Your group could then decide on the kind of information to put in the caption—a quotation of Tolstoy's about war, an excerpt from one of his war stories, or a brief summary of biographical facts, for example. Whatever you choose to write for the captions, make sure they provide important insights into the man himself. Your aim should be to portray Tolstoy as a person as well as to show him as a "great man."

Primary Print Sources Tolstoy's diaries, letters, and many writings are good places to look for quotations. You might also try Sonya Tolstoy's diary.

Secondary Print Sources There are several biographies of Tolstoy. Some include a variety of good photos. Tolstoy had a number of followers who recorded his words in books of their own, such as A. B. Goldenweizer's *Talks with Tolstoy*.

Computer Resources Many images of Tolstoy are available on the Web, including a photo tour of his estate, Yasnaya Polyana. Online encyclopedias and reliable Web sites can also give you some basic information.

Writing Options

1. **Folk Tale** Have students review **Build Background** on page 976. Then suggest that they reread the story, making a list of the essential elements in the tale. Remind them that an oral folk tale would be brief, would have simple language and sentences, and would be told in a direct style with few extra details about character or plot.
2. **Maxims for Living** Tell students that their maxims can be about different ideas from those in the story. You might have several students read aloud one or two of the guidelines for giving that they created for **Connect to Your Life** to generate ideas. You could also mention some well-known maxims, such as "The only thing we have to fear is fear itself," and "The only way to have a friend is to be one."
3. **Explanatory Essay** Remind students that they should have a clear thesis statement. You might have them work in pairs to come up with their lists of virtues and vices. Suggest that in addition to looking for virtues and vices they look for explicit morals that Tolstoy states in the stories.

Author Study Project

Creating a Photo Biography Students in each group can be assigned different aspects of the project, depending on their interests. Necessary tasks include finding a large group of photographs, choosing the photographs that are the most forceful and intriguing, deciding what aspect of Tolstoy's life each photo illustrates, finding quotations that best fit the images, writing additional material for the captions, and deciding on a final order of photographs and captions.

Secondary Print Sources *Sonya* and *The Tragedy of Tolstoy,* both noted in Inquiry & Research, have many photos of Tolstoy, including some unusual ones. Some additional photos can be found in *Tolstoy* by Henri Troyat.

Multimedia Project Instead of creating a photo biography in print form, students could make an electronic version using an authoring program such as HyperStudio or Microsoft PowerPoint.

Activities & Explorations

1. **News Display** You might have students work in small groups to discuss the theme of the story and to brainstorm ideas for appropriate articles and photos.
2. **Story Dramatization** Suggest to the students that when they are choosing their excerpts, they keep in mind that the passage should have high interest and enough action and interaction between characters to make it work well as a dramatization. Remind them that they may need to create dialogue. Suggest also that in addition to assigning the roles of the characters, they may want to have someone be a narrator.

Inquiry & Research

Biography Students can also use the following works to research Sonya Tolstoy's life:

- *The Diaries of Sophia Tolstoy,* translated by Cathy Porter
- *Sonya,* a biography, by Anne Edwards
- *The Tragedy of Tolstoy,* an account of Leo and Sonya Tolstoy by their youngest daughter, Countess Alexandra Tolstoy

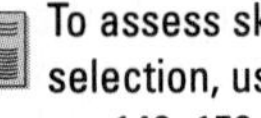
To assess skills and concepts taught in this selection, use **Formal Assessment Book,** pp. 149–150.

Assign "A Problem" by Anton Chekhov and "The Artist" by Rabindranath Tagore to prepare students for the sample writing assessment provided on page 1015. Use the **Points of Comparison** chart to guide students in identifying the similarities and differences between the two stories.

Use **Unit Six Resource Book,** p. 34, for more practice.

COMPARING LITERATURE ACROSS CULTURES

Realism in Fiction

OVERVIEW

Realistic fiction focuses on the here and now, on the everyday experiences of people. It reflects life as it is. Realistic fiction often does not have complicated plots. Instead, it concentrates on characters' behavior and reactions.

In this lesson you will read two stories that represent the realist tradition. One is by a 19th-century Russian master of realism, Anton Chekhov. The other is by a famous Indian writer of the 19th and 20th centuries, Rabindranath Tagore. The stories are set in different cultures and portray different kinds of characters and situations. In the pages that follow, you will be given the chance to compare some of the characteristics of realism that are present in each story. You will also be able to see how different realists create a fictional world.

Points of Comparison

Important characteristics of realism include the following:

- Reflects what life is like—includes details of everyday activities
- Portrays characters who are ordinary people, not heroes or villains
- Focuses on characters' motivations, circumstances, and actions, not on plot
- Is concerned with social problems and struggles that characters face
- Is not idealistic or sentimental
- Does not always have a clear resolution at the end

Analyze the Stories Create a chart like the one shown to help you in taking notes about the stories. Add any additional questions that you think would help a reader understand the realism in the two works.

Questions for Analysis	"A Problem"	"The Artist"
What real-life situations are portrayed?		
What everyday details are described?		
What are the concerns and struggles of the main characters?		
What motivates their actions and responses?		
How does the story end?		

Standardized Test Practice: Comparison-and-Contrast Essay After you have finished reading the stories, you will have the opportunity to write a comparison-and-contrast essay. Your notes will help you in planning and writing the essay.

Assessment Standardized Test Practice

COMPARISON-AND-CONTRAST ESSAY To provide practice to students in comparing two different pieces of literature from the realist tradition, have them read both stories in this **Comparing Literature** feature, rather than treating each selection separately. Have them work with the chart shown here on page 998, filling it out as they finish reading each of the two stories. (Examples of how to fill out the chart are supplied on pages 1007 and 1014.) A sample assessment writing prompt and guidelines for responding to it in writing are on page 1015.

A Problem

ANTON CHEKHOV

Anton Chekhov
1860–1904

Doctor or Writer? The Russian realist Anton Chekhov (ən-tôn' chĕk'ôf) found fame early in life. The son of a grocer and the grandson of a serf, Chekhov put himself through medical school and supported his family by selling his short stories to popular newspapers and magazines. By the time he graduated in 1884, he was well known. Chekov's work drew increasing attention, and although he did practice medicine, writing became the central focus of his life.

Literary Contribution Chekhov is considered a master of the modern short story and, along with Guy de Maupassant, had a major impact on its development. Chekhov's stories are known for their sensitive characterization and use of mood and symbolism. When Chekhov turned to writing drama, he brought the same sensitivity and insight that had graced his stories. Although failures at first, his plays soon found an eager audience at the Moscow Art Theater. In the years following the success of *The Seagull* in 1898, Chekhov established his reputation as Russia's great playwright.

Build Background

In 19th-century Europe, the upper classes had strict codes of behavior. Breaking those codes was to be avoided at all cost, and disgrace followed if a person did violate them. In "A Problem," a young man from a wealthy family has gotten in debt and forged a loan document. When he cannot pay the loan, his family finds out and faces certain scandal if the episode becomes known in society.

Connect to Your Life

In this story some of the characters are concerned with preserving their family's honor. What does the word *honor* mean to you? Can it have different meanings in different situations? Compare your ideas with those of some of your classmates.

Focus Your Reading

LITERARY ANALYSIS: IRONY

Irony exists when there is a difference between what is expected and what actually happens. For example, it is ironic that a young man from a rich family runs out of money. As you read "A Problem," look for other examples of irony.

ACTIVE READING: UNDERSTANDING CHARACTERS' VALUES

A character's values are the qualities that he or she thinks are most important in life. Examples of such qualities would be bravery, kindness, responsibility, love of money, ambition, or desire for power. Understanding a character's values helps the reader interpret the character's words and actions.

READER'S NOTEBOOK As you read "A Problem," try to identify the values that are most important to the Colonel, Ivan Markovitch, and Sasha. For each of the three characters write down the values and then note the words and actions that reflect those values.

WORDS TO KNOW **Vocabulary Preview**

assert	dissipated	inextricably	tranquilly
candid	edifying	paltry	
convention	indulgence	reprehensible	

Objectives

- understand and appreciate a **short story** in the **realist tradition (Literary Analysis)**
- identify and analyze **irony (Literary Analysis)**
- analyze words and actions of characters to **understand the characters' values (Active Reading)**

Summary

A young man, Sasha Uskov, nephew in a well-to-do family, has forged an IOU to the bank. When the IOU comes due, he can't pay his debt, so he faces public disgrace in a trial unless his family pays the debt for him. His three uncles debate what to do. One uncle, the Colonel, thinks that Sasha should be punished. A second uncle is worried about the family name being publicized in the newspapers. A third uncle, Ivan Markovitch, argues that they should help Ivan and not punish him. Sasha does little to defend himself and seems not to care what happens. After much discussion, the uncles agree to pay the debt. The Colonel is not happy, but Markovitch is overjoyed and tells Sasha that he has been spared. Sasha is relieved and immediately begins thinking about going to a party that very night. He realizes he has no money, however, so he shocks Ivan Markovitch by asking him for a loan. When Markovitch hesitates, Sasha threatens to write another false IOU and bring disgrace on the family. Markovitch, horrified, lends Sasha the money, and Sasha goes off to his party, thinking to himself that he is a criminal after all.

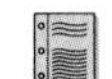
Use **Unit Six Resource Book,** p. 33, for additional support.

Thematic Link

In this story, family members debate how to teach a young man one of **life's** important **lessons.**

Use **Unit Six Resource Book,** p. 37, for practice with Words to Know.

TIME MANAGEMENT

If you wish to cover only one of the selections, use . . .

- Preparing to Read, pp. 999 or 1008
- Thinking Through the Literature, pp. 1006 or 1014

If you want to take advantage of longer blocks of class time, use . . .

- TE Teaching Options: Viewing and Representing, pp. 1001, 1011; Cross Curricular Link, pp. 1003, 1009, 1010, 1013; Vocabulary Strategy, p. 1004; Grammar, p. 1005
- Choices and Challenges, p. 1007
- Standardized Test Practice, p. 1015

5-Minute Warm-Up

Daily Language SkillBuilder

Have students **proofread** the display sentences on page 869k and write them correctly.

Reading and Analyzing

Literary Analysis IRONY

Point out that the Uskovs want to protect their family secret, but at the same time the Colonel says that lawbreakers should be punished. Ask students to explain what is ironic about this. *(If the Colonel gets his way, the family secret will be exposed in a public courtroom.)*

 Use **Unit Six Resource Book,** p. 36, for more practice.

Active Reading

UNDERSTANDING CHARACTERS' VALUES

A Ask students what the description of Ivan Markovitch tells about his values.

Possible Responses: He seems to value kindness, sympathy, and helpfulness.

Then ask students what they learn about the Colonel's values from what he says in column 2 on page 1000.

Possible Response: He seems to value honesty, strictness, and high ethical standards.

 Use **Unit Six Resource Book,** p. 35, for more practice.

A Problem

Anton Chekhov

Translated by Constance Garnett

1 The strictest measures were taken that the Uskovs'[1] family secret might not leak out and become generally known. Half of the servants were sent off to the theater or the circus; the other half were sitting in the kitchen and not allowed to leave it. Orders were given that no one was to be admitted. The wife of the Colonel, her sister, and the governess, though they had been initiated into the secret, kept up a pretense of knowing nothing; they sat in the dining-room and did not show themselves in the drawing-room or the hall.

Sasha Uskov, the young man of twenty-five who was the cause of all the commotion, had arrived some time before, and by the advice of A kind-hearted Ivan Markovitch, his uncle, who was taking his part, he sat meekly in the hall by the door leading to the study, and prepared himself to make an open, candid explanation.

The other side of the door, in the study, a family council was being held. The subject under discussion was an exceedingly disagreeable and delicate one. Sasha Uskov had cashed at one of 2 the banks a false promissory note,[2] and it had become due for payment three days before, and now his two paternal uncles[3] and Ivan Markovitch, the brother of his dead mother, were deciding the question whether they should pay the money and save the family honor, or wash their hands of it and leave the case to go for trial.

To outsiders who have no personal interest in the matter such questions seem simple; for those who are so unfortunate as to have to decide them in earnest they are extremely difficult. The uncles had been talking for a long time, but the problem seemed no nearer decision.

"My friends!" said the uncle who was a colonel, and there was a note of exhaustion and bitterness in his voice. "Who says that family honor is a mere convention? I don't say that at all. I am only warning you against a false view; I am pointing out the possibility of an unpardonable mistake. How can you fail to see it? I am not speaking Chinese; I am speaking Russian!"

"My dear fellow, we do understand," Ivan Markovitch protested mildly.

"How can you understand if you say that I don't believe in family honor? I repeat once more: fa-mil-y ho-nor false-ly un-der-stood is a 3 prejudice! Falsely understood! That's what I say: whatever may be the motives for screening a scoundrel, whoever he may be, and helping him to escape punishment, it is contrary to law and unworthy of a gentleman. It's not saving the family honor; it's civic cowardice! Take the army, for instance. . . . The honor of the army is more precious to us than any other honor, yet we don't screen our guilty members, but condemn them. And does the honor of the army suffer in

1. Uskovs (o͝o'skôfs).
2. **promissory note:** a written promise, or IOU, to pay a specific amount of money to a certain person by a certain date. In the 19th century, a person could have a bank cash an IOU made out to him or her by another person. Sasha had forged an IOU and cashed it at a bank but did not have the money to repay the bank when the note came due.
3. **paternal uncles:** uncles who are brothers of one's father.

WORDS TO KNOW

candid (kăn'dĭd) *adj.* frank; blunt; straightforward

convention (kən-vĕn'shən) *n.* a social custom

LESSON RESOURCES

UNIT SIX RESOURCE BOOK, pp. 33–41

ASSESSMENT RESOURCES

Formal Assessment, pp. 151–152

Teacher's Guide to Assessment and Portfolio Use

Test Generator

INTEGRATED TECHNOLOGY

Visit our Web site: classzone.com

ADDITIONAL RESOURCES

Lesson Planning Guide, pp. 129–130

Teacher's Sourcebook for Language Development

Double Portrait of Otto and Heinrich Benesch (1913), Egon Schiele. Neue Galerie, Linz, Austria. Photo © Art Resource, New York.

Customizing Instruction

Less Proficient Readers

1 Make sure students understand the family secret: Sasha Uskov, a nephew, has forged a financial document and now owes the bank money, which he cannot pay.

Help students identify the uncles. *(The Colonel is a brother of Sasha's father. Ivan Markovitch is a brother of Sasha's mother. There is a third uncle, also a brother of Sasha's father, who is not named.)*

Make sure students understand the conflict: the family has to decide whether to pay Sasha's debt and clear his name or else let him go to trial for forgery.

English Learners

Make sure students understand the following phrases: p. 1000, col. 1, "family council" *(members of a family meeting together to talk about a problem and figure out a solution)*; p. 1000, col. 1, "wash their hands of it" *(have nothing else to do with it)*

2 Explain that IOU stands for "I owe you." Explain that an IOU is a note that one person writes to another when borrowing money from that person. The note states how much money was borrowed and when the person will pay it back. Sasha wrote a fake IOU to himself and signed the Colonel's name (see p. 1003, col. 2). He then took it to a bank, which lent him the money with the agreement that he would pay it back by a certain date (when the signer of the IOU would pay Sasha). Since the Colonel had never signed the IOU, however, when the date came, Sasha didn't have the money and his forgery was discovered. (Sasha reveals on p. 1003, cols. 1–2, that he was expecting money from a friend but never got it.)

3 Explain to students that the phrase "fa-mil-y ho-nor false-ly un-der-stood" is written with hyphens to show how the Colonel exaggerated the words. Demonstrate for students, and then ask some of them to try it.

Advanced Learners

Have students think about what the title of the story refers to. Suggest that they consider whether there might be more than one problem.

MINI LESSON Viewing and Representing

Double Portrait of Otto and Heinrich Benesch
by Egon Schiele

ART APPRECIATION

Instruction Heinrich Benesch (hīn′rĭkн bĕn′ĕsh), though not a wealthy man, was an early patron of Egon Schiele's (ā′gôn′ shē′lə). Highly impressed with Schiele's work, he gave him loans as well as advice and encouragement.

This painting of Benesch and his son, Otto, reflects tension and some ambiguity between the two men. The son—young, unsure—is about to begin his adult life. The father appears strong and determined, with his arm held out in an expression of protection or control or perhaps both. Otto's wife later commented that Heinrich was a dominating personality who was uncomfortable with his son's growing intellectual abilities. Otto eventually became an outstanding art historian.

Application Tell students to spend some time looking at this portrait of the two men. Suggest that as they read the story, they go back to the painting from time to time and think about how it connects to the characters and to the events in the story.

Literary Analysis IRONY

Tell students to compare Ivan Markovitch's defense of Sasha with Sasha's own view of his situation. Ask them to explain any ironies they see.

Possible Responses: Markovitch is eager to help Sasha, but Sasha acts like he doesn't care what happens to him; Markovitch says that Sasha is already being punished by his conscience, but Sasha shows no remorse at all. It is ironic that Markovitch's understanding of Sasha is the opposite of Sasha's actual attitudes.

Then ask students how they would describe the relationship between Markovitch and Sasha.

Possible Response: The relationship seems superficial. Markovitch does not seem to have been involved much in Sasha's life up to this point.

Active Reading

UNDERSTANDING CHARACTERS' VALUES

Have students review Ivan Markovitch's arguments and the tone of his appeals. Ask them what they think he values most.

Possible Response: Markovitch suggests every argument he can think of to support his opinion that Sasha deserves compassion and should be offered help and kindness. Then he reminds the others about his sister, Sasha's mother, and the need to preserve family honor. He uses emotionally charged language and sounds manipulative. Although Markovitch talks a lot about compassion, his arguments and tone seem to indicate that he in fact cares more about keeping things hushed up and avoiding confrontation.

Reading Skills and Strategies
CONNECTING

You might want to have a class discussion in which students talk about how they think they would react if they were in Sasha's position.

consequence? Quite the opposite!"

The other paternal uncle, an official in the Treasury, a taciturn, dull-witted, and rheumatic man, sat silent, or spoke only of the fact that the Uskovs' name would get into the newspapers if the case went for trial. His opinion was that the case ought to be hushed up from the first and not become public property; but, apart from publicity in the newspapers, he advanced no other argument in support of this opinion.

The maternal uncle, kind-hearted Ivan Markovitch, spoke smoothly, softly, and with a tremor in his voice. He began with saying that youth has its rights and its peculiar temptations. Which of us has not been young, and who has not been led astray? To say nothing of ordinary mortals, even great men have not escaped errors and mistakes in their youth. Take, for instance, the biography of great writers. Did not every one of them gamble, drink, and draw down upon himself the anger of right-thinking people in his young days? If Sasha's error bordered upon crime, they must remember that Sasha had received practically no education; he had been expelled from the high school in the fifth class; he had lost his parents in early childhood, and so had been left at the tenderest age without guidance and good, benevolent influences. He was nervous, excitable, had no firm ground under his feet, and, above all, he had been unlucky. Even if he were guilty, anyway he deserved indulgence and the sympathy of all compassionate souls. He ought, of course, to be punished, but he was punished as it was by his conscience and the agonies he was enduring now while awaiting the sentence of his relations. The comparison with the army made by the Colonel was delightful, and did credit to his lofty intelligence; his appeal to their feeling of public duty spoke for the chivalry of his soul, but they must not forget that in each individual the citizen is closely linked with the Christian. . . .

"Shall we be false to civic duty," Ivan Markovitch exclaimed passionately, "if instead of punishing an erring boy we hold out to him a helping hand?"

Ivan Markovitch talked further of family honor. He had not the honor to belong to the Uskov family himself, but he knew their distinguished family went back to the thirteenth century; he did not forget for a minute, either, that his precious, beloved sister had been the wife of one of the representatives of that name. In short, the family was dear to him for many reasons, and he refused to admit the idea that, for the sake of a paltry fifteen hundred rubles, a blot should be cast on the escutcheon[4] that was beyond all price. If all the motives he had brought forward were not sufficiently convincing, he, Ivan Markovitch, in conclusion, begged his listeners to ask themselves what was meant by crime? Crime is an immoral act founded upon ill-will. But is the will of man free? Philosophy has not yet given a positive answer to that question. Different views were held by the learned. The latest school of Lombroso, for instance, denies the freedom of the will, and considers every crime as the product of the purely anatomical peculiarities of the individual.[5]

"Ivan Markovitch," said the Colonel, in a voice of entreaty, "we are talking seriously about an important matter, and you bring in Lombroso, you clever fellow. Think a little, what are you saying all this for? Can you imagine that all your thunderings and rhetoric will furnish an answer to the question?"

Sasha Uskov sat at the door and listened. He felt neither terror, shame, nor depression, but

4. **escutcheon** (ĭ-skŭch′ən): a shield-shaped emblem with a family's coat of arms.

5. **Lombroso** (lōm-brō′sō) . . . **of the individual:** Cesare Lombroso, an Italian criminologist of the era, tried unsuccessfully to prove a relationship between criminal behavior and an individual's physical and mental defects.

WORDS TO KNOW

indulgence (ĭn-dŭl′jəns) *n.* a giving in to someone's wishes or desires
paltry (pôl′trē) *adj.* insignificant; almost worthless

only weariness and inward emptiness. It seemed to him that it made absolutely no difference to him whether they forgave him or not; he had come here to hear his sentence and to explain himself simply because kind-hearted Ivan Markovitch had begged him to do so. He was not afraid of the future. It made no difference to him where he was: here in the hall, in prison, or in Siberia.[6]

"If Siberia, then let it be Siberia . . . !"

He was sick of life and found it insufferably hard. He was inextricably involved in debt; he had not a farthing[7] in his pocket; his family had become detestable to him; he would have to part from his friends and his women sooner or later, as they had begun to be too contemptuous of his sponging on them. The future looked black.

Sasha was indifferent, and was only disturbed by one circumstance; the other side of the door they were calling him a scoundrel and a criminal. Every minute he was on the point of jumping up, bursting into the study and shouting in answer to the detestable metallic voice of the Colonel:

"You are lying!"

"Criminal" is a dreadful word—that is what murderers, thieves, robbers are; in fact, wicked and morally hopeless people. And Sasha was very far from being all that. . . . It was true he owed a great deal and did not pay his debts. But debt is not a crime, and it is unusual for a man not to be in debt. The Colonel and Ivan Markovitch were both in debt. . . .

"What have I done wrong besides?" Sasha wondered.

He had discounted a forged note. But all the young men he knew did the same. Handrikov and Von Burst always forged IOU's from their parents or friends when their allowances were not paid at the regular time, and then when they got their money from home they redeemed[8] them before they became due. Sasha had done the same, but had not redeemed the IOU because he had not

"And it's not in my character to bring myself to commit a crime. I am soft, emotional. . . . When I have the money I help the poor. . . ."

got the money which Handrikov had promised to lend him. He was not to blame; it was the fault of circumstances. It was true that the use of another person's signature was considered reprehensible; but, still, it was not a crime but a generally accepted dodge, an ugly formality which injured no one and was quite harmless, for in forging the Colonel's signature Sasha had had no intention of causing anybody damage or loss.

"No, it doesn't mean that I am a criminal . . ." thought Sasha. "And it's not in my character to bring myself to commit a crime. I am soft, emotional. . . . When I have the money I help the poor. . . ."

Sasha was musing after this fashion while they went on talking the other side of the door.

"But, my friends, this is endless," the Colonel

6. **Siberia:** a region in north-central Russia where criminals and political prisoners were sent.

7. **farthing:** a coin worth less than a penny.

8. **redeemed:** paid off.

WORDS TO KNOW

inextricably (ĭn-ĕk'strĭ-kə-blē) *adv.* in a way that one cannot get out of

reprehensible (rĕp'rĭ-hĕn'sə-bəl) *adj.* deserving of blame

Customizing Instruction

Less Proficient Readers

Help students follow Ivan Markovitch's argument:

- Everyone makes mistakes when they are young, even great people.
- Sasha has had a difficult childhood. He is nervous and excitable and has been unlucky.
- He deserves sympathy.
- He is already being punished by his conscience.
- It is better to help the poor boy than to punish him.
- Family reputation must be preserved.
- Some philosophers think that there is no free will, so Sasha should not be blamed for what he couldn't help doing.

English Learners

- Help students with the following terms: p. 1002, col. 1, "taciturn, dull-witted, and rheumatic man" *(a person who talks very little, is rather stupid, and suffers from rheumatism, a condition of painful swelling in the muscles and joints)*; p. 1002, col. 2, "helping hand" *(help or support to a person in need)*; p. 1003, col. 1, "sponging" *(borrowing money from other people to live on)*; p. 1003, col. 1, "allowance" *(a sum of money given regularly to someone to live on)*; p. 1003, col. 2, "dodge" *(a way to cheat)*
- Review the identity of the three uncles: the two paternal uncles, brothers of Sasha's father, are the Colonel and the treasury official; the maternal uncle, brother of Sasha's mother, is Ivan Markovitch. Point out to students that both of Sasha's parents are dead.
- Point out that although dialogue is not used, the narrator is telling what Ivan Markovitch is saying on page 1002. On page 1003, the narrator describes what Sasha is thinking.

Advanced Learners

Direct students to review Sasha's thoughts as they are presented on pages 1002 to 1003. Suggest that they discuss how Sasha views himself and how realistic his self-understanding is.

Cross Curricular Link

History and Geography

SIBERIA At one point in the story, Sasha says that he doesn't care if he is sent to Siberia. If he had actually been given such a sentence, he probably would have cared very much. Siberia, which means "Sleeping Land," is a vast area of central and northern Russia. It is known for its severe weather conditions—in some places the temperature can drop to -90° F. The winters are long, and there is little snow.

Siberia was inhabited by small ethnic groups when the Russians began invading in the late 1500s. Russian rule gradually increased until it was complete in the mid-1700s. About 1754, Russia began exiling criminals and political prisoners to Siberia. They were partly settled on the land and partly used to work in the mines. The long journey was itself full of hardship, and the conditions in the prisons were brutal. Escape was virtually impossible, and many did not survive.

Unfortunately, the use of Siberia as a prison only increased in the early 20th century, when forced labor camps were established and millions were sent to Siberia under the worst conditions. It is estimated that between 15 and 30 million prisoners died before the camps were disbanded.

Reading and Analyzing

Literary Analysis
CHARACTERIZATION

Draw students' attention to the fact that although Sasha acts like he doesn't care what happens to him, he feels extreme hatred toward his uncle, the Colonel. Ask them why they think he has such strong feelings of hostility.

Possible Response: Sasha undoubtedly does care about what happens to him and wants to return to his old way of life. If the Colonel wins the argument, Sasha will not be able to do so. In his selfishness, Sasha may also be angry because it was the Colonel's signature that he forged on the IOU, and the Colonel is not willing to come up with the money. The Colonel's viewpoint also forces Sasha to look at his behavior, something he wants to avoid.

Literary Analysis IRONY

Suggest to students that by helping Sasha, Ivan Markovitch wants to give him a second chance. Ask students to explain the ironic consequences of the uncles' decision to pay Sasha's debt.

Possible Response: Sasha is thrilled that he can go to parties again and immediately tries to borrow money from Markovitch. Instead of having a change of heart, Sasha is more self-centered than ever.

Active Reading
UNDERSTANDING CHARACTERS' VALUES

A Ask students what they think Sasha reveals about himself and his values in the last two lines of the story.

Possible Response: Sasha seems to have a glimmer of insight into himself in recognizing that what he has just done could be considered criminal. But he has no intention of changing and is satisfied to act this way. Enjoying life is his most important value, and he will do anything, no matter how wrong, to make it possible.

declared, getting excited. "Suppose we were to forgive him and pay the money. You know he would not give up leading a dissipated life, squandering money, making debts, going to our tailors and ordering suits in our names! Can you guarantee that this will be his last prank? As far as I am concerned, I have no faith whatever in his reforming!"

The official of the Treasury muttered something in reply; after him Ivan Markovitch began talking blandly and suavely[9] again. The Colonel moved his chair impatiently and drowned the other's words with his detestable metallic voice. At last the door opened and Ivan Markovitch came out of the study; there were patches of red on his lean shaven face.

"Come along," he said, taking Sasha by the hand. "Come and speak frankly from your heart. Without pride, my dear boy, humbly and from your heart."

Sasha went into the study. The official of the Treasury was sitting down; the Colonel was standing before the table with one hand in his pocket and one knee on a chair. It was smoky and stifling in the study. Sasha did not look at the official or the Colonel; he felt suddenly ashamed and uncomfortable. He looked uneasily at Ivan Markovitch and muttered:

"I'll pay it . . . I'll give it back. . . ."

"What did you expect when you discounted the IOU?" he heard a metallic voice.

"I . . . Handrikov promised to lend me the money before now."

Sasha could say no more. He went out of the study and sat down again on the chair near the door. He would have been glad to go away altogether at once, but he was choking with hatred and he awfully wanted to remain, to tear the Colonel to pieces, to say something rude to him. He sat trying to think of something violent and effective to say to his hated uncle, and at that moment a woman's figure, shrouded[10] in the twilight, appeared at the drawing-room door. It was the Colonel's wife. She beckoned Sasha to her, and wringing her hands, said, weeping: "*Alexandre,*[11] I know you don't like me, but . . . listen to me; listen, I beg you. . . . But, my dear, how can this have happened? Why, it's awful, awful! For goodness' sake, beg them, defend yourself, entreat them."

Sasha looked at her quivering shoulders, at the big tears that were rolling down her cheeks, heard behind his back the hollow, nervous voices of worried and exhausted people, and shrugged his shoulders. He had not in the least expected that his aristocratic relations would raise such a tempest over a paltry fifteen hundred rubles! He could not understand her tears nor the quiver of their voices.

An hour later he heard that the Colonel was getting the best of it; the uncles were finally inclining to let the case go for trial.

"The matter's settled," said the Colonel, sighing. "Enough."

After this decision all the uncles, even the emphatic Colonel, became noticeably depressed. A silence followed.

"Merciful Heavens!" sighed Ivan Markovitch. "My poor sister!"

And he began saying in a subdued voice that most likely his sister, Sasha's mother, was present unseen in the study at that moment. He felt in his soul how the unhappy, saintly woman was weeping, grieving, and begging for her boy. For the sake of her peace beyond the grave, they ought to spare Sasha.

The sound of a muffled sob was heard. Ivan Markovitch was weeping and muttering something which it was impossible to catch through the door. The Colonel got up and paced from

9. **suavely** (swäv'lē): in a smoothly agreeable way.
10. **shrouded:** hidden from sight.
11. ***Alexandre*** (ä-lĕk-säɴ'drə): "Sasha" is short for the Russian name Aleksandr, of which "Alexandre" is the French form.

WORDS TO KNOW
dissipated (dĭs'ə-pā'tĭd) *adj.* participating excessively in sensual or foolish pleasures

MINI LESSON Vocabulary Strategy

CONTEXT CLUES

Instruction Remind students that they can infer the meaning of an unfamiliar word by using the surrounding context.

Write the following model sentence on the board:

"You know he would not give up leading a dissipated life, squandering money, making debts, going to our tailors and ordering suits in our names!" (page 1004, col. 1)

Ask a volunteer to try summarizing the meaning of the sentence. Then have students figure out the meaning of the word *dissipated* from details that are included in the sentence. Finally, ask a volunteer to use the word *dissipated* in a new sentence.

Practice In the following sentences, have students find context clues that help explain the meaning of the underlined word. Then have them give the meaning of the word. (The clues are double underlined.)

1. Becky gave Meredyth her candid opinion of the musical: she was disappointed with the singing and wouldn't recommend the show to anyone. *(honest)*
2. The job paid a paltry wage per hour, not enough to buy gas, groceries, or even a fast-food meal. *(very small)*
3. She sat tranquilly on the hill, enjoying the things that made her feel calm—the quiet, warmth, the sun, and a gentle breeze. *(peacefully)*

A lesson on using context clues appears on p. 674 of the Pupil's Edition.

corner to corner. The long conversation began over again.

But then the clock in the drawing-room struck two. The family council was over. To avoid seeing the person who had moved him to such wrath, the Colonel went from the study, not into the hall, but into the vestibule. . . . Ivan Markovitch came out into the hall. . . . He was agitated and rubbing his hands joyfully. His tear-stained eyes looked good-humored and his mouth was twisted into a smile.

"Capital,"[12] he said to Sasha. "Thank God! You can go home, my dear, and sleep tranquilly. We have decided to pay the sum, but on condition that you repent and come with me tomorrow into the country and set to work."

A minute later Ivan Markovitch and Sasha in their great-coats and caps were going down the stairs. The uncle was muttering something edifying. Sasha did not listen, but felt as though some uneasy weight were gradually slipping off his shoulders. They had forgiven him; he was free! A gust of joy sprang up within him and sent a sweet chill to his heart. He longed to breathe, to move swiftly, to live! Glancing at the street lamps and the black sky, he remembered that Von Burst was celebrating his name-day[13] that evening at the "Bear," and again a rush of joy flooded his soul. . . .

"I am going!" he decided.

But then he remembered he had not a farthing, that the companions he was going to would despise him at once for his empty pockets. He must get hold of some money, come what may!

"Uncle, lend me a hundred rubles," he said to Ivan Markovitch.

His uncle, surprised, looked into his face and backed against a lamp-post.

"Give it to me," said Sasha, shifting impatiently from one foot to the other and beginning to pant.

He longed to breathe, to move swiftly, to live!

"Uncle, I entreat you, give me a hundred rubles."

His face worked; he trembled, and seemed on the point of attacking his uncle. . . .

"Won't you?" he kept asking, seeing that his uncle was still amazed and did not understand. "Listen. If you don't, I'll give myself up tomorrow! I won't let you pay the IOU! I'll present another false note tomorrow!" 1

Petrified, muttering something incoherent in his horror, Ivan Markovitch took a hundred-ruble note out of his pocket-book and gave it to Sasha. The young man took it and walked rapidly away from him. . . .

Taking a sledge,[14] Sasha grew calmer, and felt a rush of joy within him again. The "rights of youth" of which kind-hearted Ivan Markovitch had spoken at the family council woke up and asserted themselves. Sasha pictured the drinking-party before him, and, among the bottles, the women, and his friends, the thought flashed through his mind:

"Now I see that I am a criminal; yes, I am a criminal." ❖ A

12. **capital:** very good; excellent.

13. **name day:** the feast day of the saint after whom one is named.

14. **sledge:** a sled drawn by animals.

WORDS TO KNOW

tranquilly (trăng′kwə-lē) *adv.* calmly; peacefully
edifying (ĕd′ə-fī′ĭng) *adj.* intended to improve morally; instructing **edify** *v.*
assert (ə-sûrt′) *v.* to express forcefully and positively

Customizing Instruction

Less Proficient Readers

1 Make sure students understand Sasha's threats. *(First, he threatens to give himself up to the authorities and not let the uncles pay. This would expose the family to scandal, which Markovitch has been trying to avoid. Then he threatens to write another fake IOU, the very crime he has just committed. He is showing that he cares nothing about the uncles' values or their concern about his actions and his fate.)*

English Learners

Help students with the sequence of events on these pages:

- Sasha faces the uncles and tells them he'll pay back the note.
- He goes back to the hallway, and his aunt begs him to consider the family.
- The uncles decide not to help Sasha.
- Ivan Markovitch cries, and the discussion starts all over again.
- Markovitch comes out and announces that the uncles will pay after all.
- Sasha is filled with relief and starts thinking about going out again. He asks Markovitch for a loan.
- Markovitch is shocked, Sasha makes threats, and Markovitch lends the money.
- Sasha goes on his way.

Advanced Learners

Have students reflect again on the title of this story and its possible meanings. Ask them to share their ideas with the class. *(Problems the students could identify include Sasha's forgery, the decision facing the uncles, the lack of communication between the adults and Sasha, Sasha's lack of responsibility, and how Sasha responds to having his debt paid.)*

MINI LESSON Grammar

CAPITALIZATION

Instruction Review with students the use of capitalization with titles and family names.

- Capitalize titles used with personal names.
  Professor Taylor
- Don't capitalize a title when it is used alone.
  I wrote a letter to the professor.

NOTE: Point out to students that in "A Problem," the title *colonel* is capitalized when used without the personal name, as in "the Colonel went from the study" (p. 1005, col. 1). Explain that this style of capitalization was used in England in the early 20th century, when this translation of the story was made.

- Capitalize family names used before a proper noun or used in place of the name.
  We all like Aunt Carmen's laptop.
- Don't capitalize family names preceded by articles or possessive words.
  My aunt has two computers.

Practice Have students correct the capitalization in the following sentences.

1. After she finished her speech, the Senator spoke to governor Hardy. *(senator, Governor)*
2. My Cousin gave me a gift certificate to my favorite clothing store. *(cousin)*

For more instruction and practice in capitalization, use McDougal Littell's ***Language Network:***

- Grade 10, Chapter 10, "Capitalization"
- Grade 12, Chapter 8, "Capitalization"

Connect to the Literature

1. **What Do You Think?** How do you think Ivan Markovitch feels at the end of the story? Explain your answer.

Comprehension Check
- What is the "problem"?
- Who will make the decision about Sasha's fate?
- At the end of the story, what does Sasha threaten to do if his uncle won't give him money?

Think Critically

2. **ACTIVE READING: UNDERSTANDING CHARACTERS' VALUES** Review the notes you made in your READER'S NOTEBOOK. What are the most important values for the Colonel, for Ivan Markovitch, and for Sasha? What is your opinion of each character's values?

3. What kind of person is Sasha?

- the kind of life he lives
- what his uncles say about him
- what he thinks as he listens to the uncles discuss his situation

4. How well does Ivan Markovitch understand Sasha? Explain your answer.

5. What do you think Sasha means when at the end he says, "I see that I am a criminal"?

6. How do you interpret the meaning of *honor* in this story?

Extend Interpretations

7. **What If?** Suppose that the uncles had decided not to pay Sasha's debts but rather to let his case go to trial. What do you think might have happened to him?

8. **Connect to Life** Because Sasha wants to do as he pleases, he accumulates debts and even resorts to forgery. What circumstances and expectations pressure people today to go into debt and become desperate about money?

LITERARY ANALYSIS: IRONY

Irony is the contrast between expectation and reality. Irony can surprise the reader, and it can be subtle. It can also reveal the truth about a character or situation. Irony is found in many works of realism.

Situational irony occurs when a character or the reader expects one thing to happen but something else actually does. Sometimes it springs from unexpected twists and reversals. For example, in Tolstoy's story "How Much Land Does a Man Need?" it is ironic that Pakhom dies just as he is about to get his land.

Paired Activity With a partner, find two examples of situational irony from "A Problem." Explain why each situation is ironic and what the irony reveals. Use a diagram like the one shown below to organize your ideas. Then discuss the following questions: How does irony contribute to the overall effect of the story? In what way does the title of the story prove ironic?

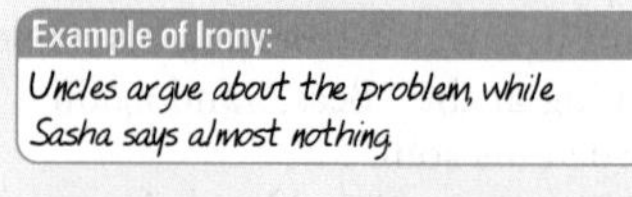

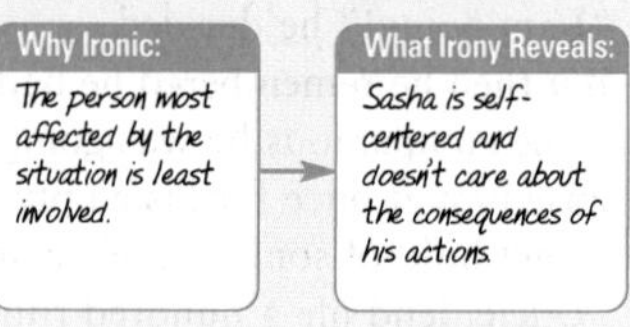

Connect to the Literature

1. **What Do You Think?** Students may say that Ivan Markovitch feels betrayed, confused, shocked, or angry.

Comprehension Check
- Sasha has forged an IOU and can't pay his debt.
- Sasha's three uncles
- He threatens to forge another note.

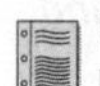
Use Selection Quiz in **Unit Six Resource Book,** p. 38.

Think Critically

2. Possible Responses: The Colonel values responsibility, the law, and justice. Ivan Markovitch values compassion and avoidance of scandal. Sasha values pleasure and ease. Many students will disapprove of Sasha's values, but opinions may vary on the values of the two uncles.
3. Possible Responses: Sasha is self-centered, irresponsible, lazy, unkind, thoughtless, and cowardly.
4. Possible Response: Ivan Markovitch does not understand Sasha well. Markovitch doesn't realize that Sasha is interested only in pursuing his party-going and shows no sign of true remorse or wanting to change. Markovitch idealizes and sentimentalizes Sasha.
5. Possible Response: Earlier in the story Sasha said that criminals are "wicked and morally hopeless people." He recognizes now that he will do anything to get his way and so is "morally hopeless."
6. Possible Responses: For the Colonel, family honor comes from doing right and obeying the law. For Ivan Markovitch, family honor comes from avoiding scandal and preserving the family's reputation.

Extend Interpretations

7. **What If?** Possible Responses: If convicted, he might have been shocked into changing his ways. If not convicted, he probably would have continued in his old ways.
8. **Connect to Life** Possible Responses: People want to have more possessions than they can afford, they want to appear successful, or they spend their money on addictions, such as drugs or gambling. Some students may note that people may also be pushed to desperation by extreme poverty.

Literary Analysis

Paired Activity Possible Responses: Sasha's statement (p. 1003) that he helps the poor when he has money is ironic because he is in debt and is trying to get money from other people. This reveals his lack of self-understanding. A second example occurs when Ivan tells Sasha the uncles will pay his debt and he immediately asks for a loan. This is ironic because he wants to carry on in his old ways instead of being sorry. The irony shows him to be irresponsible, ungrateful, and selfish.

The overall effect of the irony is to emphasize the lack of insight of the characters in the story. The irony of the title is that the story reveals many problems, not just one.

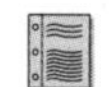
Use **Unit Six Resource Book,** p. 36, for more practice.

EXERCISE: CONTEXT CLUES Write the word that would best fill in the blank in each sentence.

1. Considering the parties, drinking, and clothes that Sasha spent all his money on, a good word to describe his life would be ______.
2. He knew that he gave in to any ______ that appealed to him.
3. He also realized that he was ______ bogged down in spending and borrowing.
4. But Sasha viewed his forgery as a harmless incident, not something ______.
5. He considered the amount he owed to be ______, too insignificant to be worth such a fuss.
6. The Colonel thought that being put on trial would be a(n) ______ experience for a young man with so little self-control.
7. The Colonel was ______ in his statements, making no attempt to hide his disapproval.
8. He felt that Sasha's behavior involved family honor and reputation, not just a trivial ______.
9. As the uncles argued, Sasha became so resigned to his fate that he felt he would go ______ wherever he was sent.
10. After he heard their decision, however, his true nature began to ______ itself.

WORDS TO KNOW

assert	dissipated	inextricably	tranquilly
candid	edifying	paltry	
convention	indulgence	reprehensible	

Building Vocabulary
For an in-depth study of context clues, see page 674.

Points of Comparison

Review the story and fill in the second column of your comparison-and-contrast chart. An example is given below.

Paired Activity Get together with a classmate and discuss the similarities and differences in your charts. Based on your discussion, you may want to make some changes in your chart.

Questions for Analysis	"A Problem"	"The Artist"
What real-life situations are portrayed?	*young man gets himself in trouble*	
What everyday details are described?		
What are the concerns and struggles of the main characters?		
What motivates their actions and responses?		
How does the story end?		

Vocabulary in Action

1. dissipated
2. indulgence
3. inextricably
4. reprehensible
5. paltry
6. edifying
7. candid
8. convention
9. tranquilly
10. assert

Points of Comparison

Point out that partners should share their charts and make changes to them only if they are persuaded that the change is a better response. Partners' charts should not be identical.

To assess skills and concepts taught in this selection, use **Formal Assessment Book,** pp. 151–152.

Objectives

- understand and appreciate an **Indian short story** in the **realist tradition (Literary Analysis)**
- compare characteristics of realism in two short stories **(Literary Analysis)**

Summary

Govinda is a wealthy man from Calcutta, India, who values money over everything. He has a brother, Mukunda, who dies and leaves behind a wife, Satyabati, and a four-year-old son, Chunilal. The two go to live with Govinda, who is in charge of their affairs. Satyabati is an artist, and when Mukunda was alive, he had supported and praised her work. Govinda despises art, however, and wants his nephew, Chunilal, to worship money. But Chunilal also loves to paint, and Satyabati encourages him, keeping their art hidden from Govinda. Satyabati's nephew Rangalal, a famous artist, comes to see their work and admires it.

One day, Govinda comes home unexpectedly and finds Satyabati and Chunilal painting. He becomes furious and tears Chunilal's picture into pieces. When the boy bursts into tears, Satyabati defends him and tells Govinda what she thinks of his love of money. Govinda then threatens to send Chunilal to a boarding school. Satyabati takes Chunilal to her nephew's house and leaves him to be raised by the artist, knowing that he will keep her son far from the worship of money.

Use **Unit Six Resource Book,** p. 40, for additional support.

Thematic Link

Two characters in this story have opposite ideas about what are **life's** most important **lessons.**

5-Minute Warm-Up

Daily Language SkillBuilder

Have students **proofread** the display sentences on page 869k and write them correctly.

PREPARING to *Read*

Now that you have read Chekhov's story, it's time to turn your attention to a story by the Indian writer Tagore. You will see some of the same characteristics of realism in his work, but look for differences as well.

Rabindranath Tagore
1861–1941

A Many-Sided Genius It is hard to imagine anyone as multitalented as Rabindranath Tagore (rə-bēn'drə-nät' tə-gôr'), one of India's greatest modern writers. A prolific poet, he also wrote novels, short stories, plays, essays, and over 2,000 popular songs. Tagore almost single-handedly brought Indian literature into the modern era. Influenced by the European realists, he introduced new ways of writing poetry and fiction, and he used everyday language rather than the traditional Sanskrit (săn'skrĭt'). He took as his subject matter the great variety of Indian life as experienced by everyone from humble villagers to intellectuals. Because Tagore traveled widely, reading from his works and arguing eloquently for Indian independence, he essentially taught the rest of the world what India was really like. He was the first Asian writer to win the Nobel Prize in Literature (1913).

Build Background

Conflicting Values People with different goals and interests may disagree strongly about what is most important in life. These people often have great difficulty understanding each other. In this story, the two main characters—one an artist and the other a businessman—come into conflict.

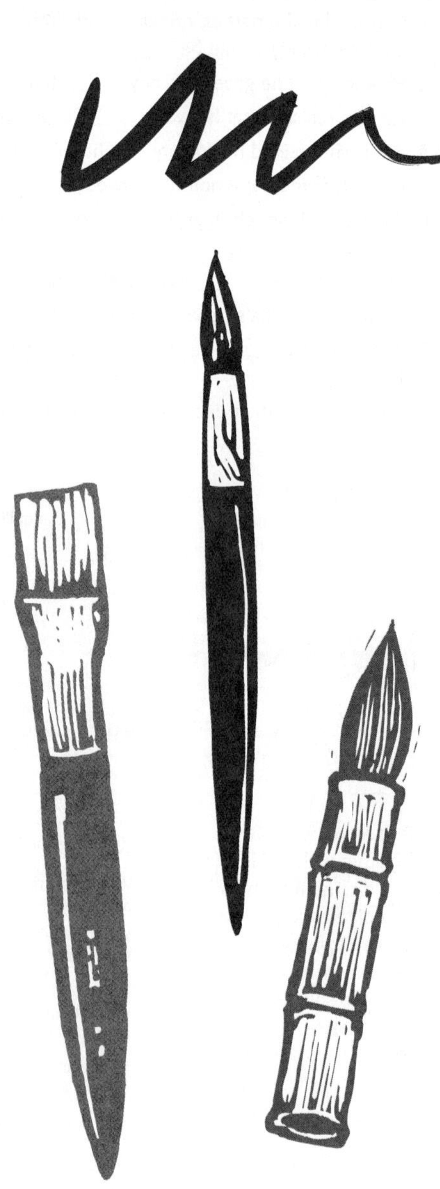

The Artist

Rabindranath Tagore

Translated by Mary Lago, Tarun Gupta, and Amiya Chakravarty

Govinda came to Calcutta after graduation from high school in Mymensingh.[1] His widowed mother's savings were meager, but his own unwavering determination was his greatest resource. "I *will* make money," he vowed, "even if I have to give my whole life to it." In his terminology, wealth was always referred to as *pice*.[2] In other words he had in mind a very concrete image of something that could be seen, touched, and smelled; he was not greatly fascinated with fame, only with the very ordinary *pice*, eroded by circulation from market to market, from hand to hand, the tarnished *pice*, the *pice* that smells of copper, the original form
1 of Kuvera,[3] who assumes the assorted guises[4] of silver, gold, securities, and wills, and keeps men's minds in a turmoil.

After traveling many tortuous roads and getting muddied repeatedly in the process, Govinda had now arrived upon the solidly paved embankment of his wide and free-flowing stream of money. He was firmly seated in the manager's chair at the MacDougal Gunnysack Company. Everyone called him MacDulal.[5]

When Govinda's lawyer-brother, Mukunda, died, he left behind a wife, a four-year-old son, a house in Calcutta, and some cash savings. In addition to this property there was some debt; therefore, provision for his family's needs depended upon frugality. Thus his son, Chunilal,[6] was brought up in circumstances that were undistinguished in comparison with those of the neighbors.

Mukunda's will gave Govinda entire responsibility for this family. Ever since Chunilal was a baby, Govinda had bestowed spiritual initiation upon his nephew with the sacred words: "Make money."

The main obstacle to the boy's initiation was his mother, Satyabati.[7] She said nothing outright; her 2
opposition showed in her behavior. Art had always been her hobby. There was no limit to her enthusiasm for creating all sorts of original and decorative things from flowers, fruits and leaves, even foodstuffs, from paper and cloth cutouts, from clay and flour, from berry juices and the juices of other fruits, from *jaba-* and *shiuli*-flower[8] stems. This activity brought her considerable grief, because anything unessential or irrational has the character of flash floods in July: it has considerable mobility,

1. **Mymensingh** (mī′mən-sĭng′): a city about 200 miles northeast of Calcutta.
2. **pice** (pīs): a very small unit of money, formerly used in India.
3. **Kuvera** (kōō-vĕ′rə): the Hindu god of wealth.
4. **guises** (gī′zĭz): outward appearances.
5. **MacDulal** (măk′dōō-läl′): The name is a play on the word *dulal*, which can mean "darling or spoiled child."
6. **Chunilal** (chōō′nē-läl′).
7. **Satyabati** (sät′yə-bə-tē′).
8. ***jaba-*** (jä′bə-) **and *shiuli*-flower** (shyōō′lē-): The jaba flower is red. The shiuli flower is white and has a sweet scent.

Cross Curricular Link History and Geography

CALCUTTA The city of Calcutta, now capital of West Bengal in India, had its beginnings in the late 1600s, when an English businessman established a trading post on the site. It is located on the Hugli (hōō′glē) River, a branch of the Ganges (găn′jēz′) River, about 100 miles upstream from the Bay of Bengal. Despite its difficult climate—temperatures can reach 108°, and summer monsoons frequently cause floods—Calcutta became an important trading center and major port as well as a center of financial and intellectual life. It was made the capital of India in 1772, and at the end of the 19th century, it was one of the largest cities in the world. The wealthy included both the elite of Indian society as well as the British who lived there as part of the ruling colonial force, known as the British Raj (räj).

Calcutta has suffered many setbacks and problems since the early 20th century. It is no longer the capital of India, and it has staggering problems of poverty and overpopulation. At the same time, however, it is still a vital intellectual and cultural center and remains the financial headquarters of eastern India. In 2001, the name of the city was changed to its Bengali form, Kolkata (käl-kŭ′tə).

Customizing Instruction

Less Proficient Readers

Make sure that students understand the family relationships in the story: Govinda and Mukunda are brothers. Mukunda is the husband of Satyabati and the father of Chunilal. When Mukunda dies, he leaves the responsibility for his wife and son's affairs to Govinda.

1 Explain that various Hindu gods will be mentioned in the story. Kuvera is thought to be able to take on the form of actual money and financial documents and so tempt people.

2 Explain that Satyabati is viewed as an "obstacle" by Govinda because he wants Chunilal to care only about money, but Satyabati disagrees with this goal and is much more interested in art.

Set a Purpose Ask students to think about who will win, Govinda or Satyabati.

English Learners

- Tell students that Govinda's referring to money as *pice* (p. 1009, col. 1) is like referring to money as *dollars, cash, or bucks* in American English.
- Explain that the word *initiation* (p. 1009, col. 2) refers to an introduction to an activity, in this case, to the idea of making money.
- Make sure students understand the following terms: p. 1009, col. 1, "frugality" *(being careful with money)*; p. 1009, col. 2, "outright" *(openly, directly)*

Advanced Learners

Remind students that verbal irony occurs when a writer says one thing but means another. Ask students to explain the verbal irony in the phrase "spiritual initiation" (p. 1009, col. 2). *(Govinda is introducing Chunilal to the love of money, a value that is the opposite of what is spiritual.)*

Point out that this ironic use of religious language gives a clue to Tagore's view of the love of money. Have students look for other uses of religious language that occur in the rest of the story.

Reading Skills and Strategies
QUESTIONING

A Ask students whether they think Satyabati was "stuck-up."

Possible Response: No. Satyabati was independent and somewhat absent-minded when she was painting. Her husband's relatives did not understand the importance of art to her or her lack of interest in family socializing.

Literary Analysis FIGURATIVE LANGUAGE

Draw students' attention to the simile "like a stalled ferry" on p. 1010, col. 1, and the metaphor "a leaky boat" on p. 1010, col. 2. Ask them to explain each of these examples of figurative language.

Possible Responses: Simile: Art, since it is not an essential, practical skill, doesn't help get things done, so it is like a ferry boat that gets stuck and can't deliver its passengers. Metaphor: A leaky boat is in danger of sinking, as a family in debt is in danger of losing its possessions and way of life.

Active Reading
UNDERSTANDING CHARACTERS' VALUES

Point out that on page 1010, the narrator goes back to describe the relationship between Mukunda and Satyabati. Have students list Mukunda's values in life.

Possible Response: His values seem to include kindness, affection, respect for others and their talents, generosity, and humility.

but in relation to the utilitarian[9] concerns of life it is like a stalled ferry. Sometimes there were invitations to visit relatives; Satyabati forgot them and spent the time in her bedroom with the door shut, kneading a lump of clay. The relatives said, "She's terribly stuck-up." **A** There was no satisfactory reply to this. Mukunda had known, even on the basis of his bookish knowledge, that value judgments can be made about art too. He had been thrilled by the noble connotations of the word "art," but he could not conceive of its having any connection with the work of his own wife.

This man's nature had been very equable.[10] When his wife squandered time on unessential whims, he had smiled at it with affectionate delight. If anyone in the household made a slighting remark, he had protested immediately. There had been a singular self-contradiction in Mukunda's makeup; he had been an expert in the practice of law, but it must be conceded that he had had no worldly wisdom with regard to his household affairs. Plenty of money had passed through his hands, but since it had not preoccupied his thoughts, it had left his mind free. Nor could he have tyrannized over his dependents in order to get his own way. His living habits had been very simple; he had never made any unreasonable demands for the attention or services of his relatives.

Mukunda had immediately silenced anyone in the household who cast an aspersion[11] upon Satyabati's disinterest in housework. Now and then, on his way home from court, he would stop at Radhabazar[12] to buy some paints, some colored silk and colored pencils, and stealthily he would go and arrange them on the wooden chest in his wife's bedroom. Sometimes, picking up one of Satyabati's drawings, he would say, "Well, this one is certainly very beautiful."

One day he had held up a picture of a man, and since he had it upside down, he had decided that the legs must be a bird's head. He had said, "Satu, this should be framed—what a marvelous picture of a stork!" Mukunda had gotten a certain delight out of thinking of his wife's art work as child's play, and the wife had taken a similar pleasure in her husband's judgment of art. Satyabati had known perfectly well that she could not hope for so much patience, so much indulgence, from any other family in Bengal. No other family would have made way so lovingly for her overpowering devotion to art. So, whenever her husband had made extravagant remarks about her painting, Satyabati could scarcely restrain her tears.

One day Satyabati lost even this rare good fortune. Before his death her husband had realized one thing quite clearly: the responsibility for his debt-ridden property must be left in the hands of someone astute[13] enough to skillfully steer even a leaky boat to the other shore. This is how Satyabati and her son came to be placed completely under Govinda's care. From the very first day Govinda made it plain to her that the *pice* was the first and foremost thing in life. There was such profound degradation[14] in his advice that Satyabati would shrink with shame.

Nevertheless, the worship of money continued in diverse forms in their daily life. If there had been some modesty about it, instead of such constant discussion, it wouldn't have been so bad. Satyabati knew in her heart that all of this lowered her son's standard of values, but there was nothing to do but endure it. Since those delicate emotions endowed[15] with uncommon dignity are

9. **utilitarian** (yo͞o-tĭl′ĭ-târ′ē-ən): practical.
10. **equable** (ĕk′wə-bəl): calm; not easily disturbed.
11. **cast an aspersion** (ə-spûr′zhən): made an unfavorable or damaging remark.
12. **Radhabazar** (rä′tə-bə-zär′): a shopping area of Calcutta.
13. **astute** (ə-sto͞ot′): shrewd; crafty.
14. **degradation** (dĕg′rə-dā′shən): disgrace or dishonor.
15. **endowed:** equipped; supplied.

Cross Curricular Link **History**

WOMEN IN INDIA In "The Artist," Mukunda encourages Satyabati in her art work and lets her make her own choices about how she spends her time. This relationship was highly unusual in Indian society until very recent times. In traditional Indian society, a woman was expected to be submissive to her husband and to fit into her husband's family. Marriages were arranged by parents, and girls were prepared from a young age to become dutiful wives and daughters-in-law. Motherhood was viewed as a woman's greatest achievement.

Marriage was meant to last for life. A woman's status was severely lowered if she became a widow, and she was forbidden to remarry. Although the legal position of women has improved, many Hindu women, especially outside of the cities, still live a life bound by the ancient traditions and limitations.

Prince taming an elephant, Mughal miniature (1609–1610), Signed by Zain al-Abidin. Opaque watercolor on paper, 19.3 cm × 13 cm. Inv I 4598 fol. 2. Museum fuer Islamische Kunst, Staatliche Museen zu Berlin, Berlin. © Bildarchiv Preussischer Kulturbesitz/Art Resource, New York.

HUMANITIES CONNECTION According to Hindu mythology, elephants once had wings and were friendly with the clouds. After the elephants lost their wings, they were still able to call upon the clouds to bring rain. These beasts are honored today in India for their association with rainfall and good crops, and they are considered good luck.

Customizing Instruction

Less Proficient Readers

- Make sure students understand the time shift that occurs on page 1010, col. 1. Explain that the narrator goes back in time to describe the relationship between Mukunda and Satyabati. Have students figure out where the time returns to the present. *(first full paragraph in col. 2)* Ask students why they think Tagore included this section at this point in the story instead of at the beginning.

Possible Response: It provides a greater contrast with Govinda.

- Review with students the basic conflict between the two brothers. *(Mukunda, though a good lawyer, did not keep careful track of his money. He paid more attention to his family. Govinda is focused entirely on making money, and nothing else has any value to him.)*

English Learners

Make sure students understand the following terms: p. 1010, col. 1, "stuck-up" *(conceited, snobby, acting like you are better than everybody else)*; p. 1010, col. 1, "whims" *(sudden unplanned thoughts or actions)*; p. 1010, col. 1, "worldly wisdom" *(knowledge of business and financial affairs)*; p. 1010, col. 2, "worship of money" *(money being more important than anything else in life)*; p. 1010, col. 2, "lowered her son's standard of values" *(influenced her son to value making money instead of valuing the most important things in life, such as love and art)*

Reading and Analyzing

Literary Analysis DESCRIPTION

Draw students' attention to the two descriptions of Satyabati and Chunilal's painting (p. 1012, col. 1, and p. 1013, col. 1). Ask students what these descriptions convey about their artwork.

Possible Response: Their painting is inventive and imaginative. The animals and other details are not realistic but are whimsical and fantastic.

Ask why this art would have especially angered Govinda. *(It would have no commercial value.)*

Active Reading

UNDERSTANDING CHARACTERS' VALUES

When students have finished reading the story, ask them to sum up Satyabati's values.

Possible Response: Most important to her are her son's well-being, creativity, and art.

Literary Analysis CHARACTER

Have students describe Rangalal.

Possible Response: He is independent, confident, successful, and decisive.

the most vulnerable, they are very easily hurt or ridiculed by rude or insensitive people.

The study of art requires all sorts of supplies. Satyabati had received these for so long without even asking that she had felt no reticence[16] with regard to them. Amid the new circumstances in the family she felt terribly ashamed to charge all these unessential items to the housekeeping budget. So she would save money by economizing on her own food and have the supplies purchased and brought in secretly. Whatever work she did was done furtively,[17] behind closed doors. She was not afraid of a scolding, but the stares of insensitive observers embarrassed her.

Now Chuni was the only spectator and critic of her artistic activity. Gradually he became a participant. He began to feel its intoxication. The child's offense could not be concealed, since it overflowed the pages of his notebook onto the walls of the house. There were stains on his face, on his hands, on the cuffs of his shirt. Indra, the king of the gods,[18] does not spare even the soul of a little boy in the effort to tempt him away from the worship of money.

On the one hand the restraint increased, on the other hand the mother collaborated in the violations. Occasionally the head of the company would take his office manager, Govinda, along on business trips out of town. Then the mother and son would get together in unrestrained joy. This was the absolute extreme of childishness!
1 They drew pictures of animals that God has yet to create. The likeness of the dog would get mixed up with that of the cat. It was difficult to distinguish between fish and fowl. There was no way to preserve all these creations; their traces had to be thoroughly obliterated before the head of the house returned. Only Brahma, the Creator, and Rudra, the Destroyer, witnessed the creative delight of these two persons; Vishnu,[19] the heavenly Preserver, never arrived.

The compulsion for artistic creation ran strong in Satyabati's family. There was an older nephew, Rangalal,[20] who rose overnight to fame as an artist. That is to say, the connoisseurs of the land roared with laughter at the unorthodoxy of his art.[21] Since their stamp of imagination did not coincide with his, they had a violent scorn for his talent. But curiously enough, his reputation thrived upon disdain and flourished in this atmosphere of opposition and mockery. Those who imitated him most took it upon themselves to prove that the man was a hoax as an artist, that there were obvious defects even in his technique.

This much maligned[22] artist came to his aunt's home one day, at a time when the office manager was absent. After persistent knocking and shoving at the door he finally got inside and found that there was nowhere to set foot on the floor.
The cat was out of the bag. 2

"It is obvious," said Rangalal, "that the image of creation has emerged anew from the soul of the artist; this is not random scribbling. He and that god who creates form[23] are the same age. Get out all the drawings and show them to me."

Where should they get the drawings? That artist who draws pictures all over the sky in
myriad[24] colors, in light and shadow, calmly dis- 3
cards his mists and mirages. Their creations had gone the same way. With an oath Rangalal said

16. **reticence** (rĕt′ĭ-səns): hesitancy to speak.
17. **furtively:** secretly.
18. **Indra, the king of the gods:** one of the chief gods of early Hinduism.
19. **Brahma** (brä′mə) . . . **Rudra** (ro͞o′drə) . . . **Vishnu** (vĭsh′no͞o): the three major gods of Hinduism. "Rudra" is another name for Shiva.
20. **Rangalal** (rän′gə-läl′).
21. **connoisseurs** (kŏn′ə-sûrz′) . . . **unorthodoxy of his art:** Those with expert knowledge in art laughed at the untraditional style of his work.
22. **maligned** (mə-līnd′): spoken about in a harmful, misleading way meant to injure.
23. **that god who creates form:** probably Brahma, understood by Tagore as the originator of all art.
24. **myriad** (mĭr′ē-əd): many; innumerable.

Now Chuni was the only spectator and critic of her artistic activity. Gradually he became a participant. He began to feel its intoxication.

to his aunt, "From now on, I'll come and get whatever you make."

There came another day when the office manager had not returned. Since morning the sky had brooded in the shadows of July; it was raining. No one monitored the hands of the clock and no one wanted to know about them. Today Chuni began to draw a picture of a sailing boat while his mother was in the prayer room. The waves of the river looked like a flock of hungry seals just on the point of swallowing the boat. The clouds seemed to cheer them on and float their shawls overhead, but the seals were not conventional seals, and it would be no exaggeration to say of the clouds: "Light and mist merge in the watery waste." In the interests of truth it must be said that if boats were built like this one, insurance companies would never assume such risks. Thus the painting continued; the sky-artist drew fanciful pictures, and inside the room the wide-eyed boy did the same.

No one realized that the door was open. The office manager appeared. He roared in a thunderous voice, "What's going on?"

The boy's heart jumped and his face grew pale. Now Govinda perceived the real reason for Chunilal's examination errors in historical dates. Meanwhile the crime became all the more evident as Chunilal tried unsuccessfully to hide the drawing under his shirt. As Govinda snatched the picture away, the design he saw on it further astonished him. Errors in historical dates would be preferable to this. He tore the picture to pieces. Chunilal burst out crying.

From the prayer room Satyabati heard the boy's weeping, and she came running. Both Chunilal and the torn pieces of the picture were on the floor. Govinda went on enumerating the reasons for his nephew's failure in the history examination and suggesting dire remedies.

Satyabati had never said a word about Govinda's behavior toward them. She had quietly endured everything, remembering that this was the person on whom her husband had relied. Now her eyes were wet with tears, and shaking with anger, she said hoarsely, "Why did you tear up Chuni's picture?"

Govinda said, "Doesn't he have to study? What will become of him in the future?"

"Even if he becomes a beggar in the street," answered Satyabati, "he'll be better off in the future. But I hope he'll never be like you. May his pride in his God-given talent be more than your pride in *pices*. This is my blessing for him, a mother's blessing."

"I can't neglect my responsibility," said Govinda. "I will not tolerate this. Tomorrow I'll send him to a boarding school; otherwise, you'll ruin him."

The office manager returned to the office. The rain fell in torrents and the streets flowed with water.

Holding her son's hand, Satyabati said, "Let's go, dear."

Chuni said, "Go where, Mother?"

"Let's get out of this place."

The water was knee-deep at Rangalal's door. Satyabati came in with Chunilal. She said, "My dear boy, you take charge of him. Keep him from the worship of money."❖

Customizing Instruction

Less Proficient Readers

Make sure students understand the following references:

- "Office manager" always refers to Govinda.
- Satyabati and Chunilal paint only when Govinda is not at home. They carefully clean up all traces of their painting so he won't know they are doing it.
- Rangalal is a nephew of Satyabati who is a well-known artist and who realizes the talent and creativity of Chunilal.
- The references to Chunilal's mistakes on the history examination infuriate Govinda because he wants Chunilal to do well on his exams so that he will have a chance to go to a university, get a good job, and make lots of money.

Have students review the predictions they made at the beginning of the story for **Set a Purpose.** Who do they think has won, Govinda or Satyabati? *(Satyabati. Even though she has had to give up Chunilal to her nephew, she has saved her son from Govinda's worship of money.)*

English Learners

1 Explain that "animals God has yet to create" means that Satyabati and Chunilal paint animals that are not like any real animals. They mixed up parts of animals, so the creatures are completely imaginary.

2 Explain that the expression "the cat was out of the bag" means that what was hidden is now known (like a cat that has been hidden in a bag and escapes).

3 Explain that the artist referred to here is the god responsible for creating all the colors of the sky, especially sunrises and sunsets.

Advanced Learners

Hold a class discussion in which students share the examples of religious language that they found and explain what they think is the meaning of this language in the story. *(The religious language is a satiric and ironic comment on Govinda's love of money.)*

Cross Curricular Link

Humanities

INDIAN ART During the 19th century, traditional Indian art was overshadowed by European influences. In the early 20th century, however, a revivalist movement emerged, spearheaded by members of the Tagore family. Two of the most influential figures were Rabindranath Tagore and his nephew, Abanindranath (ä′-bə-nĕn′drə-nät′), who some consider the father of modern Indian art.

Artists of the revivalist movement went back to earlier Indian frescoes and miniatures as well as to the myths and philosophy of India to reconnect with images, themes, and styles. They incorporated these older forms and motifs in fresh works that were clearly expressive of Indian culture.

Abanindranath Tagore influenced many other Indian artists not only as a painter but also in his role as a teacher. In particular, he was the mentor of Nandlal Bose (nənd-läl′ bōs′), an Indian painter who drew together both classical and folk traditions in his work. Bose at one time taught at Rabindranath Tagore's Visva-Bharati (vĭsh′və bä′rə-tē) University, where he was known for his ability to draw out the individual creativity of each of his students. The revivalist painters are together credited with returning Indian art to its traditional roots and bringing to it new life and energy.

Connect to the Literature

1. **What Do You Think?** Students may have different reactions. They should support their opinions with details from the story.

Comprehension Check

- with respect, affection, generosity, and pride
- Mukunda had made arrangements that when he died, Govinda would be in charge of his family's affairs.
- They love to paint.

 Use Selection Quiz in **Unit Six Resource Book,** p. 41.

Think Critically

2. Possible Response: Mukunda is a kind, gentle person. He loves and protects his family and is unconcerned about money or other people's opinions. Govinda's sole ambition in life is to make money. He has no interest in other people's concerns and is rude and thoughtless to Satyabati and Chunilal.
3. Possible Response: Satyabati loves Chunilal and encourages his love of painting. She cares about what he values in life and what kind of person he will be. She is willing to make great sacrifices for his sake.
4. Possible Response: Tagore expresses the theme that the worship of money is degrading and destructive of personal worth and of relationships. The love of art, on the other hand, generates creativity, joy, and intimacy. Tagore's use of religious language to describe Govinda's love of money is satiric and ironic. It emphasizes that Govinda is as devoted to making money as religious people would be to practicing their faith.

Points of Comparison

After students have completed their charts, initiate a class discussion about their entries. Encourage them to tell which story they liked best and to explain why.

Connect to the Literature

1. **What Do You Think?** What was your reaction to Satyabati's decision to leave Chunilal with Rangalal?

Comprehension Check

- How did Mukunda treat Satyabati?
- Why is Govinda in charge of the affairs of Satyabati and Chunilal?
- What do Satyabati and Chunilal love to do?

Think Critically

2. In what ways are Mukunda and Govinda different?
3. What kind of mother is Satyabati?
4. What idea does Tagore convey about art and the worship of money?

Points of Comparison

Paired Activity Now that you have read and studied both stories, work with a partner to compare and contrast them. First, review the answers each of you filled in on your comparison-and-contrast chart for "A Problem." Then, together, fill out the last column of your charts. An example is given at the right.

Questions for Analysis	"A Problem"	"The Artist"
What real-life situations are portrayed?	young man gets himself in trouble	mother and uncle disagree on how to raise a child
What everyday details are described?		
What are the concerns and struggles of the main characters?		
What motivates their actions and responses?		
How does the story end?		

Writing About Literature

PART 1 Reading the Prompt

In writing assessments you may be asked to compare and contrast works of literature that share certain characteristics, such as the two examples of realism that you have just read. You are now going to practice writing an essay that involves this type of comparison.

Writing Prompt

Compare and contrast the stories "A Problem" and "The Artist" ❶ as works of realism. For each story consider what the characters ❷ are like, what conflicts they face, how circumstances and situations are portrayed, and how the story ends. Point out how the two stories share aspects of realism and how they differ as examples of ❸ realism. Support your analysis with examples from the stories. ❹

STRATEGIES IN ACTION

❶ I have to **compare and contrast** two works of realism.

❷ For each story I need to discuss the **characters**, their **conflicts**, the **circumstances** and **situations**, and the **ending.**

❸ I need to explain how the stories are similar and different as works of realism.

❹ I have to support my discussion with **examples.**

PART 2 Planning a Comparison-and-Contrast Essay

- Review the comparison-and-contrast chart that you filled out for "A Problem" and "The Artist."
- Referring to your chart, find examples of similarities and differences to point out in your essay. Review the stories for other examples.
- Create an outline to help in organizing your ideas.

PART 3 Drafting Your Essay

Introduction Begin by introducing both stories as works of realism. Explain that they share important characteristics of realism but also vary in some ways.

Body Present each story's treatment of character, conflicts, situations, and so on. You can discuss each characteristic in a different paragraph, or you can first discuss the characteristics in one story and then those in the other. Point out the similarities and differences that emerge from your analysis. Consult your comparison-and-contrast chart for specific ideas and examples.

Conclusion Briefly summarize the major similarities and differences between the two stories. You might want to finish with a statement about any new understanding of realism you have gained.

Revision Check the use of signal words, such as *similarly, also, like, but,* and *while,* to make sure that your comparisons and contrasts are clear.

TEST PRACTICE

PART 1 Reading the Prompt
Model the process of reading a prompt.

- Read through the prompt in its entirety.
- List key words of the assignment on the board ("compare and contrast," "examples").
- Define each key word using **Strategies in Action** to show how students can restate the prompts in their own words.

PART 2 Planning a Comparison-and-Contrast Essay

- Students can use the chart they have been filling out for "A Problem" and "The Artist" (referenced on pages 998, 1007, and 1014).
- Encourage students to pay attention to similarities and differences in the characters, conflicts, circumstances, and endings of the two stories. They may particularly want to look for instances in which a story contains elements that are not characteristic of realism.
- In organizing their outlines, students may use a subject-by-subject order, listing all of the features in one story at a time, or a feature-by-feature order, comparing a single feature in both stories at a time.

PART 3 Drafting Your Essay

Introduction Tell students that opening their essay with a question can be an effective way of focusing their topic and getting the reader's attention.

Body Remind students that they should not switch back and forth between subject-by-subject order and feature-by-feature order. Each paragraph should flow clearly from the thesis statement.

Conclusion Suggest to students that in addition to summarizing their main ideas, they bring out any unusual comparisons they discovered in the course of writing their essay.

Revision Tell students that they should check to make sure that they have not omitted any details in their comparisons.

Use **Unit Six Resource Book,** p. 39, for additional support.

Assessment Standardized Test Practice

RESPONDING TO A WRITING PROMPT Read aloud the writing prompt at the top of this page. Discuss the **Strategies in Action** by asking students to identify the words in the prompt that tell them what to do. Suggest that they mark up their comparison-and-contrast charts, identifying points to include in their essays. When students have finished drafting their essays, have them work with a partner to see if they have accomplished the tips given in Part 3 **Drafting Your Essay.**

Additional Background

Imprisonment Dostoyevsky experienced a religious crisis during his years in Siberia. The only book he was permitted to have in prison was the New Testament, which he read constantly. Its influence was so strong that he abandoned his radical political views and became a fervent follower of Christianity. The development of his faith included a belief that the Russian Orthodox Church and the common people would be instrumental in the salvation of Russia.

Dostoyevsky actually looked on his sentence of four years of hard labor as an appropriate punishment for his actions. He endured intense spiritual struggles as he worked through his understanding of sin and suffering, and he began to have epileptic attacks, which continued for many years.

During Dostoyevsky's prison years, he also closely observed the other prisoners as they faced grinding hardship and deprivation day in and day out. He was greatly impressed by them. His fictional work, *The House of the Dead,* is a startling and compelling portrayal of Dostoyevsky's experiences in prison. What he learned of suffering, innocence, evil, and goodness fueled his imagination and his passionate search to understand the contradictions of the human mind and heart.

THE NOVELS OF

Fyodor Dostoyevsky

Imagine entering the mind of a murderer as he plots his crime against a defenseless old woman. Picture yourself as a bystander at a scandalous trial where a son is accused of murdering his father. When you open the pages of a Dostoyevsky (dŏs′tə-yĕf′skē) novel, you enter a strange and darkly fascinating world.

Both Fyodor Dostoyevsky (1821–1881) and his contemporary Leo Tolstoy have been praised as great realists. Where Tolstoy is famous for the scope of his novels, representing every level of Russian society, Dostoyevsky is known for portraying disturbed minds from the lower fringes of society. He said of his work, "I am only a realist in the highest sense. . . . I depict all the depths of the human soul."

Though Dostoyevsky was born into a respectable middle-class family, his life was marked by the very extremes that he wrote about. In his youth he was a political rebel, perhaps even a revolutionary. Later he fell prey to gambling sprees so serious that he lost his wife's dowry. For

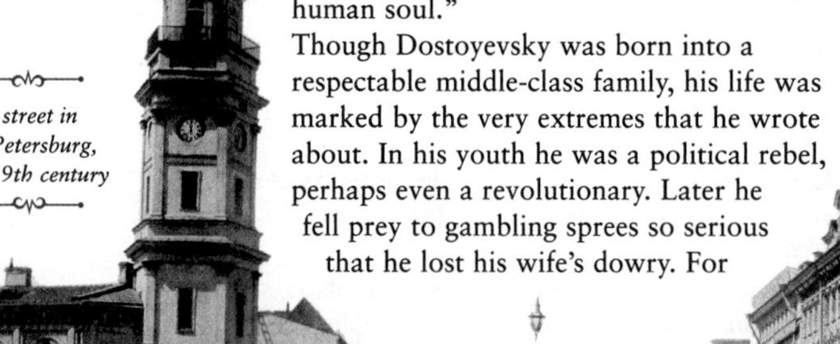

A street in St. Petersburg, late 19th century

much of his adult life, he was burdened by huge debts and subject to agonizing epileptic fits. Yet he was also a doting father, a loyal brother and husband, a patriot, and at his death a national hero.

As a young man in 1849, Dostoyevsky was imprisoned and sentenced to death for associating with political radicals. Just minutes before the prisoners' execution, a messenger announced that their lives had been spared by the czar. Dostoyevsky spent the next four years in a Siberian labor camp.

When Dostoyevsky returned from his Siberian exile, he was a changed man. His four greatest novels explore profound questions about the existence of God, the nature of freedom, and the origins of evil.

Scene from a 1998 film of Crime and Punishment, *with Ben Kingsley and Patrick Dempsey*

Crime and Punishment (1866). What happens to a poor young student who believes he is superior to everyone else? The student, Raskolnikov (rə-skôl′nĭ-kôf′), hatches a plan to kill a rich pawnbroker for money to support his family. After his crime he realizes that his motives were far more complex.

The Idiot (1868–1869). In this novel Dostoyevsky portrays "a positively beautiful person," the saintly Prince Myshkin (mĭsh′kĭn). The prince's virtue, however, proves no match for the grimy world of St. Petersburg, with all its greed, lust, and cruel ambition.

Demons (1872). In the Bible, Jesus casts out devils from a sick person, which then possess a herd of swine and proceed to drown themselves. In this political novel, inspired by the biblical story, various characters are "possessed" by the heartless ideas of revolution and atheism. The title is also translated as *The Possessed* and *Devils.*

The Brothers Karamazov (1880). What do a monk, an atheist, and a spendthrift drinker have in common? They are the Karamazov brothers, and their father is an embarrassment to everyone. When the father is murdered, one son stands accused and is put on trial. Yet all the major characters face personal trials as they search for life's meaning.

Dostoyevsky's influence continues to be felt today. His explorations into the dark recesses of the mind have influenced novelists, psychologists, artists, philosophers, and theologians. As one critic notes, "The major questions of modernity can all be traced to Dostoyevsky."

Other Fiction

Poor Folk (1846)
The House of the Dead (1860–1861)
The Insulted and the Injured (1861)
Notes from the Underground (1864)
The Gambler (1866)
An Adolescent (A Raw Youth) (1875)
"A Gentle Spirit" (1876)
"The Dream of a Ridiculous Man" (1877)

MILESTONES IN WORLD LITERATURE **1017**

Objectives

- understand and appreciate a **drama** in the **realist tradition (Literary Analysis)**
- analyze **characters, setting,** and **themes** in a **realistic drama (Literary Analysis)**
- examine **dialogue, stage directions,** and the **cast of characters** to better understand a **realistic drama (Active Reading)**

Summary

Torvald Helmer is a lawyer who is about to become a bank manager. His wife, Nora, a traditional wife and mother, is busy with Christmas preparations when an old friend, Mrs. Linde, comes to visit. Mrs. Linde, a widow, would like to get a job in Torvald's bank.

During their conversation, Nora mentions to Mrs. Linde that several years earlier she had borrowed money secretly when Torvald was seriously ill. Nora doesn't mention, however, that she had forged her father's signature to get the loan. The man who gave her the loan, Krogstad, now threatens to expose her to Torvald unless she persuades Torvald not to fire Krogstad from his bank job. But Torvald has promised Krogstad's job to Mrs. Linde.

Krogstad writes his letter, and Nora panics. Mrs. Linde, who once loved Krogstad, talks to him. They reestablish their relationship but decide not to interfere with Nora and Torvald. Torvald gets the letter and blows up at Nora. Then Krogstad returns the forged loan paper, and Torvald acts like everything is all right. Nora sees that Torvald has treated her like a child and cares only about his public image. She leaves him to find her own way in life.

 Use **Unit Six Resource Book,** pp. 42, 46, and 50, for additional support.

Thematic Link

The characters in this play come face-to-face with some of **life's** important and difficult **lessons.**

 Use **Unit Six Resource Book,** p. 53, for practice with Words to Know.

5-Minute Warm-Up

Daily Language SkillBuilder

Have students **proofread** the display sentences on page 869k and write them correctly.

A Doll House

HENRIK IBSEN

Henrik Ibsen
1828–1906

Early Life Hailed today as the father of modern drama, Henrik Ibsen (hĕn′rēk ĭb′sən) began life in a small Norwegian town. When he was seven, his father, who had been a respected merchant, went bankrupt, disgracing the family. In addition to poverty, the young Ibsen had to endure being socially outcast by the same people who used to come to his house for dinner parties. Ibsen never forgot the small-minded snobbishness that caused him such pain.

At the Theater Along with Shakespeare, Ibsen is one of very few playwrights who have had practical experience working in the theater. Starting at the age of 23, Ibsen spent approximately 11 years as a stage manager, director, and resident playwright. He eventually grew disgusted with the low-quality melodramas and silly comedies that dominated most European stages in the mid-1800s. With his wife and young son, he left Norway and began a 27-year period of wandering, mainly in Italy and Germany. During this crucial time, his genius matured as he experimented with several plays, some of them in verse. Two of them, *Brand* and *Peer Gynt* (pâr gĭnt), were popular successes. However, it was in *A Doll House,* produced in 1879, that Ibsen found his true voice. The play caused an uproar, and conventional viewers were scandalized. A small but significant audience, however, was attracted to Ibsen's work and took it seriously. As he continued to write plays that broke new ground, his audience grew, and Ibsen became established as one of the foremost dramatists of his time.

Ibsen's Art According to one biographer, Ibsen was a "man who thought romantically, but wrote realistically." Ibsen resisted being called a realist. He didn't like what he called "photographic art." Yet Ibsen shared with the realists a desire to explore the truth, for better or worse. He set out to reveal the secret inner life of his characters, where he believed the truth really lay. Audiences who watched Ibsen's characters expose their true selves were forced to reexamine their own values and moral conduct. With his searing insight, Ibsen foreshadowed the shifts in thought that were to come in the next century.

Other Works
Ghosts
An Enemy of the People
Hedda Gabler
When We Dead Awaken

LESSON RESOURCES

UNIT SIX RESOURCE BOOK,
pp. 42–54

ASSESSMENT RESOURCES
Formal Assessment, pp. 153–158
Teacher's Guide to Assessment and Portfolio Use
Test Generator

INTEGRATED TECHNOLOGY
Visit our Web site: classzone.com

ADDITIONAL RESOURCES
Lesson Planning Guide, pp. 131–136
Teacher's Sourcebook for Language Development

Build Background

Ibsen's Revolutionary Play *A Doll House* caused a sensation after its initial performance in 1879. Critics debated Ibsen's social views in newspapers and magazines. Ministers even delivered sermons on the play. Although Ibsen was sensitive to criticism, he recognized that the controversy would benefit his career: "My enemies," he declared, "have been a great help to me—their attacks have been so vicious that people come flocking to see what all the shouting was about." By the late 1880s, *A Doll House* had been produced throughout Europe, and Ibsen had become internationally famous.

Women and Society The "shouting" mainly concerned Ibsen's portrayal of a housewife who revolts against society's restrictions on women. In 19th-century Europe, husbands still had full legal authority over their wives. Married women could not carry out transactions such as taking out a loan, and they were expected to be obedient to their husbands. There was a growing movement to win political and economic rights for women. Ibsen was widely seen as a champion of women's rights after he wrote *A Doll House*. However, he denied that he had intended the play as a political statement. "I have been more the poet and less the social philosopher than people generally seem inclined to believe," Ibsen said. "My task has been the *description of humanity.*"

Realistic Drama Ibsen's exploration of women's issues wasn't the only controversial aspect of *A Doll House*. Nineteenth-century theatergoers were used to plays with fanciful plots that led to happy endings. Ibsen revolted against this tradition by presenting a simple but powerful story drawn from everyday life. Instead of creating dialogue that used formal, elevated language, he let his characters speak as ordinary people do. His prose appears to be plain and straightforward, yet he used poetic elements such as symbolism to suggest ideas. Many critics have called *A Doll House* the first modern drama.

For a humanities activity, click on:

Connect to Your Life

Think of a time when a friend or relative wasn't taking you seriously or respecting your opinion. How did this person's attitude make you feel? What steps did you take to resolve the problem? Share your experience with a classmate.

Focus Your Reading

LITERARY ANALYSIS: REALISTIC DRAMA

A Doll House is one of the first examples of **realistic drama.** As you read, notice how Ibsen develops **characters, setting,** and **themes** that reflect real life.

ACTIVE READING: STRATEGIES FOR READING REALISTIC DRAMA

The printed text of *A Doll House* consists mainly of **dialogue** spoken by the characters and **stage directions.** To better understand the play, follow these strategies.

- Read the **cast of characters** to familiarize yourself with the names and relationships.
- Pay careful attention to the stage directions. Like many realist playwrights, Ibsen offers detailed descriptions.
- **Visualize** what the characters look like.
- Use the Guide for Reading for help in keeping track of developments in the play.
- To get a better sense of what the dialogue might sound like, try reading some of it aloud.

READER'S NOTEBOOK As you read, jot down the answers to the Guide for Reading questions that occur in each act. Also note any additional strategies you used, such as visualizing characters or setting, or reading dialogue aloud.

WORDS TO KNOW **Vocabulary Preview**

calculating	inane	rash
capricious	jauntily	tactless
chronic	petty	warily
desolate		

READING FOR INFORMATION

Reading Skills and Strategies

PREVIEWING

Have students preview **Build Background** by looking at the subheads in the three paragraphs. Ask them what they think might be presented in each paragraph.

Possible Response: The first paragraph might discuss *A Doll's House* as a revolutionary play in some way, the second paragraph might discuss the position of women in society at the time of the play, and the third paragraph might discuss the characteristics of realistic drama.

Then ask students what they think they will learn about the play from **Build Background.**

Possible Response: *A Doll's House* broke new ground in its day because it portrayed a different view of women than was common, and the play was realistic in its approach, not romantic or light-hearted.

TIME MANAGEMENT

If your schedule requires that you cover the lesson objectives in a shorter time, use. . .

- Preparing to Read, pp. 1018–1019
- Thinking Through the Literature, pp. 1043, 1062, and 1081
- Vocabulary in Action, p. 1082

If you want to take advantage of longer blocks of class time, use. . .

- TE Teaching Options: Cross Curricular Link, pp. 1020, 1025, 1026, 1028–1029, 1038, 1044, 1046, 1052, 1060, 1065, 1075, 1078; Viewing and Representing, pp. 1023, 1036, 1042, 1072, 1080; Speaking and Listening, pp. 1024, 1035, 1048, 1054, 1059, 1064, 1077; Vocabulary Strategy, pp. 1040, 1057; Informal Assessment, pp. 1041, 1079; Standardized Test Practice, p. 1061; Grammar, pp. 1066–1067
- View and Compare, pp. 1042, 1080
- Translator at Work, p. 1063
- Choices and Challenges, p. 1082
- Connect to Today, p. 1083

Guide for Reading

The **Guide for Reading** notes in this selection are intended to help students read the text by dividing it into manageable sections. Each section begins with a **Focus** suggestion to help students read actively and with a purpose. Between sections, a **Pause & Reflect** question gives students an opportunity to stop and review what they have read and understood so far.

Active Reading CAST OF CHARACTERS

Remind students to read through the cast of characters and to look for each character as they read the play. Tell them that not all the characters will appear right away. Suggest that they keep notes on where each character first enters.

 Use **Unit Six Resource Book,** p. 43, for more practice.

Active Reading STAGE DIRECTIONS

Tell students that they can find important information about the characters and their relationships through the stage directions. You might want to read some of the stage directions on page 1021 with students and discuss what can be learned from them. Also, explain that Torvald Helmer is identified as Helmer whenever he speaks in the play.

Active Reading DIALOGUE

Point out to students that reading dialogue aloud will bring the play alive and make the action and characters seem real. Have students take turns reading a few lines from page 1021 to get a feel for the conversational style and pace of the play.

Literary Analysis

REALISTIC DRAMA: CHARACTERS

Ask students what they learn about the behavior and attitudes of Nora and Torvald from reading page 1021.

Possible Responses: Nora seems happy, busy, eager to please, and a little silly. Torvald seems to have a superior, condescending attitude. He acts jolly in a self-satisfied way but is also somewhat serious and moralistic.

 Use **Unit Six Resource Book,** p. 44, for more practice.

A Doll House

Henrik Ibsen

Translated by Rolf Fjelde

THE CHARACTERS

TORVALD HELMER, a lawyer	THE HELMERS' THREE SMALL CHILDREN
NORA, his wife	ANNE-MARIE, their nurse
DR. RANK	HELENE, a maid
MRS. LINDE	A DELIVERY BOY
NILS KROGSTAD, a bank clerk	

The action takes place in Helmer's *residence.*

Act One

A comfortable room, tastefully but not expensively furnished. A door to the right in the back wall leads to the entryway; another to the left leads to Helmer's *study. Between these doors, a piano. Midway in the left-hand wall a door, and further back a window. Near the window a round table with an armchair and a small sofa. In the right-hand wall, toward the rear, a door, and nearer the foreground a porcelain stove with two armchairs and a rocking chair beside it. Between the stove and the side door, a small table. Engravings on the walls. An* etagère[1] *with china figures and other small art objects; a small bookcase with richly bound books; the floor carpeted; a fire burning in the stove. It is a winter day.*

A bell rings in the entryway; shortly after we hear the door being unlocked. Nora *comes into the room, humming happily to herself; she is wearing street clothes and carries an armload of packages, which she puts down on the table to the right. She has left the hall door open; and through it a* Delivery Boy *is seen, holding a Christmas tree and a basket, which he gives to the* Maid *who let them in.*

1. **etagère** (ā′tä-zhâr′): a piece of furniture with open shelves for displaying small objects.

Cross Curricular Link History

MIDDLE-CLASS LIFE IN THE 19TH CENTURY The Industrial Revolution brought with it a rising middle class and increased wealth. A result of this wealth was that in many middle-class households, servants took care of the everyday tasks such as cooking, cleaning, and laundry. In addition, many families had live-in nurses, or nannies, to take care of the children. Parents sometimes spent only an hour a day with their children.

In the new middle-class families, there was a strict social order. The father was the head of the house and supported the family. Both wife and children were expected to defer to his judgment and wishes. For women, marriage was the ultimate goal. Being a capable housekeeper, good mother, and pleasing wife was viewed as a woman's purpose in life. She was also expected to uphold a high moral standard in her family. In fact, middle-class wives in the 19th century in western Europe were sometimes referred to as "the angel in the house," the pure and self-sacrificing woman who made life comfortable and smooth for her family.

GUIDE FOR READING

FOCUS In this part you will be introduced to the play's two main characters. As you read, look for suggestions of misunderstanding and lack of communication between them.

Nora. Hide the tree well, Helene. The children mustn't get a glimpse of it till this evening, after it's trimmed. (*To the* Delivery Boy, *taking out her purse.*) How much?

Delivery Boy. Fifty, ma'am.

Nora. There's a crown.[2] No, keep the change. (*The* Boy *thanks her and leaves.* Nora *shuts the door. She laughs softly to herself while taking off her street things. Drawing a bag of macaroons*[3] *from her pocket, she eats a couple, then steals over and listens at her husband's study door.*) Yes, he's home. (*Hums again as she moves to the table right.*)

Helmer (*from the study*). Is that my little lark twittering out there?

Nora (*busy opening some packages*). Yes, it is.

Helmer. Is that my squirrel rummaging around?

Nora. Yes!

Helmer. When did my squirrel get in?

Nora. Just now. (*Putting the macaroon bag in her pocket and wiping her mouth.*) Do come in, Torvald, and see what I've bought.

Helmer. Can't be disturbed. (*After a moment he opens the door and peers in, pen in hand.*) Bought, you say? All that there? Has the little spendthrift been out throwing money around again?

Nora. Oh, but Torvald, this year we really should let ourselves go a bit. It's the first Christmas we haven't had to economize.

Helmer. But you know we can't go squandering.

Nora. Oh yes, Torvald, we can squander a little now. Can't we? Just a tiny, wee bit. Now that you've got a big salary and are going to make piles and piles of money.

Helmer. Yes—starting New Year's. But then it's a full three months till the raise comes through.

Nora. Pooh! We can borrow that long.

Helmer. Nora! (*Goes over and playfully takes her by the ear.*) Are your scatterbrains off again? What if today I borrowed a thousand crowns, and you squandered them over Christmas week, and then on New Year's Eve a roof tile fell on my head, and I lay there—

Nora (*putting her hand on his mouth*). Oh! Don't say such things!

Helmer. Yes, but what if it happened—then what?

Nora. If anything so awful happened, then it just wouldn't matter if I had debts or not.

Helmer. Well, but the people I'd borrowed from?

Nora. Them? Who cares about them! They're strangers.

Helmer. Nora, Nora, how like a woman! No, but seriously, Nora, you know what I think about that. No debts! Never borrow! Something of freedom's lost—and something of beauty, too—from a home that's founded on borrowing and debt. We've made a brave stand up to now, the two of us; and we'll go right on like that the little while we have to.

Nora (*going toward the stove*). Yes, whatever you say, Torvald.

Helmer (*following her*). Now, now, the little lark's wings mustn't droop. Come on, don't be a sulky squirrel. (*Taking out his wallet.*) Nora, guess what I have here.

Nora (*turning quickly*). Money!

Helmer. There, see. (*Hands her some notes.*) Good grief, I know how costs go up in a house at Christmastime.

Nora. Ten—twenty—thirty—forty. Oh, thank you,

---

2. **crown:** The crown, or krone, is the basic unit of currency in Norway.

3. **macaroons** (măk′ə-ro͞onz′): sweet, chewy cookies.

Customizing Instruction

Less Proficient Readers

- Help students understand the different attitudes toward money that Nora and Torvald seem to show. *(Nora enjoys spending money and doesn't worry about keeping track of it. Torvald takes money seriously, is very careful about spending, and despises borrowing.)*
- Tell students to watch for small details that tell them something about a character. For example, draw their attention to the fact that Nora puts away the bag of macaroons and wipes her mouth when she begins to talk to Torvald. Ask them what these actions might mean.
  Possible Response: She doesn't want him to see her eating macaroons for some reason.

English Learners

- Explain the description of the setting on page 1020. You might want to make a diagram to help students visualize the room. Also suggest to them that as they read, they look for details of the setting in the photographs from movie and stage productions that are found throughout the play.
- Explain that the terms *lark* and *squirrel* are not referring to actual animals but are names Torvald uses to refer to Nora in a playful way.
- Make sure students understand the following terms: p. 1020, "nurse" *(nanny or caretaker);* p. 1021, col. 1: "trimmed" *(decorated with ornaments);* "spendthrift" *(person who spends money foolishly);* "economize" *(spend money carefully);* "squandering" *(wasting money)*
- Help students keep track of what is happening by having them give oral summaries of short passsages throughout the play.

Advanced Learners

Tell students that Ibsen makes use of foreshadowing in *A Doll House.* Remind them that foreshadowing is a writer's use of hints or clues that suggest what events will occur later. Have them look for examples as they read. Suggest that as they get farther along in the play they go back to earlier sections to check for examples of foreshadowing that they didn't recognize at their first reading. Have them keep a list, noting also how foreshadowing at times involves irony.

A DOLL HOUSE, ACT ONE **1021**

Active Reading DIALOGUE
Tell students that reading dialogue aloud can give a clearer and more vivid sense of what a character is like and how characters relate to each other. Have students work in pairs to read through the conversation between Nora and Torvald on page 1022, beginning with Nora's first complete speech. Then ask students to describe how Nora and Torvald behave with each other.
Possible Response: The two seem playful and affectionate but also somewhat manipulative. Nora acts the part of the frivolous woman, and Torvald acts like the all-knowing wise husband.

Literary Analysis FORESHADOWING
A Remind students that foreshadowing is a writer's use of hints or clues that suggest what events will occur later in a narrative. Tell students to keep these statements of Nora's in mind as they read the play.

Reading Skills and Strategies CLARIFYING
B Torvald thinks Nora is careless with money. What does he say is the cause of this fault? *(He says she inherited the behavior from her father.)*

Reading Skills and Strategies MAKING INFERENCES
Ask students who controls the money in the Helmer family. *(Torvald)*

Literary Analysis DICTION
Tell students that diction, or word choice, is an important element of style because it can convey attitudes as well as ideas. Ask students what is conveyed by Torvald's use of the words *bird* and *lark* when he is talking to Nora.
Possible Response: They are terms of affection, but they also give a sense of Torvald's superior attitude toward Nora. When he refers to her as one of "those little birds" and calls her "my sweet little lark," he sounds like he thinks of her as a child or plaything.

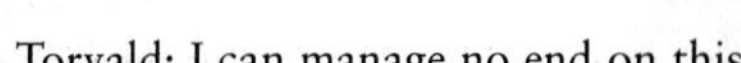

Torvald; I can manage no end on this.

Helmer. You really will have to.

Nora. Oh yes, I promise I will! But come here so I can show you everything I bought. And so cheap! Look, new clothes for Ivar[4] here—and a sword. Here a horse and a trumpet for Bob. And a doll and a doll's bed here for Emmy; they're nothing much, but she'll tear them to bits in no time anyway. And here I have dress material and handkerchiefs for the maids. Old Anne-Marie really deserves something more.

Helmer. And what's in that package there?

Nora (*with a cry*). Torvald, no! You can't see that till tonight!

Helmer. I see. But tell me now, you little prodigal,[5] what have you thought of for yourself?

A **Nora.** For myself? Oh, I don't want anything at all.

Helmer. Of course you do. Tell me just what—within reason—you'd most like to have.

Nora. I honestly don't know. Oh, listen, Torvald—

Helmer. Well?

Nora (*fumbling at his coat buttons, without looking at him*). If you want to give me something, then maybe you could—you could—

Helmer. Come on, out with it.

Nora (*hurriedly*). You could give me money, Torvald. No more than you think you can spare; then one of these days I'll buy something with it.

Helmer. But Nora—

Nora. Oh, please, Torvald darling, do that! I beg you, please. Then I could hang the bills in pretty gilt paper on the Christmas tree. Wouldn't that be fun?

Helmer. What are those little birds called that always fly through their fortunes?

Nora. Oh yes, spendthrifts; I know all that. But let's do as I say, Torvald; then I'll have time to decide what I really need most. That's very sensible, isn't it?

Helmer (*smiling*). Yes, very—that is, if you actually hung onto the money I give you, and you actually used it to buy yourself something. But it goes for the house and for all sorts of foolish things, and then I only have to lay out some more.

Nora. Oh, but Torvald—

Helmer. Don't deny it, my dear little Nora. (*Putting his arm around her waist.*) Spendthrifts are sweet, but they use up a frightful amount of money. It's incredible what it costs a man to feed such birds.

Nora. Oh, how can you say that! Really, I save everything I can.

Helmer (*laughing*). Yes, that's the truth. Everything you can. But that's nothing at all.

Nora (*humming, with a smile of quiet satisfaction*). Hm, if you only knew what expenses we larks and squirrels have, Torvald.

Helmer. You're an odd little one. Exactly the way your father was. You're never at a loss for scaring up money; but the moment you have it, it runs right out through your fingers; you never know what you've done with it. Well, one takes you as you are. It's deep in your blood. Yes, these things are hereditary, Nora. B

Nora. Ah, I could wish I'd inherited many of Papa's qualities.

Helmer. And I couldn't wish you anything but just what you are, my sweet little lark. But wait; it seems to me you have a very—what should I call it?—a very suspicious look today—

Nora. I do?

4. **Ivar** (ē′vär).

5. **prodigal** (prŏd′ĭ-gəl): a person who is foolishly extravagant.

For myself?
Oh, I don't want anything at all.

Claire Bloom as Nora and Anthony Hopkins as Torvald in a 1973 film of *A Doll's House*, directed by Patrick Garland

Customizing Instruction

English Learners

1 Explain that "bills" refers to paper money and that Nora is describing wrapping the bills in gilt, or thin gold-colored paper, and hanging them on the Christmas tree.

Make sure students understand the following terms: p. 1022, col. 1: "within reason" *(actually possible, not something wildly extravgant);*
p. 1022, col. 2: "hereditary" *(a trait inherited, or passed down, from an earlier generation);* "suspicious look" *(a facial expression that shows that the person is trying to hide something)*

Since reading dialogue aloud is especially beneficial for students learning English, you might want to have them continue to read short sections aloud from time to time as they make their way through the play. Students could choose to read the lines of the same character each time, or they could switch characters.

Less Proficient Readers

2 Make sure students understand that Torvald refers to the spendthrift as a bird in the next few speeches.

Tell students that all the action in Act One takes place during the day on Christmas Eve.

MINI LESSON Viewing and Representing

ART APPRECIATION *A Doll House* has been performed continuously since its first production in 1879. In addition to many stage productions, there also have been several film versions. The movie that this still is taken from had a stellar cast that included—in addition to Claire Bloom and Anthony Hopkins—Sir Ralph Richardson, Anna Massey, Denholm Elliott, and Dame Edith Evans.

Instruction Tell students that details of dress, facial expression, and posture can provide clues to a character's personality or attitudes. Ask students to look closely at this photograph and think about what the details tell about Nora.

Possible Response: Nora's flowered dress with lace at the neck, her jewelry, and the curls in her hair make her look feminine in a traditional way. Her facial expression looks warm and open, and the way she is leaning on Torvald and holding his hand gives a sense of ease and intimacy between them.

Reading and Analyzing

Reading Skills and Strategies
CONNECTING

A Ask students to think about how they would feel if they were Nora and Torvald scolded them and shook his finger at them.

Possible Response: Most students would feel annoyed or angry and would not tolerate such behavior.

Literary Analysis
REALISTIC DRAMA: CHARACTERS

Remind students that a writer can reveal characters through their words and actions. Ask students what they learn about Nora and about Torvald from the conversation about whether or not Nora ate some macaroons.

Possible Response: Torvald acts like he has the right to rule Nora's actions. He treats her like a naughty little child. Nora seems to be afraid of Torvald, because she lies to him and pretends she hasn't had anything sweet to eat.

Then ask what this scene reveals about their relationship. *(They are not honest with each other and do not behave as two equal adults.)*

Literary Analysis DRAMATIC IRONY

B Remind students that dramatic irony occurs when the reader or viewer knows something that a character doesn't. Ask students to explain why Nora's statement is an example of dramatic irony. *(The reader knows that Nora has in fact just gone against Torvald by eating the macaroons, but he doesn't know this.)*

Literary Analysis FOIL CHARACTER

Tell students that a foil character provides a striking contrast to another character. Suggest that they watch for ways in which Mrs. Linde might be a foil character to Nora.

Helmer. You certainly do. Look me straight in the eye.

Nora (*looking at him*). Well?

A **Helmer** (*shaking an admonitory*[6] *finger*). Surely my sweet tooth hasn't been running riot in town today, has she?

Nora. No. Why do you imagine that?

Helmer. My sweet tooth really didn't make a little detour through the confectioner's?[7]

Nora. No, I assure you, Torvald—

Helmer. Hasn't nibbled some pastry?

Nora. No, not at all.

Helmer. Not even munched a macaroon or two?

Nora. No, Torvald, I assure you, really—

Helmer. There, there now. Of course I'm only joking.

B **Nora** (*going to the table, right*). You know I could never think of going against you.

Helmer. No, I understand that; and you *have* given me your word. (*Going over to her.*) Well, you keep your little Christmas secrets to yourself, Nora darling. I expect they'll come to light this evening, when the tree is lit.

Nora. Did you remember to ask Dr. Rank?

Helmer. No. But there's no need for that; it's assumed he'll be dining with us. All the same, I'll ask him when he stops by here this morning. I've ordered some fine wine. Nora, you can't imagine how I'm looking forward to this evening.

Nora. So am I. And what fun for the children, Torvald!

Helmer. Ah, it's so gratifying to know that one's gotten a safe, secure job, and with a comfortable salary. It's a great satisfaction, isn't it?

Nora. Oh, it's wonderful!

Helmer. Remember last Christmas? Three whole weeks before, you shut yourself in every evening till long after midnight, making flowers for the Christmas tree, and all the other decorations to surprise us. Ugh, that was the dullest time I've ever lived through.

Nora. It wasn't at all dull for me.

Helmer (*smiling*). But the outcome *was* pretty sorry, Nora.

Nora. Oh, don't tease me with that again. How could I help it that the cat came in and tore everything to shreds.

Helmer. No, poor thing, you certainly couldn't. You wanted so much to please us all, and that's what counts. But it's just as well that the hard times are past.

Nora. Yes, it's really wonderful.

Helmer. Now I don't have to sit here alone, boring myself, and you don't have to tire your precious eyes and your fair little delicate hands—

Nora (*clapping her hands*). No, is it really true, Torvald, I don't have to? Oh, how wonderfully lovely to hear! (*Taking his arm.*) Now I'll tell you just how I've thought we should plan things. Right after Christmas—(*The doorbell rings.*) Oh, the bell. (*Straightening the room up a bit.*) Somebody would have to come. What a bore!

Helmer. I'm not at home to visitors, don't forget. 1

Maid (*from the hall doorway*). Ma'am, a lady to see you—

Nora. All right, let her come in.

Maid (*to* Helmer). And the doctor's just come too.

Helmer. Did he go right to my study?

Maid. Yes, he did.

(Helmer *goes into his room. The* Maid *shows in* Mrs. Linde, *dressed in traveling clothes, and shuts the door after her.*)

---

6. **admonitory** (ăd-mŏn′ĭ-tôr′ē): expressing advice or warning.

7. **confectioner's:** a store where candy and other sweets are sold.

MINI LESSON Speaking and Listening

DRAMATIC PRESENTATION

Prepare Actors use the following techniques to stress ideas and convey emotions:

- changes in volume, or loudness, of speech
- changes in speed of delivery
- changes in tone of voice
- facial expressions
- gestures or other body language

Have students work in pairs to prepare and present the scene with Nora and Torvald, beginning with Torvald's second speech on page 1024, column 1, and ending with Nora's fourth speech in column 2.

Present While each pair of students gives their dramatic presentations, have the rest of the class practice their listening skills. Encourage them to take notes, jotting down the techniques the actors use to stress ideas and convey emotions. After each presentation, invite students to share their suggestions for improvement with the actors.

This activity is particularly well suited for longer class periods.

Mrs. Linde (*in a dispirited and somewhat hesitant voice*). Hello, Nora.

Nora (*uncertain*). Hello—

Mrs. Linde. You don't recognize me.

Nora. No, I don't know—but wait, I think— (*Exclaiming.*) What! Kristine! Is it really you?

Mrs. Linde. Yes, it's me.

Nora. Kristine! To think I didn't recognize you. But then, how could I? (*More quietly.*) How you've changed, Kristine!

Mrs. Linde. Yes, no doubt I have. In nine—ten long years.

Nora. Is it so long since we met! Yes, it's all of that. Oh, these last eight years have been a happy time, believe me. And so now you've come in to town, too. Made the long trip in the winter. That took courage.

Mrs. Linde. I just got here by ship this morning.

Nora. To enjoy yourself over Christmas, of course. Oh, how lovely! Yes, enjoy ourselves, we'll do that. But take your coat off. You're not still cold? (*Helping her.*) There now, let's get cozy here by the stove. No, the easy chair there! I'll take the rocker here. (*Seizing her hands.*) Yes, now you have your old look again; it was only in that first moment. You're a bit more pale, Kristine—and maybe a bit thinner.

Mrs. Linde. And much, much older, Nora.

Nora. Yes, perhaps a bit older; a tiny, tiny bit; not much at all. (*Stopping short; suddenly serious.*) Oh, but thoughtless me, to sit here, chattering away. Sweet, good Kristine, can you forgive me?

Mrs. Linde. What do you mean, Nora?

Nora (*softly*). Poor Kristine, you've become a widow.

Mrs. Linde. Yes, three years ago.

Nora. Oh, I knew it, of course; I read it in the papers. Oh, Kristine, you must believe me; I often thought of writing you then, but I kept postponing it, and something always interfered.

Mrs. Linde. Nora dear, I understand completely.

Nora. No, it was awful of me, Kristine. You poor thing, how much you must have gone through. And he left you nothing?

Mrs. Linde. No.

Nora. And no children?

Mrs. Linde. No.

Nora. Nothing at all, then?

Mrs. Linde. Not even a sense of loss to feed on. 2

Nora (*looking incredulously at her*). But Kristine, how could that be?

Mrs. Linde (*smiling wearily and smoothing her hair*). Oh, sometimes it happens, Nora.

Nora. So completely alone. How terribly hard that must be for you. I have three lovely children. You can't see them now; they're out with the maid. But now you must tell me everything—

Mrs. Linde. No, no, no, tell me about yourself.

Nora. No, you begin. Today I don't want to be selfish. I want to think only of you today. But there *is* something I must tell you. Did you hear of the wonderful luck we had recently?

Mrs. Linde. No, what's that?

Nora. My husband's been made manager in the bank, just think!

Mrs. Linde. Your husband? How marvelous!

Nora. Isn't it? Being a lawyer is such an uncertain living, you know, especially if one won't touch any cases that aren't clean and decent. And of 3
course Torvald would never do that, and I'm with him completely there. Oh, we're simply delighted, believe me! He'll join the bank right after New Year's and start getting a huge

Customizing Instruction

Less Proficient Readers

1 Explain that in the society of the time, "not at home to visitors" meant that you would not be available to anyone who might come to see you. Although this could be intended as a snub, it was often, as in this case, simply a socially accepted practice that people understood as a convenience.

2 Explain that Mrs. Linde is indicating that she did not have a close relationship to her husband and is not experiencing grief. She apparently has no emotional connection, not even sorrow, to her husband—nothing to "feed on."

English Learners

Make sure students understand the following terms: p. 1024, col. 1: "gratifying" *(pleasing);* p. 1024, col. 2: "delicate" *(fine and beautiful);* p. 1025, col. 1: "Is it really you?" *(This is an exclamation of amazement, not a literal question. Nora is very surpised to see Mrs. Linde.);*
p. 1025, col. 2: "incredulously" *(with disbelief)*

3 Explain that Torvald has high standards and won't take on work that has any hint of being illegal.

Advanced Learners

Have students discuss Nora's conversation with Mrs. Linde on page 1025. Ask them to identify aspects of Nora's character that are revealed.

Possible Response: Nora is superficially warm and friendly, but she in fact has ignored Mrs. Linde for years and constantly interrupts her when she tries to talk. Nora speaks of Mrs. Linde's hardships but then immediately starts talking about her own good fortune. Nora is self-absorbed and doesn't understand her own behavior very clearly.

Cross Curricular Link

Geography

NORWAY Mrs. Linde travels by ship to get from her home in a rural part of Norway to the city where Nora lives. Norway has a long coastline, which is cut by deep, narrow inlets, called fjords. Scattered along the coast are about 50,000 islands. Because much of Norway is mountainous, with little farmland, most of its people live near the sea. Winds from the ocean keep the temperatures moderate along the coast, even though one-third of Norway extends north of the Arctic Circle. The harbors are navigable year-round.

Norwegians have been seafarers for many centuries. The Vikings began their invasions of western Europe about 800 A.D. They eventually made their way to Iceland, Greenland, and North America. Norway was exporting dried fish as early as 1200, and they developed their shipping industry in the 1600s. Today, Norway is a world leader in the fishing and shipping industries and is well-known for shipbuilding as well.

Norway's coasts are beautiful and are a major tourist attraction. The mountains reach right to the sea, forming sheer cliffs. They are laced with rushing rivers and high waterfalls, creating dramatic landscapes for those who travel by ship in and out of the fjords.

Reading Skills and Strategies
CLARIFYING
Ask students how Mrs. Linde views Nora.
Possible Response: Mrs. Linde thinks Nora has had an easy life with plenty of money and knows nothing of real hardship or struggle.

Active Reading STAGE DIRECTIONS
A Point out the stage direction, "Casually." Ask students what they think Ibsen is trying to suggest with this word.
Possible Response: The word seems to indicate that Nora is trying to sound as though what she is talking about has little importance. The reader gets the impression that the opposite might be true, however. The words "and such" seem to hint at something significant.

Literary Analysis
REALISTIC DRAMA: CHARACTERS
B Point out Nora's comment about Dr. Rank. Tell students to look for clues to his relationship to Nora and Torvald as the play progresses.

salary and lots of commissions. From now on we can live quite differently—just as we want. Oh, Kristine, I feel so light and happy! Won't it be lovely to have stacks of money and not a care in the world?

Mrs. Linde. Well, anyway, it would be lovely to have enough for necessities.

Nora. No, not just for necessities, but stacks and stacks of money!

Mrs. Linde (*smiling*). Nora, Nora, aren't you sensible yet? Back in school you were such a free spender.

Nora (*with a quiet laugh*). Yes, that's what Torvald still says. (*Shaking her finger.*) But "Nora, Nora" isn't as silly as you all think. Really, we've been in no position for me to go squandering. We've had to work, both of us.

Mrs. Linde. You too?

A **Nora.** Yes, at odd jobs—needlework, crocheting, embroidery, and such—(*Casually.*) and other things too. You remember that Torvald left the department when we were married? There was no chance of promotion in his office, and of course he needed to earn more money. But that first year he drove himself terribly. He took on all kinds of extra work that kept him going morning and night. It wore him down, and then he fell deathly ill. The doctors said it was essential for him to travel south.

Mrs. Linde. Yes, didn't you spend a whole year in Italy?

Nora. That's right. It wasn't easy to get away, you know. Ivar had just been born. But of course we had to go. Oh, that was a beautiful trip, and it saved Torvald's life. But it cost a frightful sum, Kristine.

Mrs. Linde. I can well imagine.

Nora. Four thousand, eight hundred crowns it cost. That's really a lot of money.

Mrs. Linde. But it's lucky you had it when you needed it.

Nora. Well, as it was, we got it from Papa.

Mrs. Linde. I see. It was just about the time your father died.

Nora. Yes, just about then. And, you know, I couldn't make that trip out to nurse him. I had to stay here, expecting Ivar any moment, and with my poor sick Torvald to care for. Dearest Papa, I never saw him again, Kristine. Oh, that was the worst time I've known in all my marriage.

Mrs. Linde. I know how you loved him. And then you went off to Italy?

Nora. Yes. We had the means now, and the doctors urged us. So we left a month after.

Mrs. Linde. And your husband came back completely cured?

Nora. Sound as a drum!

Mrs. Linde. But—the doctor?

Nora. Who?

Mrs. Linde. I thought the maid said he was a doctor, the man who came in with me. 1

Nora. Yes, that was Dr. Rank—but he's not making a sick call. He's our closest friend, and he stops by at least once a day. No, Torvald hasn't had a sick moment since, and the children are fit and strong, and I am, too. (*Jumping up and clapping her hands.*) Oh, dear God, Kristine, what a lovely thing to live and be happy! But how disgusting of me—I'm talking of nothing but my own affairs. (*Sits on a stool close by* Kristine, *arms resting across her knees.*) Oh, don't be angry with me! Tell me, is it really true that you weren't in love with your husband? Why did you marry him, then?

Mrs. Linde. My mother was still alive, but bedridden and helpless—and I had my two younger brothers to look after. In all conscience, I didn't think I could turn him down.

Science and History

MEDICINE IN THE 19TH CENTURY Nora explains to Mrs. Linde that when Torvald became seriously ill when they were first married, the doctors said he had to travel south if he was going to recover. In the 19th century, medical care was limited and inadequate. Antibiotics did not exist, and a variety of questionable remedies and practices were used to treat disease—often to little effect, and sometimes to the harm of the patient. An understanding of the germ theory of disease was only beginning to emerge. Doctors treated most people at home; hospitals were a last resort of the poor, who went there to die.

Fresh air and sunshine were often recommended for those with long-term illnesses, such as tuberculosis. For those who could afford it, travel to a warmer climate, such as Italy, was their best hope for a cure.

Nora. No, you were right there. But was he rich at the time?

Mrs. Linde. He was very well off, I'd say. But the business was shaky, Nora. When he died, it all fell apart, and nothing was left.

Nora. And then—?

Mrs. Linde. Yes, so I had to scrape up a living with a little shop and a little teaching and whatever else I could find. The last three years have been like one endless workday without a rest for me. Now it's over, Nora. My poor mother doesn't need me, for she's passed on. Nor the boys, either; they're working now and can take care of themselves.

Nora. How free you must feel—

Mrs. Linde. No—only unspeakably empty. Nothing to live for now. (*Standing up anxiously.*) That's why I couldn't take it any longer out in that desolate hole. Maybe here it'll be easier to find something to do and keep my mind occupied. If I could only be lucky enough to get a steady job, some office work—

Nora. Oh, but Kristine, that's so dreadfully tiring, and you already look so tired. It would be much better for you if you could go off to a bathing resort.

Mrs. Linde (*going toward the window*). I have no father to give me travel money, Nora.

Nora (*rising*). Oh, don't be angry with me.

Mrs. Linde (*going to her*). Nora dear, don't you be angry with me. The worst of my kind of situation is all the bitterness that's stored away. No one to work for, and yet you're always having to snap up your opportunities. You have to live; and so you grow selfish. When you told me the happy change in your lot, do you know I was delighted less for your sakes than for mine?

Nora. How so? Oh, I see. You think maybe Torvald could do something for you.

Mrs. Linde. Yes, that's what I thought.

Nora. And he will, Kristine! Just leave it to me; I'll bring it up so delicately—find something attractive to humor him with. Oh, I'm so eager to help you.

Mrs. Linde. How very kind of you, Nora, to be so concerned over me—doubly kind, considering you really know so little of life's burdens yourself.

Nora. I—? I know so little—?

Mrs. Linde (*smiling*). Well, my heavens—a little needlework and such—Nora, you're just a child.

Nora (*tossing her head and pacing the floor*). You don't have to act so superior.

Mrs. Linde. Oh?

Nora. You're just like the others. You all think I'm incapable of anything serious—

Mrs. Linde. Come now—

Nora. That I've never had to face the raw world.

Mrs. Linde. Nora dear, you've just been telling me all your troubles.

Nora. Hm! Trivia! (*Quietly.*) I haven't told you the big thing.

Mrs. Linde. Big thing? What do you mean?

Nora. You look down on me so, Kristine, but you shouldn't. You're proud that you worked so long and hard for your mother.

Mrs. Linde. I don't look down on a soul. But it *is* true: I'm proud—and happy, too—to think it was given to me to make my mother's last days almost free of care.

Nora. And you're also proud thinking of what you've done for your brothers.

Mrs. Linde. I feel I've a right to be.

Nora. I agree. But listen to this, Kristine—I've also got something to be proud and happy for.

WORDS TO KNOW

desolate (dĕs′ə-lĭt) *adj.* barren; empty; dismal

Plot Diagram

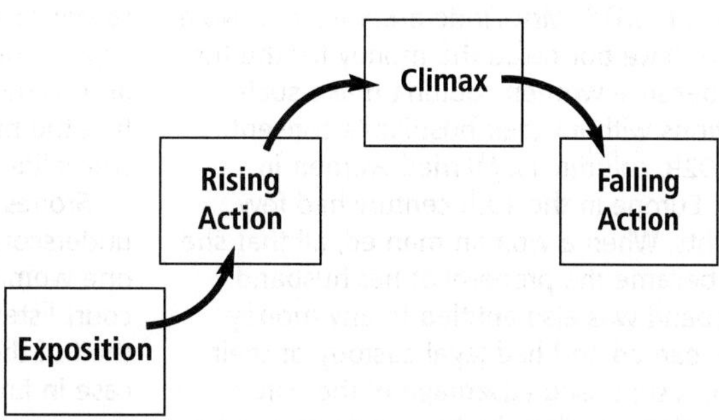

Customizing Instruction

Less Proficient Readers

1 Guide students to understand Mrs. Linde's misunderstanding about Dr. Rank. *(She thinks he has come because someone is ill.)*

2 Help students understand why Mrs. Linde is glad to hear Nora's good news. *(She hopes Torvald will give her a job now that he will be a manager at the bank.)*

Set a Purpose At the end of page 1027, Nora talks about "the big thing". Tell students to read to find out what this thing is.

English Learners

- Work with students to summarize orally Mrs. Linde's story. Make sure they understand that her primary need is to find work.
- Make sure students understand the following terms: p. 1026, col. 1: "odd jobs" *(short-term jobs that do not require professional skills);* p. 1026, col. 2: "sound as a drum" *(a common expression meaning "very healthy");* p. 1027, col. 1: "scrape up a living" *(do various low-paying jobs to get enough money to live on);* p. 1027, col. 2: "humor him" *(go along with what he likes or wants)*

Advanced Learners

Remind students that a **plot** is made up of four elements:

- **exposition** (The characters are introduced, the setting is established, and the major conflict is identified.)
- **rising action** (Suspense builds as the conflict intensifies and complications arise.)
- **climax** (The turning point often occurs when a main character makes an important discovery or decision.)
- **falling action** (The falling action shows the results of the climax and ties up the loose ends.)

Suggest that students work in pairs to begin identifying the events in Act One that belong to the exposition. Have them use a diagram like the one shown on the left, and tell them to continue to identify elements of the exposition as they read the rest of Act One.

Possible Responses: exposition: At this point in the play, three major characters have been introduced (Nora, Torvald, and Mrs. Linde), the relationship between Nora and Torvald has begun to be portrayed, and details of the setting have been given (the Christmas season in a middle-class home in 19th-century Norway).

Reading and Analyzing

Literary Analysis

REALISTIC DRAMA: CHARACTER

Ask students what new aspects of Nora's character are revealed on page 1029.

Possible Response: Nora is not as flighty as she seems. She figured out how to get money to save Torvald and arranged the trip to Italy.

Reading Skills and Strategies

CLARIFYING

Ask students why Torvald is not supposed to know about the money Nora borrowed. *(Nora says that he never knew his life was in danger and must never find out. But more importantly, since Torvald disapproves of borrowing money and since Nora did so without his consent, he mustn't discover what Nora has done.)*

I'll bet you're eaten up with curiosity, Kristine.

Anna Massey as Mrs. Linde

History

WOMEN'S RIGHTS Mrs. Linde assumes that Nora could not have borrowed the money for the trip to Italy because women couldn't make such transactions without their husband's consent (page 1029, column 1). Married women in western Europe in the 19th century had few legal rights. When a woman married, all that she owned became the property of her husband. The husband was also entitled to any money that she earned and had legal custody of their children. A supposed advantage of the wife's legal position was that the husband was legally responsible for her debts and was required to support her as long as she lived with him. This arrangement emphasized, however, the fact that the husband had legal control over his wife's life.

Stories of how the laws were carried out underscore how extreme they were. More than one woman who had her purse stolen sat in court listening to the robbery described as the theft of the property of her husband. A startling case in England involved a married woman who ran a successful hat-making business. When her

Mrs. Linde. I don't doubt it. But whatever do you mean?

Nora. Not so loud. What if Torvald heard! He mustn't, not for anything in the world. Nobody must know, Kristine. No one but you.

Mrs. Linde. But what is it, then?

Nora. Come here. (*Drawing her down beside her on the sofa.*) It's true—I've also got something to be proud and happy for. I'm the one who saved Torvald's life.

Mrs. Linde. Saved—? Saved how?

Nora. I told you about the trip to Italy. Torvald never would have lived if he hadn't gone south—

Mrs. Linde. Of course; your father gave you the means—

Nora (*smiling*). That's what Torvald and all the rest think, but—

Mrs. Linde. But—?

Nora. Papa didn't give us a pin. I was the one who raised the money.

Mrs. Linde. You? That whole amount?

Nora. Four thousand, eight hundred crowns. What do you say to that?

Mrs. Linde. But Nora, how was it possible? Did you win the lottery?

Nora (*disdainfully*). The lottery? Pooh! No art to that.

Mrs. Linde. But where did you get it from then?

Nora (*humming, with a mysterious smile*). Hmm, tra-la-la-la.

Mrs. Linde. Because you couldn't have borrowed it.

Nora. No? Why not?

Mrs. Linde. A wife can't borrow without her husband's consent.

Nora (*tossing her head*). Oh, but a wife with a little business sense, a wife who knows how to manage—

Mrs. Linde. Nora, I simply don't understand—

Nora. You don't have to. Whoever said I *borrowed* the money? I could have gotten it other ways. (*Throwing herself back on the sofa.*) I could have gotten it from some admirer or other. After all, a girl with my ravishing[8] appeal—

Mrs. Linde. You lunatic.

Nora. I'll bet you're eaten up with curiosity, Kristine.

Mrs. Linde. Now listen here, Nora—you haven't done something indiscreet?[9]

Nora (*sitting up again*). Is it indiscreet to save your husband's life?

Mrs. Linde. I think it's indiscreet that without his knowledge you—

Nora. But that's the point: he mustn't know! My Lord, can't you understand? He mustn't ever know the close call he had. It was to *me* the doctors came to say his life was in danger—that nothing could save him but a stay in the south. Didn't I try strategy then! I began talking about how lovely it would be for me to travel abroad like other young wives; I begged and I cried; I told him please to remember my condition, to be kind and indulge me; and then I dropped a hint that he could easily take out a loan. But at that, Kristine, he nearly exploded. He said I was frivolous, and it was his duty as man of the house not to indulge me in whims and fancies—as I think he called them. Aha, I thought, now you'll just have to be saved—and that's when I saw my chance.

Mrs. Linde. And your father never told Torvald the money wasn't from him?

Nora. No, never. Papa died right about then. I'd considered bringing him into my secret and

8. **ravishing:** extremely attractive.

9. **indiscreet:** not showing self-restraint or good judgment; unwise.

husband died, she learned that in his will he gave her business to his illegitimate children. She was left penniless.

Married women in the 19th century have been called non-persons in the view of the law. In addition to their husbands owning their property, they were not allowed to make contracts (the law that Mrs. Linde is referring to), they could not bear witness in court, and they could not initiate lawsuits. Divorce, which was not common in any case, was also harsh for women. No matter how cruel or dangerous a husband was, if his wife left, she still had no right to any property, and he kept custody of the children. Women began to oppose these inequities, but it took well into the 20th century for many of them to be addressed.

Customizing Instruction

Less Proficient Readers

Ask students what the "big thing" was that Nora spoke of on page 1027. *(She raised the money for the trip to Italy herself and saved Torvald's life.)*

English Learners

- Guide students through the conversation between Nora and Mrs. Linde. Make sure they understand the following:
  - Torvald needed to go to Italy to regain his health.
  - Everyone thinks that Nora's father gave the money for the trip.
  - Nora raised all of the money for the trip herself.
  - Mrs. Linde thinks Nora must have won the lottery and assumes she didn't borrow the money, because at that time it was illegal for a wife to borrow money on her own.
  - Nora pretends there might be some mysterious source of the money, and Mrs. Linde is worried.
  - Nora explains that Torvald did not know how ill he was and she had to find a way to get the money without his knowing, since he refused to borrow money.
  - Nora's father died at about that time, and Torvald never learned that the money wasn't from him.
- Make sure students understand the following terms: p. 1029, col. 2: "strategy" *(a plan of action)*; "travel abroad like other young wives" *(It was common for people in Europe to travel frequently to other parts of the continent.)*; "whims and fancies" *(silly and impractical ideas)*

Advanced Learners

Have students look back over the previous part of Act One to locate examples of foreshadowing and irony relating to the revelation that Nora raised the money for the trip herself.

Possible Responses: (Foreshadowing) p. 1021, col. 1: Torvald's comments on debts and borrowing; p. 1026, col. 2: Nora's references to her father's death, the "worst time"

(Irony) p. 1022, col. 2: Nora's comment that she saves everything she can; Torvald's criticism that she spends all the money she gets; p. 1026, col. 1: Nora's excitement about not having a care in the world

Have students note how the instances of foreshadowing also involve irony.

Reading and Analyzing

Reading Skills and Strategies
CLARIFYING

Ask students how Nora got the money to meet her loan payments. ***(She saved money out of the allowance Torvald gave her for personal spending, and she took jobs copying documents. On page 1026, col. 1, she also tells Mrs. Linde that she had had odd jobs doing needlework.)***

Literary Analysis
REALISTIC DRAMA: CHARACTER

Ask students what they learn about Nora from reading these pages.

Possible Response: She has been shrewd in figuring out ways to get money to pay the loan. She also has worked hard and made sacrifices for a long time. She seems to like to shock Mrs. Linde, as shown by her prattling on about the imaginary "rich old gentleman." She also is still insensitive to Mrs. Linde's position when she talks enthusiastically about being carefree. She becomes uneasy when Krogstad enters, however.

Active Reading STAGE DIRECTIONS

A Have students review the stage directions related to Mrs. Linde and to Nora when Krogstad enters. Ask them to discuss what they think these stage directions might suggest.

Possible Responses: The fact that Mrs. Linde is startled and turns away from Krogstad seems to indicate that there is some connection between them, apparently something uncomfortable. Nora's tensions and whispering to Krogstad seem to indicate that she has some relationship with him that she doesn't want revealed.

Literary Analysis FOIL CHARACTER

Ask students how Mrs. Linde is a foil for Nora.

Possible Response: Mrs. Linde has had a somewhat harsh life. She has been poor, has had to take care of her mother and brothers, and is now a widow. She is also a practical, serious person who faces life realistically.

begging him never to tell. But he was too sick at the time—and then, sadly, it didn't matter.

Mrs. Linde. And you've never confided in your husband since?

Nora. For heaven's sake, no! Are you serious? He's so strict on that subject. Besides—Torvald, with all his masculine pride—how painfully humiliating for him if he ever found out he was in debt to me. That would just ruin our relationship. Our beautiful, happy home would never be the same.

Mrs. Linde. Won't you ever tell him?

Nora (*thoughtfully, half smiling*). Yes—maybe sometime, years from now, when I'm no longer so attractive. Don't laugh! I only mean when Torvald loves me less than now, when he stops enjoying my dancing and dressing up and reciting for him. Then it might be wise to have something in reserve—(*Breaking off.*) How ridiculous! That'll never happen— Well, Kristine, what do you think of my big secret? I'm capable of something too, hm? You can imagine, of course, how this thing hangs over me. It really hasn't been easy meeting the payments on time. In the business world there's what they call quarterly interest and what they call amortization,[10] and these are always so terribly hard to manage. I've had to skimp a little here and there, wherever I could, you know. I could hardly spare anything from my house allowance, because Torvald has to live well. I couldn't let the children go poorly dressed; whatever I got for them, I felt I had to use up completely—the darlings!

Mrs. Linde. Poor Nora, so it had to come out of your own budget, then?

Nora. Yes, of course. But I was the one most responsible, too. Every time Torvald gave me money for new clothes and such, I never used more than half; always bought the simplest, cheapest outfits. It was a godsend that everything looks so well on me that Torvald never noticed. But it did weigh me down at times, Kristine. It *is* such a joy to wear fine things. You understand.

Mrs. Linde. Oh, of course.

Nora. And then I found other ways of making money. Last winter I was lucky enough to get a lot of copying to do. I locked myself in and sat writing every evening till late in the night. Ah, I was tired so often, dead tired. But still it was wonderful fun, sitting and working like that, earning money. It was almost like being a man.

Mrs. Linde. But how much have you paid off this way so far?

Nora. That's hard to say, exactly. These accounts, you know, aren't easy to figure. I only know that I've paid out all I could scrape together. Time and again I haven't known where to turn. (*Smiling.*) Then I'd sit here dreaming of a rich old gentleman who had fallen in love with me—

Mrs. Linde. What! Who is he?

Nora. Oh, really! And that he'd died, and when his will was opened, there in big letters it said, "All my fortune shall be paid over in cash, immediately, to that enchanting Mrs. Nora Helmer." 1

Mrs. Linde. But Nora dear—who *was* this gentleman?

Nora. Good grief, can't you understand? The old man never existed; that was only something I'd dream up time and again whenever I was at my wits' end for money. But it makes no difference now; the old fossil can go where he pleases for all I care; I don't need him or his will—because now I'm free. (*Jumping up.*)

10. **amortization** (ăm′ər-tĭ-zā′shən): the repayment of a debt by installments, with the interest on the debt decreasing from payment to payment.

Oh, how lovely to think of that, Kristine! Carefree! To know you're carefree, utterly carefree; to be able to romp and play with the children, and to keep up a beautiful, charming home—everything just the way Torvald likes it! And think, spring is coming, with big blue skies. Maybe we can travel a little then. Maybe I'll see the ocean again. Oh yes, it *is* so marvelous to live and be happy!

(*The front doorbell rings.*)

Mrs. Linde. (*rising*). There's the bell. It's probably best that I go.

Nora. No, stay. No one's expected. It must be for Torvald.

Maid (*from the hall doorway*). Excuse me, ma'am—there's a gentleman here to see Mr. Helmer, but I didn't know—since the doctor's with him—

Nora. Who is the gentleman?

Krogstad (*from the doorway*). It's me, Mrs. Helmer.

A (Mrs. Linde *starts and turns away toward the window.*)

Nora (*stepping toward him, tense, her voice a whisper*). You? What is it? Why do you want to speak to my husband?

Krogstad. Bank business—after a fashion. I have a small job in the investment bank, and I hear now your husband is going to be our chief—

Nora. In other words, it's—

Krogstad. Just dry business, Mrs. Helmer. Nothing but that.

Nora. Yes, then please be good enough to step into the study. (*She nods indifferently as she sees him out by the hall door, then returns and begins stirring up the stove.*)

Mrs. Linde. Nora—who was that man?

Nora. That was a Mr. Krogstad—a lawyer.

Mrs. Linde. Then it really was him.

Nora. Do you know that person?

Mrs. Linde. I did once—many years ago. For a time he was a law clerk in our town.

Nora. Yes, he's been that.

Mrs. Linde. How he's changed.

Nora. I understand he had a very unhappy marriage.

Mrs. Linde. He's a widower now.

Nora. With a number of children. There now, it's burning. (*She closes the stove door and moves the rocker a bit to one side.*)

Mrs. Linde. They say he has a hand in all kinds of business.

Nora. Oh? That may be true; I wouldn't know. But let's not think about business. It's so dull.

(Dr. Rank *enters from* Helmer's *study.*)

Rank (*still in the doorway*). No, no, really—I don't want to intrude, I'd just as soon talk a little while with your wife. (*Shuts the door, then notices* Mrs. Linde.) Oh, beg pardon. I'm intruding here too.

Nora. No, not at all. (*Introducing him.*) Dr. Rank, Mrs. Linde.

Rank. Well now, that's a name much heard in this house. I believe I passed the lady on the stairs as I came.

Mrs. Linde. Yes, I take the stairs very slowly. They're rather hard on me.

Rank. Uh-hm, some touch of internal weakness?

Mrs. Linde. More overexertion,[11] I'd say.

Rank. Nothing else? Then you're probably here in town to rest up in a round of parties?

Mrs. Linde. I'm here to look for work.

Rank. Is that the best cure for overexertion?

Mrs. Linde. One has to live, Doctor.

11. **overexertion:** putting out too much strenuous effort; working or exercising too hard.

Customizing Instruction

Less Proficient Readers

- Make sure students understand how Nora got the money to make her loan payments. Explain that Torvald controlled the money in the family and gave Nora specific sums for household expenses, the children's expenses, and her personal expenses. She cut back only on her personal spending in order to save money toward the loan payments. The copying work she took on involved copying legal and business documents by hand. Remind students that there were no typewriters, computers, or photocopying machines in existence at the time.

Set a Purpose Tell students to read on to find out what the relationships are between Krogstad and the Helmers and between Dr. Rank and the Helmers.

English Learners

Make sure students understand the following terms: p. 1030, col. 1: "humiliating" *(causing a loss of dignity or respect);* "your own budget" *(money given to Nora by Torvald for her personal expenses, such as clothes);* 1030, col. 2: "at my wits' end" *(completely out of ideas, not able to figure out anything);*
p. 1031, col. 1: "indifferently" *(showing no interest)*

1 Explain that the "rich old gentleman" is a fantasy of Nora's. When she was having a particularly hard time thinking of ways to get money, she would imagine that there was an old rich man who would fall in love with her, die, and leave her all his money. Also explain that Mrs. Linde misunderstands Nora and thinks there really is such an old man.

Explain that a fossil is a preserved part of a plant or animal from prehistoric times. Calling the man an old fossil is a sarcastic way of referring to his age.

Advanced Learners

Have students discuss Nora's comment about her copying work that "it was wonderful fun, working like that . . . It was almost like being a man." Suggest that they keep this comment, an example of foreshadowing, in mind as they continue to read the play.

Reading and Analyzing

Literary Analysis DRAMATIC IRONY

A Ask students to explain why Rank's statement to Nora that Krogstad is "a type you wouldn't know" is an example of dramatic irony. *(The reader knows that Nora does, in fact, know Krogstad.)*

Literary Analysis

REALISTIC DRAMA: CHARACTER

Point out that Nora lies about where she got the macaroons, (p. 1032, col. 2) and she lies about the reasons for Mrs. Linde's visit (p. 1033, col. 1). Ask students why they think she lies in these situations.

Possible Response: Nora lies about the macaroons because she is afraid of angering Torvald, who has forbidden her to eat them. She lies about Mrs. Linde's reasons in order to manipulate Torvald to get him to help Mrs. Linde.

Then ask what her behavior reveals about her relationship with Torvald. *(He thinks nothing of controlling her life, and she is not able to be direct with him.)*

Literary Analysis FORESHADOWING

B Tell students to keep Rank's description of "a type of person" in mind as they continue to read Act One. When they have finished reading the act, ask them what action in the play this description foreshadows. *(Krogstad's threatening to blackmail Nora)*

Reading Skills and Strategies ANALYZING

C Nora shocks her friends by saying she wants to swear in front of Torvald. Why do you think she has such a strong desire to do this?

Possible Response: Since such language would outrage Torvald, Nora probably wants to do it as a way of rebelling against his strict control, much as a child might rebel against a parent. She probably is not aware of her own motives, however.

Literary Analysis

REALISTIC DRAMA: CHARACTER

Ask students to describe what Dr. Rank is like.

Possible Response: He seems to know Nora very well, and he is polite with Mrs. Linde. He is serious, even somewhat gloomy, and preoccupied with questions of health.

Rank. Yes, there's a common prejudice to that effect.

Nora. Oh, come on, Dr. Rank—you really do want to live yourself.

Rank. Yes, I really do. Wretched as I am, I'll gladly prolong my torment indefinitely. All my patients feel like that. And it's quite the same, too, with the morally sick. Right at this moment there's one of those moral invalids in there with Helmer—

Mrs. Linde (*softly*). Ah!

Nora. Who do you mean?

A **Rank.** Oh, it's a lawyer, Krogstad, a type you wouldn't know. His character is rotten to the root—but even he began chattering all-importantly about how he had to *live.*

Nora. Oh? What did he want to talk to Torvald about?

Rank. I really don't know. I only heard something about the bank.

Nora. I didn't know that Krog—that this man Krogstad had anything to do with the bank.

B **Rank.** Yes, he's gotten some kind of berth down there. (*To* Mrs. Linde.) I don't know if you also have, in your neck of the woods, a type of person who scuttles about breathlessly, sniffing out hints of moral corruption, and then maneuvers his victim into some sort of key position where he can keep an eye on him. It's the healthy these days that are out in the cold.

Mrs. Linde. All the same, it's the sick who most need to be taken in.

Rank (*with a shrug*). Yes, there we have it. That's the concept that's turning society into a sanatorium.[12]

(Nora, *lost in her thoughts, breaks out into quiet laughter and claps her hands.*)

Rank. Why do you laugh at that? Do you have any real idea of what society is?

Nora. What do I care about dreary old society? I was laughing at something quite different—something terribly funny. Tell me, Doctor—is everyone who works in the bank dependent now on Torvald?

Rank. Is that what you find so terribly funny?

Nora (*smiling and humming*). Never mind, never mind! (*Pacing the floor.*) Yes, that's really immensely amusing: that we—that Torvald has so much power now over all those people. (*Taking the bag out of her pocket.*) Dr. Rank, a little macaroon on that?

Rank. See here, macaroons! I thought they were contraband[13] here.

Nora. Yes, but these are some that Kristine gave me.

Mrs. Linde. What? I—?

Nora. Now, now, don't be afraid. You couldn't possibly know that Torvald had forbidden them. You see, he's worried they'll ruin my teeth. But hmp! Just this once! Isn't that so, Dr. Rank? Help yourself! (*Puts a macaroon in his mouth.*) And you too, Kristine. And I'll also have one, only a little one—or two, at the most. (*Walking about again.*) Now I'm really tremendously happy. Now there's just one last thing in the world that I have an enormous desire to do.

Rank. Well! And what's that?

Nora. It's something I have such a consuming desire to say so Torvald could hear.

Rank. And why can't you say it?

Nora. I don't dare. It's quite shocking.

Mrs. Linde. Shocking?

Rank. Well, then it isn't advisable. But in front of us you certainly can. What do you have such a desire to say so Torvald could hear?

12. **sanatorium:** an institution for the treatment of long-term diseases.

13. **contraband:** not allowed.

C Nora. I have such a huge desire to say—to hell and be damned!

Rank. Are you crazy?

Mrs. Linde. My goodness, Nora!

Rank. Go on, say it. Here he is.

Nora (*hiding the macaroon bag*). Shh, shh, shh!

(Helmer *comes in from his study, hat in hand, overcoat over his arm.*)

Nora (*going toward him*). Well, Torvald dear, are you through with him?

Helmer. Yes, he just left.

Nora. Let me introduce you—this is Kristine, who's arrived here in town.

Helmer. Kristine—? I'm sorry, but I don't know—

Nora. Mrs. Linde, Torvald dear. Mrs. Kristine Linde.

Helmer. Of course. A childhood friend of my wife's, no doubt?

Mrs. Linde. Yes, we knew each other in those days.

Nora. And just think, she made the long trip down here in order to talk with you.

Helmer. What's this?

Mrs. Linde. Well, not exactly—

Nora. You see, Kristine is remarkably clever in office work, and so she's terribly eager to come under a capable man's supervision and add more to what she already knows—

Helmer. Very wise, Mrs. Linde.

Nora. And then when she heard that you'd become a bank manager—the story was wired out to the papers—then she came in as fast as she could and—Really, Torvald, for my sake you can do a little something for Kristine, can't you?

Helmer. Yes, it's not at all impossible. Mrs. Linde, I suppose you're a widow?

Mrs. Linde. Yes.

Helmer. Any experience in office work?

Mrs. Linde. Yes, a good deal.

Helmer. Well, it's quite likely that I can make an opening for you—

Nora (*clapping her hands*). You see, you see!

Helmer. You've come at a lucky moment, Mrs. Linde. 1

Mrs. Linde. Oh, how can I thank you?

Helmer. Not necessary. (*Putting his overcoat on.*) But today you'll have to excuse me—

Rank. Wait, I'll go with you. (*He fetches his coat from the hall and warms it at the stove.*)

Nora. Don't stay out long, dear.

Helmer. An hour; no more.

Nora. Are you going too, Kristine?

Mrs. Linde (*putting on her winter garments*). Yes, I have to see about a room now.

Helmer. Then perhaps we can all walk together.

Nora (*helping her*). What a shame we're so cramped here, but it's quite impossible for us to— 2

Mrs. Linde. Oh, don't even think of it! Good-bye, Nora dear, and thanks for everything.

Nora. Good-bye for now. Of course you'll be back this evening. And you too, Dr. Rank. What? If you're well enough? Oh, you've got to be! Wrap up tight now.

(*In a ripple of small talk the company moves out into the hall; children's voices are heard outside on the steps.*)

Nora. There they are! There they are! (*She runs to open the door. The children come in with their nurse,* Anne-Marie.) Come in, come in! (*Bends down and kisses them.*) Oh, you darlings—! Look at them, Kristine. Aren't they lovely!

Rank. No loitering in the draft here.

Customizing Instruction

Less Proficient Readers

Help students understand Rank's comments about Krogstad: Rank calls him a "moral invalid" and "rotten to the root," a person who has low moral standards and will stoop to immoral behavior. He likens Krogstad to an animal sniffing out garbage—he sniffs out failings of other people and then "maneuvers his victim"—in other words, blackmails him or her.

1 Ask students what has happened in these lines. *(Torvald has told Mrs. Linde that he can give her a job.)*

2 Explain that Nora is making excuses to Mrs. Linde for not inviting her to stay with the Helmers at their house.

English Learners

- Make sure students understand the following terms: p. 1032, col. 1: "berth" *(position, job)*; "your neck of the woods" *(the area where you live)*
- Explain that Dr. Rank and Mrs. Linde use words related to being healthy or sick to talk about people who are morally strong or weak.

Advanced Learners

In column 1 on page 1033, Dr. Rank refers to being wretched and prolonging his torment. Suggest that students keep this statement in mind as they read the next act and consider in what ways it may be an example of foreshadowing.

Pause & Reflect
Possible Responses: Torvald thinks Nora is scatterbrained and silly. He treats her like a child and has no idea that she is capable of something like taking out a loan and paying it back. Nora has avoided revealing her secret to Torvald because he is so opposed to borrowing and because he would be furious to find out what she has done behind his back.

Literary Analysis
REALISTIC DRAMA: SETTING
Remind students that the time of a play is part of its setting. Suggest that they think about why Ibsen set *A Doll's House* at Christmastime. Tell them to keep this detail in mind as they continue reading.

Active Reading STAGE DIRECTIONS
A Tell students that in this scene where Nora plays with her children, the dialogue and stage directions are blended together. Point out that only Nora talks, but a great deal of action goes on. Ask students what this passage shows about Nora.
Possible Response: This scene shows that Nora is devoted to her children and genuinely enjoys them. She enters right into their play rather than remaining aloof.

Literary Analysis
REALISTIC DRAMA: CHARACTER
Lead students in a discussion of what kind of person Krogstad seems to be as he appears in these two pages. Have students support their opinions with details and examples from the text.
Possible Response: Krogstad is somewhat threatening (his comment about the merry Christmas Nora might or might not have and his statement that he will fight with his life for his job), brusque (examples throughout), sarcastic (his comment about Torvald not being steadfast), and generally unpleasant.

Helmer. Come, Mrs. Linde—this place is unbearable now for anyone but mothers.

PAUSE & REFLECT Nora has told her secret to Mrs. Linde. How has Torvald misunderstood Nora? Why has she avoided revealing her secret to him?

FOCUS Read to find out how Nora's plans will be complicated by another visitor.

(Dr. Rank, Helmer, *and* Mrs. Linde *go down the stairs.* Anne-Marie *goes into the living room with the children.* Nora *follows, after closing the hall door.*)

Nora. How fresh and strong you look. Oh, such red cheeks you have! Like apples and roses. (*The children interrupt her throughout the following.*) And it was so much fun? That's wonderful. Really? You pulled both Emmy and Bob on the sled? Imagine, all together! Yes, you're a clever boy, Ivar. Oh, let me hold her a bit, Anne-Marie. My sweet little doll baby! (*Takes the smallest from the nurse and dances with her.*) Yes, yes, Mama will dance with Bob as well. What? Did you throw snowballs? Oh, if I'd only been there! No, don't bother, Anne-Marie—I'll undress them myself. Oh yes, let me. It's such fun. Go in and rest; you look half frozen. There's hot coffee waiting for you on the stove. (*The nurse goes into the room to the left.* Nora *takes the children's winter things off, throwing them about, while the children talk to her all at once.*) Is that so? A big dog chased you? But it didn't bite? No, dogs never bite little, lovely doll babies. Don't peek in the packages, Ivar! What is it? Yes, wouldn't you like to know. No, no, it's an ugly something. Well? Shall we play? What shall we play? Hide-and-seek? Yes, let's play hide-and-seek. Bob must hide first. I must? Yes, let me hide first. (*Laughing and shouting, she and the children play in and out of the living room and the adjoining room to the right. At last* Nora *hides under the table. The children come storming in, search, but cannot find her, then hear her muffled laughter, dash over to the table, lift the cloth up and find her. Wild shouting. She creeps forward as if to scare them. More shouts. Meanwhile, a knock at the hall door; no one has noticed it. Now the door half opens, and* Krogstad *appears. He waits a moment; the game goes on.*)

Krogstad. Beg pardon, Mrs. Helmer—

Nora (*with a strangled cry, turning and scrambling to her knees*). Oh! What do you want?

Krogstad. Excuse me. The outer door was ajar; it must be someone forgot to shut it—

Nora (*rising*). My husband isn't home, Mr. Krogstad.

Krogstad. I know that.

Nora. Yes—then what do you want here?

Krogstad. A word with you.

Nora. With—? (*To the children, quietly.*) Go in to Anne-Marie. What? No, the strange man won't hurt Mama. When he's gone, we'll play some more. (*She leads the children into the room to the left and shuts the door after them. Then, tense and nervous:*) You want to speak to me?

Krogstad. Yes, I want to.

Nora. Today? But it's not yet the first of the month—

Krogstad. No, it's Christmas Eve. It's going to be up to you how merry a Christmas you have.

Nora. What is it you want? Today I absolutely can't—

Krogstad. We won't talk about that till later. This is something else. You do have a moment to spare, I suppose?

Nora. Oh yes, of course—I do, except—

Krogstad. Good. I was sitting over at Olsen's

Nora. I have such a huge desire to say—to hell and be damned!

Rank. Are you crazy?

Mrs. Linde. My goodness, Nora!

Rank. Go on, say it. Here he is.

Nora (*hiding the macaroon bag*). Shh, shh, shh!

(Helmer *comes in from his study, hat in hand, overcoat over his arm.*)

Nora (*going toward him*). Well, Torvald dear, are you through with him?

Helmer. Yes, he just left.

Nora. Let me introduce you—this is Kristine, who's arrived here in town.

Helmer. Kristine—? I'm sorry, but I don't know—

Nora. Mrs. Linde, Torvald dear. Mrs. Kristine Linde.

Helmer. Of course. A childhood friend of my wife's, no doubt?

Mrs. Linde. Yes, we knew each other in those days.

Nora. And just think, she made the long trip down here in order to talk with you.

Helmer. What's this?

Mrs. Linde. Well, not exactly—

Nora. You see, Kristine is remarkably clever in office work, and so she's terribly eager to come under a capable man's supervision and add more to what she already knows—

Helmer. Very wise, Mrs. Linde.

Nora. And then when she heard that you'd become a bank manager—the story was wired out to the papers—then she came in as fast as she could and—Really, Torvald, for my sake you can do a little something for Kristine, can't you?

Helmer. Yes, it's not at all impossible. Mrs. Linde, I suppose you're a widow?

Mrs. Linde. Yes.

Helmer. Any experience in office work?

Mrs. Linde. Yes, a good deal.

Helmer. Well, it's quite likely that I can make an opening for you—

Nora (*clapping her hands*). You see, you see!

Helmer. You've come at a lucky moment, Mrs. Linde.

Mrs. Linde. Oh, how can I thank you?

Helmer. Not necessary. (*Putting his overcoat on.*) But today you'll have to excuse me—

Rank. Wait, I'll go with you. (*He fetches his coat from the hall and warms it at the stove.*)

Nora. Don't stay out long, dear.

Helmer. An hour; no more.

Nora. Are you going too, Kristine?

Mrs. Linde (*putting on her winter garments*). Yes, I have to see about a room now.

Helmer. Then perhaps we can all walk together.

Nora (*helping her*). What a shame we're so cramped here, but it's quite impossible for us to—

Mrs. Linde. Oh, don't even think of it! Good-bye, Nora dear, and thanks for everything.

Nora. Good-bye for now. Of course you'll be back this evening. And you too, Dr. Rank. What? If you're well enough? Oh, you've got to be! Wrap up tight now.

(*In a ripple of small talk the company moves out into the hall; children's voices are heard outside on the steps.*)

Nora. There they are! There they are! (*She runs to open the door. The children come in with their nurse,* Anne-Marie.) Come in, come in! (*Bends down and kisses them.*) Oh, you darlings—! Look at them, Kristine. Aren't they lovely!

Rank. No loitering in the draft here.

Customizing Instruction

Less Proficient Readers

Focus Help students understand the relationship between Nora and Krogstad by asking the following questions:

- Do Nora and Krogstad know each other? *(Yes. They know each other's names, Nora refers to expecting to see him on the first of the month, and she refers to "being done with the whole business" after New Year's.)*
- Does their relationship seem to be a friendly one? *(No. Nora seems upset to see him, and Krogstad makes threatening and rude remarks.)*
- What does Krogstad want from Nora? *(He wants her to persuade Torvald to keep him in his job at the bank.)*

English Learners

Make sure students understand the following terms: p. 1035, col. 1: "cross-examine" *(to question a person in a pressuring way)*; "has influence" *(has some power to affect someone's decisions or actions)*; p. 1035, col. 2: "play the innocent" *(act like you don't know anything)*; "relish" *(enjoy)*; "take me so literally" *(interpret everything I say word for word)*; "lady has spirit" *(Nora has energy and fight in her.)*

MINI LESSON Speaking and Listening

DRAMATIC INTERPRETATION

Instruction Discuss with students the impact an actor's performance can have on an audience's interpretation of a play. Explain that although stage directions give some indications about a character's feelings and reactions, the actor makes choices about how to bring that character to life.

Prepare Have students work in groups of three, with one person playing Krogstad and two people playing0 Nora. Ask them to prepare two interpretations of the scene beginning with Krogstad's first speech on page 1034, column 2, and ending with Krogstad's last complete speech on page 1035, column 2. Instruct the first actor taking Nora's part to play her as sympathetically as possible, and instruct the second actor to play her as unsympathetically as possible.

Present Have the class analyze the differences between the two performances. Ask them to discuss the effect of different tones of voice, facial expressions, and word emphasis. Then have them give their opinions about which interpretation they thought was the most convincing.

This activity is particularly well suited for longer class periods.

Literary Analysis CONFLICT
Discuss with students the developing conflict between Nora and Krogstad. Ask them to describe Krogstad's behavior toward Nora.
Possible Response: He threatens to expose Nora's actions to Torvald and then starts going over the details of the transaction and interrogating her about what she did.

Then ask students how they would describe Nora's reactions.
Possible Response: She seems unnerved and also puzzled about what Krogstad is leading up to.

Literary Analysis
REALISTIC DRAMA: CHARACTER

A Draw students' attention to Nora's statement that if Torvald finds out about the loan, he'll immediately pay what she owes and they will be through with Krogstad for good. Ask them if they think Torvald would react in this way.
Possible Response: He probably would pay the loan off, because he so despises being in debt, and they also probably would not have anymore to do with Krogstad. But that would not be the end of the matter, because Torvald would be angry with Nora for putting him in such a position.

That job in the bank
was like the first rung in my ladder.
And now your husband wants to kick me
right back down in the mud again.

Denholm Elliott as Krogstad

MINI LESSON Viewing and Representing

ART APPRECIATION
Instruction Have students look at this scene from the movie, and then ask them the following questions:

How does Nora look compared with how she looked in the scenes on pages 1023 and 1028?
Possible Response: She looks more serious and worried.

What is the effect of Krogstad being at the front of the scene with Nora in the background?
Possible Response: He seems larger than she is and in control of the situation.

How would you describe the setting in this scene?
Possible Response: The room looks pleasant and well kept, and the Christmas decorations give it a festive air.

just like all the others, of course, that once, a good many years ago, I did something rather rash.

Nora. I've heard rumors to that effect.

1 **Krogstad.** The case never got into court; but all the same, every door was closed in my face from then on. So I took up those various activities you know about. I had to grab hold somewhere; and I dare say I haven't been among the worst. But now I want to drop all that. My boys are growing up. For their sakes, I'll have to win back as much respect as possible here in town. That job in the bank was like the first rung in my ladder. And now your husband wants to kick me right back down in the mud again.

Nora. But for heaven's sake, Mr. Krogstad, it's simply not in my power to help you.

Krogstad. That's because you haven't the will to—but I have the means to make you.

Nora. You certainly won't tell my husband that I owe you money?

Krogstad. Hm—what if I told him that?

Nora. That would be shameful of you. (*Nearly in tears.*) This secret—my joy and my pride—that he should learn it in such a crude and disgusting way—learn it from you. You'd expose me to the most horrible unpleasantness—

Krogstad. Only unpleasantness?

Nora (*vehemently*). But go on and try. It'll turn out the worse for you, because then my husband will really see what a crook you are, and then you'll *never* be able to hold your job.

Krogstad. I asked if it was just domestic[17] unpleasantness you were afraid of?

A **Nora.** If my husband finds out, then of course he'll pay what I owe at once, and then we'd be through with you for good.

Krogstad (*a step closer*). Listen, Mrs. Helmer—you've either got a very bad memory, or else no head at all for business. I'd better put you a little more in touch with the facts.

Nora. What do you mean?

Krogstad. When your husband was sick, you came to me for a loan of four thousand, eight hundred crowns.

Nora. Where else could I go?

Krogstad. I promised to get you that sum—

Nora. And you got it.

Krogstad. I promised to get you that sum, on certain conditions. You were so involved in your husband's illness, and so eager to finance your trip, that I guess you didn't think out all the details. It might just be a good idea to remind you. I promised you the money on the strength of a note I drew up.

Nora. Yes, and that I signed.

Krogstad. Right. But at the bottom I added some lines for your father to guarantee the loan. He was supposed to sign down there. 2

Nora. Supposed to? He did sign.

Krogstad. I left the date blank. In other words, your father would have dated his signature himself. Do you remember that?

Nora. Yes, I think—

Krogstad. Then I gave you the note for you to mail to your father. Isn't that so?

Nora. Yes.

Krogstad. And naturally you sent it at once—because only some five, six days later you brought me the note, properly signed. And with that, the money was yours.

Nora. Well, then; I've made my payments regularly, haven't I?

Krogstad. More or less. But—getting back to the point—those were hard times for you then, Mrs. Helmer.

17. **domestic:** having to do with the family.

WORDS TO KNOW

rash (răsh) *adj.* hasty and careless

Customizing Instruction

Less Proficient Readers

1 Explain that Krogstad gives some of his background in these lines. Ask students to summarize what he says.

Possible Response: Krogstad once was involved in a crooked business deal. He was not prosecuted, but he got a bad reputation and could not get work. He then got involved in doing loan deals on the side for people who could not get them otherwise, such as Nora. Now he wants to rebuild his reputation for his sons' sake, and his job at the bank is his first step. If Torvald fires him, he will be back where he started.

2 Explain that when someone guarantees a loan, he or she co-signs the loan along with the person borrowing the money, promising to pay the loan if the person taking it out does not.

English Learners

- Explain the comparison Krogstad makes between his job and a ladder. *(The ladder represents his climb toward becoming respectable again. The job in the bank is his first step. If he loses the job, it will be like being kicked off the ladder.)*
- Explain that when Krogstad tells Nora she has "no head at all for business" (cols. 1–2), he means she doesn't understand business procedures.

Reading Skills and Strategies
ANALYZING AND EVALUATING

A Point out that Nora and Krogstad have opposite views about the act of fraud that she committed. Ask students to state the two views. *(Krogstad views Nora's action as an illegal one for which she could be prosecuted. Nora views it as a necessary act to save her husband and spare her father. She thinks it was the right thing to do.)* Then ask students' opinion of the two views.

Possible Response: Some will say that Nora should have paid more attention to the consequences of what she was doing and should not have signed her father's name. Others will say that she was in a desperate situation that called for drastic measures.

Literary Analysis
REALISTIC DRAMA: CHARACTER

Ask students to describe what Krogstad is like up to this point.

Possible Response: He has been an unlucky person who has resorted to breaking the law to try to better his situation. He now seems desperate and is willing to threaten Nora to pressure her into influencing Torvald. He seems bitter and insensitive to Nora, although he does express care for his sons.

Literary Analysis
REALISTIC DRAMA: SETTING

Remind students that the conversation between Nora and Krogstad takes place on Christmas Eve. Ask them to explain the effect of Nora's trimming the Christmas tree right after Krogstad leaves.

Possible Response: The tree trimming provides a sharp contrast to the disturbing scene that precedes it. The contrast emphasizes the difference between the ordinary life Nora leads and the secret transactions she has had with Krogstad.

Nora. Yes, they were.

Krogstad. Your father was very ill, I believe.

Nora. He was near the end.

Krogstad. He died soon after?

Nora. Yes.

Krogstad. Tell me, Mrs. Helmer, do you happen to recall the date of your father's death? The day of the month, I mean.

Nora. Papa died the twenty-ninth of September.

Krogstad. That's quite correct; I've already looked into that. And now we come to a curious thing—(*Taking out a paper.*) which I simply cannot comprehend.

Nora. Curious thing? I don't know—

Krogstad. This is the curious thing: that your father co-signed the note for your loan three days after his death.

Nora. How—? I don't understand.

1 **Krogstad.** Your father died the twenty-ninth of September. But look. Here your father dated his signature October second. Isn't that curious, Mrs. Helmer? (Nora *is silent.*) Can you explain it to me? (Nora *remains silent.*) It's also remarkable that the words "October second" and the year aren't written in your father's hand, but rather in one that I think I know. Well, it's easy to understand. Your father forgot perhaps to date his signature, and then someone or other added it, a bit sloppily, before anyone knew of his death. There's nothing wrong in that. It all comes down to the signature. And there's no question about *that,* Mrs. Helmer. It really *was* your father who signed his own name here, wasn't it?

Nora (*after a short silence, throwing her head back and looking squarely at him*). No, it wasn't. *I* signed Papa's name.

Krogstad. Wait, now—are you fully aware that this is a dangerous confession?

Nora. Why? You'll soon get your money.

Krogstad. Let me ask you a question—why didn't you send the paper to your father?

Nora. That was impossible. Papa was so sick. If I'd asked him for his signature, I also would have had to tell him what the money was for. But I couldn't tell him, sick as he was, that my husband's life was in danger. That was just impossible.

Krogstad. Then it would have been better if you'd given up the trip abroad.

Nora. I couldn't possibly. The trip was to save my husband's life. I couldn't give that up.

Krogstad. But didn't you ever consider that this was a fraud against me? A

Nora. I couldn't let myself be bothered by that. You weren't any concern of mine. I couldn't stand you, with all those cold complications you made, even though you knew how badly off my husband was.

Krogstad. Mrs. Helmer, obviously you haven't the vaguest idea of what you've involved yourself in. But I can tell you this: it was nothing more and nothing worse that I once did—and it wrecked my whole reputation.

Nora. You? Do you expect me to believe that you ever acted bravely to save your wife's life?

Krogstad. Laws don't inquire into motives. 2

Nora. Then they must be very poor laws.

Krogstad. Poor or not—if I introduce this paper in court, you'll be judged according to law.

Nora. This I refuse to believe. A daughter hasn't a right to protect her dying father from anxiety and care? A wife hasn't a right to save her husband's life? I don't know much about laws, but I'm sure that somewhere in the books these things are allowed. And you don't know anything about it—you who practice the law? You must be an awful lawyer, Mr. Krogstad.

History

BLACKMAIL When Krogstad threatens to tell Torvald about Nora's loan, he is in effect trying to blackmail her. He is trying to force her to help him get something he wants–in this case, keeping his job–by threatening to expose her forgery. Legal definitions of blackmail are complicated and cover different kinds. For example, some types are limited to using threats of physical harm to gain land. Others are broader and include any personal threat to gain money or something else of value.

The word *blackmail* originated in Scotland. *Mail* is the Scottish word for *rent,* or *payment.* In the 16th century, corrupt Scottish chieftains, or landlords, forced farmers to pay protection money or risk having their crops destroyed. This payment was referred to as blackmail for two possible reasons. One was an old association of *black* with something evil or illegal. The second was the fact that protection money was usually paid in the form of livestock instead of silver, which was known as white money. The word *blackmail* was first used as a legal term in Scotland when the Scottish parliament made it a crime to get property by writing letters threatening physical harm.

Krogstad. Could be. But business—the kind of business we two are mixed up in—don't you think I know about that? All right. Do what you want now. But I'm telling you *this:* if I get shoved down a second time, you're going to keep me company. (*He bows and goes out through the hall.*)

Nora (*pensive for a moment, then tossing her head*). Oh, really! Trying to frighten me! I'm not so silly as all that. (*Begins gathering up the children's clothes, but soon stops.*) But—? No, but that's impossible! I did it out of love.

The Children (*in the doorway, left*). Mama, that strange man's gone out the door.

Nora. Yes, yes, I know it. But don't tell anyone about the strange man. Do you hear? Not even Papa!

The Children. No, Mama. But now will you play again?

Nora. No, not now.

Maid. Oh, but Mama, you promised.

Nora. Yes, but I can't now. Go inside; I have too much to do. Go in, go in, my sweet darlings. (*She herds them gently back in the room and shuts the door after them. Settling on the sofa, she takes up a piece of embroidery and makes some stitches, but soon stops abruptly.*) No! (*Throws the work aside, rises, goes to the hall door and calls out.*) Helene! Let me have the tree in here. (*Goes to the table, left, opens the table drawer, and stops again.*) No, but that's utterly impossible!

Maid (*with the Christmas tree*). Where should I put it, ma'am?

Nora. There. The middle of the floor.

Maid. Should I bring anything else?

Nora. No, thanks. I have what I need.

(*The* Maid, *who has set the tree down, goes out.*)

Nora (*absorbed in trimming the tree*). Candles here—and flowers here. That terrible creature! Talk, talk, talk! There's nothing to it at all. The tree's going to be lovely. I'll do anything to please you, Torvald. I'll sing for you, dance for you—

(Helmer *comes in from the hall, with a sheaf of papers under his arm.*)

Nora. Oh! You're back so soon?

Helmer. Yes. Has anyone been here?

Nora. Here? No.

Helmer. That's odd. I saw Krogstad leaving the front door.

Nora. So? Oh yes, that's true. Krogstad was here a moment.

Helmer. Nora, I can see by your face that he's been here, begging you to put in a good word for him.

Nora. Yes.

Helmer. And it was supposed to seem like your own idea? You were to hide it from me that he'd been here. He asked you that, too, didn't he?

Nora. Yes, Torvald, but—

Helmer. Nora, Nora, and you could fall for that? Talk with that sort of person and promise him anything? And then in the bargain, tell me an untruth.

Nora. An untruth—?

Helmer. Didn't you say that no one had been here? (*Wagging his finger.*) My little songbird must never do that again. A songbird needs a clean beak to warble with. No false notes. (*Putting his arm about her waist.*) That's the way it should be, isn't it? Yes, I'm sure of it. (*Releasing her.*) And so, enough of that. (*Sitting by the stove.*) Ah, how snug and cozy it is here. (*Leafing among his papers.*)

Nora (*busy with the tree, after a short pause*). Torvald!

Helmer. Yes.

Customizing Instruction

Less Proficient Readers

Help students summarize what Nora's situation is by the time Krogstad leaves by asking them the following questions:

- What has Nora done? (*She has taken out a secret loan from Krogstad and committed fraud by forging her father's name on the document. She has been paying Krogstad back in secret for years.*)
- What is Krogstad afraid of? (*He is afraid that when Torvald becomes manager of the bank, he will fire Krogstad from his job.*)
- What does Krogstad do? (*He goes to Nora and threatens to tell Torvald what she has done unless she can influence Torvald to keep Krogstad on at the bank. He forces Nora to admit that she signed her father's name on the loan.*)

English Learners

1 Work through the passage in which Krogstad forces Nora to admit to the fraudulent signature. Help them understand that he is threatening toward her both in what he says and in how he says it. You might want to read the passage aloud first so that students can hear the tone of voice and see the facial expressions that would be part of Krogstad's manipulation of Nora. After working on the passage, you might want to ask for volunteers to read the passage aloud also.

Advanced Learners

2 Draw students' attention to Krogstad's statement that laws don't inquire into motives. Have students investigate and discuss exactly what this means. They then may want to debate the issue of when, if ever, it is justifiable to break the law to follow a higher good.

Active Reading DIALOGUE

Ask for volunteers to read the dialogue beginning with Nora's first speech in column 2 of page 1040 and ending with last speech in column 1 of page 1041. Tell them to pay close attention to Nora's questions and Torvald's answers. Ask them what Torvald is talking about.

Possible Response: Torvald is expressing his opinion of Krogstad and what Torvald considers his immoral behavior.

Literary Analysis DRAMATIC IRONY

Tell students that the power and tension at the end of Act One is in part related to the dramatic irony that builds. Ask them to explain the irony in this final scene.

Possible Response: The irony stems from Torvald's statements about Krogstad and his "moral breakdown." Since Nora has committed a forgery also, everything Torvald says about Krogstad also applies to her. The reader knows this, but Torvald has no idea that in judging and condemning Krogstad he is judging and condemning Nora. Almost every sentence he utters has two meanings, and the more extreme his statements are, the stronger the irony.

Reading Skills and Strategies
CLARIFYING

Ask students why Nora won't let her children come back in the room with her at the end of the act.

Possible Response: She is afraid that if what Torvald said about the influence of a bad mother is true, she shouldn't put her children in danger of being so influenced by her.

Literary Analysis
REALISTIC DRAMA: CHARACTER

Point out to students that in the beginning of the play, Nora seemed silly and impulsive. Ask them to describe how she has changed.

Possible Response: Nora seems more complicated. She has shown love, resourcefulness, and courage in financing the trip to Italy. She also has been foolish in not paying attention to the possible consequences of forgery. By the end of Act One, she faces exposure and is fearful for what might happen to her and to her family.

Nora. I'm so much looking forward to the Stenborgs' costume party, day after tomorrow.

Helmer. And I can't wait to see what you'll surprise me with.

Nora. Oh, that stupid business!

Helmer. What?

Nora. I can't find anything that's right. Everything seems so ridiculous, so inane.

Helmer. So my little Nora's come to *that* recognition?

Nora (*going behind his chair, her arms resting on its back*). Are you very busy, Torvald?

Helmer. Oh—

Nora. What papers are those?

Helmer. Bank matters.

Nora. Already?

Helmer. I've gotten full authority from the retiring management to make all necessary changes in personnel and procedure. I'll need Christmas week for that. I want to have everything in order by New Year's.

Nora. So that was the reason this poor Krogstad—

Helmer. Hm.

Nora (*still leaning on the chair and slowly stroking the nape of his neck*). If you weren't so very busy, I would have asked you an enormous favor, Torvald.

Helmer. Let's hear. What is it?

1 **Nora.** You know, there isn't anyone who has your good taste—and I want so much to look well at the costume party. Torvald, couldn't you take over and decide what I should be and plan my costume?

Helmer. Ah, is my stubborn little creature calling for a lifeguard?

Nora. Yes, Torvald, I can't get anywhere without your help.

Helmer. All right—I'll think it over. We'll hit on something.

Nora. Oh, how sweet of you. (*Goes to the tree again. Pause.*) Aren't the red flowers pretty—? But tell me, was it really such a crime that this Krogstad committed?

Helmer. Forgery. Do you have any idea what that means?

Nora. Couldn't he have done it out of need?

Helmer. Yes, or thoughtlessness, like so many others. I'm not so heartless that I'd condemn a man categorically[18] for just one mistake.

Nora. No, of course not, Torvald!

Helmer. Plenty of men have redeemed themselves by openly confessing their crimes and taking their punishment.

Nora. Punishment—?

Helmer. But now Krogstad didn't go that way. He got himself out by sharp practices, and that's the real cause of his moral breakdown. 2

Nora. Do you really think that would—?

Helmer. Just imagine how a man with that sort of guilt in him has to lie and cheat and deceive on all sides, has to wear a mask even with the nearest and dearest he has, even with his own wife and children. And with the children, Nora—that's where it's most horrible.

Nora. Why?

Helmer. Because that kind of atmosphere of lies infects the whole life of a home. Every breath the children take in is filled with the germs of something degenerate.[19]

Nora (*coming closer behind him*). Are you sure of that?

18. **categorically** (kăt′ĭ-gôr′ĭ-klē): absolutely.

19. **degenerate** (dĭ-jĕn′ər-ĭt): having inferior or undesirable moral qualities.

WORDS TO KNOW

inane (ĭn-ān′) *adj.* pointless; silly

MINI LESSON **Vocabulary Strategy**

CONTEXT CLUES

Instruction Remind students that often they can infer the meaning of an unfamiliar word by noting synonyms in the same sentence or in surrounding sentences.

Write the following passage on the board.

Nora. Oh, that stupid business!
Helmer. What?
Nora. I can't find anything that's right. Everything seems so ridiculous, so inane.

Ask students what words in the passage they think might be synonyms for the word *inane* and what they think *inane* means.

Practice Read the following sentences aloud or write them on the board. Ask students to find synonyms to help them infer the meaning of each underlined word. (The answers are double underlined.)

1. His cough was chronic. It persisted for weeks, and seemed it would linger forever.
2. I made an impulsive decision. I shouldn't have been so careless. The rash judgment was a mistake.
3. From the airplane the desert looked desolate. It was one barren, empty, dismal stretch of sand.

A lesson using context clues appears on p. 674 of the Pupil's Edition.

Helmer. Oh, I've seen it often enough as a lawyer. Almost everyone who goes bad early in life has a mother who's a chronic liar.

Nora. Why just—the mother?

Helmer. It's usually the mother's influence that's dominant, but the father's works in the same way, of course. Every lawyer is quite familiar with it. And still this Krogstad's been going home year in, year out, poisoning his own children with lies and pretense; that's why I call him morally lost. (*Reaching his hands out toward her.*) So my sweet little Nora must promise me never to plead his cause. Your hand on it. Come, come, what's this? Give me your hand. There, now. All settled. I can tell you it'd be impossible for me to work alongside of him. I literally feel physically revolted when I'm anywhere near such a person.

Nora (*withdraws her hand and goes to the other side of the Christmas tree*). How hot it is here! And I've got so much to do.

Helmer (*getting up and gathering his papers*). Yes, and I have to think about getting some of these read through before dinner. I'll think about your costume, too. And something to hang on the tree in gilt paper, I may even see about that. (*Putting his hand on her head.*) Oh you, my darling little songbird. (*He goes into his study and closes the door after him.*)

Nora (*softly, after a silence*). Oh, really! it isn't so. It's impossible. It must be impossible.

Anne-Marie (*in the doorway, left*). The children are begging so hard to come in to Mama.

Nora. No, no, no, don't let them in to me! You stay with them, Anne-Marie.

Anne-Marie. Of course, ma'am. (*Closes the door.*)

Nora (*pale with terror*). Hurt my children—! Poison my home? (*A moment's pause; then she tosses her head.*) That's not true. Never. Never in all the world.

WORDS TO KNOW

chronic (krŏn'ĭk) *adj.* lasting for a long time; continual

Customizing Instruction

Advanced Learners

1 Have students discuss why Nora makes this appeal to Torvald at this point. Tell them to look at what precedes and follows the exchange. Ask them to explain the irony in the passage.
Possible Response: Nora seems to revert to earlier behavior with Torvald, perhaps out of her sense of desperation. She also is probably trying to distract Torvald. Irony is present in her statement that she can't get anywhere without Torvald's help. She has, of course, done a great deal without his help.

Remind students to look at the plot diagram they began filling in earlier in Act One (p. 1027). Have them complete the diagram for the rest of Act One if they have not already done so.
Possible Response (for pp. 1028–1041): exposition: The other two major characters are introduced (Dr. Rank and Krogstad), and a major conflict is identified (Krogstad threatens to expose Nora's loan and forgery if he loses his job at the bank.)

Less Proficient Readers

2 Help students understand that when Nora asks questions to Torvald about Krogstad, she is really asking about herself.

English Learners

Make sure students understand the following words and phrases: p. 1040, col. 1: "lifeguard" *(a person employed to protect and rescue swimmers in danger at a beach or pool; Torvald uses it to refer to himself as Nora's protector.)*; p. 1040, col. 2: "forgery" *(a fake, or counterfeit, signature)*; "redeemed themselves" *(got back their reputation; made up for what they did)*; "sharp practices" *(deceitful business deals)*; p. 1041, col. 1: "dominant" *(strongest)*; "pretense" *(a false impression meant to deceive)*

Assessment Informal Assessment

USING A GRAPHIC Have students make a graphic like the one shown to review the relationships between Nora, Torvald, and Krogstad. Tell them to write a one-sentence description of how each character relates to each of the other two.

Possible Responses: Nora to Torvald: She is submissive and afraid of him in some ways but has also committed fraud to save his life.
Torvald to Nora: He views her like a silly child whom he needs to control and protect.
Nora to Krogstad: She has a business relationship with him, which she needs to keep secret from Torvald.
Krogstad to Nora: He knows she forged her father's signature and is using that to threaten her.
Torvald to Krogstad: Torvald despises Krogstad and is going to fire him from his job.
Krogstad to Torvald: Krogstad does not respect Torvald but is desperate to keep his job.

RUBRIC

3 Full Accomplishment Student's descriptions of the relationships are accurate and emphasize the most important points.

2 Substantial Accomplishment Student's descriptions are accurate but miss some important points.

1 Little or Partial Accomplishment Student's descriptions are inaccurate and show little understanding of the relationships.

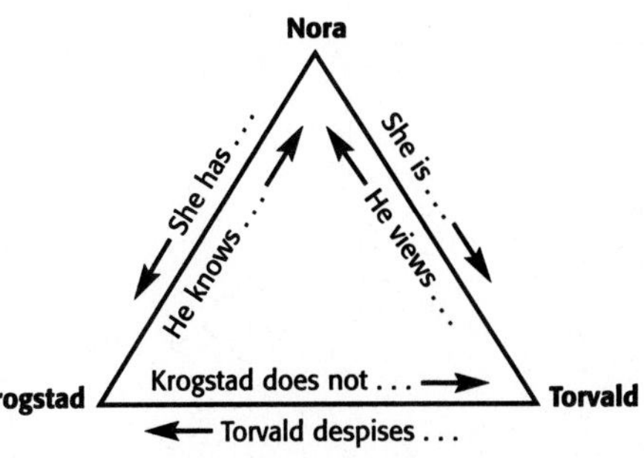

What characteristics of Nora are revealed in each of these portrayals?

Alla Nazimova, silent film, 1922

Janet McTeer, Belasco Theatre, New York City, 1997

Jane Fonda, film, 1973

Ruth Gordon, Morosco Theater, New York City, 1937

1042

MINI LESSON Viewing and Representing

COMPARING PORTRAYALS OF CHARACTER Tell students to look carefully at each photograph on the page, paying particular attention to facial expressions. Then have them discuss the question at the top of the page.

View & Compare Possible Responses: Nazimova: thoughtfulness, uncertainty, anxiety; McTeer: enthusiasm, energy, strength; Fonda: unhappiness, loneliness; Gordon: beauty, tenderness, submissiveness, proper behavior

Ask students to discuss which actress they would most like to see play the part of Nora. (You may want to include Claire Bloom in the choice.)

Connect to the Literature

1. What Do You Think? What thoughts were in your mind as you finished reading Act One?

Comprehension Check
- What good news have Torvald and Nora recently received?
- How did Nora raise money for the trip to Italy?
- Why does Krogstad threaten Nora?

Think Critically

2. **ACTIVE READING: STRATEGIES FOR READING REALISTIC DRAMA** Look over what you recorded in your  READER'S NOTEBOOK. Which strategies helped bring Act One to life for you?

3. How would you characterize Nora's and Torvald's attitudes toward each other?

THINK ABOUT
- Torvald's pet names for Nora
- Torvald's remarks about spending money
- how Nora behaves when Torvald is not present

4. What do you think are Nora's strengths and weaknesses?

5. A **foil** is a character who provides a striking contrast to another character. Why might Mrs. Linde be considered a foil for Nora?

Extend Interpretations

6. **Critic's Corner** According to the critic Harold Clurman, "Torvald owes his blissful domestic life to his thoughtlessness." What evidence in the play so far would support this statement?

7. **Connect to Life** Nora does not seem to have clear insight into herself or her relationships at this point in the play. What are some of the obstacles that prevent people from understanding what is going on in their own lives?

LITERARY ANALYSIS: CHARACTERS IN REALISTIC DRAMA

Characters are the individuals who take part in the action of a drama or narrative work. The most important ones are called **main characters.** In most realistic dramas the main characters are fully developed and possess many traits, mirroring the psychological complexity of real people. Less important figures, or **minor characters,** sometimes have only one or two dominant traits. In *A Doll House,* Anne-Marie is a minor character. In realistic drama the characters usually belong to the middle or lower class. They tend to be ordinary people dealing with everyday problems.

Paired Activity With a partner, use a chart such as the one below to record information that you learn about the five main characters. In addition, write down one or more personality traits, or qualities, that you have observed in each character.

Character	Background Information	Personality Traits
Nora	*borrowed money and forged signature*	*willing to make sacrifices for others*
Torvald		
Mrs. Linde		
Dr. Rank		
Krogstad		

Literary Analysis

Paired Activity Possible Responses: Torvald—is a successful lawyer who has just been promoted, is condescending; Mrs. Linde—is a widow who has had a hard life, is practical; Dr. Rank—is close friend of Nora and Torvald's, is serious, polite; Krogstad—has made crooked business deals, is hostile and threatening.

 Use **Unit Six Resource Book,** p. 44, for more practice.

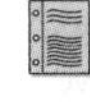 To assess skills and concepts taught in this selection, use **Formal Assessment Book,** pp. 153–154.

Connect to the Literature

1. **What Do You Think?** Accept all reasonable responses. Many students may say that they were left wondering whether Nora would be found out, and if so, what would happen to her and Torvald.

Comprehension Check
- Torvald is getting a promotion and a raise.
- She secretly got a loan by forging her father's signature.
- He wants her to persuade Torvald not to fire him from his job at the bank.

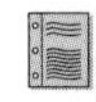 Use Selection Quiz in **Unit Six Resource Book,** p. 45.

Think Critically

2. Students will have different responses. Their answers should indicate which strategies they used and specific results of using the strategies.
3. Possible Response: Torvald is very condescending toward Nora. She gives the appearance of being submissive, but she keeps secrets and deceives him in small as well as important ways.
4. Possible Responses: Strengths: Nora is a loving person and devoted mother. Getting the loan shows that she can be resourceful, hard-working, and determined. She is energetic and enthusiastic. Weaknesses: She often isn't honest with Torvald and is manipulative to get her way. She is insensitive to Mrs. Linde's poverty and is sometimes thoughtless and silly. She is sometimes unrealistic.
5. Possible Response: Mrs. Linde is serious and practical, which contrasts with Nora's enthusiasm and disregard for the consequences of her actions.

Extend Interpretations

6. **Critic's Corner** Possible Response: Torvald doesn't give Nora credit for restoring his health by persuading him to go to Italy, he doesn't seem to have questioned how she raised the money, and he doesn't notice the sacrifices she has made to pay back the debt.
7. **Connect to Life** Possible Response: Obstacles include fear of responsibility, pressure to conform, personal background, emotional needs, and a desire to please.

Reading and Analyzing

Literary Analysis

REALISTIC DRAMA: SETTING

Tell students to review the description of the setting in the stage directions at the beginning of page 1044. Ask them what mood the setting creates.

Possible Response: The bedraggled Christmas tree with burned-down candle stubs gives a let-down feeling and conveys a sense of vague depression and loneliness.

Use **Unit Six Resource Book,** p. 48, for more practice.

Active Reading

STAGE DIRECTIONS AND CHARACTER

A Tell students to reread Nora's opening comments and the stage directions that accompany what she says. Ask students what frame of mind she seems to be in.

Possible Response: Nora seems to be trying to convince herself that nothing bad could really happen. She seems distracted and upset.

Then ask them if she seems to be in the same frame of mind toward the end of the page.

Possible Response: She seems calmer and more sober, and she seems to be thinking about serious consequences, such as being separated from her children.

Use **Unit Six Resource Book,** p. 47, for more practice.

Literary Analysis SYMBOL

B Remind students that a symbol is a person, place, object, or activity that stands for something beyond itself. Ask students in what ways going to a masquerade party symbolizes what has been happening in the play so far.

Possible Response: Nora and Torvald have both been avoiding reality. Nora has deceived Torvald about the loan, and Torvald sees Nora as a child and doesn't know what she is really like.

Act Two

GUIDE FOR READING

FOCUS In this act Nora tries to keep Torvald from finding out her secret. As you read, look for clues about her feelings for him.

Same room. Beside the piano the Christmas tree now stands stripped of ornament, burned-down candle stubs on its ragged branches. Nora'*s street clothes lie on the sofa.* Nora, *alone in the room, moves restlessly about; at last she stops at the sofa and picks up her coat.*

A **Nora** (*dropping the coat again*). Someone's coming! (*Goes toward the door, listens.*) No—there's no one. Of course—nobody's coming today, Christmas Day—or tomorrow, either. But maybe— (*Opens the door and looks out.*) No, nothing in the mailbox. Quite empty. (*Coming forward.*) What nonsense! He won't do anything serious. Nothing terrible could happen. It's impossible. Why, I have three small children.

(Anne-Marie, *with a large carton, comes in from the room to the left.*)

B **Anne-Marie.** Well, at last I found the box with the masquerade clothes.

Nora. Thanks. Put it on the table.

Anne-Marie (*does so*). But they're all pretty much of a mess.

Nora. Ahh! I'd love to rip them in a million pieces!

Anne-Marie. Oh, mercy, they can be fixed right up. Just a little patience.

Nora. Yes, I'll go get Mrs. Linde to help me.

Anne-Marie. Out again now? In this nasty weather? Miss Nora will catch cold—get sick.

Nora. Oh, worse things could happen— How are the children? 1

Anne-Marie. The poor mites are playing with their Christmas presents, but—

Nora. Do they ask for me much?

Anne-Marie. They're so used to having Mama around, you know.

Nora. Yes, but Anne-Marie, I *can't* be together with them as much as I was.

Anne-Marie. Well, small children get used to anything.

Nora. You think so? Do you think they'd forget their mother if she was gone for good?

Anne-Marie. Oh, mercy—gone for good! 2

Nora. Wait, tell me, Anne-Marie—I've wondered so often—how could you ever have the heart to give your child over to strangers?

Anne-Marie. But I had to, you know, to become little Nora's nurse.

Cross Curricular Link **Humanities**

CHRISTMAS IN NORWAY In Norway, Christmas has traditionally been celebrated on Christmas Eve. Parents trim the Christmas tree and allow their children to see it only after it has been fully decorated—which in the 19th century included real candles attached to its branches. The Christmas Eve celebration also usually includes opening presents, going to church, and having a Christmas Eve dinner. After the meal, the family forms a circle around the tree and sings Christmas carols.

Christmas Day is much quieter. Decorations are often removed from the tree, and the tree itself may be placed outdoors with nuts hanging on its branches for the birds. With the festivities largely over, people resume their usual routine. In 19th-century Norway, that routine extended to such services as mail delivery, which accounts for Nora's checking the mailbox at the beginning of Act Two.

Do you think they'd forget their mother
if she was gone for good?

Dame Edith Evans as Anne-Marie

Customizing Instruction

Less Proficient Readers

Focus Remind students to look for clues in Nora's actions as well as in her words.

Help students understand the beginning of Act Two by asking them the following questions:

- Who is Nora afraid will come? (Krogstad)
- Who is Anne-Marie? (the children's nurse, or nanny)
- How long has Anne-Marie been with Nora? (since Nora was a child herself)

Tell students that Act Two takes place on Christmas Day.

English Learners

Make sure students understand the following words and phrases: p. 1044, col. 1, "masquerade clothes," *(costumes to be worn to a party where everyone will be dressed up in disguise)*; col. 2, "mites" *(something very small, here referring to Nora's little children)*; "gone for good" *(gone away forever)*

Advanced Learners

1 Ask students to explain the dramatic irony and possible foreshadowing here. *(The reader knows what Krogstad has threatened to do, but Anne-Marie doesn't and assumes Nora is just making a general comment. The phrase "worse things could happen" might foreshadow later developments in the play.)*

2 Ask students to speculate on whether Nora's questions could involve foreshadowing.

Possible Response: Nora's second question sounds serious and somewhat shocking. It seems to suggest either that something bad will happen to her or that she will do something drastic.

A DOLL HOUSE, ACT TWO 1045

Reading Skills and Strategies
QUESTIONING

A Ask students to suggest what Nora might be thinking of here.

Possible Responses: She may be thinking that she will be punished for the forgery and have her children taken away from her. She may also be having desperate thoughts of leaving or doing harm to herself.

Active Reading
DIALOGUE AND STAGE DIRECTIONS

B Have two or three students read this passage aloud and act it out. Then ask what the reader or viewer learns about Nora's state of mind from what she says and does in this passage.

Possible Response: Nora is distracted and worried about what Krogstad will do. She tries to check on the condition of her costume but can't concentrate. She is afraid when she hears someone at the door but is relieved when it turns out to be Mrs. Linde by herself.

Reading Skills and Strategies
COMPARING

C In Act One, Torvald says that Nora inherited a tendency from her father to spend too much money (p. 1022, col. 2). Ask students what else Mrs. Linde is suggesting that Nora received from her father.

Possible Response: Mrs. Linde is complimenting Nora on her good taste in decorating and implies that Nora got her taste from her father.

Literary Analysis CHARACTERIZATION

One way a writer can develop a character is through the speech of other characters. Although Dr. Rank does not appear at this point in the play, the reader learns some facts about him through the conversation of Nora and Mrs. Linde. Have students list details about Dr. Rank that are revealed.

Possible Response: He is seriously ill and has been sickly all his life; he has been Torvald's closest friend since childhood; he comes to the Helmers' house every day, and Nora talks to him often; he has money but no family.

Active Reading DIALOGUE

D Ask students what Nora reveals about her relationship with Torvald and with Dr. Rank from this speech.

Possible Response: Torvald is a jealous person, so she has to be careful what she says to him. She can talk easily and freely with Dr. Rank, however.

Nora. Yes, but how could you *do* it?

Anne-Marie. When I could get such a good place? A girl who's poor and who's gotten in trouble is glad enough for that. Because that slippery fish, he didn't do a thing for me, you know.

Nora. But your daughter's surely forgotten you.

Anne-Marie. Oh, she certainly has not. She's written to me, both when she was confirmed and when she was married.

Nora (*clasping her about the neck*). You old Anne-Marie, you were a good mother for me when I was little.

Anne-Marie. Poor little Nora, with no other mother but me.

A **Nora.** And if the babies didn't have one, then I know that you'd— What silly talk! (*Opening the carton.*) Go in to them. Now I'll have to— Tomorrow you can see how lovely I'll look.

Anne-Marie. Oh, there won't be anyone at the party as lovely as Miss Nora. (*She goes off into the room, left.*)

B **Nora** (*begins unpacking the box, but soon throws it aside*). Oh, if I dared to go out. If only nobody would come. If only nothing would happen here while I'm out. What craziness—nobody's coming. Just don't think. This muff—needs a brushing. Beautiful gloves, beautiful gloves. Let it go. Let it go! One, two, three, four, five, six— (*With a cry.*) Oh, there they are! (*Poises to move toward the door, but remains irresolutely standing.* Mrs. Linde *enters from the hall, where she has removed her street clothes.*)

Nora. Oh, it's you, Kristine. There's no one else out there? How good that you've come.

Mrs. Linde. I hear you were up asking for me.

Nora. Yes, I just stopped by. There's something you really can help me with. Let's get settled on the sofa. Look, there's going to be a costume party tomorrow evening at the Stenborgs' right above us, and now Torvald wants me to go as a Neapolitan peasant girl and dance the tarantella that I learned in Capri.[1]

Mrs. Linde. Really, are you giving a whole performance?

Nora. Torvald says yes, I should. See, here's the dress. Torvald had it made for me down there; but now it's all so tattered that I just don't know—

Mrs. Linde. Oh, we'll fix that up in no time. It's nothing more than the trimmings—they're a bit loose here and there. Needle and thread? Good, now we have what we need.

Nora. Oh, how sweet of you!

Mrs. Linde (*sewing*). So you'll be in disguise tomorrow, Nora. You know what? I'll stop by then for a moment and have a look at you all dressed up. But listen, I've absolutely forgotten to thank you for that pleasant evening yesterday.

Nora (*getting up and walking about*). I don't think it was as pleasant as usual yesterday. You should have come to town a bit sooner, Kristine— Yes, Torvald really knows how to give a home elegance and charm.

Mrs. Linde. And you do, too, if you ask me. You're not your father's daughter for nothing. C But tell me, is Dr. Rank always so down in the mouth as yesterday?

Nora. No, that was quite an exception. But he goes around critically ill all the time—tuberculosis of the spine, poor man. You know, his father was a disgusting thing who kept mistresses and so on—and that's why the son's been sickly from birth.

1. **Neapolitan** (nē′ə-pŏl′ĭ-tən) . . . **tarantella** (tăr′ən-tĕl′ə) . . . **Capri** (kə-prē′): A Neapolitan is a person from Naples, Italy. The tarantella is a lively, whirling Italian dance. Capri is an island near Naples.

Cross Curricular Link **History**

WORKING WOMEN IN THE 19TH CENTURY The overwhelming majority of women in the 19th century had to work. Some single women were employed in factories or in such domestic industries as knitting or lace-making, but many could only obtain work as servants. The life of a servant was hard; a housemaid typically cleaned the house, carried water, and tended the fireplaces from 6 in the morning until 11 at night. Some women, particularly unmarried mothers, probably considered themselves fortunate to obtain work in a household. Like Anne-Marie, these women had to give up their children. Fortunate mothers were able to place their babies in an orphanage. Others were forced to leave their children in the workhouse, where they frequently died of malnourishment.

Most married women also had to work, at least from time to time. Wives with no special skills often worked at home. They took in laundry, rented rooms to lodgers, or did needlework. Married women were discouraged from working in factories because it was believed that such work detracted from their duties as wives and mothers. Skilled women, such as Mrs. Linde appears to have been, could hope to find better-paying jobs in offices and banks. However, most of these positions went to single or married men—at considerably higher wages.

Mrs. Linde (*lets her sewing fall to her lap*). But my dearest Nora, how do you know about such things?

Nora (*walking more jauntily*). Hmp! When you've had three children, then you've had a few visits from—from women who know something of medicine, and they tell you this and that.

Mrs. Linde (*resumes sewing; a short pause*). Does Dr. Rank come here every day?

Nora. Every blessed day. He's Torvald's best friend from childhood, and *my* good friend, too. Dr. Rank almost belongs to this house.

Mrs. Linde. But tell me—is he quite sincere? I mean, doesn't he rather enjoy flattering people?

Nora. Just the opposite. Why do you think that?

Mrs. Linde. When you introduced us yesterday, he was proclaiming that he'd often heard my name in this house; but later I noticed that your husband hadn't the slightest idea who I really was. So how could Dr. Rank—?

D **Nora.** But it's all true, Kristine. You see, Torvald loves me beyond words, and, as he puts it, he'd like to keep me all to himself. For a long time he'd almost be jealous if I even mentioned any of my old friends back home. So of course I dropped that. But with Dr. Rank I talk a lot about such things, because he likes hearing about them.

Mrs. Linde. Now listen, Nora; in many ways you're still like a child. I'm a good deal older than you, with a little more experience. I'll tell you something: you ought to put an end to all this with Dr. Rank.

Nora. What should I put an end to?

Mrs. Linde. Both parts of it, I think. Yesterday you said something about a rich admirer who'd provide you with money—

Nora. Yes, one who doesn't exist—worse luck. So?

Mrs. Linde. Is Dr. Rank well off?

Nora. Yes, he is.

Mrs. Linde. With no dependents?[2]

Nora. No, no one. But—

Mrs. Linde. And he's over here every day?

Nora. Yes, I told you that.

Mrs. Linde. How can a man of such refinement be so grasping?

Nora. I don't follow you at all.

Mrs. Linde. Now don't try to hide it, Nora. You think I can't guess who loaned you the forty-eight hundred crowns?

Nora. Are you out of your mind? How could you think such a thing! A friend of ours, who comes here every single day. What an intolerable situation that would have been!

Mrs. Linde. Then it really wasn't him.

Nora. No, absolutely not. It never even crossed my mind for a moment— And he had nothing to lend in those days; his inheritance came later.

Mrs. Linde. Well, I think that was a stroke of luck for you, Nora dear.

Nora. No, it never would have occurred to me to ask Dr. Rank— Still, I'm quite sure that if I had asked him—

Mrs. Linde. Which you won't, of course.

Nora. No, of course not. I can't see that I'd ever need to. But I'm quite positive that if I talked to Dr. Rank—

Mrs. Linde. Behind your husband's back?

Nora. I've got to clear up this other thing; *that's* also behind his back. I've *got* to clear it all up. 1

Mrs. Linde. Yes, I was saying that yesterday, but—

2. **dependents:** people whom one supports, such as a spouse or children.

WORDS TO KNOW
jauntily (jôn′tĭ-lē) *adv.* in a lively, carefree manner

Customizing Instruction

Less Proficient Readers

Explain to students Mrs. Linde's misunderstanding regarding Nora's relationship to Dr. Rank. *(Mrs. Linde jumps to conclusions. She remembers Nora's casual remark about a rich admirer, and when she learns how close Nora is to Dr. Rank and that he is rich, she assumes Dr. Rank must have lent Nora the money she borrowed.)*

1 Explain to students that "this other thing" is Krogstad's threat to tell Torvald about the secret loan and to expose her fraud.

English Learners

Help students with the following words and phrases: p. 1046, col. 1, "confirmed" *(went through a ceremony at about age 13 to become a member of a church)*; "muff," *(a warm covering for the hands in the form of a tube made of fur or thick cloth)*; col. 2, "you're not your father's daughter for nothing" *(you are very like your father)*; "down in the mouth" *(gloomy looking)*; p. 1047, col. 2, "out of your mind" *(crazy, completely mistaken)*; "behind your husband's back" *(done without your husband's knowing about it)*

Reading and Analyzing

Literary Analysis

REALISTIC DRAMA: CHARACTER

Have students describe how Nora tries to persuade Torvald not to fire Krogstad.

Possible Response: First she goes into her role of being a playful child and tries to coax Torvald. When he figures out what she is up to and resists, she becomes more direct. She tells him she is scared of Krogstad and begs him not to fire him.

Then ask students to describe what Torvald is like as he responds to Nora.

Possible Response: He is suspicious at first and then won't give in at all when he finds out what she wants. He takes a very superior attitude, making critical remarks about her father and showing that his first priority is making sure other people think well of him.

Literary Analysis DRAMATIC IRONY

A Ask students to explain the irony present in this passage. *(Nora says she is concerned for Torvald's sake, but the reader knows that she is also terrified for herself. When she says she is scared of Krogstad, the reader knows why, but Torvald doesn't.)*

Reading Skills and Strategies

PREDICTING

B Ask students whom they think the letter is for and what they think is in it.

Possible Response: It is a letter to Krogstad telling him he is fired.

Literary Analysis

REALISTIC DRAMA: SETTING

Remind students that setting includes social environment. Have students identify some of the social conventions that contribute to the setting of the play.

Possible Responses: The social conventions of the day include observing class distinctions, appearing respectable, behaving properly, and dressing appropriately.

Nora (*pacing up and down*). A man handles these problems so much better than a woman—

Mrs. Linde. One's husband does, yes.

Nora. Nonsense. (*Stopping.*) When you pay everything you owe, then you get your note back, right?

Mrs. Linde. Yes, naturally.

Nora. And can rip it into a million pieces and burn it up—that filthy scrap of paper!

Mrs. Linde (*looking hard at her, laying her sewing aside, and rising slowly*). Nora, you're hiding something from me.

Nora. You can see it in my face?

Mrs. Linde. Something's happened to you since yesterday morning. Nora, what is it?

Nora (*hurrying toward her*). Kristine! (*Listening.*) Shh! Torvald's home. Look, go in with the children a while. Torvald can't bear all this snipping and stitching. Let Anne-Marie help you.

Mrs. Linde (*gathering up some of the things*). All right, but I'm not leaving here until we've talked this out. (*She disappears into the room, left, as* Torvald *enters from the hall.*)

Nora. Oh, how I've been waiting for you, Torvald dear.

Helmer. Was that the dressmaker?

Nora. No, that was Kristine. She's helping me fix up my costume. You know, it's going to be quite attractive.

Helmer. Yes, wasn't that a bright idea I had?

Nora. Brilliant! But then wasn't I good as well to give in to you?

Helmer. Good—because you give in to your husband's judgment? All right, you little goose, I know you didn't mean it like that. But I won't disturb you. You'll want to have a fitting, I suppose.

Nora. And you'll be working?

Helmer. Yes. (*Indicating a bundle of papers.*) See. I've been down to the bank. (*Starts toward his study.*)

Nora. Torvald.

Helmer (*Stops*). Yes.

Nora. If your little squirrel begged you, with all her heart and soul, for something—?

Helmer. What's that?

Nora. Then would you do it?

Helmer. First, naturally, I'd have to know what it was.

Nora. Your squirrel would scamper about and do tricks, if you'd only be sweet and give in.

Helmer. Out with it.

Nora. Your lark would be singing high and low in every room—

Helmer. Come on, she does that anyway.

Nora. I'd be a wood nymph and dance for you in the moonlight.

Helmer. Nora—don't tell me it's that same business from this morning?

Nora (*coming closer*). Yes, Torvald, I beg you, please!

Helmer. And you actually have the nerve to drag that up again?

Nora. Yes, yes, you've got to give in to me; you *have* to let Krogstad keep his job in the bank.

Helmer. My dear Nora, I've slated his job for Mrs. Linde.

Nora. That's awfully kind of you. But you could just fire another clerk instead of Krogstad.

Helmer. This is the most incredible stubbornness! Because you go and give an impulsive promise to speak up for him, I'm expected to—

Nora. That's not the reason, Torvald. It's for your own sake. That man does writing for the worst papers; you said it yourself. He could do you any amount of harm. I'm scared to death of him— A

MINI LESSON Speaking and Listening

DRAMATIC PRESENTATION

Instruction Tell students that in the scene on these pages, Nora is working hard to change Torvald's mind about firing Krogstad. Note that despite her seeming to be submissive to Torvald, she is actually quite persistent and determined in her efforts.

Prepare Direct students to choose one part of this scene to prepare as a dramatic presentation. One possibility is from Nora's speech "Oh, how I've been waiting for you, Torvald . . . " to the end of page 1048. A second is from the beginning of page 1049 to the end of the page, just before the maid speaks. Some students may want to prepare both passages. Suggest that they read over the scenes carefully, thinking especially about how Nora and Torvald might act toward each other, what tone of voice they might use, and so on.

Present Have students work in groups of four. Each pair can practice in front of the other one, and the pair being the audience can give the performers feedback on their presentation. You might want to set aside a morning or an afternoon when all the pairs can perform their scenes for the class.

This activity is particularly well suited for longer class periods.

Helmer. Ah, I understand. It's the old memories haunting you.

Nora. What do you mean by that?

Helmer. Of course, you're thinking about your father.

Nora. Yes, all right. Just remember how those nasty gossips wrote in the papers about Papa and slandered him so cruelly. I think they'd have had him dismissed if the department hadn't sent you up to investigate, and if you hadn't been so kind and open-minded toward him.

Helmer. My dear Nora, there's a notable difference between your father and me. Your father's official career was hardly above reproach. But mine is; and I hope it'll stay that way as long as I hold my position.

Nora. Oh, who can ever tell what vicious minds can invent? We could be so snug and happy now in our quiet, carefree home—you and I and the children, Torvald! That's why I'm pleading with you so—

Helmer. And just by pleading for him you make it impossible for me to keep him on. It's already known at the bank that I'm firing Krogstad. What if it's rumored around now that the new bank manager was vetoed by his wife—

Nora. Yes, what then—?

Helmer. Oh yes—as long as our little bundle of stubbornness gets her way—! I should go and make myself ridiculous in front of the whole office—give people the idea I can be swayed by all kinds of outside pressure. Oh, you can bet I'd feel the effects of that soon enough! Besides—there's something that rules Krogstad right out at the bank as long as I'm the manager.

Nora. What's that?

Helmer. His moral failings I could maybe overlook if I had to—

Nora. Yes, Torvald, why not?

Helmer. And I hear he's quite efficient on the job. But he was a crony of mine back in my teens—one of those rash friendships that crop up again and again to embarrass you later in life. Well, I might as well say it straight out: we're on a first-name basis. And that tactless fool makes no effort at all to hide it in front of others. Quite the contrary—he thinks that entitles him to take a familiar air around me, and so every other second he comes booming out with his "Yes, Torvald!" and "Sure thing, Torvald!" I tell you, it's been excruciating[3] for me. He's out to make my place in the bank unbearable. 1

Nora. Torvald, you can't be serious about all this.

Helmer. Oh no? Why not?

Nora. Because these are such petty considerations. 2

Helmer. What are you saying? Petty? You think I'm petty!

Nora. No, just the opposite, Torvald dear. That's exactly why—

Helmer. Never mind. You call my motives petty; then I might as well be just that. Petty! All right! We'll put a stop to this for good. (*Goes to the hall door and calls.*) Helene!

Nora. What do you want?

Helmer (*searching among his papers*). *A* decision. (*The* Maid *comes in.*) Look here; take this letter; go out with it at once. Get hold of a messenger and have him deliver it. Quick now. It's already addressed. Wait, here's some money. B

Maid. Yes, sir. (*She leaves with the letter.*)

3. **excruciating** (ĭk-skrōō′shē-ā′tĭng): intensely painful.

WORDS TO KNOW

tactless (tăkt′lĭs) *adj.* not sensitive to what is appropriate in dealing with people and situations

petty (pĕt′ē) *adj.* of no importance; trivial

Customizing Instruction

Less Proficient Readers

Help students follow Torvald's arguments on page 1049 by asking the following questions:

- What does Torvald think is the reason that Nora is afraid of Krogstad? *(He thinks she is afraid that Krogstad will slander them, as her father had been slandered in the past.)*
- What does Torvald imply about Nora's father? *(that he was, in fact, crooked in some way in his business dealings)*
- What former relationship existed between Torvald and Krogstad? *(They had been friends when they were teenagers.)*
- Why is Torvald so upset at being called "petty"? *(He takes himself very seriously and cannot stand to be thought unimportant.)*

English Learners

Explain the following words and phrases: p. 1048, col. 1, "get your note back" *(get the loan agreement back from the person who lent the money);* "snipping and stitching" *(cutting and sewing);* "a fitting" *(putting on a dress and having a seamstress make adjustment to make it fit well);* p. 1049, col. 1, "above reproach" *(so good it can't be criticized);* col. 2, "rash friendships" *(friendships made quickly and without thought);* "crop up again" *(reappear)*

1 Explain that "on a first-name basis" means that Torvald and Krogstad called each other by their first names (Torvald and Nils). At the time of the play, only close friends and family members used first names. For others to do so was considered rude.

Advanced Learners

2 Point out Nora's comment about Torvald's "petty considerations" with regard to Krogstad. Then ask students why her comment is unusual. *(Nora is judging Torvald.)* What does the comment reveal about Nora?

Possible Responses: She can see Torvald for who he is; she's intelligent; she can think independently.

Active Reading VISUALIZING

A Have students try to imagine Torvald's expressions and tone of voice in this exchange with Nora. Then have them discuss their reactions to his attitudes.
Possible Responses: Students should be able to support their opinions. Most will find Torvald overbearing, condescending, and self-absorbed. He is possessive toward Nora and does not treat her as an adult.

Literary Analysis
REALISTIC DRAMA: SETTING

B Point out to students that Torvald often spends time in his study, which is offstage. Ask them how this element of the setting reflects Torvald's attitudes and position.
Possible Response: The study, with its closed door, reflects Torvald's aloofness from everyday details of the house and his view of himself as an important person. It also reflects the society of the time, which expected professional men to be separate from domestic concerns and activities.

Active Reading STAGE DIRECTIONS

C Tell students to review the stage directions given for Nora in this passage. Ask them to explain how the actions described in the stage directions relate to what Nora is thinking and saying.
Possible Response: She grips Dr. Rank's arm because she is afraid he has discovered something about the situation with Krogstad. She breathes easier when she realizes he is talking about himself.

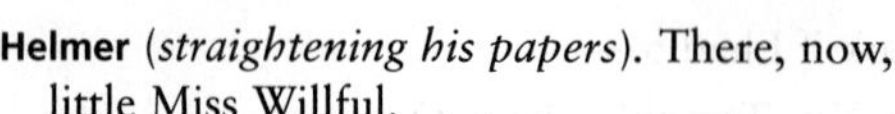

Helmer (*straightening his papers*). There, now, little Miss Willful.

Nora (*breathlessly*). Torvald, what was that letter?

Helmer. Krogstad's notice.

Nora. Call it back, Torvald! There's still time. Oh, Torvald, call it back! Do it for my sake—for your sake, for the children's sake! Do you hear, Torvald; do it! You don't know how this can harm us.

Helmer. Too late.

Nora. Yes, too late.

Helmer. Nora dear, I can forgive you this panic, even though basically you're insulting me. Yes, you are! Or isn't it an insult to think that *I* should be afraid of a courtroom hack's revenge? But I forgive you anyway, because this shows so beautifully how much you love me. (*Takes her in his arms.*) This is the way it should be, my darling Nora. Whatever comes, you'll see: when it really counts, I have strength and courage enough as a man to take on the whole weight myself.

Nora (*terrified*). What do you mean by that?

Helmer. The whole weight, I said.

Nora (*resolutely*). No, never in all the world.

Helmer. Good. So we'll share it, Nora, as man and wife. That's as it should be. (*Fondling her.*) Are you happy now? There, there, there—not these frightened dove's eyes. It's nothing at all but empty fantasies— Now you should run through your tarantella and practice your tambourine. I'll go to the inner office and shut both doors, so I won't hear a thing; you can make all the noise you like. (*Turning in the doorway.*) And when Rank comes, just tell him where he can find me. (*He nods to her and goes with his papers into the study, closing the door.*)

Nora (*standing as though rooted, dazed with fright, in a whisper*). He really could do it. He will do it. He'll do it in spite of everything. No, not that, never, never! Anything but that! Escape! A way out— (*The doorbell rings.*) Dr. Rank! Anything but that! *Anything*, whatever it is! (*Her hands pass over her face, smoothing it; she pulls herself together, goes over and opens the hall door.* Dr. Rank *stands outside, hanging his fur coat up. During the following scene, it begins getting dark.*)

Nora. Hello, Dr. Rank. I recognized your ring. But you mustn't go in to Torvald yet; I believe he's working.

Rank. And you?

Nora. For you, I always have an hour to spare—you know that. (*He has entered, and she shuts the door after him.*)

Rank. Many thanks. I'll make use of these hours while I can.

Nora. What do you mean by that? While you can?

Rank. Does that disturb you?

Nora. Well, it's such an odd phrase. Is anything going to happen?

Rank. What's going to happen is what I've been expecting so long—but I honestly didn't think it would come so soon.

Nora (*gripping his arm*). What is it you've found out? Dr. Rank, you have to tell me!

Rank (*sitting by the stove*). It's all over with me. There's nothing to be done about it.

Nora (*breathing easier*). Is it you—then—?

Rank. Who else? There's no point in lying to one's self. I'm the most miserable of all my patients, Mrs. Helmer. These past few days I've been auditing my internal accounts.[4] Bankrupt! Within a month I'll probably be

4. **auditing my internal accounts:** checking over my physical health.

There's no point in lying to one's self.
I'm the most miserable
of all my patients, Mrs. Helmer.

Sir Ralph Richardson as Dr. Rank

Customizing Instruction

Less Proficient Readers

Help students understand that Dr. Rank's comments are leading up to a revelation that he makes at the end of page 1050. Ask them what he means when he says he is bankrupt. *(He is dying.)*

English Learners

- To give students an opportunity to practice reading English, they could read aloud the conversation between Nora and Dr. Rank on page 1050, column 2.
- Help students with the following words and phrases: p. 1050, col. 1, "Krogstad's notice" *(written announcement that he is being let go from the bank)*; "courtroom hack's revenge" *(a reference to Krogstad, who took low-paying jobs writing copy for newspapers, presumably sometimes reports of court cases)*; col. 2, "an hour to spare" *(an hour of time available)*

Reading and Analyzing

Literary Analysis REALISM

A Remind students that realistic literature tries to portray life as it is lived. It focuses on fact and observation, not emotion. Ask students how this passage reflects the aims of realism.

Possible Response: Dr. Rank talks bluntly about his own coming death, as shown in his references to the churchyard, disintegration, and the sickroom.

Literary Analysis

REALISTIC DRAMA: CHARACTERS

Point out to students that through the conversation between Nora and Dr. Rank, the reader learns more about what Dr. Rank is like. Ask them to summarize what they learn about him.

Possible Response: He is open and matter-of-fact about his illness and death, although he also expresses a certain amount of bitterness and supposes that he will be forgotten quickly. But then he engages in a flirtatious, intimate exchange with Nora and reveals to her that he has deep feelings for her.

Then ask how they would describe Nora's responses to Dr. Rank.

Possible Response: At first she is talkative and flirtatious, especially with the stockings. Then, in response to his comment about not being able to show his gratitude, she hesitantly begins to ask him for a favor. When he reveals his feelings for her, however, she distances herself.

Reading Skills and Strategies

QUESTIONING

B Ask students what they think is the "big favor" Nora wants to ask.

Possible Responses: She may be going to ask him for money to pay off the loan, for help persuading Torvald not to fire Krogstad, or for help dealing with Torvald if Krogstad tells him about her loan and the forgery.

laid out and rotting in the churchyard.

Nora. Oh, what a horrible thing to say.

Rank. The thing itself is horrible. But the worst of it is all the other horror before it's over. There's only one final examination left; when I'm finished with that, I'll know about when my disintegration will begin. There's something I want to say. Helmer with his sensitivity has such a sharp distaste for anything ugly. I don't want him near my sickroom. A

Nora. Oh, but Dr. Rank—

Rank. I won't have him in there. Under no condition. I'll lock my door to him— As soon as I'm completely sure of the worst, I'll send you my calling card marked with a black cross, and you'll know then the wreck has started to come apart.

Nora. No, today you're completely unreasonable. And I wanted you so much to be in a really good humor.

Rank. With death up my sleeve? And then to suffer this way for somebody else's sins. Is there any justice in that? And in every single family, in some way or another, this inevitable retribution[5] of nature goes on—

Nora (*her hands pressed over her ears*). Oh, stuff! Cheer up! Please—be gay!

Rank. Yes, I'd just as soon laugh at it all. My poor, innocent spine, serving time for my father's gay army days.

Nora (*by the table, left*). He was so infatuated with asparagus tips and *pâté de foie gras,* wasn't that it?

Rank. Yes—and with truffles.[6]

Nora. Truffles, yes. And then with oysters, I suppose?

Rank. Yes, tons of oysters, naturally.

Nora. And then the port and champagne to go with it. It's so sad that all these delectable things have to strike at our bones.

Rank. Especially when they strike at the unhappy bones that never shared in the fun.

Nora. Ah, that's the saddest of all.

Rank (*looks searchingly at her*). Hm.

Nora (*after a moment*). Why did you smile?

Rank. No, it was you who laughed.

Nora. No, it was you who smiled, Dr. Rank!

Rank (*getting up*). You're even a bigger tease than I'd thought.

Nora. I'm full of wild ideas today.

Rank. That's obvious.

Nora (*putting both hands on his shoulders*). Dear, dear Dr. Rank, you'll never die for Torvald and me.

Rank. Oh, that loss you'll easily get over. Those who go away are soon forgotten.

Nora (*looks fearfully at him*). You believe that? 1

Rank. One makes new connections, and then—

Nora. Who makes new connections?

Rank. Both you and Torvald will when I'm gone. I'd say you're well under way already. What was that Mrs. Linde doing here last evening?

Nora. Oh, come—you can't be jealous of poor Kristine?

Rank. Oh yes, I am. She'll be my successor here in the house. When I'm down under, that woman will probably—

Nora. Shh! Not so loud. She's right in there.

Rank. Today as well. So you see.

Nora. Only to sew on my dress. Good gracious, how unreasonable you are. (*Sitting on the sofa.*) Be nice now, Dr. Rank. Tomorrow you'll see how beautifully I'll dance; and you can

5. **retribution:** punishment or return for wrongdoing.

6. ***pâté de foie gras*** (pä-tā' də fwä grä') . . . **truffles:** Pâté de foie gras is a rich meat paste made of duck or goose liver. Truffles are hard-to-find fungi that grow near certain trees and are eaten as delicacies.

Cross Curricular Link Humanities

CALLING CARDS Fashionable in high society throughout 19th-century Europe, calling cards were used for introductions, invitations, and visits. Usually, upon arriving in town, gentlemen and ladies drove to the homes of acquaintances and had their servant leave their cards at the door with the butler. The cards were placed on a tray in the front hall—with those of the most prominent visitors on top—until the mistress of the house could look through them. She was then free to either send over her own card or pay a visit in person.

Visits, or calls, were made according to a strict schedule. Casual acquaintances came between three and four o'clock; closer acquaintances arrived between four and five; and good friends appeared between five and six. Callers typically stayed for a period not longer than a half hour and left if another person came to call.

Of course, a lady or gentleman could try paying a visit without leaving a calling card at all. However, the caller then risked rejection. If the mistress of the house didn't want to receive the visitor, the butler would say that she was "not at home." It would be left to the caller to wonder whether she was truly away or simply didn't welcome the visit.

imagine then that I'm dancing only for you—yes, and of course for Torvald, too—that's understood. (*Takes various items out of the carton.*) Dr. Rank, sit over here and I'll show you something.

Rank (*sitting*). What's that?

Nora. Look here. Look.

Rank. Silk stockings.

Nora. Flesh-colored. Aren't they lovely? Now it's so dark here, but tomorrow— No, no, no, just look at the feet. Oh well, you might as well look at the rest.

Rank. Hm—

Nora. Why do you look so critical? Don't you believe they'll fit?

Rank. I've never had any chance to form an opinion on that.

Nora (*glancing at him a moment*). Shame on you. (*Hits him lightly on the ear with the stockings.*) That's for you. (*Puts them away again.*)

Rank. And what other splendors am I going to see now?

Nora. Not the least bit more, because you've been naughty. (*She hums a little and rummages among her things.*)

Rank (*after a short silence*). When I sit here together with you like this, completely easy and open, then I don't know—I simply can't imagine—whatever would have become of me if I'd never come into this house.

Nora (*smiling*). Yes, I really think you feel completely at ease with us.

Rank (*more quietly, staring straight ahead*). And then to have to go away from it all—

Nora. Nonsense, you're not going away.

Rank (*his voice unchanged*). —and not even be able to leave some poor show of gratitude behind, scarcely a fleeting regret—no more than a vacant place that anyone can fill.

Nora. And if I asked you now for—? No—

Rank. For what?

Nora. For a great proof of your friendship—

Rank. Yes, yes?

Nora. No, I mean—for an exceptionally big favor— B

Rank. Would you really, for once, make me so happy?

Nora. Oh, you haven't the vaguest idea what it is.

Rank. All right, then tell me.

Nora. No, but I can't, Dr. Rank—it's all out of reason. It's advice and help, too—and a favor—

Rank. So much the better. I can't fathom what you're hinting at. Just speak out. Don't you trust me?

Nora. Of course. More than anyone else. You're my best and truest friend, I'm sure. That's why I want to talk to you. All right, then, Dr. Rank: there's something you can help me prevent. You know how deeply, how inexpressibly dearly Torvald loves me; he'd never hesitate a second to give up his life for me.

Rank (*leaning close to her*). Nora—do you think he's the only one—

Nora (*with a slight start*). Who—?

Rank. Who'd gladly give up his life for you.

Nora (*heavily*). I see.

Rank. I swore to myself you should know this before I'm gone. I'll never find a better chance. Yes, Nora, now you know. And also you know now that you can trust me beyond anyone else.

Nora (*rising, natural and calm*). Let me by.

Rank (*making room for her, but still sitting*). Nora—

Nora (*in the hall doorway*). Helene, bring the

Customizing Instruction

Less Proficient Readers

Point out to students that the conversation between Nora and Dr. Rank has several parts: his discussion of his illness and death (p. 1052, col. 1–2); the flirtation between the two (p. 1052, col. 1–1053, col. 2); Nora's trying to ask him a favor (p. 1053, col. 2); and his revealing his feelings for her (p. 1053, col. 2).

English Learners

Make sure students understand that Dr. Rank has been ill for most of his life and that the disease is entering its final stages, which he refers to as his disintegration and the wreck starting to come apart.

Advanced Learners

1 Ask students why Nora looks fearfully at Dr. Rank.

Possible Response: Dr. Rank seems to be voicing Nora's own fears: she, too, fears that she will soon be going away and will be forgotten.

Why might Nora go away?

Possible Responses: She might be arrested; Torvald might send her away; she might run away.

Pause & Reflect
Possible Response: Nora can talk easily with Dr. Rank about everyday things, and she can relax and be herself. With Torvald, she has to be proper and do what he says. In some ways, her relationship with Dr. Rank is closer than her relationship with Torvald.

Literary Analysis FOIL CHARACTER
Remind students that a foil chararcter provides a striking contrast to another character. Have students discuss whether Dr. Rank is a foil to another character.
Possible Responses: Dr. Rank is a foil to Torvald. Rank is a professional person, but he is not preoccupied with his status or position. He is sincere in his relations with people, and he is good friends with Nora. He is not a strong person physically, which contrasts with Torvald's vigor and energy. Some students may say that Dr. Rank is a foil to Krogstad as well, because Krogstad is threatening to Nora and Dr. Rank is caring.

Reading Skills and Strategies
EVALUATING CHARACTER
Ask students what they think of Dr. Rank.
Possible Response: Students should support their opinions with details from the play. Some will feel sorry for Dr. Rank because of his illness and because of his love for Nora, which she does not or cannot respond to. Others may feel he takes advantage of Nora. Some may say he is too matter-of-fact and cynical about his own death.

Reading Skills and Strategies
CLARIFYING
A Ask students what Dr. Rank thinks Nora's "big secret" is. *(He thinks Nora has bought a new dress and wants to keep it a secret from Torvald.)*

Literary Analysis SUSPENSE
Remind students that suspense grows as the conflict intensifies and complications develop. Ask them to identify elements of suspense at this point in the play.
Possible Responses: Suspense is generated when the maid brings in the calling card; when Nora talks about the "horror"; when Krogstad implies that Torvald will find out Nora's secret; and when Krogstad says that it wouldn't do Nora any good even if she could pay off the debt.

lamp in. (*Goes over to the stove.*) Ah, dear Dr. Rank, that was really mean of you.

Rank (*getting up*). That I've loved you just as deeply as somebody else? Was *that* mean?

Nora. No, but that you came out and told me. That was quite unnecessary—

Rank. What do you mean? Have you known—?

(The Maid *comes in with the lamp, sets it on the table, and goes out again.)*

Rank. Nora—Mrs. Helmer—I'm asking you: have you known about it?

Nora. Oh, how can I tell what I know or don't know? Really, I don't know what to say—Why did you have to be so clumsy, Dr. Rank! Everything was so good.

Rank. Well, in any case, you now have the knowledge that my body and soul are at your command. So won't you speak out?

Nora (*looking at him*). After that?

Rank. Please, just let me know what it is.

Nora. You can't know anything now.

1 **Rank.** I have to. You mustn't punish me like this. Give me the chance to do whatever is humanly possible for you.

Nora. Now there's nothing you can do for me. Besides, actually, I don't need any help. You'll see—it's only my fantasies. That's what it is. Of course! (*Sits in the rocker, looks at him, and smiles.*) What a nice one you are, Dr. Rank. Aren't you a little bit ashamed, now that the lamp is here?

Rank. No, not exactly. But perhaps I'd better go—for good?

Nora. No, you certainly can't do that. You must come here just as you always have. You know Torvald can't do without you.

Rank. Yes, but *you?*

Nora. You know how much I enjoy it when you're here.

Rank. That's precisely what threw me off. You're a mystery to me. So many times I've felt you'd almost rather be with me than with Helmer.

Nora. Yes—you see, there are some people that one loves most and other people that one would almost prefer being with.

Rank. Yes, there's something to that.

Nora. When I was back home, of course I loved Papa most. But I always thought it was so much fun when I could sneak down to the maids' quarters, because they never tried to improve me, and it was always so amusing, the way they talked to each other.

Rank. Aha, so it's *their* place that I've filled.

Nora (*jumping up and going to him*). Oh, dear, sweet Dr. Rank, that's not what I meant at all. But you can understand that with Torvald it's just the same as with Papa—

(The Maid *enters from the hall.)*

Maid. Ma'am—please! (*She whispers to* Nora *and hands her a calling card.*)

Nora (*glancing at the card*). Ah! (*Slips it into her pocket.*)

Rank. Anything wrong?

Nora. No, no, not at all. It's only some—it's my new dress— 2

Rank. Really? But—there's your dress.

Nora. Oh, that. But this is another one—I ordered it—Torvald mustn't know—

Rank. Ah, now we have the big secret. A

Nora. That's right. Just go in with him—he's back in the inner study. Keep him there as long as—

Rank. Don't worry. He won't get away. (*Goes into the study.*)

PAUSE & REFLECT Why does Nora enjoy spending time with Dr. Rank? What does this suggest about her relationship with Torvald?

MINI LESSON **Speaking and Listening**

PORTRAYING A RELATIONSHIP

Instruction The conversation between Nora and Dr. Rank on page 1054 touches on complicated and deep feelings. From the moment when Nora says "Ah, dear Dr. Rank, that was really mean of you" to her speech beginning "Oh, dear, sweet Dr. Rank . . . ," there is little action, but the two characters pass through a turning point in their relationship.

Prepare Have students work in pairs to give a reading of this conversation. Tell them that they need to concentrate on portraying subtle reactions and underlying thoughts and emotions. Since there is not much action, everything must be conveyed through tone of voice, facial expression, and a few gestures.

Present Have the pairs of students take turns doing their reading for the rest of the class. Tell the other students to take notes on each reading. After all of the readings have been given, guide the class in a discussion of what aspects of the relationship between Nora and Dr. Rank were particularly brought out in the different readings and whether there were any major differences between the presentations.

This activity is particularly well suited for longer class periods.

FOCUS Nora still hasn't found a solution to her problem. As you read, notice the ways in which she shows her desperation.

Nora (*to the* Maid). And he's standing waiting in the kitchen?

Maid. Yes, he came up by the back stairs.

Nora. But didn't you tell him somebody was here?

Maid. Yes, but that didn't do any good.

Nora. He won't leave?

Maid. No, he won't go till he's talked with you, ma'am.

Nora. Let him come in, then—but quietly. Helene, don't breathe a word about this. It's a surprise for my husband.

Maid. Yes, yes, I understand— (*Goes out.*)

Nora. This horror—it's going to happen. No, no, no, it can't happen, it mustn't. (*She goes and bolts* Helmer's *door. The* Maid *opens the hall door for* Krogstad *and shuts it behind him. He is dressed for travel in a fur coat, boots, and a fur cap.*)

Nora (*going toward him*). Talk softly. My husband's home.

Krogstad. Well, good for him.

Nora. What do you want?

Krogstad. Some information.

Nora. Hurry up, then. What is it?

Krogstad. You know, of course, that I got my notice.

Nora. I couldn't prevent it, Mr. Krogstad. I fought for you to the bitter end, but nothing worked.

Krogstad. Does your husband's love for you run so thin? He knows everything I can expose you to, and all the same he dares to—

Nora. How can you imagine he knows anything about this?

Krogstad. Ah, no—I can't imagine it either, now. It's not at all like my fine Torvald Helmer to have so much guts—

Nora. Mr. Krogstad, I demand respect for my husband!

Krogstad. Why, of course—all due respect. But since the lady's keeping it so carefully hidden, may I presume to ask if you're also a bit better informed than yesterday about what you've actually done? 3

Nora. More than you ever could teach me.

Krogstad. Yes, I *am* such an awful lawyer.

Nora. What is it you want from me?

Krogstad. Just a glimpse of how you are, Mrs. Helmer. I've been thinking about you all day long. A cashier, a night-court scribbler, a—well, a type like me also has a little of what they call a heart, you know. 4

Nora. Then show it. Think of my children.

Krogstad. Did you or your husband ever think of mine? But never mind. I simply wanted to tell you that you don't need to take this thing too seriously. For the present, I'm not proceeding with any action.

Nora. Oh no, really! Well—I knew that.

Krogstad. Everything can be settled in a friendly spirit. It doesn't have to get around town at all; it can stay just among us three.

Nora. My husband must never know anything of this.

Krogstad. How can you manage that? Perhaps you can pay me the balance?

Nora. No, not right now.

Krogstad. Or you know some way of raising the money in a day or two?

Nora. No way that I'm willing to use.

Krogstad. Well, it wouldn't have done you any good, anyway. If you stood in front of me with a fistful of bills, you still couldn't buy

Customizing Instruction

Less Proficient Readers

Focus Suggest to students that they keep a list of passages in which Nora's words or actions show her anxiety.

1 Explain that the punishment Dr. Rank refers to is Nora's not being willing to ask him to do a favor for her, now that he has told her he loves her. From Nora's viewpoint, to ask his help now would be unfair and might be misinterpreted as a positive response to his feelings for her.

2 Make sure students realize that Nora doesn't really have a new dress. She says she does to make it seem that the card the maid has brought in is from a delivery person. Ask students whom they think the card is really from. *(Krogstad)*

3 Tell students that this question refers to Nora's forgery of her father's signature, which Krogstad forced her to confess in Act One (p. 1038, col. 1).

English Learners

4 Explain that because Krogstad has a bad business reputation, he has to make his money doing various kinds of low-paying jobs, such as being a clerk or writing up reports of court cases held at night—jobs most people wouldn't want.

Help students understand the following words and phrases: p. 1054, col. 1, "mean" *(unkind)*; col. 2, "tried to improve me" *(tried to make me behave properly)*; p. 1055, col. 2, "have so much guts" *(a rude way of saying that person has courage and determination)*; "action" *(legal steps taken to make an accusation)*; "balance" *(rest of the money owed)*

Reading Skills and Strategies

CLARIFYING

A Ask students what Krogstad is demanding now. *(He wants to be hired back at the bank, but in a better position than he had before.)*

Then point out that Krogstad is sure Torvald will agree to his demand. Ask: Why do you think he is so sure?

Possible Response: Krogstad thinks Torvald will agree because he knows Torvald would do anything to avoid scandal and disgrace, which is what Krogstad's revelation of the forgery would bring.

Literary Analysis FOIL CHARACTER

Have students discuss how Krogstad is a foil for Torvald.

Possible Response: Krogstad's past history and his bullying and threatening to blackmail Nora and Torvald are the opposite of Torvald's strict morality, his harsh judgments of others' weaknesses and failures, and his preoccupation with maintaining his public image.

Active Reading

STAGE DIRECTIONS AND DIALOGUE

B Ask students what the stage directions and Nora's words to herself tell about her reaction to Krogstad's visit.

Possible Reponse: She expects the worst to happen and is feeling truly desperate.

Literary Analysis SUSPENSE

Have students identify the details on page 1057 that create suspense.

Possible Response: The details include Krogstad's letter in the mailbox, Nora's hints about "something else" occurring, and the "miracle" that she says is going to take place but mustn't take place.

your signature back.

Nora. Then tell me what you're going to do with it.

Krogstad. I'll just hold onto it—keep it on file. There's no outsider who'll even get wind of it. So if you've been thinking of taking some desperate step—

Nora. I have.

Krogstad. Been thinking of running away from home—

Nora. I have!

Krogstad. Or even of something worse—

Nora. How could you guess that?

Krogstad. You can drop those thoughts.

Nora. How could you guess I was thinking of *that?*

Krogstad. Most of us think about *that* at first. I thought about it too, but I discovered I hadn't the courage—

Nora (*lifelessly*). I don't either.

Krogstad (*relieved*). That's true, you haven't the courage? You too?

Nora. I don't have it—I don't have it.

Krogstad. It would be terribly stupid, anyway. After that first storm at home blows out, why, then— I have here in my pocket a letter for your husband—

Nora. Telling everything?

Krogstad. As charitably as possible.

Nora (*quickly*). He mustn't ever get that letter. Tear it up. I'll find some way to get money.

Krogstad. Beg pardon, Mrs. Helmer, but I think I just told you—

Nora. Oh, I don't mean the money I owe you. Let me know how much you want from my husband, and I'll manage it.

Krogstad. I don't want any money from your husband.

Nora. What do you want, then?

Krogstad. I'll tell you what. I want to recoup,[7] Mrs. Helmer; I want to get on in the world—and there's where your husband can help me. For a year and a half I've kept myself clean of anything disreputable—all that time struggling with the worst conditions; but I was satisfied, working my way up step by step. Now I've been written right off, and I'm just not in the mood to come crawling back. I tell you, I want to move on. I want to get back in the bank—in a better position. Your husband can set up a job for me— **A**

Nora. He'll never do that!

Krogstad. He'll do it. I know him. He won't dare breathe a word of protest. And once I'm in there together with him, you just wait and see! Inside of a year, I'll be the manager's right-hand man. It'll be Nils Krogstad, not Torvald Helmer, who runs the bank.

Nora. You'll never see the day!

Krogstad. Maybe you think you can—

Nora. I have the courage now—for *that.*

Krogstad. Oh, you don't scare me. A smart, spoiled lady like you—

Nora. You'll see; you'll see!

Krogstad. Under the ice, maybe? Down in the freezing, coal-black water? There, till you float up in the spring, ugly, unrecognizable, with your hair falling out—

Nora. You don't frighten me.

Krogstad. Nor do you frighten me. One doesn't do these things, Mrs. Helmer. Besides, what good would it be? I'd still have him safe in my pocket.

Nora. Afterwards? When I'm no longer—?

Krogstad. Are you forgetting that *I'll* be in control then over your final reputation? (Nora

7. **recoup** (rĭ-ko͞op'): to regain a former favorable position.

stands speechless, staring at him.) Good; now I've warned you. Don't do anything stupid. When Helmer's read my letter, I'll be waiting for his reply. And bear in mind that it's your husband himself who's forced me back to my old ways. I'll never forgive him for that. Good-bye, Mrs. Helmer. (*He goes out through the hall.*)

Nora (*goes to the hall door, opens it a crack, and listens*). He's gone. Didn't leave the letter. Oh no, no, that's impossible too! (*Opening the door more and more.*) What's that? He's standing outside—not going downstairs. He's
3 thinking it over? Maybe he'll—? (*A letter falls in the mailbox; then* Krogstad's *footsteps are heard, dying away down a flight of stairs.* Nora *gives a muffled cry and runs over toward the sofa table. A short pause.*) In the mailbox. (*Slips warily over to the hall door.*) It's lying there. Torvald, Torvald—now we're lost!

Mrs. Linde (*entering with the costume from the room, left*). There now, I can't see anything else to mend. Perhaps you'd like to try—

Nora (*in a hoarse whisper*). Kristine, come here.

Mrs. Linde (*tossing the dress on the sofa*). What's wrong? You look upset.

Nora. Come here. See that letter? *There!* Look—through the glass in the mailbox.

Mrs. Linde. Yes, yes, I see it.

Nora. That letter's from Krogstad—

Mrs. Linde. Nora—it's Krogstad who loaned you the money!

Nora. Yes, and now Torvald will find out everything.

Mrs. Linde. Believe me, Nora, it's best for both of you.

Nora. There's more you don't know. I forged a name.

Mrs. Linde. But for heaven's sake—?

Nora. I only want to tell you that, Kristine, so that you can be my witness.

Mrs. Linde. Witness? Why should I—?

Nora. If I should go out of my mind—it could easily happen—

Mrs. Linde. Nora!

Nora. Or anything else occurred—so I couldn't be present here—

Mrs. Linde. Nora, Nora, you aren't yourself at all!

Nora. And someone should try to take on the whole weight, all of the guilt, you follow me— 1

Mrs. Linde. Yes, of course, but why do you think—?

Nora. Then you're the witness that it isn't true, Kristine. I'm very much myself; my mind right now is perfectly clear; and I'm telling you: nobody else has known about this; I alone did everything. Remember that.

Mrs. Linde. I will. But I don't understand all this.

Nora. Oh, how could you ever understand it? It's the miracle now that's going to take place.

Mrs. Linde. The miracle? 2

Nora. Yes, the miracle. But it's so awful, Kristine. It mustn't take place, not for anything in the world.

Mrs. Linde. I'm going right over and talk with Krogstad.

Nora. Don't go near him; he'll do you some terrible harm!

Mrs. Linde. There was a time once when he'd gladly have done anything for me.

Nora. He?

Mrs. Linde. Where does he live?

Nora. Oh, how do I know? Yes. (*Searches in her pocket.*) Here's his card. But the letter, the letter—!

Helmer (*from the study, knocking on the door*). Nora!

WORDS TO KNOW

warily (wâr'ĭ-lē) *adv.* watchfully; cautiously

Customizing Instruction

Less Proficient Readers

- Point out that part of Krogstad's threatening strategy is to prey on thoughts Nora has already had about running away or committing suicide.
- Make sure students understand that Krogstad's letter is to Torvald and reveals everything about Nora's secret loan and her forgery. Remind them that since the forgery was illegal and that it was also not legal for a wife to take out a loan on her own, Torvald would be faced with what he would view as outrageous and unacceptable behavior.

1 Explain that "someone" is an indirect way of referring to Torvald.

2 **Set a Purpose** Explain that the miracle is apparently something connected to Torvald. Tell students to look for more indications of what the miracle might be as they continue to read.

English Learners

- For practice with English, students could read aloud the conversation between Nora and Mrs. Linde on page 1057, column 1.
- Help students with the following phrases: p. 1056, col. 1, "get wind of it" *(find out anything about it);* "first storm at home blows out" *(a reference to Torvald's outrage when he finds out what Nora did);* col. 2, "crawling back" *(returning to his old job feeling shamed and embarrassed)*

MINI LESSON

Vocabulary Strategy

SUFFIXES

Instruction Remind students that sometimes they can determine the meaning of an unfamiliar word by examining its parts. Suffixes are affixes added to the ends of words. Many suffixes change the part of speech of a word.

Suffix	Suffix Meaning	Example
-less	without	odorless
-able	capable of being, or having qualities of	comfortable
-ous	full of, or having	dangerous
-ward	in the direction of	backward

Practice Have students give the meaning of the suffix in each of the following words and then give the meaning of the whole word. Students should use a dictionary for help as needed.

1. speechless *(without; not having speech)*
2. courageous *(full of; full of courage)*
3. homeward *(in the direction of; toward home)*
4. doubtless *(without; without doubt)*
5. lovable *(capable of being; capable of being loved)*

A lesson on using suffixes appears on p. 864 of the Pupil's Edition.

Reading Skills and Strategies

SUMMARIZING

Point out that Nora faces imminent disaster if Torvald looks in the mailbox. Have students summarize how she handles the situation.

Possible Response: As suggested by Mrs. Linde, she uses stalling tactics to keep Torvald from the mailbox—she begs for his help with the dance, plays her child role to flatter him, and starts playing the tarantella music to distract him from continuing to the mailbox.

Literary Analysis DRAMATIC IRONY

Tell students that because the reader knows so much more than Torvald does at this point in the play, many of the words and actions are ironic. Have students identify two examples on page 1059.

Possible Responses: col. 1: Torvald expects to see Nora's masquerade costume, but the reader knows she hasn't been doing anything with the dress; col. 2: Nora tells Torvald she needs his help practicing the dance, but the reader knows she is trying to keep him from finding Krogstad's letter; Torvald thinks Nora is worried about doing the dance well, but the reader knows she is afraid of his finding the letter.

Literary Analysis SYMBOL

A Tell students that Nora is referring to the key to the mailbox. Ask them how the key might be a symbol.

Possible Response: Torvald has controlled Nora's life in most ways, as a person who has the key to a room controls access to the room.

Literary Analysis

REALISTIC DRAMA: CHARACTER

B Ask: Why do you think Nora dances so violently?

Possible Response: The dancing reflects her inner turmoil and uncertainty and her sense that her world is in danger of falling apart.

You must give up everything this evening for me. No business —don't even touch your pen.

Nora (*with a cry of fear*). Oh! What is it? What do you want?

1 **Helmer.** Now, now, don't be so frightened. We're not coming in. You locked the door—are you trying on the dress?

Nora. Yes, I'm trying it. I'll look just beautiful, Torvald.

Mrs. Linde (*who has read the card*). He's living right around the corner.

Nora. Yes, but what's the use? We're lost. The letter's in the box.

A **Mrs. Linde.** And your husband has the key?

Nora. Yes, always.

Mrs. Linde. Krogstad can ask for his letter back unread; he can find some excuse—

Nora. But it's just this time that Torvald usually—

Mrs. Linde. Stall him. Keep him in there. I'll be back as quick as I can. (*She hurries out through the hall entrance.*)

Nora (*goes to* Helmer*'s door, opens it, and peers in*). Torvald!

Helmer (*from the inner study*). Well—does one dare set foot in one's own living room at last? Come on, Rank, now we'll get a look— (*In the doorway.*) But what's this?

Nora. What, Torvald dear?

Helmer. Rank had me expecting some grand masquerade.

Rank (*in the doorway*). That was my impression, but I must have been wrong.

Nora. No one can admire me in my splendor—not till tomorrow.

Helmer. But Nora dear, you look so exhausted. Have you practiced too hard?

Nora. No, I haven't practiced at all yet.

Helmer. You know, it's necessary—

Nora. Oh, it's absolutely necessary, Torvald. But I can't get anywhere without your help. I've forgotten the whole thing completely.

Helmer. Ah, we'll soon take care of that.

Nora. Yes, take care of me, Torvald, please! Promise me that? Oh, I'm so nervous. That big party— You must give up everything this evening for me. No business—don't even touch your pen. Yes? Dear Torvald, promise? 2

Helmer. It's a promise. Tonight I'm totally at your service—you little helpless thing. Hm—but first there's one thing I want to— (*Goes toward the hall door.*)

Nora. What are you looking for?

Helmer. Just to see if there's any mail.

Nora. No, no, don't do that, Torvald!

Helmer. Now what?

Nora. Torvald, please. There isn't any.

Helmer. Let me look, though. (*Starts out.* Nora, *at the piano, strikes the first notes of the tarantella.* Helmer, *at the door, stops.*) Aha!

Nora. I can't dance tomorrow if I don't practice with you.

Helmer (*going over to her*). Nora dear, are you really so frightened?

Nora. Yes, so terribly frightened. Let me practice right now; there's still time before dinner. Oh, sit down and play for me, Torvald. Direct me. Teach me, the way you always have.

Helmer. Gladly, if it's what you want. (*Sits at the piano.*)

Nora (*snatches the tambourine up from the box, then a long, varicolored shawl, which she throws around herself, whereupon she springs forward and cries out:*) Play for me now! Now I'll dance!

(Helmer *plays and* Nora *dances.* Rank *stands behind* Helmer *at the piano and looks on.*)

Helmer (*as he plays*). Slower. Slow down.

Nora. Can't change it. B

Helmer. Not so violent, Nora!

Nora. Has to be just like this.

Customizing Instruction

Less Proficient Readers

1 Remind students that Nora locked the study door when Krogstad arrived. Also remind them that Dr. Rank mistakenly thinks that Nora's "big secret" is ordering a new dress for the party, and he has told Torvald about it. Torvald thinks she has locked him in so he won't see the dress before she is ready. Tell students to watch how Nora handles the situation when Torvald comes out of the study.

Make sure students understand that Nora is pretending to be frightened of not being able to do the dance in order to distract Torvald and keep him from checking the mail. Also, make sure they realize that Mrs. Linde has gone to find Krogstad and try to persuade him to take his letter back.

English Learners

Explain that the expression "stall him" (p. 1059, col. 1) refers to keeping Torvald occupied so he won't go to the mailbox.

Advanced Learners

2 Ask students what Nora's plea foreshadows.

Possible Response: Nora's need for Torvald's support when the truth comes out about the loan

Why is the plea ironic?

Possible Response: Torvald thinks Nora is referring to her unpreparedness for the dance; he doesn't know what she is really frightened about.

MINI LESSON Speaking and Listening

STAGING A SCENE

Instruction Point out to students that the action on page 1059 is fast paced. Suggest to them that the action can be divided into three parts. The first ends when Mrs. Linde leaves, the second ends with Nora's speech "Torvald, please. There isn't any," and the third ends when Nora says "Has to be just like this."

Application Tell students to choose one part of the action and visualize how it might be staged. Then have them work in pairs or in groups of three, depending on which part they choose, and prepare the scene to present to the class.

Present After each presentation is given, have the class discuss whether the interpretation was clear and convincing. After all the presentations are finished, have the class share their opinions about what was the most effective staging of each part.

This activity is particularly well suited for longer class periods.

Active Reading
STAGE DIRECTIONS AND VISUALIZING

A Tell students to read these stage directions carefully and then try to picture Nora's dancing and Mrs. Linde's reaction. Ask them why Mrs. Linde is dumbfounded.

Possible Response: Nora's dancing so wildly is completely uncharacteristic behavior for her.

Literary Analysis
REALISTIC DRAMA: CHARACTER

B Ask students what Torvald's reaction shows about him.

Possible Response: He is much more concerned that Nora is doing the dance incorrectly than that she is acting out of character and is clearly experiencing strong emotion.

Literary Analysis DICTION

At the end of Act Two, Torvald starts calling Nora his "lark" again. Have students discuss the effect of his using this word.

Possible Response: It shows that Torvald still sees Nora in the way he did at the beginning of the play. It also contrasts sharply with Nora's fear and with the sense of potential disaster looming at this point in the play.

Literary Analysis FORESHADOWING

C After students have finished reading the drama, you might have them reread these lines of dialogue. Ask them to identify hints or clues that suggest what occurs at the end of *A Doll's House.*

Possible Responses: "anything ugly between us"; "before it's all over"; "Then you'll be free."

Helmer (*stopping*). No, no, that won't do at all.

Nora (*laughing and swinging her tambourine*). Isn't that what I told you?

Rank. Let me play for her.

Helmer (*getting up*). Yes, go on. I can teach her more easily then.

(Rank *sits at the piano and plays;* Nora *dances more and more wildly.* Helmer *has stationed himself by the stove and repeatedly gives her directions; she seems not to hear them; her hair loosens and falls over her shoulders; she does not notice, but goes on dancing.* Mrs. Linde *enters.*)

Mrs. Linde (*standing dumbfounded at the door*). Ah—!

Nora (*still dancing*). See what fun, Kristine!

Helmer. But Nora darling, you dance as if your life were at stake.

Nora. And it is.

Helmer. Rank, stop! This is pure madness. Stop it, I say!

(Rank *breaks off playing, and* Nora *halts abruptly.*)

Helmer (*going over to her*). I never would have believed it. You've forgotten everything I taught you.

Nora (*throwing away the tambourine*). You see for yourself.

Helmer. Well, there's certainly room for instruction here.

Nora. Yes, you see how important it is. You've got to teach me to the very last minute. Promise me that, Torvald?

Helmer. You can bet on it.

Nora. You mustn't, either today or tomorrow, think about anything else but me; you mustn't open any letters—or the mailbox—

Helmer. Ah, it's still the fear of that man—

Nora. Oh yes, yes, that too.

Helmer. Nora, it's written all over you—there's already a letter from him out there.

Nora. I don't know. I guess so. But you mustn't read such things now; there mustn't be anything ugly between us before it's all over.

Rank (*quietly to* Helmer). You shouldn't deny her.

Helmer (*putting his arm around her*). The child can have her way. But tomorrow night, after you've danced—

Nora. Then you'll be free.

Maid (*in the doorway, right*). Ma'am, dinner is served.

Nora. We'll be wanting champagne, Helene.

Maid. Very good, ma'am. (*Goes out.*)

Helmer. So—a regular banquet, hm?

Nora. Yes, a banquet—champagne till daybreak! (*Calling out.*) And some macaroons, Helene. Heaps of them—just this once.

Helmer (*taking her hands*). Now, now, now—no hysterics. Be my own little lark again.

Nora. Oh, I will soon enough. But go on in—and you, Dr. Rank. Kristine, help me put up my hair.

Rank (*whispering, as they go*). There's nothing wrong—really wrong, is there?

Helmer. Oh, of course not. It's nothing more than this childish anxiety I was telling you about.

(*They go out, right.*)

Nora. Well?

Mrs. Linde. Left town.

Nora. I could see by your face.

Mrs. Linde. He'll be home tomorrow evening. I wrote him a note.

Nora. You shouldn't have. Don't try to stop anything now. After all, it's a wonderful joy, this waiting here for the miracle.

Mrs. Linde. What is it you're waiting for?

Humanities

TARANTELLA The dance called the tarantella originated in the southern Italian city of Taranto. The tarantella is a courting dance performed by a couple as they play the tambourine and castanets. Onlookers circle the couple as they execute the fast-paced, whirling dance.

Originally, the tarantella was thought to be a symptom of a disease called tarantism, believed to be caused by a tarantula's bite. The disease made its victims dance, forcing them to jump high in the air and emit strange sounds. Oddly enough, the dance was also thought to be the only cure for the disease. Some critics have suggested that Nora's performance of the tarantella reveals her tortured mental state. Tormented by Krogstad's demands and the necessity to conceal all from Torvald, Nora dances feverishly to drive out the poison from her system.

In fact, in many productions of *A Doll's House,* Nora's dance of the tarantella is the play's most dramatic scene. Some actresses have performed the scene by dancing wildly, even hysterically. Others have used understated movements and gestures to suggest Nora's nervous exhaustion.

Nora. Oh, you can't understand that. Go in to them; I'll be along in a moment.

(Mrs. Linde *goes into the dining room.* Nora *stands a short while as if composing herself; then she looks at her watch.)*

Nora. Five. Seven hours to midnight. Twenty-four hours to the midnight after, and then the tarantella's done. Seven and twenty-four? Thirty-one hours to live.

Helmer (*in the doorway, right*). What's become of the little lark?

Nora (*going toward him with open arms*). Here's your lark!

Seven hours to midnight.
Twenty-four hours to the midnight after,
and then the tarantella's done.

Customizing Instruction

Less Proficient Readers

Tell students that at the end of Act Two, Nora is making several hints about what is to come. Explain that she is intentionally vague. She seems to be setting the stage for what might happen but does not want to explain herself at this point.

English Learners

Help students with the following terms: p. 1060, col. 1, "dumbfounded" *(completely surprised);* "as if your life were at stake" *(as though you might die);* col. 2, "hysterics," *(very excitable behavior)*

Advanced Learners

Tell students to review the elements of plot explained on page 1027. Ask them to identify the plot developments in Act Two.

Possible Response: Examples of the rising action in Act Two include Torvald's refusal to reinstate Krogstad and his sending the notice of dismissal to Krogstad; Dr. Rank's declaration of his imminent death and of his love for Nora; and Krogstad's new threat and his leaving the letter for Torvald.

Have students write a brief summary of Nora's responses to the challenges she faces in this act.

Possible Responses: She experiences great anxiety and uncertainty. She also is a strategist, however, as she balances Krogstad's threats, uses Mrs. Linde's help, and manipulates Torvald. She deals with Dr. Rank's revelation of his love for her without becoming upset. By the end of the act, although she seems excitable, she also appears resolved to face whatever comes.

Assessment Standardized Test Practice

ARRANGING EVENTS IN SEQUENTIAL ORDER

Which of the following occurs first in Act Two?

A. Krogstad sends a letter to Torvald telling him about Nora's loan and the forgery.

B. Torvald sends a letter of dismissal to Krogstad.

C. Dr. Rank tells Nora he loves her.

D. Mrs. Linde tells Nora that Krogstad is out of town.

Guide students through the process of choosing the correct answer. A is incorrect because Krogstad writes his letter in response to being fired (pp. 1055–1057). B is correct because Torvald sends the letter right after his first conversation with Nora and before either Dr. Rank or Krogstad comes. (pp. 1049–1050). C is incorrect because Dr. Rank doesn't arrive until after Torvald sends his letter to Krogstad (p. 1050). D is incorrect because Mrs. Linde goes looking for Krogstad after he has sent his letter to Torvald (p. 1059).

Connect to the Literature

1. **What Do You Think?** Most students will say that Nora has become more serious as well as more fearful and agitated as she is forced to face reality.

Comprehension Check

- She tries to persuade him not to fire Krogstad, and she distracts him from Krogstad's letter in the mailbox.
- He wants to blackmail Torvald into not firing him and giving him a new, more important job at the bank.
- Krogstad used to love her, and she hopes that she can persuade him to take back his letter.

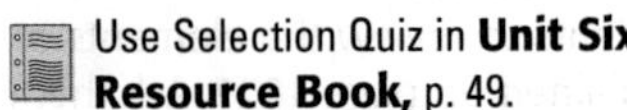
Use Selection Quiz in **Unit Six Resource Book,** p. 49.

Think Critically

2. Possible Response: Stage directions at the opening of the act, on p. 1046, col. 1, and on p. 1057, col. 1, reflect Nora's agitation and mounting anxiety. On p. 1060, col. 1, the stage directions regarding the wildness of Nora's dancing and her tone of voice suggest that she is increasingly desperate.
3. Possible Response: The miracle refers to Nora's statement on p. 1057 that "someone" would try to take on the weight of her guilt. It seems to be a hope she has that Torvald will act in some unexpected and wonderful way.
4. Possible Response: Some students may say that Krogstad's willingness to blackmail shows that Torvald's view of his character is correct. Others will respond that Krogstad is driven by his desperation to this deed, and that Torvald's main reason for firing Krogstad is petty, as even Nora points out.
5. Possible Response: The ideas of a disguise and a masquerade symbolize the relationship between Nora and Torvald. Nora has been playing the role of a submissive, childlike wife to Torvald, and he treats her like a child or a pet, choosing to respond only to the role she plays, not to what she might be like on a deeper level.

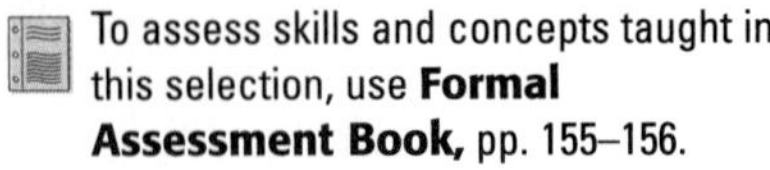
To assess skills and concepts taught in this selection, use **Formal Assessment Book,** pp. 155–156.

Connect to the Literature

1. **What Do You Think?** How has your impression of Nora changed in Act Two?

Comprehension Check

- What steps does Nora take to try to prevent Torvald from finding out her secret?
- What does Krogstad want his letter to accomplish?
- How does Mrs. Linde think she can help Nora?

Think Critically

2. **ACTIVE READING: STRATEGIES FOR READING REALISTIC DRAMA** Which stage directions give you insight into Nora's state of mind in Act Two? Explain what they suggest to you in your  **READER'S NOTEBOOK.**
3. What do you think the "miracle" might be? Support your answer with evidence from the text.
4. Krogstad says that Torvald has "forced me back to my old ways" (page 1057, col. 1). How responsible is Torvald for Krogstad's actions? Explain your answer.

THINK ABOUT
- Krogstad's past
- Krogstad's behavior in Act Two
- Torvald's attitude and actions with regard to Krogstad

5. A **symbol** is a person, a place, an object, or an activity that stands for something beyond itself. In what way are the references to disguise (page 1046, col. 2) and masquerade (page 1058, col. 1) symbolic?

Extend Interpretations

6. **What If?** Imagine that Nora does accept help from Rank. How might this affect the outcome of the play?
7. **Comparing Texts** Monna Giovanna in "Federigo's Falcon" (page 784) and Nora both take unusual measures to save the life of someone they love. What similarities and differences do you see between the two characters?
8. **Connect to Life** Good communication in marriage and in other important relationships continues to be of great concern in today's society. What do you think people can learn from Ibsen's portrayal of Nora and Torvald's relationship?

LITERARY ANALYSIS: SETTING IN REALISTIC DRAMA

The time and place of the action of a drama or narrative work is referred to as the **setting.** In a realistic drama, the setting is often described in great detail. Ibsen describes every decoration and piece of furniture in the room where the action of his play occurs. Such details can provide important clues about the characters and can help readers imagine what the stage design would look like.

In addition to time and place, setting may include the social and moral environment that forms the background for a literary work. For example, *A Doll House* is set in a middle-class environment where people place a high value on conformity and respectability.

Cooperative Learning Activity With a small group of classmates, collaborate to create a list of details that describe the setting of *A Doll House.* You might want to break the list into two sections. The first could include details of time and of place. The second could give examples of dialogue that reveals the play's social and moral environment.

Extend Interpretations

6. **What If?** Possible Response: Dr. Rank could not prevent Krogstad from using the forged note to blackmail Torvald, but as Torvald's closest friend, he might be able to break the news to Torvald and advise him on how to proceed. He might also be able to soften Torvald's reaction to Nora.
7. **Comparing Texts** Possible Response: Both women have taken daring actions to save the life of someone they loved. However, Monna Giovanna acts openly and with dignity, while Nora deceives her husband and exposes herself to blackmail.
8. **Connect to Life** Possible Response: Direct communication, honesty, and mutual respect are essential to a strong and fulfilling relationship.

Literary Analysis

Cooperative Learning Activity After students have created their lists, have them share their findings in a class discussion. Ask for volunteers to summarize the play's social and moral environment.

Use **Unit Six Resource Book,** p. 48, for more practice.

Translating Drama

Translators of drama have a complicated job. They are translating literary works that will be read, but they are also translating scripts that actors will use to create performances. Of course, it is important that the translation of a play convey the meaning of the original as closely as possible. In addition, however, its language must free the actors to interpret the actions, mood, personalities, and ideas of the work.

Below are two translations of a passage from Act One of *A Doll House*. One is from the version you have read, and the other is from another recent translation. Each is attempting to convey the freshness and naturalness of the original Norwegian; but note the differences in wording and sentence structure.

Helmer. You're an odd little one. Exactly the way your father was. You're never at a loss for scaring up money; but the moment you have it, it runs right out through your fingers; you never know what you've done with it. Well, one takes you as you are. It's deep in your blood. Yes, these things are hereditary, Nora.

Nora. Ah, I could wish I'd inherited many of Papa's qualities.

—Rolf Fjelde

Helmer. What a funny little one you are! Just like your father. Always on the look-out for money, wherever you can lay your hands on it; but as soon as you've got it, it just seems to slip through your fingers. You never seem to know what you've done with it. Well, one must accept you as you are. It's in the blood. Oh yes, it is, Nora. That sort of thing is hereditary.

Nora. Oh, I only wish I'd inherited a few more of Daddy's qualities.

—James McFarlane

Activity Imagine that you are an actor getting ready to audition for a part in *A Doll House.* Get together with a classmate and prepare readings of each of the passages above. As you work with the two translations, think about the differences between them and how those differences might affect the performance. Then tell whether you prefer one over the other and, if so, why.

The Translator at Work

READING FOR INFORMATION

Reading Skills and Strategies

COMPARING AND CONTRASTING

Point out to students that they will be comparing and contrasting two translations of a brief passage in the play. Suggest that they write down both translations on a piece of paper and then circle or underline words and phrases that they think show significant or interesting differences. Tell them to use these notations when they are preparing their readings.

Activity Suggest to students that they read the passages aloud together once or twice and then compare their ideas about the differences in the two translations. Encourage them to experiment with their readings. They might want to prepare two sets of readings, each of which would emphasize different aspects of the passages and create different interpretations.

Active Reading

STAGE DIRECTIONS AND DIALOGUE

A Remind students that stage directions give important clues about how dialogue should be spoken. Ask students to discuss how the stage directions affect the dialogue in this passage.

Possible Response: The stage directions describing Mrs. Linde's gestures and movements indicate that she is speaking in an agitated way to herself, and they give specific instruction to whisper to Krogstad.

 Use **Unit Six Resource Book,** p. 51, for more practice.

Literary Analysis
EXTENDED METAPHOR

Explain to students that in an extended metaphor, two things are compared at length and in various ways. Have them identify the extended metaphor on page 1065 and discuss the comparison that is developed. *(An extended metaphor comparing Krogstad and Mrs. Linde to half-drowned people in a shipwreck begins with Krogstad's speech in column 1, beginning "When I lost you . . ." and ends with Mrs. Linde's speech in column 2, beginning "Two on one wreck . . ." The comparison emphasizes the difficult, harsh lives both have led and the incompleteness of their lives because of being separated for many years.)*

Literary Analysis

REALISTIC DRAMA: THEME

Remind students that theme is a central idea or message in a work of literature. Remind them too that theme is not the same as the subject of the work but is a perception about life. Have them review pages 1064 and 1065 and write a theme statement about how the past influences people's lives.

Possible Responses: Decisions made in the past can have far-reaching effects and shape a person's relationships, attitudes, and security; mistakes made in the past can bring hard-earned wisdom that results in better decisions in the future.

 Use **Unit Six Resource Book,** p. 52, for more practice.

Reading Skills and Strategies
CLARIFYING

B Ask students why Mrs. Linde did come to town. *(to find Krogstad and reestablish a relationship with him)*

Act Three

GUIDE FOR READING

FOCUS In this part Mrs. Linde finally has a chance to speak with Krogstad. As you read, notice how her plans have changed since she last spoke to Nora.

Same scene. The table, with chairs around it, has been moved to the center of the room. A lamp on the table is lit. The hall door stands open. Dance music drifts down from the floor above. Mrs. Linde *sits at the table, absently paging through a book, trying to read, but apparently unable to focus her thoughts. Once or twice she pauses, tensely listening for a sound at the outer entrance.*

A **Mrs. Linde** (*glancing at her watch*). Not yet—and there's hardly any time left. If only he's not—(*Listening again.*) Ah, there he is. (*She goes out in the hall and cautiously opens the outer door. Quiet footsteps are heard on the stairs. She whispers:*) Come in. Nobody's here.

Krogstad (*in the doorway*). I found a note from you at home. What's back of all this?

Mrs. Linde. I just *had* to talk to you.

Krogstad. Oh? And it just *had* to be here in this house?

Mrs. Linde. At my place it was impossible; my room hasn't a private entrance. Come in; we're all alone. The maid's asleep, and the Helmers are at the dance upstairs.

Krogstad (*entering the room*). Well, well, the Helmers are dancing tonight? Really?

Mrs. Linde. Yes, why not?

Krogstad. How true—why not?

Mrs. Linde. All right, Krogstad, let's talk.

Krogstad. Do we two have anything more to talk about?

Mrs. Linde. We have a great deal to talk about.

Krogstad. I wouldn't have thought so.

Mrs. Linde. No, because you've never understood me, really.

Krogstad. Was there anything more to understand—except what's all too common in life? A calculating woman throws over a man the moment a better catch comes by.

Mrs. Linde. You think I'm so thoroughly calculating? You think I broke it off lightly?

Krogstad. Didn't you?

Mrs. Linde. Nils—is that what you really thought?

Krogstad. If you cared, then why did you write me the way you did?

Mrs. Linde. What else could I do? If I had to break off with you, then it was my job as well to root out everything you felt for me.

WORDS TO KNOW

calculating (kăl'kyə-lā'tĭng) *adj.* crafty; scheming

MINI LESSON **Speaking and Listening**

DRAMATIC READING

Prepare Have pairs of students work together to present a dramatic reading of the dialogue between Mrs. Linde and Krogstad. Students should begin with Mrs. Linde's line at the bottom of the first column on page 1064 ("All right, Krogstad, let's talk") and end with her line at the bottom of page 1065 ("I need to have someone to care for . . ."). Point out that the dialogue reveals the changing relationship between the two characters as they make known their feelings for each other. Tell students that they should use tone of voice and facial expressions to convey the feelings. For instance, you might suggest that students soften their tone when the characters call each other by their first names.

Present Ask students in the audience to discuss the relationship between Mrs. Linde and Krogstad. What feelings for each other do they communicate at the beginning of the dialogue? How do they seem to feel about each other by the end? Have students discuss the techniques the performers used to convey the characters' complicated relationship.

This activity is particularly well suited for longer class periods.

Krogstad (*wringing his hands*). So that was it. And this—all this, simply for money!

Mrs. Linde. Don't forget I had a helpless mother and two small brothers. We couldn't wait for you, Nils; you had such a long road ahead of you then.

Krogstad. That may be; but you still hadn't the right to abandon me for somebody else's sake.

Mrs. Linde. Yes—I don't know. So many, many times I've asked myself if I did have that right.

Krogstad (*more softly*). When I lost you, it was as if all the solid ground dissolved from under my feet. Look at me; I'm a half-drowned man now, hanging onto a wreck.

Mrs. Linde. Help may be near.

Krogstad. It was near—but then you came and blocked it off.

Mrs. Linde. Without my knowing it, Nils. Today for the first time I learned that it's you I'm replacing at the bank.

Krogstad. All right—I believe you. But now that you know, will you step aside?

Mrs. Linde. No, because that wouldn't benefit you in the slightest.

Krogstad. Not "benefit" me, hm! I'd step aside anyway.

Mrs. Linde. I've learned to be realistic. Life and hard, bitter necessity have taught me that.

Krogstad. And life's taught me never to trust fine phrases.

Mrs. Linde. Then life's taught you a very sound thing. But you do have to trust in actions, don't you?

Krogstad. What does that mean?

Mrs. Linde. You said you were hanging on like a half-drowned man to a wreck.

Krogstad. I've good reason to say that.

Mrs. Linde. I'm also like a half-drowned woman on a wreck. No one to suffer with; no one to care for.

Krogstad. You made your choice.

Mrs. Linde. There wasn't any choice then.

Krogstad. So—what of it?

Mrs. Linde. Nils, if only we two shipwrecked people could reach across to each other.

Krogstad. What are you saying?

Mrs. Linde. Two on one wreck are at least better off than each on his own.

Krogstad. Kristine!

Mrs. Linde. Why do you think I came into town? B

Krogstad. Did you really have some thought of me?

Mrs. Linde. I have to work to go on living. All my born days, as long as I can remember, I've worked, and it's been my best and my only joy. But now I'm completely alone in the world; it frightens me to be so empty and lost. To work for yourself—there's no joy in that. Nils, give me something—someone to work for.

Krogstad. I don't believe all this. It's just some hysterical feminine urge to go out and make a noble sacrifice. 1

Mrs. Linde. Have you ever found me to be hysterical?

Krogstad. Can you honestly mean this? Tell me—do you know everything about my past?

Mrs. Linde. Yes.

Krogstad. And you know what they think I'm worth around here.

Mrs. Linde. From what you were saying before, it would seem that with me you could have been another person.

Krogstad. I'm positive of that.

Mrs. Linde. Couldn't it happen still?

Krogstad. Kristine—you're saying this in all seriousness? Yes, you are! I can see it in you. And do you really have the courage, then—?

Mrs. Linde. I need to have someone to care for; and your children need a mother. We both

Customizing Instruction

Less Proficient Readers

Focus Tell students to watch for what the changed plans mean for Krogstad.

Tell students that Act Three takes place on the evening of the day after Christmas.

Ask students to explain what former relationship existed between Krogstad and Mrs. Linde. *(They apparently had been engaged to be married, but she ended the engagement to marry someone else.)*

Make sure students understand that Mrs. Linde is trying to persuade Krogstad to marry her.

1 Explain to students that when Krogstad uses the phrase "hysterical feminine urge," he is accusing Mrs. Linde of acting on an emotional impulse rather than out of true concern.

English Learners

- Help students work through the comparison of Krogstad and Mrs. Linde to half-drowned people on a shipwreck.
- Make sure students understand the following phrases: p. 1064, col. 1, "back of all this" *(the reason for what is happening)*; col. 2, "throws over a man" *(ends a relationship)*; "broke it off" *(ended it)*

Cross Curricular Link — Science

HYSTERIA Krogstad's comment about Mrs. Linde's "hysterical feminine urge" is an offhand use of language related to a psychiatric disorder called hysteria, which afflicted many middle-class women in the 19th century. The word *hysteria* comes, in fact, from the Greek word *hystera,* which means "uterus." The disease has a wide range of symptoms, from sudden fits, or seizures, to amnesia or even blindness. Nineteenth-century physicians believed hysteria affected only women and resulted from what was seen as women's natural weakness and tendency to be overly emotional and nervous. The treatments for the disorder were varied and unpleasant. Some doctors hit the patient with wet towels or threw cold water on her. Others used electrotherapy on their patients.

Today it is known that men as well as women can suffer from hysteria. Fortunately, the disease is far rarer now that it was in the 19th century, and treatment of symptoms includes appropriate medications and psychotherapy.

Reading and Analyzing

Pause & Reflect

Possible Response: Mrs. Linde doesn't want Krogstad to ask for his letter back because she realizes that Torvald needs to know the truth if he and Nora are ever to have a good relationship. She perhaps realizes that if she had been honest with Krogstad when they were young, they might have had very different lives, with much less heartache.

Reading Skills and Strategies
COMPARING CHARACTERS

Point out to students that the reader gets to see Krogstad and Mrs. Linde and Nora and Torvald as couples on these pages. Ask students what are some of the differences between the two couples.

Possible Responses: Krogstad and Mrs. Linde are open and honest with each other. Mrs. Linde takes the initiative in their conversation, they challenge each other at several points, but in the end they are able to work out a new relationship for themselves. Nora and Torvald are locked in their roles. Torvald continues to treat Nora like a child, and she acts like she is interested only in the party. In reality, she knows disaster is about to descend, but she can't tell Torvald.

Literary Analysis
REALISTIC DRAMA: THEME

A Have a volunteer read these lines. Then ask students to infer the message that Ibsen is conveying in this passage.

Possible Response: An adult, solid relationship capable of growing must be based on the truth.

Reading Skills and Strategies
EVALUATING

Ask students how they view Krogstad by the time the scene with Mrs. Linde has ended.

Possible Responses: Many students will say that they understand him better and have some sympathy for him because of what he has gone through. Others may feel that no amount of hardship justifies resorting to blackmail.

need each other. Nils, I have faith that you're good at heart—I'll risk everything together with you.

Krogstad (*gripping her hands*). Kristine, thank you, thank you— Now I know I can win back a place in their eyes. Yes—but I forgot—

Mrs. Linde. (*listening*). Shh! The tarantella. Go now! Go on!

Krogstad. Why? What is it?

Mrs. Linde. Hear the dance up there? When that's over, they'll be coming down.

Krogstad. Oh, then I'll go. But—it's all pointless. Of course, you don't know the move I made against the Helmers.

Mrs. Linde. Yes, Nils, I know.

Krogstad. And all the same, you have the courage to—?

Mrs. Linde. I know how far despair can drive a man like you.

Krogstad. Oh, if I only could take it all back.

1 **Mrs. Linde.** You easily could—your letter's still lying in the mailbox.

Krogstad. Are you sure of that?

Mrs. Linde. Positive. But—

2 **Krogstad** (*looks at her searchingly*). Is that the meaning of it, then? You'll save your friend at any price. Tell me straight out. Is that it?

Mrs. Linde. Nils—anyone who's sold herself for somebody else once isn't going to do it again.

Krogstad. I'll demand my letter back.

Mrs. Linde. No, no.

Krogstad. Yes, of course. I'll stay here till Helmer comes down; I'll tell him to give me my letter again—that it only involves my dismissal—that he shouldn't read it—

Mrs. Linde. No, Nils, don't call the letter back.

Krogstad. But wasn't that exactly why you wrote me to come here?

Mrs. Linde. Yes, in that first panic. But it's been a whole day and night since then, and in that time I've seen such incredible things in this house. Helmer's got to learn everything; this dreadful secret has to be aired; those two have to come to a full understanding; all these lies and evasions[1] can't go on.

Krogstad. Well, then, if you want to chance it. But at least there's one thing I can do, and do right away—

Mrs. Linde (*listening*). Go now, go, quick! The dance is over. We're not safe another second.

Krogstad. I'll wait for you downstairs.

Mrs. Linde. Yes, please do; take me home.

Krogstad. I can't believe it; I've never been so happy.

(*He leaves by way of the outer door; the door between the room and the hall stays open.*)

PAUSE & REFLECT Why does Mrs. Linde no longer want Krogstad to demand his letter back? How might her own experiences have influenced this change of mind?

FOCUS As you continue reading, look for signs of change in other characters.

Mrs. Linde (*straightening up a bit and getting together her street clothes*). How different now! How different! Someone to work for, to live for—a home to build. Well, it is worth the try! Oh, if they'd only come! (*Listening.*) Ah, there they are. Bundle up. (*She picks up her hat and coat.* Nora*'s and* Helmer*'s voices can be heard outside; a key turns in the lock, and* Helmer *brings* Nora *into the hall almost by force. She is wearing the Italian costume with a large black shawl about her; he has on evening dress, with a black domino*[2] *open over it.*)

1. **evasions:** avoidances.
2. **domino:** a hooded robe, usually worn at a masquerade.

MINI LESSON Grammar

NOUN CLAUSE

Instruction A noun clause is a clause that can stand in for a noun as a subject, direct object, or other sentence part. Noun clauses often begin with words such as *that, what, whatever, which, who, when, where, whether,* and *why*. Use the following examples from the play to illustrate the noun clause:

Whatever you do is always right. (noun clause as subject)

I pretend that you're my young bride. (noun clause as direct object)

Tip: Tell students that if the word *someone* or *something* can be substituted for the clause, it is probably a noun clause.

Someone is always right.

I pretend something.

Practice Ask students to make up sentences using noun clauses as follows:

- as the subject and beginning with *what*
  Possible Response: What I'm doing is making a bologna sandwich.

Nora (*struggling in the doorway*). No, no, no, not inside! I'm going up again. I don't want to leave so soon.

Helmer. But Nora dear—

Nora. Oh, I beg you, please, Torvald. From the bottom of my heart, *please*—only an hour more!

Helmer. Not a single minute, Nora darling. You know our agreement. Come on, in we go; you'll catch cold out here. (*In spite of her resistance, he gently draws her into the room.*)

Mrs. Linde. Good evening.

Nora. Kristine!

Helmer. Why, Mrs. Linde—are you here so late?

Mrs. Linde. Yes, I'm sorry, but I did want to see Nora in costume.

Nora. Have you been sitting here, waiting for me?

Mrs. Linde. Yes. I didn't come early enough; you were all upstairs; and then I thought I really couldn't leave without seeing you.

Helmer (*removing* Nora*'s shawl*). Yes, take a good look. She's worth looking at, I can tell you that, Mrs. Linde. Isn't she lovely?

Mrs. Linde. Yes, I should say—

Helmer. A dream of loveliness, isn't she? That's what everyone thought at the party, too. But she's horribly stubborn—this sweet little thing. What's to be done with her? Can you imagine, I almost had to use force to pry her away.

Nora. Oh, Torvald, you're going to regret you didn't indulge me, even for just a half hour more.

Helmer. There, you see. She danced her tarantella and got a tumultuous hand—which was well earned, although the performance may have been a bit too naturalistic—I mean it rather overstepped the proprieties[3] of art. But never mind—what's important is, she made a success, an overwhelming success. You think I could let her stay on after that and spoil the effect? Oh no; I took my lovely little Capri girl—my capricious little Capri girl, I should say—took her under my arm; one quick tour of the ballroom, a curtsy to every side, and then—as they say in novels—the beautiful vision disappeared. An exit should always be effective, Mrs. Linde, but that's what I can't get Nora to grasp. Phew, it's hot in here. (*Flings the domino on a chair and opens the door to his room.*) Why's it dark in here? Oh yes, of course. Excuse me. (*He goes in and lights a couple of candles.*)

Nora (*in a sharp, breathless whisper*). So?

Mrs. Linde (*quietly*). I talked with him.

Nora. And—?

Mrs. Linde. Nora—you must tell your husband everything.

Nora (*dully*). I knew it.

Mrs. Linde. You've got nothing to fear from Krogstad, but you have to speak out.

Nora. I won't tell.

Mrs. Linde. Then the letter will.

Nora. Thanks, Kristine. I know now what's to be done. Shh!

Helmer (*reentering*). Well, then, Mrs. Linde—have you admired her?

Mrs. Linde. Yes, and now I'll say good night.

Helmer. Oh, come, so soon? Is this yours, this knitting?

Mrs. Linde. Yes, thanks. I nearly forgot it.

Helmer. Do you knit, then?

Mrs. Linde. Oh yes.

Helmer. You know what? You should embroider instead.

Mrs. Linde. Really? Why?

3. **proprieties:** the customs of polite society.

WORDS TO KNOW

capricious (kə-prĭsh'əs) *adj.* acting on whim; unpredictable

- as the direct object and beginning with *that* **Possible Response:** She admitted that she was making a bologna sandwich.
- as the subject and beginning with *that* **Possible Response:** That farmers work hard is obvious.
- as the direct object and beginning with *what* **Possible Response:** The farmers explained what they do.

For more instruction and practice in noun clauses, use McDougal Littell's ***Language Network:***

- Grade 10, Chapter 4, "Clauses and Sentence Structure"
- Grade 12, Chapter 3, "Using Clauses"

Customizing Instruction

Less Proficient Readers

Focus Remind students that change is an important element in the development of a character.

1 Remind students what is in Krogstad's letter: It tells Torvald about Nora's taking out a loan on her own and forging her father's signature. It threatens to make this information public unless Torvald takes Krogstad back at the bank and gives him an even better position than he had before.

2 Explain to students that Krogstad is accusing Mrs. Linde of establishing a relationship with him again only to help Nora. She replies that she married her first husband for the sake of helping her mother and brothers and states firmly that she will never again deny her own happiness in that way. Her statement is an affirmation to Krogstad that she is seeking him out for her sake and his.

English Learners

- Help students with the following words: p. 1067, col. 1, "tumultuous hand" *(loud and enthusiastic applause);* "naturalistic" *(Torvald means Nora's dancing was too wild and free-spirited);* col. 2, "exit" *(leaving the stage–here referring to Nora's leaving the party after performing the dance)*
- Describe the differences between knitting and embroidering to students. You might want to bring in photos or samples of each kind of needlework.

Advanced Learners

Tell students to spend some time thinking about the title of the play. Have them think especially about how, at this point in the play, the title symbolizes Nora's life. Ask them also whether the title involves any foreshadowing or irony. Have them share their ideas in a class discussion.

Possible Responses: The title, *A Doll House,* symbolizes the role Nora has played in the marriage. It represents the emptiness and falseness of her position. The title also foreshadows what will be revealed both about and to Nora as the play continues. It is ironic as well, because it sounds like something pleasant and innocent, but it in fact represents a destructive relationship.

Reading and Analyzing

Literary Analysis

REALISTIC DRAMA: CHARACTER

A Ask students what these lines reveal about Helmer's attitude toward his wife.

Possible Response: Helmer regards his wife as a precious object for himself to enjoy rather than as a person in her own right.

Reading Skills and Strategies

MAKING INFERENCES

B Ask students what Dr. Rank implies when he mentions the results of his research.

Possible Response: Dr. Rank implies that his disease is entering its final stage. He knows he is dying.

Helmer. Yes, because it's a lot prettier. See here, one holds the embroidery so, in the left hand, and then one guides the needle with the right—so—in an easy, sweeping curve—right?

Mrs. Linde. Yes, I guess that's—

Helmer. But, on the other hand, knitting—it can never be anything but ugly. Look, see here, the arms tucked in, the knitting needles going up and down—there's something Chinese about it. Ah, that was really a glorious champagne they served.

Mrs. Linde. Yes, good night, Nora, and don't be stubborn anymore.

Helmer. Well put, Mrs. Linde!

Mrs. Linde. Good night, Mr. Helmer.

1 **Helmer** (*accompanying her to the door*). Good night, good night. I hope you get home all right. I'd be very happy to—but you don't have far to go. Good night, good night. (*She leaves. He shuts the door after her and returns.*) There, now, at last we got her out the door. She's a deadly bore, that creature.

Nora. Aren't you pretty tired, Torvald?

Helmer. No, not a bit.

Nora. You're not sleepy?

Helmer. Not at all. On the contrary, I'm feeling quite exhilarated. But you? Yes, you really look tired and sleepy.

Nora. Yes, I'm very tired. Soon now I'll sleep.

Helmer. See! You see! I was right all along that we shouldn't stay longer.

Nora. Whatever you do is always right.

Helmer (*kissing her brow*). Now my little lark talks sense. Say, did you notice what a time Rank was having tonight?

Nora. Oh, was he? I didn't get to speak with him.

Helmer. I scarcely did either, but it's a long time since I've seen him in such high spirits. (*Gazes at her a moment, then comes nearer her.*) Hm—it's marvelous, though, to be back home again—to be completely alone with you. Oh, you bewitchingly lovely young woman!

Nora. Torvald, don't took at me like that!

Helmer. Can't I look at my richest treasure? At all that beauty that's mine, mine alone—completely and utterly. A

Nora (*moving around to the other side of the table*). You mustn't talk to me that way tonight.

Helmer (*following her*). The tarantella is still in your blood, I can see—and it makes you even more enticing. Listen. The guests are beginning to go. (*Dropping his voice.*) Nora—it'll soon be quiet through this whole house.

Nora. Yes, I hope so.

Helmer. You do, don't you, my love? Do you realize—when I'm out at a party like this with you—do you know why I talk to you so little and keep such a distance away; just send you a stolen look now and then—you know why I do it? It's because I'm imagining then that you're my secret darling, my secret young bride-to-be, and that no one suspects there's anything between us.

Nora. Yes, yes; oh, yes, I know you're always thinking of me.

Helmer. And then when we leave and I place the shawl over those fine young rounded shoulders—over that wonderful curving neck—then I pretend that you're my young bride, that we're just coming from the wedding, that for the first time I'm bringing you into my house—that for the first time I'm alone with you—completely alone with you, your trembling young beauty! All this evening I've longed for nothing but you. When I saw you turn and sway in the tarantella—my blood was pounding till I couldn't stand it—that's why I brought you down here so early—

Nora. Go away, Torvald! Leave me alone. I don't want all this.

Helmer. What do you mean? Nora, you're teasing me. You will, won't you? Aren't I your husband—?

(*A knock at the outside door.*)

Nora (*startled*). What's that?

Helmer (*going toward the hall*). Who is it?

Rank (*outside*). It's me. May I come in a moment?

2 **Helmer** (*with quiet irritation*). Oh, what does he want now? (*Aloud.*) Hold on. (*Goes and opens the door.*) Oh, how nice that you didn't just pass us by!

Rank. I thought I heard your voice, and then I wanted so badly to have a look in. (*Lightly glancing about.*) Ah, me, these old familiar haunts. You have it snug and cozy in here, you two.

Helmer. You seemed to be having it pretty cozy upstairs, too.

Rank. Absolutely. Why shouldn't I? Why not take in everything in life? As much as you can, anyway, and as long as you can. The wine was superb—

Helmer. The champagne especially.

Rank. You noticed that too? It's amazing how much I could guzzle down.

Nora. Torvald also drank a lot of champagne this evening.

Rank. Oh?

Nora. Yes, and that always makes him so entertaining.

Rank. Well, why shouldn't one have a pleasant evening after a well-spent day?

Helmer. Well spent? I'm afraid I can't claim that.

Rank (*slapping him on the back*). But I can, you see!

Nora. Dr. Rank, you must have done some scientific research today.

Rank. Quite so.

Helmer. Come now—little Nora talking about scientific research!

Nora. And can I congratulate you on the results? B

Rank. Indeed you may.

Nora. Then they were good?

Rank. The best possible for both doctor and patient—certainty.

Nora (*quickly and searchingly*). Certainty?

Rank. Complete certainty. So don't I owe myself a gay evening afterwards?

Nora. Yes, you're right, Dr. Rank.

Helmer. I'm with you—just so long as you don't have to suffer for it in the morning.

Rank. Well, one never gets something for nothing in life.

Nora. Dr. Rank—are you very fond of masquerade parties?

Rank. Yes, if there's a good array of odd disguises—

Nora. Tell me, what should we two go as at the next masquerade?

Helmer. You little featherhead—already thinking of the next!

Rank. We two? I'll tell you what: you must go as Charmed Life—

Helmer. Yes, but find a costume for *that!*

Rank. Your wife can appear just as she looks every day.

Helmer. That was nicely put. But don't you know what you're going to be?

Rank. Yes, Helmer, I've made up my mind.

Helmer. Well?

Rank. At the next masquerade I'm going to be invisible.

Customizing Instruction

Less Proficient Readers

To help students understand the relationships between Nora, Torvald, and Dr. Rank at this point, have them make a graphic like the one shown. Tell them to write a sentence or two describing how each character relates to each of the other two.

Possible Responses: Nora to Torvald: She is expecting Torvald to discover and read Krogstad's letter.

Nora to Rank: She knows he is dying.

Torvald to Nora: He is feeling affectionate and possessive.

Torvald to Rank: Torvald is annoyed with Dr. Rank's interruption and makes small talk with him, oblivious of Dr. Rank's real reason for coming.

Rank to Nora: He loves her and is saying goodbye.

Rank to Torvald: Dr. Rank is saying goodbye to Torvald, although Torvald doesn't realize it.

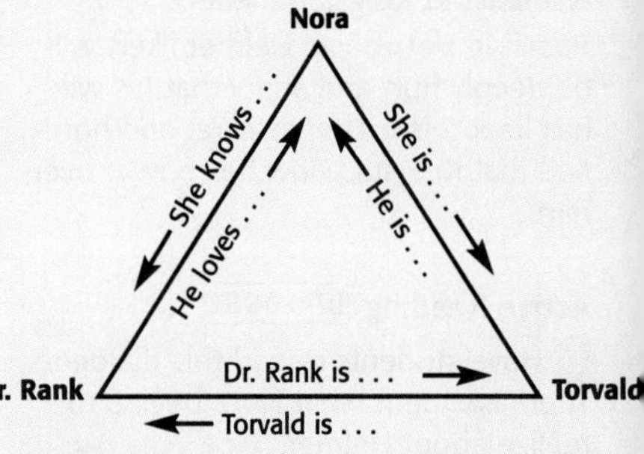

English Learners

1 2 Help students understand that Torvald is showing different attitudes in each of these two moments. He acts polite to the visitors (Mrs. Linde and then Dr. Rank) but shows his true feelings in what he says to Nora.

Explain the following terms to students: p. 1069, col. 1, "familiar haunts" *(places that a person knows well);* "snug and cozy" *(safe, warm, comfortable, pleasant);* "guzzle" *(drink down quickly);* col. 2, "array" *(variety);* "invisible" *(can't be seen)*

A DOLL HOUSE, ACT THREE **1069**

Reading and Analyzing

Literary Analysis FORESHADOWING

A Remind students that foreshadowing is a hint or clue about what will happen later. Ask students what Nora's line "Sleep well, Doctor" might foreshadow.

Possible Response: the death of Dr. Rank

Literary Analysis DRAMATIC IRONY

B Tell students that dramatic irony refers to the contrast between what a character knows and what the reader or audience knows. Then ask what Nora and the audience know that Helmer does not.

Possible Response: that Nora really is in "terrible danger," the crisis brought about by Krogstad's threat to reveal her forgery

Reading Skills and Strategies PREDICTING

C Ask students to predict how Helmer will react to Krogstad's letter.

Possible Response: Helmer likely will be deeply hurt and angry that his wife has kept this matter a secret and horrified that Krogstad now has power over him.

Active Reading DIALOGUE

D Have students reread this dialogue. Then ask them what Nora begins to realize about Helmer.

Possible Response: Nora begins to realize that Helmer is like a stranger rather than a loving husband. He questions her coldly and harshly, hurting her feelings.

Helmer. That's a funny idea.

Rank. They say there's a hat—black, huge—have you never heard of the hat that makes you invisible? You put it on, and then no one on earth can see you.

Helmer (*suppressing a smile*). Ah, of course.

Rank. But I'm quite forgetting what I came for. Helmer, give me a cigar, one of the dark Havanas.

Helmer. With the greatest pleasure. (*Holds out his case.*)

Rank. Thanks. (*Takes one and cuts off the tip.*)

Nora (*striking a match*). Let me give you a light.

Rank. Thank you. (*She holds the match for him; he lights the cigar.*) And now good-bye.

Helmer. Good-bye, good-bye, old friend.

A **Nora.** Sleep well, Doctor.

Rank. Thanks for that wish.

Nora. Wish me the same.

Rank. You? All right, if you like— Sleep well. And thanks for the light. (*He nods to them both and leaves.*)

Helmer (*his voice subdued*). He's been drinking heavily.

Nora (*absently*). Could be. (Helmer *takes his keys from his pocket and goes out in the hall.*) Torvald—what are you after?

Helmer. Got to empty the mailbox; it's nearly full. There won't be room for the morning papers.

Nora. Are you working tonight?

Helmer. You know I'm not. Why—what's this? Someone's been at the lock.

Nora. At the lock—?

Helmer. Yes, I'm positive. What do you suppose—? I can't imagine one of the maids—? Here's a broken hairpin. Nora, it's yours—

Nora (*quickly*). Then it must be the children—

Helmer. You'd better break them of that. Hm, hm—well, opened it after all. (*Takes the contents out and calls into the kitchen.*) Helene! Helene, would you put out the lamp in the hall. (*He returns to the room, shutting the hall door, then displays the handful of mail.*) Look how it's piled up. (*Sorting through them.*) Now what's this?

Nora (*at the window*). The letter! Oh, Torvald, no!

Helmer. Two calling cards—from Rank.

Nora. From Dr. Rank?

Helmer (*examining them*). "Dr. Rank, Consulting Physician." They were on top. He must have dropped them in as he left.

Nora. Is there anything on them?

Helmer. There's a black cross over the name. See? That's a gruesome notion. He could almost be announcing his own death.

Nora. That's just what he's doing.

Helmer. What! You've heard something? Something he's told you?

Nora. Yes. That when those cards came, he'd be taking his leave of us. He'll shut himself in now and die.

Helmer. Ah, my poor friend! Of course I knew he wouldn't be here much longer. But so soon— And then to hide himself away like a wounded animal.

Nora. If it has to happen, then it's best it happens in silence—don't you think so, Torvald?

Helmer (*pacing up and down*). He'd grown right into our lives. I simply can't imagine him gone. He with his suffering and loneliness—like a dark cloud setting off our sunlit happiness. Well, maybe it's best this way. For him, at least. (*Standing still.*) And maybe for us too, Nora. Now we're thrown back on each other, completely. (*Embracing her.*) Oh you, my darling wife, how can I hold you

close enough? You know what, Nora—time
B and again I've wished you were in some terrible danger, just so I could stake my life and soul and everything, for your sake.

Nora (*tearing herself away, her voice firm and decisive*). Now you must read your mail, Torvald.

Helmer. No, no, not tonight. I want to stay with you, dearest.

Nora. With a dying friend on your mind?

Helmer. You're right. We've both had a shock. There's ugliness between us—these thoughts of death and corruption. We'll have to get free of them first. Until then—we'll stay apart.

Nora (*clinging about his neck*). Torvald—good night! Good night!

Helmer (*kissing her on the cheek*). Good night,
C little songbird. Sleep well, Nora. I'll be reading my mail now. (*He takes the letters into his room and shuts the door after him.*)

Nora (*with bewildered glances, groping about, seizing* Helmer's *domino, throwing it around her, and speaking in short, hoarse, broken whispers*). Never see him again. Never, never. (*Putting her shawl over her head.*) Never see the children either—them, too. Never, never. Oh, the freezing black water! The depths—down— Oh, I wish it were over— He has it now; he's reading it—now. Oh no, no, not yet. Torvald, good-bye, you and the children—(*She starts for the hall, as she does,* Helmer
1 *throws open his door and stands with an open letter in his hand.*)

Helmer. Nora!

Nora (*screams*). Oh—!

Helmer. What is this? You know what's in this letter?

Nora. Yes, I know. Let me go! Let me out!

Helmer (*holding her back*). Where are you going?

Nora (*struggling to break loose*). You can't save me, Torvald!

Helmer (*slumping back*). True! Then it's true what he writes? How horrible! No, no, it's impossible—it can't be true.

Nora. It *is* true. I've loved you more than all this world.

Helmer. Ah, none of your slippery tricks.

Nora (*taking one step toward him*). Torvald—!

Helmer. What *is* this you've blundered into!

Nora. Just let me loose. You're not going to suffer
for my sake. You're not going to take on my D
guilt.

Helmer. No more playacting. (*Locks the hall door.*) You stay right here and give me a reckoning. You understand what you've done? Answer! You understand?

Nora (*looking squarely at him, her face hardening*). Yes. I'm beginning to understand everything now.

Helmer (*striding about*). Oh, what an awful awakening! In all these eight years—she who was my pride and joy—a hypocrite, a liar—worse, worse—a criminal! How infinitely disgusting it all is! The shame! (Nora *says nothing and goes on looking straight at him. He stops in front of her.*) I should have suspected something of the kind. I should have known. All your father's flimsy values— Be still! All your father's flimsy values have come out in you. No religion, no morals, no sense of duty— Oh, how I'm punished for letting him off! I did it for your sake, and you repay me like this.

Nora. Yes, like this.

Helmer. Now you've wrecked all my happiness—ruined my whole future. Oh, it's awful to think of. I'm in a cheap little grafter's[4] hands;

4. **grafter's:** A grafter is a person who uses his or her position dishonestly to gain something.

Customizing Instruction

Less Proficient Readers

1 Explain to students that Nora is hoping that when Torvald reads Krogstad's letter, he will realize what she has done for him and will try to take the blame on himself to protect her. She in response plans to drown herself to prevent his suffering from such shame.

English Learners

- Explain that the black hat Dr. Rank talks about at the beginning of page 1070 is a reference to death, which will make him invisible.
- Explain that the cheap grafter, or crook, that Helmer refers to at the end of page 1071 is Krogstad.
- Help students with the following word and phrase: p. 1070, col. 1, "suppressing" *(holding back)*; col. 2, "like a wounded animal" *(Dr. Rank is comparing himself to an injured animal that goes off by itself to an isolated spot to die.)*
- To help students practice reading English aloud, have them take turns reading the dialogue from Helmer's speech on page 1070, column 1, beginning "Got to empty . . ." to Nora's speech in column 2, "The letter! Oh, Torvald, no!"

Advanced Learners

After students have read the entire play, ask them to describe Dr. Rank's function in the plot.

Possible Response: Dr. Rank contrasts with Helmer. Unlike Helmer, Dr. Rank appreciates Nora as an adult and confides in her. Moreover, Dr. Rank's actions parallel Nora's in important ways. He discovers with certainty the truth about his health; she discovers with certainty the truth about her marriage. His departure from the Helmer family in the middle of Act III foreshadows Nora's at the end of the play.

A DOLL HOUSE, ACT THREE **1071**

Reading and Analyzing

Reading Skills and Strategies
EVALUATING

A Have students read aloud this passage and then evaluate Helmer's treatment of Nora.

Possible Response: Helmer treats his wife cruelly. He states that she is an unfit mother and that they never again will be happy together. He is concerned about what others will think, not about his wife's feelings.

Active Reading VISUALIZING

B Have students read this dialogue aloud. Then ask them to visualize Nora's reaction to Helmer's speech.

Possible Response: Instead of appearing relieved, Nora shows no emotion. Instead, she looks coldly at her husband, as if realizing for the first time what he is really like.

You stay right here
and give me a reckoning.
You understand what you've done?

MINI LESSON Viewing and Representing

ART APPRECIATION

Instruction Point out that the movie still on page 1072 shows Torvald speaking to Nora. Have students contrast Torvald's attitude toward Nora in this representation with his attitude toward his wife earlier in the play. Then ask students the following questions:

How would you describe Torvald's feelings for Nora up to this point?

Possible Responses: He has seemed to be loving, protective, indulgent, condescending.

How would you describe Torvald's attitude toward his wife in this still?

Possible Responses: He looks angry, accusing, upset.

What details in Torvald's facial expressions and gestures suggest his attitude?

Possible Responses: His eyes are hard and direct; his body is rigid and tense; he is pointing his finger in an accusing manner.

he can do anything he wants with me, ask for 1 anything, play with me like a puppet—and I can't breathe a word. I'll be swept down miserably into the depths on account of a featherbrained woman.

Nora. When I'm gone from this world, you'll be free.

Helmer. Oh, quit posing. Your father had a mess of those speeches too. What good would that ever do me if you were gone from this world, as you say? Not the slightest. He can still make the whole thing known; and if he does, I could be falsely suspected as your accomplice. They might even think that I was behind it—that I put you up to it. And all that I can thank you for—you that I've coddled the whole of our marriage. Can you see now what you've done to me?

Nora (*icily calm*). Yes.

Helmer. It's so incredible, I just can't grasp it. But we'll have to patch up whatever we can. Take off the shawl. I said, take it off! I've got to appease him somehow or other. The thing has to be hushed up at any cost. And as for you and me, it's got to seem like everything between us is just as it was—to the outside world, that is. You'll go right on living in this house, of course. But you can't be allowed to A bring up the children; I don't dare trust you with them— Oh, to have to say this to someone I've loved so much! Well, that's done with. From now on happiness doesn't matter; all that matters is saving the bits and pieces, the appearance— (*The doorbell rings.* Helmer *starts.*) What's that? And so late. Maybe the worst—? You think he'd—? Hide, Nora! Say you're sick. (Nora *remains standing motionless.* Helmer *goes and opens the door.*)

Maid (*half dressed, in the hall*). A letter for Mrs. Helmer.

Helmer. I'll take it. (*Snatches the letter and shuts the door.*) Yes, it's from him. You don't get it; I'm reading it myself.

Nora. Then read it.

Helmer (*by the lamp*). I hardly dare. We may be ruined, you and I. But—I've got to know. (*Rips open the letter, skims through a few lines, glances at an enclosure, then cries out joyfully.*) Nora! (Nora *looks inquiringly at him.*) Nora! Wait—better check it again— Yes, yes, it's true. I'm saved. Nora, I'm saved!

Nora. And I?

Helmer. You too, of course. We're both saved, 2 both of us. Look. He's sent back your note. He says he's sorry and ashamed—that a happy development in his life—oh, who cares what he says! Nora, we're saved! No one can hurt you. Oh, Nora, Nora—but first, this ugliness all has to go. Let me see— (*Takes a look at the note.*) No, I don't want to see it; I want the whole thing to fade like a dream. (*Tears the note and both letters to pieces, throws them into the stove and watches them burn.*) There—now there's nothing left— He wrote that since Christmas Eve you— Oh, they must have been three terrible days for you, Nora.

Nora. I fought a hard fight.

Helmer. And suffered pain and saw no escape but— No, we're not going to dwell on anything unpleasant. We'll just be grateful and keep on repeating: it's over now, it's over! You hear me, Nora? You don't seem to realize—it's B over. What's it mean—that frozen look? Oh, poor little Nora, I understand. You can't believe I've forgiven you. But I have, Nora; I swear I have. I know that what you did, you did out of love for me.

Nora. That's true.

Helmer. You loved me the way a wife ought to love her husband. It's simply the means that you couldn't judge. But you think I love you any the less for not knowing how to handle

Customizing Instruction

English Learners

1 Define the word *puppet* for students and then explain the comparison being made. *(In the same way that a puppeteer controls the puppets and can make them do any action he or she likes, so Krogstad, by theatening Torvald with exposure of Nora's loan and forgery, can force Torvald to do whatever Krogstad wants.)*

Help students with the following words and phrases: p. 1073, col. 1, "posing" *(pretending to be something or someone you are not)*; "accomplice" *(partner in carrying out a crime)*; "put you up to it" *(made you take out the loan)*; "appease" *(satisfy)*; "hushed up at any cost" *(kept secret no matter how much money or effort it takes)*; "saving . . . the appearance" *(making things look good)*; col. 2, "frozen look" *(hostile, withdrawn look)*

Less Proficient Readers

2 Explain that in Krogstad's second letter, he encloses the original note, or loan document, that Nora had signed. Make sure students understand that by returning the note, Krogstad is giving up the evidence he would have used to blackmail Torvald and therefore is making it clear that he no longer intends to be a threat to him.

A DOLL HOUSE, ACT THREE **1073**

Literary Analysis SYMBOL

A Remind students that a symbol is a person, place, or object that represents something beyond itself. Ask students what Nora's costume might represent.
Possible Response: Nora's costume represents the false roles she has been forced to play all her life. Instead of being herself, she has had to fulfill others' expectations of her.

Then ask what Nora means when she says she is getting out of her costume.
Possible Response: She implies that she will no longer play a part but will be true to herself.

Literary Analysis
REALISTIC DRAMA: CHARACTER

B Ask students what Nora realizes about herself in these lines.
Possible Response: Nora realizes that first her father and then her husband molded her in their own image, repressing her individuality.

Literary Analysis METAPHOR

C Remind students that a metaphor is a form of figurative language that makes a comparison without using the word *like* or *as*. Then ask students to explain what the metaphor "our home's been nothing but a playpen" suggests.
Possible Response: The metaphor suggests that in Helmer's household Nora has been treated as a child, not as an adult.

your affairs? No, no—just lean on me; I'll guide you and teach you. I wouldn't be a man if this feminine helplessness didn't make you twice as attractive to me. You mustn't mind those sharp words I said—that was all in the first confusion of thinking my world had collapsed. I've forgiven you, Nora; I swear I've forgiven you.

Nora. My thanks for your forgiveness. (*She goes out through the door, right.*)

Helmer. No, wait— (*Peers in.*) What are you doing in there?

A **Nora** (*inside*). Getting out of my costume.

Helmer (*by the open door*). Yes, do that. Try to calm yourself and collect your thoughts again, my frightened little songbird. You can rest easy now; I've got wide wings to shelter you with. (*Walking about close by the door.*) How snug and nice our home is, Nora. You're safe here; I'll keep you like a hunted dove I've rescued out of a hawk's claws. I'll bring peace to your poor, shuddering heart. Gradually it'll happen, Nora; you'll see. Tomorrow all this will look different to you; then everything will be as it was. I won't have to go on repeating I forgive you; you'll feel it for yourself. How can you imagine I'd ever conceivably want to disown you—or even blame you in any way? Ah, you don't know a man's heart, Nora. For a man there's something indescribably sweet and satisfying in knowing he's forgiven his wife—and forgiven her out of a full and open heart. It's as if she belongs to him in two ways now; in a sense he's given her fresh into the world again, and she's become his wife and his child as well. From now on that's what you'll be to me—you little, bewildered, helpless thing. Don't be afraid of anything, Nora; just
1 open your heart to me, and I'll be conscience and will to you both— (Nora *enters in her regular clothes.*) What's this? Not in bed? You've changed your dress?

Nora. Yes, Torvald, I've changed my dress.

Helmer. But why now, so late?

Nora. Tonight I'm not sleeping.

Helmer. But Nora dear—

Nora (*looking at her watch*). It's still not so very late. Sit down, Torvald; we have a lot to talk over. (*She sits at one side of the table.*)

Helmer. Nora—what is this? That hard expression—

Nora. Sit down. This'll take some time. I have a lot to say.

Helmer (*sitting at the table directly opposite her*). You worry me, Nora. And I don't understand you.

Nora. No, that's exactly it. You don't understand me. And I've never understood you either—until tonight. No, don't interrupt. You can just listen to what I say. We're closing out accounts, Torvald. 2

Helmer. How do you mean that?

Nora (*after a short pause*). Doesn't anything strike you about our sitting here like this?

Helmer. What's that?

Nora. We've been married now eight years. Doesn't it occur to you that this is the first time we two, you and I, man and wife, have ever talked seriously together?

Helmer. What do you mean—seriously?

Nora. In eight whole years—longer even—right from our first acquaintance, we've never exchanged a serious word on any serious thing.

Helmer. You mean I should constantly go and involve you in problems you couldn't possibly help me with?

Nora. I'm not talking of problems. I'm saying that we've never sat down seriously together and tried to get to the bottom of anything. 3

Helmer. But dearest, what good would that ever do you?

Nora. That's the point right there: you've never understood me. I've been wronged greatly, Torvald—first by Papa, and then by you.

Helmer. What! By us—the two people who've loved you more than anyone else?

Nora (*shaking her head*). You never loved me. You've thought it fun to be in love with me, that's all.

Helmer. Nora, what a thing to say!

Nora. Yes, it's true now, Torvald. When I lived at home with Papa, he told me all his opinions, so I had the same ones too; or if they were different I hid them, since he wouldn't have cared for that. He used to call me his doll-child, and he played with me the way I played with my dolls. Then I came into your house—

Helmer. How can you speak of our marriage like that?

Nora (*unperturbed*).[5] I mean, then I went from Papa's hands into yours. You arranged everything to your own taste, and so I got the same taste as you—or I pretended to; I can't remember. I guess a little of both, first one, then the other. Now when I look back, it seems as if I'd lived here like a beggar—just from hand to mouth. I've lived by doing tricks for you, Torvald. But that's the way you wanted it. It's a great sin what you and Papa did to me. You're to blame that nothing's become of me.

Helmer. Nora, how unfair and ungrateful you are! Haven't you been happy here?

Nora. No, never. I thought so—but I never have.

Helmer. Not—not happy!

Nora. No, only lighthearted. And you've always been so kind to me. But our home's been nothing but a playpen. I've been your doll-wife here, just as at home I was Papa's doll-child. And in turn the children have been my dolls. I thought it was fun when you played with me, just as they thought it fun when I played with them. That's been our marriage, Torvald.

Helmer. There's some truth in what you're saying—under all the raving exaggeration. But it'll all be different after this. Playtime's over; now for the schooling.

Nora. Whose schooling—mine or the children's?

Helmer. Both yours and the children's, dearest.

Nora. Oh, Torvald, you're not the man to teach me to be a good wife to you.

Helmer. And you can say that?

Nora. And I—how am I equipped to bring up children?

Helmer. Nora!

Nora. Didn't you say a moment ago that that was no job to trust me with?

Helmer. In a flare of temper! Why fasten on that?

Nora. Yes, but you were so very right. I'm not up to the job. There's another job I have to do first. I have to try to educate myself. You can't help me with that. I've got to do it alone. And that's why I'm leaving you now.

Helmer (*jumping up*). What's that?

Nora. I have to stand completely alone, if I'm ever going to discover myself and the world out there. So I can't go on living with you.

Helmer. Nora, Nora!

Nora. I want to leave right away. Kristine should put me up for the night—

Helmer. You're insane! You've no right! I forbid you!

Nora. From here on, there's no use forbidding me anything. I'll take with me whatever is mine. I don't want a thing from you, either now or later.

Helmer. What kind of madness is this!

Nora. Tomorrow I'm going home—I mean, home where I came from. It'll be easier up there to find something to do.

---

5. **unperturbed:** undisturbed; calm.

Cross Curricular Link — History

DIVORCE IN THE 19TH CENTURY Nora's future after she left Torvald would have been very uncertain. Women of the 19th century who broke their marriage vows had to give up everything: family, friends, children. They also found it very difficult to support themselves. Even the position of housekeeper would have been denied to a separated or divorced woman because no respectable family would have taken her in. If a woman were lucky, she might work in a clothing sweat shop or as a washerwoman. Less fortunate women were forced to turn to prostitution.

Women could find no help in the courts. Even wives who were victims of abuse and adultery could have their children taken away if they sought a divorce. Moreover, to obtain that divorce, a woman would have to produce proof of her husband's violence as well as of his infidelity. Although a man could obtain a divorce simply on the grounds of adultery, a woman could not.

Customizing Instruction

Less Proficient Readers

Help students understand the different perspectives of Nora and Torvald by asking them the following questions:

- How does Torvald view his relationship with Nora after the second letter from Krogstad arrives? *(He thinks things will go back to being just like they were before the first letter came. He thinks he is being generous in his offer to forgive Nora.)*
- How does Nora view their relationship? *(She sees through Torvald's attitudes. She understands herself better and is determined to change, even though that will be difficult.)*

English Learners

1 Explain that *conscience* refers to a person's inner sense of what is right and wrong and *will* refers to a person's ability to make decisions and follow through on them. Both are characteristics of adults. Torvald's wanting to take over Nora's conscience and will—besides being impossible—would rob her of the ability to be mature and independent.

2 Explain that "closing out accounts" refers to bringing a financial relationship, such as a bank or business account, to an end. Nora is using this comparison to refer to settling matters in a final way between her and Torvald.

3 Explain that the expression "get to the bottom of anything" refers to figuring out the cause of something.

Advanced Learners

Have students reflect again on the title of the play. Have them go back through the three acts and list details that are evidence that Nora was treated like a child and a doll in her marriage.

Possible Responses: Details include Torvald's calling her a lark, squirrel, goose, dove, and so on; his forbidding her to eat macaroons; his control of money; his references to her as a helpless child; his viewing her as a toy to dance for him; and his failure to talk to her as an equal adult.

A DOLL HOUSE, ACT THREE **1075**

Reading and Analyzing

Literary Analysis CONFLICT

A Remind students that conflict refers to a struggle between opposing forces. Then ask students to describe the conflict that now divides Helmer and Nora.
Possible Response: Helmer expresses society's beliefs about women. According to these beliefs, a woman's first duty is to others, especially her husband and her children. Nora, however, now realizes that her first duty is to herself. She must discover who she really is as a human being.

Literary Analysis
REALISTIC DRAMA: CHARACTER

B Tell students that in this passage Nora tells her husband that her illusions—or false ideas—about him have been shattered. Ask students to explain Nora's new insight about Helmer.
Possible Response: Nora once imagined that Helmer loved her so much that he would sacrifice anything for her sake. She now realizes that he would not give up his reputation to save her from public shame.

Helmer. Oh, you blind, incompetent child!

Nora. I must learn to be competent, Torvald.

Helmer. Abandon your home, your husband, your children! And you're not even thinking what people will say.

Nora. I can't be concerned about that. I only know how essential this is.

Helmer. Oh, it's outrageous. So you'll run out like this on your most sacred vows.

1 **Nora.** What do you think are my most sacred vows?

Helmer. And I have to tell you that! Aren't they your duties to your husband and children?

Nora. I have other duties equally sacred.

Helmer. That isn't true. What duties are they?

Nora. Duties to myself.

A **Helmer.** Before all else, you're a wife and a mother.

Nora. I don't believe in that anymore. I believe that, before all else, I'm a human being, no less than you—or anyway, I ought to try to become one. I know the majority thinks you're right, Torvald, and plenty of books agree with you, too. But I can't go on believing what the majority says, or what's written in books. I have to think over these things myself and try to understand them.

Helmer. Why can't you understand your place in your own home? On a point like that, isn't there one everlasting guide you can turn to? Where's your religion?

Nora. Oh, Torvald, I'm really not sure what religion is.

Helmer. What—?

Nora. I only know what the minister said when I was confirmed. He told me religion was this thing and that. When I get clear and away by myself, I'll go into that problem too. I'll see if what the minister said was right, or, in any case, if it's right for me.

Helmer. A young woman your age shouldn't talk like that. If religion can't move you, I can try to rouse[6] your conscience. You do have some moral feeling? Or, tell me—has that gone too?

Nora. It's not easy to answer that, Torvald. I simply don't know. I'm all confused about these things. I just know I see them so differently from you. I find out, for one thing, that the law's not at all what I'd thought—but I can't get it through my head that the law is fair. A woman hasn't a right to protect her dying father or save her husband's life! I can't believe that.

Helmer. You talk like a child. You don't know anything of the world you live in.

Nora. No, I don't. But now I'll begin to learn for myself. I'll try to discover who's right, the world or I.

Helmer. Nora, you're sick; you've got a fever. I almost think you're out of your head.

Nora. I've never felt more clearheaded and sure in my life.

Helmer. And—clearheaded and sure—you're leaving your husband and children?

Nora. Yes.

Helmer. Then there's only one possible reason.

Nora. What?

Helmer. You no longer love me.

Nora. No. That's exactly it.

Helmer. Nora! You can't be serious!

Nora. Oh, this is so hard, Torvald—you've been so kind to me always. But I can't help it. I don't love you anymore.

Helmer (*struggling for composure*).[7] Are you also clearheaded and sure about that?

6. **rouse:** awaken.
7. **composure:** calmness; self-control.

Nora. Yes, completely. That's why I can't go on staying here.

Helmer. Can you tell me what I did to lose your love?

Nora. Yes, I can tell you. It was this evening when the miraculous thing didn't come—then I knew you weren't the man I'd imagined.

Helmer. Be more explicit; I don't follow you.

Nora. I've waited now so patiently eight long years—for, my Lord, I know miracles don't come every day. Then this crisis broke over me, and such a certainty filled me: *now* the miraculous event would occur. While Krogstad's letter was lying out there, I never for an instant dreamed that you could give in to his terms. I was so utterly sure you'd say to him: go on, tell your tale to the whole wide world. And when he'd done that—

Helmer. Yes, what then? When I'd delivered my own wife into shame and disgrace—!

B **Nora.** When he'd done that, I was so utterly sure that you'd step forward, take the blame on yourself and say: I am the guilty one.

Helmer. Nora—!

Nora. You're thinking I'd never accept such a sacrifice from you? No, of course not. But what good would my protests be against you? That was the miracle I was waiting for, in terror and hope. And to stave that off,[8] I would have taken my life.

Helmer. I'd gladly work for you day and night, Nora—and take on pain and deprivation. But there's no one who gives up honor for love.

Nora. Millions of women have done just that.

Helmer. Oh, you think and talk like a silly child.

Nora. Perhaps. But you neither think nor talk like the man I could join myself to. When your big fright was over—and it wasn't from any threat against me, only for what might damage you—when all the danger was past, for you it was just as if nothing had happened. I was exactly the same, your little lark, your doll, that you'd have to handle with double care now that I'd turned out so brittle and frail. (*Gets up.*) Torvald—in that instant it dawned on me that for eight years I've been living here with a stranger, and that I'd even conceived three children—oh, I can't stand the thought of it! I could tear myself to bits.

Helmer (*heavily*). I see. There's a gulf that's opened between us—that's clear. Oh, but Nora, can't we bridge it somehow?

Nora. The way I am now, I'm no wife for you.

Helmer. I have the strength to make myself over.

Nora. Maybe—if your doll gets taken away.

Helmer. But to part! To part from you! No, Nora, no—I can't imagine it.

Nora (*going out, right*). All the more reason why it has to be. (*She reenters with her coat and a small overnight bag, which she puts on a chair by the table.*)

Helmer. Nora, Nora, not now! Wait till tomorrow.

Nora. I can't spend the night in a strange man's room.

Helmer. But couldn't we live here like brother and sister—

Nora. You know very well how long that would last. (*Throws her shawl about her.*) Good-bye, Torvald. I won't look in on the children. I know they're in better hands than mine. The way I am now, I'm no use to them.

Helmer. But someday, Nora—someday—?

Nora. How can I tell? I haven't the least idea what'll become of me.

Helmer. But you're my wife, now and wherever you go.

8. **stave that off:** prevent that.

Customizing Instruction

Less Proficient Learners

Make sure students understand what the miracle is. Nora was terrified of Torvald's finding out about the loan and the forgery, but at the same time she was hoping for the miracle—that he would try to protect her by taking the blame on himself and sacrificing his reputation for her sake. Also point out that although Nora wanted Torvald to offer this sacrifice, she was not willing to let him do it and was going to take her own life so that it would be clear that she was to blame.

English Learners

1 Explain that "sacred vows" are holy or religious promises and commitments.

MINI LESSON Speaking and Listening

ANALYZING MEANING

Prepare Have a pair of student volunteers prepare a reading of the dialogue from the first column of page 1077 that begins with Helmer's saying "Can you tell me what I did to lose your love?" and ends with Nora's line "Millions of women have done just that." Tell the performers to use tone of voice and facial expressions to convey Nora's meaning and Torvald's confusion. They should also use the punctuation in the text to determine phrasing and emphasis.

Present After the reading, ask students in the audience to discuss what Nora is trying to say to Torvald. What miracle was she hoping for? How did Torvald disappoint her? What do you think Nora's final line in the dialogue means?

This activity is particularly well suited for longer class periods.

Literary Analysis
REALISTIC DRAMA: THEME

A Have students use this passage to infer the theme, or main message, about marriage that the play suggests.
Possible Response: A true marriage is a relationship between partners who are absolutely free.

Reading Skills and Strategies
EVALUATING

B Tell students that at the end of the first performance of this play the audience sat in silence waiting for a conventional happy ending. They expected Nora to return to Helmer and apologize for having upset him. Then ask students to explain why Ibsen's ending of the play is so powerful.
Possible Response: A stunned Helmer is alone on stage, still reeling from Nora's dismissal of him. Nora has become a real woman, no longer Helmer's doll-wife. Abruptly, a door slams, punctuating Nora's assertions and revealing that she has indeed ended her marriage.

Oh, Torvald,
I've stopped believing in miracles.

Cross Curricular Link **Humanities**

INITIAL REACTION TO *A DOLL HOUSE* From the time the play was first performed in Denmark in 1879, it created great controversy. Most audiences and critics alike were scandalized by its portrayal of Nora and marriage. In particular, people were outraged by the idea that a woman would willingly leave her husband and children. A famous German actress refused to perform the play's final scene on stage. As a result, Ibsen wrote another ending in which Nora relents and stays for the sake of her children. For several years, this ending was adapted and performed before American audiences.

English novelist Walter Besant was so incensed by Nora's "unnatural behavior" that he published a sequel to *A Doll House*. In this sequel, Nora becomes a notorious writer, Torvald, an alcoholic, and the children, lost and suicidal. Besant's sequel prompted several writers to pen a response. One of the most famous was written by an American woman named Ednah Dow Littledale Cheney. In Mrs. Cheney's sequel, Nora becomes a doer of good works who nurses Torvald back to health after he contracts cholera. In due course, the miracle occurs: Torvald finally recognizes Nora as an independent human being and the couple is reunited.

Nora. Listen, Torvald—I've heard that when a wife deserts her husband's house just as I'm doing, then the law frees him from all responsibility. In any case, I'm freeing you from being responsible. Don't feel yourself bound, any more than I will. There has to be absolute freedom for us both. Here, take your ring back. Give me mine.

Helmer. That too?

Nora. That too.

Helmer. There it is.

Nora. Good. Well, now it's all over. I'm putting the keys here. The maids know all about keeping up the house—better than I do. Tomorrow, after I've left town, Kristine will stop by to pack up everything that's mine from home. I'd like those things shipped up to me.

Helmer. Over! All over! Nora, won't you ever think about me?

Nora. I'm sure I'll think of you often, and about the children and the house here.

Helmer. May I write you?

Nora. No—never. You're not to do that.

Helmer. Oh, but let me send you—

Nora. Nothing. Nothing.

Helmer. Or help you if you need it.

Nora. No. I accept nothing from strangers.

Helmer. Nora—can I never be more than a stranger to you?

Nora (*picking up the overnight bag*). Ah, Torvald—it would take the greatest miracle of all—

Helmer. Tell me the greatest miracle!

Nora. You and I both would have to transform ourselves to the point that— Oh, Torvald, I've stopped believing in miracles.

Helmer. But I'll believe. Tell me! Transform ourselves to the point that—?

Nora. That our living together could be a true marriage. (*She goes out down the hall.*)

Helmer (*sinks down on a chair by the door, face buried in his hands*). Nora! Nora! (*Looking about and rising.*) Empty. She's gone. (*A sudden hope leaps in him.*) The greatest miracle —?

(*From below, the sound of a door slamming shut.*) ❖

Customizing Instruction

Advanced Learners

Have students identify the plot elements in Act Three and indicate them on the plot diagram they have been completing. Next ask them to work in pairs to compare their analyses of the plot. Then draw a large plot diagram on the board. Hold a classs discussion in which the pairs of students present their ideas. Encourage all students to critique the ideas that are presented and to contribute their own ideas. Have a volunteer fill in the plot diagram with the plot elements that the class agrees on.

Possible Response: The rising action continues with the reconciliation of Mrs. Linde and Krogstad and with Dr. Rank's saying goodbye. The climax occurs when Torvald learns about the forgery and condemns Nora for her actions. The falling action includes Nora's realization of Torvald's cowardice and the emptiness of their marriage and her decision to leave him.

Assessment Informal Assessment

WRITING A RESPONSE Have students write two or three paragraphs in which they agree or disagree with the following statement. Remind them to support their response with evidence from the drama.

The change Nora undergoes throughout A Doll House *logically leads to her decision to leave Torvald.*

RUBRIC

3 Full Accomplishment Student's response is logical, well organized, and supported with evidence from the drama.

2 Substantial Accomplishment Student's response is well organized and supported with some evidence from the drama.

1 Little or Partial Accomplishment Student's response is vague and lacks adequate evidence from the drama.

What aspects of the relationship between Nora and Torvald are shown in these scenes?

Alla Nazimova and Alan Hale, silent film, 1922

Liv Strømsted and Lars Nordrum, National Theatre, Oslo, Norway, 1957

Peter Donat and Marsha Mason, American Conservatory Theatre, San Francisco, 1972–1973

Christopher Plummer, Julie Harris, and Jason Robards, Jr., Hallmark Production, 1959

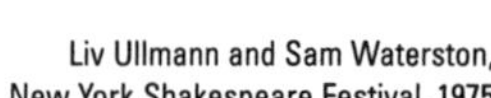

Liv Ullmann and Sam Waterston, New York Shakespeare Festival, 1975

MINI LESSON Viewing and Representing

COMPARING SCENES Encourage students to study the photographs on page 1080, paying particular attention to facial expressions, body language, and gestures. Then have students discuss the question at the top of the page.

View & Compare Possible Responses: Nazimova and Hale: The scene demonstrates Torvald's overbearing attitude toward a submissive Nora; Strømsted and Nordrum: The scene demonstrates Torvald's stern nature in the face of Nora's pleading; Donat and Mason: The scene demonstrates Torvald's tendency to treat Nora like a child; Plummer and Harris: The scene demonstrates Torvald's possessive attitude toward Nora; Ullmann and Waterston: The scene demonstrates Torvald's self-satisfaction and Nora's eagerness to please.

For each scene, ask students to suggest a line or two of dialogue that conveys the relationship shown.

Connect to the Literature

1. **What Do You Think?** How did you react to Nora's decision to leave Torvald? Explain.

Comprehension Check

- What plans does Mrs. Linde make with Krogstad?
- How does Torvald react to the first letter from Krogstad?
- What does Torvald expect to happen after he reads the second letter?

Think Critically

2. **ACTIVE READING: STRATEGIES FOR READING REALISTIC DRAMA** Look over the stage directions in this act. Which sights and sounds do you think would have the greatest impact on the audience? How do they reinforce the play's meaning?

3. Do you find Nora's actions at the end of the play to be believable?

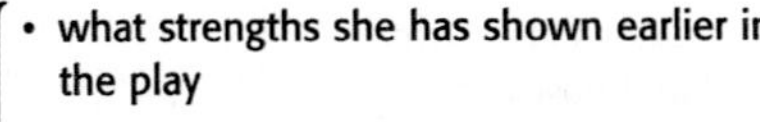

THINK ABOUT
- what strengths she has shown earlier in the play
- Torvald's reactions to Krogstad's letters
- what Nora means when she says she's "beginning to understand everything now" (page 1071, col. 2)
- what she means by "the greatest miracle of all" (page 1079, col. 2)

4. What is your opinion of Torvald?

THINK ABOUT
- the position of men in his society
- his actions and responses
- what happens at the end of the play

5. **Irony** is a contrast between what happens and what is expected. In what way is the frequent use of letters ironic in this play?

Extend Interpretations

6. **The Writer's Style** Ibsen is known for his use of **symbolism** in his plays. What do you think are the most important symbols in *A Doll House?*

7. **Different Perspectives** Suppose Torvald were the central character in the play instead of Nora. In what ways do you think the play would be different?

LITERARY ANALYSIS: THEME IN REALISTIC DRAMA

A **theme** is a central idea or message conveyed by a literary work. It is a perception about life or human nature that the writer shares with the reader. Longer works usually have more than one theme. In realistic dramas, themes usually are not stated directly. Rather, they are suggested by the action or through literary techniques such as irony and symbolism.

Paired Activity With a classmate, discuss the themes that *A Doll House* conveys about the following topics. Write a sentence stating each theme, and cite evidence from the play to support it.

- true love
- social obligations
- secrecy and deception in marriage
- women's role in society
- rigid moral views
- how the past influences people's lives

REVIEW: FORESHADOWING

Remember that **foreshadowing** is a writer's use of hints or clues to suggest what will happen later. What moments in the play are examples of foreshadowing?

Connect to the Literature

1. **What Do You Think?** Students' opinions will vary. They should be able to support their ideas with details from the play.

Comprehension Check

- She will marry him and help raise his children.
- He is furious. He plans to keep up the appearance of his marriage but cut himself and the children off from Nora.
- He expects things to go back to the way they were before this crisis.

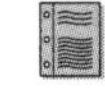

Use Selection Quiz in **Unit Six Resource Book,** p. 54.

Think Critically

2. Possible Responses: Nora's removal of her costume reinforces the idea that she is finally showing her true self to Torvald; the slamming of the door emphasizes the fact that the marriage is over and Nora is beginning a new life.
3. Possible Responses: Some students might say that Nora's actions are not believable because she makes such a drastic decision so quickly; others might say that her decision is believable because she has already shown that she can be strong and because Torvald's reaction to the first letter has destroyed the illusions that held her marriage together.
4. Possible Responses: Many students will say that Torvald is too self-centered and condescending to have a genuine relationship with anyone. Others may say that he is a product of his times and can't be blamed for some of his attitudes.
5. Possible Response: A reader would expect that if letters are being sent and received, there is communication going on between the people writing them. In the play, however, letters create misunderstandings and destroy relationships.

Extend Interpretations

6. **The Writer's Style** Possible Responses: The masquerade, the keys and locks, and a doll's house symbolize various problems in the relationship between Nora and Torvald; the slamming of the door symbolizes Nora's independence.
7. **Different Perspectives** Possible Responses: The play would be less complex and interesting because the reader would not witness Nora's conflicts with Krogstad or her internal struggles; a play that focused on Torvald would possibly be a comedy, portraying him as a buffoon, or a satire, exposing him as a shallow, unimaginative, self-important person who is bound by convention.

Literary Analysis

Paired Activity After students have written their theme statements, have them discuss which themes they think are most important in the play.

Use **Unit Six Resource Book,** p. 52, for more practice.

Foreshadowing Have students work in three groups to look for examples of foreshadowing in the three acts.

Writing Options

1. **Torvald's Response** Suggest to students that they make some notes about what Torvald's purpose is in writing this letter. Does he want to accuse or criticize Krogstad? defend himself? do both? Have them list specific points Torvald wants to make to accomplish his purpose.
2. **Nora's Diary** Encourage students to be imaginative in writing this diary entry. Tell them to write in a free-flowing style that reflects the energy and passion of Nora's actions, emotions, and decisions.
3. **Cause Analysis** Suggest to students that they can organize their essay using a cause-and-effect chain. Refer them to p. R32 of the **Writing Handbook** for an example of this type of organization.

Activities & Explorations

1. **Ibsen Improvisation** Tell students that they might want to experiment with two or three different scenarios before deciding how they want to develop their final improvisation. In addition to discussing how each character's life might have changed and how each might feel toward the other, they could think about the attitude, tone of voice, and level of honesty each adopts in this encounter.
2. **Set Design** Encourage students to be as creative as they like and to use whatever medium they want—pencil drawings, paintings, or even three-dimensional mockups if they wish. Tell them their sketches can be whimsical or precise, as long as they give a clear picture of the stage set.

Inquiry & Research

Seeking Equality Tell students that in addition to Internet resources, they should look for current books and magazines that have material related to the status of women in the country they have chosen. Encourage them to consult with the reference librarian of their public library to focus their search for materials.

Writing Options

1. Torvald's Response
Krogstad's letters to Torvald play a crucial role in Act Three. Write a letter from Torvald to Krogstad after Nora has left him. Model the style of your letter on the tone of Torvald's dialogue throughout the play.

2. Nora's Diary Imagine that you are Nora. Write a diary entry describing an important moment in the play, such as when you decide to leave Torvald. Discuss your feelings about what happened and your concerns about the future.

3. Cause Analysis Write an essay in which you explain the causes that lead to Nora's decision at the end of the play. Begin by listing important incidents and conversations from each act that have an effect on Nora. Decide which details are most critical to Nora's development. Present your ideas in a clear sequence that shows why Nora decides to leave Torvald. Place the essay in your **Working Portfolio.**

Writing Handbook
See page R32: Cause and Effect.

Activities & Explorations

1. Ibsen Improvisation With a classmate, create an improvised scene in which Nora and Torvald meet by accident several years later. Before you begin, discuss how each character's life might have changed and how each might feel toward the other.
~ **PERFORMING**

2. Set Design Sketch a design for the set of *A Doll House.* Before you begin, review Ibsen's descriptions of the set in his stage directions. Decide which act of the play you wish to represent in your sketch.
~ **VIEWING AND REPRESENTING**

Inquiry & Research

Seeking Equality With a classmate, prepare an oral report on the history of women's rights in a particular country. Find out if women may conduct business transactions, vote, and hold office, and, if so, when they gained these rights. You might also research topics such as job opportunities and marriage laws.

Vocabulary in Action

EXERCISE: WORD MEANINGS Match each situation described in the left column with the word in the right column that best fits it.

1. Quitting your job without having a new job lined up	a. chronic
2. The ruins of a building after a fire	b. calculating
3. Walking carefully on an icy sidewalk	c. rash
4. A child skipping home from school	d. capricious
5. Talking a lot about your big hiking trip to a friend who has a broken leg	e. desolate
6. Noise and pollution problems that never get cleaned up	f. tactless
7. Criticizing someone for being two minutes late to a meeting	g. inane
8. Doing things on the spur of the moment	h. warily
9. Figuring out how to turn a hobby into a money-making scheme	i. petty
10. Participating in a silly prank that you didn't even enjoy	j. jauntily

Vocabulary in Action

1. c
2. e
3. h
4. j
5. f
6. a
7. i
8. d
9. b
10. g

To assess skills and concepts taught in this selection, use **Formal Assessment Book,** pp.157–158.

Women in Society

In the years since Nora shocked her husband and conventional 19th-century society by slamming the door on her marriage, there have been changes in the status of women. Today, many women lead independent lives and pursue their own interests. During the 20th century, events occurred that laid the groundwork for this freedom. In the early part of the century, suffragists in the United States fought for and won the right to vote. In the later part, many women struggled to achieve many more social, political, and economic rights.

There has also been resistance to changes in women's status. Different cultures have varying views and expectations of women. People within a society may have different viewpoints about the kinds of lives women should lead. There continues to be discussion about what women's roles should be.

In sports such as basketball, soccer, and softball, women now play in professional leagues of their own in a number of countries. Interest in watching women's sports teams has reached an all-time high, with the 1999 Women's World Cup soccer matches playing to record crowds.

Some women today combine raising their children with building a career. Others choose to stay at home, often pursuing interests in volunteer activities. Still others return to school or work after their children are grown.

Paired or Group Discussion On balance, women have made important changes, but many people would like to see more accomplished. Do you think there are certain rights that all women should have? If so, how do you think this could be achieved? If not, explain your opinion.

Connect to Today

Use this feature to show the relevance of world literature to students. The material relates the literature selection just read to a contemporary topic connected to students' lives today.

Paired or Group Discussion Possible Responses: Most students will say that women should have all the rights that men have: the right to vote, own property, get an education, work, and so on. In addition, students may say that women should be paid as much as men for the same work. Students may say that these rights can be achieved through legal means and through education. Students who do not believe that these rights can be achieved may point to totalitarian governments, conservative religious traditions, and societal customs as potential obstacles.

Opportunities for Extension If students are interested in this topic, you might invite them to research a country, society, or religion that greatly restricts women's rights. Ask students to answer the following questions: Why are women oppressed in these countries or traditions? What are women allowed to do? What can't they do? How do the women feel about their treatment? What, if anything, should be done to help them?

Objectives
- write a Cause-and-Effect Essay
- use a written text as a model for writing
- revise a draft to include transitional words and phrases
- edit to correct any misspelled homophones

Introducing the Workshop

A Cause-and-Effect Essay Remind students that any given event, action, or trend can trigger a response. This **cause**—event, action, or trend—creates an outcome, or **effect.** Cause-and-effect writing allows a writer to examine and analyze events and their outcomes. Scientists, economists, lawyers, and other professionals are always looking at these relationships. For example, what causes smog? How do eating habits affect human health? Why does consumer spending rise and fall at certain times?

Ask students to discuss a specific event from history, such as the invention of the telephone. What caused the event? What effects did it have? Encourage students to notice cause-and-effect reporting on television news programs.

Point out that writing an effective cause-and-effect essay in their English class will help them sharpen their skills for writing essays in their history, science, and business classes.

Basics in a Box

B Using the Graphic Approach the graphic as a series of boxes that sifts ideas until they come out clearly.

C Presenting the Rubric To understand the assignment better, students can refer to the Standards for Writing a Successful Cause-and-Effect Essay. You may wish to discuss with them the complete rubric and student models in the Unit Six Resource Book on pages 60–63.

For more instruction and practice in expository writing, use McDougal Littell's ***Language Network:***
- Grade 10, Chapter 21, "Cause-and-Effect Essay"
- Grade 12, Chapter 20, "Subject Analysis"

Writing Workshop
Cause-and-Effect Essay

Looking at consequences . . .

A **From Reading to Writing** Several of the stories in this unit describe characters who suffer dramatic consequences for their actions. Every event has consequences, great or small; one way to examine the relationship between an event and its consequences is to write a **cause-and-effect essay.** You can use this type of writing to show why something happens, what its consequences are, or how events are linked.

For Your Portfolio

WRITING PROMPT Write an essay that explains the causes and/or effects of an event, or a series of events that are linked by cause and effect.

Purpose: To inform and explain

Audience: Your classmates or other interested readers

Basics in a Box

B **Cause-and-Effect Essay at a Glance**

Introduction
Introduce the subject

Body
Describe the cause and its effects*

cause → effect, effect, effect

Conclusion
Summarize the cause-and-effect relationship

* or
- present an effect and then analyze its causes
- present and analyze a chain of events related as causes and effects

RUBRIC Standards for Writing C

A successful cause-and-effect essay should
- clearly state the cause-and-effect relationship being examined
- provide any necessary background information
- present details in logical order and include transitions to show relationships between effects and causes
- summarize the cause and effect relationship in the conclusion

LESSON RESOURCES

USING PRINT RESOURCES
Unit Six Resource Book
- Prewriting, p. 55
- Drafting, p. 56
- Peer Response, pp. 57–58
- Revising, Editing, and Proofreading, p. 59
- Student Models, pp. 60–62
- Rubric, p. 63

USING MEDIA RESOURCES
Writing Coach CD-ROM
Visit our Web site: classzone.com

ADDITIONAL RESOURCES
For a complete view of Lesson Resources, see page 869h in this book.

Analyzing a Student Model

Nicholas Lilly
Oak Park and River Forest High School

RUBRIC IN ACTION

Pressure to Produce in High School

This is a stressful time for college-bound high school students, who feel increasing pressure to get good grades, impress colleges, and do well in an ever more competitive college-application process. This pressure has numerous effects on students, their quality of life, and even the quality of their education. With its emphasis on end results—grades, test scores, and high school "résumés"—this pressure ultimately causes students to pay more attention to the impression they make on colleges and less attention to what they're actually learning.

❶ Clearly states the cause-and-effect relationship being examined

A 97 percent growth rate in the last eight years . . . a record-breaking year, yielding a 23 percent increase . . . a second record-breaking year, showing a 16.5 percent annual growth rate . . . These statistics from USNews.com refer to the record increases in applications that colleges received from high school students. As the generation of Baby Boomers' children grows up and reaches the end of high school, greater numbers of students are preparing to go to college.

❷ Provides background information on the topic

D

This increased competition causes students to become anxious about their futures. This apprehension, shared by parents, is due to the belief that being a success in life and having a good job rests on a quality college education. High school students really see it as a make-or-break point in their life. No longer content to focus on the learning process, students focus on their grades and their college-entrance-test scores. They pay thousands of dollars on classes guaranteed to improve their scores. The whole process is developing into quite a business.

❸ Shows the relationship between the cause (competition) and the effect (pressure)

In addition to the push for high grades and test scores, students feel a great drive to take part in sports, clubs, volunteer work, and other extracurricular activities. While many students certainly enjoy these activities, they are also keenly aware that a full "résumé" of high school activities will make them more attractive to colleges. The student's motivation is now slightly altered: rather than doing something purely for its own sake, he or she is also doing it for the sake of appearances. Students are cramming their schedules fuller than ever. Where is the time to relax, digest, or reflect? There is none.

As a result of these pressures, students live and work in an atmosphere with an undercurrent of general unpleasantness and forced rivalry. Some students, desperate for a way to escape the dominance of competition and pressure in their lives, look for

LANGUAGE SKILLS

Teaching the Lesson

Analyzing the Model

"Pressure to Produce in High School"

D The student model looks at high school student life and examines the relationship between pressure in the college application process and academic performance.

Have students read the student model, and then discuss the Rubric in Action. Point out the key words and phrases in the model that correspond to the elements mentioned in the Rubric in Action.

1. Ask students to identify the cause and effect being examined. *(cause–students feel intense pressure to get into college; effect–students worry more about appearances and less about learning)*
2. Ask students to identify the benefit of using statistics when providing background information.
   Possible Response: Statistics give the reader a concrete impression of the situation.
3. Point out to students the use of such key words and phrases as *causes* and *due to.* These words provide a signal to readers that a cause-and-effect relationship is being discussed. Remind students that it is important to be explicit about this relationship.

4. Ask students to look at the graphic organizers on the opposite page. Which of the three graphics best reflects the progression described in this paragraph? *(The third one)*
5. Point out to students that the first sentence of this paragraph, which serves as a transition, also serves as a topic sentence for the paragraph. Remind them that a topic sentence is a helpful marking-point for readers as they make their way through an essay.
6. Point out that the writer concludes his essay by summarizing the chain of events using the pattern shown by the third graphic organizer on the opposite page.

shortcuts. Tired of the pressure, or maybe just tired, some students choose to slack off, but just slightly. They do as little as possible while still getting by with the necessary grades. Others take easier classes—if they can do it without adversely impacting their grade point average—rather than facing the challenge of the school's most difficult classes.

Finally, to various degrees, students cheat. According to USNews.com, only 20 percent of college students in 1950 said they had cheated in high school; today, surveys show that number to be between 75 percent and 98 percent. When a student first cheats—maybe by copying part of a homework assignment—it seems almost benign. Unfortunately, it soon becomes a habit, a way around time constraints. Students begin to develop a similarly lax attitude toward tests. Again, in the beginning, students convince themselves that it is fairly harmless. Perhaps, in the hallway, they ask a simple question: "So what was on the test?" For some, this behavior may progress to sharing test questions, creating "cheat sheets," or even stealing tests before exam day.

❹ Shows a logical progression of events, from mild to extreme cheating

This cheating has a damaging effect on education. When students resort to these methods as a way to achieve success, they have given up on learning the material and have reached the point where they only care about grades. Moreover, students who refuse to resort to shortcuts often do not get the grades they deserve, because they are overworked; they are left to doubt their choice to be honest. What both groups have in common, however, is that the pressure exerted on them produces a poor high school experience. There is no passion, no joy in the process of learning. There is only an obsession with an end product: grades.

❺ Having shown the causes of cheating, uses a transition to introduce the effects of cheating

It's a destructive chain of events: the increased numbers of college applications, the anxiety of added competition, the pressure for grades, the academic shortcuts, and finally the cheating. These elements together produce a considerable strain on students and can only serve to detract from their education. It may be difficult to feel sympathy for the students who engage in unethical behavior, but their behavior is a symptom of a greater problem. There is no way to decrease the number of students applying to colleges or the number of applications submitted by each student—nor should that be the goal. However, we should acknowledge the effects of this increased competition and work to keep those factors under control.

❻ Concludes by summarizing the cause-and-effect relationships and stating the importance of recognizing these relationships

1086 UNIT SIX PART 2 THE EMERGENCE OF REALISM

Writing Your Cause-and-Effect Essay

❶ Prewriting

Begin by thinking about topics for your essay. Consider events with causes or effects you don't understand. For example, perhaps you wonder why a business goes bankrupt or what happens to an ecosystem when a species becomes extinct. Any question that interests you and that has an answer of some complexity could be a suitable topic. **Brainstorm** a list of topics and then consider each one carefully, deciding which would yield the most interesting essay. See the **Idea Bank** in the margin for more suggestions. Once you have decided on a topic, follow the steps below.

Planning Your Cause-and-Effect Essay

1. **Think about the relationships between events.** Ask yourself whether these are really cause-and-effect relationships. Just because one event follows another doesn't necessarily mean that the first event caused the second. Also ask yourself whether a cause has one effect or more than one and whether an effect is the result of a single or multiple causes.
2. **Identify your audience.** What does your audience already know about your subject? What background information will you need to provide?
3. **Gather supporting information.** What will you need to learn about your topic? What sources of information can you draw on—personal observation and reflection, library research, interviews with experts?
4. **Map out your ideas.** How does the information you have collected fit together? You might create a graphic organizer to help you arrange what you already know and discover what you still need to find out.

❷ Drafting

Use drafting to explore the relationships between the events you have decided to write about. Write freely, leaving finer points and revisions for later. Be sure to clearly state the cause-and-effect relationship you're discussing. If at some point during drafting you find that you need more information, set aside your draft and conduct further research.

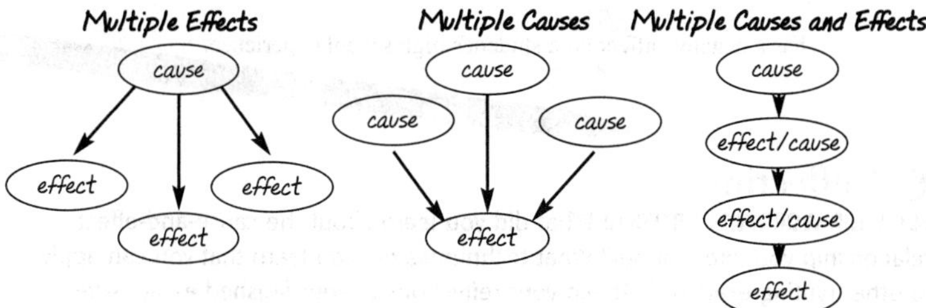

IDEABank

1. Your Working Portfolio
Look for ideas in the **Writing Option** you completed earlier in this unit:
- **Cause-and-Effect Paragraph,** p. 904

2. Acts of Nature
Make a list of natural phenomena (weather, environmental changes, natural disasters) you have experienced or heard about. Brainstorm about the causes and effects of these events.

3. Then and Now
Look through a newspaper or magazine, and make a list of current situations or events that interest or puzzle you. For each of these things, consider the various historical events that led to it.

Have questions?
See the **Writing Handbook**
Cause and Effect, pp. R32–R33

LANGUAGE SKILLS

Guiding Student Writing

Prewriting

Choosing a Subject
If after reading the Idea Bank, students are having difficulty choosing their topics, suggest they try the following:
- Make a quick list of modern inventions. Choose one and examine the effects the invention has had on people's lives.
- Think of an event that had a significant effect on your own life. Analyze the event in terms of its cause and the effect it had on you.

Planning the Cause-and-Effect Essay
1. Students may find it helpful to create a graphic representation of the causal relationships within their subject. Have students refer to the diagrams at the bottom of this page for ideas.
3. Suggest that students critically examine any information they've collected in their research for their essay. Remind them to carefully evaluate the sources they rely on for supporting information.
4. Have students create a chart with these headings: Known Effects; Known Causes; Possible Effects; Possible Causes; Possible Sources for Further Information. Caution students against using only information they already know. Encourage them to use their research skills to learn more about their topic.

Drafting

The model represents only one approach to writing a cause-and-effect essay. The writer chose to present a series of causes and effects, beginning with the first cause. He might also have begun by describing the effect in detail—students obsessed with appearances and college applications and unconcerned about learning—and then returned to explain the cause of this attitude.

Students may begin by outlining or by drawing a graphic organizer like those shown on this page to sketch their ideas.

Revising

USING TRANSITIONAL WORDS AND PHRASES

Go over the changes in the sample with students. Brainstorm with the class a list of transitional words and phrases that indicate a cause and those that indicate an effect.

Possible Response: To show cause: *after, because, since, due to,* and *as a result of.* (After the barn roof collapsed, they had nowhere to keep the hay.) To show effect: *before, therefore, consequently, for this reason,* and *as a result.* (The barn roof collapsed; consequently, they had nowhere to keep the hay.)

Have student pairs review one another's drafts to point out where transitional words and phrases could be added to make a sentence or group of sentences clearer.

Editing and Proofreading

MISSPELLED HOMOPHONES

Review the changes in the sample with students. Have them brainstorm a list of other commonly misspelled homophones.

Possible Responses: *its/it's; accept/except; capital/capitol; you're/your; foul/fowl; hurdle/hurtle; lead/led; too/two/to; whose/who's; cheep/cheap*

Reflecting

Encourage students also to consider how writing a cause-and-effect analysis will help them write other kinds of essays. What did students learn that they can use again?

Option

Managing the Paper Load

Have students choose one major question they would like you to address as you review their first drafts. Ask them to write this question at the top of their drafts. Their questions can help you focus your response.

❸ Revising

TARGET SKILL ▶ USING TRANSITIONAL WORDS AND PHRASES Transitional words and phrases play an important role in showing the relationship between causes and effects. Choose from words and phrases such as *therefore, because, as a result, in response, and consequently.*

Ask Your Peer Reader

- How would you summarize the main cause-and-effect relationship that I wrote about?
- What parts were unclear?
- What do you disagree with or want to know more about?

> *As a result of these* ~~There are~~ pressures ~~on~~ students *live and work in* ~~and~~ an atmosphere with an undercurrent of general unpleasantness and forced rivalry. Some students, desperate for a way to escape the dominance of competition and pressure in their lives, look for shortcuts.

Need revising help?

Review the **Rubric**, p. 1084

Consider **peer reader** comments

Check **Revision Guidelines,** p. R19

❹ Editing and Proofreading

TARGET SKILL ▶ MISSPELLED HOMOPHONES English is full of words that sound alike but are spelled differently and have different meanings. One very common example of near homophones is that of the words *effect* and *affect.* Their pronunciations differ only slightly, and they are commonly confused. Most of the time, *effect* is used as a noun meaning "result," and *affect* is used as a verb meaning "to have an impact on." Pay special attention to these spellings when writing about causes and effects. Misspelled homophones can confuse your readers and make a bad impression.

> This competition raises the ~~steaks~~ *stakes*, causing an increasing pressure on students not only to excel with ~~there~~ *their* grade point averages but also to make themselves peerless in the eyes of college admissions offices. This pressure, in many cases, has a negative ~~affect~~ *effect* on a student's high school experience.

Publishing IDEAS

- Submit your essay to your school or community newspaper.
- Submit your essay to an academic journal—such as a history journal—for high school students.
- Present your essay orally to your history or science class.

❺ Reflecting

FOR YOUR WORKING PORTFOLIO What did you learn about the cause-and-effect relationship you wrote about? What techniques did you learn that you can apply to other writing exercises? Attach your reflections to your finished essay. Save your essay in your **Working Portfolio.**

Read this paragraph from the first draft of a cause-and-effect essay. The underlined sections include the following kinds of errors:

- **misspelled homophones**
- **sentence fragments**
- **run-on sentences**
- **comma errors**

For each underlined section, choose the revision that most improves the writing.

When we think about technology responsible for our modern lifestyle. We often think (1) of factories automobiles and the telephones. (2) Household appliances such as the washing machine, the clothes dryer, and the refrigerator don't get that much attention these days. Although their invention had a tremendous effect on the way we live. (3) Before these labor-saving devices, laundry was an all-day chore: it had to be boiled, stirred, and rung (4) out by hand, then hung out to dry. Groceries had to be bought fresh daily or pulled in from the garden or the cellar. There was no such thing as a microwave or a refrigerator, people couldn't even save (5) a cooked meal for more than a few days, especially in hot weather. The people most directly effected (6) by these inventions, of course, were women. Relief from some of the most time-consuming household chores made it possible, eventually, for women to seek work outside the home.

1. **A.** lifestyle; we often think
B. lifestyle, we often think
C. lifestyle. We often think
D. Correct as is

2. **A.** factories automobiles, and the telephone
B. factories, automobiles; and the telephone
C. factories, automobiles, and the telephone
D. Correct as is

3. **A.** days, although their invention had a tremendous effect on the way we live.
B. days—although their invention had a tremendous effect on the way we live.
C. days, but—although their invention had a tremendous effect on the way we live.
D. Correct as is

4. **A.** wringed
B. wrung
C. rang
D. Correct as is

5. **A.** Because there was no such thing as a microwave or a refrigerator. People couldn't even save
B. There was no such thing as a microwave or a refrigerator; people couldn't even save
C. There was no such thing as a microwave or a refrigerator people couldn't even save
D. Correct as is

6. **A.** afflicted
B. affected
C. effecting
D. Correct as is

Need extra help?

See the **Grammar Handbook**
Correcting Fragments, p. R73
Correcting Run-On Sentences, p. R73
Quick Reference: Punctuation, p. R77

TEST PRACTICE

Standardized Test Practice

Demonstrate how students can eliminate incorrect choices for the first question.

A. The first choice is incorrect because it uses a semicolon to join a subordinate clause *(When we think about technology responsible for our modern lifestyle)* to an independent clause *(we often think of factories, automobiles, and the telephone).* Semicolons are used only to join two independent clauses.

B. This choice is correct because it uses a comma to join a subordinate clause and an independent clause, creating a complex sentence.

C. This choice is incorrect because it creates a fragment; "when we think about technology responsible for our modern lifestyle" is a subordinate clause, which cannot stand on its own.

D. This choice is incorrect because it creates a fragment.

Answers:
1. B; **2.** C; **3.** A; **4.** B; **5.** B; **6.** B

MINI LESSON Grammar

HOMOPHONES

Instruction Write the following sentence on the chalkboard:

The track star cleared every (hurtle, hurdle).

Ask students to discuss the difference between *hurtle* and hurdle. If they don't know, explain that *hurtle* means to move with great speed and *hurdle* is a barrier that must be leapt over in a race. Therefore, *hurdle* is correct.

Practice Have students choose the correct homonym for the following sentences. The correct word is underscored for your use.

1. The rebels engaged in (gorilla, guerrilla) warfare.
2. The bride walked slowly down the (aisle, isle).
3. The tree was struck by (lightening, lightning).
4. A (heard, herd) of buffalo crossed the plains.
5. She and her friends formed a tight (click, clique).

For more instruction and practice with common spelling errors, use McDougal Littell's ***Language Network:***

- Grade 10, "Commonly Confused Words," p. 656
- Grade 12, "Commonly Confused Words," p. 642

Objectives

- discriminate between denotative and connotative meanings of words
- interpret the connotative power of words

EXERCISE

Student responses will vary. Possible responses are provided.

1. The movie's ending caused him to weep.
   The movie's ending caused him to sob.
   Sob has a more dramatic, strongly emotional connotation than *weep*. The revised sentence depicts a stronger emotional response than the first one does.
2. The child wore an innocent expression on his face.
   The child wore a clueless expression on his face.
   The second sentence has a negative connotation, while the first is more neutral, or perhaps even positive.
3. Sally has always been fragile.
   Sally has always been hypersensitive.
   Hypersensitive is a much more critical term than *fragile*.
4. Jack is our next-door neighbor; he's very curious.
   Jack is our next-door neighbor; he's very nosy.
   Nosy has a distinctly negative connotation, while *curious* is neutral.
5. The wedding was on a humid July day.
   The wedding was on a sticky July day.
   Sticky paints a more vivid, unpleasant picture than *humid*.

Use **Unit Six Resource Book,** p. 64, for more practice.

Building Vocabulary

Recognizing Denotations and Connotations

> **Then the mother and son would get together in unrestrained joy. This was the absolute extreme of childishness! They drew pictures of animals that God has yet to create. . . . There was no way to preserve all these creations; their traces had to be thoroughly obliterated before the head of the house returned.**
>
> —Rabindranath Tagore, "The Artist"

Good writers choose their words very carefully, knowing that one word can create a different impression than another word with a similar meaning. Many words that have the same **denotations,** or literal meanings, have very different **connotations,** or implied meanings. Notice the word *obliterated* in the passage at left. What comes to mind when you hear this word?

The dictionary definition of *obliterate* is "to do away with completely, so as to leave no trace." Why didn't Tagore use the word *removed, erased,* or *destroyed?*

The word obliterate carries a connotation of great destructive force. For example, one often hears it used in describing the destruction of a city by bombing. Although Tagore is only describing the destruction of some drawings, his choice of the word *obliterated* lends great power and a sense of violence to what might otherwise seem a minor act.

Strategies for Building Vocabulary

The following strategies can help you become aware of subtle differences in meaning.

❶ Watch for Words That Create a Mood As you read, look out for words that make a particular impression on you or create a certain mood. For example, you may find words that seem funny, sad, angry, or delicate. Look for meanings that are implied but not directly stated. For example, the word *clan* denotes a large family, but it connotes a sprawling, tight-knit family, sometimes even a powerful one.

❷ Identify the Author's Purpose Consider the author's purpose and intended audience. What feelings is he or she trying to convey? How does the choice of words affect the tone of the work? For example, in the excerpt the word *meager*, which means "scanty," implies weakness and a lack of nourishment. By describing the widow's savings with this word, Tagore creates an image of her as a poor, frail creature.

> **Govinda came to Calcutta after graduation from high school in Mymensingh. His widowed mother's savings were meager, but his own unwavering determination was his greatest resource.**
>
> —Tagore, "The Artist"

❸ Choose Words Carefully When writing, remember that synonyms are not always interchangeable. They frequently have different connotations, and sometimes even different denotations. For example, the words *sing* and *conduct* are both synonyms of *perform*. Of the two, however, only the first can replace *perform* in "to perform a song," and only the second will work in "to perform surgery."

Think about the meanings implied by each of the synonyms in the following examples.

1. Lalitha can be quite **firm** in an argument. (Implies simply that she holds her ground.)
2. Lalitha can be quite **tenacious** in an argument. (Implies that she is strong, perhaps even fierce.)
3. Lalitha can be quite **obstinate** in an argument. (Implies that she is unwilling to listen to reason.)

EXERCISE For each word, write a sentence containing that word. Then rewrite the sentence, replacing the word with a synonym. Explain how the meaning of the sentence changes when you use the synonym.

1. weep
2. innocent
3. fragile
4. curious
5. humid

Sentence Crafting Using Adverb Clauses

Grammar from Literature Look at the following sentences from Guy de Maupassant's "A Piece of String." Notice the clauses highlighted in red. What kinds of information do they add to the sentences?

> **Along all the roads around Goderville the peasants and their wives were coming toward the burgh because it was market day.**
>
> **After the public crier had ceased his drum-beating, he called out in a jerky voice, speaking his phrases irregularly. . . .**

The words in red are **adverb clauses**. Like adverbs, they modify verbs, adjectives, and other adverbs. Adverb clauses answer such questions as *where, why, when,* and *to what extent.* In the sentences above, the adverb clauses modify the verbs *were coming* and *called.*

An adverb clause is a **subordinate clause**—it cannot stand alone but must be attached to an **independent clause** (also called a **main clause**). Adverb clauses are introduced by **subordinating conjunctions,** which can be classified according to the kinds of relationships they express.

Cause: *because, since, so that*
Condition: *although, as if, if, though, unless*
Place: *where, wherever*
Time: *after, as, before, since, until, when, while*

Using Adverb Clauses in Your Writing As you revise, examine how you have shown relationships between ideas. Use adverb clauses to combine sentences and make these relationships clearer.

> **Maître Hauchecome looked around. He saw accusing faces.**
>
> **Wherever Maître Hauchecome looked, he saw accusing faces.**

Usage Tip When you use a pronoun in a subordinate clause that follows an independent clause, make sure the antecedent of the pronoun is clear.

> UNCLEAR
> **Maître Malandain saw Maître Hauchecome when he picked up the string.**

In the sentence above, it is not clear who picked up the string. The problem can be solved by restructuring the sentence.

> CLEAR
> **As Maître Hauchecome picked up the string, Maître Malandain saw him do it.**

WRITING EXERCISE Combine each of the following pairs of sentences. Using a subordinating conjunction that expresses the relationship shown in parentheses, change one of the sentences into an adverb clause.

1. Maître Hauchecome was walking along the road. He saw a piece of string lying there. (time)
2. He was a frugal man. He took the string and began to roll it up. (cause)
3. He saw Maître Malandain watching him. He quickly put the string in his pocket. (time)
4. He continued to look at the ground. He was looking for something else. (condition)
5. He thought no more about it. The police questioned him. (time)

GRAMMAR EXERCISE Rewrite the sentences below so that there are no unclear pronoun antecedents.

1. When Maître Hauchecome met with the mayor, he had a very stern talk with him.
2. The mayor wanted to speak with him because of his suspicions about a theft.
3. As Pakhom's wife and her sister were talking, Pakhom overheard what she said.
4. The peasants and landlords had an agreement in which they were allowed to graze their cattle.
5. When Pakhom bought some land and another peasant wanted to pasture cattle on his land, he ran into trouble.

LANGUAGE SKILLS

Sentence Crafting

Objectives

- use adverb clauses to show relationships between ideas
- demonstrate control over grammatical elements such as pronoun-antecedent agreement

WRITING EXERCISE

Student responses will vary. Possible responses are provided.

1. As Maître Hauchecome was walking along the road, he saw a piece of string lying there.
2. Because he was a frugal man, he took the string and began to roll it up.
3. When he saw Maître Malandain watching him, he quickly put the string in his pocket.
4. He continued to look at the ground as if he was looking for something else.
5. He thought no more about it until the police questioned him.

GRAMMAR EXERCISE

1. When Maître Hauchecome met with the mayor, the mayor had a very stern talk with him.
2. The mayor had some suspicions about a theft, and he wanted to speak with Maître Hauchecome.
3. As Pakhom's wife and her sister were talking, Pakhom overheard what his wife said.
4. The landlords and the peasants had an agreement in which the peasants were allowed to graze their cattle.
5. Pakhom ran into trouble when he bought some land and another peasant wanted to pasture cattle there.

Use **Unit Six Resource Book,** p. 65, for more practice.

MINI LESSON Grammar

ADVERB CLAUSES

Practice For further practice, have students combine the following pairs of sentences. Using a subordinating conjunction that expresses the relationship shown in parentheses, change one of the sentences into an adverb clause. Student responses may vary; sample responses are given.

1. Sasha cashed a false promissory note. His family called a meeting. (time) *(When Sasha cashed a false promissory note, his family called a meeting.)*
2. They met behind closed doors. Sasha waited quietly in the hall. (time) *(While they met behind closed doors, Sasha waited quietly in the hall.)*
3. His family was furious with him. He had done this kind of thing before. (cause) *(His family was furious with him, because he had done this kind of thing before.)*
4. They came to his rescue. He simply did it again. (time) *(Whenever they came to his rescue, he simply did it again.)*
5. He promised every time to do better. He never changed his ways. *(condition)* *(Although he promised to do better, he never changed his ways.)*

For more instruction and practice with adverb clauses, use McDougal Littell's ***Language Network:***

- Grade 10, Chapter 4, "Clauses"
- Grade 12, Chapter 3, "Clauses"

Objectives
- reflect on and assess understanding of realistic literature
- identify and explain characteristics of realism found in two passages of text
- identify and analyze three examples of irony
- assess and build portfolios

Reflecting on the Literature
Suggest to students that they make a brief list of important characteristics of realistic writing before looking back at the selections. Tell them to keep their list in mind as they look for two representative passages. Each passage should reflect one characteristic of realism clearly.

 Use **Unit Six Resource Book,** page 66, for additional support.

Reviewing Literary Concepts
A successful response will
- identify three examples of irony
- explain how the irony works in each one
- point out how each instance of irony is used to develop character, plot, or theme in some way.

Building Your Portfolio
Students will use their Presentation Portfolios to file what they consider their highest quality work—the very best projects and activities from their Working Portfolios.

 For more information on using writing and assessing portfolios, see the **Teacher's Guide to Assessment and Portfolio Use,** pp. 53–74.

Part Assessment
 To assess skills and concepts taught in this unit part, use **Formal Assessment Book,** pp. 159–160.

Reflect and Assess

What understanding of realism did you gain from reading the selections in Unit Six, Part 2? Did the literature challenge you in new ways? Use the following activities to explore further what you have read.

The Peasants of Flagey Returning from the Fair (1855), Gustave Courbet. Oil on canvas, 208.5 cm × 275.cm. Musée des Beaux-Arts, Besançon, France. Photo © Erich Lessing/Art Resource, New York.

Reflecting on the Literature
Exploring Realism Realistic fiction and drama portray ordinary people in real-life settings and struggles. In these works the writers try to reveal the motivations that underly characters' actions and conflicts. Think back over the selections you have read. Choose two passages that represent some aspect of realistic writing. Briefly explain how each one shows some characteristic of realism.

Reviewing Literary Concepts
Interpreting Irony Irony is often an element in realistic literature. In this part of the book, several of the writers use irony to give insight into characters or situations. Pick three examples of irony from the selections you have read. Explain why each example is ironic. Then tell how it contributes to the development of character, plot, or theme in the selection.

Building Your Portfolio
Writing Workshop and Writing Options Look back at the cause-and-effect essay you wrote for the Writing Workshop on page 1084 and at the Writing Options you completed for this part of the book. Which piece are you most satisfied with? Put that assignment in your **Presentation Portfolio**, along with a note explaining why you think it works well.

Self ASSESSMENT
READER'S NOTEBOOK

The following list contains names and terms that relate to realism. List the words on a separate piece of paper. Next to each one, write a sentence describing or defining it. If you are uncertain about any word, review the places in this part of the book in which it is discussed or check the **Glossary of Literary Terms** (page R91).

realists	Anton Chekhov
naturalism	Fyodor Dostoyevsky
irony	Henrik Ibsen
A Doll's House	Guy de Maupassant
Leo Tolstoy	realistic drama

Setting GOALS
Several of the realist writers in this part of the book had an important influence on the writing of fiction and drama in the 20th century. As you read the literature in the next unit, look for connections to the realist works you have just read.

Assessment Self Assessment
Students can look up the listed terms in the **Glossary of Literary Terms** on page R91 or they can find them introduced in context on the text pages indicated below.

realists (pp. 942–943)
naturalism (p. 943)
irony (p. 999)
A Doll's House (p. 1019)
Leo Tolstoy (p. 954)
Anton Chekhov (p. 999)
Fyodor Dostoyevsky (p. 1016)
Henrik Ibsen (p. 1018)
Guy de Maupassant (p. 944)
realistic drama (pp. 943, 1018–1019)

Extend Your *Reading*

LITERATURE CONNECTIONS

Tess of the d'Urbervilles

THOMAS HARDY

The values of 19th-century society collide head-on with the personal life of Tess Durbeyfield, a 16-year-old girl from a poor English family. In this tragic tale of love and betrayal, a shiftless father's discovery of his aristocratic ancestry sets in motion a chain of events that spells disaster.

Here are just a few of the related readings that accompany *Tess of the d'Urbervilles:*

Life's Tragedy
BY PAUL LAURENCE DUNBAR

Disappointment Is the Lot of Woman
BY LUCY STONE

A Complaint
BY LADY CHWANG KĔANG

Five Plays

ANTON CHEKHOV; RONALD HINGLEY, TRANS.

This collection features the Russian dramatist's five greatest plays: *Ivanov, The Seagull, Uncle Vanya, The Three Sisters,* and *The Cherry Orchard.* Using simple but powerful dialogue, Chekhov deals with such themes as love, death, jealousy, and despair. His fully drawn characters try to improve their lives and relationships with others but fail, often as a result of their own sense of helplessness. Writing from a realist perspective, Chekhov exposes the resistance to change evident in Russian society in the late 1800s.

And Even *More* . . .

Books

Adam Bede GEORGE ELIOT
In this tale of destructive love, Eliot combines a deep compassion for her characters with a condemnation of a society that judges young women without helping them.

The Overcoat and Other Tales of Good and Evil
NIKOLAI V. GOGOL; DAVID MAGARSHACK, TRANS.
Mixing realism and the supernatural, Gogol expresses in these stories his frustration with the Russian government and his compassion for the poor.

Other Media

A Doll's House
The thoughtful performances in this 1973 film help bring to life Ibsen's play about a woman stifled by 19th-century society. MGM/UA Studios. (VIDEOCASSETTE)

War and Peace
Tolstoy's epic novel about family and Napoleon's invasion of Russia in 1812 is faithfully re-created in this six-part series. BBC Video. (VIDEOCASSETTE)

Great Short Works of Leo Tolstoy

LOUISE AND AYLMER MAUDE, TRANS.

The eight short novels in this volume include *The Death of Ivan Ilyich* and *The Cossacks.* In these works, Tolstoy tackles such issues as death, war, and religion.

More Recommendations for Your Students

Difficulty Level: Easy

Franck, Irene M., and David M. Brownstone. *Illustrated History of Women,* Vols. 6 and 7 (Danbury, Connecticut: Grolier Educational, 1999). These two volumes of this ten-volume series cover such topics as everyday life, social reforms, women's work, women's rights, and women's accomplishments in science, medicine, and the arts in the years 1830 to 1869 and 1870 to 1899. Discussions present developments in Europe and Asia as well as in the United States. Each volume includes a time line, interesting black-and-white illustrations, features on such women as Harriet Tubman and Florence Nightingale, and an extensive index.

Tagore, Rabindranath. Krishna Dutta and Andrew Robinson, trans. Introduction by Anita Desai. *The Post Office* (New York: St. Martin's Press, 1996). In this short, simple, but moving play, a boy's openness and hope affect all around him. Acclaimed by Elie Wiesel and W. B. Yeats, this work was performed by children in the Warsaw ghetto in the 1940s.

Difficulty Level: Average

Eliot, George. *Silas Marner* (New York: Modern Library, 2001). This novella combines elements of a moral tale with realistic fiction. The story balances the almost-miraculous transformation of the old miser Silas Marner with the gradual decline in fortune of the well-to-do Godfrey Cass.

Hardy, Thomas. *The Mayor of Casterbridge.* (New York: Modern Library, 1950). Set in Hardy's fictional region of Wessex, this novel tells the rise and fall of the tragic central character, Michael Henchard. The plot revolves around the destructive acts of Henchard and their effects on him and those around him. The setting is rich in details of the countryside and of life in the town of Casterbridge.

Pollack, Peter. *The Picture History of Photography* (New York: Harry N. Abrams, 1977). This book is a readable and informative history of photography with numerous photos included. Approximately the first half of the book covers developments in photography through the end of the 19th century.

Difficulty Level: Challenging

Dostoyevsky, Fyodor. *The House of the Dead* (New York: Penguin, 1985). This novel is a fictionalized account of Dostoyevsky's prison experience. Written as the memoirs of a man imprisoned for murdering his wife, it relates with great clarity and force the lives of the inmates whom Dostoyevsky characterized as "extraordinary people."

Ibsen, Henrik. *An Enemy of the People,* in *The Complete Major Prose Plays,* Rolf Fjelde, trans. (New York: Farrar Straus Giroux, 1978). In this comic and satiric work, the bumbling main character, Dr. Stockman, is declared an enemy of the people because he tries to expose an environmental hazard in his town. This is one of Ibsen's most popular plays.

Troyat, Henri. M. H. Heim, trans. *Chekhov* (New York: Dutton, 1986). In this accessible and sympathetic biography of Chekhov, Troyat—a novelist as well as a biographer of Tolstoy, Pushkin, and Dostoyevsky—not only presents facts and events but also portrays Chekhov's rich and creative inner life.

Modern and Contemporary Literature

This unit focuses on 20th-century literature, from the groundbreaking modernist experiments of the early decades through the works of more recent Nobel Prize winners.

Part 1

Worlds of Change: Expressions of Modernism The selections in this part reflect different aspects of modernism. Franz Kafka's surrealistic story "Metamorphosis," for example, is innovative in style and subject, reflecting a modernist concern with alienation. James Joyce's story "Eveline" breaks free of a traditional plot, exploring instead a character's psychological state. Virginia Woolf's essay "Professions for Women" discusses the female artist's need to reject limiting conceptions of womanhood. Modernist works by Asian, African, and Latin American writers are also included.

Part 2

When Worlds Collide: Responses to War and Conflict Part 2 presents literature associated with the world wars and other political conflicts of the 20th century. It includes a poem by Anna Akhmatova written shortly after the Russian Revolution, a play by Bertolt Brecht set in Nazi Germany, and a memoir by Holocaust survivor Elie Wiesel. A **Comparing Literature Across Cultures** feature lets students compare writings by Aleksandr Solzhenitsyn and Mahmud Darwish, two political prisoners. In addition, an **Author Study** focuses on Nigerian writer Chinua Achebe, whose work explores the effects of European colonialism in Africa.

Part 3

Critics and Dreamers: Contemporary Nobel Prize Winners This part includes selections by seven Nobel Prize winners who represent developments in contemporary literature. Nadine Gordimer is the best known of the many writers whose work brought attention to South Africa's cruel apartheid system. Gabriel García Márquez is a pioneer of magical realism, a style that has delighted readers and inspired a generation of writers. Naguib Mahfouz, almost singlehandedly, brought new respect to Arabic fiction. His popularity reflected growing world interest in non-Western literature.

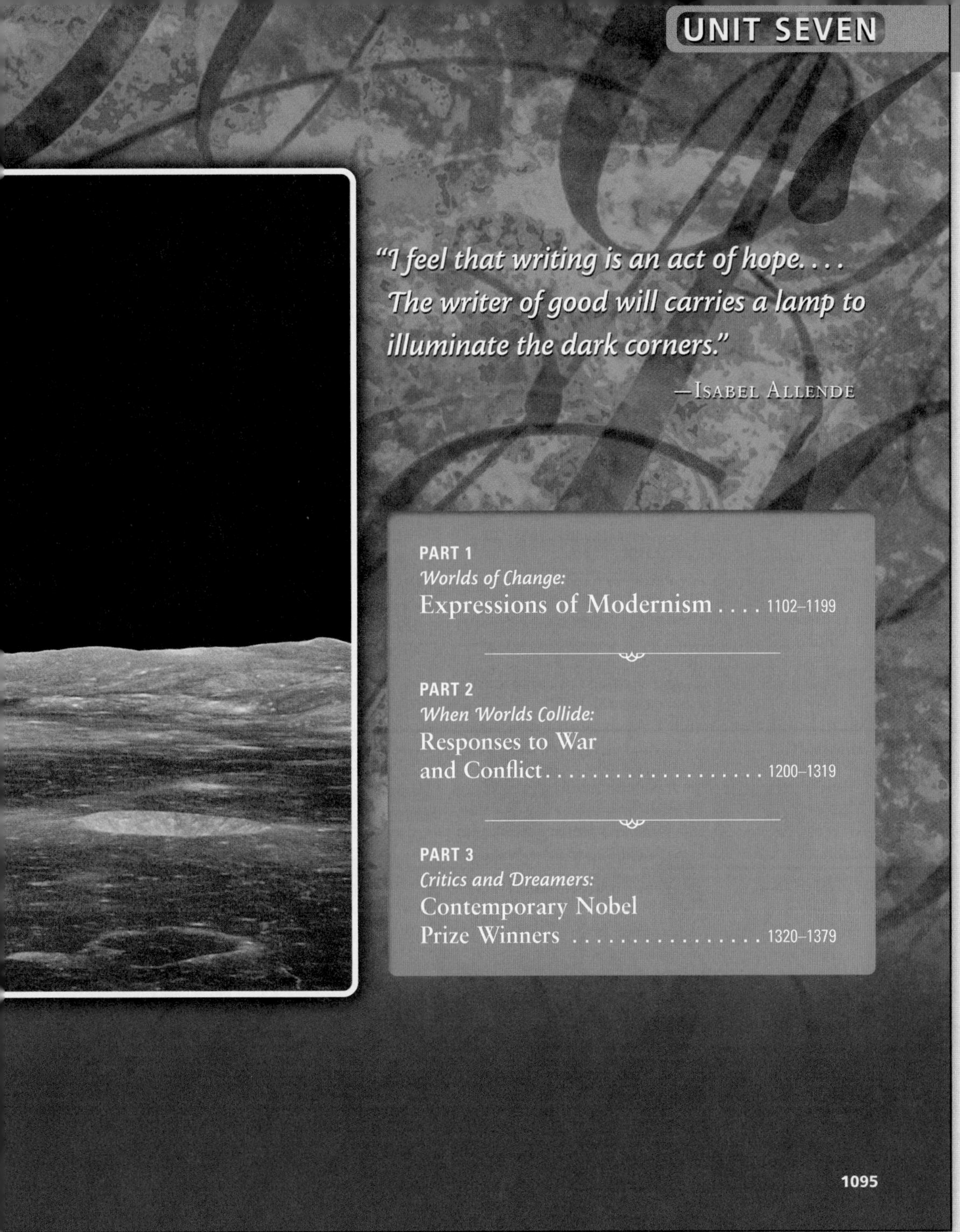

"I feel that writing is an act of hope. . . . The writer of good will carries a lamp to illuminate the dark corners."

—Isabel Allende

Making Connections

Ask: How can writing be an "act of hope"?

Possible Responses: Writing can be an act of hope when it criticizes social flaws with the intention of making people change. Writing can be an act of hope because it assumes that there will be a reader to affect—if not at that moment, then in the future. Writing can be an act of hope because it is less deadly than taking up weapons for a cause.

Features and Selections	Literary Analysis	Reading and Critical Thinking	Writing Opportunities
Modern and Contemporary Literature 1900–Present			
Worlds of Change Expressions of Modernism		Interpreting the Text, 1097, 1104	
Learning the Language of Literature Modernism	The Modernist Movement, 1106–1107	Strategies for Reading, 1107	
FICTION Metamorphosis	Point of View, 1109, 1148 Point of View, 1110, 1112, 1116, 1120, 1122, 1144	Visualizing Details, 1109, 1148 Visualizing Details, 1110, 1114, 1120, 1124, 1130, 1132, 1134 About the Translators, 1110 Surrealism, 1114 Beetles, 1123 Finance, 1127 Kafkaesque, 1146	Diary Entries, 1149 Literary Analysis, 1149 Standardized Test Practice (Writing a Short Essay Answer), 1122 Informal Assessment (Character Responses), 1135
POETRY Poems by Rainer Maria Rilke and Federico García Lorca The Panther The Guitar The Translator at Work Translating Modern Poetry	Sound Devices, 1150, 1154 Sound Devices, 1150, 1152	Connecting to Poetry, 1150, 1154 Connecting to Poetry, 1150, 1152 Paired Activity (compare and contrast), 1155	
NONFICTION Professions for Women	Diction and Audience, 1157, 1164 Diction and Audience, 1158	Recognizing Main Ideas, 1157, 1164 Recognizing Main Ideas, 1158 Professions for Women, 1158 *A Room of One's Own*, 1159	Personal Response, 1165 Definition of Male Ideal, 1165
FICTION Eveline	Internal Conflict, 1167, 1172 Internal Conflict, 1168	Analyzing Motivation, 1167, 1172 Analyzing Motivation, 1168, 1170 Informal Assessment (Identifying Main Ideas), 1169	Literary Analysis, 1173 Advice Column, 1173
FICTION The Jay	Symbol, 1175, 1180 Symbol, 1176	Clarifying Sequence, 1175, 1180 Clarifying Sequence, 1176 Animal Behavior, 1176 Marriage Customs, 1178	Character Analysis, 1181 Problem-Solution Essay, 1181
POETRY Poems by Léopold Sédar Senghor Prayer to Masks Connect to Today Appreciating Cultural Roots	Denotation and Connotation, 1183, 1186 Denotation and Connotation, 1184	Paraphrasing, 1183, 1186 Paraphrasing, 1184	
Writing Workshop Literary Interpretation Standardized Test Practice Building Vocabulary Sentence Crafting		Analyzing Student Models, 1191–1192	Literary Interpretation, 1193 Choosing a Literary Work, 1193 Planning the Literary Interpretation, 1193 Organizing the Draft, 1193

LEGEND **Black type – Pupil Edition**
Green type – Teacher's Edition
DLS – Daily Language SkillBuilder

Speaking and Listening Viewing and Representing	Inquiry and Research	Grammar, Usage, and Mechanics	Vocabulary
Using the Time Line, 1099			
Cover Illustration, 1149 Dramatic Scene, 1149 Art Appreciation, 1111, 1118, 1128, 1133, 1140 Dramatization, 1120	Story Comparison, 1149 Annotated Bibliography, 1149	DLS, 1108 Complex Sentences, 1144	Context Clues, 1149 Prefixes, 1115
Oral Performance, 1153		DLS, 1150	
Photo Essay, 1165 Words of Wisdom, 1165 Art Appreciation, 1161	Time Line of Women's History, 1165	DLS, 1156	Context Clues, 1165 Applying Root Word Meanings, 1162
Father-Daughter Dialogue, 1173 Story Illustration, 1173 Monologue, 1170	Joyce vs. the Publishers, 1173 Eveline's Prospects, 1173	DLS, 1166 Compound-Complex Sentences, 1171	
Family Tree, 1181 Reunion Dialogue, 1181	Multimedia Display: The Japanese Family, 1181	DLS, 1174	Context Clues, 1181 Context Clues, 1179
Reading a Map (Senegal), 1183 Choral Reading, 1185	Research Project, 1187	DLS, 1182	
Picturing Text Structure, 1191		Using the Active Voice, 1194 Verb Tense, 1194, 1195 Passive Voice, 1195 Verb Forms, 1195 Capitalization, 1195 Using Adjective Phrases and Clauses, 1197 Capitalizing Titles, 1195 Adjective Phrases and Clauses, 1197	Recognizing Word Families, 1196 Word Parts, 1196 Spelling, 1196

LEGEND **Black type – Pupil Edition**
Green type – Teacher's Edition
DLS – Daily Language SkillBuilder

UNIT SEVEN
PART 1 SKILLS TRACE

Features and Selections	Literary Analysis	Reading and Critical Thinking	Writing Opportunities
Reflect and Assess	Reflecting on the Literature (A Changing World), 1198 Reviewing Literary Concepts (Point of View), 1198		Building Your Portfolio, 1198

UNIT SEVEN
PART 2 SKILLS TRACE

Features and Selections	Literary Analysis	Reading and Critical Thinking	Writing Opportunities
When Worlds Collide: Responses to War and Conflict		Interpreting the Text, 1203, 1205	
FICTION War	Setting in Modern Fiction, 1207, 1212 Setting in Modern Fiction, 1208, 1210	Comparing and Contrasting Characters, 1207, 1212 Comparing and Contrasting Characters, 1208, 1210	Different Ending, 1213 Character Analysis, 1213 Personal Response, 1213
POETRY I Am Not One of Those Who Left the Land **Connect to Today** Living Dangerously: Writers in the 20th Century	Speaker and Tone, 1216, 1218 Speaker and Tone, 1216	Drawing Conclusions, 1216, 1218 Drawing Conclusions, 1216 Group Discussion, 1219	
DRAMA The Spy	Dialogue and Mood, 1221, 1230 Dialogue and Mood, 1222, 1224, 1228	Understanding Historical Context, 1221, 1230 Understanding Historical Context, 1222, 1224, 1226 Hitler and the Catholic Church, 1224	Research Plan, 1231 Top-Secret Memo, 1231
NONFICTION *from* The World Was Silent **Related Reading** When in early summer... **Connect to Today** The Holocaust and Human Rights	Author's Purpose, 1233, 1242 Author's Purpose, 1234, 1236, 1238	Connecting to the Author's Experience, 1233, 1242 Connecting to the Author's Experience, 1234, 1236, 1238 "Final Solution," 1235 Nazi Trains, 1237 Discussion Questions, 1241 Group Discussion, 1243	
FICTION The Guest	Theme, 1245, 1258 Theme, 1246, 1248, 1252, 1256	Making Inferences, 1245, 1258 Making Inferences, 1246, 1248, 1250, 1252, 1254, 1256 Existentialism, 1247 The Algerian High Plateau, 1248	Journal Entry, 1259 Story Epilogue, 1259 Literary-Analysis Essay, 1259 Informal Assessment (Comparing Characters' Relationships), 1254
Comparing Literature Across Cultures The Prison Experience		Compare and Contrast, 1260, 1264, 1268	Comparison-and-Contrast Essay, 1260 Standardized Test Practice (Comparison-and-Contrast Essay), 1260
PROSE POETRY Freedom to Breathe	Description, 1261, 1263 Description, 1262	Recognizing Sensory Details, 1261, 1263 Recognizing Sensory Details, 1262	Sensory Description, 1264
POETRY The Prison Cell			
Comparing Literature Standardized Test Practice			Comparison-and-Contrast Essay, 1269 Standardized Test Practice (Responding to a Writing Prompt), 1269

LEGEND **Black type – Pupil Edition**
Green type – Teacher's Edition
DLS – Daily Language SkillBuilder

Speaking and Listening Viewing and Representing	Inquiry and Research	Grammar, Usage, and Mechanics	Vocabulary
			Self Assessment, 1198 Self Assessment, 1198
Story Illustration, 1213 Readers Theater, 1213 Art Appreciation, 1210	The Grieving Process, 1213 World War I, 1213	DLS, 1206	Context Clues, 1213 Context Clues, 1208
Group Discussion, 1219		DLS, 1216	
Play Poster, 1231 Improvisational Performance, 1231 Dramatic Presentation, 1223 Informal Assessment (Summarizing), 1225 Dramatic Reading, 1226 Art Appreciation, 1228	Controlling Youths, 1231 Brecht's Drama, 1231	DLS, 1220 Ellipsis Points, 1229	Word Meanings, 1231 Using a Dictionary to Determine Precise Meanings, 1227
Art Appreciation, 1240	Discussion Questions, 1241 Research Project, 1243 Group Discussion, 1243	DLS, 1232 Using Semicolons to Join Independent Clauses, 1239	
Role-Playing, 1259 Landscape Drawing, 1259 Oral Reading, 1250	French Colonialism in Algeria, 1259	DLS, 1244 Distinguishing Compound Sentences from Simple Sentences with Compound Verbs, 1256–1257	Context Clues, 1259 Context Clues, 1249
Oral Interpretation, 1264 Artistic Reflection, 1264	Writers in Communist Russia, 1264	DLS, 1261	
Choral Reading, 1267		DLS, 1265	

LEGEND **Black type – Pupil Edition**
Green type – Teacher's Edition DLS – Daily Language SkillBuilder

PART 2 SKILLS TRACE

Features and Selections	Literary Analysis	Reading and Critical Thinking	Writing Opportunities
AUTHOR STUDY **Chinua Achebe**		Using the Time Line, 1271	
FICTION Dead Men's Path	Cultural Conflict, 1274, 1278 Cultural Conflict, 1276	Understanding Motivations, 1274, 1278 Understanding Motivations, 1276	Job Assessment, 1279
NONFICTION *from* An Interview with Chinua Achebe	Cultural Conflict, 1280	*Things Fall Apart,* 1282	
POETRY Keeper of the Vigil		Yusef Komunyakaa, 1284	
FICTION Civil Peace	Dialect, 1286, 1291 Dialect, 1288, 1290	Making Judgments About Characters, 1286, 1291 Making Judgments About Characters, 1288 Nigerian Civil War, 1289	News Article, 1293 Essay About the Title, 1293 Standardized Test Practice (Write a Dialogue), 1290
The Author's Style	Analysis of Style, 1292	Imitating Style, 1292 Changing Style, 1292 Comparing Styles, 1292	
Author Study Project		A Radio Program on Achebe, 1293	
NONFICTION *from* Paula	Autobiography, 1295, 1302 Autobiography, 1296, 1298	Recognizing Author's Purpose, 1295, 1302 Recognizing Author's Purpose, 1296, 1300 Latin American Women Writers, 1299	Autobiographical Essay, 1303 Mother-and-Daughter Dialogue, 1303 Letter to the Editor, 1302
Writing Workshop Research Report Standardized Test Practice Building Vocabulary Sentence Crafting		Analyzing a Student Model, 1307–1309 Teaching Tip: Drawing Conclusions, 1313	Drafting, 1313 Paragraph Building, 1314 For Your Portfolio, 1314 Choosing a Topic, 1310 Planning the Research Report, 1310
Reflect and Assess	Reflecting on the Literature (The Human Cost of Conflict), 1318 Reviewing Literary Concepts (Analyzing Tone), 1318		Building Your Portfolio, 1318

LEGEND **Black type – Pupil Edition**
Green type – Teacher's Edition
DLS – Daily Language SkillBuilder

Speaking and Listening Viewing and Representing	Inquiry and Research	Grammar, Usage, and Mechanics	Vocabulary
Artistic Interpretation, 1279 Role-Playing, 1279	Nigerian Culture, 1279	DLS, 1274	Related Words, 1279 Context Clues, 1276
		DLS, 1286	Context Clues, 1293 Analyzing Affixes and Base Words, 1288
	Primary Sources, 1293 Secondary Sources, 1293		
Human-Rights Poster, 1303 Art Appreciation, 1300	Chile After Pinochet, 1303	DLS, 1294 Colons with Independent Clauses, 1301	Meaning Clues, 1303 Prefixes and Etymologies, 1296
	Research Report, 1310–1312 Research Tip, 1310 Teaching Tip: Making Source Cards, 1311	Using Commas, 1314, 1315 Capitalization, 1315 Parallelism, 1315 Varying Sentence Length, 1317 Using Fragments, 1317 Capitalization of Organizations and Other Subjects, 1315 Problems with Sentence Fragments, 1317	Misspelled Words, 1315 Choosing Word-Attack Strategies, 1316 Context Clues, 1316 Word Families or Roots, 1316 Affixes, 1316 Reference Tools, 1316
			Self Assessment, 1318 Self Assessment, 1318

LEGEND **Black type – Pupil Edition**
Green type – Teacher's Edition
DLS – Daily Language SkillBuilder

PART 3 SKILLS TRACE

Features and Selections	Literary Analysis	Reading and Critical Thinking	Writing Opportunities
Critics and Dreamers: Contemporary Nobel Prize Winners			
FICTION Amnesty	First-Person Point of View, 1325, 1333 First-Person Point of View, 1326, 1328, 1330	Making Inferences, 1325, 1333 Making Inferences, 1326, 1328, 1330 Lobola, 1326 The Rivonia Trial, 1327 Separation from Children, 1329 Standardized Test Practice (Evaluating and Making Judgments), 1331	Comparison-and-Contrast Essay, 1334 A Daughter's Diary, 1334 Revealing Letter, 1334
Connect to Today Farm Workers in the New South Africa		Group Discussion, 1335	
POETRY After the Deluge The End and the Beginning	Tone, 1337, 1342 Tone, 1338, 1340	Evaluating, 1337, 1342 Evaluating, 1338, 1340	Poetic Portrait, 1343 Editorial on Memory, 1343 Comparison-and-Contrast Essay, 1343
Learning the Language of Literature Magical Realism	Magical Realism, 1344, 1345	Strategies for Reading, 1345	
FICTION The Handsomest Drowned Man in the World	Symbol, 1347, 1354 Symbol, 1348, 1350, 1352	Understanding Cause and Effect, 1347, 1354 Understanding Cause and Effect, 1348, 1350, 1352 Cultural Allusions, 1351	Character Biography, 1355 Interpretive Essay, 1355
POETRY Ode to the Lizard Ode to the Watermelon	Style, 1359, 1364 Style, 1360, 1362	Reading Poetry Aloud, 1359, 1364 Reading Poetry Aloud, 1360, 1362 Lizard Camouflage, 1360 About the Translator, 1362	Informal Assessment (Poetic Devices), 1361
The Translator at Work On Translating Neruda		Small Group Discussion, 1365	
FICTION Half a Day	Title and Theme, 1367, 1372 Title and Theme, 1368, 1370	Connecting with Characters, 1367, 1372 Connecting with Characters, 1368, 1370	School Memory, 1373 Interpretive Essay, 1373 Informal Assessment (Summarizing), 1370
Related Reading Counting in Sevens		Discussion Questions, 1371	
Reflect and Assess	Reflecting on the Literature (Critics and Dreamers), 1378 Reviewing Literary Concepts (Analyzing Styles), 1378		Building Your Portfolio, 1378

LEGEND **Black type – Pupil Edition**
Green type – Teacher's Edition
DLS – Daily Language SkillBuilder

Speaking and Listening Viewing and Representing	Inquiry and Research	Grammar, Usage, and Mechanics	Vocabulary
Waiting Portrait, 1334 Debate on Self-Sacrifice, 1334 Dramatic Monologue, 1328 Group Discussion, 1335	Robben Island Prisoners, 1334 Legacy of Apartheid, 1334	DLS, 1324 Participial Phrases, 1332	
Dramatic Reading, 1343 Editorial Cartoon, 1343 Personal Interview, 1343 Art Appreciation, 1339 Interpretive Reading, 1340	More by the Authors, 1343 Historical Time Line, 1343 Starting Over, 1343	DLS, 1336	
Village Diorama, 1355 Radio Recording, 1355 Oral Reading, 1348 Art Appreciation, 1350, 1353	Magical Realist Anthology, 1355	DLS, 1346	Word Meanings, 1355 Researching Word Origins, 1349
Small Group Discussion, 1365		DLS, 1358	
Life on the Line, 1373 Wordless Portrayal, 1373 Discussion Questions, 1371	Present-Day Cairo, 1373 More Mahfouz, 1373	DLS, 1366 Apostrophes and Plurals, 1371	Context Clues, 1373 Using Context Clues, 1368
			Self Assessment, 1378 Self Assessment, 1378

LEGEND **Black type – Pupil Edition**
Green type – Teacher's Edition
DLS – Daily Language SkillBuilder

RESOURCE MANAGEMENT GUIDE PART 1

	Unit Resource Book	Assessment	Integrated Technology and Media	Additional Support
Worlds of Change **Expressions of Modernism**			Humanities classzone.com	**World Art and Cultures Transparencies** • AT63 *The Fate of the Animals* • AT67 *The Twittering Machine* • AT68 *Electric Prisms*
Metamorphosis *pp. 1108–1149*	• Summary p. 4 • Active Reading p. 5 • Literary Analysis p. 6 • Words to Know p. 7 • Selection Quiz p. 8	• Selection Test, Formal Assessment pp. 161–162 • Teacher's Guide to Assessment and Portfolio Use Test Generator	Research Starter classzone.com	This selection is included in the *World Literature InterActive Reader*™. • RTC 8 visualizing • LT 17 point of view • VTC 26 prefixes • GTC 82 fragments and complete sentences • WTC 33 interpretive essay
The Panther **The Guitar** *pp. 1150–1155*	• Active Reading p. 9 • Literary Analysis p. 10	• Selection Test, Formal Assessment pp. 163–164 • Teacher's Guide to Assessment and Portfolio Use Test Generator		• LT 8 sound devices
Professions for Women *pp. 1156–1165*	• Summary p. 11 • Active Reading p. 12 • Literary Analysis p. 13 • Words to Know p. 14 • Selection Quiz p. 15	• Selection Test, Formal Assessment pp. 165–166 • Teacher's Guide to Assessment and Portfolio Use Test Generator	Research Starter classzone.com	• RTC 12 main idea and supporting detail • LT 22 style, voice, diction, purpose • VTC 83 meaning of roots • WTC 7 achieving unity
Eveline *pp. 1166–1173*	• Summary p. 16 • Active Reading p. 17 • Literary Analysis p. 18 • Selection Quiz p. 19	• Selection Test, Formal Assessment pp. 167–168 • Teacher's Guide to Assessment and Portfolio Use Test Generator	Research Starter classzone.com	• LT 12 conflict • GTC 125 compound-complex sentence • WTC 13 effective language
The Jay *pp. 1174–1181*	• Summary p. 20 • Active Reading p. 21 • Literary Analysis p. 22 • Words to Know p. 23 • Selection Quiz p. 24	• Selection Test, Formal Assessment pp. 169–170 • Teacher's Guide to Assessment and Portfolio Use Test Generator	Research Starter classzone.com	• RTC 11 chronological order • LT 21 symbols and figurative language • VTC 41 context clues • WTC 28 problem-solution
Prayer to Masks *pp. 1182–1187*	• Active Reading p. 25 • Literary Analysis p. 26	• Selection Test, Formal Assessment pp. 171–172 • Teacher's Guide to Assessment and Portfolio Use Test Generator	Research Starter classzone.com	• RTC 41 paraphrasing and summarizing, 48 cluster diagram • VTC 13 denotation and connotation

Writing Workshop: Literary Interpretation *pp. 1190–1197*

Unit Seven Resource Book
- Prewriting p. 27
- Drafting and Elaboration p. 28
- Peer Response Guide pp. 29–30
- Revising, Editing, and Proofreading p. 31
- Student Models pp. 32–36
- Rubric for Evaluation p. 37

Power Presentations CD-ROM

Publishing Options classzone.com

Teacher's Guide to Assessment and Portfolio Use

Unit Assessment
- Unit Seven, Part 1 Test, Formal Assessment pp. 173–174

Test Generator

Unit Technology

classzone.com

EasyPlanner CD-ROM

KEY

RTC = Reading and Critical Thinking Transparencies and Copymasters
LT = Literary Analysis Transparencies
WTC = Writing Transparencies and Copymasters
VTC = Vocabulary Transparencies and Copymasters
GTC = Grammar Transparencies and Copymasters

The *Grammar Transparencies and Copymasters* booklet contains extra Daily Language SkillBuilders. These are in addition to the Daily Language SkillBuilders in the Teacher's Edition. These additional exercises use examples from literature commonly read at grade ten.

RESOURCE MANAGEMENT GUIDE PART 2

	Unit Resource Book	Assessment	Integrated Technology and Media	Additional Support
When Worlds Collide **Responses to War and Conflict**			Humanities classzone.com	**World Art and Cultures Transparencies** • AT64 *L'Assault* • AT65 *Friendship of the People* • AT69 *Pillars of Society* • AT70 German and American propaganda posters • AT71 *Liberation*
War *pp. 1206–1213*	• Summary p. 41 • Active Reading p. 42 • Literary Analysis p. 43 • Words to Know p. 44 • Selection Quiz p. 45	• Selection Test, Formal Assessment pp. 175–176 • Teacher's Guide to Assessment and Portfolio Use Test Generator	Research Starter classzone.com	
Milestones in World Literature **All Quiet on the Western Front** *pp. 1214–1215*			Milestone Links classzone.com	
I Am Not One of Those Who Left the Land *pp. 1216–1219*	• Active Reading p. 46 • Literary Analysis p. 47	• Selection Test, Formal Assessment pp. 177–178 • Teacher's Guide to Assessment and Portfolio Use Test Generator		
The Spy *pp. 1220–1231*	• Summary p. 48 • Active Reading p. 49 • Literary Analysis p. 50 • Words to Know p. 51 • Selection Quiz p. 52	• Selection Test, Formal Assessment pp. 179–180 • Teacher's Guide to Assessment and Portfolio Use Test Generator	Research Starter classzone.com	
from **The World Was Silent** *pp. 1232–1243*	• Summary p. 53 • Active Reading p. 54 • Literary Analysis p. 55 • Selection Quiz p. 56	• Selection Test, Formal Assessment, pp. 181–182 • Teacher's Guide to Assessment and Portfolio Use Test Generator	Research Starter classzone.com	
The Guest *pp. 1244–1259*	• Summary p. 57 • Active Reading p. 58 • Literary Analysis p. 59 • Words to Know p. 60 • Selection Quiz p. 61	• Selection Test, Formal Assessment pp. 183–184 • Teacher's Guide to Assessment and Portfolio Use Test Generator	Research Starter classzone.com	This selection is included in the *World Literature InterActive Reader™*.
Freedom to Breathe *pp. 1260–1264* **The Prison Cell** *pp. 1265–1269*	• Points of Comparison p. 62 • Active Reading p. 63 • Literary Analysis p. 64 • Compare/contrast Essay p. 65	• Selection Test, Formal Assessment pp. 185–186 • Teacher's Guide to Assessment and Portfolio Use Test Generator	Research Starter classzone.com	
Author Study **Chinua Achebe** *pp. 1270–1273*			Author Link classzone.com NetActivities	

RESOURCE MANAGEMENT GUIDE PART 2

	Unit Resource Book	Assessment	Integrated Technology and Media	Additional Support
Dead Men's Path *pp. 1274–1279* *from* **An Interview with Chinua Achebe** *pp. 1280–1283* **Keeper of the Vigil** *pp. 1284–1285*	• Summary p. 66 • Active Reading p. 67 • Literary Analysis p. 68 • Words to Know p. 69 • Selection Quiz p. 70	• Selection Test, Formal Assessment pp. 187–188 • Teacher's Guide to Assessment and Portfolio Use Test Generator	Research Starter classzone.com	
Civil Peace *pp. 1286–1293*	• Summary p. 71 • Active Reading p. 72 • Literary Analysis p. 73 • Words to Know p. 74 • Selection Quiz p. 75	• Selection Test, Formal Assessment pp. 189–190 • Teacher's Guide to Assessment and Portfolio Use Test Generator	Research Starter classzone.com	
from **Paula** *pp. 1294–1303*	• Summary p. 76 • Active Reading p. 77 • Literary Analysis p. 78 • Words to Know p. 79 • Selection Quiz p. 80	• Selection Test, Formal Assessment pp. 191–192 • Teacher's Guide to Assessment and Portfolio Use Test Generator	Research Starter classzone.com	

Writing Workshop: Research Report *pp. 1306–1317*

Unit Seven Resource Book
- Prewriting p. 81
- Drafting and Elaboration p. 82
- Peer Response Guide pp. 83–84
- Revising, Editing, and Proofreading p. 85
- Student Models pp. 86–91
- Rubric for Evaluation p. 92

Publishing Options classzone.com

Teacher's Guide to Assessment and Portfolio Use

Unit Assessment	*Unit Technology*
• Unit Seven, Part 2 Test, Formal Assessment pp. 193–194 Test Generator • Unit Seven, Integrated Assessment Test, Integrated Assessment pp. 37–42	classzone.com NetActivities

RESOURCE MANAGEMENT GUIDE PART 3

	Unit Resource Book	Assessment	Integrated Technology and Media	Additional Support
Critics and Dreamers **Contemporary Nobel Prize Winners**			Humanities classzone.com	**World Art and Cultures Transparencies** • AT75 *After the Storm*
Amnesty *pp. 1324–1335*	• Summary p. 96 • Active Reading p. 97 • Literary Analysis p. 98 • Selection Quiz p. 99	• Selection Test, Formal Assessment pp. 195–196 • Teacher's Guide to Assessment and Portfolio Use Test Generator	Humanities Activity classzone.com Research Starter classzone.com	This selection is included in the *World Literature InterActive Reader™*.
After the Deluge **The End and the Beginning** *pp. 1336–1343*	•Active Reading p. 100 • Literary Analysis p. 101	• Selection Test, Formal Assessment pp. 197–198 • Teacher's Guide to Assessment and Portfolio Use Test Generator	Research Starter classzone.com	
The Handsomest Drowned Man in the World *pp. 1346–1355*	• Summary p. 102 • Active Reading p. 103 • Literary Analysis p. 104 • Words to Know p. 105 • Selection Quiz p. 106	• Selection Test, Formal Assessment pp. 199–200 • Teacher's Guide to Assessment and Portfolio Use Test Generator	Research Starter classzone.com	This selection is included in the *World Literature InterActive Reader™*.
Milestones in World Literature **One Hundred Years of Solitude** *pp. 1356–1357*			Milestone Links classzone.com	
Ode to the Lizard **Ode to the Watermelon** *pp. 1358–1365*	• Active Reading p. 107 • Literary Analysis p. 108	• Selection Test, Formal Assessment pp. 201–202 • Teacher's Guide to Assessment and Portfolio Use Test Generator		
Half a Day *pp. 1366–1373*	• Summary p. 109 • Active Reading p. 110 • Literary Analysis p. 111 • Words to Know p. 112 • Selection Quiz p. 113	• Selection Test, Formal Assessment pp. 203–204 • Teacher's Guide to Assessment and Portfolio Use Test Generator	Research Starter classzone.com	
		Unit Assessment	***Unit Technology***	
		• Unit Seven, Part 3 Test, Formal Assessment pp. 205–206 Test Generator	classzone.com	

DAILY LANGUAGE SKILLBUILDERS

Selection	SkillBuilder Sentences	Suggested Answers
Metamorphosis	**1.** Franz Kafka was born into a german-speaking family. **2.** The room which was emptied of furniture was now more suitable for Gregor's movements.	**1.** Franz Kafka was born into a **G**erman-speaking family. **2.** The room**,** which was emptied of furniture**,** was now more suitable for Gregor's movements.
The Panther The Guitar	**1.** Although, he was born in Prague, Rainer Maria Rilke lived in many other european cities. **2.** Among Federico García Lorca's talents were to write poetry, writing plays, and piano.	**1.** Although he was born in Prague, Rainer Maria Rilke lived in many other **E**uropean cities. [Students should remove the comma after *Although.*] **2.** Among Federico García Lorca's talents were **writing** poetry, writing plays, and **playing the** piano [or **playing** piano].
Professions for Women	**1.** Virginia Woolf was born in London to a prominent victorian family. **2.** "Face with the option of buying food and clothing or a pet, Woolf made the least sensible choice and buys a cat.	**1.** Virginia Woolf was born in London to a prominent **V**ictorian family. **2.** **Faced** with the option of buying food and clothing or a pet, Woolf made the **less** sensible choice and **bought** a cat. [Students should remove quotation marks before *Faced.*]
Eveline	**1.** James Joyce was born in Dublin Ireland he left his homeland for religious and political reasons. **2.** Eveline made the desicion to stay with her father rather than marry Frank.	**1.** James Joyce was born in Dublin**,** Ireland**;** he left his homeland for religious and political reasons. **2.** Eveline made the **decision** to stay with her father rather than marry Frank.
The Jay	**1.** Although the author was well versed in modern European literature his primary influences were japanese. **2.** Yoshiko's brother found a picture of their mother and had shown to their father.	**1.** Although the author was well versed in modern European literature**,** his primary influences were **J**apanese. **2.** Yoshiko's brother found a picture of their mother and **showed it** to their father.
Prayer to Masks	**1.** The author was born in a village in french west Africa which is now Senegal. **2.** Senghor was a teacher before he had served as the president of Senegal.	**1.** The author was born in a village in **F**rench **W**est Africa**,** which is now Senegal. **2.** Senghor was a teacher before he served as the president of Senegal. [Students should remove *had.*]
War	**1.** The woman thinks her greif is worser than him. **2.** The parents whom send their sons off to war made a huge sacrifice.	**1.** The woman thinks her **grief** is **worse** than **his grief is.** **2.** The parents **who sent** their sons off to war made a huge sacrifice.

Selection	SkillBuilder Sentences	Suggested Answers
I Am Not One of Those Who Left the Land	**1.** Writers were especialy effected by the Russian Revolution of 1917 **2.** The 20th century was a dangerous time for many writers to publish there works.	**1.** Writers were **especially affected** by the Russian Revolution of 1917. **2.** The 20th century was a dangerous time for many writers to publish **their** works.
The Spy	**1.** In The Spy, life under the Nazi goverment lead a couple to suspect their own son of spying. **2.** A husband and wife had an arguement about what their son overhears.	**1.** In The Spy, life under the Nazi **government leads** a couple to suspect their own son of spying. **2.** A husband and wife **have** an **argument** about what their son overhears.
from The World Was Silent	**1.** Elie Wiesel and his father were rounded up by Nazis, and than shipped on a cattle train to a concentration camp. **2.** The journey to the camp was even worser then the camp.	**1.** Elie Wiesel and his father were rounded up by Nazis and **then** shipped on a cattle train to a concentration camp. [Students should remove the comma after *Nazis*.] **2.** The journey to the camp was even **worse than** the camp.
The Guest	**1.** The french invaded Algeria, and set up a repressive Colonial government Albert Camus however opposed it. **2.** His students lived in such poverty that the teachers meager surroundings seems like wealth.	**1.** The **F**rench invaded Algeria and set up a repressive **c**olonial government**;** Albert Camus**,** however**,** opposed it. [Students should remove the comma after *Algeria*.] **2.** His students lived in such poverty that the teacher**'**s meager surroundings seem**ed** like wealth.
Freedom to Breathe	**1.** Alexander Solzhenitsyn wrote novels to describe the Soviet prison camps and exposing the treatment of prisoners. **2.** Solzhenitsyn felt he was denied the freedom to breath freely, imagine not being able to smell grass and flowers.	**1.** Alexander Solzhenitsyn wrote novels to describe the Soviet prison camps and **to expose** the treatment of prisoners. **2.** Solzhenitsyn felt he was denied the freedom to **breathe** freely**—**imagine not being able to smell grass and flowers. [Students may change the period to an exclamation mark.]
The Prison Cell	**1.** Mahmud Darwish is considered a principle arabic poet. **2.** Darwish was born in barweh, a vilage in Palestine.	**1.** Mahmud Darwish is considered a **principal A**rabic poet. **2.** Darwish was born in **B**arweh, a **village** in Palestine.
Dead Men's Path	**1.** The Headmaster of the school thought the villagers beliefs were redikulous. **2.** He would not reopen the path a few days later he discovered that the school grounds were ruined.	**1.** The **h**eadmaster of the school thought the villagers**'** beliefs were **ridiculous**. **2.** He would not reopen the path**. A** few days later**,** he discovered that the school grounds were ruined.

DAILY LANGUAGE SKILLBUILDERS

Selection	SkillBuilder Sentences	Suggested Answers
Keeper of the Vigil	**1.** The Poet Yusef Komunyakaa wrote a poem as a Tribute to Chinua Achebe. **2.** In it, he recognises Chinua Achebe's literary talent.	**1.** The **p**oet Yusef Komunyakaa wrote a poem as a **t**ribute to Chinua Achebe. **2.** In it, he **recognizes** Chinua Achebe's literary talent.
Civil Peace	**1.** In the story Civil Peace the main characters money is stolen. **2.** Jonathan uses every oportunity to make money.	**1.** In the story "Civil Peace," the main character's money is stolen. **2.** Jonathan uses every **opportunity** to make money.
from Paula	**1.** Salvador Allende, the uncle and Godfather of Isabel Allende, was elected president of Chile in 1970. **2.** Paula, Isabel Allende's 27 year old daughter became seriously ill and dies.	**1.** Salvador Allende, the uncle and **g**odfather of Isabel Allende, was elected president of Chile in 1970. **2.** Paula, Isabel Allende's 27-year-old daughter, became seriously ill and die**d**.
Amnesty	**1.** Born in the Transvaal province of south Africa as a young girl, Nadine Gordimer wrote short stories. **2.** Little has changed for black farm workers in South Africa since apartheid ended in 1991 however there are a few signs of progress.	**1.** Born in the Transvaal province of **S**outh Africa, Nadine Gordimer wrote short stories **as a young girl**. **2.** Little has changed for black farm workers in South Africa since apartheid ended in 1991; however, there are a few signs of progress.
After the Deluge The End and the Beginning	**1.** The nigerian author's play warned that the end of colonial rule would not neccesarily end the countrys problems. **2.** The author lived through the brutality and hardships of war, and a Communist dictatorship	**1.** The **N**igerian author's play warned that the end of colonial rule would not **necessarily** end the country's problems. **2.** The author lived through the brutality and hardships of war and a Communist dictatorship. [Students should remove the comma after *war.*]
The Handsomest Drowned Man in the World	**1.** The drowned man weren't no one the villagers knew **2.** The women covered the man's face with a hankerchief so the light wouldn't bother him.	**1.** The drowned man **wasn't anyone** the villagers knew. **2.** The women covered the man's face with a **handkerchief** so the light wouldn't bother him.
Ode to the Lizard Ode to the Watermelon	**1.** Pablo Neruda was a member of the Communist party. **2.** He wrote a epic poem about the history of latin America.	**1.** Pablo Neruda was a member of the Communist **P**arty. **2.** He wrote **an** epic poem about the history of **L**atin America.
Half a Day	**1.** Naguib Mahfouz who won the 1988 Nobel prize in literature has written many books. **2.** The main character is a young boy who's school expereinse has surprising results.	**1.** Naguib Mahfouz, who won the 1988 Nobel **P**rize in literature, has written many books. **2.** The main character is a young boy **whose** school **experience** has surprising results.

INTEGRATING GRAMMAR AND LITERATURE: GRAMMAR PLANNER

	Unit One	Unit Two	Unit Three	Unit Four	Unit Five	Unit Six	Unit Seven
Grammar Focus by Unit	Parts of Speech	The Sentence and Its Parts	Using Verbs	Using Modifiers	Using Phrases	Clauses and Sentence Structure	Clauses and Sentence Structure

The program offers several options for integrating grammar instruction and literature.

- Each unit has a grammar focus. The Teacher's Edition includes Mini Lessons for the selections that help develop the grammar focus for the unit and spring from the content of the specific literature.
- The Pupil Edition includes several full-page lessons on Sentence Crafting. These lessons are related to both the literature and the grammar focus for a unit and help students use proper grammar in their own writing.
- Daily Language SkillBuilders in the Teacher's Edition provide students with ongoing proofreading practice and reinforce correct punctuation, spelling, grammar and usage, and capitalization.

Black type — Pupil Edition
Green type — Teacher's Edition

Part 1

Clauses and Sentence Structure

Complex Sentences
"Metamorphosis," p. 1144

Compound-Complex Sentences
"Eveline," p. 1171

Adjective Clauses
Sentence Crafting, p. 1197
Sentence Crafting, p. 1197

Using Verbs

Voice of a Verb: Active Voice
Writing Workshop, p. 1194

Voice of a Verb: Passive Voice
Standardized Test Practice, p. 1195

Verb Tense
Writing Workshop, p. 1194
Standardized Test Practice, p. 1195

Principal Parts of Verbs
Standardized Test Practice, p. 1195

Capitalization

Titles
Standardized Test Practice, p. 1195
Standardized Test Practice, p. 1195

Using Phrases

Adjective Phrases
Sentence Crafting, p. 1197
Sentence Crafting, p. 1197

Part 2

Clauses and Sentence Structure

Using Semicolons to Join Independent Clauses
from *The World Was Silent*, p. 1239

Distinguishing Compound Sentences from Simple Sentences
"The Guest," pp. 1256–1257

Colons with Independent Clauses
from *Paula*, p. 1301

The Sentence and Its Parts

Sentence Fragments
Sentence Crafting, p. 1317
Sentence Crafting, p. 1317

Punctuation

Ellipsis Points
The Spy, p. 1229

Comma Uses
Writing Workshop, p. 1314
Standardized Test Practice, p. 1315

Capitalization

People and Cultures
Standardized Test Practice, p. 1315

Organizations and Other Subjects
Standardized Test Practice, p. 1315

Style

Varying Sentence Length
Sentence Crafting, p. 1317

Parallelism
Standardized Test Practice, p. 1315

Part 3

Using Phrases

Verbals: Participles
"Amnesty," p. 1332

Punctuation

Apostrophes
"Counting in Sevens," p. 1371

READING FOR INFORMATION
Reading Skills and Strategies
PREVIEWING
Give students a few moments to look over the introduction to Unit Seven. Point out that it consists of three sections: (1) an overview called **The Changing World** that describes some of the major changes in the 20th century; (2) a time line divided into two parts, **Events in World Literature and Art** and **Events in World History;** (3) a **Literary Map of the World** that matches the writers represented in the unit with their native or adoptive countries.

Reading Skills and Strategies
RECOGNIZING CONTRAST
Tell students that this overview explains both the positive and the negative results of some of the major changes in the 20th century. You might have students create a two-column chart to help them sort out the information, listing positive effects in the first column and negative ones in the second.

UNIT SEVEN
The Changing World

Perhaps no century in human history has experienced the degree of change that took place in the 1900s. At its best, the 20th century saw the spread of democracy, great scientific achievements, and marvels of technology. At its worst, it was the most violent, most destructive century in human history. Writers had no shortage of subjects.

An American astronaut stands on the surface of the moon.

Struggles for Power

The century was defined by its conflicts. In two world wars, great powers collided in struggles for economic and political domination. In the Cold War, competing systems—democratic capitalism and communism—fought for supremacy.

Indian leader Mahatma Gandhi, a key figure in India's successful revolt against British rule

During the second half of the century, independence movements against European rule sprang up throughout Africa and Asia, resulting in bloody conflicts. Later, power struggles became more localized, with terrorism and civil war taking high civilian casualties.

Triumphs–and Tragedies–of Science and Technology

In the 20th century, advances in science and technology changed life dramatically. The automobile, high-speed trains, and jet planes enabled us to travel faster and farther than ever before. A revolution in communication allowed us to send and receive information across the world in the blink of an eye. Radio, television, film, computers, cell phones, and the Internet—all were invented or flourished in the 20th century. With the flick of a switch, we could cool a house, light up a skyscraper, or heat an entire city. The same know-how made it possible to send fresh foods across continents and oceans. A

Perhaps the most beneficial achievements of the century occurred in medicine. Antibiotics, vaccines, surgery, and an arsenal of medicines now fight disease and extend life. A more nutritious diet, thanks primarily to improved methods of farming and distribution, became available to many. Life expectancy climbed steadily, especially in developed countries.

Yet science and technology have also been put to destructive uses. In World War I, for example, advanced biological and chemical weapons killed thousands. The technology of war became even more powerful in the 1940s with the invention of the atom bomb, the most powerful means of destruction ever created. Our great appetite for energy has depleted precious natural resources, while the pollution of air, soil, and water has posed a worldwide threat to health and safety. To a degree, we are victims of our own successes.

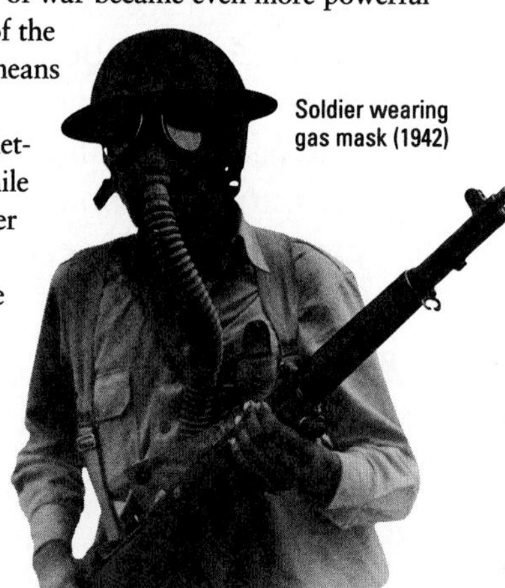
Soldier wearing gas mask (1942)

Family and friends watching their new cable television in the isolated Asian country of Bhutan

New Ways of Living

Over the century, everyday life changed at an ever-quickening pace. Industrialization, begun in Europe in the 19th century, gradually spread around the world. As a result, consumer goods became widely available, personal wealth increased, and cities grew rapidly. At the start of the 20th century, most of the world's population lived in rural areas. By century's end, more than 40 percent of that population lived in urban areas. In the cities, new economic opportunities opened, cultures mingled, and new ideas challenged traditional ways of life.

Throughout the world, many people have benefited from economic growth and progress in science, medicine, and agriculture. However, the gap between rich and poor nations is widening, and many still live in grinding poverty.

Global Interdependence

Advances in trade, technology, and communications have made the world a "smaller" place. In the first decades of the 20th century, Western countries seemed to control the fate of the world because of their power and colonial rule of nations in Asia and Africa. In recent decades, nations have become more interdependent. Former colonies welcome trade and investment from the West, while businesses in developed countries, such as Japan, Germany, and the United States, depend on international markets.

As national economies blend into one global economy, some positive and negative effects have emerged. On the one hand, cultural exchanges can enrich individual nations. On the other hand, some countries fear losing their native culture due to the influence of popular Western culture, with its rock music, jeans, and television shows.

Democracy and Education

In the last century, democracy and education became more widespread across the world.

In 1902, for example, only Australia and New Zealand allowed all adult citizens to vote. Over the next hundred years, citizen participation in government increased dramatically, especially for women and minorities. Democratic governments can now be found on every continent. Women now vote in nearly every country where men have the right to vote, and women, such as Margaret Thatcher (Great Britain) and Golda Meir (Israel), have served as elected heads of state. B

The 20th century also witnessed dramatic changes in education. At the beginning of the century, widespread formal education was common only in the West and often limited to elementary levels. By the end of the century, nearly every country of the world provided free elementary education to its young people. The number of students receiving secondary and higher education has also increased significantly worldwide. In Africa, for example, more than 40 percent of the school-age population is enrolled in secondary school.

Historical Notes

A Microchip The invention of the first integrated circuit in the late 1950s ushered in a new age of technology. By the end of the 1980s, the microchip was an integral part of major products—including automobiles, televisions, stereos, microwaves, calculators, and personal computers.

B Margaret Thatcher Margaret Thatcher (1925–) earned a chemistry degree from Oxford and studied law. As the head of the Conservative Party, she became the United Kingdom's first woman prime minister in 1979. She held this post until 1990 and then resigned, having served as prime minister longer than any other person in the 20th century. As a leader, she worked to strengthen the British economy by reducing government control over it.

MINI LESSON Interpreting the Text

Have students read pages 1096 and 1097 and then answer questions such as the following:

- Which continents saw bloody struggles for independence in the second half of the 20th century? *(Africa and Asia)*
- What might happen to native cultures in a global economy? *(Native cultures gradually might lose their distinctive characteristics and ultimately disappear.)*
- Which of the following was not a 20th-century invention: cell phones, television, automobiles, the printing press? *(the printing press)*
- What major population shift occurred in the 20th century? *(Many people migrated from rural areas to cities.)*
- In what way did women and minorities benefit in the 20th century? *(They acquired political power.)*

READING FOR INFORMATION
Reading Skills and Strategies
SEQUENCING
This time line shows major dates and events in literature, art, and history in the 20th century. The dates and events follow in sequence, moving down each column and from left to right. Help students understand that though this period spans only 100 years, it gave rise to monumental changes that were reflected in literature and in the other fine arts.

Historical Note

A **Sigmund Freud** The founder of psychoanalysis, Sigmund Freud (1856–1939) was one of the most influential thinkers of the 20th century. An Austrian neurologist, he treated people with mental illnesses. Based on his work with his patients, he created revolutionary theories about the influence of the unconscious on human behavior. He viewed the mind as composed of the id, the ego, and the superego. The id was the repository of instinctive drives; the ego was the filter through which these drives were expressed in the real world; and the superego was the conscience or the moral sense. To Freud, dreams were a symbolic language that expressed an individual's repressed drives.

Literary Note

B ***Ulysses*** Joyce's *Ulysses* is arguably the most influential novel of the 20th century. When first published, it triggered a firestorm of controversy and was banned in both Great Britain and the United States. The first U.S. edition did not appear until 1934, after a court finally ruled that the novel was not obscene. In 1998, *Ulysses* was chosen the best English-language novel of the 20th century by an editorial board of the Modern Library.

UNIT SEVEN

Time Line

EVENTS IN WORLD LITERATURE AND ART

1900

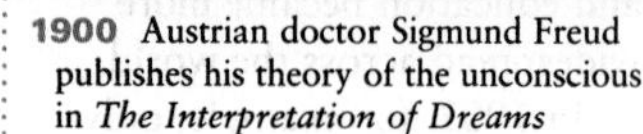

A **1900** Austrian doctor Sigmund Freud publishes his theory of the unconscious in *The Interpretation of Dreams*

1907 Pablo Picasso and Georges Braque start artistic movement called cubism in Paris

1913 Russian composer Igor Stravinsky's *The Rite of Spring* marks beginning of modernism in music

1915 Franz Kafka publishes "The Metamorphosis"

1916–1924 Dadaism, an artistic protest movement, attacks established values and ideas

1919 In Germany, Walter Gropius founds influential Bauhaus school of design that produces International style of functional, boxy architecture

1920

1920s In Jazz Age, Europeans dance to rhythms of American jazz

1921 Luigi Pirandello's innovative play *Six Characters in Search of an Author* performed

B **1922** James Joyce publishes his novel *Ulysses* in Paris

c. 1924–1937 Influenced by Freud's ideas, surrealist painters Max Ernst and Salvador Dali depict odd dream-worlds

1928 Federico García Lorca publishes his popular *Gypsy Ballads*

1929 Virginia Woolf publishes groundbreaking feminist work *A Room of One's Own*

1930s Léopold Senghor and Aimé Césaire found the Negritude movement

1940

1942 Albert Camus publishes classic novel of alienation, *The Stranger*

1944 U.S. composer Aaron Copland uses folk-song melodies and jazz rhythms in *Appalachian Spring*

1945–1960 Abstract expressionism, led by New York artist Jackson Pollock, gains respect of international art world

1948–1952 Pablo Neruda exiled from his native Chile for publicly criticizing the president

1948 Yasunari Kawabata publishes his novel *Snow Country*

1949 French writer Simone de Beauvoir publishes *The Second Sex*, arguing for an end to women's second-class status

EVENTS IN WORLD HISTORY

1900

1903 In U.S., Wright brothers make first successful airplane flight

1914–1918 World War I between Allies (Russia, France, Britain and later U.S.) and Central Powers (Germany and Austria-Hungary)

1917–1920 Russian Revolution topples czar and brings in communist government

1918 Women over 30 gain right to vote in Britain

1920

1920 World's first commercial radio station broadcasts in U.S.

1922 Benito Mussolini and Fascist Party gain control of Italy

1928 Scottish doctor Alexander Fleming discovers penicillin

1929 Stock market crash in New York soon plunges world into Great Depression

1933 Adolf Hitler and Nazi Party come to power in Germany

1937 Japan invades China

1939 Hitler invades Poland; France and Britain declare war on Germany, beginning World War II

1940

1941 Japan bombs U.S. fleet at Pearl Harbor, causing U.S. to enter war

1942 Hitler begins mass extermination of Jews

1945 Germany surrenders; Europe divided into Communist east and capitalist west

1945 U.S. drops two atomic bombs on Japan, causing Japanese surrender C

1947 Muslim Pakistan splits from Hindu India after independence from Britain, resulting in thousands of deaths

1948 State of Israel formed, angering resident Palestinians and neighboring Arab countries

1949 Mao Zedong leads Communists to victory in Chinese civil war

Gil Mayers, *The Jazz Singer*

Skyscrapers dominate skylines in cities across the world.

1950

1950s Theater of the absurd thrives with works by Samuel Beckett, Eugène Ionesco, and Edward Albee

1956 French philosopher and writer Jean-Paul Sartre explains existentialism in *Being and Nothingness*

1956–1957 Naguib Mahfouz publishes novels in his great *Cairo Trilogy*

1952 Pioneering French photojournalist Henri Cartier-Bresson publishes photo collection *The Decisive Moment*

1958 Elie Wiesel publishes *Night,* about his experiences in a Nazi death camp

1960

1962 Aleksandr Solzhenitsyn publishes *One Day in the Life of Ivan Denisovich,* based on his experiences in a Soviet prison camp

1963 Anna Akhmatova publishes her long poem *Requiem,* a moving account of Stalin's abuses

1966 Wole Soyinka's play *Kongi's Harvest* opens the first Festival of Negro Arts in Dakar, Senegal

1967 Colombian novelist Gabriel García Márquez publishes his masterpiece of magical realism, *One Hundred Years of Solitude* D

1974 Nadine Gordimer wins Booker Prize for her novel *The Conservationist*

1980

1980s Wislawa Szymborska writes under a pseudonym for an underground press in Poland

1982 Isabel Allende publishes her first novel, *The House of the Spirits*

1987 Octavio Paz publishes his collected poems from a 30-year period

1995 Writer Ken Saro-Wiwa and eight other environmental activists executed by military dictatorship in Nigeria

1950

1950–1953 War in Korea between Communist and UN forces results in division of country

1951 U.S. engineers invent first commercial digital computer, UNIVAC

1953 Scientists discover the double-helix structure of DNA

1953 Cold War escalates after U.S. and Soviet Union test the hydrogen bomb

1954 In Vietnam, French troops surrender to Ho Chi Minh's Communist forces; country is divided

1957 Ghana is first African country to win independence from British rule

1959 Fidel Castro leads Cuban Revolution

1960

1960 Nigeria wins independence from Britain

1962 Algeria gains independence from France after years of violent conflict

1965–1973 U.S. troops unsuccessfully battle Communist guerrillas in South Vietnam

1966–1976 Cultural Revolution in China stamps out intellectual and artistic activity

1971 On International Women's Day in London, women march for job opportunities and other issues

1974 First personal computer introduced in U.S.

1980

1983 Scientists discover virus that causes AIDS

1987 Palestinians in Israel begin intifada, or uprising, against Israeli rule

1989 Chinese crackdown of pro-democracy movement in Beijing's Tiananmen Square

1989 Demolition of Berlin Wall signals fall of communism in Europe E

1990 Reform begins in South Africa with repeal of apartheid laws

2001 Hijackers fly commercial planes into World Trade Center and Pentagon, killing thousands

Nelson Mandela, South African leader

1099

Historical Note

C Atomic Bomb On August 2, 1939, Albert Einstein wrote to President Franklin Roosevelt, warning him that Nazi Germany might be working to develop atomic weapons. In response to Einstein's letter, Roosevelt approved an American program—later known as the Manhattan Project—to develop an atomic bomb. On August 6, 1945, the *Enola Gay,* a B-29 bomber piloted by Colonel Paul W. Tibbets, Jr., took off from Tinian Island in the Mariana Islands. At precisely 8:16 A.M., the atomic bomb exploded above Hiroshima, a city on the Japanese island of Honshu. Tibbets described what he saw after releasing the bomb: "Down below [the mushroom cloud] the thing reminded me more of a boiling pot of tar than any other description I can give. It was black and boiling underneath with a steam haze on top of it."

Literary Note

D *One Hundred Years of Solitude* Tell students to see the feature **Milestones in World Literature** on pages 1356 and 1357 for an essay about García Márquez's novel.

Historical Note

F Berlin Wall The Communists built the Berlin Wall in 1961 to separate Communist East Berlin and non-Communist West Berlin. Patrolled by armed guards with guard dogs, the wall prevented East Germans from migrating to the West. About 26 miles long, the wall was made of concrete slabs, 12 to 15 feet high, and topped with barbed wire.

MINI LESSON Using the Time Line

SEQUENCE OF EVENTS Have students study the time line on pages 1098 and 1099 and then answer questions such as the following:

- Who came to power first, Mussolini or Hitler? *(Mussolini)*
- What classic novel did Camus write about 14 years before Sartre's *Being and Nothingness? (The Stranger)*
- Could Octavio Paz's poetry have influenced Vicente Fox? *(yes, Paz's collected poems were in print about three years before Fox became president of Mexico)*
- Did García Márquez publish *One Hundred Years of Solitude* before, during, or after the war in Vietnam? *(during)*

READING FOR INFORMATION
Reading Skills and Strategies
CLARIFYING

Make sure that students understand how to use this literary map as a source of information. The map pictures or lists the writers represented in Unit Seven. Moreover, the photographs and the lists are color coded so that students can associate writers with particular continents.

UNIT SEVEN

Literary Map of the World

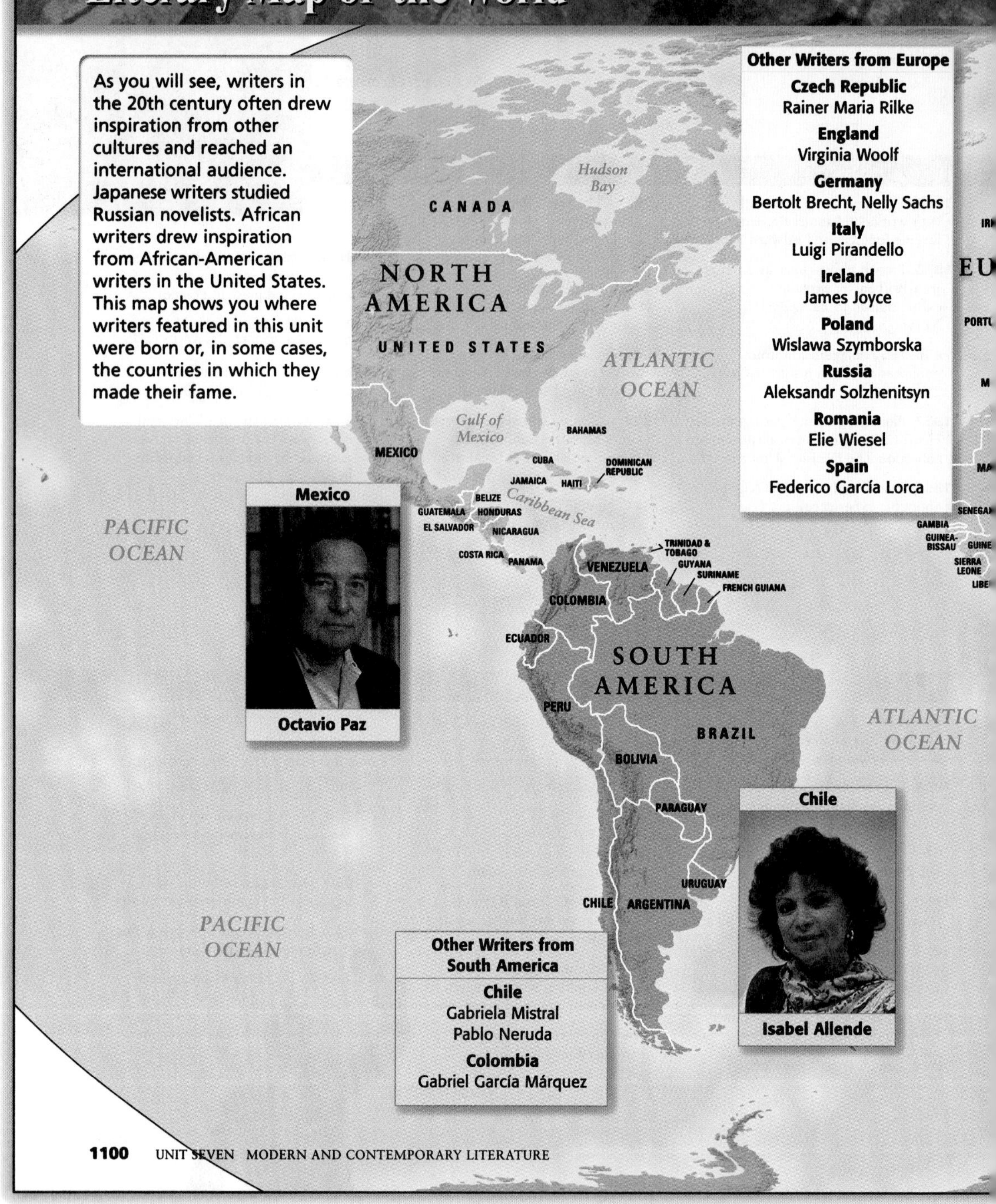

Czech Republic
Franz Kafka
Russia
Anna Akhmatova
RUSSIA
ASIA
SWEDEN
ESTONIA
LATVIA
LITH.
POLAND
BELARUS
UKRAINE
CZECH REP.
AUSTRIA
SLO.
HUNG.
MOLDOVA
ROMANIA
SLOV.
CROATIA
BOS.& HERZ.
YUGO.
BULGARIA
ITALY
ALB.
MAC.
GREECE
Black Sea
KAZAKHSTAN
MONGOLIA
Sea of Okhotsk
Caspian Sea
GEORGIA
UZBEKISTAN
KYRGYZSTAN
TURKEY
ARM.
AZER.
TURKMENISTAN
NORTH KOREA
Sea of Japan
SOUTH KOREA
JAPAN
Writers from Middle East
Israel
Yehuda Amichai
Palestine
Mahmud Darwish
CHINA
Mediterranean Sea
SYRIA
LEB.
IRAQ
ISRAEL
JORDAN
LIBYA
EGYPT
IRAN
Red Sea
BHUTAN
BANGLADESH
OMAN
MYANMAR
Arabian Sea
INDIA
Bay of Bengal
LAOS
Japan
Yasunari Kawabata
CHAD
SUDAN
ERITREA
YEMEN
VIETNAM
CAMBODIA
PHILIPPINES
DJIBOUTI
AFRICA
ETHIOPIA
CENTRAL AFRICAN REPUBLIC
SRI LANKA
MALDIVES
SOMALIA
MALAYSIA
UGANDA
KENYA
GABON
DEMOCRATIC REPUBLIC OF THE CONGO
REP. OF THE CONGO
RWANDA
BURUNDI
TANZANIA
Nigeria
Chinua Achebe
INDONESIA
PAPUA NEW GUINEA
ANGOLA
ZAMBIA
MALAWI
COMOROS
INDIAN OCEAN
MOZAMBIQUE
ZIMBABWE
NAMIBIA
MADAGASCAR
BOTSWANA
Others Writers from Africa
Algeria
Albert Camus
Egypt
Naguib Mahfouz
Nigeria
Wole Soyinka
Senegal
Léopold Sédar Senghor
South Africa
Nadine Gordimer
AUSTRALIA
Australia
Judith Wright
NTARCTICA
INTRODUCTION 1101

In Unit Seven, Part 1, you will find works by early twentieth-century writers who felt isolated or disconnected from traditional social, artistic, and religious views of the era. These writers represent an international landscape of cultures from Mexico, South America, Europe, Africa, the Middle East, and Australia.

World Art and Cultures Transparencies

AT63 *The Fate of the Animals*
AT67 *The Twittering Machine*
AT68 *Electric Prisms*

You may wish to use the listed transparencies to show the techniques some modernist artists used in their works.

READING FOR INFORMATION

Reading Skills and Strategies
IDENTIFYING MAIN IDEA

Have students read the text box labeled **Why It Matters.** Then ask: What is a modernist? *(Someone who is in love with new and provocative ideas and who seeks to create works that express these ideas.)* Tell students they will learn more about modernists and their views as they read the rest of the introduction.

Reading Skills and Strategies
SCANNING

Ask students to scan the boldfaced headings in the remaining text boxes to see what topics will be discussed. Encourage students to read each box and make connections to the accompanying photograph(s).

PART 1 Worlds of Change

Expressions of Modernism

Why It Matters As a general term, *modernism* describes much of the art, literature, and thought of the first half of the 20th century. To be a modernist is to be someone in love with what is new and provocative. As a group, modernists typically fought against traditions of all kinds and set out to create innovative works, whether in art, literature, philosophy, or other forms of expression. The next few pages will help you to understand the cultural movement that gave birth to modern literature.

For Links to Modernism, click on:
HUMANITIES CLASSZONE.COM

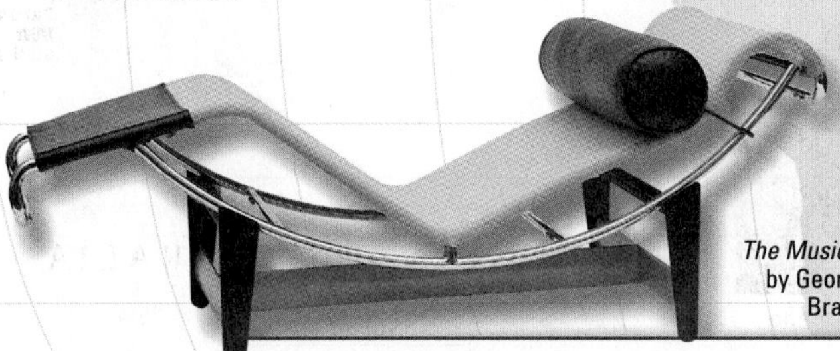

The Musician by Georges Braque

Art and Design

Many artists rebelled against earlier realistic styles. The founders of **Cubism,** Pablo Picasso of Spain and Georges Braque of France, transformed natural shapes into fragmented geometric forms. **Expressionist** painters like the Russian Wassily Kandinsky used bold colors and distorted shapes to express emotion. Sculptors experimented with new ways of portraying the human body.

Even ordinary objects, such as chairs and dinnerware, became the province of art. The chair shown above was designed in 1928 by the Swiss-born French architect and designer Le Corbusier.

1102 UNIT SEVEN PART 1: EXPRESSIONS OF MODERNISM

Movies and Photography
From the silent films of the early decades to the extravagant productions of the 1930s and 1940s, **movies** defined the 20th century. Early filmmakers such as the American D. W. Griffith and the Russian Sergei Eisenstein helped turned popular entertainment into works of art. Charlie Chaplin's silent films made him an international star. A scene from his 1936 *Modern Times* is shown here.

Photography also evolved into an art form, thanks to the efforts of such masters as the Americans Alfred Stieglitz, Edward Steichen, and Man Ray. Like painters before them, photographers held exhibitions of their work and sold photographs to bidders.

Architecture
Architects rejected traditional styles for new forms. The **International style,** popularized by the German Walter Gropius and his **Bauhaus** design school, was characterized by clean lines, open interiors, and the use of materials such as glass, steel, and concrete. The American Frank Lloyd Wright experimented with new materials and designs. Above is his Guggenheim Museum in New York City.

Music and Dance
Composers also rebelled against traditional styles. The Austrian composer Arnold Schönberg rejected traditional harmonies and musical scales. The Russian composer Igor Stravinsky relied on irregular rhythms and new sound combinations.

Modern dance reacted against the highly structured ballet of the late 19th century. The American Isadora Duncan danced barefoot in a loose tunic to express her personality. Martha Graham, shown at right, developed dance techniques to express complex emotions.

Reading Skills and Strategies
EVALUATING

Ask students whether they think the images shown on pages 1102 and 1103 are good representations of modernism. *(Most students will probably say yes; the images are bold and thought provoking.)*

READING FOR INFORMATION
Reading Skills and Strategies
EVALUATING
Have students look at the main head **Cultural Highlights of Modernism.** Then have them scan the subheads to see what these highlights are. After students have read the copy following each subhead, discuss which event or events may have had the strongest impact on the modernist movement. *(Possibly World War I)*

Cultural Highlights of Modernism

As a cultural movement, modernism began in Europe, though its influence soon spread internationally. For artists, writers, and thinkers, the world of the first half of the 20th century was both an exciting and dreadful place. Wars of furious destruction, dizzying changes in everyday life, new ideas everywhere—to modernists and ordinary people alike, the world seemed to be reinventing itself.

Sigmund Freud

Social Change in Europe

The changes begun during the Industrial Revolution of the 19th century continued into the 20th. Millions of people crowded into cities, talked on telephones, and read by electric lights. The old aristocracy, although still rich, steadily lost power, while the middle classes gained both wealth and power. Then came a war and a revolution that completely knocked Europe off its 19th-century foundation. The massive slaughter of young men in World War I—nearly half the future generation—horrified people, shaking their faith in their leaders and even in civilization itself. The Russian Revolution ushered in a new social, political, and economic order, called communism, that threatened the capitalist society built by industrialization.

In the 1920s, cars and radios helped speed up social change, as people—especially women—gained more freedom. But by the 1930s, unresolved political and economic problems boosted the rise of dictators. Mussolini (Italy), Hitler (Germany), and Stalin (Russia) unleashed the chaos and violence that led to another world war.

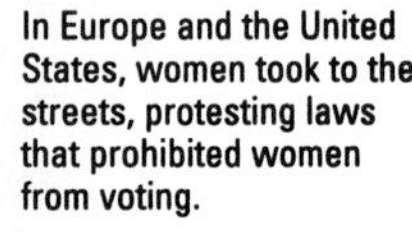

In Europe and the United States, women took to the streets, protesting laws that prohibited women from voting.

Breakdown of Traditional Beliefs

World War I shook many people's belief in the traditional virtues of reason, order, and obedience. But new ideas had begun hammering at traditional beliefs even earlier. Charles Darwin had dealt a major blow to traditional views of human nature with his theory of evolution, published in *On the Origin of Species* in 1859. In 1900, Sigmund Freud published his theory that unconscious, irrational desires rule human lives as much as reason. Soon after, the physicist Albert Einstein upset the idea of a well-ordered universe with his theory of relativity. To some, the breakdown of tradition created what T. S. Eliot called "the waste land." To others, it meant freedom.

MINI LESSON Interpreting the Text

Ask students the following questions about the information on pages 1104 and 1105:

- How did social changes in Europe and the breakdown of traditional beliefs help to create the modernist movement?

Possible Response: Social and political changes shook people's faith in their leaders. World War I also made many people question their traditional beliefs and values. To modernists, this movement away from long-held views was a chance to experiment with new ideas and new forms of expression.

- How did modernists define the word *new?*

Possible Response: Sometimes it meant shocking. Often it meant anything that the audience did not expect.

- In what city did all of the artists listed in the chart live at some point in their lives? *(Paris)*

Pablo Picasso in his Paris studio

Man Leaning on a Table (1916) by Pablo Picasso

Alienation of the Artist

Modernists sought a total break from the past and experimented constantly with new forms and ideas. But with liberation also came alienation. Modernists felt distant from society, often expressing hostility toward the very people who bought their art and read their works. In response, many heaped scorn upon the modernists, mocking what they could not understand. To advance the cause of art, artists and writers often banded together in various movements. A number of these groups published manifestos, or public statements of their views.

Search for the New

If there was one rallying cry that united the various modernists, it would have to be "Make it new!" This provocative phrase, uttered by poet Ezra Pound, was understood by all. Sometimes "new" meant shocking, such as the dislocated features in a Picasso portrait; sometimes it meant complicated, such as the experimental fiction of Virginia Woolf, James Joyce, and Marcel Proust. In music, it led to Stravinsky's dissonance, or clash of sounds, rather than a harmonious blend. In short, "new" meant anything that disrupted a reader's or audience's expectations. This constant search for the new resulted in the fragmentation of the art and literary worlds, producing many different movements and styles.

Modernism as an International Movement

Like Romanticism in the 19th century, modernism was an international movement. Modern artists and writers traveled widely and were subject to influences from many different countries, as shown by this chart.

Artist	Born in	Also resided in	Influenced by
Le Corbusier *architect*	Switzerland	Paris	Italian Renaissance architecture
Pablo Picasso *painter, sculptor*	Spain	Paris; the South of France	African masks
René Magritte *painter*	Belgium	Paris	French 19th-century symbolist poetry
Rainer Maria Rilke *poet*	Czech Republic	Paris; Munich; Berlin; Russia; Spain; Austria	Russian landscape
James Joyce *writer*	Dublin	Trieste; Paris; Zurich	French novelists
Léopold Senghor *poet*	Senegal	Paris	African tribal culture

INTRODUCTION 1105

Objectives

- compare the values of modernist writers with traditional writers of the past
- identify the characteristics of Modernist literature

The Mind as Subject

Explain to students that the focus of modernist literature on characters' thoughts and feelings reflected a change in the way people lived. The Industrial Revolution ushered in technological advances that gave people more leisure time and more time to focus on themselves. Thus, people's thoughts and feelings became more important.

Innovative Styles and Forms

Tell students that both modernist writers and artists experimented with ways to make old ideas new and exciting. Challenge students to make an old idea new. Invite students to write poems using new forms. For example, they might write poems about an object in the shape of that object. Or ask students to express their feelings about an object in a drawing without actually drawing the object.

LEARNING the Language of Literature

Modernism

The British writer Virginia Woolf (1882–1941) once declared that "in or about December, 1910, human character changed." Woolf picked that date to mark the enormous changes that occurred in her lifetime. Her bold statement sets the context for **modernism,** a literary and artistic movement that developed in the early decades of the 20th century. Woolf and other modernist writers shared a belief that their world was radically different from that of previous eras. The modernists felt disconnected from the social, religious, and artistic traditions of the past. To reflect their new and unsettling world, modernist writers experimented with daringly original literary styles and forms.

The Modernist Movement

In literature, modernism was a diverse movement that spanned Europe, the Americas, and even parts of Africa and Asia. While no two modernist writers employed the same style, the works of modernist writers do share some defining features.

The Mind as Subject Modernist writers often set out to explore the depths of the human mind. In fact, unlike the realistic novels of the 19th century, which involved many characters and settings, modernist novels often focused on the thought processes of a few main characters. Writers such as James Joyce and Virginia Woolf employed a new technique called **stream of consciousness,** in which the rapid and jumbled flow of a character's thoughts and feelings is presented as it occurs.

Innovative Styles and Forms Modernist writers typically broke new ground in style and form, following the advice of the American poet Ezra Pound to "make it new." For example, in T. S. Eliot's long poem *The Waste Land* (1922), the poet blended various styles and even languages, creating a collage of fragments. Eliot and other modern poets abandoned traditional stanza forms and meter for the more natural flow of **free verse.** In his novel *Ulysses* (1922), James Joyce tells an ingenious story modeled on Homer's *Odyssey*. Joyce's ordinary hero, Leopold Bloom, wanders the streets of Dublin on a June day in 1904. With breathtaking inventiveness, Joyce portrays the random thoughts of Bloom and others while making use of an array of styles of writing.

Writers and Artists: Modernist Allies

This painting by the French artist Marcel Duchamp caused a scandal when it was shown at the International Exhibition of Modern Art held in New York City in 1913. By throwing away the old conventions of realism, modern artists such as Duchamp and Pablo Picasso inspired writers to search for new forms of expression. In fact, Virginia Woolf's statement about the change in human character "in or about December, 1910" may have been inspired by a controversial exhibition of modern art that she viewed in London in that month and year.

Nude Descending a Staircase (No. 2) (1912), Marcel Duchamp. Philadelphia Museum of Art. © 2007 Artist Rights Society (ARS), New York/ADAGP, Paris/Succession Marcel Duchamp.

1106 UNIT SEVEN PART 1

Anxiety and Alienation In many modernist works, the world is portrayed as a wasteland marked by violence and anxiety. The characters in these works are often alienated, or emotionally withdrawn, from society and sometimes even from themselves. In Joseph Conrad's short novel *Heart of Darkness* (1902), a main character, Kurtz, becomes corrupted, and he abandons civilization for a life of isolation. In the opening line of Franz Kafka's "The Metamorphosis" (page 1108), we are introduced to a character so alienated from his world that he is transformed into a bug.

As Gregor Samsa awoke one morning from uneasy dreams he found himself transformed in his bed into a gigantic insect.

Modernists in Their Own Words

Joseph Conrad: **"My task which I am trying to achieve is, by the power of the written word, to make you hear, to make you feel—it is, before all, to make you *see*."**

Virginia Woolf: **"Let us record the atoms as they fall upon the mind in the order in which they fall, let us trace the pattern, however disconnected and incoherent in appearance."**

Rainer Maria Rilke: **"Works of art always spring from those who have faced the danger, gone to the very end of an experience, to the point beyond which no human being can go."**

Marcel Proust: **"If a little dreaming is dangerous, the cure for it is not to dream less but to dream more, to dream all the time."**

Strategies for Reading: Modernist Literature

1. Visualize as you read. Modernist writers often present details and images that will help you "see" the characters and setting.
2. Notice what is "modern" about both the subject and the style. Think about what makes the work original or distinctive.
3. Be alert to anything in the work that seems contradictory to or inconsistent with your expectations. In "Metamorphosis," you will meet a man who turns into an insect yet is worried about being late for work. Often, the **theme** or the **tone** (the writer's attitude toward his or her subject) is revealed through such surprising turns.
4. Be patient with complexity. Give yourself time to understand what you are reading. Because modernist literature relies so heavily on suggestion, you shouldn't expect everything to make sense all at once.
5. Ask yourself about the writer's view of the modern world. Is it a bleak view or an optimistic one? Why?
6. **Monitor** your reading strategies and modify them when your understanding breaks down. Remember to use the strategies for active reading: **predict, visualize, connect, question, clarify,** and **evaluate.**

Anxiety and Alienation

Tell students that it is not unusual for teenagers to feel alienated. After all, they often develop new ideas that may conflict with the traditional beliefs of their parents. Invite students to discuss some new ideas they have that conflict with traditions of older generations.

Strategies for Reading

Tell students that because of the complexities of a modernist work, not everyone will get the same meaning.

This selection is included in the **World Literature InterActive Reader™.**

Objectives

- understand and appreciate a **modern short story (Literary Analysis)**
- understand **point of view** as a literary element in a story **(Literary Analysis)**
- **visualize details** to appreciate the transformation that takes place in the story **(Active Reading)**

Summary

One morning, Gregor Samsa, a traveling salesman, awakens to find himself transformed into a giant bug. Unfortunately, Gregor cannot go to work in this condition, so he remains in his room. Regarding his tardiness as a personal affront, Gregor's boss appears at his home only an hour after Gregor would have reported for work. Gregor finally emerges and while his appearance is shocking, his family still considers him a son and a brother. However, as Gregor discovers his insect traits, the family also undergoes changes. His sister gains self-confidence as Gregor's caregiver. Faced with the loss of Gregor's income, his once sickly father becomes a robust bank messenger. The family eventually begins to think of Gregor as a bug. Once the transformation of both Gregor and his family is complete, Gregor dies and his family leaves their home.

Use **Unit Seven Resource Book,** p. 4 for additional support.

Thematic Link

In this modern tale, Kafka shows how a person's life can endure **worlds of change.**

Use **Unit Seven Resource Book,** p. 7, for practice with Words to Know.

THE METAMORPHOSIS

FRANZ KAFKA

Franz Kafka
1883–1924

A Tortured Soul "I have the true feeling of myself only when I am unbearably unhappy." Franz Kafka wrote these words in a 1913 diary entry. A lonely and brooding man, Kafka suffered in body and spirit throughout his adult life. His physical ailments included insomnia, severe headaches, and tuberculosis, which eventually killed him at age 41. Although he loved writing, it exhausted him and caused him great frustration and self-doubt.

A Double Life Despite Kafka's inner torment, outwardly he led a successful and respectable life. He was born into a German-speaking, middle-class Jewish family in Prague, a city in what is now the Czech Republic, and trained as a lawyer. From 1907 to 1922, he worked steadily in the insurance business. His friends and fellow workers knew him as charming, intelligent, kind, industrious, and even humorous. Although he was engaged three times—twice to the same woman—he could never commit to marriage. He devoted himself fiercely to the literary life, however, pursuing it after work hours. Still, only a handful of his stories were published in his lifetime.

Fear of the Father Scholars have traced many of Kafka's problems to his tyrannical father. Hermann Kafka used to bully his timid, sensitive son to be more like himself—strong, powerful, self-assured, and self-satisfied. Fear of his father haunted Kafka all his life, and he believed that it even caused his avoidance of marriage and his inability to find happiness. Yet Kafka made creative use of his fear. In many of his stories, innocent people are menaced by cruel and unreasonable authorities.

A German Jew in Prague Kafka's lifelong feeling of being an outcast can be partially explained by his position in society. Although he grew up in the Czech city of Prague, Kafka considered himself German, and he always wrote in German. Because he was Jewish, however, the German community in Prague would have nothing to do with him. Two years before his death, Kafka became involved with a small Jewish community in Berlin. Had he lived, he would probably have been killed by the Nazis. His three sisters all died in concentration camps.

Other Works

In the Penal Colony
The Castle
The Trial

5-Minute Warm-Up

Daily Language SkillBuilder

Have students **proofread** the display sentences on page 1095m and write them correctly.

LESSON RESOURCES

UNIT SEVEN RESOURCE BOOK, pp. 4–8

ASSESSMENT RESOURCES
Formal Assessment, pp. 161–162
Teacher's Guide to Assessment and Portfolio Use
Test Generator

INTEGRATED TECHNOLOGY
Visit our Web site: classzone.com

ADDITIONAL RESOURCES
Lesson Planning Guide, pp. 139–140
Teacher's Sourcebook for Language Development

Connect to Your Life

"As Gregor Samsa awoke one morning from uneasy dreams he found himself transformed in his bed into a gigantic insect." So begins Kafka's story. Imagine yourself in Gregor's situation. Write a brief description of how you would react and how your family might respond. As you read, compare the reactions of Gregor and his family to the responses that you imagined.

Focus Your Reading

LITERARY ANALYSIS: POINT OF VIEW
Point of view is the narrative method used in a story. In a story told from the **first-person point of view,** a character in the story narrates what happens in his or her own words. Such a narrator uses a first-person pronoun, such as *I* or *me,* to refer to himself or herself. In a story told from the **third-person point of view,** a narrator outside the action of the story describes events and characters. Such a narrator uses third-person pronouns, such as *he, she,* and *they,* to refer to the characters. Furthermore, the narrator never refers to himself or herself. In "Metamorphosis," Kafka primarily uses what's known as a **third-person limited point of view.** The narrator is "limited" to the thoughts and feelings of only one character, the bug Gregor Samsa. Though Gregor does not tell the story himself, we see the events through his eyes.

ACTIVE READING: VISUALIZING DETAILS
Visualizing is the act of forming mental pictures based upon what you are reading. By paying close attention to the details given by the narrator, you will be able to visualize Gregor's experiences.

READER'S NOTEBOOK As you read about the changes in Gregor's life, pause from time to time to "see" the scene being described. Form your own mental pictures from the many realistic details of Gregor's world. Make a list of the images that you can most easily visualize.

Build Background

A Famous Story of Transformation
Kafka's story draws upon the traditions of mythology and folklore, which are filled with stories of metamorphosis. A **metamorphosis** is a transformation from one state to another: a Greek god becomes a swan; a man becomes a donkey. In this story, which is Kafka's most famous one, the author blends the fantastic elements of mythology with the convincing details of realism. A mild-mannered salesperson named Gregor Samsa wakes up one morning mysteriously transformed into a giant bug. As you will see, this is only the beginning of his troubles. Although Gregor's transformation may be magical, his experience is made painfully real to the reader.

A Challenge to Readers Ever since the story was first published, readers have been challenged and puzzled by it. Many different interpretations have been offered to explain the story's message. As you read, try to build your own interpretation of what Kafka may have been trying to say.

WORDS TO KNOW **Vocabulary Preview**

amiably
chagrin
dissuade
equilibrium
imminent
intervene
lavishly
omission
refuge
unintelligible

READING FOR INFORMATION
Reading Skills and Strategies
CONNECTING
After they read **Build Background,** tell students that Kafka's story has a fairy-tale quality much like other stories that they may have been exposed to or movies they may have seen. Encourage students to think about some of the features of stories and films in which transformations have taken place, such as "Cinderella," "The Ugly Duckling," "Beauty and the Beast," "Pinocchio," and "The Fly."

TIME MANAGEMENT

If your schedule requires that you cover the lesson objectives in a shorter time, use. . .
- Preparing to Read, p. 1108
- Thinking Through the Literature, p. 1148
- Vocabulary in Action, p. 1149

If you want to take advantage of longer blocks of class time, use. . .
- TE Teaching Options: Viewing and Representing, pp. 1111, 1118, 1128, 1133, 1140; Cross Curricular Link, pp. 1110, 1114, 1123, 1127, 1146; Vocabulary Strategy, p. 1115; Grammar, p. 1144; Speaking and Listening, p. 1120; Standardized Test Practice, p. 1122; Informal Assessment, p. 1135
- Choices & Challenges, p. 1149

Reading and Analyzing

Direct student's attention to the **Guide for Reading** heading on this page. Tell students that because the selection is long, it has been divided into sections. Explain that each section begins with a **Focus** heading and ends with a **Pause & Reflect** question. The information under the Focus heading is intended to help them concentrate on a section and understand the main idea. The Pause & Reflect questions will ask them to stop and think about what they have read.

Literary Analysis POINT OF VIEW

Ask students to identify the point of view from which the story is being told and to give evidence to support their responses.
Possible Response: third person, the use of the pronoun *he* in the first few sentences

 Use **Unit Seven Resource Book,** p. 6, for more practice.

Active Reading VISUALIZING DETAILS

A Point out to students that the author describes Gregor's appearance in a very straightforward manner. Have them note that the picture of the bug may also influence the picture they create in their minds. Ask students to describe Gregor in their own words.
Possible Response: an oval-shaped bug with a hard back with panels, brown underside, six legs (since insects have that many)

 Use **Unit Seven Resource Book,** p. 5, for additional support.

The Metamorphosis

Franz Kafka

Translated by Willa and Edwin Muir

GUIDE FOR READING

FOCUS Gregor Samsa awakens to find that he has become a giant insect. Read to find out how he reacts to his situation and what he worries about.

As Gregor Samsa awoke one morning from uneasy dreams he found himself transformed in his bed into a gigantic insect. He was lying on his hard, as it were armor-plated, back and when he lifted his head a little he could see his domelike brown belly divided into stiff arched segments on top of which the bed quilt could hardly keep in position and was about to slide off completely. His numerous legs, which were pitifully thin compared to the rest of his bulk, waved helplessly before his eyes.

What has happened to me? he thought. It was no dream. His room, a regular human bedroom, only rather too small, lay quiet between the four familiar walls. Above the table on which a collection of cloth samples was unpacked and spread out—Samsa was a commercial traveler[1]—hung the picture which he had recently cut out of an illustrated magazine and put into a pretty gilt frame. It showed a lady, with a fur cap on and a fur stole, sitting upright and holding out to the spectator a huge fur muff into which the whole of her forearm had vanished!

Gregor's eyes turned next to the window, and the overcast sky—one could hear raindrops beating on the window gutter—made him quite melancholy.[2] What about sleeping a little longer and forgetting all this nonsense, he thought, but it could not be done, for he was accustomed to sleep on his right side and in his present condition he could not turn himself over. However violently he forced himself toward his right side he always rolled onto his back again. He tried it at least a hundred times, shutting his eyes to keep from seeing his struggling legs, and only desisted when he began to feel in his side a faint dull ache he had never experienced before.

Oh God, he thought, what an exhausting job I've picked on! Traveling about day in, day out. It's much more irritating work than doing the actual business in the office, and on top of that there's the trouble of constant traveling, of worrying about train connections, the bed and

1. **commercial traveler:** traveling salesperson.
2. **melancholy** (mĕl′ən-kŏl′ē): sad or depressed.

Humanities

ABOUT THE TRANSLATORS Authors Willa and Edwin Muir were both born in Scotland. After they married, the couple settled in London, England. Edwin Muir was considered one of the chief Scottish poets of his day who wrote in English. Edwin Muir believed that "Scotland can only create a national literature by writing in English." His views on Scottish literature led to the breakup of his longtime friendship with author Hugh MacDiarmid, an advocate of Lallans, a poetic language that used mainly Scottish dialect.

The Muirs were European in spirit. They traveled throughout Europe and worked together on a number of translations that introduced major European writers such as Kafka, Hermann Broch, and Lion Feuchtwanger to the English-speaking world.

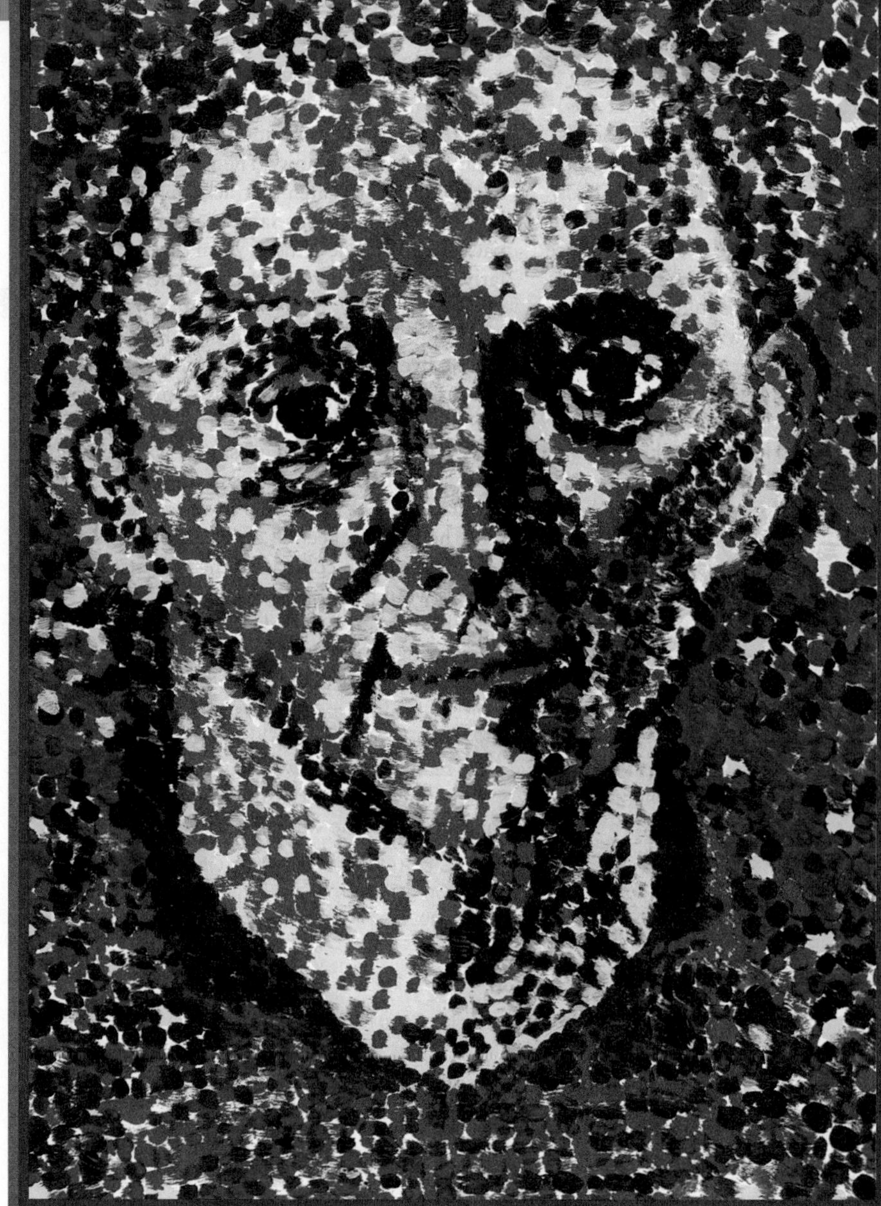

Hidden Resemblance (1991), Elizabeth Barakah Hodges. Copyright © SuperStock, Inc.

HUMANITIES CONNECTION American artist Elizabeth Barakah Hodges describes her work as magical realism. The face in this painting is drawn in a realistic manner, but the vibrant splotches of color give the image mysterious, dreamlike qualities.

Customizing Instruction

Less Proficient Readers
Help students understand that even though Gregor is a bug, his transformation is not yet complete. He still has human emotions. Have them note details on the page that suggest that Gregor is still acting human.
Possible Responses: Gregor wonders what has happened him. He thinks about sleeping longer and trying to forget his current condition. He thinks about the stressful conditions of his job.

MINI LESSON Viewing and Representing

Hidden Resemblance **by Elizabeth Barakah Hodges**

ART APPRECIATION Hodges values the hidden resemblance or the reality beyond the appearance in her art. She often paints over torn paper to create her images, so she might create a sky that is brown instead of blue. Have students study the painting and the **Humanities Connection** on page 1111. Ask students why they think Hodges may have called the painting *Hidden Resemblance.*

Possible Response: Although the painting has a mysterious quality you can still tell it is a human face.

Then ask students how the painting relates to Gregor's situation.
Possible Response: Gregor has turned into a bug, but he is still experiencing human feelings.

Reading Skills and Strategies
CLARIFYING

Ask students what things Gregor doesn't like about his job.

Possible Response: constant traveling, train schedules, uncomfortable beds, meeting new people who never become friends, getting up early, his boss

Then ask why has Gregor stayed at a job he didn't like.

Possible Response: He owes his boss money.

Literary Analysis POINT OF VIEW

A The change from the pronoun *he* in the second sentence to *I* in the fifth sentence may be jarring to students. Assure them that the point of view has not changed—the story is still being told by a narrator outside the action. Explain that the pronoun *I* signals Gregor's thoughts. Have students point out the place where the story returns to the more traditional third-person point of view. *(third paragraph on the page)*

Pause & Reflect

Possible Response: Gregor worries about his job. He thinks of all the things he doesn't like about his job, but at the same time he worries about getting to work late.

Literary Analysis MOOD

Explain to students that the mood is a feeling or atmosphere, such as happiness, horror, or sadness, that a writer creates for the reader. Writers can create mood through the use of imagery, sound, and rhythm. Kafka creates mood with extremely detailed descriptions.

Point out that the mood doesn't necessarily stay the same throughout the story. Have students note their feelings and how they change with various scenes as they read.

irregular meals, casual acquaintances that are always new and never become intimate friends. The devil take it all! He felt a slight itching up on his belly; slowly pushed himself on his back nearer to the top of the bed so that he could lift his head more easily; identified the itching place which was surrounded by many small white spots the nature of which he could not understand and made to touch it with a leg, but drew the leg back immediately, for the contact made a cold shiver run through him.

He slid down again into his former position. This getting up early, he thought, makes one quite stupid. A man needs his sleep. Other commercials
A live like harem women. For instance, when I come back to the hotel of a morning to write up the orders I've got, these others are only sitting down to the breakfast. Let me just try that with my chief; I'd be sacked on the spot. Anyhow, that might be quite a good thing for me, who can tell? If I didn't have to hold my hand[3] because of my
1 parents I'd have given notice long ago, I'd have gone to the chief and told him exactly what I think of him. That would knock him endways from his desk! It's a queer way of doing, too, this sitting on high at a desk and talking down to employees, especially when they have to come quite near because the chief is hard of hearing. Well, there's still hope; once I've saved enough money to pay back my parents' debts to him—that should take another five or six years—I'll do it without fail. I'll cut myself completely loose then. For the moment, though, I'd better get up, since my train goes at five.

He looked at the alarm clock ticking on the chest. Heavenly Father! he thought. It was half-past six o'clock and the hands were quietly moving on, it was even past the half-hour, it was getting on toward a quarter to seven. Had the alarm clock not gone off? From the bed one could see that it had been properly set for four o'clock; of course it must have gone off. Yes, but was it possible to sleep quietly through that ear-splitting noise? Well, he had not slept quietly, yet apparently all the more soundly for that. But what was he to do now? The next train went at seven o'clock; to catch that he would need to hurry like mad and his samples weren't even packed up, and he himself wasn't feeling particularly fresh and active. And even if he did catch
the train he wouldn't avoid a row[4] with the chief, 2
since the firm's porter would have been waiting for the five o'clock train and would have long since reported his failure to turn up. The porter was a creature of the chief's, spineless and stupid. Well, supposing he were to say he was sick? But that would be most unpleasant and would look suspicious, since during his five years' employment he had not been ill once. The chief himself would be sure to come with the sick-insurance doctor, would reproach his parents with their son's laziness, and would cut all excuses short by referring to the insurance doctor, who of course regarded all mankind as perfectly healthy malingerers.[5] And would he be so far wrong on this occasion? Gregor really felt quite well, apart from a drowsiness that was utterly superfluous after such a long sleep, and he was even unusually hungry.

PAUSE & REFLECT For a man who has awakened as a bug, Gregor's worries are surprising. What does he worry about?

FOCUS Read to find out what happens when Gregor's family comes to his door, and he tries to leave his bed.

As all this was running through his mind at top speed without his being able to decide to leave his bed—the alarm clock had just struck a quarter to seven—there came a cautious tap at

3. **hold my hand:** hold back.
4. **row** (rou): disagreement; fight.
5. **malingerers** (mə-lĭng′gər-ərz): people who pretend to be sick in order to avoid work.

"GREGOR, **GREGOR**," HE CALLED, "WHAT'S THE **MATTER** WITH YOU?" AND AFTER A LITTLE WHILE HE CALLED AGAIN IN A DEEPER VOICE: "GREGOR! **GREGOR!**"

the door behind the head of his bed. "Gregor," said a voice—it was his mother's—"it's a quarter to seven. Hadn't you a train to catch?" That gentle voice! Gregor had a shock as he heard his own voice answering hers, unmistakably his own voice, it was true, but with a persistent horrible twittering squeak behind it like an undertone, which left the words in their clear shape only for the first moment and then rose up reverberating around them to destroy their sense, so that one could not be sure one had heard them rightly. Gregor wanted to answer at length and explain everything, but in the circumstances he confined himself to saying: "Yes, yes, thank you, Mother, I'm getting up
3 now." The wooden door between them must have kept the change in his voice from being noticeable outside, for his mother contented herself with this statement and shuffled away. Yet this brief exchange of words had made the other members of the family aware that Gregor was still in the house, as they had not expected, and at one of the side doors his father was already knocking, gently, yet with his fist. "Gregor, Gregor," he called, "What's the matter with you?" And after a little while he called again in a deeper voice: "Gregor! Gregor!" At the other side door his sister was saying in a low, plaintive[6] tone: "Gregor? Aren't you well? Are you needing anything?" He answered them both at once: "I'm just ready," and did his best to make his voice sound as normal as possible by enunciating the words very clearly and leaving long pauses between them. So his father went back to his breakfast, but his sister whispered: "Gregor, open the door, do." However, he was not thinking of opening the door, and felt thankful for the prudent habit he had acquired in traveling of locking all doors during the night, even at home.

His immediate intention was to get up quietly without being disturbed, to put on his clothes, and above all eat his breakfast, and only then consider what else was to be done, since in bed, he was well aware, his meditations would come to no sensible conclusion. He remembered that often enough in bed he had felt small aches and pains, probably caused by awkward postures, which had proved purely imaginary once he got up, and he
looked forward eagerly to seeing this morning's 4
delusions gradually fall away. That the change in his voice was nothing but the precursor[7] of a severe chill, a standing ailment of commercial travelers, he had not the least possible doubt.

To get rid of the quilt was quite easy; he had only to inflate himself a little and it fell off by itself. But the next move was difficult, especially because he was so uncommonly broad. He would have needed arms and hands to hoist himself up; instead he had only the numerous little legs which never stopped waving in all directions and which he could not control in the least. When he tried to bend one of them it was the first to stretch itself straight; and did he succeed at last in making it do what he wanted, all the other legs meanwhile waved the more wildly in a high degree of unpleasant agitation. "But what's the use of lying idle in bed," said Gregor to himself.

6. **plaintive** (plān'tĭv): sorrowful; sad.

7. **precursor:** something that comes before; forerunner.

Customizing Instruction

Less Proficient Readers

1 Ask students to explain in their own words how Gregor feels about his job and the people he works with. *(dissatisfied, jealous, unappreciated, afraid of his boss)*

2 Make sure students understand why Gregor's worries are surprising. *(Gregor's main worry should be how he became a bug or how he can change back to a person. His job no longer matters in his present state.)*

Focus Draw students' attention to the Focus on page 1112. Explain that these directions are included to help them pay attention to important aspects of the text as they read. Then ask these questions:

3 Why is Gregor's family concerned? *(He is late for work.)*

4 Why does Gregor still think he can go to work? *(He thinks that he might be having a dream.)*

English Learners

Help students use context clues to understand the following words:

- reproach *(criticize)*
- superfluous *(unnecessary)*
- reverberate *(echo)*
- prudent *(wise)*
- delusions *(beliefs that are not true)*

Advanced Learners

Explain that while Gregor is a bug, students can learn about his character as a person through his thoughts. Have students discuss different aspects of Gregor's character and the details that reveal these traits. *(afraid to speak his mind, considerate of his parents, complaining, thinks the world is against him)*

METAMORPHOSIS **1113**

Reading and Analyzing

Active Reading VISUALIZING DETAILS

A To help students visualize Gregor's predicament, ask them to think about times they have struggled not to fall or managed to catch themselves at the last moment and remain upright.

Reading Skills and Strategies QUESTIONING

B Ask students why they think Gregor is still able to talk and understand his own speech even though he is bug.
Possible Responses: His transformation to a bug is not quite complete, so he is still able to do human things. The author may have used this device to make the story more interesting.

Reading Skills and Strategies CONNECTING

C Ask students if they agree with Gregor's assessment of how employees are treated at his job. Invite students to share how they would feel if a teacher came to their homes only an hour after they were supposed to be in school.

Pause & Reflect

Possible Response: He's on his back, an unusual position for a bug. It's hard for him to maneuver onto his stomach and gain control of his body.

He thought that he might get out of bed with the lower part of his body first, but this lower part, which he had not yet seen and of which he could form no clear conception, proved too difficult to move; it shifted so slowly; and when finally, almost wild with annoyance, he gathered his forces together and thrust out recklessly, he had miscalculated the direction and bumped heavily against the lower end of the bed, and the stinging pain he felt informed him that precisely this lower part of his body was at the moment probably the most sensitive.

A So he tried to get the top part of himself out first, and cautiously moved his head toward the edge of the bed. That proved easy enough, and despite its breadth and mass the bulk of his body at last slowly followed the movement of his head. Still, when he finally got his head free over the edge of the bed he felt too scared to go on advancing, for after all if he let himself fall in this way it would take a miracle to keep his head from being injured. And at all costs he must not lose consciousness now, precisely now; he would rather stay in bed.

But when after a repetition of the same efforts he lay in his former position again, sighing, and watched his little legs struggling against each other more wildly than ever, if that were possible, and saw no way of bringing any order into this arbitrary confusion, he told himself again that it was impossible to stay in bed and that the most sensible course was to risk everything for the smallest hope of getting away from it. At the same time he did not forget to remind himself occasionally that cool reflection, the coolest possible, was much better than desperate resolves. In such moments he focused his eyes as sharply as possible on the window, but, unfortunately, the prospect of the morning fog, which muffled even the other side of the narrow street, brought him little encouragement and comfort. "Seven o'clock already," he said to himself when the alarm clock chimed again, "seven o'clock already and still such a thick fog." And for a little while he lay quiet, breathing lightly, as if perhaps expecting such complete repose to restore all things to their real and normal condition.

But then he said to himself: "Before it strikes a quarter past seven I must be quite out of this bed, without fail. Anyhow, by that time someone will have come from the office to ask for me, since it opens before seven." And he set himself to rocking his whole body at once in a regular rhythm, with the idea of swinging it out of the bed. If he tipped himself out in that way he could keep his head from injury by lifting it at an acute angle when he fell. His back seemed to be hard and was not likely to suffer from a fall on the carpet. His biggest worry was the loud crash he would not be able to help making, which would probably cause anxiety, if not terror, behind all the doors. Still, he must take the risk. B

When he was already half out of the bed—the new method was more a game than an effort, for he needed only to hitch himself across by rocking to and fro—it struck him how simple it would be if he could get help. Two strong people—he thought of his father and the servant girl—would be amply sufficient; they would only have to thrust their arms under his convex[8] back, lever him out of the bed, bend down with their burden, and then be patient enough to let him turn himself right over onto the floor, where it was to

8. **convex:** curved outward.

Cross Curricular Link **Humanities**

SURREALISM The Surrealism movement flourished in art and literature during the early twentieth century and was characteristic of many modernist works. In surrealism, the artist or writer conveys dreamlike images in a realistic manner. Kafka was adept at describing fantastic events in a realistic way. "Metamorphosis" is an excellent example of surrealism. Although a person cannot possibly transform into a bug, Kafka's description actually makes it seem possible.

Have students discuss aspects of Kafka's style that gives the story a "surreal quality."
Possible Responses: Kafka describes what happens in a very straightforward manner. He seems to know how bugs actually live. During the story, the character actually seems to be dreaming. The reader may also be under the impression that he or she is dreaming.

be hoped his legs would then find their proper function. Well, ignoring the fact that the doors were all locked, ought he really to call for help? In spite of his misery he could not suppress a smile at the very idea of it.

He had got so far that he could barely keep his equilibrium when he rocked himself strongly, and he would have to nerve himself very soon for the final decision since in five minutes' time it would be quarter past seven—when the front doorbell rang. "That's someone from the office," he said to himself, and grew almost rigid, while his little legs only jigged about all the faster. For a moment everything stayed quiet. "They're not going to open the door," said Gregor to himself, catching at some kind of irrational hope. But then of course the servant girl went as usual to the door with her heavy tread and opened it. Gregor needed only to hear the first good morning of the visitor to know immediately who it was—the chief clerk himself. What a fate, to be condemned to work for a firm where the smallest omission at once gave rise to the gravest suspicion! Were all employees in a body nothing but scoundrels, was there not among them one single loyal devoted man who, had he wasted only an hour or so of the firm's time in a morning, was so tormented by conscience as to be driven out of his mind and actually incapable of leaving his bed? Wouldn't it really have been sufficient to send an apprentice to inquire—if any inquiry were necessary at all—did the chief clerk himself have to come and thus indicate to the entire family, an innocent family, that this suspicious circumstance could be investigated by no one less versed in affairs than himself? And more through the agitation caused by these reflections than through any act of will Gregor swung himself out of bed with all his strength. There was a loud thump, but it was not really a crash. His fall was broken to some extent by the carpet, his back, too, was less stiff than he thought, and so there was merely a dull thud, not so very startling. Only he had not lifted his head carefully enough and had hit it; he turned it and rubbed it on the carpet in pain and irritation.

PAUSE & REFLECT Why is it so hard for Gregor to get out of bed?

FOCUS Gregor has finally managed to fall out of bed. Now read about his conversation with the chief clerk.

"That was something falling down in there," said the chief clerk in the next room to the left. Gregor tried to suppose to himself that something like what had happened to him today might someday happen to the chief clerk; one really could not deny that it was possible. But as if in brusque reply to this supposition the chief clerk took a couple of firm steps in the next-door room and his patent leather boots creaked. From the right-hand room his sister was whispering to inform him of the situation: "Gregor, the chief clerk's here." "I know," muttered Gregor to himself; but he didn't dare to make his voice loud enough for his sister to hear it.

"Gregor," said his father now from the left-hand room, "the chief clerk has come and wants to know why you didn't catch the early train. We don't know what to say to him. Besides, he wants to talk to you in person. So open the door, please. He will be good enough to excuse the untidiness of your room." "Good morning, Mr. Samsa," the chief clerk was calling amiably meanwhile. "He's not well," said his mother to the visitor, while his father was still speaking through the door, "he's not well, sir, believe me. What else would make him miss a train! The boy thinks about nothing but his work. It makes me almost cross the way he never goes out in the evenings; he's been here the last eight days and 1

WORDS TO KNOW

equilibrium (ē'kwə-lĭb'rē-əm) *n.* a stable or balanced condition
omission (ō-mĭsh'ən) *n.* an act of leaving out, passing over, or neglecting
amiably (ā'mē-ə-blē) *adv.* in a friendly manner; pleasantly

Customizing Instruction

Less Proficient Readers

Focus Help students use the Focus on page 1115 by pointing out that until now there hasn't been much conversation. Explain that a conversation with the clerk signals an important development in the story.

English Learners

Ask students to use context clues to figure out the meanings of these words:

- reflection *(careful thinking)*
- resolves *(decisions)*
- scoundrels *(villains)*

Advanced Learners

1 Have students discuss the different reasons Gregor's family and the chief clerk are so concerned about his tardiness.

Possible Responses: Gregor's family doesn't want tardiness or absence to jeopardize the job that supports them all. The chief clerk doesn't want Gregor to jeopardize his position because Gregor owes him money.

MINI LESSON Vocabulary Strategy

PREFIXES

Instruction Remind students that a prefix is a word part added to the beginning of a base word or root. A prefix has its own meaning and changes the meaning of the base word. Tell students that they can use the meanings of prefixes to figure out the meanings of unfamiliar words and to create new words. Show students how prefixes influence the meanings of several words in "Metamorphosis." The word *equilibrium* applies the prefix *equi-* (which means "equal") to the Latin word *libra* (which means "balance"). Therefore, *equilibrium* means "a condition in which everything is balanced." The word *dissuade* applies the prefix *dis-* (which means "not") to the Latin word *suadere* (which means "advise"). So *dissuade* means "to advise someone not to do something." The word *intervene* applies the prefix *inter-* (which means "between") to the Latin word *venire* (which means "to come" or "to see"). Thus *intervene* means "to come between."

Practice Have students work in pairs to think of a word that uses each of these prefixes: *equi-, dis-, inter-.* Encourage students to use their knowledge of the prefix and the base word to write a definition and sentence for each word.

Possible Response: disconnect *(to stop the connection of something) If you don't pay your bill, the telephone company may* disconnect *your phone line;* international *(between or involving two or more nations) The singer was an* international *star;* equidistant *(two or more things that are equal in distance from something else) The two homes were* equidistant *from the park.*

A lesson on prefixes apears on p. 864 of the Pupil's Edition.

Reading and Analyzing

Reading Skills and Strategies
COMPARING/CONTRASTING

A Ask students to think about how Gregor describes his job as a traveling salesman on pages 1110–1111. Have students compare the aspects of his job to his life at home.

Possible Response: Although Gregor has to talk to people as a salesman, he never makes friends. At home, he doesn't interact much with his family, preferring to spend his time reading and woodworking.

Reading Skills and Strategies
DRAWING CONCLUSIONS

Ask students what conclusions they can make about Gregor from his job and his home life.

Possible Response: Gregor doesn't fit in. He seems to exist outside of normal social relationships.

Literary Analysis POINT OF VIEW

B Have students note the paragraph in which the clerk speaks to Gregor. Help students understand that the story is still being told primarily from the third-person limited point of view even though the speech includes the pronoun *I*. Point out the chief clerk's speech is introduced by the narrator who says "the chief clerk called now...."

Literary Analysis IRONY

C Irony is the difference between what is expected and what actually happens. Discuss with students the irony of the chief clerk's accusations and Gregor's response.

Possible Responses: Though the chief clerk hasn't seen Gregor, he feels no excuse would be good enough for not following the rules. Gregor is still trying to hold onto his job even though the rules have changed for him.

Pause & Reflect

Possible Response: Gregor no longer has a human voice. He can only make insect sounds.

A has stayed at home every single evening. He just sits there quietly at the table reading a newspaper or looking through railway timetables. The only amusement he gets is doing fretwork.[9] For instance, he spent two or three evenings cutting out a little picture frame; you would be surprised to see how pretty it is; it's hanging in his room; you'll see it in a minute when Gregor opens the door. I must say I'm glad you've come, sir; we should never have got him to unlock the door by ourselves; he's so obstinate; and I'm sure he's unwell, though he wouldn't have it to be so this morning." "I'm just coming," said Gregor slowly and carefully, not moving an inch for fear of losing one word of the conversation. "I can't think of any other explanation, madame," said the chief clerk, "I hope it's nothing serious. Although on the other hand I must say that we men of business—fortunately or unfortunately—very often simply have to ignore any slight indisposition,[10] since business must be attended to." "Well, can the chief clerk come in now?" asked Gregor's father impatiently, again knocking on the door. "No," said Gregor. In the left-hand room a painful silence followed this refusal, in the right-hand room his sister began to sob.

1 Why didn't his sister join the others? She was probably newly out of bed and hadn't even begun to put on her clothes yet. Well, why was she crying? Because he wouldn't get up and let the chief clerk in, because he was in danger of losing his job, and because the chief would begin dunning[11] his parents again for the old debts? Surely these were things one didn't need to worry about for the present. Gregor was still at home and not in the least thinking of deserting the family. At the moment, true, he was lying on the carpet and no one who knew the condition he was in could seriously expect him to admit the chief clerk. But for such a small discourtesy, which could plausibly be explained away somehow later on, Gregor could hardly be dismissed on the spot. And it seemed to Gregor that it would be much more sensible to leave him in peace for the present than to trouble him with tears and entreaties. Still, of course, their uncertainty bewildered them all and excused their behavior.

B "Mr. Samsa," the chief clerk called now in a louder voice, "what's the matter with you? Here you are, barricading yourself in your room, giving only 'yes' and 'no' for answers, causing your parents a lot of unnecessary trouble and neglecting—I mention this only in passing—neglecting your business duties in an incredible fashion. I am speaking here in the name of your parents and of your chief, and I beg you quite seriously to give me an immediate and precise explanation. You amaze me, you amaze me. I thought you were a quiet, dependable person, and now all at once you seem bent on making a disgraceful exhibition of yourself. The chief did hint to me early this morning a possible explanation for your disappearance—with reference to the cash payments that were entrusted to you recently—but I almost pledged my solemn word of honor that this could not be so. C But now that I see how incredibly obstinate you are, I no longer have the slightest desire to take your part at all. And your position in the firm is not so unassailable.[12] I came with the intention of telling you all this in private, but since you are wasting my time so needlessly I don't see why your parents shouldn't hear it too. For some time past your work has been most unsatisfactory; this is not the season of the year for a business boom, of course, we admit that, but a season of the year for doing no business at all, that does not exist, Mr. Samsa, must not exist."

"But, sir," cried Gregor, beside himself and in his agitation forgetting everything else, "I'm just going to open the door this very minute. A slight

9. **fretwork:** ornamental woodworking.

10. **indisposition:** minor illness.

11. **dunning:** pestering for payment.

12. **unassailable** (ŭn′ə-sā′lə-bəl): safe from question or attack.

2 illness, an attack of giddiness, has kept me from getting up. I'm still lying in bed. But I feel all right again. I'm getting out of bed now. Just give me a moment or two longer! I'm not quite so well as I thought. But I'm all right, really. How a thing like that can suddenly strike me down! Only last night I was quite well, my parents can tell you, or rather I did have a slight presentiment.[13] I must have showed some sign of it. Why didn't I report it at the office! But one always
3 thinks that an indisposition can be got over without staying in the house. Oh sir, do spare my parents! All that you're reproaching me with now has no foundation; no one has ever said a word to me about it. Perhaps you haven't looked at the last orders I sent in. Anyhow, I can still catch the eight o'clock train, I'm much better for my few hours' rest. Don't let me detain you here, sir; I'll be attending to business very soon, and do be good enough to tell the chief so and to make my excuses to him!"

4 And while all this was tumbling out pell-mell and Gregor hardly knew what he was saying, he had reached the chest quite easily, perhaps because of the practice he had had in bed, and was now trying to lever himself upright by means of it. He meant actually to open the door, actually to show himself and speak to the chief clerk; he was eager to find out what the others, after all their insistence, would say at the sight of him. If they were horrified then the responsibility was no longer his and he could stay quiet. But if they took it calmly, then he had no reason either to be upset, and could really get to the station for the eight o'clock train if he hurried. At first he slipped down a few times from the polished surface of the chest, but at length with a last heave he stood upright; he paid no more attention to the pains in the lower part of his body, however they smarted. Then he let himself fall against the back of a nearby chair, and clung with his little legs to the edges of it. That brought him into control of himself again and he stopped speaking, for now he could listen to what the chief clerk was saying.

"Did you understand a word of it?" the chief clerk was asking; "surely he can't be trying to make fools of us?" "Oh dear," cried his mother, in tears, "perhaps he's terribly ill and we're tormenting him. Grete! Grete!" she called out then. "Yes Mother?" called his sister from the other side. They were calling to each other across Gregor's room. "You must go this minute for the doctor. Gregor is ill. Go for the doctor, quick. Did you hear how he was speaking?" "That was no human voice," said the chief clerk in a voice noticeably low beside the shrillness of the mother's. "Anna! Anna!" his father was calling through the hall to the kitchen, clapping his hands, "get a locksmith at once!" And the two girls were already running through the hall with a swish of skirts—how could his sister have got dressed so quickly?—and were tearing the front door open. There was no sound of its closing again; they had evidently left it open, as one does in houses where some great misfortune has happened.

PAUSE & REFLECT When Gregor responds to the chief clerk's criticisms, everyone panics. Why are people so horrified by his voice?

FOCUS Read to find out what happens when Gregor leaves his room.

But Gregor was now much calmer. The words he uttered were no longer understandable, apparently, although they seemed clear enough to him, even clearer than before, perhaps because his ear had grown accustomed to the sound of them. Yet at any rate people now believed that something was wrong with him, and were ready to help him.

13. **presentiment** (prĭ-zĕn′tə-mənt): feeling that something is going to happen.

Customizing Instruction

Less Proficient Readers

Help students follow the chief clerk's speech. Ask students to tell why the chief clerk thinks Gregor isn't a good employee. *(Gregor is late for work; his lateness may be related to some missing cash; and his work has been unsatisfactory.)*

Focus Have students use the Focus on page 1117 to predict what will happen when Gregor emerges from his room.

Possible Responses: The chief clerk and Gregor's family will be shocked at his appearance. They may think the bug has somehow destroyed Gregor. They may try to kill the bug.

English Learners

1 Help students use context clues to figure out that obstinate means "stubborn."

2 Explain that *giddiness* means "silliness."

3 Help students use context clues to understand that *indisposition* means the same as *illness*.

4 Explain that *pell-mell* means "in a confused manner."

Advanced Learners

Remind students that sometimes irony can be playful and poke fun at someone. Irony can also be serious. Engage students in a discussion on how they view the irony in the conversation between the chief clerk and Gregor—humorous or sad. Students should give reasons to support their opinions.

METAMORPHOSIS **1117**

Reading Skills and Strategies
CLARIFYING

A Why is Gregor so determined to unlock the door?

Possible Response: He imagines that the chief clerk and his parents are encouraging him.

Reading Skills and Strategies
CONNECTING

Ask students to think about how they might react if they saw Gregor come out of the room. Have them compare their reactions with those of the clerk and Gregor's parents.

Portrait of Superintendent Trabuc in St. Paul's Hospital (1889), Vincent van Gogh. Oil on canvas, 61 cm × 46 cm. Kunstmuseum Solothurn, Switzerland. Photo © Bridgeman Art Library.

The positive certainty with which these first measures had been taken comforted him. He felt himself drawn once more into the human circle and hoped for great and remarkable results from both the doctor and the locksmith, without really distinguishing precisely between them. To make his voice as clear as possible for the decisive conversation that was now imminent he coughed a little, as quietly as he could, of course, since this noise too might not sound like a human cough for all he was able to judge. In the next room meanwhile there was complete silence. Perhaps his parents were sitting at the table with the chief clerk, whispering, perhaps they were all leaning against the door and listening.

Slowly Gregor pushed the chair toward the door, then let go of it, caught hold of the door for support—the soles at the end of his little legs were somewhat sticky—and rested against it for a

WORDS TO KNOW

imminent (ĭm′ə-nənt) *adj.* about to happen

MINI LESSON Viewing and Representing

The Asylum Attendant from Saint-Remy **by Vincent van Gogh**

ART APPRECIATION Van Gogh's work was a strong influence on the Expressionism movement in modern art. He often used striking colors and coarse brushstrokes to convey an anguish in his subjects that he himself often felt. Ask students to describe the facial expression of the man in the painting. *(Responses may include disappointed, angry, sullen, impatient, unhappy.)* Then ask them to compare the painting to their perception of Gregor's father.

Possible Response: Gregor's father may have had a similar expression as the man in the painting when he tried to get Gregor to come out of his room.

moment after his efforts. Then he set himself to turning the key in the lock with his mouth. It seemed, unhappily, that he hadn't really any teeth—what could he grip the key with?—but on the other hand his jaws were certainly very strong; with their help he did manage to set the key in motion, heedless of the fact that he was undoubtedly damaging them somewhere, since a brown fluid issued from his mouth, flowed over the key, and dripped on the floor. "Just listen to that," said the chief clerk next door; "he's turning the key." That was a great encouragement to Gregor; but they should all have shouted encouragement to him, his father and mother too: "Go on, Gregor," they should have called out, "keep going, hold on to that key!" And in the belief that they were all following his efforts intently, he clenched his jaws recklessly on the key with all the force at his command. As the turning of the key progressed he circled around the lock, holding on now only with his mouth, pushing on the key, as required, or pulling it down again with all the weight of his body. The louder click of the finally yielding lock literally quickened Gregor. With a deep breath of relief he said to himself: "So I didn't need the locksmith," and laid his head on the handle to open the door wide.

Since he had to pull the door toward him, he was still invisible when it was really wide open. He had to edge himself slowly around the near half of the double door, and to do it very carefully if he was not to fall plump upon his back just on the threshold. He was still carrying out this difficult maneuver, with no time to observe anything else, when he heard the chief clerk utter a loud "Oh!"—it seemed like a gust of wind—and now he could see the man, standing as he was nearest to the door, clapping one hand before his open mouth and slowly backing away as if driven by some invisible steady pressure. His mother—in spite of the chief clerk's being there her hair was still undone and sticking up in all directions—first clasped her hands and looked at his father, then took two steps toward Gregor and fell on the floor among her outspread skirts, her face quite hidden on her breast. His father knotted his fist with a fierce expression on his face as if he meant to knock Gregor back into his room, then looked uncertainly around the living room, covered his eyes with his hands, and wept till his great chest heaved.

Gregor did not go now into the living room, but leaned against the inside of the firmly shut wing of the door, so that only half his body was visible and his head above it bending sideways to look at the others. The light had meanwhile strengthened; on the other side of the street one could see clearly a section of the endless long, dark gray building opposite—it was a hospital—abruptly punctuated by its row of regular windows; the rain was still falling, but only in large singly discernible and literally singly splashing drops. The breakfast dishes were set out on the table lavishly, for breakfast was the most important meal of the day to Gregor's father, who lingered it out for hours over various newspapers. Right opposite Gregor on the wall hung a photograph of himself in military service, as a lieutenant, hand on sword, a carefree smile on his face, inviting one to respect his uniform and military bearing. The door leading to the hall was open, and one could see that the front

HIS FATHER KNOTTED HIS FIST WITH A FIERCE EXPRESSION ON HIS FACE AS IF HE MEANT TO KNOCK GREGOR BACK INTO HIS ROOM....

WORDS TO KNOW

lavishly (lăv′ĭsh-lē) *adv.* very freely and abundantly

Customizing Instruction

Less Proficient Readers

1 Have students describe in their own words the reactions of the chief clerk, the mother, and the father.

Advanced Learners

2 Ask students to discuss the irony of Gregor seeing his photograph as he comes out of his room.

Possible Response: Gregor's appearance is now horrifying, but he once stood proudly in uniform as a respected member of the armed forces.

Reading and Analyzing

Literary Analysis POINT OF VIEW

A Point out to students that the author is still writing in the third-person point of view. He is quoting Gregor so that the reader can experience his reaction to the situation firsthand.

Literary Analysis IRONY

B Have students discuss the irony of what Gregor is saying to the clerk.
Possible Responses: Gregor is determined to keep his job. He tries to talk to the chief clerk even though he knows his voice can't be understood. He thinks the biggest problem is that his character and work record have been questioned. He seems to think his current situation is only temporary.

Active Reading VISUALIZING DETAILS

Make sure students understand that Gregor has been holding onto the door and supporting his body on only two legs up to this point. Ask students if they can imagine how large Gregor is. Tell students to pay attention to other details that may also give hints about Gregor's size.

Pause & Reflect

Possible Response: The clerk puts his hand on his open mouth and slowly backs away. His mother faints and falls on the floor. His father clenches his fist, covers his eyes, and cries.

door stood open too, showing the landing beyond and the beginning of the stairs going down.

A "Well," said Gregor, knowing perfectly that he was the only one who had retained any composure, "I'll put my clothes on at once, pack up my samples, and start off. Will you only let me go? You see, sir, I'm not obstinate, and I'm willing to work; traveling is a hard life, but I couldn't live without it. Where are you going, sir? To the office? Yes? Will you give a true account of all this? One can be temporarily incapacitated, but that's just the moment for remembering former services and bearing in mind that later on, when B the incapacity has been got over, one will certainly work with all the more industry and concentration. I'm loyally bound to serve the chief, you know that very well. Besides, I have to provide for my parents and my sister. I'm in great difficulties, but I'll get out of them again. Don't make things any worse for me than they are. Stand up for me in the firm. Travelers are not popular there, I know. People think they earn sacks of money and just have a good time. A prejudice there's no particular reason for revis-
1 ing. But you, sir, have a more comprehensive view of affairs than the rest of the staff, yes, let me tell you in confidence, a more comprehensive view of affairs than the chief himself, who, being the owner, lets his judgment easily be swayed against one of his employees. And you know very well that the traveler, who is never seen in the office almost the whole year around, can so easily fall a victim to gossip and ill luck and unfounded complaints, which he mostly knows nothing about, except when he comes back exhausted from his rounds, and only then suffers in person from their evil consequences, which he can no longer trace back to the original causes. Sir, sir, don't go away without a word to me to show that you think me in the right at least to some extent!"

But at Gregor's very first words the chief clerk had already backed away and only stared at him with parted lips over one twitching shoulder. And while Gregor was speaking he did not stand still one moment but stole away toward the door, without taking his eyes off Gregor, yet only an inch at a time, as if obeying some secret injunction to leave the room. He was already at the hall, and the suddenness with which he took his last step out of the living room would have made one believe he had burned the sole of his foot. Once in the hall he stretched his right arm before him toward the staircase, as if some supernatural power were waiting there to deliver him.

PAUSE & REFLECT How do people respond to the sight of Gregor?

FOCUS Read to find out how Gregor is forced back into his room.

Gregor perceived that the chief clerk must on no account be allowed to go away in this frame of mind if his position in the firm were not to be endangered to the utmost. His parents did not understand this so well; they had convinced themselves in the course of years that Gregor 2
was settled for life in this firm, and besides they were so preoccupied with their immediate troubles that all foresight had forsaken them. Yet Gregor had this foresight. The chief clerk must be detained, soothed, persuaded, and finally won over; the whole future of Gregor and his family depended on it! If only his sister had been there! She was intelligent; she had begun to cry while Gregor was still lying quietly on his back. And no doubt the chief clerk, so partial to[14] ladies, would have been guided by her; she would have shut the door of the flat and in the hall talked him out of his horror. But she was not there, and

14. **partial to:** having a special liking for.

MINI LESSON Speaking and Listening

DRAMATIZATION

Prepare Help students prepare a dramatization of Gregor's attempt to keep the chief clerk from leaving the house. Have students reread the last sentence on page 1120 and all of page 1121 up to the last complete sentence which ends ". . . on the head." Point out that while there isn't much dialogue, the passage is rich with details about the physical movements of Gregor, his parents, and the chief clerk. Ask students to think about how they would portray the facial expressions and movements of each character.

Present Have groups of four students stage the scene, while other students take turns narrating the passage. If possible, have students use props (coat, hat, newspaper, chair, cane). Narrators should allow each character to recite his or her dialogue at the appropriate place in the passage. Afterward, have the class discuss which expressions and movements were the most effective in conveying the horror and chaos of the scene.

This activity is particularly well suited for longer class periods.

Gregor would have to handle the situation himself. And without remembering that he was still unaware what powers of movement he possessed, without even remembering that his words in all possibility, indeed in all likelihood, would again be unintelligible, he let go the wing of the door, pushed himself through the opening, started to walk toward the chief clerk, who was already ridiculously clinging with both hands to the railing on the landing; but immediately, as he was feeling for a support, he fell down with a little cry upon all his numerous legs. Hardly was he down when he experienced for the first time this morning a sense of physical comfort; his legs had firm ground under them; they were completely obedient, as he noted with joy; they even strove to carry him forward in whatever direction he chose; and he was inclined to believe that a final relief from all his sufferings was at hand. But in the same moment as he found himself on the floor, rocking with suppressed eagerness to move, not far from his mother, indeed just in front of her, she, who had seemed so completely crushed, sprang all at once to her feet, her arms and fingers outspread, cried: "Help, for God's sake, help!" bent her head down as if to see Gregor better, yet on the contrary kept backing senselessly away; had quite forgotten that the laden table stood behind her; sat upon it hastily, as if in absence of mind, when she bumped into it; and seemed altogether unaware that the big coffeepot beside her was upset and pouring coffee in a flood over the carpet.

"Mother, Mother," said Gregor in a low voice, and looked up at her. The chief clerk, for the moment, had quite slipped from his mind; instead, he could not resist snapping his jaws together at the sight of the streaming coffee. That made his mother scream again, she fled from the table and fell

into the arms of his father, who hastened to catch her. But Gregor had now no time to spare for his parents; the chief clerk was already on the stairs; with his chin on the banisters he was taking one last backward look. Gregor made a spring, to be as sure as possible of overtaking him; the chief clerk must have divined his intention, for he leaped down several steps and vanished; he was still yelling "Ugh!" and it echoed throughout the whole staircase.

Unfortunately, the flight of the chief clerk seemed completely to upset Gregor's father, who had remained relatively calm until now, for instead of running after the man himself, or at least not hindering Gregor in his pursuit, he seized in his right hand the walking stick that the chief clerk had left behind on a chair, together with a hat and greatcoat, snatched in his left hand a large newspaper from the table, and began stamping his feet and flourishing the stick and the newspaper to drive Gregor back into his room. No entreaty of Gregor's availed, indeed no entreaty was even understood, however humbly he bent his head his father only stamped on the floor the more loudly. Behind his father his mother had torn open a window, despite the cold weather, and was leaning far out of it with her face in her hands. A strong draught set in from the street to the staircase, the window curtains blew in, the newspapers on the table fluttered, stray pages whisked over the floor. Pitilessly Gregor's father drove him back, hissing and crying "Shoo!" like a savage. But Gregor was quite unpracticed in walking backwards, it really was a slow business. If he only had a chance to turn around he could get back to his room at once, but he was afraid of exasperating his father by the slowness of such a rotation and at any moment the stick in his father's hand might hit him a fatal blow on the back or on the head. In the end, however, nothing else was left for him to do since to his horror he observed that in moving backwards he could not even control the direction

WORDS TO KNOW

unintelligible (ŭn'ĭn-tĕl'ĭ-jə-bəl) *adj.* unable to be understood

Customizing Instruction

English Learners

1 Explain that *comprehensive* means "large in range or amount." Gregor uses the word to pay the chief clerk a compliment. He tells the clerk that he knows even more than the chief does.

Help students use context clues to figure out the meanings of these words:

- injunction *(command)*
- detained *(kept from leaving)*
- divined *(guessed)*
- draught *(wind)*

Less Proficient Readers

Set a Purpose Ask students to read to find out how Gregor responds after seeing the shocked looks of the clerk and his parents.

Focus Help students use the Focus on page 1120 by having them pay close attention to the details that describe Gregor's movements.

2 Make sure students understand that Gregor feels that his most immediate problem is not how he looks but making sure that the chief clerk doesn't leave. Ask students why he feels this way. *(He thinks the chief clerk can be persuaded to allow Gregor to keep his job.)*

Advanced Learners

Encourage students to discuss their feelings about the irony of Gregor's speech to the chief clerk. Ask them if they think Gregor's attempts to keep his job are funny or tragic. Have students support their views with examples from the text.

Literary Analysis POINT OF VIEW

Point out that Kafka may have used the third-person point of view because a narrator could make Gregor a character that readers could sympathize with. Ask students to describe how the story might change if it were narrated by one of the characters.

Possible Response: If the story were narrated by the chief clerk or a family member, the reader would not really find out about Gregor's feelings. If Gregor told the story, he might be perceived as a whiner or complainer.

Pause & Reflect

Possible Response: His father pushes him into his room with a cane.

Literary Analysis MOOD

As students read, have them describe the mood in Gregor's room. Have them point out details in the setting and the painting that contribute to the mood of this scene.

Possible Responses: dreary, sad; details from the story—electric lights casting a pale sheen, silence all around, staring into the darkness; details from the painting—sparsely furnished room

he took; and so, keeping an anxious eye on his father all the time over his shoulder, he began to turn around as quickly as he could, which was in reality very slowly. Perhaps his father noted his good intentions, for he did not interfere except every now and then to help him in the maneuver from a distance with the point of the stick. If only he would have stopped making that unbearable hissing noise! It made Gregor quite lose his head. He had turned almost completely around when the hissing noise so distracted him that he even turned a little the wrong way again. But when at last his head was fortunately right in front of the doorway, it appeared that his body was too broad simply to get through the opening. His father, of course, in his present mood was far from thinking of such a thing as opening the other half of the door, to let Gregor have enough space. He had merely the fixed idea of driving Gregor back into his room as quickly as possible. He would never have suffered Gregor to make the circumstantial preparations for standing up on end and perhaps slipping his way through the door. Maybe he was now making more noise than ever to urge Gregor forward, as if no obstacle impeded him; to Gregor, anyhow, the noise in his rear sounded no longer like the voice of one single father; this was really no joke, and Gregor thrust himself—come what might—into the doorway. One side of his body rose up, he was tilted at an angle in the doorway, his flank was quite bruised, horrid blotches stained the white door, soon he was stuck fast and, left to himself, could not have moved at all, his legs on one side fluttered trembling in the air, those on the other were crushed painfully to the floor—when from behind his father gave him a strong push which was literally a deliverance and he flew far into the room, bleeding freely. The door was slammed behind him with the stick, and then at last there was silence.

PAUSE & REFLECT How is Gregor forced back into his room?

FOCUS Read to find out how the entire household settles into a new routine and how Gregor's sister takes care of him.

Not until it was twilight did Gregor awake out of a deep sleep, more like a swoon than a sleep. He would certainly have waked up of his own accord not much later, for he felt himself sufficiently rested and well slept, but it seemed to him as if a fleeting step and a cautious shutting of the door leading into the hall had aroused him. The electric lights in the street cast a pale sheen here and there on the ceiling and the upper surfaces of the furniture, but down below, where he lay, it was dark. Slowly, awkwardly trying out his feelers, which he now first learned to appreciate, he pushed his way to the door to see what had been happening there. His left side felt like one single long, unpleasantly tense scar, and he had actually to limp on his two rows of legs. One little leg, moreover, had been severely damaged in the course of that morning's events—it was almost a miracle that only one had been damaged—and trailed uselessly behind him.

He had reached the door before he discovered what had really drawn him to it: the smell of food. For there stood a basin filled with fresh milk in which floated little sops of white bread. He could almost have laughed with joy, since he was now still hungrier than in the morning, and he dipped his head almost over the eyes straight into the milk. But soon in disappointment he withdrew it again; not only did he find it difficult to feed because of his tender left side—and he could only feed with the palpitating collaboration[15] of his whole body—he did not like the

15. **palpitating collaboration:** working together of all the parts in a trembling way.

Assessment **Standardized Test Practice**

WRITING A SHORT ESSAY ANSWER Have students write a short essay response to the following prompt: Why does Kafka tell the story mainly from Gregor's viewpoint?

RUBRIC

3 **Full Accomplishment** Students write a well-organized essay with evidence from the story. They recognize that Kafka restricts the viewpoint to show readers how the transformation affects Gregor and to show Gregor how his transformation affects others.

2 **Substantial Accomplishment** Students write a logical essay with some evidence from the story. They recognize that Kafka restricts the viewpoint in order to show how Gregor is affected by his transformation. The essay may touch on this point briefly, or it may have distracting spelling, grammar, and usage errors.

1 **Little or Partial Accomplishment** Students do not realize why Kafka restricts the viewpoint. The essay is disorganized and may be somewhat incoherent with many spelling, grammar, and usage errors.

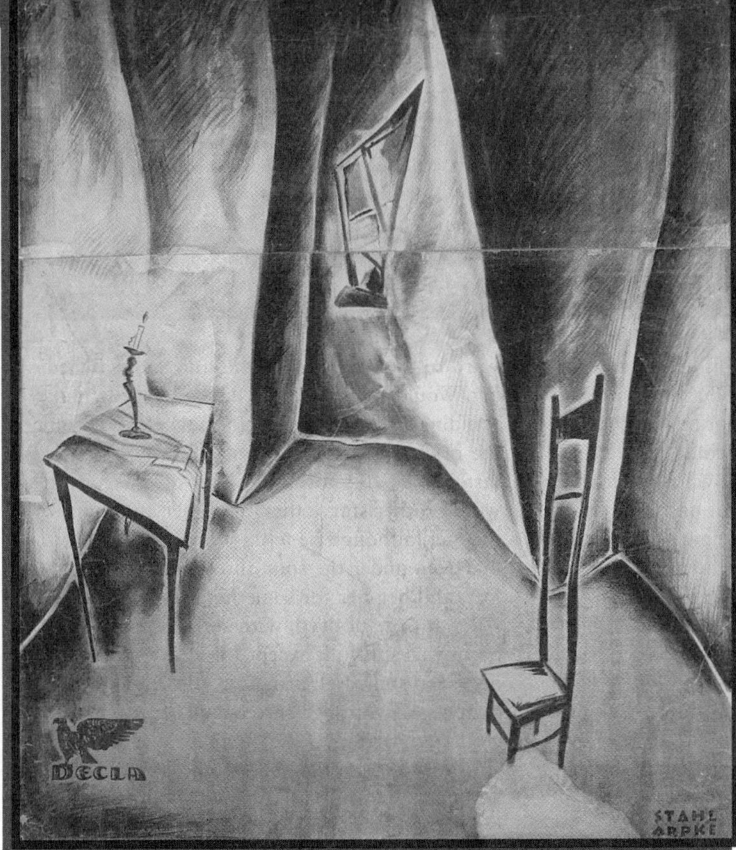

Detail of the poster for the 1920 film *Das cabinet des Dr. Caligari* [The cabinet of Dr. Caligari].

although the flat was certainly not empty of occupants. "What a quiet life our family has been leading," said Gregor to himself, and as he sat there motionless staring into the darkness he felt great pride in the fact that he had been able to provide such a life for his parents and sister in such a fine flat. But what if all the quiet, the comfort, the contentment were now to end in horror? To keep himself from being lost in such thoughts Gregor took refuge in movement and crawled up and down the room.

Once during the long evening one of the side doors was opened a little and quickly shut again, later the other side door too; someone had apparently wanted to come in and then thought better of it. Gregor now stationed himself immediately before the living-room door, determined to persuade any hesitating visitor to come in or at least to discover who it might be; but the door was not opened again and he waited in vain. In the early morning, when the doors were locked, they had all wanted to come in, now that he had opened one door and the other had apparently been opened during the day, no one came in and even the keys were on the other side of the doors.

It was late at night before the gas went out in the living room, and Gregor could easily tell that his parents and his sister had all stayed awake

milk either, although milk had been his favorite drink and that was certainly why his sister had set it there for him, indeed it was almost with repulsion that he turned away from the basin and crawled back to the middle of the room.

He could see through the crack of the door that the gas was turned on in the living room, but while usually at this time his father made a habit of reading the afternoon newspaper in a loud voice to his mother and occasionally to his sister as well, not a sound was now to be heard. Well, perhaps his father had recently given up this habit of reading aloud, which his sister had mentioned so often in conversation and in her letters. But there was the same silence all around,

WORDS TO KNOW
refuge (rĕf'yōōj) *n.* protection; comfort

Customizing Instruction

Less Proficient Readers
Point out that the words *suffered* and *flat* have different meanings from the ones students are probably used to. In this case, *suffered* means "allowed," and *flat* means "apartment."

Focus Help students use the Focus on page 1122 to note how the life of each family member, including Gregor, changes.

Advanced Learners
Remind students that characters in modernist works are often plagued with anxiety and feel alienated from society. Ask students to discuss how Gregor's time alone in his room reflects these characteristics of modernist literature.

Cross Curricular Link **Science**

BEETLES Kafka refers to Gregor as a bug, but the description he gives is most like that of a beetle, specifically a dung beetle. Beetles are not considered social insects like ants or bees. Dung beetles, in particular, do not eat fresh food. They only eat the manure of cows, sheep, horses, or camels. For this reason, Kafka may have chosen the beetle as a symbol of alienation.

Beetles are distinguished from other insects by thickened front wings, which they do not use. These wings form a shield on the insect's back. A beetle's abdomen may be made of as many as ten segments.

The beetle also has very strong legs. When a beetle walks, it is always supported by a middle leg on one side of its body and the fore and hind legs on its other side. A beetle also has cushion-like pads between the claws of its feet. These pads are covered with hairs that secrete a sticky substance. The pads allow the beetle to walk over smooth surfaces or upside down.

Active Reading VISUALIZING DETAILS

A Have students note that the author has provided yet another clue to Gregor's size. Ask students to estimate how long and how wide Gregor might be.

Reading Skills and Strategies
CLARIFYING

B Ask students if they are surprised that Gregor's sister takes care of him. Ask them if Gregor gave any clues earlier about her behavior.

Possible Responses: Most students will not be surprised. Gregor thought she would know what to do when he was trying to persuade the chief clerk not to leave the house.

Reading Skills and Strategies
SUMMARIZING

C Point out that although Gregor and his sister cannot talk to each other, she develops several signals that help her communicate with him. Have students describe what these signals are.

Possible Response: His sister leaves the room quickly and turns the key, so Gregor can eat; she turns the key slowly so that Gregor will have time to hide when she enters the room.

Reading Skills and Strategies
CLARIFYING

D Point out that Gregor reasons that his parents don't feed him or visit because they probably have too many other things to worry about. Ask students what these worries might be.

Possible Response: They are worried about others discovering his condition; they might be worried about their finances since Gregor can no longer work.

BUT THE LOFTY, EMPTY ROOM IN WHICH HE HAD TO LIE FLAT ON THE FLOOR FILLED HIM WITH AN APPREHENSION HE COULD NOT ACCOUNT FOR, SINCE IT HAD BEEN HIS VERY OWN ROOM FOR THE PAST FIVE YEARS. . . .

until then, for he could clearly hear the three of them stealing away on tiptoe. No one was likely to visit him, not until the morning, that was certain; so he had plenty of time to meditate at his leisure on how he was to arrange his life afresh. But the lofty, empty room in which he had to lie flat on the floor filled him with an apprehension he could not account for, since it had been his very own room for the past five years—and with a half-unconscious action, not without a slight feeling of shame, he scuttled under the sofa, where he felt comfortable at once, although his back was a little cramped and he could not lift his head up, and his only regret was that his body was too broad to get the whole of it under the sofa. A

He stayed there all night, spending the time partly in a light slumber, from which his hunger kept waking him up with a start, and partly in worrying and sketching vague hopes, which all led to the same conclusion, that he must lie low for the present and, by exercising patience and the utmost consideration, help the family to bear the inconvenience he was bound to cause them in his present condition.

Very early in the morning, it was still almost night, Gregor had the chance to test the strength of his new resolutions, for his sister, nearly fully dressed, opened the door from the hall and peered in. She did not see him at once, yet when she caught sight of him under the sofa—well, he had to be somewhere, he couldn't have flown away, could he?—she was so startled that without being able to help it she slammed the door shut again. B But as if regretting her behavior she opened the door again immediately and came in on tiptoe, as if she were visiting an invalid or even a stranger. Gregor had pushed his head forward to the very edge of the sofa and watched her. Would she notice that he had left the milk standing, and not for lack of hunger, and would she bring in some other kind of food more to his taste? If she did not do it of her own accord, he would rather starve than draw her attention to the fact, although he felt a wild impulse to dart out from under the sofa, throw himself at her feet, and beg her for something to eat. But his sister at once noticed, with surprise, that the basin was still full, except for a little milk that had been spilled all around it, she lifted it immediately, not with her bare hands, true, but with a cloth and carried it away. Gregor was wildly curious to know what she would bring instead, and made various speculations about it. Yet what she actually did next, in the goodness of her heart, he could never have guessed at. To find out what he liked she brought him a whole selection of food, all set out on an old newspaper. There were old, half-decayed vegetables, bones from last night's supper covered with a white sauce that had thickened; some raisins and almonds; a piece of cheese Gregor would have called uneatable two days ago; a dry roll of bread, a buttered roll, and a roll both buttered and salted. Besides all that, she set down again the same basin, into which she had poured some water, and which was apparently to be reserved for his exclusive use. And with fine tact, knowing that Gregor would not eat in her presence, she withdrew quickly and even turned the key, to let him understand that he could take his ease as much as he liked. C Gregor's legs all whizzed toward the food. His wounds must have healed completely, moreover, for he felt no disability, which amazed him and made him reflect how more than a month ago he had cut one finger a little with a knife and had still suffered pain from the wound only the day before yesterday. Am I less sensitive now? he thought, and sucked greedily at the cheese, which above all the other edibles attracted him at once and strongly. One after another and with tears of satisfaction in his eyes he quickly devoured the cheese, the vegetables, and the sauce; the fresh food, on the other hand, had no charms for him, he could not even stand the smell of it and actually dragged away to some little distance the things he could eat. He had long finished his meal and was only lying lazily on the same spot when his sister turned the key slowly as a sign for him to retreat. That roused him at once, although he was nearly asleep, and he hurried under the sofa again. But it took considerable self-control for him to stay under the sofa, even for the short time his sister was in the room, since the large meal had swollen his body somewhat and he was so cramped he could hardly breathe. Slight attacks of breathlessness afflicted him and his eyes were starting a little out of his head as he watched his unsuspecting sister sweeping together with a broom not only the remains of what he had eaten but even the things he had not touched, as if these were now of no use to anyone, and hastily shoveling it all into a bucket, which she covered with a wooden lid and carried away. Hardly had she turned her back when Gregor came from under the sofa and stretched and puffed himself out.

In this manner Gregor was fed, once in the early morning while his parents and the servant girl were still asleep, and a second time after they had all had their midday dinner, for then his parents took a short nap and the servant girl could be sent out on some errand or other by his sister. Not that they would have wanted him to starve, of course, but perhaps they could not have borne to know more about his feeding than from hearsay, perhaps too his sister wanted to spare them such little anxieties whenever possible, since they had quite enough to bear as it was. 1 D

Under what pretext the doctor and the locksmith had been got rid of on that first morning Gregor could not discover, for since what he said was not understood by the others it never struck any of them, not even his sister, that he could understand what they said, and so whenever his sister came into his room he had to content himself with hearing her utter only a sigh now and then and an occasional appeal to the saints. Later on, when she had got a little used to the situation—of course she could never get completely used to it—she sometimes threw out a remark which was kindly meant or could be so interpreted. "Well, he liked his dinner today," she would say when Gregor had made a good clearance of his food; and when he had not eaten, which gradually happened more and more often, she would say almost sadly: "Everything's been left standing again."

But although Gregor could get no news directly, he overheard a lot from the neighboring rooms, and as soon as voices were audible, he would run to the door of the room concerned and press his whole body against it. In the first few days especially there was no conversation that did not refer to him somehow, even if only indirectly. For two whole days there were family consultations at every mealtime about what should be done; but also between meals the same subject was discussed, for there were always at least two members of the family at home, since no one wanted to be alone in the flat and to leave it quite empty was unthinkable. And on the very first of these days the household cook—it was not quite clear what and how much she knew of the situation—went down on her knees to his mother

Customizing Instruction

Less Proficient Readers

1 Explain that *borne* is the past tense of *bear*, which means to "withstand or endure."

English Learners

Remind students that they can sometimes find the meaning of an unfamiliar word because the word is restated in the surrounding text. Help students find the words or phrases that are restatements to determine the meanings of *speculations (guessed)*, *retreat (hurried under the sofa again)*, and *audible (overheard)*.

Advanced Learners

After students have read page 1125, ask them if there are any conclusions they can draw about Gregor's current relationship with his family.

Possible Responses: Even though he is locked in his room, he is still considered a member of the family, because his sister feeds him. His family alters some of their routines to meet his needs, and they still talk about him.

Literary Analysis CHARACTER

Tell students that they will find out more about the family through Gregor's thoughts and feelings on these two pages. Encourage students to make notes about each character as they read. Ask students what aspects of each family member's character are revealed on these pages. Then discuss what Gregor reveals about himself.

Possible Responses: Gregor's father shows great resolve in handling the family's finances. His mother is not astute about finances, is sickly, and can't be depended on. His sister is quick-witted but only used to dressing well, sleeping late, and playing the violin. Gregor feels pride in attaining the status of a salesman to support his family. He wants to believe he is still needed or that some part of him is still human.

Reading Skills and Strategies EVALUATING

A Ask students if they think that Gregor's family's financial situation and their ability to handle it are as bad as Gregor thinks it is.

Possible Responses: Some students may say no. The family still has servants that they can dismiss, if necessary, and Gregor's sister can help with more of the housework. As their sole support for five years, Gregor wants to still feel needed by his family. Others may say yes. The father and mother are both old and incapable of producing income on a regular basis. Gregor's sister has been indulged by the rest of the family and isn't used to doing real work.

and begged leave to go, and when she departed, a quarter of an hour later, gave thanks for her dismissal with tears in her eyes as if for the greatest benefit that could have been conferred on her, and without any prompting swore a solemn oath that she would never say a single word to anyone about what had happened.

Now Gregor's sister had to cook too, helping her mother; true, the cooking did not amount to much, for they ate scarcely anything. Gregor was always hearing one of the family vainly urging another to eat and getting no answer but: "Thanks, I've had all I want," or something similar. Perhaps they drank nothing either. Time and again his sister kept asking his father if he wouldn't like some beer and offered kindly to go and fetch it herself, and when he made no answer suggested that she could ask the concierge[16] to fetch it, so that he need feel no sense of obligation, but then a round "No" came from his father and no more was said about it.

In the course of that very first day Gregor's father explained the family's financial position and prospects to both his mother and his sister. Now and then he rose from the table to get some voucher or memorandum out of the small safe he had rescued from the collapse of his business five years earlier. One could hear him opening the complicated lock and rustling papers out and shutting it again. This statement made by his father was the first cheerful information Gregor had heard since his imprisonment. He had been of the opinion that nothing at all was left over from his father's business, at least his father had never said anything to the contrary, and of course he had not asked him directly. At that time Gregor's sole desire was to do his utmost to help the family to forget as soon as possible the catastrophe that had overwhelmed the business and thrown them all into a state of complete despair. And so he had set to work with unusual ardor[17] and almost overnight had become a commercial traveler instead of a little clerk, with of

course much greater chances of earning money, and his success was immediately translated into good round coin which he could lay on the table for his amazed and happy family. These had been fine times, and they had never recurred, at least not with the same sense of glory, although later on Gregor had earned so much money that he was able to meet the expenses of the whole household and did so. They had simply got used to it, both the family and Gregor; the money was gratefully accepted and gladly given, but there was no special uprush of warm feeling. With his sister alone had he remained intimate, and it was a secret plan of his that she, who loved music, unlike himself, and could play movingly on the violin, should be sent next year to study at the Conservatorium,[18] despite the great expense that would entail, which must be made up in some other way. During his brief visits home the Conservatorium was often mentioned in the talks he had with his sister, but always merely as a beautiful dream which could never come true, and his parents discouraged even these innocent references to it; yet Gregor had made up his mind firmly about it and meant to announce the fact with due solemnity on Christmas Day.

Such were the thoughts, completely futile in his present condition, that went through his head as he stood clinging upright to the door and listening. Sometimes out of sheer weariness he had to give up listening and let his head fall negligently against the door, but he always had to pull himself together again at once, for even the slight sound his head made was audible next door and brought all conversation to a stop. "What can he be doing now?" his father would say after a while, obviously turning toward the door, and only then would the interrupted con-

16. **concierge** (kôN-syârzh'): a person in an apartment complex who serves as a doorkeeper and janitor.

17. **ardor:** eagerness; enthusiasm.

18. **Conservatorium:** school of music.

versation gradually be set going again.

Gregor was now informed as amply as he could wish—for his father tended to repeat himself in his explanations, partly because it was a long time since he had handled such matters and partly because his mother could not always grasp things at once—that a certain amount of investments, a very small amount it was true, had survived the wreck of their fortunes and had even increased a little because the dividends had not been touched meanwhile. And besides that, the money Gregor brought home every month—he had kept only a few dollars for himself—had never been quite used up and now amounted to a small capital sum. Behind the door Gregor nodded his head eagerly, rejoiced at this evidence of unexpected thrift and foresight. True, he could really have paid off some more of his father's debts to the chief with this extra money, and so brought much nearer the day on which he could quit his job, but doubtless it was better the way his father had arranged it.

Yet this capital was by no means sufficient to let the family live on the interest of it; for one year, perhaps, or at the most two, they could live on the principal, that was all. It was simply a sum that ought not to be touched and should be kept for a rainy day; money for living expenses would have to be earned. Now his father was still hale enough but an old man, and he had done no work for the past five years and could not be expected to do much; during these five years, the first years of leisure in his laborious though unsuccessful life, he had grown rather fat and become sluggish. And Gregor's old mother, how was she to earn a living with her asthma, which troubled her even when she walked through the flat and kept her lying on a sofa every other day panting for breath beside an open window? And was his sister to earn her bread, she who was still a child of seventeen and whose life hitherto had been so pleasant, consisting as it did in dressing herself nicely, sleeping long, helping in the housekeeping, going out to a few modest entertainments, and above all playing the violin? At first whenever the need for earning money was mentioned Gregor let go his hold on the door and threw himself down on the cool leather sofa beside it, he felt so hot with shame and grief.

Often he just lay there the long nights through without sleeping at all, scrabbling for hours on the leather. Or he nerved himself to the great effort of pushing an armchair to the window, then crawled up over the window sill and, braced against the chair, leaned against the windowpanes, obviously in some recollection of the sense of freedom that looking out of a window always used to give him. For in reality day by day things that were even a little way off were growing dimmer to his sight; the hospital across the street, which he used to execrate[19] for being all too often before his eyes, was now quite beyond his range of vision, and if he had not known that he lived in Charlotte Street, a quiet street but still a city street, he might have believed that his window gave on a desert waste where gray sky and gray land blended indistinguishably into each other. His quick-witted sister only needed to observe twice that the armchair stood by the window; after that whenever she had tidied the room she always pushed the chair back to the same place at the window and even left the inner casements open.

If he could have spoken to her and thanked her for all she had to do for him, he could have borne her ministrations better; as it was, they oppressed him. 2 She certainly tried to make as light as possible of whatever was disagreeable in her task, and as time went on she succeeded, of course, more and more, but time brought more

19. **execrate** (ĕk′sĭ-krāt′): declare to be hateful.

Customizing Instruction

Less Proficient Readers

Help students follow Gregor's thoughts with these questions:

- Why did Gregor work so hard to become a salesman? *(He can earn more money.)*
- Why does Gregor want to send his sister to music school? *(He enjoys her playing and is closer to her than anyone else in his family.)*
- Why is Gregor's eyesight failing? *(He is becoming more buglike.)*

English Learners

1 Tell students that one type of context clue is a contrast clue. Explain that contrast clues have a meaning that is opposite that of the unfamiliar word and are often signaled by the words *although, but,* and *however*. Have students note the contrast clues they used to figure out the meaning of *hale. (but, old)*

2 Explain that *ministrations* refers to the ways that Gregor's sister is helping him.

Advanced Learners

Tell students that modern writers often use a method of indirect characterization. That is, they show readers a character but allow the readers to interpret for themselves what kind of person the character really is. Have students use the character and physical traits mentioned on pages 1126 and 1127 to discuss their perceptions of Gregor's father.

Cross Curricular Link Economics

FINANCE Explain to students that before the father's business failed, he had probably committed some of the money he earned to something that would give him more money in the future. This type of commitment is called an *investment.* Opening bank accounts, buying stocks, or buying property are just a few of the investments that people make. *Capital* refers to the money that Gregor's father invested. The *dividends* that he mentioned probably came from a share of the profits of the company he had invested in. *Principal* refers to money the father placed in a bank account. *Interest* is the amount of money the principal earned over time.

Reading Skills and Strategies
CONNECTING

A Ask students to imagine how they might feel in the sister's situation. Have them discuss whether they would be used to Gregor's appearance after one month. Then ask students which character they sympathize with more—Gregor or his sister.

Literary Analysis CHARACTER

Ask students what the sister's refusal to look at Gregor reveals about her character. Then have them explain what Gregor's efforts to keep himself out of sight reveal about his character.
Possible Responses: Gregor's sister may feel like she has to care for him because they were once very close. Or she may just be doing it because she has now won her parent's respect. Gregor wants to maintain the bond he had with his sister. He sacrifices his own comfort by hiding under the sofa in order to spare her any discomfort.

Literary Analysis IRONY

B Ask students to explain what is ironic about the sister's respect and appreciation from her parents.
Possible Response: At one time, Gregor was the responsible, useful son who supported the entire family. The sister has gained this favored position at Gregor's expense.

Portrait of Mlle Ravoux (late-19th century), Vincent van Gogh. Photograph copyright © Christie's Images, London/SuperStock, Inc.

HUMANITIES CONNECTION Dutch artist Vincent van Gogh (1853–1890) used precise brushwork and strong colors to convey intense emotion. The dark, somber background of this portrait may be a reflection of the artist's deteriorating condition near the end of his life.

MINI LESSON Viewing and Representing

Portrait of Mlle Ravoux **by Vincent van Gogh**

ART APPRECIATION The Dutch artist van Gogh spent his last months painting mostly young women in Auvers, a small village north of Paris, France. This portrait is considered one of his most memorable. It is the teenage daughter of the owner of the inn where van Gogh stayed.

Have students study the painting and the **Humanities Connection** on page 1128. Have students discuss how the painting of the girl against the dark background enhances the story.
Possible Responses: The girl in the picture is well dressed and looks like she has lived a life with few worries, much like Gregor's sister. The dark background contrasts her "good life" with the difficult task of taking care of Gregor.

...HE OFTEN HEARD THEM EXPRESSING THEIR APPRECIATION OF HIS SISTER'S ACTIVITIES, WHEREAS FORMERLY THEY HAD FREQUENTLY SCOLDED HER FOR BEING AS THEY THOUGHT A SOMEWHAT **USELESS** DAUGHTER.

enlightenment to Gregor too. The very way she came in distressed him. Hardly was she in the room when she rushed to the window, without even taking time to shut the door, careful as she was usually to shield the sight of Gregor's room from the others, and as if she were almost suffocating tore the casements open with hasty fingers, standing then in the open draught for a while even in the bitterest cold and drawing deep breaths. This noisy scurry of hers upset Gregor twice a day; he would crouch trembling under the sofa all the time, knowing quite well that she would certainly have spared him such a disturbance had she found it at all possible to stay in his presence without opening the window.

A On one occasion, about a month after Gregor's metamorphosis, when there was surely no reason for her to be still startled at his appearance, she came a little earlier than usual and found him gazing out of the window, quite
1 motionless, and thus well placed to look like a
2 bogey. Gregor would not have been surprised had she not come in at all, for she could not immediately open the window while he was there, but not only did she retreat, she jumped back as if in alarm and banged the door shut; a stranger might well have thought that he had been lying in wait for her there meaning to bite her. Of course he hid himself under the sofa at once, but he had to wait until midday before she came again, and she seemed more ill at ease than usual. This made him realize how repulsive the sight of him still was to her, and that it was bound to go on being repulsive, and what an effort it must cost her not to run away even from the sight of the small portion of his body that stuck out from under the sofa. In order to spare her that, therefore, one day he carried a sheet on his back to the sofa—it cost him four hours' labor—and arranged it there in such a way as to hide him completely, so that even if she were to bend down she could not see him. Had she considered the sheet unnecessary, she would certainly have stripped it off the sofa again, for it was clear enough that this curtaining and confining of himself was not likely to conduce to 3
Gregor's comfort, but she left it where it was, and Gregor even fancied that he caught a thankful glance from her eye when he lifted the sheet carefully a very little with his head to see how she was taking the new arrangement.

For the first fortnight[20] his parents could not bring themselves to the point of entering his room, and he often heard them expressing their appreciation of his sister's activities, whereas formerly they had frequently scolded her for being as they thought a somewhat useless daughter. B
But now, both of them often waited outside the door, his father and his mother, while his sister tidied his room, and as soon as she came out she had to tell them exactly how things were in the room, what Gregor had eaten, how he had conducted himself this time, and whether there was not perhaps some slight improvement in his condition. His mother, moreover, began relatively soon to want to visit him, but his father and sister dissuaded her at first with arguments which Gregor listened to very attentively and altogether

20. **fortnight:** two weeks.

WORDS TO KNOW

dissuade (dĭ-swād') *v.* to persuade not to; discourage

Customizing Instruction

Less Proficient Readers

1 Ask students to describe what happens when Gregor's sister enters his room and finds him looking out the window.

Set a Purpose Have students think about how caring for Gregor has changed his sister.

English Learners

2 Explain to students that *bogey* means "an evil spirit." Some students may be more familiar with the term *bogeyman*.

3 Help students use context clues to determine that *conduce* means "contribute to" or "lead to."

METAMORPHOSIS **1129**

Reading Skills and Strategies
CLARIFYING

A Ask students what Gregor means when he thought his mother "understood things better."

Possible Response: His mother still thinks of him as her son and human. He thinks he might be able to relate to her on a human level.

Pause & Reflect

Possible Response: Gregor's sister awakens early to feed him while the servant girl is still asleep. She feeds Gregor again in the afternoon when the servant girl is sent on an errand. There are always two people at home, because no one wants to be alone with Gregor. The cook quits, so the sister also has to help cook. Gregor's sister seems to be compassionate because she is the only one willing to take care of him. Unfortunately, her inability to look at Gregor causes him much discomfort.

Active Reading VISUALIZING DETAILS

B Ask students to think about other insects they may have seen crawling on a wall or ceiling to help them visualize this scene. Have students recall what they have learned about beetles. Ask them if Kafka's description is accurate.

Literary Analysis CONFLICT

Remind students that there are two types of conflict—internal and external. An internal conflict is a conflict between opposing forces within a character. An external conflict pits a character against nature, society, or another character. Point out that both types of conflict occur on these pages. Have students describe each one.

Possible Response: Gregor has an internal conflict about the furniture. He wants it to stay because it reminds him of his old life, but he also wants it out because he will have more room to crawl. His mother and sister have an external conflict about the furniture. His mother feels that the furniture should stay as a sign of hope that Gregor will become human again. His sister knows he needs more room to crawl.

approved. Later, however, she had to be held back by main force, and when she cried out: "Do let me in to Gregor, he is my unfortunate son! Can't you understand that I must go to him?" Gregor thought that it might be well to have her come in, not every day, of course, but
A perhaps once a week; she understood things, after all, much better than his sister, who was only a child despite the efforts she was making and had perhaps taken on so difficult a task merely out of childish thoughtlessness.

PAUSE & REFLECT How has daily life changed for Gregor and the rest of his family? What do the actions of Gregor's sister reveal about her?

FOCUS To give Gregor more room for crawling, his mother and sister decide to move his furniture out. Read to find out what happens.

Gregor's desire to see his mother was soon fulfilled. During the daytime he did not want to show himself at the window, out of consideration for his parents, but he could not crawl very far around the few square yards of floor space he had, nor could he bear lying quietly at rest all during the night, while he was fast losing any interest he had ever taken in food, so that for mere recreation he had formed the habit of crawling crisscross over the walls and ceiling.
B He especially enjoyed hanging suspended from the ceiling; it was much better than lying on the floor; one could breathe more freely; one's body swung and rocked lightly; and in the almost blissful absorption induced by this suspension it could happen to his own surprise that he let go and fell plump on the floor. Yet he now had his body much better under control than formerly, and even such a big fall did him no harm. His sister at once remarked the new distraction Gregor had found for himself—he left traces behind him of the sticky stuff on his soles wherever he crawled—and she got the idea in her head of giving him as wide a field as possible to crawl in and of removing the pieces of furniture that hindered him, above all the chest of drawers and the writing desk. But that was more than she could manage all by herself; she did not dare ask her father to help her; and as for the servant girl, a young creature of sixteen who had had the courage to stay on after the cook's departure, she could not be asked to help, for she had begged as a special favor that she might keep the kitchen door locked and open it only on a definite summons; so there was nothing left but to apply to her mother at an hour when her father was out. And the old lady did come, with exclamations of joyful eagerness, which, however, died away at the door of Gregor's room. Gregor's sister, of course, went in first, to see that everything was in order before letting his mother enter. In great haste Gregor pulled the sheet lower and rucked it more in folds so that it really looked as if it had been thrown accidentally over the sofa. And this time he did not peer out from under it; he
renounced the pleasure of seeing his mother on 1
this occasion and was only glad that she had come at all. "Come in, he's out of sight," said his sister, obviously leading her mother in by the hand. Gregor could now hear the two women struggling to shift the heavy old chest from its place, and his sister claiming the greater part of the labor for herself, without listening to the admonitions of her mother, who feared she might overstrain herself. It took a long time. After at
least a quarter of an hour's tugging his mother 2
objected that the chest had better be left where it was, for in the first place it was too heavy and could never be got out before his father came home, and standing in the middle of the room like that it would only hamper Gregor's movements, while in the second place it was not at all certain that moving the furniture would be doing a service to Gregor. She was inclined to think to the contrary; the sight of the naked walls made her own heart heavy, and why shouldn't

Gregor have the same feeling, considering that he had been used to his furniture for so long and might feel forlorn without it. "And doesn't it look," she concluded in a low voice—in fact she had been almost whispering all the time as if to avoid letting Gregor, whose exact whereabouts she did not know, hear even the tones of her voice, for she was convinced that he could not understand her words—"doesn't it look as if we were showing him, by taking away his furniture, that we have given up hope of his ever getting better and are just leaving him coldly to himself? I think it would be best to keep his room exactly as it has always been, so that when he comes back to us he will find everything unchanged and be able all the more easily to forget what has happened in between."

On hearing these words from his mother Gregor realized that the lack of all direct human speech for the past two months together with the monotony of family life must have confused his mind, otherwise he could not account for the fact that he had quite earnestly looked forward to having his room emptied of furnishing. Did he really want his warm room, so comfortably fitted with old family furniture, to be turned into a naked den in which he would certainly be able to crawl unhampered in all directions but at the price of shedding simultaneously all recollection of his human background? He had indeed been so near the brink of forgetfulness that only the voice of his mother, which he had not heard for so long, had drawn him back from it. Nothing should be taken out of his room; everything must
3 stay as it was; he could not dispense with the good influence of the furniture on his state of mind; and even if the furniture did hamper him in his senseless crawling around and around, that was no drawback but a great advantage.

Unfortunately his sister was of the contrary opinion; she had grown accustomed, and not without reason, to consider herself an expert in Gregor's affairs as against her parents, and so her mother's advice was now enough to make her determined on the removal not only of the chest and the writing desk, which had been her first intention, but of all the furniture except the indispensable sofa. This determination was not, of course, merely the outcome of childish recalcitrance[21] and of the self-confidence she had recently developed so unexpectedly and at such cost; she had in fact perceived that Gregor needed a lot of space to crawl about in, while on the other hand he never used the furniture at all, so far as could be seen. Another factor might also have been the enthusiastic temperament of an adolescent girl, which seeks to indulge itself on every opportunity and which now tempted Grete to exaggerate the horror of her brother's circumstances in order that she might do all the more for him. In a room where Gregor lorded it all alone over empty walls no one save herself was likely ever to set foot.

And so she was not to be moved from her resolve by her mother, who seemed moreover to be ill at ease in Gregor's room and therefore unsure of herself, was soon reduced to silence, and helped her daughter as best she could to push the chest outside. Now, Gregor could do without the chest, if need be, but the writing desk he must retain. As soon as the two women had got the chest out of his room, groaning as they pushed it, Gregor stuck his head out from under the sofa to see how he might intervene as kindly and cautiously as possible. But as bad luck would have it, his mother was the first to return, leaving Grete clasping the chest in the room next door where she was trying to shift it all by herself, without of course moving it from the spot. His mother however was not accustomed to the sight of him, it might sicken her and so in alarm

21. **recalcitrance** (rĭ-kăl'sĭ-trəns): stubborn resistance to authority.

WORDS TO KNOW

intervene (ĭn'tər-vēn') *v.* to come between; get involved in order to help

Customizing Instruction

Less Proficient Readers

Focus Help students use the Focus on page 1130 by pointing out that they will learn a lot about the mother and sister through their attempts to remove Gregor's furniture. Guide students through the passage with these questions:

- Why does Grete decide to move the furniture out of Gregor's room? *(From the sticky trail that Gregor leaves when he crawls, she can see that he is spending a lot of time on the ceiling. He needs more floor space to crawl.)*
- Why is her mother the only person Grete can ask to help her move the furniture? *(She's afraid to ask her father, because he has never expressed interest in going into the room. She doesn't want to frighten the servant girl. Gregor's mother wants to see him.)*

English Learners

1 Explain that *renounced* means "gave up." Gregor has to give up the happiness that seeing his mother would give him because he has to hide under a sheet.

2 Explain that a "quarter of an hour" is equal to fifteen minutes.

3 Help students understand that *dispense* means "let go of." Gregor doesn't want let go of the positive effects of having the furniture in the room.

Reading Skills and Strategies
CONNECTING

A Ask students to think about how they would feel if they were in Gregor's position.

Active Reading VISUALIZING DETAILS

B Remind students of Gregor's size. Ask them what reactions they would have if they saw a bug that was Gregor's size on a wall.

Literary Analysis CHARACTER MOTIVATION

C Have students recall Gregor's internal conflict. Ask students to explain what motivates Gregor to act as if he might hurt Grete.
Possible Response: He is protecting his room—his territory.

Then ask what motivates Gregor to want to help his sister.
Possible Response: his human concern for his mother

Gregor backed quickly to the other end of the sofa, yet could not prevent the sheet from swaying a little in front. That was enough to put her on the alert. She paused, stood still for a moment, and then went back to Grete.

A Although Gregor kept reassuring himself that nothing out of the way was happening, but only a few bits of furniture were being changed around, he soon had to admit that all this trotting to and fro of the two women, their little ejaculations,[22] and the scraping of furniture along the floor affected him like a vast disturbance coming from all sides at once, and however much he tucked in his head and legs and cowered to the very floor he was bound to confess that he would not be able to stand it for long. They were clearing his room out; taking away everything he loved; the chest in which he kept his fret saw and other tools was already dragged off; they were now loosening the writing desk which had almost sunk into the floor, the desk at which he had done all his homework when he was at the commercial academy, at the grammar school before that, and, yes, even at the primary school—he had no more time to waste in weighing the good intentions of the two women, whose existence he had by now almost forgotten, for they were so exhausted that they were laboring in silence and nothing could be heard but the heavy scuffling of their feet.

And so he rushed out—the women were just leaning against the writing desk in the next room to give themselves a breather—and four times changed his direction, since he really did not know what to rescue first, then on the wall opposite, which was already otherwise cleared, he was struck by the picture of the lady muffled in so much fur and quickly crawled up to it and pressed himself to the glass, which was a good surface to hold on to and comforted his hot belly. This picture at least, which was entirely hidden beneath him, was going to be removed by nobody. He turned his head toward the door of the living room so as to observe the women when they came back.

They had not allowed themselves much of a rest and were already coming; Grete had twined her arm around her mother and was almost supporting her. "Well, what shall we take now?" said Grete, looking around. Her eyes met Gregor's from the wall. She kept her composure, presumably because of her mother, bent her head down to her mother, to keep her from looking up, and said, although in a fluttering, unpremeditated voice: "Come, hadn't we better go back to the living room for a moment?" Her intentions were clear enough to Gregor, she wanted to bestow her mother in safety and then chase him down from the wall. Well, just let her try it! He clung to his picture and would not give it up. He would rather fly in Grete's face. B

But Grete's words had succeeded in disquieting her mother, who took a step to one side, caught sight of the huge brown mass on the flowered wallpaper, and before she was really conscious that what she saw was Gregor, screamed in a loud, hoarse voice: "Oh God, oh God!" fell with outspread arms over the sofa as if giving up, and did not move. "Gregor!" cried his sister, shaking her fist and glaring at him. This was the first time she had directly addressed him since his metamorphosis. She ran into the next room for some aromatic essence[23] with which to rouse her mother from her fainting fit. Gregor wanted to help too—there was still time to rescue the picture—but he was stuck fast to the glass and had to tear himself loose; he then ran after his sister into the next room as if he could advise her, as he used to do; but then had to stand helplessly behind her; C

22. **ejaculations:** sudden, brief statements or exclamations.

23. **aromatic essence:** strong-smelling solution.

Nächtlicher lärm [Nightly noise] (1919), Georg Scholz. Oil on canvas, 56.8 cm × 50.9 cm. The Marvin and Janet Fishman Collection, Milwaukee, Wisconsin.

she meanwhile searched among various small bottles and when she turned around started in alarm at the sight of him; one bottle fell on the floor and broke; a splinter of glass cut Gregor's face and some kind of corrosive[24] medicine splashed him; without pausing a moment longer Grete gathered up all the bottles she could carry and ran to her mother with them; she banged the door shut with her foot. Gregor was now cut off from his mother, who was perhaps nearly dying because of him; he dared not open the door for fear of frightening away his sister, who had to stay with her mother; there was nothing he could do but wait; and harassed by self-reproach and worry he began now to crawl to and fro, over everything, walls, furniture, and ceiling, and finally in his despair, when the whole room seemed to be reeling around him, fell down onto the middle of the big table.

24. **corrosive** (kə-rō′sĭv): capable of eating away solid substances.

Customizing Instruction

Less Proficient Readers
Help students understand the change that has taken place in Grete. Ask them to find examples in the text that show her strength. *(She supports her mother as they walk. She shakes her fist and glares at Gregor. She rushes to help her mother when she faints.)*

MINI LESSON Viewing and Representing

Nächtlicher lärm (Nightly Noise) **by Georg Scholz**

ART APPRECIATION Georg Scholz was part of the art movement known as Expressionism, which was centered in Germany from the early to mid-twentieth century. In this style of art, the images often represented strong political views or the despair and misery of those affected by social ills. Ask students to identify as many of these images in the painting as they can. *(buildings, people who appear to be carrying bottles, a person screaming)* Then point out the English translation of the title in parentheses. Encourage students to offer their interpretations of the painting based on the title and its style.

Possible Response: The bold colors against the dark background and the person screaming suggest that the noises are not pleasant. The person screaming may be fearful of the people with bottles. The scene appears to be a neighborhood disturbance.

Then ask students how the painting enhances the story.

Possible Response: The person screaming could be Gregor because he fears losing his humanity. The painting suggests a dark, despairing mood, similar to the mood throughout most of the story.

Literary Analysis MOOD

Ask students to discuss how the mood in the story has changed.

Possible Response: The mood is very serious. Gregor's life is in danger.

Reading Skills and Strategies DRAWING CONCLUSIONS

A Ask students what conclusions they can draw about how Gregor's father felt when he first discovered Gregor was a bug.

Possible Response: He may have thought Gregor was dangerous and wanted to get rid of him when the transformation first occurred. The mother and daughter were probably against the idea.

Active Reading VISUALIZING DETAILS

B Point out that Kafka presents two different images of the father to the reader. Ask students why Gregor finds the second image so frightening.

Possible Response: Gregor's father appears very strong in his work uniform. Even though Gregor is a large bug, his father is much bigger from Gregor's vantage point on the floor.

Pause & Reflect

Possible Response: The father is angry because he always believed there was a chance that Gregor might escape and cause harm.

Literary Analysis IRONY

C Ask students to explain the irony of the father's decision to be more patient with Gregor.

Possible Response: The father's patience has limits since he never tries to remove the apple from Gregor's back.

A little while elapsed, Gregor was still lying there feebly and all around was quiet, perhaps that was a good omen. Then the doorbell rang. The servant girl was of course locked in her kitchen, and Grete would have to open the door. It was his father. "What's been happening?" were his first words; Grete's face must have told him everything. Grete answered in a muffled voice, apparently hiding her head on his breast: "Mother has been fainting, but she's better now. Gregor's broken loose." "Just what I expected," said his father, "just what I've been telling you, but you women would never listen." It was clear to Gregor that his father had taken the worst interpretation of Grete's all too brief statement and was assuming that Gregor had been guilty of some violent act. Therefore Gregor must now try to propitiate[25] his father, since he had neither time nor means for an explanation. And so he fled to the door of his own room and crouched against it, to let his father see as soon as he came in from the hall that his son had the good intention of getting back into his room immediately and that it was not necessary to drive him there, but that if only the door were opened he would disappear at once.

Yet his father was not in the mood to perceive such fine[26] distinctions. "Ah!" he cried as soon as he appeared, in a tone that sounded at once angry and exultant. Gregor drew his head back from the door and lifted it to look at his father. Truly, this was not the father he had imagined to himself; admittedly he had been too absorbed of late in his new recreation of crawling over the ceiling to take the same interest as before in what was happening elsewhere in the flat, and he ought really to be prepared for some changes. And yet, and yet, could that be his father? The man who used to lie wearily sunk in bed whenever Gregor set out on a business journey; who welcomed him back of an evening lying in a long chair in a dressing gown; who could not really rise to his feet but only lifted his arms in greeting, and on the rare occasions when he did go out with his family, on one or two Sundays a year and on highest holidays,[27] walked between Gregor and his mother, who were slow walkers anyhow, even more slowly than they did, muffled in his old greatcoat, shuffling laboriously forward with the help of his crook-handled stick which he set down most cautiously at every step and, whenever he wanted to say anything, nearly always came to a full stop and gathered his escort around him? Now he was standing there in fine shape; dressed in a smart blue uniform with gold buttons, such as bank messengers wear; his strong double chin bulged over the stiff high collar of his jacket; from under his bushy eyebrows his black eyes darted fresh and penetrating glances; his onetime tangled white hair had been combed flat on either side of a shining and carefully exact parting.[28] He pitched his cap, which bore a gold monogram, probably the badge of some bank, in a wide sweep across the whole room onto a sofa and with the tail-ends of his jacket thrown back, his hands in his trouser pockets, advanced with a grim visage[29] toward Gregor. Likely enough he did not himself know what he meant to do; at any rate he lifted his feet uncommonly high, and Gregor was dumbfounded at the enormous size of his shoe soles. But Gregor could not risk standing up to him, aware as he had been from the very first day of his new life that his father believed only the severest measures suitable for dealing with him. And so he ran before his father, stopping when he stopped and scuttling forward again when his

25. **propitiate** (prō-pĭsh′ē-āt′): calm; soothe.
26. **fine:** subtle; precise.
27. **highest holidays:** Rosh Hashanah and Yom Kippur, the Jewish New Year and Day of Atonement.
28. **parting:** part.
29. **visage:** face.

father made any kind of move. In this way they circled the room several times without anything decisive happening, indeed the whole operation did not even look like a pursuit because it was carried out so slowly. And so Gregor did not leave the floor, for he feared that his father might take as a piece of peculiar wickedness any excursion of his over the walls or the ceiling. All the same, he could not stay this course much longer, for while his father took one step he had to carry out a whole series of movements. He was already beginning to feel breathless, just as in his former life his lungs had not been very dependable. As he was staggering along, trying to concentrate his energy on running, hardly keeping his eyes open; in his dazed state never even thinking of any other escape than simply going forward; and having almost forgotten that the walls were free to him, which in this room were well provided with finely carved pieces of furniture full of knobs and crevices—suddenly something lightly flung landed close behind him and rolled before him. It was an apple; a second apple followed immediately; Gregor came to a stop in alarm; there was no point in running on, for his father was determined to bombard him. He had filled his pockets with fruit from the dish on the sideboard and was now shying apple after apple, without taking particularly good aim for the moment. The small red apples rolled about the floor as if magnetized and cannoned into each other. An apple thrown without much force grazed Gregor's back and glanced off harmlessly. But another following immediately landed right on his back and sank in; Gregor wanted to drag himself forward, as if this startling, incredible pain could be left behind him; but he felt as if nailed to the spot and flattened himself out in a
2 complete derangement of all his senses. With his last conscious look he saw the door of his room being torn open and his mother rushing out ahead of his screaming sister, in her underbodice, for her daughter had loosened her clothing to let her breathe more freely and recover from her swoon, he saw his mother rushing toward his father, leaving one after another behind her on the floor her loosened petticoats, stumbling over her petticoats straight to his father and embracing him, in complete union with him—but here Gregor's sight began to fail—with her hands clasped around his father's neck as she begged for her son's life.

PAUSE & REFLECT Why does the furniture-moving episode lead to the father's attack on Gregor?

FOCUS Gregor has been seriously wounded by the apple. Read to find out how Gregor and his family respond to his decline.

The serious injury done to Gregor, which disabled him for more than a month—the apple went on sticking in his body as a visible reminder, since no one ventured to remove it—seemed to have made even his father recollect that Gregor was a member of the family, despite his present unfortunate and repulsive shape, and ought not to be treated as an enemy, that, on the contrary, family duty required the suppression[30] of disgust and the exercise of patience, nothing but patience. C

And though his injury had impaired, probably forever, his powers of movement, and for the time being it took him long, long minutes to creep across his room like an old invalid—there was no question now of crawling up the wall—yet in his own opinion he was sufficiently compensated for this worsening of his condition by the fact that toward evening the living-room

30. **suppression** (sə-prĕsh′ən): holding back or keeping in.

Customizing Instruction

Less Proficient Readers

1 Make sure students understand what Gregor's father plans to do.
(step on Gregor with his shoe)

Focus Help students use the Focus on this page by pointing out that this is the last section of the story. Suggest they keep a list that details each character's reaction.

English Learners

2 Help students understand that the phrase "complete derangement of all his senses" means "a state of shock."

Advanced Learners

Have students discuss what the father's attack on Gregor might reveal about their relationship before the transformation.

Possible Response: His father may not have had much patience or interaction with Gregor before the transformation. Gregor spent a lot of time on the road in his job and his free time was spent on solitary activities, so he and his father probably did not have a close relationship.

Assessment Informal Assessment

CHARACTER RESPONSES Have students create direct quotations for each member of Gregor's family. Tell students that each character should express how he or she feels about Gregor. Remind students that direct quotations are the exact words of the character and should be punctuated with quotation marks. Each quote should reflect how each family member has responded so far to Gregor's transformation.

RUBRIC

3 **Full Accomplishment** Student's quotes show a thorough understanding of the events in the story and how they affect Gregor's relationship with each family member. The quotes are punctuated properly.

2 **Substantial Accomplishment** Student's quotes show a limited amount of understanding of the events in the story and may not grasp all of the dynamics of Gregor's relationships with his family. The quotes are punctuated properly.

1 **Little or Partial Accomplishment** Student's quotes show little or no understanding of the events in the story and how they affect Gregor's relationship with each family member. The quotes may not be punctuated properly.

Reading Skills and Strategies
CLARIFYING

A Ask students what the family does to make Gregor feel like he is still a part of the family.
Possible Response: They leave the living room door open so that he can see them.

CLARIFYING

B Make sure that students understand that *intercourse* means "conversation" in this passage.

Literary Analysis
CHARACTERIZATION

C One method of characterization is through a description of appearance. Ask students what changes in the father's character are revealed in this passage.
Possible Response: Because the father never bothers to change his clothes, he feels his situation is hopeless.

Reading Skills and Strategies
SUMMARIZING

Ask students to summarize how the family copes without Gregor's salary.
Possible Response: Everyone has a job. The mother makes underwear, the sister is a sales clerk, and the father is a bank messenger. They let the servant girl go, and a cleaning woman comes twice a day to do heavy work. The mother and sister sell some of their jewelry.

A door, which he used to watch intently for an hour or two beforehand, was always thrown open, so that lying in the darkness of his room, invisible to the family, he could see them all at the lamp-lit table and listen to their talk, by general consent as it were, very different from his earlier eavesdropping.

B True, their intercourse lacked the lively character of former times, which he had always called to mind with a certain wistfulness in the small hotel bedrooms where he had been wont to throw himself down, tired out, on damp bedding. They were now mostly very silent. Soon after supper his father would fall asleep in his armchair; his mother and sister would admonish each other to be silent; his mother, bending low over the lamp, stitched at fine sewing for an underwear firm; his sister, who had taken a job as a salesgirl, was learning shorthand and French in the evenings on the chance of bettering herself. Sometimes his father woke up, and as if quite unaware that he had been sleeping said to his mother: "What a lot of sewing you're doing today!" and at once fell asleep again, while the two women exchanged a tired smile.

C With a kind of mulishness his father persisted in keeping his uniform on even in the house; his dressing gown hung uselessly on its peg and he slept fully dressed where he sat, as if he were ready for service at any moment and even here only at the beck and call of his superior. As a result, his uniform, which was not brand-new to start with, began to look dirty, despite all the loving care of the mother and sister to keep it clean, and Gregor often spent whole evenings gazing at the many greasy spots on the garment, gleaming with gold buttons always in a high state of polish, in which the old man sat sleeping in extreme discomfort and yet quite peacefully.

As soon as the clock struck ten his mother tried to rouse his father with gentle words and to persuade him after that to get into bed, for sitting there he could not have a proper sleep and

Le Lessive [TheWash] (1921), Maria Blanchard. Oil on canvas. Museum of Modern Art, Paris. © SuperStock.

that was what he needed most, since he had to go on duty at six. But with the mulishness that had obsessed him since he became a bank messenger he always insisted on staying longer at the table, although he regularly fell asleep again and in the end only with the greatest trouble could be got out of his armchair and into his bed. However insistently Gregor's mother and sister kept urging him with gentle reminders, he would go on slowly

with gentle reminders, he would go on slowly shaking his head for a quarter of an hour, keeping his eyes shut, and refuse to get to his feet. The mother plucked at his sleeve, whispering endearments in his ear, the sister left her lessons to come to her mother's help, but Gregor's father was not to be caught. He would only sink down deeper in his chair. Not until the two women hoisted him up by the armpits did he open his eyes and look at them both, one after the other, usually with the remark: "This is a life. This is the peace and quiet of my old age." And leaning on the two of them he would heave himself up, with difficulty, as if he were a great burden to himself, suffer them to lead him as far as the door and then wave them off and go on alone, while the mother abandoned her needlework and the sister her pen in order to run after him and help him farther.

...A GIGANTIC BONY CHARWOMAN WITH WHITE HAIR FLYING AROUND HER HEAD CAME IN MORNING AND EVENING TO DO THE ROUGH WORK....

Who could find time, in this overworked and tired-out family, to bother about Gregor more than was absolutely needful? The household was reduced more and more; the servant girl was turned off; a gigantic bony charwoman[31] with white hair flying around her head came in morning and evening to do the rough work; everything else was done by Gregor's mother, as well as great piles of sewing. Even various family ornaments, which his mother and sister used to wear with pride at parties and celebrations, had to be sold, as Gregor discovered of an evening from hearing them all discuss the prices obtained. But what they lamented most was the fact that they could not leave the flat which was much too big for their present circumstances, because they could not think of any way to shift Gregor. Yet Gregor saw well enough that consideration for him was not the main difficulty preventing the removal, for they could have easily shifted him in some suitable box with a few air holes in it; what really kept them from moving into another flat was rather their own complete hopelessness and the belief that they had been singled out for a misfortune such as had never happened to any of their relations or acquaintances. They fulfilled to the uttermost all that the world demands of poor people, the father fetched breakfast for the small clerks in the bank, the mother devoted her energy to making underwear for strangers, the sister trotted to and fro behind the counter at the behest of customers, but more than this they had not the strength to do. And the wound in Gregor's back began to nag at him afresh when his mother and sister, after getting his father into bed, came back again, left their work lying, drew close to each other, and sat cheek by cheek; when his mother, pointing toward his room, said: "Shut that door now, Grete," and he was left again in the darkness, while next door the women mingled their tears or perhaps sat dry-eyed staring at the table.

1

Gregor hardly slept at all by night or by day. He was often haunted by the idea that next time the door opened he would take the family's affairs in hand again just as he used to do; once more, after this long interval, there appeared in his thoughts the figures of the chief and the chief clerk, the commercial travelers

31. charwoman: cleaning woman.

Customizing Instruction

Less Proficient Readers

Help students understand the change that Gregor's father undergoes after his attack on Gregor. Have them contrast his appearance with his behavior. *(When Gregor's father attacks him, he appears robust in his uniform and quite imposing. Afterwards, he spends a lot of time sleeping in his uniform and has to be helped to his room by his wife and daughter.)*

Advanced Learners

1 Gregor's family feels that they are victims of his condition. Ask students who they think is the victim in this story—Gregor or his family. Invite students with opposing views to debate this issue using examples from the text to support their arguments.

Reading and Analyzing

Literary Analysis IRONY

A Ask students to explain the irony of the family's argument about Gregor's care.

Possible Response: They have all been ignoring him but still want to argue about how his room should be cleaned.

Reading Skills and Strategies DRAWING CONCLUSIONS

B Point out that Kafka reveals the kind of bug Gregor is through the charwoman. Tell students to think about what they have learned about dung beetles. Then ask them to draw conclusions about Gregor's ability to eat food earlier in the story and his inability to eat it now.

Possible Response: Gregor was still more human earlier in the story, so he was able to eat some food. His transformation to something like a dung beetle is almost complete; therefore, he can no longer eat food because dung beetles eat only manure.

Reading Skills and Strategies SUMMARIZING

C Have students describe how Gregor's life changes when his family takes in lodgers.

Possible Response: The family pushes things in his room to make room for the guests. Because of all the junk in his room, he has no room to crawl. Because of the lodgers' presence, the door is no longer left open.

Literary Analysis FORESHADOWING

D Sometimes a writer uses clues to add suspense and to prepare the reader for future events in a story.

Ask students what future event might Kafka be preparing them for by mentioning that the lodgers like order and cleanliness.

Possible Response: Kafka is setting up a possible confrontation between Gregor and the lodgers, who are sure to react negatively because a bug represents filth.

and the apprentices, the porter who was so dull-witted, two or three friends in other firms, a chambermaid in one of the rural hotels, a sweet and fleeting memory, a cashier in a milliner's[32] shop, who he had wooed earnestly but too slowly—they all appeared, together with strangers or people he had quite forgotten, but instead of helping him and his family they were one and all unapproachable, and he was glad when they vanished. At other times he would not be in the mood to bother about his family, he was only filled with rage at the way they were neglecting him, and although he had no clear idea of what he might care to eat he would make plans for getting into the larder to take the food that was after all his due, even if he were not hungry. His sister no longer took thought to bring him what might especially please him; but in the morning and at noon before she went to business hurriedly pushed into his room with her foot any food that was available, and in the evening cleared it out again with one sweep of the broom, heedless of whether it had been merely tasted, or—as most frequently happened—left untouched. The cleaning of his room, which she now did always in the evenings, could not have been more hastily done. Streaks of dirt stretched along the walls, here and there lay balls of dust and filth. At first Gregor used to station himself in some particularly filthy corner when his sister arrived, in order to reproach her with it, so to speak. But he could have sat there for weeks without getting her to make any improvement; she could see the dirt as well as he did, but she had simply made up her mind to leave it alone. And yet, with a touchiness that was new to her, which seemed anyhow to have infected the whole family, she jealously guarded her claim to be the sole caretaker of Gregor's room. His mother once subjected his room to a thorough cleaning, which was achieved only by means of several buckets of water—all this dampness of course upset Gregor too and he lay widespread, sulky, and motionless on the sofa—but she was well punished for it. Hardly had his sister noticed the changed aspect of his room that evening than she rushed in high dudgeon[33] into the living room and, despite the imploringly raised hands of her mother, burst into a storm of weeping, while her parents—her father had of course been startled out of his chair—looked on at first in helpless amazement; then they too began to go into action; the father reproached the mother on his right for not having left the cleaning of Gregor's room to his sister; shrieked at the sister on his left that never again was she to be allowed to clean Gregor's room; while the mother tried to pull the father into his bedroom, since he was beyond himself with agitation; the sister, shaken with sobs, then beat upon the table with her small fists; and Gregor hissed loudly with rage because not one of them thought of shutting the door to spare him such a spectacle and so much noise. A

Still, even if the sister, exhausted by her daily work, had grown tired of looking after Gregor as she did formerly, there was no need for his mother's intervention or for Gregor's being neglected at all. The charwoman was there. This old widow, whose strong bony frame had enabled her to survive the worst a long life could offer, by no means recoiled from Gregor. Without being in the least curious she had once by chance opened the door of his room and at the sight of Gregor, who, taken by surprise, began to rush to and fro although no one was chasing him, merely stood there with her arms folded. From that time she never failed to open his door a little for a moment, morning and evening, to have a look at him. At first she even used to call him to her,

32. **milliner's:** hat maker's.

33. **in high dudgeon:** very angry.

with words which apparently she took to be friendly, such as: "Come along, then, you old dung beetle!" or "Look at the old dung beetle, then!" To such allocutions[34] Gregor made no answer, but stayed motionless where he was, as if the door had never been opened. Instead of being allowed to disturb him so senselessly whenever the whim took her, she should rather have been ordered to clean out his room daily, that charwoman! Once, early in the morning—heavy rain was lashing on the windowpanes, perhaps a sign that spring was on the way—Gregor was so exasperated when she began addressing him again that he ran at her, as if to attack her, although slowly and feebly enough. But the charwoman instead of showing fright merely lifted high a chair that happened to be beside the door, and as she stood there with her mouth wide open it was clear that she meant to shut it only when she brought the chair down on Gregor's back. "So you're not coming any nearer?" she asked, as Gregor turned away again, and quietly put the chair back into the corner.

Gregor was now eating hardly anything. Only when he happened to pass the food laid out for him did he take a bit of something in his mouth as a pastime, kept it there for an hour at a time, and usually spat it out again. At first he thought it was chagrin over the state of his room that prevented him from eating, yet he soon got used to the various changes in his room. It had become a habit in the family to push into his room things there was no room for elsewhere, and there were plenty of these now, since one of the rooms had been let to three lodgers. These serious gentlemen—all three of them with full beards, as Gregor once observed through a crack in the door—had a passion for order, not only in their own room but, since they were now members of the household, in all its arrangements, especially in the kitchen. Superfluous, not to say dirty, objects they could not bear. Besides, they had brought with them most of the furnishings they needed. For this reason many things could be dispensed with that it was no use trying to sell but that should not be thrown away either. All of them found their way into Gregor's room. The ash can likewise and the kitchen garbage can. Anything that was not needed for the moment was simply flung into Gregor's room by the charwoman, who did everything in a hurry; fortunately Gregor usually saw only the object, whatever it was, and the hand that held it. Perhaps she intended to take the things away again as time and opportunity offered, or to collect them until she could throw them all out in a heap, but in fact they just lay wherever she happened to throw them, except when Gregor pushed his way through the junk heap and shifted it somewhat, at first out of necessity, because he had not room enough to crawl, but later with increasing enjoyment, although after such excursions, being sad and weary to death, he would lie motionless for hours. And since the lodgers often ate their supper at home in the common living room, the living-room door stayed shut many an evening, yet Gregor reconciled himself quite easily to the shutting of the door, for often enough on evenings when it was opened he had disregarded it entirely and lain in the darkest corner of his room, quite unnoticed by the family. But on one occasion the charwoman left the door open a little and it stayed ajar even when the lodgers came in for supper and the lamp was lit. They set themselves at the top end of the table where formerly Gregor and his father and mother had eaten their meals, unfolded their napkins, and took knife and fork in hand. At once his mother appeared in the other doorway with a dish of meat and close behind her his sister with a dish of potatoes piled high. The food steamed with a thick vapor. The lodgers bent over the food set before them as if to scrutinize it before

34. **allocutions** (ăl′ə-kyo͞o′shənz): formal speeches. (The word is meant ironically here.)

WORDS TO KNOW

chagrin (shə-grĭn′) *n.* a feeling of disappointment or humiliation

Customizing Instruction

Less Proficient Readers

Set a Purpose Have students think about all the ways Gregor's life has changed as they read these pages. Suggest that they record the changes in a list.

METAMORPHOSIS **1139**

Reading and Analyzing

Literary Analysis CHARACTER

What changes occur in the family's behavior because of the lodgers?

Possible Response: They act like servants. They eat their meals in the kitchen. They are afraid to sit in their favorite chairs in the lodgers' presence.

Literary Analysis IRONY

Have students explain the irony of the family's treatment of the lodgers.

Possible Response: They make every effort to make the lodgers, who are strangers, comfortable; Gregor, a family member, starves in a room full of junk.

Literary Analysis CHARACTER MOTIVATION

(A) Have students tell what motivates Gregor's outpouring of human emotions.

Possible Response: The lodgers do not seem to care for Grete's violin playing, which Gregor has always loved.

The Skat Players (1920), Otto Dix. Oil and collage on canvas. © 2007 Artists Rights Society (ARS), New York/VG Bild-Kunst, Bonn.

seemed to pass for an authority with the other two, cut a piece of meat as it lay on the dish, obviously to discover if it were tender or should be sent back to the kitchen. He showed satisfaction, and Gregor's mother and sister, who had been watching anxiously, breathed freely and began to smile.

The family itself took its meals in the kitchen. Nonetheless, Gregor's father came into the living room before going into the kitchen and with one prolonged bow, cap in hand, made a round of the table. The lodgers all stood up and murmured something in their beards. When they were alone again they ate their food in almost complete silence. It seemed remarkable to Gregor that among the various noises coming from the table he could always distinguish the sound of their masticating[35] teeth, as if this were a sign to Gregor that one needed teeth in order to eat, and that with toothless jaws even of the finest make one could do nothing. "I'm hungry enough," said Gregor sadly to himself, "but not for that kind of food. How these lodgers are stuffing themselves, and here I am dying of starvation!"

On that very evening—during the whole of his time there Gregor could not remember ever having heard the violin—the sound of violin-playing came from the kitchen. The lodgers had already finished their supper, the one in the middle had brought out a newspaper and given the other two a page apiece, and now they were leaning back at ease reading and smoking. When the violin began to play they pricked up their ears, got to their feet, and went on tiptoe to the hall door where they stood huddled together. Their movements must have been heard in the kitchen, for Gregor's father called out: "Is the violin-playing disturbing you, gentlemen? It can be stopped at once." "On the contrary," said the middle lodger, "could not Fräulein[36] Samsa come and play in this room, beside us, where it is much more convenient and comfortable?" "Oh certainly," cried Gregor's father, as if he were the violin-player. The lodgers came back into the living room and waited. Presently Gregor's father arrived with the music stand, his mother carrying the music and his sister with the violin. His sister quietly made everything ready to start playing; his parents, who had never let rooms before and so had an exaggerated idea of the courtesy due to lodgers, did not venture to sit down on their own chairs; his father leaned against the door, the right hand thrust between two buttons of his livery coat, which was formally buttoned up; but his mother was offered a chair by one of the lodgers and, since she left the chair just where he had happened to put it, sat down in a corner to one side.

Gregor's sister began to play; the father and

35. **masticating:** chewing.

36. **Fräulein** (froi'lĭn'): the German equivalent of "Miss."

MINI LESSON Viewing and Representing

Die Skatspieler (Skat Players) **by Otto Dix**

ART APPRECIATION Otto Dix, a German artist, was part of the art movement known as Expressionism. Expressionist art was often characterized by distorted images that represented political views. Have students discuss how the men in the painting are distorted. *(The men have grotesque facial expressions. It's hard to tell their legs from the table legs. One man appears to be holding his cards between his toes. One man doesn't have an eye, while another has an eye that is much larger than the other.)* Ask students to point out other details in the painting. *(The men are playing cards. One man is wearing a medal.)* Then ask students why this painting of three men playing cards is appropriate for this story.

Possible Response: The grotesque features of the men signify that they are being portrayed as monsters. The dark background and hard edges give the impression that the card game is unfriendly and each player is trying to overpower the others. The three men may represent an oppressive Nazi government. They can be compared to the three lodgers. The lodgers are also portrayed as monsters that act as if they own the apartment that Gregor's family lives in.

"MR. SAMSA!" CRIED THE MIDDLE LODGER TO GREGOR'S FATHER, AND POINTED, WITHOUT WASTING ANY MORE WORDS, AT GREGOR, NOW WORKING HIMSELF SLOWLY FORWARD.

Gregor's sister began to play; the father and mother, from either side, intently watched the movements of her hands. Gregor, attracted by the playing, ventured to move forward a little until his head was actually inside the living room. He felt hardly any surprise at his growing lack of consideration for the others; there had been a time when he prided himself on being considerate. And yet just on this occasion he had more reason than ever to hide himself, since, owing to the amount of dust that lay thick in his room and rose into the air at the slightest movement, he too was covered with dust; fluff and hair and remnants of food trailed with him, caught on his back and along his sides; his indifference to everything was much too great for him to turn on his back and scrape himself clean on the carpet, as once he had done several times a day. And in spite of his condition, no shame deterred him from advancing a little over the spotless floor of the living room.

To be sure, no one was aware of him. The family was entirely absorbed in the violin-playing; the lodgers, however, who first of all had stationed themselves, hands in pockets, much too close behind the music stand so that they could all have read the music, which must have bothered his sister, had soon retreated to the window, half whispering with downbent heads, and stayed there while his father turned an anxious eye on them. Indeed, they were making it more than obvious that they had been disappointed in their expectation of hearing good or enjoyable violin-playing, that they had had more than enough of the performance and only out of courtesy suffered a continued disturbance of their peace. From the way they all kept blowing the smoke of their cigars high in the air through nose and mouth one could divine their irritation. And yet Gregor's sister was playing so beautifully. Her face leaned sideways, intently and sadly her eyes followed the notes of music. Gregor crawled a little farther forward and lowered his head to the ground so that it might be possible for his eyes to meet hers. Was he an animal, that music had such an effect upon him? He felt as if the way were opening before him to the unknown nourishment he craved. He was determined to push forward till he reached his sister, to pull at her skirt and so let her know that she was to come into his room with her violin, for no one here appreciated her playing as he would appreciate it. He would never let her out of his room, at least, not so long as he lived; his frightful appearance would become, for the first time, useful to him; he would watch all the doors of his room at once and spit at intruders; but his sister should need no constraint, she should stay with him out of her own free will; she should sit beside him on the sofa, bend down her ear to him, and hear him confide that he had had the firm intention of sending her to the Conservatorium, and that, but for his mishap, last Christmas—surely Christmas was long past?—he would have announced it to everybody without allowing a single objection. After this confession his sister would be so touched that she would burst into tears, and Gregor would then raise himself to her shoulder and kiss her on the neck, which, now that she went to business, she kept free of any ribbon or collar.

"Mr. Samsa!" cried the middle lodger to Gregor's father, and pointed, without wasting any more words, at Gregor, now working himself slowly forward. The violin fell silent, the middle

Customizing Instruction

Less Proficient Readers

1 Have students describe what Gregor plans to do when he reaches his sister. *(Gregor plans to pull at his sister's skirt to let her know that she is to come into his room where her violin playing will be appreciated.)*

Reading Skills and Strategies
QUESTIONING

A Ask students if they are surprised by the middle lodger's response.
Possible Response: Yes, since he and his friends like everything so orderly.

Reading Skills and Strategies
PREDICTING

Remind students of the lodgers' aversion to dirt. Have students use this clue and the middle lodger's smile to predict what might happen.

Reading Skills and Strategies
EVALUATING

B Have students discuss the significance of the speech by the middle lodger. Students will probably recognize the speech as the event that was foreshadowed by the middle lodger's unusual reaction. Ask students why the middle lodger smiles at his friends.
Possible Response: He smiles because Gregor's presence is an opportunity for him and his friends to complain about the unsanitary living conditions and thus get out of paying for their lodging.

Literary Analysis CHARACTER

Ask students why Grete has changed her attitude toward Gregor.
Possible Response: She was willing to put up with him as long as he stayed in his room. When he ventured into the living room, he ruined an otherwise pleasant evening.

Ask students how Grete shows she no longer views Gregor as her brother.
Possible Response: She refers to him as *it*.

lodger first smiled to his friends with a shake of
A the head and then looked at Gregor again. Instead of driving Gregor out, his father seemed to think it more needful to begin by soothing down the lodgers, although they were not at all agitated and apparently found Gregor more entertaining than the violin-playing. He hurried toward them and, spreading out his arms, tried to urge them back into their own room and at the same time to block their view of Gregor. They now began to be really a little angry, one
1 could not tell whether because of the old man's behavior or because it had just dawned on them that all unwittingly they had such a neighbor as Gregor next door. They demanded explanations of his father, they waved their arms like him, tugged uneasily at their beards, and only with reluctance backed toward their room. Meanwhile, Gregor's sister, who stood there as if lost when her playing was so abruptly broken off, came to life again, pulled herself together all at once after standing for a while holding violin and bow in nervelessly hanging hands and staring at her music, pushed her violin into the lap of her mother, who was still sitting in her chair fighting asthmatically for breath, and ran into the lodgers' room to which they were now being shepherded by her father rather more quickly than before. One could see the pillows and blankets on the beds flying under her accustomed fingers and being laid in order. Before the lodgers had actually reached their room she had finished making the beds and slipped out.

The old man seemed once more to be so possessed by his mulish self-assertiveness that he was forgetting all the respect he should show to his lodgers. He kept driving them on and driving them on until in the very door of the bedroom the middle lodger stamped his foot loudly on the floor and so brought him to a halt. "I beg to announce," said the lodger, lifting one hand and looking also at Gregor's mother and sister, "that because of the disgusting conditions prevailing in this household and family"—here he spat on the floor with emphatic brevity[37]—"I give you notice on the spot. Naturally I won't pay you a penny for the
days I have lived here, on the contrary I shall con- B
sider bringing an action for damages against you, based on claims—believe me—that will be easily susceptible[38] of proof." He ceased and stared straight in front of him, as if he expected something. In fact his two friends at once rushed into the breach[39] with these words: "And we too give notice on the spot." On that he seized the door handle and shut the door with a slam.

Gregor's father, groping with his hands, staggered forward and fell into his chair; it looked as if he were stretching himself there for his ordinary evening nap, but the marked jerkings of his head, which were as if uncontrollable, showed that he was far from asleep. Gregor had simply stayed quietly all the time on the spot where the lodgers had espied him. Disappointment at the failure of his plan, perhaps also the weakness arising from extreme hunger, made it impossible for him to move. He feared, with a fair degree of certainty, that at any moment the general tension would discharge itself in a combined attack upon him, and he lay waiting. He did not react even to the noise made by the violin as it fell off his mother's lap from under her trembling fingers and gave out a resonant note.

"My dear parents," said his sister, slapping her hand on the table by way of introduction, "things can't go on like this. Perhaps you don't realize that, but I do. I won't utter my brother's name in the presence of this creature, and so all I say is: we must try to get rid of it. We've tried to look after it and to put up with it as far as is

37. **brevity:** briefness; abruptness.
38. **susceptible of:** open to.
39. **breach:** gap; opening.

humanly possible, and I don't think anyone could reproach us in the slightest."

"She is more than right," said Gregor's father to himself. His mother, who was still choking for lack of breath, began to cough hollowly into her hand with a wild look in her eyes.

His sister rushed over to her and held her forehead. His father's thoughts seemed to have lost their vagueness at Grete's words, he sat more upright, fingering his service cap that lay among the plates still lying on the table from the lodgers' supper, and from time to time looked at the still form of Gregor.

"We must try to get rid of it," his sister now said explicitly to her father, since her mother was coughing too much to hear a word, "it will be the death of both of you, I can see that coming. When one has to work as hard as we do, all of us, one can't stand this continual torment at home on top of it. At least I can't stand it any longer." And she burst into such a passion of sobbing that her tears dropped on her mother's face, where she wiped them off mechanically.

"My dear," said the old man sympathetically, and with evident understanding, "but what can we do?"

Gregor's sister merely shrugged her shoulders to indicate the feeling of helplessness that had now overmastered her during her weeping fit, in contrast to her former confidence.

"If he could understand us," said her father, half questioningly; Grete, still sobbing, vehemently waved a hand to show how unthinkable that was.

"If he could understand us," repeated the old man, shutting his eyes to consider his daughter's conviction that understanding was impossible, "then perhaps we might come to some agreement with him. But as it is—"

"He must go," cried Gregor's sister, "that's the only solution, Father. You must just try to get rid of the idea that this is Gregor. The fact that we've believed it for so long is the root of all our trouble. But how can it be Gregor? If this were Gregor, he would have realized long ago that human beings can't live with such a creature, and he'd have gone away on his own accord. Then we wouldn't have any brother, but we'd be able to go on living and keep his memory in honor. As it is, this creature persecutes us, drives away our lodgers, obviously wants the whole apartment to himself, and would have us all sleep in the gutter. Just look, Father," she shrieked all at once, "he's at it again!" And in an access[40] of panic that was quite incomprehensible to Gregor she even quitted her mother, literally 2
thrusting the chair from her as if she would rather sacrifice her mother than stay so near to Gregor, and rushed behind her father, who also rose up, being simply upset by her agitation, and half spread his arms out as if to protect her.

Yet Gregor had not the slightest intention of frightening anyone, far less his sister. He had only begun to turn around in order to crawl back to his room, but it was certainly a startling operation to watch, since because of his disabled condition he could not execute the difficult turning movements except by lifting his head and then bracing it against the floor over and over again. He paused and looked around. His good

40. access: outburst.

Customizing Instruction

Less Proficient Readers

1 Ask students to describe in their own words what happens when the father tries to coax the lodgers into their bedroom.

English Learners

2 Explain to students that *quitted* doesn't mean "stop" in this instance. Here it means "left or abandoned." Grete would rather put her mother in harm's way than let Gregor get anywhere near her.

Advanced Learners

Have students discuss how Kafka shows Grete's change in character. *(He allows the narrator to quote Grete. She is so confident that her father agrees with her proposal.)*

Reading Strategies and Skills
EVALUATING

Ask students who they think is more human—Gregor or his family. Remind them to use evidence from the story to support their opinions.

Possible Response: Some students may say Gregor, because he remains loyal to his family and knows that the best thing for him in his condition is to die. Others may say his family, because each family member gets a job and changes his or her routine to accommodate his condition.

Literary Analysis POINT OF VIEW

A Have students note that there are no more of Gregor's reactions or reponses. Ask them why this happens.

Possible Response: Gregor dies, so the story can no longer tell what he is thinking.

Literary Analysis IRONY

B Ask students what is ironic about the family's failure to feed breakfast to the lodgers.

Possible Response: Gregor is now getting the attention he wanted when he was alive. The lodgers, who had been treated like royalty the night before, are being ignored.

"AND WHAT NOW?" SAID GREGOR TO HIMSELF, LOOKING AROUND IN THE DARKNESS. SOON HE MADE THE DISCOVERY THAT HE WAS NOW UNABLE TO STIR A LIMB.

intentions seemed to have been recognized; the alarm had only been momentary. Now they were all watching him in melancholy silence. His mother lay in her chair, her legs stiffly outstretched and pressed together, her eyes almost closing for sheer weariness; his father and his sister were sitting beside each other, his sister's arm around the old man's neck.

Perhaps I can go on turning around now, thought Gregor, and began his labors again. He could not stop himself from panting with the effort, and had to pause now and then to take breath. Nor did anyone harass him, he was left entirely to himself. When he had completed the turn-around he began at once to crawl straight back. He was amazed at the distance separating him from his room and could not understand how in his weak state he had managed to accomplish the same journey so recently, almost without remarking it. Intent on crawling as fast as possible, he barely noticed that not a single word, not an ejaculation from his family, interfered with his progress. Only when he was already in the doorway did he turn his head around, not completely, for his neck muscles were getting stiff, but enough to see that nothing had changed behind him except that his sister had risen to her feet. His last glance fell on his mother, who was not quite overcome by sleep.

Hardly was he well inside his room when the door was hastily pushed shut, bolted, and locked. The sudden noise in his rear startled him so much that his little legs gave beneath him. It was his sister who had shown such haste. She had been standing ready waiting and had made a light spring forward, Gregor had not even heard her coming, and she cried "At last!" to her parents as she turned the key in the lock.

"And what now?" said Gregor to himself, looking around in the darkness. Soon he made the discovery that he was now unable to stir a limb. This did not surprise him, rather it seemed unnatural that he should ever actually have been able to move on these feeble little legs. Otherwise he felt relatively comfortable. True, his whole body was aching, but it seemed that the pain was gradually growing less and would finally pass away. The rotting apple in his back and the inflamed area around it, all covered with soft dust, already hardly troubled him. He thought of his family with tenderness and love. The decision that he must disappear was one that he held to even more strongly than his sister, if that were possible. In this state of vacant and peaceful meditation he remained until the tower clock struck three in the morning. The first broadening of light in the world outside the window entered his consciousness once more. Then his head sank to the floor of its own accord and from his nostrils came the last faint flicker of his breath.

When the charwoman arrived early in the **A** morning—what between her strength and her impatience she slammed all the doors so loudly, never mind how often she had been begged not

MINI LESSON **Grammar**

COMPLEX SENTENCES

Instruction The structure of a sentence is determined by the number and kind of clauses it contains. A complex sentence contains one independent clause and one or more subordinate clauses. Remember that a clause is a group of words that may or may not be a sentence. If the clause can stand independently, it is a sentence. However, if the clause begins with a subordinating conjunction such as *since, although, after, when, where, while, because, so that, before, until,* and *if*—then it is subordinate. Because a subordinate clause does not express a complete thought, it is often attached to an independent clause to form a complex sentence. Writers use complex sentences to add variety and to supply details that explain and support their ideas.

Write the following sentences from "Metamorphosis" on the chalkboard:

1. When he had completed the turn around, he began at once to crawl straight back.
2. "It's such a long time since he's eaten anything."

Have students identify the independent clause and the subordinate clause in each sentence. Point out the comma following a subordinate clause at the beginning of a sentence.

to do so, that no one in the whole apartment could enjoy any quiet sleep after her arrival—she noticed nothing unusual as she took her customary peep into Gregor's room. She thought he was lying motionless on purpose, pretending to be in the sulks; she credited him with every kind of intelligence. Since she happened to have the long-handled broom in her hand she tried to tickle him up with it from the doorway. When that too produced no reaction she felt provoked and poked at him a little harder, and only when she had pushed him along the floor without meeting any resistance was her attention aroused. It did not take her long to establish the truth of the matter, and her eyes widened, she let out a whistle, yet did not waste much time over it but tore open the door of the Samsas' bedroom and yelled into the darkness at the top of her voice: "Just look at this, it's dead; it's lying here dead and done for!"

Mr. and Mrs. Samsa started up in their double bed and before they realized the nature of the charwoman's announcement had some difficulty in overcoming the shock of it. But then they got out of bed quickly, one on either side, Mr. Samsa throwing a blanket over his shoulders, Mrs. Samsa in nothing but her nightgown; in this array they entered Gregor's room. Meanwhile the door of the living room opened, too, where Grete had been sleeping since the advent of the lodgers; she was completely dressed as if she had not been to bed, which seemed to be confirmed also by the paleness of her face. "Dead?" said Mrs. Samsa, looking questioningly at the charwoman, although she would have investigated for herself, and the fact was obvious enough without investigation. "I should say so," said the charwoman, proving her words by pushing Gregor's corpse a long way to one side with her broomstick. Mrs. Samsa made a movement as if to stop her, but checked it. "Well," said Mr. Samsa, "now thanks be to God." He crossed himself, and the three women followed his

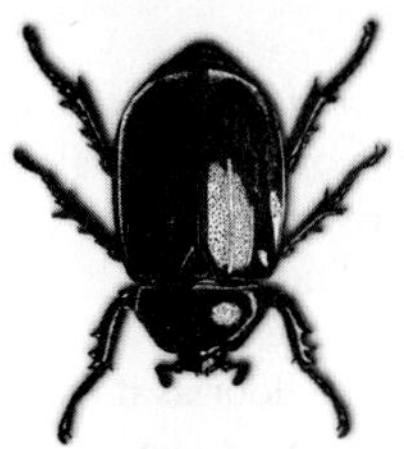

example. Grete, whose eyes never left the corpse, said: "Just see how thin he was. It's such a long time since he's eaten anything. The food came out again just as it went in." Indeed Gregor's body was completely flat and dry, as could only now be seen when it was no longer supported by the legs and nothing prevented one from looking closely at it.

"Come in beside us, Grete, for a little while," said Mrs. Samsa with a tremulous[41] smile, and Grete, not without looking back at the corpse, followed her parents into their bedroom. The charwoman shut the door and opened the window wide. Although it was so early in the morning a certain softness was perceptible in the fresh air. After all, it was already the end of March.

The three lodgers emerged from their room and were surprised to see no breakfast; they had been forgotten. "Where's our breakfast?" said the middle lodger peevishly to the charwoman. But she put her finger to her lips and hastily, without a word, indicated by gestures that they should go into Gregor's room. They did so and stood, their hands in the pockets of their somewhat shabby coats, around Gregor's corpse in the room where it was now fully light. B

At that the door of the Samsas' bedroom opened and Mr. Samsa appeared in his uniform, his wife on one arm, his daughter on the other. They all looked a little as if they had been crying; from time to time Grete hid her face on her father's arm.

"Leave my house at once!" said Mr. Samsa, and pointed to the door without disengaging himself from the women. "What do you mean by that?" said the middle lodger, taken somewhat aback, with a feeble smile. The two others put their hands behind them and kept rubbing them

41. tremulous (trĕm′yə-ləs): timid or fearful.

Less Proficient Readers
Help students understand each family member's reaction to Gregor's death. *(The mother questions his death, the father is relieved, Grete again refers to Gregor as "he;" all three go to the parents' bedroom and cry.)*

Practice Ask students to combine each pair of the following sentences by changing one into a subordinate clause. Remind them to use appropriate subordinating conjunctions and a comma if the subordinate clause begins the sentence.

1. Gregor awoke one morning. He had been transformed into a bug. *(When Gregor awoke one morning, he had been transformed into a bug.)*
2. Gregor couldn't go to work in his condition. He stayed in his room. *(Since Gregor couldn't go to work in his condition, he stayed in his room.)*
3. Gregor's appearance was shocking to his family. They tried to be understanding. *(Although Gregor's appearance was shocking to his family, they tried to be understanding.)*

For more instruction and practice in complex sentences, use McDougal Littell's ***Language Network:***

- Grade 10, Chapter 4, "Clauses and Sentence Structure"
- Grade 12, Chapter 3, "Using Clauses"

Reading Skills and Strategies
SUMMARIZING
Have students tell what changes are brought about by Gregor's death.
Possible Response: The lodgers are told to leave. The family takes the day off to rest and go for a walk. Mr. Samsa plans to fire the charwoman. The family decides to move to a smaller apartment.

Reading Skills and Strategies
EVALUATING
A Ask students what Mr. Samsa's words mean.
Possible Response: He is suggesting that they forget about the arguments they had regarding Gregor's care. He wants his wife and daughter to forgive him for his actions.

together, as if in gleeful expectation of a fine set-to in which they were bound to come off the winners. "I mean just what I say," answered Mr. Samsa, and advanced in a straight line with his two companions toward the lodger. He stood his ground at first quietly, looking at the floor as if his thoughts were taking a new pattern in his head. "Then let us go, by all means," he said, and looked up at Mr. Samsa as if in a sudden access of humility he were expecting some renewed sanction[42] for this decision. Mr. Samsa merely nodded briefly once or twice with meaning eyes. Upon that the lodger really did go with long strides into the hall, his two friends had been listening and had quite stopped rubbing their hands for some moments and now went scuttling after him as if afraid that Mr. Samsa might get into the hall before them and cut them off from their leader. In the hall they all three took their hats from the rack, their sticks from the umbrella stand, bowed in silence, and quitted the apartment. With a suspiciousness that proved quite unfounded Mr. Samsa and the two women followed them out to the landing; leaning over the banister they watched the three figures slowly but surely going down the long stairs, vanishing from sight at a certain turn of the staircase on every floor and coming into view again after a moment or so; the more they dwindled,[43] the more the Samsa family's interest in them dwindled, and when a butcher's boy met them and passed them on the stairs coming up proudly with a tray on his head, Mr. Samsa and the two women soon left the landing and as if a burden had been lifted from them went back into their apartment.

They decided to spend this day in resting and going for a stroll; they had not only deserved such a respite from work, but absolutely needed it. And so they sat down at the table and wrote three notes of excuse, Mr. Samsa to his board of management, Mrs. Samsa to her employer, and Grete to the head of her firm. While they were writing, the charwoman came in to say that she was going now, since her morning's work was finished. At first they only nodded without looking up, but as she kept hovering there they eyed her irritably. "Well?" said Mr. Samsa. The charwoman stood grinning in the doorway as if she had good news to impart to the family but meant not to say a word unless properly questioned. The small ostrich feather standing upright on her hat, which had annoyed Mr. Samsa ever since she was engaged, was waving gaily in all directions. "Well, what is it then?" asked Mrs. Samsa, who obtained more respect from the charwoman than the others. "Oh," said the charwoman, giggling so amiably that she could not at once continue, "just this, you don't need to bother about how to get rid of the thing next door. It's been seen to already." Mrs. Samsa and Grete bent over their letters again, as if preoccupied; Mr. Samsa, who perceived that she was eager to begin describing it all in detail, stopped her with a decisive hand. But since she was not allowed to tell her story, she remembered the great hurry she was in, obviously deeply huffed: "Bye, everybody," she said, whirling off violently, and departed with a frightful slamming of doors.

"She'll be given notice tonight," said Mr. Samsa, but neither from his wife nor his daughter did he get any answer, for the charwoman seemed to have shattered again the composure they had barely achieved. They rose, went to the window and stayed there, clasping each other tight. Mr. Samsa turned in his chair to look at them and quietly observed them for a little. Then he called out: "Come along, now, do. Let bygones be bygones. And you might have some consideration for me." The two of them complied at once, hastened to him, caressed him, and quickly finished their letters. A

42. **sanction** (săngk′shən): penalty; punishment.

43. **dwindled:** became smaller.

Cross Curricular Link **Humanities**

KAFKAESQUE It is not surprising that Kafka has a literary term named after him. Although he was adept at making fantastic events seem real in his writing, the term does not only apply to his own work. It refers to anything that seems surreal and nightmarish at the same time. In fact, the term is actually understood by many people who may have never read anything written by Kafka.

Then they all three left the apartment together, which was more than they had done for months, and went by train into the open country outside the town. The tram, in which they were the only passengers, was filled with warm sunshine. Leaning comfortably back in their seats they canvassed[44] their prospects for the future, and it appeared on closer inspection that these were not at all bad, for the jobs they had got, which so far they had never really discussed with each other, were all three admirable and likely to lead to better things later on. The greatest immediate improvement in their condition would of course arise from moving to another house; they wanted to take a smaller and cheaper but also better situated and more easily run apartment than the one they had, which Gregor had selected. While they were thus conversing, it struck both Mr. and Mrs. Samsa, almost at the same moment, as they became aware of their daughter's increasing vivacity, that in spite of all the sorrow of recent times, which had made her cheeks pale, she had bloomed into a pretty girl with a good figure. They grew quieter and half unconsciously exchanged glances of complete agreement, having come to the conclusion that it would soon be time to find a good husband for her. And it was like a confirmation of their new dreams and excellent intentions that at the end of their journey their daughter sprang to her feet first and stretched her young body. ❖

44. **canvassed:** carefully examined or discussed.

Customizing Instruction

Less Proficient Readers
Help students identify the feelings the family has after Gregor's death. *(They feel sadness; they're angry with the lodgers; they also feel relieved.)*

Advanced Learners
Have students compare the family's prospects for the future with the prospects that Gregor thought they had without his income. *(Everyone has jobs and thinks he or she can get even better jobs. They can save money by moving to a smaller place. Gregor felt that none of them could earn money.)* Then ask students to draw conclusions about how Gregor's situation and death changed the family. *(His situation brought out certain characteristics in each family member that seemed to strengthen each person when Gregor died.)*

Connect to the Literature

1. What Do You Think?
Students should support their reactions with examples from the text.

Comprehension Check

- Grete, Gregor's sister
- so he can have more space to crawl
- The charwoman gets rid of it.

 Use Selection Quiz in **Unit Seven Resource Book,** p. 8.

Think Critically

2. Possible Responses: Students may be more sympathetic to Gregor, because he remains loyal to his family even though they find him repulsive. Students may be least sympathetic to Gregor's father, who doesn't have much patience for Gregor's condition.
3. Possible Response: The mother has hope that Gregor will change back into human form. His father has never had much patience for Gregor and believes his transformation is an injustice against him. Grete becomes so confident and self-absorbed that she begins to neglect Gregor. Gregor struggles to remain human and be part of a family.
4. Gregor's human problems are similar to his problems as an insect. Gregor has trouble with irregular meals and with making friends before his change. As a bug, he also has trouble with getting a meal and is locked in his room away from human contact. Gregor is an outsider as a human and as a bug.
5. Possible Response: Kafka probably chose to have Gregor transformed into an insect because so many people find certain insects repulsive and are afraid of them. As the story progresses, the reader learns even more about Gregor and may be even more repelled.
6. Possible Response: The mood is often very dark and full of despair. This is best captured by the time when Gregor is first locked away in his room and feels totally isolated from his family.

Connect to the Literature

1. What Do You Think? What is your reaction to the way the story ends? Explain.

Comprehension Check

- Who takes care of Gregor?
- Why is the furniture moved out of Gregor's room?
- What happens to his body after he dies?

Think Critically

2. For which character do you have the most sympathy? For which character do you have the least sympathy? Use examples from the story to support your opinion.

3. Consider the ways in which Gregor and the other members of his family respond to his transformation. What do you learn about each of these characters as a result of his or her response?

THINK ABOUT
- why Gregor's mother won't enter his room
- what his father does to injure Gregor
- the change in his sister's treatment of Gregor
- how Gregor feels about his family

4. Compare the problems of Gregor's life as an insect to his problems before his change. Are his problems as an insect completely different from his earlier problems? Explain.

5. Why do you think Kafka chose to have Gregor transformed into an insect instead of another type of creature? Think about the characteristics of this bug, and how others react to it.

6. ACTIVE READING: VISUALIZING DETAILS Review the list of images recorded in your  READER'S NOTEBOOK. Which image do you feel best captures the emotional atmosphere, or mood, of the story? Describe that mood.

Extend Interpretations

7. Critic's Corner When a publisher intended to illustrate "The Metamorphosis," Kafka insisted that "the insect itself cannot be drawn." What do you think were Kafka's reasons?

8. The Writer's Style Kafka writes in a dry, matter-of-fact manner. Read aloud a passage that illustrates this style, then describe the effects of such a style.

9. Connect to Life Many other stories and films are about the transformation of a human being into another creature. Why do you think people find such stories interesting? Explain.

LITERARY ANALYSIS: POINT OF VIEW

The narrative method, or **point of view,** that Kafka chose for "The Metamorphosis" is mainly **third-person limited.** Though Gregor is not the narrator, the reader learns about the events from Gregor's perspective, as if seeing through his eyes. Other characters are described only as they appear to Gregor, as in this passage about his mother:

As all this was running through his mind at top speed . . . there came a cautious tap at the door behind the head of his bed. "Gregor," said a voice—it was his mother's—"it's a quarter to seven. Hadn't you a train to catch?"

After Gregor dies, the story's point of view shifts to **third-person omniscient,** a perspective in which the narrator is all-knowing and can reveal the thoughts of all the characters.

Paired Activity Working with a partner, look through the story to find two particularly striking examples that illustrate the third-person limited point of view and two that illustrate the third-person omniscient point of view. How would the story be different if it were told completely from a third-person omniscient point of view?

Extend Interpretations

7. **Critic's Corner** Possible Response: Kafka wanted the reader to imagine what kind of bug Gregor has turned into. Many readers may think Gregor is a cockroach at first.
8. **The Writer's Style** Make sure that students understand that almost any passage they select will make the events seem as though they could really happen.
9. **Connect to Life** Possible Response: People enjoy seeing how the transformed creatures try to adapt to living in a world that is designed for human comfort.

Literary Analysis

Paired Activity third-person limited point of view—Gregor wakes up and discovers he's a bug, Gregor is forced into his room with a cane; omniscient—the charwoman discovers Gregor's body, the family leaves the apartment. If the story were told from a third-person omniscient point of view, the reader would probably learn more about the other characters and not as much about Gregor.

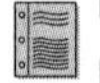 Use **Unit Seven Resource Book,** p. 6, for more practice.

Writing Options

1. Diary Entries Imagine that you are one of the characters other than Gregor. Write three diary entries from this character's point of view, describing key events in the story.

Writing Handbook
See page R27: Descriptive Writing.

2. Literary Analysis What is a central **theme,** or message, of this story? Does the story offer a lesson about the problems of modern life, a reflection about the disappointments of family relationships, or something else? Begin by completing the following sentence: "The Metamorphosis" can be interpreted as a story that _______. Use that sentence as a working draft of your thesis statement. Then review the story and arrive at three or four ideas that support your thesis. Each of these ideas can be the basis of a paragraph or two that helps to advance your thesis. Place your essay in your **Working Portfolio.**

Activities & Explorations

1. Cover Illustration Draw a cover illustration for an edition of "The Metamorphosis." Keep in mind Kafka's insistence that the insect not be portrayed. ~ **ART**

2. Dramatic Scene Get together with some of your classmates to dramatize a major scene from the story. Act out your scene or do a dramatic reading in front of the class. ~ **PERFORMANCE**

Inquiry & Research

1. Story Comparison Read another story by Kafka, such as "The Judgment" or "A Hunger Artist." Compare that story with "The Metamorphosis" in terms of point of view and symbolic meaning.

2. Annotated Bibliography Research print and online sources to find five books or articles about Kafka's life. Then draw up a list of your resources and write a sentence or two summarizing the contents of each one. Include the author, title, publisher, and date of publication for each book and the Web address for each online site.

Vocabulary in Action

EXERCISE: CONTEXT CLUES Write the Word to Know that best completes each sentence.

1. When Gregor first awoke, he had no sense that _____ disaster was about to overtake him.
2. He worried that he might neglect his duty at work or be guilty of some small _____.
3. As he tried to arise from bed, it proved hard for him to establish his _____.
4. Was he surprised that his speech was _____ and that the clerk could not understand it?
5. The stingy owner of Gregor's firm did not treat his employees _____.
6. Gregor's family might have eased his anxiety if they had talked to him _____.
7. Gregor hoped that his sister might _____ with his parents and make peace.
8. Did he think she could understand his sense of humiliation and _____?
9. Gregor felt that his only place of _____ was under the sofa.
10. Did he think that remaining out of sight would _____ the family from hating him?

WORDS TO KNOW

amiably, chagrin, dissuade, equilibrium, imminent, intervene, lavishly, omission, refuge, unintelligible

Building Vocabulary
For an in-depth lesson on context clues, see page 674.

Writing Options

1. **Diary Entries** Suggest that students pick a character that they identify with.
2. **Literary Analysis** Remind students that they should have a clear thesis statement. You might have pairs of students explore the theme by discussing how such a transformation might affect their own lives.

Activities & Explorations

1. **Cover Illustration** Have students recall the mood of the story and think about objects or scenes from the story that might convey that mood.
2. **Dramatic Scene** Remind students that most of the scenes do not have dialogue. Therefore, students must use facial expressions and movements to convey the action.

Inquiry & Research

1. **Story Comparison** Remind students that Kafka often features innocent victims of cruel characters in his stories.
2. **Annotated Bibliography** Encourage students to look for sources that offer different points of view on Kafka's life including articles or diaries by Kafka himself.

Vocabulary in Action

1. imminent
2. omission
3. equilibrium
4. unintelligible
5. lavishly
6. amiably
7. intervene
8. refuge
9. chagrin
10. dissuade

To assess skills and concepts taught in this selection, use **Formal Assessment Book,** p. 161–162.

METAMORPHOSIS 1149

Objectives

- understand and appreciate two modern **poems (Literary Analysis)**
- identify **sound devices** in poetry **(Literary Analysis)**
- make a **personal connection to poetry (Active Reading)**

Thematic Link

These two poems open up **a world of change** for readers by translating the experience of a caged panther and the sound of a flamenco guitar into human terms.

5-Minute Warm-Up

Daily Language SkillBuilder

Have students **proofread** the display sentences on page 1095m and write them correctly.

Reading and Analyzing

Active Reading CONNECTING TO POETRY

Invite students to share their observations and feelings about seeing large predators such as the big cats, wolves, or bears in a zoo.

Possible Responses: Large predators usually sleep, doze, or pace in their cages.

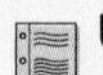 Use **Unit Seven Resource Book,** p. 9, for more practice.

Literary Analysis SOUND DEVICES

Read the poem aloud and have students identify sound devices they hear during the reading. Point out that the same line can have more than one sound effect. Then have students discuss the sound devices and their effects in the following lines.

"has grown so weary that it cannot hold"

(assonance with long o; effect—long o is a mournful sound)

"a thousand bars; and behind the bars, no world"

(consonance with a final nd or d; alliteration with initial b; effect—alternately repeating b and d sounds suggests finality, no way out)

 Use **Unit Seven Resource Book,** p. 10, for more practice.

POEMS BY RAINER MARIA RILKE AND FEDERICO GARCÍA LORCA

Rainer Maria Rilke
1875–1926

A Restless Poet Restlessness defines the life and career of Rainer Maria Rilke (rīn'ər mə-rē'ə rĭl'kə), considered one of the greatest poets of the 20th century. In his poetry he constantly experimented with new styles. Rilke moved frequently in search of places to sustain and inspire his art. After leaving his native Prague, he lived in Russia, France, Spain, Italy, Austria, and Switzerland.

Object Poetry While living in Paris in the early 1900s, Rilke became close friends with the famous sculptor Auguste Rodin (ô-gŏŏst' rō-dăn'). Inspired by Rodin and the great art collections in Paris, Rilke developed a new poetic style called object poetry. In writing an object poem, such as "The Panther," Rilke approached his subject as a visual artist would and tried to translate his precise observations into words. Rilke wrote "The Panther" after Rodin had advised him to go to the Paris zoo and look at an animal long enough to see it truly.

Modernist Experiments Rilke continued to experiment with new ways of writing. In 1910 he wrote a modernist novel about a young poet searching for his identity in Paris. After serving briefly in World War I, Rilke moved to Switzerland, where he wrote two major books of poetry—*Duino Elegies* and *Sonnets to Orpheus.* In these collections of complex and daringly original poetry, Rilke expresses his belief in the spiritual unity of all things.

Connect to Your Life

The following poems portray two different scenes that convey strong emotions. Recall a brief scene in your life that produced strong feelings of pity or sadness. Write down a list of vivid phrases to describe that scene.

Focus Your Reading

LITERARY ANALYSIS: SOUND DEVICES

When a poem is translated into another language, some of its musical qualities are lost. However, translators still use **sound devices** to appeal to the ear. If you read the following poems aloud, you should be able to hear these sound devices.

- **Alliteration** is a repetition of consonant sounds at the beginnings of words, as in "the soft sounds of the sea."
- **Assonance** is a repetition of vowel sounds in syllables that do not rhyme, as in "It is impossible."
- **Consonance** is a repetition of consonant sounds within or at the ends of words, as in "constantly passing bars."

ACTIVE READING: CONNECTING TO POETRY

When you read poetry, try to connect personally with what you are reading about. When you read "The Panther," for example, consider your own feelings about seeing caged animals at a zoo.

READER'S NOTEBOOK As you read these poems, jot down any thoughts, feelings, or memories that help to connect you to each poem.

LESSON RESOURCES

UNIT SEVEN RESOURCE BOOK, pp. 9–10

ASSESSMENT RESOURCES
Formal Assessment, pp. 163–164
Teacher's Guide to Assessment and Portfolio Use
Test Generator

INTEGRATED TECHNOLOGY
Visit our Web site: classzone.com

ADDITIONAL RESOURCES
Lesson Planning Guide, pp. 141–142
Teacher's Sourcebook for Language Development

The Panther

Rainer Maria Rilke

Translated by Stephen Mitchell

In the Jardin des Plantes, Paris

1 2 His vision, from the constantly passing bars,
has grown so weary that it cannot hold
anything else. It seems to him there are
a thousand bars; and behind the bars, no world.

As he paces in cramped circles, over and over,
the movement of his powerful soft strides
is like a ritual dance around a center
in which a mighty will stands paralyzed.

3 Only at times, the curtain of the pupils
lifts, quietly—. An image enters in,
rushes down through the tensed, arrested muscles,
plunges into the heart and is gone.

TIME MANAGEMENT

If your schedule requires that you cover the lesson objectives in a shorter time, use . . .

- Preparing to Read, pp. 1150 and 1152
- Thinking Through the Literature, p. 1154

If you want to take advantage of longer blocks of class time, use . . .

- TE Teaching Options: Speaking and Listening, p. 1153
- The Translator at Work, p. 1155

Customizing Instruction

English Learners

1 Make sure students understand that the phrase "the constantly passing bars" refers to the panther's restless pacing behind the bars of his cage (described more fully in line 5). The bars are not actually moving.

2 Explain the meaning of *hold* in relation to the panther's vision: "His vision . . . cannot hold" means "he cannot see." Point out that the choice of the word *hold* echoes other words in the poem that relate to containment, such as "cramped circles" (line 5), "ritual dance around a center" (line 7), "paralyzed" (line 8), and "arrested muscles" (line 11).

3 Ask students what they think the "curtain of the pupils" refers to? *(Literally, it could refer to the panther's eyelids; figuratively, it could mean the veil of monotony that normally clouds the panther's vision.)*

Less Proficient Readers

Have students find words that either describe or suggest characteristics of the panther in each stanza. *(The panther's weariness and boredom in the first stanza; his physical power and restlessness in the second stanza; and his momentary, instinctive visual lock on something [the "image" that makes his muscles tense] in the third stanza.)*

Advanced Learners

Have students analyze what makes this object poem different from other poems about animals that they may have read, such as William Blake's "The Tyger." Specifically, discuss the tone and point of view of the poem.

- What is the poet's attitude toward the panther? *(sympathetic but objective, not sentimental)*
- Whose point of view is expressed in the poem? *(the panther's)*
- In your opinion, is Rilke's poem the verbal equivalent of a painting?
  Possible Responses: Yes, because it tries to be true to the object—essentially, translating the panther's animal sensations and perceptions—rather than giving a subjective impression of the panther from the poet's point of view. No, because the poem is not as complete a picture of the panther as a painting could be.

Active Reading
CONNECTING TO POETRY
Have students compare the feelings that the two poems evoke. Which poem do students think is more melancholy or somber? Which has more energy? Which one do they have a stronger connection to and why?
Possible Responses: Some students may think "The Panther" is the sadder poem because they can relate more to a wild animal in captivity than to the abstract music of longing played by the guitar. Many may find "The Guitar" more energetic, however, with a driving rhythm that approximates the intensity of flamenco music.

Literary Analysis SOUND DEVICES
If necessary, review alliteration, consonance, and assonance. Remind students that several different sound devices can be used in the same line. Then have them identify the sound devices and their effects in the following lines.

"It cries repeating itself"
(consonance with t; assonance with long e; effect–repetition of sounds reinforce meaning of the line)

"It is crying for things/far off."
(assonance with short i; alliteration with f; effect–to emphasize the words)

Federico García Lorca
1898–1936

Spain's Beloved Poet
Federico García Lorca (fä-dä-rē'kō gär-sē'ə lôr'kə) became one of Spain's most revered and deeply loved poets. Also a gifted pianist and successful playwright, he counted among his friends the leading talents of his generation, such as the surrealist painter Salvador Dali and the filmmaker Luis Buñuel (lo͞o-ēs' bo͞o-nyo͞o-ĕl').

International Fame García Lorca believed that "verse is made to be recited." He began his career by giving oral readings of his poetry, often mixed with his piano performances of folk songs. His most popular collection of poetry, *Gypsy Ballads,* was inspired by folk music, stories of gypsies, and the rural life he had known as a child. His poem "The Guitar," from that collection, describes a flamenco performance. Flamenco guitar music is marked by forceful and improvised rhythms; it accompanies an equally forceful style of dance.

Violent Death Violence and death haunt much of García Lorca's work. Even though he was never very politically active, his association with socialists was considered to mark him as a leftist in Spain's bloody civil war. At the war's outbreak, he was kidnapped and brutally executed by Nationalist soldiers. His body was never found.

Other Works
Lament for the Death of a Bullfighter and Other Poems
Poet in New York
Blood Wedding

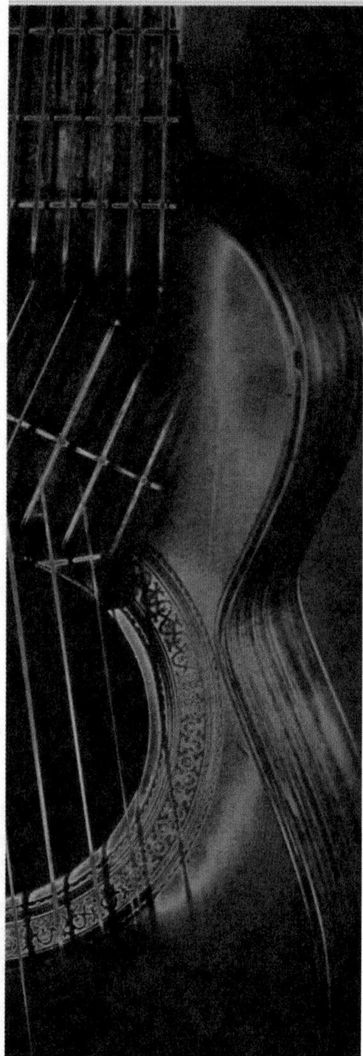

THE GUITAR

FEDERICO GARCÍA LORCA

TRANSLATED BY ROBERT BLY

The crying of the guitar
starts.
1 The goblets
of the dawn break.
The crying of the guitar
starts.
No use to stop it.
It is impossible
to stop it.
It cries repeating itself
as the water cries,
as the wind cries
over the snow.
It is impossible
to stop it.
It is crying for things
far off.
The warm sand of the South
2 that asks for white camellias.
For the arrow with nothing to hit,
the evening with no dawn coming,
and the first bird of all dead
on the branch.
Guitar!
3 Heart wounded, gravely,
by five swords.

19 camellias (kə-mēl′yəz): roselike flowers that grow on small trees.

25 gravely: very seriously.

Customizing Instruction

Less Proficient Readers

Help students understand why the guitar's sound is called "crying."

- What is the guitar's crying compared to? *(the crying of the water and wind, things from nature)*
- What does the guitar cry for? *("for things far off," things listed in lines 18–20)*
- What human emotions do the situations listed in lines 18–20 express? *(longing [the camellias], unfulfillment [the arrow], and grief [the evening and the bird])*

English Learners

1 Explain that a goblet is a glass with a stem and a base, like a wine glass. Ask if students have ever seen a singer hit a high note so powerfully that it breaks a glass or cracks a mirror. Tell them to imagine the dawn breaking like shattered wine glasses and they'll understand the image in these lines. Emphasize that the image is dynamic like the wind and water the guitar is compared to in lines 11 and 12—all are part of a headlong, unstoppable force.

2 Fragrant camellias grow in mild climates, such as France, not in the hot, dry sand of southern Spain.

Advanced Learners

3 Invite students to interpret these last two lines. Ask specifically what they think the heart and five swords refer to.

Possible Responses: The heart is the curved body of the guitar, which is "wounded," or struck, by the five fingers (i.e., the five swords) to produce the guitar's cry.

THE GUITAR 1153

MINI LESSON Speaking and Listening

ORAL PERFORMANCE

Prepare Divide students into small groups and have them prepare a performance of one of the poems. Encourage creative expression more than a simple reading. For example, students can play recorded flamenco music for a performance of "The Guitar" or a videotape of a panther pacing in his cage for "The Panther." Students can also prepare a choral reading by dividing the poem into parts for different readers and/or the group. "The Guitar" especially lends itself to alternating voices.

Present After each group presents, the class should discuss the performance, pointing out both strengths and weaknesses. Students should also explain how the performance added to their understanding of the poem. At the end of the presentations, students could vote on the two or three top performances.

This activity is particularly well suited to longer blocks of time.

Connect to the Literature

1. **What Do You Think?** What mental images did you form while reading these poems? Describe those images.

Comprehension Check
- What does the panther do in his cage?
- What kind of sound does the guitar make?

Think Critically

2. **ACTIVE READING: CONNECTING TO POETRY** How did you connect personally with these poems? Share what you wrote about in your **READER'S NOTEBOOK.**
3. From the panther's point of view, what do you think is the worst thing about being locked up?
4. The last stanza of "The Panther" tells about an image that "plunges into the [panther's] heart and is gone." What do you think the panther sees, and why does the image disappear?
5. In García Lorca's poem, why do you think the crying of the guitar cannot be stopped?
6. How would you describe the kinds of things the guitar cries for?
7. What might the guitar with its constant crying **symbolize,** or represent?

Extend Interpretations

8. **Connect to Life** Some animal-rights activists believe it is wrong to keep animals in captivity at a zoo. Does your reading of "The Panther" make you sympathetic to those views? Explain.

LITERARY ANALYSIS: SOUND DEVICES

Sound devices help make poetry pleasing to the ear. Poets use sound devices for the following purposes:
- to create musical sounds
- to emphasize certain words
- to heighten moods
- to unify passages
- to help create meaning

Three common sound devices are alliteration, assonance, and consonance.

Alliteration is a repetition of consonant sounds at the beginnings of words, **assonance** is a repetition of vowel sounds in syllables that do not rhyme, and **consonance** is a repetition of consonant sounds within or at the ends of words.

When looking for these sound devices in poetry, be sure to focus on sounds, not just letters. For example, "cramped circles" in the fifth line of "The Panther" is not an example of alliteration, because the initial *c* sounds are not the same. Likewise, "cannot hold" in the second line is not an example of assonance, because the *o* in *cannot* has a short sound, whereas the *o* in *hold* has a long sound.

Paired Activity Working with a partner, look through "The Panther" and "The Guitar" to find two examples of each sound device. Then review the list above, which identifies reasons for using sound devices. Which reasons seem to apply in the two poems? Compare your findings with those of your classmates.

Connect to the Literature

1. **What Do You Think?** Students should give details about their images and explain what in the poems sparked them.

Comprehension Check
- The panther usually paces in his cage, but sometimes he looks intently at something beyond the bars.
- The guitar makes a crying sound.

Think Critically

2. Students might share their experience looking at large predators in a zoo or hearing classical or flamenco guitar music. Some students may know about Spain or have seen a flamenco dance performance.
3. Possible Responses: the monotony, the boredom, the isolation, the loss of nature (i.e., the "world"), the lack of stimulation
4. Possible Responses: The image could be something that the panther would ordinarily consider prey that causes the instinctive reaction of tensed muscles; or it could be anything the panther sees beyond the bars that temporarily distracts him from the monotony of his cage. The image disappears because it is only momentary with no possibility for interaction.
5. Some students, citing the guitar's comparison to the wind and the water, will see the cry as an unstoppable force of nature. Others who see the guitar's cry as expressing human longing or grief may consider it as unstoppable as those human emotions.
6. Possible Response: The images in lines 18–20 are far-off things, such as the camellias, or lost things, such as the arrow's target, the dawn, and the bird.
7. Some students may see the guitar as a symbol of humanity whose grief and longing are never-ending. Others may see it as a symbol of art, which in this case transforms human suffering into music.

Extend Interpretations

8. **Connect to Life** Although most students will sympathize with the caged panther, few would advocate abolishing zoos. Some students may point out that animals have a safer life in captivity than in the wild and that most zoos now house animals in natural-looking habitats instead of cages. For some animals—tigers and pandas, for instance—their only chance of survival as a species is in a zoo.

Literary Analysis

Paired Activity

Examples of alliteration:
"soft strides" ("The Panther")
"sand of the South" ("The Guitar")
Effect: to create musical sounds

Examples of assonance:
"As he paces in cramped circles" ("The Panther")
Effect: to provide unity and emphasis
"over the snow" ("The Guitar")
Effect: to heighten mood

Examples of consonance:
"tensed, arrested muscles" ("The Panther")
"It is impossible to stop it." ("The Guitar")
Effect: to provide unity and emphasis

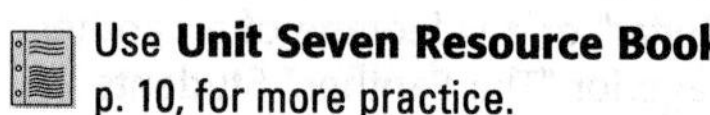
Use **Unit Seven Resource Book,** p. 10, for more practice.

To assess skills and concepts taught in this selection, use **Formal Assessment Book,** p. 163–164.

Translating Modern Poetry

All poetry is difficult to translate, but modern poetry poses special challenges. Rilke's poetry, for example, relies so much on suggestion that the poet did not even use the German words for a cage and a panther in his poem "The Panther." At the same time, he created complex sound patterns, which are often lost in translation, as illustrated by the following examples:

Rilke's Original German, from "The Panther"

Sein Blick ist vom Vorübergehn der Stäbe
so müd geworden, dass er nichts mehr hält.
Ihm ist, als ob es tausend Stäbe gäbe,
und hinter tausend Stäben keine Welt.

The German word for bars, ***Stäbe,*** is repeated three times.

Rilke makes use of an *abab* rhyme scheme. ***Stäbe*** (shtā′bə) rhymes with ***gäbe*** (gā′bə), and ***hält*** (hĕlt) rhymes with ***Welt*** (vĕlt).

The underlined *s*'s in Rilke's German illustrate his use of consonance and alliteration (the repetition of *s* and *z* sounds).

Robert Bly's Translation

From seeing the bars, his seeing is so exhausted
that it no longer holds anything anymore.
To him the world is bars, a hundred thousand
bars, and behind the bars, nothing.

Bly repeats the word ***bars*** to echo the repetition in the original. He actually repeats more words than Rilke does.

Note that Bly does not make use of rhyme. He does repeat some letter sounds, such as *b* and *s,* but he makes a more sparing use of sound devices than Rilke.

Paired Activity

With a partner, compare and contrast Bly's translation of the first stanza with the Mitchell translation of the same stanza on page 1151. What differences do you notice between the two translations? In your opinion, which version best expresses the emotions associated with the captivity of the panther?

The Translator at Work

Paired Activity Both translations capture the repetition used in the original to evoke the monotony of life in a cage. In the opening line, Bly repeats *seeing* as both a verb and a noun. Mitchell chooses *vision* but achieves repetition through the consonance of *s* sounds and the phrase "constantly passing bars," which suggests the panther's pacing. By contrast, the panther in Bly's translation seems stationary.

Both translators make use of the word *hold*. However, it can be argued that *weary* in Mitchell's translation is a more appropriate and better-sounding word than *exhausted* to express the kind of mental and emotional fatigue the caged panther must feel. Bly's choice of "a hundred thousand" seems unnecessarily precise, but his word *nothing* ends the last line with a stronger note of finality than Mitchell's "no world."

Objectives

- understand and appreciate a **speech (Literary Analysis)**
- understand the relationship between **diction and audience** in nonfiction **(Literary Analysis)**
- **recognize main ideas** in nonfiction **(Active Reading)**

Summary

For Virginia Woolf, the obstacles to becoming a professional writer are primarily internal rather than external. The first psychological hurdle is the Victorian image of woman as the "Angel in the House"—a selfless, secretly deceitful being born to serve and sympathize. The "Angel in the House" stifles the honesty and independence necessary to be a successful writer, and so Woolf has to kill her—metaphorically speaking. Another obstacle facing the woman writer is a resistance to talk about what Woolf obliquely calls "the body" or "the passions" (i.e., sex). She attributes such inhibition to a conventional male double standard that women have internalized. In closing, Woolf reminds her audience of the many hidden, internal barriers to free expression. She encourages women to work together to define the aims and the means of their freedom.

Use **Unit Seven Resource Book,** p. 11, for additional support.

Thematic Link

Women experienced a **world of change** in the 20th century. Virginia Woolf helped lead the way.

Use **Unit Seven Resource Book,** p. 14, for practice with Words to Know.

5-Minute Warm-Up

Daily Language SkillBuilder

Have students **proofread** the display sentences on page 1095m and write them correctly.

PROFESSIONS FOR WOMEN

VIRGINIA WOOLF

Virginia Woolf
1882–1941

An Unlikely Rebel "Something had to be done. . . . And so the smashing and the crashing began." These words of Virginia Woolf describe a revolution—the new literary art created by modern writers. As a leader of "the moderns," Woolf believed that the old forms of writing had outlived their usefulness; new techniques had to be invented that would capture life's complexity. Woolf was born in London into a prominent Victorian family, an unlikely setting for a rebel. Her father, Sir Leslie Stephen, was a distinguished intellectual who raised his children to appreciate the life of the mind. Like most Victorians, however, he expected more of his boys than of his girls, giving his sons a university education so that they could assume leadership roles in society.

The Bloomsbury Group After the death of both her parents, Woolf moved with her sister, Vanessa, and her two brothers to a house in an area of London called Bloomsbury. Her brothers regularly invited their friends from Cambridge University for spirited discussions of art, philosophy, and literature. Woolf and her artist sister eventually joined these social gatherings, which helped them achieve an intellectual freedom and equality with men rarely available to women at the time. Before long, those regularly attending the gatherings had become known as the Bloomsbury group, which included some of the leading writers, artists, and thinkers of Woolf's generation.

Breaking Traditions Woolf's most famous novels, *Mrs. Dalloway* (1925), *To the Lighthouse* (1927), and *The Waves* (1931), broke new ground in narrative technique and style. Woolf does not really report events as they happen but, rather, describes how those events are perceived and filtered through the minds of the characters. Her novels are made even more distinctive by her original style, which has the qualities of poetry. Besides novels, she wrote numerous reviews and critical essays. Her landmark essay, *A Room of One's Own* (1929), argues that women need to be given the same freedom as men to develop their creative potential.

A Crippling Illness Throughout her life, Woolf struggled with manic-depressive illness. Her first breakdown occurred in 1895, shortly after her beloved mother died. The second one came after her father's death nine years later. Although Woolf recovered from both episodes, the illness returned periodically. In 1941, feeling another serious episode coming on, she walked to a nearby river, put stones in her pockets, and drowned herself.

Other Works
Orlando
The Common Reader
A Writer's Diary

LESSON RESOURCES

UNIT SEVEN RESOURCE BOOK, pp. 11–15

ASSESSMENT RESOURCES
Formal Assessment, pp. 165–166
Teacher's Guide to Assessment and Portfolio Use
Test Generator

INTEGRATED TECHNOLOGY
Visit our Web site: classzone.com

ADDITIONAL RESOURCES
Lesson Planning Guide, pp. 143–144
Teacher's Sourcebook for Language Development

Connect to Your Life

In your judgment, what is most necessary for personal fulfillment? List the following items in the order of their importance to your life. Feel free to include additional items in your list.

- professional career
- family
- friends
- social service
- personal pleasure

Focus Your Reading

LITERARY ANALYSIS: DICTION AND AUDIENCE

Diction is a writer's choice of words. In many cases, a writer's diction is influenced by his or her awareness of the **audience,** the people who will read or listen to the message. Woolf originally wrote "Professions for Women" as a speech to be delivered to an organization of professional women. Like Woolf, many of these women were pioneers in their respective fields. As you read, pay attention to the words Woolf uses. Think about how her word choice might be related to her awareness of her audience.

ACTIVE READING: RECOGNIZING MAIN IDEAS

Virginia Woolf tells stories about her own professional experience to express her ideas. As a result, some of her main points are not stated directly; instead, a reader must infer them from her stories.

READER'S NOTEBOOK As you read, make two lists like the ones started at right. These lists will help you to identify Woolf's main ideas.

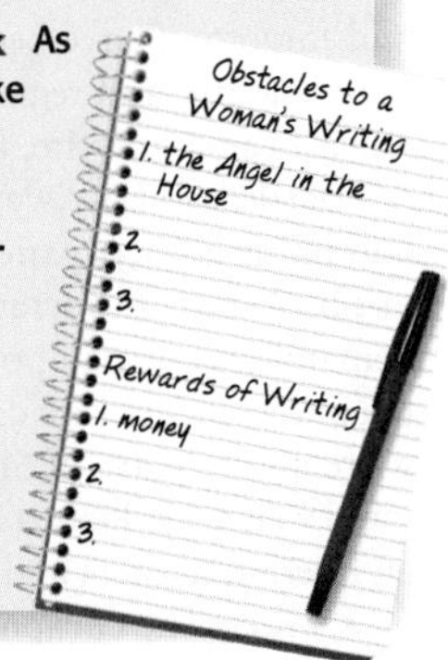

WORDS TO KNOW
Vocabulary Preview

acute
lethargy
nominally
perpetual
reputable

Build Background

Victorian Inequality To Virginia Woolf's father, and to most men in Victorian England, women's subservience to men was considered "natural." It never occurred to them that women should have equal rights, such as the rights to own property, obtain a university education, and have a career. The ideal woman was a nurturing caregiver to her husband as well as her children—a self-sacrificing "Angel in the House," according to a famous poem of the time.

Advances for Women By Woolf's generation, women's condition had improved somewhat. When Woolf wrote her speech "Professions for Women" in 1931, women in Great Britain could vote, and a few, like Woolf herself, had professional careers. But the Angel in the House proved to be a difficult stereotype to overcome, both in society at large and in a woman's self-perception.

READING FOR INFORMATION
Reading Skills and Strategies
PREVIEWING

Have students scan the headings to preview the biographical and background information on these pages. Discuss with them the information they would expect to find under each heading. Then, have students think of a brief description of Virginia Woolf based on their preview. As they read the information, they can compare their first impressions with their deeper understanding.

TIME MANAGEMENT

If your schedule requires that you cover the lesson objectives in a shorter time, use . . .

- Preparing to Read, pp. 1156 and 1157
- Thinking Through the Literature, p. 1164
- Vocabulary in Action, p. 1165

If you want to take advantage of longer blocks of class time, use . . .

- TE Teaching Options: Cross Curricular Link, pp. 1158, 1159; Viewing and Representing, p. 1161; Vocabulary Strategy, p. 1162
- Choices & Challenges, p. 1165

Literary Analysis

DICTION AND AUDIENCE

A Have students analyze Woolf's diction in the first paragraph as it relates to her audience.

- Describe the diction, or word choice, in the passage beginning "It is true I am a woman" and ending "It is difficult to say." *(conversational, casual, informal, personal)*
- How does Woolf present herself to her audience of professional women? *(She minimizes her professional experience by pointing out that writing was an accepted occupation when she entered the profession; she all but apologizes for her lack of professional experience.)*

Use **Unit Seven Resource Book,** p. 13, for more practice.

Active Reading

RECOGNIZING MAIN IDEAS

Explain to students that Woolf's paragraphs are often long and her main ideas tend to evolve rather than be stated directly.

- Have students identify the main idea in the first paragraph. *(On the surface, getting her first written work published was easy for Woolf.)*
- Then help students fill in their Reader's Notebook with notes about why the image of "Angel in the House" presents such an obstacle for Woolf's development as a writer. *(The Angel is not supposed to think of or for herself; she is supposed to help and support others; she is always sympathetic and understanding; she is the exact opposite of what a professional writer needs to be.)*

Use **Unit Seven Resource Book,** p. 12, for more practice.

Professions for Women

Virginia Woolf

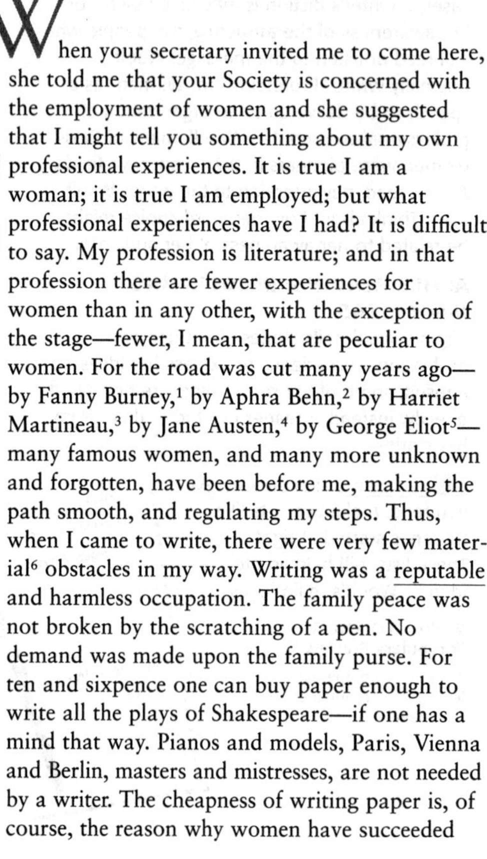

When your secretary invited me to come here, she told me that your Society is concerned with the employment of women and she suggested that I might tell you something about my own professional experiences. **A** It is true I am a woman; it is true I am employed; but what professional experiences have I had? It is difficult to say. My profession is literature; and in that profession there are fewer experiences for women than in any other, with the exception of the stage—fewer, I mean, that are peculiar to women. For the road was cut many years ago—by Fanny Burney,[1] by Aphra Behn,[2] by Harriet Martineau,[3] by Jane Austen,[4] by George Eliot[5]—many famous women, and many more unknown and forgotten, have been before me, making the path smooth, and regulating my steps. Thus, when I came to write, there were very few material[6] obstacles in my way. Writing was a reputable and harmless occupation. The family peace was not broken by the scratching of a pen. No demand was made upon the family purse. For ten and sixpence one can buy paper enough to write all the plays of Shakespeare—if one has a mind that way. Pianos and models, Paris, Vienna and Berlin, masters and mistresses, are not needed by a writer. The cheapness of writing paper is, of course, the reason why women have succeeded as writers before they have succeeded in the other professions.

But to tell you my story—it is a simple one. You have only got to figure to yourselves a girl in a bedroom with a pen in her hand. She had only to move that pen from left to right—from ten o'clock to one. Then it occurred to her to do what is simple and cheap enough after all—to slip a few of those pages into an envelope, fix a penny stamp in the corner, and drop the envelope into the red box[7] at the corner. It was thus that I became a journalist; and my effort was rewarded on the first day of the following month—a very glorious day it was for me—by a letter from an editor containing a check for one

1. **Fanny Burney:** English novelist (1752–1840).
2. **Aphra Behn:** English playwright, poet, and novelist (1640–1689); the first Englishwoman known to earn her living by writing.
3. **Harriet Martineau:** English novelist and writer on economics and history (1802–1876).
4. **Jane Austen:** English novelist (1775–1817), whose works include *Pride and Prejudice* and *Emma.*
5. **George Eliot:** pen name of Mary Ann Evans (1819–1880), English author of *Adam Bede, Silas Marner,* and *Middlemarch.*
6. **material:** significant; relevant.
7. **red box:** Mailboxes in England are characteristically red.

WORDS TO KNOW

reputable (rĕp′yə-tə-bəl) *adj.* of good reputation; honorable

Cross Curricular Link **History**

PROFESSIONS FOR WOMEN A professional woman doctor or lawyer was still a rarity in Britain and the United States in the 1930s. For the most part, the professions open to women at that time were teaching, nursing, office work, and sales. During both world wars, women gladly took over well-paying manufacturing jobs vacated by men going off to fight. But these women were just as easily relegated to their former housekeeping roles or low-wage female occupations when the men came home again.

A vivid description of the kind of work educated women could find in the early 20th century comes from Woolf herself:

I had made my living by cadging odd jobs from newspapers, by reporting a donkey show here or a wedding there; I had earned a few pounds by addressing envelopes, reading to old ladies, making artificial flowers, teaching the alphabet to small children in a kindergarten. Such were the chief occupations that were open to women before 1918. I need not, I am afraid, describe in any detail the hardness of the work, for you know perhaps women who have done it; nor the difficulty of living on the money when it was earned, for you may have tried.

–From *A Room of One's Own,* 1929

pound ten shillings and sixpence.[8] But to show you how little I deserve to be called a professional woman, how little I know of the struggles and difficulties of such lives, I have to admit that instead of spending that sum upon bread and butter, rent, shoes and stockings, or butcher's bills, I went out and bought a cat—a beautiful cat, a Persian cat, which very soon involved me in bitter disputes with my neighbors.

What could be easier than to write articles and to buy Persian cats with the profits? But wait a moment. Articles have to be about something. Mine, I seem to remember, was about a novel by a famous man. And while I was writing this review, I discovered that if I were going to review books I should need to
1 do battle with a certain phantom. And the phantom was a woman, and when I came to know her better I called her after the heroine of a famous poem, *The Angel in the House*.[9] It was she who used to come between me and my paper when I was writing reviews. It was she who bothered me and wasted my time and so tormented me that at last I killed her. You who come of a younger and happier generation may not have heard of her—you may not know what I mean by the Angel in the House. I will describe her as shortly as I can. She was intensely sympathetic. She was immensely charming. She was utterly unselfish. She excelled in the difficult arts of family life. She sacrificed herself daily. If there was chicken, she took the leg; if there was a
draught she sat 2
in it—in short she was so constituted that she never had a mind or a wish of her own, but preferred to sympathize always with the minds and wishes of others. Above all—I need not say it—she was
pure. Her purity 3
was supposed to be her chief beauty—her blushes, her great grace. In those days—the last of Queen Victoria[10]—every house had its Angel. And when I came to write I encountered her with the very first words. The shadow of her wings fell on my page; I heard the rustling of her skirts in the room. Directly, that is to say, I took my pen in hand to review that novel by a famous man, she slipped behind me and whispered: "My dear, you are a
young woman. You are writing about a book 4
that has been written by a man. Be sympathetic; be tender; flatter; deceive, use all the arts and wiles[11] of our sex. Never let anybody guess that

Virginia Woolf. Copyright © Bettmann/Corbis.

8. **one pound . . . sixpence:** Pounds, shillings, and pence are denominations of British money.
9. ***The Angel in the House:*** a long verse novel, published by the British writer Coventry Patmore in segments in the 1850s and 1860s. It presents an idealized view of a woman's role in the family.
10. **Queen Victoria:** monarch of Britain from 1837 to 1901.
11. **wiles:** tricks intended to deceive.

Customizing Instruction

English Learners

1 Students may not know that a phantom is an imaginary thing, like a ghost. Make sure they understand that the "Angel in the House" is not a real person but an ideal that women were expected to live up to.

2 Explain to students that *draught* is the British spelling of *draft*, a current of air. The "Angel in the House" would prefer to sit in the cold, drafty spot of a room rather than let someone else suffer there.

3 Explain that in this context *purity* is a kind of modesty or innocence. To live up to the ideal of the "Angel in the House," grown women were supposed to be ignorant about the larger world outside the family and especially about sexual matters. This explains the blushes and coyness that Woolf says traditionally expressed a woman's grace and beauty.

Less Proficient Readers

- Make sure students understand the image of the "Angel in the House" by having them name some of her characteristics. *(understanding, pleasant, unselfish, charming, a good wife and mother, self-sacrificing, no mind or wish of her own)*
- Have students point out the examples of behavior that the Angel demonstrates. *(taking the least desirable piece of chicken, sitting in a drafty spot in a room)*

4 Students should also understand that Woolf uses the word *sympathetic* to mean agreeable as well as understanding. Ask why being always agreeable would hinder someone from writing a book review? *(because you couldn't say anything critical about the book)*

Set a Purpose Have students read to find out why Woolf has to kill the "Angel in the House."

Advanced Learners

Ask students whether they find Woolf at all humorous or amusing in her speech so far. Ask them to point out examples of her subtle humor. *(the purchase of a Persian cat with her first paycheck; the trouble with her neighbors because of the cat; the behavior of the "Angel in the House" [i.e., preferring the chicken leg and the draft])*

Cross Curricular Link

Humanities

A ROOM OF ONE'S OWN For Virginia Woolf, economic independence was one of the most important conditions for a woman's freedom. In her famous discussion of the subject, published as *A Room of One's Own* in 1929, she explains how she achieved her own financial freedom.

My aunt, Mary Beton, I must tell you, died by a fall from her horse when she was riding out to take the air in Bombay. The news of my legacy [inheritance] reached me one night about the same time that the act was passed that gave votes to women. A solicitor's letter fell into the post-box and when I opened it I found that she had left me five hundred pounds a year for ever. Of the two—the vote and the money—the money, I own, seemed infinitely the more important.

Literary Analysis CONFLICT

A Have students discuss why Woolf has to metaphorically kill the "Angel in the House." Why is the Angel such a powerful force that Woolf calls killing her an act of "self-defense"?
Possible Response: The Angel not only represents an ideal in the society but also a personal standard of behavior that Woolf and women of her generation had internalized. The voice of the Angel is inside Woolf's head telling her what to do and not do. Woolf's struggle with the Angel is thus an internal conflict—a psychological battle between what she wants to be and what she knows is expected of her. Killing the Angel resolves Woolf's conflict by essentially removing the restrictions that she had placed on herself.

Reading Skills and Strategies VISUALIZING

Point out that Woolf uses vivid imagery and figurative language to make abstract ideas come alive for her audience. When she talks about the "Angel in the House," for example, she creates an actual character, complete with wings, a radiant halo, a "rustling" of skirts, and a sly, whispering voice. Ask students why they think Woolf created such a detailed character for the "Angel in the House." *(Woolf wanted her audience to understand that although the Angel is only a phantom, her threat is very real.)*

As students read further, help them visualize other images that Woolf uses to dramatize her ideas and experiences.

- the image of a fisherman to explain artistic creation (p. 1162)
- the imagery of explosions and clashes to illustrate disruption of the artistic process (p. 1162)

you have a mind of your own. Above all, be pure." And she made as if to guide my pen. I now record the one act for which I take some credit to myself, though the credit rightly belongs to some excellent ancestors of mine who left me

FOR, AS I FOUND, DIRECTLY I PUT PEN TO PAPER, YOU CANNOT REVIEW EVEN A NOVEL WITHOUT HAVING **A MIND OF YOUR** OWN, WITHOUT EXPRESSING WHAT YOU THINK TO BE THE TRUTH ABOUT HUMAN RELATIONS, MORALITY, SEX.

a certain sum of money—shall we say five
1 hundred pounds a year?—so that it was not necessary for me to depend solely on charm for my living. I turned upon her and caught her by the throat. I did my best to kill her. My excuse, if I were to be had up in a court of law, would be
A that I acted in self-defense. Had I not killed her she would have killed me. She would have plucked the heart out of my writing. For, as I found, directly I put pen to paper, you cannot review even a novel without having a mind of
2 your own, without expressing what you think to be the truth about human relations, morality, sex. And all these questions, according to the Angel in the House, cannot be dealt with freely and openly by women; they must charm, they must conciliate,[12] they must—to put it bluntly—tell lies if they are to succeed. Thus, whenever I felt the shadow of her wing or the radiance of her halo upon my page, I took up the inkpot and flung it at her. She died hard. Her fictitious nature was of great assistance to her. It is far harder to kill a phantom than a reality. She was always creeping back when I thought I had dispatched[13] her. Though I flatter myself that I killed her in the end, the struggle was severe; it took much time that had better have been spent upon learning Greek grammar; or in roaming the world in search of adventures. But it was a real experience; it was an experience that was bound to befall all women writers at that time. Killing the Angel in the House was part of the occupation of a woman writer.

But to continue my story. The Angel was dead; what then remained? You may say that what remained was a simple and common object—a young woman in a bedroom with an inkpot. In other words, now that she had rid herself of falsehood, that young woman had only to be herself. Ah, but what is "herself"? I mean, what is a woman? I assure you, I do not know. I do not believe that you know. I do not believe that anybody can know until she has expressed herself in all the arts and professions open to human skill. That indeed is one of the reasons why I have come here—out of respect for you, who are in process of showing us by your experiments what a woman is, who are in process of providing us, by your failures and successes, with that extremely important piece of information.

But to continue the story of my professional experiences. I made one pound ten and six by my first review; and I bought a Persian cat with the proceeds. Then I grew ambitious. A Persian cat is all very well, I said; but a Persian cat is not enough. I must have a motor car. And it was thus that I became a novelist—for it is a very

12. **conciliate:** overcome distrust of; try to gain friendship by pleasant behavior.

13. **dispatched:** sent off; sent away.

La reve II [The dream], Balthus. © 2007 Artists Rights Society (ARS), New York/ ADAGP, Paris.

HUMANITIES CONNECTION The French artist known as Balthus (1908–2001) often used realistic techniques to portray dreamlike subjects. Note the differences in the two faces portrayed here.

Customizing Instruction

English Learners

1 Tell students that a pound is British currency just as the dollar is American currency. Five hundred pounds a year in Woolf's day was enough to live on comfortably. Explain that Woolf's point here is that because she inherited money, she wasn't forced to find a husband to support her and so could financially afford to free herself from the "Angel in the House."

Less Proficient Readers

2 Make sure students understand why being an "Angel in the House" is antithetical to being a writer.

- According to Woolf, what does it take to be a writer? *(a mind of your own; honesty about "human relations, morality, sex")*
- Why can't the "Angel in the House" be open and honest about "human relations, morality, [and] sex"? *(because she always has to be agreeable, supportive, and pure)*
- How does the "Angel in the House" get her way? *(through charm, manipulation, and lies)*

MINI LESSON Viewing and Representing

La Rêve II (The Dream) **by Balthus**

ART APPRECIATION Balthus is the pseudonym of Balthazar Klossowski (b. 1908), a reclusive painter known for his mysterious landscapes and portraits of solitary adolescent girls. Helped early in his career by the French novelist André Gide and the poet Rainer Maria Rilke, Balthus gained considerable success from his unusual work. Have students study the painting and the **Humanities Connection** on page 1161. Invite them to share their interpretations of the paintings.

- Who are the two girls? *(a dreamer and a dream; a girl and a ghost; aspects of the same girl)*
- What do you think the girl on the right is doing? *(running away; protecting the other girl)*
- If you interpreted the painting in terms of Woolf's argument, which girl would be the "Angel in the House" and why? *(The sleeping girl is the Angel because of her passivity, whereas the other girl represents her potentially active self. The girl on the right is the phantom Angel whose dominant influence prevents the real girl from awakening to her true self.)*

Reading and Analyzing

Literary Analysis ANALOGY

A An analogy is an extended comparison between two things in order to make or clarify a point. Have students analyze the analogy between the creative process and the image of a fisherman.

- How is the fisherman like an artist? *(Both are fishing quietly and patiently for something nourishing—a fish for the fisherman, an idea for the artist.)*
- What qualities of the unconscious are emphasized by its comparison to a lake? *(depth, mystery, freedom of movement, the place where the big ideas ["largest fish"] slumber)*
- What point does the analogy make? *(The unconscious is the source of creative ideas. In order to mine its riches, an artist needs to be in a receptive, trance-like state.)*

Literary Analysis METAPHOR

B A metaphor is also a comparison between two things but usually not as elaborate as an analogy. Have students explain the metaphor in these lines.

- What is the "hard" obstruction—later called "a rock"—that Woolf's imagination smashes against? *(the prohibition against talking about bodily sensations or functions, such as sexuality, and "the passions," or strong feelings)*
- Why are only women writers impeded by this prohibition? *(The external prohibition amounts to a personal inhibition because it is a convention imposed but not practiced by men and internalized by women.)*

Reading Skills and Strategies SUMMARIZING

C Have students summarize the last section of Woolf's speech. Help them look for the main idea, or major point Woolf makes, and then add a few details to complete the summary.

Possible Response: Woolf closes her speech by reminding the audience of the internal obstacles to success that professional women have to overcome. One way to combat internal ghosts, she suggests, is to define and discuss them with other women. She also cautions her audience that the financial freedom of a profession is only the beginning. Women need to make decisions about their own lives every step of the way.

strange thing that people will give you a motor car if you will tell them a story. It is a still stranger thing that there is nothing so delightful in the world as telling stories. It is far pleasanter than writing reviews of famous novels. And yet, if I am to obey your secretary and tell you my professional experiences as a novelist, I must tell you about a very strange experience that befell me as a novelist. And to understand it you must try first to imagine a novelist's state of mind. I hope I am not giving away professional secrets if I say that a novelist's chief desire is to be as unconscious as possible. He has to induce in himself
1 a state of perpetual lethargy. He wants life to proceed with the utmost quiet and regularity. He wants to see the same faces, to read the same books, to do the same things day after day, month after month, while he is writing, so that nothing may break the illusion in which he is living—so that nothing may disturb or disquiet the mysterious nosings about, feelings round, darts, dashes and sudden discoveries of that very shy and illusive spirit, the imagination. I suspect that this state is the same both for men and women. Be that as it may, I want you to imagine me writing a novel in a state of trance. I want you to figure to yourselves a girl sitting with a pen in her hand, which for minutes, and indeed for hours, she never dips into the inkpot. The image that comes to my mind when I think of this girl is the image of a fisherman lying sunk in dreams on the verge[14] of a deep lake with a rod
A held out over the water. She was letting her imagination sweep unchecked round every rock and cranny of the world that lies submerged in the depths of our unconscious being.[15] Now came the experience, the experience that I believe to be far commoner with women writers than with men. The line raced through the girl's fingers. Her imagination had rushed away. It had A
sought the pools, the depths, the dark places where the largest fish slumber. And then there was a smash. There was an explosion. There was foam and confusion. The imagination had dashed itself against something hard. The girl B
was roused from her dream. She was indeed in a state of the most acute and difficult distress. To speak without figure she had thought of something, something about the body, about the 2
passions which it was unfitting for her as a woman to say. Men, her reason told her, would be shocked. The consciousness of what men will say of a woman who speaks the truth about her passions had roused her from her artist's state of unconsciousness. She could write no more. The trance was over. Her imagination could work no longer. This I believe to be a very common experience with women writers—they are impeded by the extreme conventionality[16] of the other sex.

> INDEED IT WILL BE A LONG TIME STILL, I THINK, BEFORE A WOMAN CAN SIT DOWN TO WRITE A BOOK WITHOUT FINDING A PHANTOM TO BE slain, A ROCK TO BE DASHED AGAINST.

14. **verge:** edge.
15. **the depths of our unconscious being:** Woolf is referring to that part of the mind that lies beyond our perception or control.
16. **conventionality:** a strong belief in traditional ways of thought and action.

WORDS TO KNOW

perpetual (pər-pĕch'o͞o-əl) *adj.* lasting for an indefinitely long time
lethargy (lĕth'ər-jē) *n.* inactivity; sleepy dullness
acute (ə-kyo͞ot') *adj.* intense

1162

MINI LESSON Vocabulary Strategy

APPLYING ROOT WORD MEANINGS

Instruction Remind students that a Latin word or root is often the basis for several English words that share a related meaning. Tell students that they can apply the meaning of Latin words or roots to help them figure out the definitions of meanings of unfamiliar words. Discuss these Words to Know with students: *reputable* from *reputare* (to think over), *perpetual* from *perpetuus* (continuous), and *nominally* from *nomen* (name).

Practice Ask students how the meaning of the Latin words applies to the meaning of the Words to Know. Then have students discuss the meanings of these related words and write sentences using them: *reputation, perpetuate, nominate.*

Possible Response: The company has a reputation for giving good service. The generous donation will perpetuate the organization's scholarships for students. Jennifer plans to nominate Marcel for student council president.

A lesson on analyzing Greek and Latin roots appears on p. 340 of the Pupil's Edition.

For though men sensibly allow themselves great freedom in these respects, I doubt that they realize or can control the extreme severity with which they condemn such freedom in women.

These then were two very genuine experiences of my own. These were two of the adventures of my professional life. The first—killing the Angel in the House—I think I solved. She died. But the second, telling the truth about my own experiences as a body, I do not think I solved. I doubt that any woman has solved it yet. The obstacles against her are still immensely powerful—and yet they are very difficult to define. Outwardly, what is simpler than to write books? Outwardly, what obstacles are there for a woman rather than for a man? Inwardly, I think, the case is very different; she has still many ghosts to fight, many prejudices to overcome. Indeed it will be a long time still, I think, before a woman can sit down to write a book without finding a phantom to be slain, a rock to be dashed against. And if this is so in literature, the freest of all professions for women, how is it in the new professions which you are now for the first time entering?

Those are the questions that I should like, had I time, to ask you. And indeed, if I have laid stress upon these professional experiences of mine, it is because I believe that they are, though in different forms, yours also. Even when the path is nominally open—when there is nothing to prevent a woman from being a doctor, a lawyer, a civil servant—there are many phantoms and obstacles, as I believe, looming in her way. To discuss and define them is I think of great value and importance; for thus only can the labor be shared, the difficulties be solved. But besides this, it is necessary also to discuss the ends and the aims for which we are fighting, for which we are doing battle with these formidable obstacles. Those aims cannot be taken for granted; they must be perpetually questioned and examined. The whole position, as I see it—here in this hall surrounded by women practicing for the first time in history I know not how many different professions—is one of extraordinary interest and importance. You have won rooms of your own in the house hitherto exclusively owned by men. You are able, though not without great labor and effort, to pay the rent. You are earning your five hundred pounds a year. But this freedom is only a beginning; the room is your own, but it is still bare. It has to be furnished; it has to be decorated; it has to be shared. How are you going to furnish it, how are you going to decorate it? With whom are you going to share it, and upon what terms? These, I think are questions of the utmost importance and interest. For the first time in history you are able to ask them; for the first time you are able to decide for yourselves what the answers should be. Willingly would I stay and discuss those questions and answers—but not tonight. My time is up; and I must cease. ❖

WORDS TO KNOW

nominally (nŏm′ə-nə-lē) *adv.* apparently (but usually not in reality); seemingly

Customizing Instruction

Less Proficient Readers

1 Students may need help understanding the process of artistic creation as an unconscious state of "perpetual lethargy." Explain that the process is similar to a daydream, in which you withdraw your attention from outside reality and concentrate on the workings of your own imagination. It is important not to be disturbed during this trance-like state because you can lose the story or idea you've been imagining.

2 Students may not be sure what Woolf means by "the body" or "the passions." Woolf's inhibition goes back to the purity ideal of the "Angel in the House." Victorian women were not supposed to talk about or even feel passion, especially sexual passion. Any discussion of the body or its functions in mixed company was also taboo for women.

Connect to the Literature

1. **What Do You Think?** What impression did you form of Virginia Woolf as you were reading? Explain.

Comprehension Check
- Why did Woolf have trouble reviewing a male author's novel?
- What did Woolf have to do to the Angel in the House in order to write?
- Did Woolf feel that she could tell the truth about her "experiences as a body"?

Think Critically

2. What do you think Woolf meant by the phrase "the Angel in the House," and why did this angel have such power?

- the personal qualities associated with this angel
- the expectations that Victorian men had for women
- how the Angel got in the way of writing

3. Why did Woolf believe that "killing the Angel in the House was part of the occupation of a woman writer"?

4. **ACTIVE READING: RECOGNIZING MAIN IDEAS** Review the lists that you recorded in your **READER'S NOTEBOOK**. Based on your lists, what do you think are the main ideas in Woolf's speech?

5. According to Woolf, women had to learn more about their possibilities in "the arts and professions" before any woman could truly "be herself." What do you think she meant? Do you agree with her?

6. Why did Woolf believe that she had been unable to tell the complete truth about her experiences?

7. Woolf tells her audience, "You have won rooms of your own in the house hitherto exclusively owned by men. . . . But this freedom is only a beginning. . . ." What remained to be done?

Extend Interpretations

8. **Critic's Corner** According to feminist critic Jane Marcus, "Writing, for Virginia Woolf, was a revolutionary act. . . . an act of aggression against the powerful." Does "Professions for Women" illustrate Marcus's point? Explain why or why not.

9. **Connect to Life** Do you think the Angel in the House has been permanently destroyed as an image of women? If so, what image, if any, has replaced it? Explain your opinion.

LITERARY ANALYSIS: DICTION AND AUDIENCE

Diction is a writer's choice of words. Diction can be described by the following sets of terms:
- **formal** (*an attractive sweater*) or **informal** (*an awesome sweater*)
- **technical** (*a 90-degree turn*) or **commonly understood** (*a right turn*)
- **abstract** (*justice*) or **concrete** (*a judge's gown*)
- **literal** (*running clumsily*) or **figurative** (*running like a gazelle on crutches*)

In writing her speech for a group of pathbreaking professional women, Woolf tailored her diction to suit her **audience.**

Cooperative Learning Activity
With a small group of classmates, analyze Woolf's diction. Use a chart like the one below to identify characteristics of her diction. For each pair of terms shown, circle the one that best describes Woolf's diction. Then find two examples—words, phrases, or sentences—to illustrate each term that you have circled.

Characteristics of Diction	Examples
formal / (informal)	"But to tell you my story—it is a simple one."
commonly understood/ technical	
abstract / concrete	
literal / figurative	

Connect to the Literature

What Do You Think?

1. Students may use words such as *intelligent, independent, personable, humble,* and *thoughtful* to describe their impressions of Virginia Woolf.

Comprehension Check
- She was haunted by the image of the "Angel in the House" who told her to be sympathetic and not critical.
- She had to figuratively kill her.
- No.

Use Selection Quiz in **Unit Seven Resource Book,** p. 15.

Think Critically

2. Most students will explain the "Angel in the House" as the Victorian ideal of womanhood that haunted Woolf as she first began writing. Characterized by a selfless, mindless devotion to others, the Angel has to flatter and deceive to get her way. But to be a writer, Woolf had to have a mind of her own, and most important, she had to be honest, which meant criticizing male writers at times.
3. Woolf thought all women writers had to kill the Angel to silence her voice and her influence. If not, the Angel would destroy what it takes to be a woman writer, namely, openness, honesty, and independent thinking.
4. Main ideas may include
   - obstacles to becoming a woman writer, such as the image of the "Angel in the House" and the inhibition to talk about physical sensations and functions
   - rewards of being a professional writer, such as economic independence and intellectual freedom
5. Woolf admits that after killing the "Angel in the House" she has no definition of woman to take its place. She suggests that women define who they are by expressing themselves in the arts and professions. Students may interpret that to mean women can be themselves only by living up to their own standards rather than those set for them by men.
6. Woolf says she couldn't tell the truth about her bodily experiences for fear of shocking men. Students may understand this inhibition as stemming from what men consider fit and unfit for a woman to talk about.
7. Woolf's metaphor of independence as a room of one's own is only the beginning of freedom. Students may interpret what remains to be done as determining the content of their lives (furnishing and decorating the room) and their choice of family and friends (with whom to share it and on what terms).

Extend Interpretations

8. **Critic's Corner** Some students may consider Woolf radical in her speech because she so directly challenges the assumptions and dictates that men imposed on women at the time. For others, Woolf's rhetoric seems aimed not so much against men as against the male standards that women have internalized.
9. **Connect to Life** Students may argue that the "Angel in the House" still exists in some conservative, religious homes in the West and among traditional societies of the third world. However, some students will say that in the United States the new stereotype of the Super Mom has replaced the Victorian "Angel in the House."

Writing Options

1. Personal Response Write a personal essay in which you identify Woolf's main ideas and judge whether they are still relevant today. First, make a list of her main ideas and find quotations that support those ideas. Then consider whether women continue to face the same obstacles that Woolf identified.

2. Definition of Male Ideal What ideal of manhood do men have to struggle with today? Using as a model Woolf's definition of the Angel in the House, write a paragraph defining the stereotype of the ideal male. Try to think of an interesting image that captures the essence of the stereotype.

Activities & Explorations

1. Photo Essay Create a photo essay about the roles of women in today's society. Clip photos from magazines or download images from the Internet that show those roles. Find quotations from Woolf's essay to use as captions. ~ **VIEWING AND REPRESENTING**

2. Words of Wisdom Choose a topic that your own experience qualifies you to speak about, such as competing in sports or meeting some other challenge. Then compose and deliver a speech that explains how you dealt with obstacles in your way. ~ **SPEAKING AND LISTENING**

Communication Handbook
See page R50: Giving a Speech.

Inquiry & Research

Time Line of Women's History Research the history of the women's movement in England. Then create an annotated time line of important events, such as the Married Women's Property Act of 1882, giving a brief description of each event. Also include landmark publications, such as John Stuart Mill's *The Subjection of Women* (1869).

Vocabulary in Action

EXERCISE: CONTEXT CLUES Choose the Word to Know that best completes each sentence.

1. Woolf's father was extremely industrious; he had little patience with ______.
2. With her husband, Leonard, Woolf founded the Hogarth Press, which became a(n) ______ and influential publishing house.
3. Woolf is ______ listed as a translator for some books by Russians, but scholars doubt that she truly knew Russian.
4. After completing each of her novels, Woolf's mental anguish became ______.
5. Woolf doubted her own abilities, not realizing that her greatest books would bring her ______ fame.

WORDS TO KNOW

acute
lethargy
nominally
perpetual
reputable

Building Vocabulary
For an in-depth lesson on word families, see page 1196.

Literary Analysis

Cooperative Learning Activity
Examples could be among the following:

Informal: "If there was chicken, she took the leg. . . ." and "A Persian cat is all very well, I said; but a Persian cat is not enough."

Commonly understood: "In other words, now that she had rid herself of falsehood, that young woman had only to be herself. Ah, but what is 'herself'? I mean, what is a woman?"

Concrete: "I turned upon her and caught her by the throat" and "She would have plucked the heart out of my writing."

Figurative: "[T]his girl is the image of a fisherman lying sunk in dreams on the verge of a deep lake. . . ." and "[T]he room is your own, but it is still bare. It has to be furnished; it has to be decorated; it has to be shared."

Use **Unit Seven Resource Book,** p, 13, for more practice.

Writing Options

1. **Personal Response** If necessary, help students identify Woolf's main ideas about the "Angel in the House" and her inhibition to talk about the body. Encourage students to be honest in considering today's obstacles. For example, has any female student felt it necessary or desirable to be nice and sympathetic?
2. **Definition of Male Ideal** Have students consider images of men from the media—newspapers, magazines, advertising, TV, and the movies. What kind of behavior is expected of men? What kind of men do both men and women look up to?

Activities & Explorations

1. **Photo Essay** Suggest that students include a range of roles from celebrities and sports figures to corporate executives, tradespeople, caregivers, and soccer moms.
2. **Words of Wisdom** Help students think of things they may have expertise in, such as building something, taking a test, or performing in front of an audience. Suggest that students write notes for their speech and practice in front of a mirror before delivering it to the class.

Inquiry & Research

Time Line of Women's History Suggest that students do an Internet search for information and photos about the British women's movement. Make sure they include information about Emmeline and Christabel Pankhurst and the more militant champions of women suffrage.

Vocabulary in Action

1. lethargy
2. reputable
3. nominally
4. acute
5. perpetual

To assess skills and concepts taught in this selection use **Formal Assessment Book,** p. 165–166.

Objectives

- understand and appreciate a **short story (Literary Analysis)**
- analysize a character's **internal conflict (Literary Analysis)**
- use strategies for **analyzing motivation (Active Reading)**

Summary

As day turns into evening, nineteen-year-old Eveline sits wearily by the window contemplating the upcoming change in her life. She is to elope with Frank that night and sail to Buenos Aires to begin a new life. As she sits with farewell letters to her brother and father on her lap, she inventories her life for clear reasons to go or stay. Her low-wage job certainly does not compel her to stay. Her home life, although providing food and shelter, consists of hard domestic work and caring for her younger siblings. Her father is a brute, stingy with money she herself has earned as well as cruelly manipulative and physically threatening. She remembers her mother's "life of commonplace sacrifices" that ended in madness and death. Thoughts of her mother's pitiful life ultimately spur Eveline to escape, and she leaves her home to meet Frank by the docks. But when it comes time to board the ship, Eveline freezes by the railing and refuses to follow Frank to the ship. Despite his calls to her, she remains unmoved and immovable on the dock.

Use **Unit Seven Resource Book,** p. 16, for additional support.

Thematic Link

In this story, Eveline has a chance to **change her world** dramatically if she elopes with an adventurous young man.

5-Minute Warm-Up

Daily Language SkillBuilder

Have students **proofread** the display sentences on page 1095m and write them correctly.

Eveline

JAMES JOYCE

James Joyce
1882–1941

The Writers' Writer James Joyce has been called a writers' writer because of the bold originality and artistry of his fiction. According to one critic, Joyce "published nothing but masterpieces."

Son of Ireland Joyce was born to a large family in Dublin, into an Ireland dominated by England and the Roman Catholic Church. His mother was deeply religious, and his father was a talented singer, a reckless drinker, and an indifferent worker. Though the Joyce family gradually sank into poverty, James, the oldest child, received an excellent education. As a young man, he felt stifled by the Catholic Church and the bitter divisions of Irish politics. In 1904 he left Ireland, along with the woman who would become his wife, Nora Barnacle.

Life in Exile Joyce settled in Trieste, Italy, from 1905 to 1915, teaching English to support Nora and their two children. By all accounts, Joyce's family life was a happy one. His troubles came primarily from publishers who, because of the author's frank treatment of his subjects, were unwilling to print his books for fear of violating censorship laws. Joyce had better luck publishing sections of his first novel, *A Portrait of the Artist as a Young Man,* in the *Egoist* magazine. The novel was later published in book form in 1916.

Critical Success The novel became an immediate critical success. It reveals the innermost thoughts of the young writer Stephen Dedalus, ending with his decision to leave Ireland and dedicate himself to art. The work attracted the attention of the American poet Ezra Pound, who convinced Joyce to move to Paris in 1920. By the time Joyce published his second novel, *Ulysses,* in Paris two years later, it had already become infamous for censorship troubles. The novel chronicles a single day in Dublin in 1904, making bold use of a technique called stream of consciousness, which tries to duplicate the rapid twists and turns of the mind in thought. *Ulysses* has been widely praised as the greatest novel of the 20th century.

Last Years For much of his later life, Joyce suffered from serious eye diseases. He had 25 operations and at times was completely blind. In Paris he had to rely on his increasing number of friends and followers to proofread his work. For 17 years, Joyce worked on his long final novel, *Finnegans Wake,* a complex, experimental, dreamlike work about a Dublin innkeeper and his family.

LESSON RESOURCES

UNIT SEVEN RESOURCE BOOK, pp. 16–19

ASSESSMENT RESOURCES
Formal Assessment, pp. 167–168
Teacher's Guide to Assessment and Portfolio Use
Test Generator

INTEGRATED TECHNOLOGY
Visit our Web site: classzone.com

ADDITIONAL RESOURCES
Lesson Planning Guide, pp. 145–146
Teacher's Sourcebook for Language Development

Connect to Your Life

"Eveline" tells about a woman in her late teens who considers leaving home. What are some reasons that young adults might have for contemplating such an action?

LITERARY ANALYSIS: INTERNAL CONFLICT

An **internal conflict** is a struggle between opposing forces within a person or a character. In "Professions for Women," Virginia Woolf explains a professional woman's internal conflict between the freedom she wants and the social expectations she feels obligated to fulfill. In "Eveline," the main character undergoes a similar internal struggle as she considers a major decision in her life.

ACTIVE READING: ANALYZING MOTIVATION

Motivation is the reason someone does something—the "why" behind a person's action, thought, or feeling. Since this story is about Eveline, understanding her motivation is key to understanding the entire story.

READER'S NOTEBOOK As you read, make a chart similar to the one below to help you understand Eveline's internal conflict, as well as what motivates her final decision.

Decision to Be Made: ______	
Motivations to Go:	Motivations to Stay:

Build Background

Dubliners

A Break with the Past "Eveline" is one of 15 interrelated stories collected in *Dubliners.* Although the story is one of Joyce's earliest works—it was first published in 1904—it still shows a clear break with the artificial coincidences and surprises of stories by earlier masters, such as the French writer Guy de Maupassant (gē' də mō'pə-sänt'). Very little happens in Joyce's short stories. What matters instead is the richly suggestive portraits of the main characters and the close observation of everyday life.

A "Moral History" of Irish Life In Joyce's view, these stories present a "moral history" of Ireland. Joyce was sharply critical of Irish life, because he felt that it restricted the human spirit. He set his stories in Dublin because he considered it "the center of paralysis."

Art as Revelation When Joyce was first working on these stories, he called them "epiphanies." The word *epiphany* usually refers to an experience of religious revelation. Joyce thought that art, like religion, possessed the power to reveal deep truths. He used the term *epiphany* to describe a sudden insight into the real truth of a situation or character.

READING FOR INFORMATION

Reading Skills and Strategies

MAKING INFERENCES

Remind students that an inference is an educated guess about the meaning of something. When you make an inference, you read between the lines to understand an idea that is not directly stated. After students read about Joyce's life and the background information on *Dubliners*, ask them to infer why Joyce left Dublin but chose to write about Dubliners in all of his work.

Possible Responses: Even though Joyce escaped Dublin, he was fascinated by those who stayed. Joyce needed to put a physical distance between himself and what he chose to write about. Joyce wanted to write about people in Dublin but felt too stifled to live there.

TIME MANAGEMENT

If your schedule requires that you cover the lesson objectives in a shorter time, use . . .

- Preparing to Read, pp. 1166 and 1167
- Thinking Through the Literature, p. 1172

If you want to take advantage of longer blocks of class time, use . . .

- TE Teaching Options: Informal Assessment, p. 1169; Speaking and Listening, p. 1170; Grammar, p. 1171
- Choices & Challenges, p. 1173

Literary Analysis INTERNAL CONFLICT

A As Eveline contemplates her decision to leave home, she reveals her inner conflict. Have students pay particular attention to what she does and doesn't say about her home life. For example, in this sentence, she associates home with food, shelter, and people she has known all her life. What she doesn't mention is love, companionship, pleasure, or anything else positive that you might expect someone to feel about home.

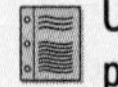 Use **Unit Seven Resource Book,** p. 18, for more practice.

Active Reading
ANALYZING MOTIVATION

B Students will find several motivations for Eveline to leave home on these two pages—namely, a lousy job, a cruel father, and an all-around hard life. But this sentence seems to undercut all her good reasons to go. Have students speculate about why she feels so ambivalent about leaving home.
Possible Responses: She's afraid of change; she clings to her known world right before she is going to leave it; she feel nostalgic about her home because she knows she may never see it again.

 Use **Unit Seven Resource Book,** p. 17, for more practice.

Eveline

James Joyce

She sat at the window watching the evening invade the avenue. Her head was leaned against the window curtains and in her nostrils was the odor of dusty cretonne.[1] She was tired.

Few people passed. The man out of the last house passed on his way home; she heard his footsteps clacking along the concrete pavement and afterwards crunching on the cinder path before the new red houses. One time there used to be a field there in which they used to play every evening with other people's children. Then a man from Belfast[2] bought the field and built houses in it—not like their little brown houses but bright brick houses with shining roofs. The children of the avenue used to play together in that field—the Devines, the Waters, the Dunns, little Keogh[3] the cripple, she and her brothers and sisters. Ernest, however, never played: he was too grown up. Her father used often to hunt them in out of the field with his blackthorn stick;[4] but usually little Keogh used to keep nix[5] and call out when he saw her father coming. Still they seemed to have been rather happy then. Her father was not so bad then; and besides, her mother was alive. That was a long time ago; she and her brothers and sisters were all grown up; her mother was dead. Tizzie Dunn was dead, too, and the Waters had gone back to England. Everything changes. Now she was going to go away like the others, to leave her home.

Home! She looked round the room, reviewing all its familiar objects which she had dusted once a week for so many years, wondering where on earth all the dust came from. Perhaps she would never see again those familiar objects from which she had never dreamed of being divided. And yet during all those years she had never found out the name of the priest whose yellowing photograph hung on the wall above the broken harmonium[6] beside the colored print of the promises made to Blessed Margaret Mary Alacoque.[7] He had been a school friend of her father. Whenever he showed the photograph to a visitor her father used to pass it with a casual word:

—He is in Melbourne[8] now.

She had consented to go away, to leave her home. Was that wise? She tried to weigh each side of the question. In her home anyway she had shelter and food; she had those whom she had known all her life about her. Of course she had to work hard both in the house and at business. What would they say of her in the Stores when they found out that she had run away with a fellow? Say she was a fool, perhaps, and her place would be filled up by advertisement. Miss Gavan would be glad. She had always had an edge on her, especially whenever there were people listening.

A

1

1. **cretonne** (krĭ-tŏn′): a heavy, colorfully printed cotton or linen fabric, often used for curtains.
2. **Belfast:** a city in Northern Ireland.
3. **Keogh** (kē′ō).
4. **blackthorn stick:** a walking stick made from the wood of the blackthorn, a type of thorny shrub.
5. **nix:** watch.
6. **harmonium:** an organlike keyboard instrument.
7. **promises made to Blessed Margaret Mary Alacoque** (ä-lä-kôk′): Many Irish Catholic households featured prints showing the Sacred Heart of Jesus and listing the promises made by God to Margaret Mary Alacoque (1647–1690), in which God vowed to honor and bless those who were faithful to the Sacred Heart.
8. **Melbourne:** a city in Australia.

Fishergirl, Newlyn, Stanhope Alexander Forbes. © Christies Images Ltd./ The Estate of Stanhope Alexander Forbes/Bridgeman Art Library.

knew it was that that had given her the palpitations.[9] When they were growing up he had never gone for her, like he used to go for Harry and Ernest, because she was a girl; but latterly he had begun to threaten her and say what he would do to her only for her dead mother's sake. And now she had nobody to protect her. Ernest was dead and Harry, who was in the church decorating business, was nearly always down somewhere in the country. Besides, the invariable squabble for money on Saturday nights had begun to weary her unspeakably. She always gave her entire wages—seven shillings[10]—and Harry always sent up what he could but the trouble was to get any money from her father. He said she used to squander the money, that she had no head, that he wasn't going to give her his hard-earned money to throw about the streets, and much more, for he was usually fairly bad of a Saturday night. In the end he would give her the money and ask her had she any intention of buying Sunday's dinner. Then she had to rush out as quickly as she could and do her marketing, holding her black leather purse tightly in her hand as she elbowed her way through the crowds and returning home late under her load of provisions. She had hard work to keep the house together and to see that the two young children who had been left to her charge went to school regularly and got their meals regularly. It was hard work—a hard life—but now that she was about to leave it she did not find it a wholly undesirable life.

—Miss Hill, don't you see these ladies are waiting?

—Look lively, Miss Hill, please.

She would not cry many tears at leaving the Stores.

But in her new home, in a distant unknown country, it would not be like that. Then she would be married—she, Eveline. People would treat her with respect then. She would not be treated as her mother had been. Even now, though she was over nineteen, she sometimes felt herself in danger of her father's violence. She

9. **palpitations:** rapid or irregular heartbeats.

10. **seven shillings:** a very small amount of money. Eveline's wages place her at poverty level.

Customizing Instruction

English Learners

1 Students may have trouble with Joyce's idiomatic phrasing. Explain that "in the Stores" indicates that Eveline's job is sales clerk at a store of some kind.

2 Make sure students understand that Eveline's father is a violent man who beat her brothers but "had never gone for her," or not hit Eveline, yet. Explain that "latterly he had begun to threaten her . . . for her dead mother's sake" means that lately he'd come close to hitting her but says the memory of her dead mother had stopped him. Of course, his reference to Eveline's mother is ironic here because the implication earlier in this paragraph is that he had abused her mother, verbally if not physically.

3 Point out that *variable* means changing or subject to change, and so *invariable* means the opposite, "unchanging or constant." The prefix *in-* frequently means "not," as in *inactive, involuntary,* and *indecisive*. A squabble is an argument over a trivial matter. "Invariable squabble" means that the argument happened over and over again.

Less Proficient Readers

4 Explain to students that Joyce is a very economical writer who doesn't waste words. This example of the cruelty of Eveline's father illustrates his manipulative, overbearing personality so precisely that few other details are necessary. First, make sure students understand that Eveline gives all of her meager wages to her father but that he is reluctant to give her any money back to buy groceries ("provisions"). Then, during their regular Saturday-night argument (the "invariable squabble") over money, he accuses her of squandering, or wasting, money. After this argument has worn her down, he relents and then deviously "asks" if she's going to buy something to cook for Sunday's dinner. Since stores in Ireland are closed on Sunday, Eveline then has to go out shopping on Saturday night and fight the crowds ("elbowed her way through"). Have students think of words that describe Eveline's father in this scene. *(brutal, overbearing, tyrannical, manipulative, mean, deceitful, devious, hypocritical, abusive, bullying)*

Assessment Informal Assessment

IDENTIFYING MAIN IDEAS To check students' understanding of Eveline's internal conflict so far, have them first list all of her obligations to her family. Then have them make a corresponding list that identifies how she feels about each of those obligations.

RUBRIC

3 Full Accomplishment Students' lists of obligations include (1) how Eveline's salary helps support her family, (2) that she shops, cooks, and cleans for her father and younger brothers, and (3) that she takes care of her younger brothers. Her feelings should include that (1) she doesn't like her job and has to hand over her salary to her father, (2) that she fears her father's violence, and (3) that she considers her life "hard" but otherwise not "wholly undesirable."

2 Substantial Accomplishment Students' lists include two of the three obligations and feelings.

1 Little or Partial Accomplishment Students' lists include one of the three obligations and feelings.

Literary Analysis CHARACTER

A Unlike Eveline's character, which is gradually revealed through her own confused thoughts and emotions, Frank's character seems much more clearly defined. Frank is such a strong presence that he brings Eveline's character into sharper focus by contrast. In literary terms, Frank is called a *foil,* a character who is meant to contrast and show off aspects of another character. Have students identify Frank's character traits as revealed in this paragraph. Then discuss the differences between Frank and Eveline.

Possible Response: According to Eveline, Frank is "kind, manly, and open-hearted." Through her description of his actions, he also shows himself to be energetic, assertive, decisive, optimistic, adventurous, and resourceful. He seems the opposite of Eveline in every way, for Eveline reveals herself to be listless, passive, indecisive, pessimistic, timid, and helpless.

Active Reading

ANALYZING MOTIVATION

B Ask students how bound they think Eveline feels by the promise she made to her mother.

Possible Responses: Some will say she feels very bound because it was a promise made at her mother's deathbed. Others may argue that Eveline doesn't seem as conflicted by her promise to her mother as she does by her fear of change in general. Some students may point out that the wording of the promise "as long as she could" gives Eveline an out.

Literary Analysis IMAGERY

C Have students identify the sound imagery in this last section of the story, when Eveline is at the docks. What is the effect of such imagery?

Possible Responses: Sounds include the "long mournful whistle" of the boat; the clanging bell "upon her heart;" Eveline's "cry of anguish;" Frank's calls and others' shouts. The sounds are not pleasant but rather either sad or harsh and disruptive. Such a confusion of sounds expresses Eveline's emotional distress.

St. Patrick's Close, Dublin, Walter Osborne.

She was about to explore another life with Frank. Frank was very kind, manly, open-hearted. She was to go away with him by the night-boat to be his wife and to live with him in Buenos Ayres[11] where he had a home waiting for her. How well she remembered the first time she had seen him; he was lodging in a house on the main road where she used to visit. It seemed a few weeks ago. He was standing at the gate, his peaked cap pushed back on his head and his hair tumbled forward over a face of bronze. Then they had come to know each other. He used to meet her outside the Stores every evening and see her home. He took her to see *The Bohemian Girl*[12] and she felt elated as she sat in an unaccustomed part of the theater with him. He was awfully fond of music and sang a little. People knew that they were courting and, when he sang about the lass that loves a sailor, she always felt pleasantly confused. He used to call her Poppens out of fun. First of all it had been an excitement for her to have a fellow and then she had begun to like him. He had tales of distant countries. He had started as a deck boy at a pound a month on a ship of the Allan Line going out to Canada. He told her the names of the ships he had been on and the names of the different services. He had sailed through the Straits of Magellan[13] and he told her stories of the terrible Patagonians.[14] He had fallen on his feet in Buenos Ayres, he said, and had come over to the old country just for a holiday. Of course, her father had found out the affair and had forbidden her to have anything to say to him.

—I know these sailor chaps, he said.

One day he had quarreled with Frank and after that she had to meet her lover secretly.

The evening deepened in the avenue. The white of two letters in her lap grew indistinct. One was to Harry; the other was to her father. Ernest had been her favorite but she liked Harry too. Her father was becoming old lately, she noticed; he would miss her. Sometimes he could be very nice. Not long before, when she had been laid up for a day, he had read her out a ghost story and made toast for her at the fire. Another day, when their mother was alive, they had all gone for a picnic to the Hill of Howth.[15] She remembered her father putting on her mother's bonnet to make the children laugh.

Her time was running out but she continued to sit by the window, leaning her head against the window curtain, inhaling the odor of dusty

11. **Buenos Ayres** (bwā′nəs âr′ēz): a city in Argentina (now spelled Buenos Aires).
12. ***The Bohemian Girl:*** a popular opera by the Irish composer Michael Balfe.
13. **Straits of Magellan:** a narrow water passage at the southern tip of South America, connecting the Atlantic and Pacific Oceans.
14. **Patagonians** (păt′ə-gō′nē-ənz): native inhabitants of Patagonia, a region in southern South America. They were traditionally thought to be of gigantic stature.
15. **Hill of Howth:** a landmark near Dublin, facing the Bay of Dublin.

MINI LESSON Speaking and Listening

MONOLOGUE

Prepare Help interested students create a monologue of Eveline's thoughts as she weighs her decision to leave. Possible passages include the paragraph beginning with "She had consented to go away" on p. 1168 to the end of p. 1169 and the beginning of p. 1170 to the break on p. 1171. Suggest that in addition to changing the pronouns from *she* to *I*, students might simplify parts of the passage by summarizing dialogue, for example.

Present Have students write up their monologues and rehearse their performance so that they do not have to read the monologue word for word. Explain that they will be evaluated on their dramatic presentation as well as on the content of the monologue.

This activity is particularly well suited to longer blocks of time.

cretonne. Down far in the avenue she could hear a street organ playing. She knew the air.[16] Strange that it should come that very night to remind her of the promise to her mother, her promise to keep the home together as long as she could. She remembered the last night of her mother's illness; she was again in the close dark room at the other side of the hall and outside she heard a melancholy air of Italy. The organ-player had been ordered to go away and given sixpence. She remembered her father strutting back into the sickroom saying:

—Damned Italians! coming over here!

As she mused the pitiful vision of her mother's life laid its spell on the very quick[17] of her being—that life of commonplace sacrifices closing in final craziness. She trembled as she heard again her mother's voice saying constantly with foolish insistence:

—Derevaun Seraun![18] Derevaun Seraun!

She stood up in a sudden impulse of terror. Escape! She must escape! Frank would save her. He would give her life, perhaps love, too. But she wanted to live. Why should she be unhappy? She had a right to happiness. Frank would take her in his arms, fold her in his arms. He would save her.

Her time was running out but she continued to sit by the window, leaning her head against the window curtain, inhaling the odor of dusty cretonne.

She stood among the swaying crowd in the station at the North Wall.[19] He held her hand and she knew that he was speaking to her, saying something about the passage over and over again. The station was full of soldiers with brown baggages. Through the wide doors of the sheds she caught a glimpse of the black mass of the boat, lying in beside the quay[20] wall, with illumined portholes. She answered nothing. She felt her cheek pale and cold and, out of a maze of distress, she prayed to God to direct her, to show her what was her duty. The boat blew a long mournful whistle into the mist. If she went, tomorrow she would be on the sea with Frank, steaming towards Buenos Ayres. Their passage had been booked. Could she still draw back after all he had done for her? Her distress awoke a nausea in her body and she kept moving her lips in silent fervent prayer.

A bell clanged upon her heart. She felt him seize her hand:

—Come!

All the seas of the world tumbled about her heart. He was drawing her into them: he would drown her. She gripped with both hands at the iron railing.

—Come!

No! No! No! It was impossible. Her hands clutched the iron in frenzy. Amid the seas she sent a cry of anguish!

—Eveline! Evvy!

He rushed beyond the barrier and called to her to follow. He was shouted at to go on but he still called to her. She set her white face to him, passive, like a helpless animal. Her eyes gave him no sign of love or farewell or recognition. ❖

16. **air:** melody; song.
17. **quick:** the most personal and sensitive part of the emotions.
18. **Derevaun Seraun:** seemingly, a misspoken phrase in Gaelic (the original language of Ireland), sometimes interpreted to mean "The end of pleasure is pain."
19. **North Wall:** a dock on the River Liffey, where passengers could board a "night-boat" to Liverpool, England. Apparently, Frank and Eveline have planned to travel to Liverpool, where they could then board a ship to Argentina.
20. **quay** (kē): a place where ships are loaded and unloaded; wharf.

Customizing Instruction

Less Proficient Readers

1 Help students understand how pitiful Eveline's mother's life must have been. In addition to hard work, an abusive husband, five children, and a life of poverty, her mother's life was one "of commonplace sacrifices closing in final craziness."

- Have students explain what that phrase means. *(She had sacrificed so much for others on a daily basis that it eventually drove her insane.)*
- Ask students if they think Eveline's life would become like her mother's if she stayed home. *(Most students will say yes because there is no evidence to suggest otherwise. Apparently, Eveline thinks so herself because in the next paragraph she feels the strong urge to escape.)*

Advanced Learners

Have students analyze the sound imagery throughout the story–from the "clacking" and "crunching" of footsteps at the beginning to Frank's singing and the street organ in the middle to the final jumble of sounds at the end. What are the different ways that Joyce uses sound imagery?

Possible Response: Sounds trigger memories twice in the story. The clacking and crunching sounds of a man's shoes on the pavement at the beginning reminds Eveline of the field that used to be there. The music of the organ grinder awakens Eveline's memory of her mother. Music is also used to express aspects of character. The amiable Frank is a singer, for example, whereas Eveline's brutal father sends the musician away from his home with a curse. The confusing sounds at the end of the story express Eveline's confusion and distress.

MINI LESSON Grammar

COMPOUND-COMPLEX SENTENCES

Instruction Review with students the definition of a compound sentence, which contains two or more independent clauses. Remind students that the clauses may be joined by a coordinating conjunction or a semicolon. Then review the definition of a complex sentence, which contains one independent clause and one or more subordinate clauses. Explain that a compound-complex sentence contains two or more independent clauses and one or more subordinate clauses.

Model Write the following sentence from page 1171 on the board:

He held her hand and she knew that he was speaking to her.

Have students identify the subordinate clause *(that he was speaking to her)*, the independent clauses *(He held her hand, she knew)*, and the coordinating conjunction *(and)*.

Practice Write the following sentences on the board and have students identify the subordinate (underlined) and independent clauses (italics):

1. When Eveline arrived at the station, *she became distressed,* and *she wavered in her decision.*
2. *Frank gripped her hand,* and *he pleaded with her* because he wanted her to join him.
3. *Eveline stood in silence; she did not even look at Frank* although he called out to her.

For more instruction and practice,, see McDougal Littell's ***Language Network:***

- Grade 10, Chapter 4, "Sentence Structure"
- Grade 12, Chapter 3, "Sentence Structure"

Connect to the Literature

1. **What Do You Think?** Some students may sympathize with Eveline's plight, while others may criticize her passivity. Students should provide reasons in the text for their opinions.

Comprehension Check

- Eveline has to decide whether to elope with Frank to Buenos Aires.
- She is poor, works hard, and cares for her younger siblings and her abusive father.
- At the last minute, Eveline refuses to go with Frank and remains frozen in a daze on the dock.

Use Selection Quiz in **Unit Seven Resource Book,** p. 19.

Think Critically

2. Some students will say that Eveline's fear of change stops her. They may interpret her fear of drowning ("he would drown her") as a fear of being overwhelmed by the unknown. Others may say that her conflicting duties to her family and to Frank as well as herself ("what was her duty") cause her to freeze at the railing.
3. Students who think Eveline's reasons for leaving far outweigh her reasons for staying will probably say that she made the wrong decision. Others may consider a move to Buenos Aires far too radical a change for Eveline—one that she may have regretted—and argue that she made the right choice in the long run.
4. For some students, the revelation will be Eveline's inability to change her life. Others may see her life as a tragic waste, caused partly by the emotional and economic poverty of her environment but also by the failure of Eveline's imagination to conceive of a better life.
5. Many students can imagine no better life for Eveline than her mother had. After her father's death, she may spend the rest of her days in loneliness. Some may argue that she could have another chance at happiness, possibly by marrying someone else or getting a better job.

Connect to the Literature

1. **What Do You Think?** What did you think of Eveline by the end of the story?

Comprehension Check

- What decision does Eveline have to make?
- Why is Eveline's life difficult?
- What happens at the end of the story?

Think Critically

2. Why do you think Eveline refuses to go with Frank? Use examples from the story to support your opinion.
3. **ACTIVE READING: ANALYZING MOTIVATION** Review the chart you made in your  READER'S NOTEBOOK. Compare Eveline's reasons for going with her reasons for staying. Do you think she made the right decision? Why or why not?
4. Joyce described his stories as epiphanies, but his readers do not always agree about what is revealed in them. In your opinion, what epiphany, or revelation, takes place at the end of this story?
5. What kind of life can Eveline expect to have now that she has decided to stay in Dublin?

THINK ABOUT
- her mother's life and death
- the way her father treats her
- the kind of job she has

Extend Interpretations

6. **What If?** What if Eveline had gone with Frank to Buenos Aires? Do you think she could have been happy? Explain your opinion.
7. **Critic's Corner** Joyce said that he chose Dublin as his setting because it was "the center of paralysis." How might this story illustrate that paralysis?
8. **Comparing Texts** How do you think Virginia Woolf would explain Eveline's problem? Apply Woolf's analysis of women's problems in "Professions for Women" to Eveline's situation.
9. **Connect to Life** When making an important decision, such as the one Eveline faced, which is more important to you, ensuring your freedom or fulfilling your responsibilities?

LITERARY ANALYSIS: INTERNAL CONFLICT

The struggle of opposing forces within a character is known as **internal conflict.** In "Eveline," the reader gets to see what's going on in Eveline's mind as she struggles with whether to leave with Frank or stay home.

Cooperative Learning Activity Working with three classmates, review the story for evidence of what causes Eveline's internal conflict. One person should focus on how Eveline's father contributes to her internal conflict; another person should focus on the role of Eveline's dead mother. A third person should study how Frank influences Eveline's internal conflict, and a fourth person should analyze Eveline's own personality. Discuss your group's findings, then give a summary of the analysis to the rest of the class.

REVIEW: POINT OF VIEW What is the narrative method, or **point of view,** in this story? Is it told from a **first-person,** a **third-person limited,** or a **third-person omniscient** point of view? What are the advantages of using this point of view in this story?

Extend Interpretations

6. **What If?** Those students who think Eveline made the wrong decision will probably think her life would have improved in another country and that she would have been happy with Frank. Some students may think that Eveline is really incapable of happiness.
7. **Critic's Corner** Most students will see Eveline's story as one of increasing paralysis. At the end, she is literally stuck to the railing—unable to move, paralyzed by her own passivity and fear.
8. **Comparing Texts** Virginia Woolf would probably diagnose Eveline's problem as the "Angel-in-the-House" syndrome. Eveline feels guilty trying to pursue her own happiness, but her self-sacrifice for her family gains her nothing. Her mother went mad trying to live up to the Angel image, and Eveline unfortunately may follow.
9. **Connect to Life** Many students will claim their freedom first, although some will feel a strong sense of family responsibility.

Writing Options

1. Literary Analysis Write a character sketch of Eveline based on what you know about her and her family life. In your analysis of her situation, explain why she ends up staying in Dublin. Use quotations from the story to support your views. Place your analysis in your **Working Portfolio.**

2. Advice Column What if Eveline had asked for help from an advice columnist? Write the letter that you imagine she would have written, and then answer the letter as you think an advice columnist would.

Activities & Explorations

1. Father-Daughter Dialogue Working with a partner, stage a dialogue between Eveline and her father that reveals not only their individual characters but also the kind of relationship they have. You may write out the dialogue ahead of time or stage an impromptu conversation.
~ SPEAKING AND LISTENING

2. Story Illustration If you had to choose one picture to accompany this story, what would it show? Look through art books to find a work of art that you think best captures the essence of the story. Show your illustration to the class and explain why you chose it.
~ VIEWING AND REPRESENTING

Inquiry & Research

1. Joyce vs. the Publishers Find out why Joyce had so much trouble getting publishers to print *Dubliners.* What did the Irish and British publishers object to? Try looking through the index of a biography of Joyce to narrow your search. Then tell the class what you found out.

2. Eveline's Prospects What prospects did young women in Dublin have at the beginning of the 20th century? What jobs could they get? What were their chances of getting married? What kind of life did single women have? The book *Joyce Annotated* by Don Gifford is a good resource for answering these questions. Report your findings to the class.

Literary Analysis

Cooperative Learning Activity
Possible findings of the group: Every person in Eveline's life gives her a reason both to stay or to leave. Eveline's father is cruel and tyrannical; but she recognizes two good things that he did (reading to her when she was sick and making the children laugh on a picnic). Eveline's mother provides an example of what can happen if she stays, but she also extracts a promise from Eveline to keep the family together. Frank is loving and attentive, but his offer to live in South America takes her too far from what she knows. Eveline herself, although she cares for Frank and feels a self-protective urge to escape, is far too passive and fearful to make the plunge into the unknown.

Use **Unit Seven Resource Book,** p. 18, for more practice.

Point of View The third person limited point of view allows the reader to learn about Eveline and her situation from her own perspective. It also increases suspense, since the reader doesn't know until the end what she's going to decide.

Writing Options

1. **Literary Analysis** Have students focus on Eveline's internal conflict in their analyses and the character traits that ultimately keep her from following Frank onto the boat.
2. **Advice Column** Remind students that the kind of advice the columnist gives would depend on his or her value system. If the columnist believes in traditional roles for women, for example, the advice would be to stay. Make sure students clarify the columnist's value system.

Activities & Explorations

1. **Father-Daughter Dialogue** Students should review the scenes between Eveline and her father on pages 1169 and 1170 before composing their dialogues. Remind them to practice before performing.
2. **Story Illustration** Suggest that students go to a public library to look through art books. Illustrated history books would also include photos and pictures from the time, as would related web sites.

Inquiry & Research

1. **Joyce vs. the Publishers** Students could begin their research with an encyclopedia article, which would also list some standard books on James Joyce, such as Richard Ellman's biography. Also, Paul Vanderham's *James Joyce and Censorship: The Trials of Ulysses* is a reliable source.
2. **Eveline's Prospects** Specific studies of Irish women's history include *Clio's Daughters: Essays on Irish Women's History 1845 to 1939* and *Women and Paid Work, 1500–1939* both edited by Bernadette Whelan.

To assess skills and concepts taught in this selection use **Formal Assessment Book,** pp. 167–168.

Objectives
- understand and appreciate a Japanese **short story (Literary Analysis)**
- understand the meaning of a **symbol (Literary Analysis)**
- use strategies for **clarifying sequence (Active Reading)**

Summary
One morning, Yoshiko notices a jay acting strangely outside the window. Her grandmother explains that the bird is a mother who had lost her chick the day before and is still looking for it. Worrying about the jay, Yoshiko prepares for a visit with her future mother-in-law whom her father and stepmother are bringing over. Yoshiko's parents divorced when she was four, and her father waited ten years before remarrying. The family then lived happily together until Yoshiko's brother announced one day that he had contacted their biological mother. Such a revelation disrupted the family, upsetting Yoshiko, her stepmother, and especially her father, who decided to live elsewhere with this second wife. Despite their separation, Yoshiko remains on good terms with her father and stepmother. While waiting for them to arrive, she finds the baby jay and reunites it with its mother.

Use **Unit Seven Resource Book,** p. 20, for more support.

Thematic Link
After suffering several **changes** and losses in her life, Yoshiko's **world** is about to become whole again.

Use **Unit Seven Resource Book,** p. 23, for practice with Words to Know.

5-Minute Warm-Up
Daily Language SkillBuilder

Have students **proofread** the display sentences on page 1095m and write them correctly.

THE JAY

yasunari **kawabata**

Yasunari Kawabata
1899–1972

Childhood Losses The Nobel Prize-winning novelist Yasunari Kawabata (yä'so͞o-nä'rē kä'wə-bä'tə) knew sadness and loss at an early age. His parents died shortly after his birth in Osaka, Japan. His grandmother, who helped raise him, died when he was seven, and his only sister died two years later. After the death of his grandfather, Kawabata found himself alone in the world at the age of 14. Many scholars have traced the sense of isolation and loneliness evident in much of Kawabata's work to these early childhood losses.

Literary Career By the time Kawabata graduated from Tokyo Imperial University in 1924, he had established a literary career. His first success was the semiautobiographical novel *The Izu Dancer*, about his youthful crush on a dancer. Kawabata's period of greatest creativity began after World War II, with the publication of his best-known novel, *Snow Country,* in 1948. In the 1950s he published two or three major works a year, including his masterpieces, *Thousand Cranes* and *The Sound of the Mountain.*

Traditional Influences Although Kawabata was well versed in modern European literature, his primary influences were Japanese. His choice of images, his use of paradoxical language, and his poetic way of telling a story all have links to traditional Buddhist thought and Japanese literary forms.

A Solitary Life Kawabata accepted his international fame with great humility and grace. Although in his later years he gave public lectures, spoke out on political issues, and actively supported aspiring writers, he always prized his solitude. For most of his life, he lived quietly with his wife in the ancient city of Kamakura, near Yokohama.

Other Works
"Of Birds and Beasts"
Beauty and Sadness
The Master of Go

LESSON RESOURCES

UNIT SEVEN RESOURCE BOOK, pp. 20–24

ASSESSMENT RESOURCES
Formal Assessment, pp. 169–170
Teacher's Guide to Assessment and Portfolio Use
Test Generator

INTEGRATED TECHNOLOGY
Visit our Web site: classzone.com

ADDITIONAL RESOURCES
Lesson Planning Guide, pp. 147–148
Teacher's Sourcebook for Language Development

Connect to Your Life

Consider how much you would be willing to give up for the sake of your family. For example, would you give up your boyfriend or girlfriend if your parents didn't approve? How about giving up your free afternoons to care for a younger sibling or an elderly grandparent? Discuss these questions with your classmates.

Build Background

The Japanese Family Traditionally, the family has held an even more important place in Japanese society than in that of the United States. Before World War II, the typical Japanese family was an extended farm family with three or more generations living together. Individual desires often took second place to family responsibilities. Marriages were arranged by parents, and the eldest son customarily brought his wife home to live with his family. A married woman's duty was not only to have children and obey her husband but also to obey her husband's parents and take care of them as they aged. Divorce was possible but rare, and children of divorced parents always stayed with their father.

After Japan's defeat in World War II, many of these extended families broke apart. Postwar Japan's rapid economic growth and urbanization contributed to an increase in smaller families consisting only of married couples and their children. By 1955, extended families made up only 44 percent of all households. In addition, the new Japanese constitution gave women rights equal to men's for the first time in Japanese history.

Kawabata's "The Jay," published in 1949, does not explicitly deal with the changes in postwar Japanese society, but it illustrates their effects in a very personal way. The story gives us a close look at a family that has been broken apart by divorce and remarriage. It also shows the difficulty individual family members have in dealing with these changes.

Focus Your Reading

LITERARY ANALYSIS: SYMBOL

A **symbol** is a person, place, or thing that stands for something beyond itself. For example, a trophy might stand for a particular victory or for a person's success in general. In "The Jay," the author uses a mother jay and her chick as symbols. As you read, think about how the jays are related to people and events in the story.

ACTIVE READING: CLARIFYING SEQUENCE

The events that have occurred in Yoshiko's family and the relationships between its various members may seem confusing at times. It will help your understanding of the story to have a clear picture of the family's history.

READER'S NOTEBOOK

As you read, create a chronology like the one started at the right, showing the key events in the life of the family.

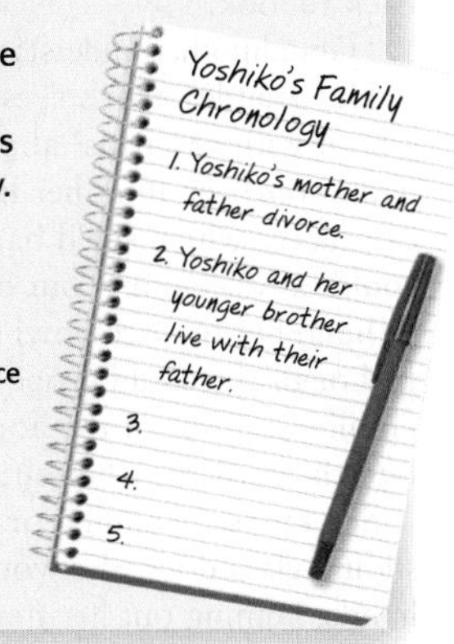

WORDS TO KNOW
Vocabulary Preview

assiduously
boundless
emaciated
intransigence
stifle

READING FOR INFORMATION
Reading Skills and Strategies
COMPARISON AND CONTRAST

After students have read the background information, have them discuss the differences between the traditional Japanese family before World War II and the traditional American family from that time.

Possible Responses: The traditional Japanese family was larger than the American family, typically including three or more generations. More Japanese families than American families lived on farms. Japanese marriages were arranged by the couple's parents rather than by the couple as in the United States. A Japanese wife had to be more obedient than an American wife. A Japanese wife was responsible for taking care of her husband's parents, while an American wife usually took care of her own parents. Divorce was less frequent in Japan than in the United States and the father got custody of the children. In the United States it was more likely that custody would be given to the mother.

TIME MANAGEMENT

If your schedule requires that you cover the lesson objectives in a shorter time, use . . .

- Preparing to Read, pp. 1174 and 1175
- Thinking Through the Literature, p. 1180
- Vocabulary in Action, p. 1181

If you want to take advantage of longer blocks of class time, use . . .

- TE Teaching Options: Cross Curricular Link, pp. 1176, 1178; Vocabulary Strategy, p. 1179
- Choices & Challenges, p. 1181

Reading and Analyzing

Literary Analysis SYMBOL

A Since the jay opens the story, students can already begin speculating about its symbolic significance. Have them discuss possible concepts that the jay and its lost chick represent. **Possible responses:** The jay could symbolize motherhood, a mother's devotion, or what a good mother is. The jay's situation could also represent the separation, loss, or disruption of a family.

Use **Unit Seven Resource Book,** p. 22, for more practice.

Active Reading

CLARIFYING SEQUENCE

Have students explain what they know about the family relationships from these two pages. *(Yoshiko lives with her brother and grandmother. Her parents have been divorced since she was four years old; her father remarried ten years later but now lives apart from Yoshiko.)*

- How does Yoshiko feel about her grandmother? *(She is awed by her grandmother's grace and wisdom.)*
- How does Yoshiko feel about her stepmother? *(She seems to like her stepmother but doesn't feel close enough to wait for her to help her dress.)*
- How does Yoshiko feel about her father? *(She is touched that he sacrificed for her by waiting to marry.)*
- Why do you think her father waited to remarry? *(so that Yoshiko could have time to adjust to the loss of her biological mother; so that she would have time with her father and not feel displaced when he married again; so that she would be older and more mature when he brought a new mother into the house)*

Use **Unit Seven Resource Book,** p. 21, for more practice.

Reading Skills and Strategies

MAKING INFERENCES

B Based on the reasons given for her parents' divorce, Yoshiko's intuition about a deeper reason, and Yoshiko's father's reaction to the photo of her mother, what can you infer is the real cause of her parents' divorce. *(the mother's infidelity)*

The Jay

Yasunari Kawabata

Translated by Lane Dunlop

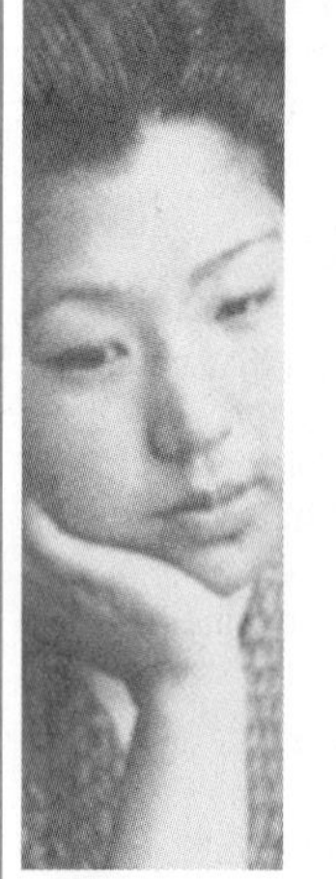

Since daybreak, the jay had been singing noisily. When they'd slid open the rain shutters, it had flown up before
A their eyes from a lower branch of the pine, but it seemed to have come back. During breakfast, there was the sound of whirring wings.

"That bird's a nuisance." The younger brother started to get to his feet.

"It's all right. It's all right." The grandmother stopped him. "It's looking for its child. Apparently the chick fell out of the nest yesterday. It was flying around until late in the evening. Doesn't she know where it is? But what a good mother. This morning she came right back to look."

"Grandmother understands well," Yoshiko[1] said.

Her grandmother's eyes were bad. Aside from a bout with nephritis[2] about ten years ago, she had never been ill in her life. But, because of her cataracts,[3] which she'd had since girlhood, she could only see dimly out of her left eye. One had to hand her the rice bowl and the chopsticks. Although she could grope her way around the familiar interior of the house, she could not go into the garden by herself.

Sometimes, standing or sitting in front of the sliding-glass door, she would spread out her hands, fanning out her fingers against the sunlight that came through the glass, and gaze out. She was concentrating all the life that was left to her into that many-angled gaze.

At such times, Yoshiko was frightened by her 1
grandmother. Though she wanted to call out to her from behind, she would furtively steal away.

This nearly blind grandmother, simply from having heard the jay's voice, spoke as if she had seen everything. Yoshiko was filled with wonder.

When, clearing away the breakfast things, Yoshiko went into the kitchen, the jay was singing from the roof of the neighbor's house.

In the back garden, there was a chestnut tree and two or three persimmon trees. When she looked at the trees, she saw that a light rain was falling. It was the sort of rain that you could not tell was falling unless you saw it against the dense foliage.

The jay, shifting its perch to the chestnut tree, then flying low and skimming the ground, returned again to its branch, singing all the while.

The mother bird could not fly away. Was it because her chick was somewhere around there?

Worrying about it, Yoshiko went to her room. She had to get herself ready before the morning was over.

In the afternoon, her father and mother were 2
coming with the mother of Yoshiko's fiancé.

Sitting at her mirror, Yoshiko glanced at the white stars under her fingernails. It was said that, when stars came out under your nails, it was a sign that you would receive something, but Yoshiko remembered having read in the newspaper that it meant a deficiency of vitamin C or

1. **Yoshiko** (yō′shē-kō′).
2. **nephritis** (nə-frī′tĭs): an inflammation of the kidneys.
3. **cataracts:** cloudiness in the lenses of the eyes, causing impairment of vision.

Science

ANIMAL BEHAVIOR The clamorous jay in Kawabata's story is related to the North American blue jay. Both are members of the crow family, which includes other noisy birds such as ravens and magpies. Although distributed world wide, jays are found primarily in woodlands of the northern hemisphere. As a species, the birds are very old, dating back 25 million years, according to fossil remains.

The most distinguishing thing about the jay is its loud voice. Although jays have several different vocalizations, some of which are quite musical, their most characteristic sound is a piercing cry. Henry David Thoreau called it an "unrelenting steel-cold scream."

Both male and female jays build a nest and care for their young. They can be aggressive at times. Some have been known to dive-bomb a marauding cat to protect their nest. In general, jays are bold, loud, and sociable birds—quite a contrast to the meek, introverted Yoshiko in Kawabata's story.

something. The job of putting on her makeup went fairly pleasantly. Her eyebrows and lips all became unbearably winsome.[4] Her kimono,[5] too, went on easily.

She'd thought of waiting for her mother to come and help with her clothes, but it was better to dress by herself, she decided.

Her father lived away from them. This was her second mother.

When her father had divorced her first mother, Yoshiko had been four and her younger brother two. The reasons given for the divorce were that her mother went around dressed in flashy clothes and spent money wildly, but Yoshiko sensed dimly that it was more than that, that the real cause lay deeper down.

Her brother, as a child, had come across a photograph of their mother and shown it to their father. The father hadn't said anything but, with a face of terrible anger, had suddenly torn the photograph to bits. B

When Yoshiko was thirteen, she had welcomed the new mother to the house. Later, Yoshiko had come to think that her father had endured his loneliness for ten years for her sake.

4. **winsome** (wĭn′səm): charming (often in a childlike way).

5. **kimono** (kə-mō′nə): a long, wide-sleeved robe, worn with a sash.

Customizing Instruction

Less Proficient Readers

1 Students may have trouble understanding why Yoshiko feels "frightened by her grandmother." Explain that her fright in this case is more like awe or alarm than fear. Thinking about her grandmother, Yoshiko is "filled with wonder." She doesn't understand her grandmother's mysterious power—how she knew the blue jay's situation even though she cannot see, for instance. On another level, people can feel frightened by God, not for fear of something specific but at the thought of his awesome power.

2 Have students recall from the **Build Background** on page 1175 how important a mother-in-law is in Japanese society at this time. *(Yoshiko's marriage is arranged by her father and her fiancé's mother; it's important that Yoshiko and her mother-in-law get along for they will be living and working closely together.)*

Reading and Analyzing

Reading Skills and Strategies
UNDERSTANDING CAUSE AND EFFECT

A Students may have trouble understanding why Yoshiko's brother's act of contacting their biological mother causes such distress and disruption in the family. Help them infer the cultural and emotional effects of the brother's act.

- How does Yoshiko's father feel about her biological mother? *(bitter, angry)*
- Why do you think the brother's attitude changes toward his stepmother after he meets his biological mother? *(He no longer feels as close to his stepmother; he no longer feels the same respect for his stepmother.)*
- Why is Yoshiko concerned for her stepmother? *(because she knows her stepmother is upset by what her brother did)*
- Why do you think the father feels he has to leave with the stepmother? *(Because the stepmother is hurt, the father sympathizes with her against his son; the father takes his son's action as a personal insult as well as defiance of his power as head of the family; the father feels betrayed because his son has rejected his wife; the father cannot tolerate his son's divided loyalties.)*

B Students should also consider psychological causes of the family's break-up. Have them discuss how this paragraph helps to explain the situation. *(Yoshiko sees the same "male intransigence" in both her father and her brother, suggesting that their conflict arises from similar character traits.)*

The second mother was a good person. A peaceful home life continued.

When the younger brother, entering upper school, began living away from home in a dormitory, his attitude toward his stepmother changed noticeably.

A "Elder sister, I've met our mother. She's married and lives in Azabu.[6] She's really beautiful. She was happy to see me."

Hearing this suddenly, Yoshiko could not say a word. Her face paled, and she began to tremble.

From the next room, her stepmother came in and sat down.

"It's a good thing, a good thing. It's not bad to meet your own mother. It's only natural. I've known for some time that this day would come. I don't think anything particular of it."

But the strength seemed to have gone out of her stepmother's body. To Yoshiko, her emaciated stepmother seemed pathetically frail and small.

Her brother abruptly got up and left. Yoshiko felt like smacking him.

"Yoshiko, don't say anything to him. Speaking to him will only make that boy go bad." Her stepmother spoke in a low voice.

Tears came to Yoshiko's eyes.

Her father summoned her brother back home from the dormitory. Although Yoshiko had thought that would settle the matter, her father had then gone off to live elsewhere with her stepmother.

1 It had frightened Yoshiko. It was as if she had been crushed by the power of masculine indignation and resentment. Did their father dislike even
B them because of their tie to their first mother? It seemed to her that her brother, who'd gotten to his feet so abruptly, had inherited the frightening male intransigence of his father.

And yet it also seemed to Yoshiko that she could now understand her father's sadness and pain during those ten years between his divorce and remarriage.

And so, when her father, who had moved away from her, came back bringing a marriage proposal, Yoshiko had been surprised.

"I've caused you a great deal of trouble. I told the young man's mother that you're a girl with these circumstances and that, rather than treating you like a bride, she should try to bring back the happy days of your childhood."

When her father said this kind of thing to her, Yoshiko wept.

If Yoshiko married, there would be no woman's hand to take care of her brother and grandmother. It had been decided that the two households would become one. With that, Yoshiko had made up her mind. She had dreaded 2
marriage on her father's account, but, when it came down to the actual talks, it was not that dreadful after all.

When her preparations were completed, Yoshiko went to her grandmother's room.

"Grandmother, can you see the red in this kimono?"[7]

"I can faintly make out some red over there. Which is it, now?" Pulling Yoshiko to her, the grandmother put her eyes close to the kimono and the sash.

"I've already forgotten your face, Yoshiko. I wish I could see what you look like now."

Yoshiko stifled a desire to giggle. She rested her hand lightly on her grandmother's head.

Wanting to go out and meet her father and the others, Yoshiko was unable just to sit there,

6. **Azabu** (ä′zä-bōō′): an area of Tokyo.

7. **the red in this kimono:** Red, a traditional color of happiness in Japan, is often included in wedding attire.

WORDS TO KNOW

emaciated (ĭ-mā′shē-ā′tĭd) *adj.* unnaturally thin **emaciate** *v.*
intransigence (ĭn-trăn′sĭ-jəns) *n.* a condition of being stubborn and uncompromising
stifle (stī′fəl) *v.* to hold back; repress

Cross Curricular Link — Humanities

MARRIAGE CUSTOMS Arranged marriages are still practiced among traditional societies, especially in Muslim countries and in India. Even where young people are free to choose their mates, the joining of two families is considered more important than the union of husband and wife. In China, for example, if the parents are not satisfied with the other family, the wedding cannot take place. Although arranged marriages declined in Japan after World War II, the custom of using a go-between is currently being revived as a practical way for compatible couples to meet.

Most traditional marriage ceremonies involve elaborate rituals and sometimes days of feasting and celebrations. In India, Pakistan, Malaysia, and the United Arab Emirates, for example, the custom of decorating the bride's hands and feet with a reddish dye called henna can last from one to two days before the wedding. The wedding ceremony itself can be highly elaborate or as minimal as a Palestinian wedding in which the religious union takes place privately weeks before the actual celebration of feasting and dancing.

Many countries share rituals similar to the West. Indian and Japanese couples, for example, exchange vows. In China, brides traditionally wear red, the color of love and joy; whereas in Japan, a white kimono is preferred. Guests customarily throw rice at newlyweds in India and Singapore. And among some African tribes, the bride and groom's hands are tied together with braided grass, similar to our custom of holding hands at the altar.

IF Yoshiko married, there would be no woman's hand to take care of her brother and grandmother. It had been decided that the two households would become one.

vaguely waiting. She went out into the garden. She held out her hand, palm upward, but the rain was so fine that it didn't wet the palm. Gathering up the skirts of her kimono, Yoshiko assiduously searched among the little trees and in the bear-grass bamboo thicket. And there, in the tall grass under the bush clover, was the baby bird.

Her heart beating fast, Yoshiko crept nearer. The baby jay, drawing its head into its neck feathers, did not stir. It was easy to take it up into her hand. It seemed to have lost its energy. Yoshiko looked around her, but the mother bird was nowhere in sight.

Running into the house, Yoshiko called out, "Grandmother! I've found the baby bird. I have it in my hand. It's very weak."

"Oh, is that so? Try giving it some water."

Her grandmother was calm.

When she ladled some water into a rice bowl and dipped the baby jay's beak in it, it drank, its little throat swelling out in an appealing way. Then—had it recovered?—it sang out, "Ki-ki-ki, Ki-ki-ki . . ."

The mother bird, evidently hearing its cry, came flying. Perching on the telephone wire, it sang. The baby bird, struggling in Yoshiko's hand, sang out again, "Ki-ki-ki . . ."

"Ah, how good that she came! Give it back to its mother, quick," her grandmother said.

Yoshiko went back out into the garden. The mother bird flew up from the telephone wire but kept her distance, looking fixedly toward Yoshiko from the top of a cherry tree.

As if to show her the baby jay in her palm, Yoshiko raised her hand, then quietly placed the chick on the ground.

As Yoshiko watched from behind the glass door, the mother bird, guided by the voice of its child singing plaintively and looking up at the sky, gradually came closer. When she'd come down to the low branch of a nearby pine, the chick flapped its wings, trying to fly up to her. Stumbling forward in its efforts, falling all over itself, it kept singing.

Still the mother bird cautiously held off from hopping down to the ground.

Soon, however, it flew in a straight line to the side of its child. The chick's joy was boundless. Turning and turning its head, its outspread wings trembling, it made up to its mother. Evidently the mother had brought it something to eat.

Yoshiko wished that her father and stepmother would come soon. She would like to show them this, she thought. ❖

WORDS TO KNOW

assiduously (ə-sĭj'o͞o-əs-lē) *adv.* diligently

boundless (bound'lĭs) *adj.* without limits; infinite

Customizing Instruction

English Learners

1 Make sure students understand that *indignation* means "anger stemming from an injustice or wrong-doing," and that *resentment* is another word for anger or bitterness. Test their understanding by asking them what Yoshiko's father feels indignant and resentful about? *(He thinks his son's action of visiting his former wife is wrong and unfair to his current wife.)*

Less Proficient Readers

2 Make sure students understand Yoshiko's initial hesitation to get married and why she ultimately decides to go ahead. *(Yoshiko is worried that if she gets married no one will take care of her grandmother and brother. But then it was agreed that "the two households would become one," that is, her grandmother and brother would go with her to live with her husband's family.)*

Advanced Learners

Have students consider the tone of the story. What is Kawabata's attitude toward the characters and events? Who, if anyone, does he blame for the disruption in the family? Who, if anyone, does he credit with restoring the family?

Possible Responses: The tone is objective, non-judgmental, and optimistic. Even though Yoshiko's father and brother cause the disruption in the family, they are not presented negatively overall. Yoshiko especially mentions her father's concern for her and his self-sacrifice in waiting to marry until she was older and could understand. Largely due to Yoshiko's efforts, the family is saved, if not actually restored, by the end. With the jays reunited and Yoshiko ready for marriage, the story concludes on an optimistic note.

MINI LESSON Vocabulary Strategy

CONTEXT CLUES

Instruction Remind students that surrounding words, phrases, or sentences may provide context clues, or hints, about the meaning of an unfamiliar word. One type of context clue is a **restatement** clue. In this kind of clue, a different word is used to say the idea again. Point out the word *emaciated* in the seventh paragraph on page 1178. Have students read the sentence containing this word and identify any words that may help them understand it.

Practice Write these sentences on the board and read them aloud. Then have students find the word(s) in each sentence that help explain the meaning of each underlined word.

1. Yoshiko put her hand over her mouth to quiet any sound and stifle her desire to laugh.
2. Yoshiko was determined to find the bird; she searched assiduously around the yard.
3. The boy's stubbornness was just one example of the intransigence he'd inherited from his father.

A lesson on using context clues appears p. 674 of the Pupil's Edition.

Connect to the Literature

1. **What Do You Think?** How did you feel about Yoshiko as you read this story? Did your feelings change? Give reasons for your responses.

Comprehension Check
- Why is Yoshiko's mother not living with the family?
- What big change is about to occur in Yoshiko's life?
- What happens to the jay chick at the end of the story?

Think Critically

2. **ACTIVE READING: CLARIFYING** Get together with a small group of classmates and compare the chronologies they wrote with the one in your own READER'S NOTEBOOK. Make revisions as needed. Then discuss the question, How do these events affect relationships within the family?

3. Why is Yoshiko closer to her grandmother than to any other member of the family?

4. Why is Yoshiko overcome with emotion when she learns that her father has asked her future mother-in-law to "try to bring back the happy days" of Yoshiko's childhood?

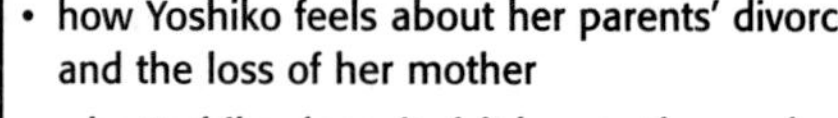

- how Yoshiko feels about her parents' divorce and the loss of her mother
- why Yoshiko doesn't visit her mother, as her brother did
- how Yoshiko reacts when her father moves away from her

5. At the end of the story, why does Yoshiko want to show her father and stepmother the mother jay reunited with her chick?

Extend Interpretations

6. **What If?** How might the story have been different if Yoshiko, like her brother, had gone to visit their mother?

7. **Connect to Life** Arranged marriages are uncommon in our society, but they still occur, particularly in ethnic groups where the custom has a long tradition. What might be some advantages and disadvantages of this way of obtaining a spouse?

LITERARY ANALYSIS: SYMBOL

A **symbol** is a person, place, or thing that stands for something beyond itself. In literature, symbols often communicate complicated, emotionally rich ideas more effectively than direct language. In "The Jay," for example, the mother jay looking for her lost chick helps the reader to understand and respond to Yoshiko's situation of being separated from her mother.

Cooperative Learning Activity With a group of classmates, brainstorm various ways the jay and her chick are related to the story of Yoshiko and her family. Then discuss this question: What ideas and feelings does Kawabata convey to the reader through the symbol of the jays? Use a chart like the one shown to record your thoughts.

How Jays Are Related to Story	Ideas Communicated	Feelings Communicated

REVIEW: MOOD

A **mood** is a feeling or atmosphere that a writer conveys in a story. How would you describe the mood of Kawabata's story?

Connect to the Literature

1. **What Do You Think?** Students should cite places in the story to support their opinions. Some who felt sorry for Yoshiko at the beginning of the story may be glad for her by the end, because she seems genuinely happy.

Comprehension Check
- Yoshiko's biological mother is divorced from her father and lives somewhere else.
- Yoshiko is about to be married.
- Yoshiko helps the jay chick reunite with its mother.

Use Selection Quiz in **Unit Seven Resource Book,** p. 24.

Think Critically

2. Students may conclude that the initial divorce has a ripple effect on the family. The father is embittered by the divorce but waits ten years to remarry, which according to Yoshiko causes him pain and loneliness. When the brother gets older, he contacts his biological mother, which then alienates him from his stepmother, angers his father, and causes his father and stepmother to live somewhere else. The family conflicts grieve Yoshiko, but her upcoming marriage promises to mend some family rifts.
3. Possible Responses: Yoshiko's grandmother has been the one constant in her life; the grandmother is wise and tender; the grandmother doesn't place any demands on Yoshiko.
4. Possible Responses: Yoshiko may be grateful that her father acknowledges her own pain ("I've caused you a great deal of trouble") and wants her to be happy.
5. Possible Responses: The reunion of the baby bird with its mother is a touching event that Yoshiko wants to show her father and stepmother, possibly to reinforce their own family bonds or to share an intimate moment.

Extend Interpretations

6. **What If?** Students may say that if she had gone to visit her mother, Yoshiko may have been less critical of her brother for doing it and more critical of her father for reacting so negatively.
7. **Connect to Life** Possible advantages: Parents might choose a better spouse for their child than their child would; joined families are more likely to get along. Possible disadvantages: Romance, love, and individual desire would be minimized; child might resent having spouse chosen for him or her.

Literary Analysis

Cooperative Learning Activity Students may say that the separation between the birds parallels Yoshiko and her brother's separation from their biological mother as well as their separation from their father and stepmother later. The reunion of the two jays is related to the brother's contacting his biological mother, the father's attempt to reconcile with Yoshiko by arranging a good marriage for her, and the joining of two households through Yoshiko's marriage. Yoshiko's role in uniting the jays also symbolizes the way she tries to hold her family together. Students might say that Kawabata sets up the jays as a natural image of a family that humans should follow. The mother jay's distress at the loss of her chick and the chick's joy at finding her again add poignancy to the story.

Use **Unit Seven Resource Book,** p. 22, for more practice.

Writing Options

1. Character Analysis
Consider the thoughts, feelings, and actions of Yoshiko in "The Jay," and write an essay analyzing her character. Begin by describing your first impressions of Yoshiko. Then explain her inner qualities and the way they are revealed in the story. Conclude by making a general statement about what kind of person you think Yoshiko is. Place your character analysis in your **Working Portfolio.**

2. Problem-Solution Essay
Yoshiko believes that her relationships with her father and brother are made more difficult by "male intransigence." What do you see as the biggest obstacle to good communication between men and women? Why does this obstacle exist? What problems does it create? What can be done to overcome it? Answer these questions in a short essay.

Writing Handbook
See page R33: Problem-Solution.

Activities & Explorations

1. Family Tree Because of her parents' divorce and her own forthcoming marriage, Yoshiko will end up with a large and complex family. A family group that includes members other than a married couple and their children is often called an extended family. Investigate some extended families that you are familiar with, and create a poster-board presentation showing a few of the many combinations of people that can make up such groups. ~ **VIEWING AND REPRESENTING**

2. Reunion Dialogue Imagine that Yoshiko and her mother are reunited. With a classmate, brainstorm the dialogue that might take place between them. Then perform your dialogue for the class. Be ready to explain why you think Yoshiko and her mother might interact in the way you have presented. ~ **SPEAKING AND LISTENING**

Inquiry & Research

Multimedia Display: The Japanese Family Find out more about how the Japanese family has changed since World War II and what it is like today. Use reference books, magazine or newspaper articles, literary works, and the Internet to find words and images that document these changes. Present your findings in the form of a multimedia display.

Communication Handbook
See page R54: Making Multimedia Presentations.

Vocabulary in Action

EXERCISE: CONTEXT CLUES On your paper, write the Word to Know that best completes each sentence.

1. Yoshiko's stepmother doesn't want to ________ her brother's desire to get to know his biological mother.
2. Yoshiko is glad to see that the baby jay has not been separated from its mother long enough to become _________.
3. The mother jay searches _________ for her chick until at last she finds it.
4. Yoshiko hopes that her father might someday forgive her mother, but she does not reckon with his _________.
5. Yoshiko feels ________ happiness when she learns that her brother and grandmother can live with her after her marriage.

WORDS TO KNOW
assiduously · emaciated · stifle
boundless · intransigence

Building Vocabulary
For an in-depth lesson on context clues, see page 674.

Mood Students may say that the mood is emotionally touching, sadly sweet, or sweetly sad.

Writing Options

1. **Character Analysis** To explain Yoshiko's inner qualities, students should look at how she responds to the jays, how understanding of her father and accepting of her stepmother she is, and what feelings she has toward her family.
2. **Problem-Solution Essay** Make sure students understand what is meant by "male intransigence." Suggest that students ground their essays in their own experience, what happens in the story, or a hypothetical example to keep from being too abstract.

Activities & Explorations

1. **Family Tree** Brainstorm with students who's included in an extended family—parents, siblings, uncles, aunts, cousins, second cousins, grandparents, great-grandparents, great uncles and aunts, in-laws, stepparents, and step-siblings.
2. **Reunion Dialogue** Remind students that they will have to imagine how Yoshiko would act around her mother. Would she be shy, emotional, or formal? Also, have students reread the only descriptions of the mother on pages 1177 and 1178.

Inquiry & Research

Multimedia Display: The Japanese Family Give students time to do their research and periodically check their progress as they work. Suggest that students look through the *Readers' Guide to Periodical Literature* to find magazine articles and newspaper indexes, such as the *New York Times Index,* to find specific news reports.

Vocabulary in Action

1. stifle
2. emaciated
3. assiduously
4. intransigence
5. boundless

To assess skills and concepets taught in this selection use **Formal Assessment Book,** pp. 169–170.

Objectives

- understand and appreciate two African **poems (Literary Analysis)**
- identify **denotation and connotation** of words and phrases in a poem **(Literary Analysis)**
- use strategies for **paraphrasing (Active Reading)**

Thematic Link

According to Senghor's poems, Africa's cultural riches can **change the world.**

5-Minute Warm-Up

Daily Language SkillBuilder

Have students **proofread** the display sentences on page 1095m and write them correctly.

Prayer to Masks

LÉOPOLD SÉDAR SENGHOR

Léopold Sédar Senghor
1906–2001

The Kingdom of Childhood Léopold Sédar Senghor (lā-ô-pôl' sā-där' sän-gôr') was born in a coastal village in French West Africa (now Senegal). As a child, he listened to folk tales and to songs of the local griots, or storytellers. He also took part in the traditions of his people, including seasonal rites and dances and visits to holy sites. Later, Senghor referred to this happy time as "the kingdom of my childhood." When Senghor was seven, his father sent him to a missionary school run by French priests. So began the Western education that eventually drew him out of Africa to Paris.

Between Two Cultures Senghor began studying in Paris in 1928 and eventually became the first black African to receive France's highest teaching certification. During his student days, he met black students from other French colonies and learned about the awakening of black awareness, both in the United States and in France. Yet, despite France's official policy of racial tolerance, he felt he was not accepted as an equal by most white Europeans.

Senghor taught at prep schools in France until he was drafted at the beginning of World War II. Although he fought bravely for France, the experience of war and his imprisonment in several German concentration camps increased his feeling of displacement.

African Identity When Senghor had begun to write poetry in the prewar years, his imagination had returned to the "kingdom" of his childhood for inspiration and subject matter. By the time his first book of poems, *Chants d'ombre* [Songs of shadow], was published in 1945, Senghor's sense of himself as an African had become fully developed.

Mr. President Senghor eventually gave up teaching to be the political leader of his people. After the war, he represented Senegal in the French government and helped draft a new constitution that gave more power to the colonies. When Senegal gained independence in 1960, Senghor served as its first president. He won reelection four times before retiring in 1980.

For a humanities activity, click on:

LESSON RESOURCES

UNIT SEVEN RESOURCE BOOK, pp. 25–26

ASSESSMENT RESOURCES
Formal Assessment, pp. 171–172
Teacher's Guide to Assessment and Portfolio Use
Test Generator

INTEGRATED TECHNOLOGY
Visit our Web site: classzone.com

ADDITIONAL RESOURCES
Lesson Planning Guide, pp. 149–150
Teacher's Sourcebook for Language Development

Build Background

The Negritude Movement Léopold Senghor's writing reflects a philosophy called Negritude that Senghor developed with writers Aimé Césaire (ā-mā' sā-zâr') of Martinique and Léon Damas (lā-ôN' dä-mä') of French Guiana during their student days in Paris in the 1930s. Césaire coined the French term *negritude,* which literally means "blackness," to designate the investigation by French-speaking black intellectuals of their African heritage, culture, and identity. The Negritude movement sought to embrace a common African heritage, to promote African cultures and values in literature and art, and to assert the dignity and freedom of all people of African descent. Negritude writers were influenced by writers of the Harlem Renaissance in the United States, especially Langston Hughes and Claude McKay.

"Prayer to Masks" In African culture, masks have religious significance and are considered sacred. They may even possess supernatural powers. In this poem, the masks represent the spirits of ancestors, which can take an active role in contemporary life.

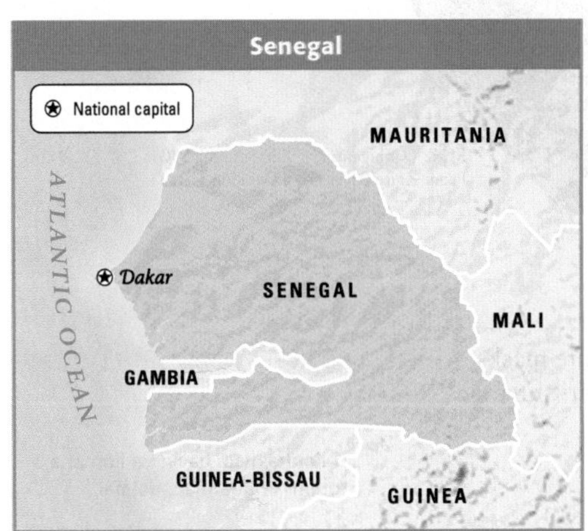

Connect to Your Life

What associations or images come to mind when you hear the word *Africa?* Do you think of wild animals, ancient traditions, modern politics, or something else? Compare your responses with those of your classmates.

Focus Your Reading

LITERARY ANALYSIS: DENOTATION AND CONNOTATION

Poets choose their words with great care, paying close attention to what is suggested by each word. The **connotation** of a word is the set of associations, images, or feelings that the word conjures up. By contrast, the **denotation** of a word is its literal meaning, a definition you would find in the dictionary. For example, a denotative meaning of *Africa* is "the second-largest continent." However, as revealed in the Connect to Your Life activity above, the word *Africa* is also rich in connotative meanings. As you read this poem, pay attention to the connotations as well as the denotations of particular words the phrases.

ACTIVE READING: PARAPHRASING

One strategy that can help you understand a poem more fully is paraphrasing. This means that you restate parts or all of the poem in your own words. When you paraphrase, you will often need to use more words than the poet uses.

READER'S NOTEBOOK As you read the poem, identify lines that seem particularly significant or whose meaning is not completely clear to you. Try paraphrasing those lines, and record your results in a chart like the one shown.

Line	Paraphrase
Now fix your immobile eyes upon your children . . .	*Focus your attention on the people of Africa*

READING FOR INFORMATION
Reading Skills and Strategies
SUMMARIZING

Remind students that a good summary states the main idea of a selection and gives a few details that explain or illustrate the main idea. Have students write a summary of the paragraph about the Negritude Movement under **Build Background.**

Possible Response: The Negritude Movement was founded in Paris in the 1930s by Léopold Senghor of Senegal, Léon Damas of French Guiana, and Aimé Césaire of Martinique. This artistic and literary movement aimed to promote the culture, values, and people of Africa.

MINI LESSON Reading a Map

SENEGAL Explain to students that on a small map such as the one on page 1183 it is important to imagine the larger context. In general, tell them to look for distinguishing landforms, such as deserts, mountain ranges, and large bodies of water. In the map of Senegal, for example, students can see that the Atlantic Ocean is on the left. Since there is no compass rose indicating direction, you can assume that the top of the map represents north. So, if students know that Senegal is in Africa and they can see that the Atlantic Ocean is west of the country, then they can infer the general location of Senegal. Have students first explain where Senegal is and then point it out on a larger map of the world.

Reading and Analyzing

Literary Analysis
DENOTATION AND CONNOTION

Have students pick out words and phrases that have strong suggestive meanings. Discuss the denotations and connotations of these words.

Possible Responses: Denotation of *rhythm* (line 15) is "a regular pattern of music"; connotations could be "heartbeat, drum beat, clapping hands, stomping feet, performance, music, and poetry." Denotation of "a new dawn" (line 16) is "a new morning"; connotations could be "a new beginning, hope for the future, new possibilities, and a better world."

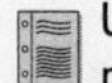
Use **Unit Seven Resource Book,** p. 26, for more practice.

Active Reading PARAPHRASING

Have students identify lines they are having trouble interpreting. Help them paraphrase the lines.

A Sample paraphrase for lines 7–8:
You masks who have no mortal marks, no dimples of childhood or wrinkles of age,
You have created my face, the one that now bends over the paper as if it were an altar to write this prayer.

Prayer to Masks

Léopold Sédar Senghor

Translated by Gerald Moore and Ulli Beier

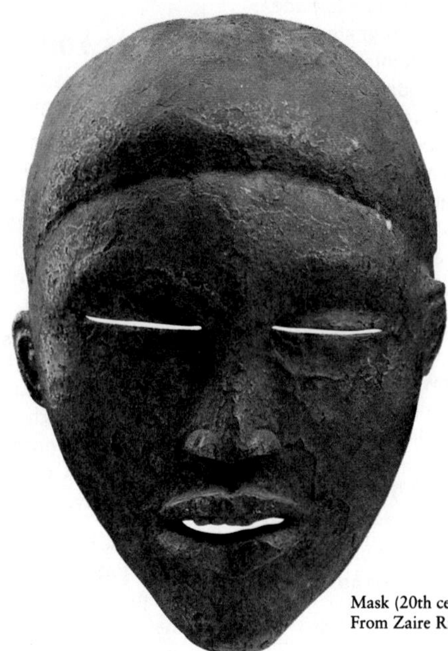

Mask (20th century), Zaire-Angola. Wood, 9" (22.8 cm). From Zaire River coastal region.

Black mask, red mask, you black and white masks,
Rectangular masks through whom the spirit breathes,
I greet you in silence!
And you too, my lionheaded ancestor

4 lionheaded: having a lion as a totem, or guardian, animal.

You guard this place, that is closed to any feminine l
aughter, to any mortal smile.
You purify the air of eternity, here where I breathe the
air of my fathers.
Masks of markless faces, free from dimples and wrinkles,
You have composed this image, this my face that bends
over the altar of white paper.
In the name of your image, listen to me!
Now while the Africa of despotism is dying—it is the
agony of a pitiable princess
Like that of Europe to whom she is connected through
the navel—
Now fix your immobile eyes upon your children who
have been called
And who sacrifice their lives like the poor man his last
garment
So that hereafter we may cry "here" at the rebirth of the
world being the leaven that the white flour needs.
For who else would teach rhythm to the world that has
died of machines and cannons?
For who else should ejaculate the cry of joy, that arouses
the dead and the wise in a new dawn?
Say, who else could return the memory of life to men
with a torn hope?
They call us cotton heads, and coffee men, and
oily men,
They call us men of death.
But we are the men of the dance whose feet only gain
power when they beat the hard soil.

9 your image: the speaker himself, who carries on the traditions and values of his ancestors.

10 despotism: government rule based on tyranny or oppression.

12 immobile: unmoving.

14 leaven: a substance, like yeast, that causes bread dough to rise.

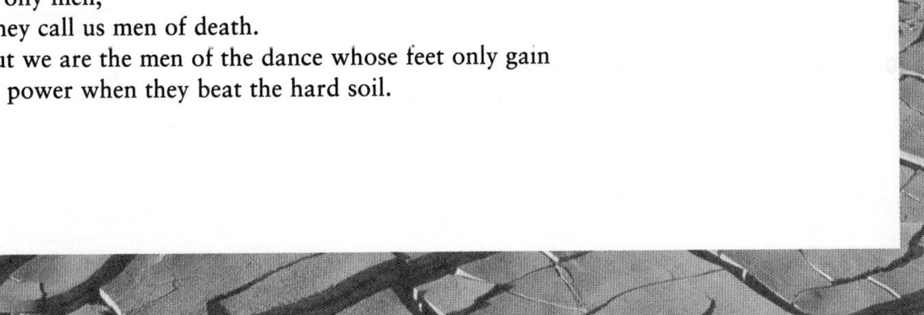

Customizing Instruction

Less Proficient Readers

Students will probably have trouble understanding "Prayer to Masks." Explain that the first ten lines of the poem are an invocation to the masks, which represent gods ("masks through whom the spirit breathes"). Lines 10–14 explain the situation: European colonization of Africa, which Senghor calls "despotism," is ending. The image he uses to illustrate this historical situation is the "pitiable princess" (Colonial Africa) who has been tied to Europe "through the navel" like an unborn child. Beginning in lines 12, Senghor argues that Africans had sacrificed for Europe by fighting in World War II (as Senghor himself had), because they wanted to have a voice, or take part, in the reorganization of the world after the defeat of Germany and Japan. Moreover, Senghor asserts that the world needs Africans like flour needs yeast to rise (line 14). The last five lines further explain why the world needs Africans.

Advanced Learners

Have students examine the imagery of birth, dying, and rebirth in "Prayer to Masks."

Possible Response: Colonial Africa is a "pitiable princess," the stillborn child of a European mother. Senghor asserts that Africans are capable of helping the rebirth of the world because they can restore life to what industrialization and war have destroyed.

MINI LESSON Speaking and Listening

CHORAL READING

Prepare Working with a partner or in small groups, have students prepare a choral reading of the poem. Suggest that students locate recordings of African music, especially the music of a khalam, and/or choral singing to accompany their reading. Public libraries often have such recordings that can be checked out. Certain web sites and encyclopedia CDs also may have samples of West African music. Students may want to dress in traditional African clothing or bring samples of artifacts, such as masks and Sudanese cloth, to enhance their performances. Encourage students to steep themselves in the presence of Africa.

Present Give students time to plan and rehearse. Before the presentations, have the class create standards for evaluating the performances that they think are fair. Then have the class judge each choral reading according to those standards.

This activity is particularly well suited to longer blocks of class time.

Connect to the Literature

1. **What Do You Think?** Students' impressions should be grounded in the text and in their own experience. Students should provide examples to support their opinions.

Think Critically

2. You may want to help groups with their paraphrases. Have volunteers read their group's paraphrases aloud to the class and discuss any differences in interpretations.
3. Students may imagine a writer (the speaker) sitting at a desk, bent over "the altar of white paper," writing. The speaker may be looking at examples of African masks and contemplating what they stand for.
4. Possible Response: The speaker asks the masks for strength, reward for the sacrifice in the war, and fulfillment of Africa's role in the rebirth of the world.
5. Possible Response: The speaker feels that colonialism was wrong, because (1) Europe tyrannically ruled over Africa and (2) the continent lost its identity.
6. Possible Response: The speaker envisions Africa as the yeast to help Europe rise again. Africans can also bring music, joy, and new hope to a world deadened by war and mechanization. Some people don't appreciate Africans because they see only Africa's material resources—cotton, coffee, and oil. But Africa has great cultural riches to offer the world as well.

Extend Interpretations

7. **Critic's Corner** Students may say that the "black personality" includes vitality, strength, joy, and a powerful spiritual heritage.
8. **Connect to Life** Student examples should be detailed enough to convey the essence of the culture they chose.

Connect to the Literature

1. **What Do You Think?** What impressions of Africa and African culture do you get from this poem?

Think Critically

2. **ACTIVE READING: PARAPHRASING** Review the paraphrases that you recorded in your READER'S NOTEBOOK. With a group of classmates, put together a paraphrase of the poem in its entirety. Discuss any lines that still seem unclear.
3. What is the speaker doing as the poem takes place?
4. In lines 1–14, the speaker addresses the masks and asks for their help. What kind of help do you think the speaker wants from the masks?
5. In lines 10–12, the speaker refers to the decline of European power in Africa, the "dying" of "the Africa of despotism." How do you think the speaker feels about the effects of colonialism on Africa? Support your opinion.
6. Reread lines 15–20. How would you describe the speaker's vision of Africa's role in the future?

- why Africans are "the leaven that the white flour needs"
- what Africans can teach the rest of the world
- why some people don't appreciate Africans (lines 18–19)

Extend Interpretations

7. **Critic's Corner** According to one scholar, Senghor's preferred English equivalent of the term *negritude* was "black personality." On the basis of this poem, how would you describe that personality?
8. **Connect to Life** Think of a culture, either your own or one you admire. If you were to write a poem about the culture, what images would you use to capture the essence of this culture? Explain your choices.

LITERARY ANALYSIS: DENOTATION AND CONNOTATION

The literal, dictionary definition of a word is its **denotation.** A word may also have one or more **connotations**—particular associations, images, or feelings the word calls to mind. Connotations often make an important contribution to the meaning of a poem. The connotations of the words and phrases Senghor chose for his descriptions of African culture in the poem convey his attitude toward and feelings about the culture.

Cooperative Learning Activity With a group of classmates, identify in the poem particular words and phrases that have strong or important connotations, and record these words and phrases in a list. Then use the list to create a word portrait of Africa like the one started here.

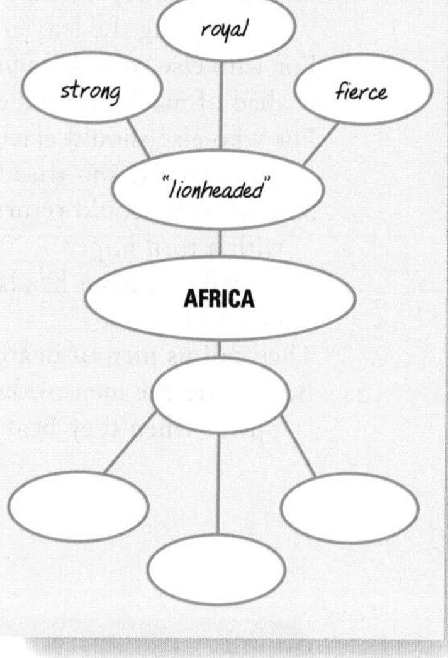

Literary Analysis

Cooperative Learning Activity Possibilities of words from the poems with strong or important connotations: somber, serene, primordial, honor, wild perfumes, leisure, singing, Soudanese cloths, black, red, lionheaded ancestor, sacrifice, rebirth, rhythm, cry of joy, dance, power.

Use **Unit Seven Resource Book,** p. 26, for more practice.

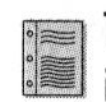
To assess skills and concepts taught in this selection use **Formal Assessment Book,** pp. 171–172.

Appreciating Cultural Roots

As you have seen, the African heritage of Léopold Sédar Senghor influenced his development as a writer. When Senghor was a student in Senegal, however, his heritage was not appreciated by his teachers, who were Europeans. He recalled one teacher in particular "who told me we were savages, that we had no traditions, no civilization." According to Senghor, that incident established his direction in life: "All this made me want to defend the civilization [my teacher] was denying us, made me want to demonstrate and illustrate it."

Diversity in U.S. Schools Most classrooms in the United States today have a very different atmosphere than the one experienced by Senghor. Yet, it is no easy task for students in schools with an increasingly diverse student body to appreciate one another's culture.

Data based on 1999 U.S. Census Bureau surveys on American diversity:

RESEARCH STARTER
CLASSZONE.COM

Research Project

To increase your appreciation of cultural diversity, choose one of the following projects. You can work either independently or in a small group.

- Create a statistical profile of students in your class. You may use the Census Bureau categories (see diagrams) or create your own categories to reflect the cultural, ethnic, and racial backgrounds of students. You may also investigate languages besides English that are spoken in students' homes. After you gather your statistics, prepare and then present an oral report on your findings, with visuals or handouts to communicate the statistics.
- Find out more about a culture that you are not familiar with that is represented in your school. Use reference works to learn more about that culture, including its art, customs, and traditions. Interview students or other people who are members of that culture. Report your findings orally or in a multimedia presentation.

Connect to Today

Use this feature to show the relevance of world literature to students. The material relates the literature selection just read to a contemporary topic connected to students' lives today.

Research Project

- For the statistical profile, suggest that students break down ethnic backgrounds further into country of origin, such as Vietnam or Guatemala. Students could also identify mixed racial or ethnic background.
- For the second research project, suggest that students investigate an Islamic country, either a non-Arabic nation, such as Pakistan, Afghanistan, Iran, Somalia, or Indonesia, or an Arabic nation, such as Iraq, Saudi Arabia, Syria, or Egypt.

Possible Objectives

This **On Your Own** featured selection may be used to achieve one or more of the following objectives:

- to give students the opportunity to read independently, either reading silently for a sustained period, reading and analyzing literature with a group, or using the Reader's Notebook to write in response to the literature
- to conduct a post-reading class discussion

Working Independently

You may want to set aside time each week for independent reading, without making an assignment related to the reading. Or once students have completed the reading, either alone or aloud in groups, you may ask them to work together on a project. If you choose to have students write responsively in their Reader's Notebook, suggest that they write about the emotions expressed in each poem and what the poems together express about the speaker's personality and values.

"I Am Not I"

Yo No Soy Yo

Juan Ramón Jiménez

Translated by Robert Bly

Juan Ramón Jiménez
1881–1958

A Literary Leader Juan Ramón Jiménez's short and intensely personal poems were an inspiration to a generation of Spanish writers in the 1920s and 1930s. Born in Spain, Jiménez briefly studied law at the University of Seville, but he eventually quit to devote himself to writing. He published his first two volumes of verse in 1900.

Spanish Classics From 1912 to 1916, Jiménez lived in Madrid, where he wrote *Platero and I* (1914), a set of prose poems about walks with a donkey. The book became a beloved Spanish classic. Also during this time, Jiménez met American-born Zenobia Camprubí Aymar, who was visiting in Spain. Jiménez's voyage to the United States to marry Camprubí inspired another successful collection, *Diary of a Newlywed Poet* (1917).

A Poet Abroad After the couple returned to Spain, Jiménez continued to devote himself to poetry. At the outbreak of the Spanish Civil War in 1936, he was sent to the United States as a representative of Spain. Eventually, Jiménez took a position at the University of Puerto Rico. The couple were in San Juan when they received word that Jiménez had won the 1956 Nobel Prize in literature.

In "I Am Not I," Jiménez explores the hidden territories of the self and its relation to the rest of the world. As you read, ask yourself these questions:

1. *How would you describe the speaker's two different selves?*
2. *Do you think that all people have an inner self that is different from the self they show the world? Explain.*

Le Reproduction Interdite (1937), René Magritte. Oil on canvas, 81 cm × 65 cm. Museum Boymans van Beuningen, Rotterdam, The Netherlands. Photo © Banque d'Images/ADAGP/ Art Resource, New York. Art © Artists Rights Society (ARS) New York.

I am not I.
I am this one
walking beside me whom I do not see,
whom at times I manage to visit,
and whom at other times I forget;
who remains calm and silent while I talk,
and forgives, gently, when I hate,
who walks where I am not,
who will remain standing when I die.

Yo no soy yo.
Soy este
que va a mi lado sin yo verlo;
que, a veces, voy a ver,
y que, a veces, olvido.
El que calla, sereno, cuando hablo,
el que perdona, dulce, cuando odio,
el que pasea por donde no estoy,
el que quedará en pie cuando yo muera.

Discussing the Selection
The two questions at the bottom of page 1188 are suitable for a post-reading class discussion. Possible responses to these questions follow:

1. How would you describe the speaker's two different selves?
   Possible Response: One is the physical self that changes, has faults, and will die; the other, the spiritual self, is virtuous and eternal.
2. Do you think that all people have an inner self that is different from the self they show the world? Explain.
   Possible Response: Encourage students to respond to this question using examples of their peers' behavior.

Objectives
- write a Literary Interpretation
- use a written text as a model
- revise a draft to eliminate awkward use of the passive voice
- use the historical present tense to write about a literary work

Introducing the Workshop

A Literary Interpretation By analyzing the elements of a literary work, students will better understand the work and may find it more interesting. Establish some criteria for what makes a literary work worth interpreting. Remind students that they will probably be asked to write a number of literary interpretations throughout their school career. Having a procedure to follow will make the task much easier.

Basics in a Box

B Using the Graphic The items in a literary interpretation work together in a specific order to create the overall piece. The introduction acquaints the reader with the literary work and the writer's interpretation of it. In the body of the paper, the image of the book shown in the graphic illustrates the importance of basing the literary interpretation on specific evidence from the literature. The conclusion wraps up important points made earlier in the paper.

C Presenting the Rubric To better understand the assignment, students can refer to the Standards for Writing a Successful Literary Interpretation. You may wish to discuss with them the complete rubric and student models in the Unit Seven Resource Book on pages 32–37.

For more instruction and practice in writing about literature, use McDougal Littell's ***Language Network:***
- Grade 10, Chapter 20: "Literary Interpretation"
- Grade 12, Chapter 19, "Critical Review of Literature."

Writing Workshop — Literary Interpretation

Making sense of it all . . .

A **From Reading to Writing** Stories like Franz Kafka's "Metamorphosis" or James Joyce's "Eveline" and poems like Federico García Lorca's "The Guitar" may leave you a little confused and wondering what to think. One way to explore a puzzling piece of literature is by writing a **literary interpretation** in which you analyze the elements that contribute to the work's meaning.

For Your Portfolio

WRITING PROMPT Write an interpretive essay about a work of literature, in which you explore the work's meaning.

Purpose: To explain your interpretation of the work
Audience: Your teacher and classmates, others who are familiar with the work

B

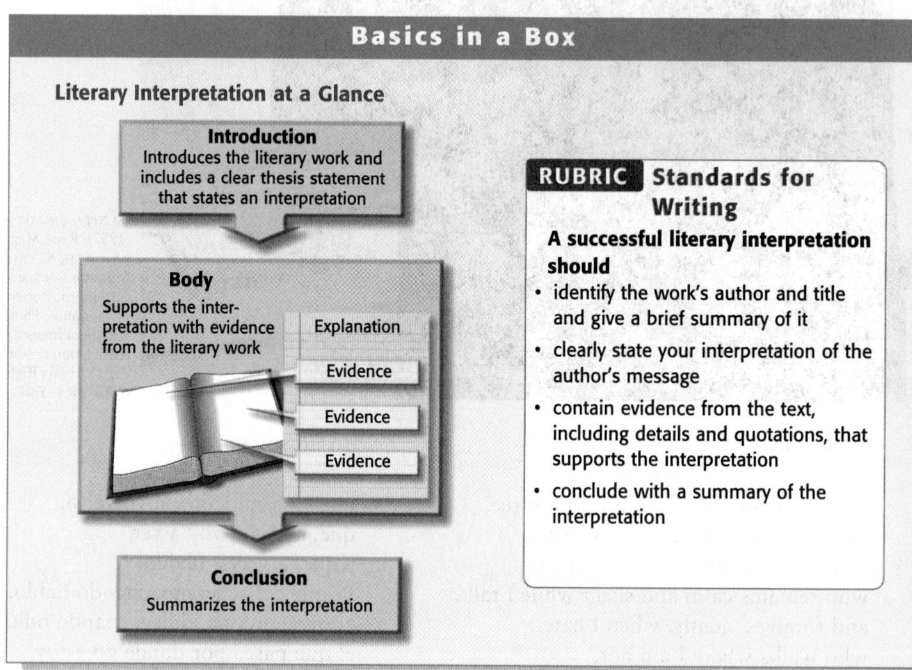

C

LESSON RESOURCES

USING PRINT RESOURCES
Unit One Resource Book
- Prewriting, p. 27
- Drafting and Elaboration, p. 28
- Peer Response, pp. 29–30
- Revising, Editing, and Proofreading, p. 31
- Student Models, pp. 32–36
- Rubric, p. 37

USING MEDIA RESOURCES
Writing Coach CD-ROM
Visit our Web site: classzone.com

ADDITIONAL RESOURCES
For a complete view of Lesson Resources, see page 1095i of this book.

Analyzing Student Models

Hannah Barker
Evanston Township
High School

RUBRIC IN ACTION

Futility and Indecision in James Joyce's "Eveline"

In his short story "Eveline," James Joyce tells a story of deep and paralyzing indecision. Eveline, a poor Irish girl, must make a choice. Should she follow her boyfriend, Frank, to Argentina, where they will be married and live a life of adventure? Or should she stay in Ireland and care for her family, as she promised her dying mother? She is torn; at the last moment she finds herself unable to act or decide, and the ship sails without her. Ultimately, Eveline's inability to decide determines her fate, keeping her at home in familiar, if bleak, surroundings. Upon first reading, it may seem that she has made a mistake—that she lets Frank go simply because she is afraid of change. However, a closer look at the story shows that Eveline's decision is far from simple. No matter what path she chooses, she'll be making a great sacrifice.

❶ In the introduction, identifies the work's author and title and provides a brief summary of it

❷ Presents the thesis statement

Certainly, her life in Ireland is miserable. She is only a little over 19, but she already has responsibility for running the household. Since her mother and her brother Ernest are dead and her brother Harry is away working, she receives little help in caring for the family. Eveline holds a job in a shop, under an unpleasant boss, but also takes responsibility for shopping, housekeeping, cooking, raising two young children, and caring for her elderly father. Her father is a curmudgeon who used to beat her brothers and now threatens to abuse her as well. He collects all of her wages and argues with her about how much she can spend on food for the family. Between work and family, Eveline lives a life of grinding struggle and boredom. If this were a fairy tale, she would be Cinderella. The reader feels sorry for Eveline and is relieved to think that she might find happiness with Frank, her Prince Charming.

D

❸ Describes the difficulty of Eveline's life, providing supporting details from the story

Frank is a sailor and not a prince, but he does promise to rescue Eveline from her dreary existence. He takes her to the opera, walks her home from work, sings to her, and tells her stories about foreign countries and his exploits at sea. She enjoys it: "People knew that they were courting and, when he sang about the lass that loves a sailor, she always felt pleasantly confused." Instead of abandoning her when his vacation in Ireland is over, Frank offers to take her back to Buenos Aires and marry her. Eveline dreams of her new life in Buenos Aires. There, she imagines, she will find love, respect, and adventure, escaping the drudgery and unhappiness that she saw in her mother's life, which was a "life of commonplace sacrifices closing in final craziness." Frank is her best hope of escaping her mother's dismal fate.

❹ Discusses the lure of life with Frank

LANGUAGE SKILLS

Teaching the Lesson

Analyzing the Model

"Futility and Indecision in James Joyce's 'Eveline'"

D The student model introduces the reader to a literary interpretation of the short story "Eveline," which is found earlier in this unit. The story is about a young woman in Ireland who is facing a difficult decision.

Have students read the model, and then discuss the Rubric in Action. Point out the key words and phrases in the student model that correspond to the elements mentioned in the Rubric in Action.

2. Point out to students that this thesis statement has two parts: first, that the message of the story is not what it first appears to be; and second, that Eveline's decision is very difficult.

3,4. Ask students whether the evidence provided in the second and third paragraphs suggest that Eveline would be better off leaving or staying. Why? *(The second paragraph shows what a hard life she has in Ireland and the third paragraph discusses the advantages of life with Frank; the two paragraphs together suggest that she would be better off leaving her family and going with him.)*

MINI LESSON Patterns of Organization

PICTURING TEXT STRUCTURE

Instruction Explain that logical structure is crucial to the success and effectiveness of a written interpretation.

Activity Have students analyze the text structure of the student model by creating a graphic organizer. The graphic should illustrate how the student writer organized her interpretation. Before students create a graphic organizer for the model, they might first work in pairs to discuss what the writer accomplished in each paragraph of the essay.

Thesis: Eveline faces a difficult decision: should she go or stay?

Evidence, Part 1: Why she should go

Evidence, Part 2: Why she should stay

Evidence, Part 3: She is paralyzed by the decision

Conclusion: There is no good choice

5. Point out to students that the fourth and fifth paragraphs present opposing evidence to that given in the second and third paragraphs; despite her difficulties at home and the potential for happiness with Frank, her life at home is not all bad and she does have very strong ties to her family.
6. Help students understand that this writer is really writing about the ambivalence of the story. In her conclusion, she reviews the difficulty of Eveline's choice and concludes that it is the futility of Eveline's decision that makes the story so sad.

However, as her departure draws near, Eveline begins to have second thoughts: "It was hard work—a hard life—but now that she was about to leave it she did not find it a wholly undesirable life." She calls up a few pleasant memories of her childhood, before her mother died and her friends moved away. She feels attached to her surroundings. Even her father is not entirely a burden; every now and then he can be sweet to her. Although many aspects of her daily life are grim, there is some comfort in being at home. After all, she's never known anything else.

And comfort or no, Eveline feels a tremendous obligation to support her family. As her mother lay dying, Eveline promised "to keep the home together as long as she could." In addition to caring for her father, she is raising two young children. If not for her, who would raise them? Her drunken father or absent brother? There is no one else who is responsible enough to run the household. Despite her terror at the thought of living a life of drudgery and dying insane like her mother, Eveline still feels bound by her familial duty, which is no small thing. Can she really desert her family, dishonor her dearly-departed mother, and leave behind the only home she's ever known? All this in pursuit of life abroad with a sailor, a man she hardly knows?

5 Shows her strong and legitimate ties to home

At first it seems that she will. Eveline goes to the boat to meet Frank, prepared to make a new life for herself. However, she thinks twice before actually stepping on board. What seemed like a sea of opportunities has become a sea of uncertainty that threatens to overwhelm her: "All the seas of the world tumbled about her heart. He was drawing her into them: he would drown her." Eveline is paralyzed with fear. Unable to decide, she does not decide. She stands rooted to the spot, allowing Frank, her rescuer, to be swept onto the boat with the other passengers.

It would be a simple story, and sad enough, if the reader knew for certain that Eveline has made a terrible mistake. As it is, one can't be so sure. What if she did climb aboard and leave Ireland forever? She would have no guarantees of a better life. She would be facing a dangerous journey, at the end of which she would spend the rest of her life in a foreign land with a strange language and culture. She would be married to a sailor who might very well spend most of his days at sea.

Eveline is in an incredibly difficult position. Whatever she chooses, she will suffer a deep loss. In the end, she opts for the loss of her unknown future—a heartbreaking decision, but perhaps no worse than the alternative. In light of this futility, her paralysis seems natural and easy to understand. She really has no good way out.

6 Concludes by summarizing the interpretation

Writing Your Literary Interpretation

❶ Prewriting

Think about stories and poems that have surprised, moved, or puzzled you. What work has really stayed with you? A work that you find especially troubling is often a good one to write about. See the **Idea Bank** in the margin for more suggestions. After you choose a story or poem to discuss, follow the steps below.

Planning Your Literary Interpretation

1. **Reread the work several times.** As you read, take notes in your Reader's Notebook. Which passages, ideas, or events confuse or trouble you? Do they become clearer when you reread the work? What questions do you still have about the work?
2. **Develop an interpretation.** Review your notes and write freely for 20 minutes or so about the literary elements of the work. What is the central conflict or image? What happens to the main character? Write a tentative thesis statement expressing your interpretation of the work.
3. **Gather evidence to support your interpretation.** In a chart, list significant passages of the text and explain how they support your interpretation.

Evidence from the Text	How It Supports Interpretation

4. **Test your interpretation.** Discuss your interpretation with others who have read the work. Are they convinced of your conclusion? Does anything in the work contradict your interpretation? How can you revise your interpretation to be more consistent with the evidence in the story or poem?

IDEABank

1. Your Working Portfolio
Look for ideas in the **Writing Options** you completed earlier in this unit:
- **Literary Analysis,** p. 1149
- **Literary Analysis,** p. 1173

2. Literary Chat
Talk with your classmates about works you particularly liked or disliked or didn't understand. Which would you like to write about?

3. Author Search
Look through this book and write down the names of authors whose work you enjoyed. Then go to the library and find some other short works by those authors.

❷ Drafting

Start by introducing the work and the author, briefly telling what the work is about. Then include a thesis statement in which you present the main point of your interpretation—the idea that the rest of your essay will support. From there, write freely about the ideas and evidence that you have gathered to support your interpretation. After you have completed the first draft, you can begin to look at how your ideas are organized.

In the main body of your essay, you will need to provide **supporting evidence** for your interpretation in the form of **details** and **quotations** from the work. You may want to explain key passages in your own words. Sum up your interpretation in the **conclusion.**

Ask Your Peer Reader

- What is the main point of my interpretation?
- What evidence did I present to support my interpretation?
- Are you convinced that my interpretation is reasonable? Why or why not?
- What other points should I include to clarify my interpretation?

LANGUAGE SKILLS

Guiding Student Writing

Prewriting

Choosing a Literary Work

If after reading the Idea Bank students are having trouble choosing a literary work, suggest they try the following:

- Look in a newspaper or magazine that publishes reviews of young adult literature. Read the reviews and choose a work that you are familiar with, or one that you think you might like to read.
- Sign on to a literary discussion group on the Internet. There are several that specialize in young adult literature.
- Work with a few classmates and brainstorm a list of books you have read. You might choose one from the list.
- Several organizations publish lists of favorite young adult books. These should be available at the library or through your teacher.

Planning the Literary Interpretation

1,2. As students reread their chosen text, have them record their questions and critical responses in their Reader's Notebook. Encourage them to write down passages from the text that strike them as significant. You might then pair students who are writing interpretations of the same piece. Allow time for them to discuss their notes and key passages from the text before writing a tentative thesis statement.

3. Have students list all the evidence they can think of that supports their thesis.

4. Remind students that they must be able to support their interpretation with evidence from the text. Encourage students to write down any evidence that disproves or contradicts their view. Have them think about how they might revise their thesis statement to take conflicting evidence into account.

Drafting

Organizing the Draft

Remind students that they should include a brief summary of the text in their literary interpretation. This writer has included the summary in her introduction. However, let students know that they can save the summary for the early part of the body of the text, and include some other discussion in the introduction, such as the explanation of an idea that is relevant to the thesis statement.

Revising

USING THE ACTIVE VOICE

If students need help with the active and passive voice, review the Grammar Mini-Lesson on page T557.

In the last unrevised sentence, the verb, *can(not) be run,* is in the passive voice. In the revised sentence the subject is *no one* and the verb is *is* (with the predicate adjective *responsible*). Now *no one* is the performer of the action, which is really the point of the sentence.

Editing and Proofreading

VERB TENSE

Remind students that verb tenses show the time of an action or state of being. The three most common tenses are the present, past, and future. The past tense is usually formed by adding *-d* or *-ed* to the present form: *watched, cooked.* Irregular verbs have a spelling change: *run, ran; forget, forgot.* The future tense is formed by using the words *shall* or *will* with the present form: *shall run; will forget.* Students must understand the different tenses in order to write their interpretations consistently in the historical present tense. Students should double-check their use of tense in order to produce an error-free final draft.

Point out that the sample, before revision, contains the past tense instead of the historical present. The last sentence is a direct quotation from the book and should be kept in the past tense as it was originally written.

Reflecting

Have students write a brief note evaluating the way in which they approached the writing assignment. You might also ask them to consider how satisfied they are with their final draft. Would they make any further changes if they were to revise their writing again? Have them attach these self-evaluations to their literary interpretations and place both in their working portfolios.

Need revising help?

Review the **Rubric,** p. 1193.

Consider **peer reader** comments.

Check **Revision Guidelines,** p. R19.

Confused about the active voice?

See the **Grammar Handbook,** Voice, p. R61

Wondering about verb tense?

See the **Grammar Handbook,** p. R60.

Publishing IDEAS

- Submit your work to a literary magazine that publishes student essays.
- Post your essay on a class Web site or another Web site for student work.

3 Revising

TARGET SKILL ▶ USING THE ACTIVE VOICE The active voice generally makes writing clearer and more graceful, so use it whenever possible. In a sentence with a verb in the active voice, the subject performs the action: *Eveline made dinner at four o'clock.* In a sentence written in the passive voice, the subject receives the action, or is acted upon: *Dinner was made at four o'clock.* Excessive or unconscious use of the passive voice may make your writing wordy, unclear, and awkward. It is, however, appropriate to use the passive voice when you don't know who performed an action or want to emphasize the action itself rather than the one performing it.

> And comfort or no, Eveline feels a tremendous obligation to support her family. As her mother lay dying, Eveline promised "to keep the home together as long as she could." ^ ~~The household cannot be run by anyone else.~~ [inserted: There is no one else who is responsible enough to run the household.]

4 Editing and Proofreading

TARGET SKILL ▶ VERB TENSE When referring to events narrated in a literary work, use the present tense. (Such a usage is called the historical present.) In other words, write about the event as if it were happening now. Do not, however, change the tenses of verbs in quotations.

> He ~~took~~ takes Eveline to the opera, ~~walked~~ walks her home from work, ~~sang~~ sings to her, and ~~told~~ tells her stories about foreign countries and his exploits at sea: "People knew that they were courting and, when he sang about the lass that loves a sailor, she always felt pleasantly confused."

5 Reflecting

FOR YOUR WORKING PORTFOLIO How did writing about a work of literature help you understand it? How did your interpretation change as you wrote? Attach your reflections to your finished essay and save it in your **Working Portfolio.**

Standardized Test Practice Revising & Editing

Read this passage from the first draft of a literary interpretation. The underlined sections may include the following kinds of errors:

- **ineffective use of passive voice**
- **errors in verb tenses**
- **incorrect verb forms**
- **capitalization errors**

For each underlined section, choose the revision that most improves the writing.

In "Metamorphosis," (1) a story of alienation and bewilderment is told by Franz Kafka (2). At the beginning of the story, Gregor Samsa woke up in the morning to find that he had turned into a large insect (3). He is puzzled by this fact, but he is mostly troubled because he has overslept and is about to miss the train. With great effort he manages to slide out of bed; by this time (4), his parents have growed (5) very worried and his employer has come to the house looking for him. They couldn't imagine (6) what could be keeping him. The odd thing is that despite his horrible transformation, Gregor is primarily worried about the inconvenience and the trouble it will cause him in getting to work.

1. **A.** in "Metamorphosis,"
   B. In "metamorphosis,"
   C. in "metamorphosis,"
   D Correct as is

2. **A.** a story by Franz Kafka, a tale is told of alienation and bewilderment
   B. a tale of alienation and bewilderment by Franz Kafka is told
   C. Franz Kafka tells a story of alienation and bewilderment
   D. Correct as is

3. **A.** Gregor Samsa wakes up in the morning to find that he had turned into a large insect
   B. Gregor Samsa wakes up in the morning to find that he has turned into a large insect
   C. Gregor Samsa woke up in the morning to find that he has turned into a large insect
   D. Correct as is

4. **A.** he manages to slide out of bed: by this time
   B. he manages to slide out of bed, by this time
   C. he manages to slide out of bed . . . by this time
   D. Correct as is

5. **A.** grew
   B. grow
   C. have grown
   D. Correct as is

6. **A.** They won't be able to imagine
   B. They can't imagine
   C. They had not been able to imagine
   D. Correct as is

Need extra help?

See the **Grammar Handbook**
Active and Passive Voice, p. R61
Verbs, p. R59
Quick Reference, p. R66

TEST PRACTICE

Standardized Test Practice

Remind students to notice the types of errors listed before they read the passage through.

Answers:
1. D; **2.** C; **3.** B; **4.** D; **5.** C; **6.** B

MINI LESSON Grammar

CAPITALIZING TITLES

Instruction Remind students that when writing the titles of books, short stories, movies, and plays, they should capitalize the first, last, and all other important words. They should not capitalize conjunctions, articles, or prepositions of fewer than five letters unless they begin the title.

Practice Write the following titles on the chalkboard without capitalization and without underscoring (letters that should be capitalized have been underscored for your viewing only). Have student volunteers describe the correct capitalization, if any, for each title.

1. the invisible man
2. harry potter and the sorcerer's stone
3. the importance of being earnest
4. the crucible
5. cat on a hot tin roof
6. from here to everywhere
7. all's well that ends well
8. the house of spirits

For more instruction and practice with capitalization, use McDougal Littell's ***Language Network:***
- Grade 10, Chapter 10, "Capitalization"
- Grade 12, Chapter 8, "Capitalization"

Building Vocabulary

Objectives

- understand that word families are groups of words with similar etymologies, or word histories
- develop strategies for identifying word roots as a means of recognizing related words
- develop strategies for using knowledge of word families to decode unfamiliar words

EXERCISE

Student responses will vary; sample responses follow.

1. *bibliography,* a list of books; *Bible,* the sacred book of Christianity, including the New Testament and the Old Testament, or Hebrew Scriptures, the sacred book of Judaism; *bibliophile,* a lover of books
2. *psychiatrist,* a physician specializing in mental health; *psychic,* one with supernatural mental powers; *psychology,* the study of mental processes and behavior
3. *benefit,* an advantage; *benefactor,* one who gives help; *benevolent,* characterized by doing good
4. *vision,* sight; *video,* having to do with television; *visor,* an eyeshade; *vista,* a view
5. *political,* having to do with government; *metropolis,* a major city; *police,* body of law enforcement
6. *orthodontist,* a dentist who straightens crooked teeth; *periodontist,* a dentist who specializes in the gums
7. *podiatry,* the branch of medicine dealing with the human foot; *arthropod,* any of a group of invertebrate animals with an exoskeleton and segmented body, such as insects or crustaceans; *podium,* a lectern for a public speaker;
8. *incredible,* unbelievable; *credulous,* too willing to believe; *credit,* a reputation for paying one's debts and general financial well-being; *creed,* a formal statement of religious belief

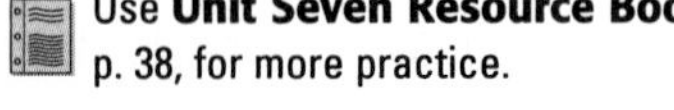
Use **Unit Seven Resource Book,** p. 38, for more practice.

Building Vocabulary

Recognizing Word Families

On pages 340 and 864 you learned about some of the Greek and Latin roots and affixes that can be found in English words. A group of words that have the same linguistic "ancestor" is called a **word family.** Knowing the etymology of a word will often help you identify and understand other words in the same family. For example, in the passage on the right from "Professions for Women," Virginia Woolf used the word *conciliate. Conciliate* contains *concil,* the root of the Latin word *concilium,* "a meeting or gathering of people." *Reconcile* contains the same root, and the word *council* is also descended from *concilium.* Knowing that these words are related will help you understand that *conciliate* has something to do with people coming together. Sure enough, if you look in a dictionary, you will find that *conciliate* means "to overcome the distrust of" or "to appease."

> **And all these questions, according to the Angel in the House, cannot be dealt with freely and openly by women; they must charm, they must *conciliate,* they must—to put it bluntly—tell lies if they are to succeed.**

Strategies for Building Vocabulary

The strategies that follow can help you use information about words' etymologies—their origins and histories—as a tool for recognizing word families, inferring meanings, and improving spelling.

❶ **Break Words into Parts** Many complex words are combinations of roots and affixes. When you see an unfamiliar word, try to break the word into its parts and then determine the meanings of the parts, as in this example:

tenacious

word parts: *ten* + *-acious*

❷ **Build Word Families** The following table shows some members of the English family of words that contain the root *ten* and are derived from the Latin verb *tenēre,* "to hold." Notice how the meanings of the words are related. Knowing the meaning of one word in a family can help you predict the meanings of related words. If you know the meaning of *detention,* for example, you may be able to guess the meaning of *tenacious.*

English Words Derived from Latin *Tenēre*

English Word	Meaning
detention	the act of **holding** in custody or temporary confinement
contents	material that is **held** or contained
tenable	capable of being maintained or **held** in an argument
tenant	one that pays rent to occupy, or **hold,** land or a building
tenure	the status of **holding** one's position (as on a faculty) on a permanent basis

❸ **Spelling** In many cases, a knowledge of word families can help you spell more accurately. The word *tributary,* for example, contains *tribut,* a Latin root meaning "give" or "grant." This root is also found in *contribute, retribution, attribute,* and *distribute.* Notice that the root's spelling is the same in all of the words, even though the emphasis in pronunciation varies.

EXERCISE List and define as many words as you can that contain the following roots.

1. *bibl* (book)
2. *psych* (mind, soul)
3. *ben, bene* (good)
4. *vis, vid* (see)
5. *poli* (city)
6. *dont* (tooth)
7. *pod* (foot)
8. *cred* (believe)

Sentence Crafting

Using Adjective Phrases and Clauses

Grammar from Literature Writers use adjectives to make their writing more accurate and colorful. Adjectives modify nouns and pronouns, answering the questions *what kind, which one, how many*, and *how much*. In addition to single-word adjectives, writers also use **adjective phrases and clauses,** which have similar functions.

Prepositional phrases, participial phrases, and infinitive phrases can all be used as adjectives. Read the following sentences from James Joyce's "Eveline," noting the adjective phrases that modify the nouns *sign* and *footsteps*.

> prepositional phrase
> **Her eyes gave him no sign** of love or farewell or recognition.
>
> **The man out of the last house passed on his way home;**
> participial phrase
> **she heard his footsteps** clacking along the concrete pavement . . .

An adjective clause also modifies a noun or pronoun, but unlike a phrase, it contains a subject and a verb. Adjective clauses are subordinate clauses, so they cannot stand alone. They begin with relative pronouns (*who, whose, that, which*) or with relative adverbs (*after, before, when, where, why*). The clauses in the following sentences from "Eveline" modify *those* and *Harry.*

> **In her home anyway she had shelter and food; she had**
> adjective clause
> **those** whom she had known all her life **about her.**
>
> adjective clause
> **Ernest was dead and Harry,** who was in the church decorating business, **was nearly always down somewhere in the country.**

Punctuation Tip An adjective clause can be **essential** or **nonessential**. An essential clause provides information that is necessary to complete the meaning of the sentence. A nonessential clause provides extra information that may be helpful but is not necessary.

> essential clause
> **Eveline headed for the ship** that was about to sail.
> *(Which ship? The one about to sail.)*
>
> nonessential clause
> **Eveline headed for the ship,** which was about to sail.
> *(There's only one ship; by the way, it's about to sail.)*

Nonessential clauses are always set off with commas; essential clauses are not. When faced with a choice between *that* and *which,* use *that* if the clause you're introducing is essential, *which* if it is nonessential. Most other relative pronouns and adverbs can be used to introduce both essential and nonessential clauses.

WRITING EXERCISE Rewrite each sentence, adding an adjective phrase or clause that modifies the underlined word. Use at least two adjective phrases and two adjective clauses. Sample answers are given for the first two sentences.

1. Eveline is planning to run away with Frank, a <u>sailor</u>.
   Sample answer: Eveline is planning to run away with Frank, a sailor *who lives in Buenos Aires.*
2. She is eager to leave behind her <u>job</u>.
   Sample answer: She is eager to leave behind her job *with Miss Gavan.*
3. Her <u>father</u> doesn't treat her very well.
4. She is looking forward to a new <u>life</u>.
5. Frank is waiting for her at the <u>ship</u>.

GRAMMAR EXERCISE For each sentence, determine whether the boldface adjective clause is essential or nonessential. Correct any errors in punctuation and in the use of *that* and *which.*

1. Eveline thinks about her mother, **who died some years before.**
2. On the day **that her mother died,** Eveline promised to take care of the children.
3. Her father who **has a very bad temper** is difficult to live with.
4. The one thing, **that gives her hope,** is the thought of a new life with Frank.
5. She is reluctant to leave her home, **which is so familiar.**

LANGUAGE SKILLS

Sentence Crafting

Objectives

- recognize how prepositional phrases, participles, and participial phrases can be used as adjectives to modify nouns and pronouns
- recognize how a subordinate clause can be used as an adjective
- revise drafts by using adjective phrases and clauses to clearly express ideas, add detail, or streamline wording
- create complex sentences by joining adjective clauses to independent clauses
- correctly punctuate essential and nonessential adjective clauses

WRITING EXERCISE

Student responses will vary. Sample responses follow.

1,2. Sample responses given on pupil page.
3. Her father, who drinks all the time, doesn't treat her very well.
4. She is looking forward to a new life with Frank.
5. Frank is waiting for her at the ship, which is docked in the harbor.

GRAMMAR EXERCISE

1. nonessential
2. essential
3. nonessential
   Her father, who has a very bad temper, is difficult to live with.
4. essential
   The one thing that gives her hope is the thought of a new life with Frank.
5. nonessential

Use **Unit Seven Resource Book,** p. 39, for more practice.

MINI LESSON Grammar

ADJECTIVE PHRASES AND CLAUSES

Practice For further practice, have students rewrite each sentence, adding an adjective phrase or clause to modify the underlined word. Student responses will vary, but a sample response is given for each sentence.

1. Yoshiko heard a bird singing in the <u>tree.</u> (. . . tree outside her window.)
2. She went into the <u>garden.</u> (. . . garden, where she looked for the bird.)
3. She found a baby bluejay under the <u>grass.</u> (. . . grass by the side of the yard.)
4. The motherless bird reminded her of her own <u>mother.</u> (. . . mother, whom she hadn't seen in many years.)
5. Her <u>father</u> almost never spoke of her mother. (Her father, who had since remarried, almost . . .)

For more instruction and practice with adjective phrases and clauses, use McDougal Littell's ***Language Network:***

- Grade 10, Chapter 3, "Phrases" and Chapter 4, "Clauses"
- Grade 12, Chapter 2, "Phrases" and Chapter 3, "Clauses"

Objectives
- reflect on and assess student understanding of the unit
- analyze how characters deal with change across texts
- review point of view and style
- assess and build portfolios

Reflecting on the Literature
Students may want to work in groups of three on this topic, each focusing on a selection, and then present their findings as a panel discussion. Make sure they emphasize the similarities and differences in the reactions to change among the selections.

Reviewing Literary Concepts
Point of View Have students identify similarities between "Eveline" and "The Jay."
- Both stories are told from a limited third person point of view.
- Both main characters are young women who have lost their mothers and are about to be married.
- Both have suspense, although to varying degrees.

Then have students consider differences between the stories.
- Eveline and Yoshiko have different personalities.
- They come from different cultures.
- Each story has a different tone and mood, partly due to the characters' different personalities.

Then have students discuss how these similarities and differences are expressed by each point of view and affect the reader's response.
Style Suggest that students write an essay on this topic.

Building Your Portfolio
If necessary, help students select their two pieces of writing. But part of this exercise is testing students' own judgment of their writing.

Part Assessment
To assess skills and concepts taught in this unit part, use, **Formal Assessment Book,** page 173.

Reflect and Assess

As you have seen, the first half of the 20th century was marked by tremendous changes in the arts and literature, which can be loosely summed up by the term *modernism.* The following options will help you to review what you have learned about this fascinating period and the literature it produced.

Reflecting on the Literature

A Changing World Modernist literature often portrays people who are struggling with great changes in the world and in their lives. Choose three selections in this part that focus on change. For each selection, consider the following questions:
- What major changes are described in the selection?
- Do these changes mainly affect individuals, or an entire society?
- Are such changes positive or negative, or a mixture of both? Why?
- What can you infer about the author's attitude toward such changes?

Compare the views of change presented by the three selections.

Reviewing Literary Concepts

Point of View Compare and contrast the point of view used in two works of fiction in this part. How does the author's use of point of view influence your reaction to the story and the judgments that you make about the characters? How would the story change if told from another point of view?

Style Compare and contrast the style of two selections in this part. What is distinctive about each author's style? Consider elements such as word choice, imagery, figurative language, sentence length, and tone.

Building Your Portfolio

Writing Workshop and Writing Options Look over the literary interpretation that you wrote for the Writing Workshop beginning on page 1190, as well as the Writing Options that you completed in this part of the book. Choose two pieces of your writing that show the most insight into the literature. Write a note explaining your choices, then add the note and both pieces of writing to your **Presentation Portfolio.**

Self ASSESSMENT

READER'S NOTEBOOK

As a way of reviewing your own knowledge of the terms below, work with a partner to create a two-column matching test. In one column, list each term from the list below; in the next column provide a phrase that defines or illustrates the term. For additional help, make use of the index or the **Glossary of Literary Terms** (beginning on page R91).

modernism
connotation
sound devices
Kafkaesque
diction
epiphany
point of view
symbol
Negritude
stream of consciousness

Setting GOALS

Make a list of your strengths and weaknesses as a reader and writer. Circle those weaknesses that you think are the easiest to correct or improve upon in the near future. Use those items that you circled as goals for your work.

Assessment Self Assessment

Students can look up the listed terms in the **Glossary of Literary Terms** on p. R91, or they can find them introduced in context on the text pages indicated below.

modernism (pp. 1106–1107)
connotation (pp. 1183 and 1186)
sound devices (pp. 1150 and 1154)
Kafkaesque
diction (pp. 1157 and 1164)
epiphany (p. 1167)
point of view (pp. 1109 and 1148)
symbol (pp. 1175 and 1180)
Negritude (p. 1183)
stream of consciousness (p. 1106)

Extend Your *Reading*

LITERATURE CONNECTIONS

1984

GEORGE ORWELL

In this novel Orwell portrays a world in which a totalitarian government controls individual thought and even reality itself. Privacy has been outlawed, and Big Brother (the government) is everywhere, spying. This classic remains timely and continues to stir the imagination while asking important questions about human nature.

Here are just a few of the related readings that accompany *1984:*

End Game
J. G. BALLARD

***from* Politics and the English Language**
GEORGE ORWELL

No One Died in Tiananmen Square
WILLIAM LUTZ

Siddhartha

HERMANN HESSE

This 1922 novel, based upon the early life of Buddha, portrays a young man's search for meaning. Born into a life of privilege in India, the man, Siddhartha, abandons his comfortable home. As he wanders throughout the land, he tries living out various answers to the problems of life, such as wealth and romance, only to realize that the truth lies deeper.

And Even *More* . . .

Books

Dubliners JAMES JOYCE
This collection of related stories, first published in 1914, asks probing questions about the Irish experience and culture.

A Room Of One's Own VIRGINIA WOOLF
In this long essay, the author eloquently makes her case for female equality.

Other Media

The Trial
A black-and-white film adaptation of Kafka's nightmarish novel, directed by Orson Welles. Zenger Media. (VIDEO)

The Shock of the New
This series of eight hour-long videos is written and hosted by the distinguished art critic Robert Hughes. He explains the revolution in art that took place during the 20th century. Time-Life. (VIDEOCASSETTE)

The Trial

FRANZ KAFKA

In this novel, a respectable bank officer, Josef K., is arrested one day for no apparent reason. Many regard his subsequent nightmare experience as a parable about modern life.

More Recommendations for Your Students

Difficulty Level: Easy

Mairowitz, David Zane, Robert Crumb. *Introducing Kafka* (New York: Totem, 1999). This book, presented in the style of a comic book, provides a fascinating introduction to the life and works of Franz Kafka. David Zane's entertaining and thought-provoking prose is augmented by the illustrations of legendary cartoonist Robert Crumb.

Chris Rodrigues, Chris Garratt, *Introducing Modernism* (New York: Totem, 2001). Fifteen basic questions about modernism are addressed in this irreverent yet thoughtful introduction. In comic book format, the writer Rodrigues and the illustrator Garrett respond to questions such as the following: What is it? How do we recognize a modernist work? Why are modernists so often exiles?

Difficult Level: Average

Yenawine, Philip. *How to Look at Modern Art* (New York: Abrams, 1991). In clear, readable language, the author explains what to look for in modern art and why. This well-illustrated book introduces major movements and artists and connects modern art to the ideas of the day.

Walter Levy, ed. *Modern Drama: Selected Plays from 1879 to the Present* (Upper Saddle River, Prentice, 1999). This anthology includes 25 modern and contemporary masterpieces from around the world. Works by Samuel Beckett, Luigi Pirandello, Bertolt Brecht, and Eugène Ionesco are included.

Difficulty Level: Challenging

Woolf, Virginia, *Mrs. Dalloway* (Orlando: Harcourt/Harvest, 1925, 1953). In this modernist classic, we enter the mind of Clarissa Dalloway and experience one day in her life. With poetic elegance and dazzling innovation, Woolf reveals Mrs. Dalloway's innermost thoughts and feelings, while recording her reaction to the chaotic sensations of London life in the 1920's.

Hughes, Robert, *The Shock of the New* (New York: Knopf, 1991). This book was originally written as companion piece for an acclaimed 1979 PBS series about modern art. Hughes provides an engaging 100 year history of modern art, explaining key artists and movements.

Unit Seven, Part 2, provides literature written in response to 20th-century wars and conflicts. This literature, representing several countries, includes works by Pirandello, Akhmatova, Brecht, Wiesel, Sachs, Camus, Solzhenitsyn, Darwish, and Allende. The feature **Milestones in World Literature** focuses on Erich Maria Remarque's classic war novel, *All Quiet on the Western Front.* In addition, the **Chinua Achebe Author Study** offers students an opportunity to explore conflicts in Nigeria as portrayed by one of Africa's greatest writers.

World Art and Cultures Transparencies

AT64 *L'Assault*

AT65 *Friendship of the People*

AT69 *Pillars of Society*

AT70 German and American propaganda posters

AT71 *Liberation*

You may use the listed transparencies to acquaint students with art created in response to modern wars and conflicts.

READING FOR INFORMATION

Reading Skills and Strategies

PREVIEWING

Give students a few moments to look over this introduction. It provides information about the major wars and conflicts of the 20th century, creating a context for the literature in this part. Tell students that the images and the captions on pages 1200 and 1201 preview major wars and conflicts in the 20th century. Point out that the feature **Historical Highlights** is divided into two parts: the first part, on pages 1202 and 1203, covers events through WWII; the second part, on pages 1204 and 1205, covers events following WWII.

Responses to War and Conflict

Why It Matters

Two world wars, regional and ethnic strife, bloody battles for independence—for all its achievements, the 20th century was one of the most violent times in history. Deeply troubled by these terrible struggles, writers often served as society's conscience. They explored the nature of war and its effects on people.

The Russian Revolution and the Cold War

Torn apart by revolution in 1917, Russia had by 1922 become part of a Communist dictatorship called the Soviet Union. It was led first by **Lenin** and later by **Stalin,** who are pictured at right. After World War II, the Soviet Union and the United States squared off as rival superpowers.

For Links to War and Conflict, click on:

American soldiers practice shooting from trenches.

The Great War

Until a second world war came along, World War I (1914–1918) was known as the Great War, for its scope was far broader and its death toll far higher than those of any previous war. In the **Battle of the Somme** in 1916, for example, more than a million soldiers were killed in four months of trench warfare.

An Even Greater War
World War II (1939–1945) surpassed World War I as history's bloodiest conflict. It was fought on land, on the sea, and in the air in many parts of the world. This war came to an end after the United States dropped atomic bombs on the cities of **Hiroshima** and **Nagasaki** in Japan.

Struggles for Independence
In the aftermath of World War II, Britain, France, and other European nations lost most of their overseas colonies. The movements for independence were often violent. By 1970, many African and Asian nations had gained their independence.

Fighting for Freedom
While many nations were throwing off the yoke of communism in the late 1980s, China remained a Communist dictatorship. In 1989, the government brutally cracked down on students demanding democracy in **Tiananmen Square** in Beijing.

READING FOR INFORMATION

Reading Skills and Strategies

NOTE TAKING AND SUMMARIZING

As students read the feature **Historical Highlights**, encourage them to use note taking as a study strategy to help them process the information. After reading, ask students to use their notes to summarize each section in their own words. The summary should include the important events in the correct sequence.

Historical Note

A **Trench Warfare** By early 1915, the opposing armies along the Western Front had dug miles of parallel trenches for protection from enemy fire. Soldiers on both sides endured miserable conditions in the trenches, which swarmed with rats. "The men slept in mud, washed in mud, ate mud, and dreamed mud," wrote one soldier. The space between the opposing trenches was known as "no man's land." When ordered to attack, soldiers leaped "over the top" of the trenches into a bombed-out landscape. There, many soldiers were mowed down by machine-gun fire. The number of dead and wounded reached staggering heights. In 1916, for example, the Germans launched an attack against the French near Verdun. More than 300,000 men on each side were slain.

Historical Note

B **Stalin's Agricultural Revolution** Unlike the well-educated and cultured Lenin, Joseph Stalin (1879–1953) was coarse and crude. Under his regime, the government in 1928 began to seize more than 25 million privately owned farms, combining them into large, government-owned, or collective, farms. Using terror and violence, Stalin forced the peasants to work on these farms and exiled about 1 million families. His brutal policies caused widespread starvation, killing between 5 million and 10 million peasants.

Historical Highlights: Through World War II

In the first half of the 20th century, two global wars and a political revolution changed the world forever. Tens of millions of soldiers and civilians lost their lives in these terrible upheavals.

Allied troops in battle in 1918

World War I

On June 28, 1914, a Serbian nationalist assassinated Archduke Franz Ferdinand, heir to the Austro-Hungarian throne, who was visiting the Bosnian capital of Sarajevo. This event ignited a war that had been smoldering for some time. On one side were the **Allied Powers** of Russia, France, and Great Britain, which were soon joined by Italy and other nations. The Allied Powers were opposed by the **Central Powers**—Germany, Austria-Hungary, Bulgaria, and the Ottoman Empire.

Stubborn leaders, patriotic propaganda, and new tools of war—poison gas, armored tanks, machine guns, and airplanes—helped make this war a horrendous struggle. It was known as "the war to end all wars." On the western front in Belgium and France, the A opposing armies dug themselves into trenches and fought to a virtual stalemate, despite terrible loss of life. Only the late U.S. entry into the war tipped the scale in the Allies' favor, so that Germany was forced to sign an **armistice** on November 11, 1918.

The Russian Revolution and Its Aftermath

In 1917, the Russian people drove their ruler, Czar Nicholas II, from power. He was replaced by a provisional government that in November 1917 fell to the **Bolsheviks,** a small group of revolutionaries led by Vladimir Lenin. He soon ended his country's involvement in World War I, signing the Treaty of Brest-Litovsk with Germany in 1918.

The former Russian empire was later renamed the Union of Soviet Socialist Republics (USSR), or Soviet Union, in 1922, and the Bolsheviks became the Communist Party. After Lenin died in 1924, a power struggle brought forth an even harsher dictator, **Joseph Stalin.** Under Stalin, the government took total control of Soviet citizens' lives. People were forced to work on collective farms and in B government-owned factories. Millions of people were executed or exiled to the frigid regions of Siberia.

The USS *West Virginia* in flames at Pearl Harbor

World War II

After World War I, economic problems in several nations led to the rise of dictators. In Italy, Benito Mussolini, who took charge in 1922, led a militant political movement called **fascism.** It stressed loyalty to the state and obedience to its leader. In Japan, a military dictatorship also came to power, though the emperor remained in nominal control. In Germany, where the Great Depression had crippled the economy, **Adolf Hitler** took control of the government in 1933.

Adolf Hitler

He led the Nazi party, which held that the "Aryan" race—Germans and certain other northern Europeans—should rule the world. In the mid-1930s, these three nations formed an alliance referred to as the **Axis.** On September 1, 1939, Germany invaded Poland, and World War II began.

With his blitzkriegs, or "lightning wars," Hitler rapidly conquered most of continental Europe, including France. In each conquered nation, the Nazis set up a dictatorship, virtually enslaved the people, and killed millions of Jews and other "non-Aryans" in a ruthless campaign now known as the Holocaust. In June 1941, Germany invaded the Soviet Union. Six months later, Japan launched a surprise attack on an American naval base at **Pearl Harbor,** Hawaii, and the United States joined the conflict. E

With the Soviets and Americans joining Britain in the fighting, the tide of war began to turn. After battling the Germans in North Africa, Allied troops moved north into Italy, where the Italians surrendered in September 1943. The Allies then mounted a massive invasion against Nazi forces in Normandy on June 6, 1944, known as **D-day.** In the next six months, the Allies liberated France, Belgium, and Luxembourg and defeated the Nazis in the **Battle of the Bulge.** Germany surrendered on May 7, 1945. After the United States dropped atomic bombs on Hiroshima and Nagasaki, Japan surrendered on September 2, 1945, thus ending the war.

History to Literature

EVENT IN HISTORY	EVENT IN LITERATURE
Millions of soldiers die fighting in Europe in World War I.	Erich Maria Remarque's novel *All Quiet on the Western Front* describes the horror of war through a German soldier's eyes. F
Nazi dictator Adolf Hitler institutes a policy of genocide against the Jewish people.	Anne Frank, Elie Wiesel, Primo Levi, and other writers provide eyewitness accounts of the horror of the Holocaust.
Soviet dictator Joseph Stalin exiles many to prison camps in Siberia.	Aleksandr Solzhenitsyn portrays the ordeal of Soviet prisoners in his novel *One Day in the Life of Ivan Denisovich.*

Historical Note

C ***Mein Kampf*** In 1923, while in prison, Adolf Hitler (1889–1945) wrote *Mein Kampf (My Struggle).* This book, which set forth his beliefs and political ideas, served as a plan of action for the Nazis. Hitler stated that the Germans, whom he incorrectly deemed "Aryans," were a "master race" and that non-Aryans—such as Jews, Slavs, and Gypsies—were subhuman. Hitler also stated that Germany needed more land. To obtain that land, he vowed to conquer Eastern Europe and Russia.

Literary Note

D **"September 1, 1939"** W. H. Auden (1907–1973) wrote a classic poem entitled "September 1, 1939." In this poem, the speaker, sitting "in one of the dives" in New York, describes his reaction to Hitler's invasion of Poland. The poem contains the haunting lines: "The unmentionable odour of death/ Offends the September night."

Historical Note

E **Pearl Harbor** On December 7, 1941, at 7:55 A.M., Japan launched a surprise attack against U.S. military installations at Pearl Harbor. Within two hours, Japanese airplanes had sunk or had damaged 21 ships, including 8 battleships, and had destroyed more than 300 American planes. The attack killed about 2,388 people and wounded about 2,000 others. The next day, in his speech to Congress, President Roosevelt described December 7 as "a date which will live in infamy." On December 11, four days after the attack, Nazi Germany declared war on the United States.

Literary Note

F ***All Quiet on the Western Front*** Tell students to see the feature **Milestones in World Literature,** on pages 1214 and 1215, for an essay about Remarque's novel.

MINI LESSON Interpreting the Text

Have students read pages 1202 and 1203 and then answer questions such as the following:

- About how long did World War I last? *(a little more than four years)*
- Did Joseph Stalin seize control of Russia before or after World War II? *(before)*
- Why was the attack on Pearl Harbor important? *(The attack brought the United States into the war against the Axis Powers.)*
- Which event happened first, the explosion of the atomic bomb over Hiroshima or the invasion of Normandy? *(the invasion of Normandy)*

Pronunciations
Sun Yat-sen (so͞on′ yät-sĕn′)
Chiang Kai-shek (jyäng′ kī-shĕk′)
Mao Zedong (mou′ dzä′dŭng′)
apartheid (ə-pärt′hīd)
Mikhail Gorbachev (mĭkн-ə-īl′ gôr′bə-chôf′)
Salvador Allende (säl-vä-dôr′ ä-yĕn′dĕ)

Historical Note

A **Cultural Revolution** Believing that the Soviet Union had betrayed the principles of the Communist Revolution, Mao Zedong launched what he called the Cultural Revolution to prevent China from following that same course. To achieve his goals, Mao urged China's young people to "learn revolution by making revolution." Millions of high school and college students heeded Mao's call, forming the Red Guards and demonstrating in large cities. They regarded peasants as heroes and intellectuals as enemies. The Red Guards shut down colleges and schools, denouncing professors, government officials, factory managers, and even their own parents. By 1976, the economy was severely damaged, and China was plunging into chaos. Mao realized that the Cultural Revolution had gone too far. He called on the army to restore order and to disband the Red Guards.

Historical Note

B **Mohandas Gandhi** Mohandas Gandhi (1869–1948) was one of the greatest spiritual leaders of the 20th century. He lived a simple life and preached tolerance and concern for others as the way to truth. His followers revered him as the Mahatma ("Great Soul"), and the people of India honored him as the father of their nation. To free India from British rule, he launched a campaign of nonviolent resistance. He urged the Indian people to refuse to buy British goods, attend government schools, pay British taxes, and vote in elections. His efforts were successful, and in 1947 India received its independence. On January 30, 1948, he was assassinated by a Hindu fanatic. Commenting on Gandhi's death, the playwright George Bernard Shaw remarked, "How dangerous it is to be good."

Historical Highlights: After World War II

No global wars occurred after World War II. Still, in the second half of the 20th century, armed conflicts raged like wildfires in several regions of the world.

In 1956, the Soviets crushed a rebellion in Hungary.

Mao Zedong

Revolution in China

China's last imperial dynasty fell in 1912, but the new Chinese republic was unstable, and civil war broke out. Within China's Nationalist Party, organized by **Sun Yat-sen,** were Communists with ties to the new Soviet Union. In 1928, **Chiang Kai-shek** took control of China's government. He forced the Communists to retreat north on the 6,000-mile Long March of 1934–1935, during which **Mao Zedong** became their leader. After World War II, there was a civil war in China. Chiang fled with his followers to the island of Taiwan, and in 1949 China became a Communist nation under Mao's control. In A 1966, Mao launched the **Cultural Revolution,** a movement to establish a society of peasants and workers. It was led by students who formed militia units called **Red Guards** and targeted those who seemed to have special privileges. Thousands were executed or died in prison.

The Collapse of Colonial Empires

After World War II, struggles for independence occurred in many of the colonies ruled by Britain and France. In India, **Mohandas** B **Gandhi,** a spiritual leader and activist, led nonviolent protests against British rule and helped India gain its independence in 1947. The West African nation of Nigeria achieved its independence from Great Britain in 1960. Algeria won its independence from France in 1962 after a long and bloody conflict.

South Africa left the British Commonwealth in 1961. After decades of pressure, **apartheid,** a policy of racial separation that denied civil rights to the nation's black majority, ended in 1991.

Crowds in Nigeria cheer election results in 1959, shortly before independence was achieved.

1204

The Cold War

The United States and the Soviet Union emerged as superpowers after World War II. They then faced off in a rivalry known as the Cold War that lasted more than 40 years. It began when the Soviet Union set up Communist governments in Eastern Europe. The British leader Winston Churchill said that an "**iron curtain**" now separated the nations of Western Europe and Eastern Europe.

To halt the spread of communism, the United States sent troops to Korea in the early 1950s and to Vietnam in the 1960s and the early 1970s. Meanwhile, the superpowers waged a nuclear–arms race and a "space race" to see which nation would land someone on the moon first (the United States did, in 1969).

In 1985, Mikhail Gorbachev's became the leader of the Soviet Union. His policy of **glasnost,** or "openness," gave the Soviet people more freedom. One by one, the nations of Eastern Europe cast off communism. The Soviet Union itself collapsed in 1991.

Palestinian and Israeli flags

Conflicts in Latin America

Throughout the 20th century, many Latin American countries were plagued with political violence. In Argentina, **Juan Perón**, a military leader, won the presidency in 1946. He and his popular wife, Eva, ruled together, setting up a dictatorship. Driven from office in 1955, Perón was again elected president in 1973, shortly before his death.

In neighboring Chile, economic troubles led many to turn to **Salvador Allende,** a Marxist who was elected president in 1970. When economic woes continued, military leaders overthrew Allende in 1973 and, in the violent aftermath, many of his supporters fled or were killed.

One of the most enduring of Latin America's leaders was **Fidel Castro.** He took control of Cuba after a revolution in 1959 and ruled as a dictator for more than four decades. In 1961, he easily repulsed a group of anti-Castro exiles who invaded Cuba at a remote beach on the Bay of Pigs.

Conflicts in the Middle East

The Middle East also has seen terrible conflicts since World War II. In 1947, the United Nations voted to partition Palestine to establish a Jewish homeland. Since then, relations between Israel and its neighbors have remained tense.

Elsewhere in the Middle East, about 1,000,000 people died in a war between Iran and Iraq before a cease-fire was declared in 1988. Two years later, **Saddam Hussein,** dictator of Iraq, invaded Kuwait. A coalition of troops led by the U.S. defeated Iraq in the **Persian Gulf War** of 1991.

After the attacks on the U.S. on September 11, 2001, the U.S. invaded Afghanistan, hunting for Osama bin Laden and his al-Qaeda terrorist network. In 2003, the war expanded to Iraq and escalated into a major world conflict.

Other Ethnic Conflicts

Ethnic conflicts erupted in Eastern Europe after Communist governments collapsed in the early 1990s. In Yugoslavia, several republics wished for an independent future. Slovenia, Croatia, Macedonia, and Bosnia-Herzegovina all voted for independence. Ethnic Serbs living in Croatia and Bosnia, however, fought to retain a portion of the land and to remain united with Serbia in a "greater Yugoslavia."

In the conflict that followed, people living in regions dominated by other ethnic groups were driven from their homes or killed. When the violence in **Bosnia** increased, the U.S. and its allies stepped in, and a peace agreement was reached in 1995. Four years later, Western nations again intervened to protect ethnic Albanians in Kosovo.

Ethnic Albanian refugees from Macedonia rest at the Kosovo-Macedonia border in 2001.

1205

Historical Note

(C) The Cuban Missile Crisis A few years after Fidel Castro seized power in Cuba, his country was involved in a crisis that brought the world to the brink of nuclear war. In July 1962, the Soviet Union, led by premier Nikita Khrushchev, began to install ballistic missiles in Cuba, an island country about 90 miles south of Florida. These missiles could easily reach several cities in the United States. In October, an American spy plane detected the missile sites. President John F. Kennedy then demanded that the Soviets remove the missiles. He also imposed a naval blockade on Cuba to prevent the shipment of more Soviet missiles. As Soviet ships headed toward Cuba, people throughout the world feared that a nuclear war was imminent. The Soviet ships, however, altered their course before reaching the blockade. The crisis was resolved when Khrushchev agreed to remove the missiles from Cuba in return for a U.S. promise never to invade that country.

Historical Note

(D) The country of Yugoslavia was created after World War I and comprised many ethnic and religious groups that were often in conflict with one another. Within the Yugoslav republic of Serbia was a region called Kosovo that was inhabited mostly by people of Albanian descent. The Kosovars sought independence, but the Serbs opposed them. War broke out as the Serbian government tried to drive the Albanians out of Kosovo. In March 1999, NATO forces began bombing Serbia. By June, the Serbs withdrew from Kosovo. In February 2003, the country of Yugoslavia became a federation known as Serbia and Montenegro. Montenegro achieved independence in June 2006. Tensions still persist between Serbs and Kosovars at this writing.

MINI LESSON Interpreting the Text

Have students read pages 1204 and 1205 and then answer questions such as the following:

- How would you describe Mao's Cultural Revolution? *(It was a movement to create a society made up of peasants and workers.)*
- In which two countries of southeastern Asia did the United States fight in an attempt to contain communism? *(Korea and Vietnam)*
- What nation in the Middle East did the United Nations help to set up after World War II? *(the nation of Israel)*
- Which dictator ruled his country for a longer time, Fidel Castro or Juan Perón? *(Fidel Castro)*

Objectives

- understand and appreciate a work of **modern fiction** about wartime sacrifice **(Literary Analysis)**
- examine how **setting** affects characters in a short story **(Literary Analysis)**
- **compare and contrast characters** to understand their response to conflict **(Active Reading)**

Summary

A husband and his distraught wife board an Italian train during the time of World War I. The woman is upset because her only son is about to be sent to the front. One of the other passengers points out that the woman is lucky because his son has been at the front since the beginning of the war. Another claims that his predicament is even worse because he has two sons at the front. Their discussion is soon interrupted by an old man who tells them that when a son dies for his country, he dies happy. Therefore, parents should not mourn their child's death. The wife, who feels encouraged by the old man's words, asks him if his son is really dead. The question forces the old man to confront the fact that his son is gone forever. He breaks down and cries uncontrollably.

Use **Unit Seven Resource Book,** p. 41, for additional support.

Thematic Link

Luigi Pirandello's short story "War" deals with parents' responses to war and conflict as their children go off to fight.

Use **Unit Seven Resource Book,** p. 44, for practice with Words to Know.

5-Minute Warm-Up

Daily Language SkillBuilder

Have students **proofread** the display sentences on page 1095m and write them correctly.

LUIGI PIRANDELLO

Luigi Pirandello
1867–1936

Dashed Dreams Luigi Pirandello (lo͞o-ē'jē pĭr'ən-dĕl'ō) was one of the most important dramatists of the 20th century. He was born in Sicily to a family of mineral merchants and studied at universities in Rome and Germany. Upon completing his studies, he settled in Rome and applied himself to writing. When a landslide in 1903 shut down the sulfur mines from which his family derived its wealth, he was left nearly penniless. To support his young family, he supplemented his writing income by teaching Italian. His wife's mental illness added to his burdens. From 1919 until her death in 1959, Antonietta Pirandello had to be kept in an institution.

From Realism to Experimentation Pirandello's early writing was realistic fiction, often wryly humorous and set in his native Sicily. In time his interest in psychology, spurred by his wife's illness, led him to focus on his characters' inner conflicts. Increasingly, he turned to drama to explore the subconscious mind. By the early 1920s, he was writing experimental plays: *Henry IV,* which examines the relation between madness and truth, and *Six Characters in Search of an Author,* which explores the boundary between fantasy and reality.

International Acclaim Later in the 1920s, Pirandello toured the world with his own theater company. In 1934 he received the Nobel Prize for Literature. One of the great innovators in modern drama, he influenced several important playwrights, including Jean Anouilh, Jean-Paul Sartre, Eugene Ionesco, Samuel Beckett, and Edward Albee.

Other Works
The Oil Jar and Other Stories
The Late Mattia Pascal
Right You Are If You Think You Are

LESSON RESOURCES

UNIT SEVEN RESOURCE BOOK, pp. 41–45

ASSESSMENT RESOURCES
Formal Assessment, pp. 175–176
Teacher's Guide to Assessment and Portfolio Use
Test Generator

INTEGRATED TECHNOLOGY
Visit our Web site: classzone.com

ADDITIONAL RESOURCES
Lesson Planning Guide, pp. 153–154
Teacher's Sourcebook for Language Development

Build Background

Wartime Italy Pirandello's short story "War" is set in Italy during World War I. At that time, Italian patriotism was put to a severe test. Italy had become a unified nation only recently, in the second half of the 19th century. Before then, it was made up of separate city-states, kingdoms, and principalities. Many Italians, therefore, continued to feel a stronger loyalty to their local region than to the nation as a whole.

In 1915, Italy declared war against its neighbor Austria-Hungary. The Italian government hoped to conquer Austrian territory where Italians lived. However, the army suffered from low morale and a lack of modern equipment. Many of those drafted were peasants who did not understand why they had to fight. The war also stirred deep resentment among civilians, who experienced severe shortages of fuel and food.

The Italian Front stretched along the frontier between Italy and Austria-Hungary. The cold weather and the mountainous terrain made it difficult for either side to launch offensives. Usually, the opposing armies were bogged down in trench warfare. Though Italy ended up on the winning side, it paid a terrible price. About 600,000 Italian soldiers died—almost 2 percent of the country's population.

WORDS TO KNOW **Vocabulary Preview**

harrowing, plight, retort, stoically, vitality

Connect to Your Life

In Unit Two, Part 2, you studied the ancient Roman poet Horace. One of his most famous sayings is "It is a great and beautiful thing to die for one's country." How do you think a young soldier going off to war might react to this statement? How might his or her parents react? Share your views with a group of classmates.

Focus Your Reading

LITERARY ANALYSIS: SETTING IN MODERN FICTION

The **setting** is the time and place in which the events of a story occur. In the opening paragraphs of this story, Pirandello uses details to establish the time and place of this story: it occurs at dawn in a second-class carriage of a local train bound for Sulmona, Italy. A story's setting may also include the historical context in which the story takes place. In this story, the historical context—World War I—is of great importance. As you read, consider how the setting affects the characters in the story.

ACTIVE READING: COMPARING AND CONTRASTING CHARACTERS

In "War," Pirandello portrays the conflicts that arise when characters respond differently to a stressful situation. To understand these conflicts, you must compare and contrast the characters' attitudes toward the war and the personal sacrifices they must make.

READER'S NOTEBOOK As you read, use a chart like the one below to take notes about the characters' attitudes.

Character	Attitude Toward War and Personal Sacrifice
Wife	*is inconsolable because her only son has gone to the front*
Husband	
First passenger	
Second passenger	
Old man	

READING FOR INFORMATION

Reading Skills and Strategies

USING VISUALS

To help students visualize the places described in **Build Background,** display a map that shows European boundaries in or around 1915. Point out Italy and Austria-Hungary on the map. Then ask a volunteer to use information in **Build Background** to locate the Italian Front. You may also want to use the map to show students the major European nations that formed the Allied Powers (Great Britain, Russia, France, Italy) and those that made up the Central Powers (Germany, Austria-Hungary, Bulgaria, Turkey) during World War I.

TIME MANAGEMENT

If your schedule requires that you cover the lesson objectives in a shorter time, use. . .

- Preparing to Read, pp. 1206–1207
- Thinking Through the Literature, p. 1212
- Vocabulary in Action, p. 1213

If you want to take advantage of longer blocks of class time, use. . .

- TE Teaching Options: Vocabulary Strategy, p. 1208; Viewing and Representing, p. 1210
- Choices & Challenges, p. 1213

Reading and Analyzing

Literary Analysis
SETTING IN MODERN FICTION

Ask students to describe the story's setting and atmosphere.

Possible Responses: The story is set in a second-class train carriage in Italy. The atmosphere in the carriage is stuffy and smoky, giving it a close and oppressive feel.

How does the setting encourage the conversation that arises?

Possible Response: The close atmosphere brings the characters face to face; speaking to each other is a natural consequence of such a setting.

 Use **Unit Seven Resource Book,** p. 43, for more practice.

Literary Analysis CHARACTERIZATION

Tell students that a writer may develop a character by describing the character's physical appearance; presenting the character's speech, thoughts, feelings, and actions; presenting other characters' speech, thoughts, feelings, and actions; and providing direct comments about the character. Have students identify details that develop the husband's character.

Possible Responses: He is described as "a tiny man, thin and weakly"; the husband has a shy and embarrassed manner of speaking; the narrator points out that the man "felt it his duty" to explain why his wife was so unhappy.

What words would students use to summarize the husband's character?

Possible Responses: shy, kind, deferential, timid, mild

Active Reading
COMPARING AND CONTRASTING CHARACTERS

Ask students to compare and contrast how the husband and wife respond to the fact that their son is about to leave for the front.

Possible Responses: The wife is so overwhelmed with sorrow that she doesn't want to speak to the other passengers; the husband is worried about his son but is able to speak about the situation.

 Use **Unit Seven Resource Book,** p. 42, for more practice.

War

Luigi Pirandello

Translated by Samuel Putnam

The passengers who had left Rome by the night express had had to stop until dawn at the small station of Fabriano[1] in order to continue their journey by the small old-fashioned "local" joining the main line with Sulmona.[2]

At dawn, in a stuffy and smoky second-class carriage in which five people had already spent the night, a bulky woman in deep mourning was hoisted in—almost like a shapeless bundle. Behind her—puffing and moaning, followed her husband—a tiny man, thin and weakly, his face death-white, his eyes small and bright and looking shy and uneasy.

Having at last taken a seat he politely thanked the passengers who had helped his wife and who had made room for her; then he turned round to the woman trying to pull down the collar of her coat and politely inquired:

"Are you all right, dear?"

The wife, instead of answering, pulled up her collar again to her eyes, so as to hide her face.

"Nasty world," muttered the husband with a sad smile.

And he felt it his duty to explain to his traveling companions that the poor woman was to be pitied for the war was taking away from her her only son, a boy of twenty to whom both had devoted their entire life, even breaking up their home at Sulmona to follow him to Rome where he had to go as a student, then allowing him to volunteer for war with an assurance, however, that at least for six months he would not be sent to the front and now, all of a sudden, receiving a wire saying that he was due to leave in three days' time and asking them to go and see him off.

The woman under the big coat was twisting and wriggling, at times growling like a wild animal, feeling certain that all those explanations would not have aroused even a shadow of sympathy from those people who—most likely—were in the same plight as herself. One of them, who had been listening with particular attention, said: 1

"You should thank God that your son is only leaving now for the front. Mine has been sent there the first day of the war. He has already come back twice wounded and been sent back again to the front."

"What about me? I have two sons and three nephews at the front," said another passenger.

"Maybe, but in our case it is our only son," ventured the husband.

"What difference can it make? You may spoil your only son with excessive attentions, but you cannot love him more than you would all your other children if you had any. Paternal love is not like bread that can be broken into pieces and split amongst the children in equal shares. A father gives all his love to each one of his children without discrimination, whether it be one or ten, and if I am suffering now for my two sons, I am not suffering half for each of them but double. . . ."

"True . . . true . . ." sighed the embarrassed husband, "but suppose (of course we all hope it will never be your case) a father has two sons at

1. **Fabriano** (fä′brē-ä′nō): a city in eastern Italy, about 100 miles northeast of Rome.

2. **Sulmona** (so͞ol-mō′nä): a city in eastern Italy, about 75 miles east of Rome.

WORDS TO KNOW

plight (plīt) *n.* a bad or unfortunate situation; predicament

MINI LESSON **Vocabulary Strategy**

CONTEXT CLUES

Instruction Remind students that context clues can often help determine the meaning of a word. Words or phrases within the sentence may provide clues to a word's meaning. Then read aloud this sentence:

". . . all those explanations would not have aroused even a shadow of sympathy from those people who–most likely–were in the same plight as herself." Context clues such as "would not have aroused . . . sympathy" and "in the same . . . as herself" suggest that *plight* means "difficult situation."

Practice Ask students to use context clues to determine the meanings of the italicized words below.

1. Jan behaved *stoically* when she heard the sad news, but her sister cried uncontrollably.
2. Demonstrating his *vitality*, the young man ran easily up the hill.
3. We were all extremely upset by the *harrowing* experience.

 Use **Unit Seven Resource Book,** p. 44, for more practice.

A lesson on using context clues appears on p. 674 of the Pupil's Edition.

Self Portrait, Käthe Kollwitz. Copyright © 2007 Artists Rights Society (ARS), New York/VG Bild-Kunst, Bonn, Germany.

AT DAWN, IN A STUFFY AND SMOKY SECOND-CLASS CARRIAGE IN WHICH FIVE PEOPLE HAD ALREADY SPENT THE NIGHT, A **BULKY WOMAN IN DEEP MOURNING WAS HOISTED IN** —ALMOST LIKE A SHAPELESS BUNDLE.

the front and he loses one of them, there is still one left to console him . . . while . . ."

"Yes," answered the other, getting cross, "a son left to console him but also a son left for whom he must survive, while in the case of the father of an only son if the son dies the father can die too and put an end to his distress. Which of the two positions is the worse? Don't you see how my case would be worse than yours?"

"Nonsense," interrupted another traveler, a fat, red-faced man with bloodshot eyes of the palest grey.

He was panting. From his bulging eyes seemed to spurt inner violence of an uncontrolled vitality which his weakened body could hardly contain.

WORDS TO KNOW

vitality (vī-tăl'ĭ-tē) *n.* strength of mind or body; energy

Customizing Instruction

Less Proficient Readers

Students may have trouble keeping track of the characters in "War"—particularly since the characters are not given names in the story. Suggest that students use a chart like the one below to jot down what the characters say or do.

Characters	What They Say or Do
Husband	*Helps his wife to board the train carriage and then tells the other passengers about his son*
Wife	
First Passenger to speak to husband	
Second Passenger to speak to husband	
Old Man	

English Learners

1 Explain that the wife's "twisting," "wriggling," and "growling" reveal her intense emotion: her impatience with her husband and her deep anxiety over her son. As students read the story, encourage them to look for other descriptions of actions or facial expressions that reveal a character's feelings.

Literary Analysis
SETTING IN MODERN FICTION

Ask students how the story's time frame—the years during World War I—affects the mood of the story.
Possible Responses: The war creates a mood of fear, apprehension, tension, sadness.

How does the time frame affect the characters and their conversation?
Possible Response: The time frame forces the characters to think and talk about how they would feel if their sons died in the war.

Literary Analysis REPETITION

Point out the old man's repetition of the phrase "I am speaking of decent boys" on page 1211. Ask students to describe the effect of the repeated phrase.
Possible Response: It emphasizes the old man's belief that "decent boys" will gladly die for their country.

What does the repetition suggest about how the old man felt about his own son?
Possible Response: The old man considered his own son a "decent boy."

Active Reading
COMPARING AND CONTRASTING CHARACTERS

Have students compare the wife with the old man. Ask: Before the old man's breakdown, how do their attitudes toward personal sacrifice appear to differ?
Possible Response: The old man is happy that his son died fighting for his country, while the wife can't bear thinking about losing her son.

After the old man's breakdown, how are the two characters' attitudes similar?
Possible Response: Both are overcome by grief and sorrow.

Reading Skills and Strategies
FORMING OPINIONS

Do students think that a parent can ever feel the way the old man claimed he did: happy that his son had died as a war hero? Why or why not?
Possible Responses: Some students may say that parents could draw some comfort from the fact that their children had died fighting for their country. Others may say—using the old man's breakdown as evidence—that these parents are only fooling themselves.

"Nonsense," he repeated, trying to cover his mouth with his hand so as to hide the two missing front teeth. "Nonsense. Do we give life to our children for our own benefit?"

The other travelers stared at him in distress. The one who had had his son at the front since the first day of the war sighed: "You are right. Our children do not belong to us, they belong to the Country. . . ."

"Bosh," retorted the fat traveler. "Do we think of the Country when we give life to our children? Our sons are born because . . . well, because they must be born and when they come to life they take our own life with them. This is the truth. We belong to them but they never belong to us. And when they reach twenty they are exactly what we were at their age. We too had a father and mother, but there were so many other things as well . . . girls, cigarettes, illusions, new ties . . . and the Country, of course, whose call we would have answered—when we were twenty—even if father and mother had said no. Now, at our age, the love of our Country is still great, of course, but stronger than it is the love for our children. Is there any one of us here who wouldn't gladly take his son's place at the front if he could?"

World War I – *"Fate tutti il vostro dovere!"* ["Everyone do your duty!"] Advertisement by Credito Italiano (an Italian Bank) for war bonds. Copyright © Jack Novak/SuperStock, Inc.

There was a silence all round, everybody nodding as to approve.

"Why then," continued the fat man, "shouldn't we consider the feelings of our children when

WORDS TO KNOW
retort (rĭ-tôrt') *v.* to reply quickly or sharply

MINI LESSON **Viewing and Representing**

War Poster

ART APPRECIATION Tell students that the young soldier in the poster on page 1210 is urging other young men to "do your duty." The text along the bottom of the poster tells the young men where they can go (an Italian bank) to sign up for the draft. Point out that the poster is an example of propaganda—the use of language or symbols to manipulate people. Nations at war frequently use propaganda to manipulate their citizens' feelings and behavior. Have students study the poster. Then ask them why the image of the soldier might appeal to young men.

Possible Responses: The soldier appears to be brave, handsome, strong, and heroic– just the sort of person many young men might aspire to be.

How might the images in the background stir a citizen's feelings of patriotism?
Possible Response: The images in the background, which show other soldiers fighting and dying, are designed to stir a citizen's feelings of duty and love of country.

they are twenty? Isn't it natural that at their age they should consider the love for their Country (I am speaking of decent boys, of course) even greater than the love for us? Isn't it natural that it should be so, as after all they must look upon us as upon old boys who cannot move any more and must stay at home? If Country exists, if Country is a natural necessity like bread, of which each of us must eat in order not to die of hunger, somebody must go to defend it. And our sons go, when they are twenty, and they don't want tears, because if they die, they die inflamed and happy (I am speaking, of course, of decent boys). Now, if one dies young and happy, without having the ugly sides of life, the boredom of it, the pettiness, the bitterness of disillusion . . . what more can we ask for him? Everyone should stop crying: everyone should laugh, as I do . . . or at least thank God—as I do—because my son, before dying, sent me a message saying that he was dying satisfied at having ended his life in the best way he could have wished. That is why, as you see, I do not even wear mourning. . . ."

He shook his light fawn[3] coat as to show it; his livid[4] lip over his missing teeth was trembling, his eyes were watery and motionless and soon after he ended with a shrill laugh which might well have been a sob.

"Quite so . . . quite so . . ." agreed the others.

The woman who, bundled in a corner under her coat, had been sitting and listening had—for the last three months—tried to find in the words of her husband and her friends something to console her in her deep sorrow, something that might show her how a mother should resign herself to send her son not even to death but to a probable danger of life. Yet not a word had she found amongst the many which had been said . . . and her grief had been greater in seeing that nobody—as she thought—could share her feelings.

But now the words of the traveler amazed and almost stunned her. She suddenly realized that it wasn't the others who were wrong and could not understand her but herself who could not rise up to the same height of those fathers and mothers willing to resign themselves, without crying, not only to the departure of their sons but even to their death.

She lifted her head, she bent over from her corner trying to listen with great attention to the details which the fat man was giving to his companions about the way his son had fallen as a hero, for his King and his Country, happy and without regrets. It seemed to her that she had stumbled into a world she had never dreamt of, a world so far unknown to her and she was so pleased to hear everyone joining in congratulating that brave father who could so stoically speak of his child's death.

Then suddenly, just as if she had heard nothing of what had been said and almost as if waking up from a dream, she turned to the old man, asking him:

"Then . . . is your son really dead?"

Everybody stared at her. The old man, too, turned to look at her, fixing his great, bulging, horribly watery light grey eyes, deep in her face. For some little time he tried to answer, but words failed him. He looked and looked at her, almost as if only then—at that silly, incongruous question—he had suddenly realized at last that his son was really dead . . . gone for ever . . . for ever. His face contracted, became horribly distorted, then he snatched in haste a handkerchief from his pocket and, to the amazement of everyone, broke into harrowing, heart-rending, uncontrollable sobs. ❖

3. **fawn:** light yellowish brown.

4. **livid:** discolored, as from a bruise.

WORDS TO KNOW

stoically (stō'ĭ-klē) *adv.* in a manner showing no emotion

harrowing (hăr'ō-ĭng) *adj.* extremely distressing

Customizing Instruction

Less Proficient Readers

Some students may be confused by the story's ending. Explain that the old man had been in denial about his son's death, hiding his true feelings behind patriotic words and a show of bravery. The woman's direct question forced the old man to confront his feelings.

English Learners

Explain the following words and usages to students:

- "bosh": an old-fashioned, usually British, expression meaning "nonsense"
- "Country" and "King": The words are capitalized to emphasize their symbolic importance during wartime. In times of war, "Country" and "King" represent everything people fight for.

Advanced Learners

Have students identify the story's surprise ending. *(The old man breaks down and cries over his son's death.)* Then ask them to explain why the ending is so powerful.

Possible Response: The ending powerfully asserts that parents do not believe "it is a great and beautiful thing" when their children die for their country.

Connect to the Literature

1. What Do You Think? How did you react to the old man's fit of grief at the end of the story?

Comprehension Check
- Why does the husband feel that the other passengers should pity his wife?
- According to the old man, how should parents react to the death of a son in the war?

Think Critically

2. **ACTIVE READING: COMPARING AND CONTRASTING CHARACTERS** Review the chart you made in your  READER'S NOTEBOOK. Which attitudes do you find reasonable? Which do you find extreme? Share your views with a classmate.
3. Why does the wife's question cause the old man to lose his composure?
4. How would you contrast the wife and the old man?
5. What do you think is the author's **theme**—his message about war and the sacrifices it entails?

   THINK ABOUT
   - the wife's inability to put her grief into words
   - the old man's statement about the loss of his son
   - the old man's breakdown

Extend Interpretations

6. **The Writer's Style** A writer's use of hints or clues to indicate later events in a story is known as **foreshadowing.** What details in the story foreshadow the old man's breakdown?
7. **Connect to Life** For most of the story, the old man hides what he really feels. Why do people sometimes try to hide their true feelings from themselves and others?

LITERARY ANALYSIS: SETTING IN MODERN FICTION

Setting is the time and place of the action of a short story, a novel, a play, a narrative poem, or narrative nonfiction. In addition to place and time frame, setting may include the larger historical and cultural contexts that form the background of a narrative. In some stories, setting can be a driving force, influencing events or affecting how the characters act and feel. In Pirandello's story the setting plays a central role. See page R29.

Cooperative Learning Activity
With a small group of classmates, discuss the following questions:
- How does the historical context—wartime in Italy—affect the characters in this story?
- Why do you think the author set this story in a train instead of in a hotel, a restaurant, a stadium, or some other place?

Have one member of the group write a brief summary of the discussion. Then share your summary with other groups.

Connect to the Literature

1. **What Do You Think?** Students will probably be surprised by the old man's grief and feel sorry for him.

Comprehension Check
- Their only son, who had volunteered to serve in the military services, was about to be sent to the front.
- Parents should not mourn because their sons have died happy, defending their country.

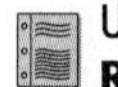 Use Selection Quiz in **Unit Seven Resource Book,** p. 45.

Think Critically

2. Possible Responses: The husband is reasonable because, although he is very worried about his son, he is still able to function. The old man's views are extreme because he insists that parents should be glad if their sons die for their country.
3. Possible Response: Her simple question surprises the old man and forces him to face the stark fact of his son's death.
4. Possible Response: The wife is indulging her fears and sorrow, while the old man is denying his grief.
5. Possible Response: Parents mourn their child's death—even when the child dies heroically.

Extend Interpretations

6. **The Writer's Style** Possible Responses: his bulging eyes, trembling lips, and shrill laugh that sounds like a sob
7. **Connect to Life** Possible Responses: They hide their feelings to avoid having to confront them; they hope they can talk themselves into feeling less; they want to show others how strong they are.

Literary Analysis

Cooperative Learning Activity Possible Responses: The war setting influences the characters' conversation and preoccupations. The setting brings the characters together by providing a common bond: the fate of their sons. The close, intimate setting of a train encourages greater interaction, forcing characters to literally face each other.

 Use **Unit Seven Resource Book,** p. 43, for more practice.

Writing Options

1. Different Ending What do you think might happen on the train after the old man suffers his emotional collapse? How might the other characters respond to his breakdown? Write a few paragraphs to extend the story.

Writing Handbook
See page R29: Narrative Writing.

2. Character Analysis In a brief essay, analyze the character of the old man. Begin by discussing the techniques that Pirandello uses to develop this character. Then discuss the old man's personality traits. Use details and quotations from the story to support your analysis.

3. Personal Response How did this story affect your views about the sacrifices war exacts of parents? Write a personal-response essay exploring your opinions.

Activities & Explorations

1. Story Illustration Create a portrait of one of the characters in the story "War." Base your drawing or painting on specific details in the story. ~ **ART**

2. Readers Theater In a Readers Theater presentation, performers read aloud, using a work of literature as a script. With a small group of classmates, prepare a dramatic reading of this story. Use the pitch, volume, and expression of your voice to suggest your character's attitudes and emotions. ~ **SPEAKING AND LISTENING**

Inquiry & Research

1. The Grieving Process Find out more about the process of grieving. What theories do psychologists use to explain this process? What stages do grieving people go through? What can help someone cope with extreme grief?

2. World War I Prepare an oral report about the fighting at the Italian Front during World War I. Include information about trench warfare and the state of military technology. Use photographs, maps, and other visual aids in your report.

Vocabulary in Action

EXERCISE: CONTEXT CLUES Choose the correct word to complete each sentence.

1. At first, the husband believed that his wife's _________ was worse than anyone else's.
2. The husband and the wife were weak and tired because their son's situation had drained much of their _________.
3. The wife in particular was so grief-stricken that she found it impossible to act _________.
4. The old man _________ angrily to the passengers carrying on their debate.
5. His troubles, it turned out, were more _________ than theirs.

WORDS TO KNOW

harrowing	retort	vitality
plight	stoically	

Building Vocabulary
For an in-depth lesson on using context clues, see page 674.

Vocabulary in Action

1. plight
2. vitality
3. stoically
4. retorted
5. harrowing

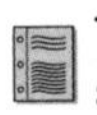
To assess skills and concepts taught in this selection, use **Formal Assessment Book,** pp. 175–176.

Writing Options

1. **Different Ending** Remind students to maintain the personalities of the characters as they write the new endings. For instance, the wife, who had gained some measure of courage and hope from the old man's words, would probably be devastated by his emotional collapse.
2. **Character Analysis** In their essays, students should include some of the following personality traits: the old man's gruffness, self-confidence, anger, sorrow, impatience.
3. **Personal Response** Students should clearly state their opinion and support it, using reasons, examples, and anecdotes. Tell students that writing about their opinion may help them clarify their ideas.

Activities & Explorations

1. **Story Illustration** Before students begin drawing their character portraits, have them identify lines of dialogue and description that reveal the character's personality.
2. **Readers Theater** Have students perform the dramatic reading before the class. During the performance, ask the audience to pay particular attention to the ways in which the readers delineate the characters' personalities and emotions. After the performance, have the class discuss what they learned about the story and its characters.

Inquiry & Research

1. **The Grieving Process** Students should discover that grief is a normal and natural reaction to loss. Some psychologists say that the stages of grief are the following: denial, anger, bargaining, depression, acceptance, and hope for the future. Writing in a journal, taking part in support groups, and keeping visual memories of the loved one are all ways to help someone cope with extreme grief.
2. **World War I** Encourage students to use a variety of sources to gather information for their report, including history books, encyclopedias, and the Internet.

Milestones in World Literature

All Quiet on the Western Front is one of the most important antiwar novels ever written. The novel was Erich Maria Remarque's first, and it brought him international acclaim at the age of 33. However, fame did not stop the author from writing about the horrors of inhumanity and war; most of his subsequent novels dealt with these themes. In his brief introduction to *All Quiet on the Western Front,* Remarque wrote: "This book is to be neither an accusation nor a confession, and least of all an adventure, for death is not an adventure to those who stand face to face with it. It will try simply to tell of a generation of men who, even though they may have escaped shells, were destroyed by the war."

Additional Background

Born in 1898 in Osnabrück, Germany, Remarque was drafted into his nation's army during World War I at the age of 18. He was assigned to a trench unit near the Western Front, where one of his friends was killed and another injured. Remarque himself suffered a severe injury and was hospitalized for much of the last year of the war.

Following the war, Remarque drifted from job to job, working variously as a substitute teacher, stonecutter, organist, and sports editor. In his spare time, he worked on a novel based on his war experiences. When it was published, *All Quiet on the Western Front* was an immediate success; it also caused a great deal of controversy. Convinced that the novel was an attack on the German nation, the Nazis tried to undermine its popularity. Bands of Hitler Youth burst into a theater where the film version of the novel was playing, throwing stink bombs and shouting "Germany, awake!" Fearing that his life was in danger, Remarque left Germany in 1931. He came to the United States in 1939 and eventually became an American citizen.

Remarque continued to write, although none of his other works achieved the popular or critical success of his first novel. He spent the years between 1939 and 1942 in Hollywood, where he became friends with many of the major actors and screenwriters of that time. After 1942, Remarque divided his time largely between the United States and Switzerland. When he died in 1970, a German journal printed his obituary but omitted the fact that Remarque had written a great novel about World War I.

Milestones in World Literature

All Quiet on the Western Front

What if you were forced to leave your family and friends to stand face to face with death on the battlefield? As you struggle to control your emotions, questions eat at your mind. Will you survive? If you do, can you ever return to the life you once knew? Will your memories of the war haunt you forever?

These are some of the disturbing questions that Erich Maria Remarque (ā′rĭKH mä-rē′ä rə-märk′) raises in *All Quiet on the Western Front,* one of the most famous novels of the 20th century. First published in 1929, this novel portrays the horrors of war as they appear to a young German soldier in World War I. Throughout the novel, the author's simple yet lyrical style creates vivid scenes.

One morning two butterflies play in front of our trench. They are brimstone-butterflies, with red spots on their yellow wings. What can they be looking for here? There is not a plant nor a flower for miles. They settle on the teeth of a skull.

Below: *German soldiers on the attack*

The narrator of the novel is Paul Bäumer, a young recruit. Behind the lines, he endures the endless drills and mindless discipline of army life. At the front, he witnesses the horrors of trench warfare—the attacks and counterattacks, the barrages of shells and rockets, the swirl of poison gas, the senseless killings, the painful wounds that bring slow death. In one gripping scene, Paul dives into a shell hole and is forced to stab a French soldier. He then dresses the soldier's wounds and watches him slowly die. In the dead man's wallet, Paul finds pictures of his wife and little girl. He is overcome by feelings of pity and guilt.

Lew Ayres in the 1930 film version

Again and again, Paul shares his deepest thoughts and feelings with the reader. To survive on the front, he realizes, he must descend to the level of an animal—relying on instinct and trusting in blind luck. He worries that he and others like him have been ruined by their experiences at the front.

> **We . . . do not know what the end may be. We know only that in some strange way we have become a waste land.**

Yet amid the swirl of blood and death, Paul realizes that one value is stronger than bombs, bayonets, and bullets. That value is comradeship, "the finest thing that arose out of the war."

No wonder this book has become a modern classic. In 1933, the Nazis, outraged at the author's realistic depiction of war, burned copies of the book in Berlin—an ironic tribute to the power of Remarque's story of a common soldier's simple heroism. Written by one who had fought as a German soldier in World War I, the novel was translated into English by an ex-soldier who had fought on the other side.

Poster for the 1930 film

Literary Chronology

1929 *All Quiet on the Western Front;* 1930 film version directed by Lewis Milestone earns Academy Awards for Best Picture and Best Director
1931 *The Road Back;* 1937 film version directed by James Whale
1937 *Three Comrades;* 1938 film version directed by Frank Borzage
1941 *Flotsam*
1946 *Arch of Triumph;* 1948 film version directed by Lewis Milestone
1952 *Spark of Life*
1954 *A Time to Love and a Time to Die;* 1958 film version directed by Douglas Sirk
1956 *The Black Obelisk*
1961 *Heaven Has No Favorites;* 1977 film version directed by Sydney Pollock
1962 *The Night in Lisbon*
1971 *Shadows in Paradise*

Objectives
- understand and appreciate a **modern poem** that deals with opposing tyranny **(Literary Analysis)**
- identify and examine **speaker and tone** in poetry **(Literary Analysis)**
- **draw conclusions** about the speaker in a poem **(Active Reading)**

Thematic Link
Anna Akhmatova wrote her poem "I Am Not One of Those Who Left the Land" in defiance of the repression in the Soviet Union. Her **response to war and conflict** was to remain in her country and continue fighting.

5-Minute Warm-Up

Daily Language SkillBuilder

Have students **proofread** the display sentences on page 1095n and write them correctly.

Reading and Analyzing

Literary Analysis SPEAKER AND TONE
Ask students whether the speaker is detached or involved with the experiences expressed in the poem. *(involved)* What details suggest the speaker's involvement?
Possible Responses: the use of the pronoun *I;* the poet's personal experiences; the poem's tone

What attitude does the speaker convey in the second stanza about "the exile"?
Possible Responses: anger, bitterness, recrimination, disdain

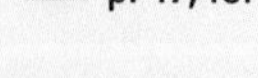
Use **Unit Seven Resource Book,** p. 47, for more practice.

Active Reading
DRAWING CONCLUSIONS
In the third stanza, what does the phrase "we, the survivors" suggest about the speaker? What conclusions can students draw about how the speaker defines herself?
Possible Response: She sees herself as a fighter.

What can you conclude about what the speaker has endured?
Possible Response: She's had to deal with and overcome very trying circumstances.

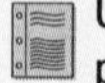
Use **Unit Seven Resource Book,** p. 46, for more practice.

I Am Not One of Those Who Left the Land

Anna Akhmatova

Translated by Stanley Kunitz with Max Hayward

Anna Akhmatova
1889–1966

Persecuted Poet "Anna Akhmatova" (ăkн-mä'tə-və) was the pen name of Anna Gorenko, one of Russia's greatest poets. By 1914, she had published two books of poetry, both widely read. Her world came apart, however, after the Russian Revolution of 1917. Civil war, famine, brutal repression, and strict censorship drove many writers into exile. In 1921, her former husband was executed for conspiracy, and Akhmatova came under suspicion. Though urged by friends to leave Russia, Akhmatova refused to do so. She wrote the following poem in 1922, when many writers had left Russia to escape its atrocities.

During the 1930s and 1940s, Akhmatova watched in horror as her friends and fellow writers were jailed and sometimes executed under the Soviet dictator Joseph Stalin.

Lasting Recognition Stalin's death in 1953 brought about an easing of government censorship, which enabled Akhmatova to publish a few volumes of her poetry. Her work earned her a place in literary history as a poet who captured the suffering of her people.

Connect to Your Life

Imagine that your own community is suddenly torn apart by violence. Buildings are damaged, the streets are unsafe, and people fear for their lives. Why might some people choose to stay in the community despite the violence?

Focus Your Reading

LITERARY ANALYSIS: SPEAKER AND TONE
The **speaker** of a poem is the voice that "talks" to the reader. This voice helps to convey the **tone,** or the writer's attitude toward his or her subject.

ACTIVE READING: DRAWING CONCLUSIONS
To **draw conclusions,** you combine what you read with what you already know in order to make logical guesses about some element in a literary work. As you read this poem, try to draw conclusions about the **speaker.** Consider the following:
- how she defines herself
- what she has endured

In your READER'S NOTEBOOK, list your conclusions about the speaker and record the evidence you used to reach them.

LESSON RESOURCES

UNIT SEVEN RESOURCE BOOK, pp. 46–47

ASSESSMENT RESOURCES
Formal Assessment, pp. 177–178
Teacher's Guide to Assessment and Portfolio Use
Test Generator

INTEGRATED TECHNOLOGY
Visit our Web site: classzone.com

ADDITIONAL RESOURCES
Lesson Planning Guide, pp. 155–156
Teacher's Sourcebook for Language Development

In Front of the Mirror, Konstantin N. Istomin. Tretyakov Gallery, Moscow, Russia. Photo © Scala/Art Resource, New York.

I am not one of those who left the land
to the mercy of its enemies.
Their flattery leaves me cold,
my songs are not for them to praise.

But I pity the exile's lot.
Like a felon, like a man half-dead,
dark is your path, wanderer;
wormwood infects your foreign bread.

But here, in the murk of conflagration,
where scarcely a friend is left to know,
we, the survivors, do not flinch
from anything, not from a single blow.

Surely the reckoning will be made
after the passing of this cloud.
We are the people without tears,
straighter than you . . . more proud . . .

8 wormwood: something bitter or extremely unpleasant.

9 conflagration: a large destructive fire.

13 reckoning: settlement of accounts.

Customizing Instruction

Less Proficient Readers

Ask students to paraphrase each stanza in their own words.

Students may need help understanding the second stanza. Explain that the speaker is comparing the situation of those who left Russia—"the exile's lot"—to that of a criminal or someone half-dead. According to the speaker, the exile is lost in a spiritual or moral sense (the reference to the "dark path"). The bitterness resulting from regret, guilt, and loss ("wormwood") will always infect the exile's life.

English Learners

Help students understand the following phrases:

- "flattery leaves me cold" (line 3): Flattery, or praise, does not please me.
- "murk of conflagration" (line 9): *Murk* means "darkness" or "gloominess." *Conflagration,* which means "large destructive fire," refers to the oppression and suspicion that the speaker is subjected to.
- "reckoning will be made" (line 13): A "reckoning" is a settlement of accounts. The speaker implies that a reckoning will reward her for her suffering.
- "passing of this cloud" (line 14): "This cloud" refers to the oppressive conditions under which the speaker lives. She is looking forward to the day when these conditions will pass, or disappear.

Advanced Learners

Ask students whether the speaker's situation would have differed if the other writers had not left Russia. Do students think the speaker's life would have been better? Why or why not?

Possible Responses: Some students will say that the speaker's life would have been better because the opposition would have been stronger and more vocal. Others will say that the other writers would have been similarly oppressed and would not have materially improved the situation.

I AM NOT ONE OF THOSE WHO LEFT THE LAND 1217

Connect to the Literature

1. **What Do You Think?** Students may discuss the poet's pride, her unwillingness to bend to her enemies, or her stoic attitude in the face of repression.

Think Critically

2. Possible Responses: loyalty, pride, love of country, freedom of expression
3. Possible Response: The poet believes that by leaving Russia, the exiles acted in a cowardly manner and were defeated. By contrast, the survivors retained their dignity and gained strength by remaining in Russia.
4. Possible Response: The survivors will be vindicated and rewarded for their sacrifices and suffering.

Extend Interpretations

5. **The Writer's Style** Possible Responses: "like a felon"; "a man half-dead"; "wormwood"; "murk of conflagration"; "people without tears"
6. **Connect to Life** Possible Responses: Some students may say that great suffering is strengthening because it teaches the person how to confront and overcome obstacles. Others may say that great suffering can overwhelm the person and cause him or her to give up.

Literary Analysis

Cooperative Learning Activity

Possible Responses: The poem's tone may be described as somber, determined, stark, serious, bitter, brave, defiant.

Use **Unit Seven Resource Book,** p. 47, for more practice.

To assess skills and concepts taught in this selection, use **Formal Assessment Book,** pp. 177–178.

Connect to the Literature

1. **What Do You Think?** What are your thoughts about the last two lines of this poem?

Think Critically

2. **ACTIVE READING: DRAWING CONCLUSIONS** Review the conclusions you listed in your  **READER'S NOTEBOOK**. What values do you think are important to the speaker?
3. Why does the speaker feel that it was better to stay in Russia than to go into exile?

   THINK ABOUT
   - the comparisons that describe the exiles
   - the suffering endured by the survivors
   - the qualities that the survivors developed

4. In line 13, the speaker mentions a "reckoning" that will be made. What do you **predict** might happen when this reckoning occurs?

Extend Interpretations

5. **The Writer's Style** Akhmatova's poetry has been praised for its precise and concrete language. Point out words in this poem that are particularly effective in conveying the poet's meaning.
6. **Connect to Life** The speaker of this poem has survived a terrible ordeal. Do you think great suffering tends to strengthen a person or break his or her spirit? Explain your opinion.

LITERARY ANALYSIS: SPEAKER AND TONE

The **speaker** of a poem, like the narrator of a story, is the voice that "talks" to the reader. The speaker of "I Am Not One of Those Who Left the Land" may be closely identified with the poet herself, who refused to leave Russia after the Communists took control. Notice that in line 11, the pronoun *we* replaces *I*. This change suggests that the speaker is the voice of an entire group—all those who remained in Russia despite the terrible suffering.

The speaker helps to convey the tone of a poem, or the writer's attitude toward his or her subject. The **tone** might be described in one or more ways—for example, as serious, bitter, playful, or detached. To identify the tone, consider the writer's diction (word choice), any revealing details, and any direct statements of his or her position.

Cooperative Learning Activity With a small group of students, create a chart like the one below. Fill in the boxes and then write down one or more words to describe the tone of "I Am Not One of Those Who Left the Land." Share your chart with other groups.

		Tone
Diction	*"like a felon"*	
Details		
Statements		

Living Dangerously: Writers in the 20th Century

As Anna Akhmatova learned, the 20th century was a dangerous time to be a writer. From 1923 to 1940, the Soviet government silenced Akhmatova, allowing no volumes of her poetry to be published. During those years, many Russian writers were imprisoned, exiled, or executed, including Osip Mandelstam, perhaps the greatest Russian poet of the 20th century, who died in a Siberian prison camp.

Although Akhmatova was allowed to publish some poetry during World War II, she fell again into disfavor. In 1946, the Central Committee of the Communist Party denounced her poetry, and a government official publicly called her a "harlot-nun." In 1949, her son was arrested and exiled to Siberia. To help gain her son's release, Akhmatova had to compromise her principles and publish a poem praising the Soviet dictator, Joseph Stalin.

The following timeline gives examples of some of the ordeals faced by modern writers:

1948 Chilean writer Pablo Neruda leaves Chile by crossing the Andes Mountains on horseback at night. Neruda had published a letter critical of Chile's president and went into exile to avoid arrest.

1956 African-raised British writer Doris Lessing is declared a "prohibited immigrant" by Southern Rhodesia (what is now Zimbabwe) because her fiction criticizes government policies of racial separation.

1967 Nigerian playwright Wole Soyinka is imprisoned for two years, allegedly for conspiring to support independence for Biafra, a region of Nigeria that formed a separate state from 1967–1970.

1974 Russian writer Aleksandr Solzhenitsyn is arrested and charged with treason for criticizing the Soviet Union. He is exiled from the Soviet Union a day later.

1989 Iranian leader Ayatollah Khomeini issues a *fatwa* (legal opinion) against Anglo-Indian writer Salman Rushdie for allegedly blaspheming Islam in a novel. A bounty is offered to anyone who would execute Rushdie, who goes into hiding under the protection of Scotland Yard.

2000 Chinese poet and editor Bei Ling is arrested and imprisoned. Copies of Ling's literary magazine are confiscated and destroyed by the government.

Group Discussion Why do you think so many governments have felt threatened by writers? Do you think a government ever has the right to limit or restrict a writer's creative work? Explain why or why not.

Connect to Today

Use this feature to show the relevance of world literature to students. The material relates the literature selection just read to a contemporary topic connected to students' lives today.

Historical Note

Share the following information on some of the writers in the time line:

- Doris Lessing: In 1994, the policy of racial separation known as apartheid was abolished in South Africa. Today, Lessing is celebrated in that country for writing that was banished in 1956.
- Wole Soyinka: Soyinka continued to write while incarcerated, publishing his volume *Poems from Prison* in 1969. He was awarded the 1986 Nobel Prize in literature, becoming the first African to receive that honor.
- Aleksandr Solzhenitsyn: In 1989, the Soviet Union began to offically approve of and publish Solzhenitsyn's work. His Soviet citizenship was restored in 1990, and the writer returned to Russia in 1994.
- Salman Rushdie: In 1998, the Iranian government no longer supported the fatwa against Rushdie and the reward for his capture was officially withdrawn. The writer emerged from hiding and currently lives in New York City.

Group Discussion Possible Responses: Some students will say that a government should never have the right to restrict a writer's creativity because society should promote free speech and freedom of expression. Restricting creativity smacks of oppression and totalitarianism. Others may believe that government should restrict creative work that is obscene, immoral, or threatens public safety. Such work would be restricted for the public good.

CONNECT TO TODAY 1219

Objectives

- understand and appreciate a **modern drama** that provides insight into life in Germany under the Nazis **(Literary Analysis)**
- notice how **dialogue** establishes **mood** in a drama **(Literary Analysis)**
- clarify incidents or references in a play using **historical context (Active Reading)**

Summary

A man and his wife are arguing about their friends and political matters. Concerned that their son may be listening, the wife gives the boy money to buy sweets. The couple keep talking, and then suddenly realize that the boy has disappeared. Worried that their son has gone to report them to his Hitler Youth leader, the man and wife try to recall what they said. They become increasingly fearful as they consider how their son might interpret their words and actions. When the boy returns, the couple brace themselves for the worst. However, the boy says that he has only been out buying chocolate. His parents wonder whether they can believe him.

Use **Unit Seven Resource Book,** p. 48, for additional support.

Thematic Link

In *The Spy,* Bertolt Brecht reveals that in many German families, the **response to war and conflict** was one of fear and suspicion of each other.

Use **Unit Seven Resource Book,** p. 51, for practice with Words to Know.

5-Minute Warm-Up

Daily Language SkillBuilder

Have students **proofread** the display sentences on page 1095n and write them correctly.

Bertolt Brecht
1898–1956

From Medicine to Writing Bertolt Brecht (brĕkt), a major playwright of the 20th century, grew up in Augsburg, a city in Bavaria. He studied medicine in Munich from 1917 to 1921, with time spent in wartime service as an orderly in an army hospital in 1918. Disillusioned with his society for the part it played in the horrors of World War I, Brecht gave up medicine and turned to writing—poetry, nonfiction, and especially drama. In all, he wrote about 35 plays.

Fame and Flight These plays, for the most part, were critical of society. For example, *Drums in the Night* (1922), Brecht's first successful play, tells of a soldier who rejects the violence of modern warfare. *The Threepenny Opera* (1928), his most popular work, explores serious issues such as poverty and crime and attacks the middle class. As a dramatist, Brecht sought to make his audience think deeply about his ideas. Many of his ideas, however, offended the Nazis. Brecht, therefore, had to flee from Germany when Adolf Hitler took control in 1933.

Exile and Return During his exile, Brecht lived first in Scandinavia and then in the United States, where he worked for a brief time on films in Hollywood. Meanwhile, in Germany, his writings were burned and his citizenship was revoked. While in exile, Brecht wrote some of the finest plays in the German language—including *Mother Courage and Her Children* (1941) and *The Life of Galileo* (1943). After World War II, he lived in Switzerland for a time before returning to Germany. There he established the Berliner Ensemble, one of the world's finest acting troupes.

Other Works
The Good Woman of Setzuan
The Caucasian Chalk Circle
The Resistible Rise of Arturo Ui

LESSON RESOURCES

UNIT SEVEN RESOURCE BOOK,
pp. 48–52

ASSESSMENT RESOURCES
Formal Assessment, pp. 179–180
Teacher's Guide to Assessment and Portfolio Use
Test Generator

INTEGRATED TECHNOLOGY
Visit our Web site: classzone.com

ADDITIONAL RESOURCES
Lesson Planning Guide, pp. 157–158
Teacher's Sourcebook for Language Development

Build Background

An Education in Hatred In Brecht's play *The Spy,* a man and his wife mistrust their only son because of his involvement with the Hitler Youth. This organization, set up by Hitler himself, promoted Nazi values and trained German youths for war. "Look at these young men and boys. What material! With them I can make a new world," Hitler thundered once in a speech. "A violently active, dominating, intrepid, brutal youth—that is what I am after."

Within a few years after Hitler's rise to power, about 60 percent of Germany's boys belonged to the Hitler Youth. They joined at age 10 and remained members until they turned 19. Their main activities included marching, playing sports and war games, and absorbing Nazi propaganda. Intellectual training was discouraged because the Nazis believed it would lead youths to question Hitler's ideas. At the same time young men were being trained in the Hitler Youth, a sister organization, the League of German Girls, sought to develop a generation of loyal Nazi women.

In 1936, participation in these youth organizations became mandatory in Germany. Any parents who failed to register their children were subject to fine or imprisonment. After a time, the Hitler Youth took on a more sinister role. Members were expected to spy on their own families in order to evaluate their parents' loyalty to the Nazis. This responsibility sometimes led boys to inform on their parents.

Hitler youth

Connect to Your Life

What do you know about life in Germany under the Nazis? What beliefs did Adolf Hitler spread among the German people? Discuss these questions with a small group of classmates.

Focus Your Reading

LITERARY ANALYSIS: DIALOGUE AND MOOD

Dialogue is written conversation between two or more characters in a literary work. In drama, the story that unfolds is told almost exclusively through dialogue. The dialogue moves the plot forward, reveals character, and helps establish the **mood**—the feeling or atmosphere that a writer creates for the reader. As you read *The Spy,* notice the feeling that the dialogue stirs in you.

ACTIVE READING: UNDERSTANDING HISTORICAL CONTEXT

To make sense of the dialogue in this play, you must have some knowledge about the play's historical context. **Historical context** refers to the period in history in which a literary work is set. *The Spy* is set in Germany after the Nazis have taken over the government and established organizations to try to influence the young.

READER'S NOTEBOOK As you read the play, record in a chart two or more incidents or references that you are able to clarify by using your knowledge of the play's historical context.

Incident or Reference	Explanation
The man's criticism of the Brown House	The Brown House refers to Hitler's headquarters, so the man is criticizing Hitler and his government.

WORDS TO KNOW Vocabulary Preview

confiscate, demoralizing, jocular, vindictive, wittingly

READING FOR INFORMATION
Reading Skills and Strategies
INTERPRETING THE TEXT

Read aloud **Build Background** on page 1221. Discuss the effect of the Hitler Youth organization on boys. Ask students why they think the Nazis wanted German boys to join the organization at the age of ten.

Possible Response: The Nazis wanted to begin indoctrinating the children when they were impressionable and eager to conform.

Why were boys willing to inform on their parents?

Possible Responses: They wanted to show their loyalty to the Nazis; they wanted to feel important; they wanted the Hitler Youth leaders to be proud of them; they wanted to hurt their parents.

What effect did a son's membership in Hitler Youth probably have on family life?

Possible Response: It probably created tension and distrust in the family.

TIME MANAGEMENT

If your schedule requires that you cover the lesson objectives in a shorter time, use. . .

- Preparing to Read, pp. 1220–1221
- Thinking Through the Literature, p. 1230
- Vocabulary in Action, p. 1231

If you want to take advantage of longer blocks of class time, use. . .

- TE Teaching Options: Speaking and Listening, pp. 1223 and 1226; Cross Curricular Link, p. 1224; Informal Assessment, p. 1225; Vocabulary Strategy, p. 1227; Viewing and Representing, p. 1228; Grammar, p. 1229
- Choices & Challenges, p. 1231

Literary Analysis
DIALOGUE AND MOOD

Ask students to identify the mood conveyed by the dialogue in these two pages.
Possible Responses: nervous, contentious

What lines of dialogue create this mood?
Possible Responses: "Are you telling me I'm a coward?"; "Do you really think it's sensible to go round making remarks like that?"

 Use **Unit Seven Resource Book,** p. 50, for more practice.

Active Reading
UNDERSTANDING HISTORICAL CONTEXT

A Point out the wife's reference to the school inspectors being "after" Klimbtsch. Then ask students to use their knowledge of historical context to explain the reference.
Possible Response: During the Nazi regime, teachers were closely scrutinized and punished if their instruction or behavior opposed Party doctrine in any way.

 Use **Unit Seven Resource Book,** p. 49, for more practice.

Reading Skills and Strategies
MAKING INFERENCES

Ask students to infer why the man and wife are silent while the maidservant is present.
Possible Response: They are afraid that she will report whatever they say to her father, the block warden.

Why is their silence ironic?
Possible Response: The man had just declared that he could say what he liked in his own home.

The Spy

Bertolt Brecht

Translated by John Willett

Cologne[1] *1935. A wet Sunday afternoon.* The Man, the Wife *and* the Boy *have finished lunch.* The Maidservant *enters.*

The Maidservant. Mr. and Mrs. Klimbtsch[2] are asking if you are at home.

The Man (*snarls*). No.

(The Maidservant *goes out.*)

The Wife. You should have gone to the phone yourself. They must know we couldn't possibly have gone out yet.

The Man. Why couldn't we?

The Wife. Because it's raining.

The Man. That's no reason.

The Wife. Where could we have gone to? That's the first thing they'll ask.

The Man. Oh, masses of places.

The Wife. Let's go then.

The Man. Where to?

The Wife. If only it wasn't raining.

The Man. And where'd we go if it wasn't raining?

The Wife. At least in the old days you could go and meet someone.

(*Pause.*)

The Wife. It was a mistake you not going to the phone. Now they'll realize we don't want to have them.

The Man. Suppose they do?

The Wife. Then it wouldn't look very nice, our dropping them just when everyone else does.

The Man. We're not dropping them.

The Wife. Why shouldn't they come here in that case?

The Man. Because Klimbtsch bores me to tears.

The Wife. He never bored you in the old days.

The Man. In the old days . . . All this talk of the old days gets me down.

The Wife. Well anyhow you'd never have cut him just because the school inspectors are after him. A

The Man. Are you telling me I'm a coward?

(*Pause.*)

The Man. All right, ring up and tell them we've just come back on account of the rain.

1. **Cologne** (kə-lōn′): a city in western Germany.
2. **Klimbtsch** (klĭmptsch).

Femme á la robe noir [Woman in a black dress], Tamara de Lempicka. Copyright © 2007 Artist Rights Society (ARS), New York/ADAGP, Paris.

(*The* Wife *remains seated.*)

The Wife. What about asking the Lemkes[3] to come over?

The Man. And have them go on telling us we're slack[4] about civil defense?

The Wife (*to the* Boy). Klaus-Heinrich, stop fiddling with the wireless.[5]

(*The* Boy *turns his attention to the newspapers.*)

The Man. It's a disaster, its raining like this. It's quite intolerable, living in a country where it's a disaster when it rains.

The Wife. Do you really think it's sensible to go round making remarks like that?

The Man. I can make what remarks I like between my own four walls. This is my home, and I shall damn well say . . .

(*He is interrupted. The* Maidservant *enters with coffee things. So long as she is present they remain silent.*)

The Man. Have we got to have a maid whose father is the block warden?[6]

The Wife. We've been over that again and again. The last thing you said was that it had its advantages.

The Man. What aren't I supposed to have said? If you mentioned anything of the sort to your mother we could land in a proper mess.

The Wife. The things I talk about to my mother . . .

3. **Lemkes** (lĕm′kəz).
4. **slack:** lacking in diligence; careless.
5. **Klaus-Heinrich** (klous′ hīn′rĭkh) . . . **wireless:** *Wireless* is an old term for radio.
6. **block warden:** someone appointed to oversee what goes on in a particular area.

Customizing Instruction

Less Proficient Readers

Students may not understand why the wife is worried about what her husband says and how people might interpret his behavior. Explain that she is afraid that someone will report them to Nazi officials. To help students gain more background, you might want to initiate a class discussion on what students know about the Nazis and their treatment of those who did not strictly conform with Party policy.

English Learners

Students may be confused by some of the following idioms in the dialogue:

- "old days": a period of time in the past; In the drama, the term probably refers to the time before the Nazis came to power.
- "dropping them": not seeing someone socially; The man and his wife no longer want to socialize with Mr. and Mrs. Klimbtsch because Mr. Klimbtsch is in trouble at the school.
- "cut him": avoid someone
- "ring up": call someone on the telephone

Advanced Learners

Ask students why they think Brecht chose to refer to the drama's main characters as The Man, The Wife, and The Boy.

Possible Responses: The characters are meant to represent a typical German family under the Nazis; the general names suggest that people lost their individuality under the Nazi regime.

MINI LESSON Speaking and Listening

DRAMATIC PRESENTATION

Prepare Have groups of students prepare dramatic presentations of the dialogue on pages 1222 and 1223. Assign lines to each group so that all of the dialogue will be performed. Share the following suggestions for the presentation:

- Use tone of voice, expressions, and gestures to bring the characters to life.
- Follow the stage directions, which sometimes provide ironic contrast with what's being said.
- Use the dialogue to convey the scene's mood.

Present After the groups practice, have them take turns performing their lines before the class. After the performances are done, invite students to discuss the characters' personalities and relationships with each other. Did the presentations help students better understand the characters?

This activity is particularly well suited for longer class periods.

Active Reading
UNDERSTANDING HISTORICAL CONTEXT

A Point out the wife's reference to "our people's recovery." Then ask students to explain the reference using historical context.
Possible Response: "Recovery" is a reference to Germany's economic recuperation after the devastation suffered in the wake of World War I.

Reading Skills and Strategies
PREDICTING
Have students pause in their reading after they finish page 1224. Then ask them to predict where the boy has gone.
Possible Responses: The boy has gone to spend the money his mother gave him; the boy has gone to inform on his parents.

Literary Analysis
DIALOGUE AND MOOD

B Invite a volunteer to read aloud the lines of dialogue on page 1225. Then ask students what mood is created by the dialogue.
Possible Responses: anxious, nervous, apprehensive

Literary Analysis CHARACTERIZATION
Remind students that characterization refers to the techniques writers use to develop characters. A character's personality can be revealed through his or her own speech and actions as well as through the speech and actions of other characters. Ask students to describe the man's personality.
Possible Responses: He's defensive, irritable, careless, and insecure.

What speeches and actions reveal the man's personality?
Possible Responses: the man's constant quarreling with his wife; her claim that he's been careless; his wondering what the boy overheard

(*Enter* the Maidservant *with the coffee.*)

The Wife. That's all right, Erna. You can go now, I'll see to it.

The Maidservant. Thank you very much, ma'am.

The Boy (*looking up from his paper*). Is that how vicars[7] always behave, dad?

The Man. How do you mean?

The Boy. Like it says here.

The Man. What's that you're reading?

(*snatches the paper from his hands*)

The Boy. Hey, our group leader[8] said it was all right for us to know about anything in that paper.

The Man. I don't have to go by what your group leader says. It's for me to decide what you can or can't read.

The Wife. There's ten pfennigs,[9] Klaus-Heinrich, run over and get yourself something.

The Boy. But it's raining.

(*He hangs round the window, trying to make up his mind.*)

The Man. If they go on reporting these cases against priests I shall cancel the paper altogether.

The Wife. Which are you going to take, then? They're all reporting them.

The Man. If all the papers are full of this kind of filth I'd sooner not read a paper at all. And I wouldn't be any worse informed about what's going on in the world.

The Wife. There's something to be said for a bit of a clean-up.

The Man. Clean-up indeed. The whole thing's politics.

The Wife. Well, it's none of our business anyway. After all, we're protestants.

The Man. It matters to our people all right if it can't hear the word vestry[10] without being reminded of dirt like this.

The Wife. But what do you want them to do when this kind of thing happens?

The Man. What do I want them to do? Suppose they looked into their own back yard. I'm told it isn't all so snowy white in that Brown House[11] of theirs.

The Wife. But that only goes to show how far our people's recovery has gone, Karl. A

The Man. Recovery! A nice kind of recovery. If that's what recovery looks like, I'd sooner have the disease any day.

The Wife. You're so on edge today. Did something happen at the school?

The Man. What on earth could have happened at school? And for God's sake don't keep saying I'm on edge, it makes me feel on edge.

The Wife. We oughtn't to keep on quarreling so, Karl. In the old days . . .

The Man. Just what I was waiting for. In the old days. Neither in the old days nor now did I wish to have my son's imagination perverted[12] for him.

The Wife. Where has he got to, anyway?

The Man. How am I to know?

The Wife. Did you see him go?

The Man. No.

The Wife. I can't think where he can have gone. (*She calls.*) Klaus-Heinrich!

(*She hurries out of the room, and is heard calling. She returns.*)

The Wife. He really has left.

7. **vicars:** priests; pastors of parishes.
8. **group leader:** a local leader in the Hitler Youth.
9. **pfennigs** (fĕn′ĭgz): A pfennig is a small unit of German money.
10. **vestry:** a room in a church where prayer meetings are held.
11. **Brown House:** Hitler's headquarters in Munich.
12. **perverted:** turned away from what is true or right.

Cross Curricular Link **History**

HITLER AND THE CATHOLIC CHURCH Hitler viewed the Catholic Church as a threat to his regime. Many Catholic activists had spoken out against Nazi laws and policies. Although Hitler had sent thousands of these activists to concentration camps, he still feared Catholic influence. To put an end to Catholic activism, Hitler and the Catholic Church signed an agreement called the Concordat in July 1933. The agreement stated that the Nazis would not interfere with the Church if the Church would stop criticizing Nazi policy.

Hitler soon broke the agreement. In 1935 and 1936, many Catholic clergy were arrested on trumped-up charges and put on trial—the so-called "Immorality" trials. Priests, monks, and nuns were accused of immoral behavior, the evidence for which was often produced by the Nazis. In one case, a priest was called to a hotel room to minister to a dying man. When the priest arrived, the caller turned out to be a prostitute, planted by government agents. Photos were taken as evidence of the priest's corruption. The trials resulted in the imprisonment of hundreds of Catholic clergy.

The Man. Why shouldn't he?

The Wife. But it's raining buckets.

The Man. Why are you so on edge at the boy's having left?

The Wife. You remember what we were talking about?

The Man. What's that got to do with it?

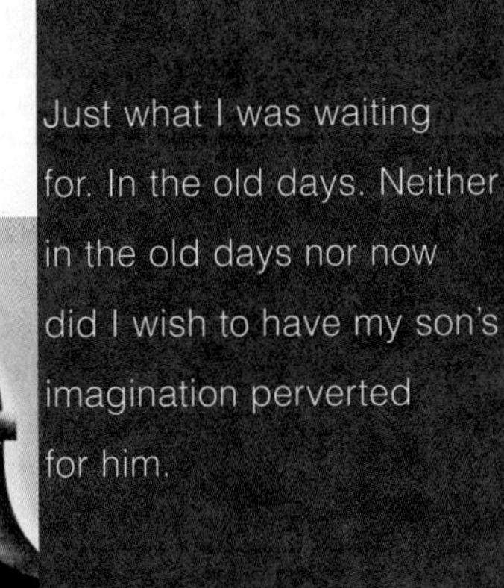

Just what I was waiting for. In the old days. Neither in the old days nor now did I wish to have my son's imagination perverted for him.

The Wife. You've been so careless lately.

The Man. I have certainly not been careless, but even if I had what's that got to do with the boy's having left?

The Wife. You know how they listen to everything.

The Man. Well?

The Wife. Well. Suppose he goes round telling people? You know how they're always dinning[13] it into them in the Hitler Youth. They deliberately encourage the kids to repeat everything. It's so odd his going off so quietly.

The Man. Rubbish.

The Wife. Didn't you see when he went?

The Man. He was hanging round the window for quite a time.

The Wife. I'd like to know how much he heard.

The Man. But he must know what happens to people who get reported.

The Wife. What about that boy the Schmulkes[14] were telling us about? They say his father's still in a concentration camp.[15] I wish we knew how long he was in the room. **B**

The Man. The whole thing's a load of rubbish.

(He hastens to the other rooms and calls the Boy.)

The Wife. I just can't see him going off somewhere without saying a word. It wouldn't be like him.

The Man. Mightn't he be with a school friend?

The Wife. Then he'd have to be at the Mummermanns'. I'll give them a ring. *(She telephones.)*

The Man. It's all a false alarm, if you ask me.

The Wife *(telephoning)*. Is that Mrs. Mummermann? It's Mrs. Furcke[16] here. Good afternoon. Is Klaus-Heinrich with you? He isn't?—Then where on earth can the boy be?—Mrs. Mummermann do you happen to know if the Hitler Youth place is open on Sunday afternoons?—It is?—Thanks a lot, I'll ask them.

(She hangs up. They sit in silence.)

The Man. What do you think he overheard?

The Wife. You were talking about the paper. You shouldn't have said what you did about the Brown House. He's so patriotic about that kind of thing.

The Man. What am I supposed to have said about the Brown House?

13. **dinning:** instilling through constant repetition.

14. **Schmulkes** (shmo͝ol'kəz).

15. **concentration camp:** prison camp where individuals are subjected to brutal treatment—including starvation and torture—and often are killed.

16. **Furcke** (fo͝or'kə).

Customizing Instruction

Less Proficient Readers

Tell students that although the man argues with his wife and tells her that there's nothing to worry about, his actions contradict his words. After he claims that his wife's worries are rubbish, the man runs to the other rooms in his home, anxiously calling his son's name. As students continue reading, encourage them to notice other instances where the man contradicts himself through his words or actions.

English Learners

Explain that the phrase "on edge," which is used several times in the dialogue on these pages, means nervous or anxious. The characters are on edge because they are constantly worried about being accused of wrongdoing. Ask students to think of words and phrases that are antonyms of "on edge."

Possible Responses: relaxed, at ease, calm

MINI LESSON Informal Assessment

SUMMARIZING Have students work in pairs to orally summarize the fears expressed by the married couple in *The Spy.* One student should play the role of the wife and express what she is afraid of and why. The other student should play the role of the man and respond to his wife's comments. Tell students that their presentation should accurately summarize what has happened in the play to this point.

RUBRIC

3 Full Accomplishment Student's summary provides an accurate and thorough explanation.

2 Substantial Accomplishment Student's summary is accurate, but some important information is missing.

1 Little or Partial Accomplishment Student's summary is missing vital information, is inaccurate, or shows little understanding of the character.

Literary Analysis CONFLICT
Remind students that a conflict is a struggle between opposing forces that moves a plot forward. Conflict may be external or internal. Ask students to identify some of the external and internal conflicts going on in the drama.
Possible Responses: External: man against his wife; man and wife against their son; man and wife against society. Internal: conflict within the man involving what he really thinks and what he thinks he should say

Literary Analysis SUSPENSE
A Point out that suspense is the tension or excitement readers feel as they are drawn into a story and become increasingly eager to learn the outcome of the plot. Suspense is created when a writer purposely leaves readers uncertain or apprehensive about what will happen. Then ask students to explain how the man's statement helps build suspense in the drama.
Possible Response: It makes readers feel that anything can happen to the couple; the Nazis do not need to have any real proof.

Active Reading
UNDERSTANDING HISTORICAL CONTEXT
B Point out the man's reference to the "winter of 1932." Ask students whether they can explain what the man is referring to.
Possible Response: In February 1932, Hitler ran for president of Germany against the current president, Paul von Hindenburg. Although Hitler did not win the election, his popularity was evident. In January 1933, he was made chancellor.

The Wife. You remember perfectly well. That things weren't all snowy white in there.

The Man. Well, nobody can take that as an attack, can they? Saying things aren't all white, or snowy white rather, as I qualified it—which makes a difference, quite a substantial one at that—well, it's more a kind of jocular remark like the man in the street makes in the vernacular,[17] sort of, and all it really means is that probably not absolutely everything even there is always exactly as the Führer[18] would like it to be. I quite deliberately emphasized that this was only "probably" so by using the phrase, as I very well remember, "I'm *told*" things aren't *all*—and that's another obvious qualification—so snowy white there. "I'm told"; that doesn't mean it's necessarily so. How could I say things aren't snowy white? I haven't any proof. Wherever there are human beings there are imperfections. That's all I was suggesting, and in very qualified form. And in any case there was a certain occasion when the Führer himself expressed the same kind of criticisms a great deal more strongly.

The Wife. I don't understand you. You don't need to talk to me in that way.

The Man. I'd like to think I don't. I wish I knew to what extent you gossip about all that's liable to be said between these four walls in the heat of the moment. Of course I wouldn't dream of accusing you of casting ill-considered aspersions on your husband, any more than I'd think my boy capable for one moment of doing anything to harm his own father. But doing harm and doing it wittingly are unfortunately two very different matters.

The Wife. You can stop that right now! What about the kind of things you say yourself? Here am I worrying myself silly whether you

Portrait of Prince Eristoff (1925), Tamara de Lempicka. Copyright © 2008 Artists Rights Society (ARS), New York/ADAGP, Paris.

made that remark about life in Nazi Germany being intolerable before or after the one about the Brown House.

The Man. I never said anything of the sort.

The Wife. You're acting absolutely as if I were the police. All I'm doing is racking my brains about what the boy may have overheard.

The Man. The term Nazi Germany just isn't in my vocabulary.

The Wife. And that stuff about the warden of our block and how the papers print nothing but lies, and what you were saying about civil defense the other day—when does the boy hear a single constructive remark? That just doesn't do any good to a child's attitude of mind, it's simply demoralizing, and at a time when the Führer keeps stressing that Germany's future lies in Germany's youth. He really isn't the kind of boy to rush off and denounce one just like that. It makes me feel quite ill.

17. **vernacular:** everyday spoken language.
18. **the Führer:** Hitler. *Führer* is German for a leader.

WORDS TO KNOW
jocular (jŏk'yə-lər) *adj.* funny; comic
wittingly (wĭt'ĭng-lē) *adv.* knowingly; intentionally
demoralizing (dĭ-môr'ə-lī'zĭng) *adj.* weakening to one's spirit or discipline; disheartening **demoralize** *v.*

MINI LESSON Speaking and Listening

DRAMATIC READING
Prepare First, discuss with students the impact an actor's performance can have on an audience's interpretation of a play. Explain that emotions and feelings are not found in the text itself but rather in the choices made by actors as they decide how to bring their dramatic characters to life. Then ask two students to perform dramatic readings of the man's long speech at the top of page 1226. Instruct one student to speak the lines in an angry tone of voice. Have the other student use a nervous tone.
Present Have the class analyze the difference between the two performances. What was the effect of the different tones of voice, facial expressions, and word emphasis? Which reading better revealed the man's state of mind?
This activity is particularly well suited for longer class periods.

The Man. He's vindictive, though.

The Wife. What on earth has he got to be vindictive about?

The Man. God knows, but there's bound to be something. The time I confiscated his tree-frog perhaps.

The Wife. But that was a week ago.

The Man. It's that kind of thing that sticks in his mind, though.

The Wife. What did you confiscate it for, anyway?

The Man. Because he wouldn't catch any flies for it. He was letting the creature starve.

The Wife. He really is run off his feet, you know.

The Man. There's not much the frog can do about that.

The Wife. But he never came back to the subject, and I gave him ten pfennigs only a moment ago. He only has to want something and he gets it.

The Man. Exactly. I call that bribery.

The Wife. What do you mean by that?

The Man. They'll simply say we were trying to bribe him to keep his mouth shut.

The Wife. What do you imagine they could do to you?

The Man. Absolutely anything. There's no limit. My God! And to think I'm supposed to be a teacher. An educator of our youth. Our youth
1 scares me stiff.

The Wife. But they've nothing against you.

The Man. They've something against everyone. Everyone's suspect. Once the suspicion's there, one's suspect.

The Wife. But a child's not a reliable witness. A child hasn't the faintest idea what it's talking about.

The Man. So you say. But when did they start
A having to have witnesses for things?

The Wife. Couldn't we work out what you could have meant by your remarks? Then he could just have misunderstood you.

The Man. Well, what did I say? I can't even remember. It's all the fault of that damned rain. It puts one in a bad mood. Actually I'm the last person to say anything against the moral resurgence[19] the German people is going
through these days. I foresaw the whole thing B
as early as the winter of 1932.

The Wife. Karl, there just isn't time to discuss that now. We must straighten everything out right away. There's not a minute to spare.

The Man. I don't believe Klaus-Heinrich's capable of it.

The Wife. Let's start with the Brown House and all the filth.

The Man. I never said a word about filth.

The Wife. You said the paper's full of filth and you want to cancel it.

The Man. Right, the paper. But not the Brown House.

The Wife. Couldn't you have been saying that you 2
won't stand for such filth in the churches? And that you think the people now being tried could quite well be the same as used to spread malicious rumors about the Brown House suggesting things weren't all that snowy white there? And that they ought to have started looking into their own place instead? And what you were telling the boy was that he should stop fiddling with the wireless and read the paper because you're firmly of the opinion that the youth of the Third Reich should have a clear view of what's happening round about them.

The Man. It wouldn't be any use.

---

19. **resurgence:** renewal; revival.

WORDS TO KNOW

vindictive (vĭn-dĭk'tĭv) *adj.* having a strong tendency toward revenge
confiscate (kŏn'fĭ-skāt') *v.* to seize by authority

Customizing Instruction

Less Proficient Readers

1 Point out the man's statement: "Our youth scares me stiff." Tell students that the statement is the central idea of the drama. The man's son—and, indeed, any child in Germany—could inform on his parents and thereby endanger their lives.

2 Students may be confused by the wife's speech. Explain that she is trying to remember what her husband said and putting it in a more favorable light. Encourage students to look back at what the man really said and then compare his comments with the wife's version.

English Learners

Explain the following idioms:

- "racking my brains": thinking very hard; The word *brains* is often used to refer to the mind or intelligence.
- "keep his mouth shut": not say anything about a particular matter
- "nothing against you": no evidence to prove your guilt

MINI LESSON Vocabulary Strategy

USING A DICTIONARY TO DETERMINE PRECISE MEANINGS

Instruction Call students' attention to the list of Words to Know on page 1221. Tell them that reference materials, such as a dictionary, can help them determine precise word meanings and usage. Remind students that the dictionary includes listings of all meanings of a word and that usage notes, synonym listings, and example sentences, which are often included, can also be very helpful in determining the proper meaning of a word.

Practice Have students work in small groups to find the meanings of each Word to Know. Students should record the definitions. When they find the term in the selection, they can determine which meaning fits the context.

Use **Unit Seven Resource Book,** p. 51, for more practice.

A lesson on using reference tools apears on p. 588 of the Pupil's Edition.

Literary Analysis
DIALOGUE AND MOOD

A Invite volunteers to read the dialogue that ensues when the phone rings. After the reading, ask students to describe the mood created by the dialogue.
Possible Responses: a mood of terror, menace, foreboding

Literary Analysis CLIMAX

Help students recall that the climax is the turning point in the plot's action, the moment when interest and intensity reach their peak. Then ask students to identify the climax of the drama.
Possible Response: the moment when the couple hear the door opening and realize their son has returned

Reading Skills and Strategies
DRAWING CONCLUSIONS

B Ask students what conclusions they draw from reading the last sentence in the drama.
Possible Responses: The man and his wife don't trust their son; they're still afraid they might be arrested; they're still going to be on guard around their son.

The Wife. Karl, you're not to give up now. You should be strong, like the Führer keeps on . . .

The Man. I'm not going to be brought before the law and have my own flesh and blood standing in the witness box and giving evidence against me.

The Wife. There's no need to take it like that.

The Man. It was a great mistake our seeing so much of the Klimbtsches.

The Wife. But nothing whatever has happened to him.

The Man. Yes, but there's talk of an inquiry.

The Wife. What would it be like if everybody got in such a panic as soon as there was talk of an inquiry?

The Man. Do you think our block warden has anything against us?

The Wife. You mean, supposing they asked him? He got a box of cigars for his birthday the other day and his Christmas box was ample.

The Man. The Gauffs gave him fifteen marks.

The Wife. Yes, but they were still taking a socialist paper in 1932, and as late as May 1933 they were hanging out the old nationalist flag.[20]

(The phone rings.)

The Man. That's the phone.

The Wife. Shall I answer it?

The Man. I don't know.

The Wife. Who could be ringing us? A

The Man. Wait a moment. If it rings again, answer it.

(They wait. It doesn't ring again.)

The Man. We can't go on living like this!

The Wife. Karl!

The Man. A Judas,[21] that's what you've borne me. Sitting at the table listening, gulping down the

20. **socialist paper . . . nationalist flag:** A socialist paper would reflect a leftist point of view, opposite to that held by the Nazis. Though not the official flag of Germany until 1935, the Nazi flag, which featured a swastika, had been in existence since about 1920.

21. **a Judas:** a traitor, such as Judas Iscariot, the betrayer of Jesus.

HUMANITIES CONNECTION Hitler set up organizations to train young people in Nazi teachings. This photograph shows children in Austria saluting the Nazi leader.

MINI LESSON **Viewing and Representing**

Photo of Children Saluting Hitler

ART APPRECIATION Tell students that at Hitler's public speeches and rallies, a young girl often presented a bouquet of flowers to the Nazi leader. The girl was typically blonde and blue-eyed, displaying the physical characteristics prized by the Nazis. Have students study the photo and the **Humanities Connection** on page 1228. Then ask them to describe the expressions on the children's faces as they salute Hitler.

Possible Responses: curious, expectant, apprehensive, awed, respectful

Why are many of the girls in the front row holding flowers?
Possible Response: They are probably preparing to give the flowers to Hitler.

soup we've given him and noting down whatever his father says, the little spy.

The Wife. That's a dreadful thing to say.

(*Pause.*)

The Wife. Do you think we ought to make any kind of preparations?

The Man. Do you think he'll bring them straight back with him?

The Wife. Could he really?

The Man. Perhaps I'd better put on my Iron Cross.[22]

The Wife. Of course you must, Karl.

(*He gets it and puts it on with shaking hands.*)

The Wife. But they've nothing against you at school, have they?

1 **The Man.** How's one to tell? I'm prepared to teach whatever they want taught; but what's that? If only I could tell . . . How am I to know what they want Bismarck[23] to have been like? When they're taking so long to publish the new text books. Couldn't you give the maid another ten marks? She's another who's always listening.

The Wife (*nodding*). And what about the picture of Hitler; shouldn't we hang it above your desk? It'd look better.

The Man. Yes, do that.

(The Wife *starts taking down the picture.*)

The Man. Suppose the boy goes and says we deliberately rehung it, though, it might look as if we had a bad conscience.

(The Wife *puts the picture back on its old hook.*)

The Man. Wasn't that the door?

The Wife. I didn't hear anything.

The Man. It was.

The Wife. Karl!

(*She embraces him.*)

The Man. Keep a grip on yourself. Pack some things for me.

(*The door of the flat opens.* Man *and* Wife *stand rigidly side by side in the corner of the room. The door opens and enter* the Boy, *a paper bag in his hand. Pause.*)

The Boy. What's the matter with you people?

The Wife. Where have you been?

(The Boy *shows her the bag, which contains chocolate.*)

The Wife. Did you simply go out to buy chocolate?

The Boy. Wherever else? Obvious, isn't it?

(*He crosses the room munching, and goes out. His parents look inquiringly after him.*)

The Man. Do you suppose he's telling the truth? 

(The Wife *shrugs her shoulders.*)

22. **Iron Cross:** a German medal awarded for bravery during wartime.

23. **Bismarck:** German statesman (1815–1898) who united the German states into an empire in 1871.

Customizing Instruction

Less Proficient Readers

Tell students that the parents are convinced now that their son is going to inform on them. The man's statement to his wife that she has borne him a Judas indicates this belief, as do the preparations the man and his wife discuss on page 1229. Putting on his Iron Cross and hanging the picture of Hitler over his desk are supposed to make the man look more patriotic and above reproach.

English Learners

1 With its fragments and disjointed sentences, the man's speech on page 1229 may be hard for some students to understand. Explain that the man is upset and worried that the Nazis may disapprove of what he teaches. The Nazis re-evaluated German history; and so, some figures considered heroes in the past were deemed traitors. The man also talks about bribing the maid to prevent her from informing on them to her father, the block warden.

Advanced Learners

Ask students how Brecht creates an atmosphere of mounting fear in *The Spy.*

Possible Responses: through the parents' increasing doubt and apprehension; through references to unsettling changes in German society; by twisting normal events and making them seem ominous

MINI LESSON Grammar

ELLIPSIS POINTS

Instruction An ellipsis (also called ellipsis points) consists of three periods preceded and followed by spaces. Three ellipsis points are used to show that one or more words have been omitted within a sentence. A period and three ellipsis points are used to show words omitted from the last part of a sentence. In fiction or informal writing, three ellipsis points may also be used to indicate a character's voice trailing off.

The maid _. . ._ is the block warden's daughter.
"He stood there for awhile _. . ._ I wonder how much he heard."
The man and his wife waited nervously as the door opened_. . . ._

Ask students to explain the use of the ellipsis points underlined in the above sentences.

Practice Have students correct errors in the use of ellipsis points in the following sentences.

1. The man. . . . hastily put on his Iron Cross. *(delete period)*
2. The couple didn't think they could trust their son . . . *(add period)*
3. The man said fearfully, "I don't know. . . . What do you think we should do?"*(delete period)*

For more instruction and practice in using ellipsis points, use McDougal Littell's ***Language Network:***

- Grade 10, Chapter 11, "Punctuation"
- Grade 12, Chapter 10, "Other Punctuation Marks"

Connect to the Literature

1. **What Do You Think?** What did you expect to happen when the door opened near the end of the play?

Comprehension Check
- What are the boy's parents talking about before he leaves?
- Why are the parents so fearful after their son goes out?

Think Critically

2. How would you describe family life under the Nazis?

THINK ABOUT
- the wife's concern over her husband's remarks
- the husband's reaction to his wife's gossiping
- their attitude toward their son

3. Do you think the boy has informed on his parents? Cite details from the play to support your opinion.
4. Explain whether the title *The Spy* is an appropriate **title** for this play.
5. **ACTIVE READING: UNDERSTANDING HISTORICAL CONTEXT** Review the chart you made in your READER'S NOTEBOOK. With a partner, discuss any incidents or references that you still have questions about.

Extend Interpretations

6. **What If?** Imagine that the play had ended with the parents' arrest. How would your reaction be different?
7. **Connect to Life** In this play, the loss of privacy is a key issue. Do you think privacy is at risk in our world today? Explain your opinion.

LITERARY ANALYSIS: DIALOGUE AND MOOD

Playwrights rely heavily on **dialogue**—written conversation between two or more characters—to develop both character and plot. For example, consider what the following lines reveal about the husband and the wife in *The Spy:*

THE MAN: It's a disaster, its raining like this. It's quite intolerable, living in a country where it's a disaster when it rains.

THE WIFE: Do you really think it's sensible to go round making remarks like that?

You might infer that the husband feels tense, threatened, and frustrated. The wife's response suggests that she feels it is better to hide one's discontent than to vent it.

The dialogue also helps to establish the **mood**—the feeling or atmosphere that a writer creates for the reader. You might describe the mood in one of several ways—for example, as romantic, gloomy, or suspenseful.

Paired Activity Draw a web and in the center write down one or more words to describe the feeling you get from the play. Then, in the surrounding circles, write down lines from the play that help create this feeling. Share your diagram with a partner.

Connect to the Literature

1. **What Do You Think?** Some students may have expected the boy to return with officials who would have arrested the parents. Others may have expected the boy to return, as he did, with a bag of candy.

Comprehension Check
- The parents are talking about friends they are avoiding for political reasons, the treatment of priests as reported in the newspaper, and Hitler's Brown House.
- They are afraid that he will inform on them.

Use Selection Quiz in **Unit Seven Resource Book,** p. 52.

Think Critically

2. Possible Responses: careful, tense, fearful, distrustful, angry
3. Possible Responses: Some students will say the boy hasn't informed on his parents because he returns home alone and seems to have gone to a candy store. Others will say that the manner in which the boy listens in on his parents' conversation and his quiet, stealthful movements suggest that he has informed on them.
4. Possible Response: The title is appropriate because the parents feel and act as if their son were a spy—whether or not he's actually spying on them.
5. You might have students share their charts and questions in a class discussion.

Extend Interpretations

6. **What If?** Possible Response: The reader would be horrified by the son's disloyalty, but the element of doubt and apprehension would be removed.
7. **Connect to Life** Possible Response: The Internet and the ease of access to personal computer files have put privacy at risk.

Literary Analysis

Paired Activity Possible Responses: Mood: tense, fearful, suspicious. Dialogue: "What do you think he overheard?"; "They've something against everyone"; "There's not a minute to spare"; "We can't go on living like this!"; "Do you suppose he's telling the truth?"

Use **Unit Seven Resource Book,** p. 50, for more practice.

Writing Options

1. Research Plan Write an outline for a research paper about family life in Nazi Germany. Begin by reviewing a few sources in order to acquire a basic understanding of the subject. Then choose a topic that is limited enough to explore in a five- to ten-page paper. Finally, write an outline of the paper, using a standard outline format. Place the outline in your **Writing Portfolio.**

Writing Handbook
See page R39: Options for Organization.

2. Top-Secret Memo Imagine that you are in a position to spy on the family portrayed in this play. Write a memo to your superiors describing your observations. Explain whether you think the parents pose a threat to the state.

Activities & Explorations

1. Play Poster Suppose that a troupe of actors will visit your school to perform *The Spy.* How would you interest other students in the play? Design a poster that suggests the play's mood. Include a powerful line or two from the play as a caption. ~ **ART**

2. Improvisational Performance With a classmate, improvise a scene between the husband and the wife after their son goes into his bedroom with the bag of chocolates. Consider whether his return home might have altered the opinions the parents expressed earlier in the play. ~ **PERFORMING**

Inquiry & Research

1. Controlling Youths The Nazi regime wasn't the only one in history to use its nation's youth in the service of the state. Find out how young people were used in other totalitarian states, such as in China during Mao Zedong's Cultural Revolution (1966–1969) and in Cambodia under Pol Pot's Khmer Rouge (1975–1979).

2. Brecht's Drama *The Spy* is part of a collection of 24 short plays by Brecht called *Fear and Misery of the Third Reich.* Read another play from this collection, and summarize its plot for the class.

Vocabulary in Action

EXERCISE: WORD MEANINGS For each sentence, write *T* if the statement is true or *F* if it is false.

1. Klaus-Heinrich showed he was **vindictive** by going out and spending his pfennigs.
2. The father felt that it was **demoralizing** to be spied on all the time.
3. He hated the rain and spoke in a **jocular** way about it.
4. The father quite **wittingly** took away his son's tree-frog.
5. The mother **confiscated** her son by calling friends to see if he was visiting them.

Building Vocabulary
For an in-depth lesson on using context clues, see page 674.

Vocabulary in Action

1. F
2. T
3. F
4. T
5. F

To assess skills and concepts taught in this selection, use **Formal Assessment Book,** pp. 179–180.

Writing Options

1. **Research Plan** You might encourage interested students to use their outlines to write a research paper.
2. **Top-Secret Memo** Before they begin, have students find evidence in the drama (dialogue, movements as described in the stage directions) that support their opinion. Then, when students write their memos, remind them to use a formal business style.

Activities & Explorations

1. **Play Poster** Students may want to use an abstract design or a scene from the play to convey its tense, fearful mood. Possible lines from the play that could serve as a caption include "What do you think he overheard?" or "They've something against everyone."
2. **Improvisational Performance** Before students perform the scene before the class, ask them to briefly discuss with their partners how they think the parents will react. Tell students to keep in mind the characters' personalities when they assume the roles. In particular, students should act out the characters' argumentative relationship.

Inquiry & Research

1. **Controlling Youths** Students should discover that young Chinese during the Cultural Revolution were urged to join the Red Guards and destroy what were considered "bourgeois" artifacts. Seen as a capitalist tool, education was also strongly discouraged. During the Khmer Rouge regime, many young people joined the army and took part in the mass killings that characterized the period. Encourage students to share their findings with the class.
2. **Brecht's Drama** You might invite students to get together in groups and perform the play they have read.

Objectives

- understand and appreciate a **personal memoir (Literary Analysis)**
- identify an author's **purpose for writing (Literary Analysis)**
- use strategies for **connecting to the author's experience (Active Reading)**

Summary

Uncertain of their final destination, 15-year-old Elie Wiesel and 119 other prisoners are herded onto one of the freezing open cars of a Nazi transport train. After the first night, S.S. guards clear the dead from the train, and young Wiesel frantically revives his father by screaming and slapping him. After three days on the train, the prisoners are starving. German civilians throw pieces of bread into the cars, and young Wiesel watches his fellow prisoners fight over them. One young man beats his dying father for a few crumbs. Later, a stranger attacks Wiesel, almost strangling him. Wiesel is saved from death through the intervention of one of his father's friends, who later freezes to death on the journey. As the train pulls into Buchenwald, the prisoners, starving and freezing, begin to scream hysterically. Out of 120 prisoners who began the journey in the train car, Wiesel and his father are among the 12 who reach the camp alive.

Use **Unit Seven Resource Book,** p. 53, for additional support.

Thematic Link

In this memoir the author, a young prisoner bound for a death camp, describes his **response** to the horrors he encounters as a victim of **war.**

5-Minute Warm-Up

Daily Language SkillBuilder

Have students **proofread** the display sentences on page 1095n and write them correctly.

FROM

THE WORLD WAS SILENT

ELIE WIESEL

Elie Wiesel
1928–

His Mission For decades, Elie Wiesel (ā'lē vē'səl) has been one of the world's most eloquent writers about the Holocaust. He himself survived the Nazi concentration camps. His mission as a writer is to keep alive the memory of the Holocaust in the hope that people will learn from the past.

Early Years Wiesel grew up in the orthodox Jewish community of Sighet (sē'gĕt), a small town in Romania. Isolated from the rest of Europe, the Jews of Sighet—about 15,000 in all—had no idea what lay in store when the Nazis rounded them up in 1944. They were shipped on a cattle train to Auschwitz (oush'vĭts'), a concentration camp in Poland. There young Elie was separated from his mother and sister, never to see them again. Later he and his father were transported to Buchenwald (bo͞o'KHən-vält'), a concentration camp in Germany. His father died in that camp shortly before the Allies set it free.

Telling the World After the war, Wiesel lived in France. He studied philosophy at the University of Paris and began a career in journalism. At first he wrote nothing about his concentration-camp experiences. Then, recognizing the need to tell the world what had happened, he drew upon his terrible ordeal to write *Night,* which appeared in French in 1958 and in English two years later. Since then, Wiesel has continued to give voice to the multitudes who perished in the Holocaust. He has also called attention to more recent human-rights violations, in countries such as South Africa, Bangladesh, and Bosnia. For his humanitarian efforts, he was awarded the Nobel Peace Prize in 1986.

Other Works
Dawn
The Accident
The Town Beyond the Wall
All Rivers Run to the Sea
And the Sea Is Never Full

For a humanities activity, click on:

LESSON RESOURCES

UNIT SEVEN RESOURCE BOOK, pp. 53–56

ASSESSMENT RESOURCES
Formal Assessment, pp. 181–182
Teacher's Guide to Assessment and Portfolio Use
Test Generator

INTEGRATED TECHNOLOGY
Visit our Web site: classzone.com

ADDITIONAL RESOURCES
Lesson Planning Guide, pp. 159–160
Teacher's Sourcebook for Language Development

Build Background

Hitler's "Final Solution" The Holocaust was the Nazis' systematic murder of millions of Jews and non-Aryans during World War II (1939–1945). The literal meaning of the word *holocaust* is "a sacrificial offering that is completely burned."

As a young man, Adolf Hitler developed a fierce hatred of the Jews. After he came to power in 1933, he targeted the Jewish people for extermination. The Nazis gradually stripped Germany's Jews of their rights, boycotted and vandalized Jewish businesses, and fired Jews from government and university posts. Within a few years Jews were barred from public facilities.

This persecution increased during World War II. As Nazi troops swept through Poland and the Soviet Union, they massacred whole populations of Jews. Then in 1942, the Nazis devised their so-called "final solution of the Jewish question": a systematic policy to murder every Jewish man, woman, and child under German rule. Multitudes of Jews were arrested, herded onto railroad cars, and transported to concentration camps. Upon arrival, some prisoners were killed immediately in gas chambers and then cremated. Others were forced to become slave laborers.

For a prisoner, the journey by train to one of the death camps was a horrendous experience. In the excerpt you are about to read, the author describes his journey. He was only 15 at the time.

Major Concentration Camps in Europe, World War II

1942 Date founded
Border, 1933

Baltic Sea
EAST PRUSSIA
Neuengamme, 1940
Bergen-Belsen 1943
Ravensbrück, 1936
Stutthof, 1939
Sachsenhausen, 1936
Treblinka 1942
Sobibor 1942
Chelmno 1941
Dora-Mittelbau 1943
GERMANY
POLAND
Buchenwald 1937
BELG.
Majdanek 1941
Theresienstadt 1941
Belzec 1942
LUX.
CZECH.
Plasow 1942
Natzweiler 1941
Auschwitz 1940
FRANCE
Dachau 1933
Mauthausen, 1938
AUSTRIA
N
Jasenovac, 1941
Jadovno, 1941
YUGOSLAVIA
Adriatic Sea
0 200 Miles
0 400 Kilometers

Connect to Your Life

Why do you think some Holocaust survivors feel the need to speak or write about their experiences in the concentration camps? What good might they accomplish by telling their stories? Discuss these questions with a small group of classmates.

Focus Your Reading

LITERARY ANALYSIS: AUTHOR'S PURPOSE

Authors write for one or more of the following purposes: to inform, to express an opinion, to entertain, and to persuade. As you read this excerpt, think about Wiesel's purpose for writing it.

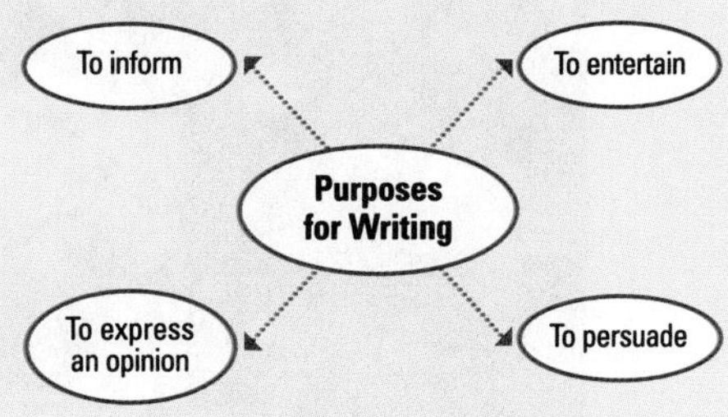

ACTIVE READING: CONNECTING TO THE AUTHOR'S EXPERIENCE

Literature that deals with disturbing events, such as Wiesel's memoir of the Holocaust, may stir intense feelings in you and lead you to reflect deeply about the world you live in. You may find yourself comparing the events retold in this excerpt with other events you have read about, heard about, or experienced. You may get so caught up as you read that you imagine yourself in the narrator's situation. These responses are ways of **connecting** with what you are reading.

READER'S NOTEBOOK As you read this excerpt, try to connect to the experiences Wiesel describes. Write down the ideas and feelings these events stir in you.

READING FOR INFORMATION

Reading Skills and Strategies

CONNECTING SETTING AND EVENTS

Have students notice the location of Buchenwald on the map on page 1233. Point out that Buchenwald is northwest of Auschwitz, the camp where young Wiesel and his father previously were imprisoned. Discuss how traveling north in winter, as the prisoners were forced to do, would have made their journey even more difficult than in other seasons. As students read, have them consider how the setting—a cramped, freezing railroad car en route to a death camp—affects what happens in this narrative.

TIME MANAGEMENT

If your schedule requires that you cover the lesson objectives in a shorter time, use. . .

- Preparing to Read, pp. 1232–1233
- Thinking Through the Literature, p. 1242

If you want to take advantage of longer blocks of class time, use. . .

- TE Teaching Options: Viewing and Representing, p. 1240; Cross-Curricular Link, pp. 1235, 1237; Grammar, p. 1239
- Related Reading, p. 1241
- Connect to Today, p. 1243

Reading and Analyzing

Literary Analysis AUTHOR'S PURPOSE

A Explain to students that in the first few paragraphs, Wiesel not only tells about the start of the journey but also conveys the prisoners' mental state. Have students identify phrases that help accomplish this purpose.

Possible Responses: "Indescribable confusion reigned," "beset by loneliness," "ominous silence," "Careworn and burdened with conflicting thoughts"

Use **Unit Seven Resource Book,** p. 55, for more practice.

Active Reading

CONNECTING TO THE AUTHOR'S EXPERIENCE

B Tell students to put themselves in young Wiesel's place as he (1) looks at the dead man, (2) fears that his own father may also be dead, and (3) struggles to revive his father. Have students discuss how they might feel in each situation.

Possible Response: Encountering the dead man might have induced horror and a feeling of revulsion. Believing that one's father had died might have caused overwhelming sadness and then a feeling of despair. Struggling to revive one's father might have instilled terror, hysteria, and finally a sense of relief when the dying man showed signs of life.

Use **Unit Seven Resource Book,** p. 54, for more practice.

from The World Was Silent

Elie Wiesel

Translated by Moshe Spiegel

Indescribable confusion reigned.

Parents searched for their children, children for their parents, and lonely captives for their friends. The people were beset[1] by loneliness. **A** Everyone feared that the outcome of the journey would be tragic and would claim its toll of lives. And so one yearned to have the companionship of someone who would stand by with a word, with a loving glance.

Afterward, an ominous silence fell upon us. We squatted on the soft snow that covered the floor of the railroad car like a carpet, and tried to keep warm by drawing closer to our neighbors.

When the train started to move, no one paid any attention to it. Careworn and burdened with conflicting thoughts, each of us wondered if he was wise to continue on the journey. But in our weari-

1. **beset:** continually troubled.

ness, whether one died today, tomorrow, a week or a generation later, hardly seemed to matter.

The night dragged on interminably, as though it were to go on to the end of time. When the gray dawn appeared in the east, I felt as though I had spent a night in a tomb haunted by evil spirits. Human beings, defeated and broken, sat like dusty tombstones in the dim light of early dawn. I looked about the subdued throng and tried to distinguish one from another. And, indeed, perhaps there was no distinction.

Careworn and burdened with conflicting thoughts, each of us wondered if he was wise to continue on the journey.

My gaze fell on one who stared blankly ahead. A wry[2] smile seemed to play on his ice-encrusted face. Those glazed eyes, whether living or dead, seemed to ensnare my gaze. A hundred and twenty captives, shadows of human lives, extinguished flames of burned-out candles lit on the anniversaries of the deaths of their loved ones.

Wrapped in a drenched blanket, his black cap pulled down over his ears, a layer of snow on his shoulders, my father sat beside me. Could it be that he, too, was dead? The thought flashed across my mind. I tried to talk to him. I wanted to shout, but all I could do was mutter. He did not reply, he did not utter a sound. I was certain that from then on I was to be all alone, all alone. Then I was filled with a numbing sense of indifference to everyone and to myself. Well, the Lord giveth and the Lord taketh away. The struggle was over. There was nothing and no one for whom to fight now.

The train ground to an abrupt halt in a snow-covered field. Awakened by the jolt, a few curious captives struggled to their feet to look out. The scene was reminiscent[3] of cattle staring stupidly from a livestock car.

German S.S. guards surrounded the human cargo, shouting, "All the dead are to be thrown out! All the dead are to be thrown out!"

The living were pleased; there would be more space. It would not be as crowded now.

Strong men appeared and examined each one who could not stand up, and rapped out, "Here's one! Get hold of him!"

Whereupon two men would pick the corpse by the shoulders and feet and fling it out of the car like a sack of flour.

From various parts of the car came such cries as, "Here's another—my neighbor! He doesn't move. Help me get rid of him!"

Two deportees[4] stepped forward and tried to lift a form beside me. It was only then that I was aroused from my stupor, and realized the seriousness of the situation. 5 And to this day I cannot understand how I summoned the strength and 6 courage to save my father from the lurking[5] death. I kneeled over him, tearing at his clothes, slapping his face, kissing him and screaming, "Daddy, B Daddy—wake up! Get up, Daddy! Don't let them throw you out of the car. . . ."

As he failed to respond, the two men said to me, "There's no use your screaming, little fellow. He's dead! Your father is dead, do you understand?"

"No! He is not dead! He's not dead!" I wailed, repeating the words over and over indefinitely. For some reason, I seemed to fear the death of my

2. **wry:** twisted.

3. **reminiscent:** awakening memories of something past.

4. **deportees:** people being deported, or sent out of a country.

5. **lurking:** waiting just out of sight.

Customizing Instruction

Less Proficient Readers

1 Make sure students understand that the "hundred and twenty captives" are the prisoners sharing the boxcar with young Wiesel and his father.

2 Explain the general structure of this memoir. Tell students that much of the narrative alternates between two types of text: descriptions of events followed by explanations of the author's feelings about them. To demonstrate, read aloud and discuss the content of this passage.

3 Tell students that *giveth* and *taketh* are old forms of "give" and "take." Explain that the line comes from the Bible.

English Learners

4 Point out that "S.S. guards" are members of an elite Nazi force particularly feared for its cruelty. Then explain the meaning of the following words:

5 *stupor:* "a condition, as of shock, in which one can barely think, act, or feel"

6 *summoned:* "called forth"

Advanced Learners

Have students note the similes and metaphors used to describe the prisoners. *("like dusty tombstones," "shadows of human lives," "cattle staring stupidly," "like a sack of flour")* Ask what general sense they convey. *(that the prisoners have become less than human)* Then ask students as they read to create their own similes and metaphors to suggest the characters of the S.S. guards, the German civilians, and the individual prisoners.

Cross Curricular Link **History**

"FINAL SOLUTION" As early as 1939, Adolf Hitler threatened the "total annihilation" of the Jews, and the gassing of prisoners began at Auschwitz Concentration Camp in 1941. The Nazis first used the term "final solution" at the Wanssee Conference in 1942 to refer to their plan to destroy every Jewish man, woman, and child in Europe. The Wanssee Conference coordinated the implementation of this plan among the upper ministries of the Nazi leadership.

Reinhard Heydrich, head of the S.S. main office in Berlin, introduced the plan at the conference. However, many other prominent Nazis were also involved in it. Heydrich was a top aide to S.S. chief Heinrich Himmler, whose special police forces had been running the concentration camps since the mid-1930s. Also involved in the plan were Hermann Goering, who with Himmler had established the camps; Adolf Eichmann, who was responsible for transporting the prisoners; and Josef Goebbels, the propaganda minister. Though no formal written order from him exists, Hitler himself originated the plan.

Literary Analysis AUTHOR'S PURPOSE

A Have students discuss Wiesel's purpose in including such horrendous attitudes and acts as the prisoners' "look[ing] forward" to bodies being dumped from the train or a young boy's biting another prisoner's ear. What does Wiesel intend to accomplish through these details?

Possible Responses: to show how the prisoners' situation has brutalized them; to shock the reader into understanding the horror of the prisoners' situation

Active Reading

CONNECTING TO THE AUTHOR'S EXPERIENCE

B Call students' attention to the two descriptions of the young divers struggling for coins. Is Wiesel's reaction to these events typical? *(Most students should agree that it is not.)* Have students discuss how Wiesel's experiences on the transport train affected his reaction to the incidents with the divers.

Possible Response: It caused him to take the divers' struggles personally and to regard them as offensive and humiliating.

father more than my own. I tried again and again to release him from the embrace of the angels of death, and I succeeded at last.

My father opened his glazed, ice-encrusted eyes, and regarded me in a dazed way, unable to understand what I was trying to convey to him or the commotion that was being made over him.

"See for yourselves, you murderers. He's alive, he's living!"

The two men eyed my father for a moment, then shrugged their shoulders and muttered, "Not for long," and turned to other silent forms.

There were some twenty-odd dead in our one car, and after they were stripped of their clothes, which the living snatched up, they were flung out of the car.

This task took several hours. Then the train chugged along, and as icy gusts shrieked about it, it seemed that through the accursed world about us could be heard the far-away, muffled wail of the naked bodies that had been abandoned on Polish snow-covered fields.

The journey was insufferable;[6] and every one who lived through it later questioned the natural laws that their survival seemed to disprove.

We were deprived of even bread and water, and snow was our only source of water. Cramped for space and thoroughly chilled, we were very weak by the third day of the journey. Days were turned into nights, and the nights cast a shadow of doom over our very souls.

The train plodded along for what seemed countless days, and the snow fell, fell, fell incessantly. And the exhausted, travel-weary unfortunates lay huddled for days on end, without uttering a word, eyes closed, waiting for one thing only—the next station, where the new yield of corpses would be got rid of. That was what we looked forward to. **A**

The journey lasted ten interminable days and nights. Each day claimed its toll of victims and each night paid its homage[7] to the Angel of Death.

We passed through German settlements, generally in the early morning hours, only in a few instances. Sometimes men on their way to work would halt in their tracks to glare at us as though we were animals in a kind of demonic circus. Once a German hurled a chunk of bread into our car and caused pandemonium to break out as scores of famished men fought each other in an effort to pounce upon it. And the German workers eyed the spectacle with sneering amusement.

Years later, I chanced to land in the Oriental port of Aden.[8] Some of the ship's passengers, looking for excitement and exotic thrills, tossed coins into the water to be retrieved by native boys who arrived on the scene to entertain the pleasure-seeking travelers by diving into the deep waters for the coins. At times the young divers would remain underwater for several minutes, and the passengers cheered the novel sport that could be enjoyed for a mere sixpence. . . .

I had once before witnessed such a scene. An elderly aristocratic woman from Paris, holding a handful of coins, stood on the deck amusing herself by throwing them one at a time to a dozen young dark-skinned swimmers. Each time she tossed a coin into the stream, a fierce fight ensued among the divers—a fact that seemed to delight her no end, judging by her peals of laughter. Revolted[9] by the scene of children trying to choke each other under water for the possession of a coin, I pleaded with the woman not to throw any more coins.

"Why not?" she replied. "I love to give charity."

She loved almsgiving—and to see six- and seven-year-old children fighting each other for a worthless coin.

Then I looked back upon that morning when

6. **insufferable:** unbearable.
7. **homage:** respect; tribute.
8. **Aden** (äd'n): a former British colony in Arabia, now part of Yemen.
9. **revolted:** disgusted.

Once a German hurled a chunk of bread into our car and caused pandemonium to break out as scores of famished men fought each other in an effort to pounce upon it.

our train, carrying its human cargo, had halted near the German city and the worker had thrown a piece of bread into our car, perhaps in compassion, although that is hard to believe. At any rate, the morsel of food caused the death of a number of men. The scramble for bread! The fight for life! The chunk of bread brought about its own kind of war to the death. The wildest instincts of the primeval[10] jungle had seized all of us, and we pounced upon the bread with all the savagery of enraged beasts. An atavistic[11] throw-back?

Unfortunately, the Torah does not relate how the children of Israel received the first manna in the wilderness.[12] Did they fight over it, and were there any casualties? And did scenes like the one in our car take place there? The German workers tarried a while, gazing at the amusing spectacle, and perhaps assuaging[13] their conscience at the same time with the thought of their benevolence in giving bread to the hungry.

All the other German workers soon followed the example of their kindhearted townsmen. Pieces of bread were cast into all the cars. Bread and victims. And they—the good, gallant[14] Germans—were pleased with themselves and smiled.

Strange, even while jotting down these words, the event seems incredible to me. I seem to be writing a horror novel—a novel that should not be read at night. It is hard to believe that what I set down in writing is really true, has actually happened to me.

And—only ten years ago!

I think to myself: if all that is alive in my memory, and that is seething in my heart, is really true, how am I able to sleep at night? How can I eat my food in peace? I can still see the scenes I experienced that early morning when the bits of bread fell from heaven. 2

Unfortunately, the bread also fell into our car. Though I was very hungry, my exhaustion was stronger. So I didn't budge from my spot, refusing to take part in what was going on. Let bread drop down—even from heaven. I would not risk my life to get it. I lacked the strength not only to fight for the hard crusts, but even to eat them. So I squatted in my corner, watching how human beings turned into animals as they attempted to snatch the morsels of food from each others' mouths.

A piece of the heavenly bread fell in a corner of the car; the next moment another corner was emptied of its occupants. Not far from me a young lad bit the ear of someone standing in front of him, in order to get to the priceless bread first. The injured person, bent only upon reaching the bread, was oblivious to the pain. I suddenly beheld a frail, elderly Jew crawling along the floor, one hand A

10. **primeval:** from the first or earliest times.
11. **atavistic:** returning to a primitive type of behavior.
12. **the Torah . . . wilderness:** The Torah is the first five books of the Hebrew scriptures (that is, the first five books of the Old Testament in Christian Bibles). The Book of Exodus contains the story of how the Israelites were given manna, a miraculous food from heaven, during their flight from Egypt.
13. **assuaging:** soothing; relieving.
14. **gallant:** noble.

Cross Curricular Link History

NAZI TRAINS The rail system in Germany was the pride of the Nazis. Great sums of money were spent on trains that could be used as mobile command centers or as secure means of transportation for high officials. Early in World War II, the well-organized train network helped move troops quickly and efficiently.

But Nazi trains also were put to more sinister use: to transport millions of Jews to concentration camps. Ever efficient, the Nazis often confined the Jews in ghettos close to train junctions. When the time came for the Jews to be transported, they were forced to walk to the trains. Usually the prisoners were told that they were going to a place where conditions were better and that they should bring with them clothing and blankets. Typically, they were then crowded into windowless cattle cars and treated in the manner that Wiesel describes—given no food, no water, and no sanitary facilities.

The journey to a camp usually lasted about four or five days, and many prisoners froze, starved, or suffocated along the way. The longest journey on record took 18 days. When the cars on that train finally were opened, everyone in them was dead.

Customizing Instruction

Less Proficient Readers

1 Have students note that these paragraphs do not relate events that occur in the railroad car. Instead, they describe events that Wiesel considers similar to the bread-throwing episode on the train. After Wiesel describes these events, he resumes telling about events on the train.

2 Explain to students that the reference to bread falling from heaven recalls the earlier reference to the Biblical manna. Make sure students understand that Wiesel is being ironic here—saying the opposite of what he means. Phrases like "kindhearted townsmen" and "good, gallant Germans" are also ironic.

English Learners

Explain the meaning of the following words:

- *abandoned* (page 1236, column 1, paragraph 5) means "left behind"
- *interminable* (page 1236, column 1, paragraph 9) means "endless"
- *pandemonium* (page 1236, column 2, paragraph 1) means "total disorder"
- *sneering* (page 1236, column 2, paragraph 1) means "looking scornfully, as by curling the upper lip"
- *ensued* (page 1236, column 2, paragraph 3) means "began"
- *benevolence* (page 1237, column 1, paragraph 1) means "kindness"
- *seething* (page 1237, column 2, continued paragraph) means "boiling"
- *oblivious* (page 1237, column 2, paragraph 2) means "not noticing"

Advanced Learners

Discuss the concept of survivor's guilt with students. Does Wiesel seem to be experiencing it? *(Responses will vary, though many students may state that he does.)* Ask students to mention other examples of survivor's guilt that they have heard or have read about. *(Students might mention the survivors of the World Trade Center attack or of other disasters.)* In what ways might survivor's guilt affect people's lives?
Possible Response: It may make people try to appreciate each day fully, but it may also make them dwell on why they—but not others—were allowed to survive.

Literary Analysis AUTHOR'S PURPOSE

A Read aloud some of the phrases that describe the father in this struggle ("sly smile," "deathly pale face," "a glint of joy in his bloodshot eyes," "his face glowed with lust," "darkened, broken teeth"). Then ask students whether Wiesel wants the reader to feel sympathy for the man.

Possible Responses: Though the phrases have negative connotations, some students may state that Wiesel is trying to arouse sympathy for the father's plight. Others may state that Wiesel felt only revulsion and wants to convey that feeling.

Active Reading

CONNECTING TO THE AUTHOR'S EXPERIENCE

B Discuss Wiesel's feelings after witnessing the fight between father and son. Ask students how they might have felt in Wiesel's place. How do they think Wiesel's age at the time might have affected his response?

Possible Response: Wiesel was only 15 years old at the time. Experiencing so much horror before having experienced much good in life may have contributed to his bitterness.

Zydowski Instytut Historyczny Instytut Naukowo-Badawczy, Warsaw, Poland. Courtesy of USHMM Photo Archives.

clutching his chest. At first I thought that he had been hurt in the fight. But then I saw him take a handful of crumbs from his bosom and devour them almost with ecstasy.

A sly smile played upon his deathly pale face for a moment, and disappeared. Then someone pounced on the old man like a phantom, and the two engaged in a death struggle, clawing, biting, trampling, kicking one another. The old man managed to raise his head, a glint of joy in his bloodshot eyes.

1 A "Little Meyer! Meyer, my son," the graybeard mumbled. "Didn't you recognize me? You have hurt me so much. . . ."

Meyer still struggled to retrieve a piece of bread from his father's bosom. Then the dying old man groaned, "Meyer, you're beating your own father . . . I brought bread for you, too. I had risked my life . . . and you're hitting, beating me—your old father. . . ."

The old man seemed on the verge of death, he no longer made any sound. Meyer had triumphed: his right hand clutched the small piece of bread, and his left wiped the blood trickling from one of his eyes. The old man held a piece of bread in his clenched fist and tried to bring it up to his mouth—to die with the taste of food in his mouth. His eyes were alert now; he was clearly aware of the situation. He was at the portals[15] of death—a condition in which one comprehends all that goes on about him. As he brought the hand with the bread closer to his half-opened mouth, his face glowed with lust for the bread. . . . It seemed as though the old man was holding back the bread intentionally, so that the pleasure of the anticipated[16] feast should last longer. The eyes seemed about to burst from their sockets. And as the old man was about to bite into the bread with his darkened, broken teeth, Meyer once

15. **portals:** doorways.

16. **anticipated:** looked forward to.

more pounced upon him and snatched the bread from him.

2 The old man muttered, "What? A last will and testament?" But, except for me, neither his son nor anyone else heard him. At last he breathed his last; and his orphaned son ate the bread. He was sprawled on the floor of the car, his right hand stretched out as though protesting to God, who had transformed Meyer into a murderer.

I could not bear to look at the old man for long. The son soon found himself engaged in a new struggle. Catching sight of the bread in his hand, others then pounced upon him. He tried to defend himself, but the furious throng, thirsting for blood in their frenzy, killed him. And so the two of them, father and son, victims of the struggle for bread, were trampled upon. Both perished, starved and alone.

Suddenly, I had the feeling that someone was laughing behind me, and I wondered who it was. But I was afraid to look around for fear of learning that the laughter was not coming from behind me, but from myself. I was fifteen years old then. Do you understand—fifteen? Is it any wonder that I, along with my generation, do not believe either in God or in man; in the feelings of a son, in the love of a father. Is it any wonder that I cannot realize that I myself experienced this thing, that my childish eyes had witnessed it?

Meir[17] Katz, a robust, energetic Jew with a thundering voice, an old friend of my father, was with us in the car. He worked as a gardener in Buna.[18] He conducted himself gallantly, both physically and morally. He was placed in command of the human cargo in our car because of his strength. It was thanks to him that I finally arrived alive in the Buchenwald concentration camp.[19]

It was during the third night of our journey—or was it some other?—we lost track of time. We squatted, trying to doze off, when I was suddenly awakened by someone choking me. With superhuman effort, I managed to shout one word—"Father!" That was all I managed to get out, as the unknown attacker was choking off my breath. Fortunately, my father awakened and tried to free me from the stranglehold. Unable to do so, however, he appealed to Meir Katz for help, whereupon the latter came to my rescue.

I didn't know the strangler or the reason for his violent act. After all, I had carried no bread with me. It may have been a sudden fit of insanity, or—just a case of mistaken identity.

Meir Katz also died during that journey. A few days before we reached Buchenwald, he said to my father, "Shloime,[20] I'm on my way out. I can't stand it any longer."

"Meir, don't give up!" my father tried to hearten him. "Bear up! You've got to! Try to have courage!"

"Shloime, it's no use—I'm washed-out," Meir muttered. "I can't go on."

Then the sturdy Meir Katz broke down and sobbed, mourning his son, who was killed in the early days of the Hitler terror.

On the last day of the journey, bitter cold, accompanied by a heavy snowfall, aggravated the situation even more. The end seemed to be near. Then someone warned, "Fellow Jews, in such weather, we've got to move about; we must not sit motionless—or we'll all freeze to death!"

So we all got up—even those who seemed to be dying—and wrapped our drenched blankets about our bodies. The scene was reminiscent of a congregation wrapped in prayer shawls,[21] swaying to and fro in prayer. The snow, the car, even the sky

17. **Meir** (mĕ-ĭr′).
18. **Buna:** a small town in eastern Germany, not far from the current Czech Republic border.
19. **Buchenwald concentration camp:** Located in eastern Germany near the city of Weimar, this camp held about 20,000 prisoners.
20. **Shloime** (shloi′mə).
21. **prayer shawls:** shawls with knotted fringe at the corners, traditionally worn by Jewish males, especially for morning prayers.

Customizing Instruction

Less Proficient Readers

1 Point out the word *graybeard* to students. Explain that the two words *gray* and *beard* form a compound word that means "an old man."

2 Explain that a *last will and testament* normally is a written document telling who should receive a person's belongings after his or her death. Here, the father may be referring to his final act of unwillingly giving the bread to his son.

3 Discuss young Wiesel's sense that someone is laughing behind him. Tell students that Wiesel is not sure what actually happened. He may have only imagined the laughter–or be laughing inside himself.

English Learners

Explain the following idioms:

- "racking my brains": thinking very hard; The word brains is often used to refer to the mind or intelligence.
- "keep his mouth shut": not say anything about a particular matter
- "cut him": avoid someone
- "nothing against you": no evidence to prove your guilt

MINI LESSON Grammar

USING SEMICOLONS TO JOIN INDEPENDENT CLAUSES

Instruction An independent clause expresses a complete thought and can stand alone as a sentence. Two or more independent clauses may form a compound sentence, joined by a semicolon or a comma followed by a coordinating conjunction, such as *and* or *but*. A semicolon indicates a stronger break than a comma does.

Activity Write the following sentence on the board:

In such terrible weather, we must move about; we must not sit motionless.

Then point out that in this sentence a semicolon joins the two independent clauses.

Practice Have students copy the following sentences and then insert a semicolon to join the independent clauses:

1. The prisoners on the train were freezing and starving never had they suffered so much.
2. Some prisoners, such as Meir Katz, were brave at first eventually they too lost heart.

For more instruction and practice in using semicolons, use McDougal Littell's ***Language Network:***

- Grade 10, Chapter 11 "Punctuation"
- Grade 12, Chapter 10 "Other Punctuation Marks"

Literary Analysis METAPHOR

A Point out the metaphor beginning "The deafening roar . . ." What is suggested by the prisoners' screams "reverberat[ing] back to earth"?
Possible Response: God is not hearing the outcries, and so the prisoners must rely on themselves.

HUMANITIES CONNECTION This photograph was taken after the Allied troops liberated Buchenwald concentration camp. Wiesel is on the second bunk from the floor, the seventh person from the left.

(heaven?)—everything and everybody seemed to be swaying, worshiping, communing[22] with God, uttering the prayer of life, the prayer of death. The sword of the Angel of Death was suspended above. A congregation of corpses at prayer.

A shout, an outcry like that of a wounded animal, suddenly rent the air in the car. The effect was terrifying and some of the people could not endure it silently, and themselves began to scream. Their outcries seemed to come from another world. Soon the rest of us joined in the uproar; screaming and shrieking filled the air. **A** The deafening roar rode the gusts of wind and amid the swirling snow soared to heaven, but, echoing from the closed gates there, reverberated back to earth.

Before long, twenty-five cars crowded with deportees joined us in the hysterical song of death. Everyone had reached the breaking point. The end was drawing near. The train was struggling up the hill of the Thyring[23] forest. The divine tragi-comedy was approaching its finale. There were no longer any illusions about surviving; the thousands of deportees were aware of their doom.

"Why don't they mow us down on the spot?" Meir Katz asked through tears. "We could at least be spared further agony."

"Reb[24] Meir, we'll soon arrive at our destination," I tried to comfort him. But the wind drowned out my words. We stood in the open car, under the falling snow, screaming hysterically.

We arrived at the Buchenwald concentration camp late at night. "Security police" of the camp came forward to unload the human cargo. The dead were left in the cars. Only those who were able to drag their feet got out. Meir Katz was left in the car; like so many others, he had frozen to death a short time before we reached our destination. The journey itself was the worst part of the ordeal. About forty of the deportees were claimed by death on that one day alone. Our car had originally started out with a hundred and twenty souls; twelve—among them my father and I—had survived the ordeal.❖

22. **communing:** talking intimately.
23. **Thyring** (tü′rĭng).
24. **Reb:** a Jewish title of respect for a man.

MINI LESSON **Viewing and Representing**

Photograph taken at Buchenwald Concentration Camp

ART APPRECIATION Have students read the **Humanities Connection** caption and study the reproduction of the photograph on page 1240. Point out that in the spring of 1945, Allied soldiers liberated concentration camps and then took photographs to document the appalling conditions they found. Moreover, camp photos taken throughout the war by S.S. photographers and others provide evidence of ongoing Nazi atrocities. Ask students what this photograph reveals about the condition of the prisoners.
Possible Response: The prisoners look gaunt and emaciated from lack of food. They are huddled in cramped quarters with little room to breathe.

When in early summer . . .

Nelly Sachs

Translated by Ruth and Matthew Mead

Nelly Sachs nearly became a Holocaust victim before escaping from Germany in 1940. Her poem opens with images of the beauty of awakening nature. A voice, however, discloses other realities—horrors perpetrated in the midst of loveliness. The sketch above was drawn by a young child in Terezin Concentration Camp.

When in early summer the moon sends out secret signs,
the chalices of lilies scent of heaven,
some ear opens to listen
beneath the chirp of the cricket
to earth turning and the language of spirits set free.

But in dreams fish fly in the air
and a forest takes firm root in the floor of the room.

But in the midst of enchantment a voice speaks clearly
and amazed:
World, how can you go on playing your games
and cheating time—
World, the little children were thrown like butterflies,
wings beating into the flames—

and your earth has not been thrown like a rotten apple
into the terror-roused abyss—

And sun and moon have gone on walking—
two cross-eyed witnesses who have seen nothing.

2 chalices: cup-shaped blossoms.

Related Reading

Nelly Sachs German poet and dramatist Nelly Sachs (1891–1970) wrote movingly about the Nazi horrors. Born and raised in Berlin, she escaped from that city to Sweden with the help of Swedish novelist Selma Lagerlöf. While in exile in Sweden, Sachs wrote one of her most admired poems, "O the Chimneys," which depicts the body of Israel as smoke drifting into the sky from the concentration camps. In 1966 Sachs was awarded the Nobel Prize for Literature.

Discussion Questions

1. At what point does a shift in thought occur in this poem? *(Most likely response is line 8, though some students may argue for line 6, where the world seems to begin turning upside down.)*
2. What effect does the poet achieve by using images from nature to describe and comment on terrible events? Give examples. *(Responses will vary. Students may note that the images of butterflies, the sun, and the moon usually have pleasant associations, so connecting them with the Holocaust conveys the sense of a disjointed universe.)*

Connect to the Literature

1. **What Do You Think?** What thoughts did you have after reading the last sentence of this selection?

Comprehension Check
- What were some specific hardships endured by the prisoners on the train?
- How did the prisoners react when bread was thrown onto the train?

Think Critically

2. **ACTIVE READING: CONNECTING TO THE AUTHOR'S EXPERIENCE** Review the notes you made in your READER'S NOTEBOOK. Which details in this memoir had the strongest effect on you?

3. How do you account for the prisoners' mental state?

- the fights to the death for bits of bread
- the attempt to strangle young Wiesel
- the terrible screaming

4. How would you contrast Meyer's and young Wiesel's treatment of their fathers?

5. In your opinion, has Wiesel come to terms with his past, or is he still haunted by it? Cite details from the selection to support your opinion.

Extend Interpretations

6. **What If?** What might have happened to young Wiesel if he had failed to save his father from being tossed off the train?

7. **Compare Texts** What connection do you see between Wiesel's choice of title, *The World Was Silent,* and the poem "When in Early Summer" (page 1241)?

8. **Connect to Life** The author writes about some of the darkest moments of his life. If you had survived a terrible ordeal, do you think you would choose to share it with others in some way? Give reasons for your response.

LITERARY ANALYSIS: AUTHOR'S PURPOSE

Authors write for one or more of these purposes: to inform, to entertain, to express opinions, and to persuade. For example, writers of editorials seek to persuade readers to do or believe something. Though an author may have several purposes, usually one is the most important. To help you in determining an author's purpose or purposes, look for the following features as you read. The purpose that each feature might signal is noted in parentheses.

- facts or explanations about people, places, or events (to inform or analyze)
- comments about facts (to express ideas, opinions, or emotions)
- statements that seem intended to convince you of something (to persuade)
- passages that you find particularly enjoyable or moving (to entertain)

Paired Activity With a classmate, go back through the excerpt and identify passages that provide clues about Wiesel's purposes for writing. Then in your notebook, list the purposes you think Wiesel had, and star the purpose you think was his most important one. Share your list with other pairs of students.

Connect to the Literature

1. **What Do You Think?** Possible Responses: Students may be appalled at the great loss of life or astonished that among those few survivors were not only young Wiesel but also his father.

Comprehension Check
- Prisoners were crowded into open railroad cars. It was bitterly cold and snow kept falling. Prisoners lacked food and water and did not know where the train was going.
- The prisoners reacted like wild beasts, grabbing food for themselves, hoarding it even from close relatives, and fighting and killing to get and keep their portions.

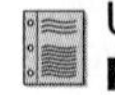

Use Selection Quiz in **Unit Seven Resource Book,** p. 56.

Think Critically

2. Responses will vary. Students may note details such as young Wiesel's seeing the dead man soon after the journey begins, his struggle to revive his father, his account of the father and son fighting over a bit of bread, and his description of the prisoners' screaming as the train nears Buchenwald.
3. Most students will agree that the prisoners are desperate. With nothing to lose, and with death probably awaiting them at the end of their train ride, they have reverted to a primitive state. When they begin screaming as they approach the camp, they are venting both terror and despair.
4. Meyer is willing to steal bread from his father even as the old man is dying. Young Wiesel, however, desperately struggles to revive his father in order to save him from being thrown from the train.
5. Responses will vary. Many students will state that Wiesel is still haunted by his past. Statements supporting this opinion include "how am I able to sleep at night?" and "Is it any wonder that I, along with my generation, do not believe either in God or in man?"

Extend Interpretations

6. **What If?** Some students may think that the death of his father would have caused young Wiesel to lose all hope, and he soon would have died in the railroad car. Other students may feel that young Wiesel shows enough resolve and strength of character (saving his father, comforting Meir Katz) to survive even without his father.
7. **Compare Texts** The message of Sachs's poem is that the world ignored—or "was silent" about—the Nazi atrocities.
8. **Connect to Life** Some students may feel that if they had survived a terrible ordeal they would want to share their experience with others in order to confront their own feelings and gain some control over them. Other students may feel that some experiences are too horrific to be shared and that it is better to try not to recall them.

Literary Analysis

Paired Activity Students should identify purposes similar to these:
- to express anger at how the prisoners were treated
- to show how frightened and desperate the prisoners were

Many students will think that the second purpose was the more important one.

Use **Unit Seven Resource Book,** p. 55, for more practice.

To assess skills and concepts taught in this selection, use **Formal Assessment Book,** pp. 181–182.

The Holocaust and Human Rights

"Wherever men or women are persecuted because of their race, religion, or political views, that place must—at that moment—become the center of the universe."

—*Elie Wiesel*

In the years since his liberation from Buchenwald, Elie Wiesel has devoted his life to preserving the memory of the Holocaust. Besides writing and speaking about his own experiences in concentration camps, Wiesel has sponsored various memorial activities and promoted the cause of human rights, as shown by the following:

- Served as Founding Chairman of the United States Holocaust Memorial Council, which built the United States Holocaust Memorial Museum in Washington, D.C.
- Worked tirelessly as a spokesperson for human rights, defending Cambodian refugees, victims of famine in Africa, victims of apartheid in South Africa, and victims of war in the former Yugoslavia.
- Established The Elie Wiesel Foundation for Humanity to advance the cause of human rights throughout the world.

Research Project and Group Discussion People can choose different ways to commemorate the Holocaust. With a partner, investigate one of the following projects or commemorations. Give an oral report about your findings and discuss with the class the best ways of commemorating the Holocaust.

- Steven Spielberg's Survivors of the Shoah Visual History Foundation
- Holocaust Memorial Day (Europe, January 27)
- The Elie Wiesel Foundation for Humanity
- Museum of Jewish Heritage: A Living Memorial to the Holocaust
- United States Holocaust Memorial Museum
- Holocaust memorial in Berlin, Germany (not yet built as of press date)

COULD THE HOLOCAUST HAVE BEEN PREVENTED?

If governments and leaders had spoken out . . .
If individuals had raised their voices . . .
If conscience had prevailed . . .
Millions of lives could have been saved.

Within weeks after this March 1944 photograph was taken of Emanuel and Avram Rosenthal in the Kovno ghetto, they were deported and killed by the Nazis.

NATIONAL DAYS OF REMEMBRANCE
Remembering the past for the sake of the future
April 15–22, 2001

REMEMBRANCE • EDUCATION • CONSCIENCE

UNITED STATES HOLOCAUST MEMORIAL MUSEUM

Above, National Days of Remembrance poster. *At left,* photos of U.S. Holocaust Memorial Museum in Washington, D.C.

RESEARCH STARTER
CLASSZONE.COM

Connect to Today

Use this feature to show the relevance of world literature to students. The material relates the literature selection just read to a contemporary topic connected to students' lives today.

Historical Update Students may wonder how the German people have faced up to the Holocaust in the years since World War II. Explain that analyzing the effects of Nazism, particularly the horrors of the Holocaust, has been part of the curriculum in West German schools since the early 1950s. (A similar curriculum was introduced into East German schools once the two Germanys were reunified in 1990.) A serious effort continues to be made to help students, and the country as a whole, to understand the forces that led to Nazism and to emphasize citizens' continued responsibility to stand up against racial or religious intolerance. Discussions of such topics often occur on television news programs and in various print media. The proposed Holocaust memorial in Berlin is one example of this ongoing remembrance.

Research Project and Group Discussion Recommend that students include the following in their reports: examples that explain the project or the commemoration; background about its founding; information on the public response; plans for continuing/strengthening/changing the project or the commemoration.

Opportunities for Extension In accepting the Nobel Peace Prize in 1986, Wiesel made reference to several other fighters for human rights. Interested students might find a copy of his speech and then research the work of the dissidents he mentions, including Lech Walesa, Andrei Sakharov, and Raoul Wallenberg.

This selection is included in the **World Literature InterActive Reader™.**

Objectives
- understand and appreciate a **short story (Literary Analysis)**
- identify the **theme** of a short story **(Literary Analysis)**
- use strategies for **making inferences (Active Reading)**

Summary
Daru, a French schoolmaster living in the Algerian desert, watches as the gendarme Balducci leads an Arab prisoner across the plateau to his schoolhouse. When Balducci arrives, he explains that the Arab has killed a cousin, and that Daru must transport him to police headquarters. Daru refuses to do it, but Balducci leaves the Arab with him anyway. Daru feeds the man and gives him a bed. In the morning he leads him out into the desert. He points out the direction to police headquarters and another route that leads to nomads who will shelter him. Leaving the Arab, Daru later sees him heading toward the police. Upon returning to his schoolhouse, Daru finds a message scrawled on the blackboard by some Arabs, saying that he will "pay" for turning in their brother.

Use **Unit Seven Resource Book,** p. 57, for additional support.

Thematic Link
As **war** looms in Algeria, a French schoolmaster is torn with **conflict** when an Arab prisoner is placed in his custody.

Use **Unit Seven Resource Book,** p. 60, for practice with Words to Know.

5-Minute Warm-Up
Daily Language SkillBuilder

Have students **proofread** the display sentences on page 1095n and write them correctly.

THE Guest

ALBERT CAMUS

Albert Camus
1913–1960

Early Years Albert Camus (ăl-bĕr′ kä-mo͞o′), a French writer, is considered one of the most important literary figures of the 20th century. He grew up in Algeria, a country in northwestern Africa, when it was still a colony of France. Several of his novels and stories are set in this region.

When Camus was only an infant, his father died in action in World War I (1914–1918), leaving his family impoverished. The young Camus was an excellent student and won a scholarship that enabled him to attend high school. There he developed a love of sports, particularly swimming, boxing, and soccer. Unfortunately, his athletic career was cut short by the onset of tuberculosis, which was to trouble him for the rest of his life. He went on to earn a degree in philosophy from the University of Algiers.

Philosophical Writer After college, Camus began working for a French-language newspaper in Algiers. Soon he was publishing personal essays, novels, and stories. Many of them show the influence of a philosophy known as existentialism (ĕg′zĭ-stĕn′shə-lĭz′əm). According to this philosophy, there is no universal meaning to life. In his writings, Camus stressed the importance of personal choice and responsibility as a way to create meaning in an otherwise absurd world.

Social Commitment Both personally and professionally, Camus took a stand against oppression. He criticized French colonialism in Africa. Moreover, after moving to Paris in 1942, he joined the French resistance against the Nazi occupation in France. He edited the underground newspaper *Combat* and narrowly escaped arrest by the Gestapo, the Nazi secret police.

Postwar Fame After Paris was freed from the Nazis, Camus continued to edit *Combat* and to win acclaim for his own fiction and nonfiction. In 1957 he was awarded the Nobel Prize for literature. Three years later, he was killed in an automobile accident.

Other Works
The Stranger
The Plague
The Rebel

LESSON RESOURCES

UNIT SEVEN RESOURCE BOOK, pp. 57–61

ASSESSMENT RESOURCES
Formal Assessment, pp. 183–184
Teacher's Guide to Assessment and Portfolio Use
Test Generator

INTEGRATED TECHNOLOGY
Visit our Web site: classzone.com

ADDITIONAL RESOURCES
Lesson Planning Guide, pp. 161–162
Teacher's Sourcebook for Language Development

Build Background

The French in Algeria In 1830, France invaded Algeria. After an easy conquest, the French set up a repressive colonial government. Large tracts of fertile land were taken from the Algerians and handed over to European settlers. The settlers strongly opposed granting rights to the native population, Arab Muslims. As a result, the vast majority of Algerians suffered political, social, and economic injustice.

After World War II, Algerian Muslims grew increasingly frustrated as efforts at reform failed to bring about needed change. In 1954 a group called the National Liberation Front launched a guerrilla war against France, which responded by sending a large army to Algeria. Roughly 10,000 French troops and as many as 250,000 Muslims died in the six years of fighting that ensued. When Algeria finally gained its independence from France in 1962, most Europeans fled the country.

The conflict in Algeria caused Albert Camus much anguish. He knew that the Muslim Algerians had suffered terribly under colonial rule. "In Algeria, as elsewhere," he said, "terrorism can be explained by a lack of hope." Yet he also feared for the safety of the European Algerians, including members of his own family. Camus argued for a peaceful solution to the conflict—one that would allow both Muslims and Europeans to live in harmony. The story you are about to read takes place in Algeria shortly before the fighting breaks out.

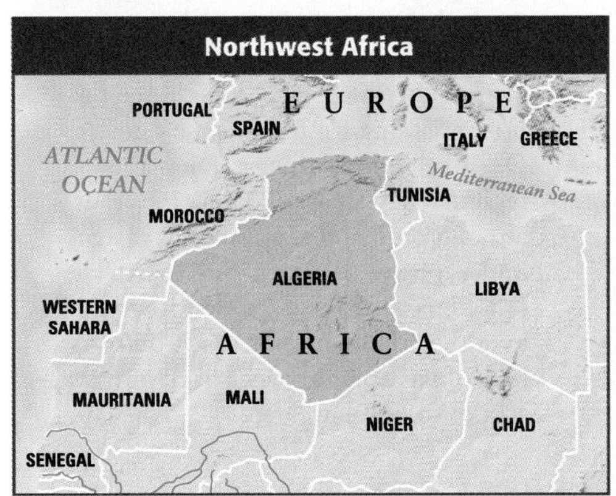

Connect to Your Life

In this story the characters are forced to make important decisions. Think about some important decisions you have made, perhaps about whether to stand up for a personal belief or to go along with the crowd. Why are some decisions so difficult to make? Share your ideas with a group of classmates.

Focus Your Reading

LITERARY ANALYSIS: THEME

A **theme** of a literary work is a central idea that the writer shares with the reader. It may be a lesson about life or human nature. Although some themes are stated directly, most must be inferred by the reader.

ACTIVE READING: MAKING INFERENCES

When you read a story, you often **make inferences** about such elements as theme, plot, and characters. That is, you "read between the lines," making logical guesses based on clues in the story. Consider, for example, what the following sentence suggests about Daru, the main character in "The Guest":

> ***Daru felt a sudden wrath against the man, against all men with their rotten spite, their tireless hates, their blood lust.***

From this sentence, you might infer that Daru has lost faith in human nature.

READER'S NOTEBOOK Make three charts like the one shown below—one for each character in the story. As you read the story, write down several actions of each character and the inferences that those actions lead you to make.

Daru	
Actions	**Inferences**
unties the Arab's hands →	*has sympathy for a stranger in pain*

WORDS TO KNOW **Vocabulary Preview**

adversary
avidly
chaotic
disconcerted
obstinate

READING FOR INFORMATION
Reading Skills and Strategies
CONNECTING FACT AND FICTION

Have a volunteer summarize the information in **Build Background.** Have the class note especially the economic and social injustices that the native Algerians suffered and Camus' conflict because of his sympathies for both sides. Then tell students to look for signs of tension between the French and the Arabs as they read "The Guest."

TIME MANAGEMENT

If your schedule requires that you cover the lesson objectives in a shorter time, use . . .

- Preparing to Read, pp. 1244–1245
- Thinking Through the Literature, p. 1258
- Vocabulary in Action, 1259

If you want to take advantage of longer blocks of class time, use . . .

- TE Teaching Options: Cross-Curricular Link, pp. 1247, 1248; Vocabulary Strategy, p. 1249; Speaking and Listening, p. 1250; Informal Assessment, p. 1254; Grammar, pp. 1256–1257
- Choices & Challenges, p. 1259

Reading and Analyzing

Tell students that this selection is broken into sections to help them understand it better and enjoy it more. At the beginning of each section, the **Focus** sets a purpose for reading. At the end of each section, the **Pause & Reflect** provides a question that checks student understanding.

Literary Analysis THEME

Remind students that the theme of a short story is the message about life that the writer shares with the reader. The theme is often related to the main character's conflicts in the story. Have students consider Daru's external and internal conflicts as they read and use them as clues to the story's theme.

 Use **Unit Seven Resource Book,** p. 59, for more practice.

Active Reading MAKING INFERENCES

A Ask students to describe Daru's attitude toward the climate and his students.

Possible Responses: He finds the climate in the area challenging and difficult, though he is satisfied with his own life there. He seems to be sensitive to his students' poverty and concerned about their welfare.

 Use **Unit Seven Resource Book,** p. 58, for more practice.

Pause & Reflect

Possible Response: The isolation and the harsh climate and landscape make it hard to grow crops or obtain goods. Thus, life is lived mostly on a subsistence level.

The Guest

Albert Camus

Translated by Justin O'Brien

Detail of *Self-Portrait* (1942), Mario Mafai.
Photo © Araldo de Luca/Corbis.

GUIDE FOR READING

FOCUS As the story begins, Daru, the schoolmaster, watches two travelers approaching in the distance. As you read, look for details that help you form impressions of Daru and the place where he lives.

The schoolmaster was watching the two men climb toward him. One was on horseback, the other on foot. They had not yet tackled the abrupt rise leading to the schoolhouse built on the hillside. They were toiling onward, making slow progress in the snow, among the stones, on the vast expanse of the high, deserted plateau.[1] From time to time the horse stumbled. Without hearing anything yet, he could see the breath issuing from the horse's nostrils. One of the men, at least, knew the region. They were following the trail although it had disappeared days ago under a layer of dirty white snow. The schoolmaster calculated that it would take them half an hour to get onto the hill. It was cold; he went back into the school to get a sweater.

1. **plateau:** an elevated, relatively level expanse of land.

Customizing Instruction

He crossed the empty, frigid classroom. On the blackboard the four rivers of France, drawn with four different colored chalks, had been flowing toward their estuaries[2] for the past three days. Snow had suddenly fallen in mid-October after eight months of drought without the transition of rain, and the twenty pupils, more or less, who lived in the villages scattered over the plateau had stopped coming. With fair weather they would return. Daru now heated only the single room that was his lodging, adjoining the classroom and giving also onto the plateau to the east. Like the class windows, his window looked to the south too. On that side the school was a few kilometers from the point where the plateau began to slope toward the south. In clear weather could be seen the purple mass of the mountain range where the gap opened onto the desert.

Somewhat warmed, Daru returned to the window from which he had first seen the two men. They were no longer visible. Hence they must have tackled the rise. The sky was not so dark, for the snow had stopped falling during the night. The morning had opened with a dirty light which had scarcely become brighter as the ceiling of clouds lifted. At two in the afternoon it seemed as if the day were merely beginning. But still this was better than those three days when the thick snow was falling amidst unbroken darkness with little gusts of wind that rattled the double door of the classroom. Then Daru had spent long hours in his room, leaving it only to go to the shed and feed the chickens or get some coal. Fortunately the delivery truck from Tadjid, the nearest village to the north, had brought his supplies two days before the blizzard. It would return in forty-eight hours.

Besides, he had enough to resist a siege, for the little room was cluttered with bags of wheat that the administration left as a stock to distribute to those of his pupils whose families had suffered from the drought. Actually they had all been victims because they were all poor. Every day Daru would distribute a ration to the children. They had missed it, he knew, during these bad days. Possibly one of the fathers or big brothers would come this afternoon and he could supply them with grain. It was just a matter of carrying them over to the next harvest. Now shiploads of wheat were arriving from France and the worst was over. But it would be hard to forget that poverty, that army of ragged ghosts wandering in the sunlight, the plateaus burned to a cinder month after month, the earth shriveled up little by little, literally scorched, every stone bursting into dust under one's foot. The sheep had died then by thousands and even a few men, here and there, sometimes without anyone's knowing. A

In contrast with such poverty, he who lived almost like a monk in his remote schoolhouse, nonetheless satisfied with the little he had and with the rough life, had felt like a lord with his whitewashed walls, his narrow couch, his unpainted shelves, his well, and his weekly provision of water and food. And suddenly this snow, without warning, without the foretaste of rain. This is the way the region was, cruel to live in, even without men—who didn't help matters either. But Daru had been born here. Everywhere else, he felt exiled.

PAUSE & REFLECT Why is life so difficult for Daru's pupils and their families?

2. **the four rivers of France . . . estuaries:** France's four major rivers are the Loire (lwär), the Seine (sān), the Marne (märn), and the Rhone (rōn). Their estuaries are the stretches near their mouths, into which ocean tides flow.

Less Proficient Readers

Explain to students that as they read this story they will need to pay attention to what Daru thinks and feels as well as to what he and the other characters say. The opening paragraphs will help students understand what Daru's life is like.

Focus Point out that not that much happens at the beginning of this story. Instead, the reader learns about the setting and the main character, Daru.

Make sure that students understand the setting and Daru's location in it. Point out that his school is near the top of a hill and that from that vantage point he can see quite far in all directions. Most of the land nearby is an empty plateau, but in the distance he can see mountains and desert. Ask students to suggest adjectives to describe this setting.

Possible Responses: harsh, lonely, and isolated

English Learners

1 Tell students that the expression *giving . . . onto* means "opening onto."

Advanced Learners

Have students note that Daru has been teaching his students about the "four rivers of France." How appropriate does this lesson seem in an Algerian school?

Possible Response: The fine points of French geography may seem rather irrelevant to poor rural students, who likely will never leave their own country.

Cross Curricular Link

Humanities

EXISTENTIALISM Existentialism is a philosophy that focuses on the nature of existence or being. Though different existentialists look at the world in somewhat different ways, existentialism's basic tenet is that individuals make themselves what they are and are responsible only to themselves.

Existentialism developed in reaction to philosophies that searched for absolute truths and beliefs. Existentialists do not think that there are any absolutes: people must make their own choices without knowing for sure whether they are correct. Only by exercising freedom of choice and taking responsibility for their decisions do people live meaningfully. Only then are they able to cope with a basically hostile or indifferent universe.

After the ravages of two world wars, existentialism became an influential philosophy in the middle decades of the 20th century. Besides Camus, well-known existentialist thinkers and writers of those years include Jean-Paul Sartre, Martin Heidegger, and Karl Jaspers.

Active Reading MAKING INFERENCES

A Ask students to describe how Balducci treats the Arab. *(Balducci treats him as a prisoner, but he is not particularly mean. He holds back his horse so as not to hurt the Arab, and later he is quite willing to untie his hands.)* Then ask students what inferences they can draw about Balducci.

Possible Response: As a gendarme Balducci is doing his job, but he is neither vicious to nor hateful of Arabs.

Literary Analysis CONFLICT AND THEME

B Remind students that the theme of a story may be suggested by the main character's conflict, or struggle. Then ask students to describe Daru's external and internal conflicts.

Possible Response: As a Frenchman, Daru is involved in the conflict between France and Algeria. Daru's internal conflict arises from the fact that the French authorities have assigned him a task that he regards as wrong.

FOCUS In this part you meet the two travelers: Balducci, a police officer, and his prisoner. Read to find out how Daru reacts to Balducci.

He stepped out onto the terrace in front of the schoolhouse. The two men were now halfway up the slope. He recognized the horseman as Balducci,[3] the old gendarme he had known for a long time. Balducci was holding on the end of a rope an Arab who was walking behind him with hands bound and head lowered.
1 The gendarme waved a greeting to which Daru did not reply, lost as he was in contemplation of the Arab dressed in a faded blue jellaba,[4] his feet in sandals but covered with socks of heavy raw wool, his head surmounted by a narrow, short *chèche.*[5] They were approaching. Balducci was holding back his horse in order not to hurt the Arab, and the group was advancing slowly. A

Within earshot, Balducci shouted: "One hour to do the three kilometers from El Ameur!"[6] Daru did not answer. Short and square in his thick sweater, he watched them climb. Not once had the Arab raised his head. "Hello," said Daru

3. **Balducci** (bäl-do͞o′chē).

4. **jellaba** (jə-lä′bə): a long, loose, hooded cloak worn by Arab men (usually spelled *djellaba*).

5. ***chèche*** (shĕsh) *French*: scarf (here, a type of scarf worn by French troops in Africa).

6. **El Ameur** (ĕl ə-mœr′): a town in northern Algeria, about 150 miles southwest of Algiers.

Cross Curricular Link **Geography**

THE ALGERIAN HIGH PLATEAU Explain to students that the setting of this story is the region of Algeria known as the High Plateau. This plateau lies roughly south of the more populated coastal section where Algiers is located and is, as described in the story, mostly barren. Typical precipitation in the High Plateau ranges between eight and sixteen inches a year. Summers are hot, and winters are usually cold. The landscape of the High Plateau is occasionally broken by large shallow basins where rain sometimes collects, though generally these basins are dry. In the western section of the region grows esparto grass, which is used for making such items as sandals and baskets.

when they got up onto the terrace. "Come in and warm up." Balducci painfully got down from his horse without letting go the rope. From under his bristling mustache he smiled at the schoolmaster. His little dark eyes, deep-set under a tanned forehead, and his mouth surrounded with wrinkles made him look attentive and studious. Daru took the bridle, led the horse to the shed, and came back to the two men, who were now waiting for him in the school. He led them into his room. "I am going to heat up the classroom," he said. "We'll be more comfortable there." When he entered the room again, Balducci was on the couch. He had undone the rope tying him to the Arab, who had squatted near the stove. His hands still bound, the *chèche* pushed back on his head, he was looking toward the window. At first Daru noticed only his huge lips, fat, smooth, almost Negroid; yet his nose was straight, his eyes were dark and full of fever. The *chèche* revealed an obstinate forehead and, under the weathered skin now rather discolored by the cold, the whole face had a restless and rebellious look that struck Daru when the Arab, turning his face toward him, looked him straight in the eyes. "Go into the other room," said the schoolmaster, "and I'll make you some mint tea." "Thanks," Balducci said. "What a chore! How I long for retirement." And addressing his prisoner in Arabic: "Come on, you." The Arab got up and, slowly, holding his bound wrists in front of him, went into the classroom.

With the tea, Daru brought a chair. But Balducci was already enthroned on the nearest pupil's desk and the Arab had squatted against the teacher's platform facing the stove, which stood between the desk and the window. When he held out the glass of tea to the prisoner, Daru hesitated at the sight of his bound hands. "He might perhaps be untied." "Sure," said Balducci. "That was for the trip." He started to get to his feet. But Daru, setting the glass on the floor, had knelt beside the Arab. Without saying anything,

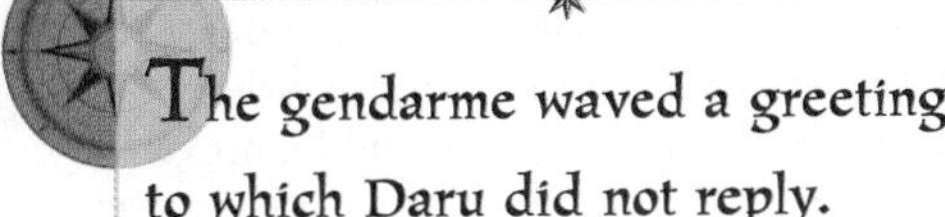

the Arab watched him with his feverish eyes. Once his hands were free, he rubbed his swollen wrists against each other, took the glass of tea, and sucked up the burning liquid in swift little sips.

"Good," said Daru. "And where are you headed?"

Balducci withdrew his mustache from the tea. "Here, son."

"Odd pupils! And you're spending the night?"

"No. I'm going back to El Ameur. And you will deliver this fellow to Tinguit. He is expected at police headquarters."

Balducci was looking at Daru with a friendly little smile.

"What's this story?" asked the schoolmaster. "Are you pulling my leg?"

"No, son. Those are the orders." 2

"The orders? I'm not . . ." Daru hesitated, not wanting to hurt the old Corsican.[7] "I mean, that's not my job." B

"What! What's the meaning of that? In wartime people do all kinds of jobs."

"Then I'll wait for the declaration of war!"

Balducci nodded.

"O.K. But the orders exist and they concern you too. Things are brewing, it appears. There is talk of a forthcoming revolt.[8] We are mobilized,[9] in a way."

Daru still had his obstinate look.

7. **Corsican** (kôr′sĭ-kən): a person from Corsica, an island to the west of Italy.

8. **forthcoming revolt:** The Arabs are preparing to fight the French in order to win their independence.

9. **mobilized:** ready for war.

WORDS TO KNOW

obstinate (ŏb′stə-nĭt) *adj.* stubborn

Customizing Instruction

Less Proficient Readers

Focus If necessary, guide students to the last paragraph on page 1248 for details about Daru's reaction to Balducci.

Make sure students understand why Daru is asked to escort the prisoner: though Daru was born in Algeria, he is French. The authorities fear that the native Algerians will revolt and need the help of French civilians living in that country. Make sure students understand that Corsica, Balducci's homeland, was also a French possession. If necessary, explain further that the Arab is Algerian.

English Learners

1 Tell students that a *gendarme* is a police officer.

2 If necessary, read through the dialogue with students to make sure that they understand who is making each statement. Explain that the expression *pulling my leg* means "playing a joke or trick on me." Also explain that *brewing* means "being plotted or planned; beginning to develop."

Make sure students understand that although Balducci calls Daru *son*, they are not related. Explain that the term *son* suggests a friendly relationship between an older and a younger man.

Advanced Learners

Share with students the information about existentialism in the mini-lesson on page 1247. Then point out that Camus, like other existentialists, emphasized the importance of freedom and responsibility in creating meaning in one's life. Then ask students how the conflict with Balducci reflects this concern.

Possible Response: Daru is deeply offended that the French authorities do not respect his freedom. They expect him to carry out their wishes.

MINI LESSON Vocabulary Strategy

CONTEXT CLUES

Instruction Remind students that they can sometimes understand the meaning of an unfamiliar word by examining the context in which the word is used and inferring its meaning. Write the following sentence on the board:

We made all her favorite foods, but the *obstinate* child refused to eat.

Have students use the meaning of the sentence to infer a meaning of the word *obstinate*. Then ask a volunteer to use the word in a sentence.

Practice Read the following sentences. Ask students to use context clues to determine the meanings of the italicized words.

1. He sat down opposite his *adversary* and prepared to do battle over a game of chess.
2. Normally calm and even-tempered, the teacher was *disconcerted* by the student's odd behavior.
3. The writer's devoted fans bought her new book and then *avidly* read every page.

Use **Unit Seven Resource Book,** p. 60, for more practice.

A lesson on using context clues appears on p. 674 of the Pupil's Edition.

Literary Analysis SETTING

A Remind students that the setting of a story may involve the social environment behind events. Point out how the backdrop of impending war affects events in this story. Have students note that the Arab's village was "beginning to stir," or get agitated, and that his people were unhappy that the French police had taken him away. Also point out that the threat of war makes Balducci feel he must quickly return to his job of patrolling the territory. Finally, Balducci isn't certain whether the Arab is "against" the French or not, but feels that they can't take any chances with him.

Active Reading MAKING INFERENCES

B Why does Daru feel "a sudden wrath" against the Arab?

Possible Responses: The man has committed a violent crime. Because of this crime, Daru will be forced to deal with him.

C Why does Daru take the revolver from the desk and put it into his pocket?

Possible Response: He does not trust the Arab enough to leave the gun where the man might be able to get to it.

Pause & Reflect

Possible Response: Daru has refused to do what Balducci has asked—that is, to agree to take the Arab to police headquarters. Moreover, Daru has acted as though he wants nothing to do with Balducci.

"Listen, son," Balducci said. "I like you and you must understand. There's only a dozen of us at El Ameur to patrol throughout the whole territory of a small department and I must get back in a hurry. I was told to hand this guy over to you and return without delay. He couldn't be kept there. His village was beginning to stir; they wanted to take him back. You must take him to Tinguit tomorrow before the day is over. Twenty kilometers shouldn't faze a husky fellow like you. After that, all will be over. You'll come back to your pupils and your comfortable life."

Behind the wall the horse could be heard snorting and pawing the earth. Daru was looking
A out the window. Decidedly, the weather was clearing and the light was increasing over the snowy plateau. When all the snow was melted, the sun would take over again and once more would burn the fields of stone. For days, still, the unchanging sky would shed its dry light on the solitary expanse where nothing had any connection with man.

"After all," he said, turning around toward Balducci, "what did he do?" And, before the gendarme had opened his mouth, he asked: "Does he speak French?"

"No, not a word. We had been looking for him for a month, but they were hiding him. He killed his cousin."

"Is he against us?"

"I don't think so. But you can never be sure."

"Why did he kill?"

"A family squabble, I think. One owed the other grain, it seems. It's not at all clear. In short, he killed his cousin with a billhook.[10] You know, like a sheep, *kreezk!*"

Balducci made the gesture of drawing a blade across his throat and the Arab, his attention attracted, watched him with a sort of anxiety.
B Daru felt a sudden wrath against the man, against all men with their rotten spite, their tireless hates, their blood lust.

Daru felt a sudden wrath against the man, against all men with their rotten spite, their tireless hates, their blood lust.

But the kettle was singing on the stove. He served Balducci more tea, hesitated, then served the Arab again, who, a second time, drank avidly. His raised arms made the jellaba fall open and the schoolmaster saw his thin, muscular chest.

"Thanks, kid," Balducci said. "And now, I'm off."

He got up and went toward the Arab, taking a small rope from his pocket.

"What are you doing?" Daru asked dryly.

Balducci, disconcerted, showed him the rope.

"Don't bother."

The old gendarme hesitated. "It's up to you. Of course, you are armed?"

"I have my shotgun."

"Where?"

"In the trunk."

"You ought to have it near your bed."

"Why? I have nothing to fear."

"You're crazy, son. If there's an uprising, no
one is safe, we're all in the same boat." 1

"I'll defend myself. I'll have time to see them coming."

Balducci began to laugh, then suddenly the mustache covered the white teeth.

"You'll have time? O.K. That's just what I was
saying. You have always been a little cracked. 2
That's why I like you, my son was like that."

10. **billhook:** an implement consisting of a curved blade attached to a handle.

WORDS TO KNOW

avidly (ăv'ĭd-lē) *adv.* eagerly

disconcerted (dĭs'kən-sûr'tĭd) *adj.* embarrassed or confused **disconcert** *v.*

1250

MINI LESSON Speaking and Listening

ORAL READING

Prepare Select three students, or have three students volunteer, to prepare an oral reading of the text beginning on page 1250, column 2, paragraph 1, and ending at the bottom of the first column on page 1251. Students can decide who will read Daru's and Balducci's lines and who will read the narrator's part. Suggest that students practice with the goal of accurately portraying the personality of each character and of conveying the tension of the scene.

Present Have students read the passage for the class. When they have finished, ask other students to critique the reading. Explain the goals that the readers were working toward and discuss whether these goals were fulfilled.

This activity is particularly well suited for longer blocks of class time.

At the same time he took out his revolver and put it on the desk.

"Keep it; I don't need two weapons from here to El Ameur."

The revolver shone against the black paint of the table. When the gendarme turned toward him, the schoolmaster caught the smell of leather and horseflesh.

3 "Listen, Balducci," Daru said suddenly, "every bit of this disgusts me, and first of all your fellow here. But I won't hand him over. Fight, yes, if I have to. But not that."

The old gendarme stood in front of him and looked at him severely.

"You're being a fool," he said slowly. "I don't like it either. You don't get used to putting a rope on a man even after years of it, and you're even ashamed—yes, ashamed. But you can't let them have their way."

"I won't hand him over," Daru said again.

"It's an order, son, and I repeat it."

"That's right. Repeat to them what I've said to you: I won't hand him over."

Balducci made a visible effort to reflect. He looked at the Arab and at Daru. At last he decided.

"No, I won't tell them anything. If you want to drop us, go ahead; I'll not denounce you. I have an order to deliver the prisoner and I'm doing so. And now you'll just sign this paper for me."

"There's no need. I'll not deny that you left him with me."

"Don't be mean with me. I know you'll tell the truth. You're from hereabouts and you are a man. But you must sign, that's the rule."

Daru opened his drawer, took out a little square bottle of purple ink, the red wooden penholder with the "sergeant-major" pen he used for making models of penmanship, and signed. The gendarme carefully folded the paper and put it into his wallet. Then he moved toward the door.

"I'll see you off," Daru said.

"No," said Balducci. "There's no use being polite. You insulted me."

He looked at the Arab, motionless in the same spot, sniffed peevishly, and turned away toward the door. "Good-by, son," he said. The door shut behind him. Balducci appeared suddenly outside the window and then disappeared. His footsteps were muffled by the snow. The horse stirred on the other side of the wall and several chickens fluttered in fright. A moment later Balducci reappeared outside the window leading the horse by the bridle. He walked toward the little rise without turning around and disappeared from sight with the horse following him. A big stone could be heard bouncing down. Daru walked back toward the prisoner, who, without stirring, never took his eyes off him. "Wait," the schoolmaster said in Arabic and went toward the bedroom. As he was going through the door, he had a second thought, went to the desk, took the revolver, and stuck it in his pocket. Then, without looking back, he went into his room. C

PAUSE & REFLECT Why does Balducci feel insulted by Daru?

FOCUS The Arab now becomes Daru's "guest" for the night. As you read, look for details that show how Daru treats him.

For some time he lay on his couch watching the sky gradually close over, listening to the silence. It was this silence that had seemed painful to him during the first days here, after the war. He had requested a post in the little town at the base of the foothills separating the upper plateaus from the desert. There, rocky walls, green and black to the north, pink and lavender to the south, marked the frontier[11] of eternal summer. He had been named to a post farther north, on the plateau itself. In the beginning, the

11. **frontier:** border.

Customizing Instruction

English Learners

Explain the meaning of the following words and expressions found in the story:

1 *all in the same boat:* "all in the same position or situation"

2 *cracked:* "crazy"

Less Proficient Readers

3 Call students' attention to this passage in which Daru and Balducci state their views about dealing with the Arab. Ask what is similar and different about the way they view the situation.

Possible Response: Daru says that the whole situation, including the Arab who caused it, "disgusts" him, and he will not participate in it. Balducci, while he is not eager to turn over the Arab either, feels that it must be done—that the French "can't let [the Arabs] have their way."

Focus You may wish to have students use their Reader's Notebook to list details that help them form opinions about Daru's treatment of the Arab.

Have students notice the reference to arriving "after the war." [page 1251, final paragraph] Explain that this is a reference to an earlier war, probably World War II.

Reading and Analyzing

Literary Analysis THEME

A Discuss with students the "decision" that troubles Daru.

Possible Response: The decision that troubles Daru is what to do about the Arab—whether to turn him in or to help him escape. Daru hopes that the Arab will run away, thereby taking the decision out of Daru's hands.

Have students consider how Daru's conflict about this decision may suggest the story's theme.

Possible Response: The story's theme may be that in some cases the freedom to choose is an agonizing responsibility.

Active Reading MAKING INFERENCES

B At the end of their conversation, the Arab says to Daru, "Come with us." What conclusion has he reached about Daru?

Possible Response: He may feel that Daru is kindly, possibly even sympathetic to his plight.

The Arab took a piece of the cake, lifted it eagerly to his mouth, and stopped short.

"And you?" he asked.

"After you. I'll eat too."

The thick lips opened slightly. The Arab hesitated, then bit into the cake determinedly.

Detail of *A Seated Arab Boy* (1858), Frederick Goodall. Oil on canvas. Copyright © Christie's Images, New York/SuperStock, Inc.

solitude and the silence had been hard for him on these wastelands peopled only by stones. Occasionally, furrows suggested cultivation, but they had been dug to uncover a certain kind of stone good for building. The only plowing here was to harvest rocks. Elsewhere a thin layer of soil accumulated in the hollows would be scraped out to enrich paltry village gardens. This is the way it was: bare rock covered three quarters of the region. Towns sprang up, flourished, then disappeared; men came by, loved one another or fought bitterly, then died. No one in this desert, neither he nor his guest, mattered. And yet, outside this desert neither of them, Daru knew, could have really lived.

When he got up, no noise came from the classroom. He was amazed at the unmixed joy he derived from the mere thought that the Arab might have fled and that he would be alone with no A decision to make. But the prisoner was there. He had merely stretched out between the stove and the desk. With eyes open, he was staring at the ceiling. In that position, his thick lips were particularly noticeable, giving him a pouting look. "Come," said Daru. The Arab got up and followed him. In the bedroom, the schoolmaster pointed to a chair near the table under the window. The Arab sat down without taking his eyes off Daru.

"Are you hungry?"

"Yes," the prisoner said.

Daru set the table for two. He took flour and oil, shaped a cake in a frying-pan, and lighted the little stove that functioned on bottled gas. While the cake was cooking, he went out to the shed to get cheese, eggs, dates, and condensed milk. When the cake was done he set it on the window sill to cool, heated some condensed milk diluted with water, and beat up the eggs into an omelette. In one of his motions he knocked against the revolver stuck in his right pocket. He set the bowl down, went into the classroom, and put the revolver in his desk drawer. When he came back
to the room, night was falling. He put on the 1
light and served the Arab. "Eat," he said. The Arab took a piece of the cake, lifted it eagerly to his mouth, and stopped short.

"And you?" he asked.

"After you. I'll eat too."

The thick lips opened slightly. The Arab hesitated, then bit into the cake determinedly.

The meal over, the Arab looked at the

schoolmaster. "Are you the judge?"

"No, I'm simply keeping you until tomorrow."

"Why do you eat with me?"

"I'm hungry."

The Arab fell silent. Daru got up and went out. He brought back a folding bed from the shed, set it up between the table and the stove, perpendicular to his own bed. From a large suitcase which, upright in a corner, served as a shelf for papers, he took two blankets and arranged them on the camp bed. Then he stopped, felt useless, and sat down on his bed. There was nothing more to do or to get ready. He had to look at this man. He looked at him,
2 therefore, trying to imagine his face bursting with rage. He couldn't do so. He could see nothing but the dark yet shining eyes and the animal mouth.

"Why did you kill him?" he asked in a voice whose hostile tone surprised him.

The Arab looked away.

"He ran away. I ran after him."

He raised his eyes to Daru again and they were full of a sort of woeful interrogation.[12] "Now what will they do to me?"

"Are you afraid?"

He stiffened, turning his eyes away.

"Are you sorry?"

The Arab stared at him openmouthed. Obviously he did not understand. Daru's annoyance was growing. At the same time he felt awkward and self-conscious with his big body wedged between the two beds.

"Lie down there," he said impatiently. "That's your bed."

The Arab didn't move. He called to Daru:

"Tell me!"

The schoolmaster looked at him.

"Is the gendarme coming back tomorrow?"

"I don't know."

"Are you coming with us?"

"I don't know. Why?"

The prisoner got up and stretched out on top of the blankets, his feet toward the window. The light from the electric bulb shone straight into his eyes and he closed them at once.

"Why?" Daru repeated, standing beside the bed.

The Arab opened his eyes under the blinding light and looked at him, trying not to blink. B

"Come with us," he said.

In the middle of the night, Daru was still not asleep. He had gone to bed after undressing completely; he generally slept naked. But when he suddenly realized that he had nothing on, he hesitated. He felt vulnerable and the temptation came to him to put his clothes back on. Then he shrugged his shoulders; after all, he wasn't a child and, if need be, he could break his adversary in two. From his bed he could observe him, lying on his back, still motionless with his eyes closed under the harsh light. When Daru turned out the light, the darkness seemed to coagulate[13] all of a sudden. Little by little, the night came back to life in the window where the starless sky was stirring gently. The schoolmaster soon made out the body lying at his feet. The Arab still did not move, but his eyes seemed open. A faint wind was prowling around the schoolhouse. Perhaps it would drive away the clouds and the sun would reappear.

During the night the wind increased. The hens fluttered a little and then were silent. The Arab turned over on his side with his back to Daru, who thought he heard him moan. Then he listened for his guest's breathing, become heavier and more regular. He listened to that breath so close to him and mused without being able to go to sleep. In this room where he had been sleeping alone for a year, this presence bothered him. But it bothered him also by imposing on him a sort of brotherhood he knew well but refused to 3
accept in the present circumstances. Men who share the same rooms, soldiers or prisoners,

12. **woeful interrogation:** sad questioning.

13. **coagulate:** thicken into a solid mass.

WORDS TO KNOW

adversary (ăd'vər-sĕr'ē)) *n.* opponent; enemy

Customizing Instruction

English Learners

1 Explain that the expression *night was falling* means "night was coming."

2 Explain that in this context *bursting* means "ready to explode in a violent way."

Less Proficient Readers

3 Discuss with students the idea of "brotherhood" described in this passage and Daru's response to it. Explain that Daru believes that men sharing a common room—even a prison cell—begin to develop a strong, close relationship. Help students understand why Daru does not want to feel this kind of closeness with the Arab. Daru resents the Arab for entangling him in a difficult situation; he is not sure what he will do with the Arab; he does not want to form a bond with the Arab because he may later decide to hand him over to the police.

Advanced Learners

Daru believes that he could not live anywhere else but in the barren desert. Have students think of other stories where the environment seems to have profoundly shaped an individual's character. Using students' examples, discuss the influence of various settings on character.

Possible Response: Answers will vary. Some students may mention some of Jack London's novels and tales set in the frigid wilderness, such as *The Call of the Wild.*

Pause & Reflect
Possible Response: Daru treats the Arab kindly, even though he is angry with him for putting him in this predicament.

Active Reading MAKING INFERENCES
A Thinking of his parting from Balducci, Daru feels "strangely empty and vulnerable." Ask students why Daru might feel this way.
Possible Responses: Daru realizes that he has injured Balducci's feelings and may never see him again. He has cut his strongest tie with France. Now Daru is alone with the Arab and is uncertain about what to do with him. Furthermore, he has heard—or imagined—"furtive steps around the schoolhouse."

Literary Analysis CONFLICT
B Ask students to describe Daru's conflict?
Possible Response: Though repelled by the Arab's violent crime, Daru feels that turning him in is dishonorable.

The Arab again stood framed in the doorway, closed the door carefully, and came back to bed without a sound.

develop a strange alliance as if, having cast off their armor with their clothing, they fraternized[14] every evening, over and above their differences,
1 in the ancient community of dream and fatigue. But Daru shook himself; he didn't like such musings, and it was essential to sleep.
2 A little later, however, when the Arab stirred slightly, the schoolmaster was still not asleep.

When the prisoner made a second move, he stiffened, on the alert. The Arab was lifting himself slowly on his arms with almost the motion of a sleepwalker. Seated upright in bed, he waited motionless without turning his head toward Daru, as if he were listening attentively. Daru did not stir; it had just occurred to him that the revolver was still in the drawer of his desk. It was better to act at once. Yet he continued to observe the prisoner, who, with the same slithery motion, put his feet on the ground, waited again, then began to stand up slowly. Daru was about to call out to him when the Arab began to walk, in a quite natural but extraordinarily silent way. He was heading toward the door at the end of the room that
opened into the shed. He lifted the latch with 3
precaution and went out, pushing the door behind him but without shutting it. Daru had not stirred. "He is running away," he merely thought. "Good riddance!" Yet he listened attentively. The hens were not fluttering; the guest must be on the plateau. A faint sound of water reached him, and he didn't know what it was until the Arab again stood framed in the doorway, closed the door carefully, and came back to bed without a sound. Then Daru turned his back on him and fell asleep. Still later he seemed, from the depths of his sleep, to hear furtive steps around the schoolhouse. "I'm dreaming! I'm dreaming!" he repeated to himself. And he went on sleeping.

PAUSE & REFLECT How would you evaluate Daru's treatment of the Arab?

14. **fraternized:** associated in a friendly, brotherly way

Assessment Informal Assessment

COMPARING CHARACTERS' RELATIONSHIPS Have students write two paragraphs in which they compare Daru's relationship with Balducci and his relationship with the Arab. Students might consider how Daru feels about each one, how well he communicates with each, and any other points of similarity or difference that they note.

RUBRIC

3 Full Accomplishment Response shows a full understanding of similarities and differences in Daru's relationship with the other two characters.

2 Substantial Accomplishment Response shows a general understanding of similarities and differences in Daru's relationship with the other two characters.

1 Little or Partial Accomplishment Response shows little understanding of similarities and differences in Daru's relationship with the other two characters.

FOCUS Daru and the Arab set out together on a journey. Each character makes a difficult decision. Read to find out about these decisions.

When he awoke, the sky was clear; the loose window let in a cold, pure air. The Arab was asleep, hunched up under the blankets now, his mouth open, utterly relaxed.
4 But when Daru shook him, he started dreadfully, staring at Daru with wild eyes as if he had never seen him and such a frightened expression that the schoolmaster stepped back. "Don't be afraid. It's me. You must eat." The Arab nodded his head and said yes. Calm had returned to his face, but his expression was vacant and listless.[15]

The coffee was ready. They drank it seated together on the folding bed as they munched their pieces of the cake. Then Daru led the Arab under the shed and showed him the faucet where he washed. He went back into the room, folded the blankets and the bed, made his own bed and put the room in order. Then he went through the classroom and out onto the terrace. The sun was already rising in the blue sky; a soft, bright light was bathing the deserted plateau. On the ridge the snow was melting in spots. The stones were about to reappear. Crouched on the edge of the plateau, the schoolmaster looked at the deserted expanse. He thought of Balducci. He had hurt him, for he had sent him off in a way as if he didn't want to
A be associated with him. He could still hear the gendarme's farewell and, without knowing why, he felt strangely empty and vulnerable. At that moment, from the other side of the schoolhouse, the prisoner coughed. Daru listened to him almost despite himself and then, furious, threw a pebble that whistled through the air before sinking into the snow. That man's stupid crime revolted him,
B but to hand him over was contrary to honor. Merely thinking of it made him smart with humiliation. And he cursed at one and the same time his own people who had sent him this Arab and the Arab too who had dared to kill and not managed to get away. Daru got up, walked in a circle on the terrace, waited motionless, and then went back into the schoolhouse.

The Arab, leaning over the cement floor of the shed, was washing his teeth with two fingers. Daru looked at him and said: "Come." He went back into the room ahead of the prisoner. He slipped a hunting-jacket on over his sweater and put on walking-shoes. Standing, he waited until the Arab had put on his *chèche* and sandals. They went into the classroom and the schoolmaster pointed to the exit, saying: "Go ahead." The fellow didn't budge. "I'm coming," said Daru. The Arab went out. Daru went back into the room and made a package of pieces of rusk,[16] dates, and sugar. In the classroom, before going out, he hesitated a second in front of his desk, then crossed the threshold and locked the door. "That's the way," he said. He started toward the east, followed by the prisoner. But, a short distance from the schoolhouse, he thought
he heard a slight sound behind them. He retraced
his steps and examined the surroundings of the 5
house; there was no one there. The Arab watched him without seeming to understand. "Come on," said Daru.

They walked for an hour and rested beside a sharp peak of limestone. The snow was melting faster and faster and the sun was drinking up the puddles at once, rapidly cleaning the plateau, which gradually dried and vibrated like the air itself. When they resumed walking, the ground rang under their feet. From time to time a bird rent the space in front of them with a joyful cry. Daru breathed in deeply the fresh morning light. He felt a sort of rapture[17] before the vast familiar

15. **listless:** lacking energy or enthusiasm.

16. **rusk:** a soft, sweet biscuit.

17. **rapture:** a strong feeling of delight or joy; ecstasy.

Customizing Instruction

English Learners

1 Tell students that *the ancient community of dream and fatigue* is a reference, continued from the previous page, to the close connection ("community") that sleep and exhaustion can sometimes bring to individuals who are not otherwise close.

2 Explain that *stirred* in the context means "changed one's position."

3 Tell students that *with precaution* means "carefully."

4 Students may not be familiar with *started* as used in this sense. Explain that here it means "move suddenly, as in surprise."

Less Proficient Readers

Focus You might ask students to predict what these difficult decisions might be.

5 Point out that this is the second time Daru thinks he hears noises around the house. (If you haven't discussed it earlier, show students the first reference, on page 1254.) Suggest that students keep these occurrences in mind as they continue reading.

Reading and Analyzing

Active Reading MAKING INFERENCES

A Ask students why the Arab seems to panic.

Possible Responses: He may never have had to make a decision about his own fate, and so he does not know what to do. He may want to run away but is afraid to do so.

Literary Analysis THEME

B Have students identify what happens to Daru in the final paragraph. *(He returns home to find a threatening message on his blackboard.)* Discuss Daru's predicament, caught between the French and the Arabs. Point out the irony in Daru's situation—though he has tried to avoid involvement in the conflict, he is now truly in the thick of it. Then ask students to infer the theme of this story.

Possible Responses: People can unwittingly get caught in struggles between large forces. Some conflicts are so large that individuals cannot escape getting entangled in them.

expanse, now almost entirely yellow under its dome of blue sky. They walked an hour more, descending toward the south. They reached a level height made up of crumbly rocks. From there on, the plateau sloped down, eastward, toward a low plain where there were a few spindly trees and, to the south, toward outcroppings of rock that gave the landscape a chaotic look.

Daru surveyed the two directions. There was nothing but the sky on the horizon. Not a man could be seen. He turned toward the Arab, who was looking at him blankly. Daru held out the package to him. "Take it," he said. "There are dates, bread, and sugar. You can hold out for two days. Here are a thousand francs too." The Arab took the package and the money but kept his full hands at chest level as if he didn't know what to do with what was being given him. "Now look," the schoolmaster said as he pointed in the direction of the east, "there's the way to Tinguit. You have a two-hour walk. At Tinguit you'll find the administration and the police. They are expecting you." The Arab looked toward the east, still holding the package and the money against his chest. Daru took his elbow and turned him rather roughly toward the south. At the foot of the height on which they stood could be seen a faint path. "That's the trail across the plateau. In a day's walk from here

WORDS TO KNOW

chaotic (kā-ŏt'ĭk) *adj.* showing great disorder or confusion

MINI LESSON **Grammar**

DISTINGUISHING COMPOUND SENTENCES FROM SIMPLE SENTENCES WITH COMPOUND VERBS

Instruction A compound sentence contains two or more independent clauses. These clauses may be joined by a semicolon or by a comma followed by a coordinating conjunction such as *and* or *but.* In contrast, a simple sentence contains only one independent clause. However, a simple sentence may have a compound verb: that is, two or more verbs or verb phrases joined by a conjunction and having the same subject.

Practice Write the following sentence on the board, and have students identify the independent clauses (clauses are underlined):

The Arab had now turned toward Daru, and a sort of panic was visible in his expression.

Now write this sentence on the board, and have students identify the compound verb (verbs are underlined).

Daru took the Arab's elbow and turned him rather roughly toward the south.

Practice Explain to students that they can distinguish a compound sentence from a simple sentence with a compound verb by trying to break the sentence into two clauses. If they cannot do so without rewording the sentence, the

> "In a day's walk from here you'll find pasturelands and the first nomads. They'll take you in and shelter you according to their law."

you'll find pasturelands and the first nomads.
1 They'll take you in and shelter you according to their law." The Arab had now turned toward
A Daru and a sort of panic was visible in his expression. "Listen," he said. Daru shook his head: "No, be quiet. Now I'm leaving you." He turned his back on him, took two long steps in the direction of the school, looked hesitantly at the motionless Arab, and started off again. For a few minutes he heard nothing but his own step resounding on the cold ground and did not turn his head. A moment later, however, he turned around. The Arab was still there on the edge of the hill, his arms hanging now, and he was looking at the schoolmaster. Daru felt something rise in his throat. But he swore with impatience, waved vaguely, and started off again. He had already gone some distance when he again stopped and looked. There was no longer anyone on the hill.

Daru hesitated. The sun was now rather high in the sky and was beginning to beat down on his head. The schoolmaster retraced his steps, at first somewhat uncertainly, then with decision. When he reached the little hill, he was bathed in sweat. He climbed it as fast as he could and stopped, out of breath, at the top. The rock-fields to the south stood out sharply against the blue sky, but on the plain to the east a steamy heat was already rising. And in that slight haze, Daru, with heavy heart, made out the Arab walking slowly on the road to prison.

A little later, standing before the window of the classroom, the schoolmaster was watching the clear light bathing the whole surface of the plateau, but he hardly saw it. Behind him B
on the blackboard, among the winding French
rivers, sprawled the clumsily chalked-up words he 2
had just read: "You handed over our brother. You will pay for this." Daru looked at the sky, the plateau, and, beyond, the invisible lands stretching all the way to the sea. In this vast landscape he had loved so much, he was alone. ❖

Customizing Instruction

Less Proficient Readers

1 Make sure students understand that Daru has tried to resolve his dilemma by making the Arab choose his own fate: he can turn himself in or seek protection elsewhere.

2 Discuss with students who wrote the message on the blackboard *(the prisoner's friends or family members).* Have them recall Daru's previous feelings that someone was prowling around.

English Learners

Explain to students that Daru is concerned about what will happen to the Arab. The following expressions help convey this concern:

- *felt something rise in his throat:* "felt unable to swallow because of a sense of pity or sorrow" [page 1257, column 1]
- *with heavy heart:* "with sadness or concern" [page 1257, column 2, paragraph 1]

Advanced Learners

Remind students that Camus as an existentialist writer values freedom and personal responsibility. Then ask students how Daru's final decision in regard to the Arab reflects this concern with personal freedom.

Possible Response: Daru chooses to remain neutral. He neither escorts the Arab to prison nor takes him to the nomads. Instead, he gives the Arab the responsibility to determine his own future.

sentence is simple. For each of the following, have students tell whether the sentence is a compound sentence or a simple sentence with a compound verb:

1. Daru had secretly hoped for the Arab's escape, but it never happened. *(compound sentence)*
2. Daru escorted the Arab for part of the way and then let him choose his direction. *(simple sentence with compound verb)*
3. The Arab looked confused and seemed uncertain about where to go. *(simple sentence with compound verb)*
4. The Arab could walk toward police headquarters, or he could seek shelter with the nomads. *(compound sentence)*
5. Daru set off in one direction, and the Arab started off in another. *(compound sentence)*

For more instruction and practice in compound sentences and compound verbs, use McDougal Littell's ***Language Network:***

- Grade 10, Chapter 2, "The Sentence and Its Parts" and Chapter 4, "Clauses and Sentence Structure"
- Grade 12, Chapter 1, "Sentence Parts" and Chapter 3, "Using Clauses"

THE GUEST 1257

Connect to the Literature

1. **What Do You Think?** What do you **predict** will happen to Daru now that the Arab's kinsmen have threatened him?

Comprehension Check
- What crime has the Arab committed?
- Why has Balducci brought the Arab to Daru?

Think Critically

2. Why do you think the Arab chooses to go to prison rather than go free? Explain your response.
3. **ACTIVE READING: MAKING INFERENCES** Review the inferences you recorded in your READER'S NOTEBOOK. How would you describe Daru's main conflict?

   THINK ABOUT
   - his duty to France
   - his attitude toward the Arab's crime
   - his reaction to the police orders
   - his growing bond with the Arab
4. Contrast Daru and Balducci in their attitude toward the Arab.
5. **Irony** is a surprising contrast between expectation and reality. What is **ironic** about what happens to Daru at the end of the story?
6. How does the **setting**—both the historical context and the desert landscape—affect the plot of this story?

Extend Interpretations

7. **What If?** Imagine that Daru had escorted the Arab to the nomads. How would your reaction to the story be different?
8. **Connect to Life** Daru is housing a murderer, yet he decides to go against the law and release his guest. How do you feel about a person's breaking the law in a situation like this?

LITERARY ANALYSIS: THEME

A **theme** is a central idea or message that a writer shares with the reader. To discover a story's theme, you might consider what happens to the main character. For example, at the end of this story, Daru has angered both Balducci—who represents the French authorities—and the local Arabs. These details suggest that the theme of this story has to do with the situation of an individual caught between larger, opposing forces.

Cooperative Learning Activity Go back through the story and list events, sentences, or phrases that provide clues about Daru's situation as a French citizen living in Algiers. Consider how Balducci and the Arab represent opposite poles of Daru's conflict. Then write a sentence that states the story's theme in your own words. Share your thematic statement with a small group of classmates. Keep in mind that different readers may state the theme of a story in different ways.

Connect to the Literature

1. **What Do You Think?** Some students will think that no harm will come to Daru as long as the French control Algeria. Others will think that Daru will be sufficiently frightened that he will want to leave the area. Still others may think that he will be killed by the Arabs.

Comprehension Check
- The Arab has killed his cousin.
- Balducci says he has orders that Daru should take the Arab to the police headquarters at Tinguit.

Use Selection Quiz in **Unit Seven Resource Book,** p. 61.

Think Critically

2. Some students will feel that the Arab knows he has done wrong and deserves punishment. Others may think that he feels he cannot escape and will be captured sooner or later.
3. Most students will agree that Daru's main conflict is whether or not he should turn the Arab over to the police.
4. Possible Response: While neither man has any personal animosity toward the Arab, Balducci believes the man must be brought to justice for his crime—that is the only way to keep order. Daru feels that turning over the Arab to the police is dishonorable. Balducci sees the Arab as just another prisoner, whereas Daru begins to feel sympathy for him.
5. Though Daru cared for the Arab and even showed him the path to freedom, the Arab's people, not knowing this, vow revenge against the teacher.
6. Possible Response: The backdrop of colonialism and impending war between the French and the Algerians is responsible for the Arab's being taken into French custody, for Daru's being assigned to deliver him to the police, and for Daru's ambivalent feelings about whose side he should be on. The desert landscape provides a sense of isolation—and perhaps no real place to escape—for Daru and the Arab.

Extend Interpretations

7. **What If?** Some students may feel that Daru, if he had helped the Arab to escape, would have been definitely in the wrong. Others may find such an action praiseworthy, as a way of taking a stand against the colonial government. Still others may believe that Camus' ambiguous ending (Did the Arab actually turn himself in or not?) is preferable.
8. **Connect to Life** Some students will feel that breaking the law in this situation is wrong. A murder was committed, and the murderer should be brought to justice. Others may feel that Daru has some justification for not turning the Arab over to the French.

Literary Analysis

Cooperative Learning Activity Students may write thematic statements similar to the following:
- Trying to do the right thing in a conflict between large forces can be thankless and futile.
- The freedom to make decisions is a heavy responsibility.
- An individual's life can be greatly altered by forces beyond his or her control.

Use **Unit Seven Resource Book,** p. 59, for more practice.

Writing Options

1. Journal Entry Write a journal entry in which Daru expresses his thoughts after finding the threat scrawled on his classroom blackboard.

2. Story Epilogue Imagine that Daru and the Arab's kinsmen meet. Write an epilogue to the story telling what happens in this encounter.

Writing Handbook
See page R29: Narrative Writing.

3. Literary-Analysis Essay In a brief essay, discuss the use of foreshadowing in this story. First define foreshadowing as a literary technique. Refer to the **Glossary of Literary Terms,** beginning on page R91, if you need help. Next describe the outcome of the story, when Daru discovers that he is a marked man. Finally, provide details from the story that hint at this outcome.

Activities & Explorations

1. Role-Playing With a classmate, role-play a conversation between Daru and Balducci after the events described in the story. Before you begin, review their dialogue in the story and discuss their manner of speaking with each other. How might Balducci react to Daru's release of the Arab? What concerns might Daru have regarding his superiors and the local Arabs? ~ **SPEAKING AND LISTENING/PERFORMING**

2. Landscape Drawing Create a drawing of the setting for this story. Before you begin, list details from the story that help you visualize the desert plateau. ~ **ART**

Inquiry & Research

French Colonialism in Algeria
Prepare an oral report that explains some aspect of Algeria's colonial history. For example, you might focus on the efforts of Muslim residents to gain legal rights or on the development of the nationalist movement. Use maps and other visual aids in your presentation.

Vocabulary in Action

EXERCISE: CONTEXT CLUES Choose the correct word to complete each sentence.

1. The starving prisoner _________ ate the food given to him.
2. He was not the least bit _________ by Daru's watching him eat greedily.
3. The prisoner was _________, stubbornly refusing to change his course of action.
4. If the situation had been _________ rather than peaceful and orderly, he might have tried to escape.
5. He knew that then Daru might have turned from friend to _________, but the idea did not frighten him.

WORDS TO KNOW

adversary	chaotic	obstinate
avidly	disconcerted	

Building Vocabulary
For an in-depth lesson on using context clues, see page 674.

Writing Options

1. **Journal Entry** Suggest that students recall everything Daru has gone through and try to put themselves in his place as they write their entries.
2. **Story Epilogue** Before students write, have them decide on the circumstances of the meeting, whether the Arab's people will believe Daru's story, and how they will respond.
3. **Literary-Analysis Essay** You may want to review with students the clues about the Arabs' attitude toward the French and the hints that intruders are watching Daru.

Activities & Explorations

1. **Role-Playing** Give students class time to plan their dialogues. Then, as various pairs present, have other students critique their content and style of presentation.
2. **Landscape Drawing** Have students note the color—or lack of it—in the descriptions of the land. Remind them that the sky is an important element in the landscape.

Inquiry & Research

French Colonialism in Algeria Suggest that students focus on a topic that takes 10 to 20 minutes to present. Recommend that they practice with their visual aids beforehand so that their presentation flows smoothly.

Vocabulary in Action

1. avidly
2. disconcerted
3. obstinate
4. chaotic
5. adversary

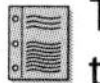
To assess skills and concepts taught in this selection, use **Formal Assessment Book,** pp. 183–184.

THE GUEST 1259

Assign the prose poem by Aleksandr Solzhenitsyn and the poem by Mahmud Darwish to prepare students for the sample writing assessment provided on page 1269. Use the **Points of Comparison** chart to guide students in identifying the similarities and differences between these two selections.

Use **Unit Seven Resource Book,** p. 62, for more practice.

COMPARING LITERATURE ACROSS CULTURES

The Prison Experience

OVERVIEW

The 20th century was marked by two world wars and numerous other armed conflicts. Millions of people were injured, slain, or uprooted from their homes. Many others suffered the horrors of prisons and concentration camps—their freedom swept away in a tidal wave of repression.

This lesson includes two selections written by 20th-century authors who suffered as political prisoners. The first selection is a prose poem by the Russian writer Aleksandr Solzhenitsyn (sōl'zhə-nēt'sĭn); the second is a poem by the Palestinian writer Mahmud Darwish (mä-mo͞od' där'wēsh). In the pages that follow, you will be asked to compare and contrast these two writers' views of the prison experience. Your comparisons will help you explore the writers' perspectives on this tragic ordeal.

Points of Comparison

Create a chart like the one shown, and fill it in after you read each selection. The topics listed will help you identify similarities and differences between the selections. Feel free to add other topics to your chart.

	"Freedom to Breathe"	"The Prison Cell"
Where is the speaker?		
How has imprisonment affected the speaker?		
What is the speaker's message about freedom?		
How strong is the speaker's spirit?		
Evidence of spiritual strength or weakness		

Standardized Test Practice: Comparison-and-Contrast Essay After you finish reading the two selections, you will be asked to write a comparison-and-contrast essay. Your chart will help you plan and develop the essay.

Assessment Standardized Test Practice

COMPARISON-AND-CONTRAST ESSAY To provide practice to students in comparing two different pieces of literature, have them read both selections in this **Comparing Literature** feature, rather than treating each selection separately. Have them work with the chart shown here on page 1260, filling it out as they finish reading each selection. (Examples of how to fill out the chart are supplied on pages 1264 and 1268 of the pupil text.) A sample assessment writing prompt and guidelines for responding to it in writing are on page 1269.

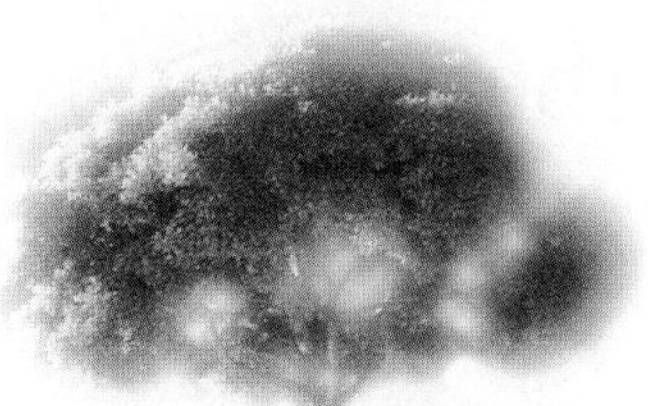

Freedom to Breathe

ALEKSANDR SOLZHENITSYN

Aleksandr Solzhenitsyn
1918–

Prisoner and Literary Giant
Aleksandr Solzhenitsyn is one of the most famous writers to come from the Soviet Union. As a young man, he joined the Soviet army to fight in World War II (1939–1945), rising to the rank of captain. In the final year of the war, however, his life took an unexpected turn. After writing a letter critical of Stalin, he was stripped of his rank and was sentenced to a Soviet prison camp. He drew upon his ordeal in writing *One Day in the Life of Ivan Denisovich.* This novella tells of a prisoner in a forced labor camp during Stalin's regime. With this work, published in 1962, Solzhenitsyn burst onto the literary scene.

To get around government censorship, Solzhenitsyn had his writings smuggled out of the Soviet Union and published abroad. They earned him the Nobel Prize in Literature in 1970. Three years later, the first volume of *The Gulag Archipelago* was published in Paris. In this nonfiction work, Solzhenitsyn described the vast network of Soviet prison camps. The government, outraged at Solzhenitsyn, expelled him from the country. Only in 1994, after the collapse of the Soviet Union, did he again set foot in Russia.

Build Background

According to one critic, Solzhenitsyn's "deepest identity is that of a former political prisoner." In "Freedom to Breathe," he describes a simple pleasure that prison took away from him.

Connect to Your Life

What freedoms do you enjoy as a member of the society you live in? Are there some freedoms that you take for granted? Share your ideas with a small group of classmates.

Focus Your Reading

LITERARY ANALYSIS: DESCRIPTION
Writing that helps a reader picture scenes, events, or people is known as **description.** Description often involves the use of precise language and vivid, original phrases, as in this passage:

A shower fell in the night and now dark clouds drift across the sky, occasionally sprinkling a fine film of rain.

Think about the effects created by the descriptive details as you read the prose poem.

ACTIVE READING: RECOGNIZING SENSORY DETAILS **Sensory details** are words and phrases that appeal to readers' senses of sight, smell, hearing, taste, or touch. For example, in the boldfaced passage above, the detail "a fine film of rain" appeals to the senses of sight and touch.

READER'S NOTEBOOK As you read, jot down sensory details and the sense or senses each appeals to.

Detail	Sense(s)
1.	1.
2	2.
3.	3.

Objectives
- compare and contrast two selections about the prison experience **(Literary Analysis)**
- analyze the technique of **description (Literary Analysis)**
- identify **sensory details (Active Reading)**

Thematic Link
In these selections two victims of political **conflicts** respond to the prison experience.

5-Minute Warm-Up

Daily Language SkillBuilder

Have students **proofread** the display sentences on page 1095n and write them correctly.

TIME MANAGEMENT

If you wish to cover only one of the selections, use . . .
- Preparing to Read, p. 1261 or p. 1265
- Thinking Through the Literature, p. 1263 or p. 1268

If you want to take advantage of longer blocks of class time, use . . .
- Choices & Challenges, p. 1264
- TE Teaching Options: Speaking and Listening, p. 1267

Reading and Analyzing

Reading Skills and Strategies
PREVIEWING
Tell students to skim, or look through, this lesson and to notice that it contains two selections about the prison experience by two different authors.

Literary Analysis DESCRIPTION

A Remind students that writers use description to help readers picture scenes, events, and characters. Then ask students to identify details that help them imagine the setting.
Possible Responses: "an apple tree in blossom," "glistens with moisture," "sweet fragrance," and "the aroma"

 Use **Unit Seven Resource Book,** p. 64, for more practice.

Active Reading
RECOGNIZING SENSORY DETAILS

B Remind students that to create description, writers often use sensory details—words and phrases that enable the reader to see, hear, smell, taste, or feel the subject described. Ask students to identify phrases that re-create what the speaker hears in the garden.
Possible Responses: "motorcycles backfiring," "radios whining," and "the burble of loudspeakers"

 Use **Unit Seven Resource Book,** p. 63, for additional support.

Freedom to Breathe

Aleksandr Solzhenitsyn

Translated by Michael Glenny

Apple Tree (1904), Kasimir Malevich. Oil on canvas. Russian State Museum, St. Petersburg, Russia. © SuperStock.

A shower fell in the night and now dark clouds drift across the sky, occasionally sprinkling a fine film of rain.

A I stand under an apple tree in blossom and I breathe. Not only the apple tree but the grass round it glistens with moisture; words cannot describe the sweet fragrance that pervades the air. I inhale as deeply as I can, and the aroma invades my whole being; I breathe with my eyes open, I breathe with my eyes closed—I cannot say which gives me the greater pleasure.

This, I believe, is the single most precious freedom that prison takes away from us: the freedom to breathe freely, as I now can. No food on earth, no wine, not even a woman's kiss is sweeter to me than this air steeped in the fragrance of flowers, of moisture and freshness.

B No matter that this is only a tiny garden, hemmed in by five-story houses like cages in a zoo. I cease to hear the motorcycles backfiring, radios whining, the burble of loudspeakers. As long as there is fresh air to breathe under an apple tree after a shower, we may survive a little longer.

LESSON RESOURCES

UNIT SEVEN RESOURCE BOOK, pp. 62–65

ASSESSMENT RESOURCES
Formal Assessment, pp. 185–186
Teacher's Guide to Assessment and Portfolio Use
Test Generator

INTEGRATED TECHNOLOGY
Visit our Web site: classzone.com

ADDITIONAL RESOURCES
Lesson Planning Guide, pp. 163–164
Teacher's Sourcebook for Language Development

Connect to the Literature

1. **What Do You Think?** What are your impressions of the speaker?

Think Critically

2. **ACTIVE READING: RECOGNIZING SENSORY DETAILS** Review the details you recorded in your  READER'S NOTEBOOK. Which sensory detail was most vivid for you? What sense or senses did it appeal to?

3. Why do you think the speaker believes that the most precious freedom is "the freedom to breathe freely"?

   THINK ABOUT
   - the sensations he experiences in the garden
   - what his experiences in prison might have been like

4. What does the last paragraph add to your understanding of this prose poem?

   THINK ABOUT
   - the setting that the speaker is in
   - whom the speaker might be referring to when he says "we" in the final sentence

Extend Interpretations

5. **Connect to Life** Think again about the freedoms you discussed for the Connect to Your Life activity on page 1261. Now that you've read the selection, have you changed your ideas about freedoms you take for granted?

LITERARY ANALYSIS: DESCRIPTION

Description is the process by which a writer creates in words a picture of a scene, an event, or a character. Good descriptive writing is rich in **sensory details,** or words and phrases that appeal to the reader's senses—sight, hearing, smell, taste, touch. Consider, for example, the phrase "glistens with moisture" in this sentence:

Not only the apple tree but the grass around it glistens with moisture.

The image appeals to the senses of sight and touch.

Paired Activity With a partner, look again at the sensory details you recorded in your  READER'S NOTEBOOK. If you took out all the details that appealed to smell, hearing, taste, and touch, leaving only visual images, how would the prose poem be affected? What couldn't it communicate about freedom?

Connect to the Literature

1. **What Do You Think?** Answers will vary. Some students may state that the speaker lives for the present moment, drinking in a simple pleasure and enjoying it to the fullest.

Think Critically

2. Answers will vary. Some students may mention "the sweet fragrance that pervades the air," a detail that appeals to the sense of smell.
3. Possible Response: The most precious freedom is the most basic: merely the freedom to breathe deeply in a tiny garden. The speaker likely was confined in a dimly lit place with stale air. No wonder he relishes filling his lungs with fresh air, a simple pleasure denied to prisoners.
4. Answers will vary. Some students may state that the last paragraph suggests that the speaker's simple pleasure is available to anyone, even those in crowded cities. The pronoun "we" might refer to others who are struggling to rebuild their lives after a terrible ordeal.

Extend Interpretations

5. **Connect to Life** Answers will vary. Some students may state that all freedoms are precious and worthy of deep appreciation.

Literary Analysis

Paired Activity Possible Responses: If the speaker used only visual images, he could neither re-create city noises—"the motorcycles backfiring, radios whining, the burble of loudspeakers"—nor convey his intense physical pleasure in the act of breathing deeply.

 Use **Unit Seven Resource Book,** p. 64, for more practice.

Writing Option

Sensory Description To get students started on this assignment, tell them to close their eyes and bring the scene to mind, imagining it with all their senses. Then have them jot down notes about the setting.

Activities & Explorations

1. **Oral Interpretation** Have students explain why they chose to emphasize certain words and phrases when reading aloud the prose poem.
2. **Artistic Reflection** Invite students to compare the visual images in their artworks with details in the prose poem. Students may state that it is more challenging in the artwork to convey the speaker's intense physical pleasure.

Inquiry & Research

Writers in Communist Russia In addition to encyclopedia articles, you might suggest that students read relevant chapters in biographies and world history textbooks.

Writing Option

Sensory Description Think about a simple pleasure you enjoy—for example, taking a walk at sunset near a pond or lake. Then write a few paragraphs to describe this pleasure, using vivid sensory details.

Writing Handbook
See page R27: Description.

Activities & Explorations

1. Oral Interpretation Prepare an oral reading of this prose poem. Use the tone, pitch, and volume of your voice to convey the speaker's sense of delight in the garden. Choose appropriate background music to enhance the mood you wish to convey. ~ **PERFORMING**

2. Artistic Reflection Create a drawing, a painting, or some other artwork to express the ideas in "Freedom to Breathe." What is more challenging to convey in the artwork than in the prose poem? ~ **ART**

Inquiry & Research

Writers in Communist Russia
Do research to find out more about conditions for writers in the Soviet Union under the totalitarian regimes of Joseph Stalin and his successors, especially Nikita Khrushchev. Share your findings in an oral report to the class.

Points of Comparison

Paired Activity With a partner, review "Freedom to Breathe," using the topics in your comparison-and-contrast chart to help you analyze the prose poem. Fill in the spaces pertaining to this selection.

	"Freedom to Breathe"	"The Prison Cell"
Where is the speaker?	*in a tiny garden in a city*	
How has imprisonment affected the speaker?		
What is the speaker's message about freedom?		
How strong is the speaker's spirit?		
Evidence of spiritual strength or weakness		

The speaker in Solzhenitsyn's prose poem—a former prisoner—is enjoying and reflecting on a freedom that was denied him in prison. In Mahmud Darwish's poem "The Prison Cell," the speaker is a prisoner struggling to cope with the conditions he is experiencing while behind bars.

Mahmud Darwish
1942–

Literary Reputation Mahmud Darwish is widely regarded as an important Arabic poet. The author of more than two dozen books, he has gained a reputation as a major voice of the Palestinian resistance to Israeli occupation in the Middle East. One reviewer has said: "Mahmud Darwish is a great poet. . . . Anyone unaware of that displays not only his ignorance of Arabic culture but also his ignorance of universal culture."

From Palestine to Exile Darwish knows firsthand the tragedy of life in a war zone. He was born in Barweh, a village in Palestine. It was raided by the Israelis when Darwish was six years old. He and his family narrowly escaped death and fled to Beirut, Lebanon. When they returned a year later, the village no longer existed. Darwish never forgot this experience. As a young man, he joined the Palestinian resistance movement, suffering arrest and imprisonment for his political activities. He left Palestine in 1971, coming home in 1996 after 25 years in exile.

His Poetry Darwish's poems are intense, dramatic, and realistic; many are controversial. Some of his poems are lyrical and have been set to music. Darwish's poetry is known throughout the Arab world and, in translation, by a larger audience.

Build Background

In the poem you are about to read, you will find details that reveal some of the conditions of the speaker's imprisonment. You will also find details that reveal how the speaker transforms these conditions through the force of his imagination. Part of the poem includes the speaker's dialogue with a prison guard. The lines of dialogue are preceded by a dash.

5-Minute Warm-Up

Daily Language SkillBuilder

Have students **proofread** the display sentences on page 1095n and write them correctly.

Reading and Analyzing

Reading Skills and Strategies
IDENTIFYING CONTRAST

A Tell students that writers sometimes use contrast, setting one element in a literary work in opposition to another. For example, in this poem the imaginative speaker and his down-to-earth prison guard are contrasted. Have students explain the contrast in lines 9 and 10.

Possible Response: The prison cell, which is narrow and constricted, contrasts with the "distant land/ Without frontiers," which is wide and expansive.

Literary Analysis IRONY

B Remind students that irony involves a contrast between expectation and reality. Then ask what is ironic about the end of this poem.

Possible Response: The prison guard—not the prisoner—feels a loss of freedom.

The Prison Cell

Mahmud Darwish

Translated by Ben Bennani

It is possible . . .
It is possible at least sometimes . . .
It is possible especially now
To ride a horse
Inside a prison cell
1 And run away . . .

It is possible for prison walls
To disappear,
For the cell to become a distant land
A Without frontiers:

2 —What did you do with the walls?
—I gave them back to the rocks.
—And what did you do with the ceiling?
—I turned it into a saddle.
—And your chain?
—I turned it into a pencil.

The prison guard got angry.
He put an end to the dialogue.
He said he didn't care for poetry,
And bolted the door of my cell.

He came back to see me
In the morning;
He shouted at me:

Wall mural with a forest and man behind bars. Copyright © 1980 Cuchi White/Corbis.

—Where did all this water come from?
—I brought it from the Nile.
—And the trees?
—From the orchards of Damascus.
—And the music?
—From my heartbeat.

The prison guard got mad;
He put an end to my dialogue.
He said he didn't like my poetry,
And bolted the door of my cell.

But he returned in the evening:

—Where did this moon come from?
—From the nights of Baghdad.
—And the wine?
—From the vineyards of Algiers.
—And this freedom?
—From the chain you tied me with last night.

B The prison guard grew so sad . . .
He begged me to give him back
His freedom.

27 Damascus: the capital of Syria (known for its apricot and nut orchards and its olive groves).

36 Baghdad (băg′dăd): the capital of Iraq (presented as a romantic setting in many literary works).

38 Algiers: the capital of Algeria (a major exporter of wine).

MINI LESSON Speaking and Listening

CHORAL READING

Prepare Have students prepare a choral reading of "The Prison Cell." Have students work in one of three groups, with one group preparing the speaker's statements and narrative; another, the guard's questions; and a third, the speaker's replies. As students rehearse their dramatic readings, they should discuss the qualities of the speaker (bold and imaginative) and the guard (curious, angry at first and then sad) and how those qualities will affect their choice of verbal and nonverbal performance techniques (tone, volume, gestures, and so on). Students also might choose appropriate background music or sound effects to accompany the reading.

Present Have the groups perform their choral reading. After the reading, ask students in the audience to evaluate how the performance enhanced their understanding and appreciation of "The Prison Cell."

This activity is particularly well suited for longer blocks of class time.

Customizing Instruction

Less Proficient Readers

Tell students that this poem falls into four parts: lines 1–10—the speaker's statements that seemingly impossible events can occur inside a prison cell; lines 11–20—the speaker's first dialogue with the guard; lines 21–33—the speaker's second dialogue with the guard; lines 34–43—the speaker's third dialogue with the guard. In each of these dialogues, the guard asks questions, and the speaker answers them. Tell students to notice that the guard's reaction after the third dialogue differs from his reaction after the first two.

1 To get students started, tell them the speaker longs to be free from his prison cell. He imagines the ultimate escape: riding a horse inside the cell as the walls vanish and the cell itself becomes a faraway land with no borders.

2 Point out that the walls of the prison are made of stones, which are hewn from rocks.

English Learners

Explain the meaning of the following words:

- *distant* (line 9) means "far off"
- *frontiers* (line 10) means "borders"
- *bolted* (line 20) means "locked"
- *orchards* (line 27) means "pieces of land where fruit trees are grown"
- *vineyards* (line 38) means "pieces of land where grapevines are grown"

Advanced Learners

Ask students to find a copy of the poem "To Althea from Prison" by the Cavalier poet Richard Lovelace (1618–1658). This poem contains the famous lines "Stone walls do not a prison make,/ Nor iron bars a cage." Then ask students to compare the speakers in the two poems.

Possible Responses: Both speakers view freedom as a spiritual, not a physical, condition that even those in prison can enjoy. To both speakers, freedom of soul is the ultimate freedom.

COMPARING LITERATURE ACROSS CULTURES 1267

Connect to the Literature

1. What Do You Think?
Thoughts or questions will vary. Some students may wonder why the guard asks the prisoner to give him back his freedom.

Comprehension Check

- The walls disappear, and the chain turns into a pencil.
- his lost freedom

Think Critically

2. Possible Response: The relationship between the guard and the prisoner develops until they figuratively change places. At first, the guard gets angry at the prisoner, scoffing at his poetry. Gradually, though, the guard is drawn into the prisoner's world of the imagination. The guard realizes that the prisoner has something priceless: a creative imagination that sets him free.
3. Responses will vary. Some students may feel that the speaker copes well with prison conditions. These students may state that by letting his imagination soar, the prisoner retreats to an inner world, a refuge from his harsh surroundings. Other students may feel that the speaker fails to cope successfully with prison life. These students may state that the prisoner lives in denial of reality—a type of madness.
4. Possible Responses: The speaker views freedom as a spiritual, not a physical, state. A strong imagination can transform harsh realities. If the mind is open and the imagination is active, even a prisoner can taste freedom.

Extend Interpretations

5. **Connect to Life** Responses will vary. Some students may agree with Einstein's statement. They may state that imagination, or the ability to wonder and see things in new ways, is the catalyst that sparks research and new knowledge. Other students may disagree with Einstein's statement. They may state that knowledge is more important than imagination. These students may point out that for centuries people imagined the earth to be the center of the universe. An increase in knowledge, however, led to an accurate picture of the solar system.

Connect to the Literature

1. **What Do You Think?** What were your thoughts or questions after reading this poem?

Comprehension Check

- Name two ways in which the speaker transforms the prison cell.
- What does the guard seek at the end of the poem?

Think Critically

2. How would you describe the relationship between the speaker and the guard?

- how the guard talks to and behaves toward the speaker
- how you interpret what the guard begs of the speaker

3. In your opinion, how well does the speaker cope with prison conditions?
4. How would you describe the speaker's view of freedom?

Extend Interpretations

5. **Connect to Life** The speaker of this poem is endowed with a vivid imagination. The famous scientist Albert Einstein once stated, "Imagination is more important than knowledge." Do you agree or disagree with Einstein's statement? Support your opinion with examples from your experience.

Points of Comparison

Paired Activity: Now that you have read and studied these two poems, work with a partner to fill in the spaces for "The Prison Cell." Use your chart to help you plan the comparison and contrast essay on page 1269.

	"Freedom to Breathe"	"The Prison Cell"
Where is the speaker?	*in a tiny garden in a city*	*inside a prison cell*
How has imprisonment affected the speaker?		
What is the speaker's message about freedom?		
How strong is the speaker's spirit?		
Evidence of spiritual strength or weakness		

To assess skills and concepts taught in this selection, use **Formal Assessment Book,** pp. 185–186.

Writing About Literature

PART 1 Reading the Prompt

In writing assessments, you may be asked to compare and contrast works of literature that treat a similar subject. You are now going to practice writing an essay that requires this type of focus.

Writing Prompt

Being imprisoned is an ordeal that tests the strength of the human spirit. Unfortunately, this ordeal was all too common in the 20th century. Think about Solzhenitsyn's "Freedom to Breathe" and Darwish's "The Prison Cell." Compare and contrast the speakers and their messages about freedom. Which speaker do you think is stronger in spirit? Support your analysis with details from the two selections. 1 2 3

STRATEGIES IN ACTION

1. I have to **compare and contrast** the speakers and also their messages about freedom.
2. I must **judge** which speaker is stronger in spirit.
3. I need to include **details** from the selections to support my analysis.

PART 2 Planning a Comparison-and-Contrast Essay

- Review the comparison-and-contrast chart that you completed for the Points of Comparison features in this lesson.
- Using your chart, find examples to use as evidence for the points you develop in your essay. If necessary, review the selections again to identify more examples.
- Create an outline to organize your main points.

PART 3 Drafting Your Essay

Introduction Introduce the topic—the response to being imprisoned—and mention that it was an important theme for many writers in the 20th century. Then explain that you will be comparing two selections in terms of the speakers' response to imprisonment.

Body You might use the topics in your comparison-and-contrast chart as a guide to the key points of your comparison. In one paragraph, for example, you might compare and contrast the effect of imprisonment on each speaker. Within each paragraph you write, give specific details to back up your points.

Conclusion Wrap up your essay with a restatement of your thesis, or main idea, and a brief summary of your main points.

Revision Check your use of transitional words and phrases to connect your ideas within and between paragraphs. Words such as *likewise, both,* and *in the same way* signal similarities. *On the other hand, instead, nevertheless,* and *however* signal differences.

TEST PRACTICE

PART 1 Reading the Prompt
Model the process of reading a prompt:

- Read through the prompt from beginning to end.
- List the key words of the assignment on the board ("Compare and contrast," "analysis," "details").
- Use **Strategies in Action** to show students how to analyze the assignment and divide it into separate tasks.

PART 2 Planning a Comparison-and-Contrast Essay
Model the process of planning a comparison-and-contrast essay:

- Read through the points listed on the chart, circling the similarities and underlining the differences.
- Star the most important similarity or difference.
- List in order of ascending importance the points you plan to develop.

PART 3 Drafting Your Essay

Introduction Tell students that the opening paragraph of an essay should not only introduce the topic but also stir interest. Students might try out different ways of beginning their essays—for example, by opening with a question, a fact, a quotation, or an opinion about freedom or imprisonment.

Body Tell students to use feature-by-feature order, comparing and contrasting one characteristic at a time.

Conclusion Tell students that writing a conclusion is somewhat like saying goodbye. A conclusion usually restates the main idea, reviews supporting points, and then leaves the reader with an interesting idea.

Revision In reviewing their drafts, students should try to strengthen the organization and clarify the phrasing.

Use **Unit Seven Resource Book,** p. 65, for additional support.

Assessment **Standardized Test Practice**

RESPONDING TO A WRITING PROMPT

Read aloud the writing prompt at the top of this page. Discuss the **Strategies in Action** by asking students to identify the words in the prompt that tell them what to do. Suggest that they mark up their comparison-and-contrast charts, identifying points to include in their essays. When students have finished drafting their essays, have them work with a partner to see if they have accomplished the tips given in **Part 3 Drafting Your Essay.**

Author Study

Objectives

- appreciate the work of a classic African writer
- understand the connection between an author's works and his philosophies and beliefs
- learn about the history and culture of Nigeria

Presenting the Author

The **Author Study** offers students the opportunity to concentrate on the works of Chinua Achebe, one of Africa's greatest writers. Students also will learn about Achebe's life and the events in African history that helped shape his works.

READING FOR INFORMATION

Reading Skills and Strategies

MONITORING READING STRATEGIES

Encourage students to monitor and modify their reading strategies as they read the **Life and Times** section. For example, students might summarize information in the running text and pay attention to the sequence of events in the time line.

The African Oral Tradition

A When Achebe was growing up in Ogidi, storytelling was used as a means to entertain young children. Achebe's mother, Janet, and his older sister, Zinobia Uzoma, told stories that stirred young Achebe's imagination. His sister also enacted the characters in the stories she told. Listening to his mother and his sister, Achebe absorbed the myths, legends, and folk tales that were part of the Ibo oral tradition.

AUTHOR STUDY

Chinua Achebe

OVERVIEW

Africa's Premier Storyteller

One of the 20th century's most honored writers, Nigeria's Chinua Achebe (chĭn′o͞o-ä ä-chā′bā) *helped pioneer native African literature written in English. His masterpiece* Things Fall Apart, *the first major novel written in English by a native African, has become a world classic. In his works, Achebe often depicts the clash of cultures and its lingering effects in his native land. His portrayal of Africa—haunting and lyrical—evokes a way of life lost forever.*

1930–

"Chinua Achebe creates . . . a coherent picture of coherence being lost, of the tragic consequences of the African-European collision."

—Robert McDowell

STUDENT OF LITERATURE Chinua Achebe was born in Ogidi, a village in Nigeria, which at the time was a colony of Great Britain. His original name was Albert Chinualumogu Achebe, the name "Albert" reflecting the cultural influence of British rule. Achebe's earliest experience with literature came from his mother, who told him folk tales from the African oral tradition. His father, who had become a Christian as a young man, taught at Ogidi's mission school, which Achebe attended as a young boy. Later, Achebe studied English A

HIS LIFE

1930 **Is born in Ogidi, an Ibo village in southeastern Nigeria**

1948 **Starts attending University College in Ibadan, Nigeria**

1930 1935 1940 1945

HIS TIMES

1929 **U.S. stock market crashes, marking the start of a worldwide economic depression.**

1939 **World War II begins when Germany invades Poland.**

1945 **World War II ends; United Nations is established.**

1948 **Mohandas Gandhi is killed by an extremist in India.**

TIME MANAGEMENT Teaching Options

If you want to present this lesson as an author study, use all the materials listed under Overview on page 1270 in the pupil edition.

If you want to teach only one of the short stories, use "Preparing to Read" on page 1274 or page 1286 and the accompanying selection:

- "Dead Men's Path," pp. 1275–1277
- "Civil Peace," pp. 1287–1290

literature at University College in Ibadan, Nigeria (where he dropped "Albert" and shortened his African name). At that time, stories about Africa were written mainly by Europeans, not by native Africans. Achebe realized the need for a new African literature. "Our story," he said, "could not be told for us by anyone else."

Nigeria's Struggle for Independence

Nigeria, Africa's most populous nation, is home to many ethnic groups, each with its own language and customs. Achebe's background is Ibo (ē'bō), or Igbo. The Ibo come from southeastern Nigeria, and their language was Achebe's first tongue. By the time Achebe was eight, however, he had begun to study English, the language introduced with British colonial rule in the 19th century. **B** Nigeria's relationship with Britain was stormy from the start, with many groups, including the Ibo, rebelling from time to time. After World War II, the pressure for self-rule grew even stronger. Finally, in 1960, Nigeria gained its independence. It became a republic three years later.

Chinua Achebe at home near Lagos in 1966

LITERARY Contributions

Fiction Achebe is best known for novels and short stories that explore the cultural conflicts of Africa, past and present. His novels and short story collections include

- ***Things Fall Apart***
- ***No Longer at Ease***
- ***The Sacrificial Egg and Other Stories***
- ***Arrow of God***
- ***A Man of the People***
- ***Girls at War and Other Stories***
- ***Anthills of the Savannah***

Poetry & Nonfiction Achebe has also published poetry volumes, essay collections, and other nonfiction works, most of which focus on African life and culture. Among them are

- ***Beware, Soul Brother and Other Poems***
- ***Christmas in Biafra and Other Poems***
- ***Morning Yet on Creation Day***
- ***The Trouble with Nigeria***
- ***Hopes and Impediments: Selected Essays, 1965–1987***
- ***Another Africa***
- ***Conversations with Chinua Achebe***
- ***Home and Exile***

1954 Joins production staff of the Nigerian Broadcasting Corporation in Lagos

1958 Publishes *Things Fall Apart*, his first novel

1962 Becomes editor of the Heinemann African Writers Series

1964 Publishes *Arrow of God*, his third novel

1967 Travels in Africa, Europe, and the United States to win support for the Biafran cause

1972 Publishes *Girls at War and Other Stories*, which includes "Dead Men's Path" and "Civil Peace"

1950 1955 1960 1965 1970

1957 Ghana becomes the first West African nation to achieve independence.

1960 Nigeria achieves independence from Great Britain.

1964 In the United States, a landmark civil rights law bans discrimination.

WE WANT BLACK POWER

1967 Civil War begins after a region in eastern Nigeria secedes as Biafra; the Nigerian poet Christopher Okigbo is killed.

1973 Rising oil prices around the world begin to bring newfound wealth to Nigeria.

Kwame Nkrumah, Ghana's first prime minister

Europeans in Nigeria

B The Portuguese were the first Europeans to arrive in what is now Nigeria, where they developed a slave trade in the late 1400s. By 1861, the area had become a British colony. At that time, European missionaries began to arrive, bringing Christianity to Nigeria. In 1914, the British joined the northern and southern regions of the country, forming the Colony and Protectorate of Nigeria. On October 1, 1960, Great Britain granted Nigeria its independence.

MINI LESSON Using the Time Line

Have students study the time line on pages 1270–1272 and then answer questions such as the following:

- Was Achebe born before or after World War II? *(before)*
- How old was Achebe when he completed his first novel, *Things Fall Apart*? *(28)*
- Did Achebe write *Home and Exile* before or after Nigeria gained its independence? *(after)*
- Which event happened first—Mohandas Gandhi's death or Achebe's publication of *Arrow of God*? *(Mohandas Gandhi's death)*

Achebe's Influence

A Known as "the father of the modern African novel," Achebe used his writing to attack racist portrayals and stereotypes of Africans. He intended his works to teach both Europeans and Africans that European colonialism in Africa was based on a false assumption: namely, that Africa was a backward and barbaric land. To challenge this assumption, Achebe described the richness of traditional African life, detailing its history, religion, and civilization. Achebe views the African writer as a teacher whose mission is to inform other Africans about their culture and traditions. As writer, editor, and publisher, he has influenced scores of younger writers.

NOVELIST FOR A NEW AFRICA Inspired by his love of language, Achebe sought to create a new African literature—one written in English by native Africans. He began writing stories and essays for his college newspaper. After graduating, he worked as a producer for the new Nigerian Broadcasting Corporation in Lagos, then Nigeria's capital. He wrote fiction in his spare time. In 1958, he published *Things Fall Apart,* a novel about a heroic Ibo leader who defies colonial rule. The novel gradually earned both critical and popular acclaim around the world.

CRUSADER FOR A LOST CAUSE Ever since Nigeria had won its independence, ethnic tensions had simmered in the new nation. In 1967, the mostly Ibo region in the east seceded from Nigeria and formed the independent republic of Biafra. A civil war erupted, involving widespread destruction and loss of life. Achebe traveled the world, trying to raise funds for the Biafran cause. After three years of bloodshed and famine, the Ibo were defeated, and the Biafran region again became part of Nigeria.

LITERARY PURSUITS After the civil war, Achebe published poetry, stories, and essays; edited *Okike,* a magazine of African literature; and taught as a visiting professor at two New England universities. In 1976, he returned home to teach literature at the University of Nigeria. Five years later, he formed the Association of Nigerian Authors and served as its first president. A

POLITICAL LIFE AND EXILE In the early 1980s, Achebe decided to take part in Nigerian politics. In 1983, he served as deputy national chairman of the People's Redemption Party (PRP). In 1985, however, a military ruler named Ibrahim Babangida (ē-brä′hēm bä-bän′gē-dä) came to power, banning many political parties, including the PRP.

In 1990, Achebe was seriously injured in a suspicious automobile accident in Nigeria, in which a military vehicle was said to have been involved. Concerned for his safety, Achebe

1975 **Begins one-year visiting professorship at the University of Connecticut**

1976 **Begins serving as professor of literature at the University of Nigeria in Nsukka**

1981 **Founds the Association of Nigerian Authors and is elected its first president**

1990 **After recuperating from a serious car accident, begins teaching at Bard College in upstate New York**

2000 **Publishes his nonfiction work *Home and Exile***

1975 1980 1985 1990 1995 2000

1989 **The Berlin Wall, which has divided East Berlin from West Berlin, comes down.**

1991 **The city of Abuja becomes Nigeria's capital.**

1994 **In South Africa's first all-race elections, Nelson Mandela is elected to lead the nation.**

decided to leave his native land. For six months he recuperated in Great Britain. He then came to the United States to teach at Bard College, in upstate New York.

Achebe has published more than 20 works—including novels, children's books, short story collections, and poetry volumes—in English, his second language. He calls language "mankind's greatest blessing," and the storyteller its "high priest." His mission as a storyteller, he says, is to enable his readers to see the world through a child's eyes. "The child . . . is new in the world, and everything is possible to him. The imagination hasn't been dulled by use and experience. Therefore, when you [write for] the adult, what you do is you give him back some of that energy and optimism of the child, that ability to be open and to expect anything."

A Literary Masterpiece: *Things Fall Apart*

B

Things Fall Apart has been called "the archetypal African novel." Achebe took the title from the opening lines of William Butler Yeats's poem "The Second Coming":

> **Turning and turning in the widening gyre**
> **The falcon cannot hear the falconer;**
> **Things fall apart; the center cannot hold;**
> **Mere anarchy is loosed upon the world,**

In this novel, Achebe describes what happens when traditional and colonial cultures collide. The novel begins with a depiction of traditional life among the Ibo people at the end of the 19th century and goes on to sketch the beginnings of European colonization and the conflicts it triggers. The main character is Okonkwo, a tribal leader. Brave, honest, and hard-working, he represents the cherished values of his culture. Clinging to his traditions, he refuses to adapt to European ways. For this hero, things do indeed fall apart, and his people's way of life is changed forever.

Ibo headdress made of carved and painted wood

Things Fall Apart

B Achebe said that this work, widely acclaimed as a world classic, was "an act of atonement with my past, the ritual return and homage of a prodigal son." Working within the conventions of the realistic novel, Achebe vividly portrayed African life in the midst of sea changes. The protagonist of the novel kills himself when he realizes that his clan will not take his side against the colonial settlers. With his death, the old order passes, and Nigeria's traditional way of life vanishes forever.

Objectives

- understand and appreciate a **short story (Literary Analysis)**
- identify the causes and effects of **cultural conflict (Literary Analysis)**
- **understand** the **motivations** of characters in conflict **(Active Reading)**

Summary

Michael Obi is thrilled at his appointment as headmaster of a village school in Nigeria. Proud, ambitious, and excited by new ideas, he wants to introduce modern reforms to the backward school. He and his wife work hard to improve the school, setting high standards and beautifying the grounds. One day, Michael notices an old village woman hobbling across the school grounds and discovers a path connecting the village and its ancestral burial grounds. He closes the path, using barbed wire to fence off the entrance and the exit to the school grounds. A village priest asks him to re-open the path, telling him that newborns use it to enter the village. Scoffing at the priest's traditional beliefs, Michael refuses to tear down the fence. A few days later, a village woman dies in childbirth. The villagers then retaliate by night, removing the fence and ruining the school grounds. As a result, a visiting supervisor writes a nasty report about Michael Obi's performance as headmaster.

 Use **Unit Seven Resource Book,** p. 66, for additional support.

Thematic Link

This short story, set in a village in colonial Nigeria, describes a **conflict** between a traditional culture and a modern one.

 Use **Unit Seven Resource Book,** p. 69, for practice with Words to Know.

5-Minute Warm-Up

Daily Language SkillBuilder

Have students **proofread** the display sentences on page 1095n and write them correctly.

PREPARING to *Read*

DEAD MEN'S PATH

Chinua Achebe

Build Background

In the 19th century, when the British began to colonize Nigeria, most of the Ibo people followed a traditional religion. They worshiped a supreme creator (called Chukwu), an earth goddess, and several lesser divinities. According to Ibo tradition, dead ancestors had the power to guard the living. These traditional beliefs were scorned by the British colonizers. Most village schools were run by Christian missionaries who taught religion along with the three R's. Thus, many Ibo villagers came to accept Christianity as a means to a modern education and a successful life. The story you are about to read takes place in an Ibo village in 1949, when Nigeria was still a British colony. The main character is the principal of a village school. He does not respect the traditional beliefs of the villagers.

Connect to Your Life

In the name of progress, historic buildings may be torn down to make room for parking lots or shopping malls. Do you think your community should preserve its landmarks or replace them to keep pace with modern life? Discuss these questions with a small group of classmates.

Focus Your Reading

LITERARY ANALYSIS: CULTURAL CONFLICT

Cultural conflict is a struggle that arises between groups of people because of their opposing values, beliefs, or customs. In "Dead Men's Path," the headmaster of a village school believes in modern methods of education. This belief triggers a conflict with the villagers.

ACTIVE READING: UNDERSTANDING MOTIVATIONS

A character's **motivations** are the reasons why he or she acts, feels, or thinks in a certain way. Often a reader must make inferences—logical guesses or conclusions based on the evidence found in a story—to determine those reasons.

READER'S NOTEBOOK Make a chart like the one shown below for Michael Obi, the main character in the story. Then make a similar chart for the village priest. As you read, list several actions of each character, the motivations you infer, and the clues you use to make your inferences.

Michael Obi		
Actions	**Motivations**	**Clues**
accepts the position of headmaster with enthusiasm	*wants to show older teachers that he can run a school better than they can*	*"outspoken in his condemnation of the narrow views of these older and often less-educated ones" (page 1275)*

WORDS TO KNOW **Vocabulary Preview**

denigration	pivotal	zeal
eradicate	skeptical	

LESSON RESOURCES

UNIT SEVEN RESOURCE BOOK, pp. 66–70

ASSESSMENT RESOURCES
Formal Assessment, pp. 187–188
Teacher's Guide to Assessment and Portfolio Use
Test Generator

INTEGRATED TECHNOLOGY
NetActivities
Visit our Web site: classzone.com

ADDITIONAL RESOURCES
Lesson Planning Guide, pp. 165–166
Teacher's Sourcebook for Language Development

Dead Men's Path

Chinua Achebe

Michael Obi's hopes were fulfilled much earlier than he had expected. He was appointed headmaster of Ndume[1] Central School in January 1949. It had always been an unprogressive school, so the Mission authorities decided to send a young and energetic man to run it. Obi accepted this responsibility with enthusiasm. He 1 had many wonderful ideas and this was an opportunity to put them into practice. He had had sound secondary school education which designated him a "pivotal teacher" in the official records and set him apart from the other headmasters in the mission field. He was outspoken in his condemnation of the narrow views of these older and often less-educated ones.

"We shall make a good job of it, shan't we?" he asked his young wife when they first heard the joyful news of his promotion.

"We shall do our best," she replied. "We shall have such beautiful gardens and everything will be just *modern* and delightful . . ." In their two years of married life she had become completely infected by his passion for "modern methods" and his denigration of "these old and superannuated[2] people in the teaching field who would be better employed as traders in the Onitsha market."[3] She began to see herself already as the admired wife of the young headmaster, the queen of the school.

The wives of the other teachers would envy her position. She would set the fashion in everything . . . Then, suddenly, it occurred to her that there might not be other wives. Wavering between hope and fear, she asked her husband, looking anxiously at him.

"All our colleagues are young and unmarried," he said with enthusiasm which for once she did 2 not share. "Which is a good thing," he continued.

"Why?"

"Why? They will give all their time and energy to the school."

Nancy was downcast. For a few minutes she 3 became skeptical about the new school; but it was only for a few minutes. Her little personal misfortune could 4 not blind her to her husband's happy prospects. She looked 5 at him as he sat folded up in a chair. He was stoop-shouldered and looked frail. But he 6 sometimes surprised people with sudden bursts of physical energy. In his present posture, however,

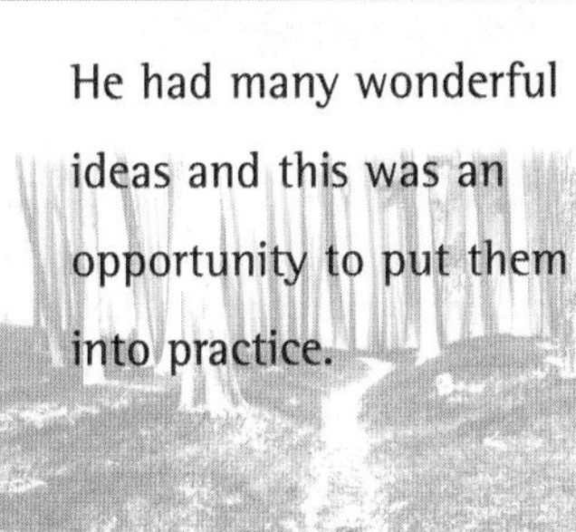

1. Ndume (ən-do͞o'mā).
2. superannuated: ready for retirement.
3. Onitsha market: The city of Onitsha, in eastern Nigeria, is known for its huge market, where many kinds of items are sold or traded.

WORDS TO KNOW

pivotal (pĭv'ə-tl) *adj.* very important
denigration (dĕn'ĭ-grā'shən) *n.* the act of speaking ill of someone; defamation
skeptical (skĕp'tĭ-kəl) *adj.* doubtful

Customizing Instruction

Less Proficient Readers

1 Have volunteers read aloud the first two paragraphs of this story and then help them form impressions of Michael Obi. Make sure that students realize that he is an African employed by Christian missionaries. He is bright, educated, enthusiastic, and eager to succeed as principal of a backward school. He believes in modern methods of education and has little respect for older teachers.

2 Make sure students understand what motivates Michael's wife. She craves admiration from the other wives whose husbands work at the school. That is why she is disappointed to learn that none of the teachers is unmarried.

English Learners

Help students use context clues to determine the meaning of the following words:

3 *downcast* means "sad"

4 *misfortune* means "bad luck"

5 *prospects* means "the likely chance of succeeding"

6 *frail* means "weak"

Advanced Learners

Ask students to predict whether Michael Obi will be successful as headmaster at Ndume Central School.

Possible Responses: Yes, because he is bright, energetic, and determined to do a good job; no, because he is rigid in his thinking and seems unwilling to compromise.

TIME MANAGEMENT

If your schedule requires that you cover the lesson objectives in a shorter time, use . . .

- Preparing to Read, p. 1274
- Thinking Through the Literature, p. 1278
- Vocabulary in Action, p. 1279

If you want to take advantage of longer blocks of class time, use . . .

- TE Teaching Options: Vocabulary Strategy, p. 1276
- Choices & Challenges, p. 1279
- *From* An Interview with Chinau Achebe, pp. 1280–1283
- Keeper of the Vigil, pp. 1284–1285

Literary Analysis FORESHADOWING

A Tell students that writers sometimes provide clues about how a story will turn out. After students have read this story, ask them how this passage foreshadows the ending.

Possible Response: The bitter conflict over the school's former attempt to close the footpath prepares the reader for the villagers' retaliation when Michael Obi actually does close it.

Literary Analysis CULTURAL CONFLICT

B Tell students that the main conflict in this story involves a clash of cultures. Then ask students to identify values, beliefs, or customs that generate this conflict.

Possible Responses: The old priest represents a traditional culture that values its tribal customs; Michael Obi, on the other hand, represents a modern culture that values efficiency and ridicules unscientific ways.

Use **Unit Seven Resource Book,** p. 68, for more practice.

Active Reading
UNDERSTANDING MOTIVATIONS

C Have students read this passage closely. Then ask them why Michael Obi is sarcastic to the old priest.

Possible Response: Michael Obi values only modern ideas of education, so he mocks the old priest's traditional beliefs.

Use **Unit Seven Resource Book,** p. 67, for more practice.

Follow (2006), Lou Wall. Photo © Lou Wall/Corbis.

all his bodily strength seemed to have retired behind his deep-set eyes, giving them an extraor-
1 dinary power of penetration. He was only twenty-six, but looked thirty or more. On the whole, he was not unhandsome.

"A penny for your thoughts, Mike," said Nancy after a while, imitating the woman's magazine she read.

"I was thinking what a grand opportunity we've got at last to show these people how a school should be run." Ndume School was backward in every sense of the word. Mr. Obi put his whole life into the work, and his wife hers too. He had two aims. A high standard of teaching
was insisted upon, and the school com- 2
pound was to be turned into a place of beauty. Nancy's dream-gardens came to life with the coming of the rains, and blossomed. Beautiful hibiscus and allamanda[4] hedges in brilliant red and yellow marked out the carefully tended school compound from the rank[5] neighborhood bushes.

One evening as Obi was admiring his
work he was scandalized to see an old 3
woman from the village hobble right across the compound, through a marigold flower-bed and the hedges. On going up there he found faint signs of an almost disused path from the village across the school compound to the bush on the other side.

"It amazes me," said Obi to one of his teachers who had been three years in the school, "that you people allowed the villagers to make use of this footpath. It is simply incredible." He shook his head.

"The path," said the teacher apologetically, "appears to be very important to them. Although it is hardly used, it connects the village shrine with their place of burial."

"And what has that got to do with the
school?" asked the headmaster. A

"Well, I don't know," replied the other with a shrug of the shoulders. "But I remember there was a big row[6] some time ago when we attempted to close it."

"That was some time ago. But it will not be used now," said Obi as he walked away. "What will the Government Education Officer think of

4. **hibiscus and allamanda:** tropical shrubs with large, showy flowers.
5. **rank:** growing wildly or excessively.
6. **row** (rou): quarrel.

MINI LESSON Vocabulary Strategy

CONTEXT CLUES Remind students that a word's context can provide clues about its meaning. Then write the following sentences on the chalkboard, and tell students to complete each sentence with the most appropriate Word to Know.

1. The scientist worked tirelessly to ________, or wipe out, the disease. *(eradicate)*
2. Because of her ______ for helping others, she devoted herself to charitable work. *(zeal)*
3. The candidate's reputation was under attack, and this ______ may have cost him the election. *(denigration)*
4. Since the offer sounded too good to be true, I was ______ of it. *(skeptical)*
5. The game is ________ for both teams because the winner will advance to the playoffs. *(pivotal)*

Use **Unit Seven Resource Book,** p. 69, for additional support.

A lesson on using context clues appears on p. 674 of the Pupil's Edition.

this when he comes to inspect the school next week? The villagers might, for all I know, decide to use the
4 schoolroom for a pagan ritual during the inspection."

Heavy sticks were planted closely across the path at the two places where it entered and left the school premises. These were further strengthened with barbed wire.

Three days later the village priest of *Ani*[7] called on the headmaster. He was an old man and walked with a slight stoop. He carried a stout walking-stick which he usually tapped on the floor, by way of emphasis, each time he made a new point in his argument.

"I have heard," he said after the usual exchange of cordialities,[8] "that our ancestral footpath has recently been closed . . ."

"Yes," replied Mr. Obi. "We cannot allow people to make a highway of our school compound."

"Look here, my son," said the priest bringing down his walking-stick, "this path was here before you were born and before your father was born. The whole life of this village depends on it.
B Our dead relatives depart by it and our ancestors visit us by it. But most important, it is the path of children coming in to be born . . ."

Mr. Obi listened with a satisfied smile on his face.

"The whole purpose of our school," he said finally, "is to eradicate just such beliefs as that. Dead men do not require footpaths. The whole idea is just fantastic. Our duty is to teach your children to laugh at such ideas."

"What you say may be true," replied the priest, "but we follow the practices of our fathers. If you re-open the path we shall have nothing to quarrel about. What I always say is: let the hawk perch and let the eagle perch." He rose to go.

> "Our dead relatives depart by it and our ancestors visit us by it. But most important, it is the path of children coming in to be born . . ."

"I am sorry," said the young headmaster. "But the school compound cannot be a 5
thoroughfare. It is against our regulations. C
I would suggest your constructing another path, skirting our premises. We can even get our boys to help in building it. I don't suppose the ancestors will find the little detour too burdensome."

"I have no more words to say," said the old priest, already outside.

Two days later a young woman in the village died in childbed. A diviner[9] was immediately consulted and he prescribed heavy sacrifices to propitiate ancestors insulted by the fence. 6

Obi woke up next morning among the ruins of his work. The beautiful hedges were torn up not just near the path but right round the school, the flowers trampled to death and one of the school buildings pulled down . . . That day, the white Supervisor came to inspect the school and wrote a nasty report on the state of the premises but more seriously about the "tribal-war situation developing between the school and the village, arising in part from the misguided zeal of 7
the new headmaster." ❖

7. *Ani* (ä′nē): In ancient Egyptian mythology, on which some African religious beliefs are based, Ani was a recorder god associated with ceremonies for the dead.
8. **cordialities:** pleasantries.
9. **diviner:** person who uses signs and omens to predict the future.

WORDS TO KNOW

eradicate (ĭ-răd′ĭ-kāt′) *v.* to get rid of; eliminate
zeal (zēl) *n.* enthusiasm; fervor

Customizing Instruction

Less Proficient Readers

Make sure that students understand the connection between the death of the woman in childbirth and the villagers' attack on the school compound. The villagers view the woman's death as a sign that their ancestors are angry at them for allowing Michael Obi's fence to close the footpath to the burial grounds. Since the footpath is closed, no new births can come to the village. With their future survival at stake, the villagers decide to take matters into their own hands.

Then use the following questions to check students' comprehension of the story:

- What is Michael Obi's position at the Ndume School? *(headmaster, or principal)*
- What does Michael Obi do to close off the footpath? *(erects a barbed-wire fence)*
- Why does the village priest visit Michael Obi? *(to ask him to re-open the path)*
- Why does the white supervisor write a nasty report about Michael Obi? *(because the school grounds are ruined and Obi's actions have created tension in the village)*

English Learners

Explain the meaning of the following words that might be difficult for students to understand:

1 *penetration* means "seeing into something"

2 *compound* means "enclosed area"

3 *scandalized* means "shocked by a shameful act"

4 *ritual* means "religious ceremony"

5 *thoroughfare* means "street or highway"

6 *propitiate* means "to keep from being angry"

7 *misguided* means "based on error"

Advanced Learners

Ask students to speculate about how Michael Obi's professional setback might affect his marriage.

Possible Response: Michael Obi's relationship with his wife likely will be damaged severely. She was swept up by his passion for modern methods of education, which seemed like the road to success. Now that his passion has ruined his career and has destroyed her gardens, she probably will be skeptical of his ideas and may lose confidence in him.

Connect to the Literature

1. **What Do You Think?** What do you **predict** will happen to Michael Obi after the supervisor files his report?

Comprehension Check
- What does the path through the school grounds connect?
- What happens to the school grounds after Michael Obi refuses to reopen the path?

Thinking Critically

2. Do you think the villagers were justified in their actions against Michael Obi? Why or why not?

3. How would you rate Michael Obi's performance as the headmaster of the village school?

THINK ABOUT
- his aims for the school
- his enthusiasm for his work
- whether he seems to care about the students
- his attitude toward the villagers' beliefs
- the ill will he creates between the village and the school

4. **ACTIVE READING: UNDERSTANDING MOTIVATIONS** Review the character charts that you made in your READER'S NOTEBOOK. In your opinion, how do Michael Obi's motivations differ from those of the village priest?

5. How would you describe the relationship between Michael Obi and his wife, Nancy?

Extend Interpretations

6. **What If?** What do you think would have happened to the school grounds if the young village woman had not died?

7. **Connect to Life** Explain the meaning of this proverb offered by the village priest: "Let the hawk perch and let the eagle perch." Then discuss how you might apply the proverb to situations in your school or community.

LITERARY ANALYSIS: CULTURAL CONFLICT

Cultural conflict occurs when customs, attitudes, or beliefs push groups of people in opposing directions. This conflict may arise from changes within a culture, from one culture's contact with other cultures, or from a combination of both. In "Dead Men's Path," contact with British culture has pushed some Nigerians—for example, Michael Obi's wife—in new directions:

> ***In their two years of married life she had become completely infected by his passion for "modern methods" and his denigration of "these old and superannuated people in the teaching field. . . ."***

Paired Activity With a partner, look through the story for clues that help you understand the causes and effects of the cultural conflict between Michael Obi and the villagers. Then write a sentence or two to describe the conflict. Finally, discuss whether or not the conflict might be resolved and, if so, how.

Connect to the Literature

1. **What Do You Think?** Students may state that Michael Obi will be severely reprimanded or might even be replaced by the Mission authorities.

Comprehension Check
- The path connects the village shrine and the ancestral burial grounds.
- The villagers destroy the school grounds, digging up bushes, trampling flowers, and tearing down a building.

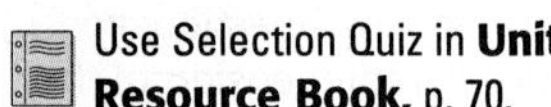
Use Selection Quiz in **Unit Seven Resource Book,** p. 70.

Think Critically

2. Possible Response: The villagers were justified because they feared that the fence threatened their survival by preventing new life.
3. Answers will vary. Most students will probably agree that while Michael Obi's enthusiasm and innovative practices might work well elsewhere, he is too insensitive and scornful of tradition to do a good job in this village. He values his accomplishments more than meeting his students' needs or building a friendly relationship with the village. Ironically, though he is convinced that his reforms will merit praise, he creates such tension in the village that he receives a nasty assessment.
4. Possible Responses: Michael Obi is motivated by ambition, self-importance, scorn for the past, and belief in modern methods of education. The priest is motivated by faith in his ancestors and his duty to protect his people's traditional way of life.
5. Possible Response: Michael Obi and his wife are well suited. Both are go-getters, who seek power and prestige.

Extend Interpretations

6. **What If?** Possible Response: The young woman's death is the catalyst that triggers the villagers' violence. But even if she had lived, tension in the village is so high that some other misfortune would have prompted the villagers to retaliate against Michael Obi. They feel threatened by his refusal to re-open the path.
7. **Connect to Life** Possible Response: The proverb means that two opposite beliefs, like two birds of prey, need not become aggressive and clash. The proverb stresses the importance of tolerance, a central theme of the story, which depicts a conflict between old ways and new—not unlike that between generations or between traditionalists and innovators. At school or in the community, groups can uphold their own views while showing respect for opposing opinions.

Literary Analysis

Paired Activity The cultural conflict in this story involves Nigerian (Ibo) traditions and modern (European-influenced) methods of education. The conflict might be resolved if each side were to respect the other's position and agree to compromise.

Use **Unit Seven Resource Book,** p. 68, for more practice.

Writing Option

Job Assessment Imagine that you are the supervisor who has just visited the village school. Write a job assessment of Michael Obi's performance as headmaster. Use your response to question 3 as a starting point.

Ndume Central School

Performance Review

Name: *Michael Obi*

Job: *Headmaster of Ndume Central School*

Starting Date: *January 1949*

Rating : ❑ excellent ❑ good ❑ fair ❑ poor

Assessment:

Suggestions for Improvement:

Activities & Explorations

1. Artistic Interpretation Draw or paint sketches depicting the school grounds before and after the destruction. ~ ART

2. Role-Playing With another student, role-play the conversation that might have taken place between the visiting supervisor and Michael Obi. ~ SPEAKING AND LISTENING

Inquiry & Research

Nigerian Culture Find out more about an aspect of Nigerian culture that interests you, such as its school system, its religions, or its literature. Share your findings in an oral report to your classmates. Use visual aids in your presentation.

Vocabulary in Action

EXERCISE: RELATED WORDS Write the letter of the word that is not related in meaning to the other words in the set.

1. (a) erase, (b) eradicate, (c) eliminate, (d) evoke
2. (a) essential, (b) unimportant, (c) pivotal, (d) crucial
3. (a) zeal, (b) enthusiasm, (c) complexity, (d) passion
4. (a) defamation, (b) denigration, (c) criticism, (d) destination
5. (a) skeptical, (b) overtired, (c) exhausted, (d) drowsy

Building Vocabulary

For an in-depth lesson on related words, see page 1196.

Writing Option

Job Assessment As students fill in Michael Obi's "report card," tell them to support their evaluations with details from the story.

Activities & Explorations

1. **Artistic Interpretation** As students display their sketches, ask them to explain the techniques they used to convey the contrast between the school grounds before and after the villagers' attack.
2. **Role-Playing** Tell students that in this dialogue the visiting supervisor should ask probing questions that elicit thoughtful responses from Michael Obi about his share of responsibility for the damage to the school grounds.

Inquiry & Research

Nigerian Culture As students conduct their research, ask them to identify some traditional Nigerian beliefs and to explain their importance to the culture.

Vocabulary in Action

1. (d)
2. (b)
3. (c)
4. (d)
5. (a)

To assess skills and concepts taught in this selection, use **Formal Assessment Book,** pp. 187–188.

Literary Analysis CULTURAL CONFLICT

A Remind students that cultural conflict involves groups of people with opposing values, beliefs, or customs. According to Achebe, the conflict between Europeans and Africans arises from the European view of Africans. Ask students to explain what Achebe means.

Possible Response: Europeans view Africans as children, not as adults. As a result, Europeans believe that Africans cannot solve their own problems.

Reading Skills and Strategies
RECOGNIZING MAIN IDEAS AND DETAILS

B Make sure students recognize the connection between these two sentences. The first sentence states the main idea—that "all kinds of mistreatment" afflict Africa. The second sentence provides evidence of that mistreatment—the dumping of toxic wastes on that continent.

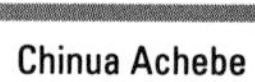
Chinua Achebe

PREPARING to *Read*

Build Background Bill Moyers has worked in the media for more than 25 years. Known especially for his documentaries on public television, he has interviewed prominent figures from all over the world. You are about to read part of a transcript of an interview with Chinua Achebe. It took place in the 1980s, when Achebe was still living in Nigeria.

MOYERS: How would you like for us to see Africa?

ACHEBE: To see Africa as a continent of people—just people, not some strange beings that demand a special kind of treatment. If you accept Africans as people, then you listen to them. They have their preferences. If you took Africa seriously as a continent of people, you would listen. You would not be able to sit back here and suggest
A that you know, for instance, what should be done in South Africa. When the majority of the people in South Africa are saying, "This is what we think will bring
1 apartheid to an end," somebody sits here and says, "No, no, that will not do it. We know what will work." Margaret Thatcher[1] sits in Britain and says, "Although the whole of Africa may think that this works, I know that what will work is something else."

That's what I want to see changed. The traditional attitude of Europe or the West is that Africa is a continent of children. A man as powerful and enlightened as Albert

1. **Margaret Thatcher:** Great Britain's first woman prime minister, who served from 1979 to 1990.

FROM AN INTERVIEW WITH

CHINUA ACHEBE

by BILL MOYERS

Schweitzer[2] was still able to say, "The black people are my brothers—but my junior brothers." We're not anybody's junior brothers.

MOYERS: There is still a lot of Robinson Crusoe.
Robinson Crusoe could never accept Friday[3]
2 as anything but a child living in a primitive
simplicity.

ACHEBE: That's right. But that's not really true, it's self-serving. What I'm suggesting is we must look at Africans as full-grown people. They may not be as wealthy or advanced in the same ways as you are here, but they're people who, in their history, also have had moments of great success—in social organization, for instance. If you grant that Africans are grown-up, a lot of other things will follow.

MOYERS: You once said that if you're an African, the world is turned upside down. Explain that.

ACHEBE: What I mean is, I look at the world, at
3 the way it is organized, and it is inadequate.
Whichever direction I look, I don't see a space
I want to stay in. On our own continent, there
B are all kinds of mistreatment. The most recent,
4 for instance, is the dumping of the toxic
wastes from the industrialized world in Africa.

MOYERS: Many American companies and Western countries are dumping their toxic wastes in African countries, and they're often bribing governments to do it.

ACHEBE: Yes. The world is not well arranged, and therefore there's no way we can be happy with it, even as writers. Sometimes our writer colleagues in the West suggest that perhaps we

2. **Albert Schweitzer** (shwīt′sər): a French physician who lived from 1875 to 1965. He spent much of his life at a missionary hospital in present-day Gabon. He was awarded the 1952 Nobel Peace Prize.

3. **Robinson Crusoe . . . Friday:** Robinson Crusoe, the hero of Daniel Defoe's 1719 novel, is an English sailor shipwrecked on an island. He befriends a native and names him Friday.

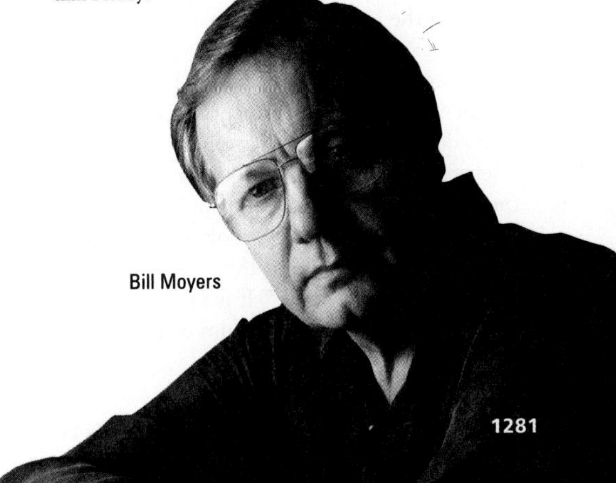

Bill Moyers

Customizing Instruction

Less Proficient Readers

Point out to students that this excerpt falls into three parts. In the first part, Achebe states his view of Africa and contrasts it with the European view; in the second part, Achebe describes the poet's function in society; in the third part, Achebe explains the power of storytelling.

1 Remind students that the term *apartheid* refers to the system of racial discrimination supported by the government in South Africa. This system, instituted in 1948, finally came to an end in 1996 when South African lawmakers passed a new constitution that guaranteed equal rights for all citizens.

English Learners

Explain the meaning of the following words that might be difficult for students to understand:

2 *primitive* means "like that of earliest times"

3 *inadequate* means "lacking"

4 *toxic* means "poisonous"

Reading Skills and Strategies
CONTRASTING

A Ask students to explain the two ways of regarding poetry.

Possible Response: According to some, poetry should express only the poet's personal thoughts and feelings and not address social concerns; according to Achebe and others, poetry should explore social issues and help bring about needed reform.

Reading Skills and Strategies
CLASSIFYING

B According to Achebe, three types of people emerge if the world is viewed in terms of storytelling. Ask students to identify each type and describe its function.

Possible Responses: drummers, who stir up the people; warriors, who fight the wars; and storytellers, who create the meaning of the survivors' ordeal

1 are too activist, we are too earnest. "Why don't you relax?" they say. "This is not really the business of poetry." About a month ago I was at an international conference of writers to celebrate the one thousandth year of Dublin. During the discussion everybody was saying that poetry has nothing to do with society or with history. Poetry is something
2 personal, private, introspective. Now, obviously, poetry can be that.

A **MOYERS:** But a poet is a member of society.

ACHEBE: Yes, yes. When you say poetry is only something personal, you are saying something
3 outrageously wrong. So I took the opportunity to state the other case. I said that poetry can be as activist as it wants, if it has the willingness and the energy. And I gave them two examples.

Toward the end of the colonial period in Angola, there was a doctor practicing his medicine and writing very delicate, very sensitive poetry in his spare time. One day he saw one of the most brutal acts of the colonial regime, and he shut down his surgery, took to the bush, and wrote a poem which had the words "I wait no more. I am the awaited." It is said that the
4 guerrillas who fought with him chanted lines from his poetry. So I'm saying that these things are possible for poetry. Of course, a poet who becomes activist risks certain dangers, such as getting into trouble with those in power.

Here's another example: Some years ago, at a conference in Stockholm, a Swedish writer and journalist said to two or three African writers, "Say, you fellows are very lucky—your governments put you in jail. Here in Sweden nobody pays any attention to us, no matter what we write."

But, you see, the point is this: A poet who sees poetry in the light I'm suggesting is likely to fall out very seriously with the emperor. Whereas the 5
poet in the West might say, "Oh no, we have no business with politics, we have no business with history, we have no business with anything—just what is in our own mind"—well, the emperor would be very, very happy.

MOYERS: So that's what you meant when you said once that storytelling is a threat to anyone in control.

ACHEBE: Yes, because a storyteller has a different agenda from the emperor.

MOYERS: And yet storytelling, poetry, literature didn't stop the brutalities that were visited on

MINI LESSON More From the Author

THINGS FALL APART In the novel *Things Fall Apart,* Chinua Achebe realistically portrays traditional African life. Instead of idealizing Okonkwo, the protagonist, Achebe creates a character with psychological complexity. This character—though strong and heroic—is deeply flawed. Achebe probes his protagonist's motives in passages like this one:

"Okonkwo ruled his household with a heavy hand. His wives, especially the youngest, lived in perpetual fear of his fiery temper, and so did his little children. Perhaps down in his heart Okonkwo was not a cruel man. But his whole life was dominated by fear, the fear of failure and of weakness. It was deeper and more intimate than the fear of evil and capricious gods and of magic, the fear of the forest, and of the forces of nature, malevolent, red in tooth and claw. Okonkwo's fear was greater than these. It was not external but lay deep within himself. It was the fear of himself, lest he should be found to resemble his father. Even as a little boy he had resented his father's failure and weakness. . . . And so Okonkwo was ruled by one passion—to hate everything that his father Unoka had loved. One of those things was gentleness and another was idleness."
(Chapter Two)

your own Ibo people in the Biafran War and didn't stop Idi Amin[4] in Uganda, or Bokassa[5] in the Central African Republic.

ACHEBE: Yes, well, there's a limit to what storytelling can achieve. We're not saying that a poet can stop a battalion with a couple of
6 lines of his poetry. But there are other forms of power. The storyteller appeals to the mind, and appeals ultimately to generations and generations and generations.

MOYERS: I love this line in *A Man of the People*—"The great thing, as the old people have told us, is reminiscence, and only those who survive can have it. Besides, if you survive, who knows? It may be your turn to eat tomorrow. Your son may bring home your share." The power of reminiscing is very important to you.

ACHEBE: If you look at the world in terms of storytelling, you have, first of all, the man who agitates, the man who drums up the people—I call him the drummer. Then you have the warrior, who goes forward and fights. But you also have the storyteller who recounts the B
event—and this is one who survives, who outlives all the others. It is the storyteller, in fact, who makes us what we are, who creates history. The storyteller creates the memory that the survivors must have—otherwise their surviving would have no meaning. ❖

4. **Idi Amin:** the military ruler of Uganda from 1971 to 1979, who killed approximately 200,000 people during his regime.
5. **Bokassa:** the president of the Central African Republic from 1966 to 1979, known as erratic and violent.

Thinking Through the Literature

1. **Comprehension Check** According to Achebe, how should Western countries regard Africa?
2. **Comparing Texts** How do the ideas in this interview influence your interpretation of Michael Obi's conduct in "Dead Men's Path"?
3. On the basis of this interview, how do you think Achebe views his role as a writer?

Customizing Instruction

English Learners

Explain the meaning of the following words and phrases:

1 *activist* means "trying to advance a cause"

2 *introspective* means "looking into one's own thoughts and feelings"

3 *outrageously* means "in a shocking way"

4 *guerrillas* means "fighters who do not belong to the regular army"

5 *to fall out very seriously with the emperor* means "to get in serious trouble with the authorities"

Less Proficient Readers

6 Make sure that students understand Achebe's views about the power of storytelling. Though storytelling does not bring about immediate, practical effects, it does exert a timeless force, influencing people down through the ages.

Thinking Through the Literature

1. **Comprehension Check** Western countries should regard Africa as a continent of people able to solve their own problems.
2. **Comparing Texts** Answers will vary. Some students may point out that both Michael Obi and the Western countries regard Africans as children needing direction.
3. Possible Response: As a writer, Achebe views his role as pointing out the meaning of events in his people's history.

INTERVIEW WITH CHINUA ACHEBE 1283

Reading and Analyzing

Literary Analysis IMAGERY AND THEME

(A) Remind students that imagery includes words and phrases that create vivid sensory experiences for the reader and that the theme is the central idea or message in a work of literature. Then have students explain how the image in these lines connects to the theme of the poem.

Possible Response: The image contrasts something living (a trembling seed) with something preserved from ages long past (the little ball made from the hardened remains of a goat's waste matter). The image suggests the poem's main message: namely, that Achebe breathed new life into Africa's decaying traditions.

Literary Analysis SPEAKER

(B) Have students read this passage slowly and carefully. Then ask them why the speaker respects Achebe.

Possible Response: The speaker believes that Achebe's works have enabled him to discover his African heritage and therefore an essential part of his identity. Though he still faces inner struggles, he has learned from Achebe to embrace his African heritage in all its aspects.

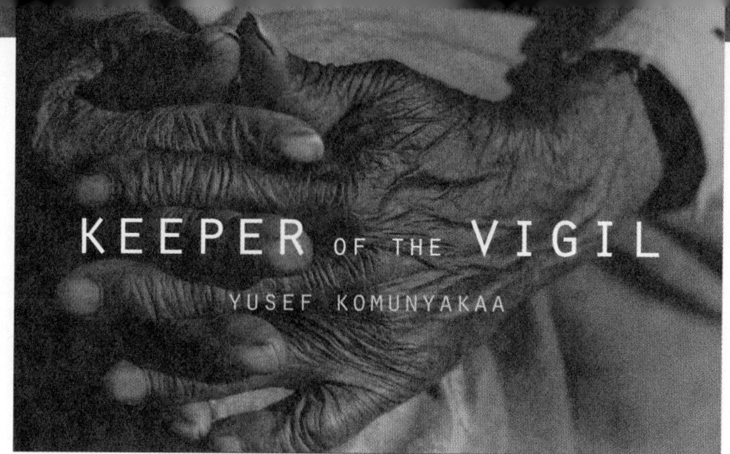

PREPARING to *Read*

Build Background Chinua Achebe is revered by many writers around the world. Yusef Komunyakaa (kō'mən-yä'kə) wrote the following poem as a tribute to Achebe's literary vision.

When the last song
  was about to leave
dust in the mouth,

where termite-eaten
  masks gazed down
in a broken repose, you

unearthed a language
  ignited by horror
& joy. A cassava

seed trembled in a pellet
  of fossilized goat dung.
The lifelines on my palms

mapped buried footprints
  along forgotten paths
into Lagos. The past

& present balanced till
  the future formed a
wishbone: Achebe,

9 cassava (kə-sä'və): any of several plants having fleshy roots that yield a nutritious starch.

11 fossilized: changed into a fossil—a trace of an organism preserved in rock or sediment.

15 Lagos (lä'gŏs'): the largest city of Nigeria.

Cross Curricular Link **Humanities**

YUSEF KOMUNYAKAA The American poet Yusef Komunyakaa (1947–) was raised in Bogalusa, Louisiana. After graduating from high school, he enlisted in the army and served in Vietnam. While there, he began to read and write poetry to escape from the violence and to cope with his feelings about the war. He was awarded the Bronze Star for his work as a reporter and an editor of the military newspaper, *The Southern Cross.*

After returning from Vietnam, he earned a fine arts degree in creative writing from the University of California at Irvine. He also published his first works of poetry, *Dedications and Other Dark Horses* (1977) and *Lost in the Bonewheel Factory* (1979). He received the 1994 Pulitzer Prize for poetry for his book *Neon Vernacular: New and Selected Poems*. He currently serves as professor of creative writing at Princeton University.

Of a writer's mission Komunyakaa has written: "The writer has to get down to the guts of the thing and rediscover the basic timbre of his or her existence."

you helped me steal
back myself. Although
sometimes the right hand

wrestles the left, you
showed me there's a time
for plaintive reed flutes

& another for machetes.
I couldn't help but see
the church & guardtower

on the same picturesque
hill. *Umuada* & *chi*
reclaimed my tongue

quick as palm wine
& kola nut, praisesongs
made of scar tissue.

—*for Chinua Achebe*

24 plaintive: sorrowful.

25 machetes (mə-shĕt′ēz): large heavy knives with broad blades.

32 kola nut: a seed of a tropical African evergreen plant.

Customizing Instruction

Less Proficient Readers

This poem is beautiful but difficult because of its diction and figurative language. Most readers will be challenged by this poem.

- Help students interpret the title. It refers to Achebe, who has kept a vigil, or has stayed alert, watching over and protecting African traditions.
- Model for students how to read the poem aloud, sentence by sentence.
- Tell students not to stop at the end of each line. Instead, they should read to the major punctuation marks, such as commas and periods. For example, students should pause briefly after the word *mouth* in line 3 and the word *repose* in line 6 and stop after the word *joy* in line 9.
- Have students work in pairs, taking turns reading sentences from the poem aloud.
- Tell students that *umuada* & *chi* in line 29 are Ibo terms. *Umuada* means "a family gathering of daughters." To participate in this gathering, Ibo women return to their native villages. *Chi* means "personal god."

English Learners

Explain the meaning of the following terms:

- *unearthed* (line 7) means "discovered or dug up"
- *plaintive* (line 24) means "sad"
- *machetes* (line 25) are "large knives with heavy blades"

KEEPER OF THE VIGIL 1285

Objectives

- understand and appreciate a **short story (Literary Analysis)**
- examine the use of **dialect** in the story **(Literary Analysis)**
- **make judgments about the characters** in the story **(Active Reading)**

Summary

Jonathan Iwegbu considers himself lucky because five of his six family members have survived the Nigerian civil war. To support his family after the war, he opens a palm-wine bar. He then exchanges his Biafran money for 20 pounds of Nigerian money from the government. That night, thieves pound at his door demanding his money. Jonathan hands them the 20 pounds. The next day, he assures his neighbors that the loss of the money is unimportant, dismissing the incident with his characteristic proverb, "Nothing puzzles God."

 Use **Unit Seven Resource Book,** p. 71, for additional support.

Thematic Link

Achebe's short story describes how a resourceful survivor of the Nigerian civil **war** responds to hardships and **conflicts** in his ruined country.

 Use **Unit Seven Resource Book,** p. 74, for practice with Words to Know.

5-Minute Warm-Up

Daily Language SkillBuilder

Have students **proofread** the display sentences on page 1095o and write them correctly.

Civil Peace

CHINUA ACHEBE

Build Background

More than 250 ethnic groups call Nigeria home. The largest groups are the Hausa and Fulani in the north, the Yoruba in the southwest, and the Ibo in the southeast. When Nigeria gained its independence in 1960, these groups began to vie for power, often violently. In 1966, anti-Ibo riots erupted in the north, where Hausa and Fulani peoples resented Ibo influence on the government. Then, in 1967, the Ibo seceded from Nigeria to form the independent republic of Biafra. A civil war followed, causing massive hardship and devastation, especially in Biafra. It is estimated that more than 1.5 million Biafrans starved to death before Biafra surrendered in 1970 and was reintegrated into Nigeria. The story you are about to read takes place shortly after the end of the civil war.

WORDS TO KNOW **Vocabulary Preview**

amenable, dissent, imperious, inaudibly, monumental

Connect to Your Life

Think about books, articles, films, or news accounts that describe the aftermath of a war. What do you think conditions are like for ordinary civilians after a war has been fought on their land?

Focus Your Reading

LITERARY ANALYSIS: DIALECT

A **dialect** is a form of a language that is spoken in a particular place or by a particular group of people. In "Civil Peace" some of the characters speak a dialect that differs markedly from standard English. Here are some words from that dialect:

am: it
commot: leave
katakata: trouble
na: is; it is
soja: soldiers
wetin: what are
wey de for inside: that went with it

Use the context to help you figure out the general meanings of sentences written in dialect. Reading these sentences aloud may help you understand them better.

ACTIVE READING: MAKING JUDGMENTS ABOUT CHARACTERS

When you read a story, you often judge the characters on the basis of what they say, do, think, or feel and how they react to events. In this story, Jonathan Iwegbu considers himself very lucky. As you read, think about whether or not you agree with him.

READER'S NOTEBOOK On a chart like the one shown below, list Jonathan's blessings and misfortunes.

Jonathan's Luck	
Blessings	**Misfortunes**
He, his wife, and three of their children survive the war.	*One of his children dies in the war.*

LESSON RESOURCES

UNIT SEVEN RESOURCE BOOK, pp. 71–75

ASSESSMENT RESOURCES
Formal Assessment, pp. 189–190
Teacher's Guide to Assessment and Portfolio Use
Test Generator

INTEGRATED TECHNOLOGY
NetActivities
Visit our Web site: classzone.com

ADDITIONAL RESOURCES
Lesson Planning Guide, pp. 167–168
Teacher's Sourcebook for Language Development

Civil Peace

Chinua Achebe

Jonathan Iwegbu[1] counted himself extraordinarily lucky. "Happy survival!" meant so much more to him than just a current fashion of greeting old friends in the first hazy days of peace. It went deep to his heart. He had come out of the war with five inestimable[2] blessings—his head, his wife Maria's head and the heads of three out of their four children. As a bonus he also had his old bicycle—a miracle too but naturally not to be compared to the safety of five human heads.

The bicycle had a little history of its own. One day at the height of the war it was commandeered "for urgent military action." Hard as its loss would have been to him he would still have let it go without a thought had he not had some doubts about the genuineness of the officer. It wasn't his disreputable[3] rags, nor the toes peeping out of one blue and one brown canvas shoes, nor yet the two stars of his rank done obviously in a hurry in biro,[4] that troubled Jonathan; many good and heroic soldiers looked the same or worse. It was rather a certain lack of grip and firmness in his manner. So Jonathan, suspecting he might be amenable to influence, rummaged in his raffia bag and produced the two pounds with which he had been going to buy firewood which his wife, Maria, retailed to camp officials for extra stock-fish and corn meal, and got his bicycle back. That night he buried it in the little clearing in the bush where the dead of the camp, including his own youngest son, were buried. When he dug it up again a year later after the surrender all it needed was a little palm-oil greasing. "Nothing puzzles God," he said in wonder.

He put it to immediate use as a taxi and accumulated a small pile of Biafran money[5] ferrying camp officials and their families across the four-mile stretch to the nearest tarred road. His standard charge per trip was six pounds and those who had the money were only glad to be

1. **Iwegbu** (ē-wĕg′bo͞o).
2. **inestimable:** priceless.
3. **disreputable:** in poor condition; not fit to be used.
4. **biro** (bîr′ō): ballpoint pen.
5. **Biafran money:** Biafra is a region in eastern Nigeria that fought unsuccessfully from 1967 to 1970 to establish itself as an independent republic.

WORDS TO KNOW

amenable (ə-mē′nə-bəl) *adj.* open to suggestion; responsive

Customizing Instruction

Less Proficient Readers

Have students read to find out why Jonathan Iwegbu considers himself a lucky man.

English Learners

Remind students that in this story they will come upon several dialect words. Point out to them the list of dialect words on page 1286, and tell them to use the context, or the surrounding words, to try to figure out the meaning of other dialect words. Have students keep a list of the dialect words they encounter as they read, along with their definitions.

Advanced Learners

Invite students to compare this story with others dealing with the effects of war on civilian populations. You might suggest that students read *Farewell to Manzanar* by Jeanne Wakatsuki Houston and James D. Houston.

TIME MANAGEMENT

If your schedule requires that you cover the lesson objectives in a shorter time, use . . .
- Preparing to Read, p. 1286
- Thinking Through the Literature, p. 1291
- Vocabulary in Action, p. 1293

If you want to take advantage of longer blocks of class time, use . . .
- TE Teaching Options: Vocabulary Strategy, p. 1288; Cross-Curricular Link, p. 1289; Standardized Test Practice, p. 1290
- Choices & Challenges, p. 1293

Active Reading

MAKING JUDGMENTS ABOUT CHARACTERS

Point out to students that readers judge characters in fiction in some of the same ways that people judge others in life; by evaluating their words and actions. Ask students what advantages a reader of fiction might have over a person in a real-life encounter in terms of judging character.

Possible Response: access to a character's thought; narrator's remarks. Tell students to look for Jonathan's words, actions, and thoughts and the narrator's remarks about him as they form judgments about his character.

Use **Unit Seven Resource Book,** p. 72, for more practice.

Literary Analysis FORESHADOWING

A Tell students that writers sometimes provide clues about a story's outcome. After students have read this story, ask them to explain how this passage foreshadows the ending.

Possible Responses: The theft prepares the reader for the robbery of Jonathan's money at the end of the story. Unlike the man in line, Jonathan is robbed at gunpoint in his home during the night. Jonathan, moreover, gets on with his life the next morning instead of collapsing into near-madness.

Literary Analysis DIALECT

B Remind students that a dialect is a variation of a language spoken in a particular place or by a particular group of people. Have students read the passage. Then ask them why a writer might use dialect in fiction.

Possible Responses: to be realistic; to show differences between characters such as class, education, or region.

Use **Unit Seven Resource Book,** p. 73, for more practice.

rid of some of it in this way. At the end of a fortnight he had made a small fortune of one hundred and fifteen pounds.

Then he made the journey to Enugu[6] and found another miracle waiting for him. It was unbelievable. He rubbed his eyes and looked again and it was still standing there before him. But, needless to say, even that monumental blessing must be accounted also totally inferior to the five heads in the family. This newest miracle was his little house in Ogui[7] Overside. Indeed nothing puzzles God! Only two houses away a huge concrete edifice some wealthy contractor had put up just before the war was a mountain of rubble. And here was Jonathan's little zinc house of no regrets built with mud blocks quite intact! Of course the doors and windows were missing and five sheets off the roof. But what was that? And anyhow he had returned to Enugu early enough to pick up bits of old zinc and wood and soggy sheets of cardboard lying around the neighborhood before thousands more came out of their forest holes looking for the same things. He got a destitute carpenter with one old hammer, a blunt plane and a few bent and rusty nails in his tool bag to turn this assortment of wood, paper and metal into door and window shutters for five Nigerian shillings or fifty Biafran pounds. He paid the pounds, and moved in with his overjoyed family carrying five heads on their shoulders.

His children picked mangoes near the military cemetery and sold them to soldiers' wives for a few pennies—real pennies this time—and his wife started making breakfast akara balls[8] for neighbors in a hurry to start life again. With his family earnings he took his bicycle to the villages around and bought fresh palm-wine which he mixed generously in his rooms with the water which had recently started running again in the public tap down the road, and opened up a bar for soldiers and other lucky people with good money.

At first he went daily, then every other day and finally once a week, to the offices of the Coal Corporation where he used to be a miner, to find out what was what. The only thing he did find out in the end was that that little house of his was even a greater blessing than he had thought. Some of his fellow examiners who had nowhere to return at the end of the day's waiting just slept outside the doors of the offices and cooked what meal they could scrounge together in Bournvita tins.[9] As the weeks lengthened and still nobody could say what was what Jonathan discontinued his weekly visits altogether and faced his palm-wine bar.

But nothing puzzles God. Came the day of the windfall when after five days of endless scuffles in queues[10] and counter-queues in the sun outside the Treasury he had twenty pounds counted into his palms as ex-gratia[11] award for the rebel money he had turned in. It was like Christmas for him and for many others like him when the payments began. They called it (since few could manage its proper official name) *egg-rasher.* 1

As soon as the pound notes were placed in his palm Jonathan simply closed it tight over them and buried fist and money inside his trouser pocket. He had to be extra careful because he had seen a man a couple of days A earlier collapse into near-madness in an instant before that oceanic crowd because no sooner had he got his twenty pounds than some heartless ruffian picked it off him. Though it was not

6. **Enugu** (ā-no͞o'go͞o): the capital city of Biafra.
7. **Ogui** (ō'go͞o-ē).
8. **akara balls:** fried batter consisting mainly of mashed black-eyed peas.
9. **Bournvita tins:** cans of a nutritional drink used to supplement children's diets.
10. **queues** (kyo͞oz): lines of waiting people.
11. **ex-gratia** (ĕks-grā'shə): as a favor rather than as a legal right.

WORDS TO KNOW

monumental (mŏn'yə-mĕn'tl) *adj.* very significant; astonishing

1288

MINI LESSON Vocabulary Strategy

ANALYZING AFFIXES AND BASE WORDS One way to figure out the meaning of a multisyllabic word is to break it down into its parts: base words, which are complete words; roots, which are the core parts of words; and affixes, which can be added to the beginning (prefixes) or the end (suffixes) of roots or base words.

Instruction

- Write the word *monumental* on the chalkboard.
- Show students how to get to the base word *monument* by removing the suffix *-al.* Since this base word means "something put up in memory of a person or an event, such as a statue or a building," students might infer that *monumental* means "having to do with a monument" or "large and important."

Practice Have students figure out the meaning of the following words:

1. abnormal *(not normal)*
2. disorderly *(not orderly)*
3. compress *(to press together)*
4. immeasurable *(unable to be measured)*
5. inaudible *(unable to be heard)*

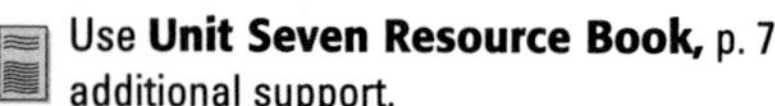
Use **Unit Seven Resource Book,** p. 74, for additional support.

A lesson on affixes appears on p. 864 of the Pupil's Edition.

Indeed nothing puzzles God!

right that a man in such an extremity of agony should be blamed yet many in the queues that day were able to remark quietly on the victim's carelessness, especially after he pulled out the innards of his pocket and revealed a hole in it big enough to pass a thief's head. But of course he had insisted that the money had been in the other pocket, pulling it out too to show its comparative wholeness. So one had to be careful.

Jonathan soon transferred the money to his left hand and pocket so as to leave his right free for shaking hands should the need arise, though by fixing his gaze at such an elevation as to miss all approaching human faces he made sure that the need did not arise, until he got home.

He was normally a heavy sleeper but that night he heard all the neighborhood noises die down one after another. Even the night watchman who knocked the hour on some metal somewhere in the distance had fallen silent after knocking one o'clock. That must have been the last thought in Jonathan's mind before he was finally carried away himself. He couldn't have been gone for long, though, when he was violently awakened again.

"Who is knocking?" whispered his wife lying beside him on the floor.

"I don't know," he whispered back breathlessly.

The second time the knocking came it was so loud and imperious that the rickety old door could have fallen down.

"Who is knocking?" he asked then, his voice parched and trembling.

"Na tief-man and him people," came the cool reply. "Make you hopen de door." This was followed by the heaviest knocking of all.

Maria was the first to raise the alarm, then he followed and all their children.

"Police-o! Thieves-o! Neighbors-o! Police-o! We are lost! We are dead! Neighbors, are you asleep? Wake up! Police-o!"

B

This went on for a long time and then stopped suddenly. Perhaps they had scared the thief away. There was total silence. But only for a short while.

"You done finish?" asked the voice outside. "Make we help you small. Oya, everybody!"

"Police-o! Tief-man-o! Neighbors-o! we done loss-o! Police-o! . . ."

There were at least five other voices besides the leader's.

Jonathan and his family were now completely paralyzed by terror. Maria and the children

WORDS TO KNOW

imperious (ĭm-pîr'ē-əs) *adj.* urgent; pressing

Customizing Instruction

English Learners

1 Pronounce *ex-gratia* for students (ex GRAY-sha). Point out the similarity in sound to *egg-rasher.* Explain that a *rasher* is a slice of bacon.

Less Proficient Readers

Use the following questions to make sure students understand the story up to this point:

- Where did Jonathan and his family live during the civil war? *(in a camp)*
- What job did Jonathan have before the civil war? *(coal miner)*
- How does Jonathan earn a living after the war? *(opens a palm-wine bar)*
- Where does Jonathan get the 20 pounds? *(from the government in return for his Biafran money)*

Cross Curricular Link **History**

NIGERIAN CIVIL WAR The Nigerian Civil War began with a coup d'etat (military takeover of the government) on January 14, 1966. Major General Johnson Aguiyi-Ironsi established control and set up a military administration. His government, however, lasted only a short time. On July 28, another coup d'etat occurred. General Yakubu Gowon emerged as the leader, but he was unable to impose order on the military. Most Ibos chose to flee to the East. Despite the attempts of Gowon and other leaders to find a viable way to govern Nigeria, the East seceded from Nigeria, declaring itself the Republic of Biafra. The Nigerian government then began military action against Biafra. The next two years saw heavy military and civilian casualties.

Literary Analysis DIALECT

A Have students paraphrase the thieves' dialect. Suggest that they try to re-create the tone, as well as the meaning, of the words. Ask students to share their paraphrases with the class and to tell why they chose the words they did.

Possible Response: This passage might be paraphrased as follows: "My friend, why don't you say something? I asked you whether you want us to call the soldiers."

Reading Skills and Strategies
DRAWING INFERENCES

B Point out that the interaction between the thieves and Jonathan is unusual, because the thieves knock on the door (rather than breaking in) and they refer to Jonathan as "friend." Ask students what they can infer about the thieves based on their somewhat polite treatment of the person they intend to rob.

Possible Response: They don't really want to be outlaws and frighten their neighbors, but the war has left them destitute, and they feel they have no choice but to steal.

Literary Analysis THEME

C Remind students that a story's theme is its central idea or message. Ask what insight about life is suggested through the repetition of the phrase "Nothing puzzles God."

Possible Response: People do not control their own fate; life is full of surprises, both good and bad.

sobbed inaudibly like lost souls. Jonathan groaned continuously.

The silence that followed the thieves' alarm vibrated horribly. Jonathan all but begged their leader to speak again and be done with it.

"My frien," said he at long last, "we don try our best for call dem but I tink say dem all done sleep-o. . . . So wetin we go do now? Sometaim you wan call soja? Or you wan make we call dem for you? Soja better pass police. No be so?"

"Na so!" replied his men. Jonathan thought he heard even more voices now than before and groaned heavily. His legs were sagging under him and his throat felt like sand-paper.

A "My frien, why you no de talk again. I de ask you say you wan make we call soja?"

"No."

"Awrighto. Now make we talk business. We no be bad tief. We no like for make trouble. Trouble done finish. War done finish and all the katakata wey de for inside. No Civil War again. This time na Civil Peace. No be so?"

"Na so!" answered the horrible chorus.

"What do you want from me? I am a poor man. Everything I had went with this war. Why do you come to me? You know people who have money. We . . ."

"Awright! We know say you no get plenty money. But we sef no get even anini."[12] So derefore make you open dis window and give us one hundred pound and we go commot. Orderwise we de come for inside now to show you guitar-boy like dis . . ."

A volley of automatic fire rang through the sky. Maria and the children began to weep aloud again.

B "Ah, missisi de cry again. No need for dat. We done talk say we na good tief. We just take our small money and go nwayorly. No molest. Abi we de molest?"

"At all!" sang the chorus.

"My friends," began Jonathan hoarsely. "I hear what you say and I thank you. If I had one hundred pounds . . ."

"Lookia my frien, no be play we come play for your house. If we make mistake and step for inside you no go like am-o. So derefore . . ."

"To God who made me; if you come inside and find one hundred pounds, take it and shoot me and shoot my wife and children. I swear to God. The only money I have in this life is this twenty-pounds egg-rasher they gave me today . . ."

"OK. Time de go. Make you open dis window and bring the twenty pound. We go manage am like dat."

There were now loud murmurs of dissent among the chorus: "Na lie de man de lie; e get plenty money. . . . Make we go inside and search properly well. . . . Wetin be twenty pound? . . ."

"Shurrup!" rang the leader's voice like a lone shot in the sky and silenced the murmuring at once. "Are you dere? Bring the money quick!"

"I am coming," said Jonathan fumbling in the darkness with the key of the small wooden box he kept by his side on the mat.

At the first sign of light as neighbors and others assembled to commiserate with him he was already strapping his five-gallon demijohn[13] to his bicycle carrier and his wife, sweating in the open fire, was turning over akara balls in a wide clay bowl of boiling oil. In the corner his eldest son was rinsing out dregs of yesterday's palm wine from old beer bottles.

"I count it as nothing," he told his sympathizers, his eyes on the rope he was tying. "What is *egg-rasher?* Did I depend on it last week? Or is it greater than other things that went with the war? I say, let *egg-rasher* perish in the flames! Let it go where everything else has gone. Nothing puzzles God." ❖ C

12. **anini:** any.

13. **demijohn:** a large glass or earthenware jar encased in wicker.

WORDS TO KNOW

inaudibly (ĭn-ô'də-blē) *adj.* in a way that cannot be heard
dissent (dĭ-sĕnt') *n.* disagreement

1290

Assessment Standardized Test Practice

WRITE A DIALOGUE For some standardized tests, students will be asked to demonstrate their ability to communicate effectively in writing on a specified topic. Ask students to invent a character who overheard the robbery. Have students write a dialogue in which the new character talks with another character about the theft.

RUBRIC

3 Full Accomplishment Student's dialogue shows complete understanding of events and characters in the story.

2 Substantial Accomplishment Student's dialogue shows some understanding of events and characters in the story.

1 Little or Partial Accomplishment Student's dialogue shows little or no understanding of events and characters in the story.

Connect to the Literature

1. **What Do You Think?** After reading the story, what are your thoughts about Jonathan?

Comprehension Check
- How does Jonathan acquire the ex-gratia award money?
- What happens to this money?

Thinking Critically

2. **ACTIVE READING: MAKING JUDGMENTS ABOUT CHARACTERS** Review the chart you created in your  READER'S NOTEBOOK. Do you agree with Jonathan's view of himself as lucky? Why or why not?

3. How would you describe Jonathan's attitude toward life?

THINK ABOUT
- the importance he places on his family's safety
- how he supports his family during and after the war
- his confrontation with the thieves
- his reaction to the loss of his money

4. How would you explain the meaning of the **aphorism** "Nothing puzzles God"?

5. What does the story say to you about the aftermath of war for ordinary civilians?

Extend Interpretations

6. **Critic's Corner** In describing Achebe's fiction, the critic G. D. Killam has observed: "Sometimes his characters meet with success, more often with defeat and despair. Through it all the spirit of man and the belief in the possibility of triumph endure." Do you think this assessment applies to Jonathan? Cite details from the story to support your opinion.

7. **Comparing Texts** Imagine that Jonathan had been in Michael Obi's situation in "Dead Men's Path." How do you think Jonathan might have handled the conflict with the village priest?

8. **Connect to Life** Do you think Jonathan's attitude in the wake of the war's destruction and tragedy is common among the survivors of wars? Give reasons for your opinion.

LITERARY ANALYSIS: DIALECT

Dialect reflects the pronunciations, vocabulary, and grammatical rules that are typical of a region. In "Civil Peace," Achebe uses two dialects of English, the Nigerian dialect of the thieves and the near-standard dialect of Jonathan and his family. The leader of the thieves first uses the Nigerian dialect when Jonathan asks who is knocking on the door:

"Na tief-man and him people," came the cool reply.

or

"The thief and his people," came the cool reply.

The thieves dialect is markedly different from standard English:

"So wetin we go do now? Sometaim you wan call soja?"

or

"So what are we going to do now? Sometime do you want to call the soldiers?"

Jonathan's own dialect is evident in this passage when he and his family raise the alarm about the thieves.

"Police-o! Thieves-o! Neighbors-o! Police-o! We are lost. We are dead! Neighbors, are you asleep? Wake up! Police-o!"

Paired Activity Working with a partner, read aloud the dialogue between Jonathan and the thieves. Then discuss why you think Achebe chose to use contrasting dialects in his story.

Connect to the Literature

1. **What Do You Think?** Possible Response: Jonathan is a survivor who values his family's welfare over material things.

Comprehension Check
- He exchanges Biafran money for Nigerian money from the government.
- Thieves steal the money from Jonathan.

 Use **Unit Seven Resource Book,** p. 75, for additional support.

Think Critically

2. Possible Responses: Yes, because he and most of his family survive the war and can support themselves afterwards; no, because Jonathan and his family are very poor and lose the little money they receive.
3. Jonathan's attitude toward life is accepting and even optimistic. He considers himself blessed because he and most of his family have lived through the civil war. He handles challenges well, finding a way to keep his bicycle during the war and afterwards to have his house rebuilt and to open a palm-wine bar. He even convinces the leader of the thieves to accept 20 pounds instead of searching the house for more money. Moreover, Jonathan puts his troubles in perspective, realizing that the loss of money is nothing compared to the loss of life.
4. Possible Response: God works in mysterious ways, and it is not for Jonathan to question lucky or unlucky events, since all are part of God's plan.
5. Possible Response: The aftermath of war presents hardships and problems that are almost as severe as those faced during the war itself.

Extend Interpretations

6. **Critic's Corner** Possible Response: Jonathan responds to adversity with a noble spirit. He knows how to cut his losses, keeping his bicycle by buying off the "officer" and convincing the leader of the thieves to settle for 20 pounds. Jonathan is resilient enough to accept the loss of his money and get on with his life.
7. **Comparing Texts** Possible Response: More flexible, perceptive, and resourceful than Michael Obi, Jonathan probably would have worked out a compromise with the village priest, allowing the path to remain open as long as the villagers were careful not to damage the school grounds.
8. **Connect to Life** In explaining their opinion, students might conclude that like Jonathan other survivors of wars must be both resourceful and lucky.

Literary Analysis

Paired Activity Students should recognize that by using contrasting dialects in the story, Achebe suggests different backgrounds and levels of education.

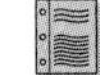 Use **Unit Seven Resource Book,** p. 73, for more practice.

Analysis of Style

A First Activity

Chike and the speaker in the passage from *Things Fall Apart* both seem to be ordinary African people, and Marcus Ibe seems like a typical politician. The diction is especially simple in the passages from *Things Fall Apart* and "Chike's School Days." The passage from *Things Fall Apart* pokes fun at the character speaking; the passage from "The Voter" pokes fun at Nigerian politics; the passage from "Chike's School Days" is ironic because it says Chike is fond of the song, but he pronounces the words in dialect and hums through many lines. In the passage from *Things Fall Apart,* the speaker quotes a proverb in his final sentence; in the passage from "The Voter," the remark about the fly and the dunghill is actually called a proverb. In the passage from "Chike's School Days," the pronunciation of the song is in dialect.

B Second Activity

Students should cite the simple characters in both stories; examples of simple diction in both stories; the irony of Jonathan's getting his new-found wealth stolen almost immediately and of Michael Obi's getting a bad report for actions he thought would earn him a good one, as well as the narrator's gentle mockery of Michael and his wife; the proverbs "Let the hawk perch and let the eagle perch" in "Dead Men's Path" and "Nothing puzzles God" in "Civil Peace"; and the dialect in "Civil Peace" in the dialogue between Jonathan and the thieves.

C Third Activity

Possible Response: Achebe's conveys his themes mainly through the use of ironic situations and African proverbs. For example, the proverb "Let the hawk perch and let the eagle perch" in "Dead Men's Path" conveys the theme, or message, that a culture can have room for two opposed belief systems. Achebe's style suggests that African village life is simple but reflects universal truths.

Achebe's Cross-Cultural Style

Though English is his second, not his native, language, Chinua Achebe writes stories about Africa in English. His style, though, is all his own, suiting his African characters, settings, and themes. Many critics have praised him for creating an authentic Ibo prose style in English.

Key Aspects of Achebe's Style

- a focus on African people and traditional African values
- simple, straightforward diction, or word choice
- the use of ironic situations and mild satire to explore social issues
- the frequent use of African proverbs and folklore to help convey character and theme
- the use of different dialects to convey cultural differences among characters

from ***Things Fall Apart***

"I know what it is to ask a man to trust another with his yams, especially these days when young men are afraid of hard work. I am not afraid of work. The lizard that jumped from the high iroko tree to the ground said he would praise himself if no one else did."

from **"The Voter"**

The village already belonged *en masse* to the People's Alliance Party, and its most illustrious son, Chief the Honorable Marcus Ibe, was Minister of Culture in the outgoing government (which was pretty certain to be the incoming one as well). Nobody doubted that the Honorable Minister would be elected in his constituency. Opposition to him was like the proverbial fly trying to move a dunghill.

from **"Chike's School Days"**

Chike was very fond of "Ten Green Bottles." They had been taught the words but they only remembered the first and the last lines. The middle was hummed and hie-ed and mumbled:

Ten grin botr angin on dar war,
Ten grin botr angin on dar war,
Hm hm hm hm hm
Hm, hm hm hm hm hm,
An ten grin botr angin on dar war.

Analysis of Style

Study the aspects of Achebe's style in the chart above and the passages from his works that appear at the right. Then complete the following activities:

- A Find in the passages examples of each aspect of Achebe's style. For examples of irony or satire, explain what Achebe targets for mockery.
- B Find additional examples of Achebe's style in "Dead Men's Path" and "Civil Peace."
- C Decide which aspects of Achebe's style help convey the themes of his work.

Applications

1. **Imitating Style** Try writing the first few paragraphs of a sequel to either "Dead Men's Path" or "Civil Peace." Make sure to imitate the style of the author.
2. **Changing Style** Rewrite the dialogue between Jonathan and the thieves in "Civil Peace," but have the thieves use standard or near-standard English instead of Nigerian dialect. What qualities, if any, do you think are lost in the rewritten version?
3. **Comparing Styles** Compare and contrast Achebe's style with the style of the West African literature in Unit Four. What influences of these older forms do you detect in Achebe's writing?

Applications

1. **Imitating Style** Remind students to revisit the **Key Aspects** box on the page before beginning their paragraphs. Especially challenging is the second bulleted item—the use of simple diction.
2. **Changing Style** In comparing their versions with Achebe's original, some students may conclude that Achebe's use of Nigerian dialect adds realism to the dialogue and sharpens the contrast between the characters in conflict.
3. **Comparing Styles** Students may conclude that although Achebe writes in English, his use of proverbs, folklore, humor, and simple diction as well as his focus on African values reflect the influence of West African literature.

Writing Options

1. News Article Write a news account—one that might appear in the local paper—describing the theft of Jonathan's money. For an effective news article, be sure to include information telling who, what, where, when, why, and how.

2. Essay About the Title In a brief essay, explain the different meanings of Achebe's title "Civil Peace." First, explain why the leader of the thieves calls the period "Civil Peace" and indicate what is ironic about the term. Then consider the other chief meaning of *civil,* and explain whether anything or anyone in the story is truly civil. Finally, explain how the title helps point to the story's central theme or themes.

Writing Handbook
See page R33: Analysis.

Vocabulary in Action

EXERCISE: CONTEXT CLUES Complete each sentence by choosing the appropriate Word to Know.

1. Jonathan was not particular; he was ____ to any plan that would help him rebuild his life.
2. He had seen _____ landowners lose their wealth in the war.
3. Though he too had suffered losses, most of his family had been saved through _____ luck.
4. In most situations, Jonathan preferred agreement rather than _____.
5. Though the thieves were murmuring _____, he became frightened and quickly gave in.

WORDS TO KNOW

amenable imperious monumental
dissent inaudibly

Building Vocabulary
For an in-depth lesson on context clues, see page 674.

Working with a group of classmates, create a radio program about Chinua Achebe's life and achievements. Begin the program with a brief oral biography of Achebe. Then present an imaginary interview with the author, in which he discusses some of his literary works and key ideas. Review Bill Moyers's interview with Chinua Achebe for examples of probing questions that elicit in-depth responses. Conclude the radio program with oral readings from some of Achebe's works, including poems as well as passages from his fiction and essays. Rehearse the program thoroughly, and then present it to the rest of the class—your "live" studio audience. Have a classmate tape-record the presentation.

Primary Sources Review several books by Achebe to find suitable poems and excerpts for the final part of the radio program. Also, to help you with the interview, find actual interviews with Achebe in books or magazine articles or at sites on the World Wide Web. *Conversations with Chinua Achebe* would be a good printed source. Reliable Web sites would include those maintained by universities and cultural societies.

Secondary Sources Obtain information about Achebe and his writing from reference works, literary biographies, and reliable online sources. Again, reliable online sources would include Web sites maintained by universities and cultural societies.

Writing Options

1. News Article Suggest that students review various newspapers for news articles to serve as models for this assignment.

2. Essay About the Title To get students started on this assignment, have them discuss the meaning of the title in small groups or as an entire class. If necessary, point out that the title contains an unusual juxtaposition—"civil peace" rather than "civil war." This title suggests the central ironical situation in this story–Jonathan endures a life-or-death crisis during peacetime, not wartime. Also point out that the word *civil* can have more than one meaning: "of a citizen or citizens" and "not rude."

Vocabulary in Action

1. amenable
2. imperious
3. monumental
4. dissent
5. inaudibly

To assess skills and concepts taught in this selection, use **Formal Assessment Book,** pp. 189–190.

Author Study Project

A Radio Program on Achebe

Remind students that to explore Achebe's life and achievements, they must include information about relevant events in Nigeria. The interviewer for the radio program should use *who, what, where, when,* and *how* questions to elicit in-depth responses. You may want to have other students serve as the radio audience, participating in an open question-and-answer section of the program.

Primary/Secondary Print Sources

Tell students to consult encyclopedia articles for biographical sketches of Achebe and information about Nigeria. Students might also refer to such works as Chinua Achebe's *The Trouble with Nigeria* (Fourth Dimension Publishers, 1983) and *Chinua Achebe: A Biography* by Ezenwa-Ohaeto (Indiana University Press, 1977). *African Writers on African Writing,* edited by G. D. Killam (Northwestern University Press, 1973), contains Achebe's important essay "The Novelist as Teacher." The reference work *Major 20th-Century Writers* is also an excellent resource for information about Achebe.

Objectives

- understand and appreciate an excerpt from an **autobiography (Literary Analysis)**
- **recognize the author's purpose** for writing **(Active Reading)**

Summary

Allende tells of the mysterious creation of her novel *Of Love and Shadows,* which describes conditions in Chile under Pinochet's reign of terror. She was inspired to write this novel by the plight of the women in Lonquén. These women searched for their loved ones, who were arrested and then murdered by the military. Allende describes her conversation with a guilt-ridden officer, who executed a political prisoner. This officer became the model for a character in her novel. After the novel was published, a priest confided to Allende that the events described in her work revealed how the bodies of the murdered men actually were discovered.

Use **Unit Seven Resource Book,** p. 76, for additional support.

Thematic Link

In this excerpt, Allende describes her process of writing a novel in response to political **conflicts** and repression in Chile.

Use **Unit Seven Resource Book,** p. 79, for practice with Words to Know.

5-Minute Warm-Up

Daily Language SkillBuilder

Have students **proofread** the display sentences on page 1095o and write them correctly.

from *Paula*

ISABEL ALLENDE

Isabel Allende
1942–

Creative Beginnings Born in Peru, Isabel Allende (ē-sä-bĕl' ä-yĕn'dĕ) moved with her mother to Santiago, Chile, at the age of three. Allende's mother recognized and nurtured her daughter's creativity from an early age, encouraging her to keep a journal and draw on a bedroom wall. The efforts paid off. Allende's love of language led her to become a journalist at the age of 17, working for Chilean television stations and magazines. However, she later claimed that her imagination was a "great handicap" in her work as a journalist because it prevented her from being objective.

Murder and Exile By the time she was 30, Allende felt settled and content with her work in Chile. In addition, her uncle and godfather, Salvador Allende, had been elected president of Chile in 1970. He died in 1973, however, during a military takeover led by General Augusto Pinochet (ou-go͞os'tô pē-nô-chĕt'). Pinochet formed a dictatorship that remained in place until 1990. For a time, Isabel Allende stayed in Chile, secretly helping those who opposed the repressive new regime. When it became clear that her own life was in danger, she fled—first to Venezuela and later to the United States.

International Acclaim While in exile, Allende began writing a letter to her grandfather, who had remained in Chile. The letter, in which she recorded many of her family's stories and legends, became the basis of Allende's first novel, *The House of the Spirits.* Published in 1982, the novel became an international bestseller. Her other works include *Of Love and Shadows* (1984), *Eva Luna* (1987), *The Stories of Eva Luna* (1990), *Paula* (1994), and *Daughter of Fortune* (1999). Allende continues to write in Spanish, but her work has been translated into many languages, including English.

LESSON RESOURCES

UNIT FIVE RESOURCE BOOK,
pp. 76–80

ASSESSMENT RESOURCES
Formal Assessment, pp. 191–192
Teacher's Guide to Assessment and Portfolio Use
Test Generator

INTEGRATED TECHNOLOGY
Visit our Web site: classzone.com

ADDITIONAL RESOURCES
Lesson Planning Guide, pp. 169–170
Teacher's Sourcebook for Language Development

Connect to Your Life

Think of a powerful world event—involving war, death, disease, or politics—that captured your attention. Then get together with a partner and discuss why the event intrigued you.

Build Background

Remembering the Dead In 1991 Allende's 27-year-old daughter Paula became seriously ill and fell into a coma. Allende stayed near her daughter's side throughout the year-long illness. During that time, she wrote the story of her own life, which she hoped that Paula herself would read one day. Tragically, the young woman never regained consciousness, dying at the age of 28. Allende later completed her autobiography, in which she interwove the story of Paula's death, and named the book after her daughter.

In this excerpt from *Paula,* Allende explains how she came to write her second novel, *Of Love and Shadows.* The novel, which takes place in an unnamed Latin American country, tells the story of a couple who find a mine filled with the dead bodies of citizens murdered by a military regime. The narrative is based on an incident that occurred after President Allende's government had been overthrown: the discovery of the bodies of 15 murdered men.

The deaths clearly had been arranged by the Chilean government. In 1973, when General Pinochet established his military dictatorship, he crushed any resistance to the government by having thousands of President Allende's supporters rounded up and secretly killed. These people became known as *desaparecidos* (dĕ-sä-pä-rĕ-sē′dôs), "the disappeared." The number of *desaparecidos* officially recognized by the Chilean government is 3,000, but many people believe the real number to be much higher.

Focus Your Reading

LITERARY ANALYSIS: AUTOBIOGRAPHY

An **autobiography** is a person's account of his or her own life. Autobiographies provide revealing insights into the characters of their writers, as well as the societies in which they lived. As you read the excerpt from *Paula,* look for details that help you learn about Isabel Allende and about conditions in Chile during Pinochet's military regime.

ACTIVE READING: RECOGNIZING AUTHOR'S PURPOSE

Recall that the term **author's purpose** refers to a writer's reason for writing something. An author's purpose may be to entertain, to inform, to express opinions, or to persuade. An author may accomplish more than one purpose in a piece of writing, but one purpose is usually the most important.

READER'S NOTEBOOK To help you recognize Allende's purpose, take notes about the following as you read the excerpt:

- the main subject of the writing
- the author's **tone,** or attitude toward the subject
- the details the author uses to develop her ideas
- what you know about why the author began writing this piece

WORDS TO KNOW **Vocabulary Preview**

implacable osmosis tedium
naive subvert

READING FOR INFORMATION
Reading Skills and Strategies
RECOGNIZING SEQUENCE

Have students read the biographical sketch of Allende on page 1294. Then have students create a time line that lists the key events in her life and the South American countries where she lived before coming to the United States—Peru, Chile, and Venezuela. Have volunteers identify these countries on a world map or a globe.

TIME MANAGEMENT

If your schedule requires that you cover the lesson objectives in a shorter time, use . . .

- Preparing to Read, pp. 1294 and 1295
- Thinking Through the Literature, p. 1302
- Vocabulary in Action, p. 1303

If you want to take advantage of longer blocks of class time, use . . .

- TE Teaching Options: Viewing and Representing, p. 1300; Vocabulary Strategy, p. 1296; Cross Curricular Link, p. 1299; Grammar, p. 1301
- Choices & Challenges, p. 1303

Reading and Analyzing

Reading Skills and Strategies
PREVIEWING
Give students a few minutes to skim, or glance through, the selection for clues about the content, using any evidence they can find, including pictures and captions in the text.

Literary Analysis AUTOBIOGRAPHY

A Remind students that an autobiography is the story of a person's life written by that person. Then ask students what is unusual about Allende's way of creating a novel.
Possible Responses: Allende believes that creating a novel is a magical process beyond her control. Instead of working from a story outline, she sits quietly, filling herself with peace and waiting for the moment of inspiration. Mysteriously, the first sentence comes to her, allowing her a glimpse of the story she will write as the characters gradually reveal it to her.

Use **Unit Seven Resource Book,** p. 78, for more practice.

Active Reading
RECOGNIZING AUTHOR'S PURPOSE

B One of Allende's purposes for writing this autobiography is to inform readers about conditions in Chile during Pinochet's regime. Ask students to evaluate these conditions.
Possible Responses: Conditions were terrible under this repressive regime. The government tolerated no opposition. Suspected people suddenly "disappeared." They were murdered by the military, and their remains were hidden. Even after their corpses were discovered, Pinochet pardoned the murderers.

Use **Unit Seven Resource Book,** p. 77, for more practice.

from Paula

Isabel Allende

Translated by Margaret Sayers Peden

I began *Of Love and Shadows* on January 8, 1983, because that day had brought me luck with *The House of the Spirits,* thus initiating a tradition I honor to this day and don't dare change; I always write the first line of my books on that date. When that time comes, I try to be alone and silent for several hours; I need a lot of time to rid my mind of the noise outside and to cleanse my memory of life's confusion. I
1 light candles to summon the muses and guardian
2 spirits, I place flowers on my desk to intimidate
tedium and the complete works of Pablo Neruda[1] beneath the computer with the hope
A they will inspire me by osmosis—if computers
can be infected with a virus, there's no reason they shouldn't be refreshed by a breath of poetry. In a secret ceremony, I prepare my mind and soul to receive the first sentence in a trance, so the door may open slightly and allow me to peer through and perceive the hazy outlines of the story waiting for me. In the following months, I will cross that threshold to explore those spaces and, little by little, if I am lucky, the characters will come alive, become more precise and more real, and reveal the narrative to me as we go
3 along. I don't know how or why I write; my
books are not born in my mind, they gestate[2] in my womb and are capricious creatures with their own lives, always ready to subvert me. I do not determine the subject, the subject chooses me, my work consists simply of providing enough time, solitude, and discipline for the book to write itself. That is what happened with my second novel. In 1978, in the area of Lonquén,[3] some fifty kilometers from Santiago, they found the bodies of fifteen campesinos[4] murdered by
the government and hidden in abandoned lime 4
kilns. The Catholic Church reported the discov- 5
ery and the scandal exploded before authorities
could muffle it; it was the first time the bodies of B
desaparecidos had been found, and the wavering finger of Chilean justice had no choice but to point to the armed forces. Several *carabineros*[5] were accused, tried, and found guilty of murder in the first degree—and immediately set free by
General Pinochet under a decree of amnesty.[6] 6
The news was published around the world,

1. **Pablo Neruda** (pä'blō nĕ-rōō'də): a Chilean poet who won the Nobel Prize for literature in 1971.
2. **gestate:** develop.
3. **Lonquén** (lôn-kĕn').
4. **campesinos** (käm'pĭ-sē'nōz): peasants.
5. ***carabineros*** (kä-rä-bē-nĕ'rôs) *Chilean Spanish:* members of the national police force.
6. **amnesty:** a general pardon granted by a government, usually for political offenses.

WORDS TO KNOW
tedium (tē'dē-əm) *n.* boredom
osmosis (ŏz-mō'sĭs) *n.* an unconscious absorbing of facts or ideas
subvert (səb-vûrt') *v.* to destroy or corrupt

1296

MINI LESSON **Vocabulary Strategy**

PREFIXES AND ETYMOLOGIES
Instruction The word *subvert* contains the prefix *sub-* (which means "below or under") and the Latin root *vert* (which means "to turn"). Remind students that they can apply the meanings of prefixes and roots to understand the meanings of words.
Practice Have students use a dictionary to look up the definition and the etymology of the following words.

1. subject: a course of study (*sub-* + *iacere,* to throw)
2. subjugate: to bring under control (*sub-* + *iugum,* yoke)
3. submerge: to put under water (*sub-* + *mergere,* to plunge)
4. submit: to surrender (*sub-* + *mittere,* to cause to go)
5. substance: the material of which something is maid (*sub-* + *stáre,* to stand)

Use **Unit Seven Resource Book,** p. 79, for additional support.

A lesson on analyzing word parts appears on p. 674 of the Pupil's Edition.

Isabel Allende. Photograph by Acey Harper.

I light candles to summon the muses and guardian spirits, I place flowers on my desk to intimidate tedium.

which was how I learned of it in Caracas.[7] By then, thousands of people had disappeared in many parts of the continent, Chile was not an exception. In Argentina, the mothers of the *desaparecidos* marched in the Plaza de Mayo[8] carrying photographs of their missing children and grandchildren; in Uruguay, the names of prisoners far exceeded physical bodies that could be counted. What happened in Lonquén was like a knife in my belly, I felt the pain for years. Five men from the same family, the Maureiras,[9] had died, murdered by *carabineros*. Sometimes I would be driving down the highway and suddenly be assaulted by the disturbing vision of the Maureira women searching for their men, years of asking their futile questions in prisons and concentration camps and hospitals and barracks, like the thousands and thousands of other persons in other places trying to find their loved ones. In Lonquén, the women were more fortunate than most; at least they knew their men had been murdered, and they could cry and pray for them—although not bury them, because the military later scattered the remains and dynamited the lime kilns to prevent their becoming a site for pilgrimages and worship. One day those women 7

---

7. **Caracas** (kə-rä′kəs): the capital of Venezuela, where Allende was living in exile.
8. **Plaza de Mayo** (plä′sä dĕ mä′yô): a main square in Buenos Aires, the Argentine capital.
9. **Maureiras** (mou-rā′räz).

Customizing Instruction

Less Proficient Readers

You may wish to have students read this selection in four parts:

- The first part (Allende's description of her preparations before sitting down to write her second novel) ends with the sentence "I do not determine the subject, . . . " (page 1296)
- the second part (Allende's account of the terrible conditions under the Pinochet regime) ends with the sentence "So by 1983 I had at my disposal . . ." (page 1298)
- the third part (Allende's story about her meeting with the officer) ends with the sentence "I jotted down those memories . . ." (page 1299)
- the fourth part (Allende's statements about the strange powers of fiction and her story about her meeting with the priest) runs to the end of the selection.

English Learners

Explain the meaning of the following words:

1 The *muses* are "spirits that are thought to give ideas and feelings to writers."

2 *intimidate* means "to make afraid"

3 *capricious* means "likely to change suddenly"

4 *abandoned* means "deserted"

5 *kilns* means "ovens"

6 *decree* means "an official order or decision"

7 Tell students that pilgrimages are journeys made to holy places. The Pinochet regime was afraid that many people would visit the mine, regarding it as a sacred place because the murdered men were buried there. So the government blew up the mine along with the corpses in it.

Advanced Learners

Ask students to contrast Allende's preparations for writing her novel with their own preparations for creative writing projects.

Possible Responses: Answers will vary. Some students may state that they too wait for the right moment before writing the first sentence; other students may state that they try to get something down on paper quickly and then revise it later.

Reading and Analyzing

Literary Analysis AUTOBIOGRAPHY

A Ask students what they can conclude about Allende from this passage.

Possible Response: Allende feels deeply committed to victims of oppression in South America. She creates her second novel out of a sense of obligation to the suffering women in Lonquén and other places.

Literary Analysis ANECDOTE

B Tell students that an anecdote is a brief story that focuses on a single episode or event in a person's life and that illustrates a particular point. Then ask students what Allende learns from her encounter with the officer.

Possible Response: Allende learns that not all of Pinochet's officers are heartless killers. This officer, though he shot to death a political prisoner, is sensitive and remorseful.

walked up and down a row of rough-hewn
1 tables, sorting through a pitiful array—keys, a comb, a shred of blue sweater, a lock of hair, or a few teeth—and said, This is my husband, This is my brother, This is my son. Every time I thought of them, I was transported with implacable clarity to the times I lived in Chile under the heavy mantle of terror: censorship and self-censorship, denunciations, curfew, soldiers with faces camouflaged so they couldn't be recognized, political police cars with tinted glass windows, arrests in the street, homes, offices, my
2 racing to help fugitives find asylum in some embassy, sleepless nights when we had someone hidden in our home, the clumsy schemes to slip information out of the country or bring money in to aid families of the imprisoned. For my second novel, I didn't have to think of a subject, the women of the Maureira family, the mothers of the Plaza de Mayo, and millions of other victims
A pursued me, obliging me to write. The story of the deaths at Lonquén had lain in my heart since 1978; I had kept every press clipping that came into my hands without knowing exactly why, since at that time I had no inkling that my steps were leading toward literature. So by 1983, I had at my disposal a thick folder of information, and knew where to find other facts; my job consisted of weaving those threads into a single cord. I was relying on my friend Francisco in Chile, whom I meant to use as model for the protagonist, a family of Spanish Republican refugees on whom to pattern the Leals,[10] and a couple of women I had worked with on the women's magazine in Santiago as inspiration for the character of Irene. I drew Gustavo Morante,[11] Irene's fiancé, from a Chilean army officer who followed me to San Cristobal Hill one noontime in the autumn of 1974. I was sitting under a tree with my mother's Swiss dog, which I used to take for walks, looking down on Santiago from the heights, when an automobile stopped a few meters away and a man in uniform got out and walked toward me. I froze with panic; for a split second I considered running, but instantly knew the futility of trying to escape and simply waited, shivering and speechless. To my surprise, the officer did not bark an order to me but removed his cap, apologized for disturbing me, and asked if he could sit down. I still was unable to speak a word, but since arrests were always made by several men it calmed me to see that he was alone. He was about thirty, tall and handsome, with a rather naive, unlined face. I noticed his distress as soon as he spoke. He told me he knew who I was; he had read some of my articles, and hadn't liked them, but he enjoyed my programs on television. He had often watched me climb the hill and had followed me that day because he had something he wanted to tell me. He said that he came from a very religious family; he was a devout Catholic and as a young man had contemplated entering the seminary, but had gone to the military academy to please his father. He soon discovered he liked that profession, and with time the army had become his true home. "I am prepared to die for my country," he said, "but I didn't know how difficult it is to kill for it." And then, after a very long pause, he described the first detail he had commanded, how he was assigned to execute a political prisoner who had been so badly tortured he couldn't stand and had to be tied in a chair, how in a frosty courtyard at five in the morning he gave the order to fire, and how when the sound of the shots faded he realized the man was still alive and staring tranquilly into his eyes, because he was beyond fear.

"I had to approach the prisoner, put my pistol to his temple, and press the trigger. The blood splattered my uniform. It's something I can't tear

10. **Leals** (lĕ-älz′): a family in *Of Love and Shadows.*

11. **Gustavo Morante** (gōōs-tä′vô mô-rän′tĕ).

WORDS TO KNOW

implacable (ĭm-plăk′ə-bəl) *adj.* unable to be appeased; unyielding
naive (nī-ēv′) *adj.* innocent or childlike

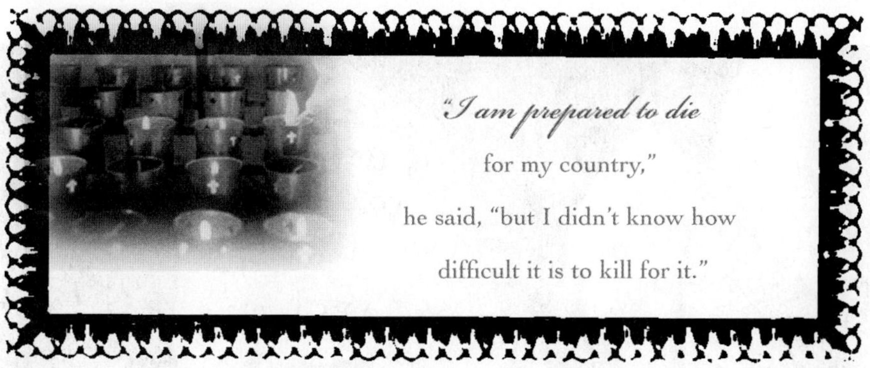

from my soul. I can't sleep, I am haunted by the memory."

"Why are you telling me this?" I asked.

"Because it isn't enough to have told my con-
B fessor, I want to share it with someone who may be able to make use of it. Not all the military are murderers, as is being said; many of us have a conscience." He stood, saluted me with a slight bow, put on his cap, and left.

Months later, another man, this one in civilian clothes, told me something similar. "Soldiers shoot at the legs to force the officers to fire the *coup de grace*[12] and stain themselves with blood, too," he said. I jotted down those memories and for nine years kept them at the bottom of a drawer, until I used them in *Of Love and Shadows.* Some critics considered the book sentimental, and too political; for me, it is filled with magic because it revealed to me the strange powers of fiction. In the slow and silent process of
7 writing, I enter a different state of consciousness in which sometimes I can draw back a veil and see the invisible, the world of my grandmother's three-legged table.[13] It is not necessary to mention all the premonitions and coincidences recorded in those pages, one will suffice. Although I had abundant information, there were large lacunae[14] in the story, because many of the military trials were conducted in secret and what was published was distorted by censorship. In addition, I was far from the scene and could not go to Chile to interrogate the involved parties as I would have done under other circumstances. My years as a journalist had taught me that it is in personal interviews that one obtains the keys, motives, and emotions of a story, no research in a library can replace the firsthand information derived from a face-to-face conversation. During those warm Caracas nights, I wrote the novel from the material in my file of clippings, a few books, some tapes from
Amnesty International,[15] and the inexhaustible 8
voices of the women of the *desaparecidos* speaking to me across distance and time. Even with all that, I had to call upon my imagination to fill in

12. ***coup de grace*** (ko͞o′ də gräs′) *French:* a death blow to a mortally wounded victim.
13. **my grandmother's three-legged table:** a table around which Allende's grandmother would sit with her friends and try to conjure up spirits of the dead.
14. **lacunae** (lə-kyo͞o′nē): gaps.
15. **Amnesty International:** a worldwide organization that works against human-rights violations and for the release of political prisoners.

Customizing Instruction

Less Proficient Readers

1 Make sure students understand that the "pitiful array" refers to all that remains of the 15 murdered men found in Lonquén.

Then check students' comprehension of the selection so far by asking the following questions:

- What does Allende place beneath her computer before writing a novel? *(a book of Pablo Neruda's poetry)*
- What was found in the deserted ovens at Lonquén? *(the remains of 15 murdered men)*
- What did the Chilean officer do to the political prisoner after the firing squad failed to kill him? *(He shot the prisoner in the head.)*

English Learners

Explain the meaning of the following words:

2 *asylum* means "a place where one is safe and secure"

3 *futility* means "uselessness"

4 *seminary* means "a place where young men study to become priests"

5 *detail* means "a special task assigned to soldiers"

6 *tranquilly* means "calmly"

7 *consciousness* means "awareness"

8 *inexhaustible* means "tireless"

Cross Curricular Link

Humanities

LATIN AMERICAN WOMEN WRITERS In recent Latin American literature, women writers have played an important role. Like the Chilean author Isabel Allende, these authors use their writing to denounce oppression and fight for human rights.

Among the most well-known of these authors is Luisa Valenzuela (1944–) of Argentina. Her collection of short stories, *Strange Things Happen Here,* vividly depicts life in Argentina under a repressive dictatorship. The autobiography of Rigoberta Menchú (1959–) of Guatemala is a gripping portrayal of the suffering of the native Indians. Claribel Alegría (1924–) of Nicaragua calls her poetry and prose "emergency or crisis writing." Her bilingual novel *Flores del volcán/Flowers from the Volcano* describes the human cost of war in her native land and in her adopted countries. Elena Poniatowska (1933–) of Mexico is widely regarded as the voice of the Mexican people. Her novel *Hasta no verte Jesús mío (Until I see you again, my Jesus)* presents events surrounding the Mexican Revolution as seen by an elderly laundry woman, who is indomitable and fiercely independent.

Reading and Analyzing

Active Reading

RECOGNIZING AUTHOR'S PURPOSE

A Ask students why Allende includes this account of her conversation with the priest.

Possible Response: to provide evidence that writing fiction increases her powers of awareness, giving her glimpses of the hidden truth

Copyright © Dave G. Houser/Corbis.

blanks. After she read the original, my mother
objected to one part that to her seemed absolutely improbable: the protagonists, at night and
during curfew, go by motorcycle to a mine sealed
off by the military; they find a break in the fence
and enter an area that is off-limits, dig into the
mouth of the mine with picks and shovels, find
the remains of the murdered, photograph them,
1 return with the proof, and deliver it to the cardinal, who finally orders the tomb opened. "That's
impossible," she said. "No one would dare run
such risks at the height of the dictatorship." "I
can't think of any other way to resolve the plot,
just think of it as literary license,"[16] I replied.
The book was published in 1984. Four years
later, the list of exiles who could not return to
2 Chile was abolished and for the first time I felt
free to go back to my country to vote in a
plebiscite[17] that finally unseated Pinochet. One
night the doorbell rang in my mother's house in
Santiago and a man insisted in talking with me
in private. In a corner of the terrace, he told me
he was a priest, that he had learned in the sanctity of the confessional about the bodies buried in
Lonquén, had gone there on his motorcycle during curfew, had opened a sealed mine with pick
and shovel, had photographed the remains and
taken the proof to the cardinal, who ordered a
group of priests, newspapermen, and diplomats
to open the clandestine tomb. 3

"No one has any knowledge of this except the cardinal and myself. If my participation in that matter had been known, I'm sure I wouldn't be here talking with you, I would be among the disappeared. How did you learn?" he asked. A

"The dead told me," I replied, but he did not believe me. ❖

16. **literary license:** a fiction writer's freedom to adjust or distort real-life situations.

17. **plebiscite** (plĕb′ĭ-sīt′): a direct vote of the people on an important issue.

Customizing Instruction

English Learners

1 Point out that a *cardinal* is a high official in the Roman Catholic Church. Then explain the meaning of the following words:

2 *abolished* means "done away with"

3 *clandestine* means "secret"

Less Proficient Readers

- Point out to students that the phrase "sanctity of the confessional" refers to the fact that a Roman Catholic priest is forbidden to reveal anything that a sinner has confessed to him.
- Make sure students understand what Allende means when she states, "The dead told me." "The dead" are the murdered men buried in the mine at Lonquén. Allende implies that they revealed to her how their bodies actually were discovered.

Advanced Learners

Ask students to recall the excerpt from the interview with Achebe, beginning on page 1280. Then ask them what Allende might say about Achebe's views of the purpose of storytelling.
Possible Response: Allende would agree with Achebe's position that writers should be activists who point out social injustices. In this essay and in her second novel, she described the brutal conditions in Chile under a military dictator.

MINI LESSON Grammar

COLONS WITH INDEPENDENT CLAUSES

Instruction Remind students that two independent clauses may be joined together by a semicolon or by a comma followed by a coordinating conjunction. A colon may also be used to join together two independent clauses. Tell students to use a colon between independent clauses when the second explains or elaborates on the first.

Activity Write the following sentence on the board:

> One part of my story seemed absolutely improbable to my mother: the protagonists, at night and during curfew, enter a mine sealed off by the military.

This sentence contains two independent clauses. The first one precedes the colon, and the second follows it. The second provides an example that shows what the mother considers improbable in the story.

Practice Have students identify the independent clauses, and then insert a colon between them:

1. As a writer, Allende prepares for the moment of inspiration she lights candles and quietly waits for the first sentence of her story to come to her. *(inspiration: she)*
2. Allende believes that writing fiction helps her discover the truth in describing the discovery of the murdered bodies, for example, she revealed how they really were found. *(truth: in)*

For more instruction and practice in using colons, use McDougal Littell's ***Language Network:***

- Grade 10, Chapter 11 "Punctuation"
- Grade 12, Chapter 10 "Other Punctuation Marks"

Connect to the Literature

1. **What Do You Think?** What is your reaction to Allende's conversation with the priest at the end of the excerpt?

Comprehension Check

- What had happened to the men whose bodies were discovered in Lonquén?
- What real events described in this selection did Allende use in *Of Love and Shadows?*

Think Critically

2. **ACTIVE READING: RECOGNIZING AUTHOR'S PURPOSE** With a small group of classmates, compare the notes you recorded in your  READER'S NOTEBOOK. As a group, decide on Allende's main **purpose** for writing the excerpt. What secondary purposes might she have had?

3. How would you describe Allende as a writer?

THINK ABOUT
- how she sets up her environment as she begins
- her decision to write about "the disappeared"
- her use of personal interviews rather than library research

4. Why do you suppose the Chilean army officer wanted Allende to write about his confession?

5. **Irony** is a surprising contrast between expectation and reality. What is ironic about the objection Allende's mother raises to the story of the sealed-off mine?

Extend Interpretations

6. **Critic's Corner** Many writers and critics believe that in order to create a good story, a writer must write about what he or she knows—that to write about events, characters, and settings not experienced at first hand almost always leads to failure. Do you agree? Could Allende have written *Of Love and Shadows* if she had never experienced Chile's political turmoil? Give reasons or examples to support your opinion.

7. **Connect to Life** Many people are working to obtain justice for "the disappeared" in Chile. What other atrocities around the world have you read or heard about? What are people doing to try to right these wrongs? If appropriate, you might want to write about the event you recalled in the Connect to Your Life on page 1295.

LITERARY ANALYSIS: AUTOBIOGRAPHY

An **autobiography** is a writer's first-person account of his or her own life. Typically, an autobiography focuses on the most significant events and people in the writer's life. The narrative reveals the writer's feelings about these events and people and provides some understanding of the society in which he or she lived. Think about what the following statement suggests about Allende and about Chile during the years of the military dictatorship:

Sometimes I would be driving down the highway and suddenly be assaulted by the disturbing vision of the Maureira women searching for their men, years of asking their futile questions in prisons and concentration camps and hospitals and barracks. . . .

Paired Activity Get together with a partner and review the excerpt from *Paula.* Identify other details that provide insights into Allende and life in Chile under Pinochet. Then think about the type of information a history text might convey about "the disappeared" in Chile. What details does Allende's autobiography contain that might not be included in a traditional history book? What additional information might you find in a history book?

Connect to the Literature

1. **What Do You Think?** Students may say that the conversation with the priest surprised them because it reveals that Allende, though she thought she was creating fiction, described what actually happened at Lonquén.

Comprehension Check

- The men were murdered by the military police.
- the murder of the missing men and the search by the Maureira women and others for their loved ones

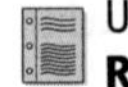 Use Selection Quiz in **Unit Seven Resource Book,** p. 80.

Think Critically

2. Possible Response: to inform readers about "the strange powers of fiction"—or the element of magic or mystery—that Allende discovered while writing her second novel.
3. Possible Response: Allende believes in mystical experience or inspiration, rather than rational control, in writing her novels. To create an atmosphere conducive to inspiration, she lights candles, arranges fresh flowers, and places a book of Neruda's poetry under her computer. Allende is convinced that she does not choose the subjects of her novels but that they choose her. For example, she attributes her decision to write about "the disappeared" to the mysterious influence of the women searching for their loved ones. She values personal interviews because they provide fresh, firsthand information.
4. Possible Response: The Chilean army officer wanted Allende to write about his confession so that her readers might regard some military officers as humans with consciences rather than monsters without feeling.
5. Possible Response: Though Allende's mother regards the story as contrived and improbable, it turns out to be true.

Extend Interpretations

6. **Critic's Corner** Responses will vary. Some students may state that if Allende had not experienced political turmoil in her own life, she would not have been able to render it so vividly. Students who challenge this opinion may cite the American writer Stephen Crane (1871–1900), who wrote one of the greatest war novels of all time—*The Red Badge of Courage*—without ever having fought a single battle.
7. **Connect to Life** Responses will vary. Some students may mention the efforts of Holocaust survivors to keep that atrocity alive in the world's memory.

Literary Analysis

Paired Activity The sentence "Every time I thought of them, . . . the imprisoned" (near the top of the first column on page 1298) describes repressive conditions in Chile under Pinochet. Allende's description of her meeting with the Chilean army officer and of her anguish for the Maureiras might not be found in a traditional history book. Instead, that book might include facts about social, political, and economic inequalities and contrast Salvador Allende and Augusto Pinochet.

 Use **Unit Seven Resource Book,** p. 78, for more practice.

Writing Options

1. Autobiographical Essay
Write an autobiographical essay in which you describe an important event, at your school or in your community, that you experienced personally. Be sure to express your feelings and opinions about the event.

Writing Handbook
See page R29: Narrative Writing.

2. Mother-and-Daughter Dialogue Write a dialogue that might have taken place between Allende and her mother after the writer's conversation with the priest.

3. Letter to the Editor Write a letter that Isabel Allende might have written to the editor of the newspaper that published the article about the deaths at Lonquén. Make sure that your letter is consistent with Allende's own feelings and opinions about the incident.

Activities & Explorations

Human-Rights Poster
Atrocities like those that Allende describes have happened—and continue to happen—around the world. Create a poster that a United Nations agency might use to promote respect for human rights. ~ **ART**

Inquiry & Research

Chile After Pinochet Do research to find out what happened in Chile after Pinochet's years in power. How was Pinochet removed from power? What happened to him? Who governs Chile now? Write a brief report in which you answer these questions.

Vocabulary in Action

EXERCISE: MEANING CLUES Use your knowledge of the Words to Know to answer the following questions.

1. If you are implacable during an argument, do you readily admit you are wrong, speak very loudly, or refuse to give in?
2. Is **tedium** likely to be a result of having nothing to do, going to an amusement park, or falling off a bicycle?
3. When you learn something by **osmosis,** have you most likely studied hard, copied someone else's work, or absorbed the information unconsciously?
4. s a **naive** person one who is very innocent, very shrewd, or very stubborn?
5. If you **subvert** someone's plan, do you carry out the plan, spoil the plan, or praise the plan?

Building Vocabulary
For an in-depth lesson on using context clues, see page 674.

Writing Options

1. Autobiographical Essay Encourage students to ask themselves questions about the event such as the following: What happened? Who was there? How did it happen? When and where did it happen? Why did it happen? Tell students to make a chart and fill in the details that answer each question.

2. Mother-and-Daughter Dialogue Suggest that students first reread Allende's conversation with the priest. In the dialogue, Allende should convey her belief that the act of writing increases her intuition, revealing mysterious truths.

3. Letter to the Editor Remind students that their goal is to persuade others to think and feel as Allende does. It is important to state Allende's position and then support it with facts and opinions.

Activities & Explorations

Human-Rights Poster Suggest that students include pictures, photographs, symbols, and colors in their poster.

Inquiry & Research

Chile After Pinochet Students might work in small groups to do this project. One student might do the research, another might write a summary, and a third might use the summary to present an oral report to the class.

Vocabulary in Action

1. refuse to give in
2. having nothing to do
3. absorbed the information unconsciously
4. very innocent
5. spoil the plan

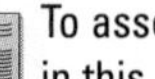
To assess skills and concepts taught in this selection, use **Formal Assessment Book,** pp. 191–192.

Possible Objectives

This **On Your Own** featured selection may be used to achieve one or more of the following objectives:

- to give students the opportunity to read independently, either reading silently on their own, reading and analyzing literature with a group, or using the Reader's Notebook to write in response to the literature
- to conduct a post-reading class discussion
- to assess students' comprehension of the selection

Working Independently

You may want to set aside time each week for independent reading, without making an assignment related to the reading. Or once students have completed the reading, either alone or aloud in groups, you may ask them to work together on a project, such as creating an illustration of the events in the poem. If you choose to have students write responsively in their Reader's Notebook, suggest that they list several phrases or images from the poem that seemed particularly strong to them. They can then write what they thought made each one effective.

Discussing the Selection

The two questions on page 1304 of the pupil edition are suitable for a post-reading class discussion. See the side column on page 1305 for possible responses to these questions.

Using the Selection for Assessment

If you want to use this selection as the basis for assessment, see **Integrated Assessment Book,** pp. 37–42, for test questions.

THE DIAMETER OF THE BOMB

YEHUDA **AMICHAI**

Translated by
CHANA BLOCH and
STEPHEN MITCHELL

Yehuda Amichai
1924–2000

Israeli Homeland Yehuda Amichai (yə-hōō'də ä'mī-ᴋʜī') is widely considered one of Israel's greatest poets. Born in Würzburg, Germany, Amichai was raised in the Orthodox Jewish tradition. To escape the persecution of Jews in Europe, his family emigrated to Jerusalem in 1936. There, Amichai became involved in Israel's struggle to win independence and define itself as a nation.

Soldier and Poet To a great extent, Amichai's poetry was influenced by his war experiences. He was a member of Britain's Jewish Brigade during World War II and fought in the Israeli army during the Arab-Israeli war of 1948. Many of his poems feature the images and terminology of warfare, and he treats such war themes as loss and destruction with ironic humor and understatement. His poetry rings true to soldiers themselves. According to one story, several Israeli students drafted to fight in the Arab-Israeli conflict of 1973 packed books of Amichai's poetry along with their rifles.

Amichai's first book of poetry was published in 1955. Over the course of his career, he wrote ten more volumes of poetry, as well as novels, short stories, and plays. Although Amichai's poetry is deeply rooted in his adopted homeland, his writing has become well-known outside Israel. His work has been translated into more than 30 languages.

In "The Diameter of the Bomb," Amichai describes the range of destruction caused by a terrorist's bomb. Like the other selections in this part of Unit Seven, the poem deals with the consequences of conflict. As you read it, ask yourself these questions:

1. *What causes the bomb's circle of destruction to keep growing?*
2. *How does Amichai's attitude toward conflict and its devastation compare with the attitudes of other writers you've read in this part?*

The diameter of the bomb was thirty centimeters
and the diameter of its effective range about seven meters,
with four dead and eleven wounded.
And around these, in a larger circle
of pain and time, two hospitals are scattered
and one graveyard. But the young woman
who was buried in the city she came from,
at a distance of more than a hundred kilometers,
enlarges the circle considerably,
and the solitary man mourning her death
at the distant shores of a country far across the sea
includes the entire world in the circle.
And I won't even mention the crying of orphans
that reaches up to the throne of God and
beyond, making
a circle with no end and no God.

Answers to questions on page 1304

1. What causes the bomb's circle of destruction to keep growing?
   Possible Response: According to the poem, the circle expands because it affects not only the people killed or injured but also those they knew or children they left behind.
2. How does Amichai's attitude toward conflict and its devastation compare with the attitudes of other writers you've read in this part?
   Possible Response: Like many of the other writers, Amichai presents a strong, vivid picture of the harm resulting from violent conflict. His particular emphasis is that the harm extends far beyond the immediate victims.

THE DIAMETER OF THE BOMB **1305**

Objectives
- write a Research Report
- use a written text as a model for writing
- revise a draft to build paragraphs
- proofread for errors in comma usage

Introducing the Workshop

A Research Report Research reports require the writer to collect and synthesize information from various sources. This skill is useful not only in school but in such professions as teaching, law, science, and business, where writers must draw on source information to support claims and develop analyses. Citing one's sources is important because it establishes credibility and provides a foundation of factual information upon which to base claims and draw conclusions.

With students, establish criteria for what makes a claim authoritative. Readers may consider a claim more valid if it comes from a credible source. A good source demonstrates expertise, knowledge, credentials, objectivity, and character.

Basics in a Box

B Using the Graphic Although the writer presents the evidence to support the thesis statement in the body of the research paper, all the parts of the paper—introduction, body, conclusion, and works cited—must be tied together to create a unified paper.

C Presenting the Rubric To better understand the assignment, students can refer to the Standards for Writing a Successful Research Report. You may wish to discuss with them the complete rubric and student models in the Unit Seven Resource Book on pages 86–92.

For more instruction and practice in writing a research report, use McDougal Littell's ***Language Network:***
- Grade 10, Chapter 25: "Research Report"
- Grade 12, Chapter 24, "Research Report"

Writing Workshop — Research Report

Researching a topic in depth . . .

A **From Reading to Writing** In this part, you have read works written in response to varying political conflicts. In coming to understand these works, a knowledge of the period's political and historical events is important. The twentieth century offers a wide range of topics for a **research report,** an academic paper in which you explore a subject and present information you have gathered and synthesized. The skills you develop in writing a research report can help you outside school—the skills involved in gathering, evaluating, and making sense of information are critical in today's world.

For Your Portfolio

WRITING PROMPT Write a short research report about a historical or political topic or another topic that interests you.

Purpose: To share information and draw a conclusion about your topic

Audience: Your classmates, your teacher, or anyone who shares your interest in the topic

B

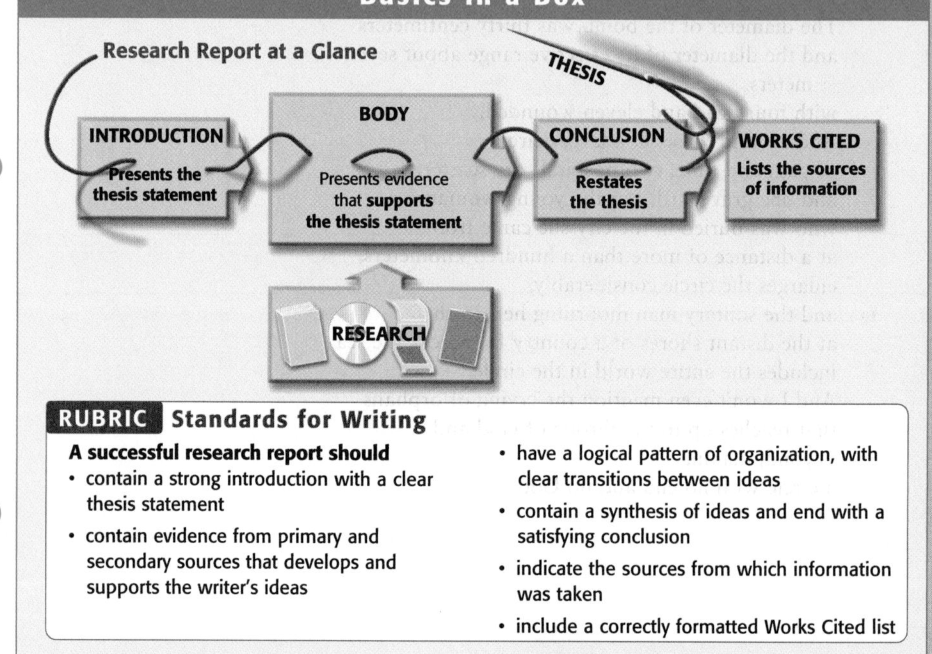

C **RUBRIC Standards for Writing**

A successful research report should
- contain a strong introduction with a clear thesis statement
- contain evidence from primary and secondary sources that develops and supports the writer's ideas
- have a logical pattern of organization, with clear transitions between ideas
- contain a synthesis of ideas and end with a satisfying conclusion
- indicate the sources from which information was taken
- include a correctly formatted Works Cited list

LESSON RESOURCES

USING PRINT RESOURCES
Unit Seven Resource Book
- Prewriting, p. 81
- Drafting and Elaboration, p. 82
- Peer Response, pp. 83–84
- Revising, Editing, and Proofreading, p. 85
- Student Models, pp. 86–91
- Rubric, p. 92

USING MEDIA RESOURCES
Writing Coach CD-ROM
Visit our Web site: classzone.com
For a complete view of Lesson Resources, see page 1095k in this book.

Analyzing a Student Model

Jones 1

Richard Jones

Mr. Martin

English, period 2

25 May

Nigeria: Independence Was Not Enough

Nigeria as we know it has existed since 1914, when Great Britain combined its protectorates of Southern Nigeria and Northern Nigeria into a single colony. The British had been in the region for almost a hundred years at that point, first as traders and missionaries and eventually as rulers. In 1960, however, they handed the country back to the Nigerian people in a remarkably peaceful transfer of power ("Western Africa" 894, 903-904). However, the Nigerian struggle for successful self-government was far from over. In fact, the gaining of independence was the easiest step in Nigeria's painful struggle for democracy, a struggle that continues today.

When Nigeria became independent, its leaders faced an entirely new situation. Before the arrival of the British in the early 19th century, there was no country called Nigeria. The region had consisted of many independent states, ranging in size from small villages and chiefdoms to powerful empires. While the different states were connected by trade and geography, and sometimes by religion, they had never shared a common identity, and certainly not a central government (Falola 19-27).

Nationalism—the desire for an independent, unified Nigeria—arose in response to British colonial rule. Many Nigerians were unhappy with colonialism; they felt that the British were racist and patronizing and that the British influence in Nigeria was damaging to traditional values. The common desire for freedom from colonial rule united people and strengthened their sense of national identity (Falola 82).

RUBRIC IN ACTION

D

1. This writer begins by giving a brief historical background.
   Other Options:
   - Begin with a provocative question.
   - Start with an anecdote.
2. Presents the thesis statement
3. Uses parenthetical documentation to credit a source

LANGUAGE SKILLS

Teaching the Lesson

Analyzing the Model

"Nigeria: Independence Was Not Enough"

D The student model analyzes the Nigerian struggle for democracy, first as it strove for freedom from British rule, and later as it has continued to strive for successful democratic self-rule in the face of a series of military coups and severe political corruption.

Have students read the model and then take turns reading aloud the Rubric in Action. Point out the key words and phrases in the student model that correspond to the elements mentioned in the Rubric.

1. Have students suggest an alternative introduction based on the other options given. Discuss the pros or cons of each alternative.
   Possible Responses: The writer could begin with an engaging fact or anecdote, which might catch the readers' attention, but also might lack context for readers unfamiliar with the subject matter; the writer could begin with an interesting and relevant quotation, which he could then use as a springboard for his discussion.
2. Point out to students that if a thesis statement is missing from a research report, the reader may have a hard time understanding where the report is going or why it contains certain information.
3. Have students note the citation in parentheses and then find the reference in the Works Cited list to see how the two are related.

4. Explain to students that chronological order is often the most appropriate organization when writing about history. However, some topics are better organized according to some other structure, such as cause-and-effect, an analysis of parts, or order of importance.
5. In an extended paper, it is important to provide readers with clues indicating relationships between paragraphs or sections. Ask students how this transitional sentence serves to connect the two topics. **Possible Response:** By saying *this independence proved difficult,* the writer indicates that he is about to elaborate on the independence that was being discussed in the previous paragraph.
6. Ask students why a writer might choose to use a direct quotation rather than a paraphrase or summary. **Possible Responses:** By quoting an expert, a writer adds to his or her credibility; a quotation can be used to vividly introduce a particular point of view; a writer can use a quotation to represent an opinion that is not necessarily his own, but is relevant to the topic.

When the British had begun to govern Nigeria, they had taken control from the traditional leaders of the independent states. Under the British government a new Nigerian elite developed—black Nigerians with a European education and Western values. It was this elite that promoted the nationalist movement. The movement gained strength during the economic depression of the 1920s and 1930s and especially during World War II, when Nigerian troops fought for the British. At this point, Nigerians realized that they were helping the British fight for freedom and democracy on an international level but that they themselves enjoyed no such benefits (Falola 81-82, 88). The nationalist movement continued to grow, and after a series of peaceful constitutional changes, the British finally granted Nigeria its independence in 1960 (Falola 89).

❹ Presents events in the rise of nationalism in chronological order

This independence proved difficult. The new Nigerian state was troubled almost from the start. Different regions of the country struggled for power, and the country saw a series of six military coups over 20 years. In 1967, three eastern states tried to establish an independent state of Biafra, and a bloody civil war ensued, lasting for almost three years. The Biafran secession failed ("Western Africa" 904).

❺ Uses a transitional phrase between paragraphs to connect ideas

In addition to ferocious ethnic and regional rivalry, Nigeria has been plagued by great corruption in government. For years, the country's leaders have diverted billions of dollars of the nation's oil wealth to increase their personal fortunes (Maier 3). The majority of Nigerians, however, have remained among the poorest people in the world (Pulsipher 348). According to Karl Meier, an American journalist, the members of the Nigerian elite have served the Nigerian people little better than the British did: "Colonial Nigeria was designed in 1914 to serve the British Empire, and the independent state serves as a tool of plunder by the country's modern rulers" (xxiii).

❻ Supports a key idea with a quotation
Other Options:
- Paraphrase a source.
- Summarize information.

What happened? "The trouble with Nigeria is simply and squarely a failure of leadership," wrote Chinua Achebe in his book The Trouble with Nigeria. "There is

Jones 3

nothing basically wrong with the Nigerian character. There is nothing wrong with the Nigerian land or climate or water or air or anything else. The Nigerian problem is the unwillingness or inability of its leaders to rise to the responsibility, to the challenge of personal example which are the hallmarks of true leadership" (1).

Jones 12

Works Cited

Achebe, Chinua. The Trouble with Nigeria. Enugu, Nigeria: Fourth Dimension, 1983.

Falola, Toyin. The History of Nigeria. Westport: Greenwood, 1999.

Maier, Karl. This House Has Fallen: Midnight in Nigeria. New York: PublicAffairs, 2000.

"Nigeria." Encyclopaedia Britannica Online. Vers. 99.1. 2000. Encyclopaedia Britannica. 16 May 2001 <http://www.eb.com:180/bol/topic?eu=120185&sctn=1&pm=1>.

Onishi, Norimitsu. "In the Oil-Rich Nigeria Delta, Deep Poverty and Grim Fires." New York Times 11 Aug. 2000, natl. ed.: A1+.

Pulsipher, Lydia Mihelič. World Regional Geography. New York: Freeman, 2000.

Soyinka, Wole. The Open Sore of a Continent: A Personal Narrative of the Nigerian Crisis. New York: Oxford UP, 1996.

"Western Africa." The New Encyclopaedia Britannica: Macropaedia. 15th ed. 1993.

Works Cited

- Identifies the information sources credited in the report
- Lists sources alphabetically, in most cases by authors' last names
- Contains complete publication information for each source
- Follows an established style for arranging and punctuating the information in entries

Need help with Works Cited?

See p. R41 in the **Writing Handbook**.

Works Cited Explain that each entry has three parts—author information, title information, and publication information—and that each part ends with a period.

Works Cited Tip

The 5th edition of the *MLA Handbook for Writers of Research Papers* was used in preparing the print and online citations that appear on the Works Cited page.

Prewriting and Exploring

Choosing a Topic

If after reading the Idea Bank students are having trouble choosing their subjects, suggest they try the following:

- Read recent newspapers and news magazines looking for problems and controversies in world events. A problem-solution essay or a cause-and-effect essay can be a good form for a research report.
- Explain to students that a question is usually the foundation of a research report; that is, many writers conduct research for the purpose of answering a question. Encourage students to develop questions about topics that interest them. When they have chosen a topic, have them use their questions to direct their research.

Planning the Research Report

1. Students may need to conduct a preliminary search in books or on the Internet to see if their topic is too broad. Looking at tables of contents and indexes can provide clues about how to break a particular topic into smaller parts.
4. Have each student write his or her thesis statement on a 3 x 5 card and tape it in a prominent place such as the front of a folder or the corner of a desk. This visual reminder can help them stay focused. Remind students that as their research progresses, they may discover new or surprising information that will cause them to change their thesis statements. Urge them to remain flexible and open to new ideas.

Researching

Students need not limit their research to the library. Encourage them to seek out interviews or use television and radio programs as sources of information. The Internet also provides sources that cannot be found elsewhere; however, students must carefully determine whether an Internet source is reliable before using the information in their report.

Research Tip

Suggest that students review the table of contents and the index of each book they find on their topic. These features can tell students whether the book is likely to be useful and direct them toward the appropriate sections of the book.

IDEABank

1. Your Working Portfolio

Build on the Writing Option you completed earlier in this unit:

- **Research Plan,** p. 1231

2. History in Literature

What literary works have made you curious about their social and historical contexts? Are you drawn to certain time periods or cultural regions? Choose one as a starting point for your research.

3. Surfing the Net

Browse the Internet for topics that interest you. Explore frequently visited sites or do a subject search, using several search engines. Choose one topic you would like to explore further.

Writing Your Research Report

1 Prewriting and Exploring

Begin by exploring topics that interest you. Look through the selections in this unit—what interesting historical, political, or literary topics do they suggest? Think about the geographic and political backgrounds of the selections. Which ones deal with real-life events or people? (See the **Idea Bank** in the margin for more suggestions for finding a topic.) Choose one topic and follow the steps below to narrow it and define your research goal.

Planning Your Research Report

1. **Focus your topic.** How broad is your topic? If it is too broad, you will find far more information on it than you can use. If it is too narrow, you might not find enough. For a too-broad topic, think about ways of dividing it into subtopics, as in this cluster diagram.

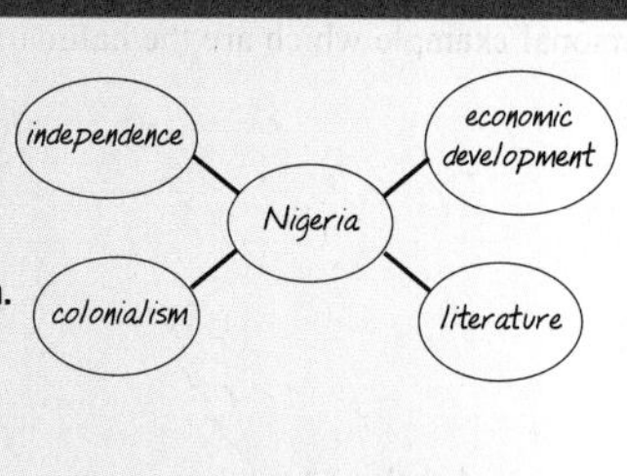

2. **Set your goals.** What do you want to accomplish in your report? Do you want to entertain your readers, prove a point, share information, or provoke a response from your readers?
3. **Identify your audience.** Who will read your report? What will interest them about your topic? What might they already know about it? What background information will you need to provide?
4. **Write a working thesis statement.** A thesis statement is a sentence that explains what your report is about. It will guide your research and help you sort through and evaluate the information that you find. For now, you simply need a working thesis, which you can revise later.

2 Researching

Begin your research by making a list of relevant, interesting, and researchable questions about your topic. Using these questions as a guide, gather and review a variety of reliable sources. You might start with general reference works (such as print or online encyclopedias) and move from there to books, periodicals, and reputable online sources for more-specific information.

Every source of information is either a primary or a secondary source. **Primary sources** provide direct, firsthand information about events. These sources include letters, journals, diaries, eyewitness accounts, and historical documents. **Secondary sources** present information derived or compiled from other sources; they offer interpretations, explanations, and comments about events. Newspapers, encyclopedias, and magazines, as well as many books, are secondary sources.

Evaluate Your Sources

Not all sources of information are equally valuable or reliable. The following questions can help you determine whether a source is a good one to use:

- **To what extent is the author's viewpoint biased**—that is, influenced by his or her position in society, political beliefs, gender, and ethnic background? Be sure to read materials from a variety of viewpoints.
- **How current is the source?** In quickly changing fields—such as technology, medicine, and present-day politics—it's particularly important to find up-to-date materials.
- **Is the source reliable?** This question is especially important when reviewing online publications.

Make Source Cards

When you have found sources of information relevant to your topic, make source cards. For each source, record the author, title, and complete publishing information on an index card. Follow the formats shown at the right, numbering the sources. You will use these cards later to credit sources in your report and to prepare your Works Cited list.

As technology begins to play a greater role in research and writing, many handbooks are beginning to recommend taking notes directly on the computer rather than using note cards; the fifth edition of the *MLA Handbook for Writers of Research Papers* has information about this approach. Ask your teacher before using this method of note taking.

Take Notes

As you read, keep your thesis statement and writing goals in mind. Take notes on any relevant information, using a separate index card for each piece of information. Write the number of the source on each note card, along with the page number on which you found the information. The example below shows two different note-taking strategies.

Internet Tip

Not all sites on the Internet are reliable: anyone can post anything, whether it's true or not. Generally, information from a government agency (".gov") or a large reputable institution will be reliable. Information from a personal Web page should not be considered reliable.

LANGUAGE SKILLS

Periodical ③

Onishi, Norimitsu. "In the Oil-Rich Nigeria Delta, Deep Poverty and Grim Fires." New York Times 11 Aug. 2000, natl. ed.: A1+

Internet ④

"Nigeria." Encyclopaedia Britannica Online. Vers. 99.1.2000 Encyclopaedia Britannica. 16 May 2001 http://www.eb.com:180/bol/topic?eu=120185&sctn=1&pm=1

Paraphrase. Restate the material in your own words. This is a good strategy to use when taking detailed notes.

Source Number.

Quotation. Copy the exact words and punctuation that appear in the source, enclosing them in quotation marks. Use a quotation when you need to emphasize a point or when the author's language is especially strong or clear.

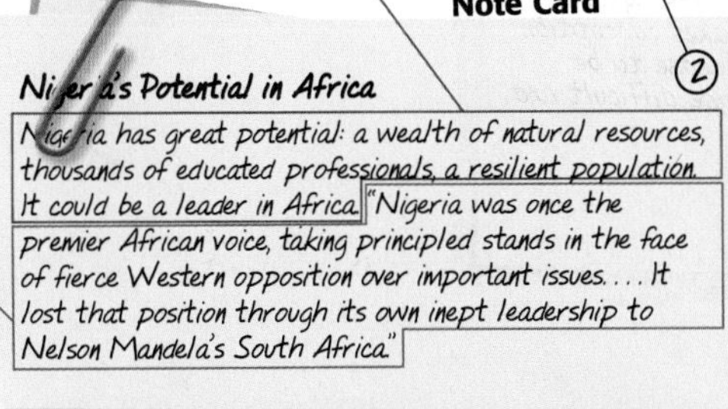

Evaluate Your Sources

To determine whether an author is a credible authority on a given subject, students may want to conduct an Internet search on that author, which may yield information about his or her career or reputation. Students can also find reputable authors by looking in bibliographies on a given topic that have been compiled by a credible source; some encyclopedia articles contain such bibliographies.

Make Source Cards

Have students compare the sample note cards on this page to an actual encyclopedia, book, periodical, and web page so that they can see where the listed information comes from.

Have students consult the *MLA Handbook for Writers of Research Papers* for information on how to document other types of sources, such as a live interview, or the foreword of a book.

Teaching Tip: Making Source Cards

Advise students to write down complete publication information immediately when they first consult a source, especially if they must leave the source at the library. If they wait to do so, they may return to find that the book or magazine they want is checked out or in use.

Take Notes

Students will have an easier time writing their research papers if they paraphrase and summarize on their note cards. Warn them against overuse of quotations. Strategically placing a few well-phrased quotations will be more effective than sprinkling their paper with numerous weak quotes.

Organize Your Material

Extra time spent at this stage of the project is time well spent. Set aside time to confer with students on the logic of their outline and report. Students who have gaps in their information will need to do additional research. Other students may have information on their outlines that is interesting but unrelated to the thesis statement. Still others may need to reorganize the information they have in order to present it more effectively. Have students revise topic outlines several times until they are tight and logically coherent.

Organize Your Material

Once you have gathered all of your information, it's time to organize your notes. A topic outline is one very good way of doing so. Begin by grouping your note cards into stacks of related ideas. Then think about how you want to arrange the ideas. You might choose chronological order for historical or biographical information, but there are other useful patterns of organization, such as cause and effect, comparison and contrast, and order of importance. Develop an outline based on the pattern you choose, and organize the notes in each stack accordingly.

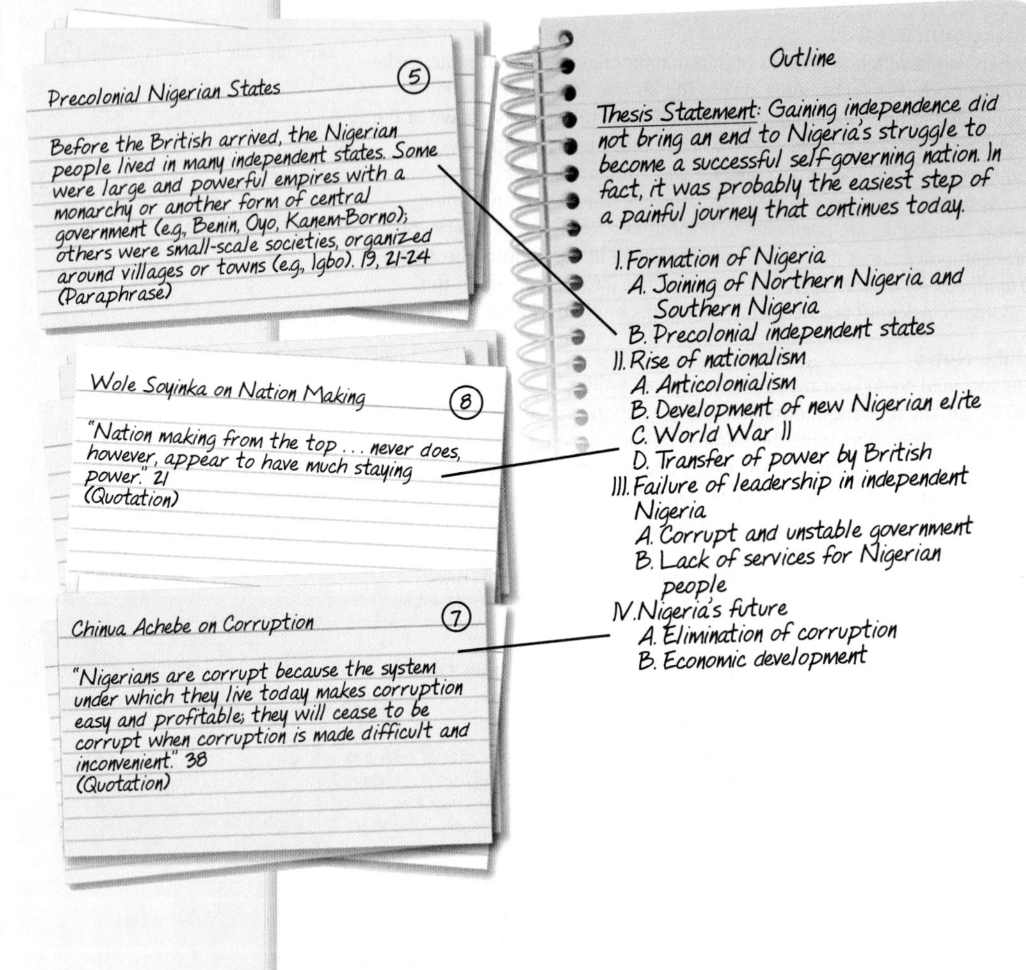

❸ Drafting

Begin drafting your report, using your outline as a guide. At the beginning of your report, you should state your main idea, or thesis; you will end with a restatement of this thesis and a summary of your main points. In the body of your report, which is the largest part, you should develop your ideas and support your thesis.

Settle on a Thesis Statement

After you've finished your research, revise your working thesis statement (if necessary) to reflect your findings.

Write Your Draft

As you draft your report, concentrate on getting your ideas on paper in clear, natural language. Follow your outline and refer to your notes as you write, keeping in mind that you may need to reorganize your material as you gather new information or discover a new way of thinking about it.

Develop your own analysis. Your report should be more than a collection of information. Analyze, synthesize, and draw conclusions from the information you've found, using facts, statistics, quotations, and examples as evidence to support your ideas.

Document your sources. After each quotation, paraphrase, or summary in your report, add (in parentheses) the name of the source's author—or its title if no author is credited—and the page number where you found the information. (If you mention the author's name in introducing the information, you need cite only the page number.) Use your note cards and source cards to identify the sources of the information you have used. If you do not credit the sources of the information in your report, you are guilty of plagiarism—the unlawful use of another's words or ideas. The Works Cited page at the end of your report will provide complete publishing information for each source.

Reread What You've Written

Take a break from your writing. Then review your draft. Ask yourself the following questions:

- How can I make my thesis statement clearer?
- What additional information would support my thesis statement?
- What information, if any, is irrelevant?
- How can I improve the organization of the ideas in my report?
- What facts and documentation do I need to check?

Ask Your Peer Reader

- What did you find most interesting in my report?
- What did you learn about my topic?
- Which ideas need more explanation?
- Does the order in which I've presented my ideas make sense? Would another type of organization work better?
- What impression were you left with when you read my conclusion?

Drafting Tip

Remember that your outline is only a tool. Feel free to reorganize your material at any time or collect new information as needed.

Need help documenting sources?

See the **Writing Handbook**, p. R40.

Drafting

To prevent students from becoming overwhelmed by their task, encourage them to develop a flow chart listing each section of the outline. As they finish writing each section, have them check it off on their flow charts.

Settle on a Thesis Statement

Have students work in pairs to revise their thesis statements to reflect the conclusions they have drawn on their topics after conducting their research.

Teaching Tip: Drawing Conclusions

Many students will need guidance in drafting a paper that goes beyond an assembly of facts to synthesize information and draw conclusions. Have volunteers share some of the conclusions they have drawn from their research. Discuss how they reached these conclusions.

Write the Draft

Remind students that their goal is not simply to report facts but to synthesize information. Ultimately, their own ideas and interpretations should be the driving force behind the paper.

Revising

PARAGRAPH BUILDING

Have a volunteer identify the main idea in the sample paragraph. Discuss why the second-to-last sentence does not belong in the paragraph.

Editing and Proofreading

USING COMMAS

Review with students some appropriate uses of the comma: to separate elements in a series; to set off introductory elements, interrupters, and nonessential phrases and clauses; to precede a coordinating conjunction joining two independent clauses; and to separate words or phrases that might otherwise be misunderstood.

Point out to students that the two commas in the first sentence of the model serve none of the above purposes. The first comma separates the verb from its direct object, which is incorrect, and the second separates a noun from an essential prepositional phrase, which is also incorrect. In the third line, a comma has been added to set off *however*, which is an interrupter.

Making a Works Cited List

Point out that the Works Cited list contains only sources that have actually been cited in the report; they need not include works that they read but did not actually refer to in the paper.

Remind students that the entries should be in alphabetical order; they should leave a double space between entries; and the first line of each entry should begin at the left margin with following lines indented.

Reflecting

Encourage students to think about how their thesis statement evolved as they conducted their research. They might also consider how the process of writing a research paper differed from the processes they used in other types of writing. Did they do enough planning before they began to write? Have students add these self-evaluations to their working portfolios.

Need revising help?

Review the **Rubric,** p. 1306.

Consider peer-reader comments.

Check **Revision Guidelines,** p. R19.

Publishing IDEAS

- Share your report with the class in an oral presentation.

❹ Revising

TARGET SKILL ▶ PARAGRAPH BUILDING Writing has unity when all the sentences in a paragraph support its central idea. As you revise your research report, delete any unrelated ideas.

> Nationalism—the desire for an independent, unified Nigeria—arose in response to British colonial rule. Many Nigerians were unhappy with colonialism; they felt that the British were racist and patronizing and that the British influence in Nigeria was damaging to traditional values. ~~The British had their own identity and traditional values.~~ The common desire for freedom from colonial rule united people and strengthened their sense of national identity (Falola 82).

❺ Editing and Proofreading

TARGET SKILL ▶ USING COMMAS Reports include a great deal of information. The correct use of commas can help your readers better understand relationships between ideas.

> For years, the country's leaders have diverted, billions of dollars, of the nation's oil wealth to increase their personal fortunes (maier 3). (CAP)
>
> The majority of Nigerians ^, however, have remained among the poorest people in the World (Pulsipher 348). (lc)

❻ Making a Works Cited List

When you have finished revising and editing your report, make a **Works Cited** list and attach it to the end of your paper. See page R41 in the **Writing Handbook** for the correct format.

❼ Reflecting

FOR YOUR PORTFOLIO What did you learn about your working style and habits as you engaged in the process of writing a research report? Is there anything more you would like to know about your topic? Write some questions for further study, then attach them to your research report and save it in your **Working Portfolio.**

Read this opening from the first draft of a research report. The underlined sections may include the following kinds of errors:

- comma errors
- capitalization errors
- misspelled words
- errors in parallelism

For each underlined section, choose the revision that most improves the writing.

When European Colonizers (1) arrived in Africa, they saw an opportunity to increase the wealth, of their empires, by (2) exploiting the natural and human resources of the African continent. There (3) first influence in Africa came through trade and Christian missionary work, eventually (4) they came to rule over African lands, either directly or ruling them indirectly (5). In the 19th century, European nations began (6) to fight among themselves for control of different African regions. They settled some of their disputes in the Berlin West Africa Conference of 1884–1885. There, European leaders decided who would have control over various parts of Africa. No African leaders were invited to participate in the conference.

1. A. European colonizers
   B. european colonizers
   C. european Colonizers
   D. Correct as is

2. A. wealth of their empires, by
   B. wealth, of their empires by
   C. wealth of their empires by
   D. Correct as is

3. A. They're
   B. Their
   C. There are
   D. Correct as is

4. A. trade and Christian missionary work, eventually,
   B. trade and Christian missionary work; eventually
   C. trade, and Christian missionary work; eventually
   D. Correct as is

5. A. either directly or indirectly
   B. either directly or to rule them indirectly
   C. either directly or without being direct
   D. Correct as is

6. A. In the 19th century, European nations, began
   B. In the 19th century—European nations began
   C. In the 19th century European nations began
   D. Correct as is

Need extra help?

See the **Grammar Handbook:**

Quick Reference: Punctuation, p. R77

Quick Reference: Capitalization, p. R79

Standardized Test Practice

Before students begin to identify errors in the passage, review the types of errors the passage contains. Remind students to carefully read the entire passage before correcting the errors.

Answers:

1. A; **2.** C; **3.** B; **4.** B; **5.** A; **6.** D

TEST PRACTICE

MINI LESSON **Grammar**

CAPITALIZATION OF ORGANIZATIONS AND OTHER SUBJECTS

Instruction Remind students that they should capitalize the names of organizations, historical events and documents, and months, days, and holidays.

Practice Write the following words and phrases on the chalkboard without capitalization and without underscoring (letters that should be capitalized are underscored for your viewing only). Have student volunteers describe the correct capitalization, if any, for each word or phrase.

1. monday, june 15
2. declaration of independence
3. grandparents
4. federal reserve
5. yesterday
6. republic of china
7. holiday
8. memorial day
9. cia
10. littleton high school

For more instruction and practice in capitalization, use McDougal Littell's ***Language Network:***

- Grade 10, Chapter 10, "Capitalization"
- Grade 12, Chapter 8, "Capitalization"

Objectives
- develop strategies for deciphering word meaning
- understand how to choose and apply strategies to decipher meaning and build vocabulary

EXERCISE
Student responses will vary; sample response is provided.
Cordialities; Based on the context clues, I think the word must mean "greetings." It might also have something to do with politeness, since it seems to be in the same word family as *cordial*, which means polite.
Cordialities is listed at the end of the dictionary entry for *cordial*, which means "warm, friendly, and sincere," as in "a cordial greeting." A cordiality must be a friendly exchange or greeting.

Use **Unit Seven Resource Book,** p. 93, for more practice.

Building Vocabulary

Choosing Word-Attack Strategies

What's the Best Approach? In this book you have learned a number of word-attack strategies for determining the meaning of unfamiliar words. When you come across a new word in your reading, you can draw on any of these strategies. However, depending on the word and its context, you may find that some strategies are more useful than others. In the passage on the right, what strategy or strategies would you use to figure out the meaning of *superannuated?*

> **In their two years of married life she had become completely infected by his passion for "modern methods" and his [criticism] of "these old and superannuated people in the teaching field who would be better employed as traders in the Onitsha market."**
> —Chinua Achebe, "Dead Men's Path"

Strategies for Building Vocabulary

Follow the steps below to evaluate and choose the appropriate word attack strategy or strategies for *superannuated.* In many cases you will find it most helpful to use a combination of strategies.

❶ Evaluate the Word and its Context When choosing word attack strategies, you can ask yourself a few quick questions to determine which strategy would be the most useful.

- Does the context help me understand the word?
- Do I recognize any parts of the word?
- Does the word resemble other words that I know?

In general, you will probably find that context clues are the most useful strategy. Even if context clues alone do not help you figure out a word's meaning, they should help you confirm or reject any guesses you make using other strategies.

❷ Consider Each Strategy Consider the usefulness of each of the following strategies for attacking the word *superannuated.*

- **Context clues** "I can see from the context that *superannuated* is used to describe old teachers who are better suited to selling goods at the market than to teaching. That gives me some idea that the word must have to do with being old or unskilled, but I'm still not sure."
- **Recognizing Word Families or Roots** "*Superannuated* sounds like it might be related to *annual,* which means 'yearly.'"
- **Recognizing Affixes** "I know the word *super,* which means 'excellent.' I also know it as a prefix meaning 'extra' or 'over and above,' as in *superfluous,* which means 'more than necessary.' If I put the prefix together with the root, I can guess that *superannuated* means 'having extra years.' That fits with the context, which suggests old age.
- **Using Reference Tools** "When I check my guess in the dictionary, I find that *superannuated* means 'retired or ineffective because of advanced age.'"

❸ Record and Use the Word To make the word a part of your permanent vocabulary, write it down and make a point of using it in class discussions or other conversations during the next few days.

Use this table as a general guide.

Strategy	When to Use
Using Context Clues	• as a first strategy
Identifying Roots	• if the word has many syllables (multisyllabic words are more likely to have Greek or Latin roots) • if you recognize the word's root
Identifying Affixes	• if the word has a familiar beginning or ending
Recognizing Word Families	• if the word resembles other familiar words
Reference Tools	• to confirm your guess • when nothing else works

EXERCISE Choose five unfamiliar words from the selections in Unit Seven. Using the strategies, write what you think each word means, and tell what strategy or strategies you used. Finally, if you haven't already done so, check the meaning in a dictionary.

Sentence Crafting Varying Sentence Length

Grammar from Literature Skilled writers add interest and rhythm to their work by writing sentences of varying length. On page 559, you learned about using variety in sentence structure. Varying your sentence length is a similar task. By varying the length of your sentences, you can improve the flow and rhythm of your writing. Read aloud the following passage from "The Guest" by Albert Camus. Listen to the rhythm created by the different sentence lengths.

> **Then he went through the classroom and out onto the terrace. The sun was already rising in the blue sky; a soft, bright light was bathing the deserted plateau. On the ridge the snow was melting in spots. The stones were about to reappear. Crouched on the edge of the plateau, the schoolmaster looked at the deserted expanse.**

The long sentences create a smoother, rolling rhythm, while shorter sentences tend to produce a stronger beat. The following passage from Elie Wiesel's *When the World Was Silent* contains two short sentences amid several much longer ones.

> **Indescribable confusion reigned.**
>
> **Parents searched for their children, children for their parents, and lonely captives for their friends. The people were beset by loneliness. Everyone feared that the outcome of the journey would be tragic and would claim its toll of lives. And so one yearned to have the companionship of someone who would stand by with a word, with a loving glance.**

The short sentences stand out against the longer ones, emphasizing the ideas of confusion and loneliness.

Pay special attention to your sentence variety during revision. Look at each paragraph. Does one paragraph contain only long sentences? Only short ones? Too many sentences of the same length can produce a rhythm that is droning or unnecessarily choppy.

Style Tip: Using Fragments for Stylistic Reasons Although sentence fragments are generally considered incorrect, writers occasionally use them deliberately. Fragments can present dialogue or thoughts in a natural way, for example, or create emphasis. In the passage below from *When the World Was Silent*, the fragment at the end of the paragraph emphasizes a single striking image.

> **So we all got up—even those who seemed to be dying—and wrapped our drenched blankets about our bodies. The scene was reminiscent of a congregation wrapped in prayer shawls, swaying to and fro in prayer. The snow, the car, even the sky (heaven?)—everything and everybody seemed to be swaying, worshipping, communing with God, uttering the prayer of life, the prayer of death. The sword of the Angel of Death was suspended above. A congregation of corpses at prayer.**

LANGUAGE SKILLS

WRITING EXERCISE The first of the following two paragraphs contains only short sentences; the second contains only long ones. Rewrite them so that they contain sentences of varying length. Feel free to change the wording in addition to combining or breaking up sentences. You might use one or two sentence fragments for effect.

Michael Obi was very proud of the new garden at Ndume Central School. His wife, Nancy, had planted it. She had used great care. She filled the school compound with beautiful flowers, hedges and trees. Then the rains came. They turned the dusty grounds into a lush, green paradise. They looked rich and refined. The plants of the village were sloppy and untended. It was a sight to behold.

Imagine Obi's surprise, then, when he discovered that the villagers were using an old footpath across the school grounds, tracking through the marigolds as if the garden were not even there. He could not believe their ignorance, and he discussed it with one of the teachers, who told him that that this was an old footpath connecting the village shrine with the burial ground. Obi found this unacceptable, and he planted heavy sticks and barbed wire across the path so that the villagers would not be able to use it ever again.

Sentence Crafting

Objectives

- recognize the effect of sentence length on style
- learn to use sentence fragments for stylistic reasons
- revise to vary sentence length

WRITING EXERCISE

Student responses will vary. Sample response is provided.

Michael Obi was very proud of the new garden at Ndume Central School. His wife, Nancy, had planted the garden with great care. She filled the school compound with beautiful flowers, hedges, and trees. When the rains came, they turned the dusty grounds into a lush, green paradise. The grounds looked rich and refined next to the plants of the village, which were sloppy and untended. Nancy's garden was a sight to behold.

Imagine Obi's surprise, then, when he discovered that the villagers were using an old footpath across the school grounds. They were tracking through the footpath as if the garden were not even there. He could not believe their ignorance. He discussed it with one of the teachers, who told him that this was an old footpath connecting the village shrine with the burial ground. Obi found this unacceptable. He planted heavy sticks and barbed wire across the path so that the villagers would not be able to use it ever again.

Use **Unit Seven Resource Book,** p. 94, for more practice.

MINI LESSON Grammar

PROBLEMS WITH SENTENCE FRAGMENTS

Instruction A sentence fragment is an incomplete sentence that is punctuated like a completed sentence. There are several types of fragments; most common are phrases and subordinate clauses. Many fragments occur because the writer has used a period to separate a phrase or clause from a complete sentence. In these cases, the fragment can be repaired by re-attaching it to the sentence.

Practice Write the following examples on the chalkboard. Ask students to identify and correct the sentence fragments.

1. I don't like to drive at night. Because I can't see well. (*Because I can't see well;* delete the period after *night* and change capital *B* to lowercase)
2. I left my sunglasses in the car. Under the back seat. (*Under the back seat;* delete the period after *car* and change capital *U* to lowercase.)
3. Whenever it rains. My brakes don't work very well. (*Whenever it rains;* change period after *rains* to a comma and change the capital *M* to lowercase.)

For more instruction and practice in correcting sentence fragments, use McDougal Littell's ***Language Network:***

- Grade 10, Chapter 5, "Sentences"
- Grade 12, Chapter 3, "Clauses"

Objectives

- reflect on and assess understanding of the literature written in response to war and conflict
- discuss the human cost of wars and conflicts
- understand important names and terms associated with modern wars and conflicts
- review tone as a literary concept and identify the tone of each selection
- assess and build portfolios
- set a reading goal

Reflecting on the Literature

The Human Cost of Conflict To help students compile their lists, have them make three-column charts. In the first column, students should list the selections and the major characters in them; in the second column, the physical effects of conflict on those characters; and in the third column, the psychological effects.

Reviewing Literary Concepts

Analyzing Tone Answers will vary. One of the selections students may choose is Pirandello's short story "War." Students may identify the tone of this story as ironic. They may read aloud the last three paragraphs of the story in which the old man breaks down at the woman's question. This fit of grief undercuts his assertions that no one should mourn for soldiers killed in the war.

 Use **Unit Seven Resource Book,** p. 47, for additional support.

Building Your Portfolio

Students will use their Presentation Portfolios to file what they consider their highest quality work—the very best projects and activities from their Working Portfolios.

 For more information on using writing and assessing portfolios, see the **Teacher's Guide to Assessment and Portfolio Use,** pp. 53–74.

Part Assessment

 To assess skills and concepts taught in this unit part, use **Formal Assessment Book,** pp. 193–194.

Reflect and Assess

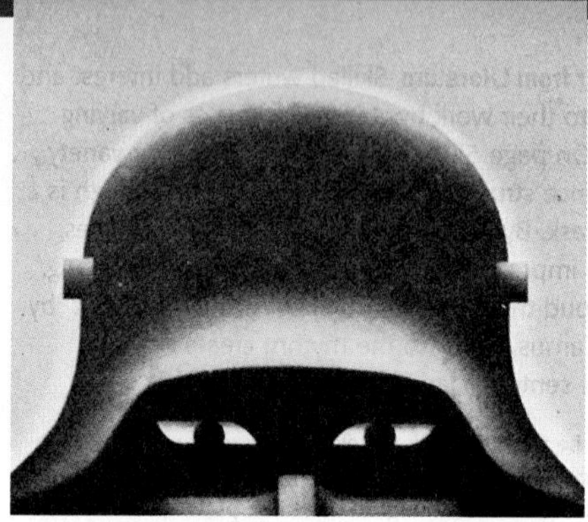

Conflict has defined much of the 20th century, from international warfare to colonial struggles for independence to civil war. The selections in this part of Unit Seven were written in response to such times of turmoil. The following options will help you to review what you have learned.

Reflecting on the Literature

The Human Cost of Conflict What do human beings lose when countries go to war or when other great conflicts erupt? Working with a partner, review the selections in this part, and make a list of all that is lost by the major characters or people in each selection. Pay attention to both the physical effects and the psychological effects of conflict. After you have finished, compare your list with those of your classmates, and discuss what you have learned about the human consequences of conflict.

Reviewing Literary Concepts

Analyzing Tone *Tone* refers to a writer's attitude toward his or her subject. Working with a partner, choose four works in this part in which you can clearly identify the author's tone. How does the author feel about the war or conflict portrayed in his or her work? What evidence can you find in the selection that helps you to identify that tone? Share the results of your work with your classmates, and read aloud passages from each of the four selections to express the tone conveyed.

Building Your Portfolio

Writing Workshop and Writing Options Review the research paper that you wrote for the Writing Workshop on page 1306. In your judgment, how successful is the paper? Attach a cover note to your research paper in which you evaluate your work, noting its strengths and weaknesses. Then review the Writing Options that you completed in this part, and choose the one that best demonstrates your ability as a writer. Attach a note to your choice, explaining your judgment. Place the research paper and the Writing Option in your **Presentation Portfolio.**

Self ASSESSMENT

READER'S NOTEBOOK

Get together with a small group of classmates to review the following terms from this part of Unit Seven. In your group, discuss the meaning of each term, using the Glossary of Literary Terms (beginning on page 000) to check your understanding. For each term, find an example from a selection that illustrates its meaning, or discuss how an entire selection helps you to understand the term. Share your findings with other groups.

setting	speaker
Holocaust	dialogue
mood	author's purpose
colonialism	theme
cultural conflict	dialect

Setting GOALS

Reflect upon the progress that you have made this year as a writer and a reader. Write down two goals for yourself that you think can be reached by the end of the year.

Assessment Self Assessment

If students need to review any of the key names or terms presented in Part 2, direct them to the pages indicated below:
setting (pages 1207 and 1212)
Holocaust (pages 1205, 1233, and 1243)
mood (pages 1221 and 1230)
colonialism (pages 1204, 1245, 1271)
cultural conflict (pages 1274 and 1278)
speaker (pages 1216 and 1218)
dialogue (pages 1221 and 1230)
author's purpose (pages 1233, 1242, 1295, and 1302)
theme (pages 1245 and 1258)
dialect (pages 1286 and 1291)

Extend Your *Reading*

LITERATURE CONNECTIONS

Things Fall Apart

CHINUA ACHEBE

This novel, set in colonial Nigeria between 1890 and 1915, explores the conflict between traditional tribal ways of life and European culture. Achebe presents two closely related tragedies, the personal tragedy of Okonkwo, a "great man" of his Ibo village, and the communal tragedy of his people.

Here are just a few of the related readings that accompany *Things Fall Apart:*

The Second Coming
WILLIAM BUTLER YEATS

Shooting an Elephant
GEORGE ORWELL

Genesis 22:1–9 The Sacrifice of Isaac
THE BIBLE

LITERATURE CONNECTIONS

When Rain Clouds Gather

BESSIE HEAD

Set in Botswana in the mid-1960s, this novel focuses on a young South African man, Makhaya, who is trying to establish a new life for himself in a poverty-stricken village. Makhaya becomes involved in the villagers' struggle to adopt new agricultural techniques and to overcome rigid customs, a corrupt chief, and the unrelenting climate.

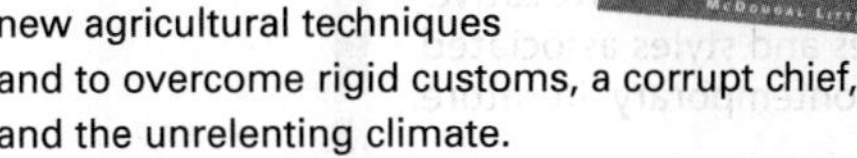

Here are just a few of the related readings that accompany *When Rain Clouds Gather:*

The Rain Came
GRACE OGOT

I Am Crying from Thirst
ALONZO LOPEZ

Some Monday for Sure
NADINE GORDIMER

And Even *More* . . .

Books

The Great War and Modern Memory PAUL FUSSELL
This landmark study of World War I focuses on the British army in the trenches, paying especially close attention to the experiences of writers.

The Stranger ALBERT CAMUS
In this short 1946 novel, a young man becomes involved in a senseless killing on a beach in Algeria. His trial reveals the absurdity of his predicament.

Other Media

The Greatest Generation
This is a compilation of Tom Brokaw's interviews with World War II veterans, as shown on *NBC Nightly News.* The interviews explore the experience of war and its effects on entire lives. (VIDEOCASSETTE)

Schindler's List
This 1993 Steven Spielberg film tells a true story about a German manufacturer during World War II who risks his life to save more than 1,000 Jews. (VIDEOCASSETTE)

One Day in the Life of Ivan Denisovich

ALEKSANDR SOLZHENITSYN

This novel provides a gripping account of the hardships of daily life in a Siberian labor camp. Based on the author's own experiences as a political prisoner in Stalinist Russia, the novel caused an international stir when published in 1962.

More Recommendations for Your Students

Difficulty Level: Easy

Ambrose, Stephen E. *The Good Fight: How World War II Was Won* (NY: Atheneum, 2001). Using photos, maps, and soldiers' letters, an honored historian examines and depicts the major events of World War II for young readers.

Heyes, Eileen. *Children of the Swastika: The Hitler Youth* (Brookfield, CT: Millbrook Press, 1993). This lively account describes the origins, activities, and importance of the Hitler Youth. Using photographs and personal interviews, the author explains how Hitler appealed to the young, making the Hitler Youth vital to the Nazi war machine.

Watkins, Yoko Kawashima. *So Far from the Bamboo Grove.* Literature Connections. (Evanston: McDougal Littell Inc., 1997). In this memoir, the author describes a Japanese family's odyssey from Korea to Japan amid the chaos at the close of WWII.

Difficulty Level: Average

Holliday, Laurel, compiler. *Children in the Holocaust and World War II: Their Secret Diaries* (NY: Pocket Books, 1995). This compilation presents diary entries from 23 young people. These entries reflect the courage and despair of life in terrible times.

Ousseini, Maria. *Caught in the Crossfire: Growing Up in a War Zone* (NY: Walker, 1995). The author, a refugee and a documentary filmmaker, examines how war affects children in countries such as Lebanon, El Salvador, Mozambique, and Bosnia-Herzegovina.

Difficulty Level: Challenging

Brokaw, Tom. *The Greatest Generation* (NY: Random House, 1998). The nationally known broadcast journalist introduces the reader to ordinary men and women inspired by duty, honor, and love of family and country. America's "greatest generation" came of age during the Great Depression, fought heroically in World War II, and returned home to rebuild their lives and their country.

Orwell, George. *1984*. Literature Connections. (Evanston: McDougal Littell Inc., 1998). First published in 1948 while the author suffered from tuberculosis, this novel is a classic attack on totalitarianism. It describes a world without privacy, ruled by a watchdog government that manipulates language and rewrites history.

Terkel, Studs. *The Good War: An Oral History of World War Two* (NY : Pantheon Books, 1984). In this Pulitzer-Prize winning book, the acclaimed writer, interviewer, and historian shows the human side of World War II through the stories of 121 participants.

In Unit Seven, Part 3, you will find short stories and poetry by Nobel Prize winners since 1970. The number of writers is necessarily limited; they were chosen for their stylistic and geographic diversity.

World Art and Cultures Transparencies

AT75 After the Storm

You may use the listed transparency to acquaint students with contemporary art.

READING FOR INFORMATION

Reading Skills and Strategies

SCANNING

Have students scan the boldfaced blue heads in the blue-outlined boxes and the images attached to the boxes. Ask students to guess what the images are without reading the black text. Then have them read the text to confirm their guesses.

PART 3 Critics and Dreamers:

Contemporary Nobel Prize Winners

Why It Matters

There is no literary award more prestigious than the Nobel Prize. The winners are considered the most important writers in the entire world, those who should be known outside of their own countries and languages. In Part 3, you will read poetry and fiction by Nobel Prize winners since 1970. Their works will introduce you to the provocative themes and styles associated with contemporary literature.

Alfred Nobel's Legacy

Dr. Alfred Bernhard Nobel (1833–1896) was a brilliant Swedish inventor and engineer who made a fortune from one of his most successful inventions—dynamite. After a newspaper mistakenly published Nobel's obituary and referred to him as a "merchant of death," Nobel decided to leave a different legacy. In his will, he established the **Nobel Prizes** to reward people "who, during the preceding year, shall have conferred the greatest benefit on mankind" in physics, chemistry, medicine, peace, and literature.

For Links to Nobel Prize Winners, click on:

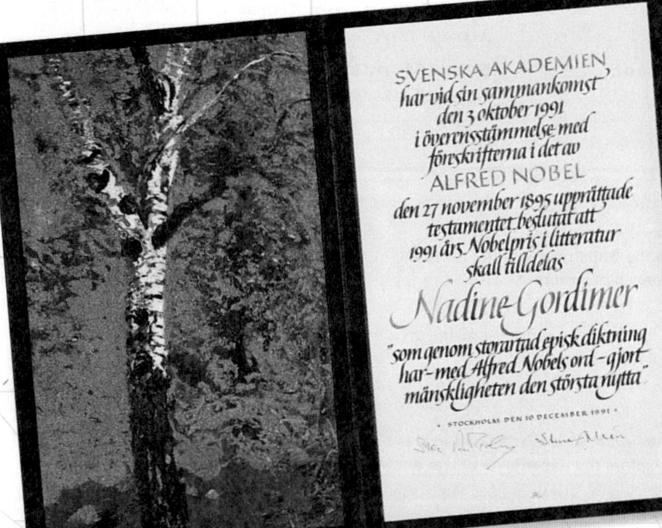

SVENSKA AKADEMIEN
har vid sin sammankomst
den 3 oktober 1991
i överensstämmelse med
föreskrifterna i det av
ALFRED NOBEL
den 27 november 1895 upprättade
testamentet beslutat att
1991 års Nobelpris i litteratur
skall tilldelas
Nadine Gordimer
"som genom storartad episk diktning
har – med Alfred Nobels ord – gjort
mänskligheten den största nytta"
• STOCKHOLM DEN 10 DECEMBER 1991 •

Benefiting Humanity

According to Nobel's will, the winner of the literature prize must have produced "the most outstanding work in an ideal direction." To select a **laureate,** a small Nobel committee judges nominations from professors, former laureates, and presidents of authors' groups. It then recommends candidates to the **Swedish Academy,** which makes the final vote. In Nadine Gordimer's Nobel diploma, the Academy acknowledged her writing's "very great benefit to humanity."

Recent Nobel Prize Winners

The names in blue are the writers whose work you will read in Part 3.

1971	Pablo Neruda	CHILE
1972	Heinrich Böll	WEST GERMANY
1976	Saul Bellow	CANADA/U.S.
1978	Isaac Bashevis Singer	POLAND/U.S.
1980	Czeslaw Milosz	POLAND/U.S.
1982	Gabriel García Márquez	COLOMBIA
1986	Wole Soyinka	NIGERIA
1987	Joseph Brodsky	U.S.S.R./U.S.
1988	Naguib Mahfouz	EGYPT
1990	Octavio Paz	MEXICO
1991	Nadine Gordimer	SOUTH AFRICA
1992	Derek Walcott	ST. LUCIA
1993	Toni Morrison	UNITED STATES
1994	Kenzaburo Oe	JAPAN
1995	Seamus Heaney	NORTHERN IRELAND
1996	Wislawa Szymborska	POLAND
1999	Günter Grass	GERMANY
2000	Gao Xingjian	CHINA
2001	V. S. Naipaul	TRINIDAD/U.K.
2002	Imre Kertész	HUNGARY
2003	J. M. Coetzee	SOUTH AFRICA
2004	Elfriede Jelinek	AUSTRIA
2005	Harold Pinter	ENGLAND
2006	Orhan Pamuk	TURKEY
2007	Doris Lessing	ZIMBABWE/U.K.

The Highest Literary Honor

One Nobel Prize is given to a poet, dramatist, or prose writer annually. In 1901, only 25 nominations were made in literature, yet today more than 200 writers are nominated each year. Not only is competition for the coveted prize fierce, but the award's value has grown since its creation. Worth about $40,000 in 1901, the prize is now worth about $1 million.

A Grand Ceremony

Writers receive the Nobel Prize in literature at a formal ceremony held in the Stockholm Concert Hall in Sweden on December 10, the anniversary of Alfred Nobel's death. The king of Sweden presents the winner with a gold medal, a diploma, and a certificate for the amount of the prize. The medal bears a portrait of Nobel on one side; on the other is a picture of a young man and a muse under a laurel tree. The laureate's diploma is a work of art that captures the spirit of his or her writings. The photo above shows the Polish poet Wislawa Szymborska receiving her prize in 1996.

Reading Skills and Strategies
READING A CHART

Tell students to study the chart on page 1321. Ask the following questions:

- What do the three columns of the chart show? *(the year the Nobel Prize was awarded, the winner of the prize, and the winner's country)*
- Which writers will be included in Part 3? *(Neruda, García Márquez, Soyinka, Mahfouz, Paz, Gordimer, Szymborska)*

READING FOR INFORMATION
Reading Skills and Strategies
CLASSIFYING
Have students read the italicized overview paragraph. Guide them to see that the columns on the rest of the spread reflect the "moral causes, political developments, and artistic movements" mentioned.

Ask students, after they read each column, to define what the term in the column head means—"Apartheid Literature," for example. Then they should note the boldfaced names of writers falling into each category.

Translation Note
The message on the poster at the bottom of page 1322 translates as "Solidarity, the Future of Poland."

The Nobel Prize and World Literature

The writing by the Nobel Prize winners in Part 3 reflects important trends and concerns in contemporary literature. Following are just some of the moral causes, political developments, and artistic movements that have shaped the pieces you will read.

Protesters demand the release of jailed antiapartheid leader Nelson Mandela.

Apartheid Literature

One important moral and political issue of the late 20th century was the struggle to end apartheid—the official system of racial segregation enforced in South Africa from 1948 to 1991.

Writers whose works carried an antiapartheid message include Nobel laureate **Nadine Gordimer,** playwrights Athol Fugard and Mbongeni Ngema, and novelist André Brink. By exposing the evils of racism, these writers helped bring change to their country.

Postcolonial Writing

The term **postcolonial writing** is often used to describe contemporary writing from India and other nations in Asia, Africa, and the Caribbean that were formerly European colonies. Usually written in colonial languages (such as English or French) instead of native languages, these works take on lingering issues within postcolonial societies—ethnic and religious conflicts, government instability, and questions of national and personal identity.

Nobel Prize winner **Wole Soyinka** and his fellow Nigerian **Chinua Achebe** are postcolonial writers who look critically at modern African society.

Eastern European Dissidents

From the end of World War II until the end of the 1980s, Eastern European nations such as Poland, Czechoslovakia, and Hungary were in the grip of the Soviet Union. In these countries, Communist leaders limited free speech. They controlled what writers could publish through censorship and the threat of imprisonment or exile. A number of writers protested against government repression and championed the causes of dignity and individuality.

Poet Czeslaw Milosz, a Nobel Prize winner in 1980, left Poland after becoming disillusioned with life under Communist rule. His countrywoman **Wislawa Szymborska** remained in Poland, publishing playful yet deeply thoughtful poems for 50 years before she, too, was awarded the Nobel Prize in 1996.

The Solidarity movement in Poland weakened Communist rule.

Egyptian writer Naguib Mahfouz

The Latin American Boom

In the 1960s, Latin American novelists gained world attention with fresh, exciting work that drew on Western literary styles, such as surrealism, yet was distinctly Latin American. Some of these writers developed a new form, **magical realism,** which mixed fantasy and realism. It blended the traditions and perspectives of the Native American, European, and African cultures that mingle in the region.

Prominent writers associated with the Latin American boom in literature include Mexico's Carlos Fuentes, Argentina's Julio Cortázar, and Colombia's **Gabriel García Márquez,** a winner of the Nobel Prize.

Poetic Innovation

In the early 20th century, poets such as Ezra Pound and T. S. Eliot rebelled against traditional forms and themes in poetry. Poets today still seek new ways to express their unique visions of the world.

For a long time, Nobel judges tended to shy away from difficult, experimental literature. However, in the past 20 years they have acknowledged innovative contemporary poets such as Chile's **Pablo Neruda,** who wrote both grand historical epics and odes to simple objects, and Mexico's **Octavio Paz,** whose complex work drew on European, Asian, and Native American philosophies.

Non-European Languages

As technology has turned the world into a "global village," readers have had more interest in foreign literature and more access to translations.

Long criticized for honoring only literature in European languages, the Nobel Prize now reflects a wider view of the world. Non-Western writers who have won in the past several years include Egyptian author **Naguib Mahfouz,** Japanese novelist Kenzaburo Oe, Chinese novelist Gao Zingjian, and Turkish writer Orhan Pamuk.

Other Literary Awards

The **Booker Prize** is awarded to the best novel in English from Britain or from other present or former Commonwealth nations. **Margaret Atwood,** Canada's foremost writer, won the prize for her complex novel within a novel, *The Blind Assassin.*

The **Prix Goncourt** is given to French-language writers. Winners have included **Jean Echenoz,** author of the art-world mystery *I'm Gone;* and **Patrick Chamoiseau,** author of *Texaco,* an imaginative history of Martinique.

The **Pulitzer Prize** is a U.S. award for journalism, literature, and music. In 2000, **Jhumpa Lahiri** won the fiction prize for *Interpreter of Maladies,* a collection of short stories set in India and the United States.

Margaret Atwood

Literary Note

Another prestigious international literary award is the Neustadt Prize, given every two years by the University of Oklahoma and the journal *World Literature Today.* The 2002 winner was Colombian novelist Alvaro Mutis, author of *The Adventures of Maqroll.* The 2008 winner was New Zealand author Patricia Grace, whose works include *Dogside Story.*

This selection is included in the **World Literature InterActive Reader™.**

Objectives

- understand and appreciate a **short story (Literary Analysis)**
- recognize and discuss **first-person point of view (Literary Analysis)**
- **make inferences** about customs and conditions in South Africa and about relationships between characters (**Active Reading**)

Summary

The narrator, a young black South African woman living on a farm, learns that her fiance has been released from prison. He had been serving a six-year sentence for antiapartheid activities. She recalls how his imprisonment kept them from getting married and kept him from seeing their young daughter. When her fiance returns home, she is happy, but she finds him unfamiliar and difficult to talk to. He immediately returns to his political work, which frequently takes him away. She gets pregnant again, but there still is no time to get married or regain their emotional closeness. Even though he is out of prison, she is still waiting for him to come back.

Use **Unit Seven Resource Book,** p. 96, for additional support.

Thematic Link

Through this story, Nadine Gordimer **criticizes** apartheid and explores the sacrifices made by people who fought it.

5-Minute Warm-Up

Daily Language SkillBuilder

Have students **proofread** the display sentences on page 1095o and write them correctly.

PREPARING to *Read*

AMNESTY

Nadine Gordimer

Nadine Gordimer
1923–

Solitary Child Nadine Gordimer, one of South Africa's most notable authors, is known for her beautifully crafted novels and short stories dealing with themes of exile, alienation, the effects of racism, and life's missed opportunities. Born into a white middle-class family in the Transvaal province of South Africa, she spent much of her childhood in solitude because her mother worried excessively about the girl's health and often kept her at home.

To relieve her loneliness, Gordimer began to write when she was 9 years old. At 15, she published her first short story in a magazine. Almost from the beginning of her career, one critic notes, her precise ear for spoken language, her keen sense of social satire, and her strong moral purpose were evident.

Critic of Apartheid Much of Gordimer's writing is set in South Africa, and her work draws on the political situation there. Many of her characters have had to grapple with the injustices of apartheid (ə-pärt'hīt')—the official system of racial segregation that was in place from 1948 to 1991—and the process of healing since the government repealed apartheid laws. Because Gordimer openly criticized apartheid and exposed its tragic consequences in her fiction, three of her novels were banned by the South African government.

Although she used her talents and influence to oppose apartheid, she refused to let her writing become propaganda. Instead, she has said, she has always tried simply to portray the society in which she lives: "I thrust my hand as deep as it will go, deep into the life around me, and I write about what comes up."

Accolades and Achievements In 1974 Gordimer won the Booker Prize, England's most prestigious literary award, for her novel *The Conservationist.* In 1991 she received the Nobel Prize in literature. In addition, she has received honorary degrees from a number of universities in the United States and has been called "one of the most gifted practitioners of the short story anywhere in English."

Other Works
Six Feet of the Country
July's People
Jump and Other Stories

For a humanities activity, click on:

LESSON RESOURCES

UNIT SEVEN RESOURCE BOOK, pp. 96–99

ASSESSMENT RESOURCES
Formal Assessment, pp. 195–196
Teacher's Guide to Assessment and Portfolio Use
Test Generator

INTEGRATED TECHNOLOGY
Visit our Web site: classzone.com

ADDITIONAL RESOURCES
Lesson Planning Guide, pp. 173–174
Teacher's Sourcebook for Language Development

Build Background

The Apartheid System "Amnesty" takes place in South Africa during the time of apartheid. Under apartheid, whites owned more than 80 percent of the land while making up less than 20 percent of the population. Black farm workers struggled to support themselves on small plots of poor farmland, some on designated tribal homelands and some on white-owned farms. In many rural families, members left home to seek industrial jobs in the towns and cities. Such jobs paid little.

Apartheid required blacks to carry passes, or identity papers, at all times and restricted where they could live and travel. In fact, this system regulated almost all aspects of the lives of blacks. It even specified the kinds of jobs blacks could hold and the schools they could attend.

Fighting Apartheid During this period many blacks, as well as some whites, actively opposed apartheid by staging boycotts, demonstrations, and strikes. To put down the resistance, the government arrested leaders in the anti-apartheid movement and imprisoned them on Robben Island, off the coast of Cape Town. Among the prisoners there was Nelson Mandela, who later became the country's first black president. In 1991 the South African government finally ended apartheid and released the political prisoners held on Robben Island. The former prisoners were given amnesty, or government pardon.

Robben Island

Connect to Your Life

In this story, a young woman waits for the man she loves to return home to her. Imagine waiting years to be with someone you love. What would you expect your relationship to be like once you were together again?

Focus Your Reading

LITERARY ANALYSIS: FIRST-PERSON POINT OF VIEW

"Amnesty" is told from the **first-person point of view,** meaning that the narrator is a character in the story who describes the action in his or her own words. As you read the story, think about how the use of this point of view affects what you learn as a reader. Consider why Gordimer might have chosen this particular narrator and point of view.

ACTIVE READING: MAKING INFERENCES

When you read a story, you form ideas about a character, a relationship, or a way of life by making **inferences,** or logical guesses based on clues. Notice what this passage from "Amnesty" suggests about the culture the characters live in:

> ***Also my parents were short of money. Two of my brothers who had gone away to work in town didn't send home; I suppose they lived with girlfriends and had to buy things for them.***

From the passage you can infer that in this culture, it is customary for sons who work in the towns to send some of the money they earn to their parents.

READER'S NOTEBOOK As you read "Amnesty," pay attention to the details that give you insight into customs and conditions in South Africa and into the relationship between the two main characters. Stop after every third or fourth paragraph and jot down some inferences you've made.

READING FOR INFORMATION
Reading Skills and Strategies
CLASSIFYING

Explain to students that the story takes place against a background of apartheid. Students should take note of the features of apartheid described in **Build Background** so that events will make sense to them.

TIME MANAGEMENT

If your schedule requires that you cover the lesson objectives in a shorter time, use. . .

- Preparing to Read, pp. 1324, 1325
- Thinking Through the Literature, p. 1333

If you want to take advantage of longer blocks of class time, use. . .

- TE Teaching Options: Cross-Curricular Link, pp. 1326, 1327, 1329; Speaking and Listening, p. 1328; Standardized Test Practice, p. 1331; Grammar, p. 1332
- Connect to Today, p. 1335

Reading and Analyzing

Literary Analysis FIRST-PERSON POINT OF VIEW

A Ask: Who is the narrator of this story? What has she revealed about herself and other characters?

Possible Responses: The narrator is a young black woman in South Africa who lives on a farm owned by a Boer. She has little education but teaches in the farm school. Her family is poor. She was to be married, but her fiance has been in prison. He is a construction worker and union activist who was jailed for fighting against apartheid but has now been released.

Use **Unit Seven Resource Book,** p. 98, for more practice.

Active Reading MAKING INFERENCES

B Ask: What inferences do you make about the narrator from her comment that she has never seen the sea?

Possible Responses: that she has never traveled; that she knows little beyond the farm

Use **Unit Seven Resource Book,** p. 97, for more practice.

Literary Analysis THEME

C Ask: What seems to be the fiance's view of religion?

Possible Response: He thinks it is used to make farm people accepting of their hard lives and unwilling to fight for change.

Amnesty

Nadine Gordimer

When we heard he was released I ran all over the farm and through the fence to our people on the next farm to tell everybody. I only saw afterwards I'd torn my dress on the barbed wire, and there was a scratch, with blood, on my shoulder.

He went away from this place nine years ago, signed up to work in town with what they call a construction company—building glass walls up to the sky. For the first two years he came home for the weekend once a month and two weeks at Christmas; that was when he asked my father for me. And he began to pay. He and I thought that in three years he would have paid enough for us to get married. But then he started wearing that T-shirt, he told us he'd joined the union, he told
1 us about the strike, how he was one of the men who went to talk to the bosses because some others had been laid off after the strike. He's always been good at talking, even in English—he was the best at the farm school, he used to read the newspapers the Indian wraps soap and sugar in when you buy at the store.

There was trouble at the hostel where he had a bed, and riots over paying rent in the townships[1] and he told me—just me, not the old ones—that wherever people were fighting against the way we are treated they were doing it for all of us, on the farms as well as the towns, and the unions were with them, he was with them, making speeches, marching. The third year, we heard he was in prison. Instead of getting married. We didn't know where to find him, until he went on trial. The case was heard in a town far away. I couldn't go often to the court because by that time I had passed my Standard 8[2] and I was working in the farm school. Also my parents were short of money. Two of my brothers who had gone away to work in town didn't send home; I suppose they lived with girl-friends and had to buy things for them. My father and other brother work here for the Boer[3] and the pay is very small, we have two goats, a few cows we're allowed to graze, and a patch of land where my mother can grow vegetables. No cash from that. A

When I saw him in the court he looked beautiful in a blue suit with a striped shirt and brown tie. All the accused—his comrades, he said—were 2
well-dressed. The union bought the clothes so that the judge and the prosecutor would know they weren't dealing with stupid *yes-baas*[4] black men who didn't know their rights. These things and everything else about the court and trial he explained to me when I was allowed to visit him in jail. Our little girl was born while the trial went on and when I brought the baby to court the first time to show him, his comrades hugged him and then hugged me across the barrier of the prisoners' dock and they had clubbed together to give me some money as a present for the baby.

1. **townships:** racially segregated areas of South Africa.
2. **Standard 8:** Standards are classes or grades in elementary schools. Standard 8 would have been the top level of elementary school.
3. **Boer:** a descendant of the Dutch colonists of South Africa.
4. ***yes-baas:*** "Yes, boss"—the words of someone who does not question authority.

Cross Curricular Link **Humanities**

LOBOLA The custom of lobola, or bride-price, is widespread among black cultures in southern Africa. A man wanting to marry must make a payment to the bride's family before the marriage is allowed. This payment is meant to compensate the bride's family for her loss and to establish the groom's right to the children of the marriage. Male relatives of the bride and groom negotiate a price; the couple themselves have no say in the amount. Traditionally the payment was in cattle—from 11 to 21 head, depending on the status of the girl. Among modern city dwellers, the payment is in cash—generally between $1000 and $4000, which is why it can take time to save the amount. There has been much debate about the practice under South Africa's new legal system, which is supposed to guarantee women's rights. Some argue that lobola makes women "property"; others feel that it shows respect for women.

We have two goats, a few cows we're allowed to graze, and a patch of land where my mother can grow vegetables.

He chose the name for her, Inkululeko.[5]

Then the trial was over and he got six years. He was sent to the Island.[6] We all knew about the Island. Our leaders had been there so long. B But I have never seen the sea except to color it in blue at school, and I couldn't imagine a piece of earth surrounded by it. I could only think of a cake of dung, dropped by the cattle, floating in a pool of rain-water they'd crossed, the water showing the sky like a looking-glass, blue. I was ashamed only to think that. He had told me how the glass walls showed the pavement trees and the other buildings in the street and the colors of the cars and the clouds as the crane lifted him on a platform higher and higher through the sky to work at the top of a building.

He was allowed one letter a month. It was my letter because his parents didn't know how to write. I used to go to them where they worked on another farm to ask what message they wanted to send. The mother always cried and put her hands on her head and said nothing, and the old man, who preached to us in the veld[7] every Sunday, said tell my son we are praying. God will make everything all right for him. Once he wrote back. That's the trouble—our people on the farms, they're told God will decide what's good for them so that they won't find the force to do anything to change their lives. C

After two years had passed, we—his parents and I—had saved up enough money to go to Cape

5. **Inkululeko** (ĭn-ko͞o′lo͞o-lā′kō): a word meaning "freedom" in the Xhosa language of South Africa.

6. **the Island:** Robben Island, the site of a maximum-security prison from the mid-1960s to 1991. Most of its inmates were black political prisoners.

7. **veld:** any open grazing area in southern Africa.

Customizing Instruction

Less Proficient Readers

Tell students that the narrator reveals information gradually. As they read, they will learn who "we," "he," and "I" are. Students shouldn't stop in frustration; they should just keep going and put together the puzzle.

English Learners

1 Explain that *union* refers to *labor union,* a group of workers who have joined together to improve their wages or working conditions. Black labor unions were very active in the anti-apartheid movement. A *strike* is a group refusal to work until some demand is met. To be *laid off* is to lose one's job.

2 Note that a *comrade* is a fellow member of a political group. The term stresses that all members of the group are equal.

Advanced Learners

After students finish reading the story, you might have them reread the first paragraph. Ask how it foreshadows themes of the story.

Possible Response: Her fiance's release causes the narrator great joy but also unexpected pain, noticed later.

Cross Curricular Link **History**

THE RIVONIA TRIAL In June 1964, Nelson Mandela and other leaders of the African National Congress (ANC) were sentenced to life imprisonment at the Rivonia Trial, named for the suburb of Johannesburg where police raided their headquarters. Ten defendants were charged with sabotage and conspiracy and faced the death sentence if convicted. This trial brought worldwide attention to the anti-apartheid struggle. Mandela did not deny the charge of sabotage; in a three-hour statement he denounced the apartheid government and defended the use of violence against it. He ended with these words:

I have cherished the ideal of a democratic and free society in which all persons live together in harmony and with equal opportunities. It is an ideal which I hope to live for and to achieve. But if needs be, it is an ideal for which I am prepared to die.

Reading and Analyzing

Literary Analysis
FIRST-PERSON POINT OF VIEW

A Ask: How does her fiance's letter make the narrator feel?
Possible Responses: guilty; ignorant
Ask: What are your own thoughts about the letter?
Possible Responses: The letter was too harsh and insensitive to narrator's feelings; the letter shows how disappointed the fiance was not to see the family; the letter shows how frustrated the fiance is by his people's lack of knowledge.

Active Reading MAKING INFERENCES

B Ask: Why is the word "power" blacked out of the letter?
Possible Response: The government is so threatened by the idea of blacks having power that it won't allow the idea even to be expressed.

Town[8] to visit him. We went by train and slept on the floor at the station and asked the way, next day, to the ferry. People were kind; they all knew that if you wanted the ferry it was because you had somebody of yours on the Island.

And there it was—there was the sea. It was green *and* blue, climbing and falling, bursting white, all the way to the sky. A terrible wind was slapping it this way and that; it hid the Island, but people like us, also waiting for the ferry, pointed where the Island must be, far out in the sea that I never thought would be like it really was.

There were other boats, and ships as big as buildings that go to other places, all over the world, but the ferry is only for the Island, it doesn't go anywhere else in the world, only to the Island. So everybody waiting there was waiting for the Island, there could be no mistake we were not in the right place. We had sweets and biscuits, trousers and a warm coat for him (a woman standing with us said we wouldn't be allowed to give him the clothes) and I wasn't wearing, any more, the old beret pulled down over my head that farm girls wear, I had bought relaxer cream[9] from the man who comes round the farms selling things out of a box on his bicycle, and my hair was combed up thick under a flowered scarf that didn't cover the gold-colored rings in my ears. His mother had her blanket tied round her waist over her dress, a farm woman, but I looked just as good as any of the other girls there. When the ferry was ready to take us, we stood all pressed together and quiet like the cattle waiting to be let through a gate. One man kept looking round with his chin moving up and down, he was counting, he must have been afraid there too many to get on and he didn't want to be left behind. We all moved up to the policeman in charge and everyone ahead of us went onto the boat. But when our turn came and he put out his hand for something, I didn't know what.

We didn't have a permit. We didn't know that 1 before you come to Cape Town, before you come to the ferry for the Island, you have to have a police permit to visit a prisoner on the Island. I tried to ask him nicely. The wind blew the voice out of my mouth.

We were turned away. We saw the ferry rock, bumping the landing where we stood, moving, lifted and dropped by all that water, getting smaller and smaller until we didn't know if we were really seeing it or one of the birds that looked black, dipping up and down, out there.

We took the train back and we never went to the Island—never saw him in the three more years he was there. Not once.

The only good thing was one of the other people took the sweets and biscuits for him. He wrote and said he got them. But it wasn't a good letter. Of course not. He was cross with me; I should have found out, I should have known about the permit. He was right—I bought the train tickets, I asked where to go for the ferry, I should have known about the permit. I have passed Standard 8. There was an advice A office to go to in town, the churches ran it, he wrote. But the farm is so far from town, we on the farms don't know about these things. It was as he said; our ignorance is the way we are kept down, this ignorance must go.

We took the train back and we never went to the Island—never saw him in the three more years he was there. Not once. We couldn't find the money for the train. His father died and I had to help his mother from my pay. For our people

8. **Cape Town:** the legislative capital of South Africa, in the extreme southeast portion of the country.

9. **relaxer cream:** cream to straighten the hair.

MINI LESSON Speaking and Listening

DRAMATIC MONOLOGUE The account of the family's fruitless visit to Cape Town could be quite moving if performed aloud.

Prepare Have one or more volunteers silently reread the section of the story that begins at the bottom of page 1327 ("After two years had passed") and ends at the bottom of page 1328 ("Not once.") They should photocopy the passage, to analyze and mark up with performance notes. What main emotion does the narrator express in each paragraph? What gestures or facial expressions would help the audience visualize what the narrator sees and feels? You might assign a director to help each performer.

Present Let performers present their monologues, either read or memorized. Encourage the audience to say which parts of a performance were particularly effective. Ask the performers what they learned by taking the role of the narrator.

This activity is especially well suited to longer blocks of class time.

Customizing Instruction

the worry is always money, I wrote. When will we ever have money? Then he sent such a good letter. That's what I'm on the Island for, far away from you, I'm here so that one day our people will have the things they need, land, food, the end of ignorance. There was something else—I could just read the word "power" the prison had blacked out. All his letters were not just for me; the prison officer read them before I could.

He was coming home after only five years! That's what it seemed to me, when I heard—the five years were suddenly disappeared—nothing!—there was no whole year still to wait. I showed my—our—little girl his photo again. That's your daddy, he's coming, you're going to see him. She told the other children at school, I've got a daddy, just as she showed off about the kid goat she had at home.

We wanted him to come at once, and at the same time we wanted time to prepare. His mother lived with one of his uncles; now that his father was dead there was no house of his father for him to take me to as soon as we married. If there had been time, my father would have cut poles, my mother and I would have baked bricks, cut thatch,[10] and built a house for him and me and the child.

We were not sure what day he would arrive. We only heard on my radio his name and the names of some others who were released. Then at the Indian's store I noticed the newspaper, *The Nation,* written by black people, and on the front a picture of a lot of people dancing and waving—I saw at once it was at that ferry. Some men were being carried on other men's shoulders. I couldn't see which one was him. We were waiting. The ferry had brought him from the Island but we remembered Cape Town is a long way from us. Then he did come. On a Saturday, no school, so I was working with my mother, hoeing and weeding round the pumpkins and mealies,[11] my hair, that I meant to keep nice, tied in an old *doek.*[12] A combi came over the veld and his comrades had brought him. I wanted to run away and wash but he stood there stretching his legs, calling, hey! hey! with his comrades making a noise around him, and my mother started shrieking in the old style aie! aie! and my father was clapping and stamping towards him. He held his arms open to us, this big man in town clothes, polished shoes, and all the time while he hugged me I was holding my dirty hands, full of mud, away from him behind his back. His teeth hit me hard through his lips, he grabbed at my mother and she struggled to hold the child up to him. I thought we would all fall down! Then everyone was quiet. The child hid behind my mother. He picked her up but she turned her head away to her shoulder. He spoke to her gently but she wouldn't speak to him. She's nearly six years old! I told her not to be a baby. She said, That's not him. 3

The comrades all laughed, we laughed, she ran off and he said, She has to have time to get used to me.

He has put on weight, yes; a lot. You couldn't believe it. He used to be so thin his feet looked too big for him. I used to feel his bones but now—that night—when he lay on me he was so heavy, I didn't remember it was like that. Such a long time. It's strange to get stronger in prison; I thought he wouldn't have enough to eat and would come out weak. Everyone said, Look at him!—he's a man, now. He laughed and banged his fist on his chest, told them how the comrades exercised in their cells, he would run three miles a day, stepping up and down on one place on the

10. **thatch:** plant stalks or leaves used to make roofs.

11. **mealies:** corn.

12. ***doek*** (do͝ok) . . . **combi:** A *doek* is a headscarf worn like a turban. A combi is a vehicle that can serve various functions.

English Learners

1 Explain that a *permit* is an official paper, given by the government, that allows one to do something. Talk about instances in which permits are needed in this culture. People need permits to hold demonstrations, or to build new homes, for example.

Less Proficient Readers

In trying to make the narrative resemble speech, Gordimer uses run-on sentences, sentence fragments, and other elements that are normally avoided in formal written English. If students get tangled up in a sentence, suggest that they read it aloud to themselves. If this doesn't work, suggest that they ask a classmate for help in interpreting it.

2 Note that the extra space and the green initial capital letter signal a break in the narration. In this case, the flashback has ended and the narrator has returned to the point where she began the story: her fiance's release.

Advanced Learners

3 Talk about why the child reacts as she does to her father. *(because he is a stranger to her)* Mention that in the United States, there is a debate about making it easier for parents in prison to see their children. Ask students how they feel about such efforts.

Cross Curricular Link **Psychology**

SEPARATION FROM CHILDREN The prisoners on Robben Island were not allowed any visitors under the age of 16. According to Ahmed Kathrada, who was held there with Nelson Mandela, their greatest deprivation was never seeing children, "because it's an unnatural world without children." At one point in their detention, the prisoners were moved to the women's section of another prison, where they heard children's voices for the first time in many years. Even hearing the children cry was "a sensational experience," Kathrada said.

Another time, a sympathetic warder smuggled Mandela's baby grandchild in to see him for a moment. Holding and kissing the child brought tears to Mandela's eyes. After his release, at his daughter's wedding, he stated, "When your life is the struggle, as mine was, there is little room left for family. That has always been my greatest regret and the most painful aspect of the choice I made."

Reading and Analyzing

Active Reading MAKING INFERENCES

A Discuss what can be inferred about the couple's relationship.

Possible Responses: They are not emotionally close; they do not talk to each other about the things most important to them; she thinks he might feel that he is beyond farm people now.

Literary Analysis THEME

B Ask students to state in their own words what the narrator now understands.

Possible Response: She understands that black people have no home in South Africa because they do not own land and have no rights or opportunities.

Literary Analysis FIRST-PERSON POINT OF VIEW

C Ask: How does the narrator view her fiance and his work? How does she think he views her?

Possible Responses: She views him and his work as very important. She thinks he views her as less important than his work but also as someone he wants to understand political ideas.

Ask students which character they feel more sympathetic toward and why.

Possible Response: Most students will probably feel more sympathetic toward the narrator because they are aware of her loneliness, her struggles to understand, and her attempts to please her fiance. Some students may feel more sympathetic toward the fiance because he is a determined fighter and makes efforts to raise the consciousness of the narrator.

Active Reading MAKING INFERENCES

D Ask students what they have inferred about the place of women in this society.

Possible Response: They lead lives very separate from men's; they are not politically active; they are not spoken to as equals; pregnancy and child-rearing are seen as their concerns and not men's.

Sometimes in the daytime I do try to tell him what it was like for me, here at home on the farm, five years.

floor of that small cell where he was kept. After we were together at night we used to whisper a long time but now I can feel he's thinking of some things I don't know and I can't worry him with talk. Also I don't know what to say. To ask him what it was like, five years shut away there; or to tell him something about school or about the child. What else has happened, here? Nothing. Just waiting. Sometimes in the daytime I do try to tell him what it was like for me, here at home on the farm, five years. He listens, he's interested, just like he's interested when people from the other farms come to visit and talk to him about little things that happened to them while he was away all that time on the Island. He smiles and nods, asks a couple of questions and then stands up and stretches. I see it's to show them it's enough, his mind is going back to something he was busy with before they came. And we farm people are very slow; we tell things slowly, he used to, too.

He hasn't signed on for another job. But he can't stay at home with us; we thought, after five years over there in the middle of that green and blue sea, so far, he would rest with us a little while. The combi or some car comes to fetch him and he says don't worry, I don't know what day I'll be back. At first I asked, what week, next week? He tried to explain to me: in the Movement it's not like it was in the union, where you do your work every day and after that you are busy with meetings; in the Movement you never know where you will have to go and what is going to come up next. And the same with money. In the Movement, it's not like a job, with regular pay—I know that, he doesn't have to tell me—it's like it was going to the Island, you do it for all our people who suffer because we haven't got money, we haven't got land—look, he said, speaking of my parents', my home, the home that has been waiting for him, with his child: look at this place where the white man owns the ground and lets you squat in mud and tin huts here only as long as you work for him—*Baba*[13] and your brother planting his crops and looking after his cattle, Mama cleaning his house and you in the school without even having the chance to train properly as a teacher. The farmer owns us, he says.

I've been thinking we haven't got a home because there wasn't time to build a house before he came from the Island; but we haven't got a home at all. Now I've understood that.

I'm not stupid. When the comrades come to this place in the combi to talk to him here I don't go away with my mother after we've brought them tea or (if she's made it for the weekend) beer. They like her beer, they talk about our culture and there's one of them who makes a point of putting his arm around my mother, calling her the mama of all of them, the mama of Africa. Sometimes they please her very much by telling her how they used to sing on the Island and getting her to sing an old song we all know from our grandmothers. Then they join in with their strong voices. My father doesn't like this noise traveling across the veld; he's afraid that if the Boer finds out my man is a political, from the Island, and he's holding meetings on the Boer's land, he'll tell my father to go, and take his family with him. But my brother says if the Boer asks anything just tell him it's a prayer meeting. Then the singing is over; my mother knows she must go away into the house.

I stay, and listen. He forgets I'm there when he's talking and arguing about something I can see is important, more important than anything we could ever have to say to each other when we're alone. But now and then, when one of the other comrades is speaking I see him look at me for a moment the way I will look up at one of my favorite children in school to encourage the child to understand. The men don't speak to me and I don't speak. One of the things they talk about is organizing the people on the farms—the workers, like my father and brother, and like his parents used to be. I learn what all these things are: minimum wage, limitation of working hours, the right to strike, annual leave, accident compensation,[14] pensions, sick and even maternity leave. I am pregnant, at last I have another child inside me, but that's women's business. When they talk about the Big Man, the Old Men,[15] I know who these are: our leaders are also back from prison. I told him about the child coming; he said, And this one belongs to a new country, he'll build the freedom we've fought for! I know he wants to get married but there's no time for that at present. There was hardly time for him to make the child. He comes to me just like he comes here to eat a meal or put on clean clothes. Then he picks up the little girl and swings her round and there!—it's done, he's getting into the combi, he's already turning to his comrade that face of his that knows only what's inside his head, those eyes that move quickly as if he's chasing something you can't see. The little girl hasn't had time to get used to this man. But I know she'll be proud of him, one day!

13. ***Baba:*** a title of respect for an aged man, here indicating the narrator's father.

14. **accident compensation:** money or medical benefits paid to someone who has been injured on a job.

15. **the Big Man, the Old Men:** Nelson Mandela and several of his elderly associates were freed from prison in the early 1990s.

Customizing Instruction

Less Proficient Readers

1 Ask students to consider the fiance's actions: does he seem interested in what people are saying to him?

Possible Response: No, he seems preoccupied.

English Learners

2 Explain these labor terms:

minimum wage–the lowest wage that a worker can be paid, by law

limitation of working hours–rule that workers can work no more than a certain number of hours

the right to strike–the right to stop work in protest without losing one's job

annual leave–paid time off every year

pensions–regular payments to a worker after he or she retires

sick leave–paid time off allowed to a worker who is sick

maternity leave–paid time off allowed to a worker who is pregnant or has just had a child

Advanced Learners

Mention that one critic of this story has said it is "patronizing" for Gordimer, as a white South African, to write in the voice of a black South African. This critic finds something "faux-naif," or falsely simple and innocent, about the narrator's speech and views. Ask students what they think of this criticism.

Possible Response: Some students may find the narrator believable and depicted respectfully; others may agree that the narrator is unconvincing. Some students may believe that there is nothing wrong with writing from the viewpoint of a character of a different race; others may believe that this is hard to do well.

Assessment Standardized Test Practice

EVALUATING AND MAKING JUDGMENTS In some standardized tests, students are asked to analyze information in order to make inferences and generalizations. Display the following question: *Why does the narrator's fiance leave home again after his release?*

A. He wants to make life better for suffering people.

B. He wants to earn money to build a house.

C. He is afraid that the Boer farmer will make his family leave.

D. He does not love the narrator.

Lead students through the possible answers. The best answer is A. The narrator's fiance explains that this is the reason he is in the Movement and must go away. B is incorrect because he says that being in the Movement is not a job with regular pay and also, he dismisses the houses that blacks are allowed to build on white land. C is the narrator's father's fear; not her fiance's. There is no evidence that D is true; the fiance encourages the narrator to understand political ideas and still wants to marry her.

Literary Analysis THEME

A Ask: How does the narrator see the land now?
Possible Response: She sees the earth as vast and belonging to no one.

Literary Analysis IMAGERY

B Ask: What do you associate with rats?
Possible Responses: ugliness, danger, fear, greed

Ask: How would you connect any of these ideas to the narrator's situation?
Possible Responses: She might be fearful about her future with a man she does not feel that close to; she may see the apartheid system as a greedy rat that is eating her life.

How can you tell that to a child six years old? But I tell her about the Big Man and the Old Men, our leaders, so she'll know that her father was with them on the Island, this man is a great man, too.

On Saturday, no school and I plant and weed with my mother, she sings but I don't; I think. On Sunday there's no work, only prayer meetings out of the farmer's way under the trees, and

> I'm watching the rat, it's losing itself, its shape, eating the sky, and I'm waiting. Waiting for him to come back.

beer drinks at the mud and tin huts where the farmers allow us to squat on their land. I go off on my own as I used to do when I was a child, making up games and talking to myself where no one would hear me or look for me. I sit on a warm stone in the late afternoon, high up, and the whole valley is a path between the hills, leading away from my feet. **A** It's the Boer's farm but that's not true, it belongs to nobody. The cattle don't know that anyone says he owns it, the sheep—they are grey stones, and then they become a thick grey snake moving—don't know. Our huts and the old mulberry tree and the little brown mat of earth that my mother dug over yesterday, way down there, and way over there the clump of trees round the chimneys and the shiny thing that is the TV mast of the farmhouse—they are nothing, on the back of this earth. It could twitch them away like a dog does a fly.

I am up with the clouds. The sun behind me is changing the colors of the sky and the clouds are changing themselves, slowly, slowly. Some are pink, some are white, swelling like bubbles. **B** Underneath is a bar of grey, not enough to make rain. It gets longer and darker, it grows a thin snout and long body and then the end of it is a tail. There's a huge grey rat moving across the sky, eating the sky.

The child remembered the photo; she said *That's not him.* I'm sitting here where I came often when he was on the Island. I came to get away from the others, to wait by myself.

I'm watching the rat, it's losing itself, its shape, eating the sky, and I'm waiting. Waiting for him to come back.

Waiting.

I'm waiting to come back home. ❖

MINI LESSON Grammar

PARTICIPIAL PHRASES

Instruction Explain that a *participle* is a verb form that functions as an adjective, modifying a noun or pronoun (the falling leaves). A *participial phrase* consists of a participle, its modifiers, and its complements (falling from the trees). Often, two sentences can be combined into a single sentence using one or more participial phrases.

Example: I go off on my own as I used to do when I was a child. I made up games and talked to myself.

Rewritten: I go off on my own as I used to do when I was a child, making up games and talking to myself.

Explain that if the participial phrase is not essential to complete the meaning of the sentence, it is set off by one or more commas.

Practice Have students use participial phrases to combine the following pair of sentences into a single sentence:

She stands in line at the ferry. She waits to visit her fiance on Robben Island.

Possible Answers: Standing in line at the ferry, she waits to visit her fiance on Robben Island. She stands in line at the ferry, waiting to visit her fiance on Robben Island.

For more instruction and practice in participial phrases, use McDougal Littell's ***Language Network:***

- Grade 10, Chapter 3, "Verbals: Participles"
- Grade 12, Chapter 2, "Verbals: Participial Phrases"

Connect to the Literature

1. **What Do You Think?** What is your impression of the narrator's life?

Comprehension Check
- Why has the narrator been separated from her fiancé for nine years?
- What does her fiancé do in the weeks after he returns home?

Think Critically

2. Describe the narrator's feelings about her fiancé.
3. How have the fiancé's political activities affected him? How have they affected the narrator and their child?
4. What is your opinion of the fiancé?

THINK ABOUT
- his commitment to the antiapartheid movement
- how he treats the narrator and their child
- how he treats the farm workers who come to talk with him

5. What do you think the narrator means at the end of the story when she says she is "waiting to come back home"?
6. **ACTIVE READING: MAKING INFERENCES** Review the list of inferences you made about customs and conditions in South Africa and about the relationship between the two main characters. What did you learn that was not directly stated in the story?

Extend Interpretations

7. **The Writer's Style** Sometimes Gordimer subtly uses description and figurative language to support themes of the story. For example, she belittles Robben Island by having the narrator compare it to a cake of cattle dung floating in a pool of rainwater. What ideas about South Africa are suggested to you by the description of the land and sky at the end of the story?
8. **Connect to Life** The narrator's fiancé tells her that he is in jail so that people's lives will be better in the future. In what way is your own life better because of someone else's effort and sacrifice for an important cause? Name the cause and, if possible, a specific person.

LITERARY ANALYSIS: FIRST-PERSON POINT OF VIEW

"Amnesty" is told from the **first-person point of view:** the narrator is a character in the story who tells everything in her own words. She is a simple country woman who at first has little political awareness. This simplicity is evident in the following description of her fiancé at a meeting of antiapartheid activists:

> ***I stay, and listen. He forgets I'm there when he's talking and arguing about something I can see is important, more important than anything we could ever have to say to each other when we're alone.***

Using the first-person point of view usually ensures that readers will feel close to the narrator, but it also restricts readers to knowing only what the narrator understands and tells them, and no more. In this story, for example, readers don't know what the narrator's fiancé feels each time he leaves his family.

Cooperative Learning Activity Gordimer could have chosen to write from the **third-person point of view,** referring to the young woman as *she*. She could have revealed only the young woman's thoughts **(third-person limited point of view).** Or she could have revealed all the characters' thoughts **(third-person omniscient point of view).** In small groups, discuss how the story would have been different if told from either of these third-person points of view. Judging by Gordimer's choice of narrator, what ideas do you think she wanted to present? How do you think she wanted to affect her readers?

Connect to the Literature

1. **What Do You Think?** Possible Responses: The narrator's life is limited and disappointing; apartheid keeps her from having a normal family life; her fiance is so involved in his political struggle that he cannot be a good husband to her.

Comprehension Check
- At first she was separated from him because he was away working in the city; then he was serving time in prison for his antiapartheid activities.
- He returns to his work in the antiapartheid movement.

Use Selection Quiz in **Unit Seven Resource Book,** p. 99.

Think Critically

2. Possible Responses: She is proud of him; she wants to please him; she finds him unfamiliar and distant; she wishes he would spend more time with her.
3. Possible Responses: They have caused him to be jailed and separated from his family; they occupy almost all his time and energy since his release. They have caused the narrator to be lonely, made the child estranged from her father, and created a financial burden. On the other hand, they make the narrator proud of her fiance and more aware of her political situation.
4. Possible Responses: Some students may fault the fiance for neglecting the narrator and their child; others may admire him for fighting to improve the condition of a whole group; others may feel sorry for him because he faces so many conflicting demands.
5. Possible Responses: She is waiting for things to be as they were before; she is waiting to have the marriage she thought she would have.
6. Possible Responses: Students may have inferred that black people on South African farms are impoverished, poorly educated, and dependent on white landowners for work and a place to live. They may have inferred that the government jails protesters, censors speech, and creates rules that make life difficult for blacks. They may also have inferred that the relationship between the narrator and her fiance is awkward and distant and that women are expected to defer to men in the culture.

Extend Interpretations

7. **The Writer's Style** Possible Responses: The observation that the cattle and sheep do not recognize the land as the Boers' suggests that people do not have to recognize land claims, either. The description of the sheep as stones that become a snake could suggest oppressed people's transformation into fighters. The description of the vastness of the earth could suggest the insignificance of man-made laws that apply to it. Changing clouds could suggest coming social change.
8. **Connect to Life** Possible Responses: Students might name people who fought to establish schools or to extend civil rights.

Literary Analysis

Cooperative Learning Activity Students might note that the third-person limited point of view might have made them feel more distant toward the main character. The third-person omniscient point of view might have made them give more weight to the fiance's thoughts and feelings. Students might feel that by choosing an ordinary woman as narrator, Gordimer could better move readers to see how the antiapartheid struggle required sacrifice from everyone, even those not imprisoned.

Use **Unit Seven Resource Book,** p. 98, for more practice.

Writing Options

1. **Comparison-and-Contrast Essay** Suggest that before students begin writing, they pair with a partner and debate the question, taking different sides.
2. **A Daughter's Diary** Suggest that students go back and reread the passages that mention how the daughter feels toward the father. Encourage them to imagine what is likely or unlikely to change and how they might feel in the daughter's situation.
3. **Revealing Letter** Tell students that this is their chance to "talk back" to a character in the story. They should list what they think the fiance believes about the narrator, then add what they know about the narrator that contradicts or expands upon these beliefs.

Activities & Explorations

1. **Waiting Portrait** As students reread the last page, they should jot down objects and colors that are mentioned. They should try to identify the mood, or overall emotional quality, of the description.
2. **Debate on Self-Sacrifice** Before students choose sides, ask them to freewrite on the following questions: What has the fiance sacrificed? Why is he sacrificing this? What would happen if he didn't sacrifice this?

Inquiry & Research

1. **Robben Island Prisoners** Students might consult Mandela's autobiography, *No Easy Walk to Freedom,* and Sobukwe's biography, *Sobukwe and Apartheid.* Others imprisoned on Robben Island include Ahmed Kathrada and Govan Mbeki (the father of Thabo Mbeki, who succeeded Mandela as president of South Africa).
2. **Legacy of Apartheid** If students have access to a computer, suggest that they go to our website, classzone.com, for links to more information on social conditions in South Africa.

To assess skills and concepts taught in this selection, use **Formal Assessment Book,** pp. 195–196.

Writing Options

1. Comparison-and-Contrast Essay Who has made the bigger sacrifices, the narrator or her fiancé? Write a brief essay comparing and contrasting the kinds of sacrifices made by the two characters.

Writing Handbook
See page R31: Compare and Contrast.

2. A Daughter's Diary Imagine that the couple's daughter is now a teenager and keeps a diary. Write an entry in which the daughter reflects on her relationship with her father and on the life he has led. Does she admire her father as her mother predicted she would?

3. Revealing Letter The narrator describes her fiancé as knowing "only what's inside his head." What does this mean? What does her fiancé fail to see and know about her? Write a letter to the fiancé telling him what he doesn't notice about the narrator.

Activities & Explorations

1. Waiting Portrait At the end of the story, the narrator describes what she sees as she sits "on a warm stone in the late afternoon" to think and to wait. Reread the passage and then draw or paint the scene you picture in your mind. In your drawing or painting, try to capture the mood of the passage. ~ ART

2. Debate on Self-Sacrifice Anyone devoted to working for a cause makes some personal sacrifices. In this story, is the fiancé sacrificing more than he should, or are all his sacrifices necessary? As a class, choose sides and debate this issue. ~ SPEECH

Inquiry & Research

1. Robben Island Prisoners Research the life of a well-known South African leader who was imprisoned on Robben Island, such as Nelson Mandela, Robert Sobukwe, or Walter Sisulu. Prepare an oral report telling about your subject's antiapartheid activities, years of imprisonment, and experiences after being freed.

2. Legacy of Apartheid Although apartheid ended in 1991, it continues to cast a long shadow over South Africa. Investigate current social problems in the country that are at least partly the legacy of apartheid and the racism it supported. Explain your findings in a cause-and-effect chart.

Connect to Today

Farm Workers in the New South Africa

How has the end of apartheid changed life for landless black farm workers in South Africa? Many new laws have been passed to benefit them, but real change has been slow in coming.

Land Rights South Africa's new national constitution, adopted in 1996, states that "everyone has the right of access to land." The government has begun a land-reform program with three objectives:

1. the return of land to blacks who had it taken away from them by whites
2. the redistribution of white-owned land to blacks, either through government-assisted purchases by individuals or through voluntary donation by owners
3. the protection of blacks against eviction from white-owned land where they have lived and worked

So far, relatively little land has changed hands. Many rural people have been unaware of their new land rights; others have not known how to complete the forms needed to apply for land. The legal process has been slow, and judges, most of whom are white, tend to favor white landowners in disputes. Land remains too expensive for most black families to buy.

Mistreatment and Murders Conditions for workers on white-owned farms are not much improved, either. For example, from January to September 1999, the South African labor department received more than 4,000 complaints from farm workers against employers, citing such mistreatment as refusing to give workers time off, unfairly evicting them from their homes, preventing them from joining unions, replacing them with lower-paid immigrants, and verbally and physically abusing them. Mutual resentment has led to a wave of racial violence in rural areas that includes murders of black workers by white farmers and murders of white farmers by black workers. More than a thousand people have been killed on farms since 1996.

A Brighter Future? Amid the violence, though, there are a few signs of progress. The Centre for Rural Legal Studies, formed in 1991, runs projects designed to improve conditions for farm workers and set a minimum wage for them. It has trained paralegals and union leaders to help farm workers obtain their rights. Also, some visionary employers have experimented with new labor arrangements. The owner of the Nelson Creek winery, for example, donated land to black workers, which they used to produce their own successful brand of wine labeled New Beginnings.

Group Discussion What more do you think could be done to improve life for farm workers in South Africa? What ways can you think of to stop the racial violence on the farms?

Connect to Today

Use this feature to show the relevance of world literature to students. The material relates the literature selection just read to a contemporary topic connected to South African life today.

Group Discussion Students might suggest more vigorous enforcement of laws, government confiscation of land, welfare payments, or retraining programs as ways to improve conditions for farm workers. They might suggest public education programs or denunciations of violence by local leaders as ways to stop the racial violence on farms.

Objectives

- appreciate modern **poetry (Literary Analysis)**
- analyze the **tone** of two poems **(Literary Analysis)**
- **evaluate** the ideas presented in poems **(Active Reading)**

Thematic Link

These poems **criticize** political corruption and examine recovery from war or political strife.

5-Minute Warm-Up

Daily Language SkillBuilder

Have students **proofread** the display sentences on page 1095o and write them correctly.

AFTER THE DELUGE

WOLE SOYINKA

THE END AND THE BEGINNING

WISLAWA SZYMBORSKA

Wole Soyinka
1934–

Playwright and Prisoner In 1986 the Nigerian writer Wole Soyinka (wō'lĕ shô-yĭng'kə) became the first African to win the Nobel Prize in literature. His work blends traditional folklore and myths from his native Yoruba culture with Western literary forms. His first major play, *A Dance of the Forests,* was commissioned as a salute to Nigeria's independence. This humorous play warned that the end of colonial rule did not necessarily promise the end of Nigeria's problems.

In the mid-1960s, Soyinka became actively involved in the civil war between the Nigerian government and the Ibo ethnic group, who wanted to form their own country, Biafra. Accused of helping the Biafrans, Soyinka was arrested in 1967 and kept in solitary confinement for more than two years. He smuggled out fragments of writing that were later published as *Poems from Prison* and *The Man Died: Prison Notes of Wole Soyinka.* Since his imprisonment, he has had long periods of exile from Nigeria. His writing has become, in his words, "more and more preoccupied with the theme of the oppressive boot, the irrelevance of the color of the foot that wears it and the struggle for individuality."

Wislawa Szymborska
1923–

Surprised to Win Wislawa Szymborska (vē-swä'vä shĭm-bôr'skə) was surprised when, one day in 1996, she learned that she had won the Nobel Prize in literature. That day the world "came crashing down" on her, she has said.

Szymborska has lived in the Polish city of Krakow since she was eight. She made her literary debut in 1945 with the publication of a poem in a newspaper. Since then, she has published 16 books of poetry, including 2 early collections she now disclaims because she was writing under pressure to praise Communism. "I really wanted to save humanity," she has said," but I chose the worst possible way. I did it out of love for mankind. Then I came to understand that you should not love mankind, but rather like people."

The poetry Szymborska has written since the loosening of Communist censorship in 1957 is praised for its sharp wit, keen observation, and simple language. Her work was largely unknown outside Poland until she won the Nobel Prize. The first English translation of her poems was *View with a Grain of Sand,* which appeared in 1995.

LESSON RESOURCES

UNIT SEVEN RESOURCE BOOK, pp. 100–101

ASSESSMENT RESOURCES
Formal Assessment, pp. 197–198
Teacher's Guide to Assessment and Portfolio Use
Test Generator

INTEGRATED TECHNOLOGY
Visit our Web site: classzone.com

ADDITIONAL RESOURCES
Lesson Planning Guide, pp. 175–176
Teacher's Sourcebook for Language Development

Connect to Your Life

We in the United States are fortunate in never having been ruled by a dictatorship and not having had a war on our own soil since the Civil War. What changes would dictatorship and war at home have brought to us? Discuss this question with classmates.

Build Background

The two poems you are about to read deal with the aftermath of catastrophic events—in "After the Deluge," a revolution, in "The End and the Beginning," a war. The authors of these poems have experienced such events firsthand. Soyinka has seen his native Nigeria torn by civil wars and ruled by military dictatorships for much of the time since the country achieved independence in 1960. Other African countries have undergone similar experiences, and Soyinka has not hesitated to criticize corrupt leaders.

Szymborska also has lived through war and dictatorship. She was a teenager when Germany invaded Poland during World War II. The war, with its brutality and hardships, was followed by a Communist dictatorship, which ruled Poland until 1989. After the end of Communist rule, people looked for new ways to organize their lives.

Warsaw, Poland, during World War II

Focus Your Reading

LITERARY ANALYSIS: TONE

The **tone** of a written work is an expression of the writer's attitude toward the work's subject. The tone of a literary work might be serious, humorous, admiring, or sarcastic, for example. Writers communicate tone largely through diction, or word choice. For example, "After every war / someone has to tidy up" has a tone different from that of the more serious "After every violent conflict / rebuilding must occur." Choice of details can also convey tone; for instance, if a poem mentioned only a leader's accomplishments and not his or her flaws, you might interpret the tone as admiring. As you read each of these poems, consider how you would describe the tone.

ACTIVE READING: EVALUATING

To evaluate is to make a judgment or form an opinion about something. As you read "After the Deluge," evaluate the former leader who is described in the poem. What kind of person is he? As you read "The End and the Beginning," evaluate the speaker's ideas about what must happen after a war. Do you agree with them?

READER'S NOTEBOOK Be aware of your evaluations, or judgments, as you read. After every stanza record your reaction in your notebook.

"After the Deluge"	
Stanza 1	*What a showoff!*

READING FOR INFORMATION

Reading Skills and Strategies

COMPARING AND CONTRASTING

In this lesson, two poems by different authors are paired. As students read the biographies, tell them to look for differences and similarities in the authors' lives. As they read **Build Background,** have them look for a similarity in the subjects of the poems.

TIME MANAGEMENT

If your schedule requires that you cover the lesson objectives in a shorter time, use. . .

- Preparing to Read, pp. 1336, 1337
- Thinking Through the Literature, p. 1342

If you want to take advantage of longer blocks of class time, use. . .

- TE Teaching Options: Viewing and Representing, p. 1339; Speaking and Listening, p. 1340
- Choices and Challenges, p. 1343

Active Reading EVALUATING

A Have students offer their opinion of the man described in the poem, based on his actions in the first stanza.
Possible Responses: Most students will probably dislike him, thinking he is vain, pretentious, and wasteful. Some may admire his wealth.

Use **Unit Seven Resource Book,** p. 100, for more practice.

Literary Analysis TONE

B Ask: What do you think is Soyinka's attitude toward this man? Have students consider whether the images in this stanza outrage them, sadden them, or make them laugh. Tell them to look closely at the last two lines in the stanza. How sincere is it to call the leader's contribution a "widow's mite"?
Possible Responses: Soyinka seems highly critical of but amused by the man he is describing. He is being sarcastic when he uses the term "widow's mite"; the leader could probably afford to give much more, and his motives are self-serving.

Ask what tone is communicated through the words "roosted" and "preying bird."
Possible Response: a critical, contemptuous tone

Use **Unit Seven Resource Book,** p. 101, for more practice.

Literary Analysis THEME

C Ask students to contrast the image of the swimming pool in the last three lines with the image of the pool in the first three lines. What thematic idea is suggested by the contrast?
Possible Response: The expensive pool used to be filled with money; now snakes and lizards live in it. The contrast suggests that excessive wealth and power pass away in time; corruption cannot last forever.

After the Deluge

Wole Soyinka

Once, for a dare,
He filled his heart-shaped swimming pool
A With bank notes, high denomination
And fed a pound of caviar to his dog.
The dog was sick; a chartered plane
Flew in replacement for the Persian rug.

He made a billion yen
Leap from Tokyo to Buenos Aires,
Turn somersaults through Brussels,
New York, Sofia and Johannesburg.
It cracked the bullion market open wide.
Governments fell, coalitions cracked
Insurrection raised its bloody flag
2 From north to south.

He knew his native land through iron gates,
His sight was radar bowls, his hearing
B Electronic beams. For flesh and blood,
Kept company with a brace of Dobermans.
But—yes—the worthy causes never lacked
His widow's mite, discreetly publicized.

He escaped the lynch days. He survives.
I dreamt I saw him on a village
Water line, a parched land where
Water is a god
That doles its favors by the drop,
And waiting is a way of life.
Rebellion gleamed yet faintly in his eye

3 denomination: value.

1 **7–10 He made . . . Johannesburg:** He transferred money through major cities of the world—probably government funds that he stole and did not want traced.

11 bullion: gold.

13 insurrection: revolt; rebellion.

18 brace of Dobermans: pair of Doberman pinschers—medium-sized dogs often trained to attack intruders.

20 widow's mite: a small contribution by one who has little.

Garbage (1924), Jose clemente Orozco. Mural. Escuela Nacional Preparatoria San Ildefonso, Mexico City, D. F., Mexico. Photo © Schalkwijk/Art Resource, New York. Art © Arists Rights Society (ARS), New York.

Traversing chrome-and-platinum retreats. There,
Hubs of commerce smoothly turn without
His bidding, and cities where he lately roosted
Have forgotten him, the preying bird
Of passage.

They let him live, but not from pity
3 Or human sufferance. He scratches life
From earth, no worse a mortal man than the rest.
Far, far away in dreamland splendor,
Creepers twine his gates of bronze relief.
The jade-lined pool is home
C To snakes and lizards; they hunt and mate
On crusted algae.

29 hubs of commerce: centers of trade.

Customizing Instruction

Less Proficient Readers

1 Warn students about the figurative language in this poem. Make sure they do not miss the explanatory sidenote for lines 7–10.

2 You might also ask students to interpret lines such as "Insurrection raised its bloody flag" *(There was violent revolt)* and "His sight was radar bowls" *(He relied on elaborate security systems to protect him from enemies).*

If you have access to a world map or globe, point out the locations of the cities mentioned in the second stanza.

English Learners

Soyinka uses difficult words, such as *discreetly, traversing,* and *sufferance* that may be unfamiliar to English learners. Encourage them to write on the board any words they are unsure of. Then, as a whole class, discuss the meanings.

Advanced Learners

3 Ask what is suggested about the reason people let the man live.

Possible Response: He now lives with as much difficulty as they do and acts no worse than they do.

Ask students what they think of the description of the man as "no worse a mortal man than the rest."

Possible Responses: Some students may think the description implies that most people are as greedy and selfish as the leader. Others may think it implies that the leader is no longer exploitive, now that he has lost his wealth and power.

MINI LESSON Viewing and Representing

Falcon's Descent on the People **by Chike Aniakor**

ART APPRECIATION Aniakor is an Igbo (Ibo) artist from Nigeria. Since the 1980s, he has used his work to comment on the political situation in his country. He feels he has no choice but to do this: "I live in a society where you turn to your left and you find people hungry. You turn to your right, you find the suffering and the helpless." Often he depicts leaders, either in human form or metaphorically as eagles or falcons. In his compositions, groups of figures are frequently huddled together.

Ask: What political message do you read into this picture? How would you relate the picture to Soyinka's poem?

Possible Response: The picture suggests that a leader is controlling and preying upon masses of helpless people. The picture and the poem are similar, both depicting a leader as a bird of prey.

Literary Analysis TONE

A Ask: How would you describe the tone of this first stanza?

Possible Responses: light, sarcastic

Active Reading EVALUATING

B Ask: How accurately does this stanza describe what happens after tragic events?

Possible Responses: The description is fairly accurate; news coverage lasts for only a short while, until the next tragic event.

Literary Analysis FIGURATIVE LANGUAGE

C Ask: What might be meant by a "rusted argument"?

Possible Responses: an argument that does not apply to the current situation; an argument that has been proved to be false or that is no longer widely believed

Active Reading EVALUATING

D Discuss whether the point made in this stanza is true, perhaps by considering what students know of the American Civil War.

The End and the Beginning

Wislawa Szymborska

Translated by Stanislaw Baranczak and Clare Cavanagh

1 A
After every war
someone has to tidy up.
Things won't pick
themselves up, after all.

Someone has to shove
the rubble to the roadsides
so the carts loaded with corpses
can get by.

Someone has to trudge
through sludge and ashes,
through the sofa springs,
the shards of glass,
the bloody rags.

Someone has to lug the post
to prop the wall,
someone has to glaze the window,
set the door in its frame.

2 B
No sound bites, no photo opportunities,
and it takes years.
All the cameras have gone
to other wars.

MINI LESSON **Speaking and Listening**

INTERPRETIVE READING To support the Literary Analysis activity on tone (p. 1342), you might have students read different stanzas aloud, with different tones.

Prepare Tell students to read the list of tones at the bottom of the Literary Analysis box. Ask ten volunteers to state simply, "My name is ______________," trying to communicate each tone.

Present Have students do the same thing with stanzas of "The End and the Beginning," trying out tones. Are there any tones that don't seem to fit the poem? Finally, ask one or two exceptional readers to perform the entire poem in a consistent tone. Can the class agree on the best interpretation?

The bridges need to be rebuilt,
the railroad stations, too.
Shirtsleeves will be rolled
to shreds.

Someone, broom in hand,
still remembers how it was.
Someone else listens, nodding
his unshattered head.
But others are bound to be bustling nearby
who'll find all that
a little boring.

From time to time someone still must
dig up a rusted argument
from underneath a bush
and haul it off to the dump.

Those who knew
what this was all about
must make way for those
who know little.
And less than that.
And at last nothing less than nothing.

Someone has to lie there
in the grass that covers up
the causes and effects
with a cornstalk in his teeth,
gawking at clouds.

Customizing Instruction

English Learners

1 Talk about the denotation and connotations of the phrase *tidy up.* It means "to put in order," but it is something one would normally say of a mildly cluttered house, not a war zone.

2 Mention that *sound bites* refers to brief quotes heard on radio or television news reports. *Photo opportunities,* often shortened to *photo ops,* are brief periods for the press to photograph people involved in a news event.

Less Proficient Readers

Encourage students, as they read, to look for words that seem odd or out of place, like "sofa springs" among the other signs of destruction in the third stanza. It is this incongruity, or out-of-place-ness, that helps make the poem effective.

THE END AND THE BEGINNING **1341**

Connect to the Literature

1. **What Do You Think?** What image from each poem stands out most in your mind?

Think Critically

2. **ACTIVE READING: EVALUATING** Give your own opinion of the former leader described in "After the Deluge." On what details is your opinion based? Look back at the reactions you recorded in your  **READER'S NOTEBOOK.**

3. Reread the last stanza of "After the Deluge." What do the images in it suggest to you?

4. What must happen after the end of a war, according to the speaker in "The End and the Beginning"? Explain the speaker's argument in your own words.

   THINK ABOUT
   - what it might mean to "tidy up" (line 2)
   - what it might mean to "dig up a rusted argument / . . . and haul it off to the dump" (lines 34–36)
   - who replaces "Those who knew / what this was all about" (lines 37–38)
   - what is suggested by the image of someone lying "in the grass that covers up / the causes and effects" and "gawking at clouds" (lines 44–47)

5. **ACTIVE READING: EVALUATING** Do you agree with the speaker's ideas about what must happen after the end of a war?

Extend Interpretations

6. **Critic's Corner** One of Szymborska's translators, Stanislaw Baranczak, has interpreted the cleaning up in "The End and the Beginning" as a metaphor for forgetting. To him, the poem implies that people "never learn from history." Do you agree or disagree that this is true of people?

7. **Comparing Texts** How similar are the messages about political regimes in these two poems?

8. **Connect to Life** What issues or conflicts in the United States are most similar to the ones described in these poems?

LITERARY ANALYSIS: TONE

Tone is an expression of a writer's attitude toward his or her subject. Reading a literary work aloud, with expression, may help you identify its tone. The emotions you convey in your reading can often give you clues.

Writers convey particular tones by means of the words and details they use. For example, Nadine Gordimer's short story "Amnesty" has a serious, thoughtful, and sad tone. In a matter-of-fact way, the narrator shares details that give a picture of the limited scope of her life. One such detail is the fact that she has never seen the sea "except to color it in blue at school."

Paired Activity Work with a partner to identify the tone of each poem you have just read. To describe a tone, you may select an adjective from the following list of words or come up with one of your own. Review each poem for examples of word choices and details that contribute to the tone you have identified. Is the tone of each poem what you would expect, considering the poem's subject?

bitter	scornful
sad	angry
humorous	sarcastic
ironic	tongue-in-cheek
lighthearted	mocking

Connect to the Literature

1. **What Do You Think?** Possible Responses: "After the Deluge"—the swimming pool full of money; the leader lonely in his fortified home; the abandoned mansion overgrown with vines, snakes, and lizards. "The End and the Beginning"—the some-one who trudges through sludge, ashes, sofa springs and more; the rusted argument hauled to the dump; the person lying on his back and staring at the clouds.

Think Critically

2. Possible Responses: Students may find the leader greedy, wasteful, corrupt, and selfish, based on his filling his swimming pool with money, feeding caviar to his dog, laundering money, hiding from people, and publicizing his charitable contributions.
3. Possible Responses: the images suggest decay, abandonment, forgotten greatness, and the processes of nature.
4. Possible Responses: After a war, people must clean up the physical damage and rebuild without attention from the rest of the world. They must get rid of outmoded or irrelevant ideas and eventually accept that future generations will not remember, understand, or care about the war.
5. Possible Responses: Some students may agree that starting over is necessary for life to go on peacefully. Others may feel that the poem is untrue because people can hold on to war-causing passions for centuries. Others may feel that some wars are just, and if people forget about the causes, then they were fought for nothing.

Extend Interpretations

6. **Critic's Corner** Possible Responses: Some students may agree, noting that people continue to make war and oppress others even though history has shown how terrible this is. Others may disagree, noting that people do try to avoid the mistakes or horrors of the past. The United Nations tries to prevent genocide, for example.
7. **Comparing Texts** Possible Responses: The poems are similar in that they suggest that political regimes are only temporary and that violent change will be followed by quieter periods.
8. **Connect to Life** Possible Responses: Students may name examples of corrupt local or national leaders or they may mention the aftermath of terrorist attacks or intense ideological conflicts.

Literary Analysis

Paired Activity The tone of "After the Deluge" might be described as scornful, mocking, and humorous. The tone of "The End and the Beginning" might be described as humorous, ironic, and tongue-in-cheek. Talk about the poets' ability to achieve a mixture of tones. Also discuss how surprising the lightness of tone is, considering that the subjects are a leader's corruption and war's aftermath.

Use **Unit Seven Resource Book,** p. 101, for more practice.

Writing Options

1. Poetic Portrait Write a poem that sharply characterizes a person, as Wole Soyinka does in "After the Deluge." Include telling details that reveal personality traits. If the person you chose is known to your classmates, leave out the name and see if they can guess who it is.

2. Editorial on Memory In an editorial, either agree or disagree with the assertion that people "never learn from history." Support your opinion with examples from world events.

Writing Handbook
See page R35: Persuasive Writing.

3. Comparison-and-Contrast Essay Write a brief essay comparing and contrasting "After the Deluge" and "The End and the Beginning." How are the poems similar or different in subject, tone, and theme?

Activities & Explorations

1. Dramatic Reading Prepare and present a dramatic reading of one of these two poems. You might work with a group to present "The End and the Beginning" as a choral reading, with separate voices speaking separate stanzas or particular lines. In your performance try to capture the tone you think the writer intended. ~ **PERFORMING**

2. Editorial Cartoon Draw an editorial cartoon mocking the leader described in "After the Deluge." You might create a caricature, a drawing in which distinctive features are deliberately exaggerated. Let images in the poem suggest ways of representing the leader. You might show him as a bird of prey, for example. ~ **ART**

3. Personal Interview If possible, interview someone who has personally witnessed a war or revolution, such as a veteran or an immigrant. Find out what the experience taught this person that he or she will never forget. ~ **SPEAKING AND LISTENING**

Communication Handbook
See page R52: Conducting an Interview.

Inquiry & Research

1. More by the Authors Find more poems by Wislawa Szymborska and choose two to share with the class. As an alternative, read a play by Wole Soyinka and present an oral review of it to the class.

2. Historical Time Line Investigate the history of either postcolonial Nigeria or postwar Poland and create a time line of major events. Do you see any connections between the events and the related poem?

3. Starting Over Investigate a country that has recently undergone a revolution or war. Report on what happened to its overthrown leaders or what rebuilding has been necessary.

Writing Options

1. **Poetic Portrait** Suggest that students write about public figures; warn them against creating unflattering portraits of their classmates.
2. **Editorial on Memory** Have students recall their own and others' answers to question 6 in preparation for this writing assignment.
3. **Comparison-and-Contrast Essay** Allow students to work in pairs to create a comparison-and-contrast chart before they begin writing their individual essays.

Activities & Explorations

1. **Dramatic Reading** This activity would be a good follow-up to the Speaking and Listening option on page 1340. Allow groups plenty of practice time before their performance.
2. **Editorial Cartoon** Bring in examples of editorial cartoons to discuss with students interested in this assignment.
3. **Personal Interview** It might be more practical to invite one person in for the whole class to interview. You could scan the archives of your local paper for possible interview subjects or ask students if they know of anyone suitable.

Inquiry & Research

1. **More by the Authors** Several collections of Szymborska's poems are available. In addition to *View with a Grain of Sand,* there is *Miracle Fair,* translated by Joanna Trzeciak. *The Lion and the Jewel* is a Soyinka play that students might enjoy.
2. **Historical Time Line** General encyclopedia articles on Nigeria and Poland should be helpful for this assignment as well as specific books on these countries. Soyinka has written his own book on Nigeria, titled *The Open Sore of a Continent.*
3. **Starting Over** You might make this a small group assignment, and suggest a specific country that has experienced war or revolution within the past five years.

To assess skills and concepts taught in this selection, use **Formal Assessment Book,** pp. 197–198.

Objectives
- identify characteristics of magical realism
- recognize strategies for reading magical realism

In Unit Seven, Part 3, students will read "The Handsomest Drowned Man in the World," a magical realist short story by Gabriel García Márquez. They will also read about his magical realist novel *One Hundred Years of Solitude.* This lesson will give them some background on magical realism as a literary style.

Mixing Reality and Fantasy
Reading Skills and Strategies
CLASSIFYING
Read aloud the excerpt from "A Very Old Man with Enormous Wings." Then ask these questions:
- What is unrealistic or fantastic about the passage? *(that a man has wings)*
- What is realistic about the passage? *(the unappealing details; Pelayo and Elisenda's initial surprise)*

Magical Realism

Mixing Reality and Fantasy
Magical realism is a category of fiction in which fantastic, unbelievable events take place in a realistic setting. Usually, magical realism is associated with Latin American fiction, but the term has been applied to writing from elsewhere.

In a magical realist work, characters accept supernatural or unlikely events without much question. To the reader, the amount of realistic detail makes the impossible seem possible. For example, in this passage from "A Very Old Man with Enormous Wings" by Gabriel García Márquez, a married couple accepts the sudden appearance of a winged man in their courtyard.

They both looked at the fallen body with mute stupor. He was dressed like a ragpicker. There were only a few faded hairs left on his bald skull and very few teeth in his mouth, and his pitiful condition of a drenched great-grandfather had taken away any sense of grandeur he might have had. His huge buzzard wings, dirty and half-plucked, were forever entangled in the mud. They looked at him so long and so closely that Pelayo and Elisenda very soon overcame their surprise and in the end found him familiar.

A Latin American Form
In Latin American fiction, Argentina's Jorge Luis Borges and Cuba's Alejo Carpentier pioneered the use of magical realism, or *"lo real maravilloso,"* as Carpentier called it. In his opinion, magical realism best captured Latin America's unique and wondrous geography, history, and culture.

In the 1950s and 1960s, magical realism flowered in novels by such authors as Julio Cortázar and Carlos Fuentes. By far the best-known example of magical realism is the 1967 novel *One Hundred Years of Solitude* by Gabriel García Márquez (see Milestones in World Literature, page 1356).

Magical realism was originally an art term applied to dreamlike paintings such as *The Philosopher's Conquest* (1914) by Giorgio de Chirico.

Characteristics of Magical Realism
Although magical realist works can differ widely, they tend to share common characteristics.

Realistic Elements Works of magical realism, as you would expect, have realistic elements. Unlike fairy tales or some fantasies, they contain recognizable characters, believable dialogue, a true-to-life setting, and, often, accounts of actual historical events. The writer will often employ a matter-of-fact tone and rely heavily on sensory details to establish credibility.

Magical Elements Drawing on folklore and myths, magical realism also contains supernatural or mysterious elements. Ghosts may appear, dreams may come true, superstitions may prove warranted, people may even fly.

Humor and Exaggeration Magical realist fiction often includes humor and exaggeration. In "The Handsomest Drowned Man in the World," for instance, García Márquez uses exaggeration in describing the drowned man: "Not only was he the tallest, strongest, most virile, and best built man they had ever seen, but even though they were looking at him there was no room for him in their imagination."

Distortions of Time and Identity In works of magical realism, readers often encounter distortions of time and identity. In *One Hundred Years of Solitude,* the same sequence of events is periodically repeated. In addition, characters may change into other characters, and the usual distinctions between living and dead characters may be blurred.

Political and Social Commentary Finally, in many works of magical realism, writers directly or indirectly address important political and social issues, such as racism, tyranny, and conformity.

YOUR TURN Identify an example of magical realism that you have read in literature or seen in a film.

Magical Realism Worldwide

Magical realism is not a purely Latin American form. Works by many world writers, including some recent Nobel Prize winners, fall into the category. The U.S. writer Toni Morrison, who received the award in 1993, is noted for weaving the supernatural into her historical novels about African-American life. In her book *Song of Solomon* is an unforgettable woman named Pilate, who has no navel—a detail that suggests her disconnection from all other humans. The plot of Morrison's later novel *Beloved* revolves around a ghost—a child killed during slavery who returns to live with her family after emancipation. The German author Günter Grass, who won the Nobel Prize in 1999, is best known for his novel *The Tin Drum.* In this novel, Nazi Germany is presented through the eyes of a young boy who wills himself not to grow up.

Strategies for Reading: Magical Realism

1. Notice realistic elements, such as recognizable characters, believable dialogue, and true-to-life settings.
2. Watch for magical elements, including bizarre or impossible events and characters with supernatural abilities.
3. Look for humor and exaggeration, and notice the mood or atmosphere they create.
4. Do not be troubled by odd shifts in time and identity. Remember that events are not always presented in chronological order and that characters' identities may change.
5. **Monitor** your reading strategies and modify them when your understanding breaks down. Remember to use the strategies for active reading: **predict, visualize, connect, question, clarify,** and **evaluate.**

Characteristics of Magical Realism

Reading Skills and Strategies

SUMMARIZING

Have students use a separate sheet to list the five characteristics of magical realism discussed, leaving space between each characteristic for taking notes. Using this list as they read "The Handsomest Drowned Man in the World" will help them understand how the story is an example of magical realism.

YOUR TURN Accept any reasonable responses. Students may have read other García Márquez stories or works by Julio Cortázar, Isabel Allende, or Louise Erdrich, for example. They may have seen the films *Like Water for Chocolate* or *Unbreakable.*

Literary Note

You might also mention that metaphors and symbols are also important in magical realist stories. The unusual events and characters are not simply entertaining; often, they represent larger ideas about the real world. For example, in *One Hundred Years of Solitude,* an entire town develops amnesia. This strange event can be seen as a metaphor for forgetting history.

This selection is included in the **World Literature InterActive Reader™.**

Objectives

- understand and appreciate a magical realist **short story (Literary Analysis)**
- analyze a **symbol** in a short story **(Literary Analysis)**
- understand **cause and effect (Active Reading)**

Summary

A drowned man washes up on the beach in a small coastal community. As the women clean his body to prepare it for burial, they are overwhelmed at his size and beauty. They imagine how magnificent he must have been when he was alive, and name him Esteban. The men just want to throw him over the cliffs quickly, but when they see his face, they are moved as well. The villagers decide to hold a splendid funeral for Esteban, choosing people to stand in for his family. After they bury him, they decide to enlarge their houses and beautify their village so that it will be worthy of him. They envision a future ship's captain pointing out their settlement as "Esteban's village."

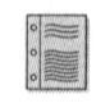

Use **Unit Seven Resource Book,** p. 102, for additional support.

Thematic Link

In this story, a mysterious drowned man makes villagers enlarge their **dreams** and lives.

Use **Unit Seven Resource Book,** p. 105, for practice with Words to Know.

5-Minute Warm-Up

Daily Language SkillBuilder

Have students **proofread** the display sentences on page 1095o and write them correctly.

GABRIEL GARCÍA MÁRQUEZ

Gabriel García Márquez
1928–

Tropical Roots Gabriel García Márquez (gär-sē'ə mär'kəs) was born in the small tropical town of Aracataca in Colombia, which he has fictionalized as the town of Macondo in his stories and novels. Raised by his grandparents until he was eight years old, García Márquez was influenced by his grandmother's unique storytelling style. She told fabulous legends and tales in a believable way, a technique García Márquez later borrowed in his writing. After his grandfather died, García Márquez returned to live with his parents and was sent away to school. Although he later enrolled in college, he abandoned his law studies to pursue a career as a journalist.

Accomplished Journalist In 1948, in the midst of political violence and riots in Colombia, García Márquez embarked on a career as a newspaper reporter. He eventually worked in France, England, and Venezuela as a freelance journalist and in 1959 helped establish a news agency for the Cuban government, working as its correspondent in Havana and New York City. Besides his novels and stories, García Márquez has published insightful works of nonfiction, such as *News of a Kidnapping* (1996). He frequently draws on his experience as a journalist in his fiction, bringing to life the political and social struggles of Latin America.

Lasting Legacy In 1982 García Márquez was awarded the Nobel Prize in literature. To date, his greatest literary achievement has been the monumental novel *One Hundred Years of Solitude,* which was published in 1967. An international success, this book traces several generations of a Colombian family and established García Márquez as a master of the style known as **magical realism.** (For more information on magical realism and *One Hundred Years of Solitude,* see Learning the Language of Literature on page 1344 and Milestones in World Literature on page 1356.)

Other Works
Chronicle of a Death Foretold
Love in the Time of Cholera

LESSON RESOURCES

UNIT SEVEN RESOURCE BOOK,
pp. 102–106

ASSESSMENT RESOURCES
Formal Assessment, pp. 199–200
Teacher's Guide to Assessment and Portfolio Use
Test Generator

INTEGRATED TECHNOLOGY
Visit our Web site: classzone.com

ADDITIONAL RESOURCES
Lesson Planning Guide, pp. 177–178
Teacher's Sourcebook for Language Development

Build Background

The Colombian Coast "The Handsomest Drowned Man in the World" was first published in 1972 as part of a collection of short stories set along the Caribbean coast of northern Colombia. The stories take place in imaginary coastal towns and villages along the Guajira Peninsula, a hot, dry, sparsely populated region. To a visitor in the 1970s, the lives of the people there would have seemed as desolate as the landscape. The inhabitants lived in wooden huts and survived largely by raising goats or working at a few trades.

The Caribbean area of Colombia is rich in folklore that reflects the region's mixture of Hispanic, African, and Indian cultures. Roaming the coastal region as a young reporter, García Márquez absorbed this folklore. Its influence shows in both his novels and his short stories.

Salt miners on the Guajira Peninsula

Connect to Your Life

Have you ever met or heard of someone who made you want to live your own life differently? If so, tell a partner about this person and how he or she affected you. In the story you are about to read, the people of an isolated fishing village react to a stranger in a surprising way.

Focus Your Reading

LITERARY ANALYSIS: SYMBOL

A **symbol** is a person, a place, or an object that stands for something beyond itself, such as an idea or a feeling. For example, a dove is a symbol of peace, and a flag can be a symbol of a country. Such visual symbols have standard interpretations. In a literary work, however, you often have to figure out a symbol's meaning by noticing what else is linked to it. As you read this story, think about what the drowned man might represent.

ACTIVE READING: UNDERSTANDING CAUSE AND EFFECT

In a story, as in real life, a single cause may have more than one effect. In "The Handsomest Drowned Man in the World," for example, one event—the discovery of a drowned man—has many effects on the people of a small village.

READER'S NOTEBOOK As you read the story, pay attention to the effects that the drowned man has on the people of the village. Jot down the effects in a chart like this one.

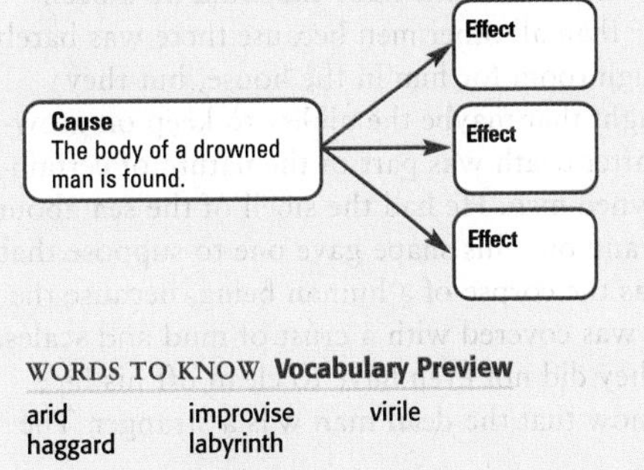

WORDS TO KNOW **Vocabulary Preview**

arid
haggard
improvise
labyrinth
virile

READING FOR INFORMATION

Reading Skills and Strategies

UNDERSTANDING CHRONOLOGICAL ORDER

As students read the author biography and **Build Background,** tell them to note the stages of García Márquez's development as a writer. Ask the following questions:

- When did he publish his most famous novel? *(1967)*
- When did he publish the story they are about to read? *(1972)*
- When did he win the Nobel Prize? *(1982)*

TIME MANAGEMENT

If your schedule requires that you cover the lesson objectives in a shorter time, use. . .

- Preparing to Read, pp. 1346, 1347
- Thinking Through the Literature, p. 1354
- Vocabulary in Action, p. 1355

If you want to take advantage of longer blocks of class time, use. . .

- TE Teaching Options: Speaking and Listening, p. 1348; Vocabulary Strategy, p. 1349; Viewing and Representing, pp. 1350, 1353; Cross-Curricular Link, p. 1351
- Choices and Challenges, p. 1355

Literary Analysis MAGICAL REALISM

A Ask: What seems unusual or not quite realistic in this passage?

Possible Responses: It seems unusual that children would play with a drowned corpse and not be frightened by it; the corpse is heavier and taller than any other man; the villagers believe that drowned men could keep growing after death.

Literary Analysis SETTING

B Ask: What are you told about the setting?

Possible Responses: Readers are told that it is a very small fishing village whose residents all know each other. There are no flowers, nor is there enough land for burial; the dead are thrown off cliffs.

Literary Analysis SYMBOL

C Ask: How do the village women think this drowned man differs from other drowned men?

Possible Responses: They think that, unlike others, he accepts his death with pride and is not lonely, haggard, or needy.

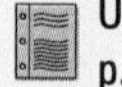
Use **Unit Seven Resource Book,** p. 104, for more practice.

Active Reading

UNDERSTANDING CAUSE AND EFFECT

D Ask: How does the drowned man affect the women, and why?

Possible Responses: They are left breathless and amazed because he is so attractive.

Use **Unit Seven Resource Book,** p. 103, for more practice.

The Handsomest Drowned Man in the World

Gabriel García Márquez

Translated by Gregory Rabassa

The first children who saw the dark and slinky bulge approaching through the sea let themselves think it was an enemy ship. Then they saw it had no flags or masts and they thought it was a whale. But when it washed up on the beach, they removed the clumps of seaweed, the jellyfish tentacles, and the remains of fish and flotsam,[1] and only then did they see that it was a drowned man.

They had been playing with him all afternoon, burying him in the sand and digging him up
A again, when someone chanced to see them and spread the alarm in the village. The men who carried him to the nearest house noticed that he weighed more than any dead man they had ever known, almost as much as a horse, and they said to each other that maybe he'd been floating too long and the water had got into his bones. When they laid him on the floor they said he'd been taller than all other men because there was barely enough room for him in the house, but they thought that maybe the ability to keep on growing after death was part of the nature of certain drowned men. He had the smell of the sea about him and only his shape gave one to suppose that it was the corpse of a human being, because the skin was covered with a crust of mud and scales.

They did not even have to clean off his face to know that the dead man was a stranger. The village was made up of only twenty-odd wooden 1
houses that had stone courtyards with no flowers and which were spread about on the end of a desertlike cape. There was so little land that mothers always went about with the fear that the wind would carry off their children and the few
dead that the years had caused among them had B
to be thrown off the cliffs. But the sea was calm and bountiful and all the men fit into seven boats. So when they found the drowned man they simply had to look at one another to see that they were all there.

That night they did not go out to work at sea. While the men went to find out if anyone was missing in neighboring villages, the women stayed behind to care for the drowned man. They took the mud off with grass swabs, they removed the underwater stones entangled in his hair, and they scraped the crust off with tools used for scaling fish. As they were doing that they noticed that the vegetation on him came from faraway oceans and deep water and that his clothes were in tatters, as if he had sailed through labyrinths of coral. They noticed too that he bore his death with pride, for he did not
have the lonely look of other drowned men who C
came out of the sea or that haggard, needy look

1. **flotsam:** wreckage or debris floating in the water.

WORDS TO KNOW

labyrinth (lăb′ə-rĭnth′) *n.* a confusing network of passages; maze

haggard (hăg′ərd) *adj.* looking worn and exhausted

MINI LESSON

Speaking and Listening

ORAL READING García Márquez has said that his writing style was influenced by his grandmother, who related unbelievable events in a matter-of-fact tone. This story has an oral, "told" quality that students can better appreciate if they read aloud.

Prepare As students read the story to themselves for the first time, have them look for passages that they particularly like. Then in class, ask for volunteers to read the story aloud, each taking a different paragraph. Emphasize that they should read as if they believe every word they're saying. Tell them also to practice smooth transitions between readers.

Present Have the performers come to the front of the room and read the story to their classmates. Ask the audience if they enjoyed the story more when it was read aloud. Ask the performers which passages were particularly fun or challenging to read.

This activity is particularly well suited to longer blocks of class time.

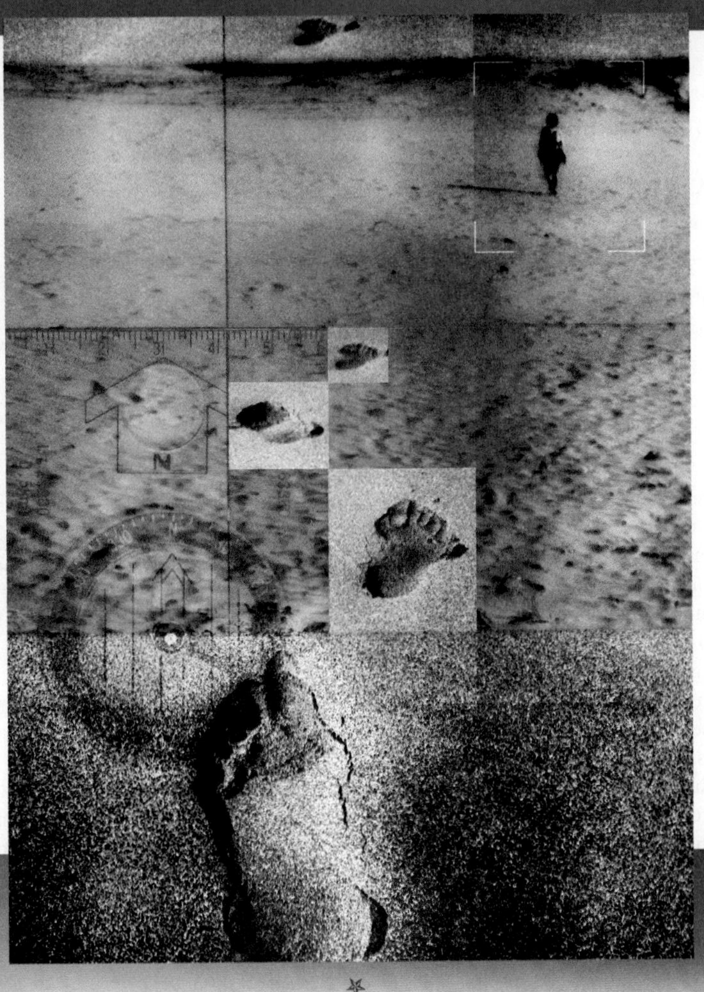

Direction, Mark Owen. Photo © Mark Owen/Illustration Works/Corbis.

of men who drowned in rivers. But only when they finished cleaning him off did they become aware of the kind of man he was and it left them breathless. Not only was he the tallest, strongest,
D most virile, and best built man they had ever seen, but even though they were looking at him there was no room for him in their imagination.

They could not find a bed in the village large enough to lay him on nor was there a table solid
2 enough to use for his wake. The tallest men's holiday pants would not fit him, nor the fattest ones' Sunday shirts, nor the shoes of the one with the biggest feet. Fascinated by his huge size and his beauty, the women then decided to make him some pants from a large piece of sail and a shirt from some bridal brabant linen[2] so that he could continue through his death with dignity. As they sewed, sitting in a circle and gazing at

2. **brabant linen:** cloth from a particular region of Belgium.

WORDS TO KNOW
virile (vîr'əl) *adj.* masculine; full of manly strength

Customizing Instruction

Less Proficient Readers
Remind students that they will have to accept descriptions that do not sound plausible. It is unlikely that any man would weigh almost as much as a horse, for example.

English Learners
1 Explain that *twenty-odd* means "slightly more than twenty." The term *-odd* is usually used to indicate a number that is not exact.

2 Explain that a *wake* is a gathering of people to watch over a dead person's body before it is buried.

MINI LESSON Vocabulary Strategy

RESEARCHING WORD ORIGINS

Instruction Call attention to the word *labyrinth*, the first one of the Words to Know listed on page 1348. Explain that *labyrinth* comes from Greek mythology; it was the maze in which the Minotaur—a monstrous half-man, half bull—was kept. Ask: How is the word's origin connected to its meaning in the story? *(In the story it means a series of passages like a maze, close and intricate enough to tear a man's clothes)*

Have students read the dictionary entry for *labyrinth*. Point out the bracketed information which traces the word's origin from the Middle English *laberinthe*, which came from the Latin *labyrinthus*, which came from the Greek *laburinthos*.

Practice Have students use dictionaries to find the derivation of other Words to Know below. Discuss how the original meaning of the word relates to its meaning in the story. Which word has the most surprising origin?

1. **haggard** *(from the Old French* hagard, *meaning "wild hawk"—students will probably think this is the most surprising origin)*
2. **virile** *(from the Latin* virilis, *derived from* vir, *"man")*
3. **arid** *(from the Latin* aridus, *derived from* arere, *"to be dry")*
4. **improvise** *(from the Latin* improvisus, *"not foreseen")*

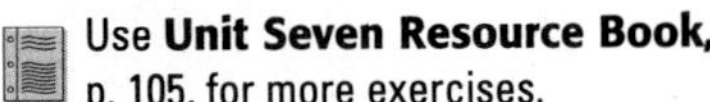

Use **Unit Seven Resource Book,** p. 105, for more exercises.

Literary Analysis SYMBOL

A Discuss what the women imagine the village would have been like if the dead man had lived there. Ask: Why do you think they imagine these particular things?

Possible Responses: They might imagine his large house because their own houses are small; they might imagine his wife's happiness because they are unhappy; they might imagine his authority because they have no leader; they might imagine his flowers because they have not planted any.

Active Reading

UNDERSTANDING CAUSE AND EFFECT

B Ask how the dead man makes the women feel about their own men. *(dissatisfied)* Discuss whether the comparisons they make are fair.

Possible Responses: The comparisons are not fair because they do not really know what the dead man was like when alive. The comparisons are fair because the dead man looks so different from their own men and is obviously extraordinary.

C Ask why the women weep, and then feel glad.

Possible Responses: They weep because they are sorry for Esteban's death; because he reminds them of their own men, and because they have turned him into a saintly figure that they know. They are glad because no one else claims Esteban and they can consider him theirs.

"He has the face of someone called Esteban."
It was true.
Most of them had only to take another look at him to see that he could not have any other name.

La Pintora de Urapan, Alfredo Ramos Martinez. Photo © Christie's Images/SuperStock.

the corpse between stitches, it seemed to them that the wind had never been so steady nor the sea so restless as on that night and they supposed that the change had something to do with the dead man. They thought that if that magnificent man had lived in the village, his house would have had the widest doors, the highest ceiling, and the strongest floor, his bedstead would have been made from a midship frame held together by iron bolts, and his wife would have been the happiest woman. They thought that he would have had so much authority that he could have drawn fish out of the sea simply by calling their names and that he would have put so much work into his land that springs would have burst forth from among the rocks so that he would have been able to plant flowers on the cliffs. They secretly compared him to their own men, thinking that for all their lives theirs were incapable of doing what he could do in one night, and they ended up dismissing them deep in their hearts as the weakest, meanest, and most useless creatures on earth. They were wandering through that maze of fantasy when the oldest woman, who as the oldest had looked upon the drowned man with more compassion than passion, sighed:

"He has the face of someone called Esteban."[3]

It was true. Most of them had only to take another look at him to see that he could not have any other name. The more stubborn among them, who were the youngest, still lived for a few hours with the illusion that when they put his clothes on and he lay among the flowers in patent leather shoes his name might be Lautaro.[4] But it was a vain illusion. There had not been enough canvas, the poorly cut and worse sewn pants were too tight, and the hidden strength of his heart popped the buttons on his shirt. After midnight the whistling of the wind died down and the sea fell into its Wednesday drowsiness. The silence put an end to any last doubts: he was Esteban. The women who had dressed him, who had combed his hair, had cut his nails and

3. **Esteban** (ĕ-stĕ'bän).
4. **Lautaro** (lou-tä'rô).

MINI LESSON Viewing and Representing

Two Women and a Child **by Diego Rivera**

ART APPRECIATION Diego Rivera (1886–1957) is considered one of the greatest Mexican painters of the 20th century. He is famous for public murals that depicted Mexican history and glorified ordinary peasants and workers. Among the many influences on his work were Renaissance frescoes and ancient Mayan and Aztec sculptures. His rounded, solid figures often have been described as "monumental."

Talk about the qualities you would ascribe to the women in this painting. Compare these to the qualities of the women in the story. How similar are Rivera's and García Márquez's attitudes toward the women they depict?

Possible Response: The women in the painting seem strong, simple, and dignified. The women in the story, on the other hand, seem emotional and a little frivolous. Rivera and García Márquez do not portray women very similarly, but they both seem to have affection for them and to put them at the center of their work.

Customizing Instruction

shaved him were unable to hold back a shudder of pity when they had to resign themselves to his being dragged along the ground. It was then that they understood how unhappy he must have been with that huge body since it bothered him even after death. They could see him in life, condemned to going through doors sideways, cracking his head on crossbeams, remaining on his feet during visits, not knowing what to do with his soft, pink, sea lion hands while the lady of the house looked for her most resistant chair and begged him, frightened to death, sit here, Esteban, please, and he, leaning against the wall, smiling, don't bother, ma'am, I'm fine where I am, his heels raw and his back roasted from having done the same thing so many times whenever he paid a visit, don't bother, ma'am, I'm fine where I am, just to avoid the embarrassment of breaking up the chair, and never knowing perhaps that the ones who said don't go, Esteban, at least wait till the coffee's ready, were the ones who later on would whisper the big boob finally left, how nice, the handsome fool has gone. That was what the women were thinking beside the body a little before dawn. Later, when they covered his face with a handkerchief so that the light would not bother him, he looked so forever dead, so defenseless, so much like their men that the first furrows of tears opened in their hearts. It was one of the younger ones who began the weeping. The others, coming to, went from sighs to wails, and the more they sobbed the more they felt like weeping, because the drowned man was becoming all the more Esteban for them, and so they wept so much, for he was the most destitute, most peaceful, and most obliging man on earth, poor Esteban. So when the men returned with the news that the drowned man was not from the neighboring villages either, the women felt an opening of jubilation in the midst of their tears.

> "Praise the Lord," they sighed, "he's ours!" The men thought the fuss was only womanish frivolity.

"Praise the Lord," they sighed, "he's ours!"

The men thought the fuss was only womanish frivolity. Fatigued because of the difficult nighttime inquiries, all they wanted was to get rid of the bother of the newcomer once and for all before the sun grew strong on that arid, windless day. They improvised a litter with the remains of foremasts and gaffs,[5] tying it together with rigging so that it would bear the weight of the body until they reached the cliffs. They wanted to tie the anchor from a cargo ship to him so that he would sink easily into the deepest waves, where fish are blind and divers die of nostalgia, and bad currents would not bring him back to shore, as had happened with other bodies. But the more they hurried, the more the women thought of ways to waste time. They walked about like startled hens, pecking with the sea charms on their breasts, some interfering on one side to put a scapular[6] of the good wind on the drowned man, some on the other side to put a wrist compass on him, and after a great deal of *get away from there, woman, stay out of the way, look, you almost made me fall on top of the dead man,* the men began to feel mistrust in their livers and started grumbling about why so many main-altar decorations for a stranger, because no

5. **gaffs:** hooks attached to poles, used for pulling fish out of the water.

6. **scapular:** a religious badge consisting of two pieces of cloth worn over the shoulders.

WORDS TO KNOW

arid (ăr'ĭd) *adj.* dry

improvise (ĭm'prə-vīz') *v.* to make on the spur of the moment, using any resources available

Advanced Learners

1 Talk about the names and their associations. If the class had found such a man, what would they have named him? What names would they have rejected immediately?

Less Proficient Readers

2 Note that in this passage, the women are imagining what Esteban must have felt like when he was alive and went visiting. The passage contains dialogue, but it is not set off by quotation marks. Suggest that students quietly read the passage aloud to themselves.

English Learners

3 Explain the meaning of *destitute* ("poor"), *obliging* ("agreeable"), and *jubilation* ("great happiness").

Cross Curricular Link Humanities

CULTURAL ALLUSIONS Critics have pointed out that the figure of Esteban alludes to other figures important in Latin American culture. The name Esteban echoes that of St. Stephen, the first Christian martyr. It also recalls Estevanico, a North African slave who explored Mexico with the Spaniard Cabeza de Vaca and amazed the native people with his appearance. Esteban also suggests the Aztec god Quetzalcoatl, who came to people from the sea and taught them how to live better lives.

Active Reading UNDERSTANDING CAUSE AND EFFECT

A Ask: How does Esteban affect the men of the village?

Possible Responses: They, too, admire him. They believe he is sincere and understanding.

Literary Analysis SYMBOL

B Ask: How do the villagers become "kinsmen"? What might this mean in a larger sense?

Possible Responses: They become kinsmen because they all adopt Esteban as a relative. In a larger sense, participating in the funeral makes the villagers feel closer to each other than they felt before.

Active Reading UNDERSTANDING CAUSE AND EFFECT

C Ask: How does the drowned man affect the way the people perceive their village?

Possible Responses: They see their surroundings as desolate and dry and see their dreams as narrow.

D Ask: What do the villagers intend to change, and why?

Possible Responses: They will build bigger and stronger houses; they will paint their houses bright colors; and they will plant flowers on the cliffs—all in Esteban's memory.

matter how many nails and holy-water jars he had on him, the sharks would chew him all the same, but the women kept piling on their junk relics,[7] running back and forth, stumbling, while they released in sighs what they did not in tears, so that the men finally exploded with *since when has there ever been such a fuss over a drifting corpse, a drowned nobody, a piece of cold*
1 *Wednesday meat.* One of the women, mortified by so much lack of care, then removed the handkerchief from the dead man's face and the men were left breathless too.

He was Esteban. It was not necessary to repeat it for them to recognize him. If they had
2 been told Sir Walter Raleigh,[8] even they might have been impressed with his gringo accent, the macaw on his shoulder, his cannibal-killing blunderbuss, but there could be only one Esteban in the world and there he was, stretched out like a sperm whale, shoeless, wearing the pants of an undersized child, and with those stony nails that had to be cut with a knife. They only had to take the handkerchief off his face to see that he was ashamed, that it was not his fault that he was so big or so heavy or so handsome, and if he had known that this was going to happen, he would have looked for a more discreet place to drown in, seriously, I even would have tied the anchor off a galleon[9] around my neck and staggered off a cliff like someone who doesn't like things in
3 order not to be upsetting people now with this Wednesday dead body, as you people say, in order not to be bothering anyone with this filthy piece of cold meat that doesn't have anything to do with me. There was so much truth in his manner that even the most mistrustful men, the ones who felt the bitterness of endless nights at sea fearing that their women would tire of
A dreaming about them and begin to dream of drowned men, even they and others who were harder still shuddered in the marrow of their bones at Esteban's sincerity.

That was how they came to hold the most splendid funeral they could conceive of for an abandoned drowned man. Some women who had gone to get flowers in the neighboring villages returned with other women who could not believe what they had been told, and those women went back for more flowers when they saw the dead man, and they brought more and more until there were so many flowers and so many people that it was hard to walk about. At the final moment it pained them to return him to the waters as an orphan and they chose a father
and mother from among the best people, and B
aunts and uncles and cousins, so that through him all the inhabitants of the village became kinsmen. Some sailors who heard the weeping from a distance went off course and people heard of one who had himself tied to the mainmast, remembering ancient fables about sirens.[10] While they fought for the privilege of carrying him on their shoulders along the steep escarpment[11] by the cliffs, men and women became aware for the first time of the desolation
of their streets, the dryness of their courtyards, C
the narrowness of their dreams as they faced the splendor and beauty of their drowned man. They let him go without an anchor so that he could come back if he wished and whenever he wished, and they all held their breath for the fraction of centuries the body took to fall into the abyss.

---

7. **relics:** objects that once belonged to a holy person.
8. **Sir Walter Raleigh . . . blunderbuss:** Sir Walter Raleigh (1552?–1618) was an English explorer. A macaw is a parrot, and a blunderbuss is a type of gun—short and not very accurate—that was used from the 1600s to the 1800s.
9. **galleon:** a type of large sailing ship in use from the 1400s through the 1600s, with three masts and two or more decks.
10. **ancient fables about sirens:** In the *Odyssey,* an ancient Greek epic, the hero Odysseus has himself tied to the mast of his ship to resist the Sirens, sweet-voiced nymphs who lure sailors to their destruction on the rocks.
11. **escarpment:** a steep slope or long cliff.

Burial of an Illustrious Man (1936), Mario Urteaga. Oil on canvas, 23″ × 32 1/2″ (58.4 cm × 82.5 cm). The Museum of Modern Art, New York. Inter-American Fund. Photograph copyright © 2001 The Museum of Modern Art, New York.

HUMANITIES CONNECTION Musicians and, likely, hired mourners are among this funeral procession of Quechua Indians in northern Peru.

They did not need to look at one another to realize that they were no longer all present, that they would never be. But they also knew that everything would be different from then on, that their houses would have wider doors, higher ceilings, and stronger floors so that Esteban's memory could go everywhere without bumping into beams and so that no one in the future would dare whisper the big boob finally died, too bad, the handsome fool has finally died, because they were going to paint their house fronts gay colors to make Esteban's memory eternal and they were going to break their backs digging for springs among the stones and planting flowers on the cliffs so that in future years at dawn the passengers on great liners would awaken, suffocated by the smell of gardens on the high seas, and the captain would have to come down from the bridge in his dress uniform, with his astrolabe, his pole star,[12] and his row of war medals and, pointing to the promontory of roses on the horizon, he would say in fourteen languages, look there, where the wind is so peaceful now that it's gone to sleep beneath the beds, over there, where the sun's so bright that the sunflowers don't know which way to turn, yes, over there, that's Esteban's village. ❖

D

12. **astrolabe** (ăs′trə-lāb′) . . . **pole star:** An astrolabe is an instrument formerly used to measure the altitude of stars, including the North Star, or pole star.

Customizing Instruction

English Learners

1 Note that a *piece of cold Wednesday meat* is not a common English idiom; it may be a way of comparing the body to food left over from Sunday dinner that nobody wants.

Advanced Learners

2 If students want to find out more about Sir Walter Raleigh, encourage them to do so and report to the class what they learned.

Less Proficient Readers

3 Note that the point of view changes in the middle of the sentence and Esteban himself is speaking here. It is not clear whether he actually is communicating these thoughts or whether the men are just imagining them.

MINI LESSON Viewing and Representing

Burial of an Illustrious Man **by Mario Urteaga**

ART APPRECIATION Mario Urteaga (1875–1957) was a Peruvian painter associated with *indigenismo*, an art and literary movement that embraced Latin America's native cultures and traditions. In his scenes of daily life among the Quechua of Peru, Urteaga portrayed native people with more dignity than other artists of his time. Have students look at the art and the **Humanities Connection** on this page. This particular work depicts the funeral procession of a real person—a respected Indian war veteran. The single-story houses in the background are typical of those found in the highlands of Peru.

Ask: How would you compare this funeral procession with Esteban's?

Possible Response: The procession in the painting is large and respectful, as was Esteban's, but it differs in that there are no women and no flowers.

Connect to the Literature

1. **What Do You Think?**
Did this story turn out the way you expected? Explain.

Comprehension Check
- What do the villagers do with the body of the drowned man?
- By the end of the story, how do they want their village to be known?

LITERARY ANALYSIS: SYMBOL

A person, a place, or an object that represents something beyond itself is known as a **symbol.** In a literary work, an element has symbolic meaning when it is used to stand for an abstract quality or idea. In the story "The Handsomest Drowned Man in the World," the drowned man comes to represent a number of qualities to the villagers. One of these qualities is beauty.

Cooperative Learning Activity
With a small group of classmates, brainstorm a list of qualities that the villagers associate with the drowned man. Then determine which two or three qualities or ideas the drowned man mainly symbolizes. Discuss the reasons for your choice.

Think Critically

2. **ACTIVE READING: UNDERSTANDING CAUSE AND EFFECT** Review the cause-and-effect chart you made in your  **READER'S NOTEBOOK.** What effects does the drowned man have on the villagers?

3. Why do you think the drowned man affects the villagers as he does?

   THINK ABOUT
   - he qualities the villagers attribute to him
   - the nature of the villagers' lives and their environment

4. What are your own theories about who the drowned man is and where he came from? Support your response.

Extend Interpretations

5. **What If?** If the villagers had found out the identity of the drowned man, how might this knowledge have affected their reaction to him?

6. **The Writer's Style** What elements in this story make it an example of **magical realism?** Be specific.

7. **Connect to Life** The Connect to Your Life activity on page 1347 asked you to discuss a person who made you want to live your life differently. How do Esteban's effects on the villagers compare with this person's effects on you?

Connect to the Literature

1. **What Do You Think?** Responses will vary. Some students may have expected that the villagers would find out the identity of the drowned man.

Comprehension Check
- The villagers clean the body, dress it, and hold an elaborate funeral before throwing it off the cliffs.
- They want the village to be known as "Esteban's village."

 Use Selection Quiz in **Unit Seven Resource Book,** p. 106.

Think Critically

2. Possible Responses: The villagers are awed by his size and beauty; they work together to prepare his body for burial; they imagine what his life might have been like; they feel deep sympathy for him; through the funeral, they feel kin to him and to each other; they vow to build bigger houses, paint them brightly, and plant flowers in his memory; they imagine the village becoming known as "Esteban's village."
3. Possible Responses: He shakes them out of their routine because he is so large, handsome, and mysterious. Because they know nothing about him, they can give their imaginations free reign. The splendor of the funeral makes them see how small and barren their village is and makes them want to enlarge and beautify it.
4. Responses will vary. Accept any for which students offer support.

Extend Interpretations

5. **What If?** Possible Responses: They might not have felt as free to imagine what his life was like, and might not have claimed him as their own. On the other hand, they might have been moved to visit Esteban's home to return his body and so still may have felt connected with him and moved to transform their village.
6. **The Writer's Style** Elements of magic realism include realistic details such as the seaweed clumps and jellyfish tentacles; magical details such as the corpse's great beauty and incredible size; exaggeration such as the claim that he would have been able to draw fish out of the sea by calling their names; the blurred distinction between living and dead created by the dead man's imagined speech; the distortions of time created by the references to both ancient galleons and modern passenger liners; and perhaps an implied social criticism of narrow perceptions and restricted imagination.
7. **Connect to Life** Responses will vary. Remind students to make a comparison.

Literary Analysis

Cooperative Learning Activity You might model analyzing a passage for symbolism; for example, the last paragraph on p. 1348. Call attention to the mud, underwater stones, and other sea details. Point out that Esteban could symbolize the sea itself or symbolize the foreign and faraway.

 Use **Unit Seven Resource Book,** p. 104, for more practice.

Writing Options

1. Character Biography Write an imaginary biography of the drowned man, telling where he's from, what his life was like, how he drowned, and how he came to wash ashore in this Caribbean fishing village.

Writing Handbook
See page R29: Narrative Writing.

2. Interpretive Essay In a brief essay, explain what the drowned man symbolizes and what the overall theme of the story might be.

Activities & Explorations

1. Village Diorama Create a diorama of "Esteban's village," emphasizing the qualities of Esteban's that the villagers wanted to honor. ~ **ART**

2. Radio Recording Work with a group to record a dramatic reading of this story for a radio broadcast. Include sound effects and background music in your recording. ~ **PERFORMING**

Inquiry & Research

Magical Realist Anthology Work with a group of classmates to find other magical realist stories from Latin America or elsewhere. For example, you might look for stories by Julio Cortázar, Isabel Allende, or Rosario Ferré. You could also use the Internet to guide you to lesser-known works. Gather your favorite stories in a class anthology. Write either a brief introduction for each story or a longer introduction for the whole collection.

Vocabulary in Action

EXERCISE: WORD MEANINGS For each sentence, write *Yes* if the italicized word seems to fit the meaning of the sentence. Write *No* if it does not seem to fit.

1. The children of the town found the body in a wide, open *labyrinth* on the beach.
2. Because of the water, the body's condition was very *arid*.
3. The man had been quite *virile*, judging from his great size and obvious strength.
4. Nothing fit him properly, so the villagers had to *improvise* in preparing him for burial.
5. The cliffs looked *haggard* after the townspeople planted them with flowers.

Building Vocabulary
For an in-depth lesson on recognizing word connotation and denotation, see page 1090.

Writing Options

1. **Character Biography** Encourage students to acknowledge the villagers' perceptions of the drowned man in some way—was he at all like they thought he was, or was he completely different?
2. **Interpretive Essay** As a starting point, students should review ideas they discussed in the Literary Analysis activity on symbols (p. 1354). Remind them to outline their essays carefully and to support their assertions with details from the story.

Activities & Explorations

1. **Village Diorama** Tell students to go back through the story to look for details about the geographical setting of the village—it is on a "desertlike cape," for example.
2. **Radio Recording** This can be an elaboration of the Speaking and Listening activity on p. 1348. As a whole class, discuss possible sound effects and music and where they should be inserted.

Inquiry & Research

Magical Realist Anthology Story collections by the authors mentioned are *Rules of the Game and Other Stories* by Julio Cortázar, *The Stories of Eva Luna* by Isabel Allende, and *The Youngest Doll and Other Stories* by Rosario Ferré.

Vocabulary in Action

1. No
2. No
3. Yes
4. Yes
5. No

To assess skills and concepts taught in this selection, use **Formal Assessment Book,** pp. 199–200.

THE HANDSOMEST DROWNED MAN IN THE WORLD 1355

One Hundred Years of Solitude may be the best-known Latin American novel and is certainly the foremost example of magical realism. In it Nobel Prize winner Gabriel García Márquez describes the unforgettable town of Macondo, settled at the edge of the jungle and wiped out by a whirlwind generations later.

Additional Background
García Márquez had been wanting to write a novel about Macondo for twenty years but had found it impossible. Suddenly in 1962, while driving his family to Acapulco for a vacation, he had a breakthrough: "I had this illumination on how to write the book. . . . I had it so completely formed, that right there I could have dictated the first chapter word by word to a typist."

He turned the car around, shut himself up in his room, and wrote eight hours a day for eighteen months. His wife had to pawn the television, radio, and other household appliances to take care of family expenses. When he finally finished, he was $10,000 in debt. But *One Hundred Years of Solitude* was the book that made his reputation. Selling out its entire first run of 8,000 copies within a week, it eventually sold 20 million copies and was translated into more than 30 languages.

MILESTONES IN WORLD LITERATURE

Gabriel García Márquez

One Hundred Years of Solitude

In Macondo, women have unearthly beauty and flowers rain from the sky.

Pablo Neruda once called *One Hundred Years of Solitude* "the greatest revelation in the Spanish language since the *Don Quixote* of Cervantes." Written by the Colombian novelist Gabriel García Márquez and first published in 1967, *One Hundred Years of Solitude* has been translated into over 30 languages and has sold more copies than any other novel from Latin America.

The book traces six generations of the Buendía family. The family's patriarch, José Arcadio, and his wife, Úrsula, establish the town of Macondo, which García Márquez based on the Colombian coastal village of Aracataca, where he was born. In successive generations, the descendants of José Arcadio and Úrsula endure hardships—such as labor strikes, political strife, and murder—as well as the joys of family and community. The novel describes not only the rise and fall of the Buendía family but also the colorful history of Macondo.

While telling the story of one family in one town, *One Hundred Years of Solitude* also reflects the social, political, and economic history of Colombia and of Latin America in general. García Márquez weaves historical facts throughout his novel and alludes to real-life events from the late 16th century to the mid-20th century. Many occurrences in the story, including violent civil wars, oppressive dictatorships, and bloody massacres, parallel actual events in Colombia's past.

García Márquez drew on many of his own experiences in writing *One Hundred Years of Solitude.* He based some characters on family members and friends, adapted African and Caribbean myths and legends he heard as a youth, and borrowed his grandmother's technique of relating outrageous events in a deadpan tone. The novel's themes, structure, and vision were also shaped by such diverse works of literature as the Bible, Greek tragedies, Kafka's "Metamorphosis," the satires of François Rabelais, the family sagas of William Faulkner, and the experimental prose of Virginia Woolf.

A complex, sprawling work, *One Hundred Years of Solitude* consists of 20 unnumbered sections. It contains more than 50 characters (some of whom have the same names) and encompasses more than 400 years of history. García Márquez creates a world in which time is cyclical, with events repeating in different generations. He often uses flashbacks and foreshadowing in his narration. Furthermore, he employs a distinctive form called **magical realism** (see Learning the Language of Literature, page 1344) to capture his view of Latin America's marvelous reality. Throughout the novel, impossible things happen: characters rise to heaven, flowers rain from the sky, and the entire population of Macondo is plagued by insomnia and amnesia.

Despite its complexity, this novel has achieved enormous popularity because of its accessible prose, lively pace, comical characters, and satirical tone. An international sensation, *One Hundred Years of Solitude* established a benchmark for magical realist fiction and gave new life to the novel form.

García Márquez wearing his masterwork

García Márquez in Sweden, receiving the 1982 Nobel Prize for his work

Literary Chronology

The following are publication dates of some of García Márquez's works:

1955 *Leaf Storm*
1961 *No One Writes to the Colonel*
1962 *In Evil Hour*
1967 *One Hundred Years of Solitude*
1970 *The Story of a Shipwrecked Sailor*
1975 *The Autumn of the Patriarch*
1981 *Chronicle of a Death Foretold*
1985 *Love in the Time of Cholera*
1989 *The General in His Labyrinth*
1992 *Strange Pilgrims*
1994 *Love and Other Demons*
1996 *News of a Kidnapping*
2003 *Chronicle of a Death Foretold*
2004 *Living to Tell the Tale*

Objectives
- understand and appreciate an **ode (Literary Analysis)**
- identify distinctive elements of a writer's **style (Literary Analysis)**
- use strategies for **reading poetry aloud (Active Reading)**

Thematic Link
These two odes use **dream-like** imagery to celebrate common things found in everyday life.

5-Minute Warm-Up
Daily Language SkillBuilder

Have students **proofread** the display sentences on page 1095o and write them correctly.

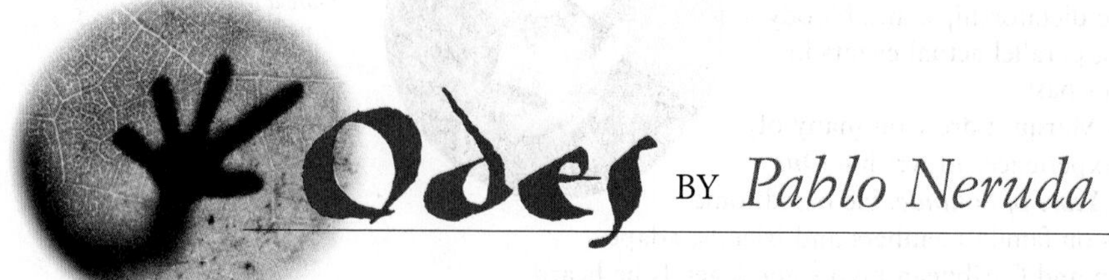

Odes BY *Pablo Neruda*

Pablo Neruda
1904–1973

Going His Own Way Pablo Neruda grew up as Neftalí Ricardo Reyes Basoalto in the rugged frontier town of Temuco, Chile. His father was a railroad worker, and his mother was a teacher who died shortly after his birth. Although Neftalí showed a talent for writing poetry by the time he was 10 years old, his friends and his father ridiculed his literary ambitions. He was encouraged instead by Gabriela Mistral (see page 1188), principal of the local girls' school, who would later become Chile's first Nobel laureate in literature. She gave him books and urged him to pursue his poetry. While still in his teens, he began to publish work under the pen name Pablo Neruda, which he took to avoid conflict with his family. Later, he made this his legal name.

Poet and Diplomat Neruda's first successful book was *Twenty Love Poems and a Song of Despair,* published when he was only 20. People still quote passionate verses from this book today. Celebrated as a poet but unable to support himself by writing, Neruda took a series of diplomatic posts in Asia and Europe. From 1927 through 1943, the Chilean government sent him as a consul to such countries as Burma, Java, Ceylon, Singapore, Cambodia, Argentina, Mexico, and Spain. In Spain, Neruda became involved in the Spanish civil war and experienced the assassination of his friend Federico García Lorca. The poems in *Residence on Earth* reflect Neruda's loneliness and sense of alienation during his time abroad.

Public Figure After returning to Chile, Neruda joined the Communist Party and was elected to the Chilean senate in 1945. After criticizing the president's policies, he was forced to leave Chile for several years to avoid arrest. He continued to write in exile and in 1950 completed his epic poem *Canto General,* about the history of Latin America. After he returned to Chile in 1952, his stature as a poet and public figure rose. He was even nominated for president in 1969. He withdrew his nomination in favor of the socialist candidate Salvador Allende but accepted an ambassadorship to France after Allende's victory.

While living in Paris, Neruda was awarded the 1971 Nobel Prize—"for a poetry that with the action of an elemental force brings alive a continent's destiny and dreams." In his acceptance speech he compared poetry to bread and a poet to a baker, an ordinary person who labors to share his product with all who need it. Two years later Neruda died of cancer, days after President Allende died during a coup. Thousands gathered in the streets for the poet's funeral, reciting his verses in defiance of surrounding government troops.

Other Works
One Hundred Love Sonnets
The House at Isla Negra

LESSON RESOURCES

UNIT SEVEN RESOURCE BOOK,
pp. 107–108

ASSESSMENT RESOURCES
Formal Assessment, pp. 201–202
Teacher's Guide to Assessment and Portfolio Use
Test Generator

INTEGRATED TECHNOLOGY
Visit our Web site: classzone.com

ADDITIONAL RESOURCES
Lesson Planning Guide, pp. 179–180
Teacher's Sourcebook for Language Development

Entryway of Neruda's home

Build Background

Exalting Simple Subjects Neruda wrote in many forms, but his "elementary odes" are especially admired. An **ode** is a lyric poem that exalts, or praises, a person, an event, or an object. This literary form dates back to classical times, when the ancient Greek poet Pindar wrote odes in praise of Greek heroes and athletes. Traditionally, the language and tone of an ode are dignified and serious, and many odes follow a fixed pattern of stanzas and rhyme.

Pablo Neruda's odes break with this tradition. Because Neruda wanted to reach a mass audience of ordinary people, he wrote odes in simple language about the most common things in daily life, such as rain and salt. But although he wrote in free verse and used conversational language, he treated these subjects with a reverence usually reserved for loftier subjects.

Connect to Your Life

What sensations or memories do you associate with a lizard? a watermelon? In your notebook, freewrite for two minutes on each subject, jotting down whatever comes to your mind. Then read Neruda's poems to see what associations these subjects held for him.

Focus Your Reading

LITERARY ANALYSIS: STYLE

The term **style** refers to the distinctive way in which a work of literature is written. Such elements as word choice, sentence length, sentence structure, tone, and imagery are all expressions of a writer's style. Notice how Neruda creates a vibrant image through the choice and arrangement of words in these lines from "Ode to the Lizard":

By the
water
you are
silent, slippery
slime.

As you read Neruda's odes, pay attention to his style of writing and think about what makes it distinctive.

ACTIVE READING: READING POETRY ALOUD

You'll notice that the lines in Neruda's odes are very short. By stretching the words out over many lines, Neruda forces the reader to focus on individual words and to savor each image. To appreciate the imagery, read the odes aloud softly and slowly to yourself, stopping every few lines to "see" what the poet is describing.

READER'S NOTEBOOK As you read each poem, copy down a passage that you especially like or one that you don't quite understand. Be prepared to examine it more closely with the class.

READING FOR INFORMATION
Reading Skills and Strategies
COMPARING AND CONTRASTING

Give students a few moments to review the **Build Background** information about the literary form of the ode. Ask students to compare and contrast the characteristics of traditional odes with those of Neruda's odes.

Suggest that students show the characteristics in a Venn diagram. In the center overlapping area, have students list the characteristics that are shared by traditional odes and Neruda's odes. In the two outer areas of the diagram, have students list the characteristics that are unique to each.

As they read "Ode to the Lizard" and "Ode to the Watermelon," students should look for examples that illustrate how Neruda's odes break from the traditional literary form.

TIME MANAGEMENT

If your schedule requires that you cover the lesson objectives in a shorter time, use. . .

- Preparing to Read, pp. 1358–1359
- Thinking Through the Literature, p. 1364

If you want to take advantage of longer blocks of class time, use. . .

- TE Teaching Options: Cross Curricular Link, pp. 1360, 1362
- The Translator at Work, p. 1365

Reading and Analyzing

Reading Skills and Strategies
PREVIEWING

Have students preview the poem and notice its form. In particular, have students take note of the ode's shape, line length, number of lines, and whether or not it has stanzas.

Literary Analysis STYLE

[A] Point out that Neruda uses imagery in the poem to help readers imagine—or visualize—the lizard. Remind students that imagery consists of words and phrases that appeal to readers' five senses. Poets use sensory details to help readers imagine how things look, feel, smell, sound, and taste. What phrases in the first two stanzas help students picture the lizard? What other image in the poem appeals to students' senses and helps them picture the lizard?

Possible Responses: first two stanzas—"a sandy tail," "a leaflike head"; other sensory image—"lizard, / cold, small / and green"

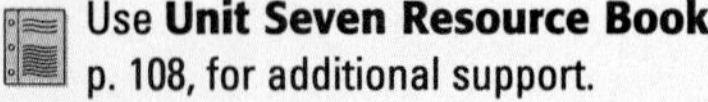
Use **Unit Seven Resource Book,** p. 108, for additional support.

Active Reading
READING POETRY ALOUD

Have volunteers take turns reading each stanza aloud. As the stanzas are read aloud, have students picture in their minds the images and/or comparisons in each stanza.

Use **Unit Seven Resource Book,** p. 107, for additional support.

Ode to the Lizard

Pablo Neruda

Translated by Margaret Sayers Peden

On the sand
a
lizard
with a sandy tail.

[A]

Beneath
a leaf,
a leaflike
head.

From what planet,
from what
[1] cold green ember
did you fall?
From the moon?
From frozen space?
Or from
the emerald
did your color
climb the vine?

On a rotting
tree trunk
you are
a living
shoot,[1]
arrow
[2] of its foliage.
On a stone
you are a stone
with two small, ancient
eyes—

1. **shoot:** a new growth on a plant.

Cross Curricular Link **Science**

LIZARD CAMOUFLAGE Neruda's poem alludes to lizards' ability to blend with their surroundings for protection. With their leaf-like shape, for example, lizards are easily hidden in leaf-litter. To give another example, the gray color and mottled pattern of the mesquite lizard blends perfectly with the bark of mesquite trees, the lizard's habitat.

One of the most distinctive lizard groups is the Chamaeleonidae—the subfamily of chameleons. A well-known feature of chameleons is the ability to change color or color pattern, which serves as protection against predators and as camouflage when stalking prey. The Malagasy chameleon *Furcifer lateralis* is usually dull green when resting in foliage. It changes its color to a threatening pattern of black, white, and yellow to warn off an attacker.

eyes of the stone.
By the
water
you are
silent, slippery
slime.
To
a fly
you are the dart
3 of an annihilating dragon.

And to me,
my childhood,
spring
beside
a lazy
river,
that's
you!
lizard,
cold, small
and green;
you are a long-ago
siesta
4 beside cool waters,
with books unopened.

The water flows and sings.

The sky, overhead, is a
warm corolla.[2]

2. **corolla** (kə-rôl′ə): the grouping of petals on a flower.

Customizing Instruction

Less Proficient Readers

Make sure students recognize and understand the use of metaphor in the ode. Remind students that a comparison that does not use the word *like or as* is called a metaphor. Tell students that metaphors help readers picture ordinary things in new ways.

Point out that in lines 21–23, the lizard is compared to "a living shoot." In lines 27–29, the lizard is compared to "a stone / with two small, ancient / eyes—."

If necessary, guide students to recognize other metaphors in the ode. Have students explain what the lizard is compared to in each metaphor.

English Learners

Explain the meaning of each of the following words:

1 *ember:* a glowing fragment from a fire

2 *foliage:* the leaves of growing plants

3 *annihilating:* the act or process of destroying

4 *siesta:* a rest, usually after a midday meal

Assessment Informal Assessment

POETIC DEVICES Have students write a paragraph in which they identify two examples of such poetic devices as simile, metaphor, alliteration, and assonance in "Ode to the Lizard" and analyze the effects created by the devices.

RUBRIC

3 Full Accomplishment Student's account identifies two examples of different poetic devices and provides an accurate and thorough analysis of the effects created by the poetic devices.

2 Substantial Accomplishment Student's account is accurate, but some important information is missing.

1 Little or Partial Accomplishment Student's account is missing vital information, is inaccurate, or shows little understanding of poetic devices.

ODE TO THE LIZARD **1361**

Reading and Analyzing

Active Reading
READING POETRY ALOUD
Ask students to listen carefully as you read aloud the first stanza of "Ode to the Watermelon." What sounds and words are repeated? What idea or feeling is created through the repetition of sounds of words?
Possible Responses: Sibilant sounds of *s* are repeated in such words as *summer, sun, cities, stones,* and *suffers.* The repetition helps create the feeling of the sizzling heat.

Literary Analysis STYLE
Have students identify examples of word choice and imagery that illustrate Neruda's distinctive style.
Possible Responses: "yellow sun, / fatigue in drops," "the thirst-tree," "green whale of the summer," "Jewel box of water, phlegmatic / queen / of the fruitshops, / warehouse / of profundity, moon / on earth!"

Literary Analysis REPETITION
A What idea or feeling is created through the use of repetition in these phrases?
Possible Response: The repetition helps convey the feeling of oppression as the heat continues to weigh upon the speaker.

Reading Skills and Strategies
VISUALIZING
Have students identify imagery describing the watermelon that appeals to their senses of sight, touch, and taste.
Possible Responses: sight: "the green whale of the summer"; touch: "the swelling / fruit"; taste: "among our longings and our teeth / you change / simply / into cool light / that slips in turn into / spring water."

Ode to the Watermelon

Pablo Neruda

Translated by Robert Bly

The tree of intense
summer,
hard,
is all blue sky,
yellow sun,
1 fatigue in drops,
a sword
above the highways,
a scorched shoe
in the cities:
the brightness and the world
weigh us down,
hit us
in the eyes
with clouds of dust,
with sudden golden blows,
they torture
our feet
with tiny thorns,
A with hot stones,
and the mouth
suffers
more than all the toes:
the throat
becomes thirsty,
the teeth,
the lips, the tongue:
we want to drink
waterfalls,
the dark blue night,
the South Pole,
and then
the coolest of all
the planets crosses
the sky,
the round, magnificent,
star-filled watermelon.

It's a fruit from the thirst-tree.
It's the green whale of the summer.

The dry universe
all at once
given dark stars
2 by this firmament of coolness
lets the swelling
fruit
come down:
3 its hemispheres open
showing a flag
green, white, red,
4 that dissolves into
wild rivers, sugar,
delight!

Cross Curricular Link **Humanities**

ABOUT THE TRANSLATOR Robert Bly, the translator of "Ode to the Watermelon," has written more than thirty books of poetry and translated more than thirty others. Through his translations, Bly has introduced many unknown European and South American poets—including Pablo Neruda—to American readers. In an interview, Bly described what happens when he translates a poem:
You feel yourself, because of the work you've done on the image, invaded by the image. You feel that it has become a part of your house like someone who's moved into your house, and your house is changed then. Your house has changed because these images have come in. So that's the way I feel about translation. It's a blessing.

As respected as Bly is for his poetry and translations, he may be even better known as a social critic and leading figure in the men's movement. His bestselling book *Iron John* (1990) drew upon myth and folklore to examine contemporary men's struggles to achieve and define manhood. His later work *The Sibling Society* (1996) argued that adults in American culture were selfish and adolescent, exerting no true authority.

Las sandias [Watermelons] (1957), Diego Rivera. Fundacion Dolores Olmedo, Mexico City. Schalkwijk/Art Resource, New York.

Jewel box of water, phlegmatic[1]
queen
5 of the fruitshops,
warehouse
of profundity,[2] moon
on earth!
You are pure,
rubies fall apart
in your abundance,
and we
want
to bite into you,
to bury our
face
in you, and
our hair, and
the soul!
When we're thirsty
we glimpse you
like
a mine or a mountain
of fantastic food,
but
among our longings and our teeth
you change
simply
into cool light
that slips in turn into
spring water
that touched us once
singing.
And that is why
you don't weigh us down
in the siesta hour
that's like an oven,
you don't weigh us down,
you just
go by
and your heart, some cold ember,
turned itself into a single
drop of water.

1. **phlegmatic** (flĕg-măt′ĭk): calm; unemotional.
2. **profundity:** great depth, especially of feeling or meaning.

Customizing Instruction

English Learners

Help students connect their own familiar experiences of summer with some of the unfamiliar concepts in the poem as conveyed through imagery or figurative language. Write the word *summer* in the center of a word web. Add words or phrases, suggested by students, that describe how summer feels to them. Then connect these descriptions, such as *hot* or *sticky,* to the sensory descriptions of summer heat in the first stanza of the poem.

Explain the meaning of the following terms:

1 *fatigue:* weariness or exhaustion

2 *firmament:* the sky

3 *hemispheres:* two half spheres, or balls

Less Proficient Readers

4 Have students state in their own words what is being described by this image.

5 Make sure students understand that each of the images included in this catalog, or list, describes the watermelon.

Advanced Learners

Ask students what effect is created by the many images, sensory details, and metaphors describing the intense summer heat. What do they think Neruda's purpose was in creating this effect?

Possible Response: The descriptive language builds to a climax, creating an overwhelming sense of thirst, which makes the watermelon all the more praiseworthy in its ability to quench such a thirst.

Connect to the Literature

1. **What Do You Think?** Responses will vary. Some students may state that they like the fresh and surprising imagery that helps them see things in new or different ways. Others may not appreciate the praise given to such ordinary things as the lizard or the watermelon. Students should cite evidence in the odes to support their opinions.

Think Critically

2. Responses will vary. Some students may cite one or more elements of style that impress them in a passage. Some students may note specific metaphors as confusing.
3. Possible Responses: The lizard is compared to "a living / shoot," "a stone / with two small, ancient / eyes," "silent, slippery / slime," "the dart / of an annihilating dragon," "a long-ago / siesta." The lizard's ancient lineage and its ability to change are evoked in the comparisons.
4. Possible Responses: Other images associate the watermelon with the heavens, cool light, and "a single / drop of water." These cool, quenching images contrast sharply with the heat and thirst of the "dry universe" described at the beginning.
5. Possible Responses: They exalt, or praise, an object. The tone of the poems is celebratory.

Extend Interpretations

6. **Critic's Corner** Possible Responses: from "Ode to the Lizard"—"you are a long-ago / siesta"; from "Ode to the Watermelon"—"Jewel box of water, phlegmatic / queen / of the fruitshops," "and we / want / to bite into you, / to bury our / face / in you, and/ our hair, and / the soul!"
7. **What If?** If "Ode to the Lizard" ended with line 39, the lizard's significance to the speaker would not be revealed. If "Ode to the Watermelon" began with line 38, the sense of desire or thirst would not be established and, therefore, the watermelon would carry far less significance.
8. **Connect to Life** Responses will vary. Many students may note that their associations with lizards and watermelons are far less passionate than Neruda's.

Connect to the Literature

1. **What Do You Think?** What do you like or dislike about these poems? Support your opinion.

Think Critically

2. **ACTIVE READING: READING POETRY ALOUD** Read aloud the passages you copied in your READER'S NOTEBOOK. Explain what impresses or confuses you about each passage.
3. What different things is a lizard compared to in the first ode? Discuss the qualities of a lizard that are brought out by these comparisons.
4. Images in the second ode associate a watermelon with a planet, stars, and what else? How do these images contrast with the images at the beginning of the poem?
5. What makes these poems **odes?**

   THINK ABOUT
   - the definition of *ode* on page 1359
   - the **tone** of the poems

Extend Interpretations

6. **Critic's Corner** According to critic René de Costa, Neruda's odes contain "an element of humor, a delicate whimsicality" that distinguishes them from odes in the classical tradition. What passages can you find to support this observation?
7. **What If?** If "Ode to the Lizard" ended with line 39, how would the poem be affected? If "Ode to the Watermelon" began with line 38, how would the poem be affected?
8. **Connect to Life** How do your associations with lizards and watermelons compare with Neruda's?

LITERARY ANALYSIS: STYLE

An author's **style** is the particular way he or she writes. The term *style* refers not to what is said but rather to *how* it is said. Many elements contribute to the style of a poem, including word choice, arrangement of lines and stanzas, tone, figurative language, and imagery. For example, consider the word choice in Neruda's odes. With a few exceptions, Neruda uses simple, everyday, concrete words.

Paired Activity Work with a partner to create a "checklist" that characterizes Neruda's style in these odes. Describe as many distinctive features of his writing style as you can. If you're having trouble recognizing these features, you may find it helpful to compare Neruda's odes with other 20th-century poems you've read in Unit Seven, such as those by Rilke, García Lorca, and Mistral (pages 1151, 1152, and 1188).

You Know It's a Neruda Ode If . . .
Word choice: *it uses mostly simple, common, concrete words*
Length of lines:
Tone:
Kind of imagery:

After you have completed your checklist, you might try to write our own ode in the style of a Neruda ode.

Literary Analysis

Paired Activity In preparation for writing their odes, have students brainstorm a list of common things in daily life that they find worthy of praise.

Use **Unit Seven Resource Book,** p. 108, for more practice.

To assess skills and concepts taught in this selection, use **Formal Assessment Book,** pp. 201–202.

On Translating Neruda

Margaret Sayers Peden

Translating poems into another language is not easy. Margaret Sayers Peden, the translator of "Ode to the Lizard," wrote that in translating odes by Neruda, she tried to follow four commandments:

1. **Respect simplicity,** keeping the same level of language as in the originals, not using fancier words.
2. **Respect sound,** keeping the musical quality of the poems.
3. **Respect sense,** preserving the content, or what each poem "tells."
4. **Respect shape,** keeping the long, narrow form of the words on the page.

Look at Peden's translation beside the original Spanish poem, and see how she followed these commandments.

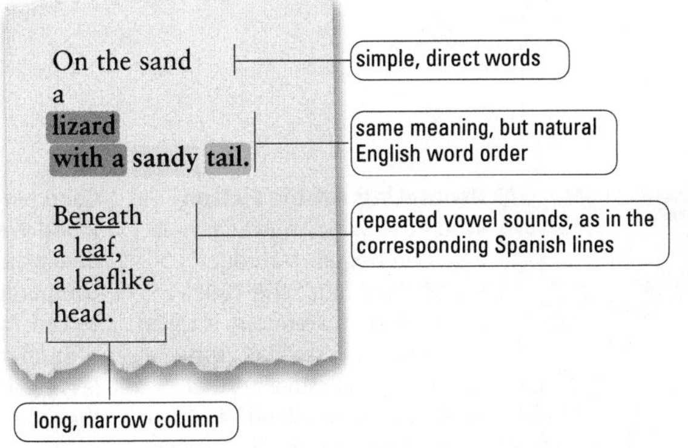

Peden said that "Respect sound" was the most difficult commandment to follow:

> ***There is little a translator can do about lost sound values except to listen constantly and to try as nearly as possible to re-create those sounds or to substitute a similar series of resonances [sounds].***

Neruda himself worried about the sound of his poetry being lost in translation:

> ***It seems to me that the English language, so different from Spanish and so much more direct, often expresses the meaning of my poetry but does not convey its atmosphere.***

Small Group Discussion Think about a poem you love. How much does the actual sound of the words contribute to the meaning or the beauty of the poem? Do you think that poem could be translated well into another language? Explain your opinion, using examples from the poem.

The Translator at Work

Reading Skills and Strategies
COMPARING

Invite a fluent Spanish speaker to read aloud the first two stanzas of Neruda's "Ode to the Lizard." Have students listen carefully to the sounds of the words. Then have another student read aloud Peden's translation. Have students compare the musical quality of the translation with the original.

Small Group Discussion As a starting point for the discussion, students might ask themselves what elements of poetry appeal the most to them—imagery, figurative language, rhyme, rhythm, or theme.

THE TRANSLATOR AT WORK 1365

Objectives

- understand and appreciate a **short story (Literary Analysis)**
- identify how a story's **title** relates to its **theme (Literary Analysis)**
- use strategies for **connecting with characters (Active Reading)**

Summary

Accompanied by his father, a young boy leaves home and walks to his first day of school. At the school gate, the father gently pushes his son toward the courtyard and promises to meet him at the end of the school day. After a while, the boy feels content at school and makes friends, with whom he plays games, sings songs, and learns about language and love. Soon, however, rivalries and hatreds arise, but it is too late to return home.

At the end of the school day, the boy waits a long time for his father. Eventually, he decides to walk home on his own. Suddenly, he notices that the gardens that had lined the streets are gone. The streets are now filled with cars. Also gone are the fields, replaced with tall buildings, loud noises, and many people. The boy wonders how so much could have changed in only half a day. He stands on the corner a long time, waiting to cross the busy street. A young boy approaches him and offers his arm, saying, "Grandpa, let me take you across."

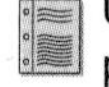 Use **Unit Seven Resource Book,** p. 109, for additional support.

Thematic Link

In this short story, time is compressed, as in a **dream.**

 Use **Unit Seven Resource Book,** p. 112, for practice with Words to Know.

5-Minute Warm-Up

Daily Language SkillBuilder

Have students **proofread** the display sentences on page 1095o and write them correctly.

PREPARING to *Read*

Half a Day

NAGUIB MAHFOUZ

Naguib Mahfouz
1911–1996

Promoting Arabic Fiction When the Swedish Academy awarded Naguib Mahfouz (nä-gēb' mä-fo͞oz') the 1988 Nobel Prize in literature, it called him a writer who "has formed an Arabian narrative art that applies to all mankind." Mahfouz, from Egypt, was the first Arabic-language writer to receive the prize. He is credited with popularizing the novel and short story as literary forms in the Arab world, where poetry has traditionally been preferred. He was little known in the rest of the world before winning the Nobel honor. Although he had written more than 50 books, few had ever been translated.

Stories of Egypt The youngest of seven children, Naguib Mahfouz was born in Cairo. After earning a degree in philosophy from the University of Cairo, he began a civil-service career and started to publish his fiction. His early works were historical novels set in ancient Egypt, but he turned his attention to modern Egypt beginning in 1945. He first gained acclaim with the 1957 publication of his "Cairo trilogy." These three books—*Palace Walk, Palace of Desire,* and *Sugar Street*—chronicle three generations of a middle-class Cairo family and serve as a history of Egypt since World War I. Full of memorable characters, precise detail, and social commentary, they have been compared to the novels of 19th-century realists such as Leo Tolstoy and Honoré de Balzac.

In the 1960s Mahfouz's style changed, becoming less realistic and more experimental, as you will see in the story "Half a Day." Still, his later works, like his earlier works, were concerned with the passage of time, the plight of the poor, and the clash of traditional and modern values—issues relevant to people worldwide.

Brutal Attack Mahfouz was not universally admired, however. At one point, certain Islamic leaders became angered by Mahfouz's support for peace with Israel and by his novel *Children of Gebalawi,* in which God and the prophets appeared as characters. These leaders called for Mahfouz's death, and in 1994, he was stabbed outside his home by an Islamic extremist. Mahfouz recovered, and his attacker was caught and executed. Afterward, Mahfouz continued to write, coming out with a new book on his 89th birthday.

Other Works
Miramar
Arabian Nights and Days

LESSON RESOURCES

UNIT SEVEN RESOURCE BOOK, pp. 109–113

ASSESSMENT RESOURCES
Formal Assessment, pp. 203–204
Teacher's Guide to Assessment and Portfolio Use
Test Generator

INTEGRATED TECHNOLOGY
Visit our Web site: classzone.com

ADDITIONAL RESOURCES
Lesson Planning Guide, pp. 181–182
Teacher's Sourcebook for Language Development

Background

A Century of Growth Nearly all of the stories that Naguib Mahfouz wrote take place in Cairo, where the author lived his entire life. In Mahfouz's lifetime, which spanned most of the 1900s, Cairo underwent vast changes, growing tremendously in both population and land area. In 1910, a year before Mahfouz was born, Cairo's population was 700,000. By the end of the century, more than 12 million people lived in the metropolitan area. Nearby cities had become absorbed as suburbs, and once-rural areas between the Nile River and the pyramids were as crowded as the city's center. In "Half a Day," Mahfouz hints, in an unusual way, at the degree of change he had seen in Cairo over his lifetime.

Because Cairo's history dates back more than 1,000 years, the city is a curious blend of the old and the new. The old quarters of the city have winding alleys with open-front shops, outdoor markets selling spices and rugs, and mosques built centuries ago. Modern sections feature Western-style high-rise apartment buildings, hotels, and shops.

Modern-day Cairo

Connect to Your Life

"Half a Day" begins with the narrator remembering his first day of school as a young boy. In what ways have you changed since your first day of school? In what ways has your community changed? Share your responses in a class discussion.

Focus Your Reading

LITERARY ANALYSIS: TITLE AND THEME

As you know, a **theme** is a central idea or message of a literary work. Often the **title** of a story or a poem gives you a clue to the work's theme. The title of Wislawa Szymborska's poem "The End and the Beginning," for example, suggests the new beginning that follows the end of a war. As you read "Half a Day," ask yourself, How does the title relate to the meaning of the story? What idea is the title referring to?

ACTIVE READING: CONNECTING WITH CHARACTERS

"Half a Day" is set in Cairo at an unspecified time in the past. Like some other stories you have read, it describes a culture that may be very different from your own. Still, you can make connections with the characters, because human beings share many of the same feelings and experiences despite cultural differences.

READER'S NOTEBOOK As you read "Half a Day," try to identify with the feelings and experiences of the main character. Then, after you've finished the story, complete the following sentence in your notebook:

____________________ in this story reminds me of a time in my life when ____________________.

WORDS TO KNOW **Vocabulary Preview**

cleave intricate majestically misgiving unmarred

READING FOR INFORMATION

Reading Skills and Strategies

IDENTIFYING MAIN IDEAS

Tell students as they read to identify the main idea of a paragraph or passage. Point out that a main idea organizes a paragraph and that all other sentences are built around that main idea. After identifying the main idea, have students identify supporting details that provide additional information about the main idea. When reading the **Build Background** feature, for example, students should look for details that support the main idea that Cairo has changed in many ways during Mahfouz's lifetime.

TIME MANAGEMENT

If your schedule requires that you cover the lesson objectives in a shorter time, use. . .

- Preparing to Read, pp. 1366–1367
- Thinking Through the Literature, p. 1372
- Vocabulary in Action, p. 1373

If you want to take advantage of longer blocks of class time, use. . .

- TE Teaching Options: Vocabulary Strategy, p. 1368; Grammar, p. 1371
- Related Reading, p. 1371
- Choices and Challenges, p. 1373

Reading and Analyzing

Literary Analysis TITLE AND THEME

A Have students read the title of the short story. Ask what ideas the title brings to mind.

Possible Response: time, the passing of time

 Use **Unit Seven Resource Book,** p. 111, for more practice.

Active Reading

CONNECTING WITH CHARACTERS

B Ask students what experiences and feelings help them immediately connect with the story's narrator.

Possible Response: childhood experiences of trying to keep up with a parent's long strides, wearing new clothes for school, and feeling a sense of dread about the first day of school

 Use **Unit Seven Resource Book,** p. 110, for more practice

Literary Analysis POINT OF VIEW

C Point out that the story is told from the first-person point of view. Ask students why they think Mahfouz chose to use a first-person narrator for this story.

Possible Response: A first-person narrator tells a story as he or she experiences it. Readers, therefore, experience events as the narrator does, which helps readers connect with the narrator.

Half a Day

Naguib Mahfouz

Translated by Denys Johnson-Davies

I proceeded alongside my father, clutching his right hand, running to keep up with the long strides he was taking. All my clothes were new: the black shoes, the green school uniform, and the red tarboosh.[1] My delight in my new clothes, however, was not altogether unmarred, for this was no feast day but the day on which I was to be cast into school for the first time.

My mother stood at the window watching our progress, and I would turn toward her from time to time, as though appealing for help. We walked along a street lined with gardens; on both sides were extensive fields planted with crops, prickly pears, henna trees,[2] and a few date palms.

"Why school?" I challenged my father openly. "I shall never do anything to annoy you."

"I'm not punishing you," he said, laughing. "School's not a punishment. It's the factory that makes useful men out of boys. Don't you want to be like your father and brothers?"

I was not convinced. I did not believe there was really any good to be had in tearing me away from the intimacy of my home and throwing me 1
into this building that stood at the end of the road like some huge, high-walled fortress, exceedingly stern and grim.

When we arrived at the gate we could see the courtyard, vast and crammed full of boys and girls. "Go in by yourself," said my father, "and join them. Put a smile on your face and be a good example to others."

I hesitated and clung to his hand, but he gently pushed me from him. "Be a man," he said. "Today you truly begin life. You will find me waiting for you when it's time to leave."

I took a few steps, then stopped and looked but saw nothing. Then the faces of boys and girls came into view. I did not know a single one of them, and none of them knew me. I felt I was a stranger who had lost his way. But glances of curiosity were directed toward me, and one boy approached and asked, "Who brought you?"

"My father," I whispered.

"My father's dead," he said quite simply.

I did not know what to say. The gate was
closed, letting out a pitiable screech. Some of the 2
children burst into tears. The bell rang. A lady

1. **tarboosh** (tär-bo͞osh′): a felt hat with a tassel on top.
2. **prickly pears, henna trees:** Prickly pears are cacti with pear-shaped, edible fruit. Henna trees are small, thorny trees with white flowers.

WORDS TO KNOW

unmarred (ŭn-märd′) *adj.* not damaged or injured

MINI LESSON **Vocabulary Strategy**

USING CONTEXT CLUES

Instruction Call attention to the Words to Know at the bottom of pages 1368 and 1369. Demonstrate the strategy of using context clues, writing the following model sentence on the board:

My delight was not *unmarred,* for it was the first day of school.

Cover up the word *unmarred* and ask volunteers to suggest possible meanings for the word, based on how they would expect a boy to feel on his first day of school. *(Possible Responses: high, great, perfect)*

Compare the guesses to the definition of *unmarred* given at the bottom of page 1368.

Practice Ask students to use context clues to determine the meaning of the italicized words.

1. Repeated rows of wide, thin, and dotted lines formed an *intricate* pattern.
2. I was perfectly content now; I had no more *misgivings.*
3. The generals, glittering with medals, rode *majestically* past the cheering crowds.
4. The jeep *cleaved* the sand dunes like a spoon dragged through sugar.

 Use **Unit Seven Resource Book,** p. 112, for more exercises.

A lesson on using context clues appears on p. 674 of the Pupil's Edition.

 3

The Village Road (1988), Ali Selim. Ramses Wissa Wassef Art Center, Cairo, Egypt. Photo © Werner Forman/Art Resource, New York.

came along, followed by a group of men. The men began sorting us into ranks. We were formed into an intricate pattern in the great courtyard surrounded on three sides by high buildings of several floors; from each floor we were overlooked by a long balcony roofed in wood.

"This is your new home," said the woman. "Here too there are mothers and fathers. Here there is everything that is enjoyable and beneficial to knowledge and religion. Dry your tears and face life joyfully."

We submitted to the facts, and this submission brought a sort of contentment. Living beings were drawn to other living beings, and from the first moments my heart made friends with such boys as were to be my friends and fell in love with such girls as I was to be in love with, so that it seemed my misgivings had had no basis. I had never imagined school would have this rich variety. We played all sorts of different games: swings, the vaulting horse, ball games. In the music room we chanted our first songs. We also had our first introduction to language. We saw a globe of the Earth, which revolved and showed
the various continents and countries. We started 4
learning the numbers. The story of the Creator of the universe was read to us, we were told of His present world and of His Hereafter, and we heard examples of what He said. We ate delicious food, took a little nap, and woke up to go on with friendship and love, play and learning.

As our path revealed itself to us, however, we did not find it as totally sweet and unclouded as we had presumed. Dust-laden winds and unexpected accidents came about suddenly, so we had

WORDS TO KNOW

intricate (ĭn′trĭ-kĭt) *adj.* complex

misgiving (mĭs-gĭv′ĭng) *n.* a feeling of doubt; concern

Customizing Instruction

English Learners

Encourage students to write down new vocabulary in a word journal. Suggest that they write the word, its definition, and a sentence using the word. Explain the meaning of each of the following words:

1 *intimacy:* friendly or warm privacy

2 *pitiable:* sorrowful

3 *contentment:* satisfaction

Less Proficient Readers

Help students keep the events in the story in chronological sequence by having them create a schedule of the narrator's "half day," beginning with the walk with his father to school.

4 Ask students what positive and negative experiences the narrator has at school.

Possible Responses: positive—plays games, learns songs, learns about language and numbers, eats delicious food, learns about friendship and love; negative—learns that accidents happen, rivalries and hatreds arise, fighting breaks out

Active Reading

CONNECTING WITH CHARACTERS

Ask students how they would feel if they found that their surroundings had suddenly completely changed.

Possible Responses: bewildered, confused, upset, angry

Reading Skills and Strategies

CLARIFYING

A Ask students what changes the narrator notices as he walks home. How does he respond to the changes?

Possible Responses: The gardens that once lined the streets are gone, the streets have been invaded by hordes of cars and people, fields have been taken over by tall buildings. The narrator responds with horror and disbelief.

Literary Analysis TITLE AND THEME

B Ask students how much time has passed in this story.

Possible Responses: In the narrator's perception, only half a day has passd. In reality, many years have passed, from his youth to his old age.

Literary Analysis SURPRISE ENDING

C Ask students to explain why the ending of the story is or is not a complete surprise. If not, what clues does Mahfouz provide to readers?

Possible Responses: Most students will suggest that the ending is not a complete surprise. Clues include a sequence of steps toward maturity: leaving home; going through the school gate on his own; accepting "the facts" at school; growing in lessons of "friendship and love, play and learning"; the forming of rivalries and hatreds; realizing that he couldn't go back home and that "Nothing lay ahead of us but exertion, struggle, and perseverance."

to be watchful, at the ready, and very patient. It was not all a matter of playing and fooling around. Rivalries could bring about pain and
4 hatred or give rise to fighting. And while the lady would sometimes smile, she would often scowl and scold. Even more frequently she would resort to physical punishment.

In addition, the time for changing one's mind was over and gone and there was no question of ever returning to the paradise of home. Nothing lay ahead of us but exertion, struggle, and perseverance. Those who were able took advantage of the opportunities for success and happiness that presented themselves amid the worries.

The bell rang announcing the passing of the day and the end of work. The throngs of children rushed toward the gate, which was opened again. I bade farewell to friends and sweethearts and passed through the gate. I peered around but found no trace of my father, who had promised to be there. I stepped aside to wait. When I had waited for a long time without avail, I decided to return home on my own. After I had taken a few steps, a middle-aged man passed by, and I realized at once that I knew him. He came toward me, smiling, and shook me by the hand, saying, "It's a long time since we last met—how are you?"

With a nod of my head, I agreed with him and in turn asked, "And you, how are you?"

"As you can see, not all that good, the Almighty be praised!"

Again he shook me by the hand and went off. I proceeded a few steps, then came to a startled halt. Good Lord! Where was the street lined with gardens? Where had it disappeared to? When did all these vehicles invade it? And when did all these hordes of humanity come to rest upon its surface? How did these hills of refuse come to cover its sides? And where were the fields that bordered it? High buildings had taken over, the street surged with children, and disturbing noises shook the air. At various points stood conjurers[3] showing off their tricks and making snakes appear from baskets. Then there was a band announcing the opening of a circus, with clowns and weight lifters walking in front. A line of trucks carrying central security troops crawled majestically by. The siren of a fire engine shrieked, and it was not clear how the vehicle would cleave its way to reach the blazing fire. A battle raged between a taxi driver and his passenger, while the passenger's wife called out for help and no one answered. Good God! I was in a daze. My head spun. I almost went crazy. How could all this have happened in half a day, between early morning and sunset? I would find the answer at home with my father. But where was my home? I could see only tall buildings and hordes of people. I hastened on to the crossroads between the gardens and Abu Khoda.[4] I had to cross Abu Khoda to reach my house, but the stream of cars would not let up. The fire engine's siren was shrieking at full pitch as it moved at a snail's pace, and I said to myself, "Let the fire take its pleasure in what it consumes." Extremely irritated, I wondered when I would be able to cross. I stood there a long time, until the young lad employed at the ironing shop on the corner came up to me. He stretched out his arm and said gallantly, "Grandpa, let me take you across." ❖

3. **conjurers** (kŏn′jər-ərz): trick players; magicians.

4. **Abu Khoda** (ə-bo͞o′ KHō′dä): a busy traffic area in Cairo.

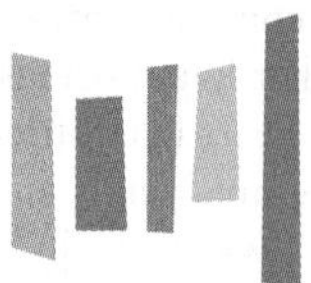

WORDS TO KNOW

majestically (mə-jĕs′tĭ-klē) *adv.* in a noble or stately way
cleave (klēv) *v.* to cut through; penetrate

1370

Assessment Informal Assessment

SUMMARIZING Ask students to write a one-paragraph summary of the short story "Half a Day." Remind students that an effective summary will present the main events in chronological order and that summaries will be judged according to their accuracy and completeness.

RUBRIC

3 Full Accomplishment Student's account provides an accurate and thorough summary of the story.

2 Substantial Accomplishment Student's account is accurate, but some important information is missing.

1 Little or Partial Accomplishment Student's account is missing vital information, is inaccurate, or shows little understanding of the story.

COUNTING IN SEVENS

JUDITH WRIGHT

Wright, a noted Australian poet, looks at the passage of time from a woman's perspective.

Seven ones are seven.
I can't remember that year
or what presents I was given.

Seven twos are fourteen.
That year I found my mind,
swore not to be what I had been.

Seven threes are twenty-one.
I was sailing my own sea,
first in love, the knots undone.

Seven fours are twenty-eight;
three false starts had come and gone;
my true love came, and not too late.

Seven fives are thirty-five.
In her cot my daughter lay,
real, miraculous, alive.

Seven sixes are forty-two.
I packed her sandwiches for school,
I loved my love and time came true.

Seven sevens are forty-nine.
Fruit loaded down my apple-tree,
near fifty years of life were mine.

Seven eights are fifty-six.
My lips still cold from a last kiss,
my fire was ash and charcoal-sticks.

Seven nines are sixty-three, seven tens are seventy,
Who would that old woman be?
She will remember being me,
but what she is I cannot see.

Yet with every added seven,
some strange present I was given.

Related Reading

Judith Wright Judith Wright, the great Australian poet, was born in 1915 in New South Wales on her family's large farm. At the age of six, Wright began writing poetry in an attempt to cheer her ill mother. By the time she was 14, Wright knew she was going to be a poet. After graduating with a B.A., Wright worked a series of secretarial jobs and continued writing. The outbreak of World War II and Wright's return home to the farm in Wallamumbi proved a turning point: "As the train panted up the foothills of the Moonbis and the haze of dust and eucalyptus vapour dimmed the drought-stricken landscape, I found myself suddenly and sharply aware of it as 'my country.' These hills and valleys were—not mine, but me." Wright's strong sense of identification with the landscape and people of Australia is echoed in the themes of her poetry. Judith Wright died in June, 2000, at the age of 85.

Discussion Questions

1. Ask students how the speaker of the poem measures and marks the passage of time.
   Possible Response: She measures it in segments of seven years. She marks the passage of each segment of years by the "strange present" she was given.
2. Have students identify some of the strange presents the speaker has been given at different ages.
   Possible Response: age 14—she found her mind; age 21—she was on her own and in love; age 28—her true love came; age 35—her daughter is born.

MINI LESSON Grammar

APOSTROPHES AND PLURALS

Instruction Call attention to the first line of Wright's poem. Explain that if she had used the numeral 1 instead of spelling out the word *one*, the correct plural form would have been "1's." An apostrophe and an s ('s) is used to form the plural of a numeral, an individual letter, a word referred to as a word, or an abbreviation containing periods. Write the following examples on the board:

1's *M*'s *and*'s Ph.D.'s

Do not use an apostrophe to form the plural of a year number or a spelled-out number. Write these examples on the board.

1960s threes

Practice Ask students to rewrite any plurals that are formed incorrectly. They should write *Correct* if the sentence is correct.

1. How many *No*s did I just hear? *(No's)*
2. The 1930's were not happy years. *(1930s)*
3. Her *i*'s look just like her *j*'s to me. *(Correct)*
4. It would be faster to count by five's. *(fives)*
5. The computer printed 2's instead of 3's. *(Correct)*

For more instruction and practice in forming plurals with apostrophes, use McDougal Littell's ***Language Network:***

- Grade 10, Chapter 11, "Hyphens and Apostrophes"
- Grade 12, Chapter 10, "Apostrophes"

COUNTING IN SEVENS **1371**

Connect to the Literature

1. **What Do You Think?** When did you first notice something unusual about the end of the story?

Comprehension Check
- How does the narrator feel about going to school for the first time?
- What is his experience at school like?
- What changes does the narrator notice after he leaves school?

Think Critically

2. How do you account for the changes the narrator witnesses after leaving school?

3. In your opinion, what does the school **symbolize** in this story?

- the schoolteacher's advice to "dry your tears and face life joyfully"
- what happens to the narrator at the school
- what has changed when the narrator leaves the school

4. Do you see any other **symbols** in the story? Explain.

5. **ACTIVE READING: CONNECTING WITH CHARACTERS** Share with a partner the sentence you completed in your READER'S NOTEBOOK. What universal human experiences does this story describe?

Extend Interpretations

6. **Critic's Corner** The critic Liz Brent has written that in "Half a Day" Mahfouz portrays the human experience of life as one "of being cast out of a paradise of early childhood into a harsh world of struggle and pain" to which we must submit. Do you agree that this is how Mahfouz portrays life?

7. **Comparing Texts** How is the narrator's experience of time in "Half a Day" similar to the speaker's in "Counting in Sevens"?

8. **Connect to Life** In your own life so far, have you experienced time as passing quickly or slowly? Explain.

LITERARY ANALYSIS: TITLE AND THEME

The **title** of a literary work often hints at the work's **theme,** or central message. One way to discover the theme of a literary work is to think about what happens to the main characters and to relate those experiences to the title. In "Half a Day," the narrator enters school as a young boy. After leaving the school at the end of the day, he discovers that the world has changed drastically. In this context, what does "half a day" represent? What does this story suggest about time and a person's life?

Cooperative Learning Activity Get together with a small group of classmates and discuss the theme of "Half a Day." See if you can come up with another title that also hints at the theme. Share your group's title with the rest of the class.

Connect to the Literature

1. **What Do You Think?** Responses will vary. Most students will probably state that they noticed something unusual when the narrator finds the changes in his neighborhood and city while walking home from school.

Comprehension Check
- anxious, unhappy, afraid
- positive experiences include friendships, games, and learning; negative experiences include developing rivalries and hatreds
- The small, quiet, picturesque, rural village has changed into a large, noisy, ugly city.

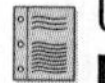
Use Selection Quiz in **Unit Seven Resource Book,** p. 113.

Think Critically

2. Possible Response: Many decades have passed.
3. Possible Responses: stages of life; lessons to be learned
4. Possible Response: Another symbol might be the gate at the school courtyard, which could symbolize a rite of passage.
5. Possible Responses: leaving home; going to school; making friends; growing old; being surprised by change

Extend Interpretations

6. **Critic's Corner** Responses will vary: Some students will agree, noting that the narrator "submits" to "the facts" at school. Others will note that acceptance and submission brought the narrator a sense of contentment. Struggle and pain emerged with the development of hatreds and the realization that it was not possible to return to the paradise of childhood.
7. **Comparing Texts** Responses will vary. Some students may note that time passes swiftly in both. Others may note that both the narrator and the speaker are surprised by the sudden arrival of old age. Both experiences of time also suggest stages of life—whether in terms of seven-year measurements or in terms of lessons learned.
8. **Connect to Life** Responses will vary. Some students may note that time seems to pass quickly when they are enjoying a special occasion or event. Others may note that time seems to pass slowly when they are anticipating something or when they are enduring an unpleasant experience or situation.

Literary Analysis

Students should realize that the half day symbolizes the passage of time, from childhood to adulthood and beyond. The story suggests that a person's lifetime passes more quickly than expected.

Cooperative Learning Activity In preparation for the small group discussion, suggest that students review the story and identify other possible symbols related to the theme that might offer new title possibilities.

Use **Unit Seven Resource Book,** p. 111, for more practice.

Writing Options

1. School Memory In a personal narrative, describe a vivid memory you have of your early school days.

2. Interpretive Essay Some critics see "Half a Day" as an allegory—a story in which characters, events, and objects represent abstract ideas. Think again about the symbols you saw in the story. Write an interpretive essay explaining how "Half a Day" is an allegory. Tell what the narrator, the school, the teacher, the ringing bell, and other elements in the story might stand for.

Writing Handbook
See page R33: Analysis.

Activities & Explorations

1. Life on the Line Create an illustrated time line that reflects how a person's sense of the passage of time varies at different stages of life. ~ **ART**

2. Wordless Portrayal Present a pantomime in which you portray the narrator as a young boy going off to school and as an old man leaving the school. ~ **PERFORMING**

Inquiry & Research

1. Present-Day Cairo Find photographs, film footage, or travelers' descriptions of present-day Cairo. Bring them to class and discuss whether they match Mahfouz's description of Cairo at the end of "Half a Day."

2. More Mahfouz Read another short story by Mahfouz, either from *God's World* or from *The Time and the Place*. Report on it to your classmates, comparing and contrasting it with "Half a Day."

Vocabulary in Action

EXERCISE: CONTEXT CLUES Write the vocabulary word that best completes each sentence.

1. The classroom floor was freshly waxed and _________ before the first students entered.
2. The first-grade teacher strode _________ into the room, like a queen.
3. One child was full of _________, fearing that he would not learn to read.
4. Could that _________ pattern of lines on the paper actually be his last name?
5. At the end of the day, he would _________ a path through a crowd to reach his mother's waiting arms.

WORDS TO KNOW

cleave intricate majestically misgiving unmarred

Building Vocabulary
For an in-depth lesson on using context clues, see page 674.

Writing Options

1. **School Memory** As a prewriting tool, suggest that students brainstorm supporting details about a vivid school memory and write those details in a web diagram.
2. **Interpretive Essay** Remind students that they should have a clear thesis statement. You might have students work in pairs to create a chart that includes each character, event, and object in the story. Beside each item listed in the chart, have students describe the abstract idea it represents.

Activities & Explorations

1. **Life on the Line** Suggest that students include significant events on their time lines.
2. **Wordless Portrayal** Remind students of the crucial importance of gestures and movements to pantomime. Have students carefully consider how certain gestures convey specific emotions.

Inquiry & Research

1. **Present-Day Cairo** Discuss ways in which the images illustrate the many contrasts of Cairo.
2. **More Mahfouz** In their comparisons, have students consider such literary elements as point of view, symbolism, theme, and setting.

Vocabulary in Action

1. unmarred
2. majestically
3. misgiving
4. intricate
5. cleave

To assess skills and concepts taught in this selection, use **Formal Assessment Book,** pp. 203–204.

Possible Objectives
This **On Your Own** featured selection may be used to achieve one or more of the following objectives:

- to give students the opportunity to read independently, either reading silently for a sustained period, reading and analyzing literature with a group, or using the Reader's Notebook to write in response to the literature
- to conduct a post-reading class discussion

ON YOUR OWN

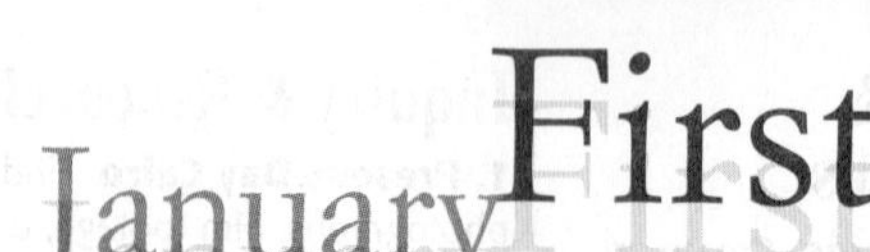

January First

OCTAVIO PAZ

Translated by *Elizabeth Bishop*

Octavio Paz
1914–1998

Early Promise Octavio Paz, who in 1990 would be the first Mexican to receive the Nobel Prize in literature, loved books from the time he was a young child. Paz was born on the outskirts of Mexico City during the Mexican Revolution. The war left his family in financial ruin, but Paz remembered his childhood as a kind of paradise: "I lived . . . in an old dilapidated house that had a junglelike garden and a great room full of books. . . . The garden soon became the center of my world; the library, an enchanted cave." He began writing as a teenager, publishing his first poem at 16 and his first book of poems, *Forest Moon,* at 19.

Mexican Voice Paz went on to become Mexico's most important modern writer in both poetry and prose. His travels to Europe, the United States, and Asia brought many influences to bear on his writing. Many of his works also reflect the influences of Spanish and Indian cultures on Mexican identity. His first prose work, *The Labyrinth of Solitude* (1950), was an exploration of Mexican culture and thought that brought him international recognition. Poetry was the most vital form of literature for Paz, however. In his poetry he sought to create unity out of the differences, divisions, and contradictions present in modern life. In his Nobel lecture, he observed, "All our ventures and exploits, all our acts and dreams, are bridges designed to overcome the separation and reunite us with the world and our fellow beings."

Other Works
Sun Stone
A Tree Within

In the poem you are about to read, the speaker faces the beginning of a new year. Paz uses familiar as well as unexpected images, words, and ideas to explore what it is like to enter a new day and year. As you read the poem, ask yourself the following questions:

1. *What does the speaker expect to do on January first?*
2. *What discoveries does the speaker make when he wakes up on the first day of the new year?*

The year's doors open
like those of language,
toward the unknown
Last night you told me:
tomorrow
we shall have to think up signs,
sketch a landscape, fabricate a plan
on the double page
of day and paper
Tomorrow, we shall have to invent,
once more,
the reality of this world.

I opened my eyes late.
For a second of a second
I felt what the Aztec felt,
on the crest of the promontory,
lying in wait
for time's uncertain return
through cracks in the horizon.

But no, the year had returned.
It filled all the room
and my look almost touched it.
Time, with no help from us,

15 the Aztec: In the 15th and 16th centuries, the Aztec people inhabited the area that is now central and southern Mexico. They developed a complex calendar based on a cycle of 52 years. The beginning of every cycle was marked with ceremonies and celebrations.

16 promontory (prŏm′ən-tôr′ē): a high point of land jutting out into a body of water.

Working Independently

You may want to set aside time each week for independent reading, without making an assignment related to the reading. Or once students have completed the reading, either alone or aloud in groups, you may ask them to work together on a project, such as a New Year Plan. If you choose to have students write responsively in their Reader's Notebook, suggest that they write about their hopes and goals for the new year.

Discussing the Selection

Use the questions at the beginning of the **On Your Own** feature to focus and/or set a purpose for students' reading. The last page of this selection provides questions you might use for a post-reading class discussion.

JANUARY FIRST **1375**

had placed
in exactly the same order as yesterday
houses in the empty street,
snow on the houses
silence on the snow.

You were beside me,
still asleep.
The day had invented you
but you hadn't yet accepted
being invented by the day.
—Nor possibly my being invented, either.
You were in another day.

You were beside me
and I saw you, like the snow,
asleep among appearances.
Time, with no help from us,
invents houses, streets, trees
and sleeping women.

When you open your eyes
we'll walk, once more,
among the hours and their inventions,
and lingering among appearances,
we'll bear witness to time and its conjugations.
We'll open the doors of the day,
and enter the unknown.

46 conjugations (kŏn'jə-gā'shənz): combinations.

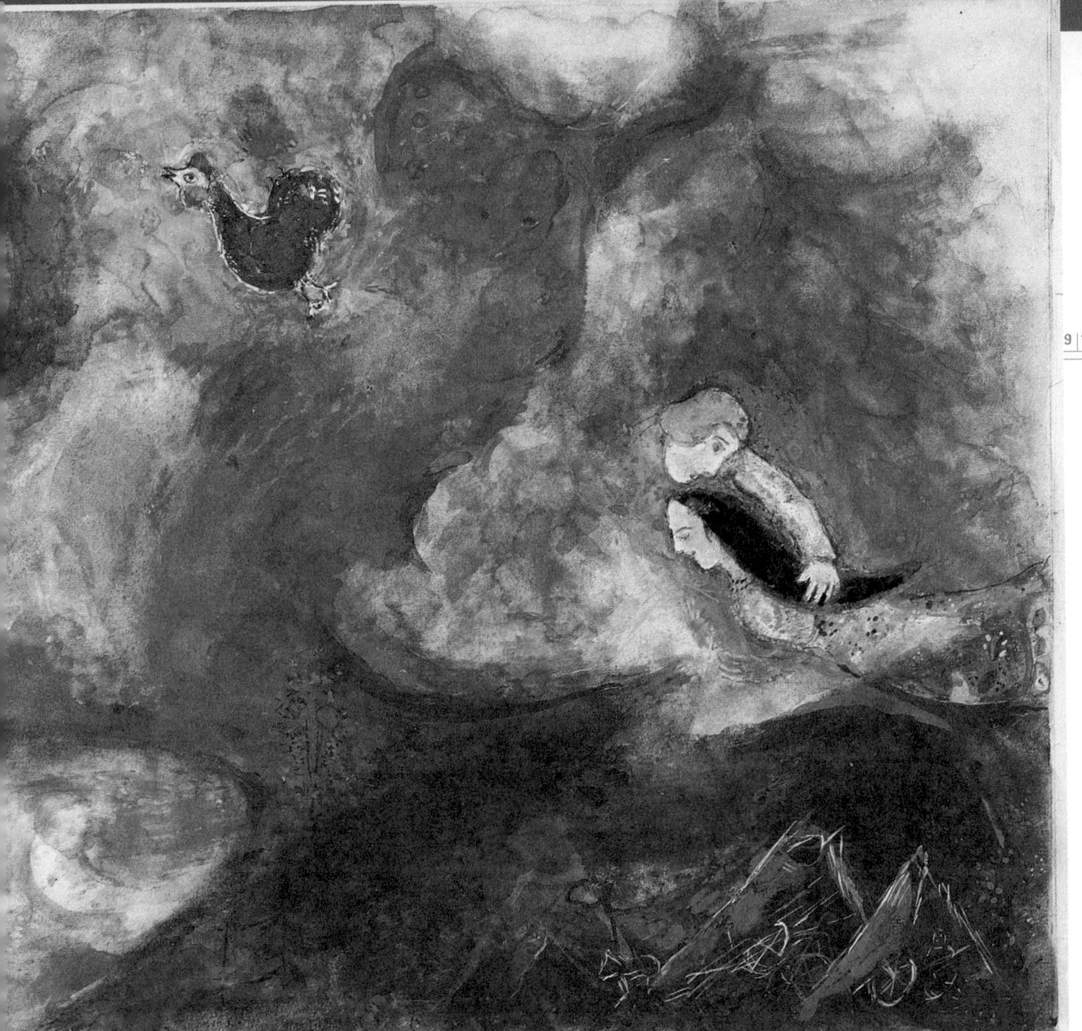

Aleko and Zemphira by Moonlight, decor for *Aleko* (Scene I) (1942), Marc Chagall. Gouache, wash, and pencil on paper, 15⅛" × 22½". Digital image © The Museum of Modern Art, New York/Licensed by Scala/Art Resource, New York. Art © 2007 Artists Rights Society (ARS), New York/ADAGP, Paris.

Discussion Questions

1. What does the speaker expect to do on January first?
   Possible Response: The speaker expects to prepare a plan for the year.
2. What discoveries does the speaker make when he wakes up on the first day of the new year?
   Possible Response: He discovers that "the year had returned" and all the familiar signs—"houses in the empty street / snow on the houses / silence on the snow"—are "in exactly the same order as yesterday."
3. What is the theme of the poem?
   Possible Response: that a new year has many possibilities; that people have no effect on the passage of time
4. What resolutions are eventually made by the speaker?
   Possible Response: "we'll walk, once more"; "we'll bear witness to time"; "We'll open the doors of the day, / and enter the unknown."
5. What action will truly begin the new year for the speaker?
   Possible Response: When his wife/lover opens her eyes.

Objectives

- reflect on and assess understanding of literature of contemporary Nobel Prize winners
- classify writers by characteristics of their work
- analyze styles across texts
- assess and build portfolios

Reflecting on the Literature

You might have students work in groups of three to classify the writers in this part as critics or dreamers.

Possible Responses: Critics–Gordimer: her story "Amnesty" criticizes South Africa's apartheid system; Soyinka: his poem "After the Deluge" criticizes corrupt leadership; Szymborska: her poem "The End and the Beginning" criticizes war. Dreamers–Neruda: his odes celebrate the ordinary objects of life and evoke surprising new ways of looking at the world; García Márquez–his imagery and use of magical realism place the reader inside a dream world; Mahfouz–his distortion of time in "Half a Day" is like the distortion perceived in dreams.

Use **Unit Seven Resource Book,** p. 114, for additional support.

Reviewing Literary Concepts

A successful response will

- identify a writer whose style appealed most to the student
- describe elements of the writer's distinctive style
- identify a writer with a contrasting writing style
- analyze how the two writing styles differ

Building Your Portfolio

Students will use their Presentation Portfolios to file what they consider their highest quality work–the very best projects and activities from their Working Portfolios.

For more information on using writing and assessing portfolios, see the **Teacher's Guide to Assessment and Portfolio Use,** pp. 53–74.

Part Assessment

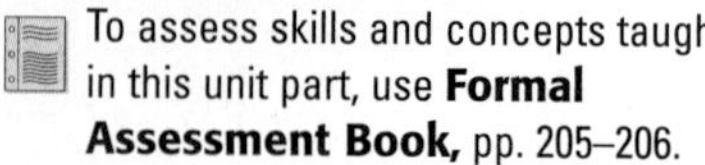
To assess skills and concepts taught in this unit part, use **Formal Assessment Book,** pp. 205–206.

End-of-Year Test

For end-of-year assessment of skills and concepts taught, use **Formal Assessment Book,** pp. 207–216.

Reflect and Assess

What did you learn about contemporary literature in Unit Seven, Part 3? Did you find the writing easier or more difficult to read than the writing of earlier eras? Use the following activities to clarify your thoughts.

Reflecting on the Literature

Critics and Dreamers This part was titled "Critics and Dreamers: Contemporary Nobel Prize Winners." Of the writers in this part, which would you classify as the critics? What are they criticizing? Which would you classify as the dreamers? What do they imagine? Create a chart that classifies the writers and explains why they belong in either category.

Reviewing Literary Concepts

Analyzing Styles Of the writers in this part, whose style appealed to you most? On a sheet of paper, name the writer and describe elements that contribute to his or her particular style, such as diction, tone, and figurative language. Then name the writer from Part 3 whose style is most different from this writer's, in your opinion. Note how their styles are different. Then compare your choices with your classmates'.

Building Your Portfolio

Writing Options Look back at the Writing Options you completed for this part, particularly any comparison-and-contrast or interpretive essays. Compare one of these with a similar assignment you did at the beginning of the year. Attach a cover sheet to the recent assignment, explaining how it shows your growth as a writer. Then place the work in your final **Presentation Portfolio.**

Self ASSESSMENT

READER'S NOTEBOOK

In your own words, define each of the following terms or names. If you are unsure of any, go back through Part 3 or consult the **Glossary of Literary Terms** (page R91).

Alfred Nobel	symbol
apartheid	ode
Wole Soyinka	tone
magical realism	Pablo Neruda
first-person point of view	
postcolonial writing	

Setting GOALS

What reading and writing goals would you like to set for yourself for next year?

Assessment Self Assessment

Students can look up the listed terms in the **Glossary of Literary Terms** on page R91 or they can find them introduced in context on the text pages indicated below.

Alfred Nobel (p. 1320)
apartheid (pp. 1322, 1325)
Wole Soyinka (p. 1336)
magical realism (pp. 1344–1345)
first-person point of view (pp. 1325, 1333)
postcolonial literature (p. 1322)
symbol (pp. 1347, 1354)
ode (p. 1359)
tone (pp. 1337, 1342)
Pablo Neruda (p. 1358)

Extend Your *Reading*

LITERATURE CONNECTIONS

Kaffir Boy

MARK MATHABANE

In this memoir, Mathabane recalls growing up under apartheid in Johannesburg in the 1960s and 1970s. After his father is arrested and forced to labor on a white-owned farm, Mathabane's mother is determined that her son will get an education. Mathabane excels in school, but it is tennis—and the inspiration of players Arthur Ashe and Stan Smith—that ultimately help him escape apartheid.

These are some of the thematically related readings that are provided along with *Kaffir Boy:*

***from* Makes Me Wanna Holler**
NATHAN MCCALL

A Message from Nelson Mandela to the Youth of America
NELSON MANDELA

LITERATURE CONNECTIONS

A Place Where the Sea Remembers

SANDRA BENÍTEZ

This best-selling magical realist novel is set in Santiago, Mexico. It consists of short, interrelated narratives, each focused on a single character. The work depicts the triumphs and tragedies of common people—a flower seller, a healer, a fisherman, a teacher, a midwife—whose lives are interwoven by fate and passion.

These are some of the thematically related readings provided along with *A Place Where the Sea Remembers:*

Talking to the Dead
JUDITH ORTIZ COFER

Death of a Young Son by Drowning
MARGARET ATWOOD

An Astrologer's Day
R. K. NARAYAN

And Even *More* . . .

Books

The Vintage Book of Contemporary World Poetry
EDITED BY J. D. MCCLATCHY
This is a collection of verse by 83 major poets, including the Nobel Prize winners in Unit 7 and others such as Czeslaw Milosz, Derek Walcott, and Seamus Heaney.

Short Stories by Latin American Women: The Magic and the Real EDITED BY CELIA C. DE ZAPATA
Isabel Allende and Luisa Valenzuela are among the contributors to this anthology of magical realist fiction.

Other Media

The García Márquez Collection
Six made-for-TV films based on stories by Gabriel García Márquez, including "A Very Old Man with Enormous Wings." In Spanish with English subtitles.
Fox Lorber (VIDEOCASSETTES)

The Nobel Prize
BURTON FELDMAN

Feldman traces the history of the Nobel Prize and examines the controversies surrounding the award. In his chapter on the Nobel Prize in literature, he groups winners by the language in which they wrote and questions why many great writers were overlooked.

More Recommendations for Your Students

Difficulty Level: Easy

Goodnough, David. *Pablo Neruda: Nobel Prize-Winning Poet* (Springfield, NJ: Enslow, 1998). Many photographs are included in this interesting biography of Neruda, written for a young-adult audience.

Rochman, Hazel, ed. *Somehow Tenderness Survives: Stories of Southern Africa* (NY: Harper & Row, 1988). A slim anthology of stories that reveal the brutality of apartheid. Nadine Gordimer and Mark Mathabane are among the writers represented.

Difficulty Level: Average

Johnson-Davies, Denis, ed. and trans. *Under the Naked Sky: Short Stories from the Arab World* (Cairo: The American University in Cairo Press, 2000). This collection of 30 modern stories from 10 Arab countries includes "Traveler with Hand Luggage," a brief, unsettling story by Naguib Mahfouz.

Milosz, Czeslaw, ed. *A Book of Luminous Things: An International Anthology of Poetry* (NY: Harcourt 1996). Milosz, a Nobel laureate, chooses 300 of his favorite ancient and modern poems, arranging them thematically under such headings as "The Secret of a Thing."

Difficulty Level: Challenging

The Kenyon Review, Vol. 23, No. 2 (Spring 2001). This special issue of the literary journal, published in collaboration with the U.K. journal *Stand,* honors the centennial of the Nobel Prizes with pieces by and about past winners.

Ross, Robert L., ed. *Colonial and Postcolonial Fiction in English: An Anthology.* (NY: Garland, 1999). A collection of 35 works by writers from Canada, Australia, New Zealand, India, Pakistan, Africa, and the Caribbean.

Zamora, Lois Parkinson, and Wendy B. Faris, eds. *Magical Realism: Theory, History, Community* (Durham, NC: Duke University Press, 1995). Critical essays on magical realism, including translations of the essays by Franz Roh and Alejo Carpentier that defined the term.

Student *Resource Bank*

Reading for Different Purposes

You read for many different reasons. In a single day, you might read a short story for fun, a textbook for information to help you pass a test, and a weather map to find out if it will rain. For every type of reading, there are specific strategies that can help you understand and remember the material. This handbook will help you become a better reader in school, at home, and on the job.

Reading Literature

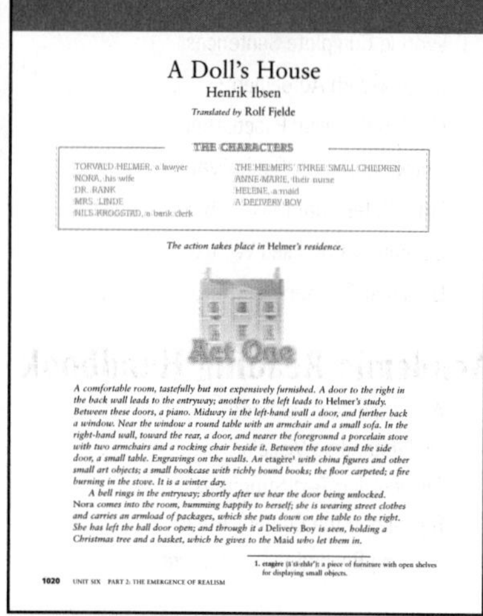

A Doll's House

Henrik Ibsen

Translated by Rolf Fjelde

THE CHARACTERS

TORVALD HELMER, a lawyer	THE HELMERS' THREE SMALL CHILDREN
NORA, his wife	ANNE-MARIE, their nurse
DR. RANK	HELENE, a maid
MRS. LINDE	A DELIVERY BOY
NILS KROGSTAD, a bank clerk	

The action takes place in Helmer's *residence.*

Act One

A comfortable room, tastefully but not expensively furnished. A door to the right in the back wall leads to the entryway; another to the left leads to Helmer's *study. Between these doors, a piano. Midway in the left-hand wall a door, and further back a window. Near the window a round table with an armchair and a small sofa. In the right-hand wall, toward the rear, a door, and nearer the foreground a porcelain stove with two armchairs and a rocking chair beside it. Between the stove and the side door, a small table. Engravings on the walls. An etagère[1] with china figures and other small art objects; a small bookcase with richly bound books; the floor carpeted; a fire burning in the stove. It is a winter day.*

A bell rings in the entryway; shortly after we hear the door being unlocked. Nora *comes into the room, humming happily to herself; she is wearing street clothes and carries an armload of packages, which she puts down on the table to the right. She has left the hall door open; and through it a* Delivery Boy *is seen, holding a Christmas tree and a basket, which he gives to the* Maid *who let them in.*

1. **etagère** (ā'tä-zhâr'): a piece of furniture with open shelves for displaying small objects.

1020 UNIT SIX PART 2: THE EMERGENCE OF REALISM

Before Reading

- Set a **purpose** for reading. What do you want to learn? Are you reading as part of an assignment or for fun? Establishing a purpose will help you focus.
- **Preview** the work by looking at the title and any images and captions. Try to **predict** what the work will be about.
- Ask yourself if you can **connect** the subject matter with what you already know.

During Reading

- **Check your understanding** of what you read. Can you restate the plot in your own words?
- Try to **connect** what you're reading to your own life. Have you experienced similar events or emotions?
- **Question** what's happening. You may wonder about events and characters' feelings.
- **Visualize,** or create a mental picture of, what the author describes.
- **Pause** from time to time to predict what will happen next.

After Reading

- **Review** your predictions. Were they correct?
- Try to **summarize** the work, expressing the **main idea** or the basic plot.
- **Reflect** on and evaluate what you have read. Did the reading fulfill your purpose?
- To **clarify** your understanding, write down opinions or thoughts about the work, or discuss it with someone.

Reading for Information

Summer Jobs Let Teens Cash In

by Kirsti MacPherson
Staff Writer

"I am so excited to be working this summer," says 15-year-old Brianna Mason. "I already have plans for the money. Some of it I'll save for college, but I'm also going to get some new clothes and CDs."

Like many teenagers, Mason will increase the number of hours she works once summer vacation begins. According to this year's Summer Jobs Survey, conducted by Junior Achievement, Inc., the most popular summer jobs for teens are in retail sales (41 percent of respondents), restaurants and fast-food establishments (20 percent), offices (14 percent), babysitting (6 percent), arts and entertainment (4 percent), and manual trades (4 percent). The survey questioned 659 teenagers nationwide.

Teenagers struggle with the desire to spend and the need to save, just as other workers do. The Junior Achievement survey found that students working during the summer saved about a third of their earnings—about 17 times what the typical adult saved! Since parents pay for most food, clothing, and shelter needs, many teens can save for higher education, cars, and other big-ticket items.

A summer job can make a teenager feel independent and accomplished—and tired. "When you work so many hours in the summer, getting back to school is kind of a relief," Mason confesses.

Students working during the summer saved about a third of their earnings.

R2 READING HANDBOOK

Set a Purpose for Reading

- Decide why you are reading the material—to study for a test, to do research, or to find out more about a topic that interests you.
- Use your **purpose** to determine how detailed your **notes** will be.

Look for Design Features

- Look at the **title** and at **subheads, boldfaced words** or phrases, **boxed text,** and any other text that is highlighted in some way.
- Use these **text organizers** to help you preview the text and identify the main ideas.
- Study photographs, maps, charts, and captions.

Notice Text Structures and Patterns

- Does the text make **comparisons?** Does it describe **causes and effects?** Is there a **sequence** of events?
- Look for **signal words** such as *same, different, because, first,* and *then* to help you see the organizational pattern.

Read Slowly and Carefully

- **Take notes** on the main ideas. State the information in your own words.
- Map the information by using a word web or another **graphic organizer.**
- Notice **unfamiliar words.** These are sometimes defined in the text.
- If there are **questions** accompanying the text, be sure that you can answer them.

Evaluate the Information

- Think about what you have read. Does the text make sense? Is it complete?
- **Summarize** the information—give the main points in just a few words.

Functional Reading

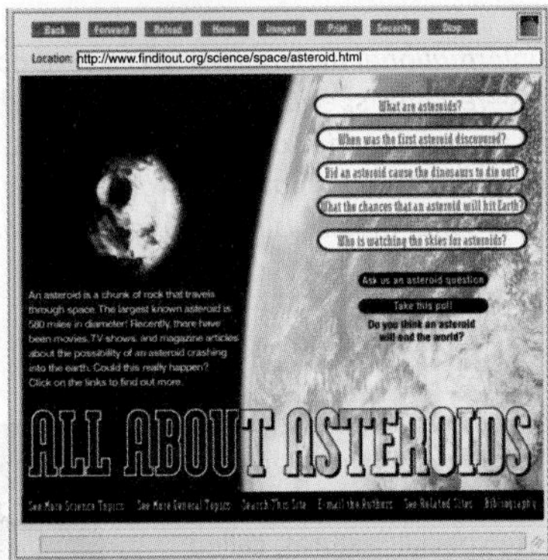

Identify the Audience, Source, and Purpose

- Look for clues that tell you whom the document is for. Is there an address or a title? Does the information in the document affect you?
- Look for clues that tell you who created the document. Is the source likely to be reliable?
- Think about the **purpose** of the document. Is it designed to show you how to do something? to warn you about something? to tell you about community events?

Read Carefully

- Notice **headings** or **rules** that separate one section from another.
- Look for numbers or letters that signal steps in a **sequence.** If you are reading directions, read them all the way through at least once before beginning the steps.
- Examine any charts, photographs, or other **graphics** and their captions.
- **Reread** complex instructions if necessary.

Evaluate the Information

- Think about whether you have found the information you need.
- Look for telephone numbers, street addresses, or e-mail addresses of places where you could find more information.

READING HANDBOOK R3

Reading for Information

Reading informational materials—such as textbooks, magazines, newspapers, and Web pages—requires special skills. As you read these materials, look for text organizers that can guide you to the main ideas, facts, terms, and names. Then think about how the information is organized. Using these strategies will help you read informational materials more quickly and with a clearer understanding.

Text Organizers

Look for headings, large or dark type, pictures, or drawings that signal the most important information on the page. These special features, called **text organizers,** help you understand and remember what you read.

Strategies for Reading

- **A** First, look at the **title** and any **subheads.** These will tell you the main ideas.
- **B** Many textbooks include a list of **objectives** or **key terms** at the start of each lesson. Keep these in mind as you read. They will help you focus on the most important facts and details.
- **C** **Key terms** are often boldfaced or underlined where they first appear in the text. Be sure that you understand what they mean.
- **D** Notice any **special features,** such as extended quotations or sidebar articles. These provide important details and can help you visualize the information.
- **E** Look at the **visuals**—photographs, illustrations, charts, maps, time lines—and read their **captions.** Visuals often give information that is not in the main text.

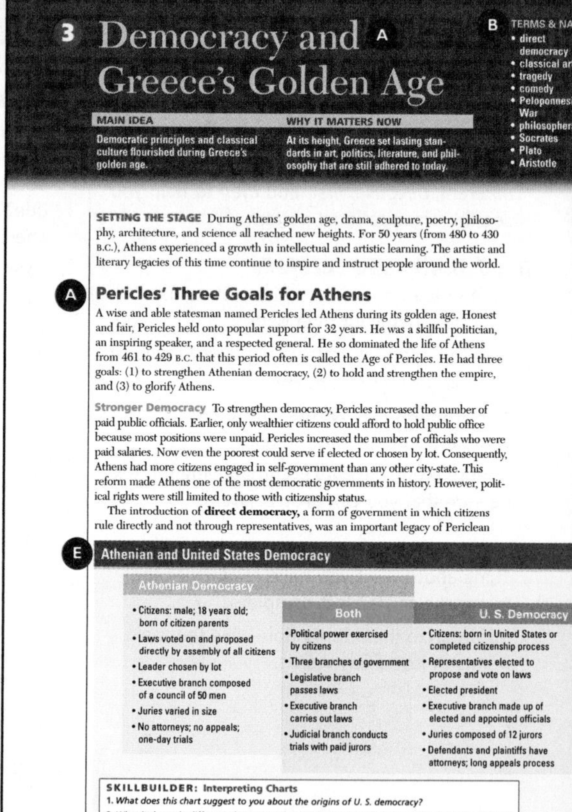

3 Democracy and Greece's Golden Age (A)

MAIN IDEA
Democratic principles and classical culture flourished during Greece's golden age.

WHY IT MATTERS NOW
At its height, Greece set lasting standards in art, politics, literature, and philosophy that are still adhered to today.

(B) TERMS & NAM
- direct democracy
- classical art
- tragedy
- comedy
- Peloponnesia War
- philosophers
- Socrates
- Plato
- Aristotle

SETTING THE STAGE During Athens' golden age, drama, sculpture, poetry, philosophy, architecture, and science all reached new heights. For 50 years (from 480 to 430 B.C.), Athens experienced a growth in intellectual and artistic learning. The artistic and literary legacies of this time continue to inspire and instruct people around the world.

(A) **Pericles' Three Goals for Athens**

A wise and able statesman named Pericles led Athens during its golden age. Honest and fair, Pericles held onto popular support for 32 years. He was a skillful politician, an inspiring speaker, and a respected general. He so dominated the life of Athens from 461 to 429 B.C. that this period often is called the Age of Pericles. He had three goals: (1) to strengthen Athenian democracy, (2) to hold and strengthen the empire, and (3) to glorify Athens.

Stronger Democracy To strengthen democracy, Pericles increased the number of paid public officials. Earlier, only wealthier citizens could afford to hold public office because most positions were unpaid. Pericles increased the number of officials who were paid salaries. Now even the poorest could serve if elected or chosen by lot. Consequently, Athens had more citizens engaged in self-government than any other city-state. This reform made Athens one of the most democratic governments in history. However, political rights were still limited to those with citizenship status.

The introduction of **direct democracy,** a form of government in which citizens rule directly and not through representatives, was an important legacy of Periclean

(E) **Athenian and United States Democracy**

Athenian Democracy	Both	U. S. Democracy
• Citizens: male; 18 years old; born of citizen parents • Laws voted on and proposed directly by assembly of all citizens • Leader chosen by lot • Executive branch composed of a council of 50 men • Juries varied in size • No attorneys; no appeals; one-day trials	• Political power exercised by citizens • Three branches of government • Legislative branch passes laws • Executive branch carries out laws • Judicial branch conducts trials with paid jurors	• Citizens: born in United States or completed citizenship process • Representatives elected to propose and vote on laws • Elected president • Executive branch made up of elected and appointed officials • Juries composed of 12 jurors • Defendants and plaintiffs have attorneys; long appeals process

SKILLBUILDER: Interpreting Charts
1. *What does this chart suggest to you about the origins of U. S. democracy?*
2. *What is the main difference between Athenian democracy and democracy in the United States?*

R4 READING HANDBOOK

More Strategies for Reading Textbooks

- Before you begin the text, read any **questions** that appear at the end of the lesson or chapter. These will help you focus your reading.
- Read slowly and carefully. If you see an unfamiliar word and can't find a definition in the text or in a marginal note, check the **glossary** or a dictionary. Look for **pronunciation guides** as you read.
- Take **notes** as you read. These will help you understand new ideas and terms. Review your notes before a test to jog your memory.
- You may want to take notes in the form of a **graphic organizer,** such as a cause-and-effect chart or a sequence chart. The graphic organizer shown in the example is a comparison-and-contrast chart.

Athens. Few other city-states practiced this style of government. In Athens, male citizens who served in the assembly established all the important government policies that affected the polis. In a speech for the slain soldiers killed in the first year of the Peloponnesian War, Pericles expressed his great pride in Athenian democracy: D

GH HISTORY
uishing
Opinion
ate do you
ericles'
that
emocracy
hands of
people"?

A VOICE FROM THE PAST

Our constitution is called a democracy because power is in the hands not of a minority but of the whole people. When it is a question of settling private disputes, everyone is equal before the law; when it is a question of putting one person before another in positions of public responsibility, what counts is not membership in a particular class, but the actual ability which the man possesses. No one, so long as he has it in him to be of service to the state, is kept in political obscurity because of poverty.

PERICLES, *Funeral Oration*

Athenian Empire Pericles tried to enlarge the wealth and power of Athens. He used the money from the Delian League's treasury to build Athens' 200-ship navy into the strongest in the Mediterranean. A strong navy was important because it helped Athens strengthen the safety of its empire. Athenian prosperity depended on gaining access to its surrounding waterways. It needed overseas trade to obtain supplies of grain and other raw materials.

Glorifying Athens Pericles also used money from the empire to beautify Athens. Without the Delian League's approval, he persuaded the Athenian assembly to vote huge sums of the league's money to buy gold, ivory, and marble. Still more money went to a small army of artisans who worked for 15 years (447–432 B.C.) to build one of architecture's noblest works—the Parthenon.

HISTORY MAKERS

Pericles
494?–429 B.C.

Pericles came from a rich and high-ranking noble family. His aristocratic father had led the Athenian assembly and fought at the Battle of Salamis in the Persian Wars. His mother was the niece of Cleisthenes, an influential statesman.

Well known for his political achievements as a leader of Athens, some historians say Pericles the man was harder to know. One historian wrote,

> [Pericles] no doubt, was a lonely man. Among the politicians, including his supporters, he had no friend. He avoided all social activity . . . [and] he only went out [of his home] for official business. . . .

Greek Styles in Art

The Parthenon, a masterpiece of craftsmanship and design, was not novel in style. Rather, Greek artisans built the 23,000-square-foot building in the traditional style that had been used to create Greek temples for 200 years. In ancient times, this temple built to honor Athena contained examples of Greek art that set standards for future generations of artists around the world.

Greek Sculpture Within the Parthenon stood a giant statue of Athena, the goddess of wisdom and the protector of Athens. Pericles entrusted much of the work on the temple, including the statue of Athena, to the sculptor Phidias (FIDH-ee-uhs). The great statue of the goddess not only contained precious materials such as gold and ivory, it stood 38 feet tall!

Phidias and other sculptors during this golden age aimed to create figures that were graceful, strong, and perfectly formed. Their faces showed neither laughter nor anger, only serenity. Greek sculptors also tried to capture the grace of the idealized human body in motion. Their values of order, balance, and proportion became the standard of what is called **classical art.** C

Classical works such as the Parthenon and the statue of Athena showcased the pride that Athenians had for their city. (See History Through Art, page 122.)

Greek Drama

The Greeks invented drama and built the first theaters in the west. Theatrical productions in Athens were both an expression of civic pride and a tribute to the gods.

Reading a Magazine Article

Strategies for Reading

- **A** Read the **title** and any other **headings** to get an idea of what the article is about and how it is organized.
- **B** As you read the main text, notice any **quotations.** Who is quoted? Is the person a reliable source on the subject?
- **C** Notice text that is set off in some way, such as a passage in a **different typeface.** A quotation or statistic that sums up the article is sometimes presented in this way.
- **D** Study **visuals,** such as graphs, charts, maps, and photographs. Read their captions and make sure you know how they relate to the main text.

A

Summer Jobs Let Teens Cash In

by Kirsti MacPherson
Staff Writer

B "I am so excited to be working this summer," says 15-year-old Brianna Mason. "I already have plans for the money. Some of it I'll save for college, but I'm also going to get some new clothes and CDs."

Like many teenagers, Mason will increase the number of hours she works once summer vacation begins. According to this year's Summer Jobs Survey, conducted by Junior Achievement, Inc., the most popular summer jobs for teens are in retail sales (41 percent of respondents), restaurants and fast-food establishments (20 percent), offices (14 percent), baby-sitting (6 percent), arts and entertainment (4 percent), and manual trades (4 percent). The survey questioned 659 teenagers nationwide.

Teenagers struggle with the desire to spend and the need to save, just as other workers do. The Junior Achievement survey found that students working during the summer saved about a third of their earnings—about 17 times what the typical adult saved! Since parents pay for most food, clothing, and shelter needs, many teens can save for higher education, cars, and other big-ticket items.

A summer job can make a teenager feel independent and accomplished—and tired. "When you work so many hours in the summer, getting back to school is kind of a relief," Mason confesses.

Students working during the summer saved about a third of their earnings. **C**

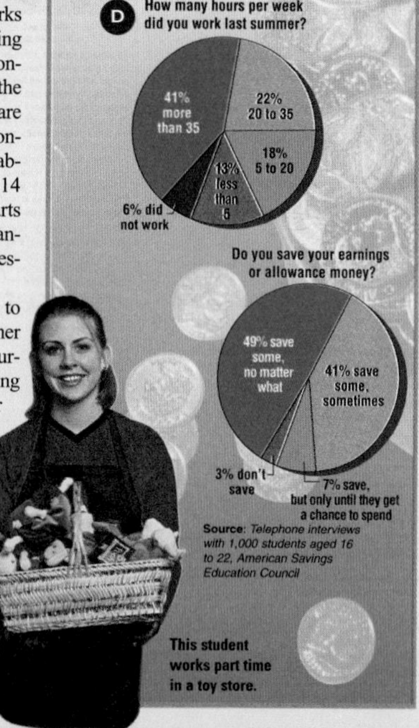

This student works part time in a toy store.

Reading a Web Page

Strategies for Reading

A Look for the page's **Web address,** sometimes called a URL. If you think you will need to return to the page, write down the address or use the Web browser to "bookmark" the page or log it as a "favorite site."

B Read the **title** of the page to find out what topics the page covers. The blue page shown here is a search-engine page. It lists pages corresponding to responses to a student's search. The other page is one of the sites the search engine identified.

C Look for **menu bars** along the top, bottom, or side of the page. These tell you about other parts of the site. Instead of printing out every page of the site, read the text carefully and decide which pages contain information you need.

D Notice any **links** to related pages. Links are sometimes buttons or underlined words.

E Some sites have **interactive areas** where you can ask questions or tell the sites' creators what you think of their work.

READING HANDBOOK R7

Patterns of Organization

Reading any type of writing is easier if you understand how it is organized. A writer organizes ideas in a sequence, or structure, that helps the reader see how the ideas are related. Five important structures are the following:

- main idea and supporting details
- chronological order
- comparison and contrast
- cause and effect
- problem and solution

This page contains an overview of the five structures, which you will learn about in more detail on pages R9–R13. Each type has been represented graphically to help you see how ideas are organized in it.

Main Idea and Supporting Details

The main idea of a paragraph or a longer piece of writing is its most important point. Supporting details give more information about the main idea.

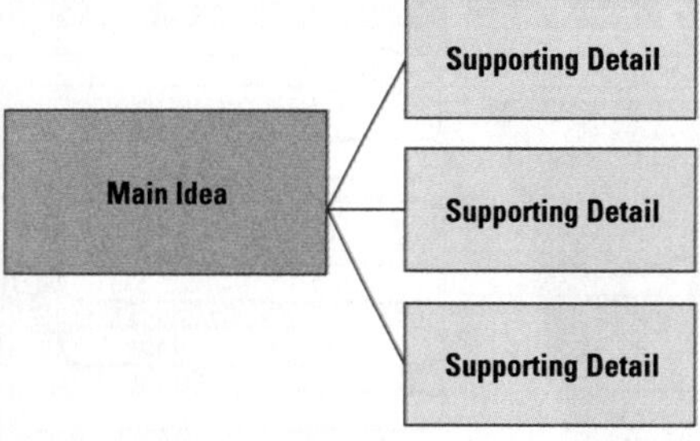

Chronological Order

Writing that is organized in chronological order presents events in the order in which they occur.

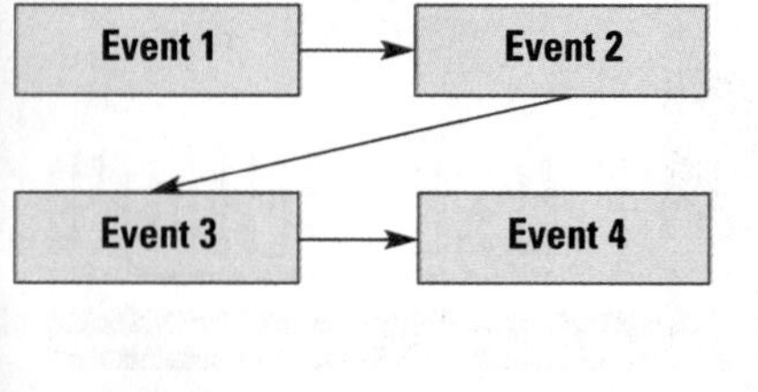

Comparison and Contrast

Comparison-and-contrast writing explains how two or more subjects are similar and how they are different.

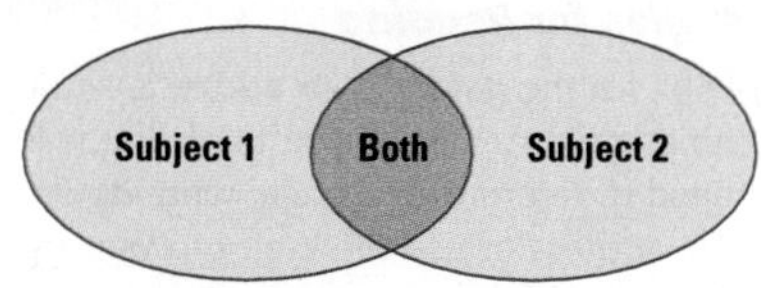

Cause and Effect

Cause-and-effect writing explains relationships between events. A cause is an event that gives rise to another event, called an effect. A cause may have more than one effect, and an effect may have more than one cause.

Single Cause with Multiple Effects

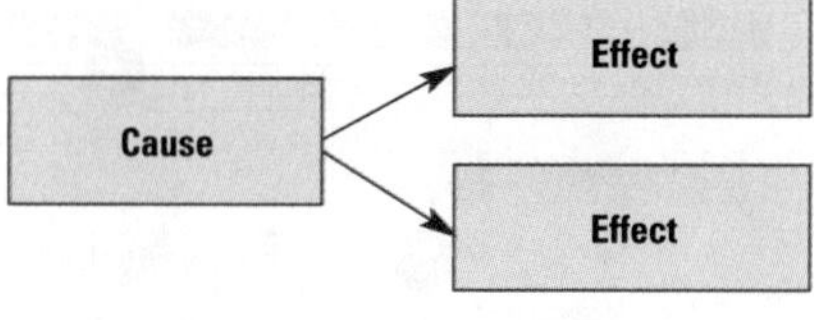

Multiple Causes with Single Effect

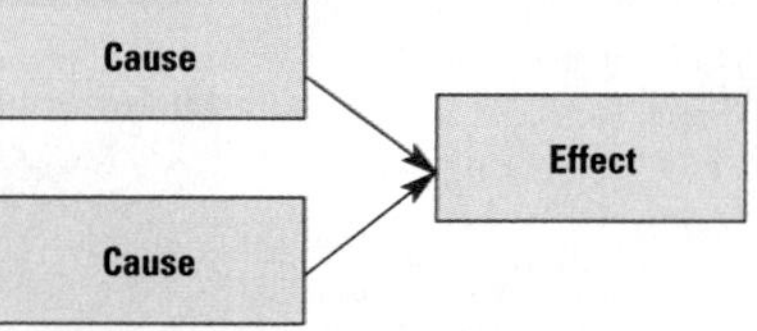

Problem and Solution

This type of writing describes a difficult issue and suggests at least one way of solving it. The writer provides reasons to support his or her solution.

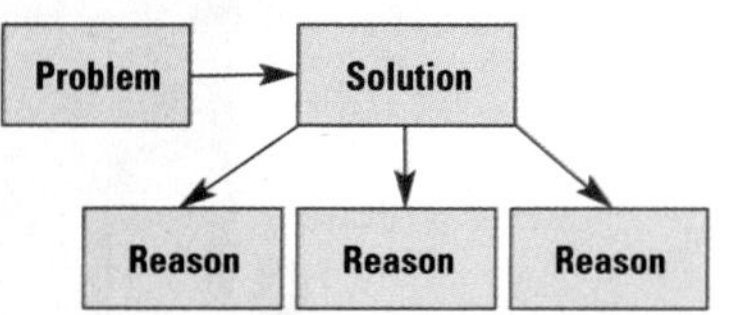

R8 READING HANDBOOK

Main Idea and Supporting Details

The **main idea** of a paragraph is the basic point you should remember from your reading. The **supporting details** give you more information about the main idea. A main idea can be stated directly, or it can be implied. If it is stated, it can appear anywhere in the paragraph. Often it will be the first or the last sentence. An implied main idea is suggested by the details that are provided.

Strategies for Reading

- To find the **main idea,** ask, What is this paragraph about?
- To find **supporting details,** ask, What else do I learn about the main idea?

MODEL

Main Idea in the First Sentence

Main idea

Supporting details

Like his chosen last name, which means "man of steel" in Russian, Joseph Stalin was hard, cold, and dangerous. He began his climb to power in 1922, by installing his followers in key positions. By 1928, he had taken control of the Communist Party. The next year, he sent his main rival, Leon Trotsky, into exile. He then transformed the Soviet Union into a totalitarian state.

MODEL

Main Idea in the Last Sentence

Supporting details

Main idea

A totalitarian government is a dictatorship in which one person has absolute control and one political party rules. The dictator uses propaganda (persuasive messages that often distort the truth) to convince people to support government policies. Citizens are expected to sacrifice their own goals for the good of the state and are severely punished if they show any opposition. A totalitarian government maintains its power by controlling every aspect of its citizens' lives.

MODEL

Implied Main Idea

Implied main idea: Totalitarianism spread across the world during the 20th century.

In the 1920s and 1930s, Benito Mussolini in Italy and Adolf Hitler in Germany began creating their own totalitarian states. Hungary, Poland, Yugoslavia, Albania, Bulgaria, and Romania also fell into the hands of dictators. In 1949, Mao Zedong followed Stalin's example and established a totalitarian dictatorship in the People's Republic of China. Neighboring North Korea became a totalitarian state in 1948 and was ruled by the dictator Kim Il Sung until 1994.

PRACTICE AND APPLY

Less than 1 percent of the German population was made up of Jews. However, the Nazis blamed them for all of Germany's troubles. This led to a wave of anti-Jewish hatred across Germany. Beginning in 1933, the Nazis passed laws depriving Jews of most of their rights. Violence against Jews increased. On the night of November 9, 1938, Nazi mobs attacked Jews in their homes and destroyed thousands of Jewish-owned businesses. This rampage was called ***Kristallnacht*** ("night of broken glass"). The Nazis used a variety of methods in their quest to eliminate Jews from German life.

Read the paragraph above and then do the following activities:

1. Identify the main idea of the paragraph. Is it stated or implied?
2. List at least two details that support or expand on the main idea.

Reading Handbook

PRACTICE AND APPLY
Possible Responses:

1. "The Nazis used a variety of methods in their quest to eliminate Jews from German life"; stated (last sentence)
2. Less than 1 percent of the German population was Jewish, but the Nazis blamed the Jews for all of Germany's troubles; there was a wave of anti-Jewish hatred across Germany; the Nazis passed laws depriving Jews of most of their rights; violence against Jews increased; during the "night of broken glass," Nazi mobs attacked Jews and destroyed thousands of Jewish-owned businesses.

Reading Handbook

Chronological Order

Events discussed in **chronological order,** also called time order, are treated in the order they happen. Historical events are usually presented in chronological order. The steps of a process may also be presented this way.

Strategies for Reading

- Look for the **individual events or steps** in the sequence.
- Look for words or phrases that identify **time,** such as *in a year, three hours earlier, in 1957,* and *later.*
- Look for words that signal **order,** such as *first, afterward, then, before, finally,* and *next.*

MODEL

Time phrases

Event

Order words

The development of language skills is one of the most important differences between humans and other living things. In an important study done in 1957, M. M. Lewis kept a record of his son's progress in understanding and speaking language—specifically, the word *flower.*

The child's mother first named and pointed to different flowers in different situations. Over a period of time, the child watched, listened, pointed, and eventually named flowers himself.

Lewis began the experiment when his son was 16 months and 12 days old. At that time, the mother brought the child close to a bowl of yellow jonquils and said, "Smell the pretty flowers." The child bent over and smelled the flowers, saying, "a . . . a . . . a." The next day, when the child was crawling around the room, his mother said, "Where are the flowers?" The child then crawled toward the jonquils and held out his hand.

Three days later, in a room with pink tulips in a bowl, the mother said, "Baby, where's flowers?" Immediately after, the child pointed to the tulips. Five weeks later, however, the child did not respond to a picture of flowers in a book.

When the child was 18 months and 14 days old, he saw a bowl of hyacinths through a window and responded, "fa, fa." When his mother wheeled him toward a bed of tulips the next day, asking "Where are the flowers?" he repeated "fa, fa" many times. Over the next week and a half, the child looked or reached toward a bowl of irises and a flowering cherry tree, naming both *fa fa.*

After another month had passed, the child followed his mother's instructions to "pick a flower and give it to Daddy." Finally, three months later, aged 22 months and 26 days, the child was able to recognize images of flowers on a sugar cookie and on embroidered slippers and name them with his word for that object—*fa fa.* Although the child could not say *flower,* he recognized flowerlike things—in bowls, in gardens, on trees, and on cookies and shoes. With correction from his parents, the child eventually replaced *fa fa* with the word *flower.*

PRACTICE AND APPLY

Reread the model and then do the following activities:

1. List at least six words or phrases in the model that show order or time. Do not include those that have been identified for you.
2. Draw a time line beginning when the child was 16 months and 12 days old and ending when he was 22 months and 26 days old. Chart each event in his acquisition of language as described in the model.

R10 READING HANDBOOK

PRACTICE AND APPLY
Possible Responses:

1. Three days later, Immediately after, Five weeks later, 18 months and 14 days old, the next day, Over the next week and a half, After another month had passed, Finally, three months later, aged 22 months and 26 days
2. 16 months 12 days—smells yellow flowers, says "a . . . a . . . a";
   16 months 13 days—crawls toward yellow flowers;
   16 months 16 days—points to pink flowers;
   17 months 23 days—does not respond to picture of flowers;
   18 months 14 days—says "fa fa" to flowers seen through window;
   18 months 15 days—repeats "fa fa" to tulips in garden;
   about 18 months 26 days—identifies irises and cherry blossoms on tree as *fa fa*;
   about 19 months 26 days—picks flower on command;
   22 months 26 days—recognizes flowers on cookie and slippers as *fa fa*

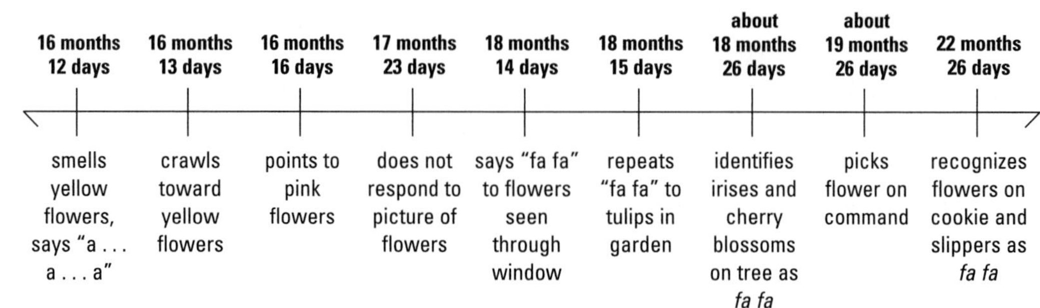

Comparison and Contrast

Comparison-and-contrast writing explains how subjects are alike and different. This type of writing is usually organized by subject or by feature. In **subject organization,** the writer discusses one subject, then discusses the other. In **feature organization,** the writer compares a feature of one subject with the same feature of the other, then compares another feature of both, and so on.

Strategies for Reading

- Look for words and phrases that signal **comparisons,** such as *like, similarly, both, also,* and *in the same way.*
- Look for words and phrases that signal **contrasts,** such as *unlike, on the other hand, in contrast,* and *however.*

MODEL

Whales are surprising creatures. Totally aquatic mammals, they belong to the order Cetacea, along with porpoises, dolphins, and narwhals. Cetaceans are divided into two main suborders, Mysticeti (baleen whales) and Odontoceti (toothed whales). Baleen whales include blue whales, humpback whales, right whales, and gray whales. Toothed whales include beaked whales, dolphins, porpoises, and narwhals.

Subjects being compared

Baleen whales and toothed whales have many similar habits and behaviors. They live in oceans, seas, and rivers. Both types of whales often travel in groups, called schools or pods. They rise to the surface of the water to breathe through blowholes on the top of their head. Out of the water they are unable to move, and their lungs may be crushed by the weight of their bodies.

Comparison words and phrases

Baleen whales and toothed whales have a number of physical differences, however. Adult baleen whales have baleen instead of teeth. Baleen is a thick curtain of hornlike plates that hang down from the roof of the whales' mouth. Some baleen whales have teeth before birth, but these disappear as the young whale grows. The baleen acts as a filter that catches the small animals and plants that make up the whales' diet. Toothed whales, on the other hand, always have teeth. These teeth have sharp edges that are good for slicing and tearing the toothed whales' food—large fish, squid, and other whales.

Contrast words and phrases

Baleen whales have two blowholes. In contrast, toothed whales have only one blowhole. Baleen whale females tend to be larger than the males, while the opposite is true for toothed whales. Baleen whales have large tongues; toothed whales have small tongues. Unlike baleen whales, which usually have four digits in their flippers, toothed whales always have five digits.

Toothed whales figure out where they are by using reflected sound waves—a process called echolocation. However, baleen whales do not seem to navigate this way. Because whales spend much of their lives underwater, they are difficult to study, and they remain a fascinating mystery.

PRACTICE AND APPLY

Reread the model and then do the following activities:

1. Tell whether the model is organized by subject or by feature.
2. Draw a chart or a Venn diagram that shows at least three features that the writer compares or contrasts. (See the top of page R8 for an example of a Venn diagram.)
3. List at least six of the comparison and contrast words and phrases that the writer uses.

PRACTICE AND APPLY
Possible Responses:

1. feature
2.

Baleen whales
- have baleen
- eat small animals and plants
- two blowholes
- females tend to be larger
- large tongues
- usually four digits in flippers
- don't seem to use echolocation

Both
- aquatic mammals
- travel in groups
- rise to the surface to breathe
- can't move when out of the water

Toothed whales
- have teeth
- eat large fish, squid, and other whales
- one blowhole
- males tend to be larger
- small tongues
- always five digits in flippers
- use echolocation

3. similar, Both, differences, however, instead of, but, on the other hand, In contrast, while the opposite is true, Unlike, However

Cause and Effect

Cause-and-effect writing explains relationships between events. A **cause** is an event that brings about another event. An **effect** is something that happens as a result of the cause. A piece of cause-and-effect writing is usually organized in one of three ways:

1. starting with a cause or causes and explaining the effect(s)
2. starting with an effect or effects and explaining the cause(s)
3. describing a chain of causes and effects

Strategies for Reading

- To find the **effect** or **effects,** ask, What happened?
- To find the **cause** or **causes,** ask, Why did it happen?
- Look for words and phrases that signal **relationships between events,** such as *because, as a result, for that reason, so, consequently,* and *since.*

MODEL

Causes

Signal words

Effects

In the 1800s, new approaches to manufacturing caused dramatic changes around the world.

These sweeping changes, usually called the Industrial Revolution, began in the 1700s in Great Britain. First, inventors discovered ways to generate power by using the energy in flowing water and plentiful supplies of coal. They then created power-driven machinery. Because of these inventions, it was possible to create large quantities of manufactured goods.

As a result of improved nutrition, sanitation, and medical care, people lived longer, healthier lives. The resulting increase in population led to an increase in the number of workers available to work in the new factories. These businesses therefore grew, and their owners were able to build more factories, fund the invention of more machines, and help industrialization spread.

One of the places where industrialization took hold was New England. This occurred because the United States had the necessary resources—rushing rivers, coal deposits, and many immigrants who were willing to work.

The first industry to be mechanized in the United States was the production of cloth. Samuel Slater, a British immigrant, established the first successful cloth mill in Rhode Island in 1793. Twenty years later, three Boston businessmen mechanized the entire process of manufacturing cloth. In 1822 they built a factory in Lowell, Massachusetts. Because of that factory, Lowell changed from a quiet village into a busy manufacturing center in only a few years.

Industrialization soon spread to other basic industries. Inventors discovered how to drill for oil and change it into fuel. A steel-making method called the Bessemer process was used to make steel from iron and coal cheaply and efficiently. These new uses for natural resources had lasting effects on the United States. A national network of railroads was established, new buildings and bridges sprang up, and new products—such as the tin-plated steel can, barbed wire, farm machinery, and the automobile—were invented.

PRACTICE AND APPLY

Reread the model and then do the following activities:

1. Identify the type of organization used in the model. (Choose from the three types listed at the beginning of this page.)
2. Create a list or chart that shows at least four causes mentioned in the model, along with their effects.
3. List at least four words and phrases the writer uses to signal causes and effects.

PRACTICE AND APPLY
Possible Responses:

1. a chain of causes and effects
2.

Cause	Effect
new approaches to manufacturing	dramatic changes around the world
power-driven machinery created	possible to create many manufactured goods
improved nutrition sanitation, medical care	People lived longer.
population increased	more workers
businesses grew	owners could build more factories, spread industrialization
United States had resources for industrialization	Industrialization took hold there.
factory built in Lowell	Lowell became busy manufacturing center
Inventors found new uses for natural resources.	U.S. changed forever—railroads, buildings, bridges, new products

3. caused, Because of, As a result of, resulting, led to, therefore, because, had lasting effects

Problem and Solution

Problem-solution writing clearly presents the various aspects of a problem and offers a solution. Logical arguments are used to convince readers that the proposed solution will solve the problem.

Strategies for Reading

- To find the **problem,** ask, What is this writing about?
- To find the **solution,** ask, What suggestions does the writer offer to remedy the problem?
- Look for the **reasons** the writer gives to support the solution. Is the thinking behind them logical? Is the evidence presented strong and convincing?

MODEL

The sun rises over the Atlantic Ocean. Peach-colored rays shimmer on the crests of the waves as they tumble against the shore. Out for a brisk morning walk along the beach, you stop to enjoy the beauty—until you stumble over a discarded soft-drink can and step down hard on a sharp bottle cap. As you gaze along the sand, you wonder if it has been snowing, until you realize that those white patches are scraps of paper and plastic left by thoughtless picnickers. Our parks and beaches are becoming garbage dumps.

Problem

It takes more than one person to create so much litter, and it will take more than one person to clean it up. One solution is to organize a group of friends and neighbors into a "save-our-favorite-spot committee." There are many advantages to this plan.

Solution

First, almost anything is more fun if it's done with people you know and like. You might want to have everyone wear the same color T-shirt or a funny hat to draw the group members together. Second, although picking up trash is work, you can make a game of it by singing songs, telling jokes, or offering prizes to the people who find the most disgusting or the most creative pieces of trash.

Reason

Also, when a group of people take responsibility for their environment, other people notice. No one may pay attention to a solitary person picking up bottles and cans and papers, but one or two dozen happy, energetic people all working together and obviously having fun are going to send a strong message to anyone who sees them. "I don't want to be left out," many onlookers will think.

The first step in organizing such a cleanup group is identifying a park or beach or river that has become overrun with litter. Be sure to choose an area that can be cleared of debris in several hours. It's more important to do a thorough job of cleaning a local playground than to barely make a mark on a national forest.

Start out by recruiting people who you know well and who share your concern for the environment. If each of those people asks one or two others along, you'll soon have a large, willing work crew. You might even make some new friends.

Nothing succeeds like success, and your cleanup efforts will give rise to others. Go ahead and take the first step.

PRACTICE AND APPLY

Reread the model and then do the following activities:

1. List two reasons the writer gives to support the plan.
2. The fifth and sixth paragraphs give tips on how to organize a cleanup group. State two of the tips the writer suggests.

Reading Handbook

PRACTICE AND APPLY
Possible Responses:

1. 1) Almost anything is more fun if it's done with people you know and like; 2) Although picking up trash is work, you can make a game of it; 3) When a group of people takes responsibility for their environment, other people notice; 4) Your cleanup efforts will give rise to others.
2. 1) Identify a site that has litter; 2) Choose an area that can be cleaned up within several hours; 3) Ask for help from people you know well and who care about the environment; 4) Have each person ask one or two more friends.

PRACTICE AND APPLY
Possible Responses:
1. to show the stops on the STA elevated/subway system
2. The station is wheelchair accessible when an agent is on duty.
3. Patrick and Halley's Square
4. north and south
5. No; both stations are closed on Sundays.

Reading Handbook

Functional Reading

Functional reading is reading to gain certain information, such as instructions for doing something. When you read a map, a memo, or a product manual, you are engaged in functional reading. These examples show how you can improve your functional-reading skills.

Transit Map

Strategies for Reading

A. Read the **title** to learn what the map shows.

B. Examine the **legend,** sometimes called a **key,** to find out what the symbols on the map mean.

C. Study **geographic labels,** such as station and town names, so that you will know the specific stops on each route.

D. Use the **compass rose** to determine direction. Some maps also include a **scale** to help you determine distance.

PRACTICE AND APPLY

Study the map and answer these questions:

1. What is the purpose of this map?
2. Explain what the symbols [station] and [wheelchair] mean when used together.
3. Which stations on the Blue Line are accessible to commuters who use wheelchairs?
4. Does the Purple Line run north and south or east and west?
5. Is it possible to take the Orange Line from Henry Street to Anthony Street on a Sunday night? Why or why not?

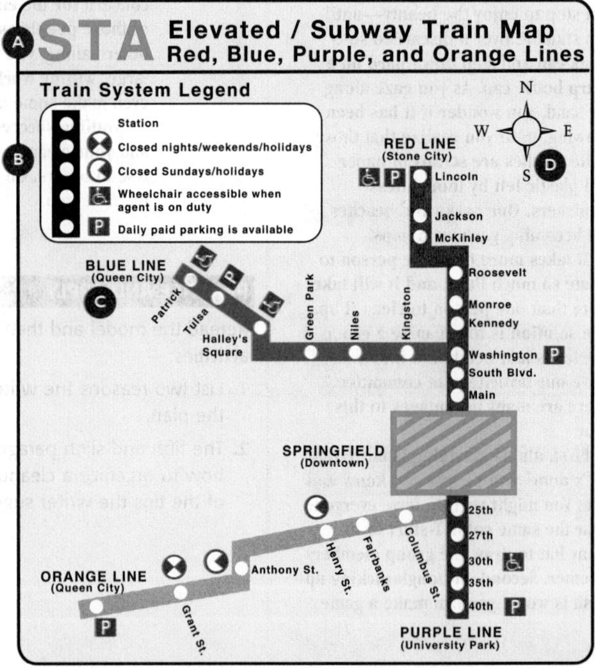

Workplace Document

Strategies for Reading

A Read the **title** to find out what the document is about. This document is a page from an employee manual.

B Notice any **introductory information** that tells who created the document or whom the document is for.

C Read any **charts** or other graphics carefully. A chart's **title** may be in the top row, in the column on the left, or in both places. The title may be in a different type size, color, or style.

D Look for **details** that explain what the document creator wants you to do.

E If you don't understand certain **terms** in the document, try to figure them out by analyzing their context (the words and sentences around the unknown terms), by breaking the words into parts, or by looking them up in a dictionary.

PRACTICE AND APPLY

Reread the document and answer these questions:

1. Who created this document?
2. Whom is the document for?
3. What is the purpose of the document?
4. What does *troubleshooting* mean?
5. According to the document, what should you do if the words you type do not appear on your computer screen?

E

A Computer Troubleshooting Guide

B All employees of the **Graziano Corporation** have access to the Computer Help Desk at extension 4315. If you have a problem with your computer or monitor, please follow these steps **BEFORE** calling the Help Desk.

Thank you,
The Help Desk Staff

C **Problem**	**What to check**
Nothing appears on computer monitor.	• Check that the power cord is properly connected. • Make sure the power switch is in the "On" position.
POWER and POWER SAVING lights are flashing.	• The monitor may have failed. Call the Help Desk immediately.
Picture is too dark.	• Adjust the dial marked "Brightness," located directly beneath the screen.
Picture is fuzzy.	• Adjust the dial marked "Contrast," located directly beneath the screen.
Picture bounces, or a wavy line moves through picture.	• Move electrical devices (heaters, fans, etc.) and magnets away from the computer. D • If there is another computer in your workstation, move it away from this computer. • Move the computer away from the wall. Electrical wiring in the wall may be causing interference.
Typed words do not appear on screen.	• Make sure the keyboard and the computer are properly connected at both points.
E-mail program refuses to accept my password.	• Be sure you are entering the correct password. • Passwords are case sensitive. The computer does not consider a password in lowercase letters (jsmith430) the same as a password in capital letters (JSMITH430). Check the "Caps Lock" light in the upper right corner of your keyboard. If the light is on, press the "Caps Lock" button once and reenter your password.

Reading Handbook

PRACTICE AND APPLY
Possible Responses:

1. the Help Desk staff
2. employees of the Graziano Corporation
3. to explain what employees should do if they have certain problems with their computers
4. getting rid of problems
5. Make sure the keyboard and the computer are properly connected at both points.

Reading Handbook

Enriching Your Vocabulary

Even the best readers sometimes see unfamiliar words. These tips will help you figure out the meaning of a challenging word or phrase.

Use Context Clues

The **context** of a word consists of the punctuation marks, words, sentences, and paragraphs that surround the word. A word's context can give you important clues about its meaning.

> When I saw that my sister had spilled nail polish on my new jacket, I wasn't just angry—I was **apoplectic.** "Cindy! Get in here right now!" I yelled.

You can figure out from the context that *apoplectic* means "enraged" or "extremely angry."

See page 674 for more information on context clues, including definition, restatement, example, comparison, contrast, and inference clues.

Break Words into Parts

Breaking a word into its parts can help you understand it. When you see an unfamiliar word, try these strategies:

- Look for any prefixes or suffixes. Then remove them to try to isolate the **root**—the word part that contains the core meaning.
- Try to think of other words containing each prefix, suffix, or root. Think about what those words mean. Do they have anything in common?
- Consider the way the word is used in the sentence. Use the context and the word parts to make a logical guess about its meaning.
- Consult a dictionary to see whether your guess is correct.

Many words have roots that come from older languages, such as Greek, Latin, and Old English. Knowing the meaning of a root can help you determine the meaning of an unfamiliar word.

Root	Meaning	Examples
ast(e)r (Greek)	star	asterisk, astronomer
bibl (Greek)	book	bible, bibliography
dynam (Greek)	power, force	dynamic, dynamite
aud (Latin)	hear	audible, auditorium
fin (Latin)	limit, end	final, finished
flor (Latin)	flower	floral, florist
gress (Latin)	step	progress, regression
lin (Old English)	flax	linen, linseed
hus (Old English)	house	husband, husbandry
mer(e) (Old English)	sea, pool	mermaid, merman

A **prefix** is a word part that appears at the beginning of a word.

Prefix	Meaning	Examples
inter-	among, between	international, Internet
mis-	bad, badly, wrong	misfire, misguided
multi-	many, much	multicolored, multimillionaire
re-	again	renew, refreshing
trans-	across	transatlantic, transcontinental
un-	not	undo, unfinished

A **suffix** is a word part that appears at the end of a word.

Suffix	Meaning	Examples
-est	most	coldest, fastest
-hood	state or quality of	motherhood, neighborhood
-ish	relating to	childish, selfish
-ize	to make	computerize, standardize
-y	being, having	jumpy, sunny

Some words come from mythology (ancient legends and stories).

Your behavior is **narcissistic.** Please stop admiring yourself in the mirror!

Aunt Amanda has the **Midas touch.** She has started three businesses, all of which have made money.

Francine, our hockey goalie, looks like a **Valkyrie** when she puts on her helmet and padding. I wouldn't dare get in her way!

You can figure out these sentences quite easily if you are familiar with mythology. Narcissus was a character in Greek and Roman legend who fell in love with his own reflection. Midas was a mythical king who turned everything he touched into gold. Valkyries were women in Norse myths who rode onto battlefields and guarded the lives of warriors. When you see a word that you think may come from a myth or legend, use a dictionary to confirm your guess.

Understand Analogies

An **analogy** is a comparison between two things that are similar in some way. Analogies are sometimes used in nonfiction when unfamiliar subjects or ideas are explained in terms of familiar ones. Analogies often appear on tests as well, usually in a format like this:

BEGIN : END : : A) complete : total
B) start : continue
C) last : only
D) create : destroy
E) finish : final

Follow these steps to determine the correct answer.

- Read the part in capital letters as *"Begin* is to *end* as . . ."
- Read the answer choices as *"complete* is to *total," "start* is to *continue,"* and so on.
- Ask yourself how the words *begin* and *end* are related. (They are opposites, or antonyms.)
- Ask yourself which of the choices shows the same relationship. (*Complete* and *total* are synonyms, not antonyms. *Start* and *continue* aren't antonyms, either. *Last* and *only* don't have opposite meanings, and neither do *finish* and *final.* Only *create* and *destroy* are opposites, so the answer is D.)

Here are some relationships that are often expressed in analogies.

Relationship	Example
Actor to action	WOLF : HOWL
Part to whole	MUSICIAN : ORCHESTRA
Word to synonym	FRIENDLY : PLEASANT
Word to antonym	BEGIN : END
Item to category	BRACELET : JEWELRY
Worker to tool	ARTIST : PAINTBRUSH
Action to object	READ : BOOK
Time sequence	DAWN : DUSK

Understand Denotations and Connotations

A word's **denotation** is its dictionary definition. Its **connotations** are the thoughts and feelings that the word evokes in people's minds. Good readers know that words can have precise shades of meaning. Make sure that you understand a word's connotations as well as denotations when you read it or use it in your writing.

Positive	Neutral	Negative
aroma	smell	stench
exotic	unusual	bizarre
bright, eye-catching	colorful	gaudy, garish, flashy

Learn Academic Vocabulary

Science, mathematics, and history have their own technical or specialized vocabularies. Use context clues and reference tools to figure out the meanings of specialized words.

This chemistry experiment will show you how to use a **catalyst,** a substance that speeds up a chemical reaction without being consumed itself.

If you cannot determine a word's meaning from its context, look for a definition or restatement of the word within the text. You can also consult a dictionary, a glossary, or an encyclopedia.

READING HANDBOOK R17

1 The Writing Process

Different writers use different processes. Try out different strategies and figure out what works best for you. For some assignments, it is best to start by figuring out what you need to end up with, make a plan or outline, and stick to it. Other writing assignments may be more successful if you start by writing everything you know about the topic, allow things to get messy, and then reshape and revise the writing so it fits the assignment. Try both approaches and get to know yourself as a writer.

Also consider whether the assignment is high-stakes or low-stakes writing. When the success of the piece is very important, such as in a test, you might choose to focus on meeting the requirements or criteria of the assignment. When the purpose of the writing is to develop your ideas, there is more opportunity to experiment and take risks. Take into account the time factor as well. In a timed writing test, you may not have time to explore and revise.

Correct grammar and spelling are very important in your final product. You don't need to focus on these as you shape your ideas and draft your piece, but be sure you allow time for a careful edit before turning in your final piece.

1.1 Prewriting

In the prewriting stage, you explore your ideas and discover what you want to write about.

Finding Ideas for Writing

Try one or more of the following techniques to help you find a writing topic.

Personal Techniques

- Practice imaging, or trying to remember mainly sensory details about a subject—its look, sound, feel, taste, and smell.
- Complete a knowledge inventory to discover what you already know about a subject.
- Browse through magazines, newspapers, and on-line bulletin boards for ideas.
- Start a clip file of articles that you want to save for future reference. Be sure to label each clip with source information.

Sharing Techniques

- With a group, brainstorm a topic by trying to come up with as many ideas as you can without stopping to critique or examine them.
- Interview someone who knows a great deal about a subject.

Writing Techniques

- After freewriting on a subject, try looping, or choosing your best idea for more freewriting. Repeat the loop at least once.
- Make a list to help you organize ideas, examine them, or identify areas for further research.

Graphic Techniques

- Create a pro-and-con chart to compare the positive and negative aspects of an idea or a course of action.
- Use a cluster map or tree diagram to explore subordinate ideas that relate to a general subject or central idea.

Determining Your Purpose

Your purpose for writing may be to express yourself, to entertain, to describe, to explain, to analyze, or to persuade. To clarify it, ask yourself questions like these:

- Why did I choose to write about my topic?
- What aspects of the topic mean the most to me?
- What do I want others to think or feel after they read my writing?

LINK TO LITERATURE One purpose for writing is to express an opinion. For example, Thomas More wrote *Utopia* (page 794) to criticize the division between the wealthy and the poor in 16th-century Europe.

Identifying Your Audience

Knowing who will read your writing can help you focus your topic and choose relevant details. As you think about your readers, ask yourself questions like these:

- What does my audience already know about my topic?
- What will they be most interested in?
- What language is most appropriate for this audience?

 Drafting

In the drafting stage, you put your ideas on paper and allow them to develop and change as you write.

Two broad approaches to this stage are discovery drafting and planned drafting.

Discovery drafting is a good approach when you are not quite sure what you think about your subject. You just plunge into your draft and let your feelings and ideas lead you where they will. After finishing a discovery draft, you may decide to start another draft, do more prewriting, or revise your first draft.

Planned drafting may work better for research reports, critical reviews, and other kinds of formal writing. Try making a writing plan or a scratch outline before you begin drafting. Then, as you write, you can fill in the details.

LINK TO LITERATURE Rarely does a successful writer achieve a final manuscript without several attempts and rewrites. Leo Tolstoy often relied on his wife, Sonya, for help with his manuscripts. As Sonya copied Leo's works in progress, she also offered opinions and suggestions on how to improve each draft. An excerpt from her diary appears on page 993.

1.3 Revising, Editing, and Proofreading

The changes you make in your writing during this stage usually fall into three categories: revising for content, revising for structure, and proofreading to correct mistakes in mechanics.

Use the questions that follow to assess problems and determine what changes would improve your work.

Revising for Content

- Does my writing have a main idea or central focus? Is my thesis clear?
- Have I incorporated adequate detail? Where might I include a telling detail, revealing statistic, or vivid example?
- Is any material unnecessary, irrelevant, or confusing?

WRITING TIP Be sure to consider the needs of your audience as you answer the questions under Revising for Content and Revising for Structure. For example, before you can determine whether any of your material is unnecessary or irrelevant, you need to identify what your audience already knows.

Revising for Structure

- Is my writing unified? Do all ideas and supporting details pertain to my main idea or advance my thesis?
- Is my writing clear and coherent? Is the flow of sentences and paragraphs smooth and logical?
- Do I need to add transitional words, phrases, or sentences to make the relationships among ideas clearer?
- Are my sentences well constructed? What sentences might I combine to improve the grace and rhythm of my writing?

Proofreading to Correct Mistakes in Grammar, Usage, and Mechanics

When you are satisfied with your revision, proofread your paper, looking for mistakes in grammar, usage, and mechanics. You may want

WRITING HANDBOOK R19

Writing Handbook

to do this several times, looking for different types of mistakes each time. The following checklist may help.

Sentence Structure and Agreement
- Are there any run-on sentences or sentence fragments?
- Do all verbs agree with their subjects?
- Do all pronouns agree with their antecedents?
- Are verb tenses correct and consistent?

Forms of Words
- Do adverbs and adjectives modify the appropriate words?
- Are all forms of *be* and other irregular verbs used correctly?
- Are pronouns used correctly?
- Are comparative and superlative forms of adjectives correct?

Capitalization, Punctuation, and Spelling
- Is any punctuation mark missing or not needed?
- Are all words spelled correctly?
- Are all proper nouns and all proper adjectives capitalized?

WRITING TIP For help with identifying and correcting problems that are listed in the proofreading checklist, see the Grammar Handbook, pages R55–R90.

You might wish to mark changes on your paper by using the proofreading symbols shown in the chart below.

Proofreading Symbols

Symbol	Meaning	Symbol	Meaning
∧	Add letters or words.	/	Make a capital letter lowercase.
⊙	Add a period.	¶	Begin a new paragraph.
≡	Capitalize a letter.	ꝭ	Delete letters or words.
⁀‿	Close up space.	∿	Switch the positions of letters or words.
∧,	Add a comma.		

1.4 Publishing and Reflecting

Always consider sharing your finished writing with a wider audience. Reflecting on your writing is another good way to bring closure to a project.

Creative Publishing Ideas

Following are some ideas for publishing and sharing your writing:

- Post your writing on an electronic bulletin board or send it to others via e-mail.
- Create a multimedia presentation and share it with classmates.
- Publish your writing in a school newspaper or literary magazine.
- Present your work orally in a report, a speech, a reading, or a dramatic performance.
- Submit your writing to a local newspaper or a magazine that publishes student writing.
- Form a writing exchange group with other students.

WRITING TIP You might work with other students to publish an anthology of class writing. Then exchange anthologies with another class or another school. Reading the work of other student writers will help you get ideas for new writing projects and find ways to improve your work.

Reflecting on Your Writing

Think about your writing process and whether you would like to add what you have written to your portfolio. You might attach a note in which you answer questions like these:

- What did I learn about myself and my subject through this writing project?
- Which parts of the writing process did I most and least enjoy?
- As I wrote, what was my biggest problem? How did I solve it?
- What did I learn that I can use the next time I write?

R20 WRITING HANDBOOK

 Using Peer Response

Peer response consists of the suggestions and comments your peers or classmates make about your writing.

You can ask a peer reader for help at any point in the writing process. For example, your peers can help you develop a topic, narrow your focus, discover confusing passages, or organize your writing.

Questions for Your Peer Readers

You can help your peer readers provide you with the most useful kinds of feedback by following these guidelines:

- Tell readers where you are in the writing process. Are you still trying out ideas, or have you completed a draft?
- Ask questions that will help you get specific information about your writing. Open-ended questions that require more than yes-or-no answers are more likely to give you information you can use as you revise.
- Give your readers plenty of time to respond thoughtfully to your writing.
- Encourage your readers to be honest when they respond to your work. It's OK if you don't agree with them—you always get to decide which changes to make.

Tips for Being a Peer Reader

Follow these guidelines when you respond to someone else's work:

- Respect the writer's feelings.
- Make sure you understand what kind of feedback the writer is looking for, and then respond accordingly.
- Use "I" statements, such as "I like . . . ," "I think . . . ," or "It would help me if . . . ." Remember that your impressions and opinions may not be the same as someone else's.

WRITING TIP Writers are better able to absorb criticism of their work if they first receive positive feedback. When you act as a peer reader, try to start your review by telling something you like about the piece.

The chart below explains different peer-response techniques to use when you are ready to share your work.

Peer-Response Techniques

Sharing Use this when you are just exploring ideas or when you want to celebrate the completion of a piece of writing.

- *Will you please read or listen to my writing without criticizing or making suggestions afterward?*

Summarizing Use this when you want to know if your main idea or goals are clear.

- *What do you think I'm saying? What's my main idea or message?*

Replying Use this strategy when you want to make your writing richer by adding new ideas.

- *What are your ideas about my topic? What do you think about what I have said in my piece?*

Responding to Specific Features Use this when you want a quick overview of the strengths and weaknesses of your writing.

- *Are the ideas supported with enough examples? Did I persuade you? Is the organization clear enough for you to follow the ideas?*

Telling Use this to find out which parts of your writing are affecting readers the way you want and which parts are confusing.

- *What did you think or feel as you read my words? Would you show me which passage you were reading when you had that response?*

Writing Handbook

WRITING HANDBOOK R21

2 Building Blocks of Good Writing

Whatever your purpose in writing, you need to capture your readers' interest, organize your ideas well, and present your thoughts clearly. Giving special attention to some particular parts of a story or an essay can make your writing more enjoyable and more effective.

2.1 Introductions

When you flip through a magazine trying to decide which articles to read, the opening paragraph is often critical. If it does not grab your attention, you are likely to turn the page.

Kinds of Introductions

Here are some introduction techniques that can capture a reader's interest:

- Make a surprising statement
- Provide a description
- Pose a question
- Relate an anecdote
- Address the reader directly
- Begin with a thesis statement

Make a Surprising Statement Beginning with a startling statement or an interesting fact can capture your reader's curiosity about the subject, as in the model below.

MODEL
September should be the seventh month, and October should be the eighth. Any Latin student knows that *septem* is "seven" and *octo* is "eight." Where did the calendar makers go wrong? The truth is that when the months acquired their names, during Roman times, the year started in March.

Provide a Description A vivid description sets a mood and brings a scene to life for your readers. Here, details about a lion observing possible prey set the tone for an essay on survival in the wild.

MODEL
Cool and cunning eyes followed the impala herd from a sturdy low-slung tree branch. The young female lion watched hungrily to see whether any of the impalas might be sickly or slower than the others. She kept every muscle quiet, though tense and ready to spring if an opportunity arose.

Pose a Question Beginning with a question can make your reader want to read on to find the answer. The following introduction asks questions about how the Holocaust could have happened.

MODEL
How could people and, indeed, entire nations stand by and allow the Holocaust to happen? As the Nazis rounded up and destroyed the Jewish populations of countless cities and towns throughout Europe, how could so many otherwise decent citizens merely watch in silence?

Relate an Anecdote Beginning with a brief anecdote, or story, can hook readers and help you make a point in a dramatic way. The anecdote below introduces an essay about the downside of self-closing shoe straps.

MODEL
My five-year old nephew, Ali, has never tied a shoelace. All his shoes have self-closing straps. Little boys already suffer because they are encouraged to develop large muscles by throwing and climbing, while little girls gain dexterity by dressing dolls and coloring in coloring books. Ali's younger sister, who has learned to tie bows on her doll clothes, may well have to stick around to tie the bows on Ali's gift packages and tie his bow tie for his tuxedo.

R22 WRITING HANDBOOK

Address the Reader Directly Speaking directly to readers establishes a friendly, informal tone and involves them in your topic.

MODEL
If you've ever wondered how to avoid using pesticides in your garden, you can get answers from Natural Gardens, Inc. It's easy to protect the environment and have pest-free plants.

Begin with a Thesis Statement A thesis statement expressing a paper's main idea may be woven into both the beginning and the end of nonfiction writing. The following is a thesis statement that introduces an essay on the relationship between caring for pets and caring for children.

MODEL
Pet owners who are casual about their pets' health and safety are likely to be the same ones who are casual about the health and safety of their children.

WRITING TIP In order to write the best introduction for your paper, you may want to try more than one of the methods and then decide which is the most effective for your purpose and audience.

2.2 Paragraphs

A paragraph is made up of sentences that work together to develop an idea or accomplish a purpose. Whether or not it contains a topic sentence stating the main idea, a good paragraph must have unity and coherence.

Unity

A paragraph has unity when all the sentences support and develop one stated or implied idea. Use the following techniques to create unity in your paragraphs.

Write a Topic Sentence A topic sentence states the main ideas of a paragraph; all other sentences in the paragraph provide supporting details. A topic sentence is often the first sentence in a paragraph. However, it may also appear later in the paragraph or at the end, to summarize or reinforce the main idea, as shown in the model that follows.

MODEL
Plastic that does not rust, rot, or shatter is useful, of course, but does add to the ever-increasing problems of waste disposal. It is possible to add chemicals to plastic that make it dissolvable by other chemicals. There are plastics that slowly disintegrate in sunlight. Biodegradable plastic is available and should be preferred over nonbiodegradable plastic.

Relate All Sentences to an Implied Main Idea A paragraph can be unified without a topic sentence as long as every sentence supports the implied, or unstated, main idea. In the example below, all the sentences work together to create a unified impression of a swim meet.

MODEL
The swimmers were lined up along the edge of the pool. Toes curled over the edge, arms swung back in the ready position, and bodies leaned forward. The swimmers' eyes looked straight ahead. Their ears were alert for the starting signal.

Coherence

A paragraph is coherent when all its sentences are related to one another and flow logically from one to the next. The following techniques will help you achieve coherence in paragraphs:

- Present your ideas in the most logical order.
- Use pronouns, synonyms, and repeated words to connect ideas.
- Use transitional devices to show relationships between ideas.

In the model below, the writer used some of these techniques to create a unified paragraph.

MODEL
As we experience day and night repeatedly, it is hard to imagine the enormous significance of that change. We have day and night because our planet rotates on its axis. We have seasons because Earth revolves around our solar system's star, the sun. Our solar system, along with many others, rotates with the Milky Way galaxy. The universe is a gigantic structure of which our daily experiences of day and night, summer and winter, are tiny parts.

Writing Handbook

WRITING HANDBOOK R23

Writing Handbook

2.3 Transitions

Transitions are words and phrases that show the connections between details. Clear transitions help show how your ideas relate to one another.

Kinds of Transitions

Transitions can help readers understand several kinds of relationships:

- Time or sequence
- Spatial relationships
- Degree of importance
- Comparison and contrast
- Cause and effect

Time or Sequence Some transitions help to clarify the sequence of events over time. When you are telling a story or describing a process, you can connect ideas with such transitional words as *first, second, always, then, next, later, soon, before, finally, after, earlier, afterward,* and *tomorrow.*

MODEL
Teaching a puppy to come when called takes patience from the owner and the puppy. First tie a lightweight rope to the dog's collar and go to a large play area. Play with the pup a while and then call to it. At the same time pull gently on the rope. Always praise the puppy for coming when called. Next allow the puppy to play again. Carry out this exercise several times a day.

Spatial Relationships Transitional words and phrases such as *in front, behind, next to, along, nearest, lowest, above, below, underneath, on the left,* and *in the middle* can help readers visualize a scene.

MODEL
On the porch, wicker chairs stand in casual disorder along the red wall of the house. Next to the red-and-white porch railing, orange day lilies nod in the breeze. Overhead, a flycatcher perches on a bare branch, alert for her next meal. Beyond the lawn, a small stream flows from beneath an arched stone bridge.

Degree of Importance Transitional words such as *mainly, strongest, weakest, first, second, most important, least important, worst,* and *best* may be used to rank ideas or to show degrees of importance, complexity, or familiarity.

MODEL
The Repertory Theater performed six plays last year. All the plays were exciting, but the most outstanding one was *Master Class.*

Comparison and Contrast Words and phrases such as *similarly, likewise, also, like, as, neither . . . nor,* and *either . . . or* show similarities between details. *However, by contrast, yet, but, unlike, instead, whereas,* and *while* show differences. Note the use of both types of transitions in the model below.

MODEL
Like running and bicycling, swimming helps you maintain aerobic fitness; however, swimming has the added benefit of exercising muscles throughout your body.

WRITING TIP Both *but* and *however* may be used to join two independent clauses. When *but* is used as a coordinating conjunction, it is preceded by a comma. When *however* is used as a conjunctive adverb, it is preceded by a semicolon and followed by a comma.

Cause and Effect When you are writing about a cause-and-effect relationship, use transitional words and phrases such as *since, because, thus, therefore, so, due to, for this reason,* and *as a result* to help clarify that relationship and to make your writing coherent.

MODEL
Because the temperature dropped to 28 degrees after it rained for five hours, car door locks froze.

R24 WRITING HANDBOOK

2.4 Conclusions

A conclusion should leave readers with a strong final impression. Try any of these approaches.

Kinds of Conclusions

Here are some effective methods for bringing your writing to a conclusion:

- Restate your thesis
- Ask a question
- Make a recommendation
- Make a prediction
- Summarize your information

Restate Your Thesis A good way to conclude an essay is by restating your thesis, or main idea, in different words. The conclusion below restates the thesis introduced on page R23.

MODEL

Although each pet has a personality of its own just as each child does, there are many ways of encouraging the best behavior in each. Love, persistence, patience, and consistency make all the difference in training pets as well as in raising children.

Ask a Question Try asking a question that sums up what you have said and gives readers something new to think about. The question below concludes an appeal to halt funding for space exploration.

MODEL

Given all the evidence, can you imagine that continued investment in the space program will benefit future generations more than the same investment in the basic needs of those living now?

Make a Recommendation When you are persuading your audience to take a position on an issue, you can conclude by recommending a specific course of action.

MODEL

Today's youth are at risk of damaging their hearing by listening to very loud music. Consider turning down the bass and turning down the volume on your headphones.

Make a Prediction Readers are concerned about matters that may affect them and therefore are moved by a conclusion that predicts the future.

MODEL

If the government continues to spend money from Social Security taxes for current operations, we will create a disastrous burden of debt for future generations.

Summarize Your Information Summarizing reinforces the writer's main ideas, leaving a strong, lasting impression. The model below is a statement that summarizes a film review.

MODEL

The movie *The Postman* shows the tremendous influence of the Chilean poet Pablo Neruda on a young Italian man—not only in his love life but also in his acquired self-confidence and his dedication to a cause.

2.5 Elaboration

Elaboration is the process of developing a writing idea by providing specific supporting details that are relevant and appropriate to the purpose and form of your writing.

- **Facts and Statistics** A fact is a statement that can be verified; a statistic is a fact expressed as a number. Make sure the facts and statistics you supply are from reliable, up-to-date sources. As in the model below, the facts and statistics you use should strongly support the statements you make.

MODEL

Our entire solar system speeds through the Milky Way galaxy at a speed of 180 miles a second. One could worry about the ability of any of us to stay in place with our feet on the ground. Or one could marvel at the magnificence of a universe that keeps everything whirling with such constancy.

Writing Handbook

WRITING HANDBOOK R25

Writing Handbook

- **Sensory Details** Details that show how something looks, sounds, tastes, smells, or feels can enliven a description, making readers feel they are actually experiencing what you are describing. Which senses does the writer appeal to in this paragraph?

MODEL

The campers lay as quiet as mice inside their tent as they considered the power of the massive beast they'd glimpsed through the tent flap. Snuffling and crackling brought news that the black bear had found something delectable inside the garbage can, probably leftover corncobs and pork-chop bones. The campfire smoke lingered, and the campers fervently hoped that the odors of grease and butter wouldn't bring the animal even closer to the tent.

- **Incidents** From our earliest years, we are interested in hearing "stories." One way to illustrate a point powerfully is to relate an incident or tell a story, as shown in the example below.

MODEL

Some of our most valuable sources of historical knowledge come from events that were disastrous for the people who were involved. The eruption of the volcano Vesuvius in A.D. 79 was a nightmare for the people of Pompeii. Many fled the city, but about 2,000 died, and their homes were buried under tons of volcanic ash. The long-buried remains have provided the modern world with detailed knowledge of everyday life in ancient Pompeii.

- **Examples** An example can help make an abstract or a complex idea concrete or can provide evidence to clarify a point for readers.

MODEL

The mere mention of the names of some writers causes distinct reactions, even from those who have not read the writers' works. For example, the mention of William Shakespeare causes many people to take in a sharp breath of admiration and others to think of something long and tedious. On the other hand, the name Edgar Allan Poe brings an involuntary shiver to almost everyone.

- **Quotations** Choose quotations that clearly support your points, and be sure that you copy each quotation word for word. Remember always to credit the source.

MODEL

In her book *How to Talk to Your Cat*, Patricia Moyes replies to certain authorities who claim that cats cannot smile: "I can only presume that these people have never owned a cat in the true sense of the word." She goes on to describe the cat's smile as a "relaxed upward tilting of the corners of the mouth" that occurs when the cat is feeling peaceful or pleased, perhaps while being stroked or while having happy dreams.

2.6 Using Language Effectively

Effective use of language can help readers to recognize the significance of an issue, to visualize a scene, or to understand a character. The specific words and phrases that you use have everything to do with how effectively you communicate meaning. This is true of all kinds of writing, from novels to office memos. Keep these particular points in mind.

- **Specific Nouns** Nouns are specific when they refer to individual or particular things. If you refer to a *city*, you are being general. If you refer to *London*, you are being specific. Specific nouns help readers identify the who, what, and where of your message.
- **Specific Verbs** Verbs are the most powerful words in sentences. They convey the action, the movement, and sometimes the drama of thoughts and observations. Verbs such as *trudged, skipped,* and *sauntered* provide more-vivid pictures of actions than the verb *walked*.
- **Specific Modifiers** Use modifiers sparingly, but when you use them, make them count. Is the building *big* or *towering*? Are your poodle's paws *small* or *petite*? Once again, it is the more specific word that carries the greater impact.

R26 WRITING HANDBOOK

3 Descriptive Writing

Descriptive writing allows you to paint word pictures about anything and everything in the world, from events of global importance to the most personal feelings. It is an essential part of almost every piece of writing, including essays, poems, letters, field notes, newspaper reports, and videos.

RUBRIC Standards for Writing

A successful description should
- have a clear focus and sense of purpose
- include sensory details and precise words that create vivid images, establish moods, or express emotions
- present details in a logical order

3.1 Key Techniques

Consider Your Goals What do you want to accomplish in writing your description? Do you want to show why something is important to you? Do you want to make a person or scene more memorable? Do you want to explain an event?

Identify Your Audience Who will read your description? How familiar are they with your subject? What background information will they need? Which details will they find most interesting?

Think Figuratively What figures of speech might help make your description vivid and interesting? What simile or metaphor comes to mind? What imaginative comparisons can you make? What living thing does an inanimate object remind you of?

MODEL

After the 10-mile hike, we pounced on the buffet table like starving lions. Some of us stuffed pieces of bread and morsels of roast beef into our mouths before we'd even finished filling our plates. By the time we flopped into chairs, we looked even more like scavenging carnivores, with our dripping hands and greasy mouths. But the predatory look in our eyes had abated somewhat.

Gather Sensory Details Which sights, smells, tastes, sounds, and textures make your subject come alive? Which details stick in your mind when you observe or recall your subject? Which senses does it most strongly affect?

MODEL

Light snowflakes brushed her cheek as she poised at the top of the mountain. After an admiring glance at the spots of bright color on the slope, she lifted both ski poles and crouched in preparation for the leap forward to start her fifth run through the powdery snow.

You might want to use a chart like the one shown here to collect sensory details about your subject.

Sights	Sounds	Textures	Smells	Tastes

Create a Mood What feelings do you want to evoke in your readers? Do you want to soothe them with comforting images? Do you want to build tension with ominous details? Do you want to evoke sadness or joy?

MODEL

It was always difficult to see the dangerous rocks just below the surface of the lake, but in the dark and without the light it was impossible. If only Guy had remembered the backup batteries. Although he had been on this lake only twice before, he had been confident he could run this fishing trip without incident. Now, as gray clouds gathered to cover even the faint light of the new moon, Guy worried not just about his summer job but also about the safety of his first paying customers.

WRITING HANDBOOK R27

3.2 Options for Organization

Spatial Order Choose one of these options to show the spatial order of a scene.

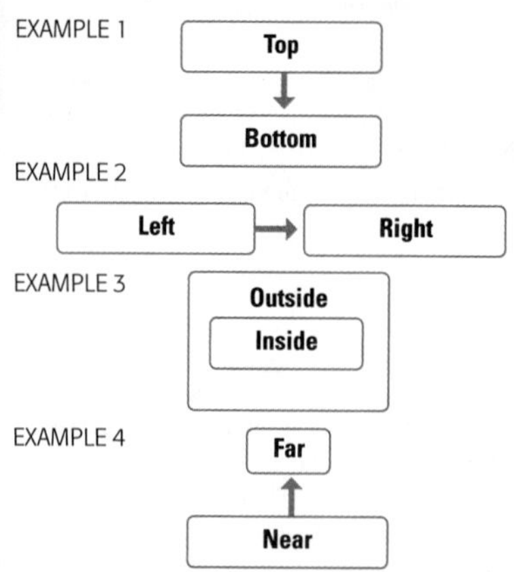

MODEL
Thunder's nostrils quivered as he was led into the barn. How would this be as a place to spend nights from now on? In the stall to the left, the straw smelled fresh. Beyond that stall a saddle hung from rough boards. To the right of his stall was another, from which a mare looked at him curiously. So far, so good. From the far right, beyond two empty stalls, strode the barn cat.

WRITING TIP Use transitions that help the reader picture the relationship among the objects you describe. Some useful transitions for showing spatial relationships are *behind, below, here, in the distance, on the left, over,* and *on top.*

Order of Impression Order of impression is how you notice details.

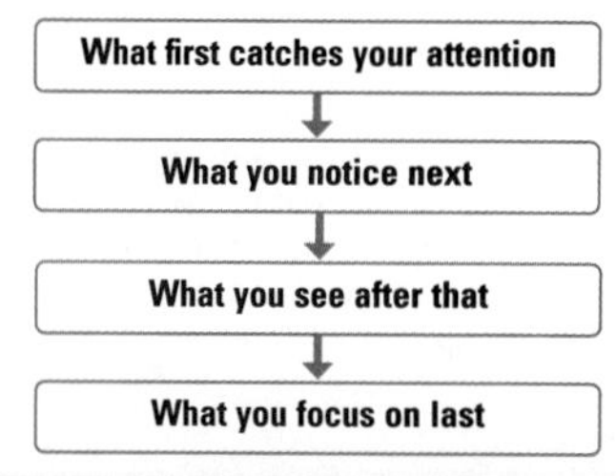

MODEL
As her foot slipped on the pebbles, her first thought was of whether she would sprain an ankle sliding into the surf. Her heart began a dangerous thumping, but soon the soft sand provided a comfortable seat so that her body responded by calming down. She realized that the water was shallow and warm. Her hat would shade her eyes and prevent sunburn. By the time she remembered she had on dry-clean-only shorts, she'd decided that sitting in the surf while her friends gathered shells was a perfectly fine way to enjoy the beach.

WRITING TIP Use transitions that help readers understand the order of the impressions you are describing. Some useful transitions are *after, next, during, first, before, finally,* and *then.*

Order of Importance You might want to use order of importance as the organizing structure for your description.

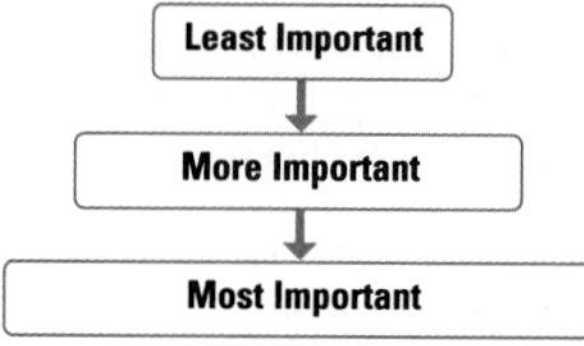

MODEL
Annaliese tried to imprint on her memory everything about the accident. She remembered unimportant details, like the song that was playing on her radio before the truck loomed up ahead. She remembered her panic as she steered into the guard rail. Gradually she recalled more important information—her conservative speed, the fact that the truck was on the wrong side of the road coming toward her, the driver's long beard. Finally, when she closed her eyes and really concentrated, she could remember the license plate number at eye level as the truck zoomed on by.

WRITING TIP Use transitions that help the reader understand the order of importance that you attach to the elements of your description. Some useful transitions are *first, second, mainly, more important, less important,* and *least important.*

R28 WRITING HANDBOOK

4 Narrative Writing

Narrative writing tells a story. If you write a story from your imagination, it is a fictional narrative. A true story about actual events is a nonfictional narrative. Narrative writing can be found in short stories, novels, news articles, and biographies.

RUBRIC Standards for Writing

A successful narrative should

- include descriptive details and dialogue to develop the characters, setting, and plot.
- have a clear beginning, middle, and end.
- have a logical organization, with clues and transitions to help the reader understand the order of events.
- maintain a consistent tone and point of view.
- use language that is appropriate for the audience.
- demonstrate the significance of events or ideas.

4.1 Key Techniques

Identify the Main Events What are the most important events in your narrative? Is each event part of the chain of events needed to tell the story? In a fictional narrative, this series of events is the story's plot.

MODEL

Event 1: **A railroad porter notices a woman boarding the train and pulling along a young child.**

Event 2: **Because the porter has the sense the child is frightened, he finds several excuses to appear at their compartment door.**

Event 3: **When he hears the child crying, he goes to the compartment and sees the glint of gunmetal inside a partially open market basket.**

Event 4: **The porter begins to plan how to identify the woman and child and to separate the child from the woman.**

Describe the Setting When do the events occur? Where do they take place? How can you use setting to create mood and to set the stage for the characters and their actions?

MODEL

Bright spring sunshine highlighted the auburn hair of the child being pulled along by the matronly woman carrying a market basket. Joshua helped her up the steps onto the train. He stooped to lift the little girl at the same moment the woman jerked the small arm, so that the child stumbled up the stairs on her own.

Depict Characters Vividly What do your characters look like? What do they think and say? How do they act? What vivid details can show readers what the characters are like?

MODEL

Joshua hardly noticed the other passengers as his eyes followed the woman and child. His instincts warned him that something was wrong here.

WRITING TIP Dialogue is an effective way of developing characters in a narrative. As you write dialogue, choose words that express your characters' personalities and show how the characters feel about one another and about the events in the plot.

MODEL

"Hello, ma'am. I'm Joshua, and I'll be in soon to get your compartment ready for the night."

The woman's whisper sent chills down Joshua's spine. "Yeah, OK."

"Are you having a nice ride?" he asked the thin little girl.

"She likes the train," answered the woman.

WRITING HANDBOOK R29

4.2 Options for Organization

Option 1: Chronological Order One way to organize a piece of narrative writing is to arrange the events in chronological order, as shown below.

MODEL

Introduction *characters and setting*: The morning after my grandfather's funeral, I wake up early and walk to the cemetery.

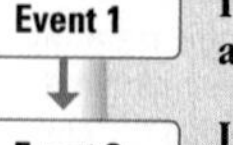

Event 1: I stand by his grave and become angry and frustrated.

Event 2: I want to find some place where I can remember my grandfather and all the good times we had together.

End *perhaps show the significance of the events*: On the beach, I sit on the huge piece of driftwood where my grandfather and I used to sit. The cool lake wind and the noise of the waves bring back my favorite memories of him.

Option 2: Flashback It is also possible in narrative writing to arrange the order of events by starting with an event that happened before the beginning of the story.

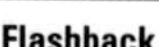

Flashback
Begin with a key event that happened before the time in which the story takes place.

↓

Introduce characters and setting.

↓

Describe the events leading up to the conflict.

Option 3: Focus on Conflict When the telling of a fictional narrative focuses on a central conflict, the story's plot may follow the model shown below.

MODEL

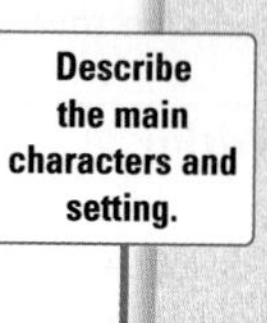

Describe the main characters and setting.: The brothers arrive at the school gym long before the rest of the basketball team. Although the twins are physically identical, their personalities couldn't be more different. Mark is outgoing and impulsive, while Matt is thoughtful and shy.

Present the conflict.: Matt realizes his brother is missing shots on purpose and believes they will lose the championship.

Relate the events that make the conflict complex and cause the characters to change.:

- Matt has a chance at a basketball scholarship if they win the championship.
- Mark needs money to buy a car.
- Matt and Mark have stood by each other no matter what.

Present the resolution or outcome of the conflict.: Matt retells a family story in which their grandfather chose honor and integrity over easy money. Mark plays to win.

R30 WRITING HANDBOOK

5 Explanatory Writing

Explanatory writing informs and explains. For example, you can use it to evaluate the effects of a new law, to compare two movies, to analyze a piece of literature, or to examine the problem of greenhouse gases in the atmosphere.

5.1 Types of Explanatory Writing

There are many types of explanatory writing. Think about your topic and select the type that presents the information most clearly.

Compare and Contrast How are two or more subjects alike? How are they different?

> MODEL
> **Achilles and Hector are both fierce in battle, but while Hector can show his enemies mercy, Achilles is often cruel and blinded by rage.**

Cause and Effect How does one event cause something else to happen? Why do certain conditions exist? What are the results of an action or a condition?

> MODEL
> **Because the goddess Athena urges Achilles to suppress his anger, the great warrior does not kill Agamemnon.**

Analysis How does something work? How can it be defined? What are its parts?

> MODEL
> **Epics, such as Homer's *Iliad*, tell about events set in a distant and glorious past and present larger-than-life heroes who perform great deeds.**

Problem-Solution How can you identify and state a problem? How would you analyze the problem and its causes? How can it be solved?

> MODEL
> **Priam desperately wishes to have the body of his dead son, Hector, returned to him, but he must beg Achilles, his son's killer, to grant his wish.**

5.2 Compare and Contrast

Compare-and-contrast writing examines the similarities and differences between two or more subjects. You might, for example, compare and contrast two short stories, the main characters in a novel, or two movies.

RUBRIC **Standards for Writing**

Successful compare-and-contrast writing should

- clearly identify the subjects that are being compared and contrasted.
- include specific, relevant details.
- follow a clear plan of organization, dealing with the same features of both subjects under discussion.
- use language and details appropriate to the audience.
- use transitional words and phrases to clarify similarities and differences.

Options for Organization
Compare-and-contrast writing can be organized in different ways. The examples that follow demonstrate feature-by-feature organization and subject-by-subject organization.

WRITING HANDBOOK R31

Option 1: Feature-by-Feature Organization

MODEL

Feature 1 — I. Temperament

Subject A. Achilles: prone to angry outbursts and violent rages

Subject B. Hector: tender with his wife and child

Feature 2 — II. Fighting ability

Subject A. Achilles: ruthless and vengeful with his enemies

Subject B. Hector: courageous but willing to show his enemies some mercy

Option 2: Subject-by-Subject Organization

MODEL

Subject A — I. Achilles

Feature 1. Temperament: prone to angry outbursts and violent rages

Feature 2. Fighting ability: ruthless and vengeful with his enemies

Subject B — II. Hector

Feature 1. Temperament: tender with his wife and child

Feature 2. Fighting ability: courageous but willing to show his enemies some mercy

WRITING TIP Remember your purpose for comparing and contrasting your subjects, and support your purpose with expressive language and specific details.

5.3 Cause and Effect

Cause-and-effect writing explains why something happened, why certain conditions exist, or what resulted from an action or a condition. You might use cause-and-effect writing to explain a character's actions, the progress of a disease, or the outcome of a war.

RUBRIC Standards for Writing

Successful cause-and-effect writing should

- clearly state the cause-and-effect relationship.
- show clear connections between causes and effects.
- present causes and effects in a logical order and use transitions effectively.
- use facts, examples, and other details to illustrate each cause and effect.
- use language and details appropriate to the audience.

Options for Organization

Your organization will depend on your topic and purpose for writing.

- If you want to explain the causes of an event such as the closing of a factory, you might first state the effect and then examine its causes.

Option 1: Effect to Cause Organization

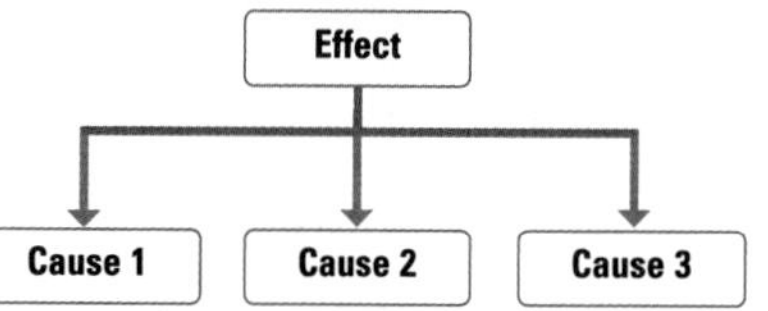

- If your focus is on explaining the effects of an event, such as the passage of a law, you might first state the cause and then explain the effects.

Option 2: Cause to Effect Organization

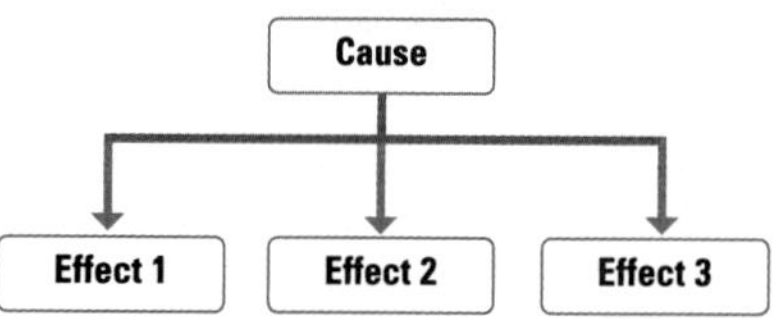

- Sometimes you'll want to describe a chain of cause-and-effect relationships to explore a topic such as the disappearance of tropical rain forests or the development of home computers.

R32 WRITING HANDBOOK

Writing Handbook

Option 3: Cause-and-Effect Chain Organization

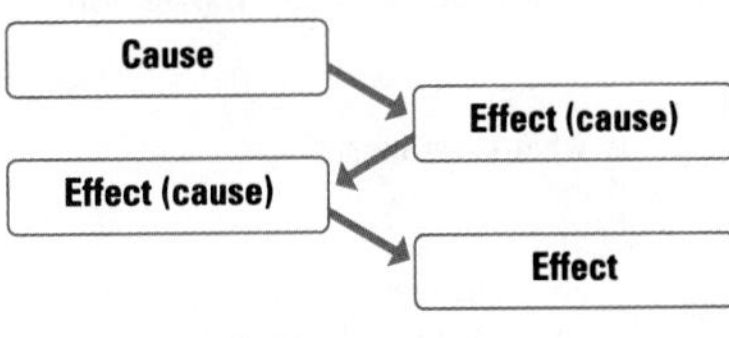

WRITING TIP Don't assume that a cause-and-effect relationship exists just because one event follows another. Look for evidence that the later event could not have happened if the first event had not caused it.

5.4 Problem-Solution

Problem-solution writing clearly states a problem, analyzes the problem, and proposes a solution to the problem. It can be used to identify and solve a conflict between characters, analyze a chemistry experiment, or explain why the home team keeps losing.

RUBRIC Standards for Writing

Successful problem-solution writing should

- identify the problem and help the reader understand the issues involved.
- analyze the causes and effects of the problem.
- integrate quotations, facts, and statistics into the text.
- explore possible solutions to the problem and recommend the best one(s).
- use language, tone, and details appropriate to the audience.

Options for Organization

Your organization will depend on the goal of your problem-solution piece, your intended audience, and the specific problem you choose to address. The organizational methods that follow are effective for different kinds of problem-solution writing.

Option 1: Simple Problem-Solution

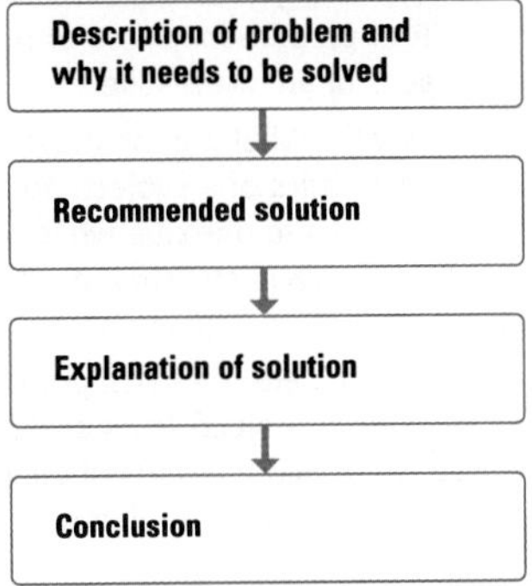

Option 2: Deciding Between Solutions

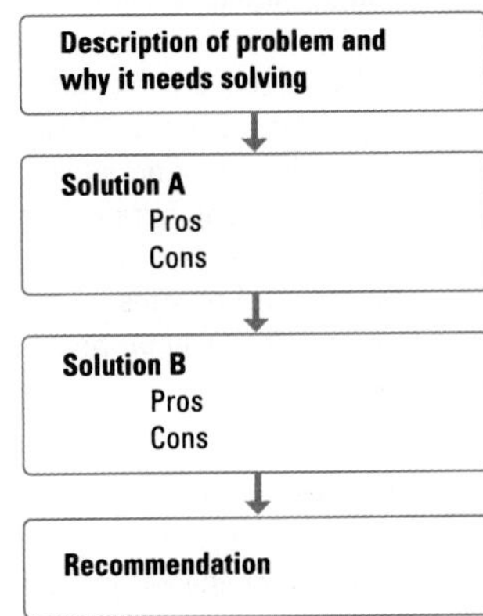

WRITING TIP Have a classmate read and respond to your problem-solution writing. Ask your peer reader: Is the problem clearly stated? Is the organization easy to follow? Do the proposed solutions seem logical?

5.5 Analysis

In writing an analysis, you explain how something works, how it is defined, or what its parts are. The details you include will depend upon the kind of analysis you write.

Process Analysis What are the major steps or stages in a process? What background information does the reader need to know—such as definitions of terms or a list of needed

WRITING HANDBOOK R33

equipment—to understand the analysis? You might use process analysis to explain how to program a VCR or prepare for a test, or to explain the stages of an insect's life.

Definition Analysis What are the most important characteristics of a subject? You might use definition analysis to describe what an insect is, explain the characteristics of a sonnet, or outline the skills of an airplane pilot.

Parts Analysis What are the parts, groups, or types that make up a subject? Parts analysis could be used to explain the parts of an insect's body or the mechanics of an airplane.

RUBRIC Standards for Writing

A successful analysis should

- hook the readers' attention with a strong introduction.
- clearly state the subject and its parts.
- use a specific organizing structure to provide a logical flow of information.
- show connections among facts and ideas through subordinate clauses and transitional words and phrases.
- use language and details appropriate for the audience.

Options for Organization

Organize your details in a logical order appropriate for the kind of analysis you're writing.

Option 1: Process Analysis A process analysis is usually organized chronologically, with steps or stages in the order they occur.

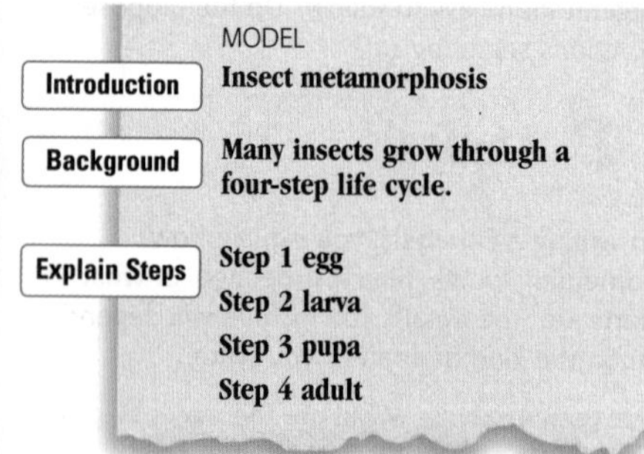

Option 2: Definition Analysis You can organize the details in a definition or parts analysis in order of importance or impression.

MODEL

Introduce Term
What is an insect?

General Definition
An insect is a small animal with an external skeleton, three body segments, and three pairs of legs.

Explain Features
Feature 1: external skeleton
Feature 2: three body segments
Feature 3: three pairs of legs

Option 3: Parts Analysis The following parts analysis describes the major parts of an insect's body.

MODEL

Introduce Subject
An insect's body is divided into three main parts.

Explain Parts
Part 1: The head includes eyes, mouth, and antennae.
Part 2: The thorax has the legs and wings attached to it.
Part 3: The abdomen contains organs for digesting food, eliminating waste, and reproducing.

WRITING TIP Try to capture your readers' interest in your introduction. You might begin with a vivid description or an interesting fact, detail, or quotation. For example, an exciting excerpt from the narrative could open the process analysis.

An effective way to conclude an analysis is to return to your thesis and restate it in different words.

R34 WRITING HANDBOOK

6 Persuasive Writing

Persuasive writing allows you to use the power of language to inform and influence others. It can take many forms, including speeches, newspaper editorials, billboards, advertisements, and critical reviews.

RUBRIC **Standards for Writing**

Successful persuasion should

- state an issue and the writer's position
- contain opinions supported by facts or reasons
- have a reasonable and respectful tone
- answer opposing views
- contain sound logic and effective language
- conclude by summing up reasons or calling for action

6.1 Key Techniques

Clarify Your Position What do you believe about the issue? How can you express your opinion most clearly?

MODEL
Our city needs to find ways to decrease pollution, especially during the workweek.

Know Your Audience Who will read your writing? What do they already know and believe about the issue? What objections to your position might they have? What additional information might they need? What tone and approach would be most effective?

MODEL
Everyone wants to breathe clean air, at least cleaner than what we've had in our city lately. The smog is heavier during the workweek, when more people drive to work, more buses run, and businesses burn more fuel to heat or cool buildings.

Support Your Opinion Why do you feel the way you do about the issue? What facts, statistics, examples, quotations, anecdotes, or opinions of authorities support your view? What reasons will convince your readers? What evidence can answer their objections?

MODEL
Climate geographers from Arizona State University report that 45 statistical analyses have shown that along the eastern seaboard rainfall is highest on Saturdays, with an average of 658 millimeters per year, and lowest on Mondays, with an average of 538 millimeters per year. The researchers have found that pollution is also highest on Saturdays and lowest on Mondays.

Ways to Support Your Argument	
Statistics	Facts that are expressed in numbers
Examples	Specific instances that explain your point
Observations	Events or situations you yourself have seen
Anecdotes	Brief stories that illustrate your point
Quotations	Direct statements from authorities

Begin and End with a Bang How can you hook your readers and make a lasting impression? What memorable quotation, anecdote, or statistic will catch their attention at the beginning or stick in their minds at the end? What strong summary or call to action can you conclude with?

BEGINNING
A recent research report states that there is more rain on weekends than during the week. Scientists attribute this to the extra pollution that builds throughout the workweek.

CONCLUSION
We need to plan for more car-pooling, efficient heating and cooling, and consolidation of some bus schedules to improve our air quality—and provide better weekend weather.

WRITING HANDBOOK R35

6.2 Options for Organization

In a two-sided persuasive essay, you want to show the weaknesses of other opinions as you explain the strengths of your own.

The example below demonstrates one method of organizing your persuasive essay to convince your audience.

Option 1: Reasons for Your Opinion

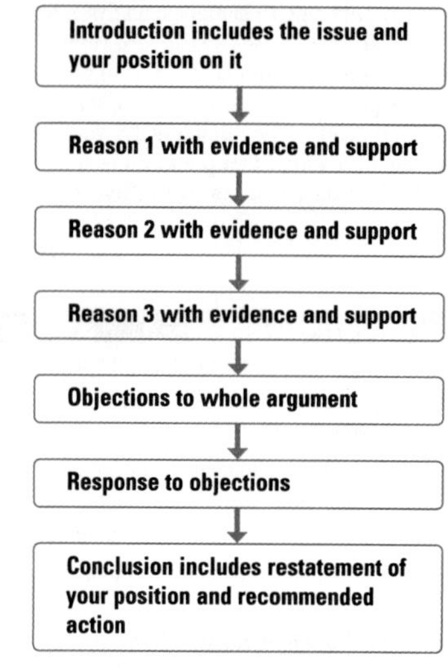

Option 2: Point-by-Point Basis
In the organization that follows, each reason and its objections are examined on a point-by-point basis.

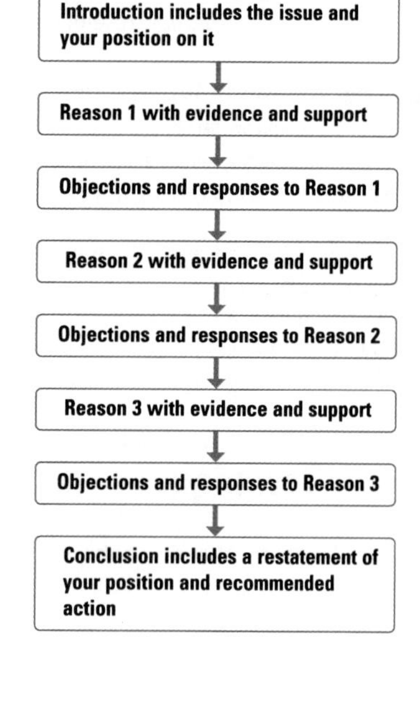

Beware of Illogical Arguments Be careful about using illogical arguments. Opponents can easily attack your argument if you present illogical material.

Circular reasoning—trying to prove a statement by just repeating it in different words

> **Precipitation is heavier on weekends because of higher rainfall then.**

Overgeneralization—making a statement that is too broad to prove

> **Nobody is doing anything to reduce air pollution.**

Either-or fallacy—stating that there are only two alternatives when there are many

> **Either we cut weekday car travel by fifty percent or pollution will make our city unlivable.**

Cause-and-effect fallacy—falsely assuming that because one event follows another, the first event caused the second

> **The growing population of our region has caused the increase in air pollution.**

R36 WRITING HANDBOOK

7 Research Report Writing

A research report explores a topic in depth, incorporating information from a variety of sources.

RUBRIC **Standards for Writing**

An effective research report should

- clearly state a main idea in a thesis statement
- contain evidence and details from a variety of sources that support the thesis
- contain only accurate and relevant information
- credit sources correctly
- develop the topic logically and include appropriate transitions
- include a properly formatted Works Cited list

7.1 Key Techniques

Develop Relevant, Interesting, and Researchable Questions Asking thoughtful questions is an ongoing part of research. Begin with a list of basic questions that are relevant to your topic. Focus on getting basic facts that answer the questions *who, what, where, when,* and *why* about your topic. If you were researching the social context of Dickens's novels, you might develop a set of questions like these.

> MODEL
> **What were living conditions like in London during the 1800s?**
>
> **What happened to orphans?**

As you become more familiar with your topic, think of questions that might provide an interesting perspective to make readers think.

> MODEL
> **How did the legal system reflect society's values?**

Check that your questions are researchable. Ask questions that will uncover facts, statistics, case studies, and other documentable evidence.

Clarify Your Thesis A thesis statement is one or two sentences clearly stating the main idea that you will develop in your report. A thesis may also indicate the organizational pattern you will follow and reflect your tone and point of view.

> MODEL
> **In *Oliver Twist*, instead of drawing clear lines between the dark underworld of London and the light of the more civilized world, Charles Dickens blurs the distinction, making good and evil in society difficult to define.**

Document Your Sources You need to document, or credit, the sources where you find your evidence. In the example below, the writer uses and documents a quotation from the novel.

> MODEL
> **In *Oliver Twist*, Dickens shows the intertwining of good and evil in the world. The narrator states, "Men who look on nature . . . and cry that all is dark and gloomy, are in the right; but the somber colours are reflections from their own jaundiced eyes and hearts. The real hues . . . need a clearer vision" (256–57).**

Support Your Ideas You should support your ideas with relevant evidence—facts, anecdotes, and statistics—from reliable sources. In the example below the writer includes a fact about the conditions of workhouses.

> MODEL
> **Oliver is condemned to a workhouse. The living conditions in workhouses were deliberately worse than those in prisons in order to discourage the poor from depending on the publicly funded institutions (Pool 245).**

WRITING HANDBOOK R37

Writing Handbook

7.2 Gathering Information: Sources

You will use a range of sources to collect the information you need to develop your research paper. These will include both print and electronic resources.

General Reference Works To clarify your thesis and begin your research, consult reference works that give quick, general overviews of a subject. General reference works include encyclopedias, almanacs and yearbooks, atlases, and dictionaries.

Specialized Reference Works Once you have a good idea of your specific topic, you are ready to look for detailed information in specialized reference works. In the library's reference section, specialized dictionaries and encyclopedias can be found for almost any field. For example, in the field of literature, you will find specialized reference sources such as *Contemporary Authors* and *Twentieth-Century Literary Criticism.*

Periodicals Journals and periodicals are a good source for detailed, up-to-date information. Periodical indexes, found in print and online catalogs in the library, will help you find articles on a topic. The *Readers' Guide to Periodical Literature* indexes many popular magazines. More specialized indexes include the *Humanities Index* and the *Social Sciences Index.*

Electronic Resources **Commercial information services** offer access to reference works such as dictionaries and encyclopedias, databases, and periodicals.

The **Internet** is a vast network of computer networks. News services, libraries, universities, researchers, organizations, and government agencies use the Internet to communicate and to distribute information. The Internet gives you access to the World Wide Web, which provides information on particular topics and links you to related topics and resources.

A **CD-ROM** is a compact disc on which information is stored. Reference works on CD-ROMs may include text, sound, images, and video.

Databases are large collections of related information stored electronically. You can scan the information or search for specific facts.

RESEARCH TIP To find books on a specific topic, check the library's online catalog. Be sure to copy the correct call numbers of books that sound promising. Also look at books shelved nearby. They may relate to your topic.

7.3 Gathering Information: Validity of Sources

When you find source material, you must determine whether it is useful and accurate.

Credibility of Author Check whether an author has written several books or articles on the subject and has published in respected newspapers or journals.

Objectivity Decide whether the information is fact, opinion, or propaganda. Reputable works credit their sources of information.

Currency Check the publication date of the source to see whether the information is current.

Credibility of Publisher Seek information from a respected newspaper or journal, not from a tabloid newspaper or popular-interest magazine.

WEB TIP Be especially skeptical of information you locate on the Internet, since virtually anyone can post anything there. Read the URL, or Internet address. Sites sponsored by government agencies (*.gov*) or educational institutions (*.edu*) are generally more reliable.

7.4 Taking Notes

As you find useful information, record bibliographic information for each source on a separate index card. Then you are ready to take notes on your sources. You will probably use these three methods of note taking.

R38 WRITING HANDBOOK

Paraphrase, or restate in your own words, the main ideas and supporting details in a passage.

Summarize, or rephrase in fewer words, the original material, trying to capture the key ideas.

Quote, or copy word for word, the original text if you think the author's own words best clarify a particular point. Use quotation marks to signal the beginning and the end of the quotation.

For more details on making source cards and taking notes, see the Writing Workshop on pages 1306–1315.

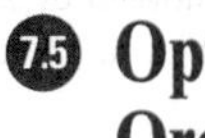 7.5 Options for Organization

Begin by reading over your note cards and sorting them into groups. The main-idea headings may help you find connections among the notes. Then arrange the groups of related note cards so that the ideas flow logically from one group to the next.

Option 1: Topic Outline

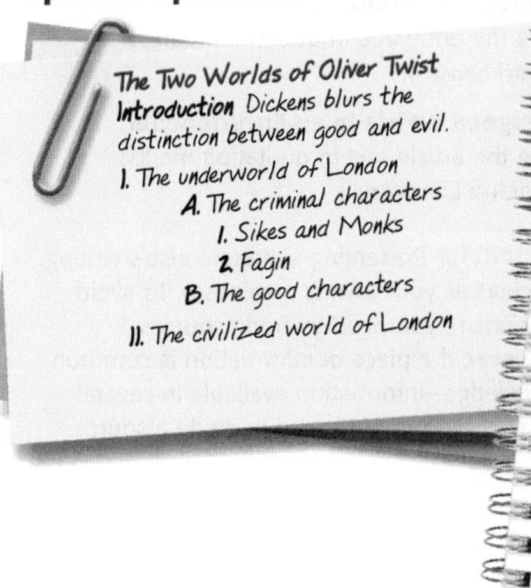

The Two Worlds of Oliver Twist
Introduction Dickens blurs the distinction between good and evil.
I. The underworld of London
A. The criminal characters
1. Sikes and Monks
2. Fagin
B. The good characters
II. The civilized world of London

Like other forms of writing, research reports can be organized in different ways. For some topics, chronological order may work. For others, you may want to compare and contrast two things. Other possibilities are a cause-and-effect organization or a least-important-to-most-important one. If your material does not lend itself to any of these organizations, try a general-to-specific approach.

Whatever your organizational pattern, making an outline can help guide the drafting process. The subtopics that you located in sorting your note cards will be the major entries in your outline, preceded by Roman numerals. Make sure that items of the same importance are parallel in form. For example, in the topic outline below, entries I and II are both phrases. So are subentries A and B.

In a second kind of outline, shown below in Option 2, complete sentences are used instead of phrases for entries and subentries.

Option 2: Sentence Outline

The Two Worlds of Oliver Twist
Introduction Dickens blurs the distinction between good and evil.
I. Dickens depicts the underworld of London by showing both evil criminal characters and those who commit crimes due to poverty or misfortune.
A. The criminal characters are cruel and brutal.
1. Sikes and Monks are characterized as men who will do anything to get what they want.
2. Fagin's amorality is shown in his manipulating children into committing crimes.
B. The good characters have believable human weaknesses and failings.
II. The civilized world of London is populated with people who are far from perfect.

WRITING HANDBOOK R39

7.6 Documenting Sources

When you quote, paraphrase, or summarize information from a source, you need to credit that source. Parenthetical documentation is the accepted method for crediting sources. You may choose to name the author in parentheses following the information, along with the page number on which the information is found.

MODEL
Workhouses were purposely made "as grim and forbidding as possible" (Pool 245).

In parenthetical documentation, you may also use the author's name in the sentence, along with the information. If you do, the parenthetical citation should consist only of the page number on which the information is found.

MODEL
According to Pool, many poor children like Oliver Twist populated London in the 1800s (31).

In either case, your reader can find out more about the source by turning to your Works Cited page, which lists complete bibliographical information for each source.

PUNCTUATION TIP When only the author and page number appear in parentheses, there is no punctuation between the two items. Also notice that the parenthetical citation comes after the closing quotation marks of a quotation, if there is one, and before the end punctuation of the sentence.

The examples above show citations for books with one author. The list that follows shows the correct way to write parenthetical citations for several kinds of sources.

Guidelines for Parenthetical Documentation

Work by One Author
Put the author's last name and the page reference in parentheses: **(Pool 191)**.

If you mention the author's name in the sentence, put only the page reference in parentheses: **(191)**.

Work by Two or Three Authors
Put the authors' last names and the page reference in parentheses: **(Mitchell and Deane 42)**.

Work by More Than Three Authors
Give the first author's last name followed by *et al.* and the page reference: **(Bentley et al. 122)**.

Work with No Author Given
Give the title or a shortened version and (if appropriate) the page reference: **("Hurried Trials" 742)**.

One of Two or More Works by Same Author
Give the author's last name, the title or a shortened version, and the page reference: **(Dunn, "But We Grow" 54)**.

Selection from a Book of Collected Essays
Give the name of the author of the essay and the page reference: **(Bayley 54)**.

Dictionary Definition
Give the entry title in quotation marks: **("Workhouse")**.

Unsigned Article in an Encyclopedia
Give the article title in quotation marks: **("English Literature")**.

WRITING TIP Presenting someone else's writing or ideas as your own is plagiarism. To avoid plagiarism, you need to credit sources. However, if a piece of information is common knowledge—information available in several sources—you do not need to credit a source.

R40 WRITING HANDBOOK

7.7 Following MLA Manuscript Guidelines

The final copy of your report should follow the Modern Language Association (MLA) guidelines for manuscript preparation.

- The heading in the upper left-hand corner of the first page should include your name, your teacher's name, the course name, and the date, each on a separate line.
- Below the heading, center the title on the page.
- Number all the pages consecutively in the upper right-hand corner, one-half inch from the top. Include your last name before each page number.
- Double-space the entire paper.
- Except for the margins above the page numbers, leave one-inch margins on all sides of every page.

The Works Cited list at the end of your report is an alphabetized list of the sources you have used and documented. In each entry all lines after the first are indented an additional one-half inch.

WRITING TIP When your report includes a quotation that is longer than four lines, set it off from the rest of the text by indenting the entire quotation one inch from the left margin. In this case, you should not use quotation marks.

Works Cited

Models for Works Cited entries

Works Cited

Bayley, John. "Oliver Twist: 'Things As They Really Are.'" Dickens and the Twentieth Century. Ed. John Gross and Gabriel Pearson. London: Routledge, 1962. 49–64.

1. Selection from a book of collected essays; note that publishers' names are shortened.

Bentley, Nicholas, et al. The Dickens Index. Oxford: Oxford UP, 1988.

2. Book with more than three authors

Collins, Philip, ed. Sikes and Nancy: A Facsimile. London: Dickens, 1982.

3. Book with editor but no single author

Dickens, Charles. Oliver Twist. New York: Bantam, 1981.

4. Book with one author

Dunn, Richard J. "'But We Grow Affecting: Let Us Proceed.'" Dickensian 62 (1966): 53–55.

5. Article in scholarly journal

---. Oliver Twist: Whole Heart and Soul. New York: Twayne, 1993.

6. Second work by same author

Mitchell, B. R., and Phyllis Deane. Abstract of British Historical Statistics. Cambridge: Cambridge UP, 1962.

7. Work with two authors

WRITING HANDBOOK R41

Writing Handbook

7.8 MLA Documentation: Electronic Sources

As with print sources, information from electronic sources, such as CD-ROMs or the Internet, must be documented in your Works Cited list. You may find a reference to a source on the Internet and then use the print version of the article. If so, document it as you do other printed works. However, if you read or print out an article on the Internet, document it as shown below for an electronic source. Although electronic sources are shown separately below, they should be included in the Works Cited list with print sources.

Internet Sources Works Cited entries for Internet sources include the same kind of information as those for print sources. They also include the dates you accessed the information and the electronic addresses of the sources. Some of the information about a source may be unavailable. Include as much as you can. For more information on how to write Works Cited entries for Internet sources, see the MLA guidelines posted on the Internet or access this document through the McDougal Littell Web site.

CD-ROMs Entries for CD-ROMs include the publication medium (CD-ROM), the distributor, and the date of publication. Some of the information shown may not always be available. Include as much as you can.

Works Cited

Models for Works Cited entries for electronic sources

Works Cited

"Charles Dickens." Britannica Online. Vers. 98.2. Apr. 1998. Encyclopaedia Britannica. 17 Sept. 1998 <http://www.eb.com:180/bol/topic?eu114623&sctn=5>.

❶ Encyclopedia entry from online version

Dickens, Charles. Oliver Twist. Ed. Andrew Lang. London, 1897. Electronic Text Center. 1993. U of Virginia Library. 14 June 1998 <http://etext.lib.virginia.edu/toc/modeng/public/DicOliv.html>.

❷ The complete text the novel, available on the Internet; includes access date

The Dickens Page. Ed. Mitsuharu Matsuoka. 1995. Nagoya U. 14 June 1998 <http://lang.nagoya-u.ac.jp/~matsuoka/Dickens. html>.

❸ Scholarly site; shows date you accessed it

Rosenberg, Brian. "Character and Contradiction in Dickens." Nineteenth Century Literature—Electronic Edition 47.2 (1992): 18 pp. 15 June 1998 <http://www-ucpress.berkeley.edu:8080/scan/ncl-e/472/articles/rosenberg.art472.html>.

❹ Article in a scholar journal available on the Internet; includes number of pages and access date

"Workhouse." The Oxford English Dictionary. 2nd ed. CD-ROM. Oxford: Oxford UP, 1992.

❺ Dictionary entry from CD-ROM version

R42 WRITING HANDBOOK

8 Business Writing

The ability to write clearly and succinctly is an essential skill in the business world. As you prepare to enter the job market, you will need to know how to create letters, memos, and résumés.

RUBRIC

Standards for Writing

Successful business writing should

- have a tone and language geared to the appropriate audience.
- state the purpose clearly in the opening sentences or paragraph.
- use precise words and avoid jargon.
- present only essential information.
- present details in a logical order.
- conclude with a summary of important points.

8.1 Key Techniques

Think About Your Purpose Why are you doing this writing? Do you want to "sell" yourself to a college admissions committee or a job interviewer? Do you want to order or complain about a product? Do you want to set up a meeting or respond to someone's ideas?

Identify Your Audience Who will read your writing? What background information will they need? What questions might they have? What tone or language is appropriate?

Support Your Points What specific details clarify your ideas? What reasons do you have for your statements? What points most strongly support them?

Finish Strongly How can you best sum up your statements? What is your main point? What action do you want others to take?

8.2 Options

Model 1: Letter

Heading *Where the letter comes from and when*

#1 Andover Lane
Sunnydale, CA 93933
July 16, ____

Inside Address *To whom the letter is being sent*

Customer Service Representative
Bionic Bikes, Inc.
12558 Industrial Drive
Schaumburg, IL 60193

Salutation *Greeting*

Dear Customer Service Representative:

Body *Text of the message*

I was really pleased to get a Bionic Bike for my birthday in March. I've ridden it every day—to school, to the rec center, and everywhere.

The bike is great, but the handlebars are not comfortable. I think you should raise the angle of the hand grips about two inches so that riders can hold them comfortably while looking straight ahead.

Thank you for considering my suggestion.

Closing

Sincerely yours,
Marisa LaPorta

WRITING HANDBOOK R43

Model 2: Memo

Heading *Whom the memo is to and from, what it's about, and when it's being sent*

To: Jeff Kniffen
From: LaDonna Ford
Re: customer letter
Date: 8/15/__

Body

Jeff, please send a brief note to this customer thanking her for her suggestion. Enclose a brochure explaining the structure of the handlebars.

Also, please forward the suggestion to the engineers.

Thanks.

Model 3: Résumé A well-written résumé is invaluable when you apply for a part-time or full-time job or to college. It should highlight your skills, accomplishments, and experience. Proofread your résumé carefully to make sure it is clear and accurate and free of errors in grammar and spelling. It is a good idea to save a copy of your résumé on your computer or on a disk so that you can easily update it.

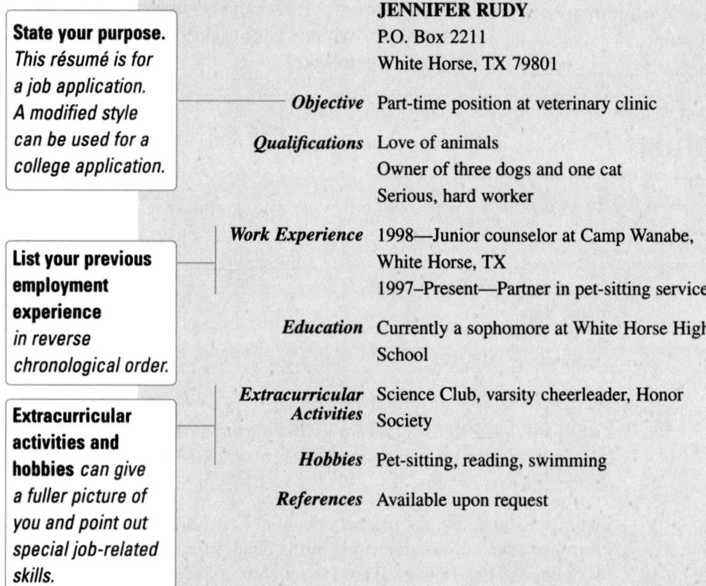

State your purpose. *This résumé is for a job application. A modified style can be used for a college application.*

List your previous employment experience *in reverse chronological order.*

Extracurricular activities and hobbies *can give a fuller picture of you and point out special job-related skills.*

JENNIFER RUDY
P.O. Box 2211
White Horse, TX 79801

Objective	Part-time position at veterinary clinic
Qualifications	Love of animals Owner of three dogs and one cat Serious, hard worker
Work Experience	1998—Junior counselor at Camp Wanabe, White Horse, TX 1997–Present—Partner in pet-sitting service
Education	Currently a sophomore at White Horse High School
Extracurricular Activities	Science Club, varsity cheerleader, Honor Society
Hobbies	Pet-sitting, reading, swimming
References	Available upon request

R44 WRITING HANDBOOK

 Inquiry and Research

In this age of information, the ability to locate and evaluate resources efficiently can spell the difference between success and failure—in both the academic and the business worlds. Make use of print and nonprint information sources.

1.1 Finding Sources

Good research involves using the wealth of resources available to answer your questions and raise new questions. Knowing where to go and how to access information can lead you to interesting and valuable sources.

Reference Works

Reference works are print and nonprint sources of information that provide quick access to both general overviews and specific facts about a subject.

Dictionaries—word definitions, pronunciations, and origins

Thesauri—lists of synonyms and antonyms of words

Glossaries—collections of specialized terms, such as those pertaining to literature, with definitions

Encyclopedias—detailed information on nearly every subject, arranged alphabetically (*Encyclopaedia Britannica*). Specialized encyclopedias concentrate on specific subjects, such as music, economics, and science (*International Encyclopedia of Economics*).

Almanacs and Yearbooks—current facts and statistics (*The World Almanac and Book of Facts, Statistical Abstract of the United States*)

Atlases—maps and information about weather, agricultural and industrial production, and other geographical topics (*National Geographic Atlas of the World*)

Specialized Reference Works—biographical data (*Who's Who, Current Biography*), literary information (*Contemporary Authors, Book Review Digest, Cyclopedia of Literary Characters, The Oxford Companion to English Literature*), and quotations (*Bartlett's Familiar Quotations*)

Electronic Sources—Many of these reference works and databases are available on CD-ROMs, which may include text, sound, photographs, and video. CD-ROMs can be used on a home or library computer. You can subscribe to services that offer access to these sources online.

Periodicals and Indexes

One kind of specialized reference is a periodical.

- Some periodicals, such as the *Atlantic Monthly* and *Psychology Today,* are intended for a general audience. They are indexed in the *Readers' Guide to Periodical Literature.*
- Many other periodicals, or journals, are intended for specialized or academic audiences. These include titles as diverse as *American Psychologist* and *Studies in Short Fiction.* These are indexed in the *Humanities Index* and the *Social Sciences Index.* In addition, most fields have their own indexes. For example, articles on literature are indexed in the *MLA International Bibliography.*

Many indexes are available in print, CD-ROM, and online forms.

Internet

The Internet is a system of networks that connect computers. News services, libraries, universities, researchers, organizations, and government agencies use the Internet to distribute information and to communicate. The Internet can provide links to library catalogs, newspapers, government sources, and many of the reference sources described above. The Internet includes two key features:

World Wide Web—source of information on specific subjects and links to related topics

Electronic mail (e-mail)—communications link to other e-mail users worldwide

COMMUNICATION HANDBOOK R45

Communication Handbook

Other Resources

In addition to reference works found in the library and over the Internet, you can get information from the following sources: corporate publications, lectures, correspondence, and media such as films, television programs, and recordings. You can also observe directly, conduct your own interviews, and collect data from polls or questionnaires that you create yourself.

 Evaluating Sources

Not all information is equal. You need to be a discriminating consumer of information and evaluate the credibility of a source, the reliability of the specific information included, and its value in answering your research needs.

Credibility of Sources

You must determine the credibility and appropriateness of each source in order to write an effective report or speech. Ask yourself the following questions:

Is the writer an authority? A writer who has written several books on a subject or whose name is included in numerous bibliographies may be considered an authoritative source.

Is the source reliable and unbiased? What is the author's motivation? For example, a defense of an industry in which the author has a financial interest may be biased. A profile of a writer or scientist written by a close relative or friend may also be biased.

WEB TIP Be especially skeptical of information you locate on the Internet, since virtually anyone can post anything there. Read the URL, or Internet address. Sites sponsored by government agencies (*.gov*) or educational institutions (*.edu*) are generally more reliable.

Is the source up-to-date? It is important to consult the most recent material, especially in fields, such as medicine and technology, in which there is constant research and development. Some authoritative sources have withstood the test of time, however, and should not be overlooked.

Is the source appropriate? For what audience is the material written? In general, look for information directed at the educated reader. Material geared to experts or to popular audiences may be too technical or too simplified and therefore not appropriate for most research projects.

Distinguishing Fact from Opinion

As you gather information, it is important to recognize facts and opinions. A **fact** can be proved to be true or false. You could verify the statement "Congress rejected the bill" by checking newspapers, magazines, or the *Congressional Record.* An **opinion** is a judgment based on facts. The statement "Congress should not have rejected the bill" is an opinion. To evaluate an opinion, check for evidence presented logically to support it.

Recognizing Bias

A writer may have a particular bias. This does not automatically make his or her point of view unreliable. However, recognizing an author's bias can help you evaluate a source. Recognizing that the author of an article about immigration is a Chinese immigrant will help you understand that author's bias. In addition, an author may have a hidden agenda that makes him or her less than objective about a topic. To avoid relying on information that may be biased, check an author's background and gather a variety of viewpoints.

 Collecting Information

People use a variety of techniques to collect information during the research process. Try out several of those suggested below and decide which ones work best for you.

Paraphrasing and Summarizing

You can adapt material from other sources by quoting it directly or by paraphrasing or summarizing it. Paraphrasing involves restating the information in your own words. A paraphrase is often a simpler version but not necessarily a

R46 COMMUNICATION HANDBOOK

shorter version. Summarizing involves extracting the main ideas and supporting details and writing a shorter version of the information.

Remember to credit the source when you paraphrase or summarize. See "Research Report Writing" in the Writing Handbook, pp. R37–R42.

Strategies for Paraphrasing
1. Select the portion of the article you want to record.
2. Read it carefully and think about those ideas you find most interesting and useful to your research. Often these will be the main ideas.
3. Retell the information in your own words.

Strategies for Summarizing
1. Read the article carefully. Determine the main ideas.
2. In your own words, write a shortened version of these main ideas.

Avoiding Plagiarism

Plagiarism is copying someone else's ideas or words and using them as if they were your own. This can happen inadvertently if you are sloppy about collecting information and documenting your sources. Plagiarism is intellectual stealing and can have serious consequences.

How to Avoid Plagiarism

1. When you paraphrase or summarize, be sure to change entirely the wording of the original by using your own words.
2. Both in notes and on your final report, enclose in quotation marks any material copied directly from other sources.
3. Indicate in your final report the sources of any ideas that are not general knowledge—including those in the visuals—that you have paraphrased or summarized.
4. Include a list of works cited with your finished report. See "Research Report Writing" in the Writing Handbook, pp. R37–R42.

2 Study Skills and Strategies

As you read an assignment for the first time, review material for a test, or search for information for a research report, you use different methods of reading and studying.

2.1 Skimming

When you run your eyes quickly over a text, paying attention to overviews, headings, topic sentences, highlighted words, and graphic features, you are skimming.

Skimming is a good technique for previewing material in a textbook or other source that you must read for an assignment. It is also useful when you are researching a self-selected topic. Skimming a source helps you determine whether it has pertinent information. For example, suppose you are writing a research report on Leo Tolstoy. Skimming an essay on the literature of Russia can help you quickly determine whether any part of it deals with your topic.

2.2 Scanning

To find a specific piece of information in a text, use scanning. To scan, place a card under the first line of a page and move it down slowly. Look for key words and phrases that signal the information you are looking for.

Scanning is useful in reviewing for a test or in finding a specific piece of information for a paper. Suppose you are looking for a discussion of Tolstoy's relationship with his family for your research report. You can scan a book chapter or an essay, looking for the key name *Sonya.*

COMMUNICATION HANDBOOK R47

2.3 In-Depth Reading

When you must thoroughly understand the material in a text, you use in-depth reading.

In-depth reading involves asking questions, taking notes, looking for main ideas, and drawing conclusions as you read slowly and carefully. For example, in researching your report on Tolstoy, you may find an essay on how Tolstoy's point of view changed in his later literature. Since this is closely related to your topic, you will read it in depth and take notes. You also should use in-depth reading for reading textbooks and literary works.

2.4 Outlining

Outlining is an efficient way of organizing ideas and is useful in taking notes.

Outlining helps you retain information as you read in depth. For example, you might outline a chapter in a history textbook, listing the main subtopics and the ideas or details that support them. An outline can also be useful for taking notes for a research report or in reading a piece of literature. The following is an example of a topic outline that summarizes, in short phrases, part of a chapter.

MAIN IDEA: **Leo Tolstoy was one of the world's greatest novelists.**

I. Early Years
- **A. First publications**
- **B. Importance of wife and family**

II. Major Novels
- **A. *War and Peace***
- **B. *Anna Karenina***

III. Later Years
- **A. Change in religious beliefs and writing style**
- **B. Abandoned by wife and daughter**

IV. Evaluations of Tolstoy
- **A. Valued everyday reality**
- **B. Wrote about varied aspects of human existence**
- **C. On a constant search for the meaning of life**

2.5 Identifying Main Ideas

To understand and remember any material you read, identify its main idea.

In informative material, the main idea is often stated. The thesis statement of an essay or article and the topic sentence of each paragraph often state the main idea. In other material, especially literary works, the main idea is implied. After reading the piece carefully, analyze the important parts, such as characters and plot. Then try to sum up in one sentence the general point that the story makes.

2.6 Taking Notes

As you listen or read in depth, take notes to help you understand the material. Look and listen for key words that point to main ideas.

One way to help you summarize the main idea and supporting details is to take notes in modified outline form. In using a modified outline form, you do not need to use numerals and letters. Unlike a formal outline, a modified outline does not require two or more points under each heading, and headings do not need to be parallel grammatically. Yet, like a formal outline, a modified outline organizes a text's main ideas and related details. The following modified outline describes methods of communication:

Preliterate Methods
- **storytelling**
- **messengers**
- **smoke signals**
- **drums**

Literate Methods
- **writing**
- **printing press**

Electronic Methods
- **telegram**
- **telephone**
- **movies**
- **television**
- **Internet**

Use abbreviations and symbols to make note taking more efficient. Following are some commonly used abbreviations for note taking.

w/	with	re	regarding
w/o	without	=	is, equals
#	number	*	important
&, +	and	def	definition
>	more than	Amer	America
<	less than	tho	although

3 Critical Thinking

Critical thinking includes the ability to analyze, evaluate, and synthesize ideas and information. Critical thinking goes beyond simply understanding something. It involves making informed judgments based on sound reasoning skills.

3.1 Avoiding Faulty Reasoning

When you write or speak for a persuasive purpose, you must make sure your logic is valid. Avoid these mistakes in reasoning, called **logical fallacies.**

Overgeneralization

Conclusions reached on the basis of too little evidence result in the fallacy called overgeneralization. A person who saw three cyclists riding bicycles without helmets might conclude, "Nobody wears bicycle helmets." That conclusion would be an overgeneralization.

Circular Reasoning

When you support an opinion by simply repeating it in different terms, you are using circular reasoning. For example, "Sport-utility vehicles are popular because more people buy them than any other category of new cars." This is an illogical statement because the second part of the sentence simply uses different words to restate the first part of the sentence.

Either-Or Fallacy

Assuming that a complex question has only two possible answers is called the either-or fallacy. "Either we raise the legal driving age or accidents caused by teenage drivers will continue to increase" is an example of the either-or fallacy. The statement ignores other ways of decreasing the automobile accident rate of teenagers.

Cause-and-Effect Fallacy

The cause-and-effect fallacy occurs when you say that event B was caused by event A just because event B occurred after event A. A person might conclude that because a city's air quality worsened two months after a new factory began operation, the new factory caused the air pollution. However, this cause-and-effect relationship would have to be supported by more specific evidence.

3.2 Identifying Modes of Persuasion

Understanding persuasive techniques can help you evaluate information, make informed decisions, and avoid persuasive techniques intended to deceive you. Some modes of persuasion appeal to your various emotions.

Loaded Language

Loaded language is words or phrases chosen to appeal to the emotions. It is often used in place of facts to shape opinion or to evoke a positive or negative reaction. For example, you might feel positive about a politician who has a *plan*. You might, however, feel negative about a politician who has a *scheme*.

Bandwagon

Bandwagon taps into the human desire to belong. This technique suggests that "everybody" is doing it, or buying it, or believing it. Phrases such as "Don't be the only one" and "Everybody is" signal bandwagon appeal.

Testimonials

Testimonials present well-known people or satisfied customers who promote and endorse a product or idea. This technique taps into the appeal of celebrities or into people's need to identify with others just like themselves.

COMMUNICATION HANDBOOK R49

3.3 Logical Thinking

Persuasive writing and speaking require good reasoning skills. Two ways of creating logical arguments are deductive reasoning and inductive reasoning.

Deductive Arguments

A deductive argument begins with a generalization, or premise, and then advances with facts and evidence that lead to a conclusion. The conclusion is the logical outcome of the premise. A false premise leads to a false conclusion; a valid premise leads to a valid conclusion provided that the specific facts are correct and the reasoning is correct.

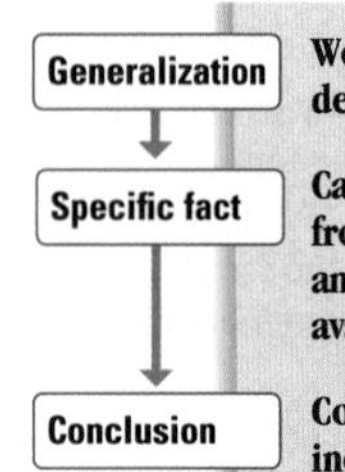

We need to reduce our dependence on fossil fuels.

Cars that get very high mileage from using a mixture of gasoline and electric power are now available in some countries.

Congress should provide tax incentives for manufacturers and consumers to use cars that use gasoline/electric power.

You may use deductive reasoning when writing a persuasive paper or speech. Your conclusion is the thesis of your paper. Facts in your paper supporting your premise should lead logically to that conclusion.

Inductive Arguments

An inductive argument begins with specific evidence that leads to a general conclusion.

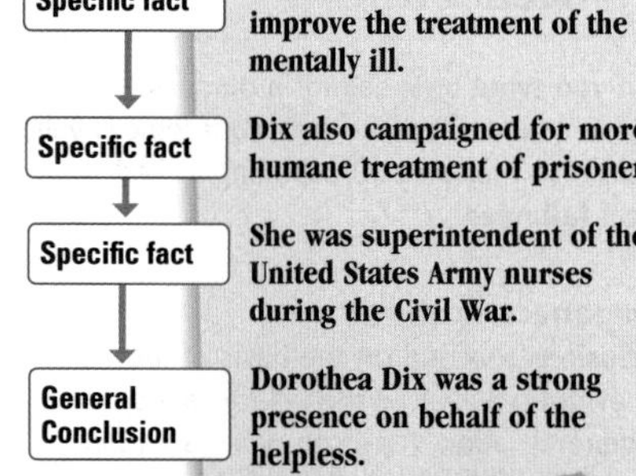

The conclusion of an inductive argument often includes a qualifying term such as *some, often,* or *most.* This usage helps to avoid the fallacy of overgeneralization.

4 Speaking and Listening

Good speakers and listeners do more than just talk and hear. They use specific techniques to present their ideas effectively, and they are attentive and critical listeners.

4.1 Giving a Speech

In school, in business, and in community life, giving a speech is one of the most effective ways of communicating. Whether you are trying to persuade, to inform, or to entertain, you may often speak before an audience.

Analyzing Audience and Purpose

In order to speak effectively, you need to know to whom you are speaking and why you are speaking. When preparing a speech, think about how much knowledge and interest your audience has in your subject. A speech has one of two main purposes: to inform or to persuade. A third purpose, to entertain, is often considered closely related to these two purposes.

A speech **to inform** gives the audience new information, provides a better understanding of information, or enables people to use information in a new way. An informative speech is presented in an objective way.

In a speech **to persuade,** a speaker tries to change the actions or beliefs of an audience.

R50 COMMUNICATION HANDBOOK

Preparing and Delivering a Speech

There are four main methods of preparing and delivering a speech.

Manuscript When you speak from **manuscript,** you prepare a complete script of your speech in advance and use it to deliver your speech.

Memory When you speak from **memory,** you prepare a written text in advance and then memorize it so you can deliver it word for word.

Impromptu When you give an **impromptu** speech, you speak on the spur of the moment without any special preparation.

Extemporaneous When you give an **extemporaneous** speech, you research and prepare your speech and then deliver it with the help of notes.

Points for Effective Speech Delivery

- Avoid speaking either too fast or too slow. Vary your **speaking rate** depending on your material. Slow down for difficult concepts. Speed up to convince your audience that you are knowledgeable about your subject.
- Speak loud enough to be heard clearly, but not so loud that your voice is overwhelming.
- Use a **conversational tone.**
- Use a change of **pitch,** or inflection, to help make your tone and meaning clear.
- Let your **facial expressions** reflect your message.
- Make **eye contact** with as many audience members as possible.
- Use **gestures** to emphasize your words. Don't make your gestures too small to be seen. On the other hand, don't gesture too frequently or wildly.
- Use **good posture**—not too relaxed and not too rigid. Avoid nervous mannerisms.

4.2 Analyzing, Evaluating and Critiquing a Speech

Evaluating speeches helps you make informed judgments about the ideas presented in a speech. It also helps you learn what makes an effective speech and delivery. Use these criteria to help you analyze, evaluate, and critique speeches.

CRITERIA How to Evaluate a Persuasive Speech

- Did the speaker have a clear goal or argument?
- Did the speaker take the audience's biases into account?
- Did the speaker support the argument with convincing facts?
- Did the speaker use sound logic in developing the argument?
- Did the speaker use voice, facial expressions, gestures, and posture effectively?
- Did the speaker hold the audience's interest?

CRITERIA How to Evaluate an Informative Speech

- Did the speaker have a specific, clearly focused topic?
- Did the speaker take the audience's previous knowledge into consideration?
- Did the speaker cite sources for the information?
- Did the speaker communicate the information objectively?
- Did the speaker present the information in an organized manner?
- Did the speaker use visual aids effectively?
- Did the speaker use voice, facial expressions, gestures, and posture effectively?

COMMUNICATION HANDBOOK R51

4.3 Using Active Listening Strategies

Listeners play an active part in the communication process. A listener has a responsibility just as a speaker does. Listening, unlike hearing, is a learned skill.

As you listen to a public speaker, use the following active listening strategies:

- Determine the **speaker's purpose.**
- Listen for the **main idea** of the message and not simply the individual details.
- **Anticipate the points** that will be made, taking into account the speaker's purpose and main idea.
- Listen with an open mind, but **identify faulty logic, unsupported facts,** and **emotional appeals.**

4.4 Conducting Interviews

Conducting a personal interview can be an effective way to get information.

Preparing for an Interview

- Read any articles by or about the person you will interview. This background information will help you get to the point during the interview.
- Prepare a list of questions. Think of more questions than you will need. Include some yes/no questions and some open-ended questions. Order your questions from most important to least important.

Participating in the Interview

- Listen interactively. Be prepared to follow up on a response you find interesting.
- Avoid arguments. Be tactful and polite.

Following Up on the Interview

- Summarize your notes while they are still fresh in your mind.
- Send a thank-you note to the interviewee.

5 Viewing and Representing

In our media-saturated world, we are immersed in visual messages that convey ideas, information, and attitudes. To understand and use visual representations effectively, you need to be aware of the techniques and the range of visuals that are commonly used.

5.1 Understanding Visual Messages

Information is communicated not only with words but with graphic devices. A **graphic device** is a visual representation of data and ideas and the relations among them.

Reading Charts and Graphs

In charts, information is organized in rows and columns. They are helpful in showing complex information clearly. When interpreting a chart, first read the title. Then analyze how the information is presented. Charts can take many different forms. The following chart compares Dante's descriptions of sinners and their punishments in the *Inferno*.

Comparison and Contrast

Sinners	Punishment
"souls unsure / whose lives earned neither honor nor bad fame"	"a blind life / So abject they envy any other fate"
those "who sinned in carnal things"	"All light is mute . . ." "hurricane of Hell"
those who betrayed their benefactors	"covered wholly by ice"

There are several different types of **graphs,** visual aids that are often used to display numerical information.

R52 COMMUNICATION HANDBOOK

- A **circle graph** shows proportions in a whole.
- A **line graph** shows changes in data over a period of time. The following line graph shows changes in the area of the United States during the 19th century.

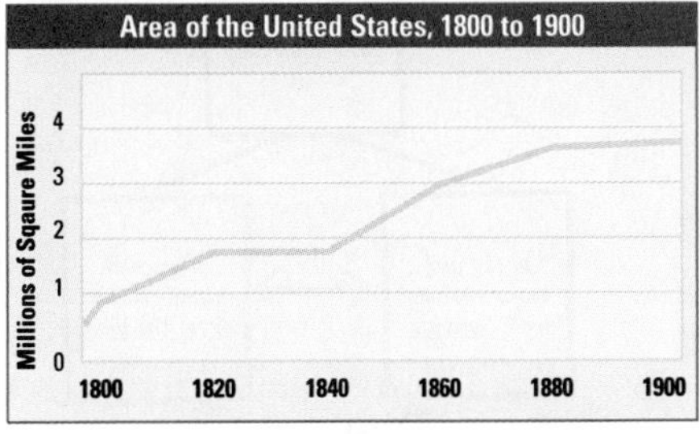

- A **bar graph** compares amounts. The following bar graph shows how many books Leo Tolstoy wrote in each period of his writing career.

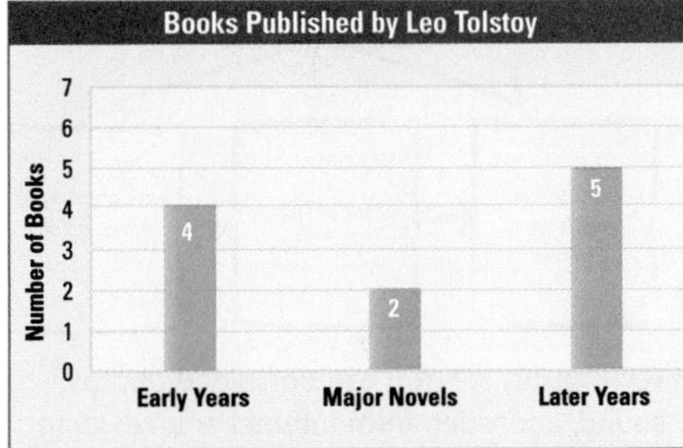

Interpreting Images

Speakers and writers often use visual aids to inform or persuade their audiences. These aids can be invaluable in helping you understand the information being communicated. However, you must interpret visual aids critically, as you do written material.

- **Examine photographs critically.** Does the camera angle or the background in the photo intentionally evoke a positive or negative response? Has the image been altered or manipulated?
- **Evaluate carefully the data presented in charts and graphs.** Some charts and graphs may exaggerate the facts. For example, a circle graph representing a sample of only ten people may be misleading if the speaker suggests that the data represent a trend.

 Evaluating Visual Messages

When you view images, whether they are cartoons, advertising art, photographs, or paintings, there are certain elements to look for.

CRITERIA **How to Analyze Images**

- Is color used realistically? Is it used to emphasize certain objects? to evoke a specific response?
- What tone is created by color and by light and dark in the picture?
- Do the background images intentionally evoke a positive or negative response?
- What is noticeable about the picture's composition—that is, the arrangement of lines, colors, and forms? Does the composition emphasize certain objects or elements in the picture?
- For graphs and charts, does the visual accurately represent the data?

 Using Visual Representations

Tables, graphs, diagrams, pictures, and animations often communicate information more effectively than words alone do.

Use visuals with written reports to illustrate complex concepts and processes or to make a page look more interesting. Computer programs, CD-ROMs, and online services can help you generate

- **graphs** that present numerical information
- **charts** and **tables** that allow easy comparison of information
- **logos** and **graphic devices** that highlight important information
- **borders** and **tints** that signal different kinds of information
- useful **illustrations**
- **interactive animations** that illustrate difficult concepts

You might want to explore ways of displaying data in more than one visual format before deciding which will work best for you.

COMMUNICATION HANDBOOK R53

5.4 Making Multimedia Presentations

A multimedia presentation is an electronically prepared combination of text, sound, and visuals (such as photographs, videos, and animations). Your audience reads, hears, and sees your presentation at a computer, following different "paths" you have created to lead them through the information you have gathered.

Planning Presentations

To create a multimedia presentation, first choose your topic and decide what you want to include. Then plan how you want the audience to move through your presentation. For a multimedia presentation on the role of the hero in literature, you might include the following items:

- text defining *hero* and discussing elements of heroes
- a taped reading from *Sundiata,* describing the "Lion King," accompanied by photo of a painting of the African leader
- a taped reading from the *Iliad,* accompanied by a sequence of slides showing various images of Achilles
- a chart comparing two descriptions of a hero: one epic, one cultural
- a video interview with an author on the role of the hero in his or her work
- a video of Troy as seen from an explorer's viewpoint, with a voice-over discussing Homer's *Iliad*
- a series of short film clips showing various heroes from epic movies

You can choose one of the following ways to organize your presentation:

step by step, with only one path, or order, in which the user can see and hear the information

a branching path that allows users to make choices about what they will see and hear, and in what order

A flow chart can help you figure out the paths a user can take through your presentation. Each box in the flow chart that follows represents something about heroes for the user to read, see, or hear. The arrows on the flow chart show the possible paths the user can follow.

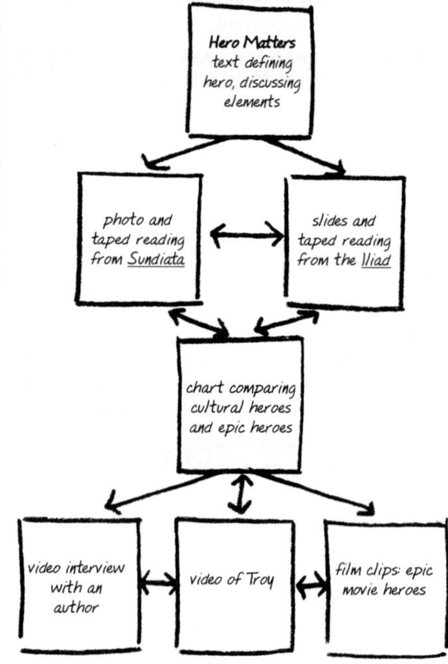

TECHNOLOGY TIP You can download photos, sound, and video from Internet sources onto your computer. This process lets you add elements that would usually require complex editing equipment.

Guiding Your User

Your user will need directions to follow the path you have planned for your multimedia presentation.

Most multimedia authoring programs allow you to create screens that include text or audio directions that guide the user from one part of your presentation to the next.

If you need help creating your multimedia presentation, ask your school's technology adviser. You may also be able to get help from your classmates or your software manual.

R54 COMMUNICATION HANDBOOK

Grammar Handbook

1 Quick Reference: Parts of Speech

Part of Speech	Definition	Examples
Noun	Names a person, place, thing, idea, quality, or action	Margaret, Texas, knuckles, nature, beauty, beginning
Pronoun	Takes the place of a noun or another pronoun	
Personal	Refers to the ones speaking, spoken to, or spoken about	I, me, my, mine, we, us, our, ours, you, your, yours, she, he, it, her, him, hers, his, its, they, them, their, theirs
Reflexive	Follows a verb or preposition and refers to a preceding noun or pronoun	myself, yourself, herself, himself, itself, ourselves, yourselves, themselves
Intensive	Emphasizes a noun or another pronoun	(Same as reflexive pronouns)
Demonstrative	Points to one or more specific persons or things	this, that, these, those
Interrogative	Signals a question	who, whom, whose, which, what
Indefinite	Refers to one or more persons or things not specifically mentioned	both, all, most, many, anyone, everybody, several, none, some
Relative	Introduces a subordinate clause and relates it to a word in the main clause	who, whom, whose, which, that
Verb	Expresses action, condition, or state of being	
Action	Tells what the subject does or did, physically or mentally	run, reaches, listened, consider, decides, dreamed
Linking	Connects a subject to that which identifies or describes it	am, is, are, was, were, sound, taste, appear, feel, become, remain, seem
Auxiliary	Precedes and introduces a main verb	be, have, do, can, could, will, would, may, might
Adjective	Modifies a noun or pronoun	**strong** women, **two** epics, **enough** time
Adverb	Modifies a verb, an adjective, or another adverb	walked **out, really** funny, **far** away
Preposition	Relates one word to another (following) word	at, by, for, from, in, of, on, to, with
Conjunction	Joins words or word groups	
Coordinating	Joins words or word groups used the same way	and, but, or, for, so, yet, nor
Correlative	Work as a pair to join words or word groups used the same way	both . . . and, either . . . or, neither . . . nor
Subordinating	Joins word groups not used the same way	although, after, as, before, because, when, if, unless
Interjection	Expresses emotion	wow, ouch, hurrah

Grammar Handbook

GRAMMAR HANDBOOK R55

GRAMMAR PRACTICE ANSWERS

Exercise A

1. common, abstract
2. common, concrete
3. proper, concrete; common, abstract
4. proper, concrete
5. common, concrete
6. proper, abstract
7. common, concrete
8. common, concrete
9. common, abstract
10. common, abstract

Exercise B

11–15. compound nouns: Mali empire, Atlantic Ocean, Niger River, storyteller; collective nouns: empire, culture, kingdom.

Exercise C

16. Sundiata's
17. kingdoms'
18. Rama's
19. tranquility's
20. values'
21. Valmiki's
22. arms'
23. strength's
24. Nigeria's
25. storytellers'

Grammar Handbook

2 Nouns

A noun is a word used to name a person, place, thing, idea, quality, or action. Nouns can be classified in several ways. All nouns can be placed in at least two classifications. They are either common or proper. All are also either abstract or concrete. Some nouns can be classified as compound, collective, or possessive as well.

2.1 *Common Nouns* are general names, common to an entire group.

EXAMPLES: *motor, tree, time, children*

2.2 *Proper Nouns* name specific, one-of-a-kind things. (See Quick Reference: Capitalization, page R79.)

EXAMPLES: *Bradbury, Eastern Standard Time, Maine*

2.3 *Concrete Nouns* name things that can be perceived by the senses.

EXAMPLES: *stadium, jacket, St. Louis, Wrigley Field*

2.4 *Abstract Nouns* name things that cannot be perceived by the senses.

EXAMPLES: *intelligence, fear, joy, loneliness*

	Common	Proper
Abstract	beauty	Enlightenment
Concrete	planet	Mars

2.5 *Compound Nouns* are formed from two or more words but express single ideas. They are written as single words, as separate words, or with hyphens. Use a dictionary to check the correct spelling of a compound noun.

EXAMPLES: *sunshine, call waiting, job-sharing*

2.6 *Collective Nouns* are singular nouns that refer to groups of people or things. (See Collective Nouns as Subjects, page R76.)

EXAMPLES: *army, flock, class, species*

2.7 *Possessive Nouns* show who or what owns something. Consult the following chart for the proper use of the possessive apostrophe.

Possessive Nouns

Category	Rule	Examples
All singular nouns	Add apostrophe plus *s*	Lily's, bass's, pitcher's, daughter-in-law's
Plural nouns not ending in *s*	Add apostrophe plus *s*	children's women's people's
Plural nouns ending in *s*	Add apostrophe only	witnesses' churches' males' Johnsons'

GRAMMAR PRACTICE

A. For each underlined noun, first tell whether it is common or proper. Then tell whether it is concrete or abstract.

1. The legend of Sundiata is loosely based on the true story of the man who established the Mali empire.
2. After he returned from years in exile, Sundiata united the kingdoms of the region.
3. The Mali territory, which eventually stretched from the Atlantic Ocean to what is now Nigeria, included part of the Niger River.
4. The tranquillity and peace established by Sundiata lasted for many years.
5. Griots, or trained storytellers, narrate the epic of Sundiata by reciting, chanting, and singing the story.
6. Valmiki, the author of the *Ramayana*, at first did not think himself worthy to tell the tale of Rama.
7. Rama, a strong and brave leader, prepares to do battle with the enemy who kidnapped Sita, Rama's wife.
8. Rama fights Ravana, a powerful demon with 10 heads and 20 arms.
9. In Indian culture, Rama represents values such as strength and leadership.
10. The *Ramayana*, while filled with action and intrigue, is a highly spiritual work as well.

B. 11–15. From the sentences above, write three compound nouns and two collective nouns.

C. Write the possessive forms of the following nouns.

16. Sundiata
17. kingdoms
18. Rama
19. tranquillity
20. values
21. Valmiki
22. arms
23. strength
24. Nigeria
25. storytellers

3 Pronouns

A pronoun is a word that is used in place of a noun or another pronoun. The word or word group to which the pronoun refers is called its antecedent.

3.1 *Personal Pronouns* are pronouns that change their form to express person, number, gender, and case. The forms of these pronouns are shown in the chart that follows.

	Nominative	Objective	Possessive
Singular			
First person	I	me	my, mine
Second person	you	you	your, yours
Third person	she, he, it	her, him, it	her, hers, his, its
Plural			
First person	we	us	our, ours
Second person	you	you	your, yours
Third person	they	them	their, theirs

3.2 *Pronoun Agreement* Pronouns should agree with their antecedents in number and person. Singular pronouns are used to replace singular nouns. Plural pronouns are used to replace plural nouns. Pronouns must also match the gender (masculine, feminine, or neuter) of the nouns they replace.

3.3 *Pronoun Case* Personal pronouns change form to show how they function in a sentence. Their forms are called *cases.* The three cases are **nominative, objective,** and **possessive.**

A nominative pronoun is used as a subject or a predicate nominative in a sentence.

An objective pronoun is used as a direct or indirect object or as an object of a preposition.

SUBJECT — OBJECT

He will lead them to us.

OBJECT OF PREPOSITION

A possessive pronoun shows ownership. The pronouns *mine, yours, hers, his, its, ours,* and *theirs* can be used in place of nouns.

EXAMPLE: *This horse is mine.*

The pronouns *my, your, her, his, its, our,* and *their* are used before nouns.

EXAMPLE: *This is my horse.*

USAGE TIP To decide which case to use in a comparison, such as *He tells better tales than (I* or *me),* fill in the missing words: *He tells better tales than I tell.*

WATCH OUT! Many spelling errors can be avoided if you watch out for *its* and *their.* Don't confuse the possessive pronoun *its* with the contraction *it's*, meaning "it is" or "it has." The homophones *they're* (contraction of *they are*) and *there* (place or expletive) are often mistakenly used for *their.*

3.4 *Reflexive and Intensive Pronouns*
These pronouns are formed by adding *-self* or *-selves* to certain personal pronouns. Their forms are the same, and they differ only in how they are used.

Reflexive pronouns follow verbs or prepositions and reflect back on an earlier noun or pronoun.

EXAMPLES: *He likes himself too much. She is now herself again.*

Intensive pronouns intensify or emphasize the nouns or pronouns to which they refer.

EXAMPLES: *They themselves will educate their children. You did it yourselves.*

GRAMMAR HANDBOOK R57

GRAMMAR PRACTICE ANSWERS

1. his = it
2. myself = himself
3. she = it
4. her = his
5. she = their

Grammar Handbook

Singular	
First person	myself
Second person	yourself
Third person	herself, himself, itself
Plural	
First person	ourselves
Second person	yourselves
Third person	themselves

WATCH OUT! Avoid using *hisself* or *theirselves.* Standard English does not include these forms.

> **NONSTANDARD:** *The children sang theirselves to sleep.*
> **STANDARD:** *The children sang themselves to sleep.*

USAGE TIP Reflexive and intensive pronouns should never be used without antecedents.

> **INCORRECT:** *Read a tale to my brother and myself.*
> **CORRECT:** *Read a tale to my brother and me.*

3.5 ***Demonstrative Pronouns*** point out things and persons near and far.

	Singular	Plural
Near	this	these
Far	that	those

WATCH OUT! Avoid using the objective pronoun *them* in place of the demonstrative *those.*

> **INCORRECT:** *Let's dramatize one of them tales.*
> **CORRECT:** *Let's dramatize one of those tales.*

3.6 ***Indefinite Pronouns*** do not refer to specific persons or things and usually have no antecedents. The chart shows some commonly used indefinite pronouns.

Singular	Plural	Singular or Plural	
each	both	all	
either	few	any	
neither	many	more	none
another	several	most	some

Here is another set of indefinite pronouns, all of which are singular. Notice that, with one exception, each is spelled as one word:

anyone	everyone	no one	someone
anybody	everybody	nobody	somebody
anything	everything	nothing	something

USAGE TIP Since all these are singular, pronouns referring to them should be singular.

> **INCORRECT:** *Did everybody play their part well?*
> **CORRECT:** *Did everybody play her part well?*

If the indefinite pronoun can denote either a male or a female, *his or her* may be used to refer to it, or the sentence may be recast.

> **EXAMPLES:** *Did everybody play his or her part well?*
> *Did all the students play their parts well?*

GRAMMAR PRACTICE

Write the correct form of each incorrect pronoun in the sentences below.

1. In "Song of P'eng-ya," a family flees rebel troops who are chasing his.
2. The speaker of the poem carries the baby girl and lets the young boy walk by myself.
3. The family travels for days in unbearable conditions until she finally reaches the marsh.
4. Sun Tsai, an old friend of the speaker, and her wife help the family.
5. The vow between Sun Tsai and the speaker reinforces she loyalty.

3.7 ***Interrogative Pronouns*** tell a reader or listener that questions are coming. The interrogative pronouns are *who, whom, whose, which,* and *what.*

> **EXAMPLES:** *Who is going to rehearse with you?*
> *From whom did you receive the script?*

USAGE TIP *Who* is used as a subject, *whom* as an object. To find out which pronoun you need to use in a question, change the question to a statement:

> **QUESTION:** *(Who/Whom) did you meet there?*
> **STATEMENT:** *You met (?) there.*

Since the verb has a subject (*you*), the needed word must be the object form, *whom.*

> **CORRECT:** *Whom did you meet there?*

WATCH OUT! A special problem arises when you use an interrupter such as *do you think* within a sentence:

EXAMPLE: *(Who/Whom) do you think will win?*

If you eliminate the interrupter, it is clear that the word you need is *who.*

3.8 *Relative Pronouns* relate, or connect, clauses to the words they modify in sentences. The noun or pronoun that a clause modifies is the antecedent of the relative pronoun. Here are the relative pronouns and their uses.

Replacing:	Subject	Object	Possessive
Persons	who	whom	whose
Things	which	which	whose
Things/persons*	that	that	whose

* *That* generally will not replace specific names, such as *Richard Wright.*

Often short sentences with related ideas can be combined by using a relative pronoun to create a more effective sentence.

SHORT SENTENCE: *Amy won a swimming contest at the age of eight.*
RELATED SENTENCE: *Amy did not plan to become a professional athlete.*
COMBINED SENTENCE: *Amy, who won a swimming contest at the age of eight, did not plan to become a professional athlete.*

GRAMMAR PRACTICE

Choose the appropriate interrogative or relative pronoun from the words in parentheses.

1. Mrs. Linde, (who/whom) is an old friend of Nora's, stops by the Helmer house for an unexpected visit.
2. When Dr. Rank tells the ladies of a morally corrupt patient, Nora asks, "(Who/Whom) do you mean?"
3. Dr. Rank, (who/whom) is in love with Nora, asks her not to tell Torvald his secret.
4. Nora knows that Torvald, (who/whom) refuses to give Krogstad a position at the bank, would be devastated by the truth.
5. Fear, pride, and love are some of the factors (that/who) prevent Nora from telling Torvald about the loan from Krogstad.
6. Finally, Nora tells Torvald about her agreement with Krogstad, (who/whom) Torvald thinks is corrupt and loathsome.
7. Nora decides to leave her home after realizing that the man to (who/whom) she devoted her life did not understand her.

4 Verbs

A verb is a word that expresses an action, a condition, or a state of being. There are two main kinds of verbs: action and linking. Other verbs, called auxiliary verbs, are sometimes used with action verbs and linking verbs.

4.1 *Action Verbs* tell what action someone or something is performing, physically or mentally.

PHYSICAL ACTION: *You hit the target.*
MENTAL ACTION: *She dreamed of me.*

4.2 *Linking Verbs* do not express actions. Linking verbs link subjects to complements that identify or describe them. Linking verbs may be divided into two groups:

FORMS OF *BE*: *She is our queen.*
VERBS THAT EXPRESS CONDITION: *The writer looked thoughtful.*

4.3 *Auxiliary Verbs,* sometimes called helping verbs, precede action or linking verbs and modify their meanings in special ways. The most commonly used auxiliary verbs are forms of the verbs *be, have,* and *do.*

Be: *am, is, are, was, were, be, being, been*
Have: *have, has, had*
Do: *do, does, did*

Other common auxiliary verbs are *can, could, will, would, shall, should, may, might,* and *must.*

EXAMPLES: *I always have admired her.*
You must listen to me.

4.4 *Transitive and Intransitive Verbs*

Action verbs can be either transitive or intransitive. A transitive verb directs the action towards someone or something. It has an object. An intransitive verb does not direct the action towards someone or something. It does not have an object. Since linking verbs convey no action, they are always intransitive.

Transitive: *The storm sank the ship.*
Intransitive: *The ship sank.*

GRAMMAR PRACTICE ANSWERS

1. who
2. Whom
3. who
4. who
5. that
6. who
7. whom

4.5 *Principal Parts* Action and linking verbs typically have four principal parts, which are used to form verb tenses. The principal parts are the *present*, the *present participle*, the *past*, and the *past participle*.

If the verb is a regular verb, the past and past participle are formed by adding the ending *-d* or *-ed* to the present part. Here is a chart showing four regular verbs.

Present	Present Participle	Past	Past Participle
risk	(is) risking	risked	(has) risked
solve	(is) solving	solved	(has) solved
drop	(is) dropping	dropped	(has) dropped
carry	(is) carrying	carried	(has) carried

Note that the present participle and past participle forms are preceded by forms of *be* and *have.* These principal parts cannot be used alone as main verbs and always need auxiliary verbs.

EXAMPLES: *She once thought her mother was wasting her time.*

Now she has stopped trying to be like everyone else.

The past and past participle of an irregular verb are not formed by adding *-d* or *-ed* to the present; they are formed in irregular ways.

Present	Present Participle	Past	Past Participle
begin	(is) beginning	began	(has) begun
break	(is) breaking	broke	(has) broken
bring	(is) bringing	brought	(has) brought
choose	(is) choosing	chose	(has) chosen
go	(is) going	went	(has) gone
lose	(is) losing	lost	(has) lost
see	(is) seeing	saw	(has) seen
swim	(is) swimming	swam	(has) swum
write	(is) writing	wrote	(has) written

4.6 *Verb Tense* The tense of a verb tells the time of the action or the state of being. An action or state of being can occur in the present, the past, or the future. There are six tenses, each expressing a different range of time.

Present tense expresses an action that is happening at the present time, occurs regularly, or is constant or generally true. Use the present part.

EXAMPLES

NOW: *This soup tastes delicious.*

REGULAR: *I make vegetable soup often.*

GENERAL: *Crops require sun, rain, and rich soil.*

Past tense expresses an action that began and ended in the past. Use the past part.

EXAMPLE: *The storyteller finished his tale.*

Future tense expresses an action (or state of being) that will occur. Use *shall* or *will* with the present part.

EXAMPLE: *They will attend the next festival.*

Present perfect tense expresses action (1) that was completed at an indefinite time in the past or (2) that began in the past and continues into the present. Use *have* or *has* with the past participle.

EXAMPLE: *Poetry has inspired readers throughout the ages.*

Past perfect tense shows an action in the past that came before another action in the past. Use *had* before the past participle.

EXAMPLE: *Before we left, we had asked him to find a place to stay.*

Future perfect tense shows an action in the future that will be completed before another action in the future. Use *shall have* or *will have* before the past participle.

EXAMPLE: *They will have finished the novel before seeing the movie version of the tale.*

4.7 *Progressive Forms* The progressive forms of the six tenses show ongoing action. Use a form of *be* with the present participle of a verb.

PRESENT PROGRESSIVE: *She is rehearsing her lines.*

PAST PROGRESSIVE: *She was rehearsing her lines.*

FUTURE PROGRESSIVE: *She will be rehearsing her lines.*

PRESENT PERFECT PROGRESSIVE: *She has been rehearsing her lines.*
PAST PERFECT PROGRESSIVE: *She had been rehearsing her lines.*
FUTURE PERFECT PROGRESSIVE: *She will have been rehearsing her lines.*

WATCH OUT! Do not shift tenses needlessly. Watch out for these special cases.

- In most compound sentences and in sentences with compound predicates, use only one tense.
  INCORRECT: *I keyed in the password, but I get an error message.*
  CORRECT: *I keyed in the password, but I got an error message.*
- If one past action happens before another, do shift tenses—from the past to the past perfect:
  INCORRECT: *They wished they started earlier.*
  CORRECT: *They wished they had started earlier.*

GRAMMAR PRACTICE

Identify the tenses of the verbs in the following sentences. If you find an unnecessary tense shift, correct it.

1. The story "Iktomi and the Wild Ducks" is a Lakota trickster tale.
2. Iktomi decided he wants some ducks for breakfast.
3. After he tells the ducks to close their eyes for a dance, Iktomi will have been killing them.
4. However, one young duck had broken Iktomi's rule and opens his eyes.
5. He tells the other ducks to take off and they flew safely into the distance.

4.8 *Active and Passive Voice*

The voice of a verb tells whether the subject of a sentence performs or receives the action expressed by the verb. When the subject performs the action, the verb is in the active voice. When the subject is the receiver of the action, the verb is in the passive voice.

Compare these two sentences:

ACTIVE: *Her sunglasses hid most of her face.*
PASSIVE: *Most of her face was hidden by her sunglasses.*

To form the passive voice, use a form of *be* with the past participle of the main verb.

WATCH OUT! Use the passive voice sparingly. It tends to make writing less forceful and less direct. It can also make the writing awkward.

AWKWARD: *She was given the handmade quilts by her mother.*
BETTER: *Her mother gave her the handmade quilts.*

There are occasions when you will choose to use the passive voice because

- you want to emphasize the receiver: *The king was shot.*
- the doer is unknown: *My books were stolen.*
- the doer is unimportant: *French is spoken here.*

4.9 *Mood*

A verb's mood conveys the manner in which the verb expresses an idea. There are three moods.

The indicative mood states a fact or asks a question. You use this mood most often.

EXAMPLE: *His trust was shattered by the betrayal.*

The imperative mood is used to give a command or make a request.

EXAMPLE: *Be there by eight o'clock sharp.*

The subjunctive mood is used to express a wish or a condition that is contrary to fact.

EXAMPLE: *If I were you, I wouldn't get my hopes up.*

GRAMMAR PRACTICE

A. Identify the boldfaced verbs as active or passive.

1. The *Epic of Gilgamesh* **was written** more than 4,000 years ago.
2. It **is considered** one of the oldest quest stories.
3. Gilgamesh **explores** both his godlike side and his human side throughout the epic.
4. The death of his friend Enkidu **causes** Gilgamesh to break down and weep.
5. Utnapishtim and his family **had been saved** from the flood.

GRAMMAR PRACTICE ANSWERS

Column 1

1. is = present
2. decided = past
   wants = present
   wants > wanted
3. tells = present
   close = present
   will have been killing = future perfect progressive
   will have been killing > kills
4. had decided = past perfect
   (had) broken = past perfect
   opens = present
   broken > to break
   opens > open
5. tells = present
   take off = present
   flew = past
   flew > fly

Column 2

1. passive
2. passive
3. active
4. active
5. passive

GRAMMAR PRACTICE ANSWERS

6. indicative
7. subjunctive
8. indicative
9. indicative
10. subjunctive

Grammar Handbook

B. Identify the boldfaced verbs as indicative or subjunctive in mood.

6. Utnapishtim **gives** Gilgamesh advice before Gilgamesh meets with the gods.
7. If Utnapishtim **were** more trusting, he wouldn't have to test Gilgamesh's word.
8. After Utnapishtim **touched** Gilgamesh, Gilgamesh thought he had slept only moments.
9. The men **were leaving** when Utnapishtim's wife called out.
10. If Gilgamesh **were** a different kind of figure, he would not learn as much as he does during his quest.

5 Modifiers

Modifiers are words or groups of words that change or limit the meanings of other words. The two kinds of modifiers are adjectives and adverbs.

5.1 *Adjectives* An adjective is a word that modifies a noun or pronoun by telling which one, what kind, how many, or how much.

WHICH ONE: *this, that, these, those*
EXAMPLE: *These tomatoes have grown quickly.*

WHAT KIND: *tiny, impressive, bold, rotten*
EXAMPLE: *The bold officer stood in front of the crowd.*

HOW MANY: *some, few, thirty, none, both, each*
EXAMPLE: *Some of us had three helpings of sweet potatoes.*

HOW MUCH: *more, less, enough, scarce*
EXAMPLE: *There was enough chicken to serve everyone.*

The **articles** *a, an,* and *the* are usually classified as adjectives. These are the most common adjectives that you will use.

EXAMPLES: *The bridge was burned before the attack.*
A group of peasants led the procession in the town.

5.2 *Predicate Adjectives* Most adjectives come before the nouns they modify, as in the examples above. Predicate adjectives, however, follow linking verbs and describe their subjects.

EXAMPLE: *My friends are very intelligent.*

Be especially careful to use adjectives (not adverbs) after such linking verbs as *look, feel, grow, taste,* and *smell.*

EXAMPLE: *The weather grows cold.*

5.3 *Adverbs* modify verbs, adjectives, and other adverbs by telling where, when, how, or to what extent.

WHERE: *The children played outside.*
WHEN: *The author spoke yesterday.*
HOW: *We walked slowly behind the leader.*
TO WHAT EXTENT: *He worked very hard.*

Unlike adjectives, adverbs tend to be mobile words; they may occur in many places in sentences.

EXAMPLES: *Suddenly the wind shifted. The wind suddenly shifted. The wind shifted suddenly.*

Changing the position of adverbs within sentences can vary the rhythm in your writing.

5.4 *Adjective or Adverb* Many adverbs are formed by adding *-ly* to adjectives.

EXAMPLES: *sweet, sweetly; gentle, gently*

However, *-ly* added to a noun will usually yield an adjective.

EXAMPLES: *friend, friendly; woman, womanly*

5.5 *Comparison of Modifiers* The form of an adjective or adverb indicates the degree of comparison that the modifier expresses. Both adjectives and adverbs have three forms, or degrees: positive, comparative, and superlative.

The positive form is used to describe individual things, groups, or actions.

EXAMPLES: *The emperor's chariots are fast. Brenda's speech was effective.*

The comparative form is used to compare two things, groups, or actions.

EXAMPLES: *The emperor's chariots are faster than the senators' chariots.*
George's speech was more effective than Brenda's speech.

R62 GRAMMAR HANDBOOK

The superlative form is used to compare more than two things, groups, or actions.

EXAMPLES: *The emperor's chariots are the fastest in the empire.*
Antony's speech was the most effective of all.

5.6 *Regular Comparisons* For one-syllable and some two-syllable adjectives and adverbs, the comparative and superlative forms are formed by adding *-er* and *-est.* All three-syllable and most two-syllable modifiers form their comparative and superlative forms by adding *more* and *most.*

Positive	Comparative	Superlative
small	smaller	smallest
thin	thinner	thinnest
sleepy	sleepier	sleepiest
useless	more useless	most useless
precisely	more precisely	most precisely

WATCH OUT! Note that spelling changes must sometimes be made to form the comparatives and superlatives of modifiers.

EXAMPLES: *friendly, friendlier* (Change *y* to *i* and add the ending.)
sad, sadder (Double the final consonant and add the ending.)

5.7 *Irregular Comparisons* Some commonly used modifiers have irregular comparative and superlative forms. You may wish to memorize them.

Positive	Comparative	Superlative
good	better	best
bad	worse	worst
far	farther *or* further	farthest *or* furthest
little	less *or* lesser	least
many	more	most
well	better	best
much	more	most

5.8 *Using Modifiers Correctly* Study the tips that follow to avoid common mistakes.

Farther* and *further *Farther* is used for distances; use *further* for everything else.

Avoiding double comparisons You make a comparison by using *-er/-est* or by using *more/most.* Using *-er* with *more* or using *-est* with *most* is incorrect.

INCORRECT: *I like her more better than she likes me.*
CORRECT: *I like her better than she likes me.*

Avoiding illogical comparisons An illogical or confusing comparison results if two unrelated things are compared or if something is compared with itself. The word *other* or the word *else* should be used in a comparison of an individual member with the rest of the group.

ILLOGICAL: *Shakespeare's plays are more popular than those of any Elizabethan writer.* (Wasn't Shakespeare an Elizabethan writer?)
LOGICAL: *Shakespeare's plays are more popular than those of any other Elizabethan writer.*

Bad* vs. *badly *Bad,* always an adjective, is used before a noun or after a linking verb to describe the subject. *Badly,* always an adverb, never modifies a noun. Be sure to use the right form after a linking verb.

INCORRECT: *Ed felt badly after his team lost.*
CORRECT: *Ed felt bad after his team lost.*

Good* vs. *well *Good* is always an adjective. It is used before a noun or after a linking verb to modify the subject. *Well* is often an adverb meaning "expertly" or "properly." *Well* can also be used as an adjective after a linking verb, when it means "in good health."

INCORRECT: *Helen writes very good.*
CORRECT: *Helen writes very well.*
CORRECT: *Yesterday I felt bad; today I feel well.*

GRAMMAR HANDBOOK R63

Double negatives If you add a negative word to a sentence that is already negative, the result will be an error known as a double negative. When using *not* or *-n't* with a verb, use *"any-"* words, such as *anybody* or *anything,* rather than *"no-"* words, such as *nobody* or *nothing,* later in the sentence.

INCORRECT: *I don't have no money.*
CORRECT: *I don't have any money.*

INCORRECT: *We haven't seen nobody.*
CORRECT: *We haven't seen anybody.*

Using *hardly, barely*, or *scarcely* after a negative word is also incorrect.

INCORRECT: *They couldn't barely see two feet ahead.*
CORRECT: *They could barely see two feet ahead.*

Misplaced modifiers A misplaced modifier is one placed so far away from the word it modifies that the intended meaning of the sentence is unclear. Place modifiers as close as possible to the words they modify.

MISPLACED: *We found the child in the park who was missing.* (The child was missing, not the park.)

CLEARER: *We found the child who was missing in the park.*

GRAMMAR PRACTICE

Choose the correct word from each pair in parentheses.

1. The *Iliad's* main character is Achilles, the (powerfulest/most powerful) soldier in the Trojan War.
2. The war begins after Paris takes Helen, the (most beautiful/beautifulest) woman in the world, away from Menelaus.
3. Paris (could/couldn't) hardly know that his rash action would cause a ten-year battle.
4. Nine years later, when the *Iliad* begins, Greek armies still hadn't defeated (no/any) Trojans.
5. Between Agamemnon and Achilles, Achilles is the (better/best) commander.
6. Achilles defects from Agamemnon, but Achilles' soldiers follow Achilles because they love him (well/good).
7. After his best friend, Patroclus, dies in battle, Achilles feels (bad/badly).
8. Achilles doesn't have (any/no) qualm about destroying Hector's body.
9. Achilles doesn't want (anyone/no one) but the Trojans to win the war.
10. Some Greeks think that Achilles is the (most good/best) leader they will ever have.

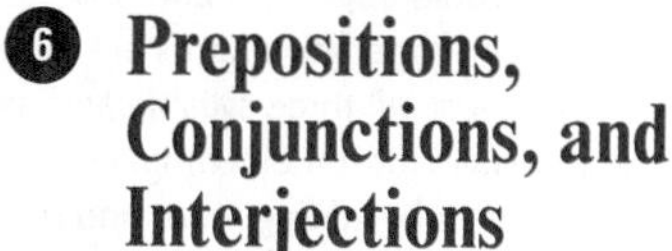

6 Prepositions, Conjunctions, and Interjections

6.1 *Prepositions* A preposition is a word used to show the relationship between a noun or a pronoun and another word in the sentence.

Commonly Used Prepositions			
above	down	near	through
at	for	of	to
before	from	on	up
below	in	out	with
by	into	over	without

The preposition is always followed by a word or group of words that serve as its object. The preposition, its object, and modifiers of the object are called a **prepositional phrase.** In each example below, the prepositional phrase is underlined and the object of the preposition is in boldface type.

EXAMPLES
*The future of the entire **kingdom** is uncertain.*
*We searched through the deepest **woods.***

Prepositional phrases may be used as adjectives or as adverbs. The phrase in the first example is used as an adjective modifying the noun *future.* In the second example, the phrase is used as an adverb modifying the verb *searched.*

WATCH OUT! A prepositional phrase must be as close as possible to the word it modifies.

MISPLACED: *We have clothes for leisure wear of many colors.*
CLEARER: *We have clothes of many colors for leisure wear.*

GRAMMAR PRACTICE ANSWERS

1. most powerful
2. most beautiful
3. could
4. any
5. better
6. well
7. bad
8. any
9. anyone
10. best

6.2 *Conjunctions* A conjunction is a word used to connect words, phrases, or sentences. There are three kinds of conjunctions: **coordinating conjunctions, correlative conjunctions,** and **subordinating conjunctions.**

Coordinating conjunctions connect words or word groups that have the same function in a sentence. These include *and, but, or, for, so, yet,* and *nor.* Coordinating conjunctions can join nouns, pronouns, verbs, adjectives, adverbs, prepositional phrases, and clauses.

These examples show coordinating conjunctions joining words of the same function:

EXAMPLES

I have many friends but few enemies. (two direct objects)

We ran out the door and into the street. (two prepositional phrases)

They are pleasant yet seem aloof. (two predicates)

We have to go now, or we will be late. (two clauses)

Correlative conjunctions are similar to coordinating conjunctions. However, correlative conjunctions are always used in pairs.

Correlative Conjunctions		
both . . . and	neither . . . nor	whether . . . or
either . . . or	not only . . . but also	

Subordinating conjunctions introduce subordinate clauses—clauses that cannot stand by themselves as complete sentences. The subordinating conjunction shows how the subordinate clause relates to the rest of the sentence. The relationships include time, manner, place, cause, comparison, condition, and purpose.

TIME	*after, as, as long as, as soon as, before, since, until, when, whenever, while*
MANNER	*as, as if*
PLACE	*where, wherever*
CAUSE	*because, since*
COMPARISON	*as, as much as, than*
CONDITION	*although, as long as, even if, even though, if, provided that, though, unless, while*
PURPOSE	*in order that, so that, that*

In the example below, the boldfaced word is the conjunction, and the underlined words are the subordinate clause:

EXAMPLE: *We sing* ***because*** *we are happy.*

We sing is an independent clause because it can stand alone as a complete sentence. *Because we are happy* cannot stand alone as a complete sentence; it is a subordinate clause.

Conjunctive adverbs are used to connect clauses that can stand by themselves as sentences. Conjunctive adverbs include *also, besides, finally, however, moreover, nevertheless, otherwise,* and *then.*

EXAMPLE: *She loved the fall; however, she also enjoyed winter.*

6.3 *Interjections* are words used to show strong emotion, such as *wow* and *cool.* Often followed by an exclamation point, they have no grammatical relationship to the rest of a sentence.

EXAMPLE: *You've written a poem? Great!*

GRAMMAR PRACTICE

Label each of the boldfaced words as a preposition, a conjunction, or an interjection.

1. Chrétien de Troyes wrote poetry about King Arthur **and** the knights of the Round Table.
2. He is well-known **for** his Arthurian romances, **but** he also wrote a tale that mocks epic **and** romance customs.
3. **In** Chrétien's romance *Perceval: The Story* ***of*** *the Grail,* the main character is searching **for** his mother.
4. Perceval feels sad **because** she fainted **when** he left home.
5. Perceval meets a man **by** a river and asks him **for** directions.
6. He finds shelter **for** the night **in** an enormous castle. **Excellent!**
7. **While** he is inside the castle, Perceval observes a ritual full **of** mystery **and** magic.
8. He is afraid **of** interrupting the ceremony, **yet** he cannot turn away.
9. **After** he leaves, he meets a girl; she tells Perceval **of** future misfortunes **for** himself **and** others.
10. **In** the end, Perceval cannot believe he saw the Holy Grail **and** didn't know it. **Wow!**

Grammar Handbook

GRAMMAR PRACTICE ANSWERS

1. conjunction
2. preposition, conjunction, conjunction
3. preposition, preposition, preposition
4. conjunction, conjunction
5. preposition, preposition
6. preposition, preposition, interjection
7. conjunction, preposition, conjunction
8. preposition, conjunction
9. conjunction, preposition, preposition, conjunction
10. preposition, conjunction, interjection

Grammar Handbook

7 Quick Reference: The Sentence and Its Parts

The diagrams that follow will give you a brief review of the essentials of the sentence—subjects and predicates—and of some of its parts.

The writer's **pen** **hit** the floor.

The **complete subject** includes all the words that identify the person, place, thing, or idea that the sentence is about.

The **complete predicate** includes all the words that tell or ask something about the subject.

pen

The **simple subject** tells exactly whom or what the sentence is about. It does not include any modifiers.

hit

The **simple predicate,** or **verb,** tells what the subject does or is. It may be one word or several, but it does not include modifiers.

For his graduation, the family **had given** the young **Buddy** money.

A **prepositional phrase** consists of a preposition, its object, and any modifiers of the object. In this phrase, *for* is the preposition and *graduation* is its object.

subject

Verbs often have more than one part. They may be made up of a **main verb,** like *given,* and one or more **auxiliary,** or **helping, verbs,** like *had.*

An **indirect object** is a word or a group of words that tells to whom or for whom or to what or for what about the verb. A sentence can have an indirect object only if it has a direct object. The indirect object always comes before the direct object in a sentence.

A **direct object** is a word or group of words that tells who or what receives the action of the verb in the sentence.

R66 GRAMMAR HANDBOOK

8 The Sentence and Its Parts

A sentence is a group of words used to express a complete thought. A complete sentence has a subject and predicate.

8.1 *Kinds of Sentences* Sentences make statements, ask questions, give commands, and show feelings. There are four basic types of sentences.

Type	Definition	Example
Declarative	States a fact, wish, intent, or feeling	I read White's essay last night.
Interrogative	Asks a question	Did you like the essay?
Imperative	Gives a command or direction	Read this paragraph aloud.
Exclamatory	Expresses strong feeling or excitement	I wish I had thought of that!

WRITING TIP One way to vary your writing is to employ a variety of different types of sentences. In the first example below, each sentence is declarative. Notice how much more interesting the revised paragraph is.

> **SAMPLE PARAGRAPH:** *You have to see Niagara Falls in person. You can truly appreciate their awesome power in no other way. You should visit them on your next vacation. They are a spectacular sight.*
>
> **REVISED PARAGRAPH:** *Have you ever seen Niagara Falls in person? You can truly appreciate their awesome power in no other way. Visit them on your next vacation. What a spectacular sight they are!*

WATCH OUT! Conversation frequently includes parts of sentences, or **fragments.** In formal writing, however, you need to be sure that every sentence is a complete thought and includes a subject and a predicate. (See Correcting Fragments, page R73.)

8.2 *Complete Subjects and Predicates*
A sentence has two parts: a subject and a predicate. The complete subject includes all the words that identify the person, place, thing, or idea that the sentence is about. The complete predicate includes all the words that tell what the subject did or what happened to the subject.

Complete Subject	Complete Predicate
The poets of the time	wrote about nature.
This new approach	was extraordinary.

8.3 *Simple Subjects and Predicates*
The simple subject is the key word in the complete subject. The simple predicate is the key word in the complete predicate. In the examples that follow they are underlined.

Simple Subject	Simple Predicate
The poets of the time	wrote about nature.
This new approach	was extraordinary.

8.4 *Compound Subjects and Predicates* A compound subject consists of two or more subjects of the same verb. They are typically joined by the coordinating conjunction *and* or *or*.

> **EXAMPLE:** *Tolstoy and Ibsen write about families.*

A compound predicate consists of two or more predicates that have the same subject. They too are usually joined by the coordinating conjunction *and, but,* or *or*.

> **EXAMPLE:** *The homeowner mowed the lawn and watered the garden.*

8.5 *Subjects in Questions* In an interrogative sentence, the subject may appear after the verb or between parts of a verb phrase.

> **INTERROGATIVE:** *Did Father get up early?*
> **INTERROGATIVE:** *Why has that book sold so well?*

GRAMMAR HANDBOOK R67

GRAMMAR PRACTICE ANSWERS

1. Sophocles wrote the play *Oedipus the King.*
2. The story begins with Oedipus ruling Thebes with his wife, Jocasta, at his side.
3. A plague causes Oedipus to search for a remedy to stop the outbreak.
4. The oracle tells the king he must find the man who murdered Jocasta's first husband, Laius.
5. As Oedipus begins to investigate, his hidden past begins to point suspicion in a startling direction.
6. The truth reveals that Oedipus himself murdered Laius.
7. Laius and Jocasta are actually Oedipus' father and mother.
8. Jocasta hangs herself to spare herself the shame of being married to her own son.
9. In a guilt stricken moment, the king blinds himself with needles.
10. Oedipus is a classic example of a tragic hero.

Grammar Handbook

8.6 *Subjects in Imperative Sentences*

Imperative sentences give commands, requests, or directions. The subject of an imperative sentence is the person spoken to. While it is not stated, it is understood to be *you.*

EXAMPLE: *(You) Please tell me what you're thinking.*

8.7 *Subjects in Sentences That Begin with* There *and* Here

When a sentence begins with *there* or *here*, the subject usually follows the verb. Remember that *there* and *here* are never the subjects of sentences. The simple subjects in the example sentences are underlined.

EXAMPLES

Here is the solution to the mystery.

There is no time to waste now.

There were too many passengers on the boat.

GRAMMAR PRACTICE

Copy each of the following sentences. Then draw one line under the complete subject and two lines under the complete predicate.

1. Sophocles wrote the play *Oedipus the King.*
2. The story begins with Oedipus ruling Thebes with his wife, Jocasta, at his side.
3. A plague causes Oedipus to search for a remedy to stop the outbreak.
4. The oracle tells the king that he must find the man who murdered Jocasta's first husband, Laius.
5. As Oedipus begins to investigate, his hidden past begins to point suspicion in a startling direction.
6. The truth is that Oedipus himself murdered Laius.
7. Laius and Jocasta are actually Oedipus' father and mother!
8. Jocasta hangs herself to spare herself the shame of being married to her own son.
9. In a guilt-stricken moment, the king blinds himself with pins.
10. Oedipus is a classic example of a tragic hero.

8.8 *Complements*

A complement is a word or group of words that completes the meaning of a predicate. A sentence may contain only a subject and a verb. Most sentences, however, require additional words placed after the verb to complete the meaning of the predicate. There are three kinds of complements: **direct objects, indirect objects,** and **subject complements.**

Direct objects are words or word groups that receive the action of action verbs. A direct object answers the question *what* or *whom.* In the examples that follow, the direct objects are underlined.

EXAMPLES

The students asked many questions. (asked what?)

The teacher quickly answered them. (answered whom?)

The school accepted girls and boys. (accepted whom?)

Indirect objects tell to or for whom or what the action of verbs is performed. Indirect objects come before direct objects. In the examples that follow, the indirect objects are underlined.

EXAMPLES

My sister usually gave her friends good advice. (gave to whom?)

Her brother sent the post office a heavy package. (sent to what?)

His kind grandfather mailed him a new tie. (mailed to whom?)

Subject complements come after linking verbs and identify or describe their subjects. Subject complements that name or identify the subjects of sentences are called **predicate nominatives.** These include **predicate nouns** and **predicate pronouns.** In the examples that follow, the subject complements are underlined.

EXAMPLES

My friends are very hard workers.

The best writer in the class is she.

Other subject complements describe the subjects of sentences. These are called **predicate adjectives.**

EXAMPLE: *The pianist appeared very energetic.*

GRAMMAR PRACTICE

Write all of the complements in the following sentences and label each as a direct object, an indirect object, a predicate noun, a predicate pronoun, or a predicate adjective.

1. The statesman Thomas More was famous in 16th-century England.
2. He gave the world many important written works.
3. *Utopia* is a respected example of social criticism.
4. The main character in the story is Raphael Hythloday.
5. With More's encouragement, Hythloday speaks glowing words about Utopia.
6. Magistrates rule the country.
7. Gold has no value, and everything is free.
8. Experienced farmers teach everyone agriculture.
9. The happiest community is theirs.
10. *Utopia* seems better than 16th-century England.

9 Phrases

A phrase is a group of related words that does not have a subject and predicate and functions in a sentence as a single part of speech.

9.1 *Prepositional Phrases* A prepositional phrase is a phrase that consists of a preposition, its object, and any modifiers of the object. Prepositional phrases that modify nouns or pronouns are called **adjective phrases.** Prepositional phrases that modify verbs, adjectives, or other adverbs are **adverb phrases.**

ADJECTIVE PHRASE: *The central character of the story is a wicked villain.*
ADVERB PHRASE: *He reveals his nature in the first scene.*

9.2 *Appositives and Appositive Phrases* An appositive is a noun or pronoun that usually comes directly after another noun or pronoun and identifies or provides further information about that word. An appositive phrase includes an appositive and all its modifiers. In the following examples, the appositive phrases are underlined.

EXAMPLES

This poem was written by Dante Alighieri, a great poet.

He wrote this poem, one of the world's most famous, as an exploration of sin and salvation.

Occasionally, an appositive phrase may precede the noun it tells about.

EXAMPLE: *A great poet, Dante Alighieri wrote one of the many poems we are studying.*

10 Verbals and Verbal Phrases

A verbal is a verb form that is used as a noun, an adjective, or an adverb. A verbal phrase consists of a verbal, all its modifiers, and all its complements. There are three kinds of verbals: infinitives, participles, and gerunds.

10.1 *Infinitives and Infinitive Phrases* An infinitive is a verb form that usually begins with *to* and functions as a noun, adjective, or adverb. The infinitive and its modifiers constitute an infinitive phrase. The examples that follow show several uses of infinitive phrases. Each infinitive phrase is underlined.

NOUN: *To know her is my only desire.* (subject)

I'm planning to walk with you. (direct object)

Her goal was to promote women's rights. (predicate nominative)

ADJECTIVE: *We saw his need to be loved.* (adjective modifying *need*)

ADVERB: *She wrote to voice her opinions.* (adverb modifying *wrote*)

Grammar Handbook

GRAMMAR PRACTICE ANSWERS

1. famous = predicate adjective
2. the world = indirect object; works = direct object
3. example = predicate noun
4. Raphael Hythloday = predicate noun
5. words = direct object
6. country = direct object
7. no value = direct object; free = predicate adjective
8. everyone = indirect object; agriculture = direct object
9. theirs = predicate pronoun
10. better = predicate adjective

GRAMMAR PRACTICE ANSWERS

1. appositive phrase
2. appositive phrase
3. infinitive phrase
4. gerund phrase
5. appositive phrase

Grammar Handbook

Like verbs themselves, infinitives can take objects (*her* in the first noun example), be made passive (*to be loved* in the adjective example), and take modifiers (*with you* in the second noun example).

Because *to*, the sign of the infinitive, precedes infinitives, it is usually easy to recognize them. However, sometimes *to* may be omitted.

EXAMPLE: *Let no one dare [to] enter this shrine.*

10.2 Participles and Participial Phrases

A participle is a verb form that functions as an adjective. Like adjectives, participles modify nouns and pronouns. Present participles end in *-ing*, and most past participles end in *-ed* or *-en*. In the examples below, the participles are underlined.

MODIFYING A NOUN: *The dying man had a smile on his face.*

MODIFYING A PRONOUN: *Frustrated, everyone abandoned the cause.*

Participial phrases are participles with all their modifiers and complements.

MODIFYING A NOUN: *The dogs searching for survivors are well trained.*

MODIFYING A PRONOUN: *Having approved your proposal, we are ready to act.*

10.3 Dangling and Misplaced Participles

A participle or participial phrase should be placed as close as possible to the word that it modifies. Otherwise the meaning of the sentence may not be clear.

MISPLACED: *The boys were looking for squirrels searching the trees.*

CLEARER: *The boys searching the trees were looking for squirrels.*

A participle or participial phrase that does not clearly modify anything in a sentence is called a **dangling participle.** A dangling participle causes confusion because it appears to modify a word that it cannot sensibly modify.

Correct a dangling participle by providing a word for the participle to modify.

CONFUSING: *Running like the wind, my hat fell off.* (The hat wasn't running.)

CLEARER: *Running like the wind, I lost my hat.*

10.4 Gerunds and Gerund Phrases

A gerund is a verb form ending in *-ing* that functions as a noun. Gerunds can perform any of the function nouns perform.

SUBJECT: *Running is my favorite pastime.*

DIRECT OBJECT: *I truly love running.*

SUBJECT COMPLEMENT: *My deepest passion is running.*

OBJECT OF PREPOSITION: *Her love of running keeps her strong.*

Gerund phrases are gerunds with all their modifiers and complements. The gerund phrases are underlined in the following examples.

SUBJECT: *Wishing on a star never got me far.*

OBJECT OF PREPOSITION: *I will finish before leaving the office.*

APPOSITIVE: *Her avocation, flying airplanes, finally led to full-time employment.*

GRAMMAR PRACTICE

Identify each underlined phrase as an appositive phrase, an infinitive phrase, a participial phrase, or a gerund phrase.

1. Born into an aristocratic family, Tolstoy was orphaned by the age of nine.
2. *War and Peace,* Tolstoy's longest novel, was published in 1869.
3. His attempt to get rid of his property brought about disagreements with his wife.
4. Seeing the naked man sitting by the shrine made Simon incredibly scared.
5. Michael gradually became a faster shoemaker than Simon, his teacher.

R70 GRAMMAR HANDBOOK

11 Clauses

A clause is a group of words that contains a subject and a verb. There are two kinds of clauses: independent clauses and subordinate clauses.

11.1 ***Independent and Subordinate Clauses*** An independent clause can stand alone as a sentence, as the word *independent* suggests.

> **INDEPENDENT CLAUSE:** *Johann Wolfgang von Goethe was one of the greatest German poets.*

A sentence may contain more than one independent clause.

> **EXAMPLE:** *Johann Wolfgang von Goethe was one of the greatest German poets, but he also produced many scientific writings.*

In the example above, the coordinating conjunction *but* joins the two independent clauses.

A subordinate clause cannot stand alone as a sentence. It is subordinate to, or dependent on, an independent clause.

> **EXAMPLE:** *Johann Wolfgang von Goethe is known as one of the greatest German poets, because his style has been widely imitated.*

Because his style has been widely imitated cannot stand by itself.

11.2 ***Adjective Clauses*** An adjective clause is a subordinate clause used as an adjective. It usually follows the noun or pronoun it modifies.

> **EXAMPLE:** *Sappho, who lived on Lesbos, wrote about intensely personal subjects.*

Adjective clauses are typically introduced by the relative pronouns *who, whom, whose, which,* and *that.* (See Relative Pronouns, page R59.) In the examples that follow, the adjective clauses are underlined.

> **EXAMPLES**
>
> *One song that we like became our theme song.*
>
> *Johann Wolfgang von Goethe, whose poems have touched many, was given a state funeral.*
>
> *The candidate whom we selected promised to serve us well.*

WATCH OUT! The relative pronouns *whom, which,* and *that* may sometimes be omitted when they are objects of their own clauses.

> **EXAMPLE:** *Sappho is a poet [whom/that] many have read.*

11.3 ***Adverb Clauses*** An adverb clause is a subordinate clause that is used as an adverb, to modify a verb, an adjective, or another adverb. It is introduced by a subordinating conjunction (see Subordinating Conjunctions, page R65).

Adverb clauses typically occur at the beginning or end of sentences. The clauses are underlined in these examples.

> **MODIFYING A VERB:** *When we need you, we will call.*
>
> **MODIFYING AN ADVERB:** *I'll stay here, where there is shelter from the rain.*
>
> **MODIFYING AN ADJECTIVE:** *Roman felt better than he had felt in days.*

11.4 ***Noun Clauses*** A noun clause is a subordinate clause that is used in a sentence as a noun. A noun clause may be used as a subject, a direct object, an indirect object, a predicate nominative, or an object of a preposition. Noun clauses are often introduced by pronouns such as *that, what, who, whoever, which,* and *whose* or by subordinating conjunctions such as *how, when, where, why,* and *whether.* (See Subordinating Conjunctions, page R65.)

USAGE TIP Because the same words may introduce adjective and noun clauses, you need to consider how the clause functions within its sentence.

To determine if a clause is a noun clause, try substituting *something* or *someone* for the clause. If you can do it, it is probably a noun clause.

> **EXAMPLES:** *I know whose woods these are.* ("I know something." The clause is a noun clause, direct object of the verb *know.*)
>
> *Give a copy to whoever wants one.* ("Give a copy to someone." The clause is a noun clause, object of the preposition *to.*)

Grammar Handbook

GRAMMAR HANDBOOK R71

GRAMMAR PRACTICE ANSWERS

1. adjective clause
2. noun clause
3. adverb clause
4. noun clause
5. adjective clause

GRAMMAR PRACTICE

Identify each underlined clause as an adjective clause, an adverb clause, or a noun clause.

1. The Hebrew God, who created the world in six days, told Adam and Eve not to eat from the tree of knowledge.
2. The serpent in the garden of Eden thought it could convince Eve to take an apple.
3. When God found out Adam and Eve had disobeyed him, he was very angry.
4. He seemed not to question whether the two of them were truly sorry.
5. God's decision, which would last forever, changed the entire fate of humankind.

12 The Structure of Sentences

When classified by their structure, there are four kinds of sentences: simple, compound, complex, and compound-complex.

12.1 *Simple Sentences* A simple sentence is a sentence that has one independent clause and no subordinate clauses. The fact that such sentences are called "simple" does not mean that they are uncomplicated. Various parts of simple sentences may be compound, and they may contain grammatical structures such as appositives and verbals.

EXAMPLES

Leo Tolstoy, a famous Russian novelist, wrote the classic War and Peace. (appositive)

Pablo Neruda, drawn to writing poetry at an early age, won celebrity at age 20. (participial and gerund phrases)

12.2 *Compound Sentences* A compound sentence contains two or more independent clauses. The clauses are joined together with a comma and a coordinating conjunction (*and, but, or, nor, yet, for, so*), a semicolon, or a conjunctive adverb with a semicolon. Like simple sentences, compound sentences do not contain any subordinate clauses.

EXAMPLES

The main character in the Inferno *goes to visit souls in Hell, but he eventually returns to where he began.*

Charles Baudelaire's poem "Invitation to the Voyage" has powerful images; however, the word voyage *does not appear anywhere in it.*

WATCH OUT! Do not confuse compound sentences with simple sentences that have compound parts.

EXAMPLE: *A subcommittee drafted a document and immediately presented it to the entire group.* (Here *and* signals a compound predicate, not a compound sentence.)

12.3 *Complex Sentences* A complex sentence contains one independent clause and one or more subordinate clauses. If a subordinate clause is used as a modifier, it usually modifies a word in the main clause, and the main clause can stand alone. However, a noun clause is a part of the independent clause; the two cannot be separated.

MODIFIER: *One should not complain unless she or he has a better solution.*

NOUN CLAUSE: *We sketched pictures of whomever we wished.* (Noun clause is the object of the preposition *of* and cannot be separated from the rest of the sentence.)

12.4 *Compound-Complex Sentences* A compound-complex sentence has two or more independent clauses and one or more subordinate clauses. Compound-complex sentences are, simply, both compound and complex. If you start with a compound sentence, all you need to do to form a compound-complex sentence is add a subordinate clause.

COMPOUND: *All the students knew the answer, yet they were too shy to volunteer.*

COMPOUND-COMPLEX: *All the students knew the answer that their teacher expected, yet they were too shy to volunteer.*

GRAMMAR PRACTICE

Tell whether each sentence is a simple sentence, a compound sentence, a complex sentence, or a compound-complex sentence.

1. Written by Heinrich Heine, "The Lorelei" is named for a cliff in Germany.
2. Legend claims a drowned maiden sings nearby, but in fact the sound is only an echo.
3. The woman's song is said to lure fishermen to their death.
4. Heine wanted to marry his cousin, but she rejected him and married another man.
5. After she refused him, Heine wrote this poem as a response.

13 Writing Complete Sentences

A sentence is a group of words that expresses a complete thought. In writing that you wish to share with a reader, try to avoid both sentence fragments and run-on sentences.

13.1 *Correcting Fragments* A sentence fragment is a group of words that is only part of a sentence. It does not express a complete thought and may be confusing to the reader or the listener. A sentence fragment may be lacking a subject, a predicate, or both.

FRAGMENT: *Waited for the boat to arrive.* (no subject)
CORRECTED: *We waited for the boat to arrive.*
FRAGMENT: *People of various races, ages, and creeds.* (no predicate)
CORRECTED: *People of various races, ages, and creeds gathered together.*
FRAGMENT: *Near the old cottage.* (neither subject nor predicate)
CORRECTED: *The burial ground is near the old cottage.*

In your writing, fragments are usually the result of haste or incorrect punctuation. Sometimes fixing a fragment will be a matter of attaching it to a preceding or following sentence.

FRAGMENT: *We saw the two girls. Waiting for the bus to arrive.*
CORRECTED: *We saw the two girls waiting for the bus to arrive.*
FRAGMENT: *Newspapers appeal to a wide audience. Including people of various races, ages, and creeds.*
CORRECTED: *Newspapers appeal to a wide audience, including people of various races, ages, and creeds.*

13.2 *Correcting Run-On Sentences*
A run-on sentence is made up of two or more sentences written as though they were one. Some run-ons have no punctuation within them. Others may use only a comma where a conjunction or stronger punctuation is necessary. Use your judgment in correcting run-on sentences, as you have choices. You can make two sentences if the thoughts are not closely connected. If the thoughts are closely related, you can keep the run-on as one sentence by adding a semicolon or a conjunction.

RUN-ON: *We found a place by a small pond for the picnic it is three miles from the village.*
MAKE TWO SENTENCES: *We found a place by a small pond for the picnic. It is three miles from the village.*
RUN-ON: *We found a place by a small pond for the picnic it was perfect.*
USE A SEMICOLON: *We found a place by a small pond for the picnic; it was perfect.*
ADD A CONJUNCTION: *We found a place by a small pond for the picnic, and it was perfect.*

WATCH OUT! When you add a conjunction, make sure you use appropriate punctuation before it: a comma for a coordinating conjunction, a semicolon for a conjunctive adverb. (See Conjunctions, page R65.) A very common mistake is to use a comma instead of a conjunction or an end mark. This error is called a **comma splice**.

INCORRECT: *He finished the apprenticeship, then he left the village.*
CORRECT: *He finished the apprenticeship, and then he left the village.*

Grammar Handbook

GRAMMAR PRACTICE ANSWERS

1. simple
2. compound-complex
3. simple
4. compound
5. complex

GRAMMAR PRACTICE ANSWERS

Omar Khayyám was born in Iran to a well-off family. He was educated in the sciences and philosophy. He later wrote a treatise on algebra. By using his knowledge of astronomy, Khayyám also helped the sultan reform the calendar. After a journey to Mecca, Khayyám returned to his hometown to teach. He wrote many works on many subjects but only his prose writing survived. *The Rubáiyát of Omar Khayyám* by Edward FitzGerald made the world aware of Khayyám's poetry. FitzGerald published his translation in 1859. *The Rubáiyát of Omar Khayyám* is a collection of quatrains. One of the most famous poems contains the lines "A Jug of Wine, a Loaf of Bread—and Thou." Khayyám uses many metaphors in his poetry to convey certain themes.

Grammar Handbook

GRAMMAR PRACTICE

Rewrite the following paragraph, correcting all fragments and run-ons.

Omar Khayyám was born in Persia. To a well-off family. He was educated in the sciences and philosophy he later wrote a treatise on algebra. By using his knowledge of astronomy. Omar also helped the sultan reform the calendar. After a journey to Mecca, Omar returned to his hometown to teach. He wrote many works on many subjects but only. His prose writing survived. *The Rubáiyát of Omar Khayyám* by Edward FitzGerald made the world aware of Khayyám's poetry FitzGerald published his translation in 1859. *The Rubáiyát of Omar Khayyám* is. A collection of quatrains. One of the most famous poems contains the lines "A Jug of Wine, a Loaf of Bread—and Thou" Khayyám uses many metaphors in his poetry to convey certain themes.

14 Subject-Verb Agreement

The subject and verb of a sentence must agree in number. When the subject is singular, the verb must be singular; when the subject is plural, the verb must be plural.

14.1 *Basic Agreement*

Fortunately, agreement between subject and verb in English is simple. Most verbs show the difference between singular and plural only in the third person of the present tense. In the present tense, the third-person singular form ends in *-s.*

Present-Tense Verb Forms	
Singular	**Plural**
I sleep	we sleep
you sleep	you sleep
she, he, it sleeps	they sleep

14.2 *Agreement of Be*

The verb *be* presents special problems in agreement because this verb does not follow the usual verb patterns.

Forms of *Be*			
Present Tense		**Past Tense**	
Singular	**Plural**	**Singular**	**Plural**
I am	we are	I was	we were
you are	you are	you were	you were
she, he, it is	they are	she, he, it was	they were

14.3 *Words Between Subject and Verb*

A verb agrees only with its subject. When words come between a subject and its verb, ignore them when considering proper agreement. Identify the subject and make sure the verb agrees with it.

EXAMPLES

A story in the newspapers tells about the 1890s.

Dad as well as Mom reads the paper daily.

14.4 *Agreement with Compound Subjects*

Use a plural verb with most compound subjects containing the word *and.*

EXAMPLE: *My father and his friends read the paper daily.*

You could substitute the plural pronoun *they* for *my father and his friends*. This shows that you need a plural verb.

If the compound subject refers to a unit, use a singular verb. Test this by substituting the singular pronoun *it.*

EXAMPLE: *Peanut butter and jelly [it] is my brother's favorite sandwich.*

Use a singular verb with a compound subject that is preceded by *each, every,* or *many a.*

EXAMPLE: *Each novel and short story seems grounded in personal experience.*

When subjects are joined by *or, nor,* or the correlative conjunctions *either . . . or* or *neither . . . nor*, make the verb agree with the noun or pronoun nearest the verb.

EXAMPLES

Cookies or ice cream is my favorite dessert.

Either Cheryl or her friends are being invited.

Neither ice storms nor snow is predicted today.

14.5 *Personal Pronouns as Subjects*

When using a personal pronoun as a subject, make sure to match it with the correct form of the verb *be*. (See the chart in section 14.2.) Note especially that the pronoun *you* takes the form *are* or *were*, regardless of whether it is singular or plural.

WATCH OUT! *You is* and *you was* are nonstandard forms and should be avoided in writing and speaking. *We was* and *they was* are also forms to be avoided.

INCORRECT: *You was helping me. They was hoping for this.*

CORRECT: *You were helping me. They were hoping for this.*

14.6 Indefinite Pronouns as Subjects

Some indefinite pronouns are always singular; some are always plural. Others may be either singular or plural.

Singular Indefinite Pronouns			
another	either	neither	one
anybody	everybody	nobody	somebody
anyone	everyone	no one	someone
anything	everything	nothing	something
each	much		

EXAMPLES

Each of the writers was given an award.

Somebody in the room upstairs is sleeping.

The indefinite pronouns that are always plural are *both, few, many, others,* and *several.* These take plural verbs.

EXAMPLES

Many of the books in our library are not in circulation.

Few have been returned recently.

Still other indefinite pronouns can be either singular or plural.

Singular or Plural Indefinite Pronouns			
all	enough	most	some
any	more	none	

The number of the indefinite pronoun *any* or *none* depends on the intended meaning.

EXAMPLES

Any of these topics has potential for a good article. (any one topic)

Any of these topics have potential for a good article. (all of the many topics)

The indefinite pronouns *all, enough, some, more, most,* and *none* are singular when they refer to quantities or parts of something. They are plural when they refer to numbers of individual things. Context will usually give a clue.

EXAMPLES

All of the flour is gone. (referring to a quantity)

All of the flowers are gone. (referring to individual items)

14.7 Inverted Sentences

Problems in agreement often occur in inverted sentences beginning with *here* or *there*; in questions beginning with *why, where,* and *what*; and in inverted sentences beginning with a phrase. Identify the subject—wherever it is—before deciding on the verb.

EXAMPLES

There clearly are far too many cooks in this kitchen.

What is the correct ingredient for this stew?

Far from the embroiled cooks stands the master chef.

GRAMMAR PRACTICE

Locate the subject of each verb. Then choose the correct verb.

1. Many scholars (think/thinks) the *Aeneid* is the finest epic of ancient Rome.
2. (Is/Are) the Trojan prince Aeneas the ideal Roman?
3. There (is/are) 16 books in the *Aeneid.*
4. Book 2 begins after the Greeks (was/were) pushed back after Achilles' death.
5. A large wooden horse full of armed men (was/were) left in front of the gates of Troy.
6. After the Greeks sailed away, their deserted camps (was/were) raided by the Trojans.
7. The Trojan people (enjoy/enjoyed) their victory but did not know it was short-lived.
8. As soon as the Trojans (was/were) asleep, the Greek army returned, let the men out of the wooden horse, and attacked the city.
9. Troy (was/were) burned to the ground
10. Virgil wanted the *Aeneid* destroyed, but it (was/were) published at the emperor's request.

Grammar Handbook

GRAMMAR PRACTICE ANSWERS

1. think
2. Is
3. are
4. were
5. was
6. were
7. enjoyed
8. were
9. was
10. was

GRAMMAR PRACTICE ANSWERS

1. involves
2. goes
3. was
4. were
5. doesn't
6. exists
7. rises
8. Does
9. finds
10. is

Grammar Handbook

14.8 Sentences with Predicate Nominatives

When a sentence contains a predicate nominative, use a verb that agrees with the subject, not the complement.

EXAMPLES

The tales of Aeneas are a great work of work literature. (*Tales* is the subject—not—and it takes the plural verb *are.*)

A great work of literature is the tales of Aeneas. (The subject is the singular noun *work.*)

14.9 Don't and Doesn't as Auxiliary Verbs

The auxiliary verb *doesn't* is used with singular subjects and with the personal pronouns *she, he,* and *it.* The auxiliary verb *don't* is used with plural subjects and with the personal pronouns *I, we, you,* and *they.*

SINGULAR

She doesn't want to be without her cane.
Doesn't the school provide help?

PLURAL

They don't know what it's like to be hungry.
Bees don't like these flowers by the door.

14.10 Collective Nouns as Subjects

Collective nouns are nouns that name a group of persons or things. *Team,* for example, is the collective name of a group of individuals. A collective noun takes a singular verb when the group acts as a single unit. It takes a plural verb when the members of the group act separately.

EXAMPLES

Our team usually wins. (The team as a whole wins.)

Our team vote differently on most issues. (The individual members vote.)

14.11 Relative Pronouns as Subjects

When a relative pronoun is used as a subject of its clause—*who, which,* and *that* can serve as subjects—the verb of the clause must agree in number with the antecedent of the pronoun.

SINGULAR: *Have you selected one of the poems that is meaningful to you?*

The antecedent of the relative pronoun *that* is the singular *one;* therefore, *that* is singular and must take the singular verb *is.*

PLURAL: *The younger redwoods, which grow in a circle around an older tree, are also very tall.*

The antecedent of the relative pronoun *which* is the plural *redwoods.* Therefore, *which* is plural, and it takes the plural verb *grow.*

GRAMMAR PRACTICE

Choose the correct verb for each of the following sentences.

1. "Metamorphosis" (involve/involves) a traveling salesman and his family.
2. Gregor (go/goes) to bed one night and wakes up the next morning changed into a bug.
3. It (was/were) a startling and unexpected transformation for both Gregor and his family.
4. They (was/were) terrified and confused by what Gregor had become.
5. Grete, Gregor's sister, (doesn't/don't) know what kind of food Gregor likes, so she brings him several choices.
6. Gregor merely (exists/exist) from day to day, gradually losing his appetite and his will to live.
7. The tension between Gregor and his family (rises/rise) with each passing day.
8. (Do/Does) everyone see Gregor as a man or as a monster?
9. The cleaning lady (finds/find) Gregor dead on the floor.
10. What do you think Franz Kafka (is/are) saying in this story?

⓯ Quick Reference: Punctuation

Punctuation	Function	Examples
End marks period, question mark, exclamation point	To end sentences	The games begin today. Who is your favorite contestant? What a play Jamie made!
	After initials and other abbreviations	Prof. Ted Bakerman, D. H. Lawrence, Houghton Mifflin Co., P.M., A.D., oz., ft., Blvd., St.
	After numerals and letters in outlines	I. Volcanoes A. Central-vent 1. Shield
	Exception: P.O. abbreviations	NE (Nebraska), NV (Nevada)
Commas	Before conjunctions in compound sentences	I have never disliked poetry, but now I really love it.
	To separate items in a series	She is brave, loyal, and kind. The slow, easy route is best.
	To set off words of address	Oh wind, if winter comes . . . Come to the front, children.
	To set off parenthetical expressions	Well, just suppose that we can't? Hard workers, as you know, don't quit. I'm not a quitter, believe me.
	After introductory phrases and clauses	At the beginning of the day, I feel fresh. While she was out, I was here. Having finished my chores, I went out.
	To set off nonessential phrases and clauses	Ed Pawn, captain of the chess team, won. Ed Pawn, who is the captain, won.
	In dates and addresses	August 18, 2002. Send it by August 18, 2002, to Cherry Jubilee, Inc., 21 Vernona St., Oakland, Minnesota.
	In letter parts	Dear Jim, Sincerely yours,
	For clarity, or to avoid confusion	By noon, time had run out. What the minister does, does matter. While cooking, Jim burned his hand.
Semicolons	In compound sentences without coordinating conjunctions	The last shall be first; the first shall be last. I read the Bible; however, I have not memorized it.
	To separate items in series that contain commas	We invited my sister, Jan; her boyfriend, Don; my uncle Jack; and Mary Dodd.
	In compound sentences whose parts contain commas	After I ran out of money, I called my parents; but only my sister was home, unfortunately.

Grammar Handbook

GRAMMAR HANDBOOK R77

Punctuation	Function	Examples
Colons	To introduce lists	**Correct:** Those we wrote were the following: Dana, John, and Will. **Incorrect:** Those we wrote were: Dana, John, and Will.
	Before long quotations	Susan B. Anthony said: "Woman must not depend upon the protection of man. . . ."
	After salutations of business letters	To Whom It May Concern: Dear Ms. Costa:
	With certain numbers	1:28 P.M., Genesis 2:5
Dashes	To indicate abrupt breaks in thought	I was thinking of my mother—who is arriving tomorrow—just as you walked in.
Parentheses	To set off less important material	Throughout her life (though some might think otherwise), she worked hard. The temperature on this July day (would you believe it?) is 45 degrees!
Hyphens	In compound adjectives before nouns	She lives in a first-floor apartment.
	In compounds with *all-, ex-, self-, -elect*	The president-elect is a respected woman.
	In compound numbers (to ninety-nine)	Today, I turn twenty-one.
	In fractions	My cup is one-third full.
	Between prefixes and words beginning with capital letters	Is this a pre-Renaissance artifact?
	With words divided at the ends of lines	Finding the right title has been a chal-lenge for the committee.
Apostrophes	In possessives of nouns and indefinite pronouns	my friend's book, my friends' books, anyone's guess, somebody else's problem
	For omitted letters in contractions or numbers in dates	don't (omitted *o*); he'd (omitted *woul*) the class of '99 (omitted *19*)
	In plurals of letters and numbers	I had two A's and no 2's on my report card.
Quotation marks	To set off a speaker's exact words	Sara said, "I'm finally ready." "I'm ready," Sara said, "finally." Did Sara say, "I'm ready"? Sara said, "I'm ready!"
	For titles of stories, short poems, essays, songs, book chapters	We read Mistral's "Time" and Joyce's "Eveline." My eyes watered when I heard "The Star-Spangled Banner."
Ellipses	For material omitted from a quotation	"Neither slavery nor involuntary servitude . . . shall exist within the United States. . . ."
Italics	For titles of books, plays, magazines, long poems, operas, films, TV series, recordings	*War and Peace, A Doll's House, Newsweek, Paradise Lost, La Bohème, ET, The Cosby Show, The Three Tenors in Concert*

R78 GRAMMAR HANDBOOK

16 Quick Reference: Capitalization

Category/Rule	Examples
People and Titles	
Names and initials of people	Alice Walker, E. B. White
Titles used with or in place of names	Professor Holmes, Senator Long, The President has arrived.
Deities and members of religious groups	Jesus, Allah, Buddha, Zeus, Baptists, Roman Catholics
Names of ethnic and national groups	Hispanics, Jews, African Americans
Geographical Names	
Cities, states, countries, continents	Charleston, Nevada, France, Asia
Regions, bodies of water, mountains	Midwest, Lake Michigan, Mount McKinley
Geographic features, parks	Continental Divide, Everglades, Yellowstone National Park
Streets and roads, planets	361 South Twenty-Third Street, Miller Avenue, Jupiter, Saturn
Organizations and Events	
Companies, organizations, teams	Monsanto, Elks, Chicago Bulls
Buildings, bridges, monuments	Alamo, Golden Gate Bridge, Lincoln Memorial
Documents, awards	Constitution, World Cup
Special named events	Super Bowl, World Series
Governmental bodies, historical periods and events	Supreme Court, Congress, Middle Ages, Boston Tea Party
Days and months, holidays	Tuesday, October, Thanksgiving, Valentine's Day
Specific cars, boats, trains, planes	Cadillac, *Titanic, Orient Express*
Proper Adjectives	
Adjectives formed from proper nouns	Doppler effect, Mexican music, Elizabethan age, Gulf coast
First Words and the Pronoun *I*	
The first word in a sentence or quotation	This is it. He said, "Let's go."
Complete sentence in parentheses	(Consult the previous chapter.)
Salutation and closing of letters	Dear Madam, Very truly yours,
First lines of most poetry The personal pronoun *I*	Then am I A happy fly If I live Or if I die.
First, last, and all important words in titles	*A Tale of Two Cities,* "The World Is Too Much with Us"

Grammar Handbook

GRAMMAR HANDBOOK R79

Grammar Handbook

17 Little Rules That Make a Big Difference

Sentences

Avoid sentence fragments. Make sure all your sentences express complete thoughts.

A sentence fragment is a group of words that does not express a grammatically complete thought. It may lack a subject, a predicate, or both. A fragment can be corrected by adding the missing element(s) or by changing the punctuation to make the fragment part of a sentence.

FRAGMENT: *One of my heroes is Barbara Jordan. A Texas senator who had an impressive record and great dedication to justice.*

COMPLETE: *One of my heroes is Barbara Jordan. She was a Texas senator who had an impressive record and great dedication to justice.* (adding a subject and a verb)

COMPLETE: *One of my heroes is Barbara Jordan, a Texas senator who had an impressive record and great dedication to justice.* (changing the punctuation)

Avoid run-on sentences. Make sure all clauses in a sentence have the proper punctuation and/or conjunctions between them.

A run-on sentence consists of two or more sentences written as though they were one. Correct a run-on by making two separate sentences, using a semicolon, adding a conjunction, or rewriting the sentence.

RUN-ON: *James Galway is a great musician, he plays the flute.*

CORRECT: *James Galway is a great musician. He plays the flute.*

CORRECT: *James Galway is a great musician; he plays the flute.*

CORRECT: *James Galway, who plays the flute, is a great musician.*

Use end marks correctly. Use a period, not a question mark, at the end of an indirect question.

An indirect question is a question that does not reproduce the exact words of the original speaker. Note the difference between the following sentences, and observe that the second sentence ends with a period, not a question mark:

DIRECT: *Lou asked, "What is that?"*

INDIRECT: *Lou asked what it was.*

Do not use quotation marks around an indirect quotation within a sentence.

A direct quotation reproduces the speaker's exact words. An indirect quotation reports a speaker's statement in other words. Compare these sentences:

DIRECT: *Jean said, "I'm going to be up all night writing my essay."* (quotation marks appropriate)

INDIRECT: *Jean said that she was going to be up all night writing her essay.* (no quotation marks)

Phrases

Place participial and prepositional phrases as close as possible to the words they modify. Participial and prepositional phrases are modifiers—that is, they tell about some other word in a sentence. To avoid confusion, they should be placed as close as possible to the words that they modify.

INCORRECT: *Tiny microphones are planted by agents called bugs.*

CORRECT: *Tiny microphones called bugs are planted by agents.*

Avoid dangling participles. Make sure a participial phrase does modify a word in the sentence.

INCORRECT: *Disappointed in love, a hermit's life seemed attractive.* (Who was disappointed?)

CORRECT: *Disappointed in love, the man became a hermit.*

R80 GRAMMAR HANDBOOK

Clauses

Use commas to set off nonessential adjective clauses.

Do you need the clause in order to indicate precisely who or what is meant? If not, it is nonessential and should be set off with commas.

USE COMMAS: *Jim's dogs, who had barked from morning until night, were suddenly quiet.*
NO COMMAS: *The dogs who had barked from morning until night were suddenly quiet.*

Verbs

Don't use a past-tense form with an auxiliary verb or a past-participle form without an auxiliary verb. (See Auxiliary Verbs, page R59.)

INCORRECT: *I have saw her somewhere before.* (*Saw* is past tense and shouldn't be used with *have*.)

CORRECT: *I have seen her somewhere before.*

INCORRECT: *I seen her somewhere before.* (*Seen* is a past participle and shouldn't be used without an auxiliary.)

Shift tenses only when necessary.

Usually, when you are writing in the present tense, you should stay in the present tense; when you are writing in the past tense, you should stay in the past tense.

INCORRECT: *When Mr. Miller spoke at the fair, we all pay attention.*

CORRECT: *When Mr. Miller spoke at the fair, we all paid attention.*

Sometimes a shift in tense is necessary to show a logical sequence of actions or the relationship of one action to another.

CORRECT: *After he had told his story, everybody went to sleep.*

Subject-Verb Agreement

Make sure subjects and verbs agree in number.

INCORRECT: *Several operas by Wagner is based on the legend of Siegfried.*

CORRECT: *Several operas by Wagner are based on the legend of Seigfried.*

INCORRECT: *Wotan, as well as others in the operas, are looking for the Ring.*

CORRECT: *Wotan, as well as others in the operas, is looking for the Ring.*

INCORRECT: *Siegmund and Sieglinde was the parents of Siegfried.*

CORRECT: *Siegmund and Sieglinde were the parents of Siegfried.*

Use a singular verb with a noun that looks plural but has a singular meaning.

Some nouns that end in -*s* are singular, even though they look plural. Examples are *measles, news, Wales,* and words ending in -*ics* that refer to school subjects, sciences, or general practices.

EXAMPLES: *Has headquarters heard from you yet?*
Physics is available to everyone who qualifies to take it.

Use a singular verb with a title.

EXAMPLE: *The* Analects *is on my summer reading list.*
"Two Springs" was written by Li Chi'ng-chao.

Use a singular verb with a word of weight, time, or measure.

EXAMPLES: *Forty pounds is what my niece weighs now.*
One hundred dollars is the price of the new equipment.

Pronouns

Use personal pronouns correctly in compounds.

Don't be confused about case when *and* joins a noun and a personal pronoun; the case of the pronoun still depends upon its function.

Grammar Handbook

GRAMMAR HANDBOOK R81

INCORRECT: *Marlene and her will conduct the interview.*

CORRECT: *Marlene and she will conduct the interview.*

INCORRECT: *She asked Sunny and I to wait for her.*

CORRECT: *She asked Sunny and me to wait for her.*

INCORRECT: *Show Anne and they how to work the video recorder.*

CORRECT: *Show Anne and them how to work the video recorder.*

Usually, if you remove the noun and *and,* the correct pronoun will be obvious.

Use *we* and *us* correctly with nouns.

When a noun directly follows *we* or *us*, the case of the pronoun depends upon its function.

INCORRECT: *Us cheerleaders have many new cheers.*

CORRECT: *We cheerleaders have many new cheers.* (*We* is the subject.)

INCORRECT: *It makes a big difference to we players.*

CORRECT: *It makes a big difference to us players.* (*Us* is the object of *to.*)

Avoid unclear pronoun reference.

The reference of a pronoun is ambiguous when the reader cannot tell which of two preceding nouns is its antecedent. The reference is indefinite when the idea to which the pronoun refers is only weakly or vaguely expressed.

AMBIGUOUS: *Pablo Neruda, not Octavio Paz, wrote "Ode to a Lizard," and he* [who?] *also wrote "Ode to a Watermelon."*

CLEARER: *Pablo Neruda, not Octavio Paz, wrote "Ode to a Lizard," and Neruda also wrote "Ode to a Watermelon."*

INDEFINITE: *Neruda won a Nobel Prize in 1971, which is a prestigious award for writers.*

CLEARER: *In 1971, Neruda won a Nobel Prize, which is a prestigious award for writers.*

Avoid changes of person.

If you are writing in the third person—using pronouns such as *she, he, it, they, them, his, her, its*—do not shift to the second person—*you.*

INCORRECT: *The feudal laborer had to obey his lord, and you needed to obey the king as well.*

CORRECT: *The feudal laborer had to obey his lord, and he needed to obey the king as well.*

Use correct pronouns in elliptical comparisons.

An elliptical comparison is a comparison from which words have been omitted. In order to choose the proper pronoun, fill in the missing words. Note the difference below:

EXAMPLES: *I like Carlos better than* (I like) *her.*
I like Carlos better than she (likes Carlos).

Don't confuse pronouns and contractions.

Possessive forms of personal pronouns do not contain apostrophes; neither does the relative pronoun *whose*. Whenever you are unsure whether to write *it's* or *its* or *who's* or *whose*, ask if you mean *it is/has* or *who is/has*. If you do, write the contraction. Do the same for *you're* and *your*, *they're* and *their*, except that the contraction in this case is for the verb *are*.

Modifiers

Avoid double comparisons.

A double comparison is a comparison made twice. In general, if you add *-er* or *-est* to a modifier, you should not also use *more* or *most* in front of it.

INCORRECT: *Juan cooks more better since he's taken the chef's course.*

CORRECT: *Juan cooks better since he's taken the chef's course.*

INCORRECT: *Now he's the most greatest cook in the class.*

CORRECT: *Now he's the greatest cook in the class.*

R82 GRAMMAR HANDBOOK

Avoid illogical comparisons.

Can you tell what is wrong with the following sentence?

Plays are more entertaining than any kind of performance art.

This sentence implies that plays are not a kind of performance art. To avoid such illogical comparisons, use *other* when comparing an individual member with the rest of its group.

Plays are more entertaining than any other kind of performance art.

To avoid another kind of illogical comparison, use *than* or *as* after the first member in a compound comparison.

ILLOGICAL: *Sophocles wrote as many great plays if not more than Aeschylus.* (*As many great plays . . . than* is incorrect.)

CLEARER: *Sophocles wrote as many great plays as Aeschylus, if not more.*

Avoid misplacing modifiers.

Modifiers of all kinds must be placed as close as possible to the words they modify. If you place them elsewhere, you risk being misunderstood.

MISPLACED: *Eveline thinks about the promise she made, before her death, to her mother.*

CLEARER: *Eveline thinks about the promise she made to her mother before her death.*

It isn't Eveline's death; it's her mother's.

Words Not to Capitalize

Do not capitalize *north, south, east,* and *west* when they are used to tell direction.

EXAMPLE: *London is east of New York City. Charleston is the capital of West Virginia.* (Here *West* is part of a proper name.)

Do not capitalize *sun* and *moon,* and capitalize *earth* only when it is used with the names of other planets.

EXAMPLES: *The sun and the moon are heavenly bodies in a solar system that includes Mars, Jupiter, and Earth.*

We now live on the earth, not in heaven.

Do not capitalize the names of seasons.

EXAMPLE: *The winter snows have nearly disappeared.*

Do not capitalize the names of most school subjects.

School subjects are capitalized only when they are names of specific courses, such as World History I. Otherwise, they are not capitalized.

EXAMPLE: *I'm taking physics, social studies, and a foreign language this year.*

Note: *English* and the names of other languages are always capitalized.

EXAMPLE: *Everybody takes English and either Spanish or French.*

GRAMMAR PRACTICE

Rewrite each sentence correctly.

1. Mrs. Kulpinsky asked Trish and I to help with the decorations.
2. Let's keep this information between we girls.
3. An award-winning collection of poems, Mary Oliver wrote *Dream Work.*
4. Babe Ruth who played for the New York Yankees hit 60 home runs in one season.
5. *The Producers,* starring Zero Mostel and Gene Wilder, are a funny movie.
6. We wanted to know what the speaker means.
7. Having written both plays and sonnets, millions of people admire William Shakespeare.
8. I like Anton Chekhov more better than Franz Kafka.
9. Preserving nature, a major concern of most citizens.
10. Stumbling forward at the finish line, the race was barely won by the shortest runner.

GRAMMAR PRACTICE ANSWERS

1. Mrs. Kulpinsky asked Trish and me to help with the decorations.
2. Let's keep this information between us girls.
3. Mary Oliver wrote *Dream Work,* an award-winning collection of poems.
4. Babe Ruth, who played for the New York Yankees, hit 60 home runs in one season.
5. *The Producers,* starring Zero Mostel and Gene Wilder, is a funny movie.
6. We wanted to know what the speaker meant.
7. Having written both plays and sonnets, William Shakespeare is admired by millions of people.
8. I like Anton Chekhov better than Franz Kafka.
9. Preserving nature is a major concern of most citizens.
10. Stumbling forward at the finish line, the shortest runner barely won the race.

Grammar Handbook

18 Commonly Confused Words

accept/except	The verb *accept* means "to receive or believe"; *except* is usually a preposition meaning "excluding."	The teams accept everyone except those who don't have at least a C average.
advice/advise	*Advise* is a verb; *advice* is a noun naming that which an adviser gives.	How did the manager advise the baseball player? Was the baseball player given good advice?
affect/effect	As a verb, *affect* means "to influence." *Effect* as a verb means "to cause." If you want a noun, you will almost always want *effect.*	How did the player's home run affect the crowd? Did it effect a change in their attitude? The effect was dramatic.
all ready/already	*All ready* is an adjective meaning "fully ready." *Already* is an adverb meaning "before or by this time."	Before the player's home run, the spectators were all ready to boo the home team. One had already talked of abandoning the team.
allusion/illusion	An allusion is an indirect reference to something. An illusion is a false picture or idea.	Modern literature has many allusions to the works of Shakespeare. The world's apparent flatness is an illusion.
among/between	*Between* is used when you are speaking of only two things. *Among* is used for three or more.	There is respect between Sally and Robert. "The Panther" is among my favorite Rilke poems.
bring/take	*Bring* is used to denote motion toward a speaker or place. *Take* is used to denote motion away from a person or place.	Bring the books over here, and I will take them to the library.
fewer/less	*Fewer* refers to a number of separate, countable units. *Less* refers to bulk quantity.	We have less literature and fewer selections in this year's curriculum.
leave/let	*Leave* means "to allow something to remain behind." *Let* means "to permit."	The librarian will leave some books on display but will not let us borrow any.
lie/lay	*Lie* means "to rest or recline." It does not take an object. *Lay* always takes an object.	Dogs love to lie in the sun. We always lay some bones next to him.
loose/lose	*Loose* (lo͞os) means "free, not restrained"; *lose* (lo͞oz) means "to misplace or fail to find."	Who turned the horses loose? I hope we won't lose any of them.
precede/proceed	*Precede* means "to go or come before." Use *proceed* for other meanings.	The drum major preceded the other band members. The band director proceeded to direct the national anthem.
than/then	Use *than* in making comparisons; use *then* on all other occasions.	I like Camus better than Kafka. We read one, then the other.
two/too/to	*Two* refers to a number. *Too* is an adverb meaning "also" or "very." Use *to* before a verb or as a preposition.	Meg had to go to town, too. We had too much reading to do. Two chapters is too much.

R84 GRAMMAR HANDBOOK

Grammar Glossary

This glossary contains various terms you need to understand when you use the Grammar Handbook. Used as a reference source, this glossary will help you explore grammar concepts and the ways they relate to one another.

Abbreviation An abbreviation is a shortened form of a word or word group; it is often made up of initials. (B.C., A.M., *Maj.*)

Active voice. *See* **Voice.**

Adjective An adjective modifies, or describes, a noun or pronoun. (*happy* camper, she is *small*)

A ***predicate adjective*** follows a linking verb and describes the subject. (The day seemed *long.*)

A ***proper adjective*** is formed from a proper noun. (*Jewish* temple, *Alaskan* husky)

The ***comparative*** form of an adjective compares two things. (*more alert, thicker*)

The ***superlative*** form of an adjective compares more than two things. (*most abundant, weakest*)

What Adjectives Tell	Examples
How many	*some* writers *all* players
What kind	*grand* plans *wider* streets
Which one(s)	*these* flowers *that* star

Adjective phrase. See **Phrase.**

Adverb An adverb modifies a verb, an adjective, or another adverb. (Clare sang *loudly.*)

The ***comparative*** form of an adverb compares two actions. (*more generously, faster*)

The ***superlative*** form of an adverb compares more than two actions. (*most sharply, closest*)

What Adverbs Tell	Examples
How	climb *carefully* chuckle *merrily*
When	arrived *late* left *early*
Where	climbed *up* moved *away*
To what extent	*extremely* upset *hardly* visible

Adverb, conjunctive. *See* **Conjunctive adverb.**

Adverb phrase. *See* **Phrase.**

Agreement Sentence parts that correspond with one another are said to be in agreement.

In ***pronoun-antecedent agreement,*** a pronoun and the word it refers to are the same in number, gender, and person. (*Bill* mailed *his* application. The *students* ate *their* lunches.)

In ***subject-verb agreement,*** the subject and verb in a sentence are the same in number. (A *child cries* for help. *They cry* aloud.)

Ambiguous reference An ambiguous reference occurs when a pronoun may refer to more than one word. (Bud asked his brother if *he* had any mail.)

Antecedent An antecedent is the noun or pronoun to which a pronoun refers. (If *Adam* forgets *his* raincoat, *he* will be late for school. *She* learned *her* lesson.)

Appositive An appositive is a noun or phrase that explains one or more words in a sentence. (Cary Grant, *an Englishman,* spent most of his adult life in America.)

An ***essential appositive*** is needed to make the sense of a sentence complete. (A comic strip inspired the musical *Annie.*)

A ***nonessential appositive*** is one that adds information to a sentence but is not necessary to its sense. (O. Henry, *a short story writer,* spent time in prison.)

Article Articles are the special adjectives *a, an,* and *the.* (*the* day, *a* fly)

The ***definite article*** (the word *the*) refers to a particular thing. (*the* cabin)

An ***indefinite article*** is used with a noun that is not unique but refers to one of many of its kind. (*a* dish, *an* otter)

Auxiliary verb. *See* **Verb.**

Clause A clause is a group of words that contains a verb and its subject. (*they slept*)

An ***adjective clause*** is a subordinate clause that modifies a noun or pronoun. (Hugh bought the sweater *that he had admired.*)

An ***adverb clause*** is a subordinate clause used to modify a verb, an adjective, or an adverb. (Ring the bell *when it is time for class to begin.*)

Grammar Handbook

Grammar Handbook

A ***noun clause*** is a subordinate clause that is used as a noun. (*Whatever you say* interests me.)

An ***elliptical clause*** is a clause from which a word or words have been omitted. (We are not as lucky as *they*.)

A ***main (independent) clause*** can stand by itself as a sentence. (*the flashlight flickered*)

A ***subordinate (dependent) clause*** does not express a complete thought and cannot stand by itself. (*while the nation watched*)

Clause	Example
Main (independent)	The hurricane struck
Subordinate (dependent)	while we were preparing to leave.

Collective noun. *See* **Noun.**

Comma splice A comma splice is an error caused when two sentences are separated with a comma instead of a correct end mark. (*The band played a medley of show tunes, everyone enjoyed the show.*)

Common noun. *See* **Noun.**

Comparative. *See* **Adjective; Adverb.**

Complement A complement is a word or group of words that completes the meaning of a verb. (The kitten finished the *milk*.) *See also* **Direct object; Indirect object.**

An ***objective complement*** is a word or a group of words that follows a direct object and renames or describes that object. (The parents of the rescued child declared Gus a *hero*.)

A ***subject complement*** follows a linking verb and renames or describes the subject. (The coach seemed *anxious*.) *See also* **Noun (predicate noun); Adjective (predicate adjective).**

Complete predicate The complete predicate of a sentence consists of the main verb plus any words that modify or complete the verb's meaning. (The student *produces work of high caliber*.)

Complete subject The complete subject of a sentence consists of the simple subject plus any words that modify or describe the simple subject. (*Students of history* believe that wars can be avoided.)

Sentence Part	Example
Complete subject	The man in the ten-gallon hat
Complete predicate	wore a pair of silver spurs.

Compound sentence part A sentence element that consists of two or more subjects, verbs, objects, or other parts is compound. (*Lou* and *Jay* helped. Laura *makes* and *models* scarves. Jill sings *opera* and *popular music*.)

Conjunction A conjunction is a word that links other words or groups of words.

A ***coordinating conjunction*** connects related words, groups of words, or sentences. (*and, but, or*)

A ***correlative conjunction*** is one of a pair of conjunctions that work together to connect sentence parts. (*either . . . or, neither . . . nor, not only . . . but also, whether . . . or, both . . . and*)

A ***subordinating conjunction*** introduces a subordinate clause. (*after, although, as, as if, as long as, as though, because, before, if, in order that, since, so that, than, though, till, unless, until, whatever, when, where, while*)

Conjunctive adverb A conjunctive adverb relates the clauses of a compound sentence. (*however, therefore, yet*)

Contraction A contraction is formed by joining two words and substituting an apostrophe for a letter or letters left out of one of the words. (*didn't, we've*)

Coordinating conjunction. *See* **Conjunction.**

Correlative conjunction. *See* **Conjunction.**

Dangling modifier A dangling modifier is one that does not clearly modify any word in the sentence. (*Dashing for the train*, the barriers got in the way.)

Demonstrative pronoun. *See* **Pronoun.**

Dependent clause. *See* **Clause.**

Direct object A direct object receives the action of a verb. Direct objects follow transitive verbs. (Jude planned the *party*.)

Direct quotation. *See* **Quotation.**

Divided quotation. *See* **Quotation.**

Double negative A double negative is the incorrect use of two negative words when only one is needed. (*Nobody didn't care*.)

End mark An end mark is any of several punctuation marks that can end a sentence. See the punctuation chart on page R77.

R86 GRAMMAR HANDBOOK

Fragment. *See* **Sentence fragment.**

Future tense. *See* **Verb tense.**

Gender The gender of a personal pronoun indicates whether the person or thing referred to is male, female, or neuter. (My cousin plays the tuba; *he* often performs in school concerts.)

Gerund A gerund is a verbal that ends in *-ing* and functions as a noun. (*Making* pottery takes patience.)

Helping verb. *See* **Verb (auxiliary verb).**

Illogical comparison An illogical comparison is a comparison that does not make sense because words are missing or illogical. (My computer is *newer than Kay.*)

Indefinite pronoun. *See* **Pronoun.**

Indefinite reference Indefinite reference occurs when a pronoun is used without a clear antecedent. (My aunt hugged me in front of my friends, and *it* was embarrassing.)

Independent clause. *See* **Clause.**

Indirect object An indirect object tells to whom or for whom (sometimes to what or for what) something is done. (Arthur wrote *Kerry* a letter.)

Indirect question An indirect question tells what someone asked without using the person's exact words. (*My friend asked me if I could go with her to the dentist.*)

Indirect quotation. *See* **Quotation.**

Infinitive An infinitive is a verbal, usually preceded by *to,* that functions as a noun, an adjective, or an adverb. (He wanted *to go* to the play.)

Intensive pronoun. *See* **Pronoun.**

Interjection An interjection is a word or phrase used to express strong feeling. (*Wow! Good grief!*)

Interrogative pronoun. *See* **Pronoun.**

Intransitive verb. *See* **Verb.**

Inverted sentence An inverted sentence is one in which the subject comes after the verb. (*How was the movie? Here come the clowns.*)

Irregular verb. *See* **Verb.**

Linking verb. *See* **Verb.**

Main clause. *See* **Clause.**

Main verb. *See* **Verb.**

Modifier A modifier makes another word more precise. Modifiers most often are adjectives or adverbs; they may also be phrases, verbals, or clauses that function as adjectives or adverbs. (*small* box, smiled *broadly,* house *by the sea,* dog *barking loudly*)

An ***essential modifier*** is one that is necessary to the meaning of a sentence. (Everybody *who has a free pass* should enter now. None *of the passengers* got on the train.)

A ***nonessential modifier*** is one that merely adds more information to a sentence that is clear without the addition. (We will use the new dishes, *which are stored in the closet.*)

Noun A noun names a person, a place, a thing, or an idea. (*auditor, shelf, book, goodness*)

An ***abstract noun*** names an idea, a quality, or a feeling. (*joy*)

A ***collective noun*** names a group of things. (*bevy*)

A ***common noun*** is a general name of a person, a place, a thing, or an idea. (*valet, hill, bread, amazement*)

A ***compound noun*** contains two or more words. (*hometown, pay-as-you-go, screen test*)

A ***noun of direct address*** is the name of a person being directly spoken to. (*Lee,* do you have the package? No, *Suki,* your letter did not arrive.)

A ***possessive noun*** shows who or what owns or is associated with something. (*Lil's* ring, a *day's* pay)

A ***predicate noun*** follows a linking verb and renames the subject. (Karen is a *writer.*)

A ***proper noun*** names a particular person, place, or thing. (*John Smith, Ohio, Sears Tower, Congress*)

Number A word is **singular** in number if it refers to just one person, place, thing, idea, or action, and **plural** in number if it refers to more than one person, place, thing, idea, or action. (The words *he, waiter,* and *is* are singular. The words *they, waiters,* and *are* are plural.)

Object of a preposition The object of a preposition is the noun or pronoun that follows a preposition. (The athletes cycled along the *route.* Jane baked a cake for *her.*)

GRAMMAR HANDBOOK R87

Object of a verb The object of a verb receives the action of the verb. (Sid told *stories.*)

P

Participle A participle is often used as part of a verb phrase. (had *written*) It can also be used as a verbal that functions as an adjective. (the *leaping* deer, the medicine *taken* for a fever)

The ***present participle*** is formed by adding *-ing* to the present form of a verb. (*Walking* rapidly, we reached the general store.)

The ***past participle*** of a regular verb is formed by adding *-d* or *-ed* to the present form. The past participles of irregular verbs do not follow this pattern. (*Startled,* they ran from the house. *Spun* glass is delicate. A *broken* cup lay there.)

Passive voice. *See* **Voice.**

Past tense. *See* **Verb tense.**

Perfect tenses. *See* **Verb tense.**

Person Person is a means of classifying pronouns.

A ***first-person*** pronoun refers to the person speaking. (*We* came.)

A ***second-person*** pronoun refers to the person spoken to. (*You* ask.)

A ***third-person*** pronoun refers to some other person(s) or thing(s) being spoken of. (*They* played.)

Personal pronoun. *See* **Pronoun.**

Phrase A phrase is a group of related words that does not contain a verb and its subject. (*noticing everything, under a chair*)

An ***adjective phrase*** modifies a noun or a pronoun. (The label *on the bottle* has faded.)

An ***adverb phrase*** modifies a verb, an adjective, or an adverb. (Come *to the fair.*)

An ***appositive phrase*** explains one or more words in a sentence. (Mary, *a champion gymnast,* won gold medals at the Olympics.)

A ***gerund phrase*** consists of a gerund and its modifiers and complements. (*Fixing the leak* will take only a few minutes.)

An ***infinitive phrase*** consists of an infinitive, its modifiers, and its complements. (*To prepare for a test,* study in a quiet place.)

A ***participial phrase*** consists of a participle and its modifiers and complements. (*Straggling to the finish line,* the last runners arrived.)

A ***prepositional phrase*** consists of a preposition, its object, and the object's modifiers. (The Saint Bernard does rescue work *in the Swiss Alps.*)

A ***verb phrase*** consists of a main verb and one or more helping verbs. (*might have ordered*)

Possessive A noun or pronoun that is possessive shows ownership or relationship. (*Dan's* story, *my* doctor)

Possessive noun. *See* **Noun.**

Possessive pronoun. *See* **Pronoun.**

Predicate The predicate of a sentence tells what the subject is or does. (The van *runs well even in winter.* The job *seems too complicated.*) *See also* **Complete predicate; Simple predicate.**

Predicate adjective. *See* **Adjective.**

Predicate nominative A predicate nominative is a noun or pronoun that follows a linking verb and renames or explains the subject. (Joan is a computer *operator.* The winner of the prize was *he.*)

Predicate pronoun. *See* **Pronoun.**

Preposition A preposition is a word that relates its object to another part of the sentence or to the sentence as a whole. (Alfredo leaped *onto* the stage.)

Prepositional phrase. *See* **Phrase.**

Present tense. *See* **Verb tense.**

Pronoun A pronoun replaces a noun or another pronoun. Some pronouns allow a writer or speaker to avoid repeating a proper noun. Other pronouns let a writer refer to an unknown or unidentified person or thing.

A ***demonstrative pronoun*** singles out one or more persons or things. (*This* is the letter.)

An ***indefinite pronoun*** refers to an unidentified person or thing. (*Everyone* stayed home. Will you hire *anybody?*)

An ***intensive pronoun*** emphasizes a noun or pronoun. (The teacher *himself* sold tickets.)

An ***interrogative pronoun*** asks a question. (*What* happened to you?)

A ***personal pronoun*** shows a distinction of person. (*I* came. *You* see. *He* knows.)

A ***possessive pronoun*** shows ownership. (*My* spaghetti is always good. Are *your* parents coming to the play?)

A ***predicate pronoun*** follows a linking verb and renames the subject. (The owners of the store were *they.*)

A ***reflexive pronoun*** reflects an action back on the subject of the sentence. (Joe helped *himself.*)

R88 GRAMMAR HANDBOOK

A ***relative pronoun*** relates a subordinate clause to the word it modifies. (The draperies, *which* had been made by hand, were ruined in the fire.)

Pronoun-antecedent agreement. *See* **Agreement.**

Pronoun forms

The ***subject form*** of a pronoun is used when the pronoun is the subject of a sentence or follows a linking verb as a predicate pronoun. (*She* fell. The star was *she.*)

The ***object form*** of a pronoun is used when the pronoun is the direct or indirect object of a verb or verbal or the object of a preposition. (We sent *him* the bill. We ordered food for *them.*)

Proper adjective. *See* **Adjective.**

Proper noun. *See* **Noun.**

Punctuation Punctuation clarifies the structure of sentences. See the punctuation chart below.

Quotation A quotation consists of words from another speaker or writer.

A ***direct quotation*** is the exact words of a speaker or writer. (Martin said, *"The homecoming game has been postponed."*)

A ***divided quotation*** is a quotation separated by words that identify the speaker. (*"The homecoming game,"* said Martin, *"has been postponed."*)

An ***indirect quotation*** reports what a person said without giving the exact words. (Martin said *that the homecoming game had been postponed.*)

Reflexive pronoun. *See* **Pronoun.**

Regular verb. *See* **Verb.**

Relative pronoun. *See* **Pronoun.**

Run-on sentence A run-on sentence consists of two or more sentences written incorrectly as one. (*The sunset was beautiful its brilliant colors lasted only a short time.*)

Sentence A sentence expresses a complete thought. The chart at the top of the next page shows the four kinds of sentences.

A ***complex sentence*** contains one main clause and one or more subordinate clauses. (*Open the windows before you go to bed. If she falls, I'll help her up.*)

A ***compound sentence*** is made up of two or more independent clauses joined by a conjunction, a colon, or a semicolon. (*The ship finally docked, and the passengers quickly left.*)

A ***simple sentence*** consists of only one main clause. (*My friend volunteers at a nursing home.*)

Punctuation	Uses	Examples
Apostrophe (')	Shows possession Indicates a contraction	Lou's garage Alva's script I'll help you. The baby's tired.
Colon (:)	Introduces a list or quotation Divides parts of some compound sentences	three colors: red, green, and yellow This was the problem: we had to find our own way home.
Comma (,)	Separates ideas Separates modifiers Separates items in series	The glass broke, and the juice spilled all over. The lively, talented cheerleaders energized the team. We visited London, Rome, and Paris.
Exclamation point (!)	Ends an exclamatory sentence	Have a wonderful time!
Hyphen (-)	Joins parts of some compound words	daughter-in-law, great-grandson
Period (.)	Ends a declarative sentence Follows many abbreviations	Swallows return to Capistrano in spring. min. qt. Blvd. Gen. Jan.
Question mark (?)	Ends an interrogative sentence	Where are you going?
Semicolon (;)	Divides parts of some compound sentences Separates items in series that contain commas	Marie is an expert dancer; she teaches a class in tap. Jerry visited Syracuse, New York; Athens, Georgia; and Tampa, Florida.

GRAMMAR HANDBOOK R89

Grammar Handbook

Kind of Sentence	Example
Declarative (statement)	Our team won.
Exclamatory (strong feeling)	I had a great time!
Imperative (request, command)	Take the next exit.
Interrogative (question)	Who owns the car?

Sentence fragment A sentence fragment is a group of words that is only part of a sentence. (*When he arrived. Merrily yodeling.*)

Simple predicate A simple predicate is the verb in the predicate. (John *collects* foreign stamps.)

Simple subject A simple subject is the key noun or pronoun in the subject. (The new *house* is empty.)

Split infinitive A split infinitive occurs when a modifier is placed between the word *to* and the verb in an infinitive. (*to quickly speak*)

Subject The subject is the part of a sentence that tells whom or what the sentence is about. (*Lou* swam.) *See* **Complete subject; Simple subject.**

Subject-verb agreement. *See* **Agreement.**

Subordinate clause. *See* **Clause.**

Subordinating conjunction. *See* **Conjunction.**

Superlative. *See* **Adjective; Adverb.**

Transitive verb. *See* **Verb.**

Unidentified reference An unidentified reference usually occurs when the word *it, they, this, which,* or *that* is used. (In California *they* have good weather most of the time.)

Verb A verb expresses an action, a condition, or a state of being.

An ***action verb*** tells what the subject does, has done, or will do. The action may be physical or mental. (Susan *trains* guide dogs.)

An ***auxiliary verb*** is added to a main verb to express tense, add emphasis, or otherwise affect the meaning of the verb. Together the auxiliary and main verb make up a verb phrase. (*will* intend, *could have* gone)

A ***linking verb*** expresses a state of being or connects the subject with a word or words that describe the subject. (The ice *feels* cold.) Linking verbs include *appear, be* (*am, are, is, was, were, been, being*), *become, feel, grow, look, remain, seem, smell, sound,* and *taste.*

A ***main verb*** expresses action or state of being; it appears with one or more auxiliary verbs. (will be *staying*)

The ***progressive form*** of a verb shows continuing action. (She *is knitting.*)

The past tense and past participle of a ***regular verb*** are formed by adding *-d* or *-ed.* (*open, opened*) An ***irregular verb*** does not follow this pattern. (*throw, threw, thrown; shrink, shrank, shrunk*)

The action of a ***transitive verb*** is directed toward someone or something, called the object of the verb. (Leo *washed* the windows.) An ***intransitive verb*** has no object. (The leaves *scattered.*)

Verbal A verbal is formed from a verb and acts as another part of speech, such as a noun, an adjective, or an adverb.

Verbal	Example
Gerund (used as a noun)	Lamont enjoys *swimming.*
Infinitive (used as an adjective, an adverb, or a noun)	Everyone wants *to help.*
Participle (used as an adjective)	The leaves *covering the drive* made it slippery.

Verb phrase. *See* **Phrase.**

Verb tense Verb tense shows the time of an action or the time of a state of being.

The ***present tense*** places an action or condition in the present. (Jan *takes* piano lessons.)

The ***past tense*** places an action or condition in the past. (We *came* to the party.)

The ***future tense*** places an action or condition in the future. (You *will understand.*)

The ***present perfect tense*** describes an action in an indefinite past time or an action that began in the past and continues in the present. (*has called, have known*)

The ***past perfect tense*** describes one action that happened before another action in the past. (*had scattered, had mentioned*)

The ***future perfect tense*** describes an event that will be finished before another future action begins. (*will have taught, shall have appeared*)

Voice The voice of a verb depends on whether the subject performs or receives the action of the verb.

In the ***active voice*** the subject of the sentence performs the verb's action. (We *knew* the answer.)

In the ***passive voice*** the subject of the sentence receives the action of the verb. (The team *has been eliminated.*)

R90 GRAMMAR HANDBOOK

Analyzing Text Features

Reading a Magazine Article

A **magazine article** is designed to catch and hold your interest. Learning how to recognize the items on a magazine page will help you read even the most complicated articles. Look at the sample magazine article as you read each strategy below.

Strategies for Reading

A. Read the **title** and other **headings** to get an idea of what the article is about. Frequently, the title presents the article's main topic. Smaller headings may introduce subtopics related to the main topic.

B. Note introductory text that is set off in some way, such as an **indented paragraph** or a passage in a **different typeface**. This text often summarizes the article.

C. Pay attention to terms in **italics** or **boldface**. Look for definitions or explanations before or after these terms.

D. Study **visuals**—photos, pictures, or maps. Visuals help bring the topic to life and enrich the text.

E. Look for **special features**, such as charts, tables, or graphs, that provide more detailed information on the topic or on a subtopic.

PRACTICE AND APPLY

Use the sample magazine page at right and the tips above to help you answer the following questions.

1. What is the article's main topic?
2. What gives fireflies their "fire"?
3. What happens soon after a firefly mates?
4. How do the visuals help you understand the article?
5. What information appears in the box?

Academic Reading Handbook

PRACTICE AND APPLY ANSWERS

1. fireflies and their characteristics
2. Their "fire" comes from luciferin (a compound that reacts with oxygen) and luciferase (an enzyme that makes this reaction possible).
3. Soon after a firefly mates, it dies.
4. (Answers will vary. A sample answer is provided.) They remind me what fireflies look like and how they light up.
5. definitions for the terms *bioluminescent* and *molt*

A

The Lure of Light

B

For humans, cosmic showers are awe-inspiring. For fireflies, lights closer to home mean it's time to mate.

Also called "lightning bugs" and "glowworms," fireflies belong to the beetle family *Lampyridae*. Their

C

bioluminescent "fire" comes from *luciferin* (a compound that reacts with oxygen) and *luciferase* (an enzyme that makes this reaction possible). Scientists are studying ways to use luciferase to "highlight" abnormal cells in people.

Most fireflies look for mates on warm summer evenings. Each species seems to have its own light signal. The male firefly flies around flashing his light signal. When the flightless female, perched on a plant, sees the appropriate signal, she responds by flashing her light. Then the male flies toward her, repeating his signal. . . .

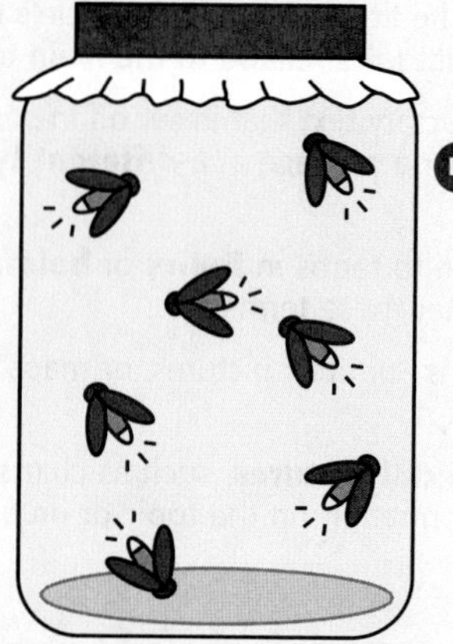

D

E

bioluminescent: emitting visible light (in a living organism)
molt: to shed a body covering

Fireflies die within days after mating. Their young hatch as wormlike larvae. They hide (on land or underwater), eat, grow, **molt,** and grow some more. After several months, each larva buries itself in an underground chamber, where it transforms into an adult firefly. The adult then chews through its chamber wall, pushes up to the surface, and searches for a mate.

The lure of light begins again.

Reading a Textbook

The first page of a **textbook** lesson introduces you to a particular topic. The page also provides important information that will guide you through the rest of the lesson. Look at the sample textbook page as you read each strategy below.

Strategies for Reading

A Preview the **title** and other **headings** to find out the lesson's main topic and related subtopics.

B Look for a list of terms or **vocabulary words**. These words will be identified and defined throughout the lesson.

C Read the **main idea**, **objectives**, or **focus**. These items summarize the lesson and establish a purpose for your reading.

D Find words set in special type, such as **italics** or **boldface**. Also look for material in **parentheses**. Boldface is often used to identify the vocabulary terms in the lesson. Material in parentheses may refer you to another page or visual in the lesson.

E Notice text on the page that is set off in some way. For example, text placed in a tinted, or colored, box may be from a **primary source** or a **quotation** that gives firsthand knowledge or historical perspective on a topic.

F Examine **visuals**, such as photos and drawings, and their captions. Visuals can help the topic come alive.

PRACTICE AND APPLY

Use the sample textbook page and the tips above to help you answer the following questions.

1. What does this lesson focus on?
2. What vocabulary terms will be defined in the lesson?
3. Review the quotation. Who is being quoted?
4. Where did the Assyrians come from?

PRACTICE AND APPLY ANSWERS

1. Assyrian domination of the Fertile Crescent
2. Assyria, Sennacherib, Ninevah, Ashurbanipal, Medes, Chaldeans, and Nebuchadnezzar
3. Lord Byron
4. The Assyrians came from the northern part of Mesopotamia.

Academic Reading Handbook

ACADEMIC READING HANDBOOK R93

Academic Reading Handbook

2 Assyria Dominates the Fertile Crescent

TERMS & NAMES
- Assyria
- Sennacherib
- Nineveh
- Ashurbanipal
- Medes
- Chaldeans
- Nebuchadnezzar

MAIN IDEA

Assyria developed a military machine, conquered an empire, and established imperial administration.

WHY IT MATTERS NOW

Some leaders still use military force to extend their rule, stamp out opposition, and gain wealth and power.

SETTING THE STAGE For more than two centuries, the Assyrian army advanced across Southwest Asia. It overwhelmed foes with its military strength. After the Assyrians seized control of Egypt, the Assyrian king Esarhaddon proclaimed, "I tore up the root of Kush, and not one therein escaped to submit to me." The last Kushite pharaoh retreated to Napata, Kush's capital city.

A Mighty Military Machine

Beginning around 850 B.C., **Assyria** (uh·SEER·ee·uh) acquired a large empire. It accomplished this by means of a sophisticated military organization and state-of-the-art weaponry. For a time, this campaign of conquest made Assyria the greatest power in Southwest Asia.

The Rise of a Warrior People The Assyrians came from the northern part of Mesopotamia. Their flat, exposed farmland made them easy to attack. Invaders swept down from the nearby mountains. The Assyrians may have developed their warlike behavior in response to these invasions. Lacking natural barriers such as mountains or deserts, they repelled invaders by developing a strong army. Through constant warfare, Assyrian kings built an empire that stretched from east and north of the Tigris River all the way to central Egypt.

One of these Assyrian kings, **Sennacherib** (sih·NAK·uhr·ihb), bragged that he had sacked 89 cities and 820 villages, burned Babylon, and ordered most of its inhabitants killed. Centuries later, in the 1800s, the English poet George Gordon, Lord Byron, romanticized the Assyrians' bloody exploits in a poem:

A VOICE ABOUT THE PAST

The Assyrian came down like a wolf on the fold,
And his cohorts were gleaming in purple and gold;
And the sheen of their spears was like stars on the sea,
When the blue wave rolls nightly on deep Galilee.

GEORGE GORDON, LORD BYRON, "The Destruction of Sennacherib"

THINK THROUGH HISTORY

A. Analyzing Causes What caused the Assyrians to develop a strong army and large empire.

Possible Answer: No natural barriers to invasion, needed strong army to repel invaders, constant warfare produced large empire.

This detail of a sandstone relief shows an Assyrian soldier with a shield and iron-tipped spear.

Military Organization and Conquest Assyria was a society which glorified military strength. Its soldiers were well equipped for conquering an empire. Making use of the iron-working technology of the time, the soldiers covered themselves in stiff leather and metal armor. They wore copper or iron helmets, padded loincloths, and leather skirts layered with metal scales. Their weapons were iron swords and iron-pointed spears. Infantry, archers, and spear throwers protected themselves with huge shields.

Advance planning and technical skill allowed the Assyrians to lay siege to enemy cities. When deep water blocked their passage, engineers would bridge the rivers with pontoons, or floating structures used to support a bridge. Tying inflated animal skins

Vocabulary

siege: a military blockade to force a city to surrender.

R94 ACADEMIC READING HANDBOOK

Understanding Visuals

Reading a Table

Tables hold a lot of information in an organized way. These tips can help you read a table quickly and accurately. Look at the example as you read each strategy in this list.

Strategies for Reading

A Read the **title** to find out the content of the table.

B Read the **introduction** to get a general overview of the information included in the table.

C Look at the **heading** of each row and column. To find specific information, find the place where a row and column intersect.

D Check the **credit** to see if the information is up-to-date and from a respected source.

A **Planets of the Solar System**

B Each planet in our solar system is unique. As the table shows, these differing traits include mass, mean distance from the sun, revolution period, and surface gravity.

C	Mass (kg)	Mean Distance from the Sun (km)	Revolution Period (Earth time)	Surface Gravity (m/s^2)
Mercury	3.3×10^{23}	57,909,175	87.97 days	3.69
Venus	4.87×10^{24}	108,208,930	224.7 days	8.86
Earth	5.9742×10^{24}	149,597,890	365.26 days	9.81
Mars	6.42×10^{23}	227,936,640	686.98 days	3.73
Jupiter	1.9×10^{27}	778,412,010	11.86 years	22.96
Saturn	5.69×10^{26}	1,426,725,400	29.46 years	11.38
Uranus	8.68×10^{25}	2,870,972,200	83.75 years	11.28
Neptune	1.02×10^{26}	4,498,252,900	163.72 years	11.67
Pluto	1.29×10^{22}	5,906,376,200	248 years	0.65

Source: National Aeronautics and Space Administration Jet Propulsion Laboratory Web site: *http://www.jpl.nasa.gov/solar_system/planets/planets_index.html* D

Academic Reading Handbook

PRACTICE AND APPLY

Answer the following questions using the table of information and tips.

1. Which planet has the strongest surface gravity?

2. Which planet is about ten times farther from the Sun than Earth?

3. Which planet is more massive: Earth or Venus?

PRACTICE AND APPLY ANSWERS

1. Jupiter
2. Saturn
3. Earth

Reading a Map

To read a **map** correctly, you have to identify and understand its elements. Look at the example below as you read each strategy in this list.

Strategies for Reading

A Scan the **title** to understand the content of the map.

B Study the **key**, or **legend**, to find out what the symbols and colors on the map stand for.

C Study **geographic labels** to understand specific places on the map.

D Look at the **pointer**, or **compass rose**, to determine direction.

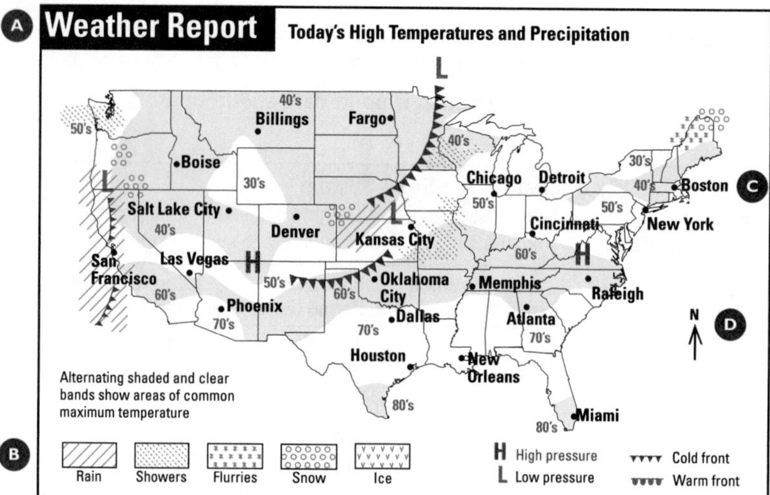

PRACTICE AND APPLY ANSWERS

1. The purpose of this map is to show the day's weather across the United States.
2. cold front
3. San Francisco and Kansas City
4. The rain always seems to be near a cold front.
5. Boston, Billings, Salt Lake City, Fargo, Boise, and Denver

PRACTICE AND APPLY

Use the map to answer the following questions.

1. What is the purpose of this map?
2. What does the symbol ▾▾▾▾ mean?
3. In which cities is rain indicated?
4. What seems to be the relationship between rain and cold fronts?
5. List the names of the coldest cities in the country.

Reading a Diagram

Diagrams combine pictures with a few words to provide a lot of information. Look at the example on the opposite page as you read each of the following strategies.

Strategies for Reading

A Look at the **title** to get a quick idea of what the diagram is about.

B Study the **images** closely to understand each part of the diagram.

C Look at the **captions** and the **labels** for more information.

Academic Reading Handbook

PRACTICE AND APPLY

Study the diagram, then answer the following questions using the strategies above.

1. What is this diagram about?
2. What is an updraft?
3. What are the two forces represented by the arrows in the Mature Stage?
4. Which force is growing stronger in this stage?
5. Why does the cloud begin to evaporate in the Dissipating Stage?

PRACTICE AND APPLY ANSWERS

1. the life cycle of a thunderstorm
2. The rising air is called an updraft.
3. The upward arrow represents the updraft and the downward arrow represents the downdraft.
4. the downdraft
5. The updraft has been weakened, reducing the supply of moist air.

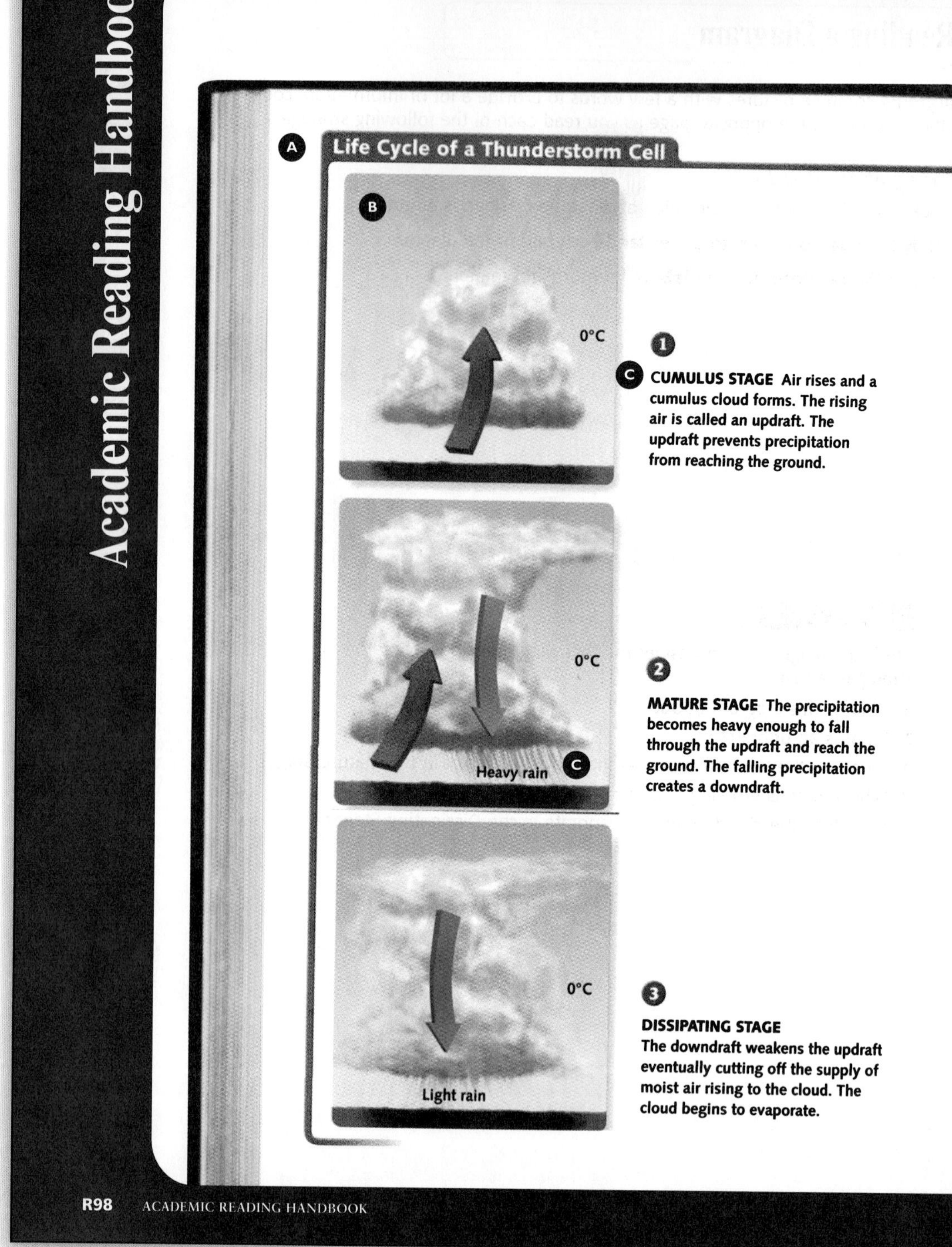
Academic Reading Handbook
A
Life Cycle of a Thunderstorm Cell
B
0°C
1
C
CUMULUS STAGE Air rises and a cumulus cloud forms. The rising air is called an updraft. The updraft prevents precipitation from reaching the ground.
0°C
Heavy rain
C
2
MATURE STAGE The precipitation becomes heavy enough to fall through the updraft and reach the ground. The falling precipitation creates a downdraft.
0°C
Light rain
3
DISSIPATING STAGE
The downdraft weakens the updraft eventually cutting off the supply of moist air rising to the cloud. The cloud begins to evaporate.
R98 ACADEMIC READING HANDBOOK

Recognizing Text Structures

Main Idea and Supporting Details

The **main idea** in a paragraph is its most important point. **Details** in the paragraph support the main idea. Identifying the main idea will help you focus on the main message the writer wants to communicate. Use the following strategies to help you identify a paragraph's main idea and supporting details.

Strategies for Reading

- Look for the **main idea**, which is often the first sentence in a paragraph.
- Use the main idea to help you **summarize** the point of the paragraph.
- Identify specific **details**, including facts and examples, that **support** the main idea.

Creatures of the Night

Main Idea — Bats are nocturnal animals—

Details — animals that are awake during the night and sleep during the day. Just before dusk, bats wake from their slumber. At dusk they begin their search for food; most eat insects, but some also eat fruit, pollen, or nectar. After feeding, bats rest, and then may eat again. Before dawn, they return to their roost for a good day's sleep.

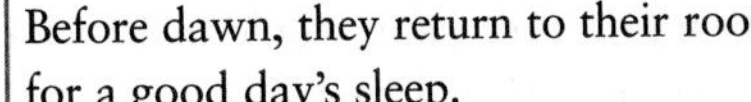

PRACTICE AND APPLY

Read the following paragraph. List the main idea and three supporting details.

When a volcano erupts, it produces a molten rock called lava. Lava is extremely hot when it first escapes but hardens as it cools. There are two kinds of lava; one kind is fast and fluid, while the other is slow and sticky.

PRACTICE AND APPLY ANSWERS

Main Idea: "When a volcano erupts, it produces a molten rock called lava." Supporting details: 1) "Lava is hot when it first escapes"; 2) "hardens as it cools"; 3) "one kind is fast and fluid"; "the other is slow and sticky."

PRACTICE AND APPLY ANSWERS

1. The city should put a stop sign at this intersection and station adult crossing guards there.
2. Students should identify one of the following statements from the second sentence of the third paragraph: "The presence of a stop sign will make sure motorists stop" or "the crossing guard will make sure that the students know when it is safe to cross."
3. (Answers will vary. Sample responses are provided.) I think the combination of the stop sign and the crossing guard is a good idea, because it would be an easy way to change people's behavior. Accidents usually happen when people aren't paying attention; the stop sign and the crossing guard would make both drivers and walkers pay attention.

   I don't think it makes much sense to put the stop sign and crossing guard at this corner. Drivers would become annoyed at having to stop, and students know how to cross the street on their own. Also, it would cost a lot of money to hire a crossing guard—too much for something that might not work, anyway.

Problem and Solution

Does the proposed **solution** to a **problem** make sense? In order to decide, you need to look at each part of the text. Use the following strategies to read the text below.

Strategies for Reading

- Look at the beginning or middle of a paragraph to find the **statement of the problem**.
- Find **details** that explain the problem and tell why it is important.
- Look for the **proposed solution**.
- Identify the **supporting details** for the proposed solution.
- Think about whether the solution is a good one.

Safer Streets *by Wanda Briggs*

Statement of problem

Explanation of solution

The intersection at Fourth and D streets, two blocks from our school, is an accident waiting to happen. Cars speed down the street while students stand at the crosswalk. Every day there are a few drivers who barely slow down, creating a dangerous situation.

Currently there is no stop sign at this intersection. Although the intersection is two blocks away from the school, many students use it because D Street connects the school with the subway station. Every morning and afternoon, hundreds of students and teachers cross the intersection at Fourth and D Streets.

The city should put a stop sign at this intersection and station adult crossing guards there. The presence of a stop sign will be a signal to motorists, and the crossing guard will make sure that students know when it is safe to cross. These safety measures would make the streets safer for students and teachers as well as drivers.

PRACTICE AND APPLY

Read the text above. Then answer these questions.

1. What is the proposed solution in the third paragraph?
2. Identify at least one detail that supports the solution.
3. Do you think the solution is a good one? Explain why or why not.

Sequence

It's important to understand the **sequence**, or order of events, in what you read. It helps you know what happens and why. Read the tips below to make sure a sequence is clear to you. Then look at the example on the opposite page.

Strategies for Reading

- Read through the passage and think about what its **main steps**, or stages, are.
- Look for **words and phrases that signal time**, such as *today, Friday, that night, later,* or *at 3 o'clock.*
- Look for **words and phrases that signal order**, such as *first, second, now, after that,* or *finally.*

PRACTICE AND APPLY

Read the article on the next page, which describes how to make your own photographic print. Use the information from the article and the tips above to answer the questions.

1. List any words or phrases that signal time.
2. List any phrases in the article that signal order.
3. A flow chart can help you understand a sequence of events. Use the information from the article to copy and complete this flow chart.

1. Load and focus the image.

Put the *negative* in the enlarger.

Adjust the ________________ knob.

2. Load and expose the paper.

Put the paper on the

____________.

Set the ____________ and push start.

3. Develop and fix the paper.

a. ______________________

b. ______________________

c. ______________________

Academic Reading Handbook

PRACTICE AND APPLY ANSWERS

1. Students should list the following phrases from the article: *five seconds, one minute, five seconds, three to five minutes.*
2. Students should list the following words and phrases from the article: *first, then, now, after, when the minute is up, then, once this time is up,* and *then.*
3. 1. negative; focus
   2. easel; timer
   3. a. Move the paper to the developer tray.
      b. Move the paper to the stop bath.
      c. Move the paper to the fix tray.

Academic Reading Handbook

How to Develop a Photograph

To make a black-and-white photographic print, you will need a photographic negative and a darkroom with an enlarger, photo paper, a printing easel to hold the paper, a clock or watch, and four trays with tongs. Each tray will contain one of four solutions: (1) developer; (2) a stop bath, or "stop"; (3) a fixing solution, or "fix"; and (4) water.

First, put the negative in the negative carrier of the enlarger. Switch the bulb on and adjust the size of the image on the easel. Then turn the focus knob until the image is sharp. Now, without moving the easel, turn off the bulb and place a sheet of photo paper on the easel. Set the timer on the enlarger to five seconds and expose the paper by pressing *start*.

After the paper has been exposed, remove it and place it in the developer tray for one minute. When the minute is up, remove the paper with tongs and place it in the stop bath for five seconds. Then move the paper to the fix tray and leave it there for three to five minutes. Once this time is up, the print has been "fixed" and you may view it in the light.

Look at the print to see whether it is too light or too dark. You may need to start again and adjust the time of exposure. Place the print in the water tray and start over with a new sheet of paper. If your first print was too dark, cut the time of exposure in half. If it was too light, double the time of exposure. Then repeat the remaining steps.

R102 ACADEMIC READING HANDBOOK

Cause and Effect

A **cause** is an event that brings about another event. An **effect** is something that happens as a result of the first event. Identifying causes and effects helps you understand how events are related. The tips below can help you find causes and effects in any reading.

Strategies for Reading

- Look for an action or event that answers the question "What happened?" This is the **effect**.
- Look for an action or event that answers the question "Why did it happen?" This is the **cause**.
- Identify words or phrases that **signal** causes and effects, such as *because, as a result, therefore, thus, consequently, since,* and *led to.*

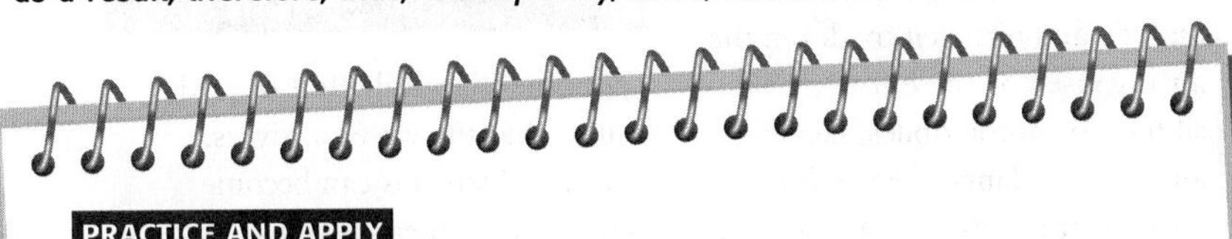

PRACTICE AND APPLY

Read the cause-and-effect passage on the next page. Then answer the following questions. Notice that the first cause and effect in the passage are highlighted.

1. List any words in the passage that signal causes and effects. The first one is highlighted for you.
2. Sometimes a cause has more than one effect. List two problems that result when acid rain destroys the waxy coating on a plant's leaves.
3. Use three of the causes and effects in the **third** paragraph to copy and complete the following diagram.

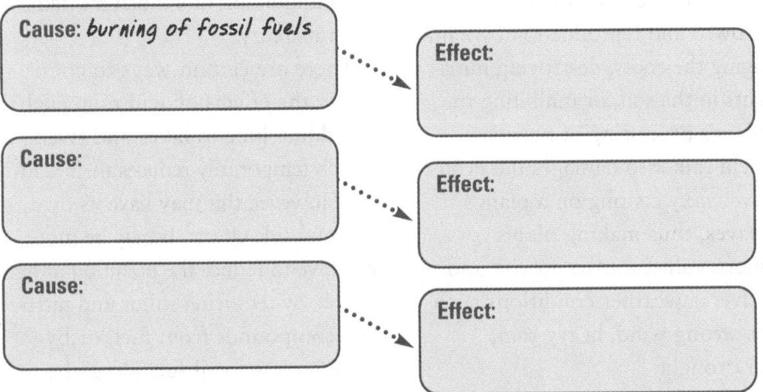

PRACTICE AND APPLY ANSWERS

1. Students should list the following words in the passage: *for this reason, thus, another harmful effect, lead to, effects, side effects,* and *effective.*
2. Students should list the following phrases from the second paragraph: "making plants more vulnerable to disease" and "subject to adverse weather conditions."
3. (Answers will vary. Sample responses are provided.)
   Cause: Acid rain
   Effect: Water in rivers, lakes, and streams can become more acidic.
   Cause: Water in rivers, lakes, and streams can become more acidic.
   Effect: Fish and other aquatic life are threatened.
   Cause: Acid rain
   Effect: Metals in soil and rocks are dissolved.
   Cause: Dissolving of metals
   Effect: These toxic elements can poison plants and wildlife.
   Cause: Acid rain
   Effect: Contaminated food or drinking water
   Cause: People eat contaminated food or drink contaminated water.
   Effect: Serious health problems

Acid Rain

One of the more serious threats to our environment is acid rain. This term refers to polluted precipitation such as rain, sleet, snow, or fog. The acid in acid rain comes from sulfur dioxide and nitrogen oxides. The presence of sulfur dioxide and nitrogen oxides in the air is caused by the burning of fossil fuels by automobiles, factories, and energy plants. Once released into the atmosphere, sulfur dioxide and nitrogen oxides react with the moisture in the air, producing nitric acid and sulfuric acid. In the last fifty years, taller smokestacks in urban areas have allowed acid pollutants to be blown great distances by the wind. For this reason acid rain has become a problem in rural as well as industrialized areas.

Effect

Signal word

Cause

Acid rain can hinder a plant's growth and reproduction by damaging the roots, destroying nutrients in the soil, or inhibiting the plant's processing of nutrients. Acid rain also damages the protective waxy coating on a plant's leaves, thus making plants more vulnerable to disease and adverse weather conditions such as strong wind, heavy rain, or drought.

Another harmful effect of acid rain is that the water in rivers, lakes, and streams can become more acidic, threatening fish and other aquatic life. It also dissolves metals such as mercury and aluminum, which are found in the surrounding soil and rocks; these toxic elements are then carried into the water supply, where they can poison plants and wildlife. Acid rain can lead to serious health problems if people drink water contaminated with aluminum or eat fish tainted with mercury.

There are certain ways to counteract the effects of acid rain, such as adding lime to lakes and rivers, which temporarily reduces their acidity. However, this may have its own harmful side effects. It may be more effective to reduce the pollution at its source by removing sulfur and nitrogen compounds from fuel, or by burning less fossil fuel altogether.

Comparison and Contrast

Comparing two things means showing how they are the same. **Contrasting** two things means showing how they are different. Comparisons and contrasts are often used in science and history books to make a subject clearer. Use these tips to help you understand comparison and contrast in reading assignments, such as the article on the opposite page.

Strategies for Reading

- Look for **direct statements** of comparison and contrast: "These things are similar because . . . " or "One major difference is. . . ."
- Pay attention to **words and phrases that signal comparisons**, such as *also, both, is the same as,* and *in the same way.*
- Notice **words and phrases that signal contrasts**. Some of these are *however, still, but,* and *on the other hand.*

PRACTICE AND APPLY

Read the essay on the opposite page. Then use the information from the article and the tips above to answer the questions.

1. List any words and phrases that signal comparisons. A sample has been highlighted for you.
2. List any words and phrases that signal contrasts. A sample has been highlighted for you.
3. A Venn diagram shows how two subjects are similar and how they are different. Copy this diagram, which uses information from the essay to compare and contrast emotional and irritant tears. Add at least one similarity to the middle part of the diagram. Add at least one difference in each outer circle.

Academic Reading Handbook

PRACTICE AND APPLY ANSWERS

1. both, both
2. Students should list the following words from the passage: differ, a little bit more complicated, different, for one thing, difference
3. Answers will vary. Sample responses are provided.
   Emotional tears: occur in response to strong feelings; mysterious; higher concentration of protein; shed more often than irritant tears
   Both: come from lacrimal glands; contain high levels of manganese
   Irritant tears: occur in response to smoke, onion vapors, or foreign bodies; have a clear purpose—to wash the eye and keep it moist.

What Are Tears?

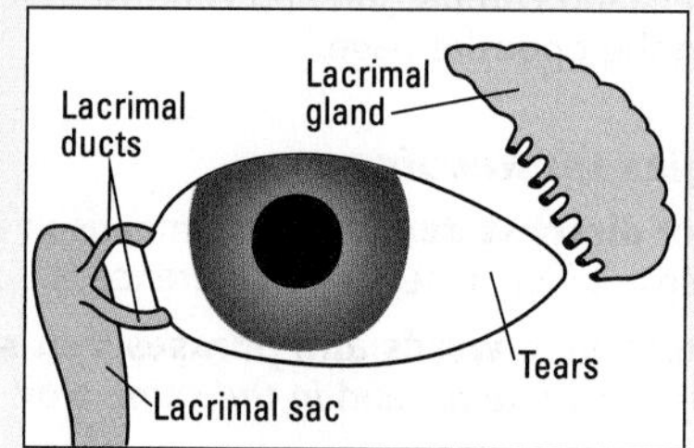

Humans shed two kinds of tears. Irritant tears occur in response to irritating physical stimuli, while emotional tears occur in response to sadness, anger, joy, or other intense emotions.

Comparison Both kinds of tears come from glands above the eyes called lacrimal glands. The fluid from the lacrimal glands moistens the eyes and keeps them clear of foreign particles. With each blink, a little bit of fluid is secreted from the glands. Tears form when the lacrimal glands produce more fluid than can drain through the available ducts.

Emotional tears occur when a strong feeling, such as grief, anger, or joy, causes the muscles around the lacrimal glands to tighten up and squeeze out excess fluid. These emotional tears differ from irritant tears, which occur in response to irritants such as smoke, onion vapors, or bits of dirt in the eye. Contrast

Irritant tears have a clear purpose —to wash the eye and keep it moist. What is the purpose of emotional tears? Scientist William Frey suspects that emotional tears might help relieve the body of chemicals that build up during stress.

He conducted a study in which he compared irritant tears with emotional tears. To produce irritant tears, he exposed people to grated onions and collected the resulting tears. Producing emotional tears was a little bit more complicated—what is the best way to make people cry without being mean to them? He finally decided to show them sad movies.

Frey found that emotional tears were in fact different from irritant tears. For one thing, people tended to shed many more emotional tears than irritant tears. And while both kinds of tears contained the element manganese, emotional tears had a much higher concentration of protein. However, the reason for this difference was not clear.

The mysterious causes and functions of tears are still being researched, but if you want to avoid shedding tears, stay away from onions and sad movies—at least that much is clear.

Argument

An **argument** is an opinion backed up with reasons and facts. Examining an opinion and the reasons and facts that back it up will help you decide if the opinion makes sense. Look at the argument on the right as you read each of these tips.

Strategies for Reading

- Look for words that **signal an opinion**: *I believe; I think; in my view; they claim, argue,* or *disagree.*
- Look for reasons, facts, or expert opinions that **support** the argument.
- Ask yourself if the argument and reasons **make sense.**
- Look for overgeneralizations or other **errors in reasoning** that may affect the argument.
- Think about the **accuracy** of the information.

PRACTICE AND APPLY

Read the argument on the next page, and then answer the questions below.

1. List any words that signal an opinion.
2. List any words or phrases that give the writer's opinion.
3. The writer presents both sides of the argument. Copy and complete the chart below to show the two sides. One example has been provided for you.

Reasons for	Reasons Against
1. Bicycles produce less air pollution than cars.	

PRACTICE AND APPLY ANSWERS

1. Students should list the following words and phrases: *I believe; In my view; those who oppose; They say; They claim; They point out; I'm not saying; I am saying.*
2. Students should list some of the following phrases: "bicyclists should have as much claim to city streets as automobiles"; "it is time to encourage bicycle riding by increasing the number of bike lanes and by shifting motorists' attitudes toward bicycle riders"; "few people would miss the constant revving of car engines and honking of horns"; "it's a safer, healthier, environmentally friendly alternative to driving."
3. (Answers will vary. Sample answers are provided.)
   Reasons For:
   2. Bicycling provides great exercise and helps keep people healthy.
   3. Bicycles are less noisy than cars.
   Reasons Against:
   1. Cars have a right to be on the streets built for them.
   2. Bicyclists make driving more dangerous because they interfere with traffic and are hard to see.
   3. Bike riding is too much trouble.

More Rights for Bikes

By Maxine Fujita

I believe bicyclists should have as much claim to city streets as automobiles. In my view, it is time to encourage bicycle riding by increasing the number of bike lanes and by changing motorists' attitudes toward bicycle riders.

The advantages of riding a bicycle rather than driving a car are clear. For one thing, automobile exhaust adds to already grave air pollution problems in our cities. By choosing to ride a bike instead of drive, we help keep our air clean. We also keep our streets quiet. Although we often forget about noise pollution, few people would miss the constant revving of car engines and honking of horns if our streets were filled with bicycles. Cycling also provides great exercise. If more people rode bikes, our population would have healthier hearts, lungs, and legs.

There are those who oppose bicycle traffic. They say the streets were made for cars, so cars have more right to be on the streets. They claim that cyclists are a nuisance and a danger because they interfere with auto traffic and are hard to see. They themselves don't want to cycle because it's too strenuous, too cold, too wet, too far, or too dangerous.

I'm not saying that bicycling is for everyone, but I am saying it's a safer, healthier, environmentally friendly alternative to driving. So join me in supporting more bike lanes and increased respect for the people who use them.

R108 ACADEMIC READING HANDBOOK

Reading in the Content Areas

Social Studies

Social studies class becomes easier when you understand how your textbook's words, pictures, and maps work together to give you information. Following these tips can make you a better reader of social studies lessons. As you read the tips, look at the sample lesson on the right-hand page.

Strategies for Reading

A First, look at any **headlines** or **subheads** on the page. These give you an idea of what each section covers.

B Make sure you know the meaning of any boldfaced or underlined **vocabulary terms**. These terms often appear on tests.

C Carefully read the text and think about **ways the information is organized**. Social studies books are full of sequence, comparison and contrast, and organization by geographic location.

D Look closely at **maps** and **map titles**. Think about how the map and the text are related.

E Read any **study tips** in the margins or at the bottom of the page. These let you check your understanding as you read.

PRACTICE AND APPLY

Carefully read the textbook page at right. Use the information from the page and from the tips above to answer these questions.

1. What are the two main subjects covered on this page? What secondary subject is covered?
2. List and define the three vocabulary terms.
3. Give three examples of uplands.
4. On the map, which river empties into the North Sea?
5. Read the "Geographic Thinking" question in the left margin. Which paragraph in the text contains the answer to this question?

PRACTICE AND APPLY ANSWERS

1. uplands and rivers; the Danube and the Rhine
2. Students should list the boldfaced terms in the first full paragraph. For *uplands,* they should write "are hills or very low mountains that may also contain mesas and high plateaus." For *Meseta,* they should write "the central plateau of Spain." For *Massif Central,* they should write "About one-sixth of French lands are located in the uplands called..."
3. Students should give three of the four following examples: the Kjølen Mountains of Scandinavia, the Scottish highlands, low mountain areas of Brittany in France, and the *Meseta.*
4. the Rhine river
5. the paragraph in the left margin under the word *Answer*

off the Balkan Peninsula from the rest of Europe. Historically, they also have isolated the peninsula's various ethnic groups from each other.

A **UPLANDS** Mountains and uplands differ from each other in their elevation. **Uplands** are hills or very low mountains that may also contain B mesas and high plateaus. Some uplands of Europe are eroded remains of ancient mountain ranges. Examples of uplands include the Kjølen (CHUR•luhn) Mountains of Scandinavia, the Scottish highlands, the low mountain areas of Brittany in France, and the central plateau of Spain called the ***Meseta*** (meh•SEH•tah). Other uplands border mountainous areas, such as the Central Uplands of Germany, which are at the base of the Alps. About one-sixth of French lands are located in the uplands called the ***Massif Central*** (ma•SEEF sahn•TRAHL).

BACKGROUND
Brittany is a region located on a peninsula in northwest France.

D

A Rivers: Europe's Links

SKILLBUILDER: Interpreting Maps

1 **MOVEMENT** Which rivers empty into the North Sea? Into the Mediterranean Sea?

2 **PLACE** What port is at the mouth of the Rhine?

Traversing Europe is a network of rivers that bring people and goods together. These rivers are used to transport goods between coastal harbors and the inland region, aiding economic growth. Historically, the rivers also have aided the movement of ideas.

C Two major castle-lined rivers—the Danube and the Rhine—have served as watery highways for centuries. The Rhine flows 820 miles from the interior of Europe north to the North Sea. The Danube cuts through the heart of Europe from west to east. Touching 9 countries over its 1,771-mile length, the Danube River links Europeans to the Black Sea.

Many other European rivers flow from the interior to the sea and are large enough for ships to traverse. Through history, these rivers helped connect Europeans to the rest of the world, encouraging both trade and travel. Europeans have explored and migrated to many other world regions.

E

Geographic Thinking
Seeing Patterns
How does the direction in which European rivers flow aid in linking Europeans to the world?
Answer: Because they flow toward seas, the rivers help Europeans to travel to other regions.

Science

Reading a **science** textbook becomes easier when you understand how the explanations, drawings, and special terms work together. Use the strategies below to help you better understand your science textbook. Look at the examples on the opposite page as you read each strategy in this list.

Strategies for Reading

- **A** Preview the **title** and **headings** on the page to see what scientific concepts will be covered.
- **B** Read the **key idea**, **objectives**, or **focus**. These items summarize the lesson and establish a purpose for your reading.
- **C** Look for **boldfaced** and **italicized** words that appear in the text. Look for **definitions** of those words.
- **D** Carefully examine any **pictures** or **diagrams**. Read the **captions** and evaluate how the graphics help to illustrate and explain the text.
- **E** Many science textbooks discuss **scientific concepts** in terms of **everyday events** or **experiences**. Look for these places and consider how they improve your understanding.

PRACTICE AND APPLY

Use the sample science page and the tips above to help you answer the following questions.

1. What scientific concepts will be covered in this lesson? Where on the page did you find this information?
2. Define the key term *fault.*
3. Why do you think the earthquake model described in the third paragraph is called the *elastic-rebound theory?*
4. What are two things the diagram tells you about earthquakes?

Academic Reading Handbook

PRACTICE AND APPLY ANSWERS

1. the causes of earthquakes; in the headline at letter A
2. a break in the lithosphere along which movement has occured
3. This model is called the *elastic-rebound theory* because the plates snap back like a rubber or elastic band.
4. (Students should include two of the following responses.) Most earth-quakes occur at faults along plate boundaries. Faults are deep breaks in the earth. The epicenter is the point on the earth's surface directly above the focus. Energy is released at the focus and travels away from it in all directions. Earthquakes displace large portions of rock.

10.1

How and Where Earthquakes Occur

KEY IDEA
Most earthquakes result from the strain that builds up at plate boundaries.

KEY VOCABULARY
- earthquake
- fault
- focus
- epicenter
- body waves
- P waves
- S waves
- surface waves

More than 3 million earthquakes occur each year, or about one earthquake every ten seconds. Most of these are too small to be noticeable. Each year, however, a number of powerful earthquakes occur. Because such earthquakes are among the most destructive of natural disasters, it is important to understand how and where earthquakes occur in order to prevent the loss of lives and property.

Causes of Earthquakes

An **earthquake** is a shaking of Earth's crust caused by a release of energy. Earthquakes can occur for many reasons. The ground may shake as a result of the eruption of a volcano, the collapse of a cavern, or even the impact of a meteor. The cause of most major earthquakes is the strain that builds up along faults at or near boundaries between lithospheric plates. A **fault** is a break in the lithosphere along which movement has occurred.

Most of the time, friction prevents the plates from moving, so strain builds up, causing the plates to deform, or change shape. Eventually, the strain becomes great enough to overcome the friction, and the plates move suddenly, causing an earthquake. The plates then snap back to the shapes they had before they were deformed, but at new locations relative to each other. This model of an earthquake is called the elastic-rebound theory.

The point at which the first movement occurs during an earthquake is called the **focus** of the earthquake. The focus is the point at which rock begins to move or break. It is where the earthquake originates and is usually many kilometers beneath the surface. The point on Earth's surface directly above the focus is the **epicenter** of the earthquake. News reports about earthquakes usually give the location of the epicenters.

EARTHQUAKE These rows of lettuce were displaced by an earthquake in California in 1979.

Focus and Epicenter of an Earthquake

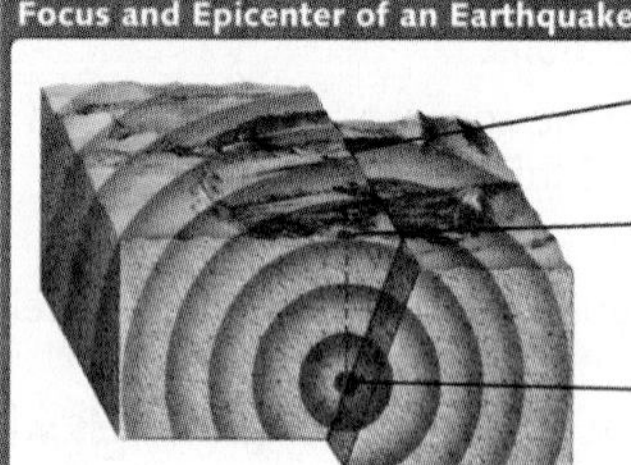

The depth at which an earthquake originates depends upon the type of plate boundary involved. At divergent boundaries, such as the Mid-Atlantic Ridge, earthquakes tend to occur within 30 kilometers of the surface. Earthquakes also tend to occur at shallow depths along transform boundaries. At subduction boundaries, however, where plates plunge beneath other plates, the focus of an earthquake can be located as far as

R112 ACADEMIC READING HANDBOOK

Mathematics

Reading in **mathematics** is different from reading in history, literature, or science. Use the strategies below to help you better understand your mathematics textbook. Look at the examples on the opposite page as you read each strategy in the list.

Strategies for Reading

A Preview the **title** and **headings** on the page to see what mathematics concepts will be covered.

B Find and read the **goals** or **objectives** for the lesson. These will tell you the most important points to know.

C Read **explanations** carefully. Sometimes a concept is explained in more than one way to make sure you understand it.

D Look for **special features**, such as study or vocabulary tips. They provide more help or information.

E Study any **worked-out solutions** to sample problems. These are the key to understanding how to do the homework assignment.

Academic Reading Handbook

PRACTICE AND APPLY

Use the sample mathematics page and the strategies above to help you answer the following questions.

1. What is the title of the lesson?
2. What learning goals should you have as you work through this lesson?
3. List and define the vocabulary words that appear in the explanation at the top of the page.
4. Why is the relation in Example 1a *not* a function?
5. Where is the origin in a coordinate plane?
6. What is the name that is given to the first number in an ordered pair?

PRACTICE AND APPLY ANSWERS

1. *Functions and Their Graphs.*
2. Goal 1: Represent relations and functions.
   Goal 2: Graph and evaluate linear functions, as applied in Exs. 55 and 56.
3. relation: a mapping, or pairing, of input values with output value
   domain: the set of input values
   range: the set of output values
   function: a relation that has exactly one output for each input
4. because not all of the input values have just one output value
5. The origin is the point where the *x-axis* and *y-axis* intersect.
6. *x-coordinate*

2.1 Functions and Their Graphs

GOAL 1 REPRESENTING RELATIONS AND FUNCTIONS

What you should learn

GOAL 1 Represent relations and functions.

GOAL 2 Graph and evaluate linear functions, as applied in **Exs. 55 and 56.**

Why you should learn it

▼ To model **real-life** quantities, such as the distance a hot air balloon travels in **Example 6.**

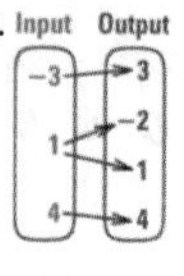

A **relation** is a *mapping*, or pairing, of input values with output values. The set of input values is the **domain**, and the set of output values is the **range**. A relation is a **function** provided there is exactly one output for each input. It is not a function if at least one input has more than one output.

Relations (and functions) between two quantities can be represented in many ways, including mapping diagrams, tables, graphs, equations, and verbal descriptions.

EXAMPLE 1 *Identifying Functions*

Identify the domain and range. Then tell whether the relation is a function.

a. Input: −3, 1, 4; Output: 3, −2, 1, 4

b. Input: −3, 1, 3, 4; Output: 3, 1, −2

SOLUTION

a. The domain consists of −3, 1, and 4, and the range consists of −2, 1, 3, and 4. The relation is not a function because the input 1 is mapped onto both −2 and 1.

b. The domain consists of −3, 1, 3, and 4, and the range consists of −2, 1, and 3. The relation is a function because each input in the domain is mapped onto exactly one output in the range.

A relation can be represented by a set of **ordered pairs** of the form (x, y). In an ordered pair the first number is the ***x*-coordinate** and the second number is the ***y*-coordinate**. To graph a relation, plot each of its ordered pairs in a **coordinate plane**, such as the one shown. A coordinate plane is divided into four **quadrants** by the ***x*-axis** and the ***y*-axis**. The axes intersect at a point called the **origin**.

Quadrant II $x < 0, y > 0$ | Quadrant I $x > 0, y > 0$ | Quadrant III $x < 0, y < 0$ | Quadrant IV $x > 0, y < 0$ | y-axis | x-axis | origin (0, 0)

STUDENT HELP

Study Tip
Although the origin O is not usually labeled, it is understood to be the point (0, 0).

Reading Beyond the Classroom

Reading an Application

Reading and understanding an **application** will help you fill it out correctly and avoid mistakes. Use the following strategies to help you understand any application. Look at the example on the next page as you read each strategy.

Strategies for Reading

- **A** **Begin at the top**. Scan the application to understand the different sections.
- **B** Look for special **instructions for filling out** the application.
- **C** Note any **request for materials** that must be attached to the application.
- **D** Watch for **sections you don't have to fill in** or **questions you don't have to answer**.
- **E** Look for difficult or confusing words or abbreviations. Look them up in a dictionary or ask someone what they mean.

PRACTICE AND APPLY

Imagine that you are applying for a Social Security card. Read the application on the next page. Then answer the following questions.

1. Where should you send the completed form?
2. Which questions can you skip if you have never before applied for or received a Social Security card?
3. In which section of the application should your phone number be entered?
4. What is the penalty for deliberately giving false information?
5. What should be written in section 8B of the application?

PRACTICE AND APPLY ANSWERS

1. any Social Security office
2. questions 11, 12, and 13
3. section 15
4. fine, imprisonment, or both
5. your mother's Social Security number

A **SOCIAL SECURITY ADMINISTRATION**
Application for a Social Security Card

Form Approved
OMB No. 0960-0066

B **STEP 1** Complete and sign the application using BLUE or BLACK ink. Do not use pencil or other colors of ink. Please print legibly.

C **STEP 2** Submit the completed and signed application with all required original documents to any Social Security office. To find out what documents are needed, please visit www.ssa.gov/online.

1	NAME → TO BE SHOWN ON CARD	First	Full Middle Name	Last
	FULL NAME AT BIRTH IF OTHER THAN ABOVE	First	Full Middle Name	Last
	OTHER NAMES USED			
2	MAILING ADDRESS → Do Not Abbreviate	Street Address, Apt. No., PO Box, Rural Route No. / City	State	Zip Code
3	CITIZENSHIP → (Check One)	☐ U.S. Citizen ☐ Legal Alien Allowed To Work	☐ Legal Alien **Not** Allowed To Work (See Instructions On Page 1)	☐ Other (See Instructions On Page 1)
4	SEX →	☐ Male	☐ Female	
5	RACE/ETHNIC DESCRIPTION → (Check One Only - Voluntary)	☐ Asian, Asian-American or Pacific Islander ☐ Hispanic	☐ Black (Not Hispanic) ☐ North American Indian or Alaskan Native	☐ White (Not Hispanic)
6	DATE OF BIRTH — Month, Day, Year	7 PLACE OF BIRTH (Do Not Abbreviate) City	State or Foreign Country	FCI; Office Use Only
8	A. MOTHER'S MAIDEN NAME →	First	Full Middle Name	Last Name At Her Birth
	B. MOTHER'S SOCIAL SECURITY NUMBER →	☐☐☐-☐☐-☐☐☐☐		
9	A. FATHER'S NAME →	First	Full Middle Name	Last
	B. FATHER'S SOCIAL SECURITY NUMBER →	☐☐☐-☐☐-☐☐☐☐		
10	Has the applicant or anyone acting on his/her behalf ever filed for or received a Social Security number card before?	☐ Yes (If "yes", answer questions 11-13.)	☐ No (If "no", go on to question 14.)	☐ Don't Know (If "don't know", go on to question 14.)
11	Enter the Social Security number previously assigned to the person listed in item 1. →	☐☐☐-☐☐-☐☐☐☐		
12 **D**	Enter the name shown on the most recent Social Security card issued for the person listed in item 1. →	First	Middle Name	Last
13	Enter any different date of birth if used on an earlier application for a card. →	Month, Day, Year		
14	TODAY'S DATE — Month, Day, Year	15 DAYTIME PHONE NUMBER ( ) Area Code	Number	

E DELIBERATELY FURNISHING (OR CAUSING TO BE FURNISHED) FALSE INFORMATION ON THIS APPLICATION IS A CRIME PUNISHABLE BY FINE OR IMPRISONMENT, OR BOTH.

16	YOUR SIGNATURE ▸	17	YOUR RELATIONSHIP TO THE PERSON IN ITEM 1 IS: ☐ Self ☐ Natural Or Adoptive Parent ☐ Legal Guardian ☐ Other (Specify)

DO NOT WRITE BELOW THIS LINE (FOR SSA USE ONLY)

EVIDENCE SUBMITTED	SIGNATURE AND TITLE OF EMPLOYEE(S) REVIEWING EVIDENCE AND/OR CONDUCTING INTERVIEW
	DCL / DATE

R116 ACADEMIC READING HANDBOOK

Reading a Public Notice

Public notices can tell you about events in your community and give you valuable information about safety. When you read a public notice, follow these tips. Each tip relates to a specific part of the notice on the opposite page.

Strategies for Reading

- **A** Read the notice's **title**, if it has one. The title often gives the main idea or purpose of the notice.
- **B** See if there is a logo, credit, or other way of telling **who created the notice**.
- **C** Ask yourself, **"Who should read this notice?"** If the information in it might be important to you or someone you know, then you should pay attention to it.
- **D** Look for **instructions**—things the notice is asking or telling you to do.
- **E** See if there are details that tell you how you can **find out more** about the topic.

Academic Reading Handbook

PRACTICE AND APPLY

The notice on the opposite page is from a state government agency. Read it carefully and answer the questions below.

1. Who is the notice from?
2. Who is the notice for?
3. What does the notice ask readers to do?
4. Where should proposals be sent?
5. What two things will be done with the proposals?
6. According to the notice, what kind of projects is the state looking to enact?

PRACTICE AND APPLY ANSWERS

1. the California State Water Control Board
2. California citizens
3. propose projects that will reduce coastal beach contamination
4. State Water Control Board
Loans & Grants Branch
P.O. Box 1234
San Pedro, CA 90202
5. They will be placed on a list and will be eligible for loans and grants, as they become available. Projects will be reviewed as they are received by staff for concurrence with the CBI's intent and completeness of information.
6. reduce coastal beach contamination

Academic Reading Handbook

B **STATE WATER CONTROL BOARD**

The energy challenge facing our state is real. Every citizen needs to take immediate action to reduce energy consumption. For a list of simple ways you can reduce demand and cut your energy costs, see our website at www.stategovxyz.gov.

A **PUBLIC NOTICE REQUESTING PROJECT PROPOSALS FOR THE BEACH CLEANUP ACT (BCA)**

C **ATTENTION:** COASTAL BIOLOGISTS, VOLUNTEER BEACH MONITORS, AND CONCERNED CITIZENS

The State's coastal beach monitoring programs indicate that beach pollution is widespread and too often exceeds acceptable levels, resulting in beach postings and closures. The major goal of the BCA is to reduce health risks and increase the public's access to clean beaches.

The State wants your proposals. The State Water Control Board (SWCB) is in the process of identifying traditional and innovative projects that will result in a reduction of coastal beach D contamination. These projects will be located in the areas of the state where beach postings and closures have been most prevalent. Project proposals that are submitted to the SWCB will be placed on a list and will be eligible for loans and grants, as they become available. During the fiscal year 2001–2002, loan moneys will be available through the State Fund for:

- development and implementation of programs to control pollution from nonpoint sources and stormwater drainage;
- publicly-owned capital improvement projects that benefit water quality;
- implementation of estuary enhancement programs.

Additionally, it is possible that a grant program may become available for local diversions, catch basins, filtration systems, and other projects that will reduce untreated runoff from reaching coastal waters. However, the SWCB will continue to seek funding for projects that will result in significant and steady decreases in beach postings and closures.

In preparing this list, we are seeking information on viable projects that will help us attain our goal of providing clean and healthy coastal beaches for all that reside in and visit our state. D Enclosed is a list of items and considerations that will be necessary for a timely review of all projects submitted. Priority will be given to projects that can be in place and in operation by July 2004. With your assistance, we plan to have an initial list of projects compiled by mid-April, 2003. Projects will be reviewed as they are received by staff for concurrence with the BCA's intent and completeness of information. We will post more information on our website at www.swcb.xyz.gov as it becomes available.

Project Proposals should be sent to:

State Water Control Board
Loans & Grants Branch
P.O. Box 1234
San Pedro, CA 90202

E If you have any questions, please contact Dr. John Smith, Clean Beaches Coordinator for the SWCB at (555) 555-1111 or jsmith@exec.swcb.xyz.gov.

Reading a Web Page

If you need information for a report, project, or hobby, the World Wide Web can probably help you. The tips below will help you understand the **Web pages** you read. As you look at the tips, notice where they match up to the sample Web page on the right.

Strategies for Reading

A Notice the page's **Web address**, or URL. You may want to write it down in case you need to access the same page at another time.

B Look for **menu bars** along the top, bottom, or side of the page. These guide you to other parts of the site that may be useful.

C Look for **links** to other parts of the site or to related pages. Links are often shown as underlined words.

D Use a **search** feature to quickly find out whether a certain kind of information is contained anywhere on the site.

E Many sites have a link that allows you to **contact** the creators with questions or feedback.

PRACTICE AND APPLY

Read the Web page on the next page. Then use the information from the page and the tips above to answer the questions.

1. What is the Web address?
2. If you wanted to know whether the ClassZone site contained any information about adjective clauses, how would you go about finding out?
3. Read the paragraph under "Topic." Then look at the thought bubbles below it. What would you expect to find if you clicked on "Write About It"?
4. What people, besides students, might find this site helpful?
5. In your own words, summarize the content under "Topic".

Academic Reading Handbook

PRACTICE AND APPLY ANSWERS

1. http://www.classzone.com/lnetwork/writing/hs_writing.htm
2. type "adjective clauses" into the box at letter D (Search this site) and click on GO
3. a space in which I could write my response
4. Answers may vary. Sample responses: teachers or anyone interested in publishing.
5. Answers may vary. Sample response: It describes the problem of Americans' lack of exercise and asks students to respond in writing.

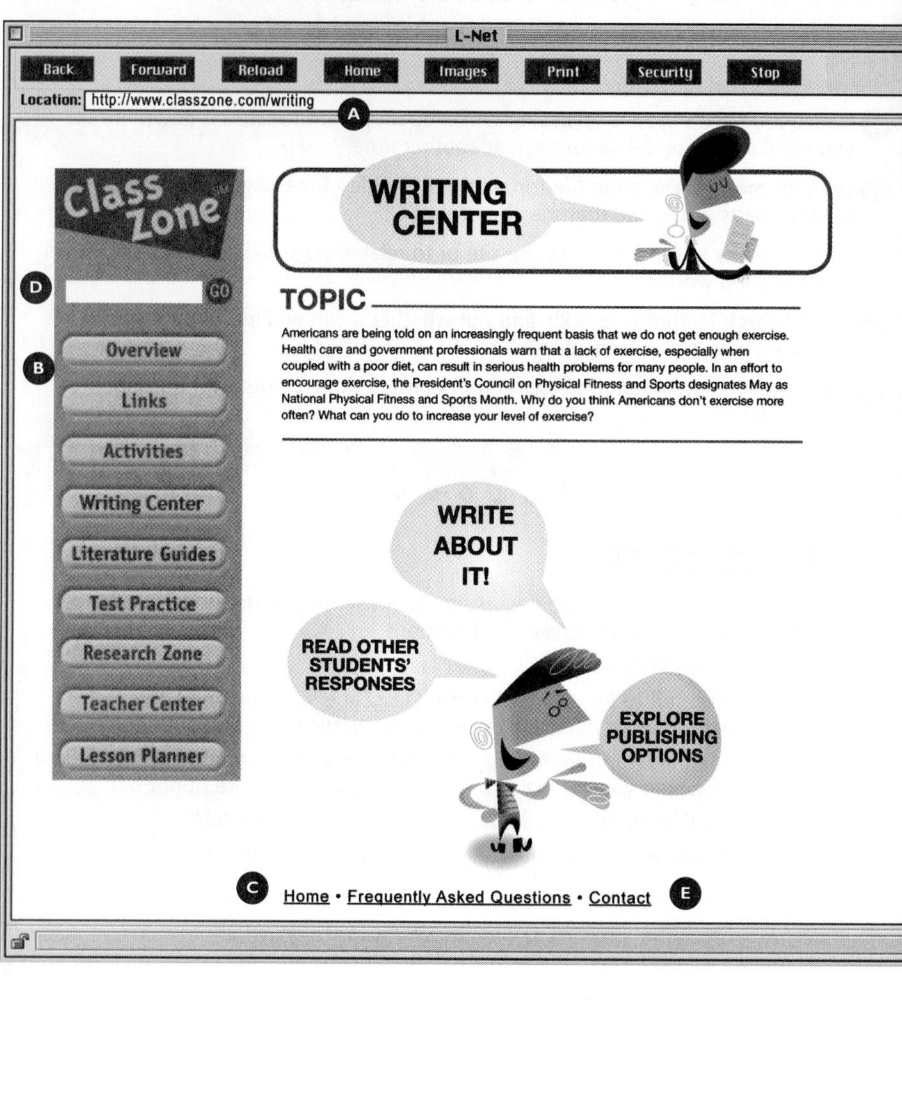
L-Net
Back
Forward
Reload
Home
Images
Print
Security
Stop
Location: http://www.classzone.com/writing
A
Class Zone
D
GO
B
Overview
Links
Activities
Writing Center
Literature Guides
Test Practice
Research Zone
Teacher Center
Lesson Planner
WRITING CENTER
TOPIC
Americans are being told on an increasingly frequent basis that we do not get enough exercise. Health care and government professionals warn that a lack of exercise, especially when coupled with a poor diet, can result in serious health problems for many people. In an effort to encourage exercise, the President's Council on Physical Fitness and Sports designates May as National Physical Fitness and Sports Month. Why do you think Americans don't exercise more often? What can you do to increase your level of exercise?
WRITE ABOUT IT!
READ OTHER STUDENTS' RESPONSES
EXPLORE PUBLISHING OPTIONS
C
Home • Frequently Asked Questions • Contact
E

Reading Technical Directions

Reading **technical directions** will help you understand how to use the products you buy. Use the following tips to help you read a variety of technical directions.

Strategies for Reading

- **A** Look carefully at any **diagrams** or **other images** of the product.
- **B** **Read all the directions** carefully at least once before using the product.
- **C** Notice **headings** or **rules** that separate one section from another.
- **D** Look for **numbers** or **letters** that give the steps in sequence.
- **E** Watch for **warnings** or **notes** with more information.

PRACTICE AND APPLY

Use the above tips and the technical directions on the next page to help you answer the following questions.

1. How will you know that the digital camera has taken a picture?
2. Into what part of the digital camera do you insert the plug labeled CAM?
3. What is the first thing you must do to download a picture?
4. What is the name of the software application that allows you to "view" and "get" images on your computer?
5. For what do you need the CD-ROM?

Academic Reading Handbook

PRACTICE AND APPLY ANSWERS

1. The camera will emit a beep
2. the camera's Serial Port
3. Turn the Mode Switch to PLAY
4. CamPics
5. to install the necessary digital camera software

Academic Reading Handbook

Digital Camera Instructions

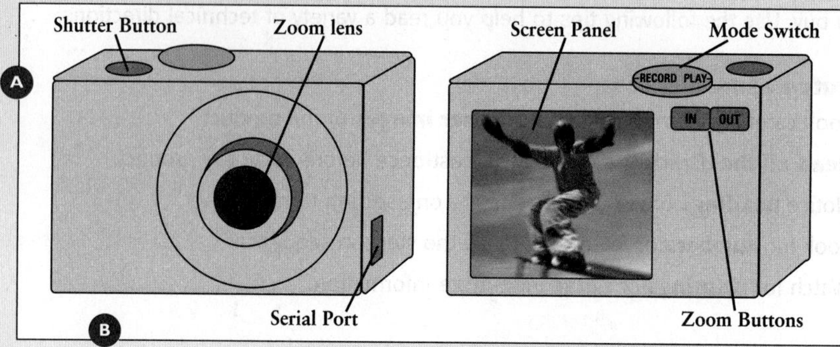

A. Taking Pictures

1. Turn the Mode Switch to RECORD.
2. Compose the image on the Screen Panel using the Zoom Buttons.
3. Press the Shutter Button halfway. This will freeze the image on the Screen Panel.
   NOTE: You will feel the button settle into a notch when it is halfway depressed.
4. If satisfied with the frozen image, press the Shutter Button fully to take the picture.
   NOTE: The camera will emit a beep to show that the picture has been taken.

B. Connecting to Your Computer

1. Locate the provided connecting cable.
2. Insert the plug labeled CAM into the camera's Serial Port.
3. Insert the plug labeled CPU into the serial port labeled CAM1 at the rear of your computer.

C. Installing Software

1. Locate the provided CD-ROM.
2. Insert the CD-ROM into your computer's CD-ROM drive and double-click on the INSTALL icon when it appears on your desktop.
3. The CD-ROM will install the necessary digital camera software over a period of up to five minutes.

D. Downloading Pictures

1. Turn the Mode Switch to PLAY.
2. Start the CamPics software by double-clicking the CamPics application icon.
3. Once the CamPics application has launched, select View Image from the Camera menu.
4. Select an image by either double-clicking on the individual image or clicking on the Get Images icon.
5. When an image has finished downloading, you may print, edit, organize, or transfer it to another host. The images are in JPEG format making them accessible to many applications.

Product Information: Safety Guidelines

Safety guidelines are facts and recommendations provided by government agencies or product manufacturers offering instructions and warnings about safe use of these products. Learning to read and follow such guidelines is important for your own safety. Look at the sample guidelines as you read each strategy below.

Strategies for Reading

A The **title** identifies what product the safety guidelines focus on.

B This section lists **recommendations** that product owners and users should follow in order to ensure safe usage of the product.

C This section lists the **hazards** associated with the product.

D This section includes the phone number and e-mail address where dangerous products or product-related injuries can be reported.

A Spa Safety Information

The U.S. Consumer Product Safety Commission (CPSC) recommends these safety precautions for spa owners and users.

B
1. Always use a locked safety cover when the spa is not in use and keep young children away from spas unless there is constant adult supervision.
2. Maintain the dual drains and covers required by current safety standards.
3. Regularly have a professional check your spa and make sure it is in safe working condition.
4. Locate the cut-off switch for your pump so you can turn it off in an emergency.
5. Be aware that consuming alcohol while using a spa could lead to drowning.
6. Keep the temperature of the water in the spa at 104° Fahrenheit or below.

C CPSC warns about these **hazards** related to spas, hot tubs, and whirlpools:
Drownings—Since 1980, the CPSC has reports of 700 deaths in spas and hot tubs. About one-third of those were drownings by children under age five.
Hair Entanglement—Since 1978, CPSC has reports of 49 incidents (including 13 deaths) in which people's hair was sucked into the suction fitting (drain) of a spa, hot tub, or whirlpool, causing the victim's head to be held under water.
Hot Tub Temperatures—CPSC knows of several deaths from extremely hot water (approximately 110 degrees Fahrenheit) in a spa. High temperatures can lead to unconsciousness.

D To report a dangerous product or a product-related injury, please contact info@cpsc.gov, or call the CPSC's hotline at (800) 638-2772.

PRACTICE AND APPLY

Read the safety guidelines to help you answer these questions.

1. What is the major cause of spa deaths?
2. What should you always do when a spa is not in use?
3. Why does the CPSC recommend that water temperature in a spa should be kept at 104 degrees Fahrenheit or below?
4. What e-mail address should you write to about a dangerous spa or a spa-related injury?
5. What temperature should the water in a spa be kept at?

Academic Reading Handbook

PRACTICE AND APPLY ANSWERS

1. drownings
2. You should always use a locked safety cover.
3. The CPSC recommends that water temperature in a spa should be kept at 104 degrees Fahrenheit or below because higher temperatures can lead to unconsciousness and even death.
4. info@cpsc.gov
5. below 104°F

Academic Reading Handbook

Reading a Television Schedule

Knowing how to read a **television schedule** accurately will help you figure out the times of your favorite programs. Look at the example as you read each strategy on this list.

Strategies for Reading

- **A** Scan the **title** to know what the schedule covers.
- **B** Look for **labels** that show **dates** or **days of the week** to help you understand how the weekly or daily schedule works.
- **C** Look for **expressions of time** to know what hours or minutes are listed on the schedule.
- **D** Study the **labels** identifying the different channels listed on the schedule.
- **E** Look at **program titles** to see what shows are playing at a given time on a given channel.

A Afternoon Programming Schedule — B July 19, 2002

C	1:00 P.M.	1:30 P.M.	2:00 P.M.	2:30 P.M.	3:00 P.M.	3:30 P.M.	4:00 P.M.
2 NMXX	Antique Timezone (E)		Trixie Bear	Ken Marx	Who's That Head?		News
D 6 NPRR	Judge Gus	Judge Edna	The Stanleys		Town Noise		News
7 NABQ	Women's Soccer (cont.)		U.S. Shot Put Finals		Infomercial	Space Time	Starmix
8 NHH	Movie: Condor's Revenge				Movie: The Road to Ruin		
11 EPS	Too Many Tomatoes		Cook Karl	Fast Times	Travel Log	Travel Log	Mexican Cuisine
13 MP&Z	My Dad	Jessica's World	Tears	Infomercial	News	News	Carrie C
18 WOW	Kids Kraft		Movie: KeeKee and Sammy				Kids News
19 PBJ	Jam City	Keevo	Behind the…	Behind the…	Storyback	Storyback	Dance Party
Pay Channels listed in **BOLD**							

PRACTICE AND APPLY

Answer the following questions using the television schedule and the strategies on this page.

1. What time span is covered by this schedule?
2. List the pay channels.
3. How many movies are listed on this schedule?
4. If you watched channel 6 from 1:30 to 2:00 and then watched channel 11 from 2:00 to 2:30, what two programs did you view?

PRACTICE AND APPLY ANSWERS

1. 1:00 to 4:30 P.M.
2. Students should list three of the following channels: *13 MP&Z, 18 WOW,* and *19 PBJ.*
3. three
4. *Judge Edna* and *Cook Karl*

Glossary of Literary Terms

Act An act is a major unit of action in a play. Acts are sometimes divided into scenes; each scene is limited to a single time and place.

Examples: Shakespeare's plays all have five acts. Many plays from the 19th century, such as Henrik Ibsen's *A Doll's House,* have three acts. Contemporary plays usually have two or three acts, although some have only one.

Allegory An allegory is a work with two levels of meaning—a literal one and a symbolic one. In an allegory, most of the characters, objects, and events stand for abstract qualities. Like a fable or parable, an allegory is often used to express generalizations about human existence and teach religious or moral lessons.

Example: Dante's *Inferno* has many allegorical elements. At the beginning of Canto I, Dante is struggling to emerge from a dark wood and reach a sun-drenched mountain. The wood represents Dante's spiritual confusion; the mountain symbolizes heaven, or paradise.

See page 759.

Alliteration Alliteration is the repetition of consonant sounds at the beginning of words. Alliteration occurs in everyday speech and in all forms of literature. Poets, in particular, use alliteration to emphasize certain words, to heighten mood, to underscore meaning, and to enhance rhythm. Notice the repeated *s* and *f* sounds in the following lines:

How craven so to strike me stricken so
Yet from you fully armed conceal his bow!
—Francesco Petrarch, "Sonnet 3"

See pages 927, 1154.
See also **Assonance; Consonance.**

Anecdote An anecdote is a brief story that focuses on a single revealing event, sometimes taken from the life of a real person. The event is meant to illustrate a particular truth or teaching.

Example: In tale 30 of Sadi's *Gulistan,* an innocent man appeals to the angry king who has condemned him to death. The man points out that if he is executed, the king will suffer from guilt forever. The anecdote teaches that people may come to regret acts committed in anger.

See page 433.

Antagonist The antagonist in a work of literature is the character or force against which the main character, or **protagonist,** is pitted. The antagonist may be another character, something in society or nature, or even an internal force within the protagonist.

Examples: In the Indian epic *Ramayana,* the antagonist is Ravana, the demon ruler of Lanka, who battles against Rama. In James Joyce's "Eveline," the main character struggles within herself to make an important decision about her future.

See also **Conflict; Protagonist.**

Aphorism *See* **Maxim.**

Assonance Assonance is the repetition of a vowel sound within nonrhyming words. *Sweet dreams* and *high and mighty* are examples of assonance. Writers of both poetry and prose use assonance to give their work a musical quality and unify stanzas and passages. Notice the examples of assonance in the following lines:

The sinking moon floods the rafters of my room
and still I seem to see it lighting your face.
—Tu Fu, "Dreaming of Li Po"

See page 1154.
See also **Alliteration; Consonance.**

Audience The audience of a piece of writing is the person or persons intended to read or listen to it. Every writer has an audience in mind when he or she is writing. The intended audience of a work influences a writer's choice of form, style, and tone and the details included.

Example: Virginia Woolf originally wrote

"Professions for Women" as a speech to be delivered to an organization of professional women. Woolf chose words that were suited to her audience.

See page 1164.

Author's Purpose Authors write for one or more of the following purposes: to inform, to express an opinion, to entertain, or to persuade. For instance, the purpose of a newspaper article is to inform; the purpose of a comic strip is to entertain.

Example: Elie Wiesel wrote *The World Was Silent* to inform readers about the horrors of the Holocaust and to persuade them to resist evil that made these horrors possible.

See pages 243, 802, 1242.

Autobiography An autobiography is a writer's account of his or her own life and is, in almost every case, told from the first-person point of view. Generally, an autobiography focuses on the most significant events and people in the writer's life over a period of time and on the ways in which those events and people affected the writer. Isabel Allende's *Paula* is an autobiography. Shorter autobiographical narratives include such private writings as **journals, diaries, memoirs,** and **letters.** Sei Shōnagon's *The Pillow Book* is a diary that provides important information about Japan during the Heian period. Elie Wiesel's *The World Was Silent* is a memoir about his experiences of the Holocaust.

See page 1302.
See also **Diary.**

Ballad A ballad is a narrative poem that was originally meant to be sung. Traditional folk ballads were composed by unknown authors and passed down orally. The ballads usually begin abruptly, focus on single tragic incidents, contain dialogue and repetition, and imply more than they actually tell. Typically, a ballad consists of four-line stanzas, with regular rhythm and rhyme. The rhythm often alternates between four-stress and three-stress lines, and the rhyme scheme usually is *abcb* or *aabb.*

A **literary ballad** is written by a single author in conscious imitation of the folk-ballad style. Heinrich Heine's "The Lorelei" is a literary ballad from the Romantic period.

See page 913.
See also **Narrative Poem; Rhyme; Rhythm.**

Biography A biography is an account of a person's life written by another person. The writer of the biography, or biographer, often researches his or her subject in order to present accurate information. A biographer may also draw upon personal knowledge of his or her subject. Although a biographer—by necessity and by inclination—presents a subject from a certain point of view, a skilled biographer strives for a balanced treatment, highlighting weaknesses as well as strengths, failures as well as achievements.

Blank Verse Blank verse is unrhymed poetry written in iambic pentameter. Each line has five metrical feet, and each foot has an unstressed syllable followed by a stressed syllable. Because iambic pentameter resembles the natural rhythm of spoken English, it has been considered the most suitable meter for dramatic verse in English. Shakespeare's plays are written largely in blank verse. The following line is an example of blank verse:

Thĕ wórld ĭs tóo mŭch wíth ŭs; láte ănd sóon
—William Wordsworth,
"The World Is Too Much with Us"

See also **Meter; Sonnet.**

Character Characters are the people who participate in the action of a work. The most important characters are the **main characters.** Less prominent characters are known as **minor characters.** In Sophocles' *Oedipus the King,* Oedipus and Jocasta are main characters; Antigone and Ismene are minor characters.

Whereas some characters are two-dimensional, with only one or two dominant traits, a fully developed character possesses many traits, mirroring the psychological complexity of a real person. In longer works of fiction, main characters often undergo change as the plot unfolds. Such characters are called **dynamic characters,** as opposed to **static**

R126 GLOSSARY OF LITERARY TERMS

characters, who remain the same. In Henrik Ibsen's *A Doll's House,* Nora is a dynamic character because she transforms from a clinging wife to an independent woman. Torvald is a static character who primarily responds to Nora's words and actions.

See pages 532, 1043.
See also **Characterization.**

Characterization *Characterization* refers to the techniques that writers use to develop characters. There are four basic methods of characterization:

1. A writer may describe the physical appearance of a character. In "The Jay," Yasunari Kawabata describes Yoshiko: "The job of putting on her makeup went fairly pleasantly. Her eyebrows and lips all became unbearably winsome. Her kimono, too, went on easily."
2. A character's nature may be revealed through his or her own speech, thoughts, feelings, or actions. In Kawabata's story, the narrator reveals Yoshiko's distress over her brother's change of attitude toward their stepmother: "Hearing this suddenly, Yoshiko could not say a word. Her face paled, and she began to tremble."
3. The speech, thoughts, feelings, and actions of other characters can be used to develop a character. The father's comments help readers understand Yoshiko better: "I've caused you a great deal of trouble. I told the young man's mother that you're a girl with these circumstances and that, rather than treating you like a bride, she should try to bring back the happy days of your childhood."
4. The narrator can make direct comments about the character's nature. The narrator of Kawabata's story comments, "She had dreaded marriage on her father's account, but, when it came down to the actual talks, it was not that dreadful after all."

See pages 126, 648, 844, 952.
See also **Character.**

Climax *See* **Plot.**

Comedy A comedy is a dramatic work that is light and often humorous in tone, usually ending happily with a peaceful resolution of the main conflict. Shakespeare's *A Midsummer Night's Dream* is a comedy.

See also **Drama.**

Conflict Conflict is a struggle between opposing forces and is the basis of plot in dramatic and narrative literature. The conflict provides the interest or suspense in a short story, drama, novel, narrative poem, or nonfiction narrative. **External conflict** occurs when a character is pitted against an outside force, such as another character, a physical obstacle, or an aspect of nature or society. **Internal conflict** occurs when the struggle takes place within a character.

Examples: In Nadine Gordimer's "Amnesty," the narrator's fiancé is in conflict with the repressive white society of South Africa. In Johann Wolfgang von Goethe's *Faust,* the main character wages an external conflict with the devil and an internal conflict with his own confused desires.

See pages 143, 640, 1172, 1278.
See also **Antagonist; Plot.**

Connotation *Connotation* refers to the particular associations, images, or feelings evoked by a word, in contrast to **denotation,** which is the literal or dictionary meaning of the word. *Kitten,* for example, is defined as "a young cat." However, the word also suggests, or connotes, images of softness, warmth, and playfulness.

Example: In Léopold Sédar Senghor's "And We Shall Be Steeped," the speaker describes some African art as "pure primordial masks distant and yet present." The word *primordial* connotes the vast culture and history of Africa.

See page 1186.

Consonance Consonance is the repetition of consonant sounds within and at the ends of words, as in "las<u>t</u> bu<u>t</u> no<u>t</u> leas<u>t</u>" and "a stro<u>k</u>e of luc<u>k</u>." Consonance is often used together with assonance, alliteration, and rhyme to create a musical quality, to emphasize certain words, or

Glossary of Literary Terms

GLOSSARY OF LITERARY TERMS R127

to unify a poem. The repetition of the *t* sound in the following lines helps create a slower, more thoughtful pace:

When to the sessions of sweet silent thought
I summon up remembrance of things past,
I sigh the lack of many a thing I sought,
—William Shakespeare, "Sonnet 30"

See page 1154.
See also **Alliteration; Assonance.**

Contrast Contrast is a stylistic device in which one element is put into opposition with another. The opposing elements might be contrasting structures, such as sentences of varying lengths or stanzas of different configurations. They could also be contrasting ideas or images juxtaposed within phrases, sentences, paragraphs, stanzas, or sections of a longer work of literature. Writers use contrast to clarify or emphasize ideas and to elicit emotional responses from the reader.

Example: Much of the power of Tu Fu's poem "Jade Flower Palace" lies in the contrast between images of a flourishing palace, with its "dancing girls" and "gold chariots," and images of a ruined palace, with its "broken tiles" and "shattered pavements."

See pages 123, 393.

Creation Story *See* **Myth.**

Cultural Hero *See* **Hero.**

Denotation *See* **Connotation.**

Denouement *See* **Plot.**

Description Description is writing that helps the reader picture scenes, events, and characters. It helps the reader understand exactly what someone or something is like. To create description, writers often use sensory images—words and phrases that enable the reader to see, hear, smell, taste, or feel the subject described—and figurative language. Effective description also relies on precise nouns, verbs, adjectives, and adverbs, as well as carefully selected details. The following passage contains clear details and images:

The snow! The hurt men struggled from the ranks,
hid in the bellies of dead horse, in stacks
of shattered caissons. By the bivouacs,
one saw the picket dying at his post,
still standing in his saddle, white with frost,
the stone lips frozen to the bugle's mouth!
—Victor Hugo, "Russia 1812"

See pages 97, 1263.
See also **Figurative Language; Imagery.**

Dialect A dialect is the form of a language spoken in a particular place by a distinct group of people. Dialects vary in pronunciation, vocabulary, colloquial expressions, and grammatical constructions. Writers use dialect to establish setting, to provide local color, and to develop characters.

Example: The thieves in Chinua Achebe's story "Civil Peace" speak in a Nigerian dialect of English, which highlights the contrast between the thieves and Jonathan Iwegbu.

See page 1291.

Dialogue Written conversation between two or more people, in either fiction or nonfiction, is called dialogue. Writers use dialogue to bring characters to life and to give readers insights into the characters' qualities, personality traits, and reactions to other people. Realistic, well-paced dialogue also advances the plot of a narrative.

Dialogue in **drama** is critical to an understanding of the playwright's story or message. How the dialogue is read or performed will determine to a great extent the reactions of the reader or audience to the play. Dramatists use **stage directions** to indicate how they intend the dialogue to be interpreted by the actors. In Henrik Ibsen's *A Doll's House,* the words *clapping her hands* and *unperturbed* are stage directions used to indicate how Nora is supposed to react to her husband at the beginning and at the end of the play.

See pages 896, 1230.
See also **Characterization; Drama.**

Diary A diary is a writer's personal day-to-day account of his or her experiences and

R128 GLOSSARY OF LITERARY TERMS

impressions. Most diaries are private and not intended to be shared. Some, however, have been published because they are well written and provide useful perspectives on historical events or on the everyday life of particular eras. Sei Shōnagon's *Pillow Book,* a sort of diary she kept while serving as lady in waiting to Empress Sadako, is a collection of character sketches, lists, anecdotes, and poems. It provides a vivid glimpse into the lives of the Japanese nobility during the Heian period.

See page 506.
See also **Autobiography.**

Diction Diction is a writer's choice of words, a significant component of style. Diction encompasses both the words used and the way the writer arranges them. Diction can be described in terms such as *formal* or *informal, technical* or *common, abstract* or *concrete, literal* or *figurative*.

Examples: The diction in Plato's *Apology* is formal, which is appropriate for a serious speech. The lofty, elevated diction in Goethe's *Faust* suits the drama's subject and themes. By contrast, the simple and concrete diction in Voltaire's *Candide* helps establish the humorous tone of the narrative.

See pages 539, 1164.
See also **Connotation; Style.**

Didactic Literature Didactic literature is literature that instructs its readers. Writers use didactic literature to teach lessons about how to live a moral life. Writers communicate their views about what is right and wrong by focusing on qualities such as honesty, courage, wisdom, and kindness. Sometimes they state their ideas directly; at other times, they present their teachings by means of examples. These teachings are expressed in various forms, including maxims, anecdotes, and parables.

See page 432.
See also **Anecdote; Maxim; Parable.**

Drama Drama is literature that develops plot and character through dialogue and action; in other words, drama is literature in play form. Dramas are meant to be performed by actors who appear on a stage, before radio microphones, or in front of television or movie cameras.

Unlike other forms of literature, such as fiction and poetry, a drama requires the collaboration of many people in order to come to life. In an important sense, a drama in printed form is an incomplete work of art. It is a skeleton that must be fleshed out by a director, actors, set designers, and others who interpret the work and stage a performance. When the members of an audience become caught up in a drama and forget to a degree the artificiality of the play, the process is called "suspension of disbelief."

Most plays are divided into acts, with each act having an emotional peak, or climax, of its own. The acts sometimes are divided into scenes; each scene is limited to a single time and place. Shakespeare's plays have five acts. Contemporary plays usually have two or three acts, although some have only one act.

Realistic drama of the 19th century is drama in which life is presented objectively and honestly. The characters usually belong to the middle or lower class, and they tend to be ordinary people dealing with everyday problems. *A Doll's House* is one of the first examples of realistic drama.

See pages 260, 1019.
See also **Act; Dialogue; Stage Directions.**

Dramatic Irony *See* **Irony.**

Epic An epic is a long narrative poem on a serious subject, presented in an elevated or formal style. It traces the adventures of a great hero. Most epics share some or all of the following characteristics:

1. The **epic hero** is a figure of high social status and often of great historical or legendary importance.
2. The actions of the hero often determine the fate of a nation or group of people.
3. The hero performs exceedingly courageous, sometimes even superhuman, deeds that reflect the ideas and values of the era.
4. Supernatural beings and events complicate the plot.
5. The setting is large in scale, involving more

GLOSSARY OF LITERARY TERMS R129

than one nation and often a long and dangerous journey through foreign lands.
6. The main character often gives long, formal speeches.
7. The poem treats universal ideas, such as good and evil, life and death.

The Epic of Gilgamesh, the *Mahabharata*, the *Ramayana*, the *Iliad*, the *Aeneid*, *Sundiata*, and *The Song of Roland* are all epics.

See pages 120, 176, 181.

Epic Hero See **Epic.**

Epic Simile See **Simile.**

Epithet An epithet is a brief phrase that points out traits associated with a particular person or thing. Homer's *Iliad* contains many examples of epithets, such as the references to Achilles as "the swift runner" and to Hector as "the gallant captain."

See pages 126, 223.

Essay An essay is a brief work of nonfiction that offers an opinion on a subject. The purpose of an essay may be to express ideas and feelings, to analyze, to inform, to entertain, or to persuade.

Some essays are formal and impersonal, and the major argument is developed systematically. Other essays are informal, personal, and less rigidly organized. The informal essay often includes anecdotes and humor.

Exposition See **Plot.**

Extended Metaphor Like any metaphor, an extended metaphor is a comparison between two essentially unlike things that nevertheless have something in common. It does not contain the word *like* or *as.* In an extended metaphor, two things are compared at length and in various ways—perhaps through a stanza, a paragraph, or even an entire work. The likening of God to a shepherd in Psalm 23 is an example of an extended metaphor.

See page 810.

See also **Figurative Language; Metaphor; Simile.**

External Conflict See **Conflict.**

Fable A fable is a brief tale, in either prose or verse, told to illustrate a moral or teach a lesson. Often, the moral of a fable appears in a distinct and memorable statement near the tale's beginning or end.

Falling Action See **Plot.**

Fantasy *Fantasy* is a term applied to works of fiction that display a disregard for the restraints of reality. The aim of a fantasy may be purely to delight or may be to make a serious comment. Some fantasies include extreme or grotesque characters. Others portray realistic characters in a realistic world who only marginally overstep the bounds of reality.

Examples: In *The Thousand and One Nights,* Sindbad voyages to islands inhabited by fantastic creatures. Gabriel García Márquez uses elements of fantasy in "The Handsomest Drowned Man in the World" to present the story's theme of the importance of heroes and great dreams.

Fiction A work of fiction is a narrative that springs from the imagination of a writer, though it may be based on actual events and real people. The writer shapes his or her narrative to capture the reader's interest and to achieve desired effects. The two major types of fiction are novels and short stories. The basic elements of fiction are characters, setting, plot, and theme.

See also **Novel; Short Story.**

Figurative Language Figurative language is language that communicates ideas beyond the literal meanings of the words. A figurative expression is not literally true, but rather creates an impression in the mind of the reader. Writers use figurative language to create effects, to emphasize ideas, and to evoke emotions. Figurative language appears in poetry and prose as well as in spoken language. Special types of figurative language, called figures of speech, include simile, metaphor, personification, and hyperbole.

Example: In Rabindranath Tagore's story "The Artist," the narrator uses a simile and personification to describe a scene in a painting: "The waves of the river looked like a flock of hungry seals just on the point of swallowing the boat. The clouds seemed to cheer them on and float their shawls overhead. . . ."

See page 903.
See also **Hyperbole; Metaphor; Personification; Simile; Understatement.**

First-Person Point of View *See* **Point of View.**

Flashback A flashback is an account of a conversation, an episode, or an event that happened before the beginning of a story. By revealing significant thoughts, experiences, or events in a character's life, a flashback can help readers understand a character's present situation. Flashbacks may take the form of reminiscences, dream sequences, or descriptions by third-person narrators; they usually interrupt the chronological flow of a story. Flashbacks may contain foreshadowing or other clues to the outcome of a story.

Folk Ballad *See* **Ballad.**

Folk Tale A folk tale is a story that is handed down, usually by word of mouth, from generation to generation. Folk tales reflect the unique characteristics of the regions they come from, showing how the inhabitants live and what their values are. Many involve supernatural events, and most suggest morals. Often, things happen in threes in folk tales. Leo Tolstoy's "What Men Live By" is a version of a Russian folk tale.

Foreshadowing Foreshadowing is a writer's use of hints or clues to indicate events that will occur later in a narrative. This technique often creates suspense and prepares readers for what is to come.

Example: In *Sundiata,* the epic hero's inability to walk foreshadows his later transformation.

See page 995.

Form When applied to poetry, the term *form* refers to all the principles of arrangement in a poem—the ways in which the words and images are organized and patterned to produce a pleasing whole, including the length and placement of lines and the grouping of lines into stanzas. Elements of form—such as the sound devices of rhythm, rhyme, alliteration, consonance, and assonance—work together with elements such as figurative language and imagery to shape a poem, convey meaning, and create a total experience for the reader. The term *form* can also refer to a type of poetry, such as the sonnet or the haiku. William Wordsworth's "The World Is Too Much with Us" and "My Heart Leaps Up" provide good examples of the poet's artful use of form.

See also **Structure.**

Frame Story A frame story exists when a story is told within a narrative setting or frame—hence, creating a story within a story.

Examples: The collection of tales in *The Thousand and One Nights* are set within a frame story. "Federigo's Falcon" and the other tales in Boccaccio's *Decameron* are presented within a similar framework.

Free Verse Free verse is poetry that does not contain regular patterns of rhyme and meter. The lines in free verse often flow more naturally than do rhymed, metrical lines and thus achieve a rhythm more like everyday speech. Much of the poetry written in the 20th century is free verse. Notice the natural flow of these free-verse lines:

> **On the sand**
> **a**
> **lizard**
> **with a sandy tail.**
> **—Pablo Neruda, "Ode to the Lizard"**

Haiku Haiku is a form of Japanese poetry that embodies three qualities greatly valued in Japanese art: precision, economy, and delicacy. Nature is a particularly important source of inspiration for Japanese haiku poets, and details from nature are often the subject of their poems. The rules of haiku are strict—in only 17 syllables, arranged in three lines of 5, 7, and 5 syllables, the poet must create a clear picture that will evoke a strong emotional response in the reader. The poems of Matsuo Bashō, Yosa Buson, and

Glossary of Literary Terms

GLOSSARY OF LITERARY TERMS **R131**

Kobayashi Issa are examples of haiku.

See page 540.
See also **Tanka.**

Hero A hero, or **protagonist,** is a central character in a work of fiction, drama, or epic poetry. A traditional hero possesses good qualities that enable him or her to triumph over an antagonist who is bad or evil in some way.

The term ***tragic hero,*** first used by the Greek philosopher Aristotle, refers to a central character in a drama who is dignified or noble. According to Aristotle, a tragic hero possesses a defect, or **tragic flaw,** that brings about or contributes to his or her downfall. This flaw may be poor judgment, pride, weakness, or an excess of an admirable quality. The tragic hero, Aristotle noted, recognizes his or her flaw and its consequences, but only after it is too late to change the course of events. Oedipus in Sophocles' *Oedipus the King* is a tragic hero.

In a quest story, a **quest hero** goes on a journey and tries to achieve a goal, such as bringing back a valuable object or acquiring knowledge. This type of hero usually has special powers or special friends that help (or hinder) him or her on the journey. Gilgamesh is a quest hero.

A **culture hero** is a larger-than-life figure who represents the values of his or her culture. Such a hero ranks somewhere between ordinary human beings and the gods. The role of a culture hero is to provide a noble image that will inspire and guide the actions of mortals. Aeneas in the *Aeneid* is a culture hero.

See pages 33, 330, 380.
See also **Epic; Protagonist; Tragedy.**

Humor In literature there are three basic types of humor, all of which may involve exaggeration or irony. **Humor of situation** is derived from the plot of a work. It usually involves exaggerated events or situational irony, which occurs when something happens that is different from what was expected. **Humor of character** is often based on exaggerated personalities or on characters who fail to recognize their own flaws, a form of dramatic irony. **Humor of language** may include sarcasm, exaggeration, puns, or verbal irony, which occurs when what is said is not what is meant. In *Candide,* Voltaire uses all three kinds of humor, including absurd situations, ridiculous characters, and ironic descriptions.

See page 856.

Hyperbole Hyperbole is a figure of speech in which the truth is exaggerated for emphasis or for humorous effect. The expression "I'm so hungry I could eat a horse" is an example of hyperbole. The following example of hyperbole has a humorous effect:

> **In short, our gentleman became so immersed in his reading that he spent whole nights from sundown to sunup and his days from dawn to dusk in poring over his books, until, finally, from so little sleeping and so much reading, his brain dried up and he went completely out of his mind.**
>
> **—Miguel de Cervantes, *Don Quixote***

Iambic Pentameter *See* **Blank Verse; Meter; Sonnet.**

Imagery Imagery consists of words and phrases that re-create vivid sensory experiences for the reader. The majority of images are visual, but imagery may also appeal to the senses of smell, hearing, taste, and touch. Effective writers of both prose and poetry frequently use imagery that appeals to more than one sense simultaneously.

Examples: The expression "I hugged her to my chest, muffling her mouth" from Tu Fu's "Song of P'eng-ya" appeals to the senses of sight, touch, and sound. In Charles Baudelaire's "Invitation to the Voyage," the lines "Flowers of rarest bloom / Proffering their perfume" appeal to the senses of sight and smell.

See pages 380, 459, 470, 546, 605, 913.

Internal Conflict *See* **Conflict.**

Irony Irony is a contrast between what is expected and what actually exists or happens. This incongruity often has the effect of surprising the reader or viewer. There are three main types of irony.

Situational irony occurs when a character or the reader expects one thing to happen but

R132 GLOSSARY OF LITERARY TERMS

something else actually happens. In Boccaccio's "Federigo's Falcon," Federigo's expectations and dreams are repeatedly overturned. In Leo Tolstoy's "How Much Land Does a Man Need?" it is ironic that Pakhom dies just as he is about to get his land.

Verbal irony occurs when a writer or character says one thing but means another. In Goethe's *Faust,* Mephisto speaks about man, claiming, "I have no wish to cause him further woe," while he intends to destroy Faust.

Dramatic irony involves a contrast between what a character knows and what the reader or audience knows. In Sophocles' *Oedipus the King,* Oedipus claims that he never saw King Laius, not realizing—as the reader does—that he is the king's son and that he killed Laius long ago.

See pages 330, 792, 1006.

Italian (Petrarchan) Sonnet *See* **Sonnet.**

Legend A legend is a story handed down from the past, especially one that is popularly believed to be based on historical fact. "The First Bard Among the Soninke" is a legend that explains about Soninke society. Though legends often incorporate supernatural elements and magical deeds, they claim to be stories of real human beings and are often set in particular times and places. These characteristics separate legends from myths.

See page 631.
See also **Myth.**

Literary Ballad *See* **Ballad.**

Lyric Poem In ancient Greece, a lyre was a musical instrument, and *lyric* became the name for a song accompanied by music. In ordinary speech, the words of a song are still called lyrics. In literature, a lyric poem is any short poem in which a single speaker expresses his or her personal thoughts and feelings. In a love lyric, such as Sappho's "He Is More Than a Hero," the speaker expresses romantic love. In other lyrics, a speaker may meditate on nature or explore personal issues, such as those addressed by Li Ch'ing-chao's "Two Springs" and "On Plum Blossoms."

See page 231.

Magical Realism *Magical realism* refers to a style of writing that often includes exaggeration, unusual humor, magical and bizarre events, dreams that come true, and superstitions that prove warranted. Magical realism differs from pure fantasy in combining fantastic elements with realistic elements, such as recognizable characters, believable dialogue, a true-to-life setting, a matter-of-fact tone, and a plot that sometimes contains historic events. Magical realism is usually associated with Latin American fiction, but the term has also been applied to writing from other parts of the world. The best-known example of magical realism is the 1967 novel *One Hundred Years of Solitude* by Gabriel García Márquez.

See page 1344.

Maxim A maxim is a short, concise statement that expresses a general truth or rule of conduct. Maxims condense important ideas into memorable language that gets the reader's attention. Some maxims are phrased in a particularly pointed and witty way. Because of their clever yet simple structure, such maxims—sometimes called **aphorisms**—are easy to recall and memorize. An example is Confucius' statement "To study without thinking is futile. To think without studying is dangerous."

See pages 432, 439.

Memoir *See* **Autobiography.**

Metaphor A metaphor is a figure of speech that makes a comparison between two things that are basically unlike but have something in common. Unlike a simile, a metaphor does not contain the word *like* or *as*. In the following lines, the phrase "preying bird of passage" is a metaphor for the poem's subject, a former leader:

> **Hubs of commerce smoothly turn without**
> **His bidding, and cities where he lately roosted**
> **Have forgotten him, the preying bird**
> **Of passage.**
>
> **—Wole Soyinka, "After the Deluge"**

See page 598.
See also **Extended Metaphor; Figurative Language; Simile.**

GLOSSARY OF LITERARY TERMS **R133**

Meter Meter is the repetition of a regular rhythmic unit in poetry. The meter of a poem emphasizes the musical quality of the language. Each unit of meter is known as a foot, consisting of one stressed syllable and one or two unstressed syllables. In representations of meter, a stressed syllable is often indicated by the symbol ´, an unstressed syllable by the symbol ˘. Four basic types of metrical feet are the **iamb,** an unstressed syllable followed by a stressed syllable (˘ ´); the **trochee,** a stressed syllable followed by an unstressed syllable (´ ˘); the **anapest,** two unstressed syllables followed by a stressed syllable (˘ ˘ ´); and the **dactyl,** a stressed syllable followed by two unstressed syllables (´ ˘ ˘).

Two words are used to identify the meter of a line of poetry. The first word describes the predominant type of metrical foot in the line. The second word describes the number of feet in the line: dimeter (two feet), trimeter (three feet), tetrameter (four feet), pentameter (five feet), hexameter (six feet), and so forth. These lines illustrate iambic pentameter, perhaps the most common meter in English poetry:

When in disgrace with Fortune and men's eyes
I all alone beweep my outcast state

—William Shakespeare, "Sonnet 29"

See page 817.
See also **Free Verse; Rhythm.**

Modernism Modernism is a literary and artistic movement that developed in the early decades of the 20th century. The modernists felt disconnected from the social, religious, and artistic traditions of the past because the modern world, with its violence, skepticism, and loss of ideals, seemed different from that of previous generations. To reflect this unsettling new world, modernist writers experimented with original literary styles and forms.

See page 1106.

Mood Mood is the feeling, or atmosphere, that a writer creates for the reader. The writer's use of connotation, imagery, and figurative language, as well as sound and rhythm, help to develop mood. Notice how the author makes use of all these techniques to create a bleak and lonely mood in the following lines:

Thin mists drift over One-Fold Mountain—
Folds of faintly dyed cloth;
In a cloudless sky a doleful wind.
Lonely mountain vista,
Remote and friendless landscape.
—Zeami Motokiyo, *The Deserted Crone*

See pages 470, 1180, 1230.
See also **Tone.**

Myth A myth is a traditional story, usually concerning some superhuman being or unlikely event, that was once widely believed to be true. Myths were passed down from one generation to the next; the original authors are unknown. Frequently, myths attempt to explain features of the natural world, to support social customs, or to guide people through life. For some peoples, myths were both a kind of science and a religion. In addition, myths served as literature and entertainment, just as they do to modern audiences.

Some of the most famous myths in the Western tradition originated among the ancient Greeks and Romans. Norse mythology, consisting of myths from Scandinavia, is also important in literature. Native Americans have produced fascinating myths of various kinds, as have the peoples of Africa and Asia.

Many Greek stories were based on myths that would have been familiar to the audience. In Ovid's *Metamorphoses,* the poet retells many of the important Greek and Roman legends and myths.

A **creation story** is a particular kind of myth that tells how the earth and human beings were created. The Fulani tale "How the World Was Created from a Drop of Milk" is an example of a creation story, as are the important Mayan work *Popol Vuh* and the opening chapters of Genesis in the Hebrew Bible.

See pages 404, 627.
See also **Legend.**

Narration *See* **Narrative; Narrator; Point of View.**

R134 GLOSSARY OF LITERARY TERMS

Narrative A narrative is any type of writing that is primarily concerned with relating an event or a series of events. A narrative can be imaginary, like a short story or a novel, or it can be factual, like a newspaper account or a work of history. Isabel Allende's autobiography *Paula* is an example of narrative nonfiction.

Narrative Poem A narrative poem tells a story. Like a short story or a novel, a narrative poem has the elements of characters, setting, plot, and point of view, all of which combine to develop a theme.

Examples: Epics, such as Homer's *Iliad* and Virgil's *Aeneid,* are narrative poems, as are ballads. Victor Hugo's "Russia 1812" is an example of a 19th-century narrative poem.

See pages 399, 920.

Narrator The narrator of a literary work is the person or voice that tells the story. The narrator can be a character in the story or a voice outside the action.

Examples: In Naguib Mahfouz's "Half a Day," the narrator takes part in the incidents he recounts. The narrator of Franz Kafka's "The Metamorphosis" is, on the other hand, observant but detached.

See also **Point of View; Speaker.**

Naturalism An extreme form of realism, naturalism in fiction involves the depiction of life objectively and precisely, without idealizing. Naturalism originated in France in the late 1800s. Like the realist, the naturalist accurately portrayed the world. However, heavily influenced by new scientific theories, the naturalist created characters who were victims of environmental forces and internal drives beyond their control. Émile Zola was the foremost writer of the naturalistic movement.

See page 943.
See also **Realism.**

Neoclassicism *Neoclassicism* refers to a movement in Europe during the late 17th and 18th centuries, marked by a revival of classical tastes and forms. Neoclassicists respected order, reason, and rules and viewed humans as limited and imperfect. They valued the intellect over emotions and society over the individual. The neoclassicists wrote tightly controlled poetry in the classical mold and witty satiric essays.

See page 878.
See also **Romanticism.**

Noh Drama Noh drama began in 14th-century Japan as religious drama and was perfected in the late 14th and early 15th centuries by Kanami Kiyotsugu and his son Zeami Motokiyo. Influenced by the simplicity and discipline of Zen Buddhism, Noh actors wear masks and use formal language, mime, and stylized gestures to express meaning. *The Deserted Crone* is an example of a Noh drama.

See page 519.

Nonfiction Nonfiction is prose writing that is about real people, places, and events. Unlike fiction, nonfiction is largely concerned with factual information, although the writer shapes the information according to his or her purposes and viewpoint. Although the subject matter of nonfiction is not imaginative, the writer's style may be individualistic and innovative. Types of nonfiction include autobiographies, biographies, letters, essays, diaries, journals, memoirs, and speeches. Examples include Sei Shōnagon's diary *The Pillow Book* and Virginia Woolf's speech "Professions for Women."

See also **Autobiography; Biography; Diary; Essay.**

Novel A novel is an extended work of fiction. Like a short story, a novel is essentially the product of a writer's imagination. The most obvious difference between a novel and a short story is length. Because the novel is considerably longer, a novelist can develop a wider range of characters and a more complex plot.

Omniscient Point of View *See* **Point of View.**

Onomatopoeia The word *onomatopoeia* literally means "name making." It is the process of creating or using words that imitate sounds. *Buzz* (of a bee), *honk* (of a car horn), and *peep* (of a chick) are onomatopoetic, or

GLOSSARY OF LITERARY TERMS R135

Glossary of Literary Terms

echoic, words. Onomatopoeia as a literary technique goes beyond the use of simple echoic words. Writers, particularly poets, choose words whose sounds suggest their denotative and connotative meanings: for example, *whisper, kick, gargle, gnash,* and *clatter.*

Parable A parable is a brief story that is meant to teach a lesson or illustrate a moral truth. A parable is more than a simple story, however. Each detail of the parable corresponds to some aspect of the problem or moral dilemma it deals with. The story of the Prodigal Son in the New Testament is a classic parable.

See pages 433, 516.

See also **Wisdom Literature.**

Paradox A paradox is a statement that seems to contradict itself but, in fact, reveals some element of truth. Religious and spiritual writings often contain paradoxes. Such paradoxes shake readers out of their normal ways of thinking and point them toward a higher level of understanding.

Examples: The sentence "There was neither death nor immortality then" in the *Rig Veda* is a paradox. The *Tao Te Ching* contains many paradoxes, including "The Tao never does anything, yet through it all things are done."

See pages 119, 445.

Parallelism Parallelism is the use of similar grammatical constructions to express ideas that are related or equal in importance. The parallel elements may be words, phrases, sentences, or paragraphs. Parallelism occurs in the following lines:

> **Did He not find you in error and guide you?**
> **Did He not find you poor and enrich you?**
> **—Koran**

See page 581.

See also **Repetition.**

Parody A parody imitates or mocks another work or type of literature. Like caricature in art, parody in literature mimics a subject or a style. The purpose of a parody may be to ridicule through broad humor. On the other hand, a parody may broaden understanding of or add insight to the original work. Some parodies are even written in tribute to a work of literature.

Example: *Don Quixote* by Miguel de Cervantes parodies the romance genre. The novel mocks romances by having Don Quixote attempt to fulfill chivalric ideals in a realistic setting.

Personification Personification is a figure of speech in which human qualities are attributed to an object, animal, or idea. Writers use personification to make feelings and images concrete for the reader. In the following lines, the winds are personified:

> **How could I leave the sound of singing winds,**
> **The strong clean scent that breathes from off**
> **the sea,**
> **Or shut my eyes forever to the spring?**
> **—Sara Teasdale, "Helen of Troy"**

See also **Figurative Language; Metaphor; Simile.**

Petrarchan (Italian) Sonnet *See* **Sonnet.**

Plot Plot is the sequence of actions and events in a narrative. Usually, the events of a plot progress because of a conflict, or struggle between opposing forces. Although there are many types of plots, most include the following stages:

1. The **exposition** lays the groundwork for the plot and provides the reader with essential background information. Characters are introduced, the setting is described, and the major conflict is identified. Although the exposition generally appears at the opening of a work, it may also occur later in the narrative.
2. In the **rising action,** complications usually arise, causing difficulties for the main characters and making the conflict more difficult to resolve. As the characters struggle to find solutions to the conflict, suspense builds.
3. The **climax** is the turning point of the action, the moment when interest and intensity reach their peak. The climax of a work usually involves an important event, decision, or discovery that affects the final outcome.
4. The **falling action** consists of the events that

R136 GLOSSARY OF LITERARY TERMS

occur after the climax. Often, the conflict is resolved, and the intensity of the action subsides. Sometimes this phase of the plot is called the **resolution** or the **denouement** (dā'no͞o-mäN'). *Denouement* is from a French word that means "untying"—in this stage the tangles of the plot are untied and mysteries are solved.

See page 589.
See also **Conflict.**

Poetry Poetry is language arranged in lines. Like other forms of literature, poetry attempts to re-create emotions and experiences. Poetry, however, is usually more compressed and suggestive than prose. Because poetry frequently does not include the kinds of explanation found in prose, it tends to leave more to the reader's imagination. Poetry also may require more work on the reader's part to unlock meaning.

Many poems are divided into stanzas, or groups of lines. The stanzas usually contain the same number of lines. Some poems have definite patterns of meter and rhyme. Others rely more on the sounds of words and less on fixed rhythms and rhyme schemes. The use of imagery and figurative language is also common in poetry.

See also **Figurative Language; Form; Free Verse; Imagery; Meter; Repetition; Rhyme; Rhythm; Stanza.**

Point of View *Point of view* refers to the narrative method used in a short story, novel, or work of nonfiction. The three most common points of view are first person, third person omniscient, and third person limited.

In **first-person point of view,** the narrator is a character in the work, narrating the action as he or she perceives and understands it. A first-person narrator tends to involve the reader in the story and to communicate a sense of immediacy and personal concern. Two short stories using first-person narration are "Amnesty" by Nadine Gordimer and "Half a Day" by Naguib Mahfouz.

In **third-person point of view,** events and characters are described by a narrator outside the action. In **third-person omniscient point of view,** the narrator is omniscient, or all-knowing, and can see into the mind of more than one character. The use of a third-person omniscient narrator gives the writer great flexibility and provides the reader with access to all the characters and to events that may be occurring simultaneously. In Boccaccio's "Federigo's Falcon," the use of a third-person omniscient narrator allows the reader insight into the private thoughts and motivations of both Federigo and Monna Giovanna.

When a writer uses a **third-person limited point of view,** the narrator tells the story from the perspective of only one of the characters. The reader learns only what that character thinks, feels, observes, and experiences. "The Guest" by Albert Camus is told from a third-person limited point of view. The writer's use of this point of view accentuates Daru's isolation and conflict.

See pages 1148, 1172, 1333.
See also **Narrator.**

Prose Generally, *prose* refers to all forms of written or spoken expression that are organized and that lack regular rhythmic patterns. Prose is characterized by logical order, continuity of thought, and individual style. Prose style varies from one writer to another, depending on such elements as word choice, sentence length and structure, use of figurative language, and tone.

Examples: Examples of prose include the Mayan *Popol Vuh,* the historical writings of Thucydides, and the fiction of Leo Tolstoy.

See also **Poetry.**

Protagonist The central character in a story, novel, or play is called the protagonist. The protagonist is always involved in the central conflict of the plot and often changes during the course of the work. The force or person who opposes the protagonist is the antagonist.

Examples: In the *Song of Roland,* the protagonist is Roland, a warrior who battles many enemies. The protagonist in Ibsen's *A Doll House* is Nora, who faces several antagonists, including her husband and the expectations and conventions of 19th-century society.

See also **Antagonist; Hero.**

GLOSSARY OF LITERARY TERMS **R137**

Proverb A proverb is a short, well-known saying that expresses a widely held belief. Proverbs, which are used in every culture, serve to warn, encourage, and console people. "Look before you leap" is an example of a familiar proverb.

Quest Hero *See* **Hero.**

Quest Story In a quest story, a hero goes on a journey, achieves a goal, or undergoes a personal transformation. A quest hero usually has special powers or special friends that help (or hinder) him or her on the journey. The quest story is common to many cultures. *The Epic of Gilgamesh* may be the oldest quest story in existence.

See page 47.

Realism In literature, *realism* has both a general meaning and a special meaning. As a general term, *realism* refers to any effort to offer an accurate and detailed portrayal of actual life. More specifically, realism refers to a literary movement of the 19th century. The realists based their writing on careful observations of ordinary life, often focusing on the middle or lower classes. They attempted to present life objectively and honestly, without the sentimentality or idealism that had characterized earlier literature, particularly fiction. Typically, realists developed their settings in great detail in an effort to re-create specific times and places for the reader. Guy de Maupassant and Leo Tolstoy are both considered realists.

See pages 942, 952, 1019.
See also **Naturalism.**

Realistic Drama *See* **Drama.**

Repetition Repetition is a technique in which a sound, word, phrase, or line is repeated for emphasis. The use of repetition often helps to reinforce meaning and to create an appealing rhythm. Repetition can also unify a poem by creating a clear structure. Note the use of repetition in the following lines:

We pick ferns, we pick ferns,
for the ferns are sprouting now:
oh to go home, to go home
before the year is over!
—"We Pick Ferns, We Pick Ferns"

See pages 451, 927.
See also **Parallelism.**

Resolution *See* **Plot.**

Rhyme Words rhyme when the sounds of their accented vowels and all succeeding sounds are identical, as in *tether* and *together.* For true rhyme, the consonants that precede the vowels must be different. Rhyme that occurs at the end of lines of poetry is called **end rhyme,** as in Dante's rhyming of *ease* and *seas* in the *Inferno*. End rhymes that are not exact but approximate are called **off rhyme,** as in the words *on* and *sun* in Heinrich Heine's "The Lorelei." Rhyme that occurs within a single line is called **internal rhyme,** as in the phrase *stunned and numb* in Rainer Maria Rilke's "The Panther."

Rhyme Scheme A rhyme scheme is the pattern of end rhyme in a poem. The pattern is charted by assigning a letter of the alphabet, beginning with the letter *a,* to each line. Lines that rhyme are given the same letter. The following example has an *abba* rhyme scheme:

What good it is to me if long ago ***a***
you eloquently praised my golden hair, ***b***
compared my eyes and beauty to the flare ***b***
of two suns where, you say, love bent the bow ***a***
—Louise Labé, "Sonnet 23"

See page 927.

Rhythm *Rhythm* refers to the pattern or beat of stressed and unstressed syllables in a line of poetry. Poets use rhythm to bring out the musical quality of language, to emphasize ideas, to create mood, to unify a work, and to reinforce subject matter.

See also **Meter.**

Rising Action *See* **Plot.**

R138 GLOSSARY OF LITERARY TERMS

Romance The romance has been a popular narrative form since the Middle Ages. Generally, the term *romance* refers to any imaginative story concerned with noble heroes, gallant love, a chivalric code of honor, daring deeds, and supernatural events. Romances usually have faraway settings, depict events unlike those of ordinary life, and idealize their heroes as well as the eras in which the heroes lived. Medieval romances are sometimes lighthearted in tone, usually consist of a number of episodes, and often involve one or more characters in a quest.

Example: Chrétien de Troyes's "Perceval: The Story of the Grail" is an example of a medieval romance. Its story of a knight who visits an unusual castle includes adventure, mysterious rituals, and a shocking supernatural secret.

See page 722.

Romanticism *Romanticism* refers to a literary movement that flourished in Europe in the first half of the 19th century. Romantic writers looked to nature for their inspiration, idealized the distant past, and celebrated the individual. In reaction against neoclassicism, their treatment of subjects was emotional rather than rational, imaginative rather than analytical.

See page 878.
See also **Neoclassicism.**

Sacred Literature *See* **Scripture.**

Satire Satire is a literary technique in which ideas, customs, behaviors, or institutions are ridiculed for the purpose of improving society. Satire may be gently witty, mildly abrasive, or bitterly critical, and exaggeration may be used in it to force readers to see something in a more critical light. Often, a satirist will distance himself or herself from a subject by creating a fictional speaker—usually a calm, and often a naive, observer—who can address the topic without revealing the true emotions of the writer. The title character of Voltaire's *Candide* is an example of such an observer.

See page 856.

Scripture Texts that convey the traditions, beliefs, and rituals of particular religions are often referred to as scriptures, or sacred literature. Scripture often has a special status in the culture from which it springs. It may be seen as divinely inspired and may be used in worship and viewed with reverence. It may also be a work of great beauty and artistry. More than many other kinds of literature, scripture is likely to have teaching as one of its main purposes. What it teaches generally has to do with a culture's most important concerns: the basic principles of morality, the meaning of human existence, and the relationship between the human and the divine. The Hebrew Bible, the *Rig Veda,* and the Koran are examples of scripture.

See page 74.

Setting Setting is the time and place of the action of a short story, novel, play, narrative poem, or nonfiction narrative. In addition to time and place, however, setting may include the larger historical and cultural contexts that form the background for a narrative. Setting is one of the main elements in fiction and often plays an important role in what happens and why.

Examples: Torvald's "tastefully but not expensively furnished" home in Ibsen's *A Doll's House* reflects the social and cultural environment of 19th-century Europe. The setting in Victor Hugo's "Russia 1812" is essential to the historical context of the narrative poem; the setting functions almost as a character.

See pages 532, 920, 1062, 1212.
See also **Fiction.**

Shakespearean (English) Sonnet *See* **Sonnet.**

Short Story A short story is a work of fiction that can be read in one sitting. Generally, a short story develops one major conflict. The basic elements of a short story are setting, character, plot, and theme.

A short story must be unified; all the elements must work together to produce a total effect. This unity of effect is reinforced through an appropriate title and through the use of symbolism, irony, and other literary devices.

Simile A simile is a figure of speech that compares two things that are basically unlike yet have something in common. Unlike a metaphor, which implies or suggests a comparison, a simile states it by means of the word *like* or *as.* Both poets and prose writers use similes to intensify emotional response, stimulate vibrant images, provide imaginative delight, and concentrate the expression of ideas. In his short story "Civil Peace," Chinua Achebe uses a simile to describe the sound of the head thief's voice:

> **"Shurrup!" rang the leader's voice like a lone shot in the sky and silenced the murmuring at once.**
>
> **—Chinua Achebe, "Civil Peace"**

An **epic simile** is a long comparison that often continues for a number of lines. Here is an example of an epic simile:

> **Like powerful stallions sweeping round the post for trophies,**
> **galloping full stretch with some fine prize at stake,**
> **a tripod, say, or woman offered up at funeral games**
> **for some brave hero fallen—so the two of them**
> **whirled three times around the city of Priam. . . .**
>
> **—Homer, *Iliad***

See also **Figurative Language; Metaphor.**

Situational Irony *See* **Irony.**

Soliloquy In a dramatic work, a soliloquy is a speech in which a character speaks his or her thoughts aloud. The character is usually on the stage alone, not speaking to other characters and perhaps not even consciously addressing the audience. (If there are other characters on stage, they are ignored temporarily.) The purpose of a soliloquy is to reveal a character's inner thoughts, feelings, and plans to the audience. In this soliloquy from Goethe's *Faust,* Mephisto reveals his ironic attitude toward the Lord:

> **I like to see the Old Man now and then**
> **And try to be not too uncivil.**
> **It's charming in a noble squire when**
> **He speaks humanely with the very Devil.**
>
> **—Johann Wolfgang von Goethe, *Faust***

See page 896.

Sonnet A sonnet is a lyric poem of 14 lines, commonly written in **iambic pentameter.** For centuries the sonnet has been a popular form because it is long enough to permit development of a complex idea yet short and structured enough to challenge any poet's skills. Sonnets written in English usually follow one of two forms.

The **Petrarchan,** or **Italian, sonnet,** introduced into English by Sir Thomas Wyatt, is named after Francesco Petrarch, the 14th-century Italian poet. This type of sonnet consists of two parts, called the **octave** (the first eight lines) and the **sestet** (the last six lines). The usual rhyme scheme for the octave is *abbaabba.* The rhyme scheme for the sestet may be *cdecde, cdccdc,* or a similar variation. The octave generally presents a problem or raises a question, and the sestet resolves or comments on the problem.

The **Shakespearean,** or **English, sonnet** is sometimes called the Elizabethan sonnet. It consists of three **quatrains,** or four-line units, and a final couplet. The typical rhyme scheme is *abab cdcd efef gg.* In the English sonnet, the rhymed couplet at the end of the sonnet provides a final commentary on the subject developed in the three quatrains. Shakespeare's sonnets are the finest examples of this type of sonnet.

Some poets have written series of related sonnets on a single subject. These are called **sonnet sequences,** or **sonnet cycles.** Toward the end of the 16th century, writing sonnet sequences became fashionable, with a common subject being love for a beautiful but unattainable woman. Petrarch wrote sonnet sequences to the mysterious Laura.

See page 804.
See also **Meter; Poetry.**

Sound Devices *See* **Alliteration; Assonance; Consonance; Onomatopoeia; Repetition; Rhyme; Rhyme Scheme; Rhythm.**

Speaker The speaker in a poem is the voice that "talks" to the reader. The speaker is not necessarily the writer; he or she may be a creation of the writer, much like a character in a play.

R140 GLOSSARY OF LITERARY TERMS

Examples: In "To Helen" by Edgar Allan Poe, the speaker may be addressing Helen of Troy or another woman who reminds the speaker of the legendary beauty. In Anna Akhmatova's poem "I Am Not One of Those Who Left the Land," the speaker may be closely identified with the poet herself, who refused to leave Russia after the Communists took control.

See pages 59, 387, 1218.

Speech A speech is a talk or public address. The purpose of a speech may be to entertain, to explain, to persuade, or to inspire, or it may be any combination of these aims. Plato's *Apology* and Virginia Woolf's "Professions for Women" are both speeches.

See page 254.

Stage Directions The stage directions in a dramatic script serve as a kind of instructional manual for the director, actors, and stage crew as well as for the general reader. Often the stage directions are printed in italic type, and they may be enclosed in parentheses or brackets.

Stage directions serve a number of important functions. They may describe the scenery or setting as well as lighting, costumes, props, music, and sound effects. Most important, the stage directions usually provide hints to the performers on how the characters look, move, and speak.

See also **Drama.**

Stanza A stanza is a group of lines that form a unit in a poem. In traditional poems, the stanzas usually have the same number of lines and often have the same rhyme scheme and meter. In the 20th century, poets have experimented more freely with stanza form, sometimes writing poems that have no stanza breaks at all.

Stream of Consciousness *Stream of consciousness* refers to a style of fiction that takes as its subject the flow of thoughts, responses, and sensations of one or more characters. A stream-of-consciousness narrative is not structured as a coherent, logical presentation of ideas. Rather, the connections between ideas are associative, with one idea suggesting another.

A character's stream of consciousness is often expressed as an interior monologue, a record of the total workings of the character's mind and emotions. An interior monologue may reveal the inner experience of the character on many levels of consciousness, often represented through a sequence of images and impressions. Virginia Woolf and James Joyce make extensive use of stream of consciousness in their fiction.

See also **Characterization; Point of View; Style.**

Structure Structure is the way in which the parts of a work of literature are put together. In poetry, structure involves the arrangement of words and lines to produce a desired effect. A common structural unit in poetry is the stanza, of which there are numerous types. In prose, structure is the arrangement of larger units or parts of a selection. Paragraphs, for example, are a basic unit in prose, as are chapters in novels and acts in plays. The structure of a poem, short story, novel, play, or nonfiction work usually emphasizes certain important aspects of content.

See also **Form.**

Style Style is the particular way in which a piece of literature is written. Style is not what is said but how it is said. It is the writer's uniquely individual way of communicating ideas. Many elements contribute to style, including word choice, sentence length, tone, figurative language, use of dialogue, and point of view. A literary style may be described in a variety of ways, such as formal, conversational, journalistic, wordy, ornate, poetic, or dynamic.

Examples: In Sei Shōnagon's *Pillow Book*, the writer uses a humorous, conversational style. In the excerpt from Elie Wiesel's *The World Was Silent*, the author uses simple words, short sentences, imagery, and dialogue to convey his horrifying experiences.

See page 1364.

Supernatural Elements Supernatural elements are beings, powers, or events that are

GLOSSARY OF LITERARY TERMS **R141**

unexplainable by known forces or laws of nature. In the *Ramayana,* Rama and Ravana battle each other with the aid of supernatural powers. In Chrétien de Troyes's narrative poem *Perceval: The Story of the Grail,* supernatural events occur in the magical castle.

Surprise Ending A surprise ending is an unexpected twist in the plot at the end of a story. The surprise may be a sudden turn in the action or a revelation that gives a different perspective to the entire story.
Example: The final paragraph of Luigi Pirandello's story "War," which provides a sudden, shattering perspective on war and loss, is an example of a surprise ending.

Suspense Suspense is the tension or excitement readers feel as they are drawn into a story and become increasingly eager to learn the outcome of the plot. Suspense is created when a writer purposely leaves readers uncertain or apprehensive about what will happen.
Example: In *The Spy,* Bertolt Brecht uses suspense-building techniques to help create doubt about the son's loyalty.

Symbol A symbol is a person, place, object, or activity that represents something beyond itself. Certain symbols are commonly used in literature, such as a journey to represent life or night to represent death. Other symbols, however, acquire their meanings within the contexts of the works in which they occur.
Examples: Torvald's house in Ibsen's *A Doll's House* may symbolize the societal restrictions from which Nora must free herself. In Federico García Lorca's poem "The Guitar," the guitar may symbolize human grief or longing.
See pages 927, 1180, 1354.

Tanka Tanka are Japanese lyric poems that express single thoughts or tell brief stories. *Tanka* means "short song," and a traditional tanka poem consists of just 31 syllables divided among five lines. The first and third lines contain 5 syllables each; the remaining lines contain 7 syllables each. Love, nature, and time are frequent themes in these poems. Tanka was the dominant form of Japanese verse from the 700s until the 1500s. Eventually, tanka inspired the more concise verse form known as haiku.
See also **Haiku.**

Theme A theme is a central idea or message in a work of literature. A theme should not be confused with a work's subject, or what the work is about. Rather, a theme is a perception about life or human nature shared with the reader. Sometimes the theme is directly stated within a work; at other times it is implied, and the reader must infer the theme. There may be more than one theme in a work. In *Oedipus the King,* for example, the themes include the immutability of fate, the blinding nature of power, and the conflict between father and son.

One way to discover the theme of a literary work is to think about what happens to the central characters. The importance of those events, stated in terms that apply to all human beings, is often the theme. In poetry, imagery and figurative language also help convey theme. In Omar Khayyám's *Rubáiyát,* for example, metaphors are used to convey such themes as time's passing quickly.
See pages 397, 598, 903, 972, 1081, 1258, 1372.

Third-Person Point of View
See **Point of View.**

Title The title of a literary work introduces readers to the piece and usually reveals something about its subject or theme. Although works are occasionally untitled or, in the case of some poems, merely identified by their first line, most literary works have been deliberately and carefully named. Some titles are straightforward, stating exactly what the reader can expect to discover in the work. Others suggest possibilities, perhaps hinting at the subject and forcing the reader to search for interpretations.
Examples: The title of Tolstoy's story "How Much Land Does a Man Need?" poses—as the reader discovers—an ironic question. "The Handsomest Drowned Man in the World," the title of a story by Gabriel García Márquez, intrigues the reader and hints at the story's magical realism.
See page 1372.

R142 GLOSSARY OF LITERARY TERMS

Tone Tone is an expression of a writer's attitude toward a subject. Unlike mood, which is intended to shape the reader's emotional response, tone reflects the feelings of the writer. The language and details a writer chooses help establish the tone, which might be playful, serious, bitter, angry, or detached, among other possibilities. To identify the tone of a work, you might find it helpful to read the work aloud. The emotions you convey in reading should give you clues to the tone of the work.

Examples: Rumi uses a joyful tone to describe a bird's song in "Birdsong from Inside the Egg." In the poem "Prayer to Masks," Léopold Sédar Senghor uses a solemn, intense tone to celebrate his African heritage.

See pages 605, 823, 1218, 1342.
See also **Mood.**

Tragedy A tragedy is a dramatic work that presents the downfall of a dignified character who is involved in historically or socially significant events. The main character, or **tragic hero,** has a **tragic flaw,** a quality that leads to his or her destruction. The events in a tragic plot are set in motion by a decision that is often an error in judgment caused by the tragic flaw. Succeeding events are linked in a cause-and-effect relationship and lead inevitably to a disastrous conclusion, usually death. A tragic hero evokes both pity and fear in readers or viewers: pity because readers or viewers feel sorry for the character, and fear because they realize that the problems and struggles faced by the character are perhaps a necessary part of human life. At the end of a tragedy, a reader or viewer generally feels a sense of waste, because humans who were in some way superior have been destroyed. Shakespeare's plays *Romeo and Juliet, Hamlet,* and *Macbeth* are tragedies, as are *Oedipus the King* and *Antigone* by the Greek dramatist Sophocles.

See page 330.
See also **Hero.**

Tragic Flaw *See* **Hero; Tragedy.**

Tragic Hero *See* **Hero; Tragedy.**

Trickster Tale A trickster tale is a humorous folk tale about an animal or person who creates mischief by trying to outwit others. Neither all good nor all bad, a trickster may be a culture hero, a clever deceiver, or a fool. Trickster tales often explain how some feature of the world or society came to be. The tales are found in West Africa and all over the world. The stories of Anansi and Iktomi are examples of trickster tales.

See page 651.

Understatement Understatement is a technique of creating emphasis by saying less than is actually or literally true. Understatement is the opposite of hyperbole, or exaggeration. One of the primary devices of irony, understatement can be used to develop a humorous effect, to create biting satire, or to achieve a restrained tone.

Verbal Irony *See* **Irony.**

Voice The term *voice* refers to a writer's unique use of language that allows a reader to "hear" a human personality in his or her writing. The elements of style that determine a writer's voice include sentence structure, diction, and tone. For example, some writers are noted for their reliance on short, simple sentences, while others make use of long, complicated ones. Certain writers use concrete words, such as *lake* or *cold,* which name things that you can see, hear, feel, taste, or smell. Others prefer abstract terms like *memory,* which name things that cannot be perceived with the senses. A writer's tone also leaves its imprint on his or her personal voice.

Wisdom Literature Wisdom literature is writing that teaches rules for living and conveys scholarly learning. Wisdom literature often takes the form of parables, brief stories that are meant to teach lessons or illustrate moral truths. Some parables contain paradoxes, or contradictions, designed to make the reader question conventional logic. Zen parables are examples of wisdom literature.

See page 516.
See also **Parable; Paradox.**

GLOSSARY OF LITERARY TERMS **R143**

Glossary of Words to Know

In English and Spanish

A

abate (ə-bāt') *v.* to lessen in intensity
abatir *v.* disminuir la intensidad

abiding (ə-bī'dĭng) *adj.* enduring
abide *v.*
duradero *adj.* perdurable; resistente **durar** *v.*

abject (ăb'jĕkt') *adj.* very low or miserable in condition
abyecto *adj.* de condición muy baja o miserable

ablution (ə-blo͞o'shən) *n.* a washing or cleansing of the body
ablución *s.* lavado o limpieza del cuerpo

acute (ə-kyo͞ot') *adj.* intense
agudo *adj.* intenso

adversary (ăd'vər-sĕr'ē) *n.* an opponent; enemy
adversario *s.* opositor; enemigo

affable (ăf'ə-bəl) *adj.* pleasant; agreeable
afable *adj.* amable; agradable

affront (ə-frŭnt') *n.* an open insult
afrenta *s.* insulto frontal

allot (ə-lŏt') *v.* to give as a share or portion
repartir *v.* dar una parte o porción

amenable (ə-mē'nə-bəl) *adj.* open to suggestion; responsive
receptivo *adj.* abierto a sugerencias; dispuesto a aceptar razones

amiably (ā'mē-ə-blē) *adv.* in a friendly manner; pleasantly
amigablemente *adv.* de manera amistosa; amablemente

anguish (ăng'gwĭsh) *n.* agony
angustia *s.* agonía

annihilation (ə-nī'ə-lā'shən) *n.* a ceasing to exist; total destruction
aniquilación *s.* destrucción total

appall (ə-pôl') *v.* to horrify
asombrar *v.* asustar; horrorizar

arid (ăr'ĭd) *adj.* dry
árido *adj.* seco

assent (ə-sĕnt') *n.* agreement
asentimiento *s.* consentimiento

assert (ə-sûrt') *v.* to express forcefully and positively
afirmar *v.* expresar fuerte y positivamente

assiduously (ə-sĭj'o͞o-əs-lē) *adv.* diligently
asiduamente *adv.* diligentemente

avail (ə-vāl') *v.* to be of use to; help
beneficiar *v.* ser de utilidad; ayudar

avidly (ăv'ĭd-lē) *adv.* eagerly
ávidamente *adv.* ansiosamente

B

banish (băn'ĭsh) *v.* to force to leave a place or country
desterrar *v.* expulsar de su tierra o del lugar donde vive

basking (băs'kĭng) *n.* warming oneself pleasantly **bask** *v.*
calentamiento *s.* asoleo **calentarse** *v.*

benediction (bĕn'ĭ-dĭk'shən) *n.* a blessing
bendición *s.* gracia

R144 GLOSSARY OF WORDS TO KNOW

benevolent (bə-nĕv'ə-lənt) *adj.* intended to promote the happiness of others; kindly
benévolo *adj.* con la intención de promover la felicidad de otros; bondadoso

bitterness (bĭt'ər-nĭs) *n.* a feeling of disgust or resentment
rencor *s.* sentimiento de repugnancia o resentimiento

blandly (blănd'lē) *adj.* in an easygoing, unconcerned way
suavemente *adj.* de modo fácil; despreocupadamente

boundless (bound'lĭs) *adj.* without limits; infinite
ilimitado *adj.* sin límites; infinito

C

calculating (kăl'kyə-lā'tĭng) *adj.* crafty; scheming
calculador *adj.* tramposo; intrigante

candid (kăn'dĭd) *adj.* frank; blunt; straightforward
cándido *adj.* franco; honesto; directo

candor (kan'dər) *n.* frankness; openness
candor *s.* franqueza; apertura

capricious (kə-prĭsh'əs) *adj.* acting on whim; unpredictable
caprichoso *adj.* que actúa por impulso; imprevisible

chagrin (shə-grĭn') *n.* a feeling of disappointment or humiliation
mortificación *s.* sentimiento de desilusión o humillación

chaotic (kā-ŏt'ĭk) *adj.* showing great disorder or confusion
caótico *adj.* que muestra gran desorden o confusión

chronic (krŏn'ĭk) *adj.* lasting for a long time; continual
crónico *adj.* que dura mucho tiempo; continuo

clandestine (klăn-dĕs'tĭn) *adj.* secret
clandestino *adj.* secreto

cleave (klēv') *v.* to cut through; penetrate
cortar *v.* partir; penetrar

commend (kə-mĕnd') to express approval of; praise
alabar *v.* expresar aprobación; halagar

compel (kəm-pĕl') *v.* to force or pressure
compeler *v.* forzar o presionar

comply (kəm-plī') *v.* to agree to a request or carry out an order; obey
cumplir *v.* aceptar una petición o llevar a cabo una orden; obedecer

compulsion (kəm-pŭl'shən) *n.* an irresistible impulse to act
compulsión *s.* impulso irresistible a actuar

compulsory (kəm-pŭl'sə-rē) *adj.* required
obligatorio *adj.* requerido

condiment (kŏn'də-mənt) *n.* a spice or other substance used as a seasoning
condimento *s.* especia u otra substancia usada para sazonar

confiscate (kŏn'fĭ-skāt') *v.* to seize by authority
confiscar *v.* tomar por la fuerza

confounded (kən-foun'dĭd) *adj.* confused; befuddled
atolondrado *adj.* confundido; aturdido

conjecture (kən-jĕk'chər) *n.* a conclusion based on guesswork
conjetura *s.* conclusión basada en suposiciones

connive (kə-nīv') *v.* to fail to take action; secretly cooperate
disimular *v.* hacerse de la vista gorda; cooperar secretamente

convention (kən-vĕn'shən) *n.* a social custom
convención *s.* costumbre social

GLOSSARY OF WORDS TO KNOW R145

credence (krēd'ns) *n.* belief; trust
crédito *s.* confianza

culmination (kŭl'mə-nā'shən) *n.* a high point or climax
culminación *s.* punto alto o clímax

culpable (kŭl'pə-bəl) *adj.* deserving of blame
culpable *adj.* que tiene la culpa

D

defile (dĭ-fīl') *v.* to treat in a shameful way; destroy the beauty or honor of
mancillar *v.* tratar de manera humillante; destruir la belleza o el honor

dejectedly (dĭ-jĕk'tĭd-lē) *adv.* sadly; in a depressed way
abatidamente *adv.* tristemente; de manera deprimida

delusion (dĭ-lo͞o'zhən) *n.* a false idea or belief
ilusión *s.* idea o creencia falsa

demoralizing (dĭ-môr'ə-lī'zĭng) *adj.* weakening to one's spirit or discipline; disheartening **demoralize** *v.*
desmoralizador *adj.* que debilita el espíritu o la disciplina; descorazonador **desmoralizar** *v.*

denigration (dĕn'ĭ-grā'shən) *n.* the act of speaking ill of someone; defamation
denigración *s.* acto de hablar mal de alguien; difamación

denounce (dĭ-nouns') *v.* to condemn publicly
denunciar *v* condenar públicamente

derisively (dĭ-rī'sĭv-lē) *adv.* in a mocking or jeering manner
burlonamente *adv.* de manera burlona, irónica

desolate (dĕs'ə-lĭt) *adj.* barren; empty; dismal
desolado *adj.* desierto; vacío; empobrecido

despair (dĭ-spâr') *n.* complete loss of hope
desesperación *s.* pérdida completa de esperanza

despondent (dĭ-spŏn'dənt) *adj.* sad; depressed
desalentado *adj.* triste; deprimido

diminish (dĭ-mĭn'ĭsh) *v.* to lessen
disminuir *v.* reducir

din (dĭn) *n.* a loud, confused noise
estrépito *s.* ruido fuerte, confuso

discern (dĭ-sûrn') *v.* to perceive with the eyes or intellect
discernir *v.* percibir con los ojos o el intelecto

disconcerted (dĭs'kən-sûr'tĭd) *adj.* embarrassed or confused **disconcert** *v.*
desconcertado *adj.* avergonzado o confundido **desconcertar** *v.*

discourse (dĭs'kôrs') *n.* talk; conversation
discurso *s.* charla; conversación

discretion (dĭ-skrĕsh'ən) *n.* a sense of carefulness and restraint in one's actions or words
discreción *s.* cuidado de las palabras o actos

disdain (dĭs-dān') *v.* to look down on or treat with contempt
desdeñar *v.* menospreciar o tratar con desprecio

disparage (dĭ-spăr'ĭj) *v.* to speak in a slighting way of; belittle
menoscabar *v.* hablar con desprecio; desacreditar

dissent (dĭ-sĕnt') *n.* disagreement
disensión *s.* desacuerdo

dissipated (dĭs'ə-pā'tĭd) *adj.* participating excessively in sensual or foolish pleasures
disipado *adj.* dedicado excesivamente a placeres sensuales o necios

R146 GLOSSARY OF WORDS TO KNOW

dissuade (dĭ-swād′) *v.* to persuade not to; discourage
disuadir *v.* convencer de no hacer algo; desalentar

docile (dŏs′əl) *adj.* obedient; easily led or managed
dócil *adj.* obediente; fácil de dirigir o manejar

donor (dō′nər) *n.* a person who gives or contributes something
donador *s.* persona que da o contribuye

E

edifying (ĕd′ə-fī′ĭng) *adj.* intended to improve morally; instructing **edify** *v.*
edificante *adj.* con la intención de mejorar moralmente; instructivo **edificar** *v.*

emaciated (ĭ-mā′shē-ā′tĭd) *adj.* unnaturally thin **emaciate** *v.*
enflaquecido *adj.* anormalmente flaco **enflaquecer** *v.*

equilibrium (ē′kwə-lĭb′rē-əm) *n.* a stable or balanced condition
equilibrio *s.* estabilidad

eradicate (ĭ-răd′ĭ-kāt′) *v.* to get rid of; eliminate
erradicar *v.* eliminar

esoteric (ĕs′ə-tĕr′ĭk) *adj.* understood by only a certain group
esotérico *adj.* entendido sólo por cierto grupo

explicit (ĭk-splĭs′ĭt) *adj.* clear; definite
explícito *adj.* claro; definido

F

fleeting (flē′tĭng) *adj.* happening or passing swiftly
efímero *adj.* que sucede o pasa rápidamente

foreboding (fôr-bō′dĭng) *n.* a sense of evil or danger to come
presentimiento *s.* sensación de que se acerca un mal o peligro

formidable (fôr′mĭ-də-bəl) *adj.* hard to overcome
formidable *adj.* difícil de superar

fortitude (fôr′tĭ-to͞od′) *n.* courage
fortaleza *s.* valentía

futile (fyo͞ot′l) *adj.* useless
futil *adj.* inútil

G

gaping (gā′pĭng) *adj.* staring open-mouthed **gape** *v.*
boquiabierto *adj.* pasmado **mirar con la boca abierta** *v.*

gaunt (gônt) *adj.* thin and drawn
demacrado *adj.* flaco y sin energía

genial (jēn′yəl) *adj.* pleasant; agreeable
genial *adj.* agradable; jovial

grave (grāv) *adj.* serious
grave *adj.* serio

H

haggard (hăg′ərd) *adj.* looking worn and exhausted
macilento *adj.* que se ve agotado

hapless (hăp′lĭs) *adj.* unfortunate
desgraciado *adj.* infortunado

harrowing (hăr′ō-ĭng) *adj.* extremely distressing
aflictivo *adj.* extremadamente inquietante

haughty (hô′tē) *adj.* overly proud; tending to look down on others
arrogante *adj.* demasiado orgulloso; tendiente a despreciar a los demás

Glossary of Words to Know

GLOSSARY OF WORDS TO KNOW R147

heedless (hēd′lĭs) *adj.* thoughtless; unmindful
desatento *adj.* descuidado; despreocupado

hinder (hĭn′dər) *v.* to keep from doing something
obstaculizar *v.* impedir que algo se haga

honed (hōnd) *adj.* finely sharpened
hone *v.*
afilado *adj.* bien pulido **afilar** *v.*

humanely (hyo͞o-mān′lē) *adv.* in a compassionate or sympathetic way
humanamente *adv.* de manera compasiva o apiadada

I

ignoramus (ĭg′nə-rā′məs) *n.* a foolish or ignorant person
ignorante *s.* tonto o sin conocimientos

illustrious (ĭ-lŭs′trē-əs) *adj.* well known and respected
ilustre *adj.* conocido y respetado

imbued (ĭm-byo͞od′) *adj.* filled or inspired
imbue *v.*
imbuido *adj.* lleno o inspirado **imbuir** *v.*

imminent (ĭm′ə-nənt) *adj.* about to happen
inminente *adj.* a punto de suceder

impassive (ĭm-păs′ĭv) *adj.* revealing no emotion; expressionless
impasible *adj.* que no revela ninguna emoción; inexpresivo

imperceptibly (ĭm′pər-sĕp′tə-blē) *adv.* in a barely noticeable way
imperceptiblemente *adv.* de manera que apenas se nota

imperious (ĭm-pîr′ē-əs) *adj.* urgent; pressing
imperioso *adj.* urgente; que presiona

impervious (ĭm-pûr′vē-əs) *adj.* unable to be affected
impenetrable *adj.* que no puede ser afectado

implacable (ĭm-plăk′ə-bəl) *adj.* unable to be appeased; unyielding
implacable *adj.* incapaz de ser apaciguado; que no cede

improvise (ĭm′prə-vīz′) *v.* to make on the spur of the moment, using any resources available
improvisar *v.* hacer en el momento, usando los recursos a la mano

inane (ĭn-ān′) *adj.* pointless; silly
anodino *adj.* sin sentido; tonto

inaudibly (ĭn-ô′də-blē) *adv.* in a way that cannot be heard
inaudiblemente *adv.* de manera que no se puede oír

incantation (ĭn′kăn-tā′shən) *n.* a set of words chanted or sung as part of a religious ritual
conjuro *s.* serie de palabras dichas o cantadas como parte de un ritual religioso

incarnation (ĭn′kär-nā′shən) *n.* a bodily form taken on by a spirit
encarnación *s.* forma corporal que toma un espíritu

incessantly (ĭn-sĕs′ənt-lē) *adv.* continually; without stopping
incesantemente *adv.* continuamente; sin parar

incompatibility (ĭn′kəm-păt′ə-bĭl′ĭ-tē) *n.* a lack of harmony; conflict
incompatibilidad *s.* falta de armonía; conflicto

incongruous (ĭn-kông′gro͞o-əs) *adj.* not appropriate; out of place
incongruente *adj.* inapropiado; fuera de lugar

incredulous (ĭn-krĕj′ə-ləs) *adj.* unwilling to believe; skeptical
incrédulo *adj.* que no desea creer; escéptico

indifferent (ĭn-dĭf′ər-ənt) *adj.* having no particular interest or concern
indiferente *adj.* que no tiene interés particular

R148 GLOSSARY OF WORDS TO KNOW

indigent (ĭn′dĭ-jənt) *adj.* without money; very poor
indigente *adj.* sin dinero; muy pobre

indignation (ĭn′dĭg-nā′shən) *n.* anger caused by something mean or unjust
indignación *s.* ira ante maldad o injusticia

indolent (ĭn′ də-lənt) *adj.* lazy
indolente *adj.* flojo

indulgence (ĭn-dŭl′jəns) *n.* a giving in to someone's wishes or desires
indulgencia *s.* ceder a los deseos de alguien

ineffectually (ĭn′ĭ-fĕk′cho͞o-ə-lē) *adv.* in a useless manner
ineficazmente *adv.* de manera inútil

inevitably (ĭn-ĕv′ĭ-tə-blē) *adv.* unavoidably
inevitablemente *adv.* de manera que no es posible evitar

inextricably (ĭn-ĕk′strĭ-kə-blē) *adv.* in a way that one cannot get out of
inextricablemente *adv.* sin posibilidad de zafarse

infatuation (ĭn-făch′o͞o-ā′shən) *n.* a foolish, unreasonable attraction
encaprichamiento *s.* atracción tonta e irracional

ingenuity (ĭn′jə-no͞o′ĭ-tē) *n.* cleverness
ingenio *s.* agudeza

inhospitable (ĭn-hŏs′pĭ-tə-bəl) *adj.* unfriendly or unwelcoming to a guest
inhospitalario *adj.* persona o lugar que no acoge

innuendo (ĭn′yo͞o-ĕn′dō) *n.* an indirect hint or reference, usually negative
alusión *s.* insinuación o referencia indirecta, generalmente negativa

insatiable (ĭn-sā′shə-bəl) *adj.* impossible to satisfy
insaciable *adj.* imposible de satisfacer

interminable (ĭn-tûr′mə-nə-bəl) *adj.* unending
interminable *adj.* sin fin

intermittently (ĭn′tər-mĭt′nt-lē) *adv.* with stops and starts; on and off
intermitentemente *adv.* con detenciones y arranques; prendido y apagado

intervene (ĭn′tər-vēn′) *v.* to come between; get involved in order to help
intervenir *v.* interponerse; involucrarse para ayudar

intransigence (ĭn-trăn′sĭ-jəns) *n.* a condition of being stubborn and uncompromising
intransigencia *s.* terquedad; rigidez

intricate (ĭn′trĭ-kĭt) *adj.* complex
intrincado *adj.* complejo

intrigue (ĭn′trēg′) *n.* a secret scheme; plot
intriga *s.* plan secreto; complot

invincible (ĭn-vĭn′sə-bəl) *adj.* unable to be conquered
invencible *adj.* que no es posible conquistar

J

jauntily (jôn′tĭ-lē) *adv.* in a lively, carefree manner
garbosamente *adv.* de manera vivaz y desenvuelta

jocular (jŏk′yə-lər) *adj.* funny; comic
jocoso *adj.* chistoso; cómico

jubilant (jo͞o′bə-lənt) *adj.* extremely joyful
jubiloso *adj.* sumamente alegre

L

labyrinth (lăb′ə-rĭnth′) *n.* a confusing network of passages; maze
laberinto *s.* red confusa de pasajes

GLOSSARY OF WORDS TO KNOW R149

Glossary of Words to Know

lament (lə-mĕnt′) *v.* to express grief or sorrow
lamentar *v.* expresar dolor o pena

lavishly (lăv′ĭsh-lē) *adv.* very freely and abundantly
copiosamente *adv.* de manera muy libre y abundante

lethargy (lĕth′ər-jē) *n.* inactivity; sleepy dullness
letargo *s.* inactividad; modorra con sueño

lithe (līth) *adj.* limber and graceful
ágil *adj.* flexible y gracioso

loathed (lōthd) *adj.* intensely hated **loathe** *v.*
aborrecido *adj.* odiado intensamente **aborrecer** *v.*

lucid (lo͞o′sĭd) *adj.* clear; easily understood
lúcido *adj.* claro; entendido fácilmente

M

majestically (mə-jĕs′tĭ-klē) *adv.* in a noble or stately way
majestuosamente *adv.* en forma noble o señorial

malicious (mə-lĭsh′əs) *adj.* evil; wicked
malicioso *adj.* malo; malvado

meagerly (mē′gər-lē) *adv.* poorly; scantily
magramente *adv.* pobremente; escasamente

menace (mĕn′ĭs) *n.* a threat
amenaza *s.* peligro

misgiving (mĭs-gĭv′ĭng) *n.* a feeling of doubt; concern
recelo *s.* sentimiento de duda; desconfianza

monumental (mŏn′yə-mĕn′tl) *adj.* very significant; astonishing
monumental *adj.* muy significativo; asombroso

mortify (môr′tə-fī′) *v.* to embarrass or humiliate
mortificar *v.* avergonzar o humillar

musing (myo͞o′zĭng) *adj.* thoughtfully questioning or meditating **muse** *v.*
meditabundo *adj.* pensativo o meditativo **meditar** *v.*

N

naive (nī-ēv′) *adj.* lacking worldliness and sophistication
ingenuo *adj.* carente de mundo y sofisticación

nominally (nŏm′ə-nə-lē) *adv.* apparently (but usually not in reality); seemingly
nominalmente *adv.* aparentemente; por cumplir las apariencias

novice (nŏv′ĭs) *n.* a beginner in a job or activity
novato *s.* nuevo en un empleo

O

oblivion (ə-blĭv′ē-ən) *n.* a state of being forgotten
olvido *s.* falta de recuerdo

oblivious (ə-blĭv′ē-əs) *adj.* not aware; unmindful
olvidadizo *adj.* abstraído; que no recuerda

obstinate (ŏb′stə-nĭt′) *adj.* stubborn
obstinado *adj.* terco

ominous (ŏm′ə-nəs) *adj.* threatening; signaling evil to come
ominoso *adj.* amenazador; que señala mal por venir

omission (ō-mĭsh′ən) *n.* an act of leaving out, passing over, or neglecting
omisión *s.* acto de dejar fuera, de olvidar o relegar

R150 GLOSSARY OF WORDS TO KNOW

ordain (ôr-dān′) *v.* to establish by decree or law
ordenar *v.* establecer por decreto o ley

osmosis (ŏz-mō′sĭs) *n.* an unconscious absorbing of facts or ideas
ósmosis *s.* forma inconsciente de absorber hechos o ideas

P

paltry (pôl′trē) *adj.* insignificant; almost worthless
miserable *adj.* insignificante; casi sin valor

parrying (păr′ē-ĭng) *n.* a warding off or turning aside **parry** *v.*
esquivador *s.* el que evita un golpe o se hace a un lado **esquivar** *v.*

peer (pîr) *n.* an equal
par *s.* igual

pensive (pĕn′sĭv) *adj.* thoughtful; moody
pensativo *adj.* abstraído; melancólico

perpetual (pər-pĕch′ōō-əl) *adj.* lasting for an indefinitely long time
perpetuo *adj.* que dura por un tiempo indefinidamente largo

petty (pĕt′ē) *adj.* of no importance; trivial
insignificante *adj.* sin importancia; trivial

pittance (pĭt′ns) *n.* a small reward; tiny amount
miseria *s.* pequeña recompensa; pequeña cantidad

pivotal (pĭv′ə-tl) *adj.* very important
axial *adj.* muy importante

plight (plīt) *n.* a bad or unfortunate situation; predicament
apuro *s.* situación mala o desafortunada

presumption (prĭ-zŭmp′shən) *n.* bold or outrageous behavior
presunción *s.* conducta atrevida o engreída

prevail (prĭ-vāl′) *v.* to hold out against; triumph over
prevalecer *v.* predominar; triunfar

prevalent (prĕv′ə-lənt) *adj.* widely or commonly occurring
frecuente *adj.* que ocurre en forma generalizada o común

primordial (prī-môr′dē-əl) *adj.* first-existing; original
primordial *adj.* que existió primero; original

pristine (prĭs′tēn′) *adj.* pure; uncorrupted
prístino *adj.* puro; incorrupto

prodigious (prə-dĭj′əs) *adj.* impressively great; stupendous
prodigioso *adj.* grandioso; estupendo

protrude (prō-trōōd′) *v.* to jut out; project
proyectar *v.* resaltar

R

rash (răsh) *adj.* hasty and careless
imprudente *adj.* temerario y descuidado

recoil (rĭ-koil′) *v.* to pull back in fear or surprise
retroceder *v.* retirarse por temor o sorpresa

reconcile (rĕk′ən-sīl′) *v.* to bring into agreement or harmony; cause to accept
reconciliar *v.* llegar a un acuerdo o armonía; llevar a aceptar

recourse (rē′kôrs′) *n.* something turned to for help or protection
recurso *s.* algo que se busca para obtener ayuda o protección

refuge (rĕf′yōōj) *n.* protection; comfort
refugio *s.* protección; amparo

reiterated (rē-ĭt′ə-rā′tĭd) *adj.* repeated **reiterate** *v*
reiterado *adj.* repetido **reiterar** *v.*

GLOSSARY OF WORDS TO KNOW R151

relinquish (rĭ-lĭng'kwĭsh) *v.* to give up; hand over
renunciar *v.* ceder; entregar

repose (rĭ-pōz') *v.* to rest
reposar *v.* descansar

reprehensible (rĕp'rĭ-hĕn'sə-bəl) *adj.* deserving of blame
reprensible *adj.* que merece reproche

reproach (rĭ-prōch') *n.* blame; criticism
reproche *s.* culpa; crítica

reprove (rĭ-pro͞ov') *v.* to scold
reprobar *v.* regañar

reputable (rĕp'yə-tə-bəl) *adj.* of good reputation; honorable
intachable *adj.* de buena reputación; honorable

resolute (rĕz'ə-lo͞ot') *adj.* resolved; determined
resuelto *adj.* decidido; determinado

respite (rĕs'pĭt) *n.* a rest
respiro *s.* descanso

retort (rĭ-tôrt') *v.* to reply quickly or sharply
replicar *v.* responder rápida o tajantemente

retract (rĭ-trăkt') *v.* to take back; withdraw
retractar *v.* revocar; retirar

revelation (rĕv'ə-lā'shən) *n.* a making known; exposure
revelación *s.* divulgación; exposición

reverberate (rĭ-vûr'bə-rāt') *v.* to reflect a noise; resound
reverberar *v.* reflejar un ruido; resonar

revile (rĭ-vīl') *v.* to abuse verbally; criticize harshly
vilipendiar *v.* insultar; criticar duramente

ruse (ro͞os) *n.* a trick
artificio *s.* truco

S

scrutinizing (skro͞ot'n-ī'zĭng) *n.* observing or inspecting with great care **scrutinize** *v.*
escrutinio *s.* observación o inspección muy cuidadosa **inspeccionar** *v.*

sinister (sĭn'ĭ-stər) *adj.* having an evil disposition or intent
siniestro *adj.* con disposición o intención mala

skeptical (skĕp'tĭ-kəl) *adj.* doubtful
escéptico *adj.* dudoso

sloth (slôth) *n.* laziness
pereza *s.* flojera

solace (sŏl'ĭs) *n.* comfort in sorrow or distress
solaz *s.* consuelo en la pena o el dolor

spurn (spûrn) *v.* to reject in a scornful way
desdeñar *v.* rechazar con desdén

stature (stăch'ər) *n.* status or importance gained by growth or achievement
estatura *s.* importancia ganada por desarrollo y logros

stifle (stī'fəl) *v.* to hold back; repress
sofocar *v.* ahogar; reprimir

stoically (stō'ĭ-klē) *adv.* in a manner showing no emotion
estoicamente *adv.* sin mostrar emoción

stupor (sto͞o'pər) *n.* a dazed condition, almost without sense or feeling
estupor *s.* embotamiento

subvert (səb-vûrt') *v.* to destroy or corrupt
subvertir *v.* destruir o corromper

suffused (sə-fyo͞ozd') *adj.* overspread; filled **suffuse** *v.*
inundado *adj.* lleno **inundar** *v.*

sumptuous (sŭmp'cho͞o-əs) *adj.* costly; magnificent
suntuoso *adj.* costoso; magnífico

R152 GLOSSARY OF WORDS TO KNOW

superfluous (so͝o-pûr′flo͞o-əs) *adj.* more than is needed; unnecessary
superfluo *adj.* más de lo necesario; innecesario

surmise (sər-mīz′) *n.* a conclusion based on little evidence; guess
suposición *s.* conclusión basada en poca evidencia; conjetura

swarthy (swôr′*th*ē) *adj.* having a dark complexion
moreno *adj.* de piel oscura

T

taciturn (tăs′ĭ-tûrn′) *adj.* not talkative
taciturno *adj.* retraído; que no habla

tactless (tăkt′lĭs) *adj.* not sensitive to what is appropriate in dealing with people and situations
imprudente *adj.* falto de tacto en el trato con personas y situaciones

tangible (tăn′jə-bəl) *adj.* capable of being felt or perceived; concrete
tangible *adj.* capaz de ser sentido o percibido; concreto

tedium (tē′dē-əm) *n.* boredom
tedio *s.* aburrimiento

teem (tēm) *v.* to be filled to overflowing
rebosar *v.* llenar más allá del tope

tenuous (tĕn′yo͞o-əs) *adj.* thin or flimsy
tenue *adj.* delgado o delicado

tranquilly (trăng′kwə-lē) *adv.* calmly; peacefully
tranquilamente *adv.* serenamente; pacíficamente

transit (trăn′sĭt) *n.* passage
tránsito *s.* pasaje

tumult (to͞o′mŭlt′) *n.* a disorderly noisiness or disturbance
tumulto *s.* ruido o disturbio desordenado

U

undeterred (ŭn′dĭ-tûrd′) *adj.* not discouraged
imparable *adj.* resuelto a seguir adelante a pesar de obstáculos

undulating (ŭn′jə-lā′tĭng) *adj.* moving with a wavelike motion **undulate** *v.*
ondulante *adj.* con movimiento como ola **ondular** *v.*

unimpeded (ŭn′ĭm-pē′dĭd) *adj.* not held back or obstructed
sin impedimento *adj.* sin detención; sin obstrucción

unintelligible (ŭn′ĭn-tĕl′ĭ-jə-bəl) *adj.* unable to be understood
ininteligible *adj.* incapaz de ser entendido

unmarred (ŭn-märd′) *adj.* not damaged or injured
intacto *adj.* sin daño; ileso

unscrupulous (ŭn-skro͞o′pyə-ləs) *adj.* lacking a sense of right and wrong
inescrupuloso *adj.* sin noción del bien y el mal

unvanquished (ŭn′văng′kwĭsht) *adj.* undefeated
inconquistable *adj.* indomable

V

versatility (vûr′sə-tĭl′ĭ-tē) *n.* an ability to do many things well
versatilidad *s.* capacidad para hacer muchas cosas bien

vindictive (vĭn-dĭk′tĭv) *adj.* having a strong tendency toward revenge
vengativo *adj.* con fuerte tendencia a la venganza

virile (vîr′əl) *adj.* masculine; full of manly strength
viril *adj.* masculino; lleno de fuerza masculina

GLOSSARY OF WORDS TO KNOW **R153**

vitality (vī-tăl′ĭ-tē) *n.* strength of mind or body; energy
vitalidad *s.* fuerza de mente y cuerpo; energía

vivacity (vĭ-văs′ĭ-tē) *n.* liveliness
vivacidad *s.* viveza; intensidad

W

waive (wāv) *v.* to voluntarily give up; abandon
ceder *v.* rendirse voluntariamente; abandonar

warily (wâr′ĭ-lē) *adv.* watchfully; cautiously
desconfiadamente *adv.* cuidadosamente; cautamente

waver (wā′vər) *v.* to have difficulty in making a decision
titubear *v.* tener dificultad para tomar una decisión

wittingly (wĭt′ĭng-lē) *adv.* knowingly; intentionally
intencionadamente *adv.* a sabiendas; a propósito

writhe (rī*th*) *v.* to twist about; squirm
retorcer *v.* torcer; enchuecar

Z

zeal (zēl) *n.* enthusiasm; fervor
fervor *s.* entusiasmo; dedicación

R154 GLOSSARY OF WORDS TO KNOW

Pronunciation Key

Symbol	Examples	Symbol	Examples	Symbol	Examples
ă	at, gas	m	man, seem	v	van, save
ā	ape, day	n	night, mitten	w	web, twice
ä	father, barn	ng	sing, anger	y	yard, lawyer
âr	fair, dare	ŏ	odd, not	z	zoo, reason
b	bell, table	ō	open, road, grow	zh	treasure, garage
ch	chin, lunch	ô	awful, bought, horse	ə	awake, even, pencil, pilot, focus
d	dig, bored	oi	coin, boy		
ĕ	egg, ten	o͝o	look, full	ər	perform, letter
ē	evil, see, meal	o͞o	root, glue, through		
f	fall, laugh, phrase	ou	out, cow		
g	gold, big	p	pig, cap		
h	hit, inhale	r	rose, star		
hw	white, everywhere	s	sit, face		
ĭ	inch, fit	sh	she, mash		
ī	idle, my, tried	t	tap, hopped		
îr	dear, here	th	thing, with		
j	jar, gem, badge	*th*	then, other		
k	keep, cat, luck	ŭ	up, nut		
l	load, rattle	ûr	fur, earn, bird, worm		

Sounds in Foreign Words

Symbol	Examples
KH	*German* ich, auch; *Scottish* loch
N	*French* entre, bon, fin
œ	*French* feu, cœur; *German* schön
ü	*French* utile, rue; *German* grün

Stress Marks

′ This mark indicates that the preceding syllable receives the primary stress. For example, in the word *language,* the first syllable is stressed: lăng′gwĭj.

′ This mark is used only in words in which more than one syllable is stressed. It indicates that the preceding syllable is stressed, but somewhat more weakly than the syllable receiving the primary stress. In the word *literature,* for example, the first syllable receives the primary stress, and the last syllable receives a weaker stress: lĭt′ər-ə-cho͝or′.

GLOSSARY OF WORDS TO KNOW R155

Index of Fine Art

x, 14–15	*Nakht hunting with his family* (18th dynasty).
xiv, 418–419	*Moonlight on the River Seba,* Ando Hiroshige.
xviii top, 684–685	*Primavera [Allegory of spring]* (1481), Sandro Botticelli.
xviii bottom	Detail of *Dante Alighieri* (1500–1503), Luca Signorelli.
xx *top,* 868–869	*Dance at the Moulin de la Galette, Montmartre* (1876), Pierre Auguste Renoir.
xxi, 954 *top*	*Portrait of Leo Tolstoy,* Ilya Yefimovich Repin.
3 *right,* 32, 44	Statue of a hero, possibly Gilgamesh, taming a lion (722–705 B.C.)
4 *bottom*	*Detail of Achilles Defeating Hector* (1630–1632), Peter Paul Rubens.
5 *top right,* 163 *bottom*	Statue of Athene (340–330 B.C.).
5 *bottom right,* 163 *bottom*	*Judgement of Paris* (1500s), Giulio Romano.
8	*Katada Bay Moon* (1800s), Yoshitoshi Taiso.
11	*Tsukiji at Akashi* (1931), Kaburagi Kiyokata.
12	*Toba (Su Tung-po)* (1820–1832), Katsushika Hokusai.
18	Mask of King Sargon of Akkad.
19	Hanging Gardens of Babylon (about 1960), Mario Larinaga.
20	Pharaoh Chephren (Fourth Dynasty).
21 *left*	Detail of Queen Ankhesenamen and King Tutankhamen (18th Dynasty).
21 *right*	Bust of Nefertiti. Museo Archeologico, Florence, Italy.
22	King Solomon. Anagni Cathedral, Italy.
23 *bottom*	Book of Esther (1800s).
26 *right*	Detail of the stele of the Law code of Hammurabi (about 1792–1750 B.C.).
27	Gold mask of Tutankhamen.
30	Detail of *Moses Receiving the Ten Commandments* (1500s), Raphael.
35	Gilgamesh and Enkidu slaying Humbaba.
38	Reconstruction of the Queen's Lyre from Ur (about 2500 B.C.).
52–53	Nakht scroll (18th Dynasty, 1350–1300 B.C.).
55	Relief of Akhenaten offers a sacrifice to Aton, the sun god (1350 B.C.).
56	Painted limestone statue of Kat-tep and his wife Hetepheres (4th dynasty).
58	Relief from the tomb of Vizier Ramose (18th Dynasty).
60	Section from *The Book of the Dead* of Nany.
61	Gray granite statue of Pady-mahes (about 700 B.C.).
64	Jonah in the fish's mouth. Illumination from the Kennicott Bible.
65	*The Creation of Adam,* Michelangelo Buonarroti.
69	*The Judgement of Adam and Eve: "So Judged He Man"* (1807), William Blake.
72, 100	The Building of the Ark (Gen. 6:13–17); The Flood (Gen. 8:6–11); Leaving the Ark (Gen. 8:18–19); The Sacrifice of Noah (Gen. 8:20–9:15) (about 1250).
76 *bottom,* 83	*The Creation of Man,* Diego Rivera.
77	Mayan cylindrical vessel decorated with mythological scene (8th century).
80	Detail of the Bonampak Fresco Cycle.
88	David, the young shepherd, plays his pipe and a bell (I Samuel 16: 5–11): French manuscript illustration.
91	Detail of *St. John the Baptist in the Wilderness,* Geertgen tot Sint Jans.
94	*Summer, or Ruth and Boaz* (1660), Nicolas Poussin.
98	*The Return of the Prodigal Son* (1773), Pompeo Batoni.

R156 INDEX OF FINE ART

INDEX OF FINE ART **R157**

R158 INDEX OF FINE ART

INDEX OF FINE ART **R159**

R160 INDEX OF FINE ART

INDEX OF FINE ART **R161**

R162 INDEX OF FINE ART

Index of Skills

Literary Concepts

INDEX OF SKILLS **R163**

R164 INDEX OF SKILLS

Reading and Critical Thinking Skills

INDEX OF SKILLS **R165**

R166 INDEX OF SKILLS

INDEX OF SKILLS **R167**

Vocabulary Skills

Grammar, Usage, and Mechanics

R168 INDEX OF SKILLS

INDEX OF SKILLS **R169**

Writing Skills, Modes, and Formats

R170 INDEX OF SKILLS

INDEX OF SKILLS **R171**

R172 INDEX OF SKILLS

Inquiry and Research

INDEX OF SKILLS **R173**

Speaking and Listening

Viewing and Representing

R174 INDEX OF SKILLS

Assessment

INDEX OF SKILLS **R175**

Index of Titles and Authors

Page numbers that appear in italics refer to biographical information.

A

B

C

D

E

F

R176 INDEX OF TITLES AND AUTHORS

G

H

I

J

K

L

M

INDEX OF TITLES AND AUTHORS **R177**

R178 INDEX OF TITLES AND AUTHORS

INDEX OF TITLES AND AUTHORS **R179**

Simon & Schuster: Excerpts from *Popol Vuh: The Mayan Book of the Dawn of Life,* translated by Dennis Tedlock. Copyright © 1985, 1996 by Dennis Tedlock. Reprinted with the permission of Simon & Schuster.

Excerpt from the Gospel According to Luke, from *The Bible, Designed to Be Read as Living Literature,* edited by Ernest Sutherland Bates. Copyright © 1936 by Simon & Schuster. Copyright renewed © 1965 by Simon & Schuster. Reprinted with the permission of Simon & Schuster.

Jewish Publication Society: The Book of Ruth, from *Tanakh, the Holy Scriptures: The New JPS Translation According to the Traditional Hebrew Text.* Copyright © 1985 by the Jewish Publication Society. Reprinted by permission of the Jewish Publication Society.

University of Chicago Press: Excerpt from "Arjuna, the Mighty Archer," from *The Mahabharata,* translated by J. A. B. van Buitenen. Copyright © 1973 by the University of Chicago. Reprinted by permission of the University of Chicago Press.

"Slow, the Weaver" and "The Brahman's Dream," from *The Panchatantra,* translated by Arthur W. Ryder. Copyright © 1925 by the University of Chicago, renewed © 1953 by Mary E. Ryder and Winifred Ryder. Reprinted by permission of the University of Chicago Press.

Bantam Books: Excerpts from *The Bhagavad-Gita,* translated by Barbara Stoler Miller. Copyright © 1986 by Barbara Stoler Miller. Reprinted by permission of Bantam Books, a division of Random House, Inc.

Viking Penguin: "Rama and Ravana in Battle," from *The Ramayana* by R. K. Narayan. Copyright © 1972 by R. K. Narayan. Used by permission of Viking Penguin, a division of Penguin Group (USA) Inc.

ICM: Excerpts from *Arrow of the Blue-Skinned God: Retracing the Ramayana Through India* by Jonah Blank. Copyright © 1992 by Jonah Blank. Reprinted by permission of International Creative Management, on behalf of the author.

Unit Two

Houghton Mifflin: Excerpt from entry s.v. "hero" in *The American Heritage Dictionary of the English Language,* fourth edition. Copyright © 2000 by Houghton Mifflin Company. Reprinted by permission of Houghton Mifflin Company.

Viking Penguin: Excerpts from the *Iliad* by Homer, translated by Robert Fagles. Copyright © 1990 by Robert Fagles. Used by permission of Viking Penguin, a division of Penguin Group (USA) Inc.

Oedipus the King, from *The Three Theban Plays* by Sophocles, translated by Robert Fagles. Copyright © 1982 by Robert Fagles. Used by permission of Viking Penguin, a division of Penguin Group (USA) Inc.

University of California Press: "He Is More Than a Hero" and "To an army wife, in Sardis:" from *Sappho: A New Translation* by Mary Barnard. Copyright © 1958 by The Regents of the University of California, renewed © 1986 by Mary Barnard. Reprinted by permission of the Regents of the University of California and the University of California Press.

Schocken Books: "To Aphrodite of the Flowers, at Knossos" by Sappho, from *Sappho and the Greek Lyric Poets,* translated by Willis Barnstone. Copyright © 1962, 1967, 1988 by Willis Barnstone. Used by permission of Schocken Books, a division of Random House, Inc.

Penguin Books: "Pericles' Funeral Oration," from *History of the Peloponnesian War* by Thucydides, translated by Rex Warner (Penguin Classics, 1954). Copyright © 1954 by Rex Warner. Reproduced by permission of Penguin Books Ltd.

Excerpt from *The Annals of Imperial Rome* by Tacitus, translated by Michael Grant (Penguin Classics, 1956; sixth revised edition, 1989). Copyright © 1956, 1959, 1971, 1973, 1977, 1989, 1996 by Michael Grant Publications, Ltd. Reproduced by permission of Penguin Books Ltd.

R180 ACKNOWLEDGMENTS

Hugh Tredennick, from *The Collected Dialogues of Plato,* edited by Edith Hamilton and Huntington Cairns. Copyright © 1961 by Princeton University Press. Reprinted by permission of Princeton University Press.

ICM: "Myth" by Muriel Rukeyser, from *The Collected Poems of Muriel Rukeyser.* Copyright © 1978 by Muriel Rukeyser. Reprinted by permission of International Creative Management, Inc.

Random House: Excerpts from the *Aeneid* by Virgil, translated by Robert Fitzgerald. Copyright © 1981, 1982, 1983 by Robert Fitzgerald. Reprinted by permission of Random House, Inc.

Scribner: "Helen of Troy" by Sara Teasdale, from *The Collected Poems of Sara Teasdale.* Copyright © 1937 by The Macmillan Company. Reprinted with the permission of Scribner, a division of Simon & Schuster. All rights reserved.

University of Michigan Press: "Seize the Day" by Horace, from *Horace's Odes and Epodes,* translated by David Mulroy (Ann Arbor: University of Michigan Press, 1994). Copyright © 1994 by the University of Michigan Press. Reprinted by permission of the University of Michigan Press.

University of Chicago Press: "Better to live, Licinius, . . ." by Horace, from *The Odes and Epodes of Horace,* translated by Joseph P. Clancy. Copyright © 1960 by the University of Chicago Press. Reprinted by permission of the University of Chicago Press.

Indiana University Press: Excerpt from *Metamorphoses* by Ovid, translated by Rolfe Humphries. Copyright © 1955 by Indiana University Press. Reprinted by permission of Indiana University Press.

New Directions: "Landscape with the Fall of Icarus," from *Collected Poems 1939–1962,* Volume II, by William Carlos Williams. Copyright © 1953 by William Carlos Williams. Reprinted by permission of New Directions Publishing Corp.

Sarah Delaney: "Ancient Greece Revived in Rome; Colosseum Reopens as Theater with Staging of *Oedipus Rex*" by Sarah Delaney, from the *Washington Post,* July 20, 2000. Copyright © 2000 by Sarah Delaney. Reprinted by permission of the author.

Unit Three

W. W. Norton & Company: Excerpts from *The Analects of Confucius,* translated by Simon Leys. Copyright © 1997 by Pierre Ryckmans. Reprinted by permission of W. W. Norton & Company, Inc.

HarperCollins Publishers: Chapters 37, 44, and 68 from *Tao Te Ching: A New English Version with Foreword and Notes* by Stephen Mitchell. Translation copyright © 1988 by Stephen Mitchell. Reprinted by permission of HarperCollins Publishers, Inc.

Four haiku by Yosa Buson and four haiku by Kobayashi Issa, from *The Essential Haiku: Versions of Bashō, Buson, and Issa,* edited and with an introduction by Robert Hass. Copyright © 1994 by Robert Hass. Translations copyright © 1994 by Robert Hass. Reprinted by permission of HarperCollins Publishers, Inc.

Pantheon Books: "The Fish Rejoice" by Chuang Tzu, from *Chinese Fairy Tales and Fantasies,* translated and edited by Moss Roberts. Copyright © 1979 by Moss Roberts. Used by permission of Pantheon Books, a division of Random House, Inc.

Grove/Atlantic: "Mulberry on the Lowland," from *The Book of Songs,* translated by Arthur Waley. Copyright © 1937 by Arthur Waley. Used by permission of Grove/Atlantic, Inc.

Columbia University Press: "We Pick Ferns, We Pick Ferns," from the *Book of Odes,* and "Dreaming of Li Po" and "Song of P'eng-ya" by Tu Fu, from *The Columbia Book of Chinese Poetry,* translated and edited by Burton Watson. Copyright © 1984 by Columbia University Press. Reprinted with permission of the publisher.

"Still Night Thoughts" by Li Po, translated by Burton Watson, from *The Columbia Anthology of Traditional Chinese Literature,* edited by Victor H. Mair. Copyright © 1994 by Columbia University Press. Reprinted with permission of the publisher.

Excerpts from *The Pillow Book of Sei Shōnagon,* translated and edited by Ivan Morris. Copyright © 1967 by Ivan Morris. Reprinted with permission of Columbia University Press.

ACKNOWLEDGMENTS **R181**

Jr., from *Twenty Plays of the Nō Theatre*, edited by Donald Keene. Copyright © 1970 by Columbia University Press. Reprinted with permission of the publisher.

New Directions Publishing Corp.: "The River-Merchant's Wife: A Letter" by Li Po, translated by Ezra Pound, from *Personae: The Collected Shorter Poems of Ezra Pound.* Copyright © 1926 by Ezra Pound. Reprinted by permission of New Directions Publishing Corp.

"Gazing at the Lu Mountain Waterfall" by Li Po, from *The Selected Poems of Li Po,* translated by David Hinton. Copyright © 1996 by David Hinton. Reprinted by permission of New Directions Publishing Corp.

"Jade Flower Palace" by Tu Fu, from *One Hundred Poems from the Chinese,* translated by Kenneth Rexroth. Copyright © 1971 by Kenneth Rexroth. Reprinted by permission of New Directions Publishing Corp.

"Two Springs" and "On Plum Blossoms" by Li Ch'ing Chao, from *Li Ch'ing-Chao: Complete Poems,* translated by Kenneth Rexroth. Copyright © 1979 by Kenneth Rexroth and Ling Chung. Reprinted by permission of New Directions Publishing Corp.

Hanging Loose Press: "Harlemite Easter" by Shakira Hightower, from *Bullseye: Stories and Poems by Outstanding High School Writers.* Copyright © 1995 by Hanging Loose Press. Reprinted by permission of Hanging Loose Press.

"Revolution" by Susan Gray, from *Bullseye: Stories and Poems by Outstanding High School Writers.* Copyright © 1995 by Hanging Loose Press. Reprinted by permission of Hanging Loose Press.

Shambhala Publications: "Aim in Life," "Contamination of Virtue," and "Hypocritical Scholars," from *Dream Conversations on Buddhism and Zen* by Musō Kokushi (Musō Soseki), translated by Thomas Cleary. Copyright © 1994 by Thomas Cleary. Reprinted by arrangement with Shambhala Publications, Inc., Boston (www.shambhala.com).

Four haiku by Matsuo Bashō, from *The Essential Bashō,* translated by Sam Hamill. Copyright © 1998 by Sam Hamill. Reprinted by arrangement with Shambhala Publications, Inc., Boston (www.shambhala.com).

Charles E. Tuttle: "Publishing the Sutras" and "Right & Wrong," translated by Nyogen Senzaki and Paul Reps, from *Zen Flesh, Zen Bones: A Collection of Zen and Pre-Zen Writings,* compiled by Paul Reps. Copyright in Japan © 1957 by Charles E. Tuttle Co., Inc. Reprinted by permission of Charles E. Tuttle Co., Inc., of Boston, Massachusetts, and Tokyo, Japan.

Doubleday: "I've gone to him" by Ono Komachi, "Spring rains weaving" by Lady Ise, "In this world" by Ki Tsurayuki, and "As I look at the moon" by Saigyō, translated by Burton Watson, and excerpt from *The Spring of My Life* by Kobayashi Issa, translated by Hiroaki Sato, from *From the Country of Eight Islands: An Anthology of Japanese Poetry* edited and translated by Hiroaki Sato and Burton Watson. Copyright © 1981 by Hiroaki Sato and Burton Watson. Used by permission of Doubleday, a division of Random House, Inc.

Dutton: "Dry Leaves" and "Flying Fish" by José Juan Tablada, translated by W. S. Merwin, from *New Poetry of Mexico* by Octavio Paz and Mark Strand. Copyright © 1970 by E. P. Dutton & Co., Inc. Copyright © 1966 by Siglo XXI Editores, S.A. Used by permission of Dutton, a division of Penguin Group (USA) Inc.

Arcade Publishing: Three haiku from *Haiku: This Other World* by Richard Wright. Copyright © 1998 by Ellen Wright. Reprinted by permission of Arcade Publishing, New York, New York.

Unit Four

Penguin Books: Excerpts from *The Koran,* translated by N. J. Dawood. Copyright © 1956, 1959, 1966, 1968, 1974, 1990, 1993, 1997, 1999, 2003, 2006 by N. J. Dawood. Reprinted by permission of Penguin Books Ltd.

"The Second Voyage of Sindbad the Sailor," from *Tales from the Thousand and One Nights,* translated by N. J. Dawood. Copyright © 1954, 1973 by N. J. Dawood. Reprinted by permission of Penguin Books Ltd.

R182 ACKNOWLEDGMENTS

from *The Essential Rumi,* translated by Coleman Barks. Copyright © 1995 by Coleman Barks. Reprinted by permission of Coleman Barks.

Reed Educational & Professional Publishing: "How the World Was Created from a Drop of Milk," from *The Origin of Life and Death: African Creation Myths,* edited by Ulli Beier. Copyright © 1966 by Heinemann Educational Books Ltd. and Ulli Beier. Reprinted by permission of Reed Educational & Professional Publishing Ltd.

The Emma Courlander Trust: "The First Bard Among the Soninke," retold by Ousmane Sako and Harold Courlander, from *The Crest and the Hide and Other African Stories of Heroes, Chiefs, Bards, Hunters, Sorcerers and Common People* by Harold Courlander. Copyright © 1982 by Harold Courlander. Reprinted by permission of The Emma Courlander Trust.

"All Stories Are Anansi's" and "Anansi Plays Dead," from *The Hat-Shaking Dance and Other Tales from the Gold Coast* by Harold Courlander. Copyright © 1957 by Harold Courlander. Reprinted by permission of The Emma Courlander Trust.

Pearson Education: Excerpt from *Sundiata: An Epic of Old Mali* by D. T. Niane, translated by G. D. Pickett. Copyright © 1965 by Longman Group Limited. Reprinted by permission of Pearson Education Limited.

Viking Penguin: "Iktomi and the Wild Ducks" and "Iktomi Takes Back a Gift," from *American Indian Trickster Tales* by Richard Erdoes and Alfonso Ortiz. Copyright © 1998 by Richard Erdoes & the Estate of Alfonso Ortiz. Used by permission of Viking Penguin, a division of Penguin Group (USA) Inc.

Hippocrene Books: Excerpts from *African Proverbs* by Gerd de Ley. Copyright © 1999 by Hippocrene Books, Inc. Reprinted by permission of Hippocrene Books.

The Free Press: Excerpts from "Edison's Curse," from *Sleep Thieves: An Eye-Opening Exploration into the Science and Mysteries of Sleep* by Stanley Coren. Copyright © 1996 by Stanley Coren. Reprinted and edited with the permission of The Free Press, a division of Simon & Schuster, Inc.

Unit Five

W. W. Norton & Company: Excerpts from *The Song of Roland,* translated by Frederick Goldin. Copyright © 1978 by W. W. Norton & Company, Inc. Reprinted by permission of W. W. Norton & Company, Inc.

Excerpt from the *Decameron* by Giovanni Boccaccio, translated by Mark Musa and Peter Bondanella. Copyright © 1982 by Mark Musa and Peter Bondanella. Used by permission of W. W. Norton & Company, Inc.

Boydell & Brewer: Excerpt from *Perceval: The Story of the Grail* by Chrétien de Troyes, translated by Nigel Bryant. Translation copyright © 1982 by Nigel Bryant. Reprinted by permission of Boydell & Brewer Ltd.

Farrar, Straus and Giroux: Excerpts from *The Inferno of Dante: A New Verse Translation* by Robert Pinsky. Translation copyright © 1994 by Robert Pinsky. Reprinted by permission of Farrar, Straus and Giroux, LLC.

Indiana University Press: Excerpts from *Dante's Vita Nuova,* translated by Mark Musa. Copyright © 1973 by Indiana University Press. Reprinted by permission by of Indiana University Press.

Columbia University Press: Excerpt from *The Art of Courtly Love* by Andreas Capellanus, translated by John Jay Parry. Copyright © 1941 by Columbia University Press. Reprinted with permission of the publisher.

Yale University Press: Excerpts from *Utopia* by St. Thomas More, edited by Edward Surtz, S.J. Copyright © 1964 by Yale University. Reprinted by permission of Yale University Press.

Oxford University Press: Excerpt from "Sonnet 3" by Francesco Petrarch, from *Selections from the Canzoniere and Other Works,* translated by Mark Musa (Oxford World's Classics, 1999). Translation copyright © 1985 by Mark Musa. Reprinted by permission of Oxford University Press.

Schocken Books: "Sonnet 23" by Louise Labé, translated by Willis Barnstone, from *A Book of Women Poets from Antiquity to Now,* edited by Aliki Barnstone and Willis Barnstone. Copyright © 1980 by Schocken Books. Used by permission of Schocken Books, a division of Random House, Inc.

ACKNOWLEDGMENTS **R183**

Obras Completas de Sor Juana Inés de la Cruz, edited by Alfonso Méndez Plancarte. Copyright © by Fondo de Cultura Económica. Reprinted by permission of Fondo de Cultura Económica.

Viking Penguin: Excerpts from *Don Quixote* by Miguel de Cervantes Saavedra, translated by Samuel Putnam. Copyright © 1949 by The Viking Press, Inc. Used by permission of Viking Penguin, a division of Penguin Group (USA) Inc.

Random House: Excerpt from *Candide* by Voltaire, translated by Richard Aldington. Copyright © 1928 by Random House, Inc. Used by permission of Random House, Inc.

Unit Six

Doubleday: Excerpts from *Goethe's Faust,* translated by Walter Kaufmann. Copyright © 1961 by Walter Kaufmann. Used by permission of Doubleday, a division of Random House, Inc.

New Directions Publishing Corp.: Excerpt from letter of March 1, 1788, by Johann Wolfgang von Goethe, translated by Berthold Biermann, from *Goethe's World as Seen in Letters and Memoirs,* edited by Berthold Biermann. Copyright © 1949 by New Directions. Reprinted by permission of New Directions Publishing Corp.

Arte Público Press: "I know of Egypt and Niger," from *Versos Sencillos/Simple Verses* by José Martí, translated by Manuel A. Tellechea (Houston: Arte Público Press—University of Houston, 1997). Copyright © 1997 by Arte Público Press. Translation copyright © 1997 by Manuel A. Tellechea. Reprinted with permission from the publisher.

HarperCollins Publishers: "Shaman Song" by Uvuvnuk, translated by Jane Hirshfield, from *Women in Praise of the Sacred,* edited by Jane Hirshfield. Copyright © 1994 by Jane Hirshfield. Reprinted by permission of HarperCollins Publishers, Inc.

Kensington Publishing: "The Lorelei" by Heinrich Heine, from *The Poetry and Prose of Heinrich Heine,* translated by Aaron Kramer. Copyright © 1948 by the Citadel Press. Reprinted by permission of Citadel Press/Kensington Publishing Corp. (www.kensingtonbooks.com). All rights reserved.

Farrar, Straus and Giroux: "Russia 1812" by Victor Hugo, translated by Robert Lowell, from *Imitations.* Copyright © 1959 by Robert Lowell. Copyright renewed © 1987 by Harriet, Sheridan, and Caroline Lowell. Reprinted by permission of Farrar, Straus and Giroux, LLC.

HMH: "L'Invitation au Voyage" ("Invitation to the Voyage") by Charles Baudelaire, translated by Richard Wilbur, from *Things of This World.* Copyright © 1956 and renewed 1984 by Richard Wilbur. Reprinted by permission of Houghton Mifflin Harcourt Publishing Company. This material may not be reproduced in any form or by any means without the prior written permission of the publisher.

Oxford University Press: "The Albatross," from *The Flowers of Evil* by Charles Baudelaire, translated and annotated by James McGowan, with an introduction by Jonathan Culler (Oxford World's Classics, 1998). Translation copyright © 1993 by James McGowan. Reprinted by permission of Oxford University Press.

Louis Simpson: "Autumn Song" by Paul Verlaine, translated by Louis Simpson. Copyright © 1988 by Louis Simpson. Reprinted by permission of the author.

Scribner: Letter to N.A. Nekrasov from Leo Tolstoy, from *Tolstoy's Letters, Volume I* edited by R.F. Christian. Copyright © 1978 by R.F. Christian. Reprinted with the permission of Scribner, an imprint of Simon & Schuster Adult Publishing Group. All rights reserved.

Dutton Signet: *A Doll's House* by Henrik Ibsen, from *Henrik Ibsen: The Complete Major Prose Plays,* translated by Rolf Fjelde. Copyright © 1965, 1970, 1978 by Rolf Fjelde. Used by permission of Dutton Signet, a division of Penguin Group (USA) Inc.

R184 ACKNOWLEDGMENTS

Schocken Books: "The Metamorphosis," from *Franz Kafka: The Complete Stories* by Franz Kafka, edited by Nahum N. Glatzer. Copyright © 1946, 1947, 1948, 1949, 1954, 1958, 1971 by Schocken Books. Used by permission of Schocken Books, a division of Random House, Inc.

Random House: "The Panther" by Rainer Maria Rilke, from *The Selected Poetry of Rainer Maria Rilke,* translated by Stephen Mitchell. Copyright © 1982 by Stephen Mitchell. Used by permission of Random House, Inc.

"After the Deluge," from *Mandela's Earth and Other Poems* by Wole Soyinka. Copyright © 1988 by Wole Soyinka. Used by permission of Random House, Inc.

Robert Bly: "The Guitar" by Federico García Lorca, from *Lorca and Jiménez: Selected Poems,* translated by Robert Bly (Boston: Beacon Press, 1973, 1997). Copyright © 1997 by Robert Bly. Reprinted by permission of Robert Bly.

"Ode to the Watermelon" by Pablo Neruda, translated by Robert Bly, from *Neruda and Vallejo: Selected Poems,* edited by Robert Bly. Copyright © 1971 by Robert Bly. Reprinted by permission of Robert Bly.

HarperCollins Publishers: Excerpt from "The Panther" by Rainer Maria Rilke, from *Selected Poems of Rainer Maria Rilke,* translated by Robert Bly. Copyright © 1981 by Robert Bly. Reprinted by permission of HarperCollins Publishers, Inc.

Excerpt from *Paula* by Isabel Allende, translated by Margaret Sayers Peden. Copyright © 1994 by Isabel Allende. Translation copyright © 1995 by Harper Collins Publishers, Inc. Reprinted by permission of HarperCollins Publishers, Inc.

"The Handsomest Drowned Man in the World," from *Leaf Storm and Other Stories* by Gabriel García Márquez, translated by Gregory Rabassa. Copyright © 1971 by Gabriel García Márquez. Reprinted by permission of HarperCollins Publishers, Inc.

Harcourt: "Professions for Women," from *The Death of the Moth and Other Essays* by Virginia Woolf. Copyright © 1942 by Harcourt, Inc., and renewed 1970 by Marjorie T. Parsons, Executrix. Reprinted by permission of the publisher.

HMH: "The End and the Beginning," from *View with a Grain of Sand* by Wislawa Szymborska, translated by Stanislaw Baranczak and Clare Cavanagh. Copyright © 1993 by Wislawa Szymborska. English translation copyright © 1995 by Houghton Mifflin Harcourt Publishing Company. Reprinted by permission of the publisher. This material may not be reproduced in any form or by any means without the prior written permission of the publisher.

Viking Penguin: "Eveline," from *Dubliners* by James Joyce. Copyright © 1916 by B. W. Huebsch. Definitive text copyright © 1967 by the Estate of James Joyce. Used by permission of Viking Penguin, a division of Penguin Group (USA) Inc.

North Point Press: "The Jay," translated by Lane Dunlop, from *Palm-of-the-Hand Stories* by Yasunari Kawabata, translated by Lane Dunlop and J. Martin Holman. Translations copyright © 1988 by Lane Dunlop and J. Martin Holman. Reprinted by permission of North Point Press, a division of Farrar, Straus and Giroux, LLC.

Penguin Books: "Prayer to Masks" by Léopold Sédar Senghor, from *The Penguin Book of Modern African Poetry,* edited by Gerald Moore and Ulli Beier (Penguin Books, 1963; third edition, 1984). Copyright © 1963, 1968, 1984 by Gerald Moore and Ulli Beier. Reprinted by permission of Penguin Books Ltd.

The Pirandello Estate and Toby Cole: "War," translated by Samuel Putnam, from *The Medals and Other Stories* by Luigi Pirandello. Copyright © 1939 by E. P. Dutton & Company. Reprinted by permission of the Pirandello Estate and Toby Cole, Agent.

Darhansoff, Verrill, Feldman Literary Agents: "I Am Not One of Those Who Left the Land," from *Poems of Akhmatova* translated by Stanley Kunitz and Max Hayward. Copyright © 1967, 1968, 1972, 1973 by Stanley Kunitz and Max Hayward. Used courtesy of Darhansoff, Verrill, Feldman Literary Agents.

Arcade Publishing: "The Spy," translated by John Willett, excerpt from the original work *Furcht und Elend des Dritten Reiches (Fear and Misery of the Third Reich)* by Bertolt Brecht. Copyright © 1957 by Suhrkamp Verlag, Frankfurt am Main. Translation copyright © 1983 by Stefan S. Brecht. Reprinted with permission of Arcade Publishing, New York, N.Y.

ACKNOWLEDGMENTS **R185**

and Matthew Mead, from *The Seeker and Other Poems* by Nelly Sachs, translated by Ruth and Matthew Mead and Michael Hamburger. Translation copyright © 1970 by Farrar, Straus & Giroux, Inc. Reprinted by permission of Farrar, Straus and Giroux, LLC.

"Freedom to Breathe," from *Stories and Prose Poems* by Alexander Solzhenitsyn, translated by Michael Glenny. Translation copyright © 1971 by Michael Glenny. Reprinted by permission of Farrar, Straus and Giroux, LLC.

"January First" by Octavio Paz, from *The Complete Poems: 1927-1979* by Elizabeth Bishop. Copyright © 1979, 1983 by Alice Helen Methfessel. Reprinted by permission of Farrar, Straus and Giroux, LLC.

Alfred A. Knopf: "The Guest," from *Exile and the Kingdom* by Albert Camus, translated by Justin O'Brien. Copyright © 1957, 1958 by Alfred A. Knopf, a division of Random House, Inc. Used by permission of Alfred A. Knopf, a division of Random House, Inc.

Ben Bennani: "The Prison Cell" by Mahmud Darwish, translated by Ben Bennani. Copyright © 1992 by Ben Bennani. Reprinted by permission of Ben Bennani.

Emma Sweeney Agency: "Dead Men's Path" and "Civil Peace," from *Girl's At War and Other Stories* by Chinua Achebe. Copyright © 1972, 1973 by Chinua Achebe. Reprinted by permissions of the Emma Sweeney Agency, LLC.

Doubleday: Excerpt from interview with Chinua Achebe, from *Bill Moyers: A World of Ideas* by Bill Moyers. Copyright © 1989 by Public Affairs Television, Inc. Used by permission of Doubleday, a division of Random House, Inc.

"Half a Day," from *The Time and the Place and Other Stories* by Naguib Mahfouz, translated by Denys Johnson-Davies. Copyright © 1991 by the American University in Cairo Press. Used by permission of Doubleday, a division of Random House, Inc.

Wesleyan University Press: "Keeper of the Vigil," from *Pleasure Dome* by Yusef Komunyakaa. Copyright © 2001 by Yusef Komunyakaa. Reprinted by permission of Wesleyan University Press.

University of California Press: "The Diameter of the Bomb" by Yehuda Amichai, from *The Selected Poetry of Yehuda Amichai,* translated by Chana Bloch and Stephen Mitchell. Copyright © 1996 by The Regents of the University of California. Reprinted by permission of the Regents of the University of California and the University of California Press and Hana Amichai.

"Ode to the Lizard" by Pablo Neruda, from *Selected Odes of Pablo Neruda,* translated by Margaret Sayers Peden. Copyright © 1990 by The Regents of the University of California, © Fundación Pablo Neruda. Reprinted by permission of the Regents of the University of California and the University of California Press.

Farrar, Straus and Giroux and Penguin Books Canada: "Amnesty," from *Jump and Other Stories* by Nadine Gordimer. Copyright © 1991 by Felix Licensing, B.V. Reprinted by permission of Farrar, Straus and Giroux, LLC, and Penguin Books Canada Limited.

Tom Thompson: "Counting in Sevens," from *A Human Pattern: Selected Poems* by Judith Wright (Sydney: ETT Imprint, 1996). Copyright © 1996 by Tom Thompson. Reprinted by permission of Tom Thompson.

The editors have made every effort to trace the ownership of all copyrighted material found in this book and to make full acknowledgment for its use. Omissions brought to our attention will be corrected in a subsequent edition.

R186 ACKNOWLEDGMENTS

Art Credits

Front Matter

x *Nakht hunting with his family* (18th Dynasty, 16th–14th centuries B.C.). From the tomb of Nakht, scribe and priest under Pharaoh Tuthmosis IV, in the cemetery of Sheikh Abd al-Qurnan, Luxor-Thebes, Egypt. Photo © Erich Lessing/Art Resource, New York; **xii** Temple E at Selinus. From *Greece: From Mycenae to the Parthenon,* Henri Stierlin. Photo by Henri Stierlin, Geneva, Switzerland; **xiv** Detail of *Moonlight on the River Sheba,* Ando Hiroshige. Musée des Arts Asiatiques-Guimet, Paris. Photo © Bridgeman-Giraudon/Art Resource, New York; **xvi** © Gerard del Vecchio/Getty Images; **xviii** *top, Primavera [Allegory of spring]* (1481), Sandro Botticelli. Uffizi, Florence, Italy. Photo © Scala/Art Resource, New York; *bottom* Detail of *Dante Alighieri* (1500–1503), Luca Signorelli. Fresco. Duomo, Orvieto, Italy. Photo © Scala/Art Resource, New York; **xx** *top* Detail of *Dance at the Moulin de la Galette, Montmartre* (1876), Auguste Renoir. Oil on canvas, 131 cm × 175 cm. Musée d'Orsay, Paris. Photo by Herve Lewandowski. Photo © Réunion des Musées Nationaux/Art Resource, New York; **xxi** *Portrait of Leo Tolstoy,* Ilya Yefimovich Repin. Tretyakov Gallery, Moscow, Russia. Photo © Scala/Art Resource, New York; **xxii** Lyndon B. Johnson Space Center/NASA; **xxiii** © Eliot Elisofon/Time & Life Pictures/Getty Images; **2** *top* © The Kobal Collection; *bottom* Detail of Rama fights Ravana (1800s). Gouache on paper. [Inv.: IM.293–1914]. Photo © Victoria & Albert Museum, London/Art Resource, New York; **3** *left* © Jacques Jangoux/Stone/Getty Images; *center* © Photofest; *right* Statue of a hero, possibly Gilgamesh, taming a lion (722–705 B.C.). Louvre, Paris. Photo © Erich Lessing/Art Resource, New York; **4** *top* The Granger Collection, New York; *bottom* Detail of *Achilles Defeating Hector* (1630–1632), Peter Paul Rubens. Oil on panel, 108 cm × 127 cm. Photo © Musée des Beaux-Arts, Pau, France/Bridgeman Art Library; **4–5** © George Hunter/Robertstock.com/Retrofile.com; **5** *top left* © Erich Lessing/Art Resource, New York; *top right* Statue of Athene (340–330 B.C.). National Archaeological Museum, Athens, Greece. Photo © Bridgeman Art Library; *bottom left, Bust of Homer*. Sala delle Muse. Museo Pio Clementino, Vatican Museums, Vatican State. Photo © Scala/Art Resource, New York; *bottom center* © The Art Archive; *bottom right, Judgement of Paris* (1500s), Giulio Romano. Ducal Palace, Mantua, Italy © SuperStock, Inc./SuperStock; **6** © Mark Douet/Getty Images; **8** *Katada Bay Moon* (19th century), Yoshitoshi Taiso. © Asian Art & Archaeology, Inc./Corbis; **11** *Tsukiji at Akashi* (1931), Kaburagi Kiyokata. Photo © Peter Harholdt/Corbis; **12** *Toba (Su Dong po)* (1820–1832), Katsushika Hokusai. Woodblock print, 516 × 227 mm. Honolulu Academy of Arts, Gift of James A. Michener, 1970 (15,943).

Unit One

14–15 *Nakht hunting with his family* (18th Dynasty, 16th–14th centuries B.C.). From the tomb of Nakht, scribe and priest under Pharaoh Tuthmose IV, in the cemetery of Sheikh Abd al-Qurnan, Luxor-Thebes, Egypt. Photo © Erich Lessing/Art Resource, New York; **16** *top* © Nik Wheeler/Corbis; *bottom* © Ray Manyley/SuperStock; **17** *left* © Zev Radovan's Bible Land Pictures; *right* © Superstock, Inc./SuperStock; **18** © Gianni Dagli Orti/Corbis; **19** *top* © Bettmann/Corbis; *bottom* © Ron Sheridan/Ancient Art and Architecture Collection Ltd.; **20** Pharaoh Chephren (Fourth Dynasty). Egyptian Museum, Cairo, Egypt. Photo © Bridgeman-Giraudon/Art Resource, New York; **21** *left* Detail of Queen Ankhesenamen and King Tutankhamen (18th Dynasty). Egyptian Museum, Cairo. © Scala/Art Resource, New York; *right* Bust of Nefertiti. Museo Archeologico, Florence, Italy. Photo © Scala/Art Resource, New York; **22** King Solomon. Anagni Cathedral, Italy. Photo © Alfredo Dagli Orti/The Art Archive; **23** *top* © Bojan Brecelj/Corbis; *bottom* Book of Esther (19th century). Scroll in filigree case of silver gilt and coral. Photo © Gianni Dagli Orti/Szapiro Collection, Paris/The Art Archive; **24** *top left* Elamite counting tokens (Calculi) (about 4000 B.C.). Terracotta. Louvre, Paris. Photo by Jérome Galland. Photo © Réunion des Musées Nationaux/Art Resource, New York; *center left* © Erich Lessing/Art Resource, New York; *bottom left* Mesopotamian cuneiform tablet (2113–2006 B.C.). Baked clay. Dagon Agricultural Collection, Haifa, Israel. © Erich Lessing/Art Resource, New York; *center right, right* © The Art Archive/Corbis; **25** *left* The Granger Collection, New York; *right* © British Museum/Art Resource, New York; **26** *left* © Getty Images; *right* Upper section of the stele of the Law code of Hammurabi (about 1792–1750 B.C.). Diorite, from Babylon (found at Susa). First Babylonian dynasty. Louvre, Paris. Photo © Hervé Lewandowki/Réunion des Musées Nationaux/Art Resource, New York; **27** © Robert Harding/Robert Harding World Imagery/Getty Images; **28–29** © Herbert Hartmann/The Image Bank/Getty Images; **28** *left* © Chromosohm Media/Stock Boston LLC; *right* © Nathan Benn/Corbis; **29** *top* © Michael St. Maur Sheil/Corbis; *bottom* © Michael Newman/PhotoEdit; **30** Detail of *Moses Receiving the Ten Commandments* (1500s), Raphael. Vatican City, Vatican State. Photo © David Lees/Corbis; **31** © Photofest; **32** Statue of a hero, possibly Gilgamesh, taming a lion (722–705 B.C.). Louvre, Paris. Photo © Erich Lessing/Art Resource, New York; **33** © G. Tortoli/Ancient Art and Architecture Collection Ltd.; **35** Cylinder seal with contest scene, perhaps Gilgamesh and Enkidu vs. Humbaba (about 700–600 B.C.). Chalcedony. 994.233.41. With permission of the Royal Ontario

ART CREDITS **R187**

Queen's Lyre from Ur (about 2500 B.C.). Wood, lapis lazuli, 112 cm high. Photo © The British Museum, London/Bridgeman Art Library; **44** Statue of a hero, possibly Gilgamesh, taming a lion (722–705 B.C.). Louvre, Paris. Photo © Erich Lessing/Art Resource, New York; **49** Fragments connected by Theodore Kwasman. Tablet with opening lines of Gilgamesh. © The Trustees of the British Museum. All rights reserved; **52–53** Papyrus from the *Book of the Dead of Nakht* (18th Dynasty, 1350–1300 B.C.). Thebes, Egypt. British Museum, London. Photo © HIP/Art Resource; **55** Akhenaten offers a sacrifice to Aton, the sun god (1350 B.C.). Relief from Amarna, Egypt. Egyptian Museum, Cairo, Egypt. Photo © Erich Lessing/Art Resource, New York; **56** Kat-tep and his wife Hetepheres (4th dynasty). Painted limestone statue. The British Museum, London. Photo © Michael Holford; **58** Relief from the tomb of Vizier Ramose (18th Dynasty), Thebes. Photo © Michael Holford; **60** Section from *The Book of the Dead* of Nany. Ca. (1040–945 B.C.) Painted and inscribed papyrus. Western Thebes. Rogers Fund, 1930. (30.3.31). Image © The Metropolitan Museum of Art/Art Resource, New York; **61** *Block Statue of Pady-mahes* (about 700 B.C.), Dynasty XXV. Gray granite, 43.3 cm high. From Tel El Moqdam. Brooklyn Museum of Art, Charles Edwin Wilbour Fund [64.146]; **64** Jonah and the whale from the Kennicott Bible (1 folio 305), Hebrew, Spain, 1476. Bodleian Library, Oxford, United Kingdom. Photo © The Art Archive; **65** *The Creation of Adam,* Michelangelo Buonarroti. Detail of the Sistine ceiling. Sistine Chapel, Vatican Palace, Vatican State. Photo © Scala/Art Resource, New York; **69** *The Judgement of Adam and Eve: "So Judged He Man"* (1807), William Blake. The Huntington Library, Art Collections, and Botanical Gardens, San Marino, California. Photo © Huntington Library/SuperStock; **72** The Building of the Ark (Gen. 6:13–17); The Flood (Gen. 8:6–11); Leaving the Ark (Gen. 8:18–19); The Sacrifice of Noah (Gen. 8:20–9:15) (about 1250). The Pierpont Morgan Library/Art Resource, New York; **76** *top* © Craig Aurness/Corbis; *bottom* Detail of *The Creation of Man,* Diego Rivera. Page from *Popol Vuh,* watercolor on paper. © 2001 Banco de México Diego Rivera and Frida Kahlo Museums Trust. Av. Cinco de Mayo No. 2, Col. Centro, Del. Cuauhtémoc 06059, México, D.F./Bridgeman Art Library; **77** Mayan cylindrical vessel decorated with mythological scene (8th century). Ceramic. Height 5/12″. The Michael C. Rockefeller Memorial Collection, Purchase, Nelson A. Rockefeller Gift, 1968. (1978.412.206). Image © The Metropolitan Museum of Art/Art Resource, New York; **78** © Craig Aurness/Corbis; **80** The Bonampak Fresco Cycle. Photo © Doug Stern/National Geographic Image Collection; **81** © Craig Aurness/Corbis; **83** Quetzalcoatl, the Plumed Serpent Diego Rivera. Page from *Popol Vuh,* watercolor on paper. © 2001 Banco de México Diego Rivera and Frida Kahlo Museums Trust. Av. Cinco de Mayo No. 2, Col. Centro, Del. Cuauhtémoc 06059, México, D.F. Photo © Bridgeman Art Library; **88, 89** David, the young shepherd, plays his pipe and a bell (I Samuel 16: 5–11): French manuscript illustration. The Granger Collection, New York; **91** Detail of *St. John the Baptist in the Wilderness,* Geertgen tot Sint Jans. 42 cm × 28 cm. Gemäldegalerie, Staatliche Museen zu Berlin. Photo © Bildarchiv Preussischer Kulturbesitz/Art Resource, New York; **94** *Summer, or Ruth and Boaz* (1660), Nicolas Poussin. Musée du Louvre, Paris. © Peter Willi/SuperStock; **98** *The Return of the Prodigal Son* (1773), Pompeo Batoni. Oil on canvas, 173 cm × 122 cm. Inv. 148 Kunthistorisches Museum Gemaldegalerie, Vienna. Photo © Erich Lessing/Art Resource, New York; **100** The Flood (Gen. 8:6–11) (about 1250). The Pierpont Morgan Library/Art Resource, New York; **102** *top* The Horse Court of the Temple of Vishnu at Srirangam, Wim Swaan. Wim Swaan Photograph Collection Research Library, Library, The Getty Research Institute, Los Angeles. (96.P.21); *bottom left* © Dinodia Photo Library, Bombay, India; *bottom center* © John and Lisa Merrill/Stone/Getty Images; *bottom right* © WIll Curtis/Getty Images; **102–103** © Robert Frerck/Odyssey Productions/ Chicago, Illinois; **103** © Alison Wright/Corbis; **104** *top* The Aryan God of War, Indra, seated on an elephant (1825). Photo © Victoria & Albert Museum, London/Art Resource, New York; *bottom* Mohenjo Daro seal. National Museum of Pakistan, Karachi, Pakistan. Photo © Scala/Art Resource, New York; **105** Head of the Buddha (400s). Buff sandstone. National Museum of India, New Delhi, India. Photo © Bridgeman Art Library; **106** *left* Detail from Ranganatha Temple Fresco. Photo © Gian Berto Vanni/Corbis; *right, Battle between armies of Arjuna and Tamradhvaia Brahma and deities in sky* (1598), Nakib Khan. Mughal. Photo © The British Library/The Art Archive; **107** *left* © Corbis; *right* Detail of Krishna playing a flute, from the *Vahula Raga* (about 1710), Basohli. Watercolor on paper. Photo © Victoria & Albert Museum, London/Bridgeman Art Library; **108** Text of the Sri Bhagavata Purana (late 1800s). Sanscrit. On a roll of silk paper. © The British Library/The Art Archive; **109** *Shiva Nataraja as The Lord of the Dance* (900s). Bronze, 67.3 cm × 48.3 cm × 17 cm. Madras, India. Victoria & Albert Museum, London, bequeathed by Mrs. L. S. Bradley [Inv.: IM.2-1934]. Photo © Victoria & Albert Museum, London/Art Resource, New York; **110** *left* Bust of a man, possibly a priest. Limestone. Height 6 7/8″. From Mohenjo Daro. Indus Valley civilizations, about 2000 B.C. National Museum of Pakistan, Karachi, Pakistan. Photo © Scala/Art Resource, New York; **111** © Araldo de Luca/Corbis; **112** *top* © Jupiterimages/Comstock Images/Alamy

R188 ART CREDITS

Sisse Brimberg/National Geographic/Getty Images; **113** © Bob Adelman/Magnum Photos; *bottom* NASA; **116** Indra, King of Three Worlds from the Temple Car (1600s), Indian. Wood carving. The Victoria & Albert Museum, London. Photo © V&A Images/Victoria & Albert Museum, London; **118** Agni (God of Fire) (1600s). Panel from Temple Car. Tak. Madras. Inv: IM.15–1929. Photo © Victoria & Albert Museum, London/Art Resource, New York; **120** Rama. Illustration from the *Ramayana* (about 1800), Indian. The Victoria & Albert Museum, London. Photo © V&A Images/Victoria and Albert Museum, London; **121** Wolverine and Spider-Man: Trademark and copyright © 2001 Marvel Characters, Inc. Used with permission; **122** © Barnaby Hall/Photonica/Getty Images; **125** Drona at the Well, Bhaktisiddhanta. From *Art Treasures of the Mahabharata,* written and illustrated by Bhaktisiddhanta. © 2000. Used with permission from Torchlight Publishing; **128** *top* © Dwarkadas Thanvi/Dinodia Picture Agency; *bottom* © Images of India/Dinodia Picture Agency; **129** *top, Henry David Thoreau* (1856), Benjamin D. Maxium. Daguerretype. Photo © National Portrait Gallery, Smithsonian Institution/Art Resource, New York; **130** © The Trustees of the British Museum. All rights reserved; **132** *Rama fighting Ravana* (1800s), Indian. Victoria and Albert Museum, London. Photo © V&A Images/Victoria and Albert Museum, London; **137** Rama cuts off Ravana's heads (1652). © The British Library/akg-images, London; **140** Rama and Sita enthroned (about 1810–1820), Indian. The Victoria & Albert Museum, London. Photo © V&A Images/The Victoria & Albert Museum, London; **141** Detail of Rama and the archer in a carrage attack Ravana (1652). © The British Library/akg-images, London; **142** *Saint George and the Dragon* (1600s). Ivory. Cavalry Museum, Pinerolo, Italy. Photo © Alfredo Dagli Orti/The Art Archive; **145** *top* Rama and Sita (1740). Pahari style, Gouache. Victoria and Albert Museum, London. Inv. IS.116-1960. Photo © Victoria and Albert Museum/Art Resource, New York; *bottom* © Batch 6/PhotosIndia.com LLC/Alamy Ltd; **148** *Kanduri* (1900), India. Cotton, 183″ × 73″. The Metropolitan Museum of Art, Purchase, Rogers Fund, Anonymous gift, in honor of W. G. and Mildred Archer, and Carolyn Kane Gift, 1986. (1986.53). Image © 2001 The Metropolitan Museum of Art; **158** Detail of illustration, Rama fights Ravana (1800s). Gouache on paper. [Inv.: IM.293–1914]. Photo © Victoria & Albert Museum, London/Art Resource, New York.

Unit Two

160–161 Temple E at Selinus. From *Greece: From Mycenae to the Parthenon,* Henri Stierlin. Photo by Henri Stierlin, Geneva, Switzerland; **162** *top* © George Hunter/New York; **163** *left* © Erich Lessing/Art Resource, New York; *right* Statue of Athene (340–330 B.C.). National Archaeological Museum, Athens, Greece. Photo © Bridgeman Art Library; **164** *Achilles and the Body of Patroclus* (*The Spoils of War*) (1986), David Ligare. Oil on canvas, 60″ × 78″. Private collection, Los Angeles; **165** Alexander Sarcophagus (333 B.C.). Archaeological Museum, Istanbul, Turkey. Photo © Erich Lessing/Art Resource, New York; **166** *left* Detail of grave stele of a youth and a little girl (about 530 B.C.). Marble, 166 11/16″ (432.4 cm). Frederick C. Hewitt Fund, 1911, Rogers Fund, 1921, Anonymous Gift, 1951 [11.185a-c, f, g]. Image © The Metropolitan Museum of Art, New York/Art Resource, New York; *center* Vase painting of Greek family (mid-fifth century B.C.), attributed to the Harrow Painter. Tampa Museum of Art, Joseph Veach Noble Collection. Purchased in part with funds donated by Mr. and Mrs. James L. Ferman, Jr. 1986.070. Photograph by Bastòn Design; *right* The Granger Collection, New York; **167** *top* Attic red-figure bell-crater (430–425 B.C.), the Komaris Painter. Greek. Photo © Ashmolean Museum, University of Oxford, United Kingdom/Bridgeman Art Library; *bottom left* Helmet and breastplate (450–400 B.C.). Ruec, Bulgaria. Bronze, Height 25 cm. Archaeological Museum, Sofia, Bulgaria. Photo © Erich Lessing/Art Resource, New York; *bottom right* White ground jug (490 B.C.) Brygo Painter. Athens, Greece. Finely dressed woman is in the act of spinning woolen thread. Photo © HIP/Art Resource, New York; **168–169** Zeus or Poseidon (460 B.C.). Bronze. National Archaeological Museum, Athens, Greece. Photo © Erich Lessing/Art Resource, New York; **169** *School of Athens* (about 1510), Raphael. Stanza della Segnatura, Stanze di Raffaello, Vatican City, Vatican State. Photo © Erich Lessing/Art Resource, New York; **170** Statue of Demosthenes. Braccio Nuovo, Vatican Museums, Vatican State. Photo © Scala/Art Resource, New York; **171** *top* © SuperStock, Inc./SuperStock; *center* © PoodlesRock/Corbis; *bottom* Apollo crowned with myrtle. White-ground kylix, about 480–470 B.C. Archaeological Museum, Delphi, Greece. Photo © Nimatallah/Art Resource, New York; **172** *top* Lekythos (oil flask) with women making woolen cloth (about 540 B.C.), Amasis Painter. Greek. Terracotta, 6 3/4″ high. Fletcher Fund, 1931 [31.11.10]. Image © The Metropolitan Museum of Art, New York/Art Resource, New York; *bottom* © Manfred Morgenstern; **173** *Aristotle.* Musei Capitolini, Rome. Photo © Scala/Art Resource, New York; **174** *left, center* © Getty Images; *right* NASA; **175** *top* © Getty Images; *bottom* © Camerique Stock Photography/H. Armstrong Roberts; **176** Detail of *Achilles Defeating Hector* (1630–1632), Peter Paul Rubens. Oil on panel, 108 cm × 127 cm. Photo © Musée des Beaux-Arts, Pau, France/Bridgeman Art Library; **178** *top, Bust of Homer.* Sala delle

ART CREDITS **R189**

State. Photo © Scala/Art Resource, New York; *bottom* © The Art Archive; **179** *Judgement of Paris* (1500s), Giulio Romano. Ducal Palace, Mantua, Italy © SuperStock, Inc./ SuperStock; **183** *foreground* Helmet and breastplate (450–400 B.C.). Ruec, Bulgaria. Bronze, Height 25 cm. Archaeological Museum, Sofia, Bulgaria. Photo © Erich Lessing/Art Resource, New York; *background* © Hugh Sitton/Stone/Getty Images; **189** © Kathleen Campbell/Stone/ Getty Images; **193** Detail of *Athena restrains Achilles from killing Agamemnon* (1757), Giambattista Tiepolo. Fresco. Villa Valmarana, Vicenza, Italy. Photo © Scala/Art Resource, New York; **196** The departure of the warrior (about 500 B.C.), Nicoxenos Vasepainter. Red-figured amphora. Louvre, Paris. Photo © Erich Lessing/Art Resource, New York; **199** *foreground* Greek bust of Zeus. National Archaelolgical Museum, Naples, Italy. © Alinari Archives/The Image Works; *background* © Steve Satushek/ Riser/Getty Images; **205** *foreground, Pallas de Velletri,* Roman marble copy of Greek original by Cresilas (about 430 B.C.). Louvre, Paris. Photo © Réunion des Musées Nationaux/Art Resource, New York; *background* © Michael Busselle/Riser/Getty Images; **208** Greek vase painting, Greek soldiers arming themselves (400s B.C.). Photo © Peter Connolly/akg-images; **214** *foreground* © Chris Hellier/Corbis; *background* © Kim Heacox/Stone/ Getty Images; **219** *foreground* © Chris Hellier/Corbis; *background* © George Grigoriou/Stone/Getty Images; **225** © Araldo de Luca/Corbis; **226** The Granger Collection, New York; **228** *right* Relief with a dancing maenad (27 B.C. to 14 A.D.). Roman, Augustan. Pentelic Marble, 56 5/16″. The Metropolitan Museum of Art, Fletcher Fund, 1935 (35.11.3). Image © 2001 The Metropolitan Museum of Art; **232** *Bust of Thucidides.* Museo Archeologico Nazionale, Naples, Italy. Photo © Scala/Art Resource, New York; **234–235** Dying Warrior (about 500). Glyptothek, Staatliche Antikensammlung, Munich, Germany. Photo © Vanni/Art Resource, New York; **237** Bust of Pericles (about 425 B.C.). Marble, 18 7/8″. The British Museum, London. Photo © JFB/The Art Archive; **238** © Michael Townsend/ Stone/Getty Images; **241** At the feet of the goddess Athena, two Greek warriors draw lots (about 490 B.C.). Red figure kylix, Kunsthistorisches Museum, Vienna. Photo © Erich Lessing/Art Resource, New York; **245** *top* AP/Wide World Photos; *bottom* Adil Bradlow/AP/Wide World Photos; **246** The Granger Collection, New York; **249** The School of Plato. Roman mosaic. Museo Archeologico Nazionale, Naples, Italy. Photo © Alinari/Art Resource, New York; **252** Socrates (first century B.C.). Fresco. Ephesus Archaeological Museum, Ephesus, Turkey. Photo © Erich Lessing/Art Resource, New York; **256** *top* © Ron Sheridan/ Ancient Art and Architecture Collection Ltd.; *bottom* Photo © Scala/Art Resource, New York; **257** *top* © Donald York; **260–261** Illustration by Stephen Conlin; **263** © Photofest; **266** © Photofest; **270** Photo © Ron Scherl/ StageImage; **277** © Merlyn Severn/Hulton Archive/Getty Images; **284** *top* © Photofest; *bottom* © Robbie Jack/ Corbis; **290, 292** Pier Paolo Cito/AP/Wide World Photos; **295** © Merlyn Severn/Hulton Archive/Getty Images; **310** Photo © Ron Scherl/StageImage; **312** Monnett-Sully in the role of Oedipus in *Oedipe Roi* (1899), Leonetto Cappiello. Pastel and gouache, 56.5 cm × 47.1 cm. Photo by Gérard Blot. Musée d'Orsay, Paris. Photo © Réunion des Musées Nationaux/Art Resource, New York © 2007 Artists Rights Society (ARS), New York; **318** © John Vickers, Vickers Theatre Collection, London. Image courtesy of the University of Bristol Theatre Collection, Old Vic Archive; **325** © Photofest; **328** *top left, top right* Courtesy of Hartford Stage. Photo by T. Charles Erickson; *bottom right* © Photofest; *bottom left* © Universal/The Kobal Collection; **329** *top* Sphinx of Taharqa. © The Trustees of the British Museum. All rights reserved; **332** © Getty Images; **342** *Minerva restrains Achilles from killing Agamemnon* (1757), Giambattista Tiepolo. Fresco. Villa Valmarana, Vicenza, Italy. Photo © Scala/Art Resource, New York; **344** © Grazia Neri/Camera Press Digital/Retna Ltd. United States of America; **345** *top* © Dennis Degnan/ Corbis; *center left, Baptism of Christ in Jordan River* (1240), unknown artist. Ancient Art & Architecture Collection Ltd.; *bottom right* Officer of the Praetorian Guard (early 100s A.D.). Roman marble relief. Louvre, Paris. Photograph by Hervé Lewandowski. © Réunion des Musées Nationaux/Art Resource, New York; **346** *top* Emperor Augustus. Bust. Musei Capitolini, Rome. Photo © SEF/Art Resource, New York; *bottom, The Founding of Rome* (1500s), Giuseppe Cesari © The Art Archive/Corbis; **347** © Elio Ciol/Corbis; **348** *left* © Araldo De Luca/Corbis; *right* Chariot. Roman bas relief, from Avignon. Museo della Civilta Romana, Rome. Photo © Scala/Art Resource, New York; **349** *top left* © Michael Holford; *top right* Gilded mummy portrait of a woman (about 165). Encaustic on limewood. British Museum, London. Photo © HIP/Art Resource, New York; *bottom* Detail of Mosaic from Cicero's Villa (0-100). Museo Archeologico Nazionale, Naples, Italy. Photo © Scala/Art Resource, New York; **350** © Alinari Archives/Corbis; **351** *top* Emperor Augustus in military dress. Marble figure. Height 204 cm. Vatican Museums, Vatican State. Photo © Erich Lessing/Art Resource, New York; *bottom, Virgil and the Muses* (200s). Roman mosaic from Sousse. Musée National du Bardo, Le Bardo, Tunisia. Photo © Bridgeman Art Library; **352, 353** *top* © Araldo de Luca/Corbis; *bottom* © Xinhua/Sovfoto; **354** *top* AP/Wide World Photos; *center* © Joseph Sohm/ Visions of America/Corbis; *bottom left* © DreamWorks SKG Photo: Jaap Buitendijk/Dreamworks/Photofest;

R190 ART CREDITS

Freeman/PhotoEdit/PictureQuest; *right* © Kevin Fleming/Corbis; **356** *left, Virgil and the Muses* (200s). Roman mosaic from Sousse. Musée National du Bardo, Le Bardo, Tunisia. Photo © Bridgeman Art Library; **361** © Photofest; **364** The Laocoon group. Roman copy. Vatican Museums, Vatican State. Photo © Nimtallah/Art Resource, New York; **367** © Bettmann/Corbis; **371** © Mimmo Jodice/Corbis; **379** © The Kobal Collection; **383** © Underwood and Underwood/Corbis; **385** Detail of *Helen of Troy* (1863), Dante Gabriel Rossetti. Oil on canvas, 38.2 cm × 27.7 cm. Inv. 2469. Hamburger Kunsthalle, Hamburg, Germany. Photo © Elke Walford/Bildarchiv Preussischer Kulturbesitz/Art Resource, New York; **388** *left* © Corbis; *right* Detail of *Helen of Troy* (1898), Evelyn De Morgan. Oil on canvas, 98 cm × 48 cm. Photo © The De Morgan Centre, London/Bridgeman Art Library; **392** *Portrait medal of Horace.* Roman. Museo Nazionale Romano, Rome. Photo © Scala/Art Resource, New York; **394** *Paquius Proculus and his wife.* Wall painting from Pompeii. Museo Archeologico Nazionale, Naples, Italy. Photo © Erich Lessing/Art Resource, New York; **395** Household Shrine: Figures with Cornucopia making sacrifice, Roman. Fresco. Pompeii, Italy. © Ronald Sheridan/Ancient Art & Architecture Collection Ltd.; **396** (Detail of) Household Shrine: Figures with Cornucopia making sacrifice, Roman. Fresco. Pompeii, Italy. © Ronald Sheridan/Ancient Art & Architecture Collection Ltd.; **398** The Granger Collection, New York; **399** *Sky and Water I* (1938), M. C. Escher © 2007 The M. C. Escher Company-Holland. All rights reserved. www.mcescher.com; **401** *The Fall of Icarus* (1600s), Jacob Peter Gowy. Oil on canvas, 195 cm × 180 cm. Museo del Prado, Madrid, Spain. Photo © The Art Archive/Corbis; **403** *top, Landscape with the Fall of Icarus,* Pieter Brueghel the Elder. Musée d'Art Ancien, Musées Royaux des Beaux-Arts, Brussels, Belgium. Photo © Scala/Art Resource, New York; **405** *left, Man in an Ornothopter,* Leonardo da Vinci. Brown ink drawing. MS B, fol 80 reacto. Bibliothèque de l'Institut de France, Paris. Photo © Bulloz/Réunion des Musées Nationaux/Art Resource, New York; *top right* © Judy MacCready; *bottom right* Photo © Steve Finberg; **406** Culver Pictures, Inc; **407** *foreground* © Art Resource, New York; *background* Illustration by Eileen Wagner; **410** *Paquius Proculus and his wife.* Wall painting from Pompeii. Museo Archeologico Nazionale, Naples, Italy. Photo © Erich Lessing/Art Resource, New York.

Unit Three

418–419 *Moonlight on the River Sheba,* Ando Hiroshige. Musée des Arts Asiatiques-Guimet, Paris. Photo © Bridgeman-Giraudon/Art Resource, New York; **420** *top* © Liu Xiaoyang/China Images/Alamy Ltd; *bottom* Pottery Shaanxi province, China. 47.5 cm. Photo © Genius of China Exhibition/The Art Archive; **421** *top* © Dallas and John Heaton/Stock Boston; *bottom* © O. Louis Mazzatenta/National Geographic Image Collection; **422** *top* Wang Lu/ChinaStock; *bottom* The Tigress, yeou vase (ritual grain alcohol container). Bronze, 12th century B.C., late Shang Dynasty (16th–11th century B.C.), China. Musée Cernuschi, Paris, France. Photo © Gianni Dagli Orti/Musée Cernuschi, Paris/The Art Archive; **424** *left* Detail of *The Thirteen Emperors* (late 600s), attributed to Yan Liben. Chinese, Tang dynasty. Ink and color on silk, 20 3/16″ × 209 1/16″. Denman Waldo Ross Collection. [31.643]. Museum of Fine Arts, Boston. Photo © 2008 Museum of Fine Arts, Boston; *right* Freer Gallery of Art, Smithsonian Institution, Washington, D.C.: Purchase, F1954.21, Section 11; **425** *top* Paper Store. Bibliothèque Nationale de France, Paris; *bottom, Equestrienne on horse* (725–750). Anonymous. Tang dynasty (618–907). Chinese. Buff earthenware with polychrome pigments, 56.2 cm × 48.2 cm × dep.: 39.0 cm. Gift of Mrs. Pauline Palmer Wood, 1970.1073. The Art Insitute of Chicago. Photo © The Art Institute of Chicago. All rights reserved; **426** © Archivo Iconographico, S.A./Corbis; **427** *top* Detail of *Nine Dragons* (1244), Chen Rong. Chinese, Southern Song dynasty. Hand scroll, ink and color on paper, 18 1/4″ × 431 5/8″. Francis Gardner Curtis Fund [17.1697]. Museum of Fine Arts, Boston. Photo © 2008 Museum of Fine Arts, Boston; *bottom, The Cold Food Observance* (Sung dynasty), Su Shih. Collection of the National Palace Museum. Taipei, Taiwan, Republic of China; **428** Cast bronze sword of the late Eastern Shou period. © The Trustees of the British Museum. All rights reserved; **429** Detail of the Bayeux Tapestry (about 1082). Wool embroidery on linen. © Musée de la Tapisserie, Bayeux, France/Bridgeman Art Library; **430** *top* © Getty Images; *center* © Burke/Triolo Productions/FoodPix/Jupiterimages Corporation; *bottom left* © Bruce Burkhardt/Corbis; *bottom right* Photo by Sharon Hoogstraten; **431** *top left* © 1996 Louis Jacobs, Jr./Mira; *right* © Jeff Hunter/Riser/Getty Images; *bottom* © Getty Images; **432** © Getty Images; **434** *bottom left* © Wang Lu/China Stock; **436** © Luca Tettoni/Corbis; **438** *A Literary Gathering,* Han Huang. Palace Museum, Beijing; **440** The Granger Collection, New York; **441** © Wolfgang Kaehler/Corbis; **442** Detail of *Lady with Fan* (mid-1800s), Ju Qing. Album leaf, ink and color on silk, 27 cm × 36.5 cm. Collection of the Art Museum of the Chinese University of Hong Kong; **443** Lao-tzu riding his ox (1500s), Zhang Lu. Hanging scroll, ink and watercolor on silk. Collection of the National Palace Museum, Taipei, Taiwan, Republic of China. Photo © Bridgeman Art Library; **444** Ming dish (1500s). Porcelain with overglaze enamel decoration.

ART CREDITS **R191**

Taiwan, Republic of China; **447** Figure of sitting woman. Imperial Museum, Beijing. Robert Harding Picture Library, London; **448** Horseman with spear (100s). Bronze. Excavated 1969 at Wu-Wei, Kansu, China. Gansu Provincial Museum, Lanzhou, China. Photo © Erich Lessing/Art Resource, New York; **450** Ink drawing, Wang Hui. From *Landscapes and Flowers,* a collaborative album with Yun Shou-p'ing. Collection of the National Palace Museum, Taipei, Taiwan, Republic of China; **452** *top* © Clive Druett/Papilio/Corbis; *bottom* © Stock Montage/SuperStock; **454** © Clive Druett/Papilio/Corbis; **455** *Beauty Viewing Flowers* (1800s), Gakutel Harunobu. © Brooklyn Museum/Corbis; **456** *Li Po* (Southern Sung Dynasty), Liang Kai. Hanging scroll, ink on paper, 31 2/3″ × 12 1/8″ (80.4 cm × 30.7 cm). Tokyo National Museum/ TNM Image Archives; **457, 458** *top* © Clive Druett/Papilio/Corbis; *bottom, Early Spring,* Kuo Hsi. Collection of the National Palace Museum, Taipei, Taiwan, Republic of China; **462** *left* © Liu Liqun/China Stock; necessary; **465** Jar (about 1430), Ming dynasty, Xuande mark and period. China. Porcelain painted in underglaze blue, 19″ × 19″. Gift of Robert E. Tod, 1937 [37.191.1]. Image © The Metropolitan Museum of Art, New York/Art Resource, New York; **466** Running horse (Han Dynasty). Bronze. Imperial Museum, Beijing. Robert Harding Picture Library, London; **467** © Gordon Gahan/National Geographic Image Collection; **469** Circular box with garden scene, Yung Lo. Collection of the National Palace Museum, Taipei, Taiwan, Republic of China; **471** *top right, center right* © Howard Davies/ Corbis; *bottom right* © Peter Turnley/Corbis; *bottom left* © Chris Hondros/Getty Images; **472** *top* © Ron Watts/ Corbis; *bottom* © Liu Liqun/China Stock; **473** *Spring Morning in the Han Palace,* Qui Ying. Collection of the National Palace Museum, Taipei, Taiwan, Republic of China; **475** Detail of *The Old Plum* (about 1647), attributed to Kano Sansetsu. Colors, ink, and gold leaf on paper, 68 3/4″ × 191 1/8″. The Harry G. C. Packard Collection of Asian Art, Gift of Harry G. C. Packard and Purchase, Fletcher, Rogers, Harris Brisbane Dick, and Louis V. Bell Funds, Joseph Pulitzer Bequest, and The Annenberg Fund, Inc. Gift, 1975 [1975.268.48a-d]. Image © The Metropolitan Museum of Art, New York/ Art Resource, New York; **484** Detail of *Spring Morning in the Han Palace.* Qui Ying. Collection of the National Palace Museum, Taiwan, Republic of China; **486** *top* © Sylvain Grandadam/Stone/Getty Images; *center* Photo © Japanese National Tourist Organization/Bridgeman Art Library; *bottom, Fisherman Netting Sole* (1853), Ando or Utagawa Hiroshige. Color woodblock print. Photo © Blackburn Museum and Art Gallery, Lancashire, United Kingdom/Bridgeman Art Library; **487** *left* © 1961 Burt London; **488–489** Tachi sword. Sword mounting is of the hyogo-gusari-tachi type. Scabbard decorated with triple triangles. Tokyo National Museum/TNM Image Archives; **489** © Ric Ergenbright/Corbis; **490** *The Emperor Go-Yozei* (early 1600s) Kano Takanobu. Kyoto National Museum, Japan; **491** *top* © Werner Forman Archive/Art Resource, New York; *bottom* Koyasan Society for the Preservation of Cultural Properties, Museum Reihokan, Koyasa, Japan; **492** *top, Moonlit Landscape* (late 1400s, Muromachi period), Saiyo. Ink and color on paper, 22 3/16″ × 8 1/2″ (56.4 cm × 21.6 cm). Eugene Fuller Memorial Collection (Acc. no. 55.55), Seattle Art Museum, Seattle, Washington. Photograph by Susan Dirk. Photo © Seattle Art Museum; *center* © Image Eye/Pacific Press Service; **493** *top* Statue of Great Buddha in Kamakura © Sakamoto Photo Research Laboratory/ Corbis; *bottom* © Bruce Burkhardt/Corbis; **494** *center, The Tale of Genji,* Lady Murasaki Shikibu. © Ancient Art & Architecture Collection Ltd.; *right* Detail of Japanese screen. Asian Art Museum of San Francisco. The Avery Brundage Collection, Chong-Moon Lee Center for Asian Art and Culture; **495** © Getty Images; **496** *top left* © Studio Eye/Corbis; *bottom left* © FoodPix; *bottom center* © Getty Images; **496–497** © 1991 Roberto Soncin Gerometta/Photo 20-20/PictureQuest/Jupiterimages Corporation; **497** *top* © Robert Holmes/Corbis; *bottom* © Karl Prouse/Catwalking/Getty Images; **498** *top* Detail of *Five Beautiful Women* (Edo period, early 1800s), Katsushika Hokusai. Ink and color on silk, 34″ × 13.5″ (86.4 cm × 34.3 cm). Margaret E. Fuller Purchase Fund (Acc. no. 56.246), Seattle Art Museum, Seattle, Washington. Photograph by Susan Dirk. Photo © Seattle Art Museum; **500** *Woman and a Cat,* Utagawa Kunimasa. Tokyo National Museum/TNM Image Archives; **502** *Three Women Reading a Letter,* Katsukawa Terushige. Tokyo National Museum/ TNM Image Archives; **505** Detail of *Five Beautiful Women* (Edo period, early 1800s), Katsushika Hokusai. Ink and color on silk, 34″ × 13.5″ (86.4 cm × 34.3 cm). Margaret E. Fuller Purchase Fund (Acc. no. 56.246), Seattle Art Museum, Seattle, Washington. Photograph by Susan Dirk. Photo © Seattle Art Museum; **508** *top* Detail of *Fan Painting (court lady)* (about 1675). Honolulu Academy of Arts, Hawaii. Gift of John Gregg Allerton, 1984; *bottom* © Archivo Iconografico, S. A./Corbis; **509** *top, Fan Painting (court lady)* (1675). Honolulu Academy of Arts, Hawaii. Gift of John Gregg Allerton, 1984; *bottom, Prince Genji with his Lover in a Boat Admiring the Snow in the Garden* (1830), Ando Hiroshige. © Bass Museum of Art/Corbis; **512** *right* © 1996 Rene Burri/Magnum Photos; **515** Carving of Zen Priest Hotto Kokushi (about 1286). Wood. Cleveland Museum of Art, Ohio. © SuperStock,

R192 ART CREDITS

Pearle/Taxi/Getty Images; *right* © Peter Turnley/Corbis; **518** *top* Momoyama Period Noh Mask © Sakamoto Photo Research Laboratory/Corbis; **520** *left* Momoyama Period Noh Mask © Sakamoto Photo Research Laboratory/Corbis; *center* Uba mask (Edo period). Polychromed wood, 8 3/8″ × 5 1/2″ (21.2 cm × 14.1 cm). Collection of the Tokyo National Museum; *right* Uba mask (Edo period, 1800s). Polychromed wood, 8″ × 5 3/8″ (20.3 cm × 13.6 cm). Collection of the Tokyo National Museum/TNM Image Archives; **521** © Morton Beebe/Corbis; **522, 523** Momoyama Period Noh Mask © Sakamoto Photo Research Laboratory/Corbis; **524** © Philadelphia Museum of Art/Corbis; **525** Uba mask (Edo period). Polychromed wood, 8 3/8″ × 5 1/2″ (21.2 cm × 14.1 cm). Collection of the Tokyo National Museum; **527** *left* Uba mask (Edo period). Polychromed wood, 8 3/8″ × 5 1/2″ (21.2 cm × 14.1 cm). Collection of the Tokyo National Museum; *right* Uba mask (Edo period, 1800s). Polychromed wood, 8″ × 5 3/8″ (20.3 cm × 13.6 cm). Collection of the Tokyo National Museum/TNM Image Archives; **528** © Sakamoto Photo Research Laboratory/Corbis; **529** Momoyama Period Noh Mask © Sakamoto Photo Research Laboratory/Corbis; **530** Tosa style fan decorated with a court scene depicting a party of noblemen (1600s). Japan. Private collection. Photo © Werner Forman/Art Resource, New York; **531** Uba mask (Edo period). Polychromed wood, 8 3/8″ × 5 1/2″ (21.2 cm × 14.1 cm). Collection of the Tokyo National Museum; **534** *The Poetess Ono no Komachi, cherry tree, full moon* (1820s), Hokkei. Woodcut, Surimono print. Acc. no. 0000.1561. William Bridges Thayer Memorial, Spencer Museum of Art, University of Kansas, Lawrence, Kansas; **536** Photo by Sharon Hoogstraten; **537** *Man and Boy Walking* (1786–1787), Egoyomi. Edo period. © Brooklyn Museum/Corbis; **538** *Poet Saigyo viewing the moon* (1637), Iwasa Katsumochi. Gunma Prefectural Museum of Modern Art, Gunma Prefecture, Japan; **541** © Shinya Yoshimori/A. collection/amanaimages; **542** © Alan Sirulnikoff/Getty Images; **543** *center* © Jane Booth Vollers/Photonica/Getty Images; *right* © David Frazier/Corbis; **544** © Kevin Schafer/Corbis; **545** © Mark Karrass/Corbis; **547** *top left, top right* © Masao Ota/Amana Images/Getty Images; *bottom left* Public Domain; *bottom right* © Hulton Archive/Getty Images; **548** *left, right* © Masao Ota/Amana Images/Getty Images; **549** *The Rhythm of a Corner* (1957). Photo by W. Eugene Smith. © W. Eugene Smith/Stockphoto.com; **560** *top* Detail of *Five Beautiful Women* (Edo period, early 1800s), Katsushika Hokusai. Ink and color on silk, 34″ × 13.5″ (86.4 cm × 34.3 cm). Margaret E. Fuller Purchase Fund (Acc. no. 56.246), Seattle Art Museum, Seattle, Washington. Photograph by Susan Dirk. Photo © Seattle Art Museum.

562–563 © Martin Norris/Alamy Ltd; **564** *top* © Archivo Iconografico, S.A./Corbis; *bottom* © Chris Bradley/Axiom; **565** *top* © Nabeel Turner/Stone/Getty Images; *bottom* © Richard Avery/Stock Boston LLC; **566** Darius I the Great giving audience (491–486 B.C.). Treasury of the Palace at Persepolis, Iran. © SEF/Art Resource, New York; **566–567** Detail of *Cavalry on Camels Fighting* (1442), Khamsa of Nizami Ganjevi. Photo © The British Library/The Art Archive; **567** Dome of south Iwan (1611–1638). Safavid dynasty. Majid-i Shah, Isfahan, Iran. Photo © SEF/Art Resource, New York; **568** *top right* By permission of the British Library (1007628.011); *bottom left* © Alistair Duncan/Dorling Kindersley; **569** *top* Bibliothèque Nationale de France, Paris; *bottom left, Persian Princess Writing Letter in a Park* (1600s). Fresco. Palace of Chihil Soutoun, Isfahan, Iran. Photo © Gianni Dagli Orti/The Art Archive; *bottom right* © Adam Woolfitt/Robert Harding Picture Library; **570** *top* The Granger Collection, New York; *bottom left* © Marvin E. Newman; *bottom right* © I. Perlman/Stock Boston; **571** *top* © Paul H. Kulper/Corbis; *bottom* © Bojan Brecelj/Corbis; **573** *top, Saladin,* Cristofano (di Papi) dell'Altissimo. Galleria degli Uffizi, Florence, Italy. Photo © Alfredo Dagli Orti/The Art Archive; *bottom* © 2000 British Library Board; **574** *top* © Bettmann/Corbis; *bottom left* © James L. Amos/Corbis; *bottom right* © Lawrence Migdale/Stone/Getty Images; **575** *left* NASA; *right* John Clarke (University of Michigan), and NASA; **577** © A. Ramey/PhotoEdit; **580** © Burstein Collection/Corbis; **582** Public Domain; **587** Illustration by Edmund Dulac; **591** *top* Photofest/Jagarts; *bottom* © Columbia Pictures/Photofest; **592** *left* Marble statue of Ferdausi, standing in the gardens at Tus where the great poet once lived. Photo by Roloff Beny (about 1974), Tus, Iran. Library and Archives Canada, Roloff Beny fonds/PA-211051. Photo © Library and Archives Canada. Reproduced with the permission of Library and Archives Canada; *right* Buzurgmihr masters the game of chess. Leaf from First Small *Shahnama* [Book of Kings] (1300–1325). Northwestern Iran or Baghdad. Ink, colors, gold and silver on paper, 7 1/2″ × 5 1/4″. The Metropolitan Museum of Art, Joseph Pulitzer Bequest, 1934 (34.24.1). Image © 1990 The Metropolitan Museum of Art; **593** Rustam Stabs Suhrab, Garrett Islamic manuscript, Mss. Third Series, no. 310 Folio: 77:2. Manuscripts Division, Department of Rare Books and Special Collections, Princeton University Library; **594** Culver Pictures, Inc.; **596** Detail of *Fête champêtre* [Picnic on the grass] (about 1610–1615), Riza. The Keir Collection, England; **599, 600** The Granger Collection, New York; **601** *Prayer in the Mosque* (1871), Jean-Léon Gérôme. Oil on canvas, 35″ × 29 1/2″. Catharine Lorillard Wolfe Collection, Bequest of Catharine Lorillard Wolfe, 1887[87.15.130]. Image © The Metropolitan

ART CREDITS **R193**

pays homage to Rumi from *The Legend of Mevlana Jalal al-Din Rumi* (1599). Topkapi Museum, Istanbul, Turkey. Photo © Gianni Dagli Orti/The Art Archive; **606** Saadi in conversation with a rich, adventurous merchant (1207–1292). Persian miniature. Bibliotheque Nationale, Paris. Photo © Visioars/akg-images, London; **609** Saadi in conversation with a rich, adventurous merchant (1207–1292). Persian miniature. Bibliotheque Nationale, Paris. Photo © Visioars/akg-images, London; **610** *top* Detail of *Fête Champêtre* [Picnic on the Grass](about 1610). The Keir Collection, England; **612** *top* © Aldona Sabalis/Photo Researchers, Inc.; *bottom* © Charles Santore/ National Geographic Image Collection; **613** *top left* © Explorer/Robert Harding; *top center* Detail of Oba Ademuwagun Adesida II, the Deji of Akure, in traditional dress. Yoruba peoples, Nigeria. EEPA EECL (2060). Photo © Eliot Elisofon, 1959. Eliot Elisofon Photographic Archives/National Museum of African Art, Smithsonian Institution, Washington, D.C.; *top right* © Nik Wheeler/ Corbis; *bottom right* Leopard (1550–1680). African, Nigeria. Edo, Court of Benin. Bronze. The Metropolitan Museum of Art, The Michael C. Rockefeller Memorial Collection, Gift of Nelson A. Rockefeller, 1972. (1978.412.321). Photo © 1983 The Metropolitan Museum of Art; **614** Detail of *Catalan Atlas* (about 1375), copy after Abraham Cresques. Photo © John Webb/The Art Archive; **615** The Granger Collection, New York; **616** *top* © Jean-Philippe Ksiazek/Getty Images; *bottom* Head of an Oba (about 1550). Nigeria. Edo, Court of Benin. Brass. Height 9 1/4″. The Michael C. Rockefeller Memorial Collection, Bequest of Nelson A. Rockefeller, 1979 (1979.206.86). Photo by Schecter Lee. The Metropolitan Museum of Art, New York. © The Metropolital Museum of Art/Art Resource, New York; **617** *left* © The Trustees of the British Museum. All rights reserved; *right* Queen Mother Head from Benin. Bronze. Benin, Nigeria. British Museum, London. Photo © Art Resource, New York; **618** © Philip Scalia/Alamy Ltd; **619** © Bryan and Cherry Alexander/Alamy Ltd; **620** *left* Courtesy of Royal Pavillion Museum and Art Gallery, Brighton, England. Photo © Geoff Dann Doring Kindersley; *right* Portrait of a King (1000s–1400s), Ife, Nigeria. Copper alloy. British Museum, London. Photo © Bridgeman Art Library; **621** Detail of *Cardinal Chigi Caring for Plague Victims* (1700s). © Gianni Dagli Orti/Corbis; **622-623** © Barbara Alper/Stock, Boston/Jupiterimages; **622** *left* © Mitchell Gerber/Corbis; *right* © Steve Vidler/eStock Photo—All rights reserved; **623** *top* © Stephen McBrady/PhotoEdit; *center right, The Smiling Spider* (before 1897), Odilon Redon. Charcoal on chamois paper, 49.5 cm × 39 cm. Inv. RF29932. Louvre, Paris. Photo by Jean-Gilles Berizzi. Fonds Orsay. Photo © Réunion des Musées Nationaux/Art Resource, New York; terracotta horseback riders. © Bernard de Grunne; **633** © Robert Gill; Papilio/Corbis; **635** Seated figure (1200s). Terracotta, 10″ (25.4 cm). Purchase, Buckeye Trust and Mr. And Mrs. Milton F. Rosenthal Gifts, Joseph Pulitzer Bequest, and Harris Brisbane Dick and Rogers Funds, 1981 [1981.218]. Image © The Metropolitan Museum of Art, New York/Art Resource, New York; **639** Terracotta horse and rider (1200–1300). Excavated in the Djenne-Mopti area, Mali. Entwistle Gallery, London. Photo © Werner Forman/Art Resource, New York; **642** *top* © Getty Images; *center* © Storm Pirate Productions/Artville/Jupiter Images; *bottom* © Peter Johnson/Corbis; **643** Henning Christoph/Das Fotoarchiv; **644** © Getty Images; **645** © Storm Pirate Productions/Artville/Jupiter Images; **646** Shango, God of Thunder. Dahomey (now Benin), Africa. Photo © Gianni Dagli Orti/Musée des Arts Africains et Océaniens/The Art Archive; **647** © Peter Johnson/Corbis; **649** © Bob Krist/Corbis; **655** Akunitam cloth (mid/late 1900s). Photo © Franko Khoury/National Museum of African Art, Smithsonian Institution, Washington, D.C.; Detail of Wrapper (mid-late 20th century), Fantes peoples. Mill-woven wool, embroidery thread, 304.2 cm × 198.7 cm (119.75″ × 78.25″). Museum purchase (84-6-10). Photo © Franko Khoury/National Museum of African Art, Smithsonian Institution, Washington, D.C.; **659** *top* © Nigel Sanndor/Illustration Works/Corbis; *bottom* © jgl247/ ShutterStock; **660** © jgl247/ShutterStock; **664–667** Public Domain; **676** Five terracotta horseback riders. © Bernard de Grunne.

Unit Five

684–685 *Primavera [Allegory of spring]* (1481), Sandro Botticelli. Uffizi, Florence, Italy. Photo © Scala/Art Resource, New York; **686** *top* Detail of *August: Mowing Wheat, Binding Sheaves* (about 1515), Simon Bening. Da Costa Hours. Bruges. Photo © The Pierpont Morgan Library/Art Resource, New York; *bottom* The Granger Collection, New York; **687** *top* © Sandro Vannini/Corbis; *bottom* © The Board of Trustees of the Armouries/Royal Armouries, Leeds, England; **688** Reliquary Bust of Charlemagne (1349). Gold and silver. World History Cathedral Treasury, Aachen, Germany © SuperStock, Inc./ SuperStock; **688–689** *The Taking of Jerusalem by the Crusaders, July 15, 1099,* Emile Signol. Chateaux de Versailles et de Trianon. Versailles, France. Photo © Réunion des Musées Nationaux/Art Resource, New York; **689** *The Wife of Bath*. Detail from *The Canterbury Tales* by Geoffrey Chaucer. The Huntington Library, Art Collections, and Botanical Gardens, San Marino, California. © Huntington Library/SuperStock; **690** *left* Detail of *January* from *Très Riches Heures du Duc de*

R194 ART CREDITS

& Albert Museum, London/Bridgeman Art Library; *right, June* from *Très Riches Heures du Duc de Berry* (early 1400s), Limbourg brothers. Photo © Victoria & Albert Museum, London/Bridgeman Art Library; **691** *top* Roundel depicting Holofernes' army crossing the Eurphrates River, from the Saint-Chapelle Chapel, Paris. Philadelphia Museum of Art. Gift of Mrs. Clement Biddle Wood in memory of her husband. Photograph by Graydon Wood, 1993. © Philadelphia Museum of Art/Corbis; *left, Golden Bull of Charles IV of Luxemburg* (about 1400). Österreichische Nationalbibliothek, Vienna, Austria © akg-images; *bottom* © Angelo Hornak/Corbis; **692** © Mark Karrass/Corbis; **693** *left* Illustration by Walter Crane in *King Arthur's Knights* by Henry Gilbert, 1911. Photo © Edwin Wallace/Mary Evans Picture Library; *right, Joan of Arc* (1400s), unknown artist. Archives Nationales, Paris. Photo © Bridgeman-Giraudon/Art Resource, New York; **694** *top* © Gregor M. Schmid/Corbis; *center, bottom* © Getty Images; **694–695** *top* Photofest; **695** *left* Ian Jones/AP/Wide World Photos; *right* Courtesy HRH The Prince of Wales; **698** Illustration of Charlemagne's army departing for Spain (1300s). Manuscript. Biblioteca Nazionale Marciana, Venice. Photo © Alfredo Dagli Orti/The Art Archive; **701, 704** The Granger Collection, New York; **708** *bottom* Illustration from medieval manuscript of Perceval at the castle of the wounded Fisher King. Bibliothèque Nationale de France, Paris; **710** *Perceval in Quest of the Holy Grail* (1912), Ferdinand Leeke. © Christie's Images Ltd.; **711** Manuscript illumination of Galahad, Boort, Perceval, and his sister arriving at an island, from *The Romance of Saint Graal* (1400s). © Gianni Dagli Orti/Corbis; **713** Bibliothèque Nationale de France, Paris; **715** Detail of *Mystery of the Holy Grail,* Wilhelm Hauschild. Neuschwanstein Castle, Germany. Photo © Alfredo Dagli Orti/The Art Archive; **719** *The Forest Crossed by Perceval to Liberate Amfortas at the Castle of the Grail,* Christian Jank. Neuschwanstein Castle, Germany. Photo © Alfredo Dagli Orti/The Art Archive; **721** *Lancelot and Guinevere: The Dawn of Love* (1867), after Gustave Doré. Steel engraving. The Granger Collection, New York; **723** © Jonathan Hession/Touchstone/Bureau L.A. Collection/Corbis; **724** *top* © Jupiterimages Corporation; *bottom* The Granger Collection, New York; **727** *The Werewolf of Eschenbach, Germany* (1685). Line engraving. The Granger Collection, New York; **728** © Jupiterimages Corporation; **730** The Granger Collection, New York; **732** *Dante Alighieri* (1500–1503), Luca Signorelli. Fresco. Duomo, Orvieto, Italy. Photo © Scala/Art Resource, New York; **733** *top* © Scala/Art Resource, New York; *bottom left, bottom right* The Granger Collection, New York; **734** Detail of *Dante and Beatrice* (1883), Henry Holiday. Oil on canvas, 142.2 cm × 203.2 cm. Photo © Walker Art *Dante and His Poem,* Domenico di Michelino. Duomo, Florence, Italy. Photo © Scala/Art Resource, New York; **736** *top foreground* © Jupiterimages Corporation; **738** The Granger Collection, New York; **740–754** © Jupiterimages Corporation; **743** *Inscription over the Gate* (1824–1827), William Blake. Illustration to *Hell,* Canto 3, of Dante's *The Divine Comedy.* Watercolor, 52.7 cm × 37.4 cm. Photo © Tate Gallery, London/Art Resource, New York; **746** The Granger Collection, New York; **751** *Dante's Dream* (1871), Dante Gabriel Rossetti. Oil on canvas, 216 cm × 312.4 cm. Photo © Walker Art Gallery, National Museums, Liverpool, United Kingdom/Bridgeman Art Library; **754** *Dante and Virgil in the Ninth Circle of the Inferno,* Gustave Doré. Photo © Christie's Images Ltd.; **757** *Beata Beatrix* (1864–1870), Dante Gabriel Rossetti. Oil on canvas, 86.4 cm × 66 cm. Tate Gallery. Photo © Tate, London/Art Resource, New York; **760** *Dante Alighieri* (1300s), unknown artist. Portraitgalerie, Schloss Ambras, Innsbruck, Austria. Photo © Erich Lessing/Art Resource, New York; **770** The Granger Collection, New York; **772** *top, Elizabeth I of England.* Miramare Palace, Trieste. Photo © Alfredo Dagli Orti/The Art Archive; © Explorer, Paris/SuperStock; **773** *top* © Bettmann/Corbis; *bottom* Detail of *David* (1501), Michelangelo Buonarotti. Marble. Galleria dell'Accademia, Florence, Italy. © SuperStock, Inc./SuperStock; **774** St. Peter's with facade by Maderno and dome by Michelangelo (1600s), Anonymous. Vatican Palace, Vatican State. Photo © Scala/Art Resource, New York; **775** *Louis XIV, King of France* (about 1700), Hyacinthe Rigaud. © Arte & Immagini srl/Corbis; **776** *top* © The Art Archive/Corbis; *bottom, Martin Luther* (1533), Lucas Cranach, the Elder. Oil on canvas. © SuperStock, Inc./SuperStock; **777** *top* © Corbis; *bottom La place de Meir a Anvers un jour de marche* © Royal Museums of Fine Arts of Belgium; **778** *Sir Isaac Newton* (1710), Sir James Thornhill. Oil on canvas, 122 cm × 101.5 cm. Trinity College, Cambridge, United Kingdom. Photo © Bridgeman Art Library; **779** *top, The Artist's Studio* (1600s), Jan Vermeer. Oil on canvas. Kunsthistorisches Museum, Vienna, Austria. © SuperStock,Inc./SuperStock; *bottom* © Christel Gerstenberg/Corbis; **780** *top, Canon's Yeoman.* Detail from *The Canterbury Tales* by Geoffrey Chaucer. The Huntington Library, Art Collections, and Botanical Gardens, San Marino, California © Huntington Library/SuperStock; *bottom* Detail of *The Last Supper,* Leonard da Vinci. © Edimédia/Corbis; **781** *Peter the Great* (1800s), Paul Delaroche. © SuperStock, Inc./SuperStock; **782** *top* © Lester Lefkowitz/Taxi/Getty Images; *bottom foreground* © Reuters/Corbis; *bottom background* The Granger Collection, New York; **783** *left* © Mehau Kulyk/Science Photo Library/Photo Researchers, Inc.; *right* © Mark Burnett/Stock Boston LLC; **784** *top* © Junko Yamada/

ART CREDITS **R195**

(1300s). Portraitgalerie, Schloss Ambras, Innsbruck, Austria. Photo © Erich Lessing/Art Resource, New York; **787** *left, La Pia de Tolommei* (1868–1880), Dante Gabriel Rossetti. Oil on canvas, 104.8 cm × 120.6 cm. Spencer Museum of Art, University of Kansas, Lawrence, Kansas. Photo © Erich Lessing/Art Resource, New York; *right* © Junko Yamada/amana images/Getty Images; **788** © Junko Yamada/amana images/Getty Images; **789** *Peregrine Falcon* (1796). Raia Serfagee of Tanjore Collection. Photo © British Library/The Art Archive; **790** © Junko Yamada/amana images/Getty Images; **794** *top* © Roy Morsch/Corbis; *left, Portrait of Sir Thomas More,* Peter Paul Rubens. Museo del Prado, Madrid. Photo © Scala/Art Resource, New York; **797** *background* © Roy Morsch/Corbis; *foreground, How Utopians Breed Chickens by Incubation,* Francois van Bleyswyck. Bibliothèque Nationale de France, Paris; **799** *background* © Roy Morsch/Corbis; *foreground, How the Island of Utopia is Shaped like a Crescent,* Francois van Bleyswyck. Bibliothèque Nationale de France, Paris; **803** *The Island of Utopia.* Illustration from a contemporary edition of *Utopia* by Thomas More. Kunstbibliothek, Staatliche Museen zu Berlin, Berlin, Germany. Photo by Dietmas Katz. © Bildarchiv Preussischer Kulturbesitz/Art Resource, New York; **804** *St. Madeleine Reading* (1500s), Master of Female Half-Lengths. © Peter Willi/Superstock; **805** *top, bottom* © Getty Images; **806** The Granger Collection, New York; **807** *Petrarch's First Sight of Laura* (1884), William Cave Thomas. Fine Art Photographic Library Ltd., London; **808** *Portrait of Pierre de Ronsard* (1600s). Photo © Giraudon/Art Resource, New York; **808–809** *Old Woman Reading* (1665), Rembrandt Harmensz van Rijn. Private collection. Photo © Bridgeman Art Library; **812** The Granger Collection, New York; **814** *Love Among the Ruins* (1894), Sir Edward Burne-Jones. Oil on canvas. Wightwick Manor, Staffordshire, United Kingdom. Photo © The Bridgeman Art Library; **815** *Sir Henry Percy, 9th Earl of Northumberland,* Nicholas Hilliard. Rijksmuseum, Amsterdam, The Netherlands. Photo © Bridgeman Art Library; **818** *top* The Granger Collection, New York; *bottom* © Miramax/Photofest; **819** Illustration by John James/Temple Rogers Artists' Agents; **821** *top, Lady with Unicorn,* Raphael. Galleria Borghese, Rome. Photo © Scala/Art Resource, New York; *bottom, Portrait of Louise Labe* (1555), Dubouchet. Engraving. Private Collection. Photo © Bridgeman Art Library; **822** *Lady with Unicorn,* Raphael. Galleria Borghese, Rome. Photo © Scala/Art Resource, New York; **824** *Sister Juana Inés de la Cruz* (1750), Miguel Cabrera. Oil on canvas, 207 cm × 148 cm. Museo Nacional de Historia, Castillo de Chapultepec, Mexico City, D.F., Mexico. Photo © Schalkwijk/Art Resource, New York; **828** *top, Don Quixote on Horseback* Neue Pinakothek, Munich, Germany. Photo © Scala/Art Resource, New York; *bottom* The Granger Collection, New York; **831** *Don Quixote on Horseback* (1870), Honoré Daumier. Oil on canvas, 51 cm × 33 cm. Neue Pinakothek, Munich, Germany. Photo © Scala/Art Resource, New York; **833** *Don Quixote in His Library* (about 1868), Gustave Doré. Engraving by Heliodore Joseph Pisan. Private collection. Photo © Bridgeman Art Library; **839** Detail of *Don Quixote and the Dead Mule* (1867), Honoré Daumier. Musée d'Orsay, Paris. Photo © Erich Lessing/Art Resource, New York; **841** *Don Quixote and the Windmill,* after Gustave Doré. Engraving by Heliodore Joseph Pisan. Bibliothèque Nationale de France, Paris. Photo © Giraudon/Art Resource, New York; **842** © Albert Normandin/Masterfile; **846, 847** *top* © The Art Archive/Corbis; *bottom* © Gianni Dagli Orti/Corbis; **848** *top* Uniforms of the Imperial calvary (1700s). Watercolor. Heeresgeschichtliches Museum, Vienna, Austria. Photo © Erich Lessing/Art Resource, New York; *bottom* The Granger Collection, New York; **850** Uniforms of the Imperial calvary (1700s). Watercolor. Heeresgeschichtliches Museum, Vienna, Austria. Photo © Erich Lessing/Art Resource, New York; **852** *The Stolen Kiss* (1785), Jean-Honoré Fragonard. Oil on canvas, 45 cm × 55 cm. The Hermitage, St. Petersburg, Russia. Photo © Erich Lessing/Art Resource, New York; **855** *Assassination of Albrecht Wallenstein, Duke of Friedland* (1700s). Watercolor. Heeresgeschichtliches Museum, Vienna, Austria. Photo © Erich Lessing/Art Resource, New York; **866** *Lady with Unicorn,* Raphael. Galleria Borghese, Rome. Photo © Scala/Art Resource, New York.

Unit Six

868–869 *Dance at the Moulin de la Galette, Montmartre* (1876), Pierre Auguste Renoir. Oil on canvas, 131 cm × 175 cm. Musée d'Orsay, Paris. Photo by Herve Lewandowski. Photo © Réunion des Musées Nationaux/Art Resource, New York; **870** *top, Portrait of Jean-Jacques Rousseau* (1700s), Maurice Quentin de la Tour. Oil on canvas. Photo © Musée de la Ville de Paris, Musée Carnavalet, Paris/Bridgeman Art Library; *bottom, Hadleigh Castle* (1829), John Constable. Oil on canvas, 122 cm × 164.5 cm. Photo © Yale Center for British Art, Paul Mellon Collection/Bridgeman Art Library; **871** *top* © Hulton-Deutsch Collection/Corbis; *bottom* Detail of *Bonaparte Crossing the Alps at Grande Saint-Bernard* (1800–1801), Jacques-Louis David. Oil on canvas. Musée National du Château de Malmaison, Rueil-Malmaison, France. © SuperStock, Inc./SuperStock; **872** © Gianni Dagli Orti/Corbis; **872–873** *Napoleon's Retreat from Moscow* (1800s), Adolf Northen. Courtesy of Sotheby's Picture Library, London; **874** *top*

R196 ART CREDITS

Caid (1837), Eugene Delacroix. Oil on canvas, 98 cm × 126 cm. Photo © Musée des Beaux-Arts, Nantes, France/ Bridgeman Art Library; **875** *top, Llanthony Abbey, Monmouthshire* (1834), Joseph Mallord William Turner. Watercolor on white wove paper, 30 cm × 42.5 cm. Photo © Indianapolis Museum of Art/Bridgeman Art Library; *bottom, Ludwig van Beethoven*, Joseph Stiele. Beethoven House, Bonn, Germany. Photo © Alfredo Dagli Orti/The Art Archive; **876** © Archiveo Iconografico, S.A./Corbis; **877** *left* Historical and Ethnological Museum of Greece; *bottom* Courtesy of the Seneca Falls (New York) Historical Society; **878** *The Wanderer Above the Sea of Fog* (1818), Caspar David Friedrich. Oil on canvas, 98.4 cm × 74.8 cm. Hamburger Kunsthalle, Hamburg, Germany. Photo © Bridgeman Art Library; **880** *top* © 1989 Ron Scherl/StageImage; *bottom, Portrait of Goethe,* Heinrich Christoph Kolbe. Goethe House and Museum, Frankfurt am Main, Germany. Photo © SEF/Art Resource, New York; **883** © 1989 Ron Scherl/StageImage; **887** Christian Nickel as Faust in 2000 stage production of Goethe's Faust. Staged in Berlin by Peter Stein. Photo © Ruth Walz; **891** Bruno Ganz as Faust and Adam Oest as Mephistopheles in 2000 stage production of Goethe's Faust. Staged in Berlin by Peter Stein. Photo © Ruth Walz; **893** Photo © Ruth Walz; **895** The Granger Collection, New York; **899** *William Wordsworth* (1818), Benjamin Robert Haydon. © National Portrait Gallery, London; **900** © HIP/Art Resource, New York; **901** *A Passing Shower* (1860), George Inness. Oil on canvas, 66 cm × 101.6 cm. Canajoharie Library and Art Gallery, Canajoharie, New York. © akg-images; **902** Silhouette of Dorothy Wordsworth, unknown artist. The Wordsworth Trust; **905** *left* The Granger Collection, New York; *right* A figurine depicting a shaman in the midst of leaving his body in spirit form to fly to other parts of the world. Eskimo art. Point Hope, Alaska. Whale vertebrae, walrus ivory, hide. Anchorage Museum of History and Art, Anchorage, Alaska. Photo © Werner Forman/Art Resource, New York; **907** *Sunset at Sea* (1906), Thomas Moran © Brooklyn Museum/Corbis; **910** The Granger Collection, New York; **911** *top* Public Domain; *bottom, Loreley* (1864), Eduard Jakob von Steinle. 213.5 cm × 135.4 cm. Schack-Galerie, Munich, Germany. Photo © Bayer & Mitko/Artothek; **912** *top* Public Domain; **914** *top* © Phil Schermeister/Corbis; *center* The Granger Collection, New York; *bottom* © Hulton-Deutsch Collection/Corbis; **915** *A Stoppage to a Stride over the Globe* (1803), English School. Private Collection. Photo © Bridgeman Art Library; **917** *On the March from Moscow* (1873), John Laslett Pott. Oil on canvas, 80.6 cm × 121.3 cm. Photo © Forbes Magazine Collection, New York/Bridgeman Art Library; **918** *Napoleon* Jean-Louis-Ernest Meissonier. Musée d'Orsay, Paris. Photo © Alfredo Dagli Orti/The Art Archive; **919** © Phil Schermeister/Corbis; **921** *top* Les Misérables, Palace Theatre, London. Photo © Ron Scherl/StageImage; *bottom left* Courtesy Everett Collection, Inc.; *bottom right* Sherrill Milnes as Rigoletto. Copyright © 1973 Ron Scherl/StageImage; **922** *top* The Granger Collection, New York; *bottom, The Absinthe Drinker* (about 1876), Edgar Degas. Oil on canvas, 36 ¼″ × 26 ¾″. Musée d'Orsay, Paris. Photo © Scala/Art Resource, New York; **924** Detail of *On Board a Sailing Ship* (1818–1819), Caspar David Friedrich. Oil on canvas, 71 cm × 56 cm. The Hermitage, St. Petersburg, Russia. Photo © Giraudon/Art Resource, New York; **926** *The Great Family (La grande famille)* (1963), René Magritte. Oil on canvas. Private collection. Photo © SuperStock. Art © 2007 C. Herscovici, Brussels/ Artists Rights Society (ARS), New York; **928** *top left* Detail of *Scene on the Tummel.* Hand-tinted engraving. © Visual Language/PunchStock; *top right* Detail of *Two Girls Among the Flowers* (about 1905), Odilon Redon. Oil on canvas. Museum of Fine Arts, Houston, Texas. © SuperStock, Inc./SuperStock; *bottom* Detail of *Coin de Table*—a group portrait of, from left: Paul Verlaine, Arthur Rimbaud, Elzear Bonnier, Leon Valade, Emile Blemont, Jean Ricard, Ernest D'Hervilly, Camille Pelletan, Henri Fantin-Latour. Oil on canvas, 160 cm × 225 cm. Musée d'Orsay, Paris. Photo © Erich Lessing/Art Resource, New York; **929** *Scene on the Tummel.* Hand-tinted engraving. © Visual Language/PunchStock; **931** *Two Girls Among the Flowers* (about 1905), Odilon Redon. Oil on canvas. Museum of Fine Arts, Houston, Texas. © SuperStock, Inc./SuperStock; **932** Detail of *On Board a Sailing Ship* (1818–1819), Caspar David Friedrich. Oil on canvas, 71 cm × 56 cm. The Hermitage, St. Petersburg, Russia. Photo © Giraudon/Art Resource, New York; **934** *top* © Barbara Galasso. Courtesy George Eastman House; *bottom* © Hulton-Deutsch Collection/ Corbis; **935** *top, The Rolling Mill (Steelmill)* (1872–1875), Adolf von Menzel. Oil on canvas, 158 cm × 254 cm. Gemaeldegalerie, Staatliche Museen zu Berlin, Germany. Photo © Erich Lessing/Art Resource, New York; *bottom* © Getty Images; **936** *bottom center* The Granger Collection, New York; **936–937** © Hulton-Deutsch Collection/Corbis; **937** *Louis Pasteur in His Laboratory* (1885), Albert Gustaf Aristides Edelfelt. Oil on canvas, 154 cm × 126 cm. Musée d'Orsay, Paris. Photo © Bridgeman Art Library; **938** *The Thinker* (1880–1881), Auguste Rodin. © Christie's Images/SuperStock; **939** *top* © Key Color/Index Stock Imagery/Jupiterimages Corporation; *bottom* © Carlyn Iverson/Photo Researchers, Inc.; **940, 941** The Granger Collection, New York; **942** *top, Paying the Harvesters* (1882), Leon

ART CREDITS **R197**

d'Orsay, Paris. Photo © Erich Lessing/Art Resource, New York; **942** *bottom left to right, Balzac* The Granger Collection, New York; *George Eliot* The Granger Collection, New York; *Flaubert* © Hulton-Deutsch Collection/Corbis; *Leo Tolstoy* © Bettman/Corbis; *Henrik Ibsen,* Erik Werenskjold. National Gallery, Oslo, Norway. Photo © Erich Lessing/Art Resource, New York. Art © 2007 Artist Rights Society (ARS), New York/BONO, Oslo; *Guy de Maupassant* (1800s). Black and white photo. Private collection. Photo © Bridgeman Art Library; *Anton Chekov* Sovfoto/Eastfoto; **944** *Portrait of Guy de Maupassant* (1800s), Francois-Nicolas Feyen-Perrin. Châteaux de Versailles et de Trianon, Versailles, France. Photo © Réunion des Musées Nationaux/Art Resource, New York; **949** *The Peasants of Flagey Returning from the Fair* (1855), Gustave Courbet. Oil on canvas, 208.5 cm × 275 cm. Musée des Beaux-Arts, Besancon, France. Photo © Erich Lessing/Art Resource, New York; **954** *top, Portrait of Leo Tolstoy,* Ilya Yefimovich Repin. Tretyakov Gallery, Moscow, Russia. Photo © Scala/Art Resource, New York; *center left* The Granger Collection, New York; *center right* © Nick Wiseman; Eye Ubiquitous/Corbis; *bottom, Queen Victoria of England* (about 1838), Sir George Hayter. Oil on canvas, 285.8 cm × 179 cm. National Portrait Gallery, London. Photo by Lutz Braun. Photo © Bildarchiv Preussischer Kulturbesitz/Art Resource, New York; **955** *left* © Bettmann/Corbis; *right* Sovfoto/Eastfoto; **956** *left* The Granger Collection, New York; *right* RIA Novosti/TopFoto/The Image Works; **957** © The State Russian Museum/Corbis; **958, 959** © Getty Images; **960** *Tolstoy in the Field of Labour* (1889), after Ilya Yefimovich Repin. Photo © Gianni Dagli Orti/Corbis; **961, 963, 964** © Getty Images; **965** *The Harvest,* Paul Serusier. Musée des Beaux-Arts, Nantes, France. Photo © Giraudon/Art Resource, New York; **966, 967, 968** © Getty Images; **969** *Vladimirka, a Street in Siberia,* Isaac Levitan. Tretyakov Gallery, Moscow. Photo © Scala/Art Resource, New York; **970** © Getty Images; **974** © C Squared Studios/Getty Images; **975** Photo by Sharon Hoogstraten; **976** © Mark Douet/Getty Images; **978** *The Grey House* (1917), Marc Chagall. Fundacion Coleccion Thyssen-Bornemisza, Madrid. Photo © Nimatallah/Art Resource, New York © 2007 Artists Rights Society (ARS), New York/ADAGP, Paris; **983** *Still-Life with Lamp* (1910), Marc Chagall. Oil on canvas, 70 cm × 45 cm. Private collection. Courtesy Galerie Rosengart, Lucerne, Switzerland © 2007 Artists Rights Society (ARS), New York/ADAGP, Paris; **987** *The Harvest,* Natalia Goncharova. Russian State Museum, St. Petersburg, Russia. Photo © Scala/Art Resource, New York © 2007 Artists Rights Society (ARS), New York/ADAGP, Paris; **991** *The Dream* (1939), Marc Chagall. Gouache on paper, 20 9/16″ × 26 3/4″. Acquired 1942. The Rights Society (ARS), New York/ADAGP, Paris; **993, 994** Photo by Sharon Hoogstraten; **996** *Portrait of Leo Tolstoy,* Ilya Yefimovich Repin. Tretyakov Gallery, Moscow, Russia. Photo © Scala/Art Resource, New York; **999** Sovfoto/Eastfoto; **1001** *Double Portrait of Otto and Heinrich Benesch* (1913), Egon Schiele. Neue Galerie, Linz, Austria. Photo © Art Resource, New York; **1008** *left* The New York Times/Redux; *right* © 1999 Visual Language; **1011** *Prince taming an elephant,* Mughal miniature (1609–1610), Signed by Zain al-Abidin. Opaque watercolor on paper, 19.3 cm × 13 cm. Inv I 4598 fol. 2. Museum fuer Islamische Kunst, Staatliche Museen zu Berlin, Berlin. © Bildarchiv Preussischer Kulturbesitz/Art Resource, New York; **1016** *top* The Granger Collection, New York; *bottom* © Bridgeman Art Library; **1017** © Oliver Upton/Hallmark/NBC/The Kobal Collection; **1018** *top* © Comstock Images/Jupiterimages Corporation; *bottom, Henrik Ibsen,* William Nicholson. © Elizabeth Banks; **1020–1022** *top* © Comstock Images/Jupiterimages Corporation; **1023** *top* © Comstock Images/Jupiterimages Corporation *bottom,* Claire Bloom as Nora and Anthony Hopkins as Torvald in Paramount Pictures' *A Doll's House* (1973), directed by Patrick Garland. Photofest; **1024–1027** © Comstock Images/Jupiterimages Corporation; **1028** *top* © Comstock Images/Jupiterimages Corporation *bottom* © The Kobal Collection; **1029–1035** © Comstock Images/Jupiterimages Corporation; **1036** *top* © Comstock Images/Jupiterimages Corporation *bottom* © Photofest; **1037–1041** © Comstock Images/Jupiterimages Corporation; **1042** © Photofest; **1043–1044** © Comstock Images/Jupiterimages Corporation; **1045** *top* © Comstock Images/Jupiterimages Corporation *bottom* © The Kobal Collection; **1046–1050** © Comstock Images/Jupiterimages Corporation; **1051** *top* © Comstock Images/Jupiterimages Corporation; *bottom* © Photofest; **1052–1057** © Comstock Images/Jupiterimages Corporation; **1058** *top* © Comstock Images/Jupiterimages Corporation *bottom* © Photofest; **1059–1060** © Comstock Images/Jupiterimages Corporation; **1061** *top* © Comstock Images/Jupiterimages Corporation *bottom* © Photofest; **1063** © Getty Images; **1064–1071** *top* © Comstock Images/Jupiterimages Corporation; **1072** *top* © Comstock Images/Jupiterimages Corporation; *bottom* © Photofest; **1073–1077** © Comstock Images/Jupiterimages Corporation; **1078** *top* © Comstock Images/Jupiterimages Corporation *bottom* © Photofest; **1079** © Comstock Images/Jupiterimages **1080** © Photofest; **1083** © Getty Images; **1092** *The Peasants of Flagey Returning from the Fair* (1855), Gustave Courbet. Oil on canvas, 208.5 cm × 275 cm. Musée des Beaux-Arts, Besancon, France. Photo © Erich Lessing/Art Resource, New York.

R198 ART CREDITS

1094–1095 Photo of Earth from the Moon. Lyndon B. Johnson Space Center/NASA; **1096** *top* NASA; *center* © Hulton-Deutsch Collection/Corbis; *bottom* © Corbis; **1097** © 2000 Jeffrey Aaronson/Still Media; **1098** *top, Jazz Singer* (1997), Gil Mayers. © Gilbert Mayers/SuperStock; *bottom* © Bettmann/Corbis; **1099** *top* © Joseph Sohm/Visions of America/Corbis; *bottom* Greg English/AP/Wide World Photos; **1100** *left* © Steve Northup/Time & Life Pictures/ Getty Images; *right* Marty Lederhandler/AP/Wide World Photos; **1101** *Kafka* © Bettman/Corbis; *Anna Andreevna Akhmatova* (1914), Natan Isaevic Altmann. Oil on canvas, 123.5 cm × 103.2 cm. State Russian Museum, St. Petersburg, Russia. Photo © Bridgeman Art Library; *Kawabata* © Bettmann/Corbis; *Wright* Courtesy ACT Heritage Library, Coward Photography Collection; *Achebe* AP/Wide World Photos; **1102** *top* © Chaplin/United Artists/The Kobal Collection; *bottom left* Chaise lounge (1928), Le Corbusier. Chrome-plated tubular steel, painted steel, fabric, and leather, 24″ × 62 5/16″ × 19 9/16″. Manufactured by Thonet Freres, Paris. The Museum of Modern Art, New York. Gift of Thonet Industries, Inc. [223.1950]. Photo © The Museum of Modern Art, New York/Licensed by Scala/Art Resource, New York. Art © 2007 Artists Rights Society (ARS), New York/ADAGP, Paris/FLC; *bottom right, The Musician* (1917–1918), Georges Braque. Oil on canvas, Kunstmuseum, Basel, Switzerland. Photo © Giraudon/Art Resource, New York. © 2008 Artists Rights Society (ARS), New York; **1103** *top* Solomon R. Guggenheim Museum, designed by Frank Lloyd Wright. © Angelo Hornak/Corbis; *bottom, Martha Graham: Letter to the World* (1940), Barbara Morgan. Gelatin silver print. Photo © Underwood Photo Archives/SuperStock. © Barbara Morgan; **1104** *top* © Bettmann/Corbis; *bottom* © Hulton-Deutsch Collection/ Corbis; **1105** *left, Pablo Picasso in his studio standing in front of Man Leaning on a Table. Paris, 1916,* Pablo Picasso. Art © 2007 Estate of Pablo Picasso/Artists Rights Society (ARS), New York; *right, Man Leaning on a Table* (1916), Pablo Picasso. Oil on canvas, 78 3/4″ × 52″ (200 cm × 132 cm). Art © 2007 Estate of Pablo Picasso/Artists Rights Society (ARS), New York; **1106** *Nude Descending a Staircase (No. 2)* (1912), Marcel Duchamp. Oil on canvas, 57 7/8″ × 35 1/8″. Philadelphia Museum of Art, The Louise and Walter Arensberg Collection, 1950. Image © Burstein Collection/Corbis, Art © 2007 Artist Rights Society (ARS), New York/ADAGP, Paris/Succession Marcel Duchamp; **1108** © Bettman/Corbis; **1111** *Hidden Resemblance* (1991), Elizabeth Barakah Hodges. Acrylic. © Elizabeth Barakah Hodges/SuperStock; **1118** *Portrait of Superintendant Trabuc in St. Paul's Hospital* (1889), Vincent van Gogh. Oil on canvas, 61 cm × 46 cm. Kunstmuseum Solothurn, Switzerland. Photo © Bridgeman Art Library; **1123** Detail of the poster for the 1920 film *Das Cabinet des Dr. Caligari* Chromolithograph. © akg-images; **1128** *Portrait of Mlle Ravoux* (1800s), Vincent Van Gogh. Christie's Images, London. Photo © Bridgeman Art Library, London/ SuperStock; **1133** *Nächtlicher Lärm* (1919), Hans Georg Scholz. Oil on canvas, 56.8 cm × 50.9 cm. The Marvin and Janet Fishman Collection, Milwaukee, Wisconsin. © akg-images; **1136** *Le Lessive* [The Wash] (1921), Maria Blanchard. Oil on canvas. Museum of Modern Art, Paris. © SuperStock, Inc./SuperStock; **1140** *The Skat Players* (1920), Otto Dix. Oil and collage on canvas, 110 cm × 87 cm. Nationalgalerie, Staatliche Museen zu Berlin, Berlin. Photo © Erich Lessing/Art Resource, New York. Art © 2007 Artists Rights Society (ARS), New York/VG Bild-Kunst, Bonn; **1150** The Granger Collection, New York; **1151** © Tim Flach/Stone/Getty Images; **1152** *left* Photograph by Rogelio Robles Romero Saavedra. Fundacion Federico García Lorca; *right* © Daniel Arsenault/ The Image Bank/Getty Images; **1156** *top* Photograph by Sharon Hoogstraten; *bottom* © Gisele Freund/Photo Researchers, Inc.; **1158** Photograph by Sharon Hoogstraten; **1159** © Bettmann/Corbis; **1160** Photograph by Sharon Hoogstraten; **1161** *La reve II* [The dream], Balthus. © 2007 Artists Rights Society (ARS), New York/ ADAGP, Paris; **1162** Photograph by Sharon Hoogstraten; **1166** The Granger Collection, New York; **1169** *Fishergirl, Newlyn,* Stanhope Alexander Forbes. © Christies Images Ltd./The Estate of Stanhope Alexander Forbes/Bridgeman Art Library; **1170** *St. Patrick's Close, Dublin,* Walter Frederick Osborne (1859–1903). Oil on canvas, 69 cm × 51 cm. Courtesy of the National Gallery of Ireland. Photo © The National Gallery of Ireland; **1174** © Bettmann/ Corbis; **1176** Detail of *Two Japanese Women,* about 1890. © Michael Maslan Historic Photographs/Corbis; **1177** *Two Japanese Women,* about 1890. © Michael Maslan Historic Photographs/Corbis; **1182** *top* © Martin B. Withers; Frank Lane Picture Agency/Corbis; *bottom* © Jean-Paul Guilloteau/Kipa/Corbis; **1184** *top* Mask (20th century). Zaire-Angola. Wood, 9″ (22.8 cm). From Zaire River coastal region. Photo by Michael Bodycomb. © Kimbell Art Museum, Fort Worth, Texas/Corbis; *bottom* © Martin B. Withers; Frank Lane Picture Agency/Corbis; **1185** © Martin B. Withers; Frank Lane Picture Agency/Corbis; **1187** © Michael Newman/PhotoEdit; **1188** *top* © Stockbyte/PictureQuest; *bottom* Culver Pictures, Inc.; **1189** *Le Reproduction Interdite* (1937), René Magritte. Oil on canvas, 81 cm × 65 cm. Musuem Boymans van Beuningen, Rotterdam, The Netherlands. Photo © Banque d'Images/ ADAGP/Art Resource, New York. Art © 2008 Artists Rights Society (ARS) New York; **1198** *Fishergirl, Newlyn,* Stanhope Alexander Forbes. © Christies Images Ltd./The Estate of Stanhope Alexander Forbes/Bridgeman Art Library; **1200** *top* Stalin and Lenin's Banner (1933), Gustav

ART CREDITS **R199**

Collection, Berlin. © akg-images; *bottom* © Underwood & Underwood/Corbis; **1201** *top* United States Air Force; *bottom* © Peter Turnley/Corbis; **1202** © Bettmann/Corbis; **1203** *top* © Bettmann/Corbis; *left* © Hulton-Deutsch Collection/Corbis; **1204** *top left* Sovfoto/Eastfoto; *top right* © Hulton Archive/Getty Images; *bottom* © Bettmann/Corbis; **1205** *top* Public Domain; *bottom* © Fehim Demir/epa/Corbis; **1206** *Portrait of the Italian Writer Luigi Pirandello* (1928), Primo Conti. Raccolta Teatrale del Burcado, Rome. Photo © Giraudon/Art Resource, New York; **1207** © Bettmann/Corbis; **1209** *Self Portrait,* Käthe Kollwitz. Art © 2007 Artists Rights Society (ARS), New York/VG Bild-Kunst, Bonn, Germany; **1210** © Jack Novak/SuperStock; **1214** *top, bottom* © Bettmann/Corbis; **1215** © Universal/The Kobal Collection; **1216** *top* © Mel Curtis/Photonica/Getty Images; *bottom, Anna Andreevna Akhmatova* (1914), Natan Isaevic Altmann. Oil on canvas, 123.5 cm × 103.2 cm. State Russian Museum, St. Petersburg, Russia. Photo © Bridgeman Art Library; **1217** *left* © Mel Curtis/Photonica/Getty Images; *right, In Front of the Mirror,* Konstantin N. Istomin. Tretyakov Gallery, Moscow, Russia. Photo © Scala/Art Resource, New York; **1219** *Soyinka* Remy de la Mauviniere/AP/Wide World Photos; *Rushdie* © Rune Hellestad/Corbis; *Lessing* © Bettmann/Corbis; *Solzhenitsyn* © Alexander Nemenov/AFP/Getty Images; **1220** *top* The Granger Collection, New York; *bottom* © akg-images; **1221** © Hulton-Deutsch Collection/Corbis; **1223** *Femme a la robe noir [Woman in a black dress],* Tamara de Lempicka. Art © 2007 Artists Rights Society (ARS), New York/ADAGP, Paris; **1225** The Granger Collection, New York; **1226** *Portrait of Prince Eristoff* (1925) Tamara de Lempicka. Private collection, New York. © 2008 Artists Rights Society (ARS), New York/ADAGP, Paris; **1228** © Hulton-Deutsch Collection/Corbis; **1229** The Granger Collection, New York; **1232** Richard Drew/AP/Wide World Photos; **1234** © Hulton Archive/Getty Images; **1238** Zydowski Instytut Historyczny Instytut Naukowo-Badawczy, Warsaw, Poland. Courtesy of USHMM Photo Archives; **1240** © Time & Life Pictures/Getty Images; **1241** Trees and butterflies. Drawing by a Jewish child made in the concentration camp at Terezin. Museum of the Old Jewish Cemetery, Prague, Czech Republic. Photo © Scala/Art Resource, New York; **1243** *left* Courtesy of USHMM Photo Archives. Photograph by Max Reid; *center* Wilfredo Lee/AP/Wide World Photos; *right* Courtesy of the United States Holocaust Memorial Museum, Washington, D.C; **1244** *top* © Visual Language/PunchStock; *bottom* © Agence France Presse/Getty Images; **1246** Detail of *Self-Portrait* (1942), Mario Mafai. Photo © Araldo de Luca/Corbis; **1248** © Adam Woolfitt/Corbis; **1249, 1250** © Visual Language/PunchStock; **1252** *left* © Visual Language/PunchStock; *right* Detail of *A Seated Arab* Images/SuperStock; **1254** *left* © Visual Language/PunchStock; *right* AP/Wide World Photos; **1256** © SuperStock, Inc./SuperStock; **1257** © Visual Language/PunchStock; **1261** *top* © Joshua Sheldon/Photonica/Getty Images; *bottom* Alexander Zemlianichenko/AP/Wide World Photos; **1262** *left* © Joshua Sheldon/Photonica/Getty Images; *right, Apple Trees* (1904), Kazimir Severinovic Malevich. Oil on canvas. Russian State Museum, St. Petersburg, Russia. © SuperStock, Inc./SuperStock.; **1265** *left* Jacqueline Larma/AP/Wide World Photos; *right* © Kamil Vojnar/Photonica/Getty Images; **1267** © Cuchi White/Corbis; **1270** *top* © Eliot Elisofon/Time & Life Pictures/Getty Images; *bottom* Courtesy of Chinua Achebe; **1271** *top* Photo © Carlo Bavagnolli/Time & Life Pictures/Getty Images; *bottom left, bottom right* AP/Wide World Photos; **1272** *left* © Time & Life Pictures/Getty Images; *right* © Jurgen Frank/Corbis; **1273** Commonwealth Institute. © Ray Moller/Dorling Kindersley; **1274, 1275** © Charles O'Rear/Corbis; **1276** *Follow* (2006), Lou Wall. Photo © Lou Wall/Corbis; **1277** © Charles O'Rear/Corbis; **1280** Bill Cramer/AP/Wide World Photos; **1281** © William Coupon/Corbis; **1283** © Jurgen Frank/Corbis; **1284** © Corbis; **1285** © Christie's Images/Corbis; **1286** Copyright © Robert Lyons; **1287** © Martin Rogers/Corbis; **1289** © Robert Lyons; **1292** Bill Cramer/AP/Wide World Photos; **1294** Marty Lederhandler/AP/Wide World Photos; **1297** © Acey Harper/Time & Life Pictures/Getty Images; **1300** © Dave G. Houser/Corbis; **1304** *top* © Gunnar Kullenberg/SuperStock; *bottom* AP/Wide World Photos; **1305** © Gunnar Kullenberg/SuperStock; **1318** The Granger Collection, New York; **1320** *top* The Granger Collection, New York; *bottom* © The Nobel Foundation 1991. Artist: Bo Larsson. Calligrapher: Annika Rücker; **1321** *top* Soren Andersson/AP/Wide World Photos; *center, bottom* AP/Wide World Photos; **1322** *top* © Robert Maass/Corbis; *bottom* © Peter Turnley/Corbis; **1323** *top* © Time & Life Pictures/Getty Images; *bottom* Jonathan Hayward/AP/Wide World Photos; **1324** Lisa Bul/AP/Wide World Photos; **1325** © Frans Lemmens/Stone/Getty Images; **1327** © Dick Durrance/National Geographic Image Collection; **1330** © SuperStock, Inc./SuperStock; **1335** © Owen Franken/Corbis; **1336** *left* Alan Mothner/AP/Wide World Photos; *right* © Hulton Archive/Getty Images; **1337** © Hulton-Deutsch Collection/Corbis; **1338** © Getty Images; **1339** *Garbage* (1924), Jose Clemente Orozco. Mural. Escuela Nacional Preparatoria San Ildefonso, Mexico City, D.F., Mexico. Photo © Schalkwijk/Art Resource, New York. Art © Artists Rights Society (ARS), New York; **1340, 1341** © Getty Images; **1344** *The Philosopher's Conquest* (1914), Giorgio de Chirico. Oil on canvas, 49 1/4″ × 39″ . The Art Institute of Chicago, Chicago, Illinois. Photo © The Art Institute of Chicago/The Art Archive. Art © 2007 Artists

R200 ART CREDITS

Banana Pancake/Alamy Ltd; *bottom* © Piero Pomponi/Getty Images; **1347** © Jeremy Horner/Corbis; **1349** © Mark Owen/Illustration Works/Corbis; **1350** *La Pintora de Urapan,* Alfredo Ramos Martinez. Photo © Christie's Images/SuperStock; **1353** *Burial of an Illustrious Man* (1936), Mario Urteaga. Oil on canvas, 23″ × 32 1/2″. Inter-American Fund. (806.1942). Digital Image © The Museum of Modern Art/Licensed by Scala/Art Resource, New York; **1356** © Piero Pomponi/Getty Images; **1357** *top* © Colita/Corbis; *center* © Thomas Woodruff; *bottom* Bjorn Elgstrand/AP/Wide World Photos; **1358** *top* © Steve Satushek/Getty Images; *bottom* Michel Lipchitz/AP/Wide World Photos; **1359** © Macduff Everton/Corbis; **1360** © Steve Satushek/Getty Images; **1365** Photo by Don Shrubshell/Columbia Daily Tribune/AP/Wide World Photos; **1366** AP/Wide World Photos; **1367** © Robert Holmes/Corbis; **1369** *The Village Road* (1988), Ali Selim. Ramses Wissa Wassef Art Center, Cairo, Egypt. Photo © Werner Forman/Art Resource, New York; **1374** AP/Wide World Photos; **1376–1377** *Aleko and Zemphira by Moonlight,* decor for *Aleko* (Scene I) (1942), Marc Chagall. Gouache, wash, and pencil on paper, 15 1/8″ × 22 1/2″. The Museum of Modern Art, New York. Acquired through the Lillie P. Bliss Bequest [137.1945.1]. Digital image © The Museum of Modern Art, New York/Licensed by Scala/Art Resource, New York. Art © 2007 Artists Rights Society (ARS), New York/ADAGP, Paris; **1378** © Dick Durrance/National Geographic Image Collection.

copyright holders of all copyrighted material in this book and to make full acknowledgment for its use. Omissions brought to our attention will be corrected in a subsequent edition.

ART CREDITS **R201**

Multicultural Advisory Board *(continued)*

Janna Rigby Clovis High School, Clovis, California

Noreen M. Rodriguez Trainer for Hillsborough County School District's Staff Development Division, Independent Consultant, Gaither High School, Tampa, Florida

Olga Y. Sanmaniego English Department Chairperson, Burges High School, El Paso, Texas

Liz Sawyer-Cunningham Los Angeles Senior High School, Los Angeles, California

Michelle Dixon Thompson Seabreeze High School, Daytona Beach, Florida

Teacher Review Panels *(continued)*

CALIFORNIA (continued)

Gail Kidd Center Middle School, Azusa School District

Corey Lay ESL Department Chairperson, Chester Nimitz Middle School, Los Angeles Unified School District

Myra LeBendig Forshay Learning Center, Los Angeles Unified School District

Dan Manske Elmhurst Middle School, Oakland Unified School District

Joe Olague Language Arts Department Chairperson, Alder Middle School, Fontana School District

Pat Salo Sixth Grade Village Leader, Hidden Valley Middle School, Escondido Elementary School District

FLORIDA

Judith H. Briant English Department Chairperson, Armwood High School, Hillsborough County School District

Beth Johnson Polk County English Supervisor, Polk County School District

Sharon Johnston Learning Resource Specialist, Evans High School, Orange County School District

Eileen Jones English Department Chairperson, Spanish River High School, Palm Beach County School District

Jan McClure Winter Park High School, Orange County School District

Wanza Murray English Department Chairperson (retired), Vero Beach Senior High School, Indian River City School District

Shirley Nichols Language Arts Curriculum Specialist Supervisor, Marion County School District

Debbie Nostro Ocoee Middle School, Orange County School District

Barbara Quinaz Assistant Principal, Horace Mann Middle School, Dade County School District

OHIO

Glyndon Butler English Department Chairperson, Glenville High School, Cleveland City School District

Ellen Geisler English/Language Arts Department Chairperson, Mentor Senior High School, Mentor School District

R202

Cleveland City School District

Loraine Hammack Executive Teacher of the English Department, Beachwood High School, Beachwood City School District

Marguerite Joyce English Department Chairperson, Woodridge High School, Woodridge Local School District

Sue Nelson Shaw High School, East Cleveland School District

Dee Phillips Hudson High School, Hudson Local School District

Carol Steiner, English Department Chairperson, Buchtel High School, Akron City School District

Nancy Strauch English Department Chairperson, Nordonia High School, Nordonia Hills City School Dictrict

Ruth Vukovich Hubbard High School, Hubbard Exempted Village School District

TEXAS

Dana Davis English Department Chairperson, Irving High School, Irving Independent School District

Susan Fratcher Cypress Creek High School, Cypress Fairbanks School District

Yolanda Garcia Abilene High School, Abilene Independent School District

Patricia Helm Lee Freshman High School, Midland Independent School District

Joanna Huckabee Moody High School, Corpus Christi Independent School District

Josie Kinard English Department Chairperson, Del Valle High School, Ysleta Independent School District

Mary McFarland Amarillo High School, Amarillo Independent School District

Gwen Rutledge English Department Chairperson, Scarborough High School, Houston Independent School District

Bunny Schmaltz Assistant Principal, Ozen High School, Beaumont Independent School District

Michael Urick A. N. McCallum High School, Austin Independent School District

Manuscript Reviewers *(continued)*

Beverly Ann Barge Wasilla High School, Wasilla, Alaska

Louann Bohman Wilbur Cross High School, New Haven, Connecticut

Rose Mary Bolden J. F. Kimball High School, Dallas, Texas

Lydia C. Bowden Boca Ciega High School, St. Petersburg, Florida

Angela Boyd Andrews High School, Andrews, Texas

Judith H. Briant Armwood High School, Seffner, Florida

Hugh Delle Broadway McCullough High School, The Woodlands, Texas

Stephan P. Clarke Spencerport High School, Spencerport, New York

Kathleen D. Crapo South Fremont High School, St. Anthony, Idaho

Dr. Shawn Eric DeNight Miami Edison Senior High School, Miami, Florida

Linda Ferguson English Department Head, Tyee High School, Seattle, Washington

Ellen Geisler Mentor Senior High School, Mentor, Ohio

Ricardo Godoy English Department Chairman, Moody High School, Corpus Christi, Texas

Meredith Gunn Secondary Language Arts Instructional Specialist, Katy, Texas

Judy Hammack English Department Chairperson, Milton High School, Alpharetta, Georgia

Robert Henderson West Muskingum High School, Zanesville, Ohio

Martha Watt Hosenfeld English Department Chairperson, Churchville-Chili High School, Churchville, New York

Janice M. Johnson Assistant Principal, Union High School, Grand Rapids, Michigan

Eileen S. Jones English Department Chair, Spanish River Community High School, Boca Raton, Florida

Paula S. L'Homme West Orange High School, Winter Garden, Florida

Bonnie J. Mansell Downey Adult School, Downey, California

Linda Maxwell MacArthur High School, Houston, Texas

Ruth McClain Paint Valley High School, Bainbridge, Ohio

Rebecca Miller Taft High School, San Antonio, Texas

Deborah Lynn Moeller Western High School, Fort Lauderdale, Florida

Bobbi Darrell Montgomery Batavia High School, Batavia, Ohio

Bettie Moody Leesburg High School, Leesburg, Florida

Margaret L. Mortenson English Department Chairperson, Timpanogos High School, Orem, Utah

Marjorie M. Nolan Language Arts Department Head, William M. Raines High School, Jacksonville, Florida

Julia Pferdehirt Freelance Writer, Former Special Education Teacher, Middleton, Wisconsin

Cindy Rogers MacArthur High School, Houston, Texas

Pauline Sahakian English Department Chairperson, San Marcos High School, San Marcos, Texas

Jacqueline Y. Schmidt Department Chairperson and Coordinator of English, San Marcos High School, San Marcos, Texas

David D. Schultz East Aurora High School, East Aurora, New York

Milinda Schwab Judson High School, Converse, Texas

John Sferro Butler High School, Vandalia, Ohio

Brad R. Smedley English Department Chairperson, Hudtloff Middle School, Lakewood, Washington

Faye S. Spangler Versailles High School, Versailles, Ohio

Rita Stecich Evergreen Park Community High School, Evergreen Park, Illinois

Ruth Vukovich Hubbard High School, Hubbard, Ohio

Kevin J. Walsh Dondero High School, Royal Oak, Michigan

Charlotte Washington Westwood Middle School, Grand Rapids, Michigan

Tom Watson Westbridge Academy, Grand Rapids, Michigan

Linda Weatherby Deerfield High School, Deerfield, Illinois

R205